DICTIONARY OF QUOTATIONS

COLLINS

DICTIONARY OF QUOTATIONS

Edited by

A. NORMAN JEFFARES & MARTIN GRAY

HarperCollinsPublishers

HarperCollins*Publishers*
P.O. Box, Glasgow G4 0NB

ISBN 0 00 434382 4
Reprint 10 9 8 7 6 5 4 3 2 1 0

A catalogue record for this book is available from the British Library.

Photoset in Linotron Garamond by
Rowland Phototypesetting Ltd
Bury St Edmunds, Suffolk.

Printed in Great Britain by
The Bath Press
Lower Bristol Road
Bath

CONTENTS

INTRODUCTION

'It is a good thing,' wrote Sir Winston Churchill in *My Early Life* (1930), 'for an uneducated man to read books of quotations.' We could extend his comment to include educated men and women as well. In addition to the obvious pleasures of recognition, dictionaries of quotations offer their readers delight in the unexpected: they contain profundities and flippancies; remarks which, once made, become inevitable; truisms which capture collective wisdom, thoughts which survive and indeed gain in strength through the years. And there are instances where the personality of the person quoted gives a richly individual and unforgettable flavour to their words.

In compiling the *Collins Dictionary of Quotations* we have sought to blend the known with the lesser known. We have ranged widely, including quotations from Australia, Canada, India, Ireland and New Zealand, as well as from Europe, the United States, Asia and the Far East, in addition to basing the *Dictionary* upon the vast reservoir of quotations created over the centuries in the United Kingdom. We have included quotations from contemporaries which will, we think, last as well as give immediate enjoyment to readers.

What is a 'quotation'?

A quotation is a phrase or collection of phrases that has become part of our cultural memory, culture comprising both 'low' and 'high'. Thus '$e=mc^2$' and 'Oh, you are awful! But I like you!' and 'a terrible beauty is born' are all included in this volume. For the purposes of compiling a dictionary of quotations, this definition has to be expanded in various ways. We have included phrases that we would delight to see enter this heritage of word and thought. Nor have we been able to resist including the occasional anecdote and joke – neither of these forms are strictly quotations – which we feel have endured the test of time. There is much poetry in this volume; we have found swathes of quotable verse; the hooks of rhyme and rhythm aid the passage of a well-turned phrase into the memory-store.

Some writers, Oscar Wilde for example, or Samuel Butler in his *Notebooks*, or Dorothy Parker, seem to have written or spoken always with an eye to the dictionary of quotations. Witty inversions of commonplace thoughts and paradoxes, both cruel and benign, make quotable material because they too have the sharp little patterns that catch in the memory.

In our postmodern world the quotation has shrunk to fragments, quips, advertisement slogans and soundbites. Some of these, of course, are witty, allusive, compressed, poetic and intelligent; certainly brilliant enough for anyone to admire and enjoy, and we have included examples of this kind in the Dictionary.

On the other hand, a collection of quotations cannot ignore even the most familiar clichés – they have to appear yet again – and they will be dazzlingly novel to some readers. Cliché is in the eye of the beholder. Above all, however, we hope that in this volume we have brought together an eclectic, memorable and heterogeneous collection of the best ideas, and the best words in the best order, from the past and the present, and from a wide variety of cultures.

The particular thanks of the Editors are due to Edwin Moore, Commissioning Editor at HarperCollins, Elaine Henderson, Project Manager, and Hazel Mills, Data Manager.

A. N. Jeffares, Fife Ness
Martin Gray, Stirling

Acknowledgements

MANAGING EDITOR: Edwin Moore
PROJECT MANAGER: Elaine Henderson
DATA MANAGER: Hazel Mills
INDEXER: Anne McCarthy
SYSTEMS ADVISERS: Douglas Cramb, Ian Prew

ADVISERS:
Dorothy Dunnett, Geoffrey Dutton, Roddy Forsyth, Dr Michael Herbert, Reginald Hill, Prof Okifumi Komesu, Iseabail McLeod

LANGUAGE ADVISERS:
Maree Airlie, Federico Bonfanti, Emmanuelle Guibé, Neil McKinlay, Hazel Mills, Robin Sowerby

EDITORIAL TEAM:
William Allan, Nancy Bailey, Kathy Brewis, Jill Campbell, Colleen Godley, Alice Goldie, Nicholas Gillard, Jane Horwood, Gordon Jarvie, Joyce Littlejohn, Catherine Lyons, Kevin McCarra, Sally Patton, Merle Read, Hanna Sambrock, Maggie Seaton, Carol Shaw, Christian Simpson, Geraldine Stoneham, Katherine Stott, Samantha Trouton, Ann Vinnicombe, Hamish Whyte

PRODUCTION:
Gordon Clark, David Hogg, Anne Rankin

How To Use This Book

Searching via keywords in the index can lead both to a specific quotation you are seeking or to a range of quotations on a particular subject. In the latter case the extract will most often include the subject word (marriage, for example). However, there is also a thematic element in the index. As well as leading the searcher to a quotation of general relevance to the theme, such entries may also provide a definition or describe an individual. They do not include the keyword.

In translations, only the English version is indexed except in a few instances where the foreign language version is likely to be at least as well known (*Gaudeamus igitur*). Then both will be indexed. Foreign words are in italics.

How To Use The Index

Index references indicate the name of the author (or category such as *Proverbs*) in a complete or abbreviated form, followed by the number of the quotation (ASCH 3).

Where there is more than one author with the same surname, identifying initials are added (HUX:A; HUX:H; HUX:JS) or, if necessary, an indication of the full forename (DOUGLAS:Alf; DOUGLAS:Arc).

Under Shakespeare, plays are listed alphabetically and each given its own range of numbers from 1. For these the index reference is to SHAK followed by an abbreviation of the name of the play (SHAK:HAM).

In locators MC (as in MCALP) denotes a Mc prefix which is arranged in the text as if it were spelled Mac.

The singular and plural of a noun are listed separately. Possessives are included under the relevant singular or plural form.

Where a noun appears both as a common noun and as a proper noun or name, these are separated (job – Job).

Archaic (ryme), elliptical (lov'd) and 'odd' (sumpshous) spellings are not used as keywords. Where these occur, they are given under the standard modern version of the word (rhyme; loved; sumptious) but with the extract cited exactly as it appears in the original. Scots language words and American English spellings *are* used as keywords.

Non-significant words (particularly a, the and oh) are almost invariably omitted from the beginning of an entry.

Thematic entries are indicated by an asterisk.

THE QUOTATIONS

Abbott, Berenice (1898–1991)
American photographer

1. Photography can never grow up if it imitates some other medium. It has to walk alone; it has to be itself.
[*Infinity*, 1951, 'It Has to Walk Alone']

Abel, Niels Henrik (1809–1829)
Norwegian mathematician

1. [Explaining how he had become a great mathematician at such a young age]
By studying the masters – not their pupils.
[In E.T. Bell, *Men of Mathematics* (1937)]

Abelard, Peter (1079–1142)
French theologian and philosopher

1. *O quanta qualia sunt illa sabbata,*
Quae semper celebrat superna curia.
O how great and how glorious are those sabbaths which the heavenly court for ever celebrates!
[*Hymnus Paraclitensis*]

2. *Quis rex, quae curia, quale palatium,*
Quae pax, quae requies, quod illud gaudium.
What a king, what a court, how fine a palace, what peace, what repose, what joy is there!
[*Hymnus Paraclitensis*]

Accius, Lucius (170–86 BC)
Roman tragic poet

1. *Oderint dum metuant.*
Let them hate provided that they fear.
[*Atreus*]

Achebe, Chinua (1930–)
Nigerian novelist, poet and critic

1. It's true that a child belongs to its father. But when a father beats his child, it seeks sympathy in its mother's hut. A man belongs to his fatherland when times are good and life is sweet. But when there is sorrow and bitterness he finds refuge in his motherland. Your mother is there to protect you. She is buried there. And that is why we say that mother is supreme.
[*Things Fall Apart* (1958)]

2. Among the Ibo the art of conversation is regarded very highly and proverbs are the palm-oil with which words are eaten.
[*Things Fall Apart* (1958)]

Acheson, Dean (1893–1971)
American Democratic politician; helped establish NATO

1. I will undoubtedly have to seek what is happily known as gainful employment, which I am glad to say does not describe holding public office.
[Remark made on leaving his post as Secretary of State, 1952]

2. Great Britain ... has lost an Empire and not yet found a role. The attempt to play a separate power role – that is, a role apart from Europe, a role based on a special relationship with the United States, a role based on being the head of a Commonwealth ... this role is about to be played out ... Her Majesty's Government is now attempting, wisely in my opinion, to re-enter Europe.
[Speech, 1962]

3. [Of the Vietnam war]
It is worse than immoral, it's a mistake.
[Quoted on Alistair Cooke's radio programme *Letter from America*. Cf. Boulay de la Meurthe: 1]

4. A memorandum is written not to inform the reader but to protect the writer.
[Attr.]

Ackerley, J.R. (1896–1967)
English writer and editor

1. I was born in 1896, and my parents were married in 1919.
[*My Father and Myself* (1968), opening words]

Acton, Eliza (1799–1859)
English authoress

1. The difference between good cookery and bad cookery can scarcely be more strikingly shown than in the manner in which sauces are prepared and served.
[*Modern Cookery for Private Families* (1845)]

Acton, First Baron (1834–1902)
English historian and moralist

1. The danger is not that a particular class is unfit to govern. Every class is unfit to govern.
[Letter to Mary Gladstone, 1881]

2. Power tends to corrupt, and absolute power corrupts absolutely. Great men are almost always bad men ... There is no worse heresy than that the office sanctifies the holder of it.
[Letter to Bishop Mandell Creighton, 1887. Cf. William Pitt [1]: 6 and Adlai Stevenson: 11]

Adamov, Arthur (1908–1970)
Russian-born French surrealist and political dramatist

1. [Remark at the International Drama Conference, Edinburgh, September 1963]
The reason why Absurdist plays take place in No Man's Land with only two characters is primarily financial.
[Attr.]

Adams, Abigail (1744–1818)
American letter-writer; wife of John Adams, second US President

1. I am more and more convinced that man is a dangerous creature and that power, whether vested in many or a few, is ever grasping, and like the grave, cries 'Give, give.'
[Letter to John Adams, 1775]

2. [Of letter-writing]
... a habit the pleasure of which increases with practice, but becomes more irksome with neglect.
[Letter to her daughter, 1808]

Adams, Charles Francis (1807–1886)
American statesman and editor

1. It would be superfluous in me to point out to your lordship that this is war.
[Dispatch to Earl Russell, September 1863]

Adams, Douglas (1952–)
English author and scriptwriter

1. The Answer to the Great Question Of ... Life, the Universe and Everything ... Is ... Forty-two.
[*The Hitch Hiker's Guide to the Galaxy* (1979)]

2. Anyone who is capable of getting themselves made President should on no account be allowed to do the job.
[*The Hitch Hiker's Guide to the Galaxy* (1979)]

3. Don't panic.
[*The Hitch Hiker's Guide to the Galaxy* (1979)]

Adams, Franklin P. (1881–1960)
American columnist, poet, translator and editor

1. The trouble with this country is that there are too many politicians who believe, with a conviction based on experience, that you can fool all of the people all of the time.
[*Nods and Becks* (1944)]

2. The rich man has his motor car,
His country and his town estate.
He smokes a fifty-cent cigar
And jeers at Fate...

3. Yet though my lamp burns low and dim,
Though I must slave for livelihood–
Think you that I would change with him?
You bet I would!
['The Rich Man']

Adams, Henry (1838–1918)
American historian and memoirist

1. Politics, as a practice, whatever its professions, has always been the systematic organization of hatreds.
[*The Education of Henry Adams* (1918)]

2. A friend in power is a friend lost.
[*The Education of Henry Adams* (1918)]

3. Every one carries his own inch-rule of taste, and amuses himself by applying it, triumphantly, wherever he travels.
[*The Education of Henry Adams* (1918)]

4. Chaos often breeds life, when order breeds habit.
[*The Education of Henry Adams* (1918)]

5. One friend in a lifetime is much; two are many; three are hardly possible. Friendship needs a certain parallelism of life, a community of thought, a rivalry of aim.
[*The Education of Henry Adams* (1918)]

6. Simplicity is the most deceitful mistress that ever betrayed man.
[*The Education of Henry Adams* (1918)]

7. They know enough who know how to learn.
[*The Education of Henry Adams* (1918)]

8. All the steam in the world could not, like the Virgin, build Chartres.
[*The Education of Henry Adams* (1918)]

Adams, John Quincy (1767–1848)
American lawyer, diplomat and sixth US President

1. Think of your forefathers! Think of your posterity!
[Speech, December 1802]

2. I inhabit a weak, frail, decayed tenement; battered by the winds and broken in on by the storms, and, from all I can learn, the landlord does not intend to repair.
[Attr.]

Adams, Phillip (1939–)
Australian writer, columnist and broadcaster

1. [On attitudes to New Zealanders]
And while we don't exactly hate New Zealanders, we're not exactly fond of each other. While they regard us as vulgar yobboes, almost Yank-like, we think of them as second-hand, recycled Poms.
[*Age*, 1977]

Adams, Richard [1] (1846–1908)
Irish journalist, barrister and judge

1. You have been acquitted by a Limerick jury and you may now leave the dock without any other stain on your character.
[In Maurice Healy, *The Old Munster Circuit*]

Adams, Richard [2] (1920–)
English novelist

1. Many human beings say that they enjoy the winter, but what they really enjoy is feeling proof against it.
[*Watership Down* (1974), 50]

Adams, Samuel (1722–1803)
American revolutionary leader and pamphleteer

1. A nation of shop-keepers are very seldom so disinterested.
[Speech supposedly made in Philadelphia, August 1776]

Adams, Sarah Flower (1805–1848)
English poet and hymn writer

1. Nearer, my God, to Thee,
Nearer to Thee.
[Hymn]

Addams, Jane (1860–1935)
American sociologist and writer; shared Nobel peace prize, 1931

1. Old-fashioned ways which no longer apply to changed conditions are a snare in which the feet of women have always become readily entangled.
[*Newer Ideals of Peace* (1907), 'Utilization of Women in City Government']

2. Civilization is a method of living, an attitude of equal respect for all men.
[Speech, Honolulu, 1933]

Addison, Joseph (1672–1719)
English essayist, poet, playwright and statesman

1. [Of Virgil]
He delivers the meanest of his precepts with a kind of grandeur, he breaks the clods and tosses the dung about with an air of gracefulness.
[*Essay on Virgil's Georgics* (1697)]

2. [Of The Georgics]
The most complete, elaborate, and finisht piece of all antiquity.
[*Essay on Virgil's Georgics* (1697)]

3. Nothing which is a phrase or saying in common talk, should be admitted into a serious poem.
[*Essay on Virgil's Georgics* (1697)]

4. 'Tis not in mortals to command success,
But we'll do more, Sempronius; we'll deserve it.
[*Cato* (1713), I]

5. 'Tis pride, rank pride, and haughtiness of soul;
I think the Romans call it stoicism.
[*Cato* (1713), I]

6. A day, an hour of virtuous liberty
Is worth a whole eternity in bondage.
[*Cato* (1713), II]

7. Content thyself to be obscurely good.
When vice prevails, and impious men bear sway,
The post of honour is a private station.
[*Cato* (1713), IV]

8. What pity is it
That we can die but once to serve our country!
[*Cato* (1713), IV]

9. The woman that deliberates is lost.
[*Cato* (1713), IV]

10. From hence, let fierce contending nations know
What dire effects from civil discord flow.
[*Cato* (1713), V]

11. I should think my self a very bad woman, if I had done what I do, for a farthing less.
[*The Drummer* (1716), Prologue]

12. There is nothing more requisite in business than dispatch.
[*Dialogues upon the Usefulness of Ancient Medals* (1721), 5]

13. It was said of Socrates that he brought philosophy down from heaven to inhabit among men; and I shall be ambitious to have it said of me that I have brought philosophy out of closets and libraries, schools and colleges, to dwell in clubs and assemblies, at tea-tables and in coffee-houses.
[*The Spectator*, March 1711, 1]

14. A reader seldom peruses a book with pleasure until he knows whether the writer of it be a black man or a fair man, of a mild or choleric disposition, married or a bachelor.
[*The Spectator*, March 1711, 1]

15. Thus I live in the world rather as a spectator of mankind, than as one of the species, by which means I have made myself a speculative statesman, soldier, merchant, and artisan, without ever meddling with any practical part in life.
[*The Spectator*, March 1711, 1]

16. A perfect tragedy is the noblest production of human nature.
[*The Spectator*, April 1711, 39]

17. The infusion of a China plant sweetened with the pith of an Indian cane.
[*The Spectator*, May, 1711, 69]

18. Sunday clears away the rust of the whole week.
[*The Spectator*, July 1711, 112]

19. Sir Roger told them, with the air of a man who would not give his judgement rashly, that much might be said on both sides.
[*The Spectator*, July 1711, 122]

20. I have often thought, says Sir Roger, it happens very well that Christmas should fall out in the Middle of Winter.
[*The Spectator*, January 1712, 269]

21. [Of Milton]
Our language sunk under him, and was unequal to that greatness of soul which furnished him with such glorious conceptions.
[*The Spectator*, February 1712, 297]

22. The Knight in the triumph of his heart made several reflections on the greatness of the British Nation; as, that one Englishman could beat three Frenchmen; that we cou'd never be in danger of Popery so long as we took care of our fleet; that the Thames was the noblest river in Europe; that London Bridge was a greater piece of work than any of the Seven Wonders of the World; with many other honest prejudices which naturally cleave to the heart of a true Englishman.
[*The Spectator*, May 1712, 383]

23. We have in England a particular bashfulness in every thing that regards religion.
[*The Spectator*, August 1712, 458]

24. A woman seldom asks advice before she has bought her wedding clothes.
[*The Spectator*, September 1712, 475]

25. Our disputants put me in mind of the skuttle fish, that when he is unable to extricate himself, blackens all the water about him, till he becomes invisible.
[*The Spectator*, September 1712, 476]

26. I value my garden more for being full of blackbirds than of cherries, and very frankly give them fruit for their songs.
[*The Spectator*, September 1712, 477]

27. If we may believe our logicians, man is distinguished from all other creatures by the faculty of laughter.
[*The Spectator*, September 1712, 494]

28. 'We are always doing,' says he, 'something for Posterity, but I would fain see Posterity do something for us.'
[*The Spectator*, August 1714, 583]

29. I consider woman as a beautiful, romantic animal, that may be adorned with furs and feathers, pearls and diamonds, ores and silks.
[*Trial of the Petticoat*]

30. Arguments out of a pretty mouth are unanswerable.
[*Women and Liberty*]

31. [Of the difference between his conversational and writing abilities]
I have but ninepence in ready money, but I can draw for a thousand pounds.
[In Boswell, *The Life of Samuel Johnson* (1791)]

32. [Remark made of the poet Cowley]
He more had pleas'd us, had he pleas'd us less.
[Attr.]

33. Music, the greatest good that mortals know,
And all of heaven we have below.
['Song for St Cecilia's Day' (1694)]

34. For whereso'er I turn my ravished eyes,
Gay gilded scenes and shining prospects rise,
Poetic fields encompass me around,
And still I seem to tread on classic ground...

35. A painted meadow, or a purling stream.
['A Letter from Italy' (1701)]

36. And, pleas'd th' Almighty's orders to perform
Rides in the whirlwind, and directs the storm...

37. And those who paint 'em truest praise 'em most.
['The Campaign' (1704)]

38. Should the whole frame of nature round him break,
In ruin and confusion hurled,
He, unconcerned, would hear the mighty crack,
And stand secure amidst a falling world.
[Translation of Horace, Odes, III]

39. The spacious firmament on high,
With all the blue ethereal sky,
And spangled heavens, a shining frame,
Their great Original proclaim.
[*The Spectator*, August 1712, 465]

40. Forever singing as they shine,
'The Hand that made us is divine.'
[*The Spectator*, August 1712, 465]

41. See in what peace a Christian can die.
[Dying words]

Ade, George (1866–1944)
American fabulist and playwright

1. 'Whom are you?' said he, for he had been to night school.
[Attr.]

2. The music teacher came twice a week to bridge the awful gap between Dorothy and Chopin.
[Attr.]

Adenauer, Konrad (1876–1967)
German Christian Democrat Chancellor

1. *Es gibt nichts, was durch Beamte nicht wieder kaputtgemacht werden kann.*
There's nothing which cannot be made a mess of again by officials.
[Attr. by Willy Brandt, and reported in *Der Spiegel*, 1975]

2. [To his doctor]
I haven't asked you to make me young again. All I want is to go on getting older.
[Attr.]

Adler, Alfred (1870–1937)
Austrian psychiatrist and psychologist

1. The truth is often a terrible weapon of aggression. It is possible to lie, and even to murder, for the truth.
[*Problems of Neurosis* (1929), 2]

2. It is easier to fight for one's principles than to live up to them.
[Attr.]

3. [On hearing that an egocentric had fallen in love]
Against whom?
[Attr.]

Adler, Polly (1900–1962)

1. A House Is Not a Home.
[Title of memoirs, 1954]

Ady, Thomas (17th century)
British poet

1. Matthew, Mark, Luke, and John,
The bed be blest that I lie on.
Four angels to my bed,
Four angels round my head,
One to watch, and one to pray,
And two to bear my soul away.
['A Candle in the Dark' (1656)]

Aeschylus (525–456 BC)
Greek dramatist and poet

1. Zeus who leads mortals on the road to understanding, Zeus who has ordained that wisdom comes through suffering.
[*Agamemnon*, 176]

2. Helen, as befits her name, a hell to ships, a hell to men and a hell to the city.
[*Agamemnon*, 689]

3. Alas, I have been struck a deep mortal blow.
[*Agamemnon*, 1343]

4. It is a fine thing even for an old man to learn wisdom.
[*Fragments*]

5. Even he who is wiser than the wise may err.
[*Fragments*]

6. The ceaseless twinkling laughter of the waves of the sea.
[*Prometheus Bound*, 89]

7. Words are physic to the distempered mind.
[*Prometheus Bound*, 378]

8. He wishes not to seem but to be the best.
[*The Seven against Thebes*, 592]

Aesop (6th century BC)
Greek fabulist

1. Grasp at the shadow and lose the substance.
[*Fables*, 'The Dog and the Shadow']

2. The grapes are sour.
[*Fables*, 'The Fox and the Grapes']

3. Thinking to get all the gold that the goose could give in one go, he killed it, and opened it only to find – nothing.
[*Fables*, 'The Goose with the Golden Eggs']

4. The gods help those who help themselves.
[*Fables*, 'Hercules and the Waggoner']

5. I see many hoof-marks going in, but I see none coming out.
[*Fables*, 'The Lion, the Fox, and the Beasts']

6. I will have nothing to do with one who blows hot and cold with the same breath.
[*Fables*, 'The Man and the Satyr']

Aga Khan III (1877–1957)
Muslim leader

1. [Justifying his liking for alcohol]
I'm so holy that when I touch wine, it turns into water.
[Attr. in Compton Miller, *Who's Really Who* (1983)]

Agar, Herbert Sebastian (1897–1980)
American journalist and diplomat

1. The truth which makes men free is for the most part the truth which men prefer not to hear.
[*A Time for Greatness* (1942)]

Agassiz, Louis (1807–1873)
Swiss zoologist, creationist and educator

1. [On lecturing for fees]
I can't afford to waste my time making money.
[Attr.]

Agate, James (1877–1947)
English dramatic critic and novelist

1. Long experience has taught me that in England nobody goes to the theatre unless he or she has bronchitis.
[Attr.]

2. The English instinctively admire any man who has no talent and is modest about it.
[Attr.]

3. Theatre director: a person engaged by the management to conceal the fact that the players cannot act.
[Attr.]

Agathon (c. 445–400 BC)
Athenian tragic poet

1. Even God is deprived of this one thing only: the power to undo what has been done.
[In Aristotle, *Nicomachean Ethics*, VI]

Agnelli, Giovanni (1921–)
Italian industrialist, Chairman of Fiat

1. *I miracoli si possono fare, ma con il sudore.*
Miracles can be made, but only by sweating.
[*Corriere della Sera*, 1994]

Agnew, Spiro T. (1918–)
American Republican politician, vice-president under Richard Nixon

1. To some extent, if you've seen one city slum you've seen them all.
[Election speech, Detroit, October 1968]

2. [On media pundits]
In the United States today we have more than our share of the nattering nabobs of negativism. They have formed their own 4-H Club: the hopeless, hysterical hypochondriacs of history.
[Speech, San Diego, 1970; written for him by William Safire]

Ailesbury, Maria, Marchioness of (d. 1902)

1. My dear, my dear, you never know when any beautiful young lady may not blossom into a Duchess!
[In the Duke of Portland, *Men, Women, and Things* (1937)]

Ainger, A.C. (1841–1919)
English schoolteacher, author of school books and hymn writer

1. God is working His purpose out as year succeeds to year,
God is working His purpose out and the time is drawing near;
Nearer and nearer draws the time, the time that shall surely be,
When the earth shall be filled with the glory of God as the waters cover the sea.
[Hymn]

Ainger, Canon (1837–1904)
English writer, lecturer and preacher

1. No flowers, by request.
[Speech, July 1897]

Akenside, Mark (1721–1770)
English poet and physician

1. O ye Northumbrian Shades, which overlook
The rocky pavement and the mossy falls
Of solitary Wensbeck's limpid streams;
How gladly I recall your well-known seats
Beloved of old, and that delightful time
When all alone, for many a summer's day,
I wandered through your calm recesses, led
In silence by some powerful hand unseen.
[*The Pleasures of Imagination* (1744)]

Alain (Emile-Auguste Chartier) (1868–1951)
French philosopher, Professor of Rhetoric and essayist

1. *Rien n'est plus dangereux qu'une idée, quand on n'a qu'une idée.*
Nothing is more dangerous than an idea, when you only have one idea.
[*Propos sur la religion* (*Remarks on Religion*, 1938), 74]

2. There are only two kinds of scholars; those who love ideas and those who hate them.
[In Alan L. Mackay, *The Harvest of a Quiet Eye* (1977)]

Alas, Leopoldo (1852–1901)
Spanish author, journalist and critic

1. *Jamás había leído* [*don Robustiano*] *a Voltaire, pero le admiraba tanto como le aborrecía Glocester, el arcediano, que no lo había leído tampoco.*
[Don Robustiano] had never read Voltaire, but he admired him as much as Glocester, the Archdeacon, detested him, who hadn't read him either.
[*La Regenta* (*The Judge's Wife*, 1884–1885), I, 12]

2. *No basta ser bueno ... para gobernar una diócesis. Ni los poetas sirven para ministros, ni los místicos para obispos.*
Being good isn't enough ... to rule a diocese. Neither are poets any use as government ministers, nor are mystics any use as bishops.
[*La Regenta* (*The Judge's Wife*, 1884–1885), I, 12]

Albee, Edward (1928–)
American dramatist

1. Who's Afraid of Virginia Woolf?
[Title of play, 1962]

2. I have a fine sense of the ridiculous, but no sense of humour.
[*Who's Afraid of Virginia Woolf?* (1962), I]

3. You gotta have a swine to show you where the truffles are.
[*Who's Afraid of Virginia Woolf?* (1962), II]

Alberoni, Francesco (1929–)

1. *La ricchezza vera si crea ogni giorno, a fatica.*
True richness is made day by day, with great effort.
[*Corriere della Sera*, 1994]

Albert, Prince Consort (1819–1861)
German-born Prince Consort of Queen Victoria

1. The works of art, by being publicly exhibited and offered for sale, are becoming articles of trade, following as such the unreasoning laws of markets and fashion; and public and even private patronage is swayed by their tyrannical influence.
[Speech to the Royal Academy, May 1851]

Albertano of Brescia (c. 1190–c. 1270)
Jurist, philosopher, magistrate and politician

1. *Iratus semper plus putat posse facere quam possit.*
The angry man always thinks he can do more than he can.
[*Liber Consolationis*]

2. *Qui omnes despicit, omnibus displicet.*
Who despises all, displeases all.
[*Liber Consolationis*]

Alcott, Bronson (1799–1888)
American educator, reformer and transcendentalist

1. A sip is the most that mortals are permitted from any goblet of delight.
[*Table Talk* (1877), 'Habits']

2. Civilization degrades the many to exalt the few.
[*Table Talk* (1877), 'Pursuits']

Alcott, Louisa May (1832–1888)
American writer and children's novelist

1. Housekeeping ain't no joke.
[*Little Women*, Part I (1868)]

2. ... girls are so queer you never know what they mean. They say No when they mean Yes, and drive a man out of his wits for the fun of it...
[*Little Women*, Part II (1869)]

3. It takes people a long time to learn the difference between talent and genius, especially ambitious young men and women.
[*Little Women*, Part II (1869)]

Alcuin (735–804)
English theologian, man of letters and educationist

1. *Nec audiendi qui solent dicere, Vox populi, vox Dei, quum tumultuositas vulgi semper insaniae proxima sit.*
Nor should those be heeded who are wont to say 'The voice of the people is the voice of God', since popular uproar is always akin to madness.
[Letter to Charlemagne]

Aldiss, Brian (1925–)
English science fiction writer

1. Science fiction is no more written for scientists than ghost stories are written for ghosts.
[*Penguin Science Fiction* (1961), Introduction]

Aldrich, Henry (1647–1710)
English scholar, divine and composer of songs

1. If all be true that I do think,
There are five reasons we should drink;
Good wine – a friend – or being dry–
Or lest we should be by and by–
Or any other reason why.
['Five Reasons for Drinking' (1689)]

Alea, Tomás Gutiérrez

1. *Humillar a Fidel es humillar a Cuba.*
To humiliate Fidel is to humiliate Cuba.
[Interview in *El País*, 1994]

Alexander the Great (356–323 BC)
Macedonian king and conquering army commander

1. [At Achilles' tomb]
O fortunate adolescens qui tuae virtutis Homerum praeconem inveneris.
O fortunate youth, to have found in Homer the herald of your valour.
[In Cicero, *Pro Archia*]

2. The earth cannot brook two suns, nor Asia two Kings.
[In Plutarch, *Sayings of Kings and Commanders*]

3. I would rather excel in the knowledge of what is excellent, than in the extent of my power.
[In Plutarch's *Lives*, 'Alexander']

4. If I were not Alexander, I would be Diogenes.
[In Plutarch's *Lives*, 'Alexander']

5. Alexander wept on hearing from Anaxarchus that there was an infinite number of worlds ... 'Do you not think it lamentable that with such an infinite number, we have not yet conquered one?'
[In Plutarch, *On the Tranquillity of the Mind*]

6. I am dying with the help of too many physicians.
[Attr.]

Alexander, Cecil Frances (1818–1895)
Irish poet and hymn writer

1. All things bright and beautiful,
All creatures great and small,
All things wise and wonderful,
The Lord God made them all...

2. The rich man in his castle,
The poor man at his gate,
God made them, high or lowly,
And order'd their estate.
[Hymn]

3. Jesus calls us; o'er the tumult
Of our life's wild restless sea.
[Hymn]

4. Once in royal David's city
Stood a lowly cattle shed,
Where a Mother laid her Baby
In a manger for His bed:
Mary was that Mother mild,
Jesus Christ her little Child.
[Hymn]

5. There is a green hill far away,
Without a city wall,
Where the dear Lord was crucified,
Who died to save us all.
[Hymn]

Alexander, Hilary
British journalist

1. To the accountants, a true work of art is an investment that hangs on the wall.
[*Sunday Telegraph*, 1993]

Alexander, Sir William, Earl of Stirling (c. 1567–1640)
Scottish poet, courtier and statesman

1. The weaker sex, to piety more prone.
[*Doomsday* (1614), Hour V]

Alfonso X (1221–1284)
King of Castile and Léon; legal reformer

1. [On the Ptolemaic system of astronomy]
If the Lord Almighty had consulted me before embarking upon Creation, I should have recommended something simpler.
[Attr.]

Algren, Nelson (1909–1981)
American writer

1. A Walk on the Wild Side.
[Title of novel, 1956]

2. Never eat at a place called Mom's. Never play cards with a man called Doc. Never go to bed with a woman whose troubles are greater than your own.
[*A Walk on the Wild Side* (1956)]

Ali, Muhammad (Cassius Clay) (1942–)
American heavyweight boxer

1. Float like a butterfly, sting like a bee.
[Catchphrase]

2. I am the greatest.
[Catchphrase]

3. You don't want no pie in the sky when you die,
You want something here on the ground while you're still around.
[Attr.]

4. [Announcing his retirement]
I want to get out with my greatness intact.
[*The Observer*, 1974]

Allainval, Abbé d' (c. 1700–1753)
French dramatist

1. *L'Embarras des Richesses.*
The embarrassment of riches.
[Title of play, 1725]

Allbeury, Ted (Theodore Edward Le Bouthillier) (1917–)
English crime writer

1. The real stuff's inside. Whether you want your porn in black and white, full-colour litho, on film or on gramophone records and in any one of five languages, this is Stockholm's place for connoisseurs. There are no pictures of old slags and tattooed sailors here. The girls in the pictures are young and pretty and even the Great Danes are registered at the Swedish Kennel Club.
[*Snowball* (1976)]

Allen, Dave (1936–)
Irish comedian and TV personality

1. New Zealanders are the most balanced people in the world – they have a chip on each shoulder.
[A regular joke during his New Zealand tour, 1978]

2. If I had a head like yours, I'd have it circumcised.
[In Gus Smith, *God's Own Comedian*]

3. The foreman says, 'You must have an intelligence test.' The Irishman says, 'All right.' So the foreman says, 'What is the difference between joist and girder?' And the Irishman says, 'Joyce wrote *Ulysses* and Goethe wrote *Faust*.'
[Re-telling the only Irish joke he really liked, quoted in Gus Smith, *God's Own Comedian*]

4. If John Major was drowning, his whole life would pass in front of him and he wouldn't be in it.
[On stage, 1991, quoted in *The Independent*, 1993]

5. I still think of myself as I was 25 years ago. Then I look in a mirror and see an old bastard and I realise it's me.
[*The Independent*, 1993]

6. [Referring to the nuns who educated him]
The Gestapo in drag.
[Attr.]

Allen, Fred (1894–1956)
American vaudeville performer and comedian

1. A celebrity is a person who works hard all his life to become known, then wears dark glasses to avoid being recognized.
[Attr.]

2. A gentleman is any man who wouldn't hit a woman with his hat on.
[Attr.]

3. [Remark to writers who had heavily edited one of his scripts]
Where were you fellows when the paper was blank?
[Attr.]

Allen, Woody (Allen Stewart Konigsberg) (1935–)
American film director, writer, actor and comedian

1. It was partially my fault that we got divorced ... I tended to place my wife under a pedestal.
[At a nightclub in Chicago, 1964]

2. Not only is there no God, but try getting a plumber on weekends.
[*Getting Even* (1971), 'My Philosophy']

3. Is sex dirty? Only if it's done right.
[*Everything You Always Wanted to Know About Sex*, film, 1972]

4. I'm short enough and ugly enough to succeed on my own.
[*Play It Again, Sam*, film, 1972]

5. I'm really a timid person – I was beaten up by Quakers.
[*Sleeper*, film, 1973]

6. My brain: it's my second favourite organ.
[*Sleeper*, film, 1973]

7. [Of God]
The worst that can be said is that he's an under-achiever.
[*Love and Death*, film, 1976]

8. It's not that I'm afraid to die. I just don't want to be there when it happens.
[*Without Feathers* (1976)]

9. The lion and the calf shall lie down together but the calf won't get much sleep.
[*Without Feathers* (1976)]

10. If only God would give me some clear sign! Like making a large deposit in my name at a Swiss bank.
[*Without Feathers* (1976)]

11. Hey, don't knock masturbation! It's sex with someone I love.
[*Annie Hall*, film, 1977]

12. [Referring to sex]
It was the most fun I ever had without laughing.
[*Annie Hall*, film, 1977]

13. And my parents finally realize that I'm kidnapped and they snap into action immediately: they rent out my room.
[In Eric Lax, *Woody Allen* (1991)]

14. I want to tell you a terrific story about oral contraception. I asked this girl to sleep with me and she said 'no'.
[Attr.]

15. I don't want to achieve immortality through my work ... I want to achieve it by not dying.
[Attr.]

Alley, Rewi (1897–1987)
New Zealand reformer and educationist, particularly concerned with the Chinese

1. [The motto of the Chinese Industrial Co-operatives Association, coined in 1938]
Gung Ho!
Work Together!
[In Geoff Chapple, *Rewi Alley of China* (1980)]

Allingham, Margery (1904–1966)
British writer of crime fiction

1. [A favourite comment of Magersfontein Lugg, his [Campion's] oldest and least presentable friend]
Up the well-known creek.
[*The Mind Readers* (1965)]

Allingham, William (1824–1889)
Irish poet and diarist

1. Up the airy mountain,
Down the rushy glen,
We daren't go a-hunting,
For fear of little men.
['The Fairies' (1883)]

2. Four ducks on a pond,
A grass-bank beyond,
A blue sky of spring,
White clouds on the wing:
What a little thing
To remember for years–
To remember with tears.
['A Memory' (1888)]

3. Two leaps the water from its race
Made to the brook below,
The first leap it was curving glass,
The second bounding snow.
[*By the Way. Verses, Fragments and Notes* (1912), 'A Mill']

4. Not men and women in an Irish street
But Catholics and Protestants you meet.
[Attr.]

Altman, Robert (1922–)
American film director

1. What's a cult? It just means not enough people to make a minority.
[*The Observer*, 1981]

Altrincham, Lord (John Grigg) (1924–)
English columnist and writer

1. [On Queen Elizabeth II's style when speaking in public]
The personality conveyed by the utterances which are put into her mouth is that of a priggish schoolgirl, captain of the hockey team, a prefect, and a recent candidate for confirmation. It is not thus that she will be able to come into her own as an independent and distinctive character.
[*National and English Review*, August 1958]

Ambrose, Saint (c. 340–397)
French-born Bishop of Milan, writer of music and hymns

1. *Ubi Petrus, ibi ergo ecclesia.*
Where Peter is, there of necessity is the Church.
[*Explanatio psalmi 40*]

2. *Si fueris Romae, Romano vivito more;*
Si fueris alibi, vivito sicut ibi.
If you are in Rome, live in the Roman fashion; if you are elsewhere, live as they do there.
[In Jeremy Taylor, *Ductor Dubitantium* (1660)]

Amery, Leo (1873–1955)
English Conservative politician, statesman and writer

1. Speak for England, Arthur!
[Interjection in House of Commons, 1939]

2. [To Neville Chamberlain, quoting Cromwell's words when he dismissed the Rump of the Long Parliament in 1653]
You have sat too long here for any good you have been doing. Depart, I say, and let us have done with you. In the name of God, go!
[Speech, House of Commons, May 1940]

Ames, Fisher (1758–1808)
American Federalist statesman and essayist

1. A monarchy is a merchantman which sails well, but will sometimes strike on a rock, and go to the bottom; a republic is a raft which will never sink, but then your feet are always in the water.
[Attr.]

Amiel, Henri-Frédéric (1821–1881)
Swiss moral philosopher, diarist and writer

1. Action is but coarsened thought – thought become concrete, obscure, and unconscious.
[*Journal*, 1850]

2. The age of great men is going; the epoch of the ant-hill, of life in multiplicity, is beginning.
[*Journal*, 1851]

3. Every life is a profession of faith, and exercises an inevitable and silent influence.
[*Journal*, 1852]

4. A belief is not true because it is useful.
[*Journal*, 1876]

Amin, Idi (1925)
Ugandan soldier, dictator and Head of State

1. [Public message to Lord Snowdon, when his marriage to Princess Margaret broke up]
Your experience will be a lesson to all of us men to be careful not to marry ladies in very high positions.
[In A. Barrow, *International Gossip* (1983)]

Amis, Kingsley (1922–)
English writer, satirical novelist, poet and critic

1. Lucky Jim.
[Title of novel, 1954]

2. [On the delusion that thousands of young people were capable of benefiting from university training but had somehow failed to find their way there]
I wish I could have a little tape-and-loudspeaker arrangement sewn into the binding of this magazine, to be triggered off by the light reflected from the reader's eyes on to this part of the page, and set to bawl out at several bels: MORE WILL MEAN WORSE.
[*Encounter*, July 1960]

3. Outside every fat man there was an even fatter man trying to close in.
[*One Fat Englishman* (1963), 3. Cf. Orwell: 7 and Evelyn Waugh: 29]

4. It was no wonder that people were so horrible when they started life as children.
[*One Fat Englishman* (1963), 14]

5. Generally, nobody behaves decently when they have power.
[*Radio Times*, 1992]

Amis, Martin (1949–)
English satirical novelist, son of writer Kingsley Amis

1. Not only are all characters and scenes in this book entirely fictitious; most of the technical, medical and psychological data are too. My working maxim here has been as follows: I may not know much about science but I know what I like.
[*Dead Babies* (1975), author's note]

Andersen, Hans Christian (1805–1875)
Danish novelist, dramatist and children's writer

1. The Ugly Duckling.
[Story title, c. 1843]

2. 'But the Emperor has nothing on at all!' cried a little child.
[*The Emperor's New Clothes* (c. 1843)]

3. Every man's life is a fairy-tale written by God's fingers.
[*Works* (c. 1843), Preface]

4. [Of the music to be played at his funeral]
Most of the people who walk after me will be children; make the beat keep time with little steps.
[In R. Godden, *Hans Christian Andersen* (1955)]

Andreotti, Giulio (1919–)
Italian statesman, former Prime Minister of Italy

1. *Se avessi delle royalties sulla frase che ho detto una volta sarei ricchissimo. Il potere logora chi non ce l'ha.*
If I had been given royalties on this statement that I once made, I would be very rich. Power wears down the man who doesn't have it.
[In E. Biagi, *Buoni e Cattivi* (*The Good and the Bad*, 1989), 'Che cosè il potere?' ('What is power?')]

Andrewes, Bishop Lancelot (1555–1626)
English preacher, writer of sermons and Bishop of Winchester

1. O! whether was greater humility or charity in Him! hard to say whether, but both unspeakable.
[*Sermon 9, Of the Nativity* (c. 1614)]

2. What gets God by *nobiscum?* Nothing He. What get we?
[*Sermon 9, Of the Nativity* (c. 1614)]

3. It was no summer progress. A cold coming they had of it, at this time of the year; just, the worst time of the year, to take a journey, and specially a long journey, in. The ways deep, the weather sharp, the days short, the sun farthest off *in solstitio brumali*, the very dead of Winter.
[*Sermon 15, Of the Nativity* (1629). Cf. T.S. Eliot: 60]

4. The nearer the Church the further from God.
[*Sermon 15, Of the Nativity* (1629)]

Andrews, Elizabeth

1. [Said when an intruder was found in Queen Elizabeth II's bedroom]
Bloody hell, Ma'am, what's he doing here?
[*Daily Mail*, 1982]

Angell, Norman (1872–1967)
English publicist, Labour politician and Nobel peace prize winner

1. The Great Illusion.
[Title of book, 1910, which argued against the concept that war was economically advantageous to a nation]

Angelou, Maya (1928–)
American novelist, poet and dramatist

1. I Know Why the Caged Bird Sings.
[Title of book, 1969; taken from Paul Lawrence Dunbar, 'Sympathy']

2. History, faced with courage, need not be lived again.
[Speech at the Inauguration of President Clinton, 1993]

Anka, Paul (1941–)
American pop singer and songwriter

1. And now the end is near
And so I face the final curtain,
My friends, I'll say it clear,
I'll state my case of which I'm certain.
I've lived a life that's full, I've travelled each and every highway
And more, much more than this, I did it my way.
['My Way', song, 1969]

Anne, the Princess Royal (1950–)
Daughter of Queen Elizabeth; horsewoman; President of Save the Children Fund

1. [In a statement to the press, a few days before her engagement to Captain Mark Phillips]
There is no romance between us. He is here solely to exercise the horses.
[Attr., 1973]

2. [Describing her first encounter with a horse]
One was presented with a small, hairy individual and, out of general curiosity, one climbed on.
[*Princess Anne and Mark Phillips Talking Horses with Genevieve Murphy* (1976)]

3. When I appear in public people expect me to neigh, grind my teeth, paw the ground and swish my tail – none of which is easy.
[*The Observer*, 'Sayings of the Week', 1977]

4. [On pregnancy]
It's a very boring time. I am not particularly maternal, it's an occupational hazard of being a wife.
[TV interview, quoted in the *Daily Express*, 1981]

5. [Remark to press photographers at the Badminton horse trials]
Why don't you naff off!
[*Daily Mirror*, 1982]

Annenberg, Walter (1908–)
American publisher and diplomat

1. [Reply to Queen Elizabeth II, when she asked him about his accommodation as Ambassador to the Court of St James]
We're in the Embassy residence, subject, of course, to some of the discomfiture as a result of a need for, uh, elements of refurbishment and rehabilitation.
[*Royal Family*, TV film, 1969]

Anonymous

Songs and hymns

1. *Ah! ça ira, ça ira, ça ira,*
Les aristocrates à la lanterne.
Oh, so it goes, so it goes, so it goes!
The aristocrats will hang.
[Refrain of the French Revolution. Cf. Vallentin: 1]

2. The animals went in one by one,
There's one more river to cross.
['One More River to Cross', song, 1865]

3. As I came down through Conroy's Gap
I heard a maiden cry,
'There goes old Bill the Bullocky,
And he's bound for Gundagai.'
A better poor old bugger
Never cracked an honest crust.
A tougher poor old bugger
Never drug a whip through dust.

Now his team got bogged on the Five-Mile Creek.
Bill lashed and swore and cried,
'If Nobby don't get me out of this,
I'll tattoo his bloody hide;'
But Nobby strained and broke his yoke,
Poked out the poler's eye,
And the dog – he *shat* in the tuckerbox,
Five miles from Gundagai!
[In Russel Ward, *A Radical Life*, 'Bullock-Driver's Song']

4. As I sat on a sunny bank,
On Christmas Day in the morning,
I spied three ships come sailing by.
['On Christmas Day in the Morning']

5. *Ave verum corpus,*
Natum ex Maria Virgine.
Hail the true body, born of the Virgin Mary.
[Eucharistic hymn, dating probably from the 14th century]

6. Begone, dull Care! I prithee begone from me!
Begone, dull Care! Thou and I shall never agree.
['Begone, Dull Care', song, 17th century]

7. The Campbells are comin', oho, oho.
['The Campbells are Comin' ', song, 1745; lyrics by Robert Burns based on earlier versions]

8. Come landlord, fill the flowing bowl,
Until it doth run over...
For tonight we'll merry, merry be,
Tomorrow we'll be sober.
['Come, Landlord, Fill the Flowing Bowl', traditional song]

9. Come lasses and lads, get leave of your dads,
And away to the Maypole hie,
For every he has got him a she,
And the fiddler's standing by.
['Come Lasses and Lads', song, c. 1670]

10. Early one morning, just as the sun was rising,
I heard a maid singing in the valley below:
'Oh, don't deceive me; Oh, never leave me!
How could you use a poor maiden so?'
['Early One Morning', traditional song]

11. Frankie and Johnny were lovers, my gawd, how they could love,
Swore to be true to each other, true as the stars above;
He was her man, but he done her wrong.
['Frankie and Johnny', song, c. 1870–1875]

12. *Gaudeamus igitur,*
Juvenes dum sumus
Post jucundam juventutem,
Post molestam senectutem,
Nos habebit humus.
Let us be happy while we are young, for after carefree youth and careworn age, the earth will hold us also.
['Gaudeamus Igitur', students' song, traced to 1267]

13. God rest you merry, gentlemen,
Let nothing you dismay;
Remember Christ our Saviour,
Who was born on Christmas Day.
['God Rest You', carol]

14. Greensleeves was all my joy,
Greensleeves was my delight,
Greensleeves was my heart of gold,
And who but my Lady Greensleeves?
['A New Courtly Sonnet of the Lady Greensleeves', possibly by King Henry VIII]

15. Here's a health unto his Majesty...
Confusion to his enemies...
And he that will not drink his health,
I wish him neither wit nor wealth,
Not yet a rope to hang himself.
['Here's a Health unto his Majesty', song]

16. Here we come a-wassailing.
['Here We Come A-Wassailing', carol]

17. Here we come gathering nuts in May
Nuts in May...
On a cold and frosty morning.
['Nuts in May', children's song]

18. He was a wight of high renown,
And thou's but of low degree.
It's pride that puts this country down:
Man, put thy old cloak about thee!
['The Old Cloak', sung in *Othello*]

19. Hitler
Has only got one ball!
Goering
Has two, but very small!
Himmler
Has something similar,
But poor old Goebbels
Has no balls at all!
[Second World War song (to the tune of Colonel Bogey)]

20. The holly and the ivy,
When they are both full grown,
Of all the trees that are in the wood,
The holly bears the crown.
The rising of the sun
And the running of the deer,
The playing of the merry organ,
Sweet singing in the choir.
['The Holly and the Ivy', carol]

21. I can not eat but little meat,
My stomach is not good:
But sure I think, that I can drink
With him that wears a hood.
Though I go bare, take ye no care,
I am nothing acold:
I stuff my skin, so full within,
Of jolly good ale and old,
Back and side go bare, go bare,
Both foot and hand go cold:
But belly God send thee good ale enough,
Whether it be new or old.
[Song from *Gammer Gurton's Needle* (1575)]

22. I'll sing you twelve O
Green grow the rushes O.
['Green Grow the Rushes O', traditional song]

23. I met wid Napper Tandy, and he took me by the hand,
And he said, 'How's poor ould Ireland, and how does she stand?'
She's the most disthressful country that iver yet was seen,
For they're hangin' men an' women there for the wearin' o' the Green.
['The Wearin' o' the Green', traditional street ballad, c. 1795]

24. In Dublin's fair city, where the girls are so pretty,
I first set my eyes on sweet Molly Malone,
As she wheeled her wheelbarrow, through streets broad and narrow,
Crying, Cockles and mussels! alive, alive, O!

She was a fishmonger, but sure 'twas no wonder,
For so were her father and mother before.
['Cockles and Mussels', song, c. 1750]

25. In good King Charles's golden days,
When loyalty no harm meant,
A zealous High Churchman was I,
And so I got preferment.

Unto my flock I daily preached,
Kings are by God appointed,
And damned are those who dare resist,
Or touch the Lord's Anointed.

And this is law, I will maintain,
Unto my dying day, Sir,
That whatsoever King shall reign,
I will be the Vicar of Bray, Sir.
['The Vicar of Bray', song, c. 1728]

26. I sing of a maiden
That is makeles;
King of all kings
To her son she ches.
[Carol]

27. It is good to be merry and wise,
It is good to be honest and true,
It is best to be off with the old love,
Before you are on with the new.
[*Songs of England and Scotland*, 'It is good to be merry and wise']

28. Like a fine old English gentleman,
All of the olden time.
[*Oxford Song Book*, 'The Fine Old English Gentleman']

29. My Bonnie lies over the ocean,
My Bonnie lies over the sea,
My Bonnie lies over the ocean,
Oh, bring back my Bonnie to me.
['My Bonnie', song, 1881]

30. My eyes are dim
I cannot see
I have not brought my specs with me.
['In the Quartermaster's Stores']

31. Now I am a bachelor, I live by myself and I work at the weaving trade,
And the only only thing that I ever did wrong
Was to woo a fair young maid.

She sighed, she cried, she damned near died: she said 'What shall I do?'
So I took her into bed and covered up her head
Just to save her from the foggy, foggy dew.
['Weaver's Song']

32. O Death, where is thy sting-a-ling-a-ling,
O Grave, thy victoree?
The bells of Hell go ting-a-ling-a-ling
For you but not for me.
[British Army song of the 1914–1918 War]

33. Oh, 'tis my delight on a shining night, in the season of the year.
['The Lincolnshire Poacher', song]

34. O, No, John! No, John! No, John! No!
['O No, John']

35. O, Shenandoah, I long to hear you
Away, you rolling river.
['Shenandoah', song, c. 1826]

36. O ye'll tak' the high road, and I'll tak' the low road,
And I'll be in Scotland afore ye,
But me and my true love will never meet again,
On the bonnie, bonnie banks o' Loch Lomon'.
['Loch Lomond', song, 1881]

37. *Salve, regina, mater misericordiae,*
Vita, dulcedo et spes nostra, salve!
Ad te clamamus exsules filii Evae,
Ad te suspiramus gementes et flentes
In hac lacrimarum valle.
Eia ergo, advocata nostra,
Illos tuos misericordes oculos ad nos converte.
Et Iesum, benedictum fructum ventris tui,
Nobis post hoc exsilium ostende,
O clemens, o pia,
O dulcis virgo Maria.
Hail holy queen, mother of mercy, hail our life, our sweetness, and our hope! To thee do we cry, poor banished children of Eve; to thee do we send up our sighs, mourning and weeping in this vale of tears. Turn then, most gracious advocate, thine eyes of mercy towards us; and after this our exile show unto us the blessed fruit of thy womb, Jesus, O clement, O loving, O sweet virgin Mary.
[Attr. to various 11th-century authors]

38. She was poor but she was honest
Victim of a rich man's game.
First he loved her, then he left her,
And she lost her maiden name.

See her on the bridge at midnight,
Saying 'Farewell, blighted love.'
Then a scream, a splash and goodness,
What is she a-doin' of?

It's the same the whole world over,
It's the poor wot gets the blame,
It's the rich wot gets the gravy.
Ain't it all a bleedin' shame?
['She was Poor but she was Honest', song of the 1914–1918 War]

39. The singer not the song.
[From a West Indian calypso; taken as title of a novel in 1959 by Audrey Erskine Lindop]

40. Some talk of Alexander, and some of Hercules,
Of Hector and Lysander, and such great names as these;
But of all the world's brave heroes there's none that can compare
With a tow, row, row, row, row, row for the British Grenadier.
['The British Grenadiers', song, c. 1750]

41. Summer is icumen in,
Lhude sing cuccu!
Groweth sed, and bloweth med,
And springeth the wude nu.
['Cuckoo Song', c. 1250. Cf. Pound:12]

42. Swing low sweet chariot,
Comin' for to carry me home,
I looked over Jordan an' what did I see?
A band of Angels coming after me,
Comin' for to carry me home.
['Swing Low, Sweet Chariot', song, 1917]

43. *Te Deum laudamus: Te Dominum confitemur...*
We praise thee, God: we own thee Lord...

44. *In te Domine, speravi: non confundar in aeternum.*
Lord, I have set my hopes in thee, I shall not be destroyed for ever.
['Te Deum', hymn]

45. Therefore let us sing and dance a galliard,
To the remembrance of the mallard:
And as the mallard dives in pool,
Let us dabble, dive, and duck in Bowl.
Oh! by the blood of Kind Edward,
Oh! by the blood of Kind Edward,
It was a swapping, swapping mallard.
[All Souls College, Oxford, song, possibly of Tudor origins]

46. There is a tavern in the town,
And there my dear love sits him down,
And drinks his wine 'mid laughter free,
And never, never thinks of me.

Fare thee well, for I must leave thee,
Do not let this parting grieve thee,
And remember that the best of friends must part.

Adieu, adieu, kind friends, adieu, adieu, adieu,
I can no longer stay with you, stay with you.
I'll hang my harp on a weeping willow-tree.
And may the world go well with thee.
['There is a Tavern in the Town', song, 1883]

47. Weep you no more, sad fountains;
What need you flow so fast?
[Lute song set to music by John Dowland]

48. We're here because we're here because we're here because we're here.
[American song of the 1914–1918 War]

49. What shall we do with the drunken sailor
Early in the morning?

Hoo-ray and up she rises
Early in the morning.
['What Shall We Do with the Drunken Sailor?', song]

50. When Israel was in Egypt land,
Let my people go,
Oppressed so hard they could not stand,
Let my people go.
Go down, Moses,
Way-down in Egypt land,
Tell old Pharaoh
To let my people go.
['Let My People Go', song]

Verse

51. [On the antiquity of Microbes]
Adam
Had 'em.
[Claimed as the shortest poem]

52. Adam lay I-bowndyn, bowndyn in a bond,
Fowre thowsand wynter thowt he not to long;
And al was for an appil, an appil that he tok,
As clerkis fyndin wretyn in here book.
['Bless the Time the Apple was Taken!']

53. Australian-born,
Australian-bred,
Long in the legs
And short in the head.
[Traditional Australian bush saying]

54. An Austrian army, awfully arrayed,
Boldly by battery besieged Belgrade.
Cossack commanders cannonading come
Dealing destruction, death's dreadful doom.
[*The Trifler*, 'Siege of Belgrade'; progressive alliterative rhyme]

55. A was an apple-pie;
B bit it;
C cut it.
[In John Eachard, *Some Observations* (1671)]

56. Beauing, belle-ing, dancing, drinking,
Breaking windows, damning,
Ever raking, never thinking
Live the rakes of Mallow.
['The Rakes of Mallow' (19th century)]

57. Boxty in the fireplace, boxty in the pan;
If you can't make boxty, you'll never get a man.
[Northern Irish rhyme]

58. Bring us in no browne bred, for that is made of brane,
Nor bring us in no white bred, for therein is no gane,
But bring us in good ale!
['Bring us in Good Ale']

59. But at the coming of the King of Heaven
All's set at six and seven:
We wallow in our sin.
Christ cannot find a chamber in the inn.
We entertain Him always like a stranger,
And as at first still lodge Him in the manger.
[From Christ Church MS]

60. Christmas is coming, the geese are getting fat,
Please to put a penny in the old man's hat;
If you haven't got a penny, a ha'penny will do,
If you haven't got a ha'penny, God bless you!
[Beggar's rhyme]

61. Dear Sir, Your astonishment's odd:
I am always about in the Quad.
And that's why the tree
Will continue to be,
Since observed by Yours faithfully, God.
[Reply to Ronald Knox, 'There was once a man']

62. Everyman, I will go with thee, and be thy guide,
In thy most need to go by thy side.
[*Everyman*]

63. Farewell all joys! O death, come close mine eyes;
More geese than men now live, more fools than wise.
[*Faber Book of Children's Verse*, 'The Silver Swan']

64. Farewell and adieu to you,
Fair Spanish Ladies,
Farewell and adieu to you, Ladies of Spain.
['Spanish Ladies']

65. The fault is great in man or woman
Who steals a goose from off a common;
But what can plead that man's excuse
Who steals a common from a goose?
[*The Tickler Magazine*, 1 February 1821. Cf. Anon.: 77]

66. God be in my head,
And in my understanding;
God be in my eyes,
And in my looking;
God be in my mouth,
And in my speaking;
God be in my heart,
And in my thinking;
God be at my end,
And at my departing.
[Sarum Missal]

67. Hark the herald angels sing
Mrs Simpson's pinched our king.
[Quoted by Clement Attlee in a letter of 26 December 1938]

68. Hath wine an oblivious power?
Can it pluck out the sting from the brain?
The draught might beguile for an hour,
But still leaves behind it the pain.
['Farewell to England'; sometimes attr. to Byron]

69. He tickles this age that can
Call Tullia's ape a marmasyte
And Leda's goose a swan.
['Fara diddle dyno']

70. I always eat peas with honey
I've done it all my life,
They do taste kind of funny,
But it keeps them on the knife.
['Peas']

71. If all the world were paper,
And all the sea were ink;
If all the trees were bread and cheese
How should we do for drink?
[17th century]

72. I feel no pain dear mother now
But oh, I am so dry!
O take me to a brewery
And leave me there to die.
[Parody of Edward Farmer, 'The Collier's Dying Child']

73. I know two things about the horse,
And one of them is rather coarse.
['The Horse']

74. *Il y avait un jeune homme de Dijon,*
Qui n'avait que peu de religion.
Il dit: 'Quant à moi,

Je déteste tous les trois,
Le Père, et le Fils, et le Pigeon.'
There was a young man from Dijon,
Who had little, if any, religion.
He said, 'As for me,
I detest all three,
The Father, the Son, and the Pigeon.'
[*The Norman Douglas Limerick Book* (1969), Introduction]

75. In his chamber, weak and dying,
While the Norman Baron lay,
Loud, without, his men were crying,
'Shorter hours and better pay.'
['A Strike among the Poets']

76. John Wayne is dead
[with a denial]:
The hell I am
[Inscription on a wall in Bermondsey Antique Market, *Evening Standard*, 1980]

77. The law doth punish man or woman
That steals the goose from off the common,
But lets the greater felon loose,
That steals the common from the goose.
[On enclosures, 18th Century. Cf. Anon.: 65]

78. Lenten ys come with love to toune, with blosmen and with briddes roune.
['Lenten is Come with Love to Town']

79. Little Willy from his mirror
Licked the mercury right off,
Thinking in his childish error,
It would cure the whooping cough.
At the funeral his mother
Smartly said to Mrs Brown:
' 'Twas a chilly day for Willie
When the mercury went down'.
['Willie's Epitaph']

80. Lizzie Borden took an axe
And gave her mother forty whacks;
When she saw what she had done
She gave her father forty-one.
['Lizzie Borden']

81. Matthew, Mark, Luke, and John,
The Bed be blest that I lie on.
Four angels to my bed,
Four angels round my head,
One to watch, and one to pray,
And two to bear my soul away.
[In Thomas Ady, *A Candle in the Dark* (1656)]

82. Miss Buss and Miss Beale
Cupid's darts do not feel.
How different from us,
Miss Beale and Miss Buss.
[Of the Headmistress of the North London Collegiate School and the Principal of the Ladies' College, Cheltenham]

83. Most Gracious Queen, we thee implore
To go away and sin no more,
But if that effort be too great,
To go away at any rate.
[Epigram on Queen Caroline, quoted in Lord Colchester's Diary, 1820]

84. Multiplication is vexation,
Division is as bad;
The rule of three doth puzzle me,
And practice drives me mad.
[Elizabethan rhyme]

85. My lover looked like an eagle from the distance, but alas
When he came nearer I saw that he was nothing but a buzzard.
[In John Robert Colombo (ed.), *Songs of the Great Land*, 'Song of a Maiden Disappointed in Love', Blackfoot poem]

86. My name is George Nathaniel Curzon,
I am a most superior person.
[*The Masque of Balliol* (c. 1870)]

87. Now I lay me down to sleep;
I pray the Lord my soul to keep.
If I should die before I wake,
I pray the Lord my soul to take.
[Traditional prayer]

88. Oh! where is my wandering boy to-night?
The boy who was bravest of all.
['Oh! Where is my Boy To-night?']

89. The rabbit has a charming face;
Its private life is a disgrace.
['The Rabbit']

90. A rainbow in the morning
Is the Shepherd's warning;
But a rainbow at night
Is the Shepherd's delight.
[Old weather rhyme]

91. A red sky at night
Is the Shepherd's delight;
But a red sky in the morning
Is the Shepherd's warning.
[Old weather rhyme, variant]

92. Roseberry to his lady says,
'My hinny and my succour,
O shall we do the thing you ken,
Or shall we take our supper?'

Wi' modest face, sae fu' o' grace,
Replied the bonny lady;
'My noble lord do as you please,
But supper is na ready.'
['Supper is na Ready'; collected by Burns and included in *The Merry Muses of Caledonia* (c. 1800)]

93. See the happy moron,
He doesn't give a damn,
I wish I were a moron,
My God! perhaps I am!
[*Eugenics Review*, 1929]

94. Seven wealthy Towns contend for Homer Dead
Through which the living Homer begged his Bread.
[*Aesop at Tunbridge* (1698). Cf. Thomas Heywood: 2]

95. The sons of the prophet were brave men and bold,
And quite unaccustomed to fear,
But the bravest by far in the ranks of the Shah
Was Abdul Abulbul Amir.
['Abdul Abulbul Amir'; also attrib. to Percy French]

96. [Of Sir Francis Drake]
The Sun himself cannot forget
His fellow traveller.
[*Wit's Recreations* (1640)]

97. There is a lady sweet and kind,
Was never face so pleased my mind;
I did but see her passing by,
And yet I love her till I die.
[Verse found on the back of leaf 53 of 'Popish Kingdome or reigne of Antichrist']

98. There is so much good in the worst of us,
And so much bad in the best of us,
That it hardly becomes any of us
To talk about the rest of us.
[Variously attr.]

99. There's a wicked wind tonight,
Wild upheaval in the sea;
No fear now that the Viking hordes
Will terrify me.
['The Viking Terror', translated by Brendan Kennelly]

100. There's a woman in the land
I won't mention her name–
And when she breaks wind,
It's like a stone from a sling.
[8th to 12th century]

101. There's a wonderful family called Stein,
There's Gert and there's Epp and there's Ein;
Gert's poems are bunk,
Epp's statues are junk,
And no one can understand Ein.
[*Good and Bad*]

102. There's nae luck about the house,
There's nae luck at a',
There's nae luck about the house
When our gudeman's awa'.
['The Mariner's Wife']

103. There was a faith-healer of Deal,
Who said, 'Although pain isn't real,
If I sit on a pin
And it punctures my skin,
I dislike what I fancy I feel.'
[*Good and Bad*]

104. There was an elopement down in Mullingar
But sad to relate the pair didn't get far;
'Oh fly,' said he, 'Darling and see how it feels.'
But the Mullingar heifer was beef to the heels.
['The Mullingar Heifer' (19th century)]

105. There was an old man from Darjeeling,
Who boarded a bus bound for Ealing,
He saw on the door:
'Please don't spit on the floor',
So he stood up and spat on the ceiling.
[*Good and Bad*]

106. There was an old man of Boulogne
Who sang a most topical song.
It wasn't the words
That frightened the birds,
But the horrible double-entendre.
[*Good and Bad*]

107. There was a young lady of Riga,
Who went for a ride on a tiger;
They returned from the ride
With the lady inside,
And a smile on the face of the tiger.
[*Good and Bad*]

108. There was a young man of Japan
Whose limericks never would scan;
When they said it was so,
He replied, 'Yes, I know,
But I always try to get as many words into the last line as ever I possibly can.'
[*Good and Bad*]

109. Thirty days hath September,
April, June and November;
All the rest have thirty-one,
Excepting February alone,
And that has twenty-eight days clear
And twenty-nine in each leap year.
[Stevins MS, c. 1555]

110. Three things one does not recover from–
oppression that knows the backing of brute force,
poverty that knows the destitution of one's home,
and being deprived of children.
[Somali poem]

111. Turn again, Whittington,
Lord Mayor of London.
[Refrain of Bow Bells heard by Dick Whittington]

112. Two men wrote a lexicon, Liddell and Scott;
Some parts were clever, but some parts were not.
Hear, all ye learned, and read me this riddle,
How the wrong part wrote Scott, and the right part wrote Liddell.
[On Henry Liddell and Robert Scott, co-authors of the *Greek Lexicon* (1843)]

113. We are the Tiger instructors
No bloody use are we.
The only time you see us
Is breakfast, dinner and tea.
And when our pupils go solo
We sing with all our might
'Per Ardua ad Astra,
Up you, Jack, I'm all right.'
[Rhyme current in the Royal Australian Air Force, in Geoffrey Dutton, *Andy*, 13]

114. Western wind, when wilt thou blow,
The small rain down can rain?
Christ, if my love were in my arms
And I in my bed again!
[*New Oxford Book of 16th-Century Verse* (1991)]

115. Wha hes gud malt and makis ill drink,
Wa mot be hir werd!
I pray to God scho rot and stink,
Sevin yeir abone the erd.
[In G.F. Maine, *A Book of Scotland*]

116. When Adam delved, and Eve span,
Who was then a gentleman?
[Attr. John Ball, 1381]

117. When he killed the Mudjokivis,
Of the skin he made him mittens,
Made them with the fur side inside,
Made them with the skin side outside.
['The Modern Hiawatha']

118. When I am dead, and laid in grave,
And all my bones are rotten,
By this may I remembered be
When I should be forgotten.
[On a girl's sampler, 1736]

119. When I was a little boy, I had but a little wit,
'Tis a long time ago, and I have no more yet;
Nor ever ever shall, until that I die,
For the longer I live the more fool am I.
[In *Wit and Mirth, an Antidote against Melancholy* (1684)]

120. Whilst Adam slept, Eve from his side arose:
Strange his first sleep should be his last repose.
['The Consequence']

121. Why, strike me pink, I'd sooner drink
With a cove sent up for arson
Than a rain-beseeching, preaching, teaching,

Blanky, cranky parson.
['I Draw the Line at Clerics', Australian bush song]

122. Would you like to sin
With Elinor Glyn
On a tiger-skin?
Or would you prefer
to err with her
on some other fur?
[In A. Glyn, *Elinor Glyn* (1955)]

123. Wowsers, whingers, ratbags, narks,
Silvertails, galahs and sharks,
Knockers, larrikins, and chromos,
Bengal lancers, bludgers, homos,
Botts and polers, spielers, lairs,
Advance Australia – you are theirs!
[In Keith Dunstan, *Knockers* (1972)]

124. Ye canny shove yer granny aff a bus.
[Scottish children's rhyme]

Epitaphs

125. All who come my grave to see
Avoid damp beds and think of me.
[Epitaph of Lydia Eason, St Michael's, Stoke]

126. God took our flour,
Our little Nell;
He thought He too
Would like a smell.
[In Thomas Wood, *Cobbers*]

127. Here lie I and my four daughters,
Killed by drinking Cheltenham waters.
Had we but stuck to Epsom salts,
We wouldn't have been in these here vaults.
['Cheltenham Waters']

128. Here lie I by the chancel door;
They put me here because I was poor.
The further in, the more you pay,
But here lie I as snug as they.
[Epitaph, Devon churchyard]

129. Here lies a child that took one peep of Life
And viewed its endless troubles with dismay,
Gazed with an anguish'd glance upon the strife
And sickening at the sight flew fast away.
What though for many the gate of Heaven is shut,
It stands wide open for this little Butt.
[Epitaph on Allena Butt, who had died when only 6 weeks old]

130. Here lies a man who was killed by lightning;
He died when his prospects seemed to be brightening.
He might have cut a flash in this world of trouble,
But the flash cut him, and he lies in the stubble.
[Epitaph, Torrington, Devon]

131. Here lies a poor woman who always was tired,
For she lived in a place where help wasn't hired.
Her last words on earth were, Dear friends I am going
Where washing ain't done nor sweeping nor sewing,
And everything there is exact to my wishes,
For there they don't eat and there's no washing of dishes...
Don't mourn for me now, don't mourn for me never,
For I'm going to do nothing for ever and ever.
[Epitaph in Bushey churchyard]

132. Here lies Fred,
Who was alive and is dead;
Had it been his father,
I had much rather;
Had it been his brother,
Still better than another;
Had it been his sister,
No one would have missed her;
Had it been the whole generation,
Still better for the nation:
But since 'tis only Fred,
Who was alive and is dead,–
There's no more to be said.
[In Horace Walpole, *Memoirs of George II* (1847)]

133. Here lies my wife,
Here lies she;
Hallelujah!
Hallelujee!
[Epitaph, Leeds churchyard]

134. Here lies the body of Mary Ann Lowder,
She burst while drinking a seidlitz powder.
Called from the world to her heavenly rest,
She should have waited till it effervesced.
[Epitaph]

135. Here lies the body of Richard Hind,
Who was neither ingenious, sober, nor kind.
[Epitaph]

136. Here lies Will Smith – and, what's something rarish,
He was born, bred, and hanged, all in the same parish.
[Epitaph]

137. Lo, Huddled up, together Lye
Gray Age, Grene youth, White Infancy.
If Death doth Nature's Laws dispence,
And reconciles All Difference
'Tis Fit, One Flesh, One House Should have
One Tombe, One Epitaph, One Grave:
And they that Liv'd and Lov'd Either,
Should Dye and Lye and Sleep together.

Good reader, whether go or stay
Thou must not hence be Long Away.
[Epitaph, of William Bartholomew (died 1662), his wife and some of their children, St John the Baptist, Burford]

138. Mary Ann has gone to rest,
Safe at last on Abraham's breast,
Which may be nuts for Mary Ann,
But is certainly rough on Abraham.
[Epitaph]

139. My sledge and anvil lie declined
My bellows too have lost their wind
My fire's extinct, my forge decayed,
And in the Dust my Vice is laid
My coals are spent, my iron's gone
My Nails are Drove, My Work is done.
[Epitaph in Nettlebed churchyard]

140. Reader, one moment stop and think,
That I am in eternity, and you are on the brink.
[Tombstone inscription at Perth, Scotland]

141. Remember man, as thou goes by,
As thou art now so once was I,
As I am now so must thou be,
Remember man that thou must die.
[Headstone in Straiton, Ayrshire]

142. Rest in peace – until we meet again.
[Widow's epitaph for husband; in Mitford, *The American Way of Death*]

143. Sacred to the memory of
Captain Anthony Wedgwood
Accidentally shot by his gamekeeper
Whilst out shooting

'Well done thou good and faithful servant'.
[Epitaph]

144. Stranger! Approach this spot with gravity!
John Brown is filling his last cavity.
[Epitaph of a dentist]

145. That we spent, we had:
That we gave, we have:
That we left, we lost.
[Epitaph of the Earl of Devonshire]

146. This is the grave of Mike O'Day
Who died maintaining his right of way.
His right was clear, his will was strong.
But he's just as dead as if he'd been wrong.
[Epitaph]

147. Warm summer sun shine kindly here:
Warm summer wind blow softly here:
Green sod above lie light, lie light:
Good-night, Dear Heart: good-night, good-night.
[Memorial to Clorinda Haywood, St Bartholomew's, Edgbaston]

Miscellaneous

148. An abomination unto the Lord, but a very present help in time of trouble.
[Definition of a lie]

149. *Ad majorem Dei gloriam.*
To the greater glory of God.
[Motto of the Society of Jesus]

150. Ah well, they say it's not as bad as they say it is.
[An Irish woman's view on the situation in Ulster]

151. The aircraft is now approaching New Zealand. Please move your watches forward two hours – and back 20 years.
[Heard from a steward on a QANTAS flight from Sydney to Auckland, 1970]

152. [Alberto] Juantorena opens wide his legs and shows his class.
[British commentator at 1976 Montreal Olympics, probably Ron Pickering; wrongly ascribed to David Coleman]

153. All human beings are born free and equal in dignity and rights.
[Universal Declaration of Human Rights, 1948, Article 1]

154. All present and correct.
[Queen's Regulations]

155. The almighty dollar is the only object of worship.
[*Philadelphia Public Ledger*, 1860]

156. Any officer who shall behave in a scandalous manner, unbecoming the character of an officer and a gentleman shall ... be CASHIERED.
[*Articles of War*, Disgraceful Conduct]

157. Anyone who isn't confused here doesn't really understand what's going on.
[Belfast citizen, 1970]

158. [Comment made by a judge in the case of a doctor who had supplied condoms at the weekend when chemists' shops were closed]
Anyone without condoms at the weekend will have to wait until Monday.
[In Michael Solomon, *Pro Life?*]

159. [A member of the Soviet Writers' Union, after the decision to urge publication of *The Gulag Archipelago*, in reply to Vladimir Karpov's comment 'I have never seen such unanimity among us']
At least, not since we voted to expel Solzhenitsyn.
[*The Independent*, 1989]

160. *Ave Maria, gratia plena, Dominus tecum: Benedicta tu in mulieribus, et benedictus fructus ventris tui, Jesus.*
Hail Mary, full of grace, the Lord is with thee: Blessed art thou among women, and blessed is the fruit of thy womb, Jesus.
['Ave Maria', also known as 'The Angelic Salutation', dating from the 11th century]

161. A beast, but a just beast.
[Description of Dr Temple, Headmaster of Rugby]

162. [Heckler's reply when Harold Wilson asked rhetorically, 'Why do I emphasize the importance of the Royal Navy?']
Because you're in Chatham.

163. Be happy while y'er leevin,
For y'er a lang time deid.
[Scottish motto]

164. The best contraceptive is a glass of cold water: not before or after, but instead.
[Remark by a delegate at International Planned Parenthood Federation Conference]

165. The best defence against the atom bomb is not to be there when it goes off.
[*The British Army Journal*, quoted in *The Observer*, 'Sayings of the Week', 1949]

166. Can't act, can't sing, slightly bald. Can dance a little.
[Comment by a Hollywood executive on Fred Astaire's first screen test]

167. Capitalism is the exploitation of man by man. Communism is the complete opposite.
[Described by Laurence J. Peter as a Polish proverb]

168. *Caveant consules ne quid res publici detrimenti caperet.*
Let the consuls see to it that no harm come to the state.
['Ultimate decree' of the Senate of Rome]

169. *Cet animal est très méchant,*
Quand on l'attaque il se défend.
This animal is very wicked,
When it is attacked it defends itself.
[*La Ménagerie* (1868)]

170. [After shooting an innocent man in Belfast, 1975]
Christ, I'm in the wrong house.
[IRA gunman, quoted in Conor O'Cleary, *Irish Political Quotations*]

171. A committee is a cul-de-sac down which ideas are lured and then quietly strangled.
[*New Scientist*, 1973]

172. A Company for carrying on an undertaking of Great Advantage, but no one to know what it is.
[The South Sea Company Prospectus]

173. Conduct ... to the prejudice of good order and military discipline.
[Army Act]

174. *Cras amet qui nunquam amavit, quique amavit cras amet!*
Let those love now, who never loved before;
Let those who always loved, now love the more.
[Pervigilium Veneris]

175. A day oot o' Aiberdeen is a day oot o' life.
[Traditional Scottish saying]

176. Defence, not defiance.
[Motto of the Volunteers Movement, 1859]

177. Difficult things take a long time; the impossible takes a little longer.
[Sometimes attributed to Nansen, and others]

178. [Term applied to Secretary Knox's activities in securing opportunities for the investment of American capital abroad, particularly in Latin America and China]
Dollar Diplomacy.
[In *Harper's Weekly*]

179. Don't call us, we'll call you.
[Polite business 'brush-off']

180. Don't tell my mother I'm in politics – she thinks I play the piano in a whorehouse.
[American saying from the Depression]

181. During the intervals [between dances] the devil is busy; yes, very busy, as sad experience proves, and on the way home in the small hours of the morning, he is busier still.
[Statement on all-night dances, by Irish bishops, quoted in *Irish Catholic*, 1933]

182. The editors are well under thirty and intend to remain so.
[Editorial, *The Canadian Mercury*, 1928]

183. The eternal triangle.
[*Daily Chronicle*, 1907]

184. [Of George Washington]
Father of his Country.
[In Francis Bailey, *Nordamericanische Kalender*]

185. Fifty million Frenchmen can't be wrong.
[Ironic expression probably originating with US servicemen in France during World War I, and later used as a song lyric]

186. [Declaration sent to Pope John XXII by the Scottish barons]
For so long as but a hundred of us remain alive, we will in no way yield ourselves to the dominion of the English. For it is not for glory, nor riches, nor honour that we fight, but for Freedom only, which no good man lays down but with his life.
[Declaration of Arbroath, 1320]

187. From ghoulies and ghosties and long leggety beasties
And things that go bump in the night,
Good Lord, deliver us!
[Traditional Cornish saying]

188. A gentleman haranguing on the perfection of our law, and that it was equally open to the poor and the rich, was answered by another, 'So is the London Tavern'.
[*Tom Paine's Jests* (1794), 23]

189. [Of America]
God's own country.
[First found in this form, 1921]

190. [Inscription in the armoury of Venice]
Happy is that city which in time of peace thinks of war.
[In Robert Burton, *Anatomy of Melancholy* (1621–1651)]

191. Has anyone here been raped and speaks English?
[BBC television reporter to Belgian civilians waiting to escape the war in the Congo, 1960]

192. He didn't love God, he just fancied him.
[On W.H. Auden]

193. He died as he lived – at sea.
[On Ramsay Macdonald who died while on a cruise in 1937]

194. Here's tae us; wha's like us?
Gey few, and they're a' deid.
[Scottish toast]

195. [Of Gladstone's Budget speeches]
He talked shop like a tenth muse.
[In G.W.E. Russell, *Collections and Recollections* (1898), 12]

196. *Hibernicis ipsis Hibernior.*
More Irish than the Irish.
[7th to 9th century]

197. *Honi soit qui mal y pense.*
Evil be to him who evil thinks.
[Motto of the Order of the Garter]

198. [Traditional description in New Zealand of a satisfactory fence]
Horse-high, bull-strong and pig-tight.
[*Standards*, 31, 9]

199. How different, how very different from the home life of our own dear Queen!
[Remark by woman at performance of Cleopatra by Sarah Bernhardt]

200. If anything can go wrong, it will.
[Murphy's Law, probably dating from the US in the 1940s. A Captain E. Murphy of the California Northrop aviation firm may have formulated it]

201. If it moves, shoot it; if it doesn't, chop it down.
[Traditional Australian bush saying]

202. If ye want a boy, dae it wi' your boots on.
[Traditional Scottish saying]

203. [A countrywoman when asked what she did in her spare time]
I go to the lavatory.
[In Jim Henderson, *Down from Marble Mountain*]

204. In particular, the State recognises that by her life within the home, woman gives to the State a support without which the common good cannot be achieved.
[*The Irish Constitution*, Article 41.2]

205. Inspiration is the act of drawing up a chair to the writing desk.

206. An intelligent Russian once remarked to us, 'Every country has its own constitution; ours is absolutism moderated by assassination.'
[In Munster, *Political Sketches of Europe* (1868)]

207. It is difficult to know, comrade, which comes first – death or glory.
['The Orkneyinga Saga']

208. It pays to advertise.
[Already current by c. 1912 when Cole Porter used it as the title of an early song]

209. King Charles the First walked and talked
Half an hour after his head was cut off.
[In Peter Puzzlewell, *A Choice Collection of Riddles, Charades, and Rebuses*]

210. The King over the Water.
[18th-century Jacobite toast]

211. Know thyself.
[Inscribed on the temple of Apollo at Delphi. Cf. Thomas Carlyle: 11]

212. *Laborare est orare.*
Work is prayer.
[Unknown origin]

213. *La grande phrase reçue, c'est* qu'il ne faut pas être plus royaliste que le roi. *Cette phrase n'est pas du moment; elle fut inventée sous Louis XVI: elle enchaîna les mains des fidèles, pour ne laisser libre que le bras du bourreau.*
The big catch-phrase is *that you mustn't be more of a royalist*

than the King. This expression is not new; it was coined under the reign of Louis XVI: it chained up the hands of the loyal, leaving free only the arm of the hangman.
[In Chateaubriand, *De la monarchie selon la charte* (1816)]

214. The longest suicide note ever penned.
[Labour Shadow Cabinet member on his party manifesto, 1983]

215. *Child*: Mamma, are Tories born wicked, or do they grow wicked afterwards?
Mother: They are born wicked, and grow worse.
[In G.W.E. Russell, *Collections and Recollections* (1898), 10]

216. The ministry of all talents.
[A name given ironically to Grenville's coalition of 1806]

217. [Description of Kingsley's doctrine]
Muscular Christianity.
[In *The Edinburgh Review*, January 1858]

218. The national territory consists of the whole island of Ireland, its islands and the territorial seas.
[*The Irish Constitution*, Article 2]

219. The nature of God is a circle of which the centre is everywhere and the circumference is nowhere.
[Attr. to Empedocles (quoted in *Roman de la Rose*)]

220. *Nemo me impune lacessit*.
Wha daur meddle wi' me.
[Motto of the Scots Crown]

221. The *noise*, my dear! And the *people*!
[On the retreat from Dunkirk, 1940]

222. Nothing in excess.
[Attributed to Thales, Solon, Cleobulus, Socrates, 7th–4th Century BC]

223. O God, if there be a God, save my soul, if I have a soul!
[Prayer of a common soldier before the Battle of Blenheim]

224. Oh dear, what a pity. Nannies are so hard to come by these days.
[Aristocratic old lady's remark to a police officer inquiring into the murder of Lord Lucan's nanny, 1974]

225. Oh no, thank you, I only smoke on special occasions.
[Labour minister when asked, while dining with King George VI, if he would like a cigar]

226. Once a clergyman always a clergyman.
[Attr. ruling in trial of Horne Tooke]

227. [On a plaque, apparently stolen by a New Zealand yachtsman in the USA, and cemented in Windsor Reserve, Devonport, Auckland, 1983]
On this site in 1897 nothing happened.
[*Auckland Star*, 1983]

228. Our company absorbs the cost.
[Useful Arab phrase in modern Arab-English phrase book for American oil engineers]

229. Overpaid, overfed, oversexed, and over here.
[Remark on GIs in Britain during World War II]

230. Oxford gave the world marmalade and a manner, Cambridge science and a sausage.
[Traditional]

231. PARAS THIRTEEN
BOGSIDE NIL.
[Derry graffiti after Bloody Sunday 1972, when thirteen people died, having been fired on by the British Paratroop regiment]

232. *Post coitum omne animal triste*.
After coition every animal is sad.
[Post-classical saying]

233. *Quidquid agas, prudenter agas, et respice finem*.
Whatever you do, do it warily, and take account of the end.
[*Gesta Romanorum*]

234. [The reply of an Italian admiral when Eva Peron complained that she had been called a 'whore' on a visit to northern Italy]
Quite so. But I have not been on a ship for fifteen years and they still call me 'Admiral'.

235. *Revenons à ces moutons*.
Let us return to our sheep [Let us get back to the subject].
[*Maistre Pierre Pathelin*, line 1191]

236. *Se non è vero, è molto ben trovato*.
If it is not true, it is a happy invention.
[16th century]

237. Shooting is a popular sport in the countryside ... Unlike many other countries, the outstanding characteristic of the sport has been that it is not confined to any one class.
[The Northern Ireland Tourist Board, in *New Statesman*, 1969]

238. The show ain't over till the fat lady sings.
[Catchphrase, originally referring to Kate Smith, a heavyweight American singer who sang 'God Bless America' at the end of performances]

239. *Sic transit gloria mundi*.
Thus passes the glory of the world.
[Spoken during the coronation of a new Pope]

240. Since wars begin in the minds of men, it is in the minds of men that the defences of peace must be constructed.
[Constitution of UNESCO]

241. *Solvitur ambulando*.
It is solved in walking.
[Quoted as epigraph by Clough, *Amours de Voyage*]

242. Spheres of influence.
[In Hertslet, *Map of Africa*]

243. *Tempora mutantur, et nos mutamur in illis*.
Times change, and we change with them.
[In William Harrison, *Description of Britain* (1577)]

244. That this house will in no circumstances fight for its King and country.
[Motion passed at Oxford Union, 1933]

245. They'll be dancing in the streets of Raith tonight.
[Falsely attributed to both Kenneth Wolstenholme and David Coleman, this reference to Raith Rovers fans dancing in a non-existent Scottish town – the team plays in Kirkcaldy – almost certainly originated in a BBC radio broadcast from London in 1963, after Raith Rovers defeated Aberdeen in a Scottish Cup tie]

246. This is a rotten argument, but it should be good enough for their lordships on a hot summer afternoon.
[Annotation in ministerial brief]

247. This must be the first time a rat has come to the aid of a sinking ship.
[BBC spokesman on the success of puppet Roland Rat at TV-am, 1983]

248. Thought shall be the harder, heart the keener, courage the greater, as our might lessens.
[In *The Battle of Maldon*, translated by R.K. Gordon from Anglo-Saxon]

249. *The Times* is a tribal noticeboard.
[Remark by a candidate for the editorship of the paper's Woman's Page in the 1960s]

250. Time wounds all heels.
[Sometimes attr. to Jane Ace]

251. Today, we were unlucky, but remember, we only have to be lucky once – you will have to be lucky always.
[IRA statement after the bombing of the Tory Party Conference in Brighton, October 1984]

252. To many people Victorian wit and humour is summed up by *Punch*, when every joke is supposed to end with 'Collapse of Stout Party', though this phrase tends to be as elusive as 'Elementary, my dear Watson' in the Sherlock Holmes sagas.
[In R. Pearsall, *Collapse of Stout Party* (1975)]

253. [Of Chiswick House]
Too small to live in and too large to hang on a watch-chain.
[In Cecil Roberts, *And so to Bath* (1940)]

254. To save the town, it became necessary to destroy it.
[American officer on the town of Ben Tre, Vietnam, during the Tet offensive, 1968]

255. *Totus mundus agit histrionem.*
The whole world plays the actor.
[Motto of Globe playhouse]

256. *Toujours perdrix!*
Always partridge!
[Said to originate in a story of Henri IV's having ordered that nothing but partridge should be served to his confessor, who had rebuked the king for his liaisons]

257. The two governments ... affirm that any change in the status of Northern Ireland would only come about with the consent of a majority of the people of Northern Ireland.
[*Anglo-Irish Agreement*, 1985, Article 1]

258. *Vox et praeterea nihil.*
A voice and nothing more.
[Description of the nightingale]

259. We get nothing and we can't go home because you can't eat sun.
[Black Liverpudlian commenting on unemployment and immigration, 1976]

260. 'Well, what sort of sport has Lord – had?'
'Oh, the young Sahib shot divinely, but God was very merciful to the birds.'
[In G.W.E. Russell, *Collections and Recollections* (1898)]

261. Whaur's yer Wully Shakespeare noo?
[Cry from audience after opening night of Home's *Douglas*, 1756]

262. Whenever God prepares evil for a man, He first damages his mind.
[Scholiast on Sophocles]

263. When you've got over the disgrace of the single life, it's more airy.
[Irish woman, quoted in broadcasts by Joyce Grenfell]

264. Where do you go when the tide comes in?
[Of New Zealand; usually attributed to an American visitor]

265. The working class can kiss my arse–
I've got the boss's job at last.
[Australian Labor movement, traditional folk saying]

266. You pays your money and you takes your choice.
[*Punch*, 1846]

Anouilh, Jean (1910–1987)
French 'theatricalist', dramatist and screenwriter

1. *Moi j'adorerais être pauvre! Seulement, je voudrais être vraiment pauvre. Tout ce qui est excessif m'enchante.*
I should love to be poor, as long as I was excessively poor! Anything in excess is quite delightful.
[*L'Invitation au château* (*Ring Round the Moon*, 1948)]

2. *Vous savez bien que l'amour, c'est avant tout le don de soi!*
Love is, above all else, the gift of oneself.
[*Ardèle ou la Marguerite* (1949)]

3. *Il y a l'amour bien sûr. Et puis il y a la vie, son ennemie.*
Oh, love exists all right. But it has an enemy – and that is life.
[*Ardèle ou la Marguerite* (1949)]

4. *C'est très jolie la vie, mais elle n'a pas de forme. L'art a pour objet de lui en donner une précisément.*
Life is very nice, but it has no shape. It is the purpose of art to give it shape.
[*La Répétition* (*The Rehearsal*, 1950)]

5. *Dieu est avec tout le monde ... Et, en fin de compte, il est toujours avec ceux qui ont beaucoup d'argent, et de grosses armées.*
God is on everyone's side ... And, in the final analysis, he is on the side of those who have plenty of money and large armies.
[*L'Alouette* (*The Lark*, 1953). Cf. Bussy-Rabutin: 3; Turenne: 1 and Voltaire: 9]

Anstey, Christopher (1724–1805)
English verse writer

1. You may go to Carlisle's, and to Almack's too;
And I'll give you my head if you find such a host,
For coffee, tea, chocolate, butter, and toast:
How he welcomes at once all the world and his wife,
And how civil to folk he ne'er saw in his life.
[*New Bath Guide* (1766), Letter 13, 'A Public Breakfast']

Anthony, Susan B. (1820–1906)
American reformer, feminist and abolitionist

1. Men their rights and nothing more; women their rights and nothing less.
[Motto of *The Revolution*, 1868]

2. There never will be complete equality until women themselves help to make laws and elect lawmakers.
[In *The Arena*, 1897, 'The Status of Women, Past, Present and Future']

3. And yet, in the schoolroom more than any other place, does the difference of sex, if there is any, need to be forgotten.
[In Theodore Stanton and Harriet Stanton Blatch (eds), *Elizabeth Cady Stanton* (1922)]

Antiphanes of Macedonia (fl. 360 BC)
Greek comic dramatist

1. Idly inquisitive tribe of grammarians, who dig up the poetry of others by the roots ... Get away, bugs that secretly bite the eloquent.
[*Greek Anthology*, 11, 322]

Antrim, Minna (1861–1950)
American prose writer

1. Experience is a good teacher, but she sends in terrific bills.
[*Naked Truth and Veiled Allusions* (1902)]

2. A fool bolts pleasure, then complains of moral indigestion.
[*Naked Truth and Veiled Allusions* (1902)]

3. A homely face and no figure have aided many women heavenward.
[*Naked Truth and Veiled Allusions* (1902)]

Apollinaire, Guillaume (1880–1918)
French modernist poet and avant-garde writer

1. *Les souvenirs sont cors de chasse*
Dont meurt le bruit parmi le vent.
Memories are hunting horns whose sound dies away in the wind.
['Cors de Chasse' (1913)]

Appius Claudius Caecus (4th–3rd century BC)
Roman censor; prose and verse writer

1. *Faber est suae quisque fortunae.*
Each man is the architect of his own destiny.
[In Sallust, *Ad Caesarem*, I]

Appleton, Sir Edward Victor (1892–1965)
English physicist; researcher of the ionosphere

1. I do not mind what language an opera is sung in so long as it is a language I don't understand.
[*The Observer*, 'Sayings of the Week', 1955]

Appleton, Thomas Gold (1812–1884)
American epigrammatist

1. Good Americans, when they die, go to Paris.
[In Oliver Wendell Holmes, *The Autocrat of the Breakfast Table* (1858)]

2. A Boston man is the east wind made flesh.
[Attr.]

Arabian Nights
Collection of stories written in Arabic

1. Who will change old lamps for new ones? ... New lamps for old ones?
['The History of Aladdin']

2. Open Sesame!
['The History of Ali Baba']

Arbuthnot, John (1667–1735)
Scottish physician, pamphleteer and wit

1. He warns the heads of parties against believing their own lies.
[*The Art of Political Lying* (1712)]

2. Law is a bottomless pit.
[*The History of John Bull* (c. 1712)]

3. Here continueth to rot the body of Francis Chartres.
[First line of epitaph]

4. [Of biography]
One of the new terrors of death.
[In Carruthers, *Life of Pope* (1857)]

Archer, Lord Jeffrey (1940–)
British Member of Parliament and popular novelist

1. An entire family of divorcees, and they're head of the Church of England. It's going to make the person out there wonder if it's all worth it.
[Comment on the Royal Family, 1992]

Archibald, John Feltham (1856–1919)
Australian journalist

1. I have nothing against Oxford men. Some of our best shearers' cooks are Oxford men.
[In R. H. Croll, *I Recall*...]

Archilochus (fl. c. 650 BC)
Early Greek lyric poet

1. The fox knows many things but the hedgehog one big one.
[In Plutarch, *Moralia*, 'The Cleverness of Animals']

Archimedes (c. 287–212 BC)
Greek mathematician, of Syracuse; physicist and inventor

1. Give me a proper standpoint and I will move the earth.
[In Pappus Alexander, *Collectio*, 8]

2. *Eureka!*
I've got it!
[In Vitruvius Pollio, *De Architectura*]

Archpoet of Cologne (fl. c. 1205)
Anonymous German poet

1. *Meum est propositum in taberna mori,*
ut sint vina proxima morientis ori.
Tunc cantabunt laetius angelorum chori:
'sit Deus propitius huic potatori!'
I am resolved to die in a tavern, so that wine will be very near to my dying mouth. Then the bands of angels will chant with greater joy 'May God forgive this drinker!'
[*The Confession of Golias* (also attr. to Walter Map and others)]

Arendt, Hannah (1906–1975)
German-born American political theorist

1. [Of Eichmann]
It was as though in those last minutes he was summing up the lessons that this long course in human wickedness had taught us – the lesson of the fearsome, word-and-thought-defying banality of evil.
[*Eichmann in Jerusalem: A Report on the Banality of Evil* (1963)]

2. It is quite gratifying to feel guilty if you haven't done anything wrong: how noble! Whereas it is rather hard and certainly depressing to admit guilt and to repent.
[*Eichmann in Jerusalem: A Report on the Banality of Evil* (1963)]

3. The defiance of established authority, religious and secular, social and political, as a world-wide phenomenon may well one day be accounted the outstanding event of the last decade.
[*Crises of the Republic* (1972), 'Civil Disobedience']

4. Under conditions of tyranny it is far easier to act than to think.
[In W.H. Auden, *A Certain World* (1970)]

Argenson, Marquis d' (1694–1757)
French politician and essayist

1. *Laisser-faire.*
No interference.
[*Mémoires* (published posthumously)]

Ariosto, Ludovico (1474–1533)
Italian epic poet and comic dramatist

1. *Natura il fece, e poi roppe la stampa.*
Nature first made him, and then smashed the mould.
[*Orlando furioso* (1516), X]

Aristophanes (c. 445–385 BC)
Greek comic dramatist and satirist

1. One may learn wisdom even from one's enemies.
[*Birds*, 382]

2. [Suggestion for the name of the Birds' capital city]
What do you think of 'Cloudcuckooland'?
[*Birds*, 819]

3. Old age is a second childhood.
[*Clouds*, 1417]

4. You will never make a crab walk straight.
[*Peace*, 1083]

Aristotle (384–322 BC)
Greek philosopher; pupil of Plato and tutor of Alexander the Great

1. All men naturally desire knowledge.
[*Metaphysics*, I]

2. The good has been well said to be that at which all things aim.
[*Nicomachean Ethics*, I]

3. One swallow does not make a summer, neither does one fine day; similarly one day or brief time of happiness does not make a person entirely happy.
[*Nicomachean Ethics*, I]

4. Just as at the Olympic games it is not the handsomest or strongest men who are crowned with victory but the successful competitors, so in life it is those who act rightly who carry off all the prizes and rewards.
[*Nicomachean Ethics*, I]

5. Moral virtue is the child of habit.
[*Nicomachean Ethics*, II]

6. Moral virtues we acquire through practice like the arts.
[*Nicomachean Ethics*, II]

7. Our actions determine our dispositions.
[*Nicomachean Ethics*, II]

8. In all things the middle state is to be praised. But it is sometimes necessary to incline towards overshooting and sometimes to shooting short of the mark, since this is the easiest way of hitting the mean and the right course.
[*Nicomachean Ethics*, II]

9. Where we are free to act, we are also free not to act, and where we are able to say No, we are also able to say Yes.
[*Nicomachean Ethics*, III]

10. The man is angry on the right grounds and with the right people, and in the right manner and at the right moment and for the right length of time, is to be praised.
[*Nicomachean Ethics*, IV]

11. Obstinate people may be subdivided into the opinionated, the ignorant, and the boorish.
[*Nicomachean Ethics*, VII]

12. The final association composed of several villages is the city state; it has now reached the limit of virtual self-sufficiency, and so while it comes into existence for the sake of life, it exists for the good life.
[*Politics*, I]

13. Man is by nature a political animal.
[*Politics*, I]

14. Revolutions may spring from trifles, but their issues are far from trifling.
[*Politics*, I]

15. A person who cannot live in society, or does not need to because he is self-sufficient, is either a beast or a god.
[*Politics*, I. Cf. Francis Bacon [1]: 65]

16. Blessed is the state in which those in power have moderate and sufficient means since where some are immoderately wealthy and others have nothing, the result will be extreme democracy or absolute oligarchy, or a tyranny may result from either of these extremes.
[*Politics*, IV]

17. Inferiors agitate in order that they may be equal and equals that they may be superior. Such is the state of mind which creates party strife.
[*Politics*, V]

18. Tragedy, then, is the imitation of an action that is serious, has magnitude, and is complete in itself ... through incidents arousing pity and fear it effects a catharsis of these and similar emotions.
[*Poetics*, VI]

19. The plot is the first principle and, as it were, the soul of tragedy; character comes second.
[*Poetics*, VI]

20. [Of the dramatic form of tragedy]
A whole is that which has a beginning, a middle, and an end.
[*Poetics*, VII]

21. The task of the poet is not to describe what actually happened, but the kind of thing that might happen according to probability or necessity ... For this reason poetry is something more philosophical and more worthy of serious attention than history.
[*Poetics*, IX]

22. Probable impossibilities are always to be preferred to improbable possibilities.
[*Poetics*, XXIV]

23. The roots of education are bitter, but the fruit is sweet.
[In Diogenes Laertius, *Lives of Philosophers: Aristotle*, V, 20]

24. On being asked what is a friend, he said 'A single soul dwelling in two bodies.'
[In Diogenes Laertius, *Lives of Philosophers: Aristotle*, V, 20]

25. *Amicus Plato, sed magis amica veritas.*
Plato is dear to me, but dearer still is truth.
[Greek original attributed to Aristotle]

Arlen, Michael (1895–1956)
Armenian-born English writer

1. There is a tale that is told in London about a nightingale, how it did this and that and, finally for no apparent reason, rested and sang in Berkeley Square.
[*These Charming people* (1924)]

Armin, Robert (fl. 1610)
British actor and dramatist

1. A flea in his ear.
[*Foole upon Foole* (1600)]

Armistead, Lewis (1817–1863)
American army officer

1. [Spoken at Gettysburg, 1863]
Give them the cold steel, boys!
[Attr.]

Armour, G.D. (1864–1949)
Scottish artist and illustrator

1. Look here, Steward, if this is coffee, I want tea; but if this is tea, then I wish for coffee.
[Punch, cartoon caption, July 1902]

Armstrong, Dr John (1709–1779)
Scottish physician, poet and essayist

1. Distrust yourself, and sleep before you fight.
'Tis not too late tomorrow to be brave.
[*The Art of Preserving Health* (1744)]

2. Of right and wrong he taught
Truths as refin'd as ever Athens heard;
And (strange to tell!) he practis'd what he preach'd.
[*The Art of Preserving Health* (1744)]

Armstrong, Louis (1900–1971)
American jazz trumpeter, singer and bandleader

1. [When asked how he felt about people copying his style]
A lotta cats copy the Mona Lisa, but people still line up to see the original.
[Attr.]

Armstrong, Neil (1930–)
American astronaut; first man on the moon

1. [First words on lunar touch-down of space module during Apollo XI mission]
Tranquillity Base here. The Eagle has landed.
[TV coverage, 20 July 1969]

2. [On stepping on to the moon]
That's one small step for a man, one giant leap for mankind.
[*New York Times*, 21 July 1969)]

Armstrong, Sir Robert (1927–)
British public servant

1. [Replying to an allegation in court that a letter he had written on behalf of the British Government had contained a lie]
It contains a misleading impression, not a lie. It was being economical with the truth.
[*The Observer*, 1986, in Jeffrey Care (ed.), *Sayings of the Eighties* (1989)]

Arno, Peter (1904–1968)
American cartoonist

1. Well, back to the old drawing board.
[*The New Yorker*, caption to cartoon of designers walking away from crashed plane]

2. Tell me about yourself, your struggles, your dreams, your telephone number.
[Caption to cartoon of man flirting with a woman]

Arnold, George (1834–1865)
American newspaperman, humorist and poet

1. The living need charity more than the dead.
[*The Jolly Old Pedagogue* (1866)]

Arnold, Matthew (1822–1888)
English poet, critic, essayist and educationist

1. Sand-strewn caverns, cool and deep,
Where the winds are all asleep;
Where the spent lights quiver and gleam;
Where the salt weed sways in the stream;
Where the sea-beasts ranged all round
Feed in the ooze of their pasture-ground...
Where great whales come sailing by,
Sail and sail, with unshut eye,
Round the world for ever and aye...

2. She left lonely for ever
The kings of the sea.
['The Forsaken Merman' (1849)]

3. Ere the parting hour go by,
Quick, thy tablets, Memory!
['A Memory Picture' (1849)]

4. Yet they, believe me, who await
No gifts from chance, have conquered fate.
['Resignation' (1849)]

5. Others abide our question. Thou art free.
We ask and ask – Thou smilest and art still,
Out-topping knowledge.
['Shakespeare' (1849)]

6. [Of Sophocles]
Who saw life steadily, and saw it whole:
The mellow glory of the Attic stage,
Singer of sweet Colonus, and its child.
['To a Friend' (1849)]

7. France, famed in all great arts, in none supreme.
['To a Republican Friend' (1849)]

8. [Of Wordsworth]
He spoke, and loosed our heart in tears.
He laid us as we lay at birth
On the cool flowery lap of earth.
['Memorial Verses' (1850)]

9. And we forget because we must
And not because we will.
['Absence' (1852)]

10. Is it so small a thing
To have enjoy'd the sun,
To have liv'd light in the spring,
To have lov'd, to have thought, to have done?
['Empedocles on Etna' (1852), I]

11. Let beam upon my inward view
Those eyes of deep, soft, lucent hue–
Eyes too expressive to be blue,
Too lovely to be grey.
['Faded Leaves' (1852), 4, On the Rhine]

12. We cannot kindle when we will
The fire which in the heart resides,
The spirit bloweth and is still,
In mystery our soul abides.
['Morality' (1852)]

13. Resolve to be thyself; and know, that he,
Who finds himself, loses his misery!
['Self-Dependence' (1852)]

14. For most men in a brazen prison live,
Where, in the sun's hot eye,
With heads bent o'er their toil, they languidly
Their lives to some unmeaning taskwork give,
Dreaming of nought beyond their prison-wall...

15. And the pale master on his spar-strewn deck
With anguish'd face and flying hair
Grasping the rudder hard,
Still bent to make some port he knows not where,
Still standing for some false, impossible shore.
And sterner comes the roar
Of sea and wind, and through the deepening gloom
Fainter and fainter wreck and helmsman loom,
And he too disappears, and comes no more.

Is there no life, but these alone?
Madman or slave, must man be one?
['A Summer Night' (1852)]

16. Yes! in the sea of life enisled,
With echoing straits between us thrown,
Dotting the shoreless watery wild,
We mortal millions live alone...

17. A God, a God their severance ruled!
And bade betwixt their shores to be
The unplumb'd, salt, estranging sea.
['To Marguerite – Continued' (1852)]

18. Strew on her roses, roses,
And never a spray of yew.
In quiet she reposes:
Ah! would that I did too.
['Requiescat' (1853)]

19. Go, for they call you, shepherd, from the hill...

20. All the live murmur of a summer's day...

21. Tired of knocking at preferment's door...

22. In hat of antique shape, and cloak of grey,
The same the gipsies wore...

23. Crossing the stripling Thames at Bab-lock-hithe,
Trailing in the cool stream thy fingers wet,
As the slow punt swings round...

24. And waiting for the spark from heaven to fall...

25. The line of festal light in Christ-Church hall...

26. Thou waitest for the spark from heaven! and we,
Light half-believers in our casual creeds...
Who hesitate and falter life away,
And lose to-morrow the ground won to-day–
Ah, do not we, wanderer, await it too?...

27. With close-lipped patience for our only friend,
Sad patience, too near neighbour to despair...

28. This strange disease of modern life...

29. Still nursing the unconquerable hope,
Still clutching the inviolable shade...

30. As some grave Tyrian trader, from the sea,
Descried at sunrise an emerging prow
Lifting the cool-hair'd creepers stealthily,
The fringes of a southward-facing brow
Among the Aegean isles;
And saw the merry Grecian coaster come,
Freighted with amber grapes, and Chian wine,
Green bursting figs, and tunnies steep'd in brine;
And knew the intruders on his ancient home,
The young light-hearted masters of the waves;
And snatched his rudder, and shook out more sail,
And day and night held on indignantly
O'er the blue Midland waters with the gale,
Betwixt the Syrtes and soft Sicily,
To where the Atlantic raves
Outside the Western Straits; and unbent sails
There, where down cloudy cliffs, through sheets of foam,
Shy traffickers, the dark Iberians come;
And on the beach undid his corded bales.
['The Scholar-Gipsy' (1853)]

31. Truth sits upon the lips of dying men...

32. But now in blood and battles was my youth,
And full of blood and battles is my age;
And I shall never end this life of blood...

33. But the majestic river floated on,
Out of the mist and hum of that low land,
Into the frosty starlight...

34. Oxus, forgetting the bright speed he had
In his high mountain-cradle in Pamere,
A foiled circuitous wanderer – till at last
The longed-for dash of waves is heard, and wide
His luminous home of waters opens, bright
And tranquil, from whose floor the new-bathed stars
Emerge, and shine upon the Aral Sea.
['Sohrab and Rustum' (1853)]

35. Wandering between two worlds, one dead,
The other powerless to be born,
With nowhere yet to rest my head,
Like these, on earth I wait forlorn...

36. Years hence, perhaps, may dawn an age,
More fortunate, alas! than we,
Which without hardness will be sage,
And gay without frivolity.
['The Grande Chartreuse' (1855)]

37. This truth – to prove, and make thine own:
'Thou hast been, shalt be, art, alone.'
['Isolation. To Marguerite' (1857)]

38. With women the heart argues, not the mind...

39. He bears the seed of ruin in himself.
[*Merope* (1858)]

40. And see all sights from pole to pole,
And glance, and nod, and bustle by;
And never once possess our soul
Before we die.
['A Southern Night' (1861)]

41. And that sweet city with her dreaming spires,
She needs not June for beauty's heightening...

42. So have I heard the cuckoo's parting cry,
From the wet field, through the vexed garden-trees,
Come with the volleying rain and tossing breeze:
'The bloom is gone, and with the bloom go I!'...

43. I know what white, what purple fritillaries
The grassy harvest of the river-fields,
Above by Ensham, down by Sandford, yields,
And what sedged brooks are Thames's tributaries...

44. The foot less prompt to meet the morning dew,
The heart less bounding at emotion new,
And hope, once crushed, less quick to spring again...

45. Roam on! The light we sought is shining still.
Dost thou ask proof? Our tree yet crowns the hill,
Our Scholar travels yet the loved hill-side.
['Thyrsis' (1866)]

46. The sea is calm to-night,
The tide is full, the moon lies fair
Upon the straits...

47. The Sea of Faith
Was once, too, at the full, and round earth's shore
Lay like the folds of a bright girdle furl'd.
But now I only hear
Its melancholy, long, withdrawing roar,
Retreating, to the breath
Of the night-wind, down the vast edges drear
And naked shingles of the world.

Ah, love, let us be true
To one another! for the world, which seems
To lie before us like a land of dreams,

So various, so beautiful, so new,
Hath really neither joy, nor love, nor light,
Nor certitude, nor peace, nor help for pain;
And we are here as on a darkling plain
Swept with confused alarms of struggle and flight
Where ignorant armies clash by night.
['Dover Beach' (1867)]

48. Creep into thy narrow bed,
Creep, and let no more be said!
Vain thy onset! all stands fast.
Thou thyself must break at last.

Let the long contention cease!
Geese are swans, and swans are geese.
Let them have it how they will!
Thou are tired; best be still.
['The Last Word' (1867)]

49. Friends who set forth at our side,
Falter, are lost in the storm,
We, we only are left!
['Rugby Chapel' (1867)]

50. Nor bring, to see me cease to live,
Some doctor full of phrase and fame,
To shake his sapient head and give
The ill he cannot cure a name.
['A Wish' (1867)]

51. Wordsworth says somewhere that wherever Virgil seems to have composed 'with his eye on the object', Dryden fails to render him. Homer invariably composes 'with his eye on the object', whether the object be a moral or a material one: Pope composes with his eye on his style, into which he translates his object, whatever it is.
[*On Translating Homer* (1861)]

52. He [the translator] will find one English book and one only, where, as in the Iliad itself, perfect plainness of speech is allied with perfect nobleness; and that book is the Bible.
[*On Translating Homer* (1861)]

53. Nothing has raised more questioning among my critics than these words – noble, the grand style ... I think it will be found that the grand style arises in poetry, when a noble nature, poetically gifted, treats with simplicity or with severity a serious subject.
[*On Translating Homer* (1861)]

54. The magnificent roaring of the young lions of the Daily Telegraph.
[*Essays in Criticism* (1865), First Series, Preface]

55. Passionate, absorbing, almost blood-thirsty clinging to life.
[*Essays in Criticism* (1865), First Series, Preface]

56. [Of Oxford]
Beautiful city! so venerable, so lovely, so unravaged by the fierce intellectual life of our century, so serene! ... whispering from her towers the last enchantments of the Middle Age ... home of lost causes, and forsaken beliefs, and unpopular names, and impossible loyalties!
[*Essays in Criticism* (1865), First Series, Preface]

57. I am bound by my own definition of criticism: a disinterested endeavour to learn and propagate the best that is known and thought in the world.
[*Essays in Criticism* (1865), First Series, 'The Function of Criticism at the Present Time']

58. The absence, in this country, of any force of educated literary and scientific opinion.
[*Essays in Criticism* (1865), First Series, 'Literary Influence of Academies']

59. Philistinism! – We have not the expression in English. Perhaps we have not the word because we have so much of the thing.
[*Essays in Criticism* (1865), First Series, 'Heinrich Heine']

60. The great apostle of the Philistines, Lord Macaulay.
[*Essays in Criticism* (1865), First Series, 'Joubert']

61. Culture being a pursuit of our total perfection by means of getting to know, on all the matters which most concern us, the best which has been thought and said in the world.
[*Culture and Anarchy* (1869), Preface]

62. Our society distributes itself into Barbarians, Philistines, and Populace; and America is just ourselves, with the Barbarians quite left out, and the Populace nearly.
[*Culture and Anarchy* (1869), Preface]

63. ... the aim which is the great aim of culture, the aim of setting ourselves to ascertain what perfection is and to make it prevail.
[*Culture and Anarchy* (1869), 1]

64. The pursuit of perfection, then, is the pursuit of sweetness and light. He who works for sweetness and light, works to make reason and the will of God prevail.
[*Culture and Anarchy* (1869), 1]

65. The men of culture are the true apostles of equality.
[*Culture and Anarchy* (1869), 1]

66. One has often wondered whether upon the whole earth there is anything so unintelligent, so unapt to perceive how the world is really going, as an ordinary young Englishman of our upper class.
[*Culture and Anarchy* (1869), 2]

67. Philistine gives the notion of something particularly stiff-necked and perverse in the resistance to light and its children; and therein it specially suits our middle class.
[*Culture and Anarchy* (1869), 3]

68. I often, therefore, when I want to distinguish clearly the aristocratic class from the Philistines proper, or middle class, name the former, in my own mind, the Barbarians.
[*Culture and Anarchy* (1869), 3]

69. But that vast portion, lastly, of the working-class which, raw and half-developed, has long lain half-hidden amidst its poverty and squalor, and is now issuing from its hiding-place to assert an Englishman's heaven-born privilege of doing as he likes, and is beginning to perplex us by marching where it likes, meeting where it likes, bawling what it likes, breaking what it likes – to this vast residuum we may with great propriety give the name of Populace.
[*Culture and Anarchy* (1869), 3]

70. Hebraism and Hellenism – between these two points of influence moves our World ... they are, each of them, contributions to human development.
[*Culture and Anarchy* (1869), 4]

71. The governing idea of Hellenism is spontaneity of consciousness; that of Hebraism, strictness of conscience.
[*Culture and Anarchy* (1869), 4]

72. Culture, the acquainting ourselves with the best that has been known and said in the world, and thus the history of the human spirit.
[*Literature and Dogma*, Preface to 1873 edition]

73. Terms like grace, new birth, justification ... terms, in short, which with St Paul are literary terms, theologians have employed as if they were scientific terms.
[*Literature and Dogma* (1873), I]

74. When we are asked further, what is conduct? – let us answer: Three fourths of life.
[*Literature and Dogma* (1873), I, 1]

75. The true meaning of religion is thus not simply morality, but morality touched by emotion.
[*Literature and Dogma* (1873), I, 2]

76. But there remains the question: what righteousness really is. The method and secret and sweet reasonableness of Jesus.
[*Literature and Dogma* (1873), XII, 2]

77. So we have the Philistine of genius in religion – Luther; the Philistine of genius in politics – Cromwell; the Philistine of genius in literature – Bunyan.
[*Mixed Essays* (1879), 'Lord Falkland']

78. Miracles do not happen.
[*Literature and Dogma*, Preface to 1883 edition]

79. [Of poetry]
A criticism of life under the conditions fixed for such a criticism by the laws of poetic truth and poetic beauty.
[*Essays in Criticism* (1888), Second Series, 'The Study of Poetry']

80. [Of Chaucer]
He lacks the high seriousness of the great classics, and therewith an important part of their virtue.
[*Essays in Criticism* (1888), Second Series, 'The Study of Poetry']

81. Dryden and Pope are not classics of our poetry, they are classics of our prose.
[*Essays in Criticism* (1888), Second Series, 'The Study of Poetry']

82. The difference between genuine poetry and the poetry of Dryden, Pope, and all their school, is briefly this: their poetry is conceived and composed in their wits, genuine poetry is conceived and composed in the soul.
[*Essays in Criticism* (1888), Second Series, 'Thomas Gray']

83. [Of Wordsworth]
His expression may often be called bald ... but it is bald as the bare mountain tops are bald, with a baldness full of grandeur.
[*Essays in Criticism* (1888), Second Series, 'Wordsworth']

84. [Quoting his own writing on Shelley]
In poetry, no less than in life, he is 'a beautiful and ineffectual angel, beating in the void his luminous wings in vain'.
[*Essays in Criticism* (1888), Second Series, 'Shelley']

85. I am past thirty, and three parts iced over.
[Letter to A.H. Clough, 1853]

86. People think that I can teach them style. What stuff it all is! Have something to say, and say it as clearly as you can. That is the only secret of style.
[In G.W.E. Russell, *Collections and Recollections* (1898)]

Arnold, Thomas (1795–1842)
English historian and educator; headmaster of Rugby School and father of Matthew Arnold

1. As for rioting, the old Roman way of dealing with that is always the right one; flog the rank and file, and fling the ringleaders from the Tarpeian rock.
[Letter, written before 1828 and quoted in *Cornhill Magazine*, August 1868]

2. My object will be, if possible, to form Christian men, for Christian boys I can scarcely hope to make.
[Letter, 1828]

3. Rather than have Physical Science the principal thing in my son's mind, I would rather have him think that the Sun went round the Earth, and the Stars were merely spangles set in a bright blue firmament.
[In Alan L. Mackay, *The Harvest of a Quiet Eye* (1977)]

Artley, Alexandra
Author and essayist

1. [On the reprocessing of foreign nuclear waste in Britain]
This is not 'polite and tidy Britain' ... It's Widow Twankey's Nuclear Laundry.
[In *Britain in the Eighties* (1989)]

Asaf, George (1880–1951)
British songwriter

1. What's the use of worrying?
It never was worth while,
So, pack up your troubles in your old kit-bag,
And smile, smile, smile.
['Pack up Your Troubles in Your Old Kit-bag', song, 1915]

Ascham, Roger (1515–1568)
English scholar, educationist and archer

1. He that will write well in any tongue, must follow this counsel of Aristotle, to speak as the common people do, to think as wise men do; and so should every man understand him, and the judgment of wise men allow him.
[*Toxophilus* (1545)]

2. *Inglese Italianato, è un diavolo incarnato,*
that is to say, you remain men in shape and fashion, but become devils in life and condition.
[*The Scholemaster* (1570)]

3. I said ... how, and why, young children, were sooner allured by love, than driven by beating, to attain good learning.
[*The Scholemaster* (1570)]

4. There is no such whetstone, to sharpen a good wit and encourage a will to learning, as is praise.
[*The Scholemaster* (1570)]

Ashbery, John (1927–)
American poet, art critic and Professor of English

1. ... Something
Ought to be written about how this affects
You when you write poetry:
The extreme austerity of an almost empty mind
Colliding with the lush, Rousseau-like foliage of its desire to communicate
Something between breaths, if only for the sake
Of others and their desire to understand you and desert you
For other centers of communication, so that understanding
May begin, and in doing so be undone.
[*Houseboat Days*, 'And *Ut Pictura Poesis* is her name']

Ashford, Daisy (1881–1972)
English child author

1. Mr Salteena was an elderly man of 42 and was fond of asking peaple to stay with him.
[*The Young Visiters* (1919), 1]

2. I do hope I shall enjoy myself with you ... I am parshial to ladies if they are nice I suppose it is my nature. I am not quite a gentleman but you would hardly notice it.
[*The Young Visiters* (1919), 1]

3. I am very pale owing to the drains in this house.
[*The Young Visiters* (1919), 2]

4. You look rather rash my dear your colors dont quite match your face.
[*The Young Visiters* (1919), 2]

5. Bernard always had a few prayers in the hall and some whiskey afterwards as he was rarther pious but Mr Salteena was not very addicted to prayers so he marched up to bed.
[*The Young Visiters* (1919), 3]

6. It was a sumpshous spot all done up in gold with plenty of looking glasses.
[*The Young Visiters* (1919), 5]

7. Oh I see said the earl but my own idear is that these things are as piffle before the wind.
[*The Young Visiters* (1919), 5]

8. My dear Clincham, The bearer of this letter is an old friend of mine not quite the right side of the blanket as they say in fact he is the son of a first rate butcher but his mother was a decent family called Hyssopps of the Glen so you see he is not so bad and is desireus of being the correct article.
[*The Young Visiters* (1919), 5]

9. I am very fond of fresh air and royalties.
[*The Young Visiters* (1919), 5]

10. Ethel patted her hair and looked very sneery.
[*The Young Visiters* (1919), 8]

11. My life will be sour grapes and ashes without you.
[*The Young Visiters* (1919), 8]

Askey, Arthur (1900–1982)
British comedian and variety artiste

1. [On pantomime]
Pantomimes – the smell of oranges and wee-wee.
[Attr.]

Asquith, Herbert Henry (Earl of Oxford and Asquith) (1852–1928)
English Liberal statesman, politician and Prime Minister

1. [Replying in 1910 to questions about whether the Government intended to coerce the House of Lords into accepting the Budget]
We had better wait and see.
[In Roy Jenkins, *Asquith* (1964)]

2. We shall never sheath the sword which we have not lightly drawn until Belgium recovers in full measure all and more than she has sacrificed, until France is adequately secured against the menace of aggression, until the rights of the smaller nationalities of Europe are placed upon an unassailable foundation, and until the military domination of Prussia is wholly and finally destroyed.
[Speech, 1914]

3. [On Bonar Law]
It is fitting that we should have buried the Unknown Prime Minister by the side of the Unknown Soldier.
[Remark supposedly made at Bonar Law's funeral, November 1923]

4. Youth would be an ideal state if it came a little later in life.
[*The Observer*, 1923]

5. [On the reason for the three sets of figures kept by the War Office]
One to mislead the public; another to mislead the Cabinet, and the third to mislead itself.
[In Alastair Horne, *The Price of Glory* (1962)]

Asquith, Margot (1864–1945)
Scottish political hostess and prose writer; wife of Herbert Asquith

1. Rich men's houses are seldom beautiful, rarely comfortable, and never original. It is a constant source of surprise to people of moderate means to observe how little a big fortune contributes to Beauty.
[*The Autobiography of Margot Asquith* (1920)]

2. To marry a man out of pity is folly; and, if you think you are going to influence the kind of fellow who has 'never had a chance, poor devil', you are profoundly mistaken. One can only influence the strong characters in life, not the weak; and it is the height of vanity to suppose that you can make an honest man of anyone.
[*The Autobiography of Margot Asquith* (1920)]

3. [Of Lady Desborough]
She tells enough white lies to ice a wedding cake.
[Quoted by Lady Violet Bonham Carter in *The Listener*, June 1953]

4. Mrs Asquith remarked indiscreetly that if Kitchener was not a great man, he was, at least, a great poster.
[In Sir Philip Magnus, *Kitchener: Portrait of an Imperialist* (1958)]

5. [Of Lloyd George]
He couldn't see a belt without hitting below it.
[Quoted by Baroness Asquith in TV programme, *As I Remember*, 30 April 1967]

6. [About a US General]
An imitation rough diamond.
[Quoted by Baroness Asquith in TV programme, *As I Remember*, 30 April 1967]

7. [On F.E. Smith]
He's very clever, but sometimes his brains go to his head.
[Quoted by Baroness Asquith in TV programme, *As I Remember*, 30 April 1967]

8. The King told me he would never have died if it had not been for that fool Dawson of Penn.
[In K. Rose, *King George V* (1983)]

9. [Of Sir Stafford Cripps]
He has a brilliant mind until he makes it up.
[In *The Wit of the Asquiths*]

Astley, Sir Jacob (1579–1652)
English soldier and royalist

1. O Lord! thou knowest how busy I must be this day; if I forget thee, do not thou forget me.
[Prayer before Battle of Edgehill, 1642]

Astor, John Jacob (1763–1848)
German-born American fur-trader and financier

1. A man who has a million dollars is as well off as if he were rich.
[Attr.]

Astor, Nancy, Viscountess (1879–1964)
American-born British Conservative politician and hostess; first woman MP

1. I married beneath me – all women do.
[*Dictionary of National Biography*]

2. [Refusing to pose for a close-up photograph]
Take a close-up of a woman past sixty! You might as well use a picture of a relief map of Ireland!
[Attr.]

Asturias, Miguel Angel (1899–1974)

1. *Para un pueblo hambriento e inactivo la sola forma en que Dios puede aparecer es en la de trabajo y comida.*
For people who are hungry and inactive, God can only appear in the form of work and food.
[*El alhajadito* (*The Little Rich Boy*, 1961), II]

Atkinson, Surgeon-Captain E.L. (1882–1929)
British polar explorer, naval officer and doctor

1. Hereabouts died a very gallant gentleman, Captain L.E.G. Oates of the Inniskilling Dragoons. In March 1912, returning from the Pole, he walked willingly to his death in a blizzard, to try and save his comrades, beset by hardships.
[Epitaph on a cairn and cross erected in the Antarctic, November 1912]

Atkinson, Ti-Grace (c. 1938–)

1. Feminism is the theory: lesbianism is the practice.
[Attr. in Kramarae and Treichler, *Amazons, Bluestockings and Crones: A Feminist Dictionary*]

Attlee, Clement (1883–1967)
English statesman, Labour politician and Prime Minister

1. I think the British have the distinction above all other nations of being able to put new wine into old bottles without bursting them.
[*Hansard*, October 1950]
2. Russian Communism is the illegitimate child of Karl Marx and Catherine the Great.
[*The Observer*, 'Sayings of the Week', 1956]
3. Democracy means government by discussion but it is only effective if you can stop people talking.
[Speech, June 1957]

Atwood, Margaret (1939–)
Canadian novelist, poet and critic

1. Marriage is not
a house or even a tent
it is before that, and colder:

the edge of the forest, the edge
of the desert . . .
2. the edge of the receding glacier

where painfully and with wonder
at having survived even
this far

we are learning to make fire
[*Procedures for Underground* (1970), 'Habitation']
3. Goddesses are possible now, and the air suffuses with desire.
[*The Handmaid's Tale* (1986), 25]
4. The north focuses our anxieties. Turning to face north, we enter our own unconscious. Always, in retrospect, the journey north has the quality of dream.
[*Saturday Night*, 1987, 'True North']
5. An eye for an eye leads only to more blindness.
[*Cat's Eye* (1988)]
6. Eating is our earliest metaphor, preceding our consciousness of gender difference, race, nationality, and language. We eat before we talk.
[*The CanLit Foodbook: From Pen to Palate – A Collection of Tasty Literary Fare* (1987)]
7. If you're not annoying somebody, you're not really alive.
[Quoted by Judith Timson in *Maclean's*, 1988]
8. Once upon a time I thought there was an old man with a grey beard somewhere who knew the truth, and if I was good enough, naturally he would tell me that this was it. That person doesn't exist, but that's who I write for. The great critic in the sky.
[In Earl G. Ingersoll (ed.), *Margaret Atwood: Conversations* (1990), interview with Graeme Gibson, 1972]
9. [Commenting on the critical comments in three countries on her novel *The Handmaid's Tale*]
The British say, 'Jolly good story!' The Canadians ask, 'Can it happen here?' And the Americans say, 'How much time have we got?'
[In Sheldon Teitelbaum, *Cinefantastique*, 1990]
10. Writing . . . is an act of faith: I believe it's also an act of hope, the hope that things can be better than they are.
[Attr.]

Auber, Daniel François Esprit (1782–1871)
French opera composer

1. [Remark made at a funeral]
This is the last time I will take part as an amateur.
[Attr.]
2. Ageing seems to be the only available way to live a long time.
[Attr.]

Aubrey, John (1626–1697)
English antiquary, folklorist and biographer

1. How these curiosities would be quite forgot, did not such idle fellows as I am put them down.
[*Brief Lives* (c. 1693), 'Venetia Digby']
2. One day going on foot to Guild-hall, with his clerk behind him, he was surprised in Cheapside with a sudden and violent looseness near the Standard. He turned up his breech against the Standard and bade his man hide his face; for they shall never see my arse again, said he.
[*Brief Lives* (c. 1693), 'Sir William Fleetwood']
3. The parliament intended to have hanged him; and he expected no less, but resolved to be hanged with the Bible under one arm and Magna Carta under the other.
[*Brief Lives* (c. 1693), 'David Jenkins']
4. He was so fair that they called him the lady of Christ's College.
[*Brief Lives* (c. 1693), 'John Milton']
5. Sciatica: he cured it, by boiling his buttock.
[*Brief Lives* (c. 1693), 'Sir Jonas Moore']
6. [Sir Thomas More's] daughters were then both together abed . . . asleep. He carries Sir [William Roper, who wished to marry one of More's daughters] into the chamber and takes the sheet by the corner and suddenly whips it off. They lay on their backs and their smocks up as high as their armpits. This awakened them, and immediately they turned on their bellies. Quoth Roper, I have seen both sides, and so gave a pat on her buttock he made choice of, saying 'Thou art mine.' Here was all the trouble of the wooing.
[*Brief Lives* (c. 1693), 'Sir Thomas More']
7. Sir Walter, being strangely surprised and put out of his countenance at so great a table, gives his son a damned blow over the face. His son, as rude as he was, would not strike his father, but strikes over the face the gentleman

that sat next to him and said 'Box about: 'twill come to my father anon.'
[*Brief Lives* (c. 1693), 'Sir Walter Raleigh']

8. He loved a wench well: and one time getting up one of the maids of honour against a tree in a wood ('twas his first lady) who seemed at first boarding to be somewhat fearful of her honour, and modest, she cried, 'Sweet Sir Walter, what do you ask me? Will you undo me? Nay, sweet Sir Walter! Sir Walter!' At last as the danger and the pleasure at the same time grew higher, she cried in the ecstasy, 'Swisser Swatter! Swisser Swatter!' She proved with child and I doubt not but this hero took care of them both, as also that the product was more than an ordinary mortal.
[*Brief Lives* (c. 1693), 'Sir Walter Raleigh']

9. He was a handsome, well-shaped man: very good company, and of a very ready and pleasant smooth wit.
[*Brief Lives* (c. 1693), 'William Shakespeare']

10. When he killed a calf he would do it in high style, and make a speech.
[*Brief Lives* (c. 1693), 'William Shakespeare']

11. He [Shakespeare] was wont to say that he 'never blotted out a line of his life'; said Ben Jonson, 'I wish he had blotted out a thousand.'
[*Brief Lives* (c. 1693), 'William Shakespeare')]

12. [Of Francis Beaumont]
There was a wonderful consimility of phansey between him and Mr John Fletcher, which caused that dearness of friendship between them ... They lived together on the Bank side, not far from the Playhouse, both bachelors; lay together; had one wench in the house between them, which they did so admire; the same clothes and cloak, &c.; between them.
[*Brief Lives* (c. 1693), 'Francis Beaumont and John Fletcher']

13. Anno 1670, not far from Cirencester, was an apparition; being demanded whether a good spirit or a bad? returned no answer, but disappeared with a curious perfume and most melodious twang. Mr W. Lilly believes it was a fairy.
[*Miscellanies* (1696), 'Apparitions']

Auden, W. H. (1907–1973)
English poet, essayist, critic, teacher and dramatist

1. 'O where are you going?' said reader to rider,
'That valley is fatal when furnaces burn,
Yonder's the midden whose odours will madden,
That gap is the grave where the tall return.'
[*Collected Poems, 1927–1932*, 'Five Songs', V]

2. Let us honour if we can
The vertical man,
Though we value none
But the horizontal one.
[*Collected Poems, 1927–1932*, 'Shorts']

3. Their fate must always be the same as yours,
To suffer the loss they were afraid of, yes,
Holders of one position, wrong for years.
[*Collected Poems, 1927–1932*, 'Venus Will Now Say a Few Words']

4. Private faces in public places
Are wiser and nicer
Than public faces in private places.
[*The Orators* (1932)]

5. Reindeer are coming to drive you away
Over the snow on an ebony sleigh,
Over the mountains and over the sea
You shall go happy and handsome and free.
[Auden and Isherwood, *The Ascent of F.6* (1936)]

6. I'll love you, dear, I'll love you
Till China and Africa meet,
And the river jumps over the mountain
And the salmon sing in the street,

I'll love you till the ocean
Is folded and hung up to dry
And the seven stars go squawking
Like geese about the sky...

7. O let not Time deceive you,
You cannot conquer Time.

In the burrows of the Nightmare
Where Justice naked is,
Time watches from the shadow
And coughs when you would kiss.

In headaches and in worry
Vaguely life leaks away,
And Time will have his fancy
To-morrow or to-day.

Into many a green valley
Drifts the appalling snow;
Time breaks the threaded dances
And the diver's brilliant bow.

O plunge your hands in water,
Plunge them in up to the wrist;
Stare, stare in the basin
And wonder what you've missed.

The glacier knocks in the cupboard,
The desert sighs in the bed,
And the crack in the tea-cup opens
A lane to the land of the dead...

8. O stand, stand at the window
As the tears scald and start;
You shall love your crooked neighbour
With your crooked heart.
[*Collected Poems, 1933–1938*, 'As I Walked Out One Evening']

9. The desires of the heart are as crooked as corkscrews,
Not to be born is the best for man;
The second-best is a formal order,
Thy dance's pattern; dance while you can.
Dance, dance, for the figure is easy,
The tune is catching and will not stop;
Dance till the stars come down from the rafters;
Dance, dance, dance till you drop.
[*Collected Poems, 1933–1938*, 'Death's Echo']

10. Perfection, of a kind, was what he was after,
And the poetry he invented was easy to understand;
He knew human folly like the back of his hand,
And was greatly interested in armies and fleets;
When he laughed, respectable senators burst with laughter,
And when he cried the little children died in the streets.
[*Collected Poems, 1933–1938*, 'Epitaph on a Tyrant']

11. Clutching a little case,
He walks out briskly to infect a city
Whose terrible future may have just arrived.
[*Collected Poems, 1933–1938*, 'Gare du Midi']

12. Look, stranger, on this island now
The leaping light for you discovers,
Stand stable here
And silent be,
That through the channels of the ear

May wander like a river
The swaying sound of the sea.
[*Collected Poems, 1933–1938*, 'On This Island']

13. Lay your sleeping head, my love,
Human on my faithless arm;
Time and fevers burn away
Individual beauty from
Thoughtful children, and the grave
Proves the child ephemeral:
But in my arms till break of day
Let the living creature lie,
Mortal, guilty, but to me
The entirely beautiful.
[*Collected Poems, 1933–1938*, 'Lullaby']

14. About suffering they were never wrong,
The Old Masters: how well they understood
Its human position; how it takes place
While someone else is eating or opening a window or just walking dully along...

15. They never forgot
That even the dreadful martyrdom must run its course
Anyhow in a corner, some untidy spot
Where the dogs go on with their doggy life and the torturer's horse
Scratches its innocent behind on a tree.
[*Collected Poems, 1933–1938*, 'Musée des Beaux Arts']

16. This is the Night Mail crossing the Border,
Bringing the cheque and the postal order,

Letters for the rich, letters for the poor,
The shop at the corner, the girl next door.

Pulling up Beattock, a steady climb:
The gradient's against her, but she's on time.

Past cotton-grass and moorland border,
Shovelling white steam over her shoulder...

17. Letters of thanks, letters from banks,
Letters of joy from girl and boy,
Receipted bills and invitations
To inspect new stock or to visit relations,
And applications for situations,
And timid lovers' declarations,
And gossip, gossip from all the nations.
[*Collected Poems, 1933–1938*, 'Night Mail']

18. O what is that sound which so thrills the ear
Down in the valley drumming, drumming?
Only the scarlet soldiers, dear,
The soldiers coming...

19. O it's broken the lock and splintered the door,
O it's the gate where they're turning, turning;
Their boots are heavy on the floor
And their eyes are burning.
[*Collected Poems, 1933–1938*, 'O What is That Sound']

20. Tomorrow for the young the poets exploding like bombs,
The walks by the lake, the weeks of perfect communion;
Tomorrow the bicycle races
Through the suburbs on summer evenings. But to-day the struggle...

21. The stars are dead. The animals will not look.
We are left alone with our day, and the time is short, and
History to the defeated
May say Alas but cannot help nor pardon.
[*Collected Poems, 1933–1938*, 'Spain 1937']

22. Out on the lawn I lie in bed,
Vega conspicuous overhead...

23. That later we, though parted then,
May still recall those evenings when
Fear gave his watch no look;
The lion griefs loped from the shade
And on our knees their muzzles laid,
And Death put down his book.
[*Collected Poems, 1933–1938*, 'A Summer Night']

24. At last the secret is out, as it always must come in the end,
The delicious story is ripe to tell to the intimate friend;
Over the tea-cups and in the square the tongue has its desire;
Still waters run deep, my dear, there's never smoke without fire...

25. For the clear voice suddenly singing, high up in the convent wall,
The scent of elder bushes, the sporting prints in the hall,
The croquet matches in summer, the handshake, the cough, the kiss,
There is always a wicked secret, a private reason for this.
[*Collected Poems, 1933–1938*, 'Twelve Songs', VIII]

26. When it comes, will it come without warning
Just as I'm picking my nose?
Will it knock on my door in the morning,
Or tread in the bus on my toes?
Will it come like a change in the weather?
Will its greeting be courteous or rough?
Will it alter my life altogether?
O tell me the truth about love.
[*Collected Poems, 1933–1938*, 'Twelve Songs', XII]

27. The sky is darkening like a stain;
Something is going to fall like rain,
And it won't be flowers.
[*Collected Poems, 1933–1938*, 'The Witnesses']

28. Only God can tell the saintly from the suburban,
Counterfeit values always resemble the true;
Neither in Life nor Art is honesty bohemian,
The free behave much as the respectable do...

29. O Unicorn among the cedars,
To whom no magic charm can lead us,
White childhood moving like a sigh
Through the green woods.
['New Year Letter' (1941)]

30. There lies that solid world
These hands can never reach;
My history, my love,
Is but a choice of speech.
['The Sea and the Mirror; Trinculo's Story' (1942–1944)]

31. Alone, alone, about a dreadful wood
Of conscious evil runs a lost mankind,
Dreading to find its Father.
['For the Time Being' (1945)]

32. Oh dear white children casual as birds,
Playing among the ruined languages,
So small beside their large confusing words,
So gay against the greater silences
Of dreadful things you did...

33. Weep for the lives your wishes never led.
[*Collected Poems, 1939–1947*, 'Anthem for St Cecilia's Day']

34. to us he is no more a person
now but a climate of opinion.
[*Collected Poems, 1939–1947*, 'In Memory of Sigmund Freud']

35. He disappeared in the dead of winter:
The brooks were frozen, the airports almost deserted,
And snow disfigured the public statues;

The mercury sank in the mouth of the dying day.
What instruments we have agree
The day of his death was a dark cold day...

36. The provinces of his body revolted,
The squares of his mind were empty,
Silence invaded the suburbs,
The current of his feeling failed; he became his admirers...

37. The words of a dead man
Are modified in the guts of the living...

38. You were silly like us; your gift survived it all:
The parish of rich women, physical decay,
Yourself...

39. Now Ireland has her madness and her weather still,
For poetry makes nothing happen...

40. Earth, receive an honoured guest:
William Yeats is laid to rest.
Let the Irish vessel lie
Emptied of its poetry...

41. Time that is intolerant
Of the brave and innocent,
And indifferent in a week
To a beautiful physique,

Worships language and forgives
Everyone by whom it lives...

42. Time that with this strange excuse
Pardoned Kipling and his views,
And will pardon Paul Claudel,
Pardons him for writing well...

43. In the deserts of the heart
Let the healing fountain start,
In the prison of his days
Teach the free man how to praise.
[*Collected Poems, 1939–1947*, 'In Memory of W.B. Yeats']

44. There is no such thing as the State
And no one exists alone.
Hunger allows no choice
To the citizen or the police;
We must love one another or die.
[*Collected Poems, 1939–1947*, 'September 1, 1939']

45. To the man-in-the-street, who, I'm sorry to say,
Is a keen observer of life,
The word intellectual suggests straight away
A man who's untrue to his wife.
[*Collected Poems, 1939–1947*, 'Shorts']

46. Thou shalt not sit
With statisticians nor commit
A social science...

47. Read *The New Yorker*, trust in God;
And take short views.
[*Collected Poems, 1939–1947*, 'Under Which Lyre']

48. Our researchers into Public Opinion are content
That he held the proper opinions for the time of year;
When there was peace, he was for peace; when there was war, he went.
[*Collected Poems, 1939–1947*,'The Unknown Citizen']

49. In an upper room at midnight
See us gathered on behalf
Of love according to the gospel
Of the radio-phonograph.
[*Nones* (1951), 'The Love Feast']

50. Altogether elsewhere, vast
Herds of reindeer move across
Miles and miles of golden moss,
Silently and very fast.
[*Collected Poems, 1948–1957*, 'The Fall of Rome']

51. Out of the air a voice without a face
Proved by statistics that some cause was just
In tones as dry and level as the place.
[*The Shield of Achilles* (1955), Title poem]

52. To save your world you asked this man to die:
Would this man, could he see you now, ask why?
['Epitaph for the Unknown Soldier' (1955)]

53. A poet's hope: to be,
like some valley cheese,
local, but prized elsewhere.
[*Collected Poems, 1958–1971*, 'Shorts II']

54. Some thirty inches from my nose
The frontier of my Person goes,
And all the untilled air between
Is private pagus and demesne.
Stranger, unless with bedroom eyes
I beckon you to fraternize,
Beware of rudely crossing it;
I have no gun, but I can spit.
[*About the House*, 'Prologue: the Birth of Architecture']

55. It is time for the destruction of error.
The chairs are being brought in from the garden,
The summer talk stopped on that savage coast
Before the storms.
['It is time']

56. It's no use raising a shout.
No, Honey, you can cut that right out.
I don't want any more hugs;
Make me some fresh tea, fetch me some rugs.
Here am I, here are you:
But what does it mean? What are we going to do?
['It's no use raising a Shout']

57. God bless the U.S.A., so large,
So friendly, and so rich.
['On the Circuit']

58. Only those in the last stages of disease could believe that children are true judges of character.
[*The Orators* (1932), 'Journals of an Airman']

59. It is a sad fact about our culture that a poet can earn much more money writing or talking about his art than he can by practising it.
[*The Dyer's Hand and Other Essays* (1963), Foreword]

60. One cannot review a bad book without showing off.
[*The Dyer's Hand and Other Essays* (1963), 'Reading']

61. Some books are undeservedly forgotten; none are undeservedly remembered.
[*The Dyer's Hand* (1963), 'Reading']

62. No poet or novelist wishes he were the only one who ever lived, but most of them wish they were the only one alive, and quite a number fondly believe their wish has been granted.
[*The Dyer's Hand* (1963), 'Writing']

63. Most people enjoy the sight of their own handwriting as they enjoy the smell of their own farts.
[*The Dyer's Hand* (1963), 'Writing']

64. The true men of action in our time, those who transform the world, are not the politicians and statesmen, but the scientists. Unfortunately, poetry cannot celebrate them,

because their deeds are concerned with things, not persons and are, therefore, speechless.
[*The Dyer's Hand* (1963), 'The Poet and the City']

65. When I find myself in the company of scientists, I feel like a shabby curate who has strayed by mistake into a drawing-room full of dukes.
[*The Dyer's Hand* (1963), 'The Poet and the City']

66. Man is a history-making creature who can neither repeat his past nor leave it behind.
[*The Dyer's Hand* (1963), 'D.H. Lawrence']

67. Political history is far too criminal and pathological to be a fit subject of study for the young. All teachers know this. In consequence, they bowdlerize, but to bowdlerize political history is not to simplify but to falsify it. Children should acquire their heroes and villains from fiction.
[*A Certain World* (1970)]

68. All sin tends to be addictive, and the terminal point of addiction is what is called damnation.
[*A Certain World* (1970)]

69. [Opening words on giving a lecture in a large hall]
If there are any of you at the back who do not hear me, please don't raise your hands because I am also nearsighted.
[Attr.]

70. A professor is one who talks in someone else's sleep.
[Attr.]

Augier, Emile (1820–1889)
French dramatist and poet; author of comedies of manners

1. *La nostalgie de la boue.*
Homesickness for the gutter.
[*Le Mariage d'Olympe* (1855), I]

Augustine, Saint (354–430)
Numidian-born Christian theologian, philosopher and scholar

1. *Fecisti nos ad te, et inquietum est cor nostrum donec requiescat in te.*
Thou hast created us for Thyself, and our heart is restless till it finds rest in Thee.
[*Confessions* (397–398), I]

2. *Veni Karthaginem, et circumstrepebat me undique sartago flagitiosorum amorum. Nondum amabam, et amare amabam ... quaerebam quid amarem, amans amare.*
I came to Carthage where a whole frying pan full of abominable loves crackled about me on every side. I was not in love yet, yet I loved to be in love ... I was looking for something to love, in love with love itself.
[*Confessions* (397–398), III]

3. *Da mihi castitatem et continentiam, sed noli modo.*
Give me chastity and continence, but not yet.
[*Confessions* (397–398), VIII]

4. *Tolle lege, tolle lege.*
Take up and read, take up and read!
[*Confessions* (397–398), VIII]

5. *Sero te amavi, pulchritudo tam antiqua et tam nova, sero te amavi! et ecce intus eras et ego foris, et ibi te quaerebam.*
Too late I came to love you, O Beauty both so ancient and so fresh, too late I came to love you. And behold, you were within me and I was out of myself, and there I was searching for you.
[*Confessions* (397–398), X]

6. *Securus iudicat orbis terrarum.*
The judgement of the world is sure.
[*Contra Epistolam Parmeniani*, III]

7. *Salus extra ecclesiam non est.*
Outside the church there is no salvation.
[*De Baptismo*, IV]

8. *Multi quidem facilius se abstinent ut non utantur, quam temperent ut bene utantur.*
Many find it easier to abstain totally than to use moderation.
[*De Bono Conjugali (On the Good of Marriage)*, XXI]

9. *Audi partem alteram.*
Hear the other side.
[*De Duabus Animabus*, XIV]

10. *Nisi credideritis, non intelligitis.*
Unless you believe, you will not understand.
[*De Libero Arbitrio*]

11. *Ama et fac quod vis.*
Love and do what you like.
[*In Joannis*, VII; popular variant of *Dilige et quod vis fac*]

12. *Roma locuta est; causa finita est.*
Rome has spoken; the case is concluded.
[*Sermons*, I]

Augustus, Caesar see CAESAR, AUGUSTUS

Aung San Suu Kyi
Burmese politician and founder of the National League for Democracy, placed under house arrest in 1989; winner of the Nobel Peace Prize, 1991

1. Concepts such as truth, justice, compassion are often the only bulwarks which stand against ruthless power.
[*Index on Censorship*, 1994]

Aurelius, Marcus (121–180)
Roman emperor and Stoic philosopher

1. This whatever this is that I am is flesh and spirit, and the ruling part.
[*Meditations*, II, 2]

2. And you will give yourself peace if you perform each act as if it were your last.
[*Meditations*, II, 5]

3. Remember that no one loses any other life than this which he now lives, nor lives any other than this which he now loses.
[*Meditations*, II, 14]

4. All things from eternity are of similar forms and come round in a circle.
[*Meditations*, II, 14]

5. That 'all that happens, happens as it should', if you observe carefully, you will find to be the case.
[*Meditations*, IV]

6. The universe is change; life is what thinking makes of it.
[*Meditations*, IV, 3]

7. Everything is ephemeral, both that which remembers and that which is remembered.
[*Meditations*, IV, 35]

8. Time is like a river made up of the things which happen, and its current is strong; no sooner does anything appear than it is carried away, and another comes in its place, and will be carried away too.
[*Meditations*, IV, 43]

9. Nothing happens to any thing which that thing is not made by nature to bear.
[*Meditations*, V, 18]

10. 'Live with the gods'. But he is living with the gods who constantly shows them that his soul is satisfied with what is assigned to him.
[*Meditations*, V, 27]

11. What is not good for the beehive, cannot be good for the bees.
[*Meditations*, VI]

12. Remember that to change your mind and follow someone who puts you right is to be none the less free than you were before.
[*Meditations*, VIII, 16]

13. Whatever may happen to you was prepared for you from all eternity; and the thread of causes was spinning from eternity both your being and this which is happening to you.
[*Meditations*, X, 5]

Austen, Jane (1775–1817)

English novelist, noted for insightful portrayal of middle-class families

1. N.B. There will be very few Dates in this History.
[*The History of England* (1791)]

2. One of Edward's Mistresses was Jane Shore, who has had a play written about her, but it is a tragedy and therefore not worth reading.
[*The History of England* (1791)]

3. Nothing can be said in his vindication, but that his abolishing Religious Houses and leaving them to the ruinous depredations of time has been of infinite use to the landscape of England in general.
[*The History of England* (1791)]

4. It was too pathetic for the feelings of Sophia and myself – we fainted Alternately on a Sofa.
[*Love and Freindship* (1791), Letter the 8th]

5. She was nothing more than a mere good-tempered, civil and obliging young woman; as such we could scarcely dislike her – she was only an Object of Contempt.
[*Love and Freindship* (1791), Letter the 13th]

6. An annuity is a very serious business; it comes over and over every year, and there is no getting rid of it.
[*Sense and Sensibility* (1811), 2]

7. On every formal visit a child ought to be of the party, by way of provision for discourse.
[*Sense and Sensibility* (1811), 6]

8. 'I am afraid,' replied Elinor, 'that the pleasantness of an employment does not always evince its propriety.'
[*Sense and Sensibility* (1811), 13]

9. Lady Middleton ... exerted herself to ask Mr Palmer if there was any news in the paper.
'No, none at all,' he replied, and read on.
[*Sense and Sensibility* (1811), 19]

10. Where so many hours have been spent in convincing myself that I am right, is there not some reason to fear I may be wrong?
[*Sense and Sensibility* (1811), 31]

11. A person and face, of strong, natural, sterling insignificance, though adorned in the first style of fashion.
[*Sense and Sensibility* (1811), 33]

12. It is a truth universally acknowledged, that a single man in possession of a good fortune, must be in want of a wife.
[*Pride and Prejudice* (1813), 1]

13. She was a woman of mean understanding, little information, and uncertain temper.
[*Pride and Prejudice* (1813), 1]

14. 'Kitty has no discretion in her coughs,' said her father; 'she times them ill.'
'I do not cough for my own amusement,' replied Kitty fretfully.
[*Pride and Prejudice* (1813), 2]

15. Happiness in marriage is entirely a matter of chance.
[*Pride and Prejudice* (1813), 6]

16. A lady's imagination is very rapid; it jumps from admiration to love, from love to matrimony, in a moment.
[*Pride and Prejudice* (1813), 6]

17. It is happy for you that you possess the talent of flattering with delicacy. May I ask whether these pleasing attentions proceed from the impulse of the moment, or are the result of previous study?
[*Pride and Prejudice* (1813), 14]

18. You have delighted us long enough.
[*Pride and Prejudice* (1813), 18]

19. An unhappy alternative is before you, Elizabeth. From this day you must be a stranger to one of your parents. – Your mother will never see you again if you do not marry Mr Collins, and I will never see you again if you do.
[*Pride and Prejudice* (1813), 20]

20. Nobody is on my side, nobody takes part with me: I am cruelly used, nobody feels for my poor nerves.
[*Pride and Prejudice* (1813), 20]

21. 'If it was not for the entail I should not mind it.'
'What should not you mind?'
'I should not mind any thing at all.'
'Let us be thankful that you are preserved from a state of such insensibility.'
[*Pride and Prejudice* (1813), 23]

22. Next to being married, a girl likes to be crossed in love a little now and then.
[*Pride and Prejudice* (1813), 24]

23. Lord, how ashamed I should be of not being married before three and twenty!
[*Pride and Prejudice* (1813), 39]

24. One cannot be always laughing at a man without now and then stumbling on something witty.
[*Pride and Prejudice* (1813), 40]

25. No arguments shall be wanting on my part, that can alleviate so severe a misfortune; or that may comfort you, under a circumstance that must be of all others most afflicting to a parent's mind. The death of your daughter would have been a blessing in comparison of this.
[*Pride and Prejudice* (1813), 48]

26. You ought certainly to forgive them as a Christian, but never to admit them in your sight, or allow their names to be mentioned in your hearing.
[*Pride and Prejudice* (1813), 57]

27. For what do we live, but to make sport for our neighbours, and laugh at them in our turn?
[*Pride and Prejudice* (1813), 57]

28. I have been a selfish being all my life, in practice, though not in principle.
[*Pride and Prejudice* (1813), 58]

29. If any young men come for Mary or Kitty, send them in, for I am quite at leisure.
[*Pride and Prejudice* (1813), 59]

30. Dear, dear Lizzy. A house in town! Every thing that is charming! Three daughters married! Ten thousand a year! Oh, Lord! What will become of me. I shall go distracted.
[*Pride and Prejudice* (1813), 59]

31. There certainly are not so many men of large fortune in the world as there are pretty women to deserve them.
[*Mansfield Park* (1814), 1]

32. You must try not to mind growing up into a pretty woman.
[*Mansfield Park* (1814), 21]

33. A large income is the best recipe for happiness I ever heard of. It certainly may secure all the myrtle and turkey part of it.
[*Mansfield Park* (1814), 22]

34. You must give my compliments to him. Yes; I think it must be compliments. Is there not a something wanted, Miss Price, in our language – a something between compliments and – and love – to suit the sort of friendly acquaintance we have had together?
[*Mansfield Park* (1814), 29]

35. We all talk Shakespeare, use his similes, and describe with his descriptions.
[*Mansfield Park* (1814), 34]

36. Let other pens dwell on guilt and misery.
[*Mansfield Park* (1814), 48]

37. She was of course only too good for him; but as nobody minds having what is too good for them, he was very steadily earnest in the pursuit of the blessing.
[*Mansfield Park* (1814), 48]

38. Matrimony, as the origin of change, was always disagreeable.
[*Emma* (1816), 1]

39. An egg boiled very soft is not unwholesome.
[*Emma* (1816), 3]

40. One half of the world cannot understand the pleasures of the other.
[*Emma* (1816), 9]

41. Nobody is healthy in London. Nobody can be.
[*Emma* (1816), 12]

42. With men he can be rational and unaffected, but when he has ladies to please, every feature works.
[*Emma* (1816), 13]

43. A man ... must have a very good opinion of himself when he asks people to leave their own fireside, and encounter such a day as this, for the sake of coming to see him. He must think himself a most agreeable fellow.
[*Emma* (1816), 13]

44. She believed he had been drinking too much of Mr Weston's good wine.
[*Emma* (1816), 15]

45. My mother's deafness is very trifling, you see, just nothing at all. By only raising my voice, and saying anything two or three times over, she is sure to hear.
[*Emma* (1816), 19]

46. Human nature is so well disposed towards those who are in interesting situations, that a young person, who either marries or dies, is sure of being kindly spoken of.
[*Emma* (1816), 22]

47. The sooner every party breaks up the better.
[*Emma* (1816), 25]

48. Perfect happiness, even in memory, is not common.
[*Emma* (1816), 27]

49. That young man ... is very thoughtless. Do not tell his father, but that young man is not quite the thing. He has been opening the doors very often this evening and keeping them open very inconsiderately. He does not think of the draught. I do not mean to set you against him, but indeed he is not quite the thing.
[*Emma* (1816), 29]

50. Open the windows! But, surely Mr Churchill, nobody would think of opening the windows at Randalls. Nobody could be so imprudent!
[*Emma* (1816), 29]

51. Fine dancing, I believe, like virtue, must be its own reward.
[*Emma* (1816), 30]

52. Why not seize the pleasure at once? How often is happiness destroyed by preparation, foolish preparation!
[*Emma* (1816), 30]

53. Business, you know, may bring money, but friendship hardly ever does.
[*Emma* (1816), 34]

54. Young ladies should take care of themselves. Young ladies are delicate plants. They should take care of their health and their complexion. My dear, did you change your stockings?
[*Emma* (1816), 34]

55. One has not great hopes from Birmingham. I always say there is something direful in the sound.
[*Emma* (1816), 36]

56. Emma denied none of it aloud, and agreed to none of it in private.
[*Emma* (1816), 42]

57. The stain of illegitimacy, unbleached by nobility or wealth, would have been a stain indeed.
[*Emma* (1816), 55]

58. 'And what are you reading, Miss —?' 'Oh! it is only a novel!' replies the young lady; while she lays down her book with affected indifference, or momentary shame. It is only *Cecilia*, or *Camilla*, or *Belinda*; or, in short, only some work in which the greatest powers of the mind are displayed, in which the most thorough knowledge of human nature, the happiest delineation of its varieties, the liveliest effusions of wit and humour, are conveyed to the world in the best chosen language.
[*Northanger Abbey* (1818), 5]

59. [Of Gothic novels]
But are they all horrid? Are you sure they are all horrid?
[*Northanger Abbey* (1818), 6]

60. Oh, Lord! not I; I never read much; I have something else to do.
[*Northanger Abbey* (1818), 7]

61. Oh! who can ever be tired of Bath?
[*Northanger Abbey* (1818), 10]

62. Real solemn history, I cannot be interested in ... The quarrels of popes and kings, with wars or pestilences, in every page; the men all so good for nothing, and hardly any women at all, it is very tiresome.
[*Northanger Abbey* (1818), 14]

63. Where people wish to attach, they should always be ignorant. To come with a well-informed mind, is to come with an inability of administering to the vanity of others, which a sensible person would always wish to avoid. A

woman especially, if she have the misfortune of knowing any thing, should conceal it as well as she can.
[*Northanger Abbey* (1818), 14]

64. From politics, it was an easy step to silence.
[*Northanger Abbey* (1818), 14]

65. Sir Walter Elliot, of Kellynch Hall, in Somersetshire, was a man who, for his own amusement, never took up any book but the Baronetage; there he found occupation for an idle hour and consolation in a distressed one ... this was the page at which the favourite volume always opened: – ELLIOT OF KELLYNCH-HALL.
[*Persuasion* (1818), 1]

66. 'My idea of good company, Mr Elliot, is the company of clever, well-informed people, who have a great deal of conversation; that is what I call good company.' 'You are mistaken,' said he gently, 'that is not good company; that is the best.'
[*Persuasion* (1818), 16]

67. My sore-throats, you know, are always worse than anybody's.
[*Persuasion* (1818), 18]

68. One does not love a place the less for having suffered in it, unless it has all been suffering, nothing but suffering.
[*Persuasion* (1818), 20]

69. All the privilege I claim for my own sex ... is that of loving longest, when existence or when hope is gone.
[*Persuasion* (1818), 23]

70. What dreadful hot weather we have! It keeps me in a continual state of inelegance.
[Letter, 1796]

71. I do not want people to be very agreeable, as it saves me the trouble of liking them a great deal.
[Letter, 1798]

72. Mrs Hall of Sherbourne was brought to bed yesterday of a dead child, some weeks before she expected, owing to a fright. I suppose she happened unawares to look at her husband.
[Letter, 1798]

73. We met ... Dr Hall in such very deep mourning that either his mother, his wife, or himself must be dead.
[Letter to Cassandra Austen, 1799]

74. I am proud to say that I have a very good eye at an Adultress, for tho' repeatedly assured that another in the same party was the She, I fixed upon the right one from the first.
[Letter to Cassandra Austen, 1801]

75. [Of the Battle of Albuera in 1811]
How horrible it is to have so many people killed! – And what a blessing that one cares for none of them!
[Letter to Cassandra Austen, 1811]

76. I think I may boast myself to be, with all possible vanity, the most unlearned and uninformed female who ever dared to be an authoress.
[Letter to James Stanier Clarke, 1815]

77. ... the little bit (two inches wide) of ivory on which I work with so fine a brush, as produces little effect after much labour.
[Letter, 1816]

78. History tells me nothing that does not either vex or weary me; the men are all so good for nothing, and hardly any women at all.
[Letter]

79. In nine cases out of ten, a woman had better show more affection than she feels.
[Letter]

Austin, Alfred (1835–1913)
English poet laureate and journalist

1. [On the illness of the Prince of Wales]
Across the wires the electric message came:
'He is no better, he is much the same.'
[Attr.]

Austin, Warren Robinson (1877–1962)
American Republican politician; first US Ambassador to the United Nations

1. [On being asked if he found long debates at the UN tiring]
It is better for aged diplomats to be bored than for young men to die.
[Attr.]

Avery, Oswald Theodore (1877–1955)
Canadian bacteriologist

1. Whenever you fall, pick up something.
[Attr.]

Ayckbourn, Alan (1939–)
English dramatist and theatre director; writer of comedies on middle-class life

1. Few women care to be laughed at and men not at all, except for large sums of money.
[*The Norman Conquests* (1975), Preface]

Ayer, A.J. (1910–1989)
English philosopher; Professor of Logic

1. The principles of logic and metaphysics are true simply because we never allow them to be anything else.
[*Language, Truth and Logic* (1936)]

2. No morality can be founded on authority, even if the authority were divine.
[*Essay on Humanism*]

Aytoun, W.E. (1813–1865)
Scottish poet, ballad writer and satirist

1. Fhairshon swore a feud
Against the clan M'Tavish;
Marched into their land
To murder and to rafish;
For he did resolve
To extirpate the vipers,
With four-and-twenty men
And five-and-thirty pipers.
['The Massacre of the Macpherson' (1844)]

2. And some that came to scoff at him
Now turned aside and wept ...

3. 'He is coming! he is coming!'
Like a bridegroom from his room,
Came the hero from his prison
To the scaffold and the doom.
['The Execution of Montrose' (1849)]

4. They bore within their breasts the grief
That fame can never heal–
The deep, unutterable woe
Which none save exiles feel.
['The Island of the Scots' (1849)]

5. The earth is all the home I have,
The heavens my wide roof-tree.
['The Wandering Jew' (1867)]

Baba, Meher (1894–1969)
Indian guru and avatar

1. Don't worry, be happy.
[Inspiration for song by Bobby McFerrin, 1988]

Babbage, Charles (1792–1871)
English mathematician and inventor of calculating machines

1. Every moment dies a man,
Every moment one and one-sixteenth is born.
[Letter to Tennyson. Cf. Tennyson: 97]

Bacon, Francis [1] (First Baron Verulam and Viscount St Albans) (1561–1626)
English philosopher, essayist, politician, lawyer and courtier

1. Knowledge itself is power.
[*Meditationes Sacrae* (*Religious Meditations*, 1597), 'Of Heresies']

2. Universities incline wits to sophistry and affectation.
[*Valerius Terminus of the Interpretation of Nature* (written 1603), 26]

3. That all things are changed, and that nothing really perishes, and that the sum of matter remains exactly the same, is sufficiently certain.
[*Cogitationes de Natura Rerum* (*Thoughts on the Nature of Things*, 1604), 5]

4. So let great authors have their due, as time, which is the author of authors, be not deprived of his due, which is, further and further to discover truth.
[*The Advancement of Learning* (1605), I, 4]

5. If a man will begin with certainties, he shall end in doubts; but if he will be content to begin with doubts, he shall end in certainties.
[*The Advancement of Learning* (1605), I, 5]

6. [Knowledge is] a rich storehouse for the glory of the Creator and the relief of man's estate.
[*The Advancement of Learning* (1605), I, 5]

7. Antiquities are history defaced, or some remnants of history which have casually escaped the shipwreck of time.
[*The Advancement of Learning* (1605), II, 2]

8. [Poesy] was ever thought to have some participation of divineness, because it doth raise and erect the mind, by submitting the shows of things to the desires of the mind; whereas reason doth buckle and bow the mind unto the nature of things.
[*The Advancement of Learning* (1605), II, 4]

9. They are ill discoverers that think there is no land, when they can see nothing but sea.
[*The Advancement of Learning* (1605), II, 7]

10. But men must know, that in this theatre of man's life it is reserved only for God and angels to be lookers on.
[*The Advancement of Learning* (1605), II, 20]

11. We are much beholden to Machiavel and others, that write what men do, and not what they ought to do.
[*The Advancement of Learning* (1605), II, 21]

12. Men must pursue things which are just in present, and leave the future to the divine Providence.
[*The Advancement of Learning* (1605), II, 21]

13. All good moral philosophy ... is but an handmaid to religion.
[*The Advancement of Learning* (1605), II, 22]

14. Man seeketh in society comfort, use, and protection.
[*The Advancement of Learning* (1605), II, 23]

15. [Paraphrasing Solomon, Ecclesiastes, II:4]
A man must make his opportunity, as oft as find it.
[*The Advancement of Learning* (1605), II, 23. Cf. Bacon: 45]

16. [Fortunes] come tumbling into some men's laps.
[*The Advancement of Learning* (1605), II, 23]

17. Books must follow sciences, and not sciences books.
['A Proposition touching the Compiling and Amendment of the Laws of England' (written 1616)]

18. A false friend is more dangerous than an open enemy.
[*A Letter of Advice ... to the Duke of Buckingham, When he became Favourite to King James* (written 1616, published 1661)]

19. I have rather studied books than men.
[*A Copy of a Letter ... to the late Duke of Buckingham when first he became a favourite to King James* (written 1616, published 1663)]

20. The ill and unfit choice of words wonderfully obstructs the understanding.
[*Novum Organum* (*The New Organon*, 1620), I, 43]

21. What a man had rather were true he more readily believes.
[*Novum Organum* (*The New Organon*, 1620), I, 49]

22. [Of natural philosophy]
That great mother of sciences.
[*Novum Organum* (*The New Organon*, 1620), I, 80]

23. I am too old, and the seas are too long, for me to double the Cape of Good Hope.
[*Memorial of Access to King James I* (c.1622, published 1763)]

24. I would live to study, and not study to live.
[*Memorial of Access to King James I* (c.1622, published 1763)]

25. Riches are a good handmaid, but the worst mistress.
[*De Dignitate et Augmentis Scientiarum* (*Of the Dignity and Advancement of Learning*, 1623), VI, 3]

26. The voice of the people has something divine, else how could so many agree in one thing?
[*De Dignitate et Augmentis Scientiarum* (*Of the Dignity and Advancement of Learning*, 1623), VI, 3]

27. Silence is the virtue of fools.
[*De Dignitate et Augmentis Scientiarum* (*Of the Dignity and Advancement of Learning*, 1623), VI, 3]

28. It is the worst solitude, to have no true friendships.
[*De Dignitate et Augmentis Scientiarum* (*Of the Dignity and Advancement of Learning*, 1623), VI, 3]

29. For as it is said of calumny, 'calumniate boldly, for some of it will stick' so it may be said of ostentation (except it be in a ridiculous degree of deformity), 'boldly sound your own praises, and some of them will stick.'
[*De Dignitate et Augmentis Scientiarum* (*Of the Dignity and Advancement of Learning*, 1623), VIII, 2]

30. One of the Seven was wont to say: 'That laws were like cobwebs; where the small flies were caught, and the great brake through.'
[*Apophthegms New and Old* (1624), 181]

31. Prosperity is the blessing of the Old Testament, adversity is the blessing of the New.
[*Essays* (1625), 'Of Adversity']

32. The pencil of the Holy Ghost hath laboured more in describing the afflictions of Job than the felicities of Solomon.
[*Essays* (1625), 'Of Adversity']

33. Prosperity is not without many fears and distastes; and adversity is not without comforts and hopes.
[*Essays* (1625), 'Of Adversity']

34. Prosperity doth best discover vice, but adversity doth best discover virtue.
[*Essays* (1625), 'Of Adversity']

35. God never wrought miracle to convince atheism, because his ordinary works convince it.
[*Essays* (1625), 'Of Atheism']

36. It is true, that a little philosophy inclineth man's mind to atheism; but depth in philosophy bringeth men's minds about to religion.
[*Essays* (1625), 'Of Atheism']

37. Virtue is like a rich stone, best plain set.
[*Essays* (1625), 'Of Beauty']

38. That is the best part of beauty, which a picture cannot express.
[*Essays* (1625), 'Of Beauty']

39. There is no excellent beauty, that hath not some strangeness in the proportion.
[*Essays* (1625), 'Of Beauty']

40. There is in human nature generally more of the fool than of the wise.
[*Essays* (1625), 'Of Boldness']

41. Mahomet made the people believe that he would call a hill to him, and from the top of it offer up his prayers for the observers of his law. The people assembled: Mahomet called the hill to come to him again and again; and when the hill stood still, he was never a whit abashed, but said, 'If the hill will not come to Mahomet, Mahomet will go to the hill.'
[*Essays* (1625), 'Of Boldness']

42. Houses are built to live in and not to look on; therefore let use be preferred before uniformity, except where both may be had.
[*Essays* (1625), 'Of Building']

43. Light gains make heavy purses.
[*Essays* (1625), 'Of Ceremonies and Respects']

44. Small matters win great commendation.
[*Essays* (1625), 'Of Ceremonies and Respects']

45. A wise man will make more opportunities than he finds.
[*Essays* (1625), 'Of Ceremonies and Respects'. Cf. Bacon: 15]

46. Books will speak plain when counsellors blanch.
[*Essays* (1625), 'Of Counsel']

47. In things that are tender and unpleasing, it is good to break the ice by some whose words are of less weight, and to reserve the more weighty voice to come in as by chance.
[*Essays* (1625), 'Of Cunning']

48. I knew one that when he wrote a letter he would put that which was most material in the postscript, as if it had been a bymatter.
[*Essays* (1625), 'Of Cunning']

49. Nothing doth more hurt in a state than that cunning men pass for wise.
[*Essays* (1625), 'Of Cunning']

50. Men fear death as children fear to go in the dark; and as that natural fear in children is increased with tales, so is the other.
[*Essays* (1625), 'Of Death']

51. There is no passion in the mind of man so weak, but it mates and masters the fear of death. And therefore death is no such terrible enemy, when a man hath so many attendants about him that can win the combat of him. Revenge triumphs over death; love slights it; honour aspireth to it; grief flieth to it.
[*Essays* (1625), 'Of Death']

52. It is as natural to die as to be born; and to a little infant, perhaps, the one is as painful as the other.
[*Essays* (1625), 'Of Death']

53. Above all, believe it, the sweetest canticle is Nunc dimittis, when a man hath obtained worthy ends and expectations. Death hath this also, that it openeth the gate to good fame, and extinguisheth envy.
[*Essays* (1625), 'Of Death']

54. Some in their discourse, desire rather commendation of wit, in being able to hold all arguments, than of judgement in discerning what is true.
[*Essays* (1625), 'Of Discourse']

55. I knew one, was wont to say in scorn; he must needs be a wise man, he speaks so much of himself.
[*Essays* (1625), 'Of Discourse']

56. I knew a wise man that had it for a by-word, when he saw men hasten to a conclusion, 'Stay a little, that we may make an end the sooner.'
[*Essays* (1625), 'Of Dispatch']

57. To choose time is to save time.
[*Essays* (1625), 'Of Dispatch']

58. It is a miserable state of mind to have few things to desire and many things to fear.
[*Essays* (1625), 'Of Empire']

59. Nothing destroyeth authority so much as the unequal and untimely interchange of power pressed too far, and relaxed too much.
[*Essays* (1625), 'Of Empire']

60. Riches are for spending.
[*Essays* (1625), 'Of Expense']

61. A man ought warily to begin charges which once begun will continue.
[*Essays* (1625), 'Of Expense']

62. There is little friendship in the world, and least of all between equals.
[*Essays* (1625), 'Of Followers and Friends']

63. Chiefly the mould of a man's fortune is in his own hands.
[*Essays* (1625), 'Of Fortune']

64. If a man look sharply, and attentively, he shall see Fortune: for though she be blind, yet she is not invisible.
[*Essays* (1625), 'Of Fortune']

65. It had been hard for him that spake it to have put more truth and untruth together, in a few words, than in that speech: 'Whosoever is delighted in solitude is either a wild beast, or a god.'
[*Essays* (1625), 'Of Friendship'. Cf. Aristotle: 15]

66. A crowd is not company, and faces are but a gallery of pictures, and talk but a tinkling cymbal, where there is no love.
[*Essays* (1625), 'Of Friendship']

67. This communicating of a man's self to his friend works two contrary effects; for it redoubleth joys, and cutteth griefs in halves.
[*Essays* (1625), 'Of Friendship']

68. As if you would call a physician, that is thought good for the cure of the disease you complain of but is unacquainted with your body, and therefore may put you in the way for a present cure but overthroweth your health in some other kind; and so cure the disease and kill the patient.
[*Essays* (1625), 'Of Friendship']

69. God Almighty first planted a garden. And indeed, it is the purest of human pleasures. It is the greatest refreshment to the spirits of man; without which, buildings and palaces are but gross handiworks: and ... when ages grow to civility and elegance, men come to build stately, sooner than to garden finely.
[*Essays* (1625), 'Of Gardens']

70. In charity there is no excess.
[*Essays* (1625), 'Of Goodness, and Goodness of Nature']

71. The inclination to goodness is imprinted deeply in the nature of man: insomuch, that if it issue not towards men, it will take unto other living creatures.
[*Essays* (1625), 'Of Goodness, and Goodness of Nature']

72. If a man be gracious and courteous to strangers, it shows he is a citizen of the world.
[*Essays* (1625), 'Of Goodness, and Goodness of Nature']

73. Men in great place are thrice servants: servants of the sovereign or state, servants of fame, and servants of business ... It is a strange desire to seek power and to lose liberty.
[*Essays* (1625), 'Of Great Place']

74. Severity breedeth fear, but roughness breedeth hate. Even reproofs from authority ought to be grave, and not taunting.
[*Essays* (1625), 'Of Great Place']

75. All rising to great place is by a winding stair.
[*Essays* (1625), 'Of Great Place']

76. Set it down to thyself, as well to create good precedents as to follow them.
[*Essays* (1625), 'Of Great Place']

77. And he that will not apply new remedies, must expect new evils; for time is the greatest innovator.
[*Essays* (1625), 'Of Innovations']

78. The speaking in a perpetual hyperbole is comely in nothing but in love.
[*Essays* (1625), 'Of Love']

79. They do best who, if they cannot but admit love, yet make it keep quarter; and sever it wholly from their serious affairs and actions of life: for if it check once with business, it troubleth men's fortunes, and maketh men, that they can no ways be true to their own ends.
[*Essays* (1625), 'Of Love']

80. He that hath wife and children, hath given hostages to fortune; for they are impediments to great enterprises, either of virtue or mischief.
[*Essays* (1625), 'Of Marriage and Single Life']

81. He was reputed one of the wise men that made answer to the question when a man should marry? 'A young man not yet, an elder man not at all.'
[*Essays* (1625), 'Of Marriage and Single Life']

82. But the most ordinary cause of a single life, is liberty; especially in certain self-pleasing and humorous minds, which are so sensible of every restraint as they will go near to think their girdles and garters to be bonds and shackles.
[*Essays* (1625), 'Of Marriage and Single Life']

83. Certainly, wife and children are a kind of discipline of humanity: and single men, though they be many times more charitable, because their means are less exhausted, yet, on the other side, they are more cruel and hard hearted ... because their tenderness is not so oft called upon.
[*Essays* (1625), 'Of Marriage and Single Life']

84. There are some other that account wife and children but as bills of charges.
[*Essays* (1625), 'Of Marriage and Single Life']

85. Wives are young men's mistresses, companions for middle age, and old men's nurses.
[*Essays* (1625), 'Of Marriage and Single Life']

86. Nature is often hidden; sometimes overcome; seldom extinguished.
[*Essays* (1625), 'Of Nature in Men']

87. A man's nature runs either to herbs, or to weeds; therefore let him seasonably water the one, and destroy the other.
[*Essays* (1625), 'Of Nature in Men']

88. It is generally better to deal by speech than by letter.
[*Essays* (1625), 'Of Negotiating']

89. It is a reverend thing to see an ancient castle or building not in decay.
[*Essays* (1625), 'Of Nobility']

90. The joys of parents are secret, and so are their griefs and fears.
[*Essays* (1625), 'Of Parents and Children']

91. Children sweeten labours, but they make misfortunes more bitter.
[*Essays* (1625), 'Of Parents and Children']

92. The noblest works and foundations have proceeded from childless men, which have sought to express the images of their minds where those of their bodies have failed.
[*Essays* (1625), 'Of Parents and Children']

93. Fame is like a river, that beareth up things light and swollen, and drowns things weighty and solid.
[*Essays* (1625), 'Of Praise']

94. Dreams and predictions of astrology ... ought to serve but for winter talk by the fireside.
[*Essays* (1625), 'Of Prophecies']

95. Age will not be defied.
[*Essays* (1625), 'Of Regimen of Health']

96. Revenge is a kind of wild justice, which the more man's nature runs to, the more ought law to weed it out.
[*Essays* (1625) 'Of Revenge']

97. Why should I be angry with a man for loving himself better than me?
[*Essays* (1625), 'Of Revenge']

98. A man that studieth revenge keeps his own wounds green.
[*Essays* (1625), 'Of Revenge']

99. Of great riches, there is no real use, except it be in distribution; the rest is but conceit.
[*Essays* (1625), 'Of Riches']

100. And money is like muck, not good except it be spread.
[*Essays* (1625), 'Of Seditions and Troubles']

101. The remedy is worse than the disease.
[*Essays* (1625), 'Of Seditions and Troubles']

102. Nakedness is uncomely as well in mind, as body.
[*Essays* (1625), 'Of Simulation and Dissimulation']

103. Studies serve for delight, for ornament, and for ability.
[*Essays* (1625), 'Of Studies']

104. To spend too much time in studies, is sloth; to use them too much for ornament, is affectation; to make judgement wholly by their rules is the humour of a scholar.
[*Essays* (1625), 'Of Studies']

105. Crafty men contemn studies; simple men admire them; and wise men use them.
[*Essays* (1625), 'Of Studies']

106. Read not to contradict and confute, nor to believe and take for granted, nor to find talk and discourse, but to weigh and consider.
[*Essays* (1625), 'Of Studies']

107. Some books are to be tasted, others to be swallowed, and some few to be chewed and digested; that is, some books are to be read only in parts; others to be read but not curiously; and some few to be read wholly, and with diligence and attention.
[*Essays* (1625), 'Of Studies']

108. Reading maketh a full man; conference a ready man; and writing an exact man.
[*Essays* (1625), 'Of Studies']

109. Histories make men wise; poets, witty; the mathematics, subtile; natural philosophy, deep; moral, grave; logic and rhetoric, able to contend.
[*Essays* (1625), 'Of Studies']

110. It were better to have no opinion of God at all, than such an opinion as is unworthy of him.
[*Essays* (1625), 'Of Superstition']

111. Suspicions amongst thoughts are like bats amongst birds, they ever fly by twilight.
[*Essays* (1625), 'Of Suspicion']

112. Travel, in the younger sort, is a part of education; in the elder, a part of experience. He that travelleth into a country before he hath some entrance into the language, goeth to school, and not to travel.
[*Essays* (1625), 'Of Travel']

113. Neither will it be, that a people overlaid with taxes should ever become valiant and martial.
[*Essays* (1625), 'Of the True Greatness of Kingdoms']

114. What is Truth? said jesting Pilate; and would not stay for an answer.
[*Essays* (1625), 'Of Truth']

115. This same truth is a naked and open daylight, that doth not show the masques and mummeries and triumphs of the world half so stately and daintily as candlelights.
[*Essays* (1625), 'Of Truth']

116. Doth any man doubt, that if there were taken out of men's minds, vain opinions, flattering hopes, false valuations, imaginations as one would, and the like; but it would leave the minds of a number of men poor shrunken things.
[*Essays* (1625), 'Of Truth']

117. But it is not the lie that passeth through the mind, but the lie that sinketh in, and settleth in it, that doth the hurt.
[*Essays* (1625), 'Of Truth']

118. To say that a man lieth, is as much to say, as that he is brave towards God, and a coward towards men.
[*Essays* (1625), 'Of Truth']

119. All colours will agree in the dark.
[*Essays* (1625), 'Of Unity in Religion']

120. It was prettily devised of Aesop, 'The fly sat upon the axletree of the chariot-wheel and said, what a dust do I raise.'
[*Essays* (1625), 'Of Vain-Glory']

121. It is a poor centre of a man's actions, himself.
[*Essays* (1625), 'Of Wisdom for a Man's Self']

122. It is the nature of extreme self-lovers, as they will set a house on fire, and it were but to roast their eggs.
[*Essays* (1625), 'Of Wisdom for a Man's Self']

123. It is the wisdom of the crocodiles, that shed tears when they would devour.
[*Essays* (1625), 'Of Wisdom for a Man's Self']

124. The end of our foundation is the knowledge of causes, and secret motions of things; and the enlarging of the bounds of human Empire, to the effecting of all things possible.
[*New Atlantis* (1627)]

125. I have often thought upon death, and I find it the least of all evils.
[*The Remaines of . . . Lord Verulam* (1648), 'An Essay on Death']

126. I do not believe that any man fears to be dead, but only the stroke of death.
[*The Remaines of . . . Lord Verulam* (1648), 'An Essay on Death']

127. Hope is a good breakfast, but it is a bad supper.
[In *Resuscitatio* (1661 edition), 'Apophthegms', 36]

128. Anger makes dull men witty, but it keeps them poor.
[In *Baconiana* (1679), 'Apophthegms', 5]

129. I have as vast contemplative ends, as I have moderate civil ends; for I have taken all knowledge to be my province.
[Letter to Burghley, 1592]

130. Opportunity makes a thief.
[Letter to Essex, 1598]

131. The world's a bubble; and the life of man
Less than a span.
[*The World* (1629). Cf. Nathaniel Ward: 1]

132. What is it then to have or have no wife,
But single thraldom, or a double strife?
[*The World* (1629)]

133. What then remains, but that we still should cry,
Not to be born, or being born, to die?
[*The World* (1629)]

Bacon, Francis [2] (1909–1993)
Irish-born expressionist painter

1. How can I take an interest in my work when I don't like it?
[Attr.]

Bacon, Sir Nicholas (1509–1579)
Father of Francis Bacon

1. [Reply to Elizabeth I who remarked on the smallness of his house]
Madam, my house is well, but it is you that have made me too great for my house.
[In Francis Bacon, *Aphophthegms, New and Old* (1624), 139]

Baedeker, Karl (1801–1859)
German editor and publisher of travel guides

1. Oxford is on the whole more attractive than Cambridge to the ordinary visitor; and the traveller is therefore recommended to visit Cambridge first, or to omit it altogether if he cannot visit both.
[*Baedeker's Great Britain* (1887)]

Baez, Joan (1941–)
American folk-singer and songwriter; known for her 'protest' songs

1. I've never had a humble opinion. If you've got an opinion, why be humble about it.
[*Scotland on Sunday*, 'Quotes of the Year', 1992]

Bagehot, Walter (1826–1877)
English economist, political philosopher and journalist

1. A constitutional statesman is in general a man of common opinions and uncommon abilities.
[*Historical Essays*, 'The Character of Sir Robert Peel'; first published in National Review, 1856]

2. [Of Sir Robert Peel]
No man has come so near our definition of a constitutional statesman – the powers of a first-rate man and the creed of a second-rate man.
[*Historical Essays*, 'The Character of Sir Robert Peel'; first published in National Review, 1856]

3. There is a glare in some men's eyes which seems to say, 'Beware, I am dangerous; Noli me tangere.' Lord Brougham's face has this. A mischievous excitability is the most obvious expression of it. If he were a horse, nobody would buy him; with that eye no one could answer for his temper.
[*Historical Essays*, 'Lord Brougham'; first published in National Review, 1857]

4. No real English gentleman, in his secret soul, was ever sorry for the death of a political economist.
[*Estimates of some Englishmen and Scotchmen* (1858), 'The First Edinburgh Reviewers']

5. Writers, like teeth, are divided into incisors and grinders.
[*Estimates of some Englishmen and Scotchmen* (1858), 'The First Edinburgh Reviewers']

6. The mystic reverence, the religious allegiance, which are essential to a true monarchy, are imaginative sentiments that no legislature can manufacture in any people.
[*The English Constitution* (1867), 'The Cabinet']

7. The Crown is, according to the saying, the 'fountain of honour'; but the Treasury is the spring of business.
[*The English Constitution* (1867), 'The Cabinet']

8. It has been said that England invented the phrase, 'Her Majesty's Opposition'; that it was the first Government which made a criticism of administration as much a part of the polity as administration itself. This critical opposition is the consequence of Cabinet government.
[*The English Constitution* (1867), 'The Cabinet']

9. [The Monarchy] gives now a vast strength to the entire Constitution, by enlisting on its behalf the credulous obedience of enormous masses.
[*The English Constitution* (1867), 'The Monarchy']

10. The best reason why Monarchy is a strong government is, that it is an intelligible government. The mass of mankind understand it, and they hardly anywhere in the world understand any other.
[*The English Constitution* (1867), 'The Monarchy']

11. Royalty is a government in which the attention of the nation is concentrated on one person doing interesting actions. A Republic is a government in which that attention is divided between many, who are all doing uninteresting actions. Accordingly, so long as the human heart is strong and the human reason weak, royalty will be strong because it appeals to diffused feeling, and Republics weak because they appeal to the understanding.
[*The English Constitution* (1867), 'The Monarchy']

12. The sovereign has, under a constitutional monarchy such as ours, three rights – the right to be consulted, the right to encourage, the right to warn.
[*The English Constitution* (1867), 'The Monarchy']

13. Women – one half the human race at least – care fifty times more for a marriage than a ministry.
[*The English Constitution* (1867), 'The Monarchy']

14. Of all nations in the world the English are perhaps the least a nation of pure philosophers.
[*The English Constitution* (1867), 'The Monarchy']

15. It has been said, not truly, but with a possible approximation to truth, 'that in 1802 every hereditary monarch was insane.'
[*The English Constitution* (1867), 'Its Supposed Checks and Balances']

16. The House of Peers has never been a House where the most important peers were most important.
[*The English Constitution* (1867), 'The House of Lords']

17. Nations touch at their summits.
[*The English Constitution* (1867), 'The House of Lords']

18. A severe though not unfriendly critic of our institutions said that 'the cure for admiring the House of Lords was to go and look at it.'
[*The English Constitution* (1867), 'The House of Lords']

19. The most melancholy of human reflections, perhaps, is that, on the whole, it is a question whether the benevolence of mankind does most good or harm.
[*Physics and Politics* (1872)]

20. One of the greatest pains to human nature is the pain of a new idea.
[*Physics and Politics* (1872)]

21. The whole history of civilization is strewn with creeds and institutions which were invaluable at first, and deadly afterwards.
[*Physics and Politics* (1872)]

22. The habit of common and continuous speech is a symptom of mental deficiency.
[*Literary Studies* (1879), 1]

23. A man who has not read Homer is like a man who has not seen the ocean. There is a great object of which he has no idea.
[*Literary Studies* (1879), 1]

24. Nothing is more unpleasant than a virtuous person with a mean mind.
[*Literary Studies* (1879), 2]

25. Poverty is an anomaly to rich people. It is very difficult to make out why people who want dinner do not ring the bell.
[*Literary Studies* (1879), 2]

26. So long as there are earnest believers in the world, they will always wish to punish opinions, even if their judgement tells them it is unwise, and their conscience that it is wrong.
[*Literary Studies* (1879), 2]

Bagnold, Enid (1889–1981)
English writer

1. The great and terrible step was taken. What else could you expect from a girl so expectant? 'Sex,' said Frank Harris, 'is the gateway to life.' So I went through the gateway in an upper room in the Café Royal.
[*Enid Bagnold's Autobiography* (1969)]

Bailey, Philip James (1816–1902)
English 'spasmodic' poet

1. America, thou half-brother of the world;
With something good and bad of every land.
[*Festus* (1839), 'The Surface']

Baillie, Joanna (1762–1851)
Scottish dramatist and poet

1. What custom hath endear'd
We part with sadly, though we prize it not.
[*Plays on the Passions* (1798), *Basil*, I]

2. But woman's grief is like a summer storm,
Short as it violent is.
[*Plays on the Passions* (1798), *Basil*, V]

Bailly, Jean Sylvain (1736–1793)
French astronomer and politician

1. [Reflection on the evening before his execution]
It's time for me to enjoy another pinch of snuff. Tomorrow my hands will be bound, so as to make it impossible.
[Attr.]

Bainbridge, Kenneth (1904–)
American nuclear physicist

1. Now we are all sons of bitches.
[Remark after directing the first atomic test, 1945]

Bairnsfather, Charles Bruce (1888–1959)
British cartoonist and army officer

1. Well, if you knows of a better 'ole, go to it.
[*Fragments from France* (1915)]

Baker, H.W. (1821–1877)
English hymn-writer and clergyman

1. The King of Love my Shepherd is,
Whose goodness faileth never;
I nothing lack if I am His
And He is mine for ever.

Perverse and foolish oft I strayed;
But yet in love He sought me.
[Hymn, 1868]

Bakewell, Joan
British journalist and television presenter

1. The BBC is full of men appointing men who remind them of themselves when young, so you get the same backgrounds, the same education, and the same programmes.
[*The Observer*, 1993]

Bakunin, Mikhail (1814–1876)
Russian anarchist and writer; member of the First International

1. *Die Lust der Zerstörung ist zugleich eine schaffende Lust!*
The desire for destruction is, at the same time, a creative desire.
[In *Jahrbuch für Wissenschaft und Kunst*, 1842, 'Die Reaktion in Deutschland', published under the pen name 'Jules Elysard']

2. [Anarchist declaration, Lyon, 1870]
We wish, in a word, equality – equality in fact as corollary, or rather, as primordial condition of liberty. From each according to his faculties, to each according to his needs; that is what we wish sincerely and energetically.
[In J. Morrison Davidson, *The Old Order and the New* (1890)
Cf. Karl Marx: 7]

Baldwin, James (1924–1987)
American essayist, novelist, short-story writer, dramatist, poet and civil rights activist

1. Money, it turned out, was exactly like sex, you thought of nothing else if you didn't have it and thought of other things if you did.
[*Nobody Knows My Name* (1961)]

2. The price one pays for pursuing any profession or calling is an intimate knowledge of its ugly side.
[*Nobody Knows My Name* (1961)]

3. Children have never been very good at listening to their elders, but they have never failed to imitate them. They must, they have no other models.
[*Nobody Knows My Name* (1961)]

4. If the concept of God has any validity or any use, it can only be to make us larger, freer, and more loving. If God cannot do this, then it is time we got rid of Him.
[*The Fire Next Time* (1963)]

5. The future is . . . black.
[*The Observer*, 'Sayings of the Week', 1963]

Baldwin, Stanley (First Earl Baldwin of Bewdley) (1867–1947)
English statesman; Conservative politician and Prime Minister, 1923–24, 1924–29, 1935–37

1. What the proprietorship of these papers is aiming at is power, and power without responsibility – the prerogative of the harlot through the ages.
[Speech at an election rally, 1931]

2. I think it is well also for the man in the street to realise that there is no power on earth that can protect him from being bombed. Whatever people may tell him, the bomber will always get through. The only defence is in offence, which means that you have to kill more women and children more quickly than the enemy if you want to save yourselves.
[Speech, 1932]

3. [On becoming Prime Minister]
I met Curzon in Downing Street, from whom I got the sort of greeting a corpse would give to an undertaker.
[Remark, 1933]

4. There is a wind of nationalism and freedom blowing round the world, and blowing as strongly in Asia as elsewhere.
[Speech, London, 4 December 1934]

5. When you think of the defence of England you no longer think of the chalk cliffs of Dover. You think of the Rhine. That is where our frontier lies today.
[Speech, 1934]

6. [On the Abyssinia crisis]
I have seldom spoken with greater regret, for my lips are not yet unsealed. Were these troubles over I would make a case, and I guarantee that not a man would go into the Lobby against me.
[Speech, House of Commons, 1935; often quoted as 'My lips are sealed.']

7. You will find in politics that you are much exposed to the attribution of false motives. Never complain and never explain.
[To Harold Nicolson, 21 July 1943, quoting Disraeli]

8. Then comes Winston with his hundred-horse-power mind and what can I do?
[In G.M. Young, *Stanley Baldwin* (1952), 11]

9. The intelligent are to the intelligentsia what a gentleman is to a gent.
[Attr.]

10. [Of the House of Commons, 1918]
A lot of hard-faced men who look as if they had done very well out of the war.
[Attr.]

11. A platitude is simply a truth repeated until people get tired of hearing it.
[Attr.]

12. There are three groups that no British Prime Minister should provoke: the Vatican, the Treasury and the miners.
[Attr.]

Balfour, Arthur James (First Earl of Balfour) (1848–1930)

Scottish statesman; Conservative politician and Prime Minister, 1902–05; philosopher

1. The energies of our system will decay, the glory of the sun will be dimmed, and the earth, tideless and inert, will no longer tolerate the race which has for a moment disturbed its solitude. Man will go down into the pit, and all his thoughts will perish.
[*The Foundations of Belief* (1895), I]

2. His Majesty's Government views with favour the establishment in Palestine of a national home for the Jewish people.
['The Balfour Declaration', 1917]

3. It is unfortunate, considering that enthusiasm moves the world, that so few enthusiasts can be trusted to speak the truth.
[Letter to Mrs Drew, 1891]

4. Frank Harris ... said ...: 'The fact is, Mr Balfour, all the faults of the age come from Christianity and journalism.' To which Arthur replied ... 'Christianity, of course ... but why journalism?'
[In Margot Asquith, *Autobiography* (1920), 10]

5. [On being asked whether he was going to marry Margot Tennant]
I rather think of having a career of my own.
[In Margot Asquith, *Autobiography* (1920), 10]

6. [Comment on Winston Churchill in 1899]
I thought he was a young man of promise; but it appears he is a young man of promises.
[In Winston Churchill, *My Early Life* (1930), 17]

7. History does not repeat itself. Historians repeat each other.
[Attr.]

8. Nothing matters very much, and very few things matter at all.
[Attr.]

Ballads

N.B. Most ballads are of uncertain date and exist in many versions.

1. 'Annan water's wading deep,
And my love Annie's wond'rous bonnie;
And I am laith she should weet her feet,
Because I love her best of ony.'
['Annan Water']

2. O cherry, cherry was her cheek,
And golden was her hair;
But claycauld were her rosy lips–
Nae spark of life was there.
['Annie of Lochryan']

3. In Scarlet town, where I was born,
There was a fair maid dwellin',
Mack every youth cry Well-a-way!
Her name was Barbara Allen.

All in the merry month of May,
When green buds they were swellin',
Young Jemmy Grove on his death-bed lay,
For love of Barbara Allen...

4. So slowly, slowly rase she up,
And slowly she came nigh him,
And when she drew the curtain by–
'Young man, I think you're dyin'!'...

5. 'O mother, mother, make my bed,
O make it saft and narrow:
My love has died for me to-day,
I'll die for him to-morrow.'...

6. 'Farewell,' she said, 'ye virgins all,
And shun the fault I fell in:
Henceforth take warning by the fall
Of cruel Barbara Allen.'
['Barbara Allen']

7. It fell about the Lammas tide,
When the muir-men win their hay,
The doughty Douglas bound him to ride
In England, to drive a prey...

8. 'But I hae dream'd a dreary dream,
Beyond the Isle of Skye;
I saw a dead man win a fight,
And I think that man was I.'
['Battle of Otterbourne']

9. There were twa sisters lived in a bower–
Binnorie, O Binnorie!
There came a knight to be their wooer,
By the bonnie mill-dams o' Binnorie...

10. He courted the eldest wi' glove an' ring,
Binnorie, O Binnorie!
But he loved the youngest above a' thing.
By the bonnie mill-dams o' Binnorie.
['Binnorie']

11. Ye Highlands and ye Lawlands,
O where hae ye been?
They hae slain the Earl of Murray,
And hae laid him on the green...

12. He was a braw gallant,
And he rid at the ring;
And the bonny Earl of Murray,
O he might hae been a king!...

13. He was a braw gallant,
And he play'd at the gluve;
And the bonny Earl of Murray,
O he was the Queen's luve!

O lang will his Lady
Look owre the Castle Downe,
Ere she see the Earl of Murray,
Come sounding through the town!
['The Bonny Earl of Murray']

14. She hadna sail'd a league, a league,
A league but barely three,
Till grim, grim grew his countenance
And gurly grew the sea.

'What hills are yon, yon pleasant hills,
The sun shines sweetly on?'–
'O yon are the hills o' Heaven,' he said,
'Where you will never won.'...

15. He strack the top-mast wi' his hand,
The fore-mast wi' his knee;

And he brake that gallant ship in twain,
And sank her in the sea.
['The Daemon Lover']

16. 'Let me have length and breadth enough,
And under my head a sod;
That they may say when I am dead,
– Here lies bold Robin Hood!'
['The Death of Robin Hood']

17. O are ye come to drink the wine,
As ye hae doon before, oh?
Or are ye come to wield the brand,
On the bonny banks o' Yarrow?
['The Dowie Houms o' Yarrow']

18. Why does your brand sae drap with bluid?
Edward! Edward!
Why does your brand sae drap with bluid,
And why sae sad gang ye, O?...

19. And what will ye leave to your ain mither dear, Edward,
Edward?
And what will ye leave to your ain mither dear,
Me dear son, now tell me, O?
The curse of hell frae me sall ye bear, Mither, Mither:
The curse of hell frae me sall ye bear:
Sic counsels ye gave to me, O.
['Edward! Edward!']

20. O well's me o' my gay goss-hawk,
That he can speak and flee!
He'll carry a letter to my love,
Bring another back to me.
['The Gay Gosshawk']

21. But ne'er a word wad ane o' them speak,
For barring of the door...

22. Goodman, you've spoken the foremost word!
Get up and bar the door.
['Get Up and Bar the Door']

23. A ship have I got in the North Country
And she goes by the name of the Golden Vanity...

24. He bored with his augur, he bored once and twice,
And some were playing cards, and some were playing dice,
When the water flowed in it dazzled their eyes,
And she sank by the Low-lands low.

So the Cabin-boy did swim all to the larboard side,
Saying 'Captain! take me in, I am drifting with the tide!'
'I will shoot you! I will kill you!' the cruel Captain cried,
'You may sink by the Low-lands low.'
['The Golden Vanity']

25. I wish I were where Helen lies,
Night and day on me she cries;
O that I were where Helen lies,
On fair Kirconnell lea!

Curst be the heart that thought the thought,
And curst the hand that fired the shot,
When in my arms burd Helen dropt,
And died to succour me!
['Helen of Kirkconnell']

26. Gae hame, gae hame, my mither dear,
Prepare my winding sheet,
And at the back o' merry Lincoln
The morn I will you meet.
['Hugh of Lincoln']

27. 'Oh, it's Hynde Horn fair, and it's Hynde Horn free;
Oh, where were you born, and in what countrie?'
'In a far distant countrie I was born;
But of home and friends I am quite forlorn.'
['Hynde Horn']

28. O Johnny was as brave a knight
As ever sailed the sea,
An he's done him to the English court,
To serve for meat and fee.
['Johnny Scott']

29. There was a May, and a weel-far'd May,
Lived high up in yon glen;
Her name was Katherine Janfarie
Weel loved by mony men.
['Katherine Janfarie']

30. O is my basnet a widow's curch?
Or my lance a wand of the willow tree?
Or my arm a lady's lily hand,
That an English lord should lightly me?
['Kinmont Willie']

31. The Laird o' Drum is a-wooing gane,
It was on a morning early,
And he has fawn in wi' a bonny may
A-shearing at her barley...

32. 'For an' I war dead, and ye war dead,
And baith in ae grave laid, O,
And ye and I war tane up again,
Wha could distain your moulds frae mine, O?'
['The Laird o' Drum']

33. 'Where hae ye been hunting, Lord Randal, my son?
Where hae ye been hunting, my handsome young man?'
'In yon wild wood, O mither; so make my bed soon,
For I'm weary wi' huntin', and fain wad lie doun.'...

34. 'What gat ye to your dinner, Lord Randal, my son?
What gat ye to your dinner, my handsome young man?'
'I gat eels boil'd in broo'; mother, make my bed soon,
For I'm weary wi' hunting, and fain wad lie doun.'
['Lord Randal']

35. There liv'd a lord on yon sea-side,
And he thought on a wile,
How he would go o'er the salt-sea,
A lady to beguile.
['Lord Thomas and Fair Annie']

36. This ae nighte, this ae nighte,
– Every nighte and alle,
Fire and fleet and candle-lighte,
And Christe receive thy saule.
['Lyke-Wake Dirge']

37. When captains courageous whom death could not daunte,
Did march to the siege of the city of Gaunt,
They mustered their soldiers by two and by three,
And the foremost in battle was Mary Ambree.
['Mary Ambree']

38. For in my mind, of all mankind
I love but you alone...

39. For I must to the greenwood go
Alone, a banished man.
['The Nut Brown Maid']

40. The ane was buried in Marie's kirk,
The other in Marie's quire;
And out of the ane there sprang a birk,
And out of the other a brier.
['Prince Robert']

41. Marie Hamilton's to the kirk gane
Wi' ribbons on her breast;

The King thought mair o' Marie Hamilton
Than he listen'd to the priest...

42. Marie Hamilton's to the kirk gane,
Wi' gloves upon her hands;
The king thought mair o' Marie Hamilton
Than the Queen and her lands...

43. Yestreen the Queen had four Maries,
The night she'll hae but three;
There was Marie Seaton, and Marie Beaton
And Mary Carmichael and me.

O little did my mother ken,
The day she cradled me,
The lands I was to travel in
Or the death I was to dee!
['The Queen's Maries']

44. She sought him east, she sought him west,
She sought him braid and narrow;
Sine, in the lifting of a craig,
She found him drown'd in Yarrow.
['Rare Willie Drowned in Yarrow']

45. There are twelve months in all the year,
As I hear many men say,
But the merriest month in all the year
Is the merry month of May.
['Robin Hood and the Widow's Three Sons']

46. Fight on, my men, sayes Sir Andrew Bartton,
I am hurt but I am not slain;
Ile lay mee downe and bleed a while
And then Ile rise and fight againe.
['Sir Andrew Bartton']

47. The king sits in Dunfermline town,
Drinking the blude-red wine;
'Oh, where will I get a gude skipper
To sail this ship of mine?'...

48. Our king has written a braid letter,
And seal'd it with his hand,
And sent it to Sir Patrick Spens,
Was walking on the strand.

'To Noroway, to Noroway,
To Noroway o'er the faem;
The king's daughter o' Noroway,
'Tis thou must bring her hame.'

The first word that Sir Patrick read
So loud, loud laughed he;
The neist word that Sir Patrick read
The tear blinded his e'e...

49. 'I saw the new moon late yestreen
Wi' the auld moon in her arm;
And if we gang to sea master,
I fear we'll come to harm.'

Go fetch a web o' the silken claith,
Another o' the twine,
And wap them into our ship's side,
And let nae the sea come in...

50. O laith, laith were our gude Scots lords
To wat their cork-heel'd shoon;
But lang or a' the play was play'd
They wat their hats aboon...

51. O lang, lang may the ladies sit,
Wi' their fans into their hand,
Before they see Sir Patrick Spens
Come sailing to the strand!

And lang, lang may the maidens sit
Wi' their gowd kames in their hair,
A-waiting for their ain dear loves!
For them they'll see nae mair.

Half-owre, half-owre to Aberdour,
'Tis fifty fathoms deep;
And there lies good Sir Patrick Spens,
Wi' the Scots lords at his feet!
['Sir Patrick Spens']

52. Then she has kilted her green kirtle
A little abune her knee;
And she has braided her yellow hair
A little abune her bree...

53. 'But when I ken this night, Tam Lin,
Gin I had kent yestreen,
I wad ta'en out thy heart o' flesh,
And put in a heart o' stane.'
['Tam Lin']

54. True Thomas lay on Huntlie bank;
A ferlie he spied wi' his e'e;
And there he saw a ladye bright,
Come riding down by the Eildon Tree...

55. She's mounted on her milk-white steed,
She's ta'en true Thomas up behind...

56. O see ye not yon narrow road,
So thick beset wi' thorns and briers?
That is the path of righteousness,
Tho' after it but few enquires.'

And see not ye yon braid, braid road,
That lies across that lily leven?
That is the path of wickedness,
Tho' some call it the road to heaven...

57. It was mirk, mirk night, there was nae starlight,
They waded thro' red blude to the knee;
For a' the blude that's shed on the earth
Rins through the springs o' that countrie.
['Thomas the Rhymer']

58. There were three ravens sat on a tree,
They were as black as they might be.
The one of them said to his make,
'Where shall we our breakfast take?'
['The Three Ravens']

59. As I was walking all alane,
I heard twa corbies making a mane:
The tane unto the tither did say,
'Whaur sall we gang and dine the day?'

'–In behint yon auld fail dyke
I wot there lies a new-slain knight;
And naebody kens that he lies there
But his hawk, his hound, and his lady fair.

'His hound is to the hunting gane,
His hawk to fetch the wild-fowl hame,
His lady's ta'en anither mate,
So we may make our dinner sweet.

'Ye'll sit on his white hause-bane,
And I'll pike out his bonny blue e'en:
Wi' ae lock o' his gowden hair
We'll theek our nest when it grows bare.'...

60. O'er his white banes, when they are bare,
The wind sall blaw for evermair.
['The Twa Corbies']

61. 'The wind doth blow to-day, my love,
And a few small drops of rain;

I never had but one true love;
In cold grave she was lain.

'I'll do as much for my true-love
As any young man may;
I'll sit and mourn all at her grave
For a twelvemonth and a day.'
['The Unquiet Grave']

62. O waly, waly, up the bank,
And waly, waly, doun the brae,
And waly, waly, yon burn-side,
Where I and my Love wont to gae!

I lean'd my back unto an aik,
I thocht it was a trustie tree;
But first it bow'd and syne it brake–
Sae my true love did lichtlie me.

O waly, waly, gin love be bonnie
A little time while it is new!
But when 'tis auld it waxeth cauld,
And fades awa' like morning dew.

O wherefore should I busk my heid,
Or wherefore should I kame my hair?
For my true Love has me forsook,
And says he'll never lo'e me mair...

63. But had I wist, before I kist,
That love had been sae ill to win,
I had lock'd my heart in a case o' gowd,
And pinn'd it wi' a siller pin.

And O! if my young babe were born,
And set upon the nurse's knee;
And I mysel' were dead and gane,
And the green grass growing over me!
['Waly, Waly']

64. 'Tom Pearse, Tom Pearse, lend me your grey mare,
All along, down along, out along, lee.
For I want for to go to Widdicombe Fair,
Wi' Bill Brewer, Jan Stewer, Peter Gurney, Peter Davey,
Dan'l Whiddon, Harry Hawk;
Old Uncle Tom Cobbleigh and all.
Old Uncle Tom Cobbleigh and all.'
['Widdicombe Fair']

65. There lived a wife at Usher's Well,
And a wealthy wife was she;
She had three stout and stalwart sons,
And sent them o'er the sea.
['The Wife of Usher's Well']

Balzac, Honoré de (1799–1850)
French realist novelist

1. *En toute chose, l'on ne reçoit qu'en raison de ce qu'on donne.*
In all things, one receives only in accordance with what one has given.
[*La Physiologie du mariage* (1826)]

2. *Le sort d'un mariage dépend de la première nuit.*
The fate of a marriage depends on the first night.
[*La Physiologie du mariage* (1826)]

3. *La fin est le retour de toutes choses à l'unite qui est Dieu.*
The end is when all things return to unity, that is to say, God.
[*Louis Lambert* (1832)]

4. *Je préfère la pensée à l'action, une idée à une affaire, la contemplation au mouvement.*
I prefer thought to action, ideas to events, meditation to movement.
[*Louis Lambert* (1832)]

5. *Penser, c'est voir.*
Thinking is seeing.
[*Louis Lambert* (1832)]

6. *Que signifie adieu, à moins de mourir? Mais la mort serait-elle un adieu?*
What does farewell mean, unless one is dying? But is death itself a farewell?
[*Louis Lambert* (1832)]

7. *L'ironie est le fond du caractère de la Providence.*
Irony is the very substance of Providence.
[*Eugénie Grandet* (1833)]

8. Equality may perhaps be a right, but no power on earth can ever turn it into a fact.
[*La Duchesse de Langeais* (1834)]

9. *Les gens généreux font de mauvais commerçants.*
Generous people make bad shopkeepers.
[*Illusions perdues* (1837–1843)]

10. *Elles doivent avoir les défauts de leurs qualités.*
They must have the weaknesses of their qualities.
[*Le Lys dans la vallée* (*The Lily in the Valley*, 1891)]

11. [Remark made on waking to find a burglar in his room]
I am laughing to think what risks you take to try to find money in a desk by night where the legal owner can never find any by day.
[Attr.]

12. It is easier to be a lover than a husband, for the same reason that it is more difficult to show a ready wit all day long than to produce an occasional bon mot.
[Attr.]

Bancroft, Richard (1544–1610)
English prelate; Archbishop of Canterbury

1. Where Christ erecteth his Church, the devil in the same churchyard will have his chapel.
[Sermon, 1588]

Banda, Dr Hastings (1905–)
Malawi politician and first president, 1966–94

1. I wish I could bring Stonehenge to Nyasaland to show there was a time when Britain had a savage culture.
[*The Observer*, 'Sayings of the Week', 1963]

Bangs, Edward (fl. 1775)
American writer of songs

1. Yankee Doodle, keep it up,
Yankee Doodle Dandy;
Mind the music and the step,
And with the girls be handy...

2. Yankee Doodle came to town
Upon a little pony;
He stuck a feather in his hat,
And called it macaroni.
['Yankee Doodle']

Bankhead, Tallulah (1903–1968)
American actress

1. I have three phobias which, could I mute them, would make my life as slick as a sonnet, but as dull as ditch water: I hate to go to bed, I hate to get up, and I hate to be alone.
[*Tallulah* (1952)]

2. It's one of the tragic ironies of the theatre that only one man in it can count on steady work – the night watchman.
[*Tallulah* (1952)]

3. I've been called many things, but never an intellectual.
[*Tallulah* (1952)]

4. I'm as pure as the driven slush.
[*The Observer*, 'Sayings of the Week', 1957]

5. [To an admirer]
I'll come and make love to you at five o'clock. If I'm late start without me.
[In E. Morgan, *Somerset Maugham* (1980)]

6. [Said on dropping fifty dollars into a tambourine held out by a Salvation Army collector]
Don't bother to thank me. I know what a perfectly ghastly season it's been for you Spanish dancers.
[Attr.]

7. Cocaine isn't habit-forming. I know, because I've been taking it for years.
[Attr.]

8. Only good girls keep diaries. Bad girls don't have the time.
[Attr.]

9. There is less in this than meets the eye.
[Attr.]

Banville, Théodore Faullain de (1823–1891)
French poet, lyricist and dramatist

1. *Vous en qui je salue une nouvelle aurore, . . .*
Jeunes hommes des temps qui ne sont pas encore.
You in whom I greet a new dawn, . . .
Young men of the times which are yet to be born.
[*Les Cariatides* (1841)]

2. *Et ceux qui ne font rien ne se trompent jamais.*
Those who do nothing are never wrong.
[*Odes funambulesques*]

Barbour, John (c. 1316–1395)
Earliest-known Scottish poet; churchman and scholar

1. A! fredome is a noble thing!
Fredome mayss man to haiff liking;
Fredome all solace to man giffis:
He levys at ess that frely levys!. . .

2. Na he that ay hass levyt free,
May nocht knaw weill the propyrtie,
The angyr, na the wrechyt dome,
That is cowpyt to foule thyrldome. . .

3. And suld think fredome mar to pryss,
Than all the gold in warld that is. . .

4. [Of loyalty]
For quhar it failyeis, na vertu
May be of price, na of value,
To mak a man sa gud, that he
May symply gud man callyt be. . .

5. For certis, I trow, thar is no man
That he ne will rew up-on woman.
[*The Bruce* (1375), I]

Bareham, Lyndsey

1. Good mashed potato is one of the great luxuries of life and I don't blame Elvis for eating it every night for the last year of his life.
[*In Praise of the Potato* (1989)]

2. [Cry of a London Victorian Potato Johnny]
Here's taters hot, my little chaps,
Now just lay out a copper,
I'm known up and down the Strand,
You won't find any hotter.
[*In Praise of the Potato* (1989)]

Barham, Rev. Richard Harris (Thomas Ingoldsby) (1788–1845)
English clergyman and comic poet

1. Though I've always considered Sir Christopher Wren,
As an architect, one of the greatest of men;
And, talking of Epitaphs, – much I admire his,
'Circumspice, si Monumentum requiris';
Which an erudite Verger translated to me,
'If you ask for his Monument, Sir-come-spy-see!'
[*The Ingoldsby Legends* (1840–1847), 'The Cynotaph']

2. A servant's too often a negligent elf;
– If it's business of consequence do it yourself!
[*The Ingoldsby Legends* (1840–1847), 'The Ingoldsby Penance! – Moral']

3. The Jackdaw sat on the Cardinal's chair!
Bishop, and abbot, and prior were there;
Many a monk, and many a friar,
Many a knight, and many a squire,
With a great many more of lesser degree, –
In sooth a goodly company;
And they served the Lord Primate on bended knee.
Never, I ween,
Was a prouder seen,
Read of in books, or dreamt of in dreams,
Than the Cardinal Lord Archbishop of Rheims!. . .

4. And six little Singing-boys – dear little souls!
In nice clean faces, and nice white stoles. . .

5. He cursed him in sleeping, that every night
He should dream of the devil, and wake in a fright. . .

6. His eye so dim,
So wasted each limb,
That, heedless of grammar, they all cried, 'That's him!'
[*The Ingoldsby Legends* (1840–1847), 'The Jackdaw of Rheims']

7. A German,
Who smoked like a chimney. . .

8. So put that in your pipe, my Lord Otto, and smoke it!
[*The Ingoldsby Legends* (1840–1847), 'A Lay of St Odille']

9. They were a little less than 'kin', and rather more than 'kind'.
[*The Ingoldsby Legends* (1840–1847), 'Nell Cook']

10. She drank Prussic acid without any water,
And died like a Duke-and-a-Duchess's daughter!
[*The Ingoldsby Legends* (1840–1847), 'The Tragedy']

Baring, Maurice (1874–1945)
English poet, novelist and journalist

1. If you would know what the Lord God thinks of money, you have only to look at those to whom He gives it.
[Attr.]

Baring-Gould, Sabine (1834–1924)
English clergyman, religious writer and folklorist

1. Now the day is over,
Night is drawing nigh,
Shadows of the evening
Steal across the sky.
[Hymn, 1865]

2. Onward! Christian soldiers,
Marching as to war,
With the Cross of Jesus
Going on before. . .

3. Like a mighty army
Moves the Church of God;
Brothers, we are treading
Where the saints have trod...

4. Onward, then ye people!
Join our happy throng;
Blend with ours your voices
In the triumph song.
[Hymn, 1865]

5. Through the night of doubt and sorrow
Onward goes the pilgrim band,
Singing songs of expectation,
Marching to the Promised Land.
[Hymn, 1867]

Barker, George (1913–1991)
English neo-Romantic poet and novelist

1. My tall dead wives with knives in their breasts
Gaze at me, I am guilty, as they roll
Like derelicts in my tempests.
[*Eros in Dogma* (1944), 'My Tall Dead Wives']

2. Seismic with laughter,
Gin and chicken helpless in her Irish hand,
Irresistible as Rabelais, but most tender for
The lame dogs and hurt birds that surround her.
[*Eros in Dogma* (1944), 'Sonnet: To My Mother']

Barker, Ronnie (1929–)
English comedian

1. The marvellous thing about a joke with a double meaning is that it can only mean one thing.
[Attr.]

Barlow, Jane (1860–1917)
Irish novelist

1. That old yahoo George Moore ... His stories impressed me as being on the whole like gruel spooned up off a dirty floor.
[Letter, 1914]

Barnard, Lady Ann (1750–1825)
Scottish poet, travel writer and literary hostess

1. My father argued sair – my mother didna speak,
But she looked in my face till my heart was like to break;
They gied him my hand but my heart was in the sea;
And so auld Robin Gray, he was gudeman to me.
['Auld Robin Gray' (1771)]

Barnard, Robert (1936–)
English crime writer

1. Early on in his stint as a junior minister a newspaper had called him 'the thinking man's Tory', and the label had stuck, possibly because there was so little competition.
[*Political Suicide* (1986)]

Barnes Barnabe, (c. 1569–1609)
English poet and dramatist

1. Ah, sweet Content! where doth thine harbour hold?
['Parthenophil and Parthenophe' (1593)]

Barnes, Clive (1927–)
British journalist; dance and theatre critic

1. [On *Oh, Calcutta!* (1969)]
This is the kind of show that gives pornography a bad name.
[Attr.]

Barnes, Julian (1946–)
British novelist and thriller-writer

1. One of these days a [British] Prime Minister will have the guts to call an election with the cry 'This is a comparatively unimportant time in our nation's history.'
[*New Yorker*, 1992, 'Letter from London']

Barnes, Peter (1931–)
English dramatist

1. I know I am God because when I pray to him I find I'm talking to myself.
[*The Ruling Class* (1968)]

Barnes, William (1801–1886)
English clergyman, teacher and scholar; the 'Dorsetshire poet'

1. An' there vor me the apple tree
Do leän down low in Linden Lea.
[*Hwomely Rhymes* (1859), 'My Orcha'd in Linden Lea']

Barnfield, Richard (1574–1627)
English poet; his work was at one time attributed to Shakespeare

1. Nothing more certain than incertainties;
Fortune is full of fresh variety:
Constant in nothing but inconstancy.
[*The Affectionate Shepherd* (1954), 'The Shepherd's Content']

2. [In memory of Sir John Hawkins]
The waters were his winding sheet, the sea was made his tomb;
Yet for his fame the ocean sea, was not sufficient room.
[*The Encomion of Lady Pecunia* (1598), 'To the Gentlemen Readers']

3. King Pandion, he is dead,
All thy friends are lapp'd in lead.
[*Poems: In Divers Humours* (1598), 'An Ode']

4. My flocks feed not, my ewes breed not,
My rams speed not, all is amiss:
Love is denying, Faith is defying,
Heart's renying, causer of this.
[In Nicholas Ling (ed.), *England's Helicon* (1600), 'The Unknown Shepherd's Complaint']

Barnum, Phineas T. (1810–1891)
American showman and author

1. There's a sucker born every minute.
[Attr.]

Barreno, Maria Isabel (1939–)
Portuguese novelist, short-story writer and essayist

1. We are still the property of men, the spoils today of warriors who pretend to be our comrades in the struggle, but who merely seek to mount us...
[*New Portuguese Letters* (1972)]

Barrie, Sir J.M. (1860–1937)
Scottish dramatist, novelist and journalist

1. I do loathe explanations.
[*My Lady Nicotine* (1890), 16]

2. If it's Heaven for climate, it's Hell for company.
[*The Little Minister* (1891), 3]

3. You canna expect to be baith grand and comfortable.
[*The Little Minister* (1891), 10]

4. What is algebra exactly; is it those three-cornered things?
[*Quality Street* (1901), II]

5. His Lordship may compel us to be equal upstairs, but there will never be equality in the servants' hall.
[*The Admirable Crichton* (1902), I]

6. When the first baby laughed for the first time, the laugh broke into a thousand pieces and they all went skipping about, and that was the beginning of fairies.
[*Peter Pan* (1904), I]

7. Every time a child says 'I don't believe in fairies,' there is a little fairy somewhere that falls down dead.
[*Peter Pan* (1904), I]

8. To die will be an awfully big adventure.
[*Peter Pan* (1904), III]

9. Do you believe in fairies? . . . If you believe, clap your hands!
[*Peter Pan* (1904), IV]

10. [On charm]
It's a sort of bloom on a woman. If you have it, you don't need to have anything else; and if you don't have it, it doesn't much matter what else you have.
[*What Every Woman Knows* (1908), I]

11. You've forgotten the grandest moral attribute of a Scotsman, Maggie, that he'll do nothing which might damage his career.
[*What Every Woman Knows* (1908), II]

12. There are few more impressive sights in the world than a Scotsman on the make.
[*What Every Woman Knows* (1908), II]

13. Every man who is high up loves to think that he has done it all himself; and the wife smiles, and lets it go at that. It's our only joke. Every woman knows that.
[*What Every Woman Knows* (1908), IV]

14. The tragedy of a man who has found himself out.
[*What Every Woman Knows* (1908), IV]

15. Facts were never pleasing to him. He acquired them with reluctance and got rid of them with relief. He was never on terms with them until he had stood them on their heads.
[*The Greenwood Hat* (1937), 'Love Me Never or For Ever']

16. But the gladness of her gladness
And the sadness of her sadness
Are as nothing, Charles,
To the badness of her badness when she's bad.
['Rosalind' (1921)]

17. Never ascribe to an opponent motives meaner than your own.
[Address, St Andrews University, 1922]

Barrington, George (1755–c. 1835)
Irish pickpocket, transported to Botany Bay; author of historical works on Australia

1. From distant climes, o'er widespread seas we come,
Though not with much éclat or beat of drum;
True patriots we; for be it understood,
We left our country for our country's good.
No private views disgraced our generous zeal,
What urged our travels was our country's weal;
And none will doubt but that our emigration
Has proved most useful to the British nation.
['Prologue' for the opening of the Playhouse, Sydney, 1796]

Barrow, Isaac (1630–1677)
English divine; professor of Greek, Geometry and Mathematics; teacher of Isaac Newton

1. Poetry is a kind of ingenious nonsense.
[In Spence, *Anecdotes*]

Barth, John (1930–)
American novelist; short-story and experimentalist writer

1. If you are a novelist of a certain type of temperament, then what you really want to do is re-invent the world. God wasn't too bad a novelist, except he was a Realist.
[Attr.]

Barth, Karl (1886–1968)
Swiss Protestant theologian

1. Men have never been good, they are not good, they never will be good.
[*Time*, 1954]

Bartlett, Charles (1921–)
American writer

1. The hawks favoured an air strike to eliminate the Cuban missile bases . . . The doves opposed the air strike and favoured a blockade.
[*Saturday Evening Post*, 1962]

Barton, Bruce (1886–1967)
US advertising agent and author

1. [Jesus] picked up twelve men from the bottom ranks of business and forged them into an organization that conquered the world.
[*The Man Nobody Knows: A Discovery of the Real Jesus* (1924)]

Baruch, Bernard M. (1870–1965)
American financier, government advisor and author

1. Let us not be deceived – we are today in the midst of a cold war.
[Speech, South Carolina, 1947]

2. I will never be an old man. To me, old age is always fifteen years older than I am.
[*The Observer*, 'Sayings of the Week', 1955]

Bashó, Matsuo (1644–1694)
Japanese haiku poet

1. Into the ancient pond
A frog dives:
A sound of the water.
['Haru-no-Hi' ('Spring Days', 1686)]

2. The din of cicadas
Seeps into the rock;
The air rings with silence.
['Oku-no-Hosomichi' ('Narrow Roads of Oku', 1703)]

3. Days and months are itinerants on an eternal journey; the years that pass by are also travellers.
['Oku-no-Hosomichi' ('Narrow Roads of Oku', 1703)]

Bateman, Edgar (fl. 19th cent.)
British songwriter

1. Wiv a ladder and some glasses,
You could see to 'Ackney Marshes,
If it wasn't for the 'ouses in between.
[Song]

Bates, Daisy May (1863–1951)
Irish-born journalist, anthropologist and reformer; 'grandmother' of the Aborigines

1. The Australian native can withstand all the reverses of nature, fiendish droughts and sweeping floods, horrors of thirst and enforced starvation – but he cannot withstand civilisation.
[*The Passing of the Aborigines*... (1938)]

2. There are a few fortunate races that have been endowed with cheerfulness as their main characteristic, the Australian Aborigine and the Irish being among these.
[*The Passing of the Aborigines*... (1938)]

Bates, Katherine Lee (1859–1929)
American poet, English teacher and editor

1. America! America!
God shed His grace on thee
And crown thy good with brotherhood
From sea to shining sea!
['America the Beautiful', song, 1895]

Batman, John (1801–1839)
Australian land speculator

1. [On 'buying' the land round Melbourne from the Aborigines]
All I can see is my own, and all I can't see is my son's.
[In John Martineau, *Letters from Australia*]

Baudelaire, Charles (1821–1867)
French lyric poet, translator and critic

1. *Le poète est semblable au prince des nuées*
Qui hante la tempête et se rit de l'archer;
Exilé sur le sol, au milieu des huées,
Ses ailes de géant l'empêchent de marcher.
The poet is like the prince of the clouds, who haunts the tempest and mocks at the archer. Exiled to the ground, an object of derision, his giant wings prevent him from walking.
[*Les Fleurs du mal* (1857), 'L'Albatros']

2. *Hypocrite lecteur, – mon semblable, – mon frère!*
Hypocrite reader, my likeness, my brother!
[*Les Fleurs du mal* (1857), 'Au Lecteur'. Cf. T.S. Eliot: 39]

3. *La nature est un temple où de vivants piliers*
Laissent parfois sortir de confuses paroles;
L'homme y passe à travers des forêts de symboles
Qui l'observent avec des regards familiers.
Nature is a temple in which living columns sometimes utter confused words. Man walks through it among forests of symbols, which watch him with knowing eyes.
[*Les Fleurs du mal* (1857), 'Correspondances']

4. *Là, tout n'est qu'ordre et beauté,*
Luxe, calme et volupté.
There, everything is order, beauty, luxury, peace and voluptuous pleasure.
[*Les Fleurs du mal* (1857), 'L'Invitation au Voyage']

5. *J'ai plus de souvenirs que si j'avais mille ans.*
I have more memories than if I had lived for a thousand years.
[*Les Fleurs du mal* (1857), 'Spleen']

6. *L'air est plein du frisson des choses qui s'enfuient,*
Et l'homme est las d'écrire et la femme d'aimer.
The air is filled with the shiver of things which flee away;
And man is weary of writing, and woman of loving.
[*Les Fleurs du mal* (1857), 'Le Crépuscule du Matin']

7. *Quelle est cette île triste et noire? C'est Cythère,*
Nous dit-on, un pays fameux dans les chansons,
Eldorado banal de tous les vieux garçons.
Regardez, après tout, c'est une pauvre terre.
What is that black and dreary island? It's Cythera, they tell us, a land celebrated in song, the banal Eldorado of all the old bachelors. You can see, after all, that it's a poor land.
[*Les Fleurs du mal* (1857), 'Un Voyage à Cythère']

8. *O Mort, vieux capitaine, il est temps! levons l'ancre!*
O Death, old captain, the time has come! Let us weigh anchor!
[*Les Fleurs du mal* (1857), 'Le Voyage']

9. *Il faut épater le bourgeois.*
One must shock the bourgeois.
[Attr. Cf. Privat-d'Anglemont: 1]

Bax, Sir Arnold (1883–1953)
English composer of romantic works

1. One should try everything once, except incest and folk-dancing.
[*Farewell My Youth* (1943)]

Baxter, James K. (1926–1972)
New Zealand poet and playwright

1. Upon the upland road
Ride easy, stranger:
Surrender to the sky
Your heart of anger.
['High Country Weather' (1945)]

2. The boy who volunteered at seventeen
At twenty-three is heavy on the booze.
['Returned Soldier' (1946)]

Baxter, Richard (1615–1691)
English Presbyterian divine; religious writer and autobiographer

1. Suppose you saw the Lord in glory continually before you; When you are hearing, praying, talking, jesting, eating, drinking, and when you are tempted to wilful sin: Suppose you saw the Lord stand over you, as verily as you see a man! Would you be godly or ungodly after it? As sure as you live, and see one another, God always seeth you.
['The Life of Faith' (1660)]

2. I preached as never sure to preach again,
And as a dying man to dying men.
[*Poetical Fragments* (1681), 'Love Breathing Thanks and Praise']

Bayard, Seigneur de (1476–1524)
French military captain

1. *Le chevalier sans peur et sans reproche.*
The knight without fear and without blame.
[Description]

Baylis, Lilian (1874–1937)
English theatrical manager

1. O God, send me some good actors – cheap.
[*The Guardian*, 1976]

2. [On a less than adequate performance in King Lear]
Quite a sweet little Goneril, don't you think?
[*The Guardian*, 1976]

Bayly, Thomas Haynes (1797–1839)
English song- and ballad-writer, novelist and dramatist

1. Oh! no! we never mention her,
Her name is never heard;

My lips are now forbid to speak
That once familiar word.
['Oh! No! We Never Mention Her', song, c. 1829]

2. Absence makes the heart grow fonder,
Isle of Beauty, Fare thee well!
['Isle of Beauty', song, 1830]

3. She wore a wreath of roses,
The night that first we met.
['She Wore a Wreath of Roses', song]

Beatty, David, (First Earl Beatty) (1871–1936)
English Admiral of the Fleet and First Sea Lord

1. [Said during the Battle of Jutland, 1916]
There's something wrong with our bloody ships to-day, Chatfield. Steer two points nearer the enemy.
[Attr.]

Beaumarchais, Pierre-Augustin Caron de (1732–1799)
French dramatist, creator of Figaro; essayist, watchmaker and spy

1. *Aujourd'hui ce qui ne vaut pas la peine d'être dit, on le chante.*
Today what is not worth saying is made into a song.
[*Le Barbier de Seville* (1775), I]

2. *Je me presse de rire de tout, de peur d'être obligé d'en pleurer.*
I make myself laugh at everything, for fear of having to cry.
[*Le Barbier de Seville* (1775), I]

3. *Boire sans soif et faire l'amour en tout temps, madame, il n'y a que ça qui nous distingue des autres bêtes.*
Drinking when we're not thirsty and making love all the time, madam, that is all there is to distinguish us from other animals.
[*Le Barbier de Seville* (1775), II]

4. *Parce que vous êtes un grand seigneur, vous vous croyez un grand génie! ... Vous vous êtes donné la peine de naître, et rien de plus.*
Because you are a great lord, you think yourself a great genius! You took the trouble to be born, but nothing more.
[*Le Mariage de Figaro* (1784), V]

5. *Tout finit par des chansons.*
Everything ends with a song.
[*Le Mariage de Figaro* (1784), V, last line]

Beaumont, Francis (1584–1616)
English dramatist and poet; wrote plays in collaboration with John Fletcher

1. Nose, nose, jolly red nose,
And who gave thee this jolly red nose?...
Nutmegs and ginger, cinnamon and cloves,
And they gave me this jolly red nose.
[*The Knight of the Burning Pestle* (1607), I]

Beaumont, Francis (1584–1616)
English dramatist and poet
and **Fletcher,** John (1579–1625)

1. It is always good
When a man has two irons in the fire.
[*The Faithful Friends* (c. 1608), I]

2. Kiss till the cow comes home.
[*The Scornful Lady* (produced 1610, published 1616), II]

3. Those have most power to hurt us, that we love.
[*The Maid's Tragedy* (produced 1611, published 1619), V]

4. As men
Do walk a mile, women should talk an hour,
After supper: 'Tis their exercise.
[*Philaster* (produced 1611, published 1620), II]

5. *Philaster*: Oh, but thou dost not know
What 'tis to die.
Bellario: Yes, I do know, my Lord:
'Tis less than to be born; a lasting sleep;
A quiet resting from all jealousy,
A thing we all pursue; I know besides,
It is but giving over of a game,
That must be lost.
[*Philaster* (produced 1611, published 1620), III]

6. All your better deeds
Shall be in water writ, but this in marble.
[*Philaster* (produced 1611, published 1620), V]

7. You are no better than you should be.
[*The Coxcomb* (produced 1612, published 1647), IV]

Beauvoir, Simone de (1908–1986)
French novelist, autobiographer, feminist, critic, teacher of philosophy and companion of Sartre

1. *L'écrivain original, tant qu'il n'est pas mort, est toujours scandaleux.*
Writers who stand out, as long as they are not dead, are always scandalous.
[*Le Deuxième Sexe* (*The Second Sex*, 1949–1950)]

2. *On ne naît pas femme: on le devient.*
One is not born a woman: one becomes a woman.
[*Le Deuxième Sexe* (*The Second Sex*, 1949–1950)]

3. *Si l'on vit assez longtemps, on voit que toute victoire se change un jour en défaite.*
If you live long enough, you'll find that every victory turns into a defeat.
[*Tous les hommes sont mortels* (*All Men are Mortal*, 1955)]

4. *Qu'est-ce qu'un adulte? Un enfant gonflé d'âge.*
What is an adult? A child blown up by age.
[*La Femme rompue* (*The Woman Destroyed*, 1969)]

Beaverbrook, Lord (Max Aitken, First Baron Beaverbrook) (1879–1964)
Canadian-born British newspaper proprietor; Conservative MP and minister; political writer

1. [Remark to Winston Churchill during the abdication crisis, 1936]
Our cock won't fight.
[In Frances Donaldson, *Edward VIII* (1974)]

2. [As Minister of Aircraft Production]
Let me say that the credit belongs to the boys in the back rooms. It isn't the man who sits in the limelight like me who should have the praise. It is not the men who sit in prominent places. It is the men in the back rooms.
[Radio broadcast, 19 March 1941]

3. [Of Earl Haig]
With the publication of his Private Papers in 1952, he committed suicide twenty-five years after his death.
[*Men and Power* (1956)]

4. [Of Lloyd George]
He did not care in which direction the car was travelling, so long as he remained in the driver's seat.
[*New Statesman*, 1963]

5. I am the cat that walks alone.
[In A.J.P. Taylor, *Beaverbrook* (1972)]

6. [To Godfrey Winn]
Go out and speak for the inarticulate and the submerged.
[In E. Morgan, *Somerset Maugham* (1980)]

7. Buy old masters. They fetch a better price than old mistresses.
[Attr.]

Becher, Johannes (1891–1958)

1. *Auferstanden aus Ruinen*
Und der Zukunft zugewandt,
Lass uns dir zum Guten dienen,
Deutschland, einig Vaterland.
Resurrected from ruins
And turned towards the future,
May our service do thee good,
Germany, united Fatherland.
['Nationalhymne der deutschen demokratischen Republik' ('National Anthem of the German Democratic Republic', 1949), opening lines]

Beckett, Samuel (1906–1989)
Irish dramatist of the Theatre of the Absurd, novelist and poet; Nobel prize 1969

1. The sun shone, having no alternative, on the nothing new.
[*Murphy* (1938)]

2. Nothing to be done.
[*Waiting for Godot* (1955), passim]

3. One of the thieves was saved. (Pause) It's a reasonable percentage.
[*Waiting for Godot* (1955), I]

4. *Estragon*: ... Let's go.
Vladimir: We can't.
Estragon: Why not?
Vladimir: We're waiting for Godot.
[*Waiting for Godot* (1955), I]

5. Nothing happens, nobody comes, nobody goes, it's awful.
[*Waiting for Godot* (1955), I]

6. *Vladimir*: That passed the time.
Estragon: It would have passed in any case.
Vladimir: Yes, but not so rapidly.
[*Waiting for Godot* (1955), I]

7. We always find something, eh, Didi, to give us the impression that we exist?
[*Waiting for Godot* (1955), II]

8. We are all born mad. Some remain so.
[*Waiting for Godot* (1955), II]

9. The air is full of our cries. But habit is a great deadener.
[*Waiting for Godot* (1955), II]

10. We could have saved sixpence. We have saved fivepence. (Pause) But at what cost?
[*All That Fall* (1957)]

11. *Clov*: Do you believe in the life to come?
Hamm: Mine was always that.
[*Endgame* (1958)]

12. Let us pray to God ... the bastard! He doesn't exist.
[*Endgame* (1958)]

13. If I had the use of my body I would throw it out of the window.
[*Malone Dies* (1958)]

14. *je voudrais que mon amour meure*
qu'il pleure sur le cimetière
et les ruelles où je vais
pleurant celle qui crut m'aimer
I would like my love to die
and the rain to be raining on the graveyard
and on me walking the streets
mourning her who thought she loved me.
['Poem', translated from the French by the author]

Beckford, William (1760–1844)
English novelist, collector, travel writer and politician

1. When he was angry, one of his eyes became so terrible, that no person could bear to behold it; and the wretch upon whom it was fixed, instantly fell backward, and sometimes expired. For fear, however, of depopulating his dominions and making his palace desolate, he but rarely gave way to his anger.
[*Vathek* (1787)]

2. He did not think with the Caliph Omar Ben Adalaziz, that it was necessary to make a hell of this world to enjoy paradise in the next.
[*Vathek* (1787)]

3. I am not over-fond of resisting temptation.
[*Vathek* (1787)]

Becon, Thomas (1512–1567)
English Protestant divine; preacher, teacher and chaplain to Cranmer

1. For when the wine is in, the wit is out.
[*Catechism* (1560)]

Beddoes, Thomas Lovell (1803–1849)
English lyric poet, dramatist and physiologist

1. If thou wilt ease thine heart
Of love and all its smart,
Then sleep, dear, sleep...

2. But wilt thou cure thine heart
Of love and all its smart,
Then die, dear, die.
[*Death's Jest Book* (1850), II]

3. Old Adam, the carrion crow.
[*Death's Jest Book* (1850), V]

4. If there were dreams to sell,
What would you buy?
Some cost a passing bell;
Some a light sigh,
That shakes from Life's fresh crown
Only a roseleaf down.
If there were dreams to sell,
Merry and sad to tell,
And the crier rung the bell,
What would you buy?
['Dream-Pedlary' (1851)]

Bede, The Venerable (673–735)
English monk, historian and scholar; author of biblical commentaries and a treatise on physical science

1. When we compare the present life of man with that time of which we have no knowledge, it seems to me like the swift flight of a lone sparrow through the banqueting-hall where you sit in the winter months ... This sparrow flies swiftly in through one door of the hall, and out through another ... Similarly, man appears on earth for a little while, but we know nothing of what went on before this life, and what follows.
[*Ecclesiastical History*, II]

Bee, Barnard Elliot (1823–1861)
American general

1. [Said at the Battle of Bull Run, 1861]
There is Jackson with his Virginians, standing like a stone

wall. Let us determine to die here, and we will conquer.
[Attr.]

Beecham, Sir Thomas (1879–1961)

English conductor and impresario; founder of the London Philharmonic Orchestra

1. [On Elgar's A Flat Symphony]
The musical equivalent of the towers of St Pancras station – neo-Gothic, you know.
[In N. Cardus, *Sir Thomas Beecham* (1961)]

2. The English may not like music – but they absolutely love the noise it makes.
[In L. Ayre, *The Wit of Music* (1966)]

3. There are two golden rules for an orchestra: start together and finish together. The public doesn't give a damn what goes on in between.
[In H. Atkins and A. Newman, *Beecham Stories: Anecdotes, Sayings and Impressions of Sir Thomas Beecham* (1978)]

4. [On Beethoven's 7th Symphony]
What can you do with it? – it's like a lot of yaks jumping about.
[In H. Atkins and A. Newman, *Beecham Stories: Anecdotes, Sayings and Impressions of Sir Thomas Beecham* (1978)]

5. [On Herbert von Karajan]
[He's a kind] of musical Malcolm Sargent.
[In H. Atkins and A. Newman, *Beecham Stories: Anecdotes, Sayings and Impressions of Sir Thomas Beecham* (1978)]

6. [Remark to Utica Welles]
I don't like your Christian name. I'd like to change it.
[Attr. She replied 'You can't, but you can change my surname.' So they were married, 1903]

7. When the history of the first half of this century comes to be written – properly written – it will be acknowledged the most stupid and brutal in the history of civilisation.
[Attr.]

8. A musicologist is a man who can read music but can't hear it.
[Attr.]

9. The sound of the harpsichord resembles that of a bird-cage played with toasting-forks.
[Attr.]

10. [Of Bruckner's 7th Symphony]
In the first movement alone, I took note of six pregnancies and at least four miscarriages.
[Attr.]

Beecher, Henry Ward (1813–1887)

American clergyman, lecturer, editor and author

1. [On receiving a note containing only one word: 'Fool']
I have known many an instance of a man writing a letter and forgetting to sign his name, but this is the only instance I have ever known of a man signing his name and forgetting to write the letter.
[Attr.]

Beeching, Rev. H.C. (1859–1919)

English theologian, preacher, poet and essayist

1. First come I; my name is Jowett.
There's no knowledge but I know it.
I am Master of this college:
What I don't know isn't knowledge.
['The Masque of Balliol' (late 1870s)]

Beer, Thomas (1889–1940)

American novelist, short-story writer and biographer

1. I agree with one of your reputable critics that a taste for drawing-rooms has spoiled more poets than ever did a taste for gutters.
[*The Mauve Decade* (1926)]

Beerbohm, Sir Max (1872–1956)

English satirist, cartoonist, dramatic critic, essayist and parodist

1. Most women are not so young as they are painted.
[*The Works of Max Beerbohm* (1896), 'A Defence of Cosmetics']

2. 'After all,' as a pretty girl once said to me, 'women are a sex by themselves, so to speak.'
[*The Works of Max Beerbohm* (1896), 'The Pervasion of Rouge']

3. None, it is said, of all who revelled with the Regent, was half so wicked as Lord George Hell.
[*The Happy Hypocrite* (1897)]

4. Not that I had any special reason for hating school . . . I was a modest, good-humoured boy. It is Oxford that has made me insufferable.
[*More* (1899), 'Going Back to School']

5. Zuleika, on a desert island, would have spent most of her time in looking for a man's foot-print.
[*Zuleika Dobson* (1911), 2]

6. The dullard's envy of brilliant men is always assuaged by the suspicion that they will come to a bad end.
[*Zuleika Dobson* (1911), 4]

7. It needs no dictionary of quotations to remind me that the eyes are the windows of the soul.
[*Zuleika Dobson* (1911), 4]

8. Women who love the same man have a kind of bitter freemasonry.
[*Zuleika Dobson* (1911), 4]

9. You will find that the woman who is really kind to dogs is always one who has failed to inspire sympathy in men.
[*Zuleika Dobson* (1911), 6]

10. You will think me lamentably crude: my experience of life has been drawn from life itself.
[*Zuleika Dobson* (1911), 7]

11. You cannot make a man by standing a sheep on its hind legs. But by standing a flock of sheep in that position you can make a crowd of men.
[*Zuleika Dobson* (1911), 9]

12. 'Ah, say that again!' she murmured. 'Your voice is music.'
He repeated his question.
'Music!' she said dreamily; and such is the force of habit that 'I don't,' she added, 'know anything about music, really. But I know what I like.'
[*Zuleika Dobson* (1911), 16]

13. The lower one's vitality, the more sensitive one is to great art.
['Enoch Soames' (1912)]

14. Enter Michael Angelo. Andrea del Sarto appears for a moment at a window. Pippa passes.
['Savonarola Brown' (1917), III, stage direction]

15. I have known no man of genius who had not to pay, in some affliction or defect either physical or spiritual, for what the gods had given him.
[*And Even Now* (1920), 'No. 2, The Pines']

16. Anything that is worth doing has been done frequently. Things hitherto undone should be given, I suspect, a wide berth.
[*Mainly on the Air* (1946)]

17. [Remark allegedly made by Benjamin Jowett, Master of Balliol, about the murals in the Oxford Union, 1916]
What were they going to do with the Grail when they found it, Mr Rossetti?
[Caption to a cartoon]

18. Great men are but life-sized. Most of them, indeed, are rather short.
[Attr.]

19. There is always something rather absurd about the past.
[Attr.]

20. To give an accurate and exhaustive account of that period would need a far less brilliant pen than mine.
[Attr.]

21. Mankind is divisible into two great classes: hosts and guests.
[Attr.]

22. Only the insane take themselves quite seriously.
[Attr.]

23. They were a tense and peculiar family, the Oedipuses, weren't they?
[Attr.]

Beers, Ethel Lynn (1827–1879)
American poet and short-story writer

1. All quiet along the Potomac to-night,
No sound save the rush of the river,
While soft falls the dew on the face of the dead–
The picket's off duty forever.
[In *Harper's Magazine*, 1861, 'The Picket Guard']

Beethoven, Ludwig Van (1770–1827)
German composer of genius; bridged classical and Romantic movements

1. *Muss es sein? Es muss sein.*
Must it be? It must be.
[Epigraph to the final movement of his String Quartet in F Major, Op. 135, 1826]

2. [Reply to Goethe, who complained about greetings from passers-by]
Machen sich Euer Exzellenz nichts draus, die Komplimente gelten vielleicht mir!
Do not worry about it, Your Excellency; perhaps the greetings are meant for me!
[In *Goethes Gespräche* (*Goethe's Conversations*, 1909), II]

3. [Said to Franz Liszt when Liszt, aged 11, had visited Beethoven and played for him]
Off with you! You're a happy fellow, for you'll give happiness and joy to many other people. There is nothing better or greater than that!
[Attr.]

4. [Said to a violinist complaining that a passage was unplayable]
When I composed that, I was conscious of being inspired by God Almighty. Do you think I can consider your puny little fiddle when He speaks to me?
[Attr.]

Beeton, Mrs (1836–1865)
Victorian author of book on cookery and household management

1. [Instructions for mistresses and servants, etc. Rule 1 from Mrs Beeton's 'Philosophy of Housekeeping']
If the mistress of a household considers that she is steward of her husband's property, and that upon her diligence, knowledge and capability depends the entire happiness of her household, she will understand how important is her post, and how any negligence on her part must necessarily repeat itself in the conduct of her domestics.
[*Every-Day Cookery and Housekeeping Book* (1861)]

Behan, Beatrice (1931–1993)
Artist and wife of Brendan Behan

1. I wonder why dreams must be broken, idylls lost and love forgotten? The transience of life has always exasperated me.
[*My Life with Brendan Behan* (1973)]

Behan, Brendan (1923–1964)
Irish dramatist, novelist and Republican

1. Never throw stones at your mother,
You'll be sorry for it when she's dead,
Never throw stones at your mother,
Throw bricks at your father instead.
[*The Hostage* (1958), I]

2. *Pat*: He was an Anglo-Irishman.
Meg: In the blessed name of God, what's that?
Pat: A Protestant with a horse.
[*The Hostage* (1958), I]

3. He was born an Englishman and remained one for years.
[*The Hostage* (1958), I]

4. When I came back to Dublin, I was courtmartialled in my absence and sentenced to death in my absence, so I said they could shoot me in my absence.
[*The Hostage* (1958), I]

5. Pound notes are the best religion in the world.
[*The Wit of Brendan Behan* (1968), 'A Daylight Atheist']

6. The English and Americans dislike only some Irish – the same Irish that the Irish themselves detest, Irish writers – the ones that think.
[*Richard's Cork Leg* (unfinished at Behan's death, completed by Alan Simpson and first staged in 1972), I]

7. I think weddings is sadder than funerals, because they remind you of your own wedding. You can't be reminded of your own funeral because it hasn't happened. But weddings always make me cry.
[*Richard's Cork Leg* (unfinished at Behan's death, completed by Alan Simpson and first staged in 1972), I]

8. Other people have a nationality. The Irish and the Jews have a psychosis.
[*Richard's Cork Leg* (unfinished at Behan's death, completed by Alan Simpson and first staged in 1972), I]

9. [Sign in the window of a Paris café, the owner of which spoke no English]
Come in, you Anglo-Saxon swine
And drink of my Algerian wine.
'Twill turn your eyeballs black and blue,
And damn well good enough for you.
[Attr.]

10. I am married to Beatrice Salkeld, a painter. We have no children, except me.
[Attr.]

11. Thank you, sister. May you be the mother of a bishop!
[Remark from his deathbed to a nun who was nursing him]

Behn, Aphra (1640–1689)
English Restoration dramatist, novelist, poet, translator and spy; first Englishwoman to live by her pen

1. Come away; poverty's catching.
[*The Rover* (1677), Part II, I]

2. Variety is the soul of pleasure.
[*The Rover* (1677), Part II, I]

3. Money speaks sense in a language all nations understand.
[*The Rover* (1677), Part II, III]

4. A brave world, Sir, full of religion, knavery, and change: we shall shortly see better days.
[*The Roundheads* (1682), I]

5. Love ceases to be a pleasure, when it ceases to be a secret.
[*The Lover's Watch* (1686), 'Four o'clock. General Conversation']

6. Of all that writ, he was the wisest bard, who spoke this mighty truth–
He that knew all that ever learning writ,
Knew only this – that he knew nothing yet.
[*The Emperor of the Moon* (1687), I]

7. Oh, what a dear ravishing thing is the beginning of an Amour!
[*The Emperor of the Moon* (1687), I]

8. Faith, Sir, we are here today and gone tomorrow.
[*The Lucky Chance* (1687), IV]

9. The soft, unhappy sex.
[*The Wandering Beauty* (c. 1694)]

Bell, Alexander Graham (1847–1922)
Scots-born American inventor of the telephone and educator of the deaf

1. Mr Watson, come here: I want you.
[First words spoken on his telephone, 1876]

2. So little done. So much to do.
[Last words, 1922]

Bell, Clive (1881–1964)
English art critic and member of the 'Bloomsbury Group'

1. It would follow that 'significant form' was form behind which we catch a sense of ultimate reality.
[*Art* (1914), I]

2. I will try to account for the degree of my aesthetic emotion. That, I conceive, is the function of the critic.
[*Art* (1914), II]

3. Only reason can convince us of those three fundamental truths without a recognition of which there can be no effective liberty: that what we believe is not necessarily true; that what we like is not necessarily good; and that all questions are open.
[*Civilisation* (1928)]

Bell, Ian
Scottish journalist

1. There is no hangover on earth like the single malt hangover. It roars in the ears, burns in the stomach and sizzles in the brain like a short circuit. Death is the easy way out.
[*The Observer*, 1991]

Belloc, Hilaire (Joseph Hilary Pierre Belloc) (1870–1953)
French-born English writer of light verse, essays, biographies and criticism; Liberal MP

1. A manner rude and wild
Is common at your age...

2. Who take their manners from the Ape,
Their habits from the Bear,
Indulge the loud unseemly jape,
And never brush their hair.
[*The Bad Child's Book of Beasts* (1896), Introduction]

3. When people call this beast to mind,
They marvel more and more
At such a little tail behind,
So large a trunk before.
[*The Bad Child's Book of Beasts* (1896), 'The Elephant']

4. I shoot the Hippopotamus
with bullets made of platinum,
Because if I use leaden ones
his hide is sure to flatten 'em.
[*The Bad Child's Book of Beasts* (1896), 'The Hippopotamus']

5. Mothers of large families (who claim to common sense)
Will find a Tiger well repays the trouble and expense.
[*The Bad Child's Book of Beasts* (1896), 'The Tiger']

6. The moon on the one hand, the dawn on the other:
The moon is my sister, the dawn is my brother.
The moon on my left and the dawn on my right.
My brother, good morning: my sister, good night.
[*Verses and Sonnets* (1896), 'The Early Morning']

7. The Microbe is so very small
You cannot make him out at all...

8. Oh! let us never, never doubt
What nobody is sure about!
[*More Beasts for Worse Children* (1897), 'The Microbe']

9. I had an Aunt in Yucatan
Who bought a Python from a man
And kept it for a pet.
She died, because she never knew
These simple little rules and few;–
The Snake is living yet.
[*More Beasts for Worse Children* (1897), 'The Python']

10. The nuisance of the tropics is
The sheer necessity of fizz...

11. Whatever happens, we have got
The Maxim Gun, and they have not.
[*Modern Traveller* (1898), Part 6]

12. The nicest child I ever knew
Was Charles Augustus Fortescue.
[*Cautionary Tales* (1907), 'Charles Augustus Fortescue']

13. Godolphin Horne was Nobly Born;
He held the Human Race in Scorn...

14. Alas! That such Affected Tricks
Should flourish in a Child of Six!
[*Cautionary Tales* (1907), 'Godolphin Horne']

15. The Chief Defect of Henry King
Was chewing little bits of String...

16. Physicians of the Utmost Fame
Were called at once; but when they came
They answered, as they took their Fees,
'There is no Cure for this Disease.'...

17. 'Oh, my Friends, be warned by me,
That Breakfast, Dinner, Lunch, and Tea

Are all the Human Frame requires...'
With that, the Wretched Child expires.
[*Cautionary Tales* (1907), 'Henry King']

18. And always keep a-hold of Nurse
For fear of finding something worse.
[*Cautionary Tales* (1907), 'Jim']

19. In my opinion, Butlers ought
To know their place, and not to play
The Old Retainer night and day...

20. We had intended you to be
The next Prime Minister but three:
The stocks were sold; the Press was squared;
The Middle Class was quite prepared.
But as it is! ... My language fails!
Go out and govern New South Wales!
[*Cautionary Tales* (1907), 'Lord Lundy']

21. Matilda told such Dreadful Lies,
It made one Gasp and Stretch one's Eyes;
Her Aunt, who, from her Earliest Youth,
Had kept a Strict Regard for Truth,
Attempted to Believe Matilda:
The effort very nearly killed her...

22. It happened that a few Weeks later
Her Aunt was off to the Theatre
To see that Interesting Play
The Second Mrs Tanqueray...

23. For every time She shouted 'Fire!'
They only answered 'Little Liar!'
[*Cautionary Tales* (1907), 'Matilda']

24. A Trick that everyone abhors
In Little Girls is slamming Doors...

25. She was not really bad at heart,
But only rather rude and wild:
She was an aggravating child.
[*Cautionary Tales* (1907), 'Rebecca']

26. It is the best of all trades, to make songs, and the second best to sing them.
[*On Everything* (1909)]

27. From quiet homes and first beginning,
Out to the undiscovered ends,
There's nothing worth the wear of winning,
But laughter and the love of friends...

28. But I will sit beside my fire,
And put my hand before my eyes,
And trace, to fill my heart's desire,
The last of all our Odysseys.
[*Verses* (1910), 'Dedicatory Ode']

29. Remote and ineffectual Don
That dared attack my Chesterton.
[*Verses* (1910), 'Lines to a Don']

30. A smell of burning fills the startled Air–
The Electrician is no longer there!
[*Verses* (1910), 'Newdigate Poem']

31. If I ever become a rich man,
Or if ever I grow to be old,
I will build a house with deep thatch
To shelter me from the cold,
And there shall the Sussex songs be sung
And the story of Sussex told.

I will hold my house in the high wood
Within a walk of the sea,
And the men that were boys when I was a boy
Shall sit and drink with me.
[*Verses* (1910), 'The South Country']

32. Lord Finchley tried to mend the Electric Light
Himself. It struck him dead: And serve him right!
It is the business of the wealthy man
To give employment to the artisan.
[*More Peers* (1911), 'Lord Finchley']

33. Child! do not throw this book about;
Refrain from the unholy pleasure
Of cutting all the pictures out!
Preserve it as your chiefest treasure.
[*The Bad Child's Book of Beasts together with More Beasts for Worse Children and Cautionary Tales* (collected ed. 1923)]

34. I'm tired of Love: I'm still more tired of Rhyme.
But Money gives me pleasure all the time.
[*Sonnets and Verse* (1923), 'Fatigue']

35. The Devil, having nothing else to do,
Went off to tempt My Lady Poltagrue.
My Lady, tempted by a private whim,
To his extreme annoyance, tempted him.
[*Sonnets and Verse* (1923), 'On Lady Poltagrue: A Public Peril']

36. When I am dead, I hope it may be said:
'His sins were scarlet, but his books were read.'
[*Sonnets and Verse* (1923), 'On His Books']

37. Do you remember an Inn,
Miranda?...

38. The fleas that tease in the High Pyrenees.
[*Sonnets and Verse* (1923), 'Tarantella']

39. Strong Brother in God and last Companion: Wine.
[*Short Talks with the Dead and Others* (1926), 'The Good Poet and the Bad Poet']

40. Like many of the Upper Class
He liked the Sound of Broken Glass.
[*New Cautionary Tales* (1930), 'About John who Lost a Fortune Throwing Stones']

41. I am a sundial, and I make a botch
Of what is done far better by a watch.
[*Sonnets and Verse* (second ed. 1938), 'On a Sundial']

42. Pale Ebenezer thought it wrong to fight,
But Roaring Bill (who killed him) thought it right.
[*Sonnets and Verse* (second ed. 1938), 'The Pacifist']

43. I am a Catholic. As far as possible I go to Mass every day. As far as possible I kneel down and tell these beads every day. If you reject me on account of my religion, I shall thank God that he has spared me the indignity of being your representative.
[Speech, 1906]

44. The Anti-Semite is a man so absorbed in his subject that he loses interest in any matter unless he can give it some association with his delusion, for delusion it is.
The Jew cannot help feeling superior, but he can help the expression of that superiority – at any rate he can modify such expression.
['The Jews' (1922)]

45. I always like to associate with a lot of priests because it makes me understand anti-clerical things so well.
[Attr.]

46. [Suggested rider to the Ten Commandments]
Candidates should not attempt more than six of these.
[Attr.]

Belloch, Juan Alberto (1950–)

1. *Los jueces se rigen por la legalidad; los políticos por la oportunidad.*
Judges are guided by the law; politicians by expediency.
[*El país: edición internacional*, 1994]

Bellow, Saul (1915–)
Canadian-born American Jewish novelist and essay writer; Nobel prize 1976

1. I feel that art has something to do with the achievement of stillness in the midst of chaos. A stillness which characterizes prayer, too, and the eye of the storm. I think that art has something to do with an arrest of attention in the midst of distraction.
[In George Plimpton (ed.), *Writers at Work* (1967)]

2. One part of mankind is in prison; another is starving to death; and those of us who are free and fed are not awake. What will it take to rouse us?
[*Critical Enquiry*, 1975, 'A World Too Much With Us']

3. If one yearns to live dangerously, is it not as dangerous to persist in the truth as to rush to the barricades? But then it is always more agreeable to play the role of a writer than to be a writer. A writer's life is solitary, often bitter. How pleasant it is to come out of one's room, to fly about the world, make speeches, and cut a swath.
[*Critical Enquiry*, 1975, 'A World Too Much With Us']

4. The great enemy of progressive ideals is not the Establishment but the limitless dullness of those who take them up.
[*To Jerusalem and Back: A Personal Account* (1976)]

5. If culture means anything, it means knowing what value to set upon human life; it's not somebody with a mortarboard reading Greek. I know a lot of facts, history. That's not culture. Culture is the openness of the individual psyche . . . to the news of being.
[*The Glasgow Herald*, 1985]

6. We are in the position of savage men who have been educated into believing there are no mysteries.
[*The Independent*, 1990]

Du Belloy, P.-L.B. (1727–1775)
French dramatist

1. *Plus je vis d'étrangers, plus j'aimai ma patrie.*
The more foreigners I saw, the more I loved my native land.
[*Le Siège de Calais* (1765)]

Benchley, Robert Charles (1889–1945)
American essayist, humorist and actor

1. I must get out of these wet clothes and into a dry martini.
[Line delivered in film *The Major and the Minor*, 1942; scriptwriters Charles Brackett and Billy Wilder]

2. [Suggesting an epitaph for an actress]
She sleeps alone at last.
[Attr.]

3. Even nowadays a man can't step up and kill a woman without feeling just a bit unchivalrous.
[Attr.]

4. [Telegram sent on arriving in Venice]
Streets flooded. Please advise.
[Attr.]

5. [Comment on being told his request for a loan had been granted]
I don't trust a bank that would lend money to such a poor risk.
[Attr.]

6. [Comment on an office shared with Dorothy Parker]
One cubic foot less of space and it would have constituted adultery.
[Attr.]

7. [Reply when asked if he realised that drinking was a slow death]
So who's in a hurry?
[Attr.]

8. I do most of my work sitting down; that's where I shine.
[Attr.]

Benda, Julien (1867–1956)
French novelist and philosopher

1. *La Trahison des clercs.*
The treachery of the intellectuals.
[Title of book, 1927]

Benes, Eduard (1884–1948)
Czech statesman; President (1935–38, 1946–48; in exile 1939–45)

1. To make peace in Europe possible, the last representative of the pre-war generation must die and take his pre-war mentality into the grave with him.
[Interview, 1929]

Benét, Stephen Vincent (1898–1943)
American poet, short-story writer and dramatist

1. I have fallen in love with American names,
The sharp gaunt names that never get fat,
The snakeskin-titles of mining-claims,
The plumed war-bonnet of Medicine Hat,
Tucson and Deadwood and Lost Mule Flat.
['American Names' (1927)]

2. Bury my heart at Wounded Knee.
['American Names' (1927)]

3. . . . the lounging mirth of cracker-barrel men,
Snowed in by winter, spitting at the fire,
And telling the disreputable truth
With the sad eye that marks the perfect liar.
['Poem']

Benjamin, Judah Philip (1811–1884)
West-Indian-born American lawyer and Confederate politician

1. [Reply to an anti-Semitic remark made by a senator of Germanic origin]
The gentleman will please remember that when his half-civilized ancestors were hunting the wild boar in Silesia, mine were princes of the earth.
[Attr.]

Benjamin, Walter (1892–1940)

1. *Bücher und Dirnen kann man ins Bett nehmen.*
Books and bimbos can be taken to bed.
[*Einbahnstrasse* (*One-way street*, 1928), Number 13, I]

Benner, Richard
Canadian screenwriter

1. Canada is a country so square that even the female impersonators are women.
[From screenplay of the film, *Outrageous*, 1977]

Bennett, Alan (1934–)
English stage, film and television dramatist; actor and diarist

1. You know life ... it's rather like opening a tin of sardines. We are all of us looking for the key.
[*Beyond the Fringe* (1962)]

2. I have never understood this liking for war. It panders to instincts already catered for within the scope of any respectable domestic establishment.
[*Forty Years On* (1969), I]

3. We started off trying to set up a small anarchist community, but people wouldn't obey the rules.
[*Getting On* (1972), I]

4. We were put to Dickens as children but it never quite took. That unremitting humanity soon had me cheesed off.
[*The Old Country* (1978), II]

5. My claim to literary fame is that I used to deliver meat to a woman who became T.S. Eliot's mother-in-law.
[*The Observer*, 'Sayings of the Year', 1992]

6. [On dogs]
It's the one species I wouldn't mind seeing vanish from the face of the earth. I wish they were like the white rhino – six of them left in the Serengeti National Park, and all males.
[Attr.]

Bennett, Arnold (1867–1931)
English novelist, dramatist and journalist

1. 'Ye can call it influenza if ye like,' said Mrs Machin. 'There was no influenza in my young days. We called a cold a cold.'
[*The Card* (1911), 8]

2. 'And yet,' demanded Councillor Barlow ... 'what great cause is he identified with?' – 'He is identified,' said the speaker, 'with the great cause of cheering us all up.'
[*The Card* (1911), 12]

3. Being a husband is a whole-time job. That is why so many husbands fail. They cannot give their entire attention to it.
[*The Title* (1918)]

4. Journalists say a thing that they know isn't true, in the hope that if they keep on saying it long enough it will be true.
[*The Title* (1918)]

5. Well, my deliberate opinion is – it's a jolly strange world.
[*The Title* (1918)]

6. Pessimism, when you get used to it, is just as agreeable as optimism.
[*Things That Have Interested Me* (1921–1925)]

7. The price of justice is eternal publicity.
[*Things That Have Interested Me* (1921–1925)]

8. The test of a first-rate work, and a test of your sincerity in calling it a first-rate work, is that you finish it.
[*Things That Have Interested Me* (1921–1925)]

9. Mr Lloyd George spoke for a hundred and seventeen minutes, in which period he was detected only once in the use of an argument.
[*Things That Have Interested Me* (1921–1925), 'After the March Offensive']

10. Habit of work is growing on me. I could get into the way of going to my desk as a man goes to whisky, or rather to chloral.
[*Journals* (1932), 5 April 1908]

11. Good taste is better than bad taste, but bad taste is better than no taste.
[*The Observer*, 'Sayings of the Week', 1930]

12. The people who live in the past must yield to the people who live in the future. Otherwise the world would begin to turn the other way round.
[Attr.]

Bennett, James Gordon (1841–1918)
American newspaper editor and supporter of African and Arctic expeditions

1. Deleted by French censor.
[Used to fill empty spaces in his papers during World War I when news was scarce]

Bennett, S. Filmore
and **Webster,** Joseph P.
Hymn writers

1. In the sweet by-and-by,
We shall meet on that beautiful shore.
[Hymn, made popular by Ira D. Sankey]

Benny, Jack (1894–1974)
American comedian

1. [Said on receiving an award]
I don't deserve this, but I have arthritis, and I don't deserve that either.
[Attr.]

Benson, A.C. (1862–1925)
English scholar, essayist, literary critic and biographer; brother of E.F. Benson

1. Land of Hope and Glory, Mother of the Free,
How shall we extol thee, who are born of thee?
Wider still and wider shall thy bounds be set;
God who made thee mighty, make thee mightier yet.
[Song, 1902]

Benson, E.F. (1867–1940)
English novelist and prose writer; brother of A.C. Benson

1. [Speaking of a fellow of King's College, Cambridge, who never emerged from his rooms except in the evening gloaming]
He then shuffled out on to the big lawn, with a stick in his hand, and he prodded with it at the worms in the grass, muttering to himself, 'Ah, damn ye: haven't got me yet.'
[*As We Were* (1930)]

Bentham, Jeremy (1748–1832)
English writer on jurisprudence and utilitarian philosopher

1. All punishment is mischief: all punishment in itself is evil.
[*An Introduction to the Principles of Morals and Legislation* (1789)]

2. It is with government as with medicine, its only business is the choice of evils. Every law is an evil, for every law is an infraction of liberty.
[*An Introduction to the Principles of Morals and Legislation* (1789)]

3. Stretching his hand out to catch the stars, he forgets the flowers at his feet.
[*Deontology* (1834)]

4. [Quoting Francis Hutcheson]
... this sacred truth – that the greatest happiness of the

greatest number is the foundation of morals and legislation.
[*Works* (1838–1843), X]

5. [Of James Mill]
He rather hated the ruling few than loved the suffering many.
[In H.N. Pym (ed.), *Memories of Old Friends, being Extracts from the Journals and Letters of Caroline Fox* (1882)]

6. Prose is when all the lines except the last go on to the end. Poetry is when some of them fall short of it.
[In M.St.J. Packe, *Life of John Stuart Mill* (1954)]

7. Lawyers are the only persons in whom ignorance of the law is not punished.
[Attr.]

Bentley, Edmund Clerihew (1875–1956)

English journalist and epigrammatist

1. The art of Biography
Is different from Geography.
Geography is about Maps,
But Biography is about chaps.

2. Chapman and Hall
Swore not at all.
Mr Chapman's yea was yea,
And Mr Hall's nay was nay.

3. What I like about Clive
Is that he is no longer alive.
There is a great deal to be said
For being dead.

4. Sir Humphrey Davy
Abominated gravy.
He lived in the odium
Of having discovered Sodium.

5. Edward the Confessor
Slept under the dresser.
When that began to pall
He slept in the hall.

6. John Stuart Mill,
By a mighty effort of will,
Overcame his natural bonhomie
And wrote 'Principles of Political Economy'.

7. Sir Christopher Wren
Said, 'I am going to dine with some men.
If anybody calls
Say I am designing St Paul's.'
[*Biography for Beginners* (1905)]

8. George the Third
Ought never to have occurred.
One can only wonder
At so grotesque a blunder.
[*More Biography* (1929)]

9. When their lordships asked Bacon
How many bribes he had taken
He had at least the grace
To get very red in the face.
[*Baseless Biography* (1939)]

10. Between what matters and what seems to matter, how should the world we know judge wisely?
[*Trent's Last Case* (1913)]

11. His judgement of persons was penetrating, but its process was internal; no one felt on good behaviour with a man who seemed always to be enjoying himself.
[*Trent's Last Case* (1913)]

Bentley, Nicolas (1907–1978)

English publisher and artist

1. [Of Henry Campbell-Bannerman]
He is remembered chiefly as the man about whom all is forgotten.
[*An Edwardian Album* (1974)]

2. His was the sort of career that made the Recording Angel think seriously about taking up shorthand.
[Attr.]

3. No news is good news; no journalists is even better.
[Attr.]

4. One should not exaggerate the importance of trifles. Life, for instance, is much too short to be taken seriously.
[Attr.]

Bentley, Richard (1662–1742)

English classical scholar, chaplain and librarian

1. It is a pretty poem, Mr Pope, but you must not call it Homer.
[In John Hawkins (ed.), *The Works of Samuel Johnson* (1787), IV, 'The Life of Pope']

2. [Of claret]
It would be port if it could.
[Attr.]

Béranger, Pierre-Jean de (1780–1857)

French lyric poet

1. *Nos amis, les ennemis.*
Our friends, the enemy.
[*Chansons de De Béranger* (1830), 'L'Opinion de ces demoiselles']

Beresford, Lord Charles (1846–1919)

English admiral and Conservative politician

1. The idea of a Commercial Alliance with England based on the integrity of China and the open door for all nations' trade.
[*The Break-Up of China* (1899)]

2. Very sorry can't come. Lie follows by post.
[Telegram to the Prince of Wales in response to an eleventh-hour summons to dine]

Bergman, Ingrid (1915–1982)

Swedish-born stage and film actress; winner of three Academy awards

1. Play it, Sam. Play 'As Time Goes By'.
[*Casablanca*, film, 1942; scriptwriters Julius and Philip Epstein and Howard Koch. Cf. Humphrey Bogart: 2]

Berkeley, Bishop George (1685–1753)

Irish philosopher, scholar of Greek and Bishop of Cloyne

1. We have first raised a dust and then complain we cannot see.
[*A Treatise Concerning the Principles of Human Knowledge* (1710), Introduction]

2. All the choir of heaven and furniture of earth – in a word, all those bodies which compose the mighty frame of the world – have not any subsistence without a mind.
[*A Treatise Concerning the Principles of Human Knowledge* (1710)]

3. [Tar water] is of a nature so mild and benign and proportioned to the human constitution, as to warm without heating, to cheer but not inebriate.
[*Siris* (1744)]

4. Truth is the cry of all, but the game of the few.
[*Siris* (1744)]

5. It is impossible that a man who is false to his friends and neighbours should be true to the public.
[*Maxims Concerning Patriotism* (1750)]

6. Westward the course of empire takes its way;
The first four acts already past,
A fifth shall close the drama with the day:
Time's noblest offspring is the last.
['On the Prospect of Planting Arts and Learning in America' (1752)]

Berlin, Irving (Israel Baline) (1888–1989)
Russian-born American writer of popular songs and Broadway musicals

1. We joined the Navy to see the world,
And what did we see? We saw the sea.
['We Saw the Sea', song, 1936; in film *Follow the Fleet*]

2. I'm dreaming of a white Christmas.
['White Christmas', song, 1942; in film *Holiday Inn*]

3. [Telegram message to Groucho Marx on his seventy-first birthday]
The world would not be in such a snarl, had Marx been Groucho instead of Karl.
[Attr.]

Berlin, Sir Isaiah (1909–)
Latvian-born British political philosopher; liberalist and moral pluralist

1. Liberty is liberty, not equality or fairness or justice or culture, or human happiness or a quiet conscience.
[*Four Essays on Liberty* (1969), 'Two Concepts of Liberty']

2. Injustice, poverty, slavery, ignorance – these may be cured by reform or revolution. But men do not live only by fighting evils. They live by positive goals, individual and collective, a vast variety of them, seldom predictable, at times incompatible.
[*Four Essays on Liberty* (1969), 'Political Ideas in the Twentieth Century']

Berlinguer, Enrico (1922–1984)
Italian political leader; advocated a moderate non-revolutionary brand of Communism

1. *Da ragazzo c'era in me un sentimento di ribellione. Contestavo, se vogliamo usare una parola di moda, tutto.*
When I was a young man I felt within me a sentiment of rebellion. I used to challenge, to use a fashionable word, everything.
[In E. Biagi, *La Geografia di Italia* (*The Geography of Italy*, 1975)]

Berlioz, Hector (1803–1869)
French Romantic composer; founder of modern orchestration

1. Time is a great teacher, but unfortunately it kills all its pupils.
[Attr.]

Berlusconi, Silvio (1936–)
Italian media baron and politician; Prime Minister (1994)

1. *Non sono stato un uomo d'affari, ma un imprenditore.*
I wasn't a businessman, but a business magnate.
[Speech delivered to the Senate on 18 May 1994]

Bernanos, Georges (1888–1948)
French novelist

1. *L'enfer, madame, c'est de ne plus aimer.*
Hell, madam, is to love no longer.
[*Journal d'un curé de campagne* (*The Diary of a Country Priest*, 1936), 2]

Bernard of Chartres (d. c. 1130)
French philosopher

1. Bernard of Chartres used to say that we are like dwarfs on the shoulders of giants, so that we can see more than they, and things at a greater distance, not by virtue of any sharpness of sight on our part, or any physical distinction, but because we are carried high and raised up by their giant size.
[In John of Salisbury, *The Metalogicon* (1159). Cf. Isaac Newton: 3]

Bernard of Cluny (fl. mid 12th century)
Benedictine monk and Latin poet

1. Jerusalem the golden,
With milk and honey blest.
[Hymn; trans. J.M. Neale]

Bernard, Jeffrey (1932–)
British columnist

1. Writers as a rule don't make fighters, although I would hate to have to square up to Taki or Andrea Dworkin.
[*Spectator*, 1992]

Bernard, Jessie

1. Women at marriage move from the status of female to that of neuter being.
[*The Future of Marriage*]

Bernard, Saint (1091–1153)
French Abbot of Clairvaux, theologian and founder of the Cistercian order

1. *Liberavi animam meam.*
I have freed my soul.
['Epistle 371']

Bernard, Tristan (1866–1947)
French comic novelist and dramatist

1. In the theatre the audience want to be surprised – but by things that they expect.
[Attr.]

Bernard, William Bayle (1807–1875)
American dramatist of rural and 'western' life

1. A Storm in a Teacup.
[Title of farce, 1854]

Berners, Lord (1883–1950)
English composer of ballets, artist and novelist

1. [Of T.E. Lawrence]
He's always backing into the limelight.
[Attr.]

Bernhardt, Sarah (Henriette Rosine Bernard) (1844–1923)
Celebrated French tragic actress

1. For the theatre one needs long arms; it is better to have them

too long than too short. An artiste with short arms can never, never make a fine gesture.
[Attr.]

2. [Remark while watching a game of football]
I do love cricket – it's so very English.
[Attr.]

Berryman, John (1914–1972)
American confessional poet, Shakespearean scholar, critic and teacher

1. Life, friends, is boring. We must not say so.
[*Dream Songs* (1964), 14]

2. I seldom go to films. They are too exciting,
Said the Honourable Possum.
[*Dream Songs* (1964), 53]

Bethell, Richard (First Baron Westbury) (1800–1873)
English judge, Liberal MP and Lord Chancellor

1. His Lordship says he will turn it over in what he is pleased to call his mind.
[In Nash, *Life of Westbury*]

Bethmann Hollweg, Theobald von (1856–1921)
Chancellor of Germany, 1909–17

1. Just for a word – 'neutrality', a word which in wartime has so often been disregarded, just for a scrap of paper – Great Britain is going to make war.
[Letter, 1914]

Bethune, Frank Pogson (1877–1942)

1. Special Orders to No. 1 Section
1. The position will be held, and the section will remain here until relieved.
2. The enemy cannot be allowed to interfere with the programme.
3. If the section cannot remain here alive, it will remain here dead, but in any case it will remain here.
4. Should any man, through shell shock or other cause, attempt to surrender, he will remain here dead.
5. Should all guns be blown out, the section will use Mills grenades, and other novelties.
6. Finally, the position, as stated, will be held.
[An order issued by Bethune to his machine gun section in France, 13 March 1918]

Betjeman, Sir John (1906–1984)
English poet laureate from 1972, writer on architecture, and broadcaster

1. Oh! chintzy, chintzy cheeriness,
Half dead and half alive!
[*Mount Zion* (1932), 'Death in Leamington']

2. Broad of Church and broad of mind,
Broad before and broad behind,
A keen ecclesiologist,
A rather dirty Wykehamist.
[*Mount Zion* (1932), 'The Wykehamist']

3. He sipped at a weak hock and seltzer
As he gazed at the London skies
Through the Nottingham lace of the curtains
Or was it his bees-winged eyes?
[*Continual Dew* (1937), 'The Arrest of Oscar Wilde at the Cadogan Hotel']

4. Spirits of well-shot woodcock, partridge, snipe
Flutter and bear him up the Norfolk sky...

5. Old men in country houses hear clocks ticking
Over thick carpets with a deadened force;

Old men who never cheated, never doubted,
Communicated monthly, sit and stare
At the new suburb stretched beyond the run-way
Where a young man lands hatless from the air.
[*Continual Dew* (1937), 'Death of King George V']

6. Come, friendly bombs, and fall on Slough
It isn't fit for humans now,
There isn't grass to graze a cow
Swarm over, Death!...

7. Come, friendly bombs, and fall on Slough
To get it ready for the plough.
[*Continual Dew* (1937), 'Slough']

8. Gracious Lord, oh bomb the Germans.
Spare their women for Thy Sake,
And if that is not too easy
We will pardon Thy Mistake.
But, gracious Lord, whate'er shall be,
Don't let anyone bomb me.
[*Old Lights for New Chancels* (1940), 'In Westminster Abbey']

9. Shall we ever, my staunch Myfanwy,
Bicycle down to North Parade?
Kant on the handle-bars, Marx in the saddlebag,
Light my touch on your shoulder-blade.
[*Old Lights for New Chancels* (1940), 'Myfanwy at Oxford']

10. Pam, I adore you, Pam, you great big mountainous sports girl,
Whizzing them over the net, full of the strength of five.
[*Old Lights for New Chancels* (1940), 'Pot Pourri from a Surrey Garden']

11. The gas was on in the Institute,
The flare was up in the gym,
A man was running a mineral line,
A lass was singing a hymn,
When Captain Webb the Dawley man,
Captain Webb from Dawley,
Came swimming along the old canal
That carried the bricks to Lawley...

12. We saw the ghost of Captain Webb,
Webb in a water sheeting,
Come dripping along in a bathing dress
To the Saturday evening meeting.
Dripping along–
Dripping along–
To the Congregational Hall;
Dripping and still he rose over the sill and faded away in a wall.
[*Old Lights for New Chancels* (1940), 'A Shropshire Lad']

13. Not yet, thank God, not yet the Night.
Oh better far those echoing hells
Half-threaten'd in the pealing bells
Than that this 'I' should cease to be–
Come quickly, Lord, come quick to me.
St Giles's bells are asking now
'And hast thou known the Lord, hast thou?'
St Giles's bells, they richly ring
'And was that Lord our Christ the King?'
St Giles's bells they hear me call
I never knew the Lord at all.
[*New Bats in Old Belfries* (1945), 'Before the Anaesthetic, or A Real Fright']

14. When shall I see the Thames again?
The prow-promoted gems again,
As beefy ATS
Without their hats

Come shooting through the bridge?
And 'cheerioh' and 'cheeri-bye'
Across the waste of waters die,
And low the mists of evening lie
And lightly skims the midge.
[*New Bats in Old Belfries* (1945), 'Henley-on-Thames']

15. 'Let us not speak, for the love we bear one another–
Let us hold hands and look.'
She, such a very ordinary little woman;
He, such a thumping crook;
But both, for a moment, little lower than the angels
In the teashop's ingle-nook.
[*New Bats in Old Belfries* (1945), 'In a Bath Teashop']

16. Where a Stone Age people breeds
The last of Europe's stone age race...

17. There in pinnacled protection,
One extinguished family waits
A Church of Ireland resurrection
By the broken, rusty gates.
Sheepswool, straw and droppings cover,
Graves of spinster, rake and lover,
Whose fantastic mausoleum
Sings its own seablown Te Deum,
In and out the slipping slates.
[*New Bats in Old Belfries* (1945), 'Ireland with Emily']

18. Belbroughton Road is bonny, and pinkly bursts the spray
Of prunus and forsythia across the public way,
For a full spring-tide of blossom seethed and departed hence,
Leaving land-locked pools of jonquils by sunny garden fence.

And a constant sound of flushing runneth from windows where
The toothbrush is airing in this new North Oxford air.
[*New Bats in Old Belfries* (1945), 'May-Day Song for North Oxford']

19. Oh the after-tram-ride quiet, when we heard a mile beyond,
Silver music from the bandstand, barking dogs by Highgate Pond;
Up the hill where stucco houses in Virginia creeper drown–
And my childish wave of pity, seeing children carrying down
Sheaves of drooping dandelions to the courts of Kentish Town.
[*New Bats in Old Belfries* (1945), 'Parliament Hill Fields']

20. Miss J. Hunter Dunn, Miss J. Hunter Dunn,
Furnish'd and burnish'd by Aldershot sun,
What strenuous singles we played after tea
We in the tournament – you against me!

Love-thirty, love-forty, oh! weakness of joy,
The speed of a swallow, the grace of a boy,
With carefullest carelessness, gaily you won,
I am weak from your loveliness, Joan Hunter Dunn.

Miss Joan Hunter Dunn, Miss Joan Hunter Dunn,
How mad I am, sad I am, glad that you won.
The warm-handled racket is back in its press,
But my shock-headed victor, she loves me no less...

21. By roads 'not adopted', by woodlanded ways,
She drove to the club in the late summer haze,
Into nine-o'clock Camberley, heavy with bells
And mushroomy, pine-woody, evergreen smells.

Miss Joan Hunter Dunn, Miss Joan Hunter Dunn,
I can hear from the car-park the dance has begun.
Oh! full Surrey twilight! importunate band!
Oh! strongly adorable tennis-girl's hand!
[*New Bats in Old Belfries* (1945), 'A Subaltern's Love Song']

22. From the geyser ventilators
Autumn winds are blowing down
On a thousand business women
Having baths in Camden Town...

23. Rest you there, poor unbelov'd ones,
Lap your loneliness in heat.
All too soon the tiny breakfast,
Trolley-bus and windy street!
[*A Few Late Chrysanthemums* (1954), 'Business Girls']

24. And girls in slacks remember Dad,
And oafish louts remember Mum,
And sleepless children's hearts are glad,
And Christmas morning bells say 'Come!'
Even to shining ones who dwell
Safe in the Dorchester Hotel.

And is it true? And is it true,
This most tremendous tale of all,
Seen in a stained-glass window's hue,
A Baby in an ox's stall?
[*A Few Late Chrysanthemums* (1954), 'Christmas']

25. Then Harrow-on-the-Hill's a rocky island
And Harrow churchyard full of sailors' graves
And the constant click and kissing of the trolley buses hissing
Is the level to the Wealdstone turned to waves.
[*A Few Late Chrysanthemums* (1954), 'Harrow-on-the-Hill']

26. Phone for the fish-knives, Norman
As Cook is a little unnerved;
You kiddies have crumpled the serviettes
And I must have things daintily served...

27. I know what I wanted to ask you;
Is trifle sufficient for sweet?...

Milk and then just as it comes dear?
I'm afraid the preserve's full of stones;
Beg pardon, I'm soiling the doileys
With afternoon tea-cakes and scones.
[*A Few Late Chrysanthemums* (1954), 'How to Get On in Society']

28. Oh wasn't it naughty of Smudges?
Oh, Mummy, I'm sick with disgust.
She threw me in front of the Judges
And my silly old collarbone's bust.
[*A Few Late Chrysanthemums* (1954), 'Hunter Trials']

29. In the Garden City Café with its murals on the wall
Before a talk on 'Sex and Civics' I meditated on the Fall.
[*A Few Late Chrysanthemums* (1954), 'Huxley Hall']

30. Gaily into Ruislip Gardens
Runs the red electric train,
With a thousand Ta's and Pardon's
Daintily alights Elaine...

31. Well cut Windsmoor flapping lightly,
Jacqmar scarf of mauve and green
Hiding hair which, Friday nightly,
Delicately drowns in Drene.
[*A Few Late Chrysanthemums* (1954), 'Middlesex']

32. There was sun enough for lazing upon beaches,
There was fun enough for far into the night.
But I'm dying now and done for,
What on earth was all the fun for?
For I'm old and ill and terrified and tight.
[*A Few Late Chrysanthemums* (1954), 'Sun and Fun']

33. I heard the church bells hollowing out the sky,
Deep beyond deep, like never-ending stars,

And turned to Archibald, my safe old bear,
Whose woollen eyes looked sad or glad at me.
[*Summoned by Bells* (1960), 1]

34. Maud was my hateful nurse who smelt of soap...
She rubbed my face in messes I had made
And was the first to tell me about Hell,
Admitting she was going there herself.
[*Summoned by Bells* (1960), 1]

35. Balkan Sobranies in a wooden box,
The college arms upon the lid; Tokay
And sherry in the cupboard; on the shelves
The University Statutes bound in blue,
Crome Yellow, Prancing Nigger, Blunden, Keats.
[*Summoned by Bells* (1960), 9]

36. You ask me what it is I do. Well actually, you know,
I'm partly a liaison man and partly P.R.O.
Essentially I integrate the current export drive
And basically I'm viable from ten o'clock till five.
[*A Nip in the Air* (1974), 'Executive']

37. I made hay while the sun shone.
My work sold.
Now, if the harvest is over
And the world cold,
Give me the bonus of laughter
As I lose hold.
[*A Nip in the Air* (1974), 'The Last Laugh']

38. Ghastly Good Taste, or A Depressing Story of the Rise and Fall of English Architecture.
[Title of book, 1933]

39. I've to prostitute myself to live comfortably and I see no point in money except to buy off anxiety. I don't want to be rich. I want to be unanxious.
[Interview with Graham Lord, *Sunday Express*, 1974]

40. [When asked if he had any regrets]
Yes, I haven't had enough sex.
[*Time With Betjeman*, BBC TV, February 1983]

Betterton, Thomas (1635–1710)
English Restoration actor and dramatist

1. [Reply to the Archbishop of Canterbury]
Actors speak of things imaginary as if they were real, while you preachers too often speak of things real as if they were imaginary.
[Attr.]

Bevan, Aneurin (1897–1960)
Welsh Labour politician and minister; miner, unionist and orator

1. This island is almost made of coal and surrounded by fish. Only an organizing genius could produce a shortage of coal and fish at the same time.
[Speech, Blackpool, 1945]

2. No amount of cajolery, and no attempts at ethical or social seduction, can eradicate from my heart a deep burning hatred for the Tory Party ... So far as I am concerned they are lower than vermin.
[Speech, 1948]

3. [Opposing unilateral nuclear disarmament]
If you carry this resolution and follow out all its implications and do not run away from it you will send a Foreign Secretary, whoever he may be, naked into the conference chamber.
[Speech, 1957]

4. [Wishing to address Harold Macmillan, the Prime Minister, rather than Selwyn Lloyd, the Foreign Secretary, in the post-Suez debate]
I am not going to spend any time whatsoever in attacking the Foreign Secretary. Quite honestly I am beginning to feel extremely sorry for him. If we complain about the tune, there is no reason to attack the monkey when the organ grinder is present.
[Speech, House of Commons, 1957]

5. Listening to a speech by Chamberlain is like paying a visit to Woolworths; everything in its place and nothing over sixpence.
[In *Tribune*, 1937]

6. We know what happens to people who stay in the middle of the road. They get run over.
[*The Observer*, 'Sayings of the Week', 1953]

7. I read the newspapers avidly. It is my one form of continuous fiction.
[*The Observer*, 'Sayings of the Week', 1960]

8. [On Churchill]
He is a man suffering from petrified adolescence.
[In Vincent Brome, *Aneurin Bevan*, 11]

9. [Of the Communist Party]
Its relationship to democratic institutions is that of the death watch beetle – it is not a Party, it is a conspiracy.
[Attr.]

10. The language of priorities is the religion of Socialism.
[Attr.]

Beven, Rodney Allan (1916–1982)

1. The people of Melbourne
Are frightfully well-born.
[*Observation Sociologique*]

Beveridge, William Henry (First Baron Beveridge) (1879–1963)
Indian-born British social reformer, economist and Liberal

1. The object of government in peace and in war is not the glory of rulers or of races, but the happiness of the common man.
[*Report on Social Insurance and Allied Services* (1942)]

2. The trouble in modern democracy is that men do not approach to leadership until they have lost the desire to lead anyone.
[*The Observer*, 'Sayings of the Week', 1934]

3. Scratch a pessimist, and you find often a defender of privilege.
[*The Observer*, 'Sayings of the Week', 1943]

Bevin, Ernest (1881–1951)
English trade unionist and Labour politician; Foreign Secretary, 1945–51

1. [On foreign policy]
My policy is to be able to take a ticket at Victoria Station and go anywhere I damn well please.
[*Spectator*, 1951]

2. [On the Council of Europe]
If you open that Pandora's Box you never know what Trojan 'orses will jump out.
[In Sir Roderick Barclay, *Ernest Bevin and the Foreign Office* (1975)]

3. [When told that another Labourite was 'his own worst enemy']
Not while I'm alive, he ain't.
[In M. Foot, *Aneurin Bevan 1945–60* (1975)]

Bhagavadgita
Religious and philosophical Sanskrit poem

1. [On the Self]
He who considers this as a slayer or he who thinks that this is slain, neither of these knows the Truth. For it does not slay, nor is it slain.
[Ch. II]

2. For that which is born death is certain, and for the dead birth is certain. Therefore grieve not over that which is unavoidable.
[Ch. II]

3. I am become death, the destroyer of worlds.
[Quoted by J. Robert Oppenheimer on seeing the first nuclear explosion]

Biagi, Enzo (1920–)

1. *La televisione ha fatto per la nostra unità più di Garibaldi e Cavour, ha dato un linguaggio e un costume comuni.*
Television has done more for the unification of Italy than Garibaldi and Cavour did; it has given us a communal custom and language.
[*Buoni e Cattivi* (*The Good and the Bad*, 1989)]

2. [On the Italians]
Allora siamo i più disonesti? Credo proprio di no: ma probabilmente i più indifferenti.
Are we then the most dishonest people? I don't really think so: but probably we are the most indifferent ones.
[*Buoni e Cattivi* (*The Good and the Bad*, 1989)]

The Bible (King James Version)

Authorized Version

1. ...upon the setting of that bright Occidental Star, Queen Elizabeth of most happy memory.
[Epistle Dedicatory]

Genesis

2. In the beginning God created the heaven and the earth.
And the earth was without form, and void; and darkness was upon the face of the deep. And the Spirit of God moved upon the face of the waters.
And God said, Let there be light: and there was light.
[1:1–3]

3. And the evening and the morning were the first day.
[1:5]

4. And God saw that it was good.
[1:10]

5. And God made two great lights; the greater light to rule the day, and the lesser light to rule the night: he made the stars also.
[1:16]

6. And God said, Let us make man in our image, after our likeness.
[1:26]

7. Male and female created he them.
[1:27]

8. Be fruitful, and multiply, and replenish the earth, and subdue it.
[1:28]

9. And the Lord God formed man of the dust of the ground, and breathed into his nostrils the breath of life; and man became a living soul.
And the Lord God planted a garden eastward in Eden.
[2:7–8]

10. And out of the ground made the Lord God to grow every tree that is pleasant to the sight, and good for food; the tree of life also in the midst of the garden, and the tree of knowledge of good and evil.
[2:9]

11. But of the tree of the knowledge of good and evil, thou shalt not eat of it: for in the day that thou eatest thereof thou shalt surely die.
[2:17]

12. It is not good that the man should be alone; I will make him an help meet for him.
[2:18]

13. And the rib, which the Lord God had taken from man, made he a woman.
[2:22]

14. This is now bone of my bones, and flesh of my flesh: she shall be called Woman, because she was taken out of Man.
[2:23. Cf. Milton: 250]

15. Therefore shall a man leave his father and his mother, and shall cleave unto his wife: and they shall be one flesh.
[2:24]

16. Now the serpent was more subtil than any beast of the field.
[3:1]

17. Ye shall be as gods, knowing good and evil.
[3:5]

18. And they sewed fig leaves together, and made themselves aprons [breeches in Genevan Bible, 1560].
And they heard the voice of the Lord God walking in the garden in the cool of the day.
[3:7–8]

19. The woman whom thou gavest to be with me, she gave me of the tree, and I did eat.
[3:12]

20. What is this that thou hast done?
[3:13]

21. The serpent beguiled me, and I did eat.
[3:13]

22. It shall bruise thy head, and thou shalt bruise his heel.
[3:15]

23. In sorrow thou shalt bring forth children.
[3:16]

24. In the sweat of thy face shalt thou eat bread.
[3:19]

25. For dust thou art, and unto dust shalt thou return.
[3:19]

26. The mother of all living.
[3:20]

27. Am I my brother's keeper?
[4:9]

28. The voice of thy brother's blood crieth unto me from the ground.
[4:10]

29. My punishment is greater than I can bear.
[4:13]

30. And the Lord set a mark upon Cain.
[4:15]

31. And Cain went out from the presence of the Lord, and dwelt in the land of Nod, on the east of Eden.
[4:16]

32. And Enoch walked with God: and he was not; for God took him.
[5:24]

33. And all the days of Methuselah were nine hundred sixty and nine years: and he died.
[5:27]

34. And Noah begat Shem, Ham, and Japheth.
[5:32]

35. There were giants in the earth in those days; and also after that, when the sons of God came in unto the daughters of men, and they bare children to them, the same became mighty men which were of old, men of renown.
[6:4]

36. There went in two and two unto Noah into the ark, the male and the female
[7:9]

37. And God remembered Noah.
[8:1]

38. But the dove found no rest for the sole of her foot.
[8:9]

39. For the imagination of man's heart is evil from his youth.
[8:21]

40. While the earth remaineth, seedtime and harvest, and cold and heat, and summer and winter, and day and night shall not cease.
[8:22]

41. At the hand of every man's brother will I require the life of man.
[9:5]

42. Whoso sheddeth man's blood, by man shall his blood be shed.
[9:6]

43. I do set my bow in the cloud, and it shall be for a token of a covenant between me and the earth.
And it shall come to pass, when I bring a cloud over the earth, that the bow shall be seen in the cloud.
[9:13–14]

44. Even as Nimrod the mighty hunter before the Lord.
[10:9]

45. Let there be no strife, I pray thee, between me and thee ... for we be brethren.
[13:8]

46. An horror of great darkness fell upon him.
[15:12]

47. Thou shalt be buried in a good old age.
[15:15]

48. His [Ishmael's] hand will be against every man, and every man's hand against him.
[16:12]

49. Now Abraham and Sarah were old and well stricken in age; and it ceased to be with Sarah after the manner of women.
[18:11]

50. But his wife looked back from behind him, and she became a pillar of salt.
[19:26]

51. Take now thy son, thine only son Isaac, whom thou lovest.
[22:2]

52. My son, God will provide himself a lamb.
[22:8]

53. Behold behind him a ram caught in a thicket by his horns.
[22:13]

54. Esau selleth his birthright for a mess of potage.
[Heading to chapter 25 in Genevan Bible of 1560]

55. Esau was a cunning hunter, a man of the field; and Jacob was a plain man, dwelling in tents.
[25:27]

56. And he sold his birthright unto Jacob.
[25:33]

57. Behold, Esau my brother is a hairy man, and I am a smooth man.
[27:11]

58. The voice is Jacob's voice, but the hands are the hands of Esau.
[27:22]

59. Thy brother came with subtilty, and hath taken away thy blessing.
[27:35]

60. And he dreamed, and behold a ladder set up on the earth, and the top of it reached to heaven: and behold the angels of God ascending and descending on it.
[28:12]

61. Surely the Lord is in this place; and I knew it not.
[28:16]

62. This is none other but the house of God, and this is the gate of heaven.
[28:17]

63. And Jacob served seven years for Rachel; and they seemed unto him but a few days, for the love he had to her.
[29:20]

64. Mizpah; for he said, The Lord watch between me and thee, when we are absent one from another.
[31:49]

65. I will not let thee go, except thou bless me.
[32:26]

66. For I have seen God face to face, and my life is preserved.
[32:30]

67. Now Israel loved Joseph more than all his children, because he was the son of his old age; and he made him a coat of many colours.
[37:3]

68. Behold, this dreamer cometh.
[37:19]

69. Some evil beast hath devoured him.
[37:20]

70. And she caught him by his garment, saying, Lie with me: and he left his garment in her hand, and fled.
[39:12]

71. And the lean and the ill favoured kine did eat up the first seven fat kine.
[41:20]

72. And the thin ears devoured the seven good ears.
[41:24]

73. Jacob saw that there was corn in Egypt.
[42:1]

74. Ye are spies; to see the nakedness of the land ye are come.
[42:9]

75. Then shall ye bring down my gray hairs with sorrow to the grave.
[42:38]

76. Ye shall eat the fat of the land.
[45:18]

77. See that ye fall not out by the way.
[45:24]

78. Few and evil have the days of the years of my life been.
[47:9]

79. Unstable as water, thou shalt not excel.
[49:4]

Exodus

80. Now there arose up a new king over Egypt, which knew not Joseph.
[1:8]

81. She took for him an ark of bulrushes, and daubed it with slime.
[2:3]

82. Who made thee a prince and a judge over us?
[2:14]

83. I have been a stranger in a strange land.
[2:22]

84. Behold, the bush burned with fire, and the bush was not consumed.
[3:2]

85. Put off thy shoes from off thy feet, for the place whereon thou standest is holy ground.
[3:5]

86. And Moses hid his face; for he was afraid to look upon God.
[3:6]

87. A land flowing with milk and honey; unto the place of the Canaanites, and the Hittites, and the Amorites, and the Perizzites, and the Hivites, and the Jebusites.
[3:8]

88. I AM THAT I AM.
[3:14]

89. The Lord God of your fathers, the God of Abraham, the God of Isaac, and the God of Jacob.
[3:15]

90. But I am slow of speech, and of a slow tongue.
[4:10]

91. And I will harden Pharaoh's heart, and multiply my signs and my wonders in the land of Egypt.
[7:3]

92. Let my people go.
[7:16]

93. A boil breaking forth with blains.
[9:10]

94. Stretch out thine hand toward heaven, that there may be darkness over the land of Egypt, even darkness which may be felt.
[10:21]

95. Your lamb shall be without blemish.
[12:5]

96. And they shall eat the flesh in that night, roast with fire, and unleavened bread; and with bitter herbs they shall eat it. Eat not of it raw, nor sodden at all with water, but roast with fire; his head with his legs, and with the purtenance thereof.
[12:8–9]

97. With your loins girded, your shoes on your feet, and your staff in your hand; and ye shall eat it in haste; it is the Lord's passover.
For I will pass through the land of Egypt this night, and will smite all the firstborn in the land of Egypt, both man and beast.
[12:11–12]

98. And Pharaoh rose up in the night, he, and all his servants, and all the Egyptians; and there was a great cry in Egypt; for there was not a house where there was not one dead.
[12:30]

99. And they spoiled the Egyptians.
[12:36]

100. And the Lord went before them by day in a pillar of a cloud, to lead them the way; and by night in a pillar of fire, to give them light.
[13:21]

101. The Lord is a man of war.
[15:3]

102. Would to God we had died by the hand of the Lord in the land of Egypt, when we sat by the flesh pots, and when we did eat bread to the full.
[16:3]

103. And God spake all these words, saying,
I am the Lord thy God, which have brought thee out of the land of Egypt, out of the house of bondage.
Thou shalt have no other gods before me.
Thou shalt not make unto thee any graven image, or any likeness of any thing that is in heaven above, or that is in the earth beneath, or that is in the water under the earth:
Thou shalt not bow down thyself to them, nor serve them: for I the Lord thy God am a jealous God, visiting the iniquity of the fathers upon the children unto the third and fourth generation of them that hate me;
And shewing mercy unto thousands of them that love me, and keep my commandments.
Thou shalt not take the name of the Lord thy God in vain; for the Lord will not hold him guiltless that taketh his name in vain.
Remember the sabbath day, to keep it holy.
Six days shalt thou labour, and do all thy work:
But the seventh day is the sabbath of the Lord thy God: in it thou shalt not do any work, thou, nor thy son, nor thy daughter, thy manservant, nor thy maidservant, nor thy cattle, nor thy stranger that is within thy gates:
For in six days the Lord made heaven and earth, the sea, and all that in them is, and rested the seventh day: wherefore the Lord blessed the sabbath day, and hallowed it.
Honour thy father and thy mother: that thy days may be long upon the land which the Lord thy God giveth thee.
Thou shalt not kill.
Thou shalt not commit adultery.
Thou shalt not steal.
Thou shalt not bear false witness against thy neighbour.
Thou shalt not covet thy neighbour's house, thou shalt not covet thy neighbour's wife, nor his manservant, nor his maidservant, nor his ox, nor his ass, nor any thing that is thy neighbour's.
[20:1–17]

104. Life for life,
Eye for eye, tooth for tooth, hand for hand, foot for foot,

Burning for burning, wound for wound, stripe for stripe.
[21:23–25]

105. Thou shalt not suffer a witch to live.
[22:18]

106. Thou shalt not seethe a kid in his mother's milk.
[23:19]

107. These be thy gods, O Israel.
[32:4]

108. And the people sat down to eat and to drink, and rose up to play.
[32:6]

109. I will not go up in the midst of thee; for thou art a stiffnecked people: lest I consume thee in the way.
[33:3]

110. There shall no man see me, and live.
[33:20]

Leviticus

111. And the swine, though he divide the hoof, and be clovenfooted, yet he cheweth not the cud; he is unclean to you.
[11:7]

112. Let him go for a scapegoat into the wilderness.
[16:10]

113. Thou shalt love thy neighbour as thyself.
[19:18]

Numbers

114. The Lord bless thee, and keep thee:
The Lord make his face shine upon thee, and be gracious unto thee.
The Lord lift up his countenance upon thee, and give thee peace.
[6:24–26]

115. These are the names of the men which Moses sent to spy out the land.
[13:16]

116. And there we saw the giants, the sons of Anak, which come of the giants: and we were in our own sight as grasshoppers, and so we were in their sight.
[13:33]

117. And Israel smote him with the edge of the sword, and possessed his land.
[21:24]

118. He whom thou blessest is blessed, and he whom thou cursest is cursed.
[22:6]

119. God is not a man, that he should lie.
[23:19]

120. What hath God wrought!
[23:23; quoted by Samuel Morse in the first electric telegraph message, Washington, 24 May 1844]

121. Be sure your sin will find you out.
[32:23]

Deuteronomy

122. For the Lord thy God is a jealous God.
[6:15]

123. Man doth not live by bread only, but by every word that proceedeth out of the mouth of the Lord doth man live.
[8:3]

124. A dreamer of dreams.
[13:1]

125. Thou shalt not muzzle the ox when he treadeth out the corn.
[25:4]

126. As thy days, so shall thy strength be.
[33:25]

127. The eternal God is thy refuge, and underneath are the everlasting arms.
[33:27]

Joshua

128. Be strong and of good courage; be not afraid, neither be thou dismayed: for the Lord thy God is with thee, whithersoever thou goest.
[1:9]

129. Let them live; but let them be hewers of wood and drawers of water.
[9:21]

130. I am going the way of all the earth.
[23:14]

Judges

131. The stars in their courses fought against Sisera.
[5:20]

132. He asked water, and she gave him milk; she brought forth butter in a lordly dish.
[5:25]

133. Why is his chariot so long in coming? why tarry the wheels of his chariots?
[5:28]

134. Out of the eater came forth meat, and out of the strong came forth sweetness.
[14:14]

135. With the jawbone of an ass, heaps upon heaps, with the jaw of an ass have I slain a thousand men.
[15:16]

136. The Philistines be upon thee, Samson.
[16:9]

137. He wist not that the Lord was departed from him.
[16:20]

138. In those days there was no king in Israel, but every man did that which was right in his own eyes.
[17:6]

Ruth

139. Intreat me not to leave thee, or to return from following after thee: for whither thou goest, I will go; and where thou lodgest, I will lodge: thy people shall be my people, and thy God my God:
Where thou diest, will I die, and there will I be buried: the Lord do so to me, and more also, if ought but death part thee and me.
[1:16–17]

I Samuel

140. Speak, Lord; for thy servant heareth.
[3:9]

141. And she named the child I-chabod, saying, The glory is departed from Israel.
[4:21]

142. Is Saul also among the prophets?
[10:11]

143. God save the king.
[10:24]

144. The Lord hath sought him a man after his own heart.
[13:14]

145. To obey is better than sacrifice, and to hearken than the fat of rams.
[15:22]

146. For the Lord seeth not as man seeth: for man looketh on the outward appearance, but the Lord looketh on the heart.
[16:7]

147. Go, and the Lord be with thee.
[17:37]

148. Am I a dog, that thou comest to me with staves?
[17:43]

149. Saul hath slain his thousands, and David his ten thousands.
[18:7]

150. Behold, I have played the fool, and have erred exceedingly.
[26:21]

II Samuel

151. Tell it not in Gath, publish it not in the streets of Askelon; lest the daughters of the Philistines rejoice, lest the daughters of the uncircumcised triumph.
[1:20]

152. Saul and Jonathan were lovely and pleasant in their lives, and in their death they were not divided.
[1:23]

153. Thy love to me was wonderful, passing the love of women.
[1:26]

154. How are the mighty fallen, and the weapons of war perished!
[1:27]

155. And David danced before the Lord with all his might.
[6:14]

156. And Nathan said to David, Thou art the man. Thus saith the Lord God of Israel, I anointed thee king over Israel, and I delivered thee out of the hand of Saul.
[12:7]

157. I shall go to him, but he shall not return to me.
[12:23]

158. Would God I had died for thee, O Absalom, my son, my son!
[18:33]

159. The sweet psalmist of Israel.
[23:1]

I Kings

160. Behold, the half was not told me.
[10:7]

161. My father hath chastised you with whips, but I will chastise you with scorpions.
[12:11]

162. An handful of meal in a barrel, and a little oil in a cruse.
[17:12]

163. How long halt ye between two opinions?
[18:21]

164. He is talking, or he is pursuing, or he is in a journey, or peradventure he sleepeth, and must be awaked.
[18:27]

165. But the Lord was not in the wind: and after the wind an earthquake: but the Lord was not in the earthquake: And after the earthquake a fire; but the Lord was not in the fire: and after the fire a still small voice.
[19:11–12]

166. Hast thou found me, O mine enemy?
[21:20]

167. And a certain man drew a bow at a venture, and smote the king of Israel between the joints of the harness.
[22:34]

II Kings

168. Go up, thou bald head.
[2:23]

169. There is death in the pot.
[4:40]

170. He shall know that there is a prophet in Israel.
[5:8]

171. Are not Abana and Pharpar, rivers of Damascus, better than all the waters of Israel?
[5:12]

172. The driving is like the driving of Jehu the son of Nimshi; for he driveth furiously.
[9:20]

I Chronicles

173. Let the heavens be glad, and let the earth rejoice: and let men say among the nations, The Lord reigneth.
[16:31]

174. And he died in a good old age, full of days, riches and honour: and Solomon his son reigned in his stead.
[29:28]

II Chronicles

175. And, behold, the one half of the greatness of thy wisdom was not told me: for thou exceedest the fame that I heard.
[9:6]

176. Be ye strong therefore, and let not your hands be weak: for your work shall be rewarded.
[15:7]

Esther

177. Let it be written among the laws of the Persians and the Medes, that it be not altered.
[1:19]

178. Thus shall it be done to the man whom the king delighteth to honour.
[6:9]

Job

179. And the Lord said unto Satan, Whence comest thou? Then Satan answered the Lord, and said, From going to and fro in the earth, and from walking up and down in it.
[1:7]

180. Doth Job fear God for nought?
[1:9]

181. The Lord gave, and the Lord hath taken away; blessed be the name of the Lord.
[1:21]

182. All that a man hath will he give for his life.
[2:4]

183. Curse God, and die.
[2:9]

184. Man is born unto trouble, as the sparks fly upward.
[5:7]

185. He shall return no more to his house, neither shall his place know him any more.
[7:10]

186. Canst thou by searching find out God?
[11:7]

187. No doubt but ye are the people, and wisdom shall die with you.
[12:2]

188. Man that is born of a woman is of few days, and full of trouble.
[14:1]

189. I know that my redeemer liveth.
[19:25]

190. I was eyes to the blind, and feet was I to the lame.
[29:15]

191. Who is this that darkeneth counsel by words without knowledge?
[38:2]

192. Where wast thou when I laid the foundations of the earth?
[38:4]

193. When the morning stars sang together, and all the sons of God shouted for joy.
[38:7]

194. Canst thou draw out leviathan with an hook?
[41:1]

195. So the Lord blessed the latter end of Job more than his beginning.
[42:12]

Psalms

196. Why do the heathen rage, and the people imagine a vain thing?
[2:1]

197. Out of the mouth of babes and sucklings hast thou ordained strength.
[8:2]

198. When I consider thy heavens, the work of thy fingers, the moon and the stars, which thou hast ordained;
What is man, that thou art mindful of him? and the son of man, that thou visitest him?
[8:3–4]

199. Thou hast made him a little lower than the angels.
[8:5]

200. The fool hath said in his heart, There is no God.
[14:1]

201. The lines are fallen unto me in pleasant places; yea, I have a goodly heritage.
[16:6]

202. The Lord is my rock, and my fortress, and my deliverer; my God, my strength, in whom I will trust.
[18:2]

203. The heavens declare the glory of God; and the firmament sheweth his handywork.
[19:1]

204. More to be desired are they than gold, yea, than much fine gold: sweeter also than honey and the honeycomb.
[19:10]

205. Strong bulls of Bashan have beset me round.
[22:12]

206. The Lord is my shepherd; I shall not want.
He maketh me to lie down in green pastures: he leadeth me beside the still waters.
He restoreth my soul: he leadeth me in the paths of righteousness for his name's sake.
Yea, though I walk through the valley of the shadow of death, I will fear no evil: for thou art with me; thy rod and thy staff they comfort me.
Thou preparest a table before me in the presence of mine enemies: thou anointest my head with oil: my cup runneth over.
Surely goodness and mercy shall follow me all the days of my life: and I will dwell in the house of the Lord for ever.
[23:1–6]

207. The earth is the Lord's, and the fulness thereof; the world, and they that dwell therein.
[24:1]

208. Lift up your heads, O ye gates; and be ye lift up, ye everlasting doors; and the King of glory shall come in.
Who is this King of glory? The Lord strong and mighty, the Lord mighty in battle.
[24:7–8]

209. I have seen the wicked in great power, and spreading himself like a green bay tree.
[37:35]

210. I waited patiently for the Lord; and he inclined unto me, and heard my cry.
[40:1]

211. Yea, mine own familiar friend, in whom I trusted, which did eat of my bread, hath lifted up his heel against me.
[41:9]

212. As the hart panteth after the water brooks, so panteth my soul after thee, O God.
[42:1]

213. Deep calleth unto deep at the noise of thy waterspouts.
[42:7]

214. My heart is inditing a good matter ... my tongue is the pen of a ready writer.
[45:1]

215. God is our refuge and strength, a very present help in trouble.
Therefore will not we fear, though the earth be removed, and though the mountains be carried into the midst of the sea.
[46:1–2]

216. Oh that I had wings like a dove!
[55:6]

217. They have digged a pit before me, into the midst whereof they are fallen themselves.
[57:6]

218. O God, thou art my God; early will I seek thee: my soul thirsteth for thee, my flesh longeth for thee in a dry and thirsty land, where no water is.
[63:1]

219. When I remember thee upon my bed, and meditate on thee in the night watches.
[63:6]

220. Then the Lord awaked as one out of sleep, and like a mighty man that shouteth by reason of wine.
And he smote his enemies in the hinder parts.
[78:65–6]

221. How amiable are thy tabernacles, O Lord of hosts!
My soul longeth, yea, even fainteth for the courts of the

Lord: my heart and my flesh crieth out for the living God.
Yea, the sparrow hath found an house, and the swallow a nest for herself, where she may lay her young, even thine altars, O Lord of hosts, my King, and my God.
Blessed are they that dwell in thy house: they will be still praising thee.
[84:1–4]

222. For a day in thy courts is better than a thousand. I had rather be a doorkeeper in the house of my God, than to dwell in the tents of wickedness.
[84:10]

223. Mercy and truth are met together; righteousness and peace have kissed each other.
[85:10]

224. For a thousand years in thy sight are but as yesterday when it is past, and as a watch in the night.
[90:4]

225. The days of our years are threescore years and ten; and if by reason of strength they be fourscore years, yet is their strength labour and sorrow.
[90:10]

226. For he shall give his angels charge over thee, to keep thee in all thy ways.
[91:11]

227. It is a good thing to give thanks unto the Lord, and to sing praises unto thy name, O most High;
To shew forth thy loving kindness in the morning, and thy faithfulness every night,
Upon an instrument of ten strings, and upon the psaltery; upon the harp with a solemn sound.
[92:1–3]

228. The righteous shall flourish like the palm tree: he shall grow like a cedar in Lebanon.
[92:12]

229. O come, let us sing unto the Lord; let us make a joyful noise to the rock of our salvation.
Let us come before his presence with thanksgiving, and make a joyful noise unto him with psalms.
For the Lord is a great God, and a great King above all gods.
In his hand are the deep places of the earth: the strength of the hills is his also.
The sea is his, and he made it: and his hands formed the dry land.
O come, let us worship and bow down: let us kneel before the Lord our maker.
[95:1–6]

230. O sing unto the Lord a new song: sing unto the Lord, all the earth.
Sing unto the Lord, bless his name; shew forth his salvation from day to day.
Declare his glory among the heathen, his wonders among all people.
For the Lord is great, and greatly to be praised: he is to be feared above all gods.
[96:1–4]

231. Bless the Lord, O my soul: and all that is within me, bless his holy name.
[103:1]

232. As for man, his days are as grass: as a flower of the field, so he flourisheth.
[103:15]

233. And wine that maketh glad the heart of man, and oil to make his face to shine.
[104:15]

234. They that go down to the sea in ships, that do business in great waters;
These see the works of the Lord, and his wonders in the deep.
[107:23–24]

235. The fear of the Lord is the beginning of wisdom.
[111:10]

236. Precious in the sight of the Lord is the death of his saints.
[116:15]

237. The stone which the builders refused is become the head stone of the corner.
[118:22]

238. Thy word is a lamp unto my feet, and a light unto my path.
[119:105]

239. I will lift up mine eyes unto the hills, from whence cometh my help.
My help cometh from the Lord, which made heaven and earth.
He will not suffer thy foot to be moved: he that keepeth thee will not slumber.
[121:1–3]

240. The Lord shall preserve thee from all evil: he shall preserve thy soul.
The Lord shall preserve thy going out and thy coming in from this time forth, and even for evermore.
[121:7–8]

241. I was glad when they said unto me,
Let us go into the house of the Lord.
[122:1]

242. They that sow in tears shall reap in joy.
[126:5]

243. Except the Lord build the house, they labour in vain that build it: except the Lord keep the city, the watchman waketh but in vain.
[127:1]

244. By the rivers of Babylon, there we sat down, yea, we wept, when we remembered Zion.
[137:1]

245. We hanged our harps upon the willows in the midst thereof.
[137:2]

246. How shall we sing the Lord's song in a strange land?
[137:4]

247. Lord, I cry unto thee: make haste unto me; give ear unto my voice, when I cry unto thee.
[141:1]

248. Put not your trust in princes, nor in the son of man, in whom there is no help.
[146: 3]

249. He delighteth not in the strength of the horse: he taketh not pleasure in the legs of a man.
[147:10]

Proverbs

250. Her ways are ways of pleasantness, and all her paths are peace.
[3:17]

251. Wisdom is the principal thing; therefore get wisdom: and with all thy getting get understanding.
[4:7]

252. The path of the just is as the shining light, that shineth more and more unto the perfect day.
[4:18]

253. Go to the ant, thou sluggard; consider her ways, and be wise.
[6:6]

254. As an ox goeth to the slaughter.
[7:22]

255. Wisdom hath builded her house, she hath hewn out her seven pillars.
[9:1]

256. Stolen waters are sweet.
[9:17]

257. A wise son maketh a glad father.
[10:1]

258. A righteous man regardeth the life of his beast.
[12:10]

259. Hope deferred maketh the heart sick.
[13:12]

260. He that spareth his rod hateth his son.
[13:24]

261. A soft answer turneth away wrath.
[15:1]

262. Better is a dinner of herbs where love is, than a stalled ox and hatred therewith.
[15:17]

263. Pride goeth before destruction, and an haughty spirit before a fall.
[16:18]

264. A merry heart doeth good like a medicine.
[17:22]

265. Wine is a mocker, strong drink is raging.
[20.1]

266. It is naught, it is naught, saith the buyer: but when he is gone his way, then he boasteth.
[20:14]

267. Train up a child in the way he should go: and when he is old, he will not depart from it.
[22:6]

268. Look not thou upon the wine when it is red.
[23:31]

269. Heap coals of fire upon his head.
[25:22]

270. Answer a fool according to his folly.
[26:5]

271. As a dog returneth to his vomit, so a fool returneth to his folly.
[26:11]

272. Boast not thyself of tomorrow; for thou knowest not what a day may bring forth.
[27:1]

273. Faithful are the wounds of a friend; but the kisses of an enemy are deceitful.
[27:6]

274. The wicked flee when no man pursueth: but the righteous are bold as a lion.
[28:1]

275. Where there is no vision, the people perish.
[29:18]

276. Who can find a virtuous woman? for her price is far above rubies.
[31:10]

277. Her children arise up, and call her blessed.
[31:28]

Ecclesiastes

278. Vanity of vanities, saith the Preacher, vanity of vanities; all is vanity.
[1:2]

279. All is vanity and vexation of spirit.
[1:14]

280. He that increaseth knowledge increaseth sorrow.
[1:18]

281. To every thing there is a season, and a time to every purpose under the heaven:
A time to be born, and a time to die; a time to plant, and a time to pluck up that which is planted;
A time to kill, and a time to heal; a time to break down, and a time to build up;
A time to weep, and a time to laugh; a time to mourn, and a time to dance;
A time to cast away stones, and a time to gather stones together; a time to embrace, and a time to refrain from embracing;
A time to get, and a time to lose; a time to keep, and a time to cast away;
A time to rend, and a time to sew; a time to keep silence, and a time to speak;
A time to love, and a time to hate; a time of war, and a time of peace.
[3:1–8]

282. God is in heaven, and thou upon earth: therefore let thy words be few.
[5:2]

283. As the crackling of thorns under a pot, so is the laughter of the fool.
[7:6]

284. Be not righteous over much.
[7:16]

285. A living dog is better than a dead lion.
[9:4]

286. Whatsoever thy hand findeth to do, do it with thy might.
[9:10]

287. The race is not to the swift, nor the battle to the strong.
[9:11]

288. Cast thy bread upon the waters: for thou shalt find it after many days.
[11:1]

289. Remember now thy Creator in the days of thy youth.
[12:1]

290. Of making many books there is no end; and much study is a weariness of the flesh.
[12:12]

291. Fear God, and keep his commandments: for this is the whole duty of man.
[12:13]

Song of Solomon

292. Let him kiss me with the kisses of his mouth: for thy love is better than wine.
[1:2]

293. I am black, but comely, O ye daughters of Jerusalem.
[1:5]

294. Stay me with flagons, comfort me with apples: for I am sick of love.
[2:5]

295. For, lo, the winter is past, the rain is over and gone;
The flowers appear on the earth; the time of the singing of birds is come, and the voice of the turtle is heard in our land.
[2:11–12]

296. Take us the foxes, the little foxes, that spoil the vines.
[2:15]

297. I sleep, but my heart waketh.
[5:2]

298. What is thy beloved more than another beloved, O thou fairest among women?
[5:9]

299. We have a little sister, and she hath no breasts.
[8:8]

Isaiah

300. Though your sins be as scarlet, they shall be as white as snow.
[1:18]

301. They shall beat their swords into plowshares, and their spears into pruninghooks: nation shall not lift up sword against nation, neither shall they learn war any more.
[2:4]

302. What mean ye that ye beat my people to pieces, and grind the faces of the poor? saith the Lord God of hosts.
[3:15]

303. Woe unto them that join house to house, that lay field to field, till there be no place, that they may be placed alone in the midst of the earth!
[5:8]

304. Woe unto them that call evil good, and good evil.
[5:20]

305. Woe is me! for I am undone; because I am a man of unclean lips, and I dwell in the midst of a people of unclean lips.
[6:5]

306. Whom shall I send, and who will go for us? Then said I, Here am I; send me.
[6:8]

307. The people that walked in darkness have seen a great light.
[9:2]

308. For unto us a child is born, unto us a son is given: and the government shall be upon his shoulder: and his name shall be called Wonderful, Counseller, The mighty God, The everlasting Father, The Prince of Peace.
[9:6]

309. And there shall come forth a rod out of the stem of Jesse, and a Branch shall grow out of his roots.
[11:1]

310. The wolf also shall dwell with the lamb, and the leopard shall lie down with the kid.
[11:6]

311. And the lion shall eat straw like the ox.
[11:7]

312. How art thou fallen from heaven, O Lucifer, son of the morning!
[14:12]

313. Watchman, what of the night?
[21:11]

314. Let us eat and drink; for to morrow we shall die.
[22:13]

315. He will swallow up death in victory; and the Lord God will wipe away tears from off all faces.
[25:8]

316. The bread of adversity, and the water of affliction.
[30:20]

317. The desert shall rejoice, and blossom as the rose.
[35:1]

318. Sorrow and sighing shall flee away.
[35:10]

319. Set thine house in order.
[38:1]

320. The voice of him that crieth in the wilderness, Prepare ye the way of the Lord, make straight in the desert a highway for our God.
Every valley shall be exalted, and every mountain and hill shall be made low: and the crooked shall be made straight, and the rough places plain:
And the glory of the Lord shall be revealed, and all flesh shall see it together: for the mouth of the Lord hath spoken it.
[40:3–5]

321. All flesh is grass, and all the goodliness thereof is as the flower of the field.
[40:6]

322. He shall feed his flock like a shepherd: he shall gather the lambs with his arm, and carry them in his bosom, and shall gently lead those that are with young.
[40:11]

323. Have ye not known? have ye not heard? hath it not been told you from the beginning?
[40:21]

324. They that wait upon the Lord shall renew their strength; they shall mount up with wings as eagles; they shall run, and not be weary; and they shall walk, and not faint.
[40:31]

325. There is no peace, saith the Lord, unto the wicked.
[48:22]

326. How beautiful upon the mountains are the feet of him that bringeth good tidings.
[52:7]

327. Who hath believed our report? and to whom is the arm of the Lord revealed?
[53:1]

328. He hath no form nor comeliness; and when we shall see him, there is no beauty that we should desire him.
He is despised and rejected of men; a man of sorrows, and acquainted with grief: and we hid as it were our faces from him; he was despised, and we esteemed him not.
Surely he hath borne our griefs, and carried our sorrows.
[53:2–4]

329. All we like sheep have gone astray; we have turned every one to his own way; and the Lord hath laid on him the iniquity of us all.
[53:6]

330. Seek ye the Lord while he may be found, call ye upon him while he is near.
[55:6]

331. For my thoughts are not your thoughts, neither are your ways my ways, saith the Lord.
[55:8]

332. Their feet run to evil, and they make haste to shed innocent blood.
[59:7]

333. He hath sent me to bind up the brokenhearted, to proclaim liberty to the captives, and the opening of the prison to them that are bound.
[61:1]

334. I have trodden the winepress alone.
[63:3]

Jeremiah

335. And they shall fight against thee; but they shall not prevail against thee; for I am with thee, saith the Lord, to deliver thee.
[1:19]

336. They were as fed horses in the morning: every one neighed after his neighbour's wife.
[5:8]

337. The harvest is past, the summer is ended, and we are not saved.
[8:20]

338. Is there no balm in Gilead?
[8:22]

339. Can the Ethiopian change his skin, or the leopard his spots?
[13:23]

340. The heart is deceitful above all things, and desperately wicked.
[17:9]

341. As the partridge sitteth on eggs, and hatcheth them not; so he that getteth riches, and not by right, shall leave them in the midst of his days, and at his end shall be a fool.
[17:11]

342. And seekest thou great things for thyself? seek them not.
[45:5]

Lamentations of Jeremiah

343. Is it nothing to you, all ye that pass by? behold, and see if there be any sorrow like unto my sorrow.
[1:12]

344. The wormwood and the gall.
[3:19]

Ezekiel

345. The fathers have eaten sour grapes, and the children's teeth are set on edge.
[18:2]

346. Son of man, can these bones live?
[37:3]

347. O ye dry bones, hear the word of the Lord.
[37:4]

Daniel

348. But if ye worship not, ye shall be cast the same hour into the midst of a burning fiery furnace.
[3:15]

349. And he commanded the most mighty men that were in his army to bind Shadrach, Meshach, and Abednego, and to cast them into the burning fiery furnace.
[3:20]

350. And this is the writing that was written, MENE, MENE, TEKEL, UPHARSIN.
[5:25]

351. Thou art weighed in the balances, and art found wanting.
[5:27]

352. Thy kingdom is divided, and given to the Medes and Persians.
[5:28]

Hosea

353. They have sown the wind, and they shall reap the whirlwind.
[8:7]

Joel

354. I will restore to you the years that the locust hath eaten.
[2:25]

355. I will pour out my spirit upon all flesh; and your sons and your daughters shall prophesy, your old men shall dream dreams, your young men shall see visions.
[2:28]

Amos

356. Can two walk together, except they be agreed?
[3:3]

357. Ye were as a firebrand plucked out of the burning.
[4:11]

Jonah

358. So they cast lots, and the lot fell upon Jonah.
[1:7]

359. Jonah was in the belly of the fish three days and three nights.
[1:17]

Micah

360. But thou, Beth-lehem Ephratah, though thou be little among the thousands of Judah, yet out of thee shall he come forth unto me that is to be ruler in Israel.
[5:2]

Habakkuk

361. Write the vision, and make it plain upon tables, that he may run that readeth it.
[2:2]

Zechariah

362. I was wounded in the house of my friends.
[13:6]

Malachi

363. Unto you that fear my name shall the Sun of righteousness arise with healing in his wings.
[4:2]

Apocrypha

364. *Magna est veritas et praevalet.*
Great is Truth, and mighty above all things.
[I Esdras, 4:41]

365. Through envy of the devil came death into the world.
[Wisdom of Solomon, 2:24]

366. He that toucheth pitch shall be defiled therewith.
[Ecclesiasticus, 13:1]

367. How agree the kettle and the earthen pot together?
[Ecclesiasticus, 13:2]

368. All wickedness is but little to the wickedness of a woman.
[Ecclesiasticus, 25:19]

369. Leave off first for manners' sake.
[Ecclesiasticus, 31:17]

370. Let us now praise famous men, and our fathers that begat us.
[Ecclesiasticus, 44:1]

371. And some there be, which have no memorial.
[Ecclesiasticus, 44:9]

372. Their bodies are buried in peace; but their name liveth for evermore.
[Ecclesiasticus, 44:14]

373. It was an holy and good thought.
[II Maccabees, 12:45]

Matthew

374. And she shall bring forth a son, and thou shalt call his name JESUS: for he shall save his people from their sins.
[1:21]

375. There came wise men from the east to Jerusalem,
Saying, Where is he that is born King of the Jews? for we have seen his star in the east, and are come to worship him.
[2:1–2]

376. They presented unto him gifts; gold, and frankincense, and myrrh.
[2:11]

377. The voice of one crying in the wilderness, Prepare ye the way of the Lord, make his paths straight.
[3:3]

378. O generation of vipers, who hath warned you to flee from the wrath to come?
[3:7]

379. This is my beloved Son, in whom I am well pleased.
[3:17]

380. Man shall not live by bread alone, but by every word that proceedeth out of the mouth of God.
[4:4. Cf. Luke 4.4]

381. Thou shalt not tempt the Lord thy God.
[4:7]

382. Angels came and ministered unto him.
[4:11]

383. Fishers of men.
[4:19]

384. Blessed are the poor in spirit: for theirs is the kingdom of heaven.
Blessed are they that mourn: for they shall be comforted.
Blessed are the meek: for they shall inherit the earth.
Blessed are they which do hunger and thirst after righteousness: for they shall be filled.
Blessed are the merciful: for they shall obtain mercy.
Blessed are the pure in heart: for they shall see God.
Blessed are the peacemakers: for they shall be called the children of God.
[5:3–9]

385. Ye are the salt of the earth: but if the salt have lost his savour, wherewith shall it be salted?
[5:13]

386. Whosoever shall compel thee to go a mile, go with him twain.
[5:41]

387. Love your enemies, bless them that curse you, do good to them that hate you, and pray for them which despitefully use you, and persecute you.
[5:44]

388. He maketh his sun to rise on the evil and on the good, and sendeth rain on the just and on the unjust.
[5:45]

389. Be ye therefore perfect, even as your Father which is in heaven is perfect.
[5:48]

390. Let not thy left hand know what thy right hand doeth.
[6:3]

391. After this manner therefore pray ye:
Our Father which art in heaven, Hallowed be thy name,
Thy Kingdom come. Thy will be done in earth, as it is in heaven.
Give us this day our daily bread.
And forgive us our debts, as we forgive our debtors.
And lead us not into temptation, but deliver us from evil:
For thine is the kingdom, and the power, and the glory, for ever. Amen.
[6:9–13]

392. Lay not up for yourselves treasures upon earth, where moth and rust doth corrupt, and where thieves break through and steal:
But lay up for yourselves treasures in heaven.
[6:19–20]

393. Where your treasure is, there will your heart be also.
[6:21]

394. No man can serve two masters: ... Ye cannot serve God and mammon.
[6:24]

395. Consider the lilies of the field, how they grow; they toil not, neither do they spin.
[6:28]

396. Seek ye first the kingdom of God, and his righteousness; and all these things shall be added unto you.
[6:33]

397. Take therefore no thought for the morrow: for the morrow shall take thought for the things of itself. Sufficient unto the day is the evil thereof.
[6:34]

398. Judge not, that ye be not judged.
[7:1]

399. Neither cast ye your pearls before swine.
[7:6]

400. Ask, and it shall be given you; seek, and ye shall find; knock, and it shall be opened unto you.
[7:7]

401. Beware of false prophets, which come to you in sheep's clothing, but inwardly they are ravening wolves.
[7:15]

402. By their fruits ye shall know them.
[7:20]

403. I have not found so great faith, no, not in Israel.
[8:10]

404. Let the dead bury their dead.
[8:22]

405. They that be whole need not a physician, but they that are sick.
[9:12]

406. I am not come to call the righteous, but sinners to repentance.
[9:13]

407. Be ye therefore wise as serpents, and harmless as doves.
[10:16]

408. Are not two sparrows sold for a farthing? and one of them shall not fall on the ground without your Father.
[10:29]

409. He that findeth his life shall lose it: and he that loseth his life for my sake shall find it.
[10:39]

410. Come unto me, all ye that labour and are heavy laden, and I will give you rest.
[11:28]

411. He that is not with me is against me.
[12:30]

412. The kingdom of heaven is like to a grain of mustard seed.
[13:31]

413. A prophet is not without honour, save in his own country, and in his own house.
[13:57]

414. Be of good cheer; it is I; be not afraid.
[14:27]

415. O thou of little faith, wherefore didst thou doubt?
[14:31]

416. If the blind lead the blind, both shall fall into the ditch.
[15:14]

417. Thou art Peter, and upon this rock I will build my church; and the gates of hell shall not prevail against it.
[16:18]

418. Get thee behind me, Satan.
[16:23]

419. What is a man profited, if he shall gain the whole world, and lose his own soul?
[16:26]

420. If thine eye offend thee, pluck it out.
[18:9]

421. For where two or three are gathered together in my name, there am I in the midst of them.
[18:20]

422. Thou shalt love thy neighbour as thyself.
[19:19]

423. With men this is impossible; but with God all things are possible.
[19:26]

424. But many that are first shall be last; and the last shall be first.
[19:30]

425. For many are called, but few are chosen.
[22:14]

426. Render therefore unto Caesar the things which are Caesar's; and unto God the things that are God's.
[22:21]

427. Ye blind guides, which strain at a gnat, and swallow a camel.
[23:24]

428. Ye shall hear of wars and rumours of wars.
[24:6]

429. Heaven and earth shall pass away, but my words shall not pass away.
[24:35]

430. Well done, thou good and faithful servant.
[25:21]

431. I was a stranger, and ye took me in:
Naked, and ye clothed me: I was sick, and ye visited me: I was in prison, and ye came unto me.
[25:35–36]

432. If it be possible, let this cup pass from me.
[26:39]

433. The spirit indeed is willing, but the flesh is weak.
[26:41]

434. All they that take the sword shall perish with the sword.
[26:52]

435. He took water, and washed his hands before the multitude, saying, I am innocent of the blood of this just person: see ye to it.
[27:24]

436. He saved others; himself he cannot save.
[27:42]

437. My God, my God, why hast thou forsaken me?
[27:46]

Mark

438. The sabbath was made for man, and not man for the sabbath.
[2:27]

439. If a house be divided against itself, that house cannot stand.
[3:25]

440. My name is Legion: for we are many.
[5:9]

441. Clothed, and in his right mind.
[5:15]

442. And they that did eat of the loaves were about five thousand men.
[6:44]

443. Lord, I believe; help thou mine unbelief.
[9:24]

444. Suffer the little children to come unto me, and forbid them not: for of such is the kingdom of God.
[10:14]

445. It is easier for a camel to go through the eye of a needle, than for a rich man to enter into the kingdom of God.
[10:25]

446. Go ye into all the world, and preach the gospel to every creature.
[16:15]

Luke

447. Because there was no room for them in the inn.
[2:7]

448. And, lo, the angel of the Lord came upon them, and the glory of the Lord shone round about them: and they were sore afraid.
[2:9]

449. Behold, I bring you good tidings of great joy.
[2:10]

450. Glory to God in the highest, and on earth peace, good will toward men.
[2:14]

451. Wist ye not that I must be about my Father's business?
[2:49]

452. Physician, heal thyself.
[4:23]

453. Love your enemies, do good to them which hate you.
[6:27]

454. No man, having put his hand to the plough, and looking back, is fit for the kingdom of God.
[9:62]

455. The labourer is worthy of his hire.
[10:7]

456. A certain man went down from Jerusalem to Jericho, and fell among thieves.
[10:30]

457. He passed by on the other side.
[10:31]

458. Go, and do thou likewise.
[10:37]

459. Thou fool, this night thy soul shall be required of thee.
[12:20]

460. I have married a wife, and therefore I cannot come.
[14:20]

461. The poor, and the maimed, and the halt, and the blind.
[14:21]

462. Joy shall be in heaven over one sinner that repenteth, more than over ninety and nine just persons, which need no repentance.
[15:7]

463. He would fain have filled his belly with the husks that the swine did eat.
[15:16]

464. Bring hither the fatted calf, and kill it.
[15:23]

465. God, I thank thee, that I am not as other men are.
[18:11]

466. If these should hold their peace, the stones would immediately cry out.
[19:40]

467. Nevertheless not my will, but thine, be done.
[22:42]

468. Father, forgive them; for they know not what they do.
[23:34]

469. Father, into thy hands I commend my spirit.
[23:46]

470. He was known of them in breaking of bread.
[24:35]

John

471. In the beginning was the Word, and the Word was with God, and the Word was God.
[1:1]

472. The light shineth in darkness; and the darkness comprehended it not.
[1:5]

473. And the Word was made flesh, and dwelt among us.
[1:14]

474. Can there any good thing come out of Nazareth?
[1:46]

475. Thou hast kept the good wine until now.
[2:10]

476. The wind bloweth where it listeth.
[3:8]

477. God so loved the world, that he gave his only begotten Son, that whosoever believeth in him should not perish, but have everlasting life.
[3:16]

478. God is a Spirit: and they that worship him must worship him in spirit and in truth.
[4:24]

479. Rise, take up thy bed, and walk.
[5:8]

480. He that is without sin among you, let him first cast a stone at her.
[8:7]

481. And ye shall know the truth, and the truth shall make you free.
[8:32]

482. The night cometh, when no man can work.
[9:4]

483. He is of age; ask him.
[9:21]

484. The good shepherd giveth his life for the sheep.
[10:11]

485. Jesus wept.
[11:35]

486. The poor always ye have with you.
[12:8]

487. Let not your heart be troubled: ye believe in God, believe also in me.
[14:1]

488. In my Father's house are many mansions.
[14:2]

489. I am the way, the truth, and the life: no man cometh unto the Father, but by me.
[14:6]

490. Greater love hath no man than this, that a man lay down his life for his friends.
[15:13]

491. Pilate saith unto him, What is truth?
[18:38]

492. What I have written I have written.
[19:22]

493. Except I shall see in his hands the print of the nails, and put my finger into the print of the nails, and thrust my hand into his side, I will not believe.
[20:25]

494. Blessed are they that have not seen, and yet have believed.
[20:29]

495. And there are also many other things which Jesus did, the which, if they should be written every one, I suppose that even the world itself could not contain the books that should be written.
[21:25]

Acts of the Apostles

496. Ye men of Galilee, why stand ye gazing up into heaven?
[1:11]

497. Silver and gold have I none; but such as I have give I thee.
[3:6]

498. Saul, Saul, why persecutest thou me?
[9:4]

499. It is hard for thee to kick against the pricks.
[9:5]

500. God is no respecter of persons.
[10:34]

501. Come over into Macedonia, and help us.
[16:9]

502. What must I do to be saved?
[16:30]

503. For in him we live, and move, and have our being.
[17:28]

504. It is more blessed to give than to receive.
[20:35]

505. A citizen of no mean city.
[21:39]

506. Paul, thou art beside thyself; much learning doth make thee mad.
[26:24]

507. Almost thou persuadest me to be a Christian.
[26:28]

Romans

508. The just shall live by faith.
[1:17]

509. Let us do evil, that good may come.
[3:8]

510. For all have sinned, and come short of the glory of God.
[3:23]

511. The wages of sin is death.
[6:23]

512. All things work together for good to them that love God.
[8:28]

513. If God be for us, who can be against us?
[8:31]

514. For I am persuaded, that neither death, nor life, nor angels, nor principalities, nor powers, nor things present, nor things to come,
Nor height, nor depth, nor any other creature, shall be able to separate us from the love of God, which is in Christ Jesus our Lord.
[8:38–39]

515. Rejoice with them that do rejoice, and weep with them that weep.
[12:15]

516. Vengeance is mine; I will repay, saith the Lord.
[12:19]

517. The powers that be are ordained of God.
[13:1]

518. The night is far spent, the day is at hand.
[13:12]

I Corinthians

519. Absent in body, but present in spirit.
[5:3]

520. It is better to marry than to burn.
[7:9]

521. I am made all things to all men.
[9:22]

522. Though I speak with the tongues of men and of angels, and have not charity, I am become as sounding brass, or a tinkling cymbal.
...and though I have all faith, so that I could remove mountains, and have not charity, I am nothing.
And though I bestow all my goods to feed the poor, and though I give my body to be burned, and have not charity, it profiteth me nothing.
Charity suffereth long, and is kind; charity envieth not; charity vaunteth not itself, is not puffed up,
Doth not behave itself unseemly, seeketh not her own, is not easily provoked, thinketh no evil;
Rejoiceth not in iniquity, but rejoiceth in the truth; Beareth all things, believeth all things, hopeth all things, endureth all things.
Charity never faileth: but whether there be prophecies, they shall fail; whether there be tongues, they shall cease; whether there be knowledge, it shall vanish away.
[13:1–8]

523. And now abideth faith, hope, charity, these three; but the greatest of these is charity.
[13:13]

524. Let all things be done decently and in order.
[14:40]

525. The last enemy that shall be destroyed is death.
[15:26]

526. Behold, I shew you a mystery; We shall not all sleep, but we shall all be changed.
[15:51]

527. O death, where is thy sting? O grave, where is thy victory?
[15:55]

II Corinthians

528. The letter killeth, but the spirit giveth life.
[3:6]

529. God loveth a cheerful giver.
[9:7]

530. There was given to me a thorn in the flesh, the messenger of Satan to buffet me.
[12:7]

Galatians

531. Be not deceived; God is not mocked: for whatsoever a man soweth, that shall he also reap.
[6:7]

Ephesians

532. ... children, tossed to and fro, and carried about with every wind of doctrine, by the sleight of men, and cunning craftiness.
[4:14]

533. We are members one of another.
[4:25]

534. Be ye angry, and sin not; let not the sun go down upon your wrath.
[4:26]

535. Be not drunk with wine, wherein is excess; but be filled with the Spirit.
[5:18]

536. Ye fathers, provoke not your children to wrath.
[6:4]

537. Put on the whole armour of God.
[6:11]

538. For we wrestle not against flesh and blood, but against principalities, against powers, against the rulers of the darkness of this world, against spiritual wickedness in high places.
[6:12]

Philippians

539. Work out your own salvation with fear and trembling.
[2:12]

540. Whose God is their belly, and whose glory is in their shame.
[3:19]

541. The peace of God, which passeth all understanding.
[4:7]

542. Whatsoever things are true, whatsoever things are honest, whatsoever things are just, whatsoever things are pure, whatsoever things are lovely, whatsoever things are of good report; if there be any virtue, and if there be any praise, think on these things.
[4:8]

543. I can do all things through Christ which strengtheneth me.
[4:13]

Colossians

544. Luke, the beloved physician.
[4:14]

I Thessalonians

545. Pray without ceasing.
[5:17]

II Thessalonians

546. If any would not work, neither should he eat.
[3:10]

I Timothy

547. Old wives' fables.
[4:7]

548. Drink no longer water, but use a little wine for thy stomach's sake and thine often infirmities.
[5:23]

549. The love of money is the root of all evil.
[6:10. Cf. Samuel Butler [2]: 5]

550. Fight the good fight of faith.
[6:12]

551. Science falsely so called.
[6:20]

II Timothy

552. The husbandman that laboureth must be first partaker of the fruits.
[2:6]

553. I have fought a good fight, I have finished my course, I have kept the faith.
[4:7]

Titus

554. Unto the pure all things are pure.
[1:15]

Hebrews

555. It is a fearful thing to fall into the hands of the living God.
[10:31]

556. Faith is the substance of things hoped for, the evidence of things not seen.
[11:1]

557. Seeing we also are compassed about with so great a cloud of witnesses.
[12:1]

558. Whom the Lord loveth he chasteneth.
[12:6]

559. Let brotherly love continue.
[13:1]

560. Be not forgetful to entertain strangers: for thereby some have entertained angels unawares.
[13:2]

561. For here have we no continuing city.
[13:14]

James

562. But be ye doers of the word, and not hearers only.
[1:22]

563. Faith without works is dead.
[2:20]

564. Resist the devil, and he will flee from you.
[4:7]

565. Let your yea be yea; and your nay, nay.
[5:12]

Peter

566. As newborn babes, desire the sincere milk of the word.
[2:2]

567. Honour all men. Love the brotherhood. Fear God. Honour the king.
[2:17]

568. Charity shall cover the multitude of sins.
[4:8]

569. Your adversary the devil, as a roaring lion, walketh about, seeking whom he may devour.
[5:8]

I John

570. He that loveth not knoweth not God; for God is love.
[4:8]

571. Perfect love casteth out fear.
[4:18]

Revelation

572. I am Alpha and Omega, the beginning and the ending, saith the Lord.
[1:8]

573. I was in the Spirit on the Lord's day.
[1:10]

574. I am he that liveth, and was dead; and, behold, I am alive for evermore, Amen.
[1:18]

575. I will not blot out his name out of the book of life.
[3:5]

576. Because thou art lukewarm, and neither cold nor hot, I will spue thee out of my mouth.
[3:16]

577. Behold, I stand at the door, and knock.
[3:20]

578. Who is worthy to open the book, and to loose the seals thereof?
[5:2]

579. And I looked, and behold a pale horse: and his name that sat on him was Death.
[6:8]

580. God shall wipe away all tears from their eyes.
[7:17]

581. When he had opened the seventh seal, there was silence in heaven about the space of half an hour.
[8:1]

582. Babylon is fallen, is fallen, that great city.
[14:8]

583. And the sea gave up the dead which were in it.
[20:13]

584. And I saw a new heaven and a new earth: for the first heaven and the first earth were passed away; and there was no more sea.
[21:1]

585. I will give unto him that is athirst of the fountain of the water of life freely.
[21:6]

586. Behold, I come quickly.
[22:12]

587. The grace of our Lord Jesus Christ be with you all. Amen.
[22:21]

The Bible (The New Testament in Scots)

The extracts from *The New Testament in Scots*, translated by W.L. Lorimer, are copyright © R.L.C. Lorimer and appear by kind permission of R.L.C. Lorimer and the Trustees of the Lorimer Trust.

588. Syne Jesus wis led awa bi the Spirit tae the muirs for tae be tempit bi the Deil. Whan he hed taen nae mait for fortie days an fortie nichts an wis fell hungrisome, the Temper cam til him an said, 'If you are the Son of God, tell these stones to turn into loaves.' Jesus answert, 'It says i the Buik: *Man sanna live on breid alane, but on ilka wurd at comes furth o God's mouth.*'
[4:1–4]

589. Gíe us our breid for this incomin day;
forgíe us the wrangs we hae wrocht,
as we hae forgíen the wrangs we hae dree'd;
an sey-us-na sairlie, but sauf us
frae the Ill Ane.
[6:11–13]

590. Nae man can sair two maisters: aither he will ill-will the tane an luve the tither, or he will grip til the tane an lichtlifie the tither. Ye canna sair God an Gowd baith.
[6:24]

591. Efterhin Jesus gaed intil the Temple an drave out aa them at bocht an sauld in it, an whummelt the tables o the money-changers an the saits o them at sauld dous: 'It says i the Bible,' qo he tae them, *'My houss sal be caa'd a houss o prayer*: but ye ar makkin it *a rubbers' howff*.
Syne some blinnd fowk an lameters cam up til him i the Temple, an he hailed them. But whan the Heid-Priests an Doctors o the Law saw the uncos at he wrocht, an heared the callans cryin i the Temple, 'Hosanna til the Son o Dauvit,' they war ill-sortit, an said til him, 'Hear ye what thir louns is sayin?' 'Ay, div I,' qo he. 'But hae ye ne'er read i your Bibles: *Thou hes lairnt the mouths o littlans an pap-bairns tae ruise thee?' Wi that he quat them, an gaed out the toun tae Bethanie, whaur he bade the nicht.*
[21:12–17]

Luke

592. Syne he tuik the Twal aside an said tae them, 'Tak tent, we ar on our gate tae Jerusalem, whaur aathing foretauld i the Prophets for the Son o Man will nou come tae pass. He will be haundit owre tae the haithen, geckit, ill-gydit, spitten on, leashed, pitten tae deith, an syne rise again the third day.' Nocht understuid the disciples o this say: the meanin o it wis hodden frae them; they war dung tae mak ocht o it.
[18:31–34]

John

593. There kythed a man, sent frae God, at his name wis John. He cam for a witness, tae beir witness tae the licht, at aa men micht win tae faith throu him. He wisna the licht himsel; he cam tae beir witness tae the licht. The true licht, at enlichtens ilka man, wis een than comin intil the warld. He was in the warld, an the warld hed come tae be throu him, but the warld miskent him. He cam tae the place at belanged him, an them at belanged him walcomed-himna. But til aa sic as walcomed him he gae the pouer tae become childer o god; een tae them at pits-faith in his name, an wis born, no o bluid or carnal desire or the will o man, but o God.
[1:6–13]

I Corinthians

594. Luve is patientfu; luve is couthie an kind; luve is nane jailous; nane sprosie; nane bowdent wi pride; nane mislaired; nane hamedrauchtit; nane toustie. Luve keeps nae nickstick o the wrangs it drees; finnds nae pleisur i the ill wark o ithers; is ey liftit up whan truith dings lies; kens ey tae keep a caum souch; is ey sweired tae misdout; ey howps the best; ey bides the warst.
Luve will ne'er fail. Prophecies, they s' een be by wi; tungs, they s' een devaul; knawledge, it s' een be by wi. Aa our knawledge is hauflin; aa our prophesiein is hauflin: but whan the perfyte is comed, the onperfyte will be by wi. In my bairn days, I hed the speech o a bairn, the mind o a bairn, the thochts o a bairn, but nou at I am grown manmuckle, I am throu wi aathing bairnlie. Nou we ar like luikin in a mirror an seein aathing athraw, but than we s' luik aathing braid i the face. Nou I ken aathing hauflinsweys, but than I will ken aathing as weill as God kens me.
In smaa: there is three things bides for ey: faith, howp, luve. But the grytest o the three is luve.
[13:4–13]

595. It is the same wi maisical instruments – chanter, like, or a hairp: gin they gie out a mixtur-maxtur o notes, wha can tell what tuin the player is playin? Or, for that pairt, gin the tout on the horn isna clair, wha will graith him for battle? It is een the same wi yoursels: whan ye moubandna your wurds plain an clair, hou is oniebodie tae uptak what ye ar sayin? Ye ar juist waistin your wind!
[14:7–9]

Titus

596. Thir men maun hae the mous o them steikit, for they ar whummlin the faith o haill faimlies wi teachin things they ochtna for the sake o ill-faured gain. Ane o themsels – a prophet o their ain, nae less – hes said: *The Cretans is ey liars, nestie bruits, sweir poke-puddins.*
[1:11–15]

The Bible (Vulgate)

597. *Dominus illuminatio mea et salus mea, quem timebo?*
The Lord is the source of my light, and my safety, so whom shall I fear?
[Psalms, 26:1]

598. *Asperges me hyssopo, et mundabor; lavabis me, et super nivem dealbabor.*
You will sprinkle me with hyssop, and I shall be made clean; you will wash me and I shall be made whiter than snow.
[Psalms, 50:9]

599. *Cantate Domino canticum novum, quia mirabilia fecit.*
Sing to the Lord a new song, because he has done marvellous things.
[Psalms, 97:1]

600. *Iubilate Domino, omnis terra, servite Domino in laetitia.*
Rejoice in the Lord, all ye lands; serve the Lord with gladness.
[Psalms, 99:2]

601. *Beatus vir, qui timet Dominum, in mandatis eius cupit nimis!*
Happy is the man who fears the Lord, who is only too willing to follow his orders.
[Psalms, 111:1]

602. *Non nobis, Domine, non nobis.*
Not unto us, Lord, not unto us.
[Psalms, 113:9 (1)]

603. *Laudate Dominum, omnes gentes.*
Praise the Lord, all nations.
[Psalms, 116:1]

604. *Nisi Dominus aedificaverit domum, in vanum laborant qui aedificant eam.*
Nisi Dominus custodierit civitatem, frustra vigilat qui custodit eam.
Unless the Lord has built the house, its builders labour in vain. Unless the Lord guards the city, it's no use its guard staying awake.
[Psalms, 126:1]

605. *De profundis clamavi ad te, Domine.*
Out of the depths I have cried to thee, Lord.
[Psalms, 129:1]

598. *Benedicite, omnia opera Domini, Domino, laudate et superexaltate eum in saecula.*
Bless the Lord, all the works of the Lord; praise him and exalt him above all things for ever.
[Daniel, 3:57]

599. *Magnificat anima mea Dominum,*
et exsultavit spiritus meus in Deo salvatore meo.
My soul doth magnify the Lord: and my spirit hath rejoiced in God my Saviour.
[St Luke, 1:46]

600. *Esurientes implevit bonis et divites dimisit inanes.*
He hath filled the hungry with good things: and the rich he hath sent away empty.
[St Luke, 1:53]

601. *Nunc dimittis servum tuum, Domine, secundum verbum tuum in pace.*
Lord, now lettest thou thy servant depart in peace: according to thy word.
[St Luke, 2:29; trans. Book of Common Prayer]

602. *Pax vobis.*
Peace be unto you.
[St Luke, 24:36]

603. *Vanitas vanitatum, et omnia vanitas.*
Vanity of vanities, and all things are vanity.
[Ecclesiastes, 1:2]

604. *Quo vadis?*
Where are you going?
[St John, 16:5]

605. *Ecce homo!*
Behold the man!
[St John, 19:5]

606. *Consummatum est!*
It is finished!
[St John, 19:30]

607. *Noli me tangere.*
Do not touch me.
[St John, 20:17]

Bickerstaffe, Isaac (c. 1733–c. 1808)
Irish comic dramatist and author of ballad operas

1. In every port he finds a wife.
[*Thomas and Sally* (1760)]

2. There was a jolly miller once,
Lived on the river Dee;
He worked and sang from morn till night;
No lark more blithe than he...

3. And this the burthen of his song,
For ever us'd to be,
I care for nobody, not I,
If no one cares for me.
[*Love in a Village* (1762), I]

4. We all love a pretty girl – under the rose.
[*Love in a Village* (1762), II]

5. Perhaps it was right to dissemble your love,
But – why did you kick me downstairs?
['An Expostulation' (1789)]

Bidault, Georges (1899–1983)
French statesman; Prime Minister, 1946, 1949–50

1. The weak have one weapon: the errors of those who think they are strong.
[*The Observer*, 1962]

Bierce, Ambrose (1842–c.1914)
American short-story writer, essayist, journalist, versifier and soldier

1. *Bore*: A person who talks when you wish him to listen.
[*The Cynic's Word Book* (1906); later republished as *The Devil's Dictionary*]

2. *Brain*: An apparatus with which we think that we think.
[*The Cynic's Word Book* (1906); later republished as *The Devil's Dictionary*]

3. *Debauchee*: One who has so earnestly pursued pleasure that he has had the misfortune to overtake it.
[*The Cynic's Word Book* (1906); later republished as *The Devil's Dictionary*]

4. *Education*: That which discloses to the wise and disguises from the foolish their lack of understanding.
[*The Cynic's Word Book* (1906); later republished as *The Devil's Dictionary*]

5. *Egotist*: A person of low taste, more interested in himself than in me.
[*The Cynic's Word Book* (1906); later republished as *The Devil's Dictionary*]

6. *Future*: That period of time in which our affairs prosper, our friends are true and our happiness is assured.
[*The Cynic's Word Book* (1906); later republished as *The Devil's Dictionary*]

7. *Lawsuit*: A machine which you go into as a pig and come out as a sausage.
[*The Cynic's Word Book* (1906); later republished as *The Devil's Dictionary*]

8. *Patience*: A minor form of despair, disguised as a virtue.
[*The Cynic's Word Book* (1906); later republished as *The Devil's Dictionary*]

9. *Peace*: In international affairs, a period of cheating between two periods of fighting.
[*The Cynic's Word Book* (1906); later republished as *The Devil's Dictionary*]

Biko, Steve (1946–1977)
Black South African civil rights leader

1. The most potent weapon in the hands of the oppressor is the mind of the oppressed.
[Address to conference on inter-racial studies, Cape Town, January 1971]

2. We wanted to remove him [the white man] from our table, strip the table of all the trappings put on it by him, decorate it in true African style, settle down and then ask him to join us if he liked.
[Address to conference on inter-racial studies, Cape Town, January 1971]

Billings, Josh (Henry Wheeler Shaw) (1818–1885)
American comic essayist, philosopher and lecturer

1. Thrice is he armed that hath his quarrel just,
But four times he who gets his blow in fust.
[*Josh Billings, his Sayings* (1865)]

Bingham, Sir Thomas (1933–)
English Master of the Rolls

1. [As Master of the Rolls, discussing the rising costs of going to law]
We cannot for ever be content to acknowledge that in England justice is open to all – like the Ritz Hotel.
[*Independent on Sunday*, 1994]

Binyon, Laurence (1869–1943)
English war poet, art historian and critic

1. They shall grow not old, as we that are left grow old:
Age shall not weary them, nor the years condemn.
At the going down of the sun and in the morning
We will remember them.
['For the Fallen' (1914)]

Bion (fl. 280 BC)
Greek bucolic poet, of Smyrna

1. Though boys throw stones at frogs in sport, the frogs do not die in sport, but in earnest.
[Quoted by Plutarch]

Birch, Nigel (later Lord Rhyl) (1906–1981)

1. For the second time the Prime Minister has got rid of a Chancellor of the Exchequer who tried to get expenditure under control. Once is more than enough.
[Letter, *The Times*, 1962]

Birkenhead, Earl of, See F.E. SMITH

Birley, Mark
Owner of fashionable London nightclub Annabel's

1. You never forget people who were kind to you when you were young.
[*The Observer*, 1989, in Jeffrey Care (ed.), *Sayings of the Eighties* (1989)]

Birrell, Augustine (1850–1933)
English essayist, Professor of Law and Liberal MP; Chief Secretary for Ireland 1907–16

1. That great dust-heap called 'history'.
[*Obiter Dicta* (1884–1887), 'Carlyle']

Birt, John (1944–)
British television producer; Director-General of the BBC

1. There is a bias in television journalism. It is not against any particular party or point of view – it is a bias against understanding.
[*The Times*, 1975]

Bismarck, Prince Otto von (1815–1898)
German statesman; first Chancellor of the German Reich, 1871–90

1. *Lieber Spitzkugeln als Spitzreden.*
Sharp bullets are preferable to sharp speeches.
[Speech, 1850]

2. *Die Politik ist keine exakte Wissenschaft.*
Politics is not a precise science.
[Speech, Prussian House of Deputies, 1863]

3. *Die Politik ist die Lehre vom Möglichen.*
Politics is the doctrine of what is possible.
[Remark to Meyer von Waldeck, editor of the St Petersburg *Zeitung*, 1863]

4. ['Going to Canossa' was seen as representing a giving way in the so-called *Kulturkampf* (Culture Struggle) with the Roman Catholic Church]
Nach Kanossa gehen wir nicht!
We won't go to Canossa!
[Speech, Reichstag, 1872]

5. [Describing Germany's role in peace negotiations]
Ich denke [mir die Macht des Deutschen Reiches] ... mehr die eines ehrlichen Maklers.
I consider [the power of the German Empire] ... to be more than that of an honest broker.
[Speech, Reichstag, 1878]

6. *Die Politik ist keine Wissenschaft ... sie ist eben eine Kunst.*
Politics is not a science ... but an art.
[Speech, Reichstag, 1884]

7. *Legt eine möglichst starke militärische Kraft, mit anderen Worten möglichst viel Blut und Eisen in die Hand des Königs von Preussen, dann wird er die Politik machen können, die Ihr wünscht; mit Reden und Schützenfesten und Liedern macht sie sich nicht, sie macht sich nur durch 'Blut und Eisen'!*
Put the strongest possible military power, in other words as much blood and iron as possible, in the hands of the King of Prussia, and then he will be able to carry out the policy you want; this cannot be achieved with speeches and shooting-matches and songs; it can only be achieved by 'blood and iron'!
[Speech, Prussian House of Deputies, 1886]

8. To youth I have but three words of counsel – work, work, work.
[Attr.]

9. [Remark made just before he died]
If there is ever another war in Europe, it will come out of some damned silly thing in the Balkans.
[Attr.]

Bissell, Claude T. (1916–)
Canadian writer and biographer; former President, University of Toronto

1. I prefer complexity to certainty, cheerful mysteries to sullen facts.
[Address, University of Toronto, 1969]

Bjelke-Petersen, Florence Isabel (1920–)
Wife of the Hon. Sir Johannes Bjelke-Petersen, politician

1. [On her husband, Premier of Queensland]
People who criticise Joh unfairly make me angry. They call him 'a racist pig' in Canberra. Joh's not a racist. Why, he's had Aborigines working for him.
[*Woman's Day*, 1975]

Bjelke-Petersen, Sir Johannes (1911–)
Australian politician, former Premier of Queensland

1. The greatest thing that could happen to the state and the nation is when we can get rid of all the media. Then we could live in peace and tranquillity, and no one would know anything.
[*Spectator*, 1987]

Black, (Cecil) John (1920–)

1. I know all about art, but I don't know what I like.
[To Stephen Murray-Smith (ed.), *The Dictionary of Australian Quotations*]

Blacker, Valentine (1778–1823)
English lieutenant-colonel; Surveyor-General of India

1. Put your trust in God, my boys, and keep your powder dry.
[*Oliver's Advice* (1856)]

Blackstone, Sir William (1723–1780)
English judge, historian of English law and politician

1. Man was formed for society.
[*Commentaries on the Laws of England* (1765–1769), Introduction]

2. The king never dies.
[*Commentaries on the Laws of England* (1765–1769), I]

3. The royal navy of England hath ever been its greatest defence and ornament; it is its ancient and natural strength; the floating bulwark of the island.
[*Commentaries on the Laws of England* (1765–1769), I]

4. That the king can do no wrong, is a necessary and fundamental principle of the English constitution.
[*Commentaries on the Laws of England* (1765–1769), III]

5. It is better that ten guilty persons escape than one innocent suffer.
[*Commentaries on the Laws of England* (1765–1769), IV]

6. Husband and wife are one, and that one is the husband.
[In Rosalind Miles, *The Women's History of the World* (1988)]

Blackwell, Antoinette Brown (1825–1921)
American feminist writer

1. Mr Darwin ... has failed to hold definitely before his mind the principle that the difference of sex, whatever it may consist in, must itself be subject to natural selection and to evolution.
[*The Sexes Throughout Nature* (1875)]

Blackwood, Helen Selina (Countess of Dufferin) (1807–1867)
English songwriter; grand-daughter of Richard Brinsley Sheridan

1. And the red was on your lip, Mary,
The love-light in your eye...

2. I'm sitting on the stile, Mary,
Where we sat, side by side...

3. They say there's bread and work for all,
And the sun shines always there:
But I'll not forget old Ireland,
Were it fifty times as fair.
['Lament of the Irish Emigrant' (1845)]

Blainey, Geoffrey Norman (1930–)

1. The physical mastering of Australia was swift and often dramatic, but the emotional conquest was slow.
[*A Land Half Won*]

2. The Tyranny of Distance: How Distance Shaped Australia's History.
[Title of book, 1963]

Blair, Robert (1699–1746)
Scottish poet and Church of Scotland minister

1. The schoolboy, with his satchel in his hand,
Whistling aloud to bear his courage up...

2. Its visits,
Like those of Angels, short, and far between.
['The Grave' (1743)]

Blake, Charles Dupee (1846–1903)
British writer of nursery rhymes

1. Rock-a-bye baby on the tree top,
When the wind blows the cradle will rock,
When the bough bends the cradle will fall,
Down comes the baby, cradle and all.
[Attr.]

Blake, Eubie (1883–1983)

1. [He died five days after his hundredth birthday]
If I'd known I was gonna live this long, I'd have taken better care of myself.
[*The Observer*, 1983]

Blake, William (1757–1827)
English Romantic poet, engraver, painter and mystic

1. How sweet I roam'd from field to field,
And tasted all the summer's pride,
'Till I the prince of love beheld,
Who in the sunny beams did glide!
[*Poetical Sketches* (1783), 'Song: How sweet I roam'd']

2. As long a-gone
When men were first a nation grown,
Lawless they liv'd – till wantonness
And liberty began t'increase;
And one man lay in another's way,
Then laws were made to keep fair play.
[*Poetical Sketches* (1783), 'Blind-Man's Buff']

3. The god of war is drunk with blood,
The earth doth faint and fail;

The stench of blood makes sick the heav'ns;
Ghosts glut the throat of hell!
[*Poetical Sketches* (1783),'Gwin, King of Norway']

4. Sweet Prince! the arts of peace are great,
And no less glorious than those of war.
[*Poetical Sketches* (1783), 'King Edward the Third', ii]

5. Ambition is the growth of ev'ry clime.
[*Poetical Sketches* (1783), 'King Edward the Third', iv]

6. Justice hath heaved a sword to plunge in Albion's breast; for Albion's sins are crimson-dy'd.
[*Poetical Sketches* (1783), 'King John', Prologue]

7. Samson, the strongest of the children of men, I sing; how he was foiled by woman's arts...

8. Ten thousand spears are like the summer grass...

9. Manoa left his fields to sit in the house, and take his evening's rest from labour – the sweetest time that God has allotted mortal man...

10. Oppression stretches his rod over our land, our country is plowed with swords, and reaped in blood!
[*Poetical Sketches* (1783), 'Samson']

11. Mans desires are limited by his perceptions; none can desire what he has not perceiv'd.
[*There is No Natural Religion* (c. 1788), First Part]

12. The desire of Man being Infinite the possession is Infinite & himself Infinite.
[*There is No Natural Religion* (c. 1788), Second Part]

13. Piping down the valleys wild,
Piping songs of pleasant glee
On a cloud I saw a child,
And he laughing said to me:

'Pipe a song about a Lamb:'
So I piped with merry chear.
'Piper pipe that song again;'
So I piped, he wept to hear.

'Drop thy pipe thy happy pipe;
Sing thy songs of happy chear:'
So I sung the same again,
While he wept with joy to hear...

14. And I made a rural pen,
And I stain'd the water clear,
And I wrote my happy songs
Every child may joy to hear.
[*Songs of Innocence* (1789), 'Introduction']

15. Little Lamb, who made thee
Dost thou know who made thee
Gave thee life & bid thee feed
By the stream & o'er the mead;
Gave thee clothing of delight,
Softest clothing wooly bright;
Gave thee such a tender voice,
Making all the vales rejoice?
[*Songs of Innocence* (1789), 'The Lamb']

16. To Mercy Pity Peace and Love,
All pray in their distress...

17. For Mercy has a human heart
Pity, a human face:
And Love, the human form divine,
And Peace, the human dress.
[*Songs of Innocence* (1789), 'The Divine Image']

18. When my mother died I was very young,
And my father sold me while yet my tongue,
Could scarcely cry, 'weep weep weep weep'
So your chimneys I sweep & in soot I sleep...

19. Hush Tom never mind it, for when your head's bare,
You know that the soot cannot spoil your white hair...

20. Tho' the morning was cold, Tom was happy & warm,
So if all do their duty, they need not fear harm.
[*Songs of Innocence* (1789), 'The Chimney Sweeper']

21. ... I have no name
I am but two days old–'
What shall I call thee?
...I happy am,
Joy is my name,–'
Sweet joy befall thee!
[*Songs of Innocence* (1789), 'Infant Joy']

22. When the voices of children are heard on the green
And laughing is heard on the hill.
[*Songs of Innocence* (1789), 'Nurse's Song']

23. 'Twas on a Holy Thursday their innocent faces clean
The children walking two & two in red & blue & green...

24. Then cherish pity, lest you drive an angel from your door.
[*Songs of Innocence* (1789), 'Holy Thursday']

25. Can I see anothers woe,
And not be in sorrow too?
Can I see anothers grief,
And not seek for kind relief?
[*Songs of Innocence* (1789), 'On Another's Sorrow']

26. When the green woods laugh with the voice of joy.
[*Songs of Innocence* (1789), 'Laughing Song']

27. My mother bore me in the southern wild,
And I am black, but O! my soul is white.
White as an angel is the English child:
But I am black, as if bereav'd of light.
[*Songs of Innocence* (1789), 'The Little Black Boy']

28. Does the Eagle know what is in the pit?
Or wilt thou go ask the Mole:
Can Wisdom be put in a silver rod?
Or Love in a golden bowl?
[*The Book of Thel* (1789), 'Thel's Motto']

29. Every thing that lives,
Lives not alone, nor for itself.
[*The Book of Thel* (1789), Plate 3]

30. Why a Tongue impress'd with honey from every wind?
Why an Ear, a whirlpool fierce to draw creations in?
Why a Nostril wide inhaling terror trembling & affright?
Why a tender curb upon the youthful burning boy!
Why a little curtain of flesh on the bed of our desire?
[*The Book of Thel* (1789), Plate 6]

31. Without Contraries is no progression. Attraction and Repulsion, Reason and Energy, Love and Hate, are necessary to Human existence.
[*The Marriage of Heaven and Hell* (c. 1790–1793), 'The Argument', Plate 3]

32. Man has no Body distinct from his Soul for that calld Body is a portion of Soul discernd by the five Senses, the chief inlets of Soul in this age.
Energy is the only life and is from the Body and Reason is the bound or outward circumference of Energy.
Energy is Eternal Delight.
Those who restrain desire, do so because theirs is weak enough to be restrained.
[*The Marriage of Heaven and Hell* (c. 1790–1793), 'The Voice of the Devil', Plate 5]

33. The reason Milton wrote in fetters when he wrote of Angels & God, and at liberty when of Devils & Hell, is because he was a true Poet and of the Devil's party without knowing it.
[*The Marriage of Heaven and Hell* (c. 1790–1793), 'The Voice of the Devil', Plate 6, note]

34. In seed time learn, in harvest teach, in winter enjoy.
Drive your cart and your plow over the bones of the dead.
The road of excess leads to the palace of wisdom.
Prudence is a rich ugly old maid courted by Incapacity.
He who desires but acts not, breeds pestilence.
The cut worm forgives the plow...

35. A fool sees not the same tree that a wise man sees...

36. Eternity is in love with the productions of time.
The busy bee has no time for sorrow...

37. All wholsom food is caught without a net or a trap...

38. No bird soars too high if he soars with his own wings...

39. The most sublime act is to set another before you.
If the fool would persist in his folly he would become wise...

40. Shame is Pride's cloke.
[*The Marriage of Heaven and Hell* (c. 1790–1793), 'Proverbs of Hell', Plate 7]

41. Prisons are built with stones of Law, Brothels with bricks of Religion.
The pride of the peacock is the glory of God.
The lust of the goat is the bounty of God.
The wrath of the lion is the wisdom of God.
The nakedness of woman is the work of God...

42. Joys impregnate. Sorrows bring forth...

43. What is now proved was once only imagin'd...

44. The cistern contains: the fountain overflows.
One thought fills immensity.
[*The Marriage of Heaven and Hell* (c. 1790–1793), 'Proverbs of Hell', Plate 8]

45. Think in the morning, Act in the noon, Eat in the evening, Sleep in the night.
He who has suffer'd you to impose on him, knows you...

46. The tygers of wrath are wiser than the horses of instruction.
Expect poison from standing water.
You never know what is enough unless you know what is more than enough...

47. The weak in courage is strong in cunning...

48. As the catterpiller chooses the fairest leaves to lay her eggs on, so the priest lays his curse on the fairest joys...

49. Damn braces: Bless relaxes.
The best wine is the oldest, the best water the newest.
[*The Marriage of Heaven and Hell* (c. 1790–1793), 'Proverbs of Hell', Plate 9]

50. Exuberance is Beauty...

51. Sooner murder an infant in its cradle than nurse unacted desires...

52. Truth can never be told so as to be understood, and not be believ'd.
[*The Marriage of Heaven and Hell* (c. 1790–1793), 'Proverbs of Hell', Plate 10]

53. If the doors of perception were cleansed every thing would appear to man as it is, infinite.
[*The Marriage of Heaven and Hell* (c. 1790–1793), 'A Memorable Fancy', Plate 14]

54. I was in a Printing house in Hell & saw the method in which knowledge is transmitted from generation to generation.
[*The Marriage of Heaven and Hell* (c. 1790–1793), 'A Memorable Fancy', Plate 15]

55. One law for the Lion & Ox is Oppression.
[*Marriage of Heaven and Hell* (c. 1790–1793), 'A Memorable Fancy', Plate 24]

56. For every thing that lives is Holy.
[*Marriage of Heaven and Hell* (c. 1790–1793), 'Chorus', Plate 27]

57. Never pain to tell thy love
Love that never told can be
For the gentle wind does move
Silently invisibly

I told my love I told my love
I told her all my heart
Trembling cold in ghastly fears
Ah she doth depart

Soon as she was gone from me
A traveller came by
Silently invisibly
He took her with a sigh.
['Never pain to tell thy Love' (c. 1793), from 'The Rossetti Manuscript']

58. Abstinence sows sand all over
The ruddy limbs & flaming hair
But Desire Gratified
Plants fruits of life & beauty there.
['Abstinence sows sand all over' (c. 1793), from 'The Rossetti Manuscript']

59. He who binds to himself a joy
Does the winged life destroy;
But he who kisses the joy as it flies
Lives in eternity's sun rise.
['Eternity' (c. 1793), from 'The Rossetti Manuscript']

60. What is it men in women do require?
The lineaments of Gratified Desire.
What is it women do in men require?
The lineaments of Gratified Desire.
['What is it men in women do require' (c. 1793), from 'The Rossetti Manuscript']

61. For every thing that lives is holy, life delights in life.
[*America: a Prophecy* (1793), Plate 10]

62. Hear the voice of the Bard!
Who Present, Past, & Future, sees.
[*Songs of Experience* (1794), Introduction]

63. Love seeketh not Itself to please,
Nor for itself hath any care;
But for another gives its ease,
And builds a Heaven in Hells despair...

64. Love seeketh only Self to please,
To bind another to Its delight;
Joys in anothers loss of ease,
And builds a Hell in Heavens despite.
[*Songs of Experience* (1794), 'The Clod & the Pebble']

65. Is this a holy thing to see,
In a rich and fruitful land,
Babes reducd to misery,
Fed with cold and usurous hand?
[*Songs of Experience* (1794), 'Holy Thursday']

66. O Rose, thou art sick,
The invisible worm,
That flies in the night
In the howling storm:

Has found out thy bed
Of crimson joy:
And his dark secret love
Does thy life destroy.
[*Songs of Experience* (1794), 'The Sick Rose']

67. Tyger Tyger, burning bright
In the forests of the night:
What immortal hand or eye
Could frame thy fearful symmetry?...

68. What the hand dare sieze the fire?

And what shoulder & what art,
Could twist the sinews of thy heart?
And when thy heart began to beat,
What dread hand? & what dread feet?...

69. When the stars threw down their spears
And water'd heaven with their tears:
Did he smile his work to see?
Did he who made the Lamb make thee?
[*Songs of Experience* (1794), 'The Tyger']

70. Ah Sun-flower! weary of time,
Who countest the steps of the Sun:
Seeking after that sweet golden clime
Where the travellers journey is done;

Where the Youth pined away with desire,
And the pale Virgin shrouded in snow:
Arise from their graves and aspire
Where my Sun-flower wishes to go.
[*Songs of Experience* (1794), 'Ah! Sun-flower']

71. I went to the Garden of Love,
And saw what I never had seen:
A Chapel was built in the midst,
Where I used to play on the green.

And the gates of this Chapel were shut,
And 'Thou shalt not' writ over the door...

72. And Priests in black gowns were walking their rounds,
And binding with briars my joys & desires.
[*Songs of Experience* (1794), 'The Garden of Love']

73. But if at the Church they would give us some Ale,
And a pleasant fire our souls to regale:
We'd sing and we'd pray all the live-long day;
Nor ever once wish from the Church to stray.
[*Songs of Experience* (1794), 'The Little Vagabond']

74. I wander thro' each charter'd street,
Near where the charter'd Thames does flow
And mark in every face I meet
Marks of weakness, marks of woe.

In every cry of every Man,
In every Infant's cry of fear,
In every voice, in every ban,
The mind-forg'd manacles I hear.

How the Chimney-sweepers cry
Every blackning Church appalls,
And the hapless Soldiers sigh
Runs in blood down Palace walls

But most thro' midnight streets I hear
How the youthful Harlots curse
Blasts the new born Infants tear,
And blights with plagues the Marriage hearse.
[*Songs of Experience* (1794), 'London']

75. My mother groand! my father wept.
Into the dangerous world I leapt:
Helpless, naked, piping loud:
Like a fiend hid in a cloud.

Struggling in my father's hands:
Striving against my swadling bands:
Bound and weary I thought best
To sulk upon by mothers breast.
[*Songs of Experience* (1794), 'Infant Sorrow']

76. I was angry with my friend:
I told my wrath, my wrath did end.
I was angry with my foe:
I told it not, my wrath did grow.
[*Songs of Experience* (1794), 'A Poison Tree']

77. Children of the future Age,
Reading this indignant page:
Know that in a former time,
Love! sweet Love! was thought a crime.
[*Songs of Experience* (1794), 'A Little Girl Lost']

78. For double the vision my Eyes do see
And a double vision is always with me.
With my inward Eye 'tis an old Man grey,
With my outward a Thistle across my way.
['Letter to Thomas Butts' (1802)]

79. O why was I born with a different face?
Why was I not born like the rest of my race?
['Letter to Thomas Butts' (1803)]

80. But vain the Sword & vain the Bow,
They never can work Wars overthrow...

81. The hand of Vengeance found the Bed
To which the Purple Tyrant fled;
The iron hand crushd the Tyrants head
And became a Tyrant in his Stead.
['The Grey Monk' (c. 1803), from 'The Pickering Manuscript']

82. To see a World in a Grain of Sand
And a Heaven in a Wild Flower
Hold Infinity in the palm of your hand
And Eternity in an hour.
A Robin Red breast in a Cage
Puts all Heaven in a Rage...

83. A dog starvd at his Masters gate
Predicts the ruin of the State.
A Horse misusd upon the Road
Calls to Heaven for Human blood.
Each outcry of the hunted Hare
A fibre from the Brain does tear.
A Skylark wounded in the wing,
A Cherubim does cease to sing...

84. Every Wolfs & Lions howl
Raises from Hell a Human Soul...

85. He who shall hurt the little Wren
Shall never be belovd by Men.
He who the Ox to wrath has movd
Shall never be by Woman lovd...

86. A truth thats told with bad intent
Beats all the Lies you can invent.
It is right it should be so
Man was made for Joy & Woe
And when this we rightly Know
Thro the World we safely go.
Joy & Woe are woven fine
A Clothing for the soul divine...

87. Every Tear from Every Eye
Becomes a Babe in Eternity...

88. The Bleat the Bark Bellow & Roar
Are Waves that Beat on Heavens Shore...

89. The Soldier armd with Sword & Gun
Palsied strikes the Summers Sun...

90. He who shall teach the Child to Doubt
The rotting Grave shall neer get out...

91. Nought can deform the Human Race
Like to the Armours iron brace...

92. He who Doubts from what he sees
Will neer Believe do what you Please.
If the Sun & Moon should doubt,
Theyd immediately Go out.
To be in a Passion you Good may do
But no Good if a Passion is in you.
The Whore & Gambler by the State
Licencd, build that Nations Fate.
The Harlots cry from Street to Street
Shall weave Old Englands winding Sheet.
['Auguries of Innocence' (c. 1803), from 'The Pickering Manuscript']

93. When a Man has Married a Wife he finds out whether
Her Knees & elbows are only glued together.
['When a Man has Married a Wife' (1800–1803), from 'The Rossetti Manuscript']

94. Such men as Goldsmith ought not to have been acquainted with such men as Reynolds.
[Annotations to Sir Joshua Reynolds' *Works* (c. 1808)]

95. To Generalize is to be an Idiot. To particularize is the Alone Distinction of Merit. General Knowledges are those Knowledges that Idiots possess.
[Annotations to Sir Joshua Reynolds' *Works* (c. 1808)]

96. When Sr Joshua Reynolds died
All Nature was degraded:
The King dropd a tear into the Queens Ear:
And all his Pictures Faded.
[Annotations to Sir Joshua Reynolds' *Works* (c. 1808)]

97. Such Artists as Reynolds, are at all times Hired by the Satans, for the Depression of Art. A Pretence of Art: To destroy Art.
[Annotations to Sir Joshua Reynolds' *Works* (c. 1808), 'Discourse 1']

98. And did those feet in ancient time
Walk upon Englands mountains green:
And was the holy Lamb of God
On Englands pleasant pastures seen!

And did the Countenance Divine
Shine forth upon our clouded hills?
And was Jerusalem builded here,
Among these dark Satanic Mills?

Bring me my Bow of burning gold:
Bring me my Arrows of desire:
Bring me my Spear: O clouds unfold:
Bring me my Chariot of Fire!

I will not cease from Mental Fight,
Nor shall my Sword sleep in my hand:
Till we have built Jerusalem
In Englands green & pleasant Land.
[*Milton* (1804–1809), Preface]

99. Great things are done when Men & Mountains meet;
This is not done by Jostling in the Street.
['Great things are done' (c. 1793–1810), from 'The Rossetti Manuscript']

100. Mock on Mock on Voltaire Rousseau,
Mock on Mock on: tis all in vain!
You throw the sand against the wind,
And the wind blows it back again...

101. The Atoms of Democritus
And Newtons Particles of light
Are sands upon the Red sea shore
Where Israels tents do shine so bright.
['Mock On' (c. 1800–1810), from 'The Rossetti Manuscript']

102. [On Hayley]
Of H – s birth this was the happy lot
His Mother on his Father him begot.
['Of Hayley's birth' (c. 1807–1810), from 'The Rossetti Manuscript']

103. [On Cromek]
A petty sneaking Knave I knew
O Mr Cr – , how do ye do?
['On Cromek' (c. 1807–1810), from 'The Rossetti Manuscript']

104. He has observd the Golden Rule
Till hes become the Golden Fool.
['He has observ'd the golden rule' (c. 1807–1810), from 'The Rossetti Manuscript']

105. Thy Friendship oft has made my heart to ake:
Do be my Enemy for Friendships sake.
['To H[ayley]' (c. 1807–1810), from 'The Rossetti Manuscript']

106. Both read the Bible day & night
But thou readst black where I read White.
['The Everlasting Gospel', (c. 1810), from 'The Rossetti Manuscript']

107. Humility is only doubt
And does the Sun & Moon blot out...

108. This lifes dim Windows of the Soul
Distorts the Heavns from Pole to Pole
And leads you to Believe a Lie
When you see with, not thro the Eye.
['The Everlasting Gospel', (c. 1810), from 'The Rossetti Manuscript']

109. I am Sure This Jesus will not do
Either for Englishman or Jew.
['The Everlasting Gospel', (c. 1810), from 'The Rossetti Manuscript']

110. Truly My Satan thou art but a Dunce
And dost not know the Garment from the Man.
Every Harlot was a Virgin once
Nor canst thou ever change Kate into Nan.

Tho thou art worshipd by the Names Divine
Of Jesus & Jehovah: thou art still
The Son of Morn in weary Nights decline,
The lost Travellers Dream under the Hill.
[*For the Sexes: The Gates of Paradise* (c. 1810), 'To The Accuser who is The God of This World']

111. When I tell any Truth it is not for the sake of Convincing those who do not know it but for the sake of defending those who Do.
[Public address, from the Notebook, c. 1810]

112. 'When the Sun rises do you not See a round Disk of fire somewhat like a Guinea?' O no no I see an Innumerable company of the Heavenly host crying 'Holy Holy Holy is the Lord God Almighty.'
['A Vision of the Last Judgment' (1810)]

113. I must Create a System, or be enslav'd by another Mans.
I will not Reason & Compare: my business is to Create.
[*Jerusalem* (1804–1820), Plate 10]

114. The fields from Islington to Marybone,
To Primrose Hill and Saint Johns Wood:
Were builded over with pillars of gold,
And there Jerusalems pillars stood.
[*Jerusalem* (1804–1820), 'To the Jews', Plate 27]

115. For a Tear is an Intellectual thing!
And a Sigh is the Sword of an Angel King
And the bitter groan of a Martyrs woe
Is an Arrow from the Almighties Bow.
[*Jerusalem* (1804–1820), 'To the Deists', Plate 52]

116. He who would do good to another must do it in Minute Particulars.
General Good is the plea of the Scoundrel hypocrite & flatterer:
For Art & Science cannot exist but in minutely organized Particulars.
[*Jerusalem* (1804–1820), Chapter 3, Plate 55]

117. I give you the end of a golden string
Only wind it into a ball:
It will lead you in at Heavens gate,
Built in Jerusalems wall...

118. England! awake! awake! awake!
Jerusalem thy Sister calls!
Why wilt thou sleep the sleep of death?
And close her from thy ancient walls?...

119. And now the time returns again:
Our souls exult & Londons towers
Receive the Lamb of God to dwell
In Englands green & pleasant bowers.
[*Jerusalem* (1804–1820), 'To the Christians', Plate 77]

120. I care not whether a Man is Good or Evil; all that I care
Is whether he is a Wise Man or a Fool. Go! put off Holiness
And put on Intellect.
[*Jerusalem* (1804–1820), Chapter 4, Plate 91]

121. Cruelty has a Human Heart
And Jealousy a Human Face,
Terror the Human Form Divine,
And Secrecy the Human Dress.
[*Songs of Experience*, Additional Poem (c. 1832), 'A Divine Image']

Blanch, Lesley (1907–)
British biographer and travel writer

1. [Of Jane Digby who was successively Lady Ellenborough, Baroness Venningen, Countess Theotoky and the wife of Sheik Abdul Medjuel El Mezrab]
She was an Amazon. Her whole life was spent riding at breakneck speed towards the wilder shores of love.
[*The Wilder Shores of Love* (1954)]

Blind Harry the Minstrel (c. 1440–c. 1492)
Scottish poet

1. Now leiff thi myrth, now leiff thi haill plesance;
Now leiff thi bliss, now leiff thi childis age;
Now leiff thi youth, now folow thi hard chance;
Now leiff thi lust, now leiff thi mariage;
Now leiff thi luff, for thou sall loss a gage
Quhilk never in erd sall be redemyt agayne.
[Attr.]

2. In thee was wyt, fredom, and hardines;
In thee was truth, manheid, and nobilnes;
In thee was rewll, in thee was governans;
In thee was wertu withoutys warians.
[Attr.]

Bliss, Philip Paul (1838–1876)
American hymn-writer and evangelist

1. Hold the fort, for I am coming.
[Hymn, 1871]

Blücher, Prince (1742–1819)

1. [Remark made on seeing London in June, 1814]
Was für Plunder!
What junk!
[Attr.]

Blue, Rabbi Lionel (1930–)
English lecturer and broadcaster on Judaism and writer

1. There is always a danger in Judaism of seeing history as a sort of poker game played between Jews and God, in which the presence of others is noted but not given much importance.
[*The Observer*, 1982, in Jeffrey Care (ed.), *Sayings of the Eighties* (1989)]

Blue Peter

1. Here's one I made earlier.
[BBC children's television programme]

Blunden, Edmund (1896–1974)
English war and pastoral poet; critic, teacher and biographer

1. All things they have in common being so poor,
And their one fear, Death's shadow at the door.
Each sundown makes them mournful, each sunrise
Brings back the brightness in their failing eyes.
[*The Waggoner and Other Poems* (1920), 'Almswomen']

2. Dance on this ball-floor thin and wan,
Use him as though you love him;
Court him, elude him, reel and pass,
And let him hate you through the glass.
[*Masks of Time* (1925), 'The Midnight Skaters']

3. I am for the woods against the world,
But are the woods for me?
[*To Themis* (1931), 'The Kiss']

Blythe, Ronald (1922–)
English writer

1. As for the British churchman, he goes to church as he goes to the bathroom, with the minimum of fuss and no explanation if he can help it.
[*The Age of Illusion* (1963)]

Boake, Barcroft Henry Thomas (1866–1892)
Australian surveyor, drover and poet

1. Out on the wastes of the Never Never,
That's where the dead men lie!
There where the heat-waves dance for ever–
That's where the dead men lie!
['Where the Dead Men Lie' (1897)]

Bocca, Giorgio (1920–)
Italian journalist and writer

1. [After the kidnapping and subsequent murder of Aldo Moro, Christian Democrat Premier, May 1978]
All'annuncio del rapimento l'Italia è come messa al tappeto da un

colpo basso: non riesce a capire che cosa sta succedendo, le pare impossibile che il terrorismo sia così forte.
At the announcement of Moro's kidnapping, Italy looked as if she had been knocked out by a blow below the belt: she doesn't understand what's happening; it seems impossible to her that terrorism could be so powerful.
[*Noi Terroristi* (*We Terrorists*, 1985)]

2. *La mafia è razionale, vuole ridurre al minimo gli omicidi.*
The mafia is rational, it wants to reduce homicides to the minimum.
[*L'Inferno* (*Hell*, 1992), 3]

Boccaccio, Giovanni (c.1313–1375)
Italian poet and celebrated writer of narrative fiction

1. Do as we say, and not as we do.
[*Decameron* (1358), 3]

Boethius (c. 475–524)
Roman statesman, scholar and philosopher

1. *In omni adversitate fortunae, infelicissimum est genus infortunii, fuisse felicem.*
At every blow of fate, the worst kind of misfortune is to have been happy.
[*De Consolatione Philosophiae* (c. 522–524), II]

2. *Nihil est miserum nisi cum putes; contraque beata sors omnis est aequanimitate tolerantis.*
Nothing is miserable unless you think it so; conversely, every lot is happy to one who is content with it.
[*De Consolatione Philosophiae* (c. 522–524), II]

3. *Quis legem dat amantibus? Major lex amor est sibi.*
Who can give a law to lovers? Love is a greater law unto itself.
[*De Consolatione Philosophiae* (c. 522–524), III]

Bogarde, Dirk (Derek van den Bogaerd) (1921–)
British film actor and writer

1. A Postillion Struck by Lightning.
[Title of book, 1988]

2. I'm not very clever, but I'm quite intelligent.
[Attr.]

Bogart, Humphrey (1899–1957)
American film actor

1. If she can stand it, I can – play it!
[*Casablanca*, film, 1942; script by Julius and Philip Epstein and Howard Koch. Cf. Bergman: 1]

2. Here's lookin' at you, kid.
[*Casablanca*, film, 1942; script by Julius and Philip Epstein and Howard Koch]

Bogart, John B. (1845–1921)
American journalist

1. When a dog bites a man that is not news, but when a man bites a dog that is news.
[Attr.]

Bohr, Niels Henrik David (1885–1962)
Danish nuclear physicist and quantum theorist; Nobel prize, 1922

1. An expert is a man who has made all the mistakes which can be made in a very narrow field.
[Attr.]

2. [Explaining why he had a horseshoe on his wall]
Of course I don't believe in it. But I understand that it brings you luck whether you believe in it or not.
[Attr.]

Boileau-Despréaux, Nicolas (1636–1711)
French poet, satirist and critic

1. *Si j'écris quatre mots, j'en effacerai trois.*
If I write four words, I shall strike out three.
[*Satires* (1666)]

2. *Le pénible fardeau de n'avoir rien à faire!*
What a terrible burden it is to have nothing to do!
[*Epitres* (c. 1690), XI]

3. *Enfin Malherbe vint, et, le premier en France,*
Fit sentir dans les vers une juste cadence.
At last came Malherbe, and, the first in France, gave poetry a proper rhythm.
[*L'Art Poétique* (1674)]

4. *Quelque sujet qu'on traite, ou plaisant, ou sublime,*
Que toujours le bon sens s'accorde avec la rime.
Be the subject lighthearted or sublime, sense always should agree with rhyme.
[*L'Art Poétique* (1674)]

5. *Qu'en un lieu, qu'en un jour, un seul fait accompli*
Tienne jusqu'à la fin le théâtre rempli.
Let a single complete action, in one place, in one day, keep a full house till the end of the play.
[*L'Art Poétique* (1674)]

6. *Qui ne sait se borner ne sut jamais écrire.*
He who does not know how to limit himself does not know how to write.
[*L'Art Poétique* (1674)]

7. *Souvent la peur d'un mal nous conduit dans un pire.*
The fear of one evil often leads us into a greater one.
[*L'Art Poétique* (1674)]

8. *Un sot trouve toujours un plus sot qui l'admire.*
A fool will always find a greater fool to admire him.
[*L'Art Poétique* (1674)]

Boland, Eavan (1944–)
Irish poet and critic

1. Poetry is defined by its energies and its eloquence, not by the passport of the poet or the editor; or the name of the nationality. That way lie all the categories, the separations, the censorships that poetry exists to dispel.
[Review of Seamus Heaney's *An Open Letter*, The Irish Times, 1983]

Boldrewood, Rolf (Thomas Alexander Browne) (1826–1915)
Australian novelist

1. Men and women, horses and dogs, are very much alike. I know which can talk best.
[*Robbery Under Arms* (1888)]

Boleyn, Anne (1507–1536)
Second queen of Henry VIII and mother of Elizabeth I

1. [Said on hearing that she was to be executed for adultery]
The king has been very good to me. He promoted me from a simple maid to be a marchioness. Then he raised me to be a queen. Now he will raise me to be a martyr.
[Attr.]

Bolingbroke, Henry St John, First Viscount (1678–1751)
English statesman, political philosopher, historian and actor

1. Truth lies within a little and certain compass, but error is immense.
[*Reflections upon Exile* (written 1716)]

2. I have read somewhere or other – in Dionysius of Halicarnassus, I think – that History is Philosophy teaching by examples.
[*Letters on Study and Use of History* (1752)]

3. Nations, like men, have their infancy.
[*Letters on Study and Use of History* (1752)]

4. [Of Thucydides and Xenophon]
They maintained the dignity of history.
[*Letters on Study and Use of History* (1752)]

5. They make truth serve as a stalking-horse to error.
[*Letters on Study and Use of History* (1752)]

6. What a world is this, and how does fortune banter us!
[Letter, 1714]

7. Plain truth will influence half a score of men at most in a nation, or an age, while mystery will lead millions by the nose.
[Letter, 1721]

Böll, Heinrich (1917–1985)
German novelist and short-story writer

1. *Sie war erstaunt, wie gelassen es in dieser Verwaltung des Todes zuging. Alles ging mechanisch, etwas gereizt ungeduldig: diese Menschen taten ihre Arbeit mit der gleichen Misslaune, wie sie jede andere Büroarbeit getan hätten, sie erfüllten lediglich eine Pflicht, eine Pflicht, die ihnen lästig war, die sie aber erfüllten.*
She was astonished how calm things were in this administration of death. Everything was done mechanically, and people were somewhat irritated and impatient: these people did their work with the same ill-humour with which they would have done any other kind of office-work, they were merely performing a duty, a duty which was a nuisance to them, but which they performed nevertheless.
[*Wo warst du, Adam?* (*Where were you, Adam?*, 1951), 4]

2. *Es gibt überhaupt keine höhere Form des Bekenntnisses zu einem Volk, als in seiner Sprache zu schreiben; selbst wenn man schlecht schreibt.*
There is absolutely no higher form of identification with a people than writing in its language; even if you write badly.
[*Eine deutsche Erinnerung. Interview mit René Wintzen* (*A German Recollection. Interview with René Wintzen*), I, 'What I call the morality of language', (1976)]

Bolt, Robert (1924–1995)
English dramatist and writer of screenplays

1. Morality's not practical. Morality's a gesture. A complicated gesture learned from books.
[*A Man for All Seasons* (1960), II]

Bolte, Sir Henry Edward (1908–1990)
Australian politician

1. [On striking teachers seeking to meet him]
I don't have a doorstep low enough for them to sit on.
[In Blazey, *Bolte*]

Bone, Sir David (1874–1959)
Scottish novelist, sailor and maritime authority

1. It's 'Damn you, Jack – I'm all right!' with you chaps.
[*The Brassbounder* (1910), 3]

Bonhoeffer, Dietrich (1906–1945)
German Lutheran theologian; executed by the Nazis

1. *Ein Gott, der sich von uns beweisen liesse, wäre ein Götze.*
A God who allowed us to prove his existence would be an idol.
[*'Glaubst du, so hast du.' Versuch eines Lutherischen Katechismus* (*'If you believe it, you have it.' Attempt at a Lutheran Catchism*), Bonhoeffer and Hildebrandt (1931)]

2. *Der Mensch hat gelernt, in allen wichtigen Fragen mit sich selbst fertig zu werden ohne Zuhilfenahme der 'Arbeitshypothese: Gott.'*
In all important questions, man has learned to cope without recourse to God as a working hypothesis.
[*Widerstand und Ergebung: Briefe und Aufzeichnungen aus der Haft* (*Resistance and Surrender: Letters and Notes from Custody*, 1951), Letter to a friend, June 1944]

Bono, Edward de (1933–)
British physician and writer; champion of 'lateral thinking'

1. Unhappiness is best defined as the difference between our talents and our expectations.
[*The Observer*, 'Sayings of the Week', 1977]

Boone, Daniel (1734–1820)
American frontiersman, hunter and explorer

1. [Reply on being asked if he had ever been lost]
I can't say I was ever lost, but I was bewildered once for three days.
[Attr.]

Boorde, Andrew (c. 1490–1549)
English traveller, physician and writer

1. Trust your no Skott.
[Letter to Thomas Cromwell, 1536]

2. The devellysche dysposicion of a Scottysh man, not to love nor favour an Englishe man.
[Letter to Thomas Cromwell, 1536]

Boorstin, Daniel J. (1914–)
American librarian; historian, lawyer and writer

1. A best-seller was a book which somehow sold well simply because it was selling well.
[*The Image* (1962)]

2. The celebrity is a person who is known for his well-knownness.
[*The Image* (1962)]

Booth, General William (1829–1912)
English founder of the Salvation Army; preacher and champion of the poor

1. This Submerged Tenth – is it, then, beyond the reach of the nine-tenths in the midst of whom they live?
[*In Darkest England* (1890)]

Borchert, Wolfgang (1921–1947)

1. *Wir sind die Generation ohne Bindung und ohne Tiefe.*
We are the generation without bonds and without depth.
['Generation ohne Abschied' ('Generation without Parting', 1946)]

Borges, Jorge Luis (1899–1986)
Argentinian magic realist short-story writer; poet and librarian

1. *Que el cielo exista, aunque mi lugar sea el infierno.*
Let heaven exist, even if my place be hell.
[*El jardín de senderos que se bifurcan* (*The Garden of Paths which Diverge*, 1941), 'La Biblioteca de Babel' ('The Library of Babel')]

2. *He conocido lo que ignoran los griegos: la incertidumbre.*
I have known what the Greeks knew not: uncertainty.
[*El jardín de senderos que se bifurcan* (*The Garden of Paths which Diverge*, 1941), 'La loteria en Babilonia' ('The Babylonian Lottery')]

3. *El visible universo era una ilusión o (más precisamente) un sofisma. Los espejos y la paternidad son abominables . . . porque lo multiplican y lo divulgan.*
The visible universe was an illusion or (more exactly) a sophism. Mirrors and fatherhood are abominable because they multiply and popularise it.
[*El jardín de senderos que se bifurcan* (*The Garden of Paths which Diverge*, 1941), 'Tlön, Uqbar, Orbis Tertius']

4. [On Henley's translation of Beckford's Vathek]
El original es infiel a la traducción.
The original is not faithful to the translation.
[*Sobre el 'Vathek' de William Beckford* (1943)]

5. [On the Falklands War of 1982]
The Falklands thing was a fight between two bald men over a comb.
[*Time*, 1983]

Borgia, Cesare (1476–1507)
Italian cardinal, politician and military leader

1. *Aut Caesar aut nihil.*
Either Caesar or nothing.
[Motto]

Borovoy, A. Alan
Canadian writer and civil liberties advocate

1. It is usually better to permit a piece of trash than to suppress a work of art.
[*When Freedoms Collide: A Case for Our Civil Liberties* (1988)]

Borrow, George (1803–1881)
English author, travel writer and linguist

1. The author of 'Amelia', the most singular genius which their island ever produced, whose works it has long been the fashion to abuse in public and to read in secret.
[*The Bible in Spain* (1843), 1]

2. My favourite, I might say, my only study, is man.
[*The Bible in Spain* (1843), 5]

3. There are no countries in the world less known by the British than these selfsame British Islands.
[*Lavengro* (1851), Preface]

4. Translation is at best an echo.
[*Lavengro* (1851)]

5. 'Life is sweet, brother.' 'Do you think so?' 'Think so! – There's night and day, brother, both sweet things; sun, moon and stars, brother, all sweet things; there's likewise a wind on the heath. Life is very sweet, brother; who would wish to die?'
[*Lavengro* (1851), 25]

6. There's the wind on the heath, brother; if I could only feel that, I would gladly live for ever.
[*Lavengro* (1851), 25]

7. A losing trade, I assure you, sir: literature is a drug.
[*Lavengro* (1851), 30]

8. Good ale, the true and proper drink of Englishmen. He is not deserving of the name of Englishman who speaketh against ale, that is good ale.
[*Lavengro* (1851), 48]

9. Youth will be served, every dog has his day, and mine has been a fine one.
[*Lavengro* (1851), 92]

10. Fear God, and take your own part.
[*The Romany Rye* (1857), 16]

Bosman, Herman Charles (1905–1951)
South African journalist and short-story writer

1. Kafirs? (said Oom Schalk Lourens), Yes, I know them. And they're all the same. I fear the Almighty, and I respect His works, but I could never understand why He made the kafir and the rinderpest.
[*Mafeking Road* (1947), 'Makapan's Caves']

Bosquet, Pierre François Joseph (1810–1861)
French general

1. [Remark on witnessing the Charge of the Light Brigade, 1854]
C'est magnifique mais ce n'est pas la guerre.
It is magnificent, but it is not war.
[Attr.]

Bossidy, John Collins (1860–1928)
American oculist

1. And this is good old Boston,
The home of the bean and the cod,
Where the Lowells talk only to Cabots,
And the Cabots talk only to God.
[Toast at Harvard dinner, 1910]

Bossuet, Jacques-Bénigne (1627–1704)
French orator, bishop and historian of philosophy

1. *L'Angleterre, ah, la perfide Angleterre, que le rempart de ses mers rendoit inaccessible aux Romains, la foi du Sauveur y est abordée.*
England, ah, perfidious England, which the bulwarks of the sea rendered inaccessible to the Romans, the faith of the Saviour made landfall even there.
[*Oeuvres de Bossuet* (1816), Sermon on the Feast of the Circumcision]

Boswell, James (1740–1795)
Scottish biographer, diarist, poet and lawyer

1. *Johnson*: Well, we had a good talk.
Boswell: Yes, Sir; you tossed and gored several persons.
[*The Life of Samuel Johnson* (1791), II]

2. A man, indeed, is not genteel when he gets drunk; but most vices may be committed very genteelly: a man may debauch his friend's wife genteelly: he may cheat at cards genteelly.
[*The Life of Samuel Johnson* (1791), II]

Botham, Ian (1955–)
English cricketer; Captain of the England team

1. [On Pakistan]
The sort of place everyone should send his mother-in-law for a month, all expenses paid.
[BBC Radio 2 interview, March 1984]

Bottomley, Gordon (1874–1948)
English poet and verse dramatist

1. When you destroy a blade of grass
You poison England at her roots:
Remember no man's foot can pass
Where evermore no green life shoots.
[*Chambers of Imagery* (1912), 'To Ironfounders and Others']

Bottomley, Horatio William (1860–1933)
English journalist, financier, politician and bankrupt

1. [When spotted sewing mailbags during his imprisonment for misappropriation of funds]
Visitor: Ah, Bottomley, sewing?
Bottomley: No, reaping.
[Attr.]

Boucicault, Dion (1822–1890)
Irish dramatist, actor and theatrical manager

1. Men talk of killing time, while time quietly kills them.
[*London Assurance* (1841), II]

Boulay de la Meurthe, Antoine (1761–1840)
French statesman, revolutionary and opponent of Jacobinism

1. [On the execution of the Duc d'Enghien, 1804]
C'est pire qu'un crime, c'est une faute.
It is worse than a crime; it is a mistake.
[Attr. Cf. Acheson: 3]

Boulton, Sir H.E. (1859–1935)
Scottish songwriter and collector

1. Speed, bonny boat, like a bird on the wing;
'Onward', the sailors cry;
Carry the lad that's born to be king
Over the sea to Skye.
['Skye Boat Song' (1908)]

Boulton, Matthew (1728–1809)
British engineer

1. [Of his steam engine]
I am selling what the whole world wants: power.
[Letter]

Bourdillon, F.W. (1852–1921)
English poet and translator

1. The night has a thousand eyes,
And the day but one;
Yet the light of the bright world dies,
With the dying sun.

The mind has a thousand eyes,
And the heart but one;
Yet the light of a whole life dies,
When love is done.
[*Among the Flowers* (1878), 'Light']

Boutros-Ghali, Boutros (1922–)
UN Secretary General from 1992; Egyptian politician and minister

1. The time of absolute and exclusive national sovereignty has passed.
[*Scotland on Sunday*, 1992]

Bowen, E.E. (1836–1901)
English schoolteacher, songwriter and sportsman

1. Follow up! Follow up! Follow up! Follow up! Follow up!
Till the field ring again and again,
With the tramp of the twenty-two men,
Follow up!
['Forty Years On', Harrow School song, 1886]

Bowen, Elizabeth (1899–1973)
Irish novelist and short-story writer

1. There is no end to the violations committed by children on children, quietly talking alone.
[*The House in Paris* (1935), I, 2]

2. Nobody speaks the truth when there's something they must have.
[*The House in Paris* (1935), I, 5]

3. Fate is not an eagle, it creeps like a rat.
[*The House in Paris* (1935), II, 2]

4. Experience isn't interesting till it begins to repeat itself – in fact, till it does that, it hardly is experience.
[*The Death of the Heart* (1938), I, 1]

5. One can live in the shadow of an idea without grasping it.
[*The Heat of the Day* (1949), 10]

6. Art is the only thing that can go on mattering once it has stopped hurting.
[*The Heat of the Day* (1949), 16]

7. No, it is not only our fate but our business to lose innocence, and once we have lost that, it is futile to attempt a picnic in Eden.
[In R. Lehmann and others (eds.), *Orion III* (1946), 'Out of a Book']

Bowen, Lord (1835–1894)
English judge and translator of Virgil

1. The rain it raineth on the just
And also on the unjust fella:
But chiefly on the just, because
The unjust steals the just's umbrella.
[In Walter Sichel, *Sands of Time* (1923)]

2. On a metaphysician: A blind man in a dark room – looking for a black hat – which isn't there.
[Attr.]

Bowen, Stella (Esther Gwendolyn) (1893–1947)

1. Any artist knows that after a good bout of work one is both too tired and too excited to be of any use to anyone ... What one wants ... is for other people to occupy themselves with one's own moods and requirements; to lie on a sofa and listen to music, and to have things brought to one on a tray!
[*Drawn from Life* (1941)]

Bowra, Sir Maurice (1898–1971)
English classical scholar and Warden of Wadham College, Oxford

1. I'm a man
More dined against than dining.
[In J. Betjeman, *Summoned by Bells* (1960)]

2. Any amusing deaths lately?
[Attr.]

Boyd, Mark Alexander (1563–1601)
Scottish Latin poet, legal scholar and soldier

1. Twa gods guides me; the ane of tham is blin',
Yea and a bairn brocht up in vanitie;
The next a wife ingenrit of the sea,
And lichter nor a dauphin with her fin.
['Sonnet']

Boyd, Martin a'Beckett (1893–1972)
Australian novelist

1. The only effect the atomic age has had on man has been to give him an underlying sense of nervous apprehension, which must also have been felt during the Black Death, and by the Christians under Diocletian.
[*Day of My Delight* (1965)]

Boyd, Robin Gerard Penleigh (1919–1971)
Australian architect

1. The Australian town-dweller spent a century in the acquisition of his toy: an emasculated garden, a five-roomed cottage of his very own, different from its neighbours by a minor contortion of window or porch – its difference significant to no one but himself.
[*Australia's Home* (1952)]
2. [On suburban homes of the 1880s]
The galvanized-iron roofs on their front verandahs dipped in a sudden curve like the brim of a sundowner's hat and were draped at the edge with cast-iron, like corks on the brim to frighten away the flies.
[*Australia's Home* (1952)]
3. The ugliness I mean is skin deep. If the visitor to Australia fails to notice it immediately, fails to respond to the surfeit of colour, the love of advertisements, the dreadful language, the ladylike euphemisms outside public lavatory doors, the technical competence, but the almost uncanny misjudgement in floral arrangements, or if he thinks that things of this sort are too trivial to dwell on, then he is unlikely to enjoy modern Australia.
[*The Australian Ugliness* (1960)]

Boyd, William (1952–)
Scottish author and scriptwriter

1. She felt weary and careworn, in the way one often does before the big job of work is tackled; that sense of premature or projected exhaustion that is the breeding-ground of all procrastination.
[*Brazzaville Beach* (1990)]
2. What now? What next? All these questions. All these doubts. So few certainties. But then I have taken new comfort and refuge in the doctrine that advises one not to seek tranquillity in certainty, but in permanently suspended judgement.
[*Brazzaville Beach* (1990)]

'Boy George' (George Alan O'Dowd) (1961–)
English pop singer and songwriter

1. I'd rather have a cup of tea than go to bed with someone – any day.
[Remark, variously expressed, 1983]

Brabazon of Tara, Derek Charles Moore-Brabazon, Baron (1910–1974)
English stockbroker and Conservative politician

1. I take the view, and always have done, that if you cannot say what you have to say in twenty minutes, you should go away and write a book about it.
[Attr.]

Bracken, Brendan, First Viscount (1901–1958)
Irish-born British journalist, publisher and Conservative politician

1. It's a good deed to forget a poor joke.
[*The Observer*, 'Sayings of the Week', 1943]

Bradbury, Malcolm (1932–)
English satirical novelist, critic and academic

1. Sympathy – for all these people, for being foreigners – lay over the gathering like a woolly blanket; and no one was enjoying it at all.
[*Eating People is Wrong* (1954), 2]
2. I like the English. They have the most rigid code of immorality in the world.
[*Eating People is Wrong* (1954), 5]
3. Reading someone else's newspaper is like sleeping with someone else's wife. Nothing seems to be precisely in the right place, and when you find what you are looking for, it is not clear then how to respond to it.
[*Stepping Westward* (1965), I, 1]
4. The English are polite by telling lies. The Americans are polite by telling the truth.
[*Stepping Westward* (1965), II, 5]
5. 'We stay together, but we distrust one another.'
'Ah, yes ... but isn't that a definition of marriage?'
[*The History Man* (1975), 3]
6. I've noticed your hostility towards him ... I ought to have guessed you were friends.
[*The History Man* (1975), 7]
7. If God had meant us to have group sex, I guess he'd have given us all more organs.
[*Who Do You Think You Are? Stories and Parodies* (1976), 'A Very Hospitable Person']

Bradford, John (c. 1510–1555)
English Protestant martyr; author of sermons and other religious works

1. [Remark on criminals going to the gallows]
But for the grace of God there goes John Bradford.
[Attr.]

Bradley, F.H. (1846–1924)
English idealist philosopher

1. Metaphysics is the finding of bad reasons for what we believe upon instinct; but to find these reasons is no less an instinct.
[*Appearance and Reality* (1893), Preface]
2. It is good to know what a man is, and also what the world takes him for. But you do not understand him until you have learnt how he understands himself.
[*Aphorisms* (1930)]
3. The propriety of some persons seems to consist in having improper thoughts about their neighbours.
[*Aphorisms* (1930)]
4. The secret of happiness is to admire without desiring. And that is not happiness.
[*Aphorisms* (1930)]
5. His mind is open; yes, it is so open that nothing is retained; ideas simply pass through him.
[Attr.]

Bradley, Omar Nelson (1893–1981)
American general

1. [On General MacArthur's proposal to carry the Korean war into China]
The wrong war, at the wrong place, at the wrong time, and with the wrong enemy.
[Senate inquiry, May 1951]

2. The way to win an atomic war is to make certain it never starts.
[*The Observer*, 'Sayings of the Week', 1952]

Bradshaw, Henry (d. 1513)
Benedictine monk and theologian

1. Proude as a pecocke.
[*The Life of Saint Werburge* (1521)]

Bradshaw, John (1602–1659)
English judge and republican; President at the trial of Charles I

1. Rebellion to tyrants is obedience to God.
[In Randall, *Life of Jefferson* (1865)]

Bradstreet, Anne (c. 1612–1672)
English-born writer; the 'first American poet'

1. I am obnoxious to each carping tongue,
Who sayes my hand a needle better fits,
A Poet's Pen, all scorne, I should thus wrong;
For such despight they cast on female wits:
If what I doe prove well, it won't advance,
They'll say it's stolne, or else, it was by chance...

2. Let Greeks be Greeks, and Women what they are,
Men have precedency, and still excell...

3. This meane and unrefined stuffe of mine,
Will make your glistering gold but more to shine.
['The Prologue' (1650)]

Brady, Nicholas (1659–1726)
Irish Anglican clergyman and poet

1. As pants the hart for cooling streams
When heated in the chase.
[*A New Version of the Psalms* (1696)]

2. Through all the changing scenes of life.
[*A New Version of the Psalms* (1696)]

Bragg, William Henry (1862–1942)
English scientist and academic

1. Going to Australia was like sunshine and fresh invigorating air.
[In G.M. Caroe, *William Henry Bragg* (1978)]

Braham, John (c. 1774–1856)
English singer and actor; leading tenor of his age

1. England, home and beauty.
['The Americans', song, 1811]

Brahms, Johannes (1833–1897)
German composer, pianist and conductor

1. [Said on leaving a gathering of friends]
If there is anyone here whom I have not insulted, I beg his pardon.
[Attr.]

Braisted, Harry (19th century)

1. If you want to win her hand,
Let the maiden understand
That's she's not the only pebble on the beach.
['You're Not the Only Pebble on the Beach']

Bramah, Ernest (Ernest Bramah Smith) (1868–1942)
English writer

1. The whole narrative is permeated with the odour of joss-sticks and honourable high-mindedness.
[*The Wallet of Kai Lung* (1900), 'Kin Yen']

2. It has been said ... that there are few situations in life that cannot be honourably settled, and without loss of time, either by suicide, a bag of gold, or by thrusting a despised antagonist over the edge of a precipice upon a dark night.
[*Kai Lung's Golden Hours* (1922), 'The Incredible Obtuseness...']

Brancusi, Constantin (1876–1957)
Romanian pioneering abstract sculptor

1. [Refusing Rodin's invitation to work in his studio]
Nothing grows well in the shade of a big tree.
[Attr.]

Brando, Marlon (1924–)
American 'method' actor of stage and screen

1. An actor's a guy who, if you ain't talking about him, ain't listening.
[*The Observer*, 'Sayings of the Week', 1956]

2. We'll make him an offer he can't refuse.
[*The Godfather*, film, 1972; script by Francis Ford Coppola and Mario Puzo]

Braque, Georges (1882–1963)
French Cubist painter

1. *L'Art est fait pour troubler, la Science rassure.*
Art is meant to disturb, science reassures.
[*Le jour et la nuit: Cahiers 1917–-52* (*Day and Night, Notebooks*, 1952)]

2. *La vérité existe; on n'invente que le mensonge.*
Truth exists; only lies are invented.
[*Le jour et la nuit: Cahiers 1917–52* (*Day and Night*, *Notebooks*, 1952)]

Brasch, Charles Orwell (1909–1973)
New Zealand poet and editor

1. [On walking on a week-day in Dunedin, 1938, when he was unemployed]
It is not only an offence against society to be seen in the streets flaunting the fact that one does not work like everyone else; it challenges the settled order of things, a threat that no right thinking New Zealander could tolerate. It makes one an object of suspicion, and more, an enemy.
[*Indirections: A Memoir 1909–1947* (1980)]

Brathwaite, Richard (c. 1588–1673)
English poet, satirist and essayist

1. To Banbury came I, O profane one!
Where I saw a Puritane-one
Hanging of his cat on Monday
For killing of a mouse on Sunday.
[*Barnabee's Journal* (1638)]

Braun, Wernher von (1912–1977)
German-born American rocket pioneer

1. [Referring to the first V2 rocket to hit London during World War II]
It was very successful, but it fell on the wrong planet.
[Attr.]

Braxfield, Lord (1722–1799)
Scottish 'hanging' judge; notoriously harsh to political prisoners

1. [To the butler who gave up his place because Lady Braxfield was always scolding him]
Lord! Ye've little to complain o': ye may be thankfu' ye're no married to her.
[In Cockburn, *Memorials* (1856)]

2. [Gerald, a political prisoner, remarked that Christ had been a reformer]
Muckle he made o' that; he was hanget.
[In Cockburn, *Memorials* (1856)]

3. [To an eloquent culprit at the bar]
Ye're a vera clever chiel, man, but ye wad be nane the waur o' a hanging.
[In Lockhart, *Life of Scott*]

4. Let them bring me prisoners, and I'll find them law.
[Attr. by Cockburn]

Bray, John Jefferson (1912–)
Australian lawyer and poet; Chief Justice, South Australia

1. A hundred canvasses and seven sons
He left, and never got a likeness once.
['Epitaph on a Portrait Painter']

2. When your grape was green you denied me.
When your grape was ripe you despised me.
Can I have a nibble at the old sultana?
['After Long Absence']

Brecht, Bertolt (1898–1956)
German experimental dramatist and poet

1. *Die Gemeinheit der Welt ist gross, und man muss sich die Beine ablaufen, damit sie einem nicht gestohlen werden.*
The wickedness of the world is so great that you have to run your legs off so you don't get them stolen from you.
[*Die Dreigroschenoper* (*The Threepenny Opera*, 1928), I.iii]

2. *Das Recht des Menschen ist's auf dieser Erden*
Da er doch nur kurz lebt, glücklich zu sein.
Man's right on this earth,
Since his days are few, is to be happy.
[*Die Dreigroschenoper* (*The Threepenny Opera*, 1928), I.iii]

3. *Erst kommt das Fressen, dann kommt die Moral.*
Feeding your face comes first, then morality.
[*Die Dreigroschenoper* (*The Threepenny Opera*, 1928), II.vi]

4. *Das Gesetz ist einzig and allein gemacht zur Ausbeutung derer, die es nicht verstehen oder die es aus nackter Not nicht befolgen können.*
The law is made solely to exploit those who don't understand it or who can't obey it because they're in desperate need.
[*Die Dreigroschenoper* (*The Threepenny Opera*, 1928), III.vii]

5. *Was ist ein Einbruch in eine Bank gegen die Gründung einer Bank?*
What is robbing a bank compared with founding a bank?
[*Die Dreigroschenoper* (*The Threepenny Opera*, 1928), III.ix]

6. Andrea*: Unglücklich das Land, das keine Helden hat!...*
Galileo*: Nein. Unglücklich das Land, das Helden nötig hat.*
Andrea: Unhappy the country that has no heroes!
Galileo: No. Unhappy the country that needs heroes.
[*Leben des Galilei* (*Life of Galileo*, 1938–1939), XII]

7. *Hier ist zu lang kein Krieg gewesen.*
It's too long since there's been a war here.
[*Mutter Courage und ihre Kinder* (*Mother Courage and her Children*, written 1939, first performed 1941), I]

8. *Da konnt [unser Herr] auch verlangen, dass man seinen Nächsten liebt, denn man war satt. Heutzutage ist das anders.*
In those days [our Lord] could demand that men love their neighbour, because they'd had enough to eat. Nowadays it's different.
[*Mutter Courage und ihre Kinder* (*Mother Courage and her Children*, written 1939, first performed 1941), II]

9. *Wenn es wo so grosse Tugenden gibt, das beweist, dass da etwas faul ist.*
Whenever there are such great virtues, it's proof that something's fishy.
[*Mutter Courage und ihre Kinder* (*Mother Courage and her Children*, written 1939, first performed 1941), II]

10. *Ich [trau] ihm nicht, wir sind befreundet.*
I'm wary of him. We're friends.
[*Mutter Courage und ihre Kinder* (*Mother Courage and her Children*, written 1939, first performed 1941), III]

11. *Der Sieg und Niederlagen der Grosskopfigen oben und der von unten fallen nämlich nicht immer zusammen.*
Victories and defeats for the bigshots at the top aren't always victories and defeats for those at the bottom.
[*Mutter Courage und ihre Kinder* (*Mother Courage and her Children*, written 1939, first performed 1941), III]

12. *Die schönsten Plän sind schon zuschanden geworden durch die Kleinlichkeit von denen, wo sie ausführen sollten, denn die Kaiser selber können ja nix machen.*
The best plans have always been wrecked by the narrow-mindedness of those who should carry them out, because after all the emperors can't do it all themselves.
[*Mutter Courage und ihre Kinder* (*Mother Courage and her Children*, written 1939, first performed 1941), VI]

13. *Einen vollkommenen Krieg, wo man sagen könnt: an dem ist nix mehr auszusetzen, wirds vielleicht nie geben.*
There'll perhaps never be a perfect war where you could say that there was nothing wrong with it.
[*Mutter Courage und ihre Kinder* (*Mother Courage and her Children*, written 1939, first performed 1941), VI]

14. *Was wird aus dem Loch, wenn der Käs gefressen ist?*
What happens to the hole when the cheese has been eaten?
[*Mutter Courage und ihre Kinder* (*Mother Courage and her Children*, written 1939, first performed 1941), VI]

15. *Der Krieg findet immer einen Ausweg.*
War always finds a solution.
[*Mutter Courage und ihre Kinder* (*Mother Courage and her Children*, written 1939, first performed 1941), VI]

16. *Sagen sie mir nicht, dass Friede ausgebrochen ist.*
Don't tell me that peace has broken out.
[*Mutter Courage und ihre Kinder* (*Mother Courage and her Children*, written 1939, first performed 1941), VIII]

17. *Ich will mit dem gehen, den ich liebe.*
Ich will nicht ausrechnen, was es kostet.
Ich will nicht nachdenken, ob es gut ist.
Ich will nicht wissen, ob er mich liebt.
Ich will mit ihm gehen, den ich liebe.
I want to go with the one I love. I don't want to count the cost. I don't want to think about whether it's good. I don't want to know if he loves me. I want to go with the man I love.
[*Der gute Mensch von Sezuan* (*The Good Person of Szechwan*, completed 1941, first performed 1943), V]

18. *Die das Glück der Mächtigen nicht teilten*
Teilen oft ihr Unglück.
Those who didn't share in the good fortune of the mighty often share in their misfortune.
[*Der kaukasische Kreidekreis* (*The Caucasian Chalk-Circle*, 1949), I]

Brenan, Gerald (1894–1987)
English travel writer and novelist

1. Those who have some means think that the most important thing in the world is love. The poor know that it is money.
[*Thoughts in a Dry Season* (1978), 'Love']

2. Religions are kept alive by heresies, which are really sudden explosions of faith. Dead religions do not produce them.
[*Thoughts in a Dry Season* (1978), 'Religion']

3. We should live as if we were going to live forever, yet at the back of our minds remember that our time is short.
[*Thoughts in a Dry Season* (1978), 'Life']

4. Intellectuals are people who believe that ideas are of more importance than values. That is to say, their own ideas and other people's values.
[*Thoughts in a Dry Season* (1978), 'Life']

5. Old age takes away from us what we have inherited and gives us what we have earned.
[*Thoughts in a Dry Season* (1978), 'Life']

6. When we attend the funerals of our friends we grieve for them, but when we go to those of other people it is chiefly our own deaths that we mourn for.
[*Thoughts in a Dry Season* (1978), 'Death']

7. The cliché is dead poetry. English, being the language of an imaginative race, abounds in clichés, so that English literature is always in danger of being poisoned by its own secretions.
[*Thoughts in a Dry Season* (1978), 'Literature']

8. [Of Henry Miller]
Miller is not really a writer but a non-stop talker to whom someone has given a typewriter.
[*Thoughts in a Dry Season* (1978), 'Literature']

9. Poets and painters are outside the class system, or rather they constitute a special class of their own, like the circus people and the gipsies.
[*Thoughts in a Dry Season* (1978), 'Writing']

Brennan, Christopher (1870–1932)
Australian symbolist poet and sometime academic

1. Fire in the heavens, and fire along the hills,
and fire made solid in the flinty stone,
thick-mass'd or scatter'd pebble, fire that fills
the breathless hour that lives in fire alone.
[*Poems* (1914)]

2. Where star-cold and the dread of space
in icy silence bind the main
I feel but vastness on my face
I sit, a mere incurious brain,
under some outcast satellite...
[*Poems* (1914)]

3. My heart was wandering in the sands,
a restless thing, a scorn apart;
Love set his fire in my hands,
I clasped the flame into my heart.
[*Poems* (1914)]

4. I am shut out of mine own heart
because my love is far from me.
['I Am Shut Out of Mine Own Heart' (1914)]

Breton, Nicholas (c. 1545–c. 1626)
English writer of satirical, pastoral, religious and romantic poetry and prose

1. I wish my deadly foe, no worse
Than want of friends, and empty purse.
['A Farewell to Town' (1577)]

2. In the merry month of May,
In a morn by break of day,
Forth I walked by the wood side,
Whenas May was in his pride:
There I spied all alone,
Phillida and Coridon.
['Phillida and Coridon' (1591)]

3. Shall we go dance the hay, the hay
Never ever pipe could play
Better Shepherd's roundelay.
['A report song']

4. A Mad World, My Masters.
[Title of dialogue, 1603]

5. He is as deaf as a door.
['Miseries of Mavillia' (1606)]

6. We rise with the lark and go to bed with the lamb.
['The Court and Country' (1618)]

Brezhnev, Leonid (1906–1982)
Soviet statesman; President of the Soviet Union, 1977–1982

1. [Diary entry from 1977]
Talked to Podgorny about football and hockey and a little bit about the constitution.
[*Newsweek*, 1993]

Bridges, Matthew (1800–1894)
English religious writer
and Thring, Godfrey (1823–1903)

1. Crown him with many crowns,
The Lamb upon his throne:
Hark how the heavenly anthem drowns
All music but its own.
[Hymn, 1851]

Bridges, Robert (1844–1930)
English poet laureate (1913); doctor, dramatist and essayist

1. For beauty being the best of all we know
Sums up the unsearchable and secret aims
Of nature.
['The Growth of Love' (1876)]

2. Awake, my heart, to be loved, awake, awake!
['Awake, My Heart, To be Loved' (1890)]

3. I heard a linnet courting
His lady in the spring.
['I heard a linnet' (1890)]

4. I love all beauteous things,
I seek and adore them;
God hath no better praise,
And man in his hasty days
Is honoured for them.

I too will something make
And joy in the making;
Altho' to-morrow it seem
Like the empty words of a dream
Remembered on waking.
['I Love All Beauteous Things' (1890)]

5. I will not let thee go.
Ends all our month-long love in this?
Can it be summed up so,
Quit in a single kiss?
I will not let thee go.
['I Will Not Let Thee Go' (1890)]

6. When men were all asleep the snow came flying,
In large white flakes falling on the city brown,
Stealthily and perpetually settling and loosely lying,
Hushing the latest traffic of the drowsy town...

7. All night it fell, and when full inches seven
It lay in depth of its uncompacted lightness,
The clouds blew off from a high and frosty heaven;
And all woke either for the unaccustomed brightness
Of the winter dawning, the strange unheavenly glare...

8. Or peering up from under the white-mossed wonder,
'O look at the trees!' they cried, 'O look at the trees!'
['London Snow' (1890)]

9. Whither, O splendid ship, thy white sails crowding,
Leaning across the bosom of the urgent West,
That fearest not sea rising, nor sky clouding,
Whither away, fair rover, and what thy quest?
['A Passer-by' (1890)]

10. So sweet love seemed that April morn,
When first we kissed beside the thorn,
So strangely sweet, it was not strange
We thought that love could never change.
But I can tell – let truth be told–
That love will change in growing old;
Though day by day is nought to see,
So delicate his motions be.
['So Sweet Love Seemed' (1890)]

11. When first we met we did not guess
That Love would prove so hard a master;
Of more than common friendliness
When first we met we did not guess
Who could foretell this sore distress,
This irretrievable disaster
When first we met? We did not guess
That Love would prove so hard a master...

12. All women born are so perverse
No man need boast their love possessing.
If nought seem better, nothing's worse:
All women born are so perverse.
From Adam's wife, that proved a curse
Though God had made her for a blessing,
All women born are so perverse
No man need boast their love possessing.
['Triolet' (1890)]

13. Rejoice ye dead, where'er your spirits dwell,
Rejoice that yet on earth your fame is bright,
And that your names, remembered day and night,
Live on the lips of those who love you well.
['Ode to Music' (1896)]

14. My delight and thy delight
Walking, like two angels white,
In the gardens of the night.
['My Delight and Thy Delight' (1925)]

15. The day begins to droop,–
Its course is done:
But nothing tells the place
Of the setting sun.
['Winter Nightfall' (1925)]

16. Man masters nature not by force but by understanding.
[Attr.]

Bridie, James (Osborne Henry Mavor) (1888–1951)
Major Scottish dramatist, autobiographer, essayist and physician

1. The Heart of Man, we are told, is deceitful and desperately wicked. However that may be, it consists of four chambers, the right ventricle, the left ventricle, the left auricle, the right auricle...
[*The Anatomist* (1931), III]

2. London! Pompous Ignorance sits enthroned there and welcomes Pretentious Mediocrity with flattery and gifts. Oh, dull and witless city! Very hell for the restless, inquiring, sensitive soul. Paradise for the snob, the parasite and the prig; the pimp, the placeman and the cheapjack.
[*The Anatomist* (1931), III]

3. Boredom is a sign of satisfied ignorance, blunted apprehension, crass sympathies, dull understanding, feeble powers of attention and irreclaimable weakness of character.
[*Mr Bolfry* (1943)]

4. Eve and the apple was the first great step in experimental science.
[*Mr Bolfry* (1943)]

Bridson, D.G. (d. 1980)

1. [On disc jockeys]
The wriggling ponces of the spoken word.
[Attr.]

Brien, Alan (1925–)
British novelist and journalist

1. I have done almost every human activity inside a taxi which does not require main drainage.
[*Punch*, 1972]

2. Violence is the repartee of the illiterate.
[*Punch*, 1973]

Bright, John (1811–1889)
English Radical statesman, Liberal politician and social reformer

1. [Referring to the Crimean War]
The angel of death has been abroad throughout the land; you may almost hear the beating of his wings.
[Speech, 1855]

2. England is the mother of Parliaments.
[Speech, 1865]

3. The right hon Gentleman ... has retired into what may be called his political Cave of Adullam – and he has called about him every one that was in distress and every one that was discontented.
[Speech, House of Commons, 1866]

4. This party of two is like the Scotch terrier that was so covered with hair that you could not tell which was the head and which was the tail.
[Speech, House of Commons, 1866]

5. Force is not a remedy.
[Speech, 1880]

6. [Of Disraeli]
He is a self-made man, and worships his creator.
[Remark, c. 1868]

7. [Comment on the American Civil War]
My opinion is that the Northern States will manage somehow to muddle through.
[Attr.]

Brigid of Kildare (453–523)
Second patron saint of Ireland

1. I should like a great lake of ale
For the King of Kings.
[*The Feast of St Brigid of Kildare*]

Brillat-Savarin, Anthelme (1755–1826)
French jurist and gastronome

1. *La découverte d'un mets nouveau fait plus pour le bonheur du genre humain que la découverte d'une étoile.*
The discovery of a new dish does more for the happiness of mankind than the discovery of a star.
[*Physiologie du Goût* (1825)]

2. *Dis-moi ce que tu manges, je te dirai ce que tu es.*
Tell me what you eat and I will tell you what you are.
[*Physiologie du Goût* (1825)]

Brittain, Vera (1893–1970)
English autobiographer, novelist, journalist and pacifist

1. The idea that it is necessary to go to a university in order to become a successful writer, or even a man or woman of letters (which is by no means the same thing), is one of those phantasies that surround authorship.
[*On Being an Author* (1948), 2]

2. It is probably true to say that the largest scope for change still lies in men's attitude to women, and in women's attitude to themselves.
[*Lady into Woman* (1953), 15]

3. Politics are usually the executive expression of human immaturity.
[*The Rebel Passion* (1964), I]

Broderick, John (1927–)

1. The city dweller who passes through a country town, and imagines it sleepy and apathetic is very far from the truth: it is watchful as the jungle.
[*The Pilgrimage*]

Brome, Alexander (1620–1666)
English poet and dramatist; Royalist and attorney

1. I have been in love, and in debt, and in drink,
This many and many a year.
['The Mad Lover' (1664)]

Brome, Richard (c. 1590–1652)
English comic dramatist, contemporary of Ben Jonson

1. You rose o' the wrong side to-day.
[*The Court Beggar* (1632)]

2. I am a gentleman, though spoiled i' the breeding. The Buzzards are all gentlemen. We came in with the Conqueror.
[*English Moor* (1637)]

3. *Doctor*: But there the maids doe woe
the Batchelors, and tis most probable,
The wives lie uppermost.
Diana: That is a trim,
upside-downe Antipodian tricke indeed.
[*The Antipodes* (1638), I.vi]

Bronowski, Jacob (1908–1974)
Polish-born British mathematician, writer and television presenter on the history of scientific achievement

1. The wish to hurt, the momentary intoxication with pain, is the loophole through which the pervert climbs into the minds of ordinary men.
[*The Face of Violence* (1954), 5]

2. The world is made of people who never quite get into the first team and who just miss the prizes at the flower show.
[*The Face of Violence* (1954), 6]

3. Every animal leaves traces of what it was; man alone leaves traces of what he created.
[*The Ascent of Man* (1973), 1]

4. That is the essence of science: ask an impertinent question, and you are on the way to the pertinent answer.
[*The Ascent of Man* (1973), 4]

5. Physics becomes in those years the greatest collective work of science – no, more than that, the great collective work of art of the twentieth century.
[*The Ascent of Man* (1973), 10]

6. Science has nothing to be ashamed of, even in the ruins of Nagasaki.
[*Science and Human Values*]

Brontë, Anne (1820–1849)
English novelist and poet, sister of Charlotte and Emily

1. The human heart is like Indian rubber: a little swells it, but a great deal will not burst it.
[*Agnes Grey* (1847), 13]

2. There is always a 'but' in this imperfect world.
[*The Tenant of Wildfell Hall* (1848), 22]

3. All our talents increase in the using, and every faculty, both good and bad, strengthens by exercise.
[*The Tenant of Wildfell Hall* (1848), 23]

4. Because the road is rough and long,
Shall we despise the skylark's song?
['Views of Life']

Brontë, Charlotte (1816–1855)
English novelist; sister of Anne and Emily

1. Had I been in anything inferior to him, he would not have hated me so thoroughly, but I knew all that he knew, and, what was worse, he suspected that I kept the padlock of silence on mental wealth in which he was no sharer.
[*The Professor* (written prior to 1847; published 1857), 4]

2. Novelists should never allow themselves to weary of the study of real life.
[*The Professor* (written prior to 1847; published 1857), 19]

3. Conventionality is not morality. Self-righteousness is not religion. To attack the first is not to assail the last. To pluck the mask from the face of the Pharisee, is not to lift an impious hand to the Crown of Thorns.
[*Jane Eyre* (1847), Preface]

4. [Of Mr Rochester]
Reader, I married him.
[*Jane Eyre* (1847), 38]

5. Of late years an abundant shower of curates has fallen upon the North of England.
[*Shirley* (1849), 1]

6. If there is one notion I hate more than another, it is that of marriage – I mean marriage in the vulgar, weak sense, as a mere matter of sentiment.
[*Shirley* (1849), 2]

7. Alfred and I intended to be married in this way almost from the first; we never meant to be spliced in the humdrum way of other people.
[*Villette* (1853), 42]

8. One day, in the autumn of 1845, I accidentally lighted on a MS volume of verse in my sister Emily's handwriting . . . I looked it over, and something more than surprise seized me, – a deep conviction that these were not common effusions,

nor at all like the poetry women generally write. I thought them condensed and terse, vigorous and genuine. To my ear, they had also a peculiar music – wild, melancholy, and elevating.
[Biographical notice]

9. Life, believe, is not a dream,
So dark as sages say;
Oft a little morning rain
Foretells a pleasant day!
['Life' (1846)]

Brontë, Emily (1818–1848)
English poet and novelist; sister of Anne and Charlotte

1. No coward soul is mine,
No trembler in the world's storm-troubled sphere:
I see Heaven's glories shine,
And faith shines equal, arming me from fear...

2. Vain are the thousand creeds
That move men's hearts: unutterably vain;
Worthless as withered weeds,
Or idlest froth amid the boundless main.
['Last Lines' (1846)]

3. Oh, for the time when I shall sleep
Without identity.
['Oh, For the Time When I Shall Sleep' (1846)]

4. Oh dreadful is the check – intense the agony–
When the ear begins to hear and the eye begins to see;
When the pulse begins to throb, the brain to think again;
The soul to feel the flesh and the flesh to feel the chain!
['The Prisoner' (1846)]

5. Once drinking deep of that divinest anguish,
How could I seek the empty world again?...

6. Cold in the earth – and fifteen wild Decembers,
From those brown hills, have melted into spring...

7. Sweet Love of youth, forgive if I forget thee
While the World's tide is bearing me along:
Sterner desires and darker hopes beset me,
Hopes which obscure but cannot do thee wrong!...

8. But when the days of golden dreams had perished,
And even Despair was powerless to destroy,
Then did I learn how existence could be cherished,
Strengthened, and fed without the aid of joy.
['Remembrance' (1846)]

9. He was, and is yet, most likely, the wearisomest, self-righteous pharisee that ever ransacked a Bible to rake the promises to himself and fling the curses on his neighbours.
[*Wuthering Heights* (1847), 5]

10. He is more myself than I am.
[*Wuthering Heights* (1847)]

11. If all else perished, and he remained, I should still continue to be; and if all else remained, and he were annihilated, the universe would turn to a mighty stranger: I should not seem a part of it. My love for Linton is like the foliage in the woods; time will change it, I'm well aware, as winter changes the trees – My love for Heathcliff resembles the eternal rocks beneath: – a source of little visible delight, but necessary.
[*Wuthering Heights* (1847), 9]

12. I lingered round them, under that benign sky: watched the moths fluttering among the heath and harebells; listened to the soft wind breathing through the grass; and wondered how anyone could ever imagine unquiet slumbers for the sleepers in that quiet earth.
[*Wuthering Heights* (1847), last lines]

Brontë, Rev. Patrick (1777–1861)
Irish author and curate of Haworth; father of Anne, Charlotte and Emily

1. [About her agreeing to write the life of Charlotte Brontë]
No quailing, Mrs Gaskell! no drawing back!
[Letter to Ellen Nussey, 1855]

2. Girls, do you know Charlotte has been writing a book, and it is much better than likely?
[In Elizabeth Gaskell, *Life of Charlotte Brontë* (1857)]

Brooke, Rupert (1887–1915)
English poet, known for his war poems and lighter verse

1. Because God put His adamantine fate
Between my sullen heart and its desire,
I swore that I would burst the Iron Gate,
Rise up, and curse Him on His throne of fire.
['Failure' (1905–1908)]

2. Oh! Death will find me long before I tire
Of watching you; and swing me suddenly
Into the shade and loneliness and mire
Of the last land!
['Oh! Death will find me' (1909)]

3. I thought when love for you died, I should die.
It's dead. Alone, mostly strangely, I live on.
['The Life Beyond' (1910)]

4. ... white Helen bears
Child on legitimate child, becomes a scold,
Haggard with virtue. Menelaus bold
Waxed garrulous, and sacked a hundred Troys
'Twixt noon and supper. And her golden voice
Got shrill as he grew deafer. And both were old.

Often he wonders why on earth he went
Troyward, or why poor Paris ever came.
Oft she weeps, gummy-eyed and impotent;
Her dry shanks twitch at Paris' mumbled name.
So Menelaus nagged; and Helen cried;
And Paris slept on by Scamander side.
[*Poems* (1911), 'Menelaus and Helen']

5. The hawthorn hedge puts forth its buds,
And my heart puts forth its pain.
['All Suddenly the Spring Comes Soft' (1912)]

6. Oh! there the chestnuts, summer through,
Beside the river make for you
A tunnel of green gloom, and sleep
Deeply above...

7. Here tulips bloom as they are told;
Unkempt about those hedges blows
An English unofficial rose...

8. Just now the lilac is in bloom
All before my little room...

9. Curates, long dust, will come and go
On lissom, clerical, printless toe;
And oft between the boughs is seen
The sly shade of a Rural Dean...

10. God! I will pack, and take a train,
And get me to England once again!...

11. For Cambridge people rarely smile,
Being urban, squat, and packed with guile...

12. They love the Good; they worship Truth;
They laugh uproariously in youth;
(And when they get to feeling old,
They up and shoot themselves, I'm told.)...

13. Stands the Church clock at ten to three?
And is there honey still for tea?
['The Old Vicarage, Grantchester' (1912)]

14. How that we've done our best and worst, and parted.
['The Busy Heart' (1913)]

15. And I shall find some girl perhaps,
And a better one than you,
With eyes as wise, but kindlier,
And lips as soft, but true
And I dare say she will do.
['The Chilterns' (1913)]

16. Fish say, they have their stream and pond;
But is there anything beyond?...

17. One may not doubt that, somehow, good
Shall come of water and of mud;
And, sure, the reverent eye must see
A purpose in liquidity...

18. Unfading moths, immortal flies,
And the worm that never dies.
And in that Heaven of all their wish,
There shall be no more land, say fish.
['Heaven' (1913)]

19. Blow out, you bugles, over the rich Dead!
There's none of these so lonely and poor of old,
But, dying, has made us rarer gifts than gold.
These laid the world away; poured out the red
Sweet wine of youth, gave up the years to be
Of work and joy, and that unhoped serene,
That men call age; and those who would have been,
Their sons, they gave, their immortality.
['The Dead' (1914)]

20. The cool kindliness of sheets, that soon
Smooth away trouble; and the rough male kiss of blankets...

21. The benison of hot water.
['The Great Lover' (1914)]

22. Now, God be thanked Who has matched us with His hour,
And caught our youth, and wakened us from sleeping...

23. Leave the sick hearts that honour could not move,
And half-men, and their dirty songs and dreary,
And all the little emptiness of love...

24. Naught broken save this body, lost but breath;
Nothing to shake the laughing heart's long peace there
But only agony, and that has ending;
And the worst friend and enemy is but Death.
['Peace' (1914)]

25. If I should die, think only this of me:
That there's some corner of a foreign field
That is for ever England. There shall be
In that rich earth a richer dust concealed;
A dust whom England bore, shaped, made aware,
Gave, once, her flowers to love, her ways to roam,
A body of England's, breathing English air,
Washed by the rivers, blest by suns of home.
And think, this heart, all evil shed away,
A pulse on the eternal mind, no less
Gives somewhere back the thoughts by England given.
Her sights and sounds; dreams happy as her day;
And laughter, learnt of friends; and gentleness,
In hearts at peace, under an English heaven.
['The Soldier' (1914)]

Brookner, Anita (1928–)
English-born novelist, of Polish parentage

1. [On the myth of the tortoise and the hare]
In real life, of course, it is the hare who wins. Every time. Look around you. And in any case it is my contention that Aesop was writing for the tortoise market ... Hares have no time to read. They are too busy winning the game.
[*Hotel du Lac* (1984)]

Brooks, Mel (Melvyn Kaminsky) (1926–)
American comic film actor and director

1. That's it, baby, if you've got it, flaunt it.
[*The Producers*, film, 1968]

2. Tragedy is if I cut my finger. Comedy is if I walk into an open sewer and die.
[*The New Yorker*, 1978]

Brooks, Phillips (1835–1893)
American Protestant bishop, orator and author

1. O little town of Bethlehem,
How still we see thee lie;
Above thy deep and dreamless sleep
The silent stars go by.
['O Little Town of Bethlemen', hymn, 1868]

Brooks, Thomas (1608–1680)
English Puritan divine and religious writer

1. For (*magna est veritas et praevalebit*) great is truth, and shall prevail.
[*The Crown and Glory of Christianity* (1662)]

Brough, Robert Barnabas (1828–1860)
English journalist and writer of burlesques

1. My Lord Tomnoddy is thirty-four;
The Earl can last but a few years more.
My Lord in the Peers will take his place:
Her Majesty's councils his words will grace.
Office he'll hold and patronage sway;
Fortunes and lives he will vote away;
And what are his qualifications? – ONE!
He's the Earl of Fitzdotterel's eldest son.
['My Lord Tomnoddy' (1855)]

Brougham, Lord Henry (1778–1868)
Scottish lawyer, politician, Lord Chancellor, abolitionist and journalist

1. The schoolmaster is abroad, and I trust more to him, armed with his primer, than I do to the soldier in full military array, for upholding and extending the liberties of his country.
[Speech, House of Commons, 1828]

2. Education makes a people easy to lead, but difficult to drive; easy to govern, but impossible to enslave.
[Attr.]

3. The great Unwashed.
[Attr.]

Brown, Ford Madox (1821–1893)
French-born English painter and designer

1. The last of England! O'er the sea, my dear,
Our homes to seek amid Australian fields.
Us, not our million-acred island yields

The space to dwell in. Thrust out, forced to hear
Low ribaldry from sots, and share rough cheer
From rudely nurtured men.
['Sonnet']

Brown, Geoff

1. Dictators needed a talking cinema to twist nations round their fingers: remove the sound from Mussolini and you are left with a puffing bullfrog.
[*The Times*, 1992]

Brown, George (1914–1985)
British statesman and Labour Party leader

1. Most British statesmen have either drunk too much or womanized too much. I never fell into the second category.
[*The Observer*, 1974]

Brown, Helen Gurley (1922–)
American writer and editor

1. [Promotional line for *Cosmopolitan* magazine]
Good girls go to heaven, bad girls go everywhere.
[Attr.]

Brown, John (1715–1766)
English dramatist, essayist and social commentator

1. Altogether upon the high horse.
[Letter to Garrick, 1765]

Brown, John Mason (1900–1969)
American literary critic

1. [On Tallulah Bankhead's performance as Shakespeare's Cleopatra in 1937]
Tallulah Bankhead barged down the Nile last night and sank. As the Serpent of the Nile she proves to be no more dangerous than a garter snake.
[In *Current Biography* (1941)]

Brown, Thomas (1663–1704)
English satirical poet, teacher, translator and pamphleteer

1. A little before you made a leap into the dark.
[*Letters from the Dead to the Living* (1702)]

2. I do not love you, Dr Fell,
But why I cannot tell;
But this I know full well,
I do not love you, Dr Fell.
[*Works* (1719), Trans. of an Epigram of Martial]

Brown, Thomas Edward (1830–1897)
Manx poet, schoolteacher and curate

1. A rich man's joke is always funny.
['The Doctor' (1887)]

2. A garden is a lovesome thing, God wot!
['My Garden' (1893)]

Browne, Cecil (1932–)
American businessman

1. But not so odd
As those who choose
A Jewish God,
But spurn the Jews.
[Reply to William Norman Ewer:
How odd/Of God/To choose/The Jews]

Browne, Coral (1913–1991)
Australian actress; worked mainly in Britain

1. [To a Hollywood writer who had criticized the work of Alan Bennett]
Listen, dear, you couldn't write fuck on a dusty venetian blind.
[Attr., in *The Sunday Times Magazine*, 1984]

Browne, Sir Thomas (1605–1682)
English physician, author and antiquary

1. At my devotion I love to use the civility of my knee, my hat, and hand.
[*Religio Medici* (1643)]

2. I could never divide my self from any man upon the difference of an opinion, or be angry with his judgment for not agreeing with me in that, from which perhaps within a few days I should dissent my self.
[*Religio Medici* (1643)]

3. Many ... have too rashly charged the troops of error, and remain as trophies unto the enemies of truth.
[*Religio Medici* (1643)]

4. A man may be in as just possession of truth as of a city, and yet be forced to surrender.
[*Religio Medici* (1643)]

5. There is another man within me, that's angry with me, rebukes, commands, and dastards me.
[*Religio Medici* (1643)]

6. As for those wingy mysteries in divinity, and airy subtleties in religion, which have unhinged the brains of better heads, they never stretched the pia mater of mine. Methinks there be not impossibilities enough in Religion for an active faith.
[*Religio Medici* (1643)]

7. I love to lose myself in a mystery; to pursue my reason to an O altitudo!
[*Religio Medici* (1643)]

8. Who can speak of eternity without a solecism, or think thereof without an ecstasy? Time we may comprehend, 'tis but five days elder than ourselves.
[*Religio Medici* (1643)]

9. I have often admired the mystical way of Pythagoras, and the secret magic of numbers.
[*Religio Medici* (1643)]

10. We carry within us the wonders we seek without us: There is all Africa and her prodigies in us.
[*Religio Medici* (1643)]

11. All things are artificial, for nature is the art of God.
[*Religio Medici* (1643)]

12. Obstinacy in a bad cause, is but constancy in a good.
[*Religio Medici* (1643)]

13. Persecution is a bad and indirect way to plant religion.
[*Religio Medici* (1643)]

14. There are many (questionless) canonized on earth, that shall never be Saints in Heaven.
[*Religio Medici* (1643)]

15. Not wrung from speculations and subtleties, but from common sense and observation – not pickt from the leaves of any author, but bred amongst the weeds and tares of mine own brain.
[*Religio Medici* (1643)]

16. I am not so much afraid of death, as ashamed thereof; 'tis the very disgrace and ignominy of our natures, that in a

moment can so disfigure us that our nearest friends, wife, and children, stand afraid and start at us.
[*Religio Medici* (1643)]

17. Certainly there is no happiness within this circle of flesh, nor is it in the optics of these eyes to behold felicity; the first day of our Jubilee is death.
[*Religio Medici* (1643)]

18. He forgets that he can die who complains of misery – we are in the power of no calamity while death is in our own.
[*Religio Medici* (1643)]

19. I have tried if I could reach that great resolution ... to be honest without a thought of Heaven or Hell.
[*Religio Medici* (1643)]

20. To believe only possibilities, is not faith, but mere Philosophy.
[*Religio Medici* (1643)]

21. There is no road or ready way to virtue.
[*Religio Medici* (1643)]

22. My desires only are, and I shall be happy therein, to be but the last man, and bring up the rear in heaven.
[*Religio Medici* (1643)]

23. I feel not in myself those common antipathies that I can discover in others; those national repugnances do not touch me, nor do I behold with prejudice the French, Italian, Spaniard, or Dutch; but where I find their actions in balance with my countrymen's, I honour, love and embrace them in the same degree.
[*Religio Medici* (1643)]

24. All places, all airs make unto me one country; I am in England, everywhere, and under any meridian.
[*Religio Medici* (1643)]

25. If there be any among those common objects of hatred I do contemn and laugh at, it is that great enemy of reason, virtue, and religion, the multitude; that numerous piece of monstrosity, which, taken asunder, seem men, and the reasonable creatures of God, but, confused together, make but one great beast, and a monstrosity more prodigious than Hydra.
[*Religio Medici* (1643)]

26. It is the common wonder of all men, how among so many millions of faces, there should be none alike.
[*Religio Medici* (1643)]

27. No man can justly censure or condemn another, because indeed no man truly knows another.
[*Religio Medici* (1643)]

28. I could be content that we might procreate like trees, without conjunction, or that there were any way to perpetuate the World without this trivial and vulgar way of coition: it is the foolishest act a wise man commits in all his life; nor is there any thing that will more deject his cool'd imagination, when he shall consider what an odd and unworthy piece of folly he hath committed.
[*Religio Medici* (1643)]

29. Sure there is music even in the beauty, and the silent note which Cupid strikes, far sweeter than the sound of an instrument. For there is a music wherever there is a harmony, order or proportion; and thus far we may maintain the music of the spheres; for those well ordered motions, and regular paces, though they give no sound unto the ear, yet to the understanding they strike a note most full of harmony.
[*Religio Medici* (1643)]

30. For even that vulgar and tavern music, which makes one man merry, another mad, strikes in me a deep fit of devotion, and a profound contemplation of the first Composer, there is something in it of divinity more than the ear discovers.
[*Religio Medici* (1643)]

31. We all labour against our own cure, for death is the cure of all diseases.
[*Religio Medici* (1643)]

32. For the world, I count it not an inn, but an hospital, and a place, not to live, but to die in.
[*Religio Medici* (1643)]

33. There is surely a piece of divinity in us, something that was before the elements, and owes no homage unto the sun.
[*Religio Medici* (1643)]

34. [Sleep is] in fine, so like death, I dare not trust it without my prayers.
[*Religio Medici* (1643)]

35. Sleep is a death, O make me try,
By sleeping what it is to die.
And as gently lay my head
On my grave, as now my bed.
[*Religio Medici* (1643). Cf. Ken: 2]

36. Charity begins at home, is the voice of the world.
[*Religio Medici* (1643). Cf. Richard Brinsley Sheridan: 27]

37. For my part, I have ever believed, and do now know, that there are witches.
[*Religio Medici* (1643)]

38. God is like a skilful Geometrician.
[*Religio Medici* (1643)]

39. Lord, deliver me from myself.
[*Religio Medici* (1643)]

40. Thus the devil played at chess with me, and yielding a pawn, thought to gain a queen of me, taking advantage of my honest endeavours.
[*Religio Medici* (1643)]

41. Thus we are men and we know not how: there is something in us that can be without us, and will be after us.
[*Religio Medici* (1643)]

42. Half our days we pass in the shadow of the earth; and the brother of death exacteth a third part of our lives.
[*Pseudodoxia Epidemica* (1646)]

43. As for that famous network of Vulcan, which enclosed Mars and Venus, and caused that unextinguishable laugh in heaven, since the gods themselves could not discern it, we shall not pry into it.
[*The Garden of Cyrus* (1658)]

44. Life itself is but the shadow of death, and souls but the shadows of the living. All things fall under this name. The sun itself is but the dark simulacrum, and light but the shadow of God.
[*The Garden of Cyrus* (1658)]

45. But the quincunx of heaven runs low, and 'tis time to close the five ports of knowledge.
[*The Garden of Cyrus* (1658)]

46. All things began in order, so shall they end, and so shall they begin again; according to the ordainer of order and mystical mathematics of the city of heaven.
[*The Garden of Cyrus* (1658)]

47. Nor will the sweetest delight of gardens afford much comfort in sleep; wherein the dullness of that sense shakes hands with delectable odours; and though in the bed of Cleopatra,

can hardly with any delight raise up the ghost of a rose.
[*The Garden of Cyrus* (1658)]

48. Old mortality, the ruins of forgotten times.
[*Hydriotaphia: Urn Burial* (1658)]

49. With rich flames, and hired tears, they solemnized their obsequies.
[*Hydriotaphia: Urn Burial* (1658)]

50. Men have lost their reason in nothing so much as their religion, wherein stones and clouts make martyrs.
[*Hydriotaphia: Urn Burial* (1658)]

51. They carried them out of the world with their feet forward.
[*Hydriotaphia: Urn Burial* (1658)]

52. Were the happiness of the next world as closely apprehended as the felicities of this, it were a martyrdom to live.
[*Hydriotaphia: Urn Burial* (1658)]

53. Time, which antiquates antiquities, and hath an art to make dust of all things, hath yet spared these minor monuments.
[*Hydriotaphia: Urn Burial* (1658)]

54. The long habit of living indisposeth us for dying.
[*Hydriotaphia: Urn Burial* (1658)]

55. What song the Sirens sang, or what name Achilles assumed when he hid himself among the women, though puzzling questions, are not beyond all conjecture.
[*Hydriotaphia: Urn Burial* (1658)]

56. But to subsist in bones, and be but pyramidally extant, is a fallacy in duration.
[*Hydriotaphia: Urn Burial* (1658)]

57. Generations pass while some tree stands, and old families last not three oaks.
[*Hydriotaphia: Urn Burial* (1658)]

58. But the iniquity of oblivion blindly scattereth her poppy, and deals with the memory of men without distinction to merit of perpetuity.
[*Hydriotaphia: Urn Burial* (1658)]

59. Herostratus lives that burnt the Temple of Diana – he is almost lost that built it.
[*Hydriotaphia: Urn Burial* (1658)]

60. The night of time far surpasseth the day, and who knows when was the equinox?
[*Hydriotaphia: Urn Burial* (1658)]

61. Diuturnity [long-lastingness] is a dream and a folly of expectation.
[*Hydriotaphia: Urn Burial* (1658)]

62. Man is a noble animal, splendid in ashes, and pompous in the grave.
[*Hydriotaphia: Urn Burial* (1658)]

63. Oblivion is a kind of Annihilation.
[*Christian Morals* (1716)]

64. He who discommendeth others obliquely commendeth himself.
[*Christian Morals* (1716)]

65. The created world is but a small parenthesis in eternity.
[*Christian Morals* (1716)]

66. They do most by Books, who could do much without them, and he that chiefly owes himself unto himself, is the substantial man.
[*Christian Morals* (1716)]

67. That children dream not in the first half year, that men dream not in some countries, are to me sick men's dreams, dreams out of the ivory gate, and visions before midnight.
[In S. Wilkin (ed.), *Sir Thomas Browne's Works* (1835), IV, 'On Dreams']

Browne, William [1] (c. 1591–1643)
English pastoral poet

1. Underneath this sable hearse
Lies the subject of all verse,
Sidney's sister, Pembroke's mother;
Death! ere thou hast slain another,
Fair and learn'd, and good as she,
Time shall throw a dart at thee.
['Epitaph on the Countess of Pembroke' (1623)]

Browne, Sir William [2] (1692–1774)
English physician and poet

1. The King to Oxford sent a troop of horse,
For Tories own no argument but force:
With equal skill to Cambridge books he sent,
For Whigs admit no force but argument.
[Reply to Trapp's Epigram. Cf. Trapp: 1]

Browning, Elizabeth Barrett (1806–1861)
English poet, noted for her sonnets; wife of Robert Browning

1. And kings crept out again to feel the sun.
['Crowned and Buried' (1844)]

2. Do you hear the children weeping, O my brothers,
Ere the sorrow comes with years?
['The Cry of the Children' (1844)]

3. And lips say, 'God be pitiful,'
Who ne'er said, 'God be praised.'
['The Cry of the Human' (1844)]

4. And that dismal cry rose slowly
And sank slowly through the air,
Full of spirit's melancholy
And eternity's despair!
And they heard the words it said–
Pan is dead! great Pan is dead!
Pan, Pan is dead!
['The Dead Pan' (1844)]

5. 'Yes,' I answered you last night;
'No,' this morning, sir, I say.
Colours seen by candle-light
Will not look the same by day.
['The Lady's Yes' (1844)]

6. I tell you, hopeless grief is passionless.
[*Sonnets* (1844), 'Grief']

7. Thou large-brained woman and large-hearted man.
['To George Sand. A Desire' (1844)]

8. There, Shakespeare, on whose forehead climb
The crowns o' the world. Oh, eyes sublime,
With tears and laughters for all time!
[*A Vision of Poets* (1844), 100]

9. Straightway I was 'ware,
So weeping, how a mystic shape did move
Behind me, and drew me backward by the hair
And a voice said in mastery while I strove...
'Guess now who holds thee?' – 'Death', I said, but there
The silver answer rang ... 'Not Death, but Love.'
[*Sonnets from the Portuguese* (1850), 1]

10. For frequent tears have run
The colours from my life.
[*Sonnets from the Portuguese* (1850), 8]

11. If thou must love me, let it be for naught
Except for love's sake only.
[*Sonnets from the Portuguese* (1850), 14]

12. God's gifts put man's best gifts to shame.
[*Sonnets from the Portuguese* (1850), 26]

13. How do I love thee? Let me count the ways,
I love thee to the depth and breadth and height
My soul can reach, when feeling out of sight
For the ends of Being and ideal Grace...

14. I love thee with a love I seemed to lose
With my lost saints – I love thee with the breath,
Smiles, tears, of all my life! – and, if God choose,
I shall but love thee better after death.
[*Sonnets from the Portuguese* (1850), 43]

15. Of writing many books there is no end.
[*Aurora Leigh* (1857), 1]

16. Near all the birds
Will sing at dawn, – and yet we do not take
The chaffering swallow for the holy lark.
[*Aurora Leigh* (1857), 1]

17. God answers sharp and sudden on some prayers,
And thrusts the thing we have prayed for in our face,
A gauntlet with a gift in't.
[*Aurora Leigh* (1857), 2]

18. Let no one till his death
Be called unhappy. Measure not the work,
Until the day's out and the labour done.
[*Aurora Leigh* (1857), 5]

19. Since when was genius found respectable?
[*Aurora Leigh* (1857), 6]

20. The devil's most devilish when respectable.
[*Aurora Leigh* (1857), 7]

21. Earth's crammed with heaven,
And every common bush afire with God;
But only he who sees, takes off his shoes,
The rest sit round it and pluck blackberries,
And daub their natural faces unaware
More and more from the first similitude.
[*Aurora Leigh* (1857), 7]

22. What was he doing, the great god Pan,
Down in the reeds by the river?
Spreading ruin and scattering ban,
Splashing and paddling with hoofs of a goat,
And breaking the golden lilies afloat
With the dragon-fly on the river.
['A Musical Instrument' (1862)]

Browning, Robert (1812–1889)

English poet, noted for his dramatic monologues; husband of Elizabeth Barrett Browning

1. [To Shelley]
Sun-treader, life and light be thine for ever!
[*Pauline, a Fragment of a Confession* (1833)]

2. Truth is within ourselves.
[*Paracelsus* (1835), I]

3. *Paracelsus*: I am he that aspired to KNOW: and thou?
Aprile: I would LOVE infinitely, and be loved!...

4. God is the perfect poet,
Who in his person acts his own creations.
[*Paracelsus* (1835), II]

5. I give the fight up: let there be an end,
A privacy, an obscure nook for me.
I want to be forgotten even by God.
[*Paracelsus* (1835), V]

6. There's heaven above, and night by night
I look right through its gorgeous roof.
['Johannes Agricola in Meditation' (1836)]

7. Who will, may hear Sordello's story told.
[*Sordello* (1840), I]

8. Any nose
May ravage with impunity a rose.
[*Sordello* (1840), VI]

9. The year's at the spring
And day's at the morn;
Morning's at seven;
The hill-side's dew-pearled;
The lark's on the wing;
The snail's on the thorn:
God's in his heaven,
All's right with the world.
[*Pippa Passes* (1841), I]

10. God must be glad one loves His world so much!...

11. A king lived long ago,
In the morning of the world,
When earth was nigher heaven than now...

12. Such grace had kings when the world begun!
[*Pippa Passes* (1841), III]

13. All service ranks the same with God–
With God, whose puppets, best and worst,
Are we: there is no last nor first.
[*Pippa Passes* (1841), Epilogue]

14. Boot, saddle, to horse, and away!
['Boot and Saddle' (1842)]

15. She should never have looked at me,
If she meant I should not love her!
['Cristina' (1842), 1]

16. The moth's kiss, first!
Kiss me as if you made believe
You were not sure, this eve,
How my face, your flower, had pursed
Its petals up...
The bee's kiss, now!
Kiss me as if you entered gay
My heart at some noonday.
['In a Gondola' (1842)]

17. 'You're wounded!' 'Nay,' the soldier's pride
Touched to the quick, he said:
'I'm killed, Sire!' And his chief beside
Smiling the boy fell dead.
['Incident of the French Camp' (1842), 5]

18. That's my last Duchess painted on the wall,
Looking as if she were alive. I call
That piece a wonder, now...

19. Never read
Strangers like you that pictured countenance,
The depth and passion of its earnest glance,
But to myself they turned (since none puts by
The curtain I have drawn for you, but I)
And seemed as they would ask me, if they durst,
How such a glance came there...

20. Sir, 'twas not
Her husband's presence only, called that spot
Of joy into the Duchess' cheek...

21. She had
A heart – how shall I say? – too soon made glad,
Too easily impressed; she liked whate'er
She looked on, and her looks went everywhere.
Sir, 'twas all one! My favour at her breast,
The dropping of the daylight in the West,
The bough of cherries some officious fool
Broke in the orchard for her, the white mule
She rode with round the terrace – all and each
Would draw from her alike the approving speech,
Or blush, at least. She thanked men, – good! but thanked
Somehow – I know not how – as if she ranked
My gift of a nine-hundred-years-old name
With anybody's gift...

22. Oh, sir, she smiled, no doubt,
Whene'er I passed her; but who passed without
Much the same smile? This grew; I gave commands;
Then all smiles stopped together. There she stands
As if alive. Will't please you rise? We'll meet
The company below, then...

23. Nay, we'll go
Together down, sir. Notice Neptune, though,
Taming a sea-horse, thought a rarity,
Which Claus of Innsbruck cast in bronze for me!
['My Last Duchess' (1842)]

24. Hamelin Town's in Brunswick,
By famous Hanover city;
The river Weser, deep and wide,
Washes its walls on the southern side.
['The Pied Piper of Hamelin' (1842), 1]

25. Rats!
They fought the dogs and killed the cats,
And bit the babies in the cradles,
And ate the cheeses out of the vats,
And licked the soup from the cooks' own ladles,
Split open the kegs of salted sprats,
Made nests inside men's Sunday hats,
And even spoiled the women's chats
By drowning their speaking
With shrieking and squeaking
In fifty different sharps and flats.
['The Pied Piper of Hamelin' (1842), 2]

26. 'Oh for a trap, a trap, a trap!'
Just as he said this, what should hap
At the chamber door but a gentle tap?
'Bless us,' cried the Mayor, 'what's that?'...

27. 'Only a scraping of shoes on the mat?
Anything like the sound of a rat
Makes my heart go pit-a-pat!'
['The Pied Piper of Hamelin' (1842), 4]

28. And the muttering grew to a grumbling
And the grumbling grew to a mighty rumbling
And out of the houses rats came tumbling...

29. Families by tens and dozens,
Brothers, sisters, husbands, wives–
Followed the Piper for their lives.
From street to street he piped advancing,
And step for step they followed dancing,
Until they came to the river Weser
Wherein all plunged and perished!
['The Pied Piper of Hamelin' (1842), 7]

30. 'You threaten us, fellow? Do your worst,
Blow your pipe there till you burst!'
['The Pied Piper of Hamelin' (1842), 11]

31. The Mayor was dumb, and the Council stood
As if they were changed into blocks of wood,
Unable to move a step, or cry
To the children merrily skipping by...

32. When, lo, as they reached the mountain side,
A wondrous portal opened wide,
As if a cavern was suddenly hollowed;
And the Piper advanced and the children followed,
And when all were in to the very last,
The door in the mountain side shut fast.
['The Pied Piper of Hamelin' (1842), 13]

33. The rain set early in to-night...

34. All her hair
In one long yellow string I wound
Three times her little throat around,
And strangled her. No pain felt she;
I am quite sure she felt no pain...

35. And all night long we have not stirred,
And yet God has not said a word!
['Porphyria's Lover' (1842)]

36. Gr-r-r there go, my heart's abhorrence!
Water your damned flower-pots, do!
If hate killed men, Brother Lawrence,
God's blood, would not mine kill you!
['Soliloquy of the Spanish Cloister' (1842), 1]

37. There's a great text in Galatians,
Once you trip on it, entails
Twenty-nine distinct damnations,
One sure, if another fails.
['Soliloquy of the Spanish Cloister' (1842), 7]

38. What's become of Waring
Since he gave us all the slip?
['Waring' (1843), 1]

39. Ichabod, Ichabod,
The glory is departed!
['Waring' (1843), 6]

40. Plague take all your pedants, say I!
['Sibrandus Schafraburgensis' (1844)]

41. Saint Praxed's ever was the church for peace...

42. Blue as a vein o'er the Madonna's breast...

43. And have I not Saint Praxed's ear to pray
Horses for ye, and brown Greek manuscripts,
And mistresses with great smooth marbly limbs?
– That's if ye carve my epitaph aright...

44. And then how I shall lie through centuries,
And hear the blessed mutter of the mass,
And see God made and eaten all day long,
And feel the steady candle-flame, and taste
Good strong thick stupefying incense-smoke!...

45. Aha, ELUCESCEBAT quoth our friend?
No Tully, said I, Ulpian at the best!
['The Bishop Orders His Tomb at Saint Praxed's Church' (1845)]

46. Where the haters meet
In the crowded city's horrible street...

47. When the liquor's out, why clink the cannikin?
['The Flight of the Duchess' (1845)]

48. I must learn Spanish, one of these days,
Only for that slow sweet name's sake.
['The Flower's Name' (1845)]

49. Oh, to be in England
Now that April's there,
And whoever wakes in England

Sees, some morning, unaware,
That the lowest boughs and the brushwood sheaf
Round the elm-tree bole are in tiny leaf,
While the chaffinch sings on the orchard bough
In England – now!

And after April, when May follows,
And the whitethroat builds, and all the swallows!...

50. That's the wise thrush; he sings each song twice over,
Lest you should think he never could recapture
The first fine careless rapture!
And though the fields look rough with hoary dew
All will be gay when noontide wakes anew
The buttercups, the little children's dower–
Far brighter than this gaudy melon-flower.
['Home-Thoughts, from Abroad' (1845)]

51. Nobly, nobly Cape St Vincent to the North-west died away;
Sunset ran, one glorious blood-red, reeking into Cadiz Bay.
['Home-Thoughts, from the Sea' (1845)]

52. I sprang to the stirrup, and Joris, and he;
I galloped, Dirck galloped, we galloped all three.
['How they brought the Good News from Ghent to Aix' (1845)]

53. Just for a handful of silver he left us,
Just for a riband to stick in his coat...

54. We that had loved him so, followed him, honoured him,
Lived in his mild and magnificent eye,
Learned his great language, caught his clear accents,
Made him our pattern to live and to die!...

55. Blot out his name, then, record one lost soul more,
One task more declined, one more footpath untrod,
One more devils'-triumph and sorrow for angels,
One wrong more to man, one more insult to God!...

56. Never glad confident morning again!...

57. Then let him receive the new knowledge and wait us,
Pardoned in heaven, the first by the throne!
['The Lost Leader' (1845)]

58. As I gain the cove with pushing prow,
And quench its speed i' the slushy sand.

Then a mile of warm sea-scented beach;
Three fields to cross till a farm appears;
A tap at the pane, a quick sharp scratch
And blue spurt of a lighted match,
And a voice less loud, thro' its joys and fears,
Than the two hearts beating each to each!
['Meeting at Night' (1845)]

59. Ah, thought which saddens while it soothes!
['Pictor Ignotus' (1845)]

60. There may be heaven; there must be hell;
Meantime, there is our earth here – well!
['Time's Revenges' (1845), last lines]

61. Oppression makes the wise man mad.
[*Luria* (1846), IV]

62. Round the cape of a sudden came the sea,
And the sun looked over the mountain's rim;
And straight was a path of gold for him,
And the need of a world of men for me.
['Parting at Morning' (1849)]

63. In the natural fog of the good man's mind...

64. In youth I looked to these very skies,
And probing their immensities,
I found God there...

65. For the loving worm within its clod,
Were diviner than a loveless god...

66. Though Rome's gross yoke
Drops off, no more to be endured,
Her teaching is not so obscured
By errors and perversities,
That no truth shines athwart the lies.
['Christmas Eve' (1850)]

67. How very hard it is
To be a Christian!...

68. 'Tis well averred
A scientific faith's absurd...

69. At last awake
From life, that insane dream we take
For waking now.
['Easter-Day' (1850)]

70. How he lies in his rights of a man!
Death has done all death can.
['After' (1855)]

71. So free we seem, so fettered fast we are!...

72. Ah, but a man's reach should exceed his grasp,
Or what's a heaven for?...

73. I am grown peaceful as old age tonight.
I regret little, I would change still less.
['Andrea del Sarto' (1855)]

74. It all comes to the same thing at the end.
['Any Wife to Any Husband' (1855), 16]

75. Why need the other women know so much?
['Any Wife to Any Husband' (1855), 17]

76. Don't you know,
I promised, if you'd watch a dinner out,
We'd see truth dawn together? – truth that peeps
Over the glass's edge when dinner's done,
And body gets its sop and holds its noise
And leaves soul free a little.
['Bishop Blougram's Apology' (1855), line 15]

77. The common problem, yours, mine, everyone's,
Is not to fancy what were fair in life
Provided it could be, – but, finding first
What may be, then find how to make it fair.
['Bishop Blougram's Apology' (1855), line 87]

78. We mortals cross the ocean of this world
Each in his average cabin of a life.
['Bishop Blougram's Apology' (1855), line 100]

79. A piano-forte is a fine resource,
All Balzac's novels occupy one shelf,
The new edition fifty volumes long.
['Bishop Blougram's Apology' (1855), line 107]

80. Just when we are safest, there's a sunset-touch,
A fancy from a flower-bell, some one's death,
A chorus-ending from Euripides,–
And that's enough for fifty hopes and fears
As old and new at once as nature's self,
To rap and knock and enter in our soul,
Take hands and dance there, a fantastic ring,
Round the ancient idol, on his base again,–
The grand Perhaps!
['Bishop Blougram's Apology' (1855), line 182]

81. All we have gained then by our unbelief
Is a life of doubt diversified by faith,
For one of faith diversified by doubt:

We called the chess-board white, – we call it black.
['Bishop Blougram's Apology' (1855), line 209]

82. If once we choose belief, on all accounts
We can't be too decisive in our faith.
['Bishop Blougram's Apology' (1855), line 271]

83. Brave with the needlework of Noodledom.
['Bishop Blougram's Apology' (1855), line 426]

84. I show you doubt, to prove that faith exists.
['Bishop Blougram's Apology' (1855), line 602]

85. And that's what all the blessed evil's for.
['Bishop Blougram's Apology' (1855), line 655]

86. No, when the fight begins within himself,
A man's worth something.
['Bishop Blougram's Apology' (1855), line 693]

87. Gigadibs the literary man,
Who played with spoons.
['Bishop Blougram's Apology' (1855), line 975]

88. He said true things, but called them by wrong names.
['Bishop Blougram's Apology' (1855), line 996]

89. How well I know what I mean to do
When the long dark autumn-evenings come.
['By the Fireside' (1855), 1]

90. I shall be found by the fire, suppose,
O'er a great wise book as beseemeth age,
While the shutters flap as the cross-wind blows
And I turn the page, and I turn the page,
Not verse now, only prose!
['By the Fireside' (1855), 2]

91. That great brow
And the spirit-small hand propping it.
['By the Fireside' (1855), 23]

92. Oh, the little more, and how much it is!
And the little less, and what worlds away!
['By the Fireside' (1855), 39]

93. If two lives join, there is oft a scar.
They are one and one, with a shadowy third;
One near one is too far.
['By the Fireside' (1855), 46]

94. As for the grass, it grew as scant as hair
In leprosy...

95. One stiff blind horse, his every bone a-stare.
['Childe Roland to the Dark Tower Came' (1855), 13]

96. I never saw a brute I hated so;
He must be wicked to deserve such pain.
['Childe Roland to the Dark Tower Came' (1855), 14]

97. Toads in a poisoned tank,
Or wild cats in a red-hot iron cage.
['Childe Roland to the Dark Tower Came' (1855), 22]

98. Dauntless the slug-horn to my lips I set,
And blew. 'Childe Roland to the Dark Tower came.'
['Childe Roland to the Dark Tower Came' (1855), 34]

99. What survives myself?
The brazen statue to o'erlook my grave,
Set on the promontory which I named...

100. There's a world of capability
For joy, spread round about us, meant for us,
Inviting us...

101. Certain slaves
Who touched on this same isle, preached him and Christ;
And (as I gather from a bystander)
Their doctrine could be held by no sane man.
['Cleon' (1855)]

102. Your ghost will walk, you lover of trees,
(If our loves remain)
In an English lane...

103. The beanflowers' boon,
And the blackbird's tune,
And May, and June!
['De Gustibus' (1855), I]

104. Italy, my Italy!
Queen Mary's saying serves for me–
(When fortune's malice
Lost her – Calais)–
Open my heart and you will see
Graved inside of it, 'Italy'.
['De Gustibus' (1855), II]

105. Karshish, the picker up of learning's crumbs,
The not-incurious in God's handiwork...

106. That puff of vapour from his mouth, man's soul...

107. The man's fantastic will is the man's law...

108. 'But love I gave thee, with myself to love.
And thou must love me who have died for thee!'
The madman saith He said so: it is strange.
['An Epistle ... of Karshish, the Arab Physician' (1855)]

109. You will wake, and remember, and understand.
['Evelyn Hope' (1855)]

110. I am poor brother Lippo, by your leave!...

111. All the Latin I construe is, 'amo' I love!...

112. Your business is to paint the souls of men...

113. If you get simple beauty and nought else,
You get about the best thing God invents...

114. You should not take a fellow eight years old,
And make him swear to never kiss the girls...

115. I always see the garden and God there
A-making man's wife...

116. This world's no blot for us,
Nor blank; it means intensely, and means good:
To find its meaning is my meat and drink.
['Fra Lippo Lippi' (1855)]

117. Yea, this in him was the peculiar grace...
That before living he'd learn how to live...

118. He said, 'What's time? Leave Now for dogs and apes!
Man has Forever.'...

119. Calculus racked him:
Leaden before, his eyes grew dross of lead:
Tussis attacked him...

120. That low man seeks a little thing to do,
Sees it and does it:
This high man, with a great thing to pursue,
Dies ere he knows it:
That low man goes on adding one to one,
His hundred's soon hit;
This high man, aiming at a million,
Misses an unit...

121. He settled Hoti's business – let it be!–
Properly based Oun–
Gave us the doctrine of the enclitic De,
Dead from the waist down...

122. Lofty designs must close in like effects:
Loftily lying,

Leave him – still loftier than the world suspects,
Living and dying.
['A Grammarian's Funeral' (1855)]

123. I liken his Grace to an acorned hog.
['Holy-Cross Day' (1855), 4]

124. We withstood Christ then? Be mindful how
At least we withstand Barabbas now!
['Holy-Cross Day' (1855), 18]

125. He took such cognizance of men and things.
['How it Strikes a Contemporary' (1855)]

126. A man can have but one life and one death,
One heaven, one hell...

127. Women hate a debt as men a gift.
['In a Balcony' (1855), I]

128. I said – Then, dearest, since 'tis so,
Since now at length my fate I know,
Since nothing all my love avails,
Since all, my life seemed meant for, fails,
Since this was written and needs must be–
My whole heart rises up to bless
Your name in pride and thankfulness!
Take back the hope you gave, – I claim
Only a memory of the same.
['The Last Ride Together' (1855), 1]

129. Who knows but the world may end to-night?
['The Last Ride Together' (1855), 2]

130. My soul
Smoothed itself out, long-cramped scroll
Freshening and fluttering in the wind...
Had I said that, had I done this,
So might I gain, so might I miss.
Might she have loved me? just as well
She might have hated, who can tell!
['The Last Ride Together' (1855), 4]

131. Look at the end of work, contrast
The petty done, the undone vast,
This present of theirs with the hopeful past!
['The Last Ride Together' (1855), 5]

132. Escape me?
Never–
Beloved!
['Life in a Love' (1855)]

133. 'Tis an awkward thing to play with souls,
And matter enough to save one's own.
['A Light Woman' (1855), 12]

134. Where the quiet-coloured end of evening smiles,
Miles and miles.
['Love among the Ruins' (1855)]

135. And find a poor devil has ended his cares
At the foot of your rotten-runged rat-riddled stairs?
Do I carry the moon in my pocket?
['Master Hugues of Saxe-Gotha' (1855), 29]

136. Ah, did you once see Shelley plain,
And did he stop and speak to you
And did you speak to him again?
How strange it seems, and new!...

137. A moulted feather, an eagle-feather!
Well, I forget the rest.
['Memorabilia' (1855)]

138. What's come to perfection perishes.
Things learned on earth, we shall practise in heaven.
Works done least rapidly, Art most cherishes.
['Old Pictures in Florence' (1855), 17]

139. There remaineth a rest for the people of God:
And I have had troubles enough, for one.
['Old Pictures in Florence' (1855), 22]

140. Dante, who loved well because he hated,
Hated wickedness that hinders loving.
['One Word More to E.B.B.' (1855), 5]

141. God be thanked, the meanest of his creatures
Boasts two soul-sides, one to face the world with,
One to show a woman when he loves her.
['One Word More to E.B.B.' (1855), 17]

142. It was roses, roses, all the way,
With myrtle mixed in my path like mad...

143. The air broke into a mist with bells.
['The Patriot' (1855)]

144. What porridge had John Keats?
['Popularity' (1855), 13]

145. Whoso mounts the throne
For beauty, knowledge, strength, should stand alone,
And mortals love the letters of his name.
['Protus' (1855)]

146. Oh, the wild joys of living! the leaping from rock up to rock,
The strong rending of boughs from the fir-tree, the cool silver shock
Of the plunge in a pool's living water...

147. How good is man's life, the mere living! how fit to employ
All the heart and the soul and the senses, for ever in joy!
['Saul', 9 (1841–1846)]

148. Leave the flesh to the fate it was fit for! the spirit be thine!
['Saul', 13 (1855)]

149. 'Tis not what man does which exalts him, but what a man would do!...

150. He who did most, shall bear most; the strongest shall stand the most weak.
['Saul', 18 (1855)]

151. She looked at him, as one who awakes:
The past was a sleep, and her life began...

152. The world and its ways have a certain worth...

153. The glory dropped from their youth and love,
And both perceived they had dreamed a dream...

154. The soldier-saints, who row on row,
Burn upward each to his point of bliss...

155. And the sin I impute to each frustrate ghost
Is, the unlit lamp and the ungirt loin,
Though the end in sight was a vice, I say.
['The Statue and the Bust' (1855)]

156. Hark, the dominant's persistence till it must be answered to!
['A Toccata of Galuppi's' (1855), 8]

157. What of soul was left, I wonder, when the kissing had to stop?
['A Toccata of Galuppi's' (1855), 14]

158. Dear dead women, with such hair, too – what's become of all the gold
Used to hang and brush their bosoms? I feel chilly and grown old.
['A Toccata of Galuppi's' (1855), 15]

159. Grand rough old Martin Luther
Bloomed fables – flowers on furze,
The better the uncouther:
Do roses stick like burrs?
['The Twins' (1855)]

160. I would that you were all to me,
You that are just so much, no more.
['Two in the Campagna' (1855), 8]

161. I pluck the rose
And love it more than tongue can speak–
Then the good minute goes.
['Two in the Campagna' (1855), 10]

162. Where is the thread now? Off again!
The old trick! only I discern–
Infinite passion, and the pain
Of finite hearts that yearn.
['Two in the Campagna' (1855), 12]

163. Had I but plenty of money, money enough and to spare,
The house for me, no doubt, were a house in the city-square...

164. Bang, whang, whang, goes the drum, tootle-te-tootle, the fife
Oh a day in the city square, there is no such pleasure in life.
['Up at a Villa – Down in the City' (1855)]

165. Let's contend no more, Love,
Strive nor weep:
All be as before, Love,
– Only sleep!
['A Woman's Last Word' (1855)]

166. On the earth the broken arcs; in the heaven, a perfect round.
['Abt Vogler' (1864), 9]

167. All we have willed or hoped or dreamed of good shall exist.
['Abt Vogler' (1864), 10]

168. But god has a few of us whom he whispers in the ear;
The rest may reason and welcome; 'tis we musicians know.
['Abt Vogler' (1864), 11]

169. I feel for the common chord again...
The C Major of this life.
['Abt Vogler' (1864), 12]

170. 'Let twenty pass, and stone the twenty-first.
Loving not, hating not, just choosing so...

171. This Quiet, all it hath a mind to do, doth.
['Caliban upon Setebos' (1864)]

172. What is he buzzing in my ears?
'Now that I come to die,
Do I view the world as a vale of tears?'
Ah, reverend sir, not I!
['Confessions' (1864), 1]

173. We loved, sir – used to meet:
How sad and bad and mad it was–
But then, how it was sweet!
['Confessions' (1864), 9]

174. Stung by the splendour of a sudden thought...

175. Such ever was love's way; to rise, it stoops.
['A Death in the Desert' (1864)]

176. The swallow has set her six young on the rail,
And looks seaward.
['James Lee's Wife' (1864), III, 1]

177. If such as came for wool, sir, went home shorn,
Where is the wrong I did them?...

178. Solomon of saloons
And philosophic diner-out...

179. My care is for myself;
Myself am whole and sole reality...

180. Why should I set so fine a gloss on things?
['Mr Sludge, The Medium' (1864)]

181. Fear death? – to feel the fog in my throat,
The mist in my face...

182. I was ever a fighter, so – one fight more,
The best and the last!
I would hate that death bandaged my eyes, and forebore,
And bade me creep past...

183. O thou soul of my soul! I shall clasp thee again,
And with God be the rest!
['Prospice' (1864)]

184. Grow old along with me!
The best is yet to be,
The last of life for which the first was made:
Our times are in His hand
Who saith, 'A whole I planned,
Youth shows but half; trust God: see all, nor be afraid!'
['Rabbi Ben Ezra' (1864), 1]

185. Irks care the crop-full bird? Frets doubt the maw-crammed beast?
['Rabbi Ben Ezra' (1864), 4]

186. I see the whole design,
I, who saw power, see now love perfect too.
['Rabbi Ben Ezra' (1864), 10]

187. Leave the fire ashes, what survives is gold.
['Rabbi Ben Ezra' (1864), 15]

188. Fancies that broke through language and escaped.
['Rabbi Ben Ezra' (1864), 25]

189. Time's wheel runs back or stops: Potter and clay endure.
['Rabbi Ben Ezra' (1864), 27]

190. My times be in Thy hand!
Perfect the cup as planned!
Let age approve of youth, and death complete the same!
['Rabbi Ben Ezra' (1864), 32]

191. I knew you once: but in Paradise,
If we meet, I will pass nor turn my face.
['The Worst of It' (1864)]

192. Well, British Public, ye who like me not.
[*The Ring and the Book* (1868–1869), I, line 410]

193. Youth means love,
Vows can't change nature, priests are only men,
And love likes stratagem and subterfuge.
[*The Ring and the Book* (1868–1869), I, line 1056]

194. O lyric Love, half-angel and half-bird
And all a wonder and wild desire.
[*The Ring and the Book* (1868–1869), I, line 1391]

195. Never may I commence my song, my due
To God who best taught song by gift of thee,
Except with bent head and beseeching hand–
That still, despite the distance and the dark,
What was, again may be.
[*The Ring and the Book* (1868–1869), I, line 1403]

196. So Pietro craved an heir,
(The story always old and always new).
[*The Ring and the Book* (1868–1869), II, line 214]

197. But facts are facts and flinch not.
[*The Ring and the Book* (1868–1869), II, line 1049]

198. In the great right of an excessive wrong.
[*The Ring and the Book* (1868–1869), III, line 1055]

199. Everyone soon or late comes round by Rome.
[*The Ring and the Book* (1868–1869), V, line 296]

200. 'T was a thief said the last kind word to Christ:
Christ took the kindness and forgave the theft.
[*The Ring and the Book* (1868–1869), VI, line 869]

201. Faultless to a fault.
[*The Ring and the Book* (1868–1869), IX, line 1175]

202. Of what I call God,
And fools call Nature.
[*The Ring and the Book* (1868–1869), X, line 1073]

203. White shall not neutralize the black, nor good
Compensate bad in man, absolve him so:
Life's business being just the terrible choice.
[*The Ring and the Book* (1868–1869), X, line 1236]

204. There's a new tribunal now
Higher than God's – the educated man's!
[*The Ring and the Book* (1868–1869), X, line 1975]

205. It is the glory and good of Art,
That Art remains the one way possible
Of speaking truth, to mouths like mine at least.
[*The Ring and the Book* (1868–1869), XII, line 838]

206. Hatred and cark and care, what place have they
In yon blue liberality of heaven?
['Aristophanes' Apology' (1875)]

207. Ignorance is not innocence but sin.
[*The Inn Album* (1875), 5]

208. I want to know a butcher paints,
A baker rhymes for his pursuit,
Candlestick-maker much acquaints
His soul with song, or, haply mute,
Blows out his brains upon the flute.
['Shop' (1876), 21]

209. Good, to forgive;
Best, to forget!
Living, we fret;
Dying, we live.
[*La Saisiaz* (1878), Dedication]

210. Never the time and the place,
And the loved one all together!
['Never the Time and the Place' (1883)]

211. A minute's success pays the failure of years.
['Apollo and the Fates' (1887)]

212. All the breath and the bloom of the year in the bag of one bee.
[*Asolando* (1890), 'Summum Bonum']

213. One who never turned his back but marched breast forward,
Never doubted clouds would break,
Never dreamed, though right were worsted, wrong would triumph
Held we fall to rise, are baffled to fight better,
Sleep to wake...

214. Greet the unseen with a cheer!...

215. Oh to love so, be so loved, yet so mistaken!
[*Asolando* (1890), Epilogue]

216. [On being asked his opinion of Austin Dobson as a poet]
Well, some people do like carved cherrystones.
[In E.F. Benson, *As We Were* (1930)]

Bruce, Lenny (1925–1966)
American comedian, prosecuted for obscenity

1. [Referring to the Crucifixion]
It was just one of those parties which got out of hand.
[*The Guardian*, 1979]

Bruce, Robert (1274–1329)
King of Scotland from 1306; secured independence from England

1. Now, God be with you, my dear children: I have breakfasted with you and shall sup with my Lord Jesus Christ.
[Oral tradition]

Brummel, Beau (George Bryan Brummell) (1778–1840)
English dandy and wit; leader of Regency fashion

1. No perfumes, but very fine linen, plenty of it, and country washing.
[In Harriette Wilson, *Memoirs* (1825), 2]

2. [Said of the Prince of Wales, 1813]
Who's your fat friend?
[In Gronow, *Reminiscences* (1862)]

3. I always like to have the morning well-aired before I get up.
[In Charles Macfarlane, *Reminiscences of a Literary Life* (1917)]

4. [To the Prince]
Shut the door, Wales.
[Attr.]

Bruno, Giordano (1548–1600)
Italian philosopher and heretic; put to death by the Inquisition

1. [Said to the cardinals who excommunicated him, 1600]
Perhaps your fear in passing judgement is greater than mine in receiving it.
[Attr.]

Bryan, William Jennings (1860–1925)
American Democratic politician, presidential candidate and editor

1. I shall not help crucify mankind upon a cross of gold. I shall not aid in pressing down upon the bleeding brow of labour this crown of thorns.
[Speech, Chicago, 1896]

2. The humblest citizen of all the land, when clad in the armour of a righteous cause is stronger than all the hosts of error.
[Speech, Chicago, 1896]

3. An orator is a man who says what he thinks and feels what he says.
[Attr.]

Bryant, William Cullen (1794–1878)
American poet and newspaper editor; member of the 'Knickerbocker School'

1. They seemed
Like old companions in adversity.
['A Winter Piece']

Buch, Hans Christoph

1. *Die Deutschen versuchen die Nazi-Vergangenheit aufzuarbeiten, indem sie besonders friedlich oder besonders grün sein wollen.*
The Germans are trying to come to terms with their Nazi past by wanting to be particularly peaceful or particularly green.
[In Ingo Roland Stoehr, 'Am Schnittpunkt mehrerer Kulturen...: ein Gespräch mit Hans Christoph Buch' ('At

the intersection of several cultures . . . : a conversation with Hans Christoph Buch') in *Dimension*, XIX, part 3, *Die Gruppe 47 in Prag 1990*]

Buchan, John (First Baron Tweedsmuir) (1875–1940)
Prolific Scottish writer; novelist, editor, critic and journalist; lawyer, Conservative politician and Governor-General of Canada 1935–40

1. 'Just so,' he said with a grin. 'It's a great life if you don't weaken.'
[*Mr Standfast* (1919), 5]

2. To live for a time close to great minds is the best kind of education.
[*Memory Hold the Door*]

3. An atheist is a man who has no invisible means of support.
[Attr.]

Buchanan, Robert Williams (1841–1901)
British poet, novelist and dramatist

1. Beauty and Truth, though never found, are worthy to be sought.
['To David in Heaven' (1865)]

2. The Fleshly School of Poetry.
[Title of article in the *Contemporary Review*, 1871]

3. She just wore
Enough for modesty – no more.
['White Rose and Red' (1873)]

4. The buying and the selling, and the strife
Of little natures . . .

5. The sweet post-prandial cigar.
['De Berney' (1874)]

6. All that is beautiful shall abide,
All that is base shall die.
['Balder the Beautiful' (1877)]

7. But his eddication to his ruination had not been over nice,
And his stupid skull was choking full of vulgar prejudice.
['Phil Blood's Leap' (1882)]

8. A race that binds
Its body in chains and calls them Liberty,
And calls each fresh link Progress.
['Titan and Avatar']

Büchner, Georg (1813–1837)
German playwright

1. *Wir sind Dickhäuter, wir strecken die Hände nacheinander aus aber es ist vergebliche Mühe, wir reiben nur das grobe Leder aneinander ab, – wir sind sehr einsam.*
We're thick-skinned, we stretch out our hands to each other but the effort is in vain, we only rub each other's coarse hide, – we are very lonely.
[*Dantons Tod* (*Danton's Death*, 1835), I.i]

2. *Puppen sind wir von unbekannten Gewalten am Draht gezogen; nichts, nichts wir selbst!*
We are puppets on strings worked by unknown forces; we ourselves are nothing, nothing!
[*Dantons Tod* (*Danton's Death*, 1835), II.v]

Buck, Pearl S. (1892–1973)
American novelist, translator from Chinese and dramatist; Nobel Prize, 1938

1. It is better to be first with an ugly woman than the hundredth with a beauty.
[*The Good Earth* (1931), 1]

2. I feel no need for any other faith than my faith in human beings.
[*I Believe* (1939)]

3. Euthanasia is a long, smooth-sounding word, and it conceals its danger as long, smooth words do, but the danger is there, nevertheless.
[*The Child Who Never Grew* (1950), 2]

4. Nothing and no one can destroy the Chinese people. They are relentless survivors. They are the oldest civilized people on earth. Their civilization passes through phases but its basic characteristics remain the same. They yield, they bend to the wind, but they never break.
[*China, Past and Present* (1972), 1]

5. Ah well, perhaps one has to be very old before one learns how to be amused rather than shocked.
[*China, Past and Present* (1972), 6]

6. No one really understood music unless he was a scientist, her father had declared, and not just a scientist, either, oh, no, only the real ones, the theoreticians, whose language was mathematics.
[*The Goddess Abides* (1972), I]

Buckingham, George Villiers, Second Duke of (1628–1687)
English courtier, member of the Cabal and comic dramatist

1. What the devil does the plot signify, except to bring in fine things?
[*The Rehearsal* (written 1663, performed c. 1671), III]

2. Ay, now the plot thickens very much upon us.
[*The Rehearsal* (written 1663, performed c. 1671), III]

Buckingham and Normanby, John Sheffield, First Duke of (1648–1721)
English poet and political leader

1. Read Homer once, and you can read no more,
For all books else appear so mean, so poor,
Verse will seem prose; but still persist to read,
And Homer will be all the books you need.
['An Essay on Poetry' (1682)]

2. Learn to write well, or not to write at all.
['Essay on Satire' (1689)]

Buckoll, H.J. (1803–1871)
English clergyman, hymn-writer and schoolteacher

1. Lord, behold us with Thy blessing
Once again assembled here . . .

2. Lord, dismiss us with Thy blessing,
Thanks for mercies past received.
[Hymn for Rugby School Chapel, 1850]

Buckstone, J.B. (1802–1879)
English comedian, writer of farces and actor–manager

1. On such an occasion as this,
All time and nonsense scorning,
Nothing shall come amiss,
And we won't go home till morning.
['Billy Taylor' (1829)]

Buddha (Gautama Siddhartha) (c. 563–483 BC)
Indian religious teacher, the 'Enlightened'; founder of Buddhism

1. All things, oh priests, are on fire . . . The eye is on fire; forms

are on fire; eye-consciousness is on fire; impressions received by the eye are on fire.
[*The Fire Sermon*]

2. This Ayrian Eightfold Path, that is to say: Right view, right aim, right speech, right action, right living, right effort, right mindfulness, right contemplation.
[In F.L. Woodward, *Some Sayings of the Buddha*]

3. Ye must leave righteous ways behind, not to speak of unrighteous ways.
[In F.L. Woodward, *Some Sayings of the Buddha*]

Budgell, Eustace (1686–1737)
English writer and journalist

1. [Lines found on his desk after his suicide]
What Cato did, and Addison approved
Cannot be wrong.
[Attr.]

Buffon, Comte de (George-Louis Leclerc) (1707–1788)
French naturalist

1. *Ces choses sont hors de l'homme, le style est l'homme même.*
These things [subject matter] are external to the man; style is the essence of man.
['Discours sur le Style' (1753)]

2. *Le génie n'est qu'une plus grande aptitude à la patience.*
Genius is merely a greater aptitude for patience.
[In Hérault de Séchelles, *Voyage à Montbar* (1803)]

Bulgakov, Mikhail (1891–1940)
Russian novelist and dramatist

1. No man should break his word of honour.
[*The White Guard* (1925)]

2. There are no evil people in the world.
[*The Master and Margarita* (1966–1967), 2]

3. Manuscripts don't burn.
[*The Master and Margarita* (1966–1967), 24]

4. Cowardice is, without a doubt, one of the greatest sins.
[*The Master and Margarita* (1966–1967), 26]

Buller, Arthur (1874–1944)
English botanist and mycologist

1. There was a young lady named Bright,
Whose speed was far faster than light;
She set out one day
In a relative way,
And returned home the previous night.
[*Punch*, 19 December 1923]

Bullock, Alan, Baron (1914–)
English historian and academic

1. The people Hitler never understood, and whose actions continued to exasperate him to the end of his life, were the British.
[*Hitler, A Study in Tyranny* (1952), 8]

2. Hitler showed surprising loyalty to Mussolini, but it never extended to trusting him.
[*Hitler, A Study in Tyranny* (1952), 11]

Bulmer-Thomas, Ivor (1905–)
Welsh politician, journalist, writer and church preservationist

1. [Of Harold Wilson]
If ever he went to school without any boots it was because he was too big for them.
[Remark, Conservative Party Conference, 1949]

Bülow, Prince Bernhard von (1849–1929)
German statesman; Chancellor 1900–1909

1. *Mit einem Worte: wir wollen niemand in den Schatten stellen, aber wir verlangen auch unseren Platz an der Sonne.*
In a word: we do not wish to put anyone in the shade, but we still demand our own place in the sun.
[Speech, Reichstag, 1897]

Bulwer-Lytton, Edward George (First Baron Lytton) (1803–1873)
English novelist, dramatist, poet and politician

1. Beneath the rule of men entirely great
The pen is mightier than the sword.
[*Richelieu* (1839)]

2. In the lexicon of youth, which Fate reserves
For a bright manhood, there is no such word
As – fail!
[*Richelieu* (1839)]

3. Poverty has strange bedfellows.
[*The Caxtons* (1849)]

4. There is no man so friendless but what he can find a friend sincere enough to tell him disagreeable truths.
[*What Will He Do With It?* (1857)]

5. In science, read, by preference, the newest works; in literature, the oldest.
[*Caxtoniana* (1863)]

Bunin, I.A. (1870–1953)
Russian novelist and poet; Nobel prize, 1933

1. Until now he had not lived, merely existed.
[*The Gentleman from San Francisco and Other Stories* (1915)]

2. Are we not born with a sense of death?
[*The Well of Days* (1933)]

Bunn, Alfred (1796–1860)
English theatrical manager, librettist and poet

1. I dreamt that I dwelt in marble halls,
With vassals and serfs at my side.
[*The Bohemian Girl* (1843), II]

Buñuel, Luis (1900–1983)
Spanish surrealist film director

1. I am still an atheist, thank God.
[Attr.]

Bunyan, John (1628–1688)
English Nonconformist preacher, pastor and writer; imprisoned for his preaching

1. As I walk'd through the wilderness of this world.
[*The Pilgrim's Progress* (1678), I]

2. Do you see yonder wicket-gate?
[*The Pilgrim's Progress* (1678), I]

3. The name of the slough was Despond.
[*The Pilgrim's Progress* (1678), I]

4. The gentleman's name that met him was Mr Worldly Wiseman.
[*The Pilgrim's Progress* (1678), I]

5. A very stately palace before him, the name of which was Beautiful.
[*The Pilgrim's Progress* (1678), I]

6. The valley of Humiliation.
[*The Pilgrim's Progress* (1678), I]

7. A foul Fiend coming over the field to meet him; his name is Apollyon.
[*The Pilgrim's Progress* (1678), I]

8. Then Apollyon straddled quite over the whole breadth of the way.
[*The Pilgrim's Progress* (1678), I]

9. It beareth the name of Vanity-Fair, because the town where 'tis kept, is lighter than vanity.
[*The Pilgrim's Progress* (1678), I]

10. So soon as the man overtook me, he was but a word and a blow.
[*The Pilgrim's Progress* (1678), I]

11. Hanging is too good for him, said Mr Cruelty.
[*The Pilgrim's Progress* (1678), I]

12. [Mr By-Ends]
Yet my great-grandfather was but a water-man, looking one way, and rowing another: and I got most of my estate by the same occupation.
[*The Pilgrim's Progress* (1678), I. Cf. Robert Burton: 4]

13. They are for religion when in rags and contempt; but I am for him when he walks in his golden slippers, in the sunshine and with applause.
[*The Pilgrim's Progress* (1678), I]

14. A castle, called Doubting-Castle, the owner whereof was Giant Despair.
[*The Pilgrim's Progress* (1678), I]

15. Now Giant Despair had a wife, and her name was Diffidence.
[*The Pilgrim's Progress* (1678), I]

16. A grievous crab-tree cudgel.
[*The Pilgrim's Progress* (1678), I]

17. They came to the Delectable Mountains.
[*The Pilgrim's Progress* (1678), I]

18. Sleep is sweet to the labouring man.
[*The Pilgrim's Progress* (1678), I]

19. A great horror and darkness fell upon Christian.
[*The Pilgrim's Progress* (1678), I]

20. Then I saw there was a way to Hell, even from the gates of heaven.
[*The Pilgrim's Progress* (1678), I]

21. So I awoke, and behold it was a dream.
[*The Pilgrim's Progress* (1678), I, last lines]

22. ... a man that could look no way but downwards, with a muck-rake in his hand ... The man did neither look up nor regard, but raked to himself the straws, the small sticks, and dust of the floor.
[*The Pilgrim's Progress* (1678), II]

23. One leak will sink a ship, and one sin will destroy a sinner.
[*The Pilgrim's Progress* (1678), II]

24. A young Woman, her name was Dull.
[*The Pilgrim's Progress* (1678), II]

25. One Great-heart.
[*The Pilgrim's Progress* (1678), II]

26. He that is down needs fear no fall,
He that is low no pride.
He that is humble ever shall
Have God to be his guide.
[*The Pilgrim's Progress* (1678), II, 'Shepherd Boy's Song']

27. [Mr Fearing]
A very zealous man ... Difficulties, Lions, or Vanity-Fair he feared not at all; 'Twas only Sin, Death, and Hell that was to him a terror.
[*The Pilgrim's Progress* (1678), II]

28. A man there was, tho' some did count him mad,
The more he cast away, the more he had.
[*The Pilgrim's Progress* (1678), II]

29. Mercy ... laboured much for the Poor ... an ornament to her profession.
[*The Pilgrim's Progress* (1678), II]

30. Who would true valour see,
Let him come hither;
One here will constant be,
Come wind, come weather.
There's no discouragement
Shall make him once relent
His first avow'd intent
To be a pilgrim.

Who so beset him round
With dismal stories,
Do but themselves confound–
His strength the more is.
[*The Pilgrim's Progress* (1678), II]

31. The last words of Mr Despondency were, Farewell night, welcome day. His daughter went through the river singing, but none could understand what she said.
[*The Pilgrim's Progress* (1678), II]

32. [Mr Valiant-for-Truth]
Though with great difficulty I am got hither, yet now I do not repent me of all the trouble I have been at to arrive where I am. My sword, I give to him that shall succeed me in my pilgrimage, and my courage and skill to him that can get it. My marks and scars I carry with me, to be a witness for me, that I have fought his battles, who will now be my rewarder. So he passed over, and the trumpets sounded for him on the other side.
[*The Pilgrim's Progress* (1678), II]

33. [Mr Standfast]
I have formerly lived by hearsay, and faith, but now I go where I shall live by sight, and shall be with Him in whose company I delight myself.
[*The Pilgrim's Progress* (1678), II]

Burchard, Rev. Samuel Dickinson (1812–1891)
American Presbyterian minister

1. We are Republicans and don't propose to leave our party and identify ourselves with the party whose antecedents are rum, Romanism, and rebellion.
[Speech, New York City, 1884]

Burchill, Julie (1960–)
English journalist

1. Sex, on the whole, was meant to be short, nasty and brutish. If what you want is cuddling, you should buy a puppy.
[*Sex and Sensibility*]

2. Once people had sex; now they have babies. In the cinema, having a baby used to be the terrible price you paid for having sex – any night of the week in the early Sixties you could find Natalie Wood contemplating suicide on some drive-in screen because of the interesting condition Steve McQueen or Warren Beatty had left her in. Now, having sex is the terrible price you pay for having a baby.
[*Sex and Sensibility*]

Burgess, Anthony (John Burgess Wilson) (1917–1993)
English novelist, critic, teacher, linguist and composer

1. Tomorrow is all like sweet flowers and turning vommy earth and the stars and the old luna up there and your old droog Alex all on his oddy knocky seeking like a mate.
[*A Clockwork Orange* (1962)]

2. Let us have no nonsensical talk about merging and melting souls, though binary suns, two spheres in a single orbit. There is the flesh and the flesh makes all. Literature is an epiphenomenon of the action of the flesh.
[*Nothing like the Sun* (1964)]

3. We're too insignificant to be attacked by either the forces of light or the forces of darkness. And yet, playing the game, we occasionally let evil in. Evil tumbles in, unaware. But there is no good to fight the evil with. That's when one grows sick of the game and wants to resign from it.
[*Tremor of Intent* (1966)]

4. Bath twice a day to be really clean, once a day to be passably clean, once a week to avoid being a public menace.
[*Inside Mr Enderby* (1968), I, 2]

5. Rome's just a city like anywhere else. A vastly overrated city, I'd say. It trades on belief just as Stratford trades on Shakespeare.
[*Inside Mr Enderby* (1968), II, 2]

6. I know how foolish critics can be, being one myself.
[*The Observer*, 1980, in Jeffrey Care (ed.), *Sayings of the Eighties* (1989)]

7. The possession of a book becomes a substitute for reading it.
[*The New York Times Book Review*]

Burgess, Gelett (1866–1951)
American humorist; writer of light verse and stories

1. I never saw a Purple Cow,
I never hope to see one;
But I can tell you, anyhow,
I'd rather see than be one!
[*The Burgess Nonsense Book* (1914), 'The Purple Cow']

Burgon, John William (1813–1888)
English clergyman and Professor of Divinity

1. Match me such marvel save in Eastern clime,
A rose-red city 'half as old as Time'!
['Petra' (1845). Cf. Plomer: 4]

Burgoyne, General Sir John (1722–1792)
English general; Tory, later Whig, politician; dramatist

1. You have only, when before your glass, to keep pronouncing to yourself nimini-pimini – the lips cannot fail of taking their plie.
[*The Heiress* (1786)]

Burke, Edmund (1729–1797)
Irish-born British Whig statesman and political philosopher

1. The fabric of superstition has in our age and nation received much ruder shocks than it had ever felt before; and through the chinks and breaches of our prison we see such glimmerings of light, and feel such refreshing airs of liberty, as daily raise our ardour for more.
[*A Vindication of Natural Society* (1756)]

2. A good parson once said, that where mystery begins, religion ends. Cannot I say, as truly at least, of human laws, that where mystery begins, justice ends? It is hard to say whether the doctors of law or divinity have made the greater advance in the lucrative business of mystery.
[*A Vindication of Natural Society* (1756)]

3. There are others so continually in the agitation of gross and merely sensual pleasures, or so occupied in the low drudgery of avarice, or so heated in the chase of honours and distinction, that their minds, which had been used continually to the storms of these violent and tempestuous passions, can hardly be put in motion by the delicate and refined play of the imagination.
[*A Philosophical Enquiry into the Origin of our Ideas of the Sublime and Beautiful* (1757), Introduction]

4. I am convinced that we have a degree of delight, and that no small one, in the real misfortunes and pains of others.
[*A Philosophical Enquiry into the Origin of our Ideas of the Sublime and Beautiful* (1757)]

5. No passion so effectually robs the mind of all its powers of acting and reasoning as fear.
[*A Philosophical Enquiry into the Origin of our Ideas of the Sublime and Beautiful* (1757)]

6. Beauty in distress is much the most affecting beauty.
[*A Philosophical Enquiry into the Origin of our Ideas of the Sublime and Beautiful* (1757)]

7. Custom reconciles us to everything.
[*A Philosophical Enquiry into the Origin of our Ideas of the Sublime and Beautiful* (1757)]

8. Darkness is more productive of sublime ideas than light.
[*A Philosophical Enquiry into the Origin of our Ideas of the Sublime and Beautiful* (1757)]

9. There is, however, a limit at which forbearance ceases to be a virtue.
[*Observations on a late Publication intituled 'The Present State of the Nation'* (2nd ed., 1769)]

10. It is a general popular error to imagine the loudest complainers for the public to be the most anxious for its welfare.
[*Observations on a late Publication intituled 'The Present State of the Nation'* (2nd ed., 1769)]

11. People not very well grounded in the principles of public morality find a set of maxims in office ready made for them, which they assume as naturally and inevitably as any of the insignia or instruments of the situation. A certain tone of the solid and practical is immediately acquired. Every former profession of public spirit is to be considered as a debauch of youth, or, at best, as a visionary scheme of unattainable perfection. The very idea of consistency is exploded. The convenience of the business of the day is to furnish the principle for doing it.
[*Observations on a late Publication intituled 'The Present State of the Nation'* (2nd ed., 1769)]

12. To complain of the age we live in, to murmur at the present possessors of power, to lament the past, to conceive extravagant hopes of the future, are the common dispositions of the greatest part of mankind.
[*Thoughts on the Cause of the Present Discontents* (1770)]

13. I am not one of those who think that the people are never in the wrong. They have been so, frequently and outrageously, both in other countries and in this. But I do say, that in all disputes between them and their rulers, the presumption is at least upon a par in favour of the people.
[*Thoughts on the Cause of the Present Discontents* (1770)]

14. The power of the crown, almost dead and rotten as

Prerogative, has grown up anew, with much more strength, and far less odium, under the name of Influence.
[*Thoughts on the Cause of the Present Discontents* (1770)]

15. The circumstances are in a great measure new. We have hardly any landmarks from the wisdom of our ancestors to guide us.
[*Thoughts on the Cause of the Present Discontents* (1770)]

16. When bad men combine, the good must associate; else they will fall, one by one, an unpitied sacrifice in a contemptible struggle.
[*Thoughts on the Cause of the Present Discontents* (1770)]

17. It is therefore our business carefully to cultivate in our minds, to rear to the most perfect vigour and maturity, every sort of generous and honest feeling that belongs to our nature. To bring the dispositions that are lovely in private life into the service and conduct of the commonwealth; so to be patriots, as not to forget we are gentlemen.
[*Thoughts on the Cause of the Present Discontents* (1770)]

18. Would twenty shillings have ruined Mr Hampden's fortune? No! but the payment of half twenty shillings, on the principle it was demanded, would have made him a slave.
[*Speech on American Taxation* (1774)]

19. It is the nature of all greatness not to be exact.
[*Speech on American Taxation* (1774)]

20. Falsehood has a perennial spring.
[*Speech on American Taxation* (1774)]

21. Great men are the guide-posts and landmarks in the state.
[*Speech on American Taxation* (1774)]

22. [Of Charles Townshend]
He had no failings which were not owing to a noble cause; to an ardent, generous, perhaps an immoderate passion for fame; a passion which is the instinct of all great souls.
[*Speech on American Taxation* (1774)]

23. To tax and to please, no more than to love and to be wise, is not given to men.
[*Speech on American Taxation* (1774)]

24. I have in general no very exalted opinion of the virtue of paper government.
[*Speech on Conciliation with America* (1775)]

25. The concessions of the weak are the concessions of fear.
[*Speech on Conciliation with America* (1775)]

26. Young man, there is America – which at this day serves for little more than to amuse you with stories of savage men, and uncouth manners; yet shall, before you taste of death, show itself equal to the whole of that commerce which now attracts the envy of the world.
[*Speech on Conciliation with America* (1775)]

27. The use of force alone is but temporary. It may subdue for a moment; but it does not remove the necessity of subduing again: and a nation is not governed, which is perpetually to be conquered.
[*Speech on Conciliation with America* (1775)]

28. Nothing less will content me, than whole America.
[*Speech on Conciliation with America* (1775)]

29. Abstract liberty, like other mere abstractions, is not to be found.
[*Speech on Conciliation with America* (1775)]

30. All protestantism, even the most cold and passive, is a sort of dissent. But the religion most prevalent in our northern colonies is a refinement on the principle of resistance; it is the dissidence of dissent, and the protestantism of the protestant religion.
[*Speech on Conciliation with America* (1775)]

31. In no country perhaps in the world is the law so general a study ... This study renders men acute, inquisitive, dexterous, prompt in attack, ready in defence, full of resources ... They augur misgovernment at a distance, and snuff the approach of tyranny in every tainted breeze.
[*Speech on Conciliation with America* (1775)]

32. I do not know the method of drawing up an indictment against an whole people.
[*Speech on Conciliation with America* (1775)]

33. It is not, what a lawyer tells me I may do; but what humanity, reason, and justice, tell me I ought to do.
[*Speech on Conciliation with America* (1775)]

34. Govern two millions of men, impatient of servitude, on the principles of freedom.
[*Speech on Conciliation with America* (1775)]

35. The march of the human mind is slow.
[*Speech on Conciliation with America* (1775)]

36. Freedom and not servitude is the cure of anarchy; as religion, and not atheism, is the true remedy for superstition.
[*Speech on Conciliation with America* (1775)]

37. All government, indeed every human benefit and enjoyment, every virtue, and every prudent act, is founded on compromise and barter.
[*Speech on Conciliation with America* (1775)]

38. Instead of a standing revenue, you will have therefore a perpetual quarrel.
[*Speech on Conciliation with America* (1775)]

39. Parties must ever exist in a free country.
[*Speech on Conciliation with America* (1775)]

40. My hold of the colonies is in the close affection which grows from common names, from kindred blood, from similar privileges, and equal protection. These are ties which, though light as air, are as strong as links of iron.
[*Speech on Conciliation with America* (1775)]

41. Slavery they can have anywhere. It is a weed that grows in every soil.
[*Speech on Conciliation with America* (1775)]

42. Deny them this participation of freedom, and you break that sole bond, which originally made, and must still preserve the unity of the empire.
[*Speech on Conciliation with America* (1775)]

43. Magnanimity in politics is not seldom the truest wisdom; and a great empire and little minds go ill together.
[*Speech on Conciliation with America* (1775)]

44. I know many have been taught to think that moderation, in a case like this, is a sort of treason.
[*Letter to the Sheriffs of Bristol on the Affairs of America* (1777)]

45. Liberty, too, must be limited in order to be possessed.
[*Letter to the Sheriffs of Bristol on the Affairs of America* (1777)]

46. Among a people generally corrupt, liberty cannot long exist.
[*Letter to the Sheriffs of Bristol on the Affairs of America* (1777)]

47. Bad laws are the worst sort of tyranny.
[*Speech at Bristol, previous to the Late Election* (1780)]

48. I flatter myself that I love a manly, moral, regulated liberty as well as any gentleman.
[*Reflections on the Revolution in France and on the Proceedings in Certain Societies in London* (1790)]

49. Whenever our neighbour's house is on fire, it cannot be amiss for the engines to play a little on our own.
[*Reflections on the Revolution in France and on the Proceedings in Certain Societies in London* (1790)]

50. Politics and the pulpit are terms that have little agreement. No sound ought to be heard in the church but the healing voice of Christian charity.
[*Reflections on the Revolution in France and on the Proceedings in Certain Societies in London* (1790)]

51. A state without the means of some change is without the means of its conservation.
[*Reflections on the Revolution in France and on the Proceedings in Certain Societies in London* (1790)]

52. Make the Revolution a parent of settlement, and not a nursery of future revolutions.
[*Reflections on the Revolution in France and on the Proceedings in Certain Societies in London* (1790)]

53. People will not look forward to posterity, who never look backward to their ancestors.
[*Reflections on the Revolution in France and on the Proceedings in Certain Societies in London* (1790)]

54. Government is a contrivance of human wisdom to provide for human wants. Men have a right that these wants should be provided for by this wisdom.
[*Reflections on the Revolution in France and on the Proceedings in Certain Societies in London* (1790)]

55. It is now sixteen or seventeen years since I saw the queen of France, then the dauphiness, at Versailles; and surely never lighted on this orb, which she hardly seemed to touch, a more delightful vision. I saw her just above the horizon, decorating and cheering the elevated sphere she just began to move in, – glittering like the morning-star, full of life, and splendour, and joy. Oh! what a revolution! and what a heart I must have, to contemplate without emotion that elevation and that fall! Little did I dream when she added titles of veneration to those of enthusiastick, distant, respectful love, that she should ever be obliged to carry the sharp antidote against disgrace concealed in that bosom; little did I dream that I should have lived to see disasters fallen upon her in a nation of gallant men, in a nation of men of honour, and of cavaliers. I thought ten thousand swords must have leaped from their scabbards to avenge even a look that threatened her with insult. But the age of chivalry is gone. That of sophisters, economists, and calculators, has succeeded; and the glory of Europe is extinguished for ever.
[*Reflections on the Revolution in France and on the Proceedings in Certain Societies in London* (1790)]

56. This barbarous philosophy, which is the offspring of cold hearts and muddy understandings.
[*Reflections on the Revolution in France and on the Proceedings in Certain Societies in London* (1790)]

57. In the groves of their academy, at the end of every vista, you see nothing but the gallows.
[*Reflections on the Revolution in France and on the Proceedings in Certain Societies in London* (1790)]

58. Kings will be tyrants from policy, when subjects are rebels from principle.
[*Reflections on the Revolution in France and on the Proceedings in Certain Societies in London* (1790)]

59. Learning will be cast into the mire, and trodden down under the hoofs of a swinish multitude.
[*Reflections on the Revolution in France and on the Proceedings in Certain Societies in London* (1790)]

60. Because half a dozen grasshoppers under a fern make the field ring with their importunate chink, whilst thousands of great cattle, reposed beneath the shadow of the British oak, chew the cud and are silent, pray do not imagine that those who make the noise are the only inhabitants of the field; that, of course, they are many in number; or that, after all, they are other than the little, shrivelled, meagre, hopping, though loud and troublesome insects of the hour.
[*Reflections on the Revolution in France and on the Proceedings in Certain Societies in London* (1790)]

61. Who now reads Bolingbroke? Who ever read him through? Ask the booksellers of London what is become of all these lights of the world.
[*Reflections on the Revolution in France and on the Proceedings in Certain Societies in London* (1790)]

62. Man is by his constitution a religious animal; ... atheism is against, not only our reason, but our instincts.
[*Reflections on the Revolution in France and on the Proceedings in Certain Societies in London* (1790)]

63. A perfect democracy is therefore the most shameless thing in the world.
[*Reflections on the Revolution in France and on the Proceedings in Certain Societies in London* (1790)]

64. Nobility is a graceful ornament to the civil order. It is the Corinthian capital of polished society.
[*Reflections on the Revolution in France and on the Proceedings in Certain Societies in London* (1790)]

65. Superstition is the religion of feeble minds.
[*Reflections on the Revolution in France and on the Proceedings in Certain Societies in London* (1790)]

66. He that wrestles with us strengthens our nerves, and sharpens our skill. Our antagonist is our helper.
[*Reflections on the Revolution in France and on the Proceedings in Certain Societies in London* (1790)]

67. Our patience will achieve more than our force.
[*Reflections on the Revolution in France and on the Proceedings in Certain Societies in London* (1790)]

68. Good order is the foundation of all good things.
[*Reflections on the Revolution in France and on the Proceedings in Certain Societies in London* (1790)]

69. The conduct of a losing party never appears right: at least it never can possess the only infallible criterion of wisdom to vulgar judgments – success.
[*Letter to a Member of the National Assembly* (1791)]

70. Those who have been once intoxicated with power, and have derived any kind of emolument from it, even though but for one year, never can willingly abandon it.
[*Letter to a Member of the National Assembly* (1791)]

71. Tyrants seldom want pretexts.
[*Letter to a Member of the National Assembly* (1791)]

72. You can never plan the future by the past.
[*Letter to a Member of the National Assembly* (1791)]

73. The cold neutrality of an impartial judge.
[Burke's Preface to J.P. Brissot, *To his Constituents* (1794)]

74. These gentle historians; on the contrary, dip their pens in nothing but the milk of human kindness.
[*A Letter to a Noble Lord* (1796)]

75. The storm has gone over me; and I lie like one of those old oaks which the late hurricane has scattered about me. I am stripped of all my honours, I am torn up by the roots, and lie prostrate on the earth!
[*A Letter to a Noble Lord* (1796)]

76. The king, and his faithful subjects, the lords and commons of this realm, – the triple cord, which no man can break.
[*A Letter to a Noble Lord* (1796)]

77. If we command our wealth, we shall be rich and free: if our wealth commands us, we are poor indeed.
[*Two Letters on the Proposals for Peace with the Regicide Directory of France* (9th ed., 1796), Letter 1]

78. All men that are ruined are ruined on the side of their natural propensities.
[*Two Letters on the Proposals for Peace with the Regicide Directory of France* (9th ed., 1796), Letter 1]

79. Example is the school of mankind, and they will learn at no other.
[*Two Letters on the Proposals for Peace with the Regicide Directory of France* (9th ed., 1796), Letter 1]

80. Well is it known that ambition can creep as well as soar.
[*Third Letter . . . on the Proposals for Peace with the Regicide Directory of France* (1797)]

81. And having looked to government for bread, on the very first scarcity they will turn and bite the hand that fed them.
[*Thoughts and Details on Scarcity* (1800)]

82. Laws, like houses, lean on one another.
[*Tracts on the Popery Laws* (1812), 3]

83. In all forms of Government the people is the true legislator.
[*Tracts on the Popery Laws* (1812), 3]

84. I would rather sleep in the southern corner of a little country church-yard, than in the tomb of the Capulets. I should like, however, that my dust should mingle with kindred dust.
[Letter to Matthew Smith, 1750]

85. People crushed by law have no hopes but from power. If laws are their enemies, they will be enemies to laws; and those who have much to hope and nothing to lose will always be dangerous more or less.
[Letter to the Hon. Charles James Fox, 1777]

86. The arrogance of age must submit to be taught by youth.
[Letter to Fanny Burney, 1782]

87. Nothing is so fatal to religion as indifference, which is, at least, half infidelity.
[Letter to William Smith, 1795]

88. The silent touches of time.
[Letter to William Smith, 1795]

89. Somebody has said, that a king may make a nobleman but he cannot make a Gentleman.
[Letter to William Smith, 1795]

90. The grand Instructor, Time.
[Letter to Sir Hercules Langrishe, 1795]

91. The greater the power, the more dangerous the abuse.
[Speech on the Middlesex election, 1771]

92. The only liberty I mean, is a liberty connected with order; that not only exists along with order and virtue, but which cannot exist at all without them.
[Speech on his arrival at Bristol, 1774]

93. Your representative owes you, not his industry only, but his judgement; and he betrays, instead of serving you, if he sacrifices it to your opinion.
[Speech to the Electors of Bristol, 1774]

94. Parliament is not a congress of ambassadors from different and hostile interests; which interests each must maintain, as an agent and advocate, against other agents and advocates; but parliament is a deliberative assembly of one nation, with one interest, that of the whole; where, not local purposes, not local prejudices ought to guide, but the general good, resulting from the general reason of the whole. You choose a member indeed; but when you have chosen him, he is not member of Bristol, but he is a member of parliament.
[Speech to the Electors of Bristol, 1774]

95. Kings are naturally lovers of low company.
[Speech, House of Commons, 1780]

96. Applaud us when we run; console us when we fall; cheer us when we recover; but let us pass on – for God's sake, let us pass on!
[Speech on the Economical Reform, 1780]

97. Every other conqueror of every other description has left some monument, either of state or beneficence, behind him. Were we to be driven out of India this day, nothing would remain to tell that it had been possessed, during the inglorious period of our dominion, by anything better than the orang-outang or the tiger.
[Speech on Fox's East India Bill, 1783]

98. The people never give up their liberties but under some delusion.
[Speech at Buckinghamshire County Meeting, 1784]

99. Religious persecution may shield itself under the guide of a mistaken and over-zealous piety.
[Speech on the impeachment of Warren Hastings, 1788]

100. A thing may look specious in theory, and yet be ruinous in practice; a thing may look evil in theory, and yet be in practice excellent.
[Speech on the impeachment of Warren Hastings, 1788]

101. An event has happened, upon which it is difficult to speak, and impossible to be silent.
[Speech on the impeachment of Warren Hastings, 1789]

102. Dangers by being despised grow great.
[Speech on the Petition of the Unitarians, 1792]

103. There is but one law for all, namely, that law which governs all law – the law of our Creator, the law of humanity, justice, equity, the law of nature, and of nations.
[Speech on the impeachment of Warren Hastings, 1794]

104. I impeach him in the name of the people of India, whose rights he has trodden under foot, and whose country he has turned into a desert. Lastly, in the name of human nature itself, in the name of both sexes, in the name of every age, in the name of every rank, I impeach the common enemy and oppressor of all!
[Impeachment of Warren Hastings, as recorded by Macaulay in his essay 'Warren Hastings' (1841)]

105. [Comment on the younger Pitt's first Speech, 1781]
Not merely a chip off the old 'block', but the old block itself.
[In N.W. Wraxall, *Historical Memoirs of My Own Time* (1904 ed.)]

106. [Remark to Boswell]
'No, no', said he, 'it is not a good imitation of Johnson; it has all his pomp, without his force; it has all the nodosities of the oak without its strength; it has all the contortions of the Sibyl without the inspiration.'
[Attr.]

107. The only thing necessary for the triumph of evil is for good men to do nothing.
[Attr.]

Burke, Johnny (1908–1964)
American songwriter

1. Don't you know each cloud contains
Pennies from Heaven?
['Pennies from Heaven', song, 1936]

Burke, Robert O'Hara (1821–1861)
First man, with William John Wills, to cross Australia from south to north

1. [To a dancing partner who spoke disparagingly of fellow-guests as fortune-seekers]
Why, my dear Mrs G–, did not you and I come out here because we could not get so good a living at home?
[In John Sadler, *Recollections of a Victorian Police Officer*]

Burleigh, William Cecil, Lord (1520–1598)
English statesman; courtier, politician and Lord High Treasurer

1. [To Queen Elizabeth, when ordered to give a pension of £100 to the poet Spenser]
What! all this for a song?
[In Birch, *Life of Spenser*]

Burne-Jones, Sir Edward (1833–1898)
English painter, illustrator and designer in the Pre-Raphaelite tradition

1. I mean by a picture a beautiful, romantic dream of something that never was, never will be – in a light better than any lights that ever shone – in a land no one can define or remember, only desire – and the forms divinely beautiful – and then I wake up, with the waking of Brynhild.
[Letter]

Burnet, Sir Frank Macfarlane (1899–1985)
Australian medical research specialist

1. The idea of man as the dominant mammal of the earth whose whole behaviour tends to be dominated by his own desire for dominance gripped me. It seemed to explain almost everything, and I applied it to everything.
[*Dominant Mammal* (1970)]

2. In an affluent society most healthy women would like to have four healthy children.
[*Dominant Mammal* (1970)]

Burney, Fanny (Mme d'Arblay) (1752–1840)
English novelist, diarist and letter-writer

1. 'Do you come to the play without knowing what it is?' 'Oh, yes, sir, yes, very frequently. I have no time to read play-bills. One merely comes to meet one's friends, and show that one's alive.'
[*Evelina* (1778), 20]

2. Nothing is so delicate as the reputation of a woman; it is at once the most beautiful and most brittle of all human things.
[*Evelina* (1778), 39]

3. Now I am ashamed of confessing that I have nothing to confess.
[*Evelina* (1778), 59]

4. Dancing? Oh, dreadful! How it was ever adopted in a civilized country I cannot find out; 'tis certainly a Barbarian exercise, and of savage origin.
[*Cecilia* (1782), 3]

5. Travelling is the ruin of all happiness! There's no looking at a building here after seeing Italy.
[*Cecilia* (1782), 4]

6. One really lives nowhere; one does but vegetate, and wish it all at an end.
[*Cecilia* (1782), 7]

7. Indeed, the freedom with which Dr Johnson condemns whatever he disapproves is astonishing.
[*Diary*, 23 August, 1778]

8. All the delusive seduction of martial music.
[*Diary*, 5–6 May, 1802]

Burns, George (1896–)
American comedian

1. Too bad all the people who know how to run the country are busy driving cabs and cutting hair.
[Attr.]

Burns, John (1858–1943)
English trade-unionist, socialist and Liberal politician

1. I have seen the Mississippi. That is muddy water. I have seen the St Lawrence. That is crystal water. But the Thames is liquid history.
[Attr.]

Burns, Robert (1759–1796)
Scottish poet, song-writer and collector; Scotland's national bard

1. There was three kings into the east,
Three kings both great and high,
And they hae sworn a solemn oath
John Barleycorn should die.
['John Barleycorn' (1782); development of an ancient folk ballad]

2. What signifies the life o' man,
An' 'twere na for the lasses, O...

3. Green grow the rashes, O;
Green grow the rashes, O;
The sweetest hours that e'er I spend,
Are spent among the lasses, O...

4. But gie me a cannie hour at e'en,
My arms about my dearie, O,
An' war'ly cares an' war'ly men
May a' gae tapsalteerie, O!...

5. The wisest man the warl' e'er saw,
He dearly lov'd the lasses, O...

   Auld nature swears, the lovely dears
Her noblest work she classes, O:
Her prentice han' she try'd on man,
An' then she made the lasses, O.
['Green Grow the Rashes' (1783)]

6. ... Nature's law,
That Man was made to mourn...

7. Man's inhumanity to man
Makes countless thousands mourn!...

8. If I'm design'd yon lordling's slave–
By Nature's law design'd–
Why was an independent wish
E'er planted in my mind?...

9. O death, the poor man's dearest friend,
The kindest and the best!
['Man was made to Mourn, a Dirge' (1784)]

10. O Thou! whatever title suit thee–
Auld Hornie, Satan, Nick, or Clootie.
['Address to the Deil' (1785)]

11. Th' expectant wee-things, toddlin, stacher through
To meet their dad, wi' flichterin' noise and glee.
His wee bit ingle, blinkin bonilie,

His clean hearth-stane, his thrifty wifie's smile,
The lisping infant, prattling on his knee,
Does a' his weary carking cares beguile,
And makes him quite forget his labor and his toil...

12. The healsome parritch, chief o' Scotia's food...

13. The sire turns o'er, wi' patriarchal grace,
The big ha'-Bible, ance his father's pride...

14. From scenes like these, old Scotia's grandeur springs
That makes her lov'd at home, rever'd abroad:
Princes and lords are but the breath of kings,
'An honest man's the noblest work of God.'
['The Cotter's Saturday Night' (1785)]

15. I was na fou, but just had plenty.
['Death and Dr Hornbook' (1785)]

16. The heart ay's the part ay
That makes us right or wrang.
['Epistle to Davie, a Brother Poet' (1785)]

17. What's a' your jargon o' your Schools,
Your Latin names for horns an' stools?
If honest Nature made you fools,
What sairs your grammers...

18. Gie me ae spark o' Nature's fire,
That's a' the learning I desire.
['First Epistle to Lapraik' (1785)]

19. O Thou that in the Heavens does dwell,
Wha, as it pleases best Thysel,
Sends ane to Heaven, an' ten to Hell,
A' for Thy glory,
And no for onie guid or ill
They've done before Thee!...

20. Yet I am here, a chosen sample,
To show Thy grace is great and ample:
I'm here a pillar o' Thy temple,
Strong as a rock,
A guide, a buckler, and example
To a' Thy flock!

But yet, O Lord! confess I must,
At times I'm fash'd wi' fleshly lust;
An' sometimes, too, in warldy trust,
Vile self gets in;
But Thou remembers we are dust,
Defiled wi' sin.
['Holy Willie's Prayer' (1785)]

21. I once was a maid, tho' I cannot tell when,
And still my delight is in proper young men...

22. Poor Andrew that tumbles for sport
Let naebody name wi' a jeer:
There's even, I'm tauld, i' the Court
A tumbler ca'd the Premier...

23. But Och! they catch'd him at the last,
And bound him in a dungeon fast.
My curse upon them every one–
They've hang'd my braw John Highlandman!...

24. Partly wi' love o'ercome sae sair,
An' partly she was drunk...

25. [Of women]
Their tricks an' craft hae put me daft,
They've taen me in, an a' that;
But clear your decks, an' here's the Sex!
I like the jads for a' that...

26. A fig for those by law protected!
Liberty's a glorious feast,
Courts for cowards were erected,
Churches built to please the priest...

27. Life is all a variorum,
We regard not how it goes;
Let them prate about decorum,
Who have character to lose.
['The Jolly Beggars' (1785); also known as 'Love and Liberty – A Cantata']

28. For thus the royal mandate ran,
When first the human race began:
'The social, friendly, honest man,
Whate'er he be,
'Tis he fulfils great Nature's plan,
And none but he.'
['Second Epistle to Lapraik' (1785)]

29. Hail, Poesie! thou nymph reserv'd!
In chase o' thee, what crowds hae swerv'd
Frae Common Sense, or sunk ennerv'd
'Mang heaps o' clavers;
And Och! o'er aft thy joes hae starv'd
'Mid a' thy favors!
['Sketch' (c. 1784–85)]

30. He'll hae misfortunes great an' sma',
But ay a heart aboon them a'.
['There was a Lad' (1785)]

31. Wee, sleekit, cowrin, tim'rous beastie,
O, what a panic's in thy breastie!
Thou need na start awa sae hasty,
Wi' bickering brattle!
I wad be laith to rin an' chase thee,
Wi' murdering pattle!

I'm truly sorry man's dominion
Has broken Nature's social union,
An' justifies that ill opinion
Which makes thee startle
At me, thy poor, earth-born companion
An' fellow mortal!...

32. The best-laid schemes o' mice an' men
Gang aft agley,
An' lea'e us nought but grief an' pain,
For promis'd joy!
['To a Mouse' (1785)]

33. Their sighin, cantin, grace-proud faces,
Their three-mile prayers, an' hauf-mile graces.
['To the Rev. John M. Math' (1785)]

34. But yet the light that led astray
Was light from Heaven.
['The Vision' (1785), Duan Second]

35. Fair fa' your honest, sonsie face,
Great chieftain o' the puddin-race!
Aboon them a' ye tak your place,
Painch, tripe, or thairm:
Weel are ye wordy of a grace
As lang's my arm...

36. His spindle shank a guid whip-lash,
His nieve a nit.
['Address to a Haggis' (1786)]

37. Then gently scan your brother man,
Still gentler sister woman;
Tho' they may gang a kennin wrang,
To step aside is human.
['Address to the Unco Guid' (1786)]

38. Freedom and whisky gang thegither,
Tak aff your dram!
['The Author's Earnest Cry and Prayer' (1786)]

39. On ev'ry hand it will allow'd be,
He's just – nae better than he should be.
['A Dedication to Gavin Hamilton' (1786)]

40. But facts are chiels that winna ding,
And downa be disputed.
['A Dream' (1786)]

41. Just now I've taen the fit o' rhyme,
My barmie noddle's working prime...

42. Some rhyme a neebor's name to lash;
Some rhyme (vain thought!) for needfu' cash;
Some rhyme to court the countra clash,
An' raise a din;
For me, an aim I never fash;
I rhyme for fun...

43. An' fareweel dear, deluding Woman,
The joy of joys!
['Epistle to James Smith' (1786)]

44. Perhaps it may turn out a sang;
Perhaps, turn out a sermon...

45. But still keep something to yoursel
Ye scarcely tell to onie...

46. I waive the quantum o' the sin,
The hazard of concealing;
But, och! it hardens a' within,
And petrifies the feeling!...

47. An atheist-laugh's a poor exchange
For Deity offended!
['Epistle to a Young Friend' (1786)]

48. Here some are thinkin' on their sins,
An' some upo' their claes...

49. Leeze me on drink! it gies us mair
Than either school or college;
It kindles wit, it waukens lear,
It pangs us fou o' knowledge...

50. There's some are fou o' love divine;
There's some are fou o' brandy;
An' monie jobs that day begin,
May end in houghmagandie
Some ither day.
['The Holy Fair' (1786)]

51. Wae worth thy power, thou cursed leaf!
Fell source of a' my woe and grief,
For lack o' thee I've lost my lass,
For lack o' thee I scrimp my glass!
['Lines written on a Bank Note' (1786)]

52. O wad some Power the giftie gie us
To see oursels as ithers see us!
It wad frae monie a blunder free us,
An' foolish notion:
What airs in dress an' gait wad lea'e us,
An' ev'n devotion!
['To a Louse' (1786)]

53. Ev'n thou who mourn'st the Daisy's fate,
That fate is thine – no distant date;
Stern Ruin's plough-share drives elate,
Full on thy bloom,
Till crush'd beneath the furrow's weight
Shall be thy doom!
['To A Mountain Daisy' (1786)]

54. His lockèd, letter'd, braw brass collar
Shew'd him the gentleman an' scholar...

55. An' there began a lang digression
About the 'lords o' the creation'...

56. I see how folk live that hae riches;
But surely poor-folk maun be wretches!...

57. But human bodies are sic fools,
For a' their colleges an' schools,
That when nae real ills perplex them,
They mak enow themsels to vex them.
['The Twa Dogs' (1786)]

58. Here lie Willie Michie's banes:
O Satan, when ye tak him,
Gie him the schulin' o' your weans,
For clever Deils he'll mak them!
['Epitaph for William Michie. Schoolmaster of Cleish Parish, Fifeshire' (1787)]

59. An idiot race, to honour lost–
Who know them best despise them most.
['On Seeing the Royal Palace at Stirling in Ruins' (1787)]

60. That I for poor auld Scotland's sake
Some usefu' plan or book could make,
Or sing a sang at least.
['To the Guidwife of Wauchope House' (1787)]

61. Cease, ye prudes, your envious railing!
Lovely Burns has charms: confess!
True it is she had ae failing:
Had ae woman ever less?
['Under the Portrait of Miss Burns' (1787)]

62. A man may drink, and no be drunk;
A man may fight, and no be slain;
A man may kiss a bonie lass,
And ay be welcome back again!
['Duncan Davison' (1788)]

63. A Gentleman who held the patent for his honours immediately from Almighty God.
['Elegy on Captain Matthew Henderson' (1788)]

64. May coward shame distain his name,
The wretch that dare not die!
['McPherson's Farewell' (1788)]

65. Of a' the airts the wind can blaw
I dearly like the west.
['Of a' the Airts' (1788)]

66. Go, fetch to me a pint o' wine,
And fill it in a silver tassie.
['The Silver Tassie' (1788)]

67. Up in the morning's no' for me,
Up in the morning early!
['Up in the Morning Early' (1788)]

68. Whistle o'er the lave o't!
['Whistle o'er the Lave o't' (1788)]

69. Should auld acquaintance be forgot,
And never brought to mind?...

70. And there's a hand, my trusty fiere!
And gie's a hand o' thine!...

71. We'll tak' a cup o' kindness yet,
For auld lang syne.
['Auld Lang Syne' (c. 1788)]

72. Flow gently, sweet Afton, among thy green braes!
Flow gently, I'll sing thee a song in thy praise!

My Mary's asleep by thy murmuring stream–
Flow gently, sweet Afton, disturb not her dream!
['Sweet Afton' (composed before February 1789)]

73. To make a happy fireside clime
To weans and wife,
That's the true pathos and sublime
Of human life.
['Epistle to Dr Blacklock' (1789)]

74. Hear, Land o' Cakes, and brither Scots...

75. A chield's amang you takin notes,
And faith he'll prent it.
['On the Late Captain Grose's Peregrinations Thro' Scotland' (1789)]

76. We are na fou, we're nae that fou,
But just a drappie in our e'e!
The cock may craw, the day may daw,
And ay we'll taste the barley-bree!
['Willie Brew'd a Peck o' Maut' (1789)]

77. Sleep I can get nane
For thinking on my dearie.
['Ay Waukin O' (1790)]

78. Some have meat and cannot eat,
Some cannot eat that want it:
But we have meat and we can eat,
Sae let the Lord be thankit.
['Burns Grace at Kirkcudbright' (1790); also known as 'The Selkirk Grace']

79. John Anderson my jo, John,
When we were first acquent,
Your locks were like the raven,
Your bonie brow was brent...

John Anderson, my jo, John,
We clamb the hills thegither;
And mony a cantie day, John,
We've had wi ane anither;
Now we maun totter down, John:
And hand in hand we'll go,
And sleep thegither at the foot,
John Anderson, my jo.
['John Anderson My Jo' (1790)]

80. My heart's in the Highlands, my heart is not here,
My heart's in the Highlands a-chasing the deer,
A-chasing the wild deer and following the roe–
My heart's in the Highlands, wherever I go!...

81. Farewell to the Highlands, farewell to the North,
The birthplace of valour, the country of worth!
['My Heart's in the Highlands' (1790)]

82. The minister kiss't the fiddler's wife–
He could na preach for thinkin o't!
['My Love she's but a Lassie yet' (1790)]

83. When chapman billies leave the street,
And drouthy neebors neebors meet;
As market days are wearing late,
An' folk begin to tak the gate;
While we sit bousing at the nappy,
An' getting fou and unco happy,
We think na on the lang Scots miles,
The mosses, waters, slaps, and styles,
That lie between us and our hame,
Whare sits our sulky, sullen dame,
Gathering her brows like gathering storm,
Nursing her wrath to keep it warm...

84. Auld Ayr, wham ne'er a town surpasses
For honest men and bonnie lasses...

85. Ah! gentle dames, it gars me greet,
To think how monie counsels sweet,
How monie lengthen'd, sage advices
The husband frae the wife despises!

But to our tale: – Ae market night,
Tam had got planted unco right;
Fast by an ingle, bleezing finely,
Wi' reaming swats, that drank divinely
And at his elbow, Souter Johnny,
His ancient, trusty, drouthy cronie:
Tam lo'ed him like a very brither;
They had been fou for weeks thegither...

86. Kings may be blest but Tam was glorious,
O'er a' the ills o' life victorious!

But pleasures are like poppies spread:
You seize the flow'r, its bloom is shed;
Or like the snow falls in the river,
A moment white – then melts for ever;
Or like the Borealis race,
That flit ere you can point their place;
Or like the rainbow's lovely form
Evanishing amid the storm.
Nae man can tether time or tide;
The hour approaches Tam maun ride;
That hour, o' night's black arch the keystane...

87. Inspiring, bold John Barleycorn!
What dangers thou canst make us scorn!
Wi' tippenny, we fear nae evil;
Wi' usquabae, we'll face the Devil!...

88. As Tammie glowr'd, amaz'd, and curious,
The mirth and fun grew fast and furious;
The piper loud and louder blew,
The dancers quick and quicker flew,
They reel'd, they set, they cross'd, they cleekit,
Till ilka carlin swat and reekit,
And coost her duddies to the wark,
And linket at it in her sark!...

89. Even Satan glowr'd, and fidg'd fu' fain,
And hotch'd and blew wi' might and main;
Till first ae caper, syne anither,
Tam tint his reason a' thegither,
And roars out, 'Weel done, Cutty-sark!'
And in an instant all was dark...

90. Ah, Tam! Ah, Tam! thou'll get thy fairin!
In hell they'll roast thee like a herrin!...

91. Now, wha this tale o' truth shall read,
Ilk man and mother's son, take heed:
Whene'er to drink you are inclin'd,
Or cutty sarks run in your mind,
Think! ye may buy the joys o'er dear,
Remember Tam o' Shanter's mare.
['Tam o' Shanter' (1790)]

92. Ae fond kiss, and then we sever!
Ae fareweel, and then forever!...

93. But to see her was to love her,
Love but her, and love for ever...

Had we never lov'd sae kindly,
Had we never lov'd sae blindly,
Never met – or never parted–
We had ne'er been broken-hearted.
['Ae Fond Kiss' (1791)]

94. I've seen sae monie changefu' years,
On earth I am a stranger grown:
I wander in the ways of men,

Alike unknowing and unknown.
['Lament for James, Earl of Glencairn' (1791)]

95. What can a young lassie,
What shall a young lassie,
What can a young lassie
Do wi' an auld man?
['What can a Young Lassie do wi' an Auld Man' (1791)]

96. Ye banks and braes o' bonny Doon,
How can ye bloom sae fresh and fair?
How can ye chant, ye little birds,
And I sae weary fu' o' care?...

97. Thou minds me o' departed joys,
Departed never to return...

98. And my fause lover stole my rose,
But ah! he left the thorn wi' me.
['Ye Banks and Braes o' Bonny Doon' (1791)]

99. But the ae best dance ere cam to the land
Was The Deil's Awa wi' th' Exciseman!
['The Deil's Awa wi' th' Exciseman' (1792)]

100. It's guid to be merry and wise,
It's guid to be honest and true,
It's guid to support Caledonia's cause
And bide by the buff and the blue.
['Here's a Health to Them that's Awa' (1792)]

101. The golden hours on angel wings
Flew o'er me and my dearie:
For dear to me as light and life
Was my sweet Highland Mary.
['Highland Mary' (1792)]

102. O Luve will venture in where it daur na weel be seen!
['The Posie' (1792)]

103. O, saw ye bonie Lesley,
As she gaed o'er the Border?
She's gane, like Alexander,
To spread her conquests farther!

To see her is to love her,
And love but her for ever;
For Nature made her what she is,
And never made anither!
['Saw Ye Bonie Lesley' (1792)]

104. Her nose and chin they threaten ither.
['Willie Wastle' (1792); alternatively known as 'Sic a Wife as Willie's Wife']

105. The wan moon sets behind the white wave,
And Time is setting with me, O.
['Open the Door to Me, O' (1793)]

106. O, whistle an' I'll come to ye, my lad!
O, whistle an' I'll come to ye, my lad!
Tho' father an' mither an' a' should gae mad,
O, whistle an' I'll come to ye, my lad!
['O, Whistle, an' I'll come to ye, my Lad' (1793)]

107. Scots, wha hae wi' Wallace bled,
Scots, wham Bruce has aften led,
Welcome to your gory bed
Or to victorie!

Now's the day, and now's the hour:
See the front o' battle lour,
See approach proud Edward's power–
Chains and slaverie!...

108. By Oppression's woes and pains,
By your sons in servile chains,
We will drain our dearest veins
But they shall be free!

Lay the proud usurpers low!
Tyrants fall in ev'ry foe!
Liberty's in every blow!
Let us do, or die!
['Scots, Wha Hae' (1793); also known as 'Robert Bruce's March to Bannockburn']

109. An' Charlie he's my darling,
My darling, my darling,
Charlie he's my darling–
The Young Chevalier!
['Charlie, He's my Darling' (1794). Cf. Hogg: 3 and Nairne: 3]

110. Contented wi' little and cantie wi' mair,
Whene'er I forgather wi' Sorrow and Care,
I gie them a skelp, as they're creepin alang,
Wi' a cog o' guid swats and an auld Scottish sang.
['Contented wi' Little and Cantie wi' Mair' (1794)]

111. It was a' for our rightfu' king
We left fair Scotland's strand...

112. The soger frae the wars returns,
The sailor frae the main,
But I hae parted frae my love
Never to meet again,
My dear–
Never to meet again.
['It was a' for our Rightfu' King' (1794)]

113. O, my luve's like a red, red, rose
That's newly sprung in June.
O, my luve's like the melodie,
That's sweetly play'd in tune.
['A Red Red Rose' (1794)]

114. Who will not sing God save the King
Shall hang as high's the steeple;
But while we sing God save the King,
We'll ne'er forget the People!
['Does Haughty Gaul Invasion Threat?' (1795)]

115. The rank is but the guinea's stamp,
The man's the gowd for a' that...

116. For a' that, an' a' that,
It's comin yet for a' that,
That man to man the world o'er
Shall brithers be for a' that.
['A Man's a Man for a' that' (1795); also known by the title 'Is There for Honest Poverty']

117. There's Death in the cup, so beware!
['On a Goblet' (1795)]

118. She draigl't a' her petticoatie,
Comin thro' the rye!...

119. Gin a body meet a body
Comin thro' the rye,
Gin a body kiss a body,
Need a body cry?
['Comin Thro' the Rye' (1796)]

120. O, gie me the lass that has acres o' charms!
O, gie me the lass wi' the weel-stockit farms!
['A Lass wi' a Tocher' (1796)]

121. O, wert thou in the cauld blast
On yonder lea, on yonder lea,
My plaidie to the angry airt,
I'd shelter thee, I'd shelter thee...

122. Or were I in the wildest waste,
Sae black and bare, sae black and bare,

The desert were a Paradise,
If thou wert there, if thou wert there.
['O, Wert Thou in the Cauld Blast' (1796)]

123. We labour soon, we labour late,
To feed the titled knave, man,
And a' the comfort we're to get,
Is that ayont the grave, man.
['The Tree of Liberty' (published 1838)]

124. As for this world I despair of ever making a figure in it – I am not formed for the bustle of the busy nor the flutter of the Gay. I shall never again be capable of it.
[Letter to his father, William Burns, 1781]

125. I am a strict economist; not, indeed, for the sake of the money; but one of the principal parts in my composition is a kind of pride of stomach; and I scorn to fear the face of any man living.
[Letter to John Murdoch, 1783]

126. The story of Wallace poured a Scottish prejudice in my veins which will boil along there till the flood-gates of life shut in eternal rest.
[Letter to Dr John Moore, 1787]

127. To be overtopped in anything else, I can bear: but in the tests of generous love, I defy all mankind!
[Letter to Clarinda (Mrs Agnes McLehose), 1788]

128. What a rocky-hearted, perfidious Succubus was that Queen Elizabeth! ... Judas Iscariot was a sad dog to be sure, but still his demerits shrink to insignificance, compared with the doings of the infernal Bess Tudor.
[Letter to Dr John Moore, 1791]

129. After all my boasted independence, curst necessity compels me to implore you for five pounds ... Do, for God's sake, send me that sum, and that by return of post ... Forgive, forgive me!
[Letter to George Thomson, 1796]

130. Don't let the awkward squad fire over me.
[In A. Cunningham, *The Works of Robert Burns; with his Life* (1834)]

131. Whatever mitigates the woes or increases the happiness of others, this is my criterion of goodness; and whatever injures society at large, or any individual in it, this is my measure of iniquity.
[Attr.]

132. I never had the least thought or inclination of turning Poet till I once got heartily in love, and then rhyme and song were, in a manner, the spontaneous language of my head.
[Attr.]

Burrows, Sir Fred (1887–1973)
English President of the National Union of Railwaymen and public servant

1. Unlike my predecessors, I have devoted more of my life to shunting and hooting than to hunting and shooting.
[Quoted in his obituary, *Daily Telegraph*, 1973]

Burt, Edward (d. 1755)
Scottish military agent and author

1. I was invited to sup at a Tavern. The cook was too filthy an Object to be described: only another English Gentleman whispered to me and said, he believed, if the fellow was to be thrown against the Wall, he would stick to it.
[*Letters from a Gentleman in the North of Scotland* (1726)]

Burton, Sir Richard (1821–1890)
English travel writer, translator, orientalist, anthropologist and poet

1. [Note to his wife, Isabel Burton, on his being replaced as Consul to Damascus in 1871]
Don't be frightened; I am recalled. Pay, pack, and follow at convenience.
[In Isabel Burton, *Life of Sir Richard Burton* (1893)]

Burton, Robert (1577–1640)
English prose writer and clergyman

1. All my joys to this are folly,
Naught so sweet as Melancholy.
[*Anatomy of Melancholy* (1621), 'Author's Abstract of Melancholy']

2. They lard their lean books with the fat of others' works.
[*Anatomy of Melancholy* (1621), 'Democritus to the Reader']

3. I had no time to lick it into form, as she [a bear] doth her young ones.
[*Anatomy of Melancholy* (1621), 'Democritus to the Reader']

4. Like watermen, that row one way and look another.
[*Anatomy of Melancholy* (1621), 'Democritus to the Reader'. Cf. Bunyan: 12]

5. Him that makes shoes go barefoot himself.
[*Anatomy of Melancholy* (1621), 'Democritus to the Reader']

6. All poets are mad.
[*Anatomy of Melancholy* (1621), 'Democritus to the Reader']

7. A loose, plain, rude writer.
[*Anatomy of Melancholy* (1621), 'Democritus to the Reader']

8. We can say nothing but what hath been said ... Our poets steal from Homer ... he that comes last is commonly best.
[*Anatomy of Melancholy* (1621), 'Democritus to the Reader']

9. Cookery is become an art, a noble science: cooks are gentlemen.
[*Anatomy of Melancholy* (1621), I]

10. I may not here omit those two main plagues, and common dotages of human kind, wine and women, which have infatuated and besotted myriads of people. They go commonly together.
[*Anatomy of Melancholy* (1621), I]

11. *Hinc quam sit calamus saevior ense patet.*
Hence it is clear how much more cruel the pen is than the sword.
[*Anatomy of Melancholy* (1621), I]

12. One was never married, and that's his hell; another is, and that's his plague.
[*Anatomy of Melancholy* (1621), I]

13. If there is a hell upon earth, it is to be found in a melancholy man's heart.
[*Anatomy of Melancholy* (1621), I]

14. Seneca thinks he takes delight in seeing thee. The gods are well pleased when they see great men contending with adversity.
[*Anatomy of Melancholy* (1621), II]

15. Who cannot give good counsel? 'tis cheap, it costs them nothing.
[*Anatomy of Melancholy* (1621), II]

16. All places are distant from Heaven alike.
[*Anatomy of Melancholy* (1621), II]

17. Tobacco, divine, rare, superexcellent tobacco, which goes far beyond all their panaceas, potable gold, and philosopher's

stones, a sovereign remedy to all diseases ... But, as it is commonly abused by most men, which take it as tinkers do ale, 'tis a plague, a mischief, a violent purger of goods, lands, health, hellish, devilish, and damned tobacco, the ruin and overthrow of body and soul.
[*Anatomy of Melancholy* (1621), II]

18. Let me not live, saith Aretine's Antonia, if I had not rather hear thy discourse than see a play!
[*Anatomy of Melancholy* (1621), III]

19. And this is that Homer's golden chain, which reacheth down from Heaven to earth, by which every creature is annexed, and depends on his Creator.
[*Anatomy of Melancholy* (1621), III]

20. To enlarge or illustrate this – is to set a candle in the sun.
[*Anatomy of Melancholy* (1621), III]

21. No chord, nor cable can so forcibly draw, or hold so fast, as love can do with a twined thread.
[*Anatomy of Melancholy* (1621), III]

22. To these crocodile's tears, they will add sobs, fiery sighs, and sorrowful countenance.
[*Anatomy of Melancholy* (1621), III]

23. Diogenes struck the father when the son swore.
[*Anatomy of Melancholy* (1621), III]

24. The fear of some divine and supreme powers, keeps men in obedience.
[*Anatomy of Melancholy* (1621), III]

25. One religion is as true as another.
[*Anatomy of Melancholy* (1621), III]

26. Be not solitary, be not idle.
[*Anatomy of Melancholy* (1621), III]

Buruma, Ian

1. Japan looks the most modern society in Asia, politically, culturally, aesthetically. It is also among the most archaic. It is one of the most open societies – foreigners can go there, live there, marry, and prosper. But it remains in many ways as exclusive as Burma. Japan is 'Westernized', yet, somehow, the country in East Asia least touched by the West.
[*God's Dust: A Modern Asian Journey* (1989), 5, 'Searching for Soul']

2. And yet Japan is hardly nondescript. Its character is overwhelming. On the surface the Japanese have achieved what all non-Western nations strive for: they are modern without being fake Westerners. The image of modern Japan, or rather the kaleidoscope of images appears unmistakably Japanese even when patterned after alien models.
[*God's Dust: A Modern Asian Journey* (1989), 5, 'Searching for Soul']

3. The more Japan imitated the West, the more national pride had to be saved by a mythology of pure national spirit.
[*God's Dust: A Modern Asian Journey* (1989), 5, 'Searching for Soul']

Busenbaum, Hermann (1600–1668)
German Jesuit theologian

1. *Cui licitus est finis, etiam licent media.*
Where the end is legitimate, the means are also legitimate, [i.e. the end justifies the means].
[*Medulla Theologiae Moralis* (1650)]

Bush, George (1924–)
US President, 1989–93

1. I do not like broccoli and I haven't liked it since I was a little kid. I am president of the United States and I am not going to eat any more.
[Attr.]

Bussy-Rabutin, Comte de (1618–1693)
French soldier, writer and memoirist

1. *L'absence est à l'amour ce qu'est au feu le vent; il éteint le petit, il allume le grand.*
Absence is to love what the wind is to fire; it extinguishes the small, it kindles the great.
[*Histoire Amoureuse des Gaules* (1665). Cf. La Rochefoucauld: 26]

2. *L'amour vient de l'aveuglement,*
L'amitié de la connaissance.
Love springs from blindness, friendship from knowledge.
[*Histoire Amoureuse des Gaules* (1665)]

3. *Comme vous savez, Dieu est d'ordinaire pour les gros escadrons contre les petits.*
As you know, God is normally on the side of the big squadrons against the small.
[Letter to the Comte de Limoges, 1677. Cf. Anouilh: 5, Turenne: 1 and Voltaire: 9]

Butler, Bishop Joseph (1692–1752)
English moral philosopher and divine

1. It has come, I know not how, to be taken for granted, by many persons, that Christianity is not so much as a subject of inquiry; but that it is, now at length, discovered to be fictitious.
[*The Analogy of Religion* (1736), Advertisement]

2. That which is the foundation of all our hopes and of all our fears; all our hopes and fears which are of any consideration: I mean a Future Life.
[*The Analogy of Religion* (1736), Introduction]

3. But to us, probability is the very guide of life.
[*The Analogy of Religion* (1736)]

4. [To John Wesley]
Sir, the pretending to extraordinary revelations and gifts of the Holy Ghost is a horrid thing, a very horrid thing.
[In Wesley, *Works*]

Butler, Nicholas Murray (1862–1947)
American teacher, lecturer, politician and author

1. ... a society like ours [USA.] of which it is truly said to be often but three generations 'from shirt-sleeves to shirt-sleeves'.
[*True and False Democracy*]

2. An expert is one who knows more and more about less and less.
[Attr.]

Butler, R.A. (Baron Butler of Saffron Walden) (1902–1982)
Indian-born British Conservative politician; held several Cabinet posts

1. Is Mr Macmillan the best prime minister we have? YES!
[Interview, London Airport; often quoted as 'Mr Macmillan is the best prime minister we have']

Butler, Samuel [1] ('Hudibras') (1612–1680)
English satirical poet

1. When civil fury first grew high,
And men fell out they knew not why...

2. Besides 'tis known he could speak Greek,
As naturally as pigs squeak...

3. For rhetoric he could not ope
His mouth, but out there flew a trope...

4. For all a rhetorician's rules
Teach nothing but to name his tools...

5. A Babylonish dialect
Which learned pedants much affect...

6. Beside, he was a shrewd philosopher,
And had read ev'ry text and gloss over...

7. What ever sceptic could inquire for;
For every why he had a wherefore...

8. He knew what's what, and that's as high
As metaphysic wit can fly...

9. Such as take lodgings in a head
That's to be let unfurnished...

10. 'Twas Presbyterian true blue...

11. Such as do build their faith upon
The holy text of pike and gun...

12. And prove their doctrine orthodox
By apostolic blows and knocks...

13. Compound for sins, they are inclin'd to
By damning those they have no mind to...

14. The trenchant blade, Toledo trusty,
For want of fighting was grown rusty,
And eat into it self, for lack
Of some body to hew and hack...

15. For rhyme the rudder is of verses,
With which like ships they steer their courses...

16. For what is Worth in anything,
But so much Money as 'twill bring...

17. He ne'er consider'd it, as loth
To look a gift-horse in the mouth.
[*Hudibras* (1663), I, canto I]

18. Through perils both of wind and limb,
Through thick and thin she follow'd him.
[*Hudibras* (1663), I, canto 2]

19. Cleric before, and Lay behind;
A lawless linsy-woolsy brother,
Half of one order, half another...

20. Learning, that cobweb of the brain,
Profane, erroneous, and vain.
[*Hudibras* (1663), I, canto 3]

21. Some have been beaten till they know
What wood a cudgel's of by th' blow;
Some kick'd, until they can feel whether
A shoe be Spanish or neats-leather...

22. She that with poetry is won
Is but a desk to write upon.
[*Hudibras* (1664), II, canto 1]

23. The sun had long since in his lap
Of Thetis, taken out his nap,
And like a lobster boil'd, the morn
From black to red began to turn...

24. Oaths are but words, and words but wind...

25. As the ancients
Say wisely, Have a care o' th' main chance,
And look before you ere you leap;
For, as you sow, you are like to reap...

26. Love is a boy, by poets styl'd,
Then spare the rod, and spoil the child.
[*Hudibras* (1664), II, canto 2]

27. Doubtless the pleasure is as great
Of being cheated, as to cheat.
As lookers-on feel most delight,
That least perceive a juggler's sleight,
And still the less they understand,
The more th' admire his sleight of hand...

28. To swallow gudgeons ere they're catched,
And count their chickens ere they're hatched.
[*Hudibras* (1664), II, canto 3]

29. Still amorous, and fond, and billing,
Like Philip and Mary on a shilling...

30. For in what stupid age or nation
Was marriage ever out of fashion?...

31. Discords make the sweetest airs...

32. What makes all doctrines plain and clear?
About two hundred pounds a year.
And that which was prov'd true before,
Prove false again?
Two hundred more.
[*Hudibras* (1678), III, canto 1]

33. For if it be but half denied,
'Tis half as good as justified.
[*Hudibras* (1678), III, canto 2]

34. For, those that fly, may fight again,
Which he can never do that's slain...

35. He that complies against his will,
Is of his own opinion still...

36. Neither have the hearts to stay,
Nor wit enough to run away...

37. For Justice, though she's painted blind,
Is to the weaker side inclin'd.
[*Hudibras* (1678), III, canto 3]

38. For money has a power above
The stars and fate, to manage love.
[*Hudibras* (1678), III, 'The Lady's Answer to the Knight']

39. The best of our actions tend
To the preposterousest end.
[*Genuine Remains* (1759), 'Satire upon the Weakness and Misery of Man']

40. The souls of women are so small,
That some believe they've none at all.
[*Miscellaneous Thoughts*]

41. For trouts are tickled best in muddy water.
[*On a Hypocritical Nonconformist*]

Butler, Samuel [2] (1835–1902)

English novelist, painter, philosopher and scholar

1. Some who had received a liberal education at the Colleges of Unreason, and taken the highest degrees in hypothetics, which are their principal study.
[*Erewhon* (1872), 9]

2. Straighteners, managers and cashiers of the Musical Banks...
[*Erewhon* (1872), 9]

3. The wish to spread those opinions that we hold conducive

to our own welfare is so deeply rooted in the English character that few of us can escape its influence.
[*Erewhon* (1872), 20]

4. An art can only be learned in the workshop of those who are winning their bread by it.
[*Erewhon* (1872), 20]

5. It has been said that the love of money is the root of all evil. The want of money is so quite as truly.
[*Erewhon* (1872), 20. Cf. Bible: 549]

6. Spontaneity is only a term for man's ignorance of the gods.
[*Erewhon* (1872), 25]

7. The most perfect humour and irony is generally quite unconscious.
[*Life and Habit* (1877)]

8. A hen is only an egg's way of making another egg.
[*Life and Habit* (1877)]

9. I am the enfant terrible of literature and science.
[*A Lecture on the Humour of Homer* (1892), 'Enfant Terrible: Myself']

10. If Bach wriggles, Wagner writhes.
[*A Lecture on the Humour of Homer* (1892), 'Handel and Music: Musical Criticism']

11. The phrase 'unconscious humour' is the one contribution I have made to the current literature of the day
[*A Lecture on the Humour of Homer* (1892), 'Homo Unius Libri: Myself and Unconscious Humour']

12. I keep my books at the British Museum and at Mudie's.
[*A Lecture on the Humour of Homer* (1892), 'Ramblings in Cheapside', 2]

13. It has been said that though God cannot alter the past, historians can; it is perhaps because they can be useful to Him in this respect that He tolerates their existence.
[*Erewhon Revisited* (1901), 14]

14. Every man's work, whether it be literature or music or pictures or architecture or anything else, is always a portrait of himself.
[*The Way of All Flesh* (1903), 14]

15. They would have been equally horrified at hearing the Christian religion doubted, and at seeing it practised.
[*The Way of All Flesh* (1903), 15]

16. That vice pays homage to virtue is notorious; we call it hypocrisy.
[*The Way of All Flesh* (1903), 19]

17. Pleasure after all is a safer guide than either right or duty.
[*The Way of All Flesh* (1903), 19]

18. The advantage of doing one's praising for oneself is that one can lay it on so thick and exactly in the right places.
[*The Way of All Flesh* (1903), 34]

19. There's many a good tune played on an old fiddle.
[*The Way of All Flesh* (1903), 61]

20. 'Tis better to have loved and lost than never to have lost at all.
[*The Way of All Flesh* (1903), 77. Cf. Tennyson: 142]

21. Life is one long process of getting tired.
[*The Note-Books of Samuel Butler* (1912), 1]

22. Life is the art of drawing sufficient conclusions from insufficient premises.
[*The Note-Books of Samuel Butler* (1912), 1]

23. All progress is based upon a universal innate desire on the part of every organism to live beyond its income.
[*The Note-Books of Samuel Butler* (1912), 1]

24. When the righteous man turneth away from his righteousness that he hath committed and doeth that which is neither quite lawful nor quite right, he will generally be found to have gained in amiability what he has lost in holiness.
[*The Note-Books of Samuel Butler* (1912), 2]

25. I believe that more unhappiness comes from this source than from any other – I mean from the attempt to prolong family connection unduly and to make people hang together artificially who would never naturally do so. The mischief among the lower classes is not so great, but among the middle and upper classes it is killing a large number daily. And the old people do not really like it much better than the young.
[*The Note-Books of Samuel Butler* (1912), 2]

26. It costs a lot of money to die comfortably.
[*The Note-Books of Samuel Butler* (1912), 2]

27. The healthy stomach is nothing if not conservative. Few radicals have good digestions.
[*The Note-Books of Samuel Butler* (1912), 6]

28. The history of art is the history of revivals.
[*The Note-Books of Samuel Butler* (1912), 8]

29. Genius ... has been defined as a supreme capacity for taking trouble ... It might be more fitly described as a supreme capacity for getting its possessors into pains of all kinds, and keeping them therein so long as the genius remains.
[*The Note-Books of Samuel Butler* (1912), 11]

30. Talking it over, we agreed that Blake was no good because he learnt Italian at over 60 to study Dante, and we knew Dante was no good because he was so fond of Virgil, and Virgil was no good because Tennyson ran him, and as for Tennyson – well, Tennyson goes without saying.
[*The Note-Books of Samuel Butler* (1912), 12]

31. An apology for the devil: it must be remembered that we have heard only one side of the case; God has written all the books.
[*The Note-Books of Samuel Butler* (1912), 14]

32. God is Love, I dare say. But what a mischievous devil Love is.
[*The Note-Books of Samuel Butler* (1912), 14]

33. To live is like love, all reason is against it, and all healthy instinct for it.
[*The Note-Books of Samuel Butler* (1912), 14]

34. I do not mind lying, but I hate inaccuracy.
[*The Note-Books of Samuel Butler* (1912), 19]

35. The world will, in the end, follow only those who have despised as well as served it.
[*The Note-Books of Samuel Butler* (1912), 24]

36. Though analogy is often misleading, it is the least misleading thing we have.
[*The Note-Books of Samuel Butler* (1912), 'Music, Pictures and Books']

37. When a man is in doubt about this or that in his writing, it will often guide him if he asks himself how it will tell a hundred years hence.
[*The Note-Books of Samuel Butler* (1912), 'Music, Pictures and Books', final note]

38. To be at all is to be religious more or less.
[*The Note-Books of Samuel Butler* (1912), 'Reconciliation: Religion']

39. Any fool can tell the truth, but it requires a man of some sense to know how to lie well.
[*The Note-Books of Samuel Butler* (1912), 'Truth and Convenience: Falsehood']

40. An honest God's the noblest work of man.
[*Further Extracts from the Note-Books of Samuel Butler* (1934). Cf. Pope: 104]

41. 'Man wants but little here below' but likes that little good – and not too long in coming.
[*Further Extracts from the Note-Books of Samuel Butler* (1934)]

42. Jesus! with all thy faults I love thee still.
[*Further Extracts from the Note-Books of Samuel Butler* (1934)]

43. My Lord, I do not believe. Help thou mine unbelief.
[In Keynes and Hill (eds), *Samuel Butler's Notebooks* (1951)]

44. Marriage is distinctly and repeatedly excluded from heaven. Is this because it is thought likely to mar the general felicity?
[In Keynes and Hill (eds), *Samuel Butler's Notebooks* (1951)]

45. Man is the only animal that can remain on friendly terms with the victims he intends to eat until he eats them.
[In Keynes and Hill (eds), *Samuel Butler's Notebooks* (1951)]

46. I would not be – not quite – so pure as you.
['A Prayer']

47. Preferrest thou the gospel of Montreal to the gospel of Hellas,
The gospel of thy connexion with Mr Spurgeon's haberdasher to the gospel of the Discobolus?
Yet none the less blasphemed he beauty saying, 'The Discobolus hath no gospel,
But my brother-in-law is haberdasher to Mr Spurgeon.'
['Psalm of Montreal' (1878)]

48. O God! O Montreal!
['Psalm of Montreal' (1878)]

49. Not on sad Stygian shore, nor in clear sheen
Of far Elysian plain, shall we meet those
Among the dead whose pupils we have been,
Nor those great shades whom we have held as foes...

50. Yet meet we shall, and part, and meet again,
Where dead men meet on lips of living men.
['The Life After Death' (1898)]

51. It was very good of God to let Carlyle and Mrs Carlyle marry one another and so make only two people miserable instead of four, besides being very amusing.
[Letter to Miss Savage, 1884]

52. When you have told anyone you have left him a legacy the only decent thing to do is to die at once.
[In Festing Jones, *Samuel Butler: A Memoir*]

53. Parents are the last people on earth who ought to have children.
[Attr.]

54. Brigands demand your money or your life; women require both.
[Attr.]

55. [Last words to his servant and friend, Alfred Cathie]
Have you brought the cheque book, Alfred?
[In P. Henderson, *Samuel Butler: The Incarnate Bachelor* (1953)]

Butler, William (1535–1618)
English physician

1. [Of the strawberry]
Doubtless God could have made a better berry, but doubtless God never did.
[In Walton, *The Compleat Angler* (1661)]

Buttiglione, Angela (1937–)
Italian journalist and broadcaster

1. *Siamo vittime di imposizioni esterne, del modello americano, mentre abbiamo doti nostre che spesso trascuriamo.*
We women are victims of external impositions, of the American kind, yet we do have our own qualities which all too often, we neglect.
[In *EPOCA*, current affairs magazine, 1994]

Buzo, Alexander John (1944–)
Australian writer and dramatist

1. *Norm*: You could have a good time out here, Ahmed. It's an easy life. Take this morning, for instance. On Sunday mornings I sit on the terrace and sip a Tia Maria and read the sports section. Lorrain's in the kitchen, smell of a roast lamb on the breeze, what more could you want? Green lawns all around, vista of the harbour, Holden in the garage, I'm sweet. No worries. See what I'm getting at? You wouldn't have that in Pakistan, now would you?
[*Norm and Ahmed* (1969)]

Buzzati, Dino (1906–1972)
Italian writer and artist

1. *'Da' qua' disse l'Onnipotente afferrando il fatale progetto. E ci mise la firma.*
'Give it to me' said the Omnipotent seizing the fatal blueprint. And he signed it.
[*Il Colombre e Altri Racconti* (*The Colombre and Other Short Stories*, 1966), 'La Creazione' ('The Creation')]

Bygraves, Max (1922–)
English singer, entertainer and TV personality

1. [Of Melbourne]
I've always wanted to see a ghost town. You couldn't even get a parachute to open here after 10 p.m.
[Melbourne *Sun*, 1965]

2. I've arrived, and to prove it, I'm here.
[In Halliwell, *Filmgoer's Book of Quotes* (1973)]

Byrom, John (1692–1763)
English poet; inventor and teacher of shorthand

1. Christians awake, salute the happy morn,
Whereon the Saviour of the world was born.
['Hymn for Christmas Day', c. 1750]

2. Some say, that Signor Bononcini,
Compar'd to Handel's a mere ninny;
Others aver, to him, that Handel
Is scarcely fit to hold a candle.
Strange! that such a high dispute shou'd be
'Twixt Tweedledum and Tweedledee.
[Epigram on the Feuds between Handel and Bononcini, 1773]

3. Bone and Skin, two millers thin,
Would starve us all, or near it;
But be it known to Skin and Bone
That Flesh and Blood can't bear it.
[Epigram on Two Monopolists, 1773]

4. Where you find
Bright passages that strike your mind,

And which perhaps you may have reason
To think on at another season,–
– Take them down in black and white.
['Hint to a Young Person' (1773)]

5. God bless the King! – I mean the Faith's Defender;
God bless (no harm in blessing) the Pretender!
But who Pretender is, or who is King,
God bless us all! – that's quite another thing.
['To an Officer in the Army' (1773)]

6. The parson leaves the Christian in the lurch
Where'er he brings his politics to church.
['On Clergymen preaching politics']

7. I shall prove it – as clear as a whistle.
[*Epistle to Lloyd*, I]

Byron, George Gordon, Lord (1788–1824)

English Romantic poet, satirist and traveller

1. Friendship is Love without his wings.
['L'amitié est l'amour sans ailes' (1806)]

2. I have tasted the sweets and the bitters of love.
['Lines Addressed to Reverend J.T. Becher' (1806)]

3. Though women are angels, yet wedlock's the devil.
['To Eliza' (1806)]

4. I only know we loved in vain–
I only feel – Farewell! – Farewell!
['Farewell! if ever fondest prayer' (1808)]

5. And wilt thou weep when I am low?
['And Wilt Thou Weep?' (c. 1808)]

6. Still must I hear? – shall hoarse Fitzgerald bawl
His creaking couplets in a tavern hall.
[*English Bards and Scotch Reviewers* (1809), line 1]

7. I'll publish, right or wrong:
Fools are my theme, let satire be my song.
[*English Bards and Scotch Reviewers* (1809), line 5]

8. 'Tis pleasant, sure, to see one's name in print;
A Book's a Book, altho' there is nothing in't.
[*English Bards and Scotch Reviewers* (1809), line 51]

9. A man must serve his time to every trade
Save censure – critics all are ready made.
Take hackney'd jokes from Miller, got by rote,
With just enough of learning to misquote.
[*English Bards and Scotch Reviewers* (1809), line 63]

10. As soon
Seek roses in December – ice in June;
Hope constancy in wind, or corn in chaff;
Believe a woman or an epitaph,
Or any other thing that's false, before
You trust in critics, who themselves are sore.
[*English Bards and Scotch Reviewers* (1809), line 75]

11. Better to err with Pope, than shine with Pye.
[*English Bards and Scotch Reviewers* (1809), line 102]

12. [Of Wordsworth]
Who, both by precept and example, shows
That prose is verse, and verse is merely prose.
[*English Bards and Scotch Reviewers* (1809), line 241]

13. Be warm, but pure: be amorous, but chaste.
[*English Bards and Scotch Reviewers* (1809), line 306]

14. Oh, Amos Cottle! – Phoebus! what a name
To fill the speaking trump of future fame!
[*English Bards and Scotch Reviewers* (1809), line 399]

15. To sanction Vice, and hunt Decorum down.
[*English Bards and Scotch Reviewers* (1809), line 621]

16. Let simple Wordsworth chime his childish verse,
And brother Coleridge lull the babe at nurse.
[*English Bards and Scotch Reviewers* (1809), line 917]

17. Glory, like the phoenix 'midst her fires,
Exhales her odours, blazes, and expires.
[*English Bards and Scotch Reviewers* (1809), line 959]

18. I too can hunt a poetaster down.
[*English Bards and Scotch Reviewers* (1809), line 1064]

19. Nor be, what man should ever be,
The friend of Beauty in distress?
['To Florence' (1809)]

20. Maid of Athens, ere we part,
Give, oh give me back my heart!
Or, since that has left my breast,
Keep it now, and take the rest!
[Song: 'Maid of Athens, ere we part' (1810)]

21. And know, whatever thou hast been,
'Tis something better not to be.
['Euthanasia' (1812)]

22. Know ye the land where the cypress and myrtle
Are emblems of deeds that are done in their clime?
Where the rage of the vulture, the love of the turtle,
Now melt into sorrow, now madden to crime?...

23. Where the virgins are soft as the roses they twine,
And all, save the spirit of man, is divine?
[*The Bride of Abydos* (1813), Canto I]

24. Mark! where his carnage and his conquests cease!
He makes a solitude, and calls it – peace!
[*The Bride of Abydos* (1813), Canto II]

25. Clime of the unforgotten brave!
Whose land from plain to mountain-cave
Was Freedom's home or Glory's grave!
['The Giaour' (1813), line 103]

26. [A cypress]
Dark tree, still sad when others' grief is fled,
The only constant mourner o'er the dead!
['The Giaour' (1813), line 286]

27. And lovelier things have mercy shown
To every failing but their own,
And every woe a tear can claim
Except an erring sister's shame.
['The Giaour' (1813), line 418]

28. I die, – but first I have possess'd,
And come what may, I have been blest.
['The Giaour' (1813), line 1114]

29. Such hath it been – shall be – beneath the sun
The many still must labour for the one.
[*The Corsair* (1814), Canto I, 8]

30. There was a laughing Devil in his sneer.
[*The Corsair* (1814), Canto I, 9]

31. Much hath been done, but more remains to do–
Their galleys blaze – why not their city too?
[*The Corsair* (1814), Canto II, 4]

32. The spirit burning but unbent,
May writhe, rebel – the weak alone repent!
[*The Corsair* (1814), Canto II, 10]

33. Oh! too convincing – dangerously dear–
In woman's eye the unanswerable tear!
[*The Corsair* (1814), Canto II, 15]

34. Slow sinks, more lovely ere his race be run,
Along Morea's hills the setting sun;
Not, as in northern climes, obscurely bright,
But one unclouded blaze of living light!
[*The Corsair* (1814), Canto III, 1 and 'The Curse of Minerva' (1812), I]

35. She for him had given
Her all on earth, and more than all in heaven!
[*The Corsair* (1814), Canto III, 17]

36. His madness was not of the head, but heart.
[*Lara* (1814), Canto I, 18]

37. [Of George Washington]
The Cincinnatus of the West.
['Ode to Napoleon Buonaparte' (1814)]

38. By headless Charles see heartless Henry lies.
['Windsor Poetics' (1814)]

39. The Assyrian came down like the wolf on the fold,
And his cohorts were gleaming in purple and gold;
And the sheen of their spears was like stars on the sea,
When the blue wave rolls nightly on deep Galilee...

40. For the Angel of Death spread his wings on the blast,
And breathed in the face of the foe as he pass'd.
['The Destruction of Sennacherib' (1815)]

41. She walks in beauty, like the night
Of cloudless climes and starry skies;
And all that's best of dark and bright
Meet in her aspect and her eyes:
Thus mellow'd to that tender light
Which heaven to gaudy day denies.
['She Walks in Beauty' (1815)]

42. The Glory and the Nothing of a Name.
['Churchill's Grave' (1816)]

43. And both were young, and one was beautiful...

44. A change came o'er the spirit of my dream.
['The Dream' (1816)]

45. Fare thee well! and if for ever,
Still for ever, fare thee well.
['Fare thee well!' (1816)]

46. It is not in the storm nor in the strife
We feel benumb'd and wish to be no more,
But in the after-silence on the shore,
When all is lost, except a little life.
['On hearing that Lady Byron was ill' (1816)]

47. Yet in my lineaments they trace
Some features of my father's face.
['Parisina' (1816)]

48. Eternal spirit of the chainless mind!
Brightest in dungeons, Liberty! thou art.
['Sonnet on Chillon' (1816)]

49. My hair is grey, but not with years,
Nor grew it white
In a single night,
As men's have grown from sudden fears.
['The Prisoner of Chillon' (1816), 1]

50. A light broke in upon my brain,–
It was the carol of a bird;
It ceased, and then it came again,
The sweetest song ear ever heard.
['The Prisoner of Chillon' (1816), 10]

51. My very chains and I grew friends,
So much a long communion tends
To make us what we are: – even I
Regain'd my freedom with a sigh.
['The Prisoner of Chillon' (1816), 14]

52. Man in portions can foresee
His own funereal destiny.
['Prometheus' (1816)]

53. Born in the garret, in a kitchen bred,
Promoted thence to deck her mistress' head.
['A Sketch from Private Life' (1816)]

54. When we two parted
In silence and tears,
Half broken-hearted
To sever for years,
Pale grew thy cheek and cold,
Colder thy kiss...

55. If I should meet thee
After long years,
How should I greet thee?–
With silence and tears.
['When we two parted' (1816)]

56. Maidens, like moths, are ever caught by glare,
And Mammon wins his way where Seraphs might despair.
[*Childe Harold's Pilgrimage* (1812–1818), Canto 1, 9]

57. Adieu, adieu! my native shore
Fades o'er the waters blue...

58. My native land – Good Night!
[*Childe Harold's Pilgrimage* (1812–1818), Canto I, 13]

59. And must they fall? the young, the proud, the brave,
To swell one bloated Chief's unwholesome reign?
[*Childe Harold's Pilgrimage* (1812–1818), Canto I, 53]

60. Here all were noble, save Nobility;
None hugg'd a conqueror's chain, save fallen Chivalry!
[*Childe Harold's Pilgrimage* (1812–1818), Canto I, 85]

61. War, war is still the cry, 'War even to the knife!'
[*Childe Harold's Pilgrimage* (1812–1818), Canto I, 86]

62. A schoolboy's tale, the wonder of an hour!
[*Childe Harold's Pilgrimage* (1812–1818), Canto II, 2]

63. Well didst thou speak, Athena's wisest son!
'All that we know is, nothing can be known.'
[*Childe Harold's Pilgrimage* (1812–1818), Canto II, 7]

64. The last, the worst, dull spoiler, who was he?
[*Childe Harold's Pilgrimage* (1812–1818), Canto II, 11]

65. The ocean queen, the free Britannia, bears
The last poor plunder from a bleeding land.
[*Childe Harold's Pilgrimage* (1812–1818), Canto II, 13]

66. Ah! happy years! once more who would not be a boy?
[*Childe Harold's Pilgrimage* (1812–1818), Canto II, 23]

67. But midst the crowd, the hum, the shock of men,
To hear, to see, to feel, and to possess.
[*Childe Harold's Pilgrimage* (1812–1818), Canto II, 26]

68. Fair Greece! Sad relic of departed worth!
Immortal, though no more; though fallen, great!
[*Childe Harold's Pilgrimage* (1812–1818), Canto II, 73]

69. Hereditary Bondsmen! know ye not
Who would be free themselves must strike the blow?
[*Childe Harold's Pilgrimage* (1812–1818), Canto II, 76]

70. Where'er we tread 'tis haunted, holy ground.
[*Childe Harold's Pilgrimage* (1812–1818), Canto II, 88]

71. Death in the front, Destruction in the rear!
[*Childe Harold's Pilgrimage* (1812–1818), Canto II, 90]

72. What is the worst of woes that wait on age?
What stamps the wrinkle deeper on the brow?
To view each loved one blotted from life's page,
And be alone on earth, as I am now.
[*Childe Harold's Pilgrimage* (1812–1818), Canto II, 98]

73. Once more upon the waters! yet once more!
And the waves bound beneath me as a steed
That knows his rider.
[*Childe Harold's Pilgrimage* (1812–1818), Canto III, 2]

74. Since my young days of passion – joy or pain–
Perchance my heart and harp have lost a string–
And both may jar.
[*Childe Harold's Pilgrimage* (1812–1818), Canto III, 4]

75. Years steal
Fire from the mind as vigour from the limb;
And life's enchanted cup but sparkles near the brim.
[*Childe Harold's Pilgrimage* (1812–1818), Canto III, 8]

76. There was a sound of revelry by night,
And Belgium's capital had gather'd then
Her Beauty and her Chivalry, and bright
The lamps shone o'er fair women and brave men;
A thousand hearts beat happily; and when
Music arose with its voluptuous swell,
Soft eyes look'd love to eyes which spake again,
And all went merry as a marriage bell;
But hush! hark! a deep sound strikes like a rising knell.
[*Childe Harold's Pilgrimage* (1812–1818), Canto III, 21]

77. Did ye not hear it? – No; 'twas but the wind,
Or the car rattling o'er the stony street;
On with the dance! let joy be unconfined;
No sleep till morn, when Youth and Pleasure meet
To chase the glowing Hours with flying feet.
[*Childe Harold's Pilgrimage* (1812–1818), Canto III, 22]

78. Within a window'd niche of that high hall
Sate Brunswick's fated chieftain...

79. He rush'd into the field, and, foremost fighting, fell.
[*Childe Harold's Pilgrimage* (1812–1818), Canto III, 23]

80. Or whispering, with white lips – 'The foe! they come! they come!'
[*Childe Harold's Pilgrimage* (1812–1818), Canto III, 25]

81. There is a very life in our despair,
Vitality of poison...

82. Life will suit
Itself to Sorrow's most detested fruit,
Like to the apples on the Dead Sea's shore,
All ashes to the taste.
[*Childe Harold's Pilgrimage* (1812–1818), Canto III, 34]

83. [Napoleon]
There sunk the greatest, nor the worst of men,
Whose spirit, antithetically mixt,
One moment of the mightiest, and again
On little objects with like firmness fixt.
[*Childe Harold's Pilgrimage* (1812–1818), Canto III, 36]

84. That untaught innate philosophy,
Which, be it wisdom, coldness, or deep pride,
Is gall and wormwood to an enemy.
[*Childe Harold's Pilgrimage* (1812–1818), Canto III, 39]

85. Quiet to quick bosoms is a hell.
[*Childe Harold's Pilgrimage* (1812–1818), Canto III, 42]

86. ... the madmen who have made men mad
By their contagion; Conquerors and Kings,
Founders of sects and systems.
[*Childe Harold's Pilgrimage* (1812–1818), Canto III, 43]

87. He who ascends to mountain-tops, shall find
The loftiest peaks most wrapt in clouds and snow;
He who surpasses or subdues mankind,
Must look down on the hate of those below.
[*Childe Harold's Pilgrimage* (1812–1818), Canto III, 45]

88. The castled crag of Drachenfels
Frowns o'er the wide and winding Rhine.
[*Childe Harold's Pilgrimage* (1812–1818), Canto III, 55]

89. But these are deeds which should not pass away,
And names that must not wither.
[*Childe Harold's Pilgrimage* (1812–1818), Canto III, 67]

90. Lake Leman woos me with its crystal face.
[*Childe Harold's Pilgrimage* (1812–1818), Canto III, 68]

91. I live not in myself, but I become
Portion of that around me; and to me
High mountains are a feeling, but the hum
Of human cities torture.
[*Childe Harold's Pilgrimage* (1812–1818), Canto III, 72]

92. Ye stars! which are the poetry of heaven!
[*Childe Harold's Pilgrimage* (1812–1818), Canto III, 88]

93. For 'tis his nature to advance or die.
[*Childe Harold's Pilgrimage* (1812–1818), Canto III, 103]

94. I have not loved the world, nor the world me;
I have not flattered its rank breath, nor bow'd
To its idolatries a patient knee,
Nor coin'd my cheek to smiles, nor cried aloud
In worship of an echo...

95. I stood
Among them, but not of them; in a shroud
Of thoughts which were not their thoughts.
[*Childe Harold's Pilgrimage* (1812–1818), Canto III, 113]

96. I stood in Venice, on the Bridge of Sighs;
A palace and a prison on each hand...

97. Where Venice sate in state, thron'd on her hundred isles!
[*Childe Harold's Pilgrimage* (1812–1818), Canto IV, 1]

98. The spouseless Adriatic mourns her lord.
[*Childe Harold's Pilgrimage* (1812–1818), Canto IV, 11]

99. The moon is up, and yet it is not night;
Sunset divides the sky with her; a sea
Of glory streams along the Alpine height
Of blue Friuli's mountains; Heaven is free
From clouds, but of all colours seems to be,–
Melted to one vast Iris of the West,–
Where the Day joins the past Eternity.
[*Childe Harold's Pilgrimage* (1812–1818), Canto IV, 27]

100. Italia! oh Italia! thou who hast
The fatal gift of beauty.
[*Childe Harold's Pilgrimage* (1812–1818), Canto IV, 42]

101. Let these describe the undescribable.
[*Childe Harold's Pilgrimage* (1812–1818), Canto IV, 53]

102. Then farewell, Horace; whom I hated so,
Not for thy faults but mine.
[*Childe Harold's Pilgrimage* (1812–1818), Canto IV, 77]

103. Oh Rome! my country! city of the soul!
[*Childe Harold's Pilgrimage* (1812–1818), Canto IV, 78]

104. The Niobe of nations! there she stands,
Childless and crownless, in her voiceless woe.
[*Childe Harold's Pilgrimage* (1812–1818), Canto IV, 79]

105. Alas! our young affections run to waste,
Or water but the desert.
[*Childe Harold's Pilgrimage* (1812–1818), Canto IV, 120]

106. Of its own beauty is the mind diseased.
[*Childe Harold's Pilgrimage* (1812–1818), Canto IV, 122]

107. Time, the avenger!
[*Childe Harold's Pilgrimage* (1812–1818), Canto IV, 130]

108. I see before me the Gladiator lie:
He leans upon his hand – his manly brow
Consents to death, but conquers agony...

109. The arena swims around him – he is gone,
Ere ceased the inhuman shout which hail'd the wretch who won.
[*Childe Harold's Pilgrimage* (1812–1818), Canto IV, 140]

110. He heard it, but he heeded not – his eyes
Were with his heart, and that was far away;
He reck'd not of the life he lost nor prize,
But where his rude hut by the Danube lay,
There were his young barbarians all at play,
There was their Dacian mother – he, their sire,
Butcher'd to make a Roman holiday.
[*Childe Harold's Pilgrimage* (1812–1818), Canto IV, 141]

111. A ruin – yet what ruin! from its mass
Walls, palaces, half-cities, have been rear'd.
[*Childe Harold's Pilgrimage* (1812–1818), Canto IV, 143]

112. While stands the Coliseum, Rome shall stand:
When falls the Coliseum, Rome shall fall;
And when Rome falls – the World.
[*Childe Harold's Pilgrimage* (1812–1818), Canto IV, 145]

113. The Lord of his unerring bow,
The God of life, and poesy, and light.
[*Childe Harold's Pilgrimage* (1812–1818), Canto IV, 161]

114. So young, so fair,
Good without effort, great without a foe.
[*Childe Harold's Pilgrimage* (1812–1818), Canto IV, 172]

115. Oh! that the Desert were my dwelling-place,
With one fair Spirit for my minister,
That I might all forget the human race,
And, hating no one, love but only her!
[*Childe Harold's Pilgrimage* (1812–1818), Canto IV, 177]

116. There is a pleasure in the pathless woods,
There is a rapture on the lonely shore,
There is society, where none intrudes,
By the deep Sea, and music in its roar:
I love not Man the less, but Nature more,
From these our interviews, in which I steal
From all I may be, or have been before,
To mingle with the Universe, and feel
What I can ne'er express, yet cannot all conceal.
[*Childe Harold's Pilgrimage* (1812–1818), Canto IV, 178]

117. Roll on, thou deep and dark blue Ocean – roll!
Ten thousand fleets sweep over thee in vain;
Man marks the earth with ruin – his control
Stops with the shore.

118. He sinks into thy depths with bubbling groan,
Without a grave, unknell'd, uncoffin'd, and unknown.
[*Childe Harold's Pilgrimage* (1812–1818), Canto IV, 179]

119. Dark-heaving – boundless, endless, and sublime,
The image of eternity.
[*Childe Harold's Pilgrimage* (1812–1818), Canto IV, 183]

120. And I have loved thee, Ocean! and my joy
Of youthful sports was on thy breast to be
Borne, like thy bubbles, onward: from a boy
I wanton'd with thy breakers.
[*Childe Harold's Pilgrimage* (1812–1818), Canto IV, 184]

121. By thy cold breast and serpent smile,
By thy unfathom'd gulfs of guile,
By that most seeming virtuous eye,
By thy shut soul's hypocrisy;
By the perfection of thine art
Which pass'd for human thine own heart;
By thy delight in others' pain,
And by thy brotherhood of Cain,
I call upon thee! and compel
Thyself to be thy proper Hell!
[*Manfred* (1817), I.i]

122. I know thee for a man of many thoughts.
[*Manfred* (1817), II.ii]

123. I pass'd
The nights of years in sciences untaught.
[*Manfred* (1817), II.ii]

124. We are the fools of time and terror: Days
Steal on us, and steal from us; yet we live,
Loathing our life, and dreading still to die.
[*Manfred* (1817), II.ii]

125. Knowledge is not happiness, and science
But an exchange of ignorance for that
Which is another kind of ignorance.
[*Manfred* (1817), II.iv]

126. There is an order
Of mortals on the earth, who do become
Old in their youth, and die ere middle age.
[*Manfred* (1817), III.i]

127. Old man! 'tis not so difficult to die.
[*Manfred* (1817), III.iv]

128. So, we'll go no more a roving
So late into the night
Though the heart be still as loving,
And the moon be still as bright...

129. Though the night was made for loving,
And the day returns too soon,
Yet we'll go no more a roving
By the light of the moon.
['So, we'll go no more a roving' (1817)]

130. My boat is on the shore,
And my bark is on the sea;
But, before I go, Tom Moore,
Here's a double health to thee!

Here's a sigh to those who love me,
And a smile to those who hate;
And, whatever sky's above me,
Here's a heart for every fate.
['To Thomas Moore' (1817)]

131. Didst ever see a Gondola?...
It glides along the water looking blackly,
Just like a coffin clapt in a canoe.
[*Beppo* (1818), 19]

132. In short, he was a perfect cavaliero,
And to his very valet seem'd a hero.
[*Beppo* (1818), 33]

133. His heart was one of those which most enamour us,
Wax to receive, and marble to retain.
[*Beppo* (1818), 34]

134. 'Tis true, your budding Miss is very charming,
But shy and awkward at first coming out,
So much alarm'd, that she is quite alarming,
All Giggle, Blush; half Pertness, and half Pout;
And glancing at Mamma, for fear there's harm in

What you, she, it, or they, may be about,
The nursery still leaps out in all they utter–
Besides, they always smell of bread and butter.
[*Beppo* (1818), 39]

135. I like the weather, when it is not rainy,
That is, I like two months of every year.
[*Beppo* (1818), 48]

136. 'Tis vain to struggle – let me perish young–
Live as I lived, and love as I have loved;
To dust if I return, from dust I sprung.
['Stanzas to the river Po' (1819)]

137. The world is a bundle of hay,
Mankind are the asses who pull;
Each tugs it a different way,
And the greatest of all is John Bull.
['Epigram' (1820)]

138. Through life's road, so dim and dirty,
I have dragg'd to three-and-thirty.
What have these years left to me?
Nothing – except thirty-three.
[Journal, 1821]

139. Who killed John Keats?
'I,' says the Quarterly,
So savage and Tartarly;
''Twas one of my feats.'
['John Keats' (c. 1821)]

140. I am the very slave of circumstance
And impulse – borne away with every breath!
[*Sardanapalus* (1821), Act IV]

141. Oh, talk not to me of a name great in story;
The days of our youth are the days of our glory;
And the myrtle and ivy of sweet two-and-twenty
Are worth all your laurels, though ever so plenty...

142. I knew it was love, and I felt it was glory.
['Stanzas Written on the Road between Florence and Pisa, November 1821']

143. And when we think we lead, we are most led.
[*The Two Foscari* (1821), II.i]

144. Saint Peter sat by the celestial gate:
His keys were rusty, and the lock was dull,
So little trouble had been given of late.
[*The Vision of Judgement* (1822), 1]

145. The angels all were singing out of tune,
And hoarse with having little else to do,
Excepting to wind up the sun and moon,
Or curb a runaway young star or two.
[*The Vision of Judgement* (1822), 2]

146. [Referring to George III]
A better farmer ne'er brush'd dew from lawn,
A worse king never left a realm undone!
[*The Vision of Judgement* (1822), 8]

147. In whom his qualities are reigning still,
Except that household virtue, most uncommon,
Of constancy to a bad, ugly woman.
[*The Vision of Judgement* (1822), 12]

148. As he drew near, he gazed upon the gate
Ne'er to be enter'd more by him or Sin,
With such a glance of supernatural hate
As made Saint Peter wish himself within;
He patter'd with his keys at a great rate,
And sweated through his apostolic skin:
Of course his perspiration was but ichor,
Or some other such spiritual liquor.
[*The Vision of Judgement* (1822), 25]

149. For by many stories,
And true, we learn the angels all are Tories.
[*The Vision of Judgement* (1822), 26]

150. Yet still between his Darkness and his Brightness
There pass'd a mutual glance of great politeness.
[*The Vision of Judgement* (1822), 35]

151. [On Southey]
He had written much blank verse, and blanker prose.
[*The Vision of Judgement* (1822), 98]

152. And when the tumult dwindled to a calm,
I left him practising the hundredth psalm.
[*The Vision of Judgement* (1822), 106]

153. The 'good old times' – all times when old are good–
Are gone.
['The Age of Bronze' (1823), 1]

154. For what were all these country patriots born?
To hunt, and vote, and raise the price of corn?
['The Age of Bronze' (1823), 14]

155. I am ashes where once I was fire.
['To the Countess of Blessington' (1823)]

156. [On Coleridge's attempt to explain metaphysics to the nation]
I wish he would explain his Explanation.
[*Don Juan* (1819–1824), Dedication, 2]

157. The intellectual eunuch Castlereagh.
[*Don Juan* (1819–24), Dedication, 11]

158. My way is to begin with the beginning.
[*Don Juan* (1819–1824), Canto I, 7]

159. In virtues nothing earthly could surpass her,
Save thine 'incomparable oil', Macassar!
[*Don Juan* (1819–1824), Canto I, 17]

160. But – Oh! ye lords of ladies intellectual,
Inform us truly, have they not hen-peck'd you all?
[*Don Juan* (1819–1824), Canto I, 22]

161. She,
Was married, charming, chaste, and twenty-three.
[*Don Juan* (1819–1824), Canto I, 59]

162. Her stature tall – I hate a dumpy woman.
[*Don Juan* (1819–1824), Canto I, 61]

163. What men call gallantry, and gods adultery,
Is much more common where the climate's sultry.
[*Don Juan* (1819–1824), Canto I, 63]

164. Even innocence itself has many a wile,
And will not dare to trust itself with truth,
And love is taught hypocrisy from youth.
[*Don Juan* (1819–1824), Canto I, 72]

165. Christians have burnt each other, quite persuaded
That all the Apostles would have done as they did.
[*Don Juan* (1819–1824), Canto I, 83]

166. Whether it was she did not see, or would not,
Or, like all very clever people, could not.
[*Don Juan* (1819–1824), Canto I, 97]

167. A little still she strove, and much repented,
And whispering 'I will ne'er consent' – consented.
[*Don Juan* (1819–1824), Canto I, 117]

168. 'Tis sweet to hear the watch-dog's honest bark
Bay deep-mouth'd welcome as we draw near home;
'Tis sweet to know there is an eye will mark

Our coming, and look brighter when we come.
[*Don Juan* (1819–1824), Canto I, 123]

169. Sweet is revenge – especially to women.
[*Don Juan* (1819–1824), Canto I, 124]

170. Pleasure's a sin, and sometimes sin's a pleasure.
[*Don Juan* (1819–1824), Canto I, 133]

171. Man's love is of man's life a thing apart,
'Tis woman's whole existence.
[*Don Juan* (1819–1824), Canto I, 194]

172. So for a good old-gentlemanly vice,
I think I must take up with avarice.
[*Don Juan* (1819–1824), Canto I, 216]

173. There's nought, no doubt, so much the spirit calms
As rum and true religion.
[*Don Juan* (1819–1824), Canto II, 34]

174. But he, poor fellow, had a wife and children,
Two things for dying people quite bewildering.
[*Don Juan* (1819–1824), Canto II, 43]

175. 'Twas twilight, and the sunless day went down
Over the waste of waters.
[*Don Juan* (1819–1824), Canto II, 49]

176. A solitary shriek, the bubbling cry
Of some strong swimmer in his agony.
[*Don Juan* (1819–1824), Canto II, 53]

177. He could, perhaps, have pass'd the Hellespont,
As once (a feat on which ourselves we prided)
Leander, Mr Ekenhead, and I did.
[*Don Juan* (1819–1824), Canto II, 105]

178. Let us have wine and women, mirth and laughter,
Sermons and soda-water the day after.
[*Don Juan* (1819–1824), Canto II, 178]

179. Man, being reasonable, must get drunk;
The best of life is but intoxication:
Glory, the grape, love, gold, in these are sunk
The hopes of all men, and of every nation.
[*Don Juan* (1819–1824), Canto II, 179]

180. Each kiss a heart-quake, – for a kiss's strength,
I think it must be reckon'd by its length.
[*Don Juan* (1819–1824), Canto II, 186]

181. A group that's quite antique,
Half naked, loving, natural, and Greek.
[*Don Juan* (1819–1824), Canto II, 194]

182. Alas! the love of women! it is known
To be a lovely and a fearful thing.
[*Don Juan* (1819–1824), Canto II, 199]

183. In her first passion woman loves her lover,
In all the others all she loves is love.
[*Don Juan* (1819–1824), Canto III, 3]

184. Romances paint at full length people's wooings,
But only give a bust of marriages:
For no one cares for matrimonial cooings.
There's nothing wrong in a connubial kiss:
Think you, if Laura had been Petrarch's wife,
He would have written sonnets all his life?
[*Don Juan* (1819–1824), Canto III, 8]

185. All tragedies are finish'd by a death,
All comedies are ended by a marriage.
[*Don Juan* (1819–1824), Canto III, 9]

186. Dreading that climax of all human ills,
The inflammation of his weekly bills.
[*Don Juan* (1819–1824), Canto III, 35]

187. He was the mildest manner'd man
That ever scuttled ship or cut a throat.
[*Don Juan* (1819–1824), Canto III, 41]

188. Cost his enemies a long repentance,
And made him a good friend, but bad acquaintance.
[*Don Juan* (1819–1824), Canto III, 54]

189. Though sages may pour out their wisdom's treasure,
There is no sterner moralist than Pleasure.
[*Don Juan* (1819–1824), Canto III, 65]

190. But Shakspeare also says, 'tis very silly
'To gild refined gold, or paint the lily.'
[*Don Juan* (1819–1824), Canto III, 76. Cf. Shakespeare, *King John*: 16]

191. Agree to a short armistice with truth.
[*Don Juan* (1819–1824), Canto III, 83]

192. The isles of Greece, the isles of Greece!
Where burning Sappho loved and sung,
Where grew the arts of war and peace,
Where Delos rose, and Phoebus sprung!
Eternal summer gilds them yet,
But all, except their sun, is set...

193. The mountains look on Marathon–
And Marathon looks on the sea;
And musing there an hour alone,
I dream'd that Greece might still be free...

194. For what is left the poet here?
For Greeks a blush – for Greece a tear...

195. Earth! render back from out thy breast
A remnant of our Spartan dead!
Of the three hundred grant but three,
To make a new Thermopylae!...

196. Fill high the cup with Samian wine!...

197. To think such breasts must suckle slaves.

Place me on Sunium's marbled steep,
Where nothing, save the waves and I,
May hear our mutual murmurs sweep;
There, swan-like, let me sing and die:
A land of slaves shall ne'er be mine–
Dash down yon cup of Samian wine!
[*Don Juan* (1819–1824), Canto III, 86]

198. Milton's the prince of poets – so we say;
A little heavy, but no less divine.
[*Don Juan* (1819–1824), Canto III, 91]

199. A drowsy frowzy poem, call'd the 'Excursion',
Writ in a manner which is my aversion.
[*Don Juan* (1819–1824), Canto III, 94]

200. Nothing so difficult as a beginning
In poesy, unless perhaps the end.
[*Don Juan* (1819–1824), Canto IV, 1]

201. Imagination droops her pinion.
[*Don Juan* (1819–1824), Canto IV, 3]

202. And if I laugh at any mortal thing,
'Tis that I may not weep.
[*Don Juan* (1819–1824), Canto IV, 4]

203. 'Whom the gods love die young' was said of yore.
[*Don Juan* (1819–1824), Canto IV, 12]

204. I've stood upon Achilles' tomb,
And heard Troy doubted; time will doubt of Rome.
[*Don Juan* (1819–1824), Canto IV, 101]

205. I thought it would appear
That there had been a lady in the case.
[*Don Juan* (1819–1824), Canto V, 19]

206. And put himself upon his good behaviour.
[*Don Juan* (1819–1824), Canto V, 47]

207. That all-softening, overpowering knell,
The tocsin of the soul – the dinner-bell.
[*Don Juan* (1819–1824), Canto V, 49]

208. A moral (like all morals) melancholy.
[*Don Juan* (1819–1824), Canto V, 63]

209. Not to admire is all the art I know.
[*Don Juan* (1819–1824), Canto V, 101]

210. The women pardon'd all except her face.
[*Don Juan* (1819–1824), Canto V, 113]

211. Why don't they knead two virtuous souls for life
Into that mortal centaur, man and wife?
[*Don Juan* (1819–1824), Canto V, 158]

212. There is a tide in the affairs of women,
Which, taken at the flood, leads – God knows where.
[*Don Juan* (1819–1824), Canto VI, 2. Cf. Shakespeare, *Julius Caesar*: 76]

213. Dudù said nothing, as
Her talents were of the more silent class.
[*Don Juan* (1819–1824), Canto VI, 49]

214. A 'strange coincidence', to use a phrase
By which such things are settled now-a-days.
[*Don Juan* (1819–1824), Canto VI, 78]

215. Must I restrain me, through the fear of strife,
From holding up the nothingness of life?
[*Don Juan* (1819–1824), Canto VII, 6]

216. 'Let there be light!' said God, 'and there was light!'
'Let there be blood!' says man, and there's a sea!
[*Don Juan* (1819–1824), Canto VII, 41]

217. Never had mortal man such opportunity,
Except Napoleon, or abused it more.
[*Don Juan* (1819–1824), Canto IX, 9]

218. He said
Little, but to the purpose.
[*Don Juan* (1819–1824), Canto IX, 83]

219. That water-land of Dutchmen and of ditches.
[*Don Juan* (1819–1824), Canto X, 63]

220. When Bishop Berkeley said 'there was no matter',
And proved it–'twas no matter what he said.
[*Don Juan* (1819–1824), Canto XI, 1]

221. But Tom's no more – and so no more of Tom.
[*Don Juan* (1819–1824), Canto XI, 20]

222. And, after all, what is a lie? 'Tis but
The truth in masquerade.
[*Don Juan* (1819–1824), Canto XI, 37]

223. John Keats, who was kill'd off by one critique,
Just as he really promised something great,
If not intelligible, without Greek
Contrived to talk about the gods of late,
Much as they might have been supposed to speak.
Poor fellow! His was an untoward fate;
'Tis strange the mind, that very fiery particle,
Should let itself be snuff'd out by an article.
[*Don Juan* (1819–1824), Canto XI, 60]

224. And hold up to the sun my little taper.
[*Don Juan* (1819–1824), Canto XII, 21]

225. For talk six times with the same single lady,
And you may get the wedding dresses ready.
[*Don Juan* (1819–1824), Canto XII, 59]

226. Merely innocent flirtation.
Not quite adultery, but adulteration.
[*Don Juan* (1819–1824), Canto XII, 63]

227. A finish'd gentleman from top to toe.
[*Don Juan* (1819–1824), Canto XII, 84]

228. Now hatred is by far the longest pleasure;
Men love in haste, but they detest at leisure.
[*Don Juan* (1819–1824), Canto XIII, 6]

229. Cervantes smiled Spain's chivalry away.
[*Don Juan* (1819–1824), Canto XIII, 11]

230. The English winter – ending in July,
To recommence in August.
[*Don Juan* (1819–1824), Canto XIII, 42]

231. Society is now one polish'd horde,
Form'd of two mighty tribes, the Bores and Bored.
[*Don Juan* (1819–1824), Canto XIII, 95]

232. I for one venerate a petticoat.
[*Don Juan* (1819–1824), Canto XIV, 26]

233. Of all the horrid, hideous notes of woe,
Sadder than owl-songs or the midnight blast,
Is that portentous phrase, 'I told you so'.
[*Don Juan* (1819–1824), Canto XIV, 50]

234. 'Tis strange – but true; for truth is always strange;
Stranger than fiction.
[*Don Juan* (1819–1824), Canto XIV, 101]

235. A lovely being, scarcely form'd or moulded,
A rose with all its sweetest leaves yet folded.
[*Don Juan* (1819–1824), Canto XV, 43]

236. Between two worlds life hovers like a star,
'Twixt night and morn, upon the horizon's verge.
How little do we know that which we are!
How less what we may be!
[*Don Juan* (1819–1824), Canto XV, 99]

237. The antique Persians taught three useful things,
To draw the bow, to ride, and speak the truth.
[*Don Juan* (1819–1824), Canto XVI, 1]

238. Not so her gracious, graceful, graceless Grace.
[*Don Juan* (1819–1824), Canto XVI, 49]

239. The loudest wit I e'er was deafen'd with.
[*Don Juan* (1819–1824), Canto XVI, 81]

240. The flower of Adam's bastards!
[*The Deformed Transformed* (1824), I.ii]

241. My days are in the yellow leaf;
The flowers and fruits of love are gone;
The worm, the canker, and the grief
Are mine alone!...

242. Seek out – less often sought than found–
A soldier's grave, for thee the best;
Then look around, and choose thy ground,
And take thy rest.
['On This Day I Complete my Thirty-sixth Year' (1824)]

243. The Impression of Parliament upon me was, that its members are not formidable as speakers, but very much so as an audience.
[*Detached Thoughts*, 11]

244. But I never see any one much improved by matrimony. All my coupled contemporaries are bald and discontented.
[Journal, 1813]

245. Cleopatra strikes me as the epitome of her sex – fond, lively, sad, tender, teasing, humble, haughty, beautiful, the devil! – coquettish to the last, as well with the 'asp' as with Antony.
[Journal, 1813]

246. The more I see of men, the less I like them. If I could but say so of women too, all would be well.
[Journal, 1814]

247. If I could always read, I should never feel the want of society.
[Journal, 1814]

248. There is something to me very softening in the presence of a woman, – some strange influence, even if one is not in love with them – which I cannot at all account for, having no very high opinion of the sex.
[Journal, 1814]

249. What is poetry? – The feeling of a Former world and Future.
[Journal, 1821]

250. When a proposal is made to emancipate or relieve, you hesitate, you deliberate for years, you temporize and tamper with the minds of men; but a death-bill must be passed off hand, without a thought of the consequences.
[Maiden speech in House of Lords, 1812]

251. [Of Annabella Milbanke]
My Princess of Parallelograms.
[Letter to Lady Melbourne, 1812]

252. Wordsworth – stupendous genius! damned fool.
[Letter to James Hogg, 1816]

253. Love in this part of the world is no sinecure.
[Letter to John Murray from Venice, 1816]

254. I am sure my bones would not rest in an English grave, or my clay mix with the earth of that country. I believe the thought would drive me mad on my deathbed, could I suppose that any of my friends would be base enough to convey my carcass back to your soil. I would not even feed your worms if I could help it.
[Letter to John Murray, 1819]

255. But I am convinced of the advantages of looking at mankind instead of reading about them, and the bitter effects of staying at home with all the narrow prejudices of an islander, that I think there should be a law amongst us, to set our young men abroad for a term, among the few allies our wars have left us.
[Letter]

256. [Remark on the instantaneous success of *Childe Harold*]
I awoke one morning and found myself famous.
[In Thomas Moore, *Letters and Journals of Lord Byron* (1830), I]

257. [To his wife]
You should have a softer pillow than my heart.
[In E.C. Mayne (ed.), *The Life and Letters of Anne Isabella, Lady Noel Byron* (1929)]

Cabell, James Branch (1879–1958)

American novelist, poet, genealogist and historian; prosecuted for obscenity

1. I am willing to taste any drink once.
[*Jurgen* (1919), 1]

2. A man possesses nothing certainly save a brief loan of his own body: and yet the body of man is capable of much curious pleasure.
[*Jurgen* (1919), 20]

3. The optimist proclaims that we live in the best of all possible worlds; and the pessimist fears this is true.
[*The Silver Stallion* (1926), IV, 26]

Cacciente, Guido

Jazz club owner

1. I've worked and slaved for years to keep this place a sewer.
[In Ian Carr, *Miles Davis: a Critical Biography* (1982)]

Caesar, Augustus (63 BC–AD14)

Roman statesman; first Roman emperor, from 27 BC

1. *Urbem ... excoluit adeo, uti iure sit gloriatus marmoream se relinquere, quam latericiam accepisset.*
He so beautified the city that he justly boasted that he found it brick and left it marble.
[In Suetonius, *Lives of the Caesars*, 'Divus Augustus', 28]

2. [Said of those who never pay their debts. The term Kalends was Roman and did not exist in Greek]
Ad Kalendas Graecas soluturos.
It will be paid at the Greek Kalends.
[In Suetonius, *Lives of the Caesars*, 'Divus Augustus', 87]

Caesar, Gaius Julius (c. 102–44 BC)

Roman statesman, historian and army commander; assassinated

1. *Gallia est omnis divisa in partes tres.*
The whole territory of Gaul is divided into three parts.
[*De Bello Gallico*, I, 1]

2. *Fere libenter homines id quod volunt credunt.*
Men generally believe what they wish.
[*De Bello Gallico*, III, 18]

3. [Remark on crossing the Rubicon]
Iacta alea est.
The die is cast.
[In Suetonius, *Lives of the Caesars*, 'Divus Julius', 32]

4. [On his triumphant Pontic campaign]
Veni, vidi, vici.
I came, I saw, I conquered.
[In Suetonius, *Lives of the Caesars*, 'Divus Julius', 37]

5. Caesar's wife must be above suspicion.
[Based on Plutarch, *Lives*, 'Julius Caesar', 10, 6]

6. I would rather be the first man here (in Gaul) than second in Rome.
[Attr. by Plutarch in *Lives*, 'Julius Caesar', 11]

7. *Et tu Brute?*
You too, Brutus?
[Attributed last words, on being stabbed by his friend]

Cage, John (1912–1992)

American experimental composer and writer

1. I have nothing to say, I am saying it, and that is poetry.
[*Silence* (1961), 'Lecture on nothing']

Cagney, James (1904–1986)

American film actor, noted for roles as gangster

1. Made it, Ma! Top of the world!
[*White Heat*, film, 1949; scriptwriters Ivan Goff and Ben Roberts]

Cahn, Sammy (Samuel Cohen) (1913–)

American songwriter

1. Love and marriage, love and marriage,
Go together like a horse and carriage.
This I tell ya, brother,

Ya can't have one without the other.
['Love and Marriage', song, 1955]

Caine, Michael (Maurice Micklewhite) (1933–)
British film actor

1. Never trust anyone who wears a beard, a bow tie, two-toned shoes, sandals or sunglasses.
[*The Times*, 1992; quoting his father]

Calderón de la Barca, Pedro (1600–1681)
Leading Spanish dramatist and poet

1. *Pues el delito mayor*
del hombre es haber nacido.
For man's greatest offence is to have been born.
[*La vida es sueño* (*Life is a Dream*, 1636), 'Primera Jornada']

2. *Pues veo estando dormido,*
que sueñe estando despierto.
For I see, since I am asleep, that I dream while I am awake.
[*La vida es sueño* (*Life is a Dream*, 1636), 'Segunda Jornada']

3. *Aun en sueños*
no se pierde el hacer bien.
Even in dreams doing good is not wasted.
[*La vida es sueño* (*Life is a Dream*, 1636), 'Segunda Jornada']

4. *¿Qué es la vida? Un frenesí.*
¿Qué es la vida? Una ilusión,
una sombra, una ficción,
y el mayor bien es pequeño;
que toda la vida es sueño,
y los sueños, sueños son.
What is life? A frenzy. What is life? An illusion, a shadow, a fiction, and the greatest good is worth little; since all of life is a dream, and dreams are dreams.
[*La vida es sueño* (*Life is a Dream*, 1636), 'Segunda Jornada']

5. Fame, like water, bears up the lighter things, and lets the weighty sink.
[Attr.]

Caligula (Gaius Julius Caesar Germanicus) (12–41)
Roman emperor (37–41), known for his cruelty

1. *Utinam populus Romanus unam cervicem haberet!*
I wish that the Roman people had only one neck!
[In Suetonius, *Lives of the Caesars*, 'Gaius Caesar Caligula', 30]

2. *Ita feri ut se mori sentiat.*
Strike him so that he may feel that he is dying.
[In Suetonius, *Lives of the Caesars*, 'Gaius Caesar Caligula', 30]

Callaghan, James, Baron Callaghan of Cardiff (1912–)
English Labour politician; Prime Minister 1976–79

1. A lie can be half-way round the world before the truth has got its boots on.
[Speech, House of Commons, 1976]

2. Either back us or sack us.
[Speech, Labour Party Conference, 1977]

Callimachus (c. 305–c. 240 BC)
Cyrene-born Alexandrian poet, grammarian, critic and epigrammatist

1. I abhor, too, the roaming lover, nor do I drink from every well; I loathe all things held in common.
[In R. Pfeiffer (ed.), *Epigrams*]

2. A great book is like great evil.
[In R. Pfeiffer (ed.), *Fragments*]

Calman, Mel (1931–1994)
English artist, news cartoonist, designer and illustrator

1. [In answer to the criticism of his cartoons that 'any child could do better']
Yes, but it takes courage for an adult to draw as badly as that.
[*The Independent*, 1994]

Calonne, Charles Alexandre de (1734–1802)
French statesman; Controller-General of France 1783–86

1. *Madame, si c'est possible, c'est fait; impossible? cela se fera.*
Madam, if it is possible, it has been done; impossible? It will be done.
[In J. Michelet, *Histoire de la Révolution Française* (1847), I, ii, 8]

Calverley, C.S. (1831–1884)
English poet, parodist, classical scholar and lawyer

1. The heart which grief hath canker'd
Hath one unfailing remedy – the Tankard.
['Beer' (1861)]

2. How they who use fusees
All grow by slow degrees
Brainless as chimpanzees,
Meagre as lizards:
Go mad, and beat their wives;
Plunge (after shocking lives)
Razors and carving knives
Into their gizzards.
['Ode to Tobacco' (1861)]

3. Yet it is better to drop thy friends, O my daughter, than to drop thy 'H's'.
['Proverbial Philosophy' (1861), 'Of Friendship']

4. The farmer's daughter hath soft brown hair
(Butter and eggs and a pound of cheese)
And I met with a ballad, I can't say where,
Which wholly consisted of lines like these.
['Ballad' (1872)]

5. I cannot sing the old songs now!
It is not that I deem them low;
'Tis that I can't remember how
They go.
['Changed' (1872)]

6. A bare-legg'd beggarly son of a gun.
['The Cock and the Bull' (1872)]

7. Friend, there be they on whom mishap
Or never or so rarely comes,
That, when they think thereof, they snap
Derisive thumbs:...

8. And fain would I be e'en as these!
Life is with such all beer and skittles;
They are not difficult to please
About their victuals...

9. And when they travel, if they find
That they have left their pocket-compass
Or Murray or thick boots behind,
They raise no rumpus.
['Contentment' (1872). Cf. George du Maurier: 1]

10. For I've read in many a novel that, unless they've souls that grovel,
Folks prefer in fact a hovel to your dreary marble halls.
['In the Gloaming' (1872)]

Calvino, Italo (1923–1985)
Italian novelist and critic

1. *Cosimo Piovasco di Rondò – Visse sugli alberi – Amò sempre la terra – – Salí in cielo–*
Cosimo Piovasco di Rondò – He lived on the trees – He always loved the earth – He ascended in the sky–
[*Il Barone Rampante* (*The Baron in the Trees*, 1957)]

Calwell, Arthur Augustus (1894–1973)
Australian Labour politician

1. [Defending the deportation of a Chinese refugee who, Calwell claimed, was not eligible to become a permanent resident of Australia]
There are many Wongs in the Chinese community, but I have to say – and I am sure that the honourable member for Balaclava will not mind me doing so – that 'two Wongs do not make a White'.
[*Commonwealth Parliamentary Debates*, 1947]
2. [To Arthur Fadden, in the House of Representatives]
I well recall the time when, for forty days and forty nights, you held the destiny of Australia in the hollow of your head.
[In Fred Daly, *The Politician who Laughed*]

Cambronne, General (Baron de Cambronne) (1770–1842)
French general

1. *La Garde meurt, et ne se rend pas.*
The Guard dies and does not surrender.
[Attr., Waterloo, June 1815]
2. ['*Le mot de Cambronne*'; said to be his reply to the call to surrender]
Merde!
[Attr., Waterloo, June 1815]

Camden, Lord (Charles Pratt, First Earl Camden) (1714–1794)
English lawyer; Lord Chancellor 1766–70

1. [Arguing that the British parliament had no right to tax the Americans.]
Taxation and representation are inseparable . . . whatever is a man's own, is absolutely his own; no man hath a right to take it from him without his consent either expressed by himself or representative; whoever attempts to do it, attempts an injury; whoever does it, commits a robbery; he throws down and destroys the distinction between liberty and slavery.
[Speech, House of Lords, 1766]

Camden, William (1551–1623)
English classical scholar, antiquary and historian

1. My friend, judge not me,
Thou seest I judge not thee.
Betwixt the stirrup and the ground
Mercy I asked, mercy I found.
[*Remains Concerning Britain* (1605), 'Epitaph for a Man Killed by Falling from His Horse']

Cameron, Simon (1799–1889)
American statesman; Republican politician and newspaper editor

1. An honest politician is one who, when he is bought, will stay bought.
[Remark]

Campbell, Alistair Te Ariki (1925–)
New Zealand poet and children's writer

1. Walk the black path
Walk the black path at noon
Walk the tilting earth
Between dream and nightmare
[*Collected Poems 1947–1981* (1981), 'Walk the Black Path']
2. Now it is water I dream of,
. . . lifting
casually on a shore
where yellow lions come out
in the early morning
and stare out to sea.
[*Collected Poems 1947–1981* (1981), 'Dreams, Yellow Lions']

Campbell, Baron (1799–1861)
Scottish lawyer and politician; Lord Chancellor 1859

1. So essential did I consider an Index to be to every book, that I proposed to bring a Bill into parliament to deprive an author who publishes a book without an Index of the privilege of copyright; and, moreover, to subject him, for his offence, to a pecuniary penalty.
[*Lives of the Chief Justices*, Preface to Vol. III]

Campbell, David Gordon (1915–1979)
Australian poet, once international rugby player and wartime pilot

1. Sweet rain, bless our windy farm,
Stepping round in skirts of storm:
Amongst the broken clods the hare
Folds his ears like hands in prayer.
['Prayer for Rain' (c. 1950)]
2. The cruel girls we loved
Are over forty,
Their subtle daughters
Have stolen their beauty;

And with a blue stare
Of cool surprise
They mock their anxious mothers
With their mothers' eyes.
['Mothers and Daughters' (c. 1965)]
3. 'Hop in,' said the Queen Mother. In I piled
Between them to lie like a stick of wood.
I couldn't find a thing to say. My blood
Beat, but like rollers at the ebb of tide.
'I hope Your Majesties sleep well,' I lied.
A hand touched mine and the Queen said, 'I am
Most grateful to you, Jock. Please call me Ma'am.'
['The Australian Dream' (c. 1965)]
4. In the heart of dew we lie
Drowned in brief immortality
And watch our fair-haired children play.
['Hearts and Children']

Campbell, Jane Montgomery (1817–1878)
English hymn-writer

1. We plough the fields, and scatter
The good seed on the land,
But it is fed and watered
By God's Almighty Hand.
He sends the snow in winter,
The warmth to swell the grain,
The breezes and the sunshine,
And soft refreshing rain.
[Hymn, 1861; trans. from the original German of Matthias Claudius (1740–1815)]

Campbell, Joseph (1879–1944)
Irish poet and republican

1. As a white candle
In a holy place,
So is the beauty
Of an aged face.
[*Irishry* (1913), 'The Old Woman']

Campbell, Menzies (1941–)
Liberal Democrat politician, lawyer and athlete

1. [Of John Smith, leader of the Labour Party]
He had all the virtues of a Scottish Presbyterian, but none of the vices.
[*The Guardian*, May 1994]

Campbell, Mrs Patrick (Beatrice Stella Tanner) (1865–1940)
English actress; friend of George Bernard Shaw

1. [To Bernard Shaw, a vegetarian]
Some day you'll eat a pork chop, Joey, and then God help all women.
[In Alexander Woollcott, *While Rome Burns* (1934), 'Some Neighbours']

2. Marriage is the result of the longing for the deep, deep peace of the double bed after the hurly-burly of the chaise-longue.
[In Cooper and Hartman, *Violets and Vinegar*]

3. I don't mind where people make love, so long as they don't do it in the street and frighten the horses.
[Attr.]

4. [To Noël Coward, after the first performance of *Private Lives*]
All your characters talk like typewriters, but I do quite like it when you do your little humming at the piano.
[Attr.]

Campbell, Roy (1901–1957)
South African poet, translator of Spanish and journalist

1. South Africa, renowned both far and wide
For politics and little else beside:
Where, having torn the land with shot and shell,
Our sturdy pioneers as farmers dwell,
And, 'twixt the hours of strenuous sleep, relax
To shear the fleeces or to fleece the blacks.
[*The Wayzgoose* (1928), I]

2. You praise the firm restraint with which they write–
I'm with you there, of course:
They use the snaffle and the curb all right,
But where's the bloody horse?
[*Adamastor* (1930), 'On Some South African Novelists']

3. The timeless, surly patience of the serf
That moves the nearest to the naked earth
And ploughs down palaces, and thrones, and towers.
[*Adamastor* (1930), 'The Serf']

4. Her body looms above him like a hill
Within whose shade a village lies at rest,
Or the first cloud so terrible and still
That bears the coming harvest in its breast.
[*Adamastor* (1930), 'The Zulu Girl']

5. Now Spring, sweet laxative of Georgian strains,
Quickens the ink in literary veins,
The Stately Homes of England ope their doors
To piping Nancy-boys and crashing Bores.
Where for weekends the scavengers of letters
Convene to chew the fat about their betters.
['The Georgiad' (1931), I]

6. Translations (like wives) are seldom strictly faithful if they are in the least attractive.
[*Poetry Review*, June – July, 1949]

Campbell, Thomas (1777–1844)
Scottish poet, ballad-writer and journalist

1. On the green banks of Shannon, when Sheelah was nigh,
No blithe Irish lad was so happy as I;
No harp like my own could so cheerily play,
And wherever I went was my poor dog Tray.
['The Harper' (1799)]

2. 'Tis distance lends enchantment to the view,
And robes the mountain in its azure hue.
[*Pleasures of Hope* (1799), I, line 7]

3. The proud, the cold untroubled heart of stone,
That never mused on sorrow but its own.
[*Pleasures of Hope* (1799), I, line 185]

4. Hope, for a season, bade the world farewell,
And Freedom shriek'd – as Kosciusko fell!
[*Pleasures of Hope* (1799), I, line 381]

5. There shall be love, when genial morn appears,
Like pensive Beauty smiling in her tears,
To watch the brightening roses of the sky
And muse on Nature with a poet's eye!
[*Pleasures of Hope* (1799), II, line 98]

6. What millions died – that Caesar might be great!
[*Pleasures of Hope* (1799), II, line 174]

7. Ye Mariners of England
That guard our native seas,
Whose flag has braved, a thousand years,
The battle and the breeze–
Your glorious standard launch again
To match another foe!
And sweep through the deep,
While the stormy winds do blow,–
While the battle rages loud and long,
And the stormy winds do blow...

8. Britannia needs no bulwarks,
No towers along the steep;
Her march is o'er the mountain waves,
Her home is on the deep.
With thunders from her native oak
She quells the floods below.
['Ye Mariners of England' (1801)]

9. Let us think of them that sleep,
Full many a fathom deep,
By thy wild and stormy steep,
Elsinore!
['Battle of the Baltic' (1809)]

10. Tomorrow let us do or die!
['Gertrude of Wyoming' (1809), III]

11. A chieftain to the Highlands bound
Cries, 'Boatman, do not tarry!
And I'll give thee a silver pound
To row us o'er the ferry.'...

12. O, I'm the chief of Ulva's isle,
And this Lord Ullin's daughter...

13. I'll meet the raging of the skies,
But not an angry father...

14. One lovely hand she stretched for aid,
And one was round her lover...

15. The waters wild went o'er his child,
And he was left lamenting.
['Lord Ullin's Daughter' (1809)]

16. Better be courted and jilted
Than never be courted at all.
['The Jilted Nymph' (1843)]

17. An original something, fair maid, you would win me
To write – but how shall I begin?
For I fear I have nothing original in me–
Excepting Original Sin.
['To a Young Lady, Who Asked Me to Write Something Original for Her Album' (1843)]

18. To live in hearts we leave behind
Is not to die.
['Hallowed Ground']

19. On Linden, when the sun was low,
All bloodless lay the untrodden snow,
And dark as winter was the flow
Of Iser, rolling rapidly...

20. The combat deepens. On, ye brave,
Who rush to glory, or the grave!
Wave, Munich! all thy banners wave,
And charge with all thy chivalry.
['Hohenlinden']

21. 'Tis the sunset of life gives me mystical lore,
And coming events cast their shadows before.
['Lochiel's Warning']

22. One moment may with bliss repay
Unnumber'd hours of pain.
['The Ritter Bann']

23. The sentinel stars set their watch in the sky.
['The Soldier's Dream']

24. [Excusing himself in proposing a toast to Napoleon at a literary dinner]
Gentlemen ... you must not mistake me. I admit that the French Emperor is a tyrant. I admit that he is a monster. I admit that he is the sworn foe of our own nation, and, if you will, of the whole human race. But, gentlemen, we must be just to our great enemy. We must not forget that he once shot a bookseller.
[Attr. in a footnote in G.O. Trevelyan, *The Life and Letters of Lord Macaulay* (1876), 12, Diary, December 12, 1848]

25. Now Barabbas was a publisher.
[Attr. in Samuel Smiles, *A Publisher and his Friends* (1891), I, 14; also attr. to Byron]

Campbell-Bannerman, Sir Henry (1836–1908)
British statesman and former Liberal Prime Minister

1. Good government could never be a substitute for government by the people themselves.
[Speech at Stirling, November 1905]

Campion, Thomas (1567–1620)
English poet, musician and doctor

1. Follow thy fair sunne, unhappy shadowe.
[*A Booke of Ayres* (1601), Part I, 4]

2. Follow your Saint, follow with accents sweet;
Haste you, sad nootes, fall at her flying feete.
There, wrapt in cloud of sorrowe pitie move,
And tell the ravisher of my soule I perish for her love.
[*A Booke of Ayres* (1601), Part I, 10]

3. The man of life upright,
Whose guiltlesse hart is free
From all dishonest deedes
Or thought of vanitie...

4. Good thoughts his onely friendes,
His wealth a well-spent age,
The earth his sober Inne
And quiet Pilgrimage.
[*A Booke of Ayres* (1601), Part I, 18]

5. Never weather-beaten sail more willing bent to shore,
Never tired pilgrim's limbs affected slumber more.
[*A Booke of Ayres* (1601)]

6. Rose-cheekt Lawra, come
Sing thou smoothly with thy beawties
Silent musick, either other
Sweetly gracing.
[*Observations on the Art of English Poesie* (1602), 'Lawra']

7. Kinde are her answeres,
But her performance keeps no day;
Breaks time, as dancers
From their own Musicke when they stray:
All her free favors and smooth words,
Wing my hopes in vaine
O did ever voice so sweet but only fain?
Can true love yeeld such delay,
Converting joy to pain?
[*The Third Booke of Ayres* (1617), 7]

8. The Summer hath his joyes,
And Winter his delights;
Though Love and all his pleasures are but toyes,
They shorten tedious nights.
[*The Third Booke of Ayres* (1617), 12]

9. There is a Garden in her face,
Where Roses and white Lillies grow;
A heav'nly paradise is that place,
Wherein all pleasant fruits doe flow.
There Cherries grow, which none may buy
Till 'Cherry ripe' themselves doe cry.

Those Cherries fayrely doe enclose
Of Orient Pearle a double row;
Which when her lovely laughter showes,
They look like Rose buds fill'd with snow.
[*The Fourth Booke of Ayres* (1617), 7]

Camus, Albert (1913–1960)
Algerian-born French novelist, dramatist and critic; Nobel prize 1957

1. *Intellectuel? Oui. Et ne jamais renier. Intellectuel = celui qui se dédouble. Ça me plaît. Je suis content d'être les deux.*
An intellectual? Yes. And never deny it. An intellectual = one who splits himself in two. I like that. I am happy to be both [halves].
[*Carnets, 1935–1942* (*Notebooks, 1935–1942*, published 1962), I, 1935–1937]

2. *La politique et le sort des hommes sont formés par des hommes sans idéal et sans grandeur. Ceux qui ont une grandeur ne font pas de politique.*
Politics and the fate of mankind are shaped by men without ideals and without greatness. Men who have greatness within them don't concern themselves with politics.
[*Carnets, 1935–1942* (*Notebooks, 1935–1942*, published 1962), II, 1937–1939]

3. *La lutte elle-même vers les sommets suffit à remplir un coeur d'homme. Il faut imaginer Sisyphe heureux.*
The struggle itself towards the heights is enough to fill a human heart. One should imagine Sisyphus happy.
[*Le Mythe de Sisyphe* (*The Myth of Sisyphus*, 1942), final words]

4. *Il semblait être l'ami de tous les plaisirs normaux, sans en être l'esclave.*
He seemed to indulge in all the usual pleasures without being a slave to any of them.
[*La Peste* (*The Plague*, 1947)]

5. *Là était la certitude, dans le travail de tous les jours ... L'essentiel était de bien faire son métier.*
That was where certainty lay, in everyday work ... The essential thing was to do one's job well.
[*La Peste* (*The Plague*, 1947)]

6. *...la peste avait enlevé à tous le pouvoir de l'amour et même de l'amitié. Car l'amour demande un peu d'avenir, et il n'y avait plus pour nous que des instants.*
The plague had deprived us all of the capacity for love and even for friendship. For love demands some future, and all we had left were moments.
[*La Peste* (*The Plague*, 1947)]

7. *Ils savaient maintenant que s'il est une chose qu'on puisse désirer toujours et obtenir quelquefois, c'est la tendresse humaine.*
They now knew that if there is one thing which can always be desired and sometimes obtained, it is human tenderness.
[*La Peste* (*The Plague*, 1947)]

8. *Tout révolutionnaire finit en oppresseur ou en hérétique.*
Every revolutionary ends as an oppressor or a heretic.
[*L'Homme révolté* (*The Rebel*, 1951)]

9. *Qu'est-ce qu'un homme révolté? Un homme qui dit non.*
What is a rebel? A man who says no.
[*L'Homme révolté* (*The Rebel*, 1951)]

10. *Toutes les révolutions modernes ont abouti à un renforcement de l'Etat.*
All modern revolutions have led to a reinforcement of the power of the State.
[*L'Homme révolté* (*The Rebel*, 1951)]

11. The future is the only kind of property that masters willingly concede to slaves.
[*L'Homme révolté* (*The Rebel*, 1951)]

12. One cannot be a part-time nihilist.
[*L'Homme révolté* (*The Rebel*, 1951)]

13. *Hélas! après un certain âge, tout homme est responsable de son visage.*
Alas! after a certain age every man is responsible for the face he has.
[*La Chute* (*The Fall*, 1956). Cf. Orwell: 40]

14. *Le style, comme la popeline, dissimule trop souvent de l'eczéma.*
Style, like sheer silk, too often hides eczema.
[*La Chute* (*The Fall*, 1956)]

15. *Combien de crimes commis simplement parce que leur auteur ne pouvait supporter d'être en faute!*
How many crimes committed simply because their authors could not endure being wrong!
[*La Chute* (*The Fall*, 1956)]

16. *N'attendez pas le jugement dernier. Il a lieu tous les jours.*
Don't wait for the Last Judgement. It is taking place every day.
[*La Chute* (*The Fall*, 1956)]

17. *C'est si vrai que nous nous confions rarement à ceux qui sont meilleurs que nous.*
It is very true that we seldom confide in those who are better than ourselves.
[*La Chute* (*The Fall*, 1956)]

Canetti, Elias (1905–1994)
Bulgarian-born English novelist, dramatist and critic; Nobel prize 1981

1. *Immer wenn man ein Tier genau betrachtet hat man das Gefühl, ein Mensch, der drin sitzt, macht sich über einen lustig.*
Whenever you observe an animal closely, you have the feeling that a person sitting inside is making fun of you.
[*Die Provinz des Menschen. Aufzeichnungen 1942–1972* (*The Human Province. Notes from 1942 to 1972*, published 1973), 1942]

2. *Die grossen Aphoristiker lesen sich so, als ob sie alle einander gut gekannt hätten.*
The great aphorists read as if they had all known each other well.
[*Die Provinz des Menschen. Aufzeichnungen 1942–1972* (*The Human Province. Notes from 1942 to 1972*, published 1973), 1943]

3. *Er legt Sätze wie Eier, aber er vergisst, sie zu bebrüten.*
He lays sentences like eggs, but he forgets to incubate them.
[*Die Provinz des Menschen. Aufzeichnungen 1942–1972* (*The Human Province. Notes from 1942 to 1972*, published 1973), 1962]

4. *Was immer ihre Tätigkeit ist, die Tätigen halten sich für besser.*
Whatever their activity is, the active think they are better.
[*Die Provinz des Menschen. Aufzeichnungen 1942–1972* (*The Human Province. Notes from 1942 to 1972*, published 1973), 1969]

5. *Ihr Berge, ihr Berge, seht ihr es alles und seid noch immer nicht auf uns gefallen.*
You mountains, you mountains, you see it all and still you have not fallen on top of us.
[*Die Provinz des Menschen. Aufzeichnungen 1942–1972* (*The Human Province. Notes from 1942 to 1972*, published 1973), section from 1969]

6. *Es ist sehr wichtig, was einer zum Schluss noch vorhat. Es gibt das Mass des Unrechts seines Todes.*
It is important what you still have planned at the end. It shows the extent of injustice in your death.
[*Die Provinz des Menschen. Aufzeichnungen 1942–1972* (*The Human Province. Notes from 1942 to 1972*, published 1973), 1972]

Canning, George (1770–1827)
English Tory statesman, orator and poet; Prime Minister 1827

1. Man, only – rash, refined, presumptuous man,
Starts from his rank, and mars creation's plan.
['Progress of Man' (1799)]

2. [Of Pitt]
Here's to the Pilot that weathered the storm.
['The Pilot', song for the inauguration of the Pitt Club, 1802]

3. Pitt is to Addington
As London is to Paddington.
['The Oracle' (c. 1803)]

4. [Of a Jacobin]
A steady patriot of the world alone,
The friend of every country but his own...

5. And finds, with keen discriminating sight,
Black's not so black; nor white so very white...

6. Give me the avowed, erect and manly foe;
Firm I can meet, perhaps return the blow;

But of all plagues, good Heaven, thy wrath can send,
Save me, oh, save me, from the candid friend.
['New Morality' (1821), I]

7. In matters of commerce the fault of the Dutch
Is offering too little and asking too much.
The French are with equal advantage content,
So we clap on Dutch bottoms just twenty per cent.
[Dispatch, in Cipher. To Sir Charles Bagot, English Ambassador to the Hague, 1826]

8. A sudden thought strikes me, let us swear an eternal friendship.
['The Rovers']

9. Whene'er with haggard eyes I view
This Dungeon, that I'm rotting in,
I think of those Companions true
Who studied with me at the U-
-NIVERSITY OF GOTTINGEN
-NIVERSITY OF GOTTINGEN.
[Song]

10. I called the New World into existence, to redress the balance of the Old.
[Speech, 1826]

Cantona, Eric (1966–)
French football player

1. [Commenting on the interest taken by the press in the outcome of his court case]
When the seagulls follow the trawler, it is because they think sardines will be thrown into the sea.
[*The Observer*, 'Sayings of the Week', 1995]

Canute, King (c. 994–1035)
Danish King of England, Denmark and Norway, and church benefactor

1. The monks were singing joyfully within Ely as King Cnut rowed past. 'Knights, row closer inshore, so we can hear the monks' song.'
[Attr. by Thomas of Ely (12th century)]

Capone, Al (1899–1947)
American gangster

1. I've been accused of every death except the casualty list of the World War.
[In Kenneth Allsop, *The Bootleggers* (1961), 11]

2. [Talking about suburban Chicago]
This is virgin territory for whorehouses.
[In Kenneth Allsop, *The Bootleggers* (1961), 16]

3. [Objecting to the US Bureau of Internal Revenue claiming large sums in unpaid back tax]
They can't collect legal taxes from illegal money.
[In J. Kobler, *Capone* (1971)]

Carew, Richard (1555–1620)
English poet and courtier

1. Take the miracle of our age, Sir Philip Sidney.
[In William Camden, *Remains concerning Britain* (1614), 'An Epistle on the Excellency of the English Tongue']

Carew, Thomas (c. 1595–1640)
English poet, musician and comic dramatist

1. Here lyes a King, that rul'd, as he thought fit
The Universal Monarchie of wit,
Here lyes two Flamens, and both those, the best,
Apollo's first, at last, the true God's Priest.
['An Elegy upon the death of Doctor Donne' (1640)]

2. Hee that loves a Rosie cheeke,
Or a corall lip admires,
Or, from star-like eyes doth seeke,
Fuel to maintaine his fires;
As old Time makes these decay,
So his flames must waste away.
['Disdaine returned' (1640)]

3. Give me more love or more disdaine;
The Torrid or the frozen Zone:
Bring equall ease unto my paine;
The temperate affords me none.
Either extreame, of love, or hate,
Is sweeter than a calme estate.
['Mediocritie in love rejected' (1640)]

4. Know, Celia (since thou art so proud,)
'Twas I that gave thee thy renowne:
Thou had'st in the forgotten crowd
Of common beauties, liv'd unknowne,
Had not my verse exhal'd thy name,
And with it imped the wings of fame.
['Ingratefull Beauty Threatened' (1640)]

5. So though a Virgin, yet a Bride
To every Grace, she justifi'd
A chaste Poligamie, and dy'd.
['Inscription on Tomb of Lady Mary Wentworth' (1640)]

6. Aske me no more where Jove bestowes,
When June is past, the fading rose:
For in your beauties orient deepe,
These Flowers as in their causes sleepe...

7. Aske me no more whither doth hast'
The Nightingale when May is past:
For in your sweet dividing throat,
She winters and keepes warme her note...

8. Aske me no more if East or West,
The Phenix builds her spicy nest:
For unto you at last shee flies,
And in your fragrant bosome dyes.
['A Song' (1640)]

9. I was foretold, your rebell sex,
Nor love, nor pitty knew.
And with what scorne, you use to vex
Poore hearts, that humbly sue.
['A deposition from love']

Carey, Henry (c. 1687–1743)
English poet, musician and comic dramatist

1. Namby-Pamby, pilly-piss,
Rhimy-pim'd on Missy Miss
Tartaretta Tartaree,
That her father's gracy grace
Might give him a placy place.
['Namby-Pamby' (1725)]

2. Of all the girls that are so smart
There's none like pretty Sally,
She is the darling of my heart,
And she lives in our alley...

3. Of all the days that's in the week
I dearly love but one day–
And that's the day that comes betwixt
A Saturday and Monday.
['Sally in our Alley' (1729)]

Carlyle, Jane Welsh (1801–1866)

Scottish letter writer, literary hostess and poet; wife of Thomas Carlyle

1. [Referring to Thomas Carlyle, before their marriage]
He has his talents, his vast and cultivated mind, his vivid imagination, his independence of soul and his high-souled principles of honour. But then – ah, these buts! – St Preux never kicked the fire-irons, nor made puddings in his tea cup.
[Letter to her cousin, Bess Stodart, 1821–1822]

2. I will be to you a true, and constant, and devoted Friend – but not a Wife.
[Letter to Thomas Carlyle, January 1822]

3. I am not at all the sort of person you and I took me for.
[Letter to Thomas Carlyle, May 1822]

4. If they had said the sun and the moon was gone out of the heavens it could not have struck me with the idea of a more awful and dreary blank in the creation than the words: Byron is dead.
[Letter to Thomas Carlyle, May 1824]

5. When one has been threatened with a great injustice, one accepts a smaller as a favour.
[*Journal*, 1855]

6. They must be comfortable people who have leisure to think about going to heaven! My most constant and pressing anxiety is to keep out of bedlam, that's all...
[*Letters and Memorials of Jane Welsh Carlyle* (1883)]

Carlyle, Thomas (1795–1881)

Scottish historian, biographer, critic, essayist, teacher and translator; husband of Jane Welsh Carlyle

1. No man who has once heartily and wholly laughed can be altogether irreclaimably bad.
[*Sartor Resartus* (1834), I, 4]

2. He who first shortened the labour of Copyists by device of Movable Types was disbanding hired Armies, and cashiering most Kings and Senates, and creating a whole new Democratic world: he had invented the Art of Printing.
[*Sartor Resartus* (1834), I, 5]

3. Man is a Tool-using Animal ... feeblest of bipeds! ... Without Tools he is nothing, with Tools he is all.
[*Sartor Resartus* (1834), I, 5]

4. Be not the slave of Words.
[*Sartor Resartus* (1834), I, 8, 'The World out of Clothes']

5. Lives there the man that can figure a naked Duke of Windlestraw addressing a naked House of Lords?
[*Sartor Resartus* (1834), I, 9]

6. Language is called the Garment of Thought: however, it should rather be, Language is the Flesh-Garment, the Body, of thought.
[*Sartor Resartus* (1834), I, 11]

7. Sarcasm I now see to be, in general, the language of the Devil.
[*Sartor Resartus* (1834), II, 4]

8. But the world is an old woman, and mistakes any gilt farthing for a gold coin; whereby being often cheated, she will thenceforth trust nothing but the common copper.
[*Sartor Resartus* (1834), II, 4]

9. The end of man is an Action and not a Thought, though it were the noblest.
[*Sartor Resartus* (1834), II, 6]

10. The everlasting No.
[*Sartor Resartus* (1834), II, title of chapter 7]

11. A certain inarticulate Self-consciousness dwells dimly in us ... Hence, too, the folly of that impossible precept, Know thyself; till it be translated into this partially possible one, Know what thou canst work at.
[*Sartor Resartus* (1834), II, 7. Cf. Anon: 211]

12. O thou who art able to write a Book, which once in the two centuries or oftener there is a man gifted to do, envy not him whom they name City-builder, and inexpressibly pity him whom they name Conqueror or City-burner!
[*Sartor Resartus* (1834), II, 8]

13. The everlasting Yea.
[*Sartor Resartus* (1834), II, title of chapter 9]

14. Man's Unhappiness, as I construe, comes of his Greatness; it is because there is an Infinite in him, which with all his cunning he cannot quite bury under the Finite.
[*Sartor Resartus* (1834), II, 9]

15. Be no longer a Chaos, but a World, or even Worldkin. Produce! Produce! Were it but the pitifullest infinitesimal fraction of a Product, produce it, in God's name!'Tis the utmost thou hast in thee: out with it, then. Up, up! Whatsoever thy hand findeth to do, do it with thy whole might.
[*Sartor Resartus* (1834), II, 9]

16. It is a mathematical fact that the casting of this pebble from my hand alters the centre of gravity of the Universe.
[*Sartor Resartus* (1834), III, 7]

17. To a shower of gold most things are penetrable.
[*History of the French Revolution* (1837), I]

18. History a distillation of rumour.
[*History of the French Revolution* (1837), I]

19. The gospel according to Jean Jacques.
[*History of the French Revolution* (1837), II]

20. The difference between Orthodoxy or My-doxy and Heterodoxy or Thy-doxy.
[*History of the French Revolution* (1837), II]

21. [Of Robespierre]
The sea-green Incorruptible.
[*History of the French Revolution* (1837), II]

22. France was long a despotism tempered by epigrams.
[*History of the French Revolution* (1837), III]

23. A well-written Life is almost as rare as a well-spent one.
[*Critical and Miscellaneous Essays* (1839), I, 'Jean Paul Friedrich Richter']

24. The three great elements of modern civilization, Gunpowder, Printing, and the Protestant Religion.
[*Critical and Miscellaneous Essays* (1839), I, 'State of German Literature']

25. Literary men are ... a perpetual priesthood.
[*Critical and Miscellaneous Essays* (1839), I, 'State of German Literature']

26. The excellence of Burns is, indeed, among the rarest, ... but ... it is plain and easily recognised: his Sincerity, his indisputable air of Truth.
[*Critical and Miscellaneous Essays* (1839), I, 'Burns']

27. A poet without love were a physical and metaphysical impossibility.
[*Critical and Miscellaneous Essays* (1839), I, 'Burns']

28. [On Locke and Milton]
The 'golden-calf of Self-love' ... was not their Deity; but

the Invisible Goodness, which alone is man's reasonable service.
[*Critical and Miscellaneous Essays* (1839), I, 'Burns']

29. It is the Age of Machinery, in every outward and inward sense of that word.
[*Critical and Miscellaneous Essays* (1839), II, 'Signs of the Times']

30. Thought, he [Dr Cabanis] is inclined to hold, is still secreted by the brain; but then Poetry and Religion (and it is really worth knowing) are 'a product of the smaller intestines'!
[*Critical and Miscellaneous Essays* (1839), II, 'Signs of the Times']

31. What is all knowledge too but recorded experience, and a product of history; of which, therefore, reasoning and belief, no less than action and passion, are essential materials?
[*Critical and Miscellaneous Essays* (1839), II, 'On History']

32. History is the essence of innumerable biographies.
[*Critical and Miscellaneous Essays* (1839), II, 'On History']

33. The barrenest of all mortals is the sentimentalist.
[*Critical and Miscellaneous Essays* (1839), III, 'Characteristics']

34. All reform except a moral one will prove unavailing.
[*Critical and Miscellaneous Essays* (1839), III, 'Corn Law Rhymes']

35. The foul sluggard's comfort: 'It will last my time.'
[*Critical and Miscellaneous Essays* (1839), IV, 'Count Cagliostro, Flight Last']

36. There is no life of a man, faithfully recorded, but is a heroic poem of its sort, rhymed or unrhymed.
[*Critical and Miscellaneous Essays* (1839), IV, 'Memoirs of the Life of Scott']

37. Under all speech that is good for anything there lies a silence that is better. Silence is deep as Eternity; speech is shallow as Time.
[*Critical and Miscellaneous Essays* (1839), IV, 'Memoirs of the Life of Scott']

38. A witty statesman said, you might prove anything by figures.
[*Chartism* (1839), 2]

39. Surely of all 'rights of man', this right of the ignorant man to be guided by the wiser, to be, gently or forcibly, held in the true course by him, is the indisputablest.
[*Chartism* (1839), 6]

40. In epochs when cash payment has become the sole nexus of man to man.
[*Chartism* (1839), 6]

41. For, as I take it, Universal History, the history of what man has accomplished in this world, is at bottom the History of the Great Men who have worked here.
[*On Heroes, Hero-Worship, and the Heroic in History* (1841), 'The Hero as Divinity']

42. The illimitable, silent, never-resting thing called Time, rolling, rushing on, swift, silent, like an all-embracing ocean-tide, on which we and all the Universe swim like exhalations, like apparitions which are, and then are not.
[*On Heroes, Hero-Worship, and the Heroic in History* (1841), 'The Hero as Divinity']

43. Worship is transcendent wonder.
[*On Heroes, Hero-Worship, and the Heroic in History* (1841), 'The Hero as Divinity']

44. No sadder proof can be given by a man of his own littleness than disbelief in great men.
[*On Heroes, Hero-Worship, and the Heroic in History* (1841), 'The Hero as Divinity']

45. No great man lives in vain. The History of the world is but the Biography of great men.
[*On Heroes, Hero-Worship, and the Heroic in History* (1841), 'The Hero as Divinity']

46. The greatest of faults, I should say, is to be conscious of none.
[*On Heroes, Hero-Worship, and the Heroic in History* (1841), 'The Hero as Prophet']

47. The Hero can be Poet, Prophet, King, Priest or what you will, according to the kind of world he finds himself born into.
[*On Heroes, Hero-Worship, and the Heroic in History* (1841), 'The Hero as Poet']

48. The true University of these days is a Collection of Books.
[*On Heroes, Hero-Worship, and the Heroic in History* (1841), 'The Hero as Man of Letters']

49. Burke said there were Three Estates in Parliament; but, in the Reporters' Gallery yonder, there sat a Fourth Estate more important far than they all.
[*On Heroes, Hero-Worship, and the Heroic in History* (1841), 'The Hero as Man of Letters']

50. Adversity is sometimes hard upon a man; but for one man who can stand prosperity, there are a hundred that will stand adversity.
[*On Heroes, Hero-Worship, and the Heroic in History* (1841), 'The Hero as Man of Letters']

51. The progress of human society consists ... in ... the better and better apportioning of wages to work.
[*Past and Present* (1843), I, 3]

52. Blessed is he who has found his work; let him ask no other blessedness.
[*Past and Present* (1843), III, 3]

53. Captains of industry.
[*Past and Present* (1843), IV, 4]

54. [Of Political Economics]
And the Social Science, – not a 'gay science', ... no, a dreary, desolate, and indeed quite abject and distressing one; what we might call ... the dismal science.
[*Latter-Day Pamphlets* (1850), 'Occasional Discourse on the Nigger Question']

55. Robert Burns never had the smallest chance to get into Parliament, much as Robert Burns deserved, for all our sakes, to have been found there.
[*Latter-Day Pamphlets* (1850), 'Downing Street']

56. [On the influence of a romantic imagination on Sterling's decision to become a priest]
Transcendental moonshine.
[*Life of John Sterling* (1851), I, 15]

57. 'Genius' (which means transcendent capacity of taking trouble, first of all).
[*History of Frederick the Great* (1858–1865), IV, 3. Cf. Jane Hopkins: 1]

58. If they could forget, for a moment, the correggiosity of Correggio, and the learned babble of the saleroom and varnishing auctioneer.
[*History of Frederick the Great* (1858–1865), VI, 6. Cf. Sterne: 19]

59. Happy the people whose annals are blank in history-books!
[*History of Frederick the Great* (1858–1865), XVI, 1]

60. [On Ralph Waldo Emerson]
A hoaryheaded and toothless baboon.
[*Collected Works* (1871)]

61. The crash of the whole solar and stellar systems could only kill you once.
[Letter to John Carlyle, 1831]

62. Work is the grand cure of all the maladies and miseries that ever beset mankind.
[Speech, Edinburgh, 1886]

63. [Epitaph for Jane Welsh Carlyle in Haddington Church]
For forty years she was the true and ever-loving helpmate of her husband, and, by act and word, unweariedly forwarded him as none else could, in all of worthy that he did or attempted. She died at London, 21st April 1866, suddenly snatched away from him, and the light of his life as if gone out.
[In Hector C. Macpherson, *Thomas Carlyle* (1896)]

64. *Margaret Fuller*: I accept the universe.
Carlyle: Gad! she'd better!
[In William James, *Varieties of Religious Experience* (1902)]

65. It were better to perish than to continue schoolmastering.
[In D.A. Wilson, *Carlyle Till Marriage* (1923)]

66. If Jesus Christ were to come to-day, people would not even crucify him. They would ask him to dinner, and hear what he had to say, and make fun of it.
[In D.A. Wilson, *Carlyle at his Zenith* (1927)]

67. [To Wm Allingham]
I don't pretend to understand the Universe – it's a great deal bigger than I am ... People ought to be modester.
[In D.A. Wilson and D. Wilson MacArthur, *Carlyle in Old Age* (1934)]

68. The Public is an old woman. Let her maunder and mumble.
[Attr.]

69. Speech is human, silence is divine, yet also brutish and dead: therefore we must learn both arts.
[Attr.]

70. [Referring to the American Civil War]
There they are cutting each other's throats, because one half of them prefer hiring their servants for life, and the other by the hour.
[Attr.]

71. [When asked what the population of England was]
Thirty millions, mostly fools.
[Attr.]

72. After two weeks of blotching and blaring I have produced two clear papers.
[Attr.]

Carnegie, Andrew (1835–1919)
Scottish-born American philanthropist and ironmaster; benefactor of public libraries

1. Surplus wealth is a sacred trust which its possessor is bound to administer in his lifetime for the good of the community.
[*The Gospel of Wealth*]

2. Of every thousand dollars spent in so-called charity today, it is probable that nine hundred and fifty dollars is unwisely spent.
[*North American Review*, June 1889, 'Wealth']

3. [What would be said of someone who had not used his surplus wealth to help others]
The man who dies thus rich dies disgraced.
[*North American Review*, June 1889, 'Wealth']

4. Pioneering does not pay.
[Attr.]

Carnegie, Dale (1888–1955)
American lecturer, teacher of public speaking and author

1. How to Win Friends and Influence People.
[Title of book, 1936]

Carney, Julia (1823–1908)

1. Little drops of water,
Little grains of sand,
Make the mighty ocean
And the beauteous land.

And the little moments,
Humble though they be,
Make the mighty ages
Of eternity...

2. Little deeds of kindness, little words of love,
Help to make earth happy, like the heaven above.
['Little Things' (1845)]

Carpenter, Joseph Edwards (1813–1885)
English songwriter and poet

1. What are the wild waves saying
Sister, the whole day long,
That ever amid our playing,
I hear but their low lone song?
['What are the Wild Waves Saying', song, 1850]

Carr, J.L. (1912–1994)
English novelist and publisher

1. We can ask and ask but we can't have again what once seemed ours forever – the way things looked, that church alone in the fields, a bed on a belfry floor, a loved face ... They'd gone, and you could only wait for the pain to pass.
[*A Month in the Country* (1980)]

Carroll, Lewis (1832–1898)
English mathematician, deacon, children's novelist and photographer

1. 'What is the use of a book,' thought Alice, 'without pictures or conversations?'
[*Alice's Adventures in Wonderland* (1865), 1]

2. Do cats eat bats? ... Do bats eat cats?
[*Alice's Adventures in Wonderland* (1865), 1]

3. 'Curiouser and curiouser!' cried Alice.
[*Alice's Adventures in Wonderland* (1865), 2]

4. How doth the little crocodile
Improve his shining tail,
And pour the waters of the Nile
On every golden scale!

How cheerfully he seems to grin,
How neatly spreads his claws,
And welcomes little fishes in
With gently smiling jaws!
[*Alice's Adventures in Wonderland* (1865), 2. Cf. Watts: 5]

5. 'Why,' said the Dodo, 'the best way to explain it is to do it.'
[*Alice's Adventures in Wonderland* (1865), 3]

6. 'I'll be judge, I'll be jury,' said cunning old Fury:
'I'll try the whole cause, and condemn you to death.'
[*Alice's Adventures in Wonderland* (1865), 3]

7. The Duchess! The Duchess! Oh my dear paws! Oh my fur and whiskers!
[*Alice's Adventures in Wonderland* (1865), 4]

8. 'I can't explain myself, I'm afraid, sir,' said Alice, 'because I'm not myself, you see.' 'I don't see,' said the Caterpillar.
[*Alice's Adventures in Wonderland* (1865), 5]

9. 'You are old, Father William,' the young man said,
'And your hair has become very white;
And yet you incessantly stand on your head–
Do you think, at your age, it is right?'

'In my youth,' Father William replied to his son,
'I feared it might injure the brain;
But now that I'm perfectly sure I have none,
Why, I do it again and again.'...

10. 'I have answered three questions, and that is enough,'
Said his father; 'don't give yourself airs!
Do you think I can listen all day to such stuff?
Be off, or I'll kick you downstairs!'
[*Alice's Adventures in Wonderland* (1865), 5. Cf. Southey: 5]

11. 'If everybody minded their own business,' said the Duchess in a hoarse growl, 'the world would go round a deal faster than it does.'
[*Alice's Adventures in Wonderland* (1865), 6]

12. Speak roughly to your little boy,
And beat him when he sneezes:
He only does it to annoy,
Because he knows it teases.
[*Alice's Adventures in Wonderland* (1865), 6]

13. 'Would you tell me, please, which way I ought to go from here?'
'That depends a good deal on where you want to get to,' said the Cat.
[*Alice's Adventures in Wonderland* (1865), 6]

14. [The Cheshire Cat]
This time it vanished quite slowly, beginning with the end of the tail, and ending with the grin, which remained some time after the rest of it had gone.
[*Alice's Adventures in Wonderland* (1865), 6]

15. 'Have some wine,' the March Hare said in an encouraging tone. Alice looked all round the table, but there was nothing on it but tea. 'I don't see any wine,' she remarked. 'There isn't any,' said the March Hare.
[*Alice's Adventures in Wonderland* (1865), 7]

16. 'Then you should say what you mean,' the March Hare went on. 'I do,' Alice hastily replied; 'at least – at least I mean what I say – that's the same thing, you know.'
[*Alice's Adventures in Wonderland* (1865), 7]

17. 'It was the best butter,' the March Hare meekly replied.
[*Alice's Adventures in Wonderland* (1865), 7]

18. Twinkle, twinkle, little bat!
How I wonder what you're at!
Up above the world you fly,
Like a teatray in the sky.
[*Alice's Adventures in Wonderland* (1865), 7. Cf. Ann and Jane Taylor: 2]

19. 'Take some more tea,' the March Hare said to Alice, very earnestly.
'I've had nothing yet,' Alice replied in an offended tone, 'so I can't take more.'
'You mean you can't take less,' said the Hatter: 'it's very easy to take more than nothing.'
[*Alice's Adventures in Wonderland* (1865), 7]

20. Let's all move one place on.
[*Alice's Adventures in Wonderland* (1865), 7]

21. The Queen was in a furious passion, and went stamping about, and shouting, 'Off with his head!' or 'Off with her head!' about once in a minute.
[*Alice's Adventures in Wonderland* (1865), 8]

22. 'A cat may look at a king,' said Alice.
[*Alice's Adventures in Wonderland* (1865), 8]

23. Everything's got a moral, if you can only find it.
[*Alice's Adventures in Wonderland* (1865), 9]

24. And the moral of that is – 'Oh, 'tis love, 'tis love that makes the world go round!'
[*Alice's Adventures in Wonderland* (1865), 9]

25. Take care of the sense, and the sounds will take care of themselves.
[*Alice's Adventures in Wonderland* (1865), 9]

26. 'Just about as much right,' said the Duchess, 'as pigs have to fly.'
[*Alice's Adventures in Wonderland* (1865), 9]

27. 'We called him Tortoise because he taught us,' said the Mock Turtle angrily. 'Really you are very dull!'
[*Alice's Adventures in Wonderland* (1865), 9]

28. 'Reeling and Writhing, of course, to begin with,' the Mock Turtle replied; 'and then the different branches of Arithmetic – Ambition, Distraction, Uglification, and Derision.'
[*Alice's Adventures in Wonderland* (1865), 9]

29. The Drawling-master was an old conger-eel, that used to come once a week: he taught Drawling, Stretching, and Fainting in Coils.
[*Alice's Adventures in Wonderland* (1865), 9]

30. 'That's the reason they're called lessons,' the Gryphon remarked: 'because they lessen from day to day.'
[*Alice's Adventures in Wonderland* (1865), 9]

31. 'Will you walk a little faster?' said a whiting to a snail,
'There's a porpoise close behind us, and he's treading on my tail.'
[*Alice's Adventures in Wonderland* (1865), 10]

32. Will you, won't you, will you, won't you, will you join the dance?
[*Alice's Adventures in Wonderland* (1865), 10]

33. The further off from England the nearer is to France–
Then turn not pale, beloved snail, but come and join the dance.
[*Alice's Adventures in Wonderland* (1865), 10]

34. 'Tis the voice of the lobster; I heard him declare,
'You have baked me too brown, I must sugar my hair.'
[*Alice's Adventures in Wonderland* (1865), 10. Cf. Watts: 14]

35. Beautiful Soup, so rich and green,
Waiting in a hot tureen!
Who for such dainties would not stoop?
Soup of the evening, beautiful Soup!
[*Alice's Adventures in Wonderland* (1865), 10]

36. The Queen of Hearts, she made some tarts,
All on a summer day:
The Knave of Hearts, he stole those tarts,
And took them quite away!
[*Alice's Adventures in Wonderland* (1865), 11]

37. 'Write that down,' the King said to the jury, and the jury eagerly wrote all three dates on their slates, and then added

them up, and reduced the answer to shillings and pence.
[Alice's Adventures in Wonderland (1865), 11]

38. 'Unimportant, of course, I meant,' the King hastily said, and went on to himself in an undertone, 'important – unimportant – unimportant – important–' as if he were trying which word sounded best.
[Alice's Adventures in Wonderland (1865), 12]

39. 'That's not a regular rule: you invented it just now.'
'It's the oldest rule in the book,' said the King. 'Then it ought to be Number One,' said Alice.
[Alice's Adventures in Wonderland (1865), 12]

40. 'Begin at the beginning,' the King said, very gravely, 'and go on till you come to the end: then stop.'
[Alice's Adventures in Wonderland (1865), 12]

41. 'No! No!' said the Queen. 'Sentence first – verdict afterwards'.
[Alice's Adventures in Wonderland (1865), 12]

42. One thing was certain, that the white kitten had had nothing to do with it: it was the black kitten's fault entirely.
[Through the Looking-Glass (and What Alice Found There) (1872), 1, opening lines]

43. 'My precious Lily! My imperial kitten!'...
'Imperial fiddlestick!'
[Through the Looking-Glass (and What Alice Found There) (1872), 1]

44. 'The horror of that moment,' the King went on, 'I shall never, never forget!'
'You will, though,' the Queen said, 'if you don't make a memorandum of it.'
[Through the Looking-Glass (and What Alice Found There) (1872), 1]

45. 'Twas brillig, and the slithy toves
Did gyre and gimble in the wabe;
All mimsy were the borogoves,
And the mome raths outgrabe.

'Beware the Jabberwock, my son!
The jaws that bite, the claws that catch!'...

46. And as in uffish thought he stood,
The Jabberwock, with eyes of flame,
Came whiffling through the tulgey wood,
And burbled as it came!

One, two! One, two! And through and through
The vorpal blade went snicker-snack!
He left it dead, and with its head
He went galumphing back.

'And hast thou slain the Jabberwock?
Come to my arms, my beamish boy!
O frabjous day! Callooh! Callay!'
He chortled in his joy.
[Through the Looking-Glass (and What Alice Found There) (1872), 1, 'Jabberwocky']

47. Curtsy while you're thinking what to say. It saves time.
[Through the Looking-Glass (and What Alice Found There) (1872), 2]

48. 'Now, here, you see, it takes all the running you can do, to keep in the same place. If you want to get somewhere else, you must run at least twice as fast as that!'
[Through the Looking-Glass (and What Alice Found There) (1872), 2]

49. Speak in French when you can't think of the English for a thing.
[Through the Looking-Glass (and What Alice Found There) (1872), 2]

50. 'If you think we're wax-works,' he said, 'you ought to pay, you know. Wax-works weren't made to be looked at for nothing. Nohow!'
[Through the Looking-Glass (and What Alice Found There) (1872), 4]

51. Tweedledum and Tweedledee
Agreed to have a battle;
For Tweedledum said Tweedledee
Had spoiled his nice new rattle.

Just then flew down a monstrous crow,
As black as a tar-barrel;
Which frightened both the heroes so,
They quite forgot their quarrel.
[Through the Looking-Glass (and What Alice Found There) (1872), 4]

52. 'Contrariwise,' continued Tweedledee, 'if it was so, it might be; and if it were so, it would be: but as it isn't, it ain't. That's logic.'
[Through the Looking-Glass (and What Alice Found There) (1872), 4]

53. The sun was shining on the sea,
Shining with all his might:
He did his very best to make
The billows smooth and bright–
And this was odd, because it was
The middle of the night...

54. 'It's very rude of him,' she said
'To come and spoil the fun!'...

55. The Walrus and the Carpenter
Were walking close at hand;
They wept like anything to see
Such quantities of sand:
'If this were only cleared away,'
They said, 'it would be grand!'

'If seven maids with seven mops
Swept it for half a year,
Do you suppose,' the Walrus said,
'That they could get it clear?'
'I doubt it,' said the Carpenter,
And shed a bitter tear...

56. And all the little Oysters stood
And waited in a row.

'The time has come,' the Walrus said,
'To talk of many things:
Of shoes – and ships – and sealing wax–
Of cabbages – and kings–
And why the sea is boiling hot–
And whether pigs have wings.'...

57. 'A loaf of bread,' the Walrus said,
'Is what we chiefly need:
Pepper and vinegar besides
Are very good indeed–
Now if you're ready, Oysters dear,
We can begin to feed.'...

58. The Carpenter said nothing but
'The butter's spread too thick!'

'I weep for you,' the Walrus said:
'I deeply sympathize.'
With sobs and tears he sorted out

Those of the largest size,
Holding his pocket-handkerchief
Before his streaming eyes...

59. But answer came there none–
And this was scarcely odd because
They'd eaten every one.
[*Through the Looking-Glass (and What Alice Found There)* (1872), 4, 'The Walrus and the Carpenter']

60. 'You know,' he added very gravely, 'it's one of the most serious things that can possibly happen to one in a battle – to get one's head cut off.'
[*Through the Looking-Glass (and What Alice Found There)* (1872), 4]

61. 'I'm very brave generally,' he went on in a low voice: 'only to-day I happen to have a headache.'
[*Through the Looking-Glass (and What Alice Found There)* (1872), 4]

62. 'Let's fight till six, and then have dinner,' said Tweedledum.
[*Through the Looking-Glass (and What Alice Found There)* (1872), 4]

63. The rule is, jam to-morrow and jam yesterday – but never jam to-day.
[*Through the Looking-Glass (and What Alice Found There)* (1872), 5]

64. 'It's a poor sort of memory that only works backwards,' the Queen remarked.
[*Through the Looking-Glass (and What Alice Found There)* (1872), 5]

65. 'There's no use trying,' she said: 'one can't believe impossible things.'
'I dare say you haven't had much practice,' said the Queen. 'When I was your age, I always did it for half an hour a day. Why, sometimes I've believed as many as six impossible things before breakfast.'
[*Through the Looking-Glass (and What Alice Found There)* (1872), 5]

66. They gave it me ... for an un-birthday present.
[*Through the Looking-Glass (and What Alice Found There)* (1872), 6]

67. 'When I use a word,' Humpty Dumpty said in rather a scornful tone, 'it means just what I choose it to mean – neither more nor less.'
[*Through the Looking-Glass (and What Alice Found There)* (1872), 6]

68. I can explain all the poems that ever were invented – and a good many that haven't been invented just yet.
[*Through the Looking-Glass (and What Alice Found There)* (1872), 6]

69. You see it's like a portmanteau – there are two meanings packed up into one word.
[*Through the Looking-Glass (and What Alice Found There)* (1872), 6]

70. 'I can repeat poetry as well as other folk if it comes to that–'
'Oh, it needn't come to that!' Alice hastily said.
[*Through the Looking-Glass (and What Alice Found There)* (1872), 6]

71. I sent a message to the fish:
I told them 'This is what I wish.'
The little fishes of the sea,
They sent an answer back to me.

The little fishes' answer was
'We cannot do it, Sir, because–'...

72. I took a kettle large and new,
Fit for the deed I had to do...

73. I said it very loud and clear;
I went and shouted in his ear.

But he was very stiff and proud;
He said 'You needn't shout so loud!'

And he was very proud and stiff;
He said 'I'd go and wake them, if–'
[*Through the Looking-Glass (and What Alice Found There)* (1872), 6]

74. He's an Anglo-Saxon Messenger – and those are Anglo-Saxon attitudes.
[*Through the Looking-Glass (and What Alice Found There)* (1872), 7]

75. The other Messenger's called Hatta. I must have two you know – to come and go. One to come, and one to go.
[*Through the Looking-Glass (and What Alice Found There)* (1872), 7]

76. 'There's nothing like eating hay when you're faint' ... 'I didn't say there was nothing better,' the King replied, 'I said there was nothing like it.'
[*Through the Looking-Glass (and What Alice Found There)* (1872), 7]

77. 'I'm sure nobody walks much faster than I do!'
'He can't do that,' said the King, 'or else he'd have been here first.'
[*Through the Looking-Glass (and What Alice Found There)* (1872), 7]

78. It's as large as life and twice as natural.
[*Through the Looking-Glass (and What Alice Found There)* (1872), 7]

79. If you'll believe in me, I'll believe in you.
[*Through the Looking-Glass (and What Alice Found There)* (1872), 7]

80. The Lion looked at Alice wearily. 'Are you animal – or vegetable – or mineral?' he said, yawning at every other word.
[*Through the Looking-Glass (and What Alice Found There)* (1872), 7]

81. I'll tell thee everything I can;
There's little to relate.
I saw an aged aged man,
A-sitting on a gate...

82. He said, 'I look for butterflies
That sleep among the wheat:
I make them into mutton-pies,
And sell them in the street...'

83. But I was thinking of a plan
To dye one's whiskers green,
And always use so large a fan
That they could not be seen...

84. And now if e'er by chance I put
My fingers into glue,
Or madly squeeze a right-hand foot
Into a left-hand shoe...

85. I weep, for it reminds me so
Of that old man I used to know.
[*Through the Looking-Glass (and What Alice Found There)* (1872), 8]

86. 'Speak when you're spoken to!' the Red Queen sharply interrupted her.
[*Through the Looking-Glass (and What Alice Found There)* (1872), 9]

87. No admittance till the week after next!
[*Through the Looking-Glass (and What Alice Found There)* (1872), 9]

88. 'You look a little shy; let me introduce you to that leg of mutton,' said the Red Queen. 'Alice – Mutton; Mutton – Alice.'
[*Through the Looking-Glass (and What Alice Found There)* (1872), 9]

89. What I tell you three times is true.
['The Hunting of the Snark' (1876), 'The Landing']

90. But oh, beamish nephew, beware of the day,
If your Snark be a Boojum! For then
You will softly and suddenly vanish away,
And never be met with again!
['The Hunting of the Snark' (1876), 'The Baker's Tale']

91. They sought it with thimbles, they sought it with care;
They pursued it with forks and hope;
They threatened its life with a railway-share;
They charmed it with smiles and soap.
['The Hunting of the Snark' (1876), 'The Beaver's Lesson']

92. For the Snark was a Boojum, you see.
['The Hunting of the Snark' (1876), 'The Vanishing']

93. He thought he saw an Elephant,
That practised on a fife:
He looked again, and found it was
A letter from his wife.
'At length I realize,' he said,
'The bitterness of life!'
[*Sylvie and Bruno* (1889), 5]

94. He thought he saw a Buffalo
Upon the chimney-piece:
He looked again, and found it was
His sister's husband's niece.
'Unless you leave this house,' he said,
'I'll send for the Police!'

He thought he saw a Rattlesnake
That questioned him in Greek,
He looked again and found it was
The Middle of Next Week.
'The one thing I regret,' he said,
'Is that it cannot speak!'
[*Sylvie and Bruno* (1889), 6]

95. He thought he saw a Banker's Clerk
Descending from the bus:
He looked again, and found it was
A Hippopotamus:
'If this should stay to dine,' he said,
'There won't be much for us.'
[*Sylvie and Bruno* (1889), 7]

96. I am fond of children (except boys).
[In Collingwood, *The Life and Letters of Lewis Carroll* (1898), Letter to Kathleen Eschwege, 1879]

Carson, Rachel Louise (1907–1964)
American marine biologist and writer

1. In its mysterious past, it encompasses all the dim origins of life and receives in the end ... the dead husks of that same life. For all at last return to the sea – to Oceanus, the ocean river, like the ever-flowing stream of time, the beginning and the end.
[*The Sea Around Us* (1951), closing words]

2. As man proceeds towards his announced goal of the conquest of nature, he has written a depressing record of destruction, directed not only against the earth he inhabits but against the life that shares it with him.
[*The Silent Spring* (1962), 7]

3. Over increasingly large areas of the United States, spring now comes unheralded by the return of the birds, and the early mornings are strangely silent where once they were filled with the beauty of bird song.
[*The Silent Spring* (1962), 8]

Carswell, Catherine (1879–1946)
Scottish novelist and biographer

1. It wasn't a woman who betrayed Jesus with a kiss.
[*The Savage Pilgrimage* (1932)]

Carter, Jimmy (1924–)
American statesman; Democratic President 1977–81

1. [Seeking to evoke the name of Hubert Horatio Humphrey]
[The] great president who might have been – Hubert Horatio Hornblower.
[Speech accepting renomination at the Democratic Convention, New York, 15 August 1980]

2. I've looked on a lot of women with lust. I've committed adultery in my heart many times. God recognizes I will do this and forgives me.
[Interview with *Playboy*, 1976]

3. [Visiting Egypt in 1979, when told that it took only twenty years to build the Great Pyramid]
I'm surprised that a government organization could do it that quickly.
[In *Time*, March 1979]

Carter, ('Miz') Lillian (1902–)
Mother of President Jimmy Carter

1. Sometimes when I look at my children I say to myself, 'Lillian, you should have stayed a virgin.'
[Remark, 1980]

2. I love all my children, but some of them I don't like.
[In *Woman*, 1977]

Cartland, Barbara (1902–)
English romantic novelist

1. [When asked in a radio interview whether she thought that British class barriers had broken down]
Of course they have, or I wouldn't be sitting here talking to someone like you.
[In J. Cooper, *Class* (1979)]

Cartwright, John (1740–1824)
English political reformer and sailor; the 'Father of Reform'

1. One man shall have one vote.
[*The People's Barrier Against Undue Influence* (1780), 1]

Caruso, Enrico (1873–1921)
Renowned Italian operatic tenor

1. You know whatta you do when you shit? Singing, it's the same thing, only up!
[In H. Brown, *Whose Little Boy Are You?*]

Cary, Joyce (Arthur Joyce Lunel Cary) (1888–1957)
Irish novelist and short-story writer

1. Sara could commit adultery at one end and weep for her sins at the other, and enjoy both operations at once.
[*The Horse's Mouth* (1944), 8]

2. Remember I'm an artist. And you know what that means in a court of law. Next worst to an actress.
[*The Horse's Mouth* (1944), 14]

Cary, Phoebe (1824–1871)
American poet

1. And though hard be the task,
'Keep a stiff upper lip.'
['Keep a Stiff Upper Lip']

Case, Phila Henrietta (fl. 1864)
British poet

1. Oh! why does the wind blow upon me so wild?–
Is it because I'm nobody's child?
['Nobody's Child']

Cassidy, Joseph (Archbishop of Tuam) (1933–)

1. What goes on in boardrooms is more important than what goes on in bedrooms.
[*The Scotsman Weekend*, 1993]

Casson, Sir Hugh (1910–)
English architect and writer

1. The British love permanence more than they love beauty.
[*The Observer*, 'Sayings of the Week', 1964]

Castle, Ted (1907–1979)
English journalist and Member of the European Parliament

1. In Place of Strife.
[Title of White Paper on industrial relations legislation, 1969]

Castro, Fidel (1927–)
Cuban Communist statesman and Prime Minister

1. All criticism is opposition. All opposition is counter-revolutionary.
[In John Newhouse, 'Socialism of Death', *The New Yorker*, 1992]

Caswall, Rev. Edward (1814–1878)
English hymn-writer

1. Jesu, the very thought of Thee
With sweetness fills the breast.
['Jesu, The Very Thought of Thee', 1849; translated from Latin]

2. Days and moments quickly flying,
Blend the living with the dead;
Soon will you and I be lying
Each within our narrow bed.
[Hymn, 1858]

Catechism
[The Shorter Catechism, approved 1648 by the General Assembly of the Church of Scotland]

1. Man's chief end is to glorify God, and to enjoy him forever.
[Question 1]

2. The Scriptures principally teach what man is to believe concerning God, and what duty God requires of man.
[Question 3]

3. All mankind by their fall lost communion with God, are under his wrath and curse, and so made liable to all the miseries in this life, to death itself, and to the pains of hell for ever.
[Question 19]

4. No mere man since the fall is able in this life perfectly to keep the commandments of God, but doth daily break them in thought, word, and deed.
[Question 82]

Cather, Willa (1873–1947)
Major American novelist; short-story writer and journalist

1. The history of every country begins in the heart of a man or a woman.
[*O Pioneers!* (1913), I, 5]

Catherine the Great (1729–1796)
German-born Empress of Russia (from 1762); patron of the arts

1. *Moi, je serai autocrate: c'est mon métier. Et le bon Dieu me pardonnera: c'est son métier.*
I shall be an autocrat: that's my job. And the good Lord will forgive me: that's his job.
[Attr. Cf. Heine: 10]

Catherwood, Mary (1847–1901)
American teacher and historical novelist

1. Two may talk together under the same roof for many years, yet never really meet; and two others at first speech are old friends.
[*Mackinac and Lake Stories*, 'Marianson']

Cato the Elder (234–149 BC)
Roman statesman, called 'the Censor'; writer and orator

1. *Delenda est Carthago.*
Carthage must be destroyed.
[In Pliny, *Naturalis Historia* (*Natural History*), XV, 74]

2. In all my life, I have never repented but of three things: that I trusted a woman with a secret, that I went by sea when I might have gone by land, and that I passed a day in idleness.
[In Pliny, *Naturalis Historia* (*Natural History*)]

3. I like to see a young man blush rather than turn pale.
[In Plutarch, *Lives*, 'Cato', XIX]

4. I would much rather have men ask why I have no statue than why I have one.
[In Plutarch, *Lives*, 'Cato', XIX]

5. Do not buy what you want, but what you need; what you do not need is dear at a farthing.
[*Reliquiae* (Remains)]

Catullus, Gaius Valerius (84–c. 54 BC)
Roman lyric poet, noted for his love poems

1. *Namque tu solebas*
Meas esse aliquid putare nugas.
For you used to think something of my scribbles.
[*Carmina*, 1, line 3]

2. *Lugete, O Veneres Cupidinesque...*
Passer mortuus est meae puellae,
Passer, deliciae meae puellae,

Passer, deliciae meae puellae,
Quem plus illa oculis suis amabat.
Mourn, you Graces and Cupids ... My beloved's sparrow is dead, the sparrow which was my beloved's darling, which she loved more than her own eyes.
[*Carmina*, 3, line 1]

3. *Qui nunc it per iter tenebricosum*
Illuc, unde negant redire quemquam.
Now he goes along the shadowy path, there, from which they say no one returns.
[*Carmina*, 3, line 11]

4. *Sed haec prius fuere.*
But these things are in the past.
[*Carmina*, 4, line 25]

5. *Vivamus, mea Lesbia, atque amemus,*
Rumoresque senum severiorum
Omnes unius aestimemus assis.
Soles occidere et redire possunt:
Nobis cum semel occidit brevis lux
Nox est perpetua una dormienda.
My sweetest Lesbia let us live and love,
And though the sager sort our deeds reprove,
Let us not weigh them: Heav'n's great lamps do dive
Into their west, and straight again revive,
But soon as once set is our little light,
Then must we sleep one ever-during night.
[*Carmina*, 5, line 1, trans. Thomas Campion]

6. *Da mi basia mille, deinde centum,*
Dein mille altera, dein secunda centum,
Deinde usque altera mille, deinde centum.
Give me a thousand kisses, then a hundred, then another thousand, then a second hundred, then yet another thousand, then a hundred.
[*Carmina*, 5, line 7]

7. *Miser Catulle, desinas ineptire,*
Et quod vides perisse perditum ducas.
Poor Catullus, stop this folly, and what you see is lost consider to be lost.
[*Carmina*, 8, line 1]

8. *Nam castum esse decet pium poetam*
Ipsum, versiculos nihil necesse est.
For the sacred poet ought to be chaste himself, but it is not necessary that his verses should be so.
[*Carmina*, 16, line 5]

9. *Paene insularum, Sirmio, insularumque*
Ocelle...
O quid solutis est beatius curis?
Cum mens onus reponit, ac peregrino
Labore fessi venimus larem ad nostrum,
Desideratoque acquiescimus lecto.
Hoc est quod unum est pro laboribus tantis.
Salve O venusta Sirmio atque hero gaude;
Gaudete vosque O Lydiae lacus undae;
Ridete quidquid est domi cachinnorum.
Sirmio, bright eye of peninsulas and islands ... O what greater happiness is there after our cares have been put aside, when the mind lays down its burden and, weary from far travel, we come to our home and find rest on the couch we have longed for? This it is which is the one thing worth such great hardships. Greetings, beautiful Sirmio, rejoice in your master, and you too, waves of the Lydian lake, laugh aloud in unison with all the laughter in my home.
[*Carmina*, 31, line 1]

10. *Nam risu inepto res ineptior nulla est.*
For there is nothing sillier than a silly laugh.
[*Carmina*, 39, line 16]

11. *Iam ver egelidos refert tepores.*
Now Spring brings back her gentle warmth.
[*Carmina*, 46, line 1]

12. [To Cicero]
Gratias tibi maximas Catullus
Agit pessimus omnium poeta,
Tanto pessimus omnium poeta,
Quanto tu optimus omnium's patronum.
Catullus gives his greatest thanks to you, Catullus the worst of all poets, by so much the worst of all poets, as you are the best of all advocates.
[*Carmina*, 49, line 4]

13. *Ille mi par esse deo videtur*
Ille, si fas est, superare divos,
Qui sedens adversus identidem te
Spectat et audit
Dulce ridentem.
He seems to me to be equal to a god, or if I may say this, to surpass the gods, who sitting opposite you again and again gazes upon you and hears you sweetly laughing.
[*Carmina*, 50, line 1]

14. *Caeli, Lesbia nostra, Lesbia illa,*
Illa Lesbia, quam Catullus unam
Plus quam se atque suos amavit omnes,
Nunc in quadriviis et angiportis
Glubit magnanimos Remi nepotes.
O Caelius, my Lesbia, that Lesbia whom Catullus has loved more than himself and all his own, now at the crossroads and in the alleyways sucks the high-minded sons of Remus.
[*Carmina*, 58, line 1]

15. *Ut flos in saeptis secretus nascitur hortis,*
Ignotus pecori, nullo contusus aratro,
Quem mulcent aurae, firmat sol, educat imber;
Multi illum pueri, multae optavere puellae:
Idem cum tenui carptus defloruit ungui,
Nulli illum pueri, nullae optavere puellae:
Sic virgo dum intacta manet, dum cara suis est;
Cum castum amisit polluto corpore florem,
Nec pueris iucunda manet nec cara suis est.
As when a flower secretly springs up in an enclosed garden, unknown to the herd, uncrushed by any plough, which the breezes caress, the sun strengthens and the rain brings out, many boys have desired it and many girls. Yet when the same flower fades nipped by a sharp hail, no boys and no girls desire it. Such is a virgin while she remains intact and is dear to her own; but when she has lost her chaste flower and her body has been sullied, she no longer remains pleasing to the boys or dear to the girls.
[*Carmina*, 62, line 39]

16. *Sed mulier cupido quod dicit amanti,*
In vento et rapida scribere oportet aqua.
But what a woman says to her eager lover, she ought to write in the wind and the running water.
[*Carmina*, 70, line 3]

17. *Desine de quoquam quicquam bene velle mereri,*
Aut aliquem fieri posse putare pium.
Stop wishing to merit anyone's gratitude or thinking that anyone can become grateful.
[*Carmina*, 73, line 1]

18. *Difficile est longum subito deponere amorem.*
It is difficult suddenly to give up a long established love.
[*Carmina*, 76, line 13]

19. *Odi et amo: quare id factum, fortasse requiris.*
Nescio, sed fieri sentio et excrucior.
I hate and I love. Perhaps you ask why I do so. I do not know, but I feel it happen and I am tormented.
[*Carmina*, 85]

20. *Multas per gentes et multa per aequora vectus*
Advenio has miseras, frater, ad inferias,
Ut te postremo donarem munere mortis
Et mutam nequiquam alloquerer cinerem.
Quandoquidem fortuna mihi tete abstulit ipsum,
Heu miser indigne frater adempte mihi,
Nunc tamen interea haec, prisco quae more parentum
Tradita sunt tristi munere ad inferias,
Accipe fraterno multum manantia fletu,
Atque in perpetuum, frater, ave atque vale.
Having journeyed through many peoples and over many a sea I come, my brother, for these sad funeral rites, that I may present to you a last gift in death and vainly address your dumb ashes, since fortune has taken you from me – alas, poor brother cruelly snatched from me – but now accept these offerings which by our parents' custom have been handed down as a funeral gift, bedewed with many fraternal tears, and for all time, my brother, hail and farewell.
[*Carmina*, 101]

21. *At non effugies meos iambos.*
But you shall not escape my iambics.
[In Mynors (ed.), *Catulli Carmina* (1958), Fragment 3]

Caudwell, Sarah (Sarah Cockburn) (1939–)
Crime fiction writer and barrister

1. I have somewhere suggested, I think, that when your fancy is taken by a young man of slender figure and pleasing profile, you should not disclose at too early a stage the true nature of your interest.
[*The Shortest Way to Hades* (1984)]

Caulfield, Sir Bernard (Mr Justice Caulfield) (1914–)
English judge

1. [Describing Mary Archer's evidence in his direction to the jury]
Remember Mary Archer in the witness box? Your vision of her probably will never disappear. Has she elegance? Has she fragrance? Would she, without the strains of this trial, have radiance?
[*The Observer*, 1987, in Jeffrey Care (ed.), *Sayings of the Eighties* (1989)]

Causley, Charles (1917–)
English poet, anthologist and school teacher

1. Ears like bombs and teeth like splinters:
A blitz of a boy is Timothy Winters.
[*Union Street* (1957), 'Timothy Winters']

Cavafy, Constantine (1863–1933)
Egyptian-born Greek poet

1. What shall become of us without any barbarians?
Those people were a kind of solution.
['Expecting the Barbarians' (1904)]

Cavell, Edith (1865–1915)
English nurse; executed by the Germans for helping Allied soldiers escape from Belgium

1. [Said on the eve of her execution]
Standing, as I do, in view of God and eternity I realize that patriotism is not enough. I must have no hatred or bitterness towards anyone.
[*The Times*, 1915]

Cavour, Count (Camillo Benso di Cavour) (1810–1861)
Italian statesman; leader of the Italian unification movement

1. *Noi siamo pronti a proclamare nell'Italia questo gran principio: Libera Chiesa in libero Stato.*
We are ready to proclaim this great principle in our united Italy: a free Church in a free State.
[Speech, 1861]

Caxton, William (c. 1421–1491)
First English printer; translator and prose writer

1. The worshipful father and first founder and embellisher of ornate eloquence in our English, I mean Master Geoffrey Chaucer.
[Epilogue to Caxton's edition (c. 1478) of Chaucer's translation of Boethius, *The Consolacion of Philosophie*]

2. It is notoriously known through the universal world that there be nine worthy and the best that ever were. That is to wit three paynims, three Jews, and three Christian men. As for the paynims they were ... the first Hector of Troy, ... the second Alexander the Great; and the third Julius Caesar ... As for the three Jews ... the first was Duke Joshua ...; the second David, King of Jerusalem; and the third Judas Maccabaeus ... And sith the said Incarnation ... was first the noble Arthur ... The second was Charlemagne or Charles the Great ...; and the third and last was Godfrey of Bouillon.
[In Malory, *Le Morte d'Arthur* (1485), original preface]

3. I, according to my copy, have done set it in imprint, to the intent that noble men may see and learn the noble acts of chivalry, the gentle and virtuous deeds that some knights used in those days.
[In Malory, *Le Morte d'Arthur* (1485), original preface]

Cecil, Lord David (1902–1986)
English literary critic and biographer

1. It does not matter that Dickens' world is not lifelike: it is alive.
[*Early Victorian Novelists* (1934), 2]

Celano, Thomas de (c. 1190–c. 1260)
Italian disciple and biographer of St Francis of Assisi

1. *Dies irae, dies illa,*
Solvet saeclum in favilla,
Teste David cum Sibylla.
The day of wrath, that day will turn the universe to ashes, as David and the Sybil foretell.
[*Dies irae*, 1]

2. *Tuba mirum sparget sonum*
Per sepulchra regionum,
Coget omnes ante thronum.

Mors stupebit et natura,
Cum resurget creatura
Iudicanti responsura.

Liber scriptus proferetur,
In quo totum continetur
Unde mundus iudicetur.
The trumpet will fling out a stupendous sound through the tombs of all regions, it will drive everyone before the throne. Death will be amazed and so will nature, when creation rises again to make answer to the judge. The written book will be brought forward, in which everything is contained whereby the world will be judged.
[*Dies irae*, 7]

3. *Inter oves locum praesta*
Et ab haedis me sequestra
Statuens in parte dextra.
Among the sheep show me a place and separate me from the goats, setting me on the right-hand side.
[*Dies irae*, 43]

Centlivre, Susannah (c. 1667–1723)
Irish dramatist, poet and actress

1. He is as melancholy as an unbrac'd drum.
[*The Wonder* (1714), II]

2. The real Simon Pure.
[*A Bold Stroke for a Wife* (1718), V]

Cernuda, Luis (1902–1963)
Spanish poet

1. *No sentía mis pies. Quise cogerlos en mi mano, y no hallé mis manos: quise gritar, y no hallé mi voz. La niebla me envolvía.*
I couldn't feel my feet. I wanted to take hold of them with my hand, but I couldn't find my hands: I wanted to shout, and I didn't find my voice. Mist enveloped me.
[*Los placeres prohibidos* (*Forbidden Pleasures*, 1931), 'En medio de la multitud' ('In the midst of the crowd'), in *La realidad y el deseo* (*Reality and Desire*, 4th Edition, 1964)]

2. *Él conocía que todo estaba muerto*
En mí, que yo era un muerto
Andando entre los muertos.
He recognised that everything in me
Was dead, that I was dead
Walking amongst the dead.
[*Las Nubes* (*The Clouds*, 1937–1940), 'Lázaro' ('Lazarus'), in *La realidad y el deseo* (*Reality and Desire*, 4th Edition, 1964)]

3. *¿Es toda acción humana, como estimas ahora,*
Fruto de imitación y de inconsciencia?
Is every human action, as you now think,
The fruit of imitation and thoughtlessness?
[*Como quien espera el alba* (*Like someone waiting for the dawn*, 1941–1944), 'La familia', in *La realidad y el deseo* (*Reality and Desire*, 4th Edition, 1964)]

4. [On leaving Glasgow, where he had lived from 1939 to 1943]
Rara vez me he ido tan a gusto de sitio alguno.
Rarely have I been so pleased to leave a place.
[*Historial de un libro* (*Chronicle of a book*, 1958)]

Cervantes, Miguel de (1547–1616)
Spanish novelist and dramatist; author of the satirical romance Don Quixote, *thought to be the first modern novel*

1. *Yo sé quién soy ... y sé que puedo ser no sólo los que he dicho, sino todos los doce Pares de Francia, y aun todos los nueve de la Fama.*
I know who I am ... and I know that I can be not only those characters I have named, but all the Twelve Peers of France, and even all the Nine Worthies too.
[*El ingenioso hidalgo don Quixote de la Mancha* (*The Ingenious Nobleman Don Quixote of La Mancha*), I (1605), 5]

2. *¿No será mejor estarse pacífico en su casa y no irse por el mundo a buscar pan de trastrigo, sin considerar que muchos van por lana y vuelven tranquilos?*
Won't it be better if you stay peacefully at home, and don't go off round the world looking for better bread than is made of wheat, without first reflecting that many go for wool and come back empty-handed?
[*Don Quixote* I (1605), 7]

3. *Mire vuestra merced ... que aquellos que allí se parecen no son gigantes, sino molinos de viento.*
Look, your worship ... those things which you see over there are not giants, but windmills.
[*Don Quixote* I (1605), 8]

4. *¿No le decía yo, señor don Quixote, que se volviese, que los que iba a acometer no eran ejércitos, sino manadas de carneros?*
Didn't I tell you to come back, Don Quixote, sir, for you weren't going to attack armies but flocks of sheep?
[*Don Quixote* I (1605), 18]

5. *El Caballero de la Triste Figura.*
The Knight of the Sad Face.
[*Don Quixote* I (1605), 19]

6. *Tiene el miedo muchos ojos, y vee las cosas debajo de tierra.*
Fear has many eyes and can see things which are underground.
[*Don Quixote* I (1605), 20]

7. *Más vale salta de mata que ruegos de hombres buenos.*
A leap over a bush is better than the prayers of good men.
[*Don Quixote* I (1605), 21]

8. *Siempre, Sancho, he oído decir, que el hacer bien a villanos es echar agua en la mar.*
I've always heard, Sancho, that to do good to rogues is to throw water into the sea.
[*Don Quixote* I (1605), 23]

9. *Con su pan se lo coman; si fueron amancebados, o no, a Dios habrán dado la cuenta; de mis viñas vengo, no sé nada; no soy amigo de saber vidas ajenas; que el compra y miente, en su bolsa lo siente. Cuanto más, que desnudo nací, desnudo me hallo: ni pierdo ni gano; mas que los fuesen, ¿qué me va a mí? Y muchos piensan que hay tocinos y no hay estacas. Mas ¿quién puede poner puertas al campo?*
Let them eat [the lie] up with their bread; whether they were lovers or not, they will have given an account of themselves to God. I've been minding my own business, I know nothing; I'm not one to poke my nose into other people's affairs. There's no point in lying about the price; your purse will have to pay out anyway. What's more, naked I was born and naked I am now: I neither lose nor win. But even if they were lovers, what does that matter to me? Many people think there's bacon and there's not even a hook to hang it on. Who can fence in Mother Nature?
[*Don Quixote* I (1605), 25]

10. [Don Quixote of his lady, Dulcinea del Toboso]
Yo imagino que todo lo que digo es así, sin que sobre ni falte nada, y píntola en mi imaginación como la deseo.
I imagine that everything is as I say it is, neither more or less, and I paint her in my imagination the way I want her to be.
[*Don Quixote* I (1605), 25]

11. *En los que escuchado le habían sobrevino nueva lástima de ver que hombre que, al parecer, tenía buen entendimiento y buen discurso en todas las cosas que trataba, le hubiese perdido tan rematadamente en tratándole de su negra y pizmienta caballería.*
Those who listened to him were filled with pity on seeing a man who was apparently of sound intellect and had understanding of all the subjects of which he spoke, and yet had lost it so hopelessly on the subject of his infernal, cursed chivalry.
[*Don Quixote* I (1605), 38]

12. *Cada uno es como Dios le hizo, y aun peor muchas veces.*
Every man is as God made him, and often even worse.
[*Don Quixote*, II (1615), 4]

13. *La mejor salsa del mundo es la hambre.*
Hunger is the best sauce in the world.
[*Don Quixote*, II (1615), 5]

14. *La mujer honrada, la pierna quebrada, y en casa; y la doncella honesta, el hacer algo es su fiesta.*
An honest woman and a broken leg should be at home; and for a decent maiden, working is her holiday.
[*Don Quixote*, II (1615), 5]

15. *Muchos pocos hacen un mucho.*
Mony a mickle maks a muckle.
[*Don Quixote*, II (1615), 7]

16. *El pan comido y la compañía deshecha.*
Once the bread has been eaten, the company breaks up.
[*Don Quixote*, II (1615), 7]

17. *Ahora bien: todas las cosas tienen remedio, si no es la muerte.*
Well, now: there's a remedy for everything, except death.
[*Don Quixote*, II (1615), 10]

18. *Él es un entreverado loco, lleno de lúcidos intervalos.*
He's an intermittent fool, full of lucid intervals.
[*Don Quixote*, II (1615), 18]

19. *Dos linajes solos hay en el mundo, como decía una agüela mía, que son el tener y el no tener.*
There are only two lineages in the world, as a grandmother of mine used to say, the Haves and the Have-nots.
[*Don Quixote*, II (1615), 20]

20. *Mucho más dañan a las honras de las mujeres las desenvolturas y libertades públicas que las maldades secretas.*
Brazenness and public liberties do much more harm to a woman's honour than secret wickedness.
[*Don Quixote*, II (1615), 22]

21. *Digo, paciencia y barajar.*
I say have patience, and shuffle the cards.
[*Don Quixote*, II (1615), 23]

22. *Dime con quién andas, decirte he quién eres.*
Tell me the company you keep, and I'll tell you who you are.
[*Don Quixote*, II (1615), 23]

23. *La diligencia es madre de la buena ventura; y la pereza, su contraria, jamás llegó al término que pide un buen deseo.*
Diligence is the mother of good fortune; and the goal of a good intention was never reached through its opposite, laziness.
[*Don Quixote*, II (1615), 43]

24. *Bien haya el que inventó el sueño, capa que cubre todos los humanos pensamientos, manjar que quita la hambre, agua que ahuyenta la sed, fuego que calienta el frío, frío que templa el ardor, y, finalmente, moneda general con que todas las cosas se compran, balanza y peso que iguala al pastor con el rey y al simple con el discreto.*
God bless whoever invented sleep, the cloak that covers all human thoughts. It is the food that satisfies hunger, the water that quenches thirst, the fire that warms cold, the cold that reduces heat, and, lastly, the common currency which can buy anything, the balance and compensating weight that makes the shepherd equal to the king, and the simpleton equal to the sage.
[*Don Quixote*, II (1615), 68]

25. *Digo que los buenos pintores imitaban a naturaleza; pero que los malos la vomitaban.*
I say that good painters imitated nature; but that bad ones vomited it.
[*Novelas ejemplares* (*Exemplary Novels*, 1613), 'El licenciado Vidriera']

26. *También se puede decir una necedad en latín como en romance.*
It's possible to say something stupid in Latin as well as in Spanish.
[*Novelas ejemplares* (*Exemplary Novels*, 1613), 'El coloquio de los perros' ('The Dialogue of the Dogs')]

Chalmers, Patrick Reginald (1872–1942)
British banker and writer on field sports

1. What's lost upon the roundabouts we pulls up on the swings!
['Green Days and Blue Days: Roundabouts and Swings' (1912)]

Chamberlain, Joseph (1836–1914)
English Liberal statesman, imperialist and orator; father of Neville Chamberlain

1. Provided that the City of London remains as it is at present, the clearing-house of the world, any other nation may be its workshop.
[Speech, London, 1904]

2. Learn to think Imperially.
[Speech, London, 1904]

3. The day of small nations has long passed away. The day of Empires has come.
[Speech, Birmingham, 1904]

4. We are not downhearted. The only trouble is, we cannot understand what is happening to our neighbours.
[Speech, Smethwick, 1906]

Chamberlain, Neville (1869–1940)
English statesman and Conservative Prime Minister 1937–40; son of Joseph Chamberlain

1. In war, whichever side may call itself the victor, there are no winners, but all are losers.
[Speech, Kettering, 1938]

2. This is the second time in our history that there has come back from Germany to Downing Street peace with honour. I believe it is peace for our time.
[Speech, Downing Street, after Munich Agreement, 1938, in Feiling, *The Life of Neville Chamberlain* (1946)]

3. [On the annexation by Germany of the Sudetenland]
How horrible, fantastic, incredible, it is that we should be digging trenches and trying on gas-masks here because of a quarrel in a far-away country between people of whom we know nothing.
[Speech, 1938, in Feiling, *The Life of Neville Chamberlain* (1946)]

4. This morning the British Ambassador in Berlin handed the German Government a final note, stating that, unless the British Government heard from them by eleven o'clock that they were prepared at once to withdraw their troops from Poland, a state of war would exist between us. I have to tell you now that no such undertaking has been received, and that consequently this country is at war with Germany.
[Radio broadcast, 3 September 1939]

5. We have resolved to finish it. It is the evil things we shall be fighting against – brute force, bad faith, injustice, oppression and persecution and against them I am certain that the right will prevail.
[Radio broadcast, 3 September 1939]

6. Whatever may be the reason, whether it was that Hitler thought he might get away with what he had got without fighting for it, or whether it was that, after all, the preparations are not sufficiently complete, one thing is certain – he missed the bus.
[Speech to Conservative Central Council, 5 April 1940]

Chambers, Haddon (1860–1921)
English dramatist

1. The long arm of coincidence.
[*Captain Swift* (1888), II]

Chamfort, Nicolas (1741–1794)
French writer, noted for his wit

1. *La plus perdue de toutes les journées est celle où l'on n'a pas ri.*
The most wasted of all days is the day one did not laugh.
[*Maximes et pensées* (1796). Cf. Chesterfield: 14]

2. Our gratitude to most benefactors is the same as our feeling for dentists who have pulled our teeth. We acknowledge the good they have done and the evil from which they have delivered us, but we remember the pain they occasioned and do not love them very much.
[*Maximes et pensées* (1796)]

3. *Vivre est une maladie dont le sommeil nous soulage toutes les 16 heures. C'est un palliatif. La mort est le remède.*
Living is an illness from which sleep provides relief every sixteen hours. It's a palliative. Death is the remedy.
[*Maximes et pensées* (1796), 2]

4. *Des qualités trop supérieures rendent souvent un homme moins propre à la société. On ne va pas au marché avec des lingots; on y va avec de l'argent ou de la petite monnaie.*
Qualities too elevated often make a man unfit for society. We don't go to market with ingots, but with silver or small change.
[*Maximes et pensées* (1796), 3]

5. *L'amour, tel qu'il existe dans la société, n'est que l'échange de deux fantaisies et le contact de deux épidermes.*
Love, as it exists in society, is nothing more than the exchange of two fantasies and the contact of two skins.
[*Maximes et pensées* (1796), 6]

6. *Je dirais volontiers des métaphysiciens ce que Scalinger disait des Basques, on dit qu'ils s'entendent, mais je n'en crois rien.*
I am tempted to say about metaphysicians what Scalinger would say about the Basques: they are said to understand one another, but I don't believe a word of it.
[*Maximes et Pensées* (1796), 7]

7. *Les pauvres sont les nègres de l'Europe.*
The poor are the negroes of Europe.
[*Maximes et Pensées* (1796), 8]

8. *Quelqu'un disait d'un homme très personnel; il brûlerait votre maison pour se faire cuire deux oeufs.*
Someone said of a great egotist: 'He would burn your house down to cook himself a couple of eggs.'
[*Caractères et anecdotes*]

9. [His interpretation of '*Fraternité ou la mort*']
Sois mon frère, ou je te tue.
Be my brother, or I shall kill you.
[In Carlyle, *History of the French Revolution* (1837), II]

Champion, Henry Hyde (1859–1928)
Australian socialist politician and writer

1. [On the Labour Party of his day]
An army of lions led by asses.
[In R.H. Croll, *I Recall*...]

Chandler, Raymond (1888–1959)
American author of crime fiction; novelist, short-story and screen writer

1. It was about eleven o'clock in the morning, mid-October, with the sun not shining and a look of hard wet rain in the clearness of the foothills. I was wearing my powder-blue suit, with dark shirt, tie and display handkerchief, black brogues, black wool socks with dark blue clocks on them. I was neat, clean, shaved and sober, and I didn't care who knew it.
[*The Big Sleep* (1939), opening lines]

2. It was a blonde. A blonde to make a bishop kick a hole in a stained glass window.
[*Farewell, My Lovely* (1940), 13]

3. She gave me a smile I could feel in my hip pocket.
[*Farewell, My Lovely* (1940), 18]

4. All men who read escape from something else ... [they] must escape at times from the deadly rhythm of their private thoughts.
[*Atlantic Monthly* (1944), 'The Simple Art of Murder']

5. Down these mean streets a man must go who is not himself mean, who is neither tarnished nor afraid.
[*Atlantic Monthly* (1944), 'The Simple Art of Murder']

6. Alcohol is like love: the first kiss is magic, the second is intimate, the third is routine. After that you just take the girl's clothes off.
[*The Long Good-bye* (1953)]

7. If my books had been any worse I should not have been invited to Hollywood, and ... if they had been any better, I should not have come.
[Letter to C.W. Morton, 1945]

8. Would you convey my compliments to the purist who reads your proofs and tell him or her that I write in a sort of broken-down patois which is something like the way a Swiss waiter talks, and that when I split an infinitive, God damn it, I split it so it will stay split.
[Letter to Edward Weeks, his English publisher, 1947]

9. When I started out to write fiction I had the great disadvantage of having absolutely no talent for it ... If more than two people were on scene I couldn't keep one of them alive.
[Letter to Paul Brooks, 1949]

Chanel, Coco (1883–1971)
French couturier and creator of perfumes

1. Youth is something very new: twenty years ago no one mentioned it.
[In Marcel Haedrich, *Coco Chanel, Her Life, Her Secrets* (1971)]

2. [When asked where one should wear perfume]
Wherever one wants to be kissed.
[In Marcel Haedrich, *Coco Chanel, Her Life, Her Secrets* (1971)]

3. Fashion is architecture: it is a matter of proportions.
[In Marcel Haedrich, *Coco Chanel, Her Life, Her Secrets* (1971)]

4. [Remark at a press conference, 1967]
Fashion is reduced to a question of hem lengths. Haute couture is finished because it's in the hands of men who don't like women.
[In Madsen, *Coco Chanel* (1990), 36]

5. [Last words]
You see, this is how you die.
[In Madsen, *Coco Chanel* (1990), 39]

Chaplin, Charlie (Sir Charles Chaplin) (1889–1977)
English comedian, film actor, director and satirist

1. *Priest*: May the Lord have mercy on your soul.
Verdoux: Why not? After all, it belongs to Him.
[*Monsieur Verdoux* (1947)]

2. All I need to make a comedy is a park, a policeman and a pretty girl.
[*My Autobiography* (1964), 10]

3. You have to believe in yourself, that's the secret. Even when I was in the orphanage, when I was roaming the street trying to find enough to eat, even then I thought of myself as the greatest actor in the world. I had to feel the exuberance

that comes from utter confidence in yourself. Without it, you go down to defeat.
[*My Autobiography* (1964)]

4. I am for people. I can't help it.
[*The Observer*, 'Sayings of the Week', 1952]

5. I remain just one thing, and one thing only – and that is a clown. It places me on a far higher plane than any politician.
[*The Observer*, 'Sayings of the Week', 1960]

6. Life is a tragedy when seen in close-up, but a comedy in long-shot.
[In *The Guardian*, Obituary, 1977]

Chapman, Arthur (1873–1935)
American poet

1. Out where the handclasp's a little stronger,
Out where the smile dwells a little longer,
That's where the West begins.
[*Out Where the West Begins* (1916)]

Chapman, George (c. 1559–c. 1634)
English poet, dramatist and translator of Greek and Latin

1. O Incredulitie, the wit of Fooles,
That slovenlie will spit on all thinges faire,
The Cowards castle, and the Sluggards cradle.
['De Guiana' (1596)]

2. For one heate (all know) doth drive out another,
One passion doth expell another still.
[*Monsieur D'Olive* (1606), V]

3. Who to himselfe is law, no law doth neede,
Offends no King, and is a King indeede.
[*Bussy D'Ambois* (1607–1608), II.i]

4. Terror of darknesse, O thou King of flames.
[*Bussy D'Ambois* (1607–1608), V.iii]

5. And let a Scholler, all earths volumes carrie,
He will be but a walking dictionarie.
[*The Teares of Peace* (1609)]

6. A Poeme, whose subject is not truth, but things like truth.
[*Revenge of Bussy D'Ambois* (1613), Dedication to Thomas Howard]

7. Danger (the spurre of all great mindes) is ever
The curbe to your tame spirits.
[*Revenge of Bussy D'Ambois* (1613), V.i]

8. His naked Ulysses, clad in eternall Fiction.
[*Homer's Odyssey* (1614), Epistle to Somerset]

9. I'me asham'd the law is such an Ass.
[*Revenge for Honour* (1654), III.ii]

Charles I (1600–1649)
Scottish-born King of Great Britain and Ireland from 1625; son of James VI of Scotland and I of England; executed

1. I will end with a rule that may serve for a statesman, a courtier, or a lover – never make a defence or apology before you be accused.
[Letter to Wentworth, 1636]

2. [Said of the Five Members of Parliament]
I see all the birds are flown.
[Speech, House of Commons, 1642]

3. Hurt not the Ax, that may hurt me.
[In King Charles His Speech Made Upon the Scaffold, 1649]

4. For the King ... the Laws of the Land will clearly instruct you for that ... For the People: And truly I desire their Liberty and Freedom as much as any body whomsoever, but I must tell you, That their Liberty and their Freedom consists in having of Government; those Laws, by which their Life and their Goods may be most their own. It is not for having share in Government (Sir) that is nothing pertaining to them; A Subject and a Sovereign are clean different things ... If I would have given way to an Arbitrary way, for to have all Laws changed according to the power of the Sword, I needed not to have come here, and therefore I tell you (and I pray God it be not laid to your charge) That I am the Martyr of the People.
[In King Charles His Speech Made Upon the Scaffold, 1649]

5. I dye a Christian, according to the profession of the Church of England, as I found it left me by my Father ... I go from a corruptible to an incorruptible Crown; where no disturbance can be, no disturbance in the world.
[In King Charles His Speech Made Upon the Scaffold, 1649]

Charles II (1630–1685)
English King of Great Britain and Ireland from 1660; son of Charles I

1. It is upon the Navy under the good Providence of God that the safety, honour, and welfare of this Realm do chiefly depend.
[Preamble to Articles of War, 1652, in Callender, *The Naval Side of British History* (1924), 8]

2. He [Charles II] said once to myself, he was no atheist, but he could not think God would make a man miserable only for taking a little pleasure out of the way. He disguised his popery to the last.
[In Burnet, *The History of His Own Time* (1724), II]

3. [Of Presbyterianism]
The king spoke to him [Lauderdale] to let that [Presbytery] go, for it was not a religion for gentlemen.
[In Burnet, *The History of His Own Time* (1724), II]

4. He told me, he had a chaplain [Woolly, later made a bishop] ... a very great blockhead ... he said he was a very silly fellow: but that, he believed, his nonsense suited their nonsense, for he had brought them all [the non-conformists] to church.
[In Burnet, *The History of His Own Time* (1724), II]

5. [Of Nell Gwyn]
Let not poor Nelly starve.
[In Burnet, *The History of His Own Time* (1724), III]

6. [To his brother James]
I am sure no man in England will take away my life to make you King.
[In William King, *Political & Literary Anecdotes* (1818)]

7. He had been, he said, a most unconscionable time dying; but he hoped that they would excuse it.
[In Macaulay, *The History of England* (1849), I, 4]

8. [Comment on Rochester's epitaph on him]
This is very true: for my words are my own, and my actions are my ministers'.
[In Thomas Hearne, *Remarks and Collections* (1885–1921). Cf. Rochester: 13]

9. [On the Debates in the House of Lords on Lord Ross's Divorce Bill, 1670]
Better than going to a play.
[In A. Bryant, *King Charles II* (1931), II, 7]

10. Brother, I am too old to go again to my travels.
[Attr.]

Charles V, Holy Roman Emperor (1500–1558)
Emperor 1519–56; King of Spain (as Charles I), 1516–56

1. An iron hand in a velvet glove.
[In Carlyle, *Latter-Day Pamphlets*]

2. [Referring to his dispute with Francis I of France over Italian territory]
My cousin Francis and I are in perfect accord – he wants Milan, and so do I.
[In W. Durant, *The Story of Civilisation*]

3. I speak Spanish to God, Italian to women, French to men, and German to my horse.
[Attr.]

4. [After the death of Martin Luther, when it was suggested that he hang the corpse on a gallows]
I make war on the living, not on the dead.
[Attr.]

Charles X, King of France (1757–1836)
King from 1824–30; brother of Louis XVIII; attempted to restore absolutism

1. I would rather hew wood than be a king under the conditions of the King of England.
[Attr.]

2. [Said to Talleyrand, who is said to have replied 'You are forgetting the postchaise']
There is no middle course between the throne and the scaffold.
[Attr.]

Charles Francis Joseph, Emperor of Austria (1887–1922)
Last ruler of the Austro-Hungarian empire; abdicated 1918

1. [On hearing of his accession to emperor]
What should I do? I think the best thing is to order a new stamp to be made with my face on it.
[In H. Hoffmeister, *Anekdotenschatz*]

Charles, Prince of Wales (1948–)
Son and heir of Elizabeth II and Prince Philip

1. All the faces here this evening seem to be bloody Poms.
[Remark at Australia Day dinner, 1973]

2. British management doesn't seem to understand the importance of the human factor.
[Speech, Parliamentary and Scientific Committee lunch, 1979]

3. [When asked, upon getting engaged, if he was 'in love']
Yes ... whatever that may mean.
[TV news interview, February 1981]

4. [On the proposed extension to the National Gallery]
A kind of vast municipal fire station ... like a monstrous carbuncle on the face of a much-loved and elegant friend.
[Speech, 1984, to the Royal Institute of British Architects]

5. I have fallen in love with all sorts of girls and I fully intend to go on doing so.
[*The Observer*, 1975]

6. What I want to know is; what is actually wrong with an élite, for God's sake?
[*The Observer*, 1985, in Jeffrey Care (ed.), *Sayings of the Eighties* (1989)]

7. The one advantage about marrying a princess – or someone from a royal family – is that they do know what happens.
[Attr.]

Charmley, John (1955–)
English historian; revisionist biographer of Winston Churchill

1. What would the man of 1938 have said of the Prime Minister of 1944?
[*Churchill: The End of Glory* (1993)]

Charron, Pierre (1541–1603)
French theologian and philosopher

1. *La vraye science et la vray estude de l'homme, c'est l'homme.*
The true science and the true study of man is man.
[*De la Sagesse* (1601), I, Preface. Cf. Pope: 89]

Chase, Salmon Portland (1808–1873)
American statesman; Chief Justice of the US under Lincoln

1. No more slave States and no more slave territory.
[Buffalo Convention resolution, 1848, in Hart, *Salmon Portland Chase* (1899), 4]

Chasen, Dave

1. Bogart's a helluva nice guy until 11.30 p.m. After that he thinks he's Bogart.
[In L. Halliwell, *The Filmgoer's Book of Quotes* (1973)]

Chateaubriand, François-René (Vicomte de Chateaubriand) (1760–1848)
French novelist, autobiographical writer and statesman

1. *L'écrivain original n'est pas celui qui n'imite personne, mais celui que personne ne peut imiter.*
The original writer is not the one who refrains from imitating others, but the one who can be imitated by none.
[*Le génie du Christianisme* (*The Beauties of Christianity*, 1802), II, 1, 3]

2. *On n'apprend pas à mourir en tuant les autres.*
One does not learn how to die by killing others.
[*Mémoires d'Outre-Tombe* (*Memoirs*, 1826–1841]

Chatterton, Thomas (1752–1770)
English poet, author of spurious medieval verse; committed suicide at 17 because of his poverty

1. O! synge untoe mie roundelaie,
O! droppe the brynie teare wythe mee,
Daunce ne moe atta hallie daie,
Lycke a reynynge ryver bee;
Mie love ys dedde,
Gon to hys death-bedde,
Al under the wyllowe-tree.
['Mynstrelles Songe' (1769)]

Chaucer, Geoffrey (c. 1340–1400)
English poet, noted for his narrative skill and humour; public servant and courtier

1. Whan that Aprill with his shoures soote
The droghte of March hath perced to the roote,
And bathed every veyne in swich licour
Of which vertu engendred is the flour...

2. And smale foweles maken melodye,
That slepen al the nyght with open ye
(So priketh hem nature in hir corages);
Thanne longen folk to goon on pilgrimages...
[*The Canterbury Tales* (1387), General Prologue]

3. [Of the Knight]
He loved chivalrie,
Trouthe and honour, fredom and curteisie...

4. He nevere yet no vileynye ne sayde
In al his lyf unto no maner wight.
He was a verray, parfit gentil knyght...

5. He was as fressh as is the month of May...

6. He koude songes make and wel endite...

7. Curteis he was, lowely, and servysable,
And carf biforn his fader at the table.
[*The Canterbury Tales* (1387), General Prologue]

8. [Of the Prioresse]
Hire gretteste ooth was but by Seinte Loy...

9. Ful weel she soong the service dyvyne,
Entuned in hir nose ful semely,
And Frenssh she spak ful faire and fetisly,
After the scole of Stratford atte Bowe,
For Frenssh of Parys was to hire unknowe...

10. She wolde wepe, if that she saugh a mous
Kaught in a trappe, if it were deed or bledde.
Of smale houndes hadde she that she fedde
With rosted flessh, or milk or wastel-breed.
But soore wepte she if oon of hem were deed...

11. Of smal coral aboute hire arm she bar
A peire of bedes, gauded al with grene,
And theron heng a brooch of gold ful sheene,
On which ther was first write a crowned A,
And after Amor vincit omnia.
[*The Canterbury Tales* (1387), General Prologue]

12. [Of the Monk]
He yaf nat of that text a pulled hen,
That seith that hunters ben nat hooly men...

13. His heed was balled, that shoon as any glas,
And eek his face, as he hadde been enoynt.
[*The Canterbury Tales* (1387), General Prologue]

14. [Of the Frere]
A Frere ther was, a wantowne and a merye...

15. He knew the tavernes wel in every toun...

16. He was the beste beggere in his hous...

17. Somwhat he lipsed, for his wantownesse,
To make his Englissh sweete upon his tonge...
[*The Canterbury Tales* (1387), General Prologue]

18. [Of the Clerk]
A Clerk ther was of Oxenford also,
That unto logyk hadde longe ygo.
As leene was his hors as is a rake,
And he nas nat right fat, I undertake,
But looked holwe, and therto sobrely...

19. For hym was levere have at his beddes heed
Twenty bookes, clad in blak or reed
Of Aristotle and his philosophie,
Than robes riche, or fithele, or gay sautrie.
But al be that he was a philosophre,
Yet hadde he but litel gold in cofre...

20. Sownynge in moral vertu was his speche,
And gladly wolde he lerne and gladly teche.
[*The Canterbury Tales* (1387), General Prologue]

21. [Of the Sergeant of the Lawe]
Nowher so bisy a man as he ther nas,
And yet he semed bisier than he was.
[*The Canterbury Tales* (1387), General Prologue]

22. [Of the Frankeleyn]
It snewed in his hous of mete and drynke.
[*The Canterbury Tales* (1387), General Prologue]

23. [Of the Doctour of Phisik]
His studie was but litel on the Bible...

24. For gold in phisik is a cordial,
Therefore he lovede gold in special.
[*The Canterbury Tales* (1387), General Prologue]

25. [Of the Wif of Bath]
She was a worthy womman al hir lyve:
Housbondes at chirche dore she hadde fyve,
Withouten oother compaignye in youthe,—
But therof nedeth nat to speke as nowthe.
And thries hadde she been at Jerusalem;
She hadde passed many a straunge strem;
At Rome she hadde been, and at Boloigne,
In Galice at Seint-Jame, and at Coloigne.
[*The Canterbury Tales* (1387), General Prologue]

26. [Of the Persoun]
This noble ensample to his sheep he yaf,
That first he wroghte, and afterward he taughte...

27. If gold ruste, what shal iren do?...

28. But Cristes loore and his apostles twelve
He taughte, but first he folwed it hymselve.
[*The Canterbury Tales* (1387), General Prologue]

29. [Of the Somonour]
A Somonour was ther with us in that place,
That hadde a fyr-reed cherubynnes face,
For saucefleem he was, with eyen narwe.
As hoot he was and lecherous as a sparwe.
With scalled browes blake and piled berd.
Of his visage children were aferd...

30. Wel loved he garleek, oynons, and eek lekes,
And for to drynken strong wyn, reed as blood.
[*The Canterbury Tales* (1387), General Prologue]

31. [Of the Pardoner]
His walet lay biforn hym in his lappe,
Bretful of pardoun, comen from Rome al hoot...

32. He hadde a croys of latoun ful of stones,
And in a glas he hadde pigges bones.
But with thise relikes, whan that he fond
A povre person dwellynge upon lond,
Upon a day he gat hym moore moneye
Than that the person gat in monthes tweye;
And thus, with feyned flaterye and japes,
He made the person and the peple his apes...

33. Well koude he rede a lessoun or a storie,
But alderbest he song an offertorie.
[*The Canterbury Tales* (1387), General Prologue]

34. Wel ofter of the welle than of the tonne
She drank...

35. Though clerkes preise wommen but a lite,
Ther kan no man in humblesse hym acquite
As womman kan.
[*The Canterbury Tales* (1387), The Clerk's Tale]

36. For o thyng, sires, saufly dar I seye,
That freendes everych oother moot obeye,
If they wol longe holden compaignye.
Love wol nat been constreyned by maistrye.
Whan maistrie comth, the God of Love anon
Beteth his wynges, and farewel, he is gon!
Love is a thyng as any spirit free.
Wommen, of kynde, desiren libertee,
And nat to been constreyned as a thral;
And so doon men, if I sooth seyen shal...

37. Til that the brighte sonne loste his hewe;
For th'orisonte hath reft the sonne his lyght,–
This is as muche to seye as it was nyght!...

38. Trouthe is the hyeste thyng that man may kepe.
[*The Canterbury Tales* (1387), The Franklin's Tale]

39. The carl spak oo thing, but he thoghte another.
[*The Canterbury Tales* (1387), The Friar's Tale]

40. Thanked be Fortune and hire false wheel,
That noon estaat assureth to be weel...

41. Wostow nat wel the olde clerkes sawe,
That 'who shal yeve a lovere any lawe?'
Love is a gretter lawe, by my pan,
Than may be yeve to an erthely man...

42. A man moot nedes love, maugree his heed...

43. And therfore, at the kynges court, my brother,
Ech man for hymself, ther is noon oother...

44. And whan a beest is deed he hath no peyne;
But man after his deeth moot wepe and pleyne...

45. The bisy larke, messager of day...

46. For pitee renneth soone in gentil herte...

47. The smylere with the knyf under the cloke...

48. Up roos the sonne, and up roos Emelye...

49. What is this world? what asketh men to have?
Now with his love, now in his colde grave...

50. This world nys but a thurghfare ful of wo,
And we been pilgrymes, passynge to and fro.
Deeth is an ende of every worldly soore...

51. To maken vertu of necessitee.
[*The Canterbury Tales* (1387), The Knight's Tale]

52. She is mirour of alle curteisye.
[*The Canterbury Tales* (1387), The Man of Law's Tale]

53. Lat take a cat, and fostre hym wel with milk
And tendre flessh, and make his couche of silk,
And lat hym seen a mous go by the wal,
Anon he weyveth milk and flessh and al,
And every deyntee that is in that hous,
Swich appetit hath he to ete a mous...

54. Kepe wel thy tonge, and thenk upon the crowe.
[*The Canterbury Tales* (1387), The Manciple's Tale]

55. What is bettre than wisedoom? Womman. And what is bettre than a good womman? Nothyng.
[*The Canterbury Tales* (1387), The Tale of Melibee]

56. A wyf wol laste, and in thyn hous endure,
Wel lenger than thee list, paraventure.
[*The Canterbury Tales* (1387),The Merchant's Tale]

57. 'Tehee!' quod she, and clapte the wyndow to.
[*The Canterbury Tales* (1387), The Miller's Tale]

58. Tragedie is to seyn a certeyn storie,
As olde bookes maken us memorie,
Of hym that stood in greet prosperitee
And is yfallen out of heigh degree
Into myserie, and endeth wrecchedly.
[*The Canterbury Tales* (1387), The Prologue of the Monk's Tale]

59. Ful wys is he that kan hymselven knowe!...

60. Redeth the grete poete of Ytaille
That highte Dant, for he kan al devyse
Fro point to point, nat o word wol he faille.
[*The Canterbury Tales* (1387), The Monk's Tale]

61. No deyntee morsel passed thurgh hir throte;
Hir diete was accordant to hir cote...

62. His coomb was redder than the fyn coral,
And batailled as it were a castel wal;
His byle was blak, and as the jeet it shoon;
Lyk asure were his legges and his toon;
His nayles whitter than the lylye flour,
And lyk the burned gold was his colour.
This gentil cok hadde in his governaunce
Sevene hennes for to doon al his plesaunce,
Whiche were his sustres and his paramours,
And wonder lyk to hym, as of colours;
Of whiche the faireste hewed on hir throte
Was cleped faire damoysele Pertelote...

63. Mordre wol out, that se we day by day...

64. Whan that the month in which the world bigan,
That highte March, whan God first maked man...

65. And daun Russell the fox stirte up atones...

66. And on a Friday fil al this meschaunce.
[*The Canterbury Tales* (1387), The Nun's Priest's Tale]

67. My theme is alwey oon, and evere was–
Radix malorum est Cupiditas...

68. Nay, I wol drynke licour of the vyne,
And have a joly wenche in every toun.
[*The Canterbury Tales* (1387), The Pardoner's Prologue]

69. O wombe! O bely! O stynkyng cod
Fulfilled of dong and of corrupcion!...

70. For dronkenesse is verray sepulture
Of mannes wit and his discrecioun...

71. 'What, carl, with sory grace!'
[*The Canterbury Tales* (1387), The Pardoner's Tale]

72. The gretteste clerkes been noght wisest men...

73. So was hir joly whistle wel ywet.
[*The Canterbury Tales* (1387), The Reeve's Tale]

74. He hadde a semely nose...

75. 'By God,' quod he, 'for pleynly, at a word,
Thy drasty rymyng is nat worth a toord!'
[*The Canterbury Tales* (1387), Sir Thopas]

76. Experience, though noon auctoritee
Were in this world, is right ynogh for me
To speke of wo that is in mariage...

77. Yblessed be God that I have wedded fyve!
Welcome the sixte, whan that evere he shal.
For sothe, I wol nat kepe me chaast in al.
Whan myn housbonde is fro the world ygon,
Som Cristen man shall wedde me anon...

78. The bacon was nat fet for hem, I trowe,
That som men han in Essex at Dunmowe...

79. But, Lord Crist! whan that it remembreth me
Upon my yowthe, and on my jolitee,
It tikleth me aboute myn herte roote.
Unto this day it dooth myn herte boote
That I have had my world as in my tyme...

80. That in his owene grece I made him frye...

81. And for to se, and eek for to be seye
Of lusty folk...

82. But yet I hadde alwey a coltes tooth.
Gat-tothed I was, and that bicam me weel...

83. I hate hym that my vices telleth me,
And so doo mo, God woot, of us than I...

84. A womman cast hir shame away,
Whan she cast of hir smok...

85. This is a long preamble of a tale!...
[*The Canterbury Tales* (1387), The Wife of Bath's Prologue]

86. As thikke as motes in the sonne-beem...

87. Of which mayde anon, maugree hir heed,
By verray force, he rafte hire maydenhed...

88. Wommen desiren to have sovereynetee
As wel over hir housbond as hir love,
And for to been in maistrie hym above...

89. That he is gentil that dooth gentil dedis.
[*The Canterbury Tales* (1387), The Wife of Bath's Tale]

90. She was so ferforth yeven hym to plese,
That al that lyked him hit dyde her ese...

91. So thirleth with the poynt of remembraunce
The swerd of sorowe, ywhet with fals plesaunce.
[*Anelida and Arcite*]

92. Venus clerk, Ovide,
That hath ysowen wonder wide
The grete god of Loves name.
[*The House of Fame*]

93. A thousand tymes have I herd men telle
That ther ys joy in hevene and peyne in helle,
And I acorde wel that it ys so;
But, natheles, yet wot I wel also
That ther nis noon dwellyng in this contree,
That eyther hath in hevene or helle ybe,
Ne may of hit noon other weyes witen,
But as he hath herd seyd, or founde it writen;
For by assay ther may no man it preve.
But God forbede but men shulde leve
Wel more thing then men han seen with ye!
Men shal not wenen every thing a lye
But yf himself yt seeth, or elles dooth;
For, God wot, thing is never the lasse sooth,
Thogh every wight ne may it nat ysee.
Bernard the monk ne saugh nat all, pardee!...

94. And as for me, though that I konne but lyte,
On bokes for to rede I me delyte,
And to hem yive I feyth and ful credence,
And in myn herte have hem in reverence
So hertely, that ther is game noon
That fro my bokes maketh me to goon,
But yt be seldom on the holyday,
Save, certeynly, whan that the month of May
Is comen, and that I here the foules synge,
And that the floures gynnen for to sprynge,
Farewel my bok, and my devocioun!...

95. Of al the floures in the mede,
Thanne love I most thise floures white and rede,
Swiche as men callen daysyes in our toun...

96. Welcome, somer, oure governour and lord!...

97. Wel by reson men it calle may
The 'dayesye', or elles the 'ye of day'.
[*The Legend of Good Women*, The Prologue]

98. And she was fayr as is the rose in May.
[*The Legend of Good Women*, 'Cleopatra']

99. The lyf so short, the craft so long to lerne,
Th'assay so hard, so sharp the conquerynge...

100. For out of olde feldes, as men seyth,
Cometh al this newe corn from yer to yere,
And out of olde bokes, in good feyth,
Cometh al this newe science that men lere...

101. Know thyself first immortal,
And loke ay besyly thow werche and wysse
To commune profit, and thow shalt not mysse
To comen swiftly to that place deere
That ful of blysse is and of soules cleere.
[*The Parliament of Fowls*]

102. The tyme, that may not sojourne,
But goth, and may never retourne,
As watir that doun renneth ay,
But never drope retourne may...

103. Povert al aloon,
That not a peny hadde in wolde,
All though she hir clothis solde,
And though she shulde anhonged be;
For nakid as a worm was she...

104. Thou shalt make castels thanne in Spayne,
And dreme of joye, all but in vayne.
[*The Romaunt of the Rose*]

105. O blynde world, O blynde entencioun!
How often falleth al the effect contraire
Of surquidrie and foul presumpcioun;
For kaught is proud, and kaught is debonaire...

106. For it is seyd, 'man maketh ofte a yerde
With which the maker is hymself ybeten.'...

107. But love a womman that she woot it nought,
And she wol quyte it that thow shalt nat fele;
Unknowe, unkist, and lost, that is unsought.
[*Troilus and Criseyde*, I]

108. O wynd, O wynd, the weder gynneth clere...

109. So longe mote ye lyve, and alle proude,
Til crowes feet be growen under youre yë.
[*Troilus and Criseyde*, II]

110. It is nought good a slepyng hound to wake...

111. For I have seyn, of a ful misty morwe
Folowen ful ofte a myrie someris day...

112. Right as an aspes leef she gan to quake...

113. For of fortunes sharpe adversitee
The worste kynde of infortune is this,
A man to han ben in prosperitee,
And it remembren, whan it passed is.
[*Troilus and Criseyde*, III]

114. Oon ere it herde, at tothir out it wente...

115. But manly sette the world on six and sevene;
And if thow deye a martyr, go to hevene!...

116. For tyme ylost may nought recovered be.
[*Troilus and Criseyde*, IV]

117. Paradis stood formed in hire yën...

118. Ye, fare wel al the snow of ferne yere!...

119. Ek gret effect men write in place lite;
Th'entente is al, and nat the lettres space...

120. Go, litel bok, go, litel myn tragedye,
Ther God thi makere yet, er that he dye,
So sende myght to make in som comedye!
But litel bok, no makyng thow n'envie,
But subgit be to alle poesye;
And kis the steppes, where as thow seest pace
Virgile, Ovide, Omer, Lucan, and Stace.

And for ther is so gret diversite
In Englissh and in writyng of oure tonge,
So prey I God that non myswrite the,
Ne the mysmetre to defaute of tonge.
And red wherso thow be, or elles songe,
That thow be understonde, God I biseche!...

121. And whan that he was slayn in this manere,
His lighte goost ful blisfully is went
Up to the holughnesse of the eighthe spere,
In convers letyng everich element;
And ther he saugh, with ful avysement,
The erratik sterres, herkenyng armonye
With sownes ful of hevenyssh melodie.

And down from thennes faste he gan avyse
This litel spot of erthe, that with the se
Embraced is, and fully gan despise
This wrecched world, and held al vanite
To respect of the pleyn felicite
That is in hevene above...

122. O yonge, fresshe folkes, he or she,
In which that love up groweth with youre age,
Repeyreth hom fro worldly vanyte,
And of youre herte up casteth the visage
To thilke God that after his ymage
Yow made, and thynketh al nys but a faire
This world, that passeth soone as floures faire.

And loveth hym, the which that right for love
Upon a crois, our soules for to beye,
First starf, and roos, and sit in hevene above;
For he nyl falsen no wight, dar I seye,
That wol his herte al holly on hym leye.
And syn he best to love is, and most meke,
What nedeth feynede loves for to seke?

Lo here, of payens corsed olde rites,
Lo here, what alle hire goddes may availle;
Lo here, thise wrecched worldes appetites;
Lo here, the fyn and guerdoun for travaille
Of Jove, Appollo, of Mars, of swich rascaille!...

123. O moral Gower, this book I directe
To the.
[*Troilus and Criseyde*, V]

124. Flee fro the prees, and dwelle with sothfastnesse...

125. Forth, pilgrim, forth! Forth, beste, out of thy stal!
Know thy contree, look up, thank God of al;
Hold the heye wey, and lat thy gost thee lede;
And trouthe thee shal delivere, it is no drede.
[*Truth: Balade de Bon Conseyl*]

Chekhov, Anton (1860–1904)
Russian short-story writer, realist dramatist and doctor

1. *Medvedenko*: Why do you always wear black?
Masha: I am in mourning for my life. I'm unhappy.
[*The Seagull* (1896), I]

2. *Nina*: It's not easy to act in your play, as there aren't any living people in it.
Treplev: Living people! Life should be shown not as it is, not as it ought to be, but as it appears in our dreams.
[*The Seagull* (1896), I]

3. Women don't forgive failure.
[*The Seagull* (1896), II]

4. *Nina*: I'm a seagull. No, that's not it ... Do you remember when you shot a seagull? A man happened to come along, saw it and, for want of something better to do, killed it. The subject for a short story.
[*The Seagull* (1896), IV]

5. Human beings have been endowed with reason and a creative power so that they can add to what thay have been given. But until now they have been not creative, but destructive. Forests are disappearing, rivers are drying up, wildlife is becoming extinct, the climate's being ruined and with every passing day the earth is becoming poorer and uglier.
[*Uncle Vanya* (1897), I]

6. A woman can only become a man's friend in this order – first she is an acquaintance, then a mistress, and only after that a friend.
[*Uncle Vanya* (1897), II]

7. *Sonya*: I'm not beautiful.
Elena Andreevna: You have lovely hair.
Sonya: No! No! When a woman isn't beautiful, people tell her, 'You have lovely eyes, you have lovely hair.'
[*Uncle Vanya* (1897), III]

8. The time has come, something huge is approaching us, a refreshing, powerful storm is brewing ... Soon it will blow away all the laziness, indifference, prejudice against work and decaying boredom from our society ... I'm going to work, and in some twenty-five or thirty years' time every one will be working. Every one!
[*The Three Sisters* (1901), I]

9. He who doesn't notice whether it is winter or summer is happy. I think that if I were in Moscow, I wouldn't notice what the weather was like.
[*The Three Sisters* (1901), II]

10. *Liubov Andreevna*: Are you really still a student?
Trofimov: I shall probably be a student forever.
[*The Cherry Orchard* (1904), I]

11. If many remedies are suggested for a disease, that means the disease is incurable.
[*The Cherry Orchard* (1904), II]

12. My God, the cherry orchard is mine! ... I've bought the estate where my grandfather and father were slaves, where they weren't even allowed inside the kitchen. I must be dreaming, I must be imagining it all.
[*The Cherry Orchard* (1904), III]

13. After all, the cynicism of real life can't be outdone by any literature: one glass won't get someone drunk when he's already had a whole barrel.
[Letter to M.V. Kiseleva, 1887]

14. Medicine is my lawful wife but literature is my mistress. When I'm bored with one, I spend the night with the other.
[Letter to A.S. Suvorin, 1888]

15. He was a rationalist, but it must be admitted, loved the ringing of church bells.
[*Notebook I* (1891–1904)]

16. The artist may not be a judge of his characters, only a dispassionate witness.
[Attr.]

17. The centre of gravity should be in two people: he and she.
[Attr.]

Cherry-Garrard, Apsley (1886–1959)
English polar explorer, zoologist and writer

1. Polar exploration is at once the cleanest and most isolated way of having a bad time which has been devised.
[*The Worst Journey in the World* (1922)]

Chesterfield, Philip Dormer Stanhope, Fourth Earl of
(1694–1773)
English politician, statesman, letter writer and orator

1. Be wiser than other people if you can; but do not tell them so.
[Letter to his son, 1745]

2. The knowledge of the world is only to be acquired in the world, and not in a closet.
[Letter to his son, 1746]

3. Custom has made dancing sometimes necessary for a young man; therefore mind it while you learn it, that you may learn to do it well, and not be ridiculous, though in a ridiculous act.
[Letter to his son, 1746]

4. An injury is much sooner forgotten than an insult.
[Letter to his son, 1746]

5. Courts and camps are the only places to learn the world in.
[Letter to his son, 1747]

6. There is a Spanish proverb, which says very justly, Tell me whom you live with, and I will tell you who you are.
[Letter to his son, 1747]

7. 'Do as you would be done by,' is the surest method that I know of pleasing.
[Letter to his son, 1747]

8. Take the tone of the company you are in.
[Letter to his son, 1747]

9. [Of William Lowndes, Secretary to the Treasury]
I knew, once, a very covetous, sordid fellow, who used frequently to say,'Take care of the pence; for the pounds will take care of themselves.' This was a just and sensible reflection in a miser.
[Letter to his son, 1747]

10. I recommend to you to take care of minutes; for hours will take care of themselves.
[Letter to his son, 1747]

11. Advice is seldom welcome; and those who want it the most, always like it the least.
[Letter to his son, 1748]

12. Speak of the moderns without contempt, and of the ancients without idolatry.
[Letter to his son, 1748]

13. Wear your learning, like your watch, in a private pocket; and do not merely pull it out and strike it merely to show you have one. If you are asked what o'clock it is, tell it; but do not proclaim it hourly and unasked like the watchman.
[Letter to his son, 1748]

14. In my mind, there is nothing so illiberal and so ill-bred, as audible laughter ... I am neither of a melancholy, nor a cynical disposition; and am as willing, and as apt, to be pleased as anybody; but I am sure that, since I have had the full use of my reason, nobody has ever heard me laugh.
[Letter to his son, 1748. Cf. Chamfort: 1]

15. If Shakespeare's genius had been cultivated, those beauties, which we so justly admire in him, would have been undisgraced by those extravagancies and that nonsense with which they are frequently accompanied.
[Letter to his son, 1748]

16. Women, then, are only children of a larger growth; they have an entertaining tattle and sometimes wit; but for solid, reasoning good-sense, I never in my life knew one that had it, or who reasoned or acted consequentially for four-and-twenty hours together.
[Letter to his son, 1748]

17. [Of women]
A man of sense only trifles with them, plays with them, humours and flatters them, as he does with a sprightly, forward child; but he neither consults them about, nor trusts them with, serious matters; though he often makes them believe that he does both.
[Letter to his son, 1748]

18. In the case of scandal, as in that of robbery, the receiver is always thought as bad as the thief.
[Letter to his son, 1748]

19. Mimickry, which is the common and favourite amusement of little, low minds, is in the utmost contempt with great ones.
[Letter to his son, 1748]

20. It must be owned that the Graces do not seem to be natives of Great Britain; and, I doubt, the best of us here have more of the rough than the polished diamond.
[Letter to his son, 1748]

21. Due attention to the inside of books, and due contempt for the outside, is the proper relation between a man of sense and his books.
[Letter to his son, 1749]

22. Idleness is only the refuge of weak minds, and the holiday of fools.
[Letter to his son, 1749]

23. Women are much more like each other than men; they have, in truth, but two passions, vanity and love; these are their universal characteristics.
[Letter to his son, 1749]

24. Putting moral virtues at the highest, and religion at the lowest, religion must still be allowed to be a collateral security, at least, to virtue; and every prudent man will sooner trust to two securities than to one.
[Letter to his son, 1750]

25. Swallow all your learning in the morning, but digest it in company in the evenings ... know everybody and endeavour to please everybody – I mean exteriorly, for fundamentally it is impossible.
[Letter to his son, 1751]

26. Have you found out that every woman is infallibly to be gained by every sort of flattery, and every man by one sort or other?
[Letter to his son, 1752]

27. The chapter of knowledge is a very short, but the chapter of accidents is a very long one.
[Letter to Solomon Dayrolles, 1753]

28. In matters of religion and matrimony I never give any advice; because I will not have anybody's torments in this world or the next laid to my charge.
[Letter to A.C. Stanhope, 1765]

29. Religion is by no means a proper subject of conversation in a mixed company ... It is too awful and respectable a subject to become a familiar one.
[Letter to his godson, c. 1766]

30. Cunning is the dark sanctuary of incapacity.
[Letter to his godson and heir (to be delivered after his own death)]

31. It is an undoubted truth, that the less one has to do, the less time one finds to do it in. One yawns, one procrastinates, one

can do it when one will, and therefore one seldom does it at all.
[Letter]

32. [On the picture of Richard Nash, between busts of Newton and Pope at Bath]
The picture plac'd the busts between,
Adds to the thought much strength;
Wisdom and Wit are little seen,
But Folly's at full length.
[*Wit and Wisdom of Lord Chesterfield*, 'Epigrams'; also attributed to Jane Brereton]

33. I assisted at the birth of that most significant word flirtation, which dropped from the most beautiful mouth in the world.
[*The World*, 1754; reprinted in *Miscellaneous Works* (1774), II]

34. [Said when Tyrawley was old and infirm]
Tyrawley and I have been dead these two years; but we don't choose to have it known.
[In Boswell, *The Life of Samuel Johnson* (1791)]

35. [When asked what could be done to control the evangelical preacher George Whitefield]
Make him a bishop, and you will silence him at once.
[Attr.]

36. [On sex]
The pleasure is momentary, the position ridiculous, and the expense damnable.
[Attr.]

Chesterton, G.K. (1874–1936)

English novelist, poet, journalist, critic and essayist

1. When fishes flew and forests walked
And figs grew upon thorn,
Some moment when the moon was blood
Then surely I was born.

With monstrous head and sickening cry
And ears like errant wings,
The devil's walking parody
On all four-footed things...

2. Fools! For I also had my hour;
One far fierce hour and sweet:
There was a shout about my ears,
And palms before my feet.
[*The Wild Knight and Other Poems* (1900), 'The Donkey']

3. This legend of an epic hour
A child I dreamed, and dream it still,
Under the great grey water-tower
That strikes the stars on Campden Hill.
[*The Napoleon of Notting Hill* (1904), dedication 'To Hilaire Belloc']

4. Before the gods that made the gods
Had seen their sunrise pass,
The White Horse of the White Horse Vale
Was cut out of the grass.
[*Ballad of the White Horse* (1911), I]

5. For the great Gaels of Ireland
Are the men that God made mad,
For all their wars are merry,
And all their songs are sad.
[*Ballad of the White Horse* (1911), II]

6. The thing on the blind side of the heart,
On the wrong side of the door,
The green plant groweth, menacing
Almighty lovers in the spring;
There is always a forgotten thing,
And love is not secure.
[*Ballad of the White Horse* (1911), III]

7. Before the Roman came to Rye or out to Severn strode,
The rolling English drunkard made the rolling English road...

8. The night we went to Birmingham by way of Beachy Head...

9. For there is good news yet to hear and fine things to be seen,
Before we go to Paradise by way of Kensal Green.
[*The Flying Inn* (1914), 'The Rolling English Road']

10. God made the wicked Grocer
For a mystery and a sign,
That men might shun the awful shops
And go to inns to dine...

11. He keeps a lady in a cage
Most cruelly all day,
And makes her count and calls her 'Miss'
Until she fades away.
[*The Flying Inn* (1914), 'The Song Against Grocers']

12. Tea, although an Oriental,
Is a gentleman at least;
Cocoa is a cad and coward,
Cocoa is a vulgar beast.
[*The Flying Inn* (1914), 'The Song of Right and Wrong']

13. And Noah he often said to his wife when he sat down to dine,
'I don't care where the water goes if it doesn't get into the wine.'...

14. And water is on the Bishop's board and the Higher Thinker's shrine,
But I don't care where the water goes if it doesn't get into the wine.
[*The Flying Inn* (1914), 'Wine and Water']

15. Are they clinging to their crosses,
F.E. Smith?...

16. Talk about the pews and steeples
And the Cash that goes therewith!
But the souls of Christian peoples...
Chuck it, Smith!
[*Poems* (1915), 'Antichrist, or the Reunion of Christendom']

17. They spoke of Progress spiring round,
Of Light and Mrs Humphrey Ward–
It is not true to say I frowned,
Or ran about the room and roared;
I might have simply sat and snored–
I rose politely in the club
And said, 'I feel a little bored;
Will someone take me to a pub?'
[*Poems* (1915), 'A Ballade of an Anti-Puritan']

18. White founts falling in the courts of the sun,
And the Soldan of Byzantium is smiling as they run...

19. Strong gongs groaning as the guns boom far,
Don John of Austria is going to the war...

20. Then the tuckets, then the trumpets, then the cannon, and he comes.
Don John laughing in the brave beard curled,
Spurning of his stirrups like the thrones of all the world,
Holding his head up for a flag of all the free.
Love-light of Spain – hurrah!
Death-light of Africa!
Don John of Austria
Is riding to the sea...

21. The walls are hung with velvet that is black and soft as sin,
And little dwarfs creep out of it and little dwarfs creep in...

22. Cervantes on his galley sets the sword back in the sheath
(Don John of Austria rides homeward with a wreath.)
[*Poems* (1915), 'Lepanto']

23. John Grubby, who was short and stout
And troubled with religious doubt,
Refused about the age of three
To sit upon the curate's knee.
[*Poems* (1915), 'The New Freethinker']

24. Smile at us, pay us, pass us; but do not quite forget.
For we are the people of England, that never have spoken yet...

25. We only know the last sad squires ride slowly towards the sea,
And a new people takes the land: and still it is not we.
[*Poems* (1915), 'The Secret People']

26. And I dream of the days when work was scrappy,
And rare in our pockets the mark of the mint,
When we were angry and poor and happy,
And proud of seeing our names in print.
[*Poems* (1915), 'A Song of Defeat']

27. The men that worked for England
They have their graves at home...

And they that rule in England,
In stately conclave met,
Alas, alas for England
They have no graves as yet.
[*The Ballad of Saint Barbara and Other Verses* (1922), 'Elegy in a Country Churchyard']

28. They died to save their country and they only saved the world.
[*The Ballad of Saint Barbara and Other Verses* (1922), 'The English Graves']

29. 'My country, right or wrong,' is a thing that no patriot would think of saying except in a desperate case. It is like saying, 'My mother, drunk or sober.'
[*The Defendant* (1901). Cf. Decatur: 1]

30. There is a road from the eye to the heart that does not go through the intellect.
[*The Defendant* (1901)]

31. All slang is metaphor, and all metaphor is poetry.
[*The Defendant* (1901), 'A Defence of Slang']

32. Individually, men may present a more or less rational appearance, eating, sleeping and scheming. But humanity as a whole is changeful, mystical, fickle and delightful. Men are men, but Man is a woman.
[*The Napoleon of Notting Hill* (1904)]

33. The human race, to which so many of my readers belong, has been playing at children's games from the beginning, and will probably do it till the end, which is a nuisance for the few people who grow up.
[*The Napoleon of Notting Hill* (1904)]

34. There is no such thing on earth as an uninteresting subject; the only thing that can exist is an uninterested person.
[*Heretics* (1905), 3]

35. Happiness is a mystery like religion, and should never be rationalized.
[*Heretics* (1905), 7]

36. A good novel tells us the truth about its hero; but a bad novel tells us the truth about its author.
[*Heretics* (1905), 15]

37. The artistic temperament is a disease that afflicts amateurs.
[*Heretics* (1905), 17]

38. The cosmos is about the smallest hole that a man can hide his head in.
[*Orthodoxy* (1908), 2, 'The Maniac']

39. Reason is itself a matter of faith. It is an act of faith to assert that our thoughts have any relation to reality at all.
[*Orthodoxy* (1908), 3, 'The Suicide of Thought']

40. Mr Shaw is (I suspect) the only man on earth who has never written any poetry.
[*Orthodoxy* (1908), 3, 'The Suicide of Thought']

41. Tradition means giving votes to the most obscure of all classes, our ancestors. It is the democracy of the dead. Tradition refuses to submit to the small and arrogant oligarchy of those who merely happen to be walking about. All democrats object to men being disqualified by the accident of birth; tradition objects to their being disqualified by the accident of death.
[*Orthodoxy* (1908), 4, 'The Ethics of Elfland']

42. All conservatism is based upon the idea that if you leave things alone you leave them as they are. But you do not. If you leave a thing alone you leave it to a torrent of change.
[*Orthodoxy* (1908), 7, 'The Eternal Revolution']

43. Angels can fly because they can take themselves lightly.
[*Orthodoxy* (1908), 7, 'The Eternal Revolution']

44. The Christian ideal has not been tried and found wanting. It has been found difficult; and left untried.
[*What's Wrong with the World* (1910)]

45. She [the elegant female] was maintaining the prime truth of woman, the universal mother: that if a thing is worth doing, it is worth doing badly.
[*What's Wrong with the World* (1910)]

46. [On fiction]
It is the art in which the conquests of woman are quite beyond controversy ... The novel of the nineteenth century was female.
[*The Victorian Age in Literature* (1913), 2]

47. Jane Austen was born before those bands which (we are told) protected woman from truth, were burst by the Brontës or elaborately untied by George Eliot. Yet the fact remains that Jane Austen knew much more about men than either of them.
[*The Victorian Age in Literature* (1913), 2]

48. Hardy went down to botanise in the swamp, while Meredith climbed towards the sun. Meredith became, at his best, a sort of daintily dressed Walt Whitman: Hardy became a sort of village atheist brooding and blaspheming over the village idiot.
[*The Victorian Age in Literature* (1913), 2]

49. The rich are the scum of the earth in every country.
[*The Flying Inn* (1914), 15]

50. To be clever enough to get all that money, one must be stupid enough to want it.
[*The Wisdom of Father Brown* (1914), 'The Paradise of Thieves']

51. One sees great things from the valley; only small things from the peak.
[*Storyteller*, 1924, 'The Hammer of God']

52. A great deal of contemporary criticism reads to me like a man saying: 'Of course I do not like green cheese; I am very fond of brown sherry.'
[*All I Survey* (1933), 'On Jonathan Swift']

53. Education is simply the soul of a society as it passes from one generation to another.
[*The Observer*, 'Sayings of the Week', 1924]

54. Democracy means government by the uneducated, while aristocracy means government by the badly educated.
[*New York Times*, 1931]

55. Is ditchwater dull? Naturalists with microscopes have told me that it teems with quiet fun.
[*The Listener*, 1936, 'The Spice of Life']

56. [On being stuck in the door of a car, he said it reminded him of an old Irishman]
'Why don't you get out sideways?'
'I have no sideways.'
[In M. Ward, *Gilbert Keith Chesterton* (1944)]

57. [Telegram to his wife; other venues have been suggested but this was the original]
Am in Market Harborough. Where ought I to be?
[In M. Ward, *Return to Chesterton* (1952)]

58. Chesterton taught me this: the only way to be sure of catching a train is to miss the one before it.
[In P. Daninos, *Vacances à tous prix* (1958), 'Le supplice de l'heure']

59. A man must love a thing very much if he not only practises it without any hope of fame and money, but even practises it without any hope of doing it well.
[In Alan L. Mackay, *The Harvest of a Quiet Eye* (1977)]

60. [Suggesting that being fat has its compensations]
Just the other day in the Underground I enjoyed the pleasure of offering my seat to three ladies.
[In W. Scholz, *Das Buch des Lachens*]

61. It's not the world that's got so much worse but the news coverage that's got so much better.
[Attr.]

62. New roads: new ruts.
[Attr.]

Chevalier, Albert (1861–1923)
English actor, music-hall singer and songwriter

1. There ain't a lady livin' in the land
As I'd 'swop' for my dear old Dutch!
['My Old Dutch', song, 1901]

2. Laugh! I thought I should 'ave died,
Knocked 'em in the Old Kent Road.
['Wot Cher!' or 'Knocked 'Em in the Old Kent Road', song, 1901]

Chevalier, Maurice (1888–1972)
French singer, film and vaudeville actor

1. Many a man has fallen in love with a girl in a light so dim he would not have chosen a suit by it.
[Attr.]

2. I prefer old age to the alternative.
[Attr.]

3. I'm over eighty in a world where the young reject the old with more intensity than ever before ... Now I'd like my old age to be my best performance. Death is the best exit.
[In Behr, *Thank Heaven for Little Girls* (1993), 19]

Chifley, Joseph Benedict (1885–1951)
Australian politician and former Prime Minister

1. My experience of gentlemen's agreements is that, when it comes to the pinch, there are rarely enough bloody gentlemen about.
[In L.F. Crisp, *Ben Chifley* (1960)]

Child, Lydia M. (1802–1880)
American novelist, abolitionist and suffragist

1. Not in vain is Ireland pouring itself all over the earth ... The Irish, with their glowing hearts and reverent credulity, are needed in this cold age of intellect and skepticism.
[*Letters from New York* (1842), I, 33]

Childers, Erskine (1870–1922)
English novelist, military historian and theoretician; Irish revolutionary politician

1. [Writing about his own execution, which took place very shortly afterwards]
It seems perfectly simple and inevitable, like lying down after a long day's work.
[Prison letter to his wife]

2. [Last words before his execution by firing squad, 24 November 1922]
Take a step forward, lads. It will be easier that way.
[In A. Boyle, *The Riddle of Erskine Childers* (1977)]

Chilebi, Katib

1. Coffee is a cold dry food, suited to the ascetic life and sedative of lust.
[In G.L. Lewis (trans.), *Anthology of Islamic Literature*]

Chillingworth, William (1602–1644)
English theologian and scholar

1. The Bible and the Bible only is the religion of Protestants.
[*The Religion of Protestants* (1637)]

2. I once knew a man out of courtesy help a lame dog over a stile, and he for requital bit his fingers.
[*The Religion of Protestants* (1637)]

Chisholm, Caroline (1808–1877)
English-born Australian humanitarian; the 'Emigrant's Friend'

1. For all the churches you can build, and all the books you can export, will never do much good without what a gentleman in that Colony very appropriately called 'God's police' – wives and little children – good and virtuous women.
[*Emigration and Transportation Relatively Considered* (1847)]

Chomsky, Noam (1928–)
Leading American linguistics scholar and political critic

1. The notion 'grammatical' cannot be identified with 'meaningful' ... in any semantic sense. Sentences (1) and (2) are equally nonsensical, but ... only the former is grammatical.
(1) Colourless green ideas sleep furiously.
(2) Furiously sleep ideas green colourless.
[*Syntactic Structures* (1957), 2]

2. As soon as questions of will or decision or reason or choice of action arise, human science is at a loss.
[Television interview, 1978]

Chonaill, Eibhlín Dhubh Ní (c. 1743–1790)

1. Till Art O'Leary returns
There will be no end to the grief
That presses down on my heart,
Closed up tight and firm

Like a trunk that is locked
And the key mislaid.
['The Lament for Arthur O'Leary']

Chopin, Kate (1851–1904)
American short-story writer and novelist

1. The voice of the sea speaks to the soul. The touch of the sea is sensuous, enfolding the body in its soft, close embrace.
[*The Awakening* (1899), 6]

2. There are some people who leave impressions not so lasting as the imprint of an oar upon the water.
[*The Awakening* (1899), 34]

Christie, Dame Agatha (1890–1976)
English crime novelist, playwright and short-story writer

1. [Hercule Poirot] tapped his forehead. 'These little grey cells, It is up to them – as you say over here.'
[*The Mysterious Affair at Styles* (1920)]

2. I believe that a well-known anecdote exists to the effect that a young writer, determined to make the commencement of his story forcible and original enough to catch the attention of the most blasé of editors, penned the first sentence: 'Hell! said the Duchess.'
[*The Murder on the Links* (1923)]

3. Curious things, habits. People themselves never knew they had them.
[*Witness for the Prosecution* (1953)]

4. One doesn't recognize in one's life the really important moments – not until it's too late.
[*Endless Night* (1967), II, 14]

5. Where large sums of money are concerned, it is advisable to trust nobody.
[*Endless Night* (1967), II, 15]

6. One is left with the horrible feeling now that war settles nothing; that to win a war is as disastrous as to lose one!
[*An Autobiography* (1977)]

7. An archaeologist is the best husband any woman can have: the older she gets, the more interested he is in her.
[News report, 8 March 1954, also quoted in *The Observer*, 1955; she denied saying it]

Chuang Tse (c. 369–286 BC)
Chinese Taoist philosopher

1. I do not know whether I was then a man dreaming I was a butterfly, or whether I am now a butterfly dreaming I am a man.
[*Chuang Tse* (1889), translated by H.A. Giles, 2]

Churchill, Charles (1731–1764)
English poet, political journalist and clergyman

1. Greatly his foes he dreads, but more his friends;
He hurts me most who lavishly commends.
['The Apology, addressed to the Critical Reviewers' (1761)]

2. Keep up appearances; there lies the test;
The world will give thee credit for the rest.
Outward be fair, however foul within;
Sin if thou wilt, but then in secret sin...

3. Stay out all night, but take especial care
That Prudence bring thee back to early prayer
As one with watching and with study faint,
Reel in a drunkard, and reel out a saint.
['Night' (1761)]

4. [Of Thomas Franklin, Professor of Greek, Cambridge]
He sicken'd at all triumphs but his own.
[*The Rosciad* (1761)]

5. [Of Alexander Wedderburn, later Lord Loughborough]
To mischief trained, e'en from his mother's womb,
Grown old in fraud, tho' yet in manhood's bloom.
Adopting arts, by which gay villains rise,
And reach the heights, which honest men despise;
Mute at the bar, and in the senate loud,
Dull 'mongst the dullest, proudest of the proud;
A pert, prim Prater of the northern race,
Guilt in his heart, and famine in his face.
[*The Rosciad* (1761)]

6. Ne'er blushed unless, in spreading Vice's snares,
She blunder'd on some virtue unawares.
[*The Rosciad* (1761)]

7. Genius is of no country.
[*The Rosciad* (1761)]

8. He mouths a sentence, as curs mouth a bone.
[*The Rosciad* (1761)]

9. Fashion – a word which knaves and fools may use,
Their knavery and folly to excuse.
[*The Rosciad* (1761)]

10. Where he falls short, 'tis Nature's fault alone;
Where he succeeds, the merit's all his own.
[*The Rosciad* (1761)]

11. The best things carried to excess are wrong.
[*The Rosciad* (1761)]

12. Thy danger chiefly lies in acting well;
No crime's so great as daring to excel...

13. By different methods different men excel;
But where is he who can do all things well?
['An Epistle to William Hogarth' (1763)]

14. Who wit with jealous eye surveys,
And sickens at another's praise.
[*The Ghost* (1763), II]

15. Just to the windward of the law.
[*The Ghost* (1763), III]

16. A joke's a very serious thing.
[*The Ghost* (1763), IV]

17. Who often, but without success, have pray'd
For apt Alliteration's artful aid.
['The Prophecy of Famine' (1763)]

18. Though by whim, envy, or resentment led,
They damn those authors whom they never read.
[*The Candidate* (1764)]

19. Be England what she will,
With all her faults, she is my country still...

20. It can't be Nature, for it is not sense.
['The Farewell' (1764)]

21. Old-age, a second child, by Nature curs'd
With more and greater evils than the first,
Weak, sickly, full of pains; in ev'ry breath
Railing at life, and yet afraid of death.
[*Gotham* (1764), I]

22. With the persuasive language of a tear.
['The Times' (1764)]

Churchill, Jennie Jerome (1854–1921)

American-born political hostess and writer; wife of Randolph and mother of Winston Churchill

1. *Alma*: I rather suspect her of being in love with him.
Martin: Her own husband? Monstrous! What a selfish woman!
[*His Borrowed Plumes* (1909)]

2. ... and we owe something to extravagance, for thrift and adventure seldom go hand in hand...
[*Pearson's*, 1915, 'Extravagance']

3. You seem to have no real purpose in life and won't realize at the age of twenty-two that for a man life means work, and hard work if you mean to succeed.
[Letter to Winston Churchill, 1897]

Churchill, Lord Randolph (1849–1894)

English Conservative politician; Chancellor of the Exchequer 1886; father of Winston Churchill

1. [Of members of the Conservative Government]
The old gang.
[Speech, 1878]

2. [Of Gladstone]
For the purposes of recreation he has selected the felling of trees, and we may usefully remark that his amusements, like his politics, are essentially destructive ... The forest laments in order that Mr Gladstone may perspire.
[Speech, 1884]

3. [Of Gladstone]
An old man in a hurry.
[Speech, 1886]

4. The duty of an opposition is to oppose.
[In W.S. Churchill, *Lord Randolph Churchill* (1906)]

5. [Of decimal points]
I never could make out what those damned dots meant.
[Attr. by Winston Churchill]

Churchill, Randolph (1911–1968)

English journalist and writer; son of Sir Winston Churchill

1. [In a letter to a hostess after ruining her dinner party with one of his displays of drunken rudeness]
I should never be allowed out in private.
[In B. Roberts, *Randolph: a Study of Churchill's Son* (1984)]

2. [During a papal audience]
I expect you know my friend, Evelyn Waugh who, like you, your holiness, is a Roman Catholic.
[Attr.]

Churchill, Sir Winston (1874–1965)

English statesman; Conservative Prime Minister 1940–45, 1951–55; historian, army officer and biographer; Nobel prize for literature 1953

1. A labour contract into which men enter voluntarily for a limited and for a brief period, under which they are paid wages which they consider adequate, under which they are not bought or sold and from which they can obtain relief ... on payment of £17.10s., the cost of their passage, may not be a desirable contract, may not be a healthy or proper contract, but it cannot in the opinion of His Majesty's Government be classified as slavery in the extreme acceptance of the word without some risk of terminological inexactitude.
[Speech, House of Commons, February 1906]

2. Men will forgive a man anything except bad prose.
[Election speech, Manchester, 1906]

3. [Of Lord Charles Beresford]
He is one of those orators of whom it was well said, 'Before they get up they do not know what they are going to say; when they are speaking, they do not know what they are saying; and when they sit down, they do not know what they have said.'
[Speech, House of Commons, December 1912]

4. The maxim of the British people is 'Business as usual'.
[Speech, November 1914]

5. Labour is not fit to govern.
[Election speech, 1920]

6. [Of the British]
They are the only people who like to be told how bad things are – who like to be told the worst.
[Speech, 1921]

7. [Of Ramsey MacDonald]
I remember, when I was a child, being taken to the celebrated Barnum's circus, which contained an exhibition of freaks and monstrosities, but the exhibit ... which I most desired to see was the one described as 'The Boneless Wonder'. My parents judged that that spectacle would be too revolting and demoralising for my youthful eyes, and I have waited 50 years to see the boneless wonder sitting on the Treasury Bench.
[Speech, House of Commons, January 1931]

8. India is a geographical term. It is no more a united nation than the Equator.
[Speech, Royal Albert Hall, 1931]

9. We have sustained a defeat without a war.
[Speech, House of Commons, 1938]

10. I cannot forecast to you the action of Russia. It is a riddle wrapped in a mystery inside an enigma.
[Broadcast, October 1939]

11. I would say to the House, as I have said to those who have joined this Government, 'I have nothing to offer but blood, toil, tears and sweat'.
[Speech, House of Commons, May 1940]

12. You ask, what is our aim? I can answer that in one word: victory at all costs, victory in spite of all terror, victory however long and hard the road may be; for without victory there is no survival.
[Speech, House of Commons, May 1940]

13. We shall not flag or fail. We shall go on to the end. We shall fight in France, we shall fight on the seas and oceans, we shall fight with growing confidence and growing strength in the air, we shall defend our island, whatever the cost may be, we shall fight on the beaches, we shall fight on the landing grounds, we shall fight in the fields and in the streets, we shall fight in the hills; we shall never surrender.
[Speech, June 1940]

14. Let us therefore brace ourselves to our duties, and so bear ourselves that, if the British Empire and its Commonwealth last for a thousand years, men will still say, 'This was their finest hour'.
[Speech, June 1940]

15. The battle of Britain is about to begin.
[Speech, July 1940]

16. [On RAF pilots in the Battle of Britain]
Never in the field of human conflict was so much owed by so many to so few.
[Speech, August 1940]

17. The British Empire and the United States will have to be somewhat mixed up together in some of their affairs for

mutual and general advantage. For my own part, looking out for the future, I do not view the process with any misgivings. I could not stop it if I wished; no one can stop it. Like the Mississippi, it just keeps rolling along. Let it roll. Let it roll on full flood, inexorable, irresistible, benignant, to broader lands and better days.
[Speech, House of Commons, August 1940]

18. We do not covet anything from any nation except their respect.
[Broadcast to the French people, October 1940]

19. We are waiting for the long-promised invasion. So are the fishes.
[Radio broadcast to the French people, October 1940]

20. I do not resent criticism, even when, for the sake of emphasis, it parts for the time with reality.
[Speech, House of Commons, January 1941]

21. [Addressing President Roosevelt]
Give us the tools, and we will finish the job.
[Broadcast, February 1941]

22. The people of London with one voice would say to Hitler, 'You do your worst, and we will do our best'.
[Speech, June 1941]

23. Do not let us speak of darker days; let us rather speak of sterner days. These are not dark days; these are great days – the greatest days our country has ever lived; and we must all thank God that we have been allowed, each of us according to our stations, to play a part in making these days memorable in the history of our race.
[Speech, October 1941]

24. When I warned them [the French Government] that Britain would fight on alone whatever they did, their Generals told their Prime Minister and his divided Cabinet, 'In three weeks England will have her neck wrung like a chicken.' Some chicken! Some neck!
[Speech, December 1941. Cf. Weygand: 1]

25. [Of Mussolini]
This whipped jackal, who, to save his own skin, has made of Italy a vassal state of Hitler's Empire, is frisking up by the side of the German tiger with yelps not only of appetite – that could be understood – but even of triumph.
[Speech, House of Commons, April 1941]

26. What kind of people do they [the Japanese] think we are?
[Speech to U.S. Congress, December 1941]

27. [On the Battle of Egypt]
This is not the end. It is not even the beginning of the end. But it is, perhaps, the end of the beginning.
[Speech, Mansion House, November 1942. Cf. Talleyrand: 2]

28. We make this wide encircling movement in the Mediterranean, having for its primary object the recovery of the command of that vital sea, but also having for its object the exposure of the underbelly of the Axis, especially of Italy, to heavy attack.
[Speech, *Hansard*, November 1942]

29. I have not become the King's First Minister in order to preside over the liquidation of the British Empire.
[Speech, Mansion House, November 1942]

30. [Of North Africa]
Not a seat but a springboard.
[Radio broadcast, November 1942]

31. The Almighty in His infinite wisdom did not see fit to create Frenchmen in the image of Englishmen.
[Speech, House of Commons, December 1942]

32. There is no finer investment for any community than putting milk into babies.
[Radio broadcast, March 1943]

33. The empires of the future are empires of the mind.
[Speech, September 1943]

34. There are few virtues that the Poles do not possess – and there are few mistakes they have ever avoided.
[Speech, House of Commons, August 1945]

35. Beware, for the time may be short. A shadow has fallen across the scenes so lately lighted by the Allied victory. Nobody knows what Soviet Russia and its Communist international organization intend to do in the immediate future. From Stettin in the Baltic to Trieste in the Adriatic an Iron Curtain has descended across the Continent.
[Speech, Fulton, Missouri, March 1946. Cf. Troubridge: 1]

36. We must build a kind of United States of Europe.
[Speech, Zurich, September 1946]

37. Many forms of government have been tried, and will be tried in this world of sin and woe. No one pretends that democracy is perfect or all-wise. Indeed, it has been said that democracy is the worst form of Government except all those other forms that have been tried from time to time.
[Speech, House of Commons, November 1947]

38. Perhaps it is better to be irresponsible and right than to be responsible and wrong.
[Party Political Broadcast, London, August 1950]

39. To jaw-jaw is better than to war-war.
[Speech, Washington, June 1954]

40. I have never accepted what many people have kindly said, namely that I inspired the nation. It was the nation and the race dwelling all round the globe that had the lion's heart. I had the luck to be called upon to give the roar.
[Speech at the Palace of Westminster, 1954, on his eightieth birthday]

41. So they told me how Mr Gladstone read Homer for fun, which I thought served him right.
[*My Early Life* (1930), 2]

42. Headmasters have powers at their disposal with which Prime Ministers have never yet been invested.
[*My Early Life* (1930), 2]

43. By being so long in the lowest form [at Harrow] I gained an immense advantage over the cleverer boys ... I got into my bones the essential structure of the normal British sentence – which is a noble thing. Naturally I am biased in favour of boys learning English; and then I would let the clever ones learn Latin as an honour, and Greek as a treat.
[*My Early Life* (1930), 2]

44. Which brings me to my conclusion upon Free Will and Predestination, namely – let the reader mark it – that they are identical.
[*My Early Life* (1930), 3]

45. It is a good thing for an uneducated man to read books of quotations.
[*My Early Life* (1930), 9]

46. Those who can win a war well can rarely make a good peace and those who could make a good peace would never have won the war.
[*My Early Life* (1930), 26]

47. Dictators ride to and fro upon tigers which they dare not dismount. And the tigers are getting hungry.
[*While England Slept* (1936)]

48. I have watched this famous island descending incontinently, fecklessly, the stairway which leads to a dark gulf. It is a fine broad stairway at the beginning, but after a bit the carpet ends. A little farther on there are only flagstones, and a little farther on still these break beneath your feet.
[*While England Slept* (1936)]

49. In war, resolution; in defeat, defiance; in victory, magnanimity; in peace, goodwill.
[*The Second World War* (1948–1954), I, The Gathering Storm, Epigraph]

50. I felt as if I were walking with destiny, and that all my past life had been but a preparation for this hour and this trial.
[*The Second World War* (1948–1954), I, The Gathering Storm]

51. On the night of the tenth of May [1940], at the outset of this mighty battle, I acquired the chief power in the State, which henceforth I wielded in ever-growing measure for five years and three months of world war, at the end of which time, all our enemies having surrendered unconditionally or being about to do so, I was immediately dismissed by the British electorate from all further conduct of their affairs.
[*The Second World War* (1948–1954), I, The Gathering Storm]

52. [Referring to the Soviet statesman Molotov]
I have never seen a human being who more perfectly represented the modern conception of a robot.
[*The Second World War* (1948–1954), I, The Gathering Storm]

53. No one can guarantee success in war, but only deserve it.
[*The Second World War* (1948–1954), II, Their Finest Hour]

54. The loyalties which centre upon number one are enormous. If he trips he must be sustained. If he makes mistakes they must be covered. If he sleeps he must not be wantonly disturbed. If he is no good he must be pole-axed.
[*The Second World War* (1948–1954), II, Their Finest Hour]

55. [Referring to Dunkirk]
Wars are not won by evacuations.
[*The Second World War* (1948–1954), II, Their Finest Hour]

56. When I look back on all these worries I remember the story of the old man who said on his deathbed that he had had a lot of trouble in his life, most of which had never happened.
[*The Second World War* (1948–1954), II, Their Finest Hour]

57. [On the ceremonial form of the declaration of war against Japan, 8 December 1941]
When you have to kill a man it costs nothing to be polite.
[*The Second World War* (1948–1954), III, The Grand Alliance]

58. I have only one purpose, the destruction of Hitler, and my life is much simplified thereby. If Hitler invaded Hell I would make at least a favourable reference to the Devil in the House of Commons.
[*The Second World War* (1948–1954), III, The Grand Alliance]

59. Before Alamein we never had a victory. After Alamein we never had a defeat.
[*The Second World War* (1948–1954), IV, The Hinge of Fate]

60. [When asked whether the Niagara Falls looked the same as when he first saw them]
Well, the principle seems the same. The water still keeps falling over.
[*The Second World War* (1948–1954), V, Closing the Ring]

61. I said that the world must be made safe for at least fifty years. If it was only for fifteen to twenty years then we should have betrayed our soldiers.
[*The Second World War* (1948–1954), V, Closing the Ring]

62. We must have a better word than 'prefabricated'. Why not 'ready-made'?
[*The Second World War* (1948–1954), V, Closing the Ring, Appendix C]

63. Peace with Germany and Japan on our terms will not bring much rest . . . As I observed last time, when the war of the giants is over the wars of the pygmies will begin.
[*The Second World War* (1948–1954), VI, Triumph and Tragedy]

64. [Said during a lunch with the Arab leader Ibn Saud, when he heard that the king's religion forbade smoking and alcohol]
I must point out that my rule of life prescribed as an absolutely sacred rite smoking cigars and also the drinking of alcohol before, after, and if need be during all meals and in the intervals between them.
[*The Second World War* (1948–1954), VI, Triumph and Tragedy]

65. [Marginal comment on a document]
This is the sort of English up with which I will not put.
[In Ernest Gowers, *Plain Words* (1948)]

66. [Of Clement Attlee]
He is a modest man who has a good deal to be modest about.
[In *Chicago Sunday Tribune Magazine of Books*, June 1954]

67. [Of Viscount Montgomery]
In defeat, unbeatable; in victory, unbearable.
[In Edward Marsh, *Ambrosia and Small Beer* (1964), 5]

68. Don't talk to me about naval tradition. It's nothing but rum, sodomy and the lash.
[In Sir Peter Gretton, *Former Naval Person* (1968), 1]

69. [Remark, December 1941]
We must just KBO ('Keep Buggering On').
[In M. Gilbert, *Finest Hour*]

70. [On the Chiefs of Staffs system, 1943]
You may take the most gallant sailor, the most intrepid airman, or the most audacious soldier, put them at a table together – what do you get? The sum of their fears.
[In H. Macmillan, *The Blast of War*, 16]

71. Everybody has a right to pronounce foreign names as he chooses.
[*The Observer*, 'Sayings of the Week', 1951]

72. An appeaser is one who feeds a crocodile – hoping that it will eat him last.
[Attr.]

73. [Describing Lord Lovat]
The handsomest man ever to cut a throat.
[Attr.]

Ciano, Count Galeazzo (1903–1944)
Italian politician; son-in-law of Mussolini

1. As always, victory finds a hundred fathers, but defeat is an orphan.
[Diary, 9 September 1942. Cf. J.F. Kennedy: 12]

Cibber, Colley (1671–1757)
English actor, dramatist and theatrical manager; poet laureate 1730

1. One had as good be out of the world, as out of the fashion.
[*Love's Last Shift* (1696), II]

2. Off with his head – so much for Buckingham.
[*Richard III* (1700), IV, adapted from Shakespeare]

3. Perish the thought!
[*Richard III* (1700), V, adapted from Shakespeare]

4. Conscience avaunt, Richard's himself again:
Hark! the shrill trumpet sounds, to horse, away,
My soul's in arms, and eager for the fray.
[*Richard III* (1700), V, adapted from Shakespeare]

5. Oh! how many torments lie in the small circle of a wedding-ring!
[*The Double Gallant* (1707), I]

6. Stolen sweets are best.
[*The Rival Fools* (1709), I. Cf. Leigh Hunt: 2]

7. What! now your fire's gone, you would knock me down with the butt-end, would you?
[*The Refusal, or, The Ladies Philosophy* (1721), I]

8. Whilst thus I sing, I am a King,
Altho' a poor blind boy.
['The Blind Boy' (1734)]

Cicero, Marcus Tullius (106–43 BC)

Roman orator, statesman, essayist and letter-writer; murdered by agents of Mark Anthony

1. *Sed nescio quo modo nihil tam absurde dici potest quod non dicatur ab aliquo philosophorum.*
But somehow there is nothing so absurd that some philosopher has not said it.
[*De Divinatione*, II, 119]

2. *Vulgo enim dicitur: 'iucundi acti labores'.*
For it is commonly said: 'hard tasks are pleasant when they are finished.'
[*De Finibus*, II, 105]

3. *Salus populi suprema est lex.*
The good of the people is the chief law.
[*De Legibus*, III, 8]

4. *Summum bonum.*
The greatest good.
[*De Officiis*, I, 5]

5. *Cedant arma togae, concedat laurea laudi.*
Let arms yield to the toga, the laurel crown to praise.
[*De Officiis*, I, 77]

6. *Numquam se minus otiosum esse quam cum otiosus, nec minus solum quam cum solus esset*
Never less idle than when free from work, nor less lonely than when completely alone.
[*De Officiis*, III, 1]

7. *Mens cuiusque is est quisque.*
The spirit is the true self.
[*De Republica*, VI, 26]

8. *O tempora! O mores!*
What times! What manners!
[*In Catilinam*, I, 1]

9. *Abiit, excessit, evasit, erupit.*
He got away, he disappeared, he escaped, he broke out.
[*In Catilinam*, II, 1]

10. *Civis Romanus sum.*
I am a Roman citizen.
[*In Verrem*, V, 147]

11. *Quod di omen avertant.*
May the gods avert this omen.
[*Philippic*, III, 35]

12. *Nervos belli, pecuniam infinitam.*
The sinews of war, unlimited money.
[*Philippic*, V, 5. Cf. Rabelais: 7]

13. *Silent enim leges inter arma.*
Laws are silent in war.
[*Pro Milone*, 11]

14. *Cui bono?*
Who stands to gain?
[*Pro Milone*, 12]

15. *Nemo enim fere saltat sobrius, nisi forte insanit.*
No sober man dances, unless he happens to be mad.
[*Pro Murena*]

16. *Id quod est praestantissimum maximeque optabile omnibus sanis et bonis et beatis, cum dignitate otium.*
The thing which is by far the best and most desirable for all who are sane and good and fortunate is 'peace with honour'.
[*Pro Sestio*, 98]

17. *Errare mehercule malo cum Platone ... quam cum istis vera sentire.*
By heaven, I prefer to be wrong with Plato than right with such men as these.
[*Tusculanae Disputationes*, I, 39]

18. *O fortunatam natam me consule Romam!*
O happy Rome, born when I was consul!
[In Juvenal, *Satires*, 10]

Clare, Dr Anthony (1942–)

Irish professor, psychiatrist and broadcaster

1. Hell is when you get what you think you want.
[*The Observer*, 1983, in Jeffrey Care (ed.), *Sayings of the Eighties* (1989)]

2. Apart from the occasional saint, it is difficult for people who have the smallest amount of power to be nice.
[*The Observer*, 1986, in Jeffrey Care (ed.), *Sayings of the Eighties* (1989)]

3. The whole notion of holding a referendum on women's access to information is such a profound disgrace for a nation such as this that I ... apologise to Irish women on behalf of what has been predominantly a male-dominated, male-driven male disgrace.
[*The Irish Times*, 1993]

Clare, John (1793–1864)

English rural poet; spent the last years of his life in an asylum

1. And what is Life? – an hour glass on the run
A mist retreating from the morning sun
A busy bustling still repeated dream
Its length? – A moment's pause, a moment's thought
And happiness? A Bubble on the stream
That in the act of seizing shrinks to nought.
[*The Englishman's Fire-side* (1820), 'What is Life?']

2. My life hath been one chain of contradictions,
Madhouses, prisons, whore-shops...

3. They took me from my wife, and to save trouble
I wed again, and made the error double...

4. Pale death, the grand physician, cures all pain;
The dead rest well who lived for joys in vain...

5. Hopeless hope hopes on and meets no end,
Wastes without springs and homes without a friend.
['Child Harold' (1841)]

6. A quiet, pilfering, unprotected race.
['Gypsies' (1841)]

7. The present is the funeral of the past,
And man the living sepulchre of life.
['The Past' (1845)]

8. I am – yet what I am, none cares or knows.
My friends forsake me like a memory lost,
I am the self-consumer of my woes–
They rise and vanish in oblivious host,
Like shadows in love's frenzied stifled throes–
And yet I am, and live – like vapours tossed

Into the nothingness of scorn and noise,
Into the living sea of waking dreams,
Where there is neither sense of life or joys,
But the vast shipwreck of my life's esteems;
Even the dearest, that I love the best,
Are strange – nay, stranger than the rest.

I long for scenes where man has never trod;
A place where woman never smiled or wept–
There to abide with my Creator, God,
And sleep as I in childhood sweetly slept,
Untroubling and untroubled where I lie,
The grass below – above the vaulted sky.
['I Am' (1848)]

9. He could not die when the trees were green,
For he loved the time too well.
['The Dying Child' (published 1873)]

10. Summers pleasures they are gone like to visions every one
And the cloudy days of autumn and of winter cometh on
I tried to call them back but unbidden they are gone
Far away from heart and eye and for ever far away.
['Remembrances' (published 1908)]

11. The crow will tumble up and down
At the first sight of spring
And in old trees around the town
Brush winter from its wing
['Crows in Spring']

12. Dear Sir, – I am in a Madhouse and quite forget your name or who you are.
[Letter, 1860]

13. If life had a second edition, how I would correct the proofs.
[Letter to a friend]

14. Language has not the power to speak what love indites:
The soul lies buried in the ink that writes.
[Attr.]

Clarendon, Edward Hyde, First Earl of (1609–1674)
English historian, statesman and advisor to Charles II

1. [Of Hampden]
Without question, when he first drew the sword, he threw away the scabbard.
[*The History of the Rebellion* (1703), III]

2. [Of Hampden]
He had a head to contrive, a tongue to persuade, and a hand to execute any mischief.
[*The History of the Rebellion* (1703), III]

3. [Of Falkland]
He ... would, with a shrill and sad accent, ingeminate the word Peace, Peace.
[*The History of the Rebellion* (1703), III]

4. [Of Falkland]
So enamoured on peace that he would have been glad the King should have bought it at any price.
[*The History of the Rebellion* (1703), III]

5. [Of Cromwell]
He will be looked upon by posterity as a brave bad man.
[*The History of the Rebellion* (1703), VI, final words]

Claribel (Mrs C.A. Barnard) (1840–1869)
English ballad-writer

1. I cannot sing the old songs
I sang long years ago,
For heart and voice would fail me,
And foolish tears would flow.
['The Old Songs' (1865)]

Clark, Lord Kenneth (1903–1983)
English art historian

1. [After speaking to a boy in the train on the way to Winchester who did not reply, as another group of boys did not. The first boy, head of the house, sent for him in the library]
He gave me three or four very painful strokes with a stick, known as a ground ash. 'That will teach you to speak to your seniors,' he said.
[*Another Part of the Wood: A Self Portrait* (1974)]

2. [On boarding schools]
This curious, and, to my mind, objectionable feature of English education was maintained solely in order that parents could get their children out of the house.
[*Another Part of the Wood: A Self Portrait* (1974)]

3. One may be optimistic, but one can't exactly be joyful at the prospect before us.
[End of TV series, *Civilization*]

Clark, Manning (1915–1991)
Australian scholar and historian

1. [On Australian war memorials]
God was rarely mentioned, Christ almost never. The past has bequeathed to Australians a long list of unmentionable words.
[*A History of Australia* (1962–1987), 6]

2. [Of the Australian writer, Henry Lawson]
He said later that the greatest pleasure he ever knew in the world was when his eyes met the eyes of a mate over the top of two foaming glasses of beer.
[*In Search of Henry Lawson* (1987)]

3. All writers are liars, and there is not the slightest chance that any writer will get into heaven.
[Speech, Melbourne, 1987]

Clark, Ralph (c. 1755–1794)
Naval officer and diarist; early emigrant to Australia

1. [On the female convicts on board the convict ship *Friendship*]
. . . the[y] are a disgrace to their Whole Sex B........s that they are I wish all the Women Wair out of the Ship–
[*The Journals and Letters of Lt. Ralph Clark 1787–1792*]

2. [From Capetown, 6 November 1787]
. . . 30 Sheep came on board this day and wair put in the Place where the women convicts Were – I think we will find much more Agreable Ship mates than they were.
[*The Journals and Letters of Lt. Ralph Clark 1787–1792*]

Clarke, Arthur C. (1917–)
English scientific and science-fiction writer; author of works on space travel

1. When a distinguished but elderly scientist states that something is possible, he is almost certainly right. When he states that something is impossible, he is very probably wrong. (Clarke's First Law.)
[*The New Yorker*, 1969]

Clarke, John (fl. 1639)
English scholar

1. He that would thrive
Must rise at five;
He that hath thriven
May lie till seven.
[*Paraemiologia Anglo-Latina* (1639), 'Diligentia']

2. Home is home, though it be never so homely.
[*Paraemiologia Anglo-Latina* (1639), 'Domi vivere']

Clarke, Marcus (Andrew Hislop) (1846–1881)
English-born Australian journalist, writer and novelist

1. In Australia alone is to be found the Grotesque, the Weird, the strange scribblings of nature learning how to write.
[Preface to A.L. Gordon, *Sea Spray and Smoke Drift* (1867)]

2. No man has a right to inflict the torture of bad wine upon his fellow-creatures.
[*The Peripatetic Philosopher* (1867–1870)]

3. A very merry Christmas, with roast beef in a violent perspiration, and the thermometer 110 in the shade!
[*Australasian*, 1868]

4. They are not a nation of Snobs like the English, or of extravagant boasters like the Americans, or of reckless profligates like the French; they are simply a nation of Drunkards.
[*Humbug*, 1869]

Clausewitz, Karl von (1780–1831)
German general and military philosopher

1. *Der Krieg ist nichts als eine Fortsetzung des politischen Verkehrs mit Einmischung anderer Mittel.*
War is nothing but a continuation of politics by other means.
[*Vom Kriege* (*On War*, 1832–1834)]

Clay, Henry (1777–1852)
American statesman and orator; Secretary of State under John Quincy Adams

1. The gentleman [Josiah Quincy] can not have forgotten his own sentiments, uttered even on the floor of this House, 'peaceably if we can, forcibly if we must'.
[Speech, 1813]

2. I had rather be right than be President.
[Remark, 1839]

Clayton, Keith (1928–)
Professor of Environmental Sciences, University of East Anglia

1. [Of sewage]
You can do far worse than putting it into a deep and well-flushed sea. As far as poisoning the fish is concerned, that's rubbish. The sewage has probably kept the poor fish alive.
[*The Times*, 1992]

Cleaver, Eldridge (1935–)
African-American writer; co-founder of the radical Black Panther movement

1. If you're not part of the solution, you're part of the problem.
[Attr.]

Cleese, John (1939–)
British 'alternative' comedian, actor and writer

1. Loving your neighbour as much as yourself is practically bloody impossible ... You might as well have a Commandment that states, 'Thou shalt fly'.
[*The Times*, 1993]

Clemenceau, Georges (1841–1929)
French statesman, known as 'The Tiger'; Prime Minister 1906–9, 1917–20, and journalist

1. *Politique intérieure: je fais la guerre; politique étrangère: je fais la guerre. Je fais toujours la guerre!*
My home policy? I wage war. My foreign policy? I wage war. Always, everywhere, I wage war.
[Speech to the Chamber of Deputies, 8 March 1918]

2. *Il est plus facile de faire la guerre que la paix.*
It is easier to make war than to make peace.
[Speech, 1919. Cf. Adlai Stevenson: 2]

3. [To General Mordacq, 11 November 1918]
We have won the war: now we have to win the peace, and it may be more difficult.
[In D.R. Watson, *Georges Clemenceau: a Political Biography* (1974)]

4. [To Lloyd George, at the Versailles peace conference, 24 January 1919, on the matter of the dominion prime ministers laying their views on mandates before the Council of Ten]
Bring your savages with you.
[In Winston Churchill, *The World Crisis* (1923–1931), IV, 'The Aftermath']

5. *La guerre! C'est une chose trop grave pour la confier à des militaires.*
War is much too serious a thing to be left to the military.
[In Suarez, *Soixante Années d'histoire française: Clemenceau* (*Sixty Years of French History: Clemenceau*)]

6. America is the only nation in history which miraculously has gone directly from barbarism to degeneration without the usual interval of civilization.
[Attr.]

Clement XIII, Pope (1693–1769)
Italian pope from 1758; defender of the Jesuits

1. [Reply to request for changes in the constitution of the Society of Jesus, 1762]
Sint ut sunt aut non sint.
Let them be as they are or let them not be at all.
[In J.A.M. Crétineau-Joly, *Clément XIV et les Jésuites* (1847)]

Cleveland, Grover (1837–1908)
American statesman; Democratic President 1885–9, 1893–97

1. [Veto of Dependent Pension Bill, 1888]
I have considered the pension list of the republic a roll of honour.
[In *A Compilation of the Messages and Papers of the Presidents* (1897)]

Cleveland, John (1613–1658)
English Cavalier poet

1. Had Cain been Scot, God would have changed his doom,
Nor forced him wander, but confined him home.
['The Rebel Scot' (1647)]

Clinton, Hillary Rodham (1947–)
US lawyer and First Lady (wife of President Bill Clinton)

1. Hardly anybody likes green peas.
[Attr.]

Clive, Lord (Robert, Baron Clive of Plassey) (1725–1774)
English general and statesman; administrator in India

1. [Said when his pistol failed to go off twice, in his attempt to commit suicide]
I feel that I am reserved for some end or other.
[In Gleig, *The Life of Robert, First Lord Clive* (1848), 1]

2. [Reply during Parliamentary cross-examination, 1773]
By God, Mr Chairman, at this moment I stand astonished at my own moderation!
[In Gleig, *The Life of Robert, First Lord Clive* (1848), 29]

Clough, Arthur Hugh (1819–1861)
English poet and letter-writer

1. Petticoats up to the knees, or even, it might be, above them,
Matching their lily-white legs with the clothes that they trod in the wash-tub!
[*The Bothie of Tober-na-Vuolich* (1848), II]

2. Sesquipedalian blackguard.
[*The Bothie of Tober-na-Vuolich* (1848), II]

3. Good, too, Logic, of course; in itself, but not in fine weather.
[*The Bothie of Tober-na-Vuolich* (1848), II]

4. Grace is given of God, but knowledge is bought in the market.
[*The Bothie of Tober-na-Vuolich* (1848), IV]

5. A world where nothing is had for nothing.
[*The Bothie of Tober-na-Vuolich* (1848), VIII]

6. As ships, becalmed at eve, that lay
With canvas drooping, side by side,
Two towers of sail at dawn of day
Are scarce long leagues apart descried.
['Qua Cursum Ventus' (1849)]

7. That out of sight is out of mind
Is true of most we leave behind.
[*Songs in Absence* (1849), 'That Out of Sight']

8. Where lies the land to which the ship would go?
Far, far ahead, is all her seamen know,
And where the land she travels from? Away,
Far, far behind, is all that they can say.
['Where lies the Land' (1852)]

9. What voice did on my spirit fall,
Peschiera, when thy bridge I crost?
''Tis better to have fought and lost,
Than never to have fought at all.'
['Peschiera' (1854)]

10. Say not, the struggle naught availeth,
The labour and the wounds are vain,
The enemy faints not, nor faileth,
And as things have been they remain.

If hopes were dupes, fears may be liars...

11. For while the tired waves, vainly breaking,
Seem here no painful inch to gain,
Far back through creeks and inlets making
Comes silent, flooding in, the main.

And not by eastern windows only,
When daylight comes, comes in the light,
In front the sun climbs slow, how slowly,
But westward, look, the land is bright.
['Say Not the Struggle Naught Availeth' (1855)]

12. Rome, believe me, my friend, is like its own Monte Testaceo,
Merely a marvellous mass of broken and castaway wine-pots...

13. The horrible pleasure of pleasing inferior people.
[*Amours de Voyage* (1858), I]

14. Am I prepared to lay down my life for the British female?
Really, who knows?...
Oh, for a child in the street I could strike; for the full-blown lady–
Somehow, Eustace, alas! I have not felt the vocation...

15. I am in love, you say; I do not think so, exactly.
[*Amours de Voyage* (1858), II]

16. But for his funeral train which the bridegroom sees in the distance,
Would he so joyfully, think you, fall in with the marriage-procession?...

17. Mild monastic faces in quiet collegiate cloisters.
[*Amours de Voyage* (1858), III]

18. Whither depart the souls of the brave that die in the battle,
Die in the lost, lost fight, for the cause that perishes with them?
[*Amours de Voyage* (1858), V]

19. Thou shalt have one God only; who
Would be at the expense of two?...

20. Thou shalt not kill; but need'st not strive
Officiously to keep alive.
Do not adultery commit;
Advantage rarely comes of it.
Thou shalt not steal, an empty feat,
When it's so lucrative to cheat...

21. Thou shalt not covet; but tradition
Approves all forms of competition.
['The Latest Decalogue' (1862)]

22. This world is bad enough, may-be,
We do not comprehend it;
But in one fact can all agree,
God won't, and we can't mend it...

23. They may talk as they please about what they call pelf,
And how one ought never to think of one's self,
And how pleasures of thought surpass eating and drinking–
My pleasure of thought is the pleasure of thinking
How pleasant it is to have money, heigh ho!
How pleasant it is to have money.
[*Dipsychus* (1865), scene v]

24. 'There is no God,' the wicked saith,
'And truly it's a blessing,
For what he might have done with us
It's better only guessing.'...

25. But country folks who live beneath
The shadow of the steeple;
The parson and the parson's wife,
And mostly married people;

Youths green and happy in first love,
So thankful for illusion;
And men caught out in what the world
Calls guilt, in first confusion;

And almost every one when age,
Disease, or sorrows strike him,
Inclines to think there is a God,
Or something very like Him.
[*Dipsychus* (1865), scene vi]

Coates, (Joseph) Gordon (1878–1943)
New Zealand statesman

1. [To a delegation of unemployed]
You can eat grass.
[Attr.]

Cobbett, William (1762–1835)
English political journalist, reformer and politician; prose writer, farmer and army officer

1. Nouns of number, or multitude, such as Mob, Parliament, Rabble, House of Commons, Regiment, Court of King's Bench, Den of Thieves and the like.
[*A Grammar of the English Language* (1818), 'Syntax as Relating to Pronouns']

2. [Of London]
But what is to be the fate of the great wen of all? The monster, called ... 'the metropolis of the empire'?
[*Political Register*, 1822, 'Rural Rides']

3. Resolve to free yourselves from the slavery of the tea and coffee and other slop-kettle.
[*Advice to Young Men* (1829)]

4. To be poor and independent is very nearly an impossibility.
[*Advice to Young Men* (1829)]

5. From a very early age, I had imbibed the opinion, that it was every man's duty to do all that lay in his power to leave his country as good as he had found it.
[*Political Register*, 1832]

6. Machines are the produce of the mind of man; and their existence distinguishes the civilized man from the savage.
[*Letter to the Luddites of Nottingham*]

Coborn, Charles (C.W. McCallum) (1852–1945)
English comedian and singer

1. Two lovely black eyes,
Oh, what a surprise!
Only for telling a man he was wrong.
Two lovely black eyes!
['Two Lovely Black Eyes', song, 1886]

Cochran, Charles B. (1872–1951)
English showman, theatrical producer and impresario

1. I still prefer a good juggler to a bad Hamlet.
[*The Observer*, 'Sayings of the Week', 1943]

Cockburn, Alison (née Rutherford) (1713–1794)
Scottish poet and songwriter; Edinburgh society hostess

1. For the flowers of the forest are a' wade away.
['The Flowers of the Forest' (1765). Cf. Jean Elliot: 1]

Cockburn, Lord Henry (1779–1854)
Scottish judge, parliamentary reformer and diarist

1. [Of Robert Dundas]
It was impossible not to like the owner of the look.
[*Memorials*, 3]

Cocteau, Jean (1889–1963)
French modernist dramatist, novelist, poet, film writer and director

1. *Le tact dans l'audace c'est de savoir jusqu'où on peut aller trop loin.*
To be tactful in audacity one has to know just how far one can go too far.
[*Le Coq et l'Arlequin* (1918) in *Le Rappel à L'Ordre* (1926)]

2. *S'il faut choisir un crucifié, la foule sauve toujours Barabbas.*
If the crowd has to choose someone to crucify, it will always save Barabbas.
[*Le Coq et l'Arlequin* (1918) in *Le Rappel à L'Ordre* (1926)]

3. *Un vrai poète se soucie peu de poésie. De même un horticulteur ne parfume pas ses roses.*
A true poet scarcely worries about poetry, just as a gardener does not scent his roses.
[*Le secret professionnel* (*Professional Secrets*, 1922)]

4. *Vivre est une chute horizontale.*
Life is falling sideways.
[*Opium* (1930)]

5. *Victor Hugo ... un fou qui se croyait Victor Hugo.*
Victor Hugo ... a madman who thought he was Victor Hugo.
[*Opium* (1930)]

Code Napoléon
The main body of French civil law, promulgated between 1804 and 1810

1. *La recherche de la paternité est interdite.*
Investigations into paternity are forbidden.
[Article 340]

Cody, Henry John (1868–1951)
Anglican Canon and President of the University of Toronto

1. Education is casting false pearls before real swine.
[Attr.]

Coetzee, John Michael (1940–)
South African novelist

1. All we can do is to uphold the laws, all of us, without allowing the memory of justice to fade.
[*Waiting for the Barbarians* (1980), V]

Coghill, Anna Louisa (1836–1907)

1. Work, for the night is coming,
When man works no more.
[Hymn, 1854]

Cohen, Sir Jack (1898–1979)
Founder of Tesco supermarkets and associated companies

1. Pile it high, sell it cheap.
[Business motto]

Cohn-Bendit, Daniel (1945–)
German political activist

1. *Europa soll aus Bosnien ein neues Westberlin machen.*
Europe should make a new West-Berlin out of Bosnia.
[Interview in *Süddeutsche Zeitung*, 1994]

Cokayne, Sir Aston (1608–1684)
English poet, dramatist and translator from Italian

1. Sydney, whom we yet admire
Lighting our little torches at his fire.
['Funeral Elegy on Mr Michael Drayton' (1658)]

Coke, Desmond (1879–1931)
English writer and school teacher

1. His blade struck the water a full second before any other ... until ... as the boats began to near the winning-post, his own was dipping into the water twice as often as any other.
[*Sandford of Merton* (1903) 12]

Coke, Sir Edward (1552–1634)
English judge, author of legal works and politician

1. How long soever it hath continued, if it be against reason, it is of no force in law.
[*The First Part of the Institutes of the Laws of England* (1628), 'Commentary upon Littleton']

2. Reason is the life of the law, nay the common law itself is nothing else but reason.
[*The First Part of the Institutes of the Laws of England* (1628), 'Commentary upon Littleton']

3. The gladsome light of Jurisprudence.
[*The First Part of the Institutes of the Laws of England* (1628), 'Commentary upon Littleton']

4. [Of corporations]
They cannot commit treason, nor be outlawed, nor excommunicate, for they have no souls.
[*The Reports of Sir Edward Coke* (1658), 'The Case of Sutton's Hospital']

5. The house of everyone is to him as his castle and fortress, as well for his defence against injury and violence, as for his repose.
[*Semayne's Case*]

6. Six hours in sleep, in law's grave study six,
Four spend in prayer, the rest on Nature fix.
[Translation of Justinian, *Pandects*, II, 4]

7. We have a maxim in the House of Commons ... that old ways are the safest and surest ways.
[Speech, 1628]

Colby, Frank Moore (1865–1925)
American editor, historian and economist

1. Men will confess to treason, murder, arson, false teeth, or a wig. How many of them will own up to a lack of humour?
[*Essays*, I]

2. I have found some of the best reasons I ever had for remaining at the bottom simply by looking at the men at the top.
[*Essays*, II]

Coleridge, Hartley (1796–1849)
English poet and prose writer; son of Samuel Taylor Coleridge

1. But what is Freedom? Rightly understood,
A universal licence to be good.
['Liberty' (1833)]

Coleridge, Mary (1861–1907)
English poet, historical novelist and teacher of working women; great-niece of Samuel Taylor Coleridge

1. Egypt's might is tumbled down
Down a-down the deeps of thought;
Greece is fallen and Troy town,
Glorious Rome hath lost her crown,
Venice' pride is nought.

But the dreams their children dreamed
Fleeting, unsubstantial, vain.
Shadowy as the shadows seemed
Airy nothing, as they deemed,
These remain.
[*Poems* (1894), 'Egypt's Might is Tumbled Down']

2. Some hang above the tombs,
Some weep in empty rooms,
I, when the iris blooms,
Remember.
[*Poems* (1897), 'On Such a Day']

3. We were young, we were merry, we were very, very wise,
And the door stood open at our feast,
When there passed us a woman with the West in her eyes,
And a man with his back to the East.
[*Poems* (1897), 'Unwelcome']

Coleridge, Samuel Taylor (1772–1834)
Leading English Romantic poet, philosopher and critic; father of Hartley Coleridge

1. Poor little Foal of an oppressed race!
I love the languid patience of thy face.
['To a Young Ass' (1794)]

2. The innumerable multitude of Wrongs
By man on man inflicted.
['Religious Musings' (1796)]

3. So for the mother's sake the child was dear,
And dearer was the mother for the child.
['Sonnet to a Friend Who Asked How I felt When the Nurse First Presented My Infant to Me' (1797)]

4. Forth from his dark and lonely hiding-place
(Portentous sight!) the owlet Atheism,
Sailing on obscene wings athwart the noon,
Drops his blue-fringèd lids, and holds them close,
And hooting at the glorious sun in Heaven,
Cries out, 'Where is it?'...

5. [Of Britain]
A vain, speech-mouthing, speech-reporting guild,
One benefit-club for mutual flattery.
['Fears in Solitude' (1798)]

6. With what deep worship I have still adored
The spirit of divinest Liberty.
['France' (1798)]

7. The frost performs its secret ministry,
Unhelped by any wind...

8. Only that film, which fluttered on the grate,
Still flutters there, a sole unquiet thing...

9. Therefore all seasons shall be sweet to thee,
Whether the summer clothe the general earth
With greenness, or the redbreast sit and sing
Betwixt the tufts of snow on the bare branch
Of mossy apple-tree, while the nigh thatch
Smokes in the sun-thaw; whether the eave-drops fall
Heard only in the trances of the blast,
Or if the secret ministry of frost
Shall hang them up in silent icicles,
Quietly shining to the quiet moon.
['Frost at Midnight' (1798)]

10. It is an ancient Mariner,
And he stoppeth one of three.
'By thy long grey beard and glittering eye,
Now wherefore stopp'st thou me?'...

11. He holds him with his skinny hand,
'There was a ship,' quoth he.
'Hold off! unhand me, grey-beard loon!'
Eftsoons his hand dropt he.

He holds him with his glittering eye–
The Wedding-Guest stood still,
And listens like a three-years' child:
The Mariner hath his will.

The Wedding-Guest sat on a stone:
He cannot choose but hear;

And thus spake on that ancient man,
The bright-eyed Mariner...

12. The sun came up upon the left,
Out of the sea came he!
And he shone bright, and on the right
Went down into the sea...

13. The Wedding-Guest here beat his breast,
For he heard the loud bassoon...

14. And ice, mast-high, came floating by,
As green as emerald...

15. The ice was here, the ice was there,
The ice was all around:
It cracked and growled, and roared and howled,
Like noises in a swound!...

16. 'God save thee, ancient Mariner!
From the fiends that plague thee thus!–
Why looks't thou so?' – With my cross-bow
I shot the Albatross.
['The Rime of the Ancient Mariner' (1798), I]

17. Nor dim nor red, like God's own head,
The glorious Sun uprist...

18. The fair breeze blew, the white foam flew,
The furrow followed free;
We were the first that ever burst
Into that silent sea...

19. As idle as a painted ship
Upon a painted ocean.

Water, water, every where,
And all the boards did shrink;
Water, water, every where
Nor any drop to drink.

The very deep did rot: O Christ!
That ever this should be!
Yea, slimy things did crawl with legs
Upon the slimy sea.
['The Rime of the Ancient Mariner' (1798), II]

20. Her lips were red, her looks were free,
Her locks were yellow as gold:
Her skin was white as leprosy,
The Nightmare LIFE-IN-DEATH was she,
Who thicks man's blood with cold...

21. 'The game is done! I've won, I've won!'
Quoth she, and whistles thrice.

The Sun's rim dips; the stars rush out:
At one stride comes the dark...

22. The hornèd Moon, with one bright star
Within the nether tip.
['The Rime of the Ancient Mariner' (1798), III]

23. 'I fear thee, ancient Mariner!
I fear thy skinny hand!
And thou art long, and lank, and brown,
As is the ribbed sea-sand.'...

24. Alone, alone, all, all alone,
Alone on a wide, wide sea!
And never a soul took pity on
My soul in agony...

25. And a thousand thousand slimy things
Lived on; and so did I...

26. The moving Moon went up the sky,
And nowhere did abide:
Softly she was going up,
And a star or two beside...

27. A spring of love gushed from my heart,
And I blessed them unawares.
['The Rime of the Ancient Mariner' (1798), IV]

28. Oh sleep! it is a gentle thing
Beloved from pole to pole!
To Mary Queen the praise be given!
She sent the gentle sleep from Heaven,
That slid into my soul...

29. Sure I had drunken in my dreams,
And still my body drank...

30. We were a ghastly crew...

31. It ceased; yet still the sails made on
A pleasant noise till noon,
A noise like of a hidden brook
In the leafy month of June,
That to the sleeping woods all night
Singeth a quiet tune...

32. Then like a pawing horse let go,
She made a sudden bound...

33. Quoth he, 'The man hath penance done,
And penance more will do.'
['The Rime of the Ancient Mariner' (1798), V]

34. Like one, that on a lonesome road
Doth walk in fear and dread,
And having once turned round walks on,
And turns no more his head;
Because he knows, a frightful fiend
Doth close behind him tread...

35. No voice; but oh! the silence sank
Like music on my heart.
['The Rime of the Ancient Mariner' (1798), VI]

36. 'Ha! ha!' quoth he, 'full plain I see,
The Devil knows how to row.'...

37. O Wedding-Guest! this soul hath been
Alone on a wide wide sea;
So lonely 'twas that God himself
Scarce seemèd there to be...

38. He prayeth best, who loveth best
All things both great and small;
For the dear God who loveth us,
He made and loveth all...

39. He went like one that hath been stunned,
And is of sense forlorn:
A sadder and a wiser man,
He rose the morrow morn.
['The Rime of the Ancient Mariner' (1798), VII]

40. From his brimstone bed at break of day
A walking the Devil is gone,
To visit his snug little farm the Earth,
And see how his stock goes on...

41. His jacket was red and his breeches were blue,
And there was a hole where the tail came through...

42. He saw a Lawyer killing a viper
On a dunghill hard by his own stable;
And the Devil smiled, for it put him in mind
Of Cain and his brother, Abel...

43. He saw a cottage with a double coach-house,
A cottage of gentility;
And the Devil did grin, for his darling sin
Is pride that apes humility...

44. As he went through Cold-Bath Fields he saw
A solitary cell;
And the Devil was pleased, for it gave him a hint
For improving his prisons in Hell.
['The Devil's Thoughts' (1799)]

45. Choose thou whatever suits the line;
Call me Sappho, call me Chloris,
Call me Lalage or Doris,
Only, only call me thine.
['Names' (1799), from Lessing's *Die Namen*]

46. In the hexameter rises the fountain's silvery column;
In the pentameter aye falling in melody back.
['Ovidian Elegiac Metre' (1799); trans. from Schiller]

47. Something Childish, but very Natural.
[Title of poem, 1799]

48. Often do the spirits
Of great events stride on before the events,
And in to-day already walks to-morrow.
['Death of Wallenstein' (1800); trans. from Schiller]

49. Swans sing before they die– 'twere no bad thing
Should certain persons die before they sing.
['Epigram on a Volunteer Singer' (1800)]

50. All thoughts, all passions, all delights,
Whatever stirs this mortal frame,
All are but ministers of Love,
And feed his sacred flame.
['Love' (1800)]

51. Well, they are gone, and here must I remain,
This lime-tree bower my prison!...

52. When the last rook
Beat its straight path along the dusky air.
['This Lime-Tree Bower my Prison' (1800)]

53. Well! If the Bard was weatherwise, who made
The grand old ballad of Sir Patrick Spence...

54. I see them all so excellently fair,
I see, not feel, how beautiful they are!...

55. I may not hope from outward forms to win
The passion and the life, whose fountains are within...

56. O Lady! we receive but what we give,
And in our life alone does Nature live.
['Dejection: an Ode' (1802)]

57. Trochee trips from long to short;
From long to long in solemn sort
Slow Spondee stalks; strong foot! yet ill able
Ever to come up with Dactyl trisyllable.
Iambics march from short to long;–
With a leap and a bound the swift Anapaests throng.
['Metrical Feet' (1806)]

58. What is an Epigram? a dwarfish whole,
Its body brevity, and wit its soul.
['Epigram' (1809). Cf. Shakespeare, *Hamlet*: 63]

59. And visited all night by troops of stars.
['Hymn before Sunrise, in the Vale of Chamouni' (1809)]

60. We ne'er can be
Made happy by compulsion.
['The Three Graves' (1809)]

61. Alas! they had been friends in youth;
But whispering tongues can poison truth;
And constancy lives in realms above;
And life is thorny; and youth is vain;
And to be wroth with one we love
Doth work like madness in the brain.
[*Christabel* (1816)]

62. On awaking he ... instantly and eagerly wrote down the lines that are here preserved. At this moment he was unfortunately called out by a person on business from Porlock.
['Kubla Khan' (1816), preliminary note]

63. In Xanadu did Kubla Khan
A stately pleasure-dome decree:
Where Alph, the sacred river, ran
Through caverns measureless to man
Down to a sunless sea.

So twice five miles of fertile ground
With walls and towers were girdled round:
And there were gardens bright with sinuous rills,
Where blossom'd many an incense-bearing tree,
And here were forests ancient as the hills,
Enfolding sunny spots of greenery.

But oh! that deep romantic chasm which slanted
Down the green hill athwart a cedarn cover!
A savage place! as holy and enchanted
As e'er beneath a waning moon was haunted
By woman wailing for her demon-lover!
And from this chasm, with ceaseless turmoil seething,
As if this earth in fast thick pants were breathing,
A mighty fountain momently was forced,
Amid whose swift half-intermittent burst
Huge fragments vaulted like rebounding hail,
Or chaffy grain beneath the thresher's flail:
And 'mid these dancing rocks at once and ever
It flung up momently the sacred river.
Five miles meandering with a mazy motion
Through wood and dale the sacred river ran,
Then reach'd the caverns measureless to man,
And sank in tumult to a lifeless ocean:
And 'mid this tumult Kubla heard from far
Ancestral voices prophesying war!

The shadow of the dome of pleasure
Floated midway on the waves;
Where was heard the mingled measure
From the fountain and the caves.
It was a miracle of rare device,
A sunny pleasure-dome with caves of ice!

A damsel with a dulcimer
In a vision once I saw:
It was an Abyssinian maid,
And on her dulcimer she played,
Singing of Mount Abora.
Could I revive within me
Her symphony and song,
To such a deep delight 'twould win me,
That with music loud and long,
I would build that dome in air,
That sunny dome! those caves of ice!
And all who heard should see them there,
And all should cry, Beware! Beware!
His flashing eyes, his floating hair!
Weave a circle round him thrice,
And close your eyes with holy dread,
For he on honey-dew hath fed,
And drunk the milk of Paradise.
['Kubla Khan' (1816)]

64. With Donne, whose muse on dromedary trots,
Wreathe iron pokers into true-love knots;
Rhyme's sturdy cripple, fancy's maze and clue,

Wit's forge and fire-blast, meaning's press and screw.
['On Donne's Poetry' (1818)]

65. In Köhln, a town of monks and bones,
And pavements fang'd with murderous stones
And rags, and hags, and hideous wenches;
I counted two and seventy stenches,
All well defined, and several stinks!
Ye Nymphs that reign o'er sewers and sinks,
The river Rhine, it is well known,
Doth wash your city of Cologne;
But tell me, Nymphs, what power divine
Shall henceforth wash the river Rhine?
['Cologne' (1828)]

66. All Nature seems at work. Slugs leave their lair–
The bees are stirring – birds are on the wing–
And Winter slumbering in the open air,
Wears on his smiling face a dream of Spring!
And I the while, the sole unbusy thing,
Nor honey make, nor pair, nor build, nor sing...

67. Work without hope draws nectar in a sieve,
And hope without an object cannot live.
['Work Without Hope' (1828)]

68. Like some poor nigh-related guest,
That may not rudely be dismist;
Yet hath outstay'd his welcome while,
And tells the jest without the smile.
['Youth and Age' (1834)]

69. From whatever place I write you will expect that part of my 'Travels' will consist of excursions in my own mind.
[*Satyrane's Letters* (1809)]

70. Reviewers are usually people who would have been poets, historians, biographers, etc., if they could; they have tried their talents at one or at the other, and have failed; therefore they turn critics.
[*Seven Lectures on Shakespeare and Milton* (delivered 1811–1812, published 1856)]

71. If a man could pass through Paradise in a dream, and have a flower presented to him as a pledge that his soul had really been there, and if he found that flower in his hand when he awoke – Aye, and what then?
[*Anima Poetae* (1816)]

72. Until you understand a writer's ignorance, presume yourself ignorant of his understanding.
[*Biographia Literaria* (1817), 12]

73. The primary imagination I hold to be the living power and prime agent of all human perception, and as a repetition in the finite mind of the eternal act of creation in the infinite I AM. The secondary imagination ... dissolves, diffuses, dissipates, in order to recreate; or where this process is rendered impossible, yet still at all events it struggles to idealize and to unify.
[*Biographia Literaria* (1817), 13]

74. Fancy, on the contrary, has no other counters to play with, but fixities and definites. The fancy is indeed no other than a mode of memory emancipated from the order of time and space.
[*Biographia Literaria* (1817)]

75. That willing suspension of disbelief for the moment, which constitutes poetic faith.
[*Biographia Literaria* (1817), 14]

76. Our myriad-minded Shakespeare.
[*Biographia Literaria* (1817), 15]

77. No man was ever yet a great poet, without being at the same time a profound philosopher.
[*Biographia Literaria* (1817)]

78. To read Dryden, Pope, etc., you need only count syllables; but to read Donne you must measure time, and discover the time of each word by the sense of passion.
[*The Friend* (1818), I]

79. The dwarf sees farther than the giant, when he has the giant's shoulder to mount on.
[*The Friend* (1818), II]

80. Poetry is not the proper antithesis to prose, but to science. Poetry is opposed to science, and prose to metre.
[*Lectures and Notes of 1818*, I]

81. He who begins by loving Christianity better than Truth will proceed by loving his own sect or church better than Christianity, and end by loving himself better than all.
[*Aids to Reflection* (1825), 'Moral and Religious Aphorisms']

82. You abuse snuff! Perhaps it is the final cause of the human nose.
[*Table Talk* (1835), 4 January 1823]

83. [Of Edmund Kean]
To see him act is like reading Shakespeare by flashes of lightning.
[*Table Talk* (1835), 27 April 1823]

84. I wish our clever young poets would remember my homely definitions of prose and poetry; that is prose = words in their best order; poetry = the best words in the best order.
[*Table Talk* (1835), 12 July 1827]

85. The man's desire is for the woman; but the woman's desire is rarely other than for the desire of the man.
[*Table Talk* (1835), 23 July 1827]

86. My mind is in a state of philosophical doubt as to animal magnetism.
[*Table Talk* (1835), 30 April 1830]

87. Poetry is certainly something more than good sense, but it must be good sense at all events; just as a palace is more than a house, but it must be a house, at least.
[*Table Talk* (1835), 9 May 1830]

88. Swift was *anima Rabelaisii habitans in sicco* – the soul of Rabelais dwelling in a dry place.
[*Table Talk* (1835), 15 June 1830]

89. In politics, what begins in fear usually ends in folly.
[*Table Talk* (1835), 5 October 1830]

90. If men could learn from history, what lessons it might teach us! But passion and party blind our eyes, and the light which experience gives is a lantern on the stern, which shines only on the waves behind us!
[*Table Talk* (1835), 18 December 1831]

91. I am glad you came in to punctuate my discourse, which I fear has gone on for an hour without any stop at all.
[*Table Talk* (1835), 29 June 1833]

92. When I was a boy, I was fondest of Aeschylus; in youth and middle-age I preferred Euripides; now in my declining years I prefer Sophocles. I can now at length see that Sophocles is the most perfect. Yet he never rises to the sublime simplicity of Aeschylus – a simplicity of design, I mean – nor diffuses himself in the passionate outpourings of Euripides.
[*Table Talk* (1835), 1 July 1833]

93. That passage is what I call the sublime dashed to pieces by

cutting too close with the fiery four-in-hand round the corner of nonsense.
[*Table Talk* (1835), 20 January 1834]

94. I believe Shakespeare was not a whit more intelligible in his own day than he is now to an educated man, except for a few local allusions of no consequence. He is of no age – nor of any religion, or party or profession. The body and substance of his works came out of the unfathomable depths of his own oceanic mind: his observation and reading, which was considerable, supplied him with the drapery of his figures.
[*Table Talk* (1835), 15 March 1834]

95. [Of Iago]
The motive-hunting of motiveless malignity.
[*The Literary Remains of Samuel Taylor Coleridge* (1836), 'Notes on the Tragedies of Shakespeare: Othello']

96. The faults of great authors are generally excellences carried to an excess.
[*Miscellanies*, 149]

97. I believe the souls of five hundred Sir Isaac Newtons would go to the making up of a Shakespeare or a Milton.
[Letter to Thomas Poole, 1801]

98. The most happy marriage I can picture or imagine to myself would be union of a deaf man to a blind woman.
[In Allsop, *Recollections* (1836)]

99. Summer has set in with its usual severity.
[In A. Ainger (ed.), *Letters of Charles Lamb* (1888), quoted in Lamb's letter to V. Novello, 1826]

100. Men, I think, have to be weighed, not counted.
[In Alan L. Mackay, *The Harvest of a Quiet Eye* (1977)]

101. What comes from the heart, goes to the heart.
[Attr.]

Colette (Sidonie-Gabrielle Colette) (1873–1954)
French novelist, noted for sensuous and descriptive writing

1. My virtue's still far too small, I don't trot it out and about yet.
[*Claudine at School* (1900)]

2. *Quand elle lève les paupières, on dirait qu'elle se déshabille.*
When she raises her eyelids she seems to be taking her clothes off at the same time.
[*Claudine s'en va* (*Claudine Goes Away*, 1903)]

3. *On ne fait bien que ce qu'on aime. Ni la science, ni la conscience ne modèlent un grand cuisinier. De quoi sert l'application où il faut l'inspiration?*
One only does well what one loves doing. Neither science nor conscience makes a great cook. What use is application where inspiration is what's needed?
[*Prisons et paradis* (1932)]

4. *Ne porte jamais de bijoux artistiques, ça déconsidère complètement une femme.*
Never wear artistic jewellery; it ruins a woman's reputation.
[*Gigi* (1944)]

5. But the past, the beautiful past striped with sunshine, grey with mist, childish, blooming with hidden joy, bruised with sweet sorrow . . . Ah! if only I could resurrect one hour of that time, one alone – but which one?
[*Paysages et portraits* (published 1958)]

6. *Une totale absence d'humour rend la vie impossible.*
A total absence of humour makes life impossible.
[*Chance Acquaintances*]

7. [Remark made to a cat which mewed at her in a New York street]
Enfin! Quelqu'un qui parle français.
At last! Someone who speaks French.
[Attr.]

Collingbourne, William (d. 1484)
English gentleman and landowner; conspirator against Richard III, executed on Tower Hill

1. [Referring to Sir William Catesby (the cat), Sir Richard Ratcliffe (the rat), Lord Lovell (whose crest was a dog), and Richard III (whose crest was a boar)]
The Cat, the Rat, and Lovell our dog,
Rule all England under a Hog.
[In R. Holinshed, *Chronicles* (1586)]

Collings, Jesse (1831–1920)
English politician, associated with land reform

1. Three acres and a cow.
[Phrase used in his land-reform propaganda of 1885, taken from J.S. Mill *Principles of Political Economy* (1848). Cf. Mill: 2]

Collingwood, Admiral (1750–1810)
English admiral; took over from Nelson at Trafalgar

1. [Said before the Battle of Trafalgar, 1805]
Now, gentlemen, let us do something today which the world may talk of hereafter.
[In G.L.N. Collingwood (ed.), *A Selection from the Correspondence of Lord Collingwood* (1828), I]

Collingwood, Robin George (1889–1943)
English philosopher, Roman archaeologist and historian

1. Perfect freedom is reserved for the man who lives by his own work and in that work does what he wants to do.
[*Speculum Mentis* (1924), Prologue]

2. So, perhaps, I may escape otherwise than by death the last humiliation of an aged scholar, when his juniors conspire to print a volume of essays and offer it to him as a sign that they now consider him senile.
[*Autobiography* (1939)]

Collins, John Churton (1848–1908)
English scholar; Professor of English Literature, critic, essayist and editor

1. To ask advice is in nine cases out of ten to tout for flattery.
[In L.C. Collins, *Life of John Churton Collins* (1912)]

Collins, Michael (1890–1922)
Irish revolutionary leader, prominent in Sinn Fein and as negotiator with Britain in 1921

1. [Said on signing the agreement with Great Britain, 1921, that established the Irish Free State; he was assassinated some months later]
Think – what have I got for Ireland? Something which she has wanted these past seven hundred years. Will anyone be satisfied at the bargain? Will anyone? I tell you this – early this morning I signed my death warrant. I thought at the time how odd, how ridiculous – a bullet may just as well have done the job five years ago.
[In T.R. Dwyer, *Michael Collins and the Treaty* (1981), Letter to John O'Kane, 1921]

Collins, Mortimer (1827–1876)
English poet, humorous novelist and essayist

1. A man is as old as he's feeling,

A woman as old as she looks.
['The Unknown Quantity']

Collins, Wilkie (1824–1889)
English novelist and dramatist; pioneer of detective fiction

1. I am not against hasty marriages, where a mutual flame is fanned by an adequate income.
[*No Name*, IV, 8]

Collins, William (1721–1759)
English poet, noted for his odes; afflicted by melancholia

1. Too nicely Jonson knew the critic's part,
Nature in him was almost lost in Art.
['Verses Addressed to Sir Thomas Hanmer' (1743)]

2. To fair Fidele's grassy tomb
Soft maids and village hinds shall bring
Each opening sweet of earliest bloom,
And rifle all the breathing spring.
['Dirge' (1744)]

3. How sleep the brave, who sink to rest,
By all their country's wishes blest!...

4. By fairy hands their knell is rung;
By forms unseen their dirge is sung;
There Honour comes, a pilgrim gray,
To bless the turf that wraps their clay;
And Freedom shall awhile repair,
To dwell a weeping hermit there!
['Ode written in the Year 1746' (1748)]

5. If aught of oaten stop, or pastoral song,
May hope, O pensive Eve, to soothe thine ear...

6. While now the bright-haired sun
Sits in yon western tent, whose cloudy skirts,
With brede ethereal wove,
O'erhang his wavy bed:

Now air is hushed, save where the weak-eyed bat,
With short shrill shriek flits by on leathern wing,
Or where the beetle winds
His small but sullen horn.

As oft he rises 'midst the twilight path,
Against the pilgrim borne in heedless hum.
['Ode to Evening' (1747)]

7. With eyes up-rais'd, as one inspir'd,
Pale Melancholy sate retir'd,
And from her wild sequester'd seat,
In notes by distance made more sweet,
Pour'd thro' the mellow horn her pensive soul...

8. Love of peace, and lonely musing,
In hollow murmurs died away.
['The Passions, an Ode for Music' (1747)]

Colman, the Elder, George (1732–1794)
English dramatist and theatrical manager, born in Florence and father of George Colman the Younger

1. Love and a cottage! Eh, Fanny! Ah, give me indifference and a coach and six!
[*The Clandestine Marriage* (1766), I]

Colman, the Younger, George (1762–1836)
English dramatist, theatrical manager and scrupulous Examiner of Plays (1824–36); son of George Colman the Elder

1. Mum's the word.
[*The Battle of Hexham* (1789)]

2. My father was an eminent button maker – but I had a soul above buttons – I panted for a liberal profession.
[*Sylvester Daggerwood: or New Hay at the Old Market* (1795)]

3. Oh, London is a fine town,
A very famous city,
Where all the streets are paved with gold,
And all the maidens pretty.
[*The Heir at Law* (1797, published 1808), I]

4. Lord help you! Tell 'em Queen Anne's dead.
[*The Heir at Law* (1797, published 1808), I]

5. Not to be sneezed at.
[*The Heir at Law* (1797, published 1808), II]

6. His heart runs away with his head.
[*Who Wants a Guinea?* (1805)]

7. Says he, 'I am a handsome man, but I'm a gay deceiver.'
[*Love Laughs at Locksmiths* (1808), II]

8. Johnson's style was grand and Gibbon's elegant; the stateliness of the former was sometimes pedantic, and the polish of the latter was occasionally finical. Johnson marched to kettle-drums and trumpets; Gibbon moved to flutes and hautboys: Johnson hewed passages through the Alps, while Gibbon levelled walks through parks and gardens.
[*Random Records* (1830), I]

Colson, Charles (1931–)
American lay minister, lawyer and writer

1. [To campaign staff, 1972]
I would walk over my grandmother if necessary to get Nixon re-elected!
[*Born Again* (1976)]

Colton, Charles Caleb (c. 1780–1832)
English clergyman, poet, satirist, essayist and gambler

1. Men will wrangle for religion; write for it; fight for it; anything but – live for it.
[*Lacon* (1820)]

2. When you have nothing to say, say nothing.
[*Lacon* (1820)]

3. Imitation is the sincerest form of flattery.
[*Lacon* (1820)]

4. Examinations are formidable even to the best prepared, for the greatest fool may ask more than the wisest man can answer.
[*Lacon* (1820)]

5. If you would be known, and not know, vegetate in a village; if you would know, and not be known, live in a city.
[*Lacon* (1820)]

6. Man is an embodied paradox, a bundle of contradictions.
[*Lacon* (1820)]

7. Friendship often ends in love; but love in friendship – never.
[*Lacon* (1820)]

8. True contentment depends not on what we have; a tub was large enough for Diogenes, but a world was too little for Alexander.
[*Lacon* (1820)]

Coltrane, Robbie (1950–)
Scottish comedian and actor

1. [On film acting]
If anyone asked me what I was doing, I'd say 'I've come 1500

miles to a foreign country to pretend to be someone else in front of a machine'.
[*Arena*, 1991]

Compton-Burnett, Dame Ivy (1884–1969)
English writer of novels concerned with upper middle-class Edwardian family life

1. 'We may as well imagine the scene.'
'No, my mind baulks at it.'
'Mine does worse. It constructs it.'
[*A Family and a Fortune* (1939)]

2. 'Know thyself' is a most superfluous direction. We can't avoid it. We can only hope that no one else knows.
[*A Family and a Fortune* (1939)]

3. 'She still seems to me in her own way a person born to command,' said Luce...
'I wonder if anyone is born to obey,' said Isabel.
'That may be why people command rather badly, that they have no suitable material to work on.'
[*Parents and Children* (1941)]

4. Well, the English have no family feelings. That is, none of the kind you mean. They have them, and one of them is that relations must cause no expense.
[*Parents and Children* (1941)]

5. Don't be too hard on parents. You may find yourself in their place.
[*Elders and Betters* (1944)]

6. My service is of a kind that cannot be paid for in money. And that means it is paid for in that way, but not very well.
[*Elders and Betters* (1944)]

7. Appearances are not held to be a clue to the truth. But we seem to have no other.
[*Manservant and Maidservant* (1947)]

8. At any time you might act for my good. When people do that, it kills something precious between them.
[*Manservant and Maidservant* (1947)]

9. 'Time has too much credit,' said Bridget. 'I never agree with the compliments paid to it. It is not a great healer. It is an indifferent and perfunctory one. Sometimes it does not heal at all. And sometimes when it seems to, no healing has been necessary.'
[*Darkness and Day* (1951), 7]

10. There is more difference within the sexes than between them.
[*Mother and Son* (1955)]

11. You must take me as I am, as people say. As though that justified their being what they are, when probably nothing could.
[*A Heritage and its History* (1959)]

12. As regards plots I find real life no help at all. Real life seems to have no plots.
[In R. Lehmann et al., *Orion I* (1945)]

13. [Describing a certain woman's age]
Pushing forty? She's clinging on to it for dear life.
[Attr.]

Comte, Auguste (1798–1857)
French philosopher, sociologist and mathematician; founder of positivism

1. M. Comte used to reproach his early English admirers with maintaining the 'conspiracy of silence' concerning his later performances.
[In J.S. Mill, *Auguste Comte and Positivism* (1865)]

Condon, Richard (1915–)
American author and dramatist

1. Writers are too self-centred to be lonely.
[Attr.]

Condorcet, Antoine-Nicolas de (Marquis de Condorcet) (1743–1794)
French mathematician and academician; President of the Legislative Assembly, 1792

1. Either none of mankind possesses genuine rights, or everyone shares them equally; whoever votes against another's rights, whatever his religion, colour or sex, forswears his own.
[In Peter Vansittart (ed.), *Voices of the Revolution* (1989), 'Sur l'admission des Femmes au Droit de Cité']

Confucius (c. 550–c. 478 BC)
Chinese philosopher and teacher of ethics, on whose system of morality Confucianism is based

1. Fine words and an insinuating appearance are seldom associated with true virtue.
[*Analects*, 1, 3]

2. Have no friends not equal to yourself.
[*Analects*, 1, 8]

3. When you have faults, do not fear to abandon them.
[*Analects*, 1, 8]

4. Learning without thought is labour lost; thought without learning is perilous.
[*Analects*, 2, 15]

5. Virtue is not left to stand alone. He who practises it will have neighbours.
[*Analects*, 4, 25]

6. The superior man is satisfied and composed; the mean man is always full of distress.
[*Analects*, 7, 36]

7. The people may be made to follow a course of action, but they may not be made to understand it.
[*Analects*, 8, 9]

8. The scholar who cherishes the love of comfort, is not fit to be deemed a scholar.
[*Analects*, 14, 3]

9. Recompense injury with justice, and recompense kindness with kindness.
[*Analects*, 14, 36]

10. The superior man is distressed by his want of ability.
[*Analects*, 15, 18]

11. What the superior man seeks is in himself: what the small man seeks is in others.
[*Analects*, 15, 20]

12. What you do not want done to yourself, do not do to others.
[*Analects*, 15, 23]

13. Men's natures are alike; it is their habits that carry them far apart.
[*Analects*, 17, 2]

14. To be able to practise five things everywhere under heaven constitutes perfect virtue ... gravity, generosity of soul, sincerity, earnestness, and kindness.
[*Analects*, 17, 6]

15. Without knowing the force of words, it is impossible to know men.
[*Analects*, 20, 3]

16. When you meet someone better than yourself, turn your thoughts to becoming his equal.
When you meet someone not as good as you are, look within and examine your own self.
[*Analects*]

17. Chi Wen Tzu always thought three times before taking action. Twice would have been quite enough.
[*Analects*]

18. True goodness springs from a man's own heart. All men are born good.
[*Analects*]

19. An oppressive government is more to be feared than a tiger.
[*Analects*]

20. Gravity is only the bark of wisdom's tree, but it preserves it.
[*Analects*]

21. Study the past, if you would divine the future.
[*Analects*]

22. The heart of the wise, like a mirror, should reflect all objects without being sullied by any.
[*Analects*]

23. In all things, success depends upon previous preparation, and without such preparation there is sure to be failure.
[*Analects*]

24. For one word a man is often deemed to be wise, and for one word he is often deemed to be foolish. We should be careful indeed what we say.
[*Analects*]

25. Everything has its beauty but not everyone sees it.
[*Analects*]

26. They must often change who would be constant in happiness or wisdom.
[*Analects*]

27. To see what is right and not to do it is want of courage.
[*Analects*]

Congreve, William (1670–1729)

English dramatist, noted for his comedies of manners and witty dialogue

1. Ah! Madam, ... you know every thing in the world but your perfections, and you only know not those, because 'tis the top of perfection not to know them.
[*Incognita* (1692)]

2. I am always of the opinion with the learned, if they speak first.
[*Incognita* (1692)]

3. In my conscience I believe the baggage loves me, for she never speaks well of me her self, nor suffers any body else to rail me.
[*The Old Bachelor* (1693), I.i]

4. One of love's April-fools.
[*The Old Bachelor* (1693), I.i]

5. The Devil watches all opportunities.
[*The Old Bachelor* (1693), II.ii]

6. Even silence may be eloquent in love.
[*The Old Bachelor* (1693), II.ii]

7. Man was by Nature Woman's cully made:
We never are, but by ourselves, betrayed.
[*The Old Bachelor* (1693), III.i]

8. Eternity was in that moment.
[*The Old Bachelor* (1693), IV.iii]

9. You were about to tell me something, child – but you left off before you began.
[*The Old Bachelor* (1693), IV.iv]

10. Now am I slap-dash down in the mouth.
[*The Old Bachelor* (1693), IV.iv]

11. *Sharper*: Thus grief still treads upon the heels of pleasure;
Marry'd in haste, we may repent at leisure.
Setter: Some by experience find those words mis-plac'd:
At leisure marry'd, they repent in haste.
[*The Old Bachelor* (1693), V.iii]

12. I could find it in my heart to marry thee, purely to be rid of thee.
[*The Old Bachelor* (1693), V.iv]

13. Courtship to marriage, as a very witty prologue to a very dull Play.
[*The Old Bachelor* (1693), V.iv]

14. It is the business of a comic poet to paint the vices and follies of human kind.
[*The Double Dealer* (1694), Epistle Dedicatory]

15. Retired to their tea and scandal, according to their ancient custom.
[*The Double Dealer* (1694), I.i]

16. There is nothing more unbecoming a man of quality than to laugh; Jesu, 'tis such a vulgar expression of the passion!
[*The Double Dealer* (1694), I.ii]

17. Tho' marriage makes man and wife one flesh, it leaves 'em still two fools.
[*The Double Dealer* (1694), II.i]

18. She lays it on with a trowel.
[*The Double Dealer* (1694), III.iii]

19. See how love and murder will out!
[*The Double Dealer* (1694), IV.ii]

20. No mask like open truth to cover lies,
As to go naked is the best disguise.
[*The Double Dealer* (1694), V.i]

21. Has he not a rogue's face? ... a hanging-look to me ... has a damn'd Tyburn-face, without the benefit o' the Clergy...
[*Love for Love* (1695), II.i]

22. I came upstairs into the world; for I was born in a cellar.
[*Love for Love* (1695), II.i]

23. What, wouldst thou have me turn pelican, and feed thee out of my own vitals?
[*Love for Love* (1695), II.i]

24. O fie miss, you must not kiss and tell.
[*Love for Love* (1695), II.ii]

25. If I marry, Sir Sampson, I'm for a good estate with any man, and for any man with a good estate.
[*Love for Love* (1695), III.iii]

26. I know that's a secret, for it's whispered everywhere.
[*Love for Love* (1695), III.iii]

27. He that first cries out stop thief, is often he that has stolen the treasure.
[*Love for Love* (1695), III.iv]

28. Women are like tricks by slight of hand,
Which, to admire, we should not understand.
[*Love for Love* (1695), IV.iii]

29. A branch of one of your antediluvian families, fellows that the flood could not wash away.
[*Love for Love* (1695), V.i]

30. To find a young fellow that is neither a wit in his own eye, nor a fool in the eye of the world, is a very hard task.
[*Love for Love* (1695), V.i]

31. Aye, 'tis well enough for a servant to be bred at an University. But the education is a little too pedantic for a gentleman.
[*Love for Love* (1695), V.ii]

32. Nay, for my part I always despised Mr Tattle of all things; nothing but his being my husband could have made me like him less.
[*Love for Love* (1695), V.ii]

33. Music has charms to soothe a savage breast.
[*The Mourning Bride* (1697), I.i]

34. Heav'n has no rage, like love to hatred turned,
Nor Hell a fury, like a woman scorn'd.
[*The Mourning Bride* (1697), III.ii]

35. Is he then dead?
What, dead at last, quite, quite for ever dead!
[*The Mourning Bride* (1697), V.iii]

36. They come together like the Coroner's Inquest, to sit upon the murdered reputations of the week.
[*The Way of the World* (1700), I.i]

37. Ay, ay, I have experience: I have a wife, and so forth.
[*The Way of the World* (1700), I.ii]

38. I always take blushing either for a sign of guilt, or of ill breeding.
[*The Way of the World* (1700), I.ii]

39. Say what you will, 'tis better to be left than never to have been loved.
[*The Way of the World* (1700), II.i]

40. O the pious friendships of the female sex!
[*The Way of the World* (1700), II.i]

41. Here she comes i' faith full sail, with her fan spread and streamers out, and a shoal of fools for tenders.
[*The Way of the World* (1700), II.ii]

42. *Millamant*: O ay, letters – I had letters – I am persecuted with letters – I hate letters – no body knows how to write letters; and yet one has 'em, one does not know why – They serve one to pin up one's hair.
Witwoud: Pray, Madam, do you pin up your hair with all your letters: I find I must keep copies.
Millamant: Only with those in verse, Mr Witwoud. I never pin up my hair with prose.
[*The Way of the World* (1700), II.ii]

43. *Millamant*: I believe I gave you some pain.
Mirabel: Does that please you?
Millamant: Infinitely; I love to give pain.
[*The Way of the World* (1700), II.ii]

44. Beauty is the lover's gift.
[*The Way of the World* (1700), II.ii]

45. Lord, what is a lover ... ? Why one makes lovers as fast as one pleases, and they live as long as one pleases, and they die as soon as one pleases: and then if one pleases one makes more.
[*The Way of the World* (1700), II.ii]

46. A little disdain is not amiss; a little scorn is alluring.
[*The Way of the World* (1700), III.i]

47. Yes, but tenderness becomes me best – a sort of dyingness – you see that picture has a sort of a – ha, Foible? A swimmingness in the eyes.
[*The Way of the World* (1700), III.i]

48. Love's but a frailty of the mind
When 'tis not with ambition join'd.
[*The Way of the World* (1700), III.iii]

49. No, I'm no enemy to learning; it hurts not me.
[*The Way of the World* (1700), III.iii]

50. O, nothing is more alluring than a levee from a couch in some confusion.
[*The Way of the World* (1700), IV.i]

51. I nauseate walking; 'tis a country diversion, I loathe the country.
[*The Way of the World* (1700), IV.i]

52. My dear liberty, shall I leave thee? My faithful solitude, my darling contemplation, must I bid you then adieu? Ay-h adieu – My morning thoughts, agreeable wakings, indolent slumbers, all ye douceurs, ye sommeils du matin, adieu – I can't do't, 'tis more than impossible.
[*The Way of the World* (1700), IV.i]

53. Don't let us be familiar or fond, nor kiss before folks, like my Lady Fadler and Sir Francis: Nor go to Hyde-Park together the first Sunday in a new chariot, to provoke eyes and whispers, and then never be seen there together again; as if we were proud of one another the first week, and asham'd of one another ever after ... Let us be very strange and well-bred: Let us be as strange as if we had been married a great while, and as well-bred as if we were not married at all.
[*The Way of the World* (1700), IV.i]

54. These articles subscrib'd, if I continue to endure you a little longer, I may by degrees dwindle into a wife.
[*The Way of the World* (1700), IV.i]

55. I hate your odious provisoes.
[*The Way of the World* (1700), IV.i]

56. I hope you do not think me prone to any iteration of nuptials.
[*The Way of the World* (1700), IV.ii]

57. You are all camphire and frankincense, all chastity and odour.
[*The Way of the World* (1700), IV.ii]

58. O, she is the antidote to desire.
[*The Way of the World* (1700), IV.ii]

59. Careless she is with artful care,
Affecting to seem unaffected...

60. She likes her self, yet others hates
For that which in herself she prizes;
And while she laughs at them, forgets
She is the thing that she despises.
['Amoret']

61. In hours of bliss we oft have met;
They could not always last;
And though the present I regret
I'm grateful for the past.
['False though she be']

62. Music alone with sudden charms can bind
The wandering sense, and calm the troubled mind.
['Hymn to Harmony']

63. Whom she refuses, she treats still
With so much sweet behaviour,
That her refusal, through her skill,
Looks almost like a favour.
['Song: Doris']

64. Wou'd I were free from this restraint,
Or else had hopes to win her;
Wou'd she cou'd make of me a saint,

Or I of her a sinner.
['Song: Pious Selinda Goes to Prayers']

65. For 'tis some virtue, virtue to commend.
['To Sir Godfrey Kneller']

66. Is there in the world a climate more uncertain than our own? And, which is a natural consequence, is there any where a people more unsteady, more apt to discontent, more saturnine, dark and melancholic than our selves? Are we not of all people the most unfit to be alone, and most unsafe to be trusted with our selves?
[*Amendments of Mr Collier's False and Imperfect Citations* (1698)]

67. I cannot help it, if I am naturally more delighted with any thing that is amiable, than with any thing that is wonderful.
[*Preface to Dryden*]

68. Alack, he's gone the way of all flesh.
['*Squire Bickerstaff Detected*]

69. I confess freely to you, I could never look long upon a monkey, without very mortifying reflections.
[Letter to Mr Dennis, concerning Humour in Comedy, 1695]

Connell, James M. (1852–1929)
Irish-born writer of socialist songs and poems

1. The people's flag is deepest red;
It shrouded oft our martyred dead,
And ere their limbs grew stiff and cold,
Their heart's blood dyed its every fold.
Then raise the scarlet standard high!
Within its shade we'll live or die.
Tho' cowards flinch and traitors sneer,
We'll keep the red flag flying here.
['The Red Flag' (1889)]

Connolly, Cyril (1903–1974)
English literary editor, journalist, critic and author of prose and verse

1. The ape-like virtues without which no one can enjoy a public school.
[*Enemies of Promise* (1938), 1]

2. Literature is the art of writing something that will be read twice; journalism what will be grasped at once.
[*Enemies of Promise* (1938), 3]

3. An author arrives at a good style when his language performs what is required of it without shyness.
[*Enemies of Promise* (1938), 3]

4. As repressed sadists are supposed to become policemen or butchers so those with irrational fear of life become publishers.
[*Enemies of Promise* (1938), 3]

5. Whom the gods wish to destroy they first call promising.
[*Enemies of Promise* (1938), 13]

6. There is no more sombre enemy of good art than the pram in the hall.
[*Enemies of Promise* (1938), 14]

7. All charming people have something to conceal, usually their total dependence on the appreciation of others.
[*Enemies of Promise* (1938), 16]

8. I have always disliked myself at any given moment; the total of such moments is my life.
[*Enemies of Promise* (1938), 18]

9. Boys do not grow up gradually. They move forward in spurts like the hands of clocks in railway stations.
[*Enemies of Promise* (1938), 18]

10. The Mandarin style ... is beloved by literary pundits, by those who would make the written word as unlike as possible to the spoken one. It is the style of those writers whose tendency is to make their language convey more than they mean or more than they feel.
[*Enemies of Promise* (1938), 20]

11. There is no fury like an ex-wife searching for a new lover.
[*The Unquiet Grave* (1944)]

12. In the sex-war thoughtlessness is the weapon of the male, vindictiveness of the female.
[*The Unquiet Grave* (1944)]

13. Life is a maze in which we take the wrong turning before we have learnt to walk.
[*The Unquiet Grave* (1944)]

14. Imprisoned in every fat man a thin one is wildly signalling to be let out.
[*The Unquiet Grave* (1944)]

15. The true index of a man's character is the health of his wife.
[*The Unquiet Grave* (1944)]

16. [Of George Orwell]
He would not blow his nose without moralizing on conditions in the handkerchief industry.
[*The Evening Colonnade* (1973)]

17. It is closing time in the gardens of the West and from now on an artist will be judged only by the resonance of his solitude or the quality of his despair.
[*Horizon*, 1949–1950]

18. Better to write for yourself and have no public, than write for the public and have no self.
[In V.S. Pritchett (ed.), *Turnstile One*]

19. The man who is master of his passions is Reason's slave.
[In V.S. Pritchett (ed.), *Turnstile One*]

20. [Of Vita Sackville-West]
She looked like Lady Chatterley above the waist and the gamekeeper below.
[Attr.]

Connolly, James (1868–1916)
Irish labour leader

1. Apostles of Freedom are ever idolised when dead, but crucified when alive.
[*Workers Republic*, 1898]

2. Governments in a capitalist society are but committees of the rich to manage the affairs of the capitalist class.
[*Irish Worker*, 1914]

Connor, William ('Cassandra') (1909–1967)
British journalist and columnist

1. [On resuming his column at the end of the Second World War]
As I was saying when I was interrupted, it is a powerful hard thing to please all the people all the time.
[*Daily Mirror*, 1946]

Conrad, Joseph (1857–1924)
Polish-born British modernist novelist and short-story writer, sailor and explorer

1. A work that aspires, however humbly, to the condition of art should carry its justification in every line.
[*The Nigger of the Narcissus* (1897), Preface]

2. In the destructive element immerse ... that was the way.
[*Lord Jim* (1900), 20]

3. You shall judge of a man by his foes as well as by his friends.
[*Lord Jim* (1900), 34]

4. Exterminate all the brutes!
[*Heart of Darkness* (1902), 2]

5. The horror! The horror!
[*Heart of Darkness* (1902), 3]

6. Mistah Kurtz – he dead.
[*Heart of Darkness* (1902), 3]

7. This could have occurred nowhere but in England, where men and sea interpenetrate, so to speak.
[*Youth* (1902)]

8. I remember my youth and the feeling that will never come back any more – the feeling that I could last for ever, outlast the sea, the earth, and all men; the deceitful feeling that lures us on to perils, to love, to vain effort – to death; the triumphant conviction of strength, the heat of life in the handful of dust, that glow in the heart that with every year grows dim, grows cold, grows small, and expires – and expires, too soon, too soon – before life itself.
[*Youth* (1902)]

9. The terrorist and the policeman both come from the same basket.
[*The Secret Agent* (1907), 4]

10. He walked frail, insignificant, shabby, miserable – and terrible in the simplicity of his idea calling madness and despair to the regeneration of the world. Nobody looked at him. He passed on unsuspected and deadly, like a pest in the street full of men.
[*The Secret Agent* (1907), closing words]

11. The scrupulous and the just, the noble, humane, and devoted natures; the unselfish and the intelligent may begin a movement – but it passes away from them. They are not the leaders of a revolution. They are its victims.
[*Under Western Eyes* (1911), II, 3]

12. The belief in a supernatural source of evil is not necessary; men alone are quite capable of every wickedness.
[*Under Western Eyes* (1911), II, 4]

13. All ambitions are lawful except those which climb upward on the miseries or credulities of mankind.
[*A Personal Record* (1912), Preface]

14. The fatal imperfection of all the gifts of life, which makes of them a delusion and a snare.
[*Victory* (1915)]

Conran, Shirley (1932–)
English journalist and novelist

1. Life is too short to stuff a mushroom.
[*Superwoman* (1975), Epigraph]

2. I make no secret of the fact that I would rather lie on a sofa than sweep beneath it. But you have to be efficient if you're going to be lazy.
[*Superwoman* (1975), 'The Reason Why']

3. [On Julie Burchill]
I cannot take seriously the criticism of someone who doesn't know how to use a semicolon.
[Attr.]

Constable, Henry (1562–1613)
English poet, noted for his sonnets

1. Diaphenia, like the daffadowndilly,
White as the sun, fair as the lily,
Heigh ho, how I do love thee!
I do love thee as my lambs
Are beloved of their dams;
How blest were I if thou wouldst prove me!
['Diaphenia']

Constable, John (1776–1837)
English landscape painer

1. The sound of water escaping from mill-dams, etc, willows, old rotten planks, slimy posts, and brickwork, I love such things ... those scenes made me a painter and I am grateful.
[Letter to John Fisher, 1821]

2. There is nothing ugly; I never saw an ugly thing in my life: for let the form of an object be what it may, – light, shade, and perspective will always make it beautiful.
[In C.R. Leslie, *Memoirs of the Life of John Constable* (1843). Cf. Emerson: 1]

3. The amiable but eccentric Blake ... said of a beautiful drawing of an avenue of fir trees ... 'Why, this is not drawing, but inspiration.' ... [Constable] replied, 'I never knew it before; I meant it for drawing'.
[In C.R. Leslie, *Memoirs of the Life of John Constable* (1843)]

4. In Claude's landscape all is lovely – all amiable – all is amenity and repose; – the calm sunshine of the heart.
[In C.R. Leslie, *Memoirs of the Life of John Constable* (1843)]

5. [Description of Watteau's 'Plaisirs du Bal']
As if painted in honey.
[In *The Times Literary Supplement*, 1993]

Constant, Benjamin (Henri Benjamin Constant de Rebecque) (1767–1834)
Swiss-born French novelist, prose writer and politician

1. *Dîner avec Robinson, écolier de Schelling. Son travail sur l'esthétique du Kant. Idées très ingénieuses. L'art pour l'art et sans but; tout but dénature l'art. Mais l'art atteint au but qu'il n'a pas.*
Dinner with Robinson, a pupil of Schelling. His work on the aesthetics of that man Kant. Very ingenious ideas. Art for art's sake, without a purpose; every purpose distorts the true nature of art. But art achieves a purpose which it does not have.
[*Journal intime*, 1804]

Constantine, Emperor (c. 288–337)
First Christian Roman emperor 306–37

1. [His motto, in memory of a vision of the Cross which appeared to him on the eve of his defeat of Maxentius and victorious entry into Rome, 312]
In hoc signo vinces.
In this sign thou shalt conquer.
[In Eusebius, *Vita Constantini*, I, 28]

Coogan, Tim Pat (1935–)
Irish journalist and biographer

1. [Describing the rulings of the Catholic Church on matters of sexual morality]
It's rather like teaching swimming from a book without ever having got wet oneself.
[*Disillusioned Decades: Ireland, 1966–87* (1987)]

Cook, A.J. (1885–1931)
English miners' leader; prominent in General Strike of 1926

1. Not a penny off the pay, not a minute on the day.
[Speech, 1926]

Cook, Captain James (1728–1779)
English navigator and explorer, responsible for the British acquisition of Australia

1. [Of the *Endeavour* expedition]
Altho' the discoveries made in this Voyage are not great, yet I flatter myself that they are such as may merit the attention of their Lordships, and altho' I have failed in discovering the so much talk'd of southern Continent (which perhaps do not exist) and which I myself had so much at heart, yet I am confident that no part of the failure of such discovery can be laid at my Charge.
[Letter, 1770]

2. [Following Cook's experiences with the natural historians on his second voyage]
Curse the scientists, and all science into the bargain.
[In J.C. Beaglehole (ed.), *The Voyage of the Resolution* (1961)]

3. [Of the Polynesians]
It would have been better for these people never to have known us.
[In Colin Bingham (ed.), *Wit and Wisdom*]

Cook, Peter (1937–1995)
English comic writer and comedian

1. [Giving an impersonation of Harold Macmillan]
We exchanged many frank words in our respective languages.
[*Beyond the Fringe*, 1961, 'T.V.P.M.']

2. I am very interested in the Universe – I am specializing in the universe and all that surrounds it.
[*Beyond the Fringe*, 1962]

3. You know, I go to the theatre to be entertained ... I don't want to see plays about rape, sodomy and drug addiction ... I can get all that at home.
[*The Observer*, caption to cartoon, 1962]

Coolidge, Calvin (1872–1933)
American statesman and lawyer; Republican President of the USA 1923–29

1. The governments of the past could fairly be characterized as devices for maintaining in perpetuity the place and position of certain privileged classes ... The Government of the United States is a device for maintaining in perpetuity the rights of the people, with the ultimate extinction of all privileged classes.
[Speech, 1924]

2. The business of America is business.
[Speech, 1925]

3. [Of the Boston police strike]
There is no right to strike against the public safety by anybody, anywhere, any time.
[Telegram to the President of the American Federation of Labour, 1919]

4. [Of Allied war debts]
They hired the money, didn't they?
[Remark, 1925]

5. [On being asked what had been said by a clergyman who preached on sin]
He said he was against it.
[Attr.]

Cooper, Derek (1925–)
British journalist, food writer and television presenter

1. [Highland saying]
One whisky is all right; two is too much; three is too few.
[*A Taste of Scotch* (1989)]

Cooper, James Fenimore (1789–1851)
American novelist and social critic; creator of the 'frontier novel'

1. The Last of the Mohicans.
[Title of novel, 1826]

Cope, Wendy (1945–)
English writer and poet

1. [Response to an Engineering Council advertisement which asked why there was no Engineers' Corner in Westminster Abbey]
We make more fuss of ballads than of blueprints–
That's why so many poets end up rich,
While engineers scrape by in cheerless garrets.
Who needs a bridge or dam? Who needs a ditch?...

2. Yes, life is hard if you choose engineering–
You're sure to need another job as well;
You'll have to plan your projects in the evenings
Instead of going out. It must be hell.
[*Making Cocoa for Kingsley Amis* (1986), 'Engineers' Corner']

3. I used to think all poets were Byronic–
Mad, bad and dangerous to know.
And then I met a few. Yes it's ironic–
I used to think all poets were Byronic.
They're mostly wicked as a ginless tonic
And wild as pension plans. Not long ago
I used to think all poets were Byronic–
Mad, bad and dangerous to know.
[*Making Cocoa for Kingsley Amis* (1986), 'Triolet']

4. There are so many kinds of awful men–
One can't avoid them all. She often said
She'd never make the same mistake again:
She always made a new mistake instead.
[*Making Cocoa for Kingsley Amis* (1986), 'Rondeau Redoublé']

5. I hardly ever tire of love or rhyme–
That's why I'm poor and have a rotten time.
['Variation on Belloc's "Fatigue"']

6. The day he moved out was terrible–
That evening she went through hell.
His absence wasn't a problem
But the corkscrew had gone as well.
[*Serious Concerns* (1992), 'Loss']

7. Bloody Christmas, here again,
Let us raise a loving cup:
Peace on earth, goodwill to men,
And make them do the washing-up.
['Another Christmas Poem']

8. 2 cures for love
1. Don't see him. Don't phone or write a letter.
2. The easy way: get to know him better.
[Attr.]

Coren, Alan (1938–)
British humorist, writer and broadcaster

1. No visit to Dove Cottage, Grasmere, is complete without examining the outhouse where Hazlitt's father, a Unitarian minister of strong liberal views, attempted to put his hand up Dorothy Wordsworth's skirt.
[*All Except the Bastard* (1969), 'Bohemia']

2. Apart from cheese and tulips, the main product of the country [Holland] is advocaat, a drink made from lawyers.
[*The Sanity Inspector* (1974), 'All You Ever Need to Know about Europe']

3. [Of Switzerland]
Since both its national products, snow and chocolate, melt, the cuckoo clock was invented solely in order to give tourists something solid to remember it by.
[*The Sanity Inspector* (1974), 'All You Ever Need to Know about Europe']

4. The Act of God designation on all insurance policies; which means, roughly, that you cannot be insured for the accidents that are most likely to happen to you.
[*The Lady from Stalingrad Museum* (1977), 'A Short History of Insurance']

5. Television is more interesting than people. If it were not, we should have people standing in the corners of our rooms.
[Attr.]

Corneille, Pierre (1606–1684)
French classical dramatist, poet and lawyer

1. *A vaincre sans péril, on triomphe sans gloire.*
When we conquer without danger our triumph is without glory.
[*Le Cid* (1637), II]

2. *Et le combat cessa, faute de combattants.*
And the battle ceased for lack of combatants.
[*Le Cid* (1637), IV]

3. *Faites votre devoir et laissez faire aux dieux.*
Do your duty, and put yourself into the hands of the gods.
[*Horace* (1640), II.viii]

4. *Et enfin la clémence est la plus belle marque*
Qui fasse à l'univers connaître un vrai monarque.
For in the end, mercy is the greatest sign by which the world may recognise a true king.
[*Cinna* (1641)]

5. *Le façon de donner vaut mieux que ce qu'on donne.*
The manner of giving is worth more than the gift.
[*Le Menteur* (1643), I.i]

6. *Il faut bonne mémoire après qu'on a menti.*
One needs a good memory after telling lies.
[*Le Menteur* (1643), IV.v]

7. *A raconter ses maux, souvent on les soulage.*
Telling one's sorrows often brings comfort.
[*Polyeucte* (1643), I.iii]

8. He who allows himself to be insulted, deserves to be.
[*Héraclius* (1646)]

Cornfeld, Bernard (1927–)
American businessman

1. Do You Sincerely Want to be Rich?
[Title of book, 1971]

Cornford, F.M. (1874–1943)
English Platonic scholar

1. Every public action which is not customary, either is wrong or, if it is right, is a dangerous precedent. It follows that nothing should ever be done for the first time.
[*Microcosmographia Academica* (1908)]

Cornford, Frances Crofts (1886–1960)
English poet and translator; granddaughter of Charles Darwin

1. O fat white woman whom nobody loves,
Why do you walk through the fields in gloves...
Missing so much and so much?
['To a Fat Lady Seen from a Train' (1910)]

2. [Of Rupert Brooke]
A young Apollo, golden-haired,
Stands dreaming on the verge of strife,
Magnificently unprepared
For the long littleness of life.
['Youth' (1910)]

3. How long ago Hector took off his plume,
Not wanting that his little son should cry,
Then kissed his sad Andromache goodbye–
And now we three in Euston waiting-room.
['Parting in Wartime' (1948)]

4. Propaganda is that branch of the art of lying which consists in nearly deceiving your friends without quite deceiving your enemies.
[*New Statesman*, 1978]

Cornuel, Madame Anne-Marie Bigot de (1605–1694)
French society hostess

1. *Il n'y a point de grand homme pour son valet de chambre.*
No man is a hero to his valet.
[In *Lettres de Mlle Aïssé à Madame C* (1787); similar sentiments attributed to Antigonus Gonatas, King of Thessaly, Madame de Sévigné, Nicolas Catinat, Goethe, and Montaigne]

Coronation Service

1. We present you with this Book, the most valuable thing that this world affords. Here is wisdom; this is the royal Law; these are the lively Oracles of God.
[In L.G. Wickham Legge, *English Coronation Records* (1901)]

Correggio (Antonio Allegri Correggio) (c. 1489–1534)
Italian painter of the High Renaissance

1. [On seeing Raphael's 'St Cecilia' in Bologna, c. 1525]
Anch' io sono pittore!
I, too, am an artist.
[In L. Pungileoni, *Memorie Istoriche de ... Correggio* (1817)]

Cory, William (born William Johnson) (1823–1892)
English lyric poet, school teacher and educational writer

1. They told me, Heraclitus, they told me you were dead,
They brought me bitter news to hear and bitter tears to shed.
I wept as I remembered how often you and I
Had tired the sun with talking and sent him down the sky.
['Heraclitus' (1858)]

2. You promise heavens free from strife,
Pure truth, and perfect change of will;
But sweet, sweet is this human life,
So sweet, I fain would breathe it still;
Your chilly stars I can forgo,
This warm kind world is all I know...

3. All beauteous things for which we live
By laws of space and time decay.
But Oh, the very reason why
I clasp them, is because they die.
['Mimnermus in Church' (1858)]

4. Jolly boating weather,
And a hay harvest breeze,
Blade on the feather,
Shade off the trees.
Swing, swing together
With your backs between your knees...

Harrow may be more clever,
Rugby may make more row,
But we'll row, row for ever,

Steady from stroke to bow.
And nothing in life shall sever
The chain that is round us now...

Others will fill our places,
Dress'd in the old light blue,
We'll recollect our races,
We'll to the flag be true,
And youth will be still in our faces
When we cheer for an Eton crew...

Twenty years hence this weather
May tempt us from office stools,
We may be slow on the feather,
And seem to the boys old fools,
But we'll still swing together
And swear by the best of schools.
['Eton Boating Song' (1865)]

Cotton, Charles (1630–1687)
English poet; noted for his translation of Montaigne's essays

1. The shadows now so long do grow,
That brambles like tall cedars show,
Molehills seem mountains, and the ant
Appears a monstrous elephant.
['Evening Quatrains' (1689)]

Coubertin, Pierre de (1863–1937)
French educationist and sportsman; founder of the International Olympic Games

1. *L'important dans la vie ce n'est point le triomphe mais le combat; l'essentiel ce n'est pas d'avoir vaincu mais de s'être bien battu.*
The most important thing in life is not the winning but the taking part ... The essential thing is not conquering but fighting well.
[Speech, Banquet for Officials of the Olympic Games, London, 1908]

Coué, Emile (1857–1926)
French psychologist, noted for his autosuggestion psychotherapy

1. *Tous les jours à tous points de vue, je vais de mieux en mieux.*
Every day, in every way, I get better and better.
[*De la suggestion et de ses applications* (1915)]

Counihan, Noel Jack (1913–1986)
Australian cartoonist and artist

1. In human society the warmth is mainly at the bottom.
[*Age*, 1986]

Cousin, Victor (1792–1867)
French eclectic philosopher and educationist

1. *Il faut de la religion pour la religion, de la morale pour la morale, comme de l'art pour l'art ... le beau ne peut être la voie ni de l'utile, ni du bien, ni du saint; il ne conduit qu'à lui-même.*
There must be religion for religion's sake, morality for morality's sake, as there is art for art's sake ... the beautiful cannot be the way to what is useful, nor to what is good, nor to what is holy; it leads only to itself.
[Lecture, 1818]

Coventry, Thomas (1578–1640)
English Attorney-General and politician

1. The dominion of the sea, as it is an ancient and undoubted right of the crown of England, so it is the best security of the land. The wooden walls are the best walls of this kingdom.
[Speech in Star Chamber, 1635]

Coward, Sir Noël (1899–1973)
English dramatist, noted for sophisticated comedies; actor, producer and composer

1. I've over-educated myself in all the things I shouldn't have known at all.
[*Mild Oats* (written 1922, published 1931)]

2. [Of the Taj Mahal]
It didn't look like a biscuit box did it? I've always felt that it might.
[*Private Lives* (1930), I]

3. Very flat, Norfolk.
[*Private Lives* (1930), I]

4. Extraordinary how potent cheap music is.
[*Private Lives* (1930), I]

5. Certain women should be struck regularly, like gongs.
[*Private Lives* (1930), III]

6. That one day this country of ours, which we love so much, will find dignity and greatness and peace again.
[The toast from *Cavalcade* (1931)]

7. There's always something fishy about the French.
[*Conversation Piece* (1934), I.vi]

8. Never mind, dear, we're all made the same, though some more than others.
[*The Café de la Paix* (1939)]

9. Life without faith is an arid business.
[*Blithe Spirit* (1941), I]

10. Time is the reef upon which all our frail mystic ships are wrecked.
[*Blithe Spirit* (1941), I]

11. I don't give a hoot about posterity. Why should I worry about what people think of me when I'm dead as a doornail anyway?
[*Present Laughter* (1943), I]

12. Everybody worships me, it's nauseating.
[*Present Laughter* (1943), I]

13. Comedies of manners swiftly become obsolete when there are no longer any manners.
[*Relative Values* (1951), I]

14. Everybody was up to something, especially, of course, those who were up to nothing.
[*Future Indefinite* (1954)]

15. Sunburn is very becoming – but only when it is even – one must be careful not to look like a mixed grill.
[*The Lido Beach*]

16. Poor little rich girl
You're a bewitched girl,
Better beware!
['Poor Little Rich Girl', song, 1925]

17. I believe that since my life began
The most I've had is just a talent to amuse.
Heigh-o,
If love were all.
['If Love Were All', song, 1929]

18. I'll see you again,
Whenever spring breaks through again.
['I'll See You Again', song, 1929]

19. A room with a view – and you
And no one to worry us
No one to hurry us.
['A Room With a View', song, 1929]

20. Mad dogs and Englishmen go out in the mid-day sun;
The Japanese don't care to, the Chinese wouldn't dare to;
Hindus and Argentines sleep firmly from twelve to one,
But Englishmen detest a
Siesta...

21. In the mangrove swamps where the python romps
There is peace from twelve till two.
Even caribous lie around and snooze,
For there's nothing else to do.
In Bengal, to move at all
Is seldom, if ever done.
['Mad Dogs and Englishmen', song, 1931]

22. Mad about the boy,
It's pretty funny but I'm mad about the boy.
He has a gay appeal
That makes me feel
There may be something sad about the boy.
['Mad about the Boy', song, 1932]

23. We're Regency Rakes
And each of us makes
A personal issue of adipose tissue.
[*Conversation Piece* (1934), I]

24. The Stately Homes of England
How beautiful they stand,
To prove the upper classes
Have still the upper hand...

25. We have been able to dispose of
Rows and rows and rows of
Gainsboroughs and Lawrences
Some sporting prints of Aunt Florence's
Some of which were rather rude...

26. And though the Van Dycks have to go
And we pawn the Bechstein grand,
We'll stand by the Stately Homes of England...

27. Tho' the pipes that supply the bathroom burst
And the lavat'ry makes you fear the worst
It was used by Charles the First
Quite informally
And later by George the Fourth
On a journey North...

28. The Stately Homes of England,
Tho' rather in the lurch,
Provide a lot of chances
For Psychical Research–
There's the ghost of a crazy younger son
Who murder'd in Thirteen Fifty-One,
An extremely rowdy Nun
Who resented it,
And people who come to call
Meet her in the hall.
['The Stately Homes of England', song, 1938. Cf. Hemans: 3]

29. They had him thrown out of a club in Bombay
For, apart from his Mess-bills exceeding his pay,
He took to pig-sticking in quite the wrong way.
I wonder what happened to him!
['I Wonder what Happened to Him', song, 1945]

30. She refused to begin the 'Beguine'
Tho' they besought her to
And with language profane and obscene
She curs'd the man who taught her to
She curs'd Cole Porter too!
['Nina', song, 1945]

31. [Written after Lawrence had retired from public life to become Aircraftsman Brown, 338171]
Dear 338171 (May I call you 338?)
[Letter to T.E. Lawrence, 1930]

32. [Reply to Laurence Olivier's five-year-old daughter, Tamsin, when she asked what two dogs were doing together]
The doggie in front has suddenly gone blind, and the other one has very kindly offered to push him all the way to St Dunstan's.
[In K. Tynan, *The Sound of Two Hands Clapping* (1975)]

33. [On child star Bonnie Langford in a musical version of *Gone with the Wind* (1972) when a horse defecated on stage]
If they'd stuffed the child's head up the horse's arse, they would have solved two problems at once.
[In N. Sherrin, *Cutting Edge, or, Back in the Knife Box Miss Sharp* (1984)]

34. [Comment on a child star, in a long-winded play]
Two things should be cut: the second act and the child's throat.
[In D. Richards, *The Wit of Noël Coward*]

35. [On a poor portrayal of Queen Victoria]
It made me feel that Albert had married beneath his station.
[In D. Richards, *The Wit of Noël Coward*]

36. Work is much more fun than fun.
[*The Observer*, 'Sayings of the Week', 1963]

37. [Of Monte Carlo]
A sunny place for shady people.
[Attr.]

38. [On Randolph Churchill]
Dear Randolph, utterly unspoiled by failure.
[Attr.]

39. [Coward had been asked, while watching the 1953 Coronation on TV, who the man was riding in a carriage with the portly Queen of Tonga]
Her lunch.
[Attr.]

40. Television is for appearing on, not looking at.
[Attr.]

Cowley, Abraham (1618–1667)
English poet and dramatist; Royalist spy

1. Love in her sunny eyes does basking play;
Love walks the pleasant mazes of her hair;
Love does on both her lips for ever stray;
And sows and reaps a thousand kisses there.
In all her outward parts Love's always seen;
But, oh, he never went within.
[*The Mistress: or ... Love Verses* (1647), 'The Change']

2. The world's a scene of changes, and to be
Constant, in Nature were inconstancy.
[*The Mistress: or ... Love Verses* (1647), 'Inconstancy']

3. Lukewarmness I account a sin
As great in love as in religion.
[*The Mistress: or ... Love Verses* (1647), 'The Request']

4. Well then; I now do plainly see
This busy world and I shall ne'er agree;
The very honey of all earthly joy
Does of all meats the soonest cloy,
And they (methinks) deserve my pity,
Who for it can endure the stings,
The crowd, and buzz, and murmurings
Of this great hive, the city...

5. Ah, yet, e'er I descend to th' grave
May I a small house, and a large garden have!
And a few friends, and many books, both true,
Both wise, and both delightful too!
And since Love ne'er will from me flee,
A Mistress moderately fair,
And good as guardian angels are,
Only belov'd, and loving me!
[*The Mistress: or ... Love Verses* (1647), 'The Wish']

6. The thirsty earth soaks up the rain,
And drinks, and gapes for drink again.
The plants suck in the earth, and are
With constant drinking fresh and fair...

7. Fill all the glasses there, for why
Should every creature drink but I,
Why man of morals, tell me why?
['Drinking' (1656)]

8. His faith perhaps in some nice tenets might
Be wrong; his life, I'm sure, was always in the right...

9. Poet and Saint! to thee alone are given
The two most sacred names of earth and Heaven.
['On the Death of Mr Crashaw' (1656)]

10. Life is an incurable disease.
['To Dr Scarborough' (1656)]

11. God the first garden made, and the first city Cain.
[*Essays in Verse and Prose* (1668), 'The Garden'. Cf. Cowper: 59]

12. Hence, ye profane; I hate ye all;
Both the great vulgar, and the small.
[*Essays in Verse and Prose* (1668), 'Of Greatness'; translated from Horace, III, ode 1]

13. This only grant me, that my means may lie
Too low for envy, for contempt too high...

14. Acquaintance I would have, but when't depends
Not on the number, but the choice of friends.
[*Essays in Verse and Prose* (1668), 'Of Myself']

Cowley, Hannah (1743–1809)
English comic dramatist and sentimental poet

1. But what is woman?–only one of Nature's agreeable blunders.
[*Who's the Dupe?* (1779), II]

2. Five minutes! Zounds! I have been five minutes too late all my life-time.
[*The Belle's Stratagem* (1780), I.i]

3. Vanity, like murder, will out.
[*The Belle's Stratagem* (1780), I.iv]

Cowper, William (1731–1800)
English poet; hymn and letter-writer

1. No dancing bear was so genteel,
Or half so dégagé.
['Of Himself' (1752)]

2. Oh! for a closer walk with God,
A calm and heav'nly frame;
A light to shine upon the road
That leads me to the Lamb!...

3. What peaceful hours I once enjoyed!
How sweet their memory still!
But they have left an aching void,
The world can never fill.
[*Olney Hymns* (1779), 1]

4. My God, till I received thy stroke,
How like a beast was I!
So unaccustomed to the yoke,
So backward to comply.
[*Olney Hymns* (1779), 12]

5. There is a fountain fill'd with blood
Drawn from Emmanuel's veins,
And sinners, plunged beneath that flood,
Lose all their guilty stains.
[*Olney Hymns* (1779), 15]

6. Hark, my soul! it is the Lord;
'Tis thy Saviour, hear his word;
Jesus speaks, and speaks to thee;
'Say, poor sinner, lov'st thou me?'...

7. Can a woman's tender care
Cease towards the child she bare?
Yes, she may forgetful be,
Yet will I remember thee.
[*Olney Hymns* (1779), 18]

8. Prayer makes the Christian's armour bright;
And Satan trembles when he sees
The weakest saint upon his knees.
[*Olney Hymns* (1779), 29]

9. I seem forsaken and alone,
I hear the lion roar;
And every door is shut but one,
And that is Mercy's door.
[*Olney Hymns* (1779), 33]

10. Judge not the Lord by feeble sense,
But trust him for his grace;
Behind a frowning providence
He hides a smiling face...

11. The bud may have a bitter taste,
But sweet will be the flower...

12. God moves in a mysterious way
His wonders to perform;
He plants his footsteps in the sea,
And rides upon the storm...

13. Blind unbelief is sure to err,
And scan his work in vain;
God is his own interpreter,
And he will make it plain.
[*Olney Hymns* (1779), 35]

14. Sometimes a light surprises
The Christian while he sings;
It is the Lord who rises
With healing in His wings.
[*Olney Hymns* (1779), 49]

15. Toll for the brave–
The brave! that are no more:
All sunk beneath the wave,
Fast by their native shore...

16. A land-breeze shook the shrouds,
And she was overset;
Down went the Royal George,
With all her crew complete...

17. His sword was in the sheath,
His fingers held the pen,
When Kempenfelt went down
With twice four hundred men.
['On the Loss of the Royal George' (1782)]

18. Oh, fond attempt to give a deathless lot
To names ignoble, born to be forgot!...

19. There goes the parson, oh! illustrious spark,
And there, scarce less illustrious, goes the clerk!
['On Observing Some Names of Little Note Recorded in the Biographia Britannica' (1782)]

20. He has no hope who never had a fear.
['Truth' (1782)]

21. Grief is itself a med'cine...

22. [Of a burglar]
He found it inconvenient to be poor.
['Charity' (1782)]

23. A fool must now and then be right, by chance.
['Conversation' (1782), line 96]

24. Contradiction for its own dear sake.
['Conversation' (1782), line 106]

25. A noisy man is always in the right.
['Conversation' (1782), line 114]

26. A tale should be judicious, clear, succinct;
The language plain, and incidents well link'd;
Tell not as new what ev'ry body knows;
And, new or old, still hasten to a close.
['Conversation' (1782), line 235]

27. The pipe, with solemn interposing puff,
Makes half a sentence at a time enough;
The dozing sages drop the drowsy strain,
Then pause, and puff – and speak, and pause again.
['Conversation' (1782), line 245]

28. Pernicious weed! whose scent the fair annoys,
Unfriendly to society's chief joys,
Thy worst effect is banishing for hours
The sex whose presence civilizes ours.
['Conversation' (1782), line 251]

29. His wit invites you by his looks to come,
But when you knock it is never at home.
['Conversation' (1782), line 303]

30. War lays a burden on the reeling state,
And peace does nothing to relieve the weight.
['Expostulation' (1782)]

31. Men deal with life as children with their play,
Who first misuse, then cast their toys away...

32. And diff'ring judgments serve but to declare
That truth lies somewhere, if we knew but where.
['Hope' (1782)]

33. Unmiss'd but by his dogs and by his groom.
['The Progress of Error' (1782), line 95]

34. Remorse, the fatal egg by pleasure laid.
['The Progress of Error' (1782), line 239]

35. As creeping ivy clings to wood or stone,
And hides the ruin that it feeds upon.
['The Progress of Error' (1782), line 285]

36. How much a dunce that has been sent to roam
Excels a dunce that has been kept at home.
['The Progress of Error' (1782), line 415]

37. Judgment drunk, and brib'd to lose his way,
Winks hard, and talks of darkness at noon-day.
['The Progress of Error' (1782), line 450]

38. Thou god of our idolatry, the press...
Thou fountain, at which drink the good and wise;
Thou ever-bubbling spring of endless lies;
Like Eden's dread probationary tree,
Knowledge of good and evil is from thee.
['The Progress of Error' (1782), line 461]

39. He likes the country, but in truth must own,
Most likes it, but he studies it in town...

40. Absence of occupation is not rest,
A mind quite vacant is a mind distress'd...

41. Beggars invention and makes fancy lame...

42. I praise the Frenchman, his remark was shrewd–
How sweet, how passing sweet, is solitude!
But grant me still a friend in my retreat,
Whom I may whisper – solitude is sweet.
['Retirement' (1782)]

43. The lie that flatters I abhor the most.
[*Table Talk* (1782), 88]

44. Freedom has a thousand charms to show,
That slaves, howe'er contented, never know.
[*Table Talk* (1782), 260]

45. [Of Pope]
But he (his musical finesse was such,
So nice his ear, so delicate his touch)
Made poetry a mere mechanic art;
And ev'ry warbler has his tune by heart.
[*Table Talk* (1782), 654]

46. I am a monarch of all I survey,
My right there is none to dispute;
From the centre all round to the sea
I am lord of the fowl and the brute.
Oh, solitude! where are the charms
That sages have seen in thy face?
Better dwell in the midst of alarms,
Than reign in this horrible place.
['Verses Supposed to be Written by Alexander Selkirk' (1782)]

47. The poplars are felled, farewell to the shade,
And the whispering sound of the cool colonnade!
['The Poplar Field' (1784)]

48. John Gilpin was a citizen
Of credit and renown,
A train-band captain eke was he
Of famous London town.
['John Gilpin' (1785), 1]

49. To-morrow is our wedding-day,
And we will then repair
Unto the Bell at Edmonton,
All in a chaise and pair.
['John Gilpin' (1785), 3]

50. My sister and my sister's child,
Myself and children three,
Will fill the chaise; so you must ride
On horseback after we.
['John Gilpin' (1785), 4]

51. O'erjoyed was he to find
That, though on pleasure she was bent,
She had a frugal mind.
['John Gilpin' (1785), 8]

52. Smack went the whip, round went the wheels,
Were never folk so glad;
The stones did rattle underneath,
As if Cheapside were mad.
['John Gilpin' (1785), 11]

53. So down he came; for loss of time,
Although it griev'd him sore,
Yet loss of pence, full well he knew,
Would trouble him much more.
['John Gilpin' (1785), 14]

54. The dogs did bark, the children screamed,
Up flew the windows all;
And every soul bawled out, Well done!
As loud as he could bawl.
['John Gilpin' (1785), 28]

55. My hat and wig will soon be here,
They are upon the road.
['John Gilpin' (1785), 44]

56. Says John, It is my wedding-day,
And all the world would stare,
If wife should dine at Edmonton,
And I should dine at Ware.
['John Gilpin' (1785), 49]

57. Nor stopp'd till where he had got up
He did again get down.
['John Gilpin' (1785), 62]

58. Now let us sing, Long live the king,
And Gilpin, long live he;
And when he next doth ride abroad,
May I be there to see!
['John Gilpin' (1785), 63]

59. God made the country, and man made the town.
[*The Task* (1785), I, 'The Sofa'. Cf. Cowley: 11]

60. Oh for a lodge in some vast wilderness,
Some boundless contiguity of shade,
Where rumour of oppression and deceit,
Of unsuccessful or successful war,
Might never reach me more!
[*The Task* (1785), II, 'The Timepiece']

61. England, with all thy faults, I love thee still–
My country!
[*The Task* (1785), II, 'The Timepiece']

62. I would not yet exchange thy sullen skies,
And fields without a flow'r, for warmer France
With all her vines.
[*The Task* (1785), II, 'The Timepiece']

63. There is a pleasure in poetic pains
Which only poets know.
[*The Task* (1785), II, 'The Timepiece']

64. Variety's the very spice of life,
That gives all its flavour.
[*The Task* (1785), II, 'The Timepiece']

65. Domestic happiness, thou only bliss
Of Paradise that has surviv'd the fall!
[*The Task* (1785), III, 'The Garden']

66. I was a stricken deer, that left the herd
Long since.
[*The Task* (1785), III, 'The Garden']

67. From reveries so airy, from the toil
Of dropping buckets into empty wells,
And growing old in drawing nothing up!
[*The Task* (1785), III, 'The Garden']

68. Riches have wings, and grandeur is a dream.
[*The Task* (1785), III, 'The Garden']

69. [Of hunting]
Detested sport,
That owes its pleasures to another's pain.
[*The Task* (1785), III, 'The Garden']

70. To combat may be glorious, and success
Perhaps may crown us; but to fly is safe.
[*The Task* (1785), III, 'The Garden']

71. How various his employments, whom the world
Calls idle.
[*The Task* (1785), III, 'The Garden']

72. Now stir the fire, and close the shutters fast,
Let fall the curtains, wheel the sofa round,
And, while the bubbling and loud-hissing urn
Throws up a steamy column, and the cups,
That cheer but not inebriate, wait on each,
So let us welcome peaceful ev'ning in.
[*The Task* (1785), IV, 'The Winter Evening']

73. I crown thee king of intimate delights,
Fire-side enjoyments, home-born happiness.
[*The Task* (1785), IV, 'The Winter Evening']

74. A Roman meal;...
a radish and an egg.
[*The Task* (1785), IV, 'The Winter Evening']

75. Shaggy, and lean, and shrewd, with pointed ears
And tail cropp'd short, half lurcher and half cur.
[*The Task* (1785), V, 'The Winter Morning Walk']

76. Great princes have great playthings.
[*The Task* (1785), V, 'The Winter Morning Walk']

77. And the first smith was the first murd'rer's son.
[*The Task* (1785), V, 'The Winter Morning Walk']

78. There is in souls a sympathy with sounds;
And, as the mind is pitched the ear is pleased
With melting airs, or martial, brisk, or grave:
Some chord in unison with what we hear
Is touched within us, and the heart replies.
[*The Task* (1785), VI, 'The Winter Walk at Noon']

79. Knowledge dwells
In heads replete with thoughts of other men;
Wisdom in minds attentive to their own.
[*The Task* (1785), VI, 'The Winter Walk at Noon']

80. Knowledge is proud that he has learn'd so much;
Wisdom is humble that he knows no more.
[*The Task* (1785), VI, 'The Winter Walk at Noon']

81. Books are not seldom talismans and spells.
[*The Task* (1785), VI, 'The Winter Walk at Noon']

82. Nature is but a name for an effect,
Whose cause is God.
[*The Task* (1785), VI, 'The Winter Walk at Noon']

83. A cheap but wholesome salad from the brook.
[*The Task* (1785), VI, 'The Winter Walk at Noon']

84. I would not enter on my list of friends
(Tho' grac'd with polish'd manners and fine sense,
Yet wanting sensibility) the man
Who needlessly sets foot upon a worm.
[*The Task* (1785), VI, 'The Winter Walk at Noon']

85. Stillest streams
Oft water fairest meadows, and the bird
That flutters least is longest on the wing.
[*The Task* (1785), VI, 'The Winter Walk at Noon']

86. Absence from whom we love is worse than death.
['Hope, like the Short-lived Ray' (1791)]

87. For 'tis a truth well known to most,
That whatsoever thing is lost–
We seek it, ere it come to light,
In every cranny but the right.
['The Retired Cat' (1791)]

88. I shall not ask Jean Jacques Rousseau,
If birds confabulate or no.
['Pairing Time Anticipated' (1795)]

89. Oh that those lips had language! Life has pass'd
With me but roughly since I heard thee last.
Those lips are thine – thy own sweet smiles I see,
The same that oft in childhood solac'd me...

90. Thy morning bounties ere I left my home,
The biscuit, or confectionary plum...

91. Perhaps a frail memorial, but sincere,
Not scorn'd in heav'n, though little notic'd here.
['On the Receipt of My Mother's Picture out of Norfolk' (1798)]

92. But misery still delights to trace
Its semblance in another's case...

93. We perished, each alone:
But I beneath a rougher sea,
And whelmed in deeper gulfs than he.
['The Castaway' (1799)]

94. [On Johnson's inadequate treatment of *Paradise Lost*]
Oh! I could thresh his old jacket till I made his pension jingle in his pockets.
[*Letters and Prose Writings of William Cowper*, Letter to the Rev. W. Unwin, 1779]

95. Our severest winter, commonly called the spring.
[*Letters and Prose Writings of William Cowper*, Letter to the Rev. W. Unwin, 1783]

96. He kissed likewise the maid in the kitchen, and seemed upon the whole a most loving, kissing, kind-hearted gentleman.
[*Letters and Prose Writings of William Cowper*, To the Rev. J. Newton, 1784]

Crabbe, George (1754–1832)

English narrative poet; clergyman, surgeon and botanist

1. Lo! the poor toper whose untutor'd sense,
Sees bliss in ale, and can with wine dispense;
Whose head proud fancy never taught to steer,
Beyond the muddy ecstasies of beer.
[*Inebriety* (1774)]

2. Lo! where the heath, with withering brake grown o'er,
Lends the light turf that warms the neighbouring poor;
From thence a length of burning sand appears,
Where the thin harvest waves its wither'd ears;
Rank weeds, that every art and care defy,
Reign o'er the land, and rob the blighted rye:
There thistles stretch their prickly arms afar,
And to the ragged infant threaten war;
There poppies, nodding, mock the hope of toil;
There the blue bugloss paints the sterile soil;
Hardy and high, above the slender sheaf,
The slimy mallow waves her silky leaf;
O'er the young shoot the charlock throws a shade,
And clasping tares cling round the sickly blade...

3. And the cold charities of man to man...

4. A potent quack, long versed in human ills,
Who first insults the victim whom he kills;
Whose murd'rous hand a drowsy Bench protect,
And whose most tender mercy is neglect.
[*The Village* (1783), I]

5. The murmuring poor, who will not fast in peace...

6. A master-passion is the love of news.
[*The Newspaper* (1785)]

7. Our farmers round, well pleased with constant gain,
Like other farmers, flourish and complain.
[*The Parish Register* (1807), 'Baptisms']

8. This, books can do – nor this alone: they give
New views to life, and teach us how to live;
They soothe the grieved, the stubborn they chastise;
Fools they admonish, and confirm the wise,
Their aid they yield to all: they never shun
The man of sorrow, nor the wretch undone;
Unlike the hard, the selfish, and the proud,
They fly not from the suppliant crowd;
Nor tell to various people various things,
But show to subjects, what they show to kings.
[*The Library* (1808), line 41]

9. With awe around these silent walks I tread:
These are the lasting mansions of the dead.
[*The Library* (1808), line 105]

10. Lo! all in silence, all in order stand,
And mighty folios first, a lordly band,
Then quartos, their well-order'd ranks maintain,
And light octavos fill a spacious plain;
See yonder, ranged in more frequented rows,
A humbler band of duodecimos.
[*The Library* (1808), line 128]

11. Coldly profane, and impiously gay.
[*The Library* (1808), line 167]

12. Books cannot always please, however good;
Minds are not ever craving for their food.
[*The Borough* (1810), 'Schools']

13. What is a church? – Our honest sexton tells,
'Tis a tall building, with a tower and bells.
[*The Borough* (1810), 'The Church']

14. Intrigues half-gather'd, conversation-scraps,
Kitchen-cabals, and nursery-mishaps...

15. Habit with him was all the test of truth,
'It must be right: I've done it from my youth.'
[*The Borough* (1810), 'The Vicar']

16. There anchoring, Peter chose from man to hide,
There hang his head, and view the lazy tide
In its hot slimy channel slowly glide;
Where the small eels that left the deeper way
For the warm shore, where the shallows play;
Where gaping mussels, left upon the mud
Slope their slow passage to the fallen flood;–
Here dull and hopeless he'd lie down and trace
How side-long crabs had scrawl'd their crooked race;
Or sadly listen to the tuneless cry
Of fishing gull or clanging golden-eye;
What time the sea-birds to the marsh would come,
And the loud bittern, from the bull-rush home,
Gave from the salt-ditch side the bellowing boom.
[*The Borough* (1810), 'Peter Grimes']

17. That all was wrong because not all was right.
[*Tales* (1812), 'The Convert']

18. Who often reads, will sometimes wish to write.
[*Tales* (1812), 'Edward Shore']

19. The wife was pretty, trifling, childish, weak;
She could not think, but would not cease to speak.
[*Tales* (1812), 'Struggle of Conscience']

20. But 'twas a maxim he had often tried,
That right was right, and there he would abide.
[*Tales* (1812), 'The Squire and the Priest']

21. The ring so worn, as you behold,
So thin, so pale, is yet of gold.
['His Mother's Wedding Ring' (1813)]

22. He tried the luxury of doing good.
[*Tales of the Hall* (1819), 'Boys at School']

23. 'The game,' he said, 'is never lost till won.'
[*Tales of the Hall* (1819), 'Gretna Green']

24. The face the index of a feeling mind.
[*Tales of the Hall* (1819), 'Lady Barbara']

25. Secrets with girls, like loaded guns with boys,
Are never valued till they make a noise.
[*Tales of the Hall* (1819), 'The Maid's Story']

26. Love warps the mind a little from the right.
[*Tales of the Hall* (1819), 'Smugglers and Poachers']

27. It is the soul that sees; the outward eyes
Present the object, but the mind descries.
[*The Lover's Journey*, 'Poems II']

Cradock, Johnny
Husband and helper of television cook, Fanny

1. And I hope all your doughnuts turn out like Fanny's.
[Attr.]

Craig, Sir Gordon (1872–1966)
English actor, artist and stage designer; son of Dame Ellen Terry

1. Farce is the essential theatre. Farce refined becomes high comedy: farce brutalized becomes tragedy.
[Attr.]

Craig, Maurice James (1919–)

1. Red bricks in the suburbs, white horse on the wall,
Eyetalian marbles in the City Hall;
O stranger from England, who stand so aghast?
May the Lord in his mercy be kind to Belfast.
['Ballad to a traditional Refrain']

Crane, Hart (1899–1932)
American poet

1. Invariably when wine redeems the sight,
Narrowing the mustard scansions of the eyes,
A leopard ranging always in the brow
Asserts a vision in the slumbering gaze.
[*White Buildings: Poems by Hart Crane* (1926), 'The Wine Menagerie']

2. O Sleepless as the river under thee,
Vaulting the sea, the prairies' dreaming sod,
Unto us lowliest sometime sweep, descend
And of the curveship lend a myth to God.
['To Brooklyn Bridge' (1930)]

Crane, Stephen (1871–1900)
American realist novelist, short-story writer and poet

1. The Red Badge of Courage.
[Title of novel, 1895]

Cranmer, Thomas (1489–1556)
English martyr; first Protestant Archbishop of Canterbury 1533–56; responsible for the Book of Common Prayer

1. [Said at the stake, 1556]
This is the hand that wrote it and therefore it shall suffer first punishment.
[In J.R. Green, *A Short History of the English People* (1874)]

Crashaw, Richard (c. 1612–1649)
English religious poet

1. *Nympha pudica Deum vidit, et erubuit.*
The modest water nymph saw her God, and blushed.
[*Epigrammata Sacra* (1634), 'Aquae in Vinum Versae']

2. I would be married, but I'd have no wife,
I would be married to a single life.
['On Marriage' (1646)]

3. Lo here a little volume, but large book...

4. It is love's great artillery
Which here contracts itself and comes to lie
Close couch'd in your white bosom.
['Prayer ... prefixed to a little Prayer-book' (1646)]

5. All is Caesar's; and what odds
So long as Caesar's self is God's?
[*Steps to the Temple* (1646), 'Mark 12']

6. To these, Whom Death again did wed,
This Grave's the second Marriage-Bed...
Peace, good Reader, doe not weepe;
Peace, the Lovers are asleepe:
They (sweet Turtles) folded lye,
In the last knot that love could tye.
[*Steps to the Temple* (1646), 'An Epitaph upon Husband and Wife, which died, and were buried together']

7. Who'er she be,
That not impossible she
That shall command my heart and me;

Where'er she lie,
Lock'd up from mortal eye,
In shady leaves of destiny...

8. A face made up,
Out of no other shop
Than what nature's white hand sets ope...

9. A Cheek where grows
More than a Morning Rose:
Which to no Box his being owes.

Lips, where all Day
A lover's kiss may play,
Yet carry nothing thence away.
['Wishes to His Supposed Mistress' (1646)]

10. Love's passives are his activ'st part.
The wounded is the wounding heart...

11. By all the eagle in thee, all the dove.
['The Flaming Heart upon the Book of Saint Teresa' (1652)]

12. Poor World (said I) what wilt thou do
To entertain this starry stranger?
Is this the best thou canst bestow?
A cold, and not too cleanly, manger?
Contend, ye powers of heav'n and earth
To fit a bed for this huge birth...

13. Welcome, all wonders in one sight!
Eternity shut in a span.
['Hymn of the Nativity' (1652)]

14. Love, thou art absolute sole Lord
Of life and death.
['Hymn to the Name and Honour of the Admirable St Teresa' (1652)]

15. Two walking baths; two weeping motions;
Portable, and compendious oceans.
['Saint Mary Magdalene, or The Weeper' (1652)]

16. And when life's sweet fable ends,
Soul and body part like friends;
No quarrels, murmurs, no delay;
A kiss, a sigh, and so away.
['Temperance' (1652)]

Crawford, Julia (fl. 1835)

1. Kathleen Mavourneen! the grey dawn is breaking,
The horn of the hunter is heard on the hill;
The lark from her light wing the bright dew is shaking;
Kathleen Mavourneen! what, slumbering still?
Oh! hast thou forgotten how soon we must sever?
Oh! hast thou forgotten this day we must part?
It may be for years, and it may be for ever,
Oh! why art thou silent, thou voice of my heart.
['Kathleen Mavourneen' (1835)]

Creighton, Mandell (1843–1901)
English historian, biographer and Bishop of London

1. No people do so much harm as those who go about doing good.
[In *The Life and Letters of Mandell Creighton* (1904)]

Crewe, Sir Ranulphe (1558–1646)
English judge

1. And yet time hath his revolution; there must be a period and an end to all temporal things, finis rerum, an end of names and dignities and whatsoever is terrene; and why not of De Vere? Where is Bohun, where's Mowbray, where's Mortimer? Nay, which is more and most of all, where is Plantagenet? They are entombed in the urns and sepulchres of mortality. And yet let the name and dignity of De Vere stand so long as it pleaseth God.
[Speech, 1625]

Crick, Francis (1916–)
British biologist

1. [On the discovery of the structure of DNA, 1953]
We have discovered the secret of life!
[In J.D. Watson, *The Double Helix* (1968)]

Crisp, Quentin (1908–)
English writer, publicist and model

1. The young always have the same problem – how to rebel and conform at the same time. They have now solved this by defying their parents and copying one another.
[*The Naked Civil Servant* (1968)]

2. Keeping up with the Joneses was a full-time job with my mother and father. It was not until many years later when I lived alone that I realized how much cheaper it was to drag the Joneses down to my level.
[*The Naked Civil Servant* (1968)]

3. There was no need to do any housework at all. After the first four years the dirt doesn't get any worse.
[*The Naked Civil Servant* (1968)]

4. Tears were to me what glass beads are to African traders.
[*The Naked Civil Servant* (1968)]

5. Vice is its own reward.
[*The Naked Civil Servant* (1968)]

6. I became one of the stately homos of England.
[*The Naked Civil Servant* (1968)]

7. I don't hold with abroad and think that foreigners speak English when our backs are turned.
[*The Naked Civil Servant* (1968)]

8. If any reader of this book is in the grip of some habit of which he is deeply ashamed, I advise him not to give way to it in secret but to do it on television. No-one will pass him with averted gaze on the other side of the street. People will cross the road at the risk of losing their own lives in order to say 'We saw you on the telly'.
[*How to Become a Virgin*]

9. It may be true that preoccupation with time has been the downfall of Western man, but it can also be argued that conjecture about eternity is a waste of time.
[In Guy Kettlehack (ed.), *The Wit and Wisdom of Quentin Crisp*]

10. I expect that rape and murder, either separately or mixed together, fill the fantasies of most men and all stylists. They are the supreme acts of ascendancy over others; they yield the only moments when a man is certain beyond all doubt that his message has been received. Of the few who live out these dreams, some preface rape with murder so as to avoid embracing a partner who might criticize their technique.
[In Guy Kettlehack (ed.), *The Wit and Wisdom of Quentin Crisp*]

Critchley, Julian (1930–)
English writer, broadcaster, journalist and Conservative MP

1. The only safe pleasure for a parliamentarian is a bag of boiled sweets.
[*The Listener*, June 1982]

Croce, Benedetto (1866–1952)
Italian philosopher, statesman and literary critic; opponent of Fascism

1. Art is ruled uniquely by the imagination.
[*Esthetic*, 1]

Croker, John Wilson (1780–1857)
Irish politician, dramatist, editor and essayist

1. [First use of the phrase 'the Conservative Party']
We now are, as we always have been, decidedly and conscientiously attached to what is called the Tory, and which might with more propriety be called the Conservative, party.
[*Quarterly Review*, 1830]

Crompton, Richmal (Richmal Crompton Lamburn) (1890–1969)
English children's writer and teacher

1. Violet Elizabeth dried her tears. She saw that they were useless and she did not believe in wasting her effects. 'All right,' she said calmly, 'I'll thcream then. I'll thcream, an' thcream, an' thcream till I'm thick.'
[*Still William* (1925)]

2. 'I don't play little girls' games,' [William] said scathingly. But Violet Elizabeth did not appear to be scathed. 'Don't you know any little girlth?' She said pityingly. 'I'll teach you little girlth gameth,' she added pleasantly. 'I don't want to,' said William. 'I don't *like* them. I don't *like* little girls' games. I don't want to know 'em.'
[*The Just William Collection* (1991), 'The Sweet Little Girl in White']

Cromwell, Oliver (1599–1658)
English general and statesman; Puritan parliamentary army leader; Lord Protector 1653

1. A few honest men are better than numbers.
[Letter to Sir William Spring, 1643]

2. Such men as had the fear of God before them and as made some conscience of what they did ... the plain russet-coated captain that knows what he fights for and loves what he knows.
[Letter to Sir William Spring, 1643]

3. I beseech you, in the bowels of Christ, think it possible you may be mistaken.
[Letter to the General Assembly of the Church of Scotland, 1650]

4. The dimensions of this mercy are above my thoughts. It is, for aught I know, a crowning mercy.
[Letter to William Lenthall, 1651]

5. The State, in choosing men to serve it, takes no notice of their opinions. If they be willing faithfully to serve it, that satisfies.
[Said before the Battle of Marston Moor, 1644]

6. You have sat too long here for any good you have been doing. Depart, I say, and let us have done with you. In the name of God, go!
[Address to the Rump Parliament, 1653]

7. Take away that fool's bauble, the mace.
[Address to the Rump Parliament, 1653]

8. Necessity hath no law. Feigned necessities, imaginary necessities, ... are the greatest cozenage that men can put upon the Providence of God, and make pretences to break known rules by.
[Speech, 1654]

9. It is not fit that you should sit here any longer! ... you shall now give place to better men.
[Speech to Parliament, 1655]

10. You have accounted yourselves happy on being environed with a great ditch from all the world beside.
[Speech to Parliament, 1658]

11. Mr Lely, I desire you would use all your skill to paint my picture freely like me, and not flatter me at all; but remark all these roughnesses, pimples, warts, and everything as you see me, otherwise I will never pay a farthing for it.
[In Horace Walpole, *Anecdotes of Painting in England* (1763)]

12. Not what they want but what is good for them.
[Attr. remark]

13. [Referring to a cheering crowd]
The people would be just as noisy if they were going to see me hanged.
[Attr.]

14. My design is to make what haste I can to be gone.
[Last words]

Cronenberg, David (1943–)
Canadian film director

1. A virus is only doing its job.
[*The Sunday Telegraph*, 1992]

Crosby, Bing (Harry Lillis Crosby) (1904–1977)
American singer and film actor

1. [Referring to fellow actor and comedian, Bob Hope]
There is nothing in the world I wouldn't do for Hope, and there is nothing he wouldn't do for me ... We spend our lives doing nothing for each other.
[*The Observer*, 'Sayings of the Week', 1950]

Cross, Richard Assheton, Viscount (1823–1914)
English Conservative statesman; Home Secretary 1874–80, 1885–86

1. [When members of the House of Lords laughed at his speech in favour of Spiritual Peers]
I hear a smile.
[In G.W.E. Russell, *Collections and Recollections* (1898)]

Crossman, Richard (1907–1974)
English politician, Labour MP and Cabinet Minister

1. [Describing his first day as a Cabinet Minister, October 1964; hence the title of the TV series, *Yes, Minister*]
Already I realize the tremendous effort it requires not to be taken over by the Civil Service. My Minister's room is like a padded cell, and in certain ways I am like a person who is suddenly certified a lunatic and put safely into this great vast room, cut off from real life ... Of course, they don't behave quite like nurses because the Civil Service is profoundly deferential – 'Yes, Minister! No, Minister! If you wish it, Minister!'
[*The Diaries of a Cabinet Minister 1964–70*, Vol. 1 (1975)]

Cumberland, Bishop Richard (1631–1718)
English philosopher, divine and translator

1. It is better to wear out than to rust out.
[In G. Horne, *The Duty of Contending for the Faith* (1786)]

cummings, e. e. (1894–1962)
American lyric poet, noted for his experimental typography, and painter

1. who knows if the moon's
a balloon, coming out of a keen city
in the sky – filled with pretty people?
[& [AND] (1925) N&: VII]

2. 'next to of course god america i
love you land of the pilgrims' and so forth oh
say can you see by the dawn's early my
country 'tis of centuries come and go
and are no more what of it we should worry
in every language even deafanddumb
thy sons acclaim your glorious name by gorry
by jingo by gee by gosh by gum
why talk of beauty what could be more beautiful than these heroic happy dead
who rushed like lions to the roaring slaughter
they did not stop to think they died instead
then shall the voice of liberty be mute?'

He spoke. And drank rapidly a glass of water.
[is 5 (1926)]

3. a politician is an arse upon
which everyone has sat except a man
[1 x 1 (1944), no. 10]

4. pity this busy monster, manunkind,
not. Progress is a comfortable disease.
[1 x 1 (1944), no. 14]

5. anyone lived in a pretty how town
(with up so floating many bells down)
spring summer autumn winter
he sang his didn't he danced his did.
[*50 Poems* (1949), no. 29]

6. a pretty girl who naked is
is worth a million statues
[*Collected Poems*, 133]

Cunard, Lady (Maud) 'Emerald' (1872–1948)
Granddaughter-in-law of Samuel Cunard, the co-founder of the Cunard Shipping Line

1. [Reply to Somerset Maugham, when he said he was leaving early 'to keep his youth']
Then why didn't you bring him with you? I should be delighted to meet him.
[In D. Fielding, *Emerald and Nancy: Lady Cunard and her Daughter* (1968)]

Cunningham, Allan (1784–1842)
Scottish poet; ballad writer, parliamentary reporter and biographer

1. It's hame and it's hame, hame fain wad I be,
O, hame, hame, hame to my ain countree!...
2. The lark shall sing me hame in my ain countree.
['It's Hame and It's Hame' (1819)]
3. Wha the deil hae we got for a King,
But a wee, wee German lairdie!
['The Wee, Wee German Lairdie' (1825)]
4. A wet sheet and a flowing sea,
A wind that follows fast
And fills the white and rustling sail
And bends the gallant mast...
5. The hollow oak our palace is,
Our heritage the sea.
['A Wet Sheet and a Flowing Sea' (1825)]

Cunningham, Peter Miller (1789–1864)
Scots-born surgeon-superintendent on convict transports

1. A young girl, when asked how she would like to go to England, replied with great naïveté, 'I should be afraid to go, from the number of thieves there,' doubtless conceiving England to be a downright hive of such, that threw off its annual swarms to people the wilds of this colony.
[*Two Years in New South Wales* (1827)]

Cuppy, Will (1884–1949)
American humorist and critic

1. The Dodo never had a chance. He seems to have been invented for the sole purpose of becoming extinct and that was all he was good for.
[*How to Become Extinct* (1941)]

Curie, Marie (1867–1934)
Polish-born French physicist; shared Nobel prize for physics for discovery of radium, 1903; for chemistry, 1911

1. After all, science is essentially international, and it is only through lack of the historical sense that national qualities have been attributed to it.
[*Memorandum*, 'Intellectual Co-operation']
2. All my life through, the new sights of Nature made me rejoice like a child.
[*Pierre Curie*]
3. [Referring to a wedding dress]
I have no dress except the one I wear every day. If you are going to be kind enough to give me one, please let it be practical and dark so that I can put it on afterwards to go to the laboratory.
[Letter to a friend, 1894]
4. One never notices what has been done; one can only see what remains to be done...
[Letter to her brother, 1894]

Curnow, Allen (1911–)
New Zealand poet and editor

1. Always to islanders danger
Is what comes over the sea...
[*Collected Poems 1933–1973* (1974), 'Landfall in Unknown Seas']
2. In your atlas two islands not in narrow seas
Like a child's kite anchored in the indifferent blue,
Two islands pointing from the Pole, upward
From the Ross Sea and the tall havenless ice:
Small trade and no triumph, men of strength
Proved at football and in wars not their own.
[*Selected Poems* (1982), 'Statement']

Curran, John Philpot (1750–1817)
Irish judge, orator, politician and reformer

1. The condition upon which God hath given liberty to man is eternal vigilance; which condition if he break, servitude is at once the consequence of his crime, and the punishment of his guilt.
[Speech concerning the election of the Lord Mayor of Dublin, 1790]
2. [Of Sir Robert Peel's smile]
...like the silver plate on a coffin.
[Quoted by Daniel O'Connell, *Hansard*, 1835]

Curtin, John (1885–1945)
Australian statesman and former Prime Minister

1. [Of R.G. Menzies]
Ah, poor Bob. It's very sad; he would rather make a point than make a friend.
[In Howard Beale, *This Inch of Time...*]

Curtiz, Michael (1888–1962)
Hungarian-born American film director

1. [Said during the filming of *The Charge of the Light Brigade*]
Bring on the empty horses!
[In David Niven, *Bring on the Empty Horses* (1975)]

Curzon, Lord (First Marquess of Kedleston) (1859–1925)
English Conservative statesman and scholar; Viceroy of India 1898–1905; Foreign Secretary 1919–24

1. I hesitate to say what the functions of the modern journalist may be; but I imagine that they do not exclude the intelligent anticipation of facts even before they occur.
[Speech, House of Commons, 1898]
2. Gentlemen do not take soup at luncheon.
[In E.L. Woodward, *Short Journey* (1942)]
3. [Referring to Stanley Baldwin on his appointment as Prime Minister]
Not even a public figure. A man of no experience. And of the utmost insignificance.
[In Harold Nicolson, *Curzon: The Last Phase*]
4. [On seeing some soldiers bathing]
I never knew the lower classes had such white skins.
[Attr.]

Cusack, Dymphna (1902–1981)
Australian novelist, dramatist and travel-writer

1. If the Spirit of the Bush walked down Martin Place it would be raped before it got ten feet.
[Remark at the Adelaide Arts Festival, March 1964]

Cuvier, Georges Léopold, Baron (1769–1832)
French comparative anatomist and politician

1. [On his deathbed when the nurse came to apply leeches]
Nurse, it was I who discovered that leeches have red blood.
[Attr.]

Cyprian, Saint (c. 200–258)
Carthaginian bishop, Father of the Church, theological writer and martyr

1. *Habere non potest Deum patrem qui ecclesiam non habet matrem.*
Who has not the Church as his mother cannot have God as his father.
[*De Unitate Ecclesiae*]

2. *Salus extra ecclesiam non est.*
There is no salvation outside the Church.
[Letter]

Cyrano de Bergerac, Savinien de (1619–1655)
French author, soldier and duellist, known for his large nose

1. *Périsse l'Univers, pourvu que je me venge.*
The universe can perish, so long as I have my revenge.
[*La Mort d'Agrippine* (1654), IV]

Dacre, Harry (d. 1922)
British songwriter

1. Daisy, Daisy, give me your answer, do!
I'm half crazy, all for the love of you!
It won't be a stylish marriage,
I can't afford a carriage,
But you'll look sweet upon the seat
Of a bicycle made for two!
['Daisy Bell', song, 1892]

Dagg, Fred (John Morrison Clarke) (1948–)
Australian writer, actor and broadcaster

1. I can see . . . why a man who lives in Colorado is so anxious for all this nuclear activity to go on in Australia, an area famed among nuclear scientists for its lack of immediate proximity to their own residential areas.
[*Dagshead Revisited* (1989)]

Dahl, Roald (1916–1990)
British short-story writer, novelist and children's author

1. Do you know what breakfast cereal is made of? It's made of all those little curly wooden shavings you find in pencil sharpeners!
[*Charlie and the Chocolate Factory* (1964), 27]

Dalai Lama (Tenzin Gyatso, the 14th Dalai Lama) (1935–)
Exiled Tibetan national and religious leader

1. The liver cannot exist without the lungs, the lungs cannot exist without the heart.
[Attr.]

Daley, Richard J. (1902–1976)

1. [To the press, concerning riots during the Democratic Convention, 1968]
Gentlemen, get the thing straight once and for all. The policeman isn't there to create disorder, the policeman is there to preserve disorder.
[Attr.]

Dali, Salvador (1904–1989)
Spanish surrealist painter and writer, also known for his religious works

1. There is only one difference between a madman and me. I am not mad.
[*The American*, July 1956]

2. I'm going to live forever. Geniuses don't die.
[*The Observer*, 1986, in Jeffrey Care (ed.), *Sayings of the Eighties* (1989)]

3. [Replying to someone who asked whether he found it hard to paint a picture]
It's either easy or impossible.
[Attr.]

D'Alpuget, (Josephine) Blanche (1944–)
Australian journalist, novelist and biographer

1. Convent girls never leave the church, they just become feminists. I learned that in Australia.
[*Turtle Beach* (1981)]

Dalton, John (1766–1844)
English chemist, natural philosopher, mathematician and meteorologist

1. [Said frequently when he was chairing scientific meetings]
This paper will no doubt be found interesting by those who take an interest in it.
[In J.J. Thomson, *Recollections and Reflections* (1890)]

D'Alton Williams, Richard (1822–1862)

1. They brought her to the city
And she faded slowly there–
Consumption has no pity
For blue eyes and golden hair.
['The Dying Girl']

Daly, Dan (1874–1937)
American marine sergeant

1. [Remark during Allied resistance at Belleau Wood, 1918]
Come on, you sons of bitches! Do you want to live for ever?
[Attr.]

Daly, Mary (1928–)

1. The liberation of language is rooted in the liberation of ourselves.
[*Beyond God The Father, Toward a Philosophy of Women's Liberation* (1973)]

2. Patriarchy is itself the prevailing religion of the entire planet, and its essential message is necrophilia.
[*Gyn/Ecology: the Metaethics of Radical Feminism* (1979)]

Damien, Father (1840–1889)
Belgian Roman Catholic missionary

1. [When asked on his deathbed whether he would leave another priest his mantle, like Elijah]
What would you do with it? It is full of leprosy.
[In H. Acton, *Memoirs of an Aesthete*]

Dana, Charles Anderson (1819–1897)
American newspaper editor and reformer

1. All the goodness of a good egg cannot make up for the badness of a bad one.
[*The Making of a Newspaper Man*]

2. When a dog bites a man that is not news, but when a man bites a dog that is news.
[*New York Sun*, 1882]

Daniel, Samuel (1562–1619)
English lyric and narrative poet, historian and dramatist; author of masques

1. Care-charmer Sleep, son of the sable Night,
Brother to Death, in silent darkness born:
Relieve my languish, and restore the light,
With dark forgetting of my care return
And let the day be time enough to mourn
The shipwreck of my ill adventured youth:
Let waking eyes suffice to wail their scorn,
Without the torment of the night's untruth.
[*Delia* (1592), Sonnet 54]

2. And who, in time, knows whither we may vent
The treasure of our tongue, to what strange shores
This gain of our best glory shall be sent,
T'enrich unknowing nations with our stores?
What worlds in th'yet unformed Occident
May come refined with th'accents that are ours?
['Musophilus' (1599)]

3. Custom that is before all law, Nature that is above all art.
['A Defence of Rhyme' (1603)]

4. But years hath done this wrong,
To make me write too much, and live too long.
[*To the Prince*, 'Philotas' (1605)]

5. Unless above himself he can
Erect himself, how poor a thing is man!
['To the Lady Margaret, Countess of Cumberland', 12]

Dante Alighieri (1265–1321)
Renowned Italian poet and political philosopher

1. *Nel mezzo del cammin di nostra vita*
Mi ritrovai per una selva oscura
Che la diritta via era smarrita.
Halfway through the journey of our life I found myself in a dark forest,
bewildered, lost and forlorn.
[*Divina Commedia* (1307), 'Inferno', Canto 1]

2. *PER ME SI VA NELLA CITTA' DOLENTE,*
PER ME SI VA NELL'ETERNO DOLORE,
PER ME SI VA TRA LA PERDUTA GENTE . . .
LASCIATE OGNI SPERANZA VOI CH'ENTRATE!
Through me one goes to the sorrowful city.
Through me one goes to eternal suffering. Through me one goes among lost people . . . Abandon all hope, you who enter!
[*Divina Commedia* (1307), 'Inferno', Canto 3]

3. *Questi non hanno speranza di morte,*
E la lor cieca vita è tanto bassa,
Che invidiosi son d'ogni altra sorte.
There is no hope of death for these souls, and their lost life is so low, that they are envious of any other kind.
[*Divina Commedia* (1307), 'Inferno', Canto 3]

4. *Non ragioniam di lor, ma guarda e passa.*
Let us not dwell on them, only look, and pass on.
[*Divina Commedia* (1307), 'Inferno', Canto 3]

5. [Of Aristotle]
Vidi il maestro di color che sanno
Seder tra filosofica famiglia.
I saw the teacher of those who know, sitting amongst the family of philosophers.
[*Divina Commedia* (1307), 'Inferno', Canto 4]

6. *Nessun maggior dolore,*
Che ricordarsi del tempo felice
Nella miseria.
No sorrow is deeper than the remembrance of happiness when in misery.
[*Divina Commedia* (1307), 'Inferno', Canto 5]

7. *Noi leggevam un giorno per diletto*
di Lancialotto, come amor lo strinse:
soli eravam, e sanza alcun sospetto.
One day we were reading and musing upon the love that constrained Lancelot: alone we were and in total innocence.
[*Divina Commedia* (1307), 'Inferno', Canto 5]

8. *Che l'arte vostra quella, quanto pote,*
Segue, come il maestro fa il discente;
Sì che vostr'arte a Dio quasi è nepote.
That your art, as far as it can, imitates nature in the way that a pupil does his master; hence your art is, as it were, God's grandchild.
[*Divina Commedia* (1307), 'Inferno', Canto 11]

9. *Onorate l'altissimo poeta.*
Honour the greatest poet.
[*Divina Commedia* (1307), 'Inferno', Canto 11]

10. [Said to the poet's friend Brunetto, whom he encountered in Hell]
Siete voi qui, ser Brunetto?
Are you here, Advocate Brunetto?
[*Divina Commedia* (1307), 'Inferno', Canto 15]

11. *Ahi fiera compagnia! ma nella chiesa*
Coi santi ed in taverna coi ghiottoni.
Ha! frightful crowd! With the saints in church and the scoundrels in taverns.
[*Divina Commedia* (1307), 'Inferno', Canto 22]

12. *Ché, seggendo in piuma,*
In fama non si vien, né sotto coltre.
For fame is not achieved by sitting on feather cushions or lying in bed.
[*Divina Commedia* (1307), 'Inferno', Canto 24]

13. *Considerate la vostra semenza:*
Fatti non foste a viver come bruti,
Ma per seguir virtute e conoscenza.
Consider your origins: you were not made to live as brutes, but to pursue virtue and knowledge.
[*Divina Commedia* (1307), 'Inferno', Canto 26]

14. *E cortesia fu lui esser villano.*
And it was an act of kindness, being rude to him.
[*Divina Commedia* (1307), 'Inferno', Canto 33]

15. *Vien dietro a me, e lascia dir le genti:*
Sta come torre ferma, che non crolla
Già mai la cima per soffiar di' venti.
Follow me and leave the world to chatter: be as steady as a tower that never bows its head, however hard the winds may blow.
[*Divina Commedia* (1307), 'Purgatorio', Canto 5]

16. *Puro e disposto a salire alle stelle.*
Cleansed and ready to ascend to the stars.
[*Divina Commedia* (1307), 'Purgatorio', Canto 33]

17. *E in la sua volontade è nostra pace.*
And in His will lies our peace.
[*Divina Commedia* (1307), 'Paradiso', Canto 3]

18. *Tu proverai sì come sa di sale*
Lo pane altrui, e com' è duro

Lo scendere e il salir per l'altrui scale.
You'll know how salty other people's bread tastes, and how hard it is to climb and descend unfamiliar stairs.
[*Divina Commedia* (1307), 'Paradiso', Canto 17]

19. *L'amor che muove il sole e l'altre stelle.*
True love that moves the sun and the universe.
[*Divina Commedia* (1307), 'Paradiso', Canto 33]

Danton, Georges (1759–1794)
French revolutionary leader; Minister of Justice (1792–94); executed

1. [Speech to the Legislative Committee of General Defence]
De l'audace, encore de l'audace, toujours de l'audace!
Boldness, more boldness, always boldness!
[*Le Moniteur*, 4 September 1792]

2. [On Louis XVI]
It's not a matter of judging him but killing him.
[In *The Guardian*, 1993]

3. [Response to formal questions during his trial in Paris, 2 April 1794]
My address will soon be Annihilation. As for my name you will find it in the Pantheon of History.
[Attr.]

4. [Remark to his executioner]
Thou wilt show my head to the people: it is worth showing.
[Attr., 1794]

Dark, Eleanor (1901–1985)
Australian novelist

1. Silence ruled this land. Out of silence mystery comes, and magic, and the delicate awareness of unreasoning things.
[*The Timeless Land* (1941), 1]

2. And that's Phyllis. Instead of being educated like a human being she has been domesticated like a cat. Her whole life was planned to that end, and she's no more to blame for the result than a goose destined to provide *pâté de foie gras* is to blame for its enlarged liver.
[*The Little Company* (1945), I, 7]

Darley, George (1795–1846)
Irish poet, mathematical writer, dramatist and art critic; uncle of Dion Boucicault

1. O blest unfabled Incense Tree,
That burns in glorious Araby.
['Nepenthe' (1835)]

2. Wash him bloodless, smooth him fair,
Stretch his limbs and sleek his hair:
Dingle-dong, the dead bells go!
Mermen swing them to and fro.
[*The Sea Bride*, 'Dirge'; also in 'Nepenthe']

Darling, Charles John, Baron (1849–1936)
English judge and Conservative politician

1. If a man stays away from his wife for seven years, the law presumes the separation to have killed him; yet according to our daily experience, it might well prolong his life.
[*Scintillae Juris* (1877)]

2. A timid question will always receive a confident answer.
[*Scintillae Juris* (1877)]

3. Much truth is spoken, that more may be concealed.
[*Scintillae Juris* (1877)]

4. Perjury is often bold and open. It is truth that is shamefaced – as, indeed, in many cases is no more than decent.
[*Scintillae Juris* (1877)]

5. The Law of England is a very strange one; it cannot compel anyone to tell the truth ... But what the Law can do is to give you seven years for not telling the truth.
[In D. Walker-Smith, *Lord Darling*, 27]

Darling, Sir James (1899–)
Australian educationalist

1. If you are going to be any good, you have got to like the little swine.
[Attr.]

Darré, Richard (1895–1953)
German Nazi Minister of Agriculture

1. [Nazi propoganda slogan promoting the concept that the people and the land are irretrievably joined, and that the survival of a nation depends on this]
Blut und Boden.
Blood and soil.
[*Neuadel aus Blut und Boden* (*New Nobility from Blood and Soil*, 1930)]

Darrow, Clarence (1857–1938)
American lawyer, reformer and writer

1. I have never killed a man, but I have read many obituaries with a lot of pleasure.
[*Medley*]

2. When I was a boy I was told that anybody could become President. I'm beginning to believe it.
[In Irving Stone, *Clarence Darrow for the Defence* (1941), 6]

3. [Remark during the trial of John Scopes in Tennessee, 1925, for teaching the theory of evolution in school]
I do not consider it an insult but rather a compliment to be called an agnostic. I do not pretend to know where many ignorant men are sure – that is all that agnosticism means.
[Attr.]

Darwin, Charles (1809–1882)
English naturalist, famous for his theory of evolution by natural selection

1. I have called this principle, by which each slight variation, if useful, is preserved, by the term of Natural Selection.
[*The Origin of Species* (1859), 3]

2. The expression often used by Mr Herbert Spencer of the Survival of the Fittest is more accurate, and is sometimes equally convenient.
[*The Origin of Species* (1859), 3]

3. We will now discuss in a little more detail the struggle for existence.
[*The Origin of Species* (1859), 3]

4. It is interesting to contemplate an entangled bank, clothed with many plants of many kinds, with birds singing on the bushes, with various insects flitting about, and with worms crawling through the damp earth, and to reflect that these elaborately constructed forms, so different from each other, and dependent upon each other in so complex a manner, have all been produced by laws acting around us ... Growth with Reproduction; Inheritance ... Variability ... a Ratio of Increase so high as to lead to a Struggle for Life, and as a consequence to Natural Selection, entailing Divergence of Character and the Extinction of less-improved forms.
[*The Origin of Species* (1859), 15]

5. The highest possible stage in moral culture is when we recognize that we ought to control our thoughts.
[*The Descent of Man* (1871), 4]

6. A hairy quadruped, furnished with a tail and pointed ears, probably arboreal in its habits.
[*The Descent of Man* (1871), 21]

7. We must, however, acknowledge, as it seems to me, that man with all his noble qualities ... still bears in his bodily frame the indelible stamp of his lowly origin.
[*The Descent of Man* (1871), conclusion]

8. I have tried lately to read Shakespeare, and found it so intolerably dull that it nauseated me.
[*Autobiography* (1877]

9. Worms do not possess any sense of hearing. They took not the least notice of the shrill notes from a metal whistle which was repeatedly sounded near them; nor did they of the deepest and loudest tones of a bassoon ... Mental Qualities. There is little to be said on this head.
[*Vegetable Mould and Earthworms* (1881)]

10. What a book a devil's chaplain might write on the clumsy, wasteful, blundering, low, and horribly cruel works of nature!
[Letter to J.D. Hooker, 1856]

11. Believing as I do that man in the distant future will be a far more perfect creature than he now is, it is an intolerable thought that he and all other sentient beings are doomed to complete annihilation after such long-continued slow progress. To those who fully admit the immortality of the human soul, the destruction of our world will not appear so dreadful.
[*Life and Letters* (1973)]

Darwin, Charles Galton (1887–1962)
English physicist; grandson of Charles Darwin

1. The evolution of the human race will not be accomplished in the ten thousand years of tame animals, but in the million years of wild animals, because man is and will always be a wild animal.
[*The Next Ten Million Years*, 4]

Darwin, Erasmus (1731–1802)
English physician, botanist and poet; grandfather of Charles Darwin

1. [Reply when asked whether he found his stammer inconvenient]
No, Sir, because I have time to think before I speak, and don't ask impertinent questions.
[In Sir Francis Darwin, *Reminiscences of My Father's Everyday Life*]

2. A fool ... is a man who never tried an experiment in his life.
[In a letter from Maria Edgeworth to Sophy Ruxton, 1792]

Daudet, Alphonse (1840–1897)
French novelist, poet, dramatist and prose writer

1. *Pour bien connaître les oranges, il faut les avoir vues chez elles, aux Iles Baléares, en Sardaigne, en Corse, en Algérie, dans l'air bleu doré, l'atmosphère tiède de la Méditerranée.*
To really know oranges one must see them in their natural setting, in the Balearic Islands, in Sardinia, in Corsica, in Algeria, in the golden blue air, the warm atmosphere of the Mediterranean.
[*Lettres de mon Moulin* (*Letters from My Mill*, 1866)]

2. *Des coups d'épée, messieurs, des coups d'épée! Mais pas de coups d'épingle!*
Strokes of the sword, gentlemen, strokes of the sword! Not pin pricks!
[*Aventures prodigieuses de Tartarin* (*The New Don Quixote*, 1872), 1]

Davenant, Charles (1656–1714)
English political economist, politician and dramatist; son of Sir William D'Avenant

1. Custom, that unwritten law,
By which the people keep even kings in awe.
[*Circe* (1677), II.iii]

D'Avenant, Sir William (1606–1668)
English poet, dramatist and theatrical manager, poet laureate (1638); father of Charles Davenant

1. In ev'ry grave make room, make room!
The world's at an end, and we come, we come.
[*The Law against Lovers* (1662). III.i]

2. I shall sleep like a top.
[*The Rivals* (1668), III]

3. Frail Life! in which, through Mists of human breath,
We grope for Truth, and make our Progress slow.
['The Christian's Reply to the Philosopher' (1673)]

4. For I must go where lazy Peace
Will hide her drowsy head;
And, for the sport of Kings, increase
The number of the Dead.
['The Soldier Going to the Field' (1673). Cf. Surtees: 3]

David, Elizabeth (1913–1992)
British cookery writer

1. Even more than long hours in the kitchen, fine meals require ingenious organization and experience which is a pleasure to acquire. A highly developed shopping sense is important, so is some knowledge of the construction of a menu with a view to the food in season, the manner of cooking, the texture and colour of the dishes to be served in relation to each other.
[*French Country Cooking* (1951)]

2. Delicious meals can, as everybody knows, be cooked with the sole aid of a blackened frying-pan over a primus stove, a camp fire, a gas-ring, or even a methylated spirit lamp.
[*French Country Cooking* (1951)]

3. To eat figs off the tree in the very early morning, when they have been barely touched by the sun, is one of the exquisite pleasures of the Mediterranean.
[*Italian Food* (1954)]

Davidson, John (1857–1909)
Scottish poet; dramatist, novelist, teacher and journalist

1. 'In shuttered rooms let others grieve,
And coffin thought in speech of lead;
I'll tie my heart upon my sleeve:
It is the Badge of Men,' he said.
['The Badge of Men' (1891)]

2. He doubted; but God said 'Even so;
Nothing is lost that's wrought with tears:
The music that you made below
Is now the music of the spheres.'
['A Ballad of Heaven' (1894)]

3. Seraphs and saints with one great voice
Welcomed the soul that knew not fear;
Amazed to find it could rejoice,
Hell raised a hoarse, half-human cheer.
['A Ballad of Hell' (1894)]

4. He cursed the canting moralist,
Who measures right and wrong.
['A Ballad of a Poet Born' (1894)]

5. 'My time is filched by toil and sleep;
My heart,' he thought, 'is clogged with dust;
My soul that flashed from out the deep,
A magic blade, begins to rust.'
['A Ballad of a Workman' (1894)]

6. A runnable stag, a kingly crop.
['A Runnable Stag' (1906)]

Davies, David (1742–1819)
Welsh divine and writer of Poor Laws

1. Though the potato is an excellent root, deserving to be brought into general use, yet it seems not likely that the use of it should ever be normal in the country.
[*The Case of the Labourers in Husbandry* (1795)]

Davies, Sir John (1569–1626)
English poet; Attorney-General for Ireland (1606–1619) and politician

1. Wit to persuade, and beauty to delight.
['Orchestra or a Poem of Dancing' (1596), 5]

2. Skill comes so slow, and life so fast doth fly,
We learn so little and forget so much.
[*Nosce Teipsum* (1599), 19]

3. I know my life's a pain and but a span,
I know my sense is mock'd in every thing;
And to conclude, I know myself a man,
Which is a proud and yet a wretched thing.
[*Nosce Teipsum* (1599), 45]

4. Wedlock indeed hath oft compared been
To public feasts where meet a public rout,
Where they that are without would fain go in
And they that are within would fain go out.
['A Contention Betwixt a Wife, a Widow, and a Maid for Precedence' (1608)]

5. Beauty's but skin deep; nay it is not so.
It floats but on the skin beneath the skin.
['A Select Second Husband, Now a Widow' (1616), 13]

Davies, Robertson (1913–)
Canadian journalist, playwright, novelist and critic

1. He turned up then, all elegance and eloquence – full of piss and vinegar like a barber's cat, to use the old expression.
[*The Lyre of Orpheus* (1988)]

2. Biography at its best is a form of fiction.
[*The Lyre of Orpheus* (1988)]

3. Better a noble lie than a miserable truth.
[In Alan Twigg, *For Openers: Conversations with Twenty-four Canadian Writers* (1981)]

4. Sex that is not an evidence of a strong human tie is just like blowing your nose; it's not a celebration of a splendid relationship.
[In J. Madison Davis (ed.), *Conversations with Robertson Davies* (1989), interview by Tom Harpur in 1974]

5. Women tell men things that men are not very likely to find out for themselves.
[In J. Madison Davis (ed.), *Conversations with Robertson Davies* (1989), interview by Terence M. Green in 1982]

6. Marriage is a framework to preserve friendship. It is valuable because it gives much more room to develop than just living together. It provides a base from which a person can work at understanding himself and another person.
[In J. Madison Davis (ed.), *Conversations with Robertson Davies* (1989), interview by John Milton Harvard in 1984]

7. No one needs a word processor if he has an efficient secretary.
[*The Toronto Star*, 1989]

Davies, Scrope Berdmore (c.1783–1852)
English conversationalist

1. Babylon in all its desolation is a sight not so awful as that of the human mind in ruins.
[Letter to Thomas Raikes, 1835]

Davies, William Henry (1871–1940)
Welsh poet, tramp and novelist

1. It was the Rainbow gave thee birth,
And left thee all her lovely hues.
[*Farewell to Poesy* (1910), 'The Kingfisher']

2. What is this life if, full of care,
We have no time to stand and stare?
[*Songs of Joy* (1911), 'Leisure']

3. Sweet Stay-at-Home, sweet Well-content...

4. I love thee for a heart that's kind–
Not for the knowledge in thy mind.
[*Foliage* (1913), 'Sweet Stay-at-Home']

5. A rainbow and a cuckoo's song
May never come together again;
May never come
This side the tomb.
[*Bird of Paradise* (1914), 'A Great Time']

6. And hear the pleasant cuckoo, loud and long–
The simple bird that thinks two notes a song.
[*Child Lovers* (1916), 'April's Charms']

Davis, Bette (1908–1989)
Leading American film actress

1. Fasten your seat belts, it's going to be a bumpy night.
[*All About Eve*, 1950; script by Joseph Mankiewicz]

2. [Of a starlet]
I see – she's the original good time that was had by all.
[In Halliwell, *Filmgoer's Book of Quotes* (1973)]

Davis, Jefferson (1808–1889)
American statesman, soldier and author; President of the Confederate States 1861–65

1. [Remark in Inaugural Address as President of Confederate States of America, 1861]
All we ask is to be let alone.
[Attr.]

Davis, Miles (1926–1991)
American jazz trumpeter and composer

1. You add to playing your instrument the running of a band and you got plenty problems.
[In Ian Carr, *Miles Davis: a Critical Biography* (1982)]

2. [On vegetarianism]
I figure if horses can eat green shit and be strong and run like motherfuckers, why shouldn't I?
[In Ian Carr, *Miles Davis: a Critical Biography* (1982)]

Davis, Sammy, Junior (1925–1990)
African-American entertainer and singer

1. Being a star has made it possible for me to get insulted in places where the average Negro could never hope to get insulted.
[*Yes I Can* (1965)]

2. [On being asked his handicap during a game of golf]
I'm a coloured, one-eyed Jew.
[Attr.]

Davis, Thomas (1814–1845)
Irish poet, patriot and newspaper editor

1. Come in the evening, or come in the morning,
Come when you're looked for, or come without warning.
['The Welcome' (1846)]

Davison, Frank Dalby (1893–1970)
Australian novelist and short story writer

1. You need a skin as thin as a cigarette paper to write a novel and the hide of an elephant to publish it.
[Letter from Marie Davison to Editor of *Meanjin*, 1982]

Davison, Sir Ronald Keith (1920–)
New Zealand lawyer and judge

1. [Giving judgement in the trial of Alain Mafart and Dominique Prieur, two French agents charged with manslaughter and wilful damage over the *Rainbow Warrior* bombing]
People who come to this country and commit terrorist activities cannot expect to have a short holiday at the expense of our government and return home as heroes.
[In Michael King, *Death of the Rainbow Warrior* (1986)]

Davy, Sir Humphry (1778–1829)
English chemist; discovered several elements and invented the Davy lamp

1. [His opinion of the art galleries in Paris]
The finest collection of frames I ever saw.
[Attr.]

Dawe, (Donald) Bruce (1930–)
Australian poet and university lecturer

1. When children are born in Victoria
they are wrapped in the club-colours, laid in beribboned cots,
having already begun a lifetime's barracking.
['Life-Cycle' (1967)]

2. Mum, you would have loved the way you went!
one moment, at a barbecue in the garden
– the next, falling out of your chair,
hamburger in one hand,
and a grandson yelling.
['Going' (1970)]

3. All day, day after day, they're bringing them home,
they're picking them up, those they can find, and bringing them home,
they're bringing them in, piled on the hulls of Grants, in trucks, in convoys,
they're zipping them up in green plastic bags,
they're tagging them now in Saigon, in the mortuary coolness,
they're giving them names, they're rolling them out of
the deep-freeze lockers – on the tarmac at Tan Son Nhut
the noble jets are whining like hounds,
they are bringing them home...

telegrams tremble like leaves from a wintering tree
and the spider grief swings in his bitter geometry
–they're bringing them home, now, too late, too early.
['Homecoming' (1971)]

Dawson of Penn, Viscount (1864–1945)
Physician-in-ordinary to King George V and Queen Mary

1. [On his patient, George V, who was dying]
The King's life is moving peacefully towards its close.
[Medical bulletin, 20 January 1936]

Day, Clarence Shepard (1874–1935)
American essayist and humorist

1. Imagine the Lord talking French! Aside from a few odd words in Hebrew, I took it completely for granted that God had never spoken anything but the most dignified English.
[*Life with Father* (1935), 'Father interferes']

2. 'If you don't go to other men's funerals,' he told Father stiffly, 'they won't go to yours.'
[*Life with Father* (1935), 'Father plans']

Day Lewis, C. (1904–1972)
Irish-born British poet, critic and author of detective fiction; poet laureate from 1968

1. Those Himalayas of the mind
Are not so easily possessed:
There's more than precipice and storm
Between you and your Everest.
[*Transitional Poem* (1924), 'Those Himalayas of the Mind']

2. Tempt me no more; for I
Have known the lightning's hour,
The poet's inward pride,
The certainty of power.
[*The Magnetic Mountain* (1933), Part 3]

3. I sang as one
Who on a tilting deck sings
To keep men's courage up, though the wave hangs
That shall cut off their sun.
['The Conflict' (1935)]

4. Now the peak of summer's past, the sky is overcast
And the love we swore would last for an age seems deceit.
['Hornpipe' (1943)]

5. It is the logic of our times,
No subject for immortal verse–
That we who lived by honest dreams
Defend the bad against the worse.
['Where are the War Poets?' (1943)]

6. Now we lament one
Who danced on a plume of words,
Sang with a fountain's panache,
Dazzled like slate roofs in sun
After rain, was flighty as birds
And alone as a mountain ash.
The ribald, inspired urchin
Leaning over the lip
Of his world, as over a rock pool
Or a lucky dip,
Found everything brilliant and virgin.
['In Memory of Dylan Thomas']

Dayan, Moshe (1915–1981)
Israeli general and politician; Minister of Defence 1967, 1969–74, and Foreign Minister 1977–79

1. [Said to Cyrus Vance during Arab-Israeli negotiations]
Whenever you accept our views we shall be in full agreement with you.
[*The Observer*, 'Sayings of the Week', 1977]

De Blank, Joost (1908–1968)
Dutch-born British churchman; Canon of Westminster from 1964

1. [Of South Africa]
Christ in this country would quite likely have been arrested under the Suppression of Communism Act.
[*The Observer*, 'Sayings of the Week', 1963]

2. I suffer from an incurable disease – colour blindness.
[Attr.]

Debray, Régis (1942–)
French journalist and writer, specialising in Marxism

1. The darkest spot in modern society is a small luminous screen.
[*Teachers, Writers, Celebrities*]

Debs, Eugene Victor (1855–1926)
American socialist, leader of the Social Democratic Party 1897–1916, and orator

1. While there is a lower class, I am in it. While there is a criminal class I am of it. While there is a soul in prison, I am not free.
[Remark made during his trial for sedition, 1918]

2. [After being pardoned by President Harding and released from prison where he was serving a sentence for sedition]
It is the government that should ask me for a pardon.
[In D. Wallechinsky, *The People's Almanac*]

Debussy, Claude (1862–1918)
French Impressionist composer and critic

1. *L'art est le plus beau des mensonges.*
Art is the most beautiful of all lies.
[*Monsieur Croche, antidilettante*]

Decatur, Stephen (1779–1820)
American naval commander

1. [Toast during a banquet to celebrate the victory over the 'barbary pirates' of Algeria, 1815]
Our country! In her intercourse with foreign nations, may she always be in the right; but our country, right or wrong.
[In Mackenzie, *Life of Decatur* (1846), 14. Cf. Chesterton: 29]

Defoe, Daniel (c. 1661–1731)
English novelist, journalist, pamphleteer and political critic

1. I was born in the year 1632, in the city of York, of a good family, though not of that country, my father being a foreigner of Bremen, who settled first at Hull.
[*The Life and Adventures of Robinson Crusoe* (1719), I]

2. He bid me observe it, and I should always find, that the calamities of life were shared among the upper and lower part of mankind; but that the middle station had the fewest disasters.
[*The Life and Adventures of Robinson Crusoe* (1719), I]

3. Robin, Robin, Robin Crusoe, poor Robin Crusoe! Where are you, Robin Crusoe? Where are you? Where have you been?
[*The Life and Adventures of Robinson Crusoe* (1719), I]

4. It happened one day, about noon, going towards my boat, I was exceedingly surprised with the print of a man's naked foot on the shore, which was very plain to be seen in the sand. I stood like one thunderstruck, or as if I had seen an apparition.
[*The Life and Adventures of Robinson Crusoe* (1719), I]

5. I takes my man Friday with me.
[*The Life and Adventures of Robinson Crusoe* (1719), I]

6. In trouble to be troubl'd
Is to have your trouble doubl'd.
[*Robinson Crusoe, The Farther Adventures* (1719)]

7. Necessity makes an honest man a knave.
[*Serious Reflections of Robinson Crusoe* (1720)]

8. The best of men cannot suspend their fate:
The good die early, and the bad die late...

9. We lov'd the doctrine for the teacher's sake.
['Character of the late Dr S. Annesley' (1697)]

10. Wherever God erects a house of prayer,
The Devil always builds a chapel there;
And 'twill be found, upon examination,
The latter has the largest congregation...

11. From this amphibious, ill-born mob began
That vain, ill-natur'd thing, an Englishman...

12. Your Roman-Saxon-Danish-Norman English.
[*The True-Born Englishman* (1701), I]

13. And of all plagues with which mankind are curst,
Ecclesiastic tyranny's the worst...

14. When kings the sword of justice first lay down,
They are no kings, though they possess the crown.
Titles are shadows, crowns are empty things,
The good of subjects is the end of kings.
[*The True-Born Englishman* (1701), II]

15. Nature has left this tincture in the blood,
That all men would be tyrants if they could.
['The Kentish Petition' (1712–1713)]

Degas, Edgar (1834–1917)
French Impressionist painter and sculptor

1. Art is vice. You don't marry it legitimately, you rape it.
[In Paul Lafond, *Degas* (1918)]

De Gaulle, Charles (1890–1970)
French statesman and general; President of France 1959–69

1. Deliberation is the work of many men. Action, of one alone.
[*War Memoirs*, Vol. 2]

2. *On ne peut rassembler les Français que sous le coup de la peur. On ne peut pas rassembler à froid un pays qui compte 265 spécialités de fromage.*
One can only unite the French under the threat of danger. One cannot simply bring together a nation that produces 265 kinds of cheese.
[Speech, 1951]

3. *Les traités, voyez-vous, sont comme les jeunes filles et comme les roses: ça dure ce que ça dure.*
You see, treaties are like young girls and roses – they last while they last.
[Speech, 1963]

4. *Vive le Québec! Vive le Québec libre!*
Long live Quebec! Long live free Quebec!
[Speech, Quebec, 1967]

5. I myself have become a Gaullist only little by little.
[*The Observer*, 'Sayings of the Year', 1963]

6. [After the death of his retarded daughter Anne]
Et maintenant elle est comme les autres.
And now she is like everyone else.
[Attr.]

7. [Replying to Jacques Soustelle's complaint that he was being attacked by his own friends]
Changez vos amis.
Change your friends.
[Attr.]

8. *Comme un homme politique ne croit jamais ce qu'il dit, il est tout étonné quand il est cru sur parole.*
Since a politician never believes what he says, he is quite surprised to be taken at his word.
[Attr.]

9. I have come to the conclusion that politics are too serious a matter to be left to the politicians.
[Attr.]

10. In order to become the master, the politician poses as the servant.
[Attr.]

11. [Explaining why he had not arrested Jean-Paul Sartre for urging French soldiers in Algeria to desert]
One does not arrest Voltaire.
[Attr.]

Dekker, Thomas (c. 1570–c. 1632)
English dramatist, and pamphleteer

1. Cold's the wind and wet's the rain,
Saint Hugh be our good speed!
Ill is the weather that bringeth no gain
Nor helps good hearts in need.

Down-a-down, hey, down-a-down
Hey derry derry down-a-down!
Ho! Well done, to me let come
Ring compass, gentle joy!
[*The Shoemaker's Holiday* (1600)]

2. Art thou poor, yet hast thou golden slumbers?
Oh sweet content!
Art thou rich, yet is thy mind perplexed?
Oh, punishment!
Dost thou laugh to see how fools are vexed
To add to golden numbers, golden numbers?
O, sweet content, O, sweet, O, sweet content!
Work apace, apace, apace, apace;
Honest labour bears a lovely face;
Then hey nonny, nonny; hey, nonny, nonny.
['Patient Grissil' (1603), I]

3. Golden slumbers kiss your eyes,
Smiles awake you when you rise:
Sleep, pretty wantons, do not cry,
And I will sing a lullaby:
Rock them, rock them, lullaby.
['Patient Grissil' (1603), IV]

4. That great fishpond (the sea).
[*The Honest Whore* (1604), I]

De La Mare, Walter (1873–1956)
English poet, novelist, anthologist and children's writer

1. I met at eve the Prince of Sleep,
His was a still and lovely face,
He wandered through a valley steep,
Lovely in a lonely place.
['I Met at Eve' (1902)]

2. What is the world, O soldiers?
It is I:
I, this incessant snow,
This northern sky;
Soldiers, this solitude
Through which we go
Is I.
['Napoleon' (1906)]

3. Oh, no man knows
Through what wild centuries
Roves back the rose...

4. Very old are we men;
Our dreams are tales
Told in dim Eden
By Eve's nightingales;
We wake and whisper awhile,
But, the day gone by,
Silence and sleep like fields
Of amaranth lie.
['All That's Past' (1912)]

5. He is crazed with the spell of far Arabia,
They have stolen his wits away.
['Arabia' (1912)]

6. 'Is there anybody there?' said the Traveller,
Knocking on the moonlit door...

7. 'Tell them I came, and no one answered,
That I kept my word,' he said...

8. Never the least stir made the listeners...

9. Ay, they heard his foot upon the stirrup,
And the sound of iron on stone,
And how the silence surged softly backward,
When the plunging hoofs were gone.
['The Listeners' (1912)]

10. Softly along the road of evening,
In a twilight dim with rose,
Wrinkled with age, and drenched with dew,
Old Nod, the shepherd, goes.
['Nod' (1912)]

11. Ann, Ann!
Come! quick as you can!
There's a fish that talks
In the frying-pan.
['Alas, Alack' (1913)]

12. In Hans' old Mill his three black cats
Watch the bins for the thieving rats.
Whisker and claw, they crouch in the night,
Their five eyes smouldering green and bright:...

Then up he climbs to his creaking mill
Out come his cats all grey with meal–
Jekkel, and Jessup, and one-eyed Jill.
['Five Eyes' (1913)]

13. Three jolly gentlemen,
In coats of red,
Rode their horses
Up to bed.
['The Huntsmen' (1913)]

14. It's a very odd thing–
As odd as can be–
That whatever Miss T eats
Turns into Miss T.
['Miss T' (1913)]

15. And there, in the moonlight, dark with dew,
Asking not wherefore nor why,
Would brood like a ghost, and as still as a post,
Old Nicholas Nye.
['Nicholas Nye' (1913)]

16. Slowly, silently, now the moon
Walks the night in her silver shoon.
['Silver' (1913)]

17. Of all the trees in England,
Oak, Elder, Elm, and Thorn,
The Yew alone burns lamps of peace
For them that lie forlorn.
['Trees' (1913)]

18. When I lie where shades of darkness
Shall no more assail mine eyes...

19. Memory fades, must the remembered
Perishing be?...

20. Look thy last on all things lovely,
Every hour. Let no night
Seal thy sense in deathly slumber
Till to delight
Thou have paid thy utmost blessing;
Since that all things thou wouldst praise
Beauty took from those who loved them
In other days.
['Fare Well' (1918)]

21. Nought but vast sorrow was there–
The sweet cheat gone.
['The Ghost' (1918)]

22. Until we learn the use of living words we shall continue to be waxworks inhabited by gramophones.
[*The Observer*, 'Sayings of the Week', 1929]

23. [On being asked, as he lay seriously ill, whether he would like fruit or flowers]
Too late for fruit, too soon for flowers.
[Attr.]

Delaney, Shelagh (1939–)

English dramatist, screenwriter for film and television and short-story writer

1. Women never have young minds. They are born three thousand years old.
[*A Taste of Honey* (1959), I.ii]

Delille, Abbé Jacques (1738–1813)

French poet and translator

1. *Le sort fait les parents, le choix fait les amis.*
Relations are made by fate, friends by choice.
[*Malheur et pitié* (1803), I]

Della Femina, Jerry (1936–)

US advertising agency executive

1. Advertising is the most fun you can have with your clothes on.
[*From those wonderful folks who gave you Pearl Harbor* (1970)]

De Mille, Cecil B. (1881–1959)

American film producer and director, known for his biblical epics

1. The public is always right.
[In Colombo, *Wit and Wisdom of the Moviemakers*]

Demosthenes (c. 384–322 BC)

Athenian statesman and orator; opponent of Macedonian power

1. There is a great deal of wishful thinking in such cases; it is the easiest thing of all to deceive one's self.
[*Olynthiac*, III, section 19]

2. There is one safeguard, which is an advantage and security for all, but especially to democracies against despots. What is it? Distrust.
[*Philippics*, II, section 24]

3. I am not going to buy repentance at the cost of ten thousand drachmas.
[In Aulus Gellius, *Noctes Atticae*, I.8]

Dempsey, Jack (1895–1983)

US boxer, World Heavyweight Champion

1. Kill the other guy before he kills you.
[Motto, quoted in *The Times*, 1983]

Denham, Sir John (1615–1669)

Irish-born English poet, royalist and Surveyor-General

1. Oh, could I flow like thee, and make thy stream
My great example, as it is my theme!
Though deep yet clear, though gentle yet not dull;
Strong without rage, without o'erflowing full.
['Cooper's Hill' (1642)]

2. Such is our pride, our folly, or our fate,
That few, but such as cannot write, translate.
['To Richard Fanshaw' (1648)]

3. Youth, what man's age is like to be doth show;
We may our ends by our beginnings know.
['Of Prudence' (1668)]

Denman, Lady (Gertrude Mary Denman) (1884–1954)

1. [Supposedly Lady Denman's words at Canberra, 12 March 1913]
I name the capital of Australia, Canberra – the accent is on the Can.
[Attr.]

Denman, Lord (Thomas, First Baron Denman) (1779–1854)

English Whig politician and Lord Chief Justice 1832–50

1. Trial by jury itself, instead of being a security to persons who are accused, will be a delusion, a mockery, and a snare.
[Speech in the House of Lords, 4 September 1844]

Denning, Lord (1899–)

English judge, Master of the Rolls

1. To every subject of this land, however powerful, I would use Thomas Fuller's words over three hundred years ago, 'Be ye never so high, the law is above you.'
[High Court ruling against the Attorney-General, January 1977]

2. [His views on the difference between a diplomat and a lady]
When a diplomat says yes, he means perhaps. When he says perhaps he means no. When he says no, he is not a diplomat. When a lady says no, she means perhaps. When she says perhaps, she means yes. But when she says yes, she is no lady.
[Speech at meeting of Magistrates Association, 14 October 1982]

Dennis, C.J. (1876–1938)

Australian journalist and poet

1. The world 'as got me snouted just a treat;
Crool Forchin's dirty left 'as smote me soul;
An' all them joys o' life I 'eld so sweet
Is up the pole.
Fer, as the poit sez, me 'eart 'as got
The pip wiv yearnin' fer – I dunno wot...

2. Me name is Mud.
[*The Sentimental Bloke* (1915), 'A Spring Song']

3. 'Young codger, sun the track,' he said.
And put his hand upon my head.
I noticed, then, that his old eyes
Were very blue and very wise.
'Ay, once I was a little lad,'
He said, and seemed to grow quite sad.
I sometimes think: When I'm a man,
I'll get a good black billy-can
And hang some corks around my hat,
And lead a jolly life like that.
['The Swagman']

4. [Definition of a wowser]
An ineffably pious person who mistakes the world for a penitentiary and himself for a warder.
[In Ross McMullin, *Will Dyson*...]

Dennis, John (1657–1734)
English critic and dramatist

1. A man who could make so vile a pun would not scruple to pick a pocket.
[*The Gentleman's Magazine*, 1781]

2. [Remark at a production of *Macbeth*, which used his new technique for producing stage thunder]
See how the rascals use me! They will not let my play run and yet they steal my thunder!
[Attr.]

Dennis, Nigel (1912–1989)
English novelist, dramatist and critic

1. This man, she reasons, as she looks at her husband, is a poor fish. But he is the nearest I can get to the big one that got away.
[*Cards of Identity* (1955)]

2. But then one is always excited by descriptions of money changing hands. It's much more fundamental than sex.
[*Cards of Identity* (1955)]

Dent, Alan (1905–1978)
Scots-born author, critic and journalist

1. This is the tragedy of a man who could not make up his mind.
[Introduction to film *Hamlet*, 1948]

De Quincey, Thomas (1785–1859)
English essayist and opium addict

1. So, then, Oxford Street, stony-hearted stepmother, thou that listenest to the sighs of orphans, and drinkest the tears of children, at length I was dismissed from thee.
[*Confessions of an English Opium Eater* (1822), II]

2. It was a Sunday afternoon, wet and cheerless: and a duller spectacle this earth of ours has not to show than a rainy Sunday in London.
[*Confessions of an English Opium Eater* (1822), II, 'The Pleasures of Opium']

3. It is most absurdly said, in popular language, of any man, that he is disguised in liquor; for, on the contrary, most men are disguised by sobriety.
[*Confessions of an English Opium Eater* (1822), II, 'The Pleasures of Opium']

4. Thou hast the keys of Paradise, oh just, subtle, and mighty opium!
[*Confessions of an English Opium Eater* (1822), II, 'The Pleasures of Opium']

5. Everlasting farewells! and again, and yet again reverberated – everlasting farewells!
[*Confessions of an English Opium Eater* (1822), II, 'The Pains of Opium']

6. Better to stand ten thousand sneers than one abiding pang, such as time could not abolish, of bitter self-reproach.
[*Confessions of an English Opium Eater* (1822)]

7. The burden of the incommunicable.
[*Confessions of an English Opium Eater* (1856 edition), I]

8. Books, we are told, propose to instruct or to amuse. Indeed! ... The true antithesis to knowledge, in this case, is not pleasure, but power. All that is literature seeks to communicate power; all that is not literature, to communicate knowledge.
[*Letters to a Young Man whose Education has been Neglected* (1823)]

9. Murder Considered as One of the Fine Arts.
[Title of Essay, 1827]

10. Even imperfection itself may have its ideal or perfect state.
['Murder Considered as One of the Fine Arts' (1839 edition)]

11. If a man once indulges himself in murder, very soon he comes to think little of robbing; and from robbing he comes next to drinking and sabbath-breaking, and from that to incivility and procrastination.
['Murder Considered as One of the Fine Arts' (1839), Supplementary Papers]

12. There is first the literature of knowledge, and secondly, the literature of power.
[*Essays on the Poets* (1848), 'Pope']

Derby, Edward Stanley, Earl of (1799–1869)
English politician; Conservative Prime Minister 1852, 1858–59, 1866–68

1. When I first came into Parliament, Mr Tierney, a great Whig authority, used always to say that the duty of an Opposition was very simple – it was, to oppose everything, and propose nothing.
[Speech, House of Commons, 1841]

2. The foreign policy of the noble Earl [Russell] ... may be summed up in two short homely but expressive words: – 'meddle and muddle'.
[Speech on the Address, House of Lords, 1864]

Descartes, René (1596–1650)
French rationalist philosopher and mathematician; founder of modern philosophy

1. *Le bon sens est la chose du monde la mieux partagée, car chacun pense en être bien pourvu.*
Common sense is the best distributed thing in the world, for we all think we possess a good share of it.
[*Discours de la Méthode* (1637)]

2. *Cogito, ergo sum.*
I think, therefore I am.
[*Discours de la Méthode* (1637)]

3. *La lecture de tous les bons livres est comme une conversation avec les plus honnêtes gens des siècles passés.*
The reading of all good books is like a conversation with the finest men of past centuries.
[*Discours de la Méthode* (1637)]

4. *Repugnare ut detur vacuum sive in quo nulla plane sit res.*
It is contrary to reason to say that there is a vacuum or space in which there is absolutely nothing.
[*Principia Philosophica* (1644), II]

Deschamps, Eustache (c. 1346–c. 1406)
French lyric poet, satirist and courtier

1. *Qui pendra la sonnette au chat?*
Who will bell the cat?
[Ballade: 'Le Chat et les souris' ('The Cat and the Mice')]

Desmoulins, Camille (1760–1794)
French pamphleteer, orator and revolutionary; guillotined

1. *La clémence aussi est une mesure révolutionnaire.*
Clemency is also a revolutionary measure.
[Speech, 1793]

2. [Reply during his trial]
My age is that of the *bon Sansculotte Jésus*; an age fatal to Revolutionists.
[Attr.]

Destouches, Philippe Néricault (1680–1754)
French dramatist, author of moralizing comedies

1. *Les absents ont toujours tort.*
The absent are always in the wrong.
[*L'Obstacle Imprévu* (1717), I.vi]

Deutsch, Babette (1895–1982)
American poet, critic and translator

1. You also, laughing one,
Tosser of balls in the sun,
Will pillow your bright head
By the incurious dead.
['A Girl']

2. Old women sit, stiffly, mosaics of pain...
Their memories: a heap of tumbling stones,
Once builded stronger than a city wall.
['Old Women']

De Valera, Eamon (1882–1975)
American-born, Irish statesman, Prime Minister, and later President of Ireland

1. Whenever I wanted to know what the Irish people wanted, I had only to examine my own heart and it told me straight off what the Irish people wanted.
[*Dáil Éireann*, 6 January 1922]

2. – a land whose countryside would be bright with cosy homesteads, whose fields and villages would be joyous with the sounds of industry, with the romping of sturdy children, the contests of athletic youths and the laughter of comely maidens, whose firesides would be forums for the wisdom of serene old age.
[Radio broadcast, St Patrick's Day, 1943]

De Valois, Dame Ninette (1898–)
Irish-born British ballerina and choreographer; founder of Sadler's Wells Ballet School, 1931

1. Ladies and gentlemen, it takes more than one to make a ballet.
[*The New Yorker*]

Devlin, Bernadette (1947–)
Founder member of the Irish Republican Socialist Party and former Northern Ireland MP

1. Among the best traitors Ireland has ever had, Mother Church ranks at the very top, a massive obstacle in the path to equality and freedom.
[*The Price of My Soul*]

Devonshire, Edward William Spencer Cavendish, Tenth Duke of (1895–1950)
English politician

1. [Referring to Stanley Baldwin's attack on newspaper proprietors]
Good God, that's done it. He's lost us the tarts' vote.
[Attr.]

Devonshire, Spencer Compton Cavendish, Eighth Duke of (1833–1908)
English statesman and Liberal politician

1. I dreamt that I was making a speech in the House. I woke up, and by Jove I was!
[In W.S. Churchill, *Thought and Adventures*]

De Vries, Peter (1910–)
American novelist and humorist

1. We know the human brain is a device to keep the ears from grating on one another.
[*Comfort me with Apples* (1956), 1]

2. Gluttony is an emotional escape, a sign something is eating us.
[*Comfort me with Apples* (1956), 7]

3. I wanted to be bored to death, as good a way to go as any.
[*Comfort me with Apples* (1956), 17]

4. It is the final proof of God's omnipotence that he need not exist in order to save us.
[*The Mackerel Plaza* (1958), 1]

5. Let us hope ... that a kind of Providence will put a speedy end to the acts of God under which we have been labouring.
[*The Mackerel Plaza* (1958), 3]

6. Everybody hates me because I'm so universally liked.
[*The Vale of Laughter* (1967), 1]

7. Anyone informed that the universe is expanding and contracting in pulsations of eighty billion years has a right to ask, 'What's in it for me?'
[*The Glory of the Hummingbird* (1974), 1]

8. I write when I'm inspired, and I see to it that I'm inspired at nine o'clock every morning.
[*The Observer*, 1980, in Jeffrey Care (ed.), *Sayings of the Eighties* (1989)]

Dewar, Lord Thomas Robert (1864–1930)
Scottish director of distilleries, Conservative politician and writer

1. The road to success is filled with women pushing their husbands along.
[Epigram]

2. Lord Dewar ... made the famous epigram about there being only two classes of pedestrians in these days of reckless motor traffic – the quick, and the dead.
[In George Robey, *Looking Back on Life*, 28]

Dewey, John (1859–1952)
American educationist, pragmatist, philosopher and reformer

1. It is strange that the one thing that every person looks forward to, namely old age, is the one thing for which no preparation is made.
[Attr.]

De Wolfe, Elsie (1865–1950)

American actress and interior designer

1. [On first sighting the Acropolis]
It's beige! My color!
[In J. Smith, *Elsie de Wolfe*]

Diaghilev, Sergei (1872–1929)

Russian ballet impresario, founder of the Ballet Russe in Paris

1. [Reply after Jean Cocteau's accusation that he rarely gave praise or encouragement]
Étonne-moi.
Surprise me.
[*The Journals of Jean Cocteau* (1956), I]

Díaz, Porfirio (1830–1915)

Mexican general and statesman; President of Mexico 1877–80, 1884–1911

1. Poor Mexico, so far from God and so near to the United States!
[Attr.]

Dibdin, Charles (1745–1814)

English songwriter, known for his sea songs; dramatist, actor and composer

1. What argufies sniv'ling and piping your eye?
['Poor Jack' (1789)]

2. In every mess I finds a friend,
In every port a wife.
['Jack in his Element' (1790)]

3. Here, a sheer hulk, lies poor Tom Bowling,
The darling of our crew...

4. Faithful, below, he did his duty;
But now he's gone aloft.
['Tom Bowling' (1790)]

5. For a soldier I listed, to grow great in fame,
And be shot at for sixpence a-day.
['Charity' (1791)]

6. Did you ever hear of Captain Wattle?
He was all for love and a little for the bottle.
['Captain Wattle and Miss Roe' (1797)]

7. What argufies pride and ambition?
Soon or late death will take us in tow:
Each bullet has got its commission,
And when our time's come we must go.
['Each Bullet has its Commission']

8. Then trust me, there's nothing like drinking
So pleasant on this side the grave;
It keeps the unhappy from thinking,
And makes e'en the valiant more brave.
['Nothing like Grog']

9. But the standing toast that pleased the most
Was – The wind that blows, the ship that goes,
And the lass that loves a sailor!
['The Round Robin']

Dibdin, Thomas (1771–1841)

English songwriter, actor and dramatist; son of Charles Dibdin

1. Oh! what a snug little Island,
A right little, tight little Island!
['The Snug Little Island' (1833)]

Dickens, Charles (1812–1870)

English novelist, noted for his narrative, characterization and criticism of social evils

1. Grief never mended no broken bones, and as good people's wery scarce, what I says is, make the most on 'em.
[*Sketches by Boz* (1836), 'Gin Shops']

2. A smattering of everything, and a knowledge of nothing.
[*Sketches by Boz* (1836), 'Sentiment']

3. He had used the word in its Pickwickian sense ... he had merely considered him a humbug in a Pickwickian point of view.
[*The Pickwick Papers* (1837), 1]

4. Heads, heads ... five children – mother – tall lady, eating sandwiches – forget the arch – crash – knock – children look round – mother's head off – sandwich in her hand – no mouth to put it in – head of a family off – shocking, shocking!
[*The Pickwick Papers* (1837), 2]

5. 'I am ruminating,' said Mr Pickwick, 'on the strange mutability of human affairs.'
'Ah, I see – in at the palace door one day, out at the window the next. Philosopher, sir?'
'An observer of human nature, sir,' said Mr Pickwick.
[*The Pickwick Papers* (1837), 2]

6. Not presume to dictate, but broiled fowl and mushrooms – capital thing!
[*The Pickwick Papers* (1837), 2]

7. Kent, sir – everybody knows Kent – apples, cherries, hops, and women.
[*The Pickwick Papers* (1837), 2]

8. 'It wasn't the wine,' murmured Mr Snodgrass, in a broken voice. 'It was the salmon.'
[*The Pickwick Papers* (1837), 8]

9. I wants to make your flesh creep.
[*The Pickwick Papers* (1837), 8]

10. 'But suppose there are two mobs?' suggested Mr Snodgrass. 'Shout with the largest,' replied Mr Pickwick.
[*The Pickwick Papers* (1837), 13]

11. 'Can I unmoved see thee dying
On a log,
Expiring frog!'
[*The Pickwick Papers* (1837), 15]

12. 'Sir,' said Mr Tupman, 'you're a fellow.' 'Sir,' said Mr Pickwick, 'you're another!'
[*The Pickwick Papers* (1837), 15]

13. Tongue; well that's a wery good thing when it an't a woman's.
[*The Pickwick Papers* (1837), 19]

14. Battledore and shuttlecock's a wery good game, vhen you an't the shuttlecock and two lawyers the battledores, in which case it gets too excitin' to be pleasant.
[*The Pickwick Papers* (1837), 20]

15. Mr Weller's knowledge of London was extensive and peculiar.
[*The Pickwick Papers* (1837), 20]

16. Take example by your father, my boy, and be wery careful o' widders all your life.
[*The Pickwick Papers* (1837), 20]

17. The wictim o' connubiality, as Blue Beard's domestic chaplain said, with a tear of pity, ven he buried him.
[*The Pickwick Papers* (1837), 20]

18. Poverty and oysters always seems to go together.
[*The Pickwick Papers* (1837), 22]

19. Wery good power o' suction, Sammy . . . You'd ha' made an uncommon fine oyster, Sammy, if you'd been born in that station o' life.
[*The Pickwick Papers* (1837), 23]

20. It's over, and can't be helped, and that's one consolation, as they always says in Turkey, ven they cuts the wrong man's head off.
[*The Pickwick Papers* (1837), 23]

21. Dumb as a drum vith a hole in it, sir.
[*The Pickwick Papers* (1837), 25]

22. Wery glad to see you, indeed, and hope our acquaintance may be a long 'un, as the gen'l'm'n said to the fi' pun' note.
[*The Pickwick Papers* (1837), 25]

23. Our noble society for providing the infant negroes in the West Indies with flannel waistcoats and moral pocket-handkerchiefs.
[*The Pickwick Papers* (1837), 27]

24. Wen you're a married man, Samivel, you'll understand a good many things as you don't understand now; but vether it's worth while goin' through so much, to learn so little, as the charity-boy said ven he got to the end of the alphabet, is a matter o' taste.
[*The Pickwick Papers* (1837), 27]

25. 'Eccentricities of genius, Sam,' said Mr Pickwick.
[*The Pickwick Papers* (1837), 30]

26. Keep yourself to yourself.
[*The Pickwick Papers* (1837), 32]

27. A double glass o' the inwariable.
[*The Pickwick Papers* (1837), 33]

28. Wot's the good o' callin' a young 'ooman a Wenus or a angel, Sammy?
[*The Pickwick Papers* (1837), 33]

29. I am afeerd that werges on the poetical, Sammy.
[*The Pickwick Papers* (1837), 33]

30. 'That's rather a sudden pull up, ain't it, Sammy?' inquired Mr Weller.
'Not a bit on it,' said Sam; 'she'll vish there wos more, and that's the great art o' letter writin'.'
[*The Pickwick Papers* (1837), 33]

31. Never sign a walentine with your own name.
[*The Pickwick Papers* (1837), 33]

32. She's a swellin' wisibly before my wery eyes.
[*The Pickwick Papers* (1837), 33]

33. It's my opinion, sir, that this meeting is drunk, sir.
[*The Pickwick Papers* (1837), 33]

34. Mr Phunky, blushing into the very whites of his eyes, tried to look as if he didn't know that everybody was gazing at him: a thing which no man ever succeeded in doing yet, or, in all reasonable probability, ever will.
[*The Pickwick Papers* (1837), 34]

35. A Being, erect upon two legs, and bearing all the outward semblance of a man, and not of a monster.
[*The Pickwick Papers* (1837), 34]

36. Chops and Tomata sauce. Yours, Pickwick.
[*The Pickwick Papers* (1837), 34]

37. 'Do you spell it with a "V" or a "W"?' inquired the judge.
'That depends upon the taste and fancy of the speller, my Lord,' replied Sam.
[*The Pickwick Papers* (1837), 34]

38. Put it down a we, my Lord, put it down a we.
[*The Pickwick Papers* (1837), 34]

39. 'Little to do, and plenty to get, I suppose?' said Sergeant Buzfuz, with jocularity.
'Oh, quite enough to get, sir, as the soldier said ven they ordered him three hundred and fifty lashes,' replied Sam.
'You must not tell us what the soldier, or any other man, said, sir,' interposed the judge; 'it's not evidence.'
[*The Pickwick Papers* (1837), 34]

40. 'Yes, I have a pair of eyes,' replied Sam, 'and that's just it. If they wos a pair o' patent double million magnifyin' gas microscopes of hextra power, p'raps I might be able to see through a flight o' stairs and a deal door; but bein' only eyes, you see my wision's limited.'
[*The Pickwick Papers* (1837), 34]

41. Oh Sammy, Sammy, vy worn't there a alleybi!
[*The Pickwick Papers* (1837), 34]

42. Miss Bolo rose from the table considerably agitated, and went straight home, in a flood of tears and a sedan-chair.
[*The Pickwick Papers* (1837), 35]

43. A friendly swarry, consisting of a boiled leg of mutton with the usual trimmings.
[*The Pickwick Papers* (1837), 37]

44. 'That 'ere young lady,' replied Sam. 'She knows wot's wot, she does.'
[*The Pickwick Papers* (1837), 37]

45. As it is, I don't think I can do with anythin' under a female markis. I might keep up with a young 'ooman o' large property as hadn't a title, if she made wery fierce love to me. Not else.
[*The Pickwick Papers* (1837), 37]

46. And we know, Mr Weller – we, who are men of the world – that a good uniform must work its way with the women, sooner or later.
[*The Pickwick Papers* (1837), 37]

47. You're a amiably-disposed young man, sir, I don't think.
[*The Pickwick Papers* (1837), 38]

48. 'It would make any one go to sleep, that bedstead would, whether they wanted to or not.'
'I should think,' said Sam, . . . 'poppies was nothing to it.'
[*The Pickwick Papers* (1837), 41]

49. They don't mind it; it's a regular holiday to them – all porter and skittles.
[*The Pickwick Papers* (1837), 41]

50. The have-his-carcase, next to the perpetual motion, is vun of the blessedest things as wos ever made.
[*The Pickwick Papers* (1837), 43]

51. Anythin' for a quiet life, as the man said wen he took the sitivation at the lighthouse.
[*The Pickwick Papers* (1837), 43]

52. Which is your partickler wanity. Vich wanity do you like the flavour on best, sir?
[*The Pickwick Papers* (1837), 45]

53. 'Never . . . see . . . a dead postboy, did you?' inquired Sam . . . 'No,' rejoined Bob, 'I never did.' 'No!' rejoined Sam triumphantly. 'Nor never vill; and there's another thing that no man never see, and that's a dead donkey.'
[*The Pickwick Papers* (1837), 51]

54. 'Vell, gov'ner, ve must all come to it, one day or another.'
'So we must, Sammy,' said Mr Weller the elder.
'There's a Providence in it all,' said Sam.
'O' course there is,' replied his father with a nod of grave

approval. 'Wot 'ud become of the undertakers vithout it, Sammy?'
[*The Pickwick Papers* (1837), 52]

55. Please, sir, I want some more.
[*Oliver Twist* (1838), 2]

56. He was better known by the sobriquet of 'The artful Dodger'.
[*Oliver Twist* (1838), 8]

57. 'Hard,' replied the Dodger. 'As Nails,' added Charley Bates.
[*Oliver Twist* (1838), 9]

58. There is a passion for hunting something deeply implanted in the human breast.
[*Oliver Twist* (1838), 10]

59. He might have brought an action against his countenance for libel, and won heavy damages.
[*Oliver Twist* (1838), 11]

60. I'll eat my head.
[*Oliver Twist* (1838), 14]

61. I only know two sorts of boys. Mealy boys, and beef-faced boys.
[*Oliver Twist* (1838), 14]

62. Oh, Mrs Corney, what a prospect this opens! What a opportunity for a joining of hearts and house-keepings!
[*Oliver Twist* (1838), 27]

63. There's light enough for wot I've got to do.
[*Oliver Twist* (1838), 47]

64. 'If the law supposes that,' said Mr Bumble ... 'the law is a ass – a idiot.'
[*Oliver Twist* (1838), 51]

65. United Metropolitan Improved Hot Muffin and Crumpet Baking and Punctual Delivery Company.
[*Nicholas Nickleby* (1839), 2]

66. EDUCATION. – At Mr Wackford Squeer's Academy, Dotheboys Hall, at the delightful village of Dotheboys, near Greta Bridge in Yorkshire, Youth are boarded, clothed, booked, furnished with pocket-money, provided with all necessaries, instructed in all languages, living and dead, mathematics, orthography, geometry, astronomy, trigonometry, the use of the globes, algebra, single stick (if required), writing, arithmetic, fortification, and every other branch of classical literature. Terms, twenty guineas per annum. No extras, no vacations, and diet unparalleled.
[*Nicholas Nickleby* (1839), 3]

67. He had but one eye, and the popular prejudice runs in favour of two.
[*Nicholas Nickleby* (1839), 4]

68. Subdue your appetites, my dears, and you've conquered human natur'.
[*Nicholas Nickleby* (1839), 5]

69. C-l-e-a-n, clean, verb active, to make bright, to scour. W-i-n, win, d-e-r, der, winder, a casement. When the boy knows this out of the book, he goes and does it.
[*Nicholas Nickleby* (1839), 8]

70. When he has learnt that bottinney means a knowledge of plants, he goes and knows 'em. That's our system, Nickleby; what do you think of it?
[*Nicholas Nickleby* (1839), 8]

71. As she frequently remarked when she made any such mistake, it would all be the same a hundred years hence.
[*Nicholas Nickleby* (1839), 9]

72. There are only two styles of portrait painting, the serious and the smirk.
[*Nicholas Nickleby* (1839), 10]

73. Oh! they're too beautiful to live, much too beautiful.
[*Nicholas Nickleby* (1839), 14]

74. SIR, My pa requests me to write to you. The doctors considering it doubtful whether he will ever recuvver the use of his legs which prevents his holding a pen.
[*Nicholas Nickleby* (1839), 15]

75. I am screaming out loud all the time I write and so is my brother which takes off my attention rather, and I hope you will excuse mistakes.
[*Nicholas Nickleby* (1839), 15]

76. This is all very well, Mr Nickleby, and very proper, so far as it goes – so far as it goes, but it doesn't go far enough.
[*Nicholas Nickleby* (1839), 16]

77. We've got a private master comes to teach us at home, but we ain't proud, because ma says it's sinful.
[*Nicholas Nickleby* (1839), 16]

78. 'It's very easy to talk,' said Mrs Mantalini. 'Not so easy when one is eating a demnition egg,' replied Mr Mantalini; 'for the yolk runs down the waistcoat, and yolk of egg does not match any waistcoat but a yellow waistcoat, demmit.'
[*Nicholas Nickleby* (1839), 17]

79. What's the demd total?
[*Nicholas Nickleby* (1839), 21]

80. Language was not powerful enough to describe the infant phenomenon.
[*Nicholas Nickleby* (1839), 23]

81. 'The unities, sir, ... are a completeness – a kind of a universal dovetailedness with regard to place and time.'
[*Nicholas Nickleby* (1839), 24]

82. She's the only sylph I ever saw, who could stand upon one leg, and play the tambourine on her other knee, like a sylph.
[*Nicholas Nickleby* (1839), 25]

83. Every baby born into the world is a finer one than the last.
[*Nicholas Nickleby* (1839), 36]

84. Bring in the bottled lightning, a clean tumbler, and a corkscrew.
[*Nicholas Nickleby* (1839), 49]

85. All is gas and gaiters!
[*Nicholas Nickleby* (1839), 49]

86. My life is one demd horrid grind!
[*Nicholas Nickleby* (1839), 64]

87. He has gone to the demnition bow-wows.
[*Nicholas Nickleby* (1839), 64]

88. Something will come of this. I hope it mayn't be human gore!
[*Barnaby Rudge* (1841), 4]

89. Polly put the ket-tle on, we'll all have tea.
[*Barnaby Rudge* (1841), 17]

90. There are strings ... in the human heart that had better not be wibrated.
[*Barnaby Rudge* (1841), 22]

91. Oh, gracious, why wasn't I born old and ugly?
[*Barnaby Rudge* (1841), 70]

92. What is the odds so long as the fire of soul is kindled at the taper of conwiviality, and the wing of friendship never moults a feather!
[*The Old Curiosity Shop* (1841), 2]

93. Fan the sinking flame of hilarity with the wing of friendship; and pass the rosy wine.
[*The Old Curiosity Shop* (1841), 7]

94. Codlin's the friend, not Short.
[*The Old Curiosity Shop* (1841), 19]

95. I never nursed a dear gazelle, to glad me with its soft black eye, but when it came to know me well, and love me, it was sure to marry a market-gardener.
[*The Old Curiosity Shop* (1841), 56]

96. 'Did you ever taste beer?' 'I had a sip of it once,' said the small servant. 'Here's a state of things!' cried Mr Swiveller, raising his eyes to the ceiling. 'She never tasted it – it can't be tasted in a sip!'
[*The Old Curiosity Shop* (1841), 57]

97. It was a maxim with Foxey – our revered father, gentlemen – 'Always suspect everybody.'
[*The Old Curiosity Shop* (1841), 66]

98. 'Bah!' said Scrooge, 'Humbug!'
[*A Christmas Carol* (1843), Stave 1]

99. In came a fiddler ... and tuned like fifty stomach-aches. In came Mrs Fezziwig, one vast substantial smile.
[*A Christmas Carol* (1843), Stave 2]

100. 'God bless us every one!' said Tiny Tim.
[*A Christmas Carol* (1843), Stave 3]

101. It *was* a Turkey! He could never have stood upon his legs, that bird. He would have snapped 'em off short in a minute, like sticks of sealing-wax.
[*A Christmas Carol* (1843), Stave 5]

102. Oh let us love our occupations,
Bless the squire and his relations,
Live upon our daily rations,
And always know our proper stations.
[*The Chimes* (1844), The Second Quarter]

103. 'The name of those fabulous animals (pagan, I regret to say) who used to sing in the water, has quite escaped me.' Mr George Chuzzlewit suggested 'Swans.' 'No,' said Mr Pecksniff. 'Not swans. Very like swans, too. Thank you.' The nephew ... propounded 'Oysters.' 'No,' said Mr Pecksniff ... 'nor oysters. But by no means unlike oysters; a very excellent idea; thank you, my dear sir, very much. Wait. Sirens. Dear me! sirens, of course.'
[*Martin Chuzzlewit* (1844), 4]

104. Any man may be in good spirits and good temper when he's well drest. There ain't much credit in that.
[*Martin Chuzzlewit* (1844), 5]

105. There might be some credit in being jolly.
[*Martin Chuzzlewit* (1844), 5]

106. A highly geological home-made cake.
[*Martin Chuzzlewit* (1844), 5]

107. 'Let us be merry.' Here he took a captain's biscuit.
[*Martin Chuzzlewit* (1844), 5]

108. With affection beaming in one eye, and calculation shining out of the other.
[*Martin Chuzzlewit* (1844), 8]

109. Charity and Mercy. Not unholy names, I hope?
[*Martin Chuzzlewit* (1844), 9]

110. Let us be moral. Let us contemplate existence.
[*Martin Chuzzlewit* (1844), 9]

111. Here's the rule, for bargains. 'Do other men, for they would do you.' That's the true business precept. All others are counterfeit.
[*Martin Chuzzlewit* (1844), 11]

112. Buy an annuity cheap, and make your life interesting to yourself and everybody else that watches the speculation.
[*Martin Chuzzlewit* (1844), 18]

113. 'Mrs Harris,' I says, 'leave the bottle on the chimley-piece, and don't ask me to take none, but let me put my lips to it when I am so dispoged.'
[*Martin Chuzzlewit* (1844), 19]

114. Some people ... may be Rooshans, and others may be Prooshans; they are born so, and will please themselves. Them which is of other naturs thinks different.
[*Martin Chuzzlewit* (1844), 19]

115. Therefore I do require it, which I makes confession, to be brought reg'lar and draw'd mild.
[*Martin Chuzzlewit* (1844), 25]

116. 'She's the sort of woman now,' said Mould ... 'one would almost feel disposed to bury for nothing: and do it neatly, too!'
[*Martin Chuzzlewit* (1844), 25]

117. He'd make a lovely corpse.
[*Martin Chuzzlewit* (1844), 25]

118. 'Sairey,' says Mrs Harris, 'sech is life. Vich likeways is the hend of all things!'
[*Martin Chuzzlewit* (1844), 29]

119. We never knows wot's hidden in each other's hearts; and if we had glass winders there, we'd need keep the shetters up, some on us, I do assure you!
[*Martin Chuzzlewit* (1844), 29]

120. Our fellow-countryman is a model of a man, quite fresh from Natur's mould! ... Rough he may be. So air our Barrs. Wild he may be. So air our Buffalers.
[*Martin Chuzzlewit* (1844), 34]

121. A lane was made; and Mrs Hominy with the aristocratic stalk, the pocket handkerchief, the clasped hands, and the classical cap, came slowly up it, in a procession of one.
[*Martin Chuzzlewit* (1844), 34]

122. 'Mind and matter,' said the lady in the wig, 'glide swift into the vortex of immensity. Howls the sublime, and softly sleeps the calm Ideal, in the whispering chambers of Imagination.'
[*Martin Chuzzlewit* (1844), 34]

123. Oh Sairey, Sairey, little do we know wot lays afore us!
[*Martin Chuzzlewit* (1844), 40]

124. No, Betsey! Drink fair, wotever you do!
[*Martin Chuzzlewit* (1844), 49]

125. 'Bother Mrs Harris!' said Betsey Prig ... 'I don't believe there's no sich a person!'
[*Martin Chuzzlewit* (1844), 49]

126. But the words she spoke of Mrs Harris, lambs could not forgive. No, ... nor worms forget!
[*Martin Chuzzlewit* (1844), 49]

127. Farewell! Be the proud bride of a ducal coronet, and forget me! ... Unalterably, never yours, Augustus.
[*Martin Chuzzlewit* (1844), 54]

128. He's tough, ma'am, tough, is J.B. Tough, and devilish sly!
[*Dombey and Son* (1848), 7]

129. I want to know what it says ... The sea, Floy, what it is that it keeps on saying?
[*Dombey and Son* (1848), 8]

130. There was no light nonsense about Miss Blimber ... She was dry and sandy with working in the graves of deceased languages. None of your live languages for Miss Blimber. They must be dead – stone dead – and then Miss Blimber dug them up like a Ghoul.
[*Dombey and Son* (1848), 11]

131. As to Mr Feeder, B.A., Doctor Blimber's assistant, he was a kind of human barrel-organ, with a little list of tunes at which he was continually working, over and over again, without any variation.
[*Dombey and Son* (1848), 11]

132. What the Waves were always saying.
[*Dombey and Son* (1848), 16, chapter heading]

133. Train up a fig-tree in the way it should go, and when you are old sit under the shade on it.
[*Dombey and Son* (1848), 19]

134. Cows are my passion.
[*Dombey and Son* (1848), 21]

135. Mr Toots devoted himself to the cultivation of those gentle arts which refine and humanize existence, his chief instructor in which was an interesting character called the Game Chicken, who was always to be heard of at the bar of the Black Badger, wore a shaggy white great-coat in the warmest weather, and knocked Mr Toots about the head three times a week, for the small consideration of ten and six per visit.
[*Dombey and Son* (1848), 22]

136. 'Oh, it's of no consequence, thank 'ee,' was the invariable reply of Mr Toots; and when he had said so, he always went away very fast.
[*Dombey and Son* (1848), 22]

137. The bearings of this observation lays in the application of it.
[*Dombey and Son* (1848), 23]

138. Say, like those wicked Turks, there is no What's-his-name but Thingummy, and What-you-may-call-it is his prophet!
[*Dombey and Son* (1848), 27]

139. I positively adore Miss Dombey; – I – I am perfectly sore with loving her.
[*Dombey and Son* (1848), 32]

140. If you could see my legs when I take my boots off, you'd form some idea of what unrequited affection is.
[*Dombey and Son* (1848), 48]

141. 'I am a lone lorn creetur',' were Mrs Gummidge's words, ... 'and everythink goes contrairy with me.'
[*David Copperfield* (1850), 3]

142. 'I feel it more than other people,' said Mrs Gummidge.
[*David Copperfield* (1850), 3]

143. I'd better go into the house, and die and be a riddance!
[*David Copperfield* (1850), 3]

144. Barkis is willin'.
[*David Copperfield* (1850), 5]

145. 'There was a gentleman here yesterday,' he said, 'a stout gentleman, by the name of Topsawyer ... He came in here, ... ordered a glass of this ale – *would* order it – I told him not – drank it, and fell dead. It was too old for him. It oughtn't to be drawn; that's the fact.'
[*David Copperfield* (1850), 5]

146. I live on broken wittles – and I sleep on the coals.
[*David Copperfield* (1850), 5]

147. 'When a man says he's willin',' said Mr Barkis ... 'it's as much as to say, that man's a waitin' for a answer.'
[*David Copperfield* (1850), 8]

148. Experientia does it – as papa used to say.
[*David Copperfield* (1850), 11]

149. [Referring to Mr Micawber]
'In case anything turned up,' which was his favourite expression.
[*David Copperfield* (1850), 11]

150. I never will desert Mr Micawber.
[*David Copperfield* (1850), 12]

151. Annual income twenty pounds, annual expenditure nineteen nineteen six, result happiness. Annual income twenty pounds, annual expenditure twenty pounds ought and six, result misery.
[*David Copperfield* (1850), 12]

152. I am well aware that I am the umblest person going ... My mother is likewise a very umble person. We live in a numble abode.
[*David Copperfield* (1850), 16]

153. We are so very umble.
[*David Copperfield* (1850), 17]

154. Uriah, with his long hands slowly twining over one another, made a ghastly writhe from the waist upwards.
[*David Copperfield* (1850), 17]

155. I only ask for information.
[*David Copperfield* (1850), 20]

156. 'It was as true,' said Mr Barkis, ' as taxes is. And nothing's truer than them.'
[*David Copperfield* (1850), 21]

157. What a world of gammon and spinnage it is, though, ain't it!
[*David Copperfield* (1850), 22]

158. Ain't I volatile?
[*David Copperfield* (1850), 22]

159. I should be happy, myself, to propose two months ... but I have a partner, Mr Jorkins.
[*David Copperfield* (1850), 23]

160. Other things are all very well in their way, but give me Blood!
[*David Copperfield* (1850), 25]

161. Accidents will occur in the best-regulated families.
[*David Copperfield* (1850), 28]

162. He told me, only the other day, that it was provided for. That was Mr Micawber's expression, 'Provided for.'
[*David Copperfield* (1850), 28]

163. 'People can't die, along the coast,' said Mr Peggotty, 'except when the tide's pretty nigh out. They can't be born, unless it's pretty nigh in – not properly born, till flood. He's a going out with the tide.'
[*David Copperfield* (1850), 30]

164. Mrs Crupp had indignantly assured him that there wasn't room to swing a cat there; but, as Mr Dick justly observed to me, sitting down on the foot of the bed, nursing his leg, 'You know, Trotwood, I don't want to swing a cat. I never do swing a cat. Therefore, what does that signify to me!'
[*David Copperfield* (1850), 35]

165. It's only my child-wife!
[*David Copperfield* (1850), 44]

166. I'm Gormed – and I can't say no fairer than that!
[*David Copperfield* (1850), 63]

167. Jarndyce and Jarndyce still drags its dreary length before the Court, perennially hopeless.
[*Bleak House* (1853), 1]

168. This is a London particular ... A fog, miss.
[*Bleak House* (1853), 3]

169. I expect a judgment. Shortly.
[*Bleak House* (1853), 3]

170. Educating the natives of Borrioboola-Gha, on the left bank of the Niger.
[*Bleak House* (1853), 4]

171. The wind's in the east ... I am always conscious of an uncomfortable sensation now and then when the wind is blowing in the east.
[*Bleak House* (1853), 6]

172. I only ask to be free. The butterflies are free. Mankind will surely not deny to Harold Skimpole what it concedes to the butterflies!
[*Bleak House* (1853), 6]

173. 'Not to put too fine a point upon it' – a favourite apology for plain-speaking with Mr Snagsby.
[*Bleak House* (1853), 11]

174. He wos wery good to me, he wos!
[*Bleak House* (1853), 11]

175. He is celebrated, almost everywhere, for his Deportment.
[*Bleak House* (1853), 14]

176. Mrs Jellyby was looking far away into Africa.
[*Bleak House* (1853), 23]

177. 'It is,' says Chadband, 'the ray of rays, the sun of suns, the moon of moons, the star of stars. It is the light of Terewth.'
[*Bleak House* (1853), 25]

178. Lo, the city is barren, I have seen but an eel.
[*Bleak House* (1853), 25]

179. It's my old girl that advises. She had the head. But I never own to it before her. Discipline must be maintained.
[*Bleak House* (1853), 27]

180. 'Old girl,' says Mr Bagnet, 'give him my opinion. You know it.'
[*Bleak House* (1853), 27]

181. It is a melancholy truth that even great men have their poor relations.
[*Bleak House* (1853), 28]

182. Never have a Mission, my dear child.
[*Bleak House* (1853), 30]

183. England has been in a dreadful state for some weeks. Lord Coodle would go out, Sir Thomas Doodle wouldn't come in, and there being nobody in Great Britain (to speak of) except Coodle and Doodle, there has been no Government.
[*Bleak House* (1853), 40]

184. She's Colour-Serjeant of the Nonpareil battalion.
[*Bleak House* (1853), 52]

185. Now, what I want is, Facts. Teach these boys and girls nothing but Facts. Facts alone are wanted in life. Plant nothing else, and root out everything else ... Stick to Facts, sir!
[*Hard Times* (1854), I, 1]

186. Whatever was required to be done, the Circumlocution Office was beforehand with all the public departments in the art of perceiving – HOW NOT TO DO IT.
[*Little Dorrit* (1857), I, 10]

187. Look here. Upon my soul you mustn't come into the place saying you want to know, you know.
[*Little Dorrit* (1857), I, 10]

188. Take a little time – count five-and-twenty, Tattycoram.
[*Little Dorrit* (1857), I, 16]

189. In company with several other old ladies of both sexes.
[*Little Dorrit* (1857), I, 17]

190. It was not a bosom to repose upon, but it was a capital bosom to hang jewels upon.
[*Little Dorrit* (1857), I, 21]

191. He won't go out, even in the back-yard, when there's no linen; but when there's linen to keep the neighbours' eyes off, he'll sit there, hours. Hours he will. Says he feels as if it was groves!
[*Little Dorrit* (1857), I, 22]

192. There's milestones on the Dover road!
[*Little Dorrit* (1857), I, 23]

193. You can't make a head and brains out of a brass knob with nothing in it. You couldn't when your Uncle George was living; much less when he's dead.
[*Little Dorrit* (1857), I, 23]

194. He proposed seven times once in a hackney-coach once in a boat once in a pew once on a donkey at Tunbridge Wells and the rest on his knees.
[*Little Dorrit* (1857), I, 24]

195. I revere the memory of Mr F. as an estimable man and most indulgent husband, only necessary to mention Asparagus and it appeared or to hint at any little delicate thing to drink and it came like magic in a pint bottle it was not ecstasy but it was comfort.
[*Little Dorrit* (1857), I, 24]

196. Papa, potatoes, poultry, prunes, and prism, are all very good words for the lips: especially prunes and prism.
[*Little Dorrit* (1857), II, 5]

197. Once a gentleman, and always a gentleman.
[*Little Dorrit* (1857), II, 28]

198. It was the best of times, it was the worst of times, it was the age of wisdom, it was the age of foolishness, it was the epoch of belief, it was the epoch of incredulity, it was the season of Light, it was the season of Darkness, it was the spring of hope, it was the winter of despair, we had everything before us, we had nothing before us, we were all going direct to Heaven, we were all going direct the other way.
[*A Tale of Two Cities* (1859), I, 1]

199. I pass my whole life, miss, in turning an immense pecuniary Mangle.
[*A Tale of Two Cities* (1859), I, 4]

200. A likely thing ... If it was ever intended that I should go across salt water, do you suppose Providence would have cast my lot in an island?
[*A Tale of Two Cities* (1859), I, 4]

201. If you must go flopping yourself down, flop in favour of your husband and child, and not in opposition to 'em.
[*A Tale of Two Cities* (1859), II, 1]

202. 'I tell thee,' said madame ... 'that although it is a long time on the road, it is on the road and coming. I tell thee it never retreats, and never stops.'
[*A Tale of Two Cities* (1859), II, 16]

203. 'It is possible – that it may not come, during our lives ... We shall not see the triumph.'
'We shall have helped it,' returned madame.
[*A Tale of Two Cities* (1859), II, 16]

204. [Sydney Carton, before his execution]
It is a far, far better thing that I do, than I have ever done;

it is a far, far better rest that I go to than I have ever known.
[*A Tale of Two Cities* (1859), III, 15]

205. There's a young man hid with me, in comparison with which young man I am a Angel. That young man hears the words I speak. That young man has a secret way pecooliar to himself, of getting at a boy, and at his heart, and at his liver.
[*Great Expectations* (1861), 1]

206. Much of my unassisted self ... I struggled through the alphabet as if it had been a bramble-bush; getting considerably worried and scratched by every letter. After that, I fell among those thieves, the nine figures, who seemed every evening to do something new to disguise themselves and baffle recognition.
[*Great Expectations* (1861), 7]

207. Your sister is given to government.
[*Great Expectations* (1861), 7]

208. He calls the knaves, Jacks, this boy! ... And what coarse hands he has! And what thick boots!
[*Great Expectations* (1861), 8]

209. I had cherished a profound conviction that her bringing me up by hand, gave her no right to bring me up by jerks.
[*Great Expectations* (1861), 8]

210. On the Rampage, Pip, and off the Rampage, Pip; such is Life!
[*Great Expectations* (1861), 15]

211. Get hold of portable property.
[*Great Expectations* (1861), 24]

212. You don't object to an aged parent, I hope?
[*Great Expectations* (1861), 25]

213. 'Have you seen anything of London, yet?'
'Why, yes, Sir ... But we didn't find that it come up to its likeness in the red bills ... it is there drawd too architectooralooral.'
[*Great Expectations* (1861), 27]

214. 'Halloa! Here's a church! ... Let's go in! ... Halloa! ... Here's Miss Skiffins! Let's have a wedding.'
[*Great Expectations* (1861), 55]

215. A literary man – *with* a wooden leg.
[*Our Mutual Friend* (1865), I, 5]

216. Decline-and-Fall-Off-The-Rooshan-Empire.
[*Our Mutual Friend* (1865), I, 5]

217. 'Mrs Boffin, Wegg,' said Boffin, 'is a highflyer at Fashion.'
[*Our Mutual Friend* (1865), I, 5]

218. Professionally he declines and falls, and as a friend he drops into poetry.
[*Our Mutual Friend* (1865), I, 8]

219. Mr Podsnap settled that whatever he put behind him he put out of existence ... Mr Podsnap had even acquired a peculiar flourish of his right arm in often clearing the world of its most difficult problems, by sweeping them behind him.
[*Our Mutual Friend* (1865), I, 11]

220. The question about everything was, would it bring a blush into the cheek of a young person?
[*Our Mutual Friend* (1865), I, 11]

221. 'This Island was Blest, Sir, to the Direct Exclusion of such Other Countries as – as there may happen to be. And if we were all Englishmen present, I would say,' added Mr Podsnap ... 'that there is in the Englishman a combination of qualities, a modesty, an independence, a responsibility, a repose, combined with an absence of everything calculated to call a blush into the cheek of a young person, which one would seek in vain among the Nations of the Earth.'
[*Our Mutual Friend* (1865), I, 11]

222. He do the Police in different voices.
[*Our Mutual Friend* (1865), I, 16]

223. [Of the House of Commons]
I think ... that it is the best club in London.
[*Our Mutual Friend* (1865), II, 3]

224. I don't care whether I am a Minx, or a Sphinx.
[*Our Mutual Friend* (1865), II, 8]

225. A slap-up gal in a bang-up chariot.
[*Our Mutual Friend* (1865), II, 8]

226. Queer Street is full of lodgers just at present!
[*Our Mutual Friend* (1865), III, 1]

227. He'd be sharper than a serpent's tooth, if he wasn't as dull as ditch water.
[*Our Mutual Friend* (1865), III, 10]

228. I want to be something so much worthier than the doll in the doll's house.
[*Our Mutual Friend* (1865), IV, 5]

229. The dodgerest of the dodgers.
[*Our Mutual Friend* (1865), IV, 8]

230. Stranger, pause and ask thyself the Question, Canst thou do likewise? If not, with a blush retire.
[*Edwin Drood* (1870), 4]

231. 'Dear me,' said Mr Grewgious, peeping in, 'it's like looking down the throat of Old Time.'
[*Edwin Drood* (1870), 9]

232. I hold my inventive faculty on the stern condition that it must master my whole life, often have complete possession of me ... and sometimes for months together put everything else away from me.
[*The Letters of Charles Dickens*, I]

Dickinson, Emily (1830–1886)
American lyric poet, little known in her lifetime

1. Success is counted sweetest
By those who ne'er succeed.
To comprehend a nectar
Requires sorest need.
['Success is counted sweetest' (c. 1859)]

2. These are the days when skies resume
The old – old sophistries of June–
A blue and gold mistake.
['These are the days when Birds come back' (c. 1859)]

3. I'm Nobody! Who are you?
Are you – Nobody – Too?
Then there's a pair of us?
Don't tell! they'd advertise – you know!

How dreary – to be – Somebody!
How public – like a Frog–
To tell one's name – the livelong June–
To an admiring Bog!
['I'm Nobody! Who are you?' (c. 1861)]

4. There's a certain Slant of light,
Winter Afternoons–
That oppresses, like the Heft
Of Cathedral Tunes–

Heavenly Hurt, it gives us–
We can find no scar,

But internal difference,
Where the Meanings, are.
['There's a certain Slant of light' (c. 1861)]

5. After great pain, a formal feeling comes–
The Nerves sit ceremonious, like Tombs–
The stiff Heart questions was it He, that bore,
And Yesterday, or Centuries before?...

6. This is the Hour of Lead–
Remembered, if outlived,
As Freezing persons, recollect the Snow–
First – Chill – then Stupor – then the letting go.
['After great pain, a formal feeling comes' (c. 1862)]

7. I heard a Fly buzz – when I died...
With Blue – uncertain stumbling Buzz–
Between the light – and me–
And then the Windows failed – and then
I could not see to see.
['I heard a Fly buzz – when I died' (c. 1862)]

8. It was not Death, for I stood up,
And all the Dead, lie down–
It was not Night, for all the Bells
Put out their Tongues, for Noon.
['It was not Death, for I stood up' (c. 1862)]

9. Our journey had advanced–
Our feet were almost come
To that odd Fork in Being's Road–
Eternity – by term.
['Our Journey had Advanced' (c. 1862)]

10. The Soul selects her own Society–
Then – shuts the Door–
To her divine Majority–
Present no more...

11. I've known her – from an ample nation–
Choose One–
Then – close the Valves of her attention–
Like Stone.
['The Soul selects her own Society' (c. 1862)]

12. What Soft – Cherubic Creatures–
These Gentlewomen are–
One would as soon assault a Plush–
Or violate a Star–

Such Dimity Convictions–
A Horror so refined
Of freckled Human Nature–
Of Deity – ashamed.
['What Soft – Cherubic Creatures' (c. 1862)]

13. Because I could not stop for Death–
He kindly stopped for me–
The Carriage held but just Ourselves–
And Immortality...

14. Since then–'tis Centuries – and yet
Feels shorter than the Day
I first surmised the Horses' Heads
Were toward Eternity.
['Because I could not stop for Death' (c. 1863)]

15. Ample make this Bed–
Make this Bed with Awe–
In it wait till Judgement break
Excellent and Fair.
['Ample make this Bed' (c. 1864)]

16. This quiet Dust was Gentlemen and Ladies
And Lads and Girls–
Was laughter and ability and Sighing
And Frocks and Curls.
['This quiet Dust was Gentlemen and Ladies' (c. 1864)]

17. I never saw a Moor–
I never saw the Sea–
Yet know I how the Heather looks
And what a Billow be.
['I never saw a Moor' (c. 1865)]

18. The Bustle in a House
The Morning after Death
Is solemnest of industries
Enacted upon Earth–

The Sweeping up the Heart
And putting Love away
We shall not want to use again
Until Eternity.
['The Bustle in a House' (c. 1866)]

19. What fortitude the Soul contains,
That it can so endure
The accent of a coming Foot–
The opening of a Door.
['Elysium is as far as to' (c. 1882)]

20. There came a Wind like a Bugle–
It quivered through the Grass...

21. How much can come
And much can go,
And yet abide the World!
['There came a Wind' (c. 1883)]

22. My life closed twice before its close–
It yet remains to see
If Immortality unveil
A third event to me

So huge, so hopeless to conceive
As these that twice befell.
Parting is all we know of heaven,
And all we need of hell.
['My life closed twice before its close' (1896)]

Dickinson, John (1732–1808)
American lawyer, politician and pamphleteer

1. Then join hand in hand, brave Americans all,–
By uniting we stand, by dividing we fall.
['The Liberty Song', 1768]

2. We have counted the cost of this contest and find nothing so dreadful as voluntary slavery ... Our cause is just. Our union is complete.
['Declaration on Taking up Arms against England', 1775]

Diderot, Denis (1713–1784)
French philosopher of the Enlightenment; encyclopaedist, novelist, dramatist and satirist

1. *Voyez-vous cet oeuf. C'est avec cela qu'on renverse toutes les écoles de théologie, et tous les temples de la terre.*
See this egg. It is with this that one overturns all the schools of theology and all the temples on earth.
[*Le Rêve de d'Alembert* (1769, published 1830)]

2. *On a dit que l'amour qui ôtait l'esprit à ceux qui en avaient en donnait à ceux qui n'en avaient pas.*
They say that love takes wit away from those who have it, and gives it to those who have none.
[*Paradoxe sur le comédien* (c. 1773–1778, published 1830)]

3. [A retort which comes to mind too late]
L'esprit de l'escalier.
Staircase wit.
[*Paradoxe sur le comédien* (c. 1773–1778, published 1830)]

4. *Oh! que ce monde-ci serait une bonne comédie si l'on n'y faisait pas un rôle.*
What a fine comedy this world would be if one did not play a part in it!
[*Letters to Sophie Volland* (1716–1784)]

5. Wandering in a vast forest at night, I have only a faint light to guide me. A stranger appears and says to me: 'My friend, you should blow out your candle in order to find your way more clearly.' This stranger is a theologian.
[*Addition aux Pensées Philosophiques*]

6. Men will never be free until the last king is strangled with the entrails of the last priest.
[*Dithyrambe sur la Fête des Rois*]

Didion, Joan (1934–)
American journalist, novelist and scriptwriter

1. Certain places seem to exist mainly because someone has written about them.
[*The White Album* (1979), 'IV Sojourns: In the Islands']

Dietrich, Marlene (1901–1992)
German-born American film actress and singer

1. Once a woman has forgiven her man, she must not reheat his sins for breakfast.
[*Marlene Dietrich's ABC* (1962), 'Forgiveness']

2. A man would prefer to come home to an unmade bed and a happy woman than to a neatly made bed and an angry woman.
[*Marlene Dietrich's ABC* (1962), 'Unmade Bed']

3. The average man is more interested in a woman who is interested in him than he is in a woman – any woman – with beautiful legs.
[News item, 1954]

4. Latins are tenderly enthusiastic. In Brazil they throw flowers at you. In Argentina they throw themselves.
[*Newsweek*, 1959]

5. Most women set out to try to change a man, and when they have changed him they do not like him.
[Attr.]

Diller, Phyllis (1917–1974)
American comedian

1. Cleaning your house while your kids are growing
Is like shoveling the walk before it stops snowing.
[*Phyllis Diller's Housekeeping Hints*]

2. Never go to bed mad. Stay up and fight.
[*Phyllis Diller's Housekeeping Hints*]

Dinning, Hector W.

1. The Australian often speaks without obviously opening his lips at all, through an immobile slit, and in extreme cases through closed teeth. This probably accounts in part for his nasal inflexion; the sound has to emerge somewhere!
[*Australian Scene*]

Diodorus Siculus (c. 1st century BC)
Sicilian-born Greek historian

1. [Inscription over library door in Alexandria]
Medicine for the soul.
[*History*, I]

Diogenes (the Cynic) (c. 400–325 BC)
Greek ascetic philosopher

1. If I were running in the stadium, ought I to slacken my pace when approaching the finish? Ought I not rather to speed up?
[In Diogenes Laertius, *Lives of Eminent Philosophers*, 'Diogenes']

2. [Asked by Alexander if he wanted anything]
Yes, stand a little out of my light.
[In Diogenes Laertius, *Lives of Eminent Philosophers*, 'Diogenes']

3. I am Diogenes the Cynic (the dog) ... fawning upon those who give me anything, barking at those who refuse, and biting rascals.
[In Diogenes Laertius, *Lives of Eminent Philosophers*, 'Diogenes']

4. [Kosmopolites: origin of the word 'cosmopolitan']
I am a citizen of the world.
[In Diogenes Laertius, *Lives of Eminent Philosophers*, 'Diogenes']

5. Education is something that tempers the young and consoles the old, gives wealth to the poor and adorns the rich.
[In Diogenes Laertius, *Lives of Eminent Philosophers*, 'Diogenes']

6. [On behaving indecently in public]
'If only it were as easy,' he said, 'to banish hunger by rubbing the belly.'
[In Diogenes Laertius, *Lives of Eminent Philosophers*, 'Diogenes']

7. I do not know whether there are gods, but there ought to be.
[In Tertullian, *Ad Nationes*]

Dionysius of Halicarnassus (fl. 30–7 BC)
Greek historian of Rome; critic and rhetorician

1. History is philosophy teaching from examples.
[*Ars Rhetorica*, 11, 2]

Di Pietro, Antonio (1947–)
Italian judge; one of the founders of the operation 'Mani pulite' which unveiled corruption in the Italian political and business world

1. [Speaking of 'Mani pulite']
L'Italia si sta tirando fuori il suo dente; che ciascuno degli altri Paesi provi a cavare il suo di dente.
Italy is pulling out her own rotten tooth, let all other countries pull out their own.
[Speech in Toronto, Canada, November 1993, reported in the magazine, *EPOCA*, 1994]

Disney, Walt (1901–1966)
US film-maker and pioneer of animated films

1. All the world owes me a living.
[*The Grasshopper and the Ant*]

2. Girls bored me – they still do. I love Mickey Mouse more than any woman I've ever known.
[In W. Wagner, *You Must Remember This* (c. 1975)]

Disraeli, Benjamin (First Earl of Beaconsfield) (1804–1881)
English statesman and novelist; Conservative Prime Minister 1868, 1874–80; son of Isaac D'Israeli

1. There is moderation even in excess.
[*Vivian Grey* (1826), II, 6]

2. Experience is the child of Thought, and Thought is the child of Action. We cannot learn men from books.
[*Vivian Grey* (1826), V, 1]

3. I repeat ... that all power is a trust – that we are accountable for its exercise – that, from the people, and for the people, all springs, and all must exist.
[*Vivian Grey* (1826), VI, 7]

4. All Paradise opens! Let me die eating ortolans to the sound of soft music!
[*The Young Duke* (1831), I, 10]

5. A dark horse, which had never been thought of, and which the careless St James had never even observed in the list, rushed past the grandstand in sweeping triumph.
[*The Young Duke* (1831), II, 5]

6. 'The age of chivalry is past,' said May Dacre. 'Bores have succeeded to dragons.'
[*The Young Duke* (1831), II,5]

7. A man may speak very well in the House of Commons, and fail very completely in the House of Lords. There are two distinct styles requisite: I intend, in the course of my career, if I have time, to give a specimen of both.
[*The Young Duke* (1831), V, 6]

8. I grew intoxicated with my own eloquence.
[*Contarini Fleming* (1832), I, 7]

9. Read no history: nothing but biography, for that is life without theory.
[*Contarini Fleming* (1832), I, 23]

10. The practice of politics in the East may be defined by one word – dissimulation.
[*Contarini Fleming* (1832), V, 10]

11. What we anticipate seldom occurs; what we least expected generally happens.
[*Henrietta Temple* (1837), II, 4]

12. Time is the great physician.
[*Henrietta Temple* (1837), VI, 9]

13. The Arch-Mediocrity who presided, rather than ruled, over this Cabinet of Mediocrities.
[*Coningsby* (1844), II, 1]

14. No Government can be long secure without a formidable opposition.
[*Coningsby* (1844), II, 1]

15. Conservatism discards Prescription, shrinks from Principle, disavows Progress: having rejected all respect for antiquity, it offers no redress for the present, and makes no preparation for the future.
[*Coningsby* (1844), II, 5]

16. A sound Conservative government ... Tory men and Whig measures.
[*Coningsby* (1844), II, 6]

17. Almost everything that is great has been done by youth.
[*Coningsby* (1844), III, 1]

18. Youth is a blunder; Manhood a struggle; Old Age a regret.
[*Coningsby* (1844), III, 1]

19. It seems to me a barren thing this Conservatism – an unhappy cross-breed, the mule of politics that engenders nothing.
[*Coningsby* (1844), III, 5]

20. I have been ever of opinion that revolutions are not to be evaded.
[*Coningsby* (1844), IV, 11]

21. Man is only truly great when he acts from the passions.
[*Coningsby* (1844), IV, 13]

22. 'I rather like bad wine,' said Mr Mountchesney; 'one gets so bored with good wine.'
[*Sybil* (1845), I, 1]

23. The Egremonts had never said anything that was remembered, or done anything that could be recalled.
[*Sybil* (1845), I, 3]

24. To do nothing and get something, formed a boy's ideal of a manly career.
[*Sybil* (1845), I, 5]

25. 'Two nations; between whom there is no intercourse and no sympathy; who are as ignorant of each other's habits, thoughts, and feelings, as if they were dwellers in different zones, or inhabitants of different planets; who are formed by a different breeding, are fed by a different food, are ordered by different manners, and are not governed by the same laws.'
'You speak of–' said Egremont, hesitatingly.
'THE RICH AND THE POOR.'
[*Sybil* (1845), II, 5]

26. Little things affect little minds.
[*Sybil* (1845), III, 2]

27. Mr Kremlin himself was distinguished for ignorance, for he had only one idea, – and that was wrong.
[*Sybil* (1845), IV, 5]

28. The Youth of a Nation are the Trustees of Posterity.
[*Sybil* (1845), VI, 13]

29. That fatal drollery called a representative government.
[*Tancred* (1847), II, 13]

30. A majority is always the best repartee.
[*Tancred* (1847), II, 14]

31. All is race; there is no other truth.
[*Tancred* (1847), II, 14]

32. London is a modern Babylon.
[*Tancred* (1847), V, 5]

33. [Of the Derby]
The blue ribbon of the turf.
[*Life of Lord George Bentinck* (1852), 26]

34. Every day when he looked into the glass, and gave the last touch to his consummate toilette, he offered his grateful thanks to Providence that his family was not unworthy of him.
[*Lothair* (1870), 1]

35. 'I could have brought you some primroses, but I do not like to mix violets with anything.'
'They say primroses make a capital salad,' said Lord St Jerome.
[*Lothair* (1870), 13]

36. A Protestant, if he wants aid or advice on any matter, can only go to his solicitor.
[*Lothair* (1870), 27]

37. London; a nation, not a city.
[*Lothair* (1870), 27]

38. [A hansom]
The gondola of London.
[*Lothair* (1870), 27]

39. When a man fell into his anecdotage it was a sign for him to retire from the world.
[*Lothair* (1870), 28]

40. I have always thought that every woman should marry – and no man.
[*Lothair* (1870), 30]

41. You know who the critics are? The men who have failed in literature and art.
[*Lothair* (1870), 35]

42. 'My idea of an agreeable person,' said Hugo Bohun, 'is a person who agrees with me.'
[*Lothair* (1870), 41]

43. St Aldegonde had a taste for marriages and public executions.
[*Lothair* (1870), 88]

44. His Christianity was muscular.
[*Endymion* (1880), 14]

45. 'Sensible men are all of the same religion.' 'And pray what is that?' inquired the prince. 'Sensible men never tell.'
[*Endymion* (1880), 81]

46. The sweet simplicity of the three per cents.
[*Endymion* (1880), 91]

47. I believe they went out, like all good things, with the Stuarts.
[*Endymion* (1880), 99]

48. Between ourselves, I could floor them all. This entre nous: I was never more confident of anything than that I could carry everything before me in that House. The time will come.
[Letters, 1833]

49. In the 'Town' yesterday, I am told 'some one asked Disraeli, in offering himself for Marylebone, on what he intended to stand. 'On my head,' was the reply'.
[Letters, 1833]

50. Marriage is the greatest earthly happiness when founded on complete sympathy.
[Letter to Gladstone]

51. Though I sit down now, the time will come when you will hear me.
[Maiden Speech in the House of Commons, 1837]

52. The Continent will not suffer England to be the workshop of the world.
[Speech, 1838]

53. A starving population, an absentee aristocracy, and an alien Church, and in addition the weakest executive in the world. That is the Irish question.
[Speech, 1844]

54. A Conservative government is an organized hypocrisy.
[Speech, 1845]

55. Protection is not a principle, but an expedient.
[Speech, House of Commons, 1845]

56. He traces the steam-engine always back to the tea-kettle.
[Speech, House of Commons, 1845]

57. Justice is truth in action.
[Speech, House of Commons, 1851]

58. [Of Sir C. Wood]
He has to learn that petulance is not sarcasm, and that insolence is not invective.
[Speech, House of Commons, 1852]

59. England does not love coalitions.
[Speech, House of Commons, 1852]

60. Finality is not the language of politics.
[Speech, 1859]

61. This shows how much easier it is to be critical than to be correct.
[Speech, House of Commons, 1860]

62. He seems to think that posterity is a pack-horse, always ready to be loaded.
[Speech, House of Commons, 1862]

63. You are not going, I hope, to leave the destinies of the British Empire to prigs and pedants.
[Speech, House of Commons, 1863]

64. Never take anything for granted.
[Speech, Salthill, 1864]

65. [Addressed to Bishop Wilberforce]
Man, my Lord, is a being born to believe.
[Speech, Meeting of Society for Increasing Endowments of Small Livings in the Diocese of Oxford, 1864]

66. Party is organized opinion.
[Speech, Meeting of Society for Increasing Endowments of Small Livings in the Diocese of Oxford, 1864]

67. Is man an ape or an angel? Now I am on the side of the angels.
[Speech, Meeting of Society for Increasing Endowments of Small Livings in the Diocese of Oxford, 1864]

68. Change is inevitable. In a progressive country change is constant.
[Speech, Edinburgh, 1867]

69. I had to prepare the mind of the country, and . . . to educate our party.
[Speech, Edinburgh, 1867]

70. We have legalized confiscation, consecrated sacrilege, and condoned high treason.
[Speech, House of Commons, 1871]

71. I believe that without party Parliamentary government is impossible.
[Speech, Manchester, 1872]

72. [Of the Treasury Bench]
You behold a range of exhausted volcanoes.
[Speech, Manchester, 1872]

73. Increased means and increased leisure are the two civilizers of man.
[Speech, Manchester, 1872]

74. An author who speaks about his own books is almost as bad as a mother who talks about her own children.
[Speech at Banquet given in Glasgow on his installation as Lord Rector, 1873]

75. Upon the education of the people of this country the fate of this country depends.
[Speech, 1874]

76. Cosmopolitan critics, men who are the friends of every country save their own.
[Speech, Guildhall, 1877]

77. The hare-brained chatter of irresponsible frivolity.
[Speech, Guildhall, 1878]

78. Lord Salisbury and myself have brought you back peace – but peace, I hope, with honour.
[Speech, 1878]

79. [Of Gladstone]
A sophistical rhetorician, inebriated with the exuberance of his own verbosity.
[Speech, 1878]

80. One of the greatest of Romans, when asked what were his

politics, replied, Imperium et Libertas. This would not make a bad programme for a British Ministry.
[Speech, Mansion House, London, 1879]

81. Protection is not only dead, but damned.
[In Monypenny and Buckle, *Life of Disraeli*, III (1914), 8]

82. Pray remember, Mr Dean, no dogma, no Dean.
[In Monypenny and Buckle, *Life of Disraeli*, IV (1916), 10]

83. [Said to a fellow peer when moving on to the House of Lords]
I am dead: dead, but in the Elysian fields.
[In Monypenny and Buckle, *Life of Disraeli*, V (1920), 13]

84. Yesterday at the racket court, sitting in the gallery among strangers, the ball ... fell at my feet. I picked it up, and observing a young rifleman excessively stiff, I humbly requested him to forward its passage into the court, as I really had never thrown a ball in my life.
[Letter to his father, quoted by André Maurois in *Disraeli: A Picture of the Victorian Age* (1927)]

85. [To Queen Victoria]
Your Majesty is the head of the literary profession.
[Attr.]

86. [To constituents, 1868]
There can be no economy where there is no efficiency.
[Attr.]

87. [Remark made to Lord Esher regarding his relationship with Queen Victoria]
I never deny; I never contradict; I sometimes forget.
[Attr.]

88. [His customary reply to those who sent him unsolicited manuscripts]
Thank you for the manuscript; I shall lose no time in reading it.
[Attr.]

89. [To Matthew Arnold]
Everyone likes flattery; and when you come to Royalty you should lay it on with a trowel.
[Attr.]

90. There are three kinds of lies: lies, damned lies and statistics.
[Attr.]

91. [Speaking to Lord Palmerston]
Your dexterity seems a happy compound of the smartness of an attorney's clerk and the intrigue of a Greek of the lower empire.
[Attr.]

92. If a traveller were informed that such a man [Lord John Russell] was leader of the House of Commons, he may well begin to comprehend how the Egyptians worshipped an insect.
[Attr.]

93. Nobody is forgotten when it is convenient to remember him.
[Attr.]

94. [In answer to Gladstone's taunt that Disraeli could make a joke of any subject, including Queen Victoria]
Her Majesty is not a subject.
[Attr.]

95. When I meet a man whose name I can't remember, I give myself two minutes; then, if it is a hopeless case, I always say, And how is the old complaint?
[Attr.]

96. Never complain, never explain.
[Attr.]

97. Damn your principles! Stick to your party.
[Attr.]

98. [To Queen Victoria]
We authors, Ma'am.
[Attr.]

99. When I want to read a novel I write one.
[Attr.]

100. Next to knowing when to seize an opportunity, the most important thing in life is to know when to forego an advantage.
[Attr.]

101. [Remark made while correcting proofs of his last Parliamentary speech, 1881]
I will not go down to posterity talking bad grammar.
[Attr.]

102. [Asked if Queen Victoria should visit him during his last illness]
No, it is better not. She would only ask me to take a message to Albert.
[Attr.]

D'Israeli, Isaac (1766–1848)
English literary critic, historian and essayist; father of Benjamin Disraeli

1. There is an art of reading, as well as an art of thinking, and an art of writing.
[*Literary Character* (1795), 11]

Dix, Dorothy (Elizabeth Meriwether Gilmer) (1870–1951)
American journalist and columnist

1. It is only the women whose eyes have been washed clear with tears who get the broad vision that makes them little sisters to all the world.
[*Dorothy Dix, Her Book* (1926), Introduction]

2. I have learned to live each day as it comes, and not to borrow trouble by dreading tomorrow. It is the dark menace of the future that makes cowards of us.
[*Dorothy Dix, Her Book* (1926), Introduction]

Dix, George Eglington Alston (Dom Gregory) (1901–1952)
English Anglican Benedictine monk; historian and liturgical scholar

1. It is no accident that the symbol of a bishop is a crook, and the sign of an archbishop is a double-cross.
[Letter to *The Times*, 1977]

Dixson, Miriam Joyce (1930–)
Australian feminist writer

1. Mateship is an informal male-bonding institution involving powerful subliminal homosexuality. Indeed some of its most ardent intellectual celebrants are slowly coming to see that mateship is deeply antipathetic to women.
[*The Real Matilda...* (1976)]

Dobbs, Kildare (1923–)
Canadian journalist and travel writer

1. My country is the English language.
[In George Galt (ed.), *The Saturday Night Traveller* (1990)]

Dobrée, Bonamy (1891–1974)
English literary critic, editor and Professor of English Literature

1. It is difficult to be humble. Even if you aim at humility,

there is no guarantee that when you have attained the state you will not be proud of the feat.
[*John Wesley*]

Dobson, Henry Austin (1840–1921)
English poet, essayist and biographer

1. I intended an Ode,
And it turned to a Sonnet.
It began à la mode,
I intended an Ode;
But Rose crossed the road
In her latest new bonnet;
I intended an Ode;
And it turned to a Sonnet.
['Rose-Leaves' (1874)]

2. Time goes, you say? Ah no!
Alas, Time stays, we go.
['The Paradox of Time' (1877)]

3. The ladies of St James's!
They're painted to the eyes,
Their white it stays for ever,
Their red it never dies:
But Phyllida, my Phyllida!
Her colour comes and goes;
It trembles to a lily,–
It wavers to a rose.
['The Ladies of St James's' (1883)]

4. And where are the galleons of Spain?
['Ballad to Queen Elizabeth' (1885)]

5. Fame is a food that dead men eat,–
I have no stomach for such meat.
['Fame is a Food' (1906)]

Dobson, Rosemary de Brissac (1920–)
Australian poet, daughter of Victorian poet and critic, Austen Dobson

1. The world is young, and you must take
Your making, breaking, shaping way:
That instant when the cord was cut
Ended by brief imperial sway.

Mine only was the being shaped
In darkness and in solitude
Moving upon the tide of dream,
Unknown, yet known beatitude.

All that is done. Now every step
You take is further still from me
Along your destined path to death,
Light, darkness or eternity.
['Child of Our Time' (1965)]

2. Life gets better
As I grow older
Not giving a damn
And looking slantwise
At everyone's morning.
['Canberra Morning']

Docherty, George M. (1911–)

1. [Remark made at a meeting on April 4, 1968 in which he expressed his fears for Martin Luther King's safety. At the close of his speech he was informed of King's assassination]
This will be a long, hot summer.
[*I've Seen the Day* (1984)]

Dodd, Ken (1931–)
English comedian, singer, entertainer and actor

1. [Commenting on Freud's theory that a good joke will lead to great relief and elation]
The trouble with Freud is that he never played the Glasgow Empire Saturday night after Rangers and Celtic had both lost.
[TV interview, 1965]

Doddridge, Philip (1702–1751)
English Nonconformist minister and hymn writer

1. O God of Bethel, by whose hand
Thy people still are fed,
Who through this weary pilgrimage
Hast all our fathers led.
[Hymn, 'O God of Bethel', 1755]]

2. 'Tis done! the great transaction's done!
I am my Lord's and He is mine.
[Hymn, 1755]

Dodington, Bubb (1691–1762)
English politician, pamphleteer and poet

1. Love thy country, wish it well,
Not with too intense a care,
'Tis enough, that when it fell,
Thou its ruin didst not share.
[In Spence, *Anecdotes* (1820)]

Donatus, Aelius (fl. 4th century AD)
Roman Latin grammarian; teacher of St Jerome

1. [Donatus was a commentator on texts]
Pereant, inquit, qui ante nos nostra dixerunt.
Confound those who have made our comments before us.
[In St. Jerome, *Commentaries on Ecclesiastes*, I]

Donleavy, J.P. (1926–)
American-born Irish novelist, short-story writer and dramatist

1. I got disappointed in human nature as well and gave it up because I found it too much like my own.
[*Fairy Tales of New York* (1961)]

2. The arrival of unpaid for goods cheers the heart.
[*The Onion Eaters* (1971)]

Donne, John (1572–1631)
English metaphysical poet and divine

1. Giddy fantastic Poets of each land.
[*Satire*, no. 1 (c. 1594)]

2. On a huge hill,
Cragged, and steep, Truth stands, and he that will
Reach her, about must, and about must go;
And what the hill's suddenness resists, win so.
[*Satire*, no. 3 (c. 1594)]

3. Love built on beauty, soon as beauty dies.
[*Elegies* (c. 1595), 2, 'The Anagram']

4. Women are like the Arts, forc'd unto none,
Open to all searchers, unpriz'd if unknown.
[*Elegies* (c. 1595), 3, 'Change']

5. O, let me not serve so, as those men serve
Whom honours smokes at once fatten and starve.
[*Elegies* (c. 1595), 6, 'Oh, let me not serve so']

6. She, and comparisons are odious.
[*Elegies* (c. 1595), 8, 'The Comparison']

7. We easily know
By this these Angels from an evil sprite,

Those set our hairs, but these our flesh upright.
Licence my roving hands, and let them go,
Before, behind, between, above, below.
O my America! my new-found-land,
My kingdom, safeliest when with one man mann'd.
[*Elegies* (c. 1595), 19, 'To His Mistress Going to Bed']

8. Sir, more than kisses, letters mingle souls...

9. And seeing the snail, which everywhere doth roam,
Carrying his own house still, still is at home,
Follow (for he is easy paced) this snail,
Be thine own palace, or the world's thy gaol.
['To Sir Henry Wotton' (1597–1598)]

10. No Spring, nor Summer Beauty hath such grace,
As I have seen in one Autumnal face.
[*Elegies* (c. 1600), 9, 'The Autumnal']

11. So, if I dream I have you, I have you,
For, all our joys are but fantastical.
[*Elegies* (c. 1600), 10, 'The Dream']

12. And must she needs be false because she's fair?...

13. May Wolves tear out his heart,
Vultures his eyes,
Swine eat his bowels, and his falser tongue,
That utter'd all, be to some Raven flung.
[*Elegies* (c. 1600), 15, 'The Expostulation']

14. By our first strange and fatal interview
By all desires which thereof did ensue...

15. Nurse, O! my love is slain; I saw him go
O'er the white Alps alone; I saw him, I,
Assail'd, fight, taken, stabb'd, bleed, fall, and die.
[*Elegies* (c. 1600), 16, 'On His Mistress']

16. How happy were our Sires in ancient times,
Who held plurality of loves no crime!
[*Elegies* (c. 1600), 17, 'Variety']

17. Who ever loves, if he do not propose
The right true end of love, he's one that goes
To sea for nothing but to make him sick...

18. The straight Hellespont between
The Sestos and Abydos of her breasts.
[*Elegies* (c. 1600), 18, 'Love's Progress']

19. I sing the progress of a deathless soul,
Whom Fate, which God made, but doth not control,
Plac'd in most shapes.
['The Progress of the Soul' (1601), 1]

20. Great Destiny the Commissary of God.
['The Progress of the Soul' (1601), 4]

21. So, of a lone unhaunted place possesst,
Did this soul's second inn, built by the guest,
This living buried man, this quiet mandrake, rest.
['The Progress of the Soul' (1601), 16]

22. Nature's great masterpiece, an Elephant,
The only harmless great thing...
Still sleeping stood; vexed not his fantasy
Black dreams; like an unbent bow, carelessly,
His sinewy proboscis did remissly lie.
['The Progress of the Soul' (1601), 39]

23. She knew treachery,
Rapine, deceit, and lust, and ills enow
To be a woman.
['The Progress of the Soul' (1601), 51]

24. Cloth'd in her virgin white integrity.
['Funeral Elegy' (1610)]

25. Twice or thrice had I loved thee,
Before I knew thy face or name;
So in a voice, so in a shapeless flame,
Angels affect us oft, and worship'd be...

26. Just such disparity
As is 'twixt Air and Angels' purity,
'Twixt women's love and men's will ever be.
[*Songs and Sonnets* (1611), 'Air and Angels']

27. All other things, to their destruction draw,
Only our love hath no decay;
This, no tomorrow hath, nor yesterday,
Running it never runs from us away,
But truly keeps his first, last, everlasting day.
[*Songs and Sonnets* (1611), 'The Anniversary']

28. Come live with me, and be my love,
And we will some new pleasures prove
Of golden sands, and crystal brooks,
With silken lines, and silver hooks.
[*Songs and Sonnets* (1611), 'The Bait']

29. A naked thinking heart, that makes no show,
Is to a woman, but a kind of ghost.
[*Songs and Sonnets* (1611), 'The Blossom']

30. For Godsake hold your tongue, and let me love.
[*Songs and Sonnets* (1611), 'The Canonization']

31. Chang'd loves are but chang'd sorts of meat,
And when he hath the kernel eat,
Who doth not fling away the shell?
[*Songs and Sonnets* (1611), 'Community']

32. Dear love, for nothing less than thee
Would I have broke this happy dream,
It was a theme
For reason, much too strong for fantasy,
Therefore thou wak'd'st me wisely; yet
My dream thou brok'st not, but continued'st it.
[*Songs and Sonnets* (1611), 'The Dream']

33. Where, like a pillow on a bed,
A pregnant bank swelled up, to rest
The violet's reclining head,
Sat we two, one another's best...

34. So to'entergraft our hands, as yet
Was all our means to make us one,
And pictures in our eyes to get
Was all our propagation...

35. And whilst our souls negotiate there,
We like sepulchral statues lay;
All day, the same our postures were,
And we said nothing, all the day...

36. But O alas! so long, so far
Our bodies why do we forbear?
They're ours, though they're not we, we are
The intelligencies, they the sphere...

37. So must pure lovers' souls descend
T'affections, and to faculties,
Which sense may reach and apprehend,
Else a great Prince in prison lies...

38. Love's mysteries in souls do grow,
But yet the body is his book.
[*Songs and Sonnets* (1611), 'The Ecstasy']

39. Who ever comes to shroud me, do not harm
Nor question much

That subtle wreath of hair, which crowns my arm;
The mystery, the sign you must not touch,
For 'tis my outward soul,
Viceroy to that, which then to heaven being gone,
Will leave this to control,
And keep these limbs, her Provinces, from dissolution...

40. What ere she meant by it, bury it with me,
For since I am
Love's martyr, it might breed idolatry,
If into other's hands these relics came;
As 'twas humility
To afford to it all that a soul can do,
So, 'tis some bravery,
That since you would save none of me, I bury some of you.
[*Songs and Sonnets* (1611), 'The Funeral']

41. I wonder by my troth, what thou, and I
Did, till we lov'd? were we not wean'd till then?
But suck'd on country pleasures, childishly?
Or snorted we in the Seven Sleepers den?...

42. And now good morrow to our waking souls,
Which watch not one another out of fear.
For love, all love of other sights controls,
And makes one little room, an everywhere...

43. Without sharp North, without declining West.
[*Songs and Sonnets* (1611), 'The Good-Morrow']

44. Rob me, but bind me not, and let me go...

45. And by Love's sweetest Part, Variety, she swore...

46. And said, alas, some two or three
Poor Heretics in love there be,
Which think to stablish dangerous constancy.
[*Songs and Sonnets* (1611), 'The Indifferent']

47. Stand still, and I will read to thee
A lecture, Love, in love's philosophy.
[*Songs and Sonnets* (1611), 'A Lecture upon the Shadow']

48. When I died last, and, Dear I die
As often as from thee I go,
Though it be but an hour ago,
And Lovers' hours be full eternity.
[*Songs and Sonnets* (1611), 'The Legacy']

49. If yet I have not all thy love,
Dear, I shall never have it all.
[*Songs and Sonnets* (1611), 'Lovers' Infiniteness']

50. I long to talk with some old lover's ghost,
Who died before the god of Love was born.
[*Songs and Sonnets* (1611), 'Love's Deity']

51. Love's not so pure, and abstract, as they use
To say, which have no Mistress but their Muse,
But as all else, being elemented too,
Love sometimes would contemplate, sometimes do.
[*Songs and Sonnets* (1611), 'Love's Growth']

52. I never stoop'd so low, as they
Which on an eye, cheek, lip can prey,
Seldom to them, which soar no higher
Then virtue or the mind to admire.
[*Songs and Sonnets* (1611), 'Negative Love']

53. 'Tis the year's midnight, and it is the day's...

54. The world's whole sap is sunk:
The general balm th' hydroptic earth hath drunk.
[*Songs and Sonnets* (1611), 'Nocturnal upon St. Lucy's Day, being the shortest day']

55. When my grave is broke up again
Some second guest to entertain,
(For graves have learnt that woman-head
To be to more than one a bed)
And he that digs it spies
A bracelet of bright hair about the bone,
Will he not let us alone?
[*Songs and Sonnets* (1611), 'The Relic']

56. Go, and catch a falling star,
Get with child a mandrake root,
Tell me, where all past years are,
Or who cleft the Devil's foot...

57. And swear
No where
Lives a woman true, and fair...

58. Though she were true, when you met her,
And last, till you write your letter,
Yet she
Will be
False, ere I come, to two, or three,
[*Songs and Sonnets* (1611), 'Song']

59. Busy old fool, unruly Sun,
Why dost thou thus,
Through windows, and through curtains call on us?...

60. Love, all alike, no season knows, nor clime,
Nor hours, days, months, which are the rags of time...

61. She is all States, and all Princes, I,
Nothing else is.
Princes do but play us...

62. This bed thy centre is, these walls, thy sphere.
[*Songs and Sonnets* (1611), 'The Sun Rising']

63. Sweetest love, I do not go,
For weariness of thee,
Nor in hope the world can show
A fitter Love for me;
But since that I
Must die at last, 'tis best
To use myself in jest,
Thus by feigned deaths to die.

Yesternight the sun went hence,
And yet is here today,
He hath no desire nor sense,
Nor half so short a way:
Then fear not me,
But believe that I shall make
Speedier journeys, since I take
More wings and spurs than he.
[*Songs and Sonnets* (1611), 'Song: Sweetest love...']

64. Send me nor this, nor that, t'increase my store,
But swear thou think'st I love thee, and no more.
[*Songs and Sonnets* (1611), 'Sonnet: The Token']

65. I am two fools, I know,
For loving, and for saying so
In whining Poetry...

66. Grief brought to numbers cannot be so fierce,
For, he tames it, that fetters it in verse.
[*Songs and Sonnets* (1611), 'The Triple Fool']

67. I have done one braver thing
Than all the Worthies did,
And yet a braver thence doth spring,
Which is, to keep that hid...

68. But he who loveliness within
Hath found, all outward loathes,
For he who colour loves, and skin,

Loves but their oldest clothes.
[*Songs and Sonnets* (1611), 'The Undertaking']

69. As virtuous men pass mildly away,
And whisper to their souls to go,
Whilst some of their sad friends do say,
The breath goes now, and some say no.

So let us melt, and make no noise,
No tear-floods, nor sigh-tempests move,
'Twere profanation of our joys
To tell the laity our love.

Moving the earth brings harm and fears,
Men reckon what it did and meant,
But trepidation of the spheres
Though greater far, is innocent.

Dull sublunary lovers love
(Whose soul is sense) cannot admit
Absence, because it doth remove
Those things which elemented it.

But we by a love, so much refin'd,
That our selves know not what it is,
Inter-assured of the mind,
Careless, eyes, lips, and hands to miss.

Our two souls therefore, which are one,
Though I must go, endure not yet
A breach, but an expansion,
Like gold to airy thinness beat.

If they be two, they are two so
As stiff twin compasses are two,
Thy soul the fixt foot makes no show
To move, but doth, if the other do.

And though it in the centre sit,
Yet when the other far doth roam,
It leans, and hearkens after it,
And grows erect, as that comes home.

Such will thou be to me, who must
Like the other foot, obliquely run;
Thy firmness makes my circle just,
And makes me end, where I begun.
[*Songs and Sonnets* (1611), 'A Valediction: Forbidding Mourning']

70. On a round ball
A workman that hath copies by, can lay
An Europe, Afrique and an Asia,
And quickly make that, which was nothing, All.
[*Songs and Sonnets* (1611), 'Valediction: Of Weeping']

71. And new philosophy calls all in doubt,
The element of fire is quite put out;
The sun is lost, and th'earth, and no man's wit
Can well direct him where to look for it.
And freely men confess that this world's spent,
When in the planets and the firmament
They seek so many new; they see that this
Is crumbled out again to his atomies.
'Tis all in pieces, all coherence gone;
All just supply and all relation...

72. She, she is dead; she's dead; when thou know'st this,
Thou know'st how dry a cinder this world is...

73. Yet, because outward storms the strongest break,
And strength itself by confidence grows weak,
This new world may be safer, being told
The dangers and diseases of the old.
[*An Anatomy of the World* (1611), 'First Anniversary']

74. Think then, my soul, that death is but a groom,
Which brings a taper to the outward room...

75. But 'twere little to have chang'd our room,
If, as we were in this our living Tomb
Oppress'd with ignorance, we still were so.
Poor soul, in this thy flesh what dost thou know?...

76. And yet one watches, starves, freezes, and sweats,
To know but Catechisms and Alphabets
Of unconcerning things, matters of fact;
How others on our stage their parts did Act;
What Caesar did, yea, and what Cicero said...

77. Her pure and eloquent blood
Spoke in her cheeks, and so distinctly wrought,
That one might almost say, her body thought...

78. Thou art the proclamation; and I am
The trumpet, at whose voice the people came.
[*Of the Progress of the Soul* (1612), 'Second Anniversary']

79. Immensity cloistered in thy dear womb,
Now leaves his well belov'd imprisonment.
[*Holy Sonnets* (1609–1617), I, 'Nativity']

80. Thou hast made me, and shall thy work decay?
[*Holy Sonnets* (1609–1617), II, 1]

81. I am a little world made cunningly
Of Elements, and an Angelic spright.
[*Holy Sonnets* (1609–1617), II, 5]

82. At the round earth's imagined corners, blow
Your trumpets, Angels, and arise, arise
From death, your numberless infinities
Of souls, and to your scattered bodies go.
All whom the flood did, and fire shall o'erthrow
All whom war, dearth, age, agues, tyrannies,
Despair, law, chance, hath slain.
[*Holy Sonnets* (1609–1617), II, 7]

83. Death be not proud, though some have called thee
Mighty and dreadful, for thou art not so,
For those whom thou think'st thou dost overthrow,
Die not, poor death, not yet canst thou kill me.
For rest and sleep, which but thy pictures be,
Much pleasure, then from thee much more must flow,
And soonest our best men with thee do go,
Rest of their bones and soul's delivery...

84. One short sleep past, we wake eternally,
And death shall be no more; death, thou shalt die.
[*Holy Sonnets* (1609–1617), II, 10]

85. Spit in my face you Jews, and pierce my side.
[*Holy Sonnets* (1609–1617), II, 11]

86. What if this present were the world's last night?
[*Holy Sonnets* (1609–1617), II, 13]

87. Batter my heart, three person'd God; for, you
As yet but knock, breathe, shine, and seek to mend...

88. I, like an usurpt town, to another due,
Labour to admit you, but Oh, to no end...

89. Take me to you, imprison me, for I
Except you enthrall me, never shall be free,
Nor ever chaste, except you ravish me.
[*Holy Sonnets* (1609–1617), II, 14]

90. Show me, dear Christ, thy spouse, so bright and clear.
[*Holy Sonnets* (1609–1617), II, 18]

91. As thou
Art jealous, Lord, so I am jealous now,
Thou lov'st not, till from loving more, thou free

My soul: whoever gives, takes liberty:
O, if thou car'st not whom I love
Alas, thou lov'st not me...

92. Seal then this bill of my Divorce to All...

93. To see God only, I go out of sight:
And to scape stormy days, I choose
An everlasting night.
['Hymn to Christ, at the Author's last going into Germany' (1619)]

94. Since I am coming to that Holy room,
Where, with thy Quire of Saints for evermore,
I shall be made thy Music; As I come
I tune the Instrument here at the door,
And what I must do then, think here before.
['Hymn to God my God, in my Sickness' (1623)]

95. Wilt thou forgive that sin, where I begun,
Which is my sin, though it were done before?
Wilt thou forgive those sins through which I run
And do them still, though still I do deplore?
When thou hast done, thou hast not done,
For I have more.

Wilt thou forgive that sin, by which I have won
Others to sin, and made my sin their door?
Wilt thou forgive that sin which I did shun
A year or two, but wallowed in a score?
When thou hast done, thou hast not done,
For I have more.
['Hymn to God the Father' (1623)]

96. Man is a lump, where all beasts kneaded be,
Wisdom makes him an Ark where all agree;
The fool, in whom these beasts do live at jar,
Is sport to others, and a Theatre.
['To Sir Edward Herbert']

97. O strong and long-liv'd death, how cam'st thou in?
[*Epicedes and Obsequies*, 'Elegy on Mrs. Boulstred']

98. So, so, break off this last lamenting kiss,
Which sucks two souls, and vapours both away,
Turn thou ghost that way, and let me turn this,
And let our selves benight our happiest day.
['The Expiration']

99. But I do nothing upon my self, and yet I am mine own Executioner.
[*Devotions upon Emergent Occasions* (1624), 'Meditation', XII]

100. No man is an Island, entire of it self; every man is a piece of Continent, a part of the main; if a clod be washed away by the sea, Europe is the less, as well as if a promontory were, as well as if a manor of thy friends or of thine own were; any man's death diminishes me, because I am involved in Mankind;
And therefore never send to know for whom the bell tolls; it tolls for thee.
[*Devotions upon Emergent Occasions* (1624), 'Meditation', XVII]

101. [On Death]
It comes equally to us all, and makes us all equal when it comes. The ashes of an Oak in the Chimney, are no epitaph of that Oak, to tell me now high or how large that was; It tells me not what flocks it sheltered while it stood, nor what men it hurt when it fell. The dust of great persons' graves is speechless too, it says nothing, it distinguishes nothing: As soon the dust of a wretch whom thou wouldest not, as of a Prince whom thou couldest not look upon, will trouble thine eyes, if the wind blow it thither; and when a whirlwind hath blown the dust of the Churchyard into the Church, and the man sweeps out the dust of the Church into the Churchyard, who will undertake to sift those dusts again, and to pronounce, This is the Patrician, this is the noble flower, and this is the yeomanly, this the Plebeian bran.
[*LXXX Sermons* (1640)]

102. There is nothing that God hath established in a constant course of nature, and which therefore is done every day, but would seem a Miracle, and exercise our admiration, if it were done but once.
[*LXXX Sermons* (1640)]

103. Poor intricated soul! Riddling, perplexed, labyrinthical soul!
[*LXXX Sermons* (1640)]

104. A day that hath no pridie, nor postridie, yesterday doth not usher it in, nor tomorrow shall not drive it out. Methusalem, with all his hundreds of years, was but a mushroom of a night's growth, to this day, And all the four Monarchies, with all their thousands of years, and all the powerful Kings and all the beautiful Queens of this world, were but as a bed of flowers, some gathered at six, some at seven, some at eight, All in one Morning, in respect of this Day.
[*LXXX Sermons* (1640), 'Eternity']

105. I throw myself down in my Chamber, and I call in, and invite God, and his Angels thither, and when they are there, I neglect God and his Angels, for the noise of a fly, for the rattling of a coach, for the whining of a door.
[*LXXX Sermons* (1640), 'At the Funeral of Sir William Cokayne']

106. A memory of yesterday's pleasures, a fear of tomorrow's dangers, a straw under my knee, a noise in mine ear, a light in mine eye, an anything, a nothing, a fancy, a Chimera in my brain, troubles me in my prayer. So certainly is there nothing, nothing in spiritual things, perfect in this world.
[*LXXX Sermons* (1640), 'At the Funeral of Sir William Cokayne']

107. All eggs are not hatched that the hens sit upon; neither could Christ himself get all the chickens that were hatched to come and stay under his wings.
[*LXXX Sermons* (1640)]

108. ... when I shall be able to stir no limbs in any other measure than a Feaver or a Palsie shall shake them, when everlasting darkness shall have an inchoation in the present dimness of mine eyes, and the everlasting gnashing in the present chattering of my teeth, and the everlasting worm in the present gnawing of the Agonies of my body and anguishes of my mind.
[*LXXX Sermons* (1640)]

109. In the beginning of the world we presume all things to have been produced in their best state; all was perfect, and yet how soon a decay! All was summer, and yet how soon the fall of the leaf!
[*LXXX Sermons* (1640)]

110. They shall awake as Jacob did, and say as Jacob said, Surely the Lord is in this place, and this is no other but the house of God, and the gate of heaven, And into that gate they shall enter, and in that house they shall dwell, where there shall be no Cloud nor Sun, no darkness nor dazzling, but one equal light, no noise nor silence, but one equal music, no fears nor hopes, but one equal possession, no foes nor friends, but one equal communion and Identity, no ends nor beginnings, but one equal eternity.
[*XXVI Sermons* (1660)]

111. The worst voluptuousness ... is an hydroptic immoderate desire of humane learning and languages.
[Letter to Sir Henry Goodyear, September 1608]

112. [On his dismissal from the service of his father-in-law]
John Donne, Anne Donne, Un-done.
[Letter to his wife]

Dors, Diana (Diana Fluck) (1931–1984)
British film star and 'sex symbol'

1. I don't think men and women were meant to live together. They are totally different animals.
[*The Observer*, 1988, in Jeffrey Care (ed.), *Sayings of the Eighties* (1989)]

2. I've had that feeling of falling in love quite a few times. It's rather like being put under anaesthetic.
[*The Observer*, 1980, in Jeffrey Care (ed.), *Sayings of the Eighties* (1989)]

Dorset, Thomas Sackville, Earl of (1536–1608)
English poet, lawyer, politician and diplomat

1. [Referring to the Duke of Buckingham]
His withered fist still knocking at Death's door.
[*Mirour for Magistrates* (1559), Induction, 334]

Dostoevsky, Fyodor (1821–1881)
Russian realist novelist, noted for his psychological insight

1. The formula 'Two and two is five' is not without its attractions.
[*Notes from the Underground* (1864)]

2. We keep imagining eternity as an idea that can't be understood, as something enormous ... instead of all that there will just be one little room, somewhat like a country bath-house, with spiders in all the corners – that's eternity.
[*Crime and Punishment* (1865)]

3. We are familiar merely with the everyday, apparent and current, and this only to the extent in which it appears to us, whereas the ends and the beginnings still constitute to man a realm of the fantastic.
[*Diary of a Writer* (1873)]

4. If you were to destroy in mankind the belief in immortality, not only love but every living force maintaining the life of the world would at once dry up. Moreover, nothing then would be immoral, everything would be lawful, even cannibalism.
[*The Brothers Karamazov* (1879–1880), Part I, II, 6]

5. I think if the devil doesn't exist, and man has created him, he has created him in his own image and likeness.
[*The Brothers Karamazov* (1879–1880), Part II, V, 4]

6. It's not God that I don't accept, Alyosha, only I most respectfully return the ticket to Him.
[*The Brothers Karamazov* (1879–1880), Part II, V, 4]

7. The mind is a tool, a machine, moved by spiritual fire.
[Letter to his brother, 1838]

8. Juridical punishment for crime scares a criminal far less than law-makers think, partly because the criminal himself requires it morally.
[Letter to Katkov, 1865]

Douglas, Lord Alfred (1870–1945)
English poet; intimate of Oscar Wilde

1. I am the Love that dare not speak its name.
['Two Loves' (1896)]

Douglas, Archibald, Fifth Earl of Angus (c. 1449–1514)
Scottish courtier; Chancellor under Charles IV, 1493–98; father of Gavin Douglas

1. [Said at a meeting of Scottish nobles, 1482, referring to his plan to capture Robert Cochrane]
I shall bell the cat.
[Attr.]

Douglas, Bishop Gavin (c. 1474–1522)
Scottish poet, bishop and courtier; translator of the Aeneid into Scots; son of Archibald Douglas

1. And all small fowlys singis on the spray:
Welcum the lord of lycht and lamp of day.
[*Eneados* (1553), XII]

Douglas, James, Earl of Morton (c. 1516–1581)
Regent of Scotland 1572–77; beheaded for his part in Darnley's murder

1. [Said during the burial of John Knox, 1572]
Here lies he who neither feared nor flattered any flesh.
[Attr.]

Douglas, Keith (1920–1944)
English war poet

1. Remember me when I am dead
And simplify me when I'm dead.
['Simplify me when I'm dead' (1941)]

2. But she would weep to see today
how on his skin the swart flies move;
the dust upon the paper eye
and the burst stomach like a cave.
For here the lover and killer are mingled
who had one body and one heart.
And death who had the soldier singled
has done the lover mortal hurt.
['Vergissmeinnicht' (1943)]

3. If at times my eyes are lenses
through which the brain explores
constellations of feeling
my ears yielding like swinging doors
admit princes to the corridors
into the mind, do not envy me.
I have a beast on my back.
['Bête Noire' (1944)]

4. And all my endeavours are unlucky explorers
come back, abandoning the expedition;
the specimens, the lilies of ambition
still spring in their climate, still unpicked:
but time, time is all I lacked
to find them, as the great collectors before me.
['On a Return from Egypt' (1946)]

Douglas, Norman (1868–1952)
Austrian-born Scottish novelist, travel writer and essayist

1. You can tell the ideals of a nation by its advertisements.
[*South Wind* (1917)]

2. Many a man who thinks to found a home discovers that he has merely opened a tavern for his friends.
[*South Wind* (1917)]

Douglas, William (c. 1672–1748)
Scottish poet

1. And for bonnie Annie Laurie
I'll lay me doun and dee.
['Annie Laurie' (c. 1700)]

Douglas-Home, Sir Alec, Baron Home of Hirsel (1903–)
Scottish statesman; Conservative Foreign Secretary (1960–63, 1970–74); Prime Minister (1963–64)

1. When I have to read economic documents I have to have a box of matches and start moving them into position to illustrate and simplify the points to myself.
[Interview in *The Observer*, 1962]

2. [In answer to a remark by Harold Wilson after Home became Prime Minister in 1963]
As far as the 14th Earl is concerned, I suppose Mr Wilson, when you come to think of it, is the 14th Mr Wilson.
[TV interview, 21 October 1963. Cf. Harold Wilson: 3]

3. There are two problems in my life. The political ones are insoluble and the economic ones are incomprehensible.
[Speech, 1964]

4. [On Stanley Baldwin]
A large pipe and thick country tweeds gave the image of a yeoman squire living close to the soil. It was very clever, because in fact he was at his happiest in a room, preferably facing north, with the windows shut, reading Mary Webb.
[*The Way the Wind Blows* (1976)]

Douglas-Home, Lady Caroline (1937–)

1. [Referring to her father's suitability for his new role as prime minister]
He is used to dealing with estate workers. I cannot see how anyone can say he is out of touch.
[*Daily Herald*, 1963]

Dow, Lorenzo (1777–1834)
American evangelist; preacher and pamphleteer

1. Observing the doctrine of Particular Election . . . and those who preached it up to make the Bible clash and contradict itself, by preaching somewhat like this: You can and you can't – You shall and you shan't – You will and you won't – And you will be damned if you do – And you will be damned if you don't.
[*Reflections on the Love of God* (1836), 6]

Dowling, Basil Cairns
New Zealand poet and pacifist

1. [On prisons]
Prisoners and warders – we are all of one blood.
They're much alike, except for a different coat
And a different hat;
And they all seem decent, kindly fellows enough
As they work and chat:
How can it be that men like this have been hanged
By men like that?
[In O.E. Burton, *In Prison* (1945)]

Dowson, Ernest (1867–1900)
English 'decadent' poet

1. I have forgot much, Cynara! gone with the wind,
Flung roses, roses riotously with the throng,
Dancing, to put thy pale, lost lilies out of mind;
But I was desolate and sick of an old passion,
Yea, all the time, because the dance was long:
I have been faithful to thee, Cynara! in my fashion . . .

2. I cried for madder music and stronger wine,
But when the feast is finish'd and the lamps expire,
Then falls thy shadow, Cynara! the night is thine;
I have been faithful to thee, Cynara! in my fashion.
['Non Sum Qualis Eram Bonae Sub Regno Cynarae' (1896)]

3. They are not long, the weeping and the laughter,
Love and desire and hate:
I think they have no portion in us after
We pass the gate.
They are not long, the days of wine and roses;
Out of a misty dream
Our path emerges for a while, then closes
Within a dream.
['Vitae Summa Brevis Spem Nos Vetat Incohare Longam' (1896). Cf. Reginald Hill: 2]

Doyle, Sir Arthur Conan (1859–1930)
Scottish novelist, short-story writer, doctor and war correspondent; creator of the detective Sherlock Holmes

1. [Dialogue between Watson and Holmes]
'Wonderful!' I ejaculated.
'Commonplace,' said Holmes.
[*A Study in Scarlet* (1887)]

2. 'I should have more faith,' he said; 'I ought to know by this time that when a fact appears opposed to a long train of deductions it invariably proves to be capable of bearing some other interpretation.'
[*A Study in Scarlet* (1887)]

3. London, that great cesspool into which all the loungers of the Empire are irresistibly drained.
[*A Study in Scarlet* (1887)]

4. Detection is, or ought to be, an exact science, and should be treated in the same cold and unemotional manner. You have attempted to tinge it with romanticism, which produces much the same effect as if you worked a love-story or an elopement into the fifth proposition of Euclid.
[*The Sign of Four* (1890)]

5. An experience of women which extends over many nations and three separate continents.
[*The Sign of Four* (1890)]

6. It is the unofficial force – the Baker Street irregulars.
[*The Sign of Four* (1890)]

7. It is an old maxim of mine that when you have excluded the impossible, whatever remains, however improbable, must be the truth.
[*The Adventures of Sherlock Holmes* (1892), 'The Beryl Coronet']

8. Singularity is almost invariably a clue. The more featureless and commonplace a crime is, the more difficult it is to bring it home.
[*The Adventures of Sherlock Holmes* (1892), 'The Boscombe Valley Mystery']

9. You know my method. It is founded upon the observance of trifles.
[*The Adventures of Sherlock Holmes* (1892), 'The Boscombe Valley Mystery']

10. A little monograph on the ashes of one hundred and forty different varieties of pipe, cigar, and cigarette tobacco.
[*The Adventures of Sherlock Holmes* (1892), 'The Boscombe Valley Mystery']

11. Depend upon it, there is nothing so unnatural as the commonplace.
[*The Adventures of Sherlock Holmes* (1892), 'A Case of Identity']

12. The husband was a teetotaller, there was no other woman, and the conduct complained of was that he had drifted into the habit of winding up every meal by taking out his false teeth and hurling them at his wife.
[*The Adventures of Sherlock Holmes* (1892), 'A Case of Identity']

13. It has long been an axiom of mine that the little things are infinitely the most important.
[*The Adventures of Sherlock Holmes* (1892), 'A Case of Identity']

14. It is my belief, Watson, founded upon my experience, that the lowest and vilest alleys of London do not present a more dreadful record of sin than does the smiling and beautiful countryside.
[*The Adventures of Sherlock Holmes* (1892), 'Copper Beeches']

15. A man should keep his little brain attic stocked with all the furniture that he is likely to use, and the rest he can put away in the lumber-room of his library, where he can get it if he wants it.
[*The Adventures of Sherlock Holmes* (1892), 'Five Orange Pips']

16. I have nothing to do to-day. My practice is never very absorbing.
[*The Adventures of Sherlock Holmes* (1892), 'The Red-Headed League']

17. It is quite a three-pipe problem, and I beg that you won't speak to me for fifty minutes.
[*The Adventures of Sherlock Holmes* (1892), 'The Red-Headed League']

18. You see, but you do not observe.
[*The Adventures of Sherlock Holmes* (1892), 'Scandal in Bohemia']

19. It is a capital mistake to theorize before one has data.
[*The Adventures of Sherlock Holmes* (1892), 'Scandal in Bohemia']

20. [Of Moriarty]
The Napoleon of crime.
[*The Adventures of Sherlock Holmes* (1893), 'The Final Problem']

21. You know my methods, Watson.
[*The Memoirs of Sherlock Holmes* (1894), 'The Crooked Man']

22. [Dialogue between Watson and Holmes]
'Excellent!' I cried.
'Elementary,' said he.
[*The Memoirs of Sherlock Holmes* (1894), 'The Crooked Man']

23. You mentioned your name as if I should recognize it, but beyond the obvious facts that you are a bachelor, a solicitor, a Freemason, and an asthmatic, I know nothing whatever about you.
[*The Memoirs of Sherlock Holmes* (1894), 'The Norwood Builder']

24. A long shot, Watson; a very long shot!
[*The Memoirs of Sherlock Holmes* (1894), 'Silver Blaze']

25. 'Is there any other point to which you would wish to draw my attention?' 'To the curious incident of the dog in the night-time.' 'The dog did nothing in the night-time.' 'That was the curious incident,' remarked Sherlock Holmes.
[*The Memoirs of Sherlock Holmes* (1894), 'Silver Blaze']

26. They were the footprints of a gigantic hound!
[*The Hound of the Baskervilles* (1904)]

27. You will remember, Watson, how the dreadful business of the Abernetty family was first brought to my notice by the depth which the parsley had sunk into the butter upon a hot day.
[*The Return of Sherlock Holmes* (1905), 'The Adventure of the Six Napoleons']

28. Now, Watson, the fair sex is your department.
[*The Return of Sherlock Holmes* (1905), 'The Second Stain']

29. The vocabulary of Bradshaw is nervous and terse, but limited.
[*The Valley of Fear* (1914)]

30. Mediocrity knows nothing higher than itself, but talent instantly recognizes genius.
[*The Valley of Fear* (1914)]

31. All other men are specialists, but his specialism is omniscience.
[*His Last Bow* (1917), 'Bruce-Partington Plans']

32. 'I [Sherlock Holmes] followed you–' 'I saw no one.' 'That is what you may expect to see when I follow you.'
[*His Last Bow* (1917), 'The Devil's Foot']

33. But here, unless I am mistaken, is our client.
[*His Last Bow* (1917), 'Wisteria Lodge']

34. There is but one step from the grotesque to the horrible.
[*His Last Bow* (1917), 'Wisteria Lodge']

35. The giant rat of Sumatra, a story for which the world is not yet prepared.
[*The Case Book of Sherlock Holmes* (1927), 'Sussex Vampire']

36. I am a brain, Watson. The rest of me is a mere appendix.
[*The Case Book of Sherlock Holmes* (1927), 'The Mazarin Stone']

37. ... one to whom ... each development comes as a perpetual surprise, and to whom the future is always a closed book.
[In Sue Bradbury, 'Economical with the Truth', The Folio Society]

Doyle, Sir Francis (1810–1888)
English Professor of Poetry, ballad writer and lawyer

1. His creed no parson ever knew,
For this was his 'simple plan,'
To have with clergymen to do
As little as a Christian can.
['The Unobtrusive Christian' (1866)]

Doyle, Roddy (1958–)
Irish writer and literary prizewinner

1. The Irish are the niggers of Europe ... An' Dubliners are the niggers of Ireland ... An' the northside Dubliners are the niggers o' Dublin – Say it loud. I'm black an' I'm proud.
[*The Commitments* (1987)]

Drake, Sir Francis (c. 1540–1596)
English navigator, sailed round the world, 1577–80; known for his role in the defeat of the Spanish Armada

1. There must be a beginning of any great matter, but the continuing unto the end until it be thoroughly finished yields the true glory.
[Dispatch to Sir Francis Walsingham, 1587]

2. [Of Cadiz, 1587]
I remember Drake, in the vaunting style of a soldier, would call the Enterprise the singeing of the King of Spain's Beard.
[In Bacon, *Considerations touching a War with Spain* (1629)]

3. I must have the gentleman to haul and draw with the mariner, and the mariner with the gentleman ... I would know him, that would refuse to set his hand to a rope, but I know there is not any such here.
[In Corbett, *Drake and the Tudor Navy* (1898)]

4. [Referring to the sighting of the Spanish Armada, during a game of bowls, 20 July 1588]
There is plenty of time to win this game, and to thrash the Spaniards too.
[Attr. in *Dictionary of National Biography*]

Drayton, Michael (1563–1631)
English poet, noted for his odes, sonnets and pastoral verse

1. When time shall turn those amber locks to grey,
My verse again shall gild and make them gay.
[*England's Heroic Epistles* (1597), 'Henry Howard, Earl of Surrey, to the Lady Geraldine']

2. Ill news hath wings, and with the wind doth go,
Comfort's a cripple and comes ever slow.
[*The Barrons' Wars* (1603), Second Canto]

3. The mind is free, whate'er afflict the man,
A King's a King, do fortune what she can.
[*The Barrons' Wars* (1603), Fifth Canto]

4. Thus when we fondly flatter our desires,
Our best conceits do prove the greatest liars.
[*The Barrons' Wars* (1603), Sixth Canto]

5. [Warwickshire]
That shire which we the heart of England well may call.
['Poly-Olbion: The Thirteenth Song' (1612)]

6. Fair stood the wind for France
When we our sails advance,
Nor now to prove our chance
Longer will tarry...

7. Upon Saint Crispin's day
Fought was this noble fray,
Which fame did not delay,
To England to carry;
O when shall English men
With such acts fill a pen?
Or England breed again
Such a King Harry?
['The Ballad of Agincourt' (1619)]

8. And Queens hereafter shall be glad to live
Upon the alms of thy superfluous praise.
['Idea', 6 (1619)]

9. Since there's no help, come let us kiss and part,
Nay, I have done: you get no more of me,
And I am glad, yea glad with all my heart,
That thus so cleanly, I myself can free,
Shake hands for ever, cancel all our vows,
And when we meet at any time again,
Be it not seen in either of our brows,
That we one jot of former love retain;
Now at the last gasp of love's latest breath,
When his pulse failing, passion speechless lies,
When faith is kneeling by his bed of death,
And innocence is closing up his eyes,
Now if thou wouldst, when all have given him over,
From death to life, thou might'st him yet recover.
['Idea', 61 (1619)]

10. I pray thee leave, love me no more,
Call home the heart you gave me,
I but in vain that saint adore,
That can, but will not, save me.
These poor half-kisses kill me quite.
Was ever man thus served?
Amidst an ocean of delight,
For pleasure to be starved.
['To His Coy Love' (1619)]

11. Neat Marlowe bathed in the Thespian springs,
Had in him those brave translunary things
That the first poets had; his raptures were
All air and fire, which made his verse clear,
For that fine madness still he did retain
Which rightly should possess a poet's brain...

12. Next these, learn'd Jonson, in this list I bring,
Who had drunk deep of the Pierian spring.
['To Henry Reynolds, Of Poets and Poesy' (1627)]

Dreiser, Theodore (1871–1945)
American naturalist novelist

1. [Proposed last words]
Shakespeare, I come!
[In S. Mayfield, *The Constant Circle*]

Drennan, William (1754–1820)
Irish poet, known for patriotic lyrics

1. Nor one feeling of vengeance presume to defile
The cause, or the men, of the Emerald Isle.
['Erin' (1795)]

Dressler, Marie (1869–1934)
American comic film actress

1. If ants are such busy workers, how come they find time to go to all the picnics?
[In Cowan, *The Wit of Women*]

Dring, Philip
Preacher of the Assembly of God Mission

1. I may commit adultery again if God moves me to it.
[*The Observer*, 1980, in Jeffrey Care (ed.), *Sayings of the Eighties* (1989)]

Drinkwater, John (1882–1937)
English 'Georgian' poet, dramatist, actor and critic

1. In the corridors under there is nothing but sleep.
And stiller than ever on orchard boughs they keep
Tryst with the moon, and deep is the silence, deep
On moon-washed apples of wonder.
['Moonlit Apples' (1917)]

Drummond, Thomas (1797–1840)
Scottish engineer and statesman; Under-Secretary for Ireland 1835–40

1. Property has its duties as well as its rights.
[Letter to the Earl of Donoughmore, 1838]

Drummond of Hawthornden, William (1585–1649)
Scottish poet, historian and military inventor

1. Phoebus, arise,
And paint the sable skies,
With azure, white, and red.
['Song: Phoebus, arise' (1614)]

2. I long to kiss the image of my death.
['Sleep, Silence Child' (1614)]

3. Only the echoes which he made relent,
Ring from their marble caves repent, repent.
['For the Baptist' (1623)]

Dryden, John (1631–1700)
English poet, noted as a satirist, heroic dramatist, critic and translator; poet laureate 1668

1. His grandeur he derived from Heaven alone,
For he was great, ere fortune made him so.
['Heroic Stanzas after Cromwell's Funeral' (1659)]

2. An horrid stillness first invades the ear,
And in that silence we the tempest fear.
['Astraea Redux' (1660)]

3. And love's the noblest frailty of the mind.
[*The Indian Emperor* (1665), II]

4. Repentance is the virtue of weak minds.
[*The Indian Emperor* (1665), III]

5. For all the happiness mankind can gain
Is not in pleasure, but in rest from pain.
[*The Indian Emperor* (1665), IV]

6. So sicken waning moons too near the sun,
And blunt their crescents on the edge of day...

7. By viewing nature, nature's handmaid art,
Makes mighty things from small beginnings grow:
Thus fishes first to shipping did impart,
Their tail the rudder, and their head the prow.
['Annus Mirabilis' (1667)]

8. For secrets are edged tools,
And must be kept from children and from fools.
[*Sir Martin Mar-All* (1667), II.ii]

9. I am resolved to grow fat and look young till forty, and then slip out of the world with the first wrinkle and the reputation of five-and-twenty.
[*The Maiden Queen* (1668), III.i]

10. All delays are dangerous in war.
[*Tyrannic Love* (1669), I.i]

11. Pains of love be sweeter far
Than all other pleasures are.
[*Tyrannic Love* (1669), IV.i]

12. I am as free as nature first made man,
Ere the base laws of servitude began,
When wild in woods the noble savage ran.
[*The Conquest of Granada* (1670), I]

13. Forgiveness to the injured does belong;
But they ne'er pardon, who have done the wrong.
[*The Conquest of Granada* (1670), I]

14. Yet dull religion teaches us content;
But when we ask it where that blessing dwells,
It points to pedant colleges and cells.
[*The Conquest of Granada* (1670), II]

15. Fair though you are
As summer mornings, and your eyes more bright
Than stars that twinkle in a winter's night.
[*The Conquest of Granada* (1670), III]

16. Treaties are but the combat of the brain,
Where still the strongest lose, the weaker gain.
[*The Conquest of Granada* (1670), III]

17. Thou strong seducer, opportunity!
[*The Conquest of Granada* (1670), IV]

18. I am to be married within these three days; married past redemption.
[*Marriage à la Mode* (1672), I]

19. So poetry, which is in Oxford made
An art, in London only is a trade.
[*Prologue to the University of Oxon* (1673)]

20. Our author by experience finds it true,
'Tis much more hard to please himself than you.
[*Aureng-Zebe* (1675), Prologue]

21. When I consider life,'tis all a cheat;
Yet, fooled with hope, men favour the deceit.
[*Aureng-Zebe* (1675), IV.i]

22. None would live past years again,
Yet all hope pleasure in what yet remain;
And, from the dregs of life, think to receive,
What the first sprightly running could not give.
[*Aureng-Zebe* (1675), IV.i]

23. Death, in itself, is nothing; but we fear,
To be we know not what, we know not where.
[*Aureng-Zebe* (1675), IV.i]

24. Errors, like straws, upon the surface flow;
He who would search for pearls must dive below.
[*All for Love* (1678), Prologue]

25. She deserves
More worlds than I can lose.
[*All for Love* (1678), I.i]

26. My love's a noble madness.
[*All for Love* (1678), II.i]

27. Fool that I was, upon my eagle's wings
I bore this wren, till I was tired with soaring,
And now he mounts above me.
[*All for Love* (1678), II.i]

28. Give, you gods,
Give to your boy, your Caesar,
The rattle of a globe to play withal,
This gewgaw world, and put him cheaply off:
I'll not be pleased with less than Cleopatra.
[*All for Love* (1678), II.i]

29. Men are but children of a larger growth;
Our appetites as apt to change as theirs,
And full as craving too, and full as vain.
[*All for Love* (1678), IV.i]

30. Your Cleopatra; Dolabella's Cleopatra; every man's Cleopatra.
[*All for Love* (1678), IV.i]

31. For, Heaven be thanked, we live in such an age,
When no man dies for love, but on the stage.
[*Mithridates* (1678), Epilogue]

32. But 'tis the talent of our English nation,
Still to be plotting some new reformation.
[*Prologue at Oxford* (1680)]

33. In pious times, ere priestcraft did begin,
Before polygamy was made a sin.
[*Absalom and Achitophel* (1681), Part I, first lines]

34. Then Israel's monarch, after Heaven's own heart,
His vigorous warmth did, variously, impart
To wives and slaves: and, wide as his command,
Scatter'd his Maker's image through the land.
[*Absalom and Achitophel* (1681), Part I, line 7]

35. Whate'er he did was done with so much ease,
In him alone 'twas natural to please.
[*Absalom and Achitophel* (1681), Part I, line 27]

36. The Jews, a headstrong, moody, murmuring race
As ever tried the extent and stretch of grace,
God's pampered people, whom, debauched with ease,
No king could govern nor no God could please.
Gods they had tried of every shape and size
That godsmiths could produce or priests devise.
[*Absalom and Achitophel* (1681), Part I, line 45]

37. Plots, true or false, are necessary things,
To raise up commonwealths and ruin kings.
[*Absalom and Achitophel* (1681), Part I, line 83]

38. Of these the false Achitophel was first:
A name to all succeeding ages curst.
For close designs and crooked counsels fit,
Sagacious, bold, and turbulent of wit,
Restless, unfixed in principles and place,

In power unpleas'd, impatient of disgrace;
A fiery soul, which working out its way,
Fretted the pigmy body to decay:
And o'er informed the tenement of clay.
A daring pilot in extremity;
Pleased with danger, when the waves went high
He sought the storms; but for a calm unfit,
Would steer too nigh the sands to boast his wit.
Great wits are sure to madness near alli'd,
And thin partitions do their bounds divide.
[*Absalom and Achitophel* (1681), Part I, line 150]

39. Why should he, with wealth and honour blest,
Refuse his age the needful hours of rest?
Punish a body which he could not please;
Bankrupt of life, yet prodigal of ease?
And all to leave what with his toil he won
To that unfeather'd two-legged thing, a son.
[*Absalom and Achitophel* (1681), Part I, line 165]

40. Born a shapeless lump, like Anarchy.
[*Absalom and Achitophel* (1681), Part I, line 172]

41. In friendship false, implacable in hate,
Resolved to ruin or to rule the state.
[*Absalom and Achitophel* (1681), Part I, line 173]

42. So easy still it proves in factious times
With public zeal to cancel private crimes.
[*Absalom and Achitophel* (1681), Part I, line 180]

43. The people's prayer, the glad diviner's theme,
The young men's vision, and the old men's dream!
[*Absalom and Achitophel* (1681), Part I, line 238]

44. All empire is no more than power in trust,
Which, when resumed, can be no longer just.
[*Absalom and Achitophel* (1681), Part I, line 411]

45. Better one suffer than a nation grieve.
[*Absalom and Achitophel* (1681), Part I, line 416]

46. But far more numerous was the herd of such
Who think too little and who talk too much.
[*Absalom and Achitophel* (1681), Part I, line 533]

47. A man so various that he seem'd to be
Not one, but all mankind's epitome.
Stiff in opinions, always in the wrong;
Was everything by starts, and nothing long:
But, in the course of one revolving moon,
Was chemist, fiddler, statesman, and buffoon.
[*Absalom and Achitophel* (1681), Part I, line 545]

48. Railing and praising were his usual themes;
And both (to show his judgement) in extremes:
So over violent, or over civil,
That every man, with him, was God or Devil.
In squandering wealth was his peculiar art:
Nothing went unrewarded, but desert.
Beggar'd by fools, whom still he found too late:
He had his jest, and they had his estate.
[*Absalom and Achitophel* (1681), Part I, line 555]

49. Did wisely from Expensive Sins refrain,
And never broke the Sabbath, but for Gain.
[*Absalom and Achitophel* (1681), Part I, line 587]

50. During his office treason was no crime,
The sons of Belial had a glorious time.
[*Absalom and Achitophel* (1681), Part I, line 597]

51. His tribe were God Almighty's gentlemen.
[*Absalom and Achitophel* (1681), Part I, line 645]

52. Youth, beauty, graceful action seldom fail;
But common interest always will prevail.
And pity never ceases to be shown
To him who makes the people's wrongs his own.
[*Absalom and Achitophel* (1681), Part I, line 723]

53. Nor is the people's judgement always true:
The most may err as grossly as the few.
[*Absalom and Achitophel* (1681), Part I, line 781]

54. Never was patriot yet, but was a fool.
[*Absalom and Achitophel* (1681), Part I, line 968]

55. Beware the fury of a patient man.
[*Absalom and Achitophel* (1681), Part I, line 1005]

56. Doeg, though without knowing how or why,
Made still a blund'ring kind of melody;
Spurr'd boldly on, and dash'd through thick and thin,
Through sense and nonsense, never out nor in;
Free from all meaning, whether good or bad,
And in one word, heroically mad.
[*Absalom and Achitophel* (1681), Part II, line 412]

57. Rhyme is the rock on which thou art to wreck.
[*Absalom and Achitophel* (1681), Part II, line 486]

58. To die for faction is a common evil,
But to be hanged for nonsense is the Devil.
[*Absalom and Achitophel* (1681), Part II, line 498]

59. There is a pleasure sure,
In being mad, which none but madmen know!
[*The Spanish Friar* (1681), I.i]

60. And, dying, bless the hand that gave the blow.
[*The Spanish Friar* (1681), II.ii]

61. They say everything in the world is good for something.
[*The Spanish Friar* (1681), III.ii]

62. All human things are subject to decay,
And, when fate summons, monarchs must obey.
[*Mac Flecknoe* (1682), line 1]

63. The rest to some faint meaning make pretence,
But Shadwell never deviates into sense.
Some beams of wit on other souls may fall,
Strike through and make a lucid interval;
But Shadwell's genuine night admits no ray,
His rising fogs prevail upon the day.
[*Mac Flecknoe* (1682), line 19]

64. Thou last great Prophet of Tautology.
[*Mac Flecknoe* (1682), line 30]

65. Thy genius calls thee not to purchase fame
In keen iambics; but mild anagram:
Leave writing plays, and choose for thy command
Some peaceful province of Acrostic Land.
There thou mayest wings display and altars raise,
And torture one poor word ten thousand ways.
[*Mac Flecknoe* (1682), line 203]

66. We loathe our manna, and we long for quails.
[*The Medal* (1682)]

67. But now the world's o'er stocked with prudent men.
[*The Medal* (1682)]

68. A man is to be cheated into passion, but to be reasoned into truth.
[*Religio Laici* (1682), Preface]

69. Dim, as the borrowed beams of moon and stars
To lonely, weary, wandering travellers
Is reason to the soul.
[*Religio Laici* (1682)]

70. How can the less the greater comprehend?
Or finite reason reach Infinity?
[*Religio Laici* (1682)]

71. But since men will believe more than they need;
And every man will make himself a creed,
In doubtful questions 'tis the safest way
To learn what unsuspected ancients say.
[*Religio Laici* (1682)]

72. And this unpolished rugged verse I chose
As fittest for discourse and nearest prose.
[*Religio Laici* (1682)]

73. Wit will shine
Through the harsh cadence of a rugged line.
['To the Memory of Mr Oldham' (1684)]

74. There are many who understand Greek and Latin, and yet are ignorant of their Mother Tongue.
[*Sylvae* (1685), Preface]

75. Happy the man, and happy he alone,
He, who can call to-day his own:
He who, secure within, can say,
Tomorrow do thy worst, for I have lived to-day.
[*Sylvae* (1685), Trans. of Horace *Odes*, III]

76. Not Heav'n itself upon the past has pow'r;
But what has been, has been, and I have had my hour.
[*Sylvae* (1685), Trans. of Horace *Odes*, III]

77. [Of Fortune]
I can enjoy her while she's kind;
But when she dances in the wind,
And shakes the wings, and will not stay,
I puff the prostitute away.
[*Sylvae* (1685), Trans. of Horace *Odes*, III]

78. Look round the habitable world! how few
Know their own good; or knowing it, pursue.
[*Sylvae* (1685), Trans. of Juvenal *Satires*, X]

79. To see and be seen, in heaps they run;
Some to undo, and some to be undone.
[*Sylvae* (1685), Trans. of Ovid *The Art of Love*, I]

80. Who, for false quantities, was whipt at school.
[*Sylvae* (1685), Trans. of Persius *Satires*, I]

81. She knows her man, and when you rant and swear,
Can draw you to her with a single hair.
[*Sylvae* (1685), Trans. of Persius *Satires*, V]

82. Arms, and the man I sing, who, forced by fate,
And haughty Juno's unrelenting hate...
[*Sylvae* (1685), Trans. of Virgil *Aeneid*, I]

83. She fear'd no danger, for she knew no sin.
[*The Hind and the Panther* (1687), Part I, line 4]

84. And doom'd to death, though fated not to die.
[*The Hind and the Panther* (1687), Part I, line 8]

85. For all have not the gift of martyrdom.
[*The Hind and the Panther* (1687), Part II, line 59]

86. Either be wholly slaves or wholly free.
[*The Hind and the Panther* (1687), Part II, line 285]

87. Much malice mingled with a little wit
Perhaps may censure this mysterious writ.
[*The Hind and the Panther* (1687), Part III, line 1]

88. For present joys are more to flesh and blood
Than a dull prospect of a distant good.
[*The Hind and the Panther* (1687), Part III, line 364]

89. By education most have been misled;
So they believe, because they so were bred.
The priest continues what the nurse began,
And thus the child imposes on the man.
[*The Hind and the Panther* (1687), Part III, line 389]

90. For those whom God to ruin has design'd,
He fits for fate, and first destroys their mind.
[*The Hind and the Panther* (1687), Part III, line 1093. Cf. Duport: 1]

91. From harmony, from heavenly harmony
This universal frame began:
From harmony to harmony
Through all the compass of the notes it ran,
The diapason closing full in Man...

92. What passion cannot Music raise and quell?...

93. The trumpet's loud clangour
Excites us to arms...

94. The soft complaining flute...

95. The trumpet shall be heard on high,
The dead shall live, the living die,
The Music shall untune the sky.
['A Song for St. Cecilia's Day' (1687)]

96. I am devilishly afraid, that's certain; but ... I'll sing, that I may seem valiant.
[*Amphitryon* (1690), II.i]

97. Whistling to keep myself from being afraid.
[*Amphitryon* (1690), III.i]

98. I never saw any good that came of telling truth.
[*Amphitryon* (1690), III.i]

99. That fairy kind of writing which depends only upon the force of imagination.
[*King Arthur* (1691), Dedication]

100. War is the trade of kings.
[*King Arthur* (1691), II]

101. Fairest Isle, all isles excelling,
Seat of pleasure, and of loves;
Venus here will choose her dwelling,
And forsake her Cyprian groves.
[*King Arthur* (1691), V, Song of Venus]

102. Ovid, the soft philosopher of love.
[*Love Triumphant* (1694), II]

103. We must beat the iron while it is hot, but we may polish it at leisure.
[*Aeneis* (1697), Dedication]

104. I trade both the living and the dead, for the enrichment of our native language.
[*Aeneis* (1697), Dedication]

105. The god-like hero sate
On his imperial throne;
His valiant peers were plac'd around;
Their brows with roses and with myrtles bound.
(So should desert in arms be crowned:)
The lovely Thais by his side,
Sate like a blooming Eastern bride
In flow'r of youth and beauty's pride.
Happy, happy, happy, pair!
None but the brave,
None but the brave,
None but the brave deserves the fair.
['Alexander's Feast' (1697), I]

106. Sound the trumpets; beat the drums;
Flush'd with a purple grace:
He shows his honest face:
Now give the hautboys breath; he comes, he comes...

107. Drinking is the soldier's pleasure;
Rich the treasure;
Sweet the pleasure;
Sweet is pleasure after pain.
['Alexander's Feast' (1697), III]

108. Fallen from his high estate,
And welt'ring in his blood:
Deserted at his utmost need
By those his former bounty fed;
On the bare earth expos'd he lies,
With not a friend to close his eyes.
['Alexander's Feast' (1697), IV]

109. Softly sweet, in Lydian measures,
Soon he sooth'd his soul to pleasures.
War, he sung, is toil and trouble;
Honour but an empty bubble.
Never ending, still beginning,
Fighting still, and still destroying,
If the world be worth thy winning,
Think, oh think, it worth enjoying.
Lovely Thais sits beside thee,
Take the good the gods provide thee...

110. The prince, unable to conceal his pain,
Gazed on the fair
Who caused his care,
And sigh'd and look'd, sigh'd and look'd
Sigh'd and look'd, and sigh'd again.
['Alexander's Feast' (1697), V]

111. At length, with love and wine at once oppressed,
The vanquished victor sunk upon her breast.
['Alexander's Feast' (1697), V, Chorus]

112. See the Furies arise!
See the snakes that they rear,
How they hiss in their hair,
And the sparkles that flash from their eyes...

113. And, like another Helen, fired another Troy.
['Alexander's Feast' (1697), VI]

114. Could swell the soul to rage, or kindle soft desire...

115. Let old Timotheus yield the prize,
Or both divide the crown:
He rais'd a mortal to the skies;
She drew an angel down.
['Alexander's Feast' (1697), VII]

116. And made almost a sin of abstinence.
['Character of a Good Parson' (1700)]

117. Old as I am, for ladies' love unfit,
The power of beauty I remember yet.
[*Cymon and Iphigenia* (1700), line 1]

118. When beauty fires the blood, how love exalts the mind.
[*Cymon and Iphigenia* (1700), line 41]

119. He trudg'd along unknowing what he sought,
And whistled as he went, for want of thought.
[*Cymon and Iphigenia* (1700), line 84]

120. Ill fortune seldom comes alone.
[*Cymon and Iphigenia* (1700), line 392]

121. Of seeming arms to make a short essay,
Then hasten to be drunk, the business of the day.
[*Cymon and Iphigenia* (1700), line 407]

122. Better to hunt in fields, for health unbought,
Than fee the doctor for a nauseous draught.
The wise, for cure, on exercise depend;
God never made his work, for man to mend.
[*Epistles* (1700), 'To John Driden of Chesterton']

123. But love's a malady without a cure.
[*Palamon and Arcite* (1700), II, line 110]

124. And Anthony, who lost the world for love.
[*Palamon and Arcite* (1700), II, line 607]

125. Repentance is but want of power to sin.
[*Palamon and Arcite* (1700), III, line 813]

126. Since ev'ry man who lives is born to die,
And none can boast sincere felicity,
With equal mind, what happens, let us bear,
Nor joy nor grieve too much for things beyond our care.
Like pilgrims to th' appointed place we tend;
The world's an inn, and death the journey's end.
[*Palamon and Arcite* (1700), III, line 883]

127. A very merry, dancing, drinking,
Laughing, quaffing, and unthinking time...

128. Joy rul'd the day, and Love the night...

129. All, all of a piece throughout;
Thy chase had a beast in view;
Thy wars brought nothing about;
Thy lovers were all untrue.
'Tis well an old age is out,
And time to begin a new.
['Secular Masque' (1700)]

130. Theirs was the giant race before the flood.
[*Epistles*, 'To Mr Congreve']

131. Heav'n, that but once was prodigal before,
To Shakespeare gave as much; she could not give him more.
[*Epistles*, 'To Mr Congreve']

132. Here lies my wife: here let her lie!
Now she's at rest, and so am I.
['Epitaph intended for his wife']

133. A thing well said will be wit in all languages.
[*Essay of Dramatic Poesy* (1668)]

134. Every age has a kind of universal genius, which inclines those that live in it to some particular studies.
[*Essay of Dramatic Poesy* (1668)]

135. [Of Shakespeare]
He was the man who of all modern, and perhaps ancient poets, had the largest and most comprehensive soul ... He was naturally learn'd; he needed not the spectacles of books to read Nature: he looked inwards, and found her there ... He is many times flat, insipid; his comic wit degenerating into clenches, his serious swelling into bombast. But he is always great.
[*Essay of Dramatic Poesy* (1668)]

136. If by the people you understand the multitude, the hoi polloi, 'tis no matter what they think; they are sometimes in the right, sometimes in the wrong: their judgement is a mere lottery.
[*Essay of Dramatic Poesy* (1668)]

137. [Of Ben Jonson]
He invades authors like a monarch; and what would be theft in other poets, is only victory in him.
[*Essay of Dramatic Poesy* (1668)]

138. [Of Ben Jonson]
He was not only a professed imitator of Horace, but a learned plagiary of all the others; you track him everywhere in their snow.
[*Essay of Dramatic Poesy* (1668)]

139. [Of Shakespeare]
He is the very Janus of poets; he wears almost everywhere two faces; and you have scarce begun to admire the one, ere you despise the other.
[*Essay on Dramatic Poetry of the Last Age* (1672)]

140. Sure the poet . . . spewed up a good lump of clotted nonsense at once.
[*Notes and Observations on the Empress of Morocco* [by E. Settle] (1674), 'The First Act']

141. How easy it is to call rogue and villain, and that wittily! But how hard to make a man appear a fool, a blockhead, or a knave, without using any of those opprobrious terms! To spare the grossness of the names, and to do the thing yet more severely, is to draw a full face, and to make the nose and cheeks stand out, and yet not to employ any depth of shadowing.
[*Of Satire* (1693)]

142. [Sarcastic reference to Jack Ketch, executioner, 1663–1686, who was notorious for his barbarity]
A man may be capable, as Jack Ketch's wife said of his servant, of a plain piece of work, a bare hanging; but to make a malefactor die sweetly was only belonging to her husband.
[*Of Satire* (1693)]

143. What judgment I had increases rather than diminishes; and thoughts, such as they are, come crowding in so fast upon me, that my only difficulty is to choose or reject; to run them into verse or to give them the other harmony of prose.
[*Fables Ancient and Modern* (1700), Preface]

144. [Of Abraham Cowley]
One of our late great poets is sunk in his reputation, because he could never forgive any conceit which came in his way; but swept like a drag-net, great and small. There was plenty enough, but the dishes were ill-sorted; whole pyramids of sweetmeats, for boys and women; but little of solid meat for men.
[*Fables Ancient and Modern* (1700), Preface]

145. [Of Chaucer]
Here is God's plenty.
[*Fables Ancient and Modern* (1700), Preface]

146. [Of Chaucer]
He is a perpetual fountain of good sense.
[*Fables Ancient and Modern* (1700), Preface]

147. Cousin Swift, you will never be a poet.
[In Samuel Johnson, *Lives of the English Poets* (1781)]

D'Souza, Dinesh (1961–)

1. If education cannot help separate truth from falsehood, beauty from vulgarity, right from wrong, then what can it teach us?
[*Atlantic Monthly*, 1991]

2. The rejection of authority can sometimes result, paradoxically, in an embrace of authoritarianism. Indeed, it can happen with insidious ease.
[*Atlantic Monthly*, 1991]

Dubcek, Alexander (1921–1992)
Czechoslovak statesman; reforming Communist Party Secretary, 1968–69

1. In the service of the people we followed such a policy that socialism would not lose its human face.
[Attr.]

Du Bellay, Joachim (1522–1560)
French poet and member of the Pléiade; known for his sonnets

1. *France, mère des arts, des armes et des lois.*
France, mother of arts, of arms, and of laws.
[*Les Regrets* (1558)]

2. *Heureux qui comme Ulysse a fait un beau voyage*
Ou comme cestuy là qui conquit la toison
Et puis est retourné, plein d'usage et raison,
Vivre entre ses parents le reste de son âge!
Happy the man who like Ulysses made a wonderful journey, or like the one who carried off the Fleece and then returned home, full of experience and good sense, to live his remaining years among his family!
[*Les Regrets* (1558)]

3. *Plus que le marbre dur me plaist l'ardoise fine,*
Plus mon Loyre Gaulois, que le Tybre Latin,
Plus mon petit Lyré, que le mont Palatin,
Et plus que l'air marin la doulceur angevine.
More than hard marble fine slate pleases me,
More than the Latin Tiber, my Gallic Loire,
More than the Palatine Hill, my little Liré,
And more than the sea breeze, the sweetness of Anjou.
[*Les Regrets* (1558)]

Dubin, Al (20th century)
American songwriter

1. You may not be an angel
'Cause angels are so few,
But until the day that one comes along
I'll string along with you.
['I'll string along with you', song, 1934]

Duby, Georges (1919–)
French historian, art critic and professor

1. Marriage, which is necessarily overt, public, ceremonious, surrounded by special words and deeds, is at the centre of any system of values, at the junction between the material and the spiritual.
[*The Knight, the Lady and the Priest* (1984); trans. Barbara Bray]

Du Deffand, Marquise (1697–1780)
French literary hostess

1. [Commenting on the legend of St Denis, who is believed to have carried his severed head for six miles after his execution]
La distance n'y fait rien; il n'y a que le premier pas qui coûte.
The distance isn't important; it is only the first step that is difficult.
[Letter to d'Alembert, 1763]

Dudley, Sir Henry Bate (1745–1824)
English journalist, prebendary and dramatist

1. Wonders will never cease.
[Letter to Garrick, 1776]

Duffield, George (1818–1888)
American Presbyterian minister

1. Stand up! stand up for Jesus,
Ye soldiers of the Cross!
[Hymn, 1858]

Duffy, Sir Charles Gavan (1816–1903)
Irish poet and editor and later Prime Minister of Victoria

1. [On his arrival in Australia in 1856]
Let me not be misunderstood. I am not here to repudiate or

apologize for any part of my past life. I am still an Irish rebel to the backbone and the spinal marrow, a rebel for the same reason that John Hampden and Algernon Sidney, George Washington and Charles Carrol of Carroltown, were rebels – because tyranny had supplanted the law.
[In Cyril Pearl, *The Three Lives of Gavan Duffy*]

Duffy, Jim

1. [Of goalkeeper Andy Murdoch]
He has an answerphone installed on his six-yard line and the message says: 'Sorry, I'm not in just now, but if you'd like to leave the ball in the back of the net, I'll get back to you as soon as I can.'
[*Umbro Book of Football Quotations* (1993)]

Duggan, Eileen May (1894–1972)
New Zealand short-story writer

1. The tides run up the Wairau
That fights against their flow.
My heart and it together
Are running salt and snow.
[*The Penguin Book of New Zealand Verse* (1985), 'The Tides Run up the Wairau']

Duhamel, Georges (1884–1966)
French novelist, poet, dramatist and physician

1. *Je respecte trop l'idée de Dieu pour la rendre responsable d'un monde aussi absurde.*
I have too much respect for the idea of God to make it responsible for such an absurd world.
[*Chronique des Pasquier* (1948), V, 'Le désert de Bièvres']

2. Courtesy is not dead – it has merely taken refuge in Great Britain.
[*The Observer*, 'Sayings of the Week', 1953]

Dukes, Ashley (1885–1959)
English dramatist, theatre manager, critic and translator

1. Adventure must be held in delicate fingers. It should be handled, not embraced. It should be sipped, not swallowed at a gulp.
[*The Man with a Load of Mischief* (1924), 1]

2. Men reason to strengthen their own prejudices, and not to disturb their adversary's convictions.
[*The Man with a Load of Mischief* (1924), 2]

3. The tender passion is much overrated by poets. They have their living to earn, poor fellows.
[*The Man with a Load of Mischief* (1924), 3]

Dulles, John Foster (1888–1959)
American statesman and lawyer; Republican Secretary of State 1953–59

1. [Reply when asked if he had ever been wrong]
Yes, once – many, many years ago. I thought I had made a wrong decision. Of course, it turned out that I had been right all along. But I was wrong to have thought that I was wrong.
[Attr.]

Dumas, Alexandre (Père) 1802–1870
French romantic historical novelist and dramatist

1. *Tous pour un, un pour tous.*
All for one, one for all.
[*Les Trois Mousquetaires* (1844)]

2. *Cherchez la femme.*
Look for the woman.
[*Les Mohicans de Paris* (1854–1855); also attributed to Joseph Fouché (1763–1820)]

Dumas, Alexandre (Fils) (1824–1895)
French dramatist, novelist and critic

1. *Si Dieu pouvait tout à coup être condamné à vivre de la vie qu'il inflige à l'homme, il se tuerait.*
If God were suddenly condemned to live the life which he had inflicted on men, He would kill Himself.
[*Pensées d'album* (1847)]

2. All generalizations are dangerous, even this one.
[Attr.]

3. It is only rarely that one can see in a little boy the promise of a man, but one can almost always see in a little girl the threat of a woman.
[Attr.]

Du Maurier, Dame Daphne (1907–1989)
English novelist, short-story writer and dramatist; granddaughter of George Du Maurier

1. Last night I dreamt I went to Manderley again.
[*Rebecca* (1938), opening lines]

2. [Referring to her house in Cornwall which was the inspiration for Manderley in *Rebecca*]
It ... was full of dry rot. An unkind visitor said that the only reason Menabilly still stood was that the woodworm obligingly held hands.
[Interview]

Du Maurier, George (1834–1896)
French-born English book and magazine illustrator and novelist

1. Life ain't all beer and skittles, and more's the pity; but what's the odds, so long as you're happy?
[*Trilby* (1894), I. Cf. Calverley: 9]

2. A little work, a little play
To keep us going – and so, good-day!
A little warmth, a little light
Of love's bestowing – and so, good-night!
A little fun, to match the sorrow
Of each day's growing – and so, good-morrow!
A little trust that when we die
We reap our sowing! and so – good-bye!
[*Trilby* (1894), I]

3. She had all the virtues but one.
[*Trilby* (1894), I]

4. [Of a husband]
Feed the brute.
[*Punch*, 1886]

Dumouriez, Charles François du Périer (1739–1823)
French general, pamphleteer and memoirist

1. [Of Louis XVIII]
Les courtisans qui l'entourent n'ont rien oublié et n'ont rien appris.
The courtiers surrounding him have forgotten nothing and learnt nothing.
[*Examen impartial d'un Ecrit intitulé Déclaration de Louis XVIII* (1795). Cf. Talleyrand: 5]

Dunbar, William (c. 1460–c. 1525)
Scottish poet, noted for his versatility; satirist and courtier

1. The Devil sa deavit was with their yell,
That in the deepest pot of hell

He smoorit them with smoke.
['The Dance of the Seven Deidly Sinnis' (1834 edition)]

2. The bank was green, the brook was full of breamis,
The stanneris clear as stern in frosty nicht.
['The Golden Targe' (1834 edition)]

3. Be merry, man! and tak nocht far in mind
The wavering of this wrechit world of sorrow;
To God be hummle, and to the friend be kind,
And with thy neebouris glaidly len' and borrow...

4. No thing is thine save only that thou spendis...

5. Without gladness availis no tresour.
['Hermes the Philosopher' (1834 edition)]

6. Flattery wearis ane furrit gown,
And falsett with the lord does roun,
And truth stands barrit at the dure.
['Into this World May None Assure' (1834 edition)]

7. I that in heill wes and gladnes
Am trublit now with gret seiknes
And feblit with infirmitie:
Timor mortis conturbat me...

8. Our plesance here is all vain glory,
This fals world is but transitory,
The flesh is bruckle, the Feynd is slee:
Timor Mortis conturbat me...

9. Unto the deid gois all Estatis,
Princis, prelatis, and potestatis,
Baith rich and poor of all degree:
Timor Mortis conturbat me.
['Lament for the Makaris' (1834 edition)]

10. London, thou art of townes A per se...

11. London, thou art the flower of cities all!
Gemme of all joy, jasper of jocunditie...

12. Fair be their wives, right lovesom, white and small.
['London' (1834 edition)]

13. I wauk, I turn, sleep may I nocht,
I vexit am with heavy thocht;
This warld all owre I cast about,
And aye the mair I am in doubt;
The mair that I remeid have socht.
['Meditation in Winter' (1834 edition)]

14. All love is lost but upon God alone.
['The Merle and the Nightingale' (1834 edition)]

15. God give to thee ane blissed chance,
And of all virtue abundance,
And grace ay for to persevere,
In hansel of this guid new year.
['New Year's Gift' (1834 edition)]

16. Gif thou has micht, be gentle and free;
And gif thou stands in povertie,
Of thine awn will to it consent;
And riches sall return to thee:
He has eneuch that is content.
['Of Content' (1834 edition)]

17. Great men for taking and oppressioun,
Are set full famous at the sessioun,
And poor takaris are hangit hie,
Shamit for ever and their successioun:
In taking suld discretioun be.
['Of Discretioun in Taking' (1834 edition)]

18. Done is a battell on the dragon blak;
Our campioun Christ counfoundit hes his force;
The yettis of hell ar brokin with a crak,
The signe triumphall rasit is of the croce.
['On the Resurrection of Christ' (1834 edition)]

Duncan, Isadora (1878–1927)
American modern dance pioneer

1. I have discovered the dance. I have discovered the art which has been lost for two thousand years.
[*My Life* (1927)]

2. [Of painful childbirth]
It is unheard of, uncivilized barbarism that any woman should still be forced to bear such monstrous torture. It should be remedied.
[*My Life* (1927)]

3. People do not live nowadays – they get about ten percent out of life.
[*This Quarter Autumn*, 'Memoirs']

4. So that ends my first experience with matrimony, which I always thought a highly overrated performance.
[*The New York Times*, 1923]

5. [Last words; she was about to test-drive a Bugatti and was strangled when her scarf caught in the spokes of a wheel]
Adieu, mes amis, je vais à la gloire.
Goodbye, my friends, I go on to glory.
[Attr.]

Dundy, Elaine (1927–)
American writer

1. The question actors most often get asked is how they can bear saying the same things over and over again night after night, but God knows the answer to that is, don't we all anyway; might as well get paid for it.
[*The Dud Avocado* (1958), 9]

Dunlop, Ian (1925–)
British art historian

1. The shock of the new: seven historic exhibitions of modern art.
[Title of book, 1972]

Dunne, Finley Peter (1867–1936)
American writer and novelist

1. There is wan thing an' on'y wan thing to be said in favour iv dhrink, an' that is that it has caused manny a lady to be loved that otherwise might've died single.
[*Mr Dooley Says* (1910), 'The Army Canteen']

Dunning, John, Baron Ashburton (1731–1783)
English lawyer and politician

1. The influence of the Crown has increased, is increasing, and ought to be diminished.
[House of Commons, 1780]

Dunstan, Keith (1925–)
Australian journalist and columnist

1. [On the opinion that Ned Kelly and his gang were homosexuals, expressed by Sidney Baker in *The Australian Language*, 1966]
It is all very well to call him a white-livered cur, a bully, a coward, a liar and a psychotic murderer but to actually name him as a queer is going too far.
[*Knockers* (1972)]

Duport, James (1606–1679)
English classical scholar; appointed King's Chaplain 1660

1. *Quem Deus vult perdere, dementat prius.*
   Whom God wishes to destroy He first sends mad.
   [*Homeri Gnomologia* (1660). Cf. Dryden: 90]

Duppa, Richard (1770–1831)
English artist and author

1. In language, the ignorant have prescribed laws to the learned.
   [*Maxims* (1830)]

Durant, Will (1885–1982)
American philosopher and writer

1. There is nothing in Socialism that a little age or a little money will not cure.
   [Attr.]

Durocher, Leo (1905–1991)
American baseball player and coach

1. [Remark at a practice ground, 1946]
   Nice guys finish last.
   [Attr.]

Durrell, Sir Gerald (1925–1995)
Author, animal-collector, founder and Director of Jersey Zoological Park

1. I said I *liked* being half-educated; you were so much more *surprised* at everything when you were ignorant.
   [*My Family and Other Animals* (1956)]

Durrell, Lawrence (1912–1990)
Indian-born British poet and novelist

1. So we learning to suffer and not condemn
   Can only wish you this great pure wind
   Condemned by Greece, and turning like a helm,
   Inland where it smokes the fires of men,
   Spins weathercocks on farms or catches
   The lovers at their quarrel in the sheets;
   Or like a walker in the darkness might,
   Knocks and disturbs the artist at his papers
   Up there alone, upon the alps of night.
   [*Collected Poems* (1960), 'Alexandria']

2. The whole Mediterranean, the sculpture, the palms, the gold beads, the bearded heroes, the wine, the ideas, the ships, the moonlight, the winged gorgons, the bronze men, the philosophers – all of it seems to rise in the sour, pungent taste of these black olives between the teeth. A taste older than meat, older than wine. A taste as old as cold water.
   [*Prospero's Cell* (1945)]

3. No one can go on being a rebel too long without turning into an autocrat.
   [*Balthazar* (1958), II]

4. No more about sex, it's too boring.
   [*Tunc* (1968)]

5. What a filthy brutal dirty culture you have in North America – with of course its obverse sentimentality.
   [Letter to Henry Miller, January 1979]

6. History is an endless repetition of the wrong way of living.
   [*The Listener*, 1978]

7. [Of the Mona Lisa]
   She has the smile of a woman who has just dined off her husband.
   [Attr.]

Dürrenmatt, Friedrich (1921–1990)
Swiss dramatist and novelist

1. *Die Gerechtigkeit ist nicht eine Hackmaschine, sondern ein Abkommen.*
   Justice is not a mincer but an agreement.
   [*Die Ehe des Herrn Mississippi* (*The Marriage of Mr Mississippi*, 1952), I]

2. *Gott ist ein unmenschlicher Begriff.*
   God is an inhuman concept.
   [*Die Ehe des Herrn Mississippi* (*The Marriage of Mr Mississippi*, 1952), I]

3. *Unsere Wissenschaft ist schrecklich geworden, unsere Forschung gefährlich, unsere Erkenntnis tödlich.*
   Our science has become terrible, our research dangerous, our knowledge fatal.
   [*Die Physiker* (*The Physicists*, 1962), II]

4. *Wer dem Paradoxen gegenübersteht, setzt sich der Wirklichkeit aus.*
   Whoever is faced with the paradoxical exposes himself to reality.
   [*Die Physiker* (*The Physicists*, 1962), '21 Points on the Physicists', no. 20]

5. *Wir haben durch die Jahrhunderte hindurch so viel dem Staat geopfert, dass es jetzt Zeit ist, dass sich der Staat für uns opfert.*
   Through the centuries we have sacrified so much for the state that it is now time for the state to sacrifice itself for us.
   [*Romulus der Grosse* (*Romulus the Great*, 1964), I]

6. *Die Gerechtigkeit ist etwas Fürchterliches.*
   Justice is something terrible.
   [*Romulus der Grosse* (*Romulus the Great*, 1964), III]

Dutton, Geoffrey (1922–)
Australian poet, novelist, historian, writer and critic

1. A dead thing, upside down,
   Never to be stirred
   Where better than a university
   For the death of a singing bird?
   [*Flowers and Fury* (1962), 'A Dead Bird in the North']

2. Those who mumble do not pray.
   Prayers grow like windless trees from silence.
   ['Twelve Sheep']

3. Hunters and lovers see best in the dark.
   ['Night Fishing']

4. Eyre was an unlucky man, and duty was his destiny and his doom.
   [*The Hero as Murderer: the Life of Edward John Eyre* (1967)]

Dworkin, Andrea (1946–)
American author and feminist

1. We imagined, in our ignorance, that we might be novelists and philosophers . . . We did not know that our professors had a system of beliefs and convictions that designated us as an inferior gender class, and that that system of beliefs and convictions was virtually universal – the cherished assumption of most of the writers, philosophers, and historians we were so ardently studying.
   [*Our Blood: Prophecies and Discourses on Sexual Politics* (1976)]

2. Intercourse as an act often expresses the power men have over women.
[*Intercourse* (1987)]

3. Sex exists on both sides of the law but the law itself creates the sides.
[*Intercourse* (1987)]

4. As a woman of letters I fight for my kind, for women, for freedom. The brazen scream distracts.
[*Mercy*]

5. Seduction is often difficult to distinguish from rape. In seduction, the rapist often bothers to buy a bottle of wine.
[*The Independent*, 1992]

6. Men love death. In everything they make, they hollow out a central place for death ... Men especially love murder. In art they celebrate it. In life, they commit it.
[*The Independent*, 1992]

Dyer, Sir Edward (c. 1540–1607)
English poet; elegist and courtier

1. My mind to me a kingdom is,
Such present joys therein I find,
That it excels all other bliss
That earth affords or grows by kind.
Though much I want which most would have,
Yet still my mind forbids to crave.
['In praise of a contented mind' (1588). Attr.]

Dyer, John [1] (c. 1700–1758)
Welsh poet; painter, traveller and cleric

1. A little rule, a little sway,
A sunbeam in a winter's day,
Is all the proud and mighty have
Between the cradle and the grave...

2. Ever charming, ever new,
When will the landscape tire the view?
[*Grongar Hill* (1726)]

Dyer, John [2] (fl. 18th century)

1. And he that will his health deny,
Down among the dead men let him lie.
[Toast: 'Here's a Health to the King' (c. 1700)]

Dylan, Bob (Robert Zimmerman) (1941–)
American singer and songwriter

1. How many roads must a man walk down
Before you call him a man?...
The answer, my friend, is blowin' in the wind,
The answer is blowin' in the wind.
['Blowin' in the Wind', song, 1962]

2. I saw ten thousand talkers whose tongues were all broken,
I saw guns and sharp swords, in the hands of young children...
And it's a hard rain's a gonna fall.
['A Hard Rain's A-Gonna Fall', song, 1963]

3. Come mothers and fathers
Throughout the land
And don't criticize
What you can't understand.
['The Times They Are A-Changin', song, 1964]

4. Money doesn't talk, it swears.
['It's Alright, Ma (I'm Only Bleeding)', song, 1965]

5. How does it feel
To be without a home
Like a complete unknown
Like a rolling stone?
['Like a Rolling Stone', song, 1965]

6. She knows there's no success like failure
And that failure's no success at all.
['Love Minus Zero/No Limit', song, 1965]

7. Hey! Mr Tambourine Man, play a song for me.
I'm not sleepy and there is no place I'm going to.
['Mr Tambourine Man', song, 1965]

8. She takes just like a woman, yes, she does
She makes love just like a woman, yes, she does
And she aches just like a woman
But she breaks just like a little girl.
['Just Like a Woman', song, 1966]

9. [On being asked if he could say something about his songs]
Yeah, some of them are about ten minutes long, others five or six.
[Interview]

Eames, Emma (1865–1952)
Chinese-born American opera singer

1. [Of her early retirement at 47]
I would rather be a brilliant memory than a curiosity.
[Attr.]

Eames, Dr Robin (1940–)
Protestant Archbishop of Armagh, Primate of All Ireland

1. [Referring to the Enniskillen bombing, 8 November 1987]
'...I see,' he said with emphasis, 'the faces of the little children who have lost a father, as they walk behind the coffin with roses in their hands. I see the faces of good, honest, decent people who have never done wrong to anyone else, who have lost a loved one, blown to bits by a terrorist bomb. And of course I weep.'
[*The Observer*, 1992]

Earhart, Amelia (1898–1937)
American aviator; first woman to fly the Atlantic

1. Courage is the price that Life exacts for granting peace.
['Courage' (1927)]

2. [Of her flight in the 'Friendship']
Of course I realized there was a measure of danger. Obviously I faced the possibility of not returning when first I considered going. Once faced and settled there really wasn't any good reason to refer to it.
[*20 Hours: 40 Minutes – Our Flight in the Friendship* (1928), 5]

Eastman, Max (1883–1969)
American author, editor and critic

1. [On chivalry]
It is but the courteous exterior of a bigot.
[*Woman Suffrage and Sentiment*]

Eastwood, Clint (1930–)
American film actor and director

1. There's only one way to have a happy marriage and as soon as I learn what it is I'll get married again.
[Attr.]

Eban, Abba (1915–)
South African-born Israeli statesman and writer; Minister of Foreign Affairs in Israel, 1966–1974

1. History teaches us that men and nations behave wisely once they have exhausted all other alternatives.
[Speech, 1970]

Ebden, Charles Hotson (1809–1867)
Australian landowner and politician

1. I fear I am becoming disgustingly rich.
[In Paul de Serville, *Port Phillip Gentlemen*]

Ebner-Eschenbach, Marie von (1830–1916)
Austrian writer

1. *Eine gescheite Frau hat Millionen geborener Feinde: – alle dummen Männer.*
A clever woman has millions of born enemies: – all stupid men.
[*Aphorismen* (*Aphorisms*, 1880)]

2. *Die stillstehende Uhr, die täglich zweimal die richtige Zeit angezeigt hat, blickt nach Jahren auf eine lange Reihe von Erfolgen zurück.*
The clock which has stopped but has twice daily indicated the right time can years later look back on a long line of successes.
[*Aphorismen* (*Aphorisms*, 1880)]

3. *Wenn zwei brave Menschen über Grundsätze streiten, haben immer beide recht.*
Whenever two good people argue over principles, both are always right.
[*Aphorismen* (*Aphorisms*, 1880)]

4. *An Rheumatismen und an wahre Liebe glaubt man erst, wenn man davon befallen wird.*
You don't believe in rheumatism and true love until they first attack you.
[*Aphorismen* (*Aphorisms*, 1880)]

5. *Wir sind so eitel, dass uns sogar an der Meinung der Leute, an denen uns nichts liegt, etwas gelegen ist.*
We are so vain that we are even concerned about the opinion of those people who are of no concern to us.
[*Aphorismen* (*Aphorisms*, 1880)]

6. *'Himmel!', ruft er, 'wenn es Kleider sind, die uns in der Welt möglich machen, wie hoch müssen wir den halten, der sie verfertigt!'*
'Goodness,' he cried, 'if it is our clothes which fit us for this world, in what high esteem must we hold those who make them!'
[*Die Zwei Komtessen, 'Komtesse Muschi'* (*The Two Countesses, 'Countess Muschi'*, 1884)]

Eco, Umberto (1932–)
Italian literary critic and novelist

1. *La TV non offre, come ideale in cui immedesimarsi, il superman ma l'everyman. La TV presenta come ideale l'uomo assolutamente medio.*
Television doesn't present, as an ideal to aspire to, the superman but the everyman. Television puts forward, as an ideal, the absolutely average man.
[Essay written in 1961, republished in the collection *Diario Minimo*, 1992]

2. [On the new Italian political system, i.e. the second Republic]
Cosí il massimo del nuovo avrà prodotto il ritorno di fiamma del vecchio.
Hence the best of the new regime will have caused a backfire of the old one.
[From his weekly column for the *Espresso*, 1994]

Eddington, Sir Arthur (1882–1944)
English astronomer, physicist and mathematician

1. We used to think that if we knew one, we knew two, because one and one are two. We are finding that we must learn a great deal more about 'and'.
[In Alan L. Mackay, *The Harvest of a Quiet Eye* (1977)]

Eddy, Mary Baker (1821–1910)
American founder of Christian Science

1. Christian Science explains all cause and effect as mental, not physical.
[*Science and Health, with Key to the Scriptures* (1875)]

2. Sin brought death, and death will disappear with the disappearance of sin.
[*Science and Health, with Key to the Scriptures* (1875)]

Eden, Anthony (1897–1977)
English statesman; Conservative Prime Minister, 1955–57

1. [When asked what effect Stalin's death would have on international affairs]
That is a good question for you to ask, not a wise question for me to answer.
[Interview, 1953]

2. We are not at war with Egypt. We are in armed conflict.
[Speech, 1956]

3. Everybody is always in favour of general economy and particular expenditure.
[*The Observer*, 'Sayings of the Week', 1956]

Eden, Clarissa (1920–1985)
English wife of Anthony Eden

1. [Of the 1956 Suez crisis]
During the last few weeks I have sometimes felt that the Suez Canal was flowing through my drawing room.
[Speech, Gateshead, 1956]

Edgar, Marriott (1880–1951)
British writer and author of monologues made famous by Stanley Holloway

1. There's a famous seaside place called Blackpool,
That's noted for fresh air and fun,
And Mr and Mrs Ramsbottom
Went there with young Albert, their son.

A grand little lad was young Albert,
All dressed in his best; quite a swell
With a stick with an 'orse's 'ead 'andle,
The finest that Woolworth's could sell.

They didn't think much to the Ocean:
The waves, they were fiddlin' and small,
There was no wrecks and nobody drownded,
Fact, nothing to laugh at at all.

So, seeking for further amusement,
They paid and went into the Zoo,
Where they'd Lions and Tigers and Camels,
And old ale and sandwiches too.

There were one great big Lion called Wallace;
His nose was all covered with scars–
He lay in a somnolent posture
With the side of his face on the bars.

Now Albert had heard about Lions,
How they was ferocious and wild–
To see Wallace lying so peaceful,
Well, it didn't seem right to the child.

So straightway the brave little feller,
Not showing a morsel of fear,

Took his stick with the 'orse's 'ead 'andle
And pushed it in Wallace's ear.

You could see that the Lion didn't like it,
For giving a kind of a roll,
He pulled Albert inside the cage, with 'im,
And swallowed the little lad 'ole...

2. The Magistrate gave his opinion
That no one was really to blame
And he said that he hoped the Ramsbottoms
Would have further sons to their name.

At that Mother got proper blazing,
'And thank you, sir, kindly,' said she,
'What, waste all our lives raising children
To feed ruddy Lions? Not me!'
[*Albert, 'Arold and Others* (1937), 'The Lion and Albert', monologue recorded by Stanley Holloway in 1932]

Edgeworth, Maria (1767–1849)
English-born Irish writer, noted for earliest 'regional novel'

1. And all the young ladies ... said ...that to be sure a love-match was the only thing for happiness, where the parties could any way afford it.
[*Castle Rackrent* (1800)]

2. We cannot judge either of the feelings or of the characters of men with perfect accuracy, from their actions or their appearance in public; it is from their careless conversations, their half-finished sentences, that we may hope with the greatest probability of success to discover their real character.
[*Castle Rackrent* (1800)]

3. Come when you're call'd;
And do as you're bid;
Shut the door after you;
And you'll never be chid.
[*Popular Tales* (1804), 'The Contrast', 1]

4. Business was his aversion; pleasure was his business.
[*Popular Tales* (1804), 'The Contrast', 1]

5. Well! some people talk of morality, and some of religion, but give me a little snug property.
[*The Absentee* (1812), 2]

6. My mother took too much, a great deal too much, care of me; she over-educated, over-instructed, over-dosed me with premature lessons of prudence: she was so afraid that I should ever do a foolish thing, or not say a wise one, that she prompted my every word, and guided my eyes, hearing with her ears, and judging with her understanding, till, at length, it was found out that I had no eyes, or understanding of my own.
[*Vivian* (1812)]

7. 'Pleasing for a moment,' said Helen smiling, 'is of some consequence; for, if we take care of the moments, the years will take care of themselves.'
[*Mademoiselle Panache*]

8. All I crave for my own part is, that if I am to have my throat cut, it may not be by a man with his face blackened by charcoal.
[Letter to Mrs Ruxton, 1795, at a time of threat from extremist secret societies]

Edison, Thomas Alva (1847–1931)
American inventor and industrialist

1. Genius is one per cent inspiration and ninety-nine per cent perspiration.
[*Life*, 1932]

2. To invent, you need a good imagination and a pile of junk.
[Attr.]

Edmeston, James (1791–1867)
English architect, surveyor and hymn writer

1. Lead us, Heavenly Father, lead us
O'er the world's tempestuous sea.
[Hymn, 1821]

Edmond, James (1859–1933)
Scots-born Australian journalist, editor and columnist

1. [Caption to a drawing by Norman Lindsay of three women seen in a Sydney street]
We walk along the gas-lit street in a dreadful row, we three,
The woman I was, the woman I am, and the woman I'll one day be.
[In William Moore, *The Story of Australian Art*]

2. I had been told by Jimmy Edmond in Australia that there were only three things against living in Britain: the place, the climate and the people.
[In David Low, *Low Autobiography*]

Edward III (1312–1377)
King of England (1327–1377); began the Hundred Years' War by claiming the French throne

1. [Of the Black Prince]
Let the boy win his spurs.
[Remark at the Battle of Crécy, 1346]

Edward VII (1841–1910)
King of Great Britain and Ireland (1901–1910); son of Queen Victoria

1. I thought everyone must know that a short jacket is always worn with a silk hat at a private view in the morning.
[In Sir P. Magnus, *Edward VII*]

Edward VIII (later Duke of Windsor) (1894–1972)
King of Great Britain and Northern Ireland in 1936 (uncrowned); abdicated to marry an American divorcée; son of George V

1. [Adopted as the Round Table movement's motto in the form 'Adopt, adapt, improve']
The young business and professional men of this country must get together round the table, adopt methods that have proved sound in the past, adapt them to the changing needs of the times and, whenever possible, improve them.
[Speech, British Industries Fair, Birmingham, 1927]

2. I have found it impossible to carry the heavy burden of responsibility and to discharge my duties as King as I would wish to do without the help and support of the woman I love.
[Radio broadcast after his abdication, 11 December 1936]

3. [Of steel works in South Wales where 9,000 men had been made unemployed]
These works brought all these people here. Something must be done to find them work.
[Speech, 1936]

4. Perhaps one of the only positive pieces of advice that I was ever given was that supplied by an old courtier who observed: 'Only two rules really count. Never miss an opportunity to relieve yourself; never miss a chance to sit down and rest your feet.'
[*A King's Story* (1951)]

5. The thing that impresses me most about America is the way parents obey their children.
[In *Look*, 1957]

6. [On receiving a large bill from a luxury hotel]
Now what do I do with this?
[Attr.]

7. [On maintaining a happy marriage]
Of course, I do have a slight advantage over the rest of you. It helps in a pinch to be able to remind your bride that you gave up a throne for her.
[Attr.]

8. [Quoting Sir William Harcourt]
We are all socialists now.
[Attr.]

Edwards, Bob (1864–1922)
Canadian publisher and newspaperman

1. One trouble with being efficient is that it makes everybody hate you so.
[*The Calgary Eye Opener*, 1916]

Edwards, Elwyn Hartley (1927–)
Equestrian writer, teacher and judge

1. [Translated from the writings of the Emir Abd-el-Kadr]
When God wanted to create the horse, he said to the South Wind, 'I want to make a creature of you. Condense.'
[*Horses: Their Role in the History of Man* (1987), 'The First Progenitor']

Edwards, Jonathan (1703–1758)
American Calvinist theologian and metaphysical philosopher

1. The bodies of those that made such a noise and tumult when alive, when dead, lie as quietly among the graves of their neighbours as any others.
[*Works* (1834), sermon on procrastination]

Edwards, Oliver (1711–1791)
English lawyer

1. For my part now, I consider supper as a turnpike through which one must pass, in order to get to bed.
[In Boswell, *The Life of Samuel Johnson* (1791), 1778]

2. I have tried too in my time to be a philosopher; but, I don't know how, cheerfulness was always breaking in.
[In Boswell, *The Life of Samuel Johnson* (1791), 1778]

Edwards, Richard (c. 1523–1566)
Welsh dramatist, poet and choirmaster

1. In going to my naked bed, as one that would have slept,
I heard a wife sing to her child, that long before had wept.
She sighed sore, and sang full sweet, to bring the babe to rest,
That would not cease, but cried still in sucking at her breast.
She was full weary of her watch and grieved with her child,
She rocked it, and rated it, till that on her it smiled.
Then did she say, 'Now have I found this proverb true to prove:
The falling out of faithful friends, renewing is of love.'
[*The Paradise of Dainty Devices* (1576), 'Amantium Irae']

Egan, Ted (1932–)

1. [Song about the struggle between the Gurindji aboriginals and the Vestey company which leased their land from 1914]
Poor bugger me, Gurindji
Me bin sit down this country
Long time before the Lord Vestey
Allabout land belongin' to we
Oh poor bugger me, Gurindji.
Poor bugger blackfeller, Gurindji
Long time work no wages, we,
Work for the good old Lord Vestey
Little bit flour, sugar and tea
For the Gurindji, from Lord Vestey
Oh poor bugger me.

Poor bugger me, Gurindji
Man called Vincent Lingiari
Talk long allabout Gurindji
'Daguragu place for we,
Home for we, Gurindji'.
But poor bugger blackfeller, Gurindji
Government boss him talk long we
'We'll build you house with electricity
But at Wave Hill, for can't you see
Wattie Creek belong to Lord Vestey'
Oh poor bugger me.
['Gurindji Blues', song, 1969]

Einstein, Albert (1879–1955)
German-born American mathematical physicist (Nobel prize 1921)

1. $E=mc^2$ (Energy = mass x the speed of light squared.)
[Statement, 1905]

2. An empty stomach is not a good political adviser.
[*Cosmic Religion* (1931)]

3. If you want to find out anything from the theoretical physicists about the methods they use, I advise you to stick closely to one principle: Don't listen to their words, fix your attention on their deeds.
[*Mein Weltbild* (*The World As I See It*, 1934)]

4. Science without religion is lame, religion without science is blind.
[*Science, Philosophy and Religion: a Symposium* (1941), 13]

5. Only a life lived for others is a life worthwhile.
['Defining Success']

6. Peace cannot be kept by force. It can only be achieved by understanding.
[*Notes on Pacifism*]

7. Imagination is more important than knowledge.
[*On Science*]

8. *Raffiniert ist der Herrgott, aber boshaft ist er nicht.*
The Lord God is crafty but he is not spiteful.
[Inscription in the Mathematical Institute at Princeton]

9. If my theory of relativity is proven successful, Germany will claim me as a German and France will declare that I am a citizen of the world. Should my theory prove untrue, France will say that I am a German and Germany will declare that I am a Jew.
[Address, Sorbonne, Paris, c. 1929]

10. I am an absolute pacifist ... It is an instinctive feeling. It is a feeling that possesses me, because the murder of men is disgusting.
[Interview, 1929]

11. I never think of the future. It comes soon enough.
[Interview, 1930]

12. Why does this magnificent applied science which saves work and makes life easier bring us so little happiness? The

simple answer runs: Because we have not yet learned to make sensible use of it.
[Address, California Institute of Technology, 1931]

13. Before God we are all equally wise – equally foolish.
[Address, Sorbonne, Paris]

14. [Of his part in the development of the atom bomb]
If only I had known, I should have become a watchmaker.
[*New Statesman*, 1965]

15. As far as the laws of mathematics refer to reality, they are not certain, and as far as they are certain, they do not refer to reality.
[In F. Capra, *The Tao of Physics* (1975), 2]

16. A theory can be proved by experiment; but no path leads from experiment to the birth of a theory.
[In Alan L. Mackay, *The Harvest of a Quiet Eye* (1977)]

17. When a man sits with a pretty girl for an hour, it seems like a minute. But let him sit on a hot stove for a minute – and it's longer than any hour. That's relativity.
[Attr.]

18. *Gott würfelt nicht.*
God does not play dice.
[Attr.]

19. Common sense is the collection of prejudices acquired by age eighteen.
[Attr.]

Eisenhower, Dwight D. (1890–1969)
American statesman, general and Republican President, 1953–61

1. Whatever America hopes to bring to pass in this world must first come to pass in the heart of America.
[Inaugural address, 1953]

2. Every gun that is made, every warship launched, every rocket fired signifies, in the final sense, a theft from those who hunger and are not fed, those who are cold and are not clothed. This world in arms is not spending money alone. It is spending the sweat of its labourers, the genius of its scientists, the hopes of its children.
[Speech in Washington, April 1953]

3. The peace we seek, founded upon decent trust and co-operative effort among nations, can be fortified, not by weapons of war but by wheat and by cotton, by milk and by wool, by meat and by timber and by rice. These are words that translate into every language on earth. These are needs that challenge this world in arms.
[Speech to the American Society of Newspaper Editors, 1953]

4. You have a row of dominoes set up. You knock over the first one and what will happen to the last one is that it will go over very quickly.
[Remark at press conference, April 1954]

5. I think that people want peace so much that one of these days governments had better get out of the way and let them have it.
[Broadcast discussion, August 1959]

6. In the councils of government, we must guard against the acquisition of unwarranted influence, whether sought or unsought, by the military-industrial complex. The potential for the disastrous rise of misplaced power exists and will persist.
[Farewell address, 17 January 1961]

7. There is one thing about being President – nobody can tell you when to sit down.
[*The Observer*, 'Sayings of the Week', 1953]

Ekland, Britt (1942–)
Swedish film and television actress and 'Bond' girl

1. As a single woman with a child, I would love to have a wife.
[*The Independent*, 1994]

2. I say I don't sleep with married men, but what I mean is that I don't sleep with happily married men.
[Attr.]

Eldershaw, M. Barnard (Marjorie Faith Barnard) (1897–1987)
Australian novelist and critic
and **Eldershaw,** Flora Sydney Patricia (1897–1956)

1. Journalists are people who take in one another's washing and then sell it.
[*Plaque with Laurel*]

Eliot, George (Mary Ann Evans) (1819–1880)
English novelist, noted for her portrayal of provincial society; poet and letter writer

1. In every parting there is an image of death.
[*Scenes of Clerical Life* (1858), 'Amos Barton', 10]

2. Animals are such agreeable friends – they ask no questions, they pass no criticisms.
[*Scenes of Clerical Life* (1858), 'Mr. Gilfil's Love-Story', 7]

3. Errors look so very ugly in persons of small means – one feels they are taking quite a liberty in going astray; whereas people of fortune may naturally indulge in a few delinquencies.
[*Scenes of Clerical Life* (1858), 'Janet's Repentance', 25]

4. A prophetess? Yea, I say unto you, and more than a prophetess – a uncommon pretty young woman.
[*Adam Bede* (1859), 1]

5. It was a pity he couldna be hatched o'er again, an' hatched different.
[*Adam Bede* (1859), 18]

6. Our deeds determine us, as much as we determine our deeds.
[*Adam Bede* (1859), 29]

7. Mrs Poyser 'has her say out'.
[*Adam Bede* (1859), 32]

8. It's them as take advantage that get advantage i' this world.
[*Adam Bede* (1859), 32]

9. A maggot must be born i' the rotten cheese to like it.
[*Adam Bede* (1859), 32]

10. He was like a cock, who thought the sun had risen to hear him crow.
[*Adam Bede* (1859), 33]

11. We hand folks over to God's mercy, and show none ourselves.
[*Adam Bede* (1859), 42]

12. I'm not one o' those as can see the cat i' the dairy, an' wonder what she's come after.
[*Adam Bede* (1859), 52]

13. I'm not denyin' the women are foolish: God Almighty made 'em to match the men.
[*Adam Bede* (1859), 53]

14. The law's made to take care o' raskills.
[*The Mill on the Floss* (1860), III, 4]

15. This is a puzzling world, and Old Harry's got a finger in it.
[*The Mill on the Floss* (1860), III, 9]

16. [Of *The Imitation of Christ*]
It was written down by a hand that waited for the heart's prompting: it is the chronicle of a solitary hidden anguish, struggle, trust and triumph.
[*The Mill on the Floss* (1860), IV, 3]

17. I've never any pity for conceited people, because I think they carry their comfort about with them.
[*The Mill on the Floss* (1860), V, 4]

18. The happiest women, like the happiest nations, have no history.
[*The Mill on the Floss* (1860), VI, 3]

19. 'Character', says Novalis, in one of his questionable aphorisms – 'character is destiny.'
[*The Mill on the Floss* (1860), VI, 6]

20. I should like to know what is the proper function of women, if it is not to make reasons for husbands to stay at home, and still stronger reasons for bachelors to go out.
[*The Mill on the Floss* (1860), VI, 6]

21. There's nothing like a dairy if folks want a bit o' worrit to make the days pass.
[*Silas Marner* (1861), 17]

22. Nothing is so good as it seems beforehand.
[*Silas Marner* (1861), 18]

23. Half the sorrows of women would be averted if they could repress the speech they know to be useless; nay, the speech they have resolved not to make.
[*Felix Holt* (1866), 2]

24. An election is coming. Universal peace is declared, and the foxes have a sincere interest in prolonging the lives of the poultry.
[*Felix Holt* (1866), 5]

25. A little daily embroidery had been a constant element in Mrs Transome's life; that soothing occupation of taking stitches to produce what neither she nor any one else wanted, was then the resource of many a well-born and unhappy woman.
[*Felix Holt* (1866), 7]

26. Speech is often barren; but silence also does not necessarily brood over a full nest. Your still fowl, blinking at you without remark, may all the while be sitting on one addled nest-egg; and when it takes to cackling, will have nothing to announce but that addled delusion.
[*Felix Holt* (1866), 16]

27. A woman can hardly ever choose ... she is dependent on what happens to her. She must take meaner things, because only meaner things are within her reach.
[*Felix Holt* (1866), 27]

28. There's many a one would be idle if hunger didn't pinch him; but the stomach sets us to work.
[*Felix Holt* (1866), 30]

29. 'Abroad', that large home of ruined reputations.
[*Felix Holt* (1866), Epilogue]

30. A woman dictates before marriage in order that she may have an appetite for submission afterwards.
[*Middlemarch* (1872), 9]

31. He said he should prefer not to know the sources of the Nile, and that there should be some unknown regions preserved as hunting-grounds for the poetic imagination.
[*Middlemarch* (1872), 9]

32. Among all forms of mistake, prophecy is the most gratuitous.
[*Middlemarch* (1872), 10]

33. Correct English is the slang of prigs who write history and essays. And the strongest slang of all is the slang of poets.
[*Middlemarch* (1872), 11]

34. A woman, let her be as good as she may, has got to put up with the life her husband makes for her.
[*Middlemarch* (1872), 25]

35. A man is seldom ashamed of feeling that he cannot love a woman so well when he sees a certain greatness in her: nature having intended greatness for men.
[*Middlemarch* (1872), 39]

36. Though, as we know, she was not fond of pets that must be held in the hands or trodden on, she was always attentive to the feelings of dogs, and very polite if she had to decline their advances.
[*Middlemarch* (1872), 39]

37. It was a room where you had no reason for sitting in one place rather than in another.
[*Middlemarch* (1872), 54]

38. Our deeds still travel with us from afar,
And what we have been makes us what we are.
[*Middlemarch* (1872), 70]

39. Gossip is a sort of smoke that comes from the dirty tobacco-pipes of those who diffuse it: it proves nothing but the bad taste of the smoker.
[*Daniel Deronda* (1876), 13]

40. A difference of taste in jokes is a great strain on the affections.
[*Daniel Deronda* (1876), 15]

41. There is a great deal of unmapped country within us which would have to be taken into account in an explanation of our gusts and storms.
[*Daniel Deronda* (1876), 24]

42. Men's men: gentle or simple, they're much of a muchness.
[*Daniel Deronda* (1876), 31]

43. Friendships begin with liking or gratitude – roots that can be pulled up.
[*Daniel Deronda* (1876), 32]

44. A blush is no language: only a dubious flag-signal which may mean either of two contradictories.
[*Daniel Deronda* (1876), 35]

45. Debasing the moral currency.
[*Theophrastus Such* (1879), title of essay]

46. Man's life was spacious in the early world:
It paused, like some slow ship with sail unfurled
Waiting in seas by scarce a wavelet curled;
Beheld the slow star-paces of the skies,
And grew from strength to strength through centuries;
Saw infant trees fill out their giant limbs,
And heard a thousand times the sweet birds' marriage hymns.
[*The Legend of Jubal* (1874)]

47. 'Tis God gives skill,
But not without men's hands: He could not make
Antonio Stradivari's violins
Without Antonio. Get thee to thy easel.
[*Complete Poems* (1888), 'Stradivarius']

48. She, stirred somewhat beyond her wont, and taking as her text the three words which have been used so often as the inspiring trumpet-calls of men – the words God, Immortality, Duty – pronounced, with terrible earnestness,

how inconceivable was the first, how unbelievable the second, and yet how peremptory and absolute the third. Never, perhaps, have sterner accents affirmed the sovereignty of impersonal and unrecompensing Law.
[In F.W.H. Myers, 'George Eliot', *Country Magazine*, 1881]

49. I am not an optimist but a meliorist.
[In Laurence Housman, A.E.H. (1937)]

Eliot, T.S. (1888–1965)

American-born British poet, verse dramatist and critic; Nobel prize for literature 1948

1. Miss Nancy Ellicot smoked
And danced all the modern dances;
And her aunts were not quite sure how they felt about it,
But they knew that it was modern.
['Cousin Nancy' (1917)]

2. Sometimes these cogitations still amaze
The troubled midnight and the noon's repose.
['La Figlia Che Piange' (1917)]

3. Let us go then, you and I,
When the evening is spread out against the sky
Like a patient etherised upon a table...

4. In the room the women come and go
Talking of Michelangelo.

The yellow fog that rubs its back upon the window-panes,
The yellow smoke that rubs its muzzle on the window-panes,
Licked its tongue into the corners of the evening.

5. There will be time, there will be time
To prepare a face to meet the faces that you meet;
There will be time to murder and create,
And time for all the works and days of hands
That lift and drop a question on your plate...

6. In a minute there is time
For decisions and revisions which a minute will reverse.

For I have known them all already, known them all–
Have known the evenings, mornings, afternoons,
I have measured out my life with coffee spoons...

7. I should have been a pair of ragged claws
Scuttling across the floors of silent seas...

8. Should I, after tea and cakes and ices,
Have the strength to force the moment to its crisis?...

9. I have seen the moment of my greatness flicker,
And I have seen the eternal Footman hold my coat, and snicker,
And in short, I was afraid...

10. No! I am not Prince Hamlet, nor was meant to be;
Am an attendant lord, one that will do
To swell a progress, start a scene or two...

11. I grow old ... I grow old...
I shall wear the bottoms of my trousers rolled.

Shall I part my hair behind? Do I dare to eat a peach?
I shall wear white flannel trousers, and walk upon the beach.
I have heard the mermaids singing, each to each.

I do not think that they will sing to me.
We have lingered in the chambers of the sea
By sea-girls wreathed with seaweed red and brown
Till human voices wake us, and we drown.
['The Love Song of J. Alfred Prufrock' (1917)]

12. They are rattling breakfast plates in the basement kitchens,
And along the trampled edges of the street
I am aware of the damp souls of housemaids
Sprouting despondently at area gates.
['Morning at the Window' (1917)]

13. When Mr Apollinax visited the United States
His laughter tinkled among the teacups.
I thought of Fragilion, that shy figure among the birch-trees,
And of Priapus in the shrubbery
Gaping at the lady in the swing.
['Mr Apollinax' (1917)]

14. Let us take the air, in a tobacco trance,
Admire the monuments,
Discuss the late events,
Correct our watches by the public clocks.
Then sit for half an hour and drink our bocks.
['Portrait of a Lady' (1917)]

15. The winter evening settles down
With smells of steaks in passageways.
Six o'clock.
The burnt-out ends of smoky days...

16. The worlds revolve like ancient women
Gathering fuel in vacant lots.
['Preludes' (1917)]

17. Every street lamp that I pass
Beats like a fatalistic drum,
And through the spaces of the dark
Midnight shakes the memory
As a madman shakes a dead geranium.

Half-past one,
The street-lamp sputtered,
The street-lamp muttered,
The street-lamp said, 'Regard that woman
Who hesitates toward you in the light of the door
Which opens on her like a grin.'...

18. 'Put your shoes at the door, sleep, prepare for life.'

The last twist of the knife.
['Rhapsody on a Windy Night' (1917)]

19. I shall not want Capital in Heaven
For I shall meet Sir Alfred Mond.
We two shall lie together, lapt
In a five per cent Exchequer Bond...

20. Where are the eagles and the trumpets?

Buried beneath some snow-deep Alps.
Over buttered scones and crumpets
Weeping, weeping multitudes
Droop in a hundred A.B.C.'s.
['A Cooking Egg' (1920)]

21. Here I am, an old man in a dry month...

22. Signs are taken for wonders. 'We would see a sign!'
The word within a word, unable to speak a word,
Swaddled with darkness. In the juvescence of the year
Came Christ the tiger

In depraved May, dogwood and chestnut, flowering judas,
To be eaten, to be divided, to be drunk
Among whispers...

23. After such knowledge, what forgiveness? Think now
History has many cunning passages, contrived corridors
And issues, deceives with whispering ambitions,
Guides us by vanities...

24. Unnatural vices
Are fathered by our heroism...

25. Thoughts of a dry brain in a dry season.
['Gerontion' (1920)]

26. Polyphiloprogenitive
The sapient sutlers of the Lord
Drift across the window-panes.
In the beginning was the Word.
['Mr Eliot's Sunday Morning Service' (1920)]

27. Paint me the bold anfractuous rocks
Faced by the snarled and yelping seas.
['Sweeney Erect' (1920)]

28. Apeneck Sweeney spreads his knees
Letting his arms hang down to laugh,
The zebra stripes along his jaw
Swelling to maculate giraffe...

29. Gloomy Orion and the Dog
Are veiled; and hushed the shrunken seas;
The person in the Spanish cape
Tries to sit on Sweeney's knees...

30. The host with someone indistinct
Converses at the door apart,
The nightingales are singing near
The Convent of the Sacred Heart,

And sang within the bloody wood
When Agamemnon cried aloud
And let their liquid siftings fall
To stain the stiff dishonoured shroud.
['Sweeney Among the Nightingales' (1920)]

31. Webster was much possessed by death
And saw the skull beneath the skin;
And breastless creatures under ground
Leaned backward with a lipless grin.

Daffodil bulbs instead of balls
Stared from the sockets of the eyes!...

32. Donne, I suppose, was such another
Who found no substitute for sense,
To seize and clutch and penetrate;
Expert beyond experience...

33. Grishkin is nice: her Russian eye
Is underlined for emphasis;
Uncorseted, her friendly bust
Gives promise of pneumatic bliss.
['Whispers of Immortality' (1920)]

34. April is the cruellest month, breeding
Lilacs out of the dead land, mixing
Memory and desire, stirring
Dull roots with spring rain.
Winter kept us warm, covering
Earth in forgetful snow, feeding
A little life with dried tubers...

35. And I will show you something different from either
Your shadow at morning striding behind you
Or your shadow at evening rising to meet you;
I will show you fear in a handful of dust...

36. Madame Sosostris, famous clairvoyante,
Had a bad cold, nevertheless
Is known to be the wisest woman in Europe,
With a wicked pack of cards. Here, said she,
Is your card, the drowned Phoenician Sailor...

37. Unreal City,
Under the brown fog of a winter dawn,
A crowd flowed over London Bridge, so many,
I had not thought death had undone so many...

38. That corpse you planted last year in your garden,
Has it begun to sprout? Will it bloom this year?...

39. Oh keep the Dog far hence, that's friend to men,
Or with his nails he'll dig it up again!
You! hypocrite lecteur! – mon semblable, – mon frère!
[*The Waste Land* (1922), 'The Burial of the Dead'. Cf. Baudelaire: 2 and John Webster: 11]

40. The Chair she sat in, like a burnished throne,
Glowed on the marble...

41. And still she cried, and still the world pursues,
'Jug Jug' to dirty ears...

42. O O O O that Shakespeherian Rag–
It's so elegant
So intelligent.
[*The Waste Land* (1922), 'A Game of Chess']

43. A rat crept softly through the vegetation
Dragging its slimy belly on the bank
While I was fishing in the dull canal
On a winter evening round behind the gashouse
Musing upon the king my brother's wreck
And on the king my father's death before him...

44. But at my back from time to time I hear
The sound of horns and motors, which shall bring
Sweeney to Mrs Porter in the spring.
O the moon shone bright on Mrs Porter
And on her daughter
They wash their feet in soda water...

45. I Tiresias, old man with wrinkled dugs
Perceived the scene, and foretold the rest–
I too awaited the expected guest.
He, the young man carbuncular, arrives,
A small house agent's clerk, with one bold stare,
One of the low on whom assurance sits
As a silk hat on a Bradford millionaire...

46. And I Tiresias have foresuffered all
Enacted on this same divan or bed...

47. When lovely woman stoops to folly and
Paces about her room again, alone,
She smoothes her hair with automatic hand,
And puts a record on the gramophone...

48. O City city, I can sometimes hear
Beside a public bar in Lower Thames Street,
The pleasant whining of a mandoline
And a clatter and a chatter from within
Where fishmen lounge at noon: where the walls
Of Magnus Martyr hold
Inexplicable splendour of Ionian white and gold...

49. Trams and dusty trees.
Highbury bore me. Richmond and Kew
Undid me. By Richmond I raised my knees
Supine on the floor of a narrow canoe.
[*The Waste Land* (1922), 'The Fire Sermon']

50. Phlebas the Phoenician, a fortnight dead,
Forgot the cry of gulls, and the deep sea swell
And the profit and loss...

51. Gentile or Jew
O you who turn the wheel and look to windward,
Consider Phlebas, who was once handsome and tall as you.
[*The Waste Land* (1922), 'Death by Water']

52. Who is the third who walks always beside you?
When I count, there are only you and I together
But when I look ahead up the white road
There is always another one walking beside you...

53. A woman drew her long black hair out tight
And fiddled whisper music on those strings
And bats with baby faces in the violet light
Whistled, and beat their wings
And crawled head downward down a blackened wall...

54. The awful daring of a moment's surrender...

55. These fragments I have shored against my ruins.
[*The Waste Land* (1922), 'What the Thunder Said']

56. We are the hollow men
We are the stuffed men
Leaning together
Headpiece filled with straw...

57. Here we go round the prickly pear
Prickly pear prickly pear...

58. Between the idea
And the reality
Between the motion
And the act
Falls the Shadow...

59. This is the way the world ends
Not with a bang but a whimper.
['The Hollow Men' (1925)]

60. 'A cold coming we had of it,
Just the worst time of the year
For a journey, and such a long journey:
The ways deep and the weather sharp,
The very dead of winter'...

61. And the cities hostile and the towns unfriendly
And the villages dirty and charging high prices...

62. And an old white horse galloped away in the meadow...

63. But set down
This set down
This: were we led all that way for
Birth or Death? There was a Birth, certainly,
We had evidence and no doubt. I had seen birth and death,
But had thought they were different; this Birth was
Hard and bitter agony for us, like Death, our death.
We returned to our places, these Kingdoms,
But no longer at ease here, in the old dispensation,
With an alien people clutching their gods.
I should be glad of another death.
['Journey of the Magi' (1927)]

64. Pray for us now and at the hour of our birth.
['Animula' (1929)]

65. Because I do not hope to turn again
Because I do not hope
Because I do not hope to turn...

66. Because these wings are no longer wings to fly
But merely vans to beat the air
The air which is now thoroughly small and dry
Smaller and dryer than the will
Teach us to care and not to care
Teach us to sit still...

67. Lady, three white leopards sat under a juniper-tree
In the cool of the day.
['Ash Wednesday' (1930)]

68. You'd be bored.
Birth, and copulation, and death.
That's all the facts when you come to brass tacks:
Birth, and copulation, and death.
I've been born, and once is enough...

69. Where the breadfruit fall
And the penguin call
And the sound is the sound of the sea
Under the bam
Under the boo
Under the bamboo tree.
[*Sweeney Agonistes* (1932), 'Fragment of an Agon']

70. Where is the Life we have lost in living?
Where is the wisdom we have lost in knowledge?
Where is the knowledge we have lost in information?
[Choruses from 'The Rock' (1934), I]

71. Every son would have his motorcycle,
And daughters ride away on casual pillions.
[Choruses from 'The Rock' (1934), II]

72. Many are engaged in writing books and printing them,
Many desire to see their names in print,
Many read nothing but the race reports...

73. In the land of lobelias and tennis flannels
The rabbit shall burrow and the thorn revisit,
The nettle shall flourish on the gravel court,
And the wind shall say: 'Here were decent godless people:
Their only monument the asphalt road
And a thousand lost golf balls.'
[Choruses from 'The Rock' (1934), III]

74. Yet we have gone on living,
Living and partly living...

75. Men will not hate you
Enough to defame or to execrate you,
But pondering the qualities that you lacked
Will only try to find the historical fact...

76. The last temptation is the greatest treason:
To do the right deed for the wrong reason.
[*Murder in the Cathedral* (1935), I]

77. However certain our expectation
The moment foreseen may be unexpected
When it arrives.
[*Murder in the Cathedral* (1935), II]

78. Why do we feel embarrassed, impatient, fretful, ill at ease,
Assembled like amateur actors who have not been assigned
their parts?
[*The Family Reunion* (1939), I.i]

79. People to whom nothing has ever happened
Cannot understand the unimportance of events.
[*The Family Reunion* (1939), I.i]

80. There is nothing at all to be done about it,
There is nothing to do about anything,
And now it is nearly time for the news.
[*The Family Reunion* (1939), II.i]

81. The clock has stopped in the dark!
[*The Family Reunion* (1939), II.iii]

82. Round and round the circle
Completing the charm
So the knot be unknotted
The crossed be uncrossed
The crooked be made straight
And the curse be ended.
[*The Family Reunion* (1939), II.iii]

83. And he'll say, as he scratches himself with his claws,
'Well, the Theatre's certainly not what it was.
These modern productions are all very well,
But there's nothing to equal, from what I hear tell,
That moment of mystery
When I made history

As Firefrorefiddle, the Fiend of the Fell.'
[*Old Possum's Book of Practical Cats* (1939), 'Gus: the Theatre Cat']

84. Macavity, Macavity, there's no one like Macavity,
There never was a Cat of such deceitfulness and suavity.
He always has an alibi, and one or two to spare:
At whatever time the deed took place – MACAVITY WASN'T THERE!
[*Old Possum's Book of Practical Cats* (1939), 'Macavity: the Mystery Cat']

85. The Naming of Cats is a difficult matter,
It isn't just one of your holiday games;
You may think at first I'm as mad as a hatter
When I tell you a cat must have THREE DIFFERENT NAMES...

86. When you notice a cat in profound meditation,
The reason, I tell you, is always the same:
His mind is engaged in a rapt contemplation
Of the thought, of the thought, of the thought of his name:
His ineffable effable
Effanineffable
Deep and inscrutable singular Name.
[*Old Possum's Book of Practical Cats* (1939), 'The Naming of Cats']

87. Time present and time past
Are both perhaps present in time future,
And time future contained in time past...

88. Human kind
Cannot bear very much reality...

89. At the still point of the turning world. Neither flesh nor fleshless;
Neither from nor towards; at the still point, there the dance is,
But neither arrest nor movement...

90. Time past and time future
Allow but a little consciousness.
To be conscious is not to be in time
But only in time can the moment in the rose-garden,
The moment in the arbour where the rain beat,
The moment in the draughty church at smokefall
Be remembered; involved with past and future.
Only through time time is conquered...

91. Words strain,
Crack and sometimes break, under the burden,
Under the tension, slip, slide, perish,
Decay with imprecision, will not stay in place,
Will not stay still.
[*Four Quartets* (1944), 'Burnt Norton']

92. In my beginning is my end...

93. That was a way of putting it – not very satisfactory:
A periphrastic study in a worn-out poetical fashion,
Leaving one still with the intolerable wrestle
With words and meanings...

94. We are only undeceived
Of that which, deceiving, could no longer harm...

95. The houses are all gone under the sea.

The dancers are all gone under the hill...

96. The wounded surgeon plies the steel
That questions the distempered part;
Beneath the bleeding hands we feel
The sharp compassion of the healer's art
Resolving the enigma of the fever chart...

97. The whole earth is our hospital
Endowed by the ruined millionaire,
Wherein, if we do well, we shall
Die of the absolute paternal care
That will not leave us, but prevents us everywhere...

98. And so each venture
Is a new beginning, a raid on the inarticulate
With shabby equipment always deteriorating
In the general mess of imprecision of feeling...

99. There is only the fight to recover what has been lost
And found and lost again and again: and now, under conditions
That seem unpropitious. But perhaps neither gain nor loss.
For us, there is only the trying. The rest is not our business...

100. In my end is my beginning.
[*Four Quartets* (1944), 'East Coker']

101. I do not know much about gods; but I think that the river
Is a strong brown god...

102. The river is within us, the sea is all about us.
[*Four Quartets* (1944), 'The Dry Salvages']

103. Ash on an old man's sleeve
Is all the ash the burnt roses leave.
Dust in the air suspended
Marks the place where a story ended...

104. Our concern was speech, and speech impelled us
To purify the dialect of the tribe...

105. From wrong to wrong the exasperated spirit
Proceeds, unless restored by that refining fire
Where you must move in measure, like a dancer...

106. We cannot revive old factions
We cannot restore old policies
Or follow an antique drum...

107. The dove descending breaks the air
With flame of incandescent terror...

108. What we call the beginning is often the end
And to make an end is to make a beginning.
The end is where we start from...

109. We shall not cease from exploration
And the end of all our exploring
Will be to arrive where we started
And know the place for the first time.
[*Four Quartets* (1944), 'Little Gidding']

110. Hell is oneself;
Hell is alone, the other figures in it
Merely projections. There is nothing to escape from
And nothing to escape to. One is always alone.
[*The Cocktail Party* (1950), I.iii]

111. You shouldn't interrupt my interruptions:
That's really worse than interrupting.
[*The Cocktail Party* (1950), III]

112. After the erection of the Chinese Wall of Milton, blank verse has suffered not only arrest but retrogression.
['Christopher Marlowe' (1919)]

113. The only way of expressing emotion in the form of art is by finding an 'objective correlative'; in other words, a set of objects, a situation, a chain of events which shall be the formula of that particular emotion; such that when the external facts, which must terminate in sensory experience, are given, the emotion is immediately evoked.
['Hamlet' (1919)]

114. No poet, no artist of any sort, has his complete meaning alone. His significance, his appreciation is the appreciation of his relation to the dead poets and artists.
['Tradition and the Individual Talent' (1919), 1]

115. The business of the poet is not to find new emotions, but to use the ordinary ones and, in working them up into poetry, to express feelings which are not in actual emotions at all.
['Tradition and the Individual Talent' (1919), 2]

116. Poetry is not a turning loose of emotion, but an escape from emotion; it is not the expression of personality, but an escape from personality.
['Tradition and the Individual Talent' (1919), 2]

117. Tennyson and Browning are poets, and they think; but they do not feel their thought as immediately as the odour of a rose. A thought to Donne was an experience; it modified his sensibility.
['The Metaphysical Poets' (1921)]

118. In the seventeenth century a dissociation of sensibility set in, from which we have never recovered.
['The Metaphysical Poets' (1921)]

119. The critic, one would suppose, if he is to justify his existence, should endeavour to discipline his personal prejudices and cranks – tares to which we are all subject – and compose his differences with as many of his fellows as possible, in the common pursuit of true judgement.
['The Function of Criticism' (1923), 1]

120. No artist produces great art by a deliberate attempt to express his own personality.
['Four Elizabethan Dramatists' (1924)]

121. We can say of Shakespeare, that never has a man turned so little knowledge to such great account.
[Lecture, 1942, 'The Classics and the Man of Letters']

122. And I am quite sure that Rosamond Vincy, in Middlemarch, frightens me far more than Goneril or Regan.
[*On Poetry and Poets* (1957), 'The Three Voices of Poetry']

123. [On his ideal of writing]
The common word exact without vulgarity, the formal word precise but not pedantic, the complete consort dancing together.
[In *The Sunday Telegraph*, 1993]

Elizabeth I (1533–1603)

Queen of England 1558–1603; Daughter of Henry VIII and Anne Boleyn; enforcer of Protestantism; scholar and letter writer

1. I am your anointed Queen. I will never be by violence constrained to do anything. I thank God I am endued with such qualities that if I were turned out of the Realm in my petticoat I were able to live in any place in Christome.
[Attr. Speech, 1566]

2. As for me, I see no such great cause why I should either be fond to live or fear to die. I have had good experience of this world, and I know what it is to be a subject and what to be a sovereign. Good neighbours I have had, and I have met with bad: and in trust I have found treason.
[Speech, 1586]

3. [Of the approaching Armada]
I know I have the body of a weak and feeble woman, but I have the heart and stomach of a king, and of a king of England too; and think foul scorn that Parma or Spain, or any prince of Europe, should dare to invade the borders of my realm.
[Speech, 1588]

4. Though God hath raised me high, yet this I count the glory of my crown: that I have reigned with your loves.
[The Golden Speech, 1601]

5. *Semper eadem.*
Ever the same.
[Motto]

6. [Of her commissioners]
Like strawberry wives, that laid two or three great strawberries at the mouth of their pot, and all the rest were little ones.
[In Bacon, *Apophthegms New and Old* (1625)]

7. If thy heart fails thee, climb not at all.
[In Thomas Fuller, *The History of the Worthies of England* (1662), I. Cf. Raleigh: 13]

8. [On being asked if she believed in Christ's presence at Holy Communion]
'Twas God the word that spake it,
He took the Bread and brake it;
And what the word did make it;
That I believe, and take it.
[In S. Clarke, *Marrow of Ecclesiastical History* (1675)]

9. The queen of Scots is lighter of a fair son, and I am but a barren stock.
[In F. Chamberlin, *The Sayings of Queen Elizabeth* (1923)]

10. [Greeting a delegation of eighteen tailors]
Good-morning, gentlemen both.
[In F. Chamberlin, *The Sayings of Queen Elizabeth* (1923)]

11. [To the Dean of St Paul's]
Leave that ungodly digression and return to your text!
[In F. Chamberlin, *The Sayings of Queen Elizabeth* (1923)]

12. [To the leaders of her Council when they opposed her policy on Mary Queen of Scots]
I will make you shorter by the head!
[In F. Chamberlin, *The Sayings of Queen Elizabeth* (1923)]

13. [Of Mary Queen of Scots]
The daughter of debate, that eke discord doth sow.
[In F. Chamberlin, *The Sayings of Queen Elizabeth* (1923)]

14. [Thanking the wife of the Archbishop of Canterbury for her hospitality. Elizabeth disapproved of married clergy.]
Madam I may not call you; mistress I am ashamed to call you; and so I know not what to call you; but, howsoever, I thank you.
[In F. Chamberlin, *The Sayings of Queen Elizabeth* (1923)]

15. [To Sir Walter Raleigh]
I have known many persons who turned their gold into smoke, but you are the first to turn smoke into gold.
[In F. Chamberlin, *The Sayings of Queen Elizabeth* (1923)]

16. [To Robert Cecil, on her death-bed in 1603]
The word 'must' is not to be used to princes. Little man, little man! if your father had lived, he durst not have said so much.
[In F. Chamberlin, *The Sayings of Queen Elizabeth* (1923)]

17. [Remark to the Countess of Nottingham]
God may pardon you, but I never can.
[Attr.]

18. [Last words]
All my possessions for a moment of time.
[Attr., 1603]

Elizabeth II (1926–)

Queen of Great Britain and Northern Ireland from 1952; daughter of George VI and Elizabeth the Queen Mother

1. I think everybody really will concede that on this, of all days, I should begin my speech with the words, 'My husband and I'.
[Speech at her Silver Wedding Banquet, Guildhall, 1972]

2. Scrutiny ... can be just as efficient, if it is made with a touch of gentleness, good humour and understanding.
[Speech at Guildhall, 1992]

3. [Speaking of 1992, in relation to the difficulties experienced by the Royal Family in that year]
Annus horribilis.
[Speech at Guildhall, 1992]

4. [Describing her life's ambition when a child]
I should like to be a horse.
[Attr.]

5. [Comment about Princess Michael of Kent]
She's more royal than we are.
[Attr., in *Sunday* magazine, 1985]

Elizabeth, the Queen Mother (1900–)
Queen of Great Britain and Northern Ireland 1936–52; wife of George VI and mother of Elizabeth II

1. [After Buckingham Palace was bombed during the Blitz in 1940]
I'm glad we've been bombed. It makes me feel I can look the East End in the face.
[Attr.]

2. [On whether, after the bombing of Buckingham Palace, her children would leave England]
The children will not leave unless I do. I shall not leave unless their father does, and the King will not leave the country in any circumstances whatever.
[Attr.]

3. My favourite programme is 'Mrs Dale's Diary'. I try never to miss it because it is the only way of knowing what goes on in a middle-class family.
[Attr.]

4. [Remark after a fishbone had lodged in her throat]
The salmon are striking back.
[Attr.]

5. [Of President Carter]
He is the only man since my dear husband died, to have the effrontery to kiss me on the lips.
[Attr.]

6. [To her daughter, the Queen, when she accepted a second glass of wine at lunch]
Do you think it's wise, darling? You know you've got to rule this afternoon.
[Attr.]

Ellerton, John (1826–1893)
English priest and writer

1. The day Thou gavest, Lord, is ended,
The darkness falls at Thy behest;
To Thee our morning hymns ascended,
Thy praise shall sanctify our rest...

2. Thy throne shall never,
Like earth's proud empires, pass away.
[Hymn, 1870]

Elliot, Jean (1727–1805)
Scottish lyricist

1. I've heard them lilting, at our yowe-milking,
Lasses a' lilting before the dawn o' day;
But now they are moaning on ilka green loaning–
The Flowers of the Forest are a' wede away.
['The Flowers of the Forest' (1756). Cf. Alison Cockburn: 1]

Elliott, Charlotte (1789–1871)
English hymn writer and religious poet

1. 'Christian! seek not yet repose,'
Hear thy guardian angel say;
Thou art in the midst of foes;
'Watch and pray.'
[Hymn]

Elliott, Ebenezer (1781–1849)
English poet and merchant; known as the 'Corn Law Rhymer'

1. When wilt thou save the people?
Oh, God of Mercy! when?
The people, Lord, the people!
Not thrones and crowns, but men!
['The People's Anthem' (1850)]

2. What is a communist? One who hath yearnings
For equal division of unequal earnings.
[Epigram, 1850]

Ellis, Bob (Robert James Keith) (1942–)
Australian dramatist

1. *King O'Malley*: Show me a Wednesday wencher and a Sunday saint, and I'll show you a Roman Catholic.
[*The Legend of King O'Malley* (1974), I, 2]

Ellis, George (1753–1815)
West Indian-born British satirist and poet

1. Snowy, Flowy, Blowy,
Showery, Flowery, Bowery,
Hoppy, Croppy, Droppy,
Breezy, Sneezy, Freezy.
['The Twelve Months']

Ellis, Havelock (1859–1939)
English sexologist and essayist

1. Every artist writes his own autobiography.
[*The New Spirit* (1890), 'Tolstoi']

2. Beauty is the child of love.
[*The New Spirit* (1890), Conclusion]

3. In many a war it has been the vanquished, not the victor, who has carried off the finest spoils.
[*The Soul of Spain* (1908)]

4. What we call 'Progress' is the exchange of one nuisance for another nuisance.
[*Impressions and Comments* (1914)]

5. God is an unutterable Sigh in the Human Heart, said the old German mystic. And therewith said the last word.
[*Impressions and Comments* (1914)]

6. The absence of flaw in beauty is itself a flaw.
[*Impressions and Comments* (1914)]

7. The whole religious complexion of the modern world is due to the absence from Jerusalem of a lunatic asylum.
[*Impressions and Comments* (1914)]

8. But for my everlasting good fortune I was flung into the wide sea of Australian bush alone, to sink or to swim.
[*My Life* (1940)]

9. Love is friendship plus sex.
[Attr.]

Ellwood, Thomas (1639–1713)
English Quaker, friend of John Milton, and poet

1. Thou hast said much here of 'Paradise Lost'; but what hast thou to say of 'Paradise found'?
[Remark to Milton, 1665]

Elstow (early 16th century)
English friar

1. [Response to being threatened with drowning by Henry VIII]
With thanks to God we know the way to heaven, to be as ready by water as by land, and therefore we care not which way we go.
[Attr.]

Éluard, Paul (Eugène Grindel) (1895–1952)
French surrealist poet

1. *Adieu tristesse*
Bonjour tristesse
Tu es inscrite dans les lignes du plafond.
Sadness, adieu, sadness, hello, you are engraved in the lines of the ceiling.
['A peine défigurée' ('Slightly Disfigured', 1932)]

El-Yezdi, Haji Abu

1. We dance along Death's icy brink,
But is the dance less full of fun?
['The Kasidah']

Emerson, Ralph Waldo (1803–1882)
American poet, essayist, transcendentalist and teacher

1. Light is the first of painters. There is no object so foul that intense light will not make it beautiful.
[*Nature* (1836), 'Beauty'. Cf. John Constable: 2]

2. We are taught by great actions that the universe is the property of every individual in it.
[*Nature* (1836), 'Beauty']

3. There is properly no history; only biography.
[*Essays, First Series* (1841), 'History']

4. To believe your own thought, to believe that what is true for you in your private heart is true for all men, – that is genius.
[*Essays, First Series* (1841), 'Self-Reliance']

5. To-morrow a stranger will say with masterly good sense precisely what we have thought and felt all the time, and we shall be forced to take with shame our own opinion from another.
[*Essays, First Series* (1841), 'Self-Reliance']

6. Society everywhere is in conspiracy against the manhood of every one of its members.
[*Essays, First Series* (1841), 'Self-Reliance']

7. Whoso would be a man must be a nonconformist.
[*Essays, First Series* (1841), 'Self-Reliance']

8. No law can be sacred to me but that of my nature. Good and bad are but names very readily transferable to that or this; the only right is what is after my own constitution, the only wrong what is against it.
[*Essays, First Series* (1841), 'Self-Reliance']

9. It is easy in the world to live after the world's opinion; it is easy in solitude after our own; but the great man is he who, in the midst of the crowd, keeps with perfect sweetness the independence of solitude.
[*Essays, First Series* (1841), 'Self-Reliance']

10. A foolish consistency is the hobgoblin of little minds, adored by little statesmen and philosophers and divines. With consistency a great soul has simply nothing to do.
[*Essays, First Series* (1841), 'Self-Reliance']

11. Is it so bad, then, to be misunderstood? Pythagoras was misunderstood, and Socrates, and Jesus, and Luther, and Copernicus, and Galileo, and Newton, and every pure and wise spirit that ever took flesh. To be great is to be misunderstood.
[*Essays, First Series* (1841), 'Self-Reliance']

12. I like the silent church before the service begins, better than any preaching.
[*Essays, First Series* (1841), 'Self-Reliance']

13. Travelling is a fool's paradise. Our first journeys discover to us the indifference of places.
[*Essays, First Series* (1841), 'Self-Reliance']

14. Fear is an instructor of great sagacity, and the herald of all revolutions.
[*Essays, First Series* (1841), 'Compensation']

15. All mankind love a lover.
[*Essays, First Series* (1841), 'Love']

16. Let the soul be assured that somewhere in the universe it should rejoin its friend, and it would be content and cheerful alone for a thousand years.
[*Essays, First Series* (1841), 'Friendship']

17. A friend is a person with whom I may be sincere. Before him I may think aloud.
[*Essays, First Series* (1841), 'Friendship']

18. A friend may well be reckoned the masterpiece of Nature.
[*Essays, First Series* (1841), 'Friendship']

19. The only reward of virtue is virtue; the only way to have a friend is to be one.
[*Essays, First Series* (1841), 'Friendship']

20. In skating over thin ice, our safety is in our speed.
[*Essays, First Series* (1841), 'Prudence']

21. It was a high counsel that I once heard given to a young person, – 'Always do what you are afraid to do.'
[*Essays, First Series* (1841), 'Heroism']

22. Beware when the great God lets loose a thinker on this planet. Then all things are at risk.
[*Essays, First Series* (1841), 'Circles']

23. Conversation is a game of circles. In conversation we pluck up the termini which bound the common of silence on every side.
[*Essays, First Series* (1841), 'Circles']

24. The virtues of society are the vices of the saint.
[*Essays, First Series* (1841), 'Circles']

25. People wish to be settled; only as far as they are unsettled is there any hope for them.
[*Essays, First Series* (1841), 'Circles']

26. Nothing great was ever achieved without enthusiasm.
[*Essays, First Series* (1841), 'Circles']

27. Though we travel the world over to find the beautiful we must carry it with us or we find it not.
[*Essays, First Series* (1841), 'Art']

28. Nothing astonishes men so much as common-sense and plain dealing.
[*Essays, First Series* (1841), 'Art']

29. Words are also actions, and actions are a kind of words.
[*Essays, Second Series* (1844), 'The Poet']

30. It is not metres, but a metre-making argument, that makes a poem.
[*Essays, Second Series* (1844), 'The Poet']

31. We are symbols, and inhabit symbols.
[*Essays, Second Series* (1844), 'The Poet']

32. Language is fossil poetry.
[*Essays, Second Series* (1844), 'The Poet']

33. To fill the hour, – that is happiness.
[*Essays, Second Series* (1844), 'Experience']

34. The wise through excess of wisdom is made a fool.
[*Essays, Second Series* (1844), 'Experience']

35. The years teach much which the days never know.
[*Essays, Second Series* (1844), 'Experience']

36. Character is nature in the highest form. It is of no use to ape it, or to contend with it.
[*Essays, Second Series* (1844), 'Character']

37. Living blood and a passion of kindness does at last distinguish God's gentlemen from Fashion's.
[*Essays, Second Series* (1844), 'Manners']

38. Good men must not obey the laws too well.
[*Essays, Second Series* (1844), 'Politics']

39. Every man is wanted, and no man is wanted much.
[*Essays, Second Series* (1844), 'Nominalist and Realist']

40. Men are conservatives when they are least vigorous, or when they are most luxurious. They are conservatives after dinner. ... when they hear music, or when they read poetry, they are radicals.
[*Essays, Second Series* (1844), 'New England Reformers']

41. The reward of a thing well done, is to have done it.
[*Essays, Second Series* (1844), 'New England Reformers']

42. Every hero becomes a bore at last.
[*Representative Men* (1850), 'Uses of Great Men']

43. Talent alone cannot make a writer. There must be a man behind the book.
[*Representative Men* (1850), 'Goethe; or, the Writer']

44. Is not marriage an open question, when it is alleged, from the beginning of the world, that such as are in the institution wish to get out and such as are out wish to get in.
[*Representative Men* (1850), 'Montaigne; or, the Skeptic']

45. [Of the English]
They think him the best dressed man, whose dress is so fit for his use that you cannot notice or remember to describe it.
[*English Traits* (1856), 5]

46. It is a lesson which all history teaches wise men, to put trust in ideas, and not in circumstances.
[*Miscellanies* (1856), 'War']

47. As there is a use in medicine for poisons, so the world cannot move without rogues.
[*Conduct of Life* (1860), 'Power']

48. The manly part is to do with might and main what you can do.
[*Conduct of Life* (1860), 'Wealth']

49. Art is a jealous mistress, and, if a man have a genius for painting, poetry, music, architecture, or philosophy, he makes a bad husband and an ill provider.
[*Conduct of Life* (1860), 'Wealth']

50. We say the cows laid out Boston. Well, there are worse surveyors.
[*Conduct of Life* (1860), 'Wealth']

51. Novels are as useful as Bibles, if they teach you the secret, that the best of life is conversation, and the greatest success is confidence.
[*Conduct of Life* (1860), 'Behavior']

52. The louder he talked of his honor, the faster we counted our spoons.
[*Conduct of Life* (1860), 'Worship']

53. A person seldom falls sick, but the bystanders are animated with a faint hope that he will die.
[*Conduct of Life* (1860), 'Considerations by the way']

54. Make yourself necessary to somebody.
[*Conduct of Life* (1860), 'Considerations by the way']

55. All sensible people are selfish, and nature is tugging at every contract to make the terms of it fair.
[*Conduct of Life* (1860), 'Considerations by the way']

56. The religions we call false were once true.
[*North American Review*, 1866, 'Character']

57. Now that is the wisdom of a man, in every instance of his labor, to hitch his wagon to a star, and see his chore done by the gods themselves.
[*Society and Solitude* (1870), 'Civilization']

58. We boil at different degrees.
[*Society and Solitude* (1870), 'Eloquence']

59. Invention breeds invention.
[*Society and Solitude* (1870), 'Works and Days']

60. The machine unmakes the man. Now that the machine is so perfect, the engineer is nobody.
[*Society and Solitude* (1870), 'Works and Days']

61. A man builds a fine house; and now he has a master, and a task for life; he is to furnish, watch, show it, and keep it in repair, the rest of his days.
[*Society and Solitude* (1870), 'Works and Days']

62. Life is good only when it is magical and musical, a perfect timing and consent, and when we do not anatomize it. You must treat the days respectfully, you must be a day yourself, and not interrogate it like a college professor ... You must hear the bird's song without attempting to render it into nouns and verbs.
[*Society and Solitude* (1870), 'Works and Days']

63. Write it on your heart that every day is the best day in the year. No man has learned anything rightly until he knows that every day is Doomsday.
[*Society and Solitude* (1870), 'Works and Days']

64. [To a person complaining that he had not enough time]
'Well,' said Red Jacket, 'I suppose you have all there is.'
[*Society and Solitude* (1870), 'Works and Days']

65. Every man is a borrower and a mimic, life is theatrical and literature a quotation.
[*Society and Solitude* (1870), 'Success']

66. Tis the good reader that makes the good book.
[*Society and Solitude* (1870), 'Success']

67. America is a country of young men.
[*Society and Solitude* (1870), 'Old Age']

68. Nature is full of freaks, and now puts an old head on young shoulders, and then a young heart beating under fourscore winters.
[*Society and Solitude* (1870), 'Old Age']

69. There is no knowledge that is not power.
[*Society and Solitude* (1870), 'Old Age']

70. It is only when the mind and character slumber that the dress can be seen.
[*Letters and Social Aims* (1875), 'Social Aims']

71. I have heard with admiring submission the experience of the lady who declared that 'the sense of being well-dressed gives a feeling of inward tranquillity which religion is powerless to bestow.'
[*Letters and Social Aims* (1875), 'Social Aims']

72. Good manners are made up of petty sacrifices.
[*Letters and Social Aims* (1875), 'Social Aims']

73. By necessity, by proclivity, – and by delight, we all quote.
[*Letters and Social Aims* (1875), 'Quotation and Originality']

74. Next to the originator of a good sentence is the first quoter of it.
[*Letters and Social Aims* (1875), 'Quotation and Originality']

75. When Shakespeare is charged with debts to his authors, Landor replies: 'Yet he was more original than his originals. He breathed upon dead bodies and brought them into life.'
[*Letters and Social Aims* (1875), 'Quotation and Originality']

76. Artists must be sacrificed to their art. Like bees, they must put their lives into the sting they give.
[*Letters and Social Aims* (1875), 'Inspiration']

77. What is a weed? A plant whose virtues have not yet been discovered.
[*Fortune of the Republic* (1878)]

78. There is a little formula, couched in pure Saxon, which you may hear in the corners of the streets and in the yard of the dame's school, from very little republicans: 'I'm as good as you be,' which contains the essence of the Massachusetts Bill of Rights and of the American Declaration of Independence.
[*Natural History of Intellect* (1893), 'Boston']

79. The bitterest tragic element in life to be derived from an intellectual source is the belief in a brute Fate or Destiny.
[*Natural History of Intellect* (1893), 'The Tragic']

80. Other world! There is no other world! Here or nowhere is the whole fact.
[*Uncollected Lectures* (1932), 'Natural Religion']

81. We are always getting ready to live, but never living.
[*Journals*]

82. I hate quotations.
[*Journals*]

83. I trust a good deal to common fame, as we all must. If a man has good corn, or wood, or boards, or pigs, to sell, or can make better chairs or knives, crucibles, or church organs, than anybody else, you will find a broad, hard-beaten road to his house, though it be in the woods.
[*Journals*]

84. Old age brings along with its ugliness the comfort that you will soon be out of it, – which ought to be a substantial relief to such discontented pendulums as we are. To be out of the war, out of debt, out of the drouth, out of the blues, out of the dentist's hands, out of the second thoughts, mortifications, and remorses that inflict such twinges and shooting pains, – out of the next winter, and the high prices, and company below your ambition, – surely these are soothing hints.
[*Journals*]

85. I pay the schoolmaster, but 'tis the schoolboys that educate my son.
[*Journals*]

86. The book written against fame and learning has the author's name on the title-page.
[*Journals*]

87. In your sane hour, you shall see that not a line has yet been written; that for all the poetry that is in the world your first sensation on entering a wood or standing on the shore of a lake has not been chanted yet . . . And yet for all this it must be owned that literature has truly told us that the cock crows in the mornings.
[*Journals*]

88. A day is a miniature eternity.
[*Journals*]

89. When divine souls appear men are compelled by their own self-respect to distinguish them.
[*Journals*]

90. The Americans have little faith. They rely on the power of a dollar.
[Lecture, 1841, 'Man the Reformer']

91. When Nature has work to be done, she creates a genius to do it.
[Lecture, 1841, 'Method of Nature']

92. He builded better than he knew;–
The conscious stone to beauty grew.
[*Poems* (1847), 'The Problem']

93. Spring still makes spring in the mind,
When sixty years are told.
[*Poems* (1847), 'The World-Soul']

94. Earth laughs in flowers.
[*Poems* (1847), 'Hamatreya']

95. Good-bye, proud world! I'm going home:
Thou art not my friend, and I'm not thine.
[*Poems* (1847), 'Good-bye']

96. The frolic architecture of the snow.
[*Poems* (1847), 'The Snow-storm']

97. Things are in the saddle,
And ride mankind.
[*Poems* (1847), 'Ode, Inscribed to W.H. Channing']

98. Here once the embattled farmers stood,
And fired the shot heard round the world.
[*Poems* (1847), Concord Hymn: sung at the Completion of the Battle Monument, 1836]

99. I am the doubter and the doubt,
And I the hymn the Brahmin sings.
[*May-Day* (1867), 'Brahma']

100. So nigh is grandeur to our dust,
So near is God to man,
When Duty whispers low, Thou must,
The youth replies, I can.
[*May-Day* (1867), 'Voluntaries']

Emery, Dick (1918–1983)
British comedian, variety artiste and writer

1. Oh, you are awful! But I like you!
[1970s catchphrase]

Emmet, Robert (1778–1803)
Irish patriot

1. [Before his execution]
When my country takes her place among the nations of the earth, then and not till then, let my epitaph be written. I have done.
[Attr.]

Emmons, Margaret

1. If while you are in school, there is a shortage of qualified personnel in a particular field, then by the time you graduate with the necessary qualifications, that field's employment market is glutted.
[Attr.]

Empedocles (c. 490–c. 430 BC)
Greek philosopher, scientist and poet

1. God is a circle whose centre is everywhere and whose circumference is nowhere.
[Attr.]

Empson, Sir William (1906–1984)
English poet and literary critic; Professor of English

1. Seven Types of Ambiguity.
[Title of book, 1930]

2. It seemed the best thing to be up and go.
['Aubade' (1934)]

3. Slowly the poison the whole blood stream fills.
It is not the effort nor the failure tires.
The waste remains, the waste remains and kills.
['Missing Dates' (1935)]

4. Waiting for the end, boys, waiting for the end.
What is there to be or do?
What's become of me or you?
Are we kind or are we true?
Sitting two and two, boys, waiting for the end.
['Just a Smack at Auden' (1940)]

Engels, Friedrich (1820–1895)
German socialist, political philosopher and co-founder (with Marx) of modern Communism

1. California and Australia are two cases which were not provided for in the Manifesto: creation of great new markets out of nothing. They must still be put into it.
[Engels to Marx, 1852, in Henry Mayer, *Marx, Engels and Australia*]

2. *Der Staat wird nicht 'abgeschafft', er stirbt ab.*
The state is not abolished, it dies away.
[*Anti-Dühring* (1878), III, 2]

3. Freedom is the recognition of necessity.
[In Alan L. Mackay, *The Harvest of a Quiet Eye* (1977)]

English, Thomas Dunn (1819–1902)
American physician, lawyer, dramatist and public official

1. Oh! don't you remember sweet Alice, Ben Bolt,
Sweet Alice, whose hair was so brown,
Who wept with delight when you gave her a smile,
And trembled with fear at your frown?
['Ben Bolt' (1885)]

Ennius, Quintus (239–169 BC)
Greek-born Roman epic poet, dramatist, satirist and teacher

1. *At tuba terribili sonitu taratantara dixit.*
And the trumpet in terrible tones went taratantara.
[*Annals*]

2. *Moribus antiquis res stat Romana virisque.*
The Roman state survives by its ancient customs and its manhood.
[*Annals*]

3. *Quem metuunt, oderunt.*
They hate whom they fear.
[*Thyestes*]

4. *Simia, quam similis turpissima bestia, nobis.*
How like us is the ape, most horrible of beasts.
[In Cicero, *De Natura Deorum*]

5. [Of Q. Fabius Maximus]
Unus homo nobis cunctando restituit rem.
One man by delaying saved the situation for us.
[In Cicero, *De Senectute*]

Epicurus (341–270 BC)
Greek philosopher and teacher; founder of Epicureanism

1. It is not so much our friends' help that helps us as the confident knowledge that they will help us.
[Attr.]

Erasmus, Desiderius (c. 1466–1536)
Dutch Renaissance scholar and humanist

1. *Scitum est inter caecos luscum regnare posse.*
It is well known, that among the blind the one-eyed man is king.
[*Adagia* (1500)]

2. *A fronte praecipitium, a tergo lupi,*
A precipice in front, wolves behind.
[*Adagia* (1500)]

3. *Dulce bellum inexpertis.*
War is sweet to those who have not tried it.
[*Adagia* (1500)]

4. *Festina lente.*
Make haste slowly.
[*Adagia* (1500)]

5. [Of his failure to fast during Lent]
I have a Catholic soul, but a Lutheran stomach.
[*Dictionnaire Encyclopédique*]

6. Is not the Turk a man and a brother?
[*Querela Pacis*]

7. [Reply to the Franciscan monks who said that he had laid an egg and Luther had hatched it]
Yes, but the egg I laid was a hen, and Luther hatched a gamecock.
[In P.S. Allen (ed.), *Works* (1906–1947)]

Ertz, Susan (1894–1985)
English writer

1. Someone has somewhere commented on the fact that millions long for immortality who don't know what to do with themselves on a rainy Sunday afternoon.
[*Anger in the Sky* (1943)]

Erwin, George Dudley (1917–1985)
Australian Cabinet Minister

1. [When asked the reason for his dismissal as Air Minister, 1969; Ms Gotto was the secretary of Prime Minister John Gorton and said to exert undue influence]
It is shapely, it wiggles, and its name is Ainslie Gotto.
[In *Dictionary of Australian Quotations*]

Essex, Robert Devereux, Earl of (1566–1601)
English soldier and courtier, beheaded for treason; writer of sonnets

1. [To Lord Willoughby]
Reasons are not like garments, the worse for wearing.
[Attr., c. 1599]

Esson, Louis (1879–1943)
Scots-born Australian dramatist

1. Australia is the only country in the world where the peasantry make the laws.
[*The Time Is Not Yet Ripe* (1912), IV]

2. [On Melbourne University]
If the science professors knew as little about their jobs as the literary ones the University would have been blown up long ago!
[In Vance Palmer, *Louis Esson and the Australian Theatre* (1948)]

Estienne, Henri (1531–1598)
French classical scholar, lexicographer, printer and publisher

1. *Si jeunesse savoit; si vieillesse pouvoit.*
If only youth knew; if only age could.
[*Les Prémices* (1594)]

Etherege, Sir George (c. 1635–1691)
English Restoration dramatist, founder of English comedy of intrigue

1. I walk within the purlieus of the law.
[*Love in a Tub* (1664), I.iii]

2. When love grows diseased, the best thing we can do is put it to a violent death; I cannot endure the torture of a lingring and consumptive passion.
[*The Man of Mode* (1676), II.ii]

3. Writing, Madam, is a mechanic part of wit; a gentleman should never go beyond a song or a billet.
[*The Man of Mode* (1676), IV.i]

4. Whate'er you say, I know all beyond High Park's a desert to you.
[*The Man of Mode* (1676), V.ii]

Euclid (fl. c. 300 BC)
Greek mathematician, founder of the mathematical school at Alexandria

1. *Quod erat demonstrandum.* [*Q.E.D.*]
Which was to be proved.
[*Elements* (Latin version)]

2. *Pons asinorum.*
The bridge of asses.
[*Elements* (Latin version)]

3. A line is length without breadth.
[*Elements*]

4. [To Ptolemy I]
There is no royal road to geometry.
[In Proclus, *Commentaria in Euclidem*]

Euripides (c. 485–406 BC)
Greek classical dramatist; tragedian and poet

1. My tongue swore, but my mind was still unpledged.
[*Hippolytus*]

2. The day is for honest men, the night for thieves.
[*Iphigenia in Tauris*]

3. Those whom God wishes to destroy, he first makes mad.
[Fragment]

Evans, Abel (1679–1737)
English divine, poet and satirist

1. Under this stone, Reader, survey
Dead Sir John Vanbrugh's house of clay.
Lie heavy on him, Earth! for he
Laid many heavy loads on thee!
['Epitaph on Sir John Vanbrugh, Architect of Blenheim Palace' (died 1726)]

Evans, Dame Edith (1888–1976)
English leading stage and film actress

1. When a woman behaves like a man, why doesn't she behave like a nice man?
[*The Observer*, 'Sayings of the Week', 1956]

2. [In Fortnum and Mason, to a salesgirl who insisted on giving her threepence change]
Keep the change, my dear. I trod on a grape as I came in.
[In B. Forbes, *Dame Edith Evans: Ned's Girl* (1977)]

3. [On being told that Nancy Mitford had been lent a villa to enable her to finish a book]
Oh really. What exactly is she reading?
[Attr.]

4. [Remark made a week before she died]
Death is my neighbour now.
[Attr.]

Evans, Harold (1928–)
English journalist and newspaper editor

1. The camera cannot lie. But it can be an accessory to untruth.
[Attr.]

Evarts, William Maxwell (1818–1901)
American lawyer and statesman

1. [Of a dinner given by US President and temperance advocate Rutherford B. Hayes]
It was a brilliant affair; water flowed like champagne.
[Attr.]

Evelyn, John (1620–1706)
English diarist and prose writer

1. A studious decliner of honours and titles.
[*Diary*, Introduction]

2. This Knight was indeede a valiant Gent; but not a little given to romance, when he spake of himselfe.
[*Diary*, 1651]

3. Mulberry Garden, now the onely place of refreshment about the Towne for persons of the best quality, to be exceedingly cheated at.
[*Diary*, 1654]

4. That miracle of a youth, Mr Christopher Wren.
[*Diary*, 1654]

5. I saw Hamlet Prince of Denmark played: but now the old playe began to disgust this refined age.
[*Diary*, 1661]

Everett, David (1769–1813)
American lawyer and writer

1. You'd scarce expect one of my age
To speak in public on the stage;
And if I chance to fall below
Demosthenes or Cicero,

Don't view me with a critic's eye,
But pass my imperfections by.
Large streams from little fountains flow,
Tall oaks from little acorns grow.
['Lines Written for a School Declamation' (at the age of 7)]

Ewart, Gavin (1916–)
English poet; author of light, comic and erotic verse and epigrams

1. Miss Twye was soaping her breasts in the bath
When she heard behind her a meaning laugh
And to her amazement she discovered
A wicked man in the bathroom cupboard.
['Miss Twye' (1939)]

2. After Cambridge – unemployment. No one wanted much to know.
Good degrees are good for nothing in the business world below.
['The Sentimental Education']

3. The Irish are great talkers
Persuasive and disarming,
You can say lots and lots
Against the Scots –
But at least they're never charming!
[*The Complete Little Ones* (1986)]

4. Good light verse is better than bad heavy verse any day of the week.
[*Penultimate Poems* (1989), 'Modest Proposal']

Ewer, William Norman (1885–1976)
English journalist

1. I gave my life for freedom – This I know:
For those who bade me fight had told me so.
[*Five Souls and Other Verses* (1917), 'The Souls']

2. How odd
Of God
To choose
The Jews.
[In *Week-End Book* (1924), 'How Odd'. Cf. Cecil Browne's reply]

Fabyan, Robert (d. 1513)
English chronicler

1. Finally he paid the debt of nature.
[*The New Chronicles of England and France* (1516), I]

2. King Henry [I] being in Normandy, after some writers, fell from or with his horse, whereof he caught his death; but Ranulphe says he took a surfeit by eating of a lamprey, and thereof died.
[*The New Chronicles of England and France* (1516), I]

3. The Duke of Clarence ... then being a prisoner in the Tower, was secretly put to death and drowned in a barrel of Malmesey wine within the said Tower.
[*The New Chronicles of England and France* (1516), II]

Fadiman, Clifton (1904–)
American writer and editor, radio and TV personality

1. [Of Gertrude Stein]
I encountered the mama of dada again.
[*Appreciations* (1955), 'Gertrude Stein']

2. We prefer to believe that the absence of inverted commas guarantees the originality of a thought, whereas it may be merely that the utterer has forgotten its source.
[*Any Number Can Play* (1957)]

3. Cheese – milk's leap toward immortality.
[*Any Number Can Play* (1957)]

4. Experience teaches you that the man who looks you straight in the eye, particularly if he adds a firm handshake, is hiding something.
[*Enter, Conversing*]

Fairbairn, Sir Nicholas (1933–1995)
Scottish Conservative MP and Queen's Counsel

1. Sex is a human activity like any other. It's a natural urge, like breathing, thinking, drinking, laughing, talking with friends, golf. They are not crimes if you plan them with someone other than your wife. Why should sex be?
[*The Independent*, 1992]

2. Most cases of rape are reported as an act of vengeance because the fellow has got himself another woman. Or guilt.
[*Daily Mail*, 1993]

3. [On women MPs]
I can't say I've ever got visually, artistically or sexually excited by any of them. They all look as though they're from the Fifth Kiev Stalinist machine-gun parade.
[*Daily Mail*, 1993]

4. [On feminism]
It's a cover for lesbian homosexuality.
[*Daily Mail*, 1993]

Fairbairn, Lady Sam (Suzanne Mary)
Second wife of Tory MP, Sir Nicholas Fairbairn

1. Behind every great man is an exhausted woman.
[*The Independent*, 1994]

Fairburn, A.R.D. (1904–1957)
New Zealand poet

1. The press: slow dripping of water on mud;
thought's daily bagwash, ironing out opinion,
scarifying the edges of ideas.
[*Collected Poems* (1966), 'Dominion']

2. What is there left to be said?
There is nothing we can say,
nothing at all to be done
to undo the time of day;
no words to make the sun
roll east, or raise the dead.
[*Collected Poems* (1966), 'A Farewell']

3. The years have stolen
all her loveliness,
her days are fallen
in the long wet grass
like petals shaken
from the lilac's bosom.
[*Collected Poems* (1966), 'An Old Woman']

Fairlie, Henry (1924–1990)

1. I have several times suggested that what I call the 'Establishment' in this country is today more powerful than ever before. By the 'Establishment' I do not mean only the centres of official power – though they are certainly part of it – but rather the whole matrix of official and social relations within which power is exercised ... the 'Establishment' can be seen at work in the activities of, not only the Prime Minister, the Archbishop of Canterbury and the Earl Marshall, but of such lesser mortals as the Chairman of the Arts Council, the Director-General of the BBC, and even

the editor of the *Times Literary Supplement*, not to mention dignitaries like Lady Violet Bonham-Carter.
[*Spectator*, 1955]

Falkland, Lucius Cary, Second Viscount (c. 1610–1643)
English politician and writer

1. When it is not necessary to change, it is necessary not to change.
[Speech concerning Episcopacy, 1641]

Fallada, Hans (1893–1947)
German author

1. *Kleiner Mann, was nun?*
Little Man, What Now?
[Title of novel]

Fanon, Frantz (1925–1961)
West Indian psychoanalyst and social philosopher

1. For the black man there is only one destiny. And it is white.
[*Black Skin, White Masks*]

Faraday, Michael (1791–1867)
English chemist and physicist; discoverer of electromagnetic induction

1. [On being offered the Presidency of the Royal Society]
Tyndall, I must remain plain Michael Faraday to the last; and let me now tell you, that if I accepted the honour which the Royal Society desires to confer upon me, I would not answer for the integrity of my intellect for a single year.
[In J. Tyndall, *Faraday as a Discoverer* (1868)]

Farjeon, Herbert (1887–1945)
English actor, dramatic critic, dramatist and theatrical manager

1. I've danced with a man, who's danced with a girl, who's danced with the Prince of Wales.
[*The Picnic* (1927)]

Farmer, Edward (c. 1809–1876)
English poet and writer

1. I have no pain, dear mother, now;
But oh! I am so dry:
Just moisten poor Jim's lips once more;
And, mother, do not cry!
['The Collier's Dying Child'. Cf. Anonymous: 72]

Farouk I (1920–1965)
Last King of Egypt, 1936–52

1. [Remark made to Lord Boyd-Orr, 1948]
There will soon be only five kings left – the Kings of England, Diamonds, Hearts, Spades and Clubs.
[Attr.]

Farquhar, George (1678–1707)
Irish comic dramatist of the Restoration period

1. Money is the sinews of love, as of war.
[*Love and a Bottle* (1698), II.i]

2. Poetry's a mere drug, Sir.
[*Love and a Bottle* (1698), III.ii]

3. He answered the description the page gave to a T, Sir.
[*Love and a Bottle* (1698), IV.iii]

4. I hate all that don't love me, and slight all that do.
[*The Constant Couple* (1699), I.ii]

5. Grant me some wild expressions, Heavens, or I shall burst – . . . Words, words or I shall burst.
[*The Constant Couple* (1699), V.iii]

6. Charming women can true converts make,
We love the precepts for the teacher's sake.
[*The Constant Couple* (1699), V.iii]

7. Crimes, like virtues, are their own rewards.
[*The Inconstant* (1702), IV.ii]

8. A lady, if undrest at Church, looks silly,
One cannot be devout in dishabilly.
[*The Stage Coach* (1704), Prologue]

9. I have fed purely upon ale; I have eat my ale, drank my ale, and I always sleep upon ale.
[*The Beaux' Stratagem* (1707), I.i]

10. My Lady Bountiful.
[*The Beaux' Stratagem* (1707), I.i]

11. Says little, thinks less, and does – nothing at all, faith.
[*The Beaux' Stratagem* (1707), I.i]

12. There's some diversion in a talking blockhead; and since a woman must wear chains, I would have the pleasure of hearing 'em rattle a little.
[*The Beaux' Stratagem* (1707), II.ii]

13. No woman can be a beauty without a fortune.
[*The Beaux' Stratagem* (1707), II.ii]

14. I believe they talked of me, for they laughed consumedly.
[*The Beaux' Stratagem* (1707), III.i]

15. 'Twas for the good of my country that I should be abroad. – Anything for the good of one's country – I'm a Roman for that.
[*The Beaux' Stratagem* (1707), III.ii]

16. *Aimwell*: Then you understand Latin, Mr Bonniface?
Bonniface: Not I, Sir, as the saying is, but he talks it so very fast that I'm sure it must be good.
[*The Beaux' Stratagem* (1707), III.ii]

17. How a little love and good company improves a woman!
[*The Beaux' Stratagem* (1707), IV.i]

18. It is a maxim that man and wife should never have it in their power to hang one another.
[*The Beaux' Stratagem* (1707), IV.ii]

19. Spare all I have, and take my life.
[*The Beaux' Stratagem* (1707), V.ii]

Farragut, David Glasgow (1801–1870)
American admiral

1. [Spoken at the battle of Mobile Bay, 1864]
Damn the torpedoes! Full speed ahead.
[Attr.]

Farrar, Frederic William, Dean of Canterbury (1831–1903)
Indian-born English clergyman; author of theological works and children's stories

1. Russell . . . acted invariably from the highest principles.
[*Eric, or Little by Little* (1858), I, 3]

2. 'What a surly devil that is,' said Eric, . . .
'A surly– ? Oh, Eric, that's the first time I ever heard you swear.'
[*Eric, or Little by Little* (1858), I, 8]

3. They all drank his health with the usual honours: – '. . . For he's a jolly good fe-el-low, which nobody can deny.'
[*Julian Home*, 21]

Faulkner, William (1897–1962)
American novelist and short-story writer, his work set in the southern states of the US; Nobel prize 1949

1. The writer's only responsibility is to his art ... If a writer has to rob his mother, he will not hesitate; the 'Ode on a Grecian Urn' is worth any number of old ladies.
[*Paris Review*, 1956]

2. [On Henry James]
The nicest old lady I ever met.
[In E. Stone, *The Battle and the Books* (c. 1964)]

3. [Of Ernest Hemingway]
He has never been known to use a word that might send the reader to the dictionary.
[Attr. Cf. Hemingway: 13]

Faust, Beatrice Eileen (1939–)
Australian writer and feminist

1. If the women's movement can be summed up in a single phrase, it is 'the right to choose'.
[*Women, Sex and Pornography* (1980)]

2. Men react impersonally to the stripper's body and sexual aura; girls react to the pop-star as a person, not as a sexy body. ... Typical pin-ups for women would be Elvis Presley or Burt Reynolds – clothed. The typical pin-up for men is Miss Big Tits, sitting on her assets.
[*Women, Sex and Pornography* (1980)]

3. Women's Liberationists are both right and wrong when they say that rape is not about sex but about power: for men, sex is power, unless culture corrects biology.
[*Women, Sex and Pornography* (1980)]

Fawcett, John (1740–1817)
English Baptist theologian and minister

1. Blest be the tie that binds
Our hearts in Jesus's love.
[Hymn]

Fawkes, Guy (1570–1606)
English Roman Catholic conspirator, executed for his part in the Gunpower Plot

1. [On being asked by the King whether he regretted his proposed plot against Parliament and the royal family]
A desperate disease requires a dangerous remedy ... one of my objects was to blow the Scots back again into Scotland.
[*Dictionary of National Biography*]

Fearon, George (1901–1972)

1. The 'angry young men' of England (who refuse to write grammatically and syntactically in order to flaunt their proletarian artistry).
[*Times Literary Supplement*, 1957]

Feather, Vic, Baron (1906–1976)
English trade unionist; General Secretary of the TUC 1969–73

1. Industrial relations are like sexual relations. It's better between two consenting parties.
[*Guardian Weekly*, 1976]

Feldman, Marty (1933–1982)
English radio, TV and film comedian and comedy writer

1. Comedy, like sodomy, is an unnatural act.
[*The Times*, 1969]

Fellini, Federico (1920–1994)
Italian film director

1. *Sono vent'anni che sempre più stancamente tento di dire che 'La dolce vita' era un titolo goffo e patetico.*
I have been trying to say for over twenty years that 'La dolce vita' was a pathetic and awkward title.
[In *Corriere della Sera*, 1993]

Fenton, James (1949–)
British poet, journalist and critic

1. How comforting it is, once or twice a year
To get together and forget the old times.
[*The Memory of War. Poems 1968–1982* (1983), 'A German Requiem']

2. I was born to a kiss and a smile,
I was born to the hopes of a prince.
I dipped my pen in the Nile
And it hasn't functioned since.
[*Out of Danger* (1993), 'An Indistinct Inscription (Meroitic Cursive)']

Ferber, Edna (1887–1968)
American novelist and dramatist

1. Being an old maid is like death by drowning, a really delightful sensation after you cease to struggle.
[In R.E. Drennan, *Wit's End* (1973), 'Completing the Circle']

Ferdinand I, Emperor (1503–1564)
Spanish-born King of Hungary and Bohemia 1526–64; became Holy Roman Emperor in 1558

1. *Fiat justitia, et pereat mundus.*
Let there be justice though the world perish.
[Attr.]

Ferdinand I, Emperor of Austria (1793–1875)
King of Hungary (1830–1848) and Emperor of Austria (1830–48); abdicated

1. I am the emperor, and I want dumplings.
[In E. Crankshaw, *The Fall of the House of Habsburg* (1963)]

Ferguson, Sir Samuel (1810–1886)
Irish poet, lawyer, antiquary and translator

1. Put your head, darling, darling, darling,
Your darling black head my heart above;
Oh, mouth of honey, with the thyme of fragrance,
Who, with heart in breast, could deny you love?
Oh, many and many a young girl for me is pining,
Letting her locks of gold to the cold wind free,
For me, the foremost of our gay young fellows;
But I'd leave a hundred, pure love, for thee!
['Cean Dubh Deelish']

Fergusson, Sir James (1832–1907)
Scottish statesman and Conservative politician

1. I have heard many arguments which influenced my opinion, but never one which influenced my vote.
[Attr.]

Fergusson, Robert (1750–1774)
Scottish poet, known for Scots poems on Edinburgh life

1. And thou, great god of Aquavitae!
Wha sway'st the empire o' this city;–
Whan fou, we're sometimes capernoity;–
Be thou prepar'd

To hedge us frae that black banditti,
The City Guard.
['The Daft Days' (1772)]

2. [Sunday]
Ane wad maist trow some people chose
To change their faces wi' their clo'es,
And fain was gar ilk neibour think
They thirst for goodness as for drink.
['Auld Reekie' (1773)]

3. So, Delia, when her beauty's flown,
Trades on a bottom not her own,
And labours to escape detection
By putting on a false complexion.
['On Seeing a Lady Paint Herself' (1773)]

Ferlinghetti, Lawrence (1920–)
American publisher, painter, poet and novelist

1. The world is a beautiful place
to be born into
if you don't mind some people dying
all the time
or maybe only starving
some of the time
which isn't half so bad
if it isn't you.
[*Pictures of the Gone World* (1955)]

Fern, Fanny (Sara Payson Parton) (1811–1872)
American essayist and children's writer

1. The way to a man's heart is through his stomach.
[*Willis Parton*]

Feuerbach, Ludwig (1804–1872)
German materialist philosopher

1. *Der Mensch ist, was er isst.*
Man is what he eats.
[In Jacob Moleschott, *Lehre der Nahrungsmittel: Für das Volk* (1850)]

Field, Eugene (1850–1895)
American columnist, children's poet, translator and humorist

1. Wynken, Blynken, and Nod one night
Sailed off in a wooden shoe–
Sailed on a river of crystal light,
Into a sea of dew.
['Wynken, Blynken, and Nod' (1889)]

2. [Of Creston Clarke as King Lear]
He played the King as though under momentary apprehension that someone else was about to play the ace.
[Attr.]

Fielding, Henry (1707–1754)
English innovative novelist, comic dramatist and political journalist

1. Love and scandal are the best sweeteners of tea.
[*Love in Several Masques* (1728), IV]

2. Yes, I had two strings to my bow; both golden ones, agad! and both cracked.
[*Love in Several Masques* (1728), V]

3. Oh! The roast beef of England,
And old England's roast beef.
[*The Grub Street Opera* (1731), III]

4. All Nature wears one universal grin.
[*Tom Thumb the Great* (1731), I]

5. To sun my self in Huncamunca's eyes.
[*Tom Thumb the Great* (1731), I]

6. When I'm not thank'd at all, I'm thank'd enough,
I've done my duty, and I've done no more.
[*Tom Thumb the Great* (1731), I]

7. The dusky night rides down the sky,
And ushers in the morn;
The hounds all join in glorious cry,
The huntsman winds his horn:
And a-hunting we will go.
[*Don Quixote in England* (1733), 'A-Hunting We Will Go']

8. I am as sober as a judge.
[*Don Quixote in England* (1733), III]

9. It hath been thought a vast commendation of a painter to say his figures seem to breathe; but surely it is much greater and nobler applause, that they appear to think.
[*Joseph Andrews* (1742), Preface]

10. For clergy are men as well as other folks.
[*Joseph Andrews* (1742), II]

11. To whom nothing is given, of him can nothing be required.
[*Joseph Andrews* (1742), II]

12. What a silly fellow must he be who would do the devil's work for nothing.
[*Joseph Andrews* (1742), II]

13. I describe not men, but manners; not an individual, but a species.
[*Joseph Andrews* (1742), III]

14. Public schools are the nurseries of all vice and immorality.
[*Joseph Andrews* (1742), III]

15. Some folks rail against other folks because other folks have what some folks would be glad of.
[*Joseph Andrews* (1742), IV]

16. He in a few minutes ravished this fair creature, or at least would have ravished her, if she had not, by a timely compliance, prevented him.
[*Jonathan Wild* (1743)]

17. There were particularly two parties ... the former were called cavaliers and tory rory ranter boys.
[*Jonathan Wild* (1743)]

18. Greatness consists in bringing all manner of mischief on mankind, and goodness in removing it from them.
[*Jonathan Wild* (1743)]

19. Never trust the man who hath reason to suspect that you know that he hath injured you.
[*Jonathan Wild* (1743)]

20. A newspaper, which consists of just the same number of words, whether there be news in it or not ... may, likewise, be compared to a stagecoach, which performs constantly the same course, empty as well as full.
[*Tom Jones* (1749), II]

21. Every physician almost hath his favourite disease.
[*Tom Jones* (1749), II]

22. When I mention religion, I mean the Christian religion; and not only the Christian religion, but the Protestant religion; and not only the Protestant religion but the Church of England.
[*Tom Jones* (1749), III]

23. Thwackum was for doing justice, and leaving mercy to Heaven.
[*Tom Jones* (1749), III]

24. What is commonly called love, namely the desire of

satisfying a voracious appetite with a certain quantity of delicate white human flesh.
[*Tom Jones* (1749), VI]

25. O! more than Gothic ignorance.
[*Tom Jones* (1749), VII]

26. 'I did not mean to abuse the cloth; I only said your conclusion was a non sequitur.'–
'You are another,' cries the sergeant, 'an you come to that, no more a sequitur than yourself.'
[*Tom Jones* (1749), IX]

27. An amiable weakness.
[*Tom Jones* (1749), X]

28. His designs were strictly honourable, as the phrase is; that is, to rob a lady of her fortune by way of marriage.
[*Tom Jones* (1749), XI]

29. Composed that monstrous animal a husband and wife.
[*Tom Jones* (1749), XV]

30. Nay, you may call me coward if you will; but if that little man there upon the stage is not frightened, I never saw any man frightened in my life.
[*Tom Jones* (1749), XVI]

31. He the best player! . . . Why, I could act as well as he myself. I am sure, if I had seen a ghost, I should have looked in the very same manner, and done just as he did . . . The king for my money! He speaks all his words distinctly, half as loud again as the other. Anybody may see he is an actor.
[*Tom Jones* (1749), XVI]

32. It hath been often said, that it is not death, but dying, which is terrible.
[*Amelia* (1751), III]

33. The devil take me, if I think anything but love to be the object of love.
[*Amelia* (1751), V]

34. When widows exclaim loudly against second marriages, I would always lay a wager, that the man, if not the wedding-day, is absolutely fixed on.
[*Amelia* (1751), VI]

35. One fool at least in every married couple.
[*Amelia* (1751), IX]

36. There is not in the universe a more ridiculous, nor a more contemptible animal, than a proud clergyman.
[*Amelia* (1751), IX]

Fields, W.C. (William Claude Dukenfield) (1880–1946)
American comic film actor

1. It ain't a fit night out for man or beast.
[*W.C. Fields by Himself* (1974)]

2. Hell, I never vote for anybody. I always vote against.
[In Robert Lewis Taylor, *W. C. Fields: His Follies and Fortunes* (1950)]

3. The best cure for insomnia is to get a lot of sleep.
[Attr.]

4. Last week, I went to Philadelphia, but it was closed.
[Attr.]

5. [His reason for not drinking water]
Fish fuck in it.
[Attr.]

6. Anybody who hates children and dogs can't be all bad.
[Attr.]

7. I am free of all prejudice. I hate everyone equally.
[Attr.]

8. On the whole, I'd rather be in Philadelphia.
[His own epitaph]

Figes, Eva (1932–)
German-born novelist and critic (now British)

1. When modern woman discovered the orgasm it was (combined with modern birth control) perhaps the biggest single nail in the coffin of male dominance.
[In Elaine Morgan, *The Descent of Woman* (1972)]

Finch, Anne, Countess of Winchilsea (1661–1720)
English poet

1. Trail all your pikes, dispirit every drum,
March in a slow procession from afar,
Ye silent, ye dejected men of war!
['All is Vanity']

Finey, George (1895–1987)
Australian war artist and cartoonist

1. The truth is always libellous.
[*Sydney Morning Herald*, 1981]

Firbank, Ronald (1886–1926)
English novelist and short-story writer

1. The world is disgracefully managed, one hardly knows to whom to complain.
[*Vainglory* (1915)]

2. There was a pause – just long enough for an angel to pass, flying slowly.
[*Vainglory* (1915)]

Firmont, Abbé Edgeworth de (1745–1807)
Irish-born confessor to Louis XVI and memoirist

1. [To Louis XVI as he climbed the steps to the guillotine]
Fils de Saint Louis, montez au ciel.
Son of Saint Louis, ascend to heaven.
[Attr., 1793]

Fish, Michael (1944–)
British television weatherman

1. [Said during the weather forecast just prior to the storm of October 1987 which proved him devastatingly wrong]
A woman rang to say she'd heard there was a hurricane on the way – well don't worry, there isn't.
[*The Sunday Telegraph*, 1989]

Fisher, H.A.L. (1856–1940)
English historian

1. One intellectual excitement has, however, been denied me. Men wiser and more learned than I have discerned in history a plot, a rhythm, a predetermined pattern. These harmonies are concealed from me. I can see only one emergency following upon another as wave follows upon wave, only one great fact with respect to which, since it is unique, there can be no generalizations, only one safe rule for the historian: that he should recognize in the development of human destinies the play of the contingent and the unforeseen.
[*History of Europe* (1935), Preface]

Fisher, John Arbuthnot (Baron Fisher) (1841–1920)
Ceylonese-born British admiral; First Sea Lord (1904–10, 1914–15)

1. This letter is not to argue with your leading article of September 2. (It's only d–d fools who argue!)
Never contradict
Never explain

Never apologize
(Those are the secrets of a happy life!)
[Letter to *The Times*, 1919]

2. [On the ruinous cost of the Fleet and those responsible for it]
You must be ruthless, relentless, and remorseless! Sack the lot!
[Letter, *The Times*, 1919]

3. The British navy always travels first class.
[In W. Churchill, *The Second World War* (1948–1954), I]

Fitzgeffrey, Charles (c. 1575–1638)
English poet and divine

1. And bold and hard adventures t' undertake,
Leaving his country for his country's sake.
['Sir Francis Drake' (1596)]

Fitzgerald, Alan John (1935–)
Australian writer, Director of Planning

1. In Canberra, even the mistakes are planned by the National Capital Development Commission.
[*Life in Canberra*]

FitzGerald, Edward (1809–1883)
English poet, translator and letter-writer

NB. Quotations are taken from the first edition and from the expanded fourth edition, and are given in the order in which they appear in the most complete version.

1. Awake! for Morning in the Bowl of Night
Has flung the Stone that puts the Stars to Flight:
And Lo! the Hunter of the East has caught
The Sultan's Turret in a Noose of Light.
[*The Rubáiyát of Omar Khayyám* (1859), 1, 1st Ed.]

2. Dreaming when Dawn's Left Hand was in the Sky
I heard a Voice within the Tavern cry,
'Awake, my Little ones, and fill the Cup
Before Life's Liquor in its Cup be dry.'
[*The Rubáiyát of Omar Khayyám* (1859), 2, 1st Ed.]

3. But in divine
High piping Pehlevi, with 'Wine! Wine! Wine!
Red Wine!' – the Nightingale cries to the Rose
That yellow Cheek of hers to incarnadine.
[*The Rubáiyát of Omar Khayyám* (1859), 6, 1st Ed.]

4. Come, fill the Cup, and in the Fire of Spring
The Winter Garment of Repentance fling:
The Bird of Time has but a little way
To fly – and Lo! the Bird is on the Wing.
[*The Rubáiyát of Omar Khayyám* (1859), 7, 1st Ed.]

5. And look – a thousand Blossoms with the Day
Woke – and a thousand scatter'd into Clay.
[*The Rubáiyát of Omar Khayyám* (1859), 8, 1st Ed.]

6. The Wine of Life keeps oozing drop by drop,
The Leaves of Life keep falling one by one.
[*The Rubáiyát of Omar Khayyám* (1879), 8, 4th Ed.]

7. Each Morn a thousand Roses brings, you say;
Yes, but where leaves the Rose of Yesterday?
And this first Summer month that brings the Rose,
Shall take Jamshyd and Kaikobad away.
[*The Rubáiyát of Omar Khayyám* (1879), 9, 4th Ed.]

8. Here with a Loaf of Bread beneath the Bough,
A Flask of Wine, a Book of Verse – and Thou
Beside me singing in the Wilderness–
And Wilderness is Paradise enow.
[*The Rubáiyát of Omar Khayyám* (1859), 11, 1st Ed.]

9. Ah, take the Cash in hand and waive the Rest;
Oh, the brave Music of a distant Drum!
[*The Rubáiyát of Omar Khayyám* (1859), 12, 1st Ed.]

10. The Worldly Hope men set their Hearts upon
Turns Ashes – or it prospers; and anon,
Like Snow upon the Desert's dusty Face,
Lighting a little Hour or two – is gone.
[*The Rubaiyat of Omar Khayyam* (1859), 14, 1st Ed.]

11. Think, in this batter'd Caravanserai
Whose Doorways are alternate Night and Day,
How Sultan after Sultan with his Pomp
Abode his Hour or two, and went his way.
[*The Rubáiyát of Omar Khayyám* (1859), 16, 1st Ed.]

12. They say the Lion and the Lizard keep
The Courts where Jamshyd gloried and drank deep:
And Bahram, that great Hunter – the Wild Ass
Stamps o'er his Head, and he lies fast asleep.
[*The Rubáiyát of Omar Khayyám* (1859), 17, 1st Ed.]

13. I sometimes think that never blows so red
The Rose as where some buried Caesar bled;
That every Hyacinth the Garden wears
Dropt in her Lap from some once lovely Head.
[*The Rubáiyát of Omar Khayyám* (1859), 18, 1st Ed.]

14. Lo! some we loved, the loveliest and best
That Time and Fate of all their Vintage prest,
Have drunk their Cup a Round or two before,
And one by one crept silently to Rest.
[*The Rubáiyát of Omar Khayyám* (1859), 21, 1st Ed.]

15. Ah, make the most of what we yet may spend,
Before we too into the Dust descend;
Dust into Dust, and under Dust, to lie,
Sans Wine, sans Song, sans Singer, and – sans End!
[*The Rubáiyát of Omar Khayyám* (1859), 23, 1st Ed.]

16. Oh, come with old Khayyám, and leave the Wise
To talk; one thing is certain, that Life flies;
One thing is certain, and the Rest is Lies;
The Flower that once hath blown for ever dies.
[*The Rubáiyát of Omar Khayyám* (1859), 26, 1st Ed.]

17. Myself when young did eagerly frequent
Doctor and Saint, and heard great argument
About it and about: but evermore
Came out by the same Door as in I went.
[*The Rubáiyát of Omar Khayyám* (1859), 27, 1st Ed.]

18. With them the Seed of Wisdom did I sow,
And with mine own hand wrought to make it grow;
And this was all the Harvest that I reap'd–
'I came like Water, and like Wind I go'.
[*The Rubáiyát of Omar Khayyám* (1859), 28, 1st Ed.]

19. There was a Door to which I found no Key:
There was a Veil past which I could not see.
[*The Rubáiyát of Omar Khayyám* (1859), 32, 1st Ed.]

20. Ah, fill the Cup: – what boots it to repeat
How Time is slipping underneath our Feet:
Unborn TOMORROW and dead YESTERDAY,
Why fret about them if TO-DAY be sweet!
[*The Rubáiyát of Omar Khayyám* (1859), 37, 1st Ed.]

21. You know, my Friends, with what a brave Carouse
I made a second Marriage in my house;
Divorced old barren Reason from my Bed,
And took the Daughter of the Vine to Spouse.
[*The Rubáiyát of Omar Khayyám* (1879), 55, 4th Ed.]

22. The Grape that can with Logic absolute
The Two-and-Seventy jarring Sects confute.
[*The Rubáiyát of Omar Khayyám* (1859), 43, 1st Ed.]

23. For in and out, above, about, below,
'Tis nothing but a Magic Shadow-show,
Played in a Box whose Candle is the Sun,
Round which we Phantom Figures come and go.
[*The Rubáiyát of Omar Khayyám* (1859), 46, 1st Ed.]

24. Strange, is it not? that of the myriads who
Before us pass'd the door of Darkness through,
Not one returns to tell us of the Road,
Which to discover we must travel too.
[*The Rubáiyát of Omar Khayyám* (1879), 64, 4th Ed.]

25. 'Tis all a Chequer-board of Nights and Days
Where Destiny with Men for Pieces plays:
Hither and thither moves, and mates, and slays,
And one by one back in the Closet lays.
[*The Rubáiyát of Omar Khayyám* (1859), 49, 1st Ed.]

26. The Moving Finger writes; and, having writ,
Moves on: nor all thy Piety nor Wit
Shall lure it back to cancel half a Line,
Nor all thy Tears wash out a Word of it.
[*The Rubáiyát of Omar Khayyám* (1859), 51, 1st Ed.]

27. And that inverted Bowl we call The Sky,
Whereunder crawling coop't we live and die,
Lift not thy hands to It for help – for It
Rolls impotently on as Thou or I.
[*The Rubáiyát of Omar Khayyám* (1859), 52, 1st Ed.]

28. Drink! for you know not whence you came, nor why:
Drink! for you know not why you go, nor where.
[*The Rubáiyát of Omar Khayyám* (1879), 74, 4th Ed.]

29. After a momentary silence spake
Some Vessel of a more ungainly Make;
'They sneer at me for leaning all awry;
What! did the Hand then of the Potter shake?'
[*The Rubáiyát of Omar Khayyám* (1879), 86, 4th Ed.]

30. 'Who is the Potter, pray, and who the Pot?'
[*The Rubáiyát of Omar Khayyám* (1859), 60, 1st Ed.]

31. Indeed the Idols I have loved so long
Have done my credit in this World much wrong:
Have drown'd my Glory in a Shallow Cup
And sold my Reputation for a Song.
[*The Rubáiyát of Omar Khayyám* (1879), 93, 4th Ed.]

32. And much as Wine has play'd the Infidel,
And robb'd me of my Robe of Honour – Well,
I often wonder what the Vintners buy
One half so precious as the Goods they sell.
[*The Rubáiyát of Omar Khayyám* (1859), 71, 1st Ed.]

33. Alas, that Spring should vanish with the Rose!
That Youth's sweet-scented Manuscript should close!
The Nightingale that in the Branches sang,
Ah, whence, and whither flown again, who knows!
[*The Rubáiyát of Omar Khayyám* (1859), 72, 1st Ed.]

34. Ah Love! Could you and I with Fate conspire
To grasp this sorry Scheme of Things entire,
Would we not shatter it to bits – and then
Re-mould it nearer to the Heart's Desire.
[*The Rubáiyát of Omar Khayyám* (1859), 73, 1st Ed.]

35. Mrs Browning's death is rather a relief to me, I must say: no more Aurora Leighs, thank God! A woman of real genius, I know; but what is the upshot of it all? She and her sex had better mind the kitchen and their children; and perhaps the poor: except in such things as little novels, they only devote themselves to what men do much better, leaving that which men do worse or not at all.
[Letter to W.H. Thompson, 1861]

36. Taste is the feminine of genius.
[Letter to J.R. Lowell, 1877]

Fitzgerald, F. Scott (1896–1940)

American novelist, short-story writer and screenwriter

1. He differed from the healthy type that was essentially middle-class – he never seemed to perspire.
[*This Side of Paradise* (1920), I, 2]

2. A big man has no time really to do anything but just sit and be big.
[*This Side of Paradise* (1920), III, 2]

3. One of those men who reach such an acute limited excellence at twenty-one that everything afterward savours of anti-climax.
[*The Great Gatsby* (1925), 1]

4. I was one of the few guests who had actually been invited. People were not invited – they went there.
[*The Great Gatsby* (1925), 3]

5. I am one of the few honest people that I have ever known.
[*The Great Gatsby* (1926), 3]

6. Americans, while willing, even eager, to be serfs, have always been obstinate about being peasantry.
[*The Great Gatsby* (1926), 5]

7. 'What'll we do with ourselves this afternoon?' cried Daisy, 'and the day after that, and the next thirty years?'
[*The Great Gatsby* (1925), 7]

8. Her voice is full of money.
[*The Great Gatsby* (1925), 7]

9. So we beat on, boats against the current, borne back ceaselessly into the past.
[*The Great Gatsby* (1925), last line]

10. Let me tell you about the very rich. They are different from you and me.
[*All the Sad Young Men* (1926), 'Rich Boy']

11. Though the Jazz Age continued, it became less and less an affair of youth. The sequel was like a children's party taken over by the elders.
[*The Crack-Up* (1945)]

12. In the real dark night of the soul it is always three o'clock in the morning.
[*The Crack-Up* (1945)]

13. *Fitzgerald*: The rich are different from us.
Hemingway: Yes, they have more money.
[*The Crack-Up* (1945), 'Notebooks, E']

14. I entertained on a cruising trip that was so much fun that I had to sink my yacht to make my guests go home.
[*The Crack-Up* (1945), 'Notebooks, K']

15. First you take a drink, then the drink takes a drink, then the drink takes you.
[In Jules Feiffer, *Ackroyd*, '1964, May 7']

16. Sometimes I don't know whether Zelda and I are real or whether we are characters in one of my novels.
[In Malcolm Cowley, *A Second Flowering*]

Fitzgerald, Zelda (1900–1948)

American novelist; wife of F. Scott Fitzgerald

1. I don't want to live – I want to love first, and live incidentally.
[Letter to F. Scott Fitzgerald, 1919]

2. Don't you think I was made for you? I feel like you had me ordered – and I was delivered to you – to be worn – I want you to wear me, like a watch-charm or a button hole bouquet – to the world.
[Letter to F. Scott Fitzgerald, 1919]

3. A vacuum can only exist, I imagine, by the things which enclose it.
[Journal, 1932]

Fitzsimmons, Robert (1862–1917)

English-born New Zealand world champion boxer

1. [Remark before a boxing match, 1900]
The bigger they come, the harder they fall.
[Attr.]

Flanagan, Bud (Robert Winthrop) (1896–1968)

English comedian

1. Underneath the arches
We dream our dreams away.
['Underneath the Arches' (1932)]

Flanders, Michael (1922–1975)

English actor and lyricist

and Swann, Donald (1923–1994)

1. Mud, mud, glorious mud,
Nothing quite like it for cooling the blood.
['The Hippopotamus Song', 1953]

2. Eating people is wrong.
['The Reluctant Cannibal', 1957]

3. If God had intended us to fly, he'd never have given us the railways.
['By Air', 1963]

Flaubert, Gustave (1821–1880)

French realist novelist

1. *Nous ferons tout ce qui nous plaira! nous laisserons pousser notre barbe!*
We'll do whatever we please! We'll grow our beards!
[*Bouvard et Pécuchet* (1881), 1]

2. *Ulysse est le plus fort type de toute la littérature ancienne, et Hamlet de toute la moderne.*
Ulysses is the strongest character in the whole of ancient literature, Hamlet the strongest character in the whole of modern literature.
[Letter to Louise Colet, 1853]

3. *Tout ce qu'on invente est vrai, soi-en sûre. La poésie est une chose aussi précise que la géométrie.*
Everything one invents is true, you can be sure of that. Poetry is as exact a science as geometry.
[Letter to Louise Colet, 1853]

4. *L'artiste doit être dans son oeuvre comme Dieu dans la création, invisible et tout-puissant; qu'on le sente partout, mais qu'on ne le voie pas.*
The artist must be in his work as God is in creation, invisible and all-powerful; his presence should be felt everywhere, but he should never be seen.
[Letter to Mlle Leroyer de Chantepie, 1857]

5. *Mais ne lisez pas, comme les enfants lisent, pour vous amuser, ni comme les ambitieux lisent, pour vous instruire. Non, lisez pour vivre.*
Do not read, as children do, for the sake of entertainment, or like the ambitious, for the purpose of instruction. No, read in order to live.
[Letter to Mlle Leroyer de Chantepie, 1857]

6. *Les livres ne se font pas comme les enfants, mais comme les pyramides ... et ça ne sert à rien! et ça reste dans le désert! ... Les chacals pissent au bas et les bourgeois montent dessus.*
Books are made not like children but like the pyramids ... and they're good for nothing! and they stay in the desert! Jackals piss at their foot and the bourgeois climb up on them.
[Letter to Ernest Feydeau, 1857]

Flecker, James Elroy (1884–1915)

English lyric poet, orientalist and translator

1. And old Maeonides the blind
Said it three thousand years ago...

2. O friend unseen, unborn, unknown,
Student of our sweet English tongue,
Read out my words at night, alone:
I was a poet, I was young.
['To a Poet a Thousand Years Hence' (1910)]

3. When the great markets by the sea shut fast
All that calm Sunday that goes on and on:
When even lovers find their peace at last,
And Earth is but a star, that once had shone.
[*The Golden Journey to Samarkand* (1913), Prologue]

4. The dragon-green, the luminous, the dark, the serpent-haunted sea.
[*The Golden Journey to Samarkand* (1913), 'The Gates of Damascus']

5. Half to forget the wandering and the pain,
Half to remember days that have gone by,
And dream and dream that I am home again!
[*The Golden Journey to Samarkand* (1913), 'Brumana']

6. West of these out to seas colder than the Hebrides I must go
Where the fleet of stars is anchored and the young star-captains glow.
[*The Golden Journey to Samarkand* (1913), 'The Dying Patriot']

7. A ship, an isle, a sickle moon–
With few but with how splendid stars
The mirrors of the sea are strewn
Between their silver bars.
[*The Golden Journey to Samarkand* (1913), 'A Ship, an Isle, and a Sickle Moon']

8. I have seen old ships sail like swans asleep
Beyond that village which men still call Tyre,
With leaden age o'ercargoed, dipping deep
For Famagusta and the hidden sun
That rings black Cyprus with a lake of fire...

9. But now through friendly seas they softly run,
Painted the mid-sea blue or the shore-sea green,
Still patterned with the vine and grapes in gold...

10. It was so old a ship – who knows, who knows?
And yet so beautiful, I watched in vain
To see the mast burst open with a rose,
And the whole deck put on its leaves again...

11. And with great lies about his wooden horse
Set the crew laughing, and forgot his course.
['The Old Ships' (1915)]

12. How splendid in the morning glows the lily; with what grace he throws
His supplication to the rose.
[*Hassan* (1922), I.ii]

13. And some to Meccah turn to pray, and I toward thy bed, Yasmin.
[*Hassan* (1922), I.ii]

14. For one night or the other night
Will come the Gardener in white, and gathered flowers are dead, Yasmin.
[*Hassan* (1922), I.ii]

15. For lust of knowing what should not be known,
We take the Golden Road to Samarkand.
[*Hassan* (1922), V.ii]

Flecknoe, Richard (d. c. 1678)
Irish priest, poet and dramatist

1. Still-born Silence! thou that art
Floodgate of the deeper heart.
['Invocation of Silence' (1653)]

Fleming, Marjory (1803–1811)
Scottish child diarist

1. A direful death indeed they had
That would put any parent mad
But she was more than usual calm
She did not give a singel dam.
[In A. Esdaile (ed.), *Journals, Letters and Verses* (1934)]

2. I hope I will be religious again but as for reganing my charecter I despare for it.
[In A. Esdaile (ed.), *Journals, Letters and Verses* (1934)]

3. My dear Isa,
I now sit down on my botom to answer all your kind and beloved letters which you was so good as to write to me.
[In A. Esdaile (ed.), *Journals, Letters and Verses* (1934), Letter to Isabella]

Fleming, Paul (1609–1640)
German lyric poet

1. *Des grossen Vaters Helm ist viel zu weit dem Sohne.*
The helm of his great father is far too broad for the son.
[*Die jetzigen Deutschen*]

Flers, Robert, Marquis de (1872–1927) and **Caillavet,** Arman de (1869–1915)

1. *Démocratie est le nom que nous donnons au peuple toutes les fois que nous avons besoin de lui.*
Democracy is the name we give the people whenever we need them.
[In *La petite illustration série théâtre*, 1913, *L'habit vert*, I.xii]

Fletcher, Andrew, of Saltoun (1655–1716)
Scottish anti-Unionist politician and reformer

1. I knew a very wise man who believed that ... if a man were permitted to make all the ballads, he need not care who should make the laws of a nation. And we find that most of the ancient legislators thought they could not well reform the manners of any city without the help of a lyric, and sometimes of a dramatic poet.
[Letter to the Marquis of Montrose, 1704]

2. Like him that lights a candle to the sun.
[Letter]

Fletcher, John (1579–1625)
English dramatist; collaborated with Francis Beaumont and Philip Massinger; cousin of Phineas Fletcher

1. It's impossible to ravish me
I'm so willing.
[*The Faithful Shepherdess* (1610), III.i]

2. Care-charming Sleep, thou easer of all woes,
Brother to Death.
[*The Tragedy of Valentinian* (produced c. 1610–1614, published 1647), V.vii, 'Song']

3. Whistle and she'll come to you.
[*Wit Without Money* (c. 1614), IV.iv]

4. Charity and beating begins at home.
[*Wit Without Money* (c. 1614), V.ii]

5. Best while you have it use your breath,
There is no drinking after death.
[*The Bloody Brother* (with Ben Jonson and others, produced 1616), II.ii]

6. And he that will go to bed sober,
Falls with the leaf still in October.
[*The Bloody Brother* (with Ben Jonson and others, produced 1616), II.ii]

7. Three merry boys, and three merry boys,
And three merry boys are we,
As ever did sing in a hempen string
Under the Gallows-Tree.
[*The Bloody Brother* (with Ben Jonson and others, produced 1616), III.ii]

8. Come, we are stark naught all, bad's the best of us.
[*The Bloody Brother* (with Ben Jonson and others, produced 1616), IV.ii]

9. I'll put a spoke among your wheels.
[*The Mad Lover* (produced before 1619), III]

10. Have you not maggots in your brains?
[*Women Pleased* (produced 1620, published 1647), III.iv]

11. Let's meet, and either do, or die.
[*The Island Princess* (1621), II.ii]

12. Come sing now, sing; for I know ye sing well,
I see ye have a singing face.
[*The Wild-Goose Chase* (produced 1621, published 1647), II.ii]

13. 'Tis virtue, and not birth that makes us noble:
Great actions speak great minds, and such should govern.
[*The Prophetess* (with Philip Massinger, produced 1622, published 1647), II.iii]

14. *Leon*: I have heard you are poetical.
Mallfort: Something given that way.
[*The Lover's Progress* (revised by Philip Massinger, produced 1623, published 1647), I.i]

15. I find the medicine worse than the malady.
[*The Lover's Progress* (revised by Philip Massinger, produced 1623, published 1647), III.ii]

16. Deeds, not words shall speak me.
[*The Lover's Progress* (revised by Philip Massinger, produced 1623, published 1647), III.vi]

17. Faith Sir, he went away with a flea in's ear.
[*The Lover's Progress* (revised by Philip Massinger, produced 1623, published 1647), IV]

18. I'll have a fling.
[*Rule a Wife and have a Wife* (produced 1624), III.v]

19. Daisies smell-less, yet most quaint,
And sweet thyme true,
Primrose first born child of Ver,
Merry Springtime's Harbinger.
[*Two Noble Kinsmen* (with Shakespeare, 1634), I.i]

20. Death hath so many doors to let out life.
[*The Custom of the Country* (with Philip Massinger, published 1647), II.ii]

21. But what is past my help is past my care.
[*The Double Marriage* (with others, published 1647), I.i]

22. Nothing's so dainty sweet as lovely melancholy.
[*The Nice Valour* (with Thomas Middleton, published 1647), III]

Fletcher, Phineas (1582–1650)

English Spenserian poet and clergyman; cousin of John Fletcher

1. Love is like linen often chang'd, the sweeter.
[*Sicelides* (1614), III.v]

2. The coward's weapon, poison.
[*Sicelides* (1614), V.iii]

3. Love's tongue is in the eyes.
['Piscatory Eclogues' (1633)]

4. Drop, drop, slow tears,
And bathe those beauteous feet,
Which brought from Heav'n
The news and Prince of Peace.
[*Poetical Miscellanies* (1633), 'An Hymn']

5. Poorly (poor man) he liv'd; poorly (poor man) he di'd.
[*The Purple Island* (1633)]

Florian, Jean-Pierre Claris de (1755–1794)

1. *Plaisir d'amour ne dure qu'un moment,*
Chagrin d'amour dure toute la vie.
Love's pleasure only lasts a moment; love's sorrow lasts one's whole life long.
['Célestine' (1784)]

Fo, Dario (1926–)

Italian playwright and actor

1. *Giusto! L'ha detto! Lo scandalo è il concime della democrazia.*
Correct! You said it! Scandal is the manure of democracy.
[*Morte accidentale di un anarchico* (*Accidental Death of an Anarchist*, 1974), II]

Foch, Ferdinand (1851–1929)

French marshal; Commander-in-Chief of Allied Forces in 1918

1. [Dispatch during the Battle of the Marne, 1914]
Mon centre cède, ma droite recule, situation excellente. J'attaque!
My centre is giving way, my right is retreating; situation excellent. I shall attack.
[Attr.]

2. [Command announcing the armistice, 1918]
Hostilities will cease along the whole front at the 11th hour, French o'clock, on Nov. 11. Allied troops will not cross, until further orders, the line reached on that date and that hour.
[Attr.]

3. None but a coward dares to boast that he has never known fear.
[Attr.]

4. [Remark on being shown the Grand Canyon]
What a marvellous place to drop one's mother-in-law!
[Attr.]

Follett, Barbara

1. It's not that I mind being married; I just object to being defined by whether I am married. I don't think my bank manager understands that.
[In *The Times*, 1992]

Fonda, Jane (1937–)

American film actress, anti-Vietnam war activist, and aerobics pioneer

1. You can run the office without a boss, but you can't run an office without the secretaries.
[*The Observer*, 1981, in Jeffrey Care (ed.), *Sayings of the Eighties* (1989)]

2. No pain, no gain.
[Attr.]

Fontaine, Jean de la (1621–1695)

French poet and fabulist

1. *De la peau du lion l'âne s'étant vêtu*
Etait craint partout à la ronde.
Et bien qu'animal sans vertu,
Il faisait trembler tout le monde.
Dressed in the skin of the lion, the ass was feared far and wide. Although an animal of no character, he made the whole world tremble.
[*Fables*, 'L'âne vêtu de la peau du lion']

2. *Aide-toi, le ciel t'aidera.*
Help yourself, and heaven will help you.
[*Fables*, 'Le Chartier Embourbé']

3. *C'est double plaisir de tromper le trompeur.*
It is a double pleasure to trick the trickster.
[*Fables*, 'Le coq et le renard']

4. *Mon bon Monsieur,*
Apprenez que tout flatteur
Vit au dépens de celui qui l'écoute.
My dear Monsieur, know that every flatterer lives at the expense of the one who listens to him.
[*Fables*, 'Le corbeau et le renard']

5. *Il connaît l'univers et ne se connaît pas.*
He knows the world and does not know himself.
[*Fables*, 'Démocrite et les Abdéritains']

6. *Aucun chemin de fleurs ne conduit à la gloire.*
No flowery path leads to glory.
[*Fables*, 'Les deux aventuriers et le talisman']

7. *Hélas! on voit que de tout temps,*
Les petits ont pâti des sottises des grands.
Alas! We see that for all time the Small have paid for the folly of the Great.
[*Fables*, 'Les deux taureaux et une grenouille']

8. *Dieu fait bien ce qu'il fait.*
What God does, He does well.
[*Fables*, 'Le gland et la citrouille']

9. *Mais les ouvrages les plus courts*
Sont toujours les meilleurs.
But the shortest works are always the best.
[*Fables, 'Les lapins'*]

10. *Il faut, autant qu'on peut, obliger tout le monde:*
On a souvent besoin d'un plus petit que soi.
We must, as much as we can, oblige everyone. We often need someone smaller than ourselves.
[*Fables*, 'Le lion et le rat']

11. *Patience et longueur de temps*
Font plus que force ni que rage.
Patience and time do more than force and rage.
[*Fables*, 'Le lion et le rat']

12. *La raison du plus fort est toujours la meilleure.*
The reason of the strongest is always the best.
[*Fables*, 'Le loup et l'agneau']

13. *Une montagne en mal d'enfant*
Jetait une clameur si haute,
Que chacun au bruit accourant,
Crut qu'elle accoucherait, sans faute,
D'une cité plus grosse que Paris:
Elle accoucha d'une souris.
A mountain in labour made such a clamour that everyone, summoned by the noise, ran up thinking that she would indeed be delivered of a city bigger than Paris; she gave birth to a mouse.
[*Fables*, 'La montagne qui accouche']

14. *Ventre affamé n'a point d'oreilles.*
A hungry stomach will not listen.
[*Fables*, 'Le milan et le rossignol']

15. *La Mort ne surprend point le sage;*
Il est toujours prêt à partir.
Death does not take the wise man by surprise, he is always prepared to leave.
[*Fables*, 'La Mort et le mourant'. Cf. Montaigne: 2]

16. *Il m'a dit qu'il ne faut jamais*
Vendre la peau de l'ours qu'on ne l'ait mis par terre.
He told me never to sell the bear's skin before killing the beast.
[*Fables*, 'L'ours et les deux compagnons'. Cf. Waller: 1]

17. *Celui-ci ne voyait pas plus loin que son nez.*
This fellow could not see further than his own nose.
[*Fables*, 'Le renard et le bouc']

18. *En toute chose il faut considérer la fin.*
In all matters one must consider the end.
[*Fables*, 'Le renard et le bouc']

Fontane, Theodor (1819–1898)
German novelist and poet

1. *... denn das Menschlichste, was wir haben, ist doch die Sprache, und wir haben sie, um zu sprechen.*
... for the most human thing that we have is language, and we've got it, so that we can speak.
[*Unwiederbringlich* (*Irretrievable*, 1891), 13]

Fontenelle, Bernard (1657–1757)
French librettist, philosopher, scientist and man of letters

1. I detest war: it ruins conversation.
[In W.H. Auden, *A Certain World* (1970)]

2. [Remark on his deathbed at the age of 99]
It is high time for me to depart, for at my age I now begin to see things as they really are.
[Attr.]

Foot, Michael (1913–)
English politician; leader of the Labour Party 1980–83

1. A Royal Commission is a broody hen sitting on a china egg.
[Speech, House of Commons, 1964]

Foote, Samuel (1720–1777)
English actor, satirical dramatist and wit

1. For as the old saying is,
When house and land are gone and spent
Then learning is most excellent.
[*Taste* (1752)]

2. Born in a cellar ... and living in a garret.
[*The Author* (1757), II]

3. [A nonsensical story made up by Foote to test the memory of the actor Charles Macklin]
So she went into the garden to cut a cabbage-leaf, to make an apple-pie; and at the same time a great she-bear, coming up the street, pops its head into the shop. 'What! no soap?' So he died, and she very imprudently married the barber; and there were present the Picninnies, and the Joblillies, and the Garyalies, and the grand Panjandrum himself, with the little round button at top, and they all fell to playing the game of catch as catch can, till the gun powder ran out at the heels of their boots.
[Attr.]

Forbes, Miss C.F. (1817–1911)
English writer

1. The sense of being well-dressed gives a feeling of inward tranquillity which religion is powerless to bestow.
[In Emerson, *Social Aims* (1876)]

Forbes, James Nicol ('Bully' Forbes) (1821–1874)

1. [Captain Forbes, of the *Marco Polo*, sailed the ship from the UK to Melbourne in 68 days and back in 76 days in 1852]
Ladies and gentlemen, last trip I astonished the world with the sailing of this ship. This trip I intend to astonish God Almighty.
[In Don Charlwood, *Wrecks and Reputations*]

Ford, Ford Madox (1873–1939)
English novelist, critic and editor

1. This is the saddest story I have ever heard.
[*The Good Soldier* (1915), first sentence]

Ford, Gerald R. (1913–)
American politician, successor to Nixon as Republican President 1974–77

1. [On taking the vice-presidential oath]
I am a Ford, not a Lincoln. My addresses will never be as eloquent as Lincoln's. But I will do my best to equal his brevity and plain speaking.
[Speech, published in Washington *Post*, 1973]

2. There is no Soviet domination of Eastern Europe and there never will be under a Ford administration.
[TV debate with Jimmy Carter, 1976]

3. [Referring to his own appointment as President]
I guess it proves that in America anyone can be President.
[In Richard Reeves, *A Ford Not a Lincoln*, 4]

Ford, Henry (1863–1947)
American car manufacturer, pioneer of mass production; pacifist

1. [Popularly remembered as 'History is bunk']
History is more or less bunk. It's tradition. We don't want tradition. We want to live in the present and the only history that is worth a tinker's damn is the history we make today.
[Chicago *Tribune*, 1916]

2. [On the Model T Ford motor car]
People can have it any colour – so long as it's black.
[In Allan Nevins, *Ford* (1957), II, 15]

3. Exercise is bunk. If you are healthy, you don't need it: if you are sick, you shouldn't take it.
[Attr.]

Ford, John [1] (c. 1586–1639)
English dramatist and poet

1. Parthenophil is lost, and I would see him;
For he is like to something I remember,
A great while since, a long, long time ago.
[*The Lover's Melancholy* (1629)]

2. Tempt not the stars, young man, thou canst not play
With the severity of fate.
[*The Broken Heart* (1633), I.iii]

3. I am ... a mushroom
On whom the dew of heaven drops now and then.
[*The Broken Heart* (1633), I.iii]

4. Green indiscretion, flattery of greatness,
Rawness of judgement, wilfulness in folly,
Thoughts vagrant as the wind, and as uncertain.
[*The Broken Heart* (1633), II.i]

5. Revenge proves its own executioner.
[*The Broken Heart* (1633), IV.i]

6. There's not a hair
Sticks on my head but, like a leaden plummet,
It sinks me to the grave: I must creep thither;
The journey is not long.
[*The Broken Heart* (1633), IV.ii]

7. He hath shook hands with time.
[*The Broken Heart* (1633), V.ii]

8. They are the silent griefs which cut the heart-strings.
[*The Broken Heart* (1633), V.iii]

9. Why, I hold fate
Clasp'd in my fist, and could command the course
Of time's eternal motion, hadst thou been
One thought more steady than an ebbing sea.
[*'Tis Pity She's a Whore* (1633), V.iv]

10. Of one so young, so rich in nature's store,
Who could not say, 'TIS PITY SHE'S A WHORE?
[*'Tis Pity She's a Whore* (1633), V.vi]

11. Tell us, pray, what devil
This melancholy is, which can transform
Men into monsters.
[*The Lady's Trial* (1639), III.i]

12. We can drink till all look blue.
[*The Lady's Trial* (1639), IV.ii]

Ford, John [2] (1895–1973)
Irish-American film director, known for his westerns; Academy Awards 1935, 1940, 1941

1. It is easier to get an actor to be a cowboy than to get a cowboy to be an actor.
[Attr.]

Ford, Lena (1870–1916)

1. Keep the home fires burning while your hearts are yearning,
Though your lads are far away, they dream of home.
There's a silver lining through the dark cloud shining:
Turn the dark cloud inside out, till the boys come home.
['Keep the Home Fires Burning' (1914)]

Forgy, Howell (1908–1983)
American naval chaplain

1. [Remark at Pearl Harbour, 1941]
Praise the Lord and pass the ammunition.
[Attr.]

Formby, George (1905–1961)
English comedian and ukulele player

1. I'm leaning on a lamp-post at the corner of the street,
In case a certain little lady walks by.
['Leaning on a Lamp-post', 1937]

2. With my little stick of Blackpool rock,
Along the Promenade I stroll.
It may be sticky but I never complain,
It's nice to have a nibble at it now and again.
['With My Little Stick of Blackpool Rock', 1937]

Forrest, Nathan Bedford (1821–1877)
American Confederate general

1. [Popular misquotation of his explanation of his success in capturing Murfreesboro; his actual words were, 'I just took the short cut and got there first with the most men.']
I got there fustest with the mostest.
[In B. Botkin, *A Civil War Treasury*]

2. [Remark to a captured enemy officer who had been tricked into surrendering]
Ah, colonel, all's fair in love and war, you know.
[In B. Botkin, *A Civil War Treasury*]

Forro, (Rev. Fr) Francis Stephen (1914–1974)

1. [Response to a journalist's comment on the scruffiness of Hungarian refugees arriving at Mascot aerodrome, Australia, in 1956]
Ah, yes, but they will make fine ancestors.
[Attr.]

Forster, E.M. (1879–1970)
English novelist, short-story writer, essayist and literary critic

1. I felt for a moment that the whole Wilcox family was a fraud, just a wall of newspapers and motor-cars and golf-clubs, and that if it fell I should find nothing behind it but panic and emptiness.
[*Howard's End* (1910), 4]

2. Beethoven's Fifth Symphony is the most sublime noise that ever penetrated into the ear of man.
[*Howard's End* (1910), 5]

3. All men are equal – all men, that is to say, who possess umbrellas.
[*Howard's End* (1910), 6]

4. Personal relations are the important thing for ever and ever, and not this outer life of telegrams and anger.
[*Howard's End* (1910), 19]

5. Only connect! That was the whole of her sermon. Only connect the prose and the passion, and both will be exalted, and human love will be seen at its highest.
[*Howard's End* (1910), 22]

6. Death destroys a man; the idea of Death saves him.
[*Howard's End* (1910), 27]

7. The so-called white races are really pinko-gray.
[*A Passage to India* (1924), 7]

8. The echo in a Marabar cave ... is entirely devoid of distinction ... Hope, politeness, the blowing of a nose, the squeak of a boot, all produce 'boum'.
[*A Passage to India* (1924), 14]

9. [Of an inscription]
One of them (composed in English to indicate His universality) consisted, by an unfortunate slip of the draughtsman, of the words, 'God si Love.' God si Love. Is this the final message of India?
[*A Passage to India* (1924), 33]

10. Yes – oh dear, yes – the novel tells a story.
[*Aspects of the Novel* (1927), 2]

11. That [the story] is the highest factor common to all novels, and I wish that it was not so, that it could be something different – melody, or perception of the truth, not this low atavistic form.
[*Aspects of the Novel* (1927), 2]

12. The historian must have ... some conception of how men who are not historians behave. Otherwise he will move in a world of the dead.
[*Abinger Harvest* (1936), 'Captain Edward Gibbon']

13. It is not that the Englishman can't feel – it is that he is afraid to feel. He has been taught at his public school that feeling is bad form. He must not express great joy or sorrow, or even open his mouth too wide when he talks – his pipe might fall out if he did.
[*Abinger Harvest* (1936), 'Notes on the English Character']

14. [Of public schoolboys]
They go forth into it [the world] with well-developed bodies, fairly developed minds, and undeveloped hearts.
[*Abinger Harvest* (1936), 'Notes on the English Character']

15. I do not believe in Belief ... Lord I disbelieve – help thou my unbelief.
[*Two Cheers for Democracy* (1951), 'What I Believe']

16. My law-givers are Erasmus and Montaigne, not Moses and St Paul.
[*Two Cheers for Democracy* (1951), 'What I Believe']

17. I hate the idea of causes, and if I had to choose between betraying my country and betraying my friend, I hope I should have the guts to betray my country.
[*Two Cheers for Democracy* (1951), 'What I Believe']

18. So Two cheers for Democracy: one because it admits variety and two because it permits criticism. Two cheers are quite enough: there is no occasion to give three. Only Love the Beloved Republic deserves that.
[*Two Cheers for Democracy* (1951), quoting Swinburne, *Hertha*]

19. Works of art, in my opinion, are the only objects in the material universe to possess internal order, and that is why, though I don't believe that only art matters, I do believe in Art for Art's sake.
[*Two Cheers for Democracy* (1951), 'Art for Art's Sake']

20. I suggest that the only books that influence us are those for which we are ready, and which have gone a little farther down our particular path than we have yet got ourselves.
[*Two Cheers for Democracy* (1951), 'Books That Influenced Me']

21. To make us feel small in the right way is a function of art. Men can only make us feel small in the wrong way.
[Attr.]

Forsyth, Bruce (1928–)
British television presenter and personality

1. Didn't they do well!
[Catchphrase used in the television show *The Generation Game*]

Foster, Charles (1828–1904)
American Republican politician; Secretary of the Treasury 1891–93

1. [At the 51st Congress; responding to a Democratic gibe about a 'million dollar Congress']
Isn't this a billion dollar country?
[Attr.]

Foster, S.C. (1826–1864)
American popular song writer and composer

1. O, Susanna! O, don't you cry for me,
I've come from Alabama, wid my banjo on my knee.
['O, Susanna', 1848]

2. Dere's no more work for poor old Ned,
He's gone whar de good niggers go.
['Uncle Ned', 1848]

3. I come down dah wid my hat caved in,
Doodah! doodah!
I go back home wid a pocket full of tin,
Oh! doodah day!
Gwine to run all night!
Gwine to run all day!
I bet my money on the bob-tail nag.
Somebody bet on the bay.
['Camptown Races', 1850]

4. 'Way down upon de Swanee Ribber,
Far, far away,
Dere's where my heart is turning ebber:
Dere's where de old folks stay.
All up and down de whole creation
Sadly I roam,
Still longing for de old plantation,
And for de old folks at home.
['The Old Folks at Home', 1851]

5. Weep no more, my lady,
Oh! weep no more today!
We will sing one song for the old Kentucky Home,
For the old Kentucky Home far away.
['My Old Kentucky Home', 1853]

6. I'm coming, I'm coming,
For my head is bending low
I hear their gentle voices calling, 'Poor old Joe'.
['Old Black Joe', 1860]

Foucault, Michel (1926–1984)
French philosopher

1. [In 1966, when *Les Mots et les choses* appeared, he was attacked for this remark]
Marxism exists in nineteenth-century thought in the same way as a fish exists in water; that is, it stops breathing anywhere else.
[In Didier Eribon, *Michel Foucault* (1989), tr. by Betsy Wing in 1991]

Fouché, Joseph (1763–1820)
French politician, revolutionary and Minister of Police 1799–1815

1. [Remark on the execution of the Duc d'Enghien, 1804]
C'est pire qu'un crime; c'est une faute.

It is worse than a crime; it is a mistake.
[Attr.; also attributed to Antoine Boulay de la Meurthe (1761–1840)]

Fourier, François Charles Marie (1772–1837)
French social theorist; founder of Fourierism

1. *L'extension des privilèges des femmes est le principe général de tous progrès sociaux.*
The extension of women's privileges is the basic principle of all social progress.
[*Théorie des Quatre Mouvements* (1808), II, 4]

2. Instead of by battles and Ecumenical Councils, the rival portions of humanity will one day dispute each other's excellence in the manufacture of little cakes.
[In Emerson, *Lectures and Biographical Sketches*]

Fowles, John (1926–)
English novelist

1. In essence the Renaissance was simply the green end of one of civilization's hardest winters.
[*The French Lieutenant's Woman* (1969), 10]

2. There are many reasons why novelists write, but they all have one thing in common – a need to create an alternative world.
[*The Sunday Times Magazine*, 1977]

Fox, Charles James (1749–1806)
English statesman; Whig politician, Foreign Secretary (1806) and abolitionist

1. [On the Fall of the Bastille]
How much the greatest event it is that ever happened in the world! and how much the best!
[Letter, 1789]

2. Kings govern by means of popular assemblies only when they cannot do without them.
[Attr.]

3. I die happy.
[Last words]

Fox, George (1624–1691)
English founder of the Society of Friends; preacher and diarist

1. I heard a voice which said, 'There is one, even Christ Jesus, that can speak to thy condition', and when I heard it, my heart did leap for joy.
[*Journal* (1674)]

2. I told them I lived in the virtue of that life and power that took away the occasion of all wars.
[*Journal* (1674)]

3. When the Lord sent me forth into the world, He forbade me to put off my hat to any high or low.
[*Journal* (1674)]

Fox, Henry Stephen (1791–1846)
English diplomat

1. [Remark after an illness]
I am so changed that my oldest creditors would hardly know me.
[Quoted by Byron in a letter to John Murray, 1817]

Foyle, Christina (1911–)
Member of famous British bookselling family

1. Animals are always loyal and love you, whereas with children you never know where you are.
[*The Times*, 1993]

Frame, Janet (1924–)
New Zealand novelist and short-story writer

1. There is no past present or future. Using tenses to divide time is like making chalk marks on water.
[*Faces in the Water* (1961)]

2. [On saying what one means]
In an age of explanation one can always choose varieties of truth.
[*Living in the Maniototo* (1979)]

France, Anatole (Jacques Anatole François Thibault) (1844–1924)
French novelist, short-story writer and critic; Nobel prize 1921

1. Man is so made that he can only find relaxation from one kind of labour by taking up another.
[*The Crime of Sylvestre Bonnard* (1881)]

2. The Arab who builds himself a hut out of the marble fragments of a temple in Palmyra is more philosophical than all the curators of the museums in London, Munich or Paris.
[*The Crime of Sylvestre Bonnard* (1881)]

3. *Le bon critique est celui qui raconte les aventures de son âme au milieu des chefs-d'oeuvre.*
A good critic is one who tells of his own soul's adventures among masterpieces.
[*La Vie Littéraire* (1888)]

4. *Il fut des temps barbares et gothiques où les mots avaient un sens; alors les écrivains exprimaient des pensées.*
It was in the times, barbarous and gothic, when words had a meaning; in those days, writers would express thoughts.
[*La Vie Littéraire* (1888)]

5. *Le hasard c'est peut-être le pseudonyme de Dieu, quand il ne veut pas signer.*
Chance might be God's pseudonym when He does not want to sign his name.
[*Le Jardin d'Epicure* (1894)]

6. *L'Ironie et la Pitié sont deux bonnes conseillères; l'une en souriant, nous rend la vie aimable; l'autre, qui pleure, nous la rend sacrée.*
Irony and Pity make two good counsellors: the one, smiling, makes life pleasant to us; the other, weeping, makes life sacred.
[*Le Jardin d'Epicure* (1894)]

7. *Le Christianisme a beaucoup fait pour l'amour en en faisant un péché.*
Christianity has done a great deal for love by making a sin of it.
[*Le Jardin d'Epicure* (1894)]

8. *La majestueuse égalité des lois, qui interdit au riche comme au pauvre de coucher sous les ponts, de mendier dans les rues et de voler du pain.*
The law, in its majestic equality, forbids the rich as well as the poor to sleep under bridges, to beg in the streets, and to steal bread.
[*Le Lys Rouge* (1894)]

9. *Désarmer les forts et armer les faibles ce serait changer l'ordre social que j'ai mission de conserver. La justice est la sanction des injustices établies.*
To disarm the strong and arm the weak would be to change

the social order which I have been commissioned to preserve. Justice is the means whereby established injustices are sanctioned.
[*Crainquebille* (1904), IV]

10. *Dans tout État policé, la richesse est chose sacrée; dans les démocraties elle est la seule chose sacrée.*
In every well-governed state, wealth is a sacred thing; in democracies it is the only sacred thing.
[*L'Ile des pingouins* (Penguin Island, 1908), VI, 2]

11. It is better to understand little than to misunderstand a lot.
[*Revolt of the Angels*]

12. It is only the poor who pay cash, and that not from virtue, but because they are refused credit.
[In J.R. Solly, *A Cynic's Breviary*]

Francis I of France (1494–1547)
King of France from 1515, rival of Charles V and patron of the arts

1. [After losing the Battle of Pavia, 1525]
Tout est perdu fors l'honneur.
All is lost save honour.
[Attr.]

Saint Francis de Sales (1567–1622)
French Bishop of Geneva, from 1602; theologian, distinguished preacher and opponent of Calvinism

1. *Ce sont les grans feux qui s'enflamment au vent, mays les petitz s'esteignent si on ne les y porte a couvert.*
Great fires flare up in the wind, but little ones are blown out if they are not sheltered.
[*Introduction à la vie dévote* (1609), III]

Franklin, Benjamin (1706–1790)
American statesman, scientist, political critic and printer

1. Remember that time is money.
[*Advice to a Young Tradesman* (1748)]

2. He's the best physician that knows the worthlessness of the most medicines.
[*Poor Richard's Almanac* (1733)]

3. To lengthen thy life, lessen thy meals.
[*Poor Richard's Almanac* (1733)]

4. Where there's marriage without love, there will be love without marriage.
[*Poor Richard's Almanac* (1734)]

5. Necessity never made a good bargain.
[*Poor Richard's Almanac* (1735)]

6. Three may keep a secret, if two of them are dead.
[*Poor Richard's Almanac* (1735)]

7. Some are weather-wise, some are otherwise.
[*Poor Richard's Almanac* (1735)]

8. Write with the learned, pronounce with the vulgar.
[*Poor Richard's Almanac* (1738)]

9. At twenty years of age, the will reigns; at thirty, the wit; and at forty, the judgement.
[*Poor Richard's Almanac* (1741)]

10. Experience keeps a dear school, but fools will learn in no other.
[*Poor Richard's Almanac* (1743)]

11. Dost thou love life? Then do not squander time, for that's the stuff life is made of.
[*Poor Richard's Almanac* (1746)]

12. Many foxes grow grey, but few grow good.
[*Poor Richard's Almanac* (1749)]

13. The golden age never was the present age.
[*Poor Richard's Almanac* (1750)]

14. Little strokes fell great oaks.
[*Poor Richard's Almanac* (1750)]

15. Old boys have their playthings as well as young ones; the difference is only in price.
[*Poor Richard's Almanac* (1752)]

16. If you would know the value of money, go and try to borrow some; for he that goes a borrowing goes a sorrowing.
[*Poor Richard's Almanac* (1754)]

17. He that lives upon hope will die fasting.
[*Poor Richard's Almanac* (1758), Preface]

18. A little neglect may breed mischief . . . for want of a nail, the shoe was lost; for want of a shoe, the horse was lost; and for want of a horse the rider was lost.
[*Poor Richard's Almanac* (1758)]

19. Early to bed and early to rise,
Makes a man healthy, wealthy and wise.
[*Poor Richard's Almanac* (1758)]

20. Creditors have better memories than debtors.
[*Poor Richard's Almanac* (1758)]

21. The body of
Benjamin Franklin, printer,
(Like the cover of an old book,
Its contents worn out,
And stript of its lettering and gilding)
Lies here, food for worms!
Yet the work itself shall not be lost,
For it will, as he believed, appear once more
In a new
And more beautiful edition,
Corrected and amended
By its Author!
[Epitaph for himself, 1728]

22. No nation was ever ruined by trade.
[*Essays*, 'Thoughts on Commercial Subjects']

23. Be in general virtuous, and you will be happy.
['On Early Marriages']

24. The having made a young girl miserable may give you frequent bitter reflection; none of which can attend the making of an old woman happy.
[*On the Choice of a Mistress*]

25. Here Skugg lies snug
As a bug in a rug.
[Letter to Miss Shipley, 1772]

26. There never was a good war, or a bad peace.
[Letter to Josiah Quincy, 1783]

27. But in this world nothing can be said to be certain, except death and taxes.
[Letter to Jean Baptiste Le Roy, 1789. Cf. Margaret Mitchell: 2]

28. We must all hang together, or, most assuredly, we shall all hang separately.
[Remark, Independence Day, 1776]

29. Man is a tool-making animal.
[In Boswell, *The Life of Samuel Johnson* (1791)]

30. [On being asked the use of a new invention]
What is the use of a new-born child?
[In J. Parton, *Life and Times of Benjamin Franklin* (1864)]

31. [On being asked what condition of man he considered the most pitiable]
A lonesome man on a rainy day who does not know how to read.
[In C. Shriner, *Wit, Wisdom, and Foibles of the Great*]

32. There are more old drunkards than old doctors.
[Attr.]

Franklin, (Stella Maria Sarah) Miles (1879–1954)
Australian novelist

1. This was life – my life – my career, my brilliant career! I was fifteen – fifteen! A few fleeting hours and I would be old as those around me. I looked at them as they stood there, weary, and turning down the other side of the hill of life. When young, no doubt they had hoped for, and dreamed of, better things – had even known them. but here they were. This had been their life; this was their career. It was, and in all probability would be, mine too. My life – my career – my brilliant career!
[*My Brilliant Career* (1901), 5]

2. Girls! girls! Those of you who have hearts, and therefore a wish for happiness, homes, and husbands by and by, never develop a reputation of being clever. It will put you out of the matrimonial running as effectually as though it had been circulated that you had leprosy.
[*My Brilliant Career* (1901), 7]

3. Men are clumsy, stupid creatures regarding little things, but in their right place they are wonderful animals.
[*My Brilliant Career* (1901), 17]

Franks, Oliver, Baron (1905–1992)
English diplomat, philosophy lecturer and banker

1. It is a secret in the Oxford sense: you may tell it to only one person at a time.
[*Sunday Telegraph*, 1977]

Fraser, George Macdonald (1925–)
Soldier, historian and novelist

1. They don't invite me to Balmoral nowadays, which is a blessing; those damned tartan carpets always put me off my food, to say nothing of the endless pictures of the Prince Consort standing knock-kneed in a kilt.
[*Flashman in the Great Game* (1975)]

2. Humanity is beastly and stupid, aye, and helpless, and there's an end to it. And that's as true for Crazy Horse as it was for Custer – and they're both long gone, thank God.
[*Flashman and the Redskins* (1982)]

Fraser, Malcolm (1930–)
Australian politician and former Prime Minister

1. Life is not meant to be easy.
[Deakin lecture, 20 July 1971; Fraser related it to Shaw, *Back to Methusaleh* (1921), 'Life is not meant to be easy, my child; but take courage: it can be delightful.']

Frayn, Michael (1933–)
English dramatist, novelist and journalist

1. No woman so naked as one you can see to be naked underneath her clothes.
[*Constructions*]

2. To be absolutely honest, what I feel really bad about is that I don't feel worse. There's the ineffectual liberal's problem in a nutshell.
[*The Observer*, 1965]

Frazer, Sir James George (1854–1941)
Scottish anthropologist, author of books on primitive religions and magic

1. The awe and dread with which the untutored savage contemplates his mother-in-law are amongst the most familiar facts of anthropology.
[*The Golden Bough* (ed. 2, 1900), I]

Frederick the Great (1712–1786)
King of Prussia 1740–86; patron of the arts

1. *Lorsque Auguste buvait, la Pologne était ivre.*
When Augustus drank, Poland became drunk.
[*Les Trois Sultanes*, III, 3]

2. *Une couronne n'est qu'un chapeau qui laisse passer la pluie.*
A crown is merely a hat that lets the rain in.
[Remark on declining a formal coronation, 1740]

3. [Command to hesitant troops]
Ihr verfluchten Kerls, wollt ihr denn ewig leben?
You damn rogues, do you want to live for ever?
[Attr.]

4. My people and I have come to an agreement which satisfies us both. They are to say what they please, and I am to do what I please.
[Attr.]

5. An army, like a serpent, goes on its belly.
[Attr.]

Freed, Arthur (1894–1973)
American film producer and lyricist

1. I'm singing in the rain, just singing in the rain;
What a wonderful feeling, I'm happy again.
['Singing in the Rain', 1929]

French, Marilyn (1929–)
American author and critic

1. There are so much easier ways to destroy a woman. You don't have to rape or kill her; you don't even have to beat her. You can just marry her.
[*The Women's Room* (1977)]

2. Whatever they may be in public life, whatever their relations with men, in their relations with women, all men are rapists, and that's all they are. They rape us with their eyes, their laws and their codes.
[*The Women's Room* (1977)]

Frere, John Hookham (1769–1846)
English diplomat and politician; poet and translator of Aristophanes

1. The feather'd race with pinions skim the air–
Not so the mackerel, and still less the bear!
['Progress of Man' (1798)]

Freud, Clement (1924–)
British Liberal politician, broadcaster, journalist and author

1. If you resolve to give up smoking, drinking and loving, you don't actually live longer; it just seems longer.
[*The Observer*, 1964]

2. [On being asked his opinion of New Zealand]
I find it hard to say, because when I was there it seemed to be shut.
[BBC radio, 1978]

Freud, Sigmund (1856–1939)
Austrian psychiatrist and founder of psychoanalysis

1. The psychic development of an individual is a short repetition of the course of development of the race.
[*Leonardo da Vinci* (1916)]

2. At bottom God is nothing more than an exalted father.
[*Totem and Taboo* (translated 1919)]

3. Religion is an illusion and it derives its strength from the fact that it falls in with our instinctual desires.
[*New Introductory Lectures on Psychoanalysis* (1933), 'A Philosophy of Life']

4. A mother is only brought unlimited satisfaction by her relation to a son; this is altogether the most perfect, the most free from ambivalence of all human relationships.
[*Freud on Women* (1990), 'Femininity']

5. The voice of the intellect is a soft one, but it does not rest till it has gained a hearing.
[*The Future of an Illusion*]

6. The great question . . . which I have not been able to answer, despite my thirty years of research into the feminine soul, is 'What does a woman want?'
[In Charles Robb, *Psychiatry in American Life*]

Freudenberg, (Norman) Graham (1934–)
Australian writer

1. Menzies never made the mistake of raising Australian expectations. It was a key to his success. His great skill lay in never despising the obvious, and in refining his technique of getting the obvious across.
[*Certain Grandeur* (1977)]

2. Calwell's three great loves were his country, his Party and his Church. With each, his relations were ambiguous and unsatisfactory.
[*Certain Grandeur* (1977)]

Friedan, Betty (1921–)
American feminist leader and writer

1. The problem that has no name – which is simply the fact that American women are kept from growing to their full human capacities.
[*The Feminine Mystique* (1963)]

2. [In an open letter to her daughter, in *Cosmopolitan*, 1978]
I hope there will come a day when you, daughter mine, or your daughter, can truly afford to say 'I'm not a feminist. I'm a person' – and a day, not too far away, I hope, when I can stop fighting for women and get onto other matters that interest me now.
[In Susan Bassnett, *Feminist Experiences: The Women's Movement in Four Cultures* (1986)]

Friedman, Milton (1912–)
US economist and advocate of free market capitalism

1. There's no such thing as a free lunch.
[An old US expression, dating back to 1840 at least; Friedman gave it new life in the 1970s, using it in articles, lectures, and as the title of a book, to support his monetarist theories]

Friel, Brian (1929–)
Irish dramatist and short-story writer

1. The result is that people with a culture of poverty suffer much less repression than we of the middle-class suffer and indeed, if I may make the suggestion with due qualification, they often have a lot more fun than we have.
[*The Freedom of the City* (1973)]

2. The hell of it seems to be, when an artist starts saving the world, he starts losing himself.
[*Extracts from a Sporadic Diary*]

Frisch, Max (1911–1991)
Swiss experimental dramatist, novelist, journalist and architect

1. *Wieso haben die Intellektuellen, wenn sie scharenweise zusammenkommen, unweigerlich etwas Komisches?*
Why is there invariably something comic about intellectuals when they meet together in crowds?
[*Tagebuch* (Diary), 1948]

2. *Jede Uniform verdirbt den Charakter.*
Every uniform corrupts one's character.
[*Tagebuch* (Diary), 1948]

Frohman, Charles (1860–1915)
American theatrical producer

1. [Last words before going down with the *Lusitania*, quoting from the play *Peter Pan* which he had produced]
Why fear death? It is the most beautiful adventure in life.
[In A. Birkin, *J. M. Barrie and the Lost Boys* (1979)]

Frost, David (1939–)
English TV personality, journalist and author

1. Television is an invention that permits you to be entertained in your living room by people you wouldn't have in your home.
[Remark, CBS Television, 1971]

Frost, Robert (1874–1963)
American lyric poet, noted for his verse on New England life

1. 'Home is the place where, when you have to go there,
They have to take you in'.
'I should have called it
Something you somehow haven't to deserve.'
['The Death of the Hired Man' (1914)]

2. Something there is that doesn't love a wall . . .

3. My apple trees will never get across
And eat the cones under his pines, I tell him.
He only says, 'Good fences make good neighbours'.
['Mending Wall' (1914)]

4. I'd like to get away from earth awhile
And then come back to it and begin over.
May no fate wilfully misunderstand me
And half grant what I wish and snatch me away
Not to return. Earth's the right place for love;
I don't know where it's likely to go better.
I'd like to go by climbing a birch tree,
And climb black branches up a snow-white trunk
Toward heaven, till the tree could bear no more,
But dipped its top and set me down again.
That would be good both going and coming back.
One could do worse than be a swinger of birches.
['Birches' (1916)]

5. Two roads diverged in a wood, and I–
I took the one less travelled by,
And that has made all the difference.
['The Road Not Taken' (1916)]

6. Some say the world will end in fire,
Some say in ice.
From what I've tasted of desire,

I hold with those who favour fire,
But if it had to perish twice,
I think I know enough of hate
To say that for destruction ice
Is also great
And would suffice.
['Fire and Ice' (1923)]

7. The woods are lovely, dark and deep,
But I have promises to keep,
And miles to go before I sleep,
And miles to go before I sleep.
['Stopping by Woods on a Snowy Evening' (1923)]

8. I have been one acquainted with the night.
I have walked out in rain – and back in rain.
I have outwalked the furthest city light.
I have looked down the saddest city lane.
I have passed by the watchman on his beat
And dropped my eyes, unwilling to explain.
['Acquainted with the Night' (1928)]

9. They cannot scare me with their empty spaces
Between stars – on stars where no human race is.
I have it in me so much nearer home
To scare myself with my own desert places.
['Desert Places' (1936)]

10. I never dared be radical when young
For fear it would make me conservative when old.
['Precaution' (1936)]

11. Whoever it is that leaves him out so late,
When other creatures have gone to stall and bin,
Ought to be told to come and take him in.
['The Runaway' (1939)]

12. The land was ours before we were the land's.
['The Gift Outright' (1942)]

13. I would have written of me on my stone:
I had a lover's quarrel with the world.
['The Lesson for Today' (1942)]

14. We dance round in a ring and suppose,
But the Secret sits in the middle and knows.
['The Secret Sits' (1942)]

15. Forgive, O Lord, my little jokes on Thee
And I'll forgive Thy great big one on me.
[*In the Clearing* (1962), 'Cluster of Faith']

16. No tears in the writer, no tears in the reader.
[*Collected Poems* (1939), Preface]

17. A poem may be worked over once it is in being, but may not be worried into being.
[*Collected Poems* (1939), 'The Figure a Poem Makes']

18. Writing free verse is like playing tennis with the net down.
[Address, 1935]

19. Poetry is a way of taking life by the throat.
[In Elizabeth Sergeant, *Robert Frost: the Trial by Existence* (1960)]

20. Poetry is what is lost in translation.
[In Untermeyer, *Robert Frost: a Backward Look* (1964)]

21. A diplomat is a man who always remembers a woman's birthday but never remembers her age.
[Attr.]

Froude, James Anthony (1818–1894)
English historian, man of letters and biographer of Carlyle

1. Men are made by nature unequal. It is vain, therefore, to treat them as if they were equal.
[*Short Studies on Great Subjects* (1877), 'Party Politics']

2. Experience teaches slowly, and at the cost of mistakes.
[*Short Studies on Great Subjects* (1877), 'Party Politics']

3. Fear is the parent of cruelty.
[*Short Studies on Great Subjects* (1877), 'Party Politics']

4. [Froude visited Australia in 1885, and this was the first recorded use of the words 'down under']
A few more hours and we were to bid adieu to the 'Australasian', her light-souled but good and clever captain, her ever kind and attentive officers. She had carried us safely down under, as the Square gardener put it to me afterwards in London, scarcely able to believe it could be reality.
[*Oceana, or England and her Colonies* (1886)]

5. Wild animals never kill for sport. Man is the only one to whom the torture and death of his fellow creatures is amusing in itself.
[*Oceana, or England and her Colonies* (1886)]

Fry, Christopher (1907–)
English verse dramatist; theatrical director and translator

1. Who should question then
Why we lean our bicycle against a hedge
And go into the house of God?
Who shall question
That coming out from our doorsteps
We have discerned a little, we have known
More than the gossip that comes to us over our gates?
[*The Boy with a Cart* (1939)]

2. I've begun to believe that the reasonable
Is an invention of man, altogether in opposition
To the facts of creation.
[*The Firstborn* (written 1945), III]

3. Life and death
Is cat and dog in this double-bed of a world.
[*A Phoenix Too Frequent* (1946)]

4. I travel light; as light,
That is, as a man can travel who will
Still carry his body around because
Of its sentimental value.
[*The Lady's not for Burning* (1949), I]

5. You bubble-mouthing, fog-blathering,
Chin-chuntering, chap-flapping, liturgical,
Turgidical, base old man!
[*The Lady's not for Burning* (1949), I]

6. Am I invisible?
Am I inaudible? Do I merely festoon
The room with my presence?
[*The Lady's not for Burning* (1949), I]

7. What, after all,
Is a halo? It's only one more thing to keep clean.
[*The Lady's not for Burning* (1949), I]

8. What is official
Is incontestable. It undercuts
The problematical world and sells us life
At a discount.
[*The Lady's not for Burning* (1949), I]

9. Using words
That are only fit for the Bible.
[*The Lady's not for Burning* (1949), II]

10. We should be like stars now that it's dark;
Use ourselves up to the last bright dregs
And vanish in the morning.
[*The Lady's not for Burning* (1949), II]

11. The moon is nothing
But a circumambulating aphrodisiac
Divinely subsidized to provoke the world
Into a rising birth-rate.
[*The Lady's not for Burning* (1949), III]

12. Oh, the unholy mantrap of love!
[*The Lady's not for Burning* (1949), III]

13. It doesn't do a man any good, daylight.
It means up and doing, and that means up to no good.
The best life is led horizontal.
[*Thor, with Angels* (1949)]

14. Over all the world
Men move unhoming, and eternally
Concerned: a swarm of bees who have lost their queen.
[*Venus Unobserved* (1950), II]

15. I know an undesirable character
When I see one; I've been one myself for years.
[*Venus Unobserved* (1950), II]

16. Try thinking of love, or something.
Amor vincit insomnia.
[*A Sleep of Prisoners* (1951)]

17. I sometimes think
His critical judgement is so exquisite
It leaves us nothing to admire except his opinion.
[*The Dark is Light Enough: a Winter Comedy* (1954), II]

18. I know your cause is lost, but in the heart
Of all right causes is a cause that cannot lose.
[*The Dark is Light Enough: a Winter Comedy* (1954), III]

19. What a minefield
Life is! One minute you're taking a stroll in the sun,
The next your legs and arms are all over the hedge.
There's no dignity in it.
[*A Yard of Sun* (1970), II]

20. There may always be another reality
To make fiction of the truth we think we've arrived at.
[*A Yard of Sun* (1970), II]

Fry, Roger (1866–1934)
English art critic, aesthetic philosopher and painter

1. Mr Fry ... brought out a screen upon which there was a picture of a circus. The interviewer was puzzled by the long waists, bulging necks and short legs of the figures. 'But how much wit there is in those figures,' said Mr Fry. 'Art is significant deformity.'
[In Virginia Woolf, *Roger Fry* (1940)]

Fry, Stephen (1957–)
British comedian and writer

1. Christmas to a child is the first terrible proof that to travel hopefully is better than to arrive.
[*Paperweight* (1992)]

2. When I was at Cambridge it was, naturally enough I felt, my ambition to be approached in some way by an elderly homosexual don and asked to spy for or against my country.
[*Paperweight* (1992)]

3. I gave coitus the red card for utilitarian reasons: the displeasure, discomfort and aggravation it caused outweighed any momentary explosions of pleasure, ease or solace.
[*Paperweight* (1992)]

4. A walk, a smile, a gait, a way of flicking the hair away from the eyes, the manner in which clothes encase the body, these can be erotic, but I would be greatly in the debt of the man who could tell me what could ever be appealing about those damp, dark, foul-smelling and revoltingly tufted areas of the body that constitute the main dishes in the banquet of love.
[*Paperweight* (1992)]

Frye, David (1934–)

1. [Of Gerald R. Ford]
He looks like the guy in a science fiction movie who is the first to see the creature.
[Attr.]

Frye, Marilyn

1. Gay men generally are in significant ways, perhaps in all important ways, more loyal to masculinity and male-supremacy than other men. The gay rights movement may be the fundamentalism of the global religion which is patriarchy.
[In Julie Burchill, *Sex and Sensibility*]

Frye, Northrop (1912–1991)
Canadian critic and academic

1. The book is the world's most patient medium.
[In NFB documentary film, *The Scholar in Society*, 1984]

2. There's only one story, the story of your life.
[In John Ayre, *Northrop Frye: A Biography* (1989)]

3. Creative culture is infinitely porous – it absorbs influences from all over the world. That is what differentiates a genuine culture from nationalism. Nationalism is the parody of the reality of cultural identity.
[Interview by Carl Mollins, *Maclean's*, 1991]

4. [Formulation of philosophy during his years as a divinity student]
Read Blake or go to hell: that's my message to the modern world.
[In his obituary by Philip Marchand in *The Toronto Star*, 1991]

Fulda, Ludwig (1862–1939)
German writer

1. *Du bleibst der König – auch in Unterhosen.*
You're still the King – even in your underpants.
[*Der Talisman* (1892), III.viii]

Fuller, Richard Buckminster (1895–1983)
American architect and engineer

1. God, to me, it seems,
is a verb
not a noun,
proper or improper.
[*No More Secondhand God* (1963)]

2. I am a passenger on the spaceship, Earth.
[*Operating Manual for Spaceship Earth* (1969)]

Fuller, Thomas [1] (1608–1661)
English divine and antiquary

1. Many have been the wise speeches of fools, though not so many as the foolish speeches of wise men.
[*The Holy State and the Profane State* (1642)]

2. A little skill in antiquity inclines a man to Popery; but depth in that study brings him about again to our religion.
[*The Holy State and the Profane State* (1642)]

3. [Of the Duke of Alva]
He was one of a lean body and visage, as if his eager soul,

biting for anger at the clog of his body, desired to fret a passage through it.
[*The Holy State and the Profane State* (1642)]

4. Learning hath gained most by those books by which the printers have lost.
[*The Holy State and the Profane State* (1642)]

5. Light (God's eldest daughter) is a principal beauty in building.
[*The Holy State and the Profane State* (1642)]

6. Anger is one of the sinews of the soul; he that wants it hath a maimed mind.
[*The Holy State and the Profane State* (1642)]

7. The pyramids themselves, doting with age, have forgotten the names of their founders.
[*The Holy State and the Profane State* (1642)]

8. It is always darkest just before the day dawneth.
[*Pisgah Sight* (1650)]

9. He was a very valiant man who first ventured on eating of oysters.
[*The History of the Worthies of England* (1662). Cf. Swift: 46]

10. [Definition of a proverb]
Much matter decocted into a few words.
[*The History of the Worthies of England* (1662)]

11. [Comparing Shakespeare and Ben Jonson]
Many were the wit-combats betwixt him and Ben Jonson, which two I behold like a Spanish great galleon, and an English man of war; Master Jonson (like the former) was built far higher in learning; solid but slow in his performances. Shakespeare was the English man of war, lesser in bulk, but lighter in sailing, could turn with all tides, tack about and take advantage of all winds, by the quickness of his wit and invention.
[*The History of the Worthies of England* (1662)]

12. There is a great difference between painting a face and not washing it.
[*Church History*, VII]

Fuller, Thomas [2] (1654–1734)
English physician and writer of maxims

1. It is a silly game where nobody wins.
[*Gnomologia* (1732)]

Funke, Alfred (b. 1869)
German writer

1. *Gott strafe England!*
God punish England!
[*Schwerte und Myrte* (1914)]

Furber, Douglas (1885–1961)
British songwriter, author of musical plays and revues and screenwriter

1. Any time you're Lambeth way,
Any evening, any day,
You'll find us all doin' the Lambeth walk.
['Doin' the Lambeth Walk', 1937]

Furphy, Joseph (Tom Collins) (1843–1912)
Australian writer of fiction and poet

1. Unemployed at last!
[*Such is Life* (1903), opening words]

2. To me the momentous variety of this interminable scrub has a charm of its own; so grave, subdued, self-centred; so alien to the genial appeal of more winsome landscape, or the assertive grandeur of mountain and gorge.
[*Such is Life* (1903), 2]

3. For there is no such thing as a democratic gentleman; the adjective and the noun are hyphenated by a drawn sword.
[*Such is Life* (1903), 3]

Fyleman, Rose (1877–1957)
English children's poet and dramatist

1. There are fairies at the bottom of our garden!
[*Fairies and Chimneys* (1918), 'Fairies']

Gable, Clark (1901–1960)
American leading film actor; Academy Award 1934

1. Frankly, my dear, I don't give a damn.
[*Gone With the Wind*, film, 1939; script by Sidney Howard from Margaret Mitchell's novel]

Gabor, Zsa-Zsa (Sari Gabor) (1919–)
Hungarian film actress; frequently married

1. I never hated a man enough to give him his diamonds back.
[*The Observer*, 'Sayings of the Week', 1957]

2. Husbands are like fires. They go out when unattended.
[*Newsweek*, 1960]

3. A man in love is incomplete until he has married. Then he's finished.
[*Newsweek*, 1960]

4. Never despise what it says in the women's magazines: it may not be subtle but neither are men.
[*The Observer*, 'Sayings of the Week', 1976]

5. [Her answer to the question 'How many husbands have you had?']
You mean apart from my own?
[Attr.]

Gaisford, Rev. Thomas (1779–1855)
English scholar of Greek and Dean of Christ Church, Oxford

1. Nor can I do better, in conclusion, than impress upon you the study of Greek literature, which not only elevates above the vulgar herd, but leads not infrequently to positions of considerable emolument.
[Christmas Day Sermon, Oxford Cathedral; in Tuckwell, *Reminiscences of Oxford* (1907)]

Gaitskell, Hugh (1906–1963)
English socialist; Labour politician (Chancellor of the Exchequer 1950–51) and party leader

1. There are some of us who will fight and fight and fight again to save the Party we love.
[Speech, Labour Party Conference, 1960]

2. [On Britain's joining the European Community]
It does mean, if this is the idea, the end of Britain as an independent European state ... it means the end of a thousand years of history.
[Speech, Labour Party Conference, 3 October 1962]

3. All terrorists, at the invitation of the Government, end up with drinks at the Dorchester.
[Letter to *The Guardian*, 1977]

Gaius (fl. c. 110–180)
Roman jurist

1. *Damnosa hereditas.*
A pernicious inheritance.
[*Institutes*, I, 163]

Galbraith, J.K. (1908–)
Canadian-born American Keynesian economist; diplomat and author

1. The Affluent Society.
[Title of book, 1958]

2. Wealth is not without its advantages, and the case to the contrary, although it has often been made, has never proved widely persuasive.
[*The Affluent Society* (1958), first sentence]

3. Wealth has never been a sufficient source of honor in itself. It must be advertised, and the normal medium is obtrusively expensive goods.
[*The Affluent Society* (1958), 7. Cf. Veblen: 1]

4. Few things are as immutable as the addiction of political groups to the ideas by which they have once won office.
[*The Affluent Society* (1958), 13]

5. In a community where public services have failed to keep abreast of private consumption things are very different. Here, in an atmosphere of private opulence and public squalor, the private goods have full sway.
[*The Affluent Society* (1958), 18]

6. In the affluent society, no sharp distinction can be made between luxuries and necessaries.
[*The Affluent Society* (1958), 21]

7. Politics is not the art of the possible. It consists in choosing between the disastrous and the unpalatable.
[*Ambassador's Journal* (1969), Letter to President Kennedy, March 1962]

8. The Australians were wise to choose such a large country, for of all the people in the world they clearly require the most space.
[*Annals of an Abiding Liberal* (1980)]

9. The salary of the chief executive of the large corporation is not a market award for achievement. It is frequently in the nature of a warm personal gesture by the individual to himself.
[*Annals of an Abiding Liberal* (1980)]

10. The Great Wall, I've been told, is the only man-made structure on earth that is visible from the moon. For the life of me I cannot see why anyone would go to the moon to look at it, when, with almost the same difficulty, it can be viewed in China.
[*The Sunday Times Magazine*]

11. Economics is extremely useful as a form of employment for economists.
[Attr.]

12. If all else fails, immortality can always be assured by spectacular error.
[Attr.]

Galileo Galilei (1564–1642)
Italian mathematician, astronomer and physicist; inventor, teacher and advocate of the Copernican system

1. [Remark made after he was forced to withdraw his assertion that the Earth moved round the Sun]
Eppur si muove.
But it does move.
[Attr., 1632 (probably apocryphal)]

2. I do not feel obliged to believe that the same God who has endowed us with sense, reason, and intellect has intended us to forgo their use.
[Attr.]

Gallacher, William (1881–1965)
Scottish politician; first Communist MP 1935–50; President of the Communist Party 1956–63

1. We are for our own people. We want to see them happy, healthy and wise, drawing strength from cooperation with the peoples of other lands, but also contributing their full share to the general well-being. Not a broken-down pauper and mendicant, but a strong, living partner in the progressive advancement of civilization.
[*The Case for Communism* (1949)]

Gallant, Mavis (1922–)
Canadian writer; moved to Paris in 1950

1. The Irish were not English. God had sent them to Canada to keep people from marrying protestants.
[*Across the Bridge* (1993), '1933']

Gallico, Paul (1897–)
American author and scriptwriter

1. The words *Liberté, Egalité, Fraternité* rimming their coins might well be replaced by the slogan 'It can be arranged'.
[*The Zoo Gang* (1971), 'The Picture Thieves']

Galsworthy, John (1867–1933)
English novelist, noted for the 'Forsyte Saga'; short-story writer and dramatist; Nobel prize 1932

1. [James Forsyte]
Nobody tells me anything.
[*The Man of Property* (1906)]

2. Oh, your precious 'lame ducks'!
[*The Man of Property* (1906)]

3. He could take nothing for dinner but a partridge, with an imperial pint of champagne.
[*The Man of Property* (1906)]

4. He [Jolyon] was afflicted by the thought that where Beauty was, nothing ever ran quite straight, which, no doubt, was why so many people looked on it as immoral.
[*In Chancery* (1920), I, 13]

5. I do wish I had the gift of writing. I really think that it is the nicest way of making money going.
[Letter to Monica Sanderson, c. 1894]

6. The French cook; we open tins.
[*Treasury of Humorous Quotations*]

Galt, John (1779–1839)
Scottish novelist, noted for observation of rural life, and Canadian pioneer

1. From the lone shieling of the misty island
Mountains divide us, and the waste of seas–
Yet still the blood is strong, the heart is Highland,
And we in dreams behold the Hebrides!
Fair these broad meads, these hoary woods are grand;
But we are exiles from our fathers' land.
[Attr. in Blackwood's *Edinburgh Magazine*, 1829]

Gambetta, Léon (1838–1882)
French statesman; Prime Minister 1881–82

1. *Les temps héroïques sont passés.*
Heroic times have passed away.
[Saying]

Gandhi, Indira (1917–1984)
Indian stateswoman and Congress Party leader; Prime Minister of India 1966–77, 1980–84; assassinated

1. You cannot shake hands with a clenched fist.
[Remark at a press conference, 1971]

2. [Said 24 hours before she was assassinated]
Even if I die in the service of this nation, I would be proud of it. Every drop of my blood, I am sure, will contribute to the growth of this nation and make it strong and dynamic.
[Speech, Bhubaneswar, Orissa, 31 October 1984]

3. There exists no politician in India daring enough to attempt to explain to the masses that cows can be eaten.
[In Oriana Fallaci, *New York Review of Books*, 'Indira's Coup']

4. To bear many children is considered not only a religious blessing but also an investment. The greater their number, some Indians reason, the more alms they can beg.
[In Oriana Fallaci, *New York Review of Books*, 'Indira's Coup']

Gandhi, Mohandas Karamchand (Mahatma Gandhi) (1869–1948)
Indian political leader, instrumental in achieving independence from Britain; sought reform by non-violent means

1. I wanted to avoid violence. Non-violence is the first article of my faith. It is also the last article of my creed.
[Speech at Shahi Bag, March 1922, in *Young India*, 1922]

2. The moment the slave resolves that he will no longer be a slave, his fetters fall. He frees himself and shows the way to others. Freedom and slavery are mental states.
[*Non-Violence in Peace and War* (1949), II, 5]

3. [When asked what he thought of Western civilization]
I think it would be an excellent idea.
[Attr.]

Garbo, Greta (Greta Louisa Gustafsson) (1905–1990)
Swedish-born American film actress of 1930s; Academy Award 1954

1. I want to be alone.
[*Grand Hotel*, film, 1932; script by William A. Drake]

2. I never said, 'I want to be alone.' I only said, 'I want to be let alone.' There is all the difference.
[In Colombo, *Wit and Wisdom of the Moviemakers*]

3. I think I go home.
[Attr.]

García Márquez, Gabriel (1928–)
Colombian novelist and short-story writer

1. *La ingratitud humana no tiene límites.*
There are no limits to human ingratitude.
[*El Coronel no tiene quien le escriba* (*No-one Writes to the Colonel*, 1961)]

2. *Un solo minuto de reconciliación tiene más mérito que toda una vida de amistad.*
One single minute of reconciliation is worth more than an entire life of friendship.
[*Cien años de soledad* (*One Hundred Years of Solitude*, 1968)]

3. *El periodismo es un género literario, muy parecido a la novela, y tiene la gran ventaja de que el reportero puede inventar cosas. Y eso el novelista lo tiene totalmente prohibido.*
Journalism is a literary genre very similar to that of the novel, and has the great advantage that the reporter can invent things. And that is completely forbidden to the novelist.
[Speech, April 1994, reported in *El País: edición internacional*, 1994]

Garel-Jones, Tristan (1941–)
English Conservative MP

1. My profession does not allow me to go swanning around buying pints of milk. I wouldn't be of sufficient service to my constituents if I went into shops.
[*The Independent*, 1994]

Garfield, James A. (1831–1881)
American soldier and politician; Republican President, 1881; assassinated

1. Fellow-citizens: God reigns, and the Government at Washington lives!
[Speech on the assassination of Lincoln, 1865]

Garibaldi, Giuseppe (1807–1882)
Italian soldier and patriot; helped establish a united Italy

1. *Soldati, io esco da Roma. Chi vuole continuare la guerra contro lo straniero venga con me. Non posso offrirgli né onori né stipendi; gli offro fame, sete, marcie forzate, battaglie e morte. Chi ama la patria mi segua.*
Men, I am leaving Rome. If you want to carry on fighting the invader, come with me. I cannot promise you either honours or wages; I can only offer you hunger, thirst, forced marches, battles and death. If you love your country, follow me.
[In G. Guerzoni, *Garibaldi* (1929), 6]

Garioch, Robert (Robert Garioch Sutherland) (1909–1981)
Scottish realist poet and translator

1. In simmer, whan aa sorts foregether
in Embro to the ploy,
fowk seek out friens to hae a blether,
or faes they'd fain annoy;
smorit wi British Railways' reek
frae Glesca or Glen Roy
or Wick, they come to hae a week
of cultivatit joy,
or three,
in Embro to the ploy.
[*Selected Poems* (1966), 'Embro to the ploy']

Garland, Judy (Frances Gumm) (1922–1969)
American film actress and singer; Academy Award 1939

1. I was born at the age of twelve on a Metro-Goldwyn-Mayer lot.
[*The Observer*, 'Sayings of the Week', 1951]

Garner, John Nance (1868–1937)
US statesman, former Vice-President

1. [The Vice-Presidency] isn't worth a pitcher of warm piss.
[Attr.]

Garrick, David (1717–1779)
Celebrated English actor, theatrical manager, dramatist and letter writer

1. Prologues precede the piece – in mournful verse;
As undertakers – walk before the hearse.
[Prologue to Arthur Murphy's *The Apprentice* (1756)]

2. I've that within – for which there are no plaisters.
[Prologue to Goldsmith's *She Stoops to Conquer* (1773)]

3. A fellow-feeling makes one wond'rous kind.
[*An Occasional Prologue on Quitting the Theatre* (1776)]

4. Come cheer up, my lads! 'tis to glory we steer,
To add something more to this wonderful year;
To honour we call you, not press you like slaves,
For who are so free as the sons of the waves?
Heart of oak are our ships,
Heart of oak are our men:
We always are ready;
Steady, boys, steady;
We'll fight and we'll conquer again and again.
['Heart of Oak' (1759)]

5. Kitty, a fair, but frozen maid,
Kindled a flame I still deplore;

The hood-wink'd boy I call'd in aid,
Much of his near approach afraid.
So fatal to my suit before.
['A Riddle' (1762)]

6. Here lies Nolly Goldsmith, for shortness call'd Noll,
Who wrote like an angel, but talk'd like poor Poll.
['Impromptu Epitaph on Goldsmith' (1774)]

Garrison, William Lloyd (1805–1879)

American abolitionist, lecturer and newspaper editor

1. I am in earnest – I will not equivocate – I will not excuse – I will not retreat a single inch – and I will be heard!
[Salutatory address of *The Liberator*, 1831]

2. Our country is the world – our countrymen are all mankind.
[Prospectus of *The Liberator*, 1837]

3. The compact which exists between the North and the South is 'a covenant with death and an agreement with hell'.
[Resolution adopted by the Massachusetts Anti-Slavery Society, 1843]

Garrod, Heathcote William (1878–1960)

English classical scholar, Professor of Poetry and essayist

1. [In response to criticism that, during World War I, he was not fighting to defend civilization]
Madam, I am the civilization they are fighting to defend.
[In D. Balsdon, *Oxford Now and Then* (1970)]

Garth, Sir Samuel (1661–1719)

English physician and poet

1. A barren superfluity of words.
['The Dispensary' (1699)]

Gaskell, Elizabeth (1810–1865)

English novelist, short-story writer and biographer of Charlotte Brontë

1. A man ... is so in the way in the house!
[*Cranford* (1853), 1]

2. [The Cranford ladies'] dress is very independent of fashion; as they observe, 'What does it signify how we dress here at Cranford, where everybody knows us?' And if they go from home, their reason is equally cogent, 'What does it signify how we dress here, where nobody knows us?'
[*Cranford* (1853), 1]

3. [Capt. Brown on Miss Betsey Barker's cow]
Get her a flannel waistcoat and flannel drawers, ma'am, if you wish to keep her alive. But my advice is, kill the poor creature at once.
[*Cranford* (1853), 1]

4. We were none of us musical, though Miss Jenkyns beat time, out of time, by way of appearing to be so.
[*Cranford* (1853), 1]

5. 'It is very pleasant dining with a bachelor,' said Miss Matty, softly, as we settled ourselves in the counting-house. 'I only hope it is not improper; so many pleasant things are!'
[*Cranford* (1853), 4]

6. Bombazine would have shown a deeper sense of her loss.
[*Cranford* (1853), 7]

7. That kind of patriotism which consists in hating all other nations.
[*Sylvia's Lovers* (1863), 1]

Gauguin, Paul (1848–1903)

French Post-Impressionist painter, developer of synthetism

1. Art is either a plagiarist or a revolutionist.
[In Huneker, *Pathos of Distance* (1913)]

2. Many excellent cooks are spoiled by going into the arts.
[In Cournos, *Modern Plutarch* (1928)]

3. Civilization is paralysis.
[In Cournos, *Modern Plutarch* (1928)]

Gautier, Théophile (1811–1872)

French Romantic poet, novelist, short-story writer and critic

1. *Oui, l'oeuvre sort plus belle*
D'une forme au travail
Rebelle,
Vers, marbre, onyx, émail.
Yes, creation comes out more beautiful from a form rebellious to work: verse, marble, onyx, enamel.
[*Emaux et camées* (1932), 'L'Art']

2. *Plutôt la barbarie que l'ennui.*
Sooner barbarity than boredom.
[Attr.]

Gavarni (Guillaume Sulpice Chevalier) (1801–1866)

French caricaturist and illustrator

1. [People given to unconventional conduct or indiscreet remarks]
Les enfants terribles.
The terrible children.
[Title of a series of prints, 1842]

Gay, John (1685–1732)

English poet, dramatist and librettist

1. I rage, I melt, I burn,
The feeble God has stab'd me to the Heart.
[*Acis and Galatea* (1718), II]

2. O ruddier than the Cherry!
O sweeter than the Berry!
O Nymph, more bright
Than Moonshine Night!
Like Kidlings blithe and merry.
[*Acis and Galatea* (1718), II]

3. Would you gain the tender Creature?
Softly, gently, kindly treat her;
Suff'ring is the Lover's Part.
Beauty by Constraint possessing,
You enjoy but half the Blessing,

Lifeless Charms, without the Heart.
[*Acis and Galatea* (1718), II]

4. Love sounds the Alarms, and Fear is a flying.
[*Acis and Galatea* (1718), II]

5. Then nature rul'd, and love, devoid of art,
Spoke the consenting language of the heart.
[*Dione* (1720), Prologue]

6. He best can pity who has felt the woe.
[*Dione* (1720), II.ii]

7. Woman's mind
Oft' shifts her passions, like th' inconstant wind;
Sudden she rages, like the troubled main,
Now sinks the storm, and all is calm again.
[*Dione* (1720), II.v]

8. A woman's friendship ever ends in love.
[*Dione* (1720), IV.vi]

9. She who has never lov'd, has never liv'd.
[*The Captives* (1724), II.ii]

10. How, like a moth, the simple maid,
Still plays about the flame!
[*The Beggar's Opera* (1728), I.iv]

11. Our Polly is a sad slut! nor heeds what we have taught her.
I wonder any man alive will ever rear a daughter!
[*The Beggar's Opera* (1728), I.viii]

12. Do you think your mother and I should have liv'd comfortably so long together, if ever we had been married?
[*The Beggar's Opera* (1728), I.viii]

13. Can Love be controll'd by advice?
[*The Beggar's Opera* (1728), I.viii]

14. Well, Polly; as far as one woman can forgive another, I forgive thee.
[*The Beggar's Opera* (1728), I.viii]

15. *Polly*: Then all my sorrows are at an end.
Mrs Peachum: A mighty likely speech in troth, for a wench who is just married!
[*The Beggar's Opera* (1728), I.viii]

16. Even butchers weep!
[*The Beggar's Opera* (1728), I.xii]

17. Pretty Polly, say,
When I was away,
Did your fancy never stray
To some newer lover?
[*The Beggar's Opera* (1728), I.xiii]

18. *Macheath*: If with me you'd fondly stray,
Polly: Over the hills and far away.
[*The Beggar's Opera* (1728), I.xiii]

19. O what pain it is to part!
[*The Beggar's Opera* (1728), I.xiii]

20. If the heart of a man is depress'd with cares,
The mist is dispell'd when a woman appears.
[*The Beggar's Opera* (1728), II.iii]

21. I must have women. There is nothing unbends the mind like them.
[*The Beggar's Opera* (1728), II.iii]

22. Youth's the season made for joys,
Love is then our duty.
[*The Beggar's Opera* (1728), II.iv]

23. To cheat a man is nothing; but the woman must have fine parts indeed who cheats a woman!
[*The Beggar's Opera* (1728), II.iv]

24. Man may escape from rope and gun;
Nay, some have out-liv'd the doctor's pill:
Who takes a woman must be undone,
That basilisk is sure to kill.
The fly that sips treacle is lost in the sweets,
So he that tastes woman, woman, woman,
He that tastes woman, ruin meets.
[*The Beggar's Opera* (1728), II.viii]

25. *Macheath*: Have you no bowels, no tenderness, my dear Lucy, to see a husband in these circumstances?
Lucy: A husband!
Macheath: In ev'ry respect but the form.
[*The Beggar's Opera* (1728), II.ix]

26. I am ready, my dear Lucy, to give you satisfaction – if you think there is any in marriage.
[*The Beggar's Opera* (1728), II.ix]

27. I think, you must do like other widows – buy your self weeds, and be cheerful.
[*The Beggar's Opera* (1728), II.xi]

28. How happy could I be with either,
Were t'other dear charmer away!
[*The Beggar's Opera* (1728), II.xiii]

29. A moment of time may make us unhappy forever.
[*The Beggar's Opera* (1728), II.xv]

30. One wife is too much for most husbands to hear,
But two at a time there's no mortal can bear.
This way, and that way, and which way I will,
What would comfort the one, t'other wife would take ill.
[*The Beggar's Opera* (1728), III.xi]

31. Whether we can afford it or no, we must have superfluities.
[*Polly* (1729), I.i]

32. No, Sir, tho' I was born and bred in England, I can dare to be poor, which is the only thing now-a-days men are asham'd of.
[*Polly* (1729), I.xi]

33. An inconstant woman, tho' she hath no chance to be very happy, can never be very unhappy.
[*Polly* (1729), I.xiv]

34. Praising all alike, is praising none.
['A Letter to a Lady' (1714)]

35. A miss for pleasure, and a wife for breed.
['The Toilette' (1716)]

36. Life is a jest; and all things show it.
I thought so once; but now I know it.
['My Own Epitaph' (1720). Cf. J.K. Stephen: 1]

37. All in the Downs the fleet was moor'd,
The streamers waving in the wind,
When black-ey'd Susan came aboard...

38. We only part to meet again.
Change, as ye list, ye winds; my heart shall be
The faithful compass that still points to thee...

39. They'll tell thee, sailors, when away,
In ev'ry port a mistress find...

40. Adieu, she cries! and waves her lily hand.
['Sweet William's Farewell to Black-Eyed Susan' (1720)]

41. She who trifles with all
Is less likely to fall
Than she who but trifles with one.
['The Coquet Mother and Coquet Daughter' (1727)]

42. Whence is thy learning? Hath thy toil
O'er books consum'd the midnight oil?
[*Fables* (1727), Introduction]

43. Where yet was ever found a mother,
Who'd give her booby for another?
[*Fables* (1727), I, 3, 'The Mother, the Nurse, and the Fairy']

44. An open foe may prove a curse,
But a pretended friend is worse.
[*Fables* (1727), I, 17, 'The Shepherd's Dog and the Wolf']

45. In ev'ry age and clime we see,
Two of a trade can ne'er agree.
[*Fables* (1727), I, 21, 'The Rat-Catcher and Cats']

46. 'While there is life, there's hope,' he cry'd;
'Then why such haste?' so groan'd and dy'd.
[*Fables* (1727), I, 27, 'The Sick Man and the Angel']

47. Those, who in quarrels interpose,
Must often wipe a bloody nose.
[*Fables* (1727), I, 34, 'The Mastiffs']

48. Fools may our scorn, not envy raise,
For envy is a kind of praise.
[*Fables* (1727), I, 44, 'The Hound and the Huntsman']

49. And when a lady's in the case,
You know, all other things give place.
[*Fables* (1727), I, 50, 'The Hare and Many Friends']

50. Give me, kind heav'n, a private station,
A mind serene for contemplation.
[*Fables* (1738), II, 2, 'The Vulture, the Sparrow, and Other Birds']

51. Studious of elegance and ease,
Myself alone I seek to please.
[*Fables* (1738), II, 8, 'The Man, the Cat, the Dog, and the Fly']

52. 'Tis a gross error, held in schools,
That Fortune always favours fools.
[*Fables* (1738), II, 12, 'Pan and Fortune']

Geddes, Sir Eric (1875–1937)
Indian-born British politician and administrator

1. The Germans, if this government is returned, are going to pay every penny; they are going to be squeezed as a lemon is squeezed – until the pips squeak.
[Speech, in Cambridge *Daily News*, 1918]

Geldof, Bob (1954–)
Irish rock musician, media personality and charity fundraiser

1. Is That It?
[Title of autobiography, 1986]

2. I'm not interested in the bloody system! Why has he no food? Why is he starving to death?
[*The Observer*, 1985, in Jeffrey Care (ed.), *Sayings of the Eighties* (1989)]

3. I'm into pop because I want to get rich, get famous and get laid.
[Attr.]

George I (1660–1727)
First Hanoverian King of Great Britain and Ireland 1714–27

1. I hate all Boets and Bainters.
[In Campbell, *Lives of the Chief Justices* (1849), 30]

George II (1683–1760)
King of Great Britain and Ireland, 1727–60; son of George I

1. [Reply to Queen Caroline who, on her deathbed, urged him to marry again]
Non, j'aurai des maîtresses.
No, I shall have mistresses.
[In Hervey, *Memoirs of the Reign of George the Second* (1848)]

2. [Reply to the Duke of Newcastle who complained that General Wolfe was a madman]
Mad, is he? Then I hope he will bite some of my other generals.
[In Wilson, *The Life and Letters of James Wolfe* (1909), 17]

George III (1738–1820)
King of Great Britain and Ireland, 1760–1820; grandson of George II

1. Born and educated in this country I glory in the name of Briton.
[Speech, 1760]

George IV (1762–1830)
King of Great Britain and Ireland 1820–30; son of George III

1. [On first meeting his future wife, Caroline of Brunswick, 1795]
Harris, I am not well; pray get me a glass of brandy.
[In the Earl of Malmesbury, *Diaries and Correspondence* (1844)]

George V (1865–1936)
King of Great Britain and Northern Ireland 1910–36; son of Edward VII

1. [Having just asked Ramsay MacDonald to form the first Labour Government]
Today, 23 years ago, dear Grandmama died. I wonder what she would have thought of a Labour Government.
[Diary, 22 January 1924]

2. [On hearing Mr Wheatley's life story]
Is it possible that my people live in such awful conditions? . . . I tell you, Mr Wheatley, that if I had to live in conditions like that I would be a revolutionary myself.
[In L. MacNeill Weir, *The Tragedy of Ramsay MacDonald* (1938), 16]

3. My father was frightened of his mother. I was frightened of my father, and I'm damned well going to make sure that my children are frightened of me.
[In R. Churchill, *Lord Derby – 'King of Lancashire': the Official Life of Edward, Seventeenth Earl of Derby 1865–1948* (1959)]

4. [On the battlefield cemeteries in Flanders, 1922]
I have many times asked myself whether there can be more potent advocates of peace upon earth through the years to come than this massed multitude of silent witnesses to the desolation of war.
[Attr.]

5. [When told he would soon be convalescing in Bognor Regis]
Bugger Bognor.
[Attr.; may date from his illness in 1929]

6. [To Lord Wigram, his secretary; sometimes quoted as his last words]
How is the Empire?
[Attr.]

George VI (1895–1952)
King of Great Britain and Northern Ireland from 1936; son of George V and father of Elizabeth II

1. Abroad is bloody.
[In Auden, *A Certain World* (1970)]

2. We're not a family; we're a firm.
[Attr. in Lane, *Our Future King*]

George, Dan (Daniel George Bunting) (1899–1982)
North American Indian Chief; film actor and author

1. O Freedom, what liberties are taken in thy name!
[In Sagittarius and D. George, *Perpetual Pessimist* (1963). Cf. Roland: 1]

2. When the white man came we had the land and they had the Bibles; now they have the land and we have the Bibles.
[Attr.]

George, Henry (1839–1897)
American economist, editor and lecturer

1. The man who gives me employment, which I must have or suffer, that man is my master, let me call him what I will.
[*Social Problems* (1884), 5]

Gerasimov, Gennady (1935–)
Former Soviet Foreign Ministry spokesman and editor of Moscow News

1. [He coined this phrase to explain the Kremlin's attitude to the 1989 revolutions in Eastern Europe]
We now have the 'Frank Sinatra Doctrine'. He had a song, 'I Had It My Way' [*sic*]. So every country decides on its own which road to take.
[On American television, 25 October 1989]

Gershwin, George (1898–1937)
American popular composer and pianist

1. [On his opera *Porgy and Bess*]
I think the music is so marvelous – I really can't believe I wrote it.
[Quoted by E. Jablonski in sleeve notes to the RCA Victor recording]

Getty, J. Paul (1892–1976)
American oil billionaire and art collector

1. If you can actually count your money you are not really a rich man.
[In A. Barrow, *Gossip*]

2. [Explaining why he refused to pay ransom money to secure his grandson's release]
I have fourteen other grandchildren and if I pay one penny now, then I'll have fourteen kidnapped grandchildren.
[Attr.]

3. The meek shall inherit the earth, but not the mineral rights.
[Attr.]

Gibbon, Edward (1737–1794)
English historian, politician and memoirist

1. The various modes of worship, which prevailed in the Roman world, were all considered by the people as equally true; by the philosopher, as equally false; and by the magistrate, as equally useful.
[*Decline and Fall of the Roman Empire* (1776–88), 2]

2. The principles of a free constitution are irrecoverably lost, when the legislative power is nominated by the executive.
[*Decline and Fall of the Roman Empire* (1776–88), 3]

3. History ... is, indeed, little more than the register of the crimes, follies, and misfortunes of mankind.
[*Decline and Fall of the Roman Empire* (1776–88), 3]

4. If a man were called to fix the period in the history of the world during which the condition of the human race was most happy and prosperous, he would, without hesitation, name that which elapsed from the death of Domitian to the accession of Commodus.
[*Decline and Fall of the Roman Empire* (1776–88), 3]

5. [Of Emperor Gordian the Younger]
Twenty-two acknowledged concubines, and a library of sixty-two thousand volumes attested the variety of his inclinations; and from the productions which he left behind him, it appears that both the one and the other were designed for use rather than for ostentation.
[*Decline and Fall of the Roman Empire* (1776–88), 7]

6. All taxes must, at last, fall upon agriculture.
[*Decline and Fall of the Roman Empire* (1776–88), 8]

7. Corruption, the most infallible symptom of constitutional liberty.
[*Decline and Fall of the Roman Empire* (1776–88), 21]

8. [Of Commenus]
In every deed of mischief he had a heart to resolve, a head to contrive, and a hand to execute.
[*Decline and Fall of the Roman Empire* (1776–88), 48]

9. Our sympathy is cold to the relation of distant misery.
[*Decline and Fall of the Roman Empire* (1776–88), 49]

10. The winds and waves are always on the side of the ablest navigators.
[*Decline and Fall of the Roman Empire* (1776–88), 68]

11. All that is human must retrograde if it does not advance.
[*Decline and Fall of the Roman Empire* (1776–88), 71]

12. The romance of *Tom Jones*, that exquisite picture of human manners, will outlive the palace of the Escurial and the imperial eagle of the house of Austria.
[*Memoirs of My Life and Writings* (1796)]

13. My early and invincible love of reading, which I would not exchange for the treasures of India.
[*Memoirs of My Life and Writings* (1796)]

14. To the University of Oxford I acknowledge no obligation; and she will as cheerfully renounce me for a son, as I am willing to disclaim her for a mother. I spent fourteen months at Magdalen College: they proved the fourteen months the most idle and unprofitable of my whole life.
[*Memoirs of My Life and Writings* (1796)]

15. If I inquire into the manufactures of the monks of Magdalen, if I extend the inquiry to the other colleges of Oxford and Cambridge, a silent blush, or a scornful frown, will be the only reply. The fellows or monks of my time were decent easy men, who supinely enjoyed the gifts of the founder.
[*Memoirs of My Life and Writings* (1796)]

16. Their dull and deep potations excused the brisk intemperance of youth.
[*Memoirs of My Life and Writings* (1796)]

17. Dr Winchester well remembered that he had a salary to receive, and only forgot that he had a duty to perform.
[*Memoirs of My Life and Writings* (1796)]

18. [After receiving the sacrament in the Church of Lausanne when he was 17 years old]
It was here that I suspended my religious inquiries.
[*Memoirs of My Life and Writings* (1796)]

19. [On Mademoiselle Curchod, his first love]
I saw and loved.
[*Memoirs of My Life and Writings* (1796)]

20. I sighed as a lover, I obeyed as a son.
[*Memoirs of My Life and Writings* (1796)]

21. [Of London]
Crowds without company, and dissipation without pleasure.
[*Memoirs of My Life and Writings* (1796)]

22. I was never less alone than when by myself.
[*Memoirs of My Life and Writings* (1796)]

23. [Referring to his own army service]
The captain of the Hampshire grenadiers ... has not been useless to the historian of the Roman empire.
[*Memoirs of My Life and Writings* (1796)]

24. It was at Rome, on the 15th of October, 1764, as I sat musing amidst the ruins of the Capitol, while the barefooted friars were singing vespers in the Temple of Jupiter, that the idea of writing the decline and fall of the city first started to my mind.
[*Memoirs of My Life and Writings* (1796)]

25. Few, perhaps, are the children who, after the expiration of some months or years, would sincerely rejoice in the resurrection of their parents.
[*Memoirs of My Life and Writings* (1796)]

26. The first of earthly blessings, independence.
[*Memoirs of My Life and Writings* (1796)]

27. I will not dissemble the first emotions of joy on the recovery of my freedom, and, perhaps, the establishment of my fame. But my pride was soon humbled, and a sober melancholy was spread over my mind, by the idea that I had taken an everlasting leave of an old and agreeable companion, and that whatsoever might be the future date of my History, the life of the historian must be short and precarious.
[*Memoirs of My Life and Writings* (1796)]

28. My English text is chaste, and all licentious passages are left in the obscurity of a learned language.
[*Memoirs of My Life and Writings* (1796)]

29. I must reluctantly observe that two causes, the abbreviation of time, and the failure of hope, will always tinge with a browner shade the evening of life.
[*Memoirs of My Life and Writings* (1796)]

Gibbon, Lewis Grassic (James Leslie Mitchell) (1901–1935)
Scottish novelist and short-story writer; journalist and soldier

1. Nothing endured at all, nothing but the land ... The land was forever, it moved and changed below you, but was forever.
[*Sunset Song* (1932), 3]

Gibbons, Orlando (1583–1625)
English organist and composer of church music and madrigals

1. The silver swan, who, living had no note,
When death approached unlocked her silent throat.
[*The First Set of Madrigals and Motets of Five Parts* (1612), 'The Silver Swan']

2. What is our life? a play of passion,
Our mirth the music of derision,
Our mothers' wombs the tiring houses be,
Where we are dressed for this short comedy...

3. Only we die in earnest, that's no jest.
[*The First Set of Madrigals and Motets of Five Parts* (1612), 'On the Life of Man']

Gibbons, Stella (1902–1989)
English novelist, poet and short-story writer

1. I saw something nasty in the woodshed.
[*Cold Comfort Farm* (1932), passim]

2. [Mrs Starkadder to her son]
'Do you want to break my heart?' 'Yes,' said Seth with an elemental simplicity.
[*Cold Comfort Farm* (1932), 3]

3. Graceless, Pointless, Feckless and Aimless awaited their turn to be milked.
[*Cold Comfort Farm* (1932), 3]

4. Every year, in the fulness o' summer, when the sukebind hangs heavy from the wains...'tes the same. And when the spring comes her hour is upon her again. 'Tes the hand of Nature, and we women cannot escape it.
[*Cold Comfort Farm* (1932), 5]

5. There's nothing like a thorn twig for clettering dishes.
[*Cold Comfort Farm* (1932), 7]

6. [Mr Mybug] said that, by God, D.H. Lawrence was right when he had said there must be a dumb, dark, dull, bitter belly-tension between a man and a woman, and how else could this be achieved save in the long monotony of marriage?
[*Cold Comfort Farm* (1932), 20]

Gibbs, Wolcott (1902–1958)
American critic, journalist and short-story writer

1. [Parody of *Time* magazine style]
Backward ran sentences until reeled the mind.
[*More in Sorrow* (1958)]

Gibran, Kahlil (1883–1931)
Lebanese poet, mystic and painter

1. Your children are not your children.
They are the sons and daughters of Life's longing for itself.
They came through you but not from you,
And though they are with you yet they belong not to you.

You may give them your love but not your thoughts,
For they have their own thoughts.
You may house their bodies but not their souls,
For their souls dwell in the house of tomorrow, which you cannot visit, not even in your dreams.
You may strive to be like them, but seek not to make them like you.
For life goes not backward nor tarries with yesterday.
You are the bows from which your children as living arrows are sent forth.
[*The Prophet* (1923), 'On Children']

2. Love has no other desire but to fulfil itself.
But if you love and must needs have desires, let these be your desires:
To melt and be like the running brook that sings its melody to the night.
To know the pain of too much tenderness.
To be wounded by your own understanding of love;
And to bleed willingly and joyfully.
To wake at dawn with a winged heart and give thanks for another day of loving;
To rest at the noon hour and meditate love's ecstasy;
To return home at eventide with gratitude;
And then to sleep with a prayer for the beloved in your heart and a song of praise upon your lips...

3. [Of marriage]
Love one another, but make not a bond of love:
Let it be rather a moving sea between the shores of your souls...

4. Let each one of you be alone,
Even as the strings of the lute are alone though they quiver with the same music...

5. Stand together yet not too near together:
For the pillars of the temple stand apart,
And the oak tree and the cypress grow not in each other's shadow.
[*The Prophet* (1923)]

Gibson, Wilfred (1878–1962)
English poet and dramatist

1. The heart-break in the heart of things.
['Lament' (1918)]

Gide, André (1869–1951)
French novelist, critic, diarist, dramatist and poet; Nobel prize 1947

1. *L'acte gratuit.*
The gratuitous action.
[*Les Caves du Vatican* (*The Vatican Cellars*, 1914), passim]

2. *M'est avis ... que le profit n'est pas toujours ce qui mène l'homme; qu'il y a des actions désintéressées. ... Par désintéressé j'entends: gratuit. Et que le mal, ce que l'on appelle: le mal, peut être aussi gratuit que le bien.*
I believe ... that profit is not always what motivates man; that there are disinterested actions. ... By disinterested I mean: gratuitous. And that evil acts, what people call evil, can be as gratuitous as good acts.
[*Les Caves du Vatican* (*The Vatican Cellars*, 1914), IV, 7]

3. Fish die belly-upward and rise to the surface; it is their way of falling.
[*Journals* (1939)]

4. [On being asked to name the greatest poet of the 19th century]
Hugo – hélas!
Hugo – alas!
[*André Gide–Paul Valéry Correspondance 1890–1942*]

Gielgud, Sir John (1904–)
English award-winning actor and Shakespearean director

1. I have never been interested in any power except my own power in the theatre, which I love.
[*The Independent*, 1994]

Gifford, William (1756–1826)
English editor, critic and satirist

1. His namby-pamby madrigals of love.
[*The Baviad*, 176]

Gilbert, Fred (1850–1903)
British songwriter

1. As I walk along the Bois Bou-long,
With an independent air,
You can hear the girls declare,
'He must be a millionaire',
You can hear them sigh and wish to die,
You can see them wink the other eye
At the man who broke the bank at Monte Carlo.
['The Man who Broke the Bank at Monte Carlo', song, 1892]

Gilbert, William Schwenck (1836–1911)
English dramatist and humorist; librettist for Arthur Sullivan's operas

1. He had often eaten oysters, but had never had enough.
[*The 'Bab' Ballads* (1869), 'Etiquette']

2. Oh, I am a cook and a captain bold,
And the mate of the Nancy brig,
And a bo'sun tight, and midshipmite,
And the crew of the captain's gig.
[*The 'Bab' Ballads* (1869), 'The Yarn of the "Nancy Bell" ']

3. The padre said, 'Whatever have you been and gone and done?'
[*The 'Bab' Ballads* (1869), 'Gentle Alice Brown']

4. Time was when Love and I were well acquainted...
[*The Sorcerer* (1877), I]

5. Oh! my name is John Wellington Wells,
I'm a dealer in magic and spells.
[*The Sorcerer* (1877), I]

6. I'm called Little Buttercup, dear Little Buttercup,
Though I could never tell why.
[*H.M.S. Pinafore* (1878), I]

7. I am the Captain of the Pinafore!
And a right good captain too!...

8. And I'm never, never sick at sea!
What, never?
No, never!
What, never?
Hardly ever!
He's hardly ever sick at sea!
Then give three cheers, and one cheer more,
For the hardy Captain of the Pinafore!...

9. You're exceedingly polite,
And I think it only right
To return the compliment.
[*H.M.S. Pinafore* (1878), I]

10. And so do his sisters, and his cousins and his aunts!
His sisters and his cousins,
Whom he reckons up by dozens,
And his aunts!
[*H.M.S. Pinafore* (1878), I]

11. When I was a lad I served a term
As office boy to an Attorney's firm.
I cleaned the windows and I swept the floor,
And I polished up the handle of the big front door.
I polished up that handle so carefullee
That now I am the Ruler of the Queen's Navee!...

12. And I copied all the letters in a big round hand...

13. I always voted at my party's call,
And I never thought of thinking for myself at all...

14. Stick close to your desks and never go to sea,
And you all may be Rulers of the Queen's Navee!
[*H.M.S. Pinafore* (1878), I]

15. Things are seldom what they seem,
Skim milk masquerades as cream.
[*H.M.S. Pinafore* (1878), II]

16. Never mind the why and wherefore.
[*H.M.S. Pinafore* (1878), II]

17. He is an Englishman!
For he himself has said it,
And it's greatly to his credit,
That he is an Englishman!...

18. For he might have been a Roosian,
A French, or Turk, or Proosian,
Or perhaps Ital-ian!
But in spite of all temptations
To belong to other nations,
He remains an Englishman!
[*H.M.S. Pinafore* (1878), II]

19. The other, upper crust,
A regular patrician.
[*H.M.S. Pinafore* (1878), II]

20. It is, it is a glorious thing
To be a Pirate King.
[*The Pirates of Penzance* (1880), I]

21. The question is, had he not been a thing of beauty,
Would she be swayed by quite as keen a sense of duty?
[*The Pirates of Penzance* (1880), I]

22. Poor wandering one,
Though thou hast surely strayed,
Take heart of grace,
Thy steps retrace,
Be not afraid...

23. Take heart, fair days will shine.
Take any heart – take mine!
[*The Pirates of Penzance* (1880), I]

24. About binomial theorem I'm teeming with a lot o' news,
With many cheerful facts about the square of the hypotenuse.
I'm very good at integral and differential calculus,
I know the scientific names of beings animalculous;
In short, in matters vegetable, animal, and mineral,
I am the very model of a modern Major-General.
[*The Pirates of Penzance* (1880), I]

25. When the foeman bares his steel,
Tarantara! tarantara!
We uncomfortable feel,
Tarantara!
[*The Pirates of Penzance* (1880), II]

26. When a felon's not engaged in his employment–
Or maturing his felonious little plans–
His capacity for innocent enjoyment–
Is just as great as any honest man's...

27. When constabulary duty's to be done,
A policeman's lot is not a happy one.
[*The Pirates of Penzance* (1880), II]

28. Twenty love-sick maidens we,
Love-sick all against our will.
[*Patience* (1881), I]

29. But the peripatetics
Of long-haired aesthetics
Are very much more to their taste.
[*Patience* (1881), I]

30. If you're anxious for to shine in the high aesthetic line as a man of culture rare...

31. You must lie upon the daisies and discourse in novel phrases of your complicated state of mind,
The meaning doesn't matter if it's only idle chatter of a transcendental kind.
And everyone will say,
As you walk your mystic way,
'If this young man expresses himself in terms too deep for me,
Why, what a very singularly deep young man this deep young man must be!'...

32. For Art stopped short in the cultivated court of the Empress Josephine...

33. Then a sentimental passion of a vegetable fashion must excite your languid spleen,
An attachment à la Plato for a bashful young potato, or a not-too-French French bean!
Though the Philistines may jostle, you will rank as an apostle in the high aesthetic band,
If you walk down Piccadilly with a poppy or a lily in your medieval hand.
And everyone will say,
As you walk your flowery way,
'If he's content with a vegetable love, which would certainly not suit me,
Why what a most particularly pure young man this pure young man must be!'
[*Patience* (1881), I]

34. Sing 'Hey to you–
Good day to you'–...
Sing 'Bah to you–
Ha! ha! to you.'
[*Patience* (1881), II]

35. 'High diddle diddle'
Will rank as an idyll,
If I pronounce it chaste!...

36. Francesca di Rimini, miminy, piminy,
Je-ne-sais-quoi young man!...

37. A very delectable, highly respectable,
Threepenny-bus young man...

38. A greenery-yallery, Grosvenor Gallery,
Foot-in-the-grave young man!
[*Patience* (1881), II]

39. I see no objection to stoutness, in moderation.
[*Iolanthe* (1882), I]

40. For I'm to be married to-day – to-day–
Yes, I'm to be married to-day!
[*Iolanthe* (1882), I]

41. Thou the singer; I the song!
[*Iolanthe* (1882), I]

42. Bow, bow, ye lower middle classes!
Bow, ye tradesmen! bow, ye masses!
[*Iolanthe* (1882), I]

43. The constitutional guardian I
Of pretty young wards in Chancery,
All very agreeable girls – and none
Are over the age of twenty-one.
A pleasant occupation for
A rather susceptible Chancellor!...

44. For I'm not so old, and not so plain,
And I'm quite prepared to marry again.
[*Iolanthe* (1882), I]

45. Spurn not the nobly born
With love affected,
Nor treat with virtuous scorn
The well connected...

46. Hearts just as pure and fair
May beat in Belgrave Square
As in the lowly air
Of Seven Dials!
[*Iolanthe* (1882), I]

47. When I went to the Bar as a very young man,
(Said I to myself – said I),

I'll work on a new and original plan,
(Said I to myself – said I).
[*Iolanthe* (1882), I]

48. When all night long a chap remains
On sentry-go, to chase monotony
He exercises of his brains,
That is, assuming that he's got any.
Though never nurtured in the lap
Of luxury, yet I admonish you,
I am an intellectual chap,
And think of things that would astonish you.
I often think it's comical
How Nature always does contrive
That every boy and every gal,
That's born into the world alive,
Is either a little Liberal,
Or else a little Conservative!
When in that House MPs divide,
If they've a brain and cerebellum, too,
They have to leave that brain outside,
And vote just as their leaders tell 'em to.
But then the prospect of a lot
Of dull MPs in close proximity,
All thinking for themselves is what
No man can face with equanimity.
[*Iolanthe* (1882), II]

49. The House of Peers, throughout the war,
Did nothing in particular,
And did it very well:
Yet Britain set the world a-blaze
In good King George's glorious days!
[*Iolanthe* (1882), II]

50. When you're lying awake with a dismal headache, and repose is taboo'd by anxiety,
I conceive you may use any language you choose to indulge in, without impropriety...

51. For you dream you are crossing the Channel, and tossing about in a steamer from Harwich–
Which is something between a large bathing-machine and a very small second-class carriage–
And you're giving a treat (penny ice and cold meat) to a party of friends and relations–
They're a ravenous horde – and they all come on board at Sloane Square and South Kensington Stations.
And bound on that journey you find your attorney (who started that morning from Devon);
He's a bit undersized, and you don't feel surprised when he tells you he's only eleven...

52. In your shirt and your socks (the black silk with gold clocks), crossing Salisbury Plain on a bicycle...

53. The night has been long – ditto ditto my song – and thank goodness they're both of them over!
[*Iolanthe* (1882), II]

54. Politics we bar,
They are not our bent;
On the whole we are
Not intelligent.
[*Princess Ida* (1884), I]

55. Yet everybody says I'm such a disagreeable man!
And I can't think why!...

56. To everybody's prejudice I know a thing or two;
I can tell a woman's age in half a minute – and I do.
[*Princess Ida* (1884), I]

57. Man is Nature's sole mistake!
[*Princess Ida* (1884), II]

58. Oh, don't the days seem lank and long
When all goes right and nothing goes wrong,
And isn't your life extremely flat
With nothing whatever to grumble at!
[*Princess Ida* (1884), III]

59. Pooh-Bah (Lord High Everything Else)
[*The Mikado* (1885), Dramatis Personae]

60. A wandering minstrel I–
A thing of shreds and patches,
Of ballads, songs and snatches,
A dreamy lullaby!
[*The Mikado* (1885), I]

61. And I am right,
And you are right,
And all is right as right can be!
[*The Mikado* (1885), I]

62. I can trace my ancestry back to a protoplasmal primordial atomic globule. Consequently, my family pride is something inconceivable.
[*The Mikado* (1885), I]

63. I a salaried minion! But I do it!
It revolts me, but I do it!
[*The Mikado* (1885), I]

64. As some day it may happen that a victim must be found,
I've got a little list – I've got a little list
Of society offenders who might well be under ground
And who never would be miss'd – who never would be miss'd!...

65. The idiot who praises, with enthusiastic tone,
All centuries but this, and ev'ry country but his own.
[*The Mikado* (1885), I]

66. I shouldn't be sufficiently degraded in my own estimation unless I was insulted with a very considerable bribe.
[*The Mikado* (1885), I]

67. Three little maids from school are we,
Pert as a schoolgirl well can be,
Filled to the brim with girlish glee...

68. Three little maids who, all unwary,
Come from a ladies' seminary.
[*The Mikado* (1885), I]

69. Modified rapture!
[*The Mikado* (1885), I]

70. Awaiting the sensation of a short, sharp shock,
From a cheap and chippy chopper on a big black block!
[*The Mikado* (1885), I]

71. Ah, pray make no mistake,
We are not shy;
We're very wide awake,
The moon and I!
[*The Mikado* (1885), II]

72. Here's a how-de-do!
[*The Mikado* (1885), II]

73. My object all sublime
I shall achieve in time–
To let the punishment fit the crime–
The punishment fit the crime...

74. On a cloth untrue
With a twisted cue,
And elliptical billiard balls!
[*The Mikado* (1885), II]

75. I drew my snickersnee!
[*The Mikado* (1885), II]

76. I have a left shoulder-blade that is a miracle of loveliness. People come miles to see it. My right elbow has a fascination that few can resist.
[*The Mikado* (1885), II]

77. Something lingering, with boiling oil in it, I fancy.
[*The Mikado* (1885), II]

78. Merely corroborative detail, intended to give artistic verisimilitude to a bald and unconvincing narrative.
[*The Mikado* (1885), II]

79. The flowers that bloom in the spring,
Tra la,
Have nothing to do with the case...

80. I've got to take under my wing,
Tra la,
A most unattractive old thing,
Tra la,
With a caricature of a face;
And that's what I mean when I say, or I sing,
'Oh bother the flowers that bloom in the spring.'
[*The Mikado* (1885), II]

81. On a tree by a river a little tom-tit
Sang 'Willow, titwillow, titwillow!'
And I said to him, 'Dicky-bird, why do you sit
Singing Willow, titwillow, titwillow?'
'Is it weakness of intellect, birdie?' I cried,
'Or a rather tough worm in your little inside?'
With a shake of his poor little head he replied,
'Oh, willow, titwillow, titwillow!'...

82. He sobbed and he sighed, and a gurgle he gave,
Then he threw himself into the billowy wave,
And an echo arose from the suicide's grave–
'Oh, willow, titwillow, titwillow!'
[*The Mikado* (1885), II]

83. There's a fascination frantic
In a ruin that's romantic;
Do you think you are sufficiently decayed?
[*The Mikado* (1885), II]

84. All baronets are bad.
[*Ruddigore* (1887), I]

85. He combines the manners of a Marquis with the morals of a Methodist.
[*Ruddigore* (1887), I]

86. If you wish in this world to advance
Your merits you're bound to enhance,
You must stir it and stump it,
And blow your own trumpet,
Or, trust me, you haven't a chance!
[*Ruddigore* (1887), I]

87. I can't say fairer than that, can I?
[*Ruddigore* (1887), I]

88. When he's excited he uses language that would make your hair curl.
[*Ruddigore* (1887), I]

89. For duty, duty must be done;
The rule applies to every one.
[*Ruddigore* (1887), I]

90. Such a bright little, tight little,
Slight little, light little,
Trim little, prim little craft!
[*Ruddigore* (1887), II]

91. If a man can't forge his own will, whose will can he forge?
[*Ruddigore* (1887), II]

92. Oh! a Baronet's rank is exceedingly nice,
But the title's uncommonly dear at the price!
[*Ruddigore* (1887), II]

93. Some word that teems with hidden meaning – like 'Basingstoke'.
[*Ruddigore* (1887), II]

94. This particularly rapid, unintelligible patter
Isn't generally heard, and if it is it doesn't matter.
[*Ruddigore* (1887), II]

95. Is life a boon?
If so, it must befall
That Death, whene'er he call,
Must call too soon.
[*The Yeoman of the Guard* (1888), I]

96. I have a song to sing O!
Sing me your song, O!...

97. It's the song of a merryman, moping mum,
Whose soul was sad, and whose glance was glum,
Who sipped no sup, and who craved no crumb,
As he sighed for the love of a ladye.
[*The Yeoman of the Guard* (1888), I]

98. Wherever valour true is found,
True modesty will there abound.
[*The Yeoman of the Guard* (1888), I]

99. 'Tis ever thus with simple folk – an accepted wit has but to say, 'Pass the mustard', and they roar their ribs out!
[*The Yeoman of the Guard* (1888), II]

100. [Of the Duke of Plaza-Toro]
He led his regiment from behind–
He found it less exciting...

101. That celebrated,
Cultivated,
Underrated
Nobleman,
The Duke of Plaza-Toro!
[*The Gondoliers* (1889), I]

102. Of that there is no manner of doubt–
No probable, possible shadow of doubt–
No possible doubt whatever...

103. A taste for drink, combined with gout,
Had doubled him up for ever.
[*The Gondoliers* (1889), I]

104. Oh, 'tis a glorious thing, I ween,
To be a regular Royal Queen!
No half-and-half affair, I mean,
But a right-down regular Royal Queen!
[*The Gondoliers* (1889), I]

105. They all shall equal be!
The Earl, the Marquis, and the Dook,
The Groom, the Butler, and the Cook,
The Aristocrat who banks with Coutts,
The Aristocrat who cleans the boots.
[*The Gondoliers* (1889), I]

106. With the gratifying feeling that our duty has been done!
[*The Gondoliers* (1889), II]

107. I am a courtier grave and serious
Who is about to kiss your hand:
Try to combine a pose imperious
With a demeanour nobly bland.
[*The Gondoliers* (1889), II]

108. Take a pair of sparkling eyes,
Hidden, ever and anon,
In a merciful eclipse...

109. Take my counsel, happy man;
Act upon it, if you can!
[*The Gondoliers* (1889), II]

110. Now, that's the kind of King for me–
He wished all men as rich as he,
So to the top of every tree
Promoted everybody...

111. Ambassadors cropped up like hay,
Prime Ministers and such as they
Grew like asparagus in May,
And Dukes were three a penny...

112. When every blessed thing you hold
Is made of silver, or of gold,
You long for simple pewter.
When you have nothing else to wear
But cloth of gold and satins rare,
For cloth of gold you cease to care–
Up goes the price of shoddy...

113. When every one is somebodee
Then no one's anybody!
[*The Gondoliers* (1889), II]

114. In all the woes that curse our race
There is a lady in the case.
[*Fallen Fairies* (1909), 2]

115. Sir, I view the proposal to hold an international exhibition at San Francisco with an equanimity bordering on indifference.
[In Hesketh Pearson, *Gilbert, His Life and Strife*]

116. [Speaking to an actor after he had given a poor performance]
My dear chap! Good isn't the word!
[Attr.]

117. [Referring to Sir Henry Irving's Hamlet]
Funny without being vulgar.
[Attr.]

Giles, Geoffrey O'Halloran (1923–)

1. The Government, in due course, acted promptly.
[*Age*, 1982]

Gill, Eric (1882–1940)
English stone-carver, engraver, typographer and author

1. That state is a state of Slavery in which a man does what he likes to do in his spare time and in his working time that which is required of him.
[*Art-nonsense and Other Essays* (1929), 'Slavery and Freedom']

Gilman, Charlotte Perkins (1860–1935)
American novelist, social reformer and feminist

1. Where young boys plan for what they will achieve and attain, young girls plan for whom they will achieve and attain.
[*Women and Economics* (1898), 5]

2. However, one cannot put a quart in a pint cup.
[*The Living of Charlotte Perkins Gilman* (1935), 4]

3. New York ... that unnatural city where every one is an exile, none more so than the American.
[*The Living of Charlotte Perkins Gilman* (1935), 20]

4. There's a whining at the threshold
There's a scratching at the floor.
To work! To work! In Heaven's name!
The wolf is at the door.
[Attr.]

Gilmore, Dame Mary (1865–1962)
Australian poet, journalist and campaigner for the disadvantaged

1. Never admit the pain,
Bury it deep;
Only the weak complain,
Complaint is cheap.
[*The Wild Swan* (1930), 'Never Admit the Pain']

2. I have grown past hate and bitterness,
I see the world as one;
But though I can no longer hate,
My son is still my son.
[*Fourteen Men* (1954), 'Nationality']

3. I never knew how wide the dark,
I never knew the depth of space,
I never knew how frail a bark,
How small is man within his place,

Not till I heard the swans go by,
Not till I marked their haunting cry,
Not till, within the vague on high,
I watched them pass across the sky.
['Swans at Night']

Gilmour, Sir Ian (1926–)
Scottish Conservative politician and Cabinet Minister

1. [Comment after being sacked by Margaret Thatcher]
It does no harm to throw the occasional man overboard, but it does not do much good if you are steering full speed ahead for the rocks.
[*Time*]

Ginsberg, Allen (1926–)
American 'Beat' poet

1. I saw the best minds of my generation destroyed by madness, starving hysterical naked.
[*Howl* (1956), first line]

2. Liverpool is at the present moment the centre of the consciousness of the human universe.
[Attr.]

Giraudoux, Jean (1882–1944)
French dramatist, poet, novelist and satirist

1. *C'est curieux comme ceux qui vous attendent se découpent moins bien que ceux que l'on attend.*
It's odd how people waiting for you stand out far less clearly than people you are waiting for.
[*La Guerre de Troie n'aura pas lieu* (1935), I; translated by Christopher Fry as *Tiger at the Gates* (1955)]

2. *Nous savons tous ici que le droit est la plus puissante des écoles de l'imagination. Jamais poète n'a interprété la nature aussi librement qu'un juriste la realité.*
All of us here know that there is no better way of exercising the imagination than the study of law. No poet has ever interpreted nature as freely as a lawyer interprets reality.
[*La Guerre de Troie n'aura pas lieu* (1935), I; translated by Christopher Fry as *Tiger at the Gates* (1955)]

Gladstone, William Ewart (1809–1898)
English statesman and reformer; Liberal Prime Minister 1868–74, 1880–85, 1892–94

1. You cannot fight against the future. Time is on our side.
[Speech on the Reform Bill, 1866]

2. [On the Bulgarian massacres of 1876]
[The Turks] one and all, bag and baggage, shall, I hope, clear out from the province they have desolated and profaned.
[Speech, House of Commons, 1877]

3. [On the Land League]
The resources of civilization against its enemies are not yet exhausted.
[Speech, 1881]

4. The domestic use of tea is a powerful champion able to encounter alcoholic drink in a fair field and throw it in a fair fight.
[Budget Speech, 1882]

5. All the world over, I will back the masses against the classes.
[Speech, Liverpool, 1886]

6. I would tell them of my own intention to keep my counsel . . . and I will venture to recommend them, as an old Parliamentary hand, to do the same.
[Speech, 1886]

7. We are part of the community of Europe, and we must do our duty as such.
[Speech, Caernarvon, 1888]

8. [On J.W. Cross's *Life of George Eliot*]
It is not a Life at all. It is a Reticence, in three volumes.
[In E.F. Benson, *As We Were* (1930)]

9. There are still two things for me to do! One is to carry Home Rule – the other is to prove the intimate connection between the Hebrew and Olympian revelations.
[In Richard Jenkyns, *The Victorians and Ancient Greece* (1980)]

Glashan, John (1931—)
Scottish artist and cartoonist

1. [Caption to cartoon of Christ descended from the cross]
On second thoughts, they knew exactly what they were doing.
[*The Spectator*, Easter 1991]

Glotz, Peter

1. *Der 'Radikal-Nationalismus' . . . ist im Deutschland von heute noch ein dünnes Rinnsal.*
'Radical Nationalism' . . . is in today's Germany still a narrow stream.
[*Der Spiegel*, 1994, 'Deutsche Gefahren' ('German Dangers')]

Gloucester, William, Duke of (1743–1805)
English Field Marshal; brother of George III

1. Another damned, thick, square book. Always scribble, scribble, scribble! Eh! Mr. Gibbon?
[In Henry Best, *Personal and Literary Memorials* (1829)]

Gloucester, William Frederick, Second Duke of Gloucester (1776–1834)
English Field Marshal; son of William, Duke of Gloucester

1. [Lending his own nickname to William IV, his nephew]
Who's Silly Billy now?
[In G. Smith, *Lectures and Essays* (1881)]

Glover, Denis (1912–1980)
New Zealand poet and printer

1. [On pioneering]
When Tom and Elizabeth took the farm
The bracken made their bed,
And Quardle oodle ardle wardle doodle
The magpies said.
[*Enter Without Knocking* (1964), 'The Magpies']

2. [Celebrating New Zealand]
What shall we sing? sings Harry.
Sing all things sweet or harsh upon
These islands in the Pacific sun,
The mountains whitened endlessly
And the white horses of the winter sea,
Sings Harry.
[*Enter Without Knocking* (1964), 'Themes']

3. [On overcrowding in Royal Navy ships]
With five or six faces in front of a mirror it sometimes becomes a problem just which one to shave.
[In John Lehmann, *I Am My Brother* (1960)]

Godard, Jean-Luc (1930–)
French 'New Wave' film director and writer

1. *La photographie, c'est la vérité. Le cinéma: la vérité vingt-quatre fois par seconde.*
Photography is truth. Cinema is truth twenty-four times a second.
[*Le Petit Soldat*, film, 1960]

2. Of course a film should have a beginning, a middle and an end. But not necessarily in that order.
[Attr.]

Godley, A.D. (1856–1925)
English classical scholar, orator and satirist

1. What is this that roareth thus?
Can it be a Motor Bus?
Yes, the smell and hideous hum
Indicate Motorem Bum!
['The Motor Bus', in a letter to C.R.L. Fletcher, 1914]

Godwin, William (1756–1836)
English political philosopher and novelist; husband of Mary Wollstonecraft and father of Mary Wollstonecraft Shelley

1. The log was burning brightly,
'Twas a night that should banish all sin,
For the bells were ringing the Old Year out,
And the New Year in.
['The Miner's Dream of Home']

Goebbels, Joseph (1897–1945)
German Nazi politician, Minister of Propaganda from 1933; committed suicide

1. *Der eiserne Vorhang.*
The Iron Curtain.
[*Das Reich*, 1945]

2. *. . . mir in Bälde einen Gesamtentwurf über die organisatorischen, sachlichen und materiellen Vorausmassnahmen zur Durchführung der angestrebten Endlösung der Judenfrage vorzulegen.*
. . . to place before me soon a complete proposal for the organisational, practical and material preliminary measures which have to be taken in order to bring about the desired Final Solution to the Jewish question.
[Letter to Reinhard Heydrich, 1941]

3. *Ohne Butter werden wir fertig, aber nicht beispielsweise ohne Kanonen. Wenn wir einmal überfallen werden, dann können wir uns nicht mit Butter, sondern nur mit Kanonen verteidigen.*
We can manage without butter but not, for example,

without guns. If we are attacked we can only defend ourselves with guns not with butter.
[Speech in Berlin, 17 January 1936]

4. [Referring to Roosevelt's death]
This was the Angel of History! We felt its wings flutter through the room. Was that not the fortune we awaited so anxiously?
[*Diary*]

Goering, Hermann (1893–1946)
German Nazi leader, military commander and founder of the Gestapo; committed suicide

1. Guns will make us powerful; butter will only make us fat.
[Broadcast, 1936]

2. When I hear anyone talk of Culture, I reach for my revolver.
[Attr.; probably derived from Hanns Johst, *Schlageter*, 1933]

Goethe, Johann Wolfgang von (1749–1832)
German Romantic poet, novelist, dramatist and scientist; greatly influenced European literature

1. *Sah ein Knab' ein Röslein stehn,*
Röslein auf der Heiden.
A boy saw a little rose growing,
Little rose on the heath.
['Heidenröslein' ('Little heath-rose', written c. 1771, published 1789)]

2. *Wer reitet so spät durch Nacht und Wind?*
Es ist der Vater mit seinem Kind.
Who rides so late through night and wind?
It is the father with his child.
['Erlkönig' ('Erlking', 1782)]

3. *Ein unnütz Leben ist ein früher Tod.*
A pointless life is an early death.
[*Iphigenie auf Tauris* (*Iphigenia on Tauris*, 1787), I.ii]

4. *Du musst herrschen und gewinnen,*
Oder dienen und verlieren,
Leiden oder triumphieren,
Amboss oder Hammer sein.
You must rule and win,
Or serve and lose,
Suffer or triumph,
Be the anvil or the hammer.
['Kophtisches Lied' ('Song of Cophta', 1787)]

5. *Es bildet ein Talent sich in der Stille,*
Sich ein Charakter in dem Strom der Welt.
Talent is formed in quiet retreat,
Character in the headlong rush of life.
[*Torquato Tasso* (1790), I.ii]

6. *Wer nie sein Brot mit Tränen ass,*
Wer nie die kummervollen Nächte
Auf seinem Bette weinend sass,
Der kennt euch nicht, ihr himmlischen Mächte.
Who never ate his bread in tears,
Who never spent the nights of sorrow
Sitting weeping on his bed,
He does not know you, you heavenly powers.
[*Wilhelm Meisters Lehrjahre*, II, 13 (*Wilhelm Meister's Apprentice Years*, 1795–1796)]

7. *Denn alle Schuld rächt sich auf Erden.*
For all guilt is avenged on earth.
[*Wilhelm Meisters Lehrjahre*, II, 13 (*Wilhelm Meister's Apprentice Years*, 1795–1796)]

8. *Kennst du das Land, wo die Zitronen blühn?*
Im dunkeln Laub die Goldorangen glühn,
Ein sanfter Wind vom blauen Himmel weht,
Die Myrte still und hoch der Lorbeer steht–
Kennst du es wohl?
Dahin! Dahin!
Möcht ich mit dir, o mein Geliebter, ziehn!
Dost thou know the land, where the lemon-trees bloom?
Where the gold oranges glow in the dark foliage,
A gentle wind wafts from the blue sky,
The myrtle is still and tall stands the laurel,
Dost thou know it well?
There! There
Would I go with thee, O my beloved!
[*Wilhelm Meisters Lehrjahre*, III, 1, (*Wilhelm Meister's Apprentice Years*, 1795–1796)]

9. *Du kannst, denn du sollst!*
You can, for you ought to!
[*Xenien* (1796), 'Ein Achter', no.88 ('An eighth'); written with Schiller]

10. *In der Beschränkung zeigt sich erst der Meister.*
The master is first seen in self-limitation.
[Sonett: 'Natur und Kunst' ('Nature and Art', 1802)]

11. *Es irrt der Mensch, solang' er strebt.*
Man errs as long as he strives.
[*Faust*, I (1808), 'Prolog im Himmel' ('Prologue in heaven')]

12. *Zwei Seelen wohnen, ach! in meiner Brust.*
There are two souls which dwell, alas! within my breast.
[*Faust*, I (1808), 'Vor dem Tor' ('Before the gate')]

13. *Ich bin der Geist, der stets verneint!*
I am the spirit that constantly denies!
[*Faust*, I (1808), 'Studierzimmer' ('Study')]

14. *Entbehren sollst du! sollst entbehren!*
Das ist der ewige Gesang.
Deny yourself! You should deny yourself! That is the eternal song.
[*Faust*, I (1808), 'Studierzimmer' ('Study')]

15. *Werd' ich zum Augenblicke sagen:*
Verweile doch! du bist so schön!
Should I say to the moment:
'Linger here! thou art so lovely!'
[*Faust*, I (1808), 'Studierzimmer' ('Study')]

16. *Denn eben wo Begriffe fehlen,*
Da stellt ein Wort zur rechten Zeit sich ein.
For precisely when concepts fail us,
A word appears at just the right time.
[*Faust*, I (1808), 'Studierzimmer' ('Study')]

17. *Grau, teurer Freund, ist alle Theorie,*
Und grün des Lebens goldner Baum.
Grey, dear friend, is all theory,
And green the golden tree of life.
[*Faust*, I (1808), 'Studierzimmer' ('Study')]

18. *Meine Ruh' ist hin,*
Mein Herz ist schwer.
My peace is lost,
My heart is heavy.
[*Faust*, I (1808), 'Gretchens Stube' ('Gretchen's Room')]

19. *Die Tat ist alles, nichts der Ruhm.*
The deed is all, the glory is naught.
[*Faust*, II (1832), Act IV, 'Hochgebirg' ('High mountains')]

20. *Alles Vergängliche*
Ist nur ein Gleichnis.
Everything transitory
Is but an image.
[*Faust*, II (1832), Act V, 'Bergschluchten' ('Mountain gorges')]

21. *Das Ewig-Weibliche*
Zieht uns hinan.
The feminine in all of us
Draws us on.
[*Faust*, II (1832), Act V, 'Bergschluchten' ('Mountain gorges')]

22. *Über allen Gipfeln*
Ist Ruh.
Over all the mountain-peaks
There is quiet.
['Wandrers Nachtlied II' ('Hiker's Night-song II', 1815)]

23. *Und so lang du das nicht hast,*
Dieses: Stirb und werde!
Bist du nur ein trüber Gast
Auf der dunklen Erde.
And as long as you have not grasped this,
Namely: 'Die and become!'
You are only a dull stranger
On the dark earth.
[*West-Östlicher Divan* (1819), 'Selige Sehnsucht' ('Holy Longing')]

24. *Mein Erbteil wie herrlich, weit und breit!*
Die Zeit ist mein Besitz, mein Acker ist die Zeit.
How marvellous, wide and broad is my inheritance!
Time is my property, my estate is time.
[*Wilhelm Meisters Wanderjahre*, I (*Wilhelm Meister's Wandering Years*, 1821)]

25. *Entzwei und gebiete! Tüchtig Wort;*
Verein' und leite! Bessrer Hort.
Divide and rule! Fine saying;
Unite and lead! Safer refuge.
[*Sprüche in Reimen*, VII.155 (*Sayings in rhyme*, 1893)]

26. *Einem bejahrten Manne verdachte man, dass er sich noch um junge Frauenzimmer bemühte. 'Es ist das einzige Mittel', versetzte er, 'sich zu verjüngen, und das will doch jedermann.'*
An elderly man was criticised for still troubling himself with young women. 'It's the only way,' he retorted, 'to rejuvenate oneself, and everyone wants to do that.'
[*Maximen und Reflexionen*, 'Erfahrung und Leben' ('Experience and Life'), no. 1263, first published in *Die Wahlverwandtschaften* (*The Elective Affinities*, 1808)]

27. *Wenn es eine Freude ist, das Gute zu geniessen, so ist es eine grössere, das Bessere zu empfinden, und in der Kunst ist das Beste gut genug. Neapel, den 3. März, 1787.*
If it is a joy to enjoy what is good, then it is a greater one to feel what is better, and in art the best is good enough. Naples, 3rd March, 1787.
[*Italienische Reise* (*Italian Journey*, published 1816–1817)]

28. *Der Aberglaube ist die Poesie des Lebens.*
Superstition is the poetry of life.
[*Maximen und Reflexionen*, 'Literatur und Sprache', 908 (*Maxims and Reflections*, 'Literature and Language'); originally published in *Über Kunst und Altertum* (*On Art and Antiquity*, 1823)]

29. *Wer fremde Sprachen nicht kennt, weiss nichts von seiner eigenen.*
Whoever is not acquainted with foreign languages knows nothing of his own.
[*Maximen und Reflexionen*, 'Literatur und Sprache' ('Literature and Language'), no. 1015, first published in *Über Kunst und Altertum* (*On Art and Antiquity*, 1818–1827)]

30. *Gewisse Bücher scheinen geschrieben zu sein, nicht damit man daraus lerne, sondern damit man wisse, dass der Verfasser etwas gewusst hat.*
Certain books seem to be written, not so that you can learn from them, but so that you know that the author knew something.
[*Maximen und Reflexionen*, 'Erkenntnis und Wissenschaft' ('Knowledge and Science'), no. 460, first published in *Über Kunst und Altertum* (*On Art and Antiquity*, 1818–1827)]

31. *Wenn man alle Gesetze studieren sollte, so hätte man gar keine Zeit, sie zu übertreten.*
If one were to study all the laws, one would have absolutely no time to break them.
[*Maximen und Reflexionen*, 'Erfahrung und Leben' ('Experience and Life'), no. 1354, first published in *Über Kunst und Altertum* (*On Art and Antiquity*, 1818–1827)]

32. *Aber Lord Byron is nur gross, wenn er dichtet; sobald er reflektiert, ist er ein Kind.*
Lord Byron is only great as a poet; as soon as he reflects, he is a child.
[*Gespräche mit Eckermann*, 1825]

33. *Im übrigen ist es zuletzt die grösste Kunst, sich zu beschränken und zu isolieren.*
Incidentally, however, ultimately the greatest art is in limiting and isolating oneself.
[*Gespräche mit Eckermann*, 1825]

34. *Nationalliteratur will jetzt nicht viel sagen, die Epoche der Weltliteratur ist an der Zeit.*
National literature does not now have much significance, it is time for the era of world literature.
[*Gespräche mit Eckermann*, 1827]

35. *Ich [nenne] die Baukunst eine erstarrte Musik.*
I [call] architecture a kind of petrified music.
[*Gespräche mit Eckermann*, 1829. Cf. Schelling: 1]

36. *Das Klassische nenne ich das Gesunde, und das Romantische das Kranke.*
Classicism I call health, and romanticism disease.
[*Gespräche mit Eckermann*, 1829]

37. *Ich kenne mich auch nicht und Gott soll mich auch davor behüten.*
I do not know myself either, and may God protect me from that.
[*Gespräche mit Eckermann*, 1829]

38. *Alles Gescheite ist schon gedacht worden, man muss nur versuchen, es noch einmal zu denken.*
Everything worth thinking has already been thought, our concern must only be to try to think it through again.
[*Maximen und Reflexionen*, 'Denken und Tun' ('Thought and Action'), no. 373, first published in *Wilhelm Meisters Wanderjahre* (*Wilhelm Meister's Wandering Years*, 1829)]

39. [On learning of his son's death]
Non ignoravi, me mortalem genuisse.
I was not unaware that I had begotten a mortal.
[F. von Müller to F. Rochlitz, quoted in *Goethes Gespräche*, 1830]

40. *Ohne Hast, ohne Rast.*
Without haste, without rest.
[Motto, etched on a seal presented to Goethe by Carlyle, 1831]

41. [Last words]
Mehr Licht!
More light!
[Attr.]

Gogarty, Oliver St John (1878–1957)

Irish poet, dramatist and prose writer; politician and surgeon

1. Only the Lion and the Cock;
As Galen says, withstand Love's shock.

So, dearest, do not think me rude
If I yield now to lassitude,
But sympathize with me. I know
You would not have me roar, or crow.
[*Collected Poems* (1951), 'After Galen']

2. I will live in Ringsend
With a red-headed whore,
And the fanlight gone in
Where it lights the hall-door;
And listen each night
For her querulous shout
As at last she streels in
And the pubs empty out.
[*Collected Poems* (1951), 'Ringsend (After reading Tolstoi)']

3. As long as there is English spoken in the home, whatever is taught in the morning will be undone in the evening by the parents, and the greatest enthusiast has not suggested the shooting of mothers of English-speaking children.
[On the Gaeltacht Commission Report in the Senate, March 1927]

4. Politics is the chloroform of the Irish people, or rather the hashish.
[*As I Was Going Down Sackville Street* (1937)]

5. In my best social accent I addressed him. I said, 'It is most extraordinary weather for this time of year!' He replied, 'Ah, it isn't this time of year at all.'
[*It Isn't This Time of Year at All* (1954)]

6. If a queen bee were crossed with a Friesian bull, would not the land flow with milk and honey?
[Attr.]

Gogol, Nicolai Vasilyevich (1809–1852)
Russian satirical novelist, short-story writer; journalist and soldier

1. Threatening, terrifying is oncoming old age, but nothing will reverse and return!
[*Dead Souls* (1835–1842)]

2. I always feel sad when I look at new buildings which are constantly being built and on which millions are spent ... Has the age of architecture passed without hope of return?
[Attr.]

Golding, William (1911–1993)
English allegorical novelist, poet and essayist; Nobel prize 1983

1. We've got to have rules and obey them. After all, we're not savages. We're English; and the English are best at everything. So we've got to do the right things.
[*Lord of the Flies* (1954), 2]

2. Ralph wept for the end of innocence, the darkness of man's heart, and the fall through the air of the true, wise friend called Piggy.
[*Lord of the Flies* (1954), 12]

Goldoni, Carlo (1707–1793)
Italian dramatist and lawyer; author of realistic comedies

1. *Bello è il rossore, ma è incomodo qualche volta.*
Blushing is becoming, yet sometimes inconvenient.
[*Pamela* (1750), I.iii]

Goldsmith, Oliver (c. 1728–1774)
Irish dramatist, poet, novelist and journalist

1. The doctor found, when she was dead,–
Her last disorder mortal.
['Elegy on Mrs Mary Blaize' (1759)]

2. Brutes never meet in bloody fray,
Nor cut each other's throats, for pay.
['Logicians Refuted' (1759)]

3. Remote, unfriended, melancholy, slow,
Or by the lazy Scheld, or wandering Po...

4. Where'er I roam, whatever realms to see,
My heart untravell'd fondly turns to thee;
Still to my brother turns, with ceaseless pain,
And drags at each remove a lengthening chain...

5. And learn the luxury of doing good...

6. Such is the patriot's boast, where'er we roam,
His first best country ever is at home...

7. Where wealth and freedom reign contentment fails,
And honour sinks where commerce long prevails...

8. At night returning, every labour sped,
He sits him down the monarch of a shed;
Smiles by his cheerful fire, and round surveys
His children's looks, that brighten at the blaze:
While his lov'd partner, boastful of her hoard,
Displays her cleanly platter on the board...

9. To men of other minds my fancy flies,
Embosom'd in the deep where Holland lies,
Methinks her patient sons before me stand,
Where the broad ocean leans against the land...

10. Pride in their port, defiance in their eye,
I see the lords of human kind pass by...

11. Laws grind the poor, and rich men rule the law...

12. In every government, though terrors reign,
Though tyrant kings, or tyrant laws restrain,
How small, of all that human hearts endure,
That part which laws or kings can cause or cure.
['The Traveller' (1764)]

13. Good people all, of every sort,
Give ear unto my song;
And if you find it wond'rous short,
It cannot hold you long...

14. And in that town a dog was found,
As many dogs there be,
Both mongrel, puppy, whelp, and hound,
And curs of low degree...

15. The dog, to gain some private ends,
Went mad and bit the man...

16. The man recovered of the bite,
The dog it was that dy'd.
['Elegy on the Death of a Mad Dog' (1766)]

17. Man wants but little here below,
Nor wants that little long.
[*The Vicar of Wakefield* (1766), 'Edwin and Angelina, or the Hermit']

18. When lovely woman stoops to folly
And finds too late that men betray,
What charm can soothe her melancholy,
What art can wash her guilt away?

The only art her guilt to cover,
To hide her shame from every eye,
To give repentance to her lover
And wring his bosom – is to die.
[*The Vicar of Wakefield* (1766), Song, 24]

19. Sweet Auburn, loveliest village of the plain,
Where health and plenty cheered the labouring swain,
Where smiling spring its earliest visit paid,

And parting summer's lingering blooms delayed...

20. The bashful virgin's side-long looks of love,
The matron's glance that would those looks reprove...

21. Ill fares the land, to hastening ills a prey,
Where wealth accumulates, and men decay;
Princes and lords may flourish, or may fade;
A breath can make them, as a breath has made;
But a bold peasantry, their country's pride,
When once destroy'd, can never be supplied.

A time there was, ere England's griefs began,
When every rood of ground maintained its man;
For him light labour spread her wholesome store,
Just gave what life required, but gave no more.
His best companions, innocence and health;
And his best riches, ignorance of wealth...

22. Trade's unfeeling train
Usurp the land and dispossess the swain...

23. How happy he who crowns in shades like these,
A youth of labour with an age of ease...

24. The watch-dog's voice that bayed the whispering wind,
And the loud laugh that spoke the vacant mind...

25. A man he was, to all the country dear,
And passing rich with forty pounds a year;
Remote from towns he ran his godly race,
Nor e'er had changed nor wish'd to change his place;
Unpractised he to fawn, or seek for power,
By doctrines fashioned to the varying hour;
Far other aims his heart had learned to prize,
More skilled to raise the wretched than to rise...

26. He chid their wanderings, but relieved their pain...

27. Truth from his lips prevailed with double sway,
And fools, who came to scoff, remained to pray...

28. A man severe he was, and stern to view,
I knew him well, and every truant knew;
Well had the boding tremblers learned to trace
The day's disasters in his morning face;
Full well they laugh'd with counterfeited glee,
At all his jokes, for many a joke had he;
Full well the busy whisper circling round,
Conveyed the dismal tidings when he frowned;
Yet he was kind, or if severe in aught,
The love he bore to learning was in fault...

29. In arguing too, the parson owned his skill,
For even tho' vanquished, he could argue still;
While words of learned length, and thundering sound,
Amazed the gazing rustics ranged around,
And still they gazed, and still the wonder grew,
That one small head could carry all he knew...

30. Where village statesmen talked with looks profound,
And news much older than their ale went round...

31. The white-washed wall, the nicely sanded floor,
The varnished clock that clicked behind the door;
The chest contrived a double debt to pay,
A bed by night, a chest of drawers by day...

32. And, even while fashion's brightest arts decoy,
The heart distrusting asks, if this be joy...

33. The man of wealth and pride,
Takes up a space that many poor supplied...

34. Ten thousand baneful arts combined
To pamper luxury, and thin mankind...

35. In all the silent manliness of grief.
[*The Deserted Village* (1770)]

36. Let school-masters puzzle their brain,
With grammar, and nonsense, and learning,
Good liquor, I stoutly maintain,
Gives genius a better discerning.
[*She Stoops to Conquer* (1773), I]

37. [Of Edmund Burke]
Who, too deep for his hearers, still went on refining,
And thought of convincing, while they thought of dining;
Tho' equal to all things, for all things unfit,
Too nice for a statesman, too proud for a wit...

38. [Of Garrick]
Here lies David Garrick, describe me who can,
An abridgment of all that was pleasant in man...

39. On the stage he was natural, simple, affecting,
'Twas only that, when he was off, he was acting...

40. He cast off his friends as a huntsman his pack,
For he knew, when he pleased, he could whistle them back...

41. [Of Reynolds]
When they talk'd of their Raphaels, Correggios and stuff,
He shifted his trumpet, and only took snuff.
['Retaliation' (1774)]

42. The true use of speech is not so much to express our wants as to conceal them.
[*The Bee* (1759), 3, 'On the Use of Language']

43. True Genius walks along a line, and, perhaps, our greatest pleasure is in seeing it so often near falling, without being ever actually down.
[*The Bee* (1759), 4, 'The Characteristics of Greatness']

44. As writers become more numerous, it is natural for readers to become more indolent.
[*The Bee* (1759), 5, 'Upon Unfortunate Merit']

45. To a philosopher, no circumstance, however trifling, is too minute.
[*The Citizen of the World* (1762), Letter 29]

46. On whatever side we regard the history of Europe, we shall perceive it to be a tissue of crimes, follies, and misfortunes.
[*The Citizen of the World* (1762), Letter 41]

47. 'Did I say so?' replied he, coolly, 'to be sure, if I said so; it was so.'
[*The Citizen of the World* (1762), Letter 52]

48. A book may be amusing with numerous errors, or it may be very dull without a single absurdity.
[*The Vicar of Wakefield* (1766), advertisement]

49. I was ever of opinion, that the honest man who married and brought up a large family, did more service than he who continued single, and only talked of population.
[*The Vicar of Wakefield* (1766), 1]

50. I ... chose my wife as she did her wedding gown, not for a fine glossy surface, but such qualities as would wear well.
[*The Vicar of Wakefield* (1766), 1]

51. The virtue which requires to be ever guarded, is scarce worth the sentinel.
[*The Vicar of Wakefield* (1766), 5]

52. It seemed to me pretty plain, that they had more of love than matrimony in them.
[*The Vicar of Wakefield* (1766), 16]

53. I ... shewed her that books were sweet unreproaching companions to the miserable, and that if they could not bring

us to enjoy life, they would at least teach us to endure it.
[*The Vicar of Wakefield* (1766), 22]

54. As ten millions of circles can never make a square, so the united voice of myriads cannot lend the smallest foundation to falsehood.
[*The Vicar of Wakefield* (1766), 27]

55. This same philosophy is a good horse in the stable, but an errant jade on a journey.
[*The Good Natur'd Man* (1768), I]

56. We must touch his weaknesses with a delicate hand. There are some faults so nearly allied to excellence, that we can scarce weed out the vice without eradicating the virtue.
[*The Good Natur'd Man* (1768), I]

57. All his faults are such that one loves him still the better for them.
[*The Good Natur'd Man* (1768), I]

58. I'm now no more than a mere lodger in my own house.
[*The Good Natur'd Man* (1768), I]

59. Friendship is a disinterested commerce between equals; love, an abject intercourse between tyrants and slaves.
[*The Good Natur'd Man* (1768), I]

60. Don't let us make imaginary evils, when you know we have so many real ones to encounter.
[*The Good Natur'd Man* (1768), I]

61. *Leontine*: An only Son, Sir, might expect more indulgence.
Croaker: An only father, Sir, might expect more obedience.
[*The Good Natur'd Man* (1768), I]

62. I'm told he makes a very handsome corpse, and becomes his coffin prodigiously.
[*The Good Natur'd Man* (1768), I]

63. Silence is become his mother tongue.
[*The Good Natur'd Man* (1768), II]

64. You, that are going to be married, think things can never be done too fast; but we, that are old, and know what we are about, must elope methodically, madam.
[*The Good Natur'd Man* (1768), IV]

65. In my time, the follies of the town crept slowly among us, but now they travel faster than a stage-coach.
[*She Stoops to Conquer* (1773), I]

66. I love every thing that's old: old friends, old times, old manners, old books, old wine.
[*She Stoops to Conquer* (1773), I]

67. As for disappointing them, I should not so much mind; but I can't abide to disappoint myself.
[*She Stoops to Conquer* (1773), I]

68. Is it one of my well looking days, child? Am I in face to-day?
[*She Stoops to Conquer* (1773), I]

69. The very pink of perfection.
[*She Stoops to Conquer* (1773), I]

70. I'll be with you in the squeezing of a lemon.
[*She Stoops to Conquer* (1773), I]

71. It's a damn'd long, dark, boggy, dirty, dangerous way.
[*She Stoops to Conquer* (1773), I]

72. The first blow is half the battle.
[*She Stoops to Conquer* (1773), II]

73. This is Liberty-Hall, gentlemen.
[*She Stoops to Conquer* (1773), II]

74. Was there ever such a cross-grained brute?
[*She Stoops to Conquer* (1773), III]

75. As for murmurs, mother, we grumble a little now and then, to be sure. But there's no love lost between us.
[*She Stoops to Conquer* (1773), IV]

76. The Scotch may be compared to a tulip planted in dung, but I never see a Dutchman in his own house, but I think of a magnificent Egyptian Temple dedicated to an ox.
[Letter from Leyden to Rev. Thomas Contarine, c. 6 May 1754]

77. There is no arguing with Johnson; for when his pistol misses fire, he knocks you down with the butt end of it.
[In Boswell, *The Life of Samuel Johnson* (1791), October 1769]

78. As I take my shoes from the shoemaker, and my coat from the tailor, so I take my religion from the priest.
[In Boswell, *The Life of Samuel Johnson* (1791), April 1773]

Goldwater, Barry (1909–)

American Republican politician; senator, presidential candidate (1964) and writer

1. [On accepting nomination for the presidency]
Extremism in the defence of liberty is no vice.
[Speech, 1964]

2. You've got to forget about this civilian. Whenever you drop bombs, you're going to hit civilians.
[Speech, New York, 1967]

3. A government that is big enough to give you all you want is big enough to take it all away.
[In M. Ivens and R. Dunstan, *Bachman's Book of Freedom Quotations*]

Goldwyn, Samuel (1882–1974)

Polish-born American film producer; Academy Award 1946

1. For years I have been known for saying 'Include me out'; but today I am giving it up for ever.
[Speech, Balliol College, Oxford, 1945]

2. Any man who goes to a psychiatrist should have his head examined.
[In Zierold, *Moguls* (1969), 3, 'Samuel Goldwyn Presents']

3. I read part of it all the way through.
[In Zierold, *Moguls* (1969), 3, 'Samuel Goldwyn Presents']

4. His [Joe Schenk's] verbal contract is worth more than the paper it's written on.
[In Zierold, *Moguls* (1969)]

5. Directors [are] always biting the hand that lays the golden egg.
[In Zierold, *Moguls* (1969)]

6. [Before the opening of his film *The Best Years of Our Lives* in 1946]
I don't care if it doesn't make a nickel, I just want every man, woman, and child in America to see it.
[In Zierold, *Moguls* (1969)]

7. [On being warned that a story was too caustic]
To hell with the cost. If it's a sound story, we'll make a picture of it.
[In Zierold, *Moguls* (1969)]

8. [In reply to a comment on his wife's beautiful hands]
Yes, I'm going to have a bust made of them.
[In Zierold, *Moguls* (1969)]

9. You've got to take the bull between the teeth.
[In Zierold, *Moguls* (1969)]

10. I'll give you a definite maybe.
[In Colombo, *Wit and Wisdom of the Moviemakers*]

11. Let's have some new clichés.
[*The Observer*, 'Sayings of the Week', 1948]

12. Why should people go out and pay money to see bad films when they can stay at home and see bad television for nothing?
[*The Observer*, 'Sayings of the Week', 1956]

13. In two words: im possible.
[Attr.; in Zierold, *Moguls* (1969), 3, 'Samuel Goldwyn Presents']

14. I am willing to admit that I may not always be right, but I am never wrong.
[Attr.]

15. If Roosevelt were alive he'd turn in his grave.
[Attr.]

16. It's more than magnificent – it's mediocre.
[Attr.]

17. Tell me, how did you love my picture?
[Attr.]

18. We have all passed a lot of water since then.
[Attr.]

19. We're overpaying him but he's worth it.
[Attr.]

20. What we want is a story that starts with an earthquake and works its way up to a climax.
[Attr.]

21. [Querying the number of disciples appearing in his film *The Last Supper*]
'Why only twelve?' 'That's the original number.' 'Well, go out and get thousands.'
[Attr.]

22. A wide screen just makes a bad film twice as bad.
[Attr.]

Goncourt, Edmond de (1822–1896)
French novelist and diarist

1. *Les historiens sont des raconteurs du passé, les romanciers des raconteurs du présent.*
Historians tell stories of the past, novelists stories of the present.
[*Journal*]

Gonne, Maud (1865–1953)
Irish patriot and philanthropist

1. To me judges seem the well paid watch-dogs of Capitalism, making things safe and easy for the devil Mammon.
[Letter to W.B. Yeats]

2. Oh how you hate old age – well so do I ... but I, who am more a rebel against man than you, rebel less against nature, and accept the inevitable and go with it gently into the unknown.
[Letter to W.B. Yeats]

Goodhart, Sir Philip (1925–)
British journalist, parliamentarian and writer

1. [On Nicholas Ridley]
I have nothing against Nick's wife or his family but I think it is time he spent more time with them.
[*Sunday Telegraph*, 1990]

Gorbachev, Mikhail (1931–)
Soviet statesman, former General Secretary of the USSR

1. [Remark, June 1988]
We have tried in this country to impose many things from above. Nothing ever comes from this. What we must do is involve the people in the processes of government, and the people will at once put everyone in his right place.
[In Peter Vansittart (ed.), *Voices of the Revolution* (1989), 'Afterthought']

Gordimer, Nadine (1923–)
South African novelist and short-story writer

1. The force of white men's wills, which dispensed and withdrew life, imprisoned and set free, fed or starved, like God himself.
[*Six Feet of the Country* (1956), 'The Smell of Death and Flowers']

2. You don't 'own' a country by signing a bit of paper the way you bought yourself the title deed to that farm.
[*The Conservationist* (1974)]

3. The tension between standing apart and being fully involved; that is what makes a writer.
[*Selected Stories* (1975), Introduction]

Gordon, Adam Lindsay (1833–1870)
Australian poet and ballad-writer

1. Life is mostly froth and bubble,
Two things stand like stone,
Kindness in another's trouble,
Courage in your own.
['Ye Wearie Wayfarer' (1866)]

2. A little season of love and laughter,
Of light and life, and pleasure and pain,
And a horror of outer darkness after,
And dust returneth to dust again.
['The Swimmer' (1870)]

3. Let me slumber in the hollow where the wattle blossoms wave,
With never stone or rail to fence my bed;
Should the sturdy station children pull the bush flowers on my grave,
I may chance to hear them romping overhead.
['The Sick Stockrider' (1870)]

Gordon, Donald (1901–1969)
Canadian businessman and President of the Canadian National Railway 1950–56

1. Nothing increases the value of a cow so much and so quickly as to get killed by a CNR train.
[*The Toronto Star*, 1966]

Gore-Booth, Eva (1870–1926)
Irish poet

1. The little waves of Breffney go
stumbling through my soul.
['The Little Waves of Breffney']

Gorky, Maxim (Aleksei Maksimovich Peshkov) (1868–1936)
Russian realist novelist, dramatist, short-story writer and revolutionary

1. Love is always a bit deceitful,
Truth always struggles with it,
We wait long for a woman worthy of it,
And we wait in vain.
[In *Samara Gazette*, 1895, 'Farewell']

2. No one can deny that clouds are once again gathering over Russia, promising great storms.
[*Russian Word*, 1913]

3. [On Germany's declaration of war against Russia]
One thing is clear; we are entering the first act of a world-wide tragedy.
[Attr., 1914]

4. Man and man alone is, I believe, the creator of all things and all ideas.
[Attr.]

5. You must write for children just as you do for adults, only better.
[Attr.]

Gorton, John Grey (1911–)
Australian retired parliamentarian

1. I am always prepared to recognize that there can be two points of view – mine, and one that is probably wrong.
[In Alan Trengove, *John Grey Gorton*]

Goschen, George, Lord (1831–1907)
English statesman; Unionist Chancellor of the Exchequer 1887–92 and First Lord of the Admiralty 1895–1900

1. I have the courage of my opinions, but I have not the temerity to give a political blank cheque to Lord Salisbury.
[Speech, House of Commons, 1884]

2. We have stood alone in that which is called isolation – our splendid isolation, as one of our colonial friends was good enough to call it.
[Speech, Lewes, 1896]

Gosse, Sir Edmund (1849–1928)
English literary critic, translator and librarian

1. [Noting his father's reply when asked to talk about 'those old Greek gods']
There is nothing in the legends of those gods, or rather devils, that it is not better for a Christian not to know.
[*Father and Son: A Study of Two Temperaments* (1907)]

2. [Referring to one of Swinburne's plays]
We were as nearly bored as enthusiasm would permit.
[In C. Hassall, *Biography of Edward Marsh*, 6]

3. [Of T. Sturge Moore]
A sheep in sheep's clothing.
[In Ferris Greenslet, *Under the Bridge*]

Goulburn, Edward, Dean of Norwich (1818–1897)
English divine, teacher and Dean of Norwich 1866–89

1. Let the scintillations of your wit be like the coruscations of summer lightning, lambent but innocuous.
[Sermon at Rugby, in Tucknell, *Reminiscences of Oxford* (1907)]

Gournay, Jean Claude Vincent de (1712–1759)
French economist and writer

1. *Laissez faire, laissez passer.*
Freedom of action, freedom of movement.
[Speech, 1758]

Gower, John (c. 1330–1408)
English poet and ballad writer; wrote in French, Latin and English

1. It hath and schal ben evermor
That love is maister wher he wile.
['Confessio Amantis' (1390)]

Gozzano, Guido (1883–1916)
Italian poet and novelist

1. *E la signora scaltra e la bambina ardita si mossero: la vita una allacciò dell'altra.*
And the shrewd lady and the daring young girl moved on: embracing each other's waist.
[*I Colloqui* (*Conversation pieces*, 1911), 'Le due strade' ('The two roads']

Grable, Betty (1916–1973)
US film star and wartime 'pin-up'

1. There are two reasons why I'm in show business, and I'm standing on both of them.
[Attr.]

Grace, W.G. (1848–1915)
Celebrated English cricketer; physician and surgeon

1. [Refusing to leave the crease after being bowled first ball in front of a large crowd]
They came to see me bat not to see you bowl.
[Attr.]

Gracián, Baltasar (1601–1658)
Spanish allegorical novelist, philosopher and Jesuit preacher

1. *No es menester arte donde basta la Naturaleza.*
Art is not essential where Nature is sufficient.
[*El héroe* (*The Hero*, 1637), section XIX]

2. *La metad del mundo se está riendo de la otra metad, con necedad de todos.*
Half the world is laughing at the other half, which shows how foolish everyone is.
[*Oráculo manual y arte de prudencia* (*Handbook-Oracle and the Art of Prudence*, 1647), no. 101]

3. *No es necio el que hace la necedad, sino el que, hecha, no la sabe encubrir.*
It is not the one who commits an act of foolishness who is foolish, but the one who, once such an act has been committed, does not know how to cover it up.
[*Oráculo manual y arte de prudencia* (*Handbook-Oracle and the Art of Prudence*, 1647), no. 126]

4. *Son tontos los que lo parecen, y la metad de los que no lo parecen.*
Those people who appear stupid are stupid, as are half of those who don't.
[*Oráculo manual y arte de prudencia* (*Handbook-Oracle and the Art of Prudence*, 1647), no. 201]

5. *Lo bueno, si breve, dos veces bueno.*
Good things, if they are short, are twice as good.
[Attr.]

Grade, Lew (Lewis Winogradsky) (1906–1994)
Russian-born British impresario; film, television and theatrical producer

1. All my shows are great. Some of them are bad. But they are all great.
[*The Observer*, 'Sayings of the Week', 1975]

2. [To Franco Zeffirelli who had explained that the high cost of the film *Jesus of Nazareth* was partly because there had to be twelve apostles]
Twelve! So who needs twelve! Couldn't we make do with six?
[*Radio Times*, 1983]

3. [On hearing that the actor portraying Christ on television was not married to the woman with whom he was living]
What about it? Do you want to crucify the boy?
[Attr.]

Graham, Billy (1918–)
American Christian Protestant evangelist

1. May the Lord bless you real good.
[Benediction]

Graham, Clementina Stirling (1782–1877)
Scottish author, lyricist and translator

1. The best way to get the better of temptation is just to yield to it.
[*Mystifications* (1859), 'Soirée at Mrs Russel's']

Graham, Harry (1874–1936)
British writer and journalist

1. O'er the rugged mountain's brow
Clara threw the twins she nursed,
And remarked, 'I wonder now
Which will reach the bottom first?'
[*Ruthless Rhymes for Heartless Homes* (1899), 'Calculating Clara']

2. Aunt Jane observed, the second time
She tumbled off a bus,
'The step is short from the Sublime
To the Ridiculous.'
[*Ruthless Rhymes for Heartless Homes* (1899), 'Equanimity']

3. 'There's been an accident!' they said,
'Your servant's cut in half; he's dead!'
'Indeed!' said Mr Jones, 'and please
Send me the half that's got my keys.'
[*Ruthless Rhymes for Heartless Homes* (1899), 'Mr Jones']

4. Billy, in one of his nice new sashes,
Fell in the fire and was burnt to ashes;
Now, although the room grows chilly,
I haven't the heart to poke poor Billy.
[*Ruthless Rhymes for Heartless Homes* (1899), 'Tender-Heartedness']

5. Weep not for little Léonie
Abducted by a French Marquis!
Though loss of honour was a wrench
Just think how it's improved her French.
[*More Ruthless Rhymes for Heartless Homes* (1930), 'Compensation']

Graham, James, Marquis of Montrose (1612–1650)
Scottish Covenanter, military campaigner, poet and Royalist; executed

1. But if thou wilt be constant then,
And faithful of thy word,
I'll make thee glorious by my pen,
And famous by my sword.
['My Dear and Only Love' (1642)]

2. [Lines written on the window of his jail the night before his execution]
Let them bestow on ev'ry Airth a Limb;
Open all my Veins, that I may swim
To thee, my Saviour, in that Crimson Lake;
Then place my pur-boil'd Head upon a Stake;
Scatter my Ashes, throw them in the Air:
Lord (since Thou know'st where all these Atoms are)
I'm hopeful, once Thou'lt recollect my Dust,
And confident Thou'lt raise me with the Just.
['His Metrical Prayer' (1650)]

3. May God have mercy upon this afflicted Kingdom.
[Last words]

Grahame, Kenneth (1859–1932)
Scottish essayist and children's writer; Secretary to the Bank of England

1. Aunt Maria flung herself on him [the curate]. 'O Mr Hodgitts!' I heard her cry, 'you are brave! for my sake do not be rash!' He was not rash.
[*The Golden Age* (1895), 'The Burglars']

2. Believe me, my young friend, there is nothing – absolutely nothing – half so much worth doing as simply messing about in boats.
[*The Wind in the Willows* (1908), 1]

3. [Toad's reaction to the motor-car which destroyed his gypsy caravan]
The *real* way to travel! Here today – in next week tomorrow! Villages skipped, towns and cities jumped – always somebody else's horizon! O bliss! O poop-poop! O my! O my!
[*The Wind in the Willows* (1908), 2]

4. The clever men at Oxford
Know all that there is to be knowed.
But they none of them know one half as much
As intelligent Mr Toad!
[*The Wind in the Willows* (1908), 10]

Grainger, James (c. 1721–1766)
Scottish poet, army surgeon and editor

1. What is fame? an empty bubble;
Gold? a transient, shining trouble.
['Solitude' (1755)]

2. Now, Muse, let's sing of rats.
[*The Sugar-Cane* (1764), MS version; quoted in Boswell, *The Life of Samuel Johnson* (1791), March 1776)]

Grainger, Percy (1882–1961)
Australian pianist and composer, particularly known for his folk song arrangements

1. Why be difficult when with a little extra effort you can make yourself impossible?
[*Anecdotes*, Index Part I, Grainger Collection]

Grant, Bruce Alexander (1925–)
Australian author, critic and civil servant

1. I recall at least two Australian ambassadors who complained to me in the past about the constraints which the inherited British style placed on Australian diplomacy, but, when their time came to resist the invitation of knighthood, their resolve buckled under the terrible strain.
[*Gods and Politicians* (1982)]

Grant, Cary (Archibald Leach) (1904–1986)
English-born American leading film actor; Academy Award 1969

1. [Responding to a telegram received by his agent inquiring: 'How old Cary Grant?']
'Old Cary Grant fine. How you?'
[In Halliwell, *Filmgoer's Book of Quotes* (1973)]

2. Nobody is ever truthful about his own life. There are always ambiguities.
[*The Observer*, 1981, in Jeffrey Care (ed.), *Sayings of the Eighties* (1989)]

Grant, Sir Robert (1779–1838)
Bengal-born British lawyer, colonial civil servant, politician and poet

1. O worship the King, all glorious above!
O gratefully sing his power and his love!
Our Shield and Defender – the Ancient of Days,
Pavilioned in splendour, and girded with praise.
[Hymn, 1833]

Grant, Ulysses S. (1822–1885)
American general, Republican President (1869–77) and memoirist

1. I purpose to fight it out on this line, if it takes all summer.
[Dispatch to Washington from headquarters in the field, 1864]

2. [Of the Whiskey Ring]
Let no guilty man escape, if it can be avoided ... No personal consideration should stand in the way of performing a public duty.
[Note on letter, 1875]

3. I know no method to secure the repeal of bad or obnoxious laws so effective as their stringent execution.
[Inaugural Address, 1869]

4. [To Simon Bolivar Buckner, whom he was besieging at Fort Donelson, 1862]
No terms except unconditional and immediate surrender can be accepted. I propose to move immediately upon your works.
[Attr.; in Headley, *The Life and Campaigns of General U.S. Grant* (1869), 6]

Granville, George, Baron Lansdowne (1666–1735)
English poet, dramatist and politician

1. Cowards in scarlet pass for men of war.
[*The She Gallants* (1696), V]

2. Bright as the day, and like the morning, fair,
Such Cloe is ... and common as the air.
['Cloe' (1712)]

3. I'll be this abject thing no more;
Love, give me back my heart again.
['Adieu l'Amour']

4. Of all the plagues with which the world is curst,
Of every ill, a woman is the worst.
[*The British Enchanters*, II.i]

5. O Love! thou bane of the most generous souls!
Thou doubtful pleasure, and thou certain pain.
['Heroic Love', II.i]

Granville-Barker, Harley (1877–1946)
English actor, dramatist, producer and critic

1. Rightly thought of there is poetry in peaches ... even when they are canned.
[*The Madras House*, I]

2. But oh, the farmyard world of sex!
[*The Madras House*, IV]

Grass, Günter (1927–)
Experimental German novelist, dramatist and poet; stone mason; Social Democrat

1. *Nur wahre Faulpelze können arbeitsparende Erfindungen machen.*
Only a real lazybones can produce labour-saving inventions.
[*Die Blechtrommel* (*The Tin Drum*, 1959)]

2. *Getauft geimpft gefirmt geschult.*
Gespielt hab ich mit Bombensplittern.
Und aufgewachsen bin ich zwischen
dem Heilgen Geist und Hitlers Bild.
Baptised innoculated confirmed educated.
I played with bomb fragments.
And I grew up between
the Holy Spirit and a picture of Hitler.
[*Ausgefragt* (*Questioned*, 1967), 'Kleckerburg']

Graves, John Woodcock (1795–1886)
British poet, inventor and huntsman

1. D'ye ken John Peel with his coat so gay?
D'ye ken John Peel at the break of the day?
D'ye ken John Peel when he's far far away
With his hounds and his horn in the morning?
'Twas the sound of his horn called me from my bed,
And the cry of his hounds has me oft-times led;
For Peel's view-hollo would waken the dead,
Or a fox from his lair in the morning.
['John Peel' (1820)]

Graves, Robert (1895–1985)
English poet, novelist, critic, autobiographer, translator and mythologist; noted for his love poetry

1. His eyes are quickened so with grief,
He can watch a grass or leaf
Every instant grow...

2. Across two counties he can hear
And catch your words before you speak.
The woodlouse or the maggot's weak
Clamour rings in his sad ear,
And noise so slight it would surpass
Credence.
['Lost Love' (1921)]

3. Children are dumb to say how hot the day is,
How hot the scent is of the summer rose.
['The Cool Web' (1927)]

4. He, of his gentleness
Thirsting and hungering
Walked in the wilderness;
Soft words of grace he spoke
Unto lost desert-folk
That listened wondering.
He heard the bittern call
From ruined palace-wall,
Answered him brotherly.
[*Collected Poems 1914–1947* (1948), 'In the Wilderness']

5. No escape,
No such thing; to dream of new dimensions,
Cheating checkmate by painting the king's robe
So that he slides like a queen.
[*Poems Selected by Himself* (1957), 'The Castle']

6. Down, wanton, down! Have you no shame
That at the whisper of Love's name,
Or Beauty's, presto! up you raise
Your angry head and stand at gaze?
['Down, Wanton Down']

7. The butterfly, a cabbage-white,
(His honest idiocy of flight)
Will never now, it is too late,
Master the art of flying straight,
Yet has – who knows so well as I?–
A just sense of how not to fly:
He lurches here and here by guess
And God and hope and hopelessness.
Even the aerobatic swift

Has not his flying-crooked gift.
['Flying Crooked']

8. Goodbye to All That.
[Title of book, 1929]

9. In love as in sport, the amateur status must be strictly maintained.
[*Occupation: Writer*]

10. The remarkable thing about Shakespeare is that he is really very good – in spite of all the people who say he is very good.
[*The Observer*, 'Sayings of the Week', 1964]

11. To be a poet is a condition rather than a profession.
[Questionnaire in *Horizon*]

Gray, Patrick, Sixth Lord (d. 1612)
Scottish courtier and ambassador at the court of Elizabeth I

1. [Advocating the execution of Mary, Queen of Scots]
A dead woman bites not.
[Oral tradition, 1587]

Gray, Thomas (1716–1771)
Renowned English 'graveyard' poet and scholar

1. And leave us leisure to be good.
['Hymn to Adversity' (1742)]

2. Ye distant spires, ye antique towers,
That crown the wat'ry glade...

3. Where once my careless childhood stray'd,
A stranger yet to pain!...

4. Who foremost now delight to cleave
With pliant arm thy glassy wave?...

5. Urge the flying ball...

6. Still as they run they look behind,
They hear a voice in every wind,
And snatch a fearful joy...

7. Alas, regardless of their doom.
The little victims play!
No sense have they of ills to come,
Nor care beyond to-day...

8. To each his suff'rings: all are men,
Condemn'd alike to groan;
The tender for another's pain,
Th' unfeeling for his own.
Yet ah! why should they know their fate?
Since sorrow never comes too late,
And happiness too swiftly flies.
Thought would destroy their paradise.
No more; where ignorance is bliss,
'Tis folly to be wise.
['Ode on a Distant Prospect of Eton College' (1742)]

9. The Attic warbler pours her throat,
Responsive to the cuckoo's note...

10. To Contemplation's sober eye
Such is the race of Man...

11. Thy sun is set, thy spring is gone–
We frolick, while 'tis May.
['Ode on the Spring' (1742)]

12. Demurest of the tabby kind,
The pensive Selima, reclin'd...

13. What female heart can gold despise?
What Cat's averse to fish?...

14. A Fav'rite has no friend!...

15. Not all that tempts your wand'ring eyes
And heedless hearts, is lawful prize;
Nor all, that glisters, gold.
['Ode on the Death of a Favourite Cat' (1747)]

16. The Curfew tolls the knell of parting day,
The lowing herd wind slowly o'er the lea,
The plowman homeward plods his weary way,
And leaves the world to darkness and to me.

Now fades the glimmering landscape on the sight,
And all the air a solemn stillness holds,
Save where the beetle wheels his droning flight,
And drowsy tinklings lull the distant folds:

Save that from yonder ivy-mantled tow'r,
The moping owl does to the moon complain
Of such as, wand'ring near her secret bow'r,
Molest her ancient solitary reign.

Beneath those rugged elms, that yew-tree's shade,
Where heaves the turf in many a mould'ring heap,
Each in his narrow cell for ever laid,
The rude Forefathers of the hamlet sleep.

The breezy call of incense-breathing Morn,
The swallow twitt'ring from the straw-built shed,
The cock's shrill clarion, or the echoing horn,
No more shall rouse them from their lowly bed...

17. Let not Ambition mock their useful toil,
Their homely joys, and destiny obscure;
Nor Grandeur hear with a disdainful smile,
The short and simple annals of the poor.

The boast of heraldry, the pomp of pow'r,
And all that beauty, all that wealth e'er gave,
Awaits alike th' inevitable hour,
The paths of glory lead but to the grave...

18. Can storied urn or animated bust
Back to its mansion call the fleeting breath?
Can Honour's voice provoke the silent dust,
Or Flatt'ry soothe the dull cold ear of Death?...

19. Hands, that the rod of empire might have sway'd,
Or wak'd to extasy the living lyre...

20. Full many a gem of purest ray serene,
The dark unfathom'd caves of ocean bear:
Full many a flower is born to blush unseen,
And waste its sweetness on the desert air.

Some village-Hampden, that with dauntless breast
The little Tyrant of his fields withstood;
Some mute inglorious Milton here may rest,
Some Cromwell guiltless of his country's blood...

21. Nor circumscrib'd alone
Their growing virtues, but their crimes confin'd;
Forbad to wade through slaughter to a throne,
And shut the gates of mercy on mankind...

22. Far from the madding crowd's ignoble strife,
Their sober wishes never learn'd to stray;
Along the cool sequester'd vale of life
They kept the noiseless tenor of their way...

23. Implores the passing tribute of a sigh...

24. For who to dumb Forgetfulness a prey,
This pleasing anxious being e'er resign'd,
Left the warm precincts of the cheerful day,
Nor cast one longing ling'ring look behind?...

25. Mindful of th' unhonour'd Dead...

26. Here rests his head upon the lap of Earth

A Youth to Fortune and to Fame unknown.
Fair Science frown'd not on his humble birth,
And Melancholy mark'd him for her own...

27. He gave to Mis'ry all he had, a tear,
He gain'd from Heav'n ('twas all he wish'd) a friend.
['Elegy Written in a Country Churchyard' (1751)]

28. Ruin seize thee, ruthless King!
Confusion on thy banners wait,
Tho' fann'd by Conquest's crimson wing
They mock the air with idle state...

29. Vocal no more, since Cambria's fatal day,
To high-born Hoël's harp, or soft Llewellyn's lay...

30. Weave the warp, and weave the woof,
The winding-sheet of Edward's race.
Give ample room, and verge enough
The characters of hell to trace...

31. Fair laughs the Morn, and soft the Zephyr blows,
While proudly riding o'er the azure realm
In gallant trim the gilded Vessel goes,
Youth on the prow, and Pleasure at the helm;
Regardless of the sweeping Whirlwind's sway,
That, hush'd in grim repose, expects his evening prey...

32. Ye Towers of Julius, London's lasting shame,
With many a foul and midnight murther fed.
['The Bard' (1757)]

33. The bloom of young Desire, and purple light of Love...

34. [On Shakespeare]
Far from the sun and summer-gale,
In thy green lap was Nature's Darling laid,
What time, where lucid Avon stray'd,
To him the mighty Mother did unveil
Her aweful face: The dauntless child
Stretch'd forth his little arms, and smiled...

35. [On Milton]
Nor second He, that rode sublime
Upon the seraph-wings of Extasy,
The secrets of th' Abyss to spy.
He pass'd the flaming bounds of Place and Time:
The living Throne, the sapphire-blaze,
Where Angels tremble, while they gaze,
He saw; but blasted with excess of light,
Closed his eyes in endless night...

36. [On himself]
Beyond the limits of a vulgar fate,
Beneath the Good how far – but far above the Great.
['The Progress of Poesy' (1757)]

37. Too poor for a bribe, and too proud to importune,
He had not the method of making a fortune.
['Sketch of his own Character' (1761)]

38. Their tears, their little triumphs o'er,
Their human passions now no more.
['Ode on the Installation of the Duke of Grafton' (1769)]

39. The meanest flowret of the vale,
The simplest note that swells the gale,
The common sun, the air, and skies,
To him are opening paradise.
['Ode on the Pleasure Arising from Vicissitude' (1771)]

40. Owls might have hooted in St Peter's Quire,
And foxes stunk and litter'd in St Paul's.
['On Lord Holland's Seat near Margate, Kent']

41. Any fool may write a most valuable book by chance, if he will only tell us what he heard and saw with veracity.
[Letter to Horace Walpole, 1768]

42. I shall be but a shrimp of an author.
[Letter to Horace Walpole, 1768]

Grayson, Victor (1881–c. 1920)

1. Never explain: your friends don't need it and your enemies won't believe it.
[Attr.]

Greeley, Horace (1811–1872)

American founding editor of the New York Tribune*; presidential candidate and supporter of Fourierism*

1. Go West, young man, and grow up with the country.
[*Hints toward Reform* (1850)]

Green, Marshall (1916–)

1. Lyndon B. Johnson always thought that Australia was the next large rectangular State beyond El Paso, and treated it accordingly.
[Interview in film *Allies*]

Green, Matthew (1696–1737)

English poet

1. To cure the mind's wrong biass, Spleen,
Some recommend the bowling green;
Some, hilly walks; all, exercise:
Fling but a stone, the giant dies.
Laugh and be well...

2. Who their ill tasted home-brew'd prayer
To the state's mellow forms prefer...

3. By happy alchemy of mind
They run to pleasure all they find.
['The Spleen' (1737)]

Greene, Graham (1904–1991)

English novelist, dramatist, screen and travel writer, his work often concerned with moral dilemmas

1. His smile explained everything; he carried it always with him as a leper carried his bell; it was a perpetual warning that he was not to be trusted.
[*England Made Me* (1935)]

2. He gave the impression that very many cities had rubbed him smooth.
[*A Gun for Sale* (1940), 4]

3. That whisky priest, I wish we had never had him in the house.
[*The Power and the Glory* (1940), I]

4. Of course, before we know he is a saint, there will have to be miracles.
[*The Power and the Glory* (1940), IV]

5. Against the beautiful and the clever and the successful, one can wage a pitiless war, but not against the unattractive.
[*The Heart of the Matter* (1948), bk I, I, 2]

6. They had been corrupted by money, and he had been corrupted by sentiment. Sentiment was the more dangerous, because you couldn't name its price. A man open to bribes was to be relied upon below a certain figure, but sentiment might uncoil in the heart at a name, a photograph, even a smell remembered.
[*The Heart of the Matter* (1948), bk I, I, 2]

7. Despair is the price one pays for setting oneself an impossible aim.
[*The Heart of the Matter* (1948), bk I, I, 2]

8. He thought: If my child had lived, she too would have been conscriptable, flung into some grim dormitory, to find her own way. After the Atlantic, the A.T.S. or the W.A.A.F., the blustering sergeant with the big bust, the cook-house and the potato peelings, the Lesbian officer with the thin lips and the tidy gold hair, and the men waiting on the Common outside the camp, among the gorse bushes...
[*The Heart of the Matter* (1948), bk II, I, 3]

9. His hilarity was like a scream from a crevasse.
[*The Heart of the Matter* (1948), bk III, I, 1]

10. Perhaps if I wanted to be understood or to understand I would bamboozle myself into belief, but I am a reporter; God exists only for leader-writers.
[*The Quiet American* (1955)]

11. Innocence is a kind of insanity.
[*The Quiet American* (1955)]

12. Those who marry God ... can become domesticated too – it's just as hum-drum a marriage as all the others.
[*A Burnt-Out Case* (1961), I, 1]

13. I have often noticed that a bribe ... has that effect – it changes a relation. The man who offers a bribe gives away a little of his own importance; the bribe once accepted, he becomes the inferior, like a man who has paid for a woman.
[*The Comedians* (1966), I, 4]

14. Catholics and Communists have committed great crimes, but at least they have not stood aside, like an established society, and been indifferent. I would rather have blood on my hands than water like Pilate.
[*The Comedians* (1966), III, 4]

15. I had left civilisation behind and entered a savage country of strange customs and inexplicable cruelties: a country in which I was a foreigner and a suspect, quite literally a hunted creature, known to have dubious associates. Was not my father the headmaster? I was like the son of a quisling in a country under occupation.
[*A Sort of Life* (1971)]

16. I slipped a bullet into a chamber and, holding the revolver behind my back, spun the chambers round ... I put the muzzle ... into my right ear and pulled the trigger. There was a minute click, and looking down the chamber I could see that the charge had moved into the firing position. I was out by one.
[*A Sort of Life* (1971)]

17. Fame is a powerful aphrodisiac.
[*Radio Times*, 1964]

18. A love affair had to begin after lunch.
[Attr.]

19. I wouldn't recommend anyone to be a Catholic, unless they had to be.
[Attr.]

20. My belief certainly seems to get stronger in the presence of people whose goodness seems of almost supernatural origin.
[Attr.]

Greene, Hughie (1920–)
Canadian former pilot and television personality

1. I mean this most sincerely, folks.
[Catchphrase from *Opportunity Knocks*; television talent contest from the 1960s]

Greene, Robert (1558–1592)
English dramatist, poet and pamphleteer

1. Ah! what is love! It is a pretty thing,
As sweet unto a shepherd as a king,
And sweeter too;
For kings have cares that wait upon a crown,
And cares can make the sweetest love to frown.
Ah then, ah then,
If country loves such sweet desires do gain,
What lady would not love a shepherd swain?
['The Shepherd's Wife's Song' (1590)]

2. [Of Shakespeare]
For there is an upstart Crow, beautified with our feathers, that with his Tyger's heart wrapt in a Player's hyde, supposes he is as well able to bombast out a blanke verse as the best of you: and being an absolute Iohannes fac totum, is in his owne conceit the onely Shake-scene in a countrey.
[*Greenes Groats-Worth of witte bought with a million of Repentance* (1592)]

Greer, Germaine (1939–)
Australian feminist, critic, English scholar and journalist

1. Probably the only place where a man can feel really secure is in a maximum security prison, except for the imminent threat of release.
[*The Female Eunuch* (1970)]

2. Mother is the dead heart of the family, spending father's earnings on consumer goods to enhance the environment in which he eats, sleeps and watches the television.
[*The Female Eunuch* (1970)]

3. Love, love, love – all the wretched cant of it, masking egotism, lust, masochism, fantasy under a mythology of sentimental postures, a welter of self induced miseries and joys, blinding and masking the essential personalities in the frozen gestures of courtship, in the kissing and the dating and the desire, the compliments and the quarrels which vivify its barrenness.
[*The Female Eunuch* (1970)]

4. The vegetable creep of women's liberation has freed some breasts from the domination of foam and wire.
[*The Female Eunuch* (1970)]

5. If you think you are emancipated, you might consider the idea of tasting your menstrual blood – if it makes you sick, you've a long way to go, baby.
[*The Female Eunuch* (1970)]

6. If women understand by emancipation the adoption of the masculine role then we are lost indeed.
[*The Female Eunuch* (1970)]

7. Nobody wants a girl whose beauty is imperceptible to all but him.
[*The Female Eunuch* (1970)]

8. A woman becomes the extension of a man's ego like his horse or his car.
[*The Female Eunuch* (1970)]

Gregory I (540–604)
Italian pope from 590, saint and Father of the Church; theologian and liturgical reformer

1. *Responsum est, quod Angli vocarentur. At ille: 'Bene' inquit, 'nam et angelicam habent faciem, et tales angelorum in caelis decet esse coheredes.'*
Answer was given that they were called Angles. But he remarked, 'They are well named, for they have the

countenance of angels, and as such should be coheirs with the angels in heaven.'
[In Bede, *Historia Ecclesiastica* (731), II, 1. Cf. Sellar and Yeatman: 3]

Gregory VII (c. 1020–1085)
Italian pope from 1073, saint and church reformer

1. [Last words]
Dilexi justitiam et odivi iniquitatem: propterea morior in exilio.
I have loved righteousness and hated iniquity: therefore I die in exile.
[In Bowden, *The Life and Pontificate of Gregory VII* (1840), II, 3, 20]

Gregory, Lady Isabella Augusta (1852–1932)
Irish dramatist, prose writer and translator

1. It's a good thing to be able to take up your money in your hand and to think no more of it when it slips away from you than you would of a trout that would slip back into the stream.
[*Twenty-Five*]
2. There's more learning than is taught in books.
[*The Jester*]
3. I am so tired of housekeeping I dreamed I was being served up for my guests and awoke only when the knife was at my throat.
[In Mary-Lou Kohfeldt, *Lady Gregory* (1985)]
4. I believe we shall meet again after death ... but if we don't you will have the worst of it, for you can't say anything to me, and if we do, I will say 'I told you so!'.
[In Mary-Lou Kohfeldt, *Lady Gregory* (1985), Letter to Wilfrid Scawen Blunt]

Grellet, Stephen (1773–1855)
French missionary

1. I expect to pass through this world but once; any good thing therefore that I can do, or any kindness that I can show to any fellow-creature, let me do it now; let me not defer or neglect it, for I shall not pass this way again.
[Attr.]

Grenfell, Julian (1888–1915)
English soldier and poet

1. The naked earth is warm with spring,
And with green grass and bursting trees
Leans to the sun's gaze glorying,
And quivers in the sunny breeze;
And life is colour and warmth and light,
And a striving evermore for these;
And he is dead who will not fight;
And who dies fighting has increase.

The fighting man shall from the sun
Take warmth, and life from the glowing earth.
['Into Battle' (1915)]

Greville, Fulke, First Baron Brooke (1554–1628)
English poet, dramatist and biographer of Sir Philip Sidney; courtier and politician

1. Silence augmenteth grief, writing increaseth rage,
Stal'd are my thoughts, which loved and lost, the wonder of our age,
Yet quick'ned now with fire, though dead with frost ere now,
Enraged I write, I know not what: dead, quick, I know not how.
['Elegy on the Death of Sir Philip Sidney' (died 1586)]
2. Oh wearisome Condition of Humanity!
Borne under one Law, to another, bound:
Vainely begot, and yet forbidden vanity,
Created sicke, commanded to be sound.
[*Mustapha* (1609), V.iv]
3. Fire and people do in this agree,
They both good servants, both ill masters be.
['An Inquisition upon Fame and Honour' (1633)]

Grey, Edward, Viscount of Fallodon (1862–1933)
English statesman; Liberal Foreign Secretary 1905–16; writer on nature

1. [To a caller at the Foreign Office in August 1914]
The lamps are going out all over Europe; we shall not see them lit again in our lifetime.
[In *Twenty-five Years*, II, 20]
2. The United States is like a gigantic boiler. Once the fire is lighted under it there is no limit to the power it can generate.
[In Winston S. Churchill, *Their Finest Hour*, 32]

Grey Owl (George Stansfield Belaney) (1888–1938)
Canadian author and naturalist

1. Civilisation says, 'Nature belongs to man.' The Indian says, 'No, man belongs to nature.'
[Address at Norwich, quoted in Donald B. Smith, *From the Land of Shadows: The Making of Grey Owl* (1990)]

Griffith, D.W. (1874–1948)
US film director

1. Out of the cradle endlessly rocking.
[Film script, *Intolerance* (1916); taken from the title of a poem by Walt Whitman]
2. [Said when directing an epic film]
Move those ten thousand horses a trifle to the right. And that mob out there, three feet forward.
[Attr.]

Griffith-Jones, Mervyn (1909–1979)
British lawyer

1. [At the trial of D.H. Lawrence's novel *Lady Chatterley's Lover*]
Is it a book you would even wish your wife or your servants to read?
[*The Times*, 1960]

Griffiths, Trevor (1935–)
British political dramatist and screenwriter

1. Comedy is medicine.
[*The Comedians* (1979), I]

Grimké, Angelina (1805–1879)
American anti-slavery activist, pamphleteer and Quaker

1. I know you do not make the laws but I also know that you are the wives and mothers, the sisters and daughters of those who do...
[*The Anti-Slavery Examiner* (1836)]

Gromyko, Andrei (1909–1989)
Soviet statesman and diplomat

1. [Proposing Mikhail Gorbachev as leader of the Soviet Communist Party]
This man has a nice smile, but he has got iron teeth.
[Speech, 1985]

Grossmith, George (1847–1912)
English singer, comic song-writer and humorous author
and **Grossmith,** Weedon (1854–1919)
English writer, painter and comic actor; brother of George Grossmith

1. What's the good of a home, if you are never in it?
[*Diary of a Nobody* (1894), 1]

2. I ... recognized her as a woman who used to work years ago for my old aunt at Clapham. It only shows how small the world is.
[*Diary of a Nobody* (1894), 2]

3. He [Gowing] suggested we should play 'Cutlets', a game we had never heard of. He sat on a chair, and asked Carrie to sit on his lap, an invitation which dear Carrie rightly declined.
[*Diary of a Nobody* (1894), 6]

4. I left the room with silent dignity, but caught my foot in the mat.
[*Diary of a Nobody* (1894), 12]

5. I am a poor man, but I would gladly give ten shillings to find out who sent me the insulting Christmas card I received this morning.
[*Diary of a Nobody* (1894), 13]

Guedalla, Philip (1889–1944)
English historian, essayist, biographer and lawyer

1. The work of Henry James has always seemed divisible by a simple dynastic arrangement into three reigns: James I, James II, and the Old Pretender.
[*Collected Essays* (1920), IV, 'Men of Letters: Mr Henry James']

2. The cheerful clatter of Sir James Barrie's cans as he went round with the milk of human kindness.
[*Supers and Supermen* (1920), 'Some Critics']

3. Any stigma, as the old saying is, will serve to beat a dogma.
[*Masters and Men* (1923), 'Ministers of State']

4. [On the evacuation of Dunkirk]
The little ships, the unforgotten Homeric catalogue of Mary Jane and Peggy IV, of Folkestone Belle, Boy Billy, and Ethel Maud, of Lady Haig and Skylark ... the little ships of England brought the Army home.
[*Mr Churchill* (1941), 7]

5. People who jump to conclusions rarely alight on them.
[*The Observer*, 'Sayings of the Week', 1924]

Guerrero, Raúl (1945–)

1. *El pensamiento y el arte sólo se desarrollan donde el artista no tiene que batallar para comer: en los países ricos. Ellos tienen eso, pero les falta el sentimiento latino.*
Thought and art only develop where the artist does not have to fight to eat: in rich countries. They're all right as far as that's concerned, but they lack Latin feelings.
[Interview in *El País*, 1994]

Guest, Edgar A.
American writer of popular verse

1. Whoe'er has paced the floor
And lived those years of fearful thoughts, and then been swept from woe
Up to the topmost height of bliss that's given man to know,
Will tell you there's no phrase so sweet, so charged with human joy
As that the doctor brings from God – that message: 'It's a boy!'
['It's a Boy']

Guillén, Jorge (1893–1984)
Spanish poet, eventually settled in US

1. *Soy, más, estoy. Respiro.*
Lo profundo es el aire.
La realidad me inventa,
Soy su leyenda. ¡Salve!
I exist, more than that, I'm alive. I'm breathing.
The profound thing is the air.
Reality invents me,
I am its legend. Hail!
[*Cántico*, (fourth edition, 1950), I, 'Más allá' ('Beyond'), I]

Guinan, Texas (1884–1933)
Canadian actress

1. [When she and her troupe were refused entry to France in 1931]
It goes to show that fifty million Frenchmen can be wrong.
[Attr.]

Guinness, Sir Alec (1914–)
British stage and film actor

1. [Vowing never to perform again in the West End when he saw the blank faces of uncomprehending tourists]
I'd rather go to the provinces where they still speak English and not Japanese.
[*Scotsman*, 1992]

Guitry, Sacha (1885–1957)
Russian-born French actor, dramatist and film director

1. [Responding to his fifth wife's jealousy of his previous wives]
The others were only my wives. But you, my dear, will be my widow.
[Attr.]

Gulbenkian, Nubar (1896–1972)
British industrialist, diplomat and philanthropist

1. The best number for a dinner party is two: myself and a damn good head waiter.
[*The Observer*, 1965]

Gunn, Jeannie (Mrs Aeneas Gunn) (1870–1961)
Australian writer

1. It is the helplessness of little women that makes them appear 'all right' in the eyes of bushmen, helplessness being foreign to snorters.
[*We of the Never-Never* (1908), 5]

2. Neither a cabbage nor a woman for five years! Think of it, townsfolk! Neither a cabbage nor a woman – with the cabbage placed first.
[*We of the Never-Never* (1908), 14]

Gunn, Thom (1929–)
Anglo-American poet, associated with the Movement

1. On motorcycles, up the road, they come:
Small, black, as flies hanging in heat, the Boys,
Until the distance throws them forth, their hum
Bulges to thunder held by calf and thigh...

2. One is always nearer by not keeping still.
['On The Move' (1957)]

3. One by one they appear in
the darkness: a few friends, and

a few with historical
names. How late they start to shine!
but before they fade they stand
perfectly embodied, all

the past lapping them like a
cloak of chaos.
['My Sad Captains' (1961)]

Gurney, Dorothy (1858–1932)
English poet

1. The kiss of the sun for pardon,
The song of the birds for mirth,
One is nearer God's Heart in a garden
Than anywhere else on earth.
['God's Garden' (1913)]

Gwenn, Edmund (1875–1959)
English stage actor

1. [Reply on his deathbed, when someone said to him, 'It must be very hard']
It is. But not as hard as farce.
[*Time*, 1984]

Gwyn, Nell (1650–1687)
English actress and mistress of Charles II

1. [On prostitution]
As for me, it is my profession, I do not pretend to anything better.
[In Rosalind Miles, *The Women's History of the World* (1988)]

2. [When surrounded in her coach by a mob during the Popish Terror in 1681]
Pray, good people, be civil. I am the Protestant whore.
[Attr.]

Gzowski, Peter
Canadian media personality

1. [Referring to the fax machine and cellular telephone]
I have seen the future and it's here.
[CBC Radio's *Morningside*, 1988]

Hadrian (AD 76–138)
Roman emperor from 117, known for strengthening imperial frontiers and as a lover of the arts

1. *Animula vagula blandula,*
Hospes comesque corporis,
Quae nunc abibis in loca
Pallidula rigida nudula,
Nec ut soles dabis iocos!
Ah fleeting Spirit! wand'ring Fire,
That long hast warm'd my tender Breast,
Must thou no more this Frame inspire?
No more a pleasing, cheerful Guest?
Whither, ah whither art thou flying!
To what dark, undiscover'd Shore?
Thou seem'st all trembling, shiv'ring, dying,
And Wit and Humour are no more!
['Ad Animam Suam', trans. Pope]

Haggard, Sir Henry Rider (1856–1925)
English writer of Romantic adventure novels and agriculturalist

1. She-who-must-be-obeyed.
[*She* (1887), passim]

Haggard, William (Richard Henry Michael Clayton) (1907–)
British civil servant and officer in the Indian army

1. Its business was security, not the convenience of the great, and that went for any government be it red or true blue or a washy pink. That was the premise and limitations followed it logically. Preventive action was like preventive war: you'd simply be destroying what you were salaried to defend.
[*The Conspirators* (1967)]

Hahnemann, C.F.S. (1755–1843)
German physician and founder of homeopathy

1. *Similia similibus curantur.*
Like cures like.
[Motto of homeopathic medicine]

Haig, Alexander (1924–)
American army officer and politician

1. [Statement after an assassination attempt on President Reagan]
As of now, I am in charge at the White House.
[*The Times*, 1981]

Haig, Douglas, First Earl of Bemersyde (1861–1928)
Scottish Commander of British forces in France and Flanders 1915–18

1. [Of Lord Derby]
A very weak-minded fellow, I'm afraid, and, like the feather pillow, bears the marks of the last person who has sat on him!
[Letter to his wife, 14 January 1918]

2. Every position must be held to the last man: there must be no retirement. With our backs to the wall, and believing in the justice of our cause, each one of us must fight on to the end.
[Order to British forces on the Western Front, 12 April 1918]

Haile Selassie (1892–1975)
Emperor of Ethiopia (1930–36, 1941–74); deposed

1. [Telegram sent to Winston Churchill mimicking his 'Give us the tools, and we will finish the job']
We have finished the job, what shall we do with the tools?
[In Edward Marsh, *Ambrosia and Small Beer*, 4]

Hailsham, Quintin Hogg, Baron (1907–)
English Conservative politician

1. [On the Profumo affair]
A great party is not to be brought down because of a squalid affair between a woman of easy virtue and a proved liar.
[Interview, BBC TV, 13 June 1963]

2. [On Labour party policy in the 1964 general election campaign]
If the British public falls for this, I say it will be stark, staring bonkers.
[Press conference, Conservative Central Office, 1964]

3. I don't see any harm in being middle class, I've been middle class all my life and have benefited from it.
[*The Observer*, 1983, in Jeffrey Care (ed.), *Sayings of the Eighties* (1989)]

4. When I'm sitting on the Woolsack in the House of Lords I amuse myself by saying 'Bollocks' *sotto voce* to the bishops.
[*The Observer*, 1985, in Jeffrey Care (ed.), *Sayings of the Eighties* (1989)]

Haines, Joe (1928–)
British journalist and editor

1. [Advising on a libel case shortly before Robert Maxwell's death]
In an unfortunate phrase, I told him not to go overboard.
[*Daily Mirror*]

Haldane, J.B.S. (1892–1964)
British biochemist, geneticist and popularizer of science

1. Einstein – the greatest Jew since Jesus. I have no doubt that Einstein's name will still be remembered and revered when Lloyd George, Foch, and William Hohenzollern share with Charlie Chaplin that ineluctable oblivion which awaits the uncreative mind.
[*Daedalus or Science and the Future* (1924)]

2. Shelley and Keats were the last English poets who were at all up-to-date in their chemical knowledge.
[*Daedalus or Science and the Future* (1924)]

3. My own suspicion is that the universe is not only queerer than we suppose, but queerer than we can suppose.
[*Possible Worlds and Other Essays* (1927), 'Possible Worlds']

4. If human beings could be propagated by cutting, like apple trees, aristocracy would be biologically sound.
[*The Inequality of Man and Other Essays* (1932), 'The Inequality of Man']

5. [Reply when asked what inferences could be drawn about the nature of God from a study of his works]
The Creator ... has a special preference for beetles.
[Lecture, 1951]

Haldeman, H.R. (1926–)
Business executive; former government official and President Nixon's Chief of Staff

1. [Comment to John Dean on Watergate affair, 1973]
Once the toothpaste is out of the tube, it is awfully hard to get it back in.
[In *Hearings Before the Select Committee on Presidential Campaign Activities of US Senate: Watergate and Related Activities* (1973), IV. Cf. Nixon: 18]

Hale, Edward Everett (1822–1909)
American preacher, Chaplain to the US Senate; short-story writer and memoirist

1. 'Do you pray for the senators, Dr Hale?' 'No, I look at the senators and I pray for the country.'
[In Van Wyck Brooks, *New England Indian Summer* (1940)]

Hale, Sir Matthew (1609–1676)
English Lord Chief Justice; writer of legal and religious works

1. Christianity is part of the laws of England.
[In Blackstone, *Commentaries on the Laws of England* (1769), IV]

Hale, Nathan (1755–1776)
American soldier and revolutionary, hanged for spying

1. [Speech before he was executed by the British]
I only regret that I have but one life to lose for my country.
[In Johnston, *Nathan Hale* (1974), 14]

Haliburton, T.C. (1796–1865)
Canadian humorist and writer on Nova Scotia

1. I want you to see Peel, Stanley, Graham, Shiel, Russell, Macaulay, Old Joe, and so on. These men are all upper crust here.
[*The Attaché, or Sam Slick in England* (1843–1844), 24]

Halifax, George Savile, First Marquis of (1633–1695)
English politician, courtier, pamphleteer and epigrammatist

1. This innocent Word Trimmer signifieth no more than this, that if men are together in a Boat, and one part of the Company would weigh it down on one side, another would make it lean as much to the contrary, it happneth there is a third Opinion, of those who conceave it would do as well, if the Boat went even, without endangering the Passengers.
[*Character of a Trimmer* (c. 1685, published 1688), Preface]

2. Love is a passion that hath friends in the Garrison.
[*The Lady's New-year's Gift: or, Advice to a Daughter* (1688), 'Behaviour and Conversation']

3. There is ... no other Fundamental, but that every Supream Power must be Arbitrary.
[*Political, Moral and Miscellaneous Thoughts and Reflections* (1750), 'Of Fundamentals']

4. Power is so apt to be insolent and Liberty to be saucy, that they are very seldom upon good Terms.
[*Political, Moral and Miscellaneous Thoughts and Reflections* (1750), 'Of Prerogative, Power and Liberty']

5. When the people contend for their Liberty, they seldom get any thing by their Victory but new Masters.
[*Political, Moral and Miscellaneous Thoughts and Reflections* (1750), 'Of Prerogative, Power and Liberty']

6. Men are not hang'd for stealing Horses, but that Horses may not be stolen.
[*Political, Moral and Miscellaneous Thoughts and Reflections* (1750), 'Of Punishment']

7. Our Vices and Virtues couple with one another, and get Children that resemble both their Parents.
[*Political, Moral and Miscellaneous Thoughts and Reflections* (1750), 'Of the World']

8. Popularity is a Crime from the Moment it is sought; it is only a Virtue where Men have it whether they will or no.
[*Political, Moral and Miscellaneous Thoughts and Reflections* (1750), 'Of Ambition']

9. Most Men make little other use of their Speech than to give evidence against their own Understanding.
[*Political, Moral and Miscellaneous Thoughts and Reflections* (1750), 'Of Folly and Fools']

10. Anger is never without an Argument, but seldom with a good one.
[*Political, Moral and Miscellaneous Thoughts and Reflections* (1750), 'Of Anger']

11. Malice is of a low Stature, but it hath very long arms.
[*Political, Moral and Miscellaneous Thoughts and Reflections* (1750), 'Of Malice and Envy']

12. It is flattering some Men to endure them.
[*Political, Moral and Miscellaneous Thoughts and Reflections* (1750), 'Of Company']

13. It is a piece of Arrogance to dare to be drunk, because a Man sheweth himself without a Vail.
[*Political, Moral and Miscellaneous Thoughts and Reflections* (1750), 'Drunkenness']

14. The best way to suppose what may come, is to remember what is past.
[*Political, Moral and Miscellaneous Thoughts and Reflections* (1750), 'Experience']

15. It is a general Mistake to think the Men we like are good for every thing, and those we do not, good for nothing.
[*Political, Moral and Miscellaneous Thoughts and Reflections* (1750), 'Partiality']

16. [On Rochester's promotion to a post of higher rank but at the same time carrying less advantage]
[Halifax] said he had heard of many kicked down stairs, but never of any that was kicked up stairs before.
[In Burnet, *The History of My Own Time* (1683–1686), III, April 1684]

Hall, Archibald (1924–)

1. [Comment after he had been convicted of five murders]
It was easy after the first one. After that I was trying for the Guinness Book of Records.
[*The Observer*, 1978]

Hall, Charles Sprague (19th century)
American songwriter

1. John Brown's body lies a-mouldering in the grave,
His soul is marching on!
['John Brown's Body', song, 1861]

Hall, Jerry (1956–)
American fashion model

1. My mother said it was simple to keep a man, you must be a maid in the living room, a cook in the kitchen and a whore in the bedroom. I said I'd hire the other two and take care of the bedroom bit.
[*The Observer*, 1985, in Jeffrey Care (ed.), *Sayings of the Eighties* (1989)]

Hall, Joseph (1574–1656)
English bishop, satirical writer and poet

1. I first adventure: follow me who list,
And be the second English Satyrist.
[*Virgidemiae* (1598), I, Prologue]

2. Perfection is the child of Time.
[*Works* (1625)]

Hall, Owen (1854–1907)
British dramatist, critic, editor and lawyer

1. Tell me, pretty maiden, are there any more at home like you?
[*Floradora*, II]

Hall, Sir Peter (1930–)
English stage director

1. We do not necessarily improve with age: for better or worse we become more like ourselves.
[*The Observer*, 1988, in Jeffrey Care (ed.), *Sayings of the Eighties* (1989)]

Hall, Radclyffe (Marguerite Radclyffe-Hall) (1883–1943)

1. I am one of those whom God marked on the forehead. Like Cain, I am marked and blemished.
[*The Well of Loneliness* (1928)]

2. Acknowledge us, oh God, before the whole world. Give us also the right to our existence!
[*The Well of Loneliness* (1928)]

Hall, Rodney (1935–)
Australian poet and novelist

1. They're dying just the same in station homesteads
they're dying in Home Beautiful apartments
in among their lovely Danish furniture
on and across the furniture they're dying
spewing blood or stiffening dry and seeming never
to have been alive.
[*Black Bagatelles* (1978), 2, 'They're Dying Just the Same in Station Homesteads']

Halleck, Fitz-Greene (1790–1867)
American poet, satirist and banker

1. Green be the turf above thee,
Friend of my better days!
None knew thee but to love thee,
Nor named thee but to praise.
['On the Death of J.R. Drake' (1820)]

Halliday, J.

1. As sure as I'm a Scot
A redshank Norland haggis-eater.
[*Rustic Bard*, quoted in F. Marian McNeill, *The Scots Kitchen* (1929)]

Halm, Friedrich (Baron von Münch-Bellinghausen) (1806–1871)
German dramatist

1. *Mein Herz, ich will dich fragen:*
Was ist denn Liebe? Sag'!–
'Zwei Seelen und ein Gedanke,
Zwei Herzen und ein Schlag!'
'My heart, I want to ask you:
What is love? Tell me!'–
'Two souls with just one thought,
Two hearts with just one beat.'
[*Der Sohn der Wildnis* (*The Son of the Wilderness*, 1842), II]

Halsey, Margaret (1910–)
American writer

1. ... it takes a great deal to produce ennui in an Englishman and if you do, he only takes it as convincing proof that you are well-bred.
[*With Malice Toward Some* (1938)]

2. The attitude of the English ... toward English history reminds one a good deal of the attitude of a Hollywood director toward love.
[*With Malice Toward Some* (1938)]

3. Living in England, provincial England, must be like being married to a stupid but exquisitely beautiful wife.
[*With Malice Toward Some* (1938)]

4. ... the English think of an opinion as something which a decent person, if he has the misfortune to have one, does all he can to hide.
[*With Malice Toward Some* (1938)]

5. All of Stratford, in fact, suggests powdered history – add hot water and stir and you have a delicious, nourishing Shakespeare.
[*With Malice Toward Some* (1938)]

Halsey, Admiral W.F. ('Bull') (1882–1959)
American naval commander, noted for his Pacific campaigns in Second World War

1. Our ships have been salvaged and are retiring at high speed toward the Japanese fleet.
[Radio message, 1944, following claims by the Japanese that most of the American Third Fleet had been sunk or were retiring]

Hamerton, P.G. (1834–1894)
British artist and essayist

1. The art of reading is to skip judiciously.
[*The Intellectual Life* (1873), IV, Letter 4]

Hamilton, Elizabeth (1758–1816)
Scottish poet, novelist and essayist

1. With expectation beating high,
Myself I now desired to spy;
And straight I in a glass surveyed
An antique lady, much decayed.
[In Sarah Hale, *Biography of Distinguished Women* (1876)]

Hamilton, Gail (Mary A. Dodge) (1838–1896)
American teacher, essayist and journalist

1. The total depravity of inanimate things.
[Epigram]

Hamilton, Sir William (1788–1856)
Scottish metaphysical philosopher

1. Truth, like a torch, the more it's shook it shines.
[*Discussions on Philosophy* (1852), title page]
2. On earth there is nothing great but man; in man there is nothing great but mind.
[Quoting Phavorinus in *Lectures on Metaphysics and Logic* (1859), I, 2]

Hamilton, William (Willie) Winter (1917–)
British Labour politician; anti-royalist and teacher

1. The tourists who come to our island take in the Monarchy along with feeding the pigeons in Trafalgar Square.
[*My Queen and I* (1975), 9]
2. Britain is not a country that is easily rocked by revolution ... In Britain our institutions evolve. We are a Fabian Society writ large.
[*My Queen and I* (1975), 9]

Hammarskjöld, Dag (1905–1961)
Swedish statesman; Secretary General of the United Nations, 1953–61, and Nobel peace prize winner 1961

1. Pray that your loneliness may spur you into finding something to live for, great enough to die for.
[*Diaries*, 1951]
2. Never let success hide its emptiness from you, achievement its nothingness, toil its desolation. And so ... keep alive the incentive to push on further, that pain in the soul which drives us beyond ourselves ... Do not look back. And do not dream about the future, either. It will neither give you back the past, nor satisfy your other daydreams. Your duty, your reward – your destiny – are here and now.
[*Markings* (1965)]

Hammerstein II, Oscar (1895–1960)
American librettist and lyricist

1. Ol' man river, dat ol' man river,
He must know sumpin', but don't say nothin',
He jus' keeps rollin',
He jus' keeps rollin' along.
['Ol' Man River', song, 1927, from *Show Boat*]
2. The last time I saw Paris,
Her heart was warm and gay,
I heard the laughter of her heart in ev'ry street café.
['The Last Time I Saw Paris', song, 1940, from *Lady Be Good*]
3. Oh, what a beautiful mornin'!
Oh, what a beautiful day!
['Oh, What a Beautiful Mornin'', song, 1943, from *Oklahoma*]
4. Hello, young lovers, wherever you are.
['Hello, Young Lovers', song, 1951, from *The King and I*]
5. The hills are alive with the sound of music
With the songs they have sung
For a thousand years.
[Title song, 1959, from *The Sound of Music*]

Hammond, Percy (1873–1936)
American drama critic

1. [Referring to the daring brevity of skirts in a musical comedy, c. 1912]
The human knee is a joint, and not an entertainment.
[In Sullivan, *Our Times, III, Pre-War America* (1930), 10]
2. I have knocked everything but the knees of the chorus-girls, and Nature has anticipated me there.
[In *The Frank Muir Book: An Irreverant Companion to Social History* (1976)]

Hampton, Christopher (1946–)
English dramatist

1. You know very well that unless you're a scientist, it's much more important for a theory to be shapely, than for it to be true.
[*The Philanthropist* (1970), Scene i]
2. You see, I always divide people into two groups. Those who live by what they know to be a lie, and those who live by what they believe, falsely, to be the truth.
[*The Philanthropist* (1970), Scene vi]
3. If I had to give a definition of capitalism I would say: the process whereby American girls turn into American women.
[*Savages* (1973), Scene xvi]
4. It's possible to disagree with someone about the ethics of non-violence without wanting to kick his face in.
[*Treats* (1976), Scene iv]
5. Asking a working writer what he thinks about critics is like asking a lamp-post how it feels about dogs.
[*The Sunday Times Magazine*, 1977]

Hancock, John (1737–1793)
American statesman

1. [Remark as first signatory of the American Declaration of Independence, 1776]
There, I guess King George will be able to read that.
[Attr.]

Hancock, Sir William Keith (1898–1988)
Australian historian

1. Were it possible to compel the prison warders of this past age to produce for our inspection a 'typical' transported convict, they would show us, not the countryman who snared rabbits, but the Londoner who stole spoons.
[*Australia* (1930)]
2. The little exclusive circles, which in Melbourne and Sydney had politely imitated English gentility, looked askance at the lucky upstarts – and intermarried with them. In the second half of the nineteenth century Australia became familiar with a new vulgarity and a new vigour.
[*Australia* (1930)]

Handke, Peter (1942–)
German playwright

1. *Der gedankenloseste aller Menschen: der in jedem Buch nur blättert.*
The most unthinking person of all: the one who only flicks through every book.
[*Das Gewicht der Welt. Ein Journal (The Weight of the World. A Diary*, March, 1977)]

Handley, Tommy (1892–1949)
See ITMA

Hankey, Kate (1834–1911)
English evangelist

1. Tell me the old, old story
Of unseen things above,
Of Jesus and His glory,
Of Jesus and His love.
Tell me the story simply,
As to a little child;
For I am weak and weary,
And helpless, and defiled.
[Hymn, 1867]

Hanover, Ernst August, Elector of (1629–1698)

1. [On seeing Louis XIV's stables at Versailles]
Les chevaux du roi de France sont mieux logés que moi.
The king of France's horses are better housed than I am.
[Attr.]

Hanrahan, Brian (1949–)
Television news correspondent and reporter

1. [Reporting the British attack on Port Stanley airport, during the Falklands War]
I'm not allowed to say how many planes joined the raid but I counted them all out and I counted them all back.
[Report broadcast by BBC, 1 May 1982]

Haraucourt, Edmond (1856–1941)
French poet

1. *Partir c'est mourir un peu,*
C'est mourir à ce qu'on aime:
On laisse un peu de soi-même
En toute heure et dans tout lieu.
Leaving is dying a little,
Dying to one's loves:
One leaves behind a little of oneself
At every moment, everywhere.
[*Seul* (1891), 'Rondel de l'Adieu']

Harbord, James Guthrie (1866–1947)
American general, Chief of Staff during First World War

1. [Referring to Colonel House]
I met the great little man, the man who can be silent in several languages.
[In Dos Passos, *Mr Wilson's War* (1962), 15]

Harburg, E.Y. ('Yip') (1896–1981)
American lyricist, librettist and writer

1. Once I built a railroad. Now it's done–
Brother can you spare a dime?
['Brother Can You Spare a Dime?', song, 1932]

2. It's only a paper moon,
Sailing over a cardboard sea,
But it wouldn't be make-believe
If you believed in me.
['It's Only a Paper Moon', song, 1932]

3. Somewhere over the rainbow,
Way up high:
There's a land that I heard of
Once in a lullaby...

4. Somewhere over the rainbow,
Skies are blue,
And the dreams that you dare to dream
Really do come true.
['Over the Rainbow', song, 1939, from the musical *The Wizard of Oz*]

Harcourt, Sir William (1827–1904)
English statesman; Liberal Party leader, Chancellor of the Exchequer and lawyer

1. We are all Socialists now.
[Attr.]

Hardie, Keir (1856–1915)
Scottish socialist politician, co-founder of the Labour Party, trade unionist and orator

1. From his childhood onward this boy [the future Edward VIII] will be surrounded by sycophants and flatterers by the score – [Cries of 'Oh, oh!'] – and will be taught to believe himself as of a superior creation. [Cries of 'Oh, oh!'] A line will be drawn between him and the people whom he is to be called upon some day to reign over. In due course, following the precedent which has already been set, he will be sent on a tour round the world, and probably rumours of a morganatic alliance will follow – [Loud cries of 'Oh, oh!' and 'Order!'] – and the end of it all will be that the country will be called upon to pay the bill. – [Cries of 'Divide!']
[Speech, House of Commons, 1894]

Hardin, Salvor

1. Violence is the last refuge of the incompetent.
[Attr.]

Harding, Gilbert (1907–1960)
English writer and broadcaster

1. Before he [Gilbert Harding] could go to New York he had to get a US visa at the American consulate in Toronto. He was called upon to fill in a long form with many questions, including 'Is it your intention to overthrow the Government of the United States by force?' By the time Harding got to that one he was so irritated that he answered: 'Sole purpose of visit.'
[In W. Reyburn, *Gilbert Harding* (1978), 2]

Harding, Warren G. (1865–1923)
US statesman and 29th President, from 1921

1. America's present need is not heroics but healing, not nostrums but normalcy.
[Speech, Boston, May 1920]

Hardwicke, Philip Yorke, Earl of (1690–1764)
English judge and Lord Chancellor, 1737; proscribed the wearing of tartan

1. [Referring to Dirleton's *Doubts*]
His doubts are better than most people's certainties.
[In Boswell, *The Life of Samuel Johnson* (1791)]

Hardwood, Edward

1. Transported with the pleasure of this wonderful scene Peter cried out – How happy will it be for us to reside in this place.
[*A Liberal Translation of the New Testament; Being an Attempt*

to translate the Sacred writing with the same Freedom, Spirit and Elegance, with which other English Translations of the Greek Classics have lately been executed..., Matthew XVII, 4]

2. He then ordered his disciples to desire the multitudes to digest themselves into regular companies and to sit down on the verdant turf.
[*A Liberal Translation of the New Testament; Being an Attempt to translate the Sacred writing with the same Freedom, Spirit and Elegance, with which other English Translations of the Greek Classics have lately been executed...*, Mark VI, 39]

Hardy, Rev. E.J. (1849–1920)
Irish army chaplain and writer

1. How To Be Happy Though Married.
[Title of book, 1885]

Hardy, Frank (1917–)
Australian writer, journalist and playwright

1. Only the poor will help the poor.
[*Legends from Benson's Valley* (1963), 'It's Moments like These']

Hardy, Oliver (1892–1957)
American comedian, known for his film partnership with Stan Laurel; Academy Award, 1932

1. Here's another fine mess you've gotten me into.
[Catchphrase from many of his films (scripts by Stan Laurel) of the 1930s and 1940s]

Hardy, Thomas (1840–1928)
English poet, novelist, short-story writer and dramatist, best known for his Wessex novels set in rural England

1. 'You left us in tatters, without shoes or socks,
Tired of digging potatoes, and spudding up docks;
And now you've gay bracelets and bright feathers three!'–
'Yes: that's how we dress when we're ruined,' said she.
['The Ruined Maid' (1866)]

2. When I set out for Lyonnesse,
A hundred miles away,
The rime was on the spray,
And starlight lit my lonesomeness
When I set out for Lyonnesse
A hundred miles away...

3. When I came back from Lyonnesse
With magic in my eyes,
All marked with mute surmise
My radiance rare and fathomless,
When I came back from Lyonnesse
With magic in my eyes!
['When I Set Out for Lyonnesse' (1870)]

4. Here's not a modest maiden elf
But dreads the final Trumpet,
Lest half of her should rise herself,
And half some sturdy strumpet!
['The Levelled Churchyard' (1882)]

5. A little ball of feather and bone.
['Shelley's Skylark' (1887)]

6. Let him in whose ears the low-voiced Best is killed by the clash of the First,
Who holds that if way to the Better there be, it exacts a full look at the Worst,
Who feels that delight is a delicate growth cramped by crookedness, custom, and fear,
Get him up and be gone as one shaped awry; he disturbs the order here.
['In Tenebris II' (1895–1896)]

7. Yet saw he something in the lives
Of those who had ceased to live
That sphered them with a majesty
Which living failed to give.
['The Casterbridge Captains' (1898)]

8. William Dewy, Tranter Reuben, Farmer Ledlow late at plough,
Robert's kin, and John's, and Ned's,
And the Squire, and Lady Susan, lie in Mellstock churchyard now!...

9. Yet at mothy curfew-tide,
And at midnight when the noon-heat breathes it back from walls and leads,

They've a way of whispering to me – fellow-wight who yet abide–
In the muted, measured note
Of a ripple under archways, or a lone cave's stillicide...

10. 'Ye mid burn the old bass-viol that I set such value by.'...

11. 'If ye break my best blue china, children, I shan't care or ho.'
['Friends Beyond' (1898)]

12. But Time, to make me grieve,
Part steals, lets part abide;
And shakes this fragile frame at eve
With throbbings of noontide.
['I Look Into My Glass' (1898)]

13. When shall the saner, softer polities,
Whereof we dream, have sway in each proud land?
['Departure' (1899)]

14. His landmark is a kopje-crest
That breaks the veldt around;
And foreign constellations west
Each night above his mound...

15. Young Hodge the Drummer never knew–
Fresh from his Wessex home–
The meaning of the broad Karoo,
The Bush, the dusty loam...

16. Yet portion of that unknown plain
Will Hodge for ever be;
His homely Northern breast and brain
Grow to some Southern tree,
And strange-eyed constellations reign
His stars eternally.
['Drummer Hodge' (1899)]

17. At once a voice arose among
The bleak twigs overhead
In a full-hearted evensong
Of joy illimited;
An aged thrush, frail, gaunt, and small,
In blast-beruffled plume,
Had chosen thus to fling his soul
Upon the growing gloom.

So little cause for carolings
Of such ecstatic sound
Was written on terrestrial things
Afar or nigh around,
That I could think there trembled through
His happy good-night air
Some blessed Hope, whereof he knew

And I was unaware.
['The Darkling Thrush' (1900)]

18. I need not go
Through sleet and snow
To where I know
She waits for me;
She will tarry me there
Till I find it fair,
To have time to spare
From company.
['I need not go' (1901)]

19. Love is lame at fifty years.
['The Revisitation' (1904)]

20. Let me enjoy the earth no less
Because the all-enacting Might
That fashioned forth its loveliness
Had other aims than my delight.
['Let Me Enjoy' (1909)]

21. In a solitude of the sea
Deep from human vanity,
And the Pride of Life that planned her, stilly couches she.

Steel chambers, late the pyres
Of her salamandrine fires,
Cold currents thrid, and turn to rhythmic tidal lyres.

Over the mirrors meant
To glass the opulent
The sea-worm crawls – grotesque, slimed, dumb,
indifferent...

22. The Immanent Will that stirs and urges everything...

23. And as the smart ship grew
In stature, grace, and hue,
In shadowy silent distance grew the Iceberg too.

Alien they seemed to be:
No mortal eye could see
The intimate welding of their later history,

Or sign that they were bent
By paths coincident
On being anon twin halves of one august event,

Till the Spinner of the Years
Said 'Now!' And each one hears,
And consummation comes, and jars two hemispheres.
['The Convergence of the Twain' (Lines on the loss of the *Titanic*) (1912)]

24. O man-projected Figure, of late
Imaged as we, thy knell who shall survive?
Whence came it we were tempted to create
One whom we can no longer keep alive?
['God's Funeral' (1912)]

25. Queer are the ways of a man I know:
He comes and stands
In a careworn craze,
And looks at the sands
And the seaward haze
With moveless hands
And face and gaze,
Then turns to go...
And what does he see when he gazes so?
['The Phantom Horsewoman' (1913)]

26. We two kept house, the Past and I.
['The Ghost of the Past' (1914)]

27. What of the faith and fire within us
Men who march away
Ere the barn-cocks say
Night is growing gray?
['Men Who March Away' (1914)]

28. And both of us, scorning parochial ways,
Had lived like the wives in the patriarchs' days.
['Over the Coffin' (1914)]

29. Good-bye is not worth while!
['Without Ceremony' (1914)]

30. Only a man harrowing clods
In a slow silent walk
With an old horse that stumbles and nods
Half asleep as they stalk.

Only thin smoke without flame
From the heaps of couch grass;
Yet this will go onward the same
Though Dynasties pass.

Yonder a maid and her wight
Come whispering by:
War's annals will cloud into night
Ere their story die.
['In Time of 'The Breaking of Nations'' (1915)]

31. Christmas Eve, and twelve of the clock.
'Now they are all on their knees,'
An elder said as we sat in a flock
By the embers in hearthside ease...

32. If someone said on Christmas Eve,
'Come; see the oxen kneel

In the lonely barton by yonder coomb
Our childhood used to know,'
I should go with him in the gloom,
Hoping it might be so.
['The Oxen' (1915)]

33. When the Present has latched its postern behind my tremulous stay,
And the May month flaps its glad green leaves like wings,
Delicate-filmed as new-spun silk, will the neighbours say,
'He was a man who used to notice such things'?...

34. Some nocturnal blackness, mothy and warm,
When the hedgehog travels furtively over the lawn.
['Afterwards' (1917)]

35. Ah, no; the years, the years;
Down their carved names the rain-drop ploughs.
['During Wind and Rain' (1917)]

36. I am the family face;
Flesh perishes, I live on.
['Heredity' (1917)]

37. In the third-class seat sat the journeying boy,
And the roof-lamp's oily flame
Played down on his listless form and face,
Bewrapt past knowing to what he was going.
Or whence he came.
['Midnight on the Great Western' (1917)]

38. 'What do you think of it, Moon,
As you go?
Is Life much, or no?'
'O, I think of it, often think of it
As a show
God ought surely to shut up soon,
As I go.'
['To the Moon' (1917)]

39. Who's in the next room? – who?
I seemed to see

Somebody in the dawning passing through,
Unknown to me.
['Who's in the Next Room' (1917)]

40. This is the weather the cuckoo likes,
And so do I;
When showers betumble the chestnut spikes,
And nestlings fly:
And the little brown nightingale bills his best,
And they sit outside at 'The Travellers' Rest'...

41. This is the weather the shepherd shuns,
And so do I...

42. And drops on gate-bars hang in a row,
And rooks in families homeward go,
And so do I.
['Weathers' (1922)]

43. A car comes up, with lamps full-glare,
That flash upon a tree:
It has nothing to do with me,
And whangs along in a world of its own,
Leaving a blacker air.
['Nobody Comes' (1924)]

44. Any little old song
Will do for me.
['Any Little Old Song' (1925)]

45. Every branch big with it,
Bent every twig with it;
Every fork like a white web-foot;
Every street and pavement mute:
Some flakes have lost their way, and grope back upward, when
Meeting those meandering down they turn and descend again.
['Snow in the Suburbs' (1925)]

46. 'Peace upon earth!' was said. We sing it,
And pay a million priests to bring it.
After two thousand years of mass
We've got as far as poison-gas.
['Christmas: 1924' (1928)]

47. Well, World, you have kept faith with me,
Kept faith with me;
Upon the whole you have proved to be
Much as you said you were.
['He Never Expected Much, A Consideration on My Eighty-Sixth birthday (1928)']

48. Good, but not religious-good.
[*Under the Greenwood Tree* (1872), I, 2]

49. I like a story with a bad moral ... all true stories have a coarse touch or a bad moral, depend upon't. If the story-tellers could ha' got decency and good morals from true stories, who'd have troubled to invent parables?
[*Under the Greenwood Tree* (1872), I, 8]

50. That man's dumbness is wonderful to listen to.
[*Under the Greenwood Tree* (1872), II, 5]

51. The sovereign brilliancy of Sirius pierced the eye with a steely glitter, the star called Capella was yellow, Aldebaran and Betelgueux shone with a fiery red.
To persons standing alone on a hill during a clear midnight such as this, the roll of the world eastward is almost a palpable movement.
[*Far From the Madding Crowd* (1874), 2]

52. Ah! stirring times we live in – stirring times.
[*Far From the Madding Crowd* (1874), 15]

53. Five decades hardly modified the cut of a gaiter, the embroidery of a smock-frock, by the breadth of a hair. Ten generations failed to alter the turn of a single phrase. In these Wessex nooks the busy outsider's ancient times are only old; his old times are still new; his present is futurity.
[*Far From the Madding Crowd* (1874), 22]

54. Of course poets have morals and manners of their own, and custom is no argument with them.
[*The Hand of Ethelberta* (1876), 2]

55. A lover without indiscretion is no lover at all.
[*The Hand of Ethelberta* (1876), 20]

56. Ethelberta breathed a sort of exclamation, not right out, but stealthily, like a parson's damn.
[*The Hand of Ethelberta* (1876), 26]

57. The heaven being spread with this pallid screen and the earth with the darkest vegetation, their meeting-line at the horizon was clearly marked. In such contrast the heath wore the appearance of an instalment of night which had taken up its place before its astronomical hour was come: darkness had to a great extent arrived hereon, while day stood distinct in the sky.
[*The Return of the Native* (1878), 1]

58. In fact, precisely at this transitional point of its nightly roll into darkness the great and particular glory of the Egdon waste began, and nobody could be said to understand the heath who had not been there at such a time.
[*The Return of the Native* (1878), 1]

59. The great inviolate place had an ancient permanence which the sea cannot claim. Who can say of a particular sea that it is old? Distilled by the sun, kneaded by the moon, it is renewed in a year, in a day, or in an hour. The sea changed, the fields changed, the rivers, the villages, and the people changed, yet Egdon remained.
[*The Return of the Native* (1878), 1]

60. ... the long, laborious road, dry, empty, and white. It was quite open to the heath on each side, and bisected that vast dark surface like the parting-line on a head of black hair, diminishing and bending away on the furthest horizon.
[*The Return of the Native* (1878), 2]

61. 'Well, pour soul; she's helpless to hinder that or anything now,' answered Mother Cuxsom. 'And all her shining keys will be took from her, and her cupboards opened, and things a' didn't wish seen, anybody will see; and her little wishes and ways will all be as nothing!'
[*The Mayor of Casterbridge* (1886), 18]

62. Dialect words – those terrible marks of the beast to the truly genteel.
[*The Mayor of Casterbridge* (1886), 20]

63. Michael Henchard's Will.
That Elizabeth-Jane Farfrae be not told of my death, or made to grieve on account of me.
& that I be not bury'd in consecrated ground.
& that no sexton be asked to toll the bell.
& that nobody is wished to see my dead body.
& that no murners walk behind me at my funeral.
& that no flours be planted on my grave.
& that no man remember me.
To this I put my name.
[*The Mayor of Casterbridge* (1886), 45]

64. You was a good man, and did good things!
[*The Woodlanders* (1887), last line]

65. A little one-eyed, blinking sort o' place.
[*Tess of the D'Urbervilles* (1891), I, 1]

66. Always washing, and never getting finished.
[*Tess of the D'Urbervilles* (1891), I, 4]

67. 'Justice' was done, and the President of the Immortals, in Aeschylean phrase, had ended his sport with Tess.
[*Tess of the D'Urbervilles* (1891), VII, 59]

68. Life's Little Ironies.
[Title of a book of stories, 1894]

69. What of the Immanent Will and Its designs?
It works unconsciously, as heretofore,
Eternal artistries in Circumstance.
[*The Dynasts*, Part I (1903), Fore Scene]

70. Like a knitter drowsed,
Whose fingers play in skilled unmindfulness,
The Will has woven with an absent heed
Since life first was; and ever will so weave.
[*The Dynasts*, Part I (1903), Fore Scene]

71. The nether sky opens, and Europe is disclosed as a prone and emaciated figure, the Alps shaping like a backbone, and the branching mountain-chains like ribs, the peninsular plateau of Spain forming a head.
[*The Dynasts*, Part I (1903), Fore Scene, stage direction]

72. A local cult called Christianity.
[*The Dynasts*, Part I (1903), I.vi]

73. My argument is that War makes rattling good history; but Peace is poor reading.
[*The Dynasts*, Part I (1903), II.v]

74. But see the intolerable antilogy
Of making figments feel.
[*The Dynasts* Part I (1903), IV.v]

75. But what's one woman's fortune more or less
Beside the schemes of kings!
[*The Dynasts*, Part II (1906), VI.iii]

76. If Galileo had said in verse that the world moved, the Inquisition might have let him alone.
[In F.E. Hardy, *The Later Years of Thomas Hardy* (1930), I, 4]

77. Clouds, mists and mountains are unimportant beside the wear on a threshold or the print of a hand.
[Attr.]

Hare, Julius (1795–1855) and **Hare,** Augustus (1792–1834)
English clergymen, writers and brothers

1. Truth, when witty, is the wittiest of all things.
[*Guesses at Truth* (1827), I]

2. Half the failures in life arise from pulling in one's horse as he is leaping.
[*Guesses at Truth* (1827), I]

3. Purity is the feminine, Truth the masculine, of Honour.
[*Guesses at Truth* (1827), I]

4. Every Irishman, the saying goes, has a potato in his head.
[*Guesses at Truth* (1827), I]

Hare, Maurice Evan (1886–1967)
English limerick writer

1. There once was a man who said, 'Damn!
It is borne in upon me I am
An engine that moves
In predestinate grooves,
I'm not even a bus, I'm a tram.'
['Limerick', 1905]

2. Alfred de Musset
Used to call his cat Pusset.
His accent was affected.
That was only to be expected.
['Byway in Biography']

Hargreaves, W.F. (1846–1919)
British songwriter

1. I'm Burlington Bertie:
I rise at ten-thirty and saunter along like a toff,
I walk down the Strand with my gloves on my hand,
Then I walk down again with them off.
['Burlington Bertie from Bow', song, 1915]

Harington, Sir John (1561–1612)
English courtier, godson of Queen Elizabeth and satirist

1. When I make a feast,
I would my guests should praise it, not the cooks.
[*Epigrams* (1618), I, 5, 'Against Writers that Carp at Other Men's Books'. Cf. Martial: 8]

2. Treason doth never prosper, what's the reason?
For if it prosper, none dare call it treason.
[*Epigrams* (1618), IV, 5, 'Of Treason']

Harkness, Richard

1. What is a committee? A group of the unwilling, picked from the unfit, to do the unnecessary.
[*New York Herald Tribune*, 1960]

Harlech, Lord (David Ormsby-Gore) (1918–1985)
English MP, ambassador and television company chairman

1. In the end it may well be that Britain will be honoured by historians more for the way she disposed of an empire than for the way in which she acquired it.
[*New York Times*, 1962]

Harlow, Jean (1911–1937)
American leading film actress and 'platinum blonde'

1. Excuse me while I slip into something more comfortable.
[*Hell's Angels*, film, 1930; script by Howard Estabrook and Harry Behn]

Harney, Bill (1895–1962)
Australian writer of the bush and the Aborigines

1. [Advice on bush cooking]
You always want to garnish it when it's orf.
[On long-playing record 'Talkabout', c. 1960]

Harold II, King of England (c. 1022–1066)
King in 1066 when defeated by William the Conqueror at the Battle of Hastings

1. [His offer to Harald, King of Norway, who invaded England shortly before William the Conqueror]
He will give him seven feet of English ground, or as much more as he may be taller than other men.
[Attr.]

Harper, Arthur P.

1. [On Lake Maporike]
[Such lakes] are all supposed by the inhabitants to be bottomless. I do not know why, except that people seem to look upon a bottomless lake as a luxury, and are very angry with the man who destroys the illusion . . . When I sounded in fourteen places, and found bottom always within 280 ft.,

many of the inhabitants of the district took it as a personal insult, and have never quite forgiven me.
[*Pioneer Work in the Alps of New Zealand* (1896)]

Harpur, Charles (1813–1868)
Australian poet

1. Not a sound disturbs the air,
There is quiet everywhere;
Over plains and over woods
What a mighty stillness broods!
All the birds and insects keep
Where the coolest shadows sleep;
Even the busy ants are found
Resting in their pebbled mound;
Even the locust clingeth now
Silent to the barky bough:
Over hills and over plains
Quiet, vast and slumbrous, reigns.
['A Midsummer Noon in the Australian Forest' (1883)]

Harris, Charles (1865–1930)
American songwriter, music publisher and autobiographer

1. Many a heart is aching, if you could read them all,
Many the hopes that have vanished, after the ball.
['After the Ball', 1892]

Harris, George (1844–1922)
American Congregational minister and educator

1. [In his address to students at the beginning of a new academic year]
I intended to give you some advice but now I remember how much is left over from last year unused.
[In Braude, *Braude's Second Encyclopedia* (1957)]

Harris, Joel Chandler (1848–1908)
American humorist; journalist, short-story writer and novelist

1. A contrapshun what he call a Tar-Baby.
[*Uncle Remus* (1881), 'Legends of the Old Plantation', 2, 'The Wonderful Tar-Baby']
2. Tar-baby ain't sayin' nuthin', en Brer Fox, he lay low.
[*Uncle Remus* (1881), 'Legends of the Old Plantation', 2, 'The Wonderful Tar-Baby']
3. Bred en bawn in a brier-patch!
[*Uncle Remus* (1881), 'Legends of the Old Plantation', 4, 'How Mr Rabbit Was Too Sharp for Mr Fox']
4. Lounjun 'roun' en suffer'n'.
[*Uncle Remus* (1881), 'Legends of the Old Plantation', 12, 'Mr Fox Tackles Old Man Tarrypin']
5. I'm de'f in one year, en I can't hear out'n de udder.
[*Uncle Remus* (1881), 'Legends of the Old Plantation', 19, 'The Fate of Mr Jack Sparrow']
6. Old man Know-All died las' year.
[*Uncle Remus* (1881), 'Plantation Proverbs']
7. Lazy fokes' stummucks don't git tired.
[*Uncle Remus* (1881), 'Plantation Proverbs']
8. Licker talks mighty loud w'en it git loose fum de jug.
[*Uncle Remus* (1881), 'Plantation Proverbs']
9. Hongry rooster don't cackle w'en he fine a wum.
[*Uncle Remus* (1881), 'Plantation Proverbs']
10. Youk'n hide de fier, but w'at you gwine do wid de smoke?
[*Uncle Remus* (1881), 'Plantation Proverbs']
11. Oh, whar shill we go w'en de great day comes,
Wid de blowin' er de trumpits en de bangin' er de drums?
How many po' sinners'll be kotched out late
En find no latch ter de golden gate?
[*Uncle Remus* (1881), 'His Songs', 1, 'Revival Hymn']
12. 'Law, Brer Tarrypin!' sez Brer Fox, sezee, 'you ain't see no trouble yit. Ef you wanter see sho' nuff trouble, you des oughter go 'longer me; I'm de man w'at kin show you trouble,' sezee.
[*Nights with Uncle Remus* (1883), 17, 'Mr Fox Figures as an Incendiary']
13. Hit look lak sparrer-grass, hit feel lak sparrer-grass, hit tas'e lak sparrer-grass, en I bless ef 'taint sparrer-grass.
[*Nights with Uncle Remus* (1883), 27, 'Brother Wolf Says Grace']
14. De wimmen, dey does de talkin' en de flyin', en de mens, dey does de walkin' en de pryin', en betwixt en betweenst um, dey ain't much dat don't come out.
[*Nights with Uncle Remus* (1883), 30, 'Brother Rabbit and His Famous Foot']
15. All by my own-alone self.
[*Nights with Uncle Remus* (1883), 36, 'Brother Wolf Falls a Victim']

Harris, Max (1921–1995)
Australian critic, poet and publisher

1. We know no mithridatum of despair
as drunks, the angry penguins of the night,
straddling the cobbles of the square,
tying a shoelace by fogged lamplight.
[*The Gift of Blood* (1940), 'Progress of Defeat']
2. In an atmosphere of reciprocal banter or rubbishing Australians can express mutual affection without running into risk of indecently exposing states of feeling.
[In Keith Dunstan, *Knockers* (1972)]
3. The Australian world is peopled with good blokes and bastards, but not heroes.
[In Peter Coleman (ed.), *Australian Civilization*]

Harris, Rolf (1930–)
Australian entertainer and TV personality

1. Play your didgeridoo, Blue,
Play your didgeridoo.
Keep playing 'til I shoot thro', Blue,
Play your didgeridoo.
Altogether now!

Tan me hide when I'm dead, Fred,
Tan me hide when I'm dead.
So we tanned his hide when he died, Clyde,
And that's it hanging on the head.

Chorus
Tie me kangaroo down, sport,
Tie me kangaroo down,
Tie me kangaroo down, sport,
Tie me kangaroo down.
['Tie Me Kangaroo Down, Sport', song]

Harrison, Tony (1937–)
British poet

1. When the chilled dough of his flesh went in an oven
not unlike those he fuelled all his life,
I thought of his cataracts ablaze with Heaven
and radiant with the sight of his dead wife,
light streaming from his mouth to shape her name,

'not Florence and not Flo but always Florrie'.
[*Continuous* (1981), 'Marked with D.']

2. Perhaps with age I've learned to let go of things and people, not to possess or confine them.
[Attr.]

Hart, Lorenz (1895–1943)
American lyricist; wrote musical shows with composer Richard Rodgers

1. I get too hungry
For dinner at eight,
I like the theatre
but never come late.
I never bother with people I hate,
That's why the lady is a tramp.
['That's Why the Lady is a Tramp', song, 1937, from *Babes in Arms*]

Harte, Bret (1836–1902)
American poet, humorist, short-story writer, editor and consul

1. If, of all words of tongue and pen,
The saddest are, 'It might have been,'
More sad are these we daily see:
'It is, but hadn't ought to be!'
['Mrs Judge Jenkins' (1867). Cf. Whittier: 2]

2. I reside at Table Mountain, and my name is Truthful James;
I am not up to small deceit, or any sinful games...

3. And he smiled a kind of sickly smile, and curled up on the floor,
And the subsequent proceedings interested him no more.
['The Society upon the Stanislaus' (1868)]

4. And on that grave where English oak and holly
And laurel wreaths entwine
Deem it not all a too presumptuous folly,–
This spray of Western pine!
['Dickens in Camp' (1870)]

5. Thar ain't no sense
In gittin' riled!
['Jim' (1870)]

Hartley, L.P. (1895–1972)
English novelist, short-story writer and critic

1. 'Should I call myself an egoist?' Miss Johnstone mused. 'Others have called me so. They merely meant I did not care for them.'
[*Simonetta Perkins* (1925)]

2. The past is a foreign country: they do things differently there.
[*The Go-Between* (1953), first sentence]

3. Once she had loved her fellow human beings; she did not love them now, she had seen them do too many unpleasant things.
[*Facial Justice* (1960)]

Harvey, William (1578–1657)
English physician; discovered the circulation of the blood

1. *Ex ovo omnia.*
Everything is from an egg.
[*Exercitationes de Generatione Animalium* (1651)]

Harwood, Gwen (1920–)
Australian poet and former music teacher

1. 'It's so sweet
to hear their chatter, watch them grow and thrive,'
she says to his departing smile. Then, nursing
the youngest child, sits staring at her feet.
To the wind she says, 'They have eaten me alive.'
[*Poems* (1968), II, 'In the Park']

2. My ghost, my self, most intimate stranger
standing beneath these lyric trees
with your one wineglass of morning
snatched from the rushing galaxies,

bright-haired and satin-lipped you offer
the youth I shall not taste again.
I know, I bear to know, your future
unlooked-for love, undreamed-of pain.
['In Brisbane']

Haskell, Arnold (1903–1980)
English balletomane and writer

1. [Of Dame Nellie Melba]
Unlike so many who find success, she remained a 'dinkum hard-swearing Aussie' to the end.
[*Waltzing Matilda* (1942)]

Haskins, Minnie Louise (1875–1957)
English teacher and writer

1. [Quoted by King George VI in his Christmas broadcast, 1939]
And I said to a man who stood at the gate of the year: 'Give me a light that I may tread safely into the unknown.' And he replied: 'Go out into the darkness and put your hand into the hand of God. That shall be to you better than a light, and safer than a known way.'
[*The Desert* (1908), 'God Knows']

Hassall, Christopher (1912–1963)
English actor, lyricist and composer

1. [On Edith Sitwell]
She's genuinely bogus.
[Attr.]

Hastings, Lady Flora (1806–1839)
Scottish poet and royal attendant

1. Grieve not that I die young. Is it not well
To pass away ere life hath lost its brightness?
['Swan Song']

Hastings, H. de Cronin (1902–1986)
British editor of architectural journals and writer

1. Worm's eye view.
[Caption to photograph in the *Architectural Review*, c. 1932 and passim]

Hattersley, Roy (1932–)
British Labour politician and author

1. Familiarity with evil breeds not contempt but acceptance.
[*The Guardian*, 1993]

Hatton, Will

1. [To his partner Ethel Manners]
Don't you know there's a war on?
[Catchphrase, 1940s]

Havel, Václav (1936–)
Czech dramatist, essayist and statesman

1. Ideology is a special way of relating to the world. It offers human beings the illusion of an identity, of dignity, and of

morality, while making it easier for them to part with it.
[*Living in Truth* (1987), 'The Power of the Powerless']

Havers, Sir Michael (1923–)
English lawyer and politician

1. [On the offer of immunity from prosecution made to the spy, Sir Anthony Blunt, in 1964]
He maintained his denial. He was offered immunity from prosecution. He sat in silence for a while. He got up, looked out of the window, poured himself a drink and after a few minutes confessed. Later he co-operated, and he continued to co-operate. That is how the immunity was given and how Blunt responded.
[Speech as Attorney-General, House of Commons, 21 November 1979]

Hawes, Stephen (d. c. 1523)
English allegorical poet and royal groom

1. Whan the lytell byrdes swetely dyde synge
Laudes to theyr maker erly in the mornynge.
[*The Passetyme of Pleasure* (1509), 33]

2. For though the day be never so longe,
At last the belles ryngeth to evensonge.
[*The Passetyme of Pleasure* (1509), 42]

Hawke, Bob (1929–)
Australian statesman; former Prime Minister

1. We are still prisoners of our colonial history.
[*The Resolution of Conflict* (1979)]

2. [On Bill Hayden, appointed by Hawke's Labor government to the position of Governor-General in 1989]
A prick with a limited future.
[Remark at ALP conference, Adelaide, 1979, quoted by Peter Couchman, ABC Television, 1986]

3. [On first entering Parliament, 1979]
Well, I don't want to be any more egotistical than possible. I have total confidence in my ability.
[In Thomson and Butel (eds), *The World According to Hawke*]

4. This stuff about the meek inheriting the earth is a lot of bullshit. The weak need the strong to look after 'em.
[In Craig McGregor, *The Australian People*]

Hawker, Robert Stephen (1803–1875)
English poet, antiquary and clergyman

1. And have they fixed the where and when?
And shall Trelawney die?
Here's twenty thousand Cornish men
Will know the reason why!
['The Song of the Western Men', based on a 17th century ballad]

Hawthorne, Nathaniel (1804–1864)
American allegorical novelist, short-story and children's writer

1. She named the infant 'Pearl', as being of great price, – purchased with all she had, – her mother's only treasure.
[*The Scarlet Letter* (1850)]

2. I have laughed in bitterness and agony of heart, at the contrast between what I seem and what I am!
[*The Scarlet Letter* (1850)]

3. Life is made up of marble and mud.
[*The House of the Seven Gables* (1851), 2]

4. What other dungeon is so dark as one's own heart! What jailer so inexorable as one's self!
[*The House of the Seven Gables* (1851), 11]

5. Dr Johnson's morality was as English an article as a beefsteak.
[*Our Old Home* (1863), 'Lichfield and Uttoxeter']

6. We sometimes congratulate ourselves at the moment of waking from a troubled dream; it may be so the moment after death.
[*American Notebooks*]

Hay, Ian (John Hay Beith) (1876–1952)
Scottish novelist and dramatist

1. Funny-peculiar or funny-ha-ha?
[*The Housemaster* (1938), III]

Hay, Will (1888–1949)
British music hall and film comedian

1. *Master*: They split the atom by firing particles at it, at 5,500 miles a second.
Boy: Good heavens. And they only split it?
[*The Fourth Form at St Michael's* (c. 1925), 'The Inkstains Theory']

Hayden, Bill (1933–)
Australian statesman

1. I'm a Christian socialist who happens to be an atheist.
[*Age*, 1983]

2. [On the Premier of New South Wales, Barry Unsworth]
If you're the sort of person who gets your simple pleasures out of life tearing wings off dying butterflies, then Barry's your man.
[*Bulletin*, 1986]

3. [Gough Whitlam] had many geniuses and one of them was that when he decided we were going to embark on one of the great national disasters, it was done with flair.
[*Sydney Morning Herald*, 1988]

Hayes, J. Milton (1884–1940)
British writer

1. There's a one-eyed yellow idol to the north of Khatmandu,
There's a little marble cross below the town;
There's a broken-hearted woman tends the grave of Mad Carew,
And the Yellow God forever gazes down.
['The Green Eye of the Yellow God' (1911)]

Hazlitt, William (1778–1830)
English essayist, critic and journalist

1. Wrong dressed out in pride, pomp, and circumstance, has more attraction than abstract right.
[*Characters of Shakespeare's Plays* (1817), 'Coriolanus']

2. There is nothing good to be had in the country, or, if there is, they will not let you have it.
[*The Round Table* (1817), 'Observations on Mr Wordsworth's Poem The Excursion']

3. The art of pleasing consists in being pleased.
[*The Round Table* (1817), 'On Manner']

4. [Of Coleridge]
He talked on for ever; and you wished him to talk on for ever.
[*Lectures on the English Poets* (1818), 'On the Living Poets'. Cf. Hazlitt: 23]

5. It is better to be able neither to read nor write than to be able to do nothing else.
[*The Edinburgh Magazine*, 1818, 'On the Ignorance of the Learned']

6. You will hear more good things on the outside of a stage-coach from London to Oxford, than if you were to pass a twelvemonth with the under-graduates, or heads of colleges, of that famous city; and more home truths are to be learnt from listening to a noisy debate in an ale-house, than from attending to a formal one in the House of Commons.
[*The Edinburgh Magazine*, 1818, 'On the Ignorance of the Learned']

7. A nickname is the heaviest stone that the devil can throw at a man.
[*The Edinburgh Magazine*, 1818, 'On Nicknames']

8. Rules and models destroy genius and art.
[*The Edinburgh Magazine*, 1818, 'Thoughts on Taste']

9. Spleen can subsist on any kind of food.
[*Lectures on the English Comic Writers* (1819), 'On Wit and Humour']

10. The love of liberty is the love of others; the love of power is the love of ourselves.
[*Political Essays* (1819), 'The Times Newspaper']

11. A person may be indebted for a nose or an eye, for a graceful carriage or a voluble discourse, to a great-aunt or uncle, whose existence he has scarcely heard of.
[*London Magazine*, 1821, 'On Personal Character'; reprinted in *The Plain Speaker* (1826)]

12. I do not think there is anything deserving the name of society to be found out of London.
[*Table-Talk* (1822), 'On Coffee-House Politicians']

13. To great evils we submit, we resent little provocations.
[*Table-Talk* (1822), 'On Great and Little Things']

14. There is not a more mean, stupid, dastardly, pitiful, selfish, spiteful, envious, ungrateful animal than the Public. It is the greatest of cowards, for it is afraid of itself.
[*Table-Talk* (1822), 'On Living to One's-self']

15. Violent antipathies are always suspicious, and betray a secret affinity.
[*Table-Talk* (1822), 'On Vulgarity and Affection']

16. One of the pleasantest things in the world is going a journey; but I like to go by myself.
[*Table-Talk* (1822), 'On Going a Journey']

17. When I am in the country, I wish to vegetate like the country.
[*Table-Talk* (1822), 'On Going a Journey']

18. Give me the clear blue sky over my head, and the green turf beneath my feet, a winding road before me, and a three hours' march to dinner – and then to thinking! It is hard if I cannot start some game on these lone heaths.
[*Table-Talk* (1822), 'On Going a Journey']

19. The incognito of an inn is one of its striking privileges.
[*Table-Talk* (1822), 'On Going a Journey']

20. The English (it must be owned) are rather a foul-mouthed nation.
[*Table-Talk* (1822), 'On Criticism']

21. Man is an intellectual animal, and therefore an everlasting contradiction to himself. His senses centre in himself, his ideas reach to the ends of the universe; so that he is torn in pieces between the two, without a possibility of its ever being otherwise.
[*Characteristics* (1823), 158]

22. If the world were good for nothing else, it is a fine subject for speculation.
[*Characteristics* (1823), 302]

23. [Of Coleridge]
The round-faced man in black entered, and dissipated all doubts on the subject by beginning to talk. He did not cease while he stayed; nor has he since, that I know of.
[*The Liberal*, 1823, 'My First Acquaintance with Poets'; reprinted in *Literary Remains* (1836), II. Cf. Hazlitt: 4]

24. So have I loitered my life away, reading books, looking at pictures, going to plays, hearing, thinking, writing on what pleased me best. I have wanted only one thing to make me happy; but wanting that, have wanted everything!
[*The Liberal*, 1823, 'My First Acquaintance with Poets'; reprinted in *Literary Remains* (1836), II]

25. He writes as fast as they can read, and he does not write himself down.
[*The Spirit of the Age* (1825), 'Sir Walter Scott']

26. His worst is better than any other person's best.
[*The Spirit of the Age* (1825), 'Sir Walter Scott']

27. His works (taken together) are almost like a new edition of human nature. This is indeed to be an author!
[*The Spirit of the Age* (1825), 'Sir Walter Scott']

28. Sir Walter would make a bad hand of a description of the Millennium, unless he could lay the scene in Scotland five hundred years ago, and then he would want facts and worm-eaten parchments to support his drooping style.
[*The Spirit of the Age* (1825), 'Sir Walter Scott']

29. We can scarcely hate any one that we know.
[*Table-Talk* (1825), 'Why Distant Objects Please']

30. [On the hatred of spiders]
It will ask another hundred years of fine writing and hard thinking to cure us of the prejudice.
[*The Plain Speaker* (1826), 'On the Pleasure of Hating']

31. The dupe of friendship, and the fool of love; have I not reason to hate and to despise myself? Indeed I do; and chiefly for not having hated and despised the world enough.
[*The Plain Speaker* (1826), 'On the Pleasure of Hating']

32. No young man believes he shall ever die.
[*Monthly Magazine*, 1827, 'On the Feeling of Immortality in Youth']

33. There is an unseemly exposure of the mind, as well as of the body.
[*Monthly Magazine*, 1827, 'On Disagreeable People']

34. The greatest offence against virtue is to speak ill of it.
[*London Weekly Review*, 1828, 'On Cant and Hypocrisy']

35. The least pain in our little finger gives us more concern and uneasiness, than the destruction of millions of our fellow-beings.
[*Edinburgh Review*, 1829, 50, 'American Literature – Dr Channing']

36. The most fluent talkers or most plausible reasoners are not always the justest thinkers.
[*Atlas* (1830), 'On Prejudice']

37. We never do anything well till we cease to think about the manner of doing it.
[*Atlas* (1830), 'On Prejudice']

38. But of all footmen the lowest class is literary footmen.
[*New Monthly Magazine*, 1830, 'Footmen']

39. Food, warmth, sleep, and a book; these are all I at present ask.
[*London Weekly Review*, 'A Farewell to Essay-Writing']

40. [Last words]
Well, I've had a happy life.
[In W.C. Hazlitt, *Memoirs of William Hazlitt* (1867), II, 18]

Hazzard, Shirley (1931–)
Australian novelist and short-story writer

1. When we are young, she thought, we worship romantic love for the wrong reasons . . . and, because of that, subsequently repudiate it. Only later, and for quite other reasons, we discover its true importance. And by then it has become tiring even to observe.
[*The Evening of a Holiday* (1966), 2]

2. Going to Europe, someone had written, was about as final as going to heaven. A mystical passage to another life, from which no one returned the same.
[*The Transit of Venus* (1980), 5]

Healey, Denis (1917–)
English Labour politician and author; Chancellor of the Exchequer 1974–79

1. I warn you there are going to be howls of anguish from the 80,000 people who are rich enough to pay over 75% on the last slice of their income.
[Speech, Labour Party Conference, 1 October 1973]

2. [On Geoffrey Howe's attack on his Budget proposals]
Like being savaged by a dead sheep.
[Speech, House of Commons, 1978]

3. Silly Billy!
[Catchphrase, invented for him by Mike Yarwood, the impressionist, and then sometimes used by him]

4. [Of Conservatives]
Their Europeanism is nothing but imperialism with an inferiority complex.
[*The Observer*, 'Sayings of the Week', 1962]

5. [Of Mrs Thatcher]
For the past few months she has been charging about like some bargain basement Boadicea.
[*The Observer*, 1982, in Jeffrey Care (ed.), *Sayings of the Eighties* (1989)]

6. Examining one's entrails while fighting a battle is a recipe for certain defeat.
[*The Observer*, 1983, in Jeffrey Care (ed.), *Sayings of the Eighties* (1989)]

7. I plan to be the Gromyko of the Labour Party.
[*Sunday Times*, 1984]

8. It is a good thing to follow the first law of holes; if you are in one, stop digging.
[*The Observer*, 1988, in Jeffrey Care (ed.), *Sayings of the Eighties* (1989)]

Heaney, Seamus (1939–)
Irish poet and critic

1. Between my finger and my thumb
The squat pen rests.
I'll dig with it.
[*Death of a Naturalist* (1966), 'Digging']

2. As a child, they could not keep me from wells
And old pumps with buckets and windlasses.
I loved the dark drop, the trapped sky, the smells
Of waterweed fungus and dank moss.
[*Death of a Naturalist* (1966), 'Personal Helicon']

3. Who would connive
in civilised outrage
yet understand the exact
and tribal, intimate revenge.
[*North* (1975), 'Punishment']

4. 'Now you're supposed to be
An educated man,'
I hear him say. 'Puzzle me
The right answer to that one.'
[*Field Work* (1979), 'Casualty']

5. Our road is steaming, the turned-up acres breathe.
Now the good life could be to cross a field
And art a paradigm of earth new from the lathe
Of ploughs. My lea is deeply tilled.
Old ploughsocks gorge the subsoil of each sense
And I am quickened with a redolence
Of farmland as a dark unblown rose.
[*Field Work* (1979), 'Glanmore Sonnets', I]

6. And in that dream I dreamt – how like you this?–
Our first night years ago in that hotel
When you came with your deliberate kiss
To raise us towards the lovely and painful
Covenants of flesh; our separateness;
The respite in our dewy dreaming faces.
[*Field Work* (1979), 'Glanmore Sonnets', X]

7. Don't be surprised
If I demur, for, be advised
My passport's green.
No glass of ours was ever raised
To toast the Queen.
[*An Open Letter*, Field Day pamphlet no. 2, 1983]

8. Her dimpled angled elbow
and intent stoop
as she aimed the smoothing iron

like a plane into linen,
like the resentment of women.
To work, her dumb lunge says,
is to move a certain mass

through a certain distance,
is to pull your weight and feel
exact and equal to it.
Feel dragged upon. And buoyant.
[*Station Island* (1984), 'Shelf Life: 2, Old Smoothing Iron']

9. To forge a poem is one thing, to forge the uncreated conscience of the race, as Stephen Dedalus put it, is quite another and places daunting pressures and responsibilities on anyone who would risk the name of poet.
[*Preoccupations, Selected Prose 1968–1978*, 'Feeling into Words']

Hearst, William Randolph (1863–1951)
American newspaper proprietor, known for his revolutionary sensationalist approach to journalism

1. [Instruction to artist Frederic Remington, who wished to return from peaceful Havana in spring 1898]
Please remain. You furnish the pictures and I'll furnish the war.
[In Winkler, *W.R. Hearst* (1928), 6; later denied by Hearst]

Heath, Sir Edward (1916–)
English statesman; Conservative Prime Minister, 1970–74, and author

1. Nor would it be in the interests of the [European] Community that its enlargement should take place except

with the full-hearted consent of the Parliament and people of the new member countries.
[Speech to the Franco-British Chamber of Commerce, Paris, 1970]

2. [On the Lonrho affair (involving tax avoidance)]
The unpleasant and unacceptable face of capitalism.
[Speech, House of Commons, 1973]

3. The real problem in life is to have sufficient time to think.
[*The Observer*, 1981, in Jeffrey Care (ed.), *Sayings of the Eighties* (1989)]

Heber, Reginald (1783–1826)

English Bishop of Calcutta, 1822–26; traveller, poet and hymn-writer

1. Brightest and best of the sons of the morning!
Dawn on our darkness and lend us Thine aid!
[Hymn, 1811, Epiphany]

2. From Greenland's icy mountains,
From India's coral strand,
Where Afric's sunny fountains
Roll down their golden sand;
From many an ancient river,
From many a palmy plain,
They call us to deliver
Their land from error's chain!...

3. Though every prospect pleases,
And only man is vile.
[Hymn, 1821]

4. Holy, holy, holy, Lord God Almighty!
Early in the morning our song shall rise to thee.
[Hymn, 1827, Trinity Sunday]

5. By cool Siloam's shady rill
How sweet the lily grows!
[Hymn, First Sunday After Epiphany, no. II]

Hegel, Georg Wilhelm (1770–1831)

Influential German idealist philosopher, noted for his dialectic

1. *Was vernünftig ist; das ist wirklich: und was wirklich ist, das ist vernünftig.*
What is rational is real, and what is real is rational.
[*Grundlinien der Philosophie des Rechts* (*Basis of Legal Philosophy*, 1820), Preface]

2. *Was die Erfahrung aber und die Geschichte lehren, ist dieses, dass Völker und Regierungen niemals etwas aus der Geschichte gelernt ... haben.*
What experience and history teach us, however, is this, that peoples and governments have never learned anything from history.
[*Vorlesungen über die Philosophie der Geschichte* (*Lectures on the Philosophy of History*, 1837), Introduction]

3. [Said on his deathbed]
Only one man ever understood me ... And he didn't understand me.
[In B. Conrad, *Famous Last Words* (1962)]

Heine, Heinrich (1797–1856)

German lyric poet; essayist and journalist

1. *Dort, wo man Bücher*
Verbrennt, verbrennt man auch am Ende Menschen.
It is there, where they
Burn books, that eventually they burn people too.
[*Almansor: A Tragedy* (1820–1821)]

2. *Auf Flügeln des Gesanges.*
On wings of song.
[*Buch der Lieder* (*Book of Songs*), 'Lyrisches Intermezzo' (1822–1823), IX, first line]

3. *Es ist eine alte Geschichte,*
Doch bleibt sie immer neu.
It is an old story, yet it remains forever new.
[*Buch der Lieder* (*Book of Songs*), 'Lyrisches Intermezzo' (1822–1823), XXXIX]

4. *Ich weiss nicht, was soll es bedeuten,*
Dass ich so traurig bin;
Ein Märchen aus alten Zeiten,
Das kommt mir nicht aus dem Sinn.
I do not know the meaning of my sadness; there is an old fairy tale that I cannot get out of my mind.
[*Buch der Lieder* (*Book of Songs*), 'Die Heimkehr' ('Homecoming', 1823–1824), II; later known as 'Die Lorelei']

5. *Hört ihr das Glöckchen klingeln? Kniet nieder – Man bringt die Sakramente einem sterbenden Gotte.*
Do you hear the little bell ringing? Kneel down – The sacraments are being brought to a dying god.
[*Zur Geschichte der Religion und Philosophie in Deutschland* (*On the History of Religion and Philosophy in Germany*, 1834), II]

6. *Sie hatten sich beide so herzlich lieb,*
Spitzbübin war sie, er war ein Dieb.
They loved each other so very deeply–
She was a slag, he was a thief.
[*Neue Gedichte*, (*New Poems*), 'Romanzen' (*Romances*, 1844), poem 1, 'Ein Weib']

7. *Gut ist der Schlaf, der Tod ist besser – freilich*
Das beste wäre, nie geboren sein.
Sleep is good, death is better; of course, it would be best never to have been born at all.
[*Nachgelesene Gedichte* (*Further Selection of Poems* from 1848–1856), III, 'Lamentationen' ('Lamentations'), poem 16, 'Morphine'. Cf. Sophocles: 5]

8. When people talk about a wealthy man of my creed, they call him an Israelite; but if he is poor they call him a Jew.
[MS. Papers]

9. It is extremely difficult for a Jew to be converted, for how can he bring himself to believe in the divinity of – another Jew?
[Attr.]

10. [Last words]
Dieu me pardonnera, c'est son métier.
God will forgive me. It is his profession.
[In Meissner, *H H Erinnerungen* (1856), 5. Cf. Catherine the Great: 1]

Heinlein, Robert A. (1907–1988)

American writer of science fiction

1. 'There ain't no such thing as a free lunch,' I added, pointing to a FREE LUNCH sign across the room. 'Or these drinks would cost half as much. Anything free costs twice as much in the long run or turns out worthless.'
[*The Moon is a Harsh Mistress* (1966)]

Heisenberg, Werner (1901–1976)

German theoretical physicist; Nobel prize 1932

1. *Ein Fachmann ist ein Mann, der einige der gröbsten Fehler kennt, die man in dem betreffenden Fach machen kann, und der sie deshalb zu vermeiden versteht.*
An expert is a man who knows some of the worst errors that

can be made in the subject in question and who therefore understands how to avoid them.
[*Der Teil und das Ganze* (*The Part and the Whole*, 1969)]

2. Natural science does not simply describe and explain nature, it is part of the interplay between nature and ourselves.
[Attr.]

Heller, Joseph (1923–)
American novelist, noted for his satire

1. He was a self-made man who owed his lack of success to nobody.
[*Catch-22* (1961), 3]

2. He had decided to live forever or die in the attempt.
[*Catch-22* (1961), 3]

3. Orr was crazy and could be grounded. All he had to do was ask; and as soon as he did, he would no longer be crazy and would have to fly more missions ... Yossarian was moved very deeply by the absolute simplicity of this clause of Catch-22 and let out a respectful whistle.
[*Catch-22* (1961), 5]

4. He knew everything about literature except how to enjoy it.
[*Catch-22* (1961), 8]

5. Some men are born mediocre, some men achieve mediocrity, and some men have mediocrity thrust upon them. With Major Major it had been all three.
[*Catch-22* (1961), 9. Cf. Shakespeare, *Twelfth Night*: 35]

6. Hungry Joe collected lists of fatal diseases and arranged them in alphabetical order so that he could put his finger without delay on any one he wanted to worry about.
[*Catch-22* (1961), 17]

7. Prostitution gives her an opportunity to meet people. It provides fresh air and wholesome exercise, and it keeps her out of trouble.
[*Catch-22* (1961), 33]

Hellman, Lillian (1905–1984)
American dramatist and screenwriter

1. Cynicism is an unpleasant way of saying the truth.
[*The Little Foxes* (1939), I]

2. I cannot and will not cut my conscience to fit this year's fashions, even though I long ago came to the conclusion that I was not a political person and could have no comfortable place in any political group.
[Letter to the US House of Representatives Committee on Un-American Activities, 1952]

3. [On being asked by *Harper's* magazine when she felt most masculine]
It makes me feel masculine to tell you that I do not answer questions like this without being paid for answering them.
[*Reader's Digest*, 1977]

Helpman, Sir Robert Murray (1909–1986)
Australian dancer, actor, choreographer, producer and director

1. I don't despair about the cultural scene in Australia because there isn't one here to despair about.
[In Keith Dunstan, *Knockers* (1972)]

2. [After the opening night of *Oh, Calcutta!*]
The trouble with nude dancing is that not everything stops when the music stops.
[In *The Frank Muir Book: An Irreverant Companion to Social History* (1976)]

3. Aren't all ballets sexy? I think they should be. I can think of nothing more kinky than a prince chasing a swan around all night.
[In Jonathon Green (ed.), *A Dictionary of Contemporary Quotations* (1982)]

Helps, Sir Arthur (1813–1875)
English historian and essayist

1. Reading is sometimes an ingenious device for avoiding thought.
[*Friends in Council* (1849), II, 1, 'Reading']

2. What a blessing this smoking is! perhaps the greatest that we owe to the discovery of America.
[*Friends in Council* (New Series, 1859), I, 1, 'Worry']

3. There is one statesman of the present day, of whom I always say, that he would have escaped making the blunders that he has made if he had only ridden more in omnibuses.
[*Friends in Council* (New Series, 1859), II, 9, 'On Government']

Helvétius, Claude Adrien (1715–1771)
French philosopher and encyclopaedist

1. *L'éducation nous faisait ce que nous sommes.*
Education made us what we are.
[*De l'esprit* (1758), 'Discours', 30]

Hemans, Felicia Dorothea (1793–1835)
Popular English poet and translator

1. The boy stood on the burning deck
Whence all but he had fled;
The flame that lit the battle's wreck
Shone round him o'er the dead...

2. There came a burst of thunder sound–
The boy – oh! where was he?
Ask of the winds that far around
With fragments strewed the sea!
['Casabianca' (1829)]

3. The stately Homes of England,
How beautiful they stand!
Amidst their tall ancestral trees,
O'er all the pleasant land!...

4. The Cottage Homes of England!
By thousands on her plains.
['The Homes of England' (1839). Cf. Coward: 24 and D.H. Lawrence: 19]

5. They grew in beauty, side by side,
They fill'd one home with glee;–
Their graves are sever'd, far and wide,
By mount, and stream, and sea.
['The Graves of a Household' (1839)]

Heming, John (1556–1630)
English editor of Shakespeare's First Folio; actor and theatrical manager
and **Condell,** Henry (d. 1627)

1. Well! it is now public, and you will stand for your privileges we know: to read, and censure. Do so, but buy it first. That doth best commend a book, the stationer says.
[Preface to the First Folio Shakespeare, 1623]

2. Who, as he was a happy imitator of Nature, was a most gentle expresser of it. His mind and hand went together: And what he thought, he uttered with that easiness, that we have scarce received from him a blot.
[Preface to the First Folio Shakespeare, 1623]

Hemingway, Ernest (1898–1961)
American novelist, short-story writer and war correspondent; Nobel prize 1954

1. The world breaks everyone and afterward many are strong at the broken places.
[*A Farewell to Arms* (1929)]

2. Bullfighting is the only art in which the artist is in danger of death and in which the degree of brilliance in the performance is left to the fighter's honour.
[*Death in the Afternoon* (1932)]

3. Prose is architecture, not interior decoration, and the Baroque is over.
[*Death in the Afternoon* (1932)]

4. [Of James Joyce]
And when you saw him he would take up a conversation interrupted three years before. It was nice to see a great writer in our time.
[*Green Hills of Africa* (1935), 4]

5. ... and always, Italy, better than any book...
[*Green Hills of Africa* (1935), 5]

6. Love is just another dirty lie. ... I know about love. Love always hangs up behind the bath-room door. It smells like lysol. To hell with love.
[*To Have and Have Not* (1937)]

7. But did thee feel the earth move?
[*For Whom the Bell Tolls* (1940), 13]

8. The world is a fine place and worth the fighting for.
[*For Whom the Bell Tolls* (1940), 43]

9. But man is not made for defeat ... A man can be destroyed but not defeated.
[*The Old Man and the Sea* (1952)]

10. If you are lucky enough to have lived in Paris as a young man, then wherever you go for the rest of your life, it stays with you, for Paris is a moveable feast.
[*A Moveable Feast* (1964), Epigraph]

11. For a true writer each book should be a new beginning, where he tries again for something that is beyond attainment.
[Speech for the presentation of the Nobel prize, 1954]

12. [When asked why he had deserted his wife Hadley for Pauline Pfeiffer in 1926]
Because I am a bastard.
[In B. Morton, *Americans in Paris* (1984)]

13. [In response to a jibe by William Faulkner]
Poor Faulkner. Does he really think big emotions come from big words? He thinks I don't know the ten-dollar words. I know them all right. But there are older and simpler and better words, and those are the ones I use.
[Attr. Cf. Faulkner: 3]

14. [Definition of 'guts']
Grace under pressure.
[Attr.; phrase first used by Dorothy Parker to describe the Hemingway hero]

Henderson, Arthur (1863–1935)
Scottish Trade Unionist, Labour politician and Cabinet member

1. The plural of conscience is conspiracy.
[*The Independent*, 1992]

Henderson, Hamish (1919–)
British translator and writer

1. There were our own, there were the others.
Their deaths were like their lives, human and animal.
There were no gods and precious few heroes.
[*Elegies for the Dead in Cyrenaica* (1948), 'First Elegy, End of a Campaign']

Henderson, Leon (1895–1986)
American economist

1. Having a little inflation is like being a little pregnant.
[Attr.]

Hendrix, Jimi (1942–1970)
US rock singer, songwriter and guitarist

1. Once you're dead, you're made for life.
[Attr.]

Henley, William Ernest (1849–1903)
English poet, dramatist, critic and editor

1. Out of the night that covers me,
Black as the Pit from pole to pole,
I thank whatever gods may be
For my unconquerable soul.

In the fell clutch of circumstance,
I have not winced nor cried aloud.
Under the bludgeonings of chance
My head is bloody, but unbowed...

2. It matters not how strait the gate,
How charged with punishments the scroll,
I am the master of my fate:
I am the captain of my soul.
[*Echoes*, 4, 'In Memoriam R.T. Hamilton Bruce' (1875)]

3. Madam Life's a piece in bloom
Death goes dogging everywhere:
She's the tenant of the room,
He's the ruffian on the stair.
[*Echoes*, 9, 'To W.R.' (1877)]

4. A late lark twitters from the quiet skies...

5. Night with her train of stars
And her great gift of sleep...

6. So be my passing!
My task accomplished and the long day done,
My wages taken, and in my heart
Some late lark singing,
Let me be gathered to the quiet west,
The sundown splendid and serene,
Death.
[*Echoes*, 35, 'In Memoriam Margaritae Sororis' (1886)]

7. Or ever the Knightly years were gone
With the old world to the grave,
I was a King in Babylon
And you were a Christian slave.
[*Echoes*, 37, 'To W.A.' (1889)]

8. What have I done for you,
England, my England?
What is there I would not do,
England, my own?
[*For England's Sake* (1900), 3, 'Pro Rege Nostro']

Henning, Rachel Biddulph (1826–1914)
Australian writer

1. [From Port Dennison, Queensland, in 1862]
You never know what thirst is unless you have travelled a whole day under an Australian sun without water.
[In David Adams (ed.), *The Letters of Rachel Henning* (1969)]

Henri IV of France (1553–1610)
Huguenot leader turned Catholic King of France, from 1589; assassinated

1. *Je veux qu'il n'y ait si pauvre paysan en mon royaume qu'il n'ait tous les dimanches sa poule au pot.*
It is my wish that in my kingdom there should be no peasant so poor that he cannot have a chicken in his pot every Sunday.
[In Hardouin de Péréfixe, *Histoire du roy Henry le Grand* (1681)]

2. [Traditional form given by Voltaire to Henri's letter to Crillon]
Pends-toi, brave Crillon; nous avons combattu à Arques et tu n'y étais pas.
Hang yourself, brave Crillon; we fought at Arques and you were not there.
[Attr.]

3. *Les grands mangeurs et les grands dormeurs sont incapables de rien faire de grand.*
Great eaters and great sleepers are not capable of doing anything great.
[Attr.]

4. *Paris vaut bien une messe.*
Paris is well worth a mass.
[Attr.; also attributed to Sully]

5. [Of James VI and I]
The wisest fool in Christendom.
[Attr.; also attributed to Sully]

6. One catches more flies with a spoonful of honey than with twenty casks of vinegar.
[Attr.]

Henry II (1133–1189)
First Plantagenet King of England

1. [Of Thomas Becket]
Will no one rid me of this turbulent priest?
[Attr., in Lyttelton, *History of the Life of King Henry* (1769), IV, 3]

Henry VIII (1491–1547)
King of England, from 1509; proclaimed himself Supreme Head of the Church of England and dissolved the monasteries; musician and poet

1. [On learning of Cranmer's suggestion that opinions on Henry's divorce should be collected]
[That man has] the sow by the right ear.
[Letter, 1529, in Scarisbrick, *Henry VIII* (1968), 9]

2. [Of Anne of Cleves]
The king ... found her so different from her picture ... that ... he swore they had brought him a Flanders mare.
[In Smollett, *History of England* (1759 edition), VI, 68]

Henry, Matthew (1662–1714)
English Nonconformist minister and commentator

1. The better day, the worse deed.
[*An Exposition of the Old and New Testament* (1706), Genesis 3: 6]

2. To their own second and sober thoughts.
[*An Exposition of the Old and New Testament* (1706), Job 6: 29]

3. Those that die by famine die by inches.
[*An Exposition of the Old and New Testament* (1706), Psalms 59: 8–17]

4. All this and heaven too.
[Attr.]

Henry, O. (William Sydney Porter) (1862–1910)
Prolific American short-story writer

1. Life is made up of sobs, sniffles, and smiles, with sniffles predominating.
[*The Four Million* (1906), 'The Gift of the Magi']

2. If men knew how women pass the time when they are alone they'd never marry.
[*The Four Million* (1906), 'Memoirs of a Yellow Dog']

3. It was beautiful and simple as all truly great swindles are.
[*The Gentle Grafter* (1908), 'The Octopus Marooned']

4. Take it from me – he's got the goods.
['The Unprofitable Servant' (1911)]

5. [Attr. last words, quoting the song 'I'm Afraid to Go Home in the Dark']
Don't turn down the light, I'm afraid to go home in the dark.
[In Leacock, 'The Amazing Genius of O. Henry', 1916]

Henry, Patrick (1736–1799)
American lawyer, orator and statesman

1. Caesar had his Brutus – Charles the First, his Cromwell – and George the Third – ['Treason,' cried the Speaker] ... may profit by their example. If this be treason, make the most of it.
[Speech in the Virginia Convention, 1765]

2. I am not a Virginian, but an American.
[Speech in the Virginia Convention, 1774]

3. Give me liberty, or give me death!
[Speech, 1775]

Henryson, Robert (c. 1425–1505)
Scottish makar; pastoral and allegorical poet, a 'Scottish Chaucerian'

1. Thar was na solace mycht his sobbing ces,
Bot cryit ay, with caris cald and kene,
'Quhar art thow gane, my luf Erudices?'
['Orpheus and Eurydice' (1508)]

2. The man that will nocht quhen he may
Sall haif nocht quhen he wald.
['Robene and Makyne' (c. 1560)]

3. Yit efter ioy oftymes cummis cair,
And troubill efter grit prosperitie.
['The Taill of the Uponlandis Mous and the Burges Mous' (1571)]

4. Nocht is your fairnes bot ane faiding flour,
Nocht is your famous laud and hie honour
Bot wind inflat in uther mennis eiris,
Your roising reid to rotting sall retour...

5. I lat yow wit, thair is richt few thairout
Quhome ye may traist to haue trew lufe agane;
Preif quhen ye will, your labour is in vaine.
Thairfoir I reid ye tak thame as ye find,
For thay ar sad as Widdercock in Wind.
['The Testament of Cresseid' (1593)]

Henshaw, Bishop Joseph (1603–1679)
English Bishop of Peterborough, 1663–79, and writer

1. One doth but breakfast here, another dines, he that liveth longest doth but sup; we must all go to bed in another world.
[*Horae Succisivae* (1631), I]

Hepburn, Katharine (1907–)
American leading film and stage actress; Academy Awards 1933, 1967, 1968 and 1981

1. I don't care what is written about me as long as it isn't true.
[In Cooper and Hartman, *Violets and Vinegar* (1980)]

Hepworth, Dame Barbara (1903–1975)
Celebrated English abstract sculptor

1. I rarely draw what I see. I draw what I feel in my body.
[Attr.]

Hepworth, John (1921–)
Australian writer

1. Most journalists of my generation died early, succumbing to one or other of the two great killers in the craft – cirrhosis or terminal alimony.
[*National Review*, 1974]

Heraclitus (c. 540–c. 480 BC)
Greek pre-Socratic philosopher of the Ionian School

1. Everything is on the move, nothing is constant.
[In Plato, *Cratylus*]

2. You cannot step twice into the same river.
[In Plato, *Cratylus*]

Herbert, Sir A.P. (1890–1971)
English humorist, novelist, dramatist and politician

1. Don't tell my mother I'm living in sin,
Don't let the old folks know:
Don't tell my twin that I breakfast on gin,
He'd never survive the blow.
[*Laughing Ann* (1925), 'Don't Tell My Mother I'm Living in Sin']

2. He didn't oughter come to bed in boots.
[*Riverside Nights* (1926), 1, 'Riverside House, Hammersmith']

3. It may be life, but ain't it slow?
[*Riverside Nights* (1926), 9, 'It May Be Life']

4. Don't let's go to the dogs tonight
For mother will be there.
[*She-Shanties* (1926), 'Don't Let's Go to the Dogs Tonight']

5. Not huffy or stuffy, nor tiny or tall,
But fluffy, just fluffy, with no brains at all.
[*Plain Jane* (1927), 'I Like them Fluffy']

6. Let's find out what everyone is doing,
And then stop everyone from doing it.
[*Ballads for Broadbrows* (1930), 'Let's Stop Somebody from Doing Something!']

7. As my poor father used to say
In 1863,
Once people start on all this Art
Good-bye, moralitee!
And what my father used to say
Is good enough for me.
[*Ballads for Broadbrows* (1930), 'Lines for a Worthy Person']

8. I'm not a jealous woman, but I can't see what he sees in her.
['I Can't Think What He Sees in Her']

9. I wouldn't be too ladylike in love if I were you.
['I Wouldn't be Too Ladylike']

10. This high official, all allow,
Is grossly overpaid;
There wasn't any Board, and now
There isn't any Trade.
['The President of the Board of Trade']

11. Well, fancy giving money to the Government!
Might as well have put it down the drain.
Fancy giving money to the Government!
Nobody will see the stuff again.
Well, they've no idea what money's for–
Ten to one they'll start another war.
I've heard a lot of silly things, but, Lor'!
Fancy giving money to the Government!
['Too Much!']

12. Holy Deadlock.
[Title of novel, 1934]

13. The Common Law of England has been laboriously built about a mythical figure – the figure of 'The Reasonable Man'.
[*Uncommon Law* (1935), 'The Reasonable Man']

14. People must not do things for fun. We are not here for fun. There is no reference to fun in any Act of Parliament.
[*Uncommon Law* (1935), 'Is it a Free Country?']

15. The critical period in matrimony is breakfast-time.
[*Uncommon Law* (1935), 'Is Marriage Lawful?']

16. The Englishman never enjoys himself except for a noble purpose.
[*Uncommon Law* (1935), 'Fox-Hunting Fun']

17. An Act of God was defined as 'something which no reasonable man could have expected'.
[*Uncommon Law* (1935), 'Act of God']

18. If elderly bishops were seen leaving the Athenaeum with jugs of stout in their hands the casual observer would form an impression of the character of that institution which would be largely unjust.
[*Uncommon Law* (1935)]

19. For any ceremonial purposes the otherwise excellent liquid, water, is unsuitable in colour and other respects.
[*Uncommon Law* (1935)]

20. Bring porridge, bring sausage, bring fish, for a start,
Bring kidneys, and mushrooms, and partridges' legs,
But let the foundation be bacon and eggs.
[In Catherine Brown, *Scottish Cookery* (1985)]

21. A highbrow is the kind of person who looks at a sausage and thinks of Picasso.
[Attr.]

Herbert, Edward, Baron Herbert of Cherbury (1583–1648)
English poet, philosopher and autobiographer; historian and diplomat; brother of George Herbert

1. Now that the April of your youth adorns
The Garden of your face.
['Ditty in imitation of the Spanish *Entre tantoque L'Avril*' (1665)]

2. O that our love might take no end,
Or never had beginning took!...

3. For where God doth admit the fair,
Think you that he excludeth Love?
['An Ode upon a Question moved, Whether Love should continue for ever?' (1665)]

Herbert, George (1593–1633)

English Metaphysical poet and priest; brother of Edward Herbert

1. Hearken unto a Verser, who may chance
Ryme thee to good, and make a bait of pleasure.
A verse may finde him who a sermon flies,
And turn delight into a sacrifice...

2. Drink not the third glasse, – which thou canst not tame
When once it is within thee...

3. The stormie working soul spits lies and froth.
Dare to be true. Nothing can need a ly.
A fault which needs it most grows two thereby...

4. O England! full of sinne, but most of sloth,
Spit out thy flegme, and fill thy brest with glorie...

5. Doe all things like a man, not sneakingly.
Think the king sees thee still; for his King does...

6. Wit's an unruly engine, wildly striking
Sometimes a friend, sometimes the engineer...

7. But love is lost, the way of friendship's gone,
Though David had his Jonathan, Christ his John...

8. Be calm in arguing; for fiercenesse makes
Errour a fault, and truth discourtesie...

9. Calmnesse is great advantage. He that lets
Another chafe, may warm him at his fire...

10. Who aimeth at the sky
Shoots higher much than he that means a tree...

11. Man is God's image, but a poore man is
Christ's stamp to boot...

12. Kneeling ne're spoil'd silk stocking. Quit thy state.
All equall are within the churches gate...

13. O, be drest,
Stay not for th' other pin. Why thou hast lost
A joy for it worth worlds...

14. Judge not the preacher; for he is thy Judge.
If thou mislike him, thou conceiv'st him not.
God calleth preaching folly. Do not grudge
To pick out treasures from an earthen pot.
The worst speak something good; if all want sense,
God takes a text, and preacheth patience...

15. Look not on pleasures as they come, but go.
[*The Temple* (1633), 'The Church-Porch']

16. Was ever grief like mine?...

17. But who does hawk at eagles with a dove?
[*The Temple* (1633), 'The Sacrifice']

18. At length I heard a ragged noise and mirth
Of theeves and murderers; there I him espied,
Who straight, Your suit is granted, said, and died.
[*The Temple* (1633), 'Redemption']

19. I got me flowers to straw thy way,
I got me boughs off many a tree,
But thou wast up by break of day,
And brought'st thy sweets along with thee.
[*The Temple* (1633), 'Easter']

20. Lord, with what care hast thou begirt us round!
Parents first season us; then schoolmasters
Deliver us to laws; they send us bound
To rules of reason, holy messengers,
Pulpits and sundayes, sorrow dogging sinne,
Afflictions sorted, anguish of all sizes,
Fine nets and stratagems to catch us in.
Bibles laid open, millions of surprises.
[*The Temple* (1633), 'Sinne' (Lord, with what care...)]

21. I reade, and sigh, and wish I were a tree,
For sure then I should grow
To fruit or shade. At least some bird would trust
Her household to me, and I should be just...

22. Ah my deare God! Though I am clean forgot,
Let me not love thee if I love thee not.
[*The Temple* (1633), 'Affliction' (When first thou didst...)]

23. Prayer the Churches banquet...
Exalted Manna, gladnesse of the best,
Heaven in ordinarie, man well drest,
The milkie way, the bird of Paradise...
The land of spices; something understood.
[*The Temple* (1633), 'Prayer' (Prayer the Churches banquet...)]

24. Let all the world in ev'ry corner sing
My God and King.

The heav'ns are not too high,
His praise may thither flie:
The earth is not too low,
His praises there may grow.

Let all the world in ev'ry corner sing
My God and King.

The Church with psalms must shout,
No door can keep them out:
But above all, the heart
Must bear the longest part.
[*The Temple* (1633), 'Antiphon' (Let all the world...)]

25. Who sayes that fictions onely and false hair
Become a verse? Is there in truth no beautie?
Is all good structure in a winding stair?...

26. I envie no man's nightingale or spring;
Nor let them punish me with losse of ryme,
Who plainly say, My God, my King.
[*The Temple* (1633), 'Jordan' (Who sayes that fictions...)]

27. Death is still working like a mole,
And digs my grave at each remove.
[*The Temple* (1633), 'Grace']

28. Lord, how can man preach thy eternall word?
He is a brittle crazie glasse:
Yet in thy temple thou dost him afford
This glorious and transcendent place,
To be a window, through thy grace.
[*The Temple* (1633), 'The Windows']

29. My God, a verse is not a crown,
No point of honour, or gay suit,
No hawk, or banquet, or renown,
Nor a good sword, nor yet a lute.
[*The Temple* (1633), 'The Quidditie']

30. He that is weary, let him sit.
My soul would stirre
And trade in courtesies and wit...

31. Oh that I were an Orenge-tree,
That busie plant!
Then should I ever laden be,
And never want
Some fruit for him that dressed me.
[*The Temple* (1633), 'Employment' (He that is weary...)]

32. Sweet day, so cool, so calm, so bright,
The bridall of the earth and skie:
The dew shall weep thy fall tonight;
For thou must die.

Sweet rose, whose hue angrie and brave
Bids the rash gazer wipe his eye,
Thy root is ever in its grave,
And thou must die.

Sweet spring, full of sweet dayes and roses,
A box where sweets compacted lie,
My musick shows ye have your closes,
And all must die.

Onely a sweet and vertuous soul,
Like season'd timber, never gives;
But though the whole world turn to coal,
Then chiefly lives.
[*The Temple* (1633), 'Vertue']

33. Man is all symmetrie,
Full of proportions, one limbe to another,
And all to all the world besides...

34. For us the windes do blow,
The earth doth rest, heav'n move, and fountains flow.
Nothing we see but means our good,
As our delight or as our treasure;
The whole is either our cupboard of food
Or cabinet of pleasure...

35. Oh mightie love! Man is one world, and hath
Another to attend him.
[*The Temple* (1633), 'Man']

36. My friend may spit upon my curious floore.
Would he have gold? I lend it instantly;
But let the poore,
And thou within them, starve at doore.
I cannot use a friend as I use Thee.
[*The Temple* (1633), 'Unkindness']

37. I made a posie while the day ran by:
Here will I smell my remnant out, and tie
My life within this band.
But time did becken to the flowers, and they
By noon most cunningly did steal away,
And wither'd in my hand.
[*The Temple* (1633), 'Life']

38. When boyes go first to bed,
They step into their voluntarie graves.
[*The Temple* (1633), 'Mortification']

39. Grasp not at much, for fear thou losest all.
[*The Temple* (1633), 'The Size']

40. I struck the board, and cry'd, 'No more.
I will abroad.'
What? shall I ever sigh and pine?
My lines and life are free; free as the rode,
Loose as the winde, as large as store.
Shall I be still in suit?
Have I no harvest but a thorn
To let me blood, and not restore
What I have lost with cordiall fruit?
Sure there was wine
Before my sighs did drie it: there was corn
Before my tears did drown it.
Is the yeare onely lost to me?
Have I no bayes to crown it?...

41. Thy rope of sands
Which pettie thoughts have made...

42. Away; take heed:
I will abroad.
Call in thy deaths head there: tie up thy fears.
He that forbears
To suit and serve his need
Deserves his load.
But as I rav'd and grew more fierce and wilde
At every worde,
Methought I heard one calling, Child!
And I replied, My Lord.
[*The Temple* (1633), 'The Collar']

43. When God at first made man,
Having a glasse of blessings standing by;
Let us (said he) poure on him all we can:
Let the world's riches, which dispersed lie,
Contract into a span...

44. Yet let him keep the rest,
But keep them with repining restlessnesse:
Let him be rich and wearie, that at least,
If goodnesse leade him not, yet wearinesse
May tosse him to my breast.
[*The Temple* (1633), 'The Pulley']

45. Who would have thought my shrivel'd heart
Could have recover'd greennesse?...

46. And now in age I bud again,
After so many deaths I live and write;
I once more smell the dew and rain,
And relish versing: O my onely light,
It cannot be
That I am he
On whom thy tempests fell all night.
[*The Temple* (1633), 'The Flower']

47. The God of love my shepherd is,
And he that doth me feed:
While he is mine, and I am his,
What can I want or need?
[*The Temple* (1633), 'The 23rd Psalme']

48. Throw away thy rod,
Throw away thy wrath:
O my God,
Take the gentle path...

49. Love is swift of foot;
Love's a man of warre,
And can shoot,
And can hit from farre.
[*The Temple* (1633), 'Discipline']

50. Teach me, my God and King,
In all things thee to see;
And what I do in any thing
To do it as for thee...

51. A man that looks on glasse,
On it may stay his eye,
Or if he pleaseth, through it passe,
And then the heav'n espie...

52. This is the famous stone
That turneth all to gold:
For that which God doth touch and own
Cannot for lesse be told.
[*The Temple* (1633), 'The Elixer']

53. Love bade me welcome; yet my soul drew back,
Guiltie of dust and sinne.
But quick-ey'd Love, observing me grow slack
From my first entrance in,

Drew nearer to me, sweetly questioning
If I lack'd any thing...

54. Love took my hand, and smiling did reply,
Who made the eyes but I?...

55. You must sit down, sayes Love, and taste my meat:
So I did sit and eat.
[*The Temple* (1633), 'Love' (Love bade me welcome...)]

56. A cheerful look makes a dish a feast.
[*Jacula Prudentum; or Outlandish Proverbs, Sentences &c.*, (1640)]

57. He that makes a good war, makes a good peace.
[*Jacula Prudentum; or Outlandish Proverbs, Sentences &c.*, (1640)]

58. Music helps not the tooth-ache.
[*Jacula Prudentum; or Outlandish Proverbs, Sentences &c.*, (1640)]

59. He that lives in hope danceth without music.
[*Jacula Prudentum; or Outlandish Proverbs, Sentences &c.*, (1640)]

60. Take heed of a young wench, a prophetess, and a Latin-bred woman.
[*Jacula Prudentum; or Outlandish Proverbs, Sentences &c.*, (1640)]

Herbert, (Alfred Francis) Xavier (1901–1984)
Australian writer, poet and social critic

1. [On returning from the war]
There's no place like home, Mum. Have me head read if ever I leave this gawd's own lovely land again. You dunno what a lovely land it is till you've seen them other crowded, foggy, frozen, furrin holes.
[*Capricornia* (1938), 12. Cf. Payne: 1]

2. Prosperity is like the tide, being able to flood one shore only by ebbing from another.
[*Capricornia* (1938), 16]

3. [On the plight of the Aborigines]
Until we give back to the Blackman just a bit of the land that was his and give it back without provisos, without strings to snatch it back, without anything but complete generosity of spirit in concession for the evil we have done him – until we do that, we shall remain what we have always been so far, a people without integrity; not a nation but a community of thieves.
[*Poor Fellow My Country* (1975)]

Herford, Oliver (1863–1935)
English-born American poet, illustrator and dramatist

1. The bubble winked at me and said,
'You'll miss me brother, when you're dead.'
[Toast: 'The Bubble Winked']

2. [When asked if he really had no ambition beyond making people laugh]
I would like to throw an egg into an electric fan.
[Attr.]

Herrick, Robert (1591–1674)
English lyric poet; royalist and clergyman

1. In Prayer the Lips ne're act the winning part,
Without the sweet concurrence of the Heart.
[*Noble Numbers* (1647), 'The Heart']

2. Lord, Thou hast given me a cell
Wherein to dwell;
A little house, whose humble Roof
Is weather-proof;
Under the sparres of which I lie
Both soft, and drie.
[*Noble Numbers* (1647), 'A Thanksgiving to God for his House']

3. If any thing delight me for to print
My book, 'tis this; that Thou, my God, art in't.
[*Noble Numbers* (1647), 'To God']

4. Here a little child I stand,
Heaving up my either hand;
Cold as Paddocks though they be,
Here I lift them up to Thee,
For a Benizon to fall
On our meat, and on us all. Amen.
[*Noble Numbers* (1647), 'Another Grace for a Child']

5. To work a wonder, God would have her shown,
At once, a Bud, and yet a Rose full-blowne.
[*Noble Numbers* (1647), 'The Virgin Mary']

6. But, for Mans fault, then was the Thorn,
Without the fragrant Rose-bud, born;
But ne're the Rose without the Thorn.
[*Noble Numbers* (1647), 'The Rose']

7. I sing of Brooks, of Blossomes, Birds, and Bowers:
Of April, May, of June and July-Flowers.
I sing of May-poles, Hock-carts, Wassails, Wakes,
Of Bride-grooms, Brides, and of their Bridall-cakes.
I write of Youth, of Love, and have Accesse
By these, to sing of cleanly-Wantonnesse.
[*Hesperides* (1648), 'The Argument of his Book']

8. Love is a circle that doth restlesse move
In the same sweet eternity of love.
[*Hesperides* (1648), 'Love What It Is']

9. More discontents I never had
Since I was born, than here;
Where I have been, and still am sad,
In this dull Devon-shire.
[*Hesperides* (1648), 'Discontents in Devon']

10. Cherrie-Ripe, Ripe, Ripe, I cry,
Full and faire ones; come and buy:
If so be, you ask me where
They doe grow? I answer, There,
Where my Julia's lips doe smile;
There's the Land, or Cherry-Ile.
[*Hesperides* (1648), 'Cherry-Ripe']

11. Now is the time, when all the lights wax dim;
And thou (Anthea) must withdraw from him
Who was thy servant...

12. For my Embalming (Sweetest) there will be
No Spices wanting, when I'm laid by thee.
[*Hesperides* (1648), 'To Anthea' (Now is the time...)]

13. So smooth, so sweet, so silv'ry is thy voice,
As, could they hear, the Damn'd would make no noise,
But listen to thee, (walking in thy chamber)
Melting melodious words, to Lutes of Amber.
[*Hesperides* (1648), 'Upon Julia's Voice']

14. Give me a kiss, add to that kiss a score;
Then to that twenty, adde an hundred more:
A thousand to that hundred: so kiss on,
To make that thousand up a million.
Treble that million, and when that is done,
Let's kiss afresh, as when we first begun.
[*Hesperides* (1648), 'To Anthea' (Ah my Anthea!...)]

15. A sweet disorder in the dresse
Kindles in cloathes a wantonnesse:

15. A sweet disorder in the dresse
Kindles in cloathes a wantonnesse:
A Lawne about the shoulders thrown
Into a fine distraction...

16. A winning wave (deserving Note)
In the tempestuous petticote:
A carelesse shooe-string, in whose tye
I see a wilde civility:
Doe more bewitch me, than when Art
Is too precise in every part.
[*Hesperides* (1648), 'Delight in Disorder']

17. With thousand such enchanting dreams, that meet
To make sleep not so sound, as sweet.
[*Hesperides* (1648), 'A Country Life: to his Brother, M. Tho. Herrick']

18. You say, to me-wards your affection's strong;
Pray love me little, so you love me long.
[*Hesperides* (1648), 'Love me little, love me long']

19. Sweet, be not proud of those two eyes,
Which Star-like sparkle in their skies...

20. That Rubie which you weare,
Sunk from the tip of your soft eare,
Will last to be a precious Stone,
When all your world of Beautie's gone.
[*Hesperides* (1648), 'To Dianeme' (Sweet, be not proud...)]

21. Get up, get up for shame, the Blooming Morne
Upon her wings presents the god unshorne...

22. Get up, sweet-Slug-a-bed, and see
The Dew-bespangling Herbe and tree...

23. Come, let us goe, while we are in our prime;
And take the harmlesse follie of the time...

24. So when or you or I are made
A fable, song, or fleeting shade;
All love, all liking, all delight
Lies drown'd with us in endlesse night.
Then while time serves, and we are but decaying;
Come, my Corinna, come, let's goe a Maying.
[*Hesperides* (1648), 'Corinna's going a Maying']

25. Welcome Maids of Honour,
You doe bring
In the Spring;
And wait upon her.
[*Hesperides* (1648), 'To Violets']

26. Gather ye Rose-buds while ye may,
Old Time is still aflying:
And this same flower that smiles today,
Tomorrow will be dying...

27. Then be not coy, but use your time;
And while ye may, goe marry:
For having lost but once your prime,
You may for ever tarry.
[*Hesperides* (1648), 'To the Virgins, to make much of Time']

28. Onely a little more
I have to write,
Then Ile give o're,
And bid the world Good-night.
[*Hesperides* (1648), 'His Poetrie his Pillar']

29. Bid me to live, and I will live
Thy Protestant to be:
Or bid me love, and I will give
A loving heart to thee...

30. Bid me to weep, and I will weep,
While I have eyes to see...

31. Bid me despaire, and Ile despaire,
Under that Cypresse tree:
Or bid me die, and I will dare
E'en Death, to die for thee.

Thou art my life, my love, my heart,
The very eyes of me:
And hast command of every part,
To live and die for thee.
[*Hesperides* (1648), 'To Anthea, who may command him Any thing']

32. Faire Daffadills, we weep to see
You haste away so soone:
As yet the early-rising Sun
Has not attain'd his Noone.
Stay, stay,
Untill the hasting day
Has run
But to the Even-song;
And, having pray'd together, we
Will goe with you along.

We have short time to stay, as you,
We have as short a Spring;
As quick a growth to meet Decay,
As you, or any thing.
[*Hesperides* (1648), 'To Daffadills']

33. Her pretty feet
Like snailes did creep
A little out, and then,
As if they started at Bo-peep,
Did soon draw in agen.
[*Hesperides* (1648), 'Upon her [Mistresse Susanna Southwell's] Feet']

34. Fain would I kiss my Julia's dainty Leg,
Which is as white and hair-lesse as an egge.
[*Hesperides* (1648), 'Her Legs']

35. And once more yet (ere I am laid out dead)
Knock at a Starre with my exalted Head.
[*Hesperides* (1648), 'The bad season makes the Poet sad']

36. I dare not ask a kisse;
I dare not beg a smile;
Lest having that, or this,
I might grow proud the while.

No, no, the utmost share
Of my desire, shall be
Onely to kisse that Aire,
That lately kissed thee.
[*Hesperides* (1648), 'To Electra' (I dare not ask...)]

37. A little streame best fits a little Boat;
A little lead best fits a little Float,
As my small Pipe best fits my little note.

A little meat best fits a little bellie,
As sweetly Lady, give me leave to tell ye,
This little Pipkin fits this little Jellie.
[*Hesperides* (1648), 'A Ternarie of littles, upon a pipkin of Jellie sent to a Lady']

38. When as in silks my Julia goes,
Then, then (me thinks) how sweetly flowes
That liquefaction of her clothes.
Next, when I cast mine eyes and see
That brave Vibration each way free;
O how that glittering taketh me!
[*Hesperides* (1648), 'Upon Julia's Clothes']

39. 'Twixt Kings & Tyrants there's this difference known;
Kings seek their Subjects good: Tyrants their owne.
[*Hesperides* (1648), 'Kings and Tyrants']

40. Night makes no difference 'twixt the Priest and Clark;
Jone as my Lady is as good i' th' dark.
[*Hesperides* (1648), 'No Difference i' th' Dark']

41. Made us nobly wild, not mad.
[*Hesperides* (1648), 'An Ode for him [Ben Jonson]']

42. Tis not the fight that crowns us, but the end.
[*Hesperides* (1648), 'The End']

43. Attempt the end, and never stand to doubt;
Nothing's so hard, but search will find it out.
[*Hesperides* (1648), 'Seeke and Finde']

Hervey, James (1714–1758)
English Methodist; devotional writer

1. Even crosses from his sovereign hand
Are blessings in disguise.
['Reflections on a Flower-Garden' (1746)]

Hervey, Lord (John, Baron Hervey of Ickworth) (1696–1743)
English politician, pamphleteer on Walpole's behalf and memoirist

1. Whoever would lie usefully should lie seldom.
[In Croker (ed.), *Memoirs of the Reign of George II* (1848), I, 19]

2. [On the inefficacy of the Riot Act, 1715]
When ... two or three hundred men are ordered by their officer to go against two or three thousand rioters, if they refuse to go it is mutiny, and they will be condemned by a court martial and shot; if they go and do not fire, they will probably be knocked on the head; and if they fire and kill anybody, they will be tried by jury and hanged. Such are the absurdities of our laws at present.
[Attr.]

Hesse, Hermann (1877–1962)
German-born Swiss novelist, short-story writer and poet; Nobel prize 1946

1. *Wenn wir einen Menschen hassen, so hassen wir in seinem Bild etwas, was in uns selber sitzt. Was nicht in uns selber ist, das regt uns nicht auf.*
If we hate a person, we hate something in our image of him that lies within ourselves. What is not within ourselves doesn't upset us.
[*Demian* (1919), 6]

Hewart, Gordon (Viscount Hewart) (1870–1943)
English Liberal politician and Lord Chief Justice of England 1922–40

1. It is not merely of some importance but is of fundamental importance that justice should not only be done, but should manifestly and undoubtedly be seen to be done.
[Rex *v.* Sussex Justices, 1923, in *King's Bench Reports* (1924), I]

2. [When taunted by F.E. Smith about the size of his stomach with, 'What's it to be – a boy or a girl?']
If it's a boy I'll call him John. If it's a girl I'll call her Mary. But if, as I suspect, it's only wind, I'll call it F.E. Smith.
[Attr.]

Hewett, Dorothy (1923–)
Australian dramatist and poet

1. O when shall we two meet again
In thunder and in lightning and in rain,
By what strange waters and by what dry docks,
By what mean streets alive with summer frocks,
And girls, and men with grease across their lips,
Who fire the boilers on what lonely ships?
['Go down Red Roses']

2. Gentlemen may remove any garment consistent with decency.
Ladies may remove any garment consistent with charm.
['Beneath the Arches']

3. My body turns to you as the earth turns.
O for such bitter need you've taken me,
To dub me lover, friend and enemy,
That neither one can set the other free.
But still there is a loveliness that burns
That burns between us two so tenderly.
['There is a Loveliness that Burns']

4. For dole bread is bitter bread
Bitter bread and sour
There's grief in the taste of it
There's weevils in the flour.
['Weevils in the Flour']

Hewitt, John (1907–1987)
Irish poet and museum and art gallery director

1. I fear their creed as we have always feared
The lifted hand between the mind and truth.
[*No Rebel Word* (1948), 'The Glens']

2. The names of a land show the heart of the race;
They move on the tongue like the lilt of a song.
You say the name and I see the place–
Drumbo, Dungannon, or Annalong.
Barony, townland, we cannot go wrong.
['Ulster Names']

Hewitt, Sir (Cyrus) Lenox Simson (1917–)
Australian company chairman and director

1. [On the inefficiency of the government drives for economy]
We've had razor gang after razor gang after razor gang, and they all end up fiddling with the tea lady.
[ABC television, 1986]

Heysen, Sir Hans William (1877–1968)
German-born Australian artist

1. Why don't they draw, draw and draw? Their one idea is to cultivate the emotional sense, under the plea that they are expressing their personality.
[In Colin Thiele, *Heysen of Hahndorf*]

Heywood, John (c. 1497–c. 1580)
English epigrammatist, dramatist and court musician

1. All a grene wyllow, wyllow;
All a grene wyllow is my garland.
['All a grene wyllow is my garland' (c. 1545). Cf. Shakespeare, *Othello*: 56]

2. Let the world slide, let the world go:
A fig for care, and a fig for woe!
If I can't pay, why I can owe,
And death makes equal the high and the low.
['Be Merry, Friends' (c. 1557)]

Heywood, Thomas (c. 1574–1641)
English dramatist, poet and translator

1. A Woman Killed with Kindness.
[Title of play; performed 1603, printed 1607]

2. Seven cities warr'd for Homer, being dead,
Who, living, had no roof to shroud his head.
['The Hierarchy of the Blessed Angels' (1635. Cf. Anon: 94]

Hicks, Sir Seymour (1871–1949)
British dramatist, actor-manager, comedian and author

1. You will recognize, my boy, the first sign of old age: it is when you go out into the streets of London and realize for the first time how young the policemen look.
[In Pulling, *They Were Singing* (1952), 7]

Hickson, William Edward (1803–1870)
English educationist; author of books on singing

1. 'Tis a lesson you should heed,
Try, try again.
If at first you don't succeed,
Try, try again.
['Try and Try Again']

Hightower, Jim (1933–)
Former Texan agriculture commissioner

1. Only things in the middle of the road are yellow lines and dead armadillos.
[Attr.]

Higinbotham, George (1826–1892)
Irish-born Australian journalist and lawyer

1. The Duke of Argyll is a nobleman of very great and cultivated intelligence, and, considering that he is a Scotchman, his cultivation has considerable breadth.
[Speech to the Victorian Legislative Assembly, 1869, in Edward E. Morris, *A Memoir of George Higinbotham* (1895)]

Higley, Brewster (19th century)
American songwriter

1. Oh give me a home where the buffalo roam,
Where the deer and the antelope play,
Where seldom is heard a discouraging word
And the skies are not cloudy all day.
['Home on the Range', song, c. 1873]

Higton, Tony
Leading Church of England evangelical; founder of Action for Biblical Witness to Our Nation

1. The church is not a mere ecclesiastical wing of the state which benignly blesses what an increasingly secular society does. Its function is primarily to represent God to the nation.
[*The Times*, 1992]

Hill, Aaron (1685–1750)
English poet, dramatist, producer and traveller

1. Tender-hearted stroke a nettle,
And it stings you for your pains;
Grasp it like a man of mettle,
And it soft as silk remains.
['Verses Written on a Window in Scotland']

Hill, Joe (Joel Hägglund) (1879–1914)
Swedish-born American songwriter and workers' organizer; convicted of murder and executed

1. You will eat (You will eat)
Bye and bye (Bye and bye)
In that glorious land above the sky (Way up high)
Work and pray (Work and pray)
Live on hay (Live on hay)
You'll get pie in the sky when you die (That's a lie.)
['The Preacher and the Slave', song, 1911]

Hill, Reginald (1936–)
British crime fiction writer and playwright

1. I have seen the future and it sucks.
[*Pictures of Perfection* (1994). Cf. Steffens: 1]

2. They were not long, the days of swine and Porsches.
[*Pictures of Perfection* (1994). Cf. Dowson: 3]

3. Nobody has ever lost money by overestimating the superstitious credulity of an English jury.
[*Pictures of Perfection* (1994)]

4. He created a man who was hard of head, blunt of speech, knew which side his bread was buttered on, and above all took no notice of women. Then God sent him forth to multiply in Yorkshire.
[*Pictures of Perfection* (1994)]

5. The first thing revolutionaries of the left or right give up is their sense of humour. The second thing is other people's rights.
[In Winks (ed.), *Colloquium on Crime* (1986), 'Looking for a Programme']

6. The ultimate stage of reputation would be to have a name so powerful in market terms it would sell anything. Well, the money would be nice, but I don't know yet if I'm ready for the irresponsibility.
[In Winks (ed.), *Colloquium on Crime* (1986), 'Looking for a Programme']

Hill, Rowland (1744–1833)
English preacher and hymn-writer

1. He did not see any reason why the devil should have all the good tunes.
[In E.W. Broome, *The Rev. Rowland Hill* (1881), 7]

Hillary, Sir Edmund (1919–)
New Zealand mountaineer, conqueror of Everest; explorer and apiarist

1. [Remark after first ascent of Mount Everest, 1953]
Well, we knocked the bastard off!
[*Nothing Venture, Nothing Win* (1975), 10]

2. [Of Tenzing Norgay, his companion during the conquest of Everest]
As far as I knew, he had never taken a photograph before, and the summit of Everest was hardly the place to show him how.
[*High Adventure*]

3. There is precious little in civilization to appeal to a Yeti.
[*The Observer*, 'Sayings of the Week', 1960]

4. Mount Everest is now littered with junk from bottom to top.
[*The Observer*, 1982, in Jeffrey Care (ed.), *Sayings of the Eighties* (1989)]

Hillel, 'The Elder' (c. 60 BC–c. 10 AD)
Babylonian rabbi; President of the Sanhedrin and renowned doctor of Jewish law

1. A name made great is a name destroyed.
[In Taylor (ed.), *Sayings of the Jewish Fathers* (1877)]

2. If I am not for myself who is for me; and being for my own self what am I? If not now when?
[In Taylor (ed.), *Sayings of the Jewish Fathers* (1877)]

Hillingdon, Lady Alice (1857–1940)

1. I am happy now that Charles calls on my bedchamber less frequently than of old. As it is, I now endure but two calls a

week and when I hear his steps outside my door I lie down on my bed, close my eyes, open my legs and think of England.
[*Journal*, 1912, cited in E. Partridge, *A Dictionary of Catch Phrases* (1985)]

Hills, Denis (1913–)
British ex-patriate

1. [These words describing President Amin of Uganda caused Hills to be sentenced to death for treason; he was freed after the intervention of the Queen and the Foreign Secretary]
A village tyrant ... a black Nero.
[*The White Pumpkin* (1975)]

Hilton, James (1900–1954)
English novelist and Hollywood screenwriter

1. Anno domini ... that's the most fatal complaint of all, in the end.
[*Goodbye, Mr Chips* (1934), 1]

Hindenburg, Paul von (1847–1934)
German general and President, 1925–34

1. An English General has said, with justice, 'The German army was stabbed in the back.'
[Statement in Reichstag, 1919; in Dorpalen, *Hindenburg and the Weimar Republic* (1964), 2]

Hippocrates (c. 460–357 BC)
Greek physician, the 'father of medicine'

1. [Of medicine]
Life is short, science is so long to learn, opportunity is elusive, experience is dangerous, judgement is difficult.
[*Aphorisms* (c. 415 BC), 1; the opening phrases are often quoted in Latin in reverse order as *Ars longa, vita brevis*]

Hirohito, Emperor (1901–1989)
Emperor of Japan

1. The war situation has developed not necessarily to Japan's advantage.
[Announcing Japan's surrender, 15 August 1945]

Hirst, Damien (1965–)
British artist

1. I sometimes feel that I have nothing to say and I want to communicate this.
[Attr.]

Hitchcock, Alfred (1899–1980)
English film director noted for his mastery of suspense and camera technique

1. What is drama but life with the dull bits cut out?
[*The Observer*, 'Sayings of the Week', 1960]

2. Television has brought murder back into the home – where it belongs.
[*The Observer*, 1965]

3. Nobody can really like an actor.
[*The New Yorker*, 1992]

4. I deny that I ever said that actors are cattle. What I said was, 'Actors should be treated like cattle'.
[Attr.]

Hitler, Adolf (1889–1945)
Austrian-born German Nazi dictator; leader of the Third Reich from 1934

1. *Nur einer tausendfachen Wiederholung einfachster Begriffe wird [die Masse] endlich ihr Gedächtnis schenken.*
[The crowd] will finally succeed in remembering only the simplest concepts repeated a thousand times.
[*Mein Kampf* (*My Struggle*), I (1925), 6]

2. *Die breite Masse eines Volkes ... [fällt] einer grossen Lüge leichter zum Opfer als einer kleinen.*
The broad mass of a people ... falls victim to a big lie more easily than to a small one.
[*Mein Kampf* (*My Struggle*), I (1925), 10]

3. *Was nicht gute Rasse ist auf dieser Welt, ist Spreu.*
Whoever is not racially pure in this world is chaff.
[*Mein Kampf* (*My Struggle*), I (1925), 11]

4. *Deutschland wird entweder Weltmacht oder überhaupt nicht sein.*
Germany will either be a world power or will not exist at all.
[*Mein Kampf* (*My Struggle*), II (1927), 14]

5. *Wesentlich ist die politische Willensbildung der gesamten Nation, sie ist der Ausgangspunkt für politische Aktionen.*
What is essential is the formation of the political will of the entire nation: that is the starting point for political actions.
[Speech, Düsseldorf, 1932, in Domarus (ed.), *Hitler: Reden und Proklamationen 1932–1945* (1962)]

6. *Ich gehe mit traumwandlerischer Sicherheit den Weg, den mich die Vorsehung gehen heisst.*
I go the way that Providence bids me go with the certainty of a sleepwalker.
[Speech, Munich, 1936, in Domarus (ed.), *Hitler: Reden und Proklamationen 1932–1945* (1962)]

7. [On the Sudeten problem]
Meine Geduld [ist] jetzt zu Ende!
My patience is now at an end!
[Speech, Berlin, 1938, in Domarus (ed.), *Hitler: Reden und Proklamationen 1932–1945* (1962)]

8. [Of Sudetenland]
Es ist die letzte territoriale Forderung, die ich Europa zu stellen habe.
It is the last territorial claim which I have to make in Europe.
[Speech, Berlin, 1938, in Domarus (ed.), *Hitler: Reden und Proklamationen 1932–1945* (1962)]

9. [Said in 1939]
In starting and waging a war it is not right that matters, but victory.
[In W.L. Shirer, *The Rise and Fall of the Third Reich* (1960), 16]

10. [Referring to the liberation of Paris, 1944]
Brennt Paris?
Is Paris burning?
[In Collins and Lapierre, *Is Paris Burning* (1965), 5]

11. [Referring to the planned invasion of the USSR, Operation Barbarossa, which began on 22 June 1941]
When Barbarossa commences, the world will hold its breath and make no comment.
[Attr.]

Hobbes, Thomas (1588–1679)
Influential English political philosopher; proponent of absolutism and nominalist

1. Laughter is nothing else but sudden glory arising from some sudden conception of some eminency in ourselves, by

comparison with infirmity of others, or with our own formerly.
[*Human Nature* (1650), IX, 13]

2. True and false are attributes of speech, not of things. And where speech is not, there is neither truth nor falsehood.
[*Leviathan* (1651), I, 4, 'Of Speech']

3. Geometry ... is the only science that it hath pleased God hitherto to bestow on mankind.
[*Leviathan* (1651), I, 4, 'Of Speech']

4. Words are wise men's counters, they do but reckon by them; but they are the money of fools.
[*Leviathan* (1651), I, 4, 'Of Speech']

5. They that approve a private opinion, call it opinion; but they that mislike it, heresy: and yet heresy signifies no more than private opinion.
[*Leviathan* (1651), I, 11, 'Of the Difference of Manners']

6. During the time men live without a common power to keep them all in awe, they are in that condition which is called war; and such a war, as is of every man, against every man ... the nature of war consisteth, not in actual fighting; but in the known disposition thereto, during all the time there is no assurance to the contrary.
[*Leviathan* (1651), I, 13, 'Of the Natural Condition of Mankind as Concerning their Felicity, and Misery']

7. No arts; no letters; no society; and which is worst of all, continual fear, and danger of violent death; and the life of man, solitary, poor, nasty, brutish, and short.
[*Leviathan* (1651), I, 13, 'Of the Natural Condition of Mankind as Concerning their Felicity, and Misery']

8. Force, and fraud, are in war the two cardinal virtues.
[*Leviathan* (1651), I, 13, 'Of the Natural Condition of Mankind as Concerning their Felicity, and Misery']

9. Covenants, without the sword, are but words, and of no strength to secure a man at all.
[*Leviathan* (1651), II, 17, 'Of the Causes, Generation, and Definition of a Commonwealth']

10. The only way to erect such a common power, as may be able to defend them from the invasion of foreigners, and the injuries of one another ... is, to confer all their power and strength upon one man, or upon one assembly of men, that may reduce all their wills, by plurality of voices, unto one will ... This is the generation of that great Leviathan, or rather, to speak more reverently, of that mortal god, to which we owe under the immortal God, our peace and defence.
[*Leviathan* (1651), II, 17, 'Of the Causes, Generation, and Definition of a Commonwealth']

11. They that are discontented under monarchy, call it tyranny; and they that are displeased with aristocracy, call it oligarchy: so also, they which find themselves grieved under a democracy, call it anarchy, which signifies want of government; and yet I think no man believes, that want of government, is any new kind of government.
[*Leviathan* (1651), II, 19, 'Of the several kinds of commonwealth by institution, and of succession to the sovereign power']

12. The Papacy is no other than the ghost of the deceased Roman empire, sitting crowned upon the grave thereof.
[*Leviathan* (1651), IV, 47, 'Of the benefit that proceedeth from such darkness, and to whom it accrueth']

13. There is nothing I distrust more than my elocution, which nevertheless I am confident, excepting the mischances of the press, is not obscure.
[*Leviathan* (1651), 'A Review, and Conclusion']

14. The praise of ancient authors, proceeds not from the reverence of the dead, but from the competition, and mutual envy of the living.
[*Leviathan* (1651), 'A Review, and Conclusion']

15. He was wont to say that if he had read as much as other men, he should have knowne no more than other men.
[In Aubrey, *Brief Lives* (c. 1693), 'Thomas Hobbes']

16. [Last words]
I am about to take my last voyage, a great leap in the dark.
[In Watkins, *Anecdotes of Men of Learning* (1808)]

Hobhouse, John Cam, Baron Broughton (1786–1869)

English statesman; Radical politician and cabinet minister

1. When I invented the phrase 'His Majesty's Opposition' [Canning] paid me a compliment on the fortunate hit.
[*Recollections of a Long Life* (1865), II, 12]

Hobson, Sir Harold (1904–1992)

British drama critic and writer

1. The United States, I believe, are under the impression that they are twenty years in advance of this country; whilst, as a matter of actual verifiable fact, of course, they are just about six hours behind it.
[*The Devil in Woodford Wells*, 8]

Hodgson, Ralph (1871–1962)

English poet, illustrator and journalist

1. Reason has moons, but moons not hers,
Lie mirror'd on her sea,
Confounding her astronomers,
But, O! delighting me.
['Reason Has Moons' (1917)]

2. I climbed a hill as light fell short,
And rooks came home in scramble sort,
And filled the trees and flapped and fought
And sang themselves to sleep...

3. When stately ships are twirled and spun
Like whipping-tops and help there's none
And mighty ships ten thousand ton
Go down like lumps of lead...

4. I heard it all, I heard the whole
Harmonious hymn of being roll
Up through the chapel of my soul
And at the altar die,
And in the awful quiet then
Myself I heard, Amen, Amen,
Amen I heard me cry!...

5. I stood upon that silent hill
And stared into the sky until
My eyes were blind with stars and still
I stared into the sky.
['The Song of Honour' (1917)]

6. Time, you old gypsy man,
Will you not stay,
Put up your caravan,
Just for one day?
['Time, You Old Gypsy Man' (1917)]

Hodson, Peregrine

British author

1. He probably doesn't understand what he's looking at but he's reluctant to ask, because this is Japan and the student doesn't ask questions but waits to be told by the teacher.
[*A Circle Round The Sun – A Foreigner in Japan*]

2. Japan is like a quicksand – the more one tries to get out of it, the more it sucks one in – or a maze without a centre – a sphinx without a riddle – or like Peer Gynt's onion, peel away the layers one after another and in the end all there is left is mush and tears.
[*A Circle Round The Sun – A Foreigner in Japan*]

3. It shows hunger for life, like the Zen parable of a man holding on to a tree root over the edge of a cliff: below him rocks, above him a tiger, and a black and white mouse nibbling at the root: the man notices a strawberry beside him and picks it.
[*A Circle Round The Sun – A Foreigner in Japan*]

Hoffer, Eric (1902–1983)
American writer, philosopher and longshoreman

1. When people are free to do as they please, they usually imitate each other.
[*The Passionate State of Mind* (1955)]

2. Passionate hatred can give meaning and purpose to an empty life.
[Attr.]

Hoffman, Elisha B. (1839–1929)

1. Have you been to Jesus for the cleansing power?
Are you washed in the blood of the Lamb?
[Hymn]

Hoffmann, Ernst Theodor Amadeus (1776–1822)
German novelist, composer and writer of fantastic stories

1. *Das ist ein böser Mann, der kommt zu den Kindern, wenn sie nicht zu Bett' gehen wollen und wirft ihnen Hände voll Sand in die Augen.*
He is an evil man who comes to children when they don't want to go to bed and throws handfuls of sand in their eyes.
[*Der Sandmann* (*The Sandman*, 1815)]

Hoffmann, Heinrich (1809–1874)
German author, illustrator and physician

1. Augustus was a chubby lad;
Fat ruddy cheeks Augustus had:
And everybody saw with joy
That plump and hearty, healthy boy.
He ate and drank as he was told,
And never let his soup get cold.
But one day, one cold winter's day,
He screamed out, 'Take the soup away!
O take the nasty soup away!
I won't have any soup today.'
[*Struwwelpeter* (1847), 'Augustus']

2. Here is cruel Frederick, see!
A horrid wicked boy was he...

3. At this, good Tray grew very red,
And growled and bit him till he bled.
[*Struwwelpeter* (1847), 'Cruel Frederick']

4. Let me see if Philip can
Be a little gentleman;
Let me see, if he is able
To sit still for once at table...

5. But fidgety Phil,
He won't sit still;
He wriggles
And giggles,
And then, I declare,
Swings backwards and forwards,
And tilts up his chair,
Just like any rocking-horse–
'Philip! I am getting cross!'
[*Struwwelpeter* (1847), 'Fidgety Philip']

6. Boys, leave the black-a-moor alone!
For if he tries with all his might,
He cannot change from black to white.
[*Struwwelpeter* (1847), 'The Inky Boys']

7. Look at little Johnny there,
Little Johnny Head-in-Air!...

8. Silly little Johnny, look,
You have lost your writing-book!
[*Struwwelpeter* (1847), 'Johnny Head-in-Air']

9. The door flew open; in he ran,
The great, long, red-legged scissor-man...

10. Snip! Snap! Snip! They go so fast.
That both his thumbs are off at last.

11. Mamma comes home: there Conrad stands,
And looks quite sad, and shows his hands.
'Ah!' said Mamma. 'I knew he'd come
To naughty little Suck-a-Thumb'
[*Struwwelpeter* (1847), 'The Little-Suck-a-Thumb']

12. He finds it hard, without a pair
Of spectacles, to shoot the hare.
The hare sits snug in leaves and grass,
And laughs to see the green man pass...

13. And while he slept like any top,
The little hare came, hop, hop, hop...

14. And now she's trying all she can,
To shoot the sleepy, green-coat man.
[*Struwwelpeter* (1847), 'The Man Who Went Out Shooting']

15. Anything to me is sweeter
Than to see Shock-headed Peter.
[*Struwwelpeter* (1847), 'Shock-headed Peter']

Hoffmann, Max (1869–1927)
German general

1. [Referring to the performance of the British army in World War I]
Ludendorff: The English soldiers fight like lions.
Hoffman: True. But don't we know that they are lions led by donkeys.
[In A. Clark, *The Donkeys* (1962), from Falkenhayn, *Memoirs*]

Hoffmann von Fallersleben, August Heinrich (1798–1874)
German poet, songwriter, philologist and librarian

1. [Adopted as the German national anthem]
Deutschland, Deutschland über alles.
Germany, Germany above all else.
[*Volksleben* (*Life of the People*, 1841), VI, 'Vaterland und Heimat' ('Fatherland and Homeland'), 'Das Lied der Deutschen' ('The German's Song)]

Hoffnung, Gerard (1925–1959)
British freelance artist, illustrator and musician

1. There is a French widow in every bedroom (affording delightful prospects).
[Speech, Oxford Union debating society, 4 December 1958]

Hogan, Paul (1939–)
Australian film actor

1. We're a nation of punters and party-goers.
[Bicentenary television programme, 'Australia Live', 1988]

Hogg, James (1770–1835)
Scottish poet, ballad writer, novelist and journalist; the 'Ettrick Shepherd'

1. For Kilmeny had been she knew not where,
And Kilmeny had seen what she could not declare.
[*The Queen's Wake* (1814), 'Kilmeny']

2. There grows a bonny brier bush in our kail-yard.
[*The Jacobite Relics of Scotland, Second Series* (1821), 'An Yon Be He']

3. And Charlie he's my darling,
The young Chevalier.
[*The Jacobite Relics of Scotland, Second Series* (1821), 'Charlie is My Darling'. Cf. Robert Burns: 109 and Nairne: 3]

4. Better lo'ed you'll never be,
And will you no come back again?
[*The Jacobite Relics of Scotland, Second Series* (1821), 'Will He No Come Back Again']

5. God bless our lord the king!
God save our lord the king!
God save the king!
Make him victorious,
Happy, and glorious,
Long to reign over us:
God save the king!
[*The Jacobite Relics of Scotland, Second Series* (1821), 'The King's Anthem']

6. We'll o'er the water, we'll o'er the sea,
We'll o'er the water to Charlie;
Come weel, come wo, we'll gather and go,
And live or die wi' Charlie.
[*The Jacobite Relics of Scotland, Second Series* (1821), 'O'er the Water to Charlie']

7. Where the pools are bright and deep,
Where the grey trout lies asleep,
Up the river and o'er the lea
That's the way for Billy and me.
['A Boy's Song' (1838)]

8. O, love, love, love!
Love is like a dizziness;
It winna let a poor body
Gang about his biziness!
['Love is Like a Dizziness']

9. How often does the evening cup of joy lead to sorrow in the morning!
[Attr.]

Hokusai (1760–1849)
Great Japanese painter, printmaker and illustrator, especially noted for his views of Mount Fuji

1. [Said on his deathbed]
If heaven had granted me five more years, I could have become a real painter.
[In B. Conrad, *Famous Last Words* (1962)]

Holberg, Ludwig, Baron (1684–1754)
Norwegian-born Danish satirical poet, comic dramatist, historian and philosopher; pioneering Scandinavian playwright

1. [In reply to 'Do you call that thing on your head a hat?']
Do you call that thing under your hat a head?
[In H. Hoffmeister, *Anekdotenschatz*]

Hölderlin, Friedrich (1770–1843)
German poet

1. *Denn, ihr Deutschen, auch ihr seid*
Tatenarm und gedankenvoll.
For, you Germans, you too are
Poor in deed and rich in thoughts.
['An die Deutschen' ('To the Germans', 1798)]

Holland, First Lord (Henry Fox) (1705–1774)
English Whig politician, notably unpopular

1. [Said during his last illness]
If Mr Selwyn calls, let him in: if I am alive I shall be very glad to see him, and if I am dead he will be very glad to see me.
[Attr.]

Holland, Canon Henry Scott (1847–1918)
English cleric, Canon of St Paul's, Professor of Divinity and Christian social reformer

1. Death is nothing at all. It does not count. I have only slipped away into the next room. Nothing has happened. Everything remains exactly as it was. I am I, and you are you, and the old life that we lived so fondly together is untouched, unchanged. Whatever we were to each other, that we are still. Call me by the old familiar name. Speak of me in the easy way which you always used. Put no difference into your tone. Wear no forced air of solemnity or sorrow. Laugh as we always laughed at the little jokes that we enjoyed together. Play, smile, think of me, pray for me. Let my name be ever the household word that it always was. Let it be spoken without an effort, without the ghost of a shadow upon it. Life means all that it ever meant. It is the same as it ever was. There is absolute and unbroken continuity. What is death but a negligible accident? Why should I be out of mind because I am out of sight? I am but waiting for you, for an interval, somewhere very near, just round the corner. All is well.
[*Facts of the faith* (1919)]

Holmes, Hugh (Lord Justice Holmes) (1840–1916)
Irish circuit judge

1. An elderly pensioner on being sentenced to fifteen years' penal servitude cried 'Ah! my Lord, I'm a very old man, and I'll never do that sentence.' The judge replied 'Well try to do as much of it as you can'.
[In Maurice Healy, *The Old Munster Circuit* (1939)]

Holmes, Rev. John H. (1879–1964)
American Unitarian minister

1. This universe is not hostile, nor yet is it friendly. It is simply indifferent.
[*A Sensible Man's View of Religion* (1932), 4]

Holmes, Oliver Wendell (1809–1894)
American physician, anatomist, poet, novelist, scientist and essayist

1. And silence, like a poultice, comes
To heal the blows of sound.
['The Music-Grinders' (1836)]

2. Lean, hungry, savage anti-everythings.
['A Modest Request' (1848)]

3. And, when you stick on conversation's burrs,
Don't strew your pathway with those dreadful urs.
['A Rhymed Lesson' (1848)]

4. Man wants but little drink below,

But wants that little strong.
['A Song of other Days' (1848)]

5. Have you heard of the wonderful one-hoss shay,
That was built in such a logical way
It ran a hundred years to the day?...

6. A general flavour of mild decay.
['The Deacon's Masterpiece' (1858)]

7. [Of Samuel Francis Smith]
Fate tried to conceal him by naming him Smith.
['The Boys' (1859)]

8. Wisdom has taught us to be calm and meek,
To take one blow, and turn the other cheek;
It is not written what a man shall do
If the rude caitiff smite the other too!
['Non-Resistance' (1861)]

9. For him in vain the envious seasons roll
Who bears eternal summer in his soul.
['The Old Player' (1861)]

10. Man has his will, – but woman has her way.
[*The Autocrat of the Breakfast-Table* (1858)]

11. A thought is often original, though you have uttered it a hundred times.
[*The Autocrat of the Breakfast-Table* (1858), 1]

12. I am omniverbivorous by nature and training. Passing by such words as are poisonous, I can swallow most others, and chew such as I cannot swallow.
[*The Autocrat of the Breakfast-Table* (1858), 11]

13. Depart, – be off, – excede, – evade, – erump!
[*The Autocrat of the Breakfast-Table* (1858), 11]

14. A moment's insight is sometimes worth a life's experience.
[*The Professor at the Breakfast-Table* (1860), 10]

15. That most wonderful object of domestic art called trifle – with its charming confusion of cream and cake and almonds and jam and jelly and wine and cinnamon and froth.
[*Elsie Venner* (1861)]

16. It is the province of knowledge to speak and it is the privilege of wisdom to listen.
[*The Poet at the Breakfast-Table* (1872), 10]

17. To be seventy years young is sometimes far more cheerful and hopeful than to be forty years old.
['On the Seventieth Birthday of Julia Ward Howe' (1889)]

Holmes, Oliver Wendell, Jr. (1841–1935)
American jurist and Supreme Court judge, 1902–32

1. [In response to Andrew Lang's enquiring if he were the son of the celebrated Oliver Wendell Holmes]
No, he was my father.
[In C. Bowen, *Yankee from Olympus* (1945)]

2. Many ideas grow better when transplanted into another mind than in the one where they sprang up.
[In C. Bowen, *Yankee from Olympus* (1945)]

3. [At the age of 86, on seeing a pretty girl]
Oh, to be seventy again!
[In C. Fadiman, *The American Treasury*]

Holst, Gustav (1874–1934)
English composer of operas, orchestral suites, choral works and ballets

1. Never compose anything unless the not composing of it becomes a positive nuisance to you.
[Letter to W.G. Whittaker]

Holt, Harold Edward (1908–1967)
Australian statesman, former Prime Minister, believed drowned

1. [Statement made by Holt, when Prime Minister, offering Australia's support to Lyndon B. Johnson, President of the United States]
All the way with L.B.J.
[Quoted on cover of *Oz*, 1965]

2. I know this beach like the back of my hand.
[Last words, *Sydney Morning Herald*, 1967]

Home, John (1722–1808)
Scottish dramatist and Church of Scotland minister

1. My name is Norval; on the Grampian hills
My father feeds his flocks; a frugal swain,
Whose constant cares were to increase his store.
[*Douglas* (1756), II]

2. He seldom errs
Who thinks the worst he can of womankind.
[*Douglas* (1756), III]

3. Like Douglas conquer, or like Douglas die.
[*Douglas* (1756), III]

4. [On the high duty on French wine, claret being 'the only wine drunk by gentlemen in Scotland']
Firm and erect the Caledonian stood,
Old was his mutton, and his claret good;
Let him drink port, an English statesman cried–
He drank the poison and his spirit died.
[In Mackenzie, *An Account of the Life and Writings of John Home, Esq.* (1822), Appendix]

Homer (fl. c. 8th century BC)
Greek epic poet

1. Achilles' wrath to Greece the direful Spring
Of Woes unnumber'd, heav'nly Goddess, sing!
That Wrath which hurl'd to Pluto's gloomy Reign
The Soul of mighty Chiefs untimely slain.
[*Iliad*, I, line 1, trans. Pope]

2. Rosy-fingered dawn.
[*Iliad*, passim]

3. Winged words.
[*Iliad*, I, passim]

4. The wine-dark sea.
[*Iliad*, I, passim]

5. He went off in silence along the shore of the sounding sea.
[*Iliad*, I, line 34]

6. [Of Helen]
It is no cause for anger that the Trojans and the well-greaved Achaeans have suffered such pains for the sake of such a woman: she is marvellously like the immortal goddesses to look upon.
[*Iliad*, III, line 156]

7. Like Leaves on Trees the Race of Man is found,
Now green in Youth, now with'ring on the Ground,
Another Race the following Spring supplies,
They fall successive, and successive rise.
[*Iliad*, VI, line 146, trans. Pope]

8. Always to excel and be distinguished above others.
[*Iliad*, VI, line 208]

9. Yet come it will, the Day decreed by Fates;
(How my Heart trembles when my Tongue relates!)
The Day when thou, imperial Troy! must bend

And see thy Warriors fall, thy Glories end.
[*Iliad*, VI, line 448, trans. Pope]

10. Laughing in spite of her tears.
[*Iliad*, VI, line 484]

11. [Hector rejects ill omens]
Without a sign, his Sword the brave Man draws,
And asks no Omen but his Country's Cause.
[*Iliad*, XII, line 243, Pope's translation]

12. The mighty man lay mightily fallen, forgetful of his horsemanship.
[*Iliad*, XII, line 776]

13. [Achilles rejects a plea for mercy]
Patroclus died, who was a better man than you.
[*Iliad*, XXI, line 107]

14. Swift was the Course, no vulgar Prize they play,
No vulgar Victim must reward the Day,
(Such as in Races crown the speedy Strife)
The Prize contended was great Hector's Life.
[*Iliad*, XXII, line 159, trans. Pope]

15. [Achilles to Priam]
Rise then: let reason mitigate our Care
To mourn avails not: Man is born to bear.
Such is alas! the Gods' severe Decree:
They, only they are blest and only free.
[*Iliad*, XXIV, line 553, trans. Pope]

16. The Man, for Wisdom's various arts renown'd,
Long exercised in woes, Oh Muse! resound.
Who, when his arms had wrought the destined fall
Of sacred Troy, and raz'd her heav'n-built wall,
Wand'ring from clime to clime, observant stray'd
Their Manners noted, and their States surveyed.
On stormy seas unnumber'd toils he bore
Safe with his friends to gain his natal shore.
[*Odyssey*, I, line 1, trans. Pope]

17. [The ghost of Achilles to Ulysses]
I would rather be a slave at another's plough, one who is poor with little means of livelihood, than rule over all the dead and departed.
[*Odyssey*, XI, line 489]

18. Alike he thwarts the hospitable end
Who drives the free or stays the hasty friend;
True friendship's laws are by this rule express'd,
Welcome the coming, speed the parting guest.
[*Odyssey*, XV, line 72, trans. Pope]

Hone, William (1780–1842)
English bookseller, journalist and satirist

1. John Jones may be described as 'one of the has beens.'
[*Every-Day Book* (1826–1827), II]

Hood, Thomas (1799–1845)
English poet, editor and humorist

1. I saw old Autumn in the misty morn
Stand shadowless like Silence, listening
To silence.
['Ode: Autumn' (1823)]

2. There is a silence where hath been no sound,
There is a silence where no sound may be,
In the cold grave – under the deep, deep sea,
Or in the wide desert where no life is found.
['Sonnet: Silence' (1823)]

3. Ben Battle was a soldier bold,
And used to war's alarms:
But a cannon-ball took off his legs,
So he laid down his arms!...

4. For here I leave my second leg,
And the Forty-second Foot!...

5. The love that loves a scarlet coat
Should be more uniform.
[*Whims and Oddities* (1826), 'Faithless Nelly Gray']

6. They went and told the sexton, and
The sexton toll'd the bell.
[*Whims and Oddities* (1826), 'Faithless Sally Brown']

7. Alas! my everlasting peace
Is broken into pieces.
[*Whims and Oddities* (1827), 'Mary's Ghost']

8. It was not in the winter
Our loving lot was cast!
It was the time of roses,
We plucked them as we passed!
['Ballad' (It was not in the winter...) (1827)]

9. I remember, I remember,
The house where I was born,
The little window where the sun
Came peeping in at morn;
He never came a wink too soon,
Nor brought too long a day,
But now, I often wish the night
Had borne my breath away!...

10. I remember, I remember,
The fir trees dark and high;
I used to think their slender tops
Were close against the sky:
It was a childish ignorance,
But now 'tis little joy
To know I'm farther off from heav'n
Than when I was a boy.
[*The Plea of the Midsummer Fairies and Other Poems* (1827), 'I Remember']

11. She stood breast high amid the corn,
Clasp'd by the golden light of morn,
Like the sweetheart of the sun,
Who many a glowing kiss had won...

12. Sure, I said, heav'n did not mean,
Where I reap thou shouldst but glean,
Lay thy sheaf adown and come,
Share my harvest and my home.
[*The Plea of the Midsummer Fairies and Other Poems* (1827), 'Ruth']

13. Much study had made him very lean,
And pale, and leaden-ey'd.
['The Dream of Eugene Aram' (1829)]

14. For that old enemy the gout
Had taken him in toe!
[*Comic Melodies* (1830), 'Lieutenant Luff']

15. And then, in the fulness of joy and hope,
Seem'd washing his hands with invisible soap,
In imperceptible water.
[*Miss Kilmansegg and her Precious Leg* (1840), 'Her Christening']

16. For one of the pleasures of having a rout,
Is the pleasure of having it over.
[*Miss Kilmansegg and her Precious Leg* (1840), 'Her Dream']

17. Home-made dishes that drive one from home.
[*Miss Kilmansegg and her Precious Leg* (1840), 'Her Misery']

18. When Eve upon the first of Men
The apple press'd with specious cant
Oh! what a thousand pities then
That Adam was not Adamant!
['A Reflection' (1842)]

19. With fingers weary and worn,
With eyelids heavy and red,
A Woman sat, in unwomanly rags,
Plying her needle and thread–
Stitch! stitch! stitch!
In poverty, hunger, and dirt...

20. O! Men with Sisters dear!
O! Men with Mothers and Wives!
It is not linen you're wearing out,
But human creatures' lives!...

21. Oh! God! that bread should be so dear,
And flesh and blood so cheap!...

22. No blessed leisure for Love or Hope,
But only time for Grief!
['The Song of the Shirt' (1843)]

23. Take her up tenderly
Lift her with care;
Fashion'd so slenderly,
Young, and so fair!...

24. Mad from life's history,
Glad to death's mystery,
Swift to be hurl'd–
Anywhere, anywhere,
Out of the world!
['The Bridge of Sighs' (1844)]

25. But evil is wrought by want of Thought,
As well as want of Heart!
['The Lady's Dream' (1844)]

26. No sun – no moon!
No morn – no noon
No dawn – no dusk – no proper time of day...

27. No warmth, no cheerfulness, no healthful ease,
No comfortable feel in any member–
No shade, no shine, no butterflies, no bees,
No fruits, no flowers, no leaves, no birds,–
November!
[*Whimsicalities* (1844), 'No!']

28. Our hands have met, but not our hearts;
Our hands will never meet again.
['To a False Friend']

29. What is a modern poet's fate?
To write his thoughts upon a slate;
The critic spits on what is done,
Gives it a wipe – and all is gone.
[In Hallam Tennyson, *Alfred Lord Tennyson, A Memoir* (1897), II, 3, 'A Joke']

30. There are three things which the public will always clamour for, sooner or later: namely, Novelty, novelty, novelty.
[Announcement of *The Comic Annual* for 1836]

31. [Of Quakers]
The sedate, sober, silent, serious, sad-coloured sect.
[*The Comic Annual* (1839), 'The Doves and the Crows']

32. 'Extremes meet', as the whiting said with its tail in its mouth.
[*The Comic Annual* (1839), 'The Doves and the Crows']

33. Holland ... lies so low they're only saved by being dammed.
[*Up the Rhine* (1840), 'Letter from Martha Penny to Rebecca Page']

Hooker, Richard (c. 1554–1600)
English theologian and prebendary; great influence on Anglican theology

1. The earth may shake, the pillars of the world may tremble under us, the countenance of the heaven may be appalled, the sun may lose his light, the moon her beauty, the stars their glory; but concerning the man that trusteth in God ... what is there in the world that shall change his heart, overthrow his faith, alter his affection towards God, or the affection of God to him?
[*Of the Laws of Ecclesiasticall Politie* (1593)]

2. He that goeth about to persuade a multitude, that they are not so well governed as they ought to be, shall never want attentive and favourable hearers.
[*Of the Laws of Ecclesiasticall Politie* (1593)]

3. Change is not made without inconvenience, even from worse to better.
[In Dr Johnson, *Dictionary of the English Language* (1755), Preface]

Hooper, Ellen Sturgis (1816–1841)
American poet and hymn-writer

1. I slept, and dreamed that life was Beauty;
I woke, and found that life was Duty.
['Beauty and Duty' (1840)]

Hooton, Harry (1908–1961)
Australian philosopher and poet

1. Psychology is the theology of the 20th century.
['Inhuman Race']

2. I fought for nothing – and I won.
['The Promised Land']

Hoover, Herbert Clark (1874–1964)
American Republican President, 1929–33; engineer, public administrator and author

1. [On the Eighteenth Amendment, enacting Prohibition]
Our country has deliberately undertaken a great social and economic experiment, noble in motive and far-reaching in purpose.
[Letter to Senator Borah, 1928]

2. The American system of rugged individualism.
[Speech, New York, 1928]

3. [Predicting the outcome if tariff protection were removed]
The grass will grow in the streets of a hundred cities, a thousand towns; the weeds will overrun the fields of millions of farms if that protection is taken away.
[Speech, 1932]

4. Older men declare war. But it is youth that must fight and die.
[Speech, Chicago, 1944]

5. Food will Win the War.
[*American Quaker*]

6. When a great many people are unable to find work, unemployment results.
[In P.F. Boller, *Presidential Anecdotes* (1981)]

Hope, Alec (Derwent) (1907–)
Australian philosophical poet and literary critic

1. And her five cities, like teeming sores,
Each drains her: a vast parasite robber-state

Where second-hand Europeans pullulate
Timidly on the edge of alien shores.
['Australia' (1939)]

2. And Adam watching too
Saw how her dumb breasts at their ripening wept,
The great pod of her belly swelled and grew,

And saw its water break, and saw, in fear,
Its quaking muscles in the act of birth,
Between her legs a pigmy face appear,
And the first murderer lay upon the earth.
['Imperial Adam' (1951)]

3. [An ironic parody of the Greek epitaph commemorating the Spartans who died at Thermopylae in 480 BC]
Go tell those old men, safe in bed,
We took their orders and are dead.
['Inscription for Any War'. Cf. Simonides: 1]

4. I expect I shall stand, looking rather out of place,
Between the mouth-organs and the didgeridoos;
Not a sheep in sight, but a goat with a puzzled face
Among all those Kangaroos.
['The Mermaid in the Zodiac (Antipodean Version)']

5. [Of Patrick White's *The Tree of Man*]
Mr White has three disastrous faults as a novelist: he knows too much, he tells too much and he talks too much.
[*Sydney Morning Herald*, 1956]

Hope, Anthony (Sir Anthony Hope Hawkins) (1863–1933)
English novelist, dramatist and lawyer

1. Economy is going without something you do want in case you should, some day, want something you probably won't want.
[*The Dolly Dialogues* (1894), 12]

2. 'You oughtn't to yield to temptation.'
'Well, somebody must, or the thing becomes absurd.'
[*The Dolly Dialogues* (1894), 14]

3. Unless one is a genius, it is best to aim at being intelligible.
[*The Dolly Dialogues* (1894), 15]

4. He is very fond of making things which he does not want, and then giving them to people who have no use for them.
[*The Dolly Dialogues* (1894), 17]

5. 'Bourgeois,' I observed, 'is an epithet which the riff-raff apply to what is respectable, and the aristocracy to what is decent.'
[*The Dolly Dialogues* (1894), 17]

6. I wish you would read a little poetry sometimes. Your ignorance cramps my conversation.
[*The Dolly Dialogues* (1894), 22]

7. Good families are generally worse than any others.
[*The Prisoner of Zenda* (1894), 1]

8. His foe was folly and his weapon wit.
[Inscription on the tablet to W.S. Gilbert, Victoria Embankment, London, 1915]

Hope, Laurence (Adela Florence Nicolson) (1865–1904)
English poet

1. Less than the dust, beneath thy Chariot wheel,
Less than the rust, that never stained thy Sword,
Less than the trust thou hast in me, Oh, Lord,
Even less than these!
Less than the weed, that grows beside thy door,
Less than the speed, of hours, spent far from thee,
Less than the need thou hast in life of me,
Even less am I.
[*The Garden of Kama* (1901), 'Less than the Dust']

2. Pale hands I loved beside the Shalimar,
Where are you now? Who lies beneath your spell?...

3. Pale hands, pink tipped, like lotus-buds that float
On those cool waters where we used to dwell,
I would have rather felt you round my throat
Crushing out life; than waving me farewell!
[*The Garden of Kama* (1901), 'Kashmiri Song']

Hopkins, Gerard Manley (1844–1889)
English poet, noted for his experimental sprung rhythm and natural imagery; classicist and Jesuit priest

1. Palate, the hutch of tasty lust,
Desire not to be rinsed with wine:
The can must be so sweet, the crust
So fresh that come in fasts divine!...

2. And you unhouse and house the Lord.
['The Habit of Perfection' (1866)]

3. I did say yes
O at lightning and lashed rod;
Thou heardst me truer than tongue confess
Thy terror, O Christ, O God...

4. How a lush-kept plush-capped sloe
Will, mouthed to flesh-burst,
Gush! – flush the man, the being with it, sour or sweet,
Brim, in a flash, full!
['The Wreck of the Deutschland' (1876)]

5. The world is charged with the grandeur of God.
It will flame out, like shining from shook foil;...
Generations have trod, have trod, have trod;
And all is seared with trade; bleared, smeared with toil;
And wears man's smudge and shares man's smell: the soil
Is bare now, nor can foot feel, being shod.
['God's Grandeur' (1877)]

6. Glory be to God for dappled things...

7. All things counter, original, spare, strange;
Whatever is fickle, freckled (who knows how?)
With swift, slow; sweet, sour; adazzle, dim;
He fathers-forth whose beauty is past change:
Praise him.
['Pied Beauty' (1877)]

8. The glassy peartree leaves and blooms, they brush
The descending blue; that blue is all in a rush
With richness.
['Spring' (1877)]

9. Look at the stars! look, look up at the skies!
Oh look at all the fire-folk sitting in the air!
The bright boroughs, the circle-citadels there!
['The Starlight Night' (1877)]

10. I caught this morning morning's minion, kingdom of daylight's dauphin, dapple-dawn-drawn Falcon, in his riding...

11. My heart in hiding
Stirred for a bird, – the achieve of, the mastery of the thing!
['The Windhover' (1877)]

12. Towery city and branchy between towers;
Cuckoo-echoing, bell-swarmèd, lark-charmèd, rook-racked, river-rounded.
['Duns Scotus' Oxford' (1879)]

13. Felix Randal the farrier, O he is dead then?...

14. Didst fettle for the great grey drayhorse his bright and battering sandal!
['Felix Randal' (1880)]

15. Margaret, are you grieving
Over Golden-grove unleaving?...

16. Ah! as the heart grows older
It will come to such sights colder
By and by, nor spare a sigh
Though worlds of wanwood leafmeal lie;
And yet you will weep and know why...

17. It is the blight man was born for,
It is Margaret you mourn for.
['Spring and Fall: To a young child' (1880)]

18. What would the world be, once bereft
Of wet and of wildness? Let them be left,
O let them be left, wildness and wet;
Long live the weeds and the wilderness yet.
['Inversnaid' (1881)]

19. As kingfishers catch fire, dragonflies draw flame;
As tumbled over rim in roundy wells
Stones ring.
['As Kingfishers Catch Fire' (c. 1882)]

20. Not, I'll not, carrion comfort, Despair, not feast on thee;
Not untwist – slack they may be – these last strands of man
In me or, most weary, cry I can no more. I can;
Can something, hope, wish day come, not choose not to be...

21. That night, that year
Of now done darkness I wretch lay wrestling with (my God!) my God.
['Carrion Comfort' (1885)]

22. No worst, there is none. Pitched past pitch of grief,
More pangs will, schooled at forepangs, wilder wring.
Comforter, where, where is your comforting?...

23. O the mind, mind has mountains; cliffs of fall
Frightful, sheer, no-man-fathomed...

24. Here! creep,
Wretch, under a comfort serves in a whirlwind: all
Life death does end and each day dies with sleep.
['No Worst, there is None' (1885)]

25. My own heart let me more have pity on; let
Me live to my sad self hereafter kind,
Charitable; not live this tormented mind
With this tormented mind tormenting yet.
['My own Heart let me more have Pity on' (c. 1885)]

26. I wake and feel the fell of dark, not day.
What hours, O what black hours we have spent
This night!...

27. I am gall, I am heartburn...

28. I see
The lost are like this, and their scourge to be
As I am mine, their sweating selves; but worse.
['I wake and Feel the Fell of dark, not day' (c. 1885)]

29. I am all at once what Christ is, since he was what I am, and
This Jack, joke, poor potsherd, patch, matchwood, immortal diamond,
Is immortal diamond.
['That Nature is a Heraclitean Fire and of the comfort of the Resurrection' (1888)]

30. Thou art indeed just, Lord, if I contend
With thee; but, sir, so what I plead is just.
Why do sinners' ways prosper? and why must
Disappointment all I endeavour end?...

31. Birds build – but not I build; no, but strain,
Time's eunuch, and not breed one work that wakes.
Mine, O thou lord of life, send my roots rain.
['Thou Art Indeed Just, Lord' (1889)]

32. A few other little things; some in sprung rhythm, with various other experiments.
[Letter to R.W. Dixon, 1878]

33. Now it is the virtue of design, pattern, or inscape to be distinctive and it is the vice of distinctiveness to become queer. This vice I cannot have escaped.
[Letter to Robert Bridges, 1879]

34. The poetical language of an age should be the current language heightened.
[Letter to Robert Bridges, 1879]

Hopkins, Jane Ellice (1836–1904)

English social reformer and writer; founder of the White Cross

1. Gift, like genius, I often think, only means an infinite capacity for taking pains.
[*Work amongst Working Men, 1870*. Cf. Thomas Carlyle: 57]

Hopper, Hedda (1890–1966)

American actress, columnist and autobiographer

1. At one time I thought he wanted to be an actor. He had certain qualifications, including no money and a total lack of responsibility.
[*From Under My Hat* (1953)]

Horace (65–8 BC)

Roman lyric poet and satirist

1. *Indocilis pauperium pati.*
Not taught to endure poverty.
[*Odes*, I, 1, line 18]

2. *Quodsi me lyricis vatibus inseres,*
Sublimi feriam sidera vertice.
But if you rank me with the lyric poets, I shall touch the stars with my exalted head.
[*Odes*, I, 1, line 35]

3. *Navis, quae tibi creditum*
Debes Vergilium; finibus Atticis
Reddas incolumen, precor,
Et serves animae dimidium meae.
O ship, you who owe us Virgil, entrusted to you, bring him back safely to Attic shores, I pray, and preserve the half of my own life.
[*Odes*, I, 3, line 5]

4. *Illi robur et aes triplex*
Circa pectus erat, qui fragilem truci
Commisit pelago ratim
Primus.
Oak and triple bronze encircled the heart of the man who first committed a frail boat to the cruel sea.
[*Odes*, I, 3, line 9]

5. *Pallida Mors, aequo pulsat pede pauperum tabernas*
Regumque turris.
Pale Death strikes with impartial foot at the cottages of the poor and the turrets of kings.
[*Odes*, I, 4, line 13]

6. *Vitae summa brevis spem nos vetat incohare longam.*
Life's brief span forbids us from entering on far-reaching hopes.
[*Odes*, I, 4, line 15]

7. *Quis multa gracilis te puer in rosa*
Perfusus liquidis urget odoribus
Grato, Pyrrha, sub antro?
Cui flavam religas comam,
Simplex munditiis?
What slender youth, amidst many a rose, steeped in scent, is courting you, Pyrrha, in some pleasant grotto? For whom are you letting down your golden hair, simple in your sophistication?
[*Odes*, I, 5, line 1]

8. *Nil desperandum Teucro duce et auspice Teucro.*
Never despair under Teucer's leadership and protection.
[*Odes*, I, 7, line 27]

9. *Nunc vino pellite curas:*
Cras ingens iterabimus aequor.
Now banish your cares with wine; tomorrow we will embark upon the mighty ocean.
[*Odes*, I, 7, line 30]

10. *Permitte divis cetera.*
Leave the rest to the gods.
[*Odes*, I, 9, line 9]

11. *Quid sit futurum cras fuge quaerere et*
Quem Fors dierum cumque dabit lucro
Appone.
Avoid enquiring into what will be tomorrow, and count as gain each day that Fortune grants you.
[*Odes*, I, 9, line 13]

12. *Tu ne quaesieris, scire nefas, quem mihi, quem tibi*
Finem di dederint.
Do not ask – it is forbidden to know – what end the gods have in store for me or for you.
[*Odes*, I, 11, line 1]

13. *Dum loquimur, fugerit invida*
Aetas: carpe diem, quam minimum credula postero.
While we speak, envious time will have sped away: pluck the fruit of today, putting as little trust as possible in tomorrow.
[*Odes*, I, 11, line 7]

14. *O matre pulchra filia pulchrior.*
O fairer daughter of a fair mother.
[*Odes*, I, 16, line 1]

15. *Integer vitae scelerisque purus.*
He who is upright and untainted by guilt.
[*Odes*, I, 22, line 1]

16. *Dulce ridentem Lalagen amabo,*
Dulce loquentem.
I will love my sweetly laughing, sweetly talking Lalage.
[*Odes*, I, 22 line 23]

17. *Persicos odi, puer, apparatus.*
I hate that Persian finery, my boy.
[*Odes*, I, 38, line 1]

18. *Mitte sectari, rosa quo locorum*
Sera moretur.
Stop searching for the place where a late rose may linger.
[*Odes*, I, 38, line 3]

19. *Aequam memento rebus in arduis*
Servare mentem.
Remember, in difficult straits, to keep a level head.
[*Odes*, II, 3, line 1]

20. *Omnes eodem cogimur, omnium*
versatur urna serius ocius
sors exitura et nos in aeternum
exsilium impositura cumbae.
We are all being gathered to the same end; the lot of every one of us is turning about in the urn doomed to come out sooner or later and to deposit us in Charon's boat in eternal exile.
[*Odes*, II, 3, line 25]

21. *Ille terrarum mihi praeter omnis*
Angulus ridet.
That corner of the world smiles for me above all others.
[*Odes*, II, 6, line 13]

22. *Auream quisquis mediocritatem*
Diligit...
Whosoever loves the golden mean...
[*Odes*, II, 10, line 5]

23. *Neque semper arcum*
Tendit Apollo.
Apollo does not always aim his bow.
[*Odes*, II, 10, line 19]

24. *Eheu fugaces, Posthume, Posthume,*
Labuntur anni.
Alas, Posthumus, Posthumus, the fleeting years are gliding by.
[*Odes*, II, 14, line 1]

25. *Nihil est ab omni*
Parte beatum.
Nothing is perfect from every point of view.
[*Odes*, II, 16, line 27]

26. *Credite posteri.*
Believe me, you who come after me!
[*Odes*, II, 19, line 2]

27. *Odi profanum vulgus et arceo;*
Favete linguis; carmina non prius
Audita Musarum sacerdos
Virginibus puerisque canto.
I hate the unholy crowd and avoid it. Pray be silent; as priest of the Muses, I sing for maiden girls and boys songs not heard before.
[*Odes*, III, 1, line 1]

28. *Post equitem sedet atra Cura.*
At the rider's back sits dismal Care.
[*Odes*, III, 1, line 40]

29. *Cur valle permutem Sabina*
Divitias operosiores?
Why should I exchange my Sabine valley for riches that bring more trouble?
[*Odes*, III, 1, line 47]

30. *Dulce et decorum est pro patria mori.*
It is sweet and honourable to die for one's country.
[*Odes*, III, 2, line 13]

31. *Iustum et tenacem propositi virum*
Non civium ardor prava iubentium,
Non vultus instantis tyranni
Mente quatit solida.
The righteous man who is tenacious of purpose is not shaken from his firm resolve by the ardour of his fellow citizens clamouring for what is wrong, or by the glare of the threatening tyrant.
[*Odes*, III, 3, line 1]

32. *Si fractus inlabitur orbis,*
Impavidum ferient ruinae.
If the world should crack and fall on him, its ruins would strike him undismayed.
[*Odes*, III, 3, line 7]

33. *Aurum inrepertum et sic melius situm.*
Gold undiscovered (and all the better for that).
[*Odes*, III, 3, line 49]

34. *Non sine dis animosus infans.*
With the gods' help, a spirited child.
[*Odes*, III, 4, line 20]

35. *Vis consili expers mole ruit sua.*
Brute force without judgement collapses under its own weight.
[*Odes*, III, 4, line 65]

36. *O magna Carthago, probrosis*
Altior Italiae ruinis!
O mighty Carthage, raised higher by Italy's shameful collapse!
[*Odes*, III, 5, line 39]

37. *Delicta maiorum immeritus lues.*
Undeservedly you will pay for the sins of your fathers.
[*Odes*, III, 6, line 1]

38. *Damnosa quid non imminuit dies?*
Aetas parentum peior avis tulit
Nos nequiores, mox daturos
Progeniem vitiosiorem.
What is undiminished by the ravages of time? Our parents' age (worse than our grandparents') has produced us, more worthless still, and destined soon to produce a generation even more vicious.
[*Odes*, III, 6, line 45]

39. *Donec gratus eram tibi.*
In the days when I was dear to you.
[*Odes*, III, 9, line 1]

40. *Tecum vivere amem, tecum obeam libens.*
With you I should love to live, with you I would willingly die.
[*Odes*, III, 9, line 24]

41. *Splendide mendax et in omne virgo*
Nobilis aevum.
A maiden gloriously false and renowned for all time.
[*Odes*, III, 11, line 35]

42. *O fons Bandusiae splendidior vitro.*
O spring of Bandusia, clearer than crystal.
[*Odes*, III, 13, line 1]

43. *Non ego hoc ferrem calidus iuventa*
Consule Planco.
I would not have borne this when I was a hot-blooded youth and Plancus was consul.
[*Odes*, III, 14, line 27]

44. *Magnas inter opes inops.*
Poverty-stricken in the midst of great riches.
[*Odes*, III, 16, line 28]

45. *O nata mecum consule Manlio*
...pia testa.
O trusty wine-jar, born with me when Manlius was consul.
[*Odes*, III, 21, line 1]

46. *Vixi puellis nuper idoneus*
Et militavi non sine gloria;
Nunc arma defunctumque bello
Barbiton hic paries habebit.
Till recently I was fit for the girls and soldiered not without glory; now on this wall will hang my weapons and my lyre that has done with the war.
[*Odes*, III, 26, line 1]

47. *Fumum et opes strepitumque Romae.*
The smoke and wealth and noise of Rome.
[*Odes*, III, 29, line 12]

48. *Exegi monumentum aere perennius.*
I have raised up a monument more lasting than bronze.
[*Odes*, III, 30, line 1]

49. *Non omnis moriar.*
I shall not wholly die.
[*Odes*, III, 30, line 6]

50. *Non sum qualis eram bonae*
Sub regno Cinarae.
I am not the man I was in the reign of my dear Cinara.
[*Odes*, IV, 1, line 3]

51. *Quod spiro et placeo, si placeo, tuum est.*
That I am inspired and please (if I do please) is because of you.
[*Odes*, IV, 3, line 24]

52. *Merses profundo: pulchrior evenit.*
Plunge it in the depths: it comes up more beautiful.
[*Odes*, IV, 4, line 65]

53. *Diffugere nives, redeunt iam gramina campis*
Arboribusque comae.
The snows have fled; now the grass is returning to the fields and the leaves are coming back to the trees.
[*Odes*, IV, 7, line 1]

54. *Immortalia ne speres, monet annus et almum*
Quae rapit hora diem.
The changing year and the passing hour that takes away the genial day warns you not to build everlasting hopes.
[*Odes*, IV, 7, line 7]

55. *Damna tamen celeres reparant caelestia lunae:*
Nos ubi decidimus
Quo pius Aeneas, quo Tullus dives et Ancus,
Pulvis et umbra sumus.
Yet moons quickly wax again after they have waned; we, when we have gone down to join good Aeneas, and Tullus who was so rich, and Ancus, we are but dust and shadow.
[*Odes*, IV, 7, line 13]

56. *Dignum laude virum Musa vetat mori.*
He who is worthy of praise the Muse forbids to die.
[*Odes*, IV, 8, line 28]

57. *Vixere fortes ante Agamemnona*
Multi; sed omnes illacrimabiles
Urgentur ignotique longa
Nocte, carent quia vate sacro.
There lived many brave men before Agammenon, but all are overwhelmed in unending night, unmourned and unknown, because they lack a poet to give them immortality.
[*Odes*, IV, 9, line 25]

58. *Non possidentem multa vocaveris*
Recte beatum: rectius occupat
Nomen beati, qui deorum
Muneribus sapienter uti
Duramque callet pauperiem pati
Peiusque leto flagitium timet.
You would not rightly call the man who has many possessions happy; he more rightly deserves to be called happy who knows how to use the gifts of the gods wisely, and can endure the hardship of poverty, and who fears dishonour more than death.
[*Odes*, IV, 9, line 45]

59. *Misce stultitiam consiliis brevem:*
Dulce est desipere in loco.
Mix a little folly with your plans: it is sweet to be silly at the right moment.
[*Odes*, IV, 12, line 27]

60. *Beatus ille, qui procul negotiis,*
Ut prisca gens mortalium
Paterna rura bobus exercet suis,
Solutus omni faenore.
Happy is the man who, far from business, like the race of men of old, works his ancestral lands with his own oxen, free from all financial dealing.
[*Epodes*, II, line 1]

61. *Qui fit, Maecenas, ut nemo, quam sibi sortem*
Seu ratio dederit seu fors obiecerit, illa
Contentus vivat, laudet diversa sequentis?
How comes it, Maecenas, that no one lives contented with his lot, whether he has planned it for himself or whether chance has thrown it in his way, but each praises those who follow other paths?
[*Satires*, I, 1, line 1]

62. *Mutato nomine de te*
Fabula narratur.
Only change the name and the story is about you.
[*Satires*, I, 1, line 69]

63. *Est modus in rebus, sunt certi denique fines,*
Quos ultra citraque nequit consistere rectum.
There is measure in all things. There are, in short, certain boundaries beyond which and short of which right can have no place.
[*Satires*, I, 1, line 106]

64. *Hoc genus omne.*
All that kind.
[*Satires*, I, 2, line 2]

65. [Describing how Tigellius would sing 'from the first course to the dessert' if the fancy took him]
Ab ovo
Usque ad mala.
From the egg right through to the apples.
[*Satires*, I, 3, line 6]

66. *Etiam disiecti membra poetae.*
Even when dismembered, the limbs of a poet.
[*Satires*, I, 4, line 62]

67. *Hic niger est, hunc tu, Romane, caveto.*
The fellow is a blackguard; be wary of him, good Roman!
[*Satires*, I, 4, line 85]

68. *Ad unguem*
Factus homo.
A man perfect to the last detail.
[*Satires*, I, 5, line 32]

69. *Credat Iudaeus Apella,*
Non ego.
Apella the Jew may believe it; I shall not.
[*Satires*, I, 5, line 100]

70. *Solventur risu tabulae, tu missus abibis.*
The case will be thrown out with a laugh. You will get off scot-free.
[*Satires*, II, 1, line 86]

71. *Hoc erat in votis: modus agri non ita magnus,*
Hortus ubi et tecto vicinus iugis aquae fons
Et paulum silvae super his foret.
This was my prayer: a piece of land not so very large, which should have a garden and near the house an ever-flowing spring, and a bit of woodland besides.
[*Satires*, II, 6, line 1]

72. *O noctes cenaeque deum!*
O nights and feasts divine!
[*Satires*, II, 6, line 65]

73. *Quisnam igitur liber? Sapiens qui sibi imperiosus,*
Quem neque pauperies neque mors neque vincula terrent,
Responsare cupidinibus, contemnere honores
Fortis, et in se ipso totus, teres, atque rotundus.
Who then is free? The wise man who commands himself, whom neither poverty nor death nor chains can terrify, who is strong enough to defy his passions and to despise distinctions, a man who is complete in himself, polished and well-rounded.
[*Satires*, II, 7, line 83]

74. *Nullius addictus iurare in verba magistri,*
Quo me cumque rapit tempestas, deferor hospes.
Sworn to no master, of no sect am I:
As drives the storm, at any door I knock.
[*Epistles*, I, 1, line 14, trans. Pope]

75. *Virtus est vitium fugere, et sapientia prima*
Stultitia caruisse.
'Tis the first virtue, vices to abhor,
And the first wisdom, to be fool no more.
[*Epistles*, I, 1, line 41, trans. Pope]

76. *Condicio dulcis sine pulvere palmae.*
The happy state of gaining victory without the dust of racing.
[*Epistles*, I, 1, line 51]

77. *Hic murus aeneus esto,*
Nil conscire sibi, nulla pallescere culpa.
This be your wall of brass, to have nothing on your conscience, no reason to grow pale with guilt.
[*Epistles*, I, 1, line 60]

78. *Rem facias, rem si possis recte, si non, quocumque modo rem.*
Make money: make it honestly if possible; if not, make it by any means.
[*Epistles*, I, 1, line 65. Cf. Pope: 150]

79. *Olim quod vulpes aegroto cauta leoni*
Respondit referam: 'quia me vestigia terrent,
Omnia te adversum spectantia, nulla retrorsum.'
I shall give the answer that the wary fox once gave to the sick lion: 'Because those footprints frighten me, all leading in your direction, none coming back!'
[*Epistles*, I, 1, line 73]

80. *Quidquid delirant reges plectuntur Achivi.*
Howsoever their kings go mad, the Greeks pay the penalty.
[*Epistles*, I, 2, line 14]

81. *Nos numerus sumus et fruges consumere nati.*
We are mere ciphers, born to consume the fruits of the earth.
[*Epistles*, I, 2, line 27]

82. *Dimidium facti qui coepit habet: sapere aude.*
To have made a beginning is half of the business; dare to be wise.
[*Epistles*, I, 2, line 40]

83. *Ira furor brevis est.*
Anger is a brief madness.
[*Epistles*, I, 2, line 62]

84. *Omnem crede diem tibi diluxisse supremum.*
Believe every day that has dawned is your last.
[*Epistles*, I, 4, line 13. Cf. Ken: 1]

85. *Nil admirari prope res est una, Numici,*
Solaque, quae possit facere et servare beatum.
Not to admire is all the art I know,

To make men happy and to keep them so.
[*Epistles*, I, 6, line 1, trans. Pope]

86. *Naturam expelles furca, tamen usque recurret.*
You may drive out Nature with a pitchfork, but she always comes hurrying back.
[*Epistles*, I, 10, line 24]

87. *Caelum, non animum, mutant qui trans mare currunt.*
Strenua nos exercet inertia; navibus atque
Quadrigis petimus bene vivere. Quod petis hic est,
Est Ulubris, animus si te non deficit aequus.
Those who rush across the sea change their clime not their frame of mind. A restless idleness occupies us. We seek happiness in boats and carriage rides. What you are looking for is here; it is at Ulubrae, if only peace of mind does not desert you.
[*Epistles*, I, 11, line 27]

88. *Concordia discors.*
Discordant harmony.
[*Epistles*, I, 12, line 19]

89. *Principibus placuisse viris non ultima laus est.*
It is not the least praise to have pleased leaders of men.
[*Epistles*, I, 17, line 35]

90. *Nam tua res agitur, paries cum proximus ardet.*
For your own safety is at stake, when your neighbour's wall catches fire.
[*Epistles*, I, 18, line 84]

91. *Fallentis semita vitae.*
The pathway of a life unnoticed.
[*Epistles*, I, 18, line 103]

92. *Prisco si credis, Maecenas docte, Cratino,*
Nulla placere diu nec vivere carmina possunt
Quae scribuntur aquae potoribus.
If you believe old Cratinus, my learned Maecenas, no poems can give pleasure for long, nor last, which are written by drinkers of water.
[*Epistles*, I, 19, line 1]

93. *O imitatores, servum pecus.*
O imitators, you slavish herd!
[*Epistles*, I, 19, line 19]

94. *Graecia capta ferum victorem cepit et artes,*
Intulit agresti Latio.
Captive Greece captivated her savage conqueror and brought the arts into rustic Latium.
[*Epistles*, II, 1, line 156]

95. *Si foret in terris, rideret Democritus.*
If he were still on earth, Democritus would laugh.
[*Epistles*, II, 1, line 194]

96. *Atque inter silvas Academi quaerere verum.*
And seek truth among the groves of Academe.
[*Epistles*, II, 2, line 45]

97. *Multa fero, ut placem genus irritabile vatum.*
I endure much to placate the sensitive race of poets.
[*Epistles*, II, 2, line 102]

98. *Quid te exempta iuvat spinis de pluribus una?*
Vivere si recte nescis, decede peritis.
Lusisti satis, edisti satis atque bibisti:
Tempus abire tibi est.
How does it help you to pluck out one thorn of many? If you don't know how to live right, make way for those who do. You have had enough fun, eaten and drunk enough: it is time for you to go.
[*Epistles*, II, 2, line 212]

99. *Pictoribus atque poetis*
Quidlibet audendi semper fuit aequa potestas.
Scimus, et hanc veniam petimusque damusque vicissim.
'Painters and poets', you say, 'have always had licence to try anything.' We know, and we poets both claim this indulgence and grant it to others in their turn.
[*Ars Poetica*, line 9]

100. *Inceptis gravibus plerumque et magna professis*
Purpureus, late qui splendeat, unus et alter
Adsuitur pannus.
In serious works and ones that promise great things, one or two purple patches are often stitched in, to glitter far and wide.
[*Ars Poetica*, line 14]

101. *Brevis esse laboro,*
Obscurus fio.
I labour to be brief, and I become obscure.
[*Ars Poetica*, line 25]

102. *Dixeris egregie notum si callida verbum*
Reddiderit iunctura novum.
You will express yourself with great distinction, if skilful positioning makes a familiar word new.
[*Ars Poetica*, line 47]

103. *Multa renascentur quae iam cecidere, cadentque*
Quae nunc sunt in honore vocabula, si volet usus,
Quem penes arbitrium est et ius et norma loquendi.
Many words which have now dropped out of favour will be revived, and many of those that are now fashionable will drop out, if usage so wills it, in whose power lies the judgement, the law and rule of speech.
[*Ars Poetica*, line 70]

104. *Grammatici certant et adhuc sub iudice lis est.*
Scholars dispute, and the case is still before the court.
[*Ars Poetica*, line 78]

105. *Proicit ampullas et sesquipedalia verba.*
Throws out his bombast and his words a foot and a half long.
[*Ars Poetica*, line 97]

106. *Difficile est proprie communia dicere.*
It is difficult to treat common things in an original way.
[*Ars Poetica*, line 128]

107. *Parturient montes, nascetur ridiculus mus.*
Mountains will be in labour, and a ridiculous mouse will be born.
[*Ars Poetica*, line 139]

108. *Semper ad eventum festinat et in medias res*
Non secus ac notas auditorem rapit.
He always hurries to the main issue and whisks his listener into the middle of things as though it were already known.
[*Ars Poetica*, line 148]

109. *Difficilis, querulus, laudator temporis acti*
Se puero, castigator censorque minorum.
Multa ferunt anni venientes commoda secum,
Multa recedentes adimunt.
Difficult, complaining, a praiser of time past when he was a boy, a critic and castigator of the young generation. The years as they come bring many blessings, but as they go by they take many away too.
[*Ars Poetica*, line 173]

110. *Vos exemplaria Graeca*
Nocturna versate manu, versate diurna.
Turn the pages of your Greek models by night, turn them by day.
[*Ars Poetica*, line 268]

111. *Grais ingenium, Grais dedit ore rotundo*
Musa loqui.

To the Greeks the Muse gave native wit, to the Greeks the gift of eloquence in well-rounded phrase.
[*Ars Poetica*, line 323]

112. *Omne tulit punctum qui miscuit utile dulci,*
Lectorem delectando pariter monendo.
He has won every vote who has mixed profit with pleasure, delighting the reader at the same time as instructing him.
[*Ars Poetica*, line 343]

113. *Indignor quandoque bonus dormitat Homerus.*
I am annoyed whenever the good Homer nods.
[*Ars Poetica*, line 359]

114. *Ut pictura poesis.*
Poetry is like painting.
[*Ars Poetica*, line 361]

115. *Mediocribus esse poetis*
Non homines, non di, non concessere columnae.
Not men, nor gods, nor booksellers have allowed that poets should be second rate.
[*Ars Poetica*, line 372]

116. *Nonumque prematur in annum,*
Membranis intus positis: delere licebit
Quod non edideris; nescit vox missa reverti.
Let it be kept back till the ninth year; the manuscript deposited within: you can destroy what you haven't published; the word once out cannot be recalled.
[*Ars Poetica*, line 388]

117. *Sit ius liceatque perire poetis,*
invitum qui servat, idem facit occidenti.
Let poets have the licence and power to destroy themselves. Whoever saves a man's life against his will does the same as murder him.
[*Ars Poetica*, line 466]

Horne, Donald Richmond (1921–)
Australian novelist, magazine contributor and university lecturer

1. Australia is a lucky country run mainly by second-rate people who share its luck.
[*The Lucky Country: Australia in the Sixties* (1964)]

2. The desire to enjoy the games of the rich became one of the most effectively expressed moods of Australian egalitarianism.
[*Southern Exposure* (1967; with David Beal)]

3. Politicians cannot help being clowns. Political activity is essentially absurd. The hopes held for it can be high, the results tragic, but the political art itself must lack dignity: it can never match our ideals of how such things should be done.
[Introduction to Boddy and Ellis, *The Legend of King O'Malley*]

4. Politics is both fraud and vision.
[Introduction to Boddy and Ellis, *The Legend of King O'Malley*]

Horne, Kenneth (1900–1969)
English radio comedian and personality

1. Read any good books, lately?
[Catchphrase in radio show *Much Binding in the Marsh*, 1940s]

Horne, Richard Henry (1803–1884)
English allegorical poet, dramatist, critic and children's writer

1. 'Tis always morning somewhere in the world.
[*Orion* (1843), III, 2]

2. Beyond, sleeps the forest, all dark; and, between,
Gold-diggings, deserted, like huge graveyards yawn
[*All the Year Round*,'The Blue Mountain Exile']

Horsley, Bishop Samuel (1733–1806)
English prelate, editor of Sir Isaac Newton and author of mathematical and theological works

1. In this country, my Lords, ... the individual subject ... 'has nothing to do with the laws but to obey them.'
[Speech, House of Lords, 1795]

Horváth, Ödön von (1901–1938)
German-Hungarian novelist

1. *Wer arm ist, darf sich was vorlügen – das ist sein Recht.*
Vielleicht sein einziges Recht.
Whoever is poor may lie to himself – that is his right.
Perhaps his only right.
[*Ein Kind unserer Zeit* (*A Child of our Time*, 1938), 'Das denkende Tier' ('The Thinking Animal')]

2. *Denken tut weh.*
Thinking hurts.
[*Ein Kind unserer Zeit* (*A Child of our Time*, 1938), 'Der verlorene Sohn' ('The Lost Son')]

Houde, Camillien (1889–1958)
Canadian politician and Mayor of Montreal

1. [Referring to his plan to open vespasiennes at Montreal thoroughfares, late 1940s]
I will erect not only urinals but also arsenals.
[Attr.]

Household, Geoffrey (Edward West) (1900–1988)
English adventure novelist and short-story writer

1. I have noticed that what cats most appreciate in a human being is not the ability to produce food which they take for granted – but his or her entertainment value.
[*Rogue Male* (1939)]

2. It's easy to make a man confess the lies he tells to himself; it's far harder to make him confess the truth.
[*Rogue Male* (1939)]

Housman, A.E. (1859–1936)
English lyric poet and leading Latin scholar

1. From Clee to heaven the beacon burns,
The shires have seen it plain,
From north and south the sign returns
And beacons burn again...

2. Oh, God will save her, fear you not:
Be you the men you've been,
Get you the sons your fathers got,
And God will save the Queen.
[*A Shropshire Lad* (1896), 1, '1887']

3. Loveliest of trees, the cherry now
Is hung with bloom along the bough,
And stands about the woodland ride
Wearing white for Eastertide.

Now, of my threescore years and ten,
Twenty will not come again,
And take from seventy springs a score,
It only leaves me fifty more.

And since to look at things in bloom
Fifty springs are little room,
About the woodlands I will go

To see the cherry hung with snow.
[*A Shropshire Lad* (1896), 2]

4. Up, lad: thews that lie and cumber
Sunlit pallets never thrive;
Morns abed and daylight slumber
Were not meant for man alive.

Clay lies still, but blood's a rover;
Breath's a ware that will not keep.
Up, lad: when the journey's over
There'll be time enough to sleep.
[*A Shropshire Lad* (1896), 4, 'Reveille']

5. They hang us now in Shrewsbury jail:
The whistles blow forlorn,
And trains all night groan on the rail
To men that die at morn...

6. And naked to the hangman's noose
The morning clocks will ring
A neck God made for other use
Than strangling in a string...

7. So here I'll watch the night and wait
To see the morning shine,
When he will hear the stroke of eight
And not the stroke of nine.
[*A Shropshire Lad* (1896), 9]

8. Lovers lying two and two
Ask not whom they sleep beside,
And the bridegroom all night through
Never turns him to the bride.
[*A Shropshire Lad* (1896), 12]

9. When I was one-and-twenty
I heard a wise man say,
'Give crowns and pounds and guineas
But not your heart away;
Give pearls away and rubies
But keep your fancy free.'
But I was one-and-twenty,
No use to talk to me.
[*A Shropshire Lad* (1896), 13]

10. Oh, when I was in love with you,
Then I was clean and brave,
And miles around the wonder grew
How well did I behave.

And now the fancy passes by,
And nothing will remain,
And miles around they'll say that I
Am quite myself again.
[*A Shropshire Lad* (1896), 18]

11. In summertime on Bredon
The bells they sound so clear;
Round both the shires they ring them
In steeples far and near,
A happy noise to hear.

Here of a Sunday morning
My love and I would lie,
And see the coloured counties,
And hear the larks so high
About us in the sky...

12. 'Come all to church, good people,'–
Oh, noisy bells, be dumb;
I hear you, I will come.
[*A Shropshire Lad* (1896), 21, 'Bredon Hill']

13. The lads in their hundreds to Ludlow come in for the fair,
There's men from the barn and the forge and the mill and the fold.
The lads for the girls and the lads for the liquor are there,
And there with the rest are the lads that will never be old...

14. They carry back bright to the coiner the mintage of man,
The lads that will die in their glory and never be old.
[*A Shropshire Lad* (1896), 23]

15. 'Is my team ploughing,
That I was used to drive
And hear the harness jingle
When I was man alive?'...

16. No change, though you lie under
The land you used to plough...

17. The goal stands up, the keeper
Stands up to keep the goal...

18. Yes, lad, I lie easy,
I lie as lads would choose;
I cheer a dead man's sweetheart,
Never ask me whose.
[*A Shropshire Lad* (1896), 27]

19. High the vanes of Shrewsbury gleam
Islanded in Severn stream.
[*A Shropshire Lad* (1896), 28, 'The Welsh Marches']

20. On Wenlock Edge the wood's in trouble,
His forest fleece the Wrekin heaves;
The gale, it plies the saplings double,
And thick on Severn snow the leaves.
[*A Shropshire Lad* (1896), 31]

21. On the idle hill of summer,
Sleepy with the flow of streams,
Far I hear the steady drummer
Drumming like a noise in dreams...

22. East and west on fields forgotten
Bleach the bones of comrades slain,
Lovely lads and dead and rotten;
None that go return again.
[*A Shropshire Lad* (1896), 35]

23. White in the moon the long road lies,
The moon stands blank above;
White in the moon the long road lies
That leads me from my love.
[*A Shropshire Lad* (1896), 36]

24. Into my heart an air that kills
From yon far country blows:
What are those blue remembered hills,
What spires, what farms are those?

That is the land of lost content,
I see it shining plain,
The happy highways where I went
And cannot come again.
[*A Shropshire Lad* (1896), 40]

25. Be still, be still, my soul; it is but for a season:
Let us endure an hour and see injustice done.
[*A Shropshire Lad* (1896), 48]

26. With rue my heart is laden
For golden friends I had,
For many a rose-lipt maiden
And many a lightfoot lad.

By brooks too broad for leaping
The lightfoot boys are laid;
The rose-lipt girls are sleeping

In fields where roses fade.
[*A Shropshire Lad* (1896), 54]

27. The man that runs away
Lives to die another day.
[*A Shropshire Lad* (1896), 56, 'The Day of Battle']

28. Say, for what were hop-yards meant,
Or why was Burton built on Trent?
Oh many a peer of England brews
Livelier liquor than the Muse,
And malt does more than Milton can
To justify God's ways to man.
Ale, man, ale's the stuff to drink
For fellows whom it hurts to think...

29. Oh I have been to Ludlow fair
And left my necktie God knows where,
And carried half way home, or near,
Pints and quarts of Ludlow beer:
Then the world seemed none so bad,
And I myself a sterling lad;
And down in lovely muck I've lain,
Happy till I woke again.
[*A Shropshire Lad* (1896), 62]

30. We'll to the woods no more,
The laurels all are cut.
[*Last Poems* (1922), Introduction]

31. The chestnut casts his flambeaux and the flowers
Stream from the hawthorn on the wind away,
The doors clap to, the pane is blind with showers.
Pass me the can, lad; there's an end of May.
[*Last Poems* (1922), 9]

32. The laws of God, the laws of man,
He may keep that will and can...

33. I, a stranger and afraid
In a world I never made...

34. And since, my soul, we cannot fly
To Saturn nor to Mercury,
Keep we must, if keep we can,
These foreign laws of God and man.
[*Last Poems* (1922), 12]

35. The candles burn their sockets,
The blinds let through the day,
The young man feels his pockets
And wonders what's to pay.
[*Last Poems* (1922), 21]

36. I sought them far and found them,
The sure, the straight, the brave,
The hearts I lost my own to,
The souls I could not save.
They braced their belts about them,
They crossed in ships the sea,
They sought and found six feet of ground,
And there they died for me.
[*Last Poems* (1922), 32]

37. These, in the day when heaven was falling,
The hour when earth's foundations fled,
Followed their mercenary calling
And took their wages and are dead.

Their shoulders held the sky suspended;
They stood, and earth's foundations stay;
What God abandoned, these defended,
And saved the sum of things for pay.
[*Last Poems* (1922), 37, 'Epitaph on an Army of Mercenaries']

38. The cuckoo shouts all day at nothing
In leafy dells alone...

39. For nature, heartless, witless nature,
Will neither care nor know
What stranger's feet may find the meadow
And trespass there and go,
Nor ask amid the dews of morning
If they are mine or no.
[*Last Poems* (1922), 40]

40. Wenlock Edge was umbered,
And bright was Abdon Burf,
And warm between them slumbered
The smooth green miles of turf.
[*Last Poems* (1922), 41, 'Fancy's Knell']

41. They say my verse is sad: no wonder;
Its narrow measure spans
Tears of eternity, and sorrow,
Not mine, but man's.

This is for all ill-treated fellows
Unborn and unbegot,
For them to read when they're in trouble
And I am not.
[*More Poems* (1936), prefatory poem]

42. When green buds hang in the elm like dust
And sprinkle the lime like rain,
Forth I wander, forth I must,
And drink of life again.
[*More Poems* (1936), 9]

43. The weeping Pleiads wester,
And the moon is under seas.
[*More Poems* (1936), 10]

44. The rainy Pleiads wester,
Orion plunges prone,
The stroke of midnight ceases,
And I lie down alone.
[*More Poems* (1936), 11]

45. Because I liked you better
Than suits a man to say,
It irked you, and I promised
To throw the thought away.
[*More Poems* (1936), 31]

46. Here dead lie we because we did not choose
To live and shame the land from which we sprung.
Life, to be sure, is nothing much to lose;
But young men think it is, and we were young.
[*More Poems* (1936), 36]

47. I did not lose my heart in summer's even,
When roses to the moonrise burst apart:
When plumes were under heel and lead was flying,
In blood and smoke and flame I lost my heart.

I lost it to a soldier and a foeman,
A chap that did not kill me, but he tried;
That took the sabre straight and took it striking
And laughed and kissed his hand to me and died.
[*More Poems* (1936), 37]

48. Oh who is that young sinner with the handcuffs on his wrists?
And what has he been after that they groan and shake their fists?
And wherefore is he wearing such a conscience-stricken air?
Oh they're taking him to prison for the colour of his hair.

'Tis a shame to human nature, such a head of hair as his;
In the good old time 'twas hanging for the colour that it is;
Though hanging isn't bad enough and flaying would be fair

For the nameless and abominable colour of his hair.
[*Collected Poems* (1939), 'Additional Poems', 18]

49. Reader, behold! this monster wild
Has gobbled up the infant child.
The infant child is not aware
It has been eaten by the bear.
[In L. Housman, *A.E.H.* (1937), 'Infant Innocence']

50. If one cannot discriminate between grammar and solecism, sequence and incoherency, sense and nonsense, one has no protection against falsehood, and believes all the lies one is told.
[*M. Manilii Astronomicon* (1903), I, Introduction]

51. Gentlemen who use MSS as drunkards use lamp-posts – not to light them on their way but to dissimulate their instability.
[*M. Manilii Astronomicon* (1903), I, Introduction]

52. Three minutes' thought would suffice to find this out; but thought is irksome and three minutes is a long time.
[*D. Iunii Iuvenalis Saturae* (1905), Preface]

53. The task of editing the classics is continually attempted by scholars who have neither enough intellect nor enough literature.
[*D. Iunii Iuvenalis Saturae* (1905), Preface]

54. The arsenals of divine vengeance, if I may so describe the Bodleian library.
[*D. Iunii Iuvenalis Saturae* (1905), Preface]

55. Good religious poetry ... is likely to be most justly appreciated and most discriminately relished by the undevout.
[The Leslie Stephen Lecture, 1933, 'The Name and Nature of Poetry']

56. Even when poetry has a meaning, as it usually has, it may be inadvisable to draw it out ... perfect understanding will sometimes almost extinguish pleasure.
[The Leslie Stephen Lecture, 1933, 'The Name and Nature of Poetry']

57. Experience has taught me, when I am shaving of a morning, to keep watch over my thoughts, because, if a line of poetry strays into my memory, my skin bristles so that the razor ceases to act.
[The Leslie Stephen Lecture, 1933, 'The Name and Nature of Poetry']

58. [Speech at farewell dinner, University College, London, before going to Cambridge as Kennedy Professor of Latin, 1911]
Cambridge has seen Wordsworth drunk, and Porson sober. Now I am a greater scholar than Wordsworth, and a greater poet than Porson; so I fall betwixt and between.
[In Watson, *A.E. Housman, A Divided Life* (1957), 9]

Howard, Michael (1922–)
English military historian and writer

1. The important thing when you are going to do something brave is to have someone on hand to witness it.
[*The Observer*, 1980, in Jeffrey Care (ed.), *Sayings of the Eighties* (1989)]

Howard, Philip (1933–)
English leader-writer and columnist

1. Every time an Englishman opens his mouth, he enables other Englishmen if not to despise him, at any rate to place him in some social and class pigeonhole.
[*The Times*, 1992]

2. The proliferation of radio and television channels has produced a wilderness of cave-dwellers instead of the promised global village.
[*The Times*, 1992]

Howe, Julia Ward (1819–1910)
American poet, suffragist, travel writer and memoirist

1. Mine eyes have seen the glory of the coming of the Lord:
He is trampling out the vintage where the grapes of wrath are stored.
['Battle Hymn of the American Republic', 1862]

Howell, John

1. The Reason why there is no table or Index added hereunto, is, that every Page in this Work is so full of Signal Remarks, that were they couched in an Index, it would make a volume as big as the Book, and so make the Postern Gate bear no proportion with the Building.
[Note in the front of *Proedria Basilike* (1664)]

Howells, W.D. (1837–1920)
American realist novelist, literary critic, editor, poet and biographer

1. Some people can stay longer in an hour than others can in a week.
[In Esar (ed.), *Treasury of Humorous Quotations* (1951)]

Howitt, Mary (1799–1888)
English novelist, translator, children's writer, editor and supporter of social reform

1. 'Will you walk into my parlour?' said a spider to a fly:
''Tis the prettiest little parlour that ever you did spy.'
['The Spider and the Fly' (1834)]

Howkins, Alun

1. CAMRA (Campaign for Real Ale), the last refuge of bearded Trotskyite Morris dancers...
[*New Statesman and Society*, 1989]

2. The English pub is, we are told from childhood, a unique institution. Nothing 'quite like it' exists anywhere else. That's true. The pub uniquely represents, even in metropolitan England, the precise inequalities of gender, race and class that construct our society. From the inconclusive white, male and proletarian 'public' of many northern pubs to the parasitic blazer and cotton dress 'locals' of the home counties, our unique institution divides our society and our social life.
[*New Statesman and Society*, 1989]

Howse, Christopher

1. It is difficult to speak about proper beer, because its friends (just like the friends of G.K. Chesterton) are its worst enemies. 'Real ale' fans are just like train-spotters – only drunk.
[*Spectator*, 1992]

Hoyle, Edmond (1672–1769)
English writer on card games, chess and backgammon; the 'Father of Whist'

1. When in doubt, win the trick.
[*Hoyle's Games* (1756), 'Whist, Twenty-four Short Rules for Learners']

Hubbard, Elbert (1856–1915)
American printer, editor, prose writer and businessman

1. Life is just one damned thing after another.
[In *Philistine*, 1909; also attributed to Frank Ward O'Malley (1875–1932), though the saying may pre-date them both]

2. Little minds are interested in the extraordinary; great minds in the commonplace.
[*A Thousand and One Epigrams* (1911)]

3. One machine can do the work of fifty ordinary men. No machine can do the work of one extraordinary man.
[*A Thousand and One Epigrams* (1911)]

4. Men are not punished for their sins, but by them.
[*A Thousand and One Epigrams* (1911)]

Hudson, Bob (1946–)

1. Girls in our town leave school at fifteen
Work at the counter or behind the machine
Spend all their money on making the scene
And plan on going to England...

2. Girls in our town are too good for the Pill
But if you keep asking they probably will
Perhaps 'cause they like you, or else for the thrill
And explain it away in the morning.
['Girls in our Town', song]

Hudson, Louise

1. Now I go to films alone
watch a silent telephone
send myself a valentine
whisper softly 'I am mine'
[In Wendy Cope (ed.), *Is That the New Moon?*, 'Men, Who Needs Them']

Hügel, Friedrich von (1852–1925)
British Roman Catholic theologian and writer; modernist; born in Florence

1. The golden rule is, to help those we love to escape from us; and never try to begin to help people, or influence them till they ask, but wait for them.
[*Letters ... to a Niece* (1928), Introduction]

Hughes, Billy (1864–1952)
Australian statesman and Prime Minister, 1915–23

1. [On being told by the Prime Minister that the new national capital would be called Myola]
It sounds like the last despairing cry of an Italian prostitute.
[Remark to Sir Eric Harrison]

2. [At the Versailles Peace Conference, answering President Wilson's query, 'Mr Hughes, I speak for very many millions of people. For whom do you speak?']
Mr President, I speak for 60,000 dead.
[In Percy Spender, *Politics and a Man*]

3. [At the Versailles Peace Conference]
Who other [than Hughes] could have told Paderewski, the pianist Prime Minister of Poland, to take his policy home and play it on the piano?
[In David Low, *Low's Autobiography*]

4. [On a rival candidate standing for election in North Sydney (Hughes's electorate) in 1931]
Oh well, I suppose it's right that the members of these old families should stick together nowadays. After all, their ancestors in those days were probably chained together.
[In David Low, *Low's Autobiography*]

5. [To his portrait painter]
My man, I don't want justice, I want mercy.
[In David Low, *Low's Autobiography*]

6. [On being asked about a challenge to his leadership of the Nationalist Party]
Look here, brother, the question of Jesus Christ as leader never arises in the midst of his apostles.
[In Jack Fingleton, *Batting from Memory*]

7. [On Enid Lyons, the first woman elected to the Australian Parliament, taking her seat]
Ah, my girl, it was very pleasant to see you here today, ah, very pleasant. But, ah, remember! Let there be no talk of the equality of the sexes! Ah, there you sat, like a bird of paradise among carrion crows!
[In Enid Lyons, *Among the Carrion Crows*]

Hughes, Langston (1902–1967)
African-American poet, playwright and short-story writer

1. Thump, thump, thump, went his foot on the floor.
He played a few chords then he sang some more–
'I got the Weary Blues
And I can't be satisfied.
Got the Weary Blues
And can't be satisfied–
I ain't happy no mo'
And I wish that I had died.'
And far into the night he crooned that tune.
The stars went out and so did the moon.
The singer stopped playing and went to bed
While the Weary Blues echoed through his head.
He slept like a rock or a man that's dead.
['The Weary Blues' (1926)]

Hughes, Sean (1966–)
Irish comedian

1. I'd like to thank God for fucking up my life and at the same time not existing, quite a special skill.
[*The Independent*, 1993]

Hughes, Ted (1930–)
English poet, children's writer, dramatist and critic; poet laureate from 1984

1. He spins from the bars, but there's no cage to him

More than to the visionary his cell:
His stride is wildernesses of freedom:
The world rolls under the long thrust of his heel.
Over the cage floor the horizons come.
[*The Hawk in the Rain* (1958), 'The Jaguar']

2. ... Now deep
In chairs, in front of the great fire, we grip
Our hearts and cannot entertain book, thought,

Or each other. We watch the fire blazing,
And feel the roots of the house move, but sit on,
Seeing the window tremble to come in,
Hearing the stones cry out under the horizons.
[*The Hawk in the Rain* (1958), 'Wind']

3. God is a good fellow, but His mother's against Him.
[*Wodwo* (1967), 'Logos']

4. Crow laughed.
He bit the Worm, God's only son,
Into two writhing halves.

He stuffed into man the tail half
With the wounded end hanging out.

He stuffed the head half headfirst into woman

And it crept in deeper and up
To peer out through her eyes
Calling its tail-half to join up quickly, quickly
Because O it was painful.

Man awoke being dragged across the grass.
Woman awoke to see him coming.
Neither knew what had happened.

God went on sleeping.

Crow went on laughing.
[*Crow* (1976), 'A Childish Prank']

5. So man cried, but with God's voice.
And God bled, but with man's blood.
[*Crow* (1976), 'Crow Blacker than Ever']

Hughes, Thomas (1822–1896)
English novelist, lawyer, Christian socialist and Liberal politician

1. Flashman was a formidable enemy for small boys ... [He] left no slander unspoken, and no deed undone, which would in any way hurt his victims, or isolate them from the rest of the house.
[*Tom Brown's Schooldays* (1857), I]

2. Life isn't all beer and skittles, – but beer and skittles, or something better of the same sort, must form a good part of every Englishman's education.
[*Tom Brown's Schooldays* (1857), I]

3. He never wants anything but what's right and fair; only when you come to settle what's right and fair, it's everything that he wants, and nothing that you want. And that's his idea of a compromise.
[*Tom Brown's Schooldays* (1857), II]

4. [Of cricket]
It's more than a game. It's an institution.
[*Tom Brown's Schooldays* (1857), II]

5. [Tom's final ambition at Rugby]
I want to leave behind me the name of a fellow who never bullied a little boy, or turned his back on a big one.
[*Tom Brown's Schooldays* (1857)]

Hugo, Victor (1802–1885)
Leading French Romantic poet, novelist and dramatist and politician

1. *La popularité? c'est la gloire en gros sous.*
Fame? It's glory in small change.
[*Ruy Blas* (1838), III.v]

2. *On résiste à l'invasion des armées; on ne résiste pas à l'invasion des idées.*
One can resist the invasion of an army; but one cannot resist the invasion of ideas.
[*Histoire d'un Crime* (1851–1852), V, 10]

3. *Car le mot, c'est le Verbe, et le Verbe, c'est Dieu.*
For the word is the Verb, and the Verb is God.
[*Contemplations* (1856), I, 8]

4. *Souffrons, mais souffrons sur les cimes.*
Let us suffer if we must, but let us suffer on the heights.
[*Contemplations* (1856), V, 26, 'Les Malheureux']

5. *La symétrie, c'est l'ennui, et l'ennui est le fond même du deuil. Le désespoir baîlle.*
Symmetry is boredom, and boredom is the very source of death. Despair yawns.
[*Les Misérables* (1862)]

6. *Le beau est aussi utile que l'utile. Plus peut-être.*
Beauty is as useful as usefulness. Maybe more so.
[*Les Misérables* (1862)]

7. *La nature est impitoyable; elle ne consent pas à retirer ses fleurs, ses musiques, ses parfums et ses rayons devant l'abomination humaine.*
Nature is unforgiving; she will not agree to withdraw her flowers, her music, her scents or her rays of light before the abominations of man.
[*Quatrevingt-treize (Ninety-three*, 1874)]

8. *Jésus a pleuré, Voltaire a souri; c'est de cette larme divine et de ce sourire humain qu'est faite la douceur de la civilisation actuelle. (Applaudissements prolongés).*
Jesus cried; Voltaire smiled. From that divine tear, from that human smile was born the sweetness of civilisation today. (Prolonged applause).
[Transcript of centenary oration on Voltaire, 1878]

9. *Vous créez un frisson nouveau.*
You create a new shiver.
[Letter to Charles Baudelaire, 1859]

10. England has two books: the Bible and Shakespeare. England made Shakespeare but the Bible made England.
[Attr.]

Hull, Josephine (1886–1957)
American stage and film actress; Academy Award 1950

1. Playing Shakespeare is very tiring. You never get to sit down, unless you're a King.
[In Cooper and Hartman, *Violets and Vinegar* (1980)]

Hulme, Keri (1947–)
New Zealand novelist, short-story writer and poet

1. Imaging a god
is the resort of the wounded
the defiance of children
the comfort of women
the strength of men.
[*The Silences Between* (1982), 'Searching for Clear Water']

2. while the whitebait with moonlight eyes
go running up the river
[*The Silences Between* (1982), 'October']

Hume, David (1711–1776)
Scottish empiricist philosopher, political economist and historian

1. We never remark any passion or principle in others, of which, in some degree or other, we may not find a parallel in ourselves.
[*A Treatise of Human Nature* (1739)]

2. Every one has observed how much more dogs are animated when they hunt in a pack, than when they pursue their game apart ... We might, perhaps, be at a loss to explain this phenomenon, if we had not experience of a similar in ourselves.
[*A Treatise of Human Nature* (1739)]

3. Grief and disappointment give rise to anger, anger to envy, envy to malice, and malice to grief again, until the whole circle be completed.
[*A Treatise of Human Nature* (1739)]

4. Philosophers never balance between profit and honesty, because their decisions are general, and neither their passions nor imaginations are interested in the objects.
[*A Treatise of Human Nature* (1739)]

5. Nothing appears more surprising to those, who consider human affairs with a philosophical eye, than the easiness

with which the many are governed by the few; and the implicit submission, with which men resign their own sentiments and passions to those of their rulers.
[*Essays, Moral, Political, and Literary*, I (1742), 4, 'Of the First Principles of Government']

6. Avarice, the spur of industry, is so obstinate a passion, and works its way through so many real dangers and difficulties, that it is not likely to be scared by an imaginary danger, which is so small, that it scarcely admits of calculation.
[*Essays, Moral, Political, and Literary*, I (1742), 12, 'Of Civil Liberty']

7. I shall tell the women what it is our sex complains of in the married state; and if they be disposed to satisfy us in this particular, all the other difficulties will easily be accommodated. If I be not mistaken, 'tis their love of dominion.
[*Essays, Moral, Political and Literary* (1742)]

8. Beauty is no quality in things themselves: It exists merely in the mind which contemplates them; and each mind perceives a different beauty.
[*Essays, Moral, Political, and Literary*, I (1742), 23, 'Of the Standard of Taste'. Cf. Hungerford: 1]

9. Custom, then, is the great guide of human life.
[*Philosophical Essays Concerning Human Understanding* (1748), 5, 'Sceptical Solutions of these Doubts']

10. We soon learn that there is nothing mysterious or supernatural in the case, but that all proceeds from the usual propensity of mankind towards the marvellous, and that, though this inclination may at intervals receive a check from sense and learning, it can never be thoroughly extirpated from human nature.
[*Philosophical Essays Concerning Human Understanding* (1748), 10, 'Of Miracles']

11. The Christian religion not only was at first attended with miracles, but even at this day cannot be believed by any reasonable person without one. Mere reason is insufficient to convince us of its veracity: and whoever is moved by Faith to assent to it, is conscious of a continued miracle in his own person, which subverts all the principles of his understanding, and gives him a determination to believe what is most contrary to custom and experience.
[*Philosophical Essays Concerning Human Understanding* (1748), 10, 'Of Miracles']

12. No testimony is sufficient to establish a miracle, unless the testimony be of such a kind that its falsehood would be more miraculous than the fact which it endeavours to establish.
[*Philosophical Essays Concerning Human Understanding* (1748), 10, 'Of Miracles']

13. If we take in our hand any volume, of divinity or school metaphysics, for instance; let us ask, Does it contain any abstract reasoning concerning quantity or number? No. Does it contain any experimental reasoning concerning matter of fact and existence? No. Commit it then to the flames; for it can contain nothing but sophistry and illusion.
[*Philosophical Essays Concerning Human Understanding* (1748), 12, 'Of the Academical or Sceptical Philosophy']

14. Opposing one species of superstition to another, set them a quarrelling; while we ourselves, during their fury and contention, happily make our escape into the calm, though obscure, regions of philosophy.
[*The Natural History of Religion* (1757), last sentence]

15. Never literary attempt was more unfortunate than my *Treatise of Human Nature*. It fell dead-born from the press.
[*My Own Life* (1777)]

16. I am dying as fast as my enemies, if I have any, could wish, and as cheerfully as my best friends could desire.
[Last words, 1776]

17. Within this circular idea
Call'd vulgarly a tomb,
The ideas and impressions lie
That constituted Hume.
[Epitaph on his monument on Calton Hill, Edinburgh]

Humphries, (John) Barry (1934–)
Australian entertainer; creator of 'Dame Edna Everage'

1. Excuse I.
[Title of show, 1965]

2. Our plate-glass picture windows,
Venetians open wide,
In the land where nothing happens
There's nothing much to hide.
['All Things Bright and Beautiful', from the show *Just a Show*, 1968]

3. Wave your gladdies, possums!
[Stock phrase, as 'Dame Edna Everage', TV show, 1970s]

4. [As 'Dame Edna Everage', on seeing a Morris Traveller in Stratford-upon-Avon]
Why, even the cars are half-timbered here!
[TV show, 1970s]

5. I think one of the highest compliments ever paid to Australia was the imminent Japanese invasion. To think the Japanese would actually [think] of coming to Australia [to] live! They did change their mind, with a little persuasion.
[*Men in Vogue*, 1976]

6. Sport is a loathsome and dangerous pursuit.
[*Sydney Morning Herald*, 1982]

7. [After posing for a nude centre-fold in *Cleo*]
Isn't it amazing what one will do for an enormous sum of money?
[*Cleo*, 1982]

8. The only people really keeping the spirit of irony alive in Australia are taxi-drivers and homosexuals.
[*Australian Women's Weekly*, 1983]

9. Look at Patty Hearst. Those parents of hers cutting those peanut butter sandwiches day after day just to turn her into an urban guerilla!
[In *A Nice Night's Entertainment* (1981)]

10. Friendship is tested in the thick years of success rather than in the thin years of struggle.
[In Jonathon Green (ed.), *A Dictionary of Contemporary Quotations* (1982)]

Hungerford, Margaret Wolfe (c. 1855–1897)
Irish novelist

1. Beauty is altogether in the eye of the beholder.
[*Molly Bawn* (1878). Cf. Hume: 8]

Hunt, G.W. (1829–1904)
British composer of music hall songs, and painter

1. We don't want to fight, but, by jingo if we do,
We've got the ships, we've got the men, we've got the money too.
We've fought the Bear before, and while Britons shall be true,
The Russians shall not have Constantinople.
[Music hall song, 1878]

Hunt, Leigh (1784–1859)
English essayist, poet, literary editor, journalist and autobiographer

1. The two divinest things this world has got,
A lovely woman in a rural spot!
[*The Story of Rimini* (1816), III]

2. Stolen sweets are always sweeter,
Stolen kisses much completer,
Stolen looks are nice in chapels,
Stolen, stolen, be your apples.
['Song of Fairies Robbing an Orchard' (1830). Cf. Cibber: 6]

3. You strange, astonished-looking, angle-faced,
Dreary-mouthed, gaping wretches of the sea.
['The Fish, the Man, and the Spirit' (1836)]

4. Abou Ben Adhem (may his tribe increase!)
Awoke one night from a deep dream of peace,
And saw, within the moonlight in his room,
Making it rich, and like a lily in bloom,
An angel writing in a book of gold:–
Exceeding peace had made Ben Adhem bold,
And to the presence in the room he said,
'What writest thou?' – The vision raised its head,
And with a look made of all sweet accord,
Answered, 'The names of those who love the Lord.'
['Abou Ben Adhem' (1838)]

5. Jenny kissed me when we met,
Jumping from the chair she sat in;
Time, you thief, who love to get
Sweets into your list, put that in:
Say I'm weary, say I'm sad,
Say that health and wealth have missed me,
Say I'm growing old, but add,
Jenny kissed me.
['Rondeau' (1838)]

6. The Earl of Liverpool, whom Madame de Staël is said to have described as having 'a talent for silence'.
[*Autobiography* (1850), 11]

7. [Of the Prince Regent]
This Adonis in Loveliness was a corpulent gentleman of fifty!
[In *The Examiner*, 1812]

8. A pleasure so exquisite as almost to amount to pain.
[Letter to Alexander Ireland, 1848. Cf. Spenser: 37]

Hunter, Anne (1742–1821)
Scottish poet

1. My mother bids me bind my hair
With bands of rosy hue,
Tie up my sleeves with ribbons rare,
And lace my bodice blue.
['My Mother Bids Me Bind My Hair' (1799)]

Hunter, William (1718–1783)
Scottish anatomist and obstetrician; author of medical works

1. Some physiologists will have it that the stomach is a mill; – others, that it is a fermenting vat; – others again that it is a stew-pan; – but in my view of the matter, it is neither a mill, a fermenting vat, nor a stew-pan – but a stomach, gentlemen, a stomach.
[MS. note from his lectures, in Paris, *A Treatise on Diet* (1826), Epigraph]

Hupfeld, Herman (1894–1951)
American songwriter

1. You must remember this, a kiss is still a kiss,
A sigh is just a sigh;–
The fundamental things apply,
As time goes by.
['As Time Goes By', song, 1931, in the film *Casablanca*, 1943]

Hurst, Sir Gerald (1877–1957)
English judge and Conservative politician; writer on history and politics

1. One of the mysteries of human conduct is why adult men and women all over England are ready to sign documents which they do not read, at the behest of canvassers whom they do not know, binding them to pay for articles which they do not want, with money which they have not got.
[*Closed Chapters* (1942)]

Huss, Jan (c. 1370–1415)
Bohemian religious reformer, preacher, defender of John Wycliffe and martyr

1. [At the stake, on seeing a peasant bringing wood]
O sancta simplicitas!
O holy simplicity!
[In Zincgreff and Weidner, *Apothegmata* (1653), III]

Hutcheson, Francis (1694–1746)
Scottish moral philosopher

1. Wisdom denotes the pursuing of the best ends by the best means.
[*An Inquiry into the Original of our Ideas of Beauty and Virtue* (1725), I, 5]

2. That action is best, which procures the greatest happiness for the greatest numbers.
[*An Inquiry into the Original of our Ideas of Beauty and Virtue* (1725), II, 3]

Hutchins, Robert M. (1899–1977)
American educationist and lawyer

1. Whenever I feel like exercise, I lie down until the feeling passes.
[Attr.]

Huxley, Aldous (1894–1963)
English novelist, essayist, poet and critic; grandson of Thomas Henry Huxley and brother of Julian Huxley

1. I can sympathize with people's pains, but not with their pleasures. There is something curiously boring about somebody else's happiness.
[*Limbo* (1920), 'Cynthia']

2. The proper study of mankind is books.
[*Crome Yellow* (1921), 28]

3. She was a machine-gun riddling her hostess with sympathy.
[*Mortal Coils* (1922), 'The Gioconda Smile']

4. Most of one's life ... is one prolonged effort to prevent oneself thinking.
[*Mortal Coils* (1922), 'Green Tunnels']

5. She was one of those indispensables of whom one makes the discovery, when they are gone, that one can get on quite as well without them.
[*Mortal Coils* (1922), 'Nuns at Luncheon']

6. There are few who would not rather be taken in adultery than in provincialism.
[*Antic Hay* (1923), 10]

7. Mr Mercaptan went on to preach a brilliant sermon on that melancholy sexual perversion known as continence.
[*Antic Hay* (1923), 18]

8. Lady Capricorn, he understood, was still keeping open bed.
[*Antic Hay* (1923), 21]

9. It is far easier to write ten passably effective Sonnets, good enough to take in the not too inquiring critic, than one effective advertisement that will take in a few thousand of the uncritical buying public.
[*On the Margin* (1923), 'Advertisement']

10. Since Mozart's day composers have learned the art of making music throatily and palpitatingly sexual.
[*Along the Road* (1925), 'Popular Music']

11. I'm afraid of losing my obscurity. Genuineness only thrives in the dark. Like celery.
[*Those Barren Leaves* (1925), I, 1]

12. In the upper and the lower churches of St Francis, Giotto and Cimabue showed that art had once worshipped something other than itself.
[*Those Barren Leaves* (1925), IV, 1]

13. It's like the question of the authorship of the Iliad ... The author of that poem is either Homer or, if not Homer, somebody else of the same name.
[*Those Barren Leaves* (1925), V, 4]

14. That all men are equal is a proposition to which, at ordinary times, no sane human being has ever given his assent.
[*Proper Studies* (1927), 'The Idea of Equality']

15. Those who believe that they are exclusively in the right are generally those who achieve something.
[*Proper Studies* (1927), 'A Note on Dogma']

16. Facts do not cease to exist because they are ignored.
[*Proper Studies* (1927), 'A Note on Dogma']

17. Defined in psychological terms, a fanatic is a man who consciously overcompensates a secret doubt.
[*Proper Studies* (1927), 'The Substitutes for Religion']

18. Success – 'The bitch-goddess, Success,' in William James's phrase – demands strange sacrifices from those who worship her.
[*Proper Studies* (1927), 'A Note on Ideals']

19. Silence is as full of potential wisdom and wit as the unhewn marble of great sculpture.
[*Point Counter Point* (1928), 1]

20. Real orgies are never so exciting as pornographic books.
[*Point Counter Point* (1928), 1]

21. [Paraphrasing Aristotle]
A little more of the possible was every instant made real; the present stood still and drew into itself the future, as a man might suck for ever at an unending piece of macaroni.
[*Point Counter Point* (1928), 11]

22. A bad book is as much of a labour to write as a good one; it comes as sincerely from the author's soul ... its sincerities will be ... uninterestingly expressed, and the labour expended on the expression will be wasted. Nature is monstrously unjust. There is no substitute for talent. Industry and all the virtues are of no avail.
[*Point Counter Point* (1928), 13]

23. Parodies and caricatures are the most penetrating of criticisms.
[*Point Counter Point* (1928), 28]

24. An admirable woman ... but rather too fond of fig-leaves – especially over the mouth.
[*Point Counter Point* (1928), 30]

25. Happiness is like coke – something you get as a by-product in the process of making something else.
[*Point Counter Point* (1928), 30]

26. Consistency is contrary to nature, contrary to life. The only completely consistent people are the dead.
[*Do What You Will* (1929)]

27. Thought must be divided against itself before it can come to any knowledge of itself.
[*Do What You Will* (1929)]

28. The aristocratic pleasure of displeasing is not the only delight that bad taste can yield. One can love a certain kind of vulgarity for its own sake.
[*Vulgarity in Literature* (1930), 4]

29. The time of Our Ford.
[*Brave New World* (1932), 3]

30. 'Going to the Feelies this evening, Henry?' enquired the Assistant Predestinator. 'I hear the new one at the Alhambra is first-rate. There's a love scene on a bearskin rug; they say it's marvellous. Every hair of the bear reproduced.'
[*Brave New World* (1932), 3]

31. Living is an art; and to practise it well, men need, not only acquired skill, but also a native tact and taste.
[*Texts and Pretexts* (1932)]

32. Official dignity tends to increase in inverse ratio to the importance of the country in which the office is held.
[*Beyond the Mexique Bay* (1934)]

33. People will insist ... on treating the mons Veneris as though it were Mount Everest.
[*Eyeless in Gaza* (1936), 30]

34. Death ... It's the only thing we haven't succeeded in completely vulgarizing.
[*Eyeless in Gaza* (1936), 31]

35. The quality of moral behaviour varies in inverse ratio to the number of human beings involved.
[*Grey Eminence* (1941), 10]

36. How appallingly thorough these Germans always managed to be, how emphatic! In sex no less than in war – in scholarship, in science. Diving deeper than anyone else and coming up muddier.
[*Time Must Have a Stop* (1944), 6]

37. There's only one corner of the universe you can be certain of improving, and that's your own self.
[*Time Must Have a Stop* (1944), 7]

38. The solemn foolery of scholarship for scholarship's sake.
[*The Perennial Philosophy* (1945)]

39. Most human beings have an almost infinite capacity for taking things for granted.
[*Themes and Variations* (1950), 'Variations on a Philosopher']

40. We participate in a tragedy; at a comedy we only look.
[*The Devils of Loudun* (1952), 11]

41. Thanks to words, we have been able to rise above the brutes; and thanks to words, we have often sunk to the level of the demons.
[*Adonis and the Alphabet* (1956)]

42. 'Bed,' as the Italian proverb succinctly puts it, 'is the poor man's opera.'
[*Heaven and Hell* (1956)]

43. A million million spermatozoa,
All of them alive:
Out of their cataclysm but one poor Noah
Dare hope to survive.
['Fifth Philosopher's Song' (1918)]

44. But when the wearied Band
Swoons to a waltz, I take her hand,
And there we sit in blissful calm,
Quietly sweating palm to palm.
['Frascati's' (1919)]

45. Your maiden modesty would float face down,
And men would weep upon your hinder parts.
['Second Philosopher's Song' (1920)]

46. Beauty for some provides escape,
Who gain a happiness in eyeing
The gorgeous buttocks of the ape
Or Autumn sunsets exquisitely dying.
['Ninth Philosopher's Song' (1920)]

47. To his dog, every man is Napoleon; hence the constant popularity of dogs.
[Attr.]

Huxley, Henrietta (née Heathorn) (1825–1915)

English writer and poet, wife of Thomas Henry Huxley

1. And if there be no meeting past the grave,
If all is darkness, silence, yet 'tis rest.
Be not afraid ye waiting hearts that weep;
For still He giveth His beloved sleep,
And if an endless sleep He wills, so best.
[Lines on the grave of her husband, 1895, in Deighton, *Huxley, His Life and Work* (1904)]

Huxley, Sir Julian Sorell (1887–1975)

English biologist, first Director General of UNESCO (1946–48) and popularizer of science; brother of Aldous Huxley

1. Operationally, God is beginning to resemble not a ruler but the last fading smile of a cosmic Cheshire cat.
[*Religion without Revelation* (1957 ed.), 3]

2. We all know how the size of sums of money appears to vary in a remarkable way according as they are being paid in or paid out.
[*Essays of a Biologist*, 5]

3. The ant herself cannot philosophize–
While man does that, and sees, and keeps a wife,
And flies, and talks, and is extremely wise.
['For a Book of Essays']

Huxley, Thomas Henry (1825–1895)

English biologist, Darwinist and agnostic

1. The chess-board is the world; the pieces are the phenomena of the universe; the rules of the game are what we call the laws of Nature. The player on the other side is hidden from us. We know that his play is always fair, just, and patient. But we also know, to our cost, that he never overlooks a mistake, or makes the smallest allowance for ignorance.
[*Macmillan's Magazine*, 1868, 'A Liberal Education; and Where to Find It']

2. If some great Power would agree to make me always think what is true and do what is right, on condition of being turned into a sort of clock and wound up every morning before I got out of bed, I should instantly close with the offer.
[*Macmillan's Magazine*, 1870, 'On Descartes' Discourse touching the Method of Using One's Reason Rightly...']

3. The great tragedy of Science – the slaying of a beautiful hypothesis by an ugly fact.
[*British Association Annual Report* (1870), 'Biogenesis and Abiogenesis']

4. Logical consequences are the scarecrows of fools and the beacons of wise men.
[*Nature*, 1874, 'On the Hypothesis that Animals are Automata, and its History']

5. The saying that a little knowledge is a dangerous thing is, to my mind, a very dangerous adage. If knowledge is real and genuine, I do not believe that it is other than a very valuable possession however infinitesimal its quantity may be. Indeed, if a little knowledge is dangerous, where is the man who has so much as to be out of danger?
[*Science and Culture* (1877), 'On Elementary Instruction in Physiology']

6. The great end of life is not knowledge but action.
[*Science and Culture* (1877), 'Technical Education']

7. Irrationally held truths may be more harmful than reasoned errors.
[*Science and Culture, and Other Essays* (1881), 'The Coming of Age of the Origin of Species']

8. It is the customary fate of new truths to begin as heresies and to end as superstitions.
[*Science and Culture and Other Essays* (1881), 'The Coming of Age of the Origin of Species']

9. Every variety of philosophical and theological opinion was represented there [the Metaphysical Society], and expressed itself with entire openness; most of my colleagues were -ists of one sort or another; and, however kind and friendly they might be, I, the man without a rag of a label to cover himself with, could not fail to have some of the uneasy feelings which must have beset the historical fox when, after leaving the trap in which his tail remained, he presented himself to his normally elongated companions. So I took thought, and invented what I conceived to be the appropriate title of 'agnostic' ... To my great satisfaction, the term took: and when the Spectator had stood godfather to it, any suspicion in the minds of respectable people ... was, of course, completely lulled.
[*Nineteenth Century*, 1889, 'Agnosticism']

10. One of the unpardonable sins, in the eyes of most people, is for a man to go about unlabelled. The world regards such a person as the police do an unmuzzled dog, not under proper control.
[*Evolution and Ethics* (1893)]

11. I doubt if the philosopher lives, or has ever lived, who could know himself to be heartily despised by a street boy without some irritation.
[*Evolution and Ethics* (1893)]

12. Some experience of popular lecturing had convinced me that the necessity of making things plain to uninstructed people was one of the very best means of clearing up the obscure corners of one's own mind.
[*Man's Place in Nature* (1894 ed.), Preface]

13. I am too much of a sceptic to deny the possibility of anything.
[Letter to Herbert Spencer, 1886]

14. [During debate on Darwin's theory of evolution]
I asserted – and I repeat – that a man has no reason to be

ashamed of having an ape for his grandfather. If there were an ancestor whom I should feel shame in recalling it would rather be a man – a man of restless and versatile intellect – who, not content with an equivocal success in his own sphere of activity, plunges into scientific questions with which he has no real acquaintance, only to obscure them by an aimless rhetoric, and distract the attention of his hearers from the real point at issue by eloquent digressions and skilled appeals to religious prejudice.
[Speech, Oxford, 1860. Cf. Wilberforce: 1]

15. [Remark to George Howell]
Posthumous fame is not particularly attractive to me, but, if I am to be remembered at all, I would rather it should be as 'a man who did his best to help the people' than by any other title.
[In L. Huxley, *Life and Letters of Thomas Henry Huxley* (1900)]

16. Try to learn something about everything and everything about something.
[Memorial stone]

Hyde, Douglas (1860–1949)
Irish scholar, poet, dramatist and first Irish President (1939–44)

1. In order to de-Anglicise ourselves we must at once arrest the decay of the language.
['The Necessity for de-Anglicising Ireland' (1892)]

Hyde, Robin (Iris Guiver Wilkinson) (1906–1939)
New Zealand writer

1. The Japanese are described as 'the most nostalgic people on earth,' but I think possibly the remark applies to all island people, who have the spirit of adventure, but also the feeling of being secure on a small place among the waters.
[*Mirror*, 1938, 'I Travel Alone: My Trans-Siberian Journey to England']

Ibárruri, Dolores ('La Pasionaria') (1895–1989)
Spanish Basque Communist leader, exiled in the Soviet Union, 1939–77; journalist and orator

1. [Referring to Franco's troops]
¡No pasarán!
They shall not pass.
[Speech, 1936; later adopted as Spanish Republican slogan]

2. *Il vaut mieux mourir debout que vivre à genoux!*
It is better to die on your feet than to live on your knees.
[Speech, Paris, 1936]

3. It is better to be the widow of a hero than the wife of a coward.
[Speech, Valencia, 1936]

Ibsen, Henrik (1828–1906)
Norwegian founder of modern prose and social drama, and poet

1. What's a man's first duty? The answer's brief: To be himself.
[*Peer Gynt* (1867), IV]

2. I am a button-moulder; and you must be popped into my casting ladle.
[*Peer Gynt* (1867), V]

3. Home life ceases to be free and beautiful as soon as it is founded on borrowing and debt.
[*A Doll's House* (1879), I]

4. In that moment it burst upon me that I had been living here these eight years with a strange man, and had borne him three children.
[*A Doll's House* (1879), III]

5. It's not just what we inherit from our mothers and fathers that haunts us. It's all kinds of old defunct theories, all sorts of old defunct beliefs, and things like that. It's not that they actually live on in us; they are simply lodged there, and we cannot get rid of them. I've only to pick up a newspaper and I seem to see ghosts gliding between the lines.
[*Ghosts* (1881), II]

6. Mother, give me the sun.
[*Ghosts* (1881), III]

7. Fools are in a terrible, overwhelming majority, all the wide world over.
[*An Enemy of the People* (1882), IV]

8. The majority has the might – more's the pity – but it hasn't right . . . The minority is always right.
[*An Enemy of the People* (1882), IV]

9. The most dangerous foe to truth and freedom in our midst is the compact majority. Yes, the damned, compact liberal majority.
[*An Enemy of the People* (1882), IV]

10. A man should never have his best trousers on when he goes out to battle for freedom and truth.
[*An Enemy of the People* (1882), V]

11. The strongest man in the world is the man who stands alone.
[*An Enemy of the People* (1882), V]

12. Take the saving lie from the average man and you take his happiness away, too.
[*The Wild Duck* (1884), V]

13. Ten o'clock . . . and back he'll come. I can just see him. With vine leaves in his hair. Flushed and confident.
[*Hedda Gabler* (1890), II]

14. [Judge Brack, on Hedda Gabler's suicide]
People don't do such things!
[*Hedda Gabler* (1890), IV]

15. Youth will come here and beat on my door, and force its way in.
[*The Master Builder* (1892), I]

16. Castles in the air – they're so easy to take refuge in. So easy to build, too.
[*The Master Builder* (1892), III]

17. [Ibsen's last words; his nurse had just remarked that he was feeling a little better]
On the contrary!
[Attr.]

Ickes, Harold L. (1874–1952)
American Republican politician; lawyer and author

1. [On his resignation as Secretary of the Interior after a dispute with President Truman]
I am against government by crony.
[Remark, 1946]

2. The trouble with Senator Long is that he is suffering from halitosis of the intellect. That's presuming Emperor Long has an intellect.
[In A.M. Schlesinger, *The Politics of Upheaval*, II, 14]

Ignatieff, Michael (1947–)
Canadian author and media personality

1. News is a genre as much as fiction or drama: it is a regime of visual authority, a coercive organization of images according to a stopwatch.
[*Daedalus*, 1988]

Illich, Ivan (1926–)
Austrian-born American educator, sociologist, writer and priest

1. Any attempt to reform the university without attending to the system of which it is an integral part is like trying to do urban renewal in New York City from the twelfth storey up.
[*Deschooling Society* (1971), 3]

2. Man must choose whether to be rich in things or in the freedom to use them.
[*Deschooling Society* (1971), 4]

3. We must rediscover the distinction between hope and expectation.
[*Deschooling Society* (1971), 7]

4. In a consumer society there are inevitably two kinds of slaves: the prisoners of addiction and the prisoners of envy.
[*Tools for Conviviality* (1973)]

Inge, William Ralph (1860–1954)
English divine, Dean of St Paul's 1911–34; writer and teacher

1. It takes in reality only one to make a quarrel. It is useless for the sheep to pass resolutions in favour of vegetarianism while the wolf remains of a different opinion.
[*Outspoken Essays: First Series* (1919), 'Patriotism']

2. The nations which have put mankind and posterity most in their debt have been small states – Israel, Athens, Florence, Elizabethan England.
[*Outspoken Essays: Second Series* (1922), 'State, visible and invisible']

3. Literature flourishes best when it is half a trade and half an art.
['The Victorian Age' (1922)]

4. Democracy is only an experiment in government, and it has the obvious disadvantage of merely counting votes instead of weighing them.
[*Possible Recovery?* (c. 1922)]

5. A man may build himself a throne of bayonets, but he cannot sit upon it.
[*Philosophy of Plotinus* (1923), Lecture 22]

6. What we know of the past is mostly not worth knowing. What is worth knowing is mostly uncertain. Events in the past may roughly be divided into those which probably never happened and those which do not matter.
[*Assessments and Anticipations* (1929), 'Prognostications']

7. Many people believe that they are attracted by God, or by Nature, when they are only repelled by man.
[*More Lay Thoughts of a Dean* (1931)]

8. The enemies of Freedom do not argue; they shout and they shoot.
[*End of an Age* (1948), 4]

9. The effect of boredom on a large scale in history is underestimated. It is a main cause of revolutions, and would soon bring to an end all the static Utopias and the farmyard civilization of the Fabians.
[*End of an Age* (1948), 6]

10. The proper time to influence the character of a child is about a hundred years before he is born.
[*The Observer*, 1929]

11. A nation is a society united by a delusion about its ancestry and by a common hatred of its neighbours.
[In Sagittarius and George, *The Perpetual Pessimist*]

Ingersoll, Robert Greene (1833–1899)
American lawyer, Republican orator, soldier, agnostic and writer

1. In nature there are neither rewards nor punishments – there are consequences.
[*Some Reasons Why* (1881)]

2. Few rich men own their own property. The property owns them.
[Address to the McKinley League, New York, 1896]

Ingrams, Richard (1937–)
British journalist; editor of the satirical magazine Private Eye, *1963–86*

1. I have come to regard the law courts not as a cathedral but rather as a casino.
[*The Guardian*, 1977]

2. [Referring to his editorship of *Private Eye*]
My own motto is publish and be sued.
[BBC radio broadcast, 1977]

3. [On the prospect of going to gaol, 1976]
The only thing I really mind about going to prison is the thought of Lord Longford coming to visit me.
[Attr.]

Ingres, J.A.D. (1780–1867)
French history and portrait painter; leading Neoclassicist

1. *Le dessin est la probité de l'art.*
Drawing is the true test of art.
[*Pensées d'Ingres* (1922)]

Innes, Hammond (1913–)
British author and traveller

1. [On growing trees]
I'm replacing some of the timber used up by my books. Books are just trees with squiggles on them.
[*Radio Times*, 1984]

Ionesco, Eugène (1912–)
Romanian-French writer and surrealist dramatist

1. Listen . . . You know I was in the country one day fishing . . . a woman fell into the water and shouted for help. As I can't swim – and anyway the fish were biting – I stayed where I was and left her to drown.
[*Amédée* (1954)]

Iphicrates (419–353 BC)
Athenian general

1. [Responding to a descendant of Harmodius (an Athenian hero), who had mocked Iphicrates for being the son of a shoemaker]
The difference between us is that my family begins with me, whereas yours ends with you.
[Attr.]

Irving, Washington (1783–1859)
American essayist, short-story writer, travel writer and diplomat

1. A woman's whole life is a history of the affections.
[*The Sketch Book* (1820), 'The Broken Heart']

2. A tart temper never mellows with age, and a sharp tongue is the only edged tool that grows keener with constant use.
[*The Sketch Book* (1820), 'Rip Van Winkle']

3. They who drink beer will think beer.
[*The Sketch Book* (1820), 'Stratford']

4. Whenever a man's friends begin to compliment him about looking young, he may be sure that they think he is growing old.
[*Bracebridge Hall* (1822), 'Bachelors']

5. I am always at a loss to know how much to believe of my own stories.
[*Tales of a Traveller* (1824)]

6. There is a certain relief in change, even though it be from bad to worse; as I have found in travelling in a stage-coach, that it is often a comfort to shift one's position and be bruised in a new place.
[*Tales of a Traveller* (1824)]

7. The almighty dollar, that great object of universal devotion throughout our land.
[*Wolfert's Roost* (1855), 'The Creole Village']

Isherwood, Christopher (1904–1986)

English-born American novelist; collaborated on plays with W.H. Auden and wrote screenplays

1. The common cormorant or shag
Lays eggs inside a paper bag
The reason you will see no doubt
It is to keep the lightning out.

But what these unobservant birds
Have never noticed is that herds
Of wandering bears may come with buns
And steal the bags to hold the crumbs.
['The Common Cormorant' (c. 1925)]

2. I am a camera with its shutter open, quite passive, recording, not thinking.
[*Goodbye to Berlin* (1939)]

ITMA

1. It's that man again.
[BBC Radio Programme, 1939–1949; scriptwriter Ted Kavanagh]

2. Can I do you now, sir?
[BBC Radio Programme, 1939–1949; scriptwriter Ted Kavanagh]

3. Don't forget the diver.
[BBC Radio Programme, 1939–1949; scriptwriter Ted Kavanagh]

4. *Cecil*: After you, Claude.
Claude: No, after you, Cecil.
[BBC Radio Programme, 1939–1949; scriptwriter Ted Kavanagh]

5. I go, I come back.
[BBC Radio Programme, 1939–1949; scriptwriter Ted Kavanagh]

6. I don't mind if I do.
[BBC Radio Programme, 1939–1949; scriptwriter Ted Kavanagh]

7. Ta-ta for now.
[BBC Radio Programme, 1939–1949; scriptwriter Ted Kavanagh]

8. What, me? In my condition?
[BBC Radio Programme, 1939–1949; scriptwriter Ted Kavanagh]

Jackson, Andrew (1767–1845)

American Democratic President, 1829–37; general and lawyer

1. You are uneasy; you never sailed with me before, I see.
[In J. Parton, *Life of Jackson* (1860), III]

2. [Order given during the Battle of New Orleans, American War of Independence]
Elevate them guns a little lower.
[Attr.]

Jackson, F.J. Foakes (1855–1941)

English divine and church historian

1. [Advice given to a new don at Jesus College, Cambridge]
It's no use trying to be clever – we are all clever here; just try to be kind – a little kind.
[Oral tradition, recorded in A.C. Benson's *Commonplace Book*]

Jackson, Glenda (1936–)

English stage and film actress and Labour MP; awarded CBE

1. [Describing her first impressions of being the new MP for Hampstead and Highgate]
People have said to me that your first week in the Commons is like your first week at school. My school was never like this. People told you what to do, they were less friendly, and there were more girls.
[*The List*, 1992]

Jackson, Robert (1946–)

English Conservative MP and writer on contemporary Europe

1. To have open government you need mature media. It is more difficult for people to discuss complex issues than it used to be because of the destructive power of the tabloids. The TV sound bite also makes it impossible to communicate complex arguments. It is all black and white, cut and dried, yaa-boo.
[*Independent on Sunday*, 1994]

Jacobs, Joe (1896–1940)

American boxing manager

1. [Remark made after Max Schmeling, whom he managed, lost his boxing title to Jack Sharkey in 1932]
We was robbed!
[Attr.]

Jacobs, W.W. (1863–1943)

English short-story writer, noted for his tales of the macabre, and novelist

1. 'Sailor men 'ave their faults,' said the night-watchman, frankly. 'I'm not denying it. I used to 'ave myself when I was at sea.'
[*The Lady of the Barge*, 'Bill's Paper Chase']

Jacomb, C.E.

1. The prevalence of men living alone has thus caused the coining of a new word in Australia: that word is 'baching'; and the word expresses vividly, if crudely, the ugly life it gives a name to.
[*God's Own Country*]

Jacopone da Todi (c. 1230–1306)

Italian religious poet and hymn writer

1. *Stabat Mater dolorosa,*
Iuxta crucem lacrimosa

Dum pendebat Filius.
The sorrowing Mother was standing beside the cross, weeping as her Son was hanging there.
[Hymn, 'Stabat Mater Dolorosa'; also attributed to Pope Innocent III and St Bonaventure]

Jago, Rev. Richard (1715–1781)

English poet

1. With leaden foot time creeps along
While Delia is away.
['Absence']

James I of Scotland (1394–1437)

King of Scots from 1424 and poet; alienated the nobility and was assassinated

1. The bird, the beast, the fish eke in the sea,
They live in freedom everich in his kind;
And I a man, and lackith liberty...

2. Worshippe, ye that loveris been, this May,
For of your blisse the Kalendis are begun,
And sing with us, away, Winter, away!
Come, Summer, come the sweet seasoun and sun...

3. So far I fallen was in loves dance,
That suddenly my wit, my countenance,
My heart, my will, my nature, and my mind
Was changit right clean in another kind.
[*The Kingis Quair*]

4. [On being introduced to a young girl proficient in Latin, Greek, and Hebrew]
These are rare attainments for a damsel, but pray tell me, can she spin?
[Attr.]

James V of Scotland (1512–1542)

King of Scots from 1513; father of Mary, Queen of Scots; 'King of the Commons'

1. [On the rule of the Stuart dynasty in Scotland]
It cam' wi' a lass, and it'll gang wi' a lass.
[Remark, 1542]

James VI of Scotland and I of England (1566–1625)

King of Scots from 1567 and of English from 1603; son of Mary, Queen of Scots; father of Charles I, essayist and patron of poetry

1. A branch of the sin of drunkenness, which is the root of all sins.
[*A Counterblast to Tobacco* (1604)]

2. A custom loathesome to the eye, hateful to the nose, harmful to the brain, dangerous to the lungs, and in the black, stinking fume thereof, nearest resembling the horrible Stygian smoke of the pit that is bottomless.
[*A Counterblast to Tobacco* (1604)]

3. Herein is not only a great vanity, but a great contempt of God's good gifts, that the sweetness of man's breath, being a good gift of God, should be wilfully corrupted by this stinking smoke.
[*A Counterblast to Tobacco* (1604)]

4. No bishop, no king.
[Attr. remark, Hampton Court Conference, 1604]

5. I will govern according to the common weal, but not according to the common will.
[Remark, 1621]

6. Dr Donne's verses are like the peace of God; they pass all understanding.
[Attr.]

James, Alice (1848–1892)

American diarist and depressive; sister of Henry and William James

1. It is so comic to hear oneself called old, even at ninety I suppose!
[In Leon Edel (ed.), *The Diary of Alice James*, 1889]

2. I suppose one has a greater sense of intellectual degradation after an interview with a doctor than from any human experience.
[In Leon Edel (ed.), *The Diary of Alice James*, 1890]

James, Brian (John Tierney) (1892–1972)

Australian short-story writer

1. A dominant personality doesn't believe in its own will. All it needs is the inability to recognise the existence of anybody else's.
[*Falling Towards England*]

2. The book of my enemy has been remaindered
And I am pleased.
['The Book of My Enemy Has Been Remaindered']

James, Henry (1843–1916)

American-born British novelist; short-story writer, critic, dramatist and letter writer

1. To kill a human being is, after all, the least injury you can do him.
[*Complete Tales* (1867), 'My Friend Bingham']

2. It takes a great deal of history to produce a little literature.
[*Hawthorne* (1879)]

3. [Of Thoreau]
Whatever question there may be of his talent, there can be none, I think, of his genius. It was a slim and crooked one; but it was eminently personal. He was imperfect, unfinished, inartistic; he was worse than provincial – he was parochial.
[*Hawthorne* (1879)]

4. Cats and monkeys, monkeys and cats – all human life is there.
[*The Madonna of the Future* (1879)]

5. The only obligation to which in advance we may hold a novel, without incurring the accusation of being arbitrary, is that it be interesting.
[*Partial Portraits* (1888), 'The Art of Fiction']

6. Experience is never limited, and it is never complete; it is an immense sensibility, a kind of huge spider-web of the finest silken threads suspended in the chamber of consciousness, and catching every air-borne particle in its tissue.
[*Partial Portraits* (1888), 'The Art of Fiction']

7. What is character but the determination of incident? What is incident but the illustration of character?
[*Partial Portraits* (1888), 'The Art of Fiction']

8. We must grant the artist his subject, his idea, his donnée: our criticism is applied only to what he makes of it.
[*Partial Portraits* (1888), 'The Art of Fiction']

9. The superiority of one man's opinion over another's is never so great as when the opinion is about a woman.
[*The Tragic Muse* (1890 edition), 9]

10. Print it as it stands – beautifully.
[*Terminations* (1895 edition), 'The Death of the Lion']

11. The fatal futility of Fact.
[*Prefaces* (1897 edition), 'The Spoils of Poynton', and elsewhere]

12. Experience was to be taken as showing that one might get a five-pound note as one got a light for a cigarette; but one had to check the friendly impulse to ask for it in the same way.
[*The Awkward Age* (1899 edition)]

13. The terrible fluidity of self-revelation.
[*Prefaces* (1903 edition), 'The Ambassadors']

14. Live all you can; it's a mistake not to. It doesn't so much matter what you do in particular, so long as you have your life. If you haven't had that then what have you had?
[*The Ambassadors* (1903 edition)]

15. She was a woman who, between courses, could be graceful with her elbows on the table.
[*The Ambassadors* (1903 edition)]

16. The deep well of unconscious cerebration.
[*The American* (1909 edition)]

17. Dramatize, dramatize!
[*Prefaces* (1909 edition), 'The Altar of the Dead']

18. The note I wanted; that of the strange and sinister embroidered on the very type of the normal and easy.
[*Prefaces* (1909 edition), 'The Altar of the Dead']

19. The historian, essentially, wants more documents than he can really use; the dramatist only wants more liberties than he can really take.
[*The Aspern Papers* (1909 edition)]

20. The black and merciless things that are behind the great possessions.
[*The Ivory Tower* (1917 edition)]

21. Poor Gissing ... struck me as quite particularly marked out for what is called in his and my profession an unhappy ending.
[Letter to Sir Sidney Colvin, 1903]

22. It is art that makes life, makes interest, makes importance, for our consideration and application of these things, and I know of no substitute whatever for the force and beauty of its process.
[Letter to H.G. Wells, 1915]

23. Summer afternoon – summer afternoon; to me those have always been the two most beautiful words in the English language.
[In Edith Wharton, *A Backward Glance* (1934), 10]

24. [Not his dying words; after having a stroke, 2 December 1915, he said he had heard a voice saying]
So here it is at last, the distinguished thing.
[In Edith Wharton, *A Backward Glance* (1934), 14]

25. I remember once saying to Henry James, in reference to a novel of the type that used euphemistically to be called 'unpleasant': 'You know, I was rather disappointed; that book wasn't nearly as bad as I expected'; to which he replied, with his incomparable twinkle: 'Ah, my dear, the abysses are all so shallow.'
[In Edith Wharton, *The House of Mirth* (1936)]

James, Dame P.D. (1920–)
British crime writer and former civil servant

1. Early this morning, 1 January 2021, three minutes after midnight, the last human being to be born on Earth was killed in a pub brawl in a suburb of Buenos Aires, aged twenty-five years two months and twelve days ... We are outraged and demoralized less by the impending end of our own species, less even by an inability to prevent it, than by our failure to discover the cause.
[*The Children of Men* (1992)]

James, William (1842–1910)
American psychologist and 'radical empiricist' philosopher; brother of Henry and Alice James

1. There is no more miserable human being than one in whom nothing is habitual but indecision.
[*Principles of Psychology* (1890)]

2. Our civilization is founded on the shambles, and every individual existence goes out in a lonely spasm of helpless agony.
[*Varieties of Religious Experience* (1902)]

3. If merely 'feeling good' could decide, drunkenness would be the supremely valid human experience.
[*Varieties of Religious Experience* (1902)]

4. The moral flabbiness born of the exclusive worship of the bitch-goddess success. That – with the squalid cash interpretation put on the word success – is our national disease.
[Letter to H.G. Wells, 1906]

5. A great many people think they are thinking when they are merely rearranging their prejudices.
[Attr.]

Jarrell, Randall (1914–1965)
American poet, literary critic and translator

1. President Robbins was so well adjusted to his environment that sometimes you could not tell which was the environment and which was President Robbins.
[*Pictures from an Institution* (1954), I, 4]

2. To Americans English manners are far more frightening than none at all.
[*Pictures from an Institution* (1954), I, 5]

3. From my mother's sleep I fell into the State,
And I hunched in its belly till my wet fur froze.
Six miles from earth, loosed from its dream of life,
I woke to black flak and the nightmare fighters.
When I died they washed me out of the turret with a hose.
['The Death of the Ball Turret Gunner' (1969)]

4. Some poetry seems to have been written on typewriters by other typewriters.
[Attr.]

Jarry, Alfred (1873–1907)
French satirical dramatist, influential on the Theatre of the Absurd, and poet

1. [On being reprimanded by a woman for firing his pistol near her child, who might have been killed]
Madame, I would have given you another!
[In A. Vollard, *Recollections of a Picture Dealer*]

Jay, Douglas (1907–)
British economist and journalist

1. For in the case of nutrition and health, just as in the case of education, the gentleman in Whitehall really does know better what is good for people than the people know themselves.
[*The Socialist Case* (1947)]

Jeans, Sir James Hopwood (1877–1946)

English mathematician, physicist, astronomer and popularizer of science

1. Life exists in the universe only because the carbon atom possesses certain exceptional properties.
[*The Mysterious Universe* (1930), 1]

2. Science should leave off making pronouncements: the river of knowledge has too often turned back on itself.
[*The Mysterious Universe* (1930), 5]

Jeffe, Sherry Bebitch

1. [A definition of the street-car theory of American politics]
To win, a candidate must be standing on the right street corner at the right time when a street-car is going in the right direction, and must have the right amount of change in their pockets.
[*The Independent on Sunday*, 1992]

Jeffers, Robinson (1887–1962)

American lyrical and narrative poet

1. I'd sooner, except the penalties, kill a man than a hawk.
[*Hunt Hawks* (1928)]

2. . . . I gave him the lead gift in the twilight. What fell was relaxed,
Owl-downy, soft feminine feathers; but what
Soared: the fierce rush: the night-heron by the flooded river cries fear at its rising
Before it was quite unsheathed from reality.
[*Hunt Hawks* (1928)]

Jefferson, Thomas (1743–1826)

American statesman; third President, 1801–09, founder of the Democratic Party

1. When in the course of human events, it becomes necessary for one people to dissolve the political bonds which have connected them with another, and to assume among the powers of the earth the separate and equal station to which the laws of nature and of Nature's God entitle them, a decent respect to the opinions of mankind requires that they should declare the causes which impel them to the separation.
[Declaration of Independence, 4 July 1776; Preamble]

2. We hold these truths to be self-evident: that all men are created equal; that they are endowed by their Creator with certain unalienable rights; that among these are life, liberty, and the pursuit of happiness.
[Declaration of Independence, 1776]

3. Indeed I tremble for my country when I reflect that God is just.
[*Notes on the State of Virginia* (1784)]

4. In the full tide of successful experiment.
[First Inaugural Address, 1801]

5. Peace, commerce, and honest friendship with all nations – entangling alliances with none.
[First Inaugural Address, 1801]

6. Error of opinion may be tolerated where reason is left free to combat it.
[First inaugural address, 1801]

7. When a man assumes a public trust, he should consider himself as public property.
[Remark, 1807]

8. Take care that you never spell a word wrong. Always before you write a word, consider how it is spelled, and, if you do not remember it, turn to a dictionary. It produces great praise to a lady to spell well.
[Letter to his wife, 1783]

9. A little rebellion now and then is a good thing.
[Letter to James Madison, 1787]

10. The tree of liberty must be refreshed from time to time with the blood of patriots and tyrants. It is its natural manure.
[Letter to W.S. Smith, 1787]

11. [On public offices]
Whenever a man has cast a longing eye on them, a rottenness begins in his conduct.
[Letter to Tenche Coxe, 1799]

12. If a due participation of office is a matter of right, how are vacancies to be obtained? Those by death are few; by resignation none.
[Letter, 1801]

13. Advertisements contain the only truths to be relied on in a newspaper.
[Letter, 1819]

14. To attain all this [universal republicanism], however, rivers of blood must yet flow, and years of desolation pass over; yet the object is worth rivers of blood, and years of desolation.
[Letter to John Adams, 1823]

15. No duty the Executive had to perform was so trying as to put the right man in the right place.
[In J.B. MacMaster, *History of the People of the U.S.* (1883–1913)]

Jeffrey, Francis, Lord (1773–1850)

Scottish critic and editor; judge and Whig politician

1. [On Wordsworth's *Excursion*]
This will never do.
[*Edinburgh Review*, 1814]

2. [Of Mrs Hamilton, author of *The Cottagers of Glenburnie*]
There was no objection to the blue stocking, provided the petticoat came low enough.
[Attr.]

Jellicoe, John Rushworth, First Earl (1859–1935)

English admiral, Commander of Grand Fleet at Battle of Jutland, 1916

1. [Referring to the Battle of Jutland, 1916]
I had always to remember that I could have lost the war in an afternoon.
[Remark]

Jenkin, Patrick (1926–)

British politician

1. [Advice to the public during the Three-Day Week, 1974, when electricity supplies were restricted]
You don't even need to do your teeth with the light on. You can do it in the dark.
[Interviewed on BBC Radio *Newsbeat*, February 1974]

Jenkins, David (1925–)

English prelate; Bishop of Durham 1984–1994

1. As I get older I seem to believe less and less and yet to believe what I do believe more and more.
[*The Observer*, 1988, in Jeffrey Care (ed.), *Sayings of the Eighties* (1989)]

Jenkins, Roy (Baron Jenkins of Hillhead) (1920–)
Welsh politician and author; Labour Home Secretary, 1965–67; 1974–76, and co-founder of the SDP, 1981

1. The permissive society has been allowed to become a dirty phrase. A better phrase is the civilized society.
[Speech, Abingdon, 19 July 1969]
2. There are always great dangers in letting the best be the enemy of the good.
[Speech, House of Commons, 1975]
3. [Used in connection with the SDP, established in 1981] Breaking the mould of British politics.
[Attr.]

Jennings, Elizabeth (1926–)
English poet, associated with the group of poets in the 1950s known as the Movement

1. Lying apart now, each in a separate bed,
He with a book, keeping the light on late,
She like a girl dreaming of childhood,
All men elsewhere – it is as if they wait
Some new event: the book he holds unread,
Her eyes fixed on the shadows overhead.

Tossed up like flotsam from a former passion,
How cool they lie. They hardly ever touch,
Or if they do it is like a confession
Of having little feeling – or too much.
Chastity faces them, a destination
For which their whole lives were a preparation.

Strangely apart, yet strangely close together,
Silence between them like a thread to hold
And not wind in. And time itself's a feather
Touching them gently. Do they know they're old,
These two who are my father and my mother
Whose fire from which I came, has now grown cold?
[*The Mind has Mountains* (1966), 'One Flesh']
2. Allow, admit the brave, attentive verb.
[*Times and Seasons* (1992), 'Grammar']
3. Now deep in my bed I turn
And the world turns on the other side.
['In the Night']

Jennings, Paul (1918–1989)
British humorous writer

1. Of all musicians, flautists are most obviously the ones who know something we don't know.
[*The Jenguin Pennings*, 'Flautists Flaunt Afflatus']

Jerome, Saint (c. 342–420)
Christian monk and scholar; translated the Bible into Latin

1. *'Quae enim communicatio luci ad tenebras? qui consensus Christo et Belial?' quid facit cum Psalterio Horatius? cum evangeliis Maro? cum apostolo Cicero? Nonne scandalizatur frater, si te vident in idolio recumbentem?'*
'For what has light to do with darkness, what agreement can there be between Christ and the Devil?' what has Horace to do with the Psalter? Virgil with the Gospels? or Cicero with Paul? Will not your brother be scandalised, if he sees you making your bed with idols?
[*Letters*, 22]
2. *Venerationi mihi semper fuit non verbosa rusticitas, sed sancta simplicitas.*
My veneration has always been for sacred simplicity rather than wordy vulgarity.
[*Letters*, 57]

Jerome, Jerome K. (1859–1927)
English humorous novelist, dramatist and journalist

1. It is impossible to enjoy idling thoroughly unless one has plenty of work to do.
[*Idle Thoughts of an Idle Fellow* (1886)]
2. Love is like the measles; we all have to go through it.
[*Idle Thoughts of an Idle Fellow* (1886)]
3. Conceit is the finest armour a man can wear.
[*Idle Thoughts of an Idle Fellow* (1886)]
4. It is easy enough to say that poverty is no crime. No; if it were men wouldn't be ashamed of it. It is a blunder, though, and is punished as such. A poor man is despised the whole world over.
[*Idle Thoughts of an Idle Fellow* (1886)]
5. If you are foolish enough to be contented, don't show it, but grumble with the rest.
[*Idle Thoughts of an Idle Fellow* (1886)]
6. George goes to sleep at a bank from ten to four each day, except Saturdays, when they wake him up and put him outside at two.
[*Three Men in a Boat* (1889), 2]
7. I like work; it fascinates me. I can sit and look at it for hours. I love to keep it by me: the idea of getting rid of it nearly breaks my heart.
[*Three Men in a Boat* (1889), 3]
8. But there, everything has its drawbacks, as the man said when his mother-in-law died, and they came down on him for the funeral expenses.
[*Three Men in a Boat* (1889), 3]

Jerrold, Douglas William (1803–1857)
English dramatist, novelist, journalist and wit

1. Religion's in the heart, not in the knees.
[*The Devil's Ducat* (1830), I]
2. Honest bread is very well – it's the butter that makes the temptation.
[*The Catspaw* (1850), III]
3. Love's like the measles – all the worse when it comes late in life.
[*Wit and Opinions of Douglas Jerrold* (1859), 'A Philanthropist']
4. The best thing I know between France and England is – the sea.
[*Wit and Opinions of Douglas Jerrold* (1859), 'The Anglo-French Alliance']
5. That fellow would vulgarize the day of judgment.
[*Wit and Opinions of Douglas Jerrold* (1859), 'A Comic Author']
6. The ugliest of trades have their moments of pleasure. Now, if I were a grave-digger, or even a hangman, there are some people I could work for with a great deal of enjoyment.
[*Wit and Opinions of Douglas Jerrold* (1859), 'Ugly Trades']
7. Some people are so fond of ill-luck that they run half-way to meet it.
[*Wit and Opinions of Douglas Jerrold* (1859), 'Meeting Troubles Half-way']
8. He was so good he would pour rose-water over a toad.
[*Wit and Opinions of Douglas Jerrold* (1859), 'A Charitable Man']

9. Talk to him of Jacob's ladder, and he would ask the number of the steps.
[*Wit and Opinions of Douglas Jerrold* (1859), 'A Matter-of-fact Man']

10. We love peace, as we abhor pusillanimity; but not peace at any price.
[*Wit and Opinions of Douglas Jerrold* (1859), 'Peace']

11. The only athletic sport I ever mastered was backgammon.
[In W. Jerrold, *Douglas Jerrold* (1914), I, 1]

12. [Remark to a small thin man who was boring him]
Sir, you are like a pin, but without either its head or its point.
[Attr.]

Jespersen, Otto (1860–1943)
Danish philologist

1. In his whole life man achieves nothing so great and so wonderful as what he achieved when he learned to talk.
[*Language* (1904), 5]

Jewsbury, Geraldine (1812–1880)
British novelist

1. I wish I had a good husband and a dozen children! Only the difficulty is that 'women of genius' require very special husbands.
[Attr. Anthony Kamm, *Biographical Dictionary of English Literature* (1993)]

Jillett, Neil (1933–)
New Zealand-born Australian film and dance critic

1. [A phrase wrongly attributed to Ava Gardner, who starred in the film *On the Beach*, adapted from Nevil Shute's novel of that name (1957)]
On the Beach is a story about the end of the world, and Melbourne sure is the right place to film it.
[Attr.]

Joad, C.E.M. (1891–1953)
English popularizer of philosophy, scholar and teacher

1. Whenever I look inside myself I am afraid.
[*The Observer*, 'Sayings of the Week', 1942]

2. There was never an age in which useless knowledge was more important than in ours.
[*The Observer*, 'Sayings of the Week', 1951]

3. It will be said of this generation that it found England a land of beauty and left it a land of beauty spots.
[*The Observer*, 'Sayings of Our Times', 1953]

4. It all depends on what you mean by...
[Response to BBC *Brains Trust* questions]

Joan of Arc (c. 1412–1431)
French patriot and military leader, against the English; burned for heresy

1. You think when you have slain me you will conquer France, but that you will never do. Though there were a hundred thousand God-dammees more in France than there are, they will never conquer that kingdom.
[Attr.]

Joffre, Joseph Jacques Césaire (1852–1931)
French marshal, Commander of French army at the Battle of the Marne

1. [Order before the first battle of the Marne]
We are about to engage in a battle on which the fate of our country depends and it is important to remind all ranks that the moment has passed for looking to the rear; all our efforts must be directed to attacking and driving back the enemy. Troops that can advance no farther must, at any price, hold on to the ground they have conquered and die on the spot rather than give way. Under the circumstances which face us, no act of weakness can be tolerated.
[*The Memoirs of Marshal Joffre* (1932)]

John XXIII (Angelo Giuseppe Roncalli) (1881–1963)
Italian Pope from 1958; promoter of ecumenicalism

1. It often happens that I wake at night and begin to think about a serious problem and decide I must tell the Pope about it. Then I wake up completely and remember I am the Pope.
[Attr.]

2. [Remark made two days before he died]
I am able to follow my own death step by step. Now I move softly towards the end.
[*The Guardian*, 1963]

St John of the Cross (1542–1591)
Spanish mystic

1. *Muero porque no muero.*
I die because I do not die.
['Coplas del alma que pena por ver a dios' (c. 1572–1577)]

John III Sobieski (1624–1696)
King of Poland from 1674 and military leader

1. [Announcing his victory over the Turks at Vienna to the pope]
I came; I saw; God conquered.
[Attr.]

John Paul II (Karol Wojtyla) (1920–)
First Polish pope, in office since 1978

1. Adultery in your heart is committed not only when you look with excessive sexual desire at a woman who is not your wife, but also if you look in the same manner at your wife.
[*The Observer*, 1980, in Jeffrey Care (ed.), *Sayings of the Eighties* (1989)]

2. *Mi stanno esaminando tutto, anche organi che neppure sapevo esistessero.*
They are examining every part of my body, even organs that I didn't know we had.
[Interview given while in hospital in Rome, in *Corriere della Sera*, 1994]

3. [Replying to the suggestion that it was inappropriate for a cardinal to ski]
It is unbecoming for a cardinal to ski badly.
[Attr.]

John, Augustus (1878–1961)
British painter

1. [To Nina Hamnet]
We have become, Nina, the sort of people our parents warned us about.
[Attr.]

Johnson, Amy (1903–1941)
English aviator; made many record flights in 1930s

1. Had I been a man I might have explored the Poles or climbed Mount Everest, but as it was my spirit found an outlet in the air...
[In Margot Asquith (ed.), *Myself When Young*]

Johnson, Hiram (1866–1945)
American Progressive Republican politician; isolationist in 1930s

1. The first casualty when war comes is truth.
[Speech, US Senate, 1917]

Johnson, Lionel (1867–1902)
English poet and critic

1. Go from me: I am one of those who fall.
What! hath no cold wind swept your heart at all,
In my sad company? Before the end,
Go from me, dear my friend!...
2. O rich and sounding voices of the air!
Interpreters and prophets of despair:
Priests of a fearful sacrament! I come,
To make with you my home.
['Mystic and Cavalier' (1889)]
3. I know you: solitary griefs,
Desolate passions, aching hours.
['The Precept of Silence' (1895)]
4. The saddest of all Kings
Crown'd, and again discrown'd...
5. Alone he rides, alone,
The fair and fatal king.
['By the Statue of King Charles I at Charing Cross' (1895)]
6. There Shelley dream'd his white Platonic dreams.
['Oxford' (1897)]

Johnson, Lyndon Baines (1908–1973)
American statesman; Democrat President 1963–69, noted for Civil Rights reform

1. We are not about to send American boys nine or ten thousand miles away from home to do what Asian boys ought to be doing for themselves.
[Broadcast address, 21 October 1964]
2. [On Vietnam]
You let a bully come into your front yard, the next day he'll be on your porch.
[A remark he made several times, quoted in *Time*, 1984]
3. Come now, let us reason together.
[Frequent exhortation, based on Isaiah 1:18]
4. If you're in politics and you can't tell when you walk into a room who's for you and who's against you, then you're in the wrong line of work.
[In B. Mooney, *The Lyndon Johnson Story* (1956)]
5. I want loyalty. I want him to kiss my ass in Macy's window at high noon and tell me it smells like roses. I want his pecker in my pocket.
[In D. Halberstam, *The Best and the Brightest* (1972)]
6. [Correct version of the frequently-misquoted: 'He couldn't walk and chew gum at the same time']
Gerry Ford is so dumb that he can't fart and chew gum at the same time.
[In R. Reeves, *A Ford, Not a Lincoln* (1975), 1]
7. [When told that he was walking towards the wrong helicopter, with the words, 'That's your helicopter over there, sir']
Son, they are all my helicopters.
[Attr.]
8. [Of J. Edgar Hoover, chief of the FBI]
I'd much rather have that fellow inside the tent pissing out, than outside pissing in.
[Attr.]

Johnson, Paul (1928–)
British editor and historical writer

1. For me this is a vital litmus test: no intellectual society can flourish where a Jew feels even slightly uneasy.
[*The Sunday Times Magazine*, 1977]

Johnson, Philander Chase (1866–1939)
American newspaperman and humorist

1. Cheer up, the worst is yet to come.
[*Everybody's Magazine*, 1920]

Johnson, Samuel (1709–1784)
English lexicographer, poet, critic, conversationalist and essayist

1. Men more frequently require to be reminded than informed.
[*The Rambler* (1750–1752)]
2. The love of life is necessary to the vigorous prosecution of any undertaking.
[*The Rambler* (1750–1752)]
3. Almost every man wastes part of his life in attempts to display qualities which he does not possess, and to gain applause which he cannot keep.
[*The Rambler* (1750–1752)]
4. I have laboured to refine our language to grammatical purity, and to clear it from colloquial barbarisms, licentious idioms, and irregular combinations.
[*The Rambler* (1750–1752)]
5. It is the fate of those who toil at the lower employments of life ... to be exposed to censure, without hope of praise; to be disgraced by miscarriage, or punished for neglect ... Among these unhappy mortals is the writer of dictionaries ... Every other author may aspire to praise; the lexicographer can only hope to escape reproach.
[*A Dictionary of the English Language* (1755), Preface]
6. I am not yet so lost in lexicography, as to forget that words are the daughters of the earth, and that things are the sons of heaven. Language is only the instrument of science, and words are but the signs of ideas: I wish, however, that the instrument might be less apt to decay, and that signs might be permanent, like the things which they denote.
[*A Dictionary of the English Language* (1755), Preface]
7. [Of citations of usage in a dictionary]
Every quotation contributes something to the stability or enlargement of the language.
[*A Dictionary of the English Language* (1755), Preface]
8. But these were the dreams of a poet doomed at last to wake a lexicographer.
[*A Dictionary of the English Language* (1755), Preface]
9. The chief glory of every people arises from its authors.
[*A Dictionary of the English Language* (1755), Preface]
10. *Dull*. 8. To make dictionaries is dull work.
[*A Dictionary of the English Language* (1755)]
11. *Excise*. A hateful tax levied upon commodities.
[*A Dictionary of the English Language* (1755)]
12. *Lexicographer*. A writer of dictionaries, a harmless drudge.
[*A Dictionary of the English Language* (1755)]
13. *Net*. Anything reticulated or decussated at equal distances, with interstices between the intersections.
[*A Dictionary of the English Language* (1755)]
14. *Oats*. A grain, which in England is generally given to horses, but in Scotland supports the people.
[*A Dictionary of the English Language* (1755)]

15. *Patron*. Commonly a wretch who supports with insolence, and is paid with flattery.
[*A Dictionary of the English Language* (1755)]

16. *Whig*. The name of a faction.
[*A Dictionary of the English Language* (1755)]

17. The reciprocal civility of authors is one of the most risible scenes in the farce of life.
[*Life of Sir Thomas Browne* (1756)]

18. A hardened and shameless tea-drinker, who has for twenty years diluted his meals with only the infusion of this fascinating plant; whose kettle has scarcely time to cool; who with tea amuses the evening, with tea solaces the midnight, and with tea welcomes the morning.
[Review in the *Literary Magazine*, 1757]

19. I shall long to see the miseries of the world, since the sight of them is necessary to happiness.
[*Rasselas* (1759), 3]

20. The business of a poet, said Imlac, is to examine, not the individual but the species; . . . he does not number the streaks of the tulip, or describe the different shades in the verdure of the forest.
[*Rasselas* (1759), 10]

21. He [the poet] must write as the interpreter of nature, and the legislator of mankind, and consider himself as presiding over the thoughts and manners of future generations; as a being superior to time and place.
[*Rasselas* (1759), 10]

22. To a poet nothing can be useless.
[*Rasselas* (1759), 10]

23. Human life is everywhere a state in which much is to be endured, and little to be enjoyed.
[*Rasselas* (1759), 11]

24. Marriage has many pains, but celibacy has no pleasures.
[*Rasselas* (1759), 26]

25. Example is always more efficacious than precept.
[*Rasselas* (1759), 29]

26. Integrity without knowledge is weak and useless, and knowledge without integrity is dangerous and dreadful.
[*Rasselas* (1759), 41]

27. The endearing elegance of female friendship.
[*Rasselas* (1759), 45]

28. Pleasure is very seldom found where it is sought; our brightest blazes of gladness are commonly kindled by unexpected sparks.
[*The Idler* (1758–1760)]

29. Every man is, or hopes to be, an idler.
[*The Idler* (1758–1760)]

30. When two Englishmen meet, their first talk is of the weather.
[*The Idler* (1758–1760)]

31. Promise, large promise, is the soul of an advertisement.
[*The Idler* (1758–1760)]

32. He is no wise man who will quit a certainty for an uncertainty.
[*The Idler* (1758–1760)]

33. In all pointed sentences, some degree of accuracy must be sacrificed to conciseness.
['The Bravery of the English Common Soldier' (1760)]

34. Nothing can please many, and please long, but just representations of general nature.
[*The Plays of William Shakespeare* (1765), Preface]

35. He that tries to recommend him by select quotations, will succeed like the pedant in Hierocles, who, when he offered his house to sale, carried a brick in his pocket as a specimen.
[*The Plays of William Shakespeare* (1765), Preface]

36. A quibble is to Shakespeare what luminous vapours are to the traveller: he follows it at all adventures; it is sure to lead him out of his way and sure to engulf him in the mire.
[*The Plays of William Shakespeare* (1765), Preface]

37. Particulars are not to be examined till the whole has been surveyed.
[*The Plays of William Shakespeare* (1765), Preface]

38. Notes are often necessary, but they are necessary evils.
[*The Plays of William Shakespeare* (1765), Preface]

39. I know not whether it be not peculiar to the Scots to have attained the liberal without the manual arts, to have excelled in ornamental knowledge, and to have wanted not only the elegancies, but the conveniences of common life.
[*A Journey to the Western Islands of Scotland* (1775)]

40. That man is little to be envied whose patriotism would not gain force upon the plain of Marathon, or whose piety would not grow warmer among the ruins of Iona.
[*A Journey to the Western Islands of Scotland* (1775)]

41. At seventy-seven it is time to be in earnest.
[*A Journey to the Western Islands of Scotland* (1775)]

42. Whatever withdraws us from the power of our senses; whatever makes the past, the distant, or the future, predominate over the present, advances us in the dignity of thinking beings.
[*A Journey to the Western Islands of Scotland* (1775)]

43. How is it that we hear the loudest yelps for liberty among the drivers of negroes?
[*Taxation No Tyranny* (1775)]

44. Whoever wishes to attain an English style, familiar but not coarse, and elegant but not ostentatious, must give his days and nights to the volumes of Addison.
[*The Lives of the Most Eminent English Poets* (1779–1781), 'Addison']

45. The great source of pleasure is variety.
[*The Lives of the Most Eminent English Poets* (1779–1781), 'Butler']

46. A man, doubtful of his dinner, or trembling at a creditor, is not much disposed to abstracted meditation, or remote enquiries.
[*The Lives of the Most Eminent English Poets* (1779–1781), 'Collins']

47. About the beginning of the seventeenth century appeared a race of writers that may be termed the metaphysical poets.
[*The Lives of the Most Eminent English Poets* (1779–1781), 'Cowley']

48. [Of metaphysical conceits]
The most heterogeneous ideas are yoked by violence together.
[*The Lives of the Most Eminent English Poets* (1779–1781), 'Cowley']

49. The true genius is a mind of large general powers, accidentally determined to some particular direction.
[*The Lives of the Most Eminent English Poets* (1779–1781), 'Cowley']

50. Language is the dress of thought.
[*The Lives of the Most Eminent English Poets* (1779–1781), 'Cowley']

51. The father of English criticism.
[*The Lives of the Most Eminent English Poets* (1779–1781), 'Dryden']

52. [Of *The Beggar's Opera*]
This play ... was first offered to Cibber and his brethren at Drury-Lane, and rejected; it being then carried to Rich, had the effect, as was ludicrously said, of making Gay rich and Rich gay.
[*The Lives of the Most Eminent English Poets* (1779–1781), 'John Gay']

53. We are perpetually moralists, but we are geometricians only by chance. Our intercourse with intellectual nature is necessary; our speculations upon matter are voluntary, and at leisure.
[*The Lives of the Most Eminent English Poets* (1779–1781), 'Milton']

54. An acrimonious and surly republican.
[*The Lives of the Most Eminent English Poets* (1779–1781), 'Milton']

55. New things are made familiar, and familiar things are made new.
[*The Lives of the Most Eminent English Poets* (1779–1781), 'Pope']

56. If Pope be not a poet, where is poetry to be found?
[*The Lives of the Most Eminent English Poets* (1779–1781), 'Pope']

57. [Of Garrick's death]
That stroke of death, which has eclipsed the gaiety of nations and impoverished the public stock of harmless pleasure.
[*The Lives of the Most Eminent English Poets* (1779–1781), 'Edmund Smith']

58. He washed himself with oriental scrupulosity.
[*The Lives of the Most Eminent English Poets* (1779–1781), 'Swift']

59. Friendship is not always the sequel of obligation.
[*The Lives of the Most Eminent English Poets*, (1779–1781) 'James Thomson']

60. The only end of writing is to enable the readers better to enjoy life, or better to endure it.
[*Works* (1787), X]

61. The power of punishment is to silence, not to confute.
[*Sermons* (1788), 23]

62. Here falling houses thunder on your head,
And here a female atheist talks you dead...

63. Of all the griefs that harrass the distress'd,
Sure the most bitter is a scornful jest;
Fate never wounds more deep the gen'rous heart,
Than when a blockhead's insult points the dart...

64. This mournful truth is ev'rywhere confess'd,
Slow rises worth by poverty depress'd.
[*London: A Poem* (1738)]

65. The stage but echoes back the public voice.
The drama's laws the drama's patrons give,
For we that live to please must please to live.
['Prologue at the Opening of Drury Lane' (1747)]

66. Let observation with extensive view,
Survey mankind, from China to Peru;
Remark each anxious toil, each eager strife,
And watch the busy scenes of crowded life.
[*The Vanity of Human Wishes* (1749), line 1]

67. Deign on the passing world to turn thine eyes,
And pause awhile from letters to be wise;
There mark what ills the scholar's life assail,
Toil, envy, want, the patron, and the jail.
See nations slowly wise, and meanly just,
To buried merit raise the tardy bust.
[*The Vanity of Human Wishes* (1749), line 157]

68. His fall was destined to a barren strand,
A petty fortress, and a dubious hand;
He left the name, at which the world grew pale,
To point a moral, or adorn a tale.
[*The Vanity of Human Wishes* (1749), line 219]

69. In life's last scene what prodigies surprise,
Fears of the brave, and follies of the wise!
From Marlb'rough's eyes the streams of dotage flow,
And Swift expires a driv'ler and a show.
[*The Vanity of Human Wishes* (1749), line 315]

70. What ills from beauty spring.
[*The Vanity of Human Wishes* (1749), line 321]

71. Must helpless man, in ignorance sedate,
Roll darkling down the torrent of his fate?
[*The Vanity of Human Wishes* (1749), line 345]

72. [Parody of a ballad]
I put my hat upon my head,
I walked into the Strand,
And there I met another man
Whose hat was in his hand.
['Parodies of the Hermit of Warkworth', in *European Magazine*, 1785, 'Anecdotes by George Steevens']

73. Grief is a species of idleness.
[Letter to Mrs. Thrale, 17 March 1773]

74. If you are idle, be not solitary; if you are solitary, be not idle.
[Letter to Boswell, 28 October 1779]

75. There is no wisdom in useless and hopeless sorrow.
[Letter to Mrs. Thrale, 12 April 1781]

76. I have, all my life long, been lying till noon; yet I tell all young men, and tell them with great sincerity, that nobody who does not rise early will ever do any good.
[In Boswell, *Journal of a Tour to the Hebrides* (1785), 14 September 1773]

77. I inherited a vile melancholy from my father, which has made me mad all my life, at least not sober.
[In Boswell, *Journal of a Tour to the Hebrides* (1785), 16 September 1773]

78. I am always sorry when any language is lost, because languages are the pedigree of nations.
[In Boswell, *Journal of a Tour to the Hebrides* (1785), 18 September 1773]

79. A fellow who makes no figure in company, and has a mind as narrow as the neck of a vinegar cruet.
[In Boswell, *Journal of a Tour to the Hebrides* (1785), 30 September 1773]

80. A cucumber should be well sliced, and dressed with pepper and vinegar, and then thrown out, as good for nothing.
[In Boswell, *Journal of a Tour to the Hebrides* (1785), 5 October 1773]

81. By seeing London, I have seen as much of life as the world can show.
[In Boswell, *Journal of a Tour to the Hebrides* (1785), 11 October 1773]

82. It is ridiculous for a Whig to pretend to be honest. He cannot hold it out.
[In Boswell, *Journal of a Tour to the Hebrides* (1785), 21 October 1773]

83. [Calling for a gill of whisky]
Come, let me know what it is that makes a Scotchman happy!
[In Boswell, *Journal of a Tour to the Hebrides* (1785), 23 October 1773]

84. Sir, are you so grossly ignorant of human nature, as not to know that a man may be very sincere in good principles without having good practice?
[In Boswell, *Journal of a Tour to the Hebrides* (1785), 25 October 1773]

85. I am sorry I have not learned to play at cards. It is very useful in life: it generates kindness and consolidates society.
[In Boswell, *Journal of a Tour to the Hebrides* (1785), 21 November 1773]

86. The rod produces an effect which terminates in itself. A child is afraid of being whipped, and gets his task, and there's an end on't; whereas, by exciting emulation and comparisons of superiority, you lay the foundation of lasting mischief; you make brothers and sisters hate each other.
[In Boswell, *The Life of Samuel Johnson* (1791), I]

87. *Johnson*: I had no notion that I was wrong or irreverent to my tutor.
Boswell: That, Sir, was great fortitude of mind.
Johnson: No, Sir; stark insensibility.
[In Boswell, *The Life of Samuel Johnson* (1791), I, 1728]

88. [Of Pembroke College, Oxford]
Sir, we are a nest of singing birds.
[In Boswell, *The Life of Samuel Johnson* (1791), I, 1730]

89. He was a vicious man, but very kind to me. If you call a dog Hervey, I shall love him.
[In Boswell, *The Life of Samuel Johnson* (1791), I, 1737]

90. [To Garrick]
I'll come no more behind your scenes, David: for the silk stockings and white bosoms of your actresses excite my amorous propensities.
[In Boswell, *The Life of Samuel Johnson* (1791), I, 1750]

91. A man may write at any time, if he will set himself doggedly to it.
[In Boswell, *The Life of Samuel Johnson* (1791), I, 1750]

92. [To Beauclerk]
Thy body is all vice, and thy mind all virtue.
[In Boswell, *The Life of Samuel Johnson* (1791), I, 1752]

93. Wretched un-idea'd girls.
[In Boswell, *The Life of Samuel Johnson* (1791), I, 1753]

94. I had done all I could; and no man is well pleased to have his all neglected, be it ever so little.
[In Boswell, *The Life of Samuel Johnson* (1791), I, Letter to Lord Chesterfield, 1755]

95. Is not a Patron, my Lord, one who looks with unconcern on a man struggling for life in the water, and, when he has reached ground, encumbers him with help? The notice which you have been pleased to take of my labours, had it been early, had been kind; but it has been delayed till I am indifferent, and cannot enjoy it; till I am solitary, and cannot impart it; till I am known, and do not want it.
[In Boswell, *The Life of Samuel Johnson* (1791), I, Letter to Lord Chesterfield, 1755]

96. A fly, Sir, may sting a stately horse and make him wince; but one is but an insect, and the other is a horse still.
[In Boswell, *The Life of Samuel Johnson* (1791), I, 1754]

97. [Of Lord Chesterfield]
This man I thought had been a Lord among wits; but, I find, he is only a wit among Lords.
[In Boswell, *The Life of Samuel Johnson* (1791), I, 1754]

98. [Of Lord Chesterfield's *Letters*]
They teach the morals of a whore, and the manners of a dancing master.
[In Boswell, *The Life of Samuel Johnson* (1791), I, 1754]

99. When the messenger who carried the last sheet [of Johnson's *Dictionary*] to Millar returned, Johnson asked him, 'Well, what did he say?' 'Sir (answered the messenger), he said, thank God I have done with him.' 'I am glad (replied Johnson, with a smile) that he thanks God for any thing.'
[In Boswell, *The Life of Samuel Johnson* (1791), I, 1755]

100. There are two things which I am confident I can do very well: one is an introduction to any literary work, stating what it is to contain, and how it should be executed in the most perfect manner; the other is a conclusion, shewing from various causes why the execution has not been equal to what the author promised himself and to the public.
[In Boswell, *The Life of Samuel Johnson* (1791), I, 1755]

101. [Asked the reason for a mistake in his dictionary]
Ignorance, madam, sheer ignorance.
[In Boswell, *The Life of Samuel Johnson* (1791), I, 1755]

102. I have protracted my work till most of those whom I wished to please have sunk into the grave, and success and miscarriage are empty sounds; I therefore dismiss it with frigid tranquillity, having little to fear or hope from censure or praise.
[In Boswell, *The Life of Samuel Johnson* (1791), I, 1755]

103. If a man does not make new acquaintance as he advances through life, he will soon find himself left alone. A man, Sir, should keep his friendship in constant repair.
[In Boswell, *The Life of Samuel Johnson* (1791), I, 1755]

104. The booksellers are generous liberal-minded men.
[In Boswell, *The Life of Samuel Johnson* (1791), I, 1756]

105. No man will be a sailor who has contrivance enough to get himself into a jail; for being in a ship is being in a jail, with the chance of being drowned ... A man in a jail has more room, better food, and commonly better company.
[In Boswell, *The Life of Samuel Johnson* (1791), I, 1759]

106. *Boswell*: I do indeed come from Scotland, but I cannot help it...
Johnson: That, Sir, I find, is what a very great many of your countrymen cannot help.
[In Boswell, *The Life of Samuel Johnson* (1791), I, 1763]

107. [On Dr Blair asking whether any man of a modern age could have written the works of Ossian]
Yes, Sir, many men, many women, and many children.
[In Boswell, *The Life of Samuel Johnson* (1791), I, 1763]

108. It was like leading one to talk of a book when the author is concealed behind the door.
[In Boswell, *The Life of Samuel Johnson* (1791), I, 1763]

109. [Of the poet, Christopher Smart, who was considered mad and confined to an asylum]
He insisted on people praying with him; and I'd as lief pray with Kit Smart as anyone else.
[In Boswell, *The Life of Samuel Johnson* (1791), I, 1763]

110. [Of Christopher Smart]
He did not love clean linen and I have no passion for it.
[In Boswell, *The Life of Samuel Johnson* (1791), I, 1763]

111. [Of literary criticism]
You may abuse a tragedy, though you cannot write one, You may scold a carpenter who has made you a bad table, though you cannot make a table. It is not your trade to make tables.
[In Boswell, *The Life of Samuel Johnson* (1791), I, 1763]

112. [Of Dr John Campbell]
I am afraid he has not been in the inside of a church for many years; but he never passes a church without pulling off his hat. This shews that he has good principles.
[In Boswell, *The Life of Samuel Johnson* (1791), I, 1763]

113. Great abilities are not requisite for an Historian ... Imagination is not required in any high degree.
[In Boswell, *The Life of Samuel Johnson* (1791), I, 1763]

114. Norway, too, has noble wild prospects; and Lapland is remarkable for prodigious noble wild prospects. But, Sir, let me tell you, the noblest prospect which a Scotchman ever sees, is the high road that leads him to England!
[In Boswell, *The Life of Samuel Johnson* (1791), I, 1763]

115. A man ought to read just as inclination leads him; for what he reads as a task will do him little good.
[In Boswell, *The Life of Samuel Johnson* (1791), I, 1763]

116. You never find people labouring to convince you that you may live very happily upon a plentiful fortune.
[In Boswell, *The Life of Samuel Johnson* (1791), I, 1763]

117. [On sceptics]
Truth, Sir, is a cow which will yield such people no more milk, and so they are gone to milk the bull.
[In Boswell, *The Life of Samuel Johnson* (1791), I, 1763]

118. Young men have more virtue than old men; they have more generous sentiments in every respect.
[In Boswell, *The Life of Samuel Johnson* (1791), I, 1763]

119. In my early years I read very hard. It is a sad reflection, but a true one, that I knew almost as much at eighteen as I do now.
[In Boswell, *The Life of Samuel Johnson* (1791), I, 1763]

120. Your levellers wish to level down as far as themselves; but they cannot bear levelling up to themselves.
[In Boswell, *The Life of Samuel Johnson* (1791), I, 1763]

121. It is no matter what you teach them [children] first, any more than what leg you shall put into your breeches first.
[In Boswell, *The Life of Samuel Johnson* (1791), I, 1763]

122. Why, Sir, Sherry [Thomas Sheridan] is dull, naturally dull; but it must have taken him a great deal of pains to become what we now see him. Such an excess of stupidity, Sir, is not in Nature.
[In Boswell, *The Life of Samuel Johnson* (1791), I, 1763]

123. [Of Thomas Sheridan's influence on the English language]
It is burning a farthing candle at Dover, to shew light at Calais.
[In Boswell, *The Life of Samuel Johnson* (1791), I, 1763]

124. I love the University of Salamanca; for when the Spaniards were in doubt as to the lawfulness of their conquering America, the University of Salamanca gave it as their opinion that it was not lawful.
[In Boswell, *The Life of Samuel Johnson* (1791), I, 1763]

125. [To a woman of the town, accosting him]
No, no, my girl ... it won't do.
[In Boswell, *The Life of Samuel Johnson* (1791), I, 1763]

126. Sir, a woman's preaching is like a dog's walking on his hinder legs. It is not done well; but you are surprised to find it done at all.
[In Boswell, *The Life of Samuel Johnson* (1791), I, 1763]

127. I look upon it, that he who does not mind his belly will hardly mind anything else.
[In Boswell, *The Life of Samuel Johnson* (1791), I, 1763]

128. This was a good dinner enough, to be sure; but it was not a dinner to ask a man to.
[In Boswell, *The Life of Samuel Johnson* (1791), I, 1763]

129. We could not have had a better dinner had there been a Synod of Cooks.
[In Boswell, *The Life of Samuel Johnson* (1791), I, 1763]

130. Don't, Sir, accustom yourself to use big words for little matters. It would not be terrible, though I were to be detained some time here.
[In Boswell, *The Life of Samuel Johnson* (1791), I, 1763]

131. [Kicking a stone in order to disprove Berkeley's theory of the non-existence of matter]
I refute it thus.
[In Boswell, *The Life of Samuel Johnson* (1791), I, 1763]

132. That all who are happy, are equally happy, is not true. A peasant and a philosopher may be equally satisfied, but not equally happy. Happiness consists in the multiplicity of agreeable consciousness.
[In Boswell, *The Life of Samuel Johnson* (1791), II, 1766]

133. It is our first duty to serve society, and, after we have done that, we may attend wholly to the salvation of our own souls. A youthful passion for abstracted devotion should not be encouraged.
[In Boswell, *The Life of Samuel Johnson* (1791), II, 1766]

134. Our tastes greatly alter. The lad does not care for the child's rattle, and the old man does not care for the young man's whore.
[In Boswell, *The Life of Samuel Johnson* (1791), II, 1766]

135. It was not for me to bandy civilities with my Sovereign.
[In Boswell, *The Life of Samuel Johnson* (1791), II, 1767]

136. Sir, if a man has a mind to prance, he must study at Christ-Church and All-Souls.
[In Boswell, *The Life of Samuel Johnson* (1791), II, 1769]

137. We know our will is free, and there's an end on't.
[In Boswell, *The Life of Samuel Johnson* (1791), II, 1769]

138. In the description of night in Macbeth, the beetle and the bat detract from the general idea of darkness, – inspissated gloom.
[In Boswell, *The Life of Samuel Johnson* (1791), II, 1769]

139. Shakespeare never had six lines together without a fault. Perhaps you may find seven, but this does not refute my general assertion.
[In Boswell, *The Life of Samuel Johnson* (1791), II, 1769]

140. I would not coddle the child.
[In Boswell, *The Life of Samuel Johnson* (1791), II, 1769]

141. Why, Sir, most schemes of political improvement are very laughable things.
[In Boswell, *The Life of Samuel Johnson* (1791), II, 1769]

142. There is no idolatry in the Mass. They believe God to be there, and they adore him.
[In Boswell, *The Life of Samuel Johnson* (1791), II, 1769]

143. It matters not how a man dies, but how he lives. The act of dying is not of importance, it lasts so short a time.
[In Boswell, *The Life of Samuel Johnson* (1791), II, 1769]

144. Burton's *Anatomy of Melancholy*, he said, was the only book that ever took him out of bed two hours sooner than he wished to rise.
[In Boswell, *The Life of Samuel Johnson* (1791), II, 1770]

145. Want of tenderness is want of parts, and is no less a proof of stupidity than of depravity.
[In Boswell, *The Life of Samuel Johnson* (1791), II, 1770]

146. That fellow seems to me to possess but one idea, and that is a wrong one.
[In Boswell, *The Life of Samuel Johnson* (1791), II, 1770]

147. Johnson observed, that 'he did not care to speak ill of any man behind his back, but he believed the gentleman was an attorney.'
[In Boswell, *The Life of Samuel Johnson* (1791), II, 1770]

148. A gentleman who had been very unhappy in marriage married immediately after his wife died. Dr Johnson said, it was the triumph of hope over experience.
[In Boswell, *The Life of Samuel Johnson* (1791), II, 1770]

149. He said that few people had intellectual resources sufficient to forgo the pleasures of wine. They would not otherwise contrive to fill the interval between dinner and supper.
[In Boswell, *The Life of Samuel Johnson* (1791), II, 1770]

150. Every man has a lurking wish to appear considerable in his native place.
[In Boswell, *The Life of Samuel Johnson* (1791), II, Letter to Sir Joshua Reynolds, 1771]

151. It is so far from being natural for a man and woman to live in a state of marriage that we find all the motives which they have for remaining in that connection, and the restraints which civilized society imposes to prevent separation, are hardly sufficient to keep them together.
[In Boswell, *The Life of Samuel Johnson* (1791), II, 1772]

152. Nobody can write the life of a man, but those who have eat and drunk and lived in social intercourse with him.
[In Boswell, *The Life of Samuel Johnson* (1791), II, 1772]

153. I would not give half a guinea to live under one form of government rather than another. It is of no moment to the happiness of an individual.
[In Boswell, *The Life of Samuel Johnson* (1791), II, 1772]

154. [To Sir Adam Ferguson]
Sir, I perceive you are a vile Whig.
[In Boswell, *The Life of Samuel Johnson* (1791), II, 1772]

155. There is more knowledge of the heart in one letter of Richardson's than in all Tom Jones.
[In Boswell, *The Life of Samuel Johnson* (1791), II, 1772]

156. Why, Sir, if you were to read Richardson for the story, your impatience would be so much fretted, that you would hang yourself. But you must read him for the sentiment, and consider the story as only giving occasion to the sentiment.
[In Boswell, *The Life of Samuel Johnson* (1791), II, 1772]

157. Much may be made of a Scotchman, if he be caught young.
[In Boswell, *The Life of Samuel Johnson* (1791), II, 1772]

158. All intellectual improvement arises from leisure.
[In Boswell, *The Life of Samuel Johnson* (1791), II, 1773]

159. *Elphinston*: What, have you not read it through?...
Johnson: No, Sir, do you read books through?
[In Boswell, *The Life of Samuel Johnson* (1791), II, 1773]

160. Read over your compositions, and where ever you meet with a passage which you think is particularly fine, strike it out.
[In Boswell, *The Life of Samuel Johnson* (1791), II, quoting a college tutor, 1773]

161. [Of Lady Diana Beauclerk]
The woman's a whore, and there's an end on't.
[In Boswell, *The Life of Samuel Johnson* (1791), II, 1773]

162. [Referring to the poetry of Ossian]
I hope I shall never be deterred from detecting what I think a cheat, by the menaces of a ruffian.
[In Boswell, *The Life of Samuel Johnson* (1791), II, Letter to Macpherson, 1775]

163. The Irish are a fair people; – they never speak well of one another.
[In Boswell, *The Life of Samuel Johnson* (1791), II, 1775]

164. [Of *Gulliver's Travels*]
When once you have thought of big men and little men, it is very easy to do all the rest.
[In Boswell, *The Life of Samuel Johnson* (1791), II, 1775]

165. There are few ways in which a man can be more innocently employed than in getting money.
[In Boswell, *The Life of Samuel Johnson* (1791), II, 1775]

166. [Of Thomas Gray]
He was dull in a new way, and that made many people think him great.
[In Boswell, *The Life of Samuel Johnson* (1791), II, 1775]

167. I never think I have hit hard, unless it rebounds.
[In Boswell, *The Life of Samuel Johnson* (1791), II, 1775]

168. The greatest part of a writer's time is spent in reading, in order to write: a man will turn over half a library to make one book.
[In Boswell, *The Life of Samuel Johnson* (1791), II, 1775]

169. Patriotism is the last refuge of a scoundrel.
[In Boswell, *The Life of Samuel Johnson* (1791), II, 1775]

170. [Of the Scots]
Their learning is like bread in a besieged town: every man gets a little, but no man gets a full meal.
[In Boswell, *The Life of Samuel Johnson* (1791), II, 1775]

171. Knowledge is of two kinds. We know a subject ourselves, or we know where we can find information upon it.
[In Boswell, *The Life of Samuel Johnson* (1791), II, 1775]

172. Politics are now nothing more than a means of rising in the world.
[In Boswell, *The Life of Samuel Johnson* (1791), II, 1775]

173. That is the happiest conversation where there is no competition, no vanity, but a calm quiet interchange of sentiments.
[In Boswell, *The Life of Samuel Johnson* (1791), II, 1775]

174. Players, Sir! I look upon them as no better than creatures set upon tables and joint stools to make faces and produce laughter, like dancing dogs.
[In Boswell, *The Life of Samuel Johnson* (1791), II, 1775]

175. In lapidary inscriptions a man is not upon oath.
[In Boswell, *The Life of Samuel Johnson* (1791), II, 1775]

176. There is now less flogging in our great schools than formerly, but then less is learned there; so that what the boys get at one end they lose at the other.
[In Boswell, *The Life of Samuel Johnson* (1791), II, 1775]

177. When men come to like a sea-life, they are not fit to live on land.
[In Boswell, *The Life of Samuel Johnson* (1791), II, 1776]

178. Nothing odd will do long. Tristram Shandy did not last.
[In Boswell, *The Life of Samuel Johnson* (1791), II, 1776]

179. There is nothing which has yet been contrived by man, by which so much happiness is produced as by a good tavern or inn.
[In Boswell, *The Life of Samuel Johnson* (1791), II, 1776]

180. Marriages would in general be as happy, and often more so, if they were all made by the Lord Chancellor ... without the parties having any choice in the matter.
[In Boswell, *The Life of Samuel Johnson* (1791), II, 1776]

181. Questioning is not the mode of conversation among gentlemen.
[In Boswell, *The Life of Samuel Johnson* (1791), II, 1776]

182. If a madman were to come into this room with a stick in his hand, no doubt we should pity the state of his mind; but our primary consideration would be to take care of ourselves. We should knock him down first, and pity him afterwards.
[In Boswell, *The Life of Samuel Johnson* (1791), III, 1776]

183. Consider, Sir, how should you like, though conscious of your innocence, to be tried before a jury for a capital crime, once a week.
[In Boswell, *The Life of Samuel Johnson* (1791), III, 1776]

184. No man but a blockhead ever wrote, except for money.
[In Boswell, *The Life of Samuel Johnson* (1791), III, 1776]

185. It is better that some should be unhappy than that none should be happy, which would be the case in a general state of equality.
[In Boswell, *The Life of Samuel Johnson* (1791), III, 1776]

186. A man who has not been in Italy, is always conscious of an inferiority, from his not having seen what it is expected a man should see. The grand object of travelling is to see the shores of the Mediterranean.
[In Boswell, *The Life of Samuel Johnson* (1791), III, 1776]

187. 'Sir, what is poetry?'
'Why Sir, it is much easier to say what it is not. We all know what light is; but it is not easy to tell what it is.'
[In Boswell, *The Life of Samuel Johnson* (1791), III, 1776]

188. Sir, you have but two topics, yourself and me. I am sick of both.
[In Boswell, *The Life of Samuel Johnson* (1791), III, 1776]

189. *Olivarii Goldsmith, Poetae, Physici, Historici, Qui nullum fere scribendi genus non tetigit, Nullum quod tetigit non ornavit.*
To Oliver Goldsmith, A Poet, Naturalist, and Historian, who left scarcely any style of writing untouched, and touched none that he did not adorn.
[In Boswell, *The Life of Samuel Johnson* (1791), III, Epitaph on Goldsmith, 1776]

190. If I had no duties, and no reference to futurity, I would spend my life in driving briskly in a post-chaise with a pretty woman.
[In Boswell, *The Life of Samuel Johnson* (1791), III, 1777]

191. Depend upon it, Sir, when a man knows he is to be hanged in a fortnight, it concentrates his mind wonderfully.
[In Boswell, *The Life of Samuel Johnson* (1791), III, 1777]

192. When a man is tired of London, he is tired of life; for there is in London all that life can afford.
[In Boswell, *The Life of Samuel Johnson* (1791), III, 1777]

193. He who praises everybody praises nobody.
[In Boswell, *The Life of Samuel Johnson* (1791), III, 1777]

194. Here's to the next insurrection of the negroes in the West Indies.
[In Boswell, *The Life of Samuel Johnson* (1791), III, 1777]

195. Round numbers are always false.
[In Boswell, *The Life of Samuel Johnson* (1791), III, 1778]

196. [Of ghosts]
All argument is against it; but all belief is for it.
[In Boswell, *The Life of Samuel Johnson* (1791), III, 1778]

197. John Wesley's conversation is good, but he is never at leisure. He is always obliged to go at a certain hour. This is very disagreeable to a man who loves to fold his legs and have out his talk, as I do.
[In Boswell, *The Life of Samuel Johnson* (1791), III, 1778]

198. Though we cannot out-vote them we will out-argue them.
[In Boswell, *The Life of Samuel Johnson* (1791), III, 1778]

199. Seeing Scotland, Madam, is only seeing a worse England. It is seeing the flower fade away to the naked stalk.
[In Boswell, *The Life of Samuel Johnson* (1791), III, 1778]

200. Every man thinks meanly of himself for not having been a soldier, or not having been at sea.
[In Boswell, *The Life of Samuel Johnson* (1791), III, 1778]

201. A mere antiquarian is a rugged being.
[In Boswell, *The Life of Samuel Johnson* (1791), III, Letter to Boswell, 1778]

202. I am willing to love all mankind, except an American.
[In Boswell, *The Life of Samuel Johnson* (1791), III, 1778]

203. Sir, the insolence of wealth will creep out.
[In Boswell, *The Life of Samuel Johnson* (1791), III, 1778]

204. All censure of a man's self is oblique praise. It is in order to shew how much he can spare.
[In Boswell, *The Life of Samuel Johnson* (1791), III, 1778]

205. I have always said, the first Whig was the Devil.
[In Boswell, *The Life of Samuel Johnson* (1791), III, 1778]

206. It is thus that mutual cowardice keeps us in peace. Were one half of mankind brave and one half cowards, the brave would be always beating the cowards. Were all brave, they would lead a very uneasy life; all would be continually fighting; but being all cowards, we go on very well.
[In Boswell, *The Life of Samuel Johnson* (1791), III, 1778]

207. Were it not for imagination, Sir, a man would be as happy in the arms of a chambermaid as of a Duchess.
[In Boswell, *The Life of Samuel Johnson* (1791), III, 1778]

208. There are innumerable questions to which the inquisitive mind can in this state receive no answer: Why do you and I exist? Why was this world created? Since it was to be created, why was it not created sooner?
[In Boswell, *The Life of Samuel Johnson* (1791), III, 1778]

209. If it rained knowledge, I'd hold out my hand; but I would not give myself the trouble to go in quest of it.
[In Boswell, *The Life of Samuel Johnson* (1791), III, 1778]

210. Claret is the liquor for boys; port for men; but he who aspires to be a hero must drink brandy.
[In Boswell, *The Life of Samuel Johnson* (1791), III, 1779]

211. A man who exposes himself when he is intoxicated, has not the art of getting drunk.
[In Boswell, *The Life of Samuel Johnson* (1791), III, 1779]

212. [Of the Giant's Causeway]
Worth seeing? yes; but not worth going to see.
[In Boswell, *The Life of Samuel Johnson* (1791), III, 1779]

213. I have got no further than this: Every man has a right to utter what he thinks truth, and every other man has a right to knock him down for it. Martyrdom is the test.
[In Boswell, *The Life of Samuel Johnson* (1791), IV, 1780]

214. A Frenchman must be always talking, whether he knows

anything of the matter or not; an Englishman is content to say nothing, when he has nothing to say.
[In Boswell, *The Life of Samuel Johnson* (1791), IV, 1780]

215. [To an abusive Thames waterman]
Sir, your wife, under pretence of keeping a bawdy-house, is a receiver of stolen goods.
[In Boswell, *The Life of Samuel Johnson* (1791), IV, 1780]

216. [Of Goldsmith]
No man was more foolish when he had not a pen in his hand, or more wise when he had.
[In Boswell, *The Life of Samuel Johnson* (1791), IV, 1780]

217. Depend upon it that if a man talks of his misfortunes there is something in them that is not disagreeable to him; for where there is nothing but pure misery there never is any recourse to the mention of it.
[In Boswell, *The Life of Samuel Johnson* (1791), IV, 1780]

218. Supposing ... a wife to be of a studious or argumentative turn, it would be very troublesome: for instance, – if a woman should continually dwell upon the subject of the Arian heresy.
[In Boswell, *The Life of Samuel Johnson* (1791), IV, 1780]

219. No man speaks concerning another, even suppose it be in his praise, if he thinks he does not hear him, exactly as he would, if he thought he was within hearing.
[In Boswell, *The Life of Samuel Johnson* (1791), IV, 1780]

220. Mrs Montagu has dropt me. Now, Sir, there are people whom one should like very well to drop, but would not wish to be dropped by.
[In Boswell, *The Life of Samuel Johnson* (1791), IV, 1781]

221. This merriment of parsons is mighty offensive.
[In Boswell, *The Life of Samuel Johnson* (1791), IV, 1781]

222. 'The woman had a bottom of good sense.' The word 'bottom' thus introduced, was so ludicrous, ... that most of us could not forbear tittering ... 'Where's the merriment? ... I say the woman was fundamentally sensible.'
[In Boswell, *The Life of Samuel Johnson* (1791), IV, 1781]

223. Classical quotation is the parole of literary men all over the world.
[In Boswell, *The Life of Samuel Johnson* (1791), IV, 1781]

224. [To Miss Monckton, afterwards Lady Corke, who said that Sterne's writings affected her]
Why, that is, because, dearest, you're a dunce.
[In Boswell, *The Life of Samuel Johnson* (1791), IV, 1781]

225. I have two very cogent reasons for not printing any list of subscribers; – one, that I have lost all the names, – the other, that I have spent all the money.
[In Boswell, *The Life of Samuel Johnson* (1791), IV, 1781]

226. Always, Sir, set a high value on spontaneous kindness. He whose inclination prompts him to cultivate your friendship of his own accord, will love you more than one whom you have been at pains to attach to you.
[In Boswell, *The Life of Samuel Johnson* (1791), IV, 1781]

227. A wise Tory and a wise Whig, I believe, will agree. Their principles are the same, though their modes of thinking are different.
[In Boswell, *The Life of Samuel Johnson* (1791), IV, 1781]

228. [On the death of Mr Levett]
Officious, innocent, sincere,
Of every friendless name the friend.
Yet still he fills affection's eye,
Obscurely wise, and coarsely kind.
[In Boswell, *The Life of Samuel Johnson* (1791), IV, 1782]

229. Resolve not to be poor: whatever you have, spend less. Poverty is a great enemy to human happiness; it certainly destroys liberty, and it makes some virtues impracticable and others extremely difficult.
[In Boswell, *The Life of Samuel Johnson* (1791), IV, Letter to Boswell, 1782]

230. I hate a fellow whom pride, or cowardice, or laziness drives into a corner, and who does nothing when he is there but sit and growl; let him come out as I do, and bark.
[In Boswell, *The Life of Samuel Johnson* (1791), IV, 1782]

231. I never have sought the world; the world was not to seek me.
[In Boswell, *The Life of Samuel Johnson* (1791), IV, 1783]

232. How few of his friends' houses would a man choose to be at when he is sick.
[In Boswell, *The Life of Samuel Johnson* (1791), IV, 1783]

233. There is a wicked inclination in most people to suppose an old man decayed in his intellects. If a young or middle-aged man, when leaving a company, does not recollect where he laid his hat, it is nothing; but if the same inattention is discovered in an old man, people will shrug up their shoulders, and say, 'His memory is going.'
[In Boswell, *The Life of Samuel Johnson* (1791), IV, 1783]

234. [On the poetry of Ossian]
A man might write such stuff for ever, if he would abandon his mind to it.
[In Boswell, *The Life of Samuel Johnson* (1791), IV, 1783]

235. [Replying to Maurice Morgann who asked him whether Derrick or Smart was the better poet]
Sir, there is no settling the point of precedency between a louse and a flea.
[In Boswell, *The Life of Samuel Johnson* (1791), IV, 1783]

236. When I observed he was a fine cat, saying, 'why yes, Sir, but I have had cats whom I liked better than this'; and then as if perceiving Hodge to be out of countenance, adding, 'but he is a very fine cat, a very fine cat indeed.'
[In Boswell, *The Life of Samuel Johnson* (1791), IV, 1783]

237. Clear your mind of cant ... You may talk in this manner; it is a mode of talking in Society: but don't think foolishly.
[In Boswell, *The Life of Samuel Johnson* (1791), IV, 1783]

238. As I know more of mankind I expect less of them, and am ready now to call a man a good man, upon easier terms than I was formerly.
[In Boswell, *The Life of Samuel Johnson* (1791), IV, 1783]

239. Boswell is a very clubbable man.
[In Boswell, *The Life of Samuel Johnson* (1791), IV, 1783]

240. [Of George Psalmanazar, whom he reverenced for his piety]
I should as soon think of contradicting a Bishop.
[In Boswell, *The Life of Samuel Johnson* (1791), IV, 1784]

241. If a man were to go by chance at the same time with [Edmund] Burke under a shed, to shun a shower, he would say – 'this is an extraordinary man.'
[In Boswell, *The Life of Samuel Johnson* (1791), IV, 1784]

242. [Of the roast mutton he had for dinner at an inn]
It is as bad as bad can be: it is ill-fed, ill-killed, ill-kept, and ill-drest.
[In Boswell, *The Life of Samuel Johnson* (1791), IV, 1784]

243. *Johnson*: As I cannot be sure that I have fulfilled the conditions on which salvation is granted, I am afraid I may be one of those who shall be damned (looking dismally).
Dr Adams: What do you mean by damned?

Johnson (passionately and loudly): Sent to Hell, Sir, and punished everlastingly.
[In Boswell, *The Life of Samuel Johnson* (1791), IV, 1784]

244. [To Miss Hannah More, who had expressed a wonder that the poet who had written *Paradise Lost* should write such poor Sonnets]
Milton, Madam, was a genius that could cut a Colossus from a rock; but could not carve heads upon cherry-stones.
[In Boswell, *The Life of Samuel Johnson* (1791), IV, 1784]

245. Don't cant in defence of savages.
[In Boswell, *The Life of Samuel Johnson* (1791), IV, 1784]

246. No man is a hypocrite in his pleasures.
[In Boswell, *The Life of Samuel Johnson* (1791), IV, 1784]

247. Dublin, though a place much worse than London, is not so bad as Iceland.
[In Boswell, *The Life of Samuel Johnson* (1791), IV, Letter to Mrs Smart, 1791]

248. Sir, I look upon every day to be lost in which I do not make a new acquaintance.
[In Boswell, *The Life of Samuel Johnson* (1791), IV, 1784]

249. [On his deathbed]
I will be conquered; I will not capitulate.
[In Boswell, *The Life of Samuel Johnson* (1791), IV, 1784]

250. Are you sick or are you sullen?
[In Boswell, *The Life of Samuel Johnson* (1791), IV, Letter to Boswell, 1784]

251. An odd thought strikes me: – we shall receive no letters in the grave.
[In Boswell, *The Life of Samuel Johnson* (1791), IV, 1784]

252. Corneille is to Shakespeare ... as a clipped hedge is to a forest.
[In Hester Lynch Piozzi, *Anecdotes of the Late Samuel Johnson* (1786)]

253. [Burlesque of Lope de Vega 'He who can conquer a lion']
If the man who turnips cries,
Cry not when his father dies,
'Tis a proof that he had rather
Have a turnip than his father.
[In Hester Lynch Piozzi, *Anecdotes of the Late Samuel Johnson* (1786)]

254. [Of Bathurst]
A man to my very heart's content: he hated a fool, and he hated a rogue, and he hated a Whig; he was a very good hater.
[In Hester Lynch Piozzi, *Anecdotes of the Late Samuel Johnson* (1786)]

255. It is very strange, and very melancholy, that the paucity of human pleasures should persuade us ever to call hunting one of them.
[In Hester Lynch Piozzi, *Anecdotes of the Late Samuel Johnson* (1786)]

256. [Of a Jamaican gentleman, then lately dead]
He will not, whither he is now gone, find much difference, I believe, either in the climate or the company.
[In Hester Lynch Piozzi, *Anecdotes of the Late Samuel Johnson* (1786)]

257. Was there ever yet anything written by mere man that was wished longer by its readers, excepting *Don Quixote*, *Robinson Crusoe* and the *Pilgrim's Progress*?
[In Hester Lynch Piozzi, *Anecdotes of the Late Samuel Johnson* (1786)]

258. Life is a pill which none of us can bear to swallow without gilding.
[In Hester Lynch Piozzi, *Anecdotes of the Late Samuel Johnson* (1786)]

259. A man seldom thinks with more earnestness of anything than he does of his dinner.
[In Hester Lynch Piozzi, *Anecdotes of the Late Samuel Johnson* (1786)]

260. Books that you may carry to the fire, and hold readily in your hand, are the most useful after all.
[In Sir John Hawkins, *Life of Samuel Johnson* (1787)]

261. A man is in general better pleased when he has a good dinner upon his table, than when his wife talks Greek.
[In Sir John Hawkins, *Life of Samuel Johnson* (1787)]

262. I would rather see the portrait of a dog that I know, than all the allegorical paintings they can shew me in the world.
[In Sir John Hawkins, *Life of Samuel Johnson* (1787)]

263. I dogmatize and am contradicted, and in this conflict of opinions and sentiments I find delight.
[In Sir John Hawkins, *Life of Samuel Johnson* (1787)]

264. Of music Dr Johnson used to say that it was the only sensual pleasure without vice.
[In *European Magazine*, 1795]

265. What is written without effort is in general read without pleasure.
[In William Seward, *Biographia* (1799)]

266. Abstinence is as easy to me as temperance would be difficult.
[In William Roberts (ed.), *Memoirs of the Life and Correspondence of Mrs Hannah More* (1834), I]

267. [Remark to Hannah More]
Madam, before you flatter a man so grossly to his face, you should consider whether or not your flattery is worth his having.
[In Charlotte Barrett (ed.), *Diary and Letters of Madame d'Arblay* (1842), I]

268. A general anarchy prevails in my kitchen.
[In Charlotte Barrett (ed.), *Diary and Letters of Madame d'Arblay* (1842), I]

269. Every man has, some time in his life, an ambition to be a wag.
[In Charlotte Barrett (ed.), *Diary and Letters of Madame d'Arblay* (1842), III]

270. Fly fishing may be a very pleasant amusement; but angling or float fishing I can only compare to a stick and a string, with a worm at one end and a fool at the other.
[Attr. in Hawker, *Instructions to Young Sportsmen* (1859)]

271. This world where much is to be done and little to be known.
[In G.B. Hill (ed.), *Johnsonian Miscellanies* (1897), I]

272. I have heard him assert, that a tavern chair was the throne of human felicity.
[In G.B. Hill (ed.), *Johnsonian Miscellanies* (1897), II, 'Extracts from Hawkins's *Life of Johnson*']

273. Sir, executions are intended to draw spectators. If they do not draw spectators, they don't answer their purpose.
[In *The Economist*, 1993]

274. No two men can be half an hour together, but one shall acquire an evident superiority over the other.
[Attr.]

275. The future is purchased by the present.
[Attr.]

Johnston, Brian (1912–1994)
Broadcaster and commentator on cricket and royal events

1. The bowler's Holding, the batsman's Willey.
[Quoted in his obituary, *Sunday Times*]

2. [When asked by his commanding officer what steps he would take if he came across a German battalion]
Long ones, backwards.
[Quoted in his obituary, *Sunday Times*]

3. We're going to see Afaq to Knight at the Nursery End.
[Quoted in his obituary, *Sunday Times*]

Johnston, Jennifer (1930–)
Irish novelist

1. I don't often eat boys. Never Celts. They're stringy.
[*The Captains and the Kings* (1972)]

Johnston, Jill (1929–)

1. Until all women are lesbians there will be no true political revolution.
[*Lesbian Nation: The Feminist Solution* (1973)]

2. Feminists who still sleep with men are delivering their most vital energies to the oppressor.
[*Lesbian Nation: The Feminist Solution* (1973)]

3. No one should have to dance backwards all their life.
[In Rosalind Miles, *The Women's History of the World* (1988)]

Johnstone, John Benn (1803–1891)
English dramatist

1. I want you to assist me in forcing her on board the lugger; once there, I'll frighten her into marriage.
[*The Gipsy Farmer* (1845); usually quoted as 'Once aboard the lugger and the maid is mine']

Johst, Hanns (1890–1978)
German dramatist

1. *Wenn ich Kultur höre ... entsichere ich meinen Browning!*
When I hear the word 'culture' ... I take the safety-catch off my Browning!
[*Schlageter* (1933). Cf. Goering: 2]

Joliot-Curie, Irène (1897–1956)
French nuclear physicist; Nobel prize, with her husband, for chemistry, 1935; daughter of Marie Curie

1. [Recalling the her mother's advice]
That one must do some work seriously and must be independent and not merely amuse oneself in life – this our mother has told us always, but never that science was the only career worth following.
[In Mary Margaret McBride, *A Long Way from Missouri*, 10]

Jolson, Al (Asa Yoelson) (1886–1950)
Russian-born American singer; famous for imitations of Negro singers

1. You ain't heard nothin' yet, folks.
[*The Jazz Singer*, film, 1927; scriptwriter Alfred A. Cohn]

Jones, Barry Owen (1932–)
Australian politician and lawyer

1. Academic economists have about the status and reliability of astrologers or the readers of Tarot cards. If the medical profession was as lacking in resources as the economics we would not have advanced very far beyond the provision of splints for broken arms.
[In John Wilkes (ed.), *The Future of Work*]

Jones, John Paul (1747–1792)
Scottish-born American naval officer and memoirist

1. [Said as his ship was sinking]
I have not yet begun to fight.
[Remark, 1779]

Jones, Peter (Peter F. Hilton-Jones)
New Zealand rugby player

1. [In a radio interview after a tremendous New Zealand win against the Springbok rugby team in 1956]
I'm absolutely buggered.
[Attr.]

Jones, Sir William (1746–1794)
English orientalist, translator and jurist

1. My opinion is, that power should always be distrusted, in whatever hands it is placed.
[In Lord Teignmouth, *Life of Sir W. Jones* (1835)]

Jonson, Ben (1572–1637)
English dramatist, poet and author of court masques; noted for 'comedy of humours'

1. Helter skelter, hang sorrow, care'll kill a cat, up-tails all, and a louse for the hangman.
[*Every Man in His Humour* (1598), I.iii]

2. Have you a stool there to be melancholy upon?
[*Every Man in His Humour* (1598), III.i]

3. Ods me, I marvel what pleasure or felicity they have in taking their roguish tobacco. It is good for nothing but to choke a man, and fill him full of smoke and embers.
[*Every Man in His Humour* (1598), III.v]

4. I do honour the very flea of his dog.
[*Every Man in His Humour* (1598), IV.ii]

5. I have it here in black and white.
[*Every Man in His Humour* (1598), IV.v]

6. There shall be no love lost.
[*Every Man out of His Humour* (1599), II.i]

7. Blind Fortune still
Bestows her gifts on such as cannot use them.
[*Every Man out of His Humour* (1599), II.ii]

8. Slow, slow, fresh fount, keep time with my salt tears:
Yet, slower, yet; O faintly, gentle springs:
List to the heavy part the music bears,
Woe weeps out her division, when she sings.
[*Cynthia's Revels* (1600), I.i]

9. So they be ill men,
If they spake worse, 'twere better: for of such
To be dispraised, is the most perfect praise.
[*Cynthia's Revels* (1600), III.ii]

10. True happiness
Consists not in the multitude of friends,
But in the worth and choice.
[*Cynthia's Revels* (1600), III.ii]

11. Queen and huntress, chaste and fair,
Now the sun is laid to sleep,
Seated in thy silver chair,
State in wonted manner keep:
Hesperus entreats thy light,

Goddess, excellently bright.
[*Cynthia's Revels* (1600), V.iii]

12. Ramp up my genius, be not retrograde;
But boldly nominate a spade a spade.
[*The Poetaster* (1601), V.i]

13. Detraction is but baseness' varlet;
And apes are apes, though clothed in scarlet.
[*The Poetaster* (1601), V.i]

14. Tell proud Jove,
Between his power and thine there is no odds:
'Twas only fear first in the world made gods.
[*Sejanus* (1603), II.ii]

15. Alas, all the castles I have, are built with air, thou know'st.
[*Eastward Ho* (1605), II.ii]

16. Good morning to the day: and next, my gold!
Open the shrine that I may see my saint.
[*Volpone* (1607), I.i]

17. Calumnies are answered best with silence.
[*Volpone* (1607), II.ii]

18. Come, my Celia, let us prove,
While we can, the sports of love.
[*Volpone* (1607), III.v]

19. Suns, that set, may rise again;
But if once we lose this light.
'Tis with us perpetual night.
[*Volpone* (1607), III.v]

20. Our drink shall be prepared gold and amber;
Which we will take, until my roof whirl around
With the vertigo: and my dwarf shall dance.
[*Volpone* (1607), III.v]

21. [To a lawyer]
You have a gift, sir, (thank your education,)
Will never let you want, while there are men,
And malice, to breed causes.
[*Volpone* (1607), V.i]

22. Mischiefs feed
Like beasts, till they be fat, and then they bleed.
[*Volpone* (1607), V.viii]

23. Still to be neat, still to be drest,
As you were going to a feast;
Still to be powder'd, still perfum'd,
Lady, it is to be presumed,
Though art's hid causes are not found,
All is not sweet, all is not sound.
Give me a look, give me a face,
That makes simplicity a grace;
Robes loosely flowing, hair as free:
Such sweet neglect more taketh me,
Than all the adulteries of art;
They strike mine eyes, but not my heart.
[*Epicoene* (1609), I]

24. Fortune, that favours fools.
[*The Alchemist* (1610), Prologue]

25. Thou look'st like Antichrist in that lewd hat.
[*The Alchemist* (1610), IV.vii]

26. Where it concerns himself,
Who's angry at a slander makes it true.
[*Catiline his Conspiracy* (1611), III.i]

27. This is the very womb and bed of enormity.
[*Bartholomew Fair* (1614), I.iv]

28. Yea, I will eat exceedingly, and prophesy.
[*Bartholomew Fair* (1614), I.vi]

29. Neither do thou lust after that tawney weed tobacco.
[*Bartholomew Fair* (1614), II.vi]

30. If he were
To be made honest by an act of parliament,
I should not alter in my faith of him.
[*The Devil is an Ass* (1616), IV.i]

31. Well, they talk we shall have no more Parliaments,
God bless us!
[*The Staple of News* (1625), III.i]

32. This is Mab, the Mistress-Fairy
That doth nightly rob the dairy.
['The Satyr' (1603)]

33. Rest in soft peace, and, ask'd say here doth lye
Ben Jonson his best piece of poetrie.
[*Epigrams* (1616), 'On My First Son']

34. Weep with me, all you that read
This little story:
And know for whom a tear you shed
Death's self is sorry.
'Twas a child that so did thrive
In grace and feature,
As Heaven and Nature seem'd to strive
Which own'd the creature.
Years he number'd scarce thirteen
When Fates turn'd cruel,
Yet three fill'd Zodiacs had he been
The stage's jewel;
And did act, what now we moan,
Old men so duly,
As sooth the Parcae thought him one,
He play'd so truly.
So, by error, to his fate
They all consented;
But viewing him since, alas, too late!
They have repented;
And have sought (to give new birth)
In baths to steep him;
But being so much too good for earth,
Heaven vows to keep him.
[*Epigrams* (1616), 'An Epitaph on Salomon Pavy, a Child of Queen Elizabeth's Chapel']

35. Follow a shadow, it still flies you,
Seem to fly it, it will pursue:
So court a mistress, she denies you;
Let her alone, she will court you.
Say, are not women truly, then,
Styl'd but the shadows of us men?
[*The Forest* (1616), 'Song: That Women are but Men's Shadows']

36. Drink to me only with thine eyes,
And I will pledge with mine;
Or leave a kiss upon the cup,
And I'll not look for wine.
The thirst that from the soul doth rise
Doth ask a drink divine;
But might I of Jove's nectar sup,
I would not change for thine.
I sent thee late a rosy wreath,
Not so much honouring thee,
As giving it a hope that there
It could not wither'd be.
[*The Forest* (1616), 'To Celia']

37. Room! room! make room for the bouncing Belly,

First father of sauce and deviser of jelly;
Prime master of arts and the giver of wit,
That found out the excellent engine, the spit,
The plough and the flail, the mill and the hopper,
The hutch and the boulter, the furnace and copper,
The oven, the bavin, the mawkin, the peel,
The hearth and the range, the dog and the wheel.
[Pleasure Reconciled to Virtue (1618), 'Song for Comus']

38. While I confess thy writings to be such,
As neither man, nor muse, can praise too much...

39. Soul of the Age!
The applause! delight! the wonder of our stage!
My Shakespeare, rise; I will not lodge thee by
Chaucer, or Spenser, or bid Beaumont lie
A little further, to make thee a room:
Thou art a monument, without a tomb,
And art alive still, while thy book doth live,
And we have wits to read, and praise to give...

40. Marlowe's mighty line...

41. And though thou hadst small Latin, and less Greek...

42. To hear thy buskin tread,
And shake a stage: or, when thy socks were on,
Leave thee alone, for the comparison
Of all that insolent Greece or haughty Rome
Sent forth, or since did from their ashes come...

43. He was not of an age, but for all time!

44. For a good poet's made as well as born...

45. Sweet Swan of Avon! what a sight it were
To see thee in our waters yet appear,
And make those flights upon the banks of Thames,
That so did take Eliza, and our James!
['To the Memory of My Beloved, the Author, Mr William Shakespeare' (1623)]

46. Have you seen but a bright lily grow,
Before rude hands have touch'd it?
Have you mark'd but the fall o' the snow
Before the soil hath smutch'd it?...
O so white! O so soft! O so sweet is she!...
[*The Underwood* (1640), 'Celebration of Charis', IV]

47. She is Venus when she smiles
But she's Juno when she walks,
And Minerva when she talks.
[*The Underwood* (1640), 'Celebration of Charis', V]

48. It is not growing like a tree
In bulk, doth make men better be;
Or standing long an oak, three hundred year,
To fall a log at last, dry, bald, and sere:
A lily of a day,
Is fairer far in May,
Although it fall and die that night;
It is the plant and flower of light.
In small proportions we just beauties see;
And in short measures, life may perfect be.
[*The Underwood* (1640), 'To the Immortal Memory ... of ... Sir Lucius Carey and Sir H. Morison']

49. The voice so sweet, the wordes so fair,
As some soft chime had stroked the air;
And though the sound were parted thence,
Still left an echo in the sense.
[*The Underwood* (1640), 'Eupheme']

50. Come, leave the loathèd stage,
And the more loathsome age,
Where pride and impudence, in faction knit,
Usurp the chair of wit!
['Ode to Himself']

51. This figure that thou here seest put,
It was for gentle Shakespeare cut,
Wherein the graver had a strife
With Nature, to out-do the life:
O could he but have drawn his wit
As well in brass, as he has hit
His face; the print would then surpass
All that was ever writ in brass:
But since he cannot, reader, look
Not on his picture, but his book.
['On the Portrait of Shakespeare, To the Reader']

52. His censure of the English poets was this...
That Donne ... deserved hanging.
That Shakespeare wanted Art.
[*Conversations with William Drummond of Hawthornden* (1619)]

53. He hath consumed a whole night in lying looking to his great toe, about which he hath seen Tartars and Turks, Romans and Carthaginians, fight in his imagination.
[*Conversations with William Drummond of Hawthornden* (1619)]

54. I remember the players have often mentioned it as an honour to Shakespeare that in his writing (whatsoever he penned) he never blotted out a line. My answer hath been 'Would he had blotted a thousand'. Which they thought a malevolent speech. I had not told posterity this, but for their ignorance, who chose that circumstance to commend their friend by wherein he most faulted; and to justify mine own candour: for I loved the man, and do honour his memory, on this side of idolatry, as much as any. He was (indeed) honest, and of an open and free nature; had an excellent phantasy, brave notions, and gentle expressions; wherein he flowed with that facility, that sometimes it was necessary he should be stopped: sufflaminandus erat, as Augustus said of Haterius. His wit was in his own power, would the rule of it had been so too ... But he redeemed his vices with his virtues. There was ever more in him to be praised than to be pardoned.
[*Timber, or Discoveries made upon Men and Matter* (1641), 'De Shakespeare Nostrati. Augustus in Haterium']

55. They say princes learn no art truly, but the art of horsemanship. The reason is, the brave beast is no flatterer. He will throw a prince as soon as his groom.
[*Timber, or Discoveries made upon Men and Matter* (1641), 'Illiteratus princeps']

56. Talking and eloquence are not the same: to speak, and to speak well, are two things.
[*Timber, or Discoveries made upon Men and Matter* (1641), 'Praecept[a] Element[aria]']

57. O rare Ben Jonson.
[Epitaph in Westminster Abbey]

Jordan, Thomas (c. 1612–1685)
English poet and dramatist

1. They pluck't communion tables down
And broke our painted glasses;
They threw our altars to the ground
And tumbled down the crosses.
They set up Cromwell and his heir–
The Lord and Lady Claypole–
Because they hated Common Prayer,
The organ and the maypole.
['How the War Began' (1664)]

2. Our God and soldier we alike adore,
Just at the brink of ruin, not before:

The danger past, both are alike requited;
God is forgotten, and our soldier slighted.
[Epigram]

Jortin, John (1698–1770)

English clergyman and ecclesiastical historian

1. *Palmam qui meruit, ferat.*
Let him who has won it bear the palm.
[*Lusus Poetici* (1748 edition), adopted by Lord Nelson as his motto]

Joseph, Michael (1897–1958)

English publisher and writer

1. Authors are easy to get on with – if you're fond of children.
[The Observer, 1949]

Jotti, Nilde (1920–)

Italian politician and first woman to become Leader of the Lower House

1. *Quali difetti attribuisce al maschio italiano: Primo è prepotente. Secondo una vittima, un prodotto che non sa badare a se stesso.*
Which faults do you attribute to the Italian male: First he's a bully. Second a victim, a product that cannot look after himself.
[In E. Biagi, *La Geografia di Italia* (*The Geography of Italy*, 1975)]

Jowett, Benjamin (1817–1893)

English scholar of Greek; translator, essayist, priest and theologian

1. The lie in the Soul is a true lie.
[From the introduction to his translation (1871) of Plato's Republic, II]
2. One man is as good as another until he has written a book.
[In E. Abbott and L. Campbell (eds), *Life and Letters of Benjamin Jowett* (1897)]
3. Nowhere probably is there more true feeling, and nowhere worse taste, than in a churchyard – both as regards the monuments and the inscriptions. Scarcely a word of the true poetry anywhere.
[In E. Abbott and L. Campbell (eds), *Life and Letters of Benjamin Jowett* (1897)]
4. Young men make great mistakes in life; for one thing, they idealize love too much.
[In E. Abbott and L. Campbell (eds), *Life and Letters of Benjamin Jowett* (1897)]
5. My dear child, you must believe in God in spite of what the clergy tell you.
[In M. Asquith, *Autobiography* (1920–1922)]
6. Research! A mere excuse for idleness; it has never achieved, and will never achieve any results of the slightest value.
[In Logan Pearsall Smith, *Unforgotten Years*]
7. The way to get things done is not to mind who gets the credit for doing them.
[Attr.]
8. [Responding to a conceited young student's assertion that he could find no evidence for a God]
If you don't find a God by five o'clock this afternoon you must leave the college.
[Attr.]

Joyce, James (1882–1941)

Irish novelist, short-story writer and poet; noted for his revolutionary 'stream of consciousness' technique and inventive language

1. A Portrait of the Artist as a Young Man.
[Title of book, 1916]
2. Once upon a time and a very good time it was there was a moocow coming down along the road and this moocow that was coming down along the road met a nicens little boy named baby tuckoo.
[*A Portrait of the Artist as a Young Man* (1916), first words]
3. Poor Parnell! he cried loudly. My dead King!
[*A Portrait of the Artist as a Young Man* (1916), 1]
4. The evening air was pale and chilly and after every charge and thud of the footballers the greasy leather orb flew like a heavy bird through the grey light. He kept on the fringe of his line, out of sight of his prefect, out of the reach of the rude feet, feigning to run now and then.
[*A Portrait of the Artist as a Young Man* (1916), 1]
5. She was alone and still, gazing out to sea: and when she felt his presence and the worship of his eyes her eyes turned to him in quiet sufferance of his gaze, without shame or wantonness.
[*A Portrait of the Artist as a Young Man* (1916), 4]
6. He drew forth a phrase from his treasure and spoke it softly to himself:
– A day of dappled seaborne clouds.
[*A Portrait of the Artist as a Young Man* (1916), 4]
7. Ireland is the old sow that eats her farrow.
[*A Portrait of the Artist as a Young Man* (1916), 5]
8. The artist, like the God of creation, remains within or behind or beyond or above his handiwork, invisible, refined out of existence, indifferent, paring his fingernails.
[*A Portrait of the Artist as a Young Man* (1916), 5]
9. April 26 … Welcome, O life! I go to encounter for the millionth time the reality of experience and to forge in the smithy of my soul the uncreated conscience of my race.
April 27. Old father, old artificer, stand me now and ever in good stead.
[*A Portrait of the Artist as a Young Man* (1916), closing words]
10. Stately, plump Buck Mulligan came from the stairhead, bearing a bowl of lather on which a mirror and a razor lay crossed. A yellow dressinggown, ungirdled, was sustained gently behind him by the mild morning air. He held the bowl aloft and intoned:
–Introibo ad altare Dei.
[*Ulysses* (1922), first sentence]
11. The snotgreen sea. The scrotumtightening sea.
[*Ulysses* (1922), I]
12. It is a symbol of Irish art. The cracked lookingglass of a servant.
[*Ulysses* (1922), I]
13. When I makes tea I makes tea, as old mother Grogan said. And when I makes water I makes water … Begob, ma'am, says Mrs. Cahill, God send you don't make them in the one pot.
[*Ulysses* (1922), I]
14. We feel in England that we have treated you [Irish] rather unfairly. It seems history is to blame.
[*Ulysses* (1922), I]

15. I fear those big words, Stephen said, which make us so unhappy.
[*Ulysses* (1922), I]

16. History is a nightmare from which I am trying to awake.
[*Ulysses* (1922), I]

17. Ineluctable modality of the visible.
[*Ulysses* (1922), I]

18. Lawn Tennyson, gentleman poet.
[*Ulysses* (1922), I]

19. Come forth, Lazarus! And he came fifth and lost the job.
[*Ulysses* (1922), II]

20. The statue of the onehandled adulterer [Nelson].
[*Ulysses* (1922), II]

21. A base barreltone voice.
[*Ulysses* (1922), II]

22. A man of genius makes no mistakes. His errors are volitional and are the portals of discovery.
[*Ulysses* (1922), II]

23. Agenbite of inwit.
[*Ulysses* (1922), II]

24. Greater love than this, he said, no man hath that a man lay down his wife for a friend. Go thou and do likewise. Thus, or words to that effect, saith Zarathustra, sometime regius professor of French letters to the University of Oxtail.
[*Ulysses* (1922), II]

25. I shall call rebutting evidence to prove up to the hilt that the hidden hand is again at its old game. When in doubt persecute Bloom.
[*Ulysses* (1922), II]

26. I regard him as the whitest man I know. He is down on his luck at present owing to the mortgaging of his extensive property at Agendath Netaim in faraway Asia Minor, slides of which will now be shown.
[*Ulysses* (1922), II]

27. The heaventree of stars hung with humid nightblue fruit.
[*Ulysses* (1922), III]

28. I was blue mouldy for the want of that pint. Declare to God I could hear it hit the pit of my stomach with a click.
[*Ulysses* (1922)]

29. And I thought well as well him as another and then I asked him with my eyes to ask again yes and then he asked me would I yes to say yes my mountain flower and first I put my arms around him yes and drew him down to me so he could feel my breasts all perfume yes and his heart was going like mad and yes I said yes I will Yes.
[*Ulysses* (1922), closing words]

30. riverrun, past Eve and Adam's, from swerve of shore to bend of bay, brings us by a commodius vicus of recirculation back to Howth Castle and Environs.
[*Finnegans Wake* (1939), first words]

31. That ideal reader suffering from an ideal insomnia.
[*Finnegans Wake* (1939), I]

32. The flushpots of Euston and the hanging garments of Marylebone.
[*Finnegans Wake* (1939), I]

33. O
tell me all about
Anna Livia! I want to hear all
about Anna Livia. Well, you know Anna Livia?
Yes, of course, we all know Anna Livia. Tell me all.
Tell me now.
[*Finnegans Wake* (1939), I]

34. If you don't like my story get out of the punt.
[*Finnegans Wake* (1939), I]

35. Can't hear with the waters of. The chittering waters of. Flittering bats, fieldmice bawk talk. Ho! Are you not gone ahome? ... Dark hawks hear us. Night! Night! My ho head halls. I feel as heavy as yonder stone ... Beside the rivering waters of, hitherandthithering waters of. Night!
[*Finnegans Wake* (1939), I]

36. Quiet takes back her folded fields.
[*Finnegans Wake* (1939), II]

37. Loud, heap miseries upon us yet entwine our arts with laughters low!
[*Finnegans Wake* (1939), II]

38. All moanday, tearsday, wailsday, thumpsday, frightday, shatterday.
[*Finnegans Wake* (1939), II]

39. Three quarks for Muster Mark!
[*Finnegans Wake* (1939), II; the word 'quark' has since been adopted by physicists for hypothetical elementary particles]

40. The Gracehoper was always jigging ajog, hoppy on akkant of his joyicity.
[*Finnegans Wake* (1939), III]

41. Soft morning, city!
[*Finnegans Wake* (1939), IV]

42. No mouth has the might to set a mearbound to the march of a landsmaul.
[*Finnegans Wake* (1939)]

43. By an epiphany he meant a sudden spiritual manifestation, whether in vulgarity of speech or of gesture or in a memorable phase of the mind itself. He believed that it was for the man of letters to record these epiphanies with extreme care, seeing that they themselves are the most delicate and evanescent of moments.
[*Stephen Hero* (1944), 25]

44. I hear an army charging upon the land
And the thunder of horses plunging,
foam about their knees.
[*Chamber Music* (1907), XXXVI]

45. Rain on Rahoon falls softly, softly falling,
Where my dark lover lies.
Sad is his voice that calls me, sadly calling,
At grey moonrise.
[*Pomes Penyeach* (1927), 'She Weeps over Rahoon']

46. A child is sleeping:
An old man gone.
O, father forsaken,
Forgive your son!
['Ecce Puer' (1936)]

47. My intention was to write a chapter of the moral history of my country and I chose Dublin for the scene because that city seemed to me the centre of paralysis.
[Letter to Grant Richards, 5 May 1905]

48. I am afraid I am more interested, Mr Connolly, in the Dublin street names than in the riddle of the universe.
[Remark to Cyril Connolly]

49. [Announcing his age on arriving at Clongowes Wood College]
Half past six.
[In Richard Ellmann, *James Joyce* (1958)]

50. [On being asked by a young admirer in Zürich, 'May I kiss the hand that wrote Ulysses?']
No, it did lots of other things too.
[In Richard Ellman, *James Joyce* (1958)]

51. [Commenting on the interruption of a music recital when a moth flew into the singer's mouth]
The desire of the moth for the star.
[In R. Ellmann, *James Joyce* (1958)]

52. [Replying to Patrick Tuohy's assertion that he wished to capture Joyce's soul in his portrait of him]
Never mind about my soul, just make sure you get my tie right.
[In R. Ellmann, *James Joyce* (1958)]

53. [On meeting W.B. Yeats]
We have met too late. You are too old for me to have any effect on you.
[In R. Ellmann, *James Joyce* (1958)]

Joyce, Nora Barnacle (1884–1951)
Wife of James Joyce, Irish author and poet

1. [Speaking of her husband]
If only Jimmy had stuck to music, we might have made some money.
[*Hindsight*, BBC Radio 4 programme, 1993]

Judge, Jack (1878–1938) and **Williams,** Harry (1874–1924)

1. Good-bye Piccadilly, Farewell Leicester Square;
It's a long, long way to Tipperary, but my heart's right there.
['It's a Long Way to Tipperary', 1912]

Julia (39 BC–14 AD)
Daughter of the emperor Augustus; died in exile

1. [On being complimented by her father on the modest dress she was wearing that day]
Today I dressed to meet my father's eyes; yesterday it was for my husband's.
[In Macrobius, *Saturnalia*]

2. [Replying to criticism of her extravagance, compared to her father's simple way of life]
He sometimes forgets that he is Caesar, but I always remember that I am Caesar's daughter.
[In Macrobius, *Saturnalia*]

Julian the Apostate (c. 332–363)
Roman emperor from 361; born at Constantinople; soldier and writer

1. *Vicisti, Galilaee.*
You have conquered, Galilean.
[Last words]

Juliana of Norwich (c. 1343–c. 1429)
English mystic and anchorite; first Englishwoman of letters

1. Sin is behovely, but all shall be well and all shall be well and all manner of things shall be well.
[*Revelations of Divine Love* (1393), 27]

2. Wouldest thou wit thy Lord's meaning in this thing? Wit it well: Love was his meaning. Who shewed it thee? Love. What shewed He thee? Love. Wherefore shewed it He? for Love . . . Thus was I learned that Love is our Lord's meaning.
[*Revelations of Divine Love* (1393), 86]

Jung, Carl Gustav (1875–1961)
Swiss psychiatrist; pupil of Freud and founder of analytic psychology

1. *Glücklicherweise hat die gütige und langmütige Natur den meisten Menschen nie die fatale Frage nach dem Sinn ihres Lebens auf die Zunge gelegt. Und wo niemand fragt, braucht keiner zu antworten.*
Fortunately Nature, kind and patient as she is, has never put the dire question as to the meaning of their lives into the mouths of most people. And where nobody asks, nobody needs to answer.
['Vom Werden der Persönlichkeit' ('On the Development of Personality', 1934)]

2. People set forth by devious paths to their destruction or salvation.
[*Psychology & Alchemy* (1944)]

3. *Das geistige Pendel schwingt zwischen Sin und Unsinn und nicht zwischen richtig und unrichtig.*
The pendulum of the mind swings between sense and nonsense, and not between what is right and what is wrong.
[*Erinnerungen, Träume, Gedanken* (*Memories, Dreams, Thoughts*, 1962), 5, 'Sigmund Freud']

4. *Ein Mensch, der nicht durch die Hölle seiner Leidenschaften gegangen ist, hat sie auch nie überwunden.*
A man who has not gone through the hell of his passions has never overcome them either.
[*Erinnerungen, Träume, Gedanken* (*Memories, Dreams, Thoughts*, 1962), 9, 'Travels: India']

5. *Soweit wir zu erkennen vermögen, ist es der einzige Sinn der menschlichen Existenz, ein Licht anzuzünden in der Finsternis des blossen Seins.*
As far as we are able to understand, the only aim of human existence is to kindle a light in the darkness of mere being.
[*Erinnerungen, Träume, Gedanken* (*Memories, Dreams, Thoughts*, 1962), 11, 'On life after death']

6. *Jede Form von Süchtigkeit ist von Übel, gleichgültig, ob es sich um Alkohol oder Morphium oder Idealismus handelt.*
Every form of addiction is a bad thing, irrespective of whether it is to alcohol, morphine or idealism.
[*Erinnerungen, Träume, Gedanken* (*Memories, Dreams, Thoughts*, 1962), 12, 'Late Thoughts']

7. Sentimentality is a superstructure covering brutality.
[*Reflections*]

8. Wherever an inferiority complex exists, there is a good reason for it. There is always something inferior there, although not just where we persuade ourselves that it is.
[Interview, 1943]

9. We need more understanding of human nature, because the only real danger that exists is man himself . . . We know nothing of man, far too little. His psyche should be studied because we are the origin of all coming evil.
[BBC television interview, 1959]

10. Show me a sane man and I will cure him for you.
[*The Observer*, 1975]

Jung Chang (1952–)
Chinese author now based in London

1. He [Mao Zedong] was, it seemed to me, really a restless fight promoter by nature and good at it. He understood ugly human instincts such as envy and resentment, and knew how to mobilize them for his ends. He ruled by getting people to hate each other.
[*Wild Swans. Three Daughters of China* (1991)]

2. Mao had managed to turn the people into the ultimate weapon of dictatorship. That was why under him there was

no real equivalent of the KGB in China. There was no need. In bringing out and nourishing the worst in people, Mao had created a moral wasteland and a land of hatred.
[*Wild Swans. Three Daughters of China* (1991)]

Junius (1769–1772)
Pen-name of anonymous author of letters criticizing ministries of George III

1. The liberty of the press is the Palladium of all the civil, political, and religious rights of an Englishman.
[*Letters* (1769–1771), Dedication]

2. To be acquainted with the merit of a ministry, we need only observe the condition of the people.
[*Letters* (1769–1771), 1]

3. The right of election is the very essence of the constitution.
[*Letters* (1769–1771), 2]

4. Is this the wisdom of a great minister? or is it the ominous vibration of a pendulum?
[*Letters* (1769–1771), 12]

5. It is not that you do wrong by design, but that you should never do right by mistake.
[*Letters* (1769–1771), 12]

6. There is a holy mistaken zeal in politics as well as in religion. By persuading others, we convince ourselves.
[*Letters* (1769–1771), 35]

7. Whether it be the heart to conceive, the understanding to direct, or the hand to execute.
[*Letters* (1769–1771), 37]

8. The injustice done to an individual is sometimes of service to the public.
[*Letters* (1769–1771), 41]

Junot, Andoche, Duc d'Abrantes (1771–1813)
Marshal of France

1. [On being made a duke]
I am my own ancestor.
[Attr.]

Justinian, Emperor (c. 482–565)
Byzantine emperor from 527, born in Illyria; had Roman law codified

1. *Justitia est constans et perpetua voluntas ius suum cuique tribuens.*
Justice is the constant and perpetual wish to give to every one his due.
[*Institutes*]

Juvenal (c. 60–130)
Roman verse satirist and Stoic

1. *Difficile est saturam non scribere. Nam quis iniquae*
Tam patiens urbis, tam ferreus, ut teneat se?
It is difficult not to write satire. For who is so tolerant of this abominable city, who so iron of soul that he can contain himself?
[*Satires*, I]

2. *Probitas laudatur et alget.*
Honesty is praised and is left out in the cold.
[*Satires*, I]

3. *Si natura negat, facit indignatio versum.*
If nature refuses, indignation will prompt my verse.
[*Satires*, I]

4. *Quidquid agunt homines, votum timor ira vuluptas*
Gaudia discursus nostri farrago libelli est.
What mankind desires, and what they shun,
Rage, passions, pleasures, impotence of will,
Shall this satirical collection fill.
[*Satires*, I; trans. Dryden]

5. *Nemo repente fuit turpissimus.*
No one ever became depraved in an instant.
[*Satires*, II]

6. *Grammaticus, rhetor, geometres, pictor, aliptes,*
Augur, schoenobates, medicus, magus, omnia novit
Graeculus esuriens: in caelum iusseris ibit.
A cook, a conjurer, a rhetorician,
A painter, a pedant, a geometrician,
A dancer on the ropes and a physician.
All things the hungry Greek exactly knows:
And bid him go to Heaven, to Heaven he goes.
[*Satires*, III; trans. Dryden]

7. *Nil habet infelix paupertas durius in se*
Quam quod ridiculos homines facit.
Nothing is harder to bear about luckless poverty than the way it exposes men to ridicule.
[*Satires*, III]

8. *Haud facile emergunt quorum virtutibus obstat*
Res angusta domi.
Rarely they rise by virtue's aid, who lie
Plung'd in the depths of helpless poverty.
[*Satires*, III; trans. Dryden]

9. *Hic vivimus ambitiosa*
Paupertate omnes.
Here we all live in a state of pretentious poverty.
[*Satires*, III]

10. *Omnia Romae*
Cum pretio.
Everything in Rome comes at a price.
[*Satires*, III]

11. *Rara avis in terris nigroque simillima cycno.*
A rare bird upon the earth, and very like a black swan.
[*Satires*, VI]

12. *Hoc volo, sic iubeo, sit pro ratione voluntas.*
I will this deed, so I order it done: let my will stand for my reason.
[*Satires*, VI]

13. *Desperanda tibi salva concordia socru.*
Despair of peace as long as your mother-in-law is alive.
[*Satires*, VI]

14. *Sed quis custodiet ipsos*
Custodes?
But who will guard the guards themselves?
[*Satires*, VI]

15. *Tenet insanabile multos*
Scribendi cacoethes et aegro in corde senescit.
The incurable itch for writing takes hold of many and becomes chronic in their distempered brains.
[*Satires*, VII]

16. *Occidit miseros crambe repetita magistros.*
Rehashed cabbage has proved fatal to many an unhappy teacher.
[*Satires*, VII]

17. *Nobilitas sola est atque unica virtus.*
The one and only true nobility is virtue.
[*Satires*, VIII]

18. *Summum crede nefas animam praeferre pudori*
Et propter vitam vivendi perdere causas.
Count it the greatest sin to put life before honour, and for the sake of life to lose the reasons for living.
[*Satires*, VIII]

19. *Cantabit vacuus coram latrone viator.*
The poure man when he goth by the weye
Bifore the theves he may synge and playe.
[*Satires*, X; trans. Chaucer]

20. *Duas tantum res anxius optat,*
Panem et circenses.
Two things only the people anxiously desire: bread and circuses.
[*Satires*, X]

21. *I, demens, et saevas curre per Alpes*
Ut pueris placeas et declamatio fias.
Go climb the Alps, ambitious fool,
To please the boys, and be a theme at school.
[*Satires*, X; trans. Dryden]

22. *Mors sola fatetur*
Quantula sint hominum corpuscula.
Death only this mysterious truth unfolds,
The mighty soul, how small a body holds.
[*Satires*, X; trans. Dryden]

23. *Orandum est ut sit mens sana in corpore sano.*
Your prayers should be for a healthy mind in a healthy body.
[*Satires*, X]

24. *Prima est haec ultio, quod se*
Iudice nemo nocens absolvitur.
The chief punishment is this: that no guilty man is acquitted in his own judgement.
[*Satires*, XIII]

25. *Maxima debetur puero reverentia, siquid*
Turpe paras, nec tu pueri contempseris annos.
If ever you have anything disgraceful in mind, you owe the greatest reverence to the young; do not disregard your son's tender years.
[*Satires*, XIV]

Kael, Pauline (1919–)
American writer and film critic

1. Kiss Kiss Bang Bang.
[Title of collected reviews of sixties films, 1968]

Kafka, Franz (1883–1924)
Influential German-speaking novelist and short-story writer; born in Prague

1. *Schriftsteller reden Gestank.*
What writers talk stinks.
[*Tagebuch* (*Diary*, 1910)]

2. *Metaphysisches Bedürfnis ist nur Todesbedürfnis.*
A metaphysical need is only a need for death.
[*Tagebuch* (*Diary*, 1912)]

3. *Nicht verzweifeln, auch darüber nicht, dass du nicht verzweifelst.*
Do not despair, not even about the fact that you do not despair.
[*Tagebuch* (*Diary*, 1913)]

4. *Sie können einwenden, dass es ja überhaupt kein Verfahren ist, Sie haben sehr recht, denn es ist ja nur ein Verfahren, wenn ich es als solches anerkenne.*
You may raise the objection that it really is not a trial at all; you are quite right, for it is only a trial if I recognise it as such.
[*Der Prozess* (*The Trial*, written 1914, published 1925), 2, 'First Interrogation']

5. *. . . dann erinnere ich Sie an den alten Rechtsspruch: für den Verdächtigen ist Bewegung besser als Ruhe, denn der, welcher ruht, kann immer, ohne es zu wissen, auf einer Waagschale sein und mit seinen Sünden gewogen werden.*
. . . then I shall remind you of the old verdict: the suspect is better to be moving than at rest, for the one that rests can, without knowing it, be in the balance being weighed with his sins.
[*Der Prozess* (*The Trial*, written 1914, published 1925), 8, 'Block the Businessman. Dismissal of the Lawyer']

6. *Es ist oft besser, in Ketten, als frei zu sein.*
It's often better to be in chains than to be free.
[*Der Prozess* (*The Trial*, written 1914, published 1925), 8, 'Block the Businessman. Dismissal of the Lawyer']

7. *'Ich bin aber nicht schuldig', sagte K., 'es ist ein Irrtum. Wie kann denn ein Mensch überhaupt schuldig sein.'*
'But I'm not guilty,' said K., 'there's been a mistake. How can a man be guilty anyway.'
[*Der Prozess* (*The Trial*, written 1914, published 1925), 9, 'In the Cathedral']

8. *Aber an K.s Gürgel legten sich die Hände des einen Herrn, während der andere das Messer ihm tief ins Herz stiess und zweimal dort drehte. Mit brechenden Augen sah noch K., wie die Herren, nahe vor seinem Gesicht, Wange an Wange aneinandergelehnt, die Entscheidung beobachteten. 'Wie ein Hund!' sagte er, es war, als sollte die Scham ihn überleben.*
But the hands of one of the gentlemen were around K.'s throat, while the other thrust the knife deep into his heart and twisted it there twice. His eyes failing, K. could still see the gentlemen just in front of his face, cheek leaning against cheek, watching the decisive act. 'Like a dog!' he said: it was as if the shame would outlive him.
[*Der Prozess* (*The Trial*, written 1914, published 1925), 10, 'End']

9. *Als Gregor Samsa eines Morgens aus unruhigen Träumen erwachte, fand er sich in seinem Bett zu einem ungeheueren Ungeziefer verwandelt.*
When Gregor Samsa awoke one morning from troubled dreams, he found himself transformed in his bed into a monstrous verminous insect.
['Die Verwandlung' ('Metamorphosis', 1915)]

10. *Im Kampf zwischen dir und der Welt sekundiere der Welt.*
In the struggle between you and the world, support the world.
[*Betrachtungen über Sünde, Leid, Hoffnung und den wahren Weg* (*Reflections on Sin, Sorrow, Hope and the True Way*, first published 1953)]

11. *Es gibt ein Ziel, aber keinen Weg; was wir Weg nennen, ist Zögern.*
There is a goal but no way of reaching it; what we call the way is hesitation.
[*Betrachtungen über Sünde, Leid, Hoffnung und den wahren Weg* (*Reflections on Sin, Sorrow, Hope and the True Way*, first published 1953)]

12. *Ich glaube, man sollte überhaupt nur solche Bücher lesen, die einen beissen und stechen.*
I think you should only read those books which bite and sting you.
[Letter to Oskar Pollak, 27 January 1904]

13. *. . . ein Buch muss die Axt sein für das gefrorene Meer in uns.*
. . . a book must be the axe for the frozen sea within us.
[Letter to Oskar Pollak, 27 January 1904]

14. *Liebe ist, dass Du mir das Messer bist, mit dem ich in mir wühle.*
Love is, that you are the knife which I plunge into myself.
[Letter to Milena Jesenká, 14 September 1920]

Kant, Immanuel (1724–1804)
German idealist philosopher, noted for his idea of the categorical imperative

1. *Aus so krummem Holze, als woraus der Mensch gemacht ist, kann nichts ganz Gerades gezimmert werden.*
No straight thing can ever be formed from timber as crooked as that from which humanity is made.
[*Idee zu einer allgemeinen Geschichte in weltbürgerlicher Absicht* (*Idea for a General History with a Cosmopolitan purpose*, 1784), proposition 6]

2. *Ich soll niemals anders verfahren als so, dass ich auch wollen könne, meine Maxime solle ein allgemeines Gesetz werden.*
I should always act in such a way that I may want my maxim to become a general law.
[*Grundlegung zur Metaphysik der Sitten* (*Outline of the Metaphysics of Morals*, 1785), I]

3. *Endlich gibt es einen Imperativ, der, ohne irgend eine andere durch ein gewisses Verhalten zu erreichende Absicht als Bedingung zum Grunde zu legen, dieses Verhalten unmittelbar gebietet. Dieser Imperativ ist* kategorisch ... *Dieser Imperativ mag der der* Sittlichkeit *heissen.*
Finally, there is an imperative which immediately dictates a certain mode of behaviour, without having as its condition any other purpose to be achieved by means of that behaviour. This imperative is *categorical* ... This imperative may be called that of *morality*.
[*Grundlegung zur Metaphysik der Sitten* (*Outline of the Metaphysics of Morals*, 1785), II]

4. *Wer den Zweck will, will (so fern die Vernunft auf seine Handlungen entscheidenden Einfluss hat) auch das dazu unentbehrlich notwendige Mittel, das in seiner Gewalt ist.*
Whoever wills the end, also wills (insofar as his reason has a decisive influence on his conduct) the indispensably necessary means which lies within his power of achieving that end.
[*Grundlegung zur Metaphysik der Sitten* (*Outline of the Metaphysics of Morals*, 1785), II]

5. *...weil Glückseligkeit nicht ein Ideal der Vernunft, sondern der Einbildungskraft ist.*
...because bliss is not an ideal of reason, but of the powers of imagination.
[*Grundlegung zur Metaphysik der Sitten* (*Outline of the Metaphysics of Morals*, 1785), II]

6. *Handle so, dass du die Menschheit, sowohl in deiner Person, als in der Person eines jeden andern, jederzeit zugleich als Zweck, niemals bloss als Mittel brauchest.*
Act in such a way that you treat humanity, both in your own person as well as in that of any other, at any time as an end withal, never merely as a means.
[*Grundlegung zur Metaphysik der Sitten* (*Outline of the Metaphysics of Morals*, 1785), II]

7. *Tue das, wodurch du würdig wirst, glücklich zu sein.*
Act in such a way that you will be worthy of being happy.
[*Kritik der reinen Vernunft* (*Critique of Pure Reason*, second edition, 1787), II, section 2, 2]

8. *Zwei Dinge erfüllen das Gemüt mit immer neuer und zunehmender Bewunderung und Ehrfurcht, je öfter und anhaltender sich das Nachdenken damit beschäftigt: der bestirnte Himmel über mir und das moralische Gesetz in mir.*
Two things fill the mind with ever-fresh and ever-increasing admiration and reverence, the more often and the more enduringly the mind is occupied with them: the starry heaven above me and the moral law within me.
[*Kritik der praktischen Vernunft* (*Critique of Practical Reason*, 1788), II, Conclusion]

9. *Es ist nur eine (wahre) Religion; aber es kann vielerlei Arten des Glaubens geben.*
There is only one (true) religion; but there can be many different kinds of belief.
[*Die Religion innerhalb der Grenzen der blossen Vernunft* (*Religion within the Boundaries of Mere Reason*, 1793), III, section V]

10. *Büchergelehrsamkeit vermehrt zwar die Kenntnisse, aber erweitert nicht den Begriff und die Einsicht, wo nicht Vernunft dazukommt.*
Book learning certainly increases knowledge, but does not broaden one's ideas and insight when it is not accompanied by reason.
[*Anthropologie in pragmatischer Hinsicht* (*Pragmatic Anthropology*, second edition, 1800), I, book 1]

11. *Der Mensch ist das einzige Geschöpf, das erzogen werden muss.*
Man is the only creature which must be educated.
[*Über Pädagogik* (*On Pedagogy*, 1803), Introduction]

12. *Ob ... der Mensch nun von Natur moralisch gut oder böse ist? Keines von beiden, denn er ist von Natur gar kein moralisches Wesen; er wird dieses nur, wenn seine Vernunft sich bis zu den Begriffen der Pflicht und des Gesetzes erhebt.*
Is man by nature morally good or evil? Neither, for he is by nature not a moral being; he only becomes such when his reason is raised to the concepts of duty and law.
[*Über Pädagogik* (*On Pedagogy*, 1803), 'Von der praktischen Erziehung' ('Practical Education')]

Karr, Alphonse (1808–1890)
French novelist, editor of Figaro and memoirist

1. *Plus ça change, plus c'est la même chose.*
The more things change, the more they remain the same.
[*Les Guêpes* (1849)]

2. *Si l'on veut abolir la peine de mort en ce cas, que MM les assassins commencent.*
If we want to abolish the death penalty, let our friends the murderers take the first step.
[*Les Guêpes* (1849)]

3. Every man has three characters: that which he exhibits, that which he has, and that which he thinks he has.
[Attr.]

Kästner, Erich (1899–1974)
German novelist, journalist and children's writer

1. *Kennst du das Land, wo die Kanonen blühn?*
Dost thou know the land, where the cannons bloom?
[Title of poem in *Herz auf Taille* (*Heart on Waist*, 1928)]

Kaufman, Jean-Claude

1. The sock is a highly sensitive conjugal object.
[*The Observer*, 'Sayings of the Year', 1992]

Kaufman, George S. (1889–1961)
American humorous journalist, scriptwriter and librettist

1. [At a rehearsal of the Marx Brothers film *Animal Crackers* (1930), for which he wrote the script]
Excuse me for interrupting but I actually thought I heard a line I wrote.
[In S. Meredith, *George S. Kaufman and the Algonquin Round Table* (1974)]

2. [On Raymond Massey's interpretation of Abraham Lincoln]
Massey won't be satisfied until somebody assassinates him.
[In S. Meredith, *George S. Kaufman and the Algonquin Round Table* (1974)]

3. [Suggestion for his own epitaph]
Over my dead body!
[Attr.]

Kavanagh, Patrick (1905–1967)
Irish poet, critic, journalist and novelist

1. My black hills have never seen the sun rising,
Eternally they look north towards Armagh...

2. 'Who owns them hungry hills
That the waterhen and snipe must have forsaken?
A poet? Then by heavens he must be poor.'
I hear and is my heart not badly shaken?
['Shancoduff']

3. ... the peasant in his little acres is tied
To a mother's womb by the wind-toughened navel-cord
Like a goat tethered to the stump of a tree–
He circles around and around wondering why it should be.
['The Great Hunger']

Kavanagh, P.J. (1931–)
English poet, novelist, journalist and scriptwriter

1. I love trees revealed, the way
Light rinses fog from colours, opens out.
[*Collected Poems* (1964), 'Edward Thomas in Heaven']

Kawabata, Yasunari (1899–1972)
Japanese journalist and Nobel prizewinning novelist

1. A single flower could impress you with more gorgeousness than one hundred such.
['Japan the Beautiful and I' (1968)]

2. Some critics say that my works are nihilistic, but the Western term 'nihilism' would not apply here. I think my writing is different deep in the heart.
['Japan the Beautiful and I' (1968)]

Kearney, Denis (1847–1907)
American labour leader, born in Ireland

1. Horny-handed sons of toil.
[Speech, c. 1878]

Keating, Paul (1944–)
Australian politician and Prime Minister

1. [On Andrew Peacock's ambitions to become leader of the Liberal Party following the 1987 elections]
Can a soufflé rise twice?
[ABC television, 1987]

Keats, John (1795–1821)
Leading English Romantic poet, noted for his passion for beauty, and letter writer

1. Sweet are the pleasures that to verse belong,
And doubly sweet a brotherhood in song.
['To George Felton Mathew' (1815)]

2. To one who has been long in city pent,
'Tis very sweet to look into the fair
And open face of heaven.
['To one who has been long in city pent' (1816)]

3. Much have I travell'd in the realms of gold,
And many goodly states and kingdoms seen...

4. Then felt I like some watcher of the skies
When a new planet swims into his ken;
Or like stout Cortez when with eagle eyes
He star'd at the Pacific – and all his men
Look'd at each other with a wild surmise–
Silent, upon a peak in Darien.
['On First Looking into Chapman's Homer' (1816)]

5. I stood tip-toe upon a little hill...

6. And then there crept
A little noiseless noise among the leaves,
Born of the very sigh that silence heaves...

7. Here are sweet peas, on tip-toe for a flight.
['I stood tip-toe upon a little hill' (1816)]

8. Stop and consider! life is but a day;
A fragile dew-drop on its perilous way
From a tree's summit; a poor Indian's sleep
While his boat hastens to the monstrous steep
Of Montmorenci...

9. O for ten years, that I may overwhelm
Myself in poesy; so I may do the deed
That my own soul has to itself decreed...

10. They sway'd about upon a rocking horse,
And thought it Pegasus...

11. A thousand handicraftsmen wore the mask
Of Poesy. Ill-fated, impious race!...

12. A drainless shower
Of light is Poesy; 'tis the supreme of power;
'Tis might half slumb'ring on its own right arm...

13. And they shall be accounted poet kings
Who simply tell the most heart-easing things.
['Sleep and Poetry' (1816)]

14. The poetry of earth is never dead:
When all the birds are faint with the hot sun,
And hide in cooling trees, a voice will run
From hedge to hedge about the new-mown mead.
['On the Grasshopper and Cricket' (1816)]

15. Happy is England! I could be content
To see no other verdure than its own;
To feel no other breezes than are blown
Through its tall woods with high romances blent...

16. To sit upon an Alp as on a throne,
And half forget what world or worldling meant.
['Happy is England! I could be content' (1816)]

17. Mortality
Weighs heavily on me like unwilling sleep.
['On Seeing the Elgin Marbles' (1817)]

18. It keeps eternal whisperings around
Desolate shores, and with its mighty swell
Gluts twice ten thousand caverns.
['On the Sea' (1817)]

19. In drear-nighted December,
Too happy, happy tree,
Thy branches ne'er remember
Their green felicity.
['In drear-nighted December' (1817)]

20. But vain is now the burning and the strife,
Pangs are in vain, until I grow high-rife
With old Philosophy.
['On Seeing a Lock of Milton's Hair' (1818)]

21. When I have fears that I may cease to be
Before my pen has glean'd my teeming brain...

22. When I behold, upon the night's starr'd face,
Huge cloudy symbols of a high romance...

23. Then on the shore
Of the wide world I stand alone, and think
Till love and fame to nothingness do sink.
['When I have fears that I may cease to be' (1818)]

24. O fret not after knowledge – I have none,
And yet my song comes native with the warmth.

O fret not after knowledge – I have none,
And yet the Evening listens.
['O thou whose face hath felt the Winter's wind' (1818)]

25. Souls of poets dead and gone,
What Elysium have ye known,
Happy field or mossy cavern,
Choicer than the Mermaid Tavern?
Have ye tippled drink more fine
Than mine host's Canary wine?
['Lines on the Mermaid Tavern' (1818)]

26. It is a flaw
In happiness, to see beyond our bourn,–
It forces us in summer skies to mourn:
It spoils the singing of the nightingale.
['To J. H. Reynolds, Esq.' (1818)]

27. Four seasons fill the measure of the year;
There are four seasons in the mind of man.
['The Human Seasons' (1818)]

28. Why were they proud? again we ask aloud.
Why in the name of Glory were they proud?...

29. So the two brothers and their murder'd man
Rode past fair Florence...

30. And she forgot the stars, the moon, and sun,
And she forgot the blue above the trees,
And she forgot the dells where waters run,
And she forgot the chilly autumn breeze;
She had no knowledge when the day was done,
And the new morn she saw not, but in peace
Hung over her sweet basil evermore...

31. 'For cruel 'tis,' said she,
'To steal my basil-pot away from me.'
['Isabella' (1818)]

32. Ay, on the shores of darkness there is light,
And precipices show untrodden green;
There is a budding morrow in midnight;
There is a triple sight in blindness keen.
['To Homer' (1818)]

33. Rich in the simple worship of a day.
['Ode to May. Fragment' (1818)]

34. A thing of beauty is a joy for ever:
Its loveliness increases; it will never
Pass into nothingness; but still will keep
A bower quiet for us, and a sleep
Full of sweet dreams, and health, and quiet breathing...

35. The inhuman dearth
Of noble natures...

36. Wherein lies happiness? In that which becks
Our ready minds to fellowship divine,
A fellowship with essence...

37. A hope beyond the shadow of a dream.
['Endymion' (1818), 1]

38. But this is human life: the war, the deeds,
The disappointment, the anxiety,
Imagination's struggles, far and nigh,
All human...

39. He ne'er is crown'd
With immortality, who fears to follow
Where airy voices lead...

40. Here is wine,
Alive with sparkles – never, I aver,
Since Ariadne was a vintager,
So cool a purple.
['Endymion' (1818), 2]

41. To Sorrow,
I bade good-morrow,
And thought to leave her far away behind;
But cheerly, cheerly,
She loves me dearly;
She is so constant to me, and so kind...

42. Their smiles,
Wan as primroses gather'd at midnight
By chilly-finger'd spring.
['Endymion' (1818), 4]

43. Deep in the shady sadness of a vale
Far sunken from the healthy breath of morn,
Far from the fiery noon, and eve's one star,
Sat gray-hair'd Saturn, quiet as a stone...

44. No stir of air was there,
Not so much life as on a summer's day
Robs not one light seed from the feather'd grass,
But where the dead leaf fell, there did it rest...

45. The Naiad 'mid her reeds
Press'd her cold finger closer to her lips...

46. That large utterance of the early Gods!...

47. O aching time! O moments big as years!...

48. As when, upon a trancèd summer-night,
Those green-rob'd senators of mighty woods,
Tall oaks, branch-charmèd by the earnest stars,
Dream, and so dream all night without a stir...

49. Unseen before by Gods or wondering men...

50. And still they were the same bright, patient stars.
['Hyperion. A Fragment' (1818), 1]

51. And only blind from sheer supremacy...

52. To bear all naked truths,
And to envisage circumstance, all calm,
That is the top of sovereignty...

53. For 'tis the eternal law
That first in beauty should be first in might.
['Hyperion. A Fragment' (1818), 2]

54. Knowledge enormous makes a God of me.
['Hyperion. A Fragment' (1818), 3]

55. Bards of Passion and of Mirth,
Ye have left your souls on earth!
Have ye souls in heaven too,
Double-lived in regions new?
['Ode' (1818)]

56. Where the nightingale doth sing
Not a senseless, trancèd thing,
But divine melodious truth.
['Ode' (1818)]

57. I had a dove and the sweet dove died;
And I have thought it died of grieving.
O, what could it grieve for? Its feet were tied,
With a silken thread of my own hand's weaving.
['Song' (1818)]

58. Ever let the Fancy roam,
Pleasure never is at home...

59. Where's the cheek that doth not fade,
Too much gaz'd at? Where's the maid
Whose lip mature is ever new?...

60. Where's the face
One would meet in every place?
['Fancy' (1819)]

61. St Agnes' Eve – Ah, bitter chill it was!
The owl, for all his feathers, was a-cold;
The hare limp'd trembling through the frozen grass,
And silent was the flock in woolly fold...

62. The sculptur'd dead, on each side, seem to freeze,
Emprison'd in black, purgatorial rails...

63. The joys of all his life were said and sung...

64. The silver, snarling trumpets 'gan to chide...

65. The music, yearning like a God in pain...

66. Sudden a thought came like a full-blown rose,
Flushing his brow...

67. A poor, weak, palsy-stricken, churchyard thing...

68. Out went the taper as she hurried in;
Its little smoke, in pallid moonshine, died...

69. A casement high and triple-arch'd there was,
All garlanded with carven imag'ries
Of fruits, and flowers, and bunches of knot-grass,
And diamonded with panes of quaint device,
Innumerable of stains and splendid dyes,
As are the tiger-moth's deep-damask'd wings...

70. Full on this casement shone the wintry moon,
And threw warm gules on Madeline's fair breast...

71. By degrees
Her rich attire creeps rustling to her knees...

72. Her soft and chilly nest...

73. As though a rose should shut, and be a bud again...

74. And still she slept an azure-lidded sleep,
In blanchèd linen, smooth, and lavender'd,
While he from forth the closet brought a heap
Of candied apple, quince, and plum, and gourd,
With jellies soother than the creamy curd,
And lucent syrops, tinct with cinnamon;
Manna and dates, in argosy transferr'd
From Fez; and spicèd dainties, every one,
From silken Samarcand to cedar'd Lebanon...

75. He play'd an ancient ditty, long since mute,
In Provence call'd, 'La belle dame sans mercy'...

76. And the long carpets rose along the gusty floor...

77. And they are gone: ay, ages long ago
These lovers fled away into the storm...

78. The Beadsman, after thousand aves told,
For aye unsought-for slept among his ashes cold.
['The Eve of St. Agnes' (1819)]

79. O what can ail thee, knight-at-arms,
Alone and palely loitering?
The sedge has wither'd from the lake,
And no birds sing...

80. I see a lily on thy brow,
With anguish moist and fever-dew;
And on thy cheek a fading rose
Fast withereth too.

I met a lady in the meads
Full beautiful – a faery's child,
Her hair was long, her foot was light,
And her eyes were wild...

81. She look'd at me as she did love,
And made sweet moan...

82. I set her on my pacing steed,
And nothing else saw all day long;
For sideways would she bend, and sing
A faery's song...

83. And sure in language strange she said–
'I love thee true'...

84. And there I shut her wild wild eyes
With kisses four...

85. La Belle Dame sans Merci
Hath thee in thrall!
['La Belle Dame Sans Merci' (1819)]

86. 'Mid hush'd, cool-rooted flowers, fragrant-eyed,
Blue, silver-white, and budded Tyrian...

87. O latest born and loveliest vision far
Of all Olympus' faded hierarchy!...

88. Nor virgin-choir to make delicious moan
Upon the midnight hours...

89. A bright torch, and a casement ope at night,
To let the warm Love in!
['Ode to Psyche' (1819)]

90. Fame, like a wayward girl, will still be coy
To those who woo her with too slavish knees.
['On Fame (1)' (1819)]

91. O soft embalmer of the still midnight,
Shutting, with careful fingers and benign,
Our gloom-pleas'd eyes.
['To Sleep' (1819)]

92. Thou still unravish'd bride of quietness,
Thou foster-child of silence and slow time,
Sylvan historian, who canst thus express
A flowery tale more sweetly than our rhyme:
What leaf-fringed legend haunts about thy shape
Of deities or mortals, or of both,
In Tempe or the dales of Arcady?
What men or gods are these? What maidens loth?
What mad pursuit? What struggle to escape?
What pipes and timbrels? What wild ecstasy?

Heard melodies are sweet, but those unheard
Are sweeter; therefore, ye soft pipes, play on;
Not to the sensual ear, but, more endear'd,
Pipe to the spirit ditties of no tone:
Fair youth, beneath the trees, thou canst not leave
Thy song, nor ever can those trees be bare;
Bold Lover, never, never canst thou kiss,
Though winning near the goal – yet, do not grieve:
She cannot fade, though thou hast not thy bliss,
For ever wilt thou love, and she be fair!

Ah, happy, happy boughs! that cannot shed
Your leaves, nor ever bid the Spring adieu;
And, happy melodist, unwearièd,
For ever piping songs for ever new;
More happy love! more happy, happy love!
For ever warm and still to be enjoy'd,
For ever panting and for ever young–
All breathing human passion far above,
That leaves a heart high-sorrowful and cloy'd,
A burning forehead, and a parching tongue.

Who are these coming to the sacrifice?
To what green altar, O mysterious priest,
Lead'st thou that heifer lowing at the skies,
And all her silken flanks with garlands drest?
What little town by river or sea shore,

Or mountain-built with peaceful citadel,
Is emptied of this folk, this pious morn?
And, little town, thy streets for evermore
Will silent be; and not a soul to tell
Why thou art desolate, can e'er return.

O Attic shape! Fair attitude! with brede
Of marble men and maidens overwrought,
With forest branches and the trodden weed;
Thou, silent form, dost tease us out of thought
As doth eternity: Cold Pastoral!
When old age shall this generation waste,
Thou shalt remain, in midst of other woe
Than ours, a friend to man, to whom thou say'st,
'Beauty is truth, truth beauty,'– that is all
Ye know on earth, and all ye need to know.
['Ode on a Grecian Urn' (1819)]

93. My heart aches, and a drowsy numbness pains
My sense, as though of hemlock I had drunk,
Or emptied some dull opiate to the drains
One minute past, and Lethe-wards had sunk:
'Tis not through envy of thy happy lot,
But being too happy in thine happiness–
That thou, light-wingèd Dryad of the trees,
In some melodious plot
Of beechen green, and shadows numberless,
Singest of summer in full-throated ease.

O, for a draught of vintage! that hath been
Cool'd a long age in the deep-delvèd earth,
Tasting of Flora and the country green,
Dance, and Provençal song, and sunburnt mirth!
O for a beaker full of the warm South,
Full of the true, the blushful Hippocrene,
With beaded bubbles winking at the brim,
And purple-stainèd mouth;
That I might drink, and leave the world unseen,
And with thee fade away into the forest dim–

Fade far away, dissolve, and quite forget
What thou among the leaves hast never known,
The weariness, the fever, and the fret,
Here, where men sit and hear each other groan;
Where palsy shakes a few, sad, last grey hairs,
Where youth grows pale, and spectre-thin, and dies;
Where but to think is to be full of sorrow
And leaden-eyed despairs;
Where Beauty cannot keep her lustrous eyes,
Or new Love pine at them beyond to-morrow.

Away! away! for I will fly to thee,
Not charioted by Bacchus and his pards,
But on the viewless wings of Poesy,
Though the dull brain perplexes and retards.
Already with thee! tender is the night,
And haply the Queen-Moon is on her throne,
Clustered around by all her starry Fays;
But here there is no light,
Save what from heaven is with the breezes blown
Through verdurous glooms and winding mossy ways.

I cannot see what flowers are at my feet,
Nor what soft incense hangs upon the boughs,
But, in embalmèd darkness, guess each sweet
Wherewith the seasonable month endows
The grass, the thicket, and the fruit-tree wild–
White hawthorn, and the pastoral eglantine;
Fast fading violets cover'd up in leaves;
And mid-May's eldest child,
The coming musk-rose, full of dewy wine,
The murmurous haunt of flies on summer eves.

Darkling I listen; and, for many a time
I have been half in love with easeful Death,
Call'd him soft names in many a musèd rhyme,
To take into the air my quiet breath;
Now more than ever seems it rich to die,
To cease upon the midnight with no pain,
While thou art pouring forth thy soul abroad
In such an ecstasy!
Still wouldst thou sing, and I have ears in vain–
To thy high requiem become a sod.

Thou wast not born for death, immortal Bird!
No hungry generations tread thee down;
The voice I hear this passing night was heard
In ancient days by emperor and clown:
Perhaps the self-same song that found a path
Through the sad heart of Ruth, when sick for home,
She stood in tears amid the alien corn;
The same that oft-times hath
Charm'd magic casements, opening on the foam
Of perilous seas, in faery lands forlorn.

Forlorn! the very word is like a bell
To toll me back from thee to my sole self!
Adieu! the fancy cannot cheat so well
As she is fam'd to do, deceiving elf.
Adieu! adieu! thy plaintive anthem fades
Past the near meadows, over the still stream,
Up the hill-side; and now 'tis buried deep
In the next valley-glades.
Was it a vision, or a waking dream?
Fled is that music – Do I wake or sleep?
['Ode to a Nightingale' (1819)]

94. No, no, go not to Lethe, neither twist
Wolf's-bane, tight-rooted, for its poisonous wine...

95. Nor let the beetle, nor the death-moth be
Your mournful Psyche...

96. But when the melancholy fit shall fall
Sudden from heaven like a weeping cloud,
That fosters the droop-headed flowers all,
And hides the green hill in an April shroud;
Then glut thy sorrow on a morning rose,
Or on the rainbow of the salt sand-wave,
Or on the wealth of globèd peonies;
Or if thy mistress some rich anger shows,
Emprison her soft hand and let her rave,
And feed deep, deep upon her peerless eyes.

She dwells with Beauty – Beauty that must die;
And Joy, whose hand is ever at his lips
Bidding adieu; and aching Pleasure nigh,
Turning to poison while the bee-mouth sips;
Ay, in the very temple of Delight
Veil'd Melancholy has her sovran shrine
Though seen of none save him whose strenuous tongue
Can burst Joy's grape against his palate fine;
His soul shall taste the sadness of her might,
And be among her cloudy trophies hung.
['Ode on Melancholy' (1819)]

97. And evenings steep'd in honied indolence...

98. For I would not be dieted with praise,
A pet-lamb in a sentimental farce!
['Ode on Indolence' (1819)]

99. Fanatics have their dreams, wherewith they weave
A paradise for a sect; the savage too
From forth the loftiest fashion of his sleep
Guesses at Heaven...

100. Every man whose soul is not a clod
Hath visions...

101. 'None can usurp this height', return'd that shade,
'But those to whom the miseries of the world
Are misery, and will not let them rest.'...

102. The poet and the dreamer are distinct,
Diverse, sheer opposite, antipodes.
The one pours out a balm upon the world,
The other vexes it.
['The Fall of Hyperion' (1819), 1]

103. She was a gordian shape of dazzling hue,
Vermilion-spotted, golden, green, and blue;
Striped like a zebra, freckled like a pard,
Eyed like a peacock, and all crimson barr'd...

104. Real are the dreams of Gods, and smoothly pass
Their pleasures in a long immortal dream.
['Lamia' (1819), 1]

105. Love in a hut, with water and a crust,
Is – Love forgive us! – cinders, ashes, dust...

106. That purple-linèd palace of sweet sin...

107. In pale contented sort of discontent...

108. Do not all charms fly
At the mere touch of cold philosophy?
There was an awful rainbow once in heaven:
We know her woof, her texture; she is given
In the dull catalogue of common things.
Philosophy will clip an Angel's wings.
['Lamia' (1819), 2]

109. Season of mists and mellow fruitfulness,
Close bosom-friend of the maturing sun;
Conspiring with him how to load and bless
With fruit the vines that round the thatch-eaves run;
To bend with apples the moss'd cottage trees,
And fill all fruit with ripeness to the core;
To swell the gourd, and plump the hazel shells
With a sweet kernel; to set budding more,
And still more, later flowers for the bees,
Until they think warm days will never cease,
For Summer has o'erbrimmed their clammy cells.

Who hath not seen thee oft amid thy store?
Sometimes whoever seeks abroad may find
Thee sitting careless on a granary floor,
Thy hair soft-lifted by the winnowing wind;
Or on a half-reap'd furrow sound asleep,
Drows'd with the fume of poppies, while thy hook
Spares the next swath and all its twinèd flowers;
And sometimes like a gleaner thou dost keep
Steady thy laden head across a brook;
Or by a cider-press, with patient look,
Thou watchest the last oozings, hours by hours.

Where are the songs of Spring? Ay, where are they?
Think not of them, thou hast thy music too–
While barrèd clouds bloom the soft-dying day,
And touch the stubble-plains with rosy hue;
Then in a wailful choir the small gnats mourn
Among the river sallows, borne aloft
Or sinking as the light wind lives or dies;
And full-grown lambs loud bleat from hilly bourn;
Hedge-crickets sing; and now with treble soft
The red-breast whistles from the garden-croft;
And gathering swallows twitter in the skies.
['To Autumn' (1819)]

110. The day is gone, and all its sweets are gone!
Sweet voice, sweet lips, soft hand, and softer breast.
['The day is gone, and all its sweets are gone!' (1819)]

111. What can I do to drive away
Remembrance from my eyes?
['What can I do to drive away' (1819)]

112. The fam'd memoirs of a thousand years,
Written by Crafticant, and published
By Parpaglion and Co.
['The Cap and Bells' (1819)]

113. Bright star, would I were steadfast as thou art–
Not in lone splendour hung aloft the night
And watching, with eternal lids apart,
Like nature's patient, sleepless Eremite,
The moving waters at their priestlike task
Of pure ablution round earth's human shores...

114. Still, still to hear her tender-taken breath,
And so live ever – or else swoon to death.
['Bright star, would I were steadfast as thou art' (1819)]

115. There is an old saying 'well begun is half done'– 'tis a bad one. I would use instead – 'Not begun at all until half done'.
[Letter to B.R. Haydon, 10–11 May, 1817]

116. I am quite disgusted with literary Men.
[Letter to Benjamin Bailey, 8 October 1817]

117. A long Poem is a test of Invention which I take to be the Polar Star of Poetry, as Fancy is the Sails, and Imagination the Rudder.
[Letter to Benjamin Bailey, 8 October 1817]

118. The Imagination may be compared to Adam's dream – he awoke and found it truth.
[Letter to Benjamin Bailey, 22 November 1817]

119. I am certain of nothing but of the holiness of the Heart's affections and the truth of Imagination – What the imagination seizes as Beauty must be truth – whether it existed before or not.
[Letter to Benjamin Bailey, 22 November 1817]

120. I have never yet been able to perceive how any thing can be known for truth by consecutive reasoning – and yet it must be.
[Letter to Benjamin Bailey, 22 November 1817]

121. O for a Life of Sensations rather than of Thoughts!
[Letter to Benjamin Bailey, 22 November 1817]

122. A man should have the fine point of his soul taken off to become fit for this world.
[Letter to J.H. Reynolds, 22 November 1817]

123. The excellence of every art is its intensity, capable of making all disagreeables evaporate, from their being in close relationship with Beauty and Truth.
[Letter to George and Tom Keats, 21 December 1817]

124. Negative Capability, that is, when a man is capable of being in uncertainties, mysteries, doubts, without any irritable reaching after fact and reason – Coleridge, for instance, would let go by a fine isolated verisimilitude caught from the Penetralium of mystery, from being incapable of remaining content with half-knowledge.
[Letter to George and Tom Keats, 21 December 1817]

125. There is nothing stable in the world; uproar's your only music.
[Letter to George and Tom Keats, 13 January 1818]

126. So I do believe ... that works of genius are the first things in this world.
[Letter to George and Tom Keats, 13 January 1818]

127. We hate poetry that has a palpable design upon us – and if we do not agree, seems to put its hand in its breeches pocket. Poetry should be great and unobtrusive, a thing

which enters into one's soul, and does not startle it or amaze it with itself, but with its subject.
[Letter to J.H. Reynolds, 3 February 1818]

128. Poetry should surprise by a fine excess and not by Singularity – it should strike the Reader as a wording of his own highest thoughts, and appear almost a Remembrance ... Its touches of Beauty should never be half way, thereby making the reader breathless instead of content: the rise, the progress, the setting of imagery should, like the Sun, come naturally to him.
[Letter to John Taylor, 27 February 1818]

129. If Poetry comes not as naturally as Leaves to a tree it had better not come at all.
[Letter to John Taylor, 27 February 1818]

130. I have great reason to be content, for thank God I can read and perhaps understand Shakespeare to his depths.
[Letter to John Taylor, 27 February 1818]

131. Scenery is fine – but human nature is finer.
[Letter to Benjamin Bailey, 13 March 1818]

132. [Of Devon]
It is impossible to live in a country which is continually under hatches ... Rain! Rain! Rain!
[Letter to J.H. Reynolds, 10 April 1818]

133. The imagination of a boy is healthy, and mature imagination of a man is healthy; but there is a space of life between, in which the soul is in a ferment, the character undecided, the way of life uncertain, the ambition thick-sighted: thence proceeds mawkishness.
['Endymion' (1818), Preface]

134. Axioms in philosophy are not axioms until they are proved upon our pulses: We read fine things but never feel them to the full until we have gone the same steps as the Author.
[Letter to J.H. Reynolds, 3 May 1818]

135. I compare human life to a large Mansion of Many Apartments, two of which I can only describe, the doors of the rest being as yet shut upon me.
[Letter to J.H. Reynolds, 3 May 1818]

136. I am in that temper that if I were under Water I would scarcely kick to come to the top.
[Letter to Benjamin Bailey, 21–25 May 1818]

137. Were it in my choice I would reject a petrarchal coronation – on account of my dying day, and because women have Cancers.
[Letter to Benjamin Bailey, 10 June 1818]

138. I do think better of Womankind than to suppose they care whether Mister John Keats five feet high likes them or not.
[Letter to Benjamin Bailey, 18 July 1818]

139. I am convinced more and more day by day that fine writing is next to fine doing, the top thing in the world.
[Letter to J. H. Reynolds, 24 August 1819]

140. I never was in love – yet the voice and the shape of a Woman has haunted me these two days.
[Letter to J.H. Reynolds, 22 September 1818]

141. There is an awful warmth about my heart like a load of Immortality.
[Letter to J.H. Reynolds, 22 September 1818]

142. I would sooner fail than not be among the greatest.
[Letter to James Hessey, 9 October 1818]

143. I think I shall be among the English Poets after my death.
[Letter to George and Georgiana Keats, 14 October 1818]

144. The roaring of the wind is my wife and the Stars through the window pane are my Children. The mighty abstract Idea I have of Beauty in all things stifles the more divided and minute domestic happiness ... the opinion I have of the generality of women – who appear to me as children to whom I would rather give a Sugar Plum than my time, forms a barrier against Matrimony which I rejoice in.
[Letter to George and Georgiana Keats, 14 October 1818]

145. A Poet is the most unpoetical of anything in existence; because he has no Identity – he is continually informing and filling some other Body.
[Letter to Richard Woodhouse, 27 October 1818]

146. I am ambitious of doing the world some good: if I should be spared, that may be the work of maturer years – in the interval I will assay to reach to as high a summit in Poetry as the nerve bestowed upon me will suffer.
[Letter to Richard Woodhouse, 27 October 1818]

147. As to the poetical Character itself (I mean that sort of which, if I am anything, I am a Member; that sort distinguished from the wordsworthian or egotistical sublime; which is a thing per se and stands alone) it is not itself – it has no self ... It has as much delight in conceiving an Iago as an Imogen.
[Letter to Richard Woodhouse, 27 October 1818]

148. I never can feel certain of any truth but from a clear perception of its Beauty.
[Letter to George and Georgiana Keats, 16 December 1818–4 January 1819]

149. I have come to this resolution – never to write for the sake of writing or making a poem, but from running over with any little knowledge or experience which many years of reflection may perhaps give me; otherwise I will be dumb.
[Letter to B.R. Haydon, 8 March 1819]

150. It is true that in the height of enthusiasm I have been cheated into some fine passages; but that is not the thing.
[Letter to B.R. Haydon, 8 March 1819]

151. I should like the window to open onto the Lake of Geneva – and there I'd sit and read all day like the picture of somebody reading.
[Letter to Fanny Keats, 13 March 1819]

152. A Man's life of any worth is a continual allegory.
[Letter to George and Georgiana Keats, 14 February–3 May 1819]

153. Shakespeare led a life of Allegory: his works are the comments on it.
[Letter to George and Georgiana Keats, 14 February–3 May 1819]

154. I go among the Fields and catch a glimpse of a Stoat or a fieldmouse peeping out of the withered grass – the creature hath a purpose and its eyes are bright with it. I go amongst the buildings of a city and I see a Man hurrying along – to what? the Creature has a purpose and his eyes are bright with it.
[Letter to George and Georgiana Keats, 14 February–3 May 1819]

155. Nothing ever becomes real till it is experienced – Even a Proverb is no proverb to you till your Life has illustrated it.
[Letter to George and Georgiana Keats, 14 February–3 May 1819]

156. Call the world if you Please 'The vale of Soul-making'.
[Letter to George and Georgiana Keats, 14 February–3 May 1819]

157. I have met with women whom I really think would like to be married to a Poem and to be given away by a Novel.
[Letter to Fanny Brawne, 8 July 1819]

158. I have two luxuries to brood over in my walks, your Loveliness and the hour of my death. O that I could have possession of them both in the same minute.
[Letter to Fanny Brawne, 25 July 1819]

159. My friends should drink a dozen of Claret on my Tomb.
[Letter to Benjamin Bailey, 14 August 1819]

160. Give me Books, fruit, french wine and fine weather and a little music out of doors, played by somebody I do not know.
[Letter to Fanny Keats, 28 August 1819]

161. The only means of strengthening one's intellect is to make up one's mind about nothing – to let the mind be a thoroughfare for all thoughts. Not a select party.
[Letter to George and Georgiana Keats, 17–27 September 1819]

162. You have ravish'd me away by a Power I cannot resist; and yet I could resist till I saw you; and even since I have seen you I have endeavoured often 'to reason against the reasons of my Love'.
[Letter to Fanny Brawne, 13 October 1819]

163. Upon the whole I dislike Mankind: whatever people on the other side of the question may advance they cannot deny that they are always surprised at hearing of a good action and never of a bad one.
[Letter to Georgiana Keats, 13–28 January, 1820]

164. 'If I should die', said I to myself, 'I have left no immortal work behind me – nothing to make my friends proud of my memory – but I have lov'd the principle of beauty in all things, and if I had had time I would have made myself remember'd.'
[Letter to Fanny Brawne, February 1820]

165. I long to believe in immortality ... If I am destined to be happy with you here – how short is the longest Life. I wish to believe in immortality – I wish to live with you for ever.
[Letter to Fanny Brawne, July 1820]

166. I wish you could invent some means to make me at all happy without you. Every hour I am more and more concentrated in you; every thing else tastes like chaff in my Mouth.
[Letter to Fanny Brawne, August 1820]

167. You, I am sure, will forgive me for sincerely remarking that you might curb your magnanimity, and be more of an artist, and load every rift of your subject with ore.
[Letter to Shelley, August 1820]

168. Is there another Life? Shall I awake and find all this a dream? There must be, we cannot be created for this sort of suffering.
[Letter to Charles Brown, 30 September 1820]

169. Here lies one whose name was writ in water.
[Epitaph for himself]

170. I shall soon be laid in the quiet grave – thank God for the quiet grave – O! I can feel the cold earth upon me – the daisies growing over me – O for this quiet – it will be my first.
[Attr.]

Keble, John (1792–1866)
English divine and poet, associated with the Oxford Movement

1. The trivial round, the common task,
Would furnish all we ought to ask;
Room to deny ourselves; a road
To bring us, daily, nearer God...

2. And help us, this and every day,
To live more nearly as we pray.
[*The Christian Year* (1827), 'Morning']

3. Abide with me from morn to eve,
For without Thee I cannot live:
Abide with me when night is nigh,
For without Thee I dare not die...

4. Be ev'ry mourner's sleep tonight
Like infant's slumbers, pure and light.
[*The Christian Year* (1827), 'Evening']

5. There is a book, who runs may read,
Which heavenly truth imparts,
And all the lore its scholars need,
Pure eyes and Christian hearts.
[*The Christian Year* (1827), 'Septuagesima Sunday']

6. The voice that breathed o'er Eden.
[*Poems* (1869), 'Holy Matrimony']

Keenan, Brian (1950–)
Irish journalist taken hostage in the Lebanon

1. I would be the voyeur of myself. This strategy I employed for the rest of my captivity. I allowed myself to do and be and say and think and feel all the things that were in me, but at the same time could stand outside observing and attempting to understand.
[*An Evil Cradling* (1992)]

2. I want to drink all the drink in the world, eat all the food in the world and make love, hopefully, to all the women in the world.
[*Sunday Telegraph*, 1990]

Keesing, Nancy Florence (1923–)
Australian author, critic and poet

1. All generations of women
Who ground the flour for bread,
And set it by their ovens
And curved strong hands to knead,

How intimately they knew
Whence man's true symbols come:
The seed, the yeast, the bread,
The child swelling in the womb.
['Bread']

Keillor, Garrison (1942–)
American writer and broadcaster

1. Lutherans are like Scottish people, only with less frivolity.
[*The Independent*, 1992]

Keith, George, Fifth Earl Marischal (1553–1623)
Scottish politician and diplomat

1. They haif said: Quhat say they? Lat thame say.
[Motto of the Earls Marischal of Scotland]

Keith, Penelope (1940–)
English stage and television actress

1. Shyness is just egotism out of its depth.
[*The Observer*, 1988, in Jeffrey Care (ed.), *Sayings of the Eighties* (1989)]

Keller, Helen (1880–1968)
American author and educator of the deaf and blind; deaf and blind herself since infancy

1. Militarism ... is one of the chief bulwarks of capitalism, and the day that militarism is undermined, capitalism will fail.
[*The Story of My Life* (1902)]

2. How reconcile this world of fact with the bright world of my imagining? My darkness has been filled with the light of intelligence, and behold, the outer day-light world was stumbling and groping in social blindness.
[In Upton Sinclair (ed.), *The Cry for Justice* (1963)]

Kellogg, Frank B. (1856–1937)

American statesman; lawyer, Republican Secretary of State, 1925–29; Nobel peace prize 1929 for Kellogg-Briand Pact

1. The high contracting parties solemnly declare in the names of their respective peoples that they condemn recourse to war for the solution of international controversies, and renounce it as an instrument of national policy in their relations with one another. The high contracting parties agree that the settlement or solution of all disputes or conflicts of whatever nature or of whatever origin they may be, which may rise among them, shall never be sought except by pacific means.
[Peace Pact, 1928; possibly based on original text by Aristide Briand]

Kelly, Bert (1912–)

Australian politician; formerly Minister for the Navy and for Works

1. Always remember that if a civil servant has the ability to . . . correctly foresee the demand situation for any product he would not be working for the government for long. He would shortly be sitting in the south of France with his feet in a bucket of champagne!
[*Economics Made Easy*]

Kelly, Ned (1855–1880)

Australian outlaw and folk hero

1. [Letter justifying his actions]
. . . is my brothers and sisters and mother not to be pitied also who has no alternative only to put up with the brutal and cowardly conduct of a parcel of big ugly fat-necked wombat headed big bellied magpie legged narrow hipped splay-footed sons of Irish Bailiffs or english landlords which is better known as officers of Justice or Victorian police . . .
['The Jerilderie Letter' (1879)]

2. There never was such a thing as justice in the English laws but any amount of injustice to be had.
[In *Overland*, 1981]

3. [On the scaffold, 11 November 1880]
'Ah well, I suppose it has come to this! . . . Such is life!'
[Attr.]

Kemble, John Philip (1757–1823)

English Shakespearian actor of renown

1. [Said during a play which was continually interrupted by a crying child]
Ladies and gentlemen, unless the play is stopped, the child cannot possibly go on.
[Attr.]

Kempis, Thomas à (c. 1380–1471)

German mystic, Augustinian monk and writer

1. *Opto magis sentire compunctionem; quam scire eius definitionem.*
I would far rather feel remorse than know how to define it.
[*De Imitatione Christi* (1892 ed.), I, 1]

2. *Humilis tui cognitio, certior via est ad Deum; quam profunda scientiae inquisitio.*
The humble knowledge of thyself is a surer way to God than the deepest search after learning.
[*De Imitatione Christi* (1892 ed.), I, 3]

3. *Certe adveniente die iudicii non quaeretur a nobis quid legimus sed quid fecimus.*
Truly, when the day of judgement comes, it will not be a question of what we have read, but what we have done.
[*De Imitatione Christi* (1892 ed.), I, 3]

4. *O quam cito transit gloria mundi.*
Oh, how quickly the glory in this world passes away.
[*De Imitatione Christi* (1892 ed.), I, 3; often quoted as Sic transit gloria mundi]

5. *Non quaeras quis hoc dixerit; sed quid dicatur attende.*
Do not ask who said this or that, but attend to what is actually said.
[*De Imitatione Christi* (1892 ed.), I, 5]

6. *Multo tutius est stare in subiectione; quam in praelatura.*
It is much safer to be in a subordinate position than in one of authority.
[*De Imitatione Christi* (1892 ed.), I, 9]

7. *Si non potes te talem facere qualem vis, quomodo poteris alium ad tuum habere beneplacitum?*
If you cannot mould yourself to such as you would wish, how can you expect others to be entirely to your liking?
[*De Imitatione Christi* (1892 ed.), I, 16]

8. *Nam homo proponit, sed Deus disponit.*
For man proposes, but God disposes.
[*De Imitatione Christi* (1892 ed.), I, 19]

9. *Numquam sis ex toto otiosus; sed aut legens, aut scribens, aut orans, aut meditans, aut aliquid utilitatis pro communi laborans.*
Never be completely idle, but be either reading, or writing, or praying, or meditating, or working at something useful for the community.
[*De Imitatione Christi* (1892 ed.), I, 19]

10. *Utinam per unam diem bene essemus conversati in hoc mundo.*
Would that we had spent one whole day well in this world!
[*De Imitatione Christi* (1892 ed.), I, 23]

11. *Passione interdum movemur; et zelum putamus.*
We are sometimes moved by passion and think it zeal.
[*De Imitatione Christi* (1892 ed.), II, 5]

12. *Si libenter crucem portas portabit te.*
If you bear the cross willingly, it will bear you.
[*De Imitatione Christi* (1892 ed.), II, 12]

13. *De duobus malis minus est semper eligendum.*
Of two evils the lesser is always to be chosen.
[*De Imitatione Christi* (1892 ed.), III, 12]

Ken, Bishop Thomas (1637–1711)

English royal chaplain, bishop and hymn-writer

1. Redeem thy mis-spent time that's past;
And live this day, as if thy last.
[Hymn. Cf. Horace: 84]

2. Teach me to live, that I may dread
The grave as little as my bed.
[Hymn. Cf. Thomas Browne: 35]

3. Praise God from whom all blessings flow,
Praise him all creatures here below,
Praise him above, Angelic host,
Praise Father, Son, and Holy Ghost.
[Hymn]

Kendall, Henry (1839–1882)

Australian poet

1. Down in the South, by the waste without sail on it–
Far from the zone of the blossom and tree–
Lieth, with winter and whirlwind and wail on it,

Ghost of a land by the ghost of a sea.
[*The Poetical Works* (1966), 'Beyond Kerguelen']

Keneally, Thomas (1935–)
Australian novelist and screenwriter

1. Pass a law to give every single wingeing bloody Pommie his fare home to England. Back to the smoke and the sun shining about ten days a year and shit in the streets. Yer can have it.
[*The Chant of Jimmie Blacksmith* (1972)]

2. It's only when you abandon your ambitions that they become possible.
[*Australian* (1983)]

Kennedy, John F. (1917–1963)
American Democratic President, 1961–63, noted for his civil rights reform programme; assassinated

1. [On his acceptance of the Democratic nomination]
We stand today on the edge of a new frontier.
[Speech, 1960]

2. And so, my fellow Americans: ask not what your country can do for you – ask what you can do for your country. My fellow citizens of the world: ask not what America will do for you, but what together we can do for the freedom of man.
[Inaugural address, 1961; these words were based on a speech given by Oliver Wendell Holmes Jr. in New Hampshire, 1884]

3. If we cannot now end our differences, at least we can help make the world safe for diversity.
[Speech, 1963]

4. [This speech caused much unintended amusement as *ein Berliner* means a jam doughnut as well as a citizen of Berlin]
As a free man, I take pride in the words *Ich bin ein Berliner*.
[Speech, 1963]

5. When power narrows the areas of man's concern, poetry reminds him of the richness and diversity of his existence.
[Speech, 1963]

6. In free society art is not a weapon . . . Artists are not engineers of the soul.
[Speech, 1963]

7. [On standing against Richard Nixon, the Republican candidate in the US Presidential election]
Do you realize the responsibility I carry? I'm the only person standing between Nixon and the White House.
[Remark to Arthur Schlesinger, 1960]

8. [At a dinner held at the White House for Nobel prizewinners]
. . . probably the greatest concentration of talent and genius in this house, except for perhaps those times when Thomas Jefferson ate alone.
[*New York Times*, 1962]

9. The United States has to move very fast to even stand still.
[*The Observer*, 'Sayings of the Week', 1963]

10. [Remark made during the Cuban missile crisis]
I guess this is the week I earn my salary.
[Attr.]

11. [Of his popularity after the failure of the US invasion of Cuba]
The worse I do, the more popular I get.
[Attr.]

12. Victory has a thousand fathers but defeat is an orphan.
[Attr. Cf. Ciano: 1]

Kennedy, Joseph P. (1888–1969)
Irish-American business executive, multi-millionaire and father of President John F. Kennedy

1. When the going gets tough, the tough get going.
[In J.H. Cutler, *Honey Fitz* (1962)]

2. If you want to make money, go where the money is.
[In A.M. Schlesinger Jr, *Robert Kennedy and his Times* (1978)]

Kennedy, Robert F. (1925–1968)
American Democrat politician and lawyer, brother of John F. Kennedy; assassinated

1. One fifth of the people are against everything all the time.
[*The Observer*, 'Sayings of the Week', 1964]

Kennelly, Brendan (1936–)
Irish poet and academic

1. 'Under it all,' Oliver said, 'The problem was simple.
How could I make Ireland work?
The Irish hate work, not knowing what it means.
I do. Work exists. It is inevitable and stark,
A dull, fierce necessity. Later ages may consider it
Superfluous but my glimpses of this world were true.
I looked, I saw, I considered, I did what
Was necessary. To live is to work. To be is to do.'
[*Cromwell* (1983), 'Therefore, I Smile']

2. What man
Knows anything of women?
If he did
He would change from being a man
As men recognise a man.
[*Antigone*, unpublished translation; play performed 1986]

3. The devil is always blaming someone.
Bricks of blame pave the floor of hell.
The girls are cold, the horses lost in the mountains
And truth is bleeding at the bottom of the well.
[*A Time for Voices* (1990), 'Blame']

4. I met a child, Eily Kilbride
Who'd never heard of marmalade,
Whose experience of breakfast
Was coldly limited,

Whose entire school day
Was a bag of crisps,
Whose parents had no work to do,

Who went, once, into the countryside,
Saw a horse with a feeding bag over its head
And thought it was sniffing glue.
[*The Book of Judas* (1991), 'Eily Kilbride']

Kenny, Mary (1944–)
Irish journalist and broadcaster

1. Decadent cultures usually fall in the end, and robust cultures rise to replace them. Our own cultural supermarket may eventually be subject to a takeover bid: the most likely challenger being, surely, Islam.
[*Sunday Telegraph*, 1993]

Kenny, Matt (1861–1942)
Irish circuit barrister and judge

1. [Said in conversation with Maurice Healy of a fellow lawyer]
'I have a great pity for the fellow. He came to consult me about his health. He told me he had been to every doctor in Munster and the best man in Dublin; he had even gone to London to see a Harley Street specialist. I felt very sorry

for the poor fellow.' 'And what advice did you give him, Matt?' 'I told him consult a vet!'
[In Maurice Healy, *The Old Munster Circuit* (1939)]

Kepler, Johannes (1571–1630)
German astronomer and mathematician, noted for his laws of planetary motion

1. [Remark made while studying astronomy]
O God, I am thinking Thy thoughts after Thee.
[Attr.]

Keppel, Mrs Alice (1869–1947)
Mistress of Edward VII

1. [On King Edward VIII's abdication]
Things were done better in my day.
[Attr.; also attributed to Maxine Elliott]

Keppel, Lady Caroline (b. 1735)
English poet

1. What's this dull town to me?
Robin's not near.
He whom I wished to see,
Wished for to hear;
Where's all the joy and mirth
Made life a heaven on earth?
O! they're all fled with thee,
Robin Adair.
['Robin Adair' (c. 1750)]

Kerouac, Jack (1922–1969)
American Beat novelist and poet

1. We're really all of us bottomly broke. I haven't had time to work in weeks.
[*On the Road* (1957), I, 7]
2. I had nothing to offer anybody except my own confusion.
[*On the Road* (1957), II, 4]
3. You know, this is really a beat generation.
[Phrase borrowed from Herbert Huncke, a drug addict, and recalled in *The Origins of the Beat Generation*]

Kerr, Jean (1923–)
American comic novelist and dramatist

1. I feel about airplanes the way I feel about diets. It seems to me that they are wonderful things for other people to go on.
[*The Snake Has All the Lines* (1958), 'Mirror, Mirror, on the Wall']

2. You don't seem to realize that a poor person who is unhappy is in a better position than a rich person who is unhappy. Because the poor person has hope. He thinks money would help.
[*Poor Richard* (1963), I]

3. Man is the only animal that learns by being hypocritical. He pretends to be polite and then, eventually, he becomes polite.
[*Finishing Touches* (1973), I]

Kerr, John
New Zealand politician

1. [Criticising a proposal to import six Venetian gondolas for the lake in the public gardens]
Why not import a pair, and then let Nature take its course.
[In G.M. Thomson, *Naturalisation of Animals and Plants in New Zealand* (1922)]

Kethe, William (d. 1594)
Scottish Protestant divine and psalmist

1. All people that on earth do dwell,
Sing to the Lord with cheerful voice.
Him serve with mirth, His praise forth tell;
Come ye before him and rejoice...

2. His truth at all times firmly stood,
And shall from age to age endure.
[Hymn]

Kettle, Thomas (1880–1916)
Irish author and academic; killed on the Somme

1. If I live, I mean to spend the rest of my life working for perpetual peace. I have seen war and faced artillery and know what an outrage it is against simple men.
[*Poems and Parodies*]

Kevans, Denis (1939–)

1. [Kevans calls himself the Poet Lorikeet; the title is a slogan on banners of the Australian Republican Association in Sydney]
I am Australia's lorikeet,
And I wrote this very fast,
You are a beaut,
I thee salute–
Elizabeth the Last.
[Australian Republican Association banner]

Key, Ellen (Karolina Sofia Key) (1849–1926)
Swedish feminist; writer and lecturer on social issues

1. ... the emancipation of women is practically the greatest egoistic movement of the nineteenth century, and the most intense affirmation of the right of the self that history has yet seen.
[*The Century of the Child* (1909), 2]

2. At every step the child should be allowed to meet the real experiences of life; the thorns should never be plucked from his roses.
[*The Century of the Child* (1909), 3]

3. Corporal punishment is as humiliating for him who gives it as for him who receives it; it is ineffective besides. Neither shame nor physical pain have any other effect than a hardening one.
[*The Century of the Child* (1909), 8]

4. Love is moral even without legal marriage, but marriage is immoral without love.
[*The Morality of Women and Other Essays* (1911), 'The Morality of Women']

5. Formerly, a nation that broke the peace did not trouble to try and prove to the world that it was done solely from higher motives ... Now war has a bad conscience. Now every nation assures us that it is bleeding for a human cause, the fate of which hangs in the balance of its victory. ... No nation will admit that it was only to insure its own safety that it declared war. No nation dares to admit the guilt of blood before the world.
[*War, Peace, and the Future* (1916), Preface]

6. Everything, everything in war is barbaric ... But the worst barbarity of war is that it forces men collectively to commit acts against which individually they would revolt with their whole being.
[*War, Peace, and the Future* (1916), 6]

Key, Francis Scott (1779–1843)
American lawyer and poet

1. 'Tis the star-spangled banner; O long may it wave
O'er the land of the free, and the home of the brave!
['The Star-Spangled Banner', 1814]

Keyes, Sidney (1922–1943)
English poet and soldier

1. At this twelfth hour of unrelenting summer
I think of those whose ready mouths are stopped,
I remember those who crouch in narrow graves,
I weep for those whose eyes are full of sand.
[*Two Offices of a Sentry* (1942), I, 'Office for Noon']

Keynes, John Maynard (1883–1946)
English economist in favour of government intervention to control the economy; co-founder of the International Monetary Fund

1. But this long run is a misleading guide to current affairs. In the long run we are all dead. Economists set themselves too easy, too useless a task if in tempestuous seasons they can only tell us that when the storm is long past the ocean will be flat again.
[*A Tract on Monetary Reform* (1923)]

2. Marxian Socialism must always remain a portent to the historians of opinion – how a doctrine so illogical and so dull can have exercised so powerful and enduring an influence over the minds of men, and, through them, the events of history.
['The End of Laissez-Faire' (1926), 3]

3. The important thing for government is not to do things which individuals are doing already, and to do them a little better or a little worse; but to do those things which at present are not done at all.
['The End of Laissez-Faire' (1926), 4]

4. I think that Capitalism, wisely managed, can probably be made more efficient for attaining economic ends than any alternative system yet in sight, but that in itself it is in many ways extremely objectionable.
['The End of Laissez-Faire' (1926), 5]

5. There are the Trade Unionists, once the oppressed, now the tyrants, whose selfish and sectional pretensions need to be bravely opposed.
['Liberalism and Labour' (1926)]

6. [Of Lloyd George]
This goat-footed bard, this half-human visitor to our age from the hag-ridden magic and enchanted woods of Celtic antiquity.
[*Essays and Sketches in Biography* (1933), 'Mr Lloyd George: A Fragment']

7. Wordly wisdom teaches that it is better for the reputation to fail conventionally than to succeed unconventionally.
[*The General Theory of Employment, Interest and Money* (1936)]

8. It is better that a man should tyrannize over his bank balance than over his fellow-citizens.
[*The General Theory of Employment, Interest and Money* (1936)]

9. Practical men, who believe themselves to be quite exempt from any intellectual influences, are usually the slaves of some defunct economist. Madmen in authority, who hear voices in the air, are distilling their frenzy from some academic scribbler of a few years back.
[*The General Theory of Employment, Interest and Money* (1936)]

10. The power of vested interests is vastly exaggerated compared with the gradual encroachment of ideas. Not, indeed, immediately ... But, soon or late, it is ideas, not vested interests, which are dangerous for good or evil.
[*The General Theory of Employment, Interest and Money* (1936)]

11. Whenever you save five shillings you put a man out of work for a day.
[*The Observer*, 'Sayings of the Week', 1931]

12. [When asked what happened when Lloyd George was alone in a room]
When he's alone in a room, there's nobody there.
[Quoted by Baroness Asquith, *As I Remember*, BBC TV, 30 April 1967]

13. [Of his refusal, while visiting Africa, to give more than a small tip to a shoe-shiner]
I will not be a party to debasing the currency.
[Attr.]

Khrushchev, Nikita (1894–1971)
Russian statesman; premier of the Soviet Union 1958–64; noted for his denunciation of Stalin

1. We had no use for the policy of the Gospels: that if someone slaps you, just turn the other cheek. We had shown that anyone who slapped our cheek would get his head kicked in.
[*Khrushchev Remembers* (1971), 2]

2. Whether you like it or not, history is on our side.
[Speech to Western ambassadors, 1956]

3. [Denouncing Stalin]
[He promoted a] cult of personality.
[Speech to 20th Party Congress, 25 February 1956]

4. Politicians are the same everywhere. They promise to build a bridge even when there's no river.
[Remark to journalists while on a visit to the USA, 1960]

5. [Remark to British businessmen]
When you are skinning your customers, you should leave some skin on to heal so that you can skin them again.
[*The Observer*, 'Sayings of the Week', 1961]

6. [Of the Cuban missile crisis]
People talk about who won and who lost. Human reason won. Mankind won.
[*The Observer*, 'Sayings of the Week', 1962]

7. If you begin throwing hedgehogs under me, I shall throw two porcupines under you.
[*The Observer*, 'Sayings of the Week', 1963]

8. [Of the Cuban missile crisis]
Only lunatics or suicides, who themselves want to perish and to destroy the whole world before they die, could want an atomic war.
[*The Independent*, 1992]

9. If you feed people with revolutionary slogans alone they will listen today, they will listen tomorrow, they will listen the day after that, but on the fourth day they will say 'To hell with you!'
[Attr.]

10. [On the possibility that the Soviet Union might one day reject communism]
Those who wait for that must wait until a shrimp learns to whistle.
[Attr.]

11. If you cannot catch a bird of paradise, better take a wet hen.
[Attr.]

Kierkegaard, Sören (1813–1855)
Danish philosopher and theologian; founder of existentialism

1. Life can only be understood backwards; but it must be lived forwards.
[*Life*]

2. Job endured everything – until his friends came to comfort him, then he grew impatient.
[*Journal*]

3. That is the road we all have to take – over the Bridge of Sighs into eternity.
[In W.H. Auden, *Kierkegaard*]

4. The Two Ways: one is to suffer; the other is to become a professor of the fact that another suffered.
[In W.H. Auden, *Kierkegaard*]

5. Dread is a sympathetic antipathy and an antipathetic sympathy.
[In W.H. Auden, *Kierkegaard*]

Kilmer, Joyce (1886–1918)
American poet, teacher, editor and soldier

1. I think that I shall never see
A poem lovely as a tree...

2. Poems are made by fools like me,
But only God can make a tree.
['Trees' (1914). Cf. Nash: 10]

Kilvert, Francis (1840–1879)
English curate and diarist

1. Of all noxious animals, too, the most noxious is a tourist. And of all tourists, the most vulgar, ill-bred, offensive and loathsome is the British tourist.
[*Diary*, 1870]

2. The Vicar of St Ives says the smell of fish there is sometimes so terrific as to stop the church clock.
[*Diary*, 1870]

3. It is a fine thing to be out on the hills alone. A man could hardly be a beast or a fool alone on a great mountain.
[*Diary*, 1871]

4. An angel satyr walks these hills.
[*Diary*, 1871]

King, Benjamin (1857–1894)
American writer of light verse

1. Nothing to do but work,
Nothing to eat but food,
Nothing to wear but clothes
To keep one from going nude.

Nothing to breathe but air,
Quick as a flash 'tis gone;
Nowhere to fall but off,
Nowhere to stand but on!
['The Pessimist']

King, Bishop Henry (1592–1669)
English royal chaplain and bishop; poet and sermonist

1. Sleep on, my Love, in thy cold bed,
Never to be disquieted!
My last good night! Thou wilt not wake
Till I thy fate shall overtake:
Till age, or grief, or sickness must
Marry my body to that dust
It so much loves; and fill the room
My heart keeps empty in thy tomb.
Stay for me there; I will not fail
To meet thee in that hollow vale...

2. But hark! My pulse like a soft drum
Beats my approach, tells thee I come.
['Exequy upon his Wife' (1651)]

3. We that did nothing study but the way
To love each other, with which thoughts the day
Rose with delight to us, and with them set,
Must learn the hateful art, how to forget.
['The Surrender' (1651)]

King, Martin Luther (1929–1968)
American civil rights leader and Baptist minister; advocated non-violence in anti-racist campaigns; Nobel peace prize 1964; assassinated

1. I have a dream that one day this nation will rise up and live out the true meaning of its creed: 'We hold these truths to be self-evident, that all men are created equal'.
[Speech, 1963]

2. Free at last, free at last, thank God Almighty, we are free at last!
[Speech, Washington civil rights demonstration, 28 August 1963, quoting an old Negro spiritual]

3. [Said the day before he was assassinated]
I've been to the mountain top ... I've looked over and I've seen the promised land. I may not get there with you, but I want you to know tonight that we as a people will get to the promised land. So, I'm happy tonight. Mine eyes have seen the glory of the coming of the Lord.
[Speech, Memphis, 3 April 1968]

4. A riot is at bottom the language of the unheard.
[*Chaos or Community* (1967), 4]

5. I want to be the white man's brother, not his brother-in-law.
[*New York Journal-American*, 1962]

King, Stoddard (1889–1933)
American columnist and writer of humorous verse

1. There's a long, long trail a-winding
Into the land of my dreams.
[Song, 1913]

King, William (1663–1712)
English judge and writer

1. Beauty from order springs.
[*Art of Cookery* (1708)]

2. Crowd not your table: let your numbers be
Not more than seven, and never less than three.
[*Art of Cookery* (1708)]

3. 'Tis by his cleanliness a cook must please.
[*Art of Cookery* (1708)]

Kinglake, Edward (Edward Rock Garnsey) (1864–1935)

1. Every Australian worships the Goddess of Sport with profound adoration, and there is no nation in the world which treats itself to so many holidays.
[*The Australian at Home*]

Kingsford-Smith, Sir Charles Edward (1897–1935)
Australian aviation pioneer

1. [On landing on Flinders Island, in Bass Strait, about 1930, and being offered a formal welcome and a handshake]
Quit the handles, mate, give us a fag.
[*Island News* (Flinders Island), 1987]

Kingsley, Charles (1819–1875)
English historical novelist, poet, lecturer and clergyman

1. We have used the Bible as if it was a constable's handbook – an opium-dose for keeping beasts of burden patient while they are being overloaded.
['Letters to Chartists' (1848), 2]

2. More ways of killing a cat than choking her with cream.
[*Westward Ho!* (1855), 20]

3. Eustace is a man no longer; he is become a thing, a tool, a Jesuit.
[*Westward Ho!* (1855), 22]

4. He did not know that a keeper is only a poacher turned outside in, and a poacher a keeper turned inside out.
[*The Water Babies* (1863), 1]

5. He was as thorough an Englishman as ever coveted his neighbour's goods.
[*The Water Babies* (1863), 4]

6. The loveliest fairy in the world; and her name is Mrs Doasyouwouldbedoneby.
[*The Water Babies* (1863), 5]

7. All the butterflies and cockyolybirds would fly past me.
[*The Water Babies* (1863), 8]

8. Truth, for its own sake, had never been a virtue with the Roman clergy.
[Review in *Macmillan's Magazine*, 1864]

9. To be discontented with the divine discontent, and to be ashamed with the noble shame, is the very germ and first upgrowth of all virtue.
[*Health and Education* (1874)]

10. [Of St Paul]
There is no sentimental melancholy in him; no pretending to be miserable; no trying to make himself miserable. He is saved, and he knows it. He is an apostle, and he stands boldly on his dignity. He is cheerful, hopeful, joyful; but whenever he speaks of his past life (and he speaks of it often) it is with noble shame and sorrow.
[*Town and Country Sermons* (1878), XVI]

11. [Comparing the cholera epidemic of 1833 to that of 1849]
But did they repent of and confess those sins which had caused the cholera? Did they repent of and confess the covetousness, the tyranny, the carelessness, which in most great towns, and in too many villages, forces the poor to lodge in undrained stifling hovels, unfit for hogs, amid vapours and smells which send forth in every breath the seeds of rickets and consumption, typhus and scarlet fever, and worse and last of all, the cholera? Did they repent of their sin in that? Not they.
[*Sermons on National Subjects*, XIII]

12. Some say that the age of chivalry is past, that the spirit of romance is dead. The age of chivalry is never past, so long as there is a wrong left unredressed on earth.
[In Mrs C. Kingsley, *Life* (1879)]

13. Airly Beacon, Airly Beacon;
Oh the pleasant sight to see
Shires and towns from Airly Beacon,
While my love climb'd up to me!
['Airly Beacon' (1847)]

14. The merry brown hares came leaping
Over the crest of the hill,
Where the clover and corn lay sleeping
Under the moonlight still.
['The Bad Squire' (1847)]

15. 'O Mary, go and call the cattle home,
And call the cattle home,
And call the cattle home
Across the sands of Dee;'
The western wind was wild and dank with foam,
And all alone went she...

16. The western tide crept up along the sand,
And o'er and o'er the sand,
And round and round the sand,
As far as eye could see.
The rolling mist came down and hid the land:
And never home came she.
['The Sands of Dee' (1849)]

17. Three fishers went sailing away to the West,
Away to the West as the sun went down;
Each thought on the woman who loved him the best,
And the children stood watching them out of the town.
For men must work, and women must weep,
And there's little to earn, and many to keep,
Though the harbour bar be moaning.
['The Three Fishers' (1851)]

18. 'Tis the hard grey weather
Breeds hard English men.
['Ode to the North-East Wind' (1854)]

19. Be good, sweet maid, and let who can be clever;
Do lovely things, not dream them, all day long;
And so make Life, and Death, and that For Ever,
One grand sweet song.
['A Farewell. To C.E.G.' (1856)]

20. What we can we will be,
Honest Englishmen.
Do the work that's nearest,
Though it's dull at whiles,
Helping, when we meet them,
Lame dogs over stiles.
['The Invitation. To Thomas Hughes' (1856)]

21. When all the world is young, lad,
And all the trees are green;
And every goose a swan, lad,
And every lass a queen;
Then hey for boot and horse, lad,
And round the world away:
Young blood must have its course, lad,
And every dog his day.
[Song from *The Water Babies* (1863), 'Young and Old']

Kingsley, Henry (1830–1876)
English novelist, brother of Charles Kingsley

1. [Phrase became widely used later in the nineteenth century]
That was what they saw, and what any man may see to-day for himself in his own village, whether in England or Australia, that working man's paradise.
[*The Recollections of Geoffrey Hamlyn* (1859), 8]

2. That touching of the hat is a very rare piece of courtesy from working men in Australia. The convicts are forced to do it, and so the free men make it a point of honour not to do so.
[*The Recollections of Geoffrey Hamlyn* (1859), 8]

Kingsmill, Hugh (Hugh Kingsmill Lunn) (1889–1949)
English literary critic, biographer and parodist

1. What, still alive at twenty-two,
A clean upstanding lad like you?
Sure, if your throat 'tis hard to slit,
Slit your girl's, and swing for it.
Like enough, you won't be glad,
When they come to hang you, lad:
But bacon's not the only thing
That's cured by hanging from a string.
[*The Table of Truth* (1933), 'Two Poems after A.E. Housman', no. 1]

2. 'Tis Summer Time on Bredon,
And now the farmers swear;
The cattle rise and listen
In valleys far and near,
And blush at what they hear.

But when the mists in autumn
On Bredon top are thick,
The happy hymns of farmers
Go up from fold and rick,
The cattle then are sick.
[*The Table of Truth* (1933), 'Two Poems after A.E. Housman', no. 2]

3. It is difficult to love mankind unless one has a reasonable private income and when one has a reasonable private income one has better things to do than loving mankind.
[In R. Ingrams, *God's Apology* (1977)]

4. Friends are God's apology for relations.
[In R. Ingrams, *God's Apology* (1977)]

Kinnock, Neil (1942–)
Welsh politician and orator; Labour party leader 1983–92

1. Compassion is not a sloppy, sentimental feeling for people who are underprivileged or sick ... it is an absolutely practical belief that, regardless of a person's background, ability or ability to pay, he should be provided with the best that society has to offer.
[Maiden speech, House of Commons, 1970]

2. [Attacking Militant members in Liverpool]
The grotesque chaos of a Labour council – a Labour council – hiring taxis to scuttle around a city handing out redundancy notices to its own workers.
[Speech, Labour Party Conference, Bournemouth, 1985]

3. The idea that there is a model Labour voter, a blue-collar council house tenant who belongs to a union and has 2.4 children, a five-year-old car and a holiday in Blackpool, is patronizing and politically immature.
[Speech, 1986]

4. [Of nuclear disarmament]
I would die for my country but I could never let my country die for me.
[Speech, 1987]

5. You cannot fashion a wit out of two half-wits.
[*The Times*, 1983]

Kipling, Rudyard (1865–1936)
Indian-born British poet, novelist, short-story and children's writer; Nobel prize 1907

1. Take my word for it, the silliest woman can manage a clever man; but it needs a very clever woman to manage a fool.
[*Plain Tales from the Hills* (1888), 'Three and – an Extra']

2. Never praise a sister to a sister, in the hope of your compliments reaching the proper ears ... Sisters are women first, and sisters afterward; and you will find that you do yourself harm.
[*Plain Tales from the Hills* (1888), 'False Dawn']

3. She was as immutable as the Hills. But not quite so green.
[*Plain Tales from the Hills* (1888), 'Venus Annodomini']

4. Every one is more or less mad on one point.
[*Plain Tales from the Hills* (1888), 'On the Strength of a Likeness']

5. Open and obvious devotion from any sort of man is always pleasant to any sort of woman.
[*Plain Tales from the Hills* (1888), 'On the Strength of a Likeness']

6. Lalun is a member of the most ancient profession in the world.
[*In Black and White* (1888), 'On the City Wall']

7. Being kissed ... by a man who didn't wax his moustache was – like eating an egg without salt.
[*The Story of the Gadsbys* (1888), 'Poor Dear Mamma']

8. Steady the Buffs!
[*The Story of the Gadsbys* (1888), 'Poor Dear Mamma']

9. A blackguard may be slow to think for himself, but he is genuinely anxious to kill, and a little punishment teaches him how to guard his own skin and perforate another's.
[*Wee Willie Winkie* (1888), 'The Drums of the Fore and Aft']

10. The Light that Failed.
[Title of novel, 1890]

11. You haf too much Ego in your Cosmos.
[*Mine Own People* (1891), 'Bertran and Bimi']

12. Asia is not going to be civilized after the methods of the West. There is too much Asia, and she is too old. You cannot reform a lady of many lovers, and Asia has been insatiable in her lifetime.
[*Mine Own People* (1891), 'The Man Who Was']

13. Some were married, which was bad, and some did other things which were worse.
[*Mine Own People* (1891), 'The Mark of the Beast']

14. We be of one blood, thou and I.
[*The Jungle Book* (1894), 'Kaa's Hunting']

15. Good hunting!
[*The Jungle Book* (1894), 'Kaa's Hunting']

16. I gloat! Hear me gloat!
[*Stalky & Co.* (1899), 'In Ambush']

17. A Jelly-bellied Flag-flapper.
[*Stalky & Co.* (1899), 'The Flag of their Country']

18. The mad all are in God's keeping.
[*Kim* (1901), 2]

19. The small 'Stute Fish said in a small 'stute voice, 'Noble and generous Cetacean, have you ever tasted Man?' 'No,' said the Whale. 'What is it like?' 'Nice,' said the small 'Stute Fish. 'Nice but nubbly.'
[*Just So Stories* (1902), 'How the Whale Got His Throat']

20. He had his Mummy's leave to paddle, or else he would never have done it, because he was a man of infinite-resource-and-sagacity.
[*Just So Stories* (1902), 'How the Whale Got His Throat']

21. The Camel came chewing milkweed most 'scruciating idle.
[*Just So Stories* (1902), 'How the Camel Got His Hump']

22. 'Humph yourself!'
And the Camel humphed himself.
[*Just So Stories* (1902), 'How the Camel Got His Hump']

23. Once upon a time ... there lived a Parsee from whose hat the rays of the sun were reflected in more-than-oriental-splendour.
[*Just So Stories* (1902), 'How the Rhinoceros Got His Skin']

24. An Elephant's Child – who was full of 'satiable curtiosity.
[*Just So Stories* (1902), 'The Elephant's Child']

25. The great, grey-green, greasy Limpopo River, all set about with fever-trees.
[*Just So Stories* (1902), 'The Elephant's Child']

26. Led go! You are hurtig be!
[*Just So Stories* (1902), 'The Elephant's Child']

27. I am the Cat who walks by himself, and all places are alike to me.
[*Just So Stories* (1902), 'The Cat That Walked by Himself']

28. And he went back through the Wet Wild Woods, waving his wild tail, and walking by his wild lone. But he never told anybody.
[*Just So Stories* (1902), 'The Cat That Walked by Himself']

29. 'Tisn't beauty, so to speak, nor good talk necessarily. It's just IT. Some women'll stay in a man's memory if they once walked down a street.
[*Traffics and Discoveries* (1904), 'Mrs Bathurst']

30. A Soldier of the Great War Known unto God.
[Inscription on the graves of unidentified soldiers, 1919]

31. And a woman is only a woman, but a good cigar is a Smoke.
[*Departmental Ditties and Other Verses* (1886), 'The Betrothed']

32. Dim dawn behind the tamarisks – the sky is saffron-yellow–
As the women from the village grind the corn,
And the parrots seek the river-side, each calling to his fellow
That the Day, the staring Eastern Day, is born...

33. High noon behind the tamarisks – the sun is hot above us–
As at Home the Christmas Day is breaking wan.
They will drink our healths at dinner – those who tell us how they love us,
And forget us till another year be gone!
[*Departmental Ditties and Other Verses* (1886), 'Christmas in India']

34. The toad beneath the harrow knows
Exactly where each tooth-point goes;
The butterfly upon the road
Preaches contentment to that toad.
[*Departmental Ditties and Other Verses* (1886), 'Pagett MP']

35. Little Tin Gods on Wheels.
[*Departmental Ditties and Other Verses* (1886), 'Public Waste']

36. The depth and dream of my desire,
The bitter paths wherein I stray–
Thou knowest Who hast made the Fire,
Thou knowest Who hast made the Clay.
[*Life's Handicap* (1888), 'My New-cut Ashlar']

37. The Three in One, the One in Three? Not so!
To my own Gods I go.
It may be they shall give me greater ease
Than your cold Christ and tangled Trinities.
[*Plain Tales from the Hills* (1888), 'The Convert']

38. Down to Gehenna or up to the Throne,
He travels the fastest who travels alone.
[*The Story of the Gadsbys* (1888), 'The Winners']

39. Oh, East is East, and West is West, and never the twain shall meet,
Till Earth and Sky stand presently at God's great Judgment Seat;
But there is neither East nor West, Border, nor Breed, nor Birth,
When two strong men stand face to face, though they come from the ends of earth!
['The Ballad of East and West' (1889)]

40. Four things greater than all things are,–
Women and Horses and Power and War.
['The Ballad of the King's Jest' (1890)]

41. And that's how it all began, my dears,
And that's how it all began.
[*The Light that Failed* (1890), 'Big Barn Stories']

42. If I were hanged on the highest hill,
Mother o' mine, O mother o' mine!
I know whose love would follow me still,
Mother o' mine, O mother o' mine!
[*The Light that Failed* (1890), 'Mother O' Mine']

43. Till the Devil whispered behind the leaves,
'It's pretty, but is it Art?'...

44. We know that the tail must wag the dog, for the horse is drawn by the cart;
But the Devil whoops, as he whooped of old: 'It's clever, but is it Art?'
['The Conundrum of the Workshops' (1890)]

45. Winds of the World, give answer! They are whimpering to and fro–
And what should they know of England who only England know?
['The English Flag' (1891)]

46. I've a head like a concertina, I've a tongue like a button-stick,
I've a mouth like an old potato, and I'm more than a little sick,
But I've had my fun o' the Corp'ral's Guard; I've made the cinders fly,
And I'm here in the Clink for thundering drink and blacking the Corporal's eye.
[*Barrack-Room Ballads and Other Verses* (1892), 'Cells']

47. 'What are the bugles blowin' for?' said Files-on-Parade.
'To turn you out, to turn you out,' the Colour-Sergeant said...

48. For they're hangin' Danny Deever, you can hear the Dead March play,
The Regiment's in 'ollow square – they're hangin' him to-day;
They've taken of 'is buttons off an' cut 'is stripes away,
An' they're hangin' Danny Deever in the mornin'.
[*Barrack-Room Ballads and Other Verses* (1892), 'Danny Deever']

49. 'E's all 'ot sand an' ginger when alive,
An' 'e's generally shammin' when 'e's dead...

50. So 'ere's to you, Fuzzy-Wuzzy, at your 'ome in the Soudan;
You're a pore benighted 'eathen but a first-class fightin' man;
An' 'ere's to you, Fuzzy-Wuzzy, with your 'ayrick 'ead of 'air–
You big black boundin' beggar – for you broke a British square!
[*Barrack-Room Ballads and Other Verses* (1892), 'Fuzzy-Wuzzy']

51. To the legion of the lost ones, to the cohort of the damned...

52. We're poor little lambs who've lost our way,
Baa! Baa! Baa!

We're little black sheep who've gone astray,
Baa – aa – aa!
Gentleman-rankers out on the spree,
Damned from here to Eternity,
God ha' mercy on such as we,
Baa! Yah! Bah!...

53. We have done with Hope and Honour, we are lost to Love and Truth,
We are dropping down the ladder rung by rung,
And the measure of our torment is the measure of our youth.
God help us, for we knew the worst too young!
[*Barrack-Room Ballads and Other Verses* (1892), 'Gentleman-Rankers']

54. You may talk o' gin and beer
When you're quartered safe out 'ere,
An' you're sent to penny-fights an' Aldershot it;
But when it comes to slaughter
You will do your work on water,
And you'll lick the bloomin' boots of 'im that's got it...

55. The uniform 'e wore
Was nothin' much before,
An' rather less than 'arf o' that be'ind...

56. An' for all 'is dirty 'ide
'E was white, clear white, inside
When 'e went to tend the wounded under fire!...

57. So I'll meet 'im later on
At the place where 'e is gone–
Where it's always double drills and no canteen.
'E'll be squattin' on the coals
Giving' drink to poor damned souls,
An' I'll get a swig in Hell from Gunga Din...

58. Though I've belted you an' flayed you,
By the livin' Gawd that made you,
You're a better man than I am, Gunga Din!
[*Barrack-Room Ballads and Other Verses* (1892), 'Gunga Din']

59. By the old Moulmein Pagoda, lookin' eastward to the sea,
There's a Burma girl a-settin', and I know she thinks o' me;
For the wind is in the palm-trees, and the temple-bells they say:
'Come you back, you British soldier; come you back to Mandalay!'
Come you back to Mandalay,
Where the old Flotilla lay:
Can't you 'ear their paddles chunkin' from Rangoon to Mandalay?
On the road to Mandalay,
Where the flyin'-fishes play,
An' the dawn comes up like thunder outer China 'crost the Bay!

'Er petticoat was yaller an' 'er little cap was green,
'An 'er name was Supi-yaw-lat – jes' the same as Theebaw's Queen,
An' I seed her first a-smokin' of a whackin' white cheroot,
An' a-wastin' Christian kisses on an 'eathen idol's foot...

60. But that's all shove be'ind me – long ago an' fur away,
An' there ain't no 'buses runnin' from the Bank to Mandalay;
An' I'm learnin' 'ere in London what the ten-year soldier tells:
'If you've 'eard the East a-callin', you won't never 'eed naught else.'...

61. I am sick o' wastin' leather on these gritty pavin'-stones,
An' the blasted Henglish drizzle wakes the fever in my bones;
Tho' I walks with fifty 'ousemaids outer Chelsea to the Strand,
An' they talks a lot o' lovin', but wot do they understand?
Beefy face an' grubby 'and–
Law! wot do they understand?
I've a neater, sweeter maiden in a cleaner, greener land!...

62. Ship me somewheres east of Suez, where the best is like the worst,
Where there aren't no Ten Commandments, an' a man can raise a thirst;
For the temple-bells are callin', an' it's there that I would be–
By the old Moulmein Pagoda, looking lazy at the sea.
[*Barrack-Room Ballads and Other Verses* (1892), 'Mandalay']

63. Shillin' a day,
Bloomin good pay–
Lucky to touch it, a shillin' a day!
[*Barrack-Room Ballads and Other Verses* (1892), 'Shillin' a Day']

64. O, it's Tommy this, an' Tommy that, an' 'Tommy, go away';
But it's 'Thank you, Mister Atkins,' when the band begins to play...

65. Then it's Tommy this, an' Tommy that, an' 'Tommy 'ow's yer soul?'
But it's 'Thin red line of 'eroes' when the drums begin to roll...

66. For it's Tommy this, an' Tommy that, an' 'Chuck him out, the brute!'
But it's 'Saviour of 'is country' when the guns begin to shoot.
[*Barrack-Room Ballads and Other Verses* (1892), 'Tommy']

67. 'Ave you 'eard o' the Widow at Windsor
With a hairy gold crown on 'er 'ead?
She 'as ships on the foam – she 'as millions at 'ome,
An' she pays us poor beggars in red...

68. Take 'old o' the Wings o' the Mornin',
An' flop round the earth till you're dead;
But you won't get away from the tune that they play
To the bloomin' old rag over 'ead.
[*Barrack-Room Ballads and Other Verses* (1892), 'The Widow at Windsor']

69. When the 'arf-made recruity goes out to the East
'E acts like a babe an' 'e drinks like a beast.
[*Barrack-Room Ballads and Other Verses* (1892), 'The Young British Soldier']

70. I have watch and ward to keep
O'er Thy wonders of the deep,
And Ye take mine honour from me if Ye take away the sea!
['The Last Chantey' (1892)]

71. Lord, Thou hast made this world below the shadow of a dream,
An', taught by time, I tak' it so – exceptin' always Steam.
From coupler-flange to spindle-guide I see Thy Hand, O God–
Predestination in the stride o' yon connectin'-rod...

72. Ye thought? Ye are not paid to think...

73. Mister McAndrew, don't you think steam spoils romance at sea?
['McAndrew's Hymn' (1893)]

74. For a man he must go with a woman, which women don't understand–
Or the sort that say they can see it, they aren't the marrying brand.
['The Mary Gloster' (1894)]

75. I'm the Prophet of the Utterly Absurd,
Of the Patently Impossible and Vain.
['The Song of the Banjo' (1894)]

76. There are nine and sixty ways of constructing tribal lays,
And – every – single – one – of – them – is – right!
['In the Neolithic Age' (1895)]

77. There's a Legion that was never 'listed,
That carries no colours or crest.
['The Lost Legion' (1895)]

78. Now this is the Law of the Jungle – as old and as true as the sky;
And the Wolf that shall keep it may prosper, but the Wolf that shall break it must die.
[*The Second Jungle Book* (1895), 'The Law of the Jungle']

79. Ere Mor the Peacock flutters, ere the Monkey People cry,
Ere Chil the Kite swoops down a furlong sheer,
Through the Jungle very softly flits a shadow and a sigh–
He is Fear, O Little Hunter, he is Fear!
[*The Second Jungle Book* (1895), 'The Song of the Little Hunter']

80. The Coastwise Lights of England watch the ships of England go!
[*The Seven Seas* (1896), 'The Coastwise Lights']

81. The 'eathen in 'is blindness bows down to wood an' stone;
'E don't obey no orders unless they is 'is own;
'E keeps 'is side-arms awful: 'e leaves 'em all about,
An' then comes up the Regiment an' pokes the 'eathen out...

82. The 'eathen in 'is blindness must end where 'e began,
But the backbone of the Army is the Non-commissioned man!
[*The Seven Seas* (1896), 'The 'Eathen']

83. Who are neither children nor Gods, but men in a world of men!
[*The Seven Seas* (1896), 'England's Answer']

84. An' I learned about women from 'er!...

85. I've taken my fun where I've found it,
An' now I must pay for my fun,
For the more you 'ave known o' the others
The less you will settle to one;
An' the end of it's sittin' and thinkin',
An' dreamin' Hell-fires to see.
So be warned by my lot (which I know you will not),
An' learn about women from me!...

86. For the Colonel's Lady an' Judy O'Grady
Are sisters under their skins!
[*The Seven Seas* (1896), 'The Ladies']

87. Cheer for the Sergeant's weddin'–
Give 'em one cheer more!
Grey gun-'orses in the lando,
An' a rogue is married to a whore.
[*The Seven Seas* (1896), 'The Sergeant's Weddin'']

88. If blood be the price of admiralty,
Lord God, we ha' paid in full!
[*The Seven Seas* (1896), 'The Song of the Dead']

89. And only The Master shall praise us, and only The Master shall blame;
And no one shall work for money, and no one shall work for fame,
But each for the joy of the working, and each, in his separate star,
Shall draw the Thing as he sees It for the God of Things as They are!
[*The Seven Seas* (1896), 'When Earth's Last Picture is Painted']

90. When 'Omer smote 'is bloomin' lyre,
He'd 'eard men sing by land an' sea;
An' what 'e thought 'e might require,
'E went an' took – the same as me!
[*The Seven Seas* (1896), 'When 'Omer Smote 'Is Bloomin' Lyre']

91. God of our fathers, known of old,
Lord of our far-flung battle-line,
Beneath whose awful Hand we hold
Dominion over palm and pine–
Lord God of Hosts, be with us yet,
Lest we forget – lest we forget!

The tumult and the shouting dies;
The Captains and the Kings depart:
Still stands Thine ancient sacrifice,
An humble and a contrite heart.
Lord God of Hosts, be with us yet,
Lest we forget – lest we forget!...

92. Lo, all our pomp of yesterday
Is one with Nineveh and Tyre!...

93. If, drunk with sight of power, we loose
Wild tongues that have not Thee in awe,
Such boastings as the Gentiles use,
Or lesser breeds without the Law.
['Recessional' (1897)]

94. A fool there was and he made his prayer
(Even as you and I!)
To a rag and a bone and a hank of hair
(We called her the woman who did not care),
But the fool he called her his lady fair
(Even as you and I!)
['The Vampire' (1897)]

95. We must go back with Policeman Day–
Back from the City of Sleep!
[*The Day's Work* (1898), 'The City of Sleep']

96. Something hidden. Go and find it, Go and look behind the Ranges–
Something lost behind the Ranges. Lost and waiting for you. Go!
['The Explorer' (1898)]

97. He's an absent-minded beggar, and his weaknesses are great–
But we and Paul must take him as we find him–
He's out on active service, wiping something off a slate–
And he's left a lot of little things behind him!
['The Absent-Minded Beggar' (1899)]

98. 'Let us now praise famous men'–
Men of little showing–
For their work continueth,
And their work continueth,
Broad and deep continueth,
Greater than their knowing!
[*Stalky and Co.* (1899), 'A School Song']

99. Take up the White Man's burden–
Send forth the best ye breed–
Go, bind your sons to exile
To serve your captives' need;
To wait in heavy harness
On fluttered folk and wild–
Your new-caught, sullen peoples,
Half devil and half child...

100. By all ye cry or whisper,
By all ye leave or do,
The silent, sullen peoples

Shall weigh your Gods and you.
['The White Man's Burden' (1899)]

101. Then ye returned to your trinkets; then ye contented your souls
With the flannelled fools at the wicket or the muddied oafs at the goals.
['The Islanders' (1902)]

102. The Camel's hump is an ugly lump
Which well you may see at the Zoo;
But uglier yet is the hump we get
From having too little to do...

103. We get the hump–
Cameelious hump–
The hump that is black and blue!...

104. The cure for this ill is not to sit still,
Or frowst with a book by the fire;
But to take a large hoe and a shovel also,
And dig till you gently perspire.

And then you will find that the sun and the wind,
And the Djinn of the Garden too,
Have lifted the hump–
The horrible hump–
The hump that is black and blue!
[*Just-So Stories* (1902), 'How the Camel Got His Hump']

105. I keep six honest serving-men
(They taught me all I knew);
Their names are What and Why and When
And How and Where and Who.
[*Just-So Stories* (1902), 'The Elephant's Child']

106. Old Man Kangaroo first, Yellow-Dog Dingo behind.
[*Just-So Stories* (1902), 'The Sing-Song of Old Man Kangaroo']

107. I've never sailed the Amazon,
I've never reached Brazil;
But the Don and Magdalena,
They can go there when they will.

Yes, weekly from Southampton,
Great steamers, white and gold,
Go rolling down to Rio
(Roll down – roll down to Rio!)
And I'd like to roll to Rio
Some day before I'm old!
[*Just-So Stories* (1902), 'The Beginning of the Armadilloes']

108. The barrow and the camp abide,
The sunlight and the sward...

109. And here the sea-fogs lap and cling
And here, each warning each,
The sheep-bells and the ship-bells ring
Along the hidden beach...

110. God gives all men all earth to love,
But, since man's heart is small,
Ordains for each one spot shall prove
Beloved over all.
['Sussex' (1902)]

111. We're foot–slog–slog–slog–sloggin' over Africa–
Foot–foot–foot–foot–sloggin' over Africa–
(Boots–boots–boots–boots–movin' up an' down again!)
There's no discharge in the war!
[*The Five Nations* (1903), 'Boots']

112. But it never really mattered till the English grew polite.
[*The Five Nations* (1903), 'Et Dona Ferentes']

113. For Allah created the English mad – the maddest of all mankind!
[*The Five Nations* (1903), 'Kitchener's School']

114. Let us admit it fairly, as a business people should,
We have had no end of a lesson: it will do us no end of good...

115. It was our fault, and our very great fault – and now we must turn it to use.
We have forty million reasons for failure, but not a single excuse.
So the more we work and the less we talk the better results we shall get–
We have had an Imperial lesson; it may make us an Empire yet!
[*The Five Nations* (1903), 'The Lesson']

116. Land of our birth, we pledge to thee
Our love and toil in the years to be;
When we are grown and take our place,
As men and women with our race...

117. That we, with Thee, may walk uncowed
By fear or favour of the crowd...

118. Teach us Delight in simple things,
And Mirth that has no bitter springs.
[*Puck of Pook's Hill* (1906), 'The Children's Song']

119. Cities and Thrones and Powers,
Stand in Time's eye,
Almost as long as flowers,
Which daily die:
But, as new buds put forth,
To glad new men,
Out of the spent and unconsidered Earth,
The Cities rise again.
[*Puck of Pook's Hill* (1906), 'Cities and Thrones and Powers']

120. What is a woman that you forsake her,
And the hearth-fire and the home-acre,
To go with the old grey Widow-maker?
[*Puck of Pook's Hill* (1906), 'Harp Song of the Dane Women']

121. If you wake at midnight, and hear a horse's feet,
Don't go drawing back the blind, or looking in the street,
Them that asks no questions isn't told a lie.
Watch the wall, my darling, while the Gentlemen go by!
Five and twenty ponies,
Trotting through the dark–
Brandy for the Parson,
'Baccy for the Clerk;
Laces for a lady, letters for a spy,
Watch the wall, my darling, while the Gentlemen go by!
[*Puck of Pook's Hill* (1906), 'A Smuggler's Song']

122. Of all the trees that grow so fair,
Old England to adorn,
Greater are none beneath the Sun,
Than Oak, and Ash, and Thorn...

123. Ellum she hateth mankind and waiteth
Till every gust be laid
To drop a limb on the head of him
That anyway trusts her shade...

124. England shall bide till Judgement Tide,
By Oak, and Ash, and Thorn!
[*Puck of Pook's Hill* (1906), 'A Tree Song']

125. [Of the English]
For undemocratic reasons and for motives not of State,
They arrive at their conclusions – largely inarticulate.
Being void of self-expression they confide their views to none;

But sometimes in a smoking-room, one learns why things were done.
[*Actions and Reactions* (1909), 'The Puzzler']

126. 'Gold is for the mistress – silver for the maid–
Copper for the craftsman, cunning at his trade.'
'Good!' said the Baron, sitting in his hall,
'But Iron – Cold Iron – is master of them all!'
[*Rewards and Fairies* (1910), 'Cold Iron']

127. If you can keep your head when all about you
Are losing theirs and blaming it on you,
If you can trust yourself when all men doubt you,
But make allowance for their doubting too;
If you can wait and not be tired by waiting,
Or being lied about, don't deal in lies,
Or being hated, don't give way to hating,
And yet don't look too good, nor talk too wise:

If you can dream – and not make dreams your master;
If you can think – and not make thoughts your aim;
If you can meet with Triumph and Disaster
And treat those two imposters just the same;
If you can bear to hear the truth you've spoken
Twisted by knaves to make a trap for fools.
Or watch the things you gave your life to, broken,
And stoop and build 'em up with worn-out tools:

If you can make one heap of all your winnings
And risk it on one turn of pitch-and-toss,
And lose, and start again at your beginnings
And never breathe a word about your loss...

128. If you can talk with crowds and keep your virtue,
Or walk with Kings – nor lose the common touch,
If neither foes nor loving friends can hurt you,
If all men count with you, but none too much;
If you can fill the unforgiving minute
With sixty seconds' worth of distance run,
Yours is the Earth and everything that's in it,
And – which is more – you'll be a Man, my son!
[*Rewards and Fairies* (1910), 'If–']

129. Valour and Innocence
Have latterly gone hence
To certain death by certain shame attended.
[*Rewards and Fairies* (1910), 'The Two Cousins']

130. No one thinks of winter when the grass is green!
[*Rewards and Fairies* (1910), 'A St Helena Lullaby']

131. They shut the road through the woods
Seventy years ago.
Weather and rain have undone it again,
And now you would never know
There was once a road through the woods...

132. You will hear the beat of a horse's feet,
And the swish of a skirt in the dew,
Steadily cantering through
The misty solitudes,
As though they perfectly knew
The old lost road through the woods–
But there is no road through the woods!
[*Rewards and Fairies* (1910), 'The Way Through the Woods']

133. When the Himalayan peasant meets the he-bear in his pride,
He shouts to scare the monster, who will often turn aside.
But the she-bear thus accosted rends the peasant tooth and nail,
For the female of the species is more deadly than the male...

134. Man propounds negotiations, Man accepts the compromise.
Very rarely will he squarely push the logic of a fact
To its ultimate conclusion in unmitigated act.
['The Female of the Species' (1911)]

135. England's on the anvil – hear the hammers ring–
Clanging from the Severn to the Tyne!
Never was a blacksmith like our Norman King–
England's being hammered, hammered, hammered into line!
[Songs written for C.R.L. Fletcher's *A History of England* (1911), 'The Anvil']

136. 'Oh, where are you going to, all you Big Steamers,
With England's own coal, up and down the salt seas?'
'We are going to fetch you your bread and your butter,
Your beef, pork, and mutton, eggs, apples, and cheese.
[Songs written for C.R.L. Fletcher's *A History of England* (1911), 'Big Steamers']

137. It is always a temptation to a rich and lazy nation,
To puff and look important and to say:–
'Though we know we should defeat you, we have not the time to meet you.
We will therefore pay you cash to go away.'

And that is called paying the Dane-geld;
But we've proved it again and again,
That if once you have paid him the Dane-geld
You never get rid of the Dane.
[Songs written for C.R.L. Fletcher's *A History of England* (1911), 'Dane-Geld']

138. Our England is a garden that is full of stately views,
Of borders, beds and shrubberies and lawns and avenues,
With statues on the terraces and peacocks strutting by;
But the Glory of the Garden lies in more than meets the eye...

139. The Glory of the Garden it abideth not in words...

140. Oh, Adam was a gardener, and God who made him sees
That half a proper gardener's work is done upon his knees,
So when your work is finished, you can wash your hands and pray
For the Glory of the Garden, that it may not pass away!
And the Glory of the Garden it shall never pass away!
[Songs written for C.R.L. Fletcher's *A History of England* (1911), 'The Glory of the Garden']

141. He wrote that monarchs were divine,
And left a son who – proved they weren't!
[Songs written for C.R.L. Fletcher's *A History of England* (1911), 'James I']

142. The Saxon is not like us Normans. His manners are not so polite.
But he never means anything serious till he talks about justice and right,
When he stands like an ox in the furrow with his sullen set eyes on your own,
And grumbles, 'This isn't fair dealing,' my son, leave the Saxon alone.
[Songs written for C.R.L. Fletcher's *A History of England* (1911), 'Norman and Saxon']

143. But remember, please, the Law by which we live,
We are not built to comprehend a lie,
We can neither love nor pity nor forgive,
If you make a slip in handling us you die!
[Songs written for C.R.L. Fletcher's *A History of England* (1911), 'The Secret of the Machines']

144. For all we have and are,
For all our children's fate,
Stand up and take the war.
The Hun is at the gate!...

145. There is but one task for all–
One life for each to give.
What stands if Freedom fall?
Who dies if England live?
['For All We Have and Are' (1914)]

146. These were our children who died for our lands...
But who shall return us the children?
['The Children' (1917)]

147. The Garden called Gethsemane
In Picardy it was,
And there the people came to see
The English soldiers pass.
We used to pass – we used to pass
Or halt, as it might be,
And ship our masks in case of gas
Beyond Gethsemane.
The Garden called Gethsemane,
It held a pretty lass,
But all the time she talked to me
I prayed my cup might pass.
The officer sat on the chair,
The men lay on the grass,
And all the time we halted there
I prayed my cup might pass.

It didn't pass – it didn't pass–
It didn't pass from me.
I drank it when we met the gas
Beyond Gethsemane!
['Gethsemane' (1914–18)]

148. There's a whisper down the field where the year has shot her yield,
And the ricks stand grey to the sun,
Singing: 'Over then, come over, for the bee has quit the clover,
'And your English summer's done.'
You have heard the beat of the off-shore wind,
And the thresh of the deep-sea rain;
You have heard the song – how long? how long?
Pull out on the trail again!
Ha' done with the Tents of Shem, dear lass,
We've seen the seasons through,
And it's time to turn on the old trail, our own trail, the out trail,
Pull out, pull out, on the Long Trail – the trail that is always new!...

149. There be triple ways to take, of the eagle or the snake,
Or the way of a man with a maid;
But the sweetest way to me is a ship's upon the sea
In the heel of the North-East Trade.
['The Long Trail' (1918)]

150. In the Carboniferous Epoch we were promised abundance for all,
By robbing selected Peter to pay for collective Paul;
But though we had plenty of money, there was nothing our money could buy,
And the Gods of the Copybook Headings said: 'If you don't work, you die'.
['The Gods of the Copybook Headings' (1919)]

151. Ah! What avails the classic bent
And what the cultured word,
Against the undoctored incident
That actually occurred?
[*The Years Between* (1919), 'The Benefactors']

152. I could not look on Death, which being known,
Men led me to him, blindfold and alone.
[*The Years Between* (1919), 'Epitaphs – The Coward']

153. 'Have you news of my boy Jack?'
Not this tide.
'When d'you think that he'll come back?'
Not with this wind blowing, and this tide.
[*The Years Between* (1919), 'My Boy Jack']

154. Oh, was there ever sailor free to choose,
That didn't settle somewhere near the sea?
[*The Years Between* (1919), 'The Virginity']

155. Father, Mother and Me,
Sister and Auntie say
All the people like us are We,
And every one else is They.
[*Debits and Credits* (1926), 'We and They']

156. Words are, of course, the most powerful drug used by mankind.
[Speech, 1923]

157. [Of newspaper barons]
Power without responsibility – the prerogative of the harlot throughout the ages.
[Remark, quoted by Stanley Baldwin in a speech, 1931. Cf. Stoppard: 1]

158. [To a magazine which incorrectly reported his death]
I've just read that I am dead. Don't forget to delete me from your list of subscribers.
[Attr.]

Kissinger, Henry (1923–)

German-born American diplomat; Republican Secretary of State 1973–77; shared Nobel peace prize 1973

1. The conventional army loses if it does not win. The guerilla wins if he does not lose.
[*Foreign Affairs*, XIII (1969), 'The Vietnam Negotiations']

2. [Of the invasion of Cambodia, 1970]
We are all the President's men.
[*The Sunday Times Magazine*, 1975]

3. Even a paranoid can have enemies.
[*Time*, 1977]

4. There cannot be a crisis next week. My schedule is already full.
[*Time*, 1977]

5. An Iranian moderate is one who has run out of ammunition.
[*The Observer*, 1987, in Jeffrey Care (ed.), *Sayings of the Eighties* (1989)]

6. Foreign policy should not be confused with missionary work.
[In *London Review of Books*, 1992, review of *Kissinger: A Biography*]

7. [On the Tiananmen Square massacre]
No government in the world would have tolerated having the main square of its capital occupied for eight weeks by tens of thousands of demonstrators.
[In *London Review of Books*, 1992, review of *Kissinger: A Biography*]

8. Power is the ultimate aphrodisiac.
[Attr.]

Kitchener, Lord (1850–1916)

Irish-born English field marshal; War Minister 1914–16; imperial administrator and army organiser

1. [Reply to the Prince of Wales' request to go to the Front]
I don't mind your being killed, but I object to your being taken prisoner.
[In Viscount Esher, *Journals and Letters*, 1914]

2. [Message to soldiers in the British Expeditionary Force, 1914]
You are ordered abroad as a soldier of the King to help our French comrades against the invasion of a common enemy. You have to perform a task which will need your courage, your energy, your patience. Remember that the honour of the British Army depends on your individual conduct. It will be your duty not only to set an example of discipline and perfect steadiness under fire but also to maintain the most friendly relations with those whom you are helping in this struggle. In this new experience you may find temptations both in wine and women. You must entirely resist both temptations, and, while treating all women with perfect courtesy, you should avoid any intimacy. Do your duty bravely. Fear God. Honour the King.
[Attr.]

Kitchiner, Dr

1. The beauty of a Poached Egg is for the yolk to be seen blushing through the white – which should only be just sufficiently hardened, to form a transparent Veil for the Egg.
[*Cook's Oracle* (1829)]

Klee, Paul (1879–1940)

Swiss painter and engraver; member of Blaue Reiter and teacher at the Bauhaus

1. *Kunst gibt nicht das Sichtbare wieder, sondern macht sichtbar.*
Art does not reproduce what is visible; it makes things visible.
['Schöpferische Konfession' ('Creative Credo', 1920)]

2. *Eine aktive Linie, die sich frei ergeht, ein Spaziergang um seiner selbst willen, ohne Ziel. Das Agens ist ein Punkt, der sich verschiebt.*
An active line going for a stroll, freely, aimlessly, a walk for its own sake. The agent is a point which moves around.
[*Pädagogisches Skizzenbuch* (*Pedagogical Sketchbook*, 1925), 1]

Klinger, Friedrich Maximilian von (1752–1831)

German dramatist

1. [Name adopted by a German literary movement of the late 18th century]
Sturm und Drang.
Storm and stress.
[Title of play, 1777]

Klopstock, Friedrich (1724–1803)

German religious and lyric poet

1. [Of one of his poems]
God and I both knew what it meant once; now God alone knows.
[Attr.]

Knight, Charles (fl.1914) and Lyle, Kenneth (20th century)

British songwriters

1. Here we are! here we are!! here we are again!!!
There's Pat and Mac and Tommy and Jack and Joe.
When there's trouble brewing,
When there's something doing,
Are we downhearted?
No! Let 'em all come!
[Song, 1914]

Knopf, Edwin H. (1899–)

1. [Said when Louis B. Mayer promoted his daughter's husband (David O. Selznick), c. 1933]
The son-in-law also rises.
[In Colombo, *Wit and Wisdom of the Moviemakers*]

Knowles, Mary (1733–1807)

English Quaker

1. [Of Dr Johnson]
He gets at the substance of a book directly; he tears out the heart of it.
[In Boswell, *The Life of Smauel Johnson* (1791), III, 1778]

Knox, John (1505–1572)

Scottish religious reformer, founder of the Presbyterian Church of Scotland (1560) and prose writer

1. The First Blast of the Trumpet Against the Monstrous Regiment of Women.
[Title of pamphlet, 1558]

2. To promote a Woman to bear rule, superiority, dominion or empire, above any Realm, Nation, or City, is repugnant to Nature; contumely to God, a thing most contrarious to his revealed will and approved ordinance; and finally it is the subversion of good Order, of all equity and justice.
['The First Blast of the Trumpet Against the Monstrous Regiment of Women', 1558]

3. *Un homme avec Dieu est toujours dans la majorité.*
A man with God is always in the majority.
[Inscription on the Reformation Monument, Geneva, Switzerland]

Knox, Philander Chase (1853–1921)

American lawyer and politician; Republican Secretary of State 1909–13

1. [Reply when Theodore Roosevelt requested legal justification for US acquisition of the Panama Canal Zone]
Oh, Mr President, do not let so great an achievement suffer from any taint of legality.
[Attr.]

Knox, Ronald (1888–1957)

English Roman Catholic priest, translator of the Bible and essayist

1. It is so stupid of modern civilization to have given up believing in the devil when he is the only explanation of it.
[Attr.]

2. There was once a man who said 'God
Must think it exceedingly odd
If he finds that this tree
Continues to be
When there's no one about in the Quad.'
[Attr. Cf. Anon.: 61]

3. O God, for as much as without Thee
We are not enabled to doubt Thee,
Help us all by Thy grace
To convince the whole race
It knows nothing whatever about Thee.
[Attr.]

4. [Definition of a baby]
A loud noise at one end and no sense of responsibility at the other.
[Attr.]

Knox, Vicesimus (1752–1821)

English clergyman, essayist and religious writer

1. Can anything be more absurd than keeping women in a state of ignorance, and yet so vehemently to insist on their resisting temptation?
[*Liberal Education* (1780), I; also attributed to Mary Wollstonecraft]

2. That learning belongs not to the female character, and that the female mind is not capable of a degree of improvement equal to that of the other sex, are narrow and unphilosophical prejudices.
[*Essays, Moral and Literary* (1782), III, 142]

Kocan, Peter Raymond (1947–)
Australian writer and poet

1. What guides the birds and fishes,
Guides simple lovers too,
– a plain trick of knowing,
The normal thing to do.
['Retarded Lovers']

Koch, Christopher John (1932–)
Australian broadcaster, novelist and poet

1. The Year of Living Dangerously.
[Title of novel, 1978]

Koestler, Arthur (1905–1983)
Hungarian-born British novelist, essayist, journalist and political refugee

1. One may not regard the world as a sort of metaphysical brothel for emotions.
[*Darkness at Noon* (1940), 'The Second Hearing']

2. Two half-truths do not make a truth, and two half-cultures do not make a culture.
[*The Ghost in the Machine* (1961), Preface]

3. God seems to have left the receiver off the hook, and time is running out.
[*The Ghost in the Machine* (1961), 18]

4. The most persistent sound which reverberates through men's history is the beating of war drums.
[*Janus: A Summing Up* (1978), Prologue]

5. A writer's ambition should be . . . to trade a hundred contemporary readers for ten readers in ten years' time and for one reader in a hundred years' time.
[*New York Times Book Review*, 1951]

6. If the creator had a purpose in equipping us with a neck, he surely meant us to stick it out.
[*Encounter*, 1970]

7. [Of the atomic bomb]
Hitherto man had to live with the idea of death as an individual; from now onward mankind will have to live with the idea of its death as a species.
[Attr.]

Koran

1. There is no doubt in this book.
[Chapter 1]

2. Let there be no violence in religion.
[Chapter 2]

3. Every age hath its book.
[Chapter 13]

Korda, Alexander (1893–1956)
Hungarian-born British film producer and director

1. It's not enough to be Hungarian, you must have talent too.
[Attr.]

Kraus, Karl (1874–1936)
Austrian satirist, critic and poet

1. *Man muss alle Schriftsteller zweimal lesen, die guten und die schlechten. Die einen wird man erkennen, die anderen entlarven.*
You must read all writers twice, both the good ones and the bad ones. You'll recognize the good ones and you'll unmask the others.
[*Sprüche und Widersprüche* (*Sayings and Contradictions*, 1909), section VI]

2. *Die Unsterblichkeit ist das einzige, was keinen Aufschub verträgt.*
Immortality is the only thing which doesn't tolerate being postponed.
[*Sprüche und Widersprüche* (*Sayings and Contradictions*, 1909), section IX]

3. *Moral ist die Tendenz, das Bad mit dem Kinde auszuschütten.*
Morality is the tendency to throw out the bath along with the baby.
[*Pro domo et mundo* (1912), section I]

4. *Keinen Gedanken haben und ihn ausdrücken können – das macht den Journalisten.*
To have no thoughts and be able to express them – that's what makes a journalist.
[*Pro domo et mundo* (1912), section III]

5. *Bildung ist das, was die meisten empfangen, viele weitergeben und wenige haben.*
Education is what most people receive, many pass on and few actually have.
[*Pro domo et mundo* (1912), section III]

6. *Künstler ist nur einer, der aus der Lösung ein Rätsel machen kann.*
The only person who is an artist is the one that can make a puzzle out of the solution.
[*Nachts* (*By Night*, 1919), section II]

7. *Die deutsche Sprache ist die tiefste, die deutsche Rede die seichteste.*
The German language is the most profound one, German speech the most shallow.
[*Nachts* (*By Night*, 1919), section V]

Kriegler, Judge Johann
Chair of South African Independent Electoral Commission

1. [On the 1994 elections in South Africa]
'Let's not get overly squeamish about it,' he said, noting that the IEC had never been asked to certify the results as 'accurate', but simply as free and fair.
[*Herald*, 1994]

Kristofferson, Kris (1936–)
American film actor and singer-songwriter

1. Freedom's just another word for nothing left to lose.
['Me and Bobby McGee', song, 1969]

Kruger, Paul (1825–1904)
Boer statesman; President of the Transvaal 1883–1900

1. A bill of indemnity . . . for raid by Dr Jameson and the British South Africa Company's troops. The amount falls under two heads – first material damage, total of claim, £577,938 3s.3d.; second, moral or intellectual damage, total of claim, £1,000,000.
[Communicated to House of Commons by Joseph Chamberlain, 1897]

Kubrick, Stanley (1928–)
American film writer, producer and director

1. The great nations have always acted like gangsters, and the small nations like prostitutes.
[*The Guardian*, 1963]

Kyd, Thomas (1558–1594)
English dramatist and tragic poet

1. What outcries pluck me from my naked bed?
[*The Spanish Tragedy* (1592), II.v]

2. Oh eyes, no eyes, but fountains fraught with tears;
Oh life, no life, but lively form of death;
Oh world, no world, but mass of public wrongs.
[*The Spanish Tragedy* (1592), III.ii]

3. I am never better than when I am mad. Then methinks I am a brave fellow; then I do wonders. But reason abuseth me, and there's the torment, there's the hell.
[*The Spanish Tragedy* (1592), III.vii]

4. My son – and what's a son? A thing begot
Within a pair of minutes, thereabout,
A lump bred up in darkness.
[*The Spanish Tragedy* (1592), III.xi]

5. Duly twice a morning
Would I be sprinkling it with fountain water.
At last it grew, and grew, and bore, and bore,
Till at the length
It grew a gallows and did bear our son,
It bore thy fruit and mine: O wicked, wicked plant.
[*The Spanish Tragedy* (1592), III.xii]

6. Why then I'll fit you.
[*The Spanish Tragedy* (1592), IV.i]

7. For what's a play without a woman in it?
[*The Spanish Tragedy* (1592), IV.i]

Labouchere, Henry (1831–1912)
English journalist and Liberal politician

1. He [Labouchere] did not object, he once said, to Gladstone's always having the ace of trumps up his sleeve, but only to his pretence that God had put it there.
[In Curzon, *Modern Parliamentary Eloquence* (1913)]

La Bruyère, Jean de (1645–1696)
French moralist, noted for satirical character studies

1. *Il y a quelques rencontres dans la vie où la vérité et la simplicité sont le meilleur manège du monde.*
There are some circumstances in life where truth and simplicity are the best strategy in the world.
[*Les caractères ou les moeurs de ce siècle* (1688), 'De la cour']

2. *Un dévot est celui qui sous un roi athée serait athée.*
A pious man is one who would be an atheist if the king were.
[*Les caractères ou les moeurs de ce siècle* (1688), 'De la mode']

3. *La plupart des hommes emploient la meilleure partie de leur vie à rendre l'autre misérable.*
Most men spend the best part of their lives in making their remaining years unhappy.
[*Les caractères ou les moeurs de ce siècle* (1688), 'De l'homme']

4. *Il n'y a pour l'homme que trois événements: naître, vivre, et mourir. Il ne se sent pas naître, il souffre à mourir, et il oublie de vivre.*
There are only three events in a man's life; birth, life, and death; he is not aware of being born, he dies in suffering, and he forgets to live.
[*Les caractères ou les moeurs de ce siècle* (1688), 'De l'homme']

5. *L'esprit de parti abaisse les plus grands hommes jusques aux petitesses du peuple.*
Party loyalty brings the greatest of men down to the petty level of the masses.
[*Les caractères ou les moeurs de ce siècle* (1688), 'De l'homme']

6. *Si la pauvreté est la mère des crimes, le défaut d'esprit en est le père.*
If poverty is the mother of crime, lack of intelligence is its father.
[*Les caractères ou les moeurs de ce siècle* (1688), 'De l'homme']

7. *Il faut rire avant que d'être heureux, de peur de mourir sans avoir ri.*
One must laugh before one is happy, for fear of dying without ever having laughed at all.
[*Les caractères ou les moeurs de ce siècle* (1688), 'Du coeur']

8. *Le commencement et le déclin de l'amour se font sentir par l'embarras où l'on est de se trouver seuls.*
The beginning and the decline of love reveal themselves in the awkwardness lovers feel in being alone together.
[*Les caractères ou les moeurs de ce siècle* (1688), 'Du coeur']

9. *Le peuple n'a guère d'esprit et les grands n'ont point d'âme ... faut-il opter, je ne balance pas, je veux être peuple.*
The people have little intelligence, the great no heart ... if I had to choose I should not hesitate: I would be of the people.
[*Les caractères ou les moeurs de ce siècle* (1688), 'Des grands']

10. *Entre le bon sens et le bon goût il y a la différence de la cause et son effet.*
Between good sense and good taste there is the same difference as between cause and effect.
[*Les caractères ou les moeurs de ce siècle* (1688), 'Des jugements']

11. *Il y a des gens qui parlent un moment avant que d'avoir pensé.*
There are people who speak one moment before they think.
[*Les caractères ou les moeurs de ce siècle* (1688), 'De la société et de la conversation']

12. *Tout est dit, et l'on vient trop tard depuis plus de sept mille ans qu'il y a des hommes et qui pensent.*
Everything has been said already; we come too late after more than seven thousand years in which men have lived and thought.
[*Les caractères ou les moeurs de ce siècle* (1688), 'Des ouvrages de l'esprit'. Cf. Terence: 4]

13. *C'est un métier que de faire un livre, comme de faire une pendule: il faut plus que de l'esprit pour être auteur.*
The making of a book, like the making of a clock, is a craft; it takes more than wit to be an author.
[*Les caractères ou les moeurs de ce siècle* (1688), 'Des ouvrages de l'esprit']

14. *Le plaisir de la critique nous ôte celui d'être vivement touchés de très belles choses.*
The pleasure of criticizing takes away from us the pleasure of being moved by some very fine things.
[*Les caractères ou les moeurs de ce siècle* (1688), 'Des ouvrages de l'esprit']

15. *Les médecins laissent mourir, les charlatans tuent.*
Doctors allow us to die; charlatans kill us.
[*Les caractères ou les moeurs de ce siècle* (1688), 'De quelques usages']

La Chaussée, Nivelle de (1692–1754)
French sentimental dramatist

1. *Quand tout le monde a tort, tout le monde a raison.*
When everyone is wrong, everyone is right.
[*La Gouvernante* (1747), I.iii]

Laforgue, Jules (1860–1887)
French poet, born in Uruguay, noted for his innovative free verse

1. *Ah! que la vie est quotidienne!*
Oh, what an everyday affair life is!
[*Les complaintes* (1885)]

Laing, R.D. (1927–1989)

Scottish pyschiatrist and psychoanalyst, noted for his social theory of mental illness; poet

1. The statesmen of the world who boast and threaten that they have Doomsday weapons are far more dangerous, and far more estranged from 'reality', than many of the people on whom the label 'psychotic' is affixed.
[*The Divided Self* (1960), Preface]

2. Schizophrenia cannot be understood without understanding despair.
[*The Divided Self* (1960), 2]

3. Few books today are forgivable.
[*The Politics of Experience* (1967), Introduction]

4. We are effectively destroying ourselves by violence masquerading as love.
[*The Politics of Experience* (1967), 13]

5. Madness need not be all breakdown. It may also be break-through. It is potential liberation and renewal as well as enslavement and existential death.
[*The Politics of Experience* (1967), 16]

Lamartine, Alphonse de (1790–1869)

French Romantic poet, historian, royalist and statesman

1. *Un seul être vous manque, et tout est dépeuplé.*
Only one being is missing, and your whole world is bereft of people.
[*Premières Méditations poétiques* (1820), 'Isolement']

Lamb, Lady Caroline (1785–1828)

English novelist and poet; her marriage to William Lamb Melbourne was marred by her infatuation with Byron

1. [Of Byron]
Mad, bad, and dangerous to know.
[*Journal*, 1812]

Lamb, Charles (1775–1834)

English essayist, critic and letter writer

1. Nothing to me is more distasteful than that entire complacency and satisfaction which beam in the countenance of a new-married couple.
[*Essays of Elia* (1823), 'A Bachelor's Complaint of Married People']

2. I even think that sentimentally I am disposed to harmony. But organically I am incapable of a tune.
[*Essays of Elia* (1823), 'A Chapter on Ears']

3. 'Presents,' I often say 'endear Absents.'
[*Essays of Elia* (1823), 'A Dissertation upon Roast Pig']

4. It argues an insensibility.
[*Essays of Elia* (1823), 'A Dissertation upon Roast Pig']

5. We are nothing; less than nothing, and dreams. We are only what might have been, and must wait upon the tedious shores of Lethe millions of ages before we have existence, and a name.
[*Essays of Elia* (1823), 'Dream Children']

6. Why have we none [i.e. no grace] for books, those spiritual repasts – a grace before Milton – a grace before Shakespeare – a devotional exercise proper to be said before reading the *Faerie Queene*?
[*Essays of Elia* (1823), 'Grace before Meat']

7. Coleridge holds that a man cannot have a pure mind who refuses apple-dumplings. I am not certain but he is right.
[*Essays of Elia* (1823), 'Grace Before Meat']

8. [Of food]
I hate a man who swallows it, affecting not to know what he is eating. I suspect his taste in higher matters.
[*Essays of Elia* (1823), 'Grace Before Meat']

9. I am, in plainer words, a bundle of prejudices – made up of likings and dislikings.
[*Essays of Elia* (1823), 'Imperfect Sympathies']

10. I have been trying all my life to like Scotchmen, and am obliged to desist from the experiment in despair.
[*Essays of Elia* (1823), 'Imperfect Sympathies']

11. In everything that relates to science, I am a whole Encyclopaedia behind the rest of the world.
[*Essays of Elia* (1823), 'The Old and the New Schoolmaster']

12. Boys are capital fellows in their own way, among their mates; but they are unwholesome companions for grown people.
[*Essays of Elia* (1823), 'The Old and the New Schoolmaster']

13. She unbent her mind afterwards – over a book.
[*Essays of Elia* (1823), 'Mrs Battle's Opinions on Whist']

14. Man is a gaming animal. He must always be trying to get the better in something or other.
[*Essays of Elia* (1823), 'Mrs Battle's Opinions on Whist']

15. The uncommunicating muteness of fishes.
[*Essays of Elia* (1823), 'A Quakers' Meeting']

16. The human species, according to the best theory I can form of it, is composed of two distinct races, *the men who borrow*, and *the men who lend*.
[*Essays of Elia* (1823), 'The Two Races of Men']

17. What a liberal confounding of those pedantic distinctions of *meum* and *tuum*!
[*Essays of Elia* (1823), 'The Two Races of Men']

18. I mean your *borrowers of books* – those mutilators of collections, spoilers of the symmetry of shelves, and creators of odd volumes.
[*Essays of Elia* (1823), 'The Two Races of Men']

19. Not many sounds in life, and I include all urban and all rural sounds, exceed in interest a knock at the door.
[*Essays of Elia* (1823), 'Valentine's Day']

20. Credulity is the man's weakness, but the child's strength.
[*Essays of Elia* (1823), 'Witches and other Night Fears']

21. Newspapers always excite curiosity. No one ever lays one down without a feeling of disappointment.
[*Last Essays of Elia* (1833), 'Detached Thoughts on Books and Reading']

22. I love to lose myself in other men's minds. When I am not walking, I am reading; I cannot sit and think. Books think for me.
[*Last Essays of Elia* (1833), 'Detached Thoughts on Books and Reading']

23. Milton almost requires a solemn service of music to be played before you enter upon him.
[*Last Essays of Elia* (1833), 'Detached Thoughts on Books and Reading']

24. A poor relation – is the most irrelevant thing in nature.
[*Last Essays of Elia* (1833), 'Poor Relations']

25. [Referring to the nature of a pun]
It is a pistol let off at the ear; not a feather to tickle the intellect.
[*Last Essays of Elia* (1833), 'Popular Fallacies']

26. How sickness enlarges the dimensions of a man's self to himself!
[*Last Essays of Elia* (1833), 'The Convalescent']

27. What a lass that were to go a-gipsying through the world with.
[*The Examiner*, 1819, 'The Jovial Crew']

28. The greatest pleasure I know, is to do a good action by stealth, and to have it found out by accident.
[*The Athenaeum*, 1834, 'Table Talk by the Late Elia']

29. Gone before
To that unknown and silent shore.
['Hester' (1803)]

30. Riddle of destiny, who can show
What thy short visit meant, or know
What thy errand here below?
['On an Infant Dying as soon as Born']

31. All, all are gone, the old familiar faces.
['The Old Familiar Faces']

32. The six weeks that finished last year and begun this, your very humble servant spent very agreeably in a madhouse at Hoxton. I am got somewhat rational now, and don't bite anyone.
[Letter to Coleridge, 1796]

33. I came home . . . hungry as a hunter.
[Letter, 1800]

34. Separate from the pleasure of your company, I don't much care if I never see another mountain in my life.
[Letter to William Wordsworth, 1801]

35. The man must have a rare recipe for melancholy, who can be dull in Fleet Street.
[Letter to Thomas Manning, 1802]

36. A little, thin, flowery border, round, neat, not gaudy.
[Letter to Wordsworth, 1806]

37. I have made a little scale, supposing myself to receive the following various accessions of dignity from the king, who is the fountain of honour – As at first, 1, Mr C. Lamb; . . . 10th, Emperor Lamb; 11th Pope Innocent, higher than which is nothing but the Lamb of God.
[Letter to Thomas Manning, 1810]

38. Nothing puzzles me more than time and space; and yet nothing troubles me less, as I never think about them.
[Letter to Thomas Manning, 1810]

39. I was at Hazlitt's marriage, and had like to have been turned out several times during the ceremony. Anything awful makes me laugh. I misbehaved once at a funeral.
[Letter to Southey, 1815]

40. This very night I am going to leave off tobacco! Surely there must be some other world in which this unconquerable purpose shall be realized. The soul hath not her generous aspirings implanted in her in vain.
[Letter to Thomas Manning, 1815]

41. [Of Coleridge]
His face when he repeats his verses hath its ancient glory, an Archangel a little damaged.
[Letter to Wordsworth, 1816]

42. How I like to be liked, and what I do to be liked!
[Letter to D. Wordsworth, 1821]

43. You are knee deep in clover.
[Letter to C.C. Clarke, 1828]

44. When my sonnet was rejected, I exclaimed, 'Damn the age; I will write for Antiquity!'
[Letter to B.W. Procter, 1829]

45. Half as sober as a judge.
[Letter to Mr and Mrs Moxon, 1833]

46. Martin, if dirt were trumps, what hands you would hold!
[In Leigh Hunt, *Lord Byron and his Contemporaries* (1828)]

47. Dr Parr . . . asked him, how he had acquired his power of smoking at such a rate? Lamb replied, 'I toiled after it, sir, as some men toil after virtue.'
[In Talfourd, *Memoirs of Charles Lamb* (1892)]

48. At Godwin's . . . they [Lamb, Holcroft, and Coleridge] were disputing fiercely which was the best – Man as he was, or man as he is to be. 'Give me,' says Lamb, 'man as he is *not* to be.'
[In Hazlitt, *English Literature*, 17]

49. May my last breath be drawn through a pipe and exhaled in a pun.
[In Wintle and Kenin, *Dictionary of Biographical Quotations*]

Lamb, Mary (1764–1847)
English prose writer; collaborated on Tales from Shakespeare *with her brother, Charles Lamb*

1. A child's a plaything for an hour.
[*Parental Recollections*; also attributed to Charles Lamb]

2. [Of Henry Crabb Robinson]
He says he never saw a man so happy in *three wives* as Mr Wordsworth is.
[Letter to Sarah Hutchinson, 1816]

Lambert, Eric (1918–1966)
English-born Australian novelist

1. [The title is taken from a phrase used to describe the Australian forces by William Joyce ('Lord Haw-Haw') in a Nazi radio broadcast during the desert war]
The Twenty Thousand Thieves.
[Title of novel, 1951]

Lambton, John, First Earl of Durham (1792–1840)
English statesman and Whig politician

1. He said he considered £40,000 a year a moderate income – such a one as a man might *jog on* with.
[In *The Creevey Papers* (1903), from a letter from Mr Creevey to Miss Elizabeth Ord, 1821]

Lampton, William James (1859–1917)
British writer

1. Same old slippers,
Same old rice,
Same old glimpse of
Paradise.
['June Weddings']

Lancaster, Sir Osbert (1908–1986)
English writer, cartoonist and stage designer

1. 'Fan vaulting' . . . an architectural device which arouses enormous enthusiasm on account of the difficulties it has all too obviously involved but which from an aesthetic standpoint frequently belongs to the 'Last-supper-carved-on-a-peach-stone' class of masterpiece.
[*Pillar to Post* (1938), 'Perpendicular']

2. A hundred and fifty accurate reproductions of Anne Hathaway's cottage, each complete with central heating and garage.
[*Pillar to Post* (1938), 'Stockbroker's Tudor']

Lanchester, Elsa (1902–1986)
British-born American stage and film actress

1. [Of Maureen O'Hara]
She looked as though butter wouldn't melt in her mouth – or anywhere else.
[Attr.]

Landers, Ann (Esther Pauline Lederer) (1918–)
Famous agony aunt and columnist

1. Women complain about sex more often than men. Their gripes fall into two major categories: (1) Not enough (2) Too much.
[*Ann Landers Says Truth Is Stranger Than*... (1968)]

Landon, Letitia Elizabeth (1802–1838)
Popular English poet and novelist

1. Few, save the poor, feel for the poor.
['The Poor']

Landor, Walter Savage (1775–1864)
English poet and prose writer

1. Ah, what avails the sceptred race!
Ah, what the form divine!
What every virtue, every grace!
Rose Aylmer, all were thine.
Rose Aylmer, whom these wakeful eyes
May weep, but never see,
A night of memories and of sighs
I consecrate to thee.
['Rose Aylmer' (1806)]

2. Past ruin'd Ilion Helen lives,
Alcestis rises from the shades;
Verse calls them forth; 'tis verse that gives
Immortal youth to mortal maids.
['To Ianthe' (1831)]

3. There is delight in singing, tho' none hear
Beside the singer.
['To Robert Browning' (1846)]

4. Death stands above me, whispering low
I know not what into my ear;
Of his strange language all I know
Is, there is not a word of fear.
[*Epigrams* (1853), 'Death']

5. George the First was always reckoned
Vile, but viler George the Second;
And what mortal ever heard
Any good of George the Third?
When from earth the Fourth descended
God be praised, the Georges ended!
[*The Atlas*, 1855, 'Epigram']

6. Around the child bent all the three
Sweet Graces: Faith, Hope, Charity.
Around the man bend other faces:
Pride, Envy, Malice, are his Graces.
['Around the Child']

7. Hail, ye indomitable heroes, hail!
Despite of all your generals ye prevail.
['The Crimean Heroes']

8. Stand close around, ye Stygian set,
With Dirce in one boat conveyed!
Or Charon, seeing, may forget
That he is old and she a shade.
['Dirce']

9. I strove with none; for none was worth my strife;
Nature I loved, and next to Nature, Art;
I warmed both hands before the fire of life;
It sinks, and I am ready to depart.
['Finis']

10. Proud word you never spoke, but you will speak
Four not exempt from pride some future day.
Resting on one white hand a warm wet cheek
Over my open volume you will say,
'This man loved *me*!' then rise and trip away.
['Proud Words You Never Spoke']

11. How many verses have I thrown
Into the fire because the one
Peculiar word, the wanted most,
Was irrevocably lost.
['Verses Why Burnt']

12. Well I remember how you smiled
To see me write your name upon
The soft sea-sand – 'O! what a child!
You think you're writing upon stone!'
I have since written what no tide
Shall ever wash away, what men
Unborn shall read o'er ocean wide
And find Ianthe's name again.
['Well I Remember How You Smiled']

13. I know not whether I am proud,
But this I know, I hate the crowd.
['With an Album']

14. Clear writers, like clear fountains, do not seem so deep as they are; the turbid look the most profound.
[*Imaginary Conversations* (1824), 'Southey and Porson']

15. Fleas know not whether they are upon the body of a giant or upon one of ordinary size.
[*Imaginary Conversations* (1824), 'Southey and Porson']

16. Laodameia died; Helen died; Leda, the beloved of Jupiter, went before.
[*Imaginary Conversations* (1824–1829), 'Aesop and Rhodope']

17. There are no fields of amaranth on this side of the grave: there are no voices, O Rhodope! that are not soon mute, however tuneful: there is no name, with whatever emphasis of passionate love repeated, of which the echo is not faint at last.
[*Imaginary Conversations* (1824–1829), 'Aesop and Rhodope']

18. He who first praises a good book becomingly, is next in merit to the author.
[*Imaginary Conversations* (1824–1829), 'Alfieri and Salomon the Florentine Jew']

19. Prose on certain occasions can bear a great deal of poetry: on the other hand, poetry sinks and swoons under a moderate weight of prose.
[*Imaginary Conversations* (1853), 'Archdeacon Hare and Walter Landor']

20. I shall dine late; but the dining-room will be well lighted, the guests few and select.
[*Imaginary Conversations* (1853), 'Archdeacon Hare and Walter Landor']

21. I hate false words, and seek with care, difficulty, and moroseness, those that fit the thing.
[*Imaginary Conversations* (1853), 'Bishop Burnet and Humphrey Hardcastle']

22. Goodness does not more certainly make men happy than happiness makes them good.
[*Imaginary Conversations* (1853), 'Lord Brooke and Sir Philip Sidney']

23. States, like men, have their growth, their manhood, their decrepitude, their decay.
[*Imaginary Conversations* (1876), 'Pollio and Calvus']

24. [Having thrown his cook out of an open window into the flowerbed below]
Good God, I forgot the violets!
[In F. Muir, *An Irreverent Companion to Social History* (1976)]

Landowska, Wanda (1877–1959)
Polish-born American harpsichordist

1. [Remark to a fellow musician]
Oh, well, you play Bach *your* way. I'll play him *his*.
[Attr.]

Landseer, Sir Edwin Henry (1802–1873)
English animal painter and engraver; sculptor of the lions at Trafalgar Square, London

1. [Said to W.P. Frith]
If people only knew as much about painting as I do, they would never buy my pictures.
[In Campbell Lennie, *Landseer the Victorian Paragon*, 12]

Lane, George Martin (1823–1897)
American Latin scholar and university lecturer

1. The waiter roars it through the hall:
'We don't give bread with one fish-ball!'
['Lay of the Lone Fish-Ball' (1855)]

Lang, Andrew (1844–1912)
Scottish poet, journalist, mythologist, anthropologist, Greek scholar and children's writer

1. And through the music of the languid hours
They hear like Ocean on a western beach
The surge and thunder of the Odyssey.
['As One That for a Weary Space has Lain' (1881)]

2. St Andrews by the Northern Sea,
A haunted town it is to me!
['Almae Matres' (1884)]

3. A mist of memory broods and floats,
The border waters flow;
The air is full of ballad notes
Borne out of long ago.
['Twilight on Tweed' (1905)]

4. There's a joy without canker or cark,
There's a pleasure eternally new,
'Tis to gloat on the glaze and the mark
Of China that's ancient and blue.
['Ballade of Blue China']

5. Our hearts are young 'neath wrinkled rind:
Life's more amusing than we thought.
['Ballade of Middle Age']

6. Golf is a thoroughly national game. It is as Scotch as haggis, cockie-leekie, high cheek-bones, or rowanberry jam.
[In W. Pett Ridge (ed.), *Daily News, Lost Leaders*, 1889]

Lang, Ian (1940–)
Conservative MP and Secretary of State for Scotland

1. History is littered with dead opinion polls.
[*The Independent*, 1994]

Langbridge, Frederick (1849–1923)
English clergyman, poet and children's writer

1. Two men look out through the same bars:
One sees the mud, and one the stars.
['A Cluster of Quiet Thoughts' (1896)]

Lange, David Russell (1942–)
New Zealand politician and lawyer

1. [A statement released during the investigations into the bombing of the Greenpeace vessel, *Rainbow Warrior*, in 1985]
We are an enemy of the nuclear threat and we are an enemy of testing nuclear weapons in the South Pacific. New Zealand did not buy into this fight. France put agents into New Zealand. France put spies into New Zealand. France lets off bombs in the Pacific. France puts its President in the Pacific to crow about it.
[In Michael King, *Death of the Rainbow Warrior* (1986)]

Langland, William (c. 1330–c. 1400)
English alliterative poet

1. [Do well, Do better, and Do best: three allegorical characters central to the search for Truth in *Piers Plowman*]
Dowel, Dobet and Dobest.
[*The Vision of William Concerning Piers the Plowman*]

2. In a somer seson whan soft was the sonne.
[*The Vision of William Concerning Piers the Plowman*, Prologue (B Text)]

3. A faire felde ful of folke fonde I there bytwene
Of all manner of men, the mene and riche,
Worchyng and wandryng as the world asketh.
[*The Vision of William Concerning Piers the Plowman*, Prologue (B Text)]

4. A glotoun of wordes.
[*The Vision of William Concerning Piers the Plowman*, Prologue (B Text)]

5. Grammere, that grounde is of alle.
[*The Vision of William Concerning Piers the Plowman*, Prologue (C Text)]

6. Ac on a May morwenyng on Maluerne hulles
Me byfel for to slepe for weyrynesse of wandryng.
[*The Vision of William Concerning Piers the Plowman* (C Text)]

7. Bakers and brewers, bouchers and cokes–
For thees men doth most harme to the mene peple.
[*The Vision of William Concerning Piers the Plowman* (C Text)]

Langton, Archbishop Stephen (d. 1228)
English theologian; Archbishop of Canterbury and witness of Magna Carta

1. *Veni, Sancte Spiritus,*
Et emitte caelitus
Lucis tuae radium.
Come, Holy Spirit, and send out from heaven the beam of your light.
[The 'Golden Sequence' for Whitsunday]

2. *Lava quod est sordidum,*
Riga quod est aridum,
Sana quod est saucium.
Flecte quod est rigidum,
Fove quod est frigidum,
Rege quod est devium.
Wash what is dirty, water what is dry, heal what is wounded. Bend what is stiff, warm what is cold, set right what is astray.
[The 'Golden Sequence' for Whitsunday]

Lao-tzu (c.604–531 BC)
Chinese philosopher, regarded as founder of Taoism

1. Acting without design, occupying oneself without making a business of it, finding the great in what is small and the many in the few, repaying injury with kindness, effecting difficult things while they are easy, and managing great things in their beginnings: this is the method of Tao.
[*Tao Te Ching*]

2. To joy in conquest is to joy in the loss of human life.
[*Tao Te Ching*]

3. The further one goes, the less one knows.
[*Tao Te Ching*]

4. Heaven and Earth have no pity; they regard all things as straw dogs.
[*Tao Te Ching*]

5. A journey of a thousand miles must begin with a single step.
[*Tao Te Ching*]

6. The Way is like an empty vessel that yet may be drawn from.
[*Tao Te Ching*]

Laplace, Pierre-Simon, Marquis de (1749–1827)
French mathematician and astronomer; formulated the nebular hypothesis, 1796

1. [Reply when asked by Napoleon why he had made no reference to God in his book about the universe, *Mécanique céleste*]
I have no need of that hypothesis.
[In E. Bell, *Men of Mathematics*]

Lardner, Ring (Ringgold Wilmer Lardner) (1885–1933)
American humorist, short-story writer and newspaperman

1. [Referring to W.H. Taft, US President 1909–-1913]
He looked at me as if I was a side dish he hadn't ordered.
[In A.K. Adams, *The Home Book of Humorous Quotations*]

2. [Speaking to a flamboyantly dressed stranger who walked into the club where he was drinking]
How do you look when I'm sober?
[In J. Yardley, *Ring*]

Larkin, Philip (1922–1985)
English poet, novelist and librarian

1. Hatless, I take off
My cycle-clips in awkward reverence.
['Church-going' (1955)]

2. Nothing, like something, happens anywhere.
['I Remember, I Remember' (1955)]

3. Why should I let the toad *work*
Squat on my life?
Can't I use my wit as a pitchfork
And drive the brute off?
['Toads' (1955)]

4. What will survive of us is love.
['An Arundel Tomb' (1964)]

5. What are days for?
Days are where we live
They come they wake us
Time and time over.
They are to be happy in;
Where can we live but days?
['Days' (1964)]

6. Get stewed:
Books are a load of crap.
['A Study of Reading Habits' (1964)]

7. Perhaps being old is having lighted rooms
Inside your head, and people in them, acting.
People you know, yet can't quite name.
['The Old Fools' (1974)]

8. They fuck you up, your mum and dad.
They may not mean to, but they do.
They fill you with the faults they had
And add some extra, just for you.
['This be the Verse' (1974)]

9. [On death]
The anaesthetic from which none come round.
[*Collected Poems* (1988), 'Aubade']

10. [Referring to modern novels]
Far too many relied on the classic formula of a beginning, a muddle, and an end.
[*New Fiction*, 1978]

11. Recognising that if you haven't got the money for something you can't have it – this is a concept that's vanished for many years.
[Interview, *The Observer*, 1979]

12. I rather think poetry has given me up, which is a great sorrow to me, but not an enormous, crushing sorrow. It's rather like going bald.
[*The Observer*, 1984, in Jeffrey Care (ed.), *Sayings of the Eighties* (1989)]

La Rochefoucauld, François, Duc de (1613–1680)
French moralist and epigrammatist

1. *On n'est jamais si malheureux qu'on croit, ni si heureux qu'on espère.*
One is never as unhappy as one thinks, or as happy as one hopes to be.
[*Sentences et Maximes de Morale* (1664), 128]

2. *Dans l'adversité de nos meilleurs amis, nous trouvons toujours quelque chose qui ne nous déplait pas.*
In the misfortunes of our closest friends, we always find something which is not displeasing to us.
[*Réflexions ou Sentences et Maximes Morales* (1665), 99]

3. *L'amour-propre est le plus grand de tous les flatteurs.*
Self-love is the greatest flatterer of all.
[*Réflexions ou Sentences et Maximes Morales* (1678), 2]

4. *Nous avons tous assez de force pour supporter les maux d'autrui.*
We are all strong enough to bear the sufferings of others.
[*Réflexions ou Sentences et Maximes Morales* (1678), 19]

5. *Il faut de plus grandes vertus pour soutenir la bonne fortune que la mauvaise.*
Greater virtues are needed to sustain good fortune than bad.
[*Réflexions ou Sentences et Maximes Morales* (1678), 25]

6. *Si nous n'avions point de défauts, nous ne prendrions pas tant de plaisir à en remarquer dans les autres.*
If we had no faults of our own, we should not take so much pleasure in noticing them in others.
[*Réflexions ou Sentences et Maximes Morales* (1678), 31]

7. *L'intérêt parle toutes sortes de langues, et joue toutes sortes de personnages, même celui de désintéressé.*
Self-interest speaks every kind of language, and plays every role, even that of disinterestedness.
[*Réflexions ou Sentences et Maximes Morales* (1678), 39]

8. *Pour s'établir dans le monde, on fait tout ce que l'on peut pour y paraître établi.*
To succeed in the world we do all we can to appear successful.
[*Réflexions ou Sentences et Maximes Morales* (1678), 56]

9. *Il n'y a guère de gens qui ne soient honteux de s'être aimés quand ils ne s'aiment plus.*
There are very few people who are not ashamed of having loved one another once they have fallen out of love.
[*Réflexions ou Sentences et Maximes Morales* (1678), 71]

10. *Si on juge de l'amour par la plupart de ses effets, il ressemble plus à la haine qu'à l'amitié.*
If love is to be judged by most of its effects, it looks more like hatred than like friendship.
[*Réflexions ou Sentences et Maximes Morales* (1678), 72]

11. *On peut trouver des femmes qui n'ont jamais eu de galanterie, mais il est rare d'en trouver qui n'en aient jamais eu qu'une.*
One can find women who have never had a love affair, but it is rare to find a woman who has only had one.
[*Réflexions ou Sentences et Maximes Morales* (1678), 73]

12. *L'amour de la justice n'est, en la plupart des hommes, que la crainte de souffrir l'injustice.*
The love of justice in most men is no more than the fear of suffering injustice.
[*Réflexions ou Sentences et Maximes Morales* (1678), 78]

13. *Le silence est le parti le plus sûr de celui qui se défie de soi-même.*
Silence is the safest policy for the man who distrusts himself.
[*Réflexions ou Sentences et Maximes Morales* (1678), 79]

14. *Il est plus honteux de se défier de ses amis que d'en être trompé.*
There is more shame in distrusting one's friends than in being deceived by them.
[*Réflexions ou Sentences et Maximes Morales* (1678), 84]

15. *Tout le monde se plaint de sa mémoire, et personne ne se plaint de son jugement.*
Everyone complains of his memory; nobody of his judgment.
[*Réflexions ou Sentences et Maximes Morales* (1678), 89]

16. *L'esprit est toujours la dupe du coeur.*
The mind is always fooled by the heart.
[*Réflexions ou Sentences et Maximes Morales* (1678), 102]

17. *On ne donne rien si libéralement que ses conseils.*
One gives nothing so generously as advice.
[*Réflexions ou Sentences et Maximes Morales* (1678), 110]

18. *Il y a de bons mariages, mais il n'y en a point de délicieux.*
There are good marriages, but no delightful ones.
[*Réflexions ou Sentences et Maximes Morales* (1678), 113]

19. *On aime mieux dire du mal de soi-même que de n'en point parler.*
One would rather speak ill of oneself than not speak of oneself at all.
[*Réflexions ou Sentences et Maximes Morales* (1678), 138]

20. *Le refus des louanges est un désir d'être loué deux fois.*
Refusal of praise reveals a desire to be praised twice over.
[*Réflexions ou Sentences et Maximes Morales* (1678), 149]

21. *La gloire des grands hommes se doit toujours mesurer aux moyens dont ils se sont servis pour l'acquérir.*
The glory of great men must always be measured by the means they have used to obtain it.
[*Réflexions ou Sentences et Maximes Morales* (1678), 157]

22. *L'hypocrisie est un hommage que le vice rend à la vertu.*
Hypocrisy is a homage that vice pays to virtue.
[*Réflexions ou Sentences et Maximes Morales* (1678), 218]

23. *Le trop grand empressement qu'on a de s'acquitter d'une obligation est une espèce d'ingratitude.*
Over-great haste to repay an obligation is a form of ingratitude.
[*Réflexions ou Sentences et Maximes Morales* (1678), 226]

24. *C'est une grande habileté que de savoir cacher son habileté.*
The height of cleverness is to be able to conceal it.
[*Réflexions ou Sentences et Maximes Morales* (1678), 245]

25. *Il n'y a guère d'homme assez habile pour connaître tout le mal qu'il fait.*
There is scarcely a single man clever enough to know all the evil he does.
[*Réflexions ou Sentences et Maximes Morales* (1678), 269]

26. *L'absence diminue les médiocres passions, et augmente les grandes, comme le vent éteint les bougies, et allume le feu.*
Absence diminishes mediocre passions and increases great ones, as the wind extinguishes candles and kindles fire.
[*Réflexions ou Sentences et Maximes Morales* (1678), 276. Cf. Bussy-Rabutin: 1]

27. *La reconnaissance de la plupart des hommes n'est qu'une secrète envie de recevoir de plus grands bienfaits.*
In most of mankind gratitude is merely a secret hope for greater favours.
[*Réflexions ou Sentences et Maximes Morales* (1678), 298]

28. *Nous n'avouons de petits défauts que pour persuader que nous n'en avons pas de grands.*
We only admit our little faults to persuade others that we have no great ones.
[*Réflexions ou Sentences et Maximes Morales* (1678), 327]

29. *L'accent du pays où l'on est né demeure dans l'esprit et dans le coeur, comme dans le langage.*
The accent of one's native country remains in the mind and the heart, as it does in one's speech.
[*Réflexions ou Sentences et Maximes Morales* (1678), 342]

30. *Nous ne trouvons guère de gens de bon sens que ceux qui sont de notre avis.*
We rarely think people have good sense unless they agree with us.
[*Réflexions ou Sentences et Maximes Morales* (1678), 347]

31. *On s'ennuie presque toujours avec les gens avec qui il n'est pas permis de s'ennuyer.*
We are almost always bored by the very people whom we are not allowed to find boring.
[*Réflexions ou Sentences et Maximes Morales* (1678), 352]

32. *On peut être plus fin qu'un autre, mais non pas plus fin que tous les autres.*
One can be more astute than another, but not more astute than all the others.
[*Réflexions ou Sentences et Maximes Morales* (1678), 394]

33. *Nous aurions souvent honte de nos plus belles actions, si le monde voyait les motifs qui les produisent.*
We would often be ashamed of our finest actions if the world could see the motives behind them.
[*Réflexions ou Sentences et Maximes Morales* (1678), 409]

34. *Rien n'empêche tant d'être naturel que l'envie de le paraître.*
Nothing prevents us from being natural so much as the desire to appear so.
[*Réflexions ou Sentences et Maximes Morales* (1678), 431]

35. *Les querelles ne dureraient pas longtemps si le tort n'était que d'un côté.*
Quarrels would not last long if the fault were on one side only.
[*Réflexions ou Sentences et Maximes Morales* (1678), 496]

La Rochefoucauld-Liancourt, Duc de (1747–1827)
French social reformer, educator and writer

1. [In reply to Louis XVI's question *'C'est une révolte?'* on hearing of the fall of the Bastille]
Non, Sire, c'est une révolution.
No, Sire, it is a revolution.
[Remark, 1789]

Laski, H.J. (1893–1950)
English political theorist, socialist and university lecturer

1. The meek do not inherit the earth unless they are prepared to fight for their meekness.
[Attr.]

Last, Nella (1890–c. 1969)
British war-time diarist

1. Who wants a woman of fifty to be sweet anyway? And besides, I suit *me* a *lot* better.
[*Nella Last's War* (1981)]

Latimer, Bishop Hugh (c. 1485–1555)
English Protestant bishop and preacher; burnt for heresy

1. *Gutta cavat lapidem, non vi sed saepe cadendo.*
The drop of rain maketh a hole in the stone, not by violence, but by oft falling.
[Sermon preached before Edward VI, 1549]

2. [Said shortly before being put to death]
Be of good comfort, Master Ridley, and play the man. We shall this day light such a candle by God's grace in England, as (I trust) shall never be put out.
[In Foxe, *Actes and Monuments* (1562–1563)]

Lauder, Sir Harry (Hugh MacLennan) (1870–1950)
Scottish comedian, entertainer and memoirist

1. Roamin' in the gloamin'
By the bonny banks of Clyde.
[Song, 1911]

2. Just a wee deoch-an-duoris
Before we gang awa'...
If y' can say
It's a braw brecht moonlecht necht,
Yer a' recht, that's a'.
[Song, 1912]

3. O! it's nice to get up in the mornin',
But it's nicer to stay in bed.
[Song, 1913]

Laurence, Margaret (1926–1987)
Canadian novelist and short-story writer

1. If, as you grow older, you feel you are also growing stupider, do not worry. This is normal, and usually occurs around the time when your children, now grown, are discovering the opposite – they now see that you aren't nearly as stupid as they had believed when they were young teenagers. Take heart from that.
[Address at Trent University, 1983, quoted in *The Globe and Mail*, 1989]

2. Women have no surnames of their own. Their names are literally sirnames. Women only have one name that is ours, our first or given name.
[*Dance on the Earth: A Memoir* (1989), ed. by her daughter, J. Laurence]

Laurence, William L. (1888–1977)
American scientific journalist, born in Lithuania

1. [Referring to the explosion of the first atomic bomb, over Hiroshima, 6 August 1945]
At first it was a giant column that soon took the shape of a supramundane mushroom.
[*The New York Times*, 1945]

Laver, James (1899–1975)
English art, costume and design historian

1. Man in every age has created woman in the image of his own desire.
[In Angela Neustater, *Hyenas in Petticoats: a Look at 20 Years of Feminism* (1989)]

Lavin, Mary (1912–)
Irish novelist and short-story writer

1. What did they know about memory? What was it but another name for dry love and barren longing?
[*In the Middle of the Fields* (1967)]

Law, Bonar (1858–1923)
Canadian-born British statesman; Conservative Prime Minister 1922–23

1. I said [in 1911] that if ever war arose between Great Britain and Germany it would not be due to inevitable causes, for I did not believe in inevitable war. I said it would be due to human folly.
[Speech, House of Commons, 1914]

2. I must follow them; I am their leader.
[In E.T. Raymond, *Mr Balfour*, 15. Cf. Ledru-Rollin: 1]

3. If I am a great man, then a good many of the great men of history are frauds.
[Attr.]

4. [Referring to Mussolini]
Look into that man's eyes. You will hear more of him later.
[Attr.]

Lawless, Emily (1845–1913)
Irish novelist and poet

1. We are all children of our environment – the good no less than the bad, – products of that particular group of habits, customs, traditions, ways of looking at things, standards of right and wrong, which chance has presented to our still growing and expanding consciousness.
[*Hurrish* (1886)]

Lawrence, D.H. (1885–1930)
English novelist, poet, short-story writer, critic, essayist and traveller

1. Be a good animal, true to your animal instincts.
[*The White Peacock* (1911), 2]

2. Therefore the dusky, golden softness of this man's sensuous flame of life, that flowed off his flesh like the flame from a candle, not baffled and gripped into incandescence by thought and spirit as her life was, seemed to her something wonderful, beyond her.
[*Sons and Lovers* (1913), 1]

3. There is no comradeship between men and women, none whatsoever, but rather a condition of battle, reserve, hostility.
[*Twilight in Italy* (1916)]

4. It is the hideous rawness of the world of men, the horrible desolating harshness of the advance of the industrial world upon the world of nature, that is so painful ... If only we

could learn to take thought for the whole world instead of for merely tiny bits of it.
[*Twilight in Italy* (1916)]

5. One realizes with horror, that the race of men is almost extinct in Europe. Only Christ-like heroes and woman-worshipping Don Juans, and rabid equality-mongrels.
[*Sea and Sardinia* (1921), 3]

6. Morality which is based on ideas, or on an ideal, is an unmitigated evil.
[*Fantasia of the Unconscious* (1922), 7]

7. And all lying mysteriously within the Australian underdark, that peculiar, lost weary aloofness of Australia. There was the vast town of Sydney. And it didn't seem to be real, it seemed to be sprinkled on the surface of a darkness into which it never penetrated.
[*Kangaroo* (1923), 1]

8. We have all lost the war. All Europe.
[*The Ladybird* (1923), 'The Ladybird']

9. Never trust the artist. Trust the tale. The proper function of a critic is to save the tale from the artist who created it.
[*Studies in Classic American Literature* (1923), 'The Spirit of Place']

10. It is as if the life had retreated eastwards. As if the Germanic life were slowly ebbing away from contact with western Europe, ebbing to the deserts of the east.
[*A Letter from Germany* (1924)]

11. The modern pantheist not only sees the god in everything, he takes photographs of it.
[*St Mawr* (1925)]

12. It was one of those places where the spirit of aboriginal England still lingers, the old savage England, whose last blood flows still in a few Englishmen, Welshmen, Cornishmen.
[*St Mawr* (1925)]

13. Ideal mankind would abolish death, multiply itself million upon million, rear up city upon city, save every parasite alive, until the accumulation of mere existence is swollen to a horror.
[*St Mawr* (1925)]

14. And suddenly she craved again for the more absolute silence of America. English stillness was so soft, like an inaudible murmur of voices, of presences.
[*St Mawr* (1925)]

15. You may have my husband, but not my horse. My husband won't need emasculating, and my horse I won't have you meddle with. I'll preserve one last male thing in the museum of this world, if I can.
[*St Mawr* (1925)]

16. There's nothing so artificial as sinning nowadays. I suppose it once was real.
[*St Mawr* (1925)]

17. 'It is sex,' she said to herself. 'How wonderful sex can be, when men keep it powerful and sacred, and it fills the world! Like sunshine through and through one!...'
[*The Plumed Serpent* (1926), 27]

18. It's all this cold-hearted fucking that is death and idiocy.
[*Lady Chatterley's Lover* (1928), 14]

19. But tha mun dress thysen, an' go back to thy stately homes of England, how beautiful they stand. Time's up! Time's up for Sir John, an' for little Lady Jane! Put thy shimmy on, Lady Chatterley!
[*Lady Chatterley's Lover* (1928), 15. Cf. Hemans: 3]

20. She is dear to me in the middle of my being. But the gold and flowing serpent is coiling up again, to sleep at the root of my tree.
[*The Man Who Died* (1931), 2]

21. To the Puritan all things are impure, as somebody says.
[*Etruscan Places* (1932), 'Cerveteri']

22. Pornography is the attempt to insult sex, to do dirt on it.
[*Phoenix* (1936), 'Pornography and Obscenity']

23. Away with all ideals. Let each individual act spontaneously from the for ever incalculable prompting of the creative wellhead within him. There is no universal law.
[*Phoenix* (1936), Preface to 'All Things are Possible' by Leo Shostov]

24. It is no good casting out devils. They belong to us, we must accept them and be at peace with them.
[*Phoenix* (1936), 'The Reality of Peace']

25. The novel is the one bright book of life.
[*Phoenix* (1936), 'Why the Novel Matters']

26. I am a man, and alive ... For this reason I am a novelist. And being a novelist, I consider myself superior to the saint, the scientist, the philosopher, and the poet, who are all great masters of different bits of man alive, but never get the whole hog.
[*Phoenix* (1936), 'Why the Novel Matters']

27. No absolute is going to make the lion lie down with the lamb unless the lamb is inside.
[*The Later D.H. Lawrence* (1951)]

28. Not I, not I, but the wind that blows through me!
[*Look! We Have Come Through!* (1917), 'Song of a man who has come through']

29. So now it is vain for the singer to burst into clamour
With the great black piano appassionato. The glamour
Of childish days is upon me, my manhood is cast
Down in the flood of remembrance, I weep like a child for the past.
[*New Poems* (1918), 'Piano']

30. A snake came to my water-trough
On a hot, hot day, and I in pyjamas for the heat,
To drink there...

31. And so, I missed my chance with one of the lords
Of life.
And I have something to expiate;
A pettiness.
[*Birds, Beasts and Flowers* (1923), 'Snake']

32. How beastly the bourgeois is
especially the male of the species.
[*Pansies* (1929), 'How Beastly the Bourgeois Is']

33. Money is our madness, our vast collective madness.
[*Pansies* (1929), 'Money-Madness']

34. Loud peace propaganda makes war seem imminent.
[*Pansies* (1929), 'Peace and War']

35. Water is H2O, hydrogen two parts, oxygen one,
but there is also a third thing, that makes it water
and nobody knows what it is.
[*Pansies* (1929), 'The Third Thing']

36. When I read Shakespeare I am struck with wonder
That such trivial people should muse and thunder
In such lovely language.
[*Pansies* (1929), 'When I Read Shakespeare']

37. Now it is autumn and the falling fruit
and the long journey towards oblivion...
Have you built your ship of death, O have you?

O build your ship of death, for you will need it.
[*Last Poems* (1932), 'The Ship of Death']

38. I like to write when I feel spiteful: it's like having a good sneeze.
[Letter to Lady Cynthia Asquith, 1913]

39. I am only half there when I am ill, and so there is only half a man to suffer. To suffer in one's whole self is so great a violation, that it is not to be endured.
[Letter to Catherine Carswell, 1916]

40. The dead don't die. They look on and help.
[Letter to J. Middleton Murry, 1923]

41. I'm not sure if a mental relation with a woman doesn't make it impossible to love her. To know the *mind* of a woman is to end in hating her. Love means the pre-cognitive flow ... it is the honest state before the apple.
[Letter to Dr Trigant Burrow, 1927]

42. [On his relationship with his mother]
We have loved each other, almost with a husband and wife love, as well as filial and maternal ... It has been rather terrible and has made me, in some respects, abnormal.
[Attr.]

Lawrence, James (1781–1813)
American naval officer

1. Don't give up the ship.
[Last words, during naval battle]

Lawrence, T.E. (1888–1935)
British soldier, Arabist (Lawrence of Arabia), archaeologist, intelligence officer, translator and prose writer

1. I loved you, so I drew these tides of men into my hands
and wrote my will across the sky in stars
To earn you Freedom, the seven pillared worthy house,
that your eyes might be shining for me
When we came.
[*The Seven Pillars of Wisdom* (1926), Epigraph]

2. All men dream: but not equally. Those who dream by night in the dusty recesses of their minds wake in the day to find that it was vanity; but the dreamers of the day are dangerous men, for they may act their dream with open eyes, to make it possible.
[*The Seven Pillars of Wisdom* (1926), 1]

Lawson, Henry (Hertzberg) (1867–1922)
Australian short-story writer and poet

1. And the sun sank on the grand Australian bush – the nurse and tutor of eccentric minds, the home of the weird, and of much that is different from things in other lands.
['Rats' (1893)]

2. The Queen has lived for seventy years, for seventy years and three;
And few have lived a flatter life, more useless life than she;
She never said a clever thing or wrote a clever line,
She never did a noble deed, in coming times to shine;
And yet we read, and still we read, in every magazine,
The praises of that woman whom the English call 'the Queen',
Whom the English call 'the Queen',
Whom the English call 'the Queen'–
That dull and brainless woman whom the English call 'the Queen'.
['The English Queen: A Birthday Ode' (1889)]

3. Our Andy's gone with cattle now–
Our hearts are out of order–
With drought he's gone to battle now
Across the Queensland border.

Oh, who shall cheek the squatter now
When he comes round us snarling?
His tongue is growing hotter now
Since Andy crossed the Darling.
[*Poetical Works* (1918), 'Andy's Gone with Cattle']

4. Droving songs are very pretty, but they call for little thanks
From the people of a country in possession of the Banks.
[*Collected Poems* (1918), 'The City Bushman']

5. Tall and freckled and sandy,
Face of a country lout;
This was the picture of Andy,
Middleton's Rouseabout.

Type of a coming nation,
In the land of cattle and sheep,
Worked on Middleton's station,
'Pound a week and his keep'.

On Middleton's wide dominions
Plied the stockwhip and shears;
Hadn't any opinion,
Hadn't any 'idears'.
['Middleton's Rouseabout']

6. Wrap me up in my stockwhip and blanket,
And bury me deep down below,
Where this piffle and sham won't disgust me,
In the land where the coolibahs grow;
For I've stayed with some well-to-do people,
And I've dined with some middle-class folk,
And I've sorrowed by clock-tower and steeple
Till my heart for the Commonwealth's broke.
['The Old Stockman's Lament']

7. Beer makes you feel as you ought to feel without beer.
[In David Low, *Low's Autobiography*]

Lazarus, Emma (1849–1887)
American poet and translator; champion of Jews

1. Give me your tired, your poor,
Your huddled masses yearning to breathe free.
['The New Colossus' (1883); verse inscribed on the Statue of Liberty]

Leach, Sir Edmund (1910–1989)
English social anthropologist

1. Far from being the basis of the good society, the family, with its narrow privacy and tawdry secrets, is the source of all our discontents.
[BBC Reith Lecture, 1967; reprinted in *The Listener*]

Leacock, Stephen Butler (1869–1944)
English-born Canadian humorist, essayist, biographer and economist

1. Get your room full of good air, then shut up the windows and keep it. It will keep for years. Anyway, don't keep using your lungs all the time. Let them rest.
[*Literary Lapses* (1910), 'How to live to be 200']

2. The landlady of a boarding-house is a parallelogram – that is, an oblong angular figure, which cannot be described, but which is equal to anything.
[*Literary Lapses* (1910), 'Boarding-House Geometry']

3. It takes a good deal of physical courage to ride a horse. This,

however, I have. I get it at about forty cents a flask, and take it as required.
[*Literary Lapses* (1910), 'Reflections on Riding']

4. Lord Ronald said nothing; he flung himself from the room, flung himself upon his horse and rode madly off in all directions.
[*Nonsense Novels* (1911), 'Gertrude the Governess']

5. The parent who could see his boy as he really is, would shake his head and say: 'Willie is no good: I'll sell him.'
[*Essays and Literary Studies* (1916), 'The Lot of a Schoolmaster']

6. Golf may be played on Sunday, not being a game within the view of the law, but being a form of moral effort.
[*Over the Footlights* (1923), 'Why I refuse to play Golf']

7. The general idea, of course, in any first-class laundry is to see that no shirt or collar ever comes back twice.
[*Winnowed Wisdom* (1926), 6]

8. Advertising may be described as the science of arresting the human intelligence long enough to get money from it.
[In Prochow, *The Public Speaker's Treasure Chest*]

9. A half truth in argument, like a half brick, carries better.
[In Flesch, *The Book of Unusual Quotations*]

Lear, Edward (1812–1888)

English nonsense poet, watercolourist, travel writer and ornithologist

1. There was an Old Man with a beard,
Who said, 'It is just as I feared!–
Two Owls and a Hen,
Four Larks and a Wren,
Have all built their nests in my beard!'
[*A Book of Nonsense* (1846)]

2. There was an old man who said, 'Hush!
I perceive a young bird in this bush!'
When they said, 'Is it small?'
He replied, 'Not at all!
It is four times as big as the bush!'
[*A Book of Nonsense* (1846)]

3. 'How pleasant to know Mr Lear!'
Who has written such volumes of stuff!
Some think him ill-tempered and queer,
But a few think him pleasant enough...

4. He has ears, and two eyes, and ten fingers,
Leastways if you reckon two thumbs;
Long ago he was one of the singers,
But now he is one of the dumbs...

5. He drinks a good deal of Marsala
But never gets tipsy at all...

6. He has many friends, laymen and clerical.
Old Foss is the name of his cat:
His body is perfectly spherical,
He weareth a runcible hat.
[*Nonsense Songs* (1871), Preface]

7. On the coast of Coromandel
Where the early pumpkins blow,
In the middle of the wood,
Lived the Yonghy-Bonghy-Bó.
Two old chairs, and half a candle;–
One old jug without a handle,–
These were all his worldly goods...

8. 'Gaze upon the rolling deep
(Fish is plentiful and cheap)
As the sea my love is deep!'
Said the Yonghy-Bonghy-Bó.
Lady Jingly answered sadly,
And her tears began to flow–
'Your proposal comes too late.'
[*Nonsense Songs* (1871), 'The Courtship of the Yonghy-Bonghy-Bó']

9. When awful darkness and silence reign
Over the great Gromboolian plain,
Through the long, long wintry nights.
When the angry breakers roar
As they beat on the rocky shore;–
When Storm-clouds brood on the towering heights
Of the Hills of the Chankly Bore...

10. And those who watch at that midnight hour
From Hall or Terrace or lofty Tower,
Cry as the wild light passes along,–
'The Dong! – the Dong!
The wandering dong through the forest goes!
The Dong! – the Dong!
The Dong with the Luminous Nose!'
[*Nonsense Songs* (1871), 'The Dong with the Luminous Nose']

11. And who so happy, – O who,
As the Duck and the Kangaroo?
[*Nonsense Songs* (1871), 'The Duck and the Kangaroo']

12. O My agéd Uncle Arly!
Sitting on a heap of Barley
Thro' the silent hours of the night,–
Close beside a leafy thicket:–
On his nose there was a Cricket,–
In his hat a Railway-Ticket;–
(But his shoes were far too tight.)
[*Nonsense Songs* (1871), 'Incidents in the Life of my Uncle Arly']

13. Far and few, far and few,
Are the lands where the Jumblies live;
Their heads are green, and their hands are blue,
And they went to sea in a Sieve...

14. They went to sea in a sieve, they did
In a sieve they went to sea...

15. In spite of all their friends could say
One winter's morn, on a stormy day,
In a Sieve they went to sea!...

16. They called aloud 'Our Sieve ain't big,
But we don't care a button! We don't care a fig!'...

17. And they brought an Owl, and a useful Cart,
And a pound of Rice, and a Cranberry Tart,
And a hive of silvery Bees.
And they brought a Pig, and some green Jack-daws,
And a lovely Monkey with lollipop paws,
And forty bottles of Ring-Bo-Ree,
And no end of Stilton Cheese.
[*Nonsense Songs* (1871), 'The Jumblies']

18. The Owl and the Pussy-Cat went to sea
In a beautiful pea-green boat.
They took some honey, and plenty of money,
Wrapped up in a five-pound note.
The Owl looked up to the Stars above
And sang to a small guitar,
'Oh lovely Pussy! – O Pussy, my love,
What a beautiful Pussy you are.'...

19. Pussy said to the Owl, 'You elegant fowl!
How charmingly sweet you sing!
O let us be married! too long we have tarried:
But what shall we do for a ring?'

They sailed away for a year and a day,
To the land where the Bong-tree grows,
And there in a wood a Piggy-wig stood
With a ring at the end of his nose...

20. 'Dear Pig, are you willing to sell for one shilling
Your ring?' Said the Piggy, 'I will.'...

21. They dined on mince, and slices of quince,
Which they ate with a runcible spoon;
And hand in hand, on the edge of the sand,
They danced by the light of the moon.
[*Nonsense Songs* (1871), 'The Owl and the Pussy-Cat']

22. Ploffskin, Pluffskin, Pelican jee!
We think no birds so happy as we!
Plumpskin, Plashkin, Pelican jill!
We think so then, and we thought so still!
[*Nonsense Songs* (1871), 'The Pelican Chorus']

23. The Pobble who has no toes
Had once as many as we;
When they said, 'Some day you may lose them all';–
He replied, – 'Fish fiddle de-dee!'
His Aunt Jobiska made him drink
Lavender water tinged with pink,
For she said, 'The world in general knows
There's nothing so good for a Pobble's toes!'...

24. For his Aunt Jobiska said, 'No harm
Can come to his toes if his nose is warm,
And it's perfectly known that a Pobble's toes
Are safe, provided he minds his nose.'...

25. When boats or ships came near him
He tinkledy-binkledy-winkled a bell...

26. He has gone to fish, for his Aunt Jobiska's
Runcible Cat with crimson whiskers!...

27. And she made him a feast at his earnest wish
Of eggs and buttercups fried with fish;
And she said, 'It's a fact the whole world knows,
That Pobbles are happier without their toes.'
[*Nonsense Songs* (1871), 'The Pobble Who Has No Toes']

28. 'But the longer I live on this Crumpetty Tree
The plainer than ever it seems to me
That very few people come this way
And that life on the whole is far from gay!'
Said the Quangle-Wangle Quee.
[*Nonsense Songs* (1871), 'The Quangle-Wangle's Hat']

29. Two old Bachelors were living in one house;
One caught a Muffin, the other caught a Mouse.
[*Nonsense Songs* (1871), 'The Two Old Bachelors']

30. There was an old person of Slough,
Who danced at the end of a bough;
But they said, 'If you sneeze,
You might damage the trees,
You imprudent old person of Slough.'
[*One Hundred Nonsense Pictures and Rhymes* (1872)]

31. There was an old person of Ware,
Who rode on the back of a bear:
When they asked, – 'Does it trot?'
He said, 'Certainly not!
He's a Moppsikon Floppsikon bear.'
[*One Hundred Nonsense Pictures and Rhymes* (1872)]

32. There was an old person of Dean,
Who dined on one pea and one bean;
For he said, 'More than that,
Would make me too fat,'
That cautious old person of Dean.
[*One Hundred Nonsense Pictures and Rhymes* (1872)]

33. Who, or why, or which, or what,
Is the Akond of Swat?...

34. Does he study the wants of his own dominion?
Or doesn't he care for public opinion a JOT?
[*Nonsense Songs* (1888 edition), 'The Akond of Swat']

35. Serve up in a clean dish, and throw the whole out of the window as fast as possible.
['To make an Amblongus Pie']

Leary, Timothy (1920–)
American psychologist, author and actor

1. Turn on, tune in, and drop out.
[*The Politics of Ecstasy* (1968)]

Lease, Mary Elizabeth (1853–1933)
American populist orator and writer on reform

1. Kansas had better stop raising corn and begin raising hell.
[Attr.]

Leavis, F.R. (1895–1978)
English literary critic, lecturer and essayist

1. Literary criticism provides the test for life and concreteness; where it degenerates, the instruments of thought degenerate too, and thinking, released from the testing and energizing contact with the full living consciousness, is debilitated, and betrayed to the academic, the abstract and the verbal.
[*Towards Standards in Criticism* (1930)]

2. The Sitwells belong to the history of publicity rather than of poetry.
[*New Bearings in English Poetry* (1932), 2]

3. [Of Rupert Brooke]
His verse exhibits ... something that is rather like Keats' vulgarity with a Public School accent.
[*New Bearings in English Poetry* (1932), 2]

Lebowitz, Fran (1950–)
American writer

1. Never judge a book by its cover.
[*Metropolitan Life* (1978)]

2. Food is an important part of a balanced diet.
[*Metropolitan Life* (1978), 'Food for Thought and Vice Versa']

Le Carré, John (1931–)
English novelist, known for his spy thrillers

1. The Spy Who Came In From the Cold.
[Title of novel, 1963]

Le Corbusier (1887–1965)
Swiss-born French architect and town planner, noted for his functionalist approach

1. *Une maison est une machine-à-habiter.*
A house is a machine for living in.
[*Vers une architecture* (1923). Cf. McGregor: 1]

Ledda, Gavino (1938–)
Italian writer

1. *Malauguratamente risultò che c'era un cucchiaio in meno delle bocche. Uno restò escluso.*
Unfortunately it resulted in there being one spoon less than the number of mouths. One man went without.
[*Padre – Padrone* (*Father and Master*, 1975)]

Ledru-Rollin, Alexandre Auguste (1807–1874)
French lawyer, politician and presidential candidate

1. [Trying to force his way through a mob during the 1848 revolution, of which he was one of the chief instigators]
Eh! je suis leur chef, il fallait bien les suivre.
Ah well! I am their leader, I really should be following them!
[In E. de Mirecourt, *Histoire Contemporaine* (1857). Cf. Law: 2]

Lee, Harper (1926–)
American novelist

1. Shoot all the bluejays you want, if you can hit 'em, but remember it's a sin to kill a mockingbird.
[*To Kill a Mockingbird* (1960), 10]

Lee, Henry (1756–1818)
American soldier, statesman and memoirist; father of Robert E. Lee

1. [Of George Washington]
A citizen, first in war, first in peace, and first in the hearts of his countrymen.
[Resolution adopted by Congress on Washington's death, 1799]

Lee, John Alexander (1891–1982)
New Zealand novelist

1. [On World War I]
The New Zealanders were a rough mob. We were going out at the line and marching past a Tommy camp. An officer came out to salute us. He was obviously a gallant officer. He had medals including a V.C. Then the silly bugger put a monocle in his eye to salute us. The boys yelled out: 'Yah, you silly bugger, why don't you get another one and stick it up your arse and turn yourself into a periscope.'
[Interview with A.J. Burns, 1978]

Lee, Nathaniel (c. 1653–1692)
English tragic dramatist

1. 'Tis beauty calls and glory leads the way.
[*The Rival Queens* (1677), I]

2. When the sun sets, shadows, that showed at noon
But small, appear most long and terrible.
[*Oedipus* (1679), IV.i]

3. Man, false man, smiling, destructive man.
[*Theodosius* (1680), III.ii]

4. [Objecting to being confined in Bedlam]
They called me mad, and I called them mad, and damn them, they outvoted me.
[In Roy Porter, *A Social History of Madness*]

Lee, Robert E. (1807–1870)
American Confederate General; Commander-in-Chief in the Civil War

1. It is well that war is so terrible – we would grow too fond of it.
[Remark made after the Battle of Fredericksburg, 1862]

2. Duty then is the sublimest word in our language. Do your duty in all things. You cannot do more. You should never wish to do less.
[Inscription in the Hall of Fame. Cf. Nelson: 14]

3. [Refusing to write his memoirs]
I should be trading on the blood of my men.
[In M. Ringo, *Nobody Said It Better*]

Lefèvre, Théo (1914–1973)
Belgian Prime Minister

1. In Western Europe there are now only small countries – those that know it and those that don't know it yet.
[*The Observer*, 'Sayings of the Week', 1963]

Le Gallienne, Richard (1866–1947)
English poet, writer, critic

1. [Of Oscar Wilde]
Paradox with him was only Truth standing on its head to attract attention.
[*The Romantic 90s*]

Lehman, Ernest (1920–)
American screenwriter

1. Sweet Smell of Success.
[Title of novel and film, 1957]

Lehmann, Rosamond (1901–1990)
English novelist

1. The trouble with Ian [Fleming] is that he gets off with women because he can't get on with them.
[Borrowing a line from Elizabeth Bowen, quoted in J. Pearson, *The Life of Ian Fleming* (1966)]

Lehrer, Tom (1928–)
American humorist, songwriter and lecturer

1. Life is like a sewer. What you get out of it depends on what you put in.
[Record album, *An Evening Wasted with Tom Lehrer* (1953)]

2. He was into animal husbandry – until they caught him at it.
[Record album, *An Evening Wasted with Tom Lehrer* (1953)]

3. It is sobering to consider that when Mozart was my age he had already been dead for a year.
[In N. Shapiro, *An Encyclopedia of Quotations about Music*]

Leigh, Fred W. (d. 1924)
British songwriter

1. There was I, waiting at the church,
Waiting at the church, waiting at the church
When I found he'd left me in the lurch,
Lor', how it did upset me!...
Can't get away to marry you today–
My wife won't let me.
['Waiting at the Church', 1906]

Leith, Prue (1940–)
English cookery writer and businesswoman

1. Cuisine is when things taste like what they are.
[Armstrong Memorial Lecture to the Royal Society of Arts, 1987, 'The Fine Art of Food']

Lemay, Curtis E. (1906–1990)

1. [Speaking of the North Vietnamese]
My solution to the problem would be to tell [them] ... they've got to draw in their horns or we're going to bomb them into the Stone Age.
[*Mission with Lemay* (1965)]

Le Mesurier, John (1912–1983)
English stage and television actor

1. John Le Mesurier wishes it to be known that he conked out on November 15th. He sadly misses family and friends.
[His death announcement in the personal column, *The Times*, 1983]

2. It's all been rather lovely.
[Last words, quoted in *The Times*, 1983]

Lenclos, Ninon de (1620–1705)
French courtesan

1. *La vieillesse est l'enfer des femmes.*
Old age is woman's hell.
[Attr.]

Lenin, V.I. (1870–1924)
Russian revolutionary, Marxist theoretician and Bolshevik leader; first Soviet Premier

1. One step forward, two steps back ... It happens in the lives of individuals, and it happens in the history of nations and in the development of parties.
[*One Step Forward, Two Steps Back* (1904)]

2. The substitution of the proletarian for the bourgeois state is impossible without a violent revolution.
[*The State and Revolution* (1917), 1]

3. Under capitalism we have a state in the proper sense of the word, that is, a special machine for the suppression of one class by another.
[*The State and Revolution* (1917), 5]

4. So long as the state exists there is no freedom. When there is freedom there will be no state.
[*The State and Revolution* (1917), 5]

5. Under socialism *all* will govern in turn and will soon become accustomed to no one governing.
[*The State and Revolution* (1917), 6]

6. [On Australia]
What sort of peculiar capitalist country is this, in which the workers' representatives predominate in the *Upper* House and, till recently, did so in the Lower House as well, and yet the capitalist system is in no danger?
[*Collected Works* (1963), 19]

7. The Australian Labour Party does not even call itself a socialist party. Actually it is a liberal-bourgeois party, while the so-called Liberals in Australia are really Conservatives.
[*Collected Works* (1963), 19]

8. We shall now proceed to construct the socialist order.
[Speech, 1917]

9. Communism is Soviet power plus the electrification of the whole country.
[Report at the eighth All-Russia Congress of Soviets on the work of the Council of People's Commissars, 1920]

10. [Of Bernard Shaw]
A good man fallen among Fabians.
[In Arthur Ransome, *Six Weeks in Russia in 1919* (1919)]

11. [Remark made to Gorky, while listening to Beethoven]
I can't listen to music too often. It affects your nerves; you want to say nice, stupid things and stroke the heads of people who could create such beauty while living in this vile hell. And now you must not stroke anyone's head – you might get your hand bitten off. You have to hit them on the head, without any mercy.
[In Lev Trotsky, trans. M. Eastman, *The History of the Russian Revolution* (1933), IV, 7]

12. [Speech in St Petersburg, 1917]
Any day now the whole of European capitalism may crash. The Russian revolution accomplished by you has prepared the way and opened a new epoch ... we shall now proceed to construct the socialist order.
[In Lev Trotsky, trans. M. Eastman, *The History of the Russian Revolution* (1933), IV, 7]

13. It is true that liberty is precious – so precious that it must be rationed.
[In Sidney and Beatrice Webb, *Soviet Communism* (1936)]

14. Any cook should be able to run the country.
[In Alexander Solzhenitzyn, *The First Circle* (1968)]

15. [Commenting on Stalin's election as General Secretary of the party, 1922]
This cook will give us nothing but spicy dishes.
[Attr.]

Lennon, John (1940–1980)
English pop singer-songwriter and guitarist, member of the Beatles 1962–70

1. She loves you, yeh, yeh, yeh,
And with a love like that you know you should be glad.
['She Loves You', song, 1963, with Paul McCartney]

2. If there's anything that you want,
If there's anything I can do,
Just call on me,
And I'll send it along with love from me to you.
['From Me to You', song, 1963, with Paul McCartney]

3. For I don't care too much for money,
For money can't buy me love.
['Can't Buy Me Love', song, 1964, with Paul McCartney]

4. It's been a hard day's night.
['A Hard Day's Night', song, 1964, with Paul McCartney]

5. Waits at the window, wearing the face that she keeps in a jar by the door
Who is it for? All the lonely people, where do they all come from?
All the lonely people, where do they all belong?
['Eleanor Rigby', song, 1966, with Paul McCartney]

6. I've got to admit it's getting better.
It's a little better all the time.
['Getting Better', song, 1967, with Paul McCartney]

7. Picture yourself in a boat on a river with tangerine trees and marmalade skies.
Somebody calls you, you answer quite slowly a girl with kaleidoscope eyes.
['Lucy in the Sky with Diamonds', song, 1967, with Paul McCartney]

8. She's leaving home after living alone for so many years.
['She's Leaving Home', song, 1967, with Paul McCartney]

9. I get by with a little help from my friends.
['With a Little Help from My Friends', song, 1967, with Paul McCartney]

10. Life is what happens to you when you're busy making other plans.
['Beautiful Boy', song, 1980]

11. Those in the cheaper seats clap. The rest of you rattle your jewellery.
[Remark, Royal Variety Performance, 15 November 1963]

12. We're more popular than Jesus Christ now. I don't know which will go first. Rock and roll or Christianity.
[*The Beatles Illustrated Lyrics*]

Lenthall, William (1591–1662)
English lawyer, politician and speaker of the Long Parliament

1. May it please Your Majesty, I have neither eye to see nor tongue to speak in this place but as this House is pleased to direct me, whose servant I am.
[Reply as Speaker of House of Commons to Charles I, 1642, when asked whether he had seen the five MPs whose arrest Charles had ordered]

Leo X (Giovanni de' Medici) (1475–1521)
Pope from 1513; patron of the Renaissance arts

1. Since God has given us the papacy, let us enjoy it.
[In T. Craven, *Men of Art*]

Léon, Fray Luis de (Luis Ponce de Léon) (c. 1527–1591)
Spanish Augustinian monk, translator and lyric poet

1. [Resuming a lecture after five years' imprisonment]
Dicebamus hesterno die.
As we were saying the other day.
[Attr.]

Leonard, Elmore (1925–)
American novelist and screenwriter

1. If porpoises were really so smart ... how come they put up with all this shit?
[*Gold Coast* (1983)]

2. Fuckin' endings, man, they weren't as easy as they looked.
[*Get Shorty* (1990)]

Leonard, Hugh (1926–)
Irish stage and screen dramatist

1. We do not squabble, fight or have rows. We collect grudges. We're in an arms race, storing up warheads for the domestic Armageddon.
[*Time Was* (1976)]

2. *Drumm*: I asked him if he had the results of the x-rays. He took me into his surgery ... He gave me one of those looks of his, redolent of the cemetery, and said that I should buy day-returns from now on instead of season tickets.
[*A Life* (1986)]

3. The problem with Ireland is that it's a country full of genius, but with absolutely no talent.
[Interview in *The Times*, 1977]

Leonardo da Vinci (1452–1519)
Italian painter, sculptor, architect, engineer, inventor, scientist and musician; outstanding Renaissance figure

1. The poet ranks far below the painter in the representation of visible things, and far below the musician in that of invisible things.
[*Selections from the Notebooks of Leonardo da Vinci* (1952 edition)]

2. While I thought that I was learning how to live, I have been learning how to die.
[*Selections from the Notebooks of Leonardo da Vinci* (1952 edition)]

3. Every man at three years old is half his height.
[*Selections from the Notebooks of Leonardo da Vinci* (1952 edition)]

Leoncavallo, Ruggiero (1858–1919)
Italian opera composer

1. *La commedia è finita.*
The comedy is over.
[*I Pagliacci*, last words. Cf. Rabelais: 9]

Leopold II (1835–1909)
King of Belgium from 1865, noted for his expansionist policy in Africa

1. [Instructing Prince Albert, the heir apparent, to pick up some papers from the floor]
A constitutional king must learn to stoop.
[In Betty Kelen, *The Mistress*]

Lermontov, Mikhail (1814–1841)
Russian poet and novelist, killed in a duel

1. What *is* the greatest good and evil? – two ends of an invisible chain which come closer together the further they move apart.
[*Vadim* (1833–1834)]

2. After all, death is the worst thing that can happen – and you can't escape it some time!
[*A Hero of our Time* (1840)]

Lerner, Alan Jay (1918–1986)
American lyricist and screenwriter; Academy Awards 1951, 1958, 1964

1. An Englishman's way of speaking absolutely classifies him.
[*My Fair Lady* (1956), I.i]

2. All I want is a room somewhere,
Far away from the cold night air;
With one enormous chair...
Oh, wouldn't it be loverly?
[*My Fair Lady* (1956), I.i]

3. I'd be equally as willing
For a dentist to be drilling
Than to ever let a woman in my life.
[*My Fair Lady* (1956), I.ii]

4. Oozing charm from every pore,
He oiled his way around the floor.
[*My Fair Lady* (1956), II.i]

5. I'm getting married in the morning!
Ding dong! the bells are gonna chime.
Pull out the stopper!
Let's have a whopper!
But get me to the church on time!
[*My Fair Lady* (1956), II.iii]

6. Why can't a woman be more like a man?
Men are so honest, so thoroughly square;
Eternally noble, historically fair.
[*My Fair Lady* (1956), II.iv]

7. I've grown accustomed to the trace
Of something in the air,
Accustomed to her face.
[*My Fair Lady* (1956), II.vi]

8. You write a hit the same way you write a flop.
[Attr.]

9. There is no greater fan of the opposite sex than me, and I have the bills to prove it.
[Attr.]

Lesage, Alain-René (1668–1747)
French novelist and dramatist

1. *On nous réconcilia: nous nous embrassâmes, et depuis ce temps-là nous sommes ennemis mortels.*
They made peace between us; we embraced, and since that time we have been mortal enemies.
[*Le Diable boiteux*, 3]

Lessing, Doris (1919–)
British novelist and short-story writer; born in Persia, brought up in Zimbabwe

1. [Referring specifically to South Africa]
When old settlers say 'One has to understand the country', what they mean is, 'You have to get used to our ideas about the native.' They are saying, in effect, 'Learn our ideas, or otherwise get out; we don't want you.'
[*The Grass is Singing* (1950), 1]

2. When a white man in Africa by accident looks into the eyes of a native and sees the human being (which it is his chief preoccupation to avoid), his sense of guilt, which he denies, fumes up in resentment and he brings down the whip.
[*The Grass is Singing* (1950), 8]

3. She was adolescent, and therefore bound to be unhappy; British, and therefore uneasy and defensive; in the fourth decade of the twentieth century, and therefore inescapably beset with problems of race and class; female, and obliged to repudiate the shackled women of the past.
[*Martha Quest* (1952), 1]

4. ... that is what learning is. You suddenly understand something you've understood all your life, but in a new way.
[*The Four-Gated City* (1969)]

Lessing, Gotthold Ephraim (1729–1781)
German dramatist, theatre critic, theologian and librarian

1. *Ein einziger dankbarer Gedanke gen Himmel ist das vollkommenste Gebet!*
A single grateful thought raised to heaven is the most perfect prayer.
[*Minna von Barnhelm* (1767), II]

2. *Gestern liebt' ich,*
Heute leid' ich,
Morgen sterb' ich.
Dennoch denk' ich
Heut und morgen
Gern an gestern.
Yesterday I loved, today I suffer, tomorrow I shall die. Nonetheless I still think with pleasure, today and tomorrow, of yesterday.
[*Vermischte Schriften* (*Miscellaneous Writings*, 1771), 'Lied aus dem Spanischen' ('Song taken from the Spanish')]

L'Estrange, Sir Roger (1616–1704)
English journalist, pamphleteer, licenser of the press, royalist, politician and translator

1. It is with our passions as it is with fire and water, they are good servants, but bad masters.
[Translation of *Aesop's Fables*, 38]

2. Though this may be play to you, 'tis death to us.
[Translation of *Aesop's Fables*, 398]

Levant, Oscar (1906–1972)
American pianist; wrote autobiographical works and made film appearances

1. *Romance on the High Seas* was Doris Day's first picture; that was before she became a virgin.
[*Memoirs of an Amnesiac* (1965)]

2. Strip the phony tinsel off Hollywood and you'll find the real tinsel underneath.
[In Halliwell, *Filmgoer's Book of Quotes* (1973)]

Leverhulme, Viscount (William Hesketh Lever) (1851–1925)
English soap manufacturer, philanthropist, Liberal politician and art collector

1. Half the money I spend on advertising is wasted, and the trouble is I don't know which half.
[In Ogilvy, *Confessions of an Advertising Man* (1963)]

Leverson, Ada Beddington (1862–1936)
English novelist, author of comedies of manners, and parodist of Oscar Wilde

1. [Of Oscar Wilde]
The last gentleman in Europe.
[*Letters to the Sphinx* (1930)]

Levi, Carlo (1902–1975)
Italian prose writer, author and painter

1. *E pensai con affettuosa angoscia a quel tempo immobile, e a quella nera civiltà che avevo abbandonato.*
And I thought with affectionate anguish of that motionless time, of that dark civilization that I had abandoned.
[*Cristo si è fermato a Eboli* (*Christ stopped at Eboli*, 1945)]

Levi, Primo (1919–1987)
Italian novelist, critic, poet and chemist; survivor of Auschwitz

1. The ascent of the privileged, not only in the Lager but in all human coexistence, is an anguishing but unfailing phenomenon: only in Utopias are they absent. It is the duty of righteous men to make war on all undeserved privilege, but one must not forget that this is a war without end.
[*The Drowned and the Saved* (1988), 2, 'The Grey Zone']

2. [Of the Nazi concentration camps]
The worst survived – that is, the fittest; the best all died.
[*The Drowned and the Saved* (1988), 3, 'Shame']

Lévi-Strauss, Claude (1908–)
French structuralist and anthropologist

1. *La langue est une raison humaine qui a ses raisons, et que l'homme ne connaît pas.*
Language is a kind of human reason, which has its own internal logic of which man knows nothing.
[*La Pensée Sauvage* (*The Savage Mind*, 1962). Cf. Pascal: 11]

2. *Le savant n'est pas l'homme qui fournit les vraies réponses; c'est celui qui pose les vraies questions.*
The wise man is not the man who gives the right answers; he is the one who asks the right questions.
[*Le Cru et le cuit* (*The Raw and the Cooked*)]

Levin, Bernard (1928–)
British journalist, author and writer for radio

1. Inflation in the Sixties was a nuisance to be endured, like varicose veins or French foreign policy.
[*The Pendulum Years* (1970), Epilogue]

2. Once, when a British Prime Minister sneezed, men half a world away would blow their noses. Now when a British Prime Minister sneezes nobody else will even say 'Bless You'.
[*The Times*, 1976]

3. Those of our own-day scientists who stir the embers of fires that went out millions of years ago may believe [their theories] but can never know. It would be better for all of us if they said as much.
[*The Times*, 1992]

Lévis, Duc de (1764–1830)
French writer and soldier

1. *Noblesse oblige.*
Nobility has its obligations.
[*Maximes et réflexions* (1812)]

2. *Gouverner, c'est choisir.*
To govern is to make choices.
[*Maximes et réflexions* (1812)]

Lewes, G.H. (1817–1878)
English biographer of Goethe, novelist, philosopher, critic and scientist; partner of George Eliot

1. Murder, like talent, seems occasionally to run in families.
[*The Physiology of Common Life* (1859), 12]

2. We must never assume that which is incapable of proof.
[*The Physiology of Common Life* (1859), 13]

Lewis, C.S. (1898–1963)
Irish-born English academic, novelist, critic, children's and popular religious writer

1. Friendship is unnecessary, like philosophy, like art ... It has no survival value; rather it is one of those things that give value to survival.
[*The Four Loves* (c. 1936), 'Friendship']

2. The coarse joke proclaims that we have here an animal which finds its own animality either objectionable or funny.
[*Miracles* (c. 1936)]

3. There is wishful thinking in Hell as well as on earth.
[*The Screwtape Letters* (1942), Preface]

4. The Future is something which everyone reaches at the rate of sixty minutes an hour, whatever he does, whoever he is.
[*The Screwtape Letters* (1942), 25]

5. She's the sort of woman who lives for others – you can tell the others by their hunted expression.
[*The Screwtape Letters* (1942), 26]

6. I am a product of long corridors, empty sunlit rooms ... attics explored in solitude, distant noises of gurgling cisterns and pipes.
[*Surprised by Joy: The Shape of an Early Life* (1955)]

7. Term, holidays, term, holidays, till we leave school, and then work, work, work till we die.
[*Surprised by Joy: The Shape of an Early Life* (1955)]

Lewis, D.B. Wyndham (1891–1969)
British writer and biographer

1. I am one of those unfortunates to whom death is less hideous than explanations.
[*Welcome to All This*]

Lewis, Sir George Cornewall (1806–1863)
English statesman; Liberal politician and writer on politics

1. Life would be tolerable but for its amusements.
[In *Dictionary of National Biography*]

Lewis, John Llewellyn (1880–1969)
American miners' leader and unionist

1. I'm not interested in classes ... Far be it from me to foster inferiority complexes among the workers by trying to make them think they belong to some special class. That has happened in Europe but it hasn't happened here yet.
[In A.M. Schlesinger Jr., *The Coming of the New Deal*]

Lewis, Norman (1914–)
English novelist and travel writer

1. Bad governments preserve nothing, and even good ones have a mediocre record in this direction, and I cannot think of any single place that I have written about that did not appear to have gone down hill – sometimes disastrously so – on a subsequent visit.
[*A View of the World* (1985 edition), Foreword]

Lewis, Sinclair (1885–1951)
American novelist, noted for his satire; Nobel prize 1930

1. In other countries, art and literature are left to a lot of shabby bums living in attics and feeding on booze and spaghetti, but in America the successful writer or picture-painter is indistinguishable from any other decent business man.
[*Babbit* (1922), 14]

2. She did her work with the thoroughness of a mind that reveres details and never quite understands them.
[*Babbit* (1922), 14]

3. It Can't Happen Here.
[Title of novel, 1935]

4. Our American professors like their literature clear, cold, pure, and very dead.
[Address to Swedish Academy, 1930]

Lewis, Wyndham (1882–1957)
American-born British painter, critic and novelist; pioneer of Vorticism

1. To give up another person's love is a mild suicide.
[*Tarr* (1918)]

2. 'Dying for an idea,' again, sounds well enough, but why not let the idea die instead of you?
[*The Art of Being Ruled* (1926), I, 1]

3. I believe that (in one form or another) castration may be the solution. And the feminization of the white European and American is already far advanced, coming in the wake of the war.
[*The Art of Being Ruled* (1926), II, 2]

4. The 'homo' is the legitimate child of the 'suffragette'.
[*The Art of Being Ruled* (1926), VIII, 4]

5. The revolutionary simpleton is everywhere.
[*Time and Western Man* (1927), I, 6]

6. The soul started at the knee-cap and ended at the navel.
[*The Apes of Gods* (1930), 12]

7. In its essence the purpose of satire – whether verse or prose – is aggression ... Satire has a great big blaring target. If successful, it blasts a great big hole in the centre.
['Note on Verse-Satire']

Ley, Robert (1890–1945)
German Nazi politician; head of Labour Front 1933

1. [Name of a leisure organisation within the German Labour Front, founded by Ley in 1933]
Kraft durch Freude.
Strength through joy.
[Attr.]

Leybourne, George (d. 1884)
English songwriter

1. He flies through the air with the greatest of ease,
This daring young man on the flying trapeze.
['The Man on the Flying Trapeze', song, 1868]

Liberace, Wladziu Valentino (1919–1987)
American pianist and showman

1. [Remark made after hostile criticism]
I cried all the way to the bank.
[*Autobiography* (1973)]

Lichtenberg, Georg Christoph (1742–1799)
German physicist, satirist and writer

1. *Sagt, ist noch ein Land ausser Deutschland, wo man die Nase eher rümpfen lernt als putzen?*
Tell me, is there a country besides Germany where you learn to turn up your nose rather than wipe it?
[*Aphorismen (Sudelbücher) (Aphorisms (Scrawlings)*, 1775–1776), E, no. 316]

2. *Zweifle an allem wenigstens einmal, und wäre es auch der Satz: zweimal zwei ist vier.*
Doubt everything at least once – even the proposition that two and two are four.
[*Vermischte Schriften (Miscellaneous Writings)*]

3. There can hardly be a stranger commodity in the world than books. Printed by people who don't understand them; sold by people who don't understand them; bound, criticized and read by people who don't understand them, and now even written by people who don't understand them.
[*A Doctrine of Scattered Occasions*]

Lie, Trygve (1896–1968)
Norwegian Labour politician; first Secretary-General of the United Nations, 1946–52

1. Now we are in a period which I can characterize as a period of cold peace.
[*The Observer*, 'Sayings of the Week', 1949]

Ligne, Charles-Joseph, Prince de (1735–1814)
Belgian-born Austrian soldier, diplomat and writer

1. [On the Congress of Vienna]
Le Congrès ne marche pas, il danse.
The Congress is going nowhere; it's just dancing.
[Attr.]

Lillie, Beatrice (Constance Sylvia Muston, Lady Peel) (1894–1989)
Canadian-born British revue singer and actress

1. I'll simply say here that I was born Beatrice Gladys Lillie at an extremely tender age because my mother needed a fourth at meals.
[*Every Other Inch a Lady* (1973), 1]

2. [Said on the *Queen Mary* in the 1940s]
When does this place get to England?
[*The New York Times*, 1967]

3. [Commenting on her childhood in Toronto]
We were located half way up the social ladder. Or half way down. It depends on which way you're looking.
[*The Toronto Star*, 1989]

Lincoln, Abraham (1809–1865)
American statesman, lawyer and abolitionist; Republican President 1861–65; assassinated

1. No man is good enough to govern another man without that other's consent.
[Speech, 1854]

2. The ballot is stronger than the bullet.
[Speech, 1856]

3. Those who deny freedom to others, deserve it not for themselves.
[Speech, 1856]

4. 'A house divided against itself cannot stand.' I believe this government cannot endure permanently, half slave and half free. I do not expect the Union to be dissolved ... but I do expect it will cease to be divided.
[Speech, 1858]

5. I leave you, hoping that the lamp of liberty will burn in your bosoms, until there shall no longer be a doubt that all men are created free and equal.
[Speech, 1858]

6. The probability that we may fail in the struggle ought not to deter us from the support of a cause we believe to be just.
[Speech, 1859]

7. What is conservatism? Is it not adherence to the old and tried, against the new and untried?
[Speech, 1860]

8. Let us have faith that right makes might; and in that faith let us to the end, dare to do our duty as we understand it.
[Speech, 1860]

9. This country, with its institutions, belongs to the people who inhabit it. Whenever they shall grow weary of the existing government, they can exercise their constitutional right of amending it, or their revolutionary right to dismember or overthrow it.
[First Inaugural Address, 1861]

10. In giving freedom to the slave, we assure freedom to the free – honourable alike in what we give and what we preserve.
[Speech, 1862]

11. Fourscore and seven years ago our fathers brought forth upon this continent a new nation, conceived in liberty, and dedicated to the proposition that all men are created equal ... In a larger sense we cannot dedicate, we cannot consecrate, we cannot hallow this ground. The brave men, living and dead, who struggled here, have consecrated it far above our power to add or detract. The world will little note, nor long remember, what we say here, but it can never forget what they did here. It is for us, the living, rather to be dedicated here to the unfinished work which they who fought here have thus far so nobly advanced. It is rather for us to be here dedicated to the great task remaining before us, that from these honoured dead we take increased devotion to that cause for which they gave the last full measure of devotion; that we here highly resolve that the dead shall not have died in vain, that this nation, under God, shall have a new birth of freedom; and that government of the people, by the people, and for the people, shall not perish from the earth.
[Address at Dedication of National Cemetery at Gettysburg, 1863]

12. It is not best to swap horses while crossing a river.
[Speech, 1864]

13. With malice toward none; with charity for all; with firmness in the right, as God gives us to see the right, let us strive on to finish the work we are in: to bind up the nation's wounds; to care for him who shall have borne the battle, and for his widow and his orphan, to do all which may achieve and cherish a just and lasting peace among ourselves, and with all nations.
[Second Inaugural Address, 1865]

14. When you have got an elephant by the hind leg, and he is trying to run away, it's best to let him run.
[Remark, 1865]

15. I think the necessity of being *ready* increases. Look to it.
[Letter to Governor Andrew Curtin of Pennsylvania, 1861]

16. If you don't want to use the army, I should like to borrow it for a while. Yours respectfully, A. Lincoln.
[Letter to General George B. McClellan during the US Civil War, 1862]

17. My paramount object in this struggle is to save the Union ... If I could save the Union without freeing any slave, I would do it; and if I could save it by freeing all the slaves, I would do it; and if I could save it by freeing some and leaving others alone, I would also do that ... I have here stated my purpose according to my views of official duty and I intend no modification of my oft-expressed personal wish that all men everywhere could be free.
[Letter to Horace Greeley, 1862]

18. I claim not to have controlled events, but confess plainly that events have controlled me.
[Letter to A.G. Hodges, 1864]

19. [Judgement on a book]
People who like this sort of thing will find this the sort of thing they like.
[In G.W.E. Russell, *Collections and Recollections* (1898), 30]

20. The Lord prefers common-looking people. That is why he makes so many of them.
[In James Morgan, *Our President* (1928)]

21. I don't know who my grandfather was; I am much more concerned to know what his grandson will be.
[In Gross, *Lincoln's Own Stories*]

22. Character is like a tree and reputation like its shadow. The shadow is what we think of it; the tree is the real thing.
[In Gross, *Lincoln's Own Stories*]

23. He reminds me of the man who murdered both his parents, and then, when sentence was about to be pronounced, pleaded for mercy on the grounds that he was an orphan.
[In Gross, *Lincoln's Own Stories*]

24. You can fool some of the people all of the time, and all of the people some of the time, but you cannot fool all of the people all the time.
[Attr.; also attributed to Phineas Barnum]

25. [Reply to the South Carolina Commissioners]
As President, I have no eyes but constitutional eyes; I cannot see you.
[Attr.]

26. Better to remain silent and be thought a fool than to speak out and remove all doubt.
[Attr.]

27. [On losing an election]
Like a little boy who has stubbed his toe in the dark ... too old to cry, but it hurt too much to laugh.
[Attr. by Adlai Stevenson]

28. [Resisting demands for the dismissal of Ulysses Grant]
I can't spare this man; he fights.
[Attr.]

29. [On meeting Harriet Beecher Stowe]
So you're the little woman who wrote the book that made this great war!
[Attr.]

Lindsay, Sir David (c. 1490–1555)

Scottish poet of the Reformation, satirist and diplomat

1. Let everie man keip weil ane toung,
And everie woman tway.
[*Satyre of the Thrie Estaitis*]

2. What vails your kingdome, and your rent,
And all your great treasure;
Without ye haif ane mirrie lyfe,
And cast aside all sturt, and stryfe.
[*Satyre of the Thrie Estaitis*]

3. We think them verray naturall fules,
That lernis ouir mekle at the sculis.
['Complaynt to the King']

Lindsay, Norman (Alfred William) (1879–1969)

Australian artist and writer

1. 'You ain't got any tobacco,' he said scornfully to Bunyip Bluegum. 'I can see that at a glance, You're one of the non-smoking sort, all fur and feathers.'
[*The Magic Pudding* (1918)]

2. [On Melbourne socialists]
They were a bloodthirsty lot, those sentimentalists who wept for the sad lot of the working classes.
[*Bohemians of the Bulletin* (1965)]

3. The best love affairs are those we never had.
[*Bohemians of the Bulletin* (1965)]

Lindsay, Vachel (1879–1931)

American poet and preacher

1. Booth died blind and still by faith he trod,
Eyes still dazzled by the ways of God.
['General William Booth Enters into Heaven' (1913)]

2. Boomlay, boomlay, boomlay, BOOM,
A roaring, epic, rag-time tune
From the mouth of the Congo
To the Mountains of the Moon...

3. Redeemed were the forests, the beasts and the men,
And only the vulture dared again
By the far, lone mountains of the moon
To cry, in the silence, the Congo tune:–
'Mumbo-Jumbo will hoo-doo you,
Mumbo-Jumbo will hoo-doo you.
Mumbo ... Jumbo ... will ... hoo-doo ... you.'
['The Congo' (1914)]

4. The flower-fed buffaloes of the spring
In the days of long ago,
Ranged where the locomotives sing
And the prairie flowers lie low:–
The tossing, blooming, perfumed grass
Is swept away by the wheat,
Wheels and wheels and wheels spin by
In the spring that still is sweet.
But the flower-fed buffaloes of the spring
Left us, long ago.
['The Flower-fed Buffaloes' (1914)]

Linklater, Eric (1899–1974)
Scottish novelist, born in Wales; satirist, short-story writer and journalist

1. With a heavy step Sir Matthew left the room and spent the morning designing mausoleums for his enemies.
[*Juan in America* (1931), Prologue]

2. There won't be any revolution in America ... The people are too clean. They spend all their time changing their shirts and washing themselves. You can't feel fierce and revolutionary in a bathroom.
[*Juan in America* (1931), V, 3]

3. While swordless Scotland, sadder than its psalms,
Fosters its sober youth on national alms
To breed a dull provincial discipline,
Commerce its god and golf its anodyne.
['Preamble to a Satire']

Linley, George (1798–1865)
English writer of ballads and farces; composer and satirist

1. Among our ancient mountains,
And from our lovely vales,
Oh, let the prayer re-echo:
'God bless the Prince of Wales!'
['God Bless the Prince of Wales', song, 1862]

Linnaeus, Carl (1707–1778)
Swedish founder of modern botany, noted for his binomial system of classification

1. *Natura non facit saltus.*
Nature does not make progress by leaps and bounds.
[*Philosophia Botanica*]

Linton, W.J. (1812–1897)
English wood engraver, editor, printer and Chartist

1. For he is one of Nature's Gentlemen, the best of every time.
[*Nature's Gentleman*]

Lippmann, Walter (1889–1974)
American journalist, teacher of philosophy and writer on politics

1. I doubt whether the student can do a greater work for his nation in this grave moment in its history than to detach himself from its preoccupations, refusing to let himself be absorbed by distractions about which, as a scholar, he can do almost nothing.
[*The Scholar in a Troubled World* (1932)]

Listen With Mother

1. Are you sitting comfortably? Then I'll begin.
[Preamble to children's stories in *Listen With Mother*, BBC radio programme, from 1950]

Litvinov, Maxim (1876–1951)
Soviet statesman and diplomat, born in Russian Poland

1. Peace is indivisible.
[Speech to League of Nations, 1936]

Livermore, Mary Ashton (c. 1820–1905)
American reformer, suffragist, editor and author

1. Other books have been written by men physicians ... One would suppose in reading them that women possess but one class of physical organs, and that these are always diseased. Such teaching is pestiferous, and tends to cause and perpetuate the very evils it professes to remedy.
[*What Shall We Do with Our Daughters*]

2. Above the titles of wife and mother, which, although dear, are transitory and accidental, there is the title human being, which precedes and out-ranks every other.
[*What Shall We Do with Our Daughters*]

Livy (Titus Livius) (59 BC–AD 17)
Roman writer, famous for his history of Rome, from its founding to 9 BC

1. *Vae victis.*
Woe to the vanquished.
[*History*, V]

2. *Pugna magna victi sumus.*
In a mighty battle were we defeated.
[*History*, XXII]

3. *In rebus asperis et tenui spe fortissima quaeque consilia tutissima sunt.*
In harsh circumstances when there is little hope, the boldest measures are the safest.
[*History*, XXV]

Llewellyn, Richard (1907–1983)
Welsh novelist

1. And there is good fresh trout for supper. My mother used to put them on a hot stone over the fire, wrapped in breadcrumbs, butter, parsley and lemon rind, all bound about with the fresh leaves of leeks. If there is better food in heaven, I am in a hurry to be there.
[*How Green was my Valley* (1939)]

Llosa, Mario Vargas (1936–)
Peruvian writer, journalist and politician; presidential candidate in 1990

1. They were half fish and half women, they lived at the bottom of lagoons waiting for people who had drowned, and as soon as a canoe tipped over they would come and grab the people and take them down to their palaces. They would put them in hammocks that were not made out of jute but made out of snakes and they would have fun with them there.
[*The Green House* (1969); first published as *La Casa Verde* (1965)]

Lloyd, Harold (1893–1971)
American silent film comedian, noted for his dangerous stunts; Academy Award 1952

1. [Reply when, aged 77, he was asked his age]
I am just turning forty and taking my time about it.
[*The Times*, 1970]

Lloyd, Marie (Matilda Alice Victoria Wood) (1870–1922)
English music-hall artiste

1. Oh, mister porter, what shall I do?
I wanted to go to Birmingham, but they've carried me on to Crewe.
['Oh, Mister Porter', song, c. 1890, made famous by Marie Lloyd]

2. [Referring to her handbag]
It's a bit of a ruin that Cromwell knocked about a bit.
[Music hall song, c. 1893, made famous by Marie Lloyd]

Lloyd, Robert (1733–1764)
English poet

1. Who teach the mind its proper face to scan,
And hold the faithful mirror up to man.
['The Actor']

2. Slow and steady wins the race.
['The Hare and the Tortoise']

Lloyd George, David (First Earl of Dwyfor) (1863–1945)
English-born Welsh Liberal statesman; Chancellor of the Exchequer 1908–15; Prime Minister 1916–22

1. [Advocating Tariff Reform]
You cannot feed the hungry on statistics.
[Speech, 1904]

2. The House of Lords is not the watchdog of the constitution: it is Mr Balfour's poodle.
[Speech, 1908]

3. A fully equipped duke costs as much to keep up as two Dreadnoughts; and dukes are just as great a terror and they last longer.
[Speech, 1909]

4. [To a deputation of ship owners urging campaigning for prohibition during the First World War]
We are fighting Germany, Austria, and drink, and so far as I can see the greatest of these deadly foes is drink.
[Speech, 1915]

5. What is our task? To make Britain a fit country for heroes to live in.
[Speech, Wolverhampton, 1918]

6. The finest eloquence is that which gets things done; the worst is that which delays them.
[Speech at Paris Peace Conference, 1919]

7. Every man has a House of Lords in his own head. Fears, prejudices, misconceptions – those are the peers, and they are hereditary.
[Speech, Cambridge, 1927]

8. Love your neighbour is not merely sound Christianity; it is good business.
[*The Observer*, 'Sayings of the Week', 1921]

9. The world is becoming like a lunatic asylum run by lunatics.
[*The Observer*, 'Sayings of Our Times', 1953]

10. [Of Neville Chamberlain]
He saw foreign policy through the wrong end of a municipal drainpipe.
[In Harris, *The Fine Art of Political Wit*, 6]

11. When they circumcised Herbert Samuel they threw away the wrong bit.
[Attr. in *The Listener*, 1978]

12. [Speech in Parliament, of Sir John Simon]
The Right Honourable gentleman has sat so long on the fence that the iron has entered his soul.
[Attr.]

13. [On being asked how he maintained his cheerfulness when beset by numerous political obstacles]
Well, I find that a change of nuisances is as good as a vacation.
[Attr.]

14. [Referring to the popular opinion that World War I would be the last major war]
This war, like the next war, is a war to end war.
[Attr.]

15. [Of Neville Chamberlain]
A good mayor of Birmingham in an off-year.
[Attr.; also attributed to Lord Hugh Cecil]

16. [Of Sir Douglas Haig]
He was brilliant to the top of his army boots.
[Attr.]

Locke, John (1632–1704)
English Liberal philosopher, founder of empiricism

1. New opinions are always suspected, and usually opposed, without any reason but because they are not already common.
[*Essay concerning Human Understanding* (1690), Dedicatory Epistle]

2. Nature never makes excellent things for mean or no uses.
[*Essay concerning Human Understanding* (1690), II, 1]

3. No man's knowledge here can go beyond his experience.
[*Essay concerning Human Understanding* (1690), II, 1]

4. It is one thing to show a man that he is in an error, and another to put him in possession of truth.
[*Essay concerning Human Understanding* (1690), IV, 4]

5. All men are liable to error; and most men are, in many points, by passion or interest, under temptation to it.
[*Essay concerning Human Understanding* (1690), IV, 20]

6. Wherever Law ends, Tyranny begins.
[*Second Treatise of Civil Government* (1690)]

Locker-Lampson, Frederick (1821–1895)
English author of light verse and civil servant

1. If you lift a guinea-pig up by the tail
His eyes drop out!
['A Garden Lyric']

Lockhart, John Gibson (1794–1854)
Scottish novelist, critic, editor and translator; biographer of Burns and Walter Scott (Lockhart's father-in-law)

1. It is a better and a wiser thing to be a starved apothecary than a starved poet; so back to the shop Mr John, back to 'plasters, pills, and ointment boxes.'
[*Blackwood's Magazine*, 1818, Review of Keats's *Endymion*]

2. Here lies that peerless peer Lord Peter,
Who broke the laws of God and man and metre.
[Epitaph for Patrick ('Peter'), Lord Robertson, 1890]

Lockier, Francis (1667–1740)
English Dean of Peterborough; friend of Dryden and Pope

1. In all my travels I have never met with any one Scotchman but what was a man of sense. I believe everybody of that country that has any, leaves it as fast as they can.
[In Joseph Spence, *Anecdotes* (1858)]

Lodge, David (1935–)
English novelist, satirist and literary critic

1. Literature is mostly about having sex and not much about having children; life is the other way round.
[*The British Museum is Falling Down* (1965), 4]

2. Rummidge ... had lately suffered the mortifying fate of most English universities of its type (civic redbrick): having competed strenuously for fifty years with two universities chiefly valued for being old, it was, at the moment of drawing level, rudely overtaken in popularity and prestige by a batch of universities chiefly valued for being new.
[*Changing Places* (1975), 1]

3. Four times, under our educational rules, the human pack is shuffled and cut – at eleven-plus, sixteen-plus, eighteen-plus and twenty-plus – and happy is he who comes top of the deck on each occasion, but especially the last. This is

called Finals, the very name of which implies that nothing of importance can happen after it. The British postgraduate student is a lonely forlorn soul ... for whom nothing had been real since the Big Push.
[*Changing Places* (1975), 1]

4. The British, he thought, must be gluttons for satire: even the weather forecast seemed to be some kind of spoof, predicting every possible combination of weather for the next twenty-four hours without actually committing itself to anything specific.
[*Changing Places* (1975), 2]

5. Walt Whitman who laid end to end words never seen in each other's company before outside of a dictionary.
[*Changing Places* (1975), 5]

Lodge, Thomas (1558–1625)
English writer of romances and lyric poetry; translator and transatlantic traveller

1. Love, in my bosom, like a bee,
Doth suck his sweet.
['Love, In My Bosom' (1590)]

2. Heigh ho, would she were mine!
['Rosalind's Description']

Loesser, Frank (1910–1969)
American writer of songs for films

1. I'd like to get you
On a slow boat to China.
['Slow Boat to China', song, 1948]

Logau, Friedrich von (1605–1655)
German epigrammatist

1. *Gottes Mühlen mahlen langsam, mahlen aber trefflich klein;*
Ob aus Langmut er sich säumet, bringt mit Schärf' er alles ein.
Though the mills of God grind slowly, yet they grind extremely small;
Though his patience makes him tarry, with exactness grinds He all.
[*Sinngedichte* (*Epigrams*, 1653), no. 638]

Lombroso, Cesare (1853–1909)
Italian physician and psychiatrist; founder of criminology

1. *L'uomo ignorante ama ciò che non capisce.*
The ignorant man always loves that which he cannot understand.
[*The Man of Genius* (1894), III, 3]

London, Jack (1876–1916)
American adventure novelist, short-story writer, journalist, sailor, socialist and goldminer

1. The Call of the Wild.
[Title of novel, 1903]

2. In an English ship, they say, it is poor grub, poor pay, and easy work; in an American ship, good grub, good pay, and hard work. And this is applicable to the working populations of both countries.
[*The People of the Abyss* (1903), 20]

Long, Huey (1893–1935)
US politician and lawyer, Governor of Louisiana

1. I looked around at the little fishes present and said, I'm the Kingfish.
[In A. Schlesinger Jr, *The Politics of Upheaval* (1961)]

2. [Slogan, 1928, quoting William Jennings Bryan]
Every man a king but no man wears a crown.
[Attr.]

Longfellow, Henry Wadsworth (1807–1882)
American poet, noted for his ballads and narrative poetry; translator and prose writer

1. Tell me not, in mournful numbers,
Life is but an empty dream!
For the soul is dead that slumbers,
And things are not what they seem.

Life is real! Life is earnest!
And the grave is not its goal;
Dust thou art, to dust returnest,
Was not spoken of the soul...

2. Art is long, and Time is fleeting,
And our hearts, though stout and brave,
Still, like muffled drums, are beating
Funeral marches to the grave...

3. Trust no Future, howe'er pleasant!
Let the dead Past bury its dead!
Act, – act in the living Present!
Heart within, and God o'erhead!...

4. Lives of great men all remind us
We can make our lives sublime,
And, departing, leave behind us
Footprints on the sands of time...

5. Let us, then, be up and doing,
With a heart for any fate;
Still achieving, still pursuing,
Learn to labour and to wait.
['A Psalm of Life' (1838)]

6. The shades of night were falling fast,
As through an Alpine village passed
A youth, who bore, 'mid snow and ice,
A banner with the strange device,
Excelsior!
['Excelsior' (1841)]

7. I like that ancient Saxon phrase, which calls
The burial-ground God's-Acre!
['God's-Acre' (1841)]

8. Standing, with reluctant feet,
Where the brook and river meet,
Womanhood and childhood fleet!
['Maidenhood' (1841)]

9. It was the schooner Hesperus,
That sailed the wintry sea;
And the skipper had taken his little daughter,
To bear him company...

10. But the father answered never a word,
A frozen corpse was he.
['The Wreck of the Hesperus' (1841)]

11. Under a spreading chestnut-tree
The village smithy stands;
The smith, a mighty man is he,
With large and sinewy hands;
And the muscles on his brawny arms
Are strong as iron bands...

12. Each morning sees some task begin,
Each evening sees it close;
Something attempted, something done,
Has earned a night's repose...

13. Looks the whole world in the face,
For he owes not any man.
['The Village Blacksmith' (1842)]

14. The cares that infest the day
Shall fold their tents, like the Arabs,
And as silently steal away...

15. The bards sublime,
Whose distant footsteps echo
Through the corridors of Time.
['The Day is Done' (1844)]

16. I shot an arrow into the air,
It fell to earth, I knew not where.
['The Arrow and the Song' (1845)]

17. Thou, too, sail on, O Ship of State!
Sail on, O Union, strong and great!
Humanity with all its fears,
With all the hopes of future years,
Is hanging breathless on thy fate!
['The Building of the Ship' (1849)]

18. You are better than all the ballads
That ever were sung or said;
For ye are living poems,
And all the rest are dead.
['Children' (1849)]

19. The heights by great men reached and kept
Were not attained by sudden flight,
But they, while their companions slept,
Were toiling upward in the night.
['The Ladder of Saint Augustine' (1850)]

20. By the shore of Gitche Gumee,
By the shining Big-Sea-Water,
Stood the wigwam of Nokomis,
Daughter of the Moon, Nokomis.
Dark behind it rose the forest,
Rose the black and gloomy pine-trees,
Rose the firs with cones upon them;
Bright before it beat the water,
Beat the clear and sunny water,
Beat the shining Big-Sea-Water.
[*The Song of Hiawatha* (1855), 'Hiawatha's Childhood']

21. From the waterfall he named her,
Minnehaha, Laughing Water.
[*The Song of Hiawatha* (1855), 'Hiawatha and Mudjekeewis']

22. As unto the bow the cord is,
So unto the man is woman;
Though she bends him, she obeys him,
Though she draws him, yet she follows;
Useless each without the other!
[*The Song of Hiawatha* (1855), 'Hiawatha's Wooing']

23. He is dead, the sweet musician!
He the sweetest of all singers!
He has gone from us for ever,
He has moved a little nearer
To the Master of all music,
To the Master of all singing!
O my brother, Chibiabos!
[*The Song of Hiawatha* (1855), 'Hiawatha's Lamentation']

24. A Lady with a Lamp shall stand
In the great history of the land,
A noble type of good,
Heroic womanhood.
['Santa Filomena' (1857)]

25. I remember the black wharves and the slips,
And the sea-tides tossing free;
And Spanish sailors with bearded lips,
And the beauty and mystery of the ships,
And the magic of the sea.
And the voice of that wayward song
Is singing and saying still:
'A boy's will is the wind's will
And the thoughts of youth are long, long thoughts.'
['My Lost Youth' (1858)]

26. Between the dark and the daylight,
When the night is beginning to lower,
Comes a pause in the day's occupations,
This is known as the Children's Hour.
['The Children's Hour' (1859)]

27. Giotto's tower,
The lily of Florence blossoming in stone.
['Giotto's Tower' (1866)]

28. A solid man of Boston.
A comfortable man, with dividends,
And the first salmon and the first green peas.
[*New England Tragedies* (1868), 'John Endicott']

29. Listen, my children, and you shall hear
Of the midnight ride of Paul Revere,
On the eighteenth of April in Seventy-five...

30. A hurry of hoofs in a village street,
A shape in the moonlight, a bulk in the dark,
And beneath, from the pebbles, in passing, a spark
Struck out from a steed flying fearless and fleet:
That was all! And yet, through the gloom and the light,
The fate of a nation was riding that night.
[*Tales of a Wayside Inn* (1863–1874), 'The Landlord's Tale: Paul Revere's Ride']

31. Ships that pass in the night, and speak each other in passing;
Only a signal shown and a distant voice in the darkness;
So on the ocean of life we pass and speak one another,
Only a look and a voice; then darkness again and a silence.
[*Tales of a Wayside Inn* (1863–1874), 'The Theologian's Tale: Elizabeth']

32. Our ingress into the world
Was naked and bare;
Our progress through the world
Is trouble and care.
[*Tales of a Wayside Inn* (1863–1874), 'The Student's Tale']

33. Not in the clamour of the crowded street,
Not in the shouts and plaudits of the throng,
But in ourselves, are triumph and defeat.
['The Poets' (1876)]

34. The secret anniversaries of the heart.
[*Sonnets* (1877), 'Holidays']

35. If you would hit the mark, you must aim a little above it;
Every arrow that flies feels the attraction of earth.
['Elegiac Verse' (1880)]

36. [Written for his second daughter when she was a baby]
There was a little girl
Who had a little curl
Right in the middle of her forehead,
When she was good
She was very, very good,
But when she was bad she was horrid.
['There was a Little Girl' (1882). Cf. Max Miller: 1 and Mae West: 5]

37. The men that women marry,
And why they marry them, will always be
A marvel and a mystery to the world.
[*Michael Angelo* (1883), I]

38. I stood on the bridge at midnight,
As the clocks were striking the hour.
['The Bridge' (1904)]

39. There is a Reaper whose name is Death,
And, by his sickle keen,
He reaps the bearded grain at a breath,
And the flowers that grow between.
['The Reaper and the Flowers' (1904)]

40. 'Wouldst thou' – so the helmsman answered. –
'Learn the secret of the sea?
Only those who brave its dangers
Comprehend its mystery!'
['The Secret of the Sea' (1904)]

Longford, Francis Aungier Pakenham, Earl of (1905–)
British politician, social reformer and biographer

1. No sex without responsibility.
[*The Observer*, 'Sayings of the Week', 1954]

2. On the whole I would not say that our Press is obscene. I would say that it trembles on the brink of obscenity.
[*The Observer*, 'Sayings of the Week', 1963]

Longworth, Alice Roosevelt (1884–1980)
American writer; daughter of Theodore Roosevelt

1. [Of John Calvin Coolidge, US President 1923–1929]
He looks as if he had been weaned on a pickle.
[*Crowded Hours* (1933)]

2. [Embroidered on a cushion at her home in Washington]
If you haven't anything nice to say about anyone, come and sit by me.
[*New York Times*, 1980]

Lonsdale, Frederick (1881–1954)
British dramatist, noted for society comedies

1. Don't keep finishing your sentences. I am not a bloody fool.
[In Frances Donaldson, *Child of the Twenties* (1959)]

Loos, Anita (1893–1981)
American humorous novelist and screenwriter

1. Gentlemen Prefer Blondes.
[Title of book, 1925]

2. A girl like I.
[*Gentlemen Prefer Blondes* (1925), passim]

3. So this gentleman said a girl with brains ought to do something with them besides think.
[*Gentlemen Prefer Blondes* (1925), 1]

4. Fate keeps on happening.
[*Gentlemen Prefer Blondes* (1925), 2]

5. Kissing your hand may make you feel very very good but a diamond and safire bracelet lasts forever.
[*Gentlemen Prefer Blondes* (1925), 4. Cf. Adlai Stevenson: 1]

6. Any girl who was a lady would not even think of having such a good time that she did not remember to hang on to her jewelry.
[*Gentlemen Prefer Blondes* (1925), 4]

7. You have got to be a Queen to get away with a hat like that.
[*Gentlemen Prefer Blondes* (1925), 4]

8. Fun is fun but no girl wants to laugh all of the time.
[*Gentlemen Prefer Blondes* (1925), 4]

9. So then Dr Froyd said that all I needed was to cultivate a few inhibitions and get some sleep.
[*Gentlemen Prefer Blondes* (1925), 5]

10. I'm furious about the Women's Liberationists. They keep getting up on soapboxes and proclaiming that women are brighter than men. That's true, but it should be kept very quiet or it ruins the whole racket.
[*The Observer*, 'Sayings of the Year', 1973]

Lorca, Federico García (1899–1936)
Leading Spanish poet and dramatist, noted for his folk plays

1. *Verde que te quiero verde.*
Verde viento. Verdes ramas.
Green I love you green. Green wind. Green branches.
[*Romancero gitano* (*The Gypsy Ballads*, 1924–27), 'Romance sonámbulo']

2. *La aurora de Nueva York tiene*
cuatro columnas de cieno
y un huracán de negras palomas
que chapotean las aguas podridas.
Dawn in New York has
four columns of mud
and a hurricane of black doves
Wet from the stagnant water.
[*Poeta en Nueva York* (1929–1930), III, 'Calles y Sueños' ('Streets and Dreams')]

3. *Ni un solo momento, viejo hermoso Walt Whitman,*
he dejado de ver tu barba llena de mariposas.
Not even for a moment, beautiful old Walt Whitman, have I stopped seeing your beard full of butterflies.
[*Poeta en Nueva York* (1929–30), VIII, 'Oda a Walt Whitman']

4. *Verte desnuda es recordar la Tierra.*
To see you naked is to recall the Earth.
[*Diván del Tamarit* (1936), 'Casida de la Mujer Tendida']

Lorenz, Konrad (1903–1989)
Austrian zoologist and psychologist; Nobel prize in physiology and medicine 1973

1. *Überhaupt ist es für den Forscher ein guter Morgensport, täglich vor dem Frühstück eine Lieblingshypothese einzustampfen – das erhält jung.*
In general it is a good morning exercise for a researcher to destroy a favourite hypothesis every day before breakfast – it keeps him young.
Das sogenannte Böse (lit: *So-called Evil*, 1963); trans. as *On Aggression*]

Lothian, Lord (Philip Henry Kerr) (1882–1940)
English journalist and Liberal statesman

1. The only lasting solution is that Europe itself should gradually find its way to an internal equilibrium and a limitation of armaments by political appeasement.
[Letter to *The Times*, 4 May 1934]

Louis XIV of France (1638–1715)
King of France from 1643 and patron of the arts; the Sun King; established absolute monarchy and waged many wars

1. [Said at the accession of his grandson to the throne of Spain]
Il n'y a plus de Pyrénées.
The Pyrenees no longer exist.
[Remark, 1700]

2. First feelings are always the most natural.
[Recorded by Mme de Sévigné, 1709]

3. *Toutes les fois que je donne une place vacante, je fais cent mécontents et un ingrat.*
Every time I make an appointment, I make a hundred men discontented and one ungrateful.
[In Voltaire, *Le Siècle de Louis XIV* (1751), 26]

4. [On hearing of the French defeat at Malplaquet]
Dieu, a-t-il donc oublié ce que j'ai fait pour lui?
Has God then forgotten what I have done for him?
[Attr.]

5. *L'État c'est moi.*
I am the State.
[Attr.]

6. *J'ai failli attendre.*
I almost had to wait.
[Attr.]

7. Ah, if I were not king, I should lose my temper.
[Attr.]

8. [Noticing as he lay on his deathbed that his attendants were crying]
Why are you weeping? Did you imagine that I was immortal?
[Attr.]

Louis XVIII of France (1755–1824)
King of France 1814–24; titular king from 1795

1. *L'exactitude est la politesse des rois.*
Punctuality is the politeness of kings.
[In Laffitte, *Souvenirs*]

Louis Philippe (1773–1850)
King of France, the Citizen King, from 1830–48; abdicated

1. [Referring to an informal understanding reached between Britain and France in 1843. The more familiar phrase 'entente cordiale' was first used in 1844]
La cordiale entente qui existe entre mon gouvernement et le sien.
The friendly understanding that exists between my government and hers [Queen Victoria's].
[Speech, 1843]

Louis, Joe (Joseph Louis Barrow) (1914–1981)
American boxer; world heavyweight champion 1937–49

1. [Referring to the speed of an opponent, Billy Conn]
He can run, but he can't hide.
[Attr.]

Lovelace, Richard (1618–1658)
English Cavalier lyric poet

1. Am not I shot
With the self-same artillery?...

2. Lucasta that bright northern star.
['Amyntor from Beyond the Sea to Alexis' (1649)]

3. When Love with unconfined wings
Hovers within my gates;
And my divine Althea brings
To whisper at the grates:
When I lie tangled in her hair,
And fettered to her eye;
The Gods, that wanton in the air,
Know no such liberty...

4. When thirsty grief in wine we steep,
When healths and draughts go free,
Fishes, that tipple in the deep,
Know no such liberty...

5. Stone walls do not a prison make
Nor iron bars a cage;
Minds innocent and quiet take
That for an hermitage;
If I have freedom in my love,
And in my soul am free;
Angels alone, that soar above,
Enjoy such liberty.
['To Althea, From Prison' (1649)]

6. If to be absent were to be
Away from thee;
Or that when I am gone,
You and I were alone;
Then my Lucasta might I crave
Pity from blust'ring wind, or swallowing wave.
['To Lucasta, Going Beyond the Seas' (1649)]

7. Tell me not (Sweet) I am unkind,
That from the nunnery
Of thy chaste breast, and quiet mind,
To war and arms I fly.

True; a new mistress now I chase,
The first foe in the field;
And with a stronger faith embrace
A sword, a horse, a shield.

Yet this inconstancy is such,
As you too shall adore;
I could not love thee (Dear) so much,
Lov'd I not honour more.
['To Lucasta, Going to the Wars' (1649)]

8. Lady, it is already Morn,
And 'twas last night I swore to thee
That fond impossibility...

9. With spoils of meaner Beauties crown'd,
I laden will return to thee.
['The Scrutiny' (1659)]

Lovell, James (1928–)
American corporate executive, former astronaut

1. [After the explosion on board Apollo XIII, which put the crew in serious danger]
OK, Houston, we have had a problem here ... Houston, we have a problem.
[Radio message, 11 April 1970]

Lovell, Maria (1803–1877)
English actress and dramatist

1. Two souls with but a single thought,
Two hearts that beat as one.
[*Ingomar the Barbarian*, II]

Lover, Samuel (1797–1868)
Irish songwriter, painter, novelist and dramatist

1. When once the itch of literature comes over a man, nothing can cure it but the scratching of a pen.
[*Handy Andy* (1842)]

Low, Sir David (1891–1963)
British political cartoonist, born in New Zealand

1. I have never met anybody who wasn't against war. Even Hitler and Mussolini were, according to themselves.
[In Jonathon Green (ed.), *A Dictionary of Contemporary Quotations* (1982)]

2. I do not know whether he draws a line himself. But I assume

that his is the direction ... It makes Disney the most significant figure in graphic art since Leonardo.
[In R. Schickel, *Walt Disney*, 20]

Lowe, Robert (Viscount Sherbrooke) (1811–1892)
English lawyer and politician; Liberal Chancellor of the Exchequer 1868–73

1. I believe it will be absolutely necessary that you should prevail on our future masters to learn their letters.
[Speech on Reform Bill, 1867]

2. The Chancellor of the Exchequer is a man whose duties make him more or less of a taxing machine. He is intrusted with a certain amount of misery which it is his duty to distribute as fairly as he can.
[Speech, House of Commons, 1870]

Lowell, Amy (1874–1925)
American imagist poet, critic and biographer

1. And the softness of my body will be guarded from embrace
By each button, hook, and lace.
For the man who should loose me is dead,
Fighting with the Duke in Flanders,
In a pattern called a war.
Christ! What are patterns for?
[*Men, Women and Ghosts* (1916), 'Patterns']

Lowell, James Russell (1819–1891)
American poet, editor and diplomat

1. No man is born into the world, whose work
Is not born with him; there is always work,
And tools to work withal, for those who will:
And blessèd are the horny hands of toil!
['A Glance Behind the Curtain' (1844)]

2. New occasions teach new duties: Time makes ancient good uncouth;
They must upward still, and onward, who would keep abreast of Truth.
['The Present Crisis' (1845)]

3. He's been true to *one* party – an' thet is himself.
[*The Biglow Papers* (First Series, 1848)]

4. An' you've gut to git up airly
Ef you want to take in God.
[*The Biglow Papers* (First Series, 1848)]

5. You've a darned long row to hoe.
[*The Biglow Papers* (First Series, 1848)]

6. I don't care how hard money is
Ez long ez mine's paid punctooal.
[*The Biglow Papers* (First Series, 1848)]

7. These pearls of thought in Persian gulfs were bred,
Each softly lucent as a rounded moon;
The diver Omar plucked them from their bed,
Fitzgerald strung them on an English thread.
['In a Copy of Omar Khayyám' (1888)]

8. The misfortunes hardest to bear are those which never come.
[*Democracy and Other Addresses* (1887), 'Democracy']

9. There is no good in arguing with the inevitable. The only argument available with an east wind is to put on your overcoat.
[*Democracy and Other Addresses* (1887), 'Democracy']

Lowell, Robert (1917–1977)
American poet and autobiographical writer

1. Sailor, can you hear
The Pequod's sea wings, beating landward, fall
Headlong and break on our Atlantic wall
Off 'Sconset.
[*Poems 1938–1949* (1950), 'The Quaker Graveyard in Nantucket', II]

2. I saw the spiders marching through the air,
Swimming from tree to tree that mildewed day
In latter August when the hay
Came creaking to the barn...

3. Let there pass
A minute, ten, ten, trillion; but the blaze
Is infinite, eternal: this is death,
To die and know it. This is the Black Widow, death.
[*Poems 1938–1949* (1950), 'Mr Edwards and the Spider']

4. The Lord survives the rainbow of His will.
[*Poems 1938–1949* (1950), 'Our Lady of Walsingham']

5. These are the tranquillized *Fifties*,
And I am forty. Ought I to regret my seedtime?
I was a fire-breathing Catholic C.O.,
and made my manic statement,
telling off the state and president, and then
set waiting sentence in the bull pen
beside a negro boy with curlicues
of marijuana in his hair.
[*Life Studies* (1956), 'Memories of West Street and Lepke']

6. One dark night,
My Tudor Ford climbed the hill's skull,
I watched for love-cars. Lights turned down,
they lay together, hull to hull,
where the graveyard shelves on the town...
My mind's not right.

A car radio bleats,
'Love, O careless Love...' I hear
my ill-spirit sob in each blood cell,
as if my hand were at its throat...
I myself am hell,
nobody's here–

only skunks, that search
in the moonlight for a bite to eat.
[*Life Studies* (1956), 'Skunk Hour']

7. The man is killing time – there's nothing else.
[*For the Union Dead* (1964), 'The Drinker']

8. Sometimes I have supposed seals
must live as long as the Scholar Gypsy...

9. Here too in Maine things bend to the wind forever.
After two years away, one must get used
to the painted soft wood staying bright and clean,
to the air blasting an all-white wall whiter,
as it blows through curtain and screen
touched with salt and evergreen...

10. The fresh paint
on the captains' houses hides softer wood...

11. Their square-riggers used to whiten
the four corners of the globe,
but it's no consolation to know
the possessors seldom outlast the possessions,
once warped and mothered by their touch.
Shed skin will never fit another wearer.
[*For the Union Dead* (1964), 'Soft Wood']

12. Their monument sticks like a fishbone
in the city's throat...

13. The Aquarium is gone. Everywhere,
giant finned cars nose forward like fish;

a savage servility
slides by on grease.
[*For the Union Dead* (1964), Title Poem]

14. O to break loose, like the chinook
salmon jumping and falling back,
nosing up to the impossible
stone and bone-crushing waterfall–
raw-jawed, weak-fleshed there, stopped by ten
steps of the roaring ladder, and then
to clear the top on the last try,
alive enough to spawn and die...

15. no rainbow smashing a dry fly
in the white run is free as I,
here squatting like a dragon on
time's hoard before the day's begun!...

16. No weekends for the gods now. Wars
flicker, earth licks its open sores,
fresh breakage, fresh promotions, chance
assassinations, no advance.
Only man thinning out his kind
sounds through the Sabbath noon, the blind
swipe of the pruner and his knife
busy about the tree of life...

Pity the planet, all joy gone
from this sweet volcanic cone;
peace to our children when they fall
in small war on the heels of small
war – until the end of time
to police the earth, a ghost
orbiting forever lost
in our monotonous sublime.
[*Near the Ocean* (1965), 'Waking Early Sunday Morning']

17. My Dolphin, you only guide me by surprise,
a captive as Racine, the man of craft,
drawn through his maze of iron composition
by the incomparable wandering voice of Phèdre.
When I was troubled in mind, you made for my body
caught in its hangman's-knot of sinking lines,
the glassy bowing and scraping of my will...
I have sat and listened to too many
words of the collaborating muse,
and plotted perhaps too freely with my life,
not avoiding injury to others,
not avoiding injury to myself–
to ask compassion ... this book, half fiction,
an eelnet made by man for the eel fighting–
my eyes have seen what my hand did.
[*The Dolphin* (1973), 'Dolphin']

18. If we see light at the end of the tunnel,
It's the light of the oncoming train.
[*Day by Day* (1977), 'Since 1939']

Lower, Lennie (1903–1947)
Australian journalist, columnist and contributor

1. She is an old lady and the age of chivalry is not dead while a Gudgeon lives. Perhaps a different son-in-law might have described her as a senseless, whining, nagging, leather-faced old whitlow not fit to cohabit with a rhinoceros beetle. But I wouldn't.
[*Here's Luck* (1930), 22]

2. The best way to tell gold is to pass the nugget around a crowded bar, and ask them if it's gold. If it comes back, it's not gold.
[*Here's Another* (1932), 'What Gold Is']

Lowry, L.S. (1887–1976)
English painter, famous for his 'matchstick' figures

1. A bachelor lives like a king and dies like a beggar.
[Attr.]

Lowry, Malcolm (1909–1957)
English novelist and poet; lived in Canada from 1939 to early 1950s

1. Where are the children I might have had? You may suppose I might have wanted them. Drowned to the accompaniment of the rattling of a thousand douche bags.
[*Under the Volcano* (1947), 10]

2. How alike are the groans of love to those of the dying.
[*Under the Volcano* (1947), 12]

Loyola, St Ignatius (1491–1556)
Spanish ecclesiastic and soldier; founder of the Society of Jesus 1534

1. Teach us, good Lord, to serve Thee as Thou deservest:
To give and not to count the cost;
To fight and not to heed the wounds;
To toil and not to seek for rest;
To labour and not to ask for any reward
Save that of knowing that we do Thy will.
['Prayer for Generosity']

Lucan (Marcus Annaeus Lucanus) (AD 39–65)
Roman epic poet, born in Spain

1. *Quis iustius induit arma*
Scire nefas, magno se iudice quisque tuetur:
Victrix causa deis placuit, sed victa Catoni.
It is not given us to know which man took up arms with more justice on his side. Each has the support of high authority: the victorious cause pleased the gods, but the vanquished pleased Cato.
[*Bellum Civile* (*Civil War*), I, line 126]

2. *Stat magni nominis umbra.*
He stands the mere shadow of a mighty name.
[*Bellum Civile* (*Civil War*), I, line 135]

3. *Nil actum credens, dum quid superesset agendum.*
Believing nothing done while anything was left undone.
[*Bellum Civile* (*Civil War*), II, line 657]

4. *Plus est quam vita salusque*
Quod perit.
More was lost there than life and safety.
[*Bellum Civile* (*Civil War*), VII, line 639]

5. *Etiam periere ruinae.*
Even the ruins have been destroyed.
[*Bellum Civile* (*Civil War*), IX, line 969]

6. *Coniunx*
Est mihi, sunt nati: dedimus tot pignora fatis.
I have a wife, I have sons: I give them as hostages to fate.
[*Works*]

Lucas, George (1944–)
American film director and producer

1. May the Force be with you.
[*Star Wars*, film, 1977]

Lucilius (Gaius Lucilius) (c. 180–102 BC)
Roman satirical poet

1. *Maior era natu; non omnia possumus omnes.*
He was of an older generation; we cannot all do everything.
[*Saturnalia*]

Lucretius (Titus Lucretius Carus) (c. 95–55 BC)
Roman poet and atomist philosopher

1. [Of Epicurus]
Ergo vivida vis animi pervicit, et extra
Processit longe flammantia moenia mundi
Atque omne immensum peragravit, mente animoque.
So the vital energy of his mind prevailed, and he ventured far beyond the flaming walls of the world and traversed the immensity of the universe in his mind and imagination.
[*De Rerum Natura*, I, line 72]

2. *Tantum religio potuit suadere malorum.*
So potent a persuasion to evil was religion.
[*De Rerum Natura*, I, line 101]

3. *Nil posse creari*
De nilo.
Nothing can be created from nothing.
[*De Rerum Natura*, I, line 155]

4. *Stillicidi casus lapidem cavat.*
The fall of drip after drip hollows out a stone.
[*De Rerum Natura*, I, line 313. Cf. Ovid: 14]

5. *Suave, mari magno turbantibus aequora ventis,*
E terra magnum alterius spectare laborem;
Non quia vexari quemquamst iucunda voluptas,
Sed quibus ipse malis careas quia cernere suave est.
Suave etiam belli certamina magna tueri
Per campos instructa tua sine parte pericli.
Sed nil dulcius est, bene quam munita tenere
Edita doctrina sapientum templa serena,
Despicere unde queas alios passimque videre
Errare atque viam palantis quaerere vitae,
Certare ingenio, contendere nobilitate,
Noctes atque dies niti praestante labore
Ad summas emergere opus rerumque potiri.
'Tis pleasant, safely to behold from shore
The rolling ship, and hear the tempest roar:
Not that another's pain is our delight;
But pains unfelt produce the pleasing sight.
'Tis pleasant also to behold from far
The moving legions mingled in the war;
But much more sweet thy lab'ring steps to guide
To virtue's heights, with wisdom well supplied,
And all the magazines of learning fortified:
From thence to look below on humankind,
Bewilder'd in the maze of life, and blind:
To see vain fools ambitiously contend
For wit and pow'r; their lost endeavours bend
T'outshine each other, waste their time and health
In search of honour, and pursuit of wealth.
[*De Rerum Natura*, II, line 1, trans. Dryden]

6. *Augescunt aliae gentes, aliae minuuntur,*
Inque brevi spatio mutantur saecla animantum
Et quasi cursores vitai lampada tradunt.
Some groups increase, others diminish, and in a short space the generations of living creatures are changed and like runners pass on the torch of life.
[*De Rerum Natura*, II, line 77]

7. *Nil igitur mors est ad nos neque pertinet hilum,*
Quandoquidem natura animi mortalis habetur.
What has this bugbear death to frighten man
If souls can die as well as bodies can?
[*De Rerum Natura*, III, line 830, trans. Dryden]

8. *Scire licet nobis nil esse in morte timendum*
Nec miserum fieri qui non est posse neque hilum
Differre an nullo fuerit iam tempore natus,
Mortalem vitam mors cum immortalis ademit.
And since the man who *is* not, feels not woe,
(For death exempts him, and wards off the blow,
Which we, the living, only feel and bear,)
What is there left for us in death to fear?
When once that pause of life has come between,
'Tis just the same as we had never been.
[*De Rerum Natura*, III, line 865, trans. Dryden]

9. *Vitaque mancipio, nulli datur, omnibus usu.*
For life is not confined to him or thee;
'Tis given to all for use, to none for property.
[*De Rerum Natura*, III, line 971, trans. Dryden]

10. *Ut quod ali cibus est aliis fuat acre venenum.*
One man's meat is another's poison.
[*De Rerum Natura*, IV, line 637]

11. *Medio de fonte leporum*
Surgit amari aliquid quod in ipsis floribus angat.
From the midst of the fountain of delights rises something bitter that is a torment even among the flowers.
[*De Rerum Natura*, IV, line 1133]

Lunt, Alfred (1892–1977)
American actor

1. [On acting]
Speak in a loud clear voice and try not to bump into the furniture.
[In Halliwell, *Filmgoer's Book of Quotes* (1973); also attributed to Noël Coward]

Luther, Martin (1483–1546)
German theologian and leader of the Protestant Reformation; translated the Bible into German

1. *Gedanken sind zollfrei.*
Thoughts are not subject to duty.
[*Von weltlicher Obrigkeit, wie weit man ihr Gehorsam schuldig sei (On worldly authority, to what extent one requires to be obedient to it*, 1523)]

2. *Wenn ich gewusst hätte, dass so viel Teufel auf mich gezielet hätten, als Ziegel auf den Dächern waren zu Worms, wäre ich dennoch eingeritten.*
If I had known that as many devils would have set on me in Worms as there are tiles on the roofs, I should nevertheless have ridden there.
[*Luthers Sämmtliche Schriften* (*Collected Writings*, 1745), XVI, written 1524]

3. *Worauf du nun ... dein Herz hängt und verlässt, das ist eigentlich dein Gott.*
Whatever your heart clings to and relies upon, that is really your God.
[*Der grosse Katechismus* (*Large Catechism*, 1529), First commandment]

4. *Ein feste Burg ist unser Gott,*
Ein gute Wehr und Waffen.
A strong castle is our God,
A good defence and weapon.
[Hymn, first extant version, *Rauscher's Hymnal* (1531)]

5. *Der alt böse Feind*
Mit Ernst er's itzt meint,
Gross Macht und viel List,
Sein grausam Rüstung ist,
Auf Erd ist nicht seins gleichen.
The ancient prince of hell
Hath risen with purpose fell;
Strong mail of craft and power
He weareth in this hour;
On earth is not his fellow.
[Hymn, c. 1527–1528; trans. Carlyle]

6. *Darum gibt unser Herr Gott gemeiniglich Reichtum den groben Eseln, denen er sonst nichts gönnt.*
For that reason our Lord God commonly gives wealth to those coarse asses to whom he grants nothing else.
[*Colloquia* or *Tischreden 1531–1546* (*Table Talk 1531–1546*), Section 11]

7. *Esto peccator et pecca fortiter, sed fortius fide et gaude in Christo.*
Be a sinner and sin strongly, but believe and rejoice in Christ even more strongly.
[Letter to Melanchton, *Epistolae* (1566), I]

8. *Hier stehe ich. Ich kann nicht anders. Gott helfe mir. Amen.*
Here I stand. I can do nothing else. God help me. Amen.
[Attr.; allegedly spoken at the Diet of Worms, 1521]

9. *Wer nicht liebt Wein, Weib und Gesang,*
Der bleibt ein Narr sein Leben lang.
Whoever does not love wine, woman and song remains a fool his whole life long.
[Attr.; taken up by Johann Gottfried Herder (1744–1803) in his poem 'Wein, Weib und Gesang']

Luthuli, Albert (1898–1967)
African resistance leader

1. The Road to Freedom is via the Cross.
[Statement, November 1952, after he was dismissed as Chief by the South African Governor-General]

Lutyens, Sir Edwin Landseer (1869–1944)
English architect, noted for his neoclassical style

1. [Comment made in a restaurant]
This piece of cod passes all understanding.
[In Robert Lutyens, *Sir Edwin Lutyens* (1942)]

2. The answer is in the plural and they bounce.
[Attr.]

Lydgate, John (c. 1370–c. 1451)
Prolific English poet, translator and monk

1. Love is mor than gold or gret richesse.
['The Story of Thebes' (c. 1420)]

2. [Of Chaucer]
Sithe off oure language he was the lodesterre...

3. Comparisouns doon offte gret greuaunce.
['The Fall of Princes' (1431–1438)]

4. Woord is but wynd; leff woord and tak the dede.
['Secrets of Old Philosophers']

Lyly, John (c. 1554–1606)
English dramatist, Euphuist and politician

1. Be valiant, but not too venturous. Let thy attire be comely, but not costly.
[*Euphues: The Anatomy of Wit* (1578)]

2. It seems to me (said she) that you are in some brown study.
[*Euphues: The Anatomy of Wit* (1578)]

3. Cupid and my Campaspe play'd
At cards for kisses, Cupid paid.
[*Campaspe* (1584), III.v]

4. At last he set her both his eyes;
She won, and Cupid blind did rise.
O Love! has she done this to thee?
What shall, alas! become of me?
[*Campaspe* (1584), III.v]

5. What bird so sings, yet does so wail?
O 'tis the ravish'd nightingale.
Jug, jug, jug, jug, tereu, she cries,
And still her woes at midnight rise.
[*Campaspe* (1584), V.i]

6. [The lark]
How at heaven's gates she claps her wings,
The morn not waking till she sings.
[*Campaspe* (1584), V.i]

7. Night hath a thousand eyes.
[*Love's Metamorphosis* (1601), III.i]

8. If all the earth were paper white
And all the sea were ink
'Twere not enough for me to write
As my poor heart doth think.
[In Bond (ed.), *The Complete Works of John Lyly* (1902)]

Lynne, Liz (1948–)
English MP

1. [On the behaviour of MPs]
It was like a bunch of 11-year-olds at their first secondary school.
[*The Independent*, 1992]

Lysander (d. 395 BC)
Spartan admiral, noted for his victories in the Peloponnesian war

1. Deceive boys with toys, but men with oaths.
[In Plutarch, *Parallel Lives*, 'Lysander']

Lyte, Henry Francis (1793–1847)
British hymn writer and clergyman

1. Abide with me; fast falls the eventide;
The darkness deepens; Lord, with me abide;
When other helpers fail, and comforts flee,
Help of the helpless, O, abide with me.

Swift to its close ebbs out life's little day;
Earth's joys grow dim, its glories pass away;
Change and decay in all around I see;
O Thou, who changest not, abide with me.
[Hymn, 1847]

Lytton, Lady Constance (1869–1923)
British suffragette, several times imprisoned, and writer; born in Vienna

1. The first time you meet Winston [Churchill] you see all his faults and the rest of your life you spend in discovering his virtues.
[In Christopher Hassall, *Edward Marsh*, 7]

McAllister, Ward (1827–1895)
American socialite

1. There are only about four hundred people in New York society.
[Interview with Charles H. Crandall in the *New York Tribune*, 1888]

McAlpine, Sir Alfred (1881–1944)
Scottish public works contractor and millionaire

1. [Last words]
Keep Paddy behind the big mixer.
[Attr.]

MacArthur, Douglas (1880–1964)
American general; Commander of Allied Forces in the Far East and SW Pacific in World War II

1. [Said on leaving the Philippines, 1942]
I shall return.
[*New York Times*, 1942]

2. In war there is no substitute for victory.
[Speech to Congress, 1951]

Macaulay, Dame Rose (1881–1958)
English novelist, essayist, journalist and travel writer

1. Decades have a delusive edge to them. They are not, of course, really periods at all, except as any other ten years would be. But we, looking at them, are caught by the different name each bears, and give them different attributes, and tie labels on them, as if they were flowers in a border.
[*Told by an Idiot* (1923), II, 1]

2. Gentlemen know that fresh air should be kept in its proper place – out of doors – and that, God having given us indoors and out-of-doors, we should not attempt to do away with this distinction.
[*Crewe Train* (1926), I, 5]

3. Owing to the weather, English Social life must always have largely occurred either indoors, or, when out of doors, in active motion.
['Life Among the English' (1942)]

4. A group of closely related persons living under one roof; it is a convenience, often a necessity, sometimes a pleasure, sometimes the reverse; but who first exalted it as admirable, an almost religious ideal?
[*The World My Wilderness* (1950), 20]

5. 'Take my camel, dear,' said my aunt Dot as she climbed down from this animal on her return from High Mass.
[*The Towers of Trebizond* (1956)]

6. Poem me no poems.
[*Poetry Review*, 1963. Cf. Shakespeare, *Romeo and Juliet*: 36]

7. The great and recurrent question about abroad is, is it worth getting there?
[Attr.]

8. It was a book to kill time for those who like it better dead.
[Attr.]

Macaulay, Thomas Babington, Lord (1800–1859)
English historian; Liberal statesman, essayist and poet

1. [Reply, aged four, after hot coffee had been spilt on his legs]
Thank you, madam, the agony is abated.
[In G.O. Trevelyan, *Life and Letters of Macaulay* (1876), 1]

2. Knowledge advances by steps, and not by leaps.
[*Essays and Biographies* (1828), 'History']

3. With the dead there is no rivalry. In the dead there is no change. Plato is never sullen. Cervantes is never petulant. Demosthenes never comes unseasonably. Dante never stays too long. No difference of political opinion can alienate Cicero. No heresy can excite the horror of Bossuet.
[*Collected Essays* (1843), 'Lord Bacon']

4. An acre in Middlesex is better than a principality in Utopia.
[*Collected Essays* (1843), 'Lord Bacon']

5. Every schoolboy knows who imprisoned Montezuma, and who strangled Atahualpa.
[*Collected Essays* (1843), 'Lord Clive']

6. The English Bible, a book which, if everything else in our language should perish, would alone suffice to show the whole extent of its beauty and power.
[*Collected Essays* (1843), 'John Dryden']

7. His imagination resembled the wings of an ostrich. It enabled him to run, though not to soar.
[*Collected Essays* (1843), 'John Dryden']

8. In order that he might rob a neighbour whom he had promised to defend, black men fought on the coast of Coromandel, and red men scalped each other by the Great Lakes of North America.
[*Collected Essays* (1843), 'Frederick the Great']

9. The gallery in which the reporters sit has become a fourth estate of the realm.
[*Collected Essays* (1843), 'Hallam']

10. The Chief Justice was rich, quiet, and infamous.
[*Collected Essays* (1843), 'Warren Hastings']

11. [Of Westminster Abbey]
That temple of silence and reconciliation where the enmities of twenty generations lie buried.
[*Collected Essays* (1843), 'Warren Hastings']

12. The old philosopher is still among us in the brown coat with the metal buttons and the shirt which ought to be at wash, blinking, puffing, rolling his head, drumming with his fingers, tearing his meat like a tiger, and swallowing his tea in oceans.
[*Collected Essays* (1843), 'Samuel Johnson']

13. Nothing is so useless as a general maxim.
[*Collected Essays* (1843), 'Machiavelli']

14. The history of England is emphatically the history of progress.
[*Collected Essays* (1843), 'Sir James Mackintosh']

15. The highest intellects, like the tops of mountains, are the first to catch and to reflect the dawn.
[*Collected Essays* (1843), 'Sir James Mackintosh']

16. Perhaps no person can be a poet, or can even enjoy poetry, without a certain unsoundness of mind.
[*Collected Essays* (1843), 'Milton']

17. The dust and silence of the upper shelf.
[*Collected Essays* (1843), 'Milton']

18. As civilization advances, poetry almost necessarily declines.
[*Collected Essays* (1843), 'Milton']

19. There is only one cure for the evils which newly acquired freedom produces; and that is freedom.
[*Collected Essays* (1843), 'Milton']

20. Many politicians of our time are in the habit of laying it down as a self-evident proposition, that no people ought to be free till they are fit to use their freedom. The maxim is worthy of the fool in the old story, who resolved not to go into the water till he had learnt to swim. If men are to wait for liberty till they become wise and good in slavery, they may indeed wait for ever.
[*Collected Essays* (1843), 'Milton']

21. [Of the Puritans]
On the rich and the eloquent, on nobles and priests, they looked down with contempt: for they esteemed themselves rich in a more precious treasure, and eloquent in a more sublime language, nobles by the right of an earlier creation, and priests by the imposition of a mightier hand.
[*Collected Essays* (1843), 'Milton']

22. We know of no spectacle so ridiculous as the British public in one of its periodical fits of morality.
[*Collected Essays* (1843), 'Moore's *Life of Byron*']

23. From the poetry of Lord Byron they drew a system of ethics, compounded of misanthropy and voluptuousness, a system in which the two great commandments were, to hate your neighbour, and to love your neighbour's wife.
[*Collected Essays* (1843), 'Moore's *Life of Byron*']

24. [Of John Hampden]
He knew that the essence of war is violence, and that moderation in war is imbecility.
[*Collected Essays* (1843), 'Lord Nugent's *Memorials of Hampden*']

25. Biographers, translators, editors, all, in short, who employ themselves in illustrating the lives or writings of others, are peculiarly exposed to the *Lues Boswelliana*, or disease of admiration.
[*Collected Essays* (1843), 'William Pitt, Earl of Chatham']

26. We have heard it said that five per cent is the natural interest of money.
[*Collected Essays* (1843), 'Southey's 'Colloquies on Society'']

27. [Of the Roman Catholic Church]
She may still exist in undiminished vigour when some traveller from New Zealand shall, in the midst of a vast solitude, take his stand on a broken arch of London Bridge to sketch the ruins of St Paul's.
[*Collected Essays* (1843), 'Von Ranke']

28. The conformation of his mind was such that whatever was little seemed to him great, and whatever was great seemed to him little.
[*Collected Essays* (1843), 'Horace Walpole']

29. The reluctant obedience of distant provinces generally costs more than it [the territory] is worth.
[*Collected Essays* (1843), 'War of the Succession in Spain']

30. I shall cheerfully bear the reproach of having descended below the dignity of history.
[*History of England* (1849), I]

31. Thus our democracy was, from an early period, the most aristocratic, and our aristocracy the most democratic in the world.
[*History of England* (1849), I]

32. [Of Puritans and Calvinists]
Persecution produced its natural effect on them. It found them a sect; it made them a faction.
[*History of England* (1849), I]

33. The Puritan hated bear-baiting, not because it gave pain to the bear, but because it gave pleasure to the spectators.
[*History of England* (1849), I]

34. There were gentlemen and there were seamen in the navy of Charles the Second. But the seamen were not gentlemen; and the gentlemen were not seamen.
[*History of England* (1849), I]

35. [Of Rumbold]
He never would believe that Providence had sent a few men into the world ready booted and spurred to ride, and millions ready saddled and bridled to be ridden.
[*History of England* (1849), I]

36. In every age the vilest specimens of human nature are to be found among demagogues.
[*History of England* (1849), I]

37. The object of oratory alone is not truth, but persuasion.
[*Works* (1898), 'Essay on Athenian Orators']

38. Obadiah Bind-their-kings-in-chains-and-their-nobles-with-links-of-iron.
['The Battle of Naseby' (1824)]

39. Attend, all ye who list to hear our noble England's praise;
I tell of the thrice famous deeds she wrought in ancient days...

40. Night sank upon the dusky beach, and on the purple sea,
Such night in England ne'er had been, nor e'er again shall be...

41. The rugged miners poured to war from Mendip's sunless caves...

42. Till Belvoir's lordly terraces the sign to Lincoln sent,
And Lincoln sped the message on o'er the wide vale of Trent;
Till Skiddaw saw the fire that burned on Gaunt's embattled pile,
And the red glare on Skiddaw roused the burghers of Carlisle.
['The Armada' (1833)]

43. One of us two, Herminius,
Shall never more go home.
I will lay on for Tusculum,
And lay thou on for Rome...

44. Let no man stop to plunder,
But slay, and slay, and slay;
The Gods who live for ever
Are on our side to-day.
[*Lays of Ancient Rome* (1842), 'The Battle of Lake Regillus']

45. Lars Porsena of Clusium
By the nine gods he swore
That the great house of Tarquin
Should suffer wrong no more.
By the Nine Gods he swore it,
And named a trysting day,
And bade his messengers ride forth,
East and west and south and north,
To summon his array.
[*Lays of Ancient Rome* (1842), 'Horatius', 1]

46. But the Consul's brow was sad,
And the Consul's speech was low,
And darkly looked he at the wall,
And darkly at the foe.
[*Lays of Ancient Rome* (1842), 'Horatius', 26]

47. Then out spake brave Horatius,
The Captain of the Gate:
'To every man upon this earth
Death cometh soon or late.
And how can man die better
Than facing fearful odds,
For the ashes of his fathers,
And the temples of his Gods?'
[*Lays of Ancient Rome* (1842), 'Horatius', 27]

48. Now who will stand on either hand,
And keep the bridge with me?
[*Lays of Ancient Rome* (1842), 'Horatius', 29]

49. Then none was for a party;
Then all were for the state;
Then the great man helped the poor,
And the poor man loved the great:
Then lands were fairly portioned;
Then spoils were fairly sold:
The Romans were like brothers
In the brave days of old.
[*Lays of Ancient Rome* (1842), 'Horatius', 31]

50. Was none who would be foremost
To lead such dire attack;
But those behind cried 'Forward!'

And those before cried 'Back!'
[*Lays of Ancient Rome* (1842), 'Horatius', 50]

51. 'Come back, come back, Horatius!'
Loud cried the Fathers all.
'Back, Lartius! back, Herminius!
Back, ere the ruin fall!'
[*Lays of Ancient Rome* (1842), 'Horatius', 53]

52. O Tiber! father Tiber!
To whom the Romans pray,
A Roman's life, a Roman's arms,
Take thou in charge this day!
[*Lays of Ancient Rome* (1842), 'Horatius', 59]

53. And even the ranks of Tuscany
Could scarce forbear to cheer.
[*Lays of Ancient Rome* (1842), 'Horatius', 60]

54. When the oldest cask is opened,
And the largest lamp is lit;...
With weeping and with laughter
Still is the story told,
How well Horatius kept the bridge
In the brave days of old.
[*Lays of Ancient Rome* (1842), 'Horatius', 69]

55. To my true king I offer'd free from stain
Courage and faith; vain faith, and courage vain...

56. By those white cliffs I never more must see,
By that dear language which I spake like thee,
Forget all feuds, and shed one English tear
O'er English dust. A broken heart lies here.
['A Jacobite's Epitaph' (1845)]

57. Ye diners-out from whom we guard our spoons.
[Letter to Hannah Macaulay, 1831]

58. The story is the old story. There are the old raptures about mountains and cataracts. The old flimsy philosophy about the effect of scenery on the mind; the old crazy mystical metaphysics; the endless wilderness of dull, flat, prosaic twaddle.
[Comment on Wordsworth's 'The Prelude' in his journal]

59. I shall not be satisfied unless I produce something which shall for a few days supersede the last fashionable novel on the tables of young ladies.
[In G.O. Trevelyan, *Life and Letters of Macaulay* (1876), 9]

McAuley, James Philip (1917–1976)
Australian poet and critic

1. The soul must feed on something for its dreams,
In those brick suburbs, and there wasn't much:
It can make do with little, so it seems.
[*Collected Poems* (1971), 'Wisteria']

2. Small things can pit the memory like a cyst:
Having seen other fathers greet their sons,
I put my childish face up to be kissed
After an absence. The rebuff still stuns

My blood. The poor man's embarrassment
At such a delicate proffer of affection
Cut like a saw. But home the lesson went:
My tenderness thenceforth escaped detection.
[*Collected Poems* (1971), 'Because']

3. Voyage within you, on the fabled ocean,
And you will find that Southern Continent,
Quiros' vision – his hidalgo heart
And mystical Australia, where reside
All things in their imagined counterpart.

It is your land of similes: the wattle
Scatters its pollen on the doubting heart;
The flowers are wide-awake; the air gives ease.
There you come home; the magpies call you Jack
And whistle like larrikins at you from the trees.
[*Collected Poems* (1971), 'Terra Australis']

4. [After his first cancer operation; to a friend]
Well, better a semi-colon than a full stop!
[In Peter Coleman, *The Heart of James McAuley* (1980)]

McAuliffe, General (1898–1975)
American army officer

1. [Reply to German demand for surrender of 101st Airborne Division men trapped at Bastogne, Belgium, 1944]
Nuts!
[*New York Times*, 1944]

MacCarthy, Sir Desmond (1878–1952)
English literary and dramatic critic

1. [Journalists are] more attentive to the minute hand of history than to the hour hand.
[In K. Tynan, *Curtains* (1961)]

McCarthy, Joseph [1] (fl. 20th century)

1. You made me love you,
I didn't want to do it.
[Song, 1913]

2. In my sweet little Alice blue gown,
When I first wandered out in the town.
['Alice Blue Gown', song, 1919]

McCarthy, Senator Joseph [2] (1908–1957)
American Republican politician, known for his investigations of alleged Communists

1. McCarthyism is Americanism with its sleeves rolled.
[Speech, 1952]

2. [Of someone alleged to have communist sympathies]
It makes me sick, sick, sick way down inside.
[In P. Lewis, *The Fifties* (1978)]

3. [On how to spot a communist]
It looks like a duck, walks like a duck, and quacks like a duck.
[Attr.]

McCarthy, Mary (1912–1989)
American novelist, critic and journalist

1. If someone tells you he is going to make 'a realistic decision', you immediately understand that he has resolved to do something bad.
[*On the Contrary* (1961), 'American Realist Playwrights']

2. When an American heiress wants to buy a man, she at once crosses the Atlantic. The only really materialistic people I have ever met have been Europeans.
[*On the Contrary* (1961), 'America the Beautiful']

3. An interviewer asked me what book I thought best represented the modern American woman. All I could think of to answer was: *Madame Bovary*.
[*On the Contrary* (1961)]

McCartney, Paul (1942–)
English pop singer-songwriter and guitarist; member of the Beatles 1962–70

1. The issues are the same. We wanted peace on earth, love,

and understanding between everyone around the world.
We have learned that change comes slowly.
[*The Observer*, 'Sayings of the Week', 1987]

McClellan, George (1826–1885)
American general, engineer, politician and memoirist

1. [Said during the American Civil War]
All quiet along the Potomac.
[Attr.]

McCormick, Peter Dodds (1834–1916)

1. [Song adopted as Australia's national anthem in 1984, with 'Australia's sons' altered to 'Australians all']
Australia's sons, let us rejoice,
For we are young and free,
We've golden soil and wealth for toil,
Our home is girt by sea;
Our land abounds in nature's gifts
Of beauty rich and rare;
In hist'ry's page, let ev'ry stage
Advance Australia fair,
In joyful strains then let us sing
Advance Australia fair.
['Advance Australia Fair', song, 1878; also attributed to John McFarlane (1825–1866)]

McCoy, Horace (1897–1955)
American short-story writer and novelist

1. They Shoot Horses, Don't They?
[Title of novel, 1935]

McCrae, John (1872–1918)
Canadian physician and poet

1. In Flanders fields the poppies blow
Between the crosses, row on row,
That mark our place...

2. Take up our quarrel with the foe:
To you from failing hands we throw
The torch; be yours to hold it high.
If ye break faith with us who die
We shall not sleep, though poppies grow
In Flanders fields.
['In Flanders Fields' (1915)]

McCuaig, Ronald (1908–1990)
Australian journalist and poet

1. Love me, and never leave me,
Love, nor ever deceive me,
And I shall always bless you
If I may undress you:
This I heard a lover say
To his sweetheart where they lay.
He, though he did undress her,
Did not always bless her;
She, though she would not leave him,
Often did deceive him;
Yet they loved, and when they died
They were buried side by side.
['Love Me and Never Leave Me' (1930)]

2. 'Girls be wary
And maids be coy;
Never you marry
A farmer's boy.'
['Habanera']

McCullough, Colleen (1937–)
Australian popular novelist

1. [On writing love scenes]
Love-making is such a non-verbal thing. I hate the explicit 'he stuck it in her' kind of thing because it is so boring. You can only say 'he stuck it in her' so many ways.
[*The Guardian*, 1977]

McDermott, John W. (20th century)
Hawaiian travel writer

1. Ninety-Mile Beach was obviously named by one of New Zealand's first advertising copywriters ... It is fifty-six miles long.
[*How to Get Lost and Found in New Zealand* (1976)]

MacDiarmid, Hugh (Christopher Murray Grieve) (1892–1978)
Leading Scottish Renaissance poet; prose writer, Nationalist and Communist

1. Oot o' the way, my senses five,
I ken a' you can tell,
Oot o' the way, my thochts, for noo
I maun face God mysel'.
['Ballad of the Five Senses' (1923)]

2. Mars is braw in crammasy,
Venus in a green silk goun,
The auld mune shak's her gowden feathers,
Their starry talk's a wheen o' blethers,
Nane for thee a thochtie sparin',
Earth, thou bonnie broukit bairn!
– But greet, an' in your tears ye'll droun
The haill clanjamfrie!
['The Bonnie Broukit Bairn' (1925)]

3. Fegs, God's no blate gin he stirs up
The men o' Crowdieknowe!
['Crowdieknowe' (1925)]

4. I amna' fou' sae muckle as tired – deid dune...

5. You canna gang to a Burns supper even
Wi'oot some wizened scrunt o' a knock-knee
Chinee turns roon to say, 'Him Haggis – velly goot!'
And ten to wan the piper is a Cockney...

6. I'll ha'e nae hauf-way hoose, but aye be whaur
Extremes meet – it's the only way I ken
To dodge the curst conceit o' bein' richt
That damns the vast majority o' men...

7. And this deid thing, whale-white obscenity,
This horror that I writhe in – is my soul!...

8. Nae doot they're sober, as a Scot ne'er was,
Each tethered to a punctual snorin' missus,
Whilst I, pure fule, owre continents unkent
And wine-dark oceans waunder like Ulysses...

9. And on my lips ye'll heed nae mair,
And in my hair forget,
The seed o' a' the men that in
My virgin womb ha'e met...

10. And as at sicna times am I,
I wad ha'e Scotland to my eye
Until I saw a timeless flame
Tak' Auchtermuchty for a name,
And kent that Ecclefechan stood
As pairt o' an eternal mood...

11. I tae ha'e heard Eternity drip water
(Aye water, water!), drap by drap

On the a'e nerve...

12. The wee reliefs we ha'e in booze,
Or wun at times in carnal states,
May hide frae us but canna cheenge
The silly horrors o' oor fates...

13. Hauf his soul a Scot maun use
Indulgin' in illusions,
And hauf in gettin' rid o' them
And comin' to conclusions...

14. And Jesus and a nameless ape
Collide and share the selfsame shape
That nocht terrestrial can escape...

15. A Scottish poet maun assume
The burden o' his people's doom,
And dee to brak' their livin' tomb...

16. O I ha'e Silence left,
–'And weel ye micht,'
Sae Jean'll say, 'efter sic a nicht!'
[*A Drunk Man Looks at the Thistle* (1926)]

17. I met ayont the cairney
A lass wi' tousie hair
Singin' till a bairnie
That was nae langer there.

Wund wi' warlds to swing
Dinna sing sae sweet,
The licht that bends owre a' thing
Is less ta'en up wi't.
['Empty Vessel' (1926)]

18. Aulder than mammoth or than mastodon
Deep i' the herts o' a' men lurk scaut-heid
Skrymmorie monsters few daur look upon.
['Gairmscoile' (1926)]

19. And I lo'e love
Wi' a scunner in't.
['Scunner' (1926)]

20. It's easier to lo'e Prince Charlie
Than Scotland – mair's the shame!
['Bonnie Prince Charlie' (1930)]

21. This Bolshevik bog! Suits me doon to the grun'!
['Tarras' (1932)]

22. There are plenty of ruined buildings in the world but no ruined stones...

23. What happens to us
Is irrelevant to the world's geology
But what happens to the world's geology
Is not irrelevant to us.
['On a Raised Beach' (1934)]

24. Poetry like politics maun cut
The cackle and pursue real ends,
Unerringly as Lenin, and to that
Its nature better tends.
['Second Hymn to Lenin' (1935)]

25. Other masters may conceivably write
Even yet in C major,
But we – we take the perhaps 'primrose path'
To the dodecaphonic bonfire.
['In Memoriam James Joyce' (1955)]

26. It is very rarely that a man loves
And when he does it is nearly always fatal.
['The International Brigade' (1957)]

27. Killing
Is the ultimate simplification of life.
['England's Double Knavery' (1969)]

28. The rose of all the world is not for me
I want for my part
Only the little white rose of Scotland
That smells sharp and sweet – and breaks the heart.
['The Little White Rose'. Cf. Mackenzie: 9]

29. Our principal writers have nearly all been fortunate in escaping regular education.
[*The Observer*, 'Sayings of the Week', 1953]

Macdonald, C.B. (1855–1939)

1. [Remark by a caddy at St Andrews to a professor who was having difficulty learning the game]
When ye come to play golf ye maun hae a heid!
[*Scotland's Gift – Golf* (1928)]

MacDonald, George (1824–1905)
Scottish novelist, poet, writer of fairy stories, journalist and preacher

1. Here lie I, Martin Elginbrodde:
Hae mercy o' my soul, Lord God;
As I wad do, were I Lord God,
And you were Martin Elginbrodde.
[*David Elginbrod* (1863), I]

2. Where did you come from, baby dear?
Out of the everywhere into here.
[*At the Back of the North Wind* (1871), 33]

MacDonald, Sir John A. (1815–1891)
Canadian politician and Prime Minister

1. [Exchange between an irate suffragette and Sir John A. MacDonald when he was Prime Minister]
Q. What is the difference between the Prime Minister and myself?
A. Madame, I cannot conceive.
[Attr.]

MacDonald, Ramsay (1866–1937)
Scottish Labour politician; Prime Minister 1924, 1929–31, 1931–35

1. Society goes on and on and on. It is the same with ideas.
[Speech, 1935]

2. We hear war called murder. It is not: it is suicide.
[*The Observer*, 'Sayings of the Week', 1930]

3. Let them [France and Germany] especially put their demands in such a way that Great Britain could say that she supported both sides.
[In A.J.P. Taylor, *The Origins of the Second World War* (1961), 3]

McEnroe, John (1959–)
US champion tennis player

1. [To an umpire at Wimbledon, 1981]
You are the pits of the world.
[*The Sunday Times*, 1984]

2. [To an umpire; this remark became a catchphrase in the early 1980s]
You cannot be serious.
[Attr.]

McGonagall, William (c. 1830–1902)
Scottish doggerel poet; tragedian and actor

1. Beautiful city of Glasgow, I now conclude my muse,

And to write in praise of thee my pen does not refuse;
And, without fear of contradiction, I will venture to say
You are the second grandest city in Scotland at the present day.
['Glasgow' (1890)]

2. Beautiful Railway Bridge of the Silv'ry Tay!
Alas, I am very sorry to say
That ninety lives have been taken away
On the last Sabbath day of 1879,
Which will be remember'd for a very long time.
['The Tay Bridge Disaster' (1890)]

McGough, Roger (1937–)
English poet and teacher

1. You will put on a dress of guilt
and shoes with broken high ideals.
['Comeclose and Sleepnow' (1967)]

McGregor, Craig (1933–)
Australian journalist, essayist and writer

1. A house is a machine for loving in.
[In Ian McKay et al., *Living and Partly Living*. Cf. Le Corbusier: 1]

Machado, Antonio (1875–1939)
Spanish poet and dramatist

1. *Yo vivo en paz con los hombres*
y en guerra con mis entrañas.
I live in peace with men and at war with my innards.
[*Campos de Castilla* (*Castilian Landscapes*, 1907–1917), 'Proverbs and Songs', 23]

Machiavelli, Niccolò di Bernardo dei (1469–1527)
Florentine statesman, political theorist and historian

1. *Dio fa gli uomini, e' s'appaiono.*
God creates men, but they choose each other.
[*La Mandragola* (*The Mandrake*, 1518), I.iii]

2. *Questi frati sono trincati, astuti; ed è ragionevole, perché e' sanno e peccati nostri.*
These friars are cunning and crafty, and it makes sense because they know our sins.
[*La Mandragola* (*The Mandrake*, 1518), III.ii]

3. *E' dicono el vero quelli che dicono che le cattive compagnie conducono li uomini alle forche.*
And they are right, those who say that bad company leads to the gallows.
[*La Mandragola* (*The Mandrake*, 1518), IV.vi]

4. *Di qui nacque che tutti e' profeti armati vinsono, e li disarmati ruinorono.*
And that is why all the armed prophets were victorious, whilst all the unarmed perished.
[*Il Principe* (*The Prince*, 1532), 6]

5. *Debbe, pertanto, uno principe non si curare della infamia di crudele, per tenere li sudditi suoi uniti e in fede.*
In order to keep his people united and faithful, a prince must not be concerned with being reputed as a cruel man.
[*Il Principe* (*The Prince*, 1532), 17]

6. *Gli uomini sidimenticano più presto la morte del padre che la perdita del patrimonio.*
Men sooner forget the death of their father than the loss of their possessions.
[*Il Principe* (*The Prince*, 1532), 17]

7. *Uno principe necessitato sapere bene usare la bestia, debbe di quelle pigliare la golpe e il lione; perché il lione non si defende da' lacci, la golpe non si defenda da' lupi. Bisogna adunque, essere golpe a conoscere e' lacci, e lione a sbigottire e' lupi.*
A prince must know how to make use of animals, and from amongst them take the attributes of the fox and the lion; because the lion doesn't protect itself from snares and the fox doesnt protect itself from wolves. Hence he must act at times as a fox that can see the snares and at times as a lion that frightens off wolves.
[*Il Principe* (*The Prince*, 1532), 18]

8. *La fortuna, come donna, è amica de giovani, perché sono meno respettivi, più feroci e con più audacia la comandano.*
Fortune, like a woman, is friendly to the young, because they show her less respect, they are more daring and command her with audacity.
[*Il Principe* (*The Prince*, 1532), 25]

9. *Gli uomini non operano mai nulla nel bene se non per necessità.*
Men never do anything good except out of necessity.
[*Dai Discorsi* (*Discourse*), I, 3]

10. *Li buoni esempi nascano dalla buona educazione; la buona educazione dalle buone leggi: e le buone leggi, da quei tumulti che molti inconsideratamente dannano.*
Good examples are borne out of good education, which is the outcome of good legislation; and good legislation is borne out of those uprisings which are unduly damned by so many people.
[*Dai Discorsi* (*Discourse*), I, 4]

MacInnes, Colin (1914–1976)
English novelist and essayist

1. England is . . . a country infested with people who love to tell us what to do, but who very rarely seem to know what's going on.
[*England, Half English*, 'Pop Songs and Teenagers']

McIver, Charles D. (1860–1906)
American educationist

1. When you educate a man you educate an individual; when you educate a woman you educate a whole family.
[Address at women's college]

Mackay, Charles (1814–1889)
Scottish poet and journalist

1. There's a good time coming, boys,
A good time coming.
['The Good Time Coming']

MacKellar, Dorothea (1885–1968)
Australian poet and novelist

1. I love a sunburnt country,
A land of sweeping plains,
Of ragged mountain ranges,
Of droughts and flooding rains.
I love her far horizons,
I love her jewel-sea,
Her beauty and her terror–
The wide brown land for me!...

2. An opal-hearted country,
A wilful, lavish land–
All you who have not loved her,
You will not understand–
Though Earth holds many splendours,
Wherever I may die,
I know to what brown country
My homing thoughts will fly.
['My Country' (1971)]

Mackenzie, Sir Compton (1883–1972)
Scottish novelist, born in England; journalist, broadcaster, nationalist and autobiographer

1. The slavery of being waited upon that is more deadening than the slavery of waiting upon other people.
[*The Adventures of Sylvia Scarlett* (1918)]

2. I don't believe in principles. Principles are only excuses for what we want to think or what we want to do.
[*The Adventures of Sylvia Scarlett* (1918)]

3. Women do not find it difficult nowadays to behave like men; but they often find it extremely difficult to behave like gentlemen.
[*Literature in My Time* (1933)]

4. From the days of Eve women have always faced sexual facts with more courage and realism than men.
[*Literature in My Time* (1933)]

5. [Of reprieve from sentence of death]
No man should be compelled to bear the burden carried by a Home Secretary.
[*On Moral Courage* (1962), 1]

6. Ever since the first World War there has been an inclination to denigrate the heroic aspect of man.
[*On Moral Courage* (1962), 3]

7. There is little to choose morally between beating up a man physically and beating him up mentally.
[*On Moral Courage* (1962), 3]

8. I told him [D.H. Lawrence] that if he was determined to convert the world to proper reverence for the sexual act ... he would always have to remember one handicap for such an undertaking – that except to the two people who are indulging in it the sexual act is a comic operation.
[*My Life and Times* (1963–1971), *Octave Five*]

9. [Of his speech at the annual commemoration of Bannockburn, June 1932]
I wound it up with the words Hugh MacDiarmid used in his lyric about the little wild rose of Scotland. In the first edition it was printed '(with acknowledgements to Compton Mackenzie)'.
[*My Life and Times* (1963–1971), *Octave Seven*. Cf. MacDiarmid: 28]

McKinney, Joyce (1950–)
US beauty queen

1. [Speaking about the Mormon ex-lover she had kidnapped]
I loved Kirk so much, I would have skied down Mount Everest in the nude with a carnation up my nose.
[Statement in British court, 1977]

Mackintosh, Sir James (1765–1832)
Scottish philosopher, historian, lawyer and Whig politician

1. The Commons, faithful to their system, remained in a wise and masterly inactivity.
[*Vindiciae Gallicae* (1791)]

2. Men are never so good or so bad as their opinions.
[*Dissertation on the Progress of Ethical Philosophy* (1830), 'Jeremy Bentham']

Macklin, Charles (c. 1697–1797)
Irish actor and dramatist

1. She looks as if butter would not melt in her mouth.
[*The Man of the World* (1781)]

MacLaine, Shirley (1934–)
American film actress

1. [On her friendship with Andrew Peacock]
I thought as long as he's Minister for Foreign Affairs I might as well give him one he'd never forget.
[Melbourne *Herald*, 1979]

McLean, Joyce
Canadian writer

1. There's an old saying which goes: Once the last tree is cut and the last river poisoned, you will find you cannot eat your money.
[*The Globe and Mail*, 1989]

McLean, Stuart
Canadian broadcaster

1. Who buys coat hangers? They breed in your closet like rattlesnakes.
[Quoted by Peter Gzowski in *The New Morningside Papers* (1987)]

MacLeish, Archibald (1892–1982)
American poet, dramatist, lawyer, teacher and librarian

1. A Poem should be palpable and mute
As a globed fruit,

Dumb
As old medallions to the thumb,

Silent as the sleeve-worn stone
Of casement ledges where the moss has grown–
A poem should be wordless
As the flight of birds...

2. A poem should not mean
But be.
['Ars poetica' (1926)]

3. We have learned the answers, all the answers:
It is the question that we do not know.
[*The Hamlet of A. MacLeish* (1935)]

McLennan, Murdoch (fl. 1715)
Scottish poet

1. There's some say that we wan, some say that they wan,
Some say that nane wan at a', man;
But one thing I'm sure, that at Sheriffmuir
A battle there was which I saw, man:
And we ran, and they ran, and they ran, and we ran,
And we ran; and they ran awa', man!
[In J. Woodfall Ebsworth (ed.), *Roxburghe Ballads* (1889), 'Sheriffmuir']

Macleod, Fiona (William Sharp) (1855–1905)
Scottish neo-Celtic poet, novelist and dramatist

1. My heart is a lonely hunter that hunts on a lonely hill.
['The Lonely Hunter' (1896)]

Macleod, Iain (1913–1970)
English Conservative politician and writer; Chancellor of the Exchequer 1970

1. History is too serious to be left to historians.
[*The Observer*, 'Sayings of the Week', 1961]

2. We now have the worst of both worlds – not just inflation on the one side or stagnation on the other side, but both of them together. We have a sort of 'stagflation' situation.
[Speech, House of Commons, 17 November 1965]

Macleod, Norman (1812–1872)
Scottish divine; royal chaplain, preacher and travel writer

1. Courage, brother! do not stumble,
Though thy path be dark as night;
There's a star to guide the humble:
'Trust in God, and do the Right'.
[Hymn, 1857]

McLuhan, Marshall (1911–1980)
Canadian communications theorist

1. For tribal man space was the uncontrollable mystery. For technological man it is time that occupies the same role.
[*The Mechanical Bridge* (1951), 'Magic that Changes Mood']

2. The new electronic interdependence recreates the world in the image of a global village.
[*The Gutenberg Galaxy* (1962)]

3. If the nineteenth century was the age of the editorial chair, ours is the century of the psychiatrist's couch.
[*Understanding Media* (1964), Introduction]

4. In a culture like ours, long accustomed to splitting and dividing all things as a means of control, it is sometimes a bit of a shock to be reminded that, in operational and practical fact, the medium is the message.
[*Understanding Media* (1964)]

5. The medium is the message. This is merely to say that the personal and social consequences of any medium ... result from the new scale that is introduced into our affairs by each extension of ourselves or by any new technology.
[*Understanding Media* (1964)]

6. The car has become the carapace, the protective and aggressive shell, of urban and suburban man.
[*Understanding Media* (1964)]

7. Ads are the cave art of the twentieth century.
[*Culture Is Our Business* (1970)]

8. Our motor car is our supreme form of privacy when away from home.
[Address, Mohawk College, Hamilton, Ontario, 1977]

9. Television brought the brutality of war into the comfort of the living room. Vietnam was lost in the living rooms of America – not on the battle fields of Vietnam.
[Montreal *Gazette*, 1975]

10. The reason universities are so full of knowledge is that the students come with so much and they leave with so little.
[*Antigonish Review*, 1988]

11. An administrator in a bureaucratic world is a man who can feel big by merging his non-entity with an abstraction. A real person in touch with real things inspires terror in him.
[In M. Molinaro, C. McLuhan and W. Toye (eds), *Letters of Marshall McLuhan*, Letter to Ezra Pound, 1951]

12. When a thing is current, it creates currency.
[In Richard Kostelanetz, *Master Minds* (1969), 'Marshall McLuhan: High Priest of the Electronic Village']

13. [Favourite conversational gambit]
For your information, let me ask you a question.
[In Philip Marchand, *Marshall McLuhan: The Medium and the Messenger* (1989)]

14. The present cannot be revealed to people until it has become yesterday.
[In Philip Marchand, *Marshall McLuhan: The Medium and the Messenger* (1989)]

15. The hydrogen bomb is history's exclamation point. It ends an age-long sentence of manifest violence.
[Attr.]

Macmahon, Marshal (1808–1893)
French army commander and royalist; President of the Third Republic 1873–79

1. [Said at the taking of the Malakoff, 1855]
J'y suis, j'y reste.
Here I am, and here I stay.
[Attr.]

MacManus, Michael (1888–1951)

1. But my work is undistinguished
And my royalties are lean
Because I never am obscure
And not at all obscene.
['An Author's Lament']

Macmillan, Harold (First Earl of Stockton) (1894–1986)
British statesman; Conservative Prime Minister 1957–63

1. The Middle Way.
[Title of book, 1938]

2. [Macmillan and Company Limited] propose to carry on their business at St Martin's Street, London W.C.2 until they are either taxed, insured, ARPd or bombed out of existence.
[Announcement, 17 September 1939, quoted in Lovat Dickson, *The House of Lords* (1963)]

3. [After a summit conference in Geneva]
There ain't gonna be no war.
[Press conference, London, 1955]

4. Let's be frank about it; most of our people have never had it so good.
[Speech, 1957]

5. On 7 January [1958] ... I made a short and carefully prepared statement ... I referred to 'some recent difficulties' in our affairs at home which had 'caused me a little anxiety'. However, 'I thought the best thing to do was to settle up these little local difficulties and then to turn to the wider vision of the Commonwealth.'
[Comment on Cabinet crisis, 1958]

6. When you're abroad you're a statesman: when you're at home you're just a politician.
[Speech, South African Parliament, 1958]

7. The most striking of all the impressions I have formed since I left London a month ago is of the strength of this African national consciousness. The wind of change is blowing through this continent.
[Speech, 1960, written by Sir David Hunt]

8. It is a good thing to be laughed at. It is better than to be ignored.
[*That Was The Week That Was*, BBC television programme, 1962]

9. [On his resignation as Prime Minister]
I hope that it will soon be possible for the customary processes of consultation to be carried on within the party about its future leadership.
[Statement (read by R.A. Butler) to Conservative Party Conference, 10 October 1963]

10. [Referring to privatization of profitable nationalized industries]
Selling the family silver.
[Speech, House of Lords, 1986]

11. [On the life of a Foreign Secretary]
Forever poised between a cliché and an indiscretion.
[*Newsweek*, 1956. Cf. Robert Runcie: 1]

12. As usual the Liberals offer a mixture of sound and original ideas. Unfortunately none of the sound ideas is original and none of the original ideas is sound.
[*The Observer*, 'Sayings of the Week', 1961]

13. If people want a sense of purpose they should get it from their archbishop. They should certainly not get it from their politicians.
[In H. Fairlie, *The Life of Politics* (1968)]

McMillan, Joyce (1952–)
Scottish journalist and critic

1. ... recognition of the suffering inflicted on peoples by their own leaders is undermining the idea of absolute national sovereignty, just as recognition of the unacceptability of domestic violence undermined the idea of absolute patriarchal rights in the family.
[*Scotland on Sunday*, 1992]

MacNally, Leonard (1752–1820)
Irish lawyer, dramatist and political informer

1. On Richmond Hill there lives a lass,
More sweet than May day morn,
Whose charms all other maids surpass,
A rose without a thorn...

2. This lass so neat, with smiles so sweet,
Has won my right good-will,
I'd crowns resign to call thee mine,
Sweet lass of Richmond Hill.
['The Lass of Richmond Hill' (1789); also attributed to W. Upton]

MacNamara, Frank (Frank the Poet) (b. 1811)
Irish-born convict poet and balladeer

1. Farewell Tasmania's isle!
I bid adieu
The possum and the kangaroo.
Farmers' Glory! Prisoners' Hell!
Land of Buggers!
Fare ye well.
['A Convict's Tour to Hell' (1839)]

MacNeice, Louis (1907–1963)
British poet, born in Belfast; radio writer and producer, translator and critic

1. World is crazier and more of it than we think,
Incorrigibly plural. I peel and portion
A tangerine and spit the pips and feel
The drunkenness of things being various.
['Snow' (1935)]

2. It's no go the merrygoround, it's no go the rickshaw,
All we want is a limousine and a ticket for the peep show...

3. It's no go the picture place, it's no go the stadium,
It's no go the country cot with a pot of pink geraniums,
It's no go the Government grants, it's no go the elections,
Sit on your arse for fifty years and hang your hat on a pension.
It's no go my honey love, it's no go my poppet;
Work your hands from day to day, the winds will blow the profit.
The glass is falling hour by hour, the glass will fall for ever,
But if you break the bloody glass, you won't hold up the weather.
['Bagpipe Music' (1938)]

4. The sunlight on the garden
Hardens and grows cold,
We cannot cage the minute
Within its nets of gold,
When all is told
We cannot beg for pardon...

5. Our freedom as free lances
Advanced towards its end;
The earth compels, upon it
Sonnets and birds descend;
And soon, my friend,
We shall have no time for dances.
['The Sunlight on the Garden' (1938)]

6. All of London littered with remembered kisses.
[*Autumn Journal* (1939), 4]

7. Better authentic mammon than a bogus god.
[*Autumn Journal* (1939), 12]

8. Good-bye now, Plato and Hegel,
The shop is closing down;
They don't want any philosopher-kings in England,
There ain't no universals in this man's town.
[*Autumn Journal* (1939), 13]

9. Crumbling between the fingers, under the feet,
Crumbling behind the eyes,
Their world gives way and dies
And something twangs and breaks at the end of the street.
['Débâcle' (1941)]

10. Time was away and somewhere else,
There were two glasses and two chairs
And two people with one pulse
(Somebody stopped the moving stairs):
Time was away and somewhere else.
['Meeting Point' (1941)]

11. So they were married – to be the more together–
And found they were never again so much together,
Divided by the morning tea,
By the evening paper,
By children and tradesmen's bills.
['Les Sylphides' (1941)]

12. I am not yet born; O fill me
With strength against those who would freeze my
humanity, would dragoon me into a lethal automaton,
would make me a cog in a machine, a thing with
one face, a thing, and against all those
who would dissipate my entirety, would
blow me like thistledown hither and
thither or hither and thither
like water held in the
hands would spill me.

Let them not make me a stone and let them not spill me.
Otherwise kill me.
['Prayer before Birth' (1944)]

13. Pride in your history is pride
In living what your fathers died,
Is pride in taking your own pulse
And counting in you someone else.
[*Collected Poems* (1966), 'Suite for Recorders']

14. It is particularly vulgar to talk about one's money – whether one has lots of it, and boasts about it, or is broke, and says so. Now I myself cannot see why a man should not talk about his money. Everybody is interested in everybody else's finances, and it seems hypocrisy to hush the subject

up in the drawing room – as if bank balances were found under gooseberry bushes.
['In Defence of Vulgarity' (1937)]

15. One must not dislike people ... because they are intransigent. For that could be only playing their own game.
[*Zoo* (1938), 'A Personal Digression']

16. Take, for instance, the question of class. There were many undergraduates like myself who theoretically conceded that all men were equal, but who, in practice, while only too willing to converse, or attempt to, with say Normandy peasants or shopkeepers, would wince away in their own college halls from those old grammar school boys who with impure vowels kept admiring Bernard Shaw or Noël Coward while grabbing their knives and forks like dumb-bells.
[*The Saturday Book* (1961), 'When I was Twenty-one: 1928']

McNeill, F. Marian (1885–1973)
Scottish author, journalist, lecturer and broadcaster

1. There are two things a Highlander likes naked, and one of them is malt whisky.
[*The Scots Cellar* (1956)]

Madan, Geoffrey (1895–1947)
English bibliophile

1. The devil finds mischief still for hands that have not learnt how to be idle.
[*Livre sans nom: Twelve Reflections* (1934)]

2. The dust of exploded beliefs may make a fine sunset.
[*Livre sans nom: Twelve Reflections* (1934)]

Madariaga, Salvador de (1886–1978)
Spanish writer, diplomat and teacher

1. First the sweetheart of the nation, then her aunt, woman governs America because America is a land where boys refuse to grow up.
['Americans are Boys']

Madden, Samuel (1686–1765)
Irish philanthropist, writer and clergyman

1. Words are men's daughters, but God's sons are things.
[*Boulter's Monument* (1745)]

Maeterlinck, Maurice (1862–1949)
Belgian poet, symbolist playwright and essayist; Nobel prize 1911

1. *Il n'y a pas de morts.*
There are no dead.
[*L'Oiseau bleu* (*The Blue Bird*, 1909), IV.ii]

2. The living are just the dead on holiday.
[Attr.]

Magee, William Connor (1821–1891)
Irish controversialist, orator and Bishop of Peterborough

1. It would be better that England should be free than that England should be compulsorily sober.
[Speech on the Intoxicating Liquor Bill, House of Lords, 1872]

Magna Carta (1215)
Charter granted by King John

1. *Quod Anglicana ecclesia libera sit.*
That the English Church shall be free.
[Clause 1]

2. *Nullus liber homo capiatur, vel imprisonetur, aut disseisiatur, aut utlagetur, aut exuletur, aut aliquo modo destruatur, nec super eum ibimus, nec super eum mittemus, nisi per legale judicium parium suorum vel per legem terrae.*
No free man shall be taken or imprisoned or dispossessed, or outlawed or exiled, or in any way destroyed, nor will we go upon him, nor will we send against him, except by the lawful judgement of his peers or by the law of the land.
[Clause 39]

3. *Nulli vendemus, nulli negabimus aut differemus, rectum aut justitiam.*
To no one will we sell, to no one will we deny, or delay, right or justice.
[Clause 40]

Mahaffy, Sir John Pentland (1839–1919)
Irish classical scholar and historian, born in Switzerland

1. My dear Oscar, you are not clever enough for us in Dublin. You had better run over to Oxford.
[In H. Montgomery Hyde, *Oscar Wilde: A Biography* (1975)]

2. [On distinguishing the Irish bull from similar freaks of language]
The Irish bull is always pregnant.
[Oral trad.]

Mahan, Alfred T. (1840–1914)
American naval historian

1. Those far distant, storm-beaten ships, upon which the Grand Army never looked, stood between it and the dominion of the world.
[*The Influence of Sea Power upon the French Revolution and Empire, 1793–1812* (1892)]

Mahler, Gustav (1860–1911)
Austrian late Romantic composer, known for his symphonies and song cycles

1. [On visiting Niagara]
Endlich fortissimo!
At last, *fortissimo!*
[In K. Blaukopf, *Gustav Mahler* (1973)]

Mailer, Norman (1923–)
American novelist, journalist and essayist; writer of faction

1. Once a newspaper touches a story, the facts are lost forever, even to the protagonists.
[*The Presidential Papers* (1976)]

2. You don't know a woman until you've met her in court.
[*The Observer*, 1983, in Jeffrey Care (ed.), *Sayings of the Eighties* (1989)]

3. Being married six times shows a degree of optimism over wisdom, but I am incorrigibly optimistic.
[*The Observer*, 1988, in Jeffrey Care (ed.), *Sayings of the Eighties* (1989)]

Maistre, Joseph de (1753–1821)
French diplomat and political philosopher

1. *Toute nation a le gouvernement qu'elle mérite.*
Each country has the government it deserves.
[*Lettres et opuscules inédits*, Letter, 1811]

2. *Les fausses opinions ressemblent à la fausse monnaie qui est frappée d'abord par de grands coupables, et dépensée ensuite par d'honnêtes gens qui perpétuent le crime sans savoir ce qu'ils font.*
Wrong opinions are like counterfeit coins, which are first minted by great wrongdoers, then spent by decent people

who perpetuate the crime without knowing what they are doing.
[*Les soirées de Saint-Pétersbourg*]

Major, John (1943–)
Conservative politician, Prime Minister from 1990

1. People with vision usually do more harm than good.
[*The Economist*, 1993]

Malamud, Bernard (1914–1986)
American novelist and short-story writer

1. Levin wanted friendship and got friendliness; he wanted steak and they offered spam.
[*A New Life* (1961), VI]

Malesherbes, Chrétien Guillaume de Lamoignonde (1721–1794)
French statesman and writer; guillotined

1. A new maxim is often a brilliant error.
[*Pensées et maximes*]

Malherbe, François de (1555–1628)
French poet, critic and classicist

1. *Et, rose, elle a vécu ce que vivent les roses,*
L'espace d'un matin.
Like a rose, she has lived as long as roses live, the space of a morning.
[*Stances (Stanzas)*]

Mallarmé, Stéphane (1842–1898)
French symbolist poet

1. *Le vierge, le vivace et le bel aujourd'hui.*
That virgin, vital, beautiful day: today.
[*Plusieurs sonnets* (1881), no. 1]

2. *La chair est triste, hélas! et j'ai lu tous les livres.*
The flesh, alas, is sad, and I have read all the books.
['Brise marine' ('Sea Breeze', 1887)]

3. *Un coup de dés jamais n'abolira le hasard.*
A throw of the dice will never eliminate chance.
[Title of work, 1897]

Mallet, David (David Malloch) (c. 1705–1765)
Scottish poet and dramatist

1. O grant me, Heaven, a middle state,
Neither too humble nor too great;
More than enough, for nature's ends,
With something left to treat my friends.
['Imitation of Horace']

Mallet, Robert (1915–)
French university rector, poet and writer

1. *Combien d'esprits pessimistes finissent par désirer ce qu'ils craignent, pour avoir raison.*
How many pessimists end up by desiring the things they fear, in order to prove that they are right.
[*Apostilles*]

Malley, Ern (Pseudonym for James McAuley and Harold Stewart) (1918–1943)
The pseudonym was the basis of a famous literary hoax: McAuley and Stewart put together a corpus of 'avant-garde' poetry in an afternoon and had it published under the name of Ern Malley. The merit of the poems was debated for two decades.

1. I had read in books that art is not easy
But no one warned that the mind repeats
In its ignorance the vision of others. I am still
The black swan of trespass on alien waters.
[Quoted as 'Old Proverb' on title page of *The Darkening Ecliptic* (1944)]

2. I have been bitter with you, my brother,
Remembering that saying of Lenin when the shadow
Was already on his face: 'The emotions are not skilled workers.'
['Colloquy with John Keats' (1944)]

3. I have remembered the chiaroscuro
Of your naked breasts and loins.
For you were wholly an admonition
That said: 'From bright to dark
Is a brief longing. To hasten is now
To delay.' But I could not obey.
['Perspective Lovesong' (1944)]

Mallory, George Leigh (1886–1924)
English mountaineer and teacher; died attempting to scale Everest

1. [Asked why he wished to climb Mt Everest]
Because it is there.
[*New York Times*, 1923]

Malory, Sir Thomas (1400–1471)
English writer, celebrated for his Arthurian prose romance translated from the French

1. Whoso pulleth out this sword of this stone and anvil is rightwise King born of all England.
[*Le Morte D'Arthur* (1470), I, 4]

2. This beast went to the well and drank, and the noise was in the beast's belly like unto the questing of thirty couple hounds, but all the while the beast drank there was no noise in the beast's belly.
[*Le Morte D'Arthur* (1470), I, 19]

3. In the midst of the lake Arthur was ware of an arm clothed in white samite, that held a fair sword in that hand.
[*Le Morte D'Arthur* (1470), I, 25]

4. Meanwhile came Sir Palomides, the good knight, following the questing beast that had in shape like a serpent's head and a body like a leopard, buttocked like a lion and footed like a hart. And in his body there was such a noise as it had been twenty couple of hounds questing [yelping], and such noise that beast made wheresomever he went.
[*Le Morte D'Arthur* (1470), IX, 12]

5. Now I thank God, said Sir Launcelot, for His great mercy of that I have seen, for it sufficeth me. For, as I suppose, no man in this world hath lived better than I have done, to achieve that I have done.
[*Le Morte D'Arthur* (1470), XVII, 16]

6. Fair lord, salute me to my lord, Sir Launcelot, my father, and as soon as ye see him, bid him remember of this unstable world.
[*Le Morte D'Arthur* (1470), XVII, 22]

7. The month of May was come, when every lusty heart beginneth to blossom, and to bring forth fruit; for like as herbs and trees bring forth fruit and flourish in May, in likewise every lusty heart that is in any manner a lover, springeth and flourisheth in lusty deeds.
[*Le Morte D'Arthur* (1470), XVIII, 25]

8. Therefore all ye that be lovers call unto your remembrance the month of May, like as did Queen Guenevere, for whom

I make here a little mention, that while she lived she was a true lover, and therefore she had a good end.
[*Le Morte D'Arthur* (1470), XVIII, 25]

9. For love that time was not as love is nowadays.
[*Le Morte d'Arthur* (1470), XX, 3]

10. Through this man and me hath all this war been wrought, and the death of the most noblest knights of the world; for through our love that we have loved together is my most noble lord slain.
[*Le Morte D'Arthur* (1470), XXI, 9]

11. Wherefore, madam, I pray you kiss me and never no more. Nay, said the queen, that shall I never do, but abstain you from such works: and they departed. But there was never so hard an hearted man but he would have wept to see the dolour that they made.
[*Le Morte D'Arthur* (1470), XXI, 10]

12. And Sir Launcelot awoke, and went and took his horse, and rode all that day and all night in a forest, weeping.
[*Le Morte D'Arthur* (1470), XXI, 10]

13. Then Sir Launcelot saw her visage, but he wept not greatly, but sighed!
[*Le Morte d'Arthur* (1470), XXI, 11]

14. Then Sir Launcelot never after ate but little meat, ne drank, till he was dead.
[*Le Morte D'Arthur* (1470), XXI, 12]

15. I saw the angels heave up Sir Launcelot unto heaven, and the gates of heaven opened against him.
[*Le Morte D'Arthur* (1470), XXI, 12]

16. Said Sir Ector ... Sir Launcelot ... thou wert never matched of earthly knight's hand; and thou wert the courteoust knight that ever bare shield; and thou wert the truest friend to thy lover that ever bestrad horse; and thou wert the truest lover of a sinful man that ever loved woman; and thou wert the kindest man that ever struck with sword; and thou wert the goodliest person that ever came among press of knights; and thou wert the meekest man and the gentlest that ever ate in hall among ladies; and thou wert the sternest knight to thy mortal foe that ever put spear in the rest.
[*Le Morte D'Arthur* (1470), XXI, 13]

Malouf, David (1934–)
Australian novelist and poet

1. I recalled what Aunt Roo had once told me: 'Actors don't pretend to be other people; they become themselves by finding other people inside them.'
[*Harland's Half Acre* (1984), 'The Island', 2]

Malthus, Thomas Robert (1766–1834)
English political economist, noted for his population theory

1. Population, when unchecked, increases in a geometrical ratio. Subsistence only increases in an arithmetical ratio.
[*Essay on the Principle of Population* (1798), 1]

2. The perpetual struggle for room and food.
[*Essay on the Principle of Population* (1798), 3]

Mandale, W.R. (19th century)

1. Up and down the City Road,
In and out the Eagle,
That's the way the money goes–
Pop goes the weasel!
['Pop Goes the Weasel', song, 1853; also attributed to Charles Twiggs]

Mandela, Nelson (1918–)
South African President from 1994; ANC politician, lawyer and former prisoner 1964–90

1. The struggle is my life.
[Letter from underground, 1961]

2. I have fought against white domination, and I have fought against black domination. I have cherished the ideal of a democratic and free society in which all persons will live together in harmony and with equal opportunities. It is an ideal which I hope to live for and achieve. But, if needs be, it is an ideal for which I am prepared to die.
[Statement in the dock, 1964; quoted by him on release from prison, 11 February 1990]

3. I cannot and will not give any undertaking at a time when I, and you, the people, are not free. Your freedom and mine cannot be separated.
[Message read by his daughter to a rally in Soweto, 1985]

4. We enter into a covenant that we shall build the society in which all South Africans, both black and white, will be able to walk tall, without any fear in their hearts, assured of their inalienable right to human dignity – a rainbow nation at peace with itself and the world.
[Speech at his inauguration as President of South Africa, 10 May 1994]

5. Never, never and never again shall it be that this beautiful land will again experience the oppression of one by another and suffer the indignity of being the skunk of the world.
[Speech at his inauguration as President of South Africa, 10 May 1994]

6. The time for the healing of the wounds has come.
[Speech at his inauguration as President of South Africa, 10 May 1994]

7. Let there be justice for all. Let there be peace for all. Let there be bread, water and salt for all. Let freedom reign. The sun shall never set on so glorious a human achievement.
[*Independent on Sunday*, 14 May 1994]

Mandela, Winnie (1934–)
Worker for civil rights in South Africa; implicated in notorious necklace killings; wife of Nelson Mandela

1. Together, hand in hand, with our boxes of matches and our necklaces, we shall liberate this country.
[Speech, 1986]

Mandelstam, Osip (1891–1938)
Russian Acmeist poet and critic

1. No, I am no one's contemporary – ever.
That would have been above my station...
How I loathe that other than my name.
He certainly never was me.
[*Poems*, 141]

Mander, Jane (1877–1949)
New Zealand novelist

1. [On early North Auckland]
Towering arrogantly above all else, on the crests and down the spurs, stood groups of the kauri, the giant timber tree of New Zealand, whose great grey trunks, like the pillars in the ancient halls of Karnak, shot up seventy and eighty feet without a knot or branch, and whose colossal heads, swelling up onto the sky, made a cipher of every tree near.
[*The Story of a New Zealand River* (1920)]

Mangan, James Clarence (1803–1849)
Irish poet and translator

1. My Dark Rosaleen!
[Title of poem]

2. In Siberia's wastes
No tears are shed,
For they freeze within the brain.
Nought is felt but the dullest pain,
Pain acute, yet dead.
['Siberia']

Manifold, John Streeter (1915–1985)
Australian editor, translator and poet

1. I wonder did my darling's mother mind
When I undressed her from behind?
['Elegy I' (1978)]

Mankiewicz, Herman J. (1897–1953)
American journalist and screenwriter; Academy Award 1944

1. [Of death]
It is the only disease you don't look forward to being cured of.
[*Citizen Kane*, film, 1941]

2. [Commenting on the fact that he had not been harmed when swimming in shark-infested waters]
I think that's what they call professional courtesy.
[Attr.]

3. [After being sick at the table of a fastidious host]
It's all right, Arthur. The white wine came up with the fish.
[Attr.]

Mrs Manley (1663–1724)
English dramatist, novelist, satirist, editor, pamphleteer and memoirist

1. No time like the present.
[*The Lost Lover* (1696), IV.i]

Mann, Horace (1796–1859)
American educationist, politician, teacher and writer

1. The object of punishment is prevention from evil; it never can be made impulsive to good.
[*Lectures and Reports on Education* (1845)]

2. Lost, yesterday, somewhere between Sunrise and Sunset, two golden hours, each set with sixty diamond minutes. No reward is offered, for they are gone for ever.
['Lost, Two Golden Hours']

Mann, Thomas (1875–1955)
German novelist, short-story writer and critic; Nobel prize 1929

1. *Wer am meisten liebt, ist der Unterlegene und muss leiden.*
He who loves most is the inferior one and must suffer.
[*Tonio Kröger* (1903), 1]

2. *Man [muss] gestorben sein, um ganz ein Schaffender zu sein.*
You have to have died in order completely to be a creator.
[*Tonio Kröger* (1903), 3]

3. *Einsamkeit zeitigt das Originale, das gewagt und befremdend Schöne, das Gedicht. Einsamkeit zeitigt aber auch das Verkehrte, das Unverhältnismässige, das Absurde und Unerlaubte.*
Solitude gives rise to what is original, to what is daringly and displeasingly beautiful, to poetry. Solitude however also gives rise to what is wrong, excessive, absurd and forbidden.
[*Der Tod in Venedig* (*Death in Venice*, 1912), 3]

4. *Was galt ihm noch Kunst und Tugend gegenüber den Vorteilen des Chaos?*
What did art and virtue matter to him compared with the advantages of chaos?
[*Der Tod in Venedig* (*Death in Venice*, 1912), 5]

5. *Der Mensch lebt nicht nur sein persönliches Leben als Einzelwesen, sondern, bewusst oder unbewusst, auch das seiner Epoche und Zeitgenossenschaft.*
Man does not only live his personal life as an individual, but also, consciously or unconsciously, the life of his era and of his contemporaries.
[*Der Zauberberg* (*The Magic Mountain*, 1924), 2]

6. *Man sollte, statt in die Kirche, zu einem Begräbnis gehen, wenn man sich ein bisschen erbauen will. Die Leute haben gutes schwarzes Zeug an und nehmen die Hüte ab und sehen auf den Sarg und halten sich ernst und andächtig, und niemand darf faule Witze machen.*
Instead of going to church you should go to a funeral when you wish to be uplifted. The people have got good black clothes on, they take their hats off, look at the coffin and are serious and reverent, and no-one dares make bad jokes.
[*Der Zauberberg* (*The Magic Mountain*, 1924), 4]

7. *Vom Tode wüsste Ihnen keiner, der wiederkäme, was Rechtes zu erzählen, denn man erlebt ihn nicht. Wir kommen aus dem Dunkel und gehen ins Dunkel, dazwischen liegen Erlebnisse, aber Anfang und Ende, Geburt und Tod, werden von uns nicht erlebt, sie haben keinen subjektiven Charakter.*
No one who could come back from death would be able to tell you anything about it, because we do not experience it. We come out of the dark and go into the dark, and in between we have experiences, but beginning and end, birth and death, are not experienced by us, they have no subjective character.
[*Der Zauberberg* (*The Magic Mountain*, 1924), 6]

8. *Was wir Trauer nennen, ist vielleicht nicht sowohl der Schmerz über die Unmöglichkeit, unsere Toten ins Leben kehren zu sehen, als darüber, dies gar nicht wünschen zu können.*
What we call mourning is perhaps not so much grief that it is impossible to see our dead return to life as grief that we are quite unable to wish to do so.
[*Der Zauberberg* (*The Magic Mountain*, 1924), 7]

Mann, W. Edward (1918–)
Canadian sociologist
and Hoffman, Edward

1. A sudden access of psychological freedom often turns from sheer excitement to deep panic.
[*The Man Who Dreamed of Tomorrow: A Conceptual Biography of Wilhelm Reich* (1980)]

Manners, Lord John, Seventh Duke of Rutland (1818–1906)
English Conservative politician and writer

1. Let wealth and commerce, laws and learning die,
But leave us still our old nobility!
[*England's Trust* (1841)]

Manning, Frederic (1882–1935)
Australian novelist

1. War is waged by men; not by beasts, or by gods. It is a peculiar human activity. To call it a crime against mankind is to miss half its significance; it is also the punishment of a crime.
[*Her Privates We* (1929), Prefatory note; also called *The Middle Parts of Fortune*]

2. [Of the men in his battalion]
These apparently rude and brutal natures comforted,

encouraged, and reconciled each other to fate, with a tenderness and tact which was more moving than anything in life.
[*Her Privates We* (1929), 15]

Mansfield, Katherine (Kathleen Mansfield Beauchamp) (1888–1923)
New Zealand-born short-story writer

1. How idiotic civilization is! Why be given a body if you have to keep it shut up in a case like a rare, rare fiddle?
[*Bliss and Other Stories* (1920), 'Bliss']
2. And after all the weather was ideal.
[*The Stories of Katherine Mansfield* (1984), 'The Garden Party', opening words]
3. But we can't possibly have a garden party with a man dead just outside the front gate.
[*The Stories of Katherine Mansfield* (1984), 'The Garden Party']
4. [To a magazine editor]
You ask for some details as to myself. I am poor – obscure – just eighteen years of age – with a rapacious appetite for everything and principles as light as my purse.
[In Vincent O'Sullivan and Margaret Scott (eds), *The Collected Letters of Katherine Mansfield 1903–1917* (1984), I]
5. [Discussing form in literature]
I hate the sort of licence that English people give themselves – to spread over and flop and roll about. I feel as fastidious as though I wrote with acid.
[In Vincent O'Sullivan and Margaret Scott (eds), *The Collected Letters of Katherine Mansfield 1903–1917* (1984), I]
6. Whenever I prepare for a journey I prepare as though for death. Should I never return, all is in order. That is what life has taught me.
[In John Middleton Murry (ed.), *Journal of Katherine Mansfield* (1954)]
7. [On human limitations]
To have the courage of your excess – to find the limit of yourself.
[In John Middleton Murry (ed.), *Journal of Katherine Mansfield* (1954)]
8. [On women's ambition]
Most women turn to salt, looking back.
[In John Middleton Murry (ed.), *Journal of Katherine Mansfield* (1954)]
9. The ostrich burying its head in the sand does at any rate wish to convey the impression that its head is the most important part of it.
[In John Middleton Murry (ed.), *Journal of Katherine Mansfield* (1954)]
10. It was an exquisite day. It was one of those days so clear, so still, so silent, you almost feel the earth itself has stopped in astonishment at its own beauty.
[In John Middleton Murry (ed.), *Journal of Katherine Mansfield* (1954)]
11. Better to write twaddle, anything, than nothing at all.
[Attr.]

Mansfield, William Murray, Earl of (1705–1793)
Scottish judge; Lord Chief Justice 1756–88

1. [Advice given to a new colonial governor]
Consider what you think justice requires, and decide accordingly. But never give your reasons; for your judgement will probably be right, but your reasons will certainly be wrong.
[In Campbell, *Lives of the Chief Justices* (1849), 40]

Mao Tse-Tung (1893–1976)
Chinese Marxist theoretician and statesman; Chairman of the Chinese Communist Party from 1949

1. Every Communist must grasp the truth. Political power grows out of the barrel of a gun.
[Speech, 1938, published in *Selected Works* (1965)]
2. Letting a hundred flowers blossom and a hundred schools of thought contend is the policy for promoting the progress of the arts and the sciences.
[Speech, 1957, 'On the Correct Handling of Contradictions']
3. The Great Leap Forward.
[Name for forced industrialization, 1958]
4. People of the world, unite and defeat the US aggressors and all their running dogs!
[Statement, 1964]
5. Imperialism is a paper tiger.
[*Quotations from Chairman Mao Tse-Tung*]
6. We are advocates of the abolition of war, we do not want war; but war can only be abolished through war, and in order to get rid of the gun it is necessary to take up the gun.
[*Quotations from Chairman Mao Tse-Tung*]
7. To read too many books is harmful.
[*The New Yorker*, 1977]
8. [To his wife and her colleagues in a conspiratorial group]
Don't be a gang of four.
[Attr.]

Map, Walter (c. 1140–c. 1209)
Welsh poet, ecclesiastic and satirical writer

1. If die I must, let me die drinking in an inn.
[*De Nugis Curialium* (1182)]

Marcuse, Herbert (1898–1979)
German-born American sociologist and political philosopher

1. Not every problem someone has with his girlfriend is necessarily due to the capitalist mode of production.
[*The Listener*]

Marcy, William (1786–1857)
American lawyer and statesman; Democrat Secretary of State 1853–57

1. [On the politicians of New York]
They see nothing wrong in the rule, that to the victor belong the spoils of the enemy.
[Speech, 1832]

Marie-Antoinette (1755–1793)
Queen of France 1774–93 and wife of Louis XVI; opposed reform and was guillotined in the French Revolution

1. [Her reply on being told the people were begging the king for bread]
Qu'ils mangent de la brioche.
Let them eat cake.
[Attr. (but much older)]

Marlborough, John Churchill, Duke of (1650–1722)
English general, Commander of British Forces in War of Spanish Succession

1. No soldier can fight unless he is properly fed on beef and beer.
[Attr.; a similar saying, 'An army, like a serpent, goes on its belly', was attributed to Frederick the Great]

Marlborough, Sarah, First Duchess of (1660–1744)

English royal attendant and memoirist

1. For painters, poets and builders have very high flights, but they must be kept down.
[Letter to the Duchess of Bedford, 1734]

2. The Duke returned from the wars today and did pleasure me in his top-boots.
[Oral trad.]

Marlowe, Christopher (1564–1593)

English poet and dramatist, noted for blank verse plays

1. From jigging veins of rhyming mother-wits,
And such conceits as clownage keeps in pay,
We'll lead you to the stately tents of war...

2. Zenocrate, lovelier than the love of Jove,
Brighter than is the silver Rhodope,
Fairer than whitest snow on Scythian Hills...

3. Not all the curses which the Furies breathe
Shall make me leave so rich a prize as this...

4. That with thy looks canst clear the darken'd sky,
And calm the rage of thundering Jupiter.
[*Tamburlaine the Great* (1590), I, Prologue]

5. Our swords shall play the orators for us.
[*Tamburlaine the Great* (1590), Part I, I.ii]

6. With Nature's pride, and richest furniture,
His looks do menace heaven and dare the Gods.
[*Tamburlaine the Great* (1590), Part I, I.ii]

7. Accurs'd be he that first invented war!
[*Tamburlaine the Great* (1590), Part I, II.iv]

8. Is it not passing brave to be a King,
And ride in triumph through Persepolis?
[*Tamburlaine the Great* (1590), Part I, II.v]

9. Nature that fram'd us of four elements,
Warring within our breasts for regiment,
Doth teach us all to have aspiring minds:
Our souls, whose faculties can comprehend
The wondrous architecture of the world:
And measure every wand'ring planet's course,
Still climbing after knowledge infinite,
And always moving as the restless Spheres,
Will us to wear ourselves and never rest,
Until we reach the ripest fruit of all,
That perfect bliss and sole felicity,
The sweet fruition of an earthly crown.
[*Tamburlaine the Great* (1590), Part I, II.vii]

10. Virtue is the fount whence honour springs.
[*Tamburlaine the Great* (1590), Part I, IV.iv]

11. Ah fair Zenocrate, divine Zenocrate,
Fair is too foul an epithet for thee.
[*Tamburlaine the Great* (1590), Part I, V.v]

12. Now walk the angels on the walls of heaven,
As sentinels to warn th' immortal souls,
To entertain divine Zenocrate.
[*Tamburlaine the Great* (1590), Part II, II.iv]

13. Yet let me kiss my Lord before I die,
And let me die with kissing of my Lord.
[*Tamburlaine the Great* (1590), Part II, II.iv]

14. Helen, whose beauty summoned Greece to arms,
And drew a thousand ships to Tenedos.
[*Tamburlaine the Great* (1590), Part II, II.iv]

15. More childish valorous than manly wise.
[*Tamburlaine the Great* (1590), Part II, IV.i]

16. Holla, ye pampered jades of Asia!
What, can ye draw but twenty miles a-day?
[*Tamburlaine the Great* (1590), Part II, IV.iii. Cf. Shakespeare, *Henry IV Pt 2*: 27]

17. Tamburlaine, the Scourge of God, must die.
[*Tamburlaine the Great* (1590), Part II, V.iii]

18. Albeit the world think Machiavel is dead,
Yet was his soul but flown beyond the Alps...

19. I count religion but a childish toy,
And hold there is no sin but ignorance.
[*The Jew of Malta* (c. 1592), Prologue]

20. Thus methinks should men of judgement frame
Their means of traffic from the vulgar trade,
And, as their wealth increaseth, so enclose
Infinite riches in a little room.
[*The Jew of Malta* (c. 1592), I.i]

21. Thus trails our fortune in by land and sea,
And thus are we on every side enrich'd.
[*The Jew of Malta* (c. 1592), I.i]

22. And better one want for a common good,
Than many perish for a private man.
[*The Jew of Malta* (c. 1592), I.i]

23. As for myself, I walk abroad o' nights
And kill sick people groaning under walls:
Sometimes I go about and poison wells.
[*The Jew of Malta* (c. 1592), II.iii]

24. Here come two religious caterpillars.
[*The Jew of Malta* (c. 1592), IV.i]

25. *Barnadine*: Thou hast committed–
Barabas: Fornication: but that was in another country;
And besides, the wench is dead.
[*The Jew of Malta* (c. 1592), IV.i]

26. My heart is an anvil unto sorrow,
Which beats upon it like the Cyclops' hammers,
And with the noise turns up my giddy brain,
And makes me frantic for my Gaveston.
[*Edward II* (1593), I]

27. Fair blows the wind for France.
[*Edward II* (1593), I]

28. My men, like satyrs grazing on the lawns,
Shall with their goat feet dance the antic hay.
[*Edward II* (1593), I]

29. Sweet Analytics, 'tis thou has ravished me.
[*Doctor Faustus* (1604), I.i]

30. I'll have them fly to India for gold,
Ransack the ocean for orient pearl.
[*Doctor Faustus* (1604), I.i]

31. I'll have them wall all Germany with brass,
And make swift Rhine circle fair Wertenberg.
I'll have them fill the public schools with silk,
Wherewith the students shall be bravely clad.
[*Doctor Faustus* (1604), I.i]

32. What doctrine call you this, *Che sera, sera*,
What will be, shall be?
[*Doctor Faustus* (1604), I.i]

33. *Faustus*: And what are you that live with Lucifer?
Mephistopheles: Unhappy spirits that fell with Lucifer,
Conspired against our God with Lucifer,
And are for ever damned with Lucifer.
[*Doctor Faustus* (1604), I.iii]

34. Why this is hell, nor am I out of it:
Thinkst thou that I who saw the face of God,
And tasted the eternal joys of heaven,
Am not tormented with ten thousand hells
In being deprived of everlasting bliss?
[*Doctor Faustus* (1604), I.iii]

35. Hell hath no limits nor is circumscrib'd
In one self place, where we are is Hell,
And where Hell is, there must we ever be.
And to be short, when all the world dissolves,
And every creature shall be purified,
All places shall be hell that are not heaven.
[*Doctor Faustus* (1604), II.i]

36. Christ cannot save thy soul, for he is just.
[*Doctor Faustus* (1604), II.ii]

37. Have I not made blind Homer sing to me?
[*Doctor Faustus* (1604), II.ii]

38. Was this the face that launch'd a thousand ships,
And burnt the topless towers of Ilium?
Sweet Helen, make me immortal with a kiss!
Her lips suck forth my soul: see, where it flies!
Come Helen, come give me my soul again.
Here will I dwell, for heaven be in these lips,
And all is dross that is not Helena.
[*Doctor Faustus* (1604), V.i]

39. O, thou art fairer than the evening's air
Clad in the beauty of a thousand stars.
[*Doctor Faustus* (1604), V.i]

40. Now hast thou but one bare hour to live,
And then thou must be damned perpetually;
Stand still you ever-moving spheres of heaven,
That time may cease, and midnight never come.
Fair nature's eye, rise, rise again and make
Perpetual day, or let this hour be but
A year, a month, a week, a natural day,
That Faustus may repent and save his soul.
O lente, lente currite noctis equi:
The stars move still, time runs, the clock will strike,
The devil will come, and Faustus must be damn'd.
O I'll leap up to my God: who pulls me down?
See, see where Christ's blood streams in the firmament,
One drop would save my soul, half a drop, ah my Christ.
[*Doctor Faustus* (1604), V.ii]

41. Ugly hell, gape not! come not, Lucifer!
I'll burn my books!
[*Doctor Faustus* (1604), V.ii]

42. Mountains and hills, come, come and fall on me,
And hide me from the heavy wrath of God.
[*Doctor Faustus* (1604), V.ii]

43. You stars that reigned at my nativity,
Whose influence hath allotted death and hell,
Now draw up Faustus like a foggy mist,
Into the entrails of yon labouring cloud,
That when you vomit forth into the air,
My limbs may issue from your smoky mouths,
So that my soul may but ascend to heaven.
[*Doctor Faustus* (1604), V.ii]

44. Ah, Pythagoras' metempsychosis, were that true,
This soul should fly from me, and I be chang'd
Unto some brutish beast.
[*Doctor Faustus* (1604), V.ii]

45. O soul, be changed into little water drops,
And fall into the ocean, ne'er to be found:
My God, my God, look not so fierce on me.
[*Doctor Faustus* (1604), V.ii]

46. Cut is the branch that might have grown full straight,
And burnèd is Apollo's laurel bough,
That some time grew within this learnèd man.
[*Doctor Faustus* (1604), Epilogue]

47. It lies not in our power to love, or hate,
For will in us is over-rul'd by fate.
When two are stripped, long ere the course begin,
We wish that one should lose, the other win;
And one especially do we affect
Of two gold ingots, like in each respect.
The reason no man knows; let it suffice,
What we behold is censured by our eyes.
Where both deliberate, the love is slight;
Who ever loved that loved not at first sight?...

48. Like untun'd golden strings all women are
Which long time lie untouch'd, will harshly jar.
[*Hero and Leander* (1598), First Sestiad]

49. Come live with me, and be my love,
And we will all the pleasures prove,
That hills and valleys, dales and fields,
Woods or steepy mountain yields...

50. By shallow rivers, to whose falls,
Melodious birds sing madrigals...

51. And I will make thee beds of roses
And a thousand fragrant posies.
['The Passionate Shepherd to his Love'; trans. of Lucan's *Pharsalia*, date unknown]

Marmion, Shackerley (1603–1639)
English dramatist and poet

1. Great joys, like griefs, are silent.
[*Holland's Leaguer* (1632), V.1]

2. Familiarity begets boldness.
[*The Antiquary* (1641)]

Maron, Monika

1. *Der Künstler als Bürger kann Demokrat sein, so gut und so schlecht wie alle anderen. Der Künstler als Künstler darf kein Demokrat sein.*
The artist as a citizen can be a democrat, just as well and as badly as everybody else. The artist as an artist may not be a democrat.
[Interview in *Der Spiegel*, 1994]

Marquis, Don (1878–1937)
American columnist, satirist and poet

1. the great open spaces
where cats are cats.
[*archy and mehitabel* (1927), 'mehitabel has an adventure']

2. girls we was all of us ladies
we was o what the hell
and once a lady always game
by crikey blood will tell.
[*archy and mehitabel* (1927) 'mehitabel dances with boreas']

3. but wotthehell archy wotthehell
jamais triste archy jamais triste
that is my motto.
[*archy and mehitabel* (1927), 'mehitabel sees paris']

4. but wotthehell wotthehell
oh i should worry and fret
death and i will coquette
there s a dance in the old dame yet
toujours gai toujours gai.
[*archy and mehitabel* (1927), 'the song of mehitabel']

5. honesty is a good
thing but
it is not profitable to
its possessor
unless it is
kept under control.
[*archys life of mehitabel* (1933), 'archygrams']

6. as i was crawling
through the holes in
a swiss cheese
the other
day it occurred to
me to wonder
what a swiss cheese
would think if
a swiss cheese
could think and after
cogitating for some
time i said to myself
if a swiss cheese
could think
it would think that
a swiss cheese
was the most important
thing in the world
just as everything that
can think at all
does think about itself...

7. now and then
there is a person born
who is so unlucky
that he runs into accidents
which started out to happen
to somebody else.
[*archys life of mehitabel* (1933), 'archy says']

8. How often when they find a sage
As great as Socrates or Plato
They hand him hemlock for his wage
Or take him like a sweet potato.
[*Taking the Longer View*]

9. An idea isn't responsible for the people who believe in it.
[*New York Sun*]

10. The art of newspaper paragraphing is to stroke a platitude until it purrs like an epigram.
[In E. Anthony, *O Rare Don Marquis* (1962)]

11. Ours is a world where people don't know what they want and are willing to go through hell to get it.
[In *Treasury of Humorous Quotations*]

Marryat, Frederick (1792–1848)
English naval officer and novelist, noted for sea stories

1. We always took care of number one.
[*Scenes and Adventures in the Life of Frank Mildmay* (1829), 19]

2. As savage as a bear with a sore head.
[*The King's Own* (1830), II, 6]

3. There's no getting blood out of a turnip.
[*Japhet in Search of a Father* (1836), 4]

4. As you are not prepared, as the Americans say, *to go the whole hog*, we will part good friends.
[*Japhet in Search of a Father* (1836), 54]

5. [Of an illegitimate baby]
If you please, ma'am, it was a very little one.
[*Mr Midshipman Easy* (1836), 3]

6. I never knows the children. It's just six of one and half-a-dozen of the other.
[*The Pirate* (1836), 4]

7. I think it much better that ... every man paddle his own canoe.
[*Settlers in Canada* (1844), 8]

Marsden, Samuel
English missionary

1. [On Christianity]
A hefty whaler, after some discussion with Marsden, remarked, 'Your religion teaches that if a man is hit on one cheek, he will turn the other.' And hit Marsden on the right cheek. Marsden obediently offered his left cheek and received a second blow. 'Now,' he said, 'I have obeyed my Master's commands. What I do next, he left to my own judgement. Take this.' And knocked the man down.
[From Mrs P.R. Woodhouse, oral tradition]

Marsh, Sir Edward Howard (1872–1953)
English patron of the arts, translator and civil servant

1. [Roger Fry (1866–1934) was an artist and art critic, who championed the Post-Impressionists]
Dear Roger Fry whom I love as a man but detest as a movement.
[In Christopher Hassall, *Edward Marsh*, 11]

Marshall, Alan John (Jock) (1911–1968)
Australian zoologist and explorer

1. Beware of people you've been kind to.
[Remark to John Morrison]

Marshall, Arthur (1910–1989)
Television personality

1. It's all part of life's rich pageant.
[*The Games Mistress*, gramophone record, 1930s]

Marshall, Thomas R. (1854–1925)
American statesman; Democrat Vice-President 1913–21

1. [Remark to the chief clerk of the Senate during a tedious debate, 1917]
What this country needs is a good five cent cigar.
[Attr.]

Martial (c. 40–c. 104)
Latin epigrammatist and poet, born in Spain

1. *Lasciva est nobis pagina, vita proba.*
My book is licentious, but my life is pure.
[*Epigrammata*, I, 4]

2. *Non est, crede mihi, sapientis dicere 'Vivam':*
Sera nimis vita est crastina: vive hodie.
Believe me, 'I shall live' is not the saying of a wise man. Tomorrow's life is too late: live today.
[*Epigrammata*, I, 15]

3. *Non amo te, Sabidi, nec possum dicere quare:*
Hoc tantum possum dicere, non amo te.
I do not like you, Sabidius, and I cannot say why; all I can say is this: I do not like you.
[*Epigrammata*, I, 32]

4. *Laudant illa sed ista legunt.*
They praise those works but they read something else.
[*Epigrammata*, IV, 49]

5. *Bonosque*
Soles effugere atque abire sentit,

Qui nobis pereunt et imputantur.
Each of us feels the good days hasten and depart, our days that perish and are counted against us.
[*Epigrammata*, V, 20]

6. *Quod tam grande sophos clamat tibi turba togata,*
Non tu, Pomponi, cena diserta tua est.
When your crowd of followers shout loudly to applaud you, Pomponius, it is not you but your dinner that is eloquent.
[*Epigrammata*, VI, 48]

7. *Non est vivere, sed valere vita est.*
It is not to live but to be healthy that makes a life.
[*Epigrammata*, VI, 70]

8. *Caenae fercula nostrae*
Malim convivis quam placuisse cocis.
I prefer that the courses at our banquet should give pleasure to the guests rather than to the cooks.
[*Epigrammata*, IX, 81. Cf. Harington: 1]

9. *Difficilis facilis, iucundus acerbus es idem:*
Nec tecum possum vivere nec sine te.
Difficult or easy-going, pleasant or bitter, you are the same you: I can neither live with you – nor without you.
[*Epigrammata*, XII, 47]

10. *Rus in urbe.*
The country in the town.
[*Epigrammata*, XII, 57]

Martineau, Harriet (1802–1876)

English writer on political economy; novelist, journalist, children's and travel writer

1. If there is any country on earth where the course of true love may be expected to run smooth, it is America.
[*Society in America* (1837), III, 'Marriage']

2. . . . the early marriages of silly children . . . where . . . every woman is married before she well knows how serious a matter human life is.
[*Society in America* (1837), III, 'Marriage']

3. Any one must see at a glance that if men and women marry those whom they do not love, they must love those whom they do not marry.
[*Society in America* (1837), III, 'Marriage']

4. Is it to be understood that the principles of the Declaration of Independence bear no relation to half of the human race?
[*Society in America* (1837), III, 'Marriage']

5. I am in truth very thankful for not having married at all.
[*Harriet Martineau's Autobiography* (1877), 1]

Marvell, Andrew (1621–1678)

English Metaphysical lyric poet and prose satirist

1. So restless Cromwell could not cease
In the inglorious arts of peace...

2. He nothing common did or mean
Upon that memorable scene:
But with his keener eye
The axe's edge did try...

3. But bowed his comely head,
Down as upon a bed.
['An Horation Ode upon Cromwell's Return from Ireland' (1650)]

4. Where the remote Bermudas ride
In th' ocean's bosom unespied...

5. He hangs in shades the orange bright,
Like golden lamps in a green night...

6. And makes the hollow seas, that roar,
Proclaim the ambergris on shore.
He cast (of which we rather boast)
The Gospel's pearls upon our coast.
['Bermudas' (c. 1653)]

7. My Love is of a birth as rare
As 'tis for object strange and high:
It was begotten by despair
Upon impossibility...

8. As lines (so loves) oblique may well
Themselves in every angle greet
But ours so truly parallel,
Though infinite can never meet.

Therefore the love which us doth bind,
But Fate so enviously debars,
Is the conjunction of the mind,
And opposition of the stars.
['The Definition of Love' (1681)]

9. Earth cannot shew so brave a Sight
As when a single Soul does fence
The Batteries of alluring Sense,
And Heaven views it with delight.
['A Dialogue between the Resolved Soul and Created Pleasure' (1681)]

10. But all resistance against her is vain,
Who has the advantage both of Eyes and Voice.
And all my Forces needs must be undone,
She having gained both the Wind and Sun.
['The Fair Singer' (1681)]

11. Engines more keen than ever yet
Adorned Tyrants Cabinet;
Of which the most tormenting are
Black Eyes, red Lips, and curled Hair.
['The Gallery' (1681)]

12. How vainly men themselves amaze
To win the palm, the oak, or bays;
And their incessant labours see
Crown'd from some single herb or tree,
Whose short and narrow vergèd shade
Does prudently their toils upbraid;
While all flowers and all trees do close
To weave the garlands of repose.
['The Garden' (1681), 1]

13. Fair quiet, have I found thee here,
And Innocence thy sister dear!...

14. Society is all but rude,
To this delicious solitude.
['The Garden' (1681), 2]

15. No white nor red was ever seen
So am'rous as this lovely green.
['The Garden' (1681), 3]

16. The Gods, that mortal beauty chase,
Still in a tree did end their race.
Apollo hunted Daphne so,
Only that she might laurel grow.
And Pan did after Syrinx speed,
Not as a nymph, but for a reed.
['The Garden' (1681), 4]

17. What wond'rous life is this I lead!
Ripe apples drop about my head;
The luscious clusters of the vine
Upon my mouth do crush their wine;
The nectarine and curious peach,
Into my hands themselves do reach;

Stumbling on melons, as I pass,
Insnar'd with flow'rs, I fall on grass.
['The Garden' (1681), 5]

18. Meanwhile the Mind, from pleasure less,
Withdraws into its happiness:
The Mind, that Ocean where each kind
Does straight its own resemblance find...

19. Annihilating all that's made
To a green Thought in a green Shade.
['The Garden' (1681), 6]

20. Here at the fountain's sliding foot,
Or at some fruit-tree's mossy root,
Casting the body's vest aside,
My soul into the boughs does glide.
['The Garden' (1681), 7]

21. Such was that happy garden-state,
While man there walk'd without a mate...

22. But 'twas beyond a mortal's share
To wander solitary there:
Two Paradises 'twere in one
To live in Paradise alone.
['The Garden' (1681), 8]

23. Ye living lamps, by whose dear light
The nightingale does sit so late,
And studying all the summer night,
Her matchless songs does meditate.

Ye country comets, that portend
No war, nor prince's funeral,
Shining unto no higher end
Than to presage the grasses' fall.
['The Mower to the Glow-worms' (1681)]

24. It is a wond'rous thing, how fleet
'Twas on those little silver feet.
With what a pretty skipping grace,
It oft would challenge me the race:
And when 't had left me far away,
'Twould stay, and run again, and stay.
For it was nimbler much than hinds;
And trod, as on the four winds...

25. I have a garden of my own,
But so with roses overgrown,
And lilies, that you would it guess
To be a little wilderness...

26. Had it liv'd long, it would have been
Lilies without, roses within.
['The Nymph Complaining for the Death of her Fawn' (1681)]

27. When I beheld the Poet blind, yet bold,
In slender Book his vast Design unfold.
['On Mr Milton's Paradise Lost' (1681)]

28. Who can foretell for what high cause
This Darling of the Gods was born!...

29. Gather the flowers, but spare the buds.
['The Picture of Little T.C. in a Prospect of Flowers' (1681)]

30. Had we but world enough, and time,
This coyness, Lady, were no crime.
We would sit down, and think which way
To walk, and pass our long love's day.
Thou by the Indian Ganges' side
Shouldst rubies find: I by the tide
Of Humber would complain. I would
Love you ten years before the Flood:
And you should if you please refuse
Till the conversion of the Jews.
My vegetable love should grow
Vaster than empires, and more slow...

31. But at my back I always hear
Time's wingèd chariot hurrying near.
And yonder all before us lie
Deserts of vast eternity.
Thy beauty shall no more be found;
Nor, in thy marble vault, shall sound
My echoing song: then worms shall try
That long preserved virginity:
And your quaint honour turn to dust;
And into ashes all my lust.
The grave's a fine and private place,
But none I think do there embrace...

32. Let us roll our strength and all
Our sweetness up into one ball,
And tear our pleasures with rough strife
Thorough the iron gates of life:
Thus, though we cannot make our sun
Stand still, yet we will make him run.
['To His Coy Mistress' (1681)]

33. Thrice happy he who, not mistook,
Hath read in Nature's mystic book...

34. But now the salmon-fishers moist
Their leathern boats begin to hoist;
And, like Antipodes in shoes,
Have shod their heads in their canoes.
How tortoise-like, but not so slow,
These rational amphibii go!
['Upon Appleton House, to my Lord Fairfax' (1681)]

35. [Of Charles II]
For though the whole world cannot shew such another,
Yet we'd better by far have him than his brother.
['The Statue in Stocks-Market' (1689)]

Marx, Chico (1886–1961)
US film comedian, eldest of the Marx Brothers

1. [Explanation given when his wife caught him kissing a chorus girl]
But I wasn't kissing her. I was whispering in her mouth.
[In G. Marx and R. Anobile, *The Marx Brothers Scrapbook* (1974)]

Marx, Groucho (1895–1977)
American film comedian

1. You're the most beautiful woman I've ever seen, which doesn't say much for you.
[*Animal Crackers*, film, 1930; scriptwriter Morrie Ryskind]

2. One morning I shot an elephant in my pajamas. How he got into my pajamas I'll never know.
[*Animal Crackers*, film, 1930; scriptwriter Morrie Ryskind]

3. What's a thousand dollars? Mere chicken feed. A poultry matter.
[*Animal Crackers*, film, 1930; scriptwriter Morrie Ryskind]

4. Look at me: I worked my way up from nothing to a state of extreme poverty.
[*Monkey Business*, film, 1931; scriptwriters Perelman, Johnstone and Sheekman]

5. I want to register a complaint. Do you know who sneaked into my room at three o'clock this morning? – Who? Nobody, and that's my complaint.
[*Monkey Business*, film, 1931; scriptwriters Perelman, Johnstone and Sheekman]

6. Sir, you have the advantage of me.
– Not yet I haven't, but wait till I get you outside.
[*Monkey Business*, film, 1931; scriptwriters Perelman, Johnstone and Sheekman]

7. There's a man outside with a big black moustache.
– Tell him I've got one.
[*Horse Feathers*, film, 1932; scriptwriters Kalmar, Ruby, Perelman and Johnstone]

8. You're a disgrace to our family name of Wagstaff, if such a thing is possible.
[*Horse Feathers*, film, 1932; scriptwriters Kalmar, Ruby, Perelman and Johnstone]

9. You've got the brain of a four-year-old boy, and I bet he was glad to get rid of it.
[*Horse Feathers*, film, 1932; scriptwriters Kalmar, Ruby, Perelman and Johnstone]

10. Remember, men, we're fighting for this woman's honour; which is probably more than she ever did.
[*Duck Soup*, film, 1933; scriptwriters Kalmar, Ruby, Sheekman and Perrin]

11. A child of five would understand this. Send somebody to fetch a child of five.
[*Duck Soup*, film, 1933; scriptwriters Kalmar, Ruby, Sheekman and Perrin]

12. My husband is dead.
– I'll bet he's just using that as an excuse.
I was with him to the end.
– No wonder he passed away.
I held him in my arms and kissed him.
– So it was murder!
[*Duck Soup*, film, 1933; scriptwriters Kalmar, Ruby, Sheekman and Perrin]

13. Go, and never darken my towels again!
[*Duck Soup*, film, 1933; scriptwriters Kalmar, Ruby, Sheekman and Perrin]

14. Do they allow tipping on the boat?
– Yes, sir.
Have you got two fives?
– Oh, yes, sir.
Then you won't need the ten cents I was going to give you.
[*A Night at the Opera*, film, 1935; scriptwriters Kaufman and Ryskind]

15. The strains of Verdi will come back to you tonight, and Mrs Claypool's cheque will come back to you in the morning.
[*A Night at the Opera*, film, 1935; scriptwriters Kaufman and Ryskind]

16. Either he's dead or my watch has stopped.
[*A Day at the Races*, film, 1937; scriptwriters Pirosh, Seaton and Oppenheimer]

17. Send two dozen roses to Room 424 and put 'Emily, I love you' on the back of the bill.
[*A Night in Casablanca*, film, 1945; scriptwriters Fields, Kibbee and Tashlin]

18. Please accept my resignation. I don't want to belong to any club that would have me as a member.
[*Groucho and Me* (1959)]

19. I never forget a face, but I'll make an exception in your case.
[*The Guardian*, 1965]

20. [When excluded, on racial grounds, from a beach club]
Since my daughter is only half-Jewish, could she go into the water up to her knees?
[*The Observer*, 1977]

21. I was so long writing my review that I never got around to reading the book.
[Attr.]

22. Time wounds all heels.
[Attr.]

23. No, Groucho is not my real name. I'm breaking it in for a friend.
[Attr.]

24. Whoever named it necking was a poor judge of anatomy.
[Attr.]

25. A man is only as old as the woman he feels.
[Attr.]

26. I eat like a vulture. Unfortunately the resemblance doesn't end there.
[Attr.]

27. Many years ago I chased a woman for almost two years, only to discover her tastes were exactly like mine: we were both crazy about girls.
[Attr.]

28. I've been around so long, I knew Doris Day before she was a virgin.
[Attr.]

29. We in this industry know that behind every successful screenwriter stands a woman. And behind her stands his wife.
[Attr.]

30. [Explaining why he didn't go to films starring Victor Mature]
I never go to movies where the hero's bust is bigger than the heroine's.
[Attr.]

Marx, Karl (1818–1883)
German political philosopher and economist; founder of Communism

1. Religion ... is the opium of the people.
[*A Contribution to the Critique of Hegel's Philosophy of Right* (1843–1844)]

2. The philosophers have merely interpreted the world in various ways; the point, however, is to change it.
[*Theses on Feuerbach* (written 1845, published 1888), 11]

3. Hegel says somewhere that all great events and personalities in world history reappear in one way or another. He forgot to add: the first time as tragedy, the second as farce.
[*The Eighteenth Brumaire of Louis Napoleon* (1852)]

4. Mankind always sets itself only those problems it can solve; since, looking at the matter more closely, one will always find that the task itself arises only when the material conditions for its solution already exist or are at least in the process of formation.
[*A Contribution to the Critique of Political Economy* (1859)]

5. Without doubt machinery has greatly increased the number of well-to-do idlers.
[*Das Kapital* (1867)]

6. Capitalist production creates, with the inexorability of a law of nature, its own negation.
[*Das Kapital* (1867)]

7. From each according to his abilities, to each according to his needs.
[*Critique of the Gotha Programme* (1875). Cf. Bakunin: 2]

8. What I did that was new was prove ... that the class struggle necessarily leads to the dictatorship of the proletariat.
[Letter, 1852]

Marx, Karl (1818–1883)
German political philosopher and Communist
and Engels, Friedrich (1820–1895)
German socialist and political philosopher

1. A spectre is haunting Europe – the spectre of Communism.
[*The Communist Manifesto* (1848)]

2. The history of all hitherto existing society is the history of class struggles.
[*The Communist Manifesto* (1848)]

3. The proletariat has nothing to lose but its chains in this revolution. It has a world to win. Workers of the world, unite!
[*The Communist Manifesto* (1848)]

Mary I (Mary Tudor) (1516–1558)
Queen of England from 1553; daughter of Henry VIII; had papal supremacy restored

1. When I am dead and opened, you shall find 'Calais' lying in my heart.
[*Holinshed's Chronicles*, IV (1808)]

Mary, Queen of Scots (1542–1587)
Queen of Scots from 1542–67; daughter of James V; forced to abdicate, imprisoned and executed

1. England is not all the world.
[Said at her trial, 1586]

2. *En ma fin git mon commencement.*
In my end is my beginning.
[Motto embroidered with her mother's emblem]

Mary, Queen Consort (1867–1953)
Queen Consort (1910–36) of George V, grandmother of the present queen

1. So *that's* what hay looks like.
[In James Pope-Hennessy, *Life of Queen Mary* (1959), 7]

2. [On the abdication crisis]
Well, Mr Baldwin! *This* is a pretty kettle of fish!
[In James Pope-Hennessy, *Life of Queen Mary* (1959), 7]

3. [On returning home after the abdication, 1936]
All *this* thrown away for *that!*
[Attr.]

4. [Remark to soldier who had exclaimed 'No more bloody wars for me']
No more bloody wars, no more bloody medals.
[Attr.]

Masefield, John (1878–1967)
English poet, novelist, critic and children's writer; poet laureate from 1930

1. I must go down to the seas again, to the lonely sea and the sky,
And all I ask is a tall ship and a star to steer her by,
And the wheel's kick and the wind's song and the white sail's shaking,
And a grey mist on the sea's face and a grey dawn breaking...

2. I must go down to the seas again, for the call of the running tide
Is a wild call and a clear call that may not be denied...

3. I must go down to the seas again, to the vagrant gypsy life,
To the gull's way and the whale's way where the wind's like a whetted knife;
And all I ask is a merry yarn from a laughing fellow rover,
And a quiet sleep and a sweet dream when the long trick's over.
['Sea Fever' (1902)]

4. It is good to be out on the road, and going one knows not where,
Going through meadow and village, one knows not whither nor why.
['Tewkesbury Road' (1902)]

5. It's a warm wind, the west wind, full of birds' cries;
I never hear the west wind but tears are in my eyes,
For it comes from the west lands, the old brown hills,
And April's in the west wind, and daffodils.
['The West Wind' (1902)]

6. I have seen dawn and sunset on moors and windy hills
Coming in solemn beauty like slow old tunes of Spain.
['Beauty' (1903)]

7. Oh some are fond of Spanish wine, and some are fond of French,
And some'll swallow tay and stuff fit only for a wench...

8. Oh some are fond of fiddles, and a song well sung,
And some are all for music for to lilt upon the tongue;
But mouths were made for tankards, and for sucking at the bung,
Says the old bold mate of Henry Morgan.
['Captain Stratton's Fancy' (1903)]

9. Quinquireme of Nineveh from distant Ophir
Rowing home to haven in sunny Palestine,
With a cargo of ivory,
And apes and peacocks,
Sandalwood, cedarwood and sweet white wine.

Dirty British coaster with a salt-caked smoke stack,
Butting through the Channel in the mad March days,
With a cargo of Tyne coal,
Road-rail, pig-lead,
Firewood, iron-ware, and cheap tin trays.
['Cargoes' (1903)]

10. One road leads to London,
One road runs to Wales,
My road leads me seawards
To the white dipping sails...

11. Most roads lead men homewards,
My road leads me forth.
['Roadways' (1903)]

12. In the dark womb where I began
My mother's life made me a man.
Through all the months of human birth
Her beauty fed my common earth.
I cannot see, nor breathe, nor stir,
But through the death of some of her.
['C.L.M.' (1910)]

13. Friends and loves we have none, nor wealth, nor blessed abode,
But the hope of the City of God at the other end of the road.
['The Seekers' (1910)]

14. To get the whole world out of bed
And washed, and dressed, and warmed, and fed,
To work, and back to bed again,
Believe me, Saul, costs worlds of pain.
['The Everlasting Mercy' (1911)]

15. The stars grew bright in the winter sky,
The wind came keen with a tang of frost,
The brook was troubled for new things lost,
The copse was happy for old things found,

The fox came home and he went to ground.
['Reynard the Fox' (1919)]

16. Death opens unknown doors. It is most grand to die.
[*Pompey the Great* (1910), II]

Mason, R.A.K. (1905–1971)
New Zealand poet

1. Though my voice is cracked and harsh
stoutly in the rear I march
Though my song have none to hear
boldly bring I up the rear.
[*Collected Poems* (1963), 'Song of Allegiance']

Mason, Walt (1862–1939)
Canadian author of prose poems and humorist

1. He's the Man Who Delivers the Goods.
[*The Man Who Delivers the Goods*]

Mass

1. *Asperges me, Domine, hyssopo, et mundabor.*
Sprinkle me with hyssop, O Lord, and I shall be cleansed.
[Anthem at Sprinkling of Holy Water]

2. *Dominus vobiscum.*
Et cum spiritu tuo.
The Lord be with you.
And with thy spirit.

3. *In Nomine Patris, et Filii, et Spiritus Sancti.*
In the Name of the Father, and of the Son, and of the Holy Ghost.
[The Ordinary of the Mass]

4. *Introibo ad altare Dei.*
I will go unto the altar of God.

5. *Gloria Patri, et Filio, et Spiritui Sancto.*
Sicut erat in principio, et nunc, et semper, et in saecula saeculorum.
Glory be to the Father, and to the Son, and to the Holy Ghost.
As it was in the beginning, is now, and ever shall be, world without end.

6. *Confiteor Deo omnipotenti, beatae Mariae semper Virgini, beato Michaeli Archangelo, beato Joanni Baptistae, sanctis Apostolis Petro et Paulo, omnibus sanctis, et tibi, Pater, quia peccavi nimis cogitatione, verbo, et opere, mea culpa, mea culpa, mea maxima culpa.*
I confess to almighty God, to blessed Mary ever Virgin, to blessed Michael the Archangel, to blessed John the Baptist, to the holy Apostles Peter and Paul, to all the saints, and to you, Father, that I have sinned exceedingly in thought, word, and deed, through my fault, through my fault, through my most grievous fault.

7. *Kyrie eleison, Kyrie eleison, Kyrie eleison.*
Christe eleison, Christe eleison, Christe eleison.
Lord, have mercy upon us.
Christ, have mercy upon us.

8. *Gloria in excelsis Deo, et in terra pax hominibus bonae voluntatis. Laudamus te, benedicimus te, adoramus te, glorificamus te.*
Glory be to God on high, and on earth peace to men of good will. We praise thee, we bless thee, we adore thee, we glorify thee.

9. *Deo gratias.*
Thanks be to God.

10. *Credo in unum Deum, Patrem onmipotentum, factorem coeli et terrae, visibilium omnium et invisibilium.*
Et in unum Dominum Jesum Christum Filium Dei unigenitum, et ex Patre natum ante omnia saecula: Deum de Deo, lumen de lumine, Deum verum de Deo vero; genitum non factum, consubstantialem Patri, per quem omnia facta sunt. Qui propter nos homines, et propter nostram salutem, descendit de coelis; et incarnatus est de Spiritu Sancto, ex Maria Virgine; ET HOMO FACTUS EST. Crucifixus etiam pro nobis, sub Pontio Pilato passus, et sepultus est. Et resurrexit tertia die, secundum Scripturas; et ascendit in coelum; sedet ad dexteram Patris; et iterum venturus est cum gloria, judicare vivos et mortuos; cuius regni non erit finis.
Et in Spiritum Sanctum, Dominum vivificantem, qui ex Patre Filioque procedit; qui cum Patre et Filio simul adoratur, et conglorificatur; qui locutus est per Prophetas. Et unam sanctam Catholicam et Apostolicam Ecclesiam. Confiteor unum Baptisma in remissionem peccatorum. Et expecto resurrectionem mortuorum, et vitam venturi saeculi.
I believe in one God, the Father almighty, maker of heaven and earth, and of all things visible and invisible.
And in one Lord Jesus Christ, the only begotten Son of God, and born of the Father before all ages; God of God, light of light; true God of true God; begotten, not made; consubstantial to the Father, by whom all things were made. Who for us men, and for our salvation, came down from heaven; and became incarnate by the Holy Ghost, of the Virgin Mary; AND WAS MADE MAN. He was crucified also for us, suffered under Pontius Pilate, and was buried. And the third day he rose again according to the Scriptures; and ascended into heaven, sitteth at the right hand of the Father; and he is to come again with glory, to judge both the living and the dead; of whose kingdom there shall be no end.
And in the Holy Ghost, the Lord and giver of life, who proceedeth from the Father and the Son; who together with the Father and the Son, is adored and glorified; who spoke by the Prophets. And one holy Catholic and Apostolic Church. I confess one Baptism for the remission of sins. And I expect the resurrection of the dead, and the life of the world to come.

11. *Oremus.*
Let us pray.

12. *Sursum corda.*
Lift up your hearts.

13. *Dignum et justum est.*
It is right and fitting.

14. *Sanctus, sanctus, sanctus, Dominus Deus Sabaoth. Pleni sunt coeli et terra gloria tua. Hosanna in excelsis. Benedictus qui venit in nomine Domini.*
Holy, holy, holy, Lord God of Hosts. Heaven and earth are full of thy glory. Hosanna in the highest. Blessed is he that cometh in the name of the Lord.

15. *Pater noster, qui es in coelis, sanctificetur nomen tuum; adveniat regnum tuum; fiat voluntas tua sicut in coelo, et in terra; panem nostrum quotidianum da nobis hodie; et dimitte nobis debita nostra, sicut et nos dimittimus debitoribus nostris; et ne nos inducas in tentationem.*
Sed libera nos a malo.
Our Father, who art in heaven, hallowed be thy name; thy kingdom come; thy will be done on earth, as it is in heaven; give us this day our daily bread; and forgive us our trespasses, as we forgive them that trespass against us; and lead us not into temptation.
But deliver us from evil.

16. *Pax Domini sit semper vobiscum.*
The peace of the Lord be always with you.

17. *Agnus Dei, qui tollis peccata mundi, miserere nobis.*
Agnus Dei, qui tollis peccata mundi, dona nobis pacem.
Lamb of God, who takest away the sins of the world, have mercy on us.

Lamb of God, who takest away the sins of the world, give us peace.

18. *Domine, non sum dignus ut intres sub tectum meum; sed tantum dic verbo, et sanabitur anima mea.*
Lord, I am not worthy that thou shouldst enter under my roof; but say only the word, and my soul shall be healed.

19. *Ite missa est.*
Go, you are dismissed.

20. *Requiem aeternam dona eis, Domine: et lux perpetua luceat eis.*
Grant them eternal rest, O Lord; and let perpetual light shine on them.
[At Requiem Masses]

21. *Requiescant in pace.*
May they rest in peace.
[At Requiem Masses]

22. *In principio erat Verbum, et Verbum erat apud Deum, et Deus erat Verbum.*
In the beginning was the Word, and the Word was with God, and the Word was God.

23. *VERBUM CARO FACTUM EST.*
THE WORD WAS MADE FLESH.

24. *O felix culpa, quae talem ac tantum meruit habere Redemptorem.*
O happy fault, which has earned such and so great a Redeemer.
['Exsultet' on Holy Saturday]

Massinger, Philip (1583–1640)

English dramatist and poet; collaborator of John Fletcher

1. Serves and fears
The fury of the many-headed monster,
The giddy multitude.
[*The Unnatural Combat* (c. 1619), III.ii]

2. Soar not too high to fall; but stoop to rise.
[*The Duke of Milan* (1623), I.ii]

3. He that would govern others, first should be
The master of himself.
[*The Bondman: an Antient Story* (1624), I.iii]

4. View yourselves
In the deceiving mirror of self-love.
[*The Parliament of Love* (1624), I.v]

5. What pity 'tis, one that can speak so well,
Should in his actions be so ill!
[*The Parliament of Love* (1624), III.iii]

6. All words,
And no performance!
[*The Parliament of Love* (1624), IV.ii]

7. Greatness, with private men
Esteem'd a blessing, is to me a curse;
And we, whom, for our high births, they conclude
The only freemen, are the only slaves.
Happy the golden mean!
[*The Great Duke of Florence* (licensed 1627), I.i]

8. I am driven
Into a desperate strait and cannot steer
A middle course.
[*The Great Duke of Florence* (licensed 1627), III.i]

9. Pray enter
You are learned Europeans and we worse
Than ignorant Americans.
[*The City Madam* (licensed 1632), III.iii]

10. Verity, you brach!
The devil turned precisian?
[*A New Way to Pay Old Debts* (1633), I.i]

11. Some undone widow sits upon my arm,
And takes away the use of 't; and my sword,
Glued to my scabbard with wrong'd orphans' tears,
Will not be drawn.
[*A New Way to Pay Old Debts* (1633), V.i]

12. Patience, the beggar's virtue.
[*A New Way to Pay Old Debts* (1633), V.i]

13. Death has a thousand doors to let out life:
I shall find one.
[*A Very Woman* (licensed 1634), V.iv. Cf. Seneca: 5]

14. Ambition, in a private man a vice,
Is, in a prince, the virtue.
[*The Bashful Lover* (licensed 1636), I.ii]

Matthews, Brander (1852–1929)

American man of letters; critic, lecturer, dramatist and autobiographer

1. A gentleman need not know Latin, but he should at least have forgotten it.
[Attr.]

Maugham, William Somerset (1874–1965)

English short-story writer, novelist, dramatist and physician; born in France

1. Like all weak men he laid an exaggerated stress on not changing one's mind.
[*Of Human Bondage* (1915), 39]

2. People ask you for criticism, but they only want praise.
[*Of Human Bondage* (1915), 50]

3. It's no use crying over spilt milk, because all the forces of the universe were bent on spilling it.
[*Of Human Bondage* (1915), 67]

4. The mystic sees the ineffable, and the psychopathologist the unspeakable.
[*The Moon and Sixpence* (1919), 1]

5. Impropriety is the soul of wit.
[*The Moon and Sixpence* (1919), 4. Cf. Shakespeare, *Hamlet*: 63]

6. You can't learn too soon that the most useful thing about a principle is that it can always be sacrificed to expediency.
[*The Circle* (1921), III]

7. A woman will always sacrifice herself if you give her the opportunity. It is her favourite form of self-indulgence.
[*The Circle* (1921), III]

8. When married people don't get on they can separate, but if they're not married it's impossible. It's a tie that only death can sever.
[*The Circle* (1921), III]

9. The right people are rude. They can afford to be.
[*Our Betters* (1923), II]

10. It was such a lovely day I thought it was a pity to get up.
[*Our Betters* (1923), II]

11. She's too crafty a woman to invent a new lie when an old one will serve.
[*The Constant Wife* (1927), II]

12. Hypocrisy is the most difficult and nerve-racking vice that any man can pursue; it needs an unceasing vigilance and a

rare detachment of spirit. It cannot, like adultery or gluttony, be practised at spare moments; it is a whole-time job.
[*Cakes and Ale* (1930), 1]

13. From the earliest times the old have rubbed it into the young that they are wiser than they, and before the young had discovered what nonsense this was they were old too, and it profited them to carry on the imposture.
[*Cakes and Ale* (1930), 11]

14. Life is too short to do anything for oneself that one can pay others to do for one.
[*The Summing Up* (1938)]

15. There is an impression abroad that everyone had it in him to write one book; but if by this is implied a good book the impression is false.
[*The Summing Up* (1938)]

16. I'll give you my opinion of the human race ... Their heart's in the right place, but their head is a thoroughly inefficient organ.
[*The Summing Up* (1938)]

17. Men have an extraordinarily erroneous opinion of their position in nature; and the error is ineradicable.
[*A Writer's Notebook* (1949)]

18. Music-hall songs provide the dull with wit, just as proverbs provide them with wisdom.
[*A Writer's Notebook* (1949)]

19. I recognize that I am made up of several persons and that the person that at the moment has the upper hand will inevitably give place to another. But which is the real one? All of them or none?
[*A Writer's Notebook* (1949)]

20. Sentimentality is only sentiment that rubs you up the wrong way.
[*A Writer's Notebook* (1949)]

21. Scotchmen seem to think it's a credit to them to be Scotch.
[*A Writer's Notebook* (1949)]

22. You know, of course, that the Tasmanians, who never committed adultery, are now extinct.
[*The Bread-Winner*]

23. I've always been interested in people, but I've never liked them.
[*The Observer*, 'Sayings of the Week', 1949]

24. The trouble with our younger authors is that they are all in their sixties.
[*The Observer*, 'Sayings of the Week', 1951]

25. Dying is a very dull, dreary affair. And my advice to you is to have nothing whatever to do with it.
[In Robin Maugham, *Escape from the Shadows* (1972)]

26. You don't just *get* a story ... You have to wait for it to come to you. I've never written a story in my life. The story has come to me *and demanded to be written*.
[In Robin Maugham, *Conversation with Willie* (1978)]

27. [Said on his ninetieth birthday]
I am sick of this way of life. The weariness and sadness of old age make it intolerable. I have walked with death in hand, and death's own hand is warmer than my own. I don't wish to live any longer.
[In M.B. Strauss, *Familiar Medical Quotations*]

Maurois, André (1885–1967)
French biographer and novelist

1. *Aucun de nous ne vit à chaque instant toutes ses idées; mais il faut juger les êtres plus par leurs dépassements que par leurs défaillances.*
None of us lives out, at every moment, all of our ideas; but one should judge human beings more by their excellence than by their weaknesses.
[*Lélia ou la vie de George Sand* (1952)]

Maxton, James (1885–1946)
Scottish socialist and orator; Labour politician and writer

1. [On a man proposing that the ILP should no longer be affiliated to the Labour Party]
If my friend cannot ride two horses – what's he doing in the bloody circus?
[In G. McAllister, *James Maxton: the Portrait of a Rebel* (1935)]

2. [Said to Ramsay MacDonald when he made his last speech in Parliament]
Sit down, man. You're a bloody tragedy.
[Attr.]

Mayakovsky, Vladimir (1893–1930)
Russian futurist poet, dramatist and artist; poet of the Revolution

1. Art is not a mirror to reflect the world, but a hammer with which to shape it.
[*The Guardian*, 1974]

Mayer, Louis B. (1885–1957)
Russian-born American film executive and producer; Academy Award 1950

1. [Comment to writers who had objected to changes in their work]
The number one book of the ages was written by a committee, and it was called The Bible.
[In Leslie Halliwell, *The Filmgoer's Book of Quotes* (1973)]

Mayhew, Christopher (1915–)
British parliamentarian and writer

1. [On the Munich Agreement]
The peace that passeth all understanding.
[Speech, Oxford Union, 1938]

2. [On the Munich Agreement]
A policy of *reculer pour mieux reculer*.
[Speech, Oxford Union, 1938]

Mayhew, Jonathan (1720–1766)
American clergyman and pamphleteer

1. Rulers have no authority from God to do mischief.
[*A Discourse Concerning Unlimited Submission and Non-Resistance to the Higher Powers* (1750)]

Maynard, Sir John (1602–1690)
English judge, politician and royalist

1. [Reply to Judge Jeffreys' suggestion that he was so old he had forgotten the law]
I have forgotten more law than you ever knew, but allow me to say, I have not forgotten much.
[Attr.]

Mayo, William James (1861–1939)
American surgeon

1. Specialist – A man who knows more and more about less and less.
[Attr.]

Mead, Margaret (1901–1978)
American anthropologist; psychologist, lecturer and writer

1. We are living beyond our means. As a people we have developed a life-style that is draining the earth of its priceless and irreplaceable resources without regard for the future of our children and people all around the world.
[*Redbook*, 'The Energy Crisis – Why Our World Will Never Again Be the Same']

2. Women want mediocre men, and men are working to be as mediocre as possible.
[*Quote Magazine*, 1958]

Mearns, Hughes (1875–1965)
American educator and writer

1. As I was going up the stair
I met a man who wasn't there.
He wasn't there again to-day.
I wish, I wish he'd stay away.
[*The Psycho-ed* (1910)]

Medawar, Sir Peter Bruin (1915–1987)
Brazilian-born British zoologist; shared Nobel prize for medicine, 1960, for work on immunology

1. Scientific discovery is a private event, and the delight that accompanies it, or the despair of finding it illusory does not travel.
[*Hypothesis and Imagination*]

2. The human mind treats a new idea the way the body treats a strange protein – it rejects it.
[Attr.]

Medici, Cosimo de' (1389–1464)
Member of prominent and cultured family of bankers, merchants and rulers of Tuscany and Florence; known as Cosimo the Great

1. We read that we ought to forgive our enemies; but we do not read that we ought to forgive our friends.
[In Francis Bacon, *Apophthegms* (1625)]

Medici, Lorenzo de' (1449–1492)
Italian statesman, poet, scholar and member of prominent family of bankers and merchants; first patron of Michelangelo; known as Lorenzo the Magnificent

1. *Quant'è bella giovinezza
che si sfugge tuttavia!
Chi vuol esser lieto, sia:
di doman non c'è certezza.*
How lovely is youth, which is always slipping away! Let him be glad who will be so: for tomorrow has no certainty.
['Trionfo di Bacco ed Arianna']

Meir, Golda (Goldie Mabovitch Myerson) (1898–1978)
Russian-born Israeli Labour stateswoman; Foreign Minister 1956–66 and Prime Minister 1969–74

1. A leader who doesn't hesitate before he sends his nation into battle is not fit to be a leader.
[Israel and Mary Shenker (eds.), *As Good as Golda* (1943)]

2. I can honestly say that I was never affected by the question of the success of an undertaking. If I felt it was the right thing to do, I was for it regardless of the possible outcome.
[In Marie Syrkin, *Golda Meir: Woman with a Cause* (1964)]

3. Being seventy is not a sin.
[*Reader's Digest*, 1971, 'The Indestructible Golda Meir']

4. We intend to remain alive. Our neighbours want to see us dead. This is not a question that leaves much room for compromise.
[*Reader's Digest*, 1971, 'The Indestructible Golda Meir']

5. Pessimism is a luxury that a Jew can never allow himself.
[*The Observer*, 'Sayings of the Week', 1974]

Melba, Dame Nellie (1861–1931)
Renowned Australian operatic soprano

1. The first rule in opera is the first rule in life: see to everything yourself.
[*Melodies and Memories* (1925)]

2. [Speaking to Clara Butt]
So you're going to Australia! I made twenty thousand pounds on my tour there, but of course *that* will never be done again. Still, it's a wonderful country, and you'll have a good time. What are you going to sing? All I can say is – sing 'em muck! It's all they can understand!
[In W.H. Ponder, *Clara Butt: Her Life Story* (1928)]

3. Melba was engaged by a socially ambitious woman to sing at a reception. When asked her fee she said it would be five hundred guineas. The woman warned her: 'I shall expect you to mix with my guests.' 'Oh,' said Melba with relief. 'Then it will only be two hundred and fifty.'
[In Martin Boyd, *Day of My Delight* (1965)]

4. [Reply to the Kaiser, who had asked if she did not think she took the Jewel Song at too fast a tempo]
No, your Imperial Majesty. I do not. I sang the part of Marguerite according to the instructions of the composer himself, M. Charles Gounod, who was pleased to express his entire satisfaction with my interpretation and to compliment me on it.
[In John Hetherington, *Melba* (1967)]

5. [To the editor of the *Argus*]
I don't care what you say, for me or against me, but for heaven's sake say something about me.
[In John Thompson, *On Lips of Living Men*]

6. [On board ship, on being offered jelly]
No thanks, there are two things I like stiff and jelly's not one of them.
[Attr.]

Melbourne, William Lamb, Second Lord (1779–1848)
English Whig politician; Prime Minister 1834, 1835–41; husband of Lady Caroline Lamb and political adviser to Queen Victoria

1. [After his dismissal by William IV]
I have always thought complaints of ill-usage contemptible, whether from a seduced disappointed girl or a turned out Prime Minister.
[In a letter from Emily Eden to Mrs Lister, 1834]

2. Now, is it to lower the price of corn, or isn't it? It is not much matter which we say, but mind, we must all say *the same*.
[Attr., in Walter Bagehot, *The English Constitution* (1867)]

3. [Of Catholic Emancipation]
What all the wise men promised has not happened, and what all the d–d fools said would happen has come to pass.
[In H. Dunckley, *Lord Melbourne* (1890)]

4. [On the Order of the Garter]
I like the Garter; there is no damned merit in it.
[In H. Dunckley, *Lord Melbourne* (1890)]

5. [On listening to an evangelical sermon]
Things have come to a pretty pass when religion is allowed to invade the sphere of private life.
[In G.W.E. Russell, *Collections and Recollections* (1898)]

6. [Replying to someone who said he would support Melbourne so long as he was right]
What I want is men who will support me when I am in the wrong.
[In Lord David Cecil, *Lord M* (1954)]

7. [Advising Queen Victoria against granting Prince Albert the title of King Consort]
For God's sake, ma'am, let's have no more of that. If you get the English people into the way of making kings, you'll get them into the way of *un*making them.
[In Lord David Cecil, *Lord M.* (1954)]

8. Damn it all, another Bishop dead – I verily believe they die to vex me
[Attr., in Lord David Cecil, *Lord M.* (1954)]

9. The worst of the present day [1835] is that men hate one another so damnably. For my part I love them all.
[Attr.]

10. [To the Queen]
I don't know, Ma'am, why they make all this fuss about education; none of the Pagets can read or write, and they get on well enough.
[Attr.]

11. While I cannot be regarded as a pillar, I must be regarded as a buttress of the church, because I support it from the outside.
[Attr.]

Melville, Herman (1819–1891)
American novelist, poet and short-story writer, noted for his sea novels

1. Call me Ishmael.
[*Moby Dick* (1851), 1, first words]

2. Better sleep with a sober cannibal than a drunken Christian.
[*Moby Dick* (1851), 3]

3. A whale ship was my Yale College and my Harvard.
[*Moby Dick* (1851), 24]

4. In youth we are, but in age we seem.
[*Pierre* (1852)]

5. I would prefer not to.
[*Bartleby* (1853)]

6. God bless Captain Vere!
[*Billy Budd* (1888)]

7. 'With mankind,' he would say 'forms, measured forms, are everything.'
[*Billy Budd* (1888)]

Ménage, Gilles (1613–1692)
French lexicographer

1. [Part of a conversation with Jean-Louis Guez de Balzac]
Comme nous nous entretenions de ce qui pouvait rendre heureux, je lui dis; Sanitas sanitatum, et omnia sanitas.
While we were talking about what could make one happy, I said to him: *Sanitas sanitatum et omnia sanitas.*
[In *Ménagiana* (1693); a play on Ecclesiastes 1:2, *vanitas vanitatum et omnia vanitas* [vanity of vanities, all is vanity], substituting 'health' for 'vanity']

Menand, Louis

1. The evil of modern society isn't that it creates racism but that it creates conditions in which people who don't suffer from injustice seem incapable of caring very much about people who do.
[*The New Yorker*, 1992]

2. Culture isn't something that comes with one's race or sex. It comes only through experience; there isn't any other way to acquire it. And in the end everyone's culture is different, because everyone's experience is different.
[*The New Yorker*, 1992]

Mencken, H.L. (1880–1956)
American journalist, critic, philologist and satirist

1. Poetry is a comforting piece of fiction set to more or less lascivious music.
[*Prejudices* (1919–1927), Third Series, 'The Poet and his Art']

2. Faith may be defined briefly as an illogical belief in the occurrence of the improbable.
[*Prejudices* (1919–1927), Third Series, 'Types of Men']

3. [Referring to the businessman]
He is the only man who is ever apologizing for his occupation.
[*Prejudices* (1919–1927), Third Series, 'Types of Men']

4. Puritanism – The haunting fear that someone, somewhere, may be happy.
[*A Mencken Chrestomathy* (1949)]

5. Conscience is the inner voice that warns us somebody may be looking.
[*A Mencken Chrestomathy* (1949)]

6. We must respect the other fellow's religion, but only in the sense and to the extent that we respect his theory that his wife is beautiful and his children smart.
[*Notebooks* (1956), 'Minority Report']

7. It is now quite lawful for a Catholic woman to avoid pregnancy by a resort to mathematics, though she is still forbidden to resort to physics and chemistry.
[*Notebooks* (1956), 'Minority Report']

8. War will never cease until babies begin to come into the world with larger cerebrums and smaller adrenal glands.
[*Notebooks* (1956), 'Minority Report']

9. One of the things that makes a Negro unpleasant to white folk is the fact that he suffers from their injustice. He is thus a standing rebuke to them.
[*Notebooks* (1956), 'Minority Report']

10. The chief contribution of Protestantism to human thought is its massive proof that God is a bore.
[*Notebooks* (1956), 'Minority Report']

11. The worst government is the most moral. One composed of cynics is often very tolerant and human. But when fanatics are on top there is no limit to oppression.
[*Notebooks* (1956), 'Minority Report']

12. God is the immemorial refuge of the incompetent, the helpless, the miserable. They find not only sanctuary in His arms, but also a kind of superiority, soothing to their macerated egos; He will set them above their betters.
[*Notebooks* (1956), 'Minority Report']

13. It takes a long while for a naturally trustful person to reconcile himself to the idea that after all God will not help him.
[*Notebooks* (1956), 'Minority Report']

14. A society made up of individuals who were all capable of original thought would probably be unendurable. The pressure of ideas would simply drive it frantic.
[*Notebooks* (1956), 'Minority Report']

15. I write in order to attain that feeling of tension relieved and function achieved which a cow enjoys on giving milk.
[*The Delights of Reading*]

16. If, after I depart this vale, you ever remember me and have thought to please my ghost, forgive some sinner and wink your eye at some homely girl.
[*Smart Set*, 1921, Epitaph]

17. [On President Calvin Coolidge]
Here, indeed, was his one really notable talent. He slept more than any other President, whether by day or by night ... Nero fiddled, but Coolidge only snored ... He had no ideas, and he was not a nuisance.
[*American Mercury*, 1933]

18. I've made it a rule never to drink by daylight and never to refuse a drink after dark.
[*New York Post*, 1945]

19. No one ever went broke underestimating the intelligence of the American people.
[Attr.]

20. The only really happy people are married women and single men.
[Attr.]

21. Opera in English is, in the main, just about as sensible as baseball in Italian.
[Attr.]

22. When women kiss, it always reminds me of prize-fighters shaking hands.
[Attr.]

Menéndez y Pelayo, Marcelino (1856–1912)
Spanish scholar, critic and poet

1. *Desde luego, es más cómodo saber poco que saber mucho.*
Of course, knowing a little is more agreeable than knowing a lot.
[*Programa de literatura española (Spanish Literature Programme*, 1934), 'Defence of the Programme']

Menzies, Sir Robert (1894–1978)
Australian statesman and Prime Minister

1. [In answer to a woman shouting, 'I wouldn't vote for you if you were the Archangel Gabriel']
If I were the Archangel Gabriel, madam, I'm afraid you would not be in my constituency.
[In Ray Robinson, *The Wit of Sir Robert Menzies* (1966)]

2. A Prime Minister exercises his greatest public influence by creating a public impression of himself, hoping all the time that the people will be generous rather than just.
[In H. Mayer and H. Nelson, *Australian Politics: A Third Reader*]

Mercer, Johnny (1909–1976)
American songwriter and composer; Academy Awards 1946, 1951, 1954

1. Jeepers Creepers – where'd you get them peepers?
['Jeepers Creepers', song, 1938]

2. That old black magic has me in its spell.
['That Old Black Magic', song, 1943]

Mercier, Louis-Sébastien (1740–1814)
French playwright and writer on drama

1. *Les extrêmes se touchent.*
Extremes meet.
[*Tableau de Paris*, IV, 348, Heading]

Meredith, George (1828–1909)
English novelist, poet and critic

1. I expect that Woman will be the last thing civilized by Man.
[*The Ordeal of Richard Feverel* (1859), 1]

2. In action Wisdom goes by majorities.
[*The Ordeal of Richard Feverel* (1859), 1]

3. Away with Systems! Away with a corrupt world! Let us breathe the air of the Enchanted island.
Golden lie the meadows; golden run the streams; red gold is on the pine-stems. The sun is coming down to earth, and walks the fields and the waters. The sun is coming down to earth, and the fields and the waters shout to him golden shouts.
[*The Ordeal of Richard Feverel* (1859), 19]

4. Kissing don't last: cookery do!
[*The Ordeal of Richard Feverel* (1859), 28]

5. Speech is the small change of silence.
[*The Ordeal of Richard Feverel* (1859), 34]

6. Much benevolence of the passive order may be traced to a disinclination to inflict pain upon oneself.
[*Vittoria* (1866), 42]

7. A dainty rogue in porcelain.
[*The Egoist* (1879), 5]

8. Cynicism is intellectual dandyism.
[*The Egoist* (1879), 7]

9. To plod on and still keep the passion fresh.
[*The Egoist* (1879), 12]

10. In ... the book of Egoism, it is written, Possession without obligation to the object possessed approaches felicity.
[*The Egoist* (1879), 14]

11. She did not seduce, she ravished.
[*Diana of the Crossways* (1885), 7]

12. She was a lady of incisive features bound in stale parchment.
[*Diana of the Crossways* (1885), 14]

13. Between the ascetic rocks and the sensual whirlpools.
[*Diana of the Crossways* (1885), 37]

14. There is nothing the body suffers the soul may not profit by.
[*Diana of the Crossways* (1885), 43]

15. None of your dam punctilio.
[*One of Our Conquerors* (1891), 1]

16. Overhead, overhead
Rushes life in a race,
As the clouds the clouds chase;
And we go,
And we drop like the fruits of the tree,
Even we,
Even so.
['Dirge in Woods' (1862)]

17. He fainted on his vengefulness, and strove
To ape the magnanimity of love.
[*Modern Love* (1862), 2]

18. Not till the fire is dying in the grate,
Look we for any kinship with the stars.
[*Modern Love* (1862), 4]

19. And if I drink oblivion of a day,
So shorten I the stature of my soul.
[*Modern Love* (1862), 12]

20. 'I play for Seasons; not Eternities!'
Says Nature.
[*Modern Love* (1862), 13]

21. A kiss is but a kiss now! and no wave
Of a great flood that whirls me to the sea.
But, as you will! we'll sit contentedly,
And eat our pot of honey on the grave.
[*Modern Love* (1862), 29]

22. That rarest gift
To Beauty, Common Sense.
[*Modern Love* (1862), 32]

23. O have a care of natures that are mute!
[*Modern Love* (1862), 35]

24. In tragic life, God wot,
No villain need be! Passions spin the plot:
We are betrayed by what is false within.
[*Modern Love* (1862), 43]

25. Love, that had robbed us of immortal things,
This little moment mercifully gave,
Where I have seen across the twilight wave
The swan sail with her young beneath her wings.
[*Modern Love* (1862), 47]

26. More brain, O Lord, more brain!...

27. Their sense is with their senses all mixed in,
Destroyed by subtleties these women are!
[*Modern Love* (1862), 48]

28. Thus piteously Love closed what he begat:
The union of this ever diverse pair!
These two were rapid falcons in a snare,
Condemned to do the flitting of a bat...

29. Ah, what a dusty answer gets the soul
When hot for certainties in this our life!
[*Modern Love* (1862), 50]

30. Under yonder beech-tree single on the greensward,
Couched with her arms behind her golden head,
Knees and tresses folded to slip and ripple idly,
Lies my young love sleeping in the shade.
['Love in the Valley' (1883), I]

31. She whom I love is hard to catch and conquer,
Hard, but O the glory of the winning were she won!
['Love in the Valley' (1883), II]

32. Lovely are the curves of the white owl sweeping
Wavy in the dusk lit by one large star.
Lone in the fir-branch, his rattle-note unvaried,
Brooding o'er the gloom, spins the brown eve-jar.
Darker grows the valley, more and more forgetting:
So were it with me if forgetting could be willed.
Tell the grassy hollow that holds the bubbling well-spring,
Tell it to forget the source that keeps it filled.
['Love in the Valley' (1883), V]

33. On a starred night Prince Lucifer uprose.
Tired of his dark dominion swung the fiend...

34. He reached a middle height, and at the stars,
Which are the brain of heaven, he looked, and sank.
Around the ancient track marched, rank on rank,
The army of unalterable law.
['Lucifer in Starlight' (1883)]

35. Enter these enchanted woods,
You who dare.
['The Woods of Westermain' (1883)]

36. Narrows the world to my neighbour's gate.
['Seed Time']

37. We spend our lives in learning pilotage,
And grow good steersmen when the vessel's crank!
['The Wisdom of Eld']

Meredith, Owen (Lord Lytton) (1831–1891)

English statesman; Viceroy of India 1876–1880 and lyric poet

1. Genius does what it must, and Talent does what it can.
['Last Words of a Sensitive Second-Rate Poet' (1868)]

Merrill, Bob (1921–1977)

American songwriter and composer

1. People who need people are the luckiest people in the world.
['People Who Need People', song, 1964]

Merritt, Dixon Lanier (1879–1972)

American editor

1. A wonderful bird is the pelican,
His bill will hold more than his belican.
He can take in his beak
Food enough for a week,
But I'm damned if I see how the helican.
[*Nashville Banner*, 1913]

Metternich, Prince Clement (1773–1859)

Austrian statesman; Chancellor of Austria 1821–48

1. *Italien ist ein geographischer Begriff.*
Italy is a geographical concept.
[Letter, 1849]

2. *L'erreur n'a jamais approché de mon esprit.*
Error has never even come close to my mind.
[Remark, 1848]

Meudell, George Dick (1860–1936)

1. Until we partially abolish poverty at home we have no right to burden ourselves with millions of paupers from abroad. What we have, we hold. AUSTRALIA FOR THE AUSTRALIANS.
[*The Pleasant Career of a Spendthrift in London*]

Mew, Charlotte (1869–1928)

English poet and short-story writer

1. She sleeps up in the attic there
Alone, poor maid. 'Tis but a stair
Betwixt us. Oh! my God! the down,
The soft young down of her, the brown,
The brown of her – her eyes, her hair, her hair!
['The Farmer's Bride' (1916)]

Meynell, Alice (1847–1922)

English lyric poet, critic, essayist, journalist and suffragist

1. My heart shall be thy garden.
['The Garden' (1875)]

2. I must not think of thee; and, tired yet strong,
I shun the thought that lurks in all delight–
The thought of thee – and in the blue heaven's height,
And in the sweetest passage of a song...

3. With the first dream that comes with the first sleep
I run, I run, I am gathered to thy heart.
['Renouncement' (1875)]

4. She walks – the lady of my delight–
A shepherdess of sheep.
['The Shepherdess' (1901)]

Meynell, Hugo (1727–1808)

1. The chief advantage of London is, that a man is always so near his burrow.
[In Boswell, *The Life of Samuel Johnson* (1791), III, 1779]

2. For anything I see, foreigners are fools.
[In Boswell, *The Life of Samuel Johnson* (1791), IV, 1780]

Michaelis, John H. (1912–1985)
American army officer

1. [Said to the 27th Infantry (Wolfhound) Regiment during the Korean War]
You're not here to die for your country. You're here to make those – die for theirs.
[Attr.]

Michelet, Jules (1798–1874)
French historian

1. [From a letter received by Dumas]
You are one of the forces of nature.
[In Alexandre Dumas, *Memoirs*]

Middleton, Thomas (c. 1580–1627)
English dramatist, poet and writer of masques; collaborated with William Rowley, among others

1. I never heard
Of any true affection, but 'twas nipt
With care.
[*Blurt, Master-Constable* (1602), III.i]

2. By many a happy accident.
[*No Wit, No Help, Like a Woman's* (c. 1613), IV.i]

3. Though I be poor, I'm honest.
[*The Witch* (1609–1616), III.ii]

4. There's no hate lost between us.
[*The Witch* (1609–1616), IV.iii]

5. When the deed's done,
I'll furnish thee with all things for thy flight;
Thou may'st live bravely in another country.
[*The Changeling* (with William Rowley, c. 1622), II.ii]

6. A woman dipp'd in blood and talk of modesty.
[*The Changeling* (with William Rowley, c. 1622), III.iv]

7. A wondrous necessary man.
[*The Changeling* (with William Rowley, c. 1622), V.i]

Mies van der Rohe, Ludwig (1886–1969)
German-born American architect; Bauhaus director 1929–33

1. Less is more.
[*New York Herald Tribune*, 1959]

Mikes, George (1912–1987)
Hungarian-born journalist and author

1. On the Continent people have good food; in England people have good table manners.
[*How to be an Alien* (1946)]

2. Continental people have sex life; the English have hot-water bottles.
[*How to be an Alien* (1946)]

3. An Englishman, even if he is alone, forms an orderly queue of one.
[*How to be an Alien* (1946)]

4. The one class you do *not* belong to and are not proud of at all is the lower-middle class. No one ever describes himself as belonging to the lower-middle class.
[*How to be an Inimitable*]

Mill, John Stuart (1806–1873)
English utilitarian philosopher; economist, reformer and politician

1. The great majority of those who speak of perfectibility as a dream, do so because they feel that it is one which would afford them no pleasure if it were realized.
[*Speech on Perfectibility* (1828)]

2. When the land is cultivated entirely by the spade and no horses are kept, a cow is kept for every three acres of land.
[*Principles of Political Economy* (1848), II, 6. Cf. Collings: 1]

3. Unearned increment.
[*Principles of Political Economy* (1848), V, 2]

4. When society requires to be rebuilt, there is no use in attempting to rebuild it on the old plan.
[*Dissertations and Discussions*, I (1859), 'Essay on Coleridge']

5. Protection, therefore, against the tyranny of the magistrate is not enough: there needs protection also against the tyranny of the prevailing opinion and feeling.
[*On Liberty* (1859), Introduction]

6. Another grand determining principle of the rules of conduct ... has been the servility of mankind towards the supposed preferences or aversions of their temporal masters, or of their gods.
[*On Liberty* (1859), Introduction]

7. The sole end for which mankind are warranted, individually or collectively, in interfering with the liberty of action of any of their number, is self-protection.
[*On Liberty* (1859), Introduction]

8. The only purpose for which power can be rightfully exercised over any member of a civilized community, against his will, is to prevent harm to others. His own good, either physical or moral, is not sufficient warrant.
[*On Liberty* (1859), 1]

9. If all mankind minus one, were of one opinion, and only one person were of the contrary opinion, mankind would be no more justified in silencing that one person, than he, if he had the power, would be justified in silencing mankind.
[*On Liberty* (1859), 2]

10. He who knows only his own side of the case knows little of that.
[*On Liberty* (1859), 2]

11. We can never be sure that the opinion we are endeavouring to stifle is a false opinion; and if we were sure, stifling it would be an evil still.
[*On Liberty* (1859), 2]

12. A party of order or stability, and a party of progress or reform, are both necessary elements of a healthy state of political life.
[*On Liberty* (1859), 2]

13. History teems with instances of truth put down by persecution ... It is a piece of idle sentimentality that truth, merely as truth, has any inherent power denied to error, of prevailing against the dungeon and the stake.
[*On Liberty* (1859), 2]

14. The liberty of the individual must be thus far limited; he must not make himself a nuisance to other people.
[*On Liberty* (1859), 3]

15. A people, it appears, may be progressive for a certain length of time, and then stop. When does it stop? When it ceases to possess individuality.
[*On Liberty* (1859), 3]

16. Whatever crushes individuality is despotism, by whatever name it may be called.
[*On Liberty* (1859), 3]

17. All good things which exist are the fruits of originality.
[*On Liberty* (1859), 3]

18. ... mere conformers to commonplace, or time-servers for truth, whose arguments on all great subjects are meant for their hearers, and are not those which have convinced themselves.
[*On Liberty* (1859), 3]

19. Persons require to possess a title, or some other badge of rank, or of the consideration of people of rank, to be able to indulge somewhat in the luxury of doing as they like without detriment to their estimation.
[*On Liberty* (1859), 3]

20. I am not aware that any community has a right to force another to be civilized.
[*On Liberty* (1859), 4]

21. Liberty consists in doing what one desires.
[*On Liberty* (1859), 5]

22. The worth of a State, in the long run, is the worth of the individuals composing it.
[*On Liberty* (1859), 5]

23. A State which dwarfs its men, in order that they may be more docile instruments in its hands even for beneficial purposes – will find that with small men no great thing can really be accomplished.
[*On Liberty* (1859), 5]

24. Were there but a few hearts and intellects like hers this earth would already become the hoped-for heaven.
[Epitaph for his wife, Harriet, 1859]

25. If we may be excused the antithesis, we should say that eloquence is *heard*, poetry is *overheard*.
[*Thoughts on Poetry and its Varieties* (1859)]

26. The Conservatives ... being by the law of their existence the stupidest party.
[*Considerations on Representative Government* (1861), 7 (footnote)]

27. As often as a study is cultivated by narrow minds, they will draw from it narrow conclusions.
[*Auguste Comte and Positivism* (1865)]

28. The principle which regulates the existing social relations between the two sexes – the legal subordination of one sex to the other – is wrong in itself, and now one of the chief hindrances to human improvement; and ... it ought to be replaced by a principle of perfect equality, admitting no power or privilege on the one side, nor disability on the other.
[*The Subjection of Women* (1869), 1]

29. The moral regeneration of mankind will only really commence, when the most fundamental of the social relations [marriage] is placed under the rule of equal justice, and when human beings learn to cultivate their strongest sympathy with an equal in rights and cultivation.
[*The Subjection of Women* (1869), 4]

30. Ask yourself whether you are happy, and you cease to be so.
[*Autobiography* (1873), 5]

31. No great improvements in the lot of mankind are possible, until a great change takes place in the fundamental constitution of their modes of thought.
[*Autobiography* (1873), 7]

32. The most important thing women have to do is to stir up the zeal of women themselves.
[Letter to Alexander Bain, 1869]

Millais, Sir John Everett (1829–1896)
English Pre-Raphaelite painter

1. One day the inspiration comes, and then it goes. It's all stomach.
[Attr.]

Millay, Edna St Vincent (1892–1950)
American poet and dramatist

1. My candle burns at both ends;
It will not last the night;
But ah, my foes, and oh my friends–
It gives a lovely light!
[*A Few Figs from Thistles* (1920), 'First Fig']

2. Was it for this I uttered prayers,
And sobbed and cursed and kicked the stairs,
That now, domestic as a plate,
I should retire at half-past eight?
[*A Few Figs from Thistles* (1920), 'Grown-up']

3. Death devours all lovely things:
Lesbia with her sparrow
Shares the darkness, – presently
Every bed is narrow...

4. After all, my erstwhile dear,
My no longer cherished,
Need we say it was not love,
Just because it perished?
[*Second April* (1921), 'Passer Mortuus Est']

5. This have I known always: Love is no more
Than the wide blossom which the wind assails,
Than the great tide that treads the shifting shore,
Strewing fresh wreckage gathered in the gales:
Pity me that the heart is slow to learn
What the swift mind beholds at every turn.
[*The Harp-Weaver and Other Poems* (1923), 'Pity me not because the light of day']

6. Euclid alone had looked on Beauty bare.
[*The Harp-Weaver and Other Poems* (1923), Sonnet 22]

7. Down, down, down into the darkness of the grave
Gently they go, the beautiful, the tender, the kind;
Quietly they go, the intelligent, the witty, the brave.
I know. But I do not approve. And I am not resigned.
[*Buck in the Snow* (1928), 'Dirge without Music']

8. Childhood is not from birth to a certain age and at a certain age
The child is grown, and puts away childish things,
Childhood is the kingdom where nobody dies.
Nobody that matters, that is.
[*Wine from these Grapes* (1934), 'Childhood is the Kingdom where Nobody dies']

9. Man has never been the same since God died.
He has taken it very hard. Why, you'd think it was only yesterday,
The way he takes it.

Not that he says much, but he laughs much louder than he used to,
And he can't bear to be left alone even for a minute, and he can't
Sit still.
[*Conversation at Midnight* (1937), IV]

Miller, Arthur (1915–)
Leading American dramatist and screenwriter

1. He's liked, but he's not well liked.
[*Death of a Salesman* (1949), I]

2. Attention, attention must finally be paid to such a person.
[*Death of a Salesman* (1949), I]

3. Nobody dast blame this man. A salesman is got to dream, boy. It comes with the territory.
[*Death of a Salesman* (1949), 'Requiem']

4. There are many who stay away from church these days because you hardly ever mention God any more.
[*The Crucible* (1952), I]

5. I am inclined to notice the ruin in things, perhaps because I was born in Italy.
[*A View from the Bridge* (1955), I]

6. Years ago a person, he was unhappy, didn't know what to do with himself – he'd go to church, start a revolution – *something*. Today you're unhappy? Can't figure it out? What is the salvation? Go shopping.
[*The Price* (1968), I]

7. A good newspaper, I suppose, is a nation talking to itself.
[*The Observer*, 'Sayings of the Week', 1961]

8. If there weren't any anti-semitism, I wouldn't think of myself as Jewish.
[*The Observer*, 'Sayings of the Week', 1995]

9. [When asked if he would attend Marilyn Monroe's funeral]
Why should I go? She won't be there.
[Attr.]

Miller, Henry (1891–1980)
American novelist and essayist; autobiographical writer; banned for obscenity

1. Sex is one of the nine reasons for reincarnation ... The other eight are unimportant.
[*Big Sur and the Oranges of Hieronymus Bosch*]

Miller, Jonathan (1934–)
English writer, director, producer and physician

1. They do those little personal things people sometimes do when they think they are alone in railway carriages; things like smelling their own armpits.
[*Beyond the Fringe* (1960)]

2. I'm not really a Jew; just Jew-ish, not the whole hog.
[*Beyond the Fringe* (1961), 'Real Class']

3. [Remark made when introducing Marshall McLuhan on British television, 1965]
McLuhan is doing for visual space what Freud did for sex.
[Quoted by McLuhan in a letter to Harold Rosenberg, 1965]

Miller, Max (Harold Sargent) (1895–1963)
British music hall and film comedian

1. There was a little girl
Who had a little curl
Right in the middle of her forehead,
When she was good she was very very good
And when she was bad she was very very popular.
[*The Max Miller Blue Book*. Cf. Longfellow: 36 and Mae West: 5]

Miller, William (1810–1872)
Scottish poet; author of nursery rhymes

1. Wee Willie Winkie rins through the town,
Up stairs and down stairs in his nicht-gown,
Tirling at the window, crying at the lock,
Are a' the weans in their bed, it's past ten o'clock?
['Willie Winkie' (1841)]

Milligan, Spike (Terence Alan Milligan) (1918–)
Irish radio, stage and screen comedian and writer

1. Money can't buy friends, but you can get a better class of enemy.
[*Puckoon* (1963), 6]

2. I shook hands with a friendly Arab ... I still have my right hand to prove it.
[*A Dustbin of Milligan*, 'Letters to Harry Secombe']

3. 'Do you come here often?'
'Only in the mating season.'
[*The Goon Show*]

4. I don't like this game.
[*The Goon Show*]

5. I'm walking backwards till Christmas.
[*The Goon Show*]

6. *Moriarty*: How are you at Mathematics?
Harry Secombe: I speak it like a native.
[*The Goon Show*]

7. You silly twisted boy.
[*The Goon Show*]

8. Contraceptives should be used on every conceivable occasion.
[*The Last Goon Show of All*]

9. Policemen are numbered in case they get lost.
[*The Last Goon Show of All*]

10. Q. Are you Jewish?
A. No, a tree fell on me.
[*Private Eye*, 1973]

11. The Army works like this: if a man dies when you hang him, keep hanging him until he gets used to it.
[Attr.]

12. [Remark made about a pre-election poll]
One day the don't-knows will get in, and then where will we be?
[Attr.]

Milman, Henry Hart (1791–1868)
English poet and historian; Dean of St Paul's from 1849

1. Ride on! ride on in majesty!
In lowly pomp ride on to die.
[Hymn, 1827]

Milne, A.A. (1882–1956)
English children's writer; dramatist, novelist, poet and journalist

1. They're changing guard at Buckingham Palace–
Christopher Robin went down with Alice.
Alice is marrying one of the guard.
'A soldier's life is terrible hard,'
Says Alice.
[*When We Were Very Young* (1924), 'Buckingham Palace']

2. James James
Morrison Morrison
Weatherby George Dupree
Took great
Care of his Mother
Though he was only three.
James James
Said to his Mother
'Mother,' he said, said he;
'You must never go down to the end of the town if you don't go down with me.'
[*When We Were Very Young* (1924), 'Disobedience']

3. The King asked
The Queen, and
The Queen asked
The Dairymaid:
'Could we have some butter for
The Royal slice of bread?'...

4. The King said
'Butter, eh?'
And bounced out of bed...

5. I do like a little bit of butter to my bread!
[*When We Were Very Young* (1924), 'The King's Breakfast']

6. And some of the bigger bears try to pretend
That they came round the corner to look for a friend;
And they'll try to pretend that nobody cares
Whether you walk on the lines or the squares.
[*When We Were Very Young* (1924), 'Lines and Squares']

7. *What* is the matter with Mary Jane?
She's perfectly well and she hasn't a pain,
And it's lovely rice pudding for dinner again,
What *is* the matter with Mary Jane?
[*When We Were Very Young* (1924), 'Rice Pudding']

8. Little Boy kneels at the foot of the bed,
Droops on the little hands, little gold head;
Hush! Hush! Whisper who dares!
Christopher Robin is saying his prayers.
[*When We Were Very Young* (1924), 'Vespers'. Cf. J.B. Morton: 1]

9. Isn't it funny
How a bear likes honey?
Buzz! Buzz! Buzz!
I wonder why he does?
[*Winnie-the-Pooh* (1926), 1]

10. Silly old Bear!
[*Winnie-the-Pooh* (1926), 2]

11. I am a Bear of Very Little Brain, and long words Bother me.
[*Winnie-the-Pooh* (1926), 4]

12. I have decided to catch a Heffalump.
[*Winnie-the-Pooh* (1926), 5]

13. Time for a little something.
[*Winnie-the-Pooh* (1926), 6]

14. 'Pathetic,' he said. 'That's what it is. Pathetic.'
[*Winnie-the-Pooh* (1926), 6]

15. On Monday, when the sun is hot,
I wonder to myself a lot:
'Now is it true, or is it not,
That what is which is which is what?'
[*Winnie-the-Pooh* (1926), 7]

16. King John was not a good man–
He had his little ways,
And sometimes no one spoke to him
For days and days and days.
[*Now We Are Six* (1927), 'King John's Christmas']

17. And nobody knows
(Tiddely pom),
How cold my toes
(Tiddely pom),
How cold my toes
(Tiddely pom),
Are growing.
[*The House at Pooh Corner* (1928), 1]

18. Tiggers don't like honey.
[*The House at Pooh Corner* (1928), 2]

19. If the English language had been properly organized ... then there would be a word which meant both 'he' and 'she', and I could write, 'If John or Mary comes heesh will want to play tennis,' which would save a lot of trouble.
[*The Christopher Robin Birthday Book*]

20. For one person who dreams of making fifty thousand pounds, a hundred people dream of being left fifty thousand pounds.
[*If I May*, 'The Future']

Milner, Alfred, First Viscount (1854–1925)
German-born British statesman and colonial administrator

1. [Of the peers' role in relation to the budget]
If we believe a thing to be bad, and if we have a right to prevent it, it is our duty to try to prevent it and to damn the consequences.
[Speech, Glasgow, 1909]

Milosz, Czeslaw (1911–)
Lithuanian-born Polish poet, novelist and critic

1. Two things cannot be reduced to rationalising: time and beauty.
[*Beginning with My Streets* (1992)]

Milton, John (1608–1674)
Great English poet; parliamentarian, libertarian and pamphleteer

1. Let us with a gladsom mind
Praise the Lord, for he is kind,
For his mercies ay endure,
Ever faithfull, ever sure.
[Psalm 136 (1623)]

2. O fairest flower no sooner blown but blasted,
Soft silken Primrose fading timelessly.
['On the Death of a Fair Infant, Dying of a Cough' (1625)]

3. This is the Month, and this the happy morn,
Wherein the Son of Heav'ns eternal King,
Of wedded Maid, and Virgin Mother born,
Our great redemption from above did bring;
For so the holy sages once did sing,
That he our deadly forfeit should release,
And with his Father work us a perpetual peace.
['On the Morning of Christ's Nativity' (1629), 1]

4. The Star-led wisards haste with odours sweet.
['On the Morning of Christ's Nativity' (1629), 4]

5. It was the Winter wilde,
While the Heav'n-born-childe,
All meanly wrapt in the rude manger lies,
Nature in aw to him
Had doff't her gawdy trim

With her great Master so to sympathize.
['On the Morning of Christ's Nativity' (1629), 'The Hymn', 1]

6. But he her fears to cease,
Sent down the meek-eyd Peace,
She crown'd with Olive green, came softly sliding
Down through the turning sphear
His ready Harbinger,
With Turtle wing the amorous clouds dividing,
And waving wide her mirtle wand,
She strikes a universall Peace through Sea and Land
['On the Morning of Christ's Nativity' (1629), 'The Hymn', 3]

7. The Stars with deep amaze
Stand fixt in stedfast gaze
Bending one way their pretious influence
And will not take their flight,
For all the morning light,
Or Lucifer that often warn'd them thence;
But in their glimmering Orbs did glow,
Untill their Lord himself bespake, and bid them go.
['On the Morning of Christ's Nativity' (1629), 'The Hymn', 6]

8. Ring out ye Crystall sphears,
Once bless our human ears,
(If ye have power to touch our senses so)
And let your silver chime
Move in melodious time;
And let the Base of Heav'ns deep Organ blow,
And with your ninefold harmony
Make up full consort to th' Angelic symphony.
['On the Morning of Christ's Nativity' (1629), 'The Hymn', 13]

9. For if such holy Song
Enwrap our fancy long,
Time will run back, and fetch the age of gold
And speckl'd vanity
Will sicken soon and die.
['On the Morning of Christ's Nativity' (1629), 'The Hymn', 14]

10. Swinges the scaly Horrour of his foulded tail.
['On the Morning of Christ's Nativity' (1629), 'The Hymn', 18]

11. The oracles are dumm,
No voice or hideous humm
Runs through the arched roof in words deceiving.
Apollo from his shrine
Can no more divine,
With hollow shreik the steep of Delphos leaving.
['On the Morning of Christ's Nativity' (1629), 'The Hymn', 19]

12. So when the Sun in bed,
Curtain'd with cloudy red,
Pillows his chin upon an Orient wave.
['On the Morning of Christ's Nativity' (1629), 'The Hymn', 26]

13. But see the Virgin blest,
Hath laid her Babe to rest.
Time is our tedious Song should here have ending.
['On the Morning of Christ's Nativity' (1629), 'The Hymn', 27]

14. What needs my Shakespear for his honour'd Bones,
The labour of an age in pilèd Stones?
Or that his hallow'd reliques should be hid
Under a Star-ypointing Pyramid?
['On Shakespear' (1630)]

15. Before the starry threshold of Joves Court
My mansion is.
[*Comus* (1637), line 1]

16. Above the smoak and stirr of this dim spot,
Which men call Earth.
[*Comus* (1637), line 5]

17. Yet som there be that by due steps aspire
To lay their just hands on that Golden Key
That ope's the Palace of Eternity.
[*Comus* (1637), line 12]

18. All the Sea-girt Iles
That, like to rich and various gemms inlay
The unadornèd bosom of the Deep.
[*Comus* (1637), line 22]

19. Bacchus that first from out the purple Grape,
Crush't the sweet poyson of mis-used Wine.
[*Comus* (1637), line 46]

20. And the gilded Car of Day
His glowing Axle doth allay
In the steep Atlantick stream.
[*Comus* (1637), line 95]

21. What hath night to do with sleep?
[*Comus* (1637), line 122]

22. Com, knit hands, and beat the ground
In a light fantastick round.
[*Comus* (1637), line 143]

23. Me thought it was the sound
Of Riot, and ill-manag'd Merriment.
[*Comus* (1637), line 171]

24. O thievish Night,
Why shouldst thou, but for some felonious end,
In thy dark lantern thus close up the stars
That Nature hung in heaven, and filled their lamps
With everlasting oil to give due light
To the misled and lonely traveller?
[*Comus* (1637), line 195]

25. Was I deceiv'd, or did a sable cloud
Turn forth her silver lining on the night?
[*Comus* (1637), line 221]

26. Sweet Echo, sweetest Nymph, that liv'st unseen
Within thy airy shell
By slow Meander's margent green,
And in the violet-imbroider'd vale.
[*Comus* (1637), line 230]

27. Such sober certainty of waking bliss
I never heard till now.
[*Comus* (1637), line 263]

28. Shepherd I take thy word,
And trust thy honest offer'd courtesie,
Which oft is sooner found in lowly sheds
With smoaky rafters, than in tap'stry Halls
And courts of princes.
[*Comus* (1637), line 321]

29. With thy long levell'd rule of streaming light.
[*Comus* (1637), line 340]

30. He that has light within his own cleer brest
May sit i' th' center and enjoy bright day;
But he that hides a dark soul and foul thoughts
Benighted walks under the mid-day Sun;

Himself is his own dungeon.
[*Comus* (1637), line 381]

31. The unsun'd heaps
Of Misers treasure.
[*Comus* (1637), line 398]

32. 'Tis chastity, my brother, chastity:
She that has that, is clad in compleat steel.
[*Comus* (1637), line 420]

33. How charming is divine Philosophy!
Not harsh, and crabbed as dull fools suppose,
But musical as is Apollo's lute,
And a perpetual feast of nectar'd sweets,
Where no crude surfeit raigns.
[*Comus* (1637), line 475]

34. What the sage Poëts taught by th' heav'nly Muse,
Storied of old in high immortal vers
Of dire Chimeras and enchanted Iles,
And rifted Rocks whose entrance leads to Hell,
For such there be, but unbelief is blind.
[*Comus* (1637), line 515]

35. Wrapt in a pleasing fit of melancholy.
[*Comus* (1637), line 546]

36. I was all eare,
And took in strains that might create a soul
Under the ribs of Death.
[*Comus* (1637), line 560]

37. O foolishness of men! that lend their ears
To those budge doctors of the Stoick furr,
And fetch their precepts from the Cynick Tub,
Praising the lean and sallow Abstinence.
[*Comus* (1637), line 706]

38. Beauty is nature's coyn, must not be hoorded,
But must be currant, and the good thereof
Consists in mutual and partak'n bliss.
[*Comus* (1637), line 739]

39. Beauty is nature's brag, and must be shown
In courts, at feasts, and high solemnities,
Where most may wonder at the workmanship;
It is for homely features to keep home,
They had their name thence; course complexions
And cheeks of sorry grain will serve to ply
The sampler, and to teize the husewife's wooll.
What need a vermeil-tinctur'd lip for that,
Love-darting eyes, or tresses like the Morn?
[*Comus* (1637), line 745]

40. Sabrina fair,
Listen where thou art sitting
Under the glassie, cool, translucent wave,
In twisted braids of Lillies knitting
The loose train of thy amber-dropping hair.
[*Comus* (1637), line 859]

41. Thus I set my printless feet
O're the Cowslip's Velvet head,
That bends not as I tread.
[*Comus* (1637), line 897]

42. Yet once more, O ye Laurels, and once more
Ye Myrtles brown, with Ivy never-sear,
I come to pluck your Berries harsh and crude,
And with forc'd fingers rude,
Shatter your leaves before the mellowing year.
Bitter constraint, and sad occasion dear,
Compels me to disturb your season due:
For Lycidas is dead, dead ere his prime,
Young Lycidas and hath not left his peer:
Who would not sing for Lycidas? he well knew
Himself to sing and build the lofty rhyme.
He must not flote upon his watry bear
Unwept, and welter to the parching wind,
Without the meed of som melodious tear.
['Lycidas' (1638), line 1]

43. Hence with denial vain, and coy excuse.
['Lycidas' (1638), line 18]

44. For we were nurst upon the self-same hill,
Fed the same flock, by fountain, shade, and rill.
['Lycidas' (1638), line 23]

45. But O the heavy change, now thou art gon,
Now thou art gon, and never must return!
['Lycidas' (1638), line 37]

46. The Woods and desert Caves,
With wild Thyme and the gadding Vine o'regrown.
['Lycidas' (1638), line 39]

47. As killing as the Canker to the Rose.
['Lycidas' (1638), line 45]

48. Where were ye Nymphs when the remorseless deep
Clos'd o're the head of your lov'd Lycidas?
['Lycidas' (1638), line 50]

49. Alas! What boots it with uncessant care
To tend the homely slighted Shepherd's trade,
And strictly meditate the thankles Muse?
Were it not better don as others use,
To sport with Amaryllis in the shade,
Or with the tangles of Neaera's hair.
Fame is the spur that the clear spirit doth raise
(That last infirmity of Noble mind)
To scorn delights, and live laborious dayes;
But the fair Guerdon when we hope to find,
And think to burst out into sudden blaze,
Comes the blind Fury with th' abhorred shears,
And slits the thin-spun life.
['Lycidas' (1638), line 64]

50. Fame is no plant that grows on mortal soil,
Nor in the glistering foil
Set off to th' world, nor in broad rumour lies.
['Lycidas' (1638), line 78]

51. It was that fatall and perfidious Bark
Built in th' eclipse, and rigg'd with curses dark,
That sunk so low that sacred head of thine.
['Lycidas' (1638), line 100]

52. Last came, and last did go,
The Pilot of the Galilean lake.
Two massy Keyes he bore of metals twain,
The Golden opes, the Iron shuts amain.
['Lycidas' (1638), line 108]

53. Blind mouthes! that scarce themselves know how to hold
A Sheep-hook, or have learn'd ought els the least
That to the faithfull Herdsman's art belongs!
['Lycidas' (1638), line 119]

54. And when they list, their lean and flashy songs
Grate on their scrannel Pipes of wretched straw,
The hungry Sheep look up, and are not fed,
But, swoln with wind, and the rank mist they draw,
Rot inwardly and foul contagion spread;
Besides what the grim Woolf with privy paw
Daily devours apace, and nothing sed,
But that two-handed engine at the door,
Stands ready to smite once, and smite no more.
Return, Alpheus, the dread voice is past,

That shrunk thy streams.
['Lycidas' (1638), line 123]

55. Bring the rathe Primrose that forsaken dies,
The tufted Crow-toe, and pale Gessamine,
The white Pink, and the Pansie freakt with jet,
The glowing Violet.
The Musk-rose, and the well-attir'd Woodbine,
With Cowslips wan that hang the pensive hed,
And every flower that sad embroidery wears:
Bid Amaranthus all his beauty shed,
And Daffadillies fill their cups with tears,
To strew the Laureat Herse where Lycid lies.
['Lycidas' (1638), line 142]

56. Whether beyond the stormy Hebrides,
Where thou perhaps under the whelming tide
Visit'st the bottom of the monstrous world;
Or whether thou, to our moist vows deny'd,
Sleep'st by the fable of Bellerus old,
Where the great vision of the guarded Mount
Looks toward Namancos and Bayona's hold;
Look homeward Angel now, and melt with ruth.
['Lycidas' (1638), line 156]

57. For Lycidas your sorrow is not dead,
Sunk though he be beneath the watry floar,
So sinks the day-star in the Ocean bed,
And yet anon repairs his drooping head,
And tricks his beams, and with new spangled Ore,
Flames in the forehead of the morning sky:
So Lycidas sunk low, but mounted high,
Through the dear might of him that walk'd the waves.
['Lycidas' (1638), line 166]

58. There entertain him all the Saints above,
In solemn troops and sweet Societies
That sing, and singing in their glory move,
And wipe the tears for ever from his eyes.
['Lycidas' (1638), line 178]

59. Thus sang the uncouth Swain to th' Okes and rills,
While the still morn went out with sandals gray;
He touch'd the tender stops of various Quills,
With eager thought warbling his Dorick lay.
['Lycidas' (1638), line 186]

60. At last he rose, and twitch'd his Mantle blew:
Tomorrow to fresh Woods, and Pastures new.
['Lycidas' (1638), line 192]

61. But headlong joy is ever on the wing,
In Wintry solstice like the shortn'd light
Soon swallow'd up in dark and long out-living night.
['The Passion' (1645)]

62. Fly envious Time, till thou run out thy race,
Call on the lazy leaden-stepping hours.
['On Time' (1645)]

63. Blest pair of Sirens, pledges of Heav'n's joy,
Sphear-born harmonious Sisters, Voice and Vers...

64. Where the bright Seraphim in burning row
Their loud up-lifted Angel trumpets blow.
['At a solemn Musick' (1645)]

65. Hence, loathed Melancholy,
Of Cerberus, and blackest midnight born,
In Stygian Cave forlorn
'Mongst horrid shapes, and shreiks, and sights unholy.
['L'Allegro' (1645), line 1]

66. So buxom, blithe, and debonair.
Haste thee Nymph, and bring with thee
Jest and youthful Jollity,
Quips and Cranks, and wanton Wiles,
Nods, and Becks, and Wreathed Smiles.
['L'Allegro' (1645), line 24]

67. Sport that wrincled Care derides,
And Laughter holding both his sides.
Com, and trip it as ye go
On the light fantastick toe,
And in thy right hand lead with thee
The Mountain Nymph, sweet Liberty.
['L'Allegro' (1645), line 31]

68. While the Cock with lively din
Scatters the rear of darknes thin,
And to the stack, or the Barn dore,
Stoutly struts his Dames before.
['L'Allegro' (1645), line 49]

69. Right against the Eastern gate,
Where the great Sun begins his state.
['L'Allegro' (1645), line 59]

70. The Plowman near at hand,
Whistles ore the Furrow'd Land,
And the Milkmaid singeth blithe,
And the Mower whets his sithe,
And every Shepherd tells his tale
Under the Hawthorn in the dale.
['L'Allegro' (1645), line 63]

71. Meadows trim with Daisies pide,
Shallow Brooks, and Rivers wide.
Towers, and Battlements it sees
Boosom'd high in tufted Trees,
Where perhaps som beauty lies,
The Cynosure of neighbouring eyes.
['L'Allegro' (1645), line 75]

72. To many a youth, and many a maid,
Dancing in the Chequer'd shade;
And young and old com forth to play
On a Sunshine Holyday,
Till the live-long day-light fail,
Then to the Spicy Nut-brown Ale.
['L'Allegro' (1645), line 95]

73. Towred Cities please us then,
And the busie humm of men.
['L'Allegro' (1645), line 117]

74. And pomp, and feast, and revelry,
With mask, and antique Pageantry,
Such sights as youthfull Poets dream,
On Summer eeves by haunted stream.
Then to the well-trod stage anon,
If Jonsons learned Sock be on,
Or sweetest Shakespear, Fancy's childe,
Warble his native Wood-notes wilde,
And ever against eating Cares,
Lap me in soft Lydian Aires,
Married to immortal verse
Such as the meeting soul may pierce
In notes, with many a winding bout
Of lincked sweetness long drawn out.
['L'Allegro' (1645), line 127]

75. The melting voice through mazes running.
['L'Allegro' (1645), line 142]

76. Such strains as would have won the ear
Of Pluto, to have quite set free
His half regain'd Eurydice.
['L'Allegro' (1645), line 148]

77. Hence vain deluding joyes,
The brood of folly without father bred.
['Il Penseroso' (1645), line 1]

78. Hail divinest Melancholy.
['Il Penseroso' (1645), line 12]

79. Com pensive Nun, devout and pure,
Sober, steadfast, and demure.
['Il Penseroso' (1645), line 31]

80. With eev'n step and musing gate,
And looks commercing with the skies,
Thy rapt soul sitting in thine eyes.
['Il Penseroso' (1645), line 38]

81. Sweet Bird, that shunn'st the noise of folly,
Most musicall, most melancholy!
['Il Penseroso' (1645), line 61]

82. I walk unseen
On the dry smooth-shaven Green,
To behold the wandering Moon,
Riding neer her highest noon,
Like one that had bin led astray
Through the Heav'n's wide pathles way;
And oft, as if her head she bow'd,
Stooping through a fleecy cloud.
Oft on a Plat of rising ground,
I hear the far-off Curfeu sound,
Over som wide-water'd shoar,
Swinging slow with sullen roar.
['Il Penseroso' (1645), line 65]

83. Where glowing Embers through the room
Teach light to counterfeit a gloom,
Far from all resort of mirth,
Save the Cricket on the hearth.
['Il Penseroso' (1645), line 79]

84. Or let my Lamp at midnight hour,
Be seen in som high lonely Towr,
Where I may oft out-watch the Bear,
With thrice great Hermes.
['Il Penseroso' (1645), line 85]

85. Somtime let Gorgeous Tragedy
In Scepter'd Pall com sweeping by,
Presenting Thebes, or Pelops' line,
Or the tale of Troy divine.
['Il Penseroso' (1645), line 97]

86. Or bid the soul of Orpheus sing
Such notes as warbled to the string,
Drew Iron tears down Pluto's cheek.
['Il Penseroso' (1645), line 105]

87. Where more is meant than meets the ear.
['Il Penseroso' (1645), line 120]

88. ... th' unseen Genius of the Wood.
['Il Penseroso' (1645), line 154]

89. But let my due feet never fail
To walk the studious Cloysters pale.
['Il Penseroso' (1645), line 155]

90. With antick Pillars massy proof,
And storied Windows richly dight,
Casting a dimm religious light.
There let the pealing Organ blow,
To the full voic'd Quire below,
In Service high, and Anthems cleer
As may, with sweetnes, through mine ear,
Dissolve me into extasies,
And bring all Heav'n before mine eyes.
['Il Penseroso' (1645), line 158]

91. Now the bright morning Star, Daye's harbinger,
Comes dancing from the East, and leads with her
The Flowry May.
['Song On May Morning' (1645)]

92. O Nightingale, that on yon bloomy Spray
Warbl'st at eeve, when all the Woods are still.
[Sonnet I, 'O Nightingale, that on yon bloomy Spray' (1645)]

93. New Presbyter is but Old Priest writ Large.
['On the new forcers of Conscience under the Long Parlament' (1645). Cf. Monro: 1]

94. How soon hath Time, the suttel theef of youth,
Stoln on his wing my three and twentith yeer!
[Sonnet VII, 'How soon hath time the suttel theef of youth' (1645)]

95. I did but prompt the age to quit their cloggs
By the known rules of antient libertie,
When straight a barbarous noise environs me
Of Owles and Cuckooes, Asses, Apes, and Doggs...

96. Licence they mean when they cry libertie;
For who loves that, must first be wise and good.
[Sonnet XII, 'I did but prompt the age to quit their cloggs' (c. 1645)]

97. For what can Warr, but endless warr still breed.
[Sonnet XV, 'On the Lord Generall Fairfax at the seige of Colchester' (1648)]

98. Help us to save free conscience from the paw
Of hireling wolves whose gospel is their maw.
[Sonnet XVI, 'To the Lord General Cromwell' (1652)]

99. Avenge O Lord thy slaughter'd Saints, whose bones
Lie scatter'd on the Alpine mountains cold,
Ev'n them who kept thy truth so pure of old
When all our Fathers worship'd Stocks and Stones.
[Sonnet XVIII, 'On the late Massacher at Piemont' (1655)]

100. [On his blindness]
When I consider how my light is spent,
Ere half my days, in this dark world and wide,
And that one Talent which is death to hide,
Lodg'd with me useless, though my Soul more bent
To serve therewith my Maker, and present
My true account, lest he returning chide,
Doth God exact day-labour, light deny'd,
I fondly ask; But patience, to prevent
That murmur, soon replies, God doth not need
Either man's work or his own gifts, who best
Bear his milde yoak, they serve him best, his State
Is Kingly. Thousands at his bidding speed
And post o're Lands and Ocean without rest:
They also serve who only stand and waite.
[Sonnet XIX, 'When I consider how my light is spent' (c. 1655)]

101. Methought I saw my late espoused Saint
Brought to me like Alcestis from the grave...

102. Love, sweetness, goodness, in her person shin'd...

103. But O as to embrace me she enclin'd,
I wak'd, she fled, and day brought back my night.
[Sonnet XXIII, 'Methought I saw my late espoused Saint' (1658)]

104. Rime being no necessary Adjunct or true Ornament of Poem or good Verse, in longer Works especially, but the Invention of a barbarous Age, to set off wretched matter and lame Meeter.
[*Paradise Lost* (1667), 'The Verse', Preface]

105. The troublesom and modern bondage of rimeing.
[*Paradise Lost* (1667), 'The Verse', Preface]

106. Of Man's First Disobedience, and the Fruit
Of that Forbidd'n Tree, whose mortal tast
Brought Death into the World, and all our woe,
With loss of Eden.
[*Paradise Lost* (1667), I, line 1]

107. Things unattempted yet in Prose or Rime.
[*Paradise Lost* (1667), I, line 16]

108. What in mee is dark
Illumin, what is low raise and support;
That to the highth of this great Argument
I may assert Eternal Providence,
And justifie the wayes of God to men.
[*Paradise Lost* (1667), I, line 22]

109. The infernal Serpent; hee it was, whose guile,
Stirrd up with Envy and Revenge, deceiv'd
The Mother of Mankinde.
[*Paradise Lost* (1667), I, line 34]

110. Him the Almighty Power
Hurld headlong flaming from th' Ethereal Skie
With hideous ruin and cumbustion down
To bottomless perdition, there to dwell
In Adamantin chains and penal Fire
Who durst defie th' Omnipotent to Arms.
[*Paradise Lost* (1667), I, line 44]

111. A Dungeon horrible, on all sides round
As one great Furnace flam'd, yet from those flames
No light, but rather darkness visible
Serv'd onely to discover sights of woe,
Regions of sorrow, doleful shades, where peace
And rest can never dwell, hope never comes
That comes to all.
[*Paradise Lost* (1667), I, line 60]

112. But O how fall'n! how chang'd
From him, who in the happy Realms of Light
Cloth'd with transcendent brightness didst outshine
Myriads though bright.
[*Paradise Lost* (1667), I, line 84]

113. United thoughts and counsels, equal hope,
And hazard in the Glorious Enterprize.
[*Paradise Lost* (1667), I, line 88]

114. Yet not for those
Nor what the Potent Victor in his rage
Can else inflict, do I repent or change,
Though chang'd in outward lustre; that fixt mind
And high disdain, from sense of injur'd merit.
[*Paradise Lost* (1667), I, line 94]

115. What though the field be lost?
All is not lost; th' unconquerable Will,
And study of revenge, immortal hate,
And courage never to submit or yeild:
And what is else not to be overcome?
[*Paradise Lost* (1667), I, line 105]

116. Vaunting aloud, but rackt with deep despaire.
[*Paradise Lost* (1667), I, line 126]

117. Fall'n Cherube, to be weak is miserable
Doing or suffering: but of this be sure,
To do aught good never will be our task,
But ever to do ill our sole delight.
[*Paradise Lost* (1667), I, line 157]

118. And out of good still to find means of evil.
[*Paradise Lost* (1667), I, line 165]

119. What reinforcement we may gain from Hope,
If not what resolution from despaire.
[*Paradise Lost* (1667), I, line 190]

120. The will
And high permission of all-ruling Heaven
Left him at large to his own dark designs,
That with reiterated crimes he might
Heap on himself damnation.
[*Paradise Lost* (1667), I, line 211]

121. Is this the Region, this the Soil, the Clime,
Said then the lost Arch-Angel, this the seat
That we must change for Heav'n, this mournful gloom
For that celestial light?
[*Paradise Lost* (1667), I, line 242]

122. Farewel happy Fields
Where Joy for ever dwells: Hail horrours, hail
Infernal World, and thou profoundest Hell
Receive thy new Possessor: One who brings
A mind not to be chang'd by Place or Time.
The mind is its own place, and in it self
Can make a Heav'n of Hell, a Hell of Heav'n.
[*Paradise Lost* (1667), I, line 249]

123. Here we may reign secure, and in my choice
To reign is worth ambition though in Hell:
Better to reign in Hell, than serve in Heav'n.
[*Paradise Lost* (1667), I, line 261]

124. His ponderous shield
Ethereal temper, massy, large and round,
Behind him cast; the broad circumference
Hung on his shoulders like the Moon, whose Orb
Through Optic Glass the Tuscan Artist views
At Ev'ning from the top of Fesole,
Or in Valdarno, to descry new Lands,
Rivers or Mountains in her spotty Globe.
His Spear, to equal which the tallest Pine
Hewn on Norwegian hills, to be the Mast
Of some great Ammiral, were but a wand,
He walkd with, to support uneasie steps
Over the burning Marle.
[*Paradise Lost* (1667), I, line 284]

125. Thick as Autumnal Leaves that strow the Brooks
In Vallombrosa, where th' Etrurian shades
High overarcht imbowr.
[*Paradise Lost* (1667), I, line 302]

126. First Moloch, horrid King, besmeard with blood
Of human sacrifice, and parents' tears.
[*Paradise Lost* (1667), I, line 392]

127. For Spirits when they please
Can either Sex assume, or both; so soft
And uncompounded is thir Essence pure,
Not tied or manacl'd with joint or limb,
Nor founded on the brittle strength of bones,
Like cumbrous flesh; but, in what shape they choose,
Dilated or condenst, bright or obscure,
Can execute thir aerie purposes.
[*Paradise Lost* (1667), I, line 423]

128. Thammuz came next behind,
Whose annual wound in Lebanon allur'd
The Syrian Damsels to lament his fate
In amorous ditties all a Summer's day,
While smooth Adonis from his native Rock
Ran purple to the Sea.
[*Paradise Lost* (1667), I, line 446]

129. And when Night
Dark'ns the Streets, then wander forth the Sons

Of Belial, flown with insolence and wine.
[*Paradise Lost* (1667), I, line 500]

130. Th' Imperial Ensign, which full high advanc't
Shon like a Meteor streaming to the Wind.
[*Paradise Lost* (1667), I, line 536]

131. Sonorous mettal blowing Martial sounds:
At which the universal Host upsent
A shout that tore Hells Concave, and beyond
Frighted the Reign of Chaos and old Night.
[*Paradise Lost* (1667), I, line 540]

132. Anon they move
In perfect phalanx to the Dorian mood
Of Flutes and soft Recorders.
[*Paradise Lost* (1667), I, line 549]

133. . . . and in stead of rage
Deliberat valour breath'd, firm and unmov'd.
[*Paradise Lost* (1667), I, line 553]

134. [Of Pygmies]
That small infantry
Warrd on by Cranes.
[*Paradise Lost* (1667), I, line 575]

135. What resounds
In Fable or Romance of Uther's Son
Begirt with British and Armoric Knights;
And all who since, Baptiz'd or Infidel
Jousted in Aspramont or Montalban,
Damasco, or Marocco, or Trebisond,
Or whom Biserta sent from Afric shore
When Charlemain with all his Peerage fell
By Fontarabbia.
[*Paradise Lost* (1667), I, line 579]

136. The Sun . . .
In dim Eclips disastrous twilight sheds
On half the Nations, and with fear of change
Perplexes Monarchs.
[*Paradise Lost* (1667), I, line 594]

137. Care
Sat on his faded cheek.
[*Paradise Lost* (1667), I, line 601]

138. Tears such as Angels weep, burst forth.
[*Paradise Lost* (1667), I, line 620]

139. For who can yet beleeve, though after loss,
That all these puissant Legions, whose exile
Hath emptied Heav'n, shall faile to re-ascend
Self-rais'd, and repossess their native seat?
[*Paradise Lost* (1667), I, line 631]

140. . . . who overcomes
By force, hath overcome but half his foe.
[*Paradise Lost* (1667), I, line 648]

141. Space may produce new Worlds.
[*Paradise Lost* (1667), I, line 650]

142. Mammon led them on,
Mammon, the least erected Spirit that fell
From Heav'n, for ev'n in Heav'n his looks and thoughts
Were always downward bent, admiring more
The riches of Heav'ns pavement, trodd'n Gold,
Than aught divine or holy else enjoyd
In vision beatific.
[*Paradise Lost* (1667), I, line 678]

143. Let none admire
That riches grow in Hell; that soile may best
Deserve the precious bane.
[*Paradise Lost* (1667), I, line 690]

144. In ancient Greece; and in Ausonian land
Men calld him Mulciber; and how he fell
From heav'n, they fabl'd, thrown by angry Jove
Sheer ore the Crystal Battlements: from Morn
To Noon he fell, from Noon to dewy Eve,
A Summer's day; and with the setting Sun
Dropd from the Zenith like a falling Starr.
[*Paradise Lost* (1667), I, line 739]

145. Nor aught availd him now
To have built in Heav'n high Towrs; nor did he scape
By all his Engins, but was headlong sent
With his industrious crew to build in Hell.
[*Paradise Lost* (1667), I, line 748]

146. Pandaemonium, the high Capitol
Of Satan and his Peers.
[*Paradise Lost* (1667), I, line 756]

147. As Bees
In spring time, when the Sun with Taurus rides,
Poure forth thir populous youth about the Hive
In clusters; they among fresh dews and flowers
Flie to and fro, or on the smoothed Plank,
The suburb of thir Straw-built Cittadel,
New rubd with Baume, expatiate and conferr
Thir State affairs.
[*Paradise Lost* (1667), I, line 768]

148. High on a Throne of Royal State, which farr
Outshon the wealth of Ormus and of Ind,
Of where the gorgeous East with richest hand
Showers on her kings Barbaric Pearl and Gold,
Satan exalted sat, by merit rais'd
To that bad eminence; and from despair
Thus high uplifted beyond hope.
[*Paradise Lost* (1667), II, line 1]

149. Where there is then no good
For which to strive, no strife can grow up there
From Faction.
[*Paradise Lost* (1667), II, line 30]

150. The strongest and the fiercest Spirit
That fought in Heav'n; now fiercer by despair.
His trust was with th' Eternal to be deemd
Equal in strength, and rather than be less
Car'd not to be at all.
[*Paradise Lost* (1667), II, line 44]

151. My sentence is for op'n warr: Of Wiles
More unexpert, I boast not.
[*Paradise Lost* (1667), II, line 51]

152. Belial, in act more graceful and humane;
A fairer person lost not Heav'n; he seemd
For dignity compos'd and high exploit:
But all was false and hollow; though his Tongue
Dropd Manna, and could make the worse appear
The better reason.
[*Paradise Lost* (1667), II, line 109]

153. For who would loose,
Though full of pain, this intellectual being,
Those thoughts that wander through Eternity,
To perish rather, swallowed up and lost
In the wide womb of uncreated night,
Devoid of sense and motion?
[*Paradise Lost* (1667), II, line 146]

154. There to converse, with everlasting groans,
Unrespited, unpitied, unrepreevd,
Ages of hopeless end.
[*Paradise Lost* (1667), II, line 184]

155. Thus Belial with words cloath'd in reasons garb
Counseld ignoble ease, and peaceful sloath.
[*Paradise Lost* (1667), II, line 226]

156. ... preferring
Hard liberty before the easie yoke
Of servil Pomp.
[*Paradise Lost* (1667), II, line 255]

157. Our torments also may in length of time
Become our Elements.
[*Paradise Lost* (1667), II, line 274]

158. With grave
Aspect he rose, and in his rising seemd
A Pillar of State; deep on his Front engraven
Deliberation sat and publick care;
And Princely counsel in his face yet shon,
Majestick though in ruin.
[*Paradise Lost* (1667), II, line 300]

159. Advise if this be worth
Attempting, or to sit in darkness here
Hatching vain Empires.
[*Paradise Lost* (1667), II, line 376]

160. But first whom shall we send
In search of this new World, whom shall we find
Sufficient? who shall tempt with wandring feet
The dark unbottomd infinite Abyss
And through the palpable obscure find out
His uncouth way?
[*Paradise Lost* (1667), II, line 402]

161. Long is the way
And hard, that out of Hell leads up to Light.
[*Paradise Lost* (1667), II, line 432]

162. O shame to men! Devil with Devil damnd
Firm concord holds: men onely disagree
Of Creatures rational, though under hope
Of heav'nly Grace; and God proclaiming peace,
Yet live in hatred, enmitie, and strife
Among themselves, and levie cruel warres,
Wasting the Earth, each other to destroy.
[*Paradise Lost* (1667), II, line 496]

163. In discourse more sweet
(For Eloquence the Soul, Song charms the Sense,)
Others apart sat on a hill retir'd,
In thoughts more elevate, and reasond high
Of Providence, Foreknowledge, Will, and Fate,
Fixt Fate, free Will, Foreknowledge absolute,
And found no end, in wandring mazes lost.
Of good and evil much they argu'd then,
Of happiness and final misery,
Passion and Apathie, and glory and shame,
Vain wisdom all, and false Philosophie.
[*Paradise Lost* (1667), II, line 555]

164. The parching Air
Burns frore, and cold performs th' effect of Fire.
[*Paradise Lost* (1667), II, line 594]

165. Feel by turns the bitter change
Of fierce extreams, extreams by change more fierce.
[*Paradise Lost* (1667), II, line 598]

166. O're many a Frozen, many a Fierie Alpe,
Rocks, Caves, Lakes, Fens, Bogs, Dens, and shades of death,
A Universe of death, which God by curse
Created evil, for evil onely good,
Where all life dies, death lives, and Nature breeds,
Perverse, all monstrous, all prodigious things,
Abominable, inutterable, and worse
Than Fables yet have feignd, or fear conceiv'd,
Gorgons and Hydras, and Chimeras dire.
[*Paradise Lost* (1667), II, line 620]

167. The other shape,
If shape it might be calld that shape had none
Distinguishable in member, joint, or limb,
Or substance might be calld that shadow seemd,
For each seemd either; black it stood as Night,
Fierce as ten Furies, terrible as Hell,
And shook a dreadful Dart; what seemd his head
The likeness of a Kingly Crown had on.
[*Paradise Lost* (1667), II, line 666]

168. Whence and what art thou, execrable shape?
[*Paradise Lost* (1667), II, line 681]

169. Incenst with indignation Satan stood
Unterrifi'd, and like a Comet burnd
That fires the length of Ophiuchus huge
In th' Arctick sky, and from his horrid hair
Shakes Pestilence and Warr.
[*Paradise Lost* (1667), II, line 707]

170. I fled, and cry'd out Death;
Hell trembl'd at the hideous Name, and sigh'd
From all her Caves, and back resounded Death.
[*Paradise Lost* (1667), II, line 787]

171. On a sudden op'n flie
With impetuous recoile and jarring sound
Th' infernal dores, and on thir hinges grate
Harsh Thunder.
[*Paradise Lost* (1667), II, line 879]

172. Chaos Umpire sits,
And by decision more imbroils the fray
By which he Reigns: next him high Arbiter
Chance governs all.
[*Paradise Lost* (1667), II, line 907]

173. Sable-vested Night, eldest of things.
[*Paradise Lost* (1667), II, line 962]

174. Confusion worse confounded.
[*Paradise Lost* (1667), II, line 996]

175. Hail holy Light, ofspring of Heav'n first-born,
Or of th' Eternal Coeternal beam.
[*Paradise Lost* (1667), III, line 1]

176. The rising world of waters dark and deep.
[*Paradise Lost* (1667), III, line 11]

177. Then feed on thoughts, that voluntarie move
Harmonious numbers; as the wakeful Bird
Sings darkling, and in shadiest Covert hid
Tunes her nocturnal Note. Thus with the Year
Seasons return, but not to mee returns
Day, or the sweet approach of Ev'n or Morn,
Or sight of vernal bloom, or Summer's Rose,
Or flocks, or herds, or human face divine;
But cloud in stead, and ever-during dark
Surrounds me, from the chearful waies of men
Cut off, and for the Book of knowledge fair
Presented with a Universal blanc
Of Nature's works to mee expung'd and ras'd,
And wisdom at one entrance quite shut out.
[*Paradise Lost* (1667), III, line 37]

178. Dark with excessive bright thy skirts appeer.
[*Paradise Lost* (1667), III, line 380]

179. So on this windie Sea of Land, the Fiend
Walkd up and down alone bent on his prey.
[*Paradise Lost* (1667), III, line 440]

180. Into a Limbo large and broad, since calld
The Paradise of Fools, to few unknown.
[*Paradise Lost* (1667), III, line 495]

181. For neither Man nor Angel can discern
Hypocrisie, the onely evil that walks
Invisible, except to God alone.
[*Paradise Lost* (1667), III, line 682]

182. At whose sight all the Starrs
Hide their diminisht heads.
[*Paradise Lost* (1667), IV, line 34]

183. Warring in Heav'n against Heav'n's matchless King.
[*Paradise Lost* (1667), IV, line 41]

184. Mee miserable! which way shall I flie
Infinite wrauth, and infinite despaire?
Which way I flie is Hell; my self am Hell;
And in the lowest deep a lower deep
Still threatening to devour me op'ns wide,
To which the Hell I suffer seems a Heav'n.
[*Paradise Lost* (1667), IV, line 73]

185. So farewel Hope, and with Hope farewel Fear,
Farewel Remorse: all Good to me is lost;
Evil be thou my Good.
[*Paradise Lost* (1667), IV, line 108]

186. When to them who saile
Beyond the Cape of Hope, and now are past
Mozambic, off at Sea North-East windes blow
Sabean odours from the spicie shoare
Of Arabie the blest, with such delay
Well pleas'd they slack thir course, and many a League
Cheard with the grateful smell old Ocean smiles.
[*Paradise Lost* (1667), IV, line 159]

187. So clomb this first grand thief into Gods Fould:
So since into his Church lewd Hirelings climbe.
Thence up he flew, and on the Tree of Life,
The middle Tree and highest there that grew,
Sat like a Cormorant.
[*Paradise Lost* (1667), IV, line 192]

188. Groves whose rich trees wept odorous gumms and balme,
Others whose fruit burnisht with Gold'n Rinde
Hung amiable, Hesperian Fables true,
If true, here onely.
[*Paradise Lost* (1667), IV, line 248]

189. Flours of all hue, and without Thorn the Rose.
[*Paradise Lost* (1667), IV, line 256]

190. The mantling Vine.
[*Paradise Lost* (1667), IV, line 258]

191. Not that faire field
Of Enna, where Proserpin gathering flours
Her self a fairer floure by gloomie Dis
Was gatherd, which cost Ceres all that pain.
[*Paradise Lost* (1667), IV, line 268]

192. For contemplation hee and valour formd;
For softness shee and sweet attractive grace,
Hee for God onely, she for God in him:
His fair large Front and Eye sublime declar'd
Absolute rule.
[*Paradise Lost* (1667), IV, line 297]

193. Which impli'd
Subjection, but requir'd with gentle sway
And by her yeilded, by him best receivd,
Yeilded with coy submission, modest pride,
And sweet reluctant amorous delay.
[*Paradise Lost* (1667), IV, line 307]

194. So hand in hand they passd, the lovliest pair
That ever since in loves imbraces met,
Adam the goodliest man of men since borne
His Sons; the fairest of her Daughters Eve.
[*Paradise Lost* (1667), IV, line 321]

195. The savourie pulp they chew, and in the rinde
Still as they thirsted scoop the brimming stream.
[*Paradise Lost* (1667), IV, line 335]

196. Sporting the Lion rampd, and in his paw,
Dandl'd the Kid; Bears, Tygers, Ounces, Pards
Gambolld before them, th' unwieldy Elephant
To make them mirth us'd all his might, and wreath'd
His Lithe Proboscis.
[*Paradise Lost* (1667), IV, line 343]

197. These two
Imparadis't in one another's arms,
The happier Eden, shall enjoy their fill
Of bliss on bliss.
[*Paradise Lost* (1667), IV, line 505]

198. Now came still Evening on, and Twilight gray
Had in her sober Liverie all things clad;
Silence accompanied, for Beast and Bird,
They to thir grassie Couch, these to thir Nests,
Were slunk, all but the wakeful Nightingale;
Shee all night long her amorous descant sung;
Silence was pleas'd: now glowd the Firmament
With living Saphirs: Hesperus that led
The starrie Host, rode brightest, till the Moon
Rising in clouded Majestie, at length
Apparent queen unvaild her peerless light,
And ore the dark her Silver Mantle threw.
[*Paradise Lost* (1667), IV, line 598]

199. God is thy Law, thou mine: to know no more
Is Woman's happiest knowledge and her praise.
With thee conversing I forget all time,
All seasons and thir change, all please alike.
Sweet is the breath of morn, her rising sweet,
With charm of earliest Birds.
[*Paradise Lost* (1667), IV, line 637]

200. Millions of spiritual Creatures walk the Earth
Unseen, both when we wake, and when we sleep.
[*Paradise Lost* (1667), IV, line 677]

201. Into thir inmost bower
Handed they went; and eas'd the putting off
These troublesom disguises which wee wear,
Strait side by side were laid, nor turned I weene
Adam from his fair Spouse, nor Eve the Rites
Mysterious of connubial Love refus'd:
Whatever Hypocrits austerely talk
Of puritie and place and innocence,
Defaming as impure what God declares
Pure, and commands to som, leaves free to all.
[*Paradise Lost* (1667), IV, line 738]

202. Hail wedded Love, mysterious Law, true sourse
Of human ofspring, sole proprietie
In Paradise of all things common else.
[*Paradise Lost* (1667), IV, line 750]

203. Sleep on,
Blest pair; and O yet happiest if ye seek
No happier state, and know to know no more.
[*Paradise Lost* (1667), IV, line 773]

204. Him there they found
Squat like a Toad, close at the eare of Eve.
[*Paradise Lost* (1667), IV, line 799]

205. Abasht the Devil stood,
And felt how awful goodness is.
[*Paradise Lost* (1667), IV, line 846]

206. But wherefore thou alone? Wherefore with thee
Came not all Hell broke loose?
[*Paradise Lost* (1667), IV, line 917]

207. The Starrie Cope of heaven.
[*Paradise Lost* (1667), IV, line 992]

208. My fairest, my espous'd, my latest found,
Heav'n's last best gift, my ever new delight.
[*Paradise Lost* (1667), V, line 18]

209. Best Image of my self and dearer half.
[*Paradise Lost* (1667), V, line 95]

210. On earth join all ye Creatures to extoll
Him first, him last, him midst, and without end.
[*Paradise Lost* (1667), V, line 164]

211. A Wilderness of sweets.
[*Paradise Lost* (1667), V, line 294]

212. So saying, with dispatchful looks in haste
She turns, on hospitable thoughts intent.
[*Paradise Lost* (1667), V, line 331]

213. Mean while our Primitive great Sire to meet
His god-like Guest walks forth, without more train
Accompni'd than with his own compleat
Perfections; in himself was all his state,
More solemn than the tedious pomp that waits
On Princes, when their rich Retinue long
Of Horses led, and Grooms besmear'd with Gold
Dazles the croud and sets them all agape.
[*Paradise Lost* (1667), V, line 350]

214. Mean while at Table Eve
Ministerd naked, and thir flowing cups
With pleasant liquors crownd.
[*Paradise Lost* (1667), V, line 443]

215. Nor jealousie
Was understood, the injur'd Lover's Hell.
[*Paradise Lost* (1667), V, line 449]

216. Freely we serve,
Because we freely love, as in our will
To love or not; in this we stand or fall.
[*Paradise Lost* (1667), V, line 538]

217. What if Earth
Be but the shaddow of Heav'n, and things therein
Each to other like, more than on Earth is thought?
[*Paradise Lost* (1667), V, line 574]

218. Hear all ye Angels, Progenie of Light,
Thrones, Dominations, Princedoms, Vertues, Powers.
[*Paradise Lost* (1667), V, line 600]

219. All seemed well pleas'd, all seemed, but were not all.
[*Paradise Lost* (1667), V, line 617]

220. Yonder starrie spheare
Of Planets and of fixt in all her Wheeles
...mazes intricate,
Eccentric, intervolv'd, yet regular
Than most, when most irregular they seem:
And in thir motions harmonie Divine
So smooths her charming tones, that God's own ear
List'ns delighted.
[*Paradise Lost* (1667), V, line 620]

221. Satan, so call him now, his former name
Is heard no more in Heav'n.
[*Paradise Lost* (1667), V, line 655]

222. But what if better counsels might erect
Our minds and teach us to cast off this Yoke?
Will ye submit your necks, and chuse to bend
The supple knee?
[*Paradise Lost* (1667), V, line 785]

223. Headlong themselves they threw
Down from the verge of Heav'n, Eternal wrauth
Burnd after them to the bottomless pit.
[*Paradise Lost* (1667), VI, line 864]

224. Standing on Earth, not rapt above the Pole,
More safe I Sing with mortal voice, unchang'd
To hoarce or mute, though fall'n on evil dayes,
On evil dayes though fall'n, and evil tongues.
[*Paradise Lost* (1667), VII, line 23]

225. Still govern thou my Song,
Urania, and fit audience find, though few.
[*Paradise Lost* (1667), VII, line 30]

226. Necessitie and Chance
Approach not mee, and what I will is Fate.
[*Paradise Lost* (1667), VII, line 172]

227. There Leviathan
Hugest of living Creatures, on the Deep
Stretcht like a Promontorie sleeps or swimmes,
And seems a moving Land, and at his Gilles
Draws in, and at his Trunck spouts out a Sea.
[*Paradise Lost* (1667), VII, line 412]

228. The Planets in thir stations list'ning stood,
While the bright Pomp ascended jubilant.
Op'n, ye everlasting Gates, they sung,
Op'n, ye Heav'ns, your living dores; let in
The great Creator from his work returnd
Magnificent, his Six Days' work, a World.
[*Paradise Lost* (1667), VII, line 563]

229. He his fabric of the Heav'ns
Hath left to thir disputes, perhaps to move
His laughter at thir quaint Opinions wide
Hereafter, when they come to model Heav'n
And calculate the Starrs, how they will weild
The mightie frame, how build, unbuild, contrive
To save appearances, how gird the sphear
With Centric and Eccentric scribbled ore,
Cycle and Epicycle, Orb in Orb.
[*Paradise Lost* (1667), VIII, line 76]

230. That Man may know he dwells not in his own;
An Edifice too large for him to fill,
Lodg'd in a small partition, and the rest
Ordaind for uses to his Lord best known.
[*Paradise Lost* (1667), VIII, line 103]

231. Heav'n is for thee too high
To know what passes there; be lowlie wise:
Think onely what concerns thee and thy being.
[*Paradise Lost* (1667), VIII, line 172]

232. Liquid Lapse of murmuring Streams.
[*Paradise Lost* (1667), VIII, line 263]

233. Tell me, how may I know him, how adore,
From whom I have that thus I move and live,
And feel that I am happier than I know?
[*Paradise Lost* (1667), VIII, line 280]

234. In solitude
What happiness, Who can enjoy alone,
Or all enjoying, what contentment find?
[*Paradise Lost* (1667), VIII, line 364]

235. . . . the sum of earthly bliss.
[*Paradise Lost* (1667), VIII, line 522]

236. Accuse not Nature, shee hath don her part;
Do thou but thine.
[*Paradise Lost* (1667), VIII, line 561]

237. Oft-times nothing profits more
Than self-esteem, grounded on just and right
Well manag'd.
[*Paradise Lost* (1667), VIII, line 571]

238. My Celestial Patroness, who deigns
Her nightly visitation unimplor'd,
And dictates to me slumbring, or inspires
Easie my unpremeditated Verse:
Since first this Subject for Heroic Song
Pleas'd me long choosing, and beginning late.
[*Paradise Lost* (1667), IX, line 21]

239. Unless an age too late, or cold
Climat, or Years damp my intended wing.
[*Paradise Lost* (1667), IX, line 44]

240. The Serpent suttl'st Beast of all the field.
[*Paradise Lost* (1667), IX, line 86]

241. Revenge, at first though sweet,
Bitter ere long back on it self recoils.
[*Paradise Lost* (1667), IX, line 171]

242. . . . nothing lovelier can be found
In Woman, than to studie household good,
And good works in her Husband to promote.
[*Paradise Lost* (1667), IX, line 232]

243. For solitude sometimes is best societie,
And short retirement urges sweet returne.
[*Paradise Lost* (1667), IX, line 249]

244. As one who long in populous City pent,
Where Houses thick and Sewers annoy the Aire,
Forth issuing on a Summer's morn to breathe
Among the pleasant Villages and Farmes
Adjoind, from each thing met conceaves delight.
[*Paradise Lost* (1667), IX, line 445]

245. Shee fair, divinely fair, fit Love for Gods.
[*Paradise Lost* (1667), IX, line 489]

246. God so commanded, and left that Command
Sole Daughter of his voice; the rest, we live
Law to our selves, our Reason is our Law.
[*Paradise Lost* (1667), IX, line 652]

247. Her rash hand in evil hour
Forth reaching to the Fruit, she pluckd, she eat:
Earth felt the wound, and Nature from her seat
Sighing through all her Works gave signs of woe
That all was lost.
[*Paradise Lost* (1667), IX, line 780]

248. O fairest of Creation, last and best
Of all God's Works! Creature in whom excelld
Whatever can to sight or thought be formd,
Holy, divine, good, amiable, or sweet!
[*Paradise Lost* (1667), IX, line 896]

249. And mee with thee hath ruined, for with thee
Certain my resolution is to Die;
How can I live without thee, how forgoe
Thy sweet Converse and Love so dearly joind,
To live again in these wilde Woods forlorn?
[*Paradise Lost* (1667), IX, line 906]

250. Flesh of Flesh,
Bone of my Bone thou art, and from thy State
Mine never shall be parted, weal or woe.
[*Paradise Lost* (1667), IX, line 914. Cf. Bible: 14]

251. What thou art is mine;
Our State cannot be severd, we are one,
One Flesh; to lose thee were to loose myself.
[*Paradise Lost* (1667), IX, line 957]

252. Yet I shall temper so
Justice with Mercie.
[*Paradise Lost* (1667), X, line 77]

253. He hears
On all sides, from innumerable tongues,
A dismal universal hiss, the sound
Of public scorn.
[*Paradise Lost* (1667), X, line 506]

254. O why did God,
Creator wise, that peopl'd highest Heav'n
With Spirits Masculine, create at last
This noveltie on Earth, this fair defect
Of Nature?
[*Paradise Lost* (1667), X, line 888]

255. Destruction with destruction to destroy.
[*Paradise Lost* (1667), X, line 1006]

256. Daemoniac Phrenzie, moping Melancholie,
And Moon-struck madness.
[*Paradise Lost* (1667), XI, line 485]

257. Nor love thy Life, nor hate; but what thou livst
Live well, how long or short permit to Heav'n.
[*Paradise Lost* (1667), XI, line 553]

258. Th' Evening Starr
Love's Harbinger.
[*Paradise Lost* (1667), XI, line 588]

259. The brazen Throat of Warr had ceast to roar,
All now was turned to jollitie and game,
The luxurie and riot, feast and dance.
[*Paradise Lost* (1667), XI, line 713]

260. For now I see
Peace to corrupt no less than Warr to waste.
[*Paradise Lost* (1667), XI, line 783]

261. They looking back, all th' Eastern side beheld
Of Paradise, so late their happie seat,
Wav'd over by that flaming Brand, the Gate
With dreadful faces throngd and fierie Arms:
Som natural tears they dropd, but wip'd them soon;
The World was all before them, where to choose
Their place of rest, and Providence thir guide:
They hand in hand with wandring steps and slow,
Through Eden took their solitarie way.
[*Paradise Lost* (1667), XII, line 641]

262. I who ere while the happy Garden sung,
By one man's disobedience lost, now sing
Recoverd Paradise to all mankind.
[*Paradise Regained* (1671), I, line 1]

263. Most men admire
Vertue, who follow not her lore.
[*Paradise Regained* (1671), I, line 482]

264. Skilld to retire, and in retiring draw
Hearts after them tangl'd in Amorous Nets.
[*Paradise Regained* (1671), II, line 161]

265. Women, when nothing else, beguil'd the heart
Of wisest Solomon, and made him build,
And made him bow to the Gods of his Wives.
[*Paradise Regained* (1671), II, line 169]

266. Beauty stands
In th' admiration onely of weak minds
Led captive.
[*Paradise Regained* (1671), II, line 220]

267. Ladies of th' Hesperides, that seemd
Fairer than feignd of old, or fabl'd since
Of Fairy Damsels met in Forest wide
By Knights of Logres, or of Lyones,
Lancelot or Pelleas, or Pellenore.
[*Paradise Regained* (1671), II, line 357]

268. Riches are needless then, both for themselves,
And for thy reason why they should be sought,
To gain a Scepter, oftest better misst.
[*Paradise Regained* (1671), II, line 484]

269. Of whom to be disprais'd were no small praise.
[*Paradise Regained* (1671), III, line 56]

270. They err who count it glorious to subdue
By Conquest farr and wide, to over-run
Large Countries, and in field great Battels win.
[*Paradise Regained* (1671), III, line 71]

271. But on Occasion's forelock watchful wait.
[*Paradise Regained* (1671), III, line 173]

272. The childhood shews the man,
As morning shews the day. Be famous then
By wisdom; as thy Empire must extend,
So let extend thy mind ore all the World.
[*Paradise Regained* (1671), IV, line 220]

273. Athens the eye of Greece, Mother of Arts
And Eloquence, native to famous wits
Or hospitable, in her sweet recess,
City or Suburban, studious walks and shades;
See there the Olive Grove of Academe,
Plato's retirement, where the Attic Bird
Trills her thick-warbl'd notes the summer long.
[*Paradise Regained* (1671), IV, line 240]

274. The first and wisest of them all professd
To know this onely, that he nothing knew.
[*Paradise Regained* (1671), IV, line 293]

275. Who reads
Incessantly, and to his reading brings not
A spirit and judgment equal or superior
(And what he brings, what needs he elsewhere seek)
Uncertain and unsettl'd still remains,
Deep verst in books and shallow in himself.
[*Paradise Regained* (1671), IV, line 322]

276. Till morning fair
Came forth with Pilgrim steps in amice gray.
[*Paradise Regained* (1671), IV, line 426]

277. A little onward lend thy guiding hand
To these dark steps, a little further on.
[*Samson Agonistes* (1671), line 1]

278. Ask for this great Deliverer now, and find him
Eyeless in Gaza, at the Mill with slaves.
[*Samson Agonistes* (1671), line 40]

279. O impotence of mind, in body strong!
But what is strength without a double share
Of wisdom.
[*Samson Agonistes* (1671), line 52]

280. O dark, dark, dark, amid the blaze of noon,
Irrecoverably dark, total Eclipse
Without all hope of day!
[*Samson Agonistes* (1671), line 80]

281. The Sun to me is dark
And silent as the Moon,
When she deserts the night
Hid in her vacant interlunar cave.
[*Samson Agonistes* (1671), line 86]

282. To live a life half dead, a living death.
[*Samson Agonistes* (1671), line 100]

283. Ran on embatteld Armies clad in Iron,
And weaponless himself,
Made Arms ridiculous.
[*Samson Agonistes* (1671), line 129]

284. For him I reck'n not in high estate
Whom long descent of birth
Or the sphear of fortune raises.
[*Samson Agonistes* (1671), line 170]

285. Wisest Men
Have errd, and by bad Women been deceiv'd;
And shall again, pretend they ne're so wise.
[*Samson Agonistes* (1671), line 210]

286. Just are the ways of God,
And justifiable to Men;
Unless ther be who think not God at all.
If any be, they walk obscure;
For of such Doctrin never was ther School,
But the heart of the Fool,
And no man therein Doctor but himself.
[*Samson Agonistes* (1671), line 293]

287. But what availd this temperance, not compleat
Against another object more enticing?
What boots it at one gate to make defence,
And at another to let in the foe?
[*Samson Agonistes* (1671), line 558]

288. My race of glory run, and race of shame,
And I shall shortly be with them that rest.
[*Samson Agonistes* (1671), line 597]

289. But who is this, what thing of Sea or Land?
Female of sex it seems,
That so bedeckt, ornate, and gay,
Comes this way sailing
Like a stately Ship
Of Tarsus, bound for th' Iles
Of Javan or Gadier
With all her bravery on, and tackle trim,
Sails filld, and streamers waving,
Courted by all the winds that hold them play,
An Amber scent of odorous perfume
Her harbinger.
[*Samson Agonistes* (1671), line 710]

290. That grounded maxim
So rife and celebrated in the mouths
Of wisest men; that to the public good
Private respects must yield.
[*Samson Agonistes* (1671), line 865]

291. Yet beauty, though injurious, hath strange power,
After offence returning, to regain
Love once possesst.
[*Samson Agonistes* (1671), line 1003]

292. Love-quarrels oft in pleasing concord end.
[*Samson Agonistes* (1671), line 1008]

293. Oh how comely it is and how reviving
To the Spirits of just men long opprest!
When God into the hands of thir deliverer
Puts invincible might

To quell the mighty of the Earth.
[*Samson Agonistes* (1671), line 1268]

294. He's gone and who knows how he may report
Thy words by adding fuel to the flame?
[*Samson Agonistes* (1671), line 1350]

295. Lords are Lordliest in thir wine.
[*Samson Agonistes* (1671), line 1418]

296. For evil news rides post, while good news baits.
[*Samson Agonistes* (1671), line 1538]

297. And as an ev'ning Dragon came,
Assailant on the perched roosts,
And nests in order rang'd
Of tame villatic Fowl.
[*Samson Agonistes* (1671), line 1692]

298. Like that self-begott'n bird
In the Arabian woods embost,
That no second knows nor third,
And lay ere while a Holocaust.
[*Samson Agonistes* (1671), line 1699]

299. And though her body die, her fame survives,
A secular bird ages of lives.
[*Samson Agonistes* (1671), line 1706]

300. Samson hath quit himself
Like Samson, and heroicly hath finisht
A life Heroic.
[*Samson Agonistes* (1671), line 1709]

301. All is best, though we oft doubt,
What th' unsearchable dispose
Of highest wisdom brings about,
And ever best found in the close.
[*Samson Agonistes* (1671), line 1745]

302. [Of writing in prose]
I should not chuse this manner of writing wherein knowing myself inferior to myself, led by the genial power of nature to another task, I have the use, as I may account it, but of my left hand.
[*The Reason of Church-government Urg'd against Prelaty* (1642), II, Introduction]

303. By labour and intent study (which I take to be my portion in this life) joyn'd with the strong propensity of nature, I might perhaps leave something so written to aftertimes, as they should not willingly let it die.
[*The Reason of Church-government Urg'd against Prelaty* (1642), II, Introduction]

304. The Land had once infranchis'd her self from this impertinent yoke of prelaty, under whose inquisitorious and tyrannical duncery no free and splendid wit can flourish.
[*The Reason of Church-government Urg'd against Prelaty* (1642), II, Introduction]

305. Beholding the bright countenance of truth in the quiet and still air of delightfull studies.
[*The Reason of Church-government Urg'd against Prelaty* (1642), II, Introduction]

306. He who would not be frustrate of his hope to write well hereafter in laudable things ought himself to bee a true Poem, that is, a composition, and patterne of the best and honourablest things.
[*An Apology against a Pamphlet . . . against Smectymnuus* (1642)]

307. His words . . . like so many nimble and airy servitors trip about him at command.
[*An Apology against a Pamphlet . . . against Smectymnuus* (1642)]

308. Let not England forget her precedence of teaching nations how to live.
[*The Doctrine and Discipline of Divorce* (1643)]

309. . . . the right path of a vertuous and noble Education, laborious indeed at the first ascent, but else so smooth, so green, so full of goodly prospect, and melodious sounds on every side, that the harp of Orpheus was not more charming.
[*Of Education: To Master Samuel Hartlib* (1644)]

310. I call therefore a compleate and generous Education that which fits a man to perform justly, skilfully and magnanimously all the offices both private and publick of peace and war.
[*Of Education: To Master Samuel Hartlib* (1644)]

311. In those vernal seasons of the yeer, when the air is calm and pleasant, it were an injury and sullennesse against nature not to go out, and see her riches, and partake in her rejoycing with heaven and earth.
[*Of Education: To Master Samuel Hartlib* (1644)]

312. As good almost kill a Man as kill a good Book; who kills a Man kills a reasonable creature, God's Image; but hee who destroyes a good Booke, kills reason it selfe, kills the Image of God, as it were in the eye. Many a man lives a burden to the Earth; but a good Booke is the pretious life-blood of a master spirit, imbalm'd and treasur'd up on purpose to a life beyond life.
[*Areopagitica* (1644)]

313. He that can apprehend and consider vice with all her baits and seeming pleasures, and yet abstain, and yet distinguish, and yet prefer that which is truly better, he is the true warfaring Christian. I cannot praise a fugitive and cloister'd vertue, unexercis'd and unbreath'd, that never sallies out and sees her adversary, but slinks out of the race, where that immortall garland is to be run for, not without dust and heat. Assuredly we bring not innocence into the world, we bring impurity much rather: that which purifies us is triall, and triall is by what is contrary.
[*Areopagitica* (1644)]

314. Our sage and serious Poet Spenser.
[*Areopagitica* (1644)]

315. If we think to regulat Printing, thereby to rectifie manners, we must regulat all recreations and pastimes, all that is delightful to man . . . It will ask more than the work of twenty licencers to examine all the lutes, the violins, and the guitars in every house . . . And who shall silence all the airs and madrigalls, that whisper softnes in chambers?
[*Areopagitica* (1644)]

316. To be still searching what we know not, by what we know, still closing up truth to truth as we find it (for all her body is homogeneal and proportionall), this is the golden rule in Theology as well as in Arithmetick, and makes up the best harmony in a Church.
[*Areopagitica* (1644)]

317. God is decreeing to begin some new and great period in his Church, ev'n to the reforming of Reformation it self. What does he then but reveal Himself to his servants, and as his manner is, first to his English-men?
[*Areopagitica* (1644)]

318. [Of London]
Behold now this vast City; a City of refuge, the mansion house of liberty, encompasst and surrounded with his protection.
[*Areopagitica* (1644)]

319. Where there is much desire to learn, there of necessity will be much arguing, much writing, many opinions; for

opinion in good men is but knowledge in the making.
[*Areopagitica* (1644)]

320. Methinks I see in my mind a noble and puissant Nation rousing herself like a strong man after sleep, and shaking her invincible locks: Methinks I see her as an Eagle mewing her mighty youth, and kindling her undazl'd eyes at the full midday beam.
[*Areopagitica* (1644)]

321. Give me the liberty to know, to utter, and to argue freely according to conscience, above all liberties.
[*Areopagitica* (1644)]

322. Though all the windes of doctrin were let loose to play upon the earth, so Truth be in the field, we do injuriously by licencing and prohibiting to misdoubt her strength. Let her and Falsehood grapple; who ever knew Truth put to the wors, in a free and open encounter.
[*Areopagitica* (1644)]

323. None can love freedom heartilie, but good men; the rest love not freedom, but licence.
[*The Tenure of Kings and Magistrates* (1649)]

324. No man who knows aught, can be so stupid to deny that all men naturally were born free.
[*The Tenure of Kings and Magistrates* (1649)]

325. [Reply when asked if he would allow his daughters to learn foreign languages]
One tongue is sufficient for a woman.
[Attr.]

Minifie, James M. (1900–1974)
Canadian broadcaster

1. The United States is the glory, jest, and terror of mankind.
[In Al Purdy (ed.), *The New Romans* (1988)]

Mirabeau, Comte de (1749–1791)
French orator and revolutionary politician; writer, essayist and memoirist

1. *La guerre est l'industrie nationale de la Prusse.*
War is Prussia's national industry.
[Attr.]

Mitchell, Joni (Roberta Joan Anderson) (1943–)
Canadian singer-songwriter

1. I've looked at life from both sides now
From win and lose and still somehow
It's life's illusions I recall
I really don't know life at all.
['Both Sides Now', song, 1968]

Mitchell, Julian (1935–)
British novelist, screenwriter and dramatist

1. The sink is the great symbol of the bloodiness of family life. All life is bad, but family life is worse.
[*As Far as You Can Go* (1963), I]

Mitchell, Margaret (1900–1949)
American novelist

1. Until you've lost your reputation, you never realize what a burden it was or what freedom really is.
[*Gone with the Wind* (1936)]

2. Death and taxes and childbirth? There's never any convenient time for any of them!
[*Gone with the Wind* (1936). Cf. Ben Franklin: 27]

3. After all, tomorrow is another day.
[*Gone with the Wind* (1936), closing words]

Mitford, Jessica Lucy (1917–)
English-born American writer and journalist; sister of Nancy Mitford

1. I have nothing against undertakers personally. It's just that I wouldn't want one to bury my sister.
[Attr. in *Saturday Review*, 1964]

Mitford, Mary Russell (1787–1855)
English essayist, dramatist, poet and letter writer

1. I have discovered that our great favourite, Miss Austen, is my country-woman ... with whom mamma before her marriage was acquainted. Mamma says that she was then the prettiest, silliest, most affected, husband-hunting butterfly she ever remembers.
[Letter to Sir William Elford, 1815]

2. [Of Jane Austen]
Perpendicular, precise and taciturn.
[In *Life and Letters of Mary R. Mitford* (1870), I]

Mitford, Nancy (1904–1973)
English novelist and biographer; sister of Jessica Mitford

1. Like all the very young we took it for granted that making love is child's play.
[*The Pursuit of Love* (1945), 3]

2. I loathe abroad, nothing would induce me to live there ... and, as for foreigners, they are all the same, and they all make me sick.
[*The Pursuit of Love* (1945), 10]

3. Abroad is unutterably bloody and foreigners are fiends.
[*The Pursuit of Love* (1945), 15]

4. Love in a Cold Climate.
[Title of novel, 1949. Cf. Southey: 24]

5. 'Twenty-three and a quarter minutes past,' Uncle Matthew was saying furiously, 'in precisely six and three-quarter minutes the damned fella will be late.'
[*Love in a Cold Climate* (1949), I, 13]

6. An aristocracy in a republic is like a chicken whose head has been cut off: it may run about in a lively way, but in fact it is dead.
[*Noblesse Oblige* (1956)]

7. I love children – especially when they cry, for then someone takes them away.
[Attr.]

Mizner, Wilson (1876–1933)
American writer, wit and dramatist

1. Be nice to people on your way up because you'll meet 'em on your way down.
[In Alva Johnston, *The Legendary Mizners* (1953); also attributed to Jimmy Durante]

Moffitt, Ian Lawson (1929–)
Australian journalist and novelist

1. The Australian's loving relationship with his car has become a commonplace: he fondles each nut and bolt in interminable conversations in the pub; strips it, lays it on the lawn, and greases its nipples while his wife wonders whether he will ever better his indoor average of one-a-month.
[*The U-Jack Society* (1972)]

Mohler, Professor Stanley (1927–)
American epidemiologist and researcher

1. Food poisoning ... probably poses a greater threat to passenger safety than hijacking.
[*The Observer*, 1989]

Mola, Emilio (1887–1937)
Spanish general

1. [Mola hoped that citizens of Madrid would take up arms, thus forming a 'fifth column' to support his 'four columns' of troops]
La quinta columna.
The fifth column.
[Remark during the Spanish Civil War, 1936]

Molière (Jean-Baptiste Poquelin) (1622–1673)
French dramatist, creator of French classical comedy; actor and director

1. *On ne meurt qu'une fois, et c'est pour si longtemps!*
One dies only once, and then for such a long time!
[*Le Dépit Amoureux* (1656), V.iii]

2. *Les gens de qualité savent tout sans avoir jamais rien appris.*
People of quality know everything without ever having learned anything.
[*Les Précieuses Ridicules* (1660), IX]

3. *Mais qui rit d'autrui*
Doit craindre qu'en revanche on rie aussi de lui.
But the man who laughs at other people must be afraid that others will laugh at him in return.
[*L'Ecole des Femmes* (1662), Scene i]

4. *Le mariage, Agnès, n'est pas un badinage.*
Marriage, Agnès, is not a joke.
[*L'Ecole des Femmes* (1662), Scene iii]

5. *C'est une étrange entreprise que celle de faire rire les honnêtes gens.*
It's a strange job, making decent people laugh.
[*L'Ecole des Femmes* (1662), Scene vi]

6. *Je voudrais bien savoir si la grande règle de toutes les règles n'est pas de plaire.*
I would like to know if, after all, the greatest rule of all is not to please.
[*L'Ecole des Femmes* (1662), Scene vi]

7. *Couvrez ce sein que je ne saurais voir:*
Par de pareils objets les âmes sont blessées,
Et cela fait venir de coupables pensées.
Cover that bosom. I must not see it. Souls are wounded by such things, and they arouse guilty thoughts.
[*Tartuffe* (1664), III]

8. *Ah, pour être dévot, je n'en suis pas moins homme.*
I am no less a man for being devout.
[*Tartuffe* (1664), III]

9. *On est aisément dupé par ce qu'on aime.*
One is easily taken in by what one loves.
[*Tartuffe* (1664), IV]

10. *Le ciel défend, de vrai, certains contentements*
Mais on trouve avec lui des accommodements.
Heaven forbids certain pleasures, it is true, but one can arrive at certain compromises.
[*Tartuffe* (1664), IV]

11. *Le scandale du monde est ce qui fait l'offense,*
Et ce n'est pas pécher que pécher en silence.
Public scandal is what constitutes offence; to sin in secret is no sin at all.
[*Tartuffe* (1664), IV]

12. *L'homme est, je vous l'avoue, un méchant animal.*
Man is, I admit it, a mediocre creature.
[*Tartuffe* (1664), V]

13. *Il faut, parmi le monde, une vertu traitable.*
Virtue, in this world, should be accommodating.
[*Le Misanthrope* (1666), I.i]

14. *C'est une folie à nulle autre seconde,*
De vouloir se mêler à corriger le monde.
The greatest folly of all is wanting to busy oneself in setting the world to rights.
[*Le Misanthrope* (1666), I.i]

15. *Si le roi m'avait donné*
Paris, sa grand' ville,
Et qu'il me fallût quitter
L'amour de ma mie,
Je dirais au roi Henri:
Reprenez votre Paris.
If the king had given me Paris, his great city, and I had to give up the love of my sweetheart, I should say to King Henry: Take back your Paris.
[*Le Misanthrope* (1666), I.iii; traditional song]

16. *L'âge amènera tout, et ce n'est pas le temps,*
Madame, comme on sait, d'être prude à vingt ans.
Everything comes with age, and everyone knows, Madame, that twenty is not the time to be a prude.
[*Le Misanthrope* (1666), III.iv]

17. *On doit se regarder soi-même un fort long temps,*
Avant que de songer à condamner les gens.
We should look long and carefully at ourselves before we consider judging others.
[*Le Misanthrope* (1666), III.vii]

18. Géronte: *Il me semble que vous les placez autrement qu'ils ne sont: que le coeur est du côté gauche, et le foie du côté droit.*
Sganarelle: *Oui, cela était autrefois ainsi, mais nous avons changé tout cela, et nous faisons maintenant la médecine d'une méthode toute nouvelle.*
Géronte: It seems to me you are locating them in the wrong place: the heart is on the left and the liver is on the right.
Sganarelle: Yes, in the old days that was so, but we changed it all, and now we practise medicine using a completely new method.
[*Le Médecin malgré lui* (1667), II.iv]

19. *Vous l'avez voulu, Georges Dandin, vous l'avez voulu.*
You asked for it, George Dandin, you asked for it.
[*Georges Dandin* (1668), I.ix]

20. *Assassiner c'est le plus court chemin.*
Assassination is the shortest way.
[*Le Sicilien* (1668), XIII]

21. *Il faut manger pour vivre et non pas vivre pour manger.*
One should eat to live, not live to eat.
[*L'Avare* (1669), III.i]

22. *C'est un homme expéditif, qui aime à dépêcher ses malades; et quand on a à mourir, cela se fait avec lui le plus vite du monde.*
He's an expeditious man, who likes to hurry his patients along; and when you have to die, he gets it over with quicker than anyone else.
[*Monsieur de Pourceaugnac* (1670), I.vii]

23. *Ils commencent ici par faire pendre un homme et puis ils lui font son procès.*
Here they have a man hanged, and then proceed to try him.
[*Monsieur de Pourceaugnac* (1670), III.ii]

24. M. Jourdain: *Quoi? quand je dis: 'Nicole, apportez-moi mes pantoufles, et me donnez mon bonnet de nuit', c'est de la prose?*
Maître de Philosophie: *Oui, Monsieur.*

M. Jourdain: *Par ma foi! il y a plus de quarante ans que je dis de la prose sans que j'en susse rien.*
M. Jourdain: What? when I say: 'Nicole, bring me my slippers, and give me my night-cap,' is that prose?
Master of Philosophy: Yes, Sir.
M. Jourdain: Good heavens! For over forty years I have been speaking prose without knowing it.
[*Le Bourgeois Gentilhomme* (1671), II.iv]

25. *Ah, la belle chose que de savoir quelque chose.*
Ah, what a fine thing it is, to know something.
[*Le Bourgeois Gentilhomme* (1671), II.vi]

26. *Je consens qu'une femme ait des clartés de tout,*
Mais je ne lui veux point la passion choquante
De se rendre savante afin d'être savante
Et j'aime que souvent, aux questions qu'on fait,
Elle sache ignorer les choses qu'elle sait.
I accept that a woman should be informed about everything, but I cannot allow her the shocking passion for acquiring learning in order to be learned. When she is asked questions, I like her often to know how not to know the things she does know.
[*Les Femmes savantes* (1672), I]

27. *La grammaire qui sait régenter jusqu'aux rois.*
Grammar, which can govern even kings.
[*Les Femmes savantes* (1672), II]

28. *Je vis de bonne soupe et non de beau langage.*
I live on good soups, not on fine words.
[*Les Femmes savantes* (1672), II]

29. *La beauté du visage est un frêle ornement,*
Une fleur passagère, un éclat d'un moment,
Et qui n'est attaché qu'à la simple épiderme.
The beauty of a face is a frail ornament, a passing flower, a moment's brightness belonging only to the skin.
[*Les Femmes savantes* (1672), III]

30. *Un sot savant est sot plus qu'un sot ignorant.*
A knowledgeable fool is more foolish than an ignorant fool.
[*Les Femmes savantes* (1672), IV]

31. *Les livres cadrent mal avec le mariage.*
Books and marriage do not go well together.
[*Les Femmes savantes* (1672), V]

Moltke, Helmuth von (1800–1891)
German field marshal; chief of Prussian general staff

1. *Der ewige Friede ist ein Traum, und nicht einmal ein schöner und der Krieg ein Glied in Gottes Weltordnung ... Ohne den Krieg würde die Welt in Materialismus versumpfen.*
Eternal peace is a dream, and not even a pleasant one; and war is an integral part of the way God has ordered the world ... Without war, the world would sink in the mire of materialism.
[Letter to Dr J.K. Bluntschli, 1880]

Monash, Sir John (1865–1931)
Australian military commander

1. Leadership counts for something, of course, but it cannot succeed without the spirit, élan and morale of those led. Therefore I count myself the most fortunate of men in having been placed at the head of the finest fighting machine the world has ever known.
[*Argus*, 1927]

2. [In France, 1917]
[War] is not a business in which one can take any pride or pleasure, or even pretend to. Its horror, its ghastly inefficiency, its unspeakable cruelty and misery has always appalled me, but there is nothing to do but to set one's teeth and stick it out as long as one can.
[In Geoffrey Serle, *John Monash* (1982)]

Monmouth, Duke of (1649–1685)
Illegitimate son of Charles II; rebelled against James II

1. [Words to his executioner]
Do not hack me as you did my Lord Russell.
[In Macaulay, *History of England* (1849), I]

Monro, David Hector (1911–)
Australian philosopher and writer

1. Others, not he, must answer Milton's charge:
New Commisar is but old Czar writ large.
[*The Sonneteer's History of Philosophy* (1981), 22, 'Karl Marx'. Cf. Milton: 93]

Monroe, Harriet (1860–1936)
American poet, editor and dramatist

1. ... poetry, 'The Cinderella of the Arts.'
[In Hope Stoddard, *Famous American Women*, 'Harriet Monroe']

Monroe, Marilyn (Norma Jean Baker) (1926–1962)
American leading film actress and model

1. [When asked if she had posed for a calendar with nothing on]
I had the radio on.
[*Time*, 1952]

2. I guess I *am* a fantasy.
[In Steinem, *Outrageous Acts and Everyday Rebellions* (1984)]

3. [On having matzo balls for supper at Arthur Miller's parents]
Isn't there another part of the matzo you can eat?
[Attr.]

Monsell, J.S.B. (1811–1875)
Irish hymn writer and clergyman

1. Fight the good fight
With all thy might.
[Hymn, 1834]

Monsarrat, Nicholas (1910–1979)
British novelist

1. You English ... think we know damn nothing *but I tell you we know damn all.*
[*The Cruel Sea* (1951)]

Montagu, Lady Mary Wortley (1689–1762)
English letter writer, poet and traveller; introduced smallpox inoculation

1. And we meet, with champagne and a chicken, at last.
[*Six Town Eclogues* (1747), 'The Lover']

2. But the fruit that can fall without shaking,
Indeed is too mellow for me.
[In J. Dodsley (ed.), *A Collection of Poems* (1758), 'Answered, for Lord William Hamilton']

3. Satire should, like a polished razor keen,
Wound with a touch that's scarcely felt or seen.
['To the Imitator of the First Satire of Horace']

4. General notions are generally wrong.
[Letter to her husband, Edward Wortley Montagu, 1710]

5. Civility costs nothing and buys everything.
[Letter to the Countess of Bute, 1756]

6. People wish their enemies dead – but I do not; I say give them the gout, give them the stone!
[In a letter from Horace Walpole to the Earl of Harcourt, 1778]

Montague, C.E. (1867–1928)
English journalist, drama critic and novelist

1. War hath no fury like a non-combatant.
[*Disenchantment* (1922), 16]

2. To be amused at what you read – that is the great spring of happy quotation.
[*A Writer's Notes on his Trade* (1930)]

Montaigne, Michel de (1533–1592)
French essayist and moralist

1. *Pour juger des choses grandes et hautes, il faut une âme de même, autrement nous leur attribuons le vice qui est le nôtre.*
To judge great and high things, one needs a soul of the same stature; otherwise we attribute to them that vice which is our own.
[*Essais* (1580), I, 14]

2. *Il faut être toujours botté et prêt à partir.*
One should always have one's boots on and be ready to leave.
[*Essais* (1580), I, 20. Cf. La Fontaine: 15]

3. *Je veux ... que la mort me trouve plantant mes choux, mais nonchalant d'elle, et encore plus de mon jardin imparfait.*
I want ... death to find me planting my cabbages, but caring little for it, and even less for my imperfect garden.
[*Essais* (1580), I, 20]

4. *Le continuel ouvrage de votre vie, c'est bâtir la mort.*
The unceasing labour of your life is to build the house of death.
[*Essais* (1580), I, 20]

5. *L'utilité de vivre n'est pas en l'espace, elle est en l'usage ... Il gît en votre volonté, non au nombre des ans, que vous ayez assez vécu.'*
The value of life does not lie in the number of years but in the use you make of them ... Whether you have lived enough depends on your will, not on the number of your years.
[*Essais* (1580), I, 20]

6. *Il faut noter, que les jeux d'enfants ne sont pas jeux: et les faut juger en eux, comme leurs plus sérieuses actions.*
It should be noted that children at play are not merely playing; their games should be seen as their most serious actions.
[*Essais* (1580), I, 23]

7. [Of his friend Étienne de la Boétie]
Si on me presse de dire pourquoi je l'aimais, je sens que cela ne se peut s'exprimer, qu'en répondant: 'Parce que c'était lui; parce que c'était moi.'
If I am pressed to say why I loved him, I feel it can only be explained by replying: 'Because it was he; because it was me.'
[*Essais* (1580), I, 28]

8. *Il n'y a guère moins de tourment au gouvernement d'une famille que d'un état entier ... et, pour être les occupations domestiques moins importantes, elles n'en sont pas moins importunes.*
There is scarcely any less trouble in running a family than in governing an entire state ... and domestic matters are no less importunate for being less important.
[*Essais* (1580), I, 39]

9. *Il se faut réserver une arrière boutique toute nôtre, toute franche, en laquelle nous établissons notre vraie liberté et principale retraite et solitude.*
We should keep for ourselves a little back shop, all our own, untouched by others, in which we establish our true freedom and chief place of seclusion and solitude.
[*Essais* (1580), I, 39]

10. *La plus grande chose du monde, c'est de savoir être à soi.*
The greatest thing in the world is to know how to belong to oneself.
[*Essais* (1580), I, 39]

11. *La gloire et le repos sont choses qui ne peuvent loger en même gîte.*
Fame and tranquillity cannot dwell under the same roof.
[*Essais* (1580), I, 39]

12. *Mon métier et mon art, c'est vivre.*
Living is both my job and my art.
[*Essais* (1580), II, 6]

13. *La vertu refuse la facilité pour compagne ... elle demande un chemin âpre et épineux.*
Virtue shuns ease as a companion ... It needs a rough and thorny path.
[*Essais* (1580), II, 11]

14. *Notre religion est faite pour extirper les vices; elle les couvre, les nourrit, les incite.*
Our religion was made to root out vices; it covers them up, nourishes them, incites them.
[*Essais* (1580), II, 12]

15. *Quand je me joue à ma chatte, qui sait si elle passe son temps de moi plus que je ne fais d'elle?*
When I play with my cat, who knows whether she isn't amusing herself with me more than I am with her?
[*Essais* (1580), II, 12]

16. *Que sais-je?*
What do I know?
[*Essais* (1580), II, 12]

17. *L'homme est bien insensé. Il ne saurait forger un ciron, et forge des Dieux à douzaines.*
Man is quite insane. He wouldn't know how to create a maggot, yet he creates Gods by the dozen.
[*Essais* (1580), II, 12]

18. *Ceux qui ont apparié notre vie à un songe, ont eu de la raison, à l'aventure plus qu'ils ne pensaient ... Nous veillons dormants, et veillants dormons.*
Those who have compared our life to a dream were, by chance, more right than they thought ... We are awake while sleeping, and sleeping while awake.
[*Essais* (1580), II, 12]

19. *Pour les affaires publiques, il n'est aucun si mauvais train, pourvu qu'il ait de l'âge et de la constance, qui ne vaille mieux que le changement et le remuement.*
There is, in public affairs, no state so bad, provided it has age and stability on its side, that is not preferable to change and disturbance.
[*Essais* (1580), II, 17]

20. *Tel a été miraculeux au monde, auquel sa femme et son valet n'ont rien vu de remarquable. Peu d'hommes ont été admirés par leurs domestiques.*
Many a man has been a wonder to the world, whose wife and valet have seen nothing in him that was remarkable. Few men have been admired by their servants.
[*Essais* (1580), III, 2. Cf. Cornuel: 1]

21. *Quelqu'un pourrait dire de moi que j'ai seulement fait ici un amas de fleurs étrangères, n'y ayant fourni du mien que le filet à les lier.*
One could say of me that in this book I have only made up a bunch of other men's flowers, providing of my own only the string to tie them together.
[*Essais* (1580), III, 12]

22. *Qui craint de souffrir, il souffre déjà de ce qu'il craint.*
A man who fears suffering is already suffering from what he fears.
[*Essais* (1580), III, 13]

Montale, Eugenio (1896–1981)
Italian poet, critic and translator

1. *... il tardo frullo*
di un piccione incapace di seguirti
sui gradini automatici che ti slittano giù.
... the delayed whirr of the wings
of a pigeon that cannot follow you
on the steps of the escalator that carries you away.
[*Di un natale metropolitano* (*On a metropolitan Christmas*, 1956), 'La bufera ed altro' ('The storm')]

Montefiore, Hugh (1920–)
English Anglican prelate

1. Why did He not marry? Could the answer be that Jesus was not by nature the marrying sort?
[At a conference, Oxford, 26 July 1967]

Montesquieu, Charles, Baron de (1689–1755)
French social and political philosopher and jurist

1. *Si les triangles faisaient un Dieu, ils lui donneraient trois côtés.*
If triangles created a god, they would give him three sides.
[*Lettres persanes* (1721)]

2. *Il n'y a jamais eu de royaume où il y ait eu tant de guerres civiles que dans celui du Christ.*
No kingdom has ever had as many civil wars as the kingdom of Christ.
[*Lettres persanes* (1721)]

3. *Un empire fondé par les armes a besoin de se soutenir par les armes.*
An empire founded by war has to maintain itself by war.
[*Considérations sur les causes de la grandeur des Romains et de leur décadence* (1734), 8]

4. *La liberté est le droit de faire tout ce que les lois permettent.*
Freedom is the right to do whatever the laws permit.
[*De l'esprit des lois* (1748), XI, 3]

5. *Les grands seigneurs ont des plaisirs, le peuple a de la joie.*
Great lords have pleasures, but the people have fun.
[*Pensées et fragments inédits* (1899)]

6. *Les Anglais sont occupés; ils n'ont pas le temps d'être polis.*
The English are busy; they don't have the time to be polite.
[*Pensées et fragments inédits* (1899)]

Montessori, Maria (1870–1952)
Italian doctor and educationist, noted for her method of nursery education

1. We teachers can only help the work going on, as servants wait upon a master.
[*The Absorbent Mind*]

Montgomery, Bernard Law, Viscount Montgomery of Alamein (1887–1976)
English field marshal, noted for his World War II campaigns in North Africa and Europe

1. [Address to the officers of the Eighth Army, 13 August 1942]
Here we will stand and fight; there will be no further withdrawal ... We are going to finish with this chap Rommel once and for all. It will be quite easy. There is no doubt about it. He is definitely a nuisance. Therefore we will hit him and crack and finish with him.
[From a post-war recording of his speech]

2. Anyone who votes Labour ought to be locked up.
[Speech, 1959]

3. [On American policy in Vietnam]
The US has broken the second rule of war. That is, don't go fighting with your land army on the mainland of Asia. Rule One is don't march on Moscow. I developed these two rules myself.
[Speech, 1962]

4. [Comment on a bill to relax the laws against homosexuals]
This sort of thing may be tolerated by the French, but we are British – thank God.
[Speech, 1965]

Montgomery, James (1771–1854)
Scottish poet, hymn writer and journalist

1. Hail to the Lord's Anointed,
Great David's greater Son!
Hail, in the time appointed,
His reign on earth begun!
[Hymn, 1821]

2. Here in the body pent,
Absent from Him I roam,
Yet nightly pitch my moving tent
A day's march nearer home.
[Hymn]

Montgomery, Robert (1807–1855)
English clergyman and poet

1. The solitary monk who shook the world.
[*Luther: a Poem* (1842), 'Man's Need and God's Supply']

Montherlant, Henry de (1896–1972)
French novelist and dramatist

1. *Les valeurs nobles, à la fin, sont toujours vaincues; l'histoire est le récit de leurs défaites renouvelées.*
Noble values, in the end, are always overcome; history tells the story of their defeat over and over again.
[*Le Maître de Santiago* (1947)]

Montrond, Casimir, Comte de (1768–1843)
French diplomat

1. *Défiez-vous des premiers mouvements parce qu'ils sont bons.*
Beware of first impulses because they are good.
[Attributed in Comte J. d'Estourmel, *Derniers souvenirs* (1860). Cf. Talleyrand: 6]

Montrose, Percy (19th century)
American songwriter

1. In a cavern, in a canyon,
Excavating for a mine
Dwelt a miner, Forty-niner,
And his daughter, Clementine.
Oh, my darling, Oh, my darling, Oh, my darling Clementine!
Thou art lost and gone for ever, dreadful sorry, Clementine...

2. Light she was and like a fairy,
And her shoes were number nine;
Herring boxes without topses,
Sandals were for Clementine...

3. But I kissed her little sister,
And forgot my Clementine.
['Clementine', song, 1884]

Monty Python's Flying Circus
BBC TV programme, 1969–74; with Graham Chapman, John Cleese, Terry Gilliam, Eric Idle, Terry Jones and Michael Palin

1. And now for something completely different.
[Catchphrase]

Moore, Brian (1921–)
Irish-born Canadian novelist

1. So the years hang like old clothes, forgotten in the wardrobe of our minds. Did I wear that? Who was I then?
[*No Other Life* (1993)]

Moore, Clement C. (1779–1863)
American Hebrew scholar and poet

1. 'Twas the night before Christmas, when all through the house
Not a creature was stirring, not even a mouse;
The stockings were hung by the chimney with care,
In hopes that St Nicholas soon would be there...

2. 'Happy Christmas to all, and to all a goodnight!'
['A Visit from St Nicholas' (1823)]

Moore, Edward (1712–1757)
English dramatist, fabulist and editor

1. This is adding insult to injuries.
[*The Foundling*, (1748), V.v]

2. I am rich beyond the dreams of avarice.
[*The Gamester* (1753), II.ii]

Moore, George (1852–1933)
Irish novelist, dramatist and critic

1. The lot of critics is to be remembered by what they failed to understand.
[*Impressions and Opinions* (1891), 'Balzac']

2. Acting is therefore the lowest of the arts, if it is an art at all.
[*Impressions and Opinions* (1891), 'Mummer-Worship']

3. Art must be parochial in the beginning to be cosmopolitan in the end.
[*Hail and Farewell: Ave* (1911)]

4. A man travels the world over in search of what he needs and returns home to find it.
[*The Brook Kerith* (1916), 11]

Moore, Marianne (1887–1972)
American poet, essayist and editor

1. Nor till the poets among us can be
'literalists of
the imagination' – above
insolence and triviality and can present
for inspection, imaginary gardens with real toads in them,
shall we have
it.
['Poetry' (1935), first version]

2. I, too, dislike it: there are things that are important beyond all this fiddle.
Reading it, however, with a perfect contempt for it, one discovers in
it after all, a place for the genuine.
['Poetry' (1935)]

3. My father used to say,
'Superior people never make long visits.'...

4. Nor was he insincere in saying, 'Make my house your inn.'
Inns are not residences...

5. Self-reliant like the cat–
that takes its prey to privacy,
the mouse's limp tail hanging like a shoelace from its mouth.
['Silence' (1935)]

6. It scarcely could be dangerous to be living
in a town like this, of simple people
who have a steeple-jack placing danger-signs by the church
where he is gilding the solid-
pointed star, which on a steeple
stands for hope.
['The Steeple-Jack' (1935)]

7. O to be a dragon
a symbol of the power of Heaven.
['O to Be a Dragon' (1959)]

Moore, Thomas (1779–1852)
Irish poet, lyricist and biographer

1. 'Twere more than woman to be wise;
'Twere more than man to wish thee so!
[*Juvenile Poems* (1882 ed.), 'The Ring']

2. To love you was pleasant enough,
And oh! 'tis delicious to hate you!
[*Juvenile Poems* (1882 ed.), 'To – When I Lov'd You']

3. Believe me, if all those endearing young charms,
Which I gaze on so fondly today,
Were to change by tomorrow, and fleet in my arms,
Like fairy gifts fading away!
Thou wouldst still be ador'd as this moment thou art,
Let thy loveliness fade as it will,
And, around the dear ruin, each wish of my heart
Would entwine itself verdantly still...

4. No, the heart that has truly lov'd never forgets,
But as truly loves on to the close,
As the sun-flower turns on her god, when he sets,
The same look which she turn'd when he rose.
[*Irish Melodies* (1807), 'Believe Me, if all those Endearing Young Charms']

5. You may break, you may shatter the vase, if you will,
But the scent of the roses will hang round it still.
[*Irish Melodies* (1807), 'Farewell! But Whenever']

6. Go where glory waits thee,
But, while fame elates thee,
Oh! still remember me.
[*Irish Melodies* (1807), 'Go Where Glory']

7. The harp that once through Tara's halls
The soul of music shed,
Now hangs as mute on Tara's walls
As if that soul were fled,–
So sleeps the pride of former days,
So glory's thrill is o'er;
And hearts, that once beat high for praise,
Now feel that pulse no more.
[*Irish Melodies* (1807), 'The Harp that Once']

8. Lesbia hath a beaming eye,
But no one knows for whom it beameth.
[*Irish Melodies* (1807), 'Lesbia Hath']

9. No, there's nothing half so sweet in life
As love's young dream.
[*Irish Melodies* (1807), 'Love's Young Dream']

10. The Minstrel Boy to the war is gone,
In the ranks of death you'll find him;
His father's sword he has girded on,
And his wild harp slung behind him.
[*Irish Melodies* (1807), 'The Minstrel Boy']

11. Oh! blame not the bard.
[*Irish Melodies* (1807), 'Oh! Blame Not']

12. Oh! breathe not his name, let it sleep in the shade,
Where cold and unhonour'd his relics are laid.
[*Irish Melodies* (1807), 'Oh, Breathe not his Name']

13. Rich and rare were the gems she wore,
And a bright gold ring on her wand she bore.
[*Irish Melodies* (1807), 'Rich and Rare']

14. She is far from the land where her young hero sleeps,
And lovers are round her, sighing:
But coldly she turns from their gaze, and weeps,
For her heart in his grave is lying.
[*Irish Melodies* (1807), 'She is Far']

15. The time I've lost in wooing,
In watching and pursuing
The light that lies
In woman's eyes,
Has been my heart's undoing.
Though wisdom oft has sought me,
I scorned the love she bought me,
My only books,
Were woman's looks,
And folly's all they've taught me.
[*Irish Melodies* (1807), 'The Time I've Lost']

16. 'Tis sweet to think, that, where'er we rove,
We are sure to find something blissful and dear,
And that, when we're far from the lips we love,
We've but to make love to the lips we are near.
[*Irish Melodies* (1807), ''Tis Sweet to Think']

17. 'Tis the last rose of summer
Left blooming alone;
All her lovely companions
Are faded and gone.
[*Irish Melodies* (1807), ''Tis the Last Rose']

18. Then awake! the heavens look bright, my dear;
'Tis never too late for delight, my dear;
And the best of all ways
To lengthen our days
Is to steal a few hours from the night, my dear!
[*Irish Melodies* (1807), 'The Young May Moon']

19. A Persian's Heaven is easily made;
'Tis but black eyes and lemonade.
[*Intercepted Letters* (1813)]

20. Oft, in the stilly night,
Ere Slumber's chain has bound me,
Fond Memory brings the light
Of other days around me...

21. I feel like one
Who treads alone
Some banquet-hall deserted,
Whose lights are fled,
Whose garlands dead
And all but he departed!
[*National Airs* (1815), 'Oft in the Stilly Night']

22. Oh! ever thus, from childhood's hour,
I've seen my fondest hopes decay;
I never lov'd a tree or flow'r,
But 'twas the first to fade away.
I never nurs'd a dear gazelle,
To glad me with its soft black eye,
But when it came to know me well,
And love me, it was sure to die!
[*Lalla Rookh* (1817), 'The Fire-Worshippers', I]

23. Like Dead Sea fruits, that tempt the eye,
But turn to ashes on the lips!
[*Lalla Rookh* (1817), 'The Fire-Worshippers', II]

24. Good at a fight, but better at a play,
Godlike in giving, but – the devil to pay!
[*Memoirs of the Life of R.B. Sheridan* (1825), 'On a Cast of Sheridan's Hand']

25. 'Come, come', said Tom's father, 'at your time of life,
'There's no longer excuse for thus playing the rake–
'It is time you should think, boy, of taking a wife'–
'Why, so it is, father – whose wife shall I take?'
[*Miscellaneous Poems* (1840), 'A Joke Versified']

26. Disguise our bondage as we will,
'Tis woman, woman, rules us still.
[*Miscellaneous Poems* (1840), 'Sovereign Woman']

Moorhouse, James (1826–1915)
English cleric, Bishop of Melbourne 1876–86

1. Don't pray for rain – dam it.
[Oral tradition]

Moravia, Alberto (Alberto Pincherle) (1907–1990)
Italian novelist and short-story writer

1. *Tutta questa gente sa dove va e cosa vuole, ha uno scopo e per questo si affretta, si tormenta è triste, allegra, io ... io ... invece nulla.*
All these people know where they are going and what they want, they have an aim in their life and that's why they hurry along, and torment themselves, they are sad, happy, whereas I... I... have nothing.
[*Gli Indifferenti* (*The Time of Indifference*, 1929)]

2. *In quel giorno gli erano stati aperti gli occhi; ma quello che aveva appreso era troppo più di quanto potesse sopportare.*
On that day his eyes had been opened; but what he had learned was far more than he could stand.
[*Agostino* (1944)]

3. *Ho avuto la malattia del ladro ... m'è venuta una crisi di furto. Cosa vuol dire una parola! Tirai avanti qualche giorno, disgustato e smanioso, finché una mattina, ricordai, ad un tratto: cleptomane. E mi sentii innocente.*
I had the thief's sickness ... I had a thieving crisis. How much meaning there can be in a word! I went along for a few days feeling disgusted and restless, until one morning I suddenly remembered: kleptomaniac. And I felt innocent.
[*Racconti romani* (*Roman Tales*, 1954), 'The Kleptomaniac']

4. *Ma è morto come potrebbe domani morire tanta gente come lui: correndo dietro al denaro e illudendosi che non ci sia che il denaro; e poi, improvvisamente, restando agghiacciato dalla paura alla vista di ciò che sta dietro il denaro.*
But he died as many people like him could die tomorrow, running after money, and believing that there is nothing but money; then he was suddenly frozen by the fear of seeing what lies behind money.
[*La Ciociara* (*Two Women*, 1957)]

5. The ratio of literacy to illiteracy is constant, but nowadays the illiterates can read and write.
[*The Observer*, 1979]

Mordaunt, Thomas Osbert (1730–1809)

1. Sound, sound the clarion, fill the fife,
Throughout the sensual world proclaim,
One crowded hour of glorious life

Is worth an age without a name.
['Verses written during the War, 1756–1763' (1791)]

More, Hannah (1745–1833)
English poet, dramatist and religious writer; member of Blue Stocking circle

1. Did not God
Sometimes withhold in mercy what we ask,
We should be ruined at our own request.
[*Moses in the Bulrushes* (1782)]

2. The sober comfort, all the peace which springs
From the large aggregate of little things;
On these small cares of daughter, wife, or friend,
The almost sacred joys of home depend.
['Sensibility' (1782)]

3. Small habits, well pursued betimes,
May reach the dignity of crimes.
[*Florio* (1786)]

4. For you'll ne'er mend your fortunes, nor help the just cause,
By breaking of windows, or breaking of laws.
['Address to the Meeting in Spa Fields' (1817)]

More, Sir Thomas (1478–1535)
English statesman and humanist; Lord Chancellor 1529–32; executed for refusing to recognize Henry VIII as head of the Church

1. *Oves inquam vestrae, quae tam mites esse, tamque exiguo solent ali, nunc (uti fertur) tam edaces atque indomitae esse coeperunt ut homines devorent ipsos; agros, domos, oppida vastant et depopulantur.*
Your sheep, that used to be so meek and tame, and so small eaters, now, as I hear say, have become so great devourers, and so wild, that they devour the very men themselves, and devastate and depopulate fields, houses and towns.
[*Utopia* (1516), I]

2. I cumber you goode Margaret muche, but I woulde be sorye, if it shoulde be any lenger than to morrowe, for it is S. Thomas evin and the vtas of Sainte Peter and therefore to morowe longe I to goe to God, it were a daye very meete and conveniente for me. I neuer liked your maner towarde me better then when you kissed me laste for I loue when doughterly loue and deere charitie hath no laisor to looke to worldly curtesye. Fare well my deere childe and praye for me, and I shall for you and all your freindes that we maie merily meete in heaven.
[Last letter to Margaret Roper, his daughter, 1535]

3. [On reading an unremarkable book recently rendered into verse by a friend]
Yea, marry, now it is somewhat, for now it is rhyme; before, it was neither rhyme nor reason.
[In Francis Bacon, *Apophthegms New and Old* (1625)]

4. [On ascending the scaffold]
I pray you, Master Lieutenant, see me safe up, and for my coming down let me shift for myself.
[In William Roper, *Life of Sir Thomas More* (1963 ed.)]

5. [To the Executioner]
Pluck up thy spirits, man, and be not afraid to do thine office; my neck is very short; take heed therefore thou strike not awry, for saving of thine honesty.
[In William Roper, *Life of Sir Thomas More* (1963 ed.)]

6. After his head was upon the block, [he] lift it up again, and gently drew his beard aside, and said, *This hath not offended the king.*
[In Francis Bacon, *Apophthegms New and Old* (1625)]

Morell, Thomas (1703–1784)
English classical scholar, librettist, editor and clergyman

1. See, the conquering hero comes!
Sound the trumpets, beat the drums!
[*Joshua* (1748)]

Morgan, Augustus de (1806–1871)
Indian-born British mathematician, logician and writer

1. Great fleas have little fleas upon their backs to bite 'em,
And little fleas have lesser fleas, and so *ad infinitum.*
['A Budget of Paradoxes'. Cf. Swift: 70]

Morgan, Elaine (1920–)
British writer

1. The trouble with specialists is that they tend to think in grooves.
[*The Descent of Woman*, 1]

Morita, Akio
Chairman, Sony Corporation

1. Curiosity is the key to creativity.
[*Made in Japan* (1986)]

2. Whereas Americans and Europeans often develop complex, large-scale solutions to problems, the Japanese constantly pare down and reduce the complexity of products and ideas to the barest minimum. They streamline the design, reduce the number of parts, and simplify the inner workings and moving parts. The influence of Zen and haiku poetry are often evident in the simplicity and utility of Japanese designs.
[*Made in Japan* (1986)]

Morley, John David
British novelist

1. For the average European a job was an income, for the average Japanese it was a home.
[*Pictures From the Water Trade – An Englishman in Japan*]

Morley, Lord (First Viscount Morley of Blackburn) (1838–1923)
English Liberal statesman; biographer, editor, essayist and critic

1. [Of letter-writing]
That most delightful way of wasting time.
[*Critical Miscellanies* (1886), 'Life of George Eliot']

Morley, Lord (Third Earl of Morley) (1843–1905)
British politician

1. I am always very glad when Lord Salisbury makes a great speech ... It is sure to contain at least one blazing indiscretion which it is a delight to remember.
[Speech, 1887]

Morley, Robert (1908–1992)
British stage and film actor

1. Beware of the conversationalist who adds 'in other words'. He is merely starting afresh.
[*The Observer*, 'Sayings of the Week', 1964]

2. There's no such thing in Communist countries as a load of old cod's wallop, the cod's wallop is always fresh made.
[*Punch*, 1974]

Morphy, Countess (Marcelle Azra Forbes) (fl. 1930–1950)
Cookery writer

1. The tragedy of English cooking is that 'plain' cooking cannot be entrusted to 'plain' cooks.
[*English Recipes* (1935)]

Morrell, Lady Ottoline (1873–1938)
Bohemian patroness of the arts and writer

1. [Of her aims at Garsington Manor]
Gather here – all who have passion and who desire to create new conditions of life – new visions of art and literature.
And new magic worlds of poetry and music.
[*Ottoline at Garsington 1915–1918* (1974)]

Morris, Charles (1745–1838)
English songwriter and soldier

1. If one must have a villa in summer to dwell,
Oh, give me the sweet shady side of Pall Mall!
['The Contrast', song, 1840]

2. A house is much more to my taste than a tree,
And for groves, oh! a good grove of chimneys for me.
['Country and Town', song, 1840]

Morris, Desmond (1928–)
English biologist and anthropologist; broadcaster and writer

1. The Naked Ape.
[Title of book, 1967]

2. Clearly, then, the city is not a concrete jungle, it is a human zoo.
[*The Human Zoo* (1969), Introduction]

Morris, George Pope (1802–1864)
American poet, editor and dramatist

1. Woodman, spare that tree!
Touch not a single bough!
In youth it sheltered me,
And I'll protect it now.
['Woodman, Spare That Tree' (1830)]

Morris, James (later Jan Morris) (1926–)
British writer, especially of travel books; underwent sex change operation

1. There's romance for you! There's the lust and dark wine of Venice! No wonder George Eliot's husband fell into the Grand Canal.
[*Venice* (1960), closing words]

Morris, William (1834–1896)
English poet, designer, craftsman, Pre-Raphaelite, artist and socialist

1. Had she come all the way for this,
To part at last without a kiss?
Yea, had she borne the dirt and rain
That her own eyes might see him slain
Beside the haystack in the floods?
['The Haystack in the Floods' (1858)]

2. There was a knight came riding by
In early spring, when the roads were dry;
And he heard that lady sing at the noon,
'Two red roses across the moon.'...

3. And ever she sung from noon to noon,
'Two red roses across the moon.'
['Two Red Roses across the Moon' (1858)]

4. Nor for my words shall ye forget your tears,
Or hope again for aught that I can say,
The idle singer of an empty day...

5. Dreamer of dreams, born out of my due time,
Why should I strive to set the crooked straight?
Let it suffice me that my murmuring rhyme
Beats with light wing against the ivory gate,
Telling a tale not too importunate
To those who in the sleepy region stay,
Lulled by the singer of an empty day.
[*The Earthly Paradise* (1868–1870), 'An Apology']

6. Forget six counties overhung with smoke,
Forget the snorting steam and piston stroke,
Forget the spreading of the hideous town;
Think rather of the pack-horse on the down,
And dream of London, small and white and clean,
The clear Thames bordered by its gardens green.
[*The Earthly Paradise* (1868–1870), 'The Wanderers']

7. Love is enough: though the world be a-waning,
And the woods have no voice but the voice of complaining.
['Love is Enough' (1872)]

8. What is this, the sound and rumour? What is this that all men hear,
Like the wind in hollow valleys when the storm is drawing near,
Like the rolling on of ocean in the eventide of fear?
'Tis the people marching on.
[*Chants for Socialists* (1885), 'The March of the Workers']

9. But lo, the old inn, and the lights, and the fire,
And the fiddler's old tune and the shuffling of feet;
Soon for us shall be quiet and rest and desire,
And to-morrow's uprising to deeds shall be sweet.
['The Message of the March Winds' (1891)]

10. Midways of a polar garden,
In the happy poplar land
Did an ancient castle stand
With an old knight for a warden.

Many scarlet bricks there were
In its walls and old grey stone
Over which red apples shone
At the right time of the year.

On the bricks the green moss grew
Yellow lichen on the stone,
Over which red apples shone
Little war that castle knew.
[*Golden Wings*]

11. If you want a golden rule that will fit everybody, this is it:
Have nothing in your houses that you do not know to be useful, or believe to be beautiful.
[*Hopes and Fears for Art* (1882), 'The Beauty of Life']

12. All their devices for cheapening labour simply resulted in increasing the burden of labour.
[*News from Nowhere* (1891)]

13. [Last words]
I want to get Mumbo-Jumbo out of the world.
[Attr.]

Morrison, Danny (1950–)

1. Who here really believes that we can win the war through the ballot box? But will anyone here object if with a ballot box in this hand and an Armalite in this hand we take power in Ireland?
[Provisional Sinn Féin Conference, November 1981, quoted in Patrick Bishop and Eamonn Mallie, *The Provisional IRA*]

Morrison, Van (1945–)
Irish singer and songwriter

1. Recall all the dreams
That you once used to know
The things you've forgotten
That took you away
To pastures not greener but meaner.
['I'm Tired Joey Boy']

Morse, Samuel (1791–1872)
American painter, inventor of electric telegraphy and memoirist

1. What God hath wrought.
[First message sent on his telegraph, 1844]

Mortimer, John (1923–)
English lawyer, dramatist and novelist

1. No brilliance is needed in the law. Nothing but common sense, and relatively clean finger nails.
[*A Voyage Round My Father* (1971), I]

2. One enlightened member said that in the past the Garrick Club excluded lunatics, gays and women: now the first two classes have been let in there's no conceivable reason to bar the third.
[Attr.]

Morton, J.B. ('Beachcomber') (1893–1979)
English journalist, humorist and author

1. Hush, hush,
Nobody cares!
Christopher Robin
Has
Fallen
Down-
Stairs.
[*By the Way* (1931), 'Now We are Sick'. Cf. Milne: 8]

2. Vegetarians have wicked, shifty eyes, and laugh in a cold and calculating manner. They pinch little children, steal stamps, drink water, favour beards ... wheeze, squeak, drawl and maunder.
[*By the Way* (1931), '4 June']

3. Dr Strabismus (Whom God Preserve) of Utrecht is carrying out research work with a view to crossing salmon with mosquitoes. He says it will mean a bite every time for fishermen.
[*By the Way* (1931), 'January Tail-piece']

4. SIXTY HORSES WEDGED IN A CHIMNEY. The story to fit this sensational headline has not turned up yet.
[*The Best of Beachcomber*]

Morton, Rogers (1914–1979)

1. [Refusing to make any last-ditch attempts to rescue President Ford's re-election campaign, 1976]
I'm not going to re-arrange the furniture on the deck of the *Titanic*.
[Attr.]

Morton, Thomas (1764–1838)
English dramatist

1. Always ding, dinging Dame Grundy into my ears – what will Mrs Grundy zay? What will Mrs Grundy think?
[*Speed the Plough* (1798), I.i]

2. I eat well, and I drink well, and I sleep well – but that's all.
[*A Roland for an Oliver* (1819), I.i]

Moses, Grandma (Anna Mary Robertson Moses) (1860–1961)
American painter of primitives; began painting at the age of 73

1. If I didn't start painting, I would have raised chickens.
[In Aotto Kallir (ed.), *Grandma Moses, My Life's History*, 3]

2. [Of painting]
I don't advise any one to take it up as a business proposition, unless they really have talent, and are crippled so as to deprive them of physical labor.
[Attr.]

Mosley, Sir Oswald (1896–1980)
English politician; founder of British Union of Fascists 1932

1. I am not, and never have been, a man of the right. My position was on the left and is now in the centre of politics.
[Letter to *The Times*, 1968]

Motion, Andrew (1952–)
English writer, biographer and critic

1. [Describing the period spent researching Philip Larkin's biography]
At times it was driving me mad. I would go upstairs and say 'Christ, why can't he just cheer up?'
[*The Guardian*, 1993]

Motley, John Lothrop (1814–1877)
American diplomat and historian

1. [Of William of Orange]
As long as he lived, he was the guiding-star of a whole brave nation, and when he died the little children cried in the streets.
[*The Rise of the Dutch Republic* (1856), VI, 7]

2. Give us the luxuries of life, and we will dispense with its necessities.
[In Oliver Wendell Holmes, *Autocrat of the Breakfast Table* (1857–1858)]

Motteux, Peter Anthony (1660–1718)
French-born English translator; journalist and dramatist

1. The devil was sick, the devil a monk would be;
The devil was well, and the devil a monk he'd be.
[Translation of Rabelais, *Gargantua and Pantagruel* (1693)]

Mountbatten of Burma, First Earl (1900–1979)
British naval commander, grandson of Queen Victoria; last Viceroy of India (1947); killed by IRA bomb

1. In my experience, I have always found that you cannot have an efficient ship unless you have a happy ship, and you cannot have a happy ship unless you have an efficient ship. That is the way I intend to start this commission, and that is the way I intend to go on – with a happy and an efficient ship.
[Initial address to crew of *HMS Kelly*, 1939, adopted verbatim by Noel Coward in the script of the film *In Which We Serve*, 1942]

2. I can't think of a more wonderful thanksgiving for the life I have had than that everyone should be jolly at my funeral.
[TV interview, shown after his death in August 1979]

3. Edwina and I spent all our married lives getting into other people's beds.
[In P. Ziegler, *Mountbatten: the Official Biography* (1985)]

Mourie, Graham (1952–)

1. Nobody ever beats Wales at rugby, they just score more points.
[In Keating, *Caught by Keating*]

Mtshali, Oswald (1940–)
South African poet

1. I trudge the city pavements
side by side with madam
who shifts her handbag
from my side to the other.
[*Sounds of a Cowhide Drum* (1971), 'Always a Suspect']

2. Boom! Boom! Boom!
I hear it far in the northern skies,
a rumble and a roar of thunder...

Boom! Boom! Boom!
That is the sound of a cowhide drum –
the Voice of Mother Africa.
[*Sounds of a Cowhide Drum* (1971), 'Sounds of a Cowhide Drum']

3. Man is
a great wall builder...
but the wall
most impregnable
has a moat
flowing with fright
around his heart.
[*Sounds of a Cowhide Drum* (1971), 'Walls']

Muggeridge, Malcolm (1903–1990)
English prose writer and journalist

1. [Of Queen Elizabeth II]
Frumpish and banal.
[Magazine article, 1957]

2. An orgy looks particularly alluring seen through the mists of righteous indignation.
[*The Most of Malcolm Muggeridge* (1966), 'Dolce Vita in a Cold Climate']

3. The orgasm has replaced the Cross as the focus of longing and the image of fulfilment.
[*The Most of Malcolm Muggeridge* (1966), 'Down with Sex']

4. Macmillan seemed, in his very person, to embody the national decay he supposed himself to be confuting. He exuded a flavour of moth-balls.
[*Tread Softly For You Tread on My Jokes* (1966)]

5. [Of Evelyn Waugh]
He looked, I decided, like a letter delivered to the wrong address.
[*Tread Softly For You Tread on My Jokes* (1966)]

6. [Of Anthony Eden]
He was not only a bore; he bored for England.
[*Tread Softly For You Tread on My Jokes* (1966)]

7. I have had my [TV] aerials removed; it's the moral equivalent of a prostate operation.
[In *Radio Times*, 1981]

8. [On *Punch*, which he once edited]
Very much like the Church of England. It is doctrinally inexplicable but it goes on.
[Attr.]

Muir, Edwin (1887–1959)
Scottish poet, critic, translator, novelist and autobiographer

1. There is a road that turning always
Cuts off the country of Again.
Archers stand there on every side
And as it runs Time's deer is slain,
And lies where it has lain.
['The Road' (1937)]

2. We have seen
Good men made evil wrangling with the evil,
Straight minds grown crooked fighting crooked minds.
Our peace betrayed us; we betrayed our peace.
Look at it well. This was the good town once.
['The Good Town' (1949)]

3. Oh these deceits are strong almost as life.
Last night I dreamt I was in the labyrinth,
And woke far on. I did not know the place.
['The Labyrinth' (1949)]

4. See him, the gentle Bible beast,
With lacquered hoofs and curling mane,
His wondering journey from the East
Half done, between the rock and plain.
['The Toy Horse' (1949)]

5. Over the sound a ship so slow would pass
That in the black hill's gloom it seemed to lie
The evening sound was smooth like sunken glass
And time seemed finished ere the ship passed by.
['Childhood' (1952)]

6. Here at the wayside station, as many a morning,
I watch the smoke torn from the fumy engine
Crawling across the field in serpent sorrow.
['The Wayside Station' (1952)]

7. The heart could never speak
But that the Word was spoken.
We hear the heart break
Here with hearts unbroken.
Time, teach us the art
That breaks and heals the heart.
['The heart could never speak' (1960)]

8. I think it possible that all Scots are illegitimate, Scotsmen being so mean and Scotswomen so generous.
[*Scottish Journey* (1935)]

Muir, Frank (1920–)
English writer, humorist and broadcaster

1. I've examined your son's head, Mr Glum, and there's nothing there.
[*Take It from Here*, BBC radio programme, 1957, with Dennis Norden]

2. It has been said that a bride's attitude towards her betrothed can be summed up in three words: Aisle. Altar. Hymn.
[*Upon My Word!*, 'A Jug of Wine', with Dennis Norden]

3. Another fact of life that will not have escaped you is that, in this country, the twenty-four-hour strike is like the twenty-four-hour flu. You have to reckon on it lasting at least five days.
[*You Can't Have Your Kayak and Heat It*, 'Great Expectations', with Dennis Norden]

4. Dogs, like horses, are quadrupeds. That is to say, they have four rupeds, one at each corner, on which they walk.
[*You Can't Have Your Kayak and Heat It*, 'Ta-ra-ra-boom-de-ay!', with Dennis Norden]

Muldoon, Paul (1951–)
Poet and radio producer, born in Northern Ireland

1. I asked her once, 'Are you asleep?'
She said, 'I am. I am.'
[*Mules* (1977), 'The Girls in the Poolroom']

Mulkerns, Val (1925–)
Irish author and journalist

1. On the last day of his life Dan decided that women who haunted you were not those whom you had enjoyed or even known remotely well, but strangers who had at one time or another troubled you with the most transient flicker of desire.
[*Loser*]

Müller, Wilhelm (1794–1827)
German lyric poet; philologist, historian, Hellenophile and librarian

1. *Vom Abendrot zum Morgenlicht*
Ward mancher Kopf zum Greise.
Wer glaubt's? Und meiner ward es nicht
Auf dieser ganzen Reise.
Between sunset and sunrise
Many a head has turned grey.
Who would believe it? And mine has not changed
Throughout this long journey.
[*Die Winterreise* (*The Winter Journey*, 1823–1824), 'Der greise Kopf' ('The Grey Head')]

Mumford, Ethel (1878–1940)
American novelist, dramatist and humorist

1. In the midst of life we are in debt.
[*Altogether New Cynic's Calendar* (1907)]
2. Don't take the will for the deed; get the deed.
[In Cowan, *The Wit of Women*]
3. Knowledge is power if you know it about the right person.
[In Cowan, *The Wit of Women*]

Murasaki, Shikibu (c. 975–1025)
Japanese woman author of classic prose novels

1. Those stories do recount what life has been since time immemorial while *The Chronicles of Japan* depicts only incidents thereof. It is in the former that the principles are treated in detail.
[*The Tale of Genji* (c. 1000)]
2. A piece of calligraphy, which, shallow as it is, indulges in cursive brushwork betraying its author's affectation, will have every appearance of adroitness and artistic accomplishment to the rash eye, but one which has achieved artistic propriety and subtlety will prove to be much superior to and more appealing than the other, though, at first sight, it may seem unattractive. If one's mind is struck thus by such a trivial matter, then how much more so should it be when confronted with a facile show of love accompanied by artificial coquetry to suit the occasion. One could never depend on such love.
[*The Tale of Genji* (c. 1000)]

Murdoch, Iris (1919–)
Irish-born British novelist, philosopher and dramatist

1. 'What are you famous *for*?'
'For nothing. I am just famous.'
[*The Flight from the Enchanter* (1955)]
2. Only lies and evil come from letting people off.
[*A Severed Head* (1961)]
3. He lives in a sort of rosy haze with Jesus and Mary and Buddha and Shiva and the Fisher King all chasing round and round dressed up as people in Chelsea.
[*The Black Prince* (1973), I]
4. He led a double life. Did that make him a liar? He did not feel a liar. He was a man of two truths.
[*The Sacred and Profane Love Machine* (1974)]
5. The cry of equality pulls everyone down.
[*The Observer*, 1987, in Jeffrey Care (ed.), *Sayings of the Eighties* (1989)]

Murdoch, Rupert (1931–)
Australian newspaperman, publisher and international businessman

1. [On the publication of the *Kinsey Report*, a survey of human sexual behaviour]
Family newspapers like ourselves gain great kudos leaving this muck alone.
[Telegram sent to the *Adelaide News*, 1953]
2. I think the important thing is that there be plenty of newspapers with plenty of people controlling them so there can be choice.
[Film interview, 1967]
3. Monopoly is a terrible thing, till you have it.
[*The New Yorker*, 1979]

Murdoch, Sir Walter Logie Forbes (1874–1970)
Scots-born academic, writer, essayist and broadcaster who lived and worked in Western Australia

1. A second-hand bookshop is the sign and symbol of a civilized community ... and the number and quality of these shops give you the exact measure of a city's right to be counted among the great cities of the world ... Show me a city's second-hand bookshops, and I will tell you what manner of citizens dwell there, and of what ancestry sprung.
[*Collected Essays* (1940)]
2. [On being asked officially if the new Western Australian university might be named after him]
Yes, if it's a good one.
[Remark, communicated to Barbara, Lady Murdoch]

Murphy, Arthur (1727–1805)
Irish-born British actor, dramatist, lawyer and author

1. Above the vulgar flight of common souls.
[*Zenobia*, V]

Murphy, C.W. (1875–1913)
British songwriter

1. Has anybody here seen Kelly?
Kelly from the Isle of Man?
['Has Anybody Here Seen Kelly?', song, 1909]

Murray, David (1888–1962)
British novelist and journalist

1. A reporter is a man who has renounced everything in life but the world, the flesh, and the devil.
[*The Observer*, 'Sayings of the Week', 1931]

Murray, Gilbert (1866–1957)
Australian classical scholar and writer

1. [Replying to Robert Graves, who asked him whether he was trying to avoid the flowers or the squares on the rug as he walked up and down]
No, it's not the flowers or the squares, it's a habit that I have got into of doing things in sevens. I take seven steps,

you see, then I change direction and go another seven steps, then I turn round.
[In Robert Graves, *Goodbye to All That* (1929)]

Murray, Jenni (1950–)
English radio and television presenter

1. Marriage is an insult and women should not touch it.
[Attr.]

Murray, Les A. (1938–)
Australian philosophical poet and prose writer

1. Men must have legends, else they die of strangeness.
['Noonday Axemen' (1965)]

2. The word goes round Repin's, the murmur goes round
Lorenzini's,
At Tattersall's, men look up from sheets of numbers,
The Stock Exchange scribblers forget the chalk in their hands
And men with bread in their pockets leave the Greek Club:
There's a fellow crying in Martin Place. They can't stop him.
['An Absolutely Ordinary Rainbow' (1969)]

3. In the defiance of fashion is the beginning of character.
[*The Boy who Stole the Funeral* (1979)]

4. The trouble
with being best man is, you don't get a chance to prove it.
[*The Boy who Stole the Funeral* (1979)]

5. Before the coming of the endless town
When I was alive, it wasn't far to go
To places where houses still stood well apart,
To places, indeed, where they stood so far apart
That from the highest hill you couldn't see one.
The idea will be quite alien, I know.
['When I was Alive']

6. Never trust a lean meritocracy
nor the leader who has been lean;
only the lifelong big have the knack of wedding
greatness with balance.

Never wholly trust the fat man
who lurks in the lean achiever
and the defeated, yearning to get out.
['Quintets for Robert Morley']

7. Much of the hostility to Australia ... shown by English people above a certain class can be traced to the fact that we are, to a large extent, the poor who got away.
[*Sydney Morning Herald*, 1974]

Murrow, Edward R. (1908–1965)
American reporter, war correspondent and news analyst

1. [Of Churchill]
He mobilized the English language and sent it into battle to steady his fellow countrymen and hearten those Europeans upon whom the long dark night of tyranny had descended.
[Broadcast, 1954]

Musset, Alfred de (1810–1857)
French Romantic poet, dramatist and novelist

1. *Mon verre n'est pas grand mais je bois dans mon verre.*
My glass is not large, but at least it is my own.
['La Coupe et les lèvres' (1832)]

2. *Malgré moi l'infini me tourmente.*
In spite of myself, infinity torments me.
['L'Espoir en Dieu' (1838)]

3. *Les plus désespérés sont les chants les plus beaux*
Et j'en sais d'immortels qui sont de purs sanglots.
The most despairing songs are the most beautiful, and I know of immortal ones which are pure tears.
['La Nuit de mai' (1840)]

4. *Le seul bien qui me rest au monde*
Est d'avoir quelquefois pleuré.
The only good things the world has left me are the times that I have wept.
['Tristesse' (1841)]

5. *Les grands artistes n'ont pas de patrie.*
Great artists have no homeland.
[*Lorenzaccio* (1834), I.v]

6. *On ne badine pas avec l'amour.*
One Must not Trifle with Love.
[Title of comedy, 1834]

Mussolini, Benito (1883–1945)
Italian fascist dictator; Prime Minister of Italy 1922–1943

1. *Ci sono le libertà; la libertà non è mai esistita.*
There are freedoms; freedom has never existed.
[Speech to the Lower House, 1923]

2. *E' l'aratro che traccia il solco, ma è la spada che lo difende.*
The plough traces the furrow, but it is the sword that defends it.
[Speech, 1934]

3. *Per noi fascisti le frontiere, tutte le frontiere, sono sacre. Non si discutono: si defendono.*
For us fascists, frontiers, all frontiers, are sacred. We do not dispute them: we defend them.
[Speech to the Lower House, 1938]

4. *Il pittoresco ci ha fregati per tre secoli.*
The picturesque has taken us in for three centuries.
[Speech to the PNF Congress (National Fascist Party), 1938]

5. *In un uomo di stato, la cosidetta 'cultura' è in fin dei conti un lusso inutile.*
In a statesman so-called 'culture' is, after all, a useless luxury.
[*Il Populo d'Italia*, 1919, 'Imponete una disciplina ('Enforce discipline')]

6. Fascism is not an article for export.
[Article in the German press, 1932]

7. [Of Hitler]
That garrulous monk.
[In W.S. Churchill, *The Second World War* (1948–1954)]

8. [On Hitler's seizing power]
Fascism is a religion; the twentieth century will be known in history as the century of Fascism.
[In George Seldes, *Sawdust Caesar*, 24]

9. We cannot change our policy now. After all, we are not political whores.
[In Alan Bullock, *Hitler*, 8]

10. I should be pleased, I suppose, that Hitler has carried out a revolution on our lines. But they are Germans. So they will end by ruining our idea.
[In C. Hibbert, *Benito Mussolini*, II, 1]

11. [Maxim to which he attributed his political success]
Keep your heart a desert.
[Attr.]

Mussolini, Vittorio (1915–)
Son of Benito Mussolini

1. [Comment on a bombing raid in Abyssinia]
I dropped an aerial torpedo right in the centre, and the group opened up like a flowering rose. It was most entertaining.
[*Voli sulle Ambe* (1937)]

Nabokov, Vladimir (1899–1977)
Russian-born American novelist, short-story writer, poet, translator and critic

1. [Remark 'of a celebrated old critic']
Poor Knight! he really had two periods, the first – a dull man writing broken English, the second – a broken man writing dull English.
[*The Real Life of Sebastian Knight* (1941), 1]

2. Yes, I was right, spring and summer did happen in Cambridge almost every year (that mysterious 'almost' was singularly pleasing).
[*The Real Life of Sebastian Knight* (1941), 5]

3. Lolita, light of my life, fire of my loins.
[*Lolita* (1955), 1]

4. Like so many ageing college people, Pnin had long ceased to notice the existence of students on the campus.
[*Pnin* (1957), 3, 6]

5. Discussion in class, which means letting twenty young blockheads and two cocky neurotics discuss something that neither their teacher nor they know.
[*Pnin* (1957), 6, 10]

6. A novelist is, like all mortals, more fully at home on the surface of the present than in the ooze of the past.
[*Strong Opinions* (1973), 20]

Nairn, Ian (1930–1983)
English writer on architecture and journalist

1. If what is called development is allowed to multiply at the present rate, then by the end of the century Great Britain will consist of isolated oases of preserved monuments in a desert of wire, concrete roads, cosy plots and bungalows ... Upon this new Britain the *Review* bestows a name in the hope that it will stick – SUBTOPIA.
[*Architectural Review*, 1955]

Nairne, Carolina, Baroness (1766–1845)
Scottish song and ballad writer

1. [Referring to Bonnie Prince Charlie]
Better lo'ed ye canna be,
Will ye no come back again?
[*Lays from Strathearn* (1846), 'Bonnie Charlie's now awa!']

2. Wha'll buy my caller herrin'?
They're bonnie fish and halesome farin'.
[*Lays from Strathearn* (1846), 'Caller Herrin'']

3. [Referring to Bonnie Prince Charlie]
Charlie is my darling, my darling, my darling,
Charlie is my darling, the young Chevalier.
[*Lays from Strathearn* (1846), 'Charlie is my Darling'. Cf. Robert Burns: 109 and Hogg: 3]

4. [A romantic glorification of the 1745 Jacobite Rebellion]
Wi' a hundred pipers an' a', an' a'.
[*Lays from Strathearn* (1846), 'The Hundred Pipers']

5. I'm wearin' awa'.
To the land o' the leal.
[*Lays from Strathearn* (1846), 'The Land o' the Leal']

Napier, Sir Charles James (1782–1853)
English general and governor of Sind, 1843–47

1. *Peccavi!*
I have sinned.
[Despatch after occupation of Sind, 1843]

Napoleon I (1769–1821)
Emperor of the French (1804–15) and much of Europe; brilliant general and reforming administrator

1. *A la guerre, les trois quarts sont des affaires morales, la balance des forces réelles n'est que pour un autre quart.*
In war, three-quarters depends on matters of character and morale; the balance of manpower and equipment counts only for the remaining quarter.
[*Correspondance de Napoléon I* (1854–1869), 27 August 1808]

2. *Quant au courage moral, il avait trouvé fort rare, disait-il, celui de deux heures après minuit; c'est-à-dire le courage de l'improviste.*
As for moral courage, he said he had very rarely encountered two o'clock in the morning courage; that is, the courage of the unprepared.
[*Mémorial de Sainte Hélène*, December 1815]

3. [On the introduction of the metric system]
Les savants conçurent une autre idée tout-à-fait étrangère au bienfait de l'unité de poids et de mesures; ils y adaptèrent la numération décimale, en prenant le mètre pour unité; ils supprimèrent tous les nombres complexes. Rien n'est plus contraire à l'organisation de l'esprit, de la mémoire et de l'imagination ... Le nouveau système de poids et mesures sera un sujet d'embarras et de difficultés pour plusieurs générations ... C'est tourmenter le peuple par des vétilles!!!
The scientists had another idea which was completely at odds with the benefits to be derived from the standardization of weights and measures; they imposed the decimal system, taking the metre as a unit, and suppressed all complicated numbers. Nothing is more contrary to the organization of the mind, the memory, and the imagination ... The new system of weights and measures will be a stumbling block and a source of difficulties for several generations to come ... It's just tormenting the people with trivialities!!!
[*Memoires ... écrits à Ste-Hélène* (1823–25), IV, xvi, 4]

4. [Speech, Battle of the Pyramids, 1798]
Soldats, songez que, du haut de ces pyramides quarante siècles vous contemplent.
Think, soldiers, from the top of these pyramids, forty centuries are looking down upon you.
[In Gourgaud, *Mémoires, Guerre d'orient*, I]

5. France has more need of me than I have need of France.
[Speech, 1813]

6. *Du sublime au ridicule il n'y a qu'un pas.*
It is only one step from the sublime to the ridiculous.
[In De Pradt, *Histoire de l'Ambassade dans le grand-duché de Varsovie en 1812* (1815). Cf. Paine: 10]

7. [Of his generals]
I made most of mine *de la boue* [out of mud]. Wherever I found talent and courage, I rewarded it. My principle was *la carrière ouverte aux talens* [*sic*] [career open to talent], without asking whether there were any quarters of nobility to show.
[In O'Meara, *Napoleon in Exile* (1822), I]

8. *Tout soldat français porte dans sa giberne le bâton de maréchal de France.*
Every French soldier carries a French marshal's baton in his knapsack.
[In E. Blaze, *La Vie Militaire sous l'Empire*, I, v]

9. [Remark made while visiting the tomb of the philosopher Jean-Jacques Rousseau, whose theories had influenced the French Revolution]
Maybe it would have been better if neither of us had been born.
[In W. Durant, *The Story of Civilisation*, II]

10. [Remark made at the Battle of Borodino, 1812; the Battle of Austerlitz, 1805, was Napoleon's great victory over the Russians and Austrians]
There rises the sun of Austerlitz.
[In W. Durant, *The Story of Civilisation*, II]

11. Charles I perished for resisting, Louis XVI for not resisting.
[In *The Guardian*, 1993]

12. Not tonight, Josephine!
[Attr.]

13. [To Josephine in 1809, on divorcing her for reasons of state]
I still love you, but in politics there is no heart, only head.
[Attr.]

14. [Referring to the carnage at the Battle of Borodino, 1812]
It's the most beautiful battlefield I've ever seen.
[Attr.]

15. [Question of potential officers]
Has he luck?
[Attr.]

16. An army marches on its stomach.
[Attr.]

17. [Answering his brother Joseph, King of Spain, who had asked whether he had ever been hit by a cannonball]
The bullet that is to kill me has not yet been moulded.
[Attr.]

18. Oh well, no matter what happens, there's always death.
[Attr.]

Napoleon III (Charles Louis Napoleon Bonaparte) (1808–1873)
Emperor of the French (1852–70); coup leader; nephew of Napoleon I

1. [On being asked to ban smoking]
This vice brings in one hundred million francs in taxes every year. I will certainly forbid it at once – as soon as you can name a virtue that brings in as much revenue.
[In H. Hoffmeister, *Anekdotenschatz*]

2. [After the narrow and bloody French victory at Solferino, 1859]
I don't care for war, there's far too much luck in it for my liking.
[In E. Crankshaw, *The Fall of the House of Habsburg*]

Narayan, R.K. (1907–)
Indian novelist, essayist and translator of Hindu scriptures

1. English is a very adaptable language. And it's so transparent it can take on the tint of any country.
[Radio conversation, 1968]

Narváez, Ramón María (1800–1868)
Spanish general and statesman

1. [On his deathbed, when asked by a priest if he forgave his enemies]
I do not have to forgive my enemies, I have had them all shot.
[Attr.]

Nash, Ogden (1902–1971)
American humorous poet

1. Let us pause to consider the English
Who when they pause to consider themselves they get all reticently thrilled and tinglish.
Englishmen are distinguished by their traditions and ceremonials,
And also by their affection for their colonies and their condescension to their colonials.
[*Collected Works* (1929), 'England Expects']

2. One would be in less danger
From the wiles of a stranger
If one's own kin and kith
Were more fun to be with.
[*Hard Lines* (1931), 'Family Court']

3. Candy
Is dandy
But liquor
Is quicker.
[*Hard Lines* (1931), 'Reflections on Ice-Breaking']

4. When I consider how my life is spent,
I hardly ever repent.
[*Hard Lines* (1931), 'Reminiscent Reflection']

5. The turtle lives 'twixt plated decks
Which practically conceal its sex.
I think it clever of the turtle
In such a fix to be so fertile.
[*Hard Lines* (1931), 'The Turtle']

6. The cow is of the bovine ilk;
One end is moo, the other, milk.
[*Free Wheeling* (1931), 'The Cow']

7. A bit of talcum
Is always walcum.
[*Free Wheeling* (1931), 'Reflection on Babies']

8. Children aren't happy with nothing to ignore,
And that's what parents were created for.
[*Happy Days* (1933), 'The Parent']

9. Any kiddie in school can love like a fool,
But hating, my boy, is an art.
[*Happy Days* (1933), 'Plea for Less Malice Toward None']

10. I think that I shall never see
A billboard lovely as a tree.
Indeed, unless the billboards fall
I'll never see a tree at all.
[*Happy Days* (1933), 'Song of the Open Road'. Cf. Kilmer: 1]

11. Home is heaven and orgies are vile
But you need an orgy, once in a while.
[*The Primrose Path* (1935), 'Home, 99.44/100% Sweet Home']

12. There was a young belle of old Natchez
Whose garments were always in patchez.
When comment arose
On the state of her clothes,
She drawled, When Ah itchez, Ah scratchez!
[*I'm a Stranger Here Myself* (1935), 'Requiem']

13. The song of canaries
Never varies,
And when they're moulting
They're pretty revolting.
[*The Face is Familiar* (1940), 'The Canary']

14. I would live my life in nonchalance and insouciance
Were it not for making a living, which is rather a nouciance.
[*The Face is Familiar* (1940), 'Introspective Reflection']

15. He who is ridden by a conscience
Worries about a lot of nonscience;
He without benefit of scruples
His fun and income soon quadruples.
[*The Face is Familiar* (1940), 'Reflection on the Fallibility of Nemesis']

16. Sure, deck your lower limbs in pants;
Yours are the limbs, my sweeting.
You look divine as you advance–
Have you seen yourself retreating?
[*The Face is Familiar* (1940), 'What's the Use?']

17. Women would rather be right than reasonable.
[*Good Intentions* (1942), 'Frailty, Thy Name is a Misnomer']

18. Beneath this slab
John Brown is stowed.
He watched the ads,
And not the road.
[*Good Intentions* (1942), 'Lather as You Go']

19. Do you think my mind is maturing late,
Or simply rotted early?
[*Good Intentions* (1942), 'Lines on Facing Forty']

20. If I could but spot a conclusion, I should race to it.
[*The Private Dining Room and Other New Verses* (1952), 'All, All Are Gone, The Old Familiar Quotations']

21. A door is what a dog is perpetually on the wrong side of.
[*The Private Dining Room and Other New Verses* (1952), 'A Dog's Best Friend Is His Illiteracy']

22. I am a conscientious man, when I throw rocks at seabirds I leave no tern unstoned.
[*The Private Dining Room and Other New Verses* (1952), 'Everybody's Mind to Me a Kingdom Is']

23. You two can be what you like, but since I am the big fromage in this family, I prefer to think of myself as the Gorgon Zola.
[*The Private Dining Room and Other New Verses* (1952), 'Medusa and the Mot Juste']

24. I prefer to forget both pairs of glasses and pass my declining years
saluting strange women and grandfather clocks.
[*The Private Dining Room and Other New Verses* (1952), 'Peekaboo, I Almost See You']

Nashe, Thomas (1567–1601)
English dramatist, satirist and pamphleteer; author of first picaresque romance in English

1. Beauty is but a flower,
Which wrinkles will devour.
Brightness falls from the air;
Queens have died young and fair;
Dust hath closed Helen's eye:
I am sick, I must die.
Lord, have mercy on us...

2. Spring, the sweet spring, is the year's pleasant king.
Then blooms each thing, then maids dance in a ring;
Cold doth not sting, the pretty birds do sing
Cuckoo, jug-jug, pu-we, to-witta-woo...

3. From winter, plague and pestilence, good Lord, deliver us!
[*Summer's Last Will and Testament* (c. 1593), Song]

4. Philemon, a Comick Poet, died with extreme laughter at the conceit of seeing an asse eat figs.
[*The Unfortunate Traveller* (1594)]

5. O, tis a precious apothegmaticall Pedant, who will finde matter inough to dilate a whole day of the first invention of Fy, fa, fum, I smell the bloud of an English-man.
[*Have with you to Saffron-walden* (1596). Cf. Shakespeare, *King Lear*: 51]

Navratilova, Martina (1956–)
Czech championship tennis player, now naturalized American

1. Do you know the difference between involvement and commitment? Think of ham and eggs. The chicken is involved. The pig is committed.
[*The Observer*, 1982, in Jeffrey Care (ed.), *Sayings of the Eighties* (1989)]

Naylor, James Ball (1860–1945)
American physician and writer

1. King David and King Solomon
Led merry, merry lives,
With many, many lady friends
And many, many wives;
But when old age crept over them,
With many, many qualms,
King Solomon wrote the Proverbs
And King David wrote the Psalms.
['King David and King Solomon' (1935)]

Neale, John Mason (1818–1866)
English divine and hymn writer

1. Good King Wenceslas looked out,
On the Feast of Stephen;
When the snow lay round about,
Deep and crisp and even...

2. Hither, page, and stand by me,
If thou know'st it, telling,
Yonder peasant, who is he?
Where and what his dwelling?
[*Carols for Christmastide* (1853), 'Good King Wenceslas']

3. Jerusalem the golden,
With milk and honey blest,
Beneath thy contemplation
Sink heart and voice oppress.
['Jerusalem the Golden' (1858)]

4. Art thou weary, art thou languid,
Art thou sore distressed?
[Hymn]

5. If I ask Him to receive me,
Will he say me nay?
[Hymn]

Neaves, Charles, Lord (1800–1876)

1. We can't for a certainty tell
What mirth may molest us on Monday;
But, at least, to begin the week well,
Let us all be unhappy on Sunday.
[*Songs and Verses*]

Needham, Joseph (1900–1995)
British biochemist, science historian and orientalist

1. *Laboratorium est oratorium*. The place where we do our scientific work is a place of prayer.
[In Alan L. Mackay, *The Harvest of a Quiet Eye* (1977)]

Needham, Richard J. (1942–)
Canadian columnist

1. I love libraries, but I will be damned if I will ever walk into a 'Resource Centre.'
[*The Wit and Wisdom of Richard Needham* (1979)]

Neilson, John Shaw (1872–1942)
Australian lyrical poet

1. Fear it has faded and the night:
The bells all peal the hour of nine.
The schoolgirls hastening through the light
Touch the unknowable Divine.
['Schoolgirls Hastening' (1922)]

2. Oh 'twas a poor country, in Autumn it was bare,
The only green was the cutting grass and the sheep found little there,
Oh, the thin wheat and the brown oats were never two foot high,
But down in the poor country no pauper was I...
['The Poor, Poor Country' (1927)]

3. Shyly the silver-hatted mushrooms make
Soft entrance through,
And undelivered lovers, half awake,
Hear noises in the dew.
[*Collected Poems* (1934), 'May']

4. Work should begin with wine and generous joking,
And in the place of penalties for smoking
Let us have fines for platitudes and croaking.
[*Collected Poems* (1934), 'To a Blonde Typist']

5. The young girl stood beside me. I
Saw not what her young eyes could see;
– A light, she said, not of the sky
Lives somewhere in the Orange Tree...

6. – Listen! the young girl said. For all
Your hapless talk you fail to see
There is a light, a step, a call
This evening on the Orange Tree.
['The Orange Tree']

Nelson, Horatio (Lord Nelson) (1758–1805)
English admiral, noted for his naval victories in the Napoleonic wars

1. I believe my arrival was most welcome, not only to the Commander of the Fleet but almost to every individual in it; and when I came to explain to them the 'Nelson touch', it was like an electric shock. Some shed tears, all approved – 'It was new – it was singular – it was simple!' ... Some may be Judas's; but the majority are much pleased with my commanding them.
[Letter to Lady Hamilton, 1805. Cf. Newbolt: 3]

2. [Advice to a young midshipman, 1793]
First, you must always implicitly obey orders, ... Secondly, you must consider every man your enemy who speaks ill of your king: and, thirdly, you must hate a Frenchman as you hate the devil.
[In Robert Southey, *The Life of Nelson* (1860 edition), 3]

3. [At the Battle of Cape St Vincent, 1797]
Westminster Abbey or victory.
[In Robert Southey, *The Life of Nelson* (1860 edition), 4]

4. [After attempt on Santa Cruz, 1797]
I know I must lose my right arm, so the sooner it is off the better.
[In Robert Southey, *The Life of Nelson* (1860 edition), 4]

5. [On the eve of the Battle of the Nile, 1798]
Before this time to-morrow I shall have gained a peerage, or Westminster Abbey.
[In Robert Southey, *The Life of Nelson* (1860 edition), 5]

6. [At the Battle of the Nile, 1798]
Victory is not a name strong enough for such a scene.
[In Robert Southey, *The Life of Nelson* (1860 edition), 5]

7. [At the Battle of Copenhagen, 1801]
It is warm work; and this day may be the last to any of us at a moment. But mark you! I would not be elsewhere for thousands.
[In Robert Southey, *The Life of Nelson* (1860 edition), 7]

8. [At the Battle of Copenhagen, 1801]
Leave off action? Now, damn me if I do! ... I have only one eye – I have a right to be blind sometimes ... I really do not see the signal! ... Damn the signal!
[In Robert Southey, *The Life of Nelson* (1860 edition), 7. Cf. Newbolt: 2]

9. [To his midshipmen]
Recollect that you must be a seaman to be an officer; and also, that you cannot be a good officer without being a gentleman.
[In Robert Southey, *The Life of Nelson* (1860 edition), 8]

10. [To Lady Hamilton at Merton, 1805]
Brave Emma! – Good Emma! – If there were more Emmas there would be more Nelsons.
[In Robert Southey, *The Life of Nelson* (1860 edition), 9]

11. [Before Trafalgar, 1805]
Friday night, (September 13), at half-past ten, I drove from dear, dear Merton; where I left all which I hold dear in this world, to go to serve my king and country.
[In Robert Southey, *The Life of Nelson* (1860 edition), 9]

12. [When asked to cover the stars on his uniform]
In honour I gained them, and in honour I will die with them.
[In Robert Southey, *The Life of Nelson* (1860 edition), 9]

13. [At the Battle of Trafalgar, 1805, as he and Hardy both escaped injury]
This is too warm work, Hardy, to last long.
[In Robert Southey, *The Life of Nelson* (1860 edition), 9]

14. [Nelson's last signal at the Battle of Trafalgar, 1805]
England expects every man to do his duty.
[In Robert Southey, *The Life of Nelson* (1860 edition), 9. Cf. Robert E. Lee: 2]

15. [Dying words at the Battle of Trafalgar, 1805]
Take care of poor Lady Hamilton.
[In Robert Southey, *The Life of Nelson* (1860 edition), 9]

16. [Last words at the Battle of Trafalgar, 1805]
Thank God, I have done my duty.
[In Robert Southey, *The Life of Nelson* (1860 edition), 9]

Nero (Nero Claudius Caesar) (37–68)
Roman emperor from 54 to 68, noted for his despotism and persecution of Christians

1. *Qualis artifex pereo!*
What a great artist dies with me!
[In Suetonius, *Lives of the Caesars*, 'Nero']

Nerval, Gérard de (1808–1855)
French poet, noted for his sonnets, and prose writer

1. *Je suis le ténébreux, – le veuf, – l'inconsolé,*
Le Prince d'Aquitaine à la tour abolie:
Ma seule étoile est morte, et mon luth constellé
Porte le soleil noir de la mélancolie.
I am the dark one, the bereaved, the unconsoled, the prince of Aquitaine, with the ruined tower. My only star is dead, and my star-strewn lute carries the black sun of melancholy.
[*Les Chimères* (1854), 'El Desdichado']

2. *Dieu est mort! le ciel est vide–*
Pleurez! enfants, vous n'avez plus de père.
God is dead! Heaven is empty – Weep, children, you no longer have a father.
['Le Christ aux Oliviers', Epigraph]

3. [Justifying his habit of walking a lobster, on a lead, in the gardens of the Palais Royal]
En quoi un homard est-il plus ridicule qu'un chien ... ou [que] toute autre bête dont on se fait suivre? J'ai le goût des homards, qui sont tranquilles, sérieux, savent les secrets de la mer, n'aboient pas et n'avalent pas la monade des gens comme les chiens, si antipathiques à Goethe, lequel pourtant n'était pas fou.
Why is a lobster any more ridiculous than a dog ... or any other creature one chooses to take for a walk? I have a liking for lobsters: they are peaceful and solemn, they know the secrets of the sea, they do not bark, and they do not eat into the essential privacy of one's soul the way dogs do. And Goethe had an aversion to dogs, and he was not mad.
[In T. Gautier, *Portraits et Souvenirs Littéraires* (1875)]

Nevill, Lady Dorothy (c. 1825–c. 1905)
Victorian traveller and writer

1. Guinea-pig, there's a tasty dish for you, but it was always a job to make your cook do it. They want bakin' same as the gipsies serve the hedgehogs. I tried eatin' donkey too, but I had to stop that, for it made me stink.
[In E.F. Benson, *As We Were* (1930)]

Nevins, Allan (1890–1971)
American historian; writer and journalist

1. The former allies had blundered in the past offering Germany too little, and offering even that too late, until finally Nazi Germany had become a menace to all mankind.
[In *Current History*, May 1935]

Newbold, H.L.

1. Sex is between the ears as well as between the legs.
[*Mega-Nutrients for Your Nerves*]

Newbolt, Sir Henry John (1862–1938)
English poet, man of letters and lawyer

1. Admirals all, for England's sake,
Honour be yours, and fame!
And honour, as long as waves shall break,
To Nelson's peerless name!...

2. He clapped the glass to his sightless eye,
And 'I'm damned if I see it', he said.
[*Admirals All and Other Verses* (1897), 'Admirals All'. Cf. Nelson: 8]

3. Whether their fame centuries long should ring
They cared not over-much,
But cared greatly to serve God and the King,
And keep the Nelson touch.
[*Admirals All and Other Verses* (1897), 'Minora Sidera'. Cf. Nelson: 1]

4. Drake he's in his hammock an' a thousand mile away
(Capten, art tha' sleepin' there below?)...

5. 'Take my drum to England, hang et by the shore,
Strike et when your powder's runnin' low;
If the Dons sight Devon, I'll quit the port o' Heaven,
An' drum them up the Channel as we drummed them long ago.'...

6. Drake he's in his hammock till the great Armadas come.
(Capten, art tha sleepin' there below?)
Slung atween the round shot, listenin' for the drum,
An' dreamin' arl the time o' Plymouth Hoe.
Call him on the deep sea, call him up the Sound,
Call him when ye sail to meet the foe;
Where the old trade's plyin' an' the old flag flyin'
They shall find him ware an' wakin', as they found him long ago.
['Drake's Drum' (1897)]

7. Now the sunset breezes shiver,
And she's fading down the river,
But in England's song for ever
She's the Fighting Téméraire.
['The Fighting Téméraire' (1897)]

8. To set the cause above renown,
To love the game beyond the prize,
To honour, while you strike him down,
The foe that comes with fearless eyes.
[*The Island Race* (1898), 'Clifton Chapel']

9. 'Ye have robb'd,' said he, 'ye have slaughter'd and made an end,
Take your ill-got plunder, and bury the dead.'
[*The Island Race* (1898), 'He Fell Among Thieves']

10. There's a breathless hush in the Close to-night–
Ten to make and the match to win–
A bumping pitch and a blinding light,
An hour to play and the last man in.
And it's not for the sake of a ribboned coat,
Or the selfish hope of a season's fame,
But his Captain's hand on his shoulder smote–
'Play up! play up! and play the game!'...

11. But the voice of the schoolboy rallies the ranks:
'Play up! play up! and play the game!'
[*The Island Race* (1898), 'Vitaï Lampada']

Newby, P.H. (1918–)
English novelist and former Director of the BBC

1. He felt that he could love this woman with the greatest brutality. The situation between them was electric. When he was in a room with her the only thing he could think of was sex.
[*A Journey to the Interior* (1945), 8]

Newcastle, Margaret, Duchess of (c. 1624–1674)
English poet, dramatist and woman of letters

1. Her name was Margaret Lucas youngest daughter of Lord Lucas, earl of Colchester, a noble family, for all the brothers were valiant, and all the sisters virtuous.
[Epitaph in Westminster Abbey; quoted by Joseph Addison]

Newman, Ernest (1868–1959)
English music critic and biographer of Wagner

1. I sometimes wonder which would be nicer – an opera without an interval, or an interval without an opera.
[In Peter Heyworth (ed.), *Berlioz, Romantic and Classic*]

Newman, John Henry, Cardinal (1801–1890)
English theologian and religious poet; associated with the Oxford Movement; appointed cardinal in 1879

1. It is as absurd to argue men, as to torture them, into believing.
[Sermon, 1831]

2. May He support us all the day long, till the shades lengthen, and the evening comes, and the busy world is hushed, and the fever of life is over, and our work is done! Then in His mercy may He give us a safe lodging, and a holy rest, and peace at the last.
[Sermon, 1834, 'Wisdom and Innocence']

3. When men understand what each other mean, they see, for the most part, that controversy is either superfluous or hopeless.
[Sermon, 1839]

4. She [the Catholic Church] holds that it were better for sun and moon to drop from heaven, for the earth to fail, and for all the many millions who are upon it to die of starvation in extremest agony, as far as temporal affliction goes, than that one soul, I will not say, should be lost, but should commit one single venial sin, should tell one wilful untruth, ... or steal one poor farthing without excuse.
[*Lectures on certain Difficulties felt by Anglicans in submitting to the Catholic Church* (1850), VIII]

5. It is almost a definition of a gentleman to say that he is one who never inflicts pain.
[*The Idea of a University* (1852), 'Knowledge and Religious Duty']

6. [In a work inspired by Charles Kingsley's assertion that Newman did not think truth a necessary virtue in the Roman clergy]
There is such a thing as legitimate warfare: war has its laws; there are things which may fairly be done, and things which may not be done ... He has attempted (as I may call it) to poison the wells.
[*Apologia pro Vita Sua* (1864), 'Mr Kingsley's Method of Disputation']

7. I will vanquish, not my Accuser, but my judges.
[*Apologia pro Vita Sua* (1864), 'True Mode of meeting Mr Kingsley']

8. Two and two only supreme and luminously self-evident beings, myself and my Creator.
[*Apologia pro Vita Sua* (1864), 'History of My Religious Opinions to the Year 1833']

9. It would be a gain to the country were it vastly more superstitious, more bigoted, more gloomy, more fierce in its religion than at present it shows itself to be.
[*Apologia pro Vita Sua* (1864), 'History of My Religious Opinions from 1833 to 1839']

10. From the age of fifteen, dogma has been the fundamental principle of my religion: I know no other religion; I cannot enter into the idea of any other sort of religion; religion, as a mere sentiment, is to me a dream and a mockery.
[*Apologia pro Vita Sua* (1864), 'History of My Religious Opinions from 1833 to 1839']

11. This is what the Church is said to want, not party men, but sensible, temperate, sober, well-judging persons, to guide it through the channel of no-meaning, between the Scylla and Charybdis of Aye and No.
[*Apologia pro Vita Sua* (1864), 'History of My Religious Opinions from 1839 to 1841']

12. Trinity had never been unkind to me. There used to be much snap-dragon growing on the walls opposite my freshman's rooms there, and I had for years taken it as the emblem of my own perpetual residence even unto death in my University. On the morning of the 23rd I left the Observatory. I have never seen Oxford since, excepting its spires, as they are seen from the railway.
[*Apologia pro Vita Sua* (1864), 'History of My Religious Opinions from 1841 to 1845']

13. Ten thousand difficulties do not make one doubt.
[*Apologia pro Vita Sua* (1864), 'Position of my Mind since 1845']

14. Whatever is the first time persons hear evil, it is quite certain that good has been beforehand with them, and they have a something within them which tells them it is evil.
[*Parochial and Plain Sermons*, VII, iv]

15. Lead, kindly Light, amid the encircling gloom,
Lead thou me on;
The night is dark, and I am far from home,
Lead thou me on.
Keep Thou my feet; I do not ask to see
The distant scene; one step enough for me...

16. And with the morn those Angel faces smile,
Which I have loved long since, and lost awhile.
[*The Pillar of Cloud* (1832–1833), 'Lead, kindly Light']

17. Praise to the Holiest in the height,
And in the depth be praise;
In all his words most wonderful,
Most sure in all His ways...

18. O wisest love! that flesh and blood
Which did in Adam fail,
Should strive afresh against their foe,
Should strive and should prevail.
[*The Dream of Gerontius* (1865)]

19. We can believe what we choose. We are answerable for what we choose to believe.
[Letter to Mrs William Froude, 1848]

20. Though you can believe what you choose, you must believe what you ought.
[Letter, 1848]

21. *Ex umbris et imaginibus in veritatem.*
From shadows and types to the reality.
[Motto]

22. *Cor ad cor loquitur.*
Heart speaks to heart.
[Motto adopted for his coat-of-arms as cardinal, 1879]

Newman, Paul (1925–)
American film actor

1. Show me a good loser and I'll show you a loser.
[*The Observer*, 1982, in Jeffrey Care (ed.), *Sayings of the Eighties* (1989)]

Newton, Sir Isaac (1642–1727)
Renowned English scientist and philosopher, noted for his study of gravity, motion, light and calculus

1. Nature is very consonant and conformable to her self.
[*Opticks* (1730 edition)]

2. Whence is it that nature doth nothing in vain; and whence arises all that Order and Beauty which we see in the World?
[*Opticks* (1730 edition)]

3. If I have seen further it is by standing on the shoulders of giants.
[Letter to Robert Hooke, 1675–1676. Cf. Bernard of Chartres: 1]

4. If I have done the public any service, it is due to patient thought.
[Letter to Dr Bentley, 1709–1713]

5. I do not know what I may appear to the world, but to myself I seem to have been only a boy playing on the sea-shore, and diverting myself in now and then finding a smoother pebble or a prettier shell than ordinary, whilst the great ocean of truth lay all undiscovered before me.
[In Brewster, *Memoirs of the Life, Writings, and Discoveries of Sir Isaac Newton* (1855)]

Newton, John (1725–1807)
English divine and hymn writer, former slave-trader

1. Glorious things of thee are spoken,
Zion, city of our God.
[*Olney Hymns* (1779), with William Cowper]

2. How sweet the Name of Jesus sounds
In a believer's ear!
It soothes his sorrows, heals his wounds,
And drives away his fear.

It makes the wounded spirit whole,
And calms the troubled breast;
'Tis manna to the hungry soul,
And to the weary rest.
[*Olney Hymns* (1779), with William Cowper]

Nichiren (1222–1282)
Japanese religious and political reformer, and writer

1. [The Lotus Sutra was one of the earlier Mahayana Buddhist texts and was venerated as the quintessence of truth by the Japanese Tendai and Nichiren sects]
One who finds faith in the Lotus Sutra is in winter: spring will surely come to him.
[Letter to Myoichi-ni, a nun, 1275]

Nichol, Dave
Canadian businessman and environmentalist

1. [Said at the Summit on the Environment, Toronto, 1989]
Incidentally, I've always heard what a practical people the Swiss are – I finally understood these comments when I found out how they dispose of their mercury batteries. They collect them, and then dump them down an abandoned mine shaft – in France!
[Attr.]

Nicholas I, Emperor of Russia (1796–1855)
Russian tsar from 1825, noted for his autocracy and military ambitions

1. Russia has two generals in whom she can trust – Generals Janvier and Février.
[Attr.]

2. [Of Turkey]
Nous avons sur les bras un homme malade – un homme gravement malade.
We have on our hands a sick man – a grievously sick man.
[Attr.]

Nicholls, Peter (1927–)
British dramatist

1. 'One advantage of *being* pregnant,' says a wife in one of my television plays, 'you don't have to worry about *getting* pregnant.'
[*Feeling You're Behind* (1984)]

Nichols, Beverley (1898–1983)
English writer and composer

1. [When reading a prize essay to the Headmaster of Marlborough]
He then proceeded casually to slide his hand down the back of my trousers and pinch me gently on the behind throughout the entire reading. This struck me as rather peculiar behaviour from a headmaster.
[*The Unforgiving Minute* (1978)]

Nicholson, Vivian (1936–)
British housewife

1. [Reply when asked what she would do with the £152,000 she won on the pools in 1961]
I'm going to spend, spend, spend, that's what I'm going to do.
[In Nicholson and Smith, *I'm Going to Spend, Spend, Spend*]

Nicias (c. 470–413 BC)
Athenian statesman, aristocrat and general; executed for military failure

1. [To the defeated Athenian army at Syracuse, 413 BC]
For a city consists of men, and not its walls or ships empty of men.
[In Thucydides, *Historiae*, VII, 77]

Niebuhr, Reinhold (1892–1971)
American Protestant theologian and writer on political morality

1. Man's capacity for justice makes democracy possible, but man's inclination to injustice makes democracy necessary.
[*The Children of Light and the Children of Darkness* (1944), Foreword]

2. God grant me the serenity to accept the things I cannot change, the courage to change the things I can, and the wisdom to distinguish the one from the other.
[Prayer adopted by Alcoholics Anonymous, attributed to but not accepted by Niebuhr]

Niemöller, Martin (1892–1984)
German Lutheran theologian, imprisoned (1938—45) for his opposition to Nazism; President of the World Council of Churches 1961–68

1. In Germany, the Nazis came for the Communists and I didn't speak up because I was not a Communist. Then they came for the Jews and I didn't speak up because I was not a Jew. Then they came for the trade unionists and I didn't speak up because I was not a trade unionist. Then they came for the Catholics and I was a Protestant so I didn't speak up. Then they came for me . . . By that time there was no one to speak up for anyone.
[In W. Neil, *Concise Dictionary of Religious Quotations*]

Nietzsche, Friedrich Wilhelm (1844–1900)
German philosopher, critic and poet, noted for his rejection of Christianity and concept of the Superman

1. *'Die Herren' sind abgetan; die Moral des gemeinen Mannes hat gesiegt.*
'The masters' have been abolished; the morality of the common man has been victorious.
[*Zur Genealogie der Moral* (*On the Genealogy of Morals*, 1881), I, 9]

2. *Auf dem Grunde aller dieser vornehmen Rassen ist das Raubtier, die prachtvolle nach Beute und Sieg lüstern schweifende* blonde Bestie *nicht zu verkennen.*
Underlying all these noble races the beast of prey is unmistakable, the magnificent *blond beast* which roams around, lecherously seeking prey and victory.
[*Zur Genealogie der Moral* (*On the Genealogy of Morals*, 1881), I, 11]

3. *Was eigentlich gegen das Leiden empört, ist nicht das Leiden an sich, sondern das Sinnlose des Leidens.*
What actually fills you with indignation as regards suffering is not suffering in itself but the pointlessness of suffering.
[*Zur Genealogie der Moral* (*On the Genealogy of Morals*, 1881), II, 7]

4. Ich lehre euch den Übermenschen. *Der Mensch ist etwas, das überwinden werden soll. Was habt ihr getan, ihn zu überwinden? Mine is the doctrine of the superman.* Man is something to be overcome. What have you done to overcome him?
[*Also Sprach Zarathustra* (*Thus Spake Zarathustra*, 1883–84), I, Prologue, 3]

5. *Keine geringe Kunst ist schlafen: es tut schon not, den ganzen Tag darauf hin zu wachen.*
Sleeping is no mean art: it is necessary to stay awake for it all day.
[*Also Sprach Zarathustra* (*Thus Spake Zarathustra*, 1883–84), I, 'Die Reden Zarathustras', 2]

6. *Alles am Weibe ist ein Rätsel, und alles am Weibe hat* eine *Lösung: sie heisst Schwangerschaft.*
Everything to do with women is a mystery, and everything to do with women has *one* solution: it's called pregnancy.
[*Also Sprach Zarathustra* (*Thus Spake Zarathustra*, 1883–84), I, 'Die Reden Zarathustras', 18]

7. *Und also sprach das alte Weiblein:*
'Du gehst zu Frauen? Vergiss die Peitsche nicht!
And thus spake the little old woman:
'You're going with women? Don't forget your whip!'
[*Also Sprach Zarathustra* (*Thus Spake Zarathustra*, 1883–84), I, 'Die Reden Zarathustras', 18]

8. *Auf* andere *warte ich ... auf Höhere, Stärkere, Sieghaftere, Wohlgemutere, solche, die rechtwinklig gebaut sind an Leib und Seele:* lachende Löwen *müssen kommen!*
I am waiting for *others* ... for higher ones, stronger ones, ones that are more confident of victory, more cheerful ones, for such that are solidly built in body and soul: *laughing lions* must come!
[*Also Sprach Zarathustra* (*Thus Spake Zarathustra*, 1883–84), IV, 11]

9. *Wer mit Ungeheurn kämpft, mag zusehn, dass er nicht dabei zum Ungeheuer wird. Und wenn du lange in einen Abgrund blickst, blickt der Abgrund auch in dich hinein.*
Whoever struggles with monsters might watch that he does not thereby become a monster. And when you stare into an abyss for a long time, the abyss also stares into you.
[*Jenseits von Gut und Böse* (*Beyond Good and Evil*, 1886), IV, no. 146. Cf. Trilling: 1]

10. *Der Gedanke an den Selbstmord ist ein starkes Trostmittel: mit ihm kommt man gut über manche böse Nacht hinweg.*
The thought of suicide is a great comfort: it's a good way of getting through many a bad night.
[*Jenseits von Gut und Böse* (*Beyond Good and Evil*, 1886), IV, no. 157]

11. *Ist das Leben nicht hundert Mal zu kurz, sich in ihm – zu langweilen?*
Is life not a hundred times too short – to get bored?
[*Jenseits von Gut und Böse* (*Beyond Good and Evil*, 1886), VII, no. 227]

12. *Es gibt* Herren-Moral *und* Sklaven-Moral.
There is *master-morality* and *slave-morality*.
[*Jenseits von Gut und Böse* (*Beyond Good and Evil*, 1886), IX, no. 260]

13. *Der Witz ist das Epigramm auf den Tod eines Gefühls.*
Wit is the epigram for the death of an emotion.
[*Menschliches, Allzumenschliches* (*Human, All too Human*, 2nd edition, 1886), II. 1, 'Vermischte Meinungen und Sprüche' ('Miscellaneous opinions and sayings'), no. 202]

14. *Mitleiden äussern wird als ein Zeichen der Verachtung empfunden, weil man ersichtlich aufgehört hat, ein Gegenstand der* Furcht *zu sein, sobald einem Mitleiden erwiesen wird.*
To show pity is felt to be a sign of scorn, because one has obviously stopped being an object of *fear* as soon as one is pitied.
[*Menschliches, Allzumenschliches* (*Human, All too Human*, 2nd edition, 1886), II, 2, 'Der Wanderer und sein Schatten' ('The Hiker and his Shadow')]

15. *Gott ist tot: aber so wie die Art der Menschen ist, wird es vielleicht noch jahrtausendelang Höhlen geben, in denen man seinen Schatten zeigt.*
God is dead: but men's natures are such that for thousands of years yet there will perhaps be caves in which his shadow will be seen.
[*Die fröhliche Wissenschaft* (*The Gay Science*, 2nd edition, 1887), III, 108]

16. *Moralität ist Herden-Instinkt im Einzelnen.*
Morality is the herd-instinct in the individual.
[*Die fröhliche Wissenschaft* (*The Gay Science*, 2nd edition, 1887), III, 116]

17. *Der christliche Entschluss, die Welt hässlich und schlecht zu finden, hat die Welt hässlich und schlecht gemacht.*
The Christian decision to find the world ugly and bad has made the world ugly and bad.
[*Die fröhliche Wissenschaft* (*The Gay Science*, 2nd edition, 1887), III, 130]

18. *Glaubt es mir! – das Geheimnis, um die grösste Fruchtbarkeit und den grössten Genuss vom Dasein einzuernten, heisst:* gefährlich leben!
Believe me! – the secret of gathering in the greatest fruitfulness and the greatest enjoyment from existence is *living dangerously!*
[*Die fröhliche Wissenschaft* (*The Gay Science*, 2nd edition, 1887), IV, 283]

19. *Dies Buch gehört den wenigsten. Vielleicht lebt selbst noch keiner von ihnen.*
This book belongs to the very few. Perhaps none of them is even alive yet.
[*Der Antichrist* (1888), Prologue]

20. *Damit* Liebe *möglich ist, muss Gott Person sein; ... Man erträgt in der Liebe mehr als sonst, man duldet alles.*
So that *love* is possible, God must be a person; ... In love, one endures more than at other times, one tolerates everything.
[*Der Antichrist* (1888), 23]

21. *Aber siehe da, auch der Mensch langweilt sich. Das Erbarmen Gottes mit der einzigen Not, die alle Paradiese an sich haben, kennt keine Grenzen: er schuf alsbald noch andre Tiere.* Erster *Fehlgriff Gottes: der Mensch fand die Tiere nich unterhaltend – er herrschte über sie, er wollte nicht einmal 'Tier' sein – Folglich schuf Gott das Weib ... Das Weib war der* zweite *Fehlgriff Gottes.*
But look, man is bored too. All paradises, by their very nature, want for one thing, and God's mercy here is boundless: he immediately created yet more animals. God's *first* mistake: man did not find the animals entertaining – he dominated them, he did not even want to be an 'animal' – Therefore God created woman ... Woman was God's *second* mistake.
[*Der Antichrist* (1888), 48]

22. *Ich heisse das Christentum den* einen *grossen Fluch, die* eine *grosse innerlichste Verdorbenheit, den* einen *grossen Instinkt der Rache, dem kein Mittel giftig, heimlich, unterirdisch,* klein *genug ist – ich heisse es den* einen *unsterblichen Schandfleck der Menschheit.*
I call Christianity the *one* great curse, the *one* great innermost form of depravity, the *one* great instinct for revenge, for which no means is poisonous, furtive, underground, *petty* enough – I call it the *one* immortal blemish of humanity.
[*Der Antichrist* (1888), 62]

23. *Als* Artist *hat man keine Heimat in Europa ausser in Paris.*
As an *artist*, one has no home in Europe except Paris.
[*Ecco Homo* (1888), 'Warum ich so klug bin' ('Why I am so clever'), 5]

24. *Ich selber bin noch nicht an der Zeit, einige werden postum geboren.*
My own time has not yet come, some are born posthumously.
[*Ecce Homo* (1888), 'Warum ich so gute Bücher schreibe' ('Why I write such good books'), I]

25. *Wie ich den Philosophen verstehe, als einen furchtbaren Explosionsstoff, vor dem Alles in Gefahr ist.*
What I understand philosophers to be: a terrible explosive, in the presence of which everything is in danger.
[*Ecce Homo* (1888), 'Die unzeitgemässen' ('The Untimely [Meditations]'), 3]

26. *Ich bin kein Mensch, ich bin Dynamit.*
I'm not a man, I'm dynamite.
[*Ecce Homo* (1888), 'Warum ich ein Schicksal bin' ('Why I am fate')]

27. *Wie? ist der Mensch nur ein Fehlgriff Gottes? Oder Gott nur ein Fehlgriff des Meschen?*
What? is man only a mistake made by God, or God only a mistake made by man?
[*Götzendämmerung* (*Twilight of the Idols*, 1889), 'Spruche und Pfeile' ('Maxims and Arrows'), 7]

28. *Wir haben die Lüge nötig, . . . um zu leben.*
We need lies . . . in order to live.
[*Nachlass* (*Fragments*, 1880–1889), 'Die Kunst in der 'Geburt der Tragödie'' ('Art in 'The Birth of Tragedy'')]

29. My doctrine is: Live that thou mayest desire to live again – that is thy duty – for in any case thou wilt live again!
[*Eternal Recurrence*]

Nightingale, Florence (1820–1910)

English nursing reformer, born in Italy; noted for her organization of hospitals during the Crimean War

1. No man, not even a doctor, ever gives any other definition of what a nurse should be than this – 'devoted and obedient'. This definition would do just as well for a porter. It might even do for a horse. It would not do for a policeman.
[*Notes on Nursing* (1860)]

2. Sir Douglas Dawson, after a short speech, stepped forward and handed the insignia of the Order [of Merit] to Miss Nightingale. Propped up by pillows, she dimly recognized that some kind of compliment was being paid her. 'Too kind – too kind,' she murmured; and she was not ironical.
[In Lytton Strachey, *Eminent Victorians* (1918), 'Florence Nightingale']

3. To understand God's thoughts we must study statistics, for these are the measure of his purpose.
[Attr.]

Nin, Anais (1903–1977)

American novelist, diarist, writer of erotica

1. Women (and I, in this Diary) have never separated sex from feeling, from love of the whole man.
[*Delta of Venus* (1977)]

Nivelle, Général Robert (1856–1924)

French general

1. *Ils ne passeront pas.*
They shall not pass.
[Statement at Battle of Verdun, 1916; often attr. to Pétain]

Nixon, Richard (1913–1994)

American politician and lawyer; Republican President 1969—74; resigned after Watergate scandal

1. You won't have Nixon to kick around any more, because, gentlemen, this is my last press conference.
[Remark to the press after losing the election for Governor of California, 1962]

2. Let us begin by committing ourselves to the truth, to see it like it is and to tell it like it is, to find the truth, to speak the truth and live with the truth. That's what we'll do.
[Nomination acceptance speech, Miami, 1968]

3. And this certainly has to be the most historic phone call ever made.
[Telephone call to astronauts on the moon, 20 July 1969]

4. This has to be the greatest week in the history of the world since the Creation.
[Speech on first moon-landing, 24 July 1969]

5. [Presidential address, attacking opponents of the Vietnam war]
If a vocal minority, however fervent its cause, prevails over reason, this nation has no future as a free society . . . And so tonight to you the great silent majority of my fellow Americans, I ask for your support.
[Speech, 1969]

6. North Vietnam cannot defeat or humiliate the United States. Only Americans can do that.
[Speech, 1969]

7. It is time for the great silent majority of Americans to stand up and be counted.
[Speech, 1970]

8. Well, I am not a crook. I've earned everything I've got.
[Speech, 1973]

9. I want you all to stonewall it.
[Advice to staff handling the Watergate scandal, 1973]

10. Always give your best, never get discouraged, never be petty. Always remember, others may hate you, but those who hate you don't win unless you hate them, and then you destroy yourself.
[Farewell speech to his White House staff three hours before formally resigning the Presidency on 9 August 1974]

11. When the President does it, that means it is not illegal.
[TV interview with David Frost, May 1977]

12. I brought myself down. I gave them a sword and they stuck it in and they twisted it with relish. And I guess if I'd been in their position I'd have done the same thing.
[TV interview with David Frost, May 1977]

13. I screwed up on Watergate and I paid the price. *Mea culpa*. But let's get on to my achievements. You'll be here in the year 2000 and we'll see how I'm regarded then.
[Speech at the Oxford Union, November 1978]

14. [Urging more generous support for Boris Yeltsin]
Without large-scale outside aid, Russia may turn to a new despotism, which could be a far more dangerous threat to peace and freedom than the old Soviet totalitarianism.
[Remark at a Washington conference, 1992]

15. There can be no whitewash at the White House.
[*The Observer*, 'Sayings of the Week', 1973]

16. I let down my friends, I let down my country. I let down our system of government.
[*The Observer*, 'Sayings of the Week', 1977]

17. Courage – or putting it more accurately, lack of fear – is a

result of discipline. By an act of will, a man refuses to think of the reasons for fear, and so concentrates entirely on winning the battle.
[*The Independent*, 1994]

18. You can't put the toothpaste back in the tube.
[Attr.; also attributed to his Chief of Staff, H.R. Haldeman, in relation to the Watergate affair]

Nolan, Sir Sidney Robert (1917–)
Australian artist

1. A successful artist would have no trouble being a successful member of the Mafia.
[*Good Weekend*, 1985]

Norfolk, Charles Howard, Eleventh Duke of (1746–1815)
English Whig politician

1. I cannot be a good Catholic; I cannot go to heaven; and if a man is to go to the devil, he may as well go thither from the House of Lords as from any other place on earth.
[In Henry Best, *Personal and Literary Memorials* (1829), 18]

Norman, Barry (1933–)
British film critic and broadcaster

1. Perhaps at fourteen every boy should be in love with some ideal woman to put on a pedestal and worship. As he grows up, of course, he will put her on a pedestal the better to view her legs.
[*The Listener*]

North, Christopher (John Wilson) (1785–1854)
Scottish poet, novelist, editor, essayist and critic

1. Tibby was for cutting it in twa bitts, but I like a saumon to be served up in its integrity.
[Blackwood's *Edinburgh Magazine*, 1822, 'Noctes Ambrosianae', 5]

2. Minds like ours, my dear James, must always be above national prejudices, and in all companies it gives me true pleasure to declare, that, as a people, the English are very little indeed inferior to the Scotch.
[Blackwood's *Edinburgh Magazine*, 1826, 'Noctes Ambrosianae', 9]

3. His Majesty's dominions, on which the sun never sets.
[Blackwood's *Edinburgh Magazine*, 1829, 'Noctes Ambrosianae', 20]

4. Laws were made to be broken.
[Blackwood's *Edinburgh Magazine*, 1830, 'Noctes Ambrosianae', 24]

5. [Of James Hogg, the Ettrick Shepherd]
Change nicht into day, and day into nicht, rinnin coonter to natur, insultin the sun, and quarrellin wi' the equawtor. That's no richt.
[Blackwood's *Edinburgh Magazine*, 1830, 'Noctes Ambrosianae', 24]

6. [To an invitation to change himself, i.e., his clothes]
A Scotticism, Sam, a palpable Scotticism. No – I will never change myself; but to the last be Christopher North.
[Blackwood's *Edinburgh Magazine*, 1834, 'Noctes Ambrosianae', 33]

7. ... if he were a Christian – nay, a man – his heart and head too would tell him that the animosities are mortal, but the Humanities live for ever.
[Blackwood's *Edinburgh Magazine*, 1834, 'Noctes Ambrosianae', 35]

8. I cannot sit still, James, and hear you abuse the shopocracy.
[Blackwood's *Edinburgh Magazine*, 1835, 'Noctes Ambrosianae', 39]

North, Lt-Col Oliver (1943–)
American marine officer, dismissed for his part in the Iran-Contra affair

1. I'm trusting in the Lord and a good lawyer.
[*The Observer*, 1986, in Jeffrey Care (ed.), *Sayings of the Eighties* (1989)]

Northcliffe, Alfred Charles William Harmsworth, Viscount (1865–1922)
Irish-born British newspaper proprietor; founder of the Daily Mail *(1896) and* Daily Mirror *(1903)*

1. [Rumoured to have been a notice to remind his staff of his opinion of the mental age of the general public]
They are only ten.
[Attr.]

2. When I want a peerage, I shall buy one like an honest man.
[Attr.]

Norton, Caroline (1808–1877)
English novelist and poet; grand-daughter of Richard Brinsley Sheridan

1. I do not love thee! – no! I do not love thee!
And yet when thou art absent I am sad;
And envy even the bright blue sky above thee,
Whose quiet stars may see thee and be glad.
[*The Sorrows of Rosalie* (1829), 'I do not love thee']

2. The Arab's Farewell to his Horse.
[*The Undying One* (1830), Title of poem]

3. For death and life, in ceaseless strife,
Beat wild on this world's shore,
And all our calm is in that balm–
Not lost but gone before.
['Not Lost but Gone Before']

Norworth, Jack (1879–1959)
American songwriter

1. Oh! shine on, shine on, harvest moon
Up in the sky.
I ain't had no lovin'
Since April, January, June or July.
['Shine On, Harvest Moon', song, 1908]

Novalis (Friedrich von Hardenberg) (1772–1801)
German Romantic poet and novelist

1. [On Spinoza]
Spinoza ist ein gotttrunkener Mensch.
Spinoza is a man intoxicated with God.
[*Fragmente und Studien 1799–1800*, no. 562, in *Schriften* (Writings), ed. Kluckhorn and Samuel, III]

2. *Oft fühl ich jetzt, wie mein Vaterland meine frühesten Gedanken mit unvergänglichen Farben angehaucht hat, und sein Bild eine seltsame Andeutung meines Gemütes geworden ist, die ich immer mehr errate, je tiefer ich einsehe, dass Schicksal und Gemüt Namen eines Begriffes sind.*
I often feel now how my homeland has tinged my earliest thoughts with immortal colours, and how the image of my homeland has become a strange indication of my feelings. I become more and more aware of these feelings the more profoundly I recognise that fate and feelings are the names of but one concept.
[*Heinrich von Ofterdingen* (1802), II; often quoted as 'Character is destiny']

Novello, Ivor (1893–1951)
Welsh actor, composer, songwriter and dramatist

1. There's something Vichy about the French.
[In Edward Marsh, *Ambrosia and Small Beer*, 4]

Noyes, Alfred (1880–1958)
English poet, critic, anti-Modernist and dramatist

1. Go down to Kew in lilac-time, in lilac-time, in lilac-time;
Go down to Kew in lilac-time (it isn't far from London!)
And you shall wander hand in hand with love in summer's wonderland;
Go down to Kew in lilac-time (it isn't far from London!)
[*Poems* (1904), 'The Barrel Organ']

2. The wind was a torrent of darkness among the gusty trees,
The moon was a ghostly galleon tossed upon cloudy seas,
The road was a ribbon of moonlight over the purple moor,
And the highwayman came riding–
Riding – riding–
The highwayman came riding, up to the old inn-door...

3. He whistled a tune to the window, and who should be waiting there
The landlord's black-eyed daughter,
Bess, the landlord's daughter,
Plaiting a dark red love-knot into her long black hair...

4. Look for me by moonlight;
Watch for me by moonlight;
I'll come to thee by moonlight, though hell should bar the way!
[*Forty Singing Seamen and Other Poems* (1908), 'The Highwayman']

Nureyev, Rudolf (1938–1993)
Russian-born Austrian ballet dancer

1. Never look backwards or you'll fall down the stairs.
[Attr.]

Nursery Rhymes
(For sources, the reader is referred to the authoritative *Oxford Dictionary of Nursery Rhymes*)

1. As I was going to St Ives,
I met a man with seven wives.
Each wife had seven sacks,
Each sack had seven cats,
Each cat had seven kits:
Kits, cats, sacks, and wives,
How many were going to St Ives?
[One or none]

2. Baa, baa, black sheep,
Have you any wool?
Yes, sir, yes, sir,
Three bags full;
One for the master,
And one for the dame,
And one for the little boy who lives down the lane.

3. Bobby Shafto's gone to sea,
Silver buckles on his knee;
He'll come back and marry me,
Bonny Bobby Shafto!

4. Boys and girls come out to play,
The moon doth shine as bright as day.

5. Bye, baby bunting,
Daddy's gone a-hunting,
Gone to get a rabbit skin
To wrap the baby bunting in.

6. Cock a doodle doo!
My dame has lost her shoe,
My master's lost his fiddling stick,
And doesn't know what to do.

7. Come, let's to bed
Says Sleepy-head;
Tarry a while, says Slow;
Put on the pan;
Says Greedy Nan,
Let's sup before we go.

8. Curly locks, Curly locks,
Wilt thou be mine?
Thou shalt not wash dishes
Nor yet feed the swine;
But sit on a cushion
And sew a fine seam,
And feed upon strawberries,
Sugar and cream.

9. Ding, dong, bell,
Pussy's in the well.
Who put her in?
Little Johnny Green.
Who pulled her out?
Little Timmy Stout.

10. Doctor Foster went to Gloucester
In a shower of rain;
He stepped in a puddle,
Right up to his middle,
And never went there again.

11. Fee, fi, fo, fum,
I smell the blood of an Englishman;
Be he alive or be he dead,
I'll grind his bones to make my bread.

12. A frog he would a-wooing go,
Heigh ho! says Rowley,
Whether his mother would let him or no.
With a rowley, powley, gammon and spinach,
Heigh ho! says Anthony Rowley.

13. Georgie Porgie, pudding and pie,
Kissed the girls and made them cry;
When the boys came out to play,
Georgie Porgie ran away.

14. Goosey, goosey gander,
Whither shall I wander?
Upstairs and downstairs
And in my lady's chamber.

There I met an old man
Who wouldn't say his prayers,
I took him by the left leg
And threw him down the stairs.

15. Here is the church, and here is the steeple;
Open the door and here are the people.

16. Hey diddle diddle,
The cat and the fiddle,
The cow jumped over the moon;
The little dog laughed
To see such sport,
And the dish ran away with the spoon.

17. Hickory, dickory, dock,
The mouse ran up the clock.
The clock struck one,
The mouse ran down,
Hickory, dickory, dock.

18. Hot cross buns!
Hot cross buns!
One a penny, two a penny,
Hot cross buns!

19. How many miles to Babylon?
Three score miles and ten.
Can I get there by candle-light?
Yes, and back again.

20. Humpty Dumpty sat on a wall,
Humpty Dumpty had a great fall.
All the king's horses,
And all the king's men,
Couldn't put Humpty together again.

21. I had a little nut tree,
Nothing would it bear
But a silver nutmeg
And a golden pear;
The King of Spain's daughter
Came to visit me,
And all for the sake
Of my little nut tree.

22. I had a little pony,
His name was Dapple Grey;
I lent him to a lady
To ride a mile away.
She whipped him, she lashed him,
She rode him though the mire;
I would not lend my pony now,
For all the lady's hire.

23. I love little pussy,
Her coat is so warm,
And if I don't hurt her,
She'll do me no harm.

24. I love sixpence, jolly little sixpence,
I love sixpence better than my life;
I spent a penny of it, I lent a penny of it,
And I took fourpence home to my wife.

25. I'm the king of the castle,
Get down, you dirty rascal!

26. I see the moon,
And the moon sees me;
God bless the moon,
And God bless me.

27. Jack and Jill went up the hill
To fetch a pail of water;
Jack fell down and broke his crown,
And Jill came tumbling after.

28. Jack Sprat could eat no fat,
His wife could eat no lean,
And so between them both, you see,
They licked the platter clean.

29. Ladybird, ladybird,
Fly away home,
Your house is on fire
And your children are gone.
All except one
And that's little Ann
And she has crept under
The warming pan.

30. Lavender's blue, dilly dilly,
Lavender's green;
When I am king, dilly dilly,
You shall be queen.

31. The lion and the unicorn
Were fighting for the crown;
The lion beat the unicorn
All around the town.

32. Little Bo-peep has lost her sheep,
And can't tell where to find them;
Leave them alone, and they'll come home,
Bringing their tails behind them.

33. Little boy blue, come blow your horn,
The sheep's in the meadow, the cow's in the corn.

34. Little Jack Horner
Sat in the corner,
Eating a Christmas pie;
He put in his thumb,
And pulled out a plum,
And said, What a good boy am I!

35. Little Miss Muffet
Sat on a tuffet,
Eating her curds and whey;
There came a big spider,
Who sat down beside her
And frightened Miss Muffet away.

36. Little Polly Flinders
Sat among the cinders,
Warming her pretty little toes;
Her mother came and caught her,
And whipped her little daughter
For spoiling her nice new clothes.

37. Little Tommy Tucker,
Sings for his supper:
What shall we give him?
White bread and butter
How shall he cut it
Without a knife?
How will he be married
Without a wife?

38. London Bridge is falling down,
My fair lady.

39. Mary had a little lamb,
Its fleece was white as snow;
And everywhere that Mary went
The lamb was sure to go.
It followed her to school one day,
That was against the rule;
It made the children laugh and play
To see a lamb at school.

40. Mary, Mary, quite contrary,
How does your garden grow?
With silver bells and cockle shells,
And pretty maids all in a row.

41. Monday's child is fair of face,
Tuesday's child is full of grace,
Wednesday's child is full of woe,
Thursday's child has far to go,
Friday's child is loving and giving,
Saturday's child works hard for a living,
And the child that is born on the Sabbath day
Is bonny and blithe, and good and gay.

42. My mother said that I never should
Play with the gypsies in the wood;
If I did, she would say,
Naughty girl to disobey.

43. The north wind doth blow,
And we shall have snow,

And what will poor robin do then?
Poor thing.

44. O dear, what can the matter be?
Dear, dear, what can the matter be,
Oh, dear, what can the matter be?
Johnny's so long at the fair.

He promised he'd buy me a fairing should please me,
And then for a kiss, oh! he vowed he would tease me,
He promised he'd buy me a bunch of blue ribbons
To tie up my bonny brown hair.

45. Oh! the grand old Duke of York
He had ten thousand men;
He marched them up to the top of the hill,
And he marched them down again.
And when they were up they were up,
And when they were down they were down,
And when they were only half way up.
They were neither up nor down.

46. Old King Cole
Was a merry old soul,
And a merry old soul was he;
He called for his pipe,
And he called for his bowl,
And he called for his fiddlers three.

47. Old Mother Hubbard
Went to the cupboard,
To fetch her poor dog a bone;
But when she came there
The cupboard was bare
And so the poor dog had none.

48. One, two, buckle my shoe;
Three, four, knock at the door;
Five, six, pick up sticks;
Seven, eight, lay them straight;
Nine, ten, big fat hen;
Eleven, twelve, dig and delve;
Thirteen, fourteen, maids a-courting;
Fifteen, sixteen, maids in the kitchen,
Seventeen, eighteen, maids in waiting;
Nineteen, twenty, my plate's empty!

49. Oranges and lemons,
Say the bells of St Clement's...

You owe me five farthings,
Say the bells of St Martin's.

When will you pay me?
Say the bells of Old Bailey.

When I grow rich
Say the bells of Shoreditch.

Pray, when will that be?
Say the bells of Stepney.

I'm sure I don't know
Says the great bell at Bow.

Here comes a candle to light you to bed,
Here comes a chopper to chop off your head!

50. Pat-a-cake, pat-a-cake, baker's man,
Bake me a cake as fast as you can;
Pat it and prick it, and mark it with B,
Put it in the oven for baby and me.

51. Peter, Peter, pumpkin eater,
Had a wife and couldn't keep her;
He put her in a pumpkin shell
And there he kept her very well.

52. Peter Piper picked a peck of pickled pepper.
A peck of pickled pepper Peter Piper picked.
If Peter Piper picked a peck of pickled pepper,
Where's the peck of pickled pepper Peter Piper picked?

53. Please to remember
The Fifth of November,
Gunpowder, treason and plot;
We know no reason
Why gunpowder treason
Should ever be forgot.

54. Polly put the kettle on,
Polly put the kettle on,
Polly put the kettle on,
We'll all have tea.
Sukey take it off again,
Sukey take it off again,
Sukey take it off again,
They've all gone away.

55. Pussy cat, pussy cat,
Where have you been?
I've been to London
To look at the queen.
Pussy cat, pussy cat,
What did you there?
I frightened a little mouse
Under her chair.

56. The Queen of Hearts
She made some tarts,
All on a summer's day;
The Knave of Hearts
He stole the tarts,
And took them clean away.

57. Rain, rain, go away,
Come again another day.

58. Ride a cock-horse to Banbury Cross,
To see a fine lady upon a white horse;
Rings on her fingers and bells on her toes,
She shall have music wherever she goes.

59. Ring-a-ring o' roses,
A pocket full of posies,
A-tishoo! A-tishoo!
We all fall down.

60. Rock-a-bye, baby, on the tree top,
When the wind blows the cradle will rock;
When the bough breaks the cradle will fall,
Down will come baby, cradle, and all.

61. Round and round the garden
Like a teddy bear;
One step, two step,
Tickle you under there!

62. Round and round the rugged rock
The ragged rascal ran.

63. Rub-a-dub-dub,
Three men in a tub,
And how do you think they got there?
The butcher, the baker,
The candlestick-maker.
They all jumped out of a rotten potato,
'Twas enough to make a man stare.

64. See-saw, Margery Daw,
Jacky shall have a new master;
Jacky shall have but a penny a day,
Because he can't work any faster.

65. Simple Simon met a pieman,
Going to the fair;
Says Simple Simon to the pieman,
Let me taste your ware.

66. Sing a song of sixpence,
A pocket full of rye;
Four and twenty blackbirds,
Baked in a pie.

When the pie was opened,
The birds began to sing;
Wasn't that a dainty dish,
To set before the king?

The king was in his counting-house,
Counting out his money;
The queen was in the parlour,
Eating bread and honey.

The maid was in the garden,
Hanging out the clothes,
When down came a blackbird
And pecked off her nose!

67. Solomon Grundy,
Born on Monday
Christened on Tuesday
Married on Wednesday
Took ill on Thursday
Worse on Friday
Died on Saturday
Buried on Sunday.
This is the end of Solomon Grundy.

68. Taffy was a Welshman, Taffy was a thief,
Taffy came to my house and stole a piece of beef.

69. Tell tale, tit!
Your tongue shall be split,
And all the dogs in town
Shall have a little bit.

70. There was a crooked man, and he walked a crooked mile,
He found a crooked sixpence against a crooked stile;
He bought a crooked cat, which caught a crooked mouse,
And they all lived together in a little crooked house.

71. There was a little girl, and she had a little curl
Right in the middle of her forehead;
When she was good, she was very, very good,
But when she was bad, she was horrid.

72. There was an old woman who lived in a shoe,
She had so many children she didn't know what to do.
She gave them some broth without any bread,
She whipped them all soundly and put them to bed.

73. Thirty days hath September,
April, June and November;
All the rest have thirty-one,
Excepting February alone
And that has twenty-eight days clear
And twenty-nine in each leap year.

74. This is the horse and the hound and the horn
That belonged to the farmer sowing his corn,
That kept the cock that crowed in the morn,
That waked the priest all shaven and shorn,
That married the man all tattered and torn,
That kissed the maiden all forlorn,
That milked the cow with the crumpled horn,
That tossed the dog,
That worried the cat,
That killed the rat,
That ate the corn,
That lay in the house that Jack built.

75. This little pig went to market,
This little pig stayed at home,
This little pig had roast beef,
This little pig had none,
And this little pig cried, Wee-wee-wee-wee-wee,
I can't find my way home.

76. Three blind mice, see how they run!
They all ran after the farmer's wife,
She cut off their tails with a carving knife,
Did ever you see such a thing in your life,
As three blind mice?

77. Three little kittens they lost their mittens,
And they began to cry.
Oh mother dear, we sadly fear
Our mittens we have lost.
What! lost your mittens,
You naughty kittens!
Then you shall have no pie.

78. Tinker,
Tailor,
Soldier,
Sailor,
Rich man,
Poor man,
Beggarman,
Thief.

79. Tom, he was a piper's son,
He learnt to play when he was young,
And all the tune that he could play
Was 'Over the hills and far away'.

80. Tom, Tom, the piper's son,
Stole a pig and away he run.
The pig was eat,
And Tom was beat,
And Tom went howling down the street.

81. The twelfth day of Christmas,
My true love sent to me
Twelve lords a-leaping,
Eleven ladies dancing,
Ten pipers piping,
Nine drummers drumming,
Eight maids a-milking,
Seven swans a-swimming,
Six geese a-laying,
Five gold rings,
Four calling birds,
Three French hens,
Two turtle doves, and
A partridge in a pear tree.

82. Two little dicky birds,
Sitting on a wall;
One named Peter,
The other named Paul,
Fly away, Peter!
Fly away, Paul!
Come back, Peter!
Come back, Paul!

83. Wee Willie Winkie runs through the town
Upstairs and downstairs and in his nightgown,
Rapping at the window, crying through the lock,
Are the children all in bed? It's past eight o'clock.

84. What are little boys made of?
Frogs and snails
And puppy-dogs' tails,
That's what little boys are made of.

What are little girls made of?
Sugar and spice
And all things nice,
That's what little girls are made of.

What are young men made of?
Sighs and leers,
And crocodile tears,
That's what young men are made of.

What are young women made of?
Ribbons and laces,
And sweet, pretty faces,
That's what young women are made of.

85. Where are you going to, my pretty maid?
I'm going a-milking, sir, she said.
What is your fortune, my pretty maid?
My face is my fortune, sir, she said.

86. Who killed Cock Robin?
I, said the Sparrow,
With my bow and arrow,
I killed Cock Robin.

Who saw him die?
I, said the Fly,
With my little eye,
I saw him die.

And all the birds of the air
Fell to sighing and sobbing,
When they heard the bell toll
For poor Cock Robin.

87. A wise old owl lived in an oak;
The more he saw the less he spoke;
The less he spoke the more he heard.
Why can't we all be like that wise old bird?

Oakeley, Frederick (1802–1880)
English clergyman, Tractarian and religious writer

1. O come, all ye faithful,
Joyful and triumphant,
O come ye, O come ye to Bethlehem.
[Hymn]

Oates, Captain Lawrence (1880–1912)
English Antarctic explorer and army captain

1. I am just going outside, and may be some time.
[Last words, quoted in Captain Scott's diary]

O'Brian, Patrick
Irish historical novelist

1. Question and answer is not a civilized form of conversation.
[*Clarissa Oakes* (1992)]

O'Brien, Conor Cruise (1917–)
Irish critic, historian, Labour politician, editor and essayist

1. If I saw Mr Haughey buried at midnight at a cross-roads, with a stake driven through his heart – politically speaking – I should continue to wear a clove of garlic round my neck, just in case.
[*The Observer*, 1982]

O'Brien, Edna (1936–)
Irish novelist, short-story writer and dramatist

1. Oh, shadows of love, inebriations of love, foretastes of love, trickles of love, but never yet the one true love.
[*Night* (1972)]

2. To Crystal, hair was the most important thing on earth. She would never get married because you couldn't wear curlers in bed.
[*Winter's Tales*, 8, 'Come into the Drawing Room, Doris']

3. The vote, I thought, means nothing to women. We should be armed.
[In Erica Jong, *Fear of Flying* (1973)]

4. I often get lonely for unrealistic things: for something absolute.
[*The Observer*, 'Sayings of the Year', 1992]

O'Brien, Flann (Myles na Gopaleen, real name Brian O'Nolan) (1911–1966)
Irish novelist and journalist

1. The pocket was the first instinct of humanity and was used long years before the human race had a trousers between them – the quiver for arrows is one example and the pocket of the kangaroo is another.
[*At Swim-Two-Birds* (1939)]

2. When things go wrong and will not come right,
Though you do the best you can,
When life looks black as the hour of night–
A PINT OF PLAIN IS YOUR ONLY MAN.
[*At Swim-Two-Birds* (1939)]

3. The dawn was contagious, spreading rapidly about the heavens. Birds were stirring and the great kingly trees were being pleasantly interfered with by the first breezes. My heart was happy and full of zest for high adventure.
[*The Third Policeman* (1967)]

4. People who spend most of their natural lives riding iron bicycles over the rocky roadsteads of this parish get their personalities mixed up with the personalities of their bicycles as a result of the interchanging of the atoms of each of them and you would be surprised at the number of people in these parts who nearly are half people and half bicycles.
[*The Third Policeman* (1967)]

5. Do engine drivers, I wonder, eternally wish they were small boys?
[*The Best of Myles na Gopaleen* (1990)]

6. [Commenting on the fact that policemen always seem to look young]
A thing of duty is a boy for ever.
[Attr.]

O'Brien, R. Barry (1847–1918)
Irish barrister and author

1. At moments he had fits of depression and melancholy. He did not wish to be alone. He would often – a most unusual thing for him – talk for talking's sake. He would walk the streets of Dublin with a follower far into the night, rather than sit in his hotel by himself.
[*The Life of Charles Stewart Parnell* (1898)]

O'Casey, Sean (1880–1964)
Irish dramatist, author of realist tragi-comedies and autobiographer

1. He's an oul' butty o' mine – oh, he's a darlin' man, a daarlin' man.
[*Juno and the Paycock* (1924), I]

2. Th' whole worl's in a terrible state o' chassis!
[*Juno and the Paycock* (1924), I]

3. I often looked up at the sky an' assed meself the question – what is the stars, what is the stars?
[*Juno and the Paycock* (1924), I]

4. Sacred Heart of the Crucified Jesus, take away our hearts o' stone ... an' give us hearts o' flesh! ... Take away this murdherin' hate ... an' give us Thine own eternal love!
[*Juno and the Paycock* (1924), II]

5. The Polis as Polis, in this city, is Null an' Void!
[*Juno and the Paycock* (1924), III]

6. There's no reason to bring religion into it. I think we ought to have as great a regard for religion as we can, so as to keep it out of as many things as possible.
[*The Plough and the Stars* (1926), I]

7. I am going where life is more like life than it is here.
[*Cock-a-Doodle Dandy* (1949), III]

8. [Of P.G. Wodehouse]
English literature's performing flea.
[In P.G. Wodehouse, *Performing Flea* (1953)]

Occam, William of (c. 1280–1349)
English nominalist philosopher and Franciscan friar

1. *Entia non sunt multiplicanda praeter necessitatem.*
Entities should not be needlessly multiplied.
[*Quodlibeta* (c. 1324), V]

Ochs, Adolph S. (1858–1935)
American newspaper publisher and editor

1. All the news that's fit to print.
[Motto of the *New York Times*]

O'Connell, Daniel (1775–1847)
Irish politician, 'The Liberator', and nationalist; founder of the Catholic Association 1823

1. The Englishman has all the qualities of a poker except its occasional warmth.
[Attr.]

O'Connor, Mark (1945–)
Australian poet, dramatist and short-story writer

1. Yet all world languages die at last:
Greek of grammar and factions; Latin
of clotted syntax and Renaissance purism;
French of bad admirals and over-subtle vowels;
English and Chinese of their written forms;
Russian of subject people's hate.
['Lingua Romana']

O'Conor, Roderic (1860–1940)

1. [On Somerset Maugham]
A bedbug on which a sensitive man refuses to stamp because of the smell and squashiness.
[Attr. in Larry Powell, 'The Discovery of a New Master, Roderic O'Conor', *Etudes Irlandaises*, 1933]

O'Faolain, Seán (John Whelan) (1900–1991)
Irish short-story writer, novelist, critic and biographer

1. I have always felt that everybody on earth goes about in disguise.
[*What it feels like to be a Writer*]

2. Then the sniper turned over the dead body and looked into his brother's face.
['The Sniper']

3. He expressed his surprise that one so cool, so ladylike in public could be so different in private. She grunted peacefully and said in her muted brogue, 'Ah, shure, dürling, everything changes in the beddaroom.'
['The Faithless Wife']

Ogden, C.K. (1889–1957)
English linguist, co-founder of Basic English
and Richards, I.A. (1893–1979)
English literary critic, linguist, poet and teacher; co-founder of Basic English

1. The belief that words have a meaning of their own account is a relic of primitive word magic, and it is still a part of the air we breathe in nearly every discussion.
[*The Meaning of Meaning* (1923)]

Ogilvy, James, First Earl of Seafield (1663–1730)
Scottish politician and lawyer; Lord Chancellor of Scotland 1702–04, 1705–07

1. [On signing the Act of Union]
Now there's an end of ane old song.
[Remark, 1707]

O'Hagan, John Francis (1898–1987)
Australian composer of popular songs, musical comedies and revues

1. There's a track winding back to an old fashioned shack.
Along the road to Gundagai,
Where the blue gums are growing and the Murrumbidgee's flowing
Beneath that sunny sky.
Where my daddy and mother are waiting for me,
And the pals of my childhood once more I will see,
Then no more will I roam, when I'm heading right for home
Along the road to Gundagai.
['The Road to Gundagai', song]

O'Hara, Geoffrey (1882–1967)
Canadian-born American songwriter, composer and writer

1. K-K-Katy, beautiful Katy,
You're the only g-g-g-girl that I adore,
When the m-m-m-moon shines over the cow shed,
I'll be waiting at the k-k-k-kitchen door.
['K-K-Katy', song, 1918]

O'Keeffe, Georgia (1887–1986)
American artist

1. My feeling about life is a curious kind of triumphant feeling about seeing it bleak, knowing it is so, and walking into it fearlessly because one has no choice.
[Attr.]

O'Keeffe, John (1747–1833)
Irish dramatist and actor

1. Amo, amas, I love a lass,
As a cedar tall and slender;
Sweet cowslip's grace
Is her nom'native case,
And she's of the feminine gender.
[*The Agreeable Surprise* (1781), II.ii]

2. You should always except the present company.
[*The London Hermit* (1793), I.ii]

3. Fat, fair and forty.
[*The Irish Mimic* (1795)]

O'Kelly, Dennis (c. 1720–1787)
Irish horse-breeder

1. Eclipse first, the rest nowhere.
[Remark at Epsom Racecourse, 1769]

Oldys, William (1696–1761)
English bibliographer, antiquary, editor and writer

1. Busy, curious, thirsty fly,
Gently drink, and drink as I;
Freely welcome to my cup.
['The Fly' (1732)]

O'Malley, Frank Ward (1875–1932)
American illustrator, journalist, dramatist and writer

1. Life is just one damned thing after another.
[Attr.; also attributed to Elbert Hubbard]

O'Malley, King (1858–1953)
Australian politician

1. [In debate in the South Australian Parliament in 1896, on the question of seating in shops for shop-assistants]
A State could no more expect to rear healthy, vigorous, manly men and womanly women from semi-crippled, exhausted, worn-out, varicose-veined, weakened-genitive-organed mothers than a studmaster could expect to raise thorough-bred racehorses from broken-down ring-boned mares.
[In A. R. Hoyle, *King O'Malley 'The American Bounder'*]

Ondaatje, Michael (1943–)
Canadian author

1. The past is still, for us, a place that is not yet safely settled.
[*The Faber Book of Contemporary Canadian Short Stories* (1990), Preface]

2. [Comment after accepting a computer at the Wang International Festival of Authors; the author writes with a fountain pen]
I think giving this computer to the last Luddite is ridiculous. It's like giving a Porsche to someone who just discovered the bicycle.
[Attr.]

O'Neill, Eugene (1888–1953)
American dramatist, noted for his experimental techniques; Nobel prize 1936

1. Our lives are merely strange dark interludes in the electric display of God the Father!
[*Strange Interlude* (1928), I.ii]

Opie, John (1761–1807)
English portrait and historical painter, and writer

1. [Asked how he mixed his colours]
I mix them with my brains, sir.
[In Samuel Smiles, *Self-Help* (1859)]

Oppenheimer, J. Robert (1904–1967)
American nuclear physicist involved in atomic bomb research

1. The physicists have known sin; and this is a knowledge which they cannot lose.
[Lecture, 1947]

2. [On the consequences of the first atomic test]
We knew the world would not be the same.
[In Giovanitti and Freed, *The Decision to Drop the Bomb* (1965)]

Orbach, Susie (1946–)
American writer and feminist

1. Fat is a Feminist Issue.
[Title of book, 1978]

Orczy, Baroness (1865–1947)
Hungarian-born British historical novelist, short-story writer and illustrator

1. We seek him here, we seek him there,
Those Frenchies seek him everywhere.
Is he in heaven? – Is he in hell?
That demmed, elusive Pimpernel?
[*The Scarlet Pimpernel* (1905), 12]

2. The weariest nights, the longest days, sooner or later must perforce come to an end.
[*The Scarlet Pimpernel* (1905), 22]

O'Reilly, Tony (1936–)
Irish industrialist and former international rugby player

1. [Commenting on the voice of Winston McCarthy, the noted rugby commentator]
The love call of two pieces of sandpaper.
[*New Zealand Listener*, 1984]

O'Rourke, P.J. (1947–)
American writer and humorist

1. [On white South Africans]
They've never learned to stand up and lie like white men.
[*The Weekend Guardian*, 1993]

2. After all, what is your hosts' purpose in having a party? Surely not for you to enjoy yourself; if that were their sole purpose, they'd have simply sent champagne and women over to your place by taxi.
[Attr.]

Orred, Meta (19th century)
Writer and poet

1. In the gloaming, O, my darling!
When the lights are dim and low,
And the quiet shadows falling
Softly come and softly go.
['In the Gloaming', song, 1877]

Ortega y Gasset, José (1883–1955)
Spanish philosopher and critic

1. *¡Santificadas sean las cosas! ¡Amadlas, amadlas!*
Hallowed be objects! Love them, love them!
[*Meditaciones del Quijote* (*Meditations on Quijote*, 1914), 'Lector...' ('Reader...')]

2. *El placer sexual parece consistir en una súbita descarga de energía nerviosa. La fruicíon estética es una súbita descarga de emociones alusivas. Análogamente es la filosofía como una súbita descarga de intelección.*
Sexual pleasure seems to consist in a sudden discharge of nervous energy. Aesthetic enjoyment is a sudden discharge of allusive emotions. Similarly, philosophy is like a sudden discharge of intellectual activity.
[*Meditaciones del Quijote* (*Meditations on Quijote*, 1914), 'Lector...' ('Reader...')]

3. *Yo soy yo y mi circunstancia, y si no la salvo a ella no me salvo yo.*
I am myself and my circumstance, and if I cannot save it I cannot save myself
[*Meditaciones del Quijote* (*Meditations on Quijote*, 1914), 'Lector...' ('Reader...')]

4. *El arte es incapaz de soportar el peso de nuestra vida. Cuando lo intenta, fracasa, perdiendo su gracia esencial.*
Art is incapable of bearing the burden of our lives. When it tries, it fails, losing its essential grace.
[*El tema de nuestro tiempo* (*The Theme of our Time*, 1923), IX]

5. *Poca cosa es la vida si no piafa en ella un afán formidable de ampliar sus fronteras. Se vive en la proporción en que se ansía vivir más.*
Life is a petty thing unless there is pounding within it an enormous desire to extend its boundaries. We live in proportion to the extent to which we yearn to live more.
[*La deshumanización del arte* (*The Dehumanization of Art*, 1925), 'Invitación a comprender' ('Invitation to understand')]

6. *Pensar es el afán de captar mediante ideas la realidad.*
Thinking is the desire to gain reality by means of ideas.
[*La deshumanización del arte* (*The Dehumanization of Art*, 1925), 'La vuelta del revés' ('About-turn')]

7. *Con el pasado no se lucha cuerpo a cuerpo. El porvenir lo vence porque se lo traga. Como deje algo de él fuera, está perdido.*
You don't fight hand-to-hand with the past. The future conquers it because it swallows it. If it leaves part of it outside, it is lost.
[*La rebelión de las masas* (*The Rebellion of the Masses*, 1930), 10]

8. *Necesitamos de la historia íntegra para ver si logramos escapar de ella, no recaer en ella.*
We need all of history in order to see if we can manage to escape from it and not fall back into it.
[*La rebelión de las masas* (*The Rebellion of the Masses*, 1930), 10]

9. *Estos años asistimos al gigantesco espectáculo de innumerables vidas humanas que marchan perdidas en el laberinto de sí mismas por no tener a que entregarse.*
These days we are witnessing the giant spectacle of innumerable human lives wandering lost in the labyrinth of their own selves because they have nothing to which they may devote themselves.
[*La rebelión de las masas* (*The Rebellion of the Masses*, 1930), 10]

Ortega Spottorno, José
Journalist and Honorary President of El Pàis *newspaper*

1. *Estoy ... convencido de que la forma actual del capitalismo dejará paso a otra más humana y menos especulativa.*
I'm convinced that the present form of capitalism will make way for another one which will be more human and less speculative.
[*El País*, 14 March 1994, 'Certezas' ('Certainties')]

Orton, Joe (1933–1967)
English comic dramatist; novelist and diarist

1. I'd the upbringing a nun would envy and that's the truth. Until I was fifteen I was more familiar with Africa than my own body.
[*Entertaining Mr Sloane* (1964), I]

2. It's all any reasonable child can expect if the dad is present at the conception.
[*Entertaining Mr Sloane* (1964), III]

3. Every luxury was lavished on you – atheism, breast-feeding, circumcision. I had to make my own way.
[*Loot* (1967), I]

4. Reading isn't an occupation we encourage among police officers. We try to keep the paper work down to a minimum.
[*Loot* (1967), II]

5. You were born with your legs apart. They'll send you to the grave in a Y-shaped coffin.
[*What the Butler Saw* (1969), I]

6. Anything worth doing is worth doing in public.
[In Julie Burchill, *Sex and Sensibility*]

Orwell, George (Eric Blair) (1903–1950)
English satirical novelist, essayist and critic, born in India

1. He was an embittered atheist (the sort of atheist who does not so much disbelieve in God as personally dislike Him).
[*Down and Out in Paris and London* (1933), 30]

2. It is brought home to you ... that it is only because miners sweat their guts out that superior persons can remain superior ... All of us really owe the comparative decency of our lives to poor drudges underground, blackened to the eyes, with their throats full of coal dust, driving their shovels forward with arms and belly muscles of steel.
[*The Road to Wigan Pier* (1937), 2]

3. I sometimes think that the price of liberty is not so much eternal vigilance as eternal dirt.
[*The Road to Wigan Pier* (1937), 4]

4. We may find in the long run that tinned food is a deadlier weapon than the machine-gun.
[*The Road to Wigan Pier* (1937), 6]

5. As with the Christian religion, the worst advertisement for Socialism is its adherents.
[*The Road to Wigan Pier* (1937), 11]

6. To the ordinary working man, the sort you would meet in any pub on Saturday night, Socialism does not mean much more than better wages and shorter hours and nobody bossing you about.
[*The Road to Wigan Pier* (1937), 11]

7. I'm fat, but I'm thin inside. Has it ever struck you that there's a thin man inside every fat man, just as they say there's a statue inside every block of stone?
[*Coming Up For Air* (1939), I, 3. Cf. Kingsley Amis: 3 and Evelyn Waugh: 29]

8. Before the war, and especially before the Boer War, it was summer all the year round.
[*Coming Up for Air* (1939), II, 1]

9. Nine times out of ten a revolutionary is merely a climber with a bomb in his pocket.
[*New English Weekly*, 1939, Review of F.C. Green, *Stendhal*]

10. ...a cult of cheeriness and manliness, beer and cricket, briar pipes and monogamy, and it was at all times possible to earn a few guineas by writing an article denouncing 'highbrows'.
['Inside the Whale' (1940), 2]

11. England is not the jewelled isle of Shakespeare's much-quoted passage, nor is it the inferno depicted by Dr Goebbels. More than either it resembles a family, a rather stuffy Victorian family, with not many black sheep in it but with all its cupboards bursting with skeletons. It has rich relations who have to be kow-towed to and poor relations who are horribly sat upon, and there is a deep conspiracy about the source of the family income. It is a family in which the young are generally thwarted and most of the power is in the hands of irresponsible uncles and bedridden aunts. Still,

it is a family ... A family with the wrong members in control.
[*The Lion and the Unicorn* (1941), 'England, Your England', 3]

12. Probably the Battle of Waterloo was won on the playing-fields of Eton, but the opening battles of all subsequent wars have been lost there.
[*The Lion and the Unicorn* (1941), 'England, Your England', 4]

13. Whatever is funny is subversive, every joke is ultimately a custard pie ... A dirty joke is not ... a serious attack upon morality, but it is a sort of mental rebellion, a momentary wish that things were otherwise.
[*Horizon*, 1941, 'The Art of Donald McGill']

14. The high sentiments always win in the end, leaders who offer blood, toil, tears and sweat always get more out of their followers than those who offer safety and a good time. When it comes to the pinch, human beings are heroic.
[*Horizon*, 1941, 'The Art of Donald McGill']

15. To a surprising extent the war-lords in shining armour, the apostles of the martial virtues, tend not to die fighting when the time comes. History is full of ignominious getaways by the great and famous.
[*Tribune*, 1941, 'Who are the War Criminals?']

16. Man is the only creature that consumes without producing.
[*Animal Farm* (1945), 1]

17. Four legs good, two legs bad.
[*Animal Farm* (1945), 3]

18. War is war. The only good human being is a dead one.
[*Animal Farm* (1945), 4]

19. He intended, he said, to devote the rest of his life to learning the remaining twenty-two letters of the alphabet.
[*Animal Farm* (1945), 9]

20. All animals are equal, but some animals are more equal than others.
[*Animal Farm* (1945), 10]

21. The creatures outside looked from pig to man, and from man to pig, and from pig to man again; but already it was impossible to say which was which.
[*Animal Farm* (1945), 10]

22. The quickest way of ending a war is to lose it.
[*Polemic* (1946), 'Second Thoughts on James Burnham']

23. To see what is in front of one's nose needs a constant struggle.
[*Tribune*, 1946, 'In Front of Your Nose']

24. No book is genuinely free from political bias. The opinion that art should have nothing to do with politics is itself a political attitude.
['Why I Write' (1946)]

25. Good prose is like a window pane.
['Why I Write' (1946)]

26. It was a bright cold day in April, and the clocks were striking thirteen.
[*Nineteen Eighty-Four* (1949), I, 1]

27. Big Brother is watching you.
[*Nineteen Eighty-Four* (1949), I, 1]

28. Only the Thought Police mattered.
[*Nineteen Eighty-Four* (1949), I, 1]

29. Newspeak was the official language of Oceania.
[*Nineteen Eighty-Four* (1949), footnote]

30. War is Peace, Freedom is Slavery, Ignorance is Strength.
[*Nineteen Eighty-Four* (1949), I, 1]

31. The Two Minutes Hate.
[*Nineteen Eighty-Four* (1949), I, 1]

32. Who controls the past ... controls the future: who controls the present controls the past.
[*Nineteen Eighty-Four* (1949), I, 3]

33. The proles are not human beings.
[*Nineteen Eighty-Four* (1949), I, 5]

34. His mind ... fetched up with a bump against the Newspeak word doublethink.
[*Nineteen Eighty-Four* (1949), footnote]

35. Doublethink means the power of holding two contradictory beliefs in one's mind simultaneously, and accepting both of them.
[*Nineteen Eighty-Four* (1949), II, 9]

36. If you want a picture of the future, imagine a boot stamping on a human face – for ever.
[*Nineteen Eighty-Four* (1949), III, 3]

37. In our time, political speech and writing are largely the defence of the indefensible.
[*Shooting an Elephant* (1950), 'Politics and the English Language']

38. Prolonged, indiscriminate reviewing of books ... not only involves praising trash ... but constantly inventing reactions towards books about which one has no spontaneous feelings whatever.
[*Shooting an Elephant* (1950), 'Confessions of a Book Reviewer']

39. Serious sport has nothing to do with fair play. It is bound up with hatred, jealousy, boastfulness, disregard for all rules and sadistic pleasure in witnessing violence; in other words it is war minus the shooting.
[*Shooting an Elephant* (1950), 'The Sporting Spirit']

40. At 50, everyone has the face he deserves.
[Closing words, notebook, 1949. Cf. Camus: 13]

41. Each generation imagines itself to be more intelligent than the one that went before it, and wiser than the one that comes after it.
[Attr.]

Osborne, Dorothy (Lady Temple) (1627–1695)
English letter writer; wife of Sir William Temple

1. All letters, methinks, should be as free and easy as one's discourse, not studied as an oration, nor made up of hard words like a charm.
[Letter to Sir William Temple, 1653]

Osborne, John (1929–1994)
English dramatist, actor and 'Angry Young Man'

1. He really deserves some sort of decoration ... a medal inscribed 'For Vaguery in the Field'.
[*Look Back in Anger* (1956), I]

2. I'm not mentioned at all because my name is a dirty word.
[*Look Back in Anger* (1956), I]

3. I keep looking back, as far as I can remember, and I can't think what it was like to feel young, really young.
[*Look Back in Anger* (1956), I]

4. I don't think one 'comes down' from Jimmy's university. According to him, it's not even red brick, but white tile.
[*Look Back in Anger* (1956), II.i]

5. They spend their time mostly looking forward to the past.
[*Look Back in Anger* (1956), II.i]

6. Poor old Daddy – just one of those sturdy old plants left over from the Edwardian Wilderness, that can't understand why the sun isn't shining any more.
[*Look Back in Anger* (1956), II.ii]

7. There aren't any good, brave causes left. If the big bang does come, and we all get killed off, it won't be in aid of the old-fashioned, grand design. It'll just be for the Brave New-nothing-very-much-thank-you.
[*Look Back in Anger* (1956), III.i]

8. The injustice of it is almost perfect! The wrong people going hungry, the wrong people being loved, the wrong people dying!
[*Look Back in Anger* (1956), III.ii]

9. Don't clap too hard – it's a very old building.
[*The Entertainer* (1957), VII]

10. Thank God we're normal, normal, normal,
Thank God we're normal,
Yes, this is our finest shower!
[*The Entertainer* (1957), VII]

11. She's like the old line about justice – not only must be done but must be seen to be done.
[*Time Present* (1968), I]

12. She's not going to walk in here ... and turn it into a Golden Sanitary Towel Award Presentation.
[*Hotel in Amsterdam* (1968)]

13. [A notice in his bathroom]
Since I gave up hope I feel so much better.
[*The Independent*, 1994]

O'Shaughnessy, Arthur (1844–1881)
English poet and herpetologist

1. We are the music makers,
And we are the dreamers of dreams,
Wandering by lone sea-breakers,
And sitting by desolate streams;
World-losers and world-forsakers,
On whom the pale moon gleams:
Yet we are the movers and shakers
Of the world for ever, it seems.

With wonderful deathless ditties
We build up the world's great cities,
And out of a fabulous story
We fashion an empire's glory:
One man with a dream, at pleasure,
Shall go forth and conquer a crown;
And three with a new song's measure
Can trample an empire down.

We, in the ages lying
In the buried past of the earth,
Built Nineveh with our sighing
And Babel itself with our mirth;
And o'erthrew them with prophesying
To the old of the new world's worth;
For each age is a dream that is dying,
Or one that is coming to birth.
['Ode' (1874)]

Osler, Sir William
Canadian physician

1. [His description of alcohol]
Milk of the elderly.
[*The Globe and Mail*, 1988]

O'Sullivan, John L. (1813–1895)
American editor and diplomat

1. Understood as a central consolidated power, managing and directing the various general interests of the society, all government is evil, and the parent of evil ... The best government is that which governs least.
[*United States Magazine and Democratic Review*, 1837, Introduction]

2. Our manifest destiny to overspread the continent allotted by Providence for the free development of our yearly multiplying millions.
[*United States Magazine and Democratic Review*, 1837, XVII]

3. [Of whisky]
A torchlight procession marching down your throat.
[Attr.]

Otis, James (1725–1783)
American lawyer, politician and pamphleteer

1. Taxation without representation is tyranny.
[Attr.]

Otway, Thomas (1652–1685)
English tragic dramatist and poet

1. You wags that judge by rote, and damn by rule.
[*Titus and Berenice* (1677), Prologue]

2. And for an apple damn'd mankind.
[*The Orphan* (1680), III.i]

3. What mighty ills have not been done by woman!
Who was't betrayed the Capitol? – A woman!
Who lost Mark Antony the world? – A woman!
Who was the cause of a long ten years' war,
And laid at last old Troy in ashes? – Woman!
Destructive, damnable, deceitful woman!
[*The Orphan* (1680), III.i]

4. Oh woman! lovely woman! Nature made thee
To temper man: we had been brutes without you;
Angels are painted fair, to look like you;
There's in you all that we believe of heav'n,
Amazing brightness, purity, and truth,
Eternal joy, and everlasting love.
[*Venice Preserv'd* (1682), I]

5. No praying, it spoils business.
[*Venice Preserv'd* (1682), II]

6. These are rogues that pretend to be of a religion now!
Well, all I say is, honest atheism for my money.
[*The Atheist* (1683), III]

Ouida (Marie Louise de la Ramée) (1839–1908)
English novelist; essayist, critic and short-story writer

1. Even of death Christianity has made a terror which was unknown to the gay calmness of the Pagan.
[*Views and Opinions* (1895), 'The Failure of Christianity']

2. A cruel story runs on wheels, and every hand oils the wheels as they run.
[*Wisdom, Wit and Pathos*, 'Moths']

Overbury, Sir Thomas (1581–1613)
English poet and courtier

1. He disdains all things above his reach, and preferreth all countries before his own.
[*Miscellaneous Works* (1632), 'An Affectate Traveller']

2. You cannot name any example in any heathen author but I will better it in Scripture.
[*Crumms Fal'n From King James's Table*, 10]

Ovid (43 BC–18 AD)
Roman poet, noted for his love poetry

1. *Procul omen abesto!*
Far from us be that fate!
[*Amores*, I, 14, line 41]

2. *Hoc quoque iussit Amor, procul hinc, procul este severae,*
Non estis teneris apta theatra modis.
This too Love has commanded of me – hence, be hence, you women who are severe; you are no fit audience for my tender strains.
[*Amores, II, 1, line 3*]

3. *Spectatum veniunt, veniunt spectentur ut ipsae.*
The women come to see, they come that they may be seen.
[*Ars Amatoria*, I, line 99]

4. *Quae dant, quaeque negant, gaudent tamen esse rogatae.*
Whether they give or refuse, women are glad that they have been asked.
[*Ars Amatoria*, I, line 345]

5. *Delectant etiam castas praeconia formae;*
Virginibus curae grataque forma sua est.
Even respectable girls delight in hearing their beauty praised; even the innocent are worried and pleased by their appearance.
[*Ars Amatoria*, I, line 623]

6. *Iuppiter ex alto periuria ridet amantum.*
Jupiter from on high smiles at lovers' perjuries.
[*Ars Amatoria*, I, line 633]

7. [*Ovid's hope for poetic fame*]
Forsitan et nostrum nomen miscebitur istis.
Perhaps our name will be linked with these.
[*Ars Amatoria*, III, line 339]

8. *Qui finem quaeris amoris,*
Cedet amor rebus; res age, tutus eris.
You who seek an end to love, love will yield to business: be busy, and you will be safe.
[*Remedia Amoris*, line 143]

9. *Virginibus cordi grataque forma sua est.*
Dear to young girls' hearts is their own beauty.
[*De Medicamine Faciei*, 32]

10. *Crede mihi, distant mores a carmine nostri–*
vita verecunda est, Musa iocosa mea.
Believe me, my moral character differs from my verse. My life is chaste, my muse is playful.
[*Tristia*, II]

11. *Sponte sua carmen numeros veniebat ad aptos,*
Et quod temptabam dicere versus erat.
Of its own accord my song used to come in the right rhythms, and what I was trying to say was verse.
[*Tristia*, IV]

12. *Adde quod ingenuas didicisse fideliter artes*
Emollit mores nec sinit esse feros.
Add the fact that to have diligently studied the liberal arts refines behaviour and does not allow it to be savage.
[*Epistulae Ex Ponto*, II, 9, line 47]

13. *Ut desint vires, tamen est laudanda voluntas.*
Though strength may be lacking, yet willingness is to be praised.
[*Epistulae Ex Ponto*, III, 4, line 29]

14. *Gutta cavat lapidem, consumitur anulus usu.*
Drops of water hollow out a stone, a ring is worn away by use.
[*Epistulae Ex Ponto*, IV, 10, line 5. Cf. Lucretius: 4]

15. *Iam seges est ubi Troia fuit.*
Now there are fields of corn where Troy once was.
[*Heroides*, I, line 53]

16. *Meminerunt omnia amantes.*
Lovers remember everything.
[*Heroides*, XV, line 43]

17. *Chaos, rudis indigestaque moles.*
Chaos, an ill-formed and unordered mass.
[*Metamorphoses*, I, line 7]

18. *Materiam superabat opus.*
The workmanship triumphed over the material.
[*Metamorphoses*, II, line 5]

19. *Medio tutissimus ibis.*
The middle way is the safest for you.
[*Metamorphoses*, II, line 137]

20. *Inopem me copia fecit.*
Plenty has made me poor.
[*Metamorphoses*, III, line 466]

21. *Ipse docet quid agam; fas est et ab hoste doceri.*
He himself teaches what I should do; it is right to learn even from an enemy.
[*Metamorphoses*, IV, line 428]

22. *Video meliora, proboque;*
Deteriora sequor.
I see the better way, and approve it, but I follow the worse.
[*Metamorphoses*, VII, line 20]

23. *Tempus edax rerum, tuque, invidiosa vetustas,*
Omnia destruitis vitiataque dentibus aevi
Paulatim lenta consumitis omnia morte.
Time, the devourer of all things, and envious age, together you destroy everything, and little by little you consume all you have corrupted with your grinding teeth in a lingering death.
[*Metamorphoses*, XV, line 234]

24. *Iamque opus exegi, quod nec Iovis ira, nec ignis,*
Nec poterit ferrum, nec edax abolere vetustas.
And now I have completed a work, which neither the wrath of Jove, nor fire, nor the sword, nor devouring age shall be able to destroy.
[*Metamorphoses*, XV, line 871]

Owen, Dr David (1938–)
English politician; Labour Foreign Secretary 1977–79, and co-founder of the SDP, 1981

1. We are fed up with fudging and nudging, with mush and slush.
[Speech, Labour Party Conference, Blackpool, 1980]

2. It was on this issue, the nuclear defence of Britain, on which I left the Labour Party, and on this issue I am prepared to stake my entire political career.
[*The Observer*, 'Sayings of the Week', 1986]

3. No general in the midst of battle has a great discussion about what he is going to do if defeated.
[*The Observer*, 'Sayings of the Week', 1987]

Owen, John (c. 1560–1622)
Welsh epigrammatist and teacher

1. God and the doctor we alike adore
But only when in danger, not before;

The danger o'er, both are alike requited,
God is forgotten, and the Doctor slighted.
[*Epigrams*]

Owen, Robert (1771–1858)
Welsh social reformer, socialist and industrialist; pioneer of co-operative societies

1. [To W. Allen, on dissolving their business partnership]
All the world is queer save thee and me, and even thou art a little queer.
[Attr., 1828]

Owen, Roderic (1921–)

1. The important thing is to know when to laugh, or since laughing is somewhat undignified, to smile.
[*The Golden Bubble*]

Owen, Wilfred (1893–1918)
English war poet

1. What passing-bells for these who die as cattle?
Only the monstrous anger of the guns.
Only the stuttering rifles' rapid rattle
Can patter out their hasty orisons...

2. And bugles calling for them from sad shires...

3. The pallor of girls' brows shall be their pall;
Their flowers the tenderness of patient minds,
And each slow dusk a drawing-down of blinds.
['Anthem for Doomed Youth' (1917)]

4. And in the happy no-time of his sleeping
Death took him by the heart.
['Asleep' (1917)]

5. If you could hear, at every jolt, the blood
Come gargling from the froth-corrupted lungs,
Obscene as cancer, bitter as the cud
Of vile, incurable sores on innocent tongues,–
My friend, you would not tell with such high zest
To children ardent for some desperate glory,
The old Lie: *Dulce et decorum est*
Pro patria mori.
['Dulce et decorum est' (1917)]

6. Move him into the sun...
If anything might rouse him now
The kind old sun will know...

7. Was it for this the clay grew tall!
– O what made fatuous sunbeams toil
To break earth's sleep at all?
['Futility' (1917)]

8. Red lips are not so red
As the stained stones kissed by the English dead.
['Greater Love' (1917)]

9. So secretly, like wrongs hushed-up, they went:
They were not ours.
We never heard to which front these were sent.
['The Send-Off' (1918)]

10. Hour after hour they ponder the warm field,–
And the far valley behind, where the buttercup
Had blessed with gold their slow boots coming up.
['Spring Offensive' (1918)]

11. It seemed that out of battle I escaped
Down some profound dull tunnel, long since scooped
Through granites which titanic wars had groined...

12. 'Strange friend,' I said, 'here is no cause to mourn.'
'None,' said the other, 'save the undone years,
The hopelessness. Whatever hope is yours,
Was my life also; I went hunting wild
After the wildest beauty in the world.'...

13. For by my glee might many men have laughed,
And of my weeping something have been left,
Which must die now. I mean the truth untold,
The pity of war, the pity war distilled.
Now men will go content with what we spoiled,
Or, discontent, boil bloody, and be spilled.
They will be swift with swiftness of the tigress,
None will break ranks, though nations trek from progress.
Courage was mine, and I had mystery,
Wisdom was mine, and I had mastery;
To miss the march of the retreating world
Into vain citadels that are not walled...

14. I am the enemy you killed, my friend.
['Strange Meeting' (1918)]

15. My subject is War, and the pity of War. The Poetry is in the pity.
[Quoted in *Poems* (1963), Preface]

16. All the poet can do today is to warn.
That is why the true Poets must be truthful.
[Quoted in *Poems* (1963), Preface]

Oxenstierna, Count Axel (1583–1654)
Swedish statesman; Chancellor from 1612

1. Do you not know, my son, with how little wisdom the world is ruled?
[Letter, 1648]

Packard, Vance (1914–)
US writer, teacher and cultural commentator

1. The Hidden Persuaders.
[Title of book, 1957]

Paglia, Camille (1947–)
American Professor of Humanities

1. If civilisation had been left in female hands, we would still be living in grass huts.
[*Sex, Art and American Culture: Essays* (1992)]

Pain, Barry (1864–1928)
English humorist, novelist and short-story writer

1. 'Come, little cottage girl, you seem
To want my cup of tea;
And will you take a little cream?
Now tell the truth to me.'
She had a rustic, woodland grin
Her cheek was soft as silk,
And she replied, 'sir, please put in
A little drop of milk.'
[*The Poets at Tea*, 'Wordsworth']

Paine, Thomas (1737–1809)
English-born American radical journalist, political theorist, deist and pamphleteer

1. Government, even in its best state, is but a necessary evil; in its worst state, an intolerable one. Government, like dress, is the badge of lost innocence; the palaces of kings are built upon the ruins of the bowers of paradise.
[*Common Sense* (1776), 1]

2. As to religion, I hold it to be the indispensable duty of government to protect all conscientious professors thereof,

and I know of no other business which government hath to do therewith.
[*Common Sense* (1776), 4]

3. These are the times that try men's souls. The summer soldier and the sunshine patriot will, in this crisis, shrink from the service of their country; but he that stands it *now*, deserves the love and thanks of men and women.
[*Pennsylvania Journal*, 1776, 'The American Crisis']

4. [Of Burke's *Reflections on the Revolution in France*]
[Burke] is not affected by the reality of distress touching his heart, but by the showy resemblance of it striking his imagination. He pities the plumage, but forgets the dying bird.
[*The Rights of Man* (1791)]

5. Lay then the axe to the root, and teach governments humanity. It is their sanguinary punishments which corrupt mankind.
[*The Rights of Man* (1791)]

6. Man is not the enemy of Man, but through the medium of a false system of government.
[*The Rights of Man* (1791)]

7. My country is the world, and my religion is to do good.
[*The Rights of Man* (1791)]

8. The final event to himself [Mr Burke] has been, that as he rose like a rocket, he fell like the stick.
[*Letter to the Addressers on the late Proclamation* (1792)]

9. It is necessary to the happiness of man that he be mentally faithful to himself. Infidelity does not consist in believing, or in disbelieving, it consists in professing to believe what one does not believe.
[*The Age of Reason*, I (1794)]

10. The sublime and the ridiculous are often so nearly related, that it is difficult to class them separately. One step above the sublime, makes the ridiculous; and one step above the ridiculous, makes the sublime again.
[*The Age of Reason*, II (1795). Cf. Napoleon: 6]

11. A share in two revolutions is living to some purpose.
[In Eric Foner, *Tom Paine and Revolutionary America* (1976)]

Paisley, Rev. Ian (1926–)
Protestant minister and Loyalist, head of Ulster Democratic Unionist Party

1. The Roman Catholic Church is getting nearer to communism every day.
[*The Irish Times*, 1969]

Palacio Valdés, Armando (1853–1938)
Spanish novelist

1. *Si quieres ser feliz, aparenta ser desgraciado.*
If you want to be happy, pretend to be miserable.
[*Papeles del doctor Angélico* (*Doctor Angélico's Papers*, 1911), 'Experiences and Outpourings']

2. *Cuando un hombre deja de ser un dios para su esposa, puede tener la seguridad de que ya es menos que un hombre.*
When a man stops being a god for his wife, he can be sure that he's now less than a man.
[*Papeles del doctor Angélico* (*Doctor Angélico's Papers*, 1911), 'Experiences and Outpourings']

3. *La oratoria política es el arte de decir vulgaridades con corrección y propiedad.*
Political oratory is the art of saying platitudes with courtesy and propriety.
[*Testamento literario* (*Literary Testament*, 1929), 'Politics']

Palafox, José de (1780–1847)
Spanish general

1. [Reply to demand for surrender at siege of Saragossa, 1808]
Guerra a cuchillo.
War to the knife.
[Attr.]

Paley, Rev. William (1743–1805)
English theologian and utilitarian philosopher

1. Who can refute a sneer?
[*Principles of Moral and Political Philosophy* (1785), V, 9]

Palmer, H.R. (1834–1907)
American composer and choir master; lecturer and writer

1. Yield not to temptation, for yielding is sin;
Each victory will help you some other to win...

2. Shun evil companions; bad language disdain;
God's name hold in reverence, nor take it in vain.
[Hymn]

Palmer, Nettie (1885–1964)
Australian literary critic

1. But is there, I wonder, any such thing as 'pure' literature? Isn't it just a conception of people who look on writing as an escape from the living world? Perhaps a painter, or musician, can cut himself off, in his work, from what's going on around him, but a writer can't.
[*Fourteen Years*..., Journal entry, 1939]

Palmer, Samuel (1805–1881)
English painter of visionary landscapes; watercolourist and etcher

1. A picture has been said to be something between a thing and a thought.
[In Arthur Symons, *Life of Blake*]

Palmer, Vance (1885–1959)
Australian novelist, short-story writer and critic

1. [On Australia in the Second World War]
I believe we will survive; that what is significant in us will survive; that we will come out of this struggle battered, stripped to the bone, but spiritually sounder than we went in, surer of our essential character, adults in a wider world than the one we lived in hitherto. These are great, tragic days. Let us accept them stoically, and make every yard of Australian earth a battle-station.
[*Meanjin Papers*, 1942]

Palmerston, Lord (Henry John Temple, Third Viscount Palmerston) (1784–1865)
English statesman; Whig Prime Minister 1855–58, 1859–65

1. I therefore fearlessly challenge the verdict which this House ... is to give ... whether, as the Roman, in days of old, held himself free from indignity, when he could say *Civis Romanus sum*; so also a British subject, in whatever land he may be, shall feel confident that the watchful eye and the strong arm of England will protect him against injustice and wrong.
[Speech, House of Commons, 1850]

2. You may call it coalition, you may call it the accidental and fortuitous concurrence of atoms.
[Speech, House of Commons, 1857]

3. What is merit? The opinion one man entertains of another.
[In Carlyle, 'Shooting Niagara and After?' (1837)]

4. [Of the Schleswig-Holstein question]
There are only three men who have ever understood it: one was Prince Albert, who is dead; the second was a German professor, who became mad. I am the third – and I have forgotten all about it.
[Attr. in Palmer, *Quotations in History*]

5. Die, my dear Doctor, that's the last thing I shall do!
[Attr. last words]

Pankhurst, Dame Christabel (1880–1958)
English suffragette and WSPU organizer; daughter of Emmeline Pankhurst

1. We are not ashamed of what we have done, because, when you have a great cause to fight for, the moment of greatest humiliation is the moment when the spirit is proudest.
[Speech, Albert Hall, London, 1908]

2. We are here to claim our right as women, not only to be free, but to fight for freedom. It is our privilege, as well as our pride and our joy, to take some part in this militant movement, which, as we believe, means the regeneration of all humanity.
[Speech, 1911]

3. What we suffragettes aspire to be when we are enfranchised is ambassadors of freedom to women in other parts of the world, who are not so free as we are.
[Speech, Carnegie Hall, New York, 1915]

4. Never lose your temper with the Press or the public is a major rule of political life.
[*Unshackled* (1959)]

Pankhurst, Emmeline (1858–1928)
English suffragette, founder of the militant Women's Social and Political Union, 1903

1. We have taken this action, because as women ... we realize that the condition of our sex is so deplorable that it is our duty even to break the law in order to call attention to the reasons why we do so.
[Speech in court, 1908]

2. Men made the moral code and they expect women to accept it.
[Speech, 1913]

3. I have no sense of guilt. I look upon myself as a prisoner of war. I am under no moral obligation to conform to, or in any way accept, the sentence imposed upon me.
[Speech in court, 1913]

4. If civilization is to advance at all in the future, it must be through the help of women, women freed of their political shackles, women with full power to work their will in society. It was rapidly becoming clear to my mind that men regarded women as a servant class in the community, and that women were going to remain in the servant class until they lifted themselves out of it.
[*My Own Story* (1914)]

5. Women had always fought for men, and for their children. Now they were ready to fight for their own human rights. Our militant movement was established.
[*My Own Story* (1914)]

6. The argument of the broken pane of glass is the most valuable argument in modern politics.
[Attr.]

Pankhurst, Sylvia (1882–1960)
English suffragette, pacifist and internationalist; daughter of Emmeline Pankhurst

1. I could not give my name to aid the slaughter in this war, fought on both sides for grossly material ends, which did not justify the sacrifice of a single mother's son. Clearly I must continue to oppose it, and expose it, to all whom I could reach with voice or pen.
[*The Home Front*, 25]

2. I have gone to war too ... I am going to fight capitalism even if it kills me. It is wrong that people like you should be comfortable and well fed while all around you people are starving.
[In David Mitchell, *The Fighting Pankhursts*]

Papprill, Ross F. (1908–1975)

1. There are two kinds of people in the world: those who believe there are two kinds of people in the world, and those who don't.
[Attr.]

Park, Mungo (1771–1806)
Scottish explorer of Africa, travel writer and physician

1. [Remark on finding a gibbet in an unexplored part of Africa]
The sight of it gave me infinite pleasure, as it proved that I was in a civilized society.
[Attr.]

Parker, Charlie (1920–1955)
American jazz alto saxophonist and composer; leading exponent of 'bepop'

1. Music is your own experience, your thoughts, your wisdom. If you don't live it, it won't come out of your horn.
[In Shapiro and Hentoff, *Hear Me Talkin' to Ya* (1955)]

Parker, Dorothy (1893–1967)
American poet, short-story writer, critic and wit

1. Where's the man could ease a heart,
Like a satin gown?
[*Not So Deep as a Well* (1937), 'The Satin Dress']

2. By the time you swear you're his,
Shivering and sighing,
And he vows his passion is
Infinite, undying–
Lady, make a note of this:
One of you is lying.
[*Not So Deep as a Well* (1937), 'Unfortunate Coincidence']

3. Four be the things I'd be better without:
Love, curiosity, freckles, and doubt.
[*Not So Deep as a Well* (1937), 'Inventory']

4. Oh, life is a glorious cycle of song,
A medley of extemporanea;
And love is a thing that can never go wrong,
And I am Marie of Roumania.
[*Not So Deep as a Well* (1937), 'Comment']

5. Razors pain you;
Rivers are damp;
Acids stain you;
And drugs cause cramp.
Guns aren't lawful;
Nooses give;
Gas smells awful;
You might as well live.
[*Not So Deep as a Well* (1937), 'Résumé']

6. Why is it no one ever sent me yet
One perfect limousine, do you suppose?
Ah no, it's always just my luck to get
One perfect rose.
[*Not So Deep as a Well* (1937), 'One Perfect Rose']

7. Men seldom make passes
At girls who wear glasses.
[*Not So Deep as a Well* (1937), 'News Item']

8. He lies below, correct in cypress wood,
And entertains the most exclusive worms.
[*Not So Deep as a Well* (1937), 'Epitaph for a Very Rich Man']

9. Sorrow is tranquillity remembered in emotion.
[*Here Lies* (1939), 'Sentiment'. Cf. William Wordsworth: 166]

10. It costs me never a stab nor squirm
To tread by chance upon a worm.
'Aha, my little dear,' I say,
'Your clan will pay me back one day.'
[*Sunset Gun*, 'Thoughts for a Sunshiny Morning']

11. [On A. A. Milne's *The House at Pooh Corner* in her column 'Constant Reader']
Tonstant Weader fwowed up.
[*The New Yorker*, 1928]

12. How do people go to sleep? I'm afraid I've lost the knack. I might try busting myself smartly over the temple with the nightlight. I might repeat to myself, slowly and soothingly, a list of quotations beautiful from minds profound; if I can remember any of the damned things.
[*Here Lies* (1939), 'The Little Hours']

13. Brevity is the soul of lingerie.
[In Alexander Woollcott, *While Rome Burns* (1934)]

14. [Of the Yale Prom]
If all the girls attending it were laid end to end, I wouldn't be at all surprised.
[In Alexander Woollcott, *While Rome Burns* (1934)]

15. [Her own epitaph]
Excuse my dust.
[In Alexander Woollcott, *While Rome Burns* (1934)]

16. I was fired from there, finally, for a lot of things, among them my insistence that the Immaculate Conception was spontaneous combustion.
[In Malcolm Cowley, *Writers at Work, First Series* (1958)]

17. [Response to news that President Calvin Coolidge had died]
How could they tell?
[In J. Keats, *You Might As Well Live* (1970), Foreword; also attributed to H.L. Mencken]

18. [Of an acquaintance]
You know, she speaks eighteen languages. And she can't say 'No' in any of them.
[In J. Keats, *You Might As Well Live* (1970), I, 5]

19. [When challenged to compose a sentence using the word 'horticulture']
You can lead a horticulture but you can't make her think.
[In J. Keats, *You Might As Well Live* (1970), I, 5]

20. [Suggesting words for tombstone]
This is on me.
[In J. Keats, *You Might As Well Live* (1970), I, 5]

21. [Comment when a man excused himself to go to the men's room]
He really needs to telephone, but he's too embarrassed to say so.
[In J. Keats, *You Might As Well Live* (1970), I, 5]

22. [Remark when someone said, 'They're ducking for apples' at a Halloween party]
There, but for a typographical error, is the story of my life.
[In J. Keats, *You Might As Well Live* (1970), I, 6]

23. [On her requirements for an apartment]
[Enough space] to lay a hat – and a few friends.
[In J. Keats, *You Might As Well Live* (1970), II, 1]

24. [Telegram sent to Mary Sherwood after her much-publicised pregnancy]
Dear Mary, We all knew you had it in you.
[In J. Keats, *You Might As Well Live* (1970), II, 2]

25. [Said on going into hospital for an abortion]
It serves me right for putting all my eggs in one bastard.
[Attr. in J. Keats, *You Might As Well Live* (1970), II, 3]

26. [Said of her husband on the day their divorce became final]
Oh, don't worry about Alan ... Alan will always land on somebody's feet.
[In J. Keats, *You Might As Well Live* (1970), IV, 1]

27. [Pressing a button marked NURSE during a stay in hospital]
That should assure us of at least forty-five minutes of undisturbed privacy.
[In James R. Gaines, *Days and Nights of the Algonquin Round Table* (1977)]

28. [Remark on a performance by Katherine Hepburn]
She ran the whole gamut of the emotions from A to B.
[In G. Carey, *Katherine Hepburn* (1985)]

29. [Quoting from *The Great Gatsby* on paying her last respects to Scott Fitzgerald]
The poor son-of-a-bitch!
[In B. Thomas, *Thalberg: Life and Legend*]

30. This is not a novel to be tossed aside lightly. It should be thrown with great force.
[In James R. Gaines, *Wit's End*]

31. You can't teach an old dogma new tricks.
[In James R. Gaines, *Wit's End*]

32. [Reply to the comment, 'Anyway, she's always very nice to her inferiors']
Where does she find them?
[In Lyttelton Hart-Davis, *Letters*]

33. [Giving her version of the two most beautiful words in the English language]
Check enclosed.
[Attr.]

34. [On naming her canary 'Onan']
Because he spills his seed on the ground.
[Attr.]

35. [Response to being described as 'very outspoken']
Outspoken by whom?
[Attr.]

36. Scratch an actor and you'll find an actress.
[Attr.]

Parker, Henry Taylor (1867–1934)
American journalist; drama and music critic

1. [Rebuking some talkative members of an audience, near whom he was sitting]
Those people on the stage are making such a noise I can't hear a word you're saying.
[In L. Humphrey, *The Humor of Music*]

Parker, Hubert Lister (Baron Parker of Waddington) (1900–1972)
English Lord Chief Justice, 1958–71

1. A judge is not supposed to know anything about the facts of life until they have been presented in evidence and explained to him at least three times.
[*The Observer*, 'Sayings of the Week', 1961]

Parker, John (1729–1775)
American revolutionary soldier

1. [Command given at the start of the Battle of Lexington]
Stand your ground. Don't fire unless fired upon, but if they mean to have a war, let it begin here!
[In J. Bartlett, *Familiar Quotations*]

Parker, Johnny

1. [On helping to free British seamen held prisoner on the German ship, *Altmark*]
The Navy's here!
[*The Times*, 1940]

Parker, Martin (c. 1600–c. 1656)
English ballad writer

1. The Man in the Moon may wear out his shoon,
By running after Charles-his-Wain,
But all's to no end; for the times will not mend
Till the King enjoys his own again.
['Upon Defacing of Whitehall' (1671)]

2. You gentlemen of England
Who live at home at ease,
How little do you think
On the dangers of the seas.
[In J.O. Halliwell (ed.), *Early Naval Ballads* (1841), 'The Valiant Sailors']

Parker, Ross (1914–1974) and Charles, Hughie (1907–)
British songwriters

1. There'll always be an England
While there's a country lane.
['There'll Always be an England', song, 1939]

Parkes, Sir Henry (1815–1896)
Australian politician, writer and poet

1. [On being congratulated when he was eighty years old on the birth of his last child]
Don't say my last, you damned fool! Say my latest.
[In Randolph Bedford, *Naught to Thirty-three*]

2. [On William Nicholas Willis]
Ho! the honourable member for Bourke, who is believed to have committed every crime in the calendar, – except the one we could so easily have forgiven him – suicide.
[In Bill Wannan, *With Malice Aforethought*]

Parkinson, Cyril Northcote (1909–1993)
English political scientist and historian

1. Work expands so as to fill the time available for its completion.
[*Parkinson's Law* (1958), 1]

2. The rise in the total of those employed is governed by Parkinson's Law and would be much the same whether the volume of work were to increase, diminish or even disappear.
[*Parkinson's Law* (1958), 1]

3. The British, being brought up on team games, enter their House of Commons in the spirit of those who would rather be doing something else. If they cannot be playing golf or tennis, they can at least pretend that politics is a game with very similar rules.
[*Parkinson's Law* (1958), 2]

4. It is now known ... that men enter local politics solely as a result of being unhappily married.
[*Parkinson's Law* (1958), 10]

Parkman, Francis (1823–1893)
American historian and horticulturalist

1. The public demands elocution rather than reason of those who address it ... On matters of the greatest interest it craves to be excited or amused.
[*The Tale of the Ripe Scholar*]

Parnell, Anna (1852–1911)

1. Two children playing by a stream
Two lovers walking in a dream
A married pair whose dream is o'er,
Two old folks who are quite a bore.
['Love's Four Ages']

Parnell, Charles Stewart (1846–1891)
Irish nationalist politician, leader of the Irish Home Rule movement

1. No man has a right to fix the boundary of the march of a nation: no man has a right to say to his country – thus far shalt thou go and no further.
[Speech, 1885]

Parr, Samuel (1747–1825)
English Latin scholar and political writer

1. [Of Dr Johnson]
Now that the old lion is dead, every ass thinks he may kick at him.
[In Boswell, *The Life of Samuel Johnson* (1791)]

Parsons, Tony (1922–)
British diplomat

1. [Of the working class in the 1980s]
They are the real class traitors, betrayers of the men who fought the Second World War, those men who fought for Churchill but voted for Clement Attlee. But in the tattooed jungle they have no sense of history. The true unruly children of Thatcherism, they know their place and wallow in their peasanthood.
[*Arena*, 1989]

2. The death of the grammar schools – those public schools without the sodomy – resulted in state education relinquishing its role of nurturing bright young working class kids.
[*Arena*, 1989]

Parton, Dolly (1946–)
American country singer and songwriter

1. You'd be surprised how much it costs to look this cheap.
[In Carole McKenzie, *Quotable Women* (1992)]

Pascal, Blaise (1623–1662)
French philosopher and scientist; mathematician, physicist, theologian and moralist

1. *Je n'ai fait celle-ci plus longue que parce que je n'ai pas eu le loisir de la faire plus courte.*
I have made this letter longer only because I have not had time to make it shorter.
[*Lettres Provinciales* (1657), 16. Cf. Thoreau: 26]

2. *A mesure qu'on a plus d'esprit, on trouve qu'il y a plus d'hommes originaux. Les gens du commun ne trouvent point de différence entre les hommes.*
The more intelligence one has the more people one finds original. Commonplace people see no difference between men.
[*Pensées* (1670), I, 7]

3. *La dernière chose qu'on trouve en faisant un ouvrage, est de savoir celle qu'il faut mettre la première.*
The last thing one finds out when constructing a work is what to put first.
[*Pensées* (1670), I, 19]

4. *Quand on voit le style naturel, on est tout étonné et ravi, car on s'attendait de voir un auteur, et on trouve un homme.*
When we see a natural style, we are quite surprised and delighted, for we expected to see an author and we find a man.
[*Pensées* (1670), I, 29]

5. *Le nez de Cléopâtre: s'il eût été plus court, toute la face de la terre aurait changé.*
If Cleopatra's nose had been shorter the whole face of the earth would have changed.
[*Pensées* (1670), II, 62]

6. *Je ne puis pardonner à Descartes: il aurait bien voulu, dans toute sa philosophie, pouvoir se passer de Dieu; mais il n'a pu s'empêcher de lui faire donner une chiquenaude, pour mettre le monde en mouvement; après celà, il n'a plus eu que faire de Dieu.*
I cannot forgive Descartes; in all his philosophy he did his best to dispense with God. But he could not avoid making Him set the world in motion with a flick of His finger; after that he had no more use for God.
[*Pensées* (1670), II, 77]

7. *Tout le malheur des hommes vient d'une seule chose, qui est de ne savoir pas demeurer en repos dans une chambre.*
All the troubles of men are caused by one single thing, which is their inability to stay quietly in a room.
[*Pensées* (1670), II, 139]

8. *Le silence éternel de ces espaces infinis m'effraie.*
The eternal silence of these infinite spaces terrifies me.
[*Pensées* (1670), III, 206]

9. *Le dernier acte est sanglant, quelque belle que soit la comédie en tout le reste.*
The last act is bloody, however delightful the rest of the play may be.
[*Pensées* (1670), III, 210]

10. *On mourra seul.*
We shall die alone.
[*Pensées* (1670), III, 211]

11. *Le coeur a ses raisons que la raison ne connaît point.*
The heart has its reasons which the mind knows nothing of.
[*Pensées* (1670), IV, 277. Cf. Lévi-Strauss: 1]

12. *L'homme n'est qu'un roseau, le plus faible de la nature; mais c'est un roseau pensant.*
Man is only a reed, the feeblest thing in nature; but he is a thinking reed.
[*Pensées* (1670), VI, 347]

13. *Se moquer de la philosophie, c'est vraiment philosopher.*
To ridicule philosophy is truly to philosophize.
[*Pensées* (1670), VI, 430]

14. *Le moi est haïssable.*
Self is hateful.
[*Pensées* (1670), VII, 455]

15. *Tu ne me chercherais pas si tu ne me possédais. Ne t'inquiète donc pas.*
You would not be looking for me if you did not possess me. So do not be anxious.
[*Pensées* (1670), VII, 553]

Pasolini, Pier Paolo (1922–1975)
Italian film director, poet, novelist and critic

1. *Ma come io possiedo la storia, essa mi possiede; ne sono illuminato: ma a che serve la luce?*
But I belong to history, as she belongs to me; and I'm enlightened, yet what's the use of light?
[*Le cenere di Gramsci* (*Gramsci's ashes*, 1957)]

2. *È attraverso lo spirito della televisione che si manifesta in concreto lo spirito del nuovo potere.*
It's through the spirit of television that the essence of the new power clearly shows itself.
[From an essay in *Corriere della sera*, 1973]

Passmore, John Arthur (1914–)

1. Never trust governments absolutely, and always do what you can to prevent them from doing too much harm.
[*The Limits of Government*]

Pasternak, Boris (1890–1960)
Russian lyric poet, novelist, short-story writer and translator; Nobel prize 1958 (declined)

1. And yet the order of the acts is planned,
The end of the way inescapable.
I am alone.
[*Doctor Zhivago* (1958)]

2. But what *is* history? It is the setting up, through the ages, of works which are consistently devoted to solving death and to overcoming it in the future.
[*Doctor Zhivago* (1958)]

3. Only real greatness can be so misplaced and so untimely.
[*Doctor Zhivago* (1958)]

Pasteur, Louis (1822–1895)
French chemist and bacteriologist, noted for his work in immunology

1. *Dans les champs de l'observation, l'hasard ne favorise que les esprits préparés.*
In the field of observation, chance favours only the prepared mind.
[Lecture, 1854]

2. *Il n'existe pas de sciences appliquées, mais seulement des applications de la science.*
There are no applied sciences, only applications of science.
[Address, 1872]

Pater, Walter (1839–1894)
English critic, essayist and lecturer, associated with the Pre-Raphaelites

1. [Of the Mona Lisa]
Hers is the head upon which all 'the ends of the world are come', and the eyelids are a little weary.
[*Studies in the History of the Renaissance* (1873), 'Leonardo da Vinci']

2. [Of the Mona Lisa]
She is older than the rocks among which she sits; like the vampire, she has been dead many times, and learned the secrets of the grave; and has been a diver in deep seas, and keeps their fallen day about her; and trafficked for strange webs with Eastern merchants: and, as Leda, was the mother

of Helen of Troy, and as Saint Anne, the mother of Mary; and all this has been to her but as the sound of lyres and flutes, and lives only in the delicacy with which it has moulded the changing lineaments, and tinged the eyelids and the hands.
[*Studies in the History of the Renaissance* (1873), 'Leonardo da Vinci']

3. All art constantly aspires towards the condition of music.
[*Studies in the History of the Renaissance* (1873), 'Giorgione']

4. To burn always with this hard, gemlike flame, to maintain this ecstasy, is success in life.
[*Studies in the History of the Renaissance* (1873), 'Conclusion']

5. Not to discriminate every moment some passionate attitude in those about us, and in the brilliancy of their gifts some tragic dividing of forces on their ways, is, on this short day of frost and sun, to sleep before evening.
[*Studies in the History of the Renaissance* (1873), 'Conclusion']

6. The love of art for art's sake.
[*Studies in the History of the Renaissance* (1873), 'Conclusion']

Paterson, Andrew
Scottish poet

1. We ca' the place Gleniffer,
It maks us feel at home,
An' yon wee, wimplin' burnie,
Ayr Watter is its name;
An' that bit hillock's Tinto–
But ca' it what ye will,
Names canna mak the heather
Bloom on a bare, bald hill...

2. Ayr Watter, Lomon', Tinto!
Scotland to me they bring,
But O, if in the gloamin'
I could hear a blackie sing.
[*Occasional Rhymes* (1959), 'A Scot Abroad']

Paterson, A.B. ('Banjo' Paterson) (1864–1941)
Australian poet, songwriter, editor and novelist

1. I had written him a letter which I had, for want of better
Knowledge, sent to where I met him down the Lachlan, years ago;
He was shearing when I knew him, so I sent the letter to him,
Just on spec, addressed as follows, 'Clancy, of The Overflow.'

And an answer came directed in a writing unexpected
(And I think the same was written with a thumb-nail dipped in tar);
'Twas his shearing mate who wrote it, and *verbatim* I will quote it:
'Clancy's gone to Queensland droving, and we don't know where he are.'...

2. And the bush has friends to meet him, and their kindly voices greet him
In the murmur of the breezes and the river on its bars,
And he sees the vision splendid of the sunlit plains extended,
And at night the wondrous glory of the everlasting stars.
['Clancy of The Overflow' (1890)]

3. Once a jolly swagman camped by a billabong
Under the shade of a coolibah tree;
And he sang, as he watched and waited while his billy boiled:
'Who'll come a-waltzing, Matilda with me?'

Waltzing Matilda, Waltzing Matilda
Who'll come a waltzing Matilda with me?
And he sang, as he watched and waited while his billy boiled:
'Who'll come a-waltzing Matilda with me?'

Down came a jumbuck to drink at that billabong
Up jumped the swagman and grabbed him with glee;
And he sang as he shoved that jumbuck in his tucker-bag,
'You'll come a-waltzing Matilda with me!'

Up rode the squatter, mounted on his thoroughbred,
Up came the troopers – one – two – three!
Whose that jolly jumbuck you've got in your tucker-bag?
'You'll come a-waltzing Matilda with me!'

Up jumped the swagman and sprang into the billabong
'You'll never take me alive!' said he,
And his ghost may be heard as you pass by that billabong,
'You'll come a-waltzing Matilda with me!'
['Waltzing Matilda', song, 1895]

4. There was movement at the station, for the word had passed around
That the colt from old Regret had got away,
And had joined the wild bush horses – he was worth a thousand pound,
So all the cracks had gathered to the fray.
All the tried and noted riders from the stations near and far
Had mustered at the homestead overnight,
For the bushmen love hard riding where the wild bush horses are,
And the stock-horse snuffs the battle with delight.
['The Man From Snowy River']

3. You had better stick to Sydney and make merry with the 'push,'
For the bush will never suit you, and you'll never suit the bush.
['In Defence Of The Bush']

Patmore, Coventry (1823–1896)
English poet and critic

1. He that but once too nearly hears
The music of forfended spheres
Is thenceforth lonely, and for all
His days as one who treads the Wall
Of China, and, on this hand, sees
Cities and their civilities
And, on the other, lions.
[*The Victories of Love* (1860), I, 2]

2. Love's perfect blossom only blows
Where noble manners veil defect.
Angels may be familiar; those
Who err each other must respect.
[*The Angel in the House* (1854–1862), I, Prelude 2]

3. I drew my bride, beneath the moon,
Across my threshold; happy hour!
But, ah, the walk that afternoon
We saw the water-flags in flower!
[*The Angel in the House* (1854–1862), I, 'The Spirit's Epochs']

4. A woman is a foreign land,
Of which, though there he settle young,
A man will ne'er quite understand
The customs, politics, and tongue.
[*The Angel in the House* (1854–1862), II, 9, Prelude 2]

5. 'I saw you take his kiss!' ''Tis true.'
'O modesty!' ''Twas strictly kept:
He thought me asleep; at least, I knew
He thought I thought he thought I slept.'
[*The Angel in the House* (1854–1862), II, 'The Kiss']

6. So, till to-morrow eve, my Own, adieu!
Parting's well-paid with soon again to meet,

Soon in your arms to feel so small and sweet,
Sweet to myself that am so sweet to you!
[*The Unknown Eros* (1877), 'The Azalea']

7. With all my will, but much against my heart,
We two now part.
My Very Dear,
Our solace is, the sad road lies so clear.
It needs no art,
With faint, averted feet
And many a tear,
In our opposed paths to persevere.
[*The Unknown Eros* (1877), 'A Farewell']

8. It was not like your great and gracious ways!
Do you, that have nought other to lament,
Never, my Love, repent
Of how, that July afternoon,
You went,
With sudden, unintelligible phrase, – and frightened eye,
Upon your journey of so many days,
Without a single kiss or a good-bye?
[*The Unknown Eros* (1877), I, 'Departure']

9. For want of me the world's course will not fail:
When all its work is done, the lie shall rot;
The truth is great, and shall prevail,
When none cares whether it prevail or not.
[*The Unknown Eros* (1877), I, 12]

10. Some dish more sharply spiced than this
Milk-soup men call domestic bliss.
[*Olympus*]

Paton, Alan (1903–1988)
South African novelist

1. There is a lovely road that runs from Ixopo into the hills. These hills are grass-covered and rolling, and they are lovely beyond any singing of it.
[*Cry, the Beloved Country* (1948), I, 1]

2. I have one great fear in my heart, that one day when they [whites] are turned to loving, they will find we [blacks] are turned to hating.
[*Cry, the Beloved Country* (1948), I, 7]

3. By liberalism I don't mean the creed of any party or any century. I mean a generosity of spirit, a tolerance of others, an attempt to comprehend otherness, a commitment to the rule of law, a high ideal of the worth and dignity of man, a repugnance for authoritarianism and a love of freedom.
[Lecture on South Africa at Yale University, 1973]

4. Black schoolchildren started rioting in the great black city of Soweto on June 16, 1976, on the day after which, of all the hundred thousand days of our written history, nothing would be the same again.
[*Towards the Mountain* (1980), 32]

5. It was on Wednesday 16 June 1976 that an era came to an end in South Africa. That was the day when black South Africans said to white, 'You can't do this to us any more'. It had taken three hundred years for them to say that.
[*Journey Continued* (1988), Epilogue]

Patten, Brian (1946–)
British poet

1. Death is the only grammatically correct full-stop...

2. Between himself and the grave his parents stand,
monuments that will crumble.
[*Grinning Jack* (1990), 'Schoolboy']

3. When I went out I stole an orange
It was a safeguard against imagining there was nothing
bright or special in the world.
['The stolen orange']

4. We pass–
And lit briefly by one another's light
Think the way we go is right.
['One another's light']

5. Death does not necessarily diminish us,
it also deepens our awareness of what it means to be alive.
['Grave gossip']

Patterson, Johnny (1840–1889)

1. Have you ever been in love, me boys
Oh! have you felt the pain,
I'd rather be in jail, I would,
Than be in love again.
['The Garden where the Praties Grow']

Pattison, Mark (1813–1884)
English educationist, memoirist and priest

1. In research the horizon recedes as we advance, and is no nearer at sixty than it was at twenty. As the power of endurance weakens with age, the urgency of the pursuit grows more intense ... And research is always incomplete.
[*Isaac Casaubon* (1875), 10]

Patton, George Smith, Jr. (1885–1945)
American general of both World Wars

1. [Message to Eisenhower after Patton crossed the Seine in World War II]
Dear Ike, Today I spat in the Seine.
[In C. Fadiman, *The American Treasury*]

Paul, Leslie (1905–1985)
Irish author and teacher, poet and lecturer; founder of the Woodcraft Folk

1. Angry Young Man.
[Title of book, 1951]

Pavese, Cesare (1908–1950)
Italian realist novelist, short-story writer and translator

1. One stops being a child when one realizes that telling one's trouble does not make it better.
[*The Business of Living: Diaries 1935–50*]

Pavlova, Anna (1881–1931)
World-famous Russian ballerina

1. Although one may fail to find happiness in theatrical life, one never wishes to give it up after having once tasted its fruits. To enter the School of the Imperial Ballet is to enter a convent whence frivolity is banned, and where merciless discipline reigns.
[In Franks (ed.), *Pavlova: A Biography*, 'Pages of My Life']

2. As is the case in all branches of art, success depends in a very large measure upon individual initiative and exertion, and cannot be achieved except by dint of hard work.
[In Franks (ed.), *Pavlova: A Biography*, 'Pages of My Life']

Payn, James (1830–1898)
Prolific English novelist; editor and poet

1. I had never had a piece of toast
Particularly long and wide,
But fell upon the sanded floor,
And always on the buttered side.
[*Chamber's Journal*, 1884]

Payne, J.H. (1791–1852)
American dramatist, poet and actor

1. Mid pleasures and palaces though we may roam,
Be it ever so humble, there's no place like home;
A charm from the skies seems to hallow us there,
Which, seek through the world, is ne'er met with elsewhere.
Home, home, sweet, sweet home!
There's no place like home! there's no place like home!
['Home, Sweet Home', song, 1823, from the opera *Clari, the Maid of Milan*. Cf. Xavier Herbert: 1]

Paz, Octavio (1914–)
Mexican poet and critic

1. *Las diferencias entre el idioma hablado o escrito y los otros – plásticos o musicales – son muy profundas, pero no tanto que nos hagan olvidar que todos son, esencialmente, lenguaje: sistemas expresivos dotados de poder significativo.*
The differences between the spoken or written language and the other ones – plastic or musical – are very profound, but not to such an extent that they make us forget that essentially they are all language: expressive systems which possess a significative power.
[*El arco y la lira* (*The Bow and the Lyre*, 1956), Introduction]

2. *La poesía no es nada sino tiempo, ritmo perpetuamente creador.*
Poetry is nothing but time, ceaselessly creative rhythm.
[*El arco y la lira* (*The Bow and the Lyre*, 1956), Introduction]

Peabody, Elizabeth (1804–1894)
American teacher, educationist and writer

1. [Giving a Transcendentalist explanation for her accidentally walking into a tree]
I saw it, but I did not realize it.
[In L. Tharp, *The Peabody Sisters of Salem*]

Peacock, Thomas Love (1785–1866)
English satirical novelist, essayist and lyric poet

1. Nothing can be more obvious than that all animals were created solely and exclusively for the use of man.
[*Headlong Hall* (1816), 2]

2. 'I distinguish the picturesque and the beautiful, and I add to them, in the laying out of grounds, a third and distinct character, which I call *unexpectedness*.'
'Pray, sir,' said Mr Milestone, 'by what name do you distinguish this character, when a person walks round the grounds for the second time?'
[*Headlong Hall* (1816), 4]

3. Marriage may often be a stormy lake, but celibacy is almost always a muddy horse-pond.
[*Melincourt* (1817)]

4. There are two reasons for drinking; one is, when you are thirsty, to cure it; the other, when you are not thirsty, to prevent it ... Prevention is better than cure.
[*Melincourt* (1817)]

5. He was sent, as usual, to a public school, where a little learning was painfully beaten into him, and from thence to the university, where it was carefully taken out of him.
[*Nightmare Abbey* (1818), 1]

6. Laughter is pleasant, but the exertion is too much for me.
[*Nightmare Abbey* (1818), 5]

7. Sir, I have quarrelled with my wife; and a man who has quarrelled with his wife is absolved from all duty to his country.
[*Nightmare Abbey* (1818), 11]

8. Respectable means rich, and decent means poor. I should die if I heard my family called decent.
[*Crotchet Castle* (1831), 3]

9. Ancient sculpture is the true school of modesty. But where the Greeks had modesty, we have cant; where they had poetry, we have cant; where they had patriotism, we have cant; where they had anything that exalts, delights, or adorns humanity, we have nothing but cant, cant, cant.
[*Crotchet Castle* (1831), 7]

10. A book that furnishes no quotations is, *me judice*, no book – it is a plaything.
[*Crotchet Castle* (1831), 9]

11. The march of mind has marched in through my back parlour shutters, and out again with my silver spoons, in the dead of night. The policeman, who was sent down to examine, says my house has been broken open on the most scientific principles.
[*Crotchet Castle* (1831), 17]

12. I almost think it is the ultimate destiny of science to exterminate the human race.
[*Gryll Grange* (1861)]

13. A Sympathizer would seem to imply a certain degree of benevolent feeling. Nothing of the kind. It signifies a ready-made accomplice in any species of political villainy.
[*Gryll Grange* (1861)]

14. Seamen three! What men be ye?
Gotham's three Wise Men we be.
[*Nightmare Abbey* (1818), 11, 'Three Men of Gotham']

15. The mountain sheep are sweeter,
But the valley sheep are fatter;
We therefore deemed it meeter
To carry off the latter.
[*The Misfortunes of Elphin* (1823), 'The War-Song of Dinas Vawr']

16. He remembered too late on his thorny green bed,
Much that well may be thought cannot wisely be said.
[*Crotchet Castle* (1831), 'The Priest and the Mulberry Tree']

17. Long night succeeds thy little day
Oh blighted blossom! can it be,
That this gray stone and grassy clay
Have closed our anxious care of thee?
[In Henry Cole (ed.), *Works of Peacock* (1875), 'Epitaph on his Daughter']

18. If ifs and ands were pots and pans
There'd be no work for the tinkers.
['Manley']

Peale, Norman Vincent (1898–)
American clergyman, television presenter, secular and religious writer

1. The Power of Positive Thinking.
[Title of book, 1952]

Pearson, Hesketh (1887–1964)
English biographer

1. A widely-read man never quotes accurately ... Misquotation is the pride and privilege of the learned.
[*Common Misquotations* (1937)]

2. Misquotations are the only quotations that are never misquoted.
[*Common Misquotations* (1937)]

Pearson, Lester B. (1897–1972)
Canadian diplomat and Prime Minister

1. Diplomacy is letting someone else have your way.
[*The Observer*, 1965]

Peary, Robert Edwin (1856–1920)
American Arctic explorer, admiral and writer

1. The Eskimo had his own explanation. Said he: 'The devil is asleep or having trouble with his wife, or we should never have come back so easily.'
[*The North Pole* (1910)]

Peck, Gregory (1916–)
American leading film actor; Academy Award 1963

1. [On the fact that no-one in a crowded restaurant recognized him]
If you have to tell them who you are, you aren't anybody.
[In S. Harris, *Pieces of Eight*]

Pedro I, Emperor of Brazil (Pedro IV of Portugal) (1798–1834)
First Emperor of Brazil (1822–31) and, briefly, King of Portugal; abdicated

1. [In response to popular support, and in defiance of a decree from Lisbon requiring his return]
Como é para o bem de todos e a felicidade geral da nação, estou pronto: diga ao povo que fico.
Since it is for the good of everyone and the general happiness of the nation, I am ready. Tell the people I'm staying.
[Speech, 1822, in R.J. Barman, *Brazil: The Forging of a Nation, 1798–1852* (1988)]

Peel, Arthur Wellesley, First Viscount (1829–1912)
English Liberal politician; Speaker of the House, 1884–95; son of Robert Peel

1. [Protesting against his arrest by the police, recently established by his father]
My father didn't create you to arrest me.
[Attr.]

Peel, Sir Robert (1788–1850)
English statesman; Conservative Prime Minister 1834–35, 1841–46; founder of the Metropolitan Police

1. I may be a Tory. I may be an illiberal – but ... Tory as I am, I have the further satisfaction of knowing that there is not a single law connected with my name which has not had as its object some mitigation of the criminal law; some prevention of abuse in the exercise of it; and some security for its impartial administration.
[Speech, House of Commons, 1827]

Peele, George (c. 1558–c. 1597)
English dramatist and lyric poet

1. Fair and fair, and twice so fair,
As fair as any may be;
The fairest shepherd on our green,
A love for any lady.
[*The Arraignment of Paris* (1584), 'Song of Oenone and Paris']

2. His golden locks time hath to silver turn'd;
O time too swift, O swiftness never ceasing!
His youth 'gainst time and age hath ever spurn'd
But spurn'd in vain; youth waneth by increasing:
Beauty, strength, youth, are flowers but fading seen;
Duty, faith, love, are roots, and ever green.
His helmet now shall make a hive for bees,
And, lovers' sonnets turn'd to holy psalms,
A man-at-arms must now serve on his knees,
And feed on prayers, which are age his alms:
But though from court to cottage he depart,
His saint is sure of his unspotted heart...
Goddess, allow this aged man his right,
To be your beadsman now that was your knight.
['Sonnet. A Farewell to Arms' (1590)]

3. What thing is love for (well I wot) love is a thing.
It is a prick, it is a sting,
It is a pretty, pretty thing;
It is a fire, it is a coal
Whose flame creeps in at every hole.
['The Hunting of Cupid' (c. 1591)]

4. When as the rye reach to the chin,
And chopcherry, chopcherry ripe within,
Strawberries swimming in the cream,
And schoolboys playing in the stream,
Then O, then O, then O, my true love said,
Till that time come again,
She could not live a maid.
[*The Old Wives' Tale* (c. 1595), 'Song']

Péguy, Charles (1873–1914)
French Catholic socialist, poet, political writer, publisher and nationalist

1. *La mémoire et l'habitude sont les fourriers de la mort.*
Memory and habit are the harbingers of death.
[*Note conjointe sur M. Descartes*]

Pembroke, Henry Herbert, Second Earl of (c. 1534–1601)
Welsh courtier and President of Wales (from 1586); cultural patron

1. A parliament can do any thing but make a man a woman, and a woman a man.
[Quoted in speech made by his son, the Fourth Earl, 1648]

Pembroke, Henry Herbert, Tenth Earl of (1734–1794)
English general

1. Dr Johnson's sayings would not appear so extraordinary, were it not for his *bow-wow way*.
[In Boswell, *The Life of Samuel Johnson* (1791)]

Peniakoff, Vladimir (1897–1951)
Belgian-born soldier in the British army and writer

1. A message came on the wireless to me. It said 'SPREAD ALARM AND DESPONDENCY' ... The date was, I think, May 18th, 1942.
[*Popski's Private Army* (1950), II]

Penn, William (1644–1718)
English Quaker, founder of Pennsylvania; religious and political writer

1. No pain, no palm; no thorns, no throne; no gall, no glory; no cross, no crown.
[*No Cross, No Crown* (1669)]

2. It is a reproach to religion and government to suffer so much poverty and excess.
[*Some Fruits of Solitude, in Reflections and Maxims relating to the Conduct of Humane Life* (1693), I, 52]

3. Men are generally more careful of the breed of their horses and dogs than of their children.
[*Some Fruits of Solitude, in Reflections and Maxims relating to the Conduct of Humane Life* (1693), I, 85]

4. The taking of a Bribe or Gratuity, should be punished with as severe Penalties as the defrauding of the State.
[*Some Fruits of Solitude, in Reflections and Maxims relating to the Conduct of Humane Life* (1693), I, 384]

Pepys, Samuel (1633–1703)
English diarist (1660–69), naval administrator and politician

1. I stayed up till the bell-man came by with his bell just under my window as I was writing of this very line, and cried, 'Past one of the clock, and a cold, frosty, windy morning.'
[*Diary*, 1659–1660]

2. And so home, weary to bed.
[*Diary*, July 1660]

3. A silk suit, which cost me much money, and I pray God to make me able to pay for it.
[*Diary*, July 1660]

4. I went out to Charing Cross, to see Major-General Harrison hanged, drawn and quartered; which was done there, he looking as cheerful as any man could do in that condition.
[*Diary*, October 1660]

5. Very merry, and the best fritters that ever I eat in my life.
[*Diary*, February (Shrove Tuesday) 1660–61]

6. A good, honest and painful sermon.
[*Diary*, March 1661]

7. But methought it lessened my esteem of a king, that he should not be able to command the rain.
[*Diary*, July 1662]

8. I see it is impossible for the King to have things done as cheap as other men.
[*Diary*, July 1662]

9. But Lord! to see the absurd nature of Englishmen, that cannot forbear laughing and jeering at everything that looks strange.
[*Diary*, November 1662]

10. My wife, who, poor wretch, is troubled with her lonely life.
[*Diary*, December 1662]

11. Went to hear Mrs Turner's daughter ... play on the harpsichon; but, Lord! it was enough to make any man sick to hear her; yet was I forced to commend her highly.
[*Diary*, May 1663]

12. [Referring to a comment from his cousin, who was looking for a wife]
A woman sober, and no high flyer, as he calls it.
[*Diary*, May 1663]

13. Most of their discourse was about hunting, in a dialect I understand very little.
[*Diary*, November 1663]

14. While we were talking came by several poor creatures carried by, by constables, for being at a conventicle ... I would to God they would either conform, or be more wise, and not be catched!
[*Diary*, August 1664]

15. Strange to see how a good dinner and feasting reconciles everybody.
[*Diary*, November 1665]

16. Strange to say what delight we married people have to see these poor fools decoyed into our condition.
[*Diary*, December 1665]

17. Music and women I cannot but give way to, whatever my business is.
[*Diary*, March 1666]

18. Home, and, being washing-day, dined upon cold meat.
[*Diary*, April 1666]

19. And mighty proud I am (and ought to be thankful to God Almighty) that I am able to have a spare bed for my friends.
[*Diary*, August 1666]

20. I bless God I do find that I am worth more than ever I yet was, which is £6,200, for which the Holy Name of God be praised!
[*Diary*, October 1666]

21. To church; and with my mourning, very handsome, and new periwig, make a great show.
[*Diary*, March 1667]

22. But it is pretty to see what money will do.
[*Diary*, March 1667]

23. My wife has something in her gizzard, that only waits an opportunity of being provoked to bring up.
[*Diary*, June 1668]

24. This day my wife made it appear to me that my late entertainment this week cost me above £12, an expense which I am almost ashamed of, though it is but once in a great while, and is the end for which, in the most part, we live, to have such a merry day once or twice in a man's life.
[*Diary*, March 1669]

25. And so I betake myself to that course, which is almost as much as to see myself go into my grave – for which, and all the discomforts that will accompany my being blind, the good God prepare me!
[*Diary*, closing words, May 1669]

Perelman, S.J. (1904–1979)
American humorist, journalist and dramatist

1. I'll dispose of my teeth as I see fit, and after they've gone, I'll get along. I started off living on gruel, and by God, I can always go back to it again.
[*Crazy Like a Fox* (1944), 'Nothing but the Tooth']

2. I tried to resist his overtures, but he plied me with symphonies, quartets, chamber music and cantatas.
[*Crazy Like a Fox* (1944), 'The Love Decoy']

3. He bit his lip in a manner which immediately awakened my maternal sympathy, and I helped him bite it.
[*Crazy Like a Fox* (1944), 'The Love Decoy']

4. I've got Bright's disease and he's got mine.
[Attr.]

5. [Giving his reasons for refusing to see a priest as he lay dying]
I am curious to see what happens in the next world to one who dies unshriven.
[Attr.]

Pérez Galdos, Benito (1843–1920)
Spanish novelist and dramatist

1. *Adquirí cierta presunción pedantesca y un airecillo de autoridad de que posteriormente, a Dios gracias, me he curado por completo.*
I acquired a certain pedantic presumption and the slightest touch of ostentation, which subsequently, thank goodness, I've completely cured myself of.
[*El amigo Manso* (*Friend Manso*, 1882), 2]

2. *El hombre de pensamiento descubre la Verdad; pero quien goza de ella y utiliza sus celestiales dones es el hombre de acción.*
The man of reflection discovers Truth; but the one who enjoys it and makes use of its heavenly gifts is the man of action.
[*El amigo Manso* (*Friend Manso*, 1882), 39]

Pericles (c. 495–429)
Athenian statesman; democratic leader, general, orator and cultural patron

1. We enjoy a constitution that does not follow the customs of our neighbours; we are rather an example to them than they to us. Our government is called a democracy because power is in the hands not of the few but of the many.
[In Thucydides, *Histories*, II, 37]

2. Our love of beauty does not lead to extravagance, and our love of wisdom does not make us soft.
[In Thucydides, *Histories*, II, 40]

3. In short, I declare that our city as a whole is the school of Hellas, and that its individuals in all the various aspects of type are able to show themselves masters of their own persons and to do this moreover with exceptional grace and versatility.
[In Thucydides, *Histories*, II, 41]

4. For the whole earth is the sepulchre of famous men.
[In Thucydides, *Histories*, II, 43]

5. The greatest glory of a woman is to be least talked about by men, in praise or blame.
[In Thucydides, *Histories*, II, 46]

6. Wait for that wisest of counsellors, Time.
[In Plutarch, *Life*]

Perkins, Frances (1882–1965)
American government official

1. [Alleged to have been her reply when asked, as the first woman to hold Cabinet rank in the US, how she wished to be addressed. In fact a man's words to the effect that 'Madam Secretary' would be in order were put into her mouth]
Call me madam.
[In G. Martin, *Madam Secretary – Frances Perkins* (1976)]

Persius Flaccus, Aulus (AD 34–62)
Roman satirical poet

1. *Nec te quaesiveris extra.*
Do not look for opinions beyond your own.
[*Satires*, I, 7]

2. *Virtutem videant intabescantque relicta.*
Let them see virtue and pine away for having lost it.
[*Satires*, III, 38]

3. *Venienti occurrite morbo.*
Confront disease at its onset.
[*Satires*, III, 64]

4. *Tecum habita: noris quam sit tibi curta supellex.*
Live in your own house, and recognise how sparsely furnished it is.
[*Satires*, IV, 52]

Pessoa, Fernando (1888–1935)
Portuguese poet

1. *Ser poeta não é una ambição minha.*
É a minha maneira de estar sozinho.
Being a poet is not an ambition of mine.
It is my way of being alone.
[*O guardador de rebanhos* (*The Guardian of Flocks*, 1914), I]

Pétain, Henri Philippe (1856–1951)
French marshal; led the Vichy administration 1940–44

1. *On les aura!*
We shall have them!
[From an order at the Battle of Verdun, 1916]

Peter, Laurence J. (1919–1990)
Canadian educationist and writer

1. In a hierarchy every employee tends to rise to his level of incompetence.
[*The Peter Principle – Why Things Always Go Wrong* (1969), with R. Hull]

2. The noblest of all dogs is the hot-dog; it feeds the hand that bites it.
[*Quotations for Our Time* (1977)]

3. A pessimist is a man who looks both ways before crossing a one-way street.
[Attr.]

Peters, Ellis (Edith Mary Pargeter) (b. 1913–)
English crime writer

1. 'It may well be,' said Cadfael, 'that our justice sees as in a mirror image, left where right should be, evil reflected back as good, good as evil, your angel as her devil. But God's justice, if it makes no haste, makes no mistakes.'
[*The Potter's Field. The Seventeenth Chronicle of Brother Cadfael* (1989)]

Petronius Arbiter (d. AD 66)
Roman prose and verse satirist

1. *Canis ingens, catena vinctus, in pariete erat pictus superque quadrata littera scriptum 'Cave canem.'*
A huge dog, tied by a chain, was painted on the wall and above it was written in capital letters 'Beware of the dog'.
[*Satyricon*]

2. [Speaking of someone who had died]
Abiit ad plures.
He has joined the great majority.
[*Satyricon*]

3. *Scimus te prae litteras fatuum esse.*
We know that you are mad with too much reading.
[*Satyricon*]

4. *Litteratum esse, quos odisse divites solent.*
A man of letters, of the kind that rich men usually hate.
[*Satyricon*]

5. *Foeda est in coitu et brevis voluptas*
Et taedet Veneris statim peractae.
Pleasure in coupling is gross and brief. Once sated, desire begins to pall.
[In A. Baehrens, *Poetae Latini Minores*]

Pevsner, Sir Nikolaus (1902–1983)
German-born British architectural historian; teacher and writer

1. No part of the walls is left undecorated. From everywhere the praise of the Lord is drummed into you.
[*London, except the Cities of London and Westminster* (1951–1974)]

Pheidippides or Phidippides (d. 490 BC)
Athenian athlete

1. [His last words, after he had run to Athens with news of the Battle of Marathon]
Greetings, we have won.
[In Lucian, 'Pro lapsu inter salutandum' ('A Slip of the Tongue in Greeting'), 3]

Phelps, E.J. (1822–1900)
American lawyer, diplomat and Democrat politician

1. The man who makes no mistakes does not usually make anything.
[Speech, 1899]

Philip, Prince, Duke of Edinburgh (1921–)
British consort of Queen Elizabeth II, born in Greece

1. I include 'pidgin-English' ... even though I am referred to in that splendid language as 'Fella belong Mrs Queen'.
[Speech, English-Speaking Union Conference, Ottawa, 1958]

2. ... the biggest waste of water in the country by far. You spend half a pint and flush two gallons.
[Speech, 1965]

3. [Speaking to Edinburgh University students studying Chinese in Xian, China]
If you stay here much longer you'll all be slitty-eyed.
[*The Times*, 1986]

4. I don't think a prostitute is more moral than a wife, but they are doing the same thing.
[*The Observer*, 1988, in Jeffrey Care (ed.), *Sayings of the Eighties* (1989)]

5. The art world thinks of me as an uncultured, polo-playing clod.
[*The Independent*, 1994]

6. Dentopedology is the science of opening your mouth and putting your foot in it. I've been practising it for years.
[Attr.]

7. [Opening a new annexe, Vancouver City Hall]
I declare this thing open – whatever it is.
[Attr.]

8. A man can be forgiven a lot if he can quote Shakespeare in an economic crisis.
[Attr.]

Philip, John Woodward (1840–1900)
American naval officer

1. [Said at the Battle of Santiago, 1898]
Don't cheer, men; those poor devils are dying.
[In *Dictionary of American Biography* (1934)]

Philip, Sir Robert (1857–1939)
Scottish physician and bacteriologist

1. Mankind is responsible for tuberculosis. What an ignorant civilisation has introduced, an educated civilisation can remove.
[Attr.]

Philippe, Charles-Louis (1874–1909)
French novelist, noted for his portrayal of poverty

1. *On a toujours l'air de mentir quand on parle à des gendarmes.*
One always seems to be lying when one speaks to the police.
[*Les Chroniques du canard sauvage*]

Philips, Ambrose (c. 1675–1749)
English poet and politician

1. The flowers anew, returning seasons bring!
But beauty faded has no second spring.
[*The First Pastoral* (1710), 'Lobbin']

2. Dimply damsel, sweetly smiling,
All caressing, none beguiling.
Bud of beauty, fairly blowing,
Every charm to nature owing.
['To Miss Margaret Pultenay' (1727)]

Philips, John (1676–1709)
English poet

1. Happy the man, who void of cares and strife,
In silken, or in leathern purse retains
A splendid shilling.
['The Splendid Shilling' (1701), parody of Milton]

Phillip, Arthur (1738–1814)
English Royal Navy Captain of the First Fleet; founder and Colony Governor

1. [From a letter to Lord Sydney, 1788]
Nor do I doubt but that this country will prove the most valuable acquisition Great Britain ever made.
[*Historical Records of New South Wales*, I, 2]

2. [To Under Secretary Nepean, 1790]
Dismal accounts will, I make no doubt, be sent to England, but we shall not starve, though seven-eighth of the colony deserves nothing better.
[*Historical Records of New South Wales*, I, 2]

Phillips, Arthur Angell (1900–1985)
Australian critic and editor

1. Above our writers – and other artists – looms the intimidating mass of Anglo-Saxon culture. Such a situation almost inevitably produces the characteristic Australian Cultural Cringe – appearing either as the Cringe Direct, or as the Cringe Inverted, in the attitude of the Blatant Blatherskite, the God's-Own-Country and I'm-a-better-man-than-you-are Australian bore.
[*Meanjin*, 1950, 'The Cultural Cringe']

2. I believe that progress will quicken when we articulately recognise two facts: that the Cringe is a worse enemy to our cultural development than our isolation, and that the opposite of the Cringe is not the Strut, but a relaxed erectness of carriage.
[*Meanjin*, 1950, 'The Cultural Cringe']

Phillips, Wendell (1811–1884)
American abolitionist and reformer, lawyer and orator

1. Every man meets his Waterloo at last.
[Lecture, 1859]

Phillpotts, Eden (1862–1960)
English realist novelist, dramatist and poet, born in India

1. His father's sister had bats in the belfry and was put away.
[*Peacock House*, 'My First Murder']

Picasso, Pablo (1881–1973)
Spanish painter, sculptor and graphic artist; pioneer of Cubism

1. Painting is a blind man's profession. He paints not what he sees, but what he feels, what he tells himself about what he has seen.
[In Jean Cocteau, *Journals* (1929), 'Childhood']

2. [Remark made at an exhibition of children's drawings]
When I was their age, I could draw like Raphael, but it took me a lifetime to learn to draw like them.
[In Roland Penrose, *Picasso: His Life and Work* (1958)]

3. [Explaining why a Renoir in his apartment was hung crooked]
It's better like that, if you want to kill a picture all you have to do is to hang it beautifully on a nail and soon you will

see nothing of it but the frame. When it's out of place you see it better.
[In Roland Penrose, *Picasso: His Life and Work* (1958)]

4. God is really only another artist. He invented the giraffe, the elephant, and the cat. He has no real style. He just goes on trying other things.
[In Gilot and Lake, *Life with Picasso* (1964), 1]

5. I hate that aesthetic game of the eye and the mind, played by these connoisseurs, these mandarins who 'appreciate' beauty. What *is* beauty, anyway? There's no such thing. I never 'appreciate', any more than I 'like'. I love or I hate.
[In Gilot and Lake, *Life with Picasso* (1964), 2]

6. There's no such thing as a bad Picasso, but some are less good than others.
[In A. Whitman, *Come to Judgement*]

7. Age only matters when one is ageing. Now that I have arrived at a great age, I might just as well be twenty.
[In John Richardson, *The Observer, Shouts and Murmurs*, 'Picasso in Private']

8. *Je ne cherche pas; je trouve.*
I do not search; I find.
[Attr.]

Piccolomini, Enea (1405–1464)
Pope (Pius II 1458–64), essayist and orator

1. [Comment after a visit to Scotland in 1435]
There is nothing the Scots like better to hear than abuse of the English.
[Attr.]

Pickles, Wilfred (1904–1978)
British broadcaster and radio actor

1. [Said to Barney Colehan]
Give him the money, Barney.
[*Have a Go*, BBC radio programme, passim]

Piddington, Albert Bathurst (1862–1945)
Australian publisher and campaigner for constitutional reform

1. [Satirising Sir Edmund Barton's way with a deputation]
Gentlemen, I hope I have made myself sufficiently ambiguous.
[*Argus*, 1920]

Piggy, Miss
Puppet character from The Muppets, *created by Jim Henson*

1. Never eat anything at one sitting that you can't lift.
[*Woman's Hour*, BBC Radio Programme, 1992]

Pike, Douglas Henry (1904–1974)
Australian academic, editor and writer

1. Paradise of Dissent.
[Title of book on the early history of South Australia, 1957]

Pindar (518–438 BC)
Greek lyric poet, known for his victory odes

1. Water is best, but gold like fire blazing in the night shines more brightly than all other lordly wealth.
[*Olympian Odes*, I, 1]

2. Strive not, my soul, for an immortal life, but make the most of what is possible.
[*Pythian Odes*, III, 61]

Pindar, Peter (John Wolcot) (1738–1819)
English satirical poet and physician

1. What rage for fame attends both great and small!
Better be damned than mentioned not at all!
['To the Royal Academicians' (1782–1785)]

Pinero, Sir Arthur Wing (1855–1934)
English dramatist and actor

1. While there's tea there's hope.
[*The Second Mrs Tanqueray* (1893), I]

2. From forty to fifty a man is at heart either a stoic or a satyr.
[*The Second Mrs Tanqueray* (1893), I]

Pinter, Harold (1930–)
English dramatist, poet and screenwriter, noted for his use of dialogue

1. I can't drink Guinness from a thick mug. I only like it out of a thin glass.
[*The Caretaker* (1960), I]

2. If only I could get down to Sidcup! I've been waiting for the weather to break. He's got my papers, this man I left them with.
[*The Caretaker* (1960), I]

3. In other words, apart from the known and the unknown, what else is there.
[*The Homecoming* (1965), II]

4. I tend to believe that cricket is the greatest thing that God ever created on earth ... certainly greater than sex, although sex isn't too bad either.
[Interview in *The Observer*, 1980]

5. I've never regarded myself as the one authority on my plays just because I wrote the damned things.
[*The Observer*, 'Sayings of the Week', 1993]

6. [Asked what his plays are about]
The weasel under the cocktail cabinet.
[In J. Russell Taylor, *Anger and After* (1962)]

7. [On being asked why he did not include a character representing himself in *The Birthday Party*]
I had – I have – nothing to say about myself, directly. I wouldn't know where to begin. Particularly since I often look at myself in the mirror and say 'Who the hell's that?'
[Attr.]

Pirsig, Robert (1928–)
American author

1. You are never dedicated to something you have complete confidence in. No one is fanatically shouting that the sun is going to rise tomorrow. They *know* it's going to rise tomorrow. When people are fanatically dedicated to political or religious faiths or any other kind of dogmas or goals, it's always because these dogmas or goals are in doubt.
[*Zen and the Art of Motorcycle Maintenance* (1974), II, 13]

2. Traditional scientific method had always been at the very *best*, 20–20 hindsight. It's good for seeing where you've been.
[*Zen and the Art of Motorcycle Maintenance* (1974), III, 24]

3. We keep passing unseen through little moments of other people's lives.
[*Zen and the Art of Motorcycle Maintenance* (1974), III, 24]

4. That's the classical mind at work, runs fine inside but looks dingy on the surface.
[*Zen and the Art of Motorcycle Maintenance* (1974), III, 25]

Pitkin, William B. (1878–1953)
American psychologist, journalist and editor

1. Life Begins at Forty.
[Title of book, 1932]

Pitt, William [1], First Earl of Chatham (1708–1778)
English Whig politician; Prime Minister 1756–61, 1766–68

1. The atrocious crime of being a young man . . . I shall neither attempt to palliate nor deny.
[Speech, House of Commons, 1741]

2. The poorest man may in his cottage bid defiance to all the forces of the Crown. It may be frail – its roof may shake – the wind may blow through it – the rain may enter – but the King of England cannot enter – all his force dares not cross the threshold of the ruined tenement!
[Speech, c. 1763]

3. I rejoice that America has resisted. Three millions of people, so dead to all the feelings of liberty, as voluntarily to submit to be slaves, would have been fit instruments to make slaves of the rest.
[Speech, House of Commons, 1766]

4. I cannot give them my confidence; pardon me, gentlemen, confidence is a plant of slow growth in an aged bosom: youth is the season of credulity.
[Speech, House of Commons, 1766]

5. Where law ends, there tyranny begins.
[Speech, 1770]

6. Unlimited power is apt to corrupt the minds of those who possess it.
[Speech, House of Commons, 1770. Cf. First Baron Acton: 2 and Adlai Stevenson: 11]

7. There is something behind the throne greater than the King himself.
[Speech, House of Commons, 1770]

8. We have a Calvinistic creed, a Popish liturgy, and an Arminian clergy.
[Speech, House of Commons, 1772]

9. If I were an American, as I am an Englishman, while a foreign troop was landed in my country, I never would lay down my arms, – never – never – never!
[Speech, House of Commons, 1777]

10. You cannot conquer America.
[Speech, 1777]

11. I invoke the genius of the Constitution!
[Speech, 1777]

12. [Of its parks]
The lungs of London.
[Quoted by William Windham, in a speech in the House of Commons, 1808]

13. Our watchword is security.
[Attr.]

Pitt, William [2] (1759–1806)
English Tory politician and fiscal reformer; Prime Minister 1783–1801, 1804–1806; son of William Pitt, Earl of Chatham

1. Necessity is the plea for every infringement of human freedom. It is the argument of tyrants; it is the creed of slaves.
[Speech, 1783]

2. England has saved herself by her exertions, and will, as I trust, save Europe by her example.
[Speech, 1805]

3. [Commenting on the map of Europe, after the Battle of Austerlitz, 1805]
Roll up that map; it will not be wanted these ten years.
[In Lord Stanhope, *Life of the Rt. Hon. William Pitt*, (1862)]

4. I think I could eat one of Bellamy's veal pies.
[Attr. last words]

Pitter, Ruth (1897–1992)
English anti-modernist poet

1. The seldom female in a world of males!
[*On Cats* (1947), 'The Kitten's Eclogue']

Pitts, William Ewart (1900–1980)
British Chief Constable

1. It is the overtakers who keep the undertakers busy.
[*The Observer*, 'Sayings of the Week', 1963]

Planché, James Robinson (1796–1880)
English dramatist, librettist, translator and antiquary

1. It would have made a cat laugh.
[*The Queen of the Frogs* (1879), I.iv]

Plath, Sylvia (1932–1963)
American poet and novelist; short-story writer, essayist and diarist

1. [On seeing her newborn baby]
What did my fingers do before they held him?
What did my heart do, with its love?
I have never seen a thing so clear.
His lids are like the lilac flower
And soft as a moth, his breath.
I shall not let go.
There is no guile or warp in him. May he keep so.
['Three Women: A Poem for Three Voices' (1962)]

2. Every woman adores a Fascist,
The boot in the face, the brute
Brute heart of a brute like you.
['Daddy' (1963)]

3. Dying
Is an art, like everything else.
I do it exceptionally well.
['Lady Lazarus' (1963)]

4. Tomorrow I will be sweet God, I will set them free.
The box is only temporary.
['The Arrival of the Bee Box' (1966)]

Plato (c. 429–347 BC)
Greek philosopher, noted for his concept of forms; founder of the Academy, pupil of Socrates and teacher of Aristotle

1. That man is wisest who, like Socrates, has realized that in truth his wisdom is worth nothing.
[*The Apology of Socrates*, 23b]

2. You must consider this too, that we are born, each of us, not for ourselves alone but partly for our country, partly for our parents and partly for our friends.
[*Epistles*, IX]

3. Time brings everything.
[*Greek Anthology*, IX, 51]

4. The good is the beautiful.
[*Lysis*, 216d]

5. [Spoken by Socrates' jailor]
Socrates, I shall not find fault with you as I find fault with others for getting angry and cursing me when I tell them to drink the poison imposed by the authorities. No, I have found you in your time here to be the noblest and gentlest and best man of all who have ever come here; and now I am sure you are not angry with me, but with them, for you know who are to blame.
[*Phaedo*, 116c]

6. [Of Socrates' death]
This was the end, Echecrates, of our friend; who was, we may say, of all whom we have known, the best, the wisest and the most upright man.
[*Phaedo*, 118]

7. It is the rulers of the state, if anybody, who may lie in dealing with citizens or enemies, for reasons of state.
[*Republic*, II, 389b]

8. How then might we contrive one of those convenient falsehoods of which we were speaking just now, some magnificent myth that might be credited by the rulers themselves or failing that the rest of the city?
[*Republic*, III, 414c]

9. Our object in the establishment of the state is the greatest happiness of the whole, and not that of any one class.
[*Republic*, IV, 420b]

10. Unless either philosophers become kings in our states, or those who are now called kings and rulers become to a serious and sufficient degree philosophers ... there will be no fewer ills afflicting our states or indeed the whole of the human race.
[*Republic*, V, 473d]

11. Do you think that these men would have seen anything of themselves or of one another, except the shadows cast from the fire on to the wall in front of them?
[*Republic*, VII, 515a]

12. Tyranny comes from no other form of government but democracy.
[*Republic*, VIII, 564a]

13. The only poetry we can admit into our city consists of hymns to the gods and the praises of good men.
[*Republic*, X, 607a]

14. Let us be persuaded ... to consider that the soul is immortal and capable of enduring all evil and all good, and so we shall always hold to the upward way and pursue justice with wisdom.
[*Republic*, X, 621c]

15. But, my dearest Agathon, it is truth which you cannot contradict; you can easily contradict Socrates.
[*Symposium*, 201]

16. [Inscription written over the entrance to the Academy]
Let no one ignorant of mathematics enter here.
[Attr.]

Platt, Ken (1922–)
British comedian

1. [Of a person]
Daft as a brush.
[Catchphrase, from 1940s onwards, adapted from the northern saying, 'Soft as a brush']

2. I won't take me coat off – I'm not stopping.
[Catchphrase, from 1951 onwards]

Plautus, Titus Maccius (c. 254–184 BC)
Roman comic dramatist and poet

1. *Lupus est homo homini.*
Man is a wolf to man.
[*Asinaria*, 495]

2. *Quem di diligunt*
Adulescens moritur.
He whom the gods love dies young.
[*Bacchides*, 816]

3. *Miles gloriosus.*
The boastful soldier.
[Title of play]

4. *Simul flare sorbereque haud factu facilest.*
To blow and whistle at the same time is not an easy thing to do.
[*Mostellaria*, 791]

5. *Dictum sapienti sat est.*
A word to the wise is enough.
[*Persa*, 729]

6. *Tetigisti acu.*
You've hit the nail on the head. (*lit.* You have touched it with a needle.)
[*Rudens*, 1306]

Pliny the Elder (AD 23–79)
Roman scientist, historian and soldier

1. *Ex Africa semper aliquid novi.*
There is always something new out of Africa.
[*Historia Naturalis*, VIII (altered), 6]

2. *In vino veritas.*
Wine brings out the truth!
[*Historia Naturalis*, XIV]

3. *Cum grano salis.*
With a grain of salt.
[*Historia Naturalis*, XXIII]

4. *Sal Atticum.*
Attic wit.
[*Historia Naturalis*, XXXI]

Plomer, William (1903–1973)
South African-born British novelist, poet, librettist and editor

1. Out of that bungled, unwise war
An alp of unforgiveness grew.
[*The Fivefold Screen* (1932), 'The Boer War']

2. Limpopo and Tugela churned
In flood for brown and angry miles...

3. That was the Africa we knew,
Where, wandering alone,
We saw, heraldic in the heat,
A scorpion on a stone.
[*The Fivefold Screen* (1932), 'The Scorpion']

4. A rose-red sissy half as old as time.
['The Playboy of the Demi-World: 1938' (1945). Cf. Burgon: 1]

5. A pleasant old buffer, nephew to a lord,
Who believed that the bank was mightier than the sword,
And that an umbrella might pacify barbarians abroad:
Just like an old liberal
Between the wars.
['Father and Son: 1939' (1945)]

6. On a sofa upholstered in panther skin

Mona did research in original sin.
['Mews Flat Mona' (1960)]

7. Men being absent, Africa is good.
['The Wild Doves at Louis Trichardt' (1960)]

8. [In memory of the South African writers Ingrid Jonker and Nathaniel Nakasa, who committed suicide in 1965]
Her blood and his
Fed the slow, tormented
Tree that is destined
To bear what will be
Bough-bending plenty.

Let those who savour
Ripeness and sweetness,
Let them taste and remember
Him, her, and all others
Secreted in the juices.
[*Taste and Remember* (1966), 'The Taste of the Fruit']

9. The warm heart of any human that saw the black man first not as a black but as a man.
[*Turbott Wolfe* (1926), I, 10]

10. Africa is not the white man's country.
[*Turbott Wolfe* (1926), II, 10]

11. Patriotism is the last refuge of the sculptor.
[Attr.]

Plotinus (205–270)
Greek neo-Platonist philosopher

1. To Real Being we go back, all that we have and are; to that we return, and to its first offshoot (Soul).
[*The Enneads*, VI.5.7, in Stephen MacKenna (trans.), *Plotinus The Enneads: Vol. 5* (1930)]

Plutarch (c. AD 46–c. 120)
Greek biographer and philosopher

1. A visitor to Sparta, standing for a long time upon one leg, said to a Spartan, 'I do not believe you can do as much.' 'True,' said he, 'but every goose can.'
[*Laconic Apothegms*, 260]

2. He who triumphs by breaking an oath confesses that he fears his enemy, but despises God.
[*Lives*, 'Lysander', VIII]

3. The great god Pan is dead.
[*The Obsolescence of Oracles*, 419]

Poe, Edgar Allan (1809–1849)
American poet, author of often macabre short stories, and editor

1. Helen, thy beauty is to me
Like those Nicean barks of yore,
That gently, o'er a perfumed sea,
The weary, wayworn wanderer bore
To his own native shore.

On desperate seas long wont to roam,
Thy hyacinth hair, thy classic face,
Thy Naiad airs have brought me home,
To the glory that was Greece
And the grandeur that was Rome.
['To Helen' (1831)]

2. The play is the tragedy, 'Man,'
And its hero the Conqueror Worm.
['The Conqueror Worm' (1843)]

3. Once upon a midnight dreary, while I pondered, weak and weary,
Over many a quaint and curious volume of forgotten lore,
While I nodded, nearly napping, suddenly there came a tapping,
As of some one gently rapping, rapping at my chamber door...

4. Eagerly I wished the morrow, – vainly had I sought to borrow
From my books surcease of sorrow – sorrow for the lost Lenore–
For the rare and radiant maiden whom the angels name Lenore–
Nameless here for evermore...

5. Take thy beak from out my heart, and take thy form from off my door!
Quoth the Raven, 'Nevermore'.
['The Raven' (1845)]

6. The skies they were ashen and sober;
The leaves they were crispèd and sere–
The leaves they were withering and sere;
It was night in the lonesome October
Of my most immemorial year.
['Ulalume' (1847)]

7. It was many and many a year ago,
In a kingdom by the sea,
That a maiden there lived whom you may know
By the name of Annabel Lee;
And this maiden she lived with no other thought
Than to love and be loved by me...

8. I was a child and she was a child,
In this kingdom by the sea;
But we loved with a love which was more than love–
I and my Annabel Lee...

9. And so, all the night-tide, I lie down by the side
Of my darling, my darling, my life and my bride
In her sepulchre there by the sea,
In her tomb by the side of the sea.
['Annabel Lee' (1849)]

10. Keeping time, time, time,
In a sort of Runic rhyme,
To the tintinnabulation that so musically wells
From the bells, bells, bells, bells.
['The Bells' (1849)]

11. All that we see or seem
Is but a dream within a dream.
['A Dream within a Dream' (1849)]

12. The fever call'd 'Living'
Is conquered at last.
['For Annie' (1849)]

13. To be buried while alive is, beyond question, the most terrific of these extremes which has ever fallen to the lot of mere mortality.
[*Tales of Mystery and Imagination* (1908), 'The Premature Burial']

Marco Polo (c. 1254–1324)
Venetian merchant, traveller and writer

1. [Last words]
I have not told half of what I saw.
[In W. Durant, *The Story of Civilization*, I]

Polybius (c. 204–122 BC)
Greek historian of Rome

1. On any occasion when one can discover the cause of events, one should not resort to the gods.
[Attr.]

Pomfret, John (1667–1702)
English poet and clergyman

1. Near some fair town, I'd have a private Seat,
Built uniform, not little, nor too great.
['The Choice' (1700)]

2. We live and learn, but not the wiser grow.
['Reason' (1700)]

Pompadour, Madame de (1721–1764)
French mistress of Louis XV; patron of the arts

1. [Remark after Battle of Rossbach, 1757]
Après nous le déluge.
After us the flood.
[In Madame du Hausset, *Mémoires* (1824)]

Pompidou, Georges (1911–1974)
French statesman; Premier of the Fifth French Republic 1962–68; President from 1969

1. A statesman is a politician who places himself at the service of a nation. A politician is a statesman who places the nation at his service.
[*The Observer*, 'Sayings of the Year', 1973]

Poole, John (c. 1786–1872)
English dramatist and writer

1. I hope I don't intrude?
[*Paul Pry* (1825), I.ii]

Poole, Shona Crawford (1943–)
Cookery writer

1. Ice cream is the most evocative of puddings. It brings back summer holidays and the bicycle bell call of the hokey-cokey man with his tricycle cart, and rushing down the garden path with grandpa's big mug to have it filled for the ice cream sodas which were invariably constructed in tall sundae glasses.
[*The New Times Cookbook*]

Pope, Alexander (1688–1744)
English satirical poet; translator and editor

1. Happy the man, whose wish and care
A few paternal acres bound,
Content to breathe his native air,
In his own ground...

2. Thus let me live, unseen, unknown;
Thus unlamented let me die;
Steal from the world, and not a stone
Tell where I lie.
['Ode on Solitude' (c. 1700)]

3. Where'er you walk, cool gales shall fan the glade,
Trees, where you sit, shall crowd into a shade:
Where'er you tread, the blushing flow'rs shall rise,
And all things flourish where you turn your eyes.
[*Pastorals* (1709), 'Summer']

4. 'Tis hard to say, if great want of skill
Appear in writing or in judging ill.
[*An Essay on Criticism* (1711), line 1]

5. 'Tis with our judgements as our watches, none
Go just alike, yet each believes his own.
[*An Essay on Criticism* (1711), line 9]

6. Let such teach others who themselves excel,
And censure freely who have written well.
[*An Essay on Criticism* (1711), line 15]

7. Some are bewilder'd in the maze of schools,
And some made coxcombs Nature meant but fools.
[*An Essay on Criticism* (1711), line 26]

8. Some have at first for Wits, then Poets pass'd,
Turned Critics next, and proved plain fools at last.
[*An Essay on Criticism* (1711), line 36]

9. Pride, the never-failing vice of fools.
[*An Essay on Criticism* (1711), line 204]

10. A little learning is a dangerous thing;
Drink deep, or taste not the Pierian spring:
There shallow draughts intoxicate the brain,
And drinking largely sobers us again.
[*An Essay on Criticism* (1711), line 215]

11. Hills peep o'er hills, and Alps on Alps arise!
[*An Essay on Criticism* (1711), line 232]

12. Whoever thinks a faultless piece to see,
Thinks what ne'er was, nor is, nor e'er shall be.
[*An Essay on Criticism* (1711), line 253]

13. Poets, like painters, thus, unskill'd to trace
The naked nature and the living grace,
With gold and jewels cover ev'ry part,
And hide with ornaments their want of art.
[*An Essay on Criticism* (1711), line 293]

14. True Wit is Nature to advantage dress'd,
What oft was thought, but ne'er so well express'd.
[*An Essay on Criticism* (1711), line 297]

15. Words are like leaves; and where they most abound,
Much fruit of sense beneath is rarely found.
[*An Essay on Criticism* (1711), line 309]

16. Such labour'd nothings, in so strange a style,
Amaze th' unlearn'd, and make the learned smile.
[*An Essay on Criticism* (1711), line 326]

17. Be not the first by whom the new are try'd,
Nor yet the last to lay the old aside.
[*An Essay on Criticism* (1711), line 335]

18. As some to Church repair,
Not for the doctrine, but the music there.
These equal syllables alone require,
Though oft the ear the open vowels tire;
While expletives their feeble aid do join;
And ten low words oft creep in one dull line.
[*An Essay on Criticism* (1711), line 342]

19. Where'er you find 'the cooling western breeze,'
In the next line, it 'whispers thro' the trees;'
If crystal streams 'with pleasing murmurs creep,'
The reader's threatened (not in vain) with 'sleep.'
Then, at the last and only couplet fraught
With some unmeaning thing they call a thought,
A needless Alexandrine ends the song,
That, like a wounded snake, drags its slow length along.
[*An Essay on Criticism* (1711), line 350]

20. True ease in writing comes from art, not chance,
As those move easiest who have learn'd to dance.
'Tis not enough no harshness gives offence,
The sound must seem an echo to the sense.
[*An Essay on Criticism* (1711), line 362]

21. But when loud surges lash the sounding shore,
The hoarse, rough verse should like a torrent roar.
When Ajax strives, some rock's vast weight to throw,
The line too labours, and the words move slow.
[*An Essay on Criticism* (1711), line 368]

22. Yet let not each gay turn thy rapture move;
For fools admire, but men of sense approve.
[*An Essay on Criticism* (1711), line 390]

23. Some praise at morning what they blame at night;
But always think the last opinion right.
[*An Essay on Criticism* (1711), line 430]

24. Fondly we think we honour merit then,
When we but praise ourselves in other men.
[*An Essay on Criticism* (1711), line 454]

25. Nor in the Critic let the Man be lost.
Good-nature and good-sense must ever join;
To err is human, to forgive, divine.
[*An Essay on Criticism* (1711), line 523. Cf. Proverbs: 395]

26. All seems infected that th' infected spy,
As all looks yellow to the jaundic'd eye.
[*An Essay on Criticism* (1711), line 558]

27. The bookful blockhead, ignorantly read,
With loads of learned lumber in his head.
[*An Essay on Criticism* (1711), line 612]

28. For Fools rush in where Angels fear to tread.
[*An Essay on Criticism* (1711), line 625]

29. And the same age saw Learning fall, and Rome.
[*An Essay on Criticism* (1711), line 686]

30. A brave man struggling in the storms of fate,
And greatly falling with a falling state.
While Cato gives his little senate laws,
What bosom beats not in his Country's cause?
['Prologue to Addison's *Cato*' (1713)]

31. Here hills and vales, the woodland and the plain,
Here earth and water seem to strive again,
Not Chaos-like together crush'd and bruis'd,
But as the world, harmoniously confus'd:
Where order in variety we see,
And where though all things differ, all agree...

32. The fox obscene to gaping tombs retires,
And savage howlings fill the sacred quires...

33. See! from the brake the whirring pheasant springs,
And mounts exulting on triumphant wings:
Short is his joy; he feels the fiery wound,
Flutters in blood, and panting beats the ground.
Ah! what avail his glossy, varying dyes,
His purple crest, and scarlet-circled eyes,
The vivid green his shining plumes unfold,
His painted wings and breast that flames with gold?...

34. Oft, as the mounting larks their notes prepare,
They fall, and leave their little lives in air...

35. And seas but join the regions they divide.
['Windsor Forest' (1713)]

36. What dire offence from am'rous causes springs,
What mighty contests rise from trivial things,
I sing.
[*The Rape of the Lock* (1714), I, line1]

37. Now lap-dogs give themselves the rousing shake,
And sleepless lovers, just at twelve, awake:
Thrice rung the bell, the slipper knock'd the ground,
And the press'd watch return'd a silver sound.
[*The Rape of the Lock* (1714), I, line 15]

38. They shift the moving Toyshop of their heart.
[*The Rape of the Lock* (1714), I, line 100]

39. Here files of Pins extend their shining rows,
Puffs, Powders, Patches, Bibles, Billet-doux.
[*The Rape of the Lock* (1714), I, line 137]

40. On her white breast a sparkling Cross she wore,
Which Jews might kiss, and Infidels adore.
[*The Rape of the Lock* (1714), II, line 7]

41. Favours to none, to all she smiles extends;
Oft she rejects, but never once offends.
[*The Rape of the Lock* (1714), II, line 11]

42. Bright as the sun, her eyes the gazers strike,
And, like the sun, they shine on all alike.
[*The Rape of the Lock* (1714), II, line 13]

43. If to her share some female errors fall,
Look on her face, and you'll forget 'em all.
[*The Rape of the Lock* (1714), II, line 17]

44. Fair tresses man's imperial race insnare,
And beauty draws us with a single hair.
[*The Rape of the Lock* (1714), II, line 27]

45. Or stain her honour, or her new brocade;
Forget her pray'rs, or miss a masquerade;
Or lose her heart, or necklace, at a ball.
[*The Rape of the Lock* (1714), II, line 107]

46. Here thou, great Anna! whom three realms obey,
Dost sometimes counsel take – and sometimes Tea.
[*The Rape of the Lock* (1714), III, line 7]

47. At ev'ry word a reputation dies.
[*The Rape of the Lock* (1714), III, line 16]

48. The hungry Judges soon the sentence sign,
And wretches hang that jury-men may dine
[*The Rape of the Lock* (1714), III, line 21]

49. Let Spades be trumps! she said, and trumps they were.
[*The Rape of the Lock* (1714), III, line 46]

50. For lo! the board with cups and spoons is crown'd,
For berries crackle, and the mill turns round;
On shining Altars of Japan they raise
The silver lamp; the fiery spirits blaze:
From silver spouts the grateful liquors glide,
While China's earth receives the smoking tide:
At once they gratify their scent and taste,
And frequent cups prolong the rich repast.
[*The Rape of the Lock* (1714), III, line 105]

51. Coffee, (which makes the politician wise,
And see thro' all things with his half-shut eyes)
Sent up in vapours to the Baron's brain
New stratagems, the radiant Lock to gain.
[*The Rape of the Lock* (1714), III, line 117]

52. The peer now spreads the glitt'ring forfex wide,
T' inclose the lock; now joins it, to divide.
Ev'n then, before the fatal engine closed,
A wretched sylph too fondly interposed;
Fate urged the shears, and cut the sylph in twain,
(But airy substance soon unites again)
The meeting points the sacred hair dissever
From the fair head, for ever, and for ever!
Then flash'd the living lightning from her eyes,
And screams of horror rend th' affrighted skies.
Not louder shrieks to pitying Heaven are cast,
When husbands, or when lap-dogs breathe their last;
Or when rich China vessels fall'n from high,
In glitt'ring dust and painted fragments lie!
[*The Rape of the Lock* (1714), III, line 147]

53. Oh hadst thou, cruel! been content to seize
Hairs less in sight, or any hairs but these!
[*The Rape of the Lock* (1714), IV, line 175]

54. Good-humour can prevail,
When airs, and flights, and screams, and scolding fail.

Beauties in vain their pretty eyes may roll;
Charms strike the sight, but merit wins the soul.
[*The Rape of the Lock* (1714), V, line 31]

55. Then teach me, Heav'n! to scorn the guilty bays,
Drive from my breast that wretched lust of praise,
Unblemished let me live, or die unknown;
Oh grant an honest fame, or grant me none!
[*The Temple of Fame* (1715)]

56. What beck'ning ghost, along the moonlight shade
Invites my step, and points to yonder glade?...

57. Is it, in heav'n, a crime to love too well?...

58. Is there no bright reversion in the sky,
For those who greatly think, or bravely die?...

59. On all the line a sudden vengeance waits,
And frequent hearses shall besiege your gates...

60. By foreign hands thy dying eyes were clos'd,
By foreign hands thy decent limbs compos'd,
By foreign hands thy humble grave adorn'd,
By strangers honour'd, and by strangers mourn'd!...

61. A heap of dust alone remains of thee;
'Tis all thou art, and all the proud shall be!
['Elegy to the Memory of an Unfortunate Lady' (1717)]

62. Of all affliction taught a lover yet,
'Tis sure the hardest science to forget!
How shall I lose the sin, yet keep the sense,
And love the offender, yet detest th' offence?
How the dear object from the crime remove,
Or how distinguish penitence from love?...

63. How happy is the blameless Vestal's lot?
The world forgetting, by the world forgot...

64. One thought of thee puts all the pomp to flight,
Priests, tapers, temples, swim before my sight;
In seas of flame my plunging soul is drown'd,
While altars blaze, and angels tremble round.
['Eloisa to Abelard' (1717)]

65. She went, to plain-work, and to purling brooks,
Old-fashion'd halls, dull aunts, and croaking rooks:
She went from Op'ra, park, assembly, play,
To morning-walks, and pray'rs three hours a day;
To part her time 'twixt reading and Bohea,
To muse, and spill her solitary Tea,
Or o'er cold coffee trifle with the spoon,
Count the slow clock, and dine exact at noon;
Divert her eyes with pictures in the fire,
Hum half a tune, tell stories to the squire.
Up to her godly garret after sev'n,
There starve and pray, for that's the way to heav'n.
['Epistle to Miss Blount, on her leaving the Town after the Coronation' (1717)]

66. True friendship's laws are by this rule express'd,
Welcome the coming, speed the parting guest.
[*The Odyssey* (1725–1726), XV]

67. Fame is at best an unperforming cheat;
But 'tis substantial happiness, to *eat*.
['Prologue for Mr D'Urfey's Last Play' (1727)]

68. Vital spark of heav'nly flame!
Quit, oh quit this mortal frame:
Trembling, hoping, ling'ring, flying,
Oh the pain, the bliss of dying!...

69. Tell me, my Soul, can this be death?...

70. I mount! I fly!
O Grave! where is thy victory?
O Death! where is thy sting?
['The Dying Christian to his Soul' (1730)]

71. Nature, and Nature's laws lay hid in night:
God said, *Let Newton be!* and all was light.
['Epitaph for Sir Isaac Newton' (1730). Cf. Squire: 2]

72. To rest, the Cushion and soft Dean invite,
Who never mentions Hell to ears polite...

73. Another age shall see the golden Ear
Imbrown the Slope, and nod on the Parterre,
Deep Harvests bury all his pride had planned,
And laughing Ceres reassume the land.
['Epistle to Lord Burlington' (1731)]

74. Sir, I admit your gen'ral Rule
That every Poet is a Fool;
But you yourself may serve to show it,
That every Fool is not a Poet.
['Epigram from the French' (1732)]

75. You beat your Pate, and fancy Wit will come;
Knock as you please, there's nobody at home.
['Epigram' (1732)]

76. Who shall decide, when Doctors disagree,
And soundest Casuists doubt, like you and me?...

77. But thousands die, without or this or that,
Die, and endow a College, or a Cat...

78. The ruling Passion, be it what it will,
The ruling Passion conquers Reason still.
['Epistle to Lord Bathurst' (1733)]

79. Eye Nature's walks, shoot folly as it flies,
And catch the Manners living as they rise.
Laugh where we must, be candid where we can;
But vindicate the ways of God to Man.
Say first, of God above or Man below,
What can we reason, but from what we know?
[*An Essay on Man*, I (1733), line 13]

80. Observe how system into system runs,
What other planets circle other suns.
[*An Essay on Man*, I (1733), line 25]

81. Then say not man's imperfect, Heav'n in fault;
Say rather, Man's as perfect as he ought.
[*An Essay on Man*, I (1733), line 69]

82. Who sees with equal eye, as God of all,
A hero perish, or a sparrow fall,
Atoms or systems into ruin hurl'd,
And now a bubble burst, and now a world.
[*An Essay on Man*, I (1733), line 87]

83. Hope springs eternal in the human breast;
Man never Is, but always To be blest:
The soul, uneasy, and confin'd from home,
Rests and expatiates in a life to come.
Lo! the poor Indian, whose untutor'd mind
Sees God in clouds, or hears him in the wind;
His soul proud Science never taught to stray
Far as the solar walk, or milky way;
Yet simple Nature to his hope has giv'n,
Behind the cloud-topp'd hill, an humbler Heav'n.
[*An Essay on Man*, I (1733), line 95]

84. Men would be Angels, Angels would be Gods.
Aspiring to be Gods, if Angels fell,
Aspiring to be Angels, Men rebel.
[*An Essay on Man*, I (1733), line 126]

85. Why has not Man a microscopic eye?
For this plain reason, Man is not a fly.

Say what the use, were finer optics giv'n,
T' inspect a mite, not comprehend the heav'n?
[*An Essay on Man*, I (1733), line 193]

86. The spider's touch, how exquisitely fine!
Feels at each thread, and lives along the line.
[*An Essay on Man*, I (1733), line 217]

87. All are but parts of one stupendous whole,
Whose body Nature is, and God the soul.
[*An Essay on Man*, I (1733), line 267]

88. All Nature is but Art, unknown to thee;
All Chance, Direction which thou canst not see;
All Discord, Harmony, not understood;
All partial Evil, universal Good;
And, spite of Pride, in erring Reason's spite,
One truth is clear, 'Whatever is, is right.'
[*An Essay on Man*, I (1733), line 289]

89. Know then thyself, presume not God to scan;
The proper study of Mankind is Man.
Plac'd on this isthmus of a middle state,
A being darkly wise, and rudely great:
With too much knowledge for the Sceptic side,
With too much weakness for the Stoic's pride,
He hangs between; in doubt to act or rest,
In doubt to deem himself a God, or Beast;
In doubt his Mind or Body to prefer,
Born but to die, and reas'ning but to err;
Alike in ignorance, his reason such,
Whether he thinks too little or too much.
[*An Essay on Man*, II (1733), line 1. Cf. Charron: 1]

90. Created half to rise, and half to fall;
Great lord of all things, yet a prey to all;
Sole judge of truth, in endless error hurl'd:
The glory, jest, and riddle of the world!
[*An Essay on Man*, II (1733), line 15]

91. Go, teach Eternal Wisdom how to rule–
Then drop into thyself, and be a fool!
[*An Essay on Man*, II (1733), line 29]

92. Fixed like a plant on his peculiar spot,
To draw nutrition, propagate, and rot.
[*An Essay on Man*, II (1733), line 63]

93. Nor God alone in the still calm we find,
He mounts the storm, and walks upon the wind.
[*An Essay on Man*, II (1733), line 109]

94. Pleasures are ever in our hands or eyes,
And when in act they cease, in prospect rise;
Present to grasp, and future still to find,
The whole employ of body and of mind.
[*An Essay on Man*, II (1733), line 123]

95. Vice is a monster of so frightful mien,
As, to be hated, needs but to be seen;
Yet soon too oft, familiar with her face,
We first endure, then pity, then embrace.
But where th' extreme of vice, was ne'er agreed:
Ask where's the North? at York, 'tis on the Tweed;
In Scotland, at the Orcades; and there,
At Greenland, Zembla, or the Lord knows where.
[*An Essay on Man*, II (1733), line 217]

96. The learned is happy Nature to explore,
The fool is happy that he knows no more.
[*An Essay on Man*, II (1733), line 263]

97. Behold the child, by Nature's kindly law,
Pleas'd with a rattle, tickled with a straw.
[*An Essay on Man*, II (1733), line 275]

98. Scarfs, garters, gold, amuse his riper stage;
And beads and pray'r-books are the toys of age:
Pleas'd with this bauble still, as that before;
Till tir'd, he sleeps, and Life's poor play is o'er.
[*An Essay on Man*, II (1733), line 279]

99. For Forms of Government let fools contest;
Whate'er is best administer'd is best:
For Modes of Faith, let graceless zealots fight;
His can't be wrong whose life is in the right:
In Faith and Hope the world will disagree,
But all Mankind's concern is Charity.
[*Essay on Man*, III (1733), line 303]

100. Thus God and Nature link'd the gen'ral frame,
And bade Self-love and Social be the same.
[*Essay on Man*, III (1733), line 317]

101. Oh Happiness! our being's end and aim!
[*Essay on Man*, IV (1734), line 1]

102. Order is Heav'n's first law.
[*Essay on Man*, IV (1734), line 49]

103. Go, like the Indian, in another life
Expect thy dog, thy bottle, and thy wife.
[*Essay on Man*, IV (1734), line 177]

104. A Wit's a feather, and a Chief a rod;
An honest Man's the noblest work of God.
[*Essay on Man*, IV (1734), line 247. Cf. Samuel Butler [2]: 40]

105. If parts allure thee, think how Bacon shin'd,
The wisest, brightest, meanest of mankind:
Or ravish'd with the whistling of a name,
See Cromwell, damn'd to everlasting fame!
[*Essay on Man*, IV (1734), line 281]

106. Slave to no sect, who takes no private road,
But looks through Nature, up to Nature's God.
[*Essay on Man*, IV (1734), line 331]

107. Shall then this verse to future age pretend
Thou wert my guide, philosopher, and friend?
That urg'd by thee, I turn'd the tuneful art
From sounds to things, from fancy to the heart;
For Wit's false mirror held up Nature's light;
Shewed erring Pride, whatever is, is right;
That reason, passion, answer one great aim;
That true self-love and social are the same;
That virtue only makes our bliss below;
And all our knowledge is, ourselves to know.
[*Essay on Man*, IV (1734), line 389]

108. To observations which ourselves we make,
We grow more partial for th' Observer's sake...

109. All manners take a tincture from our own;
Or come discolour'd through our Passions shown...

110. Alas! in truth the man but chang'd his mind,
Perhaps was sick, in love, or had not dined...

111. 'Tis from high Life high Characters are drawn;
A Saint in Crape is twice a Saint in Lawn...

112. 'Tis Education forms the common mind,
Just as the Twig is bent, the Tree's inclined...

113. Search then the ruling passion: there, alone,
The Wild are constant and the Cunning known;
The Fool consistent, and the False sincere;
Priests, Princes, Women, no dissemblers here.
This clue once found, unravels all the rest...

114. Old Politicians chew on wisdom past,
And totter on in bus'ness to the last...

115. Odious! in woollen! 'twould a saint provoke!...

116. One would not, sure, be frightful when one's dead–
And – Betty – give this Cheek a little Red.
['Epistle to Lord Cobham' (1734)]

117. Shut, shut the door, good John! fatigu'd I said,
Tye up the knocker; say I'm sick, I'm dead.
The Dog-star rages!
['Epistle to Dr Arbuthnot' (1735), line 1]

118. Destroy his fib or sophistry; in vain,
The creature's at his dirty work again.
['Epistle to Dr Arbuthnot' (1735), line 91]

119. As yet a child, nor yet a fool to fame,
I lisp'd in numbers, for the numbers came.
I left no calling for this idle trade,
No duty broke, no father disobey'd.
The Muse but serv'd to ease some friend, not Wife,
To help me thro' this long disease, my Life.
['Epistle to Dr Arbuthnot' (1735), line 131]

120. Pretty! in amber to observe the forms
Of hairs, or straws, or dirt, or grubs, or worms!
The things, we know, are neither rich nor rare,
But wonder how the devil they got there?
['Epistle to Dr Arbuthnot' (1735), line 169]

121. [Of Addison]
Were there One whose fires
True Genius kindles, and fair Fame inspires;
Blest with each talent and each art to please,
And born to write, converse, and live with ease:
Should such a man, too fond to rule alone,
Bear, like the Turk, no brother near the throne,
View him with scornful, yet with jealous eyes,
And hate for arts that caused himself to rise;
Damn with faint praise, assent with civil leer,
And, without sneering, teach the rest to sneer;
Willing to wound, and yet afraid to strike,
Just hint a fault, and hesitate dislike.
Alike reserv'd to blame, or to commend,
A tim'rous foe, and a suspicious friend;
Dreading ev'n fools, by Flatterers besieged,
And so obliging, that he ne'er oblig'd;
Like Cato, give his little Senate laws,
And sit attentive to his own applause.
['Epistle to Dr Arbuthnot' (1735), line 193]

122. [Of Addison]
Who but must laugh, if such a man there be?
Who would not weep, if Atticus were he!
['Epistle to Dr Arbuthnot' (1735), line 213]

123. [Of a noble patron]
But still the Great have kindness in reserve,
He help'd to bury whom he help'd to starve.
['Epistle to Dr Arbuthnot' (1735), line 247]

124. Cursed be the verse, how well soe'er it flow,
That tends to make one worthy man my foe.
['Epistle to Dr Arbuthnot' (1735), line 282]

125. [Of Lord Hervey]
Let Sporus tremble – 'What? that thing of silk,
Sporus, that mere white curd of Ass's milk?
Satire or sense, alas! can Sporus feel?
Who breaks a butterfly upon a wheel?'
Yet let me flap this bug with gilded wings,
This painted child of dirt, that stinks and stings.
['Epistle to Dr Arbuthnot' (1735), line 309]

126. [Of Lord Hervey]
Eternal smiles his emptiness betray,
As shallow streams run dimpling all the way.
['Epistle to Dr Arbuthnot' (1735), line 315]

127. [Of Lord Hervey]
His wit all see-saw, between that and this,
Now high, now low, now Master up, now Miss,
And he himself one vile Antithesis.
['Epistle to Dr Arbuthnot' (1735), line 325]

128. [Of Lord Hervey]
Eve's tempter thus the Rabbins have express'd,
A Cherub's face, a reptile all the rest.
['Epistle to Dr Arbuthnot' (1735), line 331]

129. [Of his own father]
Unlearn'd, he knew no schoolman's subtle art,
No language, but the language of the heart.
By Nature honest, by Experience wise,
Healthy by temp'rance, and by exercise.
['Epistle to Dr Arbuthnot' (1735), line 398]

130. Most Women have no Characters at all...

131. A very Heathen in the carnal part,
Yet still a sad, good Christian at her heart...

132. Chaste to her Husband, frank to all beside,
A teeming Mistress, but a barren Bride...

133. Wise Wretch! with Pleasures too refin'd to please,
With too much Spirit to be e'er at ease,
With too much Quickness ever to be taught;
With too much Thinking to have common Thought:
You purchase Pain with all that Joy can give,
And die of nothing but a Rage to live...

134. 'With ev'ry pleasing, ev'ry prudent part,
Say, what can Cloe want?' – She wants a Heart...

135. Virtue she finds too painful an endeavour,
Content to dwell in Decencies for ever...

136. In Men, we various Ruling Passions find,
In Women, two almost divide the kind;
Those, only fix'd, they first or last obey,
The Love of Pleasure, and the Love of Sway...

137. Men, some to business, some to pleasure take;
But every Woman is at heart a rake:
Men, some to quiet, some to public strife;
But every lady would be queen for life...

138. Still round and round the Ghosts of Beauty glide,
And haunt the places where their Honour dy'd.
See how the World its Veterans rewards!
A Youth of Frolics, an old Age of Cards...

139. She who ne'er answers till a Husband cools,
Or, if she rules him, never shows she rules;
Charms by accepting, by submitting sways,
Yet has her humour most, when she obeys...

140. And Mistress of herself, tho' China fall...

141. Woman's at best a Contradiction still.
['Epistle to a Lady' (1735)]

142. Shakespeare (whom you and ev'ry Play-house bill
Style the divine, the matchless, what you will)
For gain, not glory, wing'd his roving flight,
And grew Immortal in his own despite...

143. Who now reads Cowley? if he pleases yet,
His Moral pleases, not his pointed wit...

144. The People's Voice is odd,
It is, and it is not, the voice of God...

145. Waller was smooth; but Dryden taught to join
The varying verse, the full-resounding line,

The long majestic March, and Energy divine...

146. Ev'n copious Dryden, wanted, or forgot,
The last and greatest Art, the Art to blot...

147. There still remains, to mortify a Wit,
The many-headed Monster of the Pit.
[*Imitations of Horace* (1737–1738), 'To Augustus']

148. Our Gen'rals now, retir'd to their estates,
Hang their old Trophies o'er the Garden gates,
In Life's cool ev'ning satiate of applause...

149. Not to go back, is somewhat to advance,
And men must walk at least before they dance...

150. Get Place and Wealth, if possible, with Grace;
If not, by any means get Wealth and Place.
[*Imitations of Horace* (1737–1738), 'To Lord Bolingbroke'. Cf. Horace: 78]

151. For Virtue's self may too much zeal be had;
The worst of Madmen is a Saint run mad.
[*Imitations of Horace* (1737–1738), 'To Mr Murray']

152. Let humble Allen, with an awkward Shame,
Do good by stealth, and blush to find it Fame.
[*Imitations of Horace* (1737–1738), 'Epilogue to the Satires', I]

153. Ask you what Provocation I have had?
The strong Antipathy of Good to Bad...

154. Yes, I am proud; I must be proud to see
Men not afraid of God, afraid of me.
[*Imitations of Horace* (1737–1738), 'Epilogue to the Satires', II]

155. [On the collar of a dog given to Frederick, Prince of Wales]
I am his Highness' dog at Kew;
Pray, tell me sir, whose dog are you?
['Epigram' (1738)]

156. Teach me to feel another's Woe,
To hide the Fault I see;
That Mercy I to others show,
That Mercy show to me.
['The Universal Prayer' (1738)]

157. Books and the man I sing, the first who brings
The Smithfield muses to the Ear of kings.
[*The Dunciad* (1742), I, first lines]

158. Still Dunce the second reigns like Dunce the first.
[*The Dunciad* (1742), I, line 6]

159. Maggots half-form'd in rhyme exactly meet,
And learn to crawl upon poetic feet.
[*The Dunciad* (1742), I, line 61]

160. While pensive Poets painful vigils keep,
Sleepless themselves, to give their readers sleep.
[*The Dunciad* (1742), I, line 93]

161. Sinking from thought to thought, a vast profound!
[*The Dunciad* (1742), I, line 118]

162. Some Daemon stole my pen (forgive th' offence)
And once betray'd me into common sense.
[*The Dunciad* (1742), I, line 187]

163. For thee explain a thing till all men doubt it,
And write about it, and about it.
[*The Dunciad* (1742), I, line 251]

164. Glory, and gain, th' industrious tribe provoke;
And gentle Dullness ever loves a joke.
[*The Dunciad* (1742), II, line 34]

165. A brain of feathers, and a heart of lead.
[*The Dunciad* (1742), II, line 44]

166. Peel'd, patch'd, and pyebald, linsey-wolsey brothers,
Grave Mummers! sleeveless some, and shirtless others.
[*The Dunciad* (1742), III, line 115]

167. Each Songster, Riddler, ev'ry nameless name,
All crowd, who foremost shall be damn'd to Fame.
[*The Dunciad* (1742), III, line 158]

168. Flow, Welsted, flow! like thine inspirer, Beer,
Tho' stale, not ripe; tho' thin, yet never clear;
So sweetly mawkish, and so smoothly dull;
Heady, not strong; o'erflowing, tho' not full.
[*The Dunciad* (1742), III, line 169]

169. May you, may Cam, and Isis, preach it long,
The Right Divine of kings to govern wrong.
[*The Dunciad* (1742), IV, line 186]

170. Turn what they will to Verse, their toil is vain,
Critics like me shall make it Prose again.
[*The Dunciad* (1742), IV, line 213]

171. To happy Convents, bosom'd deep in vines,
Where slumber Abbots, purple as their wines.
[*The Dunciad* (1742), IV, line 301]

172. All Classic learning lost on Classic ground;
And last turn'd Air, the Echo of a Sound!
[*The Dunciad* (1742), IV, line 321]

173. She marked thee there,
Stretch'd on the rack of a too easy chair,
And heard thy everlasting yawn confess
The Pains and Penalties of idleness.
[*The Dunciad* (1742), IV, line 341]

174. Religion blushing veils her sacred fires,
And unawares Morality expires.
[*The Dunciad* (1742), IV, line 649]

175. Lo! thy dread empire, Chaos! is restor'd;
Light dies before thy uncreating word:
Thy hand, great Anarch! lets the curtain fall;
And Universal Darkness buries All.
[*The Dunciad* (1742), IV, last lines]

176. To endeavour to work upon the vulgar with fine sense, is like attempting to hew blocks with a razor.
[*Miscellanies* (1727), 'Thoughts on Various Subjects']

177. A man should never be ashamed to own he has been in the wrong, which is but saying, in other words, that he is wiser today than he was yesterday.
[*Miscellanies* (1727), 'Thoughts on Various Subjects']

178. When men grow virtuous in their old age, they only make a sacrifice to God of the devil's leavings.
[*Miscellanies* (1727), 'Thoughts on Various Subjects']

179. It is with narrow-souled people as with narrow-necked bottles: the less they have in them, the more noise they make in pouring it out.
[*Miscellanies* (1727), 'Thoughts on Various Subjects']

180. The most positive men are the most credulous.
[*Miscellanies* (1727), 'Thoughts on Various Subjects']

181. I never knew any man in my life, who could not bear another's misfortunes perfectly like a Christian.
[*Miscellanies* (1727), 'Thoughts on Various Subjects']

182. Party-spirit, which at best is but the madness of many for the gain of a few.
[Letter to Edward Blount, 1714]

183. 'Blessed is the man who expects nothing, for he shall never be disappointed,' was the ninth beatitude which a man of wit (who like a man of wit was a long time in gaol) added to the eighth.
[Letter to William Fortescue, 1725]

184. How often are we to die before we go quite off this stage? In every friend we lose a part of ourselves, and the best part.
[Letter to Swift, 1732]

185. Here am I, dying of a hundred good symptoms.
[In Spence, *Anecdotes*]

Popper, Sir Karl (1902–1994)
Austrian-born British philosopher of science and logic

1. The Open Society and its Enemies.
[Title of book, 1945]

2. Our civilization ... has not yet fully recovered from the shock of its birth – the transition from the tribal or 'closed society', with its submission to magical forces, to the 'open society' which sets free the critical powers of man.
[*The Open Society and its Enemies* (1945)]

3. There is no history of mankind, there are only many histories of all kinds of aspects of human life. And one of these is the history of political power. This is elevated into the history of the world.
[*The Open Society and its Enemies* (1945)]

4. We must plan for freedom, and not only for security, if for no other reason than that only freedom can make security secure.
[*The Open Society and its Enemies* (1945)]

5. Our knowledge can only be finite, while our ignorance must necessarily be infinite.
[*Conjectures and Refutations* (1963)]

6. We may become the makers of our fate when we have ceased to pose as its prophets.
[*The Observer*, 1975]

7. Science may be described as the art of systematic oversimplification.
[*The Observer*, 1982, in Jeffrey Care (ed.), *Sayings of the Eighties* (1989)]

8. Science must begin with myths, and with the criticism of myths.
[In C.A. Mace (ed.), *British Philosophy in the Mid-Century* (1957)]

Porson, Richard (1759–1808)
English scholar of Greek, noted for his study of Euripides

1. [Giving his opinion of the poems of Robert Southey]
Your works will be read after Shakespeare and Milton are forgotten – and not till then.
[In L. Meissen, *Quotable Anecdotes*]

Porter, Cole (1891–1964)
American composer and lyricist of musical comedies

1. Birds do it, bees do it
Even educated fleas do it
Let's do it, let's fall in love.
['Let's Fall in Love', song, 1928, from *Paris*]

2. Night and day, you are the one,
Only you beneath the moon and under the sun.
['Night and Day', song, 1932, from *The Gay Divorcee*]

3. Now, heaven knows, anything goes.
[Title song, 1934, from *Anything Goes*]

4. Miss Otis regrets she's unable to lunch today.
['Miss Otis Regrets', song, 1934, from *Hi Diddle Diddle*]

5. And we suddenly know, what heaven we're in,
When they begin the beguine.
['Begin the Beguine', song, 1935, from *Jubilee*]

6. But I'm always true to you, darlin', in my fashion
Yes I'm always true to you, darlin', in my way.
['Always True to You in My Fashion', song, 1948, from *Kiss Me, Kate*]

7. I love Paris in the springtime.
['I Love Paris', song, 1953, from *Can-Can*]

8. *He*: Have you heard it's in the stars
Next July we collide with Mars?
She: Well, did you evah! What a swell party this is.
['Well, Did you Evah!', song, 1956, from *High Society*]

9. Who Wants to Be a Millionaire? I don't.
[Title song, 1956, from *Who Wants to be a Millionaire?*]

Porter, Sir George (1920–)
English chemist; co-winner of the Nobel prize, 1967, for his work on flash photolysis

1. Should we force science down the throats of those that have no taste for it? Is it our duty to drag them kicking and screaming into the twenty-first century? I am afraid that it is.
[Speech, 1986]

Porter, Hal (1911–1984)
Australian novelist, short-story writer, dramatist and poet

1. How ruthless and hard and vile and right the young are.
[*The Watcher on the Cast-iron Balcony* (1963)]

Porter, Peter Neville Frederick (1929–)
Australian poet, who lives in London

1. All man's regret is no more
than Attila with a cold
and no Saviour here or
in Science Fiction will come
without a Massacre of the Innocents
and a Rape of El Dorado.
[*Collected Poems* (1983), 'The Sadness of the Creatures']

2. Moving one paw out and yawning,
he closes his eyes. Everywhere
people are in despair. And he is dancing.
[*Collected Poems* (1983), 'My Old Cat Dances']

3. Language of the liberal dead speaks
From the soil of Highgate, tears
Show a great water table is intact.
You cannot leave England, it turns
A planet majestically in the mind.
['The Last of England']

Porteus, Beilby (1731–1808)
English Bishop of London, preacher and religious writer

1. One murder made a villain,
Millions a hero...

2. War its thousands slays, Peace its ten thousands...

3. Teach him how to live,
And, oh! still harder lesson! how to die.
['Death' (1759). Cf. Jean Rostand: 1]

Portland, William John Arthur Charles James Cavendish-Bentinck, Sixth Duke of (1857–1943)
British aristocrat; Privy Councillor and writer

1. [On being told to reduce his expenses by dispensing with one of his two Italian pastry cooks]
What! Can't a fellow even enjoy a biscuit any more?
[In S. Winchester, *Their Noble Lordships*]

Post, Emily (1873–1960)
American novelist and journalist

1. Ideal conversation must be an exchange of thought, and not, as many of those who worry most about their shortcomings believe, an eloquent exhibition of wit or oratory.
[*Etiquette* (1922), 6]

2. To the old saying that man built the house but woman made of it a 'home' might be added the modern supplement that woman accepted cooking as a chore but man has made of it a recreation.
[*Etiquette* (1922), 34]

Potter, Beatrix (1866–1943)
English writer and illustrator of children's stories; sheep farmer

1. Once upon a time there were four little Rabbits, and their names were Flopsy, Mopsy, Cottontail, and Peter.
[*The Tale of Peter Rabbit* (1902)]

2. You may go into the field or down the lane, but don't go into Mr McGregor's garden: your Father had an accident there; he was put in a pie by Mrs McGregor.
[*The Tale of Peter Rabbit* (1902)]

3. 'No teeth, no teeth, no teeth!' said Mr Jackson.
[*The Tale of Mrs Tittlemouse* (1910)]

Potter, Stephen (1900–1969)
English humorous writer, radio producer, critic and lecturer

1. Gamesmanship or, The Art of Winning Games without actually Cheating.
[Title of book, 1947]

2. *How to be one up* – how to make the other man feel that something has gone wrong, however slightly.
[*Lifemanship* (1950)]

3. *Donsmanship* – the art of criticizing without actually listening.
[*Lifemanship* (1950)]

4. It is an important general rule always to refer to your friend's country establishment as a 'cottage'.
[*Lifemanship* (1950)]

5. [A blocking phrase for conversation]
Yes, but not in the South, with slight adjustments will do for any argument about any place, if not about any person.
[*Lifemanship* (1950)]

6. It is WRONG to do what everyone else does – namely, to hold the wine list just out of sight, look for the second cheapest claret on the list, and say, 'Number 22, please'.
[*One-Upmanship* (1952)]

7. A good general rule is to state that the bouquet is better than the taste, and vice versa.
[*One-Upmanship* (1952)]

Pottier, Eugène (1816–1887)
French politician

1. *Debout! les damnés de la terre!*
Debout! les forçats de la faim!
La raison tonne en son cratère,
C'est l'éruption de la fin.
Du passé faisons table rase,
Foule esclave, debout, debout,
Le monde va changer de base,
Nous ne sommes rien, soyons tout!
C'est la lutte finale
Groupons-nous, et, demain,
L'Internationale
Sera le genre humain.
Rise up, you damned souls of the earth! Rise up, inmates of hunger's prison! Reason is thundering in its crater, and its final eruption is coming. Let us wipe clean the slate of the past – on your feet, you enslaved multitude, on your feet – the world is going to change: we are nothing, let us be everything! This is the final struggle: let us form up and, tomorrow, the International will be the human race.
['L'Internationale' (1871)]

Pound, Ezra (1885–1972)
American imagist poet, translator and critic; indicted for treason 1945

1. Bah! I have sung women in three cities,
But it is all the same;
And I will sing of the sun.
['Cino' (1908)]

2. Nay, whatever comes
One hour was sunlit and the most high gods
May not make boast of any better thing
Than to have watched that hour as it passed.
['Erat Hora' (1908)]

3. Free us, for we perish
In this ever-flowing monotony
Of ugly print marks, black
Upon white parchment.
['The Eyes' (1908)]

4. So many thousand beauties are gone down to Avernus,
Ye might let one remain above with us.
['Prayer for his Lady's Life' (1908)]

5. There come now no kings nor Caesars
Nor gold-giving lords like those gone.
Howe'er in mirth most magnified,
Whoe'er lived in life most lordliest,
Drear all this excellence, delights undurable!
Waneth the watch, but the world holdeth.
Tomb hideth trouble. The blade is layed low.
Earthly glory ageth and seareth.
['The Seafarer' (1912); from the Anglo-Saxon original]

6. The leaves fall early this autumn, in wind.
The paired butterflies are already yellow with August
Over the grass in the West garden;
They hurt me. I grow older.
If you are coming down through the narrows of the river Kiang,
Please let me know beforehand,
And I will come out to meet you
As far as Cho-fu-sa.
['The River Merchant's Wife: A Letter' (1915); from the Chinese of Rihaku]

7. And if you ask how I regret that parting:
It is like the flowers falling at Spring's end
Confused, whirled in a tangle.
What is the use of talking, and there is no end of talking,
There is no end of things in the heart.
['Exile's Letter'; from the Chinese of Rihaku (1915)]

8. Blue, blue is the grass about the river
And the willows have overfilled the close garden.
And within, the mistress, in the midmost of her youth,
White, white of face, hesitates, passing the door.
Slender, she puts forth a slender hand;
And she was a courtesan in the old days,
And she has married a sot,
Who now goes drunkenly out
And leaves her too much alone.
['The Beautiful Toilet'; from the Chinese of Mei Sheng (1915)]

9. And we knew all that stream,
And our two horses had traced out the valleys;
Knew the low flooded lands squared out with poplars,
In the young days when the deep sky befriended.
And great wings beat above us in the twilight,
And the great wheels in heaven
Bore us together ... surging ... and apart...
Believing we should meet with lips and hands,
High, high and sure ... and then the counter-thrust:
'Why do you love me? Will you always love me?
But I am like the grass, I cannot love you.'
['Near Perigord' (1915)]

10. Suddenly discovering in the eyes of the very beautiful
Normande cocotte
The eyes of the very learned British Museum assistant.
['Pagani's, November 8' (1915)]

11. I had over-prepared the event,
that much was ominous.
With middle-ageing care
I had laid out just the right books.
I had almost turned down the pages.
['Villanelle: the psychological hour' (1915)]

12. Winter is icummen in,
Lhude sing Goddamn,
Raineth drop and staineth slop,
And how the wind doth ramm!
Sing: Goddamn.
['Ancient Music' (1916). Cf. Anon.: 41]

13. As a bathtub lined with white porcelain,
When the hot water gives out or goes tepid,
So is the slow cooling of our chivalrous passion,
O my much praised but-not-altogether-satisfactory lady.
['The Bath Tub' (1916)]

14. Oh how hideous it is
To see three generations of one house gathered together!
It is like an old tree with shoots,
And with some branches rotted and falling.
['Commission' (1916)]

15. Come, let us pity those who are better off than we are.
Come, my friend, and remember that the rich have butlers
and no friends,
And we have friends and no butlers.
Come, let us pity the married and unmarried.
['The Garret' (1916)]

16. I'd seen a lot of his lot...
ever since Rhodez,
Coming down from the fair
of St John,
With caravans, but never an ape or a bear.
['The Gipsy' (1916)]

17. The apparition of these faces in the crowd;
Petals on a wet, black bough.
['In a Station of the Metro' (1916)]

18. O God, O Venus, O Mercury, patron of thieves,
Give me in due time, I beseech you, a little tobacco-shop...
And a pair of scales not too greasy,
And the whores dropping in for a word or two in passing,
For a flip word, and to tidy their hair a bit.

O God, O Venus, O Mercury, patron of thieves,
Lend me a little tobacco-shop,
or install me in any profession
Save this damn'd profession of writing,
where one needs one's brains all the time.
['The Lake Isle' (1916)]

19. The rustling of the silk is discontinued,
Dust drifts over the court-yard,
There is no sound of foot-fall, and the leaves
Scurry into heaps and lie still,
And she the rejoicer of the heart is beneath them:

A wet leaf clings to the threshold.
['Liu Ch'e' (1916)]

20. When I carefully consider the curious habits of dogs
I am compelled to conclude
That man is the superior animal.

When I consider the curious habits of man
I confess, my friend, I am puzzled.
['Meditatio' (1916)]

21. I make a pact with you, Walt Whitman–
I have detested you long enough...
It was you that broke the new wood,
Now it is a time for carving.
We have one sap and one root–
Let there be commerce between us.
['A Pact' (1916)]

22. O generation of the thoroughly smug and thoroughly
uncomfortable.
['Salutation' (1916)]

23. Come, my songs, let us speak of perfection–
We shall get ourselves rather disliked.
['Salvationists' (1916)]

24. Will people accept them?
(i.e. these songs).
As a timorous wench from a centaur
(or a centurion),
Already they flee, howling in terror.
['Tenzone' (1916)]

25. For three years, out of key with his time,
He strove to resuscitate the dead art
Of poetry; to maintain 'the sublime'
In the old sense. Wrong from the start...

26. His true Penelope was Flaubert,
He fished by obstinate isles;
Observed the elegance of Circe's hair
Rather than the mottoes on sundials.
[*Hugh Selwyn Mauberley* (1920), 'E.P. Ode pour l'élection de son sépulcre', 1]

27. Better mendacities
Than the classics in paraphrase!
[*Hugh Selwyn Mauberley* (1920), 'E.P. Ode pour l'élection de son sépulcre', 2]

28. The tea-rose tea-gown, etc.
Supplants the *mousseline* of Cos,
The pianola 'replaces'
Sappho's barbitos.

Christ follows Dionysus,
Phallic and ambrosial

Made way for macerations;
Caliban casts out Ariel.

All things are a flowing,
Sage Heracleitus says;
But a tawdry cheapness
Shall outlast our days.
[*Hugh Selwyn Mauberley* (1920), 'E.P. Ode pour l'élection de son sépulcre', 3]

29. There died a myriad,
And of the best, among them,
For an old bitch gone in the teeth,
For a botched civilization.
[*Hugh Selwyn Mauberley* (1920), 'E.P. Ode pour l'élection de son sépulcre', 5]

30. And give up verse, my boy,
There's nothing in it.
[*Hugh Selwyn Mauberley* (1920), 'Mr Nixon']

31. Palace in smoky light,
Troy but a heap of smouldering boundary stones.
[*Draft of XXX Cantos* (1930), 4]

32. And even I can remember
A day when the historians left blanks in their writings,
I mean for things they didn't know.
[*Draft of XXX Cantos* (1930), 13]

33. Yet you ask on what account I write so many love-lyrics
And whence this soft book comes into my mouth.
Neither Calliope nor Apollo sung these things into my ear,
My genius is no more than a girl.
If she with ivory fingers drive a tune through the lyre,
We look at the process.
How easy the moving fingers; if hair is mussed on her forehead,
If she goes in a gleam of Cos, in a slither of dyed stuff,
There is a volume in the matter.
[*Homage to Sextus Propertius* (1934), V]

34. What thou lovest well remains,
the rest is dross
What thou lov'st well shall not be reft from thee
What thou lov'st well is thy true heritage...

35. The ant's a centaur in his dragon world.
Pull down thy vanity, it is not man
Made courage, or made order, or made grace.
Pull down thy vanity, I say pull down.
Learn of the green world what can be thy place
In scaled invention or true artistry,
Pull down thy vanity,
Paquin pull down!
The green casque has outdone your elegance...

36. Pull down thy vanity
Thou art a beaten dog beneath the hail,
A swollen magpie in a fitful sun,
Half black half white
Not knowst 'ou wing from tail
Pull down thy vanity...

37. But to have done instead of not doing
this is not vanity
To have, with decency, knocked
That a Blunt should open
To have gathered from the air a live tradition
or from a fine old eye the unconquered flame
This is not vanity.
Here error is all in the not done,
all in the diffidence that faltered.
[*Pisan Cantos* (1948), 81]

38. With usura hath no man a house of good stone
each block cut smooth and well fitting
that design might cover their face...

39. WITH USURA
wool comes not to market
sheep bringeth no gain with usura
Usura is a murrain, usura
blunteth the needle in the maid's hand
and stoppeth the spinner's cunning...

40. Usura rusteth the chisel
It rusteth the craft and the craftsman...

41. Azure hath a canker by usura; cramoisi is unbroidered
Emerald findeth no Memling
Usura slayeth the child in the womb
It stayeth the young man's courting
It hath brought palsey to bed, lyeth
between the young bride and her bridegroom
CONTRA NATURA
They have brought whores for Eleusis
Corpses are set to banquet
at behest of usura.
[*Cantos* (1954), 45]

42. Great Literature is simply language charged with meaning to the utmost possible degree.
[*How to Read* (1931)]

43. Music begins to atrophy when it departs too far from the dance; ... poetry begins to atrophy when it gets too far from music.
[*ABC of Reading* (1934)]

44. One of the pleasures of middle age is to *find out* that one WAS right, and that one was much righter than one knew at say 17 or 23.
[*ABC of Reading* (1934)]

45. Literature is news that STAYS news.
[*ABC of Reading* (1934)]

46. The difference between a gun and a tree is a difference of tempo. The tree explodes every spring.
[*Criterion* (1937)]

Powell, Anthony (1905–)
English novelist, critic and memoirist

1. He fell in love with himself at first sight and it is a passion to which he has always remained faithful. Self-love seems so often unrequited.
[*A Dance to the Music of Time: The Acceptance World* (1955), 1]

2. Dinner at the Huntercombes' possessed 'only two dramatic features – the wine was a farce and the food a tragedy'.
[*A Dance to the Music of Time: The Acceptance World* (1955), 4]

3. All men are brothers, but, thank God, they aren't all brothers-in-law.
[*A Dance to the Music of Time: At Lady Molly's* (1957), 4]

4. It must be generations since anyone but highbrows lived in this cottage ... I imagine most of the agricultural labourers round here commute from London.
[*A Dance to the Music of Time: The Kindly Ones* (1962), 2]

5. One of the worst things about life is not how nasty the nasty people are. You know that already. It is how nasty the nice people can be.
[*A Dance to the Music of Time: The Kindly Ones* (1962), 4]

6. Books Do Furnish a Room.
[Title of novel, 1971]

7. Growing old is like being increasingly penalized for a crime you haven't committed.
[*A Dance to the Music of Time: Temporary Kings* (1973), 1]

8. People think that because a novel's invented, it isn't true. Exactly the reverse is the case. Biography and memoirs can never be wholly true, since they cannot include every conceivable circumstance of what happened. The novel can do that.
[*A Dance to the Music of Time: Hearing Secret Harmonies* (1975), 3]

Powell, Enoch (1912–)
English Conservative, later Ulster Unionist, politician and Greek scholar

1. [On race relations in Britain]
As I look ahead I am filled with foreboding. Like the Roman I seem to see 'The River Tiber foaming with much blood.'
[Speech, Birmingham, 1968]

2. Above any other position of eminence, that of Prime Minister is filled by fluke.
[*The Observer*, 'Sayings of the Week', 1987]

Powell, Sir John (1645–1713)
English judge

1. Let us consider the reason of the case. For nothing is law that is not reason.
[In Lord Raymond's *Reports* (1765), Coggs v. Bernard, 2]

Powell, Sandy (1900–1982)
British light entertainer

1. Can you hear me, mother?
[Catchphrase, from mid-1930s]

Power, John O'Connor (b. 1846)
British lawyer and politician

1. [Of the Liberal Unionists]
The mules of politics: without pride of ancestry, or hope of posterity.
[In H.H. Asquith, *Memories and Reflections* (1928), I, 16]

Power, Marguerite, Countess of Blessington (1789–1849)
English writer

1. ... it is better to die young than to outlive all one loved, and all that rendered one lovable.
[*The Confessions of an Elderly Gentleman* (1836)]

2. Tears fell from my eyes – yes, weak and foolish as it now appears to me, I wept for my departed youth; and for that beauty of which the faithful mirror too plainly assured me, no remnant existed.
[*The Confessions of an Elderly Lady* (1838)]

Power, Sir William James Tyrone

1. [Definition of a kiwi]
The Kiwi is the ugliest bird one can well imagine – stilted up on long, thick, clumsy legs, with scarcely the rudiments of wings, with an overgrown head and long beak. It was, not unaptly, described by a facetious subaltern, who saw one for the first time, as a cross between a snipe and a monkey. It is a solitary night-bird, and feeds on worms and grubs, for which it goes sniffling about, with an unpleasant noise as if afflicted with a bad cold in the head.
[*Sketches in New Zealand* (1849)]

Powys, John Cowper (1872–1963)
English novelist, poet and essayist

1. He combined scepticism of everything with credulity about everything ... and I am convinced this is the true Shakespearian way wherewith to take life.
[*Autobiography*]

Pratchett, Terry (1948–)
British writer of science fiction and fantasy

1. Unlike wizards, who like nothing better than a complicated hierarchy, witches don't go in much for the structural approach to career progression.
[*Wyrd Sisters* (1988)]

Book of Common Prayer

1. A Table of the Moveable Feasts.
[Introductory pages]

2. There was never any thing by the wit of man so well devised, or so sure established, which in continuance of time hath not been corrupted.
[*The Preface* Concerning the Service of the Church]

3. Dearly beloved brethren, the Scripture moveth us in sundry places to acknowledge and confess our manifold sins and wickedness; and that we should not dissemble nor cloke them before the face of Almighty God our heavenly Father; but confess them with an humble, lowly, penitent, and obedient heart ... I pray and beseech you, as many as are here present, to accompany me with a pure heart, and humble voice, unto the throne of the heavenly grace.
[*The Order for Morning Prayer* Sentences of the Scriptures]

4. We have erred, and strayed from thy ways like lost sheep. We have followed too much the devices and desires of our own hearts ... We have left undone those things which we ought to have done; And we have done those things which we ought not to have done.
[*The Order for Morning Prayer* General Confession]

5. Restore thou them that are penitent; According to thy promises declared unto mankind in Christ Jesu our Lord. And grant, O most merciful Father, for his sake; That we may hereafter live a godly, righteous, and sober life.
[*The Order for Morning Prayer* General Confession]

6. Our Father, which art in heaven. Hallowed be thy Name. Thy kingdom come. Thy will be done, in earth as it is in heaven. Give us this day our daily bread. And forgive us our trespasses, As we forgive them that trespass against us. And lead us not into temptation; But deliver us from evil: For thine is the kingdom, The power and the glory, For ever and ever, Amen.
[*The Order for Morning Prayer* The Lord's Prayer]

7. [Priest] Glory be to the Father, and to the Son: and to the Holy Ghost.
[Answer] As it was in the beginning, is now, and ever shall be: world without end. Amen.
[*The Order for Morning Prayer* Gloria]

8. We praise thee, O God: we acknowledge thee to be the Lord.
All the earth doth worship thee: the Father everlasting.
To thee all Angels cry aloud: the Heavens, and all the Powers therein.
To thee Cherubin, and Seraphin: continually do cry,
Holy, Holy, Holy: Lord God of Sabaoth;
Heaven and earth are full of the Majesty: of thy Glory.
The glorious company of the Apostles: praise thee.
The goodly fellowship of the Prophets: praise thee.
The noble army of Martyrs: praise thee.
[*The Order for Morning Prayer* Te Deum Laudamus]

BOOK OF COMMON PRAYER

9. An infinite Majesty.
[*The Order for Morning Prayer* Te Deum Laudamus]

10. When thou hadst overcome the sharpness of death: thou didst open the Kingdom of Heaven to all believers.
[*The Order for Morning Prayer* Te Deum Laudamus]

11. Day by day: we magnify thee;
And we worship thy Name: ever world without end.
Vouchsafe, O Lord: to keep us this day without sin.
O Lord, have mercy upon us: have mercy upon us.
O Lord, let thy mercy lighten upon us: as our trust is in thee.
O Lord, in thee have I trusted: let me never be confounded.
[*The Order for Morning Prayer* Te Deum Laudamus]

12. O all ye Works of the Lord, bless ye the Lord.
[*The Order for Morning Prayer* Benedicite, Omnia Opera]

13. O ye Waters that be above the Firmament, bless ye the Lord.
[*The Order for Morning Prayer* Benedicite, Omnia Opera]

14. O ye Showers and Dew, bless ye the Lord: praise him, and magnify him for ever.
O ye Winds of God, bless ye the Lord: praise him, and magnify him for ever.
[*The Order for Morning Prayer* Benedicite, Omnia Opera]

15. O ye Dews and Frosts, bless ye the Lord: praise him, and magnify him for ever.
O ye Frost and Cold, bless ye the Lord: praise him, and magnify him for ever.
O ye Ice and Snow, bless ye the Lord: praise him, and magnify him for ever.
O ye Nights and Days, bless ye the Lord: praise him, and magnify him for ever.
[*The Order for Morning Prayer* Benedicite, Omnia Opera]

16. O let the Earth bless the Lord: yea, let it praise him, and magnify him for ever.
[*The Order for Morning Prayer* Benedicite, Omnia Opera]

17. O all ye Green Things upon the Earth, bless ye the Lord: praise him, and magnify him for ever.
[*The Order for Morning Prayer* Benedicite, Omnia Opera]

18. O ye Whales, and all that move in the Waters, bless ye the Lord: praise him, and magnify him for ever.
[*The Order for Morning Prayer* Benedicite, Omnia Opera]

19. I believe in God the Father Almighty, Maker of heaven and earth:
And in Jesus Christ his only Son our Lord, Who was conceived by the Holy Ghost, Born of the Virgin Mary, Suffered under Pontius Pilate, Was crucified, dead, and buried, He descended into hell; The third day he rose again from the dead, He ascended into heaven, And sitteth on the right hand of God the Father Almighty; From thence he shall come to judge the quick and the dead.
I believe in the Holy Ghost; The holy Catholick Church; The Communion of Saints; The Forgiveness of sins; The Resurrection of the body, And the life everlasting. Amen.
[*The Order for Morning Prayer* The Apostles' Creed]

20. Lord, have mercy upon us.
Christ, have mercy upon us.
[*The Order for Morning Prayer* Prayers following the Apostles' Creed]

21. [Priest] Give peace in our time, O Lord.
[Answer] Because there is none other that fighteth for us, but only thou, O God.
[*The Order for Morning Prayer* Versicle]

22. O God, who art the author of peace and lover of concord, in knowledge of whom standeth our eternal life, whose service is perfect freedom; Defend us thy humble servants in all assaults of our enemies.
[*The Order for Morning Prayer* The Second Collect, for Peace]

23. Grant that this day we fall into no sin, neither run into any kind of danger.
[*The Order for Morning Prayer* The Third Collect, for Grace]

24. Endue her plenteously with heavenly gifts; grant her in health and wealth long to live.
[*The Order for Morning Prayer* A Prayer for the Queen's Majesty]

25. Almighty God, the fountain of all goodness.
[*The Order for Morning Prayer* A Prayer for the Royal Family]

26. Almighty and everlasting God, who alone workest great marvels; Send down upon our Bishops, and Curates, and all Congregations committed to their charge, the healthful Spirit of thy grace; and that they may truly please thee, pour upon them the continual dew of thy blessing.
[*The Order for Morning Prayer* A Prayer for the Clergy and People]

27. Almighty God, who hast given us grace at this time with one accord to make our common supplications unto thee, and dost promise, that when two or three are gathered together in thy Name thou wilt grant their requests: Fulfil now, O Lord, the desires and petitions of thy servants, as may be most expedient for them.
[*The Order for Morning Prayer* A Prayer of St Chrysostom]

28. O God, from whom all holy desires, all good counsels, and all just works do proceed; Give unto thy servants that peace which the world cannot give.
[*The Order for Evening Prayer* The Second Collect at Evening Prayer]

29. Lighten our darkness, we beseech thee, O Lord; and by thy great mercy defend us from all perils and dangers of this night.
[*The Order for Evening Prayer* The Third Collect, For Aid Against All Perils]

30. And the Catholick Faith is this: That we worship one God in Trinity, and Trinity in Unity;
Neither confounding the Persons: nor dividing the Substance.
[*At Morning Prayer* The Creed of Saint Athanasius]

31. They are not three Gods: but one God.
[*At Morning Prayer* The Creed of Saint Athanasius]

32. Have mercy upon us miserable sinners.
[*The Litany*]

33. From all evil and mischief; from sin, from the crafts and assaults of the devil; from thy wrath, and from everlasting damnation,
Good Lord, deliver us.
From all blindness of heart; from pride, vain-glory, and hypocrisy; from envy, hatred, and malice, and all uncharitableness,
Good Lord, deliver us.
From fornication, and all other deadly sin; and from all the deceits of the world, the flesh, and the devil,
Good Lord, deliver us.
From lightning and tempest; from plague, pestilence, and famine; from battle and murder, and from sudden death,
Good Lord, deliver us.
[*The Litany*]

34. By thine Agony and bloody Sweat; by thy Cross and Passion; by thy precious Death and Burial; by thy glorious Resurrection and Ascension; and by the coming of the Holy Ghost,
Good Lord, deliver us.

In all time of our tribulation; in all time of our wealth; in the hour of death, and in the day of judgment,
Good Lord, deliver us.
[*The Litany*]

35. That it may please thee to strengthen such as do stand; and to comfort and help the weak-hearted; and to raise up them that fall; and finally to beat down Satan under our feet;
We beseech thee to hear us, good Lord.
[*The Litany*]

36. That it may please thee to preserve all that travel by land or by water, all women labouring of child, all sick persons, and young children; and to shew thy pity upon all prisoners and captives;
We beseech thee to hear us, good Lord.
That it may please thee to defend, and provide for, the fatherless children, and widows, and all that are desolate and oppressed;
We beseech thee to hear us, good Lord.
[*The Litany*]

37. That it may please thee to give and preserve to our use the kindly fruits of the earth, so as in due time we may enjoy them;
We beseech thee to hear us, good Lord.
[*The Litany*]

38. O God, the Creator and Preserver of all mankind, we humbly beseech thee for all sorts and conditions of men.
[*Prayers and Thanksgivings upon Several Occasions* A Collect or Prayer for all Conditions of Men]

39. We commend to thy fatherly goodness all those, who are any ways afflicted, or distressed, in mind, body, or estate; that it may please thee to comfort and relieve them, according to their several necessities, giving them patience under their sufferings, and a happy issue out of all their afflictions.
[*Prayers and Thanksgivings upon Several Occasions* A Collect or Prayer for all Conditions of Men]

40. We bless thee for our creation, preservation, and all the blessings of this life; but above all, for thine inestimable love in the redemption of the world by our Lord Jesus Christ; for the means of grace, and for the hope of glory.
[*Prayers and Thanksgivings upon Several Occasions* A General Thanksgiving]

41. O God our heavenly Father, who by thy gracious providence dost cause the former and the latter rain to descend upon the earth, that it may bring forth fruit for the use of man; We give thee humble thanks that it hath pleased thee, in our great necessity, to send us at the last a joyful rain upon thine inheritance, and to refresh it when it was dry.
[*Prayers and Thanksgivings upon Several Occasions* Thanksgiving for Rain]

42. Almighty God, give us grace that we may cast away the works of darkness, and put upon us the armour of light, now in the time of this mortal life, in which thy Son Jesus Christ came to visit us in great humility.
[*The Collects* The First Sunday in Advent]

43. Blessed Lord, who hast caused all holy Scriptures to be written for our learning; Grant that we may in such wise hear them, read, mark, learn, and inwardly digest them, that by patience, and comfort of thy holy Word, we may embrace, and ever hold fast the blessed hope of everlasting life.
[*The Collects* The Second Sunday in Advent]

44. The glory that shall be revealed.
[*The Collects* St Stephen's Day]

45. O Lord, we beseech thee mercifully to receive the prayers of thy people which call upon thee; and grant that they may both perceive and know what things they ought to do, and also may have grace and power faithfully to fulfil the same.
[*The Collects* The First Sunday after the Epiphany]

46. All our doings without charity are nothing worth, . . . pour into our hearts that most excellent gift of charity.
[*The Collects* The Sunday called Quinquagesima]

47. Have mercy upon all Jews, Turks, Infidels, and Hereticks.
[*The Collects* The Third Collect for Good Friday]

48. Grant us so to put away the leaven of malice and wickedness, that we may alway serve thee in pureness of living and truth.
[*The Collects* The First Sunday after Easter]

49. O Almighty God, who alone canst order the unruly wills and affections of sinful men; Grant unto thy people, that they may love the thing which thou commandest, and desire that which thou dost promise; that so, among the sundry and manifold changes of the world, our hearts may surely there be fixed, where true joys are to be found.
[*The Collects* The Fourth Sunday after Easter]

50. We beseech thee, leave us not comfortless; but send to us thine Holy Ghost to comfort us, and exalt us unto the same place whither our Saviour Christ is gone before.
[*The Collects* Sunday after Ascension Day]

51. Because through the weakness of our mortal nature we can do no good thing without thee, grant us the help of thy grace, that in keeping of thy commandments we may please thee, both in will and deed.
[*The Collects* The First Sunday after Trinity]

52. O God, the protector of all that trust in thee, without whom nothing is strong, nothing is holy; Increase and multiply upon us thy mercy; that, thou being our ruler and guide, we may so pass through things temporal, that we finally lose not the things eternal.
[*Collects* The Fourth Sunday after Trinity]

53. Grant, O Lord, we beseech thee, that the course of this world may be so peaceably ordered by thy governance, that thy Church may joyfully serve thee in all godly quietness.
[*The Collects* The Fifth Sunday after Trinity]

54. O God, who hast prepared for them that love thee such good things as pass man's understanding; Pour into our hearts such love toward thee, that we, loving thee above all things, may obtain thy promises, which exceed all that we can desire.
[*The Collects* The Sixth Sunday after Trinity]

55. Lord of all power and might, who art the author and giver of all good things; Graft in our hearts the love of thy Name, increase in us true religion, nourish us with all goodness, and of thy great mercy keep us in the same.
[*The Collects* The Seventh Sunday after Trinity]

56. O God, forasmuch as without thee we are not able to please thee; Mercifully grant, that thy Holy Spirit may in all things direct and rule our hearts.
[*The Collects* The Nineteenth Sunday after Trinity]

57. Grant, we beseech thee, merciful Lord, to thy faithful people pardon and peace, that they may be cleansed from all their sins, and serve thee with a quiet mind.
[*The Collects* The Twenty-first Sunday after Trinity]

58. Stir up, we beseech, O Lord, the wills of thy faithful people; that they, plenteously bringing forth the fruit of good works, may of thee be plenteously rewarded.
[*The Collects* The Twenty-fifth Sunday after Trinity]

BOOK OF COMMON PRAYER

59. O Almighty God, whom truly to know is everlasting life.
[*The Collects* St Philip and St James's Day]

60. O Almighty God, who has knit together thine elect in one communion and fellowship, in the mystical body of thy Son Christ our Lord; Grant us grace so to follow thy blessed Saints in all virtuous and godly living, that we may come to those unspeakable joys, which thou hast prepared for them that unfeignedly love thee.
[*The Collects* All Saints' Day]

61. So many as intend to be partakers of the holy Communion shall signify their names to the Curate, at least some time the day before.
And if any of those be an open and notorious evil liver, or have done any wrong to his neighbours by word or deed, so that the Congregation be thereby offended; the Curate, having knowledge thereof, shall call him and advertise him, that in any wise he presume not to come to the Lord's Table, until he have openly declared himself to have truly repented and amended his former naughty life.
[*Holy Communion* Introductory rubric]

62. The Table at the Communion-time having a fair white linen cloth upon it, shall stand in the Body of the Church, or in the Chancel.
[*Holy Communion* Introductory rubric]

63. Almighty God, unto whom all hearts be open, all desires known, and from whom no secrets are hid; Cleanse the thoughts of our hearts by the inspiration of thy Holy Spirit, that we may perfectly love thee, and worthily magnify thy holy Name.
[*Holy Communion* The Collect]

64. Lord, have mercy upon us, and incline our hearts to keep this law.
[*Holy Communion* The Ten Commandments (response)]

65. Thou shalt do no murder.
[*Holy Communion* The Ten Commandments]

66. I believe in one God the Father Almighty, Maker of heaven and earth, And of all things visible and invisible:
And in one Lord Jesus Christ, the only-begotten Son of God, Begotten of his Father before all worlds, God of God, Light of Light, Very God of very God, Begotten, not made, Being of one substance with the Father, By whom all things were made ... And I believe in the Holy Ghost, The Lord and giver of life, Who proceedeth from the Father and the Son, Who with the Father and the Son together is worshipped and glorified, Who spake by the Prophets. And I believe one Catholick and Apostolick Church.
[*Holy Communion* Nicene Creed]

67. Let us pray for the whole state of Christ's Church militant here in earth.
[*Holy Communion* Prayer for the Church Militant]

68. We humbly beseech thee most mercifully to accept our alms and oblations, and to receive these our prayers, which we offer unto thy Divine Majesty; beseeching thee to inspire continually the universal Church with the spirit of truth, unity, and concord: And grant, that all they that do confess thy holy Name may agree in the truth of thy holy Word, and live in unity, and godly love.
[*Holy Communion* Prayer for the Church Militant]

69. [Of the Queen's government]
Grant unto her whole Council, and to all that are put in authority under her, that they may truly and indifferently minister justice.
[*Holy Communion* Prayer for the Church Militant]

70. Give grace, O heavenly Father, to all Bishops and Curates, that they may both by their life and doctrine set forth thy true and lively Word.
[*Holy Communion* Prayer for the Church Militant]

71. Ye that do truly and earnestly repent you of your sins, and are in love and charity with your neighbours, and intend to lead a new life ... Draw near with faith.
[*Holy Communion* The Invitation]

72. Hear what comfortable words our Saviour Christ saith unto all that truly turn to him.
[*Holy Communion* Comfortable Words]

73. It is very meet, right, and our bounden duty, that we should at all times, and in all places, give thanks unto thee, O Lord.
[*Holy Communion* Hymn of Praise]

74. I should renounce the devil and all his works, the pomps and vanity of this wicked world, and all the sinful lusts of the flesh.
[*A Catechism*]

75. In their Mother Tongue.
[*A Catechism* Final rubric]

76. Laying on of Hands.
[*The Order of Confirmation* Subtitle]

77. Being now come to the years of discretion.
[*The Order of Confirmation* Preface]

78. [Bishop] Our help is in the Name of the Lord;
[Answer] Who hath made heaven and earth...
[Bishop] Lord, hear our prayers.
[Answer] And let our cry come unto thee.
[*The Order of Confirmation*]

79. If any of you know cause, or just impediment, why these two persons should not be joined together in holy Matrimony, ye are to declare it. This is the first time of asking.
[*The Form of Solemnization of Matrimony* The Banns]

80. Dearly beloved, we are gathered together here in the sight of God, and in the face of this congregation, to join together this Man and this Woman in holy Matrimony.
[*The Form of Solemnization of Matrimony* Exhortation]

81. [Marriage] is not by any to be enterprised, nor taken in hand, unadvisedly, lightly, or wantonly, to satisfy men's carnal lusts and appetites, like brute beasts that have no understanding; but reverently, discreetly, advisedly, soberly, and in the fear of God.
[*The Form of Solemnization of Matrimony* Exhortation]

82. If any man can shew any just cause, why they may not lawfully be joined together, let him now speak, or else hereafter for ever hold his peace.
[*The Form of Solemnization of Matrimony* Exhortation]

83. Wilt thou have this Woman to thy wedded wife, to live together after God's ordinance in the holy estate of Matrimony? Wilt thou love her, comfort her, honour, and keep her in sickness and in health; and, forsaking all other, keep thee only unto her, so long as ye both shall live?
[*The Form of Solemnization of Matrimony* Betrothal]

84. To have and to hold from this day forward, for better for worse, for richer for poorer, in sickness and in health, to love and to cherish, till death us do part, according to God's holy ordinance; and thereto I plight thee my troth.
[*The Form of Solemnization of Matrimony* Betrothal]

85. To love, cherish, and to obey.
[*The Form of Solemnization of Matrimony* Betrothal]

86. With this Ring I thee wed, with my body I thee worship, and with all my worldly goods I thee endow.
[*The Form of Solemnization of Matrimony* Wedding]

87. Those whom God hath joined together let no man put asunder.
[*The Form of Solemnization of Matrimony* Prayer]

88. Forasmuch as – and – have consented together in holy wedlock, and have witnessed the same before God and this company, and thereto have given and pledged their troth either to other, and have declared the same by giving and receiving of a Ring, and by joining of hands; I pronounce that they be Man and Wife together.
[*The Form of Solemnization of Matrimony* Minister's Declaration]

89. Peace be to this house, and to all that dwell in it.
[*The Order for the Visitation of the Sick*]

90. The more the outward man decayeth, strengthen him, we beseech thee, so much the more continually with thy grace and Holy Spirit in the inner man.
[*The Order for the Visitation of the Sick* A Prayer ... when there appeareth small hope of recovery]

91. Man that is born of a woman hath but a short time to live, and is full of misery. He cometh up, and is cut down, like a flower; he fleeth as it were a shadow, and never continueth in one stay. In the midst of life we are in death.
[*The Order for the Burial of the Dead* First Anthem]

92. Forasmuch as it hath pleased Almighty God of his great mercy to take unto himself the soul of our dear brother here departed, we therefore commit his body to the ground; earth to earth, ashes to ashes, dust to dust; in sure and certain hope of the Resurrection to eternal life, through our Lord Jesus Christ; who shall change our vile body, that it may be like unto his glorious body.
[*The Order for the Burial of the Dead* Interment]

93. Forasmuch as it hath pleased Almighty God of his goodness to give you safe deliverance, and hath preserved you in the great danger of Child-birth: you shall therefore give hearty thanks unto God.
[*The Churching of Women*]

94. O suffer us not to sink under the weight of our sins, or the violence of the enemy.
[*Forms of Prayer to be Used at Sea* Special Prayers with Respect to the Enemy]

95. We therefore commit his body to the deep, to be turned into corruption, looking for the resurrection of the body, (when the Sea shall give up her dead).
[*Forms of Prayer to be Used at Sea* At the Burial of their Dead at Sea]

Prévert, Jacques (1900–1977)
French poet, noted for his song poems, satirist and screen writer

1. *Notre Père qui êtes aux cieux*
Restez-y
Et nous nous resterons sur la terre.
Our Father which art in heaven, stay there; and as for us, we shall stay on earth.
[*Paroles* (1946), 'Pater Noster']

2. *Je suis comme je suis*
Je suis faite comme ça.
I am the way I am. That's the way I'm made.
[*Paroles* (1946), 'Je suis comme je suis']

Previn, André (1929–)
German-born American conductor, composer and popularizer of classical music

1. The basic difference between classical music and jazz is that in the former the music is always greater than its performance – whereas the way jazz is performed is always more important than what is being played.
[In Nat Shapiro, *An Encyclopedia of Quotations about Music*]

Priestley, J.B. (1894–1984)
English novelist, dramatist, critic, essayist and autobiographical writer

1. Comedy, we may say, is society protecting itself – with a smile.
[*George Meredith* (1926)]

2. If there was a little room somewhere in the British Museum that contained only about twenty exhibits and good lighting, easy chairs, and a notice imploring you to smoke, I believe I should become a museum man.
[*Self-Selected Essays* (1932), 'In the British Museum']

3. I am always surprised when I am told that somebody likes me.
[*Instead of the Trees: A Final Chapter of Autobiography* (1977)]

4. They will review a book by a writer much older than themselves as if it were an over-ambitious essay by a second-year student ... It is the little dons I complain about, like so many corgis trotting up, hoping to nip your ankles.
[*Outcries and Asides*]

5. [Of politicians]
A number of anxious dwarfs trying to grill a whale.
[*Outcries and Asides*]

6. Our trouble is that we drink too much tea. I see in this the slow revenge of the Orient, which has diverted the Yellow River down our throats.
[*The Observer*, 'Sayings of the Week', 1949]

7. God can stand being told by Professor Ayer and Marghanita Laski that He doesn't exist.
[*The Listener*, 1965, 'The BBC's Duty to Society']

Pringle, John Martin Douglas (1912–)
Scots-born Australian journalist and essayist

1. [On Sydney Opera House]
There it stands, like Santa Maria della Salute on the lagoon in Venice, a perfect symbol linking the city to the sea ... I believe it is a building of which all Australians may rightly be proud, perhaps the only true work of architecture on this continent.
[*On Second Thoughts* (1971)]

Pringle, Thomas (1789–1834)
Scottish poet, lived in and wrote about South Africa

1. Afar in the desert I love to ride,
With the silent Bush-boy alone by my side;
Away, away in the wilderness vast,
Where the white man's foot hath never passed...

2. Man is distant, but God is near.
[*African Sketches* (1834), 'Afar in the Desert']

3. But *I* brought the handsomest bride of them all–
Brown Dinah, the bondmaid who sat in our hall...

4. Shall the Edict of Mercy be sent forth at last,
To break the harsh fetters of Colour and Caste?
[*Poetical Works* (1838), 'The Forester of the Neutral Ground: A South African Border-Ballad']

Prior, Matthew (1664–1721)
English poet, epigrammatist and diplomat

1. The song too daring, and the theme too great!
['Carmen Seculare' (1700)]

2. For the idiom of words very little she heeded,
Provided the matter she drove at succeeded,
She took and gave languages just as she needed.
['Jinny the Just' (after 1700)]

3. For as our diff'rent ages move,
'Tis so ordained, would Fate but mend it,
That I shall be past making love,
When she begins to comprehend it.
['To a Child of Quality of Five Years Old' (1704)]

4. Be to her virtues very kind;
Be to her faults a little blind;
Let all her ways be unconfin'd;
And clap your padlock – on her mind.
['An English Padlock' (1705)]

5. And oft the pangs of absence to remove
By letters, soft interpreters of love.
['Henry and Emma' (1708)]

6. The merchant, to secure his treasure,
Conveys it in a borrowed name:
Euphelia serves to grace my measure:
But Chloe is my real flame.
['An Ode' (1709)]

7. He's half absolv'd who has confess'd.
[*Alma* (1718), II]

8. Salads, and eggs, and lighter fare,
Tune the Italian spark's guitar.
And, if I take Dan Congreve right,
Pudding and beef make Britons fight.
[*Alma* (1718), III]

9. Dear Cloe, how blubber'd is that pretty face!...

10. Odds life! must one swear to the truth of a song?...

11. I court others in verse: but I love thee in prose:
And they have my whimsies, but thou hast my heart.
['A Better Answer' (1718)]

12. For hope is but a dream of those that wake.
[*Solomon* (1718), II]

13. No, no, for my virginity,
When I lose that, says Rose, I'll die;
Behind the elms last night, cry'd Dick,
Rose, were you not extremely sick?
['A True Maid' (1718)]

14. I never strove to rule the roast,
She ne'er refus'd to pledge my toast.
['The Turtle and the Sparrow' (1723)]

15. Cur'd yesterday of my disease,
I died last night of my physician.
['The Remedy Worse than the Disease' (1727)]

16. They never taste who always drink;
They always talk, who never think.
['Upon this Passage in Scaligerana' (1740)]

Privat d'Anglemont, Alexandre (c. 1820–1859)
French man of letters

1. *Je les ai épatés, les bourgeois.*
I shocked them, the *bourgeois*.
[Attr. Cf. Baudelaire: 9]

Procter, Ann Adelaide (1825–1864)
English popular poet and hymn writer

1. Seated one day at the organ,
I was weary and ill at ease,
And my fingers wandered idly
Over the noisy keys...

2. But I struck one chord of music,
Like the sound of a great Amen.
[*Legends and Lyrics* (1858), 'A Lost Chord']

Propertius, Sextus Aurelius (c. 50–c. 15 BC)
Roman elegiac poet, noted for his love poetry

1. *Navita de ventis, de tauris narrat arator,*
Enumerat miles vulnera, pastor oves.
The sailor tells stories of winds, the ploughman of bulls; the soldier counts his wounds, the shepherd his sheep.
[*Elegies*, II, 1, line 43]

2. *Quod si deficiant vires, audacia certe*
Laus erit: in magnis et voluisse sat est.
Even if my strength should fail, my daring will win me praise: in mighty enterprises even the will to succeed is enough.
[*Elegies*, II, 10, line 5]

3. [On Virgil's Aeneid]
Cedite Romani scriptores, cedite Grai!
Nescioquid maius nascitur Iliade.
Yield, Roman writers, yield, Greeks! Something greater than the Iliad is born.
[*Elegies*, II, 34, line 65]

4. *Magnum iter ascendo, sed dat mihi gloria vires.*
Great is the height that I must scale, but the prospect of glory gives me strength.
[*Elegies*, IV, 10, line 3]

Protagoras (c. 485–c. 410 BC)
First Greek Sophist

1. Man is the measure of all things.
[In Plato, *Theaetetus*]

Proudhon, Pierre-Joseph (1809–1865)
French social reformer and anarchist; politician and writer, imprisoned for his beliefs

1. *Si j'avais à répondre à la question suivante: qu'est-ce que l'esclavage? et que d'un seul mot je répondisse: c'est l'assassinat, ma pensée serait aussitôt comprise ... Pourquoi donc à cette autre demande: qu'est-ce que la propriété? ne puis-je répondre de même: c'est le vol!*
If I were asked to answer the following question: 'What is slavery?' and I replied in one word, 'Murder!' my meaning would be understood at once ... Why, then, to this other question: 'What is property?' may I not likewise answer 'Theft'?
[*Qu'est-ce que la propriété?* (1840), 1]

Proust, Marcel (1871–1922)
Great French novelist; critic and letter writer

1. *Le désir fleurit, la possession flétrit toutes choses.*
Desire makes everything blossom; possession makes everything wither and fade.
[*Les Plaisirs et les Jours* (1896)]

2. *Longtemps, je me suis couché de bonne heure.*
For a long time I used to go to bed early.
[*A la recherche du temps perdu, Du côté de chez Swann* (1913), first sentence]

3. *Et tout d'un coup le souvenir m'est apparu. Ce goût c'était celui du petit morceau de madeleine que le dimanche matin à Combray ... ma tante Léonie m'offrait après l'avoir trempé dans son infusion de thé ou de tilleul.*
And suddenly the memory came back to me. The taste was that of the little piece of madeleine which on Sunday mornings at Combray ... my aunt Léonie used to give me, after dipping it first in her cup of tea or *tisane*.
[*A la recherche du temps perdu, Du côté de chez Swann* (1913)]

4. *Et il ne fut plus question de Swann chez les Verdurin.*
After that there was no more talk of Swann at the Verdurins'.
[*A la recherche du temps perdu, Du côté de chez Swann* (1913)]

5. *Nous appelons notre avenir l'ombre de lui-même que notre passé projette devant nous.*
What we call our future is the shadow which our past throws in front of us.
[*A la recherche du temps perdu, A l'ombre des jeunes filles en fleurs* (1918)]

6. *On devient moral dès qu'on est malheureux.*
One becomes moral as soon as one is unhappy.
[*A la recherche du temps perdu, A l'ombre des jeunes filles en fleurs* (1918)]

7. Une dame prétentieuse: *Que pensez-vous de l'amour?*
Mme Leroi: *L'amour? Je le fais souvent, mais je n'en parle jamais.*
A pretentious lady: What are your views on love?
Mme Leroi: I often make love but I never talk about it.
[*A la recherche du temps perdu, Le Côté de Guermantes* (1921)]

8. *Tout ce que nous connaissons de grand nous vient des nerveux. Ce sont eux et non pas d'autres qui ont fondé les religions et composé les chefs-d'oeuvre.*
Everything great in the world is done by neurotics; they alone founded our religions and composed our masterpieces.
[*A la recherche du temps perdu, Le Côté de Guermantes* (1921)]

9. *On a même pu dire que la louange la plus haute de Dieu est dans la négation de l'athée qui trouve la Création assez parfaite pour se passer d'un créateur.*
It has been said that the highest praise of God consists in the denial of Him by the atheist, who finds creation so perfect that that it has no need of a creator.
[*A la recherche du temps perdu, Le Côté de Guermantes* (1921)]

10. *Il n'y a rien comme le désir pour empêcher les choses qu'on dit d'avoir aucune ressemblance avec ce qu'on a dans la pensée.*
There is nothing like desire for preventing the things one says from bearing any resemblance to what one has in mind.
[*A la recherche du temps perdu, Le Côté de Guermantes* (1921)]

11. *J'ai horreur des couchers du soleil, c'est romantique, c'est opéra.*
I have a horror of sunsets, they're so romantic, so operatic.
[*A la recherche du temps perdu, Sodome et Gomorrhe* (1922)]

12. *On a tort de parler en amour de mauvais choix, puisque dès qu'il y a choix il ne peut être que mauvais.*
It is wrong to speak of making a bad choice in love, since as soon as there is choice, it can only be bad.
[*A la recherche du temps perdu, La Fugitive* (1923)]

13. *On l'enterra, mais toute la nuit funèbre, aux vitrines éclairées, ses livres disposés trois par trois veillaient comme des anges aux ailes éployées et semblaient, pour celui qui n'était plus, le symbole de sa résurrection.*
They buried him, but all through the night of mourning, in lighted windows, his books arranged three by three kept watch like angels with outspread wings and seemed, for him who was no more, the symbol of his resurrection.
[*A la recherche du temps perdu, La Prisonnière* (1923)]

14. *Les vrais paradis sont les paradis qu'on a perdus.*
The true paradises are the paradises we have lost.
[*A la recherche du temps perdu, Le Temps retrouvé* (1926)]

15. *Le bonheur seul est salutaire pour le corps, mais c'est le chagrin qui développe les forces de l'esprit.*
Happiness alone is beneficial for the body, but it is grief that develops the powers of the mind.
[*A la recherche du temps perdu, Le Temps retrouvé* (1926)]

16. *Une de ces dépêches dont M. de Guermantes avait spirituellement fixé le modèle: 'Impossible venir, mensonge suit'.*
One of those telegrams of which M. de Guermantes had wittily fixed the formula: 'Cannot come, lie follows'.
[*A la recherche du temps perdu, Le Temps retrouvé* (1926)]

17. *Une vérité clairement comprise ne peut plus être écrite avec sincérité.*
A truth which is clearly understood can no longer be written with sincerity.
[*Essais et articles*, 'Senancour c'est moi']

Proverbs

1. Absence makes the heart grow fonder.
2. Accidents will happen in the best regulated families.
3. Actions speak louder than words.
4. After a storm comes a calm.
5. All are not saints that go to church.
6. All bread is not baked in one oven.
7. All cats are grey in the dark.
8. All good things must come to an end.
9. All is fair in love and war.
10. All men are mortal.
11. All roads lead to Rome.
12. All's grist that comes to the mill.
13. All's well that ends well.
14. All that glitters is not gold.
15. All the world loves a lover.
16. All work and no play make Jack a dull boy.
17. Any port in a storm.
18. Any publicity is good publicity.
19. Appearances are deceptive.
20. An apple a day keeps the doctor away.
21. An apple-pie without some cheese is like a kiss without a squeeze.
22. Ask a silly question and you'll get a silly answer.
23. Ask no questions and hear no lies.
24. Attack is the best form of defence.
25. Bad news travels fast.
26. A bad penny always turns up.
27. A bad workman always blames his tools.
28. Barking dogs seldom bite.
29. The beak of the goose is no longer than that of the gander.
30. Beauty is in the eye of the beholder.
31. Beauty is only skin-deep.
32. Beggars can't be choosers.
33. Believe nothing of what you hear, and only half of what you see.
34. The best of friends must part.

35. The best things come in small parcels.
36. The best things in life are free.
37. Better a lie that heals than a truth that wounds.
38. Better be a fool than a knave.
39. Better be an old man's darling than a young man's slave.
40. Better be envied than pitied.
41. Better bend the neck than bruise the forehead.
42. Better be safe than sorry.
43. Better late than never.
44. Better salt than sour.
45. A bird in the hand is worth two in the bush.
46. Birds of a feather flock together.
47. A blessing will not feed the stomach.
48. Blood is thicker than water.
49. Books and friends should be few but good.
50. Bread is the staff of life.
51. Caesar's wife must be above suspicion.
52. A cat has nine lives.
53. A cat may look at a king.
54. A chain is no stronger than its weakest link.
55. Charity begins at home.
56. Christmas comes but once a year.
57. Civility costs nothing.
58. Cold hands, warm heart.
59. Come for your inheritance and you may have to pay for the funeral.
60. Constant dripping wears away the stone.
61. Craft maun hae claes, but truth goes naked.
62. Curiosity killed the cat.
63. Cut your coat according to your cloth.
64. The darkest hour is just before the dawn.
65. Dead men tell no tales.
66. Death is the great leveller.
67. Desperate cuts must have desperate cures.
68. The devil finds work for idle hands to do.
69. The devil is not so black as he is painted.
70. The devil looks after his own.
71. Divide and rule.
72. Do as I say, not as I do.
73. Do as you would be done by.
74. Dog does not eat dog.
75. Do not use a hatchet to remove a fly from a friend's forehead.
76. Don't count your chickens before they are hatched.
77. Don't cross the bridge till you come to it.
78. Don't cut off your nose to spite your face.
79. Don't meet troubles half way.
80. Don't put all your eggs in one basket.
81. Don't spoil the ship for a ha'porth of tar.
82. Don't teach your grandmother to suck eggs.
83. Don't throw the baby out with the bathwater.
84. Don't wash your dirty linen in public.
85. A drowning man will clutch at a straw.
86. Dry bread at home is better than roast meat abroad.
87. The early bird catches the worm.
88. Early to bed and early to rise, makes a man healthy, wealthy and wise.
89. Easier said than done.
90. East, west, home's best.
91. Easy come, easy go.
92. Eat to live and not live to eat.
93. Empty vessels make the most noise.
94. The end justifies the means.
95. An Englishman's home is his castle.
96. An Englishman's word is his bond
97. Even a worm can turn.
98. Every cloud has a silver lining.
99. Every dog has his day.
100. Every family has a skeleton in the cupboard.
101. Every little helps.
102. Every man after his fashion.
103. Every man is his own worst enemy.
104. Every man to his trade.
105. Every one is innocent until he is proved guilty.
106. Every one to his taste.
107. Every picture tells a story.
108. Everything comes to him who waits.
109. The exception proves the rule.
110. Experience is the best teacher.
111. Experience is the mother of wisdom.
112. The eye is bigger than the belly.
113. The eyes are the window of the soul.
114. Faith will move mountains.
115. Familiarity breeds contempt.
116. Fear of death is worse than death itself.
117. Fight fire with fire.
118. Finders keepers, losers weepers.
119. Fine feathers make fine birds.
120. Fine words butter no parsnips.
121. Fingers were made before forks, and hands before knives.
122. First come, first served.
123. The first day a guest, the second day a guest, the third day a calamity.
124. First impressions are the most lasting.
125. The first step is the hardest.
126. First things first.
127. Fish and guests smell in three days.

128. A fool and his money are soon parted.

129. A fool at forty is a fool indeed.

130. Fools build houses, and wise men buy them.

131. Forbidden fruits are sweet.

132. Forewarned is forearmed.

133. Forgive and forget.

134. Fortune favours fools.

135. For want of a nail the shoe was lost; for want of a shoe the horse was lost; for want of a horse the rider was lost.

136. A friend in need is a friend indeed.

137. From clogs to clogs takes only three generations.

138. From small beginnings come great things.

139. From the sublime to the ridiculous is only a step.

140. The full man doesn't understand the wants of the hungry.

141. A fu' man's a true man.

142. Genius is an infinite capacity for taking pains.

143. Give a dog a bad name and hang him.

144. Give a thief enough rope and he'll hang himself.

145. Give him an inch and he'll take a yard.

146. Give me a child for the first seven years, and he is mine forever.

147. God defend me from my friends; from my enemies I can defend myself.

148. God helps them that help themselves.

149. God is always on the side of the big battalions.

150. God is kind to fou folk and bairns.

151. The good die young.

152. A good dog deserves a good bone.

153. Good fences make good neighbours.

154. Go to bed with the lamb, and rise with the lark.

155. Great oaks from little acorns grow.

156. A guest always brings pleasure: if not the arrival, the departure.

157. Half a loaf is better than no bread.

158. Handsome is as handsome does.

159. The hand that rocks the cradle rules the world.

160. Haste makes waste.

161. Health is better than wealth.

162. A hedge between keeps friendship green.

163. He that fights and runs away, may live to fight another day.

164. He that lives long suffers much.

165. He travels fastest who travels alone.

166. He who hesitates is lost.

167. He who lives by the sword dies by the sword.

168. He who pays the piper calls the tune.

169. He who rides a tiger is afraid to dismount.

170. He who sups with the devil should have a long spoon.

171. History repeats itself.

172. Hoist your sail when the wind is fair.

173. Home is home, though it be never so homely.

174. Home is where the heart is.

175. An honest man's word is as good as his bond.

176. Honesty is the best policy.

177. Hope for the best.

178. An hour in the morning is worth two in the evening.

179. Hunger finds no fault with the cookery.

180. Hunger is the best sauce.

181. If a job's worth doing, it's worth doing well.

182. If anything *can* go wrong, it will.

183. If at first you don't succeed, try, try, try again.

184. If ifs and ands were pots and pans, there'd be no trade for tinkers.

185. If the dog bark, go in; if the bitch bark, go out.

186. If the mountain will not come to Mahomet, Mahomet must go to the mountain.

187. If there's a hen or a goose, it's on the priest's table you'll find it.

188. If the rich could hire other people to die for them, the poor could make a wonderful living.

189. If wishes were horses, beggars would ride.

190. If you can't be good, be careful.

191. If you don't like the heat, get out of the kitchen.

192. If you play with fire you get burnt.

193. If you want a thing well done, do it yourself.

194. If you want to know what a man is really like, take notice how he acts when he loses money.

195. I hate a man with a memory at a drinking bout.

196. Imitation is the sincerest form of flattery.

197. An overfilled belly will not study willingly.

198. In for a penny, in for a pound.

199. In love, there is always one who kisses, and one who offers his cheek.

200. Innocence itself sometimes hath need of a mask.

201. In the country of the blind, the one-eyed man is king.

202. It is a long lane that has no turning.

203. It is better to be born lucky than rich.

204. It is easy to bear the misfortunes of others.

205. It is easy to be wise after the event.

206. It is no use crying over spilt milk.

207. It never rains but it pours.

208. It's an ill wind that blows nobody any good.

209. It's a small world.

210. It's too late to shut the stable door after the horse has bolted.

211. It takes all sorts to make a world.

212. It takes two to make a quarrel.

213. It takes two to tango.

214. It will all come right in the wash.

215. It will be all the same in a hundred years.

216. Jack of all trades, master of none.

217. A judge knows nothing unless it has been explained to him three times.

218. Keep something for a rainy day.

219. Keep your mouth shut and your eyes open.

220. Keep your weather-eye open.

221. Kill not the goose that lays the golden egg.

222. Knowledge is power.

223. Know thyself.

224. The last straw breaks the camel's back.

225. Laugh and grow fat.

226. Laugh before breakfast, you'll cry before supper.

227. Laughter is brightest where food is best.

228. Laughter is the best medicine.

229. The law does not concern itself about trifles.

230. Least said soonest mended.

231. Leave well alone.

232. Lend only what you can afford to lose.

233. Let bygones be bygones.

234. Let sleeping dogs lie.

235. Let the cobbler stick to his last.

236. A liar is worse than a thief.

237. Life begins at forty.

238. Life is just a bowl of cherries.

239. Life is not all beer and skittles.

240. Life is sweet.

241. Like breeds like.

242. Like father, like son.

243. Listeners never hear good of themselves.

244. Live and learn.

245. Long absent, soon forgotten.

246. Look after number one.

247. Look before you leap.

248. Look on the bright side.

249. Love conquers all.

250. Love is blind.

251. Love laughs at locksmiths.

252. Love makes the world go round.

253. Love me, love my dog.

254. Love will find a way.

255. Love your neighbour, but don't pull down the fence.

256. Lucky at cards, unlucky in love.

257. Mackerel sky and mares' tails make lofty ships carry low sails.

258. Make hay while the sun shines.

259. A man can die but once.

260. A man is as old as he feels, and a woman as old as she looks.

261. Manners maketh man.

262. Man proposes, God disposes.

263. Many a mickle makes a muckle.

264. Many a true word is spoken in jest.

265. Many hands make light work.

266. Many irons in the fire, some must cool.

267. March comes in like a lion and goes out like a lamb.

268. March winds and April showers bring forth May flowers.

269. Marriages are made in heaven.

270. Marry in haste, and repent at leisure.

271. Marry in Lent, and you'll live to repent.

272. Marry in May, rue for aye.

273. Mind your own business.

274. A miss is as good as a mile.

275. Moderation in all things.

276. More haste, less speed.

277. The more the merrier; the fewer the better fare.

278. Music is the food of love.

279. The nearer the bone, the sweeter the flesh.

280. Necessity is the mother of invention.

281. Needs must when the devil drives.

282. Ne'er cast a clout till May be out.

283. Never do things by halves.

284. Never judge from appearances.

285. Never look a gift horse in the mouth.

286. Never put off till tomorrow what you can do today.

287. Never say die.

288. Never speak ill of the dead.

289. Never too late to learn.

290. Ninety per cent of inspiration is perspiration.

291. No bees, no honey; no work, no money.

292. A nod is as good as a wink to a blind horse.

293. No love like the first love.

294. No man is infallible.

295. No names, no pack-drill.

296. No news is good news.

297. No pleasure without pain.

298. The north wind does blow, and we shall have snow.

299. Nothing is certain but death and taxes.

300. Nothing so bad but it might have been worse.

301. Nothing succeeds like success.

302. Nothing ventured, nothing gained.

303. No time like the present.

304. Old habits die hard.

305. Old sins cast long shadows.

306. Old soldiers never die, they simply fade away.

307. Once a parson always a parson.

308. One chops the wood, the other does the grunting.

309. [Referring to magpies or crows; there are numerous variants] One for sorrow, two for mirth; three for a wedding, four for a birth; five for silver, six for gold; seven for a secret, never to be told; eight for heaven, nine for hell; and ten for the devil's own sel'.

310. One good turn deserves another.

311. One hour's sleep before midnight, is worth two after.

312. One man's meat is another man's poison.

313. One swallow does not make a summer.

314. Opportunity seldom knocks twice.

315. Out of sight, out of mind.

316. Patience is a virtue.

317. Peel a fig for your friend, a peach for your enemy.

318. A penny saved is a penny earned.

319. Penny wise, pound foolish.

320. Pigs might fly, if they had wings.

321. Possession is nine points of the law.

322. Poverty is not a crime.

323. Practise what you preach.

324. Prevention is better than cure.

325. Punctuality is the politeness of princes.

326. Put off the evil hour as long as you can.

327. Every month one should get drunk at least once.

328. Rain before seven: fine before eleven.

329. A rainbow in the morning is the shepherd's warning; a rainbow at night is the shepherd's delight.

330. Rain, rain, go away, come again another day.

331. Red sky at night, shepherd's delight; red sky in the morning, shepherd's warning.

332. Revenge is a dish that tastes better cold.

333. Revenge is sweet.

334. The road to hell is paved with good intentions.

335. Rome was not built in a day.

336. Sailors have a port in every storm.

337. Save your breath to cool your porridge.

338. Saying is one thing, and doing another.

339. Scratch my back and I'll scratch yours.

340. See a pin and pick it up, all the day you'll have good luck; see a pin and let it lie, you'll want a pin before you die.

341. Seeing is believing.

342. See Naples and die.

343. Self-praise is no recommendation.

344. Send a fool to the market and a fool he will return again.

345. The shoemaker's son always goes barefoot.

346. Silence is golden.

347. Slow but sure wins the race.

348. Small is beautiful.

349. Soon learnt, soon forgotten.

350. Spare the rod and spoil the child.

351. Speak when you are spoken to.

352. Speech is silver, silence is golden.

353. Sticks and stones may break my bones, but words will never hurt me.

354. A still tongue makes a wise head.

355. Still waters run deep.

356. A stitch in time saves nine.

357. The streets of London are paved with gold.

358. Strike while the iron is hot.

359. St Swithin's Day, if thou dost rain, for forty days it will remain: St Swithin's Day, if thou be fair, for forty days 'twill rain no more.

360. The style is the man.

361. Take a hair of the dog that bit you.

362. Take care of the pence, and the pounds will take care of themselves.

363. Take things as they come.

364. A tale never loses in the telling.

365. Talk of the devil, and he is bound to appear.

366. Tell the truth and shame the devil.

367. There are more old drunkards than old doctors.

368. There are only twenty-four hours in the day.

369. There is a time and place for everything.

370. There is honour among thieves.

371. There is more than one way to skin a cat.

372. There is much meat in God's storehouse.

373. There is no accounting for tastes.

374. There is safety in numbers.

375. There's a black sheep in every flock.

376. There's always room at the top.

377. There's better fish in the sea than any that've been caught.

378. There's many a good tune played on an old fiddle.

379. There's many a slip 'twixt cup and lip.

380. There's no fool like an old fool.

381. There's no place like home.

382. There's no smoke without fire.

383. There's nowt so queer as folk.

384. There's one law for the rich, and another for the poor.

385. There's only one pretty child in the world, and every mother has it.

386. There will be sleeping enough in the grave.

387. Things are not always what they seem.

388. Third time lucky.

389. Those whom the gods love die young.

390. Throw dirt enough, and some will stick.

391. Throw out a sprat to catch a mackerel.

392. Time and tide wait for no man.

393. Time is a great healer.

394. Time will tell.

395. To err is human; to forgive divine. [Cf. Pope: 25]

396. Tomorrow is another day.

397. Tomorrow never comes.

398. Too many cooks spoil the broth.

399. Travel broadens the mind.

400. A trouble shared is a trouble halved.

401. True love never grows cold.

402. Truth fears no trial.

403. Truth is stranger than fiction.

404. Truth is the safest lie.

405. Truth will out.

406. Two heads are better than one.

407. Two wrongs do not make a right.

408. Union is strength.

409. United we stand, divided we fall.

410. Vice is often clothed in virtue's habit.

411. Walls have ears.

412. Waste not, want not.

413. A watched pot never boils.

414. The way to a man's heart is through his stomach.

415. The weakest goes to the wall.

416. We must learn to walk before we can run.

417. What can't be cured, must be endured.

418. What must be, must be.

419. What's done cannot be undone.

420. What was hard to endure is sweet to recall.

421. What you don't know can't hurt you.

422. What you lose on the swings you gain on the roundabouts.

423. When a father gives to his son, both laugh; when a son gives to his father, both cry.

424. When one door shuts, another opens.

425. When poverty comes in at the door, love flies out of the window.

426. When the cat's away, the mice will play.

427. When the wine is in, the wit is out.

428. Where there's a will there's a way.

429. While there's life there's hope.

430. Who spits against the wind, it falls in his face.

431. Why buy a cow when milk is so cheap?

432. Why keep a dog and bark yourself?

433. With a Scotsman or a priest, don't begin a lawsuit.

434. A woman's place is in the home.

435. A woman's work is never done.

436. You can have too much of a good thing.

437. You can lead a horse to water, but you can't make him drink.

438. You cannot run with the hare and hunt with the hounds.

439. You can't get a quart into a pint pot.

440. You can't get blood out of a stone.

441. You can't make an omelette without breaking eggs.

442. You can't make bricks without straw.

443. You can't please everyone.

444. You can't take it with you when you go.

445. You can't teach an old dog new tricks.

446. You can't tell a book by its cover.

Psalms

1. And from the sword (Lord) save my soule
By thy myght and thy power:
And keepe my soule, thy darling deare,
From dogs that would devour

And from the Lion's mouth that would
Me all in sunder shiver:
And from the hornes of Unicornes,
Lord safely me deliver.
[Psalm XXII from the 1569 Book of Psalms published in Geneva by Sternhod I. Hopkins and others]

2. And then the Lord began to wake
Lyke one that slept a time
Or lyke a valiant man of warre,
Refreshed after wyne.
With Emeroides in the hinder part,
He strake his enmies all:
And put them unto a shame,
That was perpetuall.
[Psalm LXXIX from the 1569 Book of Psalms published in Geneva by Sternhod I. Hopkins and others]

Publilius, Syrus (1st century BC)
Roman writer of mimes and apophthegms

1. *Formosa facies muta commendatio est.*
A pretty face is a dumb recommendation.
[*Sententiae*]

2. *Inopi beneficium bis dat qui dat celeriter.*
He does the poor man two favours who gives quickly.
[*Sententiae*]

3. *Iudex damnatur ubi nocens absolvitur.*
The judge is condemned when the guilty party is acquitted.
[*Sententiae*]

4. *Necessitas dat legem non ipsa accipit.*
Necessity gives the law without itself recognizing any.
[*Sententiae*]

Pudney, John (1909–1977)
English poet, journalist and novelist

1. Do not despair
For Johnny head-in-air;
He sleeps as sound
As Johnny underground...

2. Better by far
For Johnny-the-bright-star,
To keep your head
And see his children fed.
['For Johnny' (1942)]

Pulteney, William, Earl of Bath (1684–1764)
English Whig politician and pamphleteer

1. Since twelve honest men have decided the cause,
And were judges of fact, though not judges of laws.
['The Honest Jury' (1729)]

Punch

British humorous periodical, founded 1841

1. Advice to persons about to marry – 'Don't!'
[1845]

2. You pays your money and you takes your choice.
[1846]

3. The Half-Way House to Rome, Oxford.
[1849]

4. What is better than presence of mind in a railway accident? Absence of body.
[1849]

5. Never do to-day what you can put off till tomorrow.
[1849]

6. 'Who's 'im, Bill?' 'A stranger!' ''Eave 'arf a brick at 'im.'
[1854]

7. What is Matter? – Never mind.
What is Mind? – No matter.
[1855]

8. '*Peccavi* – I've Scinde' wrote Lord Ellen so proud.
More briefly Dalhousie wrote – '*Vovi* – I've Oude'.
[1856]

9. Mun, a had na' been the-erre abune two hours when – *bang* – went saxpence!!!
[1868]

10. Cats is 'dogs' and rabbits is 'dogs' and so's Parrats, but this 'ere 'Tortis' is an insect, and there ain't no charge for it.
[1869]

11. Nothink for nothink 'ere, and precious little for sixpence.
[1869]

12. Sure, the next train has gone ten minutes ago.
[1871]

13. It appears the Americans have taken umbrage. The deuce they have! Whereabouts is that?
[1872]

14. Go directly – see what she's doing, and tell her she mustn't.
[1872]

15. There was one poor tiger that hadn't *got* a Christian.
[1875]

16. What did you take out of the bag, Mamma? *I* only got sixpence.
[1876]

17. It's worse than wicked, my dear, it's vulgar.
[1876]

18. I never read books – I *write* them.
[1876]

19. I am not hungry; but thank goodness, I am greedy.
[1878]

20. *Bishop*: Who is it that sees and hears all we do, and before whom even I am but as a crushed worm?
Page: The Missus my Lord.
[1880]

21. Ah whiles hae ma doots aboot the meenister.
[1880]

22. What sort of a doctor is he?
Oh, well, I don't know very much about his ability; but he's got a very good bedside manner!
[1884]

23. I used your soap two years ago; since then I have used no other.
[1884]

24. Don't look at me, Sir, with – ah – in that tone of voice.
[1884]

25. Oh, yes! I'm sure he's not so fond of me as at first. He's away so much, neglects me dreadfully, and he's so cross when he comes home. What *shall* I do?
Feed the brute!
[1885]

26. Nearly all our best men are dead! Carlyle, Tennyson, Browning, George Eliot! – I'm not feeling very well myself.
[1893]

27. Botticelli isn't a wine, you Juggins! Botticelli's a *cheese*!
[1894]

28. 'I'm afraid you've got a bad egg, Mr Jones.' 'Oh no, my Lord, I assure you! Parts of it are excellent!'
[1895]

Pushkin, Aleksandr (1799–1837)

Russian poet, novelist and playwright; fatally wounded in a duel

1. I remember a wonderful moment:
Before me you appeared,
Like a fleeting apparition,
Like a spirit of pure beauty.
['To–' (1825)]

2. I loved you: love still, it's possible,
Has not quite died away in my soul.
But let it trouble you no longer;
I don't want to sadden you at all.

I loved you without words, without hope,
Now by shyness, now by jealousy tormented;
I loved you so sincerely, so gently,
As God grant you may be loved by another.
['I loved you' (1829)]

3. The less we love a woman,
The easier we're liked,
We're more certain of her ruin
In our seductive nets.
[*Eugene Onegin: a Novel in Verse* (1823–1831), IV, 7]

4. Where, where have you gone,
Golden days of my springtime?
[*Eugene Onegin: a Novel in Verse* (1823–1831), VI, 21]

5. The poet's memory has fled
Like smoke across an azure sky,
[*Eugene Onegin: a Novel in Verse* (1823–1831), VII, 14]

6. Here [in St Petersburg] we are fated by Nature
To hack through a window on Europe . . .

7. Beautify yourself, city of Peter, and stand
Steadfast, like Russia.
['The Bronze Horseman' (1833), Introduction]

8. My heart asks for peace–
Day after day flies by, and every hour takes away
A little piece of life; but you and I, we two,
We contemplate living . . . And then suddenly we die.
['It's time, my friend, it's time' (1834)]

Putnam, Israel (1718–1790)
American Revolutionary general and writer

1. [Said at the Battle of Bunker Hill, 1775]
Men, you are all marksmen – don't one of you fire until you see the whites of their eyes.
[In R. Frothingham, *History of the Siege of Boston*(1873); also attributed to William Prescott]

Puzo, Mario (1920–)
American writer; creator of the 'Godfather' novels portraying the American Mafia

1. He's a businessman. I'll make him an offer he can't refuse.
[*The Godfather* (1969)]

2. A lawyer with his briefcase can steal more than a thousand men with guns.
[*The Godfather* (1969)]

Pym, Barbara (1928–1980)
English writer, noted for comedies of English middle-class society

1. [Comment on the rejection of a novel]
What is the future of my kind of writing? ... Perhaps in retirement ... a quieter, narrower kind of life can be worked out and adopted. Bounded by English literature and the Anglican Church and small pleasures like sewing and choosing dress material for this uncertain summer.
[Diary, entry for 6 March 1972]

Pyrrhus (319–272 BC)
King of Epirus from 306 BC and army commander

1. [After a hard-won battle]
If we are victorious against the Romans in one more battle we shall be utterly ruined.
[In Plutarch, *Lives*, 'Pyrrhus', XXI]

Quarles, Francis (1592–1644)
English poet, prose writer and royalist

1. He teaches to deny that faintly prays.
[*A Feast for Worms* (1620), VII]

2. No man is born unto himself alone;
Who lives unto himself, he lives to none.
['Esther' (1621), I]

3. Our God and soldiers we alike adore
Ev'n at the brink of danger; not before:
After deliverance, both alike requited,
Our God's forgotten, and our soldiers slighted.
[*Divine Fancies*(1632), 'Of Common Devotion']

4. I wish thee as much pleasure in the reading, as I had in the writing.
[*Emblems* (1635), 'To the Reader']

5. The heart is a small thing, but desireth great matters.
It is not sufficient for a kite's dinner, yet the whole world is not sufficient for it.
[*Emblems*, I (1635), 'Hugo de Anima']

6. My soul, sit thou a patient looker-on;
Judge not the play before the play is done:
Her plot has many changes; every day
Speaks a new scene; the last act crowns the play.
[*Emblems*, I (1635),'Respice Finem']

7. We spend our midday sweat, our midnight oil;
We tire the night in thought, the day in toil.
[*Emblems*, II (1635)]

8. Be wisely worldly, not worldly wise.
[*Emblems*, II (1635)]

9. Man is Heaven's masterpiece.
[*Emblems*, II (1635)]

10. Man is man's A.B.C. There is none that can
Read God aright, unless he first spell Man.
[*Hieroglyphics of the Life of Man* (1638), I]

11. He that begins to live, begins to die.
[*Hieroglyphics of the Life of Man* (1638), I]

12. Physicians of all men are most happy; what good success soever they have, the world proclaimeth, and what faults they commit, the earth covereth.
[*Hieroglyphics of the Life of Man* (1638), IV]

13. Thou art my way; I wander, if thou fly;
Thou art my light; if hid, how blind am I!
Thou art my life; if thou withdraw, I die.
[*Emblems*, III (1643)]

14. The road to resolution lies by doubt:
The next way home's the farthest way about.
[*Emblems*, IV (1643)]

15. We'll cry both arts and learning down,
And hey! then up go we!
[*The Shepherd's Oracles* (1646)]

Quasimodo, Salvatore (1901–1968)
Italian poet

1. *Ognuno sta solo sul cuor della terra trafitto da un raggio di sole: ed è subito sera.*
We are all alone on the earth's heart pierced by a sun-ray: and the evening has already drawn in.
[*Acque e Terre* (*Land and Waters*, 1920–1929)]

Quennell, Peter (1905–)
English writer and biographer

1. I'm apt to forget my age. The other day I saw Kingsley Amis and asked how well he knew D.H. Lawrence. His eyes bulged and his face grew purple.
[*The Observer*, 1988, in Jeffrey Care (ed.), *Sayings of the Eighties* (1989)]

Quesnay, François (1694–1774)
French political economist, encyclopaedist and physician

1. *Vous ne connaissez qu'une seule règle du commerce; c'est (pour me servir de vos propres termes) de laisser passer et de laisser faire tous les acheteurs et tous les vendeurs quelconques.*
You recognize only one rule of commerce; that is (to avail myself of your own terms) to allow free passage and freedom of action to all buyers and sellers whoever they may be.
[In L. Salleron, *François Quesnay et la Physiocratie*, Letter from M. Alpha to de Quesnay, 1767]

2. [Of government interference]
Laissez faire, laissez passer.
Leave it alone, and let it happen.
[Attr.]

Quevedo y Villegas, Francisco Gómez de (1580–1645)
Spanish poet and writer

1. *Tan ciego estoy a mi mortal enredo
que no te oso llamar, Señor, de miedo
de que querrás sacarme de pecado.*
So blind am I to my mortal entanglement
that I dare not call upon thee, Lord, for fear
that thou wouldst take me away from my sin.
[*Heráclito Cristiano* (*Christian Heraclitus*, 1613), 'Psalm 6']

Quiller-Couch, Sir Arthur ('Q') (1863–1944)
English novelist, poet, critic, anthologist and academic

1. The best is the best, though a hundred judges have declared it so.
[*Oxford Book of English Verse* (1900), Preface]

2. Does it or does it not strike you as queer that the people who set you 'courses of study' in English Literature never include the Authorised Version, which not only intrinsically but historically is out and away the greatest book of English prose? Perhaps they pay you the compliment of supposing that you are perfectly acquainted with it? ... I wonder.
[*On the Art of Writing* (1916), 'On the Capital Difficulty of Prose']

Quincy, Josiah (1772–1864)
American lawyer, Federalist politician, orator and writer

1. As it will be the right of all, so it will be the duty of some, definitely to prepare for a separation, amicably if they can, violently if they must.
[Speech on states' rights, 1811]

Quintilian (Marcus Fabius Quintilianus) (c. 35–c. 100)
Roman rhetorician and teacher

1. *Mendacem memorem esse oportere.*
A liar must have a good memory.
[*Institutio Oratoria*, IV, 2, 91]

2. [Comparing Roman with Greek]
Satura quidem tota nostra est.
Verse satire indeed is all our own.
[*Institutio Oratoria*, X, 1, 93]

Rabelais, François (c. 1494–c. 1553)
French satirist; humanist, physician and monk

1. *Quaestio subtilissima, utrum chimera in vacuo bombinans possit comedere secundas intentiones.*
A most subtle question; whether a chimera bombinating in a vacuum can devour second intentions.
[*Pantagruel* (1532), II, 7]

2. *Je boy pour la soif advenir.*
I drink for the thirst to come.
[*Gargantua* (1534), 5]

3. *L'appétit vient en mangeant ... la soif s'en va en beuvant.*
Appetite comes with eating ... thirst goes with drinking.
[*Gargantua* (1534), 5]

4. *Natura abhorret vacuum.*
Nature abhors a vacuum.
[*Gargantua* (1534), 5]

5. *Lever matin n'est poinct bon heur;*
Boire matin est le meilleur.
Getting up in the morning is no pleasure;
Drinking in the morning is the best.
[*Gargantua* (1534), 21]

6. *Jamais homme noble ne hayst le bon vin.*
No noble man ever hated good wine.
[*Gargantua* (1534), 27]

7. *Guerre faicte sans bonne provision d'argent n'a qu'un souspirail de vigueur. Les nerfs des batailles sont les pécunes.*
The strength of a war waged without a good supply of money is as fleeting as a breath. Money is the sinews of battle.
[*Gargantua* (1534), 46. Cf. Cicero: 12]

8. [Referring to the fictional Abbey of Thélème]
En leur règle n'estoit que ceste clause: 'fay ce que vouldra.'
In their rules there was only this one clause: 'Do what you will.'
[*Gargantua* (1534), 57]

9. [Last words]
Je vais quérir un grand peut-être ... Tirez le rideau, la farce est jouée.
I am going to seek a great perhaps ... Bring down the curtain, the farce is played out.
[Attr. Cf. Leoncavallo: 1]

Rachmaninov, Sergei (1873–1943)
Russian pianist and Romantic composer, noted for his piano music

1. [When told he had cancer]
My dear hands. Farewell, my poor hands.
[Attr.]

Racine, Jean (1639–1699)
Great French classical tragedian and poet

1. *Ah! je l'ai trop aimé pour ne le point haïr!*
Ah, I have loved him too much not to hate him!
[*Andromaque* (1667), II.i]

2. *Mon innocence enfin commence à me peser.*
My innocence is at last becoming a burden to me.
[*Andromaque* (1667), II.i]

3. *Je t'aimais inconstant, qu'aurais-je fait fidèle?*
I loved you inconstant; what would I have done had you been faithful?
[*Andromaque* (1667), IV.v]

4. *Sans argent l'honneur n'est qu'une maladie.*
Without money, honour is no more than a disease.
[*Les Plaideurs* (1668), I.i]

5. *Tel qui rit vendredi, dimanche pleurera.*
He who laughs on Friday will cry on Sunday.
[*Les Plaideurs* (1668), I.i]

6. *Ce n'est plus une ardeur dans mes veines cachée:*
C'est Vénus tout entière à sa proie attachée.
It is no longer an ardour hidden in my veins: it's Venus in all her power fastening on her prey.
[*Phèdre* (1677), I.iii]

7. *Ainsi que la vertu, le crime a ses degrés.*
Crime has its degrees, as virtue does.
[*Phèdre* (1677), IV.ii]

8. *C'était pendant l'horreur d'une profonde nuit.*
It happened during the horror of a profoundly dark night.
[*Athalie* (1691), II.v]

9. *Elle flotte, elle hésite; en un mot, elle est femme.*
She wavers, she hesitates; in a word, she is a woman.
[*Athalie* (1691), III.iii]

10. *Elle s'endormit du sommeil des justes.*
She fell asleep and slept the sleep of the just.
[*Abrégé de l'Histoire de Port Royal* (written c. 1699, published 1742)]

Radcliffe-Brown, Alfred Reginald (1881–1935)

1. [On the anthropologist and reformer, Daisy Bates]
The contents of her mind ... were somewhat similar to the contents of a well-stored sewing-basket after half a dozen kittens had been playing there undisturbed for a few days.
[In E.L. Grant Watson, *But to What Purpose*]

Rae, John (1931–)
English educationist and writer

1. War is, after all, the universal perversion. We are all tainted: if we cannot experience our perversion at first hand we spend our time reading war stories, the pornography of war; or seeing war films, the blue films of war; or titillating our senses with the imagination of great deeds, the masturbation of war.
[*The Custard Boys* (1960), 13]

Raglan, FitzRoy James Henry Somerset, First Baron (1788–1855)
English general; Commander-in-Chief in the Crimean War; politician

1. [Said after his arm had been amputated at Waterloo, 1815]
Don't carry away that arm till I have taken off my ring.
[In *Dictionary of National Biography*]

Rainborowe, Thomas (d. 1648)
English Parliamentarian and soldier

1. The poorest he that is in England hath a life to live as the greatest he.
[Speech in Army debates, 1647]

Rains, Claude (1889–1967)
English-born film actor, noted for his character roles

1. Major Strasser has been shot. Round up the usual suspects.
[*Casablanca*, film, 1942; scriptwriters Julius J. Epstein, Philip G. Epstein and Howard Koch]

Raleigh, Sir Walter (c. 1552–1618)
English courtier, explorer, military commander, poet, historian and essayist; beheaded after a failed expedition

1. If all the world and love were young,
And truth in every shepherd's tongue,
These pretty pleasures might me move
To live with thee, and be thy love.
['The Nymph's Reply to the Shepherd' (c. 1590). Cf. Marlowe: 49]

2. Give me my scallop-shell of quiet,
My staff of faith to walk upon,
My scrip of joy, immortal diet,
My bottle of salvation,
My gown of glory, hope's true gage,
And thus I'll make my pilgrimage.
['The Passionate Man's Pilgrimage' (1604)]

3. Go, Soul, the body's guest,
Upon a thankless arrant:
Fear not to touch the best;
The truth shall be thy warrant:
Go, since I needs must die,
And give the world the lie.
['The Lie' (1608)]

4. Now what is love? I pray thee, tell.
It is that fountain and that well,
Where pleasure and repentance dwell.
It is perhaps that sauncing bell,
That tolls all in to heaven or hell:
And this is love, as I hear tell.
['A Description of Love']

5. Only we die in earnest, that's no jest.
['On the Life of Man']

6. As you came from the holy land
Of Walsinghame,
Met you not with my true love
By the way as you came?
How shall I know your true love,
That have met many one
As I went to the holy land,
That have come, that have gone?
['Walsinghame']

7. My body in the walls captived
Feels not the wound of spiteful envy...

8. But now close kept, as captives wonted are:
That food, that heat, that light I find no more;
Despair bolts up my doors, and I alone
Speak to dead walls, but those hear not my moan.
[Untitled poem]

9. [Written the night before his execution]
Even such is Time, which takes in trust
Our youth, our joys, and all we have,
And pays us but with age and dust;
Who in the dark and silent grave,
When we have wandered all our ways,
Shuts up the story of our days:
And from which earth, and grave, and dust,
The Lord shall raise me up, I trust.
[Untitled poem (1618)]

10. O eloquent, just and mighty Death! ... thou hast drawn together all the far-stretched greatness, all the pride, cruelty, and ambition of man, and covered it all over with these two narrow words, *Hic jacet* [Here lies].
[*The History of the World* (1614), V, 6]

11. [Reply when asked which way he would like to lay his head on the block]
So the heart be right, it is no matter which way the head lies.
[In W. Stebbing, *Sir Walter Raleigh* (1891)]

12. I have a long journey to take, and must bid the company farewell.
[In Edward Thompson, *Sir Walter Raleigh* (1935)]

13. [Written on a window-pane, and referring to his ambitions at the court of Elizabeth I]
Fain would I climb, yet fear I to fall.
[Attr. Cf. Elizabeth I: 7]

14. [Said after his trial for treason, 1603]
The world itself is but a large prison, out of which some are daily led to execution.
[Attr.]

15. [On feeling the edge of the axe before his execution]
'Tis a sharp remedy, but a sure one for all ills.
[Attr.]

Ralph, Julian (1853–1903)
American journalist, short-story writer and autobiographer

1. [The first recorded use of this phrase]
News value.
[Lecture, Columbia University, 1892]

Ramanujan, Srinivasa (1887–1920)
Outstanding Indian mathematician

1. [Reply to the mathematician, G.H. Hardy, who remarked that a cab's number – 1729 – was dull]
No, it is a very interesting number; it is the smallest number expressible as a sum of two cubes in two different ways.
[*Proceedings of the London Mathematical Society* (1921); the two ways are $1^3 + 12^3$, and $9^3 + 10^3$]

Rame, Franca (1929–)
Italian actress and playwright; wife and collaborator of playwright Dario Fo

1. [On the role of her theatre in Italian society]
Per pulire dentro gli animi, per ritrovare una vita vivibile. Non sono mica Dio, ci provo con il teatro insieme a queste donne.
To cleanse our souls, to find again a livable life. I am not God but I do try with the theatre, together with these women.
[From an interview given to the *Corriere della Sera*, 1994]

Ramey, Estelle (1917–)
American physiologist, educator, feminist

1. More and more it appears that, biologically, men are designed for short, brutal lives and women for long miserable ones.
[*The Observer*, 1985, in Jeffrey Care (ed.), *Sayings of the Eighties* (1989)]

Ramos, Graciliano (1892–1953)
Brazilian writer

1. *Então mete-se um homem na cadeia porque ele não sabe falar direito?*
So you put a man in jail because he can't talk properly?
[*Vidas secas* (*Dry Lives*, 1938), 'Cadeia' ('Prison')]

Ramsay, Allan (1686–1758)
Scottish poet, satirist, dramatist, song collector and bookseller; founded first circulating library in Britain

1. Farewell to Lochaber, and farewell my Jean,
Where heartsome wi' thee I hae mony day been.
['Lochaber No More' (1724)]

2. Bannocks and a share of cheese
Will make a breakfast that a laird might please.
['The Gentle Shepherd' (1725)]

3. Ane canna wive an' thrive baith in ae year.
[*A Collection of Scots Proverbs* (1737)]

4. A Scots mist will weet an Englishman to the skin.
[*A Collection of Scots Proverbs* (1737)]

5. Better a finger aff than aye wagging.
[*A Collection of Scots Proverbs* (1737)]

Randolph, David

1. [On *Parsifal*]
The kind of opera that starts at six o'clock and after it has been going three hours, you look at your watch and it says 6.20.
[In F. Muir, *An Irreverant Companion to Social History* (1976)]

Rankin, J.E. (1828–1904)
American clergyman and hymn writer

1. God be with you till we meet again.
[Hymn, 1882]

Ransom, John Crowe (1888–1974)
American poet, critic, editor and teacher

1. Two evils, monstrous either one apart,
Possessed me, and were long and loath at going:
A cry of Absence, Absence, in the heart,
And in the wood the furious winter blowing...

2. Dear love, these fingers that had known your touch,
And tied our separate forces first together,
Were ten poor idiot fingers not worth much,
Ten frozen parsnips hanging in the weather.
['Winter Remembered' (1945)]

Raphael, Frederic (1931–)
British novelist and screenwriter; Academy Award 1965

1. [Of Cambridge]
This is the city of perspiring dreams.
[*The Glittering Prizes* (1976), 'An Early Life']

2. I come from suburbia ... I don't ever want to go back. It's the one place in the world that's further away than anywhere else.
[*The Glittering Prizes* (1976), 'A Sex Life']

Rattigan, Terence (1911–1977)
English dramatist and screenwriter

1. *Brian*: *Elle a des idées au-dessus de sa gare.* [She has ideas above her station]
Kenneth: You can't do it like that. You can't say *au-dessus de sa gare*. It isn't that sort of station.
[*French Without Tears* (1937), I]

2. A nice, respectable, middle-class, middle-aged, maiden lady, with time on her hands and the money to help her pass it ... Let us call her Aunt Edna ... Aunt Edna is universal, and to those who might feel that all the problems of the modern theatre might be solved by her liquidation, let me add that ... she is also immortal.
[*Collected Plays* (1953), II, Preface]

3. You can be in the Horse Guards and still be common, dear.
[*Separate Tables* (1955), 'Table Number Seven']

Reade, Charles (1814–1884)
English novelist and dramatist; collaborated with Dion Boucicault

1. She wrenched from her brow a diamond and eyed it with contempt, took from her pocket a sausage and contemplated it with respect and affection.
[*Peg Woffington* (1852)]

2. [Programme for a serial novel]
Make 'em laugh; make 'em cry; make 'em wait.
[Attr.]

Reagan, Ronald (1911–)
American politician and former film actor; Republican President 1981–89

1. Politics is supposed to be the second oldest profession. I have come to understand that it bears a very close resemblance to the first.
[Remark at a conference, 1977]

2. [During a microphone test prior to a radio broadcast]
My fellow Americans, I am pleased to tell you that I have signed legislation to outlaw Russia for ever. We begin bombing in five minutes.
[Audio recording, 1984]

3. [On his challenger, Walter Mondale, in the 1984 election campaign]
I will not make age an issue of this campaign. I am not going to exploit for political purposes my opponent's youth and inexperience.
[TV debate, 1984]

4. [After the hi-jack of a US plane by Shiite Muslims]
We are not going to tolerate these attacks from outlaw states run by the strangest collection of misfits, looney tunes and squalid criminals since the advent of the Third Reich.
[Speech, 1985]

5. I am delighted to be with you. In fact, at my age, I am delighted to be anywhere.
[Speech at the Oxford Union, 1992]

6. You can tell a lot about a fellow's character by the way he eats jelly beans.
[*Daily Mail*, 1981]

7. [When told by an aide that the Government was running normally, after an attempt to assassinate him]
What makes you think I'd be happy about that?
[*Time*, 1981]

8. [In his victory speech, 1984, and during the preceding campaign]
You ain't seen nothing yet!
[*Daily Express*, 1984]

9. [To the American Business Conference]
I have my veto pen drawn and ready for any tax increase that Congress might even think of sending up. And I have only one thing to say to the tax increasers. Go ahead – make my day.
[*Time*, 1985]

10. You know, by the time you reach my age, you've made plenty of mistakes if you've lived your life properly.
[*The Observer*, 'Sayings of the Week', 1987]

11. [To the surgeons about to operate on him after he was wounded in an assassination attempt]
Please assure me that you are all Republicans!
[In P. Boller, *Presidential Anecdotes* (1981)]

12. They say hard work never hurt anybody, but I figure why take the chance.
[Attr.]

Reed, Henry (1914–1986)
English poet, radio dramatist and translator

1. As we get older we do not get any younger.
Seasons return, and today I am fifty-five,
And this time last year I was fifty-four,
And this time next year I shall be sixty-two...

2. It is, we believe,
Idle to hope that the simple stirrup-pump
Can extinguish hell.
['Chard Whitlow (Mr Eliot's Sunday Evening Postscript)' (1941)]

3. Today we have naming of parts. Yesterday,
We had daily cleaning. And tomorrow morning,
We shall have what to do after firing. But today,
Today we have naming of parts...

4. And this you can see is the bolt. The purpose of this
Is to open the breech, as you see. We can slide it
Rapidly backwards and forwards: we call this
Easing the spring. And rapidly backwards and forwards
The early bees are assaulting and fumbling the flowers:
They call it easing the Spring.

They call it easing the Spring: it is perfectly easy
If you have any strength in your thumb: like the bolt,
And the breech, and the cocking-piece, and the point of balance,
Which in our case we have not got; and the almond-blossom
Silent in all of the gardens and the bees going backwards and forwards,
For today we have naming of parts.
[*Lessons of War* (1946), I, 'Naming of Parts']

5. And the various holds and rolls and throws and breakfalls
Somehow or other I always seemed to put
In the wrong place. And as for war, my wars
Were global from the start.
[*Lessons of War* (1946), III, 'Unarmed Combat']

6. I have known her pass the whole evening without mentioning a single book, or *in fact anything unpleasant*, at all.
[*A Very Great Man Indeed* (1953)]

7. In a civil war, the general must know – and I'm afraid it's a thing rather of instinct than of practice – he must know exactly when to move over to the other side.
[*Not a Drum was Heard: The War Memoirs of General Gland* (1959)]

Reed, John (1887–1920)
American journalist and war correspondent; founder of the Communist Party in America

1. [Of the October Revolution in Russia]
Ten Days that Shook the World.
[Title of book, 1919]

Reed, Joseph (1741–1785)
American lawyer, Revolutionary statesman and soldier

1. [Reply on being offered money to act on behalf of the British Crown]
I am not worth purchasing, but such as I am, the King of Great Britain is not rich enough to do it.
[In W.B. Reed, *Life and Correspondence of Joseph Reed* (1847)]

Reed, Rex (1938–)
American film and music critic and columnist

1. In Hollywood, if you don't have happiness you send out for it.
[In J.R. Colombo, *Colombo's Hollywood*]

2. Cannes is where you lie on the beach and stare at the stars – or vice versa.
[Attr.]

Reinhardt, Gottfried (1911–)
Austrian film producer

1. Money is good for bribing yourself through the inconveniences of life.
[In Lillian Ross, *Picture*]

Reith, John Charles Walsham, Baron (1889–1971)
Scottish public servant; first Director-General of the BBC 1927–38; wartime minister, administrator and diarist

1. It was in fact the combination of public service motive, sense of moral obligation, assured finance and the brute force of monopoly which enabled the BBC to make of broadcasting what no other country has made of it.
[*Into the Wind* (1949)]

2. You can't think rationally on an empty stomach, and a whole lot of people can't do it on a full one either.
[Attr.]

Remarque, Erich Maria (1898–1970)
German-born novelist, became an American citizen in 1947

1. *Im Westen nichts Neues.*
All Quiet on the Western Front.
[Title of book, 1929]

Renan, J. Ernest (1823–1892)
French philologist, religious writer and historian

1. *'Savoir c'est pouvoir' est le plus beau mot qu'on ait dit.*
'Knowledge is power' is the finest idea ever put into words.
[*Dialogues et fragments philosophiques* (1876)]

2. *La femme nous remet en communication avec l'éternelle source où Dieu se mire.*
Woman puts us back into communication with the eternal spring in which God looks at his reflection.
[*Souvenirs d'enfance et de jeunesse* (1883)]

Renard, Jules (1894–1910)
French novelist, dramatist and diarist

1. *Les bourgeois, ce sont les autres.*
The bourgeois are other people.
[*Journal*, 1890]

2. *Il faut dompter la vie par la douceur.*
Life should be tamed with tenderness.
[*Journal*, 1892]

3. *L'ironie est la pudeur de l'humanité.*
Irony is humanity's sense of propriety.
[*Journal*, 1892]

4. *Un mauvais style, c'est une pensée imparfaite.*
Poor style reflects imperfect thought.
[*Journal*, 1898]

Rendall, Montague John (1862–1950)
English teacher and BBC administrator

1. Nation shall speak peace unto nation.
[Motto of BBC]

Rendell, Ruth (1930–)
British crime author, also writes as Barbara Vine

1. 'All one needs,' he said, 'is an electric kettle in the bathroom and a fridge somewhere else.' He added rather obscurely, 'Eating out keeps you thin because it is so expensive.'
[*The Copper Peacock* (1991), Title story]

Renoir, Jean (1894–1979)
Distinguished French film director; son of Pierre-Auguste Renoir

1. *Est-il possible de réussir sans trahir?*
Is it possible to succeed without betrayal?
[*Ma Vie et mes films* (*My Life and My Films*, 1974), 'Nana']

Renoir, Pierre Auguste (1841–1919)
French Impressionist painter; father of Jean Renoir

1. [Of the men of the French Commune]
C'étaient des fous, mais ils avaient cette petite flamme qui ne s'éteint pas.
They were madmen; but they had in them that little flame which does not go out.
[In Jean Renoir, *Renoir, My Father* (1962)]

2. [On why he still painted although he had arthritis of his hands]
The pain passes, but the beauty remains.
[Attr.]

3. [Of the lifelike flesh tones of his nudes]
I just keep painting till I feel like pinching. Then I know it's right.
[Attr.]

Reuben, David (1933–)

1. Everything You Always Wanted to Know About Sex, But Were Afraid to Ask.
[Title of book, 1969]

Revson, Charles (1906–1975)
American cosmetic company executive

1. In the factory we make cosmetics. In the store we sell hope.
[In A. Tobias, *Fire and Ice* (1976)]

Rexford, Eben (1848–1916)
American poet and writer on gardening

1. Darling, I am growing old,
Silver threads among the gold.
['Silver Threads Among the Gold' (1873)]

Reynolds, Sir Joshua (1723–1792)
English portrait painter, and writer on art; first President of the Royal Academy, 1768

1. If you have great talents, industry will improve them: if you have but moderate abilities, industry will supply their deficiency.
[*Discourses on Art*, II (1769)]

2. A mere copier of nature can never produce anything great.
[*Discourses on Art*, III (1770)]

3. He who resolves never to ransack any mind but his own, will be soon reduced, from mere barrenness, to the poorest of all imitations; he will be obliged to imitate himself, and to repeat what he has before often repeated.
[*Discourses on Art*, VI (1774)]

4. I should desire that the last words which I should pronounce in this Academy, and from this place, might be the name of – Michael Angelo.
[*Discourses on Art*, XV (1790)]

5. Taste does not come by chance: it is a long and laborious task to acquire it.
[In James Northcote, *Life of Sir Joshua Reynolds* (1818 edition)]

Reynolds, Malvina (1900–1978)
American singer-songwriter

1. [Describing newly built houses south of San Francisco]
They're all made out of ticky-tacky,
And they all look just the same.
['Little Boxes', song, 1962]

Rhodes, Cecil (1853–1902)
English imperialist, financier and statesman in South Africa; Prime Minister of Cape Colony 1890–96

1. The unctuous rectitude of my countrymen.
[Speech, 1896]

2. Remember that you are an Englishman, and have consequently won first prize in the lottery of life.
[In Peter Ustinov, *Dear Me* (1977)]

3. [Replying to Queen Victoria who remarked that he disliked women]
How can I possibly dislike a sex to which Your Majesty belongs?
[Attr.]

4. [Last words]
So little done, so much to do!
[In Lewis Mitchell, *Life of Rhodes* (1910)]

Rhondda, Viscountess (1883–1958)
English founder and editor of Time and Tide *and suffragette*

1. Women must come off the pedestal. Men put us up there to get us out of the way.
[*The Observer*, 'Sayings of the Week', 1920]

Rhys, Jean (Ella Gwendolen Rees Williams) (1894–1979)
West Indian-born British novelist and short-story writer

1. The feeling of Sunday is the same everywhere, heavy, melancholy, standing still. Like when they say, 'As it was in the beginning, is now, and ever shall be, world without end.'
[*Voyage in the Dark* (1934), 4]

2. Next week, or next month, or next year I'll kill myself. But I might as well last out my month's rent, which has been paid up, and my credit for breakfast in the morning.
[*Good Morning, Midnight* (1939), II]

3. I often want to cry. That is the only advantage women have over men – at least they can cry.
[*Good Morning, Midnight* (1939), II]

Ribblesdale, Lord (1854–1925)
British army officer and courtier

1. It [is] gentlemanly to get one's quotations very slightly wrong. In that way one unprigs oneself and allows the company to correct one.
[In Lady D. Cooper, *The Light of Common Day* (1959)]

Rice, Grantland (1880–1954)
American sports journalist and poet

1. For when the One Great Scorer comes to mark against your name,
He marks – not that you won or lost – but how you played the Game.
['Alumnus Football' (1941)]

Rice, Sir Stephen (1637–1715)
Irish lawyer; Chief Baron of the Exchequer in Ireland

1. I will drive a coach and six horses through the Act of Settlement.
[In W. King, *State of the Protestants of Ireland* (1672)]

Rice, Tim (1944–)
English songwriter and broadcaster

1. [Herod to Christ]
Prove to me that you're no fool,
Walk across my swimming pool.
['King Herod's Song', 1970, from *Jesus Christ Superstar!*]

Rice-Davies, Mandy (1944–)
Welsh model, nightclub performer and owner

1. [Remark during the Profumo Affair, 1963, in response to Lord Astor's denial that they had been lovers]
He would, wouldn't he?
[*The Guardian*, 1963]

Rich, Adrienne (1929–)
American poet and critic

1. Aunt Jennifer's tigers prance across a screen,
Bright topaz denizens of a world of green.
They do not fear the men beneath the tree;
They pace in sleek chivalric certainty.

Aunt Jennifer's fingers fluttering through her wool
Find even the ivory needle hard to pull.
The massive weight of Uncle's wedding band
Sits heavily upon Aunt Jennifer's hand.

When Aunt is dead, her terrified hands will lie
Still ringed with ordeals she was mastered by.
The tigers in the panel that she made
Will go on prancing, proud and unafraid.
[*A Change of World* (1951), 'Aunt Jennifer's Tigers']

2. *To have in this uncertain world some stay*
which cannot be undermined,
is of the utmost consequence.'
Thus wrote
a woman, partly brave and partly good,
who fought with what she partly understood.
Few men about her would or could do more,
hence she was labeled harpy, shrew and whore.
[*Snapshots of a Daughter-in-Law: Poems* (1956), Title poem]

Richard I (1157–1199)
King of England from 1189 and a leader of the Third Crusade, 1191; son of Henry II and known as 'Lionheart'; poet

1. *Dieu et mon droit.*
God and my right.
[Attr., 1198]

2. [Remark on sighting Jerusalem]
Lord, I pray Thee to suffer me not to see Thy Holy City, since I cannot deliver it from the hands of Thy enemies.
[Attr.]

Richards, Frank (1875–1961)
English children's writer (creator of Billy Bunter) and scriptwriter

1. [Cries of Billy Bunter]
Yarooh! . . . I say you fellows! . . . You beast!
[Billy Bunter stories (1908–1940), passim]

2. The rottenfulness is terrific!
[Billy Bunter stories (1908–1940), passim]

Richards, Sir Gordon (1904–1986)
British champion jockey, trainer and racing manager

1. [Referring to his height, when he learned of his knighthood]
Mother always told me my day was coming, but I never realized I'd end up being the shortest knight of the year.
[Attr.]

Richards, I.A. (1893–1979)
English literary critic, linguist, poet and teacher; co-founder of Basic English with C.K. Ogden

1. [Of poetry]
It is a perfectly possible means of overcoming chaos.
[*Science and Poetry* (1926), 7]

Richardson, Henry Handel (Ethel Florence Lindesay Richardson) (1870–1946)
Australian novelist

1. [On a beach holiday]
When, however, on your way to the beach you had laboriously attained the summit of the great dune, the sight that met you almost took your breath away: as far as the eye could reach, the bluest of skies melting into the bluest of seas, which broke its foam-flecked edge against the flat, brown reefs that fringed the shore.
[*The Getting of Wisdom* (1910), 19]

Richardson, Sir Ralph (1902–1983)
English actor of stage and screen

1. The most precious things in speech are pauses.
[Attr.]

Richardson, Samuel (1689–1761)
English author of influential epistolary novels; printer and publisher

1. Desert and reward, I can assure her, seldom keep company.
[*Clarissa* (1747–1748), IV]

2. Pity is but one remove from love.
[*The History of Sir Charles Grandison* (1754), I]

3. That's the beauty of it; to offend and make up at pleasure.
[*The History of Sir Charles Grandison* (1754), III]

Richelieu, Armand Jean du Plessis, Cardinal de (1585–1642)
French statesman and cardinal; Chief Minister from 1624; strengthened the French Crown and the role of France in Europe

1. *Faire une loi et ne pas la faire exécuter, c'est autoriser la chose qu'on veut défendre.*
To pass a law and not have it enforced is to authorize the very thing you wish to prohibit.
[*Mémoires*]

2. If you give me six lines written by the most honest man, I will find something in them to hang him.
[Attr.]

Richelieu, Armand-Emmanuel du Plessis, Duc de (1766–1822)
French courtier, soldier and Prime Minister 1815–18, 1820–21

1. [On discovering his wife with her lover]
Madame, you must really be more careful. Suppose it had been someone else who found you like this.
[In D. Wallechinsky, *The Book of Lists* (1977)]

Ridding, Bishop George (1828–1904)
English headmaster and first Bishop of Southwell, from 1884

1. I feel a feeling which I feel you all feel.
[Sermon, 1885]

Rifkin, Jeremy
American bioethicist

1. When the Iroquois made a decision, they said, 'How does it affect seven generations in the future?'
[*The New York Times Magazine*, 1988]

Rilke, Rainer Maria (1875–1926)
Austrian poet, born in Prague; noted for his visionary lyrics

1. *Frühling ist wiedergekommen. Die Erde*
ist wie ein Kind, das Gedichte weiss.
Spring has come again. The earth is like a child who knows poems.
[*Die Sonette an Orpheus* (*The Sonnets to Orpheus*, 1923), I, 21]

2. *Wunderlich nah ist der Held doch den jugendlichen Toten.*
Wondrous close is the hero to those who die young.
[*Duineser Elegien* (*Duino Elegies*, 1923), 6]

3. *So leben wir und nehmen immer Abschied.*
And so we live and forever take our leave.
[*Duineser Elegien* (*Duino Elegies*, 1923), 8]

4. *Eines ... Tages wird das Mädchen da sein und die Frau, deren Name nicht mehr nur einen Gegensatz zum Männlichen bedeuten wird, sondern etwas für sich, etwas, wobei man an keine Ergänzung und Grenze denkt, nur an Leben und Dasein, – der weibliche Mensch. Dieser Fortschritt wird das Liebe-Erleben ... zu einer Beziehung umbilden, die von Mensch zu Mensch gemeint ist, nicht mehr von Mann und Weib. Und diese menschlichere Liebe ... wird jener ähneln, ... die darin besteht, dass zwei Einsamkeiten einander schützen, grenzen und grüssen.*
One day ... there will be the girl and the woman, whose name will no longer signify merely a contrast to masculinity, but something of value in itself, something in respect of which one thinks not of a complement and a limitation, but only of life and existence: the female person. This progress will make the experience of love ... become a relationship which is one of person to person, no longer one of man and wife. And this more human love ... will resemble one ... which consists in this, that two solitary people protect and limit and greet each other.
[*Briefe an einen jungen Dichter* (*Letters to a Young Poet*, written 1904, published 1929)]

Rimbaud, Arthur (1854–1891)
French poet, influential on Symbolism; abandoned writing at the age of twenty, after an affair with Paul Verlaine

1. *Je me suis baigné dans le Poème*
De la Mer, infusé d'astres, et lactescent,
Dévorant les azurs verts.
I have bathed in the Poem
Of the Sea, steeped in stars, milky,
Devouring the green azures.
['Le Bâteau ivre' (1870)]

2. *Je m'en allais, les poings dans mes poches crevées;*
Mon paletot aussi devenait idéal.
I was walking along, fists in my torn pockets; my overcoat also was entering the realm of the ideal.
['Ma Bohème' (1870)]

3. *O saisons, ô châteaux!*
Quelle âme est sans défauts?
O seasons, O castles! What soul is without faults?
['O saisons, ô châteaux' (1872)]

Rimsky-Korsakov, Nikolai (1844–1908)
Russian composer noted for his orchestration

1. [Of Debussy's music]
I have already heard it. I had better not go: I will start to get accustomed to it and finally like it.
[In Robert Craft and Igor Stravinsky, *Conversations with Stravinsky* (1959)]

Ripley, R.L. (1893–1949)
American cartoonist

1. Believe it or not.
[Title of newspaper feature, from 1918]

Rippon, Geoffrey (1924–)
English Conservative politician and Cabinet member

1. Governments don't retreat, they simply advance in another direction.
[*The Observer*, 1981, in Jeffrey Care (ed.), *Sayings of the Eighties* (1989)]

Rivarol, Antoine de (1753–1801)
French satirist, wit and pamphleteer

1. *Ce qui n'est pas clair n'est pas français.*
What is not clear is not French.
[*Discours sur l'Universalité de la Langue Française* (1784)]

2. [On a couplet by a mediocre poet]
C'est bien, mais il y a des longueurs.
Very good, but it has its *longueurs*.
[*Rivaroliana*]

Rivera, Antoine de (d. 1936)
Spanish Nationalist hero

1. [Giving the order to open fire at the siege of the Alcázar, a fortress above Toledo, occupied by the Nationalists in the Spanish Civil War]
Fire – without hatred.
[In C. Eby, *The Siege of the Alcázar* (1965)]

Robbins, Tom (1936–)
American novelist

1. Human beings were invented by water as a device for transporting itself from one place to another.
[*Another Roadside Attraction* (1971)]

Robespierre, Maximilien (1758–1794)
French revolutionary, leader of the Jacobin Reign of Terror; executed

1. *Toute loi qui viole les droits imprescriptibles de l'homme, est essentiellement injuste et tyrannique; elle n'est point une loi.*
Any law which violates the indefeasible rights of man is in essence unjust and tyrannical; it is no law.
[*Déclaration des Droits de l'homme* (1793), Article 6]

2. *Toute institution qui ne suppose pas le peuple bon, et le magistrat corruptible, est vicieuse.*
Any institution which does not suppose the people good, and the magistrate corruptible, is a vicious one.
[*Déclaration des Droits de l'homme* (1793), Article 25]

Robey, Sir George (1869–1954)
English comedian

1. The Prime Minister of Mirth.
[Handbill]

Robinson, Edwin Arlington (1869–1935)
American lyric and narrative poet

1. I shall have more to say when I am dead.
[*The Three Taverns* (1920), 'John Brown']

Robinson, James Harvey (1863–1936)
American historian, teacher and writer

1. Partisanship is our great curse. We too readily assume that everything has two sides and that it is our duty to be on one or the other.
[*The Mind in the Making* (1921)]

Robinson, Mary (1944–)
Irish barrister and politician, President of Ireland from 1990

1. As the elected choice of the people of this part of our island I want to extend the hand of friendship and of love to both communities in the other part.
[Inaugural speech as President, 1991]

Robinson, Robert (1927–)
English journalist, television and radio broadcaster

1. Certain people are born with natural false teeth.
[*Stop the Week*, BBC radio programme, 1977]

Robinson, Roland Edward (1912–1992)
Irish-born Australian poet

1. Where does imagination start
but from primeval images
in man's barbaric heart?
['Mopoke']

Robson, Bobby (1933–)
English footballer and manager of the England team

1. The first ninety minutes are the most important.
[Quoted as the title of a TV documentary, 1983]

Roche, Sir Boyle (1743–1807)
Irish politician and soldier

1. What has posterity done for us?
[Speech, 1780]

2. Mr Speaker, I smell a rat; I see him forming in the air and darkening the sky; but I'll nip him in the bud.
[Attr.]

3. He regretted that he was not a bird, and could not be in two places at once.
[Attr.]

Rochester, John Wilmot, Second Earl of (1647–1680)
English lyric poet, satirist, courtier and libertine

1. [Of love]
That cordial drop heaven in our cup has thrown
To make the nauseous draught of life go down.
['A letter from Artemisa in the Town to Chloe in the Country' (1679)]

2. Reason, an *ignis fatuus* of the mind,
Which leaving the light of nature, sense, behind...

3. Then Old Age, and Experience, hand in hand,
Lead him to Death, and make him understand,
After a search so painful, and so long,
That all his life he has been in the wrong.
Huddled in dirt the reasoning engine lies,
Who was so proud, so witty, and so wise...

4. For all men would be cowards if they durst...

5. Most men are cowards, all men should be knaves.
['A Satire Against Reason and Mankind' (1679)]

6. The best good man, with the worst-natur'd muse.
['An Allusion to Horace' (1680)]

7. 'Is there then no more?'
She cries. 'All this to love and rapture's due;
Must we not pay a debt to pleasure too?'
['The Imperfect Enjoyment' (1680)]

8. Love a woman? You're an ass!
['Song' (1680)]

9. Since 'tis Nature's law to change,
Constancy alone is strange.
['A Dialogue between Strephon and Daphne' (1691)]

10. An age in her embraces passed,
Would seem a winter's day.
['The Mistress: A Song' (1691)]

11. Ancient person, for whom I
All the flattering youth defy,
Long be it ere thou grow old,
Aching, shaking, crazy, cold;
But still continue as thou art,
Ancient person of my heart.
['A Song of a Young Lady to her Ancient Lover' (1691)]

12. A merry monarch, scandalous and poor.
['A Satire on King Charles II' (1697)]

13. Here lies our sovereign lord the King
Whose word no man relies on,
Who never said a foolish thing,
Nor ever did a wise one.
[Epitaph written for Charles II (1706). Cf. Charles II: 8]

14. What vain, unnecessary things are men!
How well we do without 'em!
['Fragment' (published 1953)]

Rockefeller, Nelson (1908–1979)
US politician, Governor of New York state

1. The brotherhood of man under the fatherhood of God.
[*Time*, 1982]

Rockne, Knut (1888–1931)
American football player and coach

1. Show me a good and gracious loser and I'll show you a failure.
[Attr.]

Rodó, José Enrique (1872–1917)
Uruguayan writer and critic

1. *Lo bello nace de la muerte de lo útil; lo útil se convierte en bello cuando ha caducado su utilidad.*
What is beautiful has its origin in the death of what is useful; what is useful becomes beautiful when it has outlived its usefulness.
[Letter to Miguel de Unamuno, 19 July 1903]

Roethke, Theodore (1908–1963)
American poet

1. I wake to sleep, and take my waking slow,
I feel my fate in what I cannot fear.
I learn by going where I have to go.
['The Waking' (1953)]

2. I knew a woman, lovely in her bones,
When small birds sighed, she would sigh back at them;
Ah, when she moved, she moved more ways than one:
The shapes a bright container can contain!
['I Knew a Woman' (1958)]

Rogers, E.W. (1864–1913)

1. Ev'ry member of the force
Has a watch and chain, of course;
If you want to know the time,
Ask a P'liceman!
['Ask a P'liceman', song, 1889]

Rogers, Samuel (1763–1855)
English poet, wit and banker

1. Oh! she was good as she was fair.
None – none on earth above her!
As pure in thought as angels are,
To know her was to love her.
[*Jacqueline* (1814)]

2. Go – you may call it madness, folly;
You shall not chase my gloom away.
There's such a charm in melancholy,
I would not, if I could, be gay.
['To –, 1814']

3. Think nothing done while aught remains to do...

4. But there are moments which he calls his own,
Then, never less alone than when alone,
Those whom he loved so long and sees no more,
Loved and still loves – not dead – but gone before,
He gathers round him.
['Human Life' (1819)]

5. ... many a temple half as old as time.
[*Italy* (1838)]

6. It doesn't much signify whom one marries, for one is sure to find next morning that it was someone else.
[*Recollections of the Table-Talk of Samuel Rogers* (1856)]

7. Sheridan was listened to with such attention that you might have heard a pin drop.
[*Recollections of the Table-Talk of Samuel Rogers* (1856)]

Rogers, Thorold (1823–1890)
English economic historian

1. Sir, to be facetious it is not necessary to be indecent.
[In John Bailey, *Dr Johnson and his Circle* (1913)]

Rogers, Will (1879–1935)
American humorist, comic actor, rancher, writer and wit

1. Income tax has made more liars out of American people than golf.
[*The Illiterate Digest* (1924), 'Helping the Girls with their Income Taxes']

2. Everything is funny as long as it is happening to someone else.
[*The Illiterate Digest* (1924), 'Warning to Jokers: lay off the Prince']

3. You can't say civilization don't advance, however, for in every war they kill you a new way.
[*The New York Times*, 1929]

4. Half our life is spent trying to find something to do with the time we have rushed through life trying to save.
[*The New York Times*, 1930]

5. The more you read ... about this Politics thing, you got to admit that each party is worse than the other.
[*Autobiography of Will Rogers* (1949), 6]

6. Communism is like prohibition, it's a good idea but it won't work.
[*Weekly Articles* (1981), III]

7. Heroing is one of the shortest-lived professions there is.
[In Grove, *The Will Rogers Book* (1961)]

8. The movies are the only business where you can go out front and applaud yourself.
[In Halliwell, *Filmgoer's Book of Quotes* (1973)]

9. [Message to his niece on a postcard of the Venus de Milo]
See what will happen to you if you don't stop biting your fingernails.
[Attr.]

10. I don't make jokes – I just watch the government and report the facts.
[Attr.]

Roland, Madame (1754–1793)
French revolutionary; memoirist and letter writer; executed

1. [Remark on mounting the scaffold]
O liberté! O liberté! que de crimes on commet en ton nom!
O liberty! O liberty! how many crimes are committed in your name!
[In A. de Lamartine, *Histoire des Girondins* (1847). Cf. Dan George: 1]

Rolfe, Frederick William ('Baron Corvo') (1860–1913)
English novelist

1. Pray for the repose of His soul. He was so tired.
[*Hadrian VII* (1904), 24]

Rolleston, Sir Humphrey (1862–1944)
English consultant physician; editor and author of medical books

1. [Of physicians]
First they get *on*, then they get *honour*, then they get *honest*.
[In David Ogilvy, *Confessions of an Advertising Man* (1963)]

Rolleston, T.W. (1857–1920)
Irish journalist and writer on Celtic mythology

1. In a quiet watered land, a land of roses,
Stands Saint Kieran's City fair;
And the warriors of Erin in their famous generations
Slumber there.
[*Lyra Celtica* (1896), 'The Dead at Clonmacnois'; trans. from the Irish of Enoch O'Gillan]

Rolmaz, James (19th century)
British songwriter

1. Where did you get that hat?
Where did you get that tie?
['Where Did You Get That Hat?', song, 1888]

Ronsard, Pierre de (1524–1585)
French poet; leading member of the Pléiade

1. *Quand vous serez bien vieille, au soir, à la chandelle,*
Assise auprès du feu, dévidant et filant,
Direz, chantant mes vers, en vous émerveillant,
Ronsard me célébrait du temps que j'étais belle.
When you are very old, at night, in the candle-light, sitting spinning by the fire, you will say as you sing my verses, marvelling, 'Ronsard sang of me in the time of my beauty.'
[*Sonnets pour Hélène* (1578), II, 42. Cf. Yeats: 14]

Roosevelt, Eleanor (1884–1962)
American diplomat, social activist and writer; wife of Franklin Delano Roosevelt and niece of Theodore Roosevelt

1. I used to tell my husband that, if he could make *me* understand something, it would be clear to all the other people in the country.
[Newspaper column, 'My Day', 1947]

2. No one can make you feel inferior without your consent.
[*Catholic Digest*, 1960]

3. I think if the people of this country can be reached with the truth, their judgment will be in favour of the many, as against the privileged few.
[*Ladies' Home Journal*]

4. I have spent many years of my life in opposition and I rather like the role.
[Letter to Bernard Baruch, 1952]

Roosevelt, Franklin Delano (1882–1945)
American lawyer and statesman; Democrat President 1933–1945, noted for his New Deal reforms and wartime leadership

1. I confess to pride in this coming generation. You are working out your own salvation; you are more in love with life; you play with fire openly, where we did in secret, and few of you are burned!
[Address, 1926]

2. To stand upon the ramparts and die for our principles is heroic, but to sally forth to battle and win for our principles is something more than heroic.
[Speech, 1928]

3. . . . the forgotten man at the bottom of the economic pyramid.
[Radio broadcast, 1932]

4. I pledge you – I pledge myself – to a New Deal for the American people.
[Speech, 1932]

5. The only thing we have to fear is fear itself.
[First Inaugural Address, 1933]

6. We have always known that heedless self-interest was bad morals; we know now that it is bad economics.
[First Inaugural Address, 1933]

7. I would dedicate this nation to the policy of the good neighbour.
[First Inaugural Address, 1933]

8. I see one-third of a nation ill-housed, ill-clad, ill-nourished.
[Second Inaugural Address, 1937]

9. A radical is a man with both feet firmly planted in the air.
[Radio broadcast, 1939]

10. When peace has been broken anywhere, the peace of all countries everywhere is in danger.
[Radio broadcast, 1939]

11. We must be the great arsenal of democracy.
[Radio broadcast, 1940]

12. In the future days, which we seek to make secure, we look forward to a world founded upon four essential human freedoms. The first is freedom of speech and expression – everywhere in the world. The second is freedom of every person to worship God in his own way – everywhere in the world. The third is freedom from want . . . The fourth is freedom from fear.
[Address to Congress, 1941]

13. More than an end to war, we want an end to the beginnings of all wars.
[Speech broadcast on the day after he died, 1945]

14. I ask you to judge me by the enemies I have made.
[*The Observer*, 'Sayings of the Week', 1932]

15. We all know that books burn – yet we have the greater knowledge that books cannot be killed by fire. People die, but books never die. No man and no force can abolish memory . . . In this war, we know, books are weapons.
[*Publisher's Weekly*, 1942, 'Message to the American Booksellers Association']

16. Defeat of Germany means the defeat of Japan, probably without firing a shot or losing a life.
[In Winston S. Churchill, *The Hinge of Fate* (1951)]

17. The best immediate defence of the United States is the success of Great Britain in defending itself.
[In Winston S. Churchill, *Their Finest Hour* (1951)]

Roosevelt, Theodore (1858–1919)
American statesman, soldier and writer; Republican President 1901–09; Nobel peace prize 1906 for mediating in the Russo-Japanese war; distant cousin of Franklin Delano Roosevelt

1. The first requisite of a good citizen in this republic of ours is that he shall be able and willing to pull his weight.
[Speech, 1902]

2. There is a homely old adage which runs, 'Speak softly and carry a big stick; you will go far.'
[Speech, 1903]

3. A man who is good enough to shed his blood for the country is good enough to be given a square deal afterwards. More

than that no man is entitled to, and less than that no man shall have.
[Speech, 1903]

4. No man needs sympathy because he has to work ... Far and away the best prize that life offers is the chance to work hard at work worth doing.
[Address, 1903]

5. The men with the muck-rakes are often indispensable to the well-being of society; but only if they know when to stop raking the muck.
[Speech, 1906]

6. There is no room in this country for hyphenated Americanism.
[Speech, 1915]

7. Nine-tenths of wisdom is being wise in time.
[Speech, 1917]

8. I want to see you shoot the way you shout.
[Speech, 1917]

9. There can be no fifty-fifty Americanism in this country. There is room here for only hundred per cent Americanism, only for those who are Americans and nothing else.
[Speech, 1918]

10. [When standing for the Vice-Presidency]
I am as strong as a bull moose and you can use me to the limit.
[Letter to Mark Hanna, 1900]

11. No man is justified in doing evil on the ground of expediency.
[*The Strenuous Life* (1900)]

12. We demand that big business give the people a square deal; in return we must insist that when any one engaged in big business honestly endeavors to do right he shall himself be given a square deal.
[*Theodore Roosevelt: an Autobiography* (1913)]

13. ... men who form the lunatic fringe in all reform movements.
[*Theodore Roosevelt: an Autobiography* (1913)]

14. Don't hit at all if it is honourably possible to avoid hitting; but *never* hit soft!
[In J.B. Bishop, *Theodore Roosevelt and his time, shown in his own letters* (1920)]

15. [Dismissing a cowboy who had put Roosevelt's brand on a steer belonging to a neighbouring ranch]
A man who will steal *for* me will steal *from* me.
[In Herman Hagedorn, *Roosevelt in the Bad Lands* (1921)]

16. We have room in this country for but one flag, the Stars and Stripes ... We have room for but one loyalty, loyalty to the United States ... We have room for but one language, the language of the Declaration of Independence and the Gettysburg speech.
[In Lord Charnwood, *Theodore Roosevelt* (1923)]

17. [On asking President Wilson for permission to raise a division of volunteers to serve in France, 1917]
Peace is not the end. Righteousness is the end ... If I must choose between righteousness and peace I choose righteousness.
[In Lord Charnwood, *Theodore Roosevelt* (1923)]

18. Kings and such like are just as funny as politicians.
[In John Dos Passos, *Mr Wilson's War* (1963), 1]

19. The poorest way to face life is to face it with a sneer.
[Attr.]

Ros, Amanda McKittrick (1860–1939)
Irish novelist and poet

1. Holy Moses! Have a look!
Flesh decayed in every nook.
Some rare bits of brain lie here,
Mortal loads of beef and beer.
['Lines on Westminster Abbey']

Roscommon, Fourth Earl of (1633–1685)
Irish translator, critic and poet

1. But words once spoke can never be recall'd.
[*Horace's Art of Poetry Made English* (1680). Cf. Horace: 116]

2. Immodest words admit of no defence,
For want of Decency is want of Sense.
[*An Essay on Translated Verse* (1684)]

Rosebery, Earl of (1847–1929)
English statesman, orator and writer; Liberal Prime Minister 1894–95

1. The Empire is a Commonwealth of Nations.
[Speech, Adelaide, 1884]

2. It is beginning to be hinted that we are a nation of amateurs.
[Speech, 1900]

3. I must plough my furrow alone.
[Speech, 1901]

Ross, Alan S.C. (1907–1980)
British linguistics scholar and editor

1. U and Non-U. An Essay in Sociological Linguistics.
[In Nancy Mitford (ed.), *Noblesse Oblige* (1956), Title of essay]

Ross, Harold W. (1892–1951)
American founder editor of The New Yorker *(from 1825)*

1. [Customary query when he found a name he did not know in an article]
Who he?
[In J. Thurber, *The Years With Ross* (1957)]

Ross, Sir Ronald (1857–1932)
Indian-born British physician; discoverer of the malaria parasite; Nobel prize for medicine 1902, writer and memoirist

1. O Death, where is thy sting?
Thy victory, O Grave?
[*Philosophies* (1910), 'In Exile']

Rossetti, Christina (1830–1894)
English Pre-Raphaelite poet, noted for her lyric and religious verse; sister of Dante Gabriel Rossetti

1. 'Come cheer up, my lads, 'tis to glory we steer!'
As the soldier remarked whose post lay in the rear.
[Untitled couplet (c. 1845)]

2. My heart is like a singing bird
Whose next is in a watered shoot;
My heart is like an apple-tree
Whose boughs are bent with thickset fruit;
My heart is like a rainbow shell
That paddles in a halcyon sea;
My heart is gladder than all these
Because my love is come to me...

3. Because the birthday of my life
Is come, my love is come to me.
['A Birthday' (1862)]

4. Come to me in the silence of the night;
Come in the speaking silence of a dream;
Come with soft rounded cheeks and eyes as bright
As sunlight on a stream;
Come back in tears,
O memory, hope, love of finished years.
['Echo' (1862)]

5. For there is no friend like a sister
In calm or stormy weather;
To cheer one on the tedious way,
To fetch one if one goes astray,
To lift one if one totters down,
To strengthen whilst one stands.
['Goblin Market' (1862)]

6. The hope I dreamed of was a dream,
Was but a dream; and now I wake,
Exceeding comfortless, and worn, and old,
For a dream's sake.
['Mirage' (1862)]

7. Remember me when I am gone away,
Gone far away into the silent land...

8. Better by far you should forget and smile
Than you should remember and be sad.
['Remember' (1862)]

9. O Earth, lie heavily upon her eyes;
Seal her sweet eyes weary of watching, Earth...

10. Silence more musical than any song.
['Rest' (1862)]

11. Oh roses for the flush of youth,
And laurel for the perfect prime;
But pluck an ivy branch for me
Grown old before my time.
['Oh Roses for the Flush of Youth' (1862)]

12. When I am dead, my dearest,
Sing no sad songs for me;
Plant thou no roses at my head,
Nor shady cypress tree:
Be the green grass above me
With showers and dewdrops wet;
And if thou wilt, remember,
And if thou wilt, forget...

13. And dreaming through the twilight
That doth not rise nor set,
Haply I may remember,
And haply may forget.
['Song: When I am Dead' (1862)]

14. Does the road wind up-hill all the way?
Yes, to the very end.
Will the day's journey take the whole long day?
From morn to night, my friend...

15. Will there be beds for me and all who seek?
Yea, beds for all who come.
['Up-Hill' (1862)]

16. Who has seen the wind?
Neither you nor I:
But when the trees bow down their heads,
The wind is passing by.
['Who Has Seen the Wind?' (1872)]

17. This downhill path is easy, but there's no turning back.
['Amor Mundi' (1875)]

18. In the bleak mid-winter
Frosty wind made moan,
Earth stood hard as iron,
Water like a stone;
Snow had fallen, snow on snow,
Snow on snow,
In the bleak mid-winter,
Long ago.
['A Christmas Carol' (1875)]

Rossetti, Dante Gabriel (1828–1882)

English poet and painter; co-founder of the Pre-Raphaelite Brotherhood; translator and letter writer

1. The blessed damozel leaned out
From the gold bar of Heaven;
Her eyes were deeper than the depth
Of waters stilled at even;
She had three lilies in her hand,
And the stars in her hair were seven...

2. Her hair that lay along her back
Was yellow like ripe corn...

3. As low as where this earth
Spins like a fretful midge...

4. And the souls mounting up to God
Went by her like thin flames.
['The Blessed Damozel' (1870)]

5. I have been here before,
But when or how I cannot tell:
I know the grass beyond the door,
The sweet keen smell,
The sighing sound, the lights around the shore.
['Sudden Light' (1870)]

6. From perfect grief there need not be
Wisdom or even memory:
One thing then learnt remains to me,–
The woodspurge has a cup of three.
['The Woodspurge' (1870)]

7. A sonnet is a moment's monument,–
Memorial from the Soul's eternity
To one dead deathless hour.
[*The House of Life* (1881), I, Introduction]

8. 'Tis visible silence, still as the hour-glass...

9. Deep in the sun-searched growths the dragon-fly
Hangs like a blue thread loosened from the sky:–
So this winged hour is dropt to us from above.
Oh! clasp we to our hearts, for deathless dower,
This close-companioned inarticulate hour
When twofold silence was the song of love.
[*The House of Life* (1881), I, 'Silent Noon']

10. I do not see them here; but after death
God knows I know the faces I shall see,
Each one a murdered self, with low last breath.
'I am thyself, – what hast thou done to me?'
'And I – and I – thyself', (lo! each one saith,)
'And thou thyself to all eternity!'
[*The House of Life* (1881), II, 'Lost Days']

11. When vain desire at last and vain regret
Go hand in hand to death, and all is vain,
What shall assuage the unforgotten pain
And teach the unforgetful to forget?
[*The House of Life* (1881), II, 'The One Hope']

12. Look in my face; my name is Might-have-been
I am also called No-more, Too-Late, Farewell...

13. Then shalt thou see me smile, and turn apart
Thy visage to mine ambush at my heart
Sleepless with cold commemorative eyes.
[*The House of Life* (1881), II, 'A Superscription']

14. The worst moment for the atheist is when he is really thankful and has nobody to thank.
[Attr.]

Rossini, Gioacchino (1792–1868)
Italian composer, noted for his operas

1. *Monsieur Wagner a de beaux moments, mais de mauvais quart d'heures.*
Wagner has beautiful moments but awful quarters of an hour.
[In E. Naumann, *Italienische Tondichter* (1883)]

2. Give me a laundry-list and I will set it to music.
[Attr.]

Rostand, Edmond (1868–1918)
French Romantic poet and dramatist

1. *Le seul rêve intéresse,*
Vivre sans rêve, qu'est-ce?
Et j'aime la Princesse
Lointaine.
Only dreaming is of interest. What is life, without dreams? And I love the Far-away Princess.
[*La Princesse Lointaine* (1895), I.iv]

2. *Énorme, mon nez!*
– Vil camus, sot camard, tête plate, apprenez
Que je m'enorgueillis d'un pareil appendice,
Attendu qu'un grand nez est proprement l'indice
D'un homme affable, bon, courtois, spirituel,
Libéral, courageux, tel que je suis.
Enormous, my nose! Vile pug-nose, flat-nose, flat-head, let me inform you that I pride myself in such an appendage, considering that a big nose is the proper sign of a friendly, good, courteous, witty, liberal, courageous man, such as I am.
[*Cyrano de Bergerac* (1897), I.iv]

3. Cyrano: *Il y a malgré vous quelque chose*
Que j'emporte, et ce soir, quand j'entrerai chez Dieu,
Mon salut balaiera largement le seuil bleu,
Quelque chose que sans un pli, sans une tache,
J'emporte malgré vous ... et c'est ...
Roxane: *C'est? ...*
Cyrano: *Mon panache!*
Cyrano: There is, in spite of you, something which I shall take with me. And tonight, when I enter God's house, my bow will make a wide sweep across the blue threshold. Something which, without a crease, without a mark, I'm taking away in spite of you ... and it's...
Roxane: It's...
Cyrano: My panache!
[*Cyrano de Bergerac* (1897), V.iv]

Rostand, Jean (1894–1977)
French biologist

1. *Tue un homme, on est un assassin. On tue des millions d'hommes, on est conquérant. On les tue tous, on est un dieu.*
Kill one man, and you are a murderer. Kill millions of men, and you are a conqueror. Kill them all, and you are a god.
[*Pensées d'un biologiste* (*Thoughts of a Biologist*, 1939). Cf. Porteous: 1]

2. *Etre adulte, c'est être seul.*
To be an adult is to be alone.
[*Pensées d'un biologiste* (*Thoughts of a Biologist*, 1939)]

3. *Il est dans la tolérance un degré qui confine à l'injure.*
There is a degree of tolerance which borders on insult.
[*Pensées d'un biologiste* (*Thoughts of a Biologist*, 1939)]

Rosten, Leo (Leonard Q. Ross) (1908–)
Polish-born American social scientist, writer and humorist

1. [Of W.C. Fields; often attributed to him]
Any man who hates dogs and babies can't be all bad.
[Speech, 1939]

Roth, Philip (1933–)
American novelist, short-story writer and essayist; noted for his portrayal of Jewish-American life

1. A Jewish man with parents alive is a fifteen-year-old boy, and will remain a fifteen-year-old boy until *they die*.
[*Portnoy's Complaint* (1969)]

2. Doctor, my doctor, what do you say – LET'S PUT THE ID BACK IN YID!
[*Portnoy's Complaint* (1969)]

Rouget de Lisle, Claude-Joseph (1760–1836)
French army officer and essayist

1. *Allons, enfants de la patrie,*
Le jour de gloire est arrivé...
Let us go, children of this land, the day of glory has arrived!...

2. *Aux armes, citoyens!*
To arms, citizens!
['La Marseillaise' (now French national Anthem), 1792]

Rourke, M.E. (20th century)
American songwriter

1. And when I told them how beautiful you are
They didn't believe me! They didn't believe me!
['They Didn't Believe Me', song, 1914]

Rousseau, Émile (1929–)
Agent General in London for Saskatchewan

1. *Les grands mangeurs de viande sont en général cruels et féroces plus que les autres hommes ... La barbarie anglaise est connue.*
Great eaters of meat are in general more cruel and ferocious than other men ... The English are known for their cruelty.
[Attr.]

Rousseau, Jean-Jacques (1712–1778)
Influential French social and political philosopher, educationist and essayist; born in Switzerland

1. *L'homme est né libre, et partout il est dans les fers.*
Man was born free, and everywhere he is in chains.
[*Du Contrat Social* (1762)]

2. *Les lois sont toujours utiles à ceux qui possèdent et nuisibles à ceux qui n'ont rien.*
Laws are always useful to those who have possessions, and harmful to those who have nothing.
[*Du Contrat Social* (1762)]

3. *On n'est curieux qu'à proportion qu'on est instruit.*
One is only curious in proportion to one's level of education.
[*Émile ou De l'éducation* (1762)]

4. *La feinte charité du riche n'est en lui qu'un luxe de plus; il nourrit les pauvres comme des chiens et des chevaux.*
The feigned charity of the rich man is for him no more than another luxury; he feeds the poor as he feeds dogs and horses.
[*Correspondance* (1753–1764), Letter to M. Moulton]

5. *La nature a fait l'homme heureux et bon, mais ... la société le dép
rave et le rend misérable.*
Nature made man happy and good, but ... society corrupts him and makes him miserable.
[*Rousseau juge de Jean-Jacques*]

Routh, Martin Joseph (1755–1854)
English divine and patristic scholar

1. You will find it a very good practice always to verify your references, sir!
[Attr.]

Roux, Joseph (1834–1886)

1. Science is for those who learn; poetry, for those who know.
[*Meditations of a Parish Priest* (1886), 1]

2. We love justice greatly, and just men but little.
[*Meditations of a Parish Priest* (1886), 4]

3. The egoist does not tolerate egoism.
[*Meditations of a Parish Priest* (1886), 9]

Rowbotham, David Harold (1924–)
Australian journalist, critic and poet

1. Let some of the tranquillity of the cat
Curl into me. The creature, curled in my lap,
Has the world like a ball of wool in its purring eyes.
How many men, for the labour they are at,
Want the shapes of a caress or the gentle reward
Of curled-up animal generosities!
['The Creature in the Chair']

Rowe, Nicholas (1674–1718)
English tragic dramatist, poet and translator; poet laureate from 1715

1. At length the morn and cold indifference came.
[*The Fair Penitent* (1703), I]

2. That false Lothario!
[*The Fair Penitent* (1703), II]

3. ... the evening of my age.
[*The Fair Penitent* (1703), IV]

4. I feel thy pangs of disappointed love.
[*The Fair Penitent* (1703), IV]

5. Death is the privilege of human nature,
And life without it were not worth our taking.
[*The Fair Penitent* (1703), V]

Rowland, Edward (20th century)
British songwriter

1. Mademoiselle from Armentiers,
Hasn't been kissed for forty years,
Hinky, dinky, par-lee-voo.
['Mademoiselle from Armentiers', song, 1918]

Rowland, Helen (1875–1950)
American writer

1. When you see what some girls marry, you realize how they must hate to work for a living.
[*Reflections of a Bachelor Girl* (1909)]

2. It takes a woman twenty years to make a man of her son, and another woman twenty minutes to make a fool of him.
[*Reflections of a Bachelor Girl* (1909)]

3. The follies which a man regrets most in his life are those which he didn't commit when he had the opportunity.
[*A Guide to Men* (1922)]

4. Never trust a husband too far, nor a bachelor too near.
[*The Rubaiyat of a Bachelor* (1925)]

5. Before marriage, a man will lie awake thinking about something you said; after marriage, he'll fall asleep before you finish saying it.
[In Cowan, *The Wit of Women*]

Rowland, Richard (c. 1881–1947)

1. [When United Artists was established in 1919 by Mary Pickford, Douglas Fairbanks, Charlie Chaplin and D.W. Griffith]
The lunatics have taken over the asylum.
[Attr.]

Royce, Phillip

1. ... as an Australian I was brought up in an Anglo-Irish country – part of the weirdness of our personality is that inside every Australian there's an Irishman fighting an Englishman.
[*The Independent*, 1992]

Rubens, Paul Alfred (1875–1917)
English songwriter, composer and dramatist

1. We don't want to lose you but we think you ought to go.
['Your King and Country Want You', song, 1914]

Rubin, Jerry (1936–)

1. Dont trust anyone over thirty.
[In S.B. Flexner, *Listening to America*]

Rubinstein, Helena (c. 1872–1965)
Polish-born American businesswoman and cosmetics manufacturer

1. I have always felt that a woman has a right to treat the subject of her age with ambiguity until, perhaps, she passes into the realm of over ninety. Then it is better she be candid with herself and with the world.
[*My Life for Beauty* (1965), I]

2. There are no ugly women, only lazy ones.
[*My Life for Beauty* (1965), I]

Rückriem, Ulrich (1938–)

1. People don't want art, they want football.
[*Scala*, 1992]

Runcie, Robert (1921–)
English prelate and Archbishop of Canterbury

1. [On his discussions with the Prince and Princess of Wales prior to marrying them]
My advice was delicately poised between the cliché and the indiscretion.
[*The Times*, 1981. Cf. Harold Macmillan: 11]

Runcie, Rosalind (1932–)
Wife of Robert Runcie, Archbishop of Canterbury

1. Too much religion makes me go pop.
[In M. Duggan, *Runcie: The Making of an Archbishop* (1983)]

Runciman, Sir Steven (1903–)
British scholar and academic; authority on Byzantine and Greek history and archaeology

1. Unlike Christianity, which preached a peace that it never achieved, Islam unashamedly came with a sword.
[*A History of the Crusades* (1951–1954), 'The First Crusade']

Runyon, Damon (1884–1946)
American journalist and short-story writer, known for his Broadway stories

1. More than Somewhat.
[Title of book, 1937]

2. And you cannot tell by the way a party looks or how he lives in this town, if he has any scratch, because many a party who is around in automobiles, and wearing good clothes, and chucking quite a swell is nothing but a phonus bolonus and does not have any real scratch whatever.
[*More than Somewhat* (1937), 'The Snatching of Bookie Bob']

3. All she has to do is to walk around and about Georgie White's stage with only a few light bandages on, and everybody considers her very beautiful, especially from the neck down.
[*Furthermore* (1938), 'A Very Honourable Guy']

4. Always try to rub up against money, for if you rub up against money long enough, some of it may rub off on you.
[*Furthermore* (1938), 'A Very Honourable Guy']

5. Her stomach thinks her throat is cut.
[*Furthermore* (1938), 'Little Miss Marker']

6. He is without doubt strictly a Hoorah Henry, and he is generally figured as nothing but a lob as far as doing anything useful in this world is concerned.
[*Take It Easy* (1938), 'Tight Shoes']

7. These citizens are always willing to bet that what Nicely-Nicely dies of will be over-feeding and never anything small like pneumonia, for Nicely-Nicely is known far and wide as a character who dearly loves to commit eating.
[*Take it Easy* (1938), 'Lonely Heart']

8. She is a smart old broad. It is a pity she is so nefarious.
[*Runyon à la carte* (1944), 'Broadway Incident']

9. At such an hour the sinners are still in bed resting up from their sinning of the night before, so they will be in good shape for more sinning a little later on.
[*Runyon à la carte* (1944), 'The Idyll of Miss Sarah Brown']

10. A free-loader is a confirmed guest. He is the man who is always willing to come to dinner.
[*Short Takes* (1946), 'Free-Loading Ethics']

Rusk, Dean (1909–)
American politician and diplomat; Democrat Secretary of State 1961–69

1. [Of the Cuban missile crisis]
We're eye-ball to eye-ball and I think the other fellow just blinked.
[Remark, 1962]

Ruskin, John (1819–1900)
English art critic, social philosopher and reformer; essayist and champion of the Pre-Raphaelites

1. I believe the right question to ask, respecting all ornament, is simply this: Was it done with enjoyment – was the carver happy while he was about it?
[*The Seven Lamps of Architecture* (1849), 'The Lamp of Life']

2. Better the rudest work that tells a story or records a fact, than the richest without meaning. There should not be a single ornament put upon great civic buildings, without some intellectual intention.
[*The Seven Lamps of Architecture* (1849), 'The Lamp of Memory']

3. When we build, let us think that we build for ever.
[*The Seven Lamps of Architecture* (1849), 'The Lamp of Memory']

4. Remember that the most beautiful things in the world are the most useless; peacocks and lilies for instance.
[*The Stones of Venice*, I (1851)]

5. The purest and most thoughtful minds are those which love colour the most.
[*The Stones of Venice*, II (1853)]

6. What is poetry? ... The suggestion, by the imagination, of noble grounds for the noble emotions.
[*Modern Painters* (1856), III, 4, 1]

7. All violent feelings ... produce in us a falseness in all our impressions of external things, which I would generally characterize as the 'Pathetic Fallacy'.
[*Modern Painters* (1856), III, 4, 12]

8. Mountains are the beginning and the end of all natural scenery.
[*Modern Painters* (1856), IV, 5, 20]

9. Fine art is that in which the hand, the head, and the heart of man go together.
[*The Two Paths* (1859), 2]

10. Not only is there but one way of *doing* things rightly, but there is only one way of *seeing* them, and that is, seeing the whole of them.
[*The Two Paths* (1859), 2]

11. Nobody cares much at heart about Titian; only there is a strange undercurrent of everlasting murmur about his name, which means the deep consent of all great men that he is greater than they.
[*The Two Paths* (1859), 2]

12. No human being, however great, or powerful, was ever so free as a fish.
[*The Two Paths* (1859), 5]

13. Soldiers of the ploughshare as well as soldiers of the sword.
[*Unto this Last* (1862), Preface]

14. It ought to be quite as natural and straightforward a matter for a labourer to take his pension from his parish, because he has deserved well of his parish, as for a man in higher rank to take his pension from his country, because he has deserved well of his country.
[*Unto this Last* (1862), Preface]

15. Government and cooperation are in all things the laws of life; anarchy and competition, the laws of death.
[*Unto this Last* (1862), 3]

16. Whereas it has long been known and declared that the poor have no right to the property of the rich, I wish it also to be known and declared that the rich have no right to the property of the poor.
[*Unto this Last* (1862), 3]

17. There is no wealth but life.
[*Unto this Last* (1862), 4]

18. But whether thus submissively or not, at least be sure that you go to the author to get at *his* meaning, not to find yours.
[*Sesame and Lilies* (1865), 'Of Kings' Treasuries']

19. Which of us ... is to do the hard and dirty work for the rest – and for what pay? Who is to do the pleasant and clean work, and for what pay?
[*Sesame and Lilies* (1865), 'Of Kings' Treasuries']

20. What do we, as a nation, care about books? How much do you think we spend altogether on our libraries, public or

private, as compared with what we spend on our horses?
[*Sesame and Lilies* (1865), 'Of Kings' Treasuries']

21. We call ourselves a rich nation, and we are filthy and foolish enough to thumb each other's books out of circulating libraries!
[*Sesame and Lilies* (1865), 'Of Kings' Treasuries']

22. How long most people would look at the best book before they would give the price of a large turbot for it!
[*Sesame and Lilies* (1865), 'Of Kings' Treasuries']

23. If a book is worth reading, it is worth buying.
[*Sesame and Lilies* (1865), 'Of Kings' Treasuries']

24. Labour without joy is base. Labour without sorrow is base. Sorrow without labour is base. Joy without labour is base.
[*Time and Tide by Weare and Tyne* (1867), Letter 5]

25. Your honesty is *not* to be based either on religion or policy. Both your religion and policy must be based on *it*. Your honesty must be based, as the sun is, in vacant heaven; poised, as the lights in the firmament, which have rule over the day and over the night.
[*Time and Tide by Weare and Tyne* (1867), Letter 8]

26. To make your children *capable of honesty* is the beginning of education.
[*Time and Tide by Weare and Tyne* (1867), Letter 8]

27 I hold it for indisputable, that the first duty of a State is to see that every child born therein shall be well housed, clothed, fed and educated, till it attain years of discretion.
[*Time and Tide by Weare and Tyne* (1867), Letter 13]

28. Life without industry is guilt, and industry without art is brutality.
[*Lectures on Art* (1870), 'The Relation of Art to Morals']

29. Thackeray settled like a meat-fly on whatever one had got for dinner, and made one sick of it.
[*Fors Clavigera* (1871–1884), Letter 31, 1873]

30. [Of one of Whistler's works]
I have seen, and heard, much of Cockney impudence before now; but never expected to hear a coxcomb ask two hundred guineas for flinging a pot of paint in the public's face.
[*Fors Clavigera* (1871–1884), Letter 79, 1877]

31. There was a rocky valley between Buxton and Bakewell, ... divine as the vale of Tempe; you might have seen the gods there morning and evening, – Apollo and the sweet Muses of the Light ... You enterprised a railroad, ... you blasted its rocks away ... And now, every fool in Buxton can be at Bakewell in half-an-hour, and every fool in Bakewell at Buxton.
[*Praeterita* (1889), III, 'Joanna's Cave']

32. There is really no such thing as bad weather, only different kinds of good weather.
[Attr.]

Russell, Bertrand (1872–1970)

English philosopher, logician, mathematician, controversialist, essayist and social reformer; Nobel prize for literature 1950

1. This method is, to define as the number of a class the class of all classes similar to the given class.
[*The Principles of Mathematics* (1903), II, 11]

2. Mathematics, rightly viewed, possesses not only truth, but supreme beauty – a beauty cold and austere, like that of sculpture.
[*Mysticism and Logic* (1918), 4]

3. Mathematics may be defined as the subject in which we never know what we are talking about, nor whether what we are saying is true.
[*Mysticism and Logic* (1918), 4]

4. Pure mathematics consists entirely of assertions to the effect that, if such and such a proposition is true of *anything*, then such and such another proposition is true of that thing. It is essential not to discuss whether the first proposition is really true, and not to mention what the anything is, of which it is supposed to be true.
[*Mysticism and Logic* (1918), 5]

5. Organic life, we are told, has developed gradually from the protozoon to the philosopher, and this development, we are assured, is indubitably an advance. Unfortunately it is the philosopher, not the protozoon, who gives us this assurance.
[*Mysticism and Logic* (1918), 6]

6. Brief and powerless is Man's life; on him and all his race the slow, sure doom falls pitiless and dark.
[*Mysticism and Logic* (1918), 'A Free Man's Worship']

7. No one gossips about other people's secret virtues.
[*On Education, especially in early childhood* (1926)]

8. Matter ... a convenient formula for describing what happens where it isn't.
[*An Outline of Philosophy* (1927)]

9. It is undesirable to believe a proposition when there is no ground whatever for supposing it true.
[*Sceptical Essays* (1928), 'On the Value of Scepticism']

10. Every man, wherever he goes, is encompassed by a cloud of comforting convictions, which move with him like flies on a summer day.
[*Sceptical Essays* (1928), 'Dreams and Facts']

11. Machines are worshipped because they are beautiful, and valued because they confer power; they are hated because they are hideous, and loathed because they impose slavery.
[*Sceptical Essays* (1928), 'Machines and Emotions']

12. We have, in fact, two kinds of morality side by side: one which we preach but do not practise, and another which we practise but seldom preach.
[*Sceptical Essays* (1928), 'Eastern and Western Ideals of Happiness']

13. America ... where law and custom alike are based upon the dreams of spinsters.
[*Marriage and Morals* (1929)]

14. Of all forms of caution, caution in love is perhaps the most fatal to true happiness.
[*Marriage and Morals* (1929)]

15. The megalomaniac differs from the narcissist by the fact that he wishes to be powerful rather than charming, and seeks to be feared rather than loved. To this type belong many lunatics and most of the great men of history.
[*The Conquest of Happiness* (1930)]

16. There are two motives for reading a book: one, that you enjoy it, the other that you can boast about it.
[*The Conquest of Happiness* (1930)]

17. Drunkenness is temporary suicide: the happiness that it brings is merely negative, a momentary cessation of unhappiness.
[*The Conquest of Happiness* (1930)]

18. Man is not a solitary animal, and so long as social life survives, self-realization cannot be the supreme principle of ethics.
[*A History of Western Philosophy* (1946), 'The Romantic Movement']

19. In America everybody is of the opinion that he has no social superiors, since all men are equal, but he does not admit that he has no social inferiors.
[*Unpopular Essays* (1950), 'Ideas that have harmed mankind']

20. Aristotle maintained that women have fewer teeth than men; although he was twice married, it never occurred to him to verify this statement by examining his wives' mouths.
[*The Impact of Science upon Society* (1952), 1]

21. ... the nuns who never take a bath without wearing a bathrobe all the time. When asked why, since no man can see them, the reply 'Oh, but you forget the good God.'
[*The Basic Writings of Bertrand Russell* (1961), II, 7]

22. Three passions, simple but overwhelmingly strong, have governed my life: the longing for love, the search for knowledge, and unbearable pity for the suffering of mankind.
[*The Autobiography of Bertrand Russell* (1967–1969), Prologue]

23. I was told that the Chinese say they would bury me by the Western Lake and build a shrine to my memory. I have some slight regret that this did not happen, as I might have become a god, which would have been very *chic* for an atheist.
[*The Autobiography of Bertrand Russell* (1967–1969)]

24. I have never but once succeeded in making [G.E. Moore] tell a lie, that was by a subterfuge. 'Moore,' I said, 'do you *always* speak the truth?' 'No,' he replied. I believe this to be the only lie he had ever told.
[*The Autobiography of Bertrand Russell* (1967–1969)]

25. The collection of prejudices which is called political philosophy is useful provided that it is not called philosophy.
[*The Observer*, 'Sayings of the Year', 1962]

26. People don't seem to realize that it takes time and effort and preparation to think. Statesmen are far too busy making speeches to think.
[In Kenneth Harris, *Kenneth Harris Talking To:* (1971), 'Bertrand Russell']

27. There's a Bible on that shelf there. But I keep it next to Voltaire – poison and antidote.
[In Kenneth Harris, *Kenneth Harris Talking To:* (1971), 'Bertrand Russell']

28. [On the possibility of nuclear war between the USA and the USSR]
You may reasonably expect a man to walk a tightrope safely for ten minutes; it would be unreasonable to do so without accident for two hundred years.
[In Desmond Bagley, *The Tightrope Men* (1973)]

29. Many people would sooner die than think. In fact they do.
[In Anthony Flew, *Thinking about Thinking* (1975)]

30. [Of Anthony Eden]
Not a gentleman; dresses too well.
[In Alistair Cooke, *Six Men* (1977)]

31. One of the symptoms of approaching nervous breakdowns is the belief that one's work is terribly important. If I were a medical man, I should prescribe a holiday to any patient who considered his work important.
[Attr.]

32. Few people can be happy unless they hate some other person, nation or creed.
[Attr.]

33. Patriots always talk of dying for their country, and never of killing for their country.
[Attr.]

34. [On being asked if he would be willing to die for his beliefs]
Of course not. After all, I may be wrong.
[Attr.]

35. Every time I talk to a savant I feel quite sure that happiness is no longer a possibility. Yet when I talk to my gardener, I'm convinced of the opposite.
[Attr.]

Russell, George William (1867–1935)
Irish poet; painter, editor, journalist and writer on economics

1. In ancient shadows and twilights
Where childhood had strayed
The worlds great sorrows were born
And its heroes were made.
In the lost boyhood of Judas
Christ was betrayed.
[*Vale and Other Poems* (1931), Germinal]

Russell, John [1] (1919–)
British art critic

1. Certain phrases stick in the throat, even if they offer nothing that is analytically improbable. 'A dashing Swiss officer' is one such.
[*Paris* (1960), 11]

Russell, Lord John [2] (1792–1878)
English statesman, associated with 1832 reform act; Liberal Prime Minister 1846–52, 1865–66, and writer

1. [After the Reform Bill was rejected in the House of Lords]
It is impossible that the whisper of a faction should prevail against the voice of a nation.
[Letter to T. Attwood, 1831]

2. If peace cannot be maintained with honour, it is no longer peace.
[Speech, 1853]

3. Among the defects of the Bill, which were numerous, one provision was conspicuous by its presence and another by its absence.
[Speech, 1859]

4. A proverb is one man's wit and all men's wisdom.
[In R.J. Mackintosh, *Sir James Mackintosh* (1835)]

5. [When asked to describe a suitable punishment for bigamy]
Two mothers-in-law.
[Attr.]

Russell, Sir William Howard (1820–1907)
Irish war correspondent and travel writer

1. [Of the Russian charge on the 93rd Highlanders at the Battle of Balaclava]
They dashed on towards that thin red line tipped with steel.
[*The British Expedition to the Crimea* (1877)]

Rutherford, Ernest (First Baron Rutherford of Nelson) (1871–1937)
New Zealand-born British physicist, noted for his atomic research; Nobel prize for chemistry 1908

1. We haven't the money, so we've got to think!
[In *Bulletin of the Institute of Physics*, 1962]

2. [Joking about the atom's enormous potential energy]
Some fool in a laboratory might blow up the universe unawares.
[In Mark Oliphant, *Rutherford Recollections of the Cambridge Days* (1972)]

3. [On bureaucrats and scientists]
It is essential for men of science to take an interest in the administration of their own affairs or else the professional civil servant will step in – and then the Lord help you.
[In Alan L. Mackay (ed.), *The Harvest of a Quiet Eye* (1977)]

Rutskoi, Alexander (1947–)
Russian politician

1. The dollar is Russia's national currency now, the rouble is just a sweetie paper. We've handed our sword to America.
[*Newsweek*, 1994]

Ryle, Gilbert (1900–1976)
English metaphysical philosopher

1. A myth is, of course, not a fairy story. It is the presentation of facts belonging to one category in the idioms appropriate to another. To explode a myth is accordingly not to deny the facts but to re-allocate them.
[*The Concept of Mind* (1949), Introduction]

2. Philosophy is the replacement of category-habits by category-disciplines.
[*The Concept of Mind* (1949), Introduction]

3. The dogma of the Ghost in the Machine.
[*The Concept of Mind* (1949), 1]

Sabatini, Rafael (1875–1950)
Italian-born English novelist

1. Born with the gift of laughter and a sense that the world was mad.
[*Scaramouche*, film, 1921; scriptwriter Ronald Miller]

Sabia, Laura
Canadian journalist and feminist

1. I'm a Roman Catholic and I take a dim view of 2,500 celibates shuffling back and forth to Rome to discuss birth control and not one woman to raise a voice.
[*The Toronto Star*, 1975]

Sackville-West, Vita (Victoria) (1892–1962)
English novelist, poet and biographer; writer on travel and gardening

1. Travel is the most private of pleasures. There is no greater bore than the travel bore. We do not in the least want to hear what he has seen in Hong Kong.
[*Passenger to Tehran* (1926), 1]

2. Those who have never dwelt in tents have no idea either of the charm or of the discomfort of a nomadic existence. The charm is purely romantic, and consequently very soon proves to be fallacious.
[*Twelve Days* (1928), 6]

3. The greater cats with golden eyes
Stare out between the bars.
Deserts are there, and different skies,
And night with different stars.
[*The King's Daughter* (1929), II, 1]

Sade, Donatien Alphonse François, Marquis de (1740–1814)
French soldier and novelist, known for his sexually explicit writing; imprisoned for sexual offences

1. All universal moral principles are idle fancies.
[*The 120 Days of Sodom* (1784)]

2. *La tolérance est la vertu du faible.*
Tolerance is the virtue of the weak.
[*La nouvelle Justine* (1797)]

3. *Il n'y a d'autre enfer pour l'homme que la bêtise ou la méchanceté de ses semblables.*
There is no other hell for man than the stupidity and wickedness of his own kind.
[*Histoire de Juliette* (1797)]

Sadleir, Michael (1888–1957)
English publisher and book collector; author of bibliographical and biographical works

1. Fanny by Gaslight.
[Title of book, 1940]

Sagan, Françoise (1935–)
French novelist

1. *Quel mur s'impose donc toujours entre les êtres humains et leur désir le plus intime, leur effroyable volonté de bonheur? ... Est-ce une nostalgie cultivée depuis l'enfance?*
What is that wall that always rises up between human beings and their most intimate desire, their frightening will to be happy? ... Is it a nostalgia nurtured from childhood?
[*Le Garde du coeur* (1968), 9]

2. Every little girl knows about love. It is only her capacity to suffer because of it that increases.
[*Daily Express*]

Sahl, Mort (1927–)
American comedian, born in Canada

1. Washington could not tell a lie; Nixon could not tell the truth; Reagan cannot tell the difference.
[*The Observer*, 1987, in Jeffrey Care (ed.), *Sayings of the Eighties* (1989)]

2. [Of President Nixon]
Would you buy a second-hand car from this man?
[Attr.]

Saikaku, Ihara (1642–1693)
Japanese novelist, satirist and poet, noted for his haiku

1. Marrying off your daughter is a piece of business you may expect to do only once in a lifetime, and, bearing in mind that none of the losses are recoverable later, you should approach the matter with extreme caution.
[*The Japanese Family Storehouse* (1688)]

2. And why do people wilfully exhaust their strength in promiscuous living, when their wives are on hand from bridal night till old age – to be taken when required, like fish from a private pond.
[*The Japanese Family Storehouse* (1688)]

Sainte-Beuve, Charles-Augustin (1804–1869)
French literary critic; essayist and poet

1. *Du déclin de l'automne, il est souvent des jours*
Où l'année, on dirait, va se tromper de cours.
As autumn comes to an end, there is often a day
When the year, so it seems, is going to lose its way.
[*Poésies* (1840)]

2. [On the habit of literary men and politicians of constantly improvising and expressing their thoughts in public]
Les pensées nées devant tous sont comme ces beautés qui passent leur vie dans les bals ... elles n'ont pas de teint. Tâchez que les pensées en se produisant aient leur rougeur naturelle, c'est la vraie couleur.
Thoughts which are born in front of everyone are like beautiful women who spend their lives at balls ... they have no colouring. Try to produce thoughts which have their natural colour, their true colour, which is red.
[*Cahiers* (*Notebooks*, 1834–1847), I, 'Le cahier vert']

3. *Une des plus vraies satisfactions de l'homme, c'est quand la femme qu'il a passionément désirée et qui s'est refusée opiniâtrement à lui cesse d'être belle.*
One of the greatest satisfactions for a man is when the woman he passionately desired and who obstinately refused to give herself to him ceases to be beautiful.
[*Cahiers* (*Notebooks*, 1834–1847), I, 'Le cahier vert']

Saint-Exupéry, Antoine de (1900–1944)
French novelist, prose writer and aviator

1. *L'expérience nous montre qu'aimer ce n'est point nous regarder l'un l'autre mais regarder ensemble dans la même direction.*
Experience shows us that love is not looking into one another's eyes but looking together in the same direction.
[*Terre des Hommes* (*Wind, Sand and Stars*, 1939)]

2. *C'est tellement mystérieux, le pays des larmes.*
It is such a mysterious place, the land of tears.
[*Le Petit Prince* (*The Little Prince*, 1943)]

3. *On ne voit bien qu'avec le coeur. Les choses importantes sont invisibles à l'oeil nu.*
It is only with the heart that one can see clearly. The important things are invisible to the naked eye.
[*Le Petit Prince* (*The Little Prince*, 1943)]

Saint-Lambert, Jean François, Marquis de (1716–1803)
French poet and encyclopaedist

1. *Souvent j'écoute encor quand le chant a cessé.*
Often I am still listening when the song has ended.
[*Les Saisons*, 'Le Printemps']

St Leger, Warham (1850–c. 1915)

1. There is a fine stuffed chavender,
A chavender, or chub,
That decks the rural pavender,
The pavender, or pub,
Wherein I eat my gravender,
My gravender, or grub.
['The Chavender, or Chub']

Saint-Pierre, Bernardin de (1737–1814)
French writer, influenced by Rousseau

1. *Les femmes sont fausses dans les pays où les hommes sont des tyrans. Partout la violence produit la ruse.*
Women are false in countries where men are tyrants. Violence everywhere leads to deception.
[*Paul et Virginie* (1788)]

Saintsbury, George Edward Bateman (1845–1933)
English literary critic and historian, professor

1. [From an examination paper]
Without remarking that the thing became a trumpet in his hands, say something relevant about Milton's sonnets.
[In Stephen Potter, *The Muse in Chains* (1937)]

2. It is the unbroken testimony of all history that alcoholic liquors have been used by the strongest, wisest, handsomest, and in every way best races of all times.
[Attr.]

Saki (Hector Hugh Munro) (1870–1916)
Burmese-born British journalist, novelist and writer of humorous and macabre short stories

1. People may say what they like about the decay of Christianity; the religious system that produced green Chartreuse can never really die.
[*Reginald* (1904), 'Reginald on Christmas Presents']

2. I always say beauty is only sin deep.
[*Reginald* (1904), 'Reginald's Choir Treat']

3. I think she must have been very strictly brought up, she's so desperately anxious to do the wrong thing correctly.
[*Reginald* (1904), 'Reginald on Worries']

4. Even the Hooligan was probably invented in China centuries before we thought of him.
[*Reginald* (1904), 'Reginald on House-Parties']

5. The young have aspirations that never come to pass, the old have reminiscences of what never happened. It's only the middle-aged who are really conscious of their limitations.
[*Reginald* (1904), 'Reginald at the Carlton']

6. There may have been disillusionments in the lives of the mediaeval saints, but they would scarcely have been better pleased if they could have foreseen that their names would be associated nowadays chiefly with racehorses and the cheaper clarets.
[*Reginald* (1904), 'Reginald at the Carlton']

7. The cook was a good cook, as cooks go; and as cooks go she went.
[*Reginald* (1904), 'Reginald on Besetting Sins']

8. Women and elephants never forget an injury.
[*Reginald* (1904), 'Reginald on Besetting Sins']

9. The Western custom of one wife and hardly any mistresses.
[*Reginald in Russia* (1910), 'A Young Turkish Catastrophe']

10. But, good gracious, you've got to educate him first. You can't expect a boy to be vicious till he's been to a good school.
[*Reginald in Russia* (1910), 'The Baker's Dozen']

11. He's simply got the instinct for being unhappy highly developed.
[*The Chronicles of Clovis* (1911), 'The Match-Maker']

12. All decent people live beyond their incomes nowadays, and those who aren't respectable live beyond other people's. A few gifted individuals manage to do both.
[*The Chronicles of Clovis* (1911), 'The Match-Maker']

13. His shoes exhaled the right *soupçon* of harness-room; his socks compelled one's attention without losing one's respect.
[*The Chronicles of Clovis* (1911), 'Ministers of Grace']

14. By insisting on having your bottle pointing to the north when the cork is being drawn, and calling the waiter Max, you may induce an impression on your guests which hours of laboured boasting might be powerless to achieve. For this purpose, however, the guests must be chosen as carefully as the wine.
[*The Chronicles of Clovis* (1911), 'The Chaplet']

15. There are so many things to complain of in this household that it would never have occurred to me to complain of rheumatism.
[*The Chronicles of Clovis* (1911), 'The Quest']

16. A woman whose dresses are made in Paris and whose marriage has been made in heaven might be equally biased for and against free imports.
[*The Unbearable Bassington* (1912), 9]

17. Sherard Blaw, the dramatist who had discovered himself, and who had given so ungrudgingly of his discovery to the world.
[*The Unbearable Bassington* (1912), 13]

18. Romance at short notice was her speciality.
[*Beasts and Super-Beasts* (1914), 'The Open Window']

19. 'The man is a common murderer.'
'A common murderer, possibly, but a very uncommon cook.'
[*Beasts and Super-Beasts* (1914), 'The Blind Spot']

20. When she inveighed eloquently against the evils of capitalism at drawing-room meetings and Fabian conferences she was conscious of a comfortable feeling that the system, with all its inequalities and iniquities, would probably last her time. It is one of the consolations of middle-aged reformers that the good they inculcate must live after them if it is to live at all.
[*Beasts and Super-Beasts* (1914), 'The Byzantine Omelette']

21. Waldo is one of those people who would be enormously improved by death.
[*Beasts and Super-Beasts* (1914), 'The Feast of Nemesis']

22. 'I believe I take precedence,' he said coldly; 'you are merely the club Bore; I am the club Liar.'
[*Beasts and Super-Beasts* (1914), 'A Defensive Diamond']

23. Children with Hyacinth's temperament don't know better as they grow older; they merely know more.
[*The Toys of Peace* (1919), 'Hyacinth']

24. A little inaccuracy sometimes saves tons of explanation.
[*The Square Egg* (1924), 'Clovis on the Alleged Romance of Business']

25. In baiting a mouse-trap with cheese, always leave room for the mouse.
[*The Square Egg* (1924), 'The Infernal Parliament']

Salinger, J.D. (1919–)
American novelist and short-story writer

1. If you really want to hear about it, the first thing you'll probably want to know is where I was born and what my lousy childhood was like, and how my parents were occupied and all before they had me, and all that David Copperfield kind of crap.
[*The Catcher in the Rye* (1951), opening words]

2. Sex is something I really don't understand too hot. You never know *where* the hell you are. I keep making up these sex rules for myself, and then I break them right away.
[*The Catcher in the Rye* (1951), 9]

3. They didn't act like people and they didn't act like actors. It's hard to explain. They acted more like they knew they were celebrities and all. I mean they were good, but they were *too* good.
[*The Catcher in the Rye* (1951), 17]

4. What I have to do, I have to catch everybody if they start to go over the cliff – I mean if they're running and they don't look where they're going I have to come out from somewhere and *catch* them ... I'd just be the catcher in the rye and all.
[*The Catcher in the Rye* (1951), 22]

Salisbury, Lord (Robert Cecil, Third Marquess of Salisbury) (1830–1903)
English statesman, known for his foreign policy; Conservative Prime Minister 1885–86, 1886–92, 1895–1902

1. No lesson seems to be so deeply inculcated by the experience of life as that you never should trust experts. If you believe the doctors, nothing is wholesome: if you believe the theologians, nothing is innocent: if you believe the soldiers, nothing is safe. They all require to have their strong wine diluted by a very large admixture of insipid common sense.
[Letter to Lord Lytton, 1877]

2. We are part of the community of Europe and we must do our duty as such.
[Speech, 1888]

3. Our first duty is towards the people of this country, to maintain their interests and their rights; our second duty is to all humanity.
[Speech, 1896]

4. [Of the *Daily Mail*]
By office boys for office boys.
[In Fyfe, *Northcliffe, an Intimate Biography* (1930), 4]

Salk, Jonas E. (1914–)
American virologist; developed a poliomyelitis vaccine in 1954

1. [On being asked who owned the patent on his antipolio vaccine]
The people – could you patent the sun?
[Attr.]

Sallust (Gaius Sallustius Crispus) (86–c. 34 BC)
Roman historian and statesman

1. *Alieni appetens, sui profusus.*
Covetous of others' possessions, prodigal of his own.
[*Catiline*, 5, 4]

2. *Idem velle atque idem nolle, ea demum firma amicitia est.*
To like and dislike the same things, this in the end is the basis of true friendship.
[*Catiline*, 20, 4]

3. *Quieta movere magna merces videbatur.*
Just to disturb the peace seemed a great reward in itself.
[*Catiline*, 21, 1]

4. *Psallere et saltare elegantius, quam necesse est probae.*
To play the lyre and dance more beautifully than a virtuous woman need.
[*Catiline*, 25, 2]

5. [Of Cato]
Esse quam videri bonus malebat.
He preferred to be rather than to seem good.
[*Catiline*, 54, 6]

6. *Se pro patria, pro liberis, pro aris atque focis suis certare.*
To fight for their country, children, altars, and hearths.
[*Catiline*, 59, 5]

7. *Dux atque imperator vitae mortalium animus est.*
The mind is the guide and ruler of men's lives.
[*Jugurtha*, 1]

8. *Omne bellum sumi facile, ceterum aegerrime desinere, non in ejusdem potestate initium ejus et finem esse.*
Every war is easy to begin but difficult to stop; its beginning and end are not in the control of the same person.
[*Jugurtha*, 83]

9. *Punica fide.*
With Punic faith [i.e. treachery].
[*Jugurtha*, 108]

Salmon, George (1819–1904)
Provost of Trinity College, Dublin

1. [Remark at the unveiling of a portrait of a colleague]
Excellent, excellent, you can just hear the lies trickling out of his mouth.
[Attr.]

2. [On hearing a colleague claiming to have been caned only once in his life, and that, for telling the truth]
Well, it certainly cured you, Mahaffy.
[Attr.]

Salvandy, Narcisse Achille (1795–1856)
French statesman, man of letters and soldier

1. *Nous dansons sur un volcan.*
We are dancing on a volcano.
[Remark made before July Revolution, 1830]

Sampson, Anthony (1926–)
British writer and journalist

1. [Of the Civil Service]
Members rise from CMG (known sometimes in Whitehall as 'Call Me God') to the KCMG ('Kindly Call Me God') to . . . the GCMG ('God Calls Me God').
[*The Anatomy of Britain* (1962), 18]

Samuel, Herbert (First Viscount Samuel) (1870–1963)
English Liberal statesman; Home Secretary 1916, 1932–33; philosopher and administrator

1. Without doubt the greatest injury of all was done by basing morals on myth. For, sooner or later, myth is recognized for what it is, and disappears. Then morality loses the foundation on which it has been built.
[Romanes Lecture, 1947]

2. To help the unemployed is not the same thing as dealing with unemployment.
[*The Observer*, 'Sayings of the Week', 1933]

3. Hansard is history's ear, already listening.
[*The Observer*, 'Sayings of the Week', 1949]

4. A library is thought in cold storage.
[*A Book of Quotations* (1947)]

5. It takes two to make a marriage a success and only one a failure.
[*A Book of Quotations* (1947)]

6. [Referring to the Civil Service]
A difficulty for every solution.
[Attr.]

Sand, George (Aurore Dupin) (1804–1876)
French novelist, dramatist, autobiographical and letter writer

1. *L'art n'est pas une étude de la réalité positive; c'est une recherche de la vérité idéale.*
Art is not a study of positive reality; it is a search for ideal truth.
[*La Mare au diable* (*The Devil's Pond*, 1846), I]

2. *Il faut s'avouer impuissant devant cette fatalité politique d'un nouvel ordre dans l'histoire:* le suffrage universel.
One must admit one is powerless in the face of the political inevitability of this new order in history: *universal suffrage.*
[Letter to Joseph Mazzini, 1848]

3. *Le vrai est trop simple, il faut y arriver toujours par le compliqué.*
The truth is too simple, it must always be arrived at through complication.
[Letter to Armand Barbès, 1867]

Sandburg, Carl (1878–1967)
American poet, noted for his free verse; journalist, song collector and biographer of Lincoln

1. The fog comes
on little cat feet.

It sits looking
over harbor and city
on silent haunches
and then moves on.
[*Chicago Poems* (1916), 'Fog']

2. Pile the bodies high at Austerlitz and Waterloo.
Shovel them under and let me work–
I am the grass; I cover all.
[*Cornhuskers* (1918), 'Grass']

3. The people will live on.
The learning and blundering people will live on.
[*The People, Yes* (1936), 107]

Sanger, Margaret (1879–1966)
American social reformer

1. No woman can call herself free who does not own and control her own body.
[In Rosalind Miles, *The Women's History of the World* (1988)]

Santayana, George (1863–1952)
Spanish-born American philosopher, poet, critic and novelist

1. Fanaticism consists in redoubling your effort when you have forgotten your aim.
[*The Life of Reason* (1905–1906), I, Introduction]

2. Those who cannot remember the past are condemned to repeat it.
[*The Life of Reason* (1905–1906), I, 12]

3. Music is essentially useless, as life is: but both have an ideal extension which lends utility to its conditions.
[*The Life of Reason* (1905–1906), IV, 4]

4. Nothing is really so poor and melancholy as art that is interested in itself and not in its subject.
[*The Life of Reason* (1905–1906), IV, 8]

5. For an idea ever to be fashionable is ominous, since it must afterwards be always old-fashioned.
[*Winds of Doctrine* (1913), 'Modernism and Christianity']

6. To be interested in the changing seasons is, in this middling zone, a happier state of mind than to be hopelessly in love with spring.
[*Little Essays* (1920)]

7. There is no cure for birth and death save to enjoy the interval.
[*Soliloquies in England* (1922), 'War Shrines']

8. It is a great advantage for a system of philosophy to be substantially true.
[*The Unknowable* (1923)]

9. The young man who has not wept is a savage, and the old man who will not laugh is a fool.
[*Dialogues in Limbo* (1925), 3]

10. The working of great institutions is mainly the result of a vast mass of routine, petty malice, self interest, carelessness, and sheer mistake. Only a residual fraction is thought.
[*The Crime of Galileo*]

11. The Bible is literature, not dogma.
[Introduction to Spinoza's *Ethics*]

12. If all the arts aspire to the condition of music, all the sciences aspire to the condition of mathematics.
[*The Observer*, 'Sayings of the Week', 1928]

13. [On being asked why he always travelled third class]
Because there's no fourth class.
[In H. Thomas, *Living Biographies of the Great Philosophers*]

14. Life is not a spectacle or a feast; it is a predicament.
[In Sagittarius and George, *The Perpetual Pessimist*]

Sappho (fl. 7th–6th centuries BC)
Greek lyric poet, known for her love poetry

1. He seems equal to the gods to me,
the man who sits opposite you
and closely listens to you talking sweetly

and your lovely laugh – this excites the heart
in my breast, for when I see you fleetingly
my voice fails me

instead, my tongue is frozen, instantly
a gentle fire flickers under my skin,
my eyes see nothing, I hear throbbing,

a sweat runs down me, a trembling
seizes my whole person, I am paler than grass,
and I feel not far from death.
[In D.L. Page (ed.), *Lyrica Selecta Graeca* (1968)]

2. [Of a girl before her marriage]
Just as the sweet-apple reddens on the high branch, on the top of the topmost bough, and the apple-pickers missed it, or rather did not miss it altogether, but could not reach it.
[In D.L. Page (ed.), *Lyrica Selecta Graeca* (1968)]

3. Beauty endures for only as long as it can be seen; goodness, beautiful today, will remain so tomorrow.
[In Naim Attallah, *Women* (1987)]

Sarasate (y Navascués) Pablo (1844–1908)
Spanish violinist and composer

1. [On being hailed as a genius by a critic]
A genius! For thirty-seven years I've practised fourteen hours a day, and now they call me a genius!
[Attr.]

Sargent, Epes (1813–1880)
American writer

1. A life on the ocean wave,
A home on the rolling deep.
['A Life on the Ocean Wave', song, 1838]

Sargent, John Singer (1856–1925)
American painter, born in Florence; noted for his society portraits

1. Every time I paint a portrait I lose a friend.
[In N. Bentley and E. Esar, *Treasury of Humorous Quotations* (1951)]

Sargent, Sir Malcolm (1895–1967)
English conductor

1. [Rehearsing a female chorus in 'For Unto Us a Child is Born' from Handel's *Messiah*]
Just a little more reverence, please, and not so much astonishment.
[Attr.]

Sargeson, Frank (1903–1982)
New Zealand short-story writer, novelist and critic

1. [A childhood memory of the Northland coast]
It was my first beach picnic (and the best of all my years). The flames of the driftwood fire were very hot, yet because of the bright sunlight they were no-colour, barely to be seen: potatoes in their jackets were cooked in sea-water, oysters were eaten raw from the shell, and mussels were put into embers from the fire until they opened.
[*Never Enough! Places and People Mainly* (1977)]

2. [A notice to callers, said to be on his house door]
Frank Sargeson works in the mornings. Do you?
[*Islands*, 1978, 'A Sort of Poet Too']

Saroyan, William (1908–1981)
American short-story writer, dramatist and novelist

1. [Last words]
Everybody has got to die, but I have always believed an exception would be made in my case. Now what?
[*Time*, 1984]

Sarton, May (1912–)
American poet, novelist and essayist

1. Loneliness is the poverty of self; solitude is the richness of self.
[*Mrs Stevens Hears the Mermaids Singing* (1993)]

2. Old age is not an illness, it is a timeless ascent. As power diminishes, we grow toward the light.
[*Ms* magazine, 1982]

Sartre, Jean-Paul (1905–1980)
French existentialist, philosopher, novelist, dramatist, critic and left-wing intellectual; declined Nobel prize 1964; companion of Simone de Beauvoir

1. *Les choses sont tout entières ce qu'elles paraissent* – et derrière elles *... il n'y a rien.*
Things are entirely what they appear to be and *behind them* ... there is nothing.
[*La Nausée* (*Nausea*, 1938)]

2. *Ma pensée, c'est moi: voilà pourquoi je ne peux pas m'arrêter. J'existe par ce que je pense ... et je ne peux pas m'empêcher de penser.*
My thought is *me*: that is why I cannot stop. I exist by what I think ... and I can't prevent myself from thinking.
[*La Nausée* (*Nausea*, 1938)]

3. *Je sais très bien que je ne veux rien faire: faire quelque chose, c'est créer de l'existence – et il y a bien assez d'existence comme ça.*
I know perfectly well that I don't want to do anything; to do something is to create existence – and there is quite enough existence as it is.
[*La Nausée* (*Nausea*, 1938)]

4. *On ne peut vaincre le mal que par un autre mal.*
One can only overcome evil by means of another evil.
[*Les Mouches* (*The Flies*, 1943)]

5. *Quand une fois la liberté a explosé dans une âme d'homme, les Dieux ne peuvent plus rien contre lui.*
Once freedom has exploded in the soul of a man, the gods have no more power over him.
[*Les Mouches* (*The Flies*, 1943)]

6. *Alors, c'est ça l'enfer. Je n'aurais jamais cru ... Vous vous rappelez: le soufre, le bûcher, le gril ... Ah! quelle plaisanterie. Pas besoin de gril, l'enfer, c'est les Autres.*
So that's what Hell is. I'd never have believed it ... Do you remember, brimstone, the stake, the gridiron? ... What a joke! No need of a gridiron, Hell is other people.
[*Huis Clos* (*In Camera*, 1944)]

7. *Ainsi, il n'y a pas de nature humaine, puisqu'il n'y a pas de Dieu pour la concevoir.*
So there is no human nature, since there is no God to conceive it.
[*L'Existentialisme est un humanisme* (*Existentialism and Humanism*, 1946)]

8. *L'absence c'est Dieu. Dieu, c'est la solitude des hommes.*
God is absence. God is the solitude of man.
[*Le Diable et le Bon Dieu* (1951)]

9. *Je déteste les victimes quand elles respectent leurs bourreaux.*
I hate victims who respect their executioners.
[*Les Séquestrés d'Altona* (1960), I.i]

10. *Elle ne croyait à rien; seul, son scepticisme l'empêchait d'être athée.*
She didn't believe in anything; only her scepticism kept her from being an atheist.
[*Les Mots* (*Words*, 1964), 'Lire']

11. *Il est toujours facile d'obéir, si l'on rêve de commander.*
It is always easy to obey, if one dreams of being in command.
[*Situations*, I]

12. *Le monde peut fort bien se passer de la littérature. Mais il peut se passer de l'homme encore mieux.*
The world can survive very well without literature. But it can survive even more easily without man.
[*Situations*, II]

Sassoon, Siegfried (1886–1967)

English poet, novelist and autobiographical writer, noted for his anti-war poems

1. Safe with his wound, a citizen of life,
He hobbled blithely through the garden gate,
And thought: 'Thank God they had to amputate!'
['The One-Legged Man' (1916)]

2. I'd like to see a Tank come down the stalls,
Lurching to rag-time tunes, or 'Home, sweet Home,'–
And there'd be no more jokes in Music-halls
To mock the riddled corpses round Bapaume.
['Blighters' (1917)]

3. The place was rotten with dead: green clumsy legs
High-booted, sprawled and grovelled along the saps
And trunks, face downward, in the sucking mud
Wallowed like trodden sandbags loosely filled;
And naked sodden buttocks, mats of hair,
Bulged, clotted heads slept in the plastering slime.
And then the rain began – the jolly old rain!
['Counter-Attack' (1917)]

4. If I were fierce and bald and short of breath,
I'd live with scarlet Majors at the Base,
And speed glum heroes up the line to death...

5. And when the war is done and youth stone dead
I'd toddle safely home and die – in bed.
['Base Details' (1917)]

6. Does it matter? – losing your legs?...
For people will always be kind,
And you need not show that you mind
When others come in after hunting
To gobble their muffins and eggs.

Does it matter? – losing your sight?...
There's such splendid work for the blind;
And people will always be kind,
As you sit on the terrace remembering
And turning your face to the light.
['Does it Matter?' (1917)]

7. Soldiers are citizens of death's gray land,
Drawing no dividend from time's tomorrows...

8. Soldiers are dreamers; when the guns begin
They think of firelit homes, clean beds, and wives.
I see them in foul dug-outs, gnawed by rats,
And in the ruined trenches, lashed with rain,
Dreaming of things they did with balls and bats.
['Dreamers' (1917)]

9. 'Good morning; good morning!' the general said
When we met him last week on our way to the line.
Now the soldiers he smiled at are most of 'em dead,
And we're cursing his staff for incompetent swine.
'He's a cheery old card,' grunted Harry to Jack
As they slogged up to Arras with rifle and pack...

But he did for them both with his plan of attack.
['The General' (1917)]

10. Why do you lie with your legs ungainly huddled,
And one arm bent across your sullen, cold
Exhausted face?...

11. You are too young to fall asleep for ever;
And when you sleep you remind me of the dead.
['The Dug-Out' (1918)]

12. Everyone suddenly burst out singing;
And I was filled with such delight
As prisoned birds must find in freedom
Winging wildly across the white
Orchards and dark green fields; on – on – and out of sight.
['Everyone Sang' (1919)]

13. They have spoken lightly of my deathless friends,
(Lamps for my gloom, hands guiding where I stumble),
Quoting, for shallow conversational ends,
What Shelley shrilled, what Blake once wildly muttered...

14. How can they use such names and not be humble?
I have sat silent; angry at what they uttered.
The dead bequeathed them life; the dead have said
What these can only memorize and mumble.
['Grandeur of Ghosts' (1928)]

15. In me the tiger sniffs the rose.
[*The Heart's Journey* (1928), VIII]

16. *Alone* ... The word is life endured and known.
It is the stillness where our spirits walk
And all but inmost faith is overthrown.
[*The Heart's Journey* (1928), XI]

17. Here sleeps the Silurist; the loved physician;
The face that left no portraiture behind;
The skull that housed white angels and had vision
Of daybreak through the gateways of the mind.
[*The Heart's Journey* (1928), XXIII, 'At the Grave of Henry Vaughan']

18. Stumbling along the trench in the dusk, dead men and living lying against the sides of the trenches – one never knew which

were dead and which living. Dead and living were nearly one, for death was in all our hearts.
[*Diary*, April 1917]

19. The simplicity that I see in some of the men is the one candle in my darkness. The one flower in all this arid sunshine.
[*Diary*, April 1918]

20. Man, it seemed, had been created to jab the life out of Germans.
[*Memoirs of an Infantry Officer* (1930), I, 1]

21. [From the statement sent to his commanding officer, 6 July 1917]
I am making this statement as an act of wilful defiance of military authority, because I believe that the War is being deliberately prolonged by those who have the power to end it ... I have seen and endured the sufferings of the troops, and I can no longer be a party to prolong these sufferings for ends which I believe to be evil and unjust.
[*Memoirs of an Infantry Officer* (1930), X, 5]

Satie, Erik (1866–1925)
French experimental composer

1. *Mon médecin m'a toujours dit de fumer. Il ajoute à ses conseils: 'Fumez, mon ami: sans cela, un autre fumera à votre place.'*
My doctor has always told me to smoke. He explains himself thus: 'Smoke, my friend. If you don't, someone else will smoke in your place.'
[*Mémoires d'un amnésique* (1924)]

2. When I was young, I was told: 'You'll see, when you're fifty.' I am fifty and I haven't seen a thing.
[In Pierre-Daniel Templier, *Erik Satie*, 2, Letter to his brother]

3. [Direction on one of his piano pieces]
To be played with both hands in the pocket.
[Attr.]

Saunders, Ernest (1935–)
British businessman and company director; jailed for his role in the Guinness takeover scandal

1. I was on a basic £100,000 a year. You don't make many savings on that.
[*The Observer*, 1987, in Jeffrey Care (ed.), *Sayings of the Eighties* (1989)]

Savage, Michael Joseph (1872–1940)
New Zealand statesman and Prime Minister

1. [When asked to restrain Hon. P.C. Webb's amorous affairs]
Have you ever tried to lasso a kangaroo?
[In Barry Gustafson, *From the Cradle to the Grave* (1986)]

Sayers, Dorothy L. (1893–1957)
English novelist, noted for her detective stories; dramatist, essayist and translator of Dante

1. I admit it is better fun to punt than to be punted, and that a desire to have all the fun is nine-tenths of the law of chivalry.
[*Gaudy Night* (1935), 14]

2. My impression is that I was thinking about writing a detective story, and that he walked in, complete with spats.
[*Harcourt Brace News*, 1936, 'How I came to Invent the Character of Lord Peter']

3. I can't see that she could have found anything nastier to say if she'd thought it out with both hands for a fortnight.
[*Busman's Honeymoon* (1937)]

4. As I grow older and older,
And totter towards the tomb,
I find that I care less and less
Who goes to bed with whom.
[In Hitchman, *Such a Strange Lady* (1975), 12, 'That's Why I Never Read Modern Novels']

5. [On *Whose Body?*, 1923, her first book]
One cannot write a novel unless one has something to say about life, and I had nothing to say about it, because I knew nothing.
[In Hone, *Dorothy L. Sayers: A Literary Biography* (1979), 'The Art of the Mystery Story']

Sayle, Alexei (1952–)
English comedian, producer and columnist

1. [On compèring]
I remember once telling Robin Williams he could only do 10 minutes. He offered to buy the club.
[*The Independent*, 1992]

Scanlon, Hugh, Baron (1913–)
British trade union leader

1. [Referring to his union's attitude to the Common Market]
Here we are again with both feet firmly planted in the air.
[*The Observer*, 'Sayings of the Year', 1973]

Scarron, Paul (1610–1660)
French comic dramatist, picaresque novelist and poet

1. [As he lay dying]
At last I am going to be well!
[Attr.]

Schacht, Hjalmar (1877–1970)
German financier, President of the Reichsbank

1. I wouldn't believe Hitler was dead, even if he told me so himself.
[Attr. remark on 8 May 1945]

Schelling, Friedrich von (1775–1854)
German philosopher

1. *Die Architektur ... [ist] gleichsam die erstarrte Musik.*
Architecture is, as it were, petrified music.
[*Philosophie der Kunst* (*Philosophy of Art*, 1802–1803), II. Cf. Goethe: 35]

Schiller, Johann Christoph Friedrich (1759–1805)
Leading writer of German Romanticism; dramatist, critic, lyric poet and historian

1. *Die Weltgeschichte ist das Weltgericht.*
The history of the world is its judgement.
['Resignation' (1786)]

2. *Die Könige sind nur Sklaven ihres Standes,*
Dem eignen Herzen dürfen sie nicht folgen.
Kings are but slaves of their rank,
They may not follow their own heart.
[*Maria Stuart* (1800), II.ii]

3. *Ernst ist das Leben, heiter ist die Kunst.*
Life is serious, art is serene.
[*Wallenstein I* (1798–1801), Prologue]

4. *Das Herz und nicht die Meinung ehrt den Mann.*
Man is honoured by his heart and not by his opinions.
[*Wallenstein II: Wallensteins Tod* (1798–1801), IV.viii]

5. *Gehorsam ist des Weibes Pflicht auf Erden,*
Das harte Dulden ist ihr schweres Los.
Obedience is woman's earthly duty,

Harsh suffering is her sorry fate.
[*Die Jungfrau von Orleans* (*The Maid of Orleans*, 1801), I.x]

6. *Mit der Dummheit kämpfen Götter selbst vergebens.*
Gods themselves struggle in vain with stupidity.
[*Die Jungfrau von Orleans* (*The Maid of Orleans*, 1801), III.vi]

7. *Freude, schöner Götterfunken,*
Tochter aus Elysium,
Wir betreten feuertrunken
Himmlische, dein Heiligtum.
Deine Zauber binden wieder,
Was die Mode streng geteilt,
Alle Menschen werden Brüder,
Wo dein sanfter Flügel weilt.
Joy, fair ray of the gods,
Daughter of Elysium,
Dazzled we enter,
Heavenly one, thy shrine.
Again thy charms join together
What custom has harshly divided,
All men become brothers,
Under thy gentle wing.
['An die Freude' ('To Joy', revised 1803); set to music by Beethoven in the last movement of his Ninth Symphony]

8. *Der zahlreichere Teil der Menschen wird durch den Kampf mit der Not viel zu sehr ermüdet und abgespannt, als dass er sich zu einem neuen und härtern Kampf mit dem Irrtum aufraffen sollte.*
The greater part of humanity is far too weary and worn down by the struggle with want to rouse itself for a new and harder struggle with error.
[*Über die ästhetische Erziehung des Menschen* (*On the Aesthetic Education of Man*, 1793–1795), 8]

9. *Die Wahrheit lebt in der Täuschung fort.*
Truth lives on in deception.
[*Über die ästhetische Erziehung des Menschen* (*On the Aesthetic Education of Man*, 1793–1795), 9]

10. *Es gibt Augenblicke in unserm Leben, wo wir der Natur in Pflanzen, Mineralen, Tieren, Landschaften sowie der menschliche Natur in Kindern, in den Sitten des Landvolks und der Urwelt, nicht weil sie unsern Sinnen wohltut, auch nicht weil sie unsern Verstand oder Geschmack befriedigt ... sondern bloss* weil sie Natur ist, *eine Art von Liebe und von rührender Achtung widmen.*
There are moments in our life when we accord a kind of love and touching respect to nature in plants, minerals, the countryside, as well as human nature in children, in the customs of country folk and the primitive world, not because it is beneficial for our senses, and not because it satisfies our understanding or taste either ... but simply *because it is nature.*
['Über naive und sentimentalische Dichtung' ('On Naive and Sentimental Poetry', 1795–1796)]

11. *Die Schönheit ist das Produkt der Zusammenstimmung zwischen dem Geist und den Sinnen.*
Beauty is the product of harmony between the mind and the senses.
['Über naive und sentimentalische Dichtung' ('On Naive and Sentimental Poetry', 1795–1796)]

Schlegel, Friedrich von (1772–1829)
A founder of German Romanticism; critic and philosopher

1. *Anfang und Ende der Geschichte ist* prophetisch, *kein Objekt mehr der reinen Historie.*
The beginning and end of history are *prophetic*, they are no longer the object of pure history.
[*Fragmente zur Literatur und Poesie* (*Fragments on Literature and Poetry*, 1797–1801), 448]

2. *Der Historiker ist ein rückwärts gekehrter Prophet.*
A historian is a prophet in reverse.
[*Athenäum – Fragmente* (1802–1804)]

Von Schlieffen, Alfred, Graf (1833–1913)
German field marshal

1. [Referring to the Schlieffen plan, a German military strategy to enter France by first going through Belgium]
When you march into France, let the last man on the right brush the Channel with his sleeve.
[In Barbara Tuchman, *The Guns of August 1914* (1964), 2]

Schliemann, Heinrich (1822–1890)
German archaeologist, known for his excavations at Troy and Mycenae

1. [On discovering a gold death mask at an excavation in Mycenae]
I have looked upon the face of Agamemnon.
[In W. Durant, *The Story of Civilization: The Life of Greece* (1939)]

Schnabel, Artur (1882–1951)
Austrian pianist and composer; noted interpreter of Beethoven, Mozart and Schubert

1. The notes I handle no better than many pianists. But the pauses between the notes – ah, that is where the art resides.
[*Chicago Daily News*, 1958]

2. The sonatas of Mozart are unique; they are too easy for children, and too difficult for artists.
[In Nat Shapiro (ed.), *An Encyclopaedia of Quotations about Music* (1978)]

3. [Advice given to the pianist Vladimir Horowitz]
When a piece gets difficult make faces.
[Attr.]

Schoenberg, Arnold (1874–1951)
Austrian composer and musical theorist

1. [When told that his violin concerto would need a soloist with six fingers]
Very well, I can wait.
[Attr.]

Schopenhauer, Arthur (1788–1860)
German pessimist philosopher

1. *Aus seiner Individualität kann Keiner heraus.*
No-one can escape from his individuality.
[*Parerga und Paralipomena* (1851), 'Aphorismen zur Lebensweisheit' ('Aphorisms for Wisdom'), 1]

2. *Einsamkeit ist das Los aller hervorragenden Geister: sie werden solche bisweilen beseufzen; aber stets sie als das kleinere von zwei Übeln erwählen.*
Solitude is the fate of all outstanding minds: it will at times be deplored; but it will always be chosen as the lesser of two evils.
[*Parerga und Paralipomena* (1851), 'Aphorismen zur Lebensweisheit' ('Aphorisms for Wisdom'), 5]

3. *Das Schicksal mischt die Karten und wir spielen.*
Fate shuffles the cards and we play.
[*Parerga und Paralipomena* (1851), 'Aphorismen zur Lebensweisheit' ('Aphorisms for Wisdom'), 5]

4. *Der Wille in uns ist allerdings Ding an sich, für sich bestehend ... Dennoch ist er keiner Selbsterkenntnis fähig; weil er an und für sich ein bloss Wollendes, kein* Erkennendes, *ist.*
The will in us is certainly a thing-in-itself, existing for itself ... It is nonetheless not capable of self-knowledge; because it

is actually something that merely wills, not something that *knows*.
[*Parerga und Paralipomena* (1851), II, 3]

5. *Ein eigentümlicher Fehler der Deutschen ist, dass sie, was vor ihren Füssen liegt, in den Wolken suchen.*
It is a curious failing in the German people that they search in the clouds for what lies at their feet.
[*Parerga und Paralipomena* (1851), II, 9]

6. *Die Gelehrten aber, wie sie in der Regel sind, studieren zu dem Zweck, lehren und schreiben zu können. Daher gleicht ihr Kopf einem Magen und Gedärmen, daraus die Speisen unverdaut wieder abgehn.*
Scholars, however, as a rule study with the aim of being able to teach and write. That is why their heads are like a stomach and intestines from which food passes out again undigested.
[*Parerga und Paralipomena* (1851), II, 21]

7. *Jede Trennung gibt einen Vorschmack des Todes, – und jedes Wiedersehen einen Vorschmack der Auferstehung.*
Every separation gives a foretaste of death, – and every reunion a foretaste of resurrection.
[*Parerga und Paralipomena* (1851), II, 26]

8. *Demgemäss wird man als den Grundfehler des weiblichen Charakters* Ungerechtigkeit *finden.*
Correspondingly it will be found that *injustice* is the fundamental fault of the female character.
[*Parerga und Paralipomena* (1851), II, 27]

9. *Es gibt nur* einen *angeborenen Irrtum, und es ist der, dass wir dasind, um glücklich zu sein.*
There is only *one* innate error, and that is that we are here in order to be happy.
[*Die Welt als Wille und Vorstellung* (*The World as Will and Idea*, 1859 edition), II, 49]

Schreiner, Olive (1855–1920)
South African novelist and writer

1. She thought of the narrowness of the limits within which a human soul may speak and be understood by its nearest of mental kin, of how soon it reaches that solitary land of the individual experience in which no fellow footfall is ever heard.
[*The Story of an African Farm* (1884)]

2. It is delightful to be a woman; but every man thanks the Lord devoutly that he isn't one.
[*The Story of an African Farm* (1884)]

Schroeder, Congresswoman Patricia (1940–)
American politician

1. We've got the kind of President who thinks arms control means some kind of deodorant.
[*The Observer*, 1987, in Jeffrey Care (ed.), *Sayings of the Eighties* (1989)]

Schubert, Franz (1797–1828)
Austrian composer, supreme exponent of the modern German lied

1. My compositions spring from my sorrows. Those that give the world the greatest delight were born of my deepest griefs.
[*Diary*, 27 March 1824]

Schulz, Charles (1922–)
American cartoonist

1. I love mankind – it's people I can't stand.
[*Go Fly a Kite, Charlie Brown*]

Schumacher, E.F. (1911–1977)
German-born British economist, essayist and lecturer; noted for work in developing countries

1. Small is Beautiful. A study of economics as if people mattered.
[Title of book, 1973]

Schurz, Carl (1829–1906)
German-born American lawyer, soldier, Republican politician, journalist and writer

1. Our country, right or wrong! When right, to be kept right; when wrong, to be put right!
[Speech, US Senate, 1872]

Schwarzenberg, Felix, Prince (1800–1852)
Austrian statesman and diplomat

1. [On being asked whether Austria was under any obligation to Russia for help received previously]
Austria will astonish the world by the magnitude of her ingratitude.
[In E. Crankshaw, *The Fall of the House of Habsburg* (1963), 4, 2]

Schweitzer, Albert (1875–1965)
Alsatian medical missionary, Protestant theologian, philosopher, physician and organist; Nobel peace prize 1952

1. *'Heda, Kamerad', rufe ich, 'willst du uns nicht ein wenig helfen?' 'Ich bin ein Intellektueller und trage kein Holz', lautete die Antwort. 'Hast du Glück', erwiderte ich; 'auch ich wollte ein Intellektueller werden, aber es ist mir nicht gelungen.'*
'Hello, friend,' I shout, 'Won't you help us?' 'I am an intellectual and don't carry wood around,' came the answer. 'You're lucky,' I replied. 'I too wanted to become an intellectual, but I didn't manage it.'
[*Mitteilungen aus Lambarene* (1928); translated as *More from the Primeval Forest* (1931)]

Scott, Alexander (c. 1525–c. 1584)
Scottish lyric poet and musician

1. Luve is ane fervent fire,
Kendillit without desire;
Short pleisure, lang displeisure,
Repentence is the hire;
Ane puir treisure without meisure.
Luve is ane fervent fire.
['A Rondel of Luve' (c. 1568)]

Scott, C.P. (1846–1932)
English editor of the Manchester Guardian *1872–1929; Liberal politician*

1. A newspaper is of necessity something of a monopoly, and its first duty is to shun the temptations of monopoly. Its primary office is the gathering of news. At the peril of its soul it must see that the supply is not tainted. Neither in what it gives, nor in what it does not give, nor in the mode of presentation, must the unclouded face of truth suffer wrong. Comment is free, but facts are sacred.
[*Manchester Guardian*, 1921]

2. Television? The word is half Latin and half Greek. No good can come of it.
[Attr.]

Scott, Captain Robert Falcon (1868–1912)
English naval officer, antarctic explorer and writer

1. [Of the South Pole]
Great God! this is an awful place.
[*Journal*, 17 January 1912]

2. For God's sake look after our people.
[*Journal*, 25 March 1912]

3. Had we lived, I should have had a tale to tell of the hardihood, endurance, and courage of my companions which would have stirred the heart of every Englishman. These rough notes and our dead bodies must tell the tale.
[Message to the Public, 1912]

Scott, Rose (1847–1925)
Australian suffragette and reformer

1. Don't do anything for people until you know what they want.
[In Flora S. Eldershaw (ed.), *The Peaceful Army* (1938)]

Scott, Valerie
Canadian prostitute and feminist

1. [Toronto prostitute-by-choice, who prefers the term 'whore', spokesperson for the Canadian Organization for the Rights of Prostitutes (CORP)]
We don't sell our bodies. Housewives do that. What we do is *rent* our bodies for sexual services.
[*The Toronto Star*, 1989]

Scott, Sir Walter (1771–1832)
Scottish Romantic novelist, poet, short-story writer, historian, folklorist, dramatist, editor, critic and translator

1. The way was long, the wind was cold,
The Minstrel was infirm and old;
His wither'd cheek, and tresses gray,
Seemed to have known a better day...

2. The last of all the Bards was he,
Who sung of Border chivalry;
For, welladay! their date was fled,
His tuneful brethren all were dead;
And he, neglected and oppress'd,
Wish'd to be with them, and at rest.
[*The Lay of the Last Minstrel* (1805), Introduction]

3. Vengeance, deep-brooding o'er the slain,
Had lock'd the source of softer woe;
And burning pride and high disdain
Forbade the rising tear to flow...

4. What shall be the maiden's fate?
Who shall be the maiden's mate?
[*The Lay of the Last Minstrel* (1805), I]

5. If thou would'st view fair Melrose aright,
Go visit it by the pale moonlight;
For the gay beams of lightsome day
Gild, but to flout, the ruins grey...

6. Strange sounds along the chancel pass'd,
The banner waved without a blast...

7. I cannot tell how the truth may be;
I say the tale as 'twas said to me.
[*The Lay of the Last Minstrel* (1805), II]

8. In peace, Love tunes the shepherd's reed;
In war, he mounts the warrior's steed;
In halls, in gay attire is seen;
In hamlets, dances on the green.
Love rules the court, the camp, the grove,
And men below, and saints above;
For love is heaven, and heaven is love.
[*The Lay of the Last Minstrel* (1805), III]

9. True love's the gift which God has given
To man alone beneath the heaven:
It is the secret sympathy,
The silver link, the silken tie,
Which heart to heart, and mind to mind,
In body and in soul can bind.
[*The Lay of the Last Minstrel* (1805), V]

10. Breathes there the man, with soul so dead,
Who never to himself hath said,
This is my own, my native land!
Whose heart hath ne'er within him burned,
As home his footsteps he hath turned,
From wandering on a foreign strand!...

11. Despite those titles, power, and pelf,
The wretch, concentred all in self,
Living, shall forfeit fair renown,
And, doubly dying, shall go down
To the vile dust, from whence he sprung,
Unwept, unhonoured and unsung.

O Caledonia! stern and wild,
Meet nurse for a poetic child!
Land of brown heath and shaggy wood,
Land of the mountain and the flood,
Land of my sires! what mortal hand
Can e'er untie the filial band,
That knits me to thy rugged strand!
[*The Lay of the Last Minstrel* (1805), VI]

12. November's sky is chill and drear,
November's leaf is red and sear...

13. [Of Pitt]
Had'st thou but liv'd, though stripp'd of power,
A watchman on the lonely tower...

14. Now is the stately column broke,
The beacon-light is quenched in smoke,
The trumpet's silver sound is still,
The warder silent on the hill!...

15. But search the land of living men,
Where wilt thou find their like agen?
[*Marmion* (1808), 'Introduction to Canto First']

16. And come he slow, or come he fast,
It is but Death who comes at last.
[*Marmion* (1808), II, 'The Convent']

17. Still is thy name in high account,
And still thy verse has charms,
Sir David Lindesay of the Mount,
Lord Lion King-at-arms!
[*Marmion* (1808), IV, 'The Camp']

18. O young Lochinvar is come out of the west
Through all the wide Border his steed was the best;
And save his good broadsword, he weapons had none,
He rode all unarm'd, and he rode all alone.
So faithful in love, and so dauntless in war,
There never was knight like the young Lochinvar...

19. For a laggard in love, and a dastard in war,
Was to wed the fair Ellen of brave Lochinvar...

20. 'O come ye in peace here, or come ye in war,
Or to dance at our bridal, young Lord Lochinvar?'...

21. 'To lead but one measure, drink one cup of wine.'...

22. She look'd down to blush, and she look'd up to sigh,

With a smile on her lips and a tear in her eye,
He took her soft hand, ere her mother could bar,–
'Now tread we a measure!' said young Lochinvar...

23. 'She is won! we are gone, over bank, bush, and scaur;
They'll have fleet steeds that follow,' quoth young Lochinvar.
[*Marmion* (1808), V, 'The Court']

24. Heap on more wood! – the wind is chill;
But let it whistle as it will,
We'll keep our Christmas merry still...

25. England was merry England, when
Old Christmas brought his sports again.
'Twas Christmas broach'd the mightiest ale;
'Twas Christmas told the merriest tale;
A Christmas gambol oft could cheer
The poor man's heart through half the year.
[*Marmion* (1808), 'Introduction to Canto Sixth']

26. 'And dar'st thou then
To beard the lion in his den,
The Douglas in his hall?
And hop'st thou thence unscathed to go?
No, by Saint Bride of Bothwell, no!
Up, drawbridge, grooms – what, warder, ho!
Let the portcullis fall.'...

27. O what a tangled web we weave,
When first we practise to deceive!...

28. And such a yell was there,
Of sudden and portentous birth,
As if men fought upon the earth,
And fiends in upper air...

29. O Woman! in our hours of ease,
Uncertain, coy, and hard to please,
And variable as the shade
By the light quivering aspen made,
When pain and anguish wring the brow,
A ministering angel thou!...

30. 'Charge, Chester, charge! On, Stanley, on!'
Were the last words of Marmion...

31. O, for a blast of that dread horn,
On Fontarabian echoes borne!...

32. The stubborn spear-men still made good
Their dark impenetrable wood,
Each stepping where his comrade stood,
The instant that he fell...

33. Still from the sire the son shall hear
Of the stern strife, and carnage drear,
Of Flodden's fatal field,
Where shiver'd was fair Scotland's spear,
And broken was her shield!
[*Marmion* (1808), VI, 'The Battle']

34. To all, to each, a fair good-night,
And pleasing dreams, and slumbers light!
[*Marmion* (1808), 'L'envoy']

35. The stag at eve had drunk his fill,
Where danced the moon on Monan's rill,
And deep his midnight lair had made
In lone Glenartney's hazel shade...

36. His ready speech flow'd fair and free,
In phrase of gentlest courtesy;
Yet seem'd that tone, and gesture bland,
Less used to sue than to command...

37. Soldier, rest! thy warfare o'er,
Sleep the sleep that knows not breaking;
Dream of battled fields no more,
Days of danger, nights of waking.

Huntsman, rest! thy chase is done,
Think not of the rising sun,
For at dawning to assail ye
Here no bugles sound reveillé.
[*The Lady of the Lake* (1810), I, 'The Chase']

38. Hail to the Chief who in triumph advances!
[*The Lady of the Lake* (1810), II, 'The Island']

39. Like the dew on the mountain,
Like the foam on the river,
Like the bubble on the fountain,
Thou art gone, and for ever!...

40. Ave Maria! maiden mild!
Listen to a maiden's prayer!
[*The Lady of the Lake* (1810), III, 'The Gathering']

41. These are Clan-Alpine's warriors true;
And, Saxon, – I am Roderick Dhu!...

42. Respect was mingled with surprise,
And the stern joy which warriors feel
In foemen worthy of their steel.
[*The Lady of the Lake* (1810), V, 'The Combat']

43. Where, where was Roderick then?
One blast upon his bugle-horn
Were worth a thousand men!
[*The Lady of the Lake* (1810), VI, 'The Guard-Room']

44. The valiant Knight of Triermain
Rung forth his challenge-blast again
But answer came there none.
[*The Bridal of Triermain* (1813), III]

45. See yon pale stripling! when a boy,
A mother's pride, a father's joy!
[*Rokeby* (1813), III]

46. There is mist on the mountain, and night on the vale,
But more dark is the sleep of the sons of the Gael.
A stranger commanded – it sunk on the land,
It has frozen each heart, and benumb'd every hand!
[*Waverley* (1814), 22, 'Flora MacIvor's Song']

47. My heart's in the Highlands, my heart is not here,
My heart's in the Highlands a-chasing the deer.
[*Waverley* (1814), 28]

48. Gin by pailfuls, wine in rivers,
Dash the window-glass to shivers!
For three wild lads were we, brave boys,
And three wild lads were we;
Thou on the land, and I on the sand,
And Jack on the gallows-tree!
[*Guy Mannering* (1815), 34]

49. O hush thee, my babie, thy sire was a knight,
Thy mother a lady, both lovely and bright...

50. Then hush thee, my darling, take rest while you may,
For strife comes with manhood, and waking with day.
['Lullaby of an Infant Chief' (1815)]

51. Thus, then, my noble foe I greet;
Health and high fortune till we meet
And then – what pleases Heaven.
[*The Lord of the Isles* (1815), III]

52. O! many a shaft, at random sent,
Finds mark the archer little meant!
And many a word, at random spoken,

May soothe or wound a heart that's broken.
[*The Lord of the Isles* (1815), V]

53. To that dark inn, the grave!
[*The Lord of the Isles* (1815), VI]

54. Pibroch of Donuil Dhu,
Pibroch of Donuil,
Wake thy wild voice anew,
Summon Clan-Conuil.
Come away, come away,
Hark to the summons!
Come in your war array,
Gentles and commons...

55. Leave untended the herd,
The flock without shelter;
Leave the corpse uninterr'd,
The bride at the altar.
['Pibroch of Donuil Dhu' (1816)]

56. Come fill up my cup, come fill up my cann,
Come saddle my horses, and call up my man;
Come open your gates, and let me gae free,
I daurna stay langer in bonny Dundee.
[*Rob Roy* (1817), 23]

57. Proud Maisie is in the wood,
Walking so early;
Sweet Robin sits in the bush,
Singing so rarely.
[*The Heart of Midlothian* (1818), 40]

58. Look not thou on beauty's charming,
Sit thou still when kings are arming,
Taste not when the wine-cup glistens,
Speak not when the people listens,
Stop thine ear against the singer,
From the red gold keep thy finger;
Vacant heart and hand and eye,
Easy live and quiet die.
[*The Bride of Lammermoor* (1819), 2]

59. March, march, Ettrick and Teviotdale,
Why the deil dinna ye march forward in order?
March, march, Eskdale and Liddesdale,
All the Blue Bonnets are bound for the Border.
[*The Monastery* (1820), 25, 'Border March']

60. Ah! County Guy, the hour is nigh,
The sun has left the lea,
The orange flower perfumes the bower,
The breeze is on the sea.
[*Quentin Durward* (1823), 4, 'County Guy']

61. Come weal, come woe, we'll gather and go,
And live or die with Charlie.
[*Redgauntlet* (1824), 11]

62. Widow'd wife, and wedded maid,
Betrothed, betrayer, and betray'd!
[*The Betrothed* (1825), 15]

63. Woman's faith, and woman's trust–
Write the characters in dust.
[*The Betrothed* (1825), 20]

64. Now change the scene – and let the trumpets sound,
For we must rouse the lion from his lair.
[*The Talisman* (1825), 6]

65. A man may drink and not be drunk;
A man may fight and not be slain;
A man may kiss a bonny lass,
And yet be welcome home again.
[*Woodstock* (1826), 27]

66. From the lone shieling of the misty island
Mountains divide us and the waste of the seas–
Yet still the blood is strong, the heart is Highland,
And we in dreams behold the Hebrides!
['Canadian Boat Song' (1829); authorship doubtful]

67. To the Lords of Convention 'twas Claver'se who spoke,
'Ere the King's crown shall fall there are crowns to be broke;
So let each Cavalier who loves honour and me,
Come follow the bonnet of Bonny Dundee.
[*The Doom of Devorgoil* (1830), II, ii, 'Song']

68. Abel Sampson, probationer of divinity ... was ever after designated as a 'stickit minister'.
[*Guy Mannering* (1815), 2]

69. *Mrs Bertram*: That sounds like nonsense, my dear.
Mr Bertram: May be so, my dear; but it may be very good law for all that.
[*Guy Mannering* (1815), 9]

70. The frolicsome company had begun to practise the ancient and now forgotten pastime of *High Jinks*.
[*Guy Mannering* (1815), 36]

71. You ... whirl'd them to the back o' beyont.
[*The Antiquary* (1816), 2]

72. It's no fish ye're buying – it's men's lives.
[*The Antiquary* (1816), 11]

73. But with the morning cool repentance came.
[*Rob Roy* (1817), 12]

74. There's a gude time coming.
[*Rob Roy* (1817), 32]

75. Speak out, sir, and do not Maister or Campbell me – my foot is on my native heath, and my name is Macgregor!
[*Rob Roy* (1817), 34]

76. When we had a king, and a chancellor, and Parliament men o' our ain, we could aye pebble them wi' stanes when they werena gude bairns – but naebody's nails can reach the length o' Lunnon.
[*The Heart of Midlothian* (1818), 4]

77. [Traditional words of the kelpie, or water sprite, in a swollen stream]
The hour is come, but not the man.
[*The Heart of Midlothian* (1818), 4]

78. Jock, when ye hae naething else to do, ye may be aye sticking in a tree; it will be growing, Jock, when ye're sleeping.
[*The Heart of Midlothian* (1818), 8]

79. I live by twa trades, sir, ... fiddle, sir, and spade; filling the world, and emptying of it.
[*The Bride of Lammermoor* (1819), 24]

80. Her winding-sheet is up as high as her throat already.
[*The Bride of Lammermoor* (1819), 34]

81. The spell lies in two words ... *Pax vobiscum* will answer all queries. If you go or come, eat or drink, bless or ban, *Pax vobiscum* carries you through it all ... speak it but thus, in a deep grave tone – *Pax vobiscum* – it is irresistible.
[*Ivanhoe* (1819), 26]

82. His morning walk was beneath the elms in the churchyard; 'for death,' he said, 'had been his next-door neighbour for so many years, that he had no apology for dropping the acquaintance.'
[*A Legend of Montrose* (1819), Introduction]

83. There is a southern proverb, – fine words butter no parsnips.
[*A Legend of Montrose* (1819), 3]

84. But no one shall find me rowing against the stream. I care not who knows it – I write for the general amusement.
[*The Fortunes of Nigel* (1822), Introductory Epistle]

85. It's ill taking the breeks aff a wild Highlandman.
[*The Fortunes of Nigel* (1822), 5]

86. Fat, fair, and forty.
[*St Ronan's Well* (1823)]

87. Man is a cooking animal.
[*St Ronan's Well* (1823)]

88. And it's ill speaking between a fou man and a fasting.
[*Redgauntlet* (1824), Letter 11, 'Wandering Willie's Tale']

89. The ae half of the warld thinks the tither daft.
[*Redgauntlet* (1824), 'Journal of Darsie Latimer']

90. The play-bill, which is said to have announced the tragedy of Hamlet, the character of the Prince of Denmark being left out.
[*The Talisman* (1825), Introduction]

91. I never saw a richer company or to speak my mind a finer people. The worst of them is the bitter and envenomed dislike which they have to each other; their factions have been so long envenomed and have so little ground to fight their battle in that they are like people fighting with daggers in a hogshead.
[Letter to Joanna Baillie, 1825]

92. We shall never learn to feel and respect our real calling and destiny, unless we have taught ourselves to consider every thing as moonshine, compared with the education of the heart.
[Letter to J.G. Lockhart, 1825]

93. [Comment on the Union of Scotland with England in 1707]
We have become the caterpillars of the island, instead of its pillars.
[Letter to the Editor of *The Edinburgh Weekly Journal*, 1826]

94. All men who have turned out worth anything have had the chief hand in their own education.
[Letter to J.G. Lockhart, 1830]

95. [On Jane Austen]
The Big Bow-Wow strain I can do myself like any now going; but the exquisite touch, which renders ordinary commonplace things and characters interesting, from the truth of the description and the sentiment, is denied to me.
[Journal, 14 March 1826]

96. I would like to be there, were it but to see how the cat jumps.
[Journal, 7 October 1826]

97. The blockheads talk of my being like Shakespeare – not fit to tie his brogues.
[Journal, 11 December 1826]

98. [Refusing offers of help following his bankruptcy in 1826]
No! this right hand shall work it all off!
[In Lord Cockburn, *Memorials of His Time* (1856), 7]

99. Here lies one who might be trusted with untold gold, but not with unmeasured whisky.
[Epitaph for his favourite servant, Tom Purdie]

Scottish Metrical Psalms (1650)

1. The Lord's my shepherd, I'll not want.
He makes me down to lie
In pastures green: he leadeth me
the quiet waters by.
My soul he doth restore again;
and me to walk doth make
Within the paths of righteousness,
ev'n for his own name's sake.

Yea, though I walk in death's dark vale,
yet will I fear none ill:
For thou art with me; and thy rod
and staff me comfort still.
My table thou hast furnished
in presence of my foes;
My head thou dost with oil anoint,
and my cup overflows.
[Psalm 23]

2. I to the hills will lift mine eyes
from whence doth come mine aid.
[Psalm 121]

3. The race that long in darkness pin'd
have seen a glorious light.
[Paraphrase 19; *Isaiah* 9:2]

Scriven, Joseph (1820–1886)

1. What a Friend we have in Jesus,
All our sins and griefs to bear!
What a privilege to carry
Everything to God in prayer!
[Hymn, c. 1855, with Charles C. Converse]

Searle, Ronald William Fordham (1920–)
English illustrator and cartoonist

1. The Terror of St Trinian's.
[Title of book, 1952, based on Searle's cartoons; text by Timothy Shy (Dominic Bevan Wyndham Lewis)]

2. Though loaded firearms were strictly forbidden at St Trinian's to all but Sixth-Formers ... one or two of them carried automatics acquired in the holidays, generally the gift of some indulgent relative.
[*The Terror of St Trinian's* (1952), 3]

3. In the spring ... your lovely Chloë lightly turns to one mass of spots.
[*The Terror of St Trinian's* (1952), 3]

4. Maidens of St Trinian's
Gird your armour on.
Grab the nearest weapon
Never mind which one!
The battle's to the strongest
Might is always right,
Trample on the weakest
Glory in their plight!
['St Trinian's School Song', words by Sidney Gilliat; theme song for the film *Blue Murder at St Trinian's*]

Sears, E.H. (1810–1876)
American Unitarian minister and writer

1. It came upon the midnight clear,
That glorious song of old,
From Angels bending near the earth
To touch their harps of gold;
'Peace on the earth; good will to man
From Heaven's all gracious King.'
The world in solemn stillness lay
To hear the angels sing.
[Hymn, c. 1850]

Secombe, Sir Harry (1921–)
Welsh comedian and singer

1. My advice if you insist on slimming: Eat as much as you like – just don't swallow it.
[*Daily Herald*, 1962]

Sedgwick, Catharine Maria (1789–1867)

American novelist, biographer and feminist

1. [Comparing heaven with her home town of Stockbridge, Massachussetts]
I expect no very violent transition.
[Attr.]

Sedley, Sir Charles (c. 1639–1701)

English poet, dramatist, courtier and wit

1. Phyllis is my only joy,
Faithless as the winds or seas;
Sometimes coming, sometimes coy,
Yet she never fails to please...

2. Phyllis, without frown or smile,
Sat and knotted all the while.
['Song' (1694)]

3. She deceiving,
I believing;
What need lovers wish for more?
['Song']

4. Love still has something of the Sea
From whence his Mother rose.
['Song: Love still has Something']

5. Not, Celia, that I juster am
Or better than the rest,
For I would change each hour like them,
Were not my heart at rest...

6. Why then should I seek farther store,
And still make love anew;
When change itself can give no more,
'Tis easy to be true.
['To Celia']

Seeger, Pete (1919–)

American folk singer-songwriter, noted for his protest songs

1. Where have all the flowers gone?
The girls have picked them every one.
Oh, when will you ever learn?
['Where Have All the Flowers Gone?', song, 1961]

Seeley, Sir John Robert (1834–1895)

English historian, essayist and Latin scholar

1. We [the English] seem as it were to have conquered and peopled half the world in a fit of absence of mind.
[*The Expansion of England* (1883), Lecture 1]

2. [Quoting E.A. Freeman]
History is past politics, and politics present history.
[*The Growth of British Policy* (1895)]

Segal, Erich (1937–)

American scholar, lecturer, novelist, screenwriter and essayist

1. Love means never having to say you're sorry.
[*Love Story* (1970)]

2. The OED database is one of the wonders of the modern world – to paraphrase Christopher Marlowe, 'infinite riches in a little ROM'.
[*Times Literary Supplement*, 1992]

Selden, John (1584–1654)

English historian, antiquary, jurist, orientalist and politician; imprisoned for his opposition to King James

1. *Scrutamini scripturas.* [Let us look at the Scriptures]. These two words have undone the world.
[*Table Talk* (1689), 'Bible Scripture']

2. Old friends are best. King James used to call for his old shoes; they were easiest for his feet.
[*Table Talk* (1689), 'Friends']

3. 'Tis not the drinking that is to be blamed, but the excess.
[*Table Talk* (1689), 'Humility']

4. A king is a thing men have made for their own sakes, for quietness' sake. Just as in a family one man is appointed to buy the meat.
[*Table Talk* (1689), 'Of a King']

5. Ignorance of the law excuses no man; not that all men know the law, but because 'tis an excuse every man will plead, and no man can tell how to confute him.
[*Table Talk* (1689), 'Law']

6. Take a straw and throw it up into the air, you shall see by that which way the wind is.
[*Table Talk* (1689), 'Libels']

7. Marriage is nothing but a civil contract.
[*Table Talk* (1689), 'Marriage']

8. There never was a merry world since the fairies left off dancing, and the Parson left conjuring.
[*Table Talk* (1689), 'Parson']

9. There is not anything in the world so much abused as this sentence, *Salus populi suprema lex esto.* [Let public safety be the supreme law]
[*Table Talk* (1689), 'People']

10. Philosophy is nothing but discretion.
[*Table Talk* (1689), 'Philosophy']

11. Pleasure is nothing else but the intermission of pain, the enjoyment of something I am in great trouble for till I have it.
[*Table Talk* (1689), 'Pleasure']

12. Preachers say, Do as I say, not as I do.
[*Table Talk* (1689), 'Preaching']

Selfridge, H. Gordon (1858–1947)

American-born British businessman, founder of London's first large department store

1. 'Business as usual' must be the order of the day.
[Speech, 26 August 1914]

2. There are ... shopping days to Christmas.
[In A.H. Williams, *No Name on the Door: A Memoir of Gordon Selfridge* (1956)]

Sellar, Walter Carruthers (1898–1951)

British writer and teacher

and **Yeatman,** Robert Julian (1897–1968)

British humorous writer

1. 1066 And All That.
[Title of book, 1930]

2. The Roman Conquest was, however, a *Good Thing*, since the Britons were only natives at that time.
[*1066 And All That* (1930), 1]

3. Pope Gregory ... made the memorable joke – *'Non Angli, sed Angeli'* (*'not* Angels, but *Anglicans'*).
[*1066 And All That* (1930), 3. Cf. Gregory I: 1]

4. The Venomous Bead (author of *The Rosary*).
[*1066 And All That* (1930), 3]

5. Magna Charter was ... the cause of Democracy in England, and thus a *Good Thing* for everyone (except the Common People).
[*1066 And All That* (1930), 19]

6. The Cavaliers (Wrong but Wromantic) and the Roundheads (Right but Repulsive).
[*1066 And All That* (1930), 35]

7. Charles II was always very merry and was therefore not so much a king as a Monarch.
[*1066 And All That* (1930), 36]

8. The National Debt is a very Good Thing and it would be dangerous to pay it off, for fear of Political Economy.
[*1066 And All That* (1930), 38]

9. Napoleon's armies always used to march on their stomachs, shouting: 'Vive l'Intérieur!' and so moved about very slowly.
[*1066 And All That* (1930), 48]

10. A Bad Thing: America was thus clearly top nation, and History came to a .
[*1066 And All That* (1930), 62]

11. Do not on any account attempt to write on both sides of the paper at once.
[*1066 And All That* (1930), Test Paper 5]

12. *For* Pheasant *read* Peasant, throughout.
[*1066 And All That* (1930), Errata, page 50]

13. For every person wishing to teach there are thirty not wanting to be taught.
[*And Now All This* (1932), Introduction]

Semple, Robert (1873–1955)
New Zealand Labour politician

1. [Allegedly said on the occasion of the Fordell tunnel botch, 1944]
As minister I accept the responsibility but not the blame.
[In Richard Long, *Dominion* (1984)]

2. [A favourite term of abuse for whingeing complainants or opponents]
Snivelling snufflebusters.
[A Semple-ism, first recorded 1905]

3. [On being accused of having building or property interests in Australia]
(1) I don't own enough timber in Australia to build a lavatory for a cockroach.
(2) I haven't enough property in Sydney to make a square meal for a borer.
[Attr.]

Seneca (Lucius Annaeus Seneca) (c. 4 BC–AD 65)
Roman Stoic philosopher, tragic poet and dramatist; essayist, rhetorician, statesman and tutor of Nero

1. *Homines dum docent discunt.*
Even while they teach, men learn.
[*Epistulae Morales*, 7, 8]

2. *Nil melius aeterna lex fecit, quam quod unum introitum nobis ad vitam dedit, exitus multos.*
Eternal law has arranged nothing better than this, that it has given us one way in to life, but many ways out.
[*Epistulae Morales*, 70, 14]

3. Live among men as if God beheld you; speak to God as if men were listening.
[*Epistles*]

4. Conversation has a kind of charm about it, an insinuating and insidious something that elicits secrets from us just like love or liquor.
[*Epistles*]

5. *Eripere vitam nemo non homini potest,*
At nemo mortem; mille ad hanc aditus patent.
Anyone can take away a man's life, but no one his death; to this a thousand doors lie open.
[*Phoenissae*, line 152. Cf. Massinger: 13]

6. *Qui genus joctat suum*
Aliena laudat.
Who boasts his ancestry, praises others' worth.
[*Hercules Furens*, line 340]

7. *Victima haud ulla amplior*
Potest magisque opima mactari Iovi
Quam rex iniquus.
There can be slain
No sacrifice to God more acceptable
Than an unjust and wicked king.
[*Hercules Furens*, line 922, trans. Milton]

8. *Illi mors gravis incubat*
Qui notus nimis omnibus
Ignotus moritur sibi.
For him death grippeth right hard by the crop
That know of all, but to himself, alas
Doth die unknown, dazed with dreadful face.
[*Thyestes*, line 401, Chorus, trans. Wyatt]

Servetus, Michael (1511–1553)
Spanish Anabaptist theologian and physician, discoverer of pulmonary blood circulation; burnt for heresy

1. [Comment to the judges of the Inquisition after being condemned to be burned at the stake]
I will burn, but this is a mere incident. We shall continue our discussion in eternity.
[Attr.]

Service, Robert W. (1874–1958)
British-born Canadian poet, novelist, journalist and autobiographical writer

1. This is the Law of the Yukon, that only the Strong shall thrive;
That surely the Weak shall perish, and only the Fit survive.
Dissolute, damned and despairful, crippled and palsied and slain,
This is the Will of the Yukon, – Lo, how she makes it plain!
['The Law of the Yukon' (1907)]

2. Back of the bar, in a solo game, sat Dangerous Dan McGrew,
And watching his luck was his light-o'-love, the lady that's known as Lou.
['The Shooting of Dan McGrew' (1907)]

3. A promise made is a debt unpaid.
['The Cremation of Sam McGee' (1907)]

4. Ah! the clock is always slow;
It is later than you think.
['It is Later than You Think' (1921)]

5. When we, the Workers, all demand: 'What are we fighting for?'...
Then, then we'll end that stupid crime, that devil's madness – War.
['Michael' (1921)]

Seth, Vikram (1952–)
Poet and novelist who trained as an economist

1. 'You will marry a boy I choose,' said Mrs Rupa Mehra firmly to her younger daughter.
[*A Suitable Boy* (1993)]

Sévigné, Marie de Rabutin-Chantal, Marquise de (1626–1696)
French letter writer

1. *Je trouve la mort si terrible, que je hais plus la vie parce qu'elle m'y mène, que par les épines qui s'y rencontrent.*
I find death so terrible that I hate life more for leading me towards it than for the thorns encountered on the way.
[*Correspondance*, Letter to Mme de Grignan, 1672]

2. The more I see of men, the more I admire dogs.
[Attr.]

Seward, William (1801–1872)
American statesman and orator; Republican Secretary of State 1861–69

1. I know, and all the world knows, that revolutions never go backward.
[Speech at Rochester on the Irrepressible Conflict, 1858]

Sexby, Edward (d. 1658)
English soldier and conspirator

1. Killing noe Murder. Briefly Discourst in three quaestions.
[Title of pamphlet, 1657]

Sexton, Anne (1928–1974)
American poet and critic

1. In a dream you are never eighty.
['Old' (1962)]

Sforza, Francesco, Duke of Milan (1401–1466)

1. [On his secretary Cecco Siminotta]
If I lose him, I must have another Cecco in his place, even if I have to make him out of wax.
[Attr.]

Shadbolt, Tim (1932–)
New Zealand novelist

1. [On teenage pleasures, c. 1960]
I used to love sitting in the gutter with bare feet, a chrome-studded chair-covered leather jacket and filthy jeans. Eatin' chips. People look at you with such disgust and hate. It was terrific.
[*Bullshit & Jellybeans* (1971)]

Shadwell, Thomas (c. 1642–1692)
English dramatist, poet and writer of operas; poet laureate from 1689

1. Words may be false and full of Art,
Sighs are the natural language of the heart.
[*Psyche* (1675), III]

2. The haste of a Fool is the slowest thing in the World.
[*A True Widow* (1679), III]

3. I am out of the Lady's company like a Fish out of the water.
[*A True Widow* (1679), III]

4. Every Man loves what he is good at.
[*A True Widow* (1679), V]

Shaffer, Peter (1926–)
English dramatist

1. All my wife had ever taken from the Mediterranean – from that whole vast intuitive culture – are four bottles of Chianti to make into lamps, and two china condiment donkeys labelled Sally and Peppy.
[*Equus* (1973), I.xviii]

2. Passion, you see, can be destroyed by a doctor. It cannot be created.
[*Equus* (1973), II.xxxv]

3. Rehearsing a play is making the word flesh. Publishing a play is reversing the process.
[*Equus* (1973), Note]

Shaftesbury, First Earl of, Anthony Ashley Cooper (1621–1683)
English statesman; Chancellor of the Exchequer 1661–72 and Lord Chancellor 1672–73; organizer of Whig opposition to Charles II

1. 'People differ in their discourse and profession about these matters, but men of sense are really but of one religion.' ... 'Pray, my Lord, what religion is that which men of sense agree in?' 'Madam,' says the earl immediately, 'men of sense never tell it.'
[In Bishop Burnet's *History of His Own Time* (1823), I]

Shahn, Ben (1898–1969)
American social realist painter and muralist, born in Lithuania

1. [Outlining the difference between professional and amateur painters]
An amateur is an artist who supports himself with outside jobs which enable him to paint. A professional is someone whose wife works to enable him to paint.
[Attr.]

Shakespeare, William (1564–1616)
Greatest English dramatist and poet; author of comedies, tragedies, historical plays and sonnets; actor

All's Well That Ends Well

1. 'Twere all one
That I should love a bright particular star
And think to wed it, he is so above me.
[I.i]

2. The hind that would be mated by the lion
Must die for love.
[I.i]

3. Your virginity, your old virginity, is like one of our French wither'd pears: it looks ill, it eats drily.
[I.i]

4. Our remedies oft in ourselves do lie,
Which we ascribe to heaven.
[I.i]

5. It is like a barber's chair, that fits all buttocks.
[II.ii]

6. To th' wars, my boy, to th' wars!
He wears his honour in a box unseen
That hugs his kicky-wicky here at home,
Spending his manly marrow in her arms,
Which should sustain the bound and high curvet
Of Mars's fiery steed.
[II.iii]

7. A young man married is a man that's marr'd.
[II.iii]

8. I know a man that had this trick of melancholy sold a goodly manor for a song.
[III.ii]

9. The flow'ry way that leads to the broad gate and the great fire.
[IV.v]

10. Praising what is lost
Makes the remembrance dear.
[V.iii]

11. Th' inaudible and noiseless foot of Time.
[V.iii]

Antony and Cleopatra

1. The triple pillar of the world transform'd
Into a strumpet's fool.
[I.i]

2. *Cleopatra*: If it be love indeed, tell me how much.
Antony: There's beggary in the love that can be reckon'd.
Cleopatra: I'll set a bourn how far to be belov'd.
Antony: Then must thou needs find out new heaven, new earth.
[I.i]

3. Kingdoms are clay; our dungy earth alike
Feeds beast as man. The nobleness of life
Is to do thus, when such a mutual pair
And such a twain can do't.
[I.i]

4. In nature's infinite book of secrecy
A little I can read.
[I.ii]

5. You shall be yet far fairer than you are.
[I.ii]

6. Mine, and most of our fortunes, to-night, shall be – drunk to bed.
[I.ii]

7. On the sudden
A Roman thought hath struck him.
[I.ii]

8. The nature of bad news infects the teller.
[I.ii]

9. These strong Egyptian fetters I must break,
Or lose myself in dotage.
[I.ii]

10. I must from this enchanting queen break off.
Ten thousand harms, more than the ills I know,
My idleness doth hatch.
[I.ii]

11. I have seen her die twenty times upon far poorer moment. I do think there is mettle in death, which commits some loving act upon her, she hath such a celerity in dying.
[I.ii]

12. O sir, you had then left unseen a wonderful piece of work, which not to have been blest withal would have discredited your travel.
[I.ii]

13. Indeed the tears live in an onion that should water this sorrow.
[I.ii]

14. If you find him sad,
Say I am dancing; if in mirth, report
That I am sudden sick.
[I.iii]

15. *Charmian*: In each thing give him way; cross him in nothing.
Cleopatra: Thou teachest like a fool – the way to lose him.
[I.iii]

16. In time we hate that which we often fear.
[I.iii]

17. Eternity was in our lips and eyes,
Bliss in our brows' bent.
[I.iii]

18. Though age from folly could not give me freedom,
It does from childishness.
[I.iii]

19. Courteous lord, one word.
Sir, you and I must part – but that's not it.
Sir, you and I have lov'd – but there's not it.
That you know well. Something it is I would–
O, my oblivion is a very Antony,
And I am all forgotten!
[I.iii]

20. Give me to drink mandragora...
That I might sleep out this great gap of time
My Antony is away.
[I.v]

21. O happy horse, to bear the weight of Antony!
Do bravely, horse; for wot'st thou whom thou mov'st?
The demi-Atlas of this earth, the arm
And burgonet of men. He's speaking now,
Or murmuring 'Where's my serpent of old Nile?'
[I.v]

22. Think on me,
That am with Phoebus' amorous pinches black,
And wrinkled deep in time? Broad-fronted Caesar,
When thou wast here above the ground, I was
A morsel for a monarch; and great Pompey
Would stand and make his eyes grow in my brow;
There would he anchor his aspect and die
With looking on his life.
[I.v]

23. My salad days,
When I was green in judgment, cold in blood,
To say as I said then.
[I.v]

24. I do not much dislike the matter, but
The manner of his speech.
[II.ii]

25. The barge she sat in, like a burnish'd throne,
Burn'd on the water. The poop was beaten gold;
Purple the sails, and so perfumed that
The winds were love-sick with them; the oars were silver,
Which to the tune of flutes kept stroke, and made
The water which they beat to follow faster,
As amorous of their strokes. For her own person,
It beggar'd all description. She did lie
In her pavilion, cloth-of-gold, of tissue,
O'erpicturing that Venus where we see
The fancy out-work nature. On each side her
Stood pretty dimpled boys, like smiling Cupids,
With divers-colour'd fans, whose wind did seem
To glow the delicate cheeks which they did cool,
And what they undid did.
[II.ii]

26. Her gentlewomen, like the Nereides,
So many mermaids, tended her i' th' eyes,
And made their bends adornings. At the helm
A seeming mermaid steers. The silken tackle
Swell with the touches of those flower-soft hands
That yarely frame the office. From the barge
A strange invisible perfume hits the sense
Of the adjacent wharfs. The city cast
Her people out upon her; and Antony,
Enthron'd i' th' market-place, did sit alone,
Whistling to th' air; which, but for vacancy,
Had gone to gaze on Cleopatra too,
And made a gap in nature.
[II.ii]

27. I saw her once
Hop forty paces through the public street;
And, having lost her breath, she spoke, and panted,
That she did make defect perfection,
And, breathless, pow'r breathe forth.
[II.ii]

28. Age cannot wither her, nor custom stale
Her infinite variety. Other women cloy
The appetites they feed, but she makes hungry
Where most she satisfies; for vilest things
Become themselves in her, that the holy priests
Bless her when she is riggish.
[II.ii]

29. I' th' East my pleasure lies.
[II.iii]

30. Give me mine angle – we'll to th' river. There,
My music playing far off, I will betray
Tawny-finn'd fishes; my bended hook shall pierce
Their slimy jaws; and as I draw them up
I'll think them every one an Antony,
And say 'Ah ha!' Y'are caught'.
[II.v]

31. I laugh'd him out of patience; and that night
I laugh'd him into patience; and next morn,
Ere the ninth hour, I drunk him to his bed.
[II.v]

32. There is gold, and here
My bluest veins to kiss – a hand that kings
Have lipp'd, and trembled kissing.
[II.v]

33. Though it be honest, it is never good
To bring bad news. Give to a gracious message
An host of tongues; but let ill tidings tell
Themselves when they be felt.
[II.v]

34. I will praise any man that will praise me.
[II.vi]

35. *Lepidus*: What manner o' thing is your crocodile?
Antony: It is shap'd, sir, like itself, and it is as broad as it hath breadth; it is just so high as it is, and moves with it own organs. It lives by that which nourisheth it, and the elements once out of it, it transmigrates.
Lepidus: What colour is it of?
Antony: Of its own colour too.
Lepidus: 'Tis a strange serpent.
Antony: 'Tis so. And the tears of it are wet.
[II.vii]

36. We have kiss'd away
Kingdoms and provinces.
[III.x]

37. He wears the rose
Of youth upon him.
[III.xiii]

38. Yet he that can endure
To follow with allegiance a fall'n lord
Does conquer him that did his master conquer,
And earns a place i' th' story.
[III.xiii]

39. I found you as a morsel cold upon
Dead Caesar's trencher.
[III.xiii]

40. Let's have one other gaudy night. Call to me
All my sad captains; fill our bowls once more;
Let's mock the midnight bell.
[III.xiii]

41. Since my lord
Is Antony again, I will be Cleopatra.
[III.xiii]

42. To business that we love we rise betime,
And go to't with delight.
[IV.iv]

43. O, my fortunes have
Corrupted honest men!
[IV.v]

44. I am alone the villain of the earth,
And feel I am so most.
[IV.vi]

45. *Cleopatra*: Lord of lords!
O infinite virtue, com'st thou smiling from
The world's great snare uncaught?
Antony: Mine nightingale,
We have beat them to their beds.
[IV.viii]

46. O sovereign mistress of true melancholy,
The poisonous damp of night disponge upon me,
That life, a very rebel to my will,
May hang no longer on me.
[IV.ix]

47. The hearts
That spaniel'd me at heels, to whom I gave
Their wishes, do discandy, melt their sweets
On blossoming Caesar.
[IV.xii]

48. The soul and body rive not more in parting
Than greatness going off.
[IV.xiii]

49. Sometime we see a cloud that's dragonish;
A vapour sometime like a bear or lion,
A tower'd citadel, a pendent rock,
A forked mountain, or blue promontory
With trees upon't that nod unto the world
And mock our eyes with air. Thou hast seen these signs;
They are black vesper's pageants.
[IV.xiv]

50. That which is now a horse, even with a thought
The rack dislimns, and makes it indistinct,
As water is in water.
[IV.xiv]

51. Unarm, Eros; the long day's task is done,
And we must sleep.
[IV.xiv]

52. Lie down, and stray no farther. Now all labour
Mars what it does; yea, very force entangles

Itself with strength...
Stay for me;
Where souls do couch on flowers, we'll hand in hand,
And with our sprightly port make the ghosts gaze.
Dido and her Aeneas shall want troops,
And all the haunt be ours.
[IV.xiv]

53. I will be
A bridegroom in my death, and run into't
As to a lover's bed.
[IV.xiv]

54. All strange and terrible events are welcome,
But comforts we despise.
[IV.xv]

55. *Antony*: Not Caesar's valour hath o'erthrown Antony,
But Antony's hath triumph'd on itself.
Cleopatra: So it should be, that none but Antony
Should conquer Antony.
[IV.xv]

56. I am dying, Egypt, dying; only
I here importune death awhile, until
Of many thousand kisses the poor last
I lay upon thy lips.
[IV.xv]

57. The miserable change now at my end
Lament nor sorrow at; but please your thoughts
In feeding them with those my former fortunes
Wherein I liv'd the greatest prince o' th' world,
The noblest; and do now not basely die,
Not cowardly put off my helmet to
My countryman – a Roman by a Roman
Valiantly vanquish'd.
[IV.xv]

58. Hast thou no care of me? Shall I abide
In this dull world, which in thy absence is
No better than a sty? O, see, my women,
The crown o' th' earth doth melt. My lord!
O, wither'd is the garland of the war,
The soldier's pole is fall'n! Young boys and girls
Are level now with men. The odds is gone,
And there is nothing left remarkable
Beneath the visiting moon.
[IV.xv]

59. No more but e'en a woman, and commanded
By such poor passion as the maid that milks
And does the meanest chares.
[IV.xv]

60. What's brave, what's noble,
Let's do it after the high Roman fashion,
And make death proud to take us.
[IV.xv]

61. A rarer spirit never
Did steer humanity. But you gods will give us
Some faults to make us men.
[V.i]

62. My desolation does begin to make
A better life. 'Tis paltry to be Caesar:
Not being Fortune, he's but Fortune's knave,
A minister of her will; and it is great
To do that thing that ends all other deeds,
Which shackles accidents and bolts up change,
Which sleeps, and never palates more the dug,
The beggar's nurse and Caesar's.
[V.ii]

63. Nor once be chastis'd with the sober eye
Of dull Octavia. Shall they hoist me up,
And show me to the shouting varletry
Of censuring Rome? Rather a ditch in Egypt
Be gentle grave unto me! Rather on Nilus' mud
Lay me stark-nak'd, and let the water-flies
Blow me into abhorring!
[V.ii]

64. His legs bestrid the ocean; his rear'd arm
Crested the world. His voice was propertied
As all the tuned spheres, and that to friends;
But when he meant to quail and shake the orb,
He was as rattling thunder. For his bounty,
There was no winter in't; an autumn 'twas
That grew the more by reaping. His delights
Were dolphin-like: they show'd his back above
The element they liv'd in. In his livery
Walk'd crowns and crownets; realms and islands were
As plates dropp'd from his pocket.
[V.ii]

65. He words me, girls, he words me, that I should not
Be noble to myself.
[V.ii]

66. Finish, good lady; the bright day is done,
And we are for the dark.
[V.ii]

67. Antony
Shall be brought drunken forth, and I shall see
Some squeaking Cleopatra boy my greatness
I' th' posture of a whore.
[V.ii]

68. My resolution's plac'd, and I have nothing
Of woman in me. Now from head to foot
I am marble-constant; now the fleeting moon
No planet is of mine.
[V.ii]

69. His biting is immortal; those that do die of it do seldom or never recover.
[V.ii]

70. A very honest woman, but something given to lie.
[V.ii]

71. I know that a woman is a dish for the gods, if the devil dress her not.
[V.ii]

72. Give me my robe, put on my crown; I have
Immortal longings in me.
[V.ii]

73. Husband, I come.
Now to that name my courage prove my title!
I am fire and air; my other elements
I give to baser life.
[V.ii]

74. If thou and nature can so gently part,
The stroke of death is as a lover's pinch,
Which hurts and is desir'd.
[V.ii]

75. *Cleopatra*: If she first meet the curled Antony,
He'll make demand of her, and spend that kiss
Which is my heaven to have. Come, thou mortal wretch,
With thy sharp teeth this knot intrinsicate
Of life at once untie. Poor venomous fool,
Be angry, and dispatch. O couldst thou speak,
That I might hear thee call great Caesar ass
Unpolicied!

Charmian: O Eastern star!
Cleopatra: Peace, peace!
Dost thou not see my baby at my breast
That sucks the nurse asleep?
[V.ii]

76. Now boast thee, death, in thy possession lies
A lass unparallel'd.
[V.ii]

77. It is well done, and fitting for a princess
Descended of so many royal kings.
[V.ii]

78. She looks like sleep,
As she would catch another Antony
In her strong toil of grace.
[V.ii]

79. She hath pursu'd conclusions infinite
Of easy ways to die.
[V.ii]

80. She shall be buried by her Antony;
No grave upon the earth shall clip in it
A pair so famous.
[V.ii]

As You Like It

1. Fleet the time carelessly, as they did in the golden world.
[I.i]

2. Let us sit and mock the good housewife Fortune from her wheel, that her gifts may henceforth be bestowed equally.
[I.ii]

3. Well said; that was laid on with a trowel.
[I:ii]

4. Thus men may grow wiser every day. It is the first time that ever I heard breaking of ribs was sport for ladies.
[I.ii]

5. Only in the world I fill up a place, which may be better supplied when I have made it empty.
[I.ii]

6. Sir, you have wrestled well, and overthrown
More than your enemies.
[I.ii]

7. Hereafter, in a better world than this,
I shall desire more love and knowledge of you.
[I.ii]

8. O, how full of briers is this working-day world!
[I.iii]

9. Alas, what danger will it be to us,
Maids as we are, to travel forth so far!
Beauty provoketh thieves sooner than gold.
[I.iii]

10. We'll have a swashing and a martial outside,
As many other mannish cowards have
That do outface it with their semblances.
[I.iii]

11. Hath not old custom made this life more sweet
Than that of painted pomp? Are not these woods
More free from peril than the envious court?
Here feel we but the penalty of Adam,
The seasons' difference; as the icy fang
And churlish chiding of the winter's wind,
Which when it bites and blows upon my body,
Even till I shrink with cold, I smile and say
'This is no flattery'.
[II.i]

12. Sweet are the uses of adversity;
Which, like the toad, ugly and venomous,
Wears yet a precious jewel in his head;
And this our life, exempt from public haunt,
Finds tongues in trees, books in the running brooks,
Sermons in stones, and good in everything.
[II.i]

13. The big round tears
Cours'd one another down his innocent nose
In piteous chase.
[II.i]

14. I love to cope him in these sullen fits,
For then he's full of matter.
[II.i]

15. Unregarded age in corners thrown.
[II.iii]

16. Though I look old, yet I am strong and lusty;
For in my youth I never did apply
Hot and rebellious liquors in my blood.
[II.iii]

17. Therefore my age is as a lusty winter,
Frosty, but kindly.
[II.iii]

18. O good old man, how well in thee appears
The constant service of the antique world,
When service sweat for duty, not for meed!
Thou art not for the fashion of these times,
Where none will sweat but for promotion,
And having that do choke their service up
Even with the having.
[II.iii]

19. I had rather bear with you than bear you.
[II:iv]

20. Ay, now am I in Arden; the more fool I; when I was at home
I was in a better place; but travellers must be content.
[II.iv]

21. In thy youth thou wast as true a lover
As ever sigh'd upon a midnight pillow.
[II.iv]

22. If thou remembr'rest not the slightest folly
That ever love did make thee run into,
Thou hast not lov'd.
[II.iv]

23. We that are true lovers run into strange capers.
[II.iv]

24. Under the greenwood tree
Who loves to lie with me,
And turn his merry note
Unto the sweet bird's throat,
Come hither, come hither, come hither.
Here shall he see
No enemy
But winter and rough weather.
[II.v]

25. I can suck melancholy out of a song, as a weasel sucks eggs.
[II.v]

26. Who doth ambition shun,
And loves to live i' th' sun,
Seeking the food he eats,
And pleas'd with what he gets.
[II.v]

27. I'll go sleep, if I can; if I cannot, I'll rail against all the first-born of Egypt.
[II.v]

28. A fool, a fool! I met a fool i' th' forest,
A motley fool. A miserable world!
As I do live by food, I met a fool,
Who laid him down and bask'd him in the sun,
And rail'd on Lady Fortune in good terms,
In good set terms – and yet a motley fool.
'Good morrow, fool,' quoth I; 'No, sir,' quoth he
'Call me not fool till heaven hath sent me fortune.'
[II.vii]

29. And so, from hour to hour, we ripe and ripe,
And then, from hour to hour, we rot and rot;
And thereby hangs a tale.
[II.vii]

30. My lungs began to crow like chanticleer
That fools should be so deep contemplative;
And I did laugh sans intermission
An hour by his dial. O noble fool!
A worthy fool! Motley's the only wear.
[II.vii]

31. O worthy fool! One that hath been a courtier,
And says, if ladies be but young and fair,
They have the gift to know it; and in his brain,
Which is as dry as the remainder biscuit
After a voyage, he hath strange places cramm'd
With observation, the which he vents
In mangled forms.
[II.vii]

32. I must have liberty
Withal, as large a charter as the wind,
To blow on whom I please.
[II.vii]

33. If ever you have look'd on better days,
If ever been where bells have knoll'd to church,
If ever sat at any good man's feast,
If ever from your eyelids wip'd a tear,
And know what 'tis to pity and be pitied,
Let gentleness my strong enforcement be.
[II.vii]

34. All the world's a stage,
And all the men and women merely players;
They have their exits and their entrances;
And one man in his time plays many parts,
His acts being seven ages. At first the infant,
Mewling and puking in the nurse's arms;
Then the whining school-boy, with his satchel
And shining morning face, creeping like snail
Unwillingly to school. And then the lover,
Sighing like furnace, with a woeful ballad
Made to his mistress' eyebrow. Then a soldier,
Full of strange oaths, and bearded like the pard,
Jealous in honour, sudden and quick in quarrel,
Seeking the bubble reputation
Even in the cannon's mouth. And then the justice,
In fair round belly with good capon lin'd,
With eyes severe and beard of formal cut,
Full of wise saws and modern instances;
And so he plays his part. The sixth age shifts
Into the lean and slipper'd pantaloon,
With spectacles on nose and pouch on side,
His youthful hose, well sav'd, a world too wide
For his shrunk shank; and his big manly voice,
Turning again toward childish treble, pipes
And whistles in his sound. Last scene of all,
That ends this strange eventful history,
Is second childishness and mere oblivion;
Sans teeth, sans eyes, sans taste, sans every thing.
[II.vii]

35. Blow, blow, thou winter wind,
Thou art not so unkind
As man's ingratitude;
Thy tooth is not so keen,
Because thou art not seen,
Although thy breath be rude.
Heigh-ho! sing heigh-ho! unto the green holly:
Most friendship is feigning, most loving mere folly.
Then, heigh-ho, the holly!
This life is most jolly.

Freeze, freeze, thou bitter sky,
That dost not bite so nigh
As benefits forgot;
Though thou the waters warp,
Thy sting is not so sharp
As friend rememb'red not.
[II.vii]

36. Run, run, Orlando; carve on every tree,
The fair, the chaste, and unexpressive she.
[III.ii]

37. He that wants money, means, and content, is without three good friends.
[III.ii]

38. I earn that I eat, get that I wear; owe no man hate, envy no man's happiness; glad of other men's good, content with my harm.
[III.ii]

39. From the east to western Inde,
No jewel is like Rosalinde.
[III.ii]

40. Let us make an honourable retreat; though not with bag and baggage, yet with scrip and scrippage.
[III.ii]

41. O wonderful, wonderful, and most wonderful wonderful! and yet again wonderful, and after that, out of all whooping!
[III.ii]

42. It is as easy to count atomies as to resolve the propositions of a lover.
[III.ii]

43. Do you not know I am a woman? When I think, I must speak.
[III.ii]

44. I do desire we may be better strangers.
[III.ii]

45. *Jaques*: I do not like her name.
Orlando: There was no thought of pleasing you when she was christen'd.
[III.ii]

46. You have a nimble wit; I think 'twas made of Atalanta's heels.
[III.ii]

47. *Rosalind*: Time travels in divers paces with divers persons…
Orlando: Who stays it still withal?
Rosalind: With lawyers in the vacation; for they sleep between term and term.
[III.ii]

48. Truly, I would the gods had made thee poetical.
[III.iii]

49. The truest poetry is the most feigning.
[III:iii]

50. I am not a slut, though I thank the gods I am foul.
[III.iii]

51. Down on your knees,
And thank heaven, fasting, for a good man's love.
[III.v]

52. I pray you do not fall in love with me,
For I am falser than vows made in wine.
[III.v]

53. Dead shepherd, now I find thy saw of might:
'Who ever lov'd that lov'd not at first sight?'
[III.v. Cf. Marlowe: 47]

54. I had rather have a fool to make me merry than experience to make me sad.
[IV.i]

55. *Jaques*: Nay, then, God buy you, an you talk in blank verse.
Rosalind: Farewell, Monsieur Traveller; look you lisp and wear strange suits, disable all the benefits of your own country, be out of love with your nativity, and almost chide God for making you that countenance you are; or I will scarce think you have swam in a gondola.
[IV.i]

56. Come, woo me, woo me; for now I am in a holiday humour, and like enough to consent.
[IV.i]

57. You were better speak first; and when you were gravell'd for lack of matter, you might take occasion to kiss.
[IV.i]

58. Men have died from time to time, and worms have eaten them, but not for love.
[IV.i]

59. Men are April when they woo, December when they wed: maids are May when they are maids, but the sky changes when they are wives.
[IV.i]

60. O coz, coz, coz, my pretty little coz, that thou didst know how many fathom deep I am in love!
[IV.i]

61. The horn, the horn, the lusty horn,
Is not a thing to laugh to scorn.
[IV.ii]

62. Chewing the food of sweet and bitter fancy.
[IV.iii]

63. Your brother and my sister no sooner met but they look'd; no sooner look'd but they lov'd; no sooner lov'd but they sigh'd; no sooner sigh'd but they ask'd one another the reason; no sooner knew the reason but they sought the remedy – and in these degrees have they made a pair of stairs to marriage, which they will climb incontinent, or else be incontinent before marriage.
[V.ii]

64. O, how bitter a thing it is to look into happiness through another man's eyes!
[V.ii]

65. *Phebe*: Good shepherd, tell this youth what 'tis to love.
Silvius: It is to be all made of sighs and tears...
It is to be all made of faith and service...
It is to be all made of fantasy,
All made of passion, and all made of wishes;
All adoration, duty, and observance,
All humbleness, all patience, and impatience;
All purity, all trial, all obedience.
[V.ii]

66. 'Tis like the howling of Irish wolves against the moon.
[V.ii]

67. It was a lover and his lass,
With a hey, and a ho, and a hey nonino,
That o'er the green corn-field did pass
In the spring time, the only pretty ring time,
When birds do sing, hey ding a ding, ding.
Sweet lovers love the spring.

Between the acres of the rye,
With a hey, and a ho, and a hey nonino,
These pretty country folks would lie,
In the spring time, &c.

This carol they began that hour,
With a hey, and a ho, and a hey nonino,
How that a life was but a flower,
In the spring time, &c.

And therefore take the present time,
With a hey, and a ho, and a hey nonino,
For love is crowned with the prime,
In the spring time, &c.
[V.iii]

68. Here comes a pair of very strange beasts which in all tongues are call'd fools.
[V.iv]

69. A poor virgin, sir, an ill-favour'd thing, sir, but mine own; a poor humour of mine, sir, to take that that no man else will. Rich honesty dwells like a miser, sir, in a poor house; as your pearl in your foul oyster.
[V.iv]

70. The Retort Courteous ... the Quip Modest ... the Reply Churlish ... the Reproof Valiant ... the Countercheck Quarrelsome ... the Lie Circumstantial ... the Lie Direct.
[V.iv]

71. Your If is the only peace-maker; much virtue in If.
[V.iv]

72. He uses his folly like a stalking-horse, and under the presentation of that he shoots his wit.
[V.iv]

73. If it be true that good wine needs no bush, 'tis true that a good play needs no epilogue.
[Epilogue]

The Comedy of Errors

1. There's nothing situate under heaven's eye
But hath his bound, in earth, in sea, in sky.
The beasts, the fishes, and the winged fowls,
Are their males' subjects, and at their controls.
Man, more divine, the master of all these,
Lord of the wide world and wild wat'ry seas,
Indu'd with intellectual sense and souls,
Of more pre-eminence than fish and fowls,
Are masters to their females, and their lords;
Then let your will attend on their accords.
[II.i]

2. Am I so round with you, as you with me,
That like a football you do spurn me thus?
[II.i]

3. Since that my beauty cannot please his eye,
I'll weep what's left away, and weeping die.
[II.i]

4. Marry, sir, she's the kitchen-wench, and all grease; and I know not what use to put her to but to make a lamp of her and run from her by her own light. I warrant, her rags and the tallow in them will burn a Poland winter. If she lives till doomsday, she'll burn a week longer than the whole world.
[III.ii]

5. Marry, he must have a long spoon that must eat with the devil.
[IV.iii]

6. The venom clamours of a jealous woman
Poisons more deadly than a mad dog's tooth.
[V.i]

7. They brought one Pinch, a hungry lean-fac'd villain,
A mere anatomy, a mountebank,
A threadbare juggler, and a fortune-teller,
A needy, hollow-ey'd, sharp-looking wretch,
A living dead man.
[V.i]

8. Though now this grained face of mine be hid
In sap-consuming winter's drizzled snow,
And all the conduits of my blood froze up,
Yet hath my night of life some memory.
[V.i]

Coriolanus

1. He's a very dog to the commonalty.
[I.i]

2. What's the matter, you dissentious rogues
That, rubbing the poor itch of your opinion,
Make yourselves scabs?
[I.i]

3. They threw their caps
As they would hang them on the horns o' th' moon,
Shouting their emulation.
[I.i]

4. I am known to be . . . one that loves a cup of hot wine with not a drop of allaying Tiber in't.
[II.i]

5. Bid them wash their faces
And keep their teeth clean.
[II.iii]

6. Custom calls me to't.
What custom wills, in all things should we do't,
The dust on antique time would lie unswept,
And mountainous error be too highly heap'd
For truth to o'erpeer.
[II.iii]

7. I thank you for your voices. Thank you,
Your most sweet voices.
[II.iii]

8. For the mutable, rank-scented many, let them
Regard me as I do not flatter, and
Therein behold themselves.
[III.i]

9. Hear you this Triton of the minnows? Mark you
His absolute 'shall'?
[III.i]

10. You common cry of curs, whose breath I hate
As reek o' th' rotten fens, whose loves I prize
As the dead carcasses of unburied men
That do corrupt my air – I banish you.
[III.iii]

11. Despising
For you the city, thus I turn my back;
There is a world elsewhere.
[III.iii]

12. The beast
With many heads butts me away.
[IV.i]

13. Thou hast a grim appearance, and thy face
Bears a command in't; though thy tackle's torn,
Thou show'st a noble vessel. What's thy name?
[IV.v]

14. Let me have war, say I; it exceeds peace as far as day does night; it's spritely, waking, audible, and full of vent. Peace is a very apoplexy, lethargy; mull'd, deaf, sleepy, insensible; a getter of more bastard children than war's a destroyer of men.
[IV.v]

15. I'll never
Be such a gosling to obey instinct, but stand
As if a man were author of himself
And knew no other kin.
[V.iii]

16. Like a dull actor now,
I have forgot my part and I am out,
Even to a full disgrace.
[V.iii]

17. O, a kiss
Long as my exile, sweet as my revenge!
Now, by the jealous queen of heaven, that kiss
I carried from thee, dear, and my true lip
Hath virgin'd it e'er since.
[V.iii]

18. Chaste as the icicle
That's curdied by the frost from purest snow,
And hangs on Dian's temple.
[V.iii]

19. The god of soldiers,
With the consent of supreme Jove, inform
Thy thoughts with nobleness, that thou mayst prove
To shame unvulnerable, and stick i' th' wars
Like a great sea-mark, standing every flaw,
And saving those that eye thee!
[V.iii]

20. Thou hast never in thy life
Show'd thy dear mother any courtesy,
When she, poor hen, fond of no second brood,
Has cluck'd thee to the wars, and safely home
Loaden with honour.
[V.iii]

21. He wants nothing of a god but eternity, and a heaven to throne in.
[V.iv]

22. If you have writ your annals true, 'tis there
That, like an eagle in a dove-cote, I
Flutter'd your Volscians in Corioli.
Alone I did it.
[V.vi]

23. Thou hast done a deed whereat valour will weep.
[V.vi]

Cymbeline

1. If she be furnish'd with a mind so rare,
She is alone th' Arabian bird, and I
Have lost the wager. Boldness be my friend!
Arm me, audacity.
[I.vi]

2. Cytherea,
How bravely thou becom'st thy bed! fresh lily,
And whiter than the sheets! That I might touch!
But kiss; one kiss! Rubies unparagon'd,
How dearly they do't! 'Tis her breathing that
Perfumes the chamber thus. The flame o' th' taper
Bows toward her and would under-peep her lids
To see th' enclosed lights, now canopied
Under these windows white and azure, lac'd
With blue of heaven's own tinct.
[II.ii]

3. On her left breast
A mole cinque-spotted, like the crimson drops
I' th' bottom of a cowslip.
[II.ii]

4. Hark, hark! the lark at heaven's gate sings,
And Phoebus 'gins arise,
His steeds to water at those springs
On chalic'd flow'rs that lies;
And winking Mary-buds begin
To ope their golden eyes.
With everything that pretty is,
My lady sweet, arise.
[II.iii]

5. Is there no way for men to be, but women
Must be half-workers?
[II.v]

6. I thought her
As chaste as unsunn'd snow.
[II.v]

7. There be many Caesars
Ere such another Julius. Britain is
A world by itself, and we will nothing pay
For wearing our own noses.
[III.i]

8. The natural bravery of your isle, which stands
As Neptune's park, ribb'd and pal'd in
With rocks unscalable, and roaring waters.
[III.i]

9. O for a horse with wings!
[III.ii]

10. O, this life
Is nobler than attending for a check,
Richer than doing nothing for a bribe,
Prouder than rustling in unpaid-for silk.
[III:iii]

11. What should we speak of
When we are old as you? When we shall hear
The rain and wind beat dark December, how,
In this our pinching cave, shall we discourse
The freezing hours away? We have seen nothing.
[III.iii]

12. Hath Britain all the sun that shines?
[III.iv]

13. Weariness
Can snore upon the flint, when resty sloth
Finds the down pillow hard.
[III.vi]

14. Society is no comfort
To one not sociable.
[IV:ii]

15. Great griefs, I see, med'cine the less.
[IV.ii]

16. Thersites' body is as good as Ajax',
When neither are alive.
[IV.ii]

17. Fear no more the heat o' th' sun
Nor the furious winter's rages;
Thou thy worldly task hast done,
Home art gone, and ta'en thy wages.
Golden lads and girls all must,
As chimney-sweepers, come to dust.

Fear no more the frown o' th' great;
Thou art past the tyrant's stroke.
Care no more to clothe and eat;
To thee the reed is as the oak.
The sceptre, learning, physic, must
All follow this, and come to dust.

Fear no more the lightning flash,
Nor th' all-dreaded thunder-stone;
Fear not slander, censure rash;
Thou hast finish'd joy and moan.
All lovers young, all lovers must
Consign to thee and come to dust.

No exorciser harm thee!
Nor no witchcraft charm thee!
Ghost unlaid forbear thee!
Nothing ill come near thee!
Quiet consummation have,
And renowned be thy grave!
[IV.ii]

18. Every good servant does not all commands.
[V.i]

19. He that sleeps feels not the toothache.
[V.iv]

20. He spake of her as Dian had hot dreams
And she alone were cold.
[V.v]

Hamlet

1. You come most carefully upon your hour.
[I.i]

2. Not a mouse stirring.
[I.i]

3. But, in the gross and scope of mine opinion,
This bodes some strange eruption to our state.
[I.i]

4. This sweaty haste
Doth make the night joint-labourer with the day.
[I.i]

5. In the most high and palmy state of Rome,
A little ere the mightiest Julius fell,
The graves stood tenantless, and the sheeted dead
Did squeak and gibber in the Roman streets.
[I.i]

6. The moist star
Upon whose influence Neptune's empire stands
Was sick almost to doomsday with eclipse.
[I.i]

7. I'll cross it, though it blast me.
[I.i]

8. We do it wrong, being so majestical,
To offer it the show of violence;
For it is, as the air, invulnerable,
And our vain blows malicious mockery.
[I.i]

9. And then it started like a guilty thing
Upon a fearful summons.
[I.i]

10. It faded on the crowing of the cock.
Some say that ever 'gainst that season comes
Wherein our Saviour's birth is celebrated,
This bird of dawning singeth all night long;
And then, they say, no spirit dare stir abroad,
The nights are wholesome, then no planets strike,
No fairy takes, nor witch hath power to charm,
So hallowed and so gracious is that time.
[I.i]

11. But look, the morn, in russet mantle clad,
Walks o'er the dew of yon high eastward hill.
[I.i]

12. Though yet of Hamlet our dear brother's death
The memory be green...
Therefore our sometime sister, now our queen,...
Have we, as 'twere with a defeated joy,
With an auspicious and a dropping eye,
With mirth in funeral, and with dirge in marriage,
In equal scale weighing delight and dole,
Taken to wife.
[I.ii]

13. The head is not more native to the heart,
The hand more instrumental to the mouth,
Than is the throne of Denmark to thy father.
[I.ii]

14. A little more than kin, and less than kind.
[I.ii]

15. Not so, my lord; I am too much in the sun.
[I.ii]

16. Good Hamlet, cast thy nighted colour off,
And let thine eye look like a friend on Denmark.
[I.ii]

17. *Queen*: Thou know'st 'tis common – all that lives must die,
Passing through nature to eternity.
Hamlet: Ay, madam, it is common.
[I.ii]

18. Seems, madam! Nay, it is; I know not seems.
'Tis not alone my inky cloak, good mother,
Nor customary suits of solemn black,
Nor windy suspiration of forc'd breath,
No, nor the fruitful river in the eye,
Nor the dejected haviour of the visage,
Together with all forms, moods, shapes of grief,
That can denote me truly. These, indeed, seem;
For they are actions that a man might play;
But I have that within which passes show–
These but the trappings and the suits of woe.
[I.ii]

19. But to persever
In obstinate condolement is a course
Of impious stubbornness; 'tis unmanly grief;
It shows a will most incorrect to heaven,
A heart unfortified, a mind impatient.
[I.ii]

20. *Hamlet*: I shall in all my best obey you, madam.
King: Why, 'tis a loving and a fair reply.
[I.ii]

21. O, that this too too solid flesh would melt,
Thaw, and resolve itself into a dew!
Or that the Everlasting had not fix'd
His canon 'gainst self-slaughter! O God! God!
How weary, stale, flat, and unprofitable,
Seem to me all the uses of this world!
Fie on't! Ah, fie! 'tis an unweeded garden,
That grows to seed; things rank and gross in nature
Possess it merely. That it should come to this!
But two months dead! Nay, not so much, not two.
So excellent a king that was to this
Hyperion to a satyr; so loving to my mother,
That he might not beteem the winds of heaven
Visit her face too roughly. Heaven and earth!
Must I remember? Why, she would hang on him
As if increase of appetite had grown
By what it fed on; and yet, within a month–
Let me not think on't. Frailty, thy name is woman!–
A little month, or ere those shoes were old
With which she followed my poor father's body,
Like Niobe, all tears – why she, even she–
O God! a beast that wants discourse of reason
Would have mourn'd longer – married with my uncle,
My father's brother; but no more like my father
Than I to Hercules.
[I.ii]

22. It is not, nor it cannot come to good.
But break, my heart, for I must hold my tongue.
[I.ii]

23. A truant disposition, good my lord.
[I.ii]

24. Thrift, thrift, Horatio! The funeral bak'd-meats
Did coldly furnish forth the marriage tables.
Would I had met my dearest foe in heaven
Or ever I had seen that day, Horatio!
[I.ii]

25. 'A was a man, take him for all in all,
I shall not look upon his like again.
[I.ii]

26. Give it an understanding, but no tongue.
[I.ii]

27. Foul deeds will rise,
Though all the earth o'erwhelm them, to men's eyes.
[I.ii]

28. And keep you in the rear of your affection,
Out of the shot and danger of desire.
The chariest maid is prodigal enough
If she unmask her beauty to the moon.
[I.iii]

29. Do not, as some ungracious pastors do,
Show me the steep and thorny way to heaven,
Whiles, like a puff'd and reckless libertine,
Himself the primrose path of dalliance treads
And recks not his own rede.
[I.iii]

30. And these few precepts in thy memory
Look thou character. Give thy thoughts no tongue,
Nor any unproportion'd thought his act.
Be thou familiar, but by no means vulgar.
Those friends thou hast, and their adoption tried,
Grapple them to thy soul with hoops of steel;
But do not dull thy palm with entertainment

Of each new-hatch'd, unfledg'd courage. Beware
Of entrance to a quarrel; but, being in,
Bear't that th' opposed may beware of thee.
Give every man thy ear, but few thy voice;
Take each man's censure, but reserve thy judgment.
Costly thy habit as thy purse can buy,
But not express'd in fancy; rich, not gaudy;
For the apparel oft proclaims the man;
And they in France of the best rank and station
Are of a most select and generous choice in that.
Neither a borrower nor a lender be;
For loan oft loses both itself and friend,
And borrowing dulls the edge of husbandry.
This above all – to thine own self be true,
And it must follow, as the night the day,
Thou canst not then be false to any man.
[I.iii]

31. You speak like a green girl,
Unsifted in such perilous circumstance.
[I.iii]

32. Ay, springes to catch woodcocks! I do know,
When the blood burns, how prodigal the soul
Lends the tongue vows. These blazes, daughter,
Giving more light than heat – extinct in both,
Even in their promise, as it is a-making–
You must not take for fire.
[I.iii]

33. Be something scanter of your maiden presence.
[I.iii]

34. *Hamlet*: The air bites shrewdly; it is very cold.
Horatio: It is a nipping and an eager air.
[I.iv]

35. But to my mind, though I am native here
And to the manner born, it is a custom
More honour'd in the breach than the observance.
[I.iv]

36. Angels and ministers of grace defend us!
Be thou a spirit of health or goblin damn'd,
Bring with thee airs from heaven or blasts from hell,
Be thy intents wicked or charitable,
Thou com'st in such a questionable shape
That I will speak to thee. I'll call thee Hamlet,
King, father, royal Dane. O, answer me!
Let me not burst in ignorance, but tell
Why thy canoniz'd bones, hearsed in death,
Have burst their cerements; why the sepulchre
Wherein we saw thee quietly enurn'd
Hath op'd his ponderous and marble jaws
To cast thee up again. What may this mean
That thou, dead corse, again in complete steel
Revisits thus the glimpses of the moon,
Making night hideous, and we fools of nature
So horridly to shake our disposition
With thoughts beyond the reaches of our souls?
[I.iv]

37. I do not set my life at a pin's fee;
And for my soul, what can it do to that,
Being a thing immortal as itself?
[I.iv]

38. Unhand me, gentlemen.
By heaven, I'll make a ghost of him that lets me.
[I.iv]

39. Something is rotten in the state of Denmark.
[I.iv]

40. Alas, poor ghost!
[I.v]

41. I am thy father's spirit,
Doom'd for a certain term to walk the night.
[I.v]

42. But that I am forbid
To tell the secrets of my prison-house,
I could a tale unfold whose lightest word
Would harrow up thy soul, freeze thy young blood,
Make thy two eyes, like stars, start from their spheres,
Thy knotted and combined locks to part,
And each particular hair to stand an end,
Like quills upon the fretful porpentine.
But this eternal blazon must not be
To ears of flesh and blood. List, list, O, list!
[I.v]

43. Revenge his foul and most unnatural murder.
[I.v]

44. Murder most foul, as in the best it is;
But this most foul, strange, and unnatural.
[I.v]

45. And duller shouldst thou be than the fat weed
That roots itself in ease on Lethe wharf,
Wouldst thou not stir in this.
[I.v]

46. O my prophetic soul!
My uncle!
[I.v]

47. But soft! methinks I scent the morning air.
[I.v]

48. Thus was I, sleeping, by a brother's hand
Of life, of crown, of queen, at once dispatch'd;
Cut off even in the blossoms of my sin,
Unhous'led, disappointed, unanel'd;
No reck'ning made, but sent to my account
With all my imperfections on my head.
O, horrible! O, horrible! most horrible!
If thou hast nature in thee, bear it not.
[I.v]

49. Leave her to heaven,
And to those thorns that in her bosom lodge
To prick and sting her.
[I.v]

50. The glowworm shows the matin to be near,
And 'gins to pale his uneffectual fire.
[I.v]

51. Remember thee!
Ay, thou poor ghost, whiles memory holds a seat
In this distracted globe. Remember thee!
Yea, from the table of my memory
I'll wipe away all trivial fond records,
All saws of books, all forms, all pressures past,
That youth and observation copied there.
[I.v]

52. O most pernicious woman!
O villain, villain, smiling, damned villain!
My tables – meet it is I set it down
That one may smile, and smile, and be a villain;
At least I am sure it may be so in Denmark.
[I.v]

53. *Hamlet*: There's never a villain dwelling in all Denmark
But he's an arrant knave.
Horatio: There needs no ghost, my lord, come from the grave

To tell us this.
[I.v]

54. It is an honest ghost, that let me tell you.
[I.v]

55. Well said, old mole! Canst work i' th' earth so fast?
[I.v]

56. O day and night, but this is wondrous strange!
[I.v]

57. There are more things in heaven and earth, Horatio,
Than are dreamt of in your philosophy.
[I.v]

58. As I perchance hereafter shall think meet
To put an antic disposition on.
[I.v]

59. Rest, rest, perturbed spirit!
[I.v]

60. The time is out of joint. O cursed spite,
That ever I was born to set it right!
[I.v. Cf. Strachey: 1]

61. Lord Hamlet, with his doublet all unbrac'd,
No hat upon his head, his stockings fouled,
Ungart'red and down-gyved to his ankle.
[II.i]

62. This is the very ecstasy of love.
[II.i]

63. Brevity is the soul of wit.
[II.ii. Cf. Maugham: 5 and S.T. Coleridge: 58]

64. To define true madness,
What is't but to be nothing else but mad?
[II.ii]

65. That he's mad, 'tis true: 'tis true 'tis pity;
And pity 'tis 'tis true. A foolish figure!
But farewell it, for I will use no art.
[II.ii]

66. That's an ill phrase, a vile phrase; 'beautified' is a vile phrase.
[II.ii]

67. Doubt thou the stars are fire;
Doubt that the sun doth move;
Doubt truth to be a liar;
But never doubt I love.
[II.ii]

68. Lord Hamlet is a prince out of thy star.
[II.ii]

69. And he repelled, a short tale to make,
Fell into a sadness, then into a fast,
Thence to a watch, thence into a weakness,
Thence to a lightness, and, by this declension,
Into the madness wherein now he raves
And all we mourn for.
[II.ii]

70. Let me be no assistant for a state,
But keep a farm and carters.
[II.ii]

71. *Polonius*: Do you know me, my lord?
Hamlet: Excellent well; you are a fishmonger.
[II.ii]

72. *Polonius*: What do you read, my lord?
Hamlet: Words, words, words.
[II.ii]

73. The satirical rogue says here that old men have grey beards; that their faces are wrinkled; their eyes purging thick amber and plum-tree gum; and that they have a plentiful lack of wit, together with most weak hams – all of which, sir, though I most powerfully and potently believe, yet I hold it not honesty to have it thus set down.
[II.ii]

74. Though this be madness, yet there is method in't.
[II.ii]

75. *Polonius*: My lord, I will take my leave of you.
Hamlet: You cannot, sir, take from me anything that I will more willingly part withal – except my life, except my life, except my life.
[II.ii]

76. *Guildenstern*: On fortune's cap we are not the very button.
Hamlet: Nor the soles of her shoe?
Rosencrantz: Neither, my lord.
Hamlet: Then you live above her waist, or in the middle of her favours?
Guildenstern: Faith, her privates we.
Hamlet: In the secret parts of Fortune? O, most true; she is a strumpet. What news?
Rosencrantz: None, my lord, but that the world's grown honest.
Hamlet: Then is doomsday near.
[II.ii]

77. There is nothing either good or bad, but thinking makes it so.
[II.ii]

78. O God, I could be bounded in a nutshell and count myself a king of infinite space, were it not that I have bad dreams.
[II.ii]

79. Beggar that I am, I am even poor in thanks.
[II.ii]

80. It goes so heavily with my disposition that this goodly frame, the earth, seems to me a sterile promontory; this most excellent canopy the air, look you, this brave o'erhanging firmament, this majestical roof fretted with golden fire – why, it appeareth no other thing to me than a foul and pestilent congregation of vapours. What a piece of work is a man! How noble in reason! how infinite in faculties! in form and moving, how express and admirable! in action, how like an angel! in apprehension, how like a god! the beauty of the world! the paragon of animals! And yet, to me, what is this quintessence of dust? Man delights not me – no, nor woman neither, though by your smiling you seem to say so.
[II.ii]

81. There is something in this more than natural, if philosophy could find it out.
[II.ii]

82. I am but mad north-north-west; when the wind is southerly I know a hawk from a handsaw.
[II.ii]

83. That great baby you see there is not yet out of his swaddling clouts.
[II.ii]

84. The best actors in the world, either for tragedy, comedy, history, pastoral, pastoral-comical, historical-pastoral, tragical-historical, tragical-comical-historical-pastoral, scene individable, or poem unlimited. Seneca cannot be too heavy nor Plautus too light.
[II.ii]

85. One fair daughter, and no more,
The which he loved passing well.
[II.ii]

86. The play, I remember, pleas'd not the million; 'twas caviary to the general.
[II.ii]

87. But who, ah, who had seen the mobled queen.
[II.ii]

88. Good my lord, will you see the players well bestowed? Do you hear: let them be well used; for they are the abstract and brief chronicles of the time; after your death you were better have a bad epitaph than their ill report while you live.
[II.ii]

89. Use every man after his desert, and who shall scape whipping?
[II.ii]

90. O, what a rogue and peasant slave am I!
Is it not monstrous that this player here,
But in a fiction, in a dream of passion,
Could force his soul so to his own conceit
That from her working all his visage wann'd;
Tears in his eyes, distraction in's aspect,
A broken voice, and his whole function suiting
With forms to his conceit? And all for nothing!
For Hecuba!
What's Hecuba to him or he to Hecuba,
That he should weep for her?
[II.ii]

91. He would drown the stage with tears,
And cleave the general ear with horrid speech;
Make mad the guilty, and appal the free,
Confound the ignorant, and amaze indeed
The very faculties of eyes and ears.
[II.ii]

92. I,
A dull and muddy-mettl'd rascal, peak,
Like John-a-dreams, unpregnant of my cause,
And can say nothing.
[II.ii]

93. But I am pigeon-liver'd, and lack gall
To make oppression bitter, or ere this
I should 'a fatted all the region kites
With this slave's offal. Bloody, bawdy villain!
Remorseless, treacherous, lecherous, kindless villain!
[II.ii]

94. I have heard
That guilty creatures, sitting at a play,
Have by the very cunning of the scene
Been struck so to the soul that presently
They have proclaim'd their malefactions;
For murder, though it have no tongue, will speak
With most miraculous organ.
[II.ii]

95. The play's the thing
Wherein I'll catch the conscience of the King.
[II.ii]

96. 'Tis too much prov'd, that with devotion's visage
And pious action we do sugar o'er
The devil himself.
[III.i]

97. To be, or not to be – that is the question;
Whether 'tis nobler in the mind to suffer
The slings and arrows of outrageous fortune,
Or to take arms against a sea of troubles,
And by opposing end them? To die, to sleep–
No more; and by a sleep to say we end
The heart-ache and the thousand natural shocks
That flesh is heir to. 'Tis a consummation
Devoutly to be wish'd. To die, to sleep;
To sleep, perchance to dream. Ay, there's the rub;
For in that sleep of death what dreams may come,
When we have shuffled off this mortal coil,
Must give us pause. There's the respect
That makes calamity of so long life;
For who would bear the whips and scorns of time,
Th' oppressor's wrong, the proud man's contumely,
The pangs of despis'd love, the law's delay,
The insolence of office, and the spurns
That patient merit of th' unworthy takes,
When he himself might his quietus make
With a bare bodkin? Who would these fardels bear,
To grunt and sweat under a weary life,
But that the dread of something after death–
The undiscover'd country, from whose bourn
No traveller returns – puzzles the will,
And makes us rather bear those ills we have
Than fly to others that we know not of?
Thus conscience does make cowards of us all;
And thus the native hue of resolution
Is sicklied o'er with the pale cast of thought,
And enterprises of great pitch and moment,
With this regard, their currents turn awry
And lose the name of action.
[III.i]

98. Nymph, in thy orisons
Be all my sins rememb'red.
[III.i]

99. For to the noble mind
Rich gifts wax poor when givers prove unkind.
[III.i]

100. Get thee to a nunnery. Why wouldst thou be a breeder of sinners? I am myself indifferent honest, but yet I could accuse me of such things that it were better my mother had not borne me: I am very proud, revengeful, ambitious; with more offences at my beck than I have thoughts to put them in, imagination to give them shape, or time to act them in. What should such fellows as I do crawling between earth and heaven? We are arrant knaves, all; believe none of us.
[III.i]

101. Be thou as chaste as ice, as pure as snow, thou shalt not escape calumny. Get thee to a nunnery, go, farewell.
[III.i]

102. I have heard of your paintings too, well enough; God hath given you one face, and you make yourselves another.
[III.i]

103. I say we will have no more marriage.
[III.i]

104. O, what a noble mind is here o'erthrown!
The courtier's, soldier's, scholar's, eye, tongue, sword;
Th' expectancy and rose of the fair state,
The glass of fashion and the mould of form,
Th' observ'd of all observers – quite, quite down!
And I, of ladies most deject and wretched,
That suck'd the honey of his music vows,
Now see that noble and most sovereign reason,
Like sweet bells jangled, out of time and harsh;
That unmatch'd form and feature of blown youth
Blasted with ecstasy. O, woe is me
T' have seen what I have seen, see what I see!
[III.i]

105. Madness in great ones must not unwatch'd go.
[III:i]

106. Speak the speech, I pray you, as I pronounc'd it to you, trippingly on the tongue; but if you mouth it, as many of our players do, I had as lief the town-crier spoke my lines. Nor do not saw the air too much with your hand, thus, but use all gently; for in the very torrent, tempest, and, as I may say, whirlwind of your passion, you must acquire and beget a temperance that may give it smoothness. O, it offends me to the soul to hear a robustious periwig-pated fellow tear a passion to tatters, to very rags, to split the ears of the groundlings, who, for the most part, are capable of nothing but inexplicable dumb shows and noise. I would have such a fellow whipp'd for o'erdoing Termagant; it out-herods Herod. Pray you avoid it.
[III.ii]

107. Be not too tame neither, but let your own discretion be your tutor. Suit the action to the word, the word to the action; with this special observance, that you o'erstep not the modesty of nature; for anything so o'erdone is from the purpose of playing, whose end, both at the first and now, was and is to hold, as 'twere, the mirror up to nature; to show virtue her own feature, scorn her own image, and the very age and body of the time his form and pressure. Now, this overdone or come tardy off, though it makes the unskilful laugh, cannot but make the judicious grieve; the censure of the which one must, in your allowance, o'erweigh a whole theatre of others. O, there be players that I have seen play – and heard others praise, and that highly – not to speak it profanely, that, neither having th' accent of Christians, nor the gait of Christian, pagan, nor man, have so strutted and bellowed that I have thought some of Nature's journeymen had made men, and not made them well, they imitated humanity so abominably.
[III.ii]

108. A man that Fortune's buffets and rewards
Hast ta'en with equal thanks; and blest are those
Whose blood and judgment are so well comeddled
That they are not a pipe for Fortune's finger
To sound what stop she please. Give me that man
That is not passion's slave, and I will wear him
In my heart's core, ay, in my heart of heart,
As I do thee.
[III.ii]

109. It is a damned ghost that we have seen,
And my imaginations are as foul
As Vulcan's stithy.
[III.ii]

110. ... the chameleon's dish. I eat the air, promise-cramm'd; you cannot feed capons so.
[III.ii]

111. That's a fair thought to lie between maids' legs.
[III.ii]

112. Die two months ago, and not forgotten yet? Then there's hope a great man's memory may outlive his life half a year; but, by'r lady, 'a must build churches, then.
[III.ii]

113. For O, for O, the hobby-horse is forgot!
[III.ii]

114. Marry, this is miching mallecho; it means mischief.
[III.ii]

115. *Ophelia*: 'Tis brief, my lord.
Hamlet: As woman's love.
[III.ii]

116. The lady doth protest too much, methinks.
[III.ii]

117. *Hamlet*: No, no; they do but jest, poison in jest; no offence i' th' world.
King: What do you call the play?
Hamlet: 'The Mouse-trap.'
[III.ii]

118. We that have free souls, it touches us not. Let the galled jade wince, our withers are unwrung.
[III.ii]

119. The story is extant, and written in very choice Italian.
[III.ii]

120. What, frighted with false fire!
[III.ii]

121. Why, let the stricken deer go weep,
The hart ungalled play;
For some must watch, while some must sleep;
Thus runs the world away.
[III.ii]

122. We shall obey, were she ten times our mother.
[III.ii]

123. The proverb is something musty.
[III.ii]

124. You would play upon me; you would seem to know my stops; you would pluck out the heart of my mystery; you would sound me from my lowest note to the top of my compass.
[III.ii]

125. Do you think I am easier to be play'd on than a pipe? Call me what instrument you will, though you can fret me, yet you cannot play upon me.
[III.ii]

126. *Hamlet*: Do you see yonder cloud that's almost in shape of a camel?
Polonius: By th' mass, and 'tis like a camel indeed.
Hamlet: Methinks it is like a weasel.
Polonius: It is back'd like a weasel.
Hamlet: Or like a whale?
Polonius: Very like a whale.
[III.ii]

127. They fool me to the top of my bent.
[III.ii]

128. 'Tis now the very witching time of night,
When churchyards yawn, and hell itself breathes out
Contagion to this world. Now could I drink hot blood,
And do such bitter business as the day
Would quake to look upon.
[III.ii]

129. Let me be cruel, not unnatural:
I will speak daggers to her, but use none.
[III.ii]

130. O, my offence is rank, it smells to heaven.
[III.iii]

131. O wretched state! O bosom black as death!
O limed soul, that, struggling to be free,
Art more engag'd!
[III.iii]

132. Now might I do it pat, now 'a is a-praying.
[III.iii]

133. My words fly up, my thoughts remain below.
Words without thoughts never to heaven go.
[III.iii]

134. Tell him his pranks have been too broad to bear with.
[III.iv]

135. You go not till I set you up a glass
Where you may see the inmost part of you.
[III.iv]

136. How now! a rat? Dead, for a ducat, dead!
[III.iv]

137. A bloody deed! – almost as bad, good mother,
As kill a king and marry with his brother.
[III.iv]

138. Thou wretched, rash, intruding fool, farewell!
I took thee for thy better.
[III.iv]

139. Ay me, what act,
That roars so loud and thunders in the index?
[III.iv]

140. You cannot call it love; for at your age
The heyday in the blood is tame, it's humble,
And waits upon the judgment.
[III.iv]

141. Speak no more!
Thou turn'st my eyes into my very soul.
[III.iv]

142. Nay, but to live
In the rank sweat of an enseamed bed,
Stew'd in corruption, honeying and making love
Over the nasty sty!
[III.iv]

143. A cutpurse of the empire and the rule,
That from a shelf the precious diadem stole
And put it in his pocket!
[III.iv]

144. A king of shreds and patches.
[III.iv]

145. Lay not that flattering unction to your soul.
[III.iv]

146. *Queen*: O Hamlet, thou hast cleft my heart in twain.
Hamlet: O, throw away the worser part of it,
And live the purer with the other half.
[III.iv]

147. Assume a virtue, if you have it not.
That monster custom, who all sense doth eat,
Of habits devil, is angel yet in this.
[III.iv]

148. I must be cruel, only to be kind.
[III.iv]

149. For 'tis the sport to have the engineer
Hoist with his own petar; and't shall go hard
But I will delve one yard below their mines
And blow them at the moon.
[III.iv]

150. I'll lug the guts into the neighbour room.
[III.iv]

151. He keeps them, like an ape an apple in the corner of his jaw; first mouth'd, to be last swallowed.
[IV.ii]

152. Diseases desperate grown
By desperate appliance are reliev'd,
Or not at all.
[IV.iii]

153. A certain convocation of politic worms are e'en at him. Your worm is your only emperor for diet.
[IV.iii]

154. A man may fish with the worm that hath eat of a king, and eat of the fish that hath fed of that worm.
[IV.iii]

155. We go to gain a little patch of ground
That hath in it no profit but the name.
[IV.iv]

156. How all occasions do inform against me,
And spur my dull revenge! What is a man,
If his chief good and market of his time
Be but to sleep and feed? A beast, no more!
Sure he that made us with such large discourse,
Looking before and after, gave us not
That capability and godlike reason
To fust in us unus'd.
[IV.iv]

157. Rightly to be great
Is not to stir without great argument,
But greatly to find quarrel in a straw,
When honour's at the stake.
[IV.iv]

158. How should I your true love know
From another one?
By his cockle hat and staff,
And his sandal shoon.
[IV.v]

159. He is dead and gone, lady,
He is dead and gone;
At his head a grass-green turf,
At his heels a stone.
[IV.v]

160. White his shroud as the mountain snow...
Larded with sweet flowers;
Which bewept to the grave did go
With true-love showers.
[IV.v]

161. Lord, we know what we are, but know not what we may be.
[IV.v]

162. Come, my coach! Good night, ladies; good night, sweet ladies, good night, good night.
[IV.v]

163. When sorrows come, they come not single spies,
But in battalions.
[IV.v]

164. We have done but greenly
In hugger-mugger to inter him.
[IV.v]

165. There's such divinity doth hedge a king
That treason can but peep to what it would.
[IV.v]

166. To hell, allegiance! Vows, to the blackest devil!
Conscience and grace, to the profoundest pit!
I dare damnation.
[IV.v]

167. Nature is fine in love; and where 'tis fine
It sends some precious instance of itself
After the thing it loves.
[IV.v]

168. They bore him barefac'd on the bier;
Hey non nonny, nonny, hey nonny;

And in his grave rain'd many a tear.
[IV.v]

169. There's rosemary, that's for remembrance; pray you, love, remember. And there is pansies, that's for thoughts.
[IV.v]

170. There's fennel for you, and columbines. There's rue for you; and here's some for me. We may call it herb of grace a Sundays. O, you must wear your rue with a difference. There's a daisy. I would give you some violets, but they wither'd all when my father died. They say 'a made a good end.
For bonny sweet Robin is all my joy.
[IV.v]

171. No, no, he is dead,
Go to thy death-bed,
He never will come again.
[IV.v]

172. He is gone, he is gone,
And we cast away moan:
God-a-mercy on his soul!
[IV.v]

173. His means of death, his obscure funeral–
No trophy, sword, nor hatchment, o'er his bones,
No noble rite nor formal ostentation.
[IV.v]

174. It warms the very sickness in my heart
That I shall live and tell him to his teeth
'Thus didest thou'.
[IV.vii]

175. A very riband in the cap of youth,
Yet needful too; for youth no less becomes
The light and careless livery that it wears
Than settled age his sables and his weeds,
Importing health and graveness.
[IV.vii]

176. There is a willow grows aslant the brook
That shows his hoar leaves in the glassy stream;
Therewith fantastic garlands did she make
Of crowflowers, nettles, daisies, and long purples
That liberal shepherds give a grosser name,
But our cold maids do dead men's fingers call them.
There, on the pendent boughs her coronet weeds
Clamb'ring to hang, an envious sliver broke;
When down her weedy trophies and herself
Fell in the weeping brook. Her clothes spread wide
And, mermaid-like, awhile they bore her up;
Which time she chanted snatches of old lauds,
As one incapable of her own distress.
[IV.vii]

177. Too much of water hast thou, poor Ophelia,
And therefore I forbid my tears; but yet
It is our trick; nature her custom holds,
Let shame say what it will.
[IV.vii]

178. Is she to be buried in Christian burial when she wilfully seeks her own salvation?
[V.i]

179. There is no ancient gentlemen but gard'ners, ditchers, and grave-makers; they hold up Adam's profession.
[V.i]

180. *First Clown*: What is he that builds stronger than either the mason, the shipwright, or the carpenter?
Second Clown: The gallows-maker; for that frame outlives a thousand tenants.
[V.i]

181. How absolute the knave is! We must speak by the card, or equivocation will undo us.
[V.i]

182. The age is grown so picked that the toe of the peasant comes so near the heel of the courtier, he galls his kibe.
[V.i]

183. Alas, poor Yorick! I knew him, Horatio: a fellow of infinite jest, of most excellent fancy; he hath borne me on his back a thousand times. And now how abhorred in my imagination it is! My gorge rises at it. Here hung those lips that I have kiss'd I know not how oft. Where be your gibes now, your gambols, your songs, your flashes of merriment that were wont to set the table on a roar? Not one now to mock your own grinning – quite chap-fall'n? Now get you to my lady's chamber, and tell her, let her paint an inch thick, to this favour she must come; make her laugh at that.
[V.i]

184. To what base uses we may return, Horatio!
[V.i]

185. Imperious Caesar, dead and turn'd to clay,
Might stop a hole to keep the wind away.
[V.i]

186. Lay her i' th' earth;
And from her fair and unpolluted flesh
May violets spring! I tell thee, churlish priest,
A minist'ring angel shall my sister be
When thou liest howling.
[V.i]

187. I thought thy bride-bed to have deck'd, sweet maid,
And not have strew'd thy grave.
[V.i]

188. I lov'd Ophelia: forty thousand brothers
Could not, with all their quantity of love,
Make up my sum.
[V.i]

189. And thus awhile the fit will work on him;
Anon, as patient as the female dove
When that her golden couplets are disclos'd,
His silence will sit drooping.
[V.i]

190. Let Hercules himself do what he may,
The cat will mew, and dog will have his day.
[V.i]

191. There's a divinity that shapes our ends,
Rough-hew them how we will.
[V.ii]

192. I once did hold it, as our statists do,
A baseness to write fair, and labour'd much
How to forget that learning; but, sir, now
It did me yeoman's service.
[V.ii]

193. Not a whit, we defy augury: there is a special providence in the fall of a sparrow. If it be now, 'tis not to come; if it be not to come, it will be now; if it be not now, yet it will come – the readiness is all.
[V.ii]

194. I have shot my arrow o'er the house
And hurt my brother.
[V.ii]

195. Why, as a woodcock, to mine own springe, Osric;
I am justly kill'd with mine own treachery.
[V.ii]

196. O, villainy! Ho! let the door be lock'd.
Treachery! seek it out.
[V.ii]

197. This fell sergeant Death
Is strict in his arrest.
[V.ii]

198. I am more an antique Roman than a Dane.
[V.ii]

199. If thou didst ever hold me in thy heart,
Absent thee from felicity awhile,
And in this harsh world draw thy breath in pain,
To tell my story.
[V.ii]

200. The rest is silence.
[V.ii]

201. Now cracks a noble heart. Good night, sweet prince,
And flights of angels sing thee to thy rest!
[V.ii]

202. The ears are senseless that should give us hearing
To tell him his commandment is fulfill'd,
That Rosencrantz and Guildenstern are dead.
[V.ii]

203. Let four captains
Bear Hamlet like a soldier to the stage;
For he was likely, had he been put on,
To have prov'd most royal.
[V.ii]

Henry IV, Part 1

1. So shaken as we are, so wan with care.
[I.i]

2. In those holy fields
Over whose acres walk'd those blessed feet
Which fourteen hundred years ago were nail'd
For our advantage on the bitter cross.
[I.i]

3. Unless hours were cups of sack, and minutes capons, and clocks the tongues of bawds, and dials the signs of leaping-houses, and the blessed sun himself a fair hot wench in flame-coloured taffeta, I see no reason why thou shouldst be so superfluous to demand the time of the day.
[I.ii]

4. Let us be Diana's foresters, gentlemen of the shade, minions of the moon.
[I.ii]

5. *Falstaff*: And is not my hostess of the tavern a most sweet wench?
Prince: As the honey of Hybla, my old lad of the castle.
[I.ii]

6. What, in thy quips and thy quiddities?
[I.ii]

7. Shall there be gallows standing in England when thou art king, and resolution thus fubb'd as it is with the rusty curb of old father antic the law?
[I.ii]

8. Thou hast the most unsavoury similes.
[I.ii]

9. I would to God thou and I knew where a commodity of good names were to be bought.
[I.ii]

10. O! thou hast damnable iteration, and art indeed able to corrupt a saint.
[I.ii]

11. Now am I, if a man should speak truly, little better than one of the wicked.
[I.ii]

12. I'll be damn'd for never a king's son in Christendom.
[I.ii]

13. [Of stealing]
Why, Hal, 'tis my vocation, Hal; 'tis no sin for a man to labour in his vocation.
[I.ii]

14. How agrees the devil and thee about thy soul, that thou soldest him on Good Friday last for a cup of Madeira and a cold capon's leg?
[I.ii]

15. I know you all, and will awhile uphold
The unyok'd humour of your idleness.
[I.ii]

16. If all the year were playing holidays,
To sport would be as tedious as to work;
But when they seldom come, they wish'd-for come.
[I.ii]

17. And as the soldiers bore dead bodies by,
He call'd them untaught knaves, unmannerly,
To bring a slovenly unhandsome corse
Betwixt the wind and his nobility.
With many holiday and lady terms
He questioned me.
[I.iii]

18. So pest'red with a popinjay.
[I.iii]

19. It was great pity, so it was,
This villainous saltpetre should be digg'd
Out of the bowels of the harmless earth,
Which many a good tall fellow had destroy'd
So cowardly; and but for these vile guns
He would himself have been a soldier.
[I.iii]

20. To put down Richard, that sweet lovely rose,
And plant this thorn, this canker, Bolingbroke?
[I.iii]

21. O, the blood more stirs
To rouse a lion than to start a hare!
[I.iii]

22. By heaven, methinks it were an easy leap
To pluck bright honour from the pale-fac'd moon;
Or dive into the bottom of the deep,
Where fathom-line could never touch the ground,
And pluck up drowned honour by the locks.
[I.iii]

23. Why, what a candy deal of courtesy
This fawning greyhound then did proffer me!
[I.iii]

24. I know a trick worth two of that.
[II.i]

25. At hand, quoth pick-purse.
[II.i]

26. We have the receipt of fern-seed, we walk invisible.
[II.i]

27. I am bewitch'd with the rogue's company. If the rascal have not given me medicines to make me love him, I'll be hang'd.
[II.ii]

28. Hang thyself in thine own heir-apparent garters.
[II.ii]

29. It would be argument for a week, laughter for a month, and a good jest for ever.
[II.ii]

30. Falstaff sweats to death
And lards the lean earth as he walks along.
[II.ii]

31. Out of this nettle, danger, we pluck this flower, safety.
[II.iii]

32. A good plot, good friends, and full of expectation; an excellent plot, very good friends.
[II.iii]

33. Away, you trifler! Love, I love thee not,
I care not for thee, Kate; this is no world
To play with mammets and to tilt with lips:
We must have bloody noses and crack'd crowns.
[II.iii]

34. Constant you are,
But yet a woman; and for secrecy,
No lady closer; for I well believe
Thou wilt not utter what thou dost not know.
[II.iii]

35. I am not yet of Percy's mind, the Hotspur of the north; he that kills me some six or seven dozen of Scots at a breakfast, washes his hands, and says to his wife 'Fie upon this quiet life! I want work'.
[II.iv]

36. There lives not three good men unhang'd in England, and one of them is fat and grows old.
[II.iv]

37. Call you that backing of your friends?
A plague upon such backing! Give me them that will face me.
[II.iv]

38. A plague of all cowards, still say I.
[II.iv]

39. I am a Jew else, an Ebrew Jew.
[II.iv]

40. Nay, that's past praying for: I have pepper'd two of them; two I am sure I have paid – two rogues in buckram suits. I tell thee what, Hal, if I tell thee a lie, spit in my face, call me horse. Thou knowest my old ward: here I lay, and thus I bore my point. Four rogues in buckram let drive at me.
[II.iv]

41. O monstrous! eleven buckram men grown out of two!
[II.iv]

42. Give you a reason on compulsion! If reasons were as plentiful as blackberries, I would give no man a reason upon compulsion, I.
[II.iv]

43. Mark now, how a plain tale shall put you down.
[II.iv]

44. What a slave art thou to hack thy sword as thou hast done, and then say it was in fight!
[II.iv]

45. Instinct is a great matter: I was now a coward on instinct.
[II.iv]

46. Ah, no more of that, Hal, an thou lovest me!
[II.iv]

47. What doth gravity out of his bed at midnight?
[II.iv]

48. A plague of sighing and grief! it blows a man up like a bladder.
[II.iv]

49. Shall the blessed sun of heaven prove a micher and eat blackberries? A question not to be ask'd.
[II.iv]

50. There is a devil haunts thee in the likeness of an old fat man; a tun of man is thy companion.
[II.iv]

51. That roasted Manningtree ox with the pudding in his belly, that reverend vice, that grey iniquity, that father ruffian, that vanity in years?
[II.iv]

52. If sack and sugar be a fault, God help the wicked!
[II.iv]

53. No, my good lord: banish Peto, banish Bardolph, banish Poins; but, for sweet Jack Falstaff, kind Jack Falstaff, true Jack Falstaff, valiant Jack Falstaff – and therefore more valiant, being, as he is, old Jack Falstaff – banish not him thy Harry's company, banish not him thy Harry's company. Banish plump Jack, and banish all the world.
[II.iv]

54. O monstrous! but one halfpennyworth of bread to this intolerable deal of sack!
[II.iv]

55. *Glendower*: At my nativity
The front of heaven was full of fiery shapes,
Of burning cressets; and at my birth
The frame and huge foundation of the earth
Shaked like a coward.
Hotspur: Why, so it would have done at the same season if your mother's cat had but kitten'd.
[III.i]

56. And all the courses of my life do show
I am not in the roll of common men.
[III.i]

57. *Glendower*: I can call spirits from the vasty deep.
Hotspur: Why, so can I, or so can any man;
But will they come when you do call for them?
[III.i]

58. O, while you live, tell truth, and shame the devil!
[III.i]

59. I'll have the current in this place damm'd up,
And here the smug and silver Trent shall run
In a new channel, fair and evenly.
[III.i]

60. I had rather be a kitten and cry mew
Than one of these same metre ballad-mongers.
[III.i]

61. That would set my teeth nothing on edge,
Nothing so much as mincing poetry.
'Tis like the forc'd gait of a shuffling nag.
[III.i]

62. And such a deal of skimble-skamble stuff
As puts me from my faith.
[III.i]

63. O, he is as tedious
As a tired horse, a railing wife;
Worse than a smoky house; I had rather live
With cheese and garlic in a windmill, far,
Than feed on cates and have him talk to me
In any summer house in Christendom.
[III.i]

64. I understand thy kisses, and thou mine,
And that's a feeling disputation.
[III.i]

65. Now I perceive the devil understands Welsh.
[III.i]

66. You swear like a comfit-maker's wife.
[III.i]

67. Swear me, Kate, like a lady as thou art,
A good mouth-filling oath.
[III.i]

68. The skipping King, he ambled up and down
With shallow jesters and rash bavin wits.
[III.ii]

69. Being daily swallowed by men's eyes,
They surfeited with honey and began
To loathe the taste of sweetness, whereof a little
More than a little is by much too much.
So, when he had occasion to be seen,
He was but as the cuckoo is in June,
Heard, not regarded.
[III.ii]

70. My nearest and dearest enemy?
[III.ii]

71. Well, I'll repent, and that suddenly, while I am in some liking; I shall be out of heart shortly, and then I shall have no strength to repent.
[III.iii]

72. Company, villainous company, hath been the spoil of me.
[III.iii]

73. Shall I not take mine ease in mine inn but I shall have my pocket pick'd?
[III.iii]

74. Thou knowest in the state of innocency Adam fell; and what should poor Jack Falstaff do in the days of villainy? Thou seest I have more flesh than another man, and therefore more frailty.
[III.iii]

75. Where is his son,
That nimble-footed madcap Prince of Wales,
And his comrades that daff'd the world aside
And bid it pass?
[IV.i]

76. I saw young Harry with his beaver on,
His cushes on his thighs, gallantly arm'd,
Rise from the ground like feathered Mercury,
And vaulted with such ease into his seat
As if an angel dropp'd down from the clouds
To turn and wind a fiery Pegasus,
And witch the world with noble horsemanship.
[IV.i]

77. Doomsday is near; die all, die merrily.
[IV.i]

78. I have misused the King's press damnably.
[IV.ii]

79. I am as vigilant as a cat to steal cream.
[IV.ii]

80. Food for powder; they'll fill a pit as well as better: tush, man, mortal men, mortal men.
[IV.ii]

81. Greatness knows itself.
[IV.iii]

82. For mine own part, I could be well content
To entertain the lag-end of my life
With quiet hours.
[V.i]

83. Rebellion lay in his way, and he found it.
[V.i]

84. I do not think a braver gentleman,
More active-valiant or more valiant-young,
More daring or more bold, is now alive
To grace this latter age with noble deeds.
For my part, I may speak it to my shame,
I have a truant been to chivalry.
[V.i]

85. *Falstaff*: I would 'twere bed-time, Hal, and all well.
Prince: Why, thou owest God a death.
[V.i]

86. Honour pricks me on. Yea, but how if honour prick me off when I come on? How then? Can honour set to a leg? No. Or an arm? No. Or take away the grief of a wound? No. Honour hath no skill in surgery, then? No. What is honour? A word. What is in that word? Honour. What is that honour? Air. A trim reckoning! Who hath it? He that died o' Wednesday. Doth he feel it? No. Doth he hear it? No. 'Tis insensible, then? Yea, to the dead. But will it not live with the living? No. Why? Detraction will not suffer it. Therefore I'll none of it. Honour is a mere scutcheon. And so ends my catechism.
[V.i]

87. O gentlemen, the time of life is short!
To spend that shortness basely were too long.
[V.ii]

88. I like not such grinning honour as Sir Walter hath. Give me life, which if I can save, so; if not, honour comes unlook'd for, and there's an end.
[V.iii]

89. But thoughts, the slaves of life, and life, time's fool,
And time, that takes survey of all the world,
Must have a stop.
[V.iv]

90. Fare thee well, great heart!
Ill-weav'd ambition, how much art thou shrunk!
When that this body did contain a spirit,
A kingdom for it was too small a bound;
But now two paces of the vilest earth
Is room enough. This earth that bears thee dead
Bears not alive so stout a gentleman.
[V.iv]

91. Thy ignominy sleep with thee in the grave,
But not rememb'red in thy epitaph!
What, old acquaintance! Could not all this flesh
Keep in a little life? Poor Jack, farewell!
I could have better spar'd a better man.
[V.iv]

92. The better part of valour is discretion; in the which better part I have saved my life.
[V.iv]

93. Full bravely hast thou flesh'd
Thy maiden sword.
[V.iv]

94. Lord, Lord, how this world is given to lying! I grant you I was down and out of breath, and so was he; but we rose both at an instant, and fought a long hour by Shrewsbury clock.
[V.iv]

95. For my part, if a lie may do thee grace,
I'll gild it with the happiest terms I have.
[V.iv]

96. I'll purge, and leave sack, and live cleanly, as a nobleman should do.
[V.iv]

Henry IV, Part 2

1. I speak of peace while covert enmity,
Under the smile of safety, wounds the world.
[Induction]

2. Rumour is a pipe
Blown by surmises, jealousies, conjectures,
And of so easy and so plain a stop
That the blunt monster with uncounted heads,
The still-discordant wav'ring multitude,
Can play upon it.
[Induction]

3. Even such a man, so faint, so spiritless,
So dull, so dead in look, so woe-begone,
Drew Priam's curtain in the dead of night
And would have told him half his Troy was burnt.
[I.i]

4. Yet the first bringer of unwelcome news
Hath but a losing office, and his tongue
Sounds ever after as a sullen bell,
Rememb'red tolling a departing friend.
[I.i]

5. The brain of this foolish-compounded clay, man, is not able to invent anything that intends to laughter, more than I invent or is invented on me. I am not only witty in myself, but the cause that wit is in other men. I do here walk before thee like a sow that hath overwhelm'd all her litter but one.
[I.ii]

6. Your lordship, though not clean past your youth, hath yet some smack of age in you, some relish of the saltness of time.
[I.ii]

7. This apoplexy, as I take it, is a kind of lethargy, an 't please your lordship, a kind of sleeping in the blood, a whoreson tingling.
[I.ii]

8. It is the disease of not listening, the malady of not marking, that I am troubled withal.
[I.ii]

9. I am as poor as Job, my lord, but not so patient.
[I.ii]

10. The young Prince hath misled me. I am the fellow with the great belly, and he my dog.
[I.ii]

11. Well, I am loath to gall a new-heal'd wound.
[I.ii]

12. Have you not a moist eye, a dry hand, a yellow cheek, a white beard, a decreasing leg, an increasing belly? Is not your voice broken, your wind short, your chin double, your wit single, and every part about you blasted with antiquity? And will you yet call yourself young? Fie, fie, fie, Sir John!
[I.ii]

13. My lord, I was born about three of the clock in the afternoon, with a white head and something a round belly. For my voice – I have lost it with hallooing and singing of anthems.
[I.ii]

14. *Chief Justice*: God send the Prince a better companion!
Falstaff: God send the companion a better prince! I cannot rid my hands of him.
[I.ii]

15. Well, I cannot last ever; but it was alway yet the trick of our English nation, if they have a good thing, to make it too common.
[I.ii]

16. I would to God my name were not so terrible to the enemy as it is. I were better to be eaten to death with a rust than to be scoured to nothing with perpetual motion.
[I.ii]

17. I can get no remedy against this consumption of the purse; borrowing only lingers and lingers it out, but the disease is incurable.
[I.ii]

18. When we mean to build,
We first survey the plot, then draw the model;
And when we see the figure of the house,
Then must we rate the cost of the erection;
Which if we find outweighs ability,
What do we then but draw anew the model
In fewer offices, or at least desist
To build at all?
[I.iii]

19. Past and to come seems best; things present, worst.
[I.iii]

20. A hundred mark is a long one for a poor lone woman to bear; and I have borne, and borne, and borne; and have been fubb'd off, and fubb'd off, and fubb'd off, from this day to that day, that it is a shame to be thought on
[II.i]

21. Away, you scullion! you rampallian! you fustilarian! I'll tickle your catastrophe.
[II.i]

22. He hath eaten me out of house and home.
[II.i]

23. Thou didst swear to me upon a parcel-gilt goblet, sitting in my Dolphin chamber, at the round table, by a sea-coal fire, upon Wednesday in Wheeson week.
[II.i]

24. Doth it not show vilely in me to desire small beer?
[II.ii]

25. I do now remember the poor creature, small beer.
[II.ii]

26. He was indeed the glass
Wherein the noble youth did dress themselves.
[II.iii]

27. Shall packhorses,
And hollow pamper'd jades of Asia,
Which cannot go but thirty mile a day,
Compare with Caesars, and with Cannibals,
And Troiant Greeks? Nay, rather damn them with

King Cerberus; and let the welkin roar.
[II.iv. Cf. Marlowe:16]

28. Thou whoreson little tidy Bartholomew boar-pig, when wilt thou leave fighting a days and foining a nights, and begin to patch up thine old body for heaven?
[II.iv]

29. Is it not strange that desire should so many years outlive performance?
[II.iv]

30. O sleep, O gentle sleep,
Nature's soft nurse, how have I frighted thee,
That thou no more wilt weigh my eyelids down,
And steep my senses in forgetfulness?
Why rather, sleep, liest thou in smoky cribs,
Upon uneasy pallets stretching thee,
And hush'd with buzzing night-flies to thy slumber,
Than in the perfum'd chambers of the great,
Under the canopies of costly state,
And lull'd with sound of sweetest melody?
[III.i]

31. Uneasy lies the head that wears a crown.
[III.i]

32. O God! that one might read the book of fate,
And see the revolution of the times
Make mountains level, and the continent,
Weary of solid firmness, melt itself
Into the sea.
[III.i]

33. O, if this were seen,
The happiest youth, viewing his progress through,
What perils past, what crosses to ensue,
Would shut the book and sit him down and die.
[III.i]

34. There is a history in all men's lives,
Figuring the natures of the times deceas'd;
The which observ'd, a man may prophesy,
With a near aim, of the main chance of things
As yet not come to life, who in their seeds
And weak beginning lie intreasured.
[III.i]

35. Death, as the Psalmist saith, is certain to all; all shall die.
How a good yoke of bullocks at Stamford Fair?
[III.ii]

36. Care I for the limb, the thews, the stature, bulk, and big assemblance of a man! Give me the spirit.
[III.ii]

37. Lord, Lord, how subject we old men are to this vice of lying!
[III.ii]

38. When a' was naked, he was for all the world like a fork'd radish, with a head fantastically carved upon it with a knife.
[III.ii]

39. Against ill chances men are ever merry;
But heaviness foreruns the good event.
[IV.ii]

40. That I may justly say with the hook-nos'd fellow of Rome – I came, saw, and overcame.
[IV.iii]

41. A man cannot make him laugh – but that's no marvel; he drinks no wine.
[IV.iii]

42. A good sherris-sack hath a twofold operation in it. It ascends me into the brain; dries me there all the foolish and dull and crudy vapours which environ it; makes it apprehensive, quick, forgetive, full of nimble, fiery, and delectable shapes; which delivered o'er to the voice, the tongue, which is the birth, becomes excellent wit. The second property of your excellent sherris is the warming of the blood; which before, cold and settled, left the liver white and pale, which is the badge of pusillanimity and cowardice; but the sherris warms it, and makes it course from the inwards to the parts extreme. It illumineth the face, which, as a beacon, gives warning to all the rest of this little kingdom, man, to arm; and then the vital commoners and inland petty spirits muster me all to their captain, the heart, who, great and puff'd up with this retinue, doth any deed of courage – and this valour comes of sherris. So that skill in the weapon is nothing without sack, for that sets it a-work; and learning, a mere hoard of gold kept by a devil till sack commences it and sets it in act and use.
[IV.iii]

43. If I had a thousand sons, the first humane principle I would teach them should be to forswear thin potations, and to addict themselves to sack.
[IV.iii]

44. O polish'd perturbation! golden care!
That keep'st the ports of slumber open wide
To many a watchful night! Sleep with it now!
Yet not so sound and half so deeply sweet
As he whose brow with homely biggen bound
Snores out the watch of night.
[IV.v]

45. This sleep is sound indeed; this is a sleep
That from this golden rigol hath divorc'd
So many English kings.
[IV.v]

46. Commit
The oldest sins the newest kind of ways?
[IV.v]

47. It hath been prophesied to me many years,
I should not die but in Jerusalem;
Which vainly I suppos'd the Holy Land.
But bear me to that chamber; there I'll lie;
In that Jerusalem shall Harry die.
[IV.v]

48. This is the English, not the Turkish court;
Not Amurath an Amurath succeeds,
But Harry Harry.
[V.ii]

49. My father is gone wild into his grave.
[V.ii]

50. A foutra for the world and worldlings base!
I speak of Africa and golden joys.
[V.iii]

51. Under which king, Bezonian? Speak, or die.
[V.iii]

52. Let us take any man's horses: the laws of England are at my commandment.
[V.iii]

53. I know thee not, old man. Fall to thy prayers.
How ill white hairs become a fool and jester!
I have long dreamt of such a kind of man,
So surfeit-swell'd, so old, and so profane.
[V.v]

54. Make less thy body hence, and more thy grace;
Leave gormandizing; know the grave doth gape

For thee thrice wider than for other men.
[V.v]

55. Presume not that I am the thing I was.
[V.v]

Henry V

1. O for a Muse of fire, that would ascend
The brightest heaven of invention,
A kingdom for a stage, princes to act,
And monarchs to behold the swelling scene!
[Prologue]

2. Can this cockpit hold
The vasty fields of France? Or may we cram
Within this wooden O the very casques
That did affright the air at Agincourt?
[Prologue]

3. Consideration like an angel came
And whipp'd th' offending Adam out of him.
[I.i]

4. When he speaks,
The air, a charter'd libertine, is still.
[I.i]

5. O noble English, that could entertain
With half their forces the full pride of France,
And let another half stand laughing by,
All out of work and cold for action!
[I.ii]

6. And make her chronicle as rich with praise
As is the ooze and bottom of the sea
With sunken wreck and sumless treasuries.
[I.ii]

7. For so work the honey bees,
Creatures that by a rule in nature teach
The act of order to a peopled kingdom.
They have a king, and officers of sorts,
Where some like magistrates correct at home;
Others like merchants venture trade abroad;
Others like soldiers, armed in their stings,
Make boot upon the summer's velvet buds,
Which pillage they with merry march bring home
To the tent-royal of their emperor;
Who, busied in his majesty, surveys
The singing masons building roofs of gold,
The civil citizens kneading up the honey,
The poor mechanic porters crowding in
Their heavy burdens at his narrow gate,
The sad-ey'd justice, with his surly hum,
Delivering o'er to executors pale
The lazy yawning drone.
[I.ii]

8. *King Henry*: What treasure, uncle?
Exeter: Tennis-balls, my liege.
[I.ii]

9. His present and your pains we thank you for.
When we have match'd our rackets to these balls,
We will in France, by God's grace, play a set
Shall strike his father's crown into the hazard.
[I.ii]

10. Now all the youth of England are on fire,
And silken dalliance in the wardrobe lies;
Now thrive the armourers, and honour's thought
Reigns solely in the breast of every man;
They sell the pasture now to buy the horse,
Following the mirror of all Christian kings
With winged heels, as English Mercuries.
For now sits Expectation in the air,
And hides a sword from hilts unto the point
With crowns imperial, crowns, and coronets,
Promis'd to Harry and his followers.
[II, Prologue]

11. I dare not fight; but I will wink and hold out mine iron.
[II.i]

12. Though patience be a tired mare, yet she will plod.
[II.i]

13. He's in Arthur's bosom, if ever man went to Arthur's bosom. 'A made a finer end, and went away an it had been any christom child; 'a parted ev'n just between twelve and one, ev'n at the turning o' th' tide; for after I saw him fumble with the sheets, and play with flowers, and smile upon his fingers' end, I knew there was but one way; for his nose was as sharp as a pen, and 'a babbl'd of green fields.
[II.iii]

14. So 'a cried out 'God, God, God!' three or four times. Now I, to comfort him, bid him 'a should not think of God; I hop'd there was no need to trouble himself with any such thoughts yet. So 'a bade me lay more clothes on his feet; I put my hand into the bed and felt them, and they were as cold as any stone; then I felt to his knees, and so upward and upward, and all was as cold as any stone.
[II.iii]

15. *Boy*: Yes, that 'a did, and said they were devils incarnate.
Hostess: 'A could never abide carnation; 'twas a colour he never lik'd.
Boy: 'A said once the devil would have him about women.
[II.iii]

16. Trust none;
For oaths are straws, men's faiths are wafer-cakes,
And Holdfast is the only dog, my duck.
[II.iii]

17. Once more unto the breach, dear friends, once more;
Or close the wall up with our English dead.
In peace there's nothing so becomes a man
As modest stillness and humility;
But when the blast of war blows in our ears,
Then imitate the action of the tiger:
Stiffen the sinews, summon up the blood,
Disguise fair nature with hard-favour'd rage;
Then lend the eye a terrible aspect.
[III.i]

18. On, on, you noblest English,
Whose blood is fet from fathers of war-proof–
Fathers that like so many Alexanders
Have in these parts from morn till even fought,
And sheath'd their swords for lack of argument.
[III.i]

19. And you, good yeomen,
Whose limbs were made in England, show us here
The mettle of your pasture.
[III.i]

20. I see you stand like greyhounds in the slips,
Straining upon the start. The game's afoot:
Follow your spirit; and upon this charge
Cry 'God for Harry, England, and Saint George!'
[III.i]

21. Would I were in an alehouse in London! I would give all my fame for a pot of ale and safety.
[III.ii]

22. Men of few words are the best men.
[III.ii]

23. 'A never broke any man's head but his own, and that was against a post when he was drunk.
[III.ii]

24. Give them great meals of beef and iron and steel; they will eat like wolves and fight like devils.
[III.vii]

25. Now entertain conjecture of a time
When creeping murmur and the poring dark
Fills the wide vessel of the universe.
From camp to camp, through the foul womb of night,
The hum of either army stilly sounds,
That the fix'd sentinels almost receive
The secret whispers of each other's watch.
Fire answers fire, and through their paly flames
Each battle sees the other's umber'd face;
Steed threatens steed, in high and boastful neighs
Piercing the night's dull ear; and from the tents
The armourers accomplishing the knights,
With busy hammers closing rivets up,
Give dreadful note of preparation.
[IV, Prologue]

26. Gloucester, 'tis true that we are in great danger;
The greater therefore should our courage be.
[IV.i]

27. Thus may we gather honey from the weed,
And make a moral of the devil himself.
[IV.i]

28. Discuss unto me: art thou officer,
Or art thou base, common and popular?
[IV.i]

29. The King's a bawcock and a heart of gold,
A lad of life, an imp of fame;
Of parents good, of fist most valiant.
I kiss his dirty shoe, and from heart-string
I love the lovely bully.
[IV.i]

30. Though it appear a little out of fashion,
There is much care and valour in this Welshman.
[IV.i]

31. I think the King is but a man as I am: the violet smells to him as it doth to me.
[IV.i]

32. I am afeard there are few die well that die in a battle; for how can they charitably dispose of anything when blood is their argument?
[IV.i]

33. Every subject's duty is the King's; but every subject's soul is his own.
[IV.i]

34. What infinite heart's ease
Must kings neglect that private men enjoy!
And what have kings that privates have not too,
Save ceremony – save general ceremony?
[IV.i]

35. 'Tis not the balm, the sceptre, and the ball,
The sword, the mace, the crown imperial,
The intertissued robe of gold and pearl,
The farced title running fore the king,
The throne he sits on, nor the tide of pomp
That beats upon the high shore of this world–
No, not all these, thrice gorgeous ceremony,
Not all these, laid in bed majestical,
Can sleep so soundly as the wretched slave
Who, with a body fill'd and vacant mind,
Gets him to rest, cramm'd with distressful bread;
Never sees horrid night, the child of hell;
But, like a lackey, from the rise to set
Sweats in the eye of Phoebus, and all night
Sleeps in Elysium.
[IV.i]

36. O God of battles, steel my soldiers' hearts,
Possess them not with fear! Take from them now
The sense of reck'ning, if th' opposed numbers
Pluck their hearts from them!
[IV.i]

37. O that we now had here
But one ten thousand of those men in England
That do no work to-day!
[IV.iii]

38. If we are mark'd to die, we are enow
To do our country loss; and if to live,
The fewer men, the greater share of honour.
[IV.iii]

39. But if it be a sin to covet honour,
I am the most offending soul alive.
[IV.iii]

40. He which hath no stomach to this fight,
Let him depart; his passport shall be made,
And crowns for convoy put into his purse;
We would not die in that man's company
That fears his fellowship to die with us.
This day is call'd the feast of Crispian.
He that outlives this day, and comes safe home,
Will stand a tip-toe when this day is nam'd,
And rouse him at the name of Crispian.
He that shall live this day, and see old age,
Will yearly on the vigil feast his neighbours,
And say 'To-morrow is Saint Crispian'.
Then will he strip his sleeve and show his scars,
And say 'These wounds I had on Crispian's day'.
Old men forget; yet all shall be forgot,
But he'll remember, with advantages,
What feats he did that day. Then shall our names,
Familiar in his mouth as household words–
Harry the King, Bedford and Exeter,
Warwick and Talbot, Salisbury and Gloucester–
Be in their flowing cups freshly rememb'red.
This story shall the good man teach his son;
And Crispin Crispian shall ne'er go by,
From this day to the ending of the world,
But we in it shall be remembered–
We few, we happy few, we band of brothers;
For he to-day that sheds his blood with me
Shall be my brother; be he ne'er so vile,
This day shall gentle his condition;
And gentlemen in England now a-bed
Shall think themselves accurs'd they were not here,
And hold their manhoods cheap whiles any speaks
That fought with us upon Saint Crispin's day.
[IV.iii]

41. Thou damned and luxurious mountain-goat.
[IV.iv]

42. But now behold
In the quick forge and working-house of thought,
How London doth pour out her citizens!
[V, Prologue]

43. There is occasions and causes why and wherefore in all things.
[V.i]

44. I pray you fall to; if you can mock a leek, you can eat a leek.
[V.i]

45. Let it not disgrace me
If I demand, before this royal view,
What rub or what impediment there is
Why that the naked, poor, and mangled Peace,
Dear nurse of arts, plenties, and joyful births,
Should not in this best garden of the world,
Our fertile France, put up her lovely visage?
[V.ii]

46. For these fellows of infinite tongue, that can rhyme themselves into ladies' favours, they do always reason themselves out again.
[V.ii]

47. Shall not thou and I, between Saint Denis and Saint George, compound a boy, half French, half English, that shall go to Constantinople and take the Turk by the beard?
[V.ii]

48. It is not a fashion for the maids in France to kiss before they are married.
[V.ii]

Henry VI, Part 1

1. Hung be the heavens with black, yield day to night!
[I.i]

2. *Plantagenet*: Let him that is a true-born gentleman
And stands upon the honour of his birth,
If he suppose that I have pleaded truth,
From off this brier pluck a white rose with me.
Somerset: Let him that is no coward nor no flatterer,
But dare maintain the party of the truth,
Pluck a red rose from off this thorn with me.
[II.iv]

3. So doth the swan her downy cygnets save,
Keeping them prisoner underneath her wings.
[V.iii]

4. She's beautiful, and therefore to be woo'd;
She is a woman, therefore to be won.
[V.iii]

Henry VI, Part 2

1. She bears a duke's revenues on her back,
And in her heart she scorns our poverty.
[I.iii]

2. Could I come near your beauty with my nails,
I could set my ten commandments in your face.
[I.iii]

3. Smooth runs the water where the brook is deep.
[III.i]

4. What stronger breastplate than a heart untainted?
Thrice is he arm'd that hath his quarrel just;
And he but naked, though lock'd up in steel,
Whose conscience with injustice is corrupted.
[III.ii]

5. Forbear to judge, for we are sinners all.
Close up his eyes, and draw the curtain close;
And let us all to meditation.
[III.iii]

6. The gaudy, blabbing, and remorseful day
Is crept into the bosom of the sea.
[IV.i]

7. True nobility is exempt from fear:
More can I bear than you dare execute.
[IV.i]

8. I say it was never merry world in England since gentlemen came up.
[IV.ii]

9. *Cade*: There shall be in England seven halfpenny loaves sold for a penny; the three-hoop'd pot shall have ten hoops; and I will make it felony to drink small beer. All the realm shall be in common, and in Cheapside shall my palfrey go to grass. And when I am king – as king I will be – ... there shall be no money; all shall eat and drink on my score, and I will apparel them all in one livery, that they may agree like brothers and worship me their lord.
Dick: The first thing we do, let's kill all the lawyers.
[IV.ii]

10. Is not this a lamentable thing, that of the skin of an innocent lamb should be made parchment? That parchment, being scribbl'd o'er, should undo a man?
[IV.ii]

11. Thou hast most traitorously corrupted the youth of the realm in erecting a grammar school; and whereas, before, our forefathers had no other books but the score and the tally, thou hast caused printing to be us'd, and, contrary to the King, his crown, and dignity, thou hast built a paper-mill.
[IV.vii]

12. Away with him, away with him! He speaks Latin.
[IV.vii]

Henry VI, Part 3

1. O tiger's heart wrapp'd in a woman's hide!
[I.iv]

2. This battle fares like to the morning's war,
When dying clouds contend with growing light,
What time the shepherd, blowing of his nails,
Can neither call it perfect day nor night.
[II.v]

3. O God! methinks it were a happy life
To be no better than a homely swain;
To sit upon a hill, as I do now,
To carve out dials quaintly, point by point,
Thereby to see the minutes how they run–
How many makes the hour full complete,
How many hours brings about the day,
How many days will finish up the year,
How many years a mortal man may live.
[II.v]

4. Gives not the hawthorn bush a sweeter shade
To shepherds looking on their silly sheep,
Than doth a rich embroider'd canopy
To kings that fear their subjects' treachery?
[II.v]

5. Peace, impudent and shameless Warwick,
Proud setter up and puller down of kings!
[III.iii]

6. A little fire is quickly trodden out,
Which, being suffer'd, rivers cannot quench.
[IV.viii]

7. Lo now my glory smear'd in dust and blood!
My parks, my walks, my manors, that I had,
Even now forsake me; and of all my lands
Is nothing left me but my body's length.
Why, what is pomp, rule, reign, but earth and dust?
And live we how we can, yet die we must.
[V.ii]

8. Suspicion always haunts the guilty mind:
The thief doth fear each bush an officer.
[V.vi]

9. Down, down to hell; and say I sent thee thither.
[V.vi]

Henry VIII

1. Heat not a furnace for your foe so hot
That it do singe yourself.
[I.i]

2. If I chance to talk a little wild, forgive me;
I had it from my father.
[I.iv]

3. Go with me like good angels to my end;
And as the long divorce of steel falls on me
Make of your prayers one sweet sacrifice,
And lift my soul to heaven.
[II.i]

4. *Chamberlain*: It seems the marriage with his brother's wife
Has crept too near his conscience.
Suffolk: No, his conscience
Has crept too near another lady.
[II.ii]

5. Heaven will one day open
The King's eyes, that so long have slept upon
This bold bad man.
[II.ii]

6. I swear 'tis better to be lowly born
And range with humble livers in content
Than to be perk'd up in a glist'ring grief
And wear a golden sorrow.
[II.iii]

7. Orpheus with his lute made trees,
And the mountain tops that freeze,
Bow themselves when he did sing;
To his music plants and flowers
Ever sprung, as sun and showers
There had made a lasting spring.

Every thing that heard him play,
Even the billows of the sea,
Hung their heads and then lay by.
In sweet music is such art,
Killing care and grief of heart
Fall asleep or hearing die.
[III.i]

8. Heaven is above all yet: there sits a Judge
That no king can corrupt.
[III.i]

9. I shall fall
Like a bright exhalation in the evening,
And no man see me more.
[III.ii]

10. Farewell, a long farewell, to all my greatness!
This is the state of man: to-day he puts forth
The tender leaves of hopes; to-morrow blossoms
And bears his blushing honours thick upon him;
The third day comes a frost, a killing frost,
And when he thinks, good easy man, full surely
His greatness is a-ripening, nips his root,
And then he falls, as I do. I have ventur'd,
Like little wanton boys that swim on bladders,
This many summers in a sea of glory;
But far beyond my depth. My high-blown pride
At length broke under me, and now has left me,
Weary and old with service, to the mercy
Of a rude stream, that must for ever hide me.
Vain pomp and glory of this world, I hate ye;
I feel my heart new open'd. O, how wretched
Is that poor man that hangs on princes' favours!
There is betwixt that smile we would aspire to,
That sweet aspect of princes, and their ruin
More pangs and fears than wars or women have;
And when he falls, he falls like Lucifer,
Never to hope again.
[III.ii]

11. A peace above all earthly dignities,
A still and quiet conscience.
[III.ii]

12. Cromwell, I charge thee, fling away ambition:
By that sin fell the angels. How can man then,
The image of his Maker, hope to win by it?
Love thyself last; cherish those hearts that hate thee;
Corruption wins not more than honesty.
Still in thy right hand carry gentle peace
To silence envious tongues. Be just, and fear not;
Let all the ends thou aim'st at be thy country's,
Thy God's, and truth's; then, if thou fall'st, O Cromwell,
Thou fall'st a blessed martyr!
[III.ii]

13. Had I but serv'd my God with half the zeal
I serv'd my King, he would not in mine age
Have left me naked to mine enemies.
[III.ii]

14. An old man, broken with the storms of state,
Is come to lay his weary bones among ye;
Give him a little earth for charity!
[IV.ii]

15. He gave his honours to the world again,
His blessed part to heaven, and slept in peace.
[IV.ii]

16. So may he rest; his faults lie gently on him!
[IV.ii]

17. His promises were, as he then was, mighty;
But his performance, as he is now, nothing.
[IV.ii]

18. Men's evil manners live in brass: their virtues
We write in water.
[IV.ii]

19. He was a scholar, and a ripe and good one;
Exceeding wise, fair-spoken, and persuading;
Lofty and sour to them that lov'd him not,
But to those men that sought him sweet as summer.
[IV.ii]

20. Those about her
From her shall read the perfect ways of honour.
[V.v]

21. Nor shall this peace sleep with her; but as when
The bird of wonder dies, the maiden phoenix,
Her ashes new create another heir
As great in admiration as herself.
[V.v]

Julius Caesar

1. Hence! home, you idle creatures, get you home.
Is this a holiday? What! know you not,
Being mechanical, you ought not walk
Upon a labouring day without the sign

Of your profession?
[I.i]

2. You blocks, you stones, you worse than senseless things!
O you hard hearts, you cruel men of Rome,
Knew you not Pompey?
[I.i]

3. *Caesar*: Who is it in the press that calls on me?
I hear a tongue, shriller than all the music,
Cry 'Caesar!' Speak. Caesar is turn'd to hear.
Soothsayer: Beware the ides of March.
[I.ii]

4. He is a dreamer; let us leave him. Pass.
[I.ii]

5. I am not gamesome: I do lack some part
Of that quick spirit that is in Antony.
[I.ii]

6. Poor Brutus, with himself at war,
Forgets the shows of love to other men.
[I.ii]

7. Set honour in one eye and death i' th' other,
And I will look on both indifferently.
[I.ii]

8. Well, honour is the subject of my story.
I cannot tell what you and other men
Think of this life; but, for my single self,
I had as lief not be as live to be
In awe of such a thing as I myself.
I was born free as Caesar; so were you.
We both have fed as well, and we can both
Endure the winter's cold as well as he.
For once, upon a raw and gusty day,
The troubled Tiber chafing with her shores,
Caesar said to me 'Dar'st thou, Cassius, now
Leap in with me into this angry flood,
And swim to yonder point?' Upon the word,
Accoutred as I was, I plunged in
And bade him follow . . .
But ere we could arrive the point propos'd,
Caesar cried, 'Help me, Cassius, or I sink!'
I, as Aeneas, our great ancestor,
Did from the flames of Troy upon his shoulder
The old Anchises bear, so from the waves of Tiber
Did I the tired Caesar. And this man
Is now become a god.
[I.ii]

9. He had a fever when he was in Spain,
And when the fit was on him I did mark
How he did shake. 'Tis true, this god did shake.
His coward lips did from their colour fly,
And that same eye, whose bend doth awe the world,
Did lose his lustre.
[I.ii]

10. Ye gods! it doth amaze me
A man of such a feeble temper should
So get the start of the majestic world,
And bear the palm alone.
[I.ii]

11. Why, man, he doth bestride the narrow world
Like a Colossus, and we petty men
Walk under his huge legs, and peep about
To find ourselves dishonourable graves.
Men at some time are masters of their fates:
The fault, dear Brutus, is not in our stars,
But in ourselves, that we are underlings.
[I.ii]

12. 'Brutus' will start a spirit as soon as 'Caesar'.
Now, in the names of all the gods at once,
Upon what meat doth this our Caesar feed,
That he is grown so great?
[I.ii]

13. When could they say, till now, that talk'd of Rome,
That her wide walls encompass'd but one man?
Now is it Rome indeed, and room enough,
When there is in it but one only man.
[I.ii]

14. Let me have men about me that are fat;
Sleek-headed men, and such as sleep o' nights.
Yond Cassius has a lean and hungry look;
He thinks too much. Such men are dangerous.
[I.ii]

15. Would he were fatter! But I fear him not.
Yet if my name were liable to fear,
I do not know the man I should avoid
So soon as that spare Cassius. He reads much,
He is a great observer, and he looks
Quite through the deeds of men. He loves no plays,
As thou dost, Antony; he hears no music.
Seldom he smiles, and smiles in such a sort
As if he mock'd himself, and scorn'd his spirit
That could be mov'd to smile at anything.
Such men as he be never at heart's ease
Whiles they behold a greater than themselves,
And therefore are they very dangerous.
I rather tell thee what is to be fear'd
Than what I fear; for always I am Caesar.
[I.ii]

16. *Cassius*: Did Cicero say anything?
Casca: Ay, he spoke Greek.
Cassius: To what effect?
Casca: Nay, an I tell you that, I'll ne'er look you i' th' face again. But those that understood him smil'd at one another, and shook their heads; but for mine own part, it was Greek to me.
[I.ii]

17. Yesterday the bird of night did sit,
Even at noon-day, upon the market-place,
Hooting and shrieking.
[I.iii]

18. But men may construe things after their fashion,
Clean from the purpose of the things themselves.
[I.iii]

19. It is the bright day that brings forth the adder,
And that craves wary walking.
[II.i]

20. 'Tis a common proof
That lowliness is young ambition's ladder,
Whereto the climber-upward turns his face;
But when he once attains the upmost round,
He then unto the ladder turns his back,
Looks in the clouds, scorning the base degrees
By which he did ascend.
[II.i]

21. Between the acting of a dreadful thing
And the first motion, all the interim is
Like a phantasma or a hideous dream.
The genius and the mortal instruments
Are then in council; and the state of man,
Like to a little kingdom, suffers then
The nature of an insurrection.
[II.i]

22. O conspiracy,
Sham'st thou to show thy dang'rous brow by night,
When evils are most free?
[II.i]

23. Let's be sacrificers, but not butchers, Caius.
[II.i]

24. Let's carve him as a dish fit for the gods,
Not hew him as a carcase fit for hounds.
[II.i]

25. But when I tell him he hates flatterers,
He says he does, being then most flattered.
[II.i]

26. What, is Brutus sick,
And will he steal out of his wholesome bed,
To dare the vile contagion of the night?
[II.i]

27. *Portia*: Dwell I but in the suburbs
Of your good pleasure? If it be no more,
Portia is Brutus' harlot, not his wife.
Brutus: You are my true and honourable wife,
As dear to me as are the ruddy drops
That visit my sad heart.
[II.i]

28. I grant I am a woman; but withal
A woman that Lord Brutus took to wife.
I grant I am a woman; but withal
A woman well reputed, Cato's daughter.
Think you I am no stronger than my sex,
Being so father'd and so husbanded?
[II.i]

29. A lioness hath whelped in the streets,
And graves have yawn'd and yielded up their dead.
[II.ii]

30. *Calphurnia*: When beggars die there are no comets seen:
The heavens themselves blaze forth the death of princes.
Caesar: Cowards die many times before their deaths:
The valiant never taste of death but once.
Of all the wonders that I yet have heard,
It seems to me most strange that men should fear,
Seeing that death, a necessary end,
Will come when it will come.
[II.ii]

31. Danger knows full well
That Caesar is more dangerous than he:
We are two lions litter'd in one day,
And I the elder and more terrible;
And Caesar shall go forth.
[II.ii]

32. *Caesar*: The ides of March are come.
Soothsayer: Ay, Caesar, but not gone.
[III.i]

33. Be not fond
To think that Caesar bears such rebel blood
That will be thaw'd from the true quality
With that which melteth fools – I mean, sweet words,
Low-crooked curtsies, and base spaniel fawning.
Thy brother by decree is banished;
If thou dost bend, and pray, and fawn for him,
I spurn thee like a cur out of my way.
[III.i]

34. If I could pray to move, prayers would move me;
But I am constant as the northern star,
Of whose true-fix'd and resting quality
There is no fellow in the firmament.
The skies are painted with unnumb'red sparks,
They are all fire, and every one doth shine;
But there's but one in all doth hold his place.
So in the world: 'tis furnish'd well with men,
And men are flesh and blood, and apprehensive;
Yet in the number I do know but one
That unassailable holds on his rank,
Unshak'd of motion; and that I am he,
Let me a little show it, even in this–
That I was constant Cimber should be banish'd,
And constant do remain to keep him so.
[III.i]

35. Et tu, Brute? – Then fall, Caesar!
[III.i]

36. That we shall die, we know; 'tis but the time,
And drawing days out, that men stand upon.
[III.i]

37. He that cuts off twenty years of life
Cuts off so many years of fearing death.
[III.i]

38. *Cassius*: How many ages hence
Shall this our lofty scene be acted over
In states unborn and accents yet unknown!
Brutus: How many times shall Caesar bleed in sport.
[III.i]

39. O mighty Caesar! dost thou lie so low?
Are all thy conquests, glories, triumphs, spoils,
Shrunk to this little measure?
[III.i]

40. Your swords, made rich
With the most noble blood of all this world.
[III.i]

41. The choice and master spirits of this age.
[III.i]

42. Had I as many eyes as thou hast wounds,
Weeping as fast as they stream forth thy blood,
It would become me better than to close
In terms of friendship with thine enemies.
[III.i]

43. O, pardon me, thou bleeding piece of earth,
That I am meek and gentle with these butchers!
Thou art the ruins of the noblest man
That ever lived in the tide of times.
[III.i]

44. Caesar's spirit, ranging for revenge,
With Até by his side come hot from hell,
Shall in these confines with a monarch's voice
Cry 'Havoc!' and let slip the dogs of war,
That this foul deed shall smell above the earth
With carrion men, groaning for burial.
[III.i]

45. Not that I lov'd Caesar less, but that I lov'd Rome more.
[III.ii]

46. As he was valiant, I honour him; but – as he was ambitious, I slew him.
[III.ii]

47. Who is here so base that would be a bondman? If any, speak; for him have I offended. Who is here so rude that would not be a Roman? If any, speak; for him have I offended. Who is here so vile that will not love his country? If any, speak; for him have I offended. I pause for a reply.
[III.ii]

48. Friends, Romans, countrymen, lend me your ears;
I come to bury Caesar, not to praise him.
The evil that men do lives after them;
The good is oft interred with their bones;
So let it be with Caesar. The noble Brutus
Hath told you Caesar was ambitious.
If it were so, it was a grievous fault;
And grievously hath Caesar answer'd it.
Here, under leave of Brutus and the rest–
For Brutus is an honourable man;
So are they all, all honourable men–
Come I to speak in Caesar's funeral.
[III.ii]

49. He was my friend, faithful and just to me;
But Brutus says he was ambitious,
And Brutus is an honourable man.
[III.ii]

50. When that the poor have cried, Caesar hath wept;
Ambition should be made of sterner stuff.
[III.ii]

51. On the Lupercal
I thrice presented him a kingly crown,
Which he did thrice refuse. Was this ambition?
[III.ii]

52. O judgment, thou art fled to brutish beasts,
And men have lost their reason!
[III.ii]

53. You are not wood, you are not stones, but men;
And being men, hearing the will of Caesar,
It will inflame you, it will make you mad.
[III.ii]

54. If you have tears, prepare to shed them now.
You all do know this mantle. I remember
The first time ever Caesar put it on;
'Twas on a summer's evening, in his tent,
That day he overcame the Nervii.
[III.ii]

55. This was the most unkindest cut of all;
For when the noble Caesar saw him stab,
Ingratitude, more strong than traitors' arms,
Quite vanquish'd him. Then burst his mighty heart;
And in his mantle muffling up his face,
Even at the base of Pompey's statua,
Which all the while ran blood, great Caesar fell.
O, what a fall was there, my countrymen!
Then I, and you, and all of us fell down,
Whilst bloody treason flourish'd over us.
O, now you weep, and I perceive you feel
The dint of pity. These are gracious drops.
[III.ii]

56. I come not, friends, to steal away your hearts;
I am no orator, as Brutus is,
But, as you know me all, a plain blunt man,
That love my friend.
[III.ii]

57. For I have neither wit, nor words, nor worth,
Action, nor utterance, nor the power of speech,
To stir men's blood; I only speak right on.
I tell you that which you yourselves do know.
[III.ii]

58. But were I Brutus,
And Brutus Antony, there were an Antony
Would ruffle up your spirits, and put a tongue
In every wound of Caesar, that should move
The stones of Rome to rise and mutiny.
[III.ii]

59. He hath left you all his walks,
His private arbours, and new-planted orchards,
On this side Tiber; he hath left them you,
And to your heirs for ever – common pleasures,
To walk abroad and recreate yourselves.
Here was a Caesar! When comes such another?
[III.ii]

60. Now let it work. Mischief, thou art afoot,
Take thou what course thou wilt!
[III.ii]

61. Fortune is merry,
And in this mood will give us any thing.
[III.ii]

62. *First Plebeian*: Tear him to pieces; he's a conspirator!
Cinna: I am Cinna the poet, I am Cinna the poet.
Fourth Plebeian: Tear him for his bad verses, tear him for his bad verses!
[III.iii]

63. He shall not live; look, with a spot I damn him.
[IV.i]

64. This is a slight unmeritable man,
Meet to be sent on errands. Is it fit,
The threefold world divided, he should stand
One of the three to share it?
[IV.i]

65. A barren-spirited fellow; one that feeds
On abjects, orts, and imitations.
[IV.i]

66. When love begins to sicken and decay,
It useth an enforced ceremony.
There are no tricks in plain and simple faith.
[IV.ii]

67. Let me tell you, Cassius, you yourself
Are much condemn'd to have an itching palm.
[IV.iii]

68. Shall we now
Contaminate our fingers with base bribes?
[IV.iii]

69. I had rather be a dog and bay the moon
Than such a Roman.
[IV.iii]

70. I'll use you for my mirth, yea, for my laughter,
When you are waspish.
[IV.iii]

71. You wrong me every way; you wrong me, Brutus;
I said an elder soldier, not a better.
Did I say 'better'?
[IV.iii]

72. By heaven, I had rather coin my heart,
And drop my blood for drachmas, than to wring
From the hard hands of peasants their vile trash
By any indirection.
[IV.iii]

73. Cassius is aweary of the world:
Hated by one he loves; brav'd by his brother;
Check'd like a bondman; all his faults observ'd,
Set in a notebook, learn'd, and conn'd by rote,
To cast into my teeth.
[IV.iii]

74. O Cassius, you are yoked with a lamb,
That carries anger as the flint bears fire;
Who, much enforced, shows a hasty spark,

And straight is cold again.
[IV.iii]

75. Good reasons must, of force, give place to better.
[IV.iii]

76. The enemy increaseth every day:
We, at the height, are ready to decline.
There is a tide in the affairs of men
Which, taken at the flood, leads on to fortune;
Omitted, all the voyage of their life
Is bound in shallows and in miseries.
On such a full sea are we now afloat,
And we must take the current when it serves,
Or lose our ventures.
[IV.iii. Cf. Byron: 212]

77. The deep of night is crept upon our talk,
And nature must obey necessity.
[IV.iii]

78. *Brutus*: Then I shall see thee again?
Ghost: Ay, at Philippi.
Brutus: Why, I will see thee at Philippi, then.
[IV.iii]

79. But for your words, they rob the Hybla bees,
And leave them honeyless.
[V.i]

80. If we do meet again, why, we shall smile;
If not, why then this parting was well made.
[V.i]

81. O that a man might know
The end of this day's business ere it come!
But it sufficeth that the day will end,
And then the end is known.
[V.i]

82. This day I breathed first. Time is come round,
And where I did begin there shall I end;
My life is run his compass.
[V.iii]

83. O hateful error, melancholy's child,
Why dost thou show to the apt thoughts of men
The things that are not?
[V.iii]

84. O Julius Caesar, thou art mighty yet!
Thy spirit walks abroad and turns our swords
In our own proper entrails.
[V.iii]

85. Thou seest the world, Volumnius, how it goes:
Our enemies have beat us to the pit;
It is more worthy to leap in ourselves
Than tarry till they push us.
[V.v]

86. Thou art a fellow of a good respect;
Thy life hath had some smatch of honour in it.
Hold then my sword, and turn away thy face,
While I do run upon it.
[V.v]

87. Caesar, now be still.
I kill'd not thee with half so good a will.
[V.v]

88. This was the noblest Roman of them all.
All the conspirators save only he
Did that they did in envy of great Caesar;
He only in a general honest thought
And common good to all made one of them.
His life was gentle; and the elements
So mix'd in him that Nature might stand up
And say to all the world 'This was a man!'
[V.v]

King John

1. Hadst thou rather be a Faulconbridge,
And like thy brother, to enjoy thy land,
Or the reputed son of Coeur-de-lion,
Lord of thy presence and no land beside?
[I.i]

2. And if his name be George, I'll call him Peter;
For new-made honour doth forget men's names.
[I.i]

3. Sweet, sweet, sweet poison for the age's tooth.
[I.i]

4. Courage mounteth with occasion.
[II.i]

5. Saint George, that swing'd the dragon, and e'er since
Sits on's horse back at mine hostess' door.
[II.i]

6. Mad world! mad kings! mad composition!
[II.i]

7. That smooth-fac'd gentleman, tickling commodity,
Commodity, the bias of the world.
[II.i]

8. Well, whiles I am a beggar, I will rail
And say there is no sin but to be rich;
And being rich, my virtue then shall be
To say there is no vice but beggary.
[II.i]

9. Thou wear a lion's hide! Doff it for shame,
And hang a calf's-skin on those recreant limbs.
[III.i]

10. Old Time the clock-setter, that bald sexton Time.
[III.i]

11. Bell, book, and candle, shall not drive me back,
When gold and silver becks me to come on.
[III.iii]

12. Grief fills the room up of my absent child,
Lies in his bed, walks up and down with me,
Puts on his pretty looks, repeats his words,
Remembers me of all his gracious parts,
Stuffs out his vacant garments with his form;
Then have I reason to be fond of grief.
[III.iv]

13. Life is as tedious as a twice-told tale
Vexing the dull ear of a drowsy man.
[III.iv]

14. Methinks no body should be sad but I;
Yet, I remember, when I was in France,
Young gentlemen would be as sad as night,
Only for wantonness.
[IV.i]

15. Will you put out mine eyes,
These eyes that never did nor never shall
So much as frown on you?
[IV.i]

16. To be possess'd with double pomp,
To guard a title that was rich before,
To gild refined gold, to paint the lily,
To throw a perfume on the violet,
To smooth the ice, or add another hue

Unto the rainbow, or with taper-light
To seek the beauteous eye of heaven to garnish,
Is wasteful and ridiculous excess.
[IV.ii. Cf. Byron: 190]

17. Another lean unwash'd artificer
Cuts off his tale, and talks of Arthur's death.
[IV.ii]

18. How oft the sight of means to do ill deeds
Make deeds ill done!
[IV.ii]

19. Heaven take my soul, and England keep my bones!
[IV.iii]

20. None of you will bid the winter come
To thrust his icy fingers in my maw,
Nor let my kingdom's rivers take their course
Through my burn'd bosom, nor entreat the north
To make his bleak winds kiss my parched lips
And comfort me with cold. I do not ask you much;
I beg cold comfort; and you are so strait
And so ingrateful you deny me that.
[V.vii]

21. This England never did, nor never shall,
Lie at the proud foot of a conqueror,
But when it first did help to wound itself.
Now these her princes are come home again,
Come the three corners of the world in arms,
And we shall shock them. Nought shall make us rue,
If England to itself do rest but true.
[V.vii]

King Lear

1. Nothing will come of nothing. Speak again.
[I.i]

2. *Lear*: So young and so untender?
Cordelia: So young, my lord, and true.
Lear: Let it be so! Thy truth, then, be thy dower!
For, by the sacred radiance of the sun,
The mysteries of Hecat and the night;
By all the operation of the orbs
From whom we do exist and cease to be;
Here I disclaim all my paternal care,
Propinquity and property of blood,
And as a stranger to my heart and me
Hold thee from this for ever.
[I.i]

3. Come not between the dragon and his wrath.
[I.i]

4. I want that glib and oily art
To speak and purpose not, since what I well intend
I'll do't before I speak.
[I.i]

5. Love's not love
When it is mingled with regards that stands
Aloof from th' entire point.
[I.i]

6. Fairest Cordelia, that art most rich, being poor;
Most choice, forsaken; and most lov'd, despis'd!
[I.i]

7. Why bastard? Wherefore base?
When my dimensions are as well compact,
My mind as generous, and my shape as true,
As honest madam's issue? Why brand they us
With base? with baseness? bastardy? base, base?
Who, in the lusty stealth of nature, take
More composition and fierce quality
Than doth, within a dull, stale, tired bed,
Go to th' creating a whole tribe of fops
Got 'tween asleep and wake?
[I.ii]

8. I grow; I prosper.
Now, gods, stand up for bastards.
[I.ii]

9. This is the excellent foppery of the world, that, when we are sick in fortune, often the surfeits of our own behaviour, we make guilty of our disasters the sun, the moon, and stars; as if we were villains on necessity; fools by heavenly compulsion; knaves, thieves, and treachers, by spherical predominance; drunkards, liars, and adulterers, by an enforc'd obedience of planetary influence; and all that we are evil in, by a divine thrusting on – an admirable evasion of whoremaster man, to lay his goatish disposition on the charge of a star! My father compounded with my mother under the Dragon's tail, and my nativity was under Ursa Major, so that it follows I am rough and lecherous. Fut, I should have been that I am, had the maidenliest star in the firmament twinkled on my bastardizing.
[I.ii]

10. Pat! He comes like the catastrophe of the old comedy. My cue is villainous melancholy, with a sigh like Tom o' Bedlam.
[I.ii]

11. *Lear*. Dost thou know me, fellow?
Kent: No, sir; but you have that in your countenance which I would fain call master.
Lear: What's that?
Kent: Authority.
[I.iv]

12. Not so young, sir, to love a woman for singing, nor so old to dote on her for anything.
[I.iv]

13. *Lear*: Do you bandy looks with me, you rascal!
Oswald: I'll not be strucken, my lord.
Kent: Nor tripp'd neither, you base football player.
[I.iv]

14. *Lear*: Take heed, sirrah – the whip.
Fool: Truth's a dog must to kennel; he must be whipp'd out, when Lady the brach may stand by th' fire and stink.
[I.iv]

15. Have more than thou showest,
Speak less than thou knowest,
Lend less than thou owest.
[I.iv]

16. *Lear*: Dost thou call me fool, boy?
Fool: All thy other titles thou hast given away; that thou wast born with.
Kent: This is not altogether fool, my lord.
[I.iv]

17. Not only, sir, this your all-licens'd fool,
But other of your insolent retinue
Do hourly carp and quarrel, breaking forth
In rank and not-to-be-endured riots.
[I.iv]

18. The hedge-sparrow fed the cuckoo so long
That it's had it head bit off by it young.
So, out went the candle, and we were left darkling.
[I.iv]

19. Ingratitude, thou marble-hearted fiend,
More hideous when thou show'st thee in a child

Than the sea-monster!
[I.iv]

20. Into her womb convey sterility;
Dry up in her the organs of increase.
[I.iv]

21. How sharper than a serpent's tooth it is
To have a thankless child.
[I.iv]

22. O, let me not be mad, not mad, sweet heaven!
Keep me in temper; I would not be mad!
[I.v]

23. Thou whoreson zed! thou unnecessary letter! My lord, if you will give me leave, I will tread this unbolted villain into mortar, and daub the wall of a jakes with him. – Spare my grey beard, you wagtail?
[II.ii]

24. Goose, if I had you upon Sarum plain,
I'd drive ye cackling home to Camelot.
[II.ii]

25. This is some fellow
Who, having been prais'd for bluntness, doth affect
A saucy roughness, and constrains the garb
Quite from his nature. He cannot flatter, he,
An honest mind and plain – he must speak truth.
An they will take it, so; if not, he's plain.
These kind of knaves I know, which in this plainness
Harbour more craft and more corrupter ends
Than twenty silly ducking observants
That stretch their duties nicely.
[II.ii]

26. *Hysterica passio* – down, thou climbing sorrow,
Thy element's below.
[II.iv]

27. Cry to it, nuncle, as the cockney did to the eels when she put 'em i' th' paste alive; she knapp'd 'em o' th' coxcombs with a stick, and cried 'Down, wantons, down'. 'Twas her brother that, in pure kindness to his horse, butter'd his hay.
[II.iv]

28. O, sir, you are old;
Nature in you stands on the very verge
Of her confine.
[II.iv]

29. O, reason not the need! Our basest beggars
Are in the poorest thing superfluous.
Allow not nature more than nature needs,
Man's life is cheap as beast's.
[II.iv]

30. You see me here, you gods, a poor old man,
As full of grief as age; wretched in both.
[II.iv]

31. Touch me with noble anger,
And let not women's weapons, water-drops,
Stain my man's cheeks! No, you unnatural hags,
I will have such revenges on you both
That all the world shall – I will do such things–
What they are yet I know not; but they shall be
The terrors of the earth. You think I'll weep.
No, I'll not weep.
I have full cause of weeping; but this heart
Shall break into a hundred thousand flaws
Or ere I'll weep. O fool, I shall go mad!
[II.iv]

32. Blow, winds, and crack your cheeks; rage, blow.
You cataracts and hurricanoes, spout
Till you have drench'd our steeples, drown'd the cocks.
You sulph'rous and thought-executing fires,
Vaunt-couriers of oak-cleaving thunderbolts,
Singe my white head. And thou, all-shaking thunder,
Strike flat the thick rotundity o' th' world;
Crack nature's moulds, all germens spill at once,
That makes ingrateful man!
[III.ii]

33. Rumble thy bellyful. Spit, fire; spout, rain.
Nor rain, wind, thunder, fire, are my daughters.
I tax not you, you elements, with unkindness;
I never gave you kingdom, call'd you children;
You owe me no subscription. Then let fall
Your horrible pleasure. Here I stand, your slave,
A poor, infirm, weak and despis'd old man.
[III.ii]

34. There was never yet fair woman but she made mouths in a glass.
[III.ii]

35. Marry, here's grace and a cod-piece; that's a wise man and a fool.
[III.ii]

36. Things that love night
Love not such nights as these.
[III.ii]

37. Close pent-up guilts,
Rive your concealing continents, and cry
These dreadful summoners grace. I am a man
More sinn'd against than sinning.
[III.ii]

38. The art of our necessities is strange
That can make vile things precious.
[III.ii]

39. He that has and a little tiny wit
With heigh-ho, the wind and the rain–
Must make content with his fortunes fit,
Though the rain it raineth every day.
[III.ii]

40. When the mind's free
The body's delicate.
[III.iv]

41. O, that way madness lies; let me shun that.
[III.iv]

42. Poor naked wretches, wheresoe'er you are,
That bide the pelting of this pitiless storm,
How shall your houseless heads and unfed sides,
Your loop'd and window'd raggedness, defend you
From seasons such as these? O, I have ta'en
Too little care of this! Take physic, pomp;
Expose thyself to feel what wretches feel.
[III.iv]

43. Pillicock sat on Pillicock-hill.
Alow, alow, loo, loo!
[III.iv]

44. A serving-man, proud in heart and mind: that curl'd my hair; wore gloves in my cap; serv'd the lust of my mistress' heart, and did the act of darkness with her; swore as many oaths as I spake words, and broke them in the sweet face of heaven; one that slept in the contriving of lust, and wak'd to do it. Wine lov'd I deeply, dice dearly; and in woman out-paramour'd the Turk.
[III.iv]

45. Keep thy foot out of brothels, thy hand out of plackets, thy pen from lenders' books, and defy the foul fiend.
[III.iv]

46. Thou art the thing itself; unaccommodated man is no more but such a poor, bare, forked animal as thou art. Off, off, you lendings! Come, unbutton here.
[III.iv]

47. This is the foul fiend Flibbertigibbet; he begins at curfew, and walks till the first cock; he gives the web and the pin, squenes the eye, and makes the hare-lip; mildews the white wheat, and hurts the poor creature of earth.
[III.iv]

48. The prince of darkness is a gentleman.
[III.iv]

49. Poor Tom's a-cold.
[III.iv]

50. I will keep still with my philosopher.
[III.iv]

51. Child Rowland to the dark tower came,
His word was still 'Fie, foh, and fum,
I smell the blood of a British man'.
[III.iv. Cf. Nashe: 5]

52. He's mad that trusts in the tameness of a wolf, a horse's health, a boy's love, or a whore's oath.
[III.vi]

53. By the kind gods, 'tis most ignobly done
To pluck me by the beard.
[III.vii]

54. *Cornwall*: Out vile jelly!
Where is thy lustre now?
Gloucester: All dark and comfortless.
[III.vii]

55. Yet better thus and known to be contemn'd,
Than still contemn'd and flatter'd. To be worst,
The lowest and most dejected thing of fortune,
Stands still in esperance, lives not in fear.
The lamentable change is from the best;
The worst returns to laughter.
[IV.i]

56. I have no way, and therefore want no eyes;
I stumbled when I saw.
[IV.i]

57. Might I but live to see thee in my touch,
I'd say I had eyes again!
[IV.i]

58. The worst is not
So long as we can say 'This is the worst'.
[IV.i]

59. As flies to wanton boys are we to th' gods–
They kill us for their sport.
[IV.i]

60. You are not worth the dust which the rude wind
Blows in your face.
[IV.ii]

61. Wisdom and goodness to the vile seem vile;
Filths savour but themselves. What have you done?
Tigers, not daughters, what have you perform'd?
[IV.ii]

62. It will come
Humanity must perforce prey on itself,
Like monsters of the deep.
[IV.ii]

63. It is the stars,
The stars above us, govern our conditions.
[IV.iii]

64. He was met even now
As mad as the vex'd sea, singing aloud,
Crown'd with rank fumiter and furrow weeds,
With hardocks, hemlock, nettles, cuckoo-flow'rs,
Darnel, and all the idle weeds that grow
In our sustaining corn.
[IV.iv]

65. How fearful
And dizzy 'tis to cast one's eyes so low!
The crows and choughs that wing the midway air
Show scarce so gross as beetles. Half-way down
Hangs one that gathers samphire – dreadful trade!
Methinks he seems no bigger than his head.
The fishermen that walk upon the beach
Appear like mice; and yond tall anchoring bark
Diminish'd to her cock; her cock, a buoy
Almost too small for sight. The murmuring surge
That on th' unnumb'red idle pebble chafes
Cannot be heard so high.
[IV.vi]

66. They told me I was everything; 'tis a lie – I am not ague-proof.
[IV.vi]

67. *Gloucester*: Is't not the King?
Lear: Ay, every inch a king.
When I do stare, see how the subject quakes.
I pardon that man's life. What was thy cause?
Adultery?
Thou shalt not die. Die for adultery? No.
The wren goes to't, and the small gilded fly
Does lecher in my sight.
Let copulation thrive.
[IV.vi]

68. *Lear*: The fitchew nor the soiled horse goes to't
With a more riotous appetite.
Down from the waist they are centaurs,
Though women all above;
But to the girdle do the gods inherit,
Beneath is all the fiends';
There's hell, there's darkness, there is the sulphurous pit–
Burning, scalding, strench, consumption. Fie, fie, fie! pah, pah! Give me an ounce of civet, good apothecary, to sweeten my imagination. There's money for thee.
Gloucester: O, let me kiss that hand!
Lear: Let me wipe it first; it smells of mortality.
Gloucester: O ruin'd piece of nature! This great world
Shall so wear out to nought.
[IV.vi]

69. A man may see how this world goes with no eyes. Look with thine ears. See how yond justice rails upon yond simple thief. Hark, in thine ear: change places and, handy-dandy, which is the justice, which is the thief?
[IV.vi]

70. Thou rascal beadle, hold thy bloody hand.
Why dost thou lash that whore? Strip thy own back;
Thou hotly lusts to use her in that kind
For which thou whip'st her.
[IV.vi]

71. Through tatter'd clothes small vices do appear;
Robed and furr'd gowns hide all.
[IV.vi]

72. Plate sin with gold,
And the strong lance of justice hurtless breaks;
Arm it in rags, a pigmy's straw does pierce it.
[IV.vi]

73. Get thee glass eyes,
And, like a scurvy politician, seem
To see the things thou dost not.
[IV.vi]

74. I know thee well enough; thy name is Gloucester.
Thou must be patient; we came crying hither.
Thou know'st the first time that we smell the air
We wawl and cry.
[IV.vi]

75. When we are born, we cry that we are come
To this great stage of fools.
[IV.vi]

76. Thou art a soul in bliss; but I am bound
Upon a wheel of fire, that mine own tears
Do scald like molten lead.
[IV.vii]

77. I am a very foolish fond old man,
Fourscore and upward, not an hour more nor less;
And, to deal plainly,
I fear I am not in my perfect mind.
[IV.vii]

78. Men must endure
Their going hence, even as their coming hither:
Ripeness is all.
[V.ii]

79. Come, let's away to prison.
We two alone will sing like birds i' th' cage;
When thou dost ask me blessing, I'll kneel down
And ask of thee forgiveness; so we'll live,
And pray, and sing, and tell old tales, and laugh
At gilded butterflies, and hear poor rogues
Talk of court news; and we'll talk with them too–
Who loses and who wins; who's in, who's out–
And take upon's the mystery of things
As if we were God's spies; and we'll wear out
In a wall'd prison packs and sects of great ones
That ebb and flow by th' moon.
[V.iii]

80. Upon such sacrifices, my Cordelia,
The gods themselves throw incense.
[V.iii]

81. *Edgar*: My name is Edgar, and thy father's son.
The gods are just, and of our pleasant vices
Make instruments to plague us:
The dark and vicious place where thee he got
Cost him his eyes.
Edmund: Thou hast spoken right, 'tis true;
The wheel is come full circle; I am here.
[V.iii]

82. His flaw'd heart–
Alack, too weak the conflict to support!–
'Twixt two extremes of passion, joy and grief,
Burst smilingly.
[V.iii]

83. Howl, howl, howl, howl! O, you are men of stones!
Had I your tongues and eyes, I'd use them so
That heaven's vault should crack. She's gone for ever.
[V.iii]

84. Her voice was ever soft,
Gentle, and low – an excellent thing in woman.
[V.iii]

85. And my poor fool is hang'd! No, no, no life!
Why should a dog, a horse, a rat have life,
And thou no breath at all? Thou'lt come no more,
Never, never, never, never, never.
Pray you undo this button.
[V.iii]

86. Vex not his ghost. O, let him pass! He hates him
That would upon the rack of this tough world
Stretch him out longer.
[V.iii]

87. The weight of this sad time we must obey;
Speak what we feel, not what we ought to say.
The oldest hath borne most; we that are young
Shall never see so much nor live so long.
[V.iii]

Love's Labour's Lost

1. Let fame, that all hunt after in their lives,
Live regist'red upon our brazen tombs,
And then grace us in the disgrace of death;
When, spite of cormorant devouring Time,
Th' endeavour of this present breath may buy
That honour which shall bate his scythe's keen edge,
And make us heirs of all eternity.
[I.i]

2. At Christmas I no more desire a rose
Than wish a snow in May's new-fangled shows;
But like of each thing that in season grows.
[I.i]

3. Assist me, some extemporal god of rhyme, for I am sure I shall turn sonnet. Devise, wit; write, pen; for I am for whole volumes in folio.
[I.ii]

4. Your wit 's too hot, it speeds too fast, 'twill tire.
[II.i]

5. Thy own wish wish I thee in every place.
[II.i]

6. Warble, child; make passionate my sense of hearing.
[III.i]

7. Remuneration! O, that's the Latin word for three farthings.
[III.i]

8. This wimpled, whining, purblind, wayward boy,
This senior-junior, giant-dwarf, Dan Cupid;
Regent of love-rhymes, lord of folded arms,
Th' anointed sovereign of sighs and groans,
Liege of all loiterers and malcontents,
Dread prince of plackets, king of codpieces,
Sole imperator, and great general
Of trotting paritors. O my little heart!
[III.i]

9. A whitely wanton with a velvet brow,
With two pitch balls stuck in her face for eyes;
Ay, and, by heaven, one that will do the deed,
Though Argus were her eunuch and her guard.
And I to sigh for her! to watch for her!
To pray for her!
[III.i]

10. He hath never fed of the dainties that are bred in a book; he hath not eat paper, as it were; he hath not drunk ink.
[IV.ii]

11. Old Mantuan! old Mantuan! Who understandeth thee not, loves thee not.
[IV.ii]

12. Here are only numbers ratified; but, for the elegancy, facility, and golden cadence of poesy, caret. Ovidius Naso was the man. And why, indeed, 'Naso' but for smelling out the odoriferous flowers of fancy, the jerks of invention?
[IV.ii]

13. Thou for whom Jove would swear
Juno but an Ethiope were;
And deny himself for Jove,
Turning mortal for thy love.
[IV.iii]

14. From women's eyes this doctrine I derive:
They are the ground, the books, the academes,
From whence doth spring the true Promethean fire.
[IV.iii]

15. For where is any author in the world
Teaches such beauty as a woman's eye?
[IV.iii]

16. But love, first learned in a lady's eyes,
Lives not alone immured in the brain,
But with the motion of all elements
Courses as swift as thought in every power,
And gives to every power a double power,
Above their functions and their offices.
It adds a precious seeing to the eye.
A lover's eyes will gaze an eagle blind.
A lover's ear will hear the lowest sound,
When the suspicious head of theft is stopp'd.
Love's feeling is more soft and sensible
Than are the tender horns of cockled snails;
Love's tongue proves dainty Bacchus gross in taste.
For valour, is not Love a Hercules,
Still climbing trees in the Hesperides?
Subtle as Sphinx; as sweet and musical
As bright Apollo's lute, strung with his hair.
And when Love speaks, the voice of all the gods
Make heaven drowsy with the harmony.
Never durst poet touch a pen to write
Until his ink were temp'red with Love's sighs.
[IV.iii]

17. From women's eyes this doctrine I derive.
They sparkle still the right Promethean fire;
They are the books, the arts, the academes,
That show, contain, and nourish, all the world.
[IV.iii]

18. He draweth out the thread of his verbosity finer than the staple of his argument.
[V.i]

19. *Moth*: They have been at a great feast of languages and stol'n the scraps.
Costard: O, they have liv'd long on the alms-basket of words. I marvel thy master hath not eaten thee for a word, for thou art not so long by the head as honorificabilitudinitatibus; thou art easier swallowed than a flap-dragon.
[V.i]

20. The posteriors of this day; which the rude multitude call the afternoon.
[V.i]

21. Taffeta phrases, silken terms precise,
Three-pil'd hyperboles, spruce affectation,
Figures pedantical – these summer-flies
Have blown me full of maggot ostentation.
I do forswear them.
[V.ii]

22. Henceforth my wooing mind shall be express'd
In russet yeas, and honest kersey noes.
And, to begin, wench – so God help me, law!–
My love to thee is sound, sans crack or flaw.
[V.ii]

23. A jest's prosperity lies in the ear
Of him that hears it, never in the tongue
Of him that makes it.
[V.ii]

24. When daisies pied and violets blue
And lady-smocks all silver-white
And cuckoo-buds of yellow hue
Do paint the meadows with delight,
The cuckoo then on every tree
Mocks married men, for thus sings he:
'Cuckoo;
Cuckoo, cuckoo' – O word of fear,
Unpleasing to a married ear!
[V.ii]

25. When icicles hang by the wall,
And Dick the shepherd blows his nail,
And Tom bears logs into the hall,
And milk comes frozen home in pail,
When blood is nipp'd, and ways be foul.
Then nightly sings the staring owl:
'Tu-who;
Tu-whit, Tu-who' – A merry note,
While greasy Joan doth keel the pot.

When all aloud the wind doth blow,
And coughing drowns the parson's saw,
And birds sit brooding in the snow,
And Marian's nose looks red and raw,
When roasted crabs hiss in the bowl,
Then nightly sings the staring owl:
'Tu-who;
Tu-whit, Tu-who' – A merry note,
While greasy Joan doth keel the pot.
[V.ii]

26. The words of Mercury are harsh after the songs of Apollo.
[V.ii]

Macbeth

1. *First Witch*: When shall we three meet again?
In thunder, lightning, or in rain?
Second Witch: When the hurlyburly's done,
When the battle's lost and won.
Third Witch: That will be ere the set of sun.
First Witch: Where the place?
Second Witch: Upon the heath.
Third Witch: There to meet with Macbeth.
First Witch: I come, Greymalkin.
Second Witch: Paddock calls.
Third Witch: Anon!
All: Fair is foul, and foul is fair:
Hover through the fog and filthy air.
[I.i]

2. What bloody man is that?
[I.ii]

3. Brave Macbeth – well he deserves that name–
Disdaining Fortune, with his brandish'd steel
Which smok'd with bloody execution,
Like valour's minion, carv'd out his passage
Till he fac'd the slave;
Which ne'er shook hands, nor bade farewell to him,

Till he unseam'd him from the nave to th' chaps,
And fix'd his head upon our battlements.
[I.ii]

4. They doubly redoubled strokes upon the foe.
Except they meant to bathe in reeking wounds,
Or memorize another Golgotha,
I cannot tell.
[I.ii]

5. A sailor's wife had chestnuts in her lap,
And mounch'd, and mounch'd, and mounch'd.
'Give me' quoth I.
'Aroint thee, witch!' the rump-fed ronyon cries.
Her husband's to Aleppo gone, master o' th' Tiger;
But in a sieve I'll thither sail
And, like a rat without a tail,
I'll do, I'll do, and I'll do.
[I.iii]

6. Sleep shall neither night nor day
Hang upon his pent-house lid;
He shall live a man forbid;
Weary sev'nights, nine times nine,
Shall he dwindle, peak, and pine.
Though his bark cannot be lost,
Yet it shall be tempest-tost.
[I.iii]

7. So foul and fair a day I have not seen.
[I.iii]

8. What are these,
So wither'd, and so wild in their attire,
That look not like th' inhabitants o' th' earth,
And yet are on't? Live you, or are you aught
That man may question? You seem to understand me,
By each at once her choppy finger laying
Upon her skinny lips. You should be women,
And yet your beards forbid me to interpret
That you are so.
[I.iii]

9. If you can look into the seeds of time
And say which grain will grow and which will not,
Speak then to me, who neither beg nor fear
Your favours nor your hate.
[I.iii]

10. Stay, you imperfect speakers, tell me more.
[I.iii]

11. Were such things here as we do speak about?
Or have we eaten on the insane root
That takes the reason prisoner?
[I.iii]

12. What, can the devil speak true?
[I.iii]

13. The Thane of Cawdor lives; why do you dress me
In borrowed robes?
[I.iii]

14. Oftentimes to win us to our harm,
The instruments of darkness tell us truths,
Win us with honest trifles, to betray's
In deepest consequence.
[I.iii]

15. Two truths are told,
As happy prologues to the swelling act
Of the imperial theme.
[I.iii]

16. This supernatural soliciting
Cannot be ill; cannot be good. If ill,
Why hath it given me earnest of success,
Commencing in a truth? I am Thane of Cawdor.
If good, why do I yield to that suggestion
Whose horrid image doth unfix my hair
And make my seated heart knock at my ribs
Against the use of nature? Present fears
Are less than horrible imaginings.
My thought, whose murder yet is but fantastical,
Shakes so my single state of man
That function is smother'd in surmise,
And nothing is but what is not.
[I.iii]

17. Come what come may,
Time and the hour runs through the roughest day.
[I.iii]

18. *Malcolm*: Nothing in his life
Became him like the leaving it: he died
As one that had been studied in his death
To throw away the dearest thing he ow'd
As 'twere a careless trifle.
Duncan: There's no art
To find the mind's construction in the face.
He was a gentleman on whom I built
An absolute trust.
[I.iv]

19. Glamis thou art, and Cawdor; and shalt be
What thou art promis'd. Yet do I fear thy nature;
It is too full o' th' milk of human kindness
To catch the nearest way. Thou wouldst be great;
Art not without ambition, but without
The illness should attend it. What thou wouldst highly,
That wouldst thou holily; wouldst not play false,
And yet wouldst wrongly win.
[I.v]

20. The raven himself is hoarse
That croaks the fatal entrance of Duncan
Under my battlements. Come, you spirits
That tend on mortal thoughts, unsex me here;
And fill me, from the crown to the toe, top-full
Of direst cruelty. Make thick my blood,
Stop up th' access and passage to remorse,
That no compunctious visitings of nature
Shake my fell purpose nor keep peace between
Th' effect and it. Come to my woman's breasts,
And take my milk for gall, you murd'ring ministers,
Wherever in your sightless substances
You wait on nature's mischief. Come, thick night,
And pall thee in the dunnest smoke of hell,
That my keen knife see not the wound it makes,
Nor heaven peep through the blanket of the dark
To cry 'Hold, hold'.
[I.v]

21. Your face, my thane, is as a book where men
May read strange matters. To beguile the time,
Look like the time; bear welcome in your eye,
Your hand, your tongue; look like th' innocent flower,
But be the serpent under 't.
[I.v]

22. *Duncan*: This castle hath a pleasant seat; the air
Nimbly and sweetly recommends itself
Unto our gentle senses.
Banquo: This guest of summer,
The temple-haunting martlet, does approve
By his lov'd mansionry that the heaven's breath
Smells wooingly here; no jutty, frieze,
Buttress, nor coign of vantage, but this bird

Hath made her pendent bed and procreant cradle.
Where they most breed and haunt, I have observ'd
The air is delicate.
[I.vi]

23. If it were done when 'tis done, then 'twere well
It were done quickly. If th' assassination
Could trammel up the consequence, and catch,
With his surcease, success; that but this blow
Might be the be-all and the end-all here–
But here upon this bank and shoal of time–
We'd jump the life to come. But in these cases
We still have judgment here, that we but teach
Bloody instructions, which being taught return
To plague th' inventor. This even-handed justice
Commends th' ingredience of our poison'd chalice
To our own lips.
[I.vii]

24. Besides, this Duncan
Hath borne his faculties so meek, hath been
So clear in his great office, that his virtues
Will plead like angels, trumpet-tongu'd, against
The deep damnation of his taking-off;
And pity, like a naked new-born babe,
Striding the blast, or heaven's cherubin hors'd
Upon the sightless couriers of the air,
Shall blow the horrid deed in every eye,
That tears shall drown the wind. I have no spur
To prick the sides of my intent, but only
Vaulting ambition, which o'er-leaps itself,
And falls on th' other.
[I.vii]

25. We will proceed no further in this business.
He hath honour'd me of late; and I have bought
Golden opinions from all sorts of people.
[I.vii]

26. Was the hope drunk
Wherein you dress'd yourself? Hath it slept since,
And wakes it now to look so green and pale
At what it did so freely? From this time
Such I account thy love. Art thou afeard
To be the same in thine own act and valour
As thou art in desire? Wouldst thou have that
Which thou esteem'st the ornament of life,
And live a coward in thine own esteem,
Letting 'I dare not' wait upon 'I would',
Like the poor cat i' th' adage?
[I.vii]

27. I dare do all that may become a man;
Who dares do more is none.
[I.vii]

28. *Lady Macbeth*: I have given suck, and know
How tender 'tis to love the babe that milks me–
I would, while it was smiling in my face,
Have pluck'd my nipple from his boneless gums,
And dash'd the brains out, had I so sworn
As you have done to this.
Macbeth: If we should fail?
Lady Macbeth: We fail!
But screw your courage to the sticking place,
And we'll not fail.
[I.vii]

29. Bring forth men-children only;
For thy undaunted mettle should compose
Nothing but males.
[I.vii]

30. False face must hide what the false heart doth know.
[I.vii]

31. There's husbandry in heaven;
Their candles are all out.
[II.i]

32. A heavy summons lies like lead upon me,
And yet I would not sleep.
[II.i]

33. Is this a dagger which I see before me,
The handle toward my hand? Come, let me clutch thee.
I have thee not, and yet I see thee still.
Art thou not, fatal vision, sensible
To feeling as to sight? or art thou but
A dagger of the mind, a false creation,
Proceeding from the heat-oppressed brain?
[II.i]

34. Now o'er the one half-world
Nature seems dead, and wicked dreams abuse
The curtain'd sleep; now witchcraft celebrates
Pale Hecate's offerings; and wither'd murder,
Alarum'd by his sentinel, the wolf,
Whose howl's his watch, thus with his stealthy pace,
With Tarquin's ravishing strides, towards his design
Moves like a ghost. Thou sure and firm-set earth,
Hear not my steps which way they walk, for fear
The very stones prate of my whereabout
And take the present horror from the time,
Which now suits with it. Whiles I threat, he lives;
Words to the heat of deeds too cold breath gives.
I go, and it is done; the bell invites me.
Hear it not, Duncan, for it is a knell
That summons thee to heaven or to hell.
[II.i]

35. It was the owl that shriek'd, the fatal bellman,
Which gives the stern'st good-night.
[II.ii]

36. Th' attempt, and not the deed,
Confounds us.
[II.ii]

37. Had he not resembled
My father as he slept, I had done't.
[II.ii]

38. Macbeth: I have done the deed. Didst thou not hear a noise?
Lady Macbeth: I heard the owl scream and the crickets cry.
[II.ii]

39. But wherefore could not I pronounce 'Amen'?
I had most need of blessing, and 'Amen'
Stuck in my throat.
[II.ii]

40. Methought I heard a voice cry 'Sleep no more;
Macbeth does murder sleep' – the innocent sleep,
Sleep that knits up the ravell'd sleave of care,
The death of each day's life, sore labour's bath,
Balm of hurt minds, great nature's second course,
Chief nourisher in life's feast.
[II.ii]

41. Glamis hath murder'd sleep; and therefore Cawdor
Shall sleep no more – Macbeth shall sleep no more.
[II.ii]

42. You do unbend your noble strength to think
So brainsickly of things.
[II.ii]

43. *Macbeth*: I am afraid to think what I have done;
Look on't again I dare not.

Lady Macbeth: Infirm of purpose!
Give me the daggers. The sleeping and the dead
Are but as pictures; 'tis the eye of childhood
That fears a painted devil. If he do bleed,
I'll gild the faces of the grooms withal,
For it must seem their guilt.
[II.ii]

44. Whence is that knocking?
How is't with me, when every noise appals me?
[II.ii]

45. Will all great Neptune's ocean wash this blood
Clean from my hand? No; this my hand will rather
The multitudinous seas incarnadine,
Making the green one red.
[II.ii]

46. A little water clears us of this deed.
How easy is it then!
[II.ii]

47. Wake Duncan with thy knocking! I would thou couldst!
[II.ii]

48. Here's a knocking indeed! If a man were porter of hell-gate, he should have old turning the key. Knock, knock, knock! Who's there, i' th' name of Beelzebub? Here's a farmer that hanged himself on th' expectation of plenty.
[II.iii]

49. Who's there, i' th' other devil's name? Faith, here's an equivocator, that could swear in both the scales against either scale; who committed treason enough for God's sake, yet could not equivocate to heaven. O, come in, equivocator.
[II.iii]

50. This place is too cold for hell. I'll devil-porter it no further. I had thought to have let in some of all professions that go the primrose way to th' everlasting bonfire.
[II.iii]

51. *Porter*: Drink, sir, is a great provoker of three things.
Macduff: What three things does drink especially provoke?
Porter: Marry, sir, nose-painting, sleep, and urine. Lechery, sir, it provokes, and unprovokes: it provokes the desire, but it takes away the performance.
[II.iii]

52. The night has been unruly. Where we lay,
Our chimneys were blown down; and, as they say,
Lamentings heard i' th' air, strange screams of death,
And prophesying, with accents terrible,
Of dire combustion and confus'd events
New hatch'd to th' woeful time; the obscure bird
Clamour'd the livelong night. Some say the earth
Was feverous and did shake.
[II.iii]

53. O horror, horror, horror! Tongue nor heart
Cannot conceive nor name thee.
[II.iii]

54. Confusion now hath made his masterpiece.
Most sacrilegious murder hath broke ope
The Lord's anointed temple, and stole thence
The life o' th' building.
[II.iii]

55. Shake off this downy sleep, death's counterfeit,
And look on death itself. Up, up, and see
The great doom's image!
[II.iii]

56. Had I but died an hour before this chance,
I had liv'd a blessed time; for, from this instant,
There's nothing serious in mortality–
All is but toys; renown and grace is dead;
The wine of life is drawn, and the mere lees
Is left this vault to brag of.
[II.iii]

57. Who can be wise, amaz'd, temp'rate, and furious,
Loyal and neutral, in a moment? No man.
[II.iii]

58. Where we are,
There's daggers in men's smiles; the near in blood,
The nearer bloody.
[II.iii]

59. A falcon, tow'ring in her pride of place,
Was by a mousing owl hawk'd at and kill'd.
[II.iv]

60. Thou hast it now – King, Cawdor, Glamis, all
As the weird women promis'd; and I fear
Thou play'dst most foully for't.
[III.i]

61. *First Murderer*: We are men, my liege.
Macbeth: Ay, in the catalogue ye go for men;
As hounds, and greyhounds, mongrels, spaniels, curs,
Shoughs, water-rugs, and demi-wolves, are clept
All by the name of dogs.
[III.i]

62. *Second Murderer*: I am one, my liege,
Whom the vile blows and buffets of the world
Have so incens'd that I am reckless what
I do to spite the world.
First Murderer: And I another,
So weary with disasters, tugg'd with fortune,
That I would set my life on any chance,
To mend it or be rid on't.
[III.i]

63. Leave no rubs nor botches in the work.
[III.i]

64. Nought's had, all's spent,
Where our desire is got without content.
'Tis safer to be that which we destroy,
Than by destruction dwell in doubtful joy.
[III.ii]

65. *Lady Macbeth*: Things without all remedy
Should be without regard. What's done is done.
Macbeth: We have scotch'd the snake, not kill'd it;
She'll close, and be herself, whilst our poor malice
Remains in danger of her former tooth.
But let the frame of things disjoint, both the worlds suffer,
Ere we will eat our meal in fear and sleep
In the affliction of these terrible dreams
That shake us nightly. Better be with the dead,
Whom we, to gain our peace, have sent to peace,
Than on the torture of the mind to lie
In restless ecstasy. Duncan is in his grave;
After life's fitful fever he sleeps well;
Treason has done his worst; nor steel, nor poison,
Malice domestic, foreign levy, nothing,
Can touch him further.
[III.ii]

66. Ere the bat hath flown
His cloister'd flight; ere to black Hecate's summons
The shard-borne beetle with his drowsy hums
Hath rung night's yawning peal, there shall be done
A deed of dreadful note.
[III.ii]

67. Be innocent of the knowledge, dearest chuck,
Till thou applaud the deed. Come, seeling night,
Scarf up the tender eye of pitiful day,
And with thy bloody and invisible hand
Cancel and tear to pieces that great bond
Which keeps me pale. Light thickens, and the crow
Makes wing to th' rooky wood;
Good things of day begin to droop and drowse,
Whiles night's black agents to their preys do rouse.
[III.ii]

68. The west yet glimmers with some streaks of day;
Now spurs the lated traveller apace
To gain the timely inn.
[III.iii]

69. But now I am cabin'd, cribb'd, confin'd, bound in
To saucy doubts and fears.
[III.iv]

70. Now good digestion wait on appetite,
And health on both!
[III.iv]

71. Thou canst not say I did it; never shake
Thy gory locks at me.
[III.iv]

72. What man dare, I dare.
Approach thou like the rugged Russian bear,
The arm'd rhinoceros, or th' Hyrcan tiger;
Take any shape but that, and my firm nerves
Shall never tremble.
[III.iv]

73. Stand not upon the order of your going,
But go at once.
[III.iv]

74. *Macbeth*: It will have blood; they say blood will have blood.
Stones have been known to move, and trees to speak;
Augurs and understood relations have
By maggot-pies and choughs and rooks brought forth
The secret'st man of blood. What is the night?
Lady Macbeth: Almost at odds with morning, which is which.
[III.iv]

75. I am in blood
Stepp'd in so far that, should I wade no more,
Returning were as tedious as go o'er.
[III.iv]

76. You lack the season of all natures, sleep.
[III.iv]

77. Security
Is mortals' chiefest enemy.
[III.v]

78. Round about the cauldron go;
In the poison'd entrails throw.
Toad that under cold stone
Days and nights hast thirty-one
Swelt'red venom sleeping got
Boil thou first i' th' charmed pot.
Double, double toil and trouble;
Fire burn, and cauldron bubble.
[IV.i]

79. Eye of newt, and toe of frog,
Wool of bat, and tongue of dog,
Adder's fork, and blind-worm's sting,
Lizard's leg, and howlet's wing–
For a charm of pow'rful trouble,
Like a hell-broth boil and bubble.
[IV.i]

80. Liver of blaspheming Jew,
Gall of goat, and slips of yew
Sliver'd in the moon's eclipse,
Nose of Turk, and Tartar's lips,
Finger of birth-strangled babe
Ditch-deliver'd by a drab–
Make the gruel thick and slab.
[IV.i]

81. *Second Witch*: By the pricking of my thumbs,
Something wicked this way comes.
Open, locks, whoever knocks.
Macbeth: How now, you secret, black, and midnight hags!
What is't you do?
Witches: A deed without a name.
[IV.i]

82. Be bloody, bold, and resolute; laugh to scorn
The pow'r of man, for none of woman born
Shall harm Macbeth.
[IV.i]

83. But yet I'll make assurance double sure
And take a bond of fate.
[IV.i]

84. Macbeth shall never vanquish'd be until
Great Birnam wood to high Dunsinane Hill
Shall come against him.
[IV.i]

85. Show his eyes, and grieve his heart;
Come like shadows, so depart!
[IV.i]

86. What, will the line stretch out to th' crack of doom?
[IV.i]

87. He loves us not;
He wants the natural touch; for the poor wren,
The most diminutive of birds, will fight,
Her young ones in her nest, against the owl.
[IV.ii]

88. I have done no harm. But I remember now
I am in this earthly world, where to do harm
Is often laudable, to do good sometime
Accounted dangerous folly.
[IV.ii]

89. *Son*: Thou liest, thou shag-ear'd villain.
First Murderer: What, you egg?
Young fry of treachery!
[IV.ii]

90. Each new morn
New widows howl, new orphans cry; new sorrows
Strike heaven on the face, that it resounds
As if it felt with Scotland and yell'd out
Like syllable of dolour.
[IV.iii]

91. Angels are bright still, though the brightest fell.
[IV.iii]

92. I think our country sinks beneath the yoke;
It weeps, it bleeds; and each new day a gash
Is added to her wounds.
[IV.iii]

93. *Macduff*: Not in the legions
Of horrid hell can come a devil more damn'd
In evils to top Macbeth.
Malcolm: I grant him bloody,
Luxurious, avaricious, false, deceitful,

Sudden, malicious, smacking of every sin
That has a name; but there's no bottom, none,
In my voluptuousness. Your wives, your daughters,
Your matrons, and your maids, could not fill up
The cistern of my lust.
[IV.iii]

94. Nay, had I pow'r, I should
Pour the sweet milk of concord into hell,
Uproar the universal peace, confound
All unity on earth.
[IV.iii]

95. *Macduff*: Stands Scotland where it did?
Ross: Alas, poor country,
Almost afraid to know itself! It cannot
Be call'd our mother, but our grave.
[IV.iii]

96. What, man! Ne'er pull your hat upon your brows;
Give sorrow words. The grief that does not speak
Whispers the o'erfraught heart and bids it break.
[IV.iii]

97. *Malcolm*: Let's make us med'cines of our great revenge
To cure this deadly grief.
Macduff: He has no children. All my pretty ones?
Did you say all? O hell-kite! All?
What, all my pretty chickens and their dam
At one fell swoop?
[IV.iii]

98. *Malcolm*: Dispute it like a man.
Macduff: I shall do so;
But I must also feel it as a man.
[IV.iii]

99. *Doctor*: You see her eyes are open.
Gentlewoman: Ay, but their sense is shut.
[V.i]

100. Out, damned spot! out, I say! One, two; why then 'tis time to do't. Hell is murky. Fie, my lord, fie! a soldier, and afeard? What need we fear who knows it, when none can call our pow'r to account? Yet who would have thought the old man to have had so much blood in him?
[V.i]

101. The Thane of Fife had a wife; where is she now? What, will these hands ne'er be clean? No more o' that, my lord, no more o' that; you mar all with this starting.
[V.i]

102. Here's the smell of the blood still. All the perfumes of Arabia will not sweeten this little hand. Oh, oh, oh!
[V.i]

103. I would not have such a heart in my bosom for the dignity of the whole body.
[V.i]

104. Wash your hands, put on your nightgown, look not so pale.
[V.i]

105. What's done cannot be undone. To bed, to bed, to bed.
[V.i]

106. Foul whisp'rings are abroad. Unnatural deeds
Do breed unnatural troubles; infected minds
To their deaf pillows will discharge their secrets.
More needs she the divine than the physician.
[V.i]

107. Those he commands move only in command,
Nothing in love. Now does he feel his title
Hang loose about him, like a giant's robe
Upon a dwarfish thief.
[V.ii]

108. Bring me no more reports; let them fly all.
Till Birnam wood remove to Dunsinane
I cannot taint with fear.
[V.iii]

109. The devil damn thee black, thou cream-fac'd loon!
Where got'st thou that goose look?
[V.iii]

110. I have liv'd long enough. My way of life
Is fall'n into the sear, the yellow leaf;
And that which should accompany old age,
As honour, love, obedience, troops of friends,
I must not look to have; but, in their stead,
Curses not loud but deep, mouth-honour, breath,
Which the poor heart would fain deny, and dare not.
[V.iii]

111. *Macbeth*: Canst thou not minister to a mind diseas'd,
Pluck from the memory a rooted sorrow,
Raze out the written troubles of the brain,
And with some sweet oblivious antidote
Cleanse the stuff'd bosom of that perilous stuff
Which weighs upon the heart?
Doctor: Therein the patient
Must minister to himself.
Macbeth: Throw physic to the dogs – I'll none of it.
[V.iii]

112. I have almost forgot the taste of fears.
The time has been my senses would have cool'd
To hear a night-shriek, and my fell of hair
Would at a dismal treatise rouse and stir
As life were in't. I have supp'd full with horrors;
Direness, familiar to my slaughterous thoughts,
Cannot once start me.
[V.v]

113. She should have died hereafter;
There would have been a time for such a word.
To-morrow, and to-morrow, and to-morrow,
Creeps in this petty pace from day to day
To the last syllable of recorded time,
And all our yesterdays have lighted fools
The way to dusty death. Out, out, brief candle!
Life's but a walking shadow, a poor player,
That struts and frets his hour upon the stage,
And then is heard no more; it is a tale
Told by an idiot, full of sound and fury,
Signifying nothing.
[V.v]

114. If this which he avouches does appear,
There is nor flying hence nor tarrying here.
I gin to be aweary of the sun,
And wish th' estate o' th' world were now undone.
Ring the alarum bell. Blow wind, come wrack;
At least we'll die with harness on our back.
[V.v]

115. *Macbeth*: I bear a charmed life, which must not yield
To one of woman born.
Macduff: Despair thy charm;
And let the angel whom thou still hast serv'd
Tell thee Macduff was from his mother's womb
Untimely ripp'd.
[V.viii]

116. Lay on, Macduff;
And damn'd be him that first cries 'Hold, enough!'
[V.viii]

Measure For Measure

1. Now, as fond fathers,
Having bound up the threat'ning twigs of birch,
Only to stick it in their children's sight
For terror, not to use, in time the rod
Becomes more mock'd than fear'd; so our decrees,
Dead to infliction, to themselves are dead;
And liberty plucks justice by the nose;
The baby beats the nurse, and quite athwart
Goes all decorum.
[I.iii]

2. Lord Angelo is precise;
Stands at a guard with envy; scarce confesses
That his blood flows, or that his appetite
Is more to bread than stone. Hence shall we see,
If power change purpose, what our seemers be.
[I.iii]

3. I hold you as a thing enskied and sainted,
By your renouncement an immortal spirit,
And to be talk'd with in sincerity,
As with a saint.
[I.iv]

4. A man whose blood
Is very snow-broth, one who never feels
The wanton stings and motions of the sense,
But doth rebate and blunt his natural edge
With profits of the mind, study and fast.
[I.iv]

5. We must not make a scarecrow of the law,
Setting it up to fear the birds of prey,
And let it keep one shape till custom make it
Their perch, and not their terror.
[II.i]

6. 'Tis one thing to be tempted, Escalus,
Another thing to fall. I not deny
The jury, passing on the prisoner's life,
May in the sworn twelve have a thief or two
Guiltier than him they try.
[II.i]

7. Some rise by sin, and some by virtue fall.
[II.i]

8. This will last out a night in Russia,
When nights are longest there.
[II.i]

9. Condemn the fault and not the actor of it!
[II.ii]

10. No ceremony that to great ones 'longs,
Not the king's crown nor the deputed sword,
The marshal's truncheon nor the judge's robe,
Become them with one half so good a grace
As mercy does.
[II.ii]

11. The law hath not been dead, though it hath slept.
[II.ii]

12. O, it is excellent
To have a giant's strength! But it is tyrannous
To use it like a giant.
[II.ii]

13. Man, proud man,
Dress'd in a little brief authority,
Most ignorant of what he's most assur'd,
His glassy essence, like an angry ape,
Plays such fantastic tricks before high heaven
As makes the angels weep.
[II.ii]

14. That in the captain's but a choleric word
Which in the soldier is flat blasphemy.
[II.ii]

15. Is this her fault or mine?
The tempter or the tempted, who sins most?
Ha!
Not she; nor doth she tempt; but it is I
That, lying by the violet in the sun,
Do as the carrion does, not as the flow'r,
Corrupt with virtuous season. Can it be
That modesty may more betray our sense
Than woman's lightness? Having waste ground enough,
Shall we desire to raze the sanctuary,
And pitch our evils there? O, fie, fie, fie!
What dost thou, or what art thou, Angelo?
Dost thou desire her foully for those things
That make her good? O, let her brother live!
Thieves for their robbery have authority
When judges steal themselves.
[II.ii]

16. O cunning enemy, that, to catch a saint,
With saints dost bait thy hook! Most dangerous
Is that temptation that doth goad us on
To sin in loving virtue. Never could the strumpet,
With all her double vigour, art and nature,
Once stir my temper; but this virtuous maid
Subdues me quite. Ever till now
When men were fond, I smil'd and wond'red.
[II.ii]

17. Might there not be a charity in sin
To save this brother's life?
[II.iv]

18. *Claudio*: The miserable have no other medicine
But only hope:
I have hope to live, and am prepar'd to die.
Duke: Be absolute for death; either death or life
Shall thereby be the sweeter. Reason thus with life.
If I do lose thee, I do lose a thing
That none but fools would keep. A breath thou art,
Servile to all the skyey influences,
That dost this habitation where thou keep'st,
Hourly afflict. Merely, thou art Death's fool;
For him thou labour'st by thy flight to shun
And yet run'st toward him still.
[III.i]

19. If thou art rich, thou'rt poor;
For, like an ass whose back with ingots bows,
Thou bear'st thy heavy riches but a journey,
And Death unloads thee.
[III.i]

20. Thou hast nor youth nor age,
But, as it were, an after-dinner's sleep,
Dreaming on both; for all thy blessed youth
Becomes as aged, and doth beg the alms
Of palsied eld.
[III.i]

21. Dar'st thou die?
The sense of death is most in apprehension;
And the poor beetle that we tread upon
In corporal sufferance finds a pang as great
As when a giant dies.
[III.i]

22. If I must die,
I will encounter darkness as a bride
And hug it in mine arms.
[III.i]

23. Sure it is no sin;
Or of the deadly seven it is the least.
[III.i]

24. *Claudio*: Death is a fearful thing.
Isabella: And shamed life a hateful.
Claudio: Ay, but to die, and go we know not where;
To lie in cold obstruction, and to rot;
This sensible warm motion to become
A kneaded clod; and the delighted spirit
To bathe in fiery floods or to reside
In thrilling region of thick-ribbed ice;
To be imprison'd in the viewless winds,
And blown with restless violence round about
The pendent world; or to be worse than worst
Of those that lawless and incertain thought
Imagine howling–'tis too horrible.
The weariest and most loathed worldly life
That age, ache, penury, and imprisonment,
Can lay on nature is a paradise
To what we fear of death.
[III.i]

25. The hand that hath made you fair hath made you good.
[III.i]

26. Virtue is bold, and goodness never fearful.
[III.i]

27. It was a mad fantastical trick of him to steal from the state and usurp the beggary he was never born to. Lord Angelo dukes it well in his absence.
[III.ii]

28. Some report a sea-maid spawn'd him; some, that he was begot between two stock-fishes. But it is certain that when he makes water his urine is congeal'd ice.
[III.ii]

29. Why, what a ruthless thing is this in him, for the rebellion of a codpiece to take away the life of a man! Would the Duke that is absent have done this? Ere he would have hang'd a man for the getting a hundred bastards, he would have paid for the nursing of a thousand. He had some feeling of the sport; he knew the service, and that instructed him to mercy.
[III.ii]

30. Take, O, take those lips away,
That so sweetly were forsworn;
And those eyes, the break of day,
Lights that do mislead the morn;
But my kisses bring again, bring again;
Seals of love, but seal'd in vain, seal'd in vain.
[IV.i]

31. Music oft hath such a charm
To make bad good and good provoke to harm.
[IV.i]

32. Every true man's apparel fits your thief.
[IV.ii]

33. A man that apprehends death no more dreadfully but as a drunken sleep; careless, reckless, and fearless, of what's past, present, or to come; insensible of mortality and desperately mortal.
[IV.ii]

34. O, death's a great disguiser.
[IV.ii]

35. The old fantastical Duke of dark corners.
[IV.iii]

36. Nay, friar, I am a kind of burr;
I shall stick.
[IV.iii]

37. O, your desert speaks loud; and I should wrong it
To lock it in the wards of covert bosom,
When it deserves, with characters of brass,
A forted residence 'gainst the tooth of time
And razure of oblivion.
[V.i]

38. Let the devil
Be sometime honour'd for his burning throne!
[V.i]

39. Haste still pays haste, and leisure answers leisure;
Like doth quit like, and Measure still for Measure.
[V.i]

40. They say best men are moulded out of faults;
And, for the most, become much more the better
For being a little bad; so may my husband.
[V.i]

41. Marrying a punk, my lord, is pressing to death, whipping and hanging.
[V.i]

42. What's mine is yours, and what is yours is mine.
[V.i]

The Merchant of Venice

1. *Antonio*: In sooth I know not why I am so sad.
It wearies me; you say it wearies you;
But how I caught it, found it, or came by it,
What stuff 'tis made of, whereof it is born,
I am to learn;
And such a want-wit sadness makes of me
That I have much ado to know myself.
Salerio: Your mind is tossing on the ocean;
There where your argosies, with portly sail–
Like signiors and rich burghers on the flood,
Or as it were the pageants of the sea–
Do overpeer the petty traffickers,
That curtsy to them, do them reverence,
As they fly by them with their woven wings.
[I.i]

2. You have too much respect upon the world;
They lose it that do buy it with much care.
[I.i]

3. I hold the world but as the world, Gratiano–
A stage, where every man must play a part,
And mine a sad one.
[I.i]

4. Why should a man whose blood is warm within
Sit like his grandsire cut in alabaster?
[I.i]

5. There are a sort of men whose visages
Do cream and mantle like a standing pond,
And do a wilful stillness entertain,
With purpose to be dress'd in an opinion
Of wisdom, gravity, profound conceit;
As who should say, 'I am Sir Oracle,
And when I ope my lips let no dog bark'.
O my Antonio, I do know of these
That therefore only are reputed wise
For saying nothing.
[I.i]

6. Fish not with this melancholy bait
For this fool gudgeon, this opinion.
[I.i]

7. Silence is only commendable
In a neat's tongue dried, and a maid not vendible.
[I.i]

8. Gratiano speaks an infinite deal of nothing, more than any man in all Venice. His reasons are as two grains of wheat hid in two bushels of chaff: you shall seek all day ere you find them, and when you have them they are not worth the search.
[I.i]

9. My purse, my person, my extremest means,
Lie all unlock'd to your occasions.
[I.i]

10. In Belmont is a lady richly left,
And she is fair and, fairer than that word,
Of wondrous virtues. Sometimes from her eyes
I did receive fair speechless messages.
[I.i]

11. They are as sick that surfeit with too much as they that starve with nothing. It is no mean happiness, therefore, to be seated in the mean: superfluity comes sooner by white hairs, but competency lives longer.
[I.ii]

12. If to do were as easy as to know what were good to do, chapels had been churches, and poor men's cottages princes' palaces. It is a good divine that follows his own instructions; I can easier teach twenty what were good to be done than to be one of the twenty to follow mine own teaching.
[I.ii]

13. I think he bought his doublet in Italy, his round hose in France, his bonnet in Germany, and his behaviour everywhere.
[I.ii]

14. I will buy with you, sell with you, talk with you, walk with you, and so following; but I will not eat with you, drink with you, nor pray with you.
[I.iii]

15. How like a fawning publican he looks!
I hate him for he is a Christian;
But more for that in low simplicity
He lends out money gratis, and brings down
The rate of usance here with us in Venice.
If I can catch him once upon the hip,
I will feed fat the ancient grudge I bear him.
He hates our sacred nation; and he rails,
Even there where merchants most do congregate,
On me, my bargains, and my well-won thrift,
Which he calls interest.
[I.iii]

16. The devil can cite Scripture for his purpose.
An evil soul producing holy witness
Is like a villain with a smiling cheek,
A goodly apple rotten at the heart.
O, what a goodly outside falsehood hath!
[I.iii]

17. Signior Antonio, many a time and oft
In the Rialto you have rated me
About my moneys and my usances;
Still have I borne it with a patient shrug,
For suff'rance is the badge of all our tribe;
You call me misbeliever, cut-throat dog,
And spit upon my Jewish gaberdine,
And all for use of that which is mine own.
[I.iii]

18. You that did void your rheum upon my beard
And foot me as you spurn a stranger cur
Over your threshold; moneys is your suit.
What should I say to you? Should I not say
'Hath a dog money? Is it possible
A cur can lend three thousand ducats?' Or
Shall I bend low and, in a bondman's key,
With bated breath and whisp'ring humbleness,
Say this:
'Fair sir, you spit on me Wednesday last,
You spurn'd me such a day; another time
You call'd me dog; and for these courtesies
I'll lend you thus much moneys'?
[I.iii]

19. O father Abram, what these Christians are,
Whose own hard dealings teaches them suspect
The thoughts of others!
[I.iii]

20. The boy was the very staff of my age, my very prop.
[II.ii]

21. It is a wise father that knows his own child.
[II.ii]

22. Truth will come to light; murder cannot be hid long.
[II.ii]

23. There is some ill a-brewing towards my rest,
For I did dream of money-bags to-night.
[II.v]

24. Love is blind, and lovers cannot see
The pretty follies that themselves commit.
[II.vi]

25. What! must I hold a candle to my shames?
[II.vi]

26. Men that hazard all
Do it in hope of fair advantages.
A golden mind stoops not to shows of dross.
[II.vii]

27. All that glisters is not gold,
Often have you heard that told.
[II.vii]

28. Had you been as wise as bold,
Young in limbs, in judgment old,
Your answer had not been inscroll'd.
[II.vii]

29. What many men desire – that 'many' may be meant
By the fool multitude, that choose by show,
Not learning more than the fond eye doth teach;
Which pries not to th' interior, but, like the martlet,
Builds in the weather on the outward wall,
Even in the force and road of casualty.
I will not choose what many men desire,
Because I will not jump with common spirits
And rank me with the barbarous multitudes.
[II.ix]

30. The portrait of a blinking idiot.
[II.ix]

31. Thus hath the candle sing'd the moth.
O, these deliberate fools!
[II.ix]

32. Hath not a Jew eyes? Hath not a Jew hands, organs, dimensions, senses, affections, passions, fed with the same

food, hurt with the same weapons, subject to the same diseases, healed by the same means, warmed and cooled by the same winter and summer, as a Christian is? If you prick us, do we not bleed? If you tickle us, do we not laugh? If you poison us, do we not die? And if you wrong us, shall we not revenge? If we are like you in the rest, we will resemble you in that.
[III.i]

33. He makes a swan-like end,
Fading in music.
[III.ii]

34. Tell me where is fancy bred,
Or in the heart or in the head,
How begot, how nourished?
Reply, reply.
It is engend'red in the eyes,
With gazing fed; and fancy dies
In the cradle where it lies.
Let us all ring fancy's knell:
I'll begin it – Ding, dong, bell.
[III.ii]

35. Ornament is but the guiled shore
To a most dangerous sea; the beauteous scarf
Veiling an Indian beauty; in a word,
The seeming truth which cunning times put on
To entrap the wisest.
[III.ii]

36. How all the other passions fleet to air,
As doubtful thoughts, and rash-embrac'd despair,
And shudd'ring fear, and green-ey'd jealousy!
[III.ii]

37. Here are a few of the unpleasant'st words
That ever blotted paper!
[III.ii]

38. How every fool can play upon the word!
[III.v]

39. You'll ask me why I rather choose to have
A weight of carrion flesh than to receive
Three thousand ducats. I'll not answer that,
But say it is my humour – is it answer'd?
[IV.i]

40. Some men there are love not a gaping pig;
Some that are mad if they behold a cat;
And others, when the bagpipe sings i' th' nose,
Cannot contain their urine.
[IV.i]

41. What judgment shall I dread, doing no wrong?
[IV.i]

42. The pound of flesh which I demand of him
Is dearly bought, 'tis mine, and I will have it.
[IV.i]

43. I am a tainted wether of the flock,
Meetest for death; the weakest kind of fruit
Drops earliest to the ground.
[IV.i]

44. *Portia*: Then must the Jew be merciful.
Shylock: On what compulsion must I? Tell me that.
Portia: The quality of mercy is not strain'd;
It droppeth as the gentle rain from heaven
Upon the place beneath. It is twice blest:
It blesseth him that gives and him that takes.
'Tis mightiest in the mightiest; it becomes
The throned monarch better than his crown;
His sceptre shows the force of temporal power,
The attribute to awe and majesty,
Wherein doth sit the dread and fear of kings;
But mercy is above this sceptred sway,
It is enthroned in the hearts of kings,
It is an attribute to God himself;
And earthly power doth then show likest God's
When mercy seasons justice. Therefore, Jew,
Though justice be thy plea, consider this–
That in the course of justice none of us
Should see salvation; we do pray for mercy,
And that same prayer doth teach us all to render
The deeds of mercy.
[IV.i]

45. Wrest once the law to your authority;
To do a great right do a little wrong.
[IV.i]

46. The court awards it and the law doth give it.
[IV.i]

47. Thyself shalt see the act;
For, as thou urgest justice, be assur'd
Thou shalt have justice, more than thou desir'st.
[IV.i]

48. Nay, take my life and all, pardon not that.
You take my house when you do take the prop
That doth sustain my house; you take my life
When you do take the means whereby I live.
[IV.i]

49. He is well paid that is well satisfied.
[IV.i]

50. How sweet the moonlight sleeps upon this bank!
Here will we sit and let the sounds of music
Creep in our ears; soft stillness and the night
Become the touches of sweet harmony.
Sit, Jessica. Look how the floor of heaven
Is thick inlaid with patines of bright gold;
There's not the smallest orb which thou behold'st
But in his motion like an angel sings,
Still quiring to the young-ey'd cherubins;
Such harmony is in immortal souls,
But whilst this muddy vesture of decay
Doth grossly close it in, we cannot hear it.
[V.i]

51. The man that hath no music in himself,
Nor is not mov'd with concord of sweet sounds,
Is fit for treasons, stratagems, and spoils;
The motions of his spirit are dull as night,
And his affections dark as Erebus.
Let no such man be trusted.
[V.i]

52. How far that little candle throws his beams!
So shines a good deed in a naughty world.
[V.i]

53. The crow doth sing as sweetly as the lark
When neither is attended; and I think
The nightingale, if she should sing by day,
When every goose is cackling, would be thought
No better a musician than the wren.
How many things by season season'd are
To their right praise and true perfection!
[V.i]

54. This night methinks is but the daylight sick.
[V.i]

55. Let me give light, but let me not be light,
For a light wife doth make a heavy husband.
[V.i]

The Merry Wives of Windsor

1. I will make a Star Chamber matter of it.
[I.i]

2. I had rather than forty shillings I had my Book of Songs and Sonnets here.
[I.i]

3. 'Convey' the wise it call. 'Steal' foh! A fico for the phrase!
[I.iii]

4. Here will be an old abusing of God's patience and the King's English.
[I.iv]

5. We burn daylight.
[II.i]

6. Faith, thou hast some crotchets in thy head now.
[II.i]

7. Why, then the world's mine oyster,
Which I with sword will open.
[II.ii]

8. Marry, this is the short and the long of it.
[II.ii]

9. *Falstaff*: Of what quality was your love, then?
Ford: Like a fair house built on another man's ground; so that I have lost my edifice by mistaking the place where I erected it.
[II.ii]

10. I cannot tell what the dickens his name is.
[III.ii]

11. He capers, he dances, he has eyes of youth, he writes verses, he speaks holiday, he smells April and May.
[III.ii]

12. O, what a world of vile ill-favour'd faults
Looks handsome in three hundred pounds a year!
[III.iii]

13. If I be serv'd such another trick, I'll have my brains ta'en out and butter'd, and give them to a dog for a new year's gift.
[III.v]

14. You may know by my size that I have a kind of alacrity in sinking.
[III.v]

15. A man of my kidney.
[III.v]

A Midsummer Night's Dream

1. Question your desires,
Know of your youth, examine well your blood,
Whether, if you yield not to your father's choice,
You can endure the livery of a nun,
For aye to be in shady cloister mew'd,
To live a barren sister all your life,
Chanting faint hymns to the cold fruitless moon.
Thrice-blessed they that master so their blood
To undergo such maiden pilgrimage;
But earthlier happy is the rose distill'd
Than that which withering on the virgin thorn
Grows, lives, and dies, in single blessedness.
[I.i]

2. Ay me! for aught that I could ever read,
Could ever hear by tale or history,
The course of true love never did run smooth.
[I.i]

3. O hell! to choose love by another's eyes.
[I.i]

4. Your eyes are lode-stars and your tongue's sweet air
More tuneable than lark to shepherd's ear,
When wheat is green, when hawthorn buds appear.
[I.i]

5. How happy some o'er other some can be!
Through Athens I am thought as fair as she.
But what of that? Demetrius thinks not so;
He will not know what all but he do know.
And as he errs, doting on Hermia's eyes,
So I, admiring of his qualities.
Things base and vile, holding no quantity,
Love can transpose to form and dignity.
Love looks not with the eyes, but with the mind;
And therefore is wing'd Cupid painted blind.
[I.i]

6. The most Lamentable Comedy and most Cruel Death of Pyramus and Thisby.
[I.ii]

7. I could play Ercles rarely, or a part to tear a cat in, to make all split.
[I.ii]

8. Nay, faith, let not me play a woman; I have a beard coming.
[I.ii]

9. I will roar that I will do any man's heart good to hear me; I will roar that I will make the Duke say 'Let him roar again, let him roar again'.
[I.ii]

10. I will roar you as gently as any sucking dove; I will roar you an 'twere any nightingale.
[I.ii]

11. Pyramus is a sweet-fac'd man; a proper man, as one shall see in a summer's day.
[I.ii]

12. *Puck*: How now, spirit! whither wander you?
Fairy: Over hill, over dale,
Thorough bush, thorough brier,
Over park, over pale,
Thorough flood, thorough fire,
I do wander every where,
Swifter than the moon's sphere;
And I serve the Fairy Queen,
To dew her orbs upon the green.
The cowslips tall her pensioners be;
In their gold coats spots you see;
Those be rubies, fairy favours,
In those freckles live their savours.
I must go seek some dewdrops here,
And hang a pearl in every cowslip's ear.
[II.i]

13. The wisest aunt, telling the saddest tale,
Sometime for three-foot stool mistaketh me;
Then slip I from her bum, down topples she,
And 'tailor' cries, and falls into a cough;
And then the whole quire hold their hips and laugh.
[II.i]

14. Ill met by moonlight, proud Titania.
[II.i]

15. The fold stands empty in the drowned field,
And crows are fatted with the murrion flock;
The nine men's morris is fill'd up with mud.
[II.i]

16. Therefore the moon, the governess of floods,
Pale in her anger, washes all the air,
That rheumatic diseases do abound.
And thorough this distemperature we see
The seasons alter: hoary-headed frosts
Fall in the fresh lap of the crimson rose.
[II.i]

17. Since once I sat upon a promontory,
And heard a mermaid on a dolphin's back
Uttering such dulcet and harmonious breath
That the rude sea grew civil at her song,
And certain stars shot madly from their spheres
To hear the sea-maid's music.
[II.i]

18. But I might see young Cupid's fiery shaft
Quench'd in the chaste beams of the wat'ry moon;
And the imperial vot'ress passed on,
In maiden meditation, fancy-free.
Yet mark'd I where the bolt of Cupid fell.
It fell upon a little western flower,
Before milk-white, now purple with love's wound,
And maidens call it Love-in-idleness.
[II.i]

19. I'll put a girdle round about the earth
In forty minutes.
[II.i]

20. I know a bank where the wild thyme blows,
Where oxlips and the nodding violet grows,
Quite over-canopied with luscious woodbine,
With sweet musk-roses, and with eglantine;
There sleeps Titania sometime of the night,
Lull'd in these flowers with dances and delight;
And there the snake throws her enamell'd skin,
Weed wide enough to wrap a fairy in.
[II.i]

21. You spotted snakes with double tongue,
Thorny hedgehogs, be not seen;
Newts and blind-worms, do no wrong,
Come not near our fairy Queen.
[II.ii]

22. Weaving spiders, come not here;
Hence, you long-legg'd spinners, hence.
Beetles black, approach not near;
Worm nor snail do no offence.
[II.ii]

23. God shield us! – a lion among ladies is a most dreadful thing; for there is not a more fearful wild-fowl than your lion living.
[III.i]

24. Look in the almanack; find out moonshine, find out moonshine.
[III.i]

25. What hempen homespuns have we swagg'ring here,
So near the cradle of the Fairy Queen?
[III.i]

26. Bless thee, Bottom, bless thee! Thou art translated.
[III.i]

27. *Bottom*: The ousel cock, so black of hue,
With orange-tawny bill,
The throstle with his note so true,
The wren with little quill.
Titania: What angel wakes me from my flow'ry bed?
[III.i]

28. As wild geese that the creeping fowler eye,
Or russet-pated choughs, many in sort,
Rising and cawing at the gun's report,
Sever themselves and madly sweep the sky,
So at his sight away his fellows fly.
[III.ii]

29. Lord, what fools these mortals be!
[III.ii]

30. So we grew together,
Like to a double cherry, seeming parted,
But yet an union in partition,
Two lovely berries moulded on one stem;
So, with two seeming bodies, but one heart.
[III.ii]

31. Ay, do – persever, counterfeit sad looks,
Make mouths upon me when I turn my back.
[III.ii]

32. O! when she is angry, she is keen and shrewd;
She was a vixen when she went to school;
And, though she be but little, she is fierce.
[III.ii]

33. Night's swift dragons cut the clouds full fast;
And yonder shines Aurora's harbinger,
At whose approach ghosts, wand'ring here and there,
Troop home to churchyards.
[III.ii]

34. Cupid is a knavish lad,
Thus to make poor females mad.
[III.ii]

35. Jack shall have Jill;
Nought shall go ill;
The man shall have his mare again, and all shall be well.
[III.ii]

36. I must to the barber's, mounsieur; for methinks I am marvellous hairy about the face.
[IV.i]

37. I have a reasonable good ear in music. Let's have the tongs and the bones.
[IV.i]

38. Methinks I have a great desire to a bottle of hay. Good hay, sweet hay, hath no fellow.
[IV.i]

39. I pray you, let none of your people stir me; I have an exposition of sleep come upon me.
[IV.i]

40. My Oberon! What visions have I seen!
Methought I was enamour'd of an ass.
[IV.i]

41. I was with Hercules and Cadmus once
When in a wood of Crete they bay'd the bear
With hounds of Sparta; never did I hear...
So musical a discord, such sweet thunder.
[IV.i]

42. The eye of man hath not heard, the ear of man hath not seen, man's hand is not able to taste, his tongue to conceive, nor his heart to report, what my dream was.
[IV.i]

43. The lunatic, the lover, and the poet,
Are of imagination all compact.
One sees more devils than vast hell can hold;

That is the madman. The lover, all as frantic,
Sees Helen's beauty in a brow of Egypt.
The poet's eye, in a fine frenzy rolling,
Doth glance from heaven to earth, from earth to heaven;
And as imagination bodies forth
The forms of things unknown, the poet's pen
Turns them to shapes, and gives to airy nothing
A local habitation and a name.
Such tricks hath strong imagination
That, if it would but apprehend some joy,
It comprehends some bringer of that joy;
Or in the night, imagining some fear,
How easy is a bush suppos'd a bear?
[V.i]

44. What revels are in hand? Is there no play
To ease the anguish of a torturing hour?
[V.i]

45. A tedious brief scene of young Pyramus
And his love Thisby; very tragical mirth.
[V.i]

46. If we offend, it is with our good will.
That you should think, we come not to offend,
But with good will. To show our simple skill,
That is the true beginning of our end.
Consider then, we come but in despite.
We do not come, as minding to content you,
Our true intent is. All for your delight
We are not here.
[V.i]

47. Whereat with blade, with bloody blameful blade,
He bravely broach'd his boiling bloody breast.
[V.i]

48. I see a voice; now will I to the chink,
To spy an I can hear my Thisby's face.
[V.i]

49. The best in this kind are but shadows; and the worst are no worse, if imagination amend them.
[V.i]

50. The iron tongue of midnight hath told twelve.
Lovers, to bed; 'tis almost fairy time.
[V.i]

51. Now the hungry lion roars,
And the wolf behowls the moon;
Whilst the heavy ploughman snores,
All with weary task fordone.
[V.i]

52. Not a mouse
Shall disturb this hallowed house.
I am sent with broom before,
To sweep the dust behind the door.
[V.i]

53. If we shadows have offended,
Think but this, and all is mended,
That you have but slumb'red here
While these visions did appear.
[V.i]

Much Ado About Nothing

1. I thank God, and my cold blood, I am of your humour for that: I had rather hear my dog bark at a crow than a man swear he loves me.
[I.i]

2. Prove that ever I lose more blood with love than I will get again with drinking, pick out mine eyes with a ballad-maker's pen, and hang me up at the door of a brothel-house for the sign of blind Cupid.
[I.i]

3. In time the savage bull doth bear the yoke.
[I.i]

4. Would it not grieve a woman to be over-master'd with a piece of valiant dust, to make an account of her life to a clod of wayward marl?
[II.i]

5. I have a good eye, uncle; I can see a church by daylight.
[II.i]

6. Friendship is constant in all other things
Save in the office and affairs of love.
[II.i]

7. She speaks poniards, and every word stabs; if her breath were as terrible as her terminations, there were no living near her; she would infect to the north star.
[II.i]

8. Silence is the perfectest herald of joy: I were but little happy if I could say how much. Lady, as you are mine, I am yours; I give away myself for you, and dote upon the exchange.
[II.i]

9. *Don Pedro*: Will you have me, lady?
Beatrice: No, my lord, unless I might have another for working-days; your Grace is too costly to wear every day.
[II.i]

10. *Don Pedro*: Out o' question, you were born in a merry hour.
Beatrice: No, sure, my lord, my mother cried; but then there was a star danc'd, and under that was I born.
[II.i]

11. She is never sad but when she sleeps, and not ever sad then; for I have heard my daughter say she hath often dreamt of unhappiness, and wak'd herself with laughing.
[II.i]

12. Now, divine air! now is his soul ravish'd. Is it not strange that sheeps' guts should hale souls out of men's bodies?
[II.iii]

13. Sigh no more, ladies, sigh no more,
Men were deceivers ever,
One foot in sea and one on shore,
To one thing constant never.
Then sigh not so, but let them go,
And be you blithe and bonny;
Converting all your sounds of woe
Into Hey nonny nonny.
[II.iii]

14. Sits the wind in that corner?
[II.iii]

15. Doth not the appetite alter? A man loves the meat in his youth that he cannot endure in his age.
[II.iii]

16. The world must be peopled. When I said I would die a bachelor, I did not think I should live till I were married.
[II.iii]

17. He hath a heart as sound as a bell, and his tongue is the clapper; for what his heart thinks, his tongue speaks.
[III.ii]

18. Every one can master a grief but he that has it.
[III.ii]

19. To be a well-favoured man is the gift of fortune; but to write and read comes by nature.
[III.iii]

20. For for the watch to babble and to talk is most tolerable and not to be endured.
[III.iii]

21. *Dogberry*: Goodman Verges, sir, speaks a little off the matter – an old man, sir, and his wits are not so blunt as, God help, I would desire they were; but, in faith, honest as the skin between his brows.
Verges: Yes, I thank God I am as honest as any man living that is an old man and no honester than I.
Dogberry: Comparisons are odorous; palabras, neighbour Verges.
Leonato: Neighbours, you are tedious.
[III.v]

22. A good old man, sir, he will be talking; as they say 'When the age is in the wit is out.'
[III.v]

23. O, what men dare do! What men may do! What men daily do, not knowing what they do!
[IV.i]

24. There, Leonato, take her back again;
Give not this rotten orange to your friend;
She's but the sign and semblance of her honour.
Behold how like a maid she blushes here.
O, what authority and show of truth
Can cunning sin cover itself withal!
[IV.i]

25. She knows the heat of a luxurious bed;
Her blush is guiltiness, not modesty.
[IV.i]

26. I do love nothing in the world so well as you. Is not that strange?
[IV.i]

27. O God, that I were a man! I would eat his heart in the market-place.
[IV.i]

28. O that he were here to write me down an ass! But, masters, remember that I am an ass; though it be not written down, yet forget not that I am an ass.
[IV.ii]

29. Patch grief with proverbs.
[V.i]

30. I will be flesh and blood;
For there was never yet philosopher
That could endure the toothache patiently.
[V.i]

31. In a false quarrel there is no true valour.
[V.i]

32. Though care kill'd a cat, thou hast mettle enough in thee to kill care.
[V.i]

33. Leander the good swimmer, Troilus the first employer of panders, and a whole bookful of these quondam carpet-mongers, whose names yet run smoothly in the even road of a blank verse, why, they were never so truly turn'd over and over as my poor self in love.
[V.ii]

34. No, I was not born under a rhyming planet.
[V.ii]

Othello

1. A fellow almost damn'd in a fair wife.
[I.i]

2. In following him I follow but myself.
[I.i]

3. But I will wear my heart upon my sleeve
For daws to peck at: I am not what I am.
[I.i]

4. Even now, now, very now, an old black ram
Is tupping your white ewe.
[I.i]

5. 'Zounds, sir, you are one of those that will not serve God if the devil bid you.
[I.i]

6. Keep up your bright swords, for the dew will rust them.
[I.ii]

7. *Othello*: Most potent, grave, and reverend signiors,
My very noble and approv'd good masters:
That I have ta'en away this old man's daughter,
It is most true; true, I have married her–
The very head and front of my offending
Hath this extent, no more. Rude am I in my speech,
And little blest with the soft phrase of peace;
For since these arms of mine had seven years' pith,
Till now some nine moons wasted, they have us'd
Their dearest action in the tented field;
And little of this great world can I speak
More than pertains to feats of broil and battle;
And therefore little shall I grace my cause
In speaking for myself. Yet, by your gracious patience,
I will a round unvarnish'd tale deliver
Of my whole course of love – what drugs, what charms,
What conjuration, and what mighty magic,
For such proceedings am I charg'd withal,
I won his daughter.
Brabantio: A maiden never bold,
Of spirit so still and quiet that her motion
Blush'd at herself.
[I.iii]

8. Her father lov'd me, oft invited me;
Still question'd me the story of my life
From year to year – the battles, sieges, fortunes,
That I have pass'd.
I ran it through, even from my boyish days
To th' very moment that he bade me tell it;
Wherein I spake of most disastrous chances,
Of moving accidents by flood and field;
Of hairbreadth scapes i' th' imminent deadly breach;
Of being taken by the insolent foe
And sold to slavery; of my redemption thence,
And portance in my travel's history;
Wherein of antres vast and deserts idle,
Rough quarries, rocks, and hills whose heads touch heaven,
It was my hint to speak – such was the process;
And of the Cannibals that each other eat,
The Anthropophagi, and men whose heads
Do grow beneath their shoulders. This to hear
Would Desdemona seriously incline.
[I.iii]

9. And often did beguile her of her tears,
When I did speak of some distressful stroke
That my youth suffer'd. My story being done,
She gave me for my pains a world of sighs;
She swore, in faith, 'twas strange, 'twas passing strange;
'Twas pitiful, 'twas wondrous pitiful.
She wish'd she had not heard it, yet she wish'd

That heaven had made her such a man. She thank'd me;
And bade me, if I had a friend that lov'd her,
I should but teach him how to tell my story,
And that would woo her. Upon this hint I spake;
She lov'd me for the dangers I had pass'd;
And I lov'd her that she did pity them.
This only is the witchcraft I have us'd.
[I.iii]

10. I do perceive here a divided duty.
[I.iii]

11. The robb'd that smiles steals something from the thief.
[I.iii]

12. But words are words: I never yet did hear
That the bruis'd heart was pierced through the ear.
[I.iii]

13. The tyrant custom, most grave senators,
Hath made the flinty and steel couch of war
My thrice-driven bed of down.
[I.iii]

14. Virtue? A fig! 'Tis in ourselves that we are thus or thus. Our bodies are our gardens to the which our wills are gardeners.
[I.iii]

15. Put money in thy purse; follow thou the wars; defeat thy favour with an usurp'd beard. I say, put money in thy purse.
[I.iii]

16. These Moors are changeable in their wills – fill thy purse with money. The food that to him now is as luscious as locusts shall be to him shortly as acerbe as the coloquintida.
[I.iii]

17. He hath a person and a smooth dispose
To be suspected – fram'd to make women false.
[I.iii]

18. The Moor is of a free and open nature
That thinks men honest that but seem to be so;
And will as tenderly be led by th' nose
As asses are.
I ha't – it is engender'd. Hell and night
Must bring this monstrous birth to the world's light.
[I.iii]

19. You are pictures out a-doors, bells in your parlours, wildcats in your kitchens, saints in your injuries, devils being offended, players in your huswifery, and huswives in your beds.
[II.i]

20. I am not merry; but I do beguile
The thing I am by seeming otherwise.
[II.i]

21. *Iago*: She that was ever fair, and never proud;
Had tongue at will, and yet was never loud;
Never lack'd gold, and yet went never gay;
Fled from her wish, and yet said 'Now I may';
She that, being ang'red, her revenge being nigh,
Bade her wrong stay and her displeasure fly;
She that in wisdom never was so frail
To change the cod's head for the salmon's tail;
She that could think, and ne'er disclose her mind;
See suitors following, and not look behind:
She was a wight, if ever such wight were–
Desdemona: To do what?
Iago: To suckle fools and chronicle small beer.
Desdemona: O most lame and impotent conclusion!
[II.i]

22. *Othello*: If it were now to die,
'Twere now to be most happy; for I fear
My soul hath her content so absolute
That not another comfort like to this
Succeeds in unknown fate.
Desdemona: The heavens forbid
But that our loves and comforts should increase
Even as our days do grow!
[II.i]

23. Make the Moor thank me, love me, and reward me,
For making him egregiously an ass,
And practising upon his peace and quiet
Even to madness.
[II.i]

24. I have very poor and unhappy brains for drinking; I could well wish courtesy would invent some other custom of entertainment.
[II.iii]

25. My boat sails freely, both with wind and stream.
[II.iii]

26. But men are men; the best sometimes forget.
[II.iii]

27. Reputation, reputation, reputation! O, I have lost my reputation! I have lost the immortal part of myself, and what remains is bestial. My reputation, Iago, my reputation!
[II.iii]

28. O God, that men should put an enemy in their mouths to steal away their brains! That we should with joy, pleasance, revel and applause, transform ourselves into beasts!
[II.iii]

29. Come, come, good wine is a good familiar creature if it be well us'd; exclaim no more against it.
[II.iii]

30. How poor are they that have not patience!
What wound did ever heal but by degrees?
[II.iii]

31. Excellent wretch! Perdition catch my soul
But I do love thee; and when I love thee not
Chaos is come again.
[III.iii]

32. By heaven, he echoes me,
As if there were some monster in his thought
Too hideous to be shown.
[III.iii]

33. Men should be that they seem.
[III.iii]

34. Good name in man and woman, dear my lord,
Is the immediate jewel of their souls:
Who steals my purse steals trash; 'tis something, nothing;
'Twas mine, 'tis his, and has been slave to thousands;
But he that filches from me my good name
Robs me of that which not enriches him
And makes me poor indeed.
[III.iii]

35. O, beware, my lord, of jealousy;
It is the green-ey'd monster which doth mock
The meat it feeds on.
[III.iii]

36. In Venice they do let God see the pranks
They dare not show their husbands; their best conscience
Is not to leave't undone, but keep't unknown.
[III.iii]

37. Not to affect many proposed matches
Of her own clime, complexion, and degree,
Whereto we see in all things nature tends–
Foh! one may smell in such a will most rank,
Foul disproportion, thoughts unnatural.
[III.iii]

38. If I do prove her haggard,
Though that her jesses were my dear heart-strings,
I'd whistle her off and let her down the wind
To prey at fortune. Haply, for I am black
And have not those soft parts of conversation
That chamberers have, or for I am declin'd
Into the vale of years – yet that's not much–
She's gone; I am abus'd; and my relief
Must be to loathe her. O curse of marriage,
That we can call these delicate creatures ours,
And not their appetites! I had rather be a toad,
And live upon the vapour of a dungeon,
Than keep a corner in the thing I love
For others' uses.
[III.iii]

39. If she be false, O, then heaven mocks itself!
I'll not believe it.
[III.iii]

40. Trifles light as air
Are to the jealous confirmations strong
As proofs of holy writ.
[III.iii]

41. Not poppy, nor mandragora,
Nor all the drowsy syrups of the world,
Shall ever medicine thee to that sweet sleep
Which thou owed'st yesterday.
[III.iii]

42. He that is robb'd, not wanting what is stol'n,
Let him not know't, and he's not robb'd at all.
[III.iii]

43. I had been happy if the general camp,
Pioneers and all, had tasted her sweet body,
So I had nothing known. O, now for ever
Farewell the tranquil mind! farewell content!
Farewell the plumed troops, and the big wars
That makes ambition virtue! O, farewell!
Farewell the neighing steed and the shrill trump,
The spirit-stirring drum, th' ear-piercing fife,
The royal banner, and all quality,
Pride, pomp, and circumstance, of glorious war!
And O ye mortal engines whose rude throats
Th' immortal Jove's dread clamours counterfeit,
Farewell! Othello's occupation's gone.
[III.iii]

44. Villain, be sure thou prove my love a whore–
Be sure of it; give me the ocular proof.
[III.iii]

45. O wretched fool,
That liv'st to make thine honesty a vice!
O monstrous world! Take note, take note, O world,
To be direct and honest is not safe.
[III.iii]

46. Jealous souls will not be answer'd so;
They are not ever jealous for the cause,
But jealous for they are jealous.
[III.iv]

47. My heart is turn'd to stone; I strike it, and it hurts my hand. O, the world hath not a sweeter creature; she might lie by an emperor's side and command him tasks.
[IV.i]

48. An admirable musician – O, she will sing the savageness out of a bear!
[IV.i]

49. But yet the pity of it, Iago! O, Iago, the pity of it, Iago!
[IV.i]

50. O, well-painted passion!
[IV.i]

51. Is this the nature
Whom passion could not shake, whose solid virtue
The shot of accident nor dart of chance
Could neither graze nor pierce?
[IV.i]

52. Had it pleas'd heaven
To try me with affliction; had they rain'd
All kind of sores and shames on my bare head,
Steep'd me in poverty to the very lips,
Given to captivity me and my utmost hopes,
I should have found in some place of my soul
A drop of patience; but, alas, to make me
The fixed figure for the time of scorn
To point his slow and unmoving finger at! – O, O!
Yet could I bear that too; well, very well;
But there, where I have garner'd up my heart,
Where either I must live or bear no life,
The fountain from the which my current runs,
Or else dries up – to be discarded thence!
Or keep it as a cistern for foul toads
To knot and gender in! Turn thy complexion there,
Patience, thou young and rose-lipp'd cherubin–
Ay, here, look grim as hell.
[IV.ii]

53. I cry you mercy, then.
I took you for that cunning whore of Venice
That married with Othello. – You, mistress,
That have the office opposite to Saint Peter
And keeps the gate of hell!
[IV.ii]

54. *Emilia*: I would you had never seen him.
Desdemona: So would not I: my love doth so approve him
That even his stubbornness, his checks, his frowns...
Have grace and favour in them.
[IV.iii]

55. My mother had a maid call'd Barbary:
She was in love; and he she lov'd prov'd mad,
And did forsake her. She had a song of 'willow';
An old thing 'twas, but it express'd her fortune,
And she died singing it. That song to-night
Will not go from my mind.
[IV.iii]

56. The poor soul sat sighing by a sycamore tree,
Sing all a green willow;
Her hand on her bosom, her head on her knee.
Sing willow, willow, willow.
The fresh streams ran by her, and murmur'd her moans;
Sing willow, willow, willow;
Her salt tears fell from her and soft'ned the stones;
Sing willow ... willow, willow...
Sing all a green willow must be my garland.
[IV.iii. Cf. John Heywood: 1]

57. *Desdemona*: Mine eyes do itch;
Doth that bode weeping?
Emilia: 'Tis neither here nor there.
[IV.iii]

58. Who would not make her husband a cuckold to make him a monarch?
[IV.iii]

59. He hath a daily beauty in his life
That makes me ugly.
[V.i]

60. It is the cause, it is the cause, my soul–
Let me not name it to you, you chaste stars–
It is the cause. Yet I'll not shed her blood,
Nor scar that whiter skin of hers than snow,
And smooth as monumental alabaster.
Yet she must die, else she'll betray more men.
Put out the light, and then put out the light.
If I quench thee, thou flaming minister,
I can again thy former light restore,
Should I repent me; but once put out thy light,
Thou cunning'st pattern of excelling nature,
I know not where is that Promethean heat
That can thy light relume. When I have pluck'd thy rose,
I cannot give it vital growth again;
It needs must wither. I'll smell thee on the tree.
O balmy breath, that dost almost persuade
Justice to break her sword! One more, one more.
Be thus when thou art dead, and I will kill thee,
And love thee after. One more, and that's the last:
So sweet was ne'er so fatal. I must weep,
But they are cruel tears. This sorrow's heavenly;
It strikes where it doth love.
[V.ii]

61. Alas, why gnaw you so your nether lip?
Some bloody passion shakes your very frame.
These are portents; but yet I hope, I hope,
They do not point on me.
[V.ii]

62. Kill me to-morrow; let me live to-night.
[V.ii]

63. It is the very error of the moon;
She comes more nearer earth than she was wont,
And makes men mad.
[V.ii]

64. *Othello*: She's like a liar gone to burning hell:
'Twas I that kill'd her.
Emilia: O, the more angel she,
And you the blacker devil!
[V.ii]

65. Nay, had she been true,
If heaven would make me such another world
Of one entire and perfect chrysolite,
I'd not have sold her for it.
[V.ii]

66. Thou hast not half that power to do me harm
As I have to be hurt.
[V.ii]

67. I will play the swan,
And die in music.
[V.ii]

68. O ill-starr'd wench!
Pale as thy smock! When we shall meet at compt,
This look of thine will hurl my soul from heaven,
And fiends will snatch at it. Cold, cold, my girl!
Even like thy chastity. O cursed, cursed slave!
Whip me, ye devils,
From the possession of this heavenly sight.
Blow me about in winds, roast me in sulphur,
Wash me in steep-down gulfs of liquid fire.
O Desdemona! Dead! Desdemona! Dead!
[V.ii]

69. An honourable murderer, if you will;
For nought I did in hate, but all in honour.
[V.ii]

70. I have done the state some service, and they know't–
No more of that. I pray you, in your letters,
When you shall these unlucky deeds relate,
Speak of me as I am; nothing extenuate,
Nor set down aught in malice. Then must you speak
Of one that lov'd not wisely, but too well;
Of one not easily jealous, but, being wrought,
Perplexed in the extreme; of one whose hand,
Like the base Indian, threw a pearl away
Richer than all his tribe; of one whose subdu'd eyes,
Albeit unused to the melting mood,
Drop tears as fast as the Arabian trees
Their med'cinable gum. Set you down this:
And say besides that in Aleppo once,
Where a malignant and a turban'd Turk
Beat a Venetian and traduc'd the state,
I took by th' throat the circumcised dog,
And smote him – thus.
[V.ii]

71. *Gratiano*: All that is spoke is marr'd.
Othello: I kiss'd thee ere I kill'd thee. No way but this–
Killing my self, to die upon a kiss.
[V.ii]

Pericles, Prince of Tyre

1. See where she comes, apparell'd like the spring.
[I.i]

2. Few love to hear the sins they love to act.
[I.i]

3. Kings are earth's gods; in vice their law's their will.
[I.i]

4. *Third Fisherman*: I marvel how the fishes live in the sea.
First Fisherman: Why, as men do a-land – the great ones eat up the little ones.
[II.i]

Richard II

1. Old John of Gaunt, time-honoured Lancaster.
[I.i]

2. Let's purge this choler without letting blood.
[I.i]

3. The purest treasure mortal times afford
Is spotless reputation; that away,
Men are but gilded loam or painted clay.
A jewel in a ten-times barr'd-up chest
Is a bold spirit in a loyal breast.
Mine honour is my life; both grow in one;
Take honour from me, and my life is done.
[I.i]

4. We were not born to sue, but to command.
[I.i]

5. The language I have learnt these forty years,
My native English, now I must forgo;
And now my tongue's use is to me no more
Than an unstringed viol or a harp.
[I.iii]

6. I am too old to fawn upon a nurse,
Too far in years to be a pupil now.
[I.iii]

7. But what thou art, God, thou, and I, do know;
And all too soon, I fear, the King shall rue.
[I.iii]

8. How long a time lies in one little word!
Four lagging winters and four wanton springs
End in a word: such is the breath of Kings.
[I.iii]

9. Things sweet to taste prove in digestion sour.
[I.iii]

10. Must I not serve a long apprenticehood
To foreign passages; and in the end,
Having my freedom, boast of nothing else
But that I was a journeyman to grief?
[I.iii]

11. All places that the eye of heaven visits
Are to a wise man ports and happy havens.
Teach thy necessity to reason thus:
There is no virtue like necessity.
[I.iii]

12. O, who can hold a fire in his hand
By thinking on the frosty Caucasus?
Or cloy the hungry edge of appetite
By bare imagination of a feast?
Or wallow naked in December snow
By thinking on fantastic summer's heat?
O, no! the apprehension of the good
Gives but the greater feeling to the worse.
[I.iii]

13. Off goes his bonnet to an oyster-wench;
A brace of draymen bid God speed him well
And had the tribute of his supple knee,
With 'Thanks, my countrymen, my loving friends';
As were our England in reversion his,
And he our subjects' next degree in hope.
[I.iv]

14. Now put it, God, in the physician's mind
To help him to his grave immediately!
The lining of his coffers shall make coats
To deck our soldiers for these Irish wars.
[I.iv]

15. More are men's ends mark'd than their lives before.
The setting sun, and music at the close,
As the last taste of sweets, is sweetest last,
Writ in remembrance more than things long past.
[II.i]

16. Methinks I am a prophet new inspir'd,
And thus expiring do foretell of him:
His rash fierce blaze of riot cannot last,
For violent fires soon burn out themselves;
Small showers last long, but sudden storms are short;
He tires betimes that spurs too fast betimes.
[II.i]

17. This royal throne of kings, this scept'red isle,
This earth of majesty, this seat of Mars,
This other Eden, demi-paradise,
This fortress built by Nature for herself
Against infection and the hand of war,
This happy breed of men, this little world,
This precious stone set in the silver sea,
Which serves it in the office of a wall,
Or as a moat defensive to a house,
Against the envy of less happier lands;
This blessed plot, this earth, this realm, this England,
This nurse, this teeming womb of royal kings,
Fear'd by their breed, and famous by their birth,
Renowned for their deeds as far from home,
For Christian service and true chivalry,
As is the sepulchre in stubborn Jewry
Of the world's ransom, blessed Mary's Son;
This land of such dear souls, this dear dear land,
Dear for her reputation through the world,
Is now leas'd out – I die pronouncing it–
Like to a tenement or pelting farm.
England, bound in with the triumphant sea,
Whose rocky shore beats back the envious siege
Of wat'ry Neptune, is now bound in with shame,
With inky blots and rotten parchment bonds;
That England, that was wont to conquer others,
Hath made a shameful conquest of itself.
[II.i]

18. Lay aside life-harming heaviness
And entertain a cheerful disposition.
[II.ii]

19. *Green*: Here comes the Duke of York.
Queen: With signs of war about his aged neck.
O, full of careful business are his looks!
[II.ii]

20. I count myself in nothing else so happy
As in a soul rememb'ring my good friends.
[II.iii]

21. The caterpillars of the commonwealth.
[II.iii]

22. Things past redress are now with me past care.
[II.iii]

23. Not all the water in the rough rude sea
Can wash the balm off from an anointed king;
The breath of worldly men cannot depose
The deputy elected by the Lord.
For every man that Bolingbroke hath press'd
To lift shrewd steel against our golden crown,
God for his Richard hath in heavenly pay
A glorious angel. Then, if angels fight,
Weak men must fall; for heaven still guards the right.
[III.ii]

24. The worst is death, and death will have his day.
[III.ii]

25. White-beards have arm'd their thin and hairless scalps
Against thy majesty; boys, with women's voices,
Strive to speak big, and clap their female joints
In stiff unwieldy arms against thy crown;
Thy very beadsmen learn to bend their bows
Of double-fatal yew against thy state;
Yea, distaff-women manage rusty bills
Against thy seat: both young and old rebel,
And all goes worse than I have power to tell.
[III.ii]

26. O villains, vipers, damn'd without redemption!
Dogs, easily won to fawn on any man!
Snakes, in my heart-blood warm'd, that sting my heart!
Three Judases, each one thrice worse than Judas!
Would they make peace? Terrible hell make war
Upon their spotted souls for this offence!
[III.ii]

27. Of comfort no man speak.
Let's talk of graves, of worms, and epitaphs;
Make dust our paper, and with rainy eyes
Write sorrow on the bosom of the earth.
Let's choose executors and talk of wills.
[III.ii]

28. For God's sake let us sit upon the ground
And tell sad stories of the death of kings:
How some have been depos'd, some slain in war,
Some haunted by the ghosts they have depos'd,
Some poison'd by their wives, some sleeping kill'd,
All murder'd – for within the hollow crown
That rounds the mortal temples of a king
Keeps Death his court; and there the antic sits,
Scoffing his state and grinning at his pomp;
Allowing him a breath, a little scene,
To monarchize, be fear'd, and kill with looks;
Infusing him with self and vain conceit,
As if this flesh which walls about our life
Were brass impregnable; and, humour'd thus,
Comes at the last, and with a little pin
Bores through his castle wall, and farewell, king!
[III.ii]

29. See, see, King Richard doth himself appear,
As doth the blushing discontented sun
From out the fiery portal of the east.
[III.iii]

30. O that I were as great
As is my grief, or lesser than my name!
Or that I could forget what I have been!
Or not remember what I must be now!
[III.iii]

31. What must the King do now? Must he submit?
The King shall do it. Must he be depos'd?
The King shall be contented. Must he lose
The name of king? A God's name, let it go.
I'll give my jewels for a set of beads,
My gorgeous palace for a hermitage,
My gay apparel for an almsman's gown,
My figur'd goblets for a dish of wood,
My sceptre for a palmer's walking staff,
My subjects for a pair of carved saints,
And my large kingdom for a little grave,
A little little grave, an obscure grave–
Or I'll be buried in the king's high way,
Some way of common trade, where subjects' feet
May hourly trample on their sovereign's head;
For on my heart they tread now whilst I live,
And buried once, why not upon my head?
[III.iii]

32. Shall we play the wantons with our woes
And make some pretty match with shedding tears?
[III.iii]

33. Down, down I come, like glist'ring Phaethon,
Wanting the manage of unruly jades.
[III.iii]

34. Here did she fall a tear; here in this place
I'll set a bank of rue, sour herb of grace.
Rue, even for ruth, here shortly shall be seen,
In the remembrance of a weeping queen.
[III.iv]

35. Here, cousin,
On this side my hand, and on that side thine.
Now is this golden crown like a deep well
That owes two buckets, filling one another;
The emptier ever dancing in the air,
The other down, unseen, and full of water.
That bucket down and full of tears am I,
Drinking my griefs, whilst you mount up on high.
[IV.i]

36. You may my glories and my state depose,
But not my griefs; still am I king of those.
[IV.i]

37. Mine eyes are full of tears; I cannot see.
And yet salt water blinds them not so much
But they can see a sort of traitors here.
Nay, if I turn mine eyes upon myself,
I find myself a traitor with the rest.
[IV.i]

38. O that I were a mockery king of snow.
[IV.i]

39. A brittle glory shineth in this face;
As brittle as the glory is the face.
[IV.i]

40. I am sworn brother, sweet,
To grim Necessity; and he and I
Will keep a league till death.
[V.i]

41. In winter's tedious nights sit by the fire
With good old folks, and let them tell thee tales
Of woeful ages long ago betid;
And ere thou bid good night, to quit their griefs,
Tell thou the lamentable tale of me,
And send the hearers weeping to their beds.
[V.i]

42. As in a theatre the eyes of men
After a well-grac'd actor leaves the stage
Are idly bent on him that enters next,
Thinking his prattle to be tedious;
Even so, or with much more contempt, men's eyes
Did scowl on gentle Richard.
[V.ii]

43. Who are the violets now
That strew the green lap of the new come spring?
[V.ii]

44. I have been studying how I may compare
This prison where I live unto the world;
And, for because the world is populous
And here is not a creature but myself,
I cannot do it. Yet I'll hammer it out.
My brain I'll prove the female to my soul,
My soul the father; and these two beget
A generation of still-breeding thoughts,
And these same thoughts people this little world.
[V.v]

45. How sour sweet music is
When time is broke and no proportion kept!
So is it in the music of men's lives.
[V.v]

46. I wasted time, and now doth time waste me.
[V.v]

47. Mount, mount, my soul! thy seat is up on high;
Whilst my gross flesh sinks downward, here to die.
[V.v]

Richard III

1. Now is the winter of our discontent
Made glorious summer by this sun of York.
[I.i]

2. Grim-visag'd war hath smooth'd his wrinkled front,
And now, instead of mounting barbed steeds
To fright the souls of fearful adversaries,
He capers nimbly in a lady's chamber
To the lascivious pleasing of a lute.

But I – that am not shap'd for sportive tricks,
Nor made to court an amorous looking-glass–
I – that am rudely stamp'd, and want love's majesty
To strut before a wanton ambling nymph–
I – that am curtail'd of this fair proportion,
Cheated of feature by dissembling nature,
Deform'd, unfinish'd, sent before my time
Into this breathing world scarce half made up,
And that so lamely and unfashionable
That dogs bark at me as I halt by them–
Why, I, in this weak piping time of peace,
Have no delight to pass away the time.
[I.i]

3. And therefore, since I cannot prove a lover
To entertain these fair well-spoken days,
I am determined to prove a villain
And hate the idle pleasures of these days.
[I.i]

4. No beast so fierce but knows some touch of pity.
[I.ii]

5. Cannot a plain man live and think no harm
But thus his simple truth must be abus'd
With silken, sly, insinuating Jacks?
[I.iii]

6. Since every Jack became a gentleman,
There's many a gentle person made a Jack.
[I.iii]

7. And thus I clothe my naked villainy
With odd old ends stol'n forth of holy writ,
And seem a saint when most I play the devil.
[I.iii]

8. O, I have pass'd a miserable night,
So full of fearful dreams, of ugly sights,
That, as I am a Christian faithful man,
I would not spend another such a night
Though 'twere to buy a world of happy days–
So full of dismal terror was the time!
[I.iv]

9. O Lord, methought what pain it was to drown,
What dreadful noise of waters in my ears,
What sights of ugly death within my eyes!
Methought I saw a thousand fearful wrecks,
A thousand men that fishes gnaw'd upon,
Wedges of gold, great anchors, heaps of pearl,
Inestimable stones, unvalued jewels,
All scatt'red in the bottom of the sea;
Some lay in dead men's skulls, and in the holes
Where eyes did once inhabit there were crept,
As 'twere in scorn of eyes, reflecting gems,
That woo'd the slimy bottom of the deep
And mock'd the dead bones that lay scatt'red by.
[I.iv]

10. So wise so young, they say, do never live long.
[III.i]

11. Thou art a traitor.
Off with his head!
[III.iv]

12. Cousin, thou wast not wont to be so dull.
Shall I be plain? I wish the bastards dead.
[IV.ii]

13. I am not in the giving vein to-day.
[IV.ii]

14. Thou cam'st on earth to make the earth my hell.
A grievous burden was thy birth to me;
Tetchy and wayward was thy infancy;
Thy school-days frightful, desp'rate, wild, and furious;
Thy prime of manhood daring, bold, and venturous;
Thy age confirm'd, proud, subtle, sly, and bloody,
More mild, but yet more harmful-kind in hatred.
What comfortable hour canst thou name
That ever grac'd me with thy company?
[IV.iv]

15. An honest tale speeds best being plainly told.
[IV.iv]

16. True hope is swift and flies with swallow's wings;
Kings it makes gods, and meaner creatures kings.
[V.ii]

17. My conscience hath a thousand several tongues,
And every tongue brings in a several tale,
And every tale condemns me for a villain.
[V.iii]

18. I shall despair. There is no creature loves me;
And if I die no soul will pity me:
And wherefore should they, since that I myself
Find in myself no pity to myself?
[V.iii]

19. Conscience is but a word that cowards use,
Devis'd at first to keep the strong in awe.
[V.iii]

20. A horse! a horse! my kingdom for a horse!
[V.iv]

21. Slave, I have set my life upon a cast
And I will stand the hazard of the die.
[V.iv]

Romeo and Juliet

1. From forth the fatal loins of these two foes
A pair of star-cross'd lovers take their life.
[Prologue]

2. The fearful passage of their death-mark'd love,
And the continuance of their parents' rage,
Which, but their children's end, nought could remove,
Is now the two hours' traffic of our stage.
[Prologue]

3. She will not stay the siege of loving terms,
Nor bide th' encounter of assailing eyes,
Nor ope her lap to saint-seducing gold.
[I.i]

4. And 'tis not hard, I think,
For men so old as we to keep the peace.
[I.ii]

5. O, then I see Queen Mab hath been with you.
She is the fairies' midwife, and she comes
In shape no bigger than an agate stone
On the fore-finger of an alderman,
Drawn with a team of little atomies
Athwart men's noses as they lie asleep;
Her waggon-spokes made of long spinners' legs;
The cover, of the wings of grasshoppers;
Her traces, of the smallest spider's web;
Her collars, of the moonshine's wat'ry beams;
Her whip, of cricket's bone; the lash, of film;
Her waggoner, a small grey-coated gnat,
Not half so big as a round little worm
Prick'd from the lazy finger of a maid.
Her chariot is an empty hazel-nut,
Made by the joiner squirrel or old grub,
Time out o' mind the fairies' coachmakers.
And in this state she gallops night by night

Through lovers' brains, and then they dream of love;
O'er courtiers' knees, that dream on curtsies straight;
O'er lawyers' fingers, who straight dream on fees;
O'er ladies' lips, who straight on kisses dream,
Which oft the angry Mab with blisters plagues,
Because their breaths with sweetmeats tainted are.
Sometimes she gallops o'er a courtier's nose,
And then dreams he of smelling out a suit;
And sometimes comes she with a tithe-pig's tail,
Tickling a parson's nose as 'a lies asleep,
Then dreams he of another benefice.
Sometime she driveth o'er a soldier's neck,
And then dreams he of cutting foreign throats,
Of breaches, ambuscadoes, Spanish blades,
Of healths five fathom deep; and then anon
Drums in his ear, at which he starts and wakes,
And, being thus frighted, swears a prayer or two,
And sleeps again. This is that very Mab
That plats the manes of horses in the night;
And bakes the elf-locks in foul sluttish hairs,
Which once untangled much misfortune bodes.
This is the hag, when maids lie on their backs,
That presses them and learns them first to bear,
Making them women of good carriage.
[I.iv]

6. You and I are past our dancing days.
[I.v]

7. O, she doth teach the torches to burn bright!
It seems she hangs upon the cheek of night
As a rich jewel in an Ethiop's ear–
Beauty too rich for use, for earth too dear!
[I.v]

8. He jests at scars that never felt a wound.
But, soft! What light through yonder window breaks?
It is the east, and Juliet is the sun.
[II.ii]

9. See how she leans her cheek upon her hand!
O that I were a glove upon that hand,
That I might touch that cheek!
[II.ii]

10. O Romeo, Romeo! wherefore art thou Romeo?
Deny thy father and refuse thy name;
Or, if thou wilt not, be but sworn my love,
And I'll no longer be a Capulet.
[II.ii]

11. What's in a name? That which we call a rose
By any other name would smell as sweet.
[II.ii]

12. With love's light wings did I o'er-perch these walls,
For stony limits cannot hold love out;
And what love can do, that dares love attempt.
[II.ii]

13. Thou knowest the mask of night is on my face,
Else would a maiden blush bepaint my cheek
For that which thou hast heard me speak to-night.
Fain would I dwell on form, fain, fain deny
What I have spoke; but farewell compliment!
[II.ii]

14. *Romeo*: Lady, by yonder blessed moon I vow,
That tips with silver all these fruit-tree tops–
Juliet: O, swear not by the moon, th' inconstant moon,
That monthly changes in her circled orb,
Lest that thy love prove likewise variable.
Romeo: What shall I swear by?
Juliet: Do not swear at all;
Or, if thou wilt, swear by thy gracious self,
Which is the god of my idolatry.
[II.ii]

15. It is too rash, too unadvis'd, too sudden;
Too like the lightning, which doth cease to be
Ere one can say 'It lightens'. Sweet, good night!
This bud of love, by summer's ripening breath,
May prove a beauteous flow'r when next we meet.
[II.ii]

16. My bounty is as boundless as the sea,
My love as deep: the more I give to thee,
The more I have, for both are infinite.
[II.ii]

17. Love goes toward love as school-boys from their books;
But love from love, toward school with heavy looks.
[II.ii]

18. *Juliet*: O, for a falc'ner's voice,
To lure this tassel-gentle back again!
Bondage is hoarse, and may not speak aloud;
Else would I tear the cave where Echo lies,
And make her airy tongue more hoarse than mine
With repetition of my Romeo's name.
Romeo!
Romeo: It is my soul that calls upon my name.
How silver-sweet sound lovers' tongues by night,
Like softest music to attending ears!
[II.ii]

19. *Juliet*: 'Tis almost morning. I would have thee gone;
And yet no farther than a wanton's bird,
That lets it hop a little from her hand,
Like a poor prisoner in his twisted gyves,
And with a silk thread plucks it back again,
So loving-jealous of his liberty.
Romeo: I would I were thy bird.
Juliet: Sweet, so would I.
Yet I should kill thee with much cherishing.
Good night, good night! Parting is such sweet sorrow
That I shall say good night till it be morrow.
Romeo: Sleep dwell upon thine eyes, peace in thy breast!
Would I were sleep and peace, so sweet to rest!
[II.ii]

20. Wisely and slow; they stumble that run fast.
[II.iii]

21. O flesh, flesh, how art thou fishified!
[II.iv]

22. I am the very pink of courtesy.
[II.iv]

23. These violent delights have violent ends.
[II.vi]

24. O, so light a foot
Will ne'er wear out the everlasting flint.
[II.vi]

25. Thy head is as full of quarrels as an egg is full of meat.
[III.i]

26. Men's eyes were made to look, and let them gaze;
I will not budge for no man's pleasure, I.
[III.i]

27. A plague a both your houses!
They have made worms' meat of me.
[III.i]

28. O, I am fortune's fool!
[III.i]

29. Gallop apace, you fiery-footed steeds,
Towards Phoebus' lodging; such a waggoner
As Phaethon would whip you to the west,
And bring in cloudy night immediately.
Spread thy close curtain, love-performing night,
That runaway's eyes may wink, and Romeo
Leap to these arms, untalk'd of and unseen.
Lovers can see to do their amorous rites
By their own beauties; or if love be blind,
It best agrees with night. Come, civil night,
Thou sober-suited matron, all in black.
[III.ii]

30. Come, night; come, Romeo; come, thou day in night;
For thou wilt lie upon the wings of night
Whiter than new snow on a raven's back.
Come, gentle night, come, loving, black-brow'd night,
Give me my Romeo; and, when he shall die,
Take him and cut him out in little stars,
And he will make the face of heaven so fine
That all the world will be in love with night,
And pay no worship to the garish sun.
[III.ii]

31. He was not born to shame:
Upon his brow shame is asham'd to sit.
[III.ii]

32. Romeo, come forth; come forth, thou fearful man;
Affliction is enamour'd of thy parts,
And thou art wedded to calamity.
[III.iii]

33. Thou cut'st my head off with a golden axe,
And smilest upon the stroke that murders me.
[III.iii]

34. Adversity's sweet milk, philosophy.
[III.iii]

35. *Juliet*: Wilt thou be gone? It is not yet near day;
It was the nightingale, and not the lark,
That pierc'd the fearful hollow of thine ear;
Nightly she sings on yond pomegranate tree.
Believe me, love, it was the nightingale.
Romeo: It was the lark, the herald of the morn,
No nightingale. Look, love, what envious streaks
Do lace the severing clouds in yonder east;
Night's candles are burnt out, and jocund day
Stands tiptoe on the misty mountain tops.
I must be gone and live, or stay and die.
[III.v]

36. Thank me no thankings, nor proud me no prouds.
[III.v. Cf. Rose Macaulay: 6]

37. Is there no pity sitting in the clouds
That sees into the bottom of my grief?
[III.v]

38. 'Tis an ill cook that cannot lick his own fingers.
[IV.ii]

39. Farewell! God knows when we shall meet again.
I have a faint cold fear thrills through my veins,
That almost freezes up the heat of life.
[IV.iii]

40. Out, alas! she's cold;
Her blood is settled, and her joints are stiff.
Life and these lips have long been separated.
Death lies on her like an untimely frost
Upon the sweetest flower of all the field.
[IV.v]

41. Tempt not a desp'rate man.
[V.iii]

42. How oft when men are at the point of death
Have they been merry! Which their keepers call
A lightning before death.
[V.iii]

43. Beauty's ensign yet
Is crimson in thy lips and in thy cheeks,
And death's pale flag is not advanced there.
[V.iii]

44. Shall I believe
That unsubstantial Death is amorous,
And that the lean abhorred monster keeps
Thee here in dark to be his paramour?
For fear of that I still will stay with thee,
And never from this palace of dim night
Depart again. Here, here will I remain
With worms that are thy chambermaids. O, here
Will I set up my everlasting rest,
And shake the yoke of inauspicious stars
From this world-wearied flesh. Eyes, look your last.
Arms, take your last embrace. And, lips, O you
The doors of breath, seal with a righteous kiss
A dateless bargain to engrossing death!
[V.iii]

The Taming of the Shrew

1. No profit grows where is no pleasure ta'en;
In brief, sir, study what you most affect.
[I.i]

2. There's small choice in rotten apples.
[I.i]

3. Why, give him gold enough and marry him to a puppet or an aglet-baby, or an old trot with ne'er a tooth in her head, though she have as many diseases as two and fifty horses. Why, nothing comes amiss, so money comes withal.
[I.ii]

4. O this learning, what a thing it is!
[I.ii]

5. She is your treasure, she must have a husband;
I must dance bare-foot on her wedding day,
And for your love to her lead apes in hell.
[II.i]

6. Say that she rail; why, then I'll tell her plain
She sings as sweetly as a nightingale.
Say that she frown; I'll say she looks as clear
As morning roses newly wash'd with dew.
Say she be mute, and will not speak a word;
Then I'll commend her volubility,
And say she uttereth piercing eloquence.
[II.i]

7. You are call'd plain Kate,
And bonny Kate, and sometimes Kate the curst;
But, Kate, the prettiest Kate in Christendom,
Kate of Kate Hall, my super-dainty Kate,
For dainties are all Kates, and therefore, Kate,
Take this of me, Kate of my consolation.
[II.i]

8. Your father hath consented
That you shall be my wife; your dowry 'greed on;
And will you, nill you, I will marry you.
[II.i]

9. Kiss me, Kate; we will be married a Sunday.
[II.i]

10. She shall watch all night;
And if she chance to nod I'll rail and brawl
And with the clamour keep her still awake.
This is a way to kill a wife with kindness,
And thus I'll curb her mad and headstrong humour.
He that knows better how to tame a shrew,
Now let him speak.
[IV.i]

11. What's this? A sleeve? 'Tis like a demi-cannon.
What, up and down, carv'd like an apple-tart?
Here's snip and nip and cut and slish and slash,
Like to a censer in a barber's shop.
[IV.iii]

12. *Petruchio*: It shall be what o'clock I say it is.
Hortensio: Why, so this gallant will command the sun.
[IV.iii]

13. I cannot tarry. I knew a wench married in an afternoon as she went to the garden for parsley to stuff a rabbit.
[IV.iv]

14. A woman mov'd is like a fountain troubled–
Muddy, ill-seeming, thick, bereft of beauty.
[V.ii]

15. Thy husband is thy lord, thy life, thy keeper,
Thy head, thy sovereign; one that cares for thee,
And for thy maintenance commits his body
To painful labour both by sea and land.
[V.ii]

16. Such duty as the subject owes the prince,
Even such a woman oweth to her husband.
[V.ii]

17. I am asham'd that women are so simple
To offer war where they should kneel for peace.
[V.ii]

The Tempest

1. What cares these roarers for the name of king?
[I.i]

2. He hath no drowning mark upon him; his complexion is perfect gallows.
[I.i]

3. Now would I give a thousand furlongs of sea for an acre of barren ground – long heath, brown furze, any thing. The wills above be done, but I would fain die a dry death.
[I.i]

4. What seest thou else
In the dark backward and abysm of time?
[I.ii]

5. Your tale, sir, would cure deafness.
[I.ii]

6. My library
Was dukedom large enough.
[I.ii]

7. *Prospero*: Thou most lying slave,
Whom stripes may move, not kindness! I have us'd thee,
Filth as thou art, with human care, and lodg'd thee
In mine own cell, till thou didst seek to violate
The honour of my child.
Caliban: O ho, O ho! Would 't had been done.
Thou didst prevent me; I had peopl'd else
This isle with Calibans.
[I.ii]

8. You taught me language, and my profit on't
Is, I know how to curse. The red plague rid you
For learning me your language!
[I.ii]

9. Come unto these yellow sands,
And then take hands;
Curtsied when you have and kiss'd,
The wild waves whist,
Foot it featly here and there,
And, sweet sprites, the burden bear.
[I.ii]

10. This music crept by me upon the waters,
Allaying both their fury and my passion
With its sweet air.
[I.ii]

11. Full fathom five thy father lies;
Of his bones are coral made;
Those are pearls that were his eyes;
Nothing of him that doth fade
But doth suffer a sea-change
Into something rich and strange.
Sea-nymphs hourly ring his knell:
Ding-dong.
Hark! now I hear them – Ding-dong, bell.
[I.ii]

12. The fringed curtains of thine eye advance,
And say what thou seest yond.
[I.ii]

13. He receives comfort like cold porridge.
[II.i]

14. Look, he's winding up the watch of his wit; by and by it will strike.
[II.i]

15. What's past is prologue.
[II.i]

16. Open-ey'd conspiracy
His time doth take.
[II.i]

17. Misery acquaints a man with strange bedfellows.
[II.ii]

18. Well, here's my comfort.

The master, the swabber, the boatswain and I,
The gunner, and his mate,
Lov'd Mall, Meg, and Marian, and Margery,
But none of us car'd for Kate;
For she had a tongue with a tang,
Would cry to a sailor 'Go hang!'
[II.ii]

19. 'Ban 'Ban, Ca – Caliban,
Has a new master – Get a new man.
[II.ii]

20. *Ferdinand*: Wherefore weep you?
Miranda: At mine unworthiness, that dare not offer
What I desire to give, and much less take
What I shall die to want.
[III.i]

21. *Miranda*: I am your wife, if you will marry me;
If not, I'll die your maid. To be your fellow
You may deny me; but I'll be your servant,
Whether you will or no.
Ferdinand: My mistress, dearest;
And I thus humble ever.
Miranda: My husband, then?
Ferdinand: Ay, with a heart as willing
As bondage e'er of freedom. Here's my hand.

Miranda: And mine, with my heart in't.
[III.i]

22. Flout 'em and scout 'em,
And scout 'em and flout 'em;
Thought is free.
[III.ii]

23. He that dies pays all debts.
[III.ii]

24. Be not afeard. The isle is full of noises,
Sounds, and sweet airs, that give delight, and hurt not.
Sometimes a thousand twangling instruments
Will hum about mine ears; and sometime voices,
That, if I then had wak'd after long sleep,
Will make me sleep again; and then, in dreaming,
The clouds methought would open and show riches
Ready to drop upon me, that, when I wak'd,
I cried to dream again.
[III.ii]

25. If thou dost break her virgin-knot before
All sanctimonious ceremonies may
With full and holy rite be minist'red,
No sweet aspersion shall the heavens let fall
To make this contract grow; but barren hate,
Sour-ey'd disdain, and discord, shall bestrew
The union of your bed with weeds so loathly
That you shall hate it both. Therefore take heed,
As Hymen's lamps shall light you.
[IV.i]

26. The murkiest den,
The most opportune place, the strong'st suggestion
Our worser genius can, shall never melt
Mine honour into lust.
[IV.i]

27. Our revels now are ended. These our actors,
As I foretold you, were all spirits, and
Are melted into air, into thin air;
And, like the baseless fabric of this vision,
The cloud-capp'd towers, the gorgeous palaces,
The solemn temples, the great globe itself,
Yea, all which it inherit, shall dissolve,
And, like this insubstantial pageant faded,
Leave not a rack behind. We are such stuff
As dreams are made on; and our little life
Is rounded with a sleep.
[IV.i]

28. The rarer action is
In virtue than in vengeance.
[V.i]

29. Ye elves of hills, brooks, standing lakes, and groves;
And ye that on the sands with printless foot
Do chase the ebbing Neptune, and do fly him
When he comes back; you demi-puppets that
By moonshine do the green sour ringlets make,
Whereof the ewe not bites.
[V.i]

30. This rough magic
I here abjure...
I'll break my staff,
Bury it certain fathoms in the earth,
And, deeper than did ever plummet sound
I'll drown my book.
[V.i]

31. Where the bee sucks, there suck I;
In a cowslip's bell I lie;
There I couch when owls do cry.
On the bat's back I do fly
After summer merrily.
Merrily, merrily shall I live now
Under the blossom that hangs on the bough.
[V.i]

32. How many goodly creatures are there here!
How beauteous mankind is! O brave new world
That has such people in't!
[V.i]

33. Retire me to my Milan, where
Every third thought shall be my grave.
[V.i]

Timon of Athens

1. 'Tis not enough to help the feeble up,
But to support him after.
[I.i]

2. He that loves to be flattered is worthy o' th' flatterer.
[I.i]

3. The strain of man's bred out
Into baboon and monkey.
[I.i]

4. Faults that are rich are fair.
[I.ii]

5. I wonder men dare trust themselves with men.
[I.ii]

6. Like madness is the glory of this life.
[I.ii]

7. Men shut their doors against a setting sun.
[I.ii]

8. Nothing emboldens sin so much as mercy.
[III.v]

9. You fools of fortune, trencher friends, time's flies.
[III.vi]

10. We have seen better days.
[IV.ii]

11. O the fierce wretchedness that glory brings us!
[IV.ii]

12. [He] has almost charm'd me from my profession by persuading me to it.
[IV.iii]

13. Timon hath made his everlasting mansion
Upon the beached verge of the salt flood,
Who once a day with his embossed froth
The turbulent surge shall cover.
[V.i]

Titus Andronicus

1. What, man! more water glideth by the mill
Than wots the miller of.
[II.i]

2. Come and take choice of all my library,
And so beguile thy sorrow.
[IV.i]

3. The eagle suffers little birds to sing,
And is not careful what they mean thereby.
[IV.iv]

4. If one good deed in all my life I did,
I do repent it from my very soul.
[V.iii]

Troilus and Cressida

1. O, that her hand,
In whose comparison all whites are ink
Writing their own reproach; to whose soft seizure
The cygnet's down is harsh, and spirit of sense
Hard as the palm of ploughman!
[I.i]

2. Women are angels, wooing:
Things won are done; joy's soul lies in the doing.
That she belov'd knows nought that knows not this:
Men prize the thing ungain'd more than it is.
[I.ii]

3. The heavens themselves, the planets, and this centre,
Observe degree, priority, and place,
Insisture, course, proportion, season, form,
Office, and custom, in all line of order.
[I.iii]

4. O, when degree is shak'd,
Which is the ladder of all high designs,
The enterprise is sick!
[I.iii]

5. Take but degree away, untune that string,
And hark what discord follows! Each thing melts
In mere oppugnancy.
[I.iii]

6. The general's disdain'd
By him one step below, he by the next,
That next by him beneath; so every step,
Exampl'd by the first pace that is sick
Of his superior, grows to an envious fever
Of pale and bloodless emulation.
[I.iii]

7. Achilles ... who wears his wit in his belly and his guts in his head – I'll tell you what I say of him.
[II.i]

8. 'Tis mad idolatry
To make the service greater than the god.
[II.ii]

9. All the argument is a whore and a cuckold.
[II.iii]

10. I am giddy; expectation whirls me round.
Th' imaginary relish is so sweet
That it enchants my sense.
[III.ii]

11. This is the monstruosity in love, lady, that the will is infinite, and the execution confin'd; that the desire is boundless, and the act a slave to limit.
[III.ii]

12. To be wise and love
Exceeds man's might.
[III.ii]

13. I am as true as truth's simplicity,
And simpler than the infancy of truth.
[III.ii]

14. Time hath, my lord, a wallet at his back,
Wherein he puts alms for oblivion,
A great-siz'd monster of ingratitudes.
Those scraps are good deeds past, which are devour'd
As fast as they are made, forgot as soon
As done.
[III.iii]

15. Perseverance, dear my lord,
Keeps honour bright. To have done is to hang
Quite out of fashion, like a rusty mail
In monumental mock'ry.
[III.iii]

16. Beauty, wit,
High birth, vigour of bone, desert in service,
Love, friendship, charity, are subjects all
To envious and calumniating Time.
One touch of nature makes the whole world kin–
That all with one consent praise new-born gawds,
Though they are made and moulded of things past,
And give to dust that is a little gilt
More laud than gilt o'er-dusted.
[III.iii]

17. A plague of opinion! A man may wear it on both sides, like a leather jerkin.
[III.iii]

18. How my achievements mock me!
[IV.ii]

19. My love admits no qualifying dross.
[IV.iv]

20. We two, that with so many thousand sighs
Did buy each other, must poorly sell ourselves
With the rude brevity and discharge of one.
Injurious time now with a robber's haste
Crams his rich thievery up, he knows not how.
As many farewells as be stars in heaven,
With distinct breath and consign'd kisses to them,
He fumbles up into a loose adieu,
And scants us with a single famish'd kiss,
Distasted with the salt of broken tears.
[IV.iv]

21. Fie, fie upon her!
There's language in her eye, her cheek, her lip,
Nay, her foot speaks; her wanton spirits look out
At every joint and motive of her body.
[IV.v]

22. What's past and what's to come is strew'd with husks
And formless ruin of oblivion.
[IV.v]

23. The end crowns all;
And that old common arbitrator, Time,
Will one day end it.
[IV.v]

24. Lechery, lechery! Still wars and lechery! Nothing else holds fashion.
[V.ii]

25. Words, words, mere words, no matter from the heart.
[V.iii]

26. Hector is dead; there is no more to say.
[V.x]

27. O world! world! world! thus is the poor agent despis'd! O traitors and bawds, how earnestly are you set a work, and how ill requited! Why should our endeavour be so lov'd, and the performance so loathed?
[V.x]

Twelfth Night

1. If music be the food of love, play on,
Give me excess of it, that, surfeiting,
The appetite may sicken and so die.
That strain again! It had a dying fall;
O, it came o'er my ear like the sweet sound
That breathes upon a bank of violets,
Stealing and giving odour! Enough, no more;

'Tis not so sweet now as it was before.
O spirit of love, how quick and fresh art thou!
That, notwithstanding thy capacity
Receiveth as the sea, nought enters there,
Of what validity and pitch soe'er,
But falls into abatement and low price
Even in a minute. So full of shapes is fancy,
That it alone is high fantastical.
[I.i]

2. O, when mine eyes did see Olivia first,
Methought she purg'd the air of pestilence!
That instant was I turn'd into a hart,
And my desires, like fell and cruel hounds,
E'er since pursue me.
[I.i]

3. Methinks sometimes I have no more wit than a Christian or an ordinary man has; but I am a great eater of beef, and I believe that does harm to my wit.
[I.iii]

4. *Sir Andrew*: I would I had bestowed that time in the tongues that I have in fencing, dancing, and bear-baiting. O, had I but followed the arts!
Sir Toby: Then hadst thou had an excellent head of hair.
[I.iii]

5. Is it a world to hide virtues in?
[I.iii]

6. They shall yet belie thy happy years
That say thou art a man: Diana's lip
Is not more smooth and rubious; thy small pipe
Is as the maiden's organ, shrill and sound,
And all is semblative a woman's part.
[I.iv]

7. Many a good hanging prevents a bad marriage.
[I.v]

8. What says Quinapalus? 'Better a witty fool than a foolish wit.'
[I.v]

9. Virtue that transgresses is but patch'd with sin, and sin that amends is but patch'd with virtue.
[I.v]

10. Misprision in the highest degree! Lady, 'Cucullus non facit monachum'; that's as much to say as I wear not motley in my brain.
[I.v]

11. O, you are sick of self-love, Malvolio, and taste with a distemper'd appetite. To be generous, guiltless, and of free disposition, is to take those things for bird-bolts that you deem cannon bullets. There is no slander in an allow'd fool, though he do nothing but rail; nor no railing in a known discreet man, though he do nothing but reprove.
[I.v]

12. Not yet old enough for a man, nor young enough for a boy; as a squash is before 'tis a peascod, or a codling when 'tis almost an apple; 'tis with him in standing water, between boy and man. He is very well-favour'd, and he speaks very shrewishly; one would think his mother's milk were scarce out of him.
[I.v]

13. I would be loath to cast away my speech; for, besides that it is excellently well penn'd, I have taken great pains to con it.
[I.v]

14. I can say little more than I have studied, and that question's out of my part.
[I.v]

15. *Olivia*: Have you any commission from your lord to negotiate with my face? . . . we will draw the curtain and show you the picture. Look you, sir, such a one I was this present. Is't not well done?
Viola: Excellently done, if God did all.
Olivia: 'Tis in grain, sir; 'twill endure wind and weather.
Viola: 'Tis beauty truly blent, whose red and white
Nature's own sweet and cunning hand laid on.
Lady, you are the cruell'st she alive,
If you will lead these graces to the grave,
And leave the world no copy.
Olivia: O, sir, I will not be so hard-hearted; I will give out divers schedules of my beauty. It shall be inventoried, and every particle and utensil labell'd to my will: as – item, two lips indifferent red; item, two grey eyes with lids to them; item, one neck, one chin, and so forth.
[I.v]

16. Make me a willow cabin at your gate,
And call upon my soul within the house;
Write loyal cantons of contemned love
And sing them loud even in the dead of night;
Halloo your name to the reverberate hills,
And make the babbling gossip of the air
Cry out 'Olivia!' O, you should not rest
Between the elements of air and earth
But you should pity me!
[I.v]

17. *Olivia*: What is your parentage?
Viola: Above my fortunes, yet my state is well:
I am a gentleman.
[I.v]

18. O Time, thou must untangle this, not I;
It is too hard a knot for me t' untie!
[II.ii]

19. O mistress mine, where are you roaming?
O, stay and hear; your true love's coming,
That can sing both high and low.
Trip no further, pretty sweeting;
Journeys end in lovers meeting,
Every wise man's son doth know . . .

What is love? 'Tis not hereafter;
Present mirth hath present laughter;
What's to come is still unsure.
In delay there lies no plenty,
Then come kiss me, sweet and twenty;
Youth's a stuff will not endure.
[II.iii]

20. He does it with a better grace, but I do it more natural.
[II.iii]

21. My masters, are you mad? Or what are you? Have you no wit, manners, nor honesty, but to gabble like tinkers at this time of night? Do ye make an ale-house of my lady's house, that ye squeak out your coziers' catches without any mitigation or remorse of voice? Is there no respect of place, persons, nor time, in you?
[II.iii]

22. Dost thou think, because thou art virtuous, there shall be no more cakes and ale?
[II.iii]

23. My purpose is, indeed, a horse of that colour.
[II.iii]

24. Now, good Cesario, but that piece of song,
That old and antique song we heard last night;
Methought it did relieve my passion much,
More than light airs and recollected terms
Of these most brisk and giddy-paced times.
Come, but one verse.
[II.iv]

25. *Duke*: If ever thou shalt love,
In the sweet pangs of it remember me;
For such as I am all true lovers are,
Unstaid and skittish in all motions else
Save in the constant image of the creature
That is belov'd. How dost thou like this tune?
Viola: It gives a very echo to the seat
Where love is thron'd.
[II.iv]

26. Let still the woman take
An elder than herself; so wears she to him,
So sways she level in her husband's heart.
For, boy, however we do praise ourselves,
Our fancies are more giddy and unfirm,
More longing, wavering, sooner lost and won,
Than women's are.
[II.iv]

27. Then let thy love be younger than thyself,
Or thy affection cannot hold the bent.
[II.iv]

28. Mark it, Cesario; it is old and plain;
The spinsters and the knitters in the sun,
And the free maids that weave their thread with bones,
Do use to chant it; it is silly sooth,
And dallies with the innocence of love,
Like the old age.
[II.iv]

29. Come away, come away, death;
And in sad cypress let me be laid;
Fly away, fly away, breath,
I am slain by a fair cruel maid.
My shroud of white, stuck all with yew,
O, prepare it!
My part of death no one so true
Did share it.
[II.iv]

30. Now the melancholy god protect thee; and the tailor make thy doublet of changeable taffeta, for thy mind is a very opal.
[II.iv]

31. *Viola*: My father had a daughter lov'd a man,
As it might be perhaps, were I a woman,
I should your lordship.
Duke: And what's her history?
Viola: A blank, my lord. She never told her love,
But let concealment, like a worm i' th' bud,
Feed on her damask cheek. She pin'd in thought;
And with a green and yellow melancholy
She sat like Patience on a monument,
Smiling at grief. Was not this love indeed?
We men may say more, swear more, but indeed
Our shows are more than will; for still we prove
Much in our vows, but little in our love.
[II.iv]

32. I am all the daughters of my father's house,
And all the brothers too.
[II.iv]

33. Contemplation makes a rare turkey-cock of him; how he jets under his advanc'd plumes!
[II.v]

34. I may command where I adore.
[II.v]

35. Be not afraid of greatness. Some are born great, some achieve greatness, and some have greatness thrust upon 'em.
[II.v. Cf. Heller: 5]

36. Let thy tongue tang arguments of state; put thyself into the trick of singularity. She thus advises thee that sighs for thee. Remember who commended thy yellow stockings, and wish'd to see thee ever cross-garter'd.
[II.v]

37. This fellow is wise enough to play the fool;
And to do that well craves a kind of wit.
[III.i]

38. Taste your legs, sir; put them to motion.
[III.i]

39. Most excellent accomplish'd lady, the heavens rain odours on you!
[III.i]

40. O world, how apt the poor are to be proud!
[III.i]

41. O, what a deal of scorn looks beautiful
In the contempt and anger of his lip!
[III.i]

42. Love sought is good, but given unsought is better.
[III.i]

43. You are now sail'd into the north of my lady's opinion; where you will hang like an icicle on a Dutchman's beard.
[III.ii]

44. As many lies as will lie in thy sheet of paper, although the sheet were big enough for the bed of Ware in England, set 'em down.
[III.ii]

45. If he were open'd and you find so much blood in his liver as will clog the foot of a flea, I'll eat the rest of th' anatomy.
[III.ii]

46. He does smile his face into more lines than is in the new map with the augmentation of the Indies.
[III.ii]

47. What, man, defy the devil; consider, he's an enemy to mankind.
[III.iv]

48. If this were play'd upon a stage now,
I could condemn it as an improbable fiction.
[III.iv]

49. Still you keep o' th' windy side of the law.
[III.iv]

50. Fare thee well; and God have mercy upon one of our souls! He may have mercy upon mine; but my hope is better, and so look to thyself.
[III.iv]

51. I am one that would rather go with sir priest than sir knight. I care not who knows so much of my mettle.
[III.iv]

52. I hate ingratitude more in a man
Than lying, vainness, babbling drunkenness,
Or any taint of vice whose strong corruption
Inhabits our frail blood.
[III.iv]

53. In nature there's no blemish but the mind:
None can be call'd deform'd but the unkind.
[III.iv]

54. Out, hyperbolical fiend! How vexest thou this man! Talkest thou nothing but of ladies?
[IV.ii]

55. *Clown*: What is the opinion of Pythagoras concerning wild fowl?
Malvolio: That the soul of our grandam might haply inhabit a bird.
Clown: What think'st thou of his opinion?
Malvolio: I think nobly of the soul, and no way approve his opinion.
[IV.ii]

56. Why have you suffer'd me to be imprison'd,
Kept in a dark house, visited by the priest,
And made the most notorious geck and gull
That e'er invention play'd on? Tell me why.
[V.i]

57. And thus the whirligig of time brings in his revenges.
[V.i]

58. I'll be reveng'd on the whole pack of you.
[V.i]

59. When that I was and a little tiny boy,
With hey, ho, the wind and the rain,
A foolish thing was but a toy,
For the rain it raineth every day.

But when I came to man's estate,
With hey, ho, the wind and the rain,
'Gainst knaves and thieves men shut their gate,
For the rain it raineth every day.

But when I came, alas! to wive,
With hey, ho, the wind and the rain,
By swaggering could I never thrive,
For the rain it raineth every day.

But when I came unto my beds,
With hey, ho, the wind and the rain,
With toss-pots still had drunken heads,
For the rain it raineth every day.

A great while ago the world begun,
With hey, ho, the wind and the rain,
But that's all one, our play is done,
And we'll strive to please you every day.
[V.i]

The Two Gentlemen of Verona

1. Home-keeping youth have ever homely wits.
[I.i]

2. He was more than over shoes in love.
[I.i]

3. I have no other but a woman's reason:
I think him so, because I think him so.
[I.ii]

4. Fie, fie, how wayward is this foolish love,
That like a testy babe will scratch the nurse,
And presently, all humbled, kiss the rod!
[I.ii]

5. O, how this spring of love resembleth
The uncertain glory of an April day,
Which now shows all the beauty of the sun,
And by and by a cloud takes all away!
[I.iii]

6. O jest unseen, inscrutable, invisible,
As a nose on a man's face, or a weather-cock on a steeple!
[II.i]

7. Even as one heat another heat expels
Or as one nail by strength drives out another,
So the remembrance of my former love
Is by a newer object quite forgotten.
[II.iv]

8. Now can I break my fast, dine, sup, and sleep,
Upon the very naked name of love.
[II.iv]

9. Win her with gifts, if she respect not words:
Dumb jewels often in their silent kind
More than quick words do move a woman's mind.
[III.i]

10. For Orpheus' lute was strung with poets' sinews,
Whose golden touch could soften steel and stones,
Make tigers tame, and huge leviathans
Forsake unsounded deeps to dance on sands.
[III.ii]

11. A man I am cross'd with adversity.
[IV.i]

12. Who is Sylvia? What is she,
That all our swains commend her?
Holy, fair, and wise is she;
The heaven such grace did lend her,
That she might admired be.

Is she kind as she is fair?
For beauty lives with kindness.
Love doth to her eyes repair,
To help him of his blindness;
And, being help'd, inhabits there.

Then to Silvia let us sing
That Silvia is excelling;
She excels each mortal thing
Upon the dull earth dwelling.
To her let us garlands bring.
[IV.ii]

13. But since she did neglect her looking-glass
And threw her sun-expelling mask away,
The air hath starv'd the roses in her cheeks
And pinch'd the lily-tincture of her face,
That now she is become as black as I.
[IV.iv]

14. How use doth breed a habit in a man!
[V.iv]

15. It is the lesser blot, modesty finds,
Women to change their shapes than men their minds.
[V.iv]

16. O heaven, were man
But constant, he were perfect!
[V.iv]

The Winter's Tale

1. We were as twinn'd lambs that did frisk i' th' sun
And bleat the one at th' other. What we chang'd
Was innocence for innocence; we knew not
The doctrine of ill-doing, nor dream'd
That any did.
[I.ii]

2. But to be paddling palms and pinching fingers,
As now they are, and making practis'd smiles
As in a looking-glass.
[I.ii]

3. How like, methought, I then was to this kernel,
This squash, this gentleman.
[I.ii]

4. I may be negligent, foolish, and fearful:
In every one of these no man is free.
[I.ii]

5. A sad tale's best for winter. I have one
Of sprites and goblins.
[II.i]

6. It is an heretic that makes the fire,
Not she which burns in't.
[II.iii]

7. What's gone and what's past help
Should be past grief.
[III.ii]

8. Exit, pursued by a bear.
[III.iii, stage direction]

9. I would there were no age between ten and three and twenty, or that youth would sleep out the rest; for there is nothing in the between but getting wenches with child, wronging the ancientry, stealing, fighting.
[III.iii]

10. But to make an end of the ship – to see how the sea flap-dragon'd it; but first, how the poor souls roared, and the sea mock'd them; and how the poor gentleman roared, and the bear mock'd him, both roaring louder than the sea or weather.
[III.iii]

11. Thou met'st with things dying, I with things new-born.
[III.iii]

12. When daffodils begin to peer,
With heigh! the doxy over the dale,
Why, then comes in the sweet o' the year,
For the red blood reigns in the winter's pale.

The white sheet bleaching on the hedge,
With heigh! the sweet birds, O, how they sing!
Doth set my pugging tooth on edge,
For a quart of ale is a dish for a king.

The lark, that tirra-lirra chants,
With heigh! with heigh! the thrush and the jay,
Are summer songs for me and my aunts,
While we lie tumbling in the hay.
[IV.iii]

13. My father nam'd me Autolycus; who, being, as I am, litter'd under Mercury, was likewise a snapper-up of unconsidered trifles.
[IV.iii]

14. For the life to come, I sleep out the thought of it.
[IV.iii]

15. Jog on, jog on, the footpath way,
And merrily hent the stile-a;
A merry heart goes all the day,
Your sad tires in a mile-a.
[IV.iii]

16. For you there's rosemary and rue; these keep
Seeming and savour all the winter long.
[IV.iv]

17. The fairest flow'rs o' th' season
Are our carnations and streak'd gillyvors,
Which some call nature's bastards.
[IV.iv]

18. This is an art
Which does mend nature – change it rather; but
The art itself is nature.
[IV.iv]

19. Here's flow'rs for you:
Hot lavender, mints, savory, marjoram;
The marigold, that goes to bed wi' th' sun,
And with him rises weeping.
[IV.iv]

20. O Proserpina,
For the flowers now that, frighted, thou let'st fall
From Dis's waggon! – daffodils,
That come before the swallow dares, and take
The winds of March with beauty; violets dim,
But sweeter than the lids of Juno's eyes
Or Cytherea's breath; pale primroses,
That die unmarried ere they can behold
Bright Phoebus in his strength – a malady
Most incident to maids; bold oxlips, and
The crown-imperial; lilies of all kinds,
The flow'r-de-luce being one.
[IV.iv]

21. When you do dance, I wish you
A wave o' th' sea, that you might ever do
Nothing but that; move still, still so,
And own no other function.
[IV.iv]

22. Good sooth, she is
The queen of curds and cream.
[IV.iv]

23. Lawn as white as driven snow.
[IV.iv]

24. *Mopsa*: I love a ballad in print a-life, for then we are sure they are true.
Autolycus: Here's one to a very doleful tune: how a usurer's wife was brought to bed of twenty money-bags at a burden, and how she long'd to eat adders' heads and toads carbonado'd.
[IV.iv]

25. The self-same sun that shines upon his court
Hides not his visage from our cottage, but
Looks on alike.
[IV.iv]

26. Being now awake, I'll queen it no inch farther,
But milk my ewes and weep.
[IV.iv]

27. Prosperity's the very bond of love,
Whose fresh complexion and whose heart together
Affliction alters.
[IV.iv]

28. Ha, ha! what a fool Honesty is! and Trust, his sworn brother, a very simple gentleman!
[IV.iv]

29. Though I am not naturally honest, I am so sometimes by chance.
[IV.iv]

30. Though authority be a stubborn bear, yet he is oft led by the nose with gold.
[IV.iv]

31. Stars, stars,
And all eyes else dead coals!
[V.i]

32. Still, methinks,
There is an air comes from her. What fine chisel
Could ever yet cut breath?
[V.iii]

33. O, she's warm!
If this be magic, let it be an art
Lawful as eating.
[V.iii]

Poetry

1. Crabbed age and youth cannot live together:
Youth is full of pleasance, age is full of care...

2. Age, I do abhor thee; youth, I do adore thee.
[*The Passionate Pilgrim*, xii]

3. Let the bird of loudest lay,
On the sole Arabian tree,
Herald sad and trumpet be,
To whose sound chaste wings obey.
[*The Phoenix and the Turtle*, first lines]

4. Beauty itself doth of itself persuade
The eyes of men without an orator.
[*The Rape of Lucrece*, line 29]

5. Who buys a minute's mirth to wail a week?
Or sells eternity to get a toy?
For one sweet grape who will the vine destroy?
[*The Rape of Lucrece*, line 213]

6. Time's glory is to calm contending kings,
To unmask falsehood, and bring truth to light.
[*The Rape of Lucrece*, line 939]

7. And now this pale swan in her wat'ry nest
Begins the sad dirge of her certain ending.
[*The Rape of Lucrece*, line 1611]

8. If the first heire of my invention prove deformed, I shall be sorie it had so noble a god-father.
[*Venus and Adonis*, Dedication]

9. Hunting he lov'd, but love he laugh'd to scorn.
[*Venus and Adonis*, line 4]

10. Bid me discourse, I will enchant thine ear,
Or, like a fairy, trip upon the green,
Or, like a nymph, with long dishevelled hair,
Dance on the sands, and yet no footing seen.
Love is a spirit all compact of fire,
Not gross to sink, but light, and will aspire.
[*Venus and Adonis*, line 145]

11. Round-hoof'd, short-jointed, fetlocks shag and long,
Broad breast, full eye, small head, and nostril wide,
High crest, short ears, straight legs and passing strong,
Thin mane, thick tail, broad buttock, tender hide;
Look what a horse should have he did not lack,
Save a proud rider on so proud a back.
[*Venus and Adonis*, line 295]

12. By this, poor Wat, far off upon a hill,
Stands on his hinder legs with list'ning ear,
To hearken if his foes pursue him still.
[*Venus and Adonis*, line 697]

Sonnets

1. From fairest creatures we desire increase,
That thereby beauty's rose might never die.
[Sonnet 1]

2. When forty winters shall besiege thy brow,
And dig deep trenches in thy beauty's field.
[Sonnet 2]

3. Thou art thy mother's glass, and she in thee
Calls back the lovely April of her prime.
[Sonnet 3]

4. Music to hear, why hear'st thou music sadly?
Sweets with sweets war not, joy delights in joy.
Why lov'st thou that which thou receiv'st not gladly,
Or else receiv'st with pleasure thine annoy?
If the true concord of well-tuned sounds,
By unions married, do offend thine ear,
They do but sweetly chide thee.
[Sonnet 8]

5. If I could write the beauty of your eyes
And in fresh numbers number all your graces,
The age to come would say 'This poet lies;
Such heavenly touches ne'er touch'd earthly faces'.
So should my papers, yellowed with their age,
Be scorn'd, like old men of less truth than tongue;
And your true rights be term'd a poet's rage,
And stretched metre of an antique song.
[Sonnet 17]

6. Shall I compare thee to a summer's day?
Thou art more lovely and more temperate.
Rough winds do shake the darling buds of May,
And summer's lease hath all too short a date:
Sometimes too hot the eye of heaven shines,
And often is his gold complexion dimm'd;
And every fair from fair some time declines,
By chance, or nature's changing course, untrimm'd;
But thy eternal summer shall not fade
Nor lose possession of that fair thou ow'st;
Nor shall Death brag thou wand'rest in his shade,
When in eternal lines to time thou grow'st.
So long as men can breathe or eyes can see,
So long lives this, and this gives life to thee.
[Sonnet 18]

7. A woman's face, with Nature's own hand painted,
Hast thou, the Master Mistress of my passion.
[Sonnet 20]

8. My glass shall not persuade me I am old
So long as youth and thou are of one date;
But when in thee time's furrows I behold,
Then look I death my days should expiate.
[Sonnet 22]

9. O, let my books be then the eloquence
And dumb presagers of my speaking breast.
[Sonnet 23]

10. Weary with toil, I haste me to my bed,
The dear repose for limbs with travel tired;
But then begins a journey in my head
To work my mind when body's work's expired.
[Sonnet 27]

11. When in disgrace with Fortune and men's eyes,
I all alone beweep my outcast state,
And trouble deaf heaven with my bootless cries,
And look upon myself, and curse my fate,
Wishing me like to one more rich in hope,
Featur'd like him, like him with friends possess'd,
Desiring this man's art, and that man's scope,
With what I most enjoy contented least;
Yet in these thoughts myself almost despising,
Haply I think on thee, and then my state,
Like to the lark at break of day arising
From sullen earth, sings hymns at heaven's gate;
For thy sweet love remember'd such wealth brings
That then I scorn to change my state with kings.
[Sonnet 29]

12. When to the sessions of sweet silent thought
I summon up remembrance of things past,
I sigh the lack of many a thing I sought,
And with old woes new wail my dear time's waste.
Then can I drown an eye, unus'd to flow,
For precious friends hid in death's dateless night,
And weep afresh love's long since cancell'd woe,
And moan th' expense of many a vanish'd sight.
Then can I grieve at grievances foregone,
And heavily from woe to woe tell o'er
The sad account of fore-bemoaned moan,
Which I new pay as if not paid before.
But if the while I think on thee, dear friend,
All losses are restor'd, and sorrows end.
[Sonnet 30]

13. But since he died, and poets better prove,
Theirs for their style I'll read, his for his love.
[Sonnet 32]

14. Full many a glorious morning have I seen
Flatter the mountain-tops with sovereign eye,
Kissing with golden face the meadows green,
Gilding pale streams with heavenly alchemy...

15. But out, alack! he was but one hour mine,
The region cloud hath mask'd him from me now.
Yet him for this my love no whit disdaineth;
Suns of the world may stain when heaven's sun staineth.
[Sonnet 33]

16. Why didst thou promise such a beauteous day,
And make me travel forth without my cloak,
To let base clouds o'ertake me in my way,
Hiding thy brav'ry in their rotten smoke?
[Sonnet 34]

17. Roses have thorns, and silver fountains mud;
Clouds and eclipses stain both moon and sun,
And loathsome canker lives in sweetest bud.
All men make faults.
[Sonnet 35]

18. Mine eye and heart are at a mortal war
How to divide the conquest of thy sight.
[Sonnet 46]

19. Against that time when thou shalt strangely pass
And scarcely greet me with that sun, thine eye,
When love, converted from the thing it was,
Shall reasons find of settled gravity.
[Sonnet 49]

20. What is your substance, whereof are you made,
That millions of strange shadows on you tend?
[Sonnet 53]

21. Not marble nor the gilded monuments
Of princes shall outlive this pow'rful rhyme;
But you shall shine more bright in these contents
Than unswept stone, besmear'd with sluttish time.
[Sonnet 55]

22. Being your slave, what should I do but tend
Upon the hours and times of your desire?
I have no precious time at all to spend,
Nor services to do, till you require.
Nor dare I chide the world-without-end hour,
Whilst I, my sovereign, watch the clock for you,
Nor think the bitterness of absence sour,
When you have bid your servant once adieu;
Nor dare I question with my jealous thought
Where you may be, or your affairs suppose,
But, like a sad slave, stay and think of nought
Save where you are how happy you make those.
So true a fool is love that in your will,
Though you do anything, he thinks no ill.
[Sonnet 57]

23. Like as the waves make towards the pebbled shore,
So do our minutes hasten to their end...

24. Time doth transfix the flourish set on youth,
And delves the parallels in beauty's brow.
[Sonnet 60]

25. Sin of self-love possesseth all mine eye,
And all my soul, and all my every part.
[Sonnet 62]

26. When I have seen by Time's fell hand defaced
The rich proud cost of outworn buried age...

27. When I have seen the hungry ocean gain
Advantage on the kingdom of the shore...

28. This thought is as a death, which cannot choose
But weep to have that which it fears to lose.
[Sonnet 64]

29. Since brass, nor stone, nor earth, nor boundless sea,
But sad mortality o'ersways their power,
How with this rage shall beauty hold a plea,
Whose action is no stronger than a flower?
[Sonnet 65]

30. Tir'd with all these, for restful death I cry:
As, to behold desert a beggar born,
And needy nothing trimm'd in jollity,
And purest faith unhappily forsworn,
And gilded honour shamefully misplac'd,
And maiden virtue rudely strumpeted,
And right perfection wrongfully disgrac'd,
And strength by limping sway disabled,
And art made tongue-tied by authority,
And folly, doctor-like, controlling skill,
And simple truth miscall'd simplicity,
And captive good attending captain ill–
Tir'd with all these, from these would I be gone,
Save that, to die, I leave my love alone.
[Sonnet 66]

31. Those parts of thee that the world's eye doth view
Want nothing that the thought of hearts can mend.
All tongues, the voice of souls, give thee that due,
Utt'ring bare truth, even so as foes commend.
[Sonnet 69]

32. No longer mourn for me when I am dead
Than you shall hear the surly sullen bell
Give warning to the world that I am fled
From this vile world, with vilest worms to dwell.
[Sonnet 71]

33. That time of year thou mayst in me behold
When yellow leaves, or none, or few, do hang
Upon those boughs which shake against the cold,
Bare ruin'd choirs where late the sweet birds sang.
In me thou seest the twilight of such day
As after sunset fadeth in the west,
Which by and by black night doth take away,
Death's second self, that seals up all in rest.
[Sonnet 73]

34. O, know, sweet love, I always write of you,
And you and love are still my argument;
So all my best is dressing old words new,
Spending again what is already spent.
[Sonnet 76]

35. Time's thievish progress to eternity.
[Sonnet 77]

36. Your monument shall be my gentle verse,
Which eyes not yet created shall o'er-read;
And tongues to be your being shall rehearse,
When all the breathers of this world are dead.
You still shall live, such virtue hath my pen,
Where breath most breathes, even in the mouths of men.
[Sonnet 81]

37. Was it the proud full sail of his great verse,
Bound for the prize of all-too-precious you,
That did my ripe thoughts in my brain inhearse,
Making their tomb the womb wherein they grew?
[Sonnet 86]

38. Farewell! thou art too dear for my possessing,
And like enough thou know'st thy estimate.
The charter of thy worth gives thee releasing;
My bonds in thee are all determinate.
For how do I hold thee but by thy granting?
And for that riches where is my deserving?
The cause of this fair gift in me is wanting,
And so my patent back again is swerving.
Thy self thou gav'st, thy own worth then not knowing,
Or me, to whom thou gav'st it, else mistaking;
So thy great gift, upon misprision growing,
Comes home again, on better judgment making.
Thus have I had thee, as a dream doth flatter:
In sleep a king, but waking no such matter.
[Sonnet 87]

39. For thee, against myself I'll vow debate,
For I must ne'er love him whom thou dost hate.
[Sonnet 89]

40. Ah, do not, when my heart hath scap'd this sorrow,
Come in the rearward of a conquer'd woe;
Give not a windy night a rainy morrow,
To linger out a purpos'd overthrow.
[Sonnet 90]

41. They that have power to hurt and will do none,
That do not do the thing they most do show,
Who, moving others, are themselves as stone,
Unmoved, cold, and to temptation slow–
They rightly do inherit Heaven's graces,
And husband nature's riches from expense;
They are the lords and owners of their faces,
Others but stewards of their excellence.
The summer's flow'r is to the summer sweet
Though to itself it only live and die;
But if that flow'r with base infection meet,
The basest weed outbraves his dignity.
For sweetest things turn sourest by their deeds;
Lilies that fester smell far worse than weeds.
[Sonnet 94]

42. How like a winter hath my absence been
From thee, the pleasure of the fleeting year!
What freezings have I felt, what dark days seen!
What old December's bareness everywhere!
[Sonnet 97]

43. From you have I been absent in the spring,
When proud-pied April, dress'd in all his trim,
Hath put a spirit of youth in every thing.
[Sonnet 98]

44. O truant Muse, what shall be thy amends
For thy neglect of truth in beauty dy'd?
Both truth and beauty on my love depends;
So dost thou too, and therein dignified.
[Sonnet 101]

45. For to no other pass my verses tend
Than of your graces and your gifts to tell;
And more, much more, than in my verse can sit
Your own glass shows you, when you look in it.
[Sonnet 103]

46. To me, fair friend, you never can be old,
For as you were when first your eye I ey'd,
Such seems your beauty still. Three winters cold
Have from the forests shook three summers' pride,
Three beauteous springs to yellow autumn turn'd
In process of the seasons have I seen,
Three April perfumes in three hot Junes burn'd,
Since first I saw you fresh, which yet are green.
Ah, yet doth beauty, like a dial-hand,
Steal from his figure, and no pace perceiv'd;
So your sweet hue, which methinks still doth stand,
Hath motion, and mine eye may be deceiv'd.
For fear of which, hear this, thou age unbred:
Ere you were born was beauty's summer dead.
[Sonnet 104]

47. Fair, kind, and true, have often liv'd alone,
Which three, till now, never kept seat in one.
[Sonnet 105]

48. When in the chronicle of wasted time
I see descriptions of the fairest wights,
And beauty making beautiful old rhyme
In praise of ladies dead and lovely knights...

49. For we, which now behold these present days,
Have eyes to wonder, but lack tongues to praise.
[Sonnet 106]

50. Not mine own fears, nor the prophetic soul
Of the wide world dreaming on things to come,
Can yet the lease of my true love control,
Suppos'd as forfeit to a confin'd doom.
The mortal moon hath her eclipse endur'd,
And the sad augurs mock their own presage...
And thou in this shalt find thy monument,
When tyrants' crests and tombs of brass are spent.
[Sonnet 107]

51. Alas, 'tis true I have gone here and there
And made myself a motley to the view,
Gor'd mine own thoughts, sold cheap what is most dear,
Made old offences of affections new.
Most true it is that I have look'd on truth
Askance and strangely; but, by all above,
These blenches gave my heart another youth,
And worse essays prov'd thee my best of love.
[Sonnet 110]

52. Let me not to the marriage of true minds
Admit impediments. Love is not love
Which alters when it alteration finds,
Or bends with the remover to remove.
O, no! it is an ever-fixed mark,
That looks on tempests and is never shaken;
It is the star to every wand'ring bark,
Whose worth's unknown, although his height be taken.
Love's not Time's fool, though rosy lips and cheeks
Within his bending sickle's compass come;
Love alters not with his brief hours and weeks,
But bears it out even to the edge of doom.
If this be error, and upon me prov'd,
I never writ, nor no man ever lov'd.
[Sonnet 116]

53. What potions have I drunk of Siren tears,
Distill'd from limbecks foul as hell within,
Applying fears to hopes, and hopes to fears,
Still losing when I saw my self to win!
[Sonnet 119]

54. 'Tis better to be vile than vile esteemed,
When not to be receives reproach of being,
And the just pleasure lost, which is so deemed
Not by our feeling, but by others' seeing.
[Sonnet 121]

55. No, Time, thou shalt not boast that I do change.
Thy pyramids built up with newer might
To me are nothing novel, nothing strange;
They are but dressings of a former sight.
[Sonnet 123]

56. Th' expense of spirit in a waste of shame
Is lust in action; and till action, lust
Is perjur'd, murd'rous, bloody, full of blame,
Savage, extreme, rude, cruel, not to trust;
Enjoyed no sooner but despised straight;
Past reason hunted; and, no sooner had,
Past reason hated, as a swallowed bait,
On purpose laid to make the taker mad–
Mad in pursuit, and in possession so;
Had, having, and in quest to have, extreme;
A bliss in proof, and prov'd, a very woe;
Before, a joy propos'd; behind, a dream.
All this the world well knows; yet none knows well
To shun the heaven that leads men to this hell.
[Sonnet 129]

57. Make but my name thy love, and love that still,
And then thou lov'st me, for my name is Will.
[Sonnet 136]

58. Thou blind fool, Love, what dost thou to mine eyes
That they behold, and see not what they see?
[Sonnet 137]

59. When my love swears that she is made of truth,
I do believe her, though I know she lies.
[Sonnet 138]

60. Two loves I have, of comfort and despair,
Which like two spirits do suggest me still:
The better angel is a man right fair,
The worser spirit a woman colour'd ill.
[Sonnet 144]

61. Poor soul, the centre of my sinful earth,
[My sinful earth] these rebel pow'rs that thee array,
Why dost thou pine within and suffer dearth,
Painting thy outward walls so costly gay?
Why so large cost, having so short a lease,
Dost thou upon thy fading mansion spend?...

62. So shalt thou feed on Death, that feeds on men,
And, Death once dead, there's no more dying then.
[Sonnet 146]

63. Past cure I am, now reason is past care,
And frantic mad with evermore unrest;
My thoughts and my discourse as mad men's are,
At random from the truth vainly express'd;
For I have sworn thee fair, and thought thee bright,
Who art as black as hell, as dark as night.
[Sonnet 147]

64. For I have sworn thee fair – more perjur'd I,
To swear against the truth so foul a lie!
[Sonnet 152]

65. Love's fire heats water, water cools not love.
[Sonnet 154]

Miscellaneous

1. [Contained in his will]
Item, I give unto my wife my second best bed.
[Attr.]

2. [Epitaph on his tomb]
Good friend, for Jesu's sake forbear,
To dig the dust enclosed here.
Blest be the man that spares these stones,
And curst be he that moves my bones.
[Attr.]

Shankly, Bill (1914–1981)

Scottish footballer and manager

1. Some people think football is a matter of life and death. I don't like that attitude. I can assure them it is much more serious than that.
[Remark on BBC TV, 1981]

Sharpe, Tom (1928–)

English comic novelist

1. The South African Police would leave no stone unturned to see that nothing disturbed the even tenor of their lives.
[*Indecent Exposure* (1973), 1]

2. Skullion had little use for contraceptives at the best of times. Unnatural, he called them, and placed them in the lower social category of things along with elastic-sided boots and made-up bow ties. Not the sort of attire for a gentleman.
[*Porterhouse Blue* (1974), 9]

3. His had been an intellectual decision founded on his conviction that if a little knowledge was a dangerous thing, a lot was lethal.
[*Porterhouse Blue* (1974), 18]

Shaw, George Bernard (1856–1950)

Irish novelist, dramatist, essayist, critic, pamphleteer, socialist and letter writer; Nobel prize 1925

1. A day's work is a day's work, neither more nor less, and the man who does it needs a day's sustenance, a night's repose, and due leisure, whether he be painter or ploughman.
[*An Unsocial Socialist* (1887), 5]

2. The Gospel of Getting On.
[*Mrs Warren's Profession* (1898), IV]

3. You can always tell an old soldier by the inside of his holsters and cartridge boxes. The young ones carry pistols and cartridges: the old ones, grub.
[*Arms and the Man* (1898), I]

4. You are a very poor soldier: a chocolate cream soldier!
[*Arms and the Man* (1898), I]

5. I never apologise.
[*Arms and the Man* (1898), III]

6. You're not a man: you're a machine.
[*Arms and the Man* (1898), III]

7. We have no more right to consume happiness without producing it than to consume wealth without producing it.
[*Candida* (1898), I]

8. Do you think that the things people make fools of themselves about are any less real and true than the things they behave sensibly about?
[*Candida* (1898), I]

9. It is easy – terribly easy – to shake a man's faith in himself. To take advantage of that to break a man's spirit is devil's work.
[*Candida* (1898), I]

10. Man can climb to the highest summits; but he cannot dwell there long.
[*Candida* (1898), III]

11. I'm only a beer teetotaller, not a champagne teetotaller.
[*Candida* (1898), III]

12. There is no satisfaction in hanging a man who does not object to it.
[*The Man of Destiny* (1898)]

13. There is only one universal passion: fear.
[*The Man of Destiny* (1898)]

14. There is nothing so bad or so good that you will not find Englishmen doing it; but you will never find an Englishman in the wrong. He does everything on principle. He fights you on patriotic principles; he robs you on business principles; he enslaves you on imperial principles; he bullies you on manly principles; he supports his king on loyal principles and cuts off his king's head on republican principles.
[*The Man of Destiny* (1898)]

15. The fickleness of the women I love is only equalled by the infernal constancy of the women who love me.
[*The Philanderer* (1898), II]

16. Man is a creature of habit. You cannot write three plays and then stop.
[*Plays Pleasant and Unpleasant* (1898), Preface]

17. There is only one religion, though there are a hundred versions of it.
[*Plays Pleasant and Unpleasant* (1898), Preface]

18. We're from Madeira, but perfectly respectable, so far.
[*You Never Can Tell* (1898), I]

19. We don't bother much about dress and manners in England, because, as a nation, we don't dress well and we've no manners.
[*You Never Can Tell* (1898), I]

20. Well, sir, you never can tell. That's a principle in life with me, sir, if you'll excuse my having such a thing, sir.
[*You Never Can Tell* (1898), II]

21. He [the Briton] is a barbarian, and thinks that the custom of his tribe and island are the laws of nature.
[*Caesar and Cleopatra* (1901), II]

22. When a stupid man is doing something he is ashamed of, he always declares that it is his duty.
[*Caesar and Cleopatra* (1901), III]

23. He who has never hoped can never despair.
[*Caesar and Cleopatra* (1901), IV]

24. An Englishman reading [Caesar's books] would say that Caesar was a man of great common sense and good taste, meaning thereby a man without originality or moral courage.
[*Caesar and Cleopatra* (1901), Notes, 'Julius Caesar']

25. The worst sin towards our fellow creatures is not to hate them, but to be indifferent to them: that's the essence of inhumanity.
[*The Devil's Disciple* (1901), II]

26. I never expect a soldier to think.
[*The Devil's Disciple* (1901), III]

27. Give women the vote, and in five years there will be a crushing tax on bachelors.
[*Man and Superman* (1903), Epistle Dedicatory]

28. Our political experiment of democracy, the last refuge of cheap misgovernment.
[*Man and Superman* (1903), Epistle Dedicatory]

29. A lifetime of happiness! No man alive could bear it: it would be hell on earth.
[*Man and Superman* (1903), I]

30. We are ashamed of everything that is real about us; ashamed of ourselves, of our relatives, of our incomes, of our accents, of our opinions, of our experience, just as we are ashamed of our naked skins ... The more things a man is ashamed of, the more respectable he is.
[*Man and Superman* (1903), I]

31. The true artist will let his wife starve, his children go barefoot, his mother drudge for his living at seventy, sooner than work at anything but his art.
[*Man and Superman* (1903), I]

32. There is no love sincerer than the love of food.
[*Man and Superman* (1903), I]

33. Is the devil to have all the passions as well as all the good tunes?
[*Man and Superman* (1903), I]

34. Very nice sort of place, Oxford, I should think, for people that like that sort of place.
[*Man and Superman* (1903), II]

35. You think that you are Ann's suitor; that you are the pursuer and she the pursued; that it is your part to woo, to persuade, to prevail, to overcome. Fool: it is you who are the pursued, the marked down quarry, the destined prey.
[*Man and Superman* (1903), II]

36. It is a woman's business to get married as soon as possible, and a man's to keep unmarried as long as he can.
[*Man and Superman* (1903), II]

37. Marry Ann; and at the end of a week you'll find no more inspiration in her than in a plate of muffins.
[*Man and Superman* (1903), II]

38. You can be as romantic as you please about love, Hector; but you mustn't be romantic about money.
[*Man and Superman* (1903), II]

39. I am a gentleman: I live by robbing the poor.
[*Man and Superman* (1903), III]

40. At every one of those concerts in England you will find rows of weary people who are there, not because they really like classical music, but because they think they ought to like it.
[*Man and Superman* (1903), III]

41. An Englishman thinks he is moral when he is only uncomfortable.
[*Man and Superman* (1903), III]

42. As an old soldier I admit the cowardice: it's as universal as sea sickness, and matters just as little.
[*Man and Superman* (1903), III]

43. This creature Man, who in his own selfish affairs is a coward to the backbone, will fight for an idea like a hero.
[*Man and Superman* (1903), III]

44. When the military man approaches, the world locks up its spoons and packs off its womankind.
[*Man and Superman* (1903), III]

45. What is virtue but the Trade Unionism of the married?
[*Man and Superman* (1903), III]

46. Those who talk most about the blessings of marriage and the constancy of its vows are the very people who declare that if the chain were broken and the prisoners left free to choose, the whole social fabric would fly asunder. You cannot have the argument both ways. If the prisoner is happy, why lock him in? If he is not, why pretend that he is?
[*Man and Superman* (1903), III]

47. There are two tragedies in life. One is to lose your heart's desire. The other is to gain it.
[*Man and Superman* (1903), IV]

48. Do not do unto others as you would they should do unto you. Their tastes may not be the same.
[*Man and Superman* (1903), 'Maxims for Revolutionists: The Golden Rule']

49. The golden rule is that there are no golden rules.
[*Man and Superman* (1903), 'Maxims for Revolutionists: The Golden Rule']

50. The populace cannot understand the bureaucracy: it can only worship the national idols.
[*Man and Superman* (1903), 'Maxims for Revolutionists: Idolatry']

51. Democracy substitutes election by the incompetent many for appointment by the corrupt few.
[*Man and Superman* (1903), 'Maxims for Revolutionists: Democracy']

52. Liberty means responsibility. That is why most men dread it.
[*Man and Superman* (1903), 'Maxims for Revolutionists: Liberty and Equality']

53. He who can, does. He who cannot, teaches.
[*Man and Superman* (1903), 'Maxims for Revolutionists: Education']

54. Activity is the only road to knowledge.
[*Man and Superman* (1903), 'Maxims for Revolutionists: Education']

55. Marriage is popular because it combines the maximum of temptation with the maximum of opportunity.
[*Man and Superman* (1903), 'Maxims for Revolutionists: Marriage']

56. Titles distinguish the mediocre, embarrass the superior, and are disgraced by the inferior.
[*Man and Superman* (1903), 'Maxims for Revolutionists: Titles']

57. When domestic servants are treated as human beings it is not worth while to keep them.
[*Man and Superman* (1903), 'Maxims for Revolutionists: Servants']

58. If you strike a child, take care that you strike it in anger, even at the risk of maiming it for life. A blow in cold blood neither can nor should be forgiven.
[*Man and Superman* (1903), 'Maxims for Revolutionists: How to Beat Children']

59. Beware of the man whose god is in the skies.
[*Man and Superman* (1903), 'Maxims for Revolutionists: Religion']

60. Self-denial is not a virtue: it is only the effect of prudence on rascality.
[*Man and Superman* (1903), 'Maxims for Revolutionists: Virtues and Vices']

61. In heaven an angel is nobody in particular.
[*Man and Superman* (1903), 'Maxims for Revolutionists: Greatness']

62. The reasonable man adapts himself to the world: the unreasonable one persists in trying to adapt the world to himself. Therefore all progress depends on the unreasonable man.
[*Man and Superman* (1903), 'Maxims for Revolutionists: Reason']

63. The man who listens to Reason is lost: Reason enslaves all whose minds are not strong enough to master her.
[*Man and Superman* (1903), 'Maxims for Revolutionists: Reason']

64. Decency is Indecency's Conspiracy of Silence.
[*Man and Superman* (1903), 'Maxims for Revolutionists: Decency']

65. Life levels all men: death reveals the eminent.
[*Man and Superman* (1903), 'Maxims for Revolutionists: Fame']

66. Home is the girl's prison and the woman's workhouse.
[*Man and Superman* (1903), 'Maxims for Revolutionists: Women in the Home']

67. Every man over forty is a scoundrel.
[*Man and Superman* (1903), 'Maxims for Revolutionists: Stray Sayings']

68. Youth, which is forgiven everything, forgives itself nothing: age, which forgives itself everything, is forgiven nothing.
[*Man and Superman* (1903), 'Maxims for Revolutionists: Stray Sayings']

69. Beware of the man who does not return your blow: he neither forgives you nor allows you to forgive yourself.
[*Man and Superman* (1903), 'Maxims for Revolutionists: Stray Sayings']

70. Money is indeed the most important thing in the world; and all sound and successful personal and national morality should have this fact for its basis.
[*The Irrational Knot* (1905), Preface]

71. Though the Life Force supplies us with its own purpose, it has no other brains to work with than those it has painfully and imperfectly evolved in our heads.
[*The Irrational Knot* (1905), Preface]

72. Reminiscences make one feel so deliciously aged and sad.
[*The Irrational Knot* (1905), 14]

73. A man who has no office to go to – I don't care who he is – is a trial of which you can have no conception.
[*The Irrational Knot* (1905), 18]

74. With the single exception of Homer, there is no eminent writer, not even Sir Walter Scott, whom I can despise so entirely as I despise Shakespeare when I measure my mind against his ... it would positively be a relief to me to dig him up and throw stones at him.
[*Dramatic Opinions and Essays* (1906), 'Blaming the Bard']

75. An Irishman's heart is nothing but his imagination.
[*John Bull's Other Island* (1907), I]

76. My way of joking is to tell the truth. It's the funniest joke in the world.
[*John Bull's Other Island* (1907), II]

77. What really flatters a man is that you think him worth flattering.
[*John Bull's Other Island* (1907), IV]

78. There are only two qualities in the world: efficiency and inefficiency; and only two sorts of people: the efficient and the inefficient.
[*John Bull's Other Island* (1907), IV]

79. The greatest of our evils and the worst of our crimes is poverty.
[*Major Barbara* (1907), Preface]

80. The universal regard for money is the one hopeful fact in our civilization, the one sound spot in our social conscience. Money is the most important thing in the world. It represents health, strength, honour, generosity and beauty as conspicuously and undeniably as the want of it represents illness, weakness, disgrace, meanness and ugliness.
[*Major Barbara* (1907), Preface]

81. All men are anarchists with regard to laws which are against their consciences ... In London our worst anarchists are the magistrates, because many of them are so old and ignorant that when they are called upon to administer any law that is based on ideas or knowledge less than half a century old, they disagree with it, and ... naively set the example of violating it.
[*Major Barbara* (1907), Preface]

82. Cusins is a very nice fellow, certainly: nobody would ever guess that he was born in Australia.
[*Major Barbara* (1907), I]

83. Nobody can say a word against Greek: it stamps a man at once as an educated gentleman.
[*Major Barbara* (1907), I]

84. I am a Millionaire. That is my religion.
[*Major Barbara* (1907), II]

85. I am a sort of collector of religions; and the curious thing is that I find I can believe in them all.
[*Major Barbara* (1907), II]

86. I can't talk religion to a man with bodily hunger in his eyes.
[*Major Barbara* (1907), II]

87. Wot prawce selvytion nah?
[*Major Barbara* (1907), II]

88. Alcohol is a very necessary article ... It enables Parliament to do things at eleven at night that no sane person would do at eleven in the morning.
[*Major Barbara* (1907), II]

89. You daren't handle high explosives; but you're all ready to handle honesty and truth and justice and the whole duty of man, and kill one another at that game. What a country! What a world!
[*Major Barbara* (1907), III]

90. He knows nothing; and he thinks he knows everything. That points clearly to a political career.
[*Major Barbara* (1907), III]

91. *Cusins*: Do you call poverty a crime?
Undershaft: The worst of crimes. All the other crimes are virtues beside it: all the other dishonours are chivalry itself by comparison.
[*Major Barbara* (1907), IV]

92. There is at bottom only one genuinely scientific treatment for all diseases, and that is to stimulate the phagocytes.
[*The Doctor's Dilemma* (1908), I]

93. All professions are conspiracies against the laity.
[*The Doctor's Dilemma* (1908), I]

94. I believe in Michael Angelo, Velasquez, and Rembrandt; in the might of design, the mystery of colour, the redemption of all things by Beauty everlasting, and the message of Art that has made these hands blessed. Amen.
[*The Doctor's Dilemma* (1908), IV]

95. If you are going to have doctors you had better have doctors well off; just as if you are going to have a landlord you had better have a rich landlord. Taking all the round of professions and occupations, you will find that every man is the worse for being poor; and the doctor is a specially dangerous man when poor.
[*The Socialist Criticism of the Medical Profession* (1909)]

96. It's all that the young can do for the old, to shock them and keep them up to date.
[*Fanny's First Play* (1911), Induction]

97. The one point on which all women are in furious secret rebellion against the existing law is the saddling of the right to a child with the obligation to become the servant of a man.
[*Getting Married* (1911), Preface]

98. What God hath joined together no man ever shall put asunder: God will take care of that.
[*Getting Married* (1911)]

99. We possessed all the universe together; and you ask me to give you my scanty wages as well. I have given you the greatest of all things; and you ask me to give you little things. I gave you your own soul: you ask me for my body as a plaything. Was it not enough? Was it not enough?
[*Getting Married* (1911)]

100. Assassination is the extreme form of censorship.
[*The Shewing-Up of Blanco Posnet* (1911), Preface, 'The Rejected Statement']

101. Optimistic lies have such immense therapeutic value that a doctor who cannot tell them convincingly has mistaken his profession.
[*Misalliance* (1914), Preface, 'Parents and Children']

102. Heaven, as conventionally conceived, is a place so inane, so dull, so useless, so miserable, that nobody has ever ventured to describe a whole day in heaven, though plenty of people have described a day at the seaside.
[*Misalliance* (1914), Preface, 'Parents and Children']

103. The secret of being miserable is to have leisure to bother about whether you are happy or not.
[*Misalliance* (1914), Preface, 'Parents and Children']

104. Whether you think Jesus was God or not, you must admit that he was a first-rate political economist.
[*Androcles and the Lion* (1915), Preface, 'John']

105. The English have no respect for their language, and will not teach their children to speak it ... It is impossible for an Englishman to open his mouth without making some other Englishman hate or despise him.
[*Pygmalion* (1916), Preface]

106. He's a gentleman: look at his boots.
[*Pygmalion* (1916), I]

107. *Pickering*: Have you no morals, man?
Doolittle: Can't afford them, Governor.
[*Pygmalion* (1916), II]

108. I'm one of the undeserving poor: that's what I am. Think of what that means to a man. It means that he's up agen middle class morality all the time ... What is middle class morality? Just an excuse for never giving me anything.
[*Pygmalion* (1916), II]

109. My aunt died of influenza: so they said ... But it's my belief they done the old woman in.
[*Pygmalion* (1916), III]

110. Gin was mother's milk to her.
[*Pygmalion* (1916), III]

111. Walk! Not bloody likely. I am going in a taxi.
[*Pygmalion* (1916), III]

112. I have never sneered in my life. Sneering doesn't become either the human face or the human soul.
[*Pygmalion* (1916), V]

113. I am a woman of the world, Hector; and I can assure you that if you will only take the trouble always to do the perfectly correct thing, and to say the perfectly correct thing, you can do just what you like.
[*Heartbreak House* (1919), I]

114. Old men are dangerous: it doesn't matter to them what is going to happen to the world.
[*Heartbreak House* (1919), II]

115. All great truths begin as blasphemies.
[*Annajanska* (1919)]

116. If ever I utter an oath again may my soul be blasted to eternal damnation!
[*Saint Joan* (1924), Scene ii]

117. How can what an Englishman believes be heresy? It is a contradiction in terms.
[*Saint Joan* (1924), Scene iv]

118. Must then a Christ perish in torment in every age to save those that have no imagination?
[*Saint Joan* (1924), Epilogue]

119. O God that madest this beautiful earth, when will it be ready to receive Thy saints? How long, O Lord, how long?
[*Saint Joan* (1924), Epilogue]

120. One man that has a mind and knows it can always beat ten men who haven't and don't.
[*The Apple Cart* (1930), I]

121. What Englishman will give his mind to politics as long as he can afford to keep a motor car?
[*The Apple Cart* (1930), I]

122. I never resist temptation, because I have found that things that are bad for me do not tempt me.
[*The Apple Cart* (1930), Interlude]

123. The play is now virtually over; but the characters will discuss it at great length for two acts more. The exit doors are all in order. Goodnight.
[*Too True to be Good* (1932), I]

124. Parentage is a very important profession; but no test of fitness for it is ever imposed in the interest of the children.
[*Everybody's Political What's What* (1944), 9]

125. A government which robs Peter to pay Paul can always depend on the support of Paul.
[*Everybody's Political What's What* (1944), 30]

126. England and America are two countries separated by the same language.
[*Reader's Digest*, 1942]

127. I often quote myself. It adds spice to the conversation.
[*Reader's Digest*, 1943]

128. A dramatic critic ... leaves no turn unstoned.
[*The New York Times*, 1950]

129. It is the sexless novel that should be distinguished: the sex novel is now normal.
[In Henderson, *Table Talk of G.B.S.* (1925), 4]

130. The trouble, Mr Goldwyn, is that you are only interested in art and I am only interested in money.
[In Johnson, *The Great Goldwyn* (1937), 3]

131. [On youth]
Far too good to waste on children.
[Attr. in Copeland, *10,000 Jokes, Toasts, & Stories* (1939)]

132. [Responding to Oscar Wilde's advice to avoid fashion]
I am too much in advance of the time to be interested in fashion.
[In Winsten, *Jesting Apostle* (1956), 6]

133. Every busy man should go to bed for a year when he is forty.
[In Michael Holroyd, *Shaw*, II, (1989)]

134. If you want to bore an Irishman, play him an Irish melody, or introduce him to another Irishman.
[In Michael Holroyd, *Shaw*, II, (1989)]

135. I've been offered titles, but I think they get one into disreputable company.
[In Barrow, *Gossip*]

136. [On refusing an invitation to a vegetarian gala dinner]
The thought of two thousand people crunching celery at the same time horrified me.
[In Lieberman, *The Greatest Laughs of All Time*]

137. [On a bust sculpted of him by Rodin]
It's a funny thing about that bust. As time goes on it seems to get younger and younger.
[In Edwards, *More Things I Wish I'd Said*]

138. [Responding to a solitary boo amongst the mid-act applause at the first performance of *Arms and the Man* in 1894]
I quite agree with you, sir, but what can two do against so many?
[In Sir James Sutherland (ed.), *Oxford Book of Literary Anecdotes*]

139. A perpetual holiday is a good working definition of hell.
[Attr.]

Shaw-Lefevre, Charles, Viscount Eversley (1794–1888)
English lawyer and Liberal politician; Speaker 1839–57

1. [As a child on hearing Charles James Fox speak in the Commons]
What is that fat gentleman in such a passion about?
[In G.W.E. Russell, *Collections and Recollections* (1898), 11]

Shawcross, Sir Hartley (Lord Shawcross) (1902–)
English lawyer and Labour politician, born in Germany; chief British prosecutor at Nuremberg Trials

1. We are the masters at the moment, and not only at the moment, but for a very long time to come.
[Speech, House of Commons, 1946; usually quoted as 'We are the masters now']

Sheale, Richard (fl. 16th century)

1. For Witherington needs must I wail,
As one in doleful dumps;
For when his legs were smitten off,
He fought upon his stumps.
['Ballad of Chevy Chase', II]

Sheen, J. Fulton (1895–1979)
American Roman Catholic archbishop and religious writer

1. [Referring to his contract for a television appearance]
The big print giveth and the fine print taketh away.
[Attr.]

Sheldon, A.F. (1868–1935)
American business writer and teacher

1. He profits most who serves best.
[Motto of International Rotary]

Shelley, Mary Wollstonecraft (1797–1851)
English novelist; letter writer, diarist and editor of her husband, Percy Bysshe Shelley; daughter of Mary Wollstonecraft and William Godwin

1. Mrs Shelley was choosing a school for her son, and asked the advice of this lady, who gave for advice ... Just the sort of banality, you know, one does come out with: 'Oh, send him somewhere where they will teach him to think for himself!' ... Mrs Shelley answered: 'Teach him to think for himself? Oh, my God, teach him rather to think like other people!'
[In Matthew Arnold, *Essays in Criticism, Second Series* (1888), 'Shelley']

Shelley, Percy Bysshe (1792–1822)
English Romantic poet and dramatist, known for his lyrics; essayist and letter writer; husband of Mary Wollstonecraft Shelley

1. But what was he who taught them that the God
Of nature and benevolence hath given
A special sanction to the trade of blood?
[*Queen Mab* (1813), 2]

2. Many faint with toil,
That few may know the cares and woe of sloth.
[*Queen Mab* (1813), 3]

3. Yet every heart contains perfection's germ.
[*Queen Mab* (1813), 5]

4. But human pride
Is skilful to invent most serious names
To hide its ignorance.
[*Queen Mab* (1813), 7]

5. Earth groans beneath religion's iron age,
And priests dare babble of a God of peace,
Even whilst their hands are red with guiltless blood.
[*Queen Mab* (1813), 7]

6. That sweet bondage which is Freedom's self.
[*Queen Mab* (1813), 9]

7. The fountains of divine philosophy
Fled not his thirsting lips.
[*Alastor* (1815), 4]

8. Day after day a weary waste of hours.
[*Alastor* (1815), 7]

9. How wonderful is Death,
Death and his brother Sleep!
One pale as the yonder wan and hornèd moon,
With lips of lurid blue,
The other glowing like the vital morn,
When throned on ocean's wave
It breathes over the world:
Yet both so passing strange and wonderful!
['The Daemon of the World' (1816); also the opening lines of *Queen Mab*)]

10. I hated thee, fallen tyrant! I did groan
To think that a most unambitious slave,
Like thou, shouldst dance and revel on the grave
Of Liberty...

11. Virtue owns a more eternal foe
Than Force or Fraud: old Custom, legal Crime,
And bloody Faith the foulest birth of Time.
['Feelings of a Republican on the Fall of Bonaparte' (1816)]

12. The awful shadow of some unseen Power
Floats though unseen among us, – visiting
This various world with as inconstant wing
As summer winds that creep from flower to flower...

13. Spirit of Beauty, that dost consecrate
With thine own hues all thou dost shine upon
Of human thought or form...

14. While yet a boy I sought for ghosts, and sped
Through many a listening chamber, cave and ruin,
And starlight wood, with fearful steps pursuing
Hopes of high talk with the departed dead.
['Hymn to Intellectual Beauty' (1816)]

15. Some say that gleams of a remoter world
Visit the soul in sleep, – that death is slumber...

16. Power dwells apart in its tranquillity,
Remote, serene, and inaccessible.
['Mont Blanc' (1816)]

17. Nought may endure but Mutability.
['Mutability' (1816)]

18. In honoured poverty thy voice did weave
Songs consecrate to truth and liberty,–
Deserting these, thou leavest me to grieve,
Thus having been, that thou shouldst cease to be.
['To Wordsworth' (1816)]

19. My spirit like a charmèd bark doth swim
Upon the liquid waves of thy sweet singing.
['Fragment: To One Singing' (1817)]

20. A hater he came and sat by a ditch,
And he took an old cracked lute;
And he sang a song that was more of a screech
'Gainst a woman that was a brute.
['A Hate-Song' (1817)]

21. I met a traveller from an antique land
Who said: Two vast and trunkless legs of stone
Stand in the desert ... Near them, on the sand,
Half sunk, a shattered visage lies, whose frown,
And wrinkled lip, and sneer of cold command,
Tell that its sculptor well those passions read
Which yet survive, stamped on these lifeless things...

22. 'My name is Ozymandias, king of kings:
Look on my works, ye Mighty, and despair!'
Nothing beside remains. Round the decay
Of that colossal wreck, boundless and bare
The lone and level sands stretch far away.
['Ozymandias' (1817)]

23. I love all waste
And solitary places; where we taste
The pleasures of believing what we see
Is boundless, as we wish our souls to be...

24. Thou Paradise of exiles, Italy!...

25. Most wretched men
Are cradled into poetry by wrong,
They learn in suffering what they teach in song.
['Julian and Maddalo' (1818)]

26. Many a green isle needs must be
In the deep wide sea of Misery...

27. Beneath is spread like a green sea
The waveless plain of Lombardy,
Bounded by the vaporous air,
Islanded by cities fair;
Underneath Day's azure eyes
Ocean's nursling, Venice lies,
A peopled labyrinth of walls,
Amphitrite's destined halls...

28. Sun-girt City, thou hast been
Ocean's child, and then his queen;
Now is come a darker day,
And thou soon must be his prey.
['Lines written among the Euganean Hills' (1818)]

29. With hue like that when some great painter dips
His pencil in the gloom of earthquake and eclipse.
[*The Revolt of Islam* (1818), V, 23]

30. Lift not the painted veil which those who live
Call Life.
['Sonnet' (1818)]

31. I see the waves upon the shore,
Like light dissolved in star-showers, thrown...

32. Alas! I have nor hope nor health,
Nor peace within nor calm around,
Nor that content surpassing wealth
The sage in meditation found,
And walked with inward glory crowned.
['Stanzas Written in Dejection, near Naples' (1818)]

33. Chameleons feed on light and air:
Poets' food is love and fame...

34. Fame is love disguised.
['An Exhortation' (1819)]

35. I arise from dreams of thee
In the first sweet sleep of night.
When the winds are breathing low,
And the stars are shining bright...

36. Oh lift me from the grass!
I die! I faint! I fail!
Let thy love in kisses rain
On my lips and eyelids pale.
['The Indian Serenade' (1819)]

37. I met Murder on the way–
He had a mask like Castlereagh...

38. His big tears, for he wept well,
Turned to mill-stones as they fell.

And the little children, who
Round his feet played to and fro,
Thinking every tear a gem,
Had their brains knocked out by them...

39. Rise like Lions after slumber
In unvanquishable number–
Shake your chains to earth like dew
Which in sleep had fallen on you–
Ye are many – they are few.
['The Mask of Anarchy' (1819)]

40. O wild West Wind, thou breath of Autumn's being,
Thou, from whose unseen presence the leaves dead
Are driven, like ghosts from an enchanter fleeing,

Yellow, and black, and pale, and hectic red,
Pestilence-stricken multitudes: O thou,
Who chariotest to their dark wintry bed

The wingèd seeds, where they lie cold and low,
Each like a corpse within its grave, until
Thine azure sister of the Spring shall blow

Her clarion o'er the dreaming earth, and fill
(Driving sweet buds like flocks to feed in air)
With living hues and odours plain and hill:

Wild Spirit, which art moving everywhere;
Destroyer and preserver; hear, oh, hear!...

41. There are spread
On the blue surface of thine aëry surge,
Like the bright hair uplifted from the head

Of some fierce Maenad, even from the dim verge
Of the horizon to the zenith's height,
The locks of the approaching storm. Thou dirge

Of the dying year, to which this closing night
Will be the dome of a vast sepulchre...

42. Thou who didst waken from his summer dreams
The blue Mediterranean, where he lay,
Lulled by the coil of his crystàlline streams,

Beside a pumice isle in Baiae's bay,
And saw in sleep old palaces and towers
Quivering within the wave's intenser day,

All overgrown with azure moss and flowers
So sweet, the sense faints picturing them!...

43. Far below
The sea-blooms and the oozy woods which wear
The sapless foliage of the ocean, know

Thy voice, and suddenly grow gray with fear,
And tremble and despoil themselves: oh, hear!...

44. If I were a dead leaf thou mightest bear;
If I were a swift cloud to fly with thee;
A wave to pant beneath thy power, and share

The impulse of thy strength, only less free
Than thou, O uncontrollable! If even
I were as in my boyhood, and could be

The comrade of thy wanderings over Heaven.

45. Oh, lift me as a wave, a leaf, a cloud!
I fall upon the thorns of life! I bleed!

A heavy weight of hours has chained and bowed
One too like thee: tameless, and swift, and proud.

Make me thy lyre, even as the forest is:
What if my leaves are falling like its own!
The tumult of thy mighty harmonies

Will take from both a deep, autumnal tone,
Sweet though in sadness...

46. And, by the incantation of this verse,

Scatter, as from an unextinguished hearth
Ashes and sparks, my words among mankind!
Be through my lips to unawakened earth

The trumpet of a prophecy! O, Wind,
If Winter comes, can Spring be far behind?
['Ode to the West Wind' (1819)]

47. Its horror and its beauty are divine.
['On the Medusa of Leonardo da Vinci' (1819)]

48. Hell is a city much like London–
A populous and a smoky city.
['Peter Bell the Third' (1819), III, 1]

49. Teas,
Where small talk dies in agonies.
['Peter Bell the Third' (1819), III, 12]

50. But from the first 'twas Peter's drift
To be a kind of moral eunuch,
He touched the hem of Nature's shift,
Felt faint – and never dared uplift
The closest, all-concealing tunic.
['Peter Bell the Third' (1819) IV, 11]

51. Men of England, wherefore plough
For the lords who lay ye low?...

52. The seed ye sow, another reaps;
The wealth ye find, another keeps;
The robes ye weave, another wears;
The arms ye forge, another bears.

Sow seed, – but let no tyrant reap;
Find wealth, – let no imposter heap;
Weave robes, – let not the idle wear;
Forge arms, – in your defence to bear.
['Song to the Men of England' (1819)]

53. [Of George III]
An old, mad, blind, despised, and dying king.
['Sonnet: England in 1819' (1819)]

54. I wield the flail of the lashing hail,
And whiten the green plains under,
And then again I dissolve it in rain,
And laugh as I pass in thunder...

55. That orbèd maiden, with white fire laden,
Whom mortals call the Moon,
Glides glimmering o'er my fleece-like floor,
By the midnight breezes strewn;
And wherever the beat of her unseen feet,
Which only the angels hear,
May have broken the woof of my tent's thin roof,
The stars peep behind her and peer;
And I laugh to see them whirl and flee,
Like a swarm of golden bees,
When I widen the rent in my wind-built tent,
Till the calm rivers, lakes, and seas,
Like strips of the sky fallen through me on high,
Are each paved with the moon and these...

56. I am the daughter of Earth and Water,
And the nursling of the Sky;
I pass through the pores of the ocean and shores;
I change, but I cannot die.
For after the rain when with never a stain
The pavilion of Heaven is bare,
And the winds and sunbeams with their convex gleams
Build up the blue dome of air,
I silently laugh at my own cenotaph,
And out of the caverns of rain,
Like a child from the womb, like a ghost from the tomb,
I arise and unbuild it again.
['The Cloud' (1820)]

57. Good-night? ah! no; the hour is ill
Which severs those it should unite;
Let us remain together still,
Then it will be good night.
['Good Night' (1820)]

58. I pursued a maiden and clasped a reed.
Gods and men, we are all deluded thus!
It breaks in our bosom and then we bleed.
['Hymn of Pan' (1820)]

59. The self-impelling steam-wheels of the mind.
['Letter to Maria Gisborne' (1820), line 108]

60. We watched the ocean and the sky together,
Under the roof of blue Italian weather.
['Letter to Maria Gisborne' (1820), line 146]

61. London, that great sea, whose ebb and flow
At once is deaf and loud, and on the shore
Vomits its wrecks, and still howls on for more.
['Letter to Maria Gisborne' (1820), line 193]

62. You will see Coleridge – he who sits obscure
In the exceeding lustre and the pure
Intense irradiation of a mind,
Which, with its own internal lightning blind,
Flags wearily through darkness and despair–
A cloud-encircled meteor of the air,
A hooded eagle among blinking owls.–
You will see Hunt – one of those happy souls
Which are the salt of the earth, and without whom
This world would smell like what it is – a tomb.
['Letter to Maria Gisborne' (1820), line 202]

63. Have you not heard
When a man marries, dies, or turns Hindoo,
His best friends hear no more of him?
['Letter to Maria Gisborne' (1820), line 235]

64. [Of T.L. Peacock]
His fine wit
Makes such a wound, the knife is lost in it.
['Letter to Maria Gisborne' (1820), line 240]

65. Alas, good friend, what profit can you see
In hating such a hateless thing as me?
['Lines to a Reviewer' (1820)]

66. Ere Babylon was dust,
The Magus Zoroaster, my dead child,
Met his own image walking in the garden.
That apparition, sole of men, he saw.
[*Prometheus Unbound* (1820), I, line 191]

67. Cruel he looks, but calm and strong,
Like one who does, not suffers wrong.
[*Prometheus Unbound* (1820), I, line 238]

68. It doth repent me: words are quick and vain;
Grief for awhile is blind, and so was mine.
I wish no living thing to suffer pain.
[*Prometheus Unbound* (1820), I, line 303]

69. Kingly conclaves stern and cold,
Where blood with guilt is bought and sold.
[*Prometheus Unbound* (1820), I, line 530]

70. The heaven around, the earth below
Was peopled with thick shapes of human death,
All horrible, and wrought by human hands,
And some appeared the work of human hearts,
For men were slowly killed by frowns and smiles.
[*Prometheus Unbound* (1820), I, line 587]

71. Peace is in the grave.
The grave hides all things beautiful and good:
I am a God and cannot find it there.
[*Prometheus Unbound* (1820), I, line 638]

72. From the dust of creeds outworn.
[*Prometheus Unbound* (1820), I, line 697]

73. On a poet's lips I slept
Dreaming like a love-adept
In the sound his breathing kept.
[*Prometheus Unbound* (1820), I, line 737]

74. He will watch from dawn to gloom
The lake-reflected sun illume
The yellow bees in the ivy-bloom,
Nor heed, nor see, what things they be;
But from these create he can
Forms more real than living man,
Nurslings of immortality!
[*Prometheus Unbound* (1820), I, line 743]

75. To know nor faith, nor love, nor law; to be
Omnipotent but friendless is to reign.
[*Prometheus Unbound* (1820), II.iv, line 47]

76. He gave man speech, and speech created thought,
Which is the measure of the universe;
And Science struck the thrones of earth and heaven.
[*Prometheus Unbound* (1820), II.iv, line 72]

77. All spirits are enslaved which serve things evil.
[*Prometheus Unbound* (1820), II.iv, line 110]

78. Fate, Time, Occasion, Chance, and Change? To these
All things are subject but eternal Love.
[*Prometheus Unbound* (1820), II.iv, line 119]

79. All love is sweet,
Given or returned. Common as light is love,
And its familiar voice wearies not ever.
[*Prometheus Unbound* (1820), II.v, line 39]

80. My soul is an enchanted boat,
Which, like a sleeping swan, doth float
Upon the silver waves of thy sweet singing.
[*Prometheus Unbound* (1820), II.v, line 72]

81. We have passed Age's icy caves,
And Manhood's dark and tossing waves,
And Youth's smooth ocean, smiling to betray:
Beyond the glassy gulfs we flee
Of shadow-peopled Infancy,
Through Death and Birth, to a diviner day.
[*Prometheus Unbound* (1820), II.v, line 98]

82. The soul of man, like unextinguished fire,
Yet burns towards heaven with fierce reproach.
[*Prometheus Unbound* (1820), III.i, line 5]

83. Death is the veil which those who live call life:
They sleep, and it is lifted.
[*Prometheus Unbound* (1820), III.iii, line 113]

84. The loathsome mask has fallen, the man remains
Sceptreless, free, uncircumscribed, but man
Equal, unclassed, tribeless, and nationless,
Exempt from awe, worship, degree, the king
Over himself; just, gentle, wise: but man
Passionless? – no, yet free from guilt or pain,
Which were, for his will made or suffered them,
Nor yet exempt, though ruling them like slaves,
From chance, and death, and mutability,
The clogs of that which else might oversoar
The loftiest star of unascended heaven,
Pinnacled dim in the intense inane.
[*Prometheus Unbound* (1820), III.iv, line 193]

85. Familiar acts are beautiful through love.
[*Prometheus Unbound* (1820), IV, line 403]

86. A traveller from the cradle to the grave
Through the dim night of this immortal day.
[*Prometheus Unbound* (1820), IV, line 551]

87. To suffer woes which Hope thinks infinite;
To forgive wrongs darker than death or night;
To defy Power, which seems omnipotent;
To love, and bear; to hope till Hope creates
From its own wreck the thing it contemplates;
Neither to change, nor falter, nor repent;
This, like thy glory, Titan, is to be
Good, great and joyous, beautiful and free;
This is alone Life, Joy, Empire and Victory.
[*Prometheus Unbound* (1820), IV, line 570]

88. I dreamed that, as I wandered by the way,
Bare Winter suddenly was changed to Spring,
And gentle odours led my steps astray,
Mixed with a sound of water's murmuring
Along a shelving bank of turf, which lay
Under a copse, and hardly dared to fling
Its green arms round the bosom of the stream,
But kissed it and then fled, as thou mightest in dream...

89. There grew pied wind-flowers and violets,
Daisies, those pearled Arcturi of the earth,
The constellated flower that never sets...

90. And in the warm hedge grew lush eglantine,
Green cowbind and the moonlight-coloured may,
And cherry-blossoms, and white cups, whose wine
Was the bright dew, yet drained not by the day;
And wild roses, and ivy serpentine,
With its dark buds and leaves, wandering astray;
And flowers azure, black, and streaked with gold,
Fairer than any wakened eyes behold...

91. And nearer to the river's trembling edge
There grew broad flag-flowers, purple pranked with white,
And starry river buds among the sedge,
And floating water-lilies, broad and bright.
['The Question' (1820)]

92. A Sensitive Plant in a garden grew...

93. And the rose like a nymph to the bath addressed,
Which unveiled the depth of her glowing breast,
Till, fold after fold, to the fainting air
The soul of her beauty and love lay bare.
['The Sensitive Plant' (1820), I]

94. It is a modest creed, and yet
Pleasant if one considers it,
To own that death itself must be,
Like all the rest, a mockery.
['The Sensitive Plant' (1820), III]

95. Hail to thee, blithe Spirit!
Bird thou never wert,
That from Heaven, or near it,
Pourest thy full heart
In profuse strains of unpremeditated art...

96. And singing still dost soar, and soaring ever singest...

97. Like an unbodied joy whose race is just begun...

98. Like a Poet hidden
In the light of thought,
Singing hymns unbidden,
Till the world is wrought
To sympathy with hopes and fears it heeded not...

99. With thy clear keen joyance
Languor cannot be:
Shadow of annoyance
Never came near thee:
Thou lovest – but ne'er knew love's sad satiety...

100. We look before and after,
And pine for what is not:
Our sincerest laughter
With some pain is fraught;
Our sweetest songs are those that tell of saddest thought...

101. Better than all measures
Of delightful sound,
Better than all treasures
That in books are found,
Thy skill to poet were, thou scorner of the ground!

Teach me half the gladness
That thy brain must know,
Such harmonious madness
From my lips would flow
The world should listen then – as I am listening now.
['To a Skylark' (1820)]

102. Art thou pale for weariness
Of climbing heaven and gazing on the earth,
Wandering companionless
Among the stars that have a different birth, –
And ever changing, like a joyless eye
That finds no object worth its constancy?
['To the Moon' (1820)]

103. And like a dying lady, lean and pale,
Who totters forth, wrapped in a gauzy veil.
['The Waning Moon' (1820)]

104. For she was beautiful – her beauty made
The bright world dim, and everything beside
Seemed like the fleeting image of a shade...

105. The rapid, blind
And fleeting generations of mankind.
['The Witch of Atlas' (1820)]

106. The cemetery is an open space among the ruins, covered in winter with violets and daisies. It might make one in love with death, to think that one should be buried in so sweet a place.
[*Adonais* (1821), Preface]

107. I weep for Adonais – he is dead!
O, weep for Adonais! though our tears
Thaw not the frost which binds so dear a head!
[*Adonais* (1821), 1]

108. Most musical of mourners, weep again!
Lament anew, Urania! – He died,
Who was the Sire of an immortal strain,
Blind, old and lonely.
[*Adonais* (1821), 4]

109. To that high Capital, where kingly Death
Keeps his pale court in beauty and decay,
He came.
[*Adonais* (1821), 7]

110. The quick Dreams,
The passion-wingèd Ministers of thought.
[*Adonais* (1821), 9]

111. Lost Angel of a ruined Paradise!
She knew not 'twas her own; as with no stain
She faded, like a cloud which had outwept its rain.
[*Adonais* (1821), 10]

112. Desires and Adorations,
Wingèd Persuasions and veiled Destinies,
Splendours, and Glooms, and glimmering Incarnations
Of hopes and fears, and twilight Phantasies;
And Sorrow, with her family of Sighs,
And Pleasure, blind with tears, led by the gleam
Of her own dying smile instead of eyes,
Came in slow pomp.
[*Adonais* (1821), 13]

113. Ah, woe is me! Winter is come and gone,
But grief returns with the revolving year.
[*Adonais* (1821), 18]

114. The great morning of the world when first
God dawned on Chaos.
[*Adonais* (1821), 19]

115. Alas! that all we loved of him should be,
But for our grief, as if it had not been,
And grief itself be mortal! Woe is me!
Whence are we, and why are we? Of what scene
The actors or spectators?
[*Adonais* (1821), 21]

116. Why didst thou leave the trodden paths of men
Too soon, and with weak hands though mighty heart
Dare the unpastured dragon in his den?
[*Adonais* (1821), 27]

117. The herded wolves, bold only to pursue;
The obscene ravens, clamorous o'er the dead.
[*Adonais* (1821), 28]

118. A pard-like Spirit, beautiful and swift–
A Love in desolation masked; – a Power
Girt round with weakness; – it can scarce uplift
The weight of the superincumbent hour;
It is a dying lamp, a falling shower,
A breaking billow; – even whilst we speak
Is it not broken?
[*Adonais* (1821), 32]

119. Our Adonais has drunk poison – oh!
What deaf and viperous murderer could crown
Life's early cup with such a draught of woe?
[*Adonais* (1821), 36]

120. He wakes or sleeps with the enduring dead;
Thou canst not soar where he is sitting now. –
Dust to the dust! but the pure spirit shall flow
Back to the burning fountain whence it came,
A portion of the Eternal.
[*Adonais* (1821), 38]

121. He hath awakened from the dream of life–
'Tis we, who lost in stormy visions, keep
With phantoms an unprofitable strife,
And in mad trance, strike with our spirit's knife
Invulnerable nothings.
[*Adonais* (1821), 39]

122. He has outsoared the shadow of our night;
Envy and calumny and hate and pain,
And that unrest which men miscall delight,
Can touch him not and torture not again;
From the contagion of the world's slow stain
He is secure, and now can never mourn
A heart grown cold, a head grown gray in vain.
[*Adonais* (1821), 40]

123. He lives, he wakes– 'tis Death is dead, not he.
[*Adonais* (1821), 41]

124. He is made one with Nature: there is heard
His voice in all her music, from the moan
Of thunder, to the song of night's sweet bird.
[*Adonais* (1821), 42]

125. He is a portion of the loveliness
Which once he made more lovely.
[*Adonais* (1821), 43]

126. What Adonais is, why fear we to become?
[*Adonais* (1821), 51]

127. The One remains, the many change and pass;
Heaven's light forever shines, Earth's shadows fly;
Life, like a dome of many-coloured glass,

Stains the white radiance of Eternity,
Until Death tramples it to fragments.
[*Adonais* (1821), 52]

128. The soul of Adonais, like a star,
Beacons from the abode where the Eternal are.
[*Adonais* (1821), 55, last words]

129. My last delight! tell them that they are dull,
And bid them own that thou art beautiful.
['Epipsychidion' (1821), Advertisement]

130. We – are we not formed, as notes of music are,
For one another, though dissimilar?
['Epipsychidion' (1821), line 142]

131. I never was attached to that great sect,
Whose doctrine is, that each one should select
Out of the crowd a mistress or a friend,
And all the rest, though fair and wise, commend
To cold oblivion, though it is in the code
Of modern morals, and the beaten road
Which those poor slaves with weary footsteps tread,
Who travel to their home among the dead
By the broad highway of the world, and so
With one chained friend, perhaps a jealous foe,
The dreariest and the longest journey go.
['Epipsychidion' (1821), line 149]

132. The breath of her false mouth was like faint flowers,
Her touch was as electric poison.
['Epipsychidion' (1821), line 258]

133. A ship is floating in the harbour now,
A wind is hovering o'er the mountain's brow;
There is a path on the sea's azure floor,
No keel has ever ploughed that path before.
['Epipsychidion' (1821), line 408]

134. An isle under Ionian skies,
Beautiful as a wreck of Paradise.
['Epipsychidion' (1821), line 422]

135. One Heaven, one Hell, one immortality
And one annihilation.
['Epipsychidion' (1821), line 586]

136. I pant, I sink, I tremble, I expire!
['Epipsychidion' (1821), line 591]

137. O world! O life! O time!
On whose last steps I climb,
Trembling at that where I had stood before;
When will return the glory of your prime?
No more – Oh, never more!
['A Lament' (1821)]

138. The flower that smiles to-day
To-morrow dies.
['Mutability' (1821)]

139. Rarely, rarely, comest thou,
Spirit of Delight!...

140. I love all that thou lovest,
Spirit of Delight!
The fresh Earth in new leaves dressed,
And the starry night;
Autumn evening, and the morn
When the golden mists are born...

141. I love snow, and all the forms
Of the radiant frost...

142. I love tranquil solitude,
And such society
As is quiet, wise, and good;
Between thee and me
What difference? but thou dost possess
The things I seek, not love them less.
['Song: Rarely, rarely, Comest Thou' (1821)]

143. The worm beneath the sod
May lift itself in homage of the God.
['Sonnet to Byron' (1821)]

144. Music, when soft voices die,
Vibrates in the memory–
Odours, when sweet violets sicken,
Live within the sense they quicken.

Rose leaves, when the rose is dead,
Are heaped for the beloved's bed;
And so thy thoughts, when thou art gone,
Love itself shall slumber on.
['To–: Music, When Soft Voices Die' (1821)]

145. The desire of the moth for the star,
Of the night for the morrow,
The devotion to something afar
From the sphere of our sorrow.
['To–: One Word is too often Profaned' (1821)]

146. Swiftly walk o'er the western wave,
Spirit of Night!
Out of the misty eastern cave,
Where, all the long and lone daylight,
Thou wovest dreams of joy and fear,
Which make thee terrible and dear,
Swift be thy flight!...

147. Blind with thine hair the eyes of Day;
Kiss her until she be wearied out,
Then wander o'er city, and sea, and land,
Touching all with thine opiate wand–
Come, long-sought!...

148. Thy brother Death came, and cried,
Wouldst thou me?
Thy sweet child Sleep, the filmy-eyed,
Murmured like a noontide bee,
Shall I nestle near thy side?...

149. Death will come when thou art dead,
Soon, too soon–
Sleep will come when thou art fled;
Of neither would I ask the boon
I ask of thee, beloved Night–
Swift be thine approaching flight,
Come soon, soon!
['To Night' (1821)]

150. England, farewell! thou, who hast been my cradle,
Shalt never be my dungeon or my grave!
[*Charles the First* (1822), Scene iv]

151. A widow bird sate mourning for her love
Upon a wintry bough;
The frozen wind crept on above,
The freezing stream below.

There was no leaf upon the forest bare,
No flower upon the ground,
And little motion in the air
Except the mill-wheel's sound.
[*Charles the First* (1822), Scene v, Fool's song]

152. Youth will stand foremost ever.
['Scenes from the Faust of Goethe' (1822), Scene ii]

153. Let there be light! said Liberty,
And like sunrise from the sea,
Athens arose!
[*Hellas* (1822), line 682]

154. The world's great age begins anew,
The golden years return,
The earth doth like a snake renew
Her winter weeds outworn:
Heaven smiles, and faiths and empires gleam,
Like wrecks of a dissolving dream.
[*Hellas* (1822), line 1060]

155. A loftier Argo cleaves the main,
Fraught with a later prize;
Another Orpheus sings again,
And loves, and weeps, and dies.
A new Ulysses leaves once more
Calypso for his native shore.
[*Hellas* (1822), line 1072]

156. Oh, write no more the tale of Troy.
[*Hellas* (1822), line 1078]

157. Although a subtler Sphinx renew
Riddles of death Thebes never knew.
[*Hellas* (1822), line 1082]

158. Another Athens shall arise,
And to remoter time
Bequeath, like sunset to the skies,
The splendour of its prime;
And leave, if nought so bright may live,
All earth can take or Heaven can give.
[*Hellas* (1822), line 1084]

159. O cease! must hate and death return?
Cease! must men kill and die?
Cease! drain not to its dregs the urn
Of bitter prophecy.
The world is weary of the past,
Oh, might it die or rest at last!
[*Hellas* (1822), line 1096]

160. When the lamp is shattered
The light in the dust lies dead–
When the cloud is scattered
The rainbow's glory is shed.
When the lute is broken,
Sweet tones are remembered not;
When the lips have spoken,
Loved accents are soon forgot...

161. When hearts have once mingled
Love first leaves the well-built nest;
The weak one is singled
To endure what it once possessed.
O Love! who bewailest
The frailty of things here,
Why choose you the frailest
For your cradle, your home, and your bier?
['Lines: When the Lamp is Shattered' (1822)]

162. I am gone into the fields
To take what this sweet hour yields;–
Reflection, you may come to-morrow,
Sit by the fireside with Sorrow.–
You with the unpaid bill, Despair,–
You, tiresome verse-reciter, Care,–
I will pay you in the grave,–
Death will listen to your stave.
['To Jane: The Invitation' (1822)]

163. Less oft is peace in Shelley's mind,
Than calm in waters, seen.
['To Jane: The Recollection' (1822)]

164. A single word even may be a spark of inextinguishable thought.
[*A Defence of Poetry* (1821)]

165. [Poetry] lifts the veil from the hidden beauty of the world, and makes familiar objects be as if they were not familiar.
[*A Defence of Poetry* (1821)]

166. Poetry is the record of the happiest and best moments of the happiest and best minds.
[*A Defence of Poetry* (1821)]

167. The rich have become richer, and the poor have become poorer; and the vessel of the state is driven between the Scylla and Charybdis of anarchy and despotism.
[*A Defence of Poetry* (1821)]

168. Poets are ... the trumpets which sing to battle and feel not what they inspire ... Poets are the unacknowledged legislators of the world.
[*A Defence of Poetry* (1821)]

169. When it was a matter of wonder how Keats, who was ignorant of Greek, could have written his 'Hyperion', Shelley, whom envy never touched, gave as a reason, 'Because he was a Greek'.
[In W.S. Landor, *Imaginary Conversations. Southey and Landor*]

Shenstone, William (1714–1763)
English poet, essayist and letter writer

1. Whoe'er has travell'd life's dull round,
Where'er his stages may have been,
May sigh to think he still has found
The warmest welcome, at an inn.
['At an Inn at Henley' (1758)]

2. Beneath a church-yard yew
Decay'd and worn with age,
At dusk of eve methought I spy'd
Poor Slender's ghost, that whimpering cry'd
O sweet, O sweet Anne Page!
['Slender's Ghost']

3. Laws are generally found to be nets of such a texture, as the little creep through, the great break through, and the middle-sized are alone entangled in.
[*Works in Verse and Prose* (1764), 'On Politics'. Cf. Solon: 1 and Swift: 10]

4. People in high or in distinguished life ought to have a greater circumspection in regard to their most trivial actions. For instance, I saw Mr Pope ... to the best of my memory, he was picking his nose.
[*The Selected Works in Verse and Prose of William Shenstone* (1770), 'On Writing and Books']

Sheridan, Philip Henry (1831–1888)
American Union general in the Civil War

1. The only good Indian is a dead Indian.
[Attr.]

Sheridan, Richard Brinsley (1751–1816)
Irish comic dramatist and theatre manager; politician and orator

1. I was struck all of a heap.
[*The Duenna* (1775), II.ii]

2. Conscience has no more to do with gallantry than it has with politics.
[*The Duenna* (1775), II.iv]

3. I don't know any business you have to think at all – thought does not become a young woman.
[*The Rivals* (1775), I.ii]

4. Illiterate him, I say, quite from your memory.
[*The Rivals* (1775), I.ii]

5. 'Tis safest in matrimony to begin with a little aversion.
[*The Rivals* (1775), I.ii]

6. Madam, a circulating library in a town is an ever-green tree of diabolical knowledge! – It blossoms through the year! – And depend on it, Mrs Malaprop, that they who are so fond of handling the leaves, will long for the fruit at last.
[*The Rivals* (1775), I.ii]

7. A progeny of learning.
[*The Rivals* (1775), I.ii]

8. He is the very pine-apple of politeness!
[*The Rivals* (1775), III.iii]

9. It gives me the hydrostatics to such a degree.
[*The Rivals* (1775), III.iii]

10. An aspersion upon my parts of speech! ... If I reprehend anything in this world, it is the use of my oracular tongue, and a nice derangement of epitaphs!
[*The Rivals* (1775), III.iii]

11. She's as headstrong as an allegory on the banks of the Nile.
[*The Rivals* (1775), III.iii]

12. *Acres*: Do, Sir Lucius, let me begin with a damme.
Sir Lucius O'Trigger: Pho! pho! do the thing *decently* and like a Christian. Begin now, – 'Sir'–
Acres: That's too civil by half.
[*The Rivals* (1775), III.iv]

13. No caparisons, Miss, if you please! – Caparisons don't become a young woman.
[*The Rivals* (1775), IV.ii]

14. The quarrel is a very pretty quarrel as it stands – we should only spoil it by trying to explain it.
[*The Rivals* (1775), IV.iii]

15. My valour is certainly going! – it is sneaking off! – I feel it oozing out as it were at the palms of my hands!
[*The Rivals* (1775), V.iii]

16. I own the soft impeachment.
[*The Rivals* (1775), V.iii]

17. Through all the drama – whether damned or not–
Love gilds the scene, and women guide the plot.
[*The Rivals* (1775), Epilogue]

18. Tale-bearers are as bad as the tale-makers.
[*The School for Scandal* (1777), I.i]

19. You shall see them on a beautiful quarto page, where a neat rivulet of text shall murmur through a meadow of margin.
[*The School for Scandal* (1777), I.i]

20. You had no taste when you married me.
[*The School for Scandal* (1777), II.i]

21. *Mrs Candour*: I'll swear her colour is natural – I have seen it come and go–
Lady Teazle: I dare swear you have ma'am – it goes of a night, and comes again in the morning.
[*The School for Scandal* (1777), II.ii]

22. Here is the whole set! a character dead at every word.
[*The School for Scandal* (1777), II.ii]

23. I'm called away by particular business. But I leave my character behind me.
[*The School for Scandal* (1777), II.ii]

24. Here's to the maiden of bashful fifteen;
Here's to the widow of fifty;
Here's to the flaunting, extravagant quean;
And here's to the housewife that's thrifty.
Let the toast pass–
Drink to the lass–
I'll warrant she'll prove an excuse for the glass!
[*The School for Scandal* (1777), III.iii]

25. Here's to the charmer whose dimples we prize!
Now to the maid who has none, sir;
Here's to the girl with the pair of blue eyes,
And here's to the nymph with but one, sir!
[*The School for Scandal* (1777), III.iii]

26. An unforgiving eye, and a damned disinheriting countenance!
[*The School for Scandal* (1777), IV.i]

27. *Rowley*: I believe there is no sentiment he has more faith in than that 'charity begins at home'.
Sir Oliver Surface: And his, I presume, is of that domestic sort which never stirs abroad at all.
[*The School for Scandal* (1777), V.i. Cf. Thomas Browne: 36]

28. There is no trusting appearances.
[*The School for Scandal* (1777), V.ii]

29. The newspapers! Sir, they are the most villainous – licentious – abominable – infernal – Not that I ever read them – No – I make it a rule never to look into a newspaper.
[*The Critic* (1779), I.i]

30. If it is abuse, – why one is always sure to hear of it from one damned good-natured friend or another!
[*The Critic* (1779), I.i]

31. Egad, I think the interpreter is the hardest to be understood of the two!
[*The Critic* (1779), I.ii]

32. Yes, sir, puffing is of various sorts; the principal are, the puff direct, the puff preliminary, the puff collateral, the puff collusive, and the puff oblique, or puff by implication.
[*The Critic* (1779), I.ii]

33. No scandal about Queen *Elizabeth*, I hope?
[*The Critic* (1779), II.i]

34. I open with a clock striking, to beget an awful attention in the audience: it also marks the time, which is four o'clock in the morning, and saves a description of the rising sun, and a great deal about gilding the eastern hemisphere.
[*The Critic* (1779), II.ii]

35. The Spanish fleet thou *canst* not see – because
– It is not yet in sight!
[*The Critic* (1779), II.ii]

36. All that can be said is, that two people happened to hit on the same thought – and Shakespeare made use of it first, that's all.
[*The Critic* (1779), III.i]

37. *Burleigh comes forward, shakes his head, and exit.*
Sneer: He is very perfect indeed. Now pray, what did he mean by that?
Puff: Why, by that shake of the head, he gave you to understand that even though they had more justice in their cause and wisdom in their measures, yet, if there was not a greater spirit shown on the part of the people, the country would at last fall a sacrifice to the hostile ambition of the Spanish monarchy.
Sneer: The devil! – did he mean all that by shaking his head?
Puff: Every word of it. If he shook his head as I taught him.
[*The Critic* (1779), III.i]

38. O Lord, sir, when a heroine goes mad she always goes into white satin.
[*The Critic* (1779), III.i]

39. An oyster may be crossed in love!
[*The Critic* (1779), III.i]

40. You write with ease, to show your breeding;
But easy writing's vile hard reading.
['Clio's Protest' (1771)]

41. [At a coffee house, during the fire which destroyed his Drury Lane theatre, 1809]
A man may surely be allowed to take a glass of wine by his own fireside.
[In Moore, *Memoirs of the Life of Sheridan* (1825), 20]

42. [Reply to Mr Dundas]
The Right Honourable Gentleman is indebted to his memory for his jests, and to his imagination for his facts.
[Speech, House of Commons, in Moore, *Memoirs of the Life of Sheridan* (1825), 21]

43. [Handing one of his creditors an IOU]
Thank God, that's settled.
[In C. Shriner, *Wit, Wisdom, and Foibles of the Great* (1918)]

44. [On being warned that his drinking would destroy the coat of his stomach]
Well, then, my stomach must just digest in its waistcoat.
[In L. Harris, *The Fine Art of Political Wit* (1965)]

45. [On a notice fixed to his door when he was a Secretary to the Treasury]
No applications can be received here on Sundays, nor any business done during the remainder of the week.
[Attr. in Morwood, *The Life and Works of Richard Brinsley Sheridan* (1985), 6]

46. [After being refused a loan of £25 from a friend who asked him to repay the £500 he had already borrowed]
My dear fellow, be reasonable; the sum you ask me for is a very considerable one, whereas I only ask you for twenty-five pounds.
[Attr.]

47. [To his tailor when he requested payment of a debt, or at least the interest on it]
It is not my interest to pay the principal, nor my principle to pay the interest.
[Attr.]

48. [On being asked to apologize for calling a fellow MP a liar]
Mr Speaker, I said the honourable member was a liar it is true and I am sorry for it. The honourable member may place the punctuation where he pleases.
[Attr.]

Sheridan, Tom (1775–1817)
English colonial administrator and poet; son of Richard Brinsley Sheridan, father of Caroline Norton

1. [To his father, after learning that he was to be cut out of his will with a shilling]
I'm sorry to hear that, sir, you don't happen to have the shilling about you now, do you?
[In L. Harris, *The Fine Art of Political Wit* (1965)]

Sherman, William Tecumseh (1820–1891)
American Union general in the Civil War; army Chief of Staff 1869–83

1. There is many a boy here today who looks on war as all glory, but, boys, it is all hell.
[Speech, Columbus, Ohio, 1880]

2. I will not accept if nominated, and will not serve if elected.
[Telegram refusing Presidential nomination, 1884]

3. I would not for a million dollars subject myself and family to the ordeal of a political canvass and afterwards to a four years' service in the White House.
[Letter to his brother, 1884]

Shinran (1173–1263)
Japanese reformer of Buddhism

1. Even good people achieve their rebirth in the Land of Perfect Bliss; then how much more so should the case be with evil persons!
[*Tannishó* (c. 1290)]

Shinwell, Emanuel (1884–1986)
British Labour politician and Cabinet Minister

1. We know that you, the organized workers of the country, are our friends ... As for the rest, they do not matter a tinker's curse.
[Speech at the Electrical Trades Union Conference, Margate, 1947]

Shirley, James (1596–1666)
English dramatic poet; author of tragedies, comedies and masques

1. How little room
Do we take up in death that living know
No bounds!
[*The Wedding* (1629), IV.iv]

2. I presume you're mortal, and may err.
[*The Lady of Pleasure* (1637), II.ii]

3. The glories of our blood and state
Are shadows, not substantial things;
There is no armour against fate;
Death lays his icy hand on kings:
Sceptre and crown
Must tumble down,
And in the dust be equal made
With the poor crooked scythe and spade.
[*The Contention of Ajax and Ulysses* (1659), I.iii]

4. Only the actions of the just
Smell sweet, and blossom in their dust.
[*The Contention of Ajax and Ulysses* (1659), I.iii]

Shorthouse, J.H. (1834–1903)
English novelist

1. 'The Church of England,' I said, seeing that Mr Inglesant paused, 'is no doubt a compromise.'
[*John Inglesant* (1880), 40]

Shortis, Gregory Brien (1945–)

1. I'm observing the golden mean and living frugally
In the country without plumbing and only
A smoky, open fire, and things would be perfect
If my wife wasn't an intellectual.
['To Malcolm from an Unemployed Youth']

Shuter, Edward (1728–1776)
English comic actor and wit

1. [Explaining why he did not mend the holes in his stocking]
A hole is the accident of a day, but a darn is premeditated poverty.
[*Dictionary of National Biography* (1897), III]

Sibelius, Jean (1865–1957)
Finnish composer

1. Pay no attention to what the critics say. No statue has ever been put up to a critic.
[Attr.]

Sickert, Walter (1860–1942)
British Impressionist painter and writer on art, born in Germany; known for his urban subject matter

1. Nothing knits man to man ... like the frequent passage from hand to hand of cash.
[*New Age*, 1910, 'The Language of Art']

2. [To Denton Welch]
Come again when you can't stay so long.
[In D. Welch, 'Sickert at St Peter's', *Horizon*, 1942]

Siddique, Dr Kalim
Spokesman for British Muslims

1. We cannot live in this country together with *The Satanic Verses* and Salman Rushdie. They will have to go.
[*The Independent*, 1989]

Sidney, Algernon (1622–1683)
English politician and republican; executed for treason

1. Liars ought to have good memories.
[*Discourses Concerning Government* (1698), 2, 15]

Sidney, Sir Philip (1554–1586)
English poet, critic, soldier, courtier and diplomat

1. Leave me, O Love, which reaches but to dust,
And thou, my mind, aspire to higher things;
Grow rich in that which never taketh rust;
What ever fades, but fading pleasure brings.
[*Certain Sonnets* (1577–1581), 'The Farewell to Desire']

2. Shallow brookes murmur moste, Depe sylent slyde away.
[*Old Arcadia* (1581), 'The Firste Eclogues']

3. My true Love hathe my harte and I have his,
By just exchaunge one for the other given,
I holde his deare, and myne hee can not misse,
There never was a better Bargayne driven.
[*Old Arcadia* (1581), 3]

4. Byting my tongue and penne, beating my selfe for spite:
'Foole,' saide My muse to mee, 'looke in thy heart and write'.
[*Astrophel and Stella* (1591), 1]

5. With how sad steps O Moone thou clim'st the skyes,
How silently, and with how meane a face,
What may it be, that even in heavenly place,
That busie Archer his sharpe Arrowes tryes?
[*Astrophel and Stella* (1591), 31]

6. Come, Sleepe, O Sleepe, the certaine knot of peace,
The bathing place of wits, the balm of woe,
The poore man's wealth, the prysoner's release,
The indifferent Judge betweene the hie and lowe.
[*Astrophel and Stella* (1591), 38]

7. They love indeede who dare not say they love.
[*Astrophel and Stella* (1591), 53]

8. O heavenly Foole, thy most kisse worthy face
Anger invests with such a lovely grace,
That Anger's selfe I needes must kisse againe.
[*Astrophel and Stella* (1591), 72]

9. I never dranke of Aganippe well,
Nor never did in shade of Tempe sit,
And Muses scorne with vulgar braines to dwell;
Poore Lay-man I, for sacred rites unfit...
I am no Pickepurse of an other's wit.
[*Astrophel and Stella* (1591), 73]

10. High way, since you my chiefe Parnassus be,
And that my Muse to some eares not unmeete,
Tempers hir words to trampling horses' feete,
More often than a Chamber mellodie,
Now blessed you beare onwards blessed me,
To hir where my heart safeliest shall meete.
[*Astrophel and Stella* (1591), 83]

11. Doubt you to whom my Muse these notes intendeth,
Which now my brest surcharged with musick lendeth?
To you, to you, all song of praise is due,
Onely in you my song begins and endeth.
[*Astrophel and Stella* (1591), 'First sonnet']

12. Who shoots at the midday sun, though he be sure he shall never hit the mark, yet as sure he is he shall shoot higher than who aims but at a bush.
[*New Arcadia* (1590), 2]

13. The Poet ... lifted up with the vigor of his own invention, doth grow, in effect, into an other nature.
[*The Defence of Poesie* (1595)]

14. Nature never set foorth the earth inso rich Tapistry as diverse Poets have done ... her world is brasen, the Poets only deliver a golden.
[*The Defence of Poesie* (1595)]

15. With a tale forsooth he commeth unto you, with a tale, which holdeth children from play, and olde men from the Chimney corner.
[*The Defence of Poesie* (1595)]

16. Certainly I must confesse mine owne barbarousnesse, I never heard the old Song of Percy and Douglas, that I founde not my heart mooved more than with a Trumpet.
[*The Defence of Poesie* (1595)]

17. Though I will not wish unto you the Ass's eares of Midas, nor to be driven by a Poet's verses as Bubonax was, to hang himselfe, nor to be rimed to death as is said to be done in Ireland; yet thus much Curse I must send you in the behalfe of all Poets, that while you live, you live in love, and never get favour, for lacking skill of a Sonet, and when you die, your memorie die from the earth for want of an Epitaphe.
[*The Defence of Poesie* (1595)]

18. [Offering his water-bottle, despite his own injuries, to a dying soldier on the battlefield near Zutphen, 1586]
Thy necessity is yet greater than mine.
[In Sir Fulke Greville, *Life of Sir Philip Sidney* (1652), 12]

Sieyès, Abbé Emmanuel Joseph (1748–1836)
French statesman, political theorist, pamphleteer and priest

1. [Reply when asked what he did during the French Revolution]
J'ai vécu.
I lived.
[In F.A.M. Mignet, *Notice historique sur la vie et les travaux de M. le Comte de Sieyès* (1836)]

2. [On voting for the death of Louis XVI in 1793]
La mort, sans phrases.
Death, without more words.
[Attr., although he denied having said it]

Sigismund (1368–1437)
Holy Roman Emperor from 1411; King of Hungary from 1387 and of Bohemia from 1419; opposed by the Hussites

1. [Responding to criticism of his Latin]
I am the Roman Emperor, and am above grammar.
[Attr.]

Simenon, Georges (1903–1989)
Belgian novelist, creator of the Maigret detective stories

1. [His wife later said: 'The true figure is no more than twelve hundred']
I have made love to ten thousand women.
[*Die Tat*, 1977]

Simeon, Charles (1759–1836)
English evangelical clergyman

1. Standing up, he announced his text ('Will a man rob God?' Malachi 3:8). With much deliberation repeating his text, he then looked round on the assembled multitude, said in tones as only Simeon [could], 'You have all robbed Him'; and, pointing with his finger in various directions, said, 'You! and You! and You!!!'
[In A. Pollard (ed.), *Let Wisdom Judge*]

Simmons, John (1937–)
British horticulturalist and Curator of Kew Gardens

1. A weed is simply a plant that you don't want.
[*The Observer*, 1983, in Jeffrey Care (ed.), *Sayings of the Eighties* (1989)]

Simon, Guy (1944–)

1. Jimmy Carter had the air of a man who had never taken any decisions in his life. They had always taken him.
[*The Sunday Times*, 1978]

Simon, Neil (1927–)
American playwright and scriptwriter

1. New York ... is not Mecca. It just smells like it.
[*California Suite* (1976)]

Simon, Paul (1941–)
American singer-songwriter

1. People talking without speaking,
People listening without hearing,
People writing songs that voices never shared.
['Sound of Silence', song, 1964]

2. Here's to you, Mrs Robinson,
Jesus loves you more than you will know.
['Mrs Robinson', song, 1967]

3. Like a bridge over troubled water,
I will ease your mind.
['Bridge Over Troubled Water', song, 1970]

Simonides (c. 556–468 BC)
Greek lyric poet and epigrammatist, known for his elegies and choral odes

1. [Epitaph for the three hundred Spartans under Leonidas who died at Thermopylae in 480]
Go, tell the Spartans, thou who passest by,
That here, obedient to their laws, we lie.
[In Herodotus, *Histories*, VII, 228. Cf. Alec Hope: 3]

Simple, Peter (Michael Wharton) (1913–)
British author, journalist and columnist

1. Rentacrowd Ltd, the enterprising firm which supplies crowds for all occasions and has done so much to keep progressive causes in the public eye.
[*Daily Telegraph*, 1962]

Simpson, N.F. (1919–)
English comic dramatist, associated with the Theatre of the Absurd

1. Each of us as he receives his private trouncings at the hands of fate is kept in good heart by the moth in his brother's parachute, and the scorpion in his neighbour's underwear.
[*A Resounding Tinkle* (1958), I.ii]

2. Knocked down a doctor? With an ambulance? How could she? It's a contradiction in terms!
[*One-Way Pendulum* (1960), I]

Simpson, Ronald Albert (1929–)
Australian poet

1. She cannot say just when
The cooking first began within her mind–
But here she knows ... like cakes or bread, a wife
Must lie content as if within a hand
And feel the teeth of time upon her life.
['Wife']

Sims, George R. (1847–1922)
English journalist, dramatist and novelist

1. It is Christmas Day in the Workhouse.
['In the Workhouse – Christmas Day' (1879)]

Singer, Isaac Bashevis (1904–1991)
American Yiddish novelist and short-story writer, born in Poland; Nobel prize 1978

1. We have to believe in free will. We've got no choice.
[*The Times*, 1982]

2. When I was a little boy they called me a liar but now that I am a grown up they call me a writer.
[*The Observer*, 1983, in Jeffrey Care (ed.), *Sayings of the Eighties* (1989)]

Sitting Bull (c. 1834–1890)
Sioux chief, known for his defeat of General Custer in 1876

1. The white man knows how to make everything, but he does not know how to distribute it.
[Attr.]

Sitwell, Dame Edith (1887–1964)
English poet, anthologist, critic and biographer; sister of Sir Osbert Sitwell

1. The fire was furry as a bear.
['Dark Song' (1922)]

2. Another little drink wouldn't do us any harm.
['Scotch Rhapsody' (1922)]

3. Jane, Jane,
Tall as a crane,
The morning light creaks down again.
['Aubade' (1923)]

4. When
Sir
Beelzebub called for his syllabub in the hotel in Hell
Where Proserpine first fell.
['Sir Beelzebub' (1923)]

5. Daisy and Lily,
Lazy and silly,
Walk by the shore of the wan grassy sea–
Talking once more 'neath a swan-bosomed tree.
['Waltz' (1923)]

6. 'See me dance the polka,'
Said Mr Wagg like a bear.
['Polka' (1923)]

7. Lily O'Grady,
Silly and shady,
Longing to be
A lazy lady.
['Popular Song' (1923)]

8. Still falls the Rain–
Dark as the world of man, black as our loss–
Blind as the nineteen hundred and forty nails
Upon the Cross.
['Still Falls the Rain' (1942)]

9. Who dreamed that Christ has died in vain?
He walks again on the Seas of Blood, he comes in the terrible Rain.
[*The Shadow of Cain* (1947)]

10. My poems are hymns of praise to the glory of Life.
[*Selected Poems* (1952), 'Some Notes on My Poetry']

11. During the writing ... of this book, I realized that the public will believe anything – so long as it is not founded on truth.
[*Taken Care Of* (1965), Preface]

12. A pompous woman of his acquaintance, complaining that the head-waiter of a restaurant had not shown her and her husband immediately to a table, said 'We had to tell him who we were.' Gerald, interested, enquired, 'And who were you?'
[*Taken Care Of* (1965), 15]

13. [Of Virginia Woolf]
I enjoyed talking to her, but thought *nothing* of her writing. I considered her 'a beautiful little knitter'.
[Letter to G. Singleton, 1955]

14. Would you please substitute *Dame* Edith for Dr Sitwell. The Queen has honoured my poetry by making me a Dame, so that is now my name.
[Letter to G. Singleton, 1955]

15. I have often wished I had time to cultivate modesty ... But I am too busy thinking about myself.
[*The Observer*, 'Sayings of the Week', 1950]

16. Why not be oneself? That is the whole secret of a successful appearance. If one is a greyhound, why try to look like a Pekingese?
[*Sunday Graphic*, 1955, 'Why I look the Way I do']

17. [Commenting on William Burroughs' novel, *The Naked Lunch* (1963)]
As the author of *Gold Coast Customs* I can scarcely be accused of shirking reality, but I do not wish to spend the rest of my life with my nose nailed to other people's lavatories.
[*The Independent*, 1994]

18. [On novelist Ethel Mannin]
I do not want Miss Mannin's feelings to be hurt by the fact that I have never heard of her ... At the moment I am debarred from the pleasure of putting her in her place by the fact that she has not got one.
[In J. Pearson, *Façades* (1978)]

Sitwell, Sir Osbert (1892–1969)

English poet, novelist, short-story and autobiographical writer; brother of Edith Sitwell

1. The British Bourgeoisie
Is not born,
And does not die,
But, if it is ill,
It has a frightened look in its eyes.
['At the House of Mrs Kinfoot' (1921)]

2. In reality, *killing time*
Is only the name for another of the multifarious ways
By which Time kills us.
['Milordo Inglese' (1958)]

Skelton, John (c. 1460–1529)

English satirical poet; clergyman, tutor of the future Henry VIII and poet laureate

1. For the sowle of Phyllyp Sparowe,
That was late slayn at Carowe
Among the Nones Blake.
For that swete soule's sake,
And for all sparowes' soules
Set in our bede rolles,
Pater noster qui,
With an *Ave Mari*...

2. Vengeaunce I aske and crye,
By way of exclamacyon,
On all the hole nacyon
Of cattes wylde and tame;
God send them sorowe and shame!...

3. And Robyn Redbrest
He shall be the preest
The requiem masse to synge,
Softly warbelynge.
['Phyllyp Sparowe' (c. 1505)]

4. With solace and gladnes,
Moche mirthe and no madnes,
All good and no badnes,
So joyously,
So maydenly,
So womanly
Her demenyng...

5. Far may be sought
Erst that ye can fynde
So corteise, so kynde,
As merry Margarete,
This midsomer flowre,
Jentyll as fawcoun
Or hawke of the towre.
[*Garlande or Chapelet of Laurel* (1523), 'To maystres Margaret Hussey']

6. She is the vyolet,
The daysy delectable,
The columbyn commendable
This jelofer amyable;
For this most goodly floure,
This blossom of fressh colour,
So Jupiter me succour,
She florysheth new and new
In beautie and vertew.
['Phyllyp Sparowe: The Commendacions']

Skelton, Robin (1925–)

British-born Canadian critic, editor and poet

1. Anything said off the cuff has usually been written on it first.
[Attr.]

Skinner, B.F. (1904–1990)

American behavioural psychologist and writer, noted for his study of 'conditioning'

1. Indeed one of the ultimate advantages of an education is simply coming to the end of it.
[*The Technology of Teaching* (1968)]

2. Education is what survives when what has been learned has been forgotten.
[*New Scientist*, 1964, 'New Methods and New Aims in Teaching']

Skinner, Cornelia Otis (1901–1979)
American stage and film actress, and humorist

1. Woman's virtue is man's greatest invention.
[Attr.]

Skyhooks (fl. mid 1970s)
Australian Rock Band

1. I'm living in the seventies
Eating fake food under plastic trees
My face gets dirty just a walking around
I need another pill to calm me down.
['Living in the Seventies', song]

Slessor, Kenneth (1901–1971)
Australian poet and journalist

1. All through the night-time, clock talked to clock,
In the captain's cabin, tock-tock-tock,
One ticked fast and one ticked slow,
And Time went over them a hundred years ago.
['Five Visions of Captain Cook' (1931), 2]

2. Two chronometers the captain had,
One by Arnold that ran like mad,
One by Kendal in a walnut case,
Poor devoted creature with a hangdog face.

Arnold always hurried with a crazed click-click
Dancing over Greenwich like a lunatic,
Kendal panted faithfully his watch-dog beat,
Climbing out of Yesterday with sticky little feet.
['Five Visions of Captain Cook' (1931), 3]

3. After the whey-faced anonymity
Of river-gums and scribbly-gums and bush,
After the rubbing and the hit of brush,
You come to the South Country

As if the argument of trees were done,
The doubts and quarrelling, the plots and pains,
All ended by those clear and gliding planes
Like an abrupt solution.

And over the flat earth of empty farms
The monstrous continent of air floats back
Coloured by rotting sunlight and the black,
Bruised flesh of thunderstorms:

Air arched, enormous, pounding the bony ridge,
Ditches and hutches, with a drench of light,
So huge, from such infinities of height,
You walk in the sky's beach

While even the dwindled hills are small and bare,
As if, rebellious, buried, pitiful,
Something below pushed up a knob of skull,
Feeling its way to air.
['South Country' (1933–1939)]

4. *Time that is moved by little fidget wheels
Is not my Time, the flood that does not flow.
Between the double and the single bell
Of a ship's hour, between a round of bells
From the dark warship riding there below,
I have lived many lives, and this one life
Of Joe, long dead, who lives between five bells.*

Deep and dissolving verticals of light
Ferry the falls of moonshine down. Five bells
Coldly rung out in a machine's voice. Night and water
Pour to one rip of darkness, the Harbour floats
In air, the Cross hangs upside-down in water...

5. But I hear nothing, nothing ... only bells,
Five bells, the bumpkin calculus of Time.
Your echoes die, your voice is dowsed by Life,
There's not a mouth can fly the pygmy strait–
Nothing except the memory of some bones
Long shoved away, and sucked away, in mud.
['Five Bells' (1939)]

6. Softly and humbly to the Gulf of Arabs
The convoys of dead sailors come;
At night they sway and wander in the waters far under,
But morning rolls them in the foam.
['Beach Burial' (1942)]

7. When the iceman doesn't cater
For the idle millionaire
With his private Kelvinator
And his faithful Frigidaire,
Where the windows gleam with money
And the wine is never sly,
And the world is always sunny
And the rent is always high,
And the landlord says with passion
The locality is 'choice',
In a condescending fashion
Goes the green Rolls Royce.
Where the Black Marias clatter,
And peculiar ladies nod,
And the flats are rather flatter,
And the lodgers rather odd,
Where the night is full of dangers
And the darkness full of fear,
And eleven hundred strangers
Live on aspirin and beer,
Where the gas-lights flare and flutter
And the phonographs rejoice,
Like an archduke in the gutter
Goes the green Rolls Royce.
['The Green Rolls Royce']

8. [On Sydney's ferry-boats]
At sunset, when the Harbour is glazed with pebbles of gold and white, and the sun is burning out like a bushfire behind Balmain, the ferry-boats put on their lights. They turn into luminous water-beetles, filed with a gliding, sliding reflected glitter that bubbles on the water like phosphorus.
[*Bread and Wine* (1970), 'A Portrait of Sydney']

Slezak, Leo (1873–1946)
Austrian-born American tenor

1. [When the mechanical swan left the stage without him during a performance of *Lohengrin*]
What time is the next swan?
[In W. Slezak, *What Time's the Next Swan?* (1962)]

Small, Diogenes

1. Be it ever so humble there's no place like home for sending one slowly crackers.
[*Obiter Dicta*]

Smart, Christopher (1722–1771)
English poet and translator, noted for his religious lyrics

1. [On his cat]
For he counteracts the powers of darkness by his electrical skin and glaring eyes.

For he counteracts the Devil, who is death, by brisking about the life.
[*Jubilate Agno* (c. 1758–1763), Fragment B2]

2. Strong is the horse upon his speed;
Strong in pursuit the rapid glede,
Which makes at once his game:
Strong the tall ostrich on the ground;
Strong thro' the turbulent profound
Shoots xiphias to his aim.

Strong is the lion – like a coal
His eye-ball – like a bastion's mole
His chest against his foes:
Strong, the gier-eagle on his sail,
Strong against tide, th' enormous whale
Emerges as he goes...

3. Glorious the sun in mid career;
Glorious th' assembled fires appear;
Glorious the comet's train:
Glorious the trumpet and alarm;
Glorious th' almighty stretch'd-out arm;
Glorious th' enraptur'd main:
Glorious the northern lights astream;
Glorious the song, when God's the theme;
Glorious the thunder's roar:
Glorious hosanna from the den;
Glorious the catholic amen;
Glorious the martyr's gore:

Glorious – more glorious is the crown
Of Him that brought salvation down
By meekness, call'd thy Son;
Thou that stupendous truth believ'd,
And now the matchless deed's achiev'd,
Determined, dared, and done.
[*A Song to David* (1763)]

Smedley, Francis Edward (1818–1864)
English novelist, editor and poet

1. You are looking as fresh as paint!
[*Frank Fairlegh* (1850), 41]

Smiles, Samuel (1812–1904)
Scottish social reformer, biographer, editor and physician

1. Cecil's despatch of business was extraordinary, his maxim being, 'The shortest way to do many things is to do only one thing at once.'
[*Self-Help* (1859), 9]

2. We often discover what *will* do, by finding out what will not do; and probably he who never made a mistake never made a discovery.
[*Self-Help* (1859), 11]

3. A place for everything, and everything in its place. Order is wealth.
[*Thrift* (1875), 5]

Smith, Adam (1723–1790)
Scottish economist, moral philosopher and essayist; founder of modern political economy

1. And thus, place, that great object which divides the wives of aldermen, is the end of half the labours of human life; and is the cause of all the tumult and bustle, all the rapine and injustice, which avarice and ambition have introduced into this world.
[*The Theory of Moral Sentiments* (1759), I, 3]

2. The rich only select from the heap what is most precious and agreeable. They consume little more than the poor, and in spite of their natural selfishness and rapacity ... they divide with the poor the produce of all their improvements. They are led by an invisible hand to make nearly the same distribution of the necessaries of life, which would have been made, had the earth been divided into equal portions among all its inhabitants.
[*The Theory of Moral Sentiments* (1759), IV, 1]

3. No society can surely be flourishing and happy, of which the far greater part of the members are poor and miserable.
[*Wealth of Nations* (1776), I, 8, 'Of the Wages of Labour']

4. Poverty, though it does not prevent the generation, is extremely unfavourable to the rearing of children. The tender plant is produced, but in so cold a soil and so severe a climate, soon withers and dies.
[*Wealth of Nations* (1776), I, 8, 'Of the Wages of Labour']

5. People of the same trade seldom meet together, even for merriment and diversion, but the conversation ends in a conspiracy against the public, or in some contrivance to raise prices.
[*Wealth of Nations* (1776), I, 10, Part 2, 'Inequalities occasioned by the Policy of Europe']

6. With the greater part of rich people, the chief enjoyment of riches consists in the parade of riches, which in their eyes is never so complete as when they appear to possess those decisive marks of opulence which nobody can possess but themselves.
[*Wealth of Nations* (1776), I, 11, Part 2, 'Of the Produce of the Land']

7. To found a great empire for the sole purpose of raising up a people of customers, may at first sight appear a project fit only for a nation of shopkeepers. It is, however, a project altogether unfit for a nation of shopkeepers; but extremely fit for a nation whose government is influenced by shopkeepers.
[*Wealth of Nations* (1776), IV, 7, Part 3, 'Of the Advantages which Europe has derived from the Discovery of America']

8. The discipline of colleges and universities is in general contrived, not for the benefit of the students, but for the interest, or more properly speaking, for the ease of the masters.
[*Wealth of Nations* (1776), V, 1, Article 2, 'Of the Expense of the Institutions for the Education of Youth']

9. [Of universities]
Several of those learned societies have chosen to remain ... the sanctuaries in which exploded systems and obsolete prejudices found shelter and protection, after they had been hunted out of every other corner of the world.
[*Wealth of Nations* (1776), V, 1, Article 2, 'Of the Expense of the Institutions for the Education of Youth']

10. There are no public institutions for the education of women, and there is accordingly nothing useless, absurd, or fantastical in the common course of their education.
[*Wealth of Nations* (1776), V, 1, Article 2, 'Of the Expense of the Institutions for the Education of Youth']

11. It is the interest of every man to live as much at his ease as he can; and if his emoluments are to be precisely the same whether he does, or does not perform some very laborious duty, it is certainly his interest, at least as interest is vulgarly understood, either to neglect it altogether, or, if he is subject to some authority which will not suffer him to do this, to perform it in as careless and slovenly a manner as that authority will permit.
[*Wealth of Nations* (1776), V, 1, Article 2, 'Of the Expense of the Institutions for the Education of Youth']

12. There is no art which one government sooner learns of another than that of draining money from the pockets of the people.
[*Wealth of Nations* (1776), V, 2, 'Appendix, Taxes upon the capital Value of Land, Houses, and Stock']

13. In England the different poll-taxes never produced the sum which had been expected of them, or which, it was supposed, they might have produced, had they been exactly levied.
[*Wealth of Nations* (1776), V, 2, 'Article 4, Capitation Taxes']

14. If any of the provinces of the British empire cannot be made to contribute towards the support of the whole empire, it is surely time that Great Britain should free herself from the expense of defending those provinces in time of war, and of supporting any part of their civil or military establishments in time of peace, and endeavour to accommodate her future views and designs to the real mediocrity of her circumstances.
[*Wealth of Nations* (1776), V, 3, final words]

15. I believe we must adjourn this meeting to some other place.
[Last words]

Smith, Alexander (1830–1867)
Scottish 'Spasmodic' poet and prose writer

1. Like a pale martyr in his shirt of fire.
[*A Life Drama* (1853), II]

2. City! I am true son of thine;
Ne'er dwelt I where great mornings shine
Around the bleating pens;
Ne'er by the rivulets I strayed,
And ne'er upon my childhood weighed
The silence of the glens.
Instead of shores where ocean beats,
I hear the ebb and flow of streets.
Thou hast my kith and kin:
My childhood, youth, and manhood brave;
Thou hast that unforgotten grave
Within thy central din.
A sacredness of love and death
Dwells in thy noise and smoky breath.
[*City Poems* (1857), 'Glasgow']

3. Nature, who makes the perfect rose and bird,
Has never made the full and perfect man.
[*City Poems* (1857), 'Horton']

Smith, Alfred Emanuel (1873–1944)
American Democrat politician and presidential candidate in 1928

1. [On William Randolph Hearst's support in 1926 for Ogden L. Mills' Republican candidacy]
The kiss of death.
[*Up to Now* (1929), 22]

2. [About the folly of attacking Government benefit programmes]
Nobody shoots at Santa Claus.
[Campaign speeches, 1936]

3. No matter how thin you slice it, it's still baloney.
[Campaign speeches, 1936]

Smith, Sir Cyril (1928–)
British Liberal politician

1. [On the House of Commons]
The longest running farce in the West End.
[Remark to foreign press, 1973]

2. If the fence is strong enough I'll sit on it.
[*The Observer*, 1974]

Smith, Delia
British cookery writer

1. I truly have tried and we had a microwave to heat things in the filming – but, actually, we mainly use it to keep the ashtrays in. I think it takes the soul out of food. Cooking is about ingredients being put together, and having time to amalgamate.
[Interview by Libby Purves, *The Times*, 1990]

Smith, F.E. (First Earl of Birkenhead) 1872–1930
English Conservative politician; Lord Chancellor 1919–22

1. We have the highest authority for believing that the meek shall inherit the Earth; though I have never found any particular corroboration of this aphorism in the records of Somerset House.
[*Contemporary Personalities* (1924), 'Marquess Curzon']

2. [On Bolshevism]
Nature has no cure for this sort of madness, though I have known a legacy from a rich relative work wonders.
[*Law, Life and Letters* (1927), II, 19]

3. The world continues to offer glittering prizes to those who have stout hearts and sharp swords.
[Rectorial Address, Glasgow University, 1923]

4. *Judge Willis*: You are extremely offensive, young man.
F.E. Smith: As a matter of fact, we both are, and the only difference between us is that I am trying to be, and you can't help it.
[In Birkenhead, *Frederick Elwin, Earl of Birkenhead* (1933), I, 9]

5. *Judge Willis*: What do you suppose I am on the Bench for, Mr Smith?
F.E. Smith: It is not for me to attempt to fathom the inscrutable workings of Providence.
[In Birkenhead, *Frederick Elwin, Earl of Birkenhead* (1933), I, 9]

6. [To a judge who asked who George Robey was]
Mr George Robey is the Darling of the music-halls, m'lud.
[In W. Churchill, *Great Contemporaries* (1942)]

7. [To a judge who complained that he was no wiser at the end than at the start of one of Smith's cases]
Possibly not, My Lord, but far better informed.
[In Birkenhead, *Life of F.E. Smith* (1959)]

8. [When the Labour MP J.H. Thomas complained he ''ad a 'eadache']
Try taking a couple of aspirates.
[Attr.]

9. Winston [Churchill] has devoted the best years of his life to preparing his impromptu speeches.
[Attr.]

Smith, Ian (1919–)
Prime Minister of Rhodesia (now Zimbabwe) 1964–79

1. I don't believe in black majority rule in Rhodesia ... not in a thousand years.
[Speech, 1976]

Smith, John (1938–1994)
Scottish politician, leader of the Labour Party 1992–94

1. The opportunity to serve our country – that is all we ask.
[Attr.]

Smith, Joseph (1805–1844)
American religious leader; founder of the Mormon Church in 1830

1. No man knows my history.
[Funeral sermon, written by himself]

Smith, Logan Pearsall (1865–1946)
American-born British epigrammatist, essayist, critic and short-story writer

1. There are two things to aim at in life: first, to get what you want; and, after that, to enjoy it. Only the wisest of mankind achieve the second.
[*Afterthoughts* (1931), 1, 'Life and Human Nature']

2. There are few sorrows, however poignant, in which a good income is of no avail.
[*Afterthoughts* (1931), 1, 'Life and Human Nature']

3. I cannot forgive my friends for dying; I do not find these vanishing acts of theirs at all amusing.
[*Afterthoughts* (1931), 2, 'Age and Death']

4. Most people sell their souls, and live with a good conscience on the proceeds.
[*Afterthoughts* (1931), 3, 'Other People']

5. When people come and talk to you of their aspirations, before they leave you had better count your spoons.
[*Afterthoughts* (1931), 3, 'Other People']

6. Married women are kept women, and they are beginning to find it out.
[*Afterthoughts* (1931), 3, 'Other People']

7. It is the wretchedness of being rich that you have to live with rich people.
[*Afterthoughts* (1931), 4, 'In the World']

8. Eat with the rich, but go to the play with the Poor, who are capable of Joy.
[*Afterthoughts* (1931), 4, 'In the World']

9. I love money; just to be in the room with a millionaire makes me less forlorn.
[*Afterthoughts* (1931), 4, 'In the World']

10. I might give my life for my friend, but he had better not ask me to do up a parcel.
[*Afterthoughts* (1931), 6, 'Myself']

11. People say that life is the thing, but I prefer reading.
[*Afterthoughts* (1931), 6, 'Myself']

12. How often my soul visits the National Gallery, and how seldom I go there myself!
[*Afterthoughts* (1931), 6, 'Myself']

13. The old know what they want; the young are sad and bewildered.
[*All Trivia* (1933), 'Last Words']

14. Thank heavens, the sun has gone in, and I don't have to go out and enjoy it.
[*All Trivia* (1933), 'Last Words']

15. There is more felicity on the far side of baldness than young men can possibly imagine.
[*All Trivia* (1933), 'Last Words']

16. [Contemplating whether life has any meaning, shortly before his death]
Yes, there is a meaning, at least for me, there is one thing that matters – to set a chime of words tinkling in the minds of a few fastidious people.
[*New Statesman*, 1946]

Smith, Robert (1634–1716)

1. [Referring to a Puritan preacher]
One of those fellows pouring out his extempore stuff amongst his ignorant, whining, factious followers.
[Sermon, 'Against Long Extempore Prayers']

Smith, Samuel Francis (1808–1895)
American Baptist clergyman and poet

1. My country, 'tis of thee,
Sweet land of liberty,
Of thee I sing:
Land where my fathers died,
Land of the pilgrims' pride,
From every mountain-side
Let freedom ring.
['America' (1832)]

Smith, Stevie (Florence Margaret Smith) (1902–1971)
English novelist, poet and illustrator of her verse

1. A Good Time Was Had By All.
[Title of book, 1937]

2. This Englishwoman is so refined
She has no bosom and no behind.
['This Englishwoman' (1937)]

3. Private Means is dead,
God rest his soul, officers and fellow-rankers said.
['Private Means is Dead' (1937)]

4. Nobody heard him, the dead man,
But still he lay moaning:
I was much further out than you thought
And not waving but drowning.
['Not Waving But Drowning' (1957)]

5. Oh I am a cat that likes to
Gallop about doing good.
['The Galloping Cat' (1972)]

6. If there wasn't death, I think you couldn't go on.
[*The Observer*, 1969]

Smith, Sydney [1] (1771–1845)
English clergyman, essayist, journalist, wit and lecturer on philosophy

1. The moment the very name of Ireland is mentioned, the English seem to bid adieu to common feeling, common prudence, and to common sense, and to act with the barbarity of tyrants, and the fatuity of idiots.
[*Letters of Peter Plymley* (1807), Letter 2]

2. The schoolboy whips his taxed top – the beardless youth manages his taxed horse, with a taxed bridle, on a taxed road: – and the dying Englishman, pouring his medicine, which has paid seven per cent., into a spoon that has paid fifteen per cent. – flings himself back upon his chintz bed, which has paid twenty-two per cent. – and expires in the arms of an apothecary who has paid a licence of a hundred pounds for the privilege of putting him to death.
[*Edinburgh Review*, 1820, 'America']

3. A Curate – there is something which excites compassion in the very name of a Curate!!!
[*Edinburgh Review*, 1822, 'Persecuting Bishops']

4. What Bishops like best in their Clergy is a droppingdown-deadness of manner.
[*The Works of the Rev. Sydney Smith* (1839), III, 'First Letter to Archdeacon Singleton']

5. There is not a better man in England than Lord John Russell; but his worst failure is, that he is utterly ignorant of all

moral fear; there is nothing he would not undertake. I believe he would perform the operation for the stone – build St Peter's – or assume (with or without ten minutes' notice) the command of the Channel Fleet; and no one would discover by his manner that the patient had died – the Church tumbled down – and the Channel Fleet been knocked to atoms.
[*The Works of the Rev. Sydney Smith* (1839), III, 'Second Letter to Archdeacon Singleton']

6. I like, my dear Lord, the road you are travelling, but I don't like the pace you are driving; too similar to that of the son of Nimshi. I always feel myself inclined to cry out, Gently, John, gently down hill. Put on the drag.
[*The Works of the Rev. Sydney Smith* (1839), III, 'A Letter to Lord John Russell']

7. Bishop Berkeley destroyed this world in one volume octavo; and nothing remained, after his time, but mind; which experienced a similar fate from the hand of Mr Hume in 1739.
[*Sketches of Moral Philosophy* (1849), Introduction]

8. We shall generally find that the triangular person has gone into the square hole, the oblong into the triangular, and a square person has squeezed himself into the round hole. The officer and the office, the doer and the thing done, seldom fit so exactly that we can say they were almost made for each other.
[*Sketches of Moral Philosophy* (1849)]

9. I never could find any man who could think for two minutes together.
[*Sketches of Moral Philosophy* (1849)]

10. Mankind are always happy for having been happy, so that if you make them happy now, you make them happy twenty years hence by the memory of it.
[*Sketches of Moral Philosophy* (1849)]

11. [Commenting on the attempt of the Lords to stop the progress of the Reform Bill]
Dame Partington ... was seen ... with mop and pattens ... vigorously pushing away the Atlantic Ocean. ... The Atlantic Ocean beat Mrs Partington. She was excellent at a slop, or a puddle, but she should not have meddled with a tempest.
[Speech, Taunton, 1831]

12. I am better in health ... and drinking nothing but London water, with a million insects in every drop. He who drinks a tumbler of London water has literally in his stomach more animated beings than there are men, women, and children on the face of the globe.
[Letter to Countess Grey, 1834]

13. I am convinced digestion is the great secret of life.
[Letter to Arthur Kinglake, 1837]

14. I have no relish for the country; it is a kind of healthy grave.
[Letter to Miss G. Harcourt, 1838]

15. You must not think me necessarily foolish because I am facetious, nor will I consider you necessarily wise because you are grave.
[Open letter to *The Times*, addressed to Bishop Blomfield, 1840]

16. [On his convalescent diet]
If you hear of sixteen or eighteen pounds of human flesh, they belong to me. I look as if a curate has been taken out of me.
[Letter to Lady Carlisle, 1844]

17. It requires a surgical operation to get a joke well into a Scotch understanding. Their only idea of wit ... is laughing immoderately at stated intervals.
[In Holland, *A Memoir of the Reverend Sydney Smith* (1855), I, 2]

18. [Of Scotland]
That knuckle-end of England – that land of Calvin, oat-cakes, and sulphur.
[In Holland, *A Memoir of the Reverend Sydney Smith* (1855), I, 2]

19. Take short views, hope for the best, and trust in God.
[In Holland, *A Memoir of the Reverend Sydney Smith* (1855), I, 6]

20. No furniture so charming as books, even if you never open them, or read a single word.
[In Holland, *A Memoir of the Reverend Sydney Smith* (1855), I, 9]

21. Most London dinners evaporate in whispers to one's next-door neighbour. I make it a rule never to speak a word to mine, but fire across the table; though I broke it once ... I turned suddenly round and said, 'Madam, I have been looking for a person who disliked gravy all my life; let us swear eternal friendship.'
[In Holland, *A Memoir of the Reverend Sydney Smith* (1855), I, 9]

22. How can a bishop marry? How can he flirt? The most he can say is, 'I will see you in the vestry after service.'
[In Holland, *A Memoir of the Reverend Sydney Smith* (1855), I, 9]

23. Not body enough to cover his mind decently with; his intellect is improperly exposed.
[In Holland, *A Memoir of the Reverend Sydney Smith* (1855), I, 9]

24. We naturally lose illusions as we get older, like teeth, but there is no Cartwright to fit a new set into our understandings. I have, alas, only one illusion left, and that is the Archbishop of Canterbury.
[In Holland, *A Memoir of the Reverend Sydney Smith* (1855), I, 9]

25. As the French say, there are three sexes – men, women, and clergymen.
[In Holland, *A Memoir of the Reverend Sydney Smith* (1855), I, 9]

26. Praise is the best diet for us, after all.
[In Holland, *A Memoir of the Reverend Sydney Smith* (1855), I, 9]

27. [Discussing the recent hot weather]
Heat, Ma'am! It was so dreadful here, that I found there was nothing left for it but to take off my flesh and sit in my bones.
[In Holland, *A Memoir of the Reverend Sydney Smith* (1855), I, 9]

28. [On marriage]
It resembles a pair of shears, so joined that they cannot be separated; often moving in opposite directions, yet always punishing anyone who comes between them.
[In Holland, *A Memoir of the Reverend Sydney Smith* (1855), I, 11]

29. [Of Macaulay]
He is like a book in breeches.
[In Holland, *A Memoir of the Reverend Sydney Smith* (1855), I, 11]

30. [Of Macaulay]
He has occasional flashes of silence, that make his conversation perfectly delightful.
[In Holland, *A Memoir of the Reverend Sydney Smith* (1855), I, 11]

31. [From his recipe for salads]
Serenely full, the epicure would say,
Fate cannot harm me, I have dined today.
[In Holland, *A Memoir of the Reverend Sydney Smith* (1855), I, 11]

32. [Of an unnamed Dean]
Deserves to be preached to death by wild curates.
[In Holland, *A Memoir of the Reverend Sydney Smith* (1855), I, 11]

33. [Of William Whewell]
Science is his forte and omniscience is his foible.
[In Isaac Todhunter, *William Whewell* (1876), I, 21]

34. Poverty is no disgrace to a man, but it is confoundedly inconvenient.
[In J. Potter Briscoe (ed.), *Sydney Smith* (1900)]

35. I never read a book before reviewing it; it prejudices a man so.
[In H. Pearson, *The Smith of Smiths* (1934), 3]

36. Minorities ... are almost always in the right.
[In H. Pearson, *The Smith of Smiths* (1934), 9]

37. My idea of heaven is, eating *pâté de foie gras* to the sound of trumpets.
[In H. Pearson, *The Smith of Smiths* (1934), 10]

38. What a pity it is that we have no amusements in England but vice and religion!
[In H. Pearson, *The Smith of Smiths* (1934), 10]

39. I always let it be inferred that I am the son of Adam Smith.
[In H. Pearson, *The Smith of Smiths* (1934), 11]

40. [To 'Bobus' Smith]
Brother, you and I are the exceptions to the laws of nature. You have risen by your gravity and I have sunk by my levity.
[In H. Pearson, *The Smith of Smiths* (1934), 11]

41. Death must be distinguished from dying, with which it is often confused.
[In H. Pearson, *The Smith of Smiths* (1934), 11]

42. [To Monkton Milnes]
I am just going to pray for you at St Paul's, but with no very lively hope of success.
[In H. Pearson, *The Smith of Smiths* (1934), 13]

43. Thank God for tea! What would the world do without tea? How did it exist? I am glad I was not born before tea.
[Attr.]

Smith, Sir Sydney [2] (1883–1969)
New Zealand-born British Professor of Forensic Medicine and writer

1. No child is born a criminal: no child is born an angel: he's just born.
[Remark]

Smith, Thorne (1892–1934)
American humorous novelist

1. Steven's mind was so tolerant that he could have attended a lynching every day without becoming critical.
[*The Jovial Ghosts* (1933), 11]

Smithers, Alan Jack (1919–)

1. [Of Sir John Monash, Australian military commander]
He was, above all, the first twentieth-century general, a man with petrol in his veins and a computer in his head.
[*Sir John Monash*]

Smollett, Tobias (1721–1771)
Scottish author of picaresque novels; editor, satirist, translator, historian, traveller and physician

1. Some folks are wise, and some are otherwise.
[*The Adventures of Roderick Random* (1748), 6]

2. He was formed for the ruin of our sex.
[*The Adventures of Roderick Random* (1748), 22]

3. I consider the world as made for me, not me for the world: it is my maxim therefore to enjoy it while I can, and let futurity shift for itself.
[*The Adventures of Roderick Random* (1748), 45]

4. [On being tongue-tied when alone with one's object of desire]
'Tis very surprising that love should act so inconsistent with itself, as to deprive its votaries of the use of their faculties, when they have most occasion for them.
[*The Adventures of Roderick Random* (1748), 56]

5. The painful ceremony of receiving and returning visits.
[*The Adventures of Peregrine Pickle* (1751), 5]

6. Finding her importance in the family greatly diminished, her attractions neglected by all the male sex in the neighbourhood, and the withering hand of time hang threateningly over her head, [Mrs Grizzle] began to feel the horror of eternal virginity, and ... resolved ... to rescue herself from that reproachful and uncomfortable situation.
[*The Adventures of Peregrine Pickle* (1751), 5]

7. Any man of humane sentiments ... would have been prompted to offer his services to the forlorn stranger: but ... our hero was devoid of all these infirmities of human nature.
[*The Adventures of Ferdinand Count Fathom* (1753), 25]

8. I think for my part one half of the nation is mad – and the other not very sound.
[*The Adventures of Sir Launcelot Greaves* (1762), 6]

9. True Patriotism is of no Party.
[*The Adventures of Sir Launcelot Greaves* (1762), 9]

10. A seafaring man may have a sweetheart in every port; but he should steer clear of a wife, as he would avoid a quicksand.
[*The Adventures of Sir Launcelot Greaves* (1762), 21]

11. You that live in the country have no deception of our doings at Bath.
[*The Expedition of Humphry Clinker* (1771), Letter to Mrs Mary Jones ... Bath, April 26]

12. Hark ye, Clinker, you are a most notorious offender. You stand convicted of sickness, hunger, wretchedness, and want.
[*The Expedition of Humphry Clinker* (1771), Letter to Sir Watkin Phillips ... London, May 24]

13. What is life but a veil of affliction?
[*The Expedition of Humphry Clinker* (1771), Letter to Mrs Mary Jones ... London, June 14]

14. I have met with so many axidents, suprisals, and terrifications, that I am in a pafeck fantigo, and I believe I shall never be my own self again.
[*The Expedition of Humphry Clinker* (1771), Letter to Mrs Mary Jones ... London, October 14]

15. That great Cham of literature, Samuel Johnson.
[In Boswell, *The Life of Samuel Johnson* (1793 edition), Letter to John Wilkes, 1759]

Snagge, John (1904–)
British television broadcaster and commentator

1. I don't know who's ahead – it's either Oxford or Cambridge.
[Radio commentary on the Oxford and Cambridge University Boat Race, 1949]

Snow, C.P. (Baron Snow of Leicester) (1905–1980)
English novelist, critic, physicist, biographer and public administrator

1. The official world, the corridors of power, the dilemmas of conscience and egotism – she disliked them all.
[*Homecomings* (1956), 22]

2. A good many times I have been present at gatherings of people who, by the standards of the traditional culture, are thought highly educated and who have with considerable gusto been expressing their incredulity at the illiteracy of scientists. Once or twice I have been provoked and have asked the company how many of them could describe the Second Law of Thermodynamics. The response was cold: it was also negative.
[*The Two Cultures and the Scientific Revolution* (1959), 1]

3. [On people who say that it will take five hundred years for Asians or Africans to catch up with Western technology]
They are both suicidal and technologically illiterate. Particularly when said ... by someone looking as though it wouldn't take Neanderthal Man five years to catch up with *him*.
[*The Two Cultures and the Scientific Revolution* (1959), 4]

4. [On industrialisation]
Common men can show astonishing fortitude in chasing jam tomorrow. Jam today, and men aren't at their most exciting: jam tomorrow, and one often sees them at their noblest.
[*The Two Cultures and the Scientific Revolution* (1959), 4]

5. 'I grant you that he's not two-faced,' I said, 'But what's the use of that, when the one face he has got is so peculiarly unpleasant?'
[*The Affair* (1960), 4]

6. Corridors of Power.
[Title of novel, 1964]

Snyder, Gary (1930–)
American mystical poet and researcher

1. A clear, attentive mind
Has no meaning but that
Which sees is truly seen.
[*Riprap* (1959), 'Piute Creek']

2. My political position is to be a spokesman for wild nature. I take that as a primary constituency.
[*The Real Work, Interviews and Talks 1964–1979* (1980), 'Knots in the Grain']

Socrates (469–399 BC)
Athenian philosopher, noted for his method of instruction, recorded by Plato; condemned to death for impiety

1. I am not an Athenian nor a Greek, but a citizen of the world.
[Attr. in Plutarch, *On Exile*, 600]

2. [Looking at goods for sale]
How many things I have no need of!
[Attr. in Diogenes Laertius, *Lives of the Eminent Philosophers*, 'Socrates', 24]

3. The unexamined life is not a life worth living for a human being.
[Attr. in Plato, *Apology*, 38a]

4. Death is one of two things. Either it is nothingness, and the dead have no consciousness of anything; or, as people say, it is a change and migration of the soul from this place to another.
[Attr. in Plato, *Apology*, 40]

5. No evil can befall a good man either in life or death.
[Attr. in Plato, *Apology*, 41]

6. But now it is time to depart, for me to die and for you to go on living; but which of us has the better lot, is unknown to anyone but God.
[Attr. in Plato, *Apology*, 42a]

7. A man should feel confident concerning his soul, who in his life has rejected those pleasures and fineries that go with the body as being alien to him, considering them to result more in harm than in good, and has eagerly sought the pleasures that go with learning and adorned his soul with no alien but rather with its own proper refinements, moderation and justice and courage and freedom and truth; thus he awaits his journey to the world below, ready whenever fate calls him.
[Attr. in Plato, *Phaedo*, 114d]

8. 'What do you say about pouring a libation to some god from this cup? Is it allowed or not?'
'We only prepare what we think is the right measure to drink, Socrates,' [the jailor] said.
'I understand,' he went on; 'but it is allowed and necessary to pray to the gods, that my departure from hence may be fortunate; thus I pray, and may it be granted.'
[Attr. in Plato, *Phaedo*, 117b]

9. [Last words]
Crito, we owe a cock to Asclepius. Pay it and do not neglect it.
[Attr. in Plato, *Phaedo*, 118]

Solanis, Valerie (1940–)

1. [SCUM (Society for Cutting Up Men), manifesto, 1968]
Every man, deep down, knows he's a worthless piece of shit.
[In Susan Bassnett, *Feminist Experiences: The Women's Movement in Four Cultures* (1986)]

Solon (c. 638–c. 559 BC)
Athenian statesman, noted for his legal, political and economic reforms, and poet

1. Laws are like spider's webs, which hold firm when any light, yielding object falls upon them, while a larger thing breaks through them and escapes.
[In Diogenes Laertius, *Lives of the Eminent Philosophers*, I, 58. Cf. Shenstone: 3 and Swift: 10]

2. Until [a man] dies, be careful to call him not happy but lucky.
[In Herodotus, *Histories*, I, 32]

3. I grow old ever learning many things.
[In Theodor Bergk (ed.), *Poetae Lyrici Graeci*, 'Solon', 18]

4. Wrongdoing can only be avoided if those who are not wronged feel the same indignation at it as those who are.
[Attr.]

Solzhenitsyn, Alexander (1918–)
Russian novelist, dramatist and historian; Nobel prize 1970; a critic of the Soviet regime, expelled from the USSR in 1974

1. The whole of his life had prepared Podduyev for living, not dying.
[*Cancer Ward* (1968), I, 8]

2. Nowadays we don't think much of a man's love for an animal; we mock people who are attached to cats. But if we stop loving animals, aren't we bound to stop loving humans too?
[*Cancer Ward* (1968), I, 20]

3. If decade after decade the truth cannot be told, each person's mind starts to roam irretrievably. One's fellow countrymen become harder to understand than Martians.
[*Cancer Ward* (1968), II, 11]

4. You took my freedom away long ago and you can't give it back to me because you haven't got it yourself.
[*The First Circle* (1968), 17]

5. You only have power over people as long as you don't take *everything* away from them. But when you've robbed a man of *everything* he's no longer in your power – he's free again.
[*The First Circle* (1968), 17]

6. Their teacher had advised them not to read Tolstoy's novels, because they were very long and would only confuse the clear ideas which they had acquired from reading critical studies about him.
[*The First Circle* (1968), 40]

7. The salvation of mankind lies only in making everything the concern of everyone.
[Nobel Lecture, 1970]

8. This universal, compulsory, force-feeding with lies is now the most agonizing aspect of existence in our country – worse than all our material miseries, worse than any lack of civil liberties.
[*Letter to Soviet Leaders* (1974), 6]

9. In our country the lie has become not just a moral category but a pillar of the State. In recoiling from the lie we are performing a moral act, not a political act.
[Interview in *Time* magazine, 1974]

10. For us in Russia, communism is a dead dog, while for many people in the West, it is still a living lion.
[*The Listener*, 1979]

Somerville, William (1675–1742)
English poet

1. My hoarse-sounding horn
Invites thee to the chase, the sport of kings;
Image of war, without its guilt...

2. Hail, happy Britain! highly favoured isle,
And Heaven's peculiar care!
[*The Chase* (1735), I]

Somoza, Anastasio (1925–1980)
President of Nicaragua, 1937–47

1. You won the elections. But I won the count.
[*The Guardian*, 1977]

Sontag, Susan (1933–)
American critic, essayist, novelist and short-story writer

1. Interpretation is the revenge of the intellect upon art.
[*Evergreen Review*, 1964, 'Against Interpretation']

2. A photograph is not only an image (as a painting is an image), an interpretation of the real; it is also a trace, something directly stencilled off the real, like a footprint or a death mask.
[*New York Review of Books*, 1977, 'Photography Unlimited']

3. Social misery has inspired the comfortably-off with the urge to take pictures, the gentlest of predations, in order to document a hidden reality, that is, a reality hidden from *them*.
[*New York Review of Books*, 1977, 'Photography Unlimited']

4. Illness is the night-side of life, a more onerous citizenship. Everyone who is born holds dual citizenship, in the kingdom of the well and in the kingdom of the sick. Although we all prefer to use only the good passport, sooner or later each of us is obliged, at least for a spell, to identify ourselves as citizens of that other place.
[*Illness as Metaphor* (1978)]

Sophocles (496–406 BC)
Classical Greek dramatist and poet, known for his seven surviving tragedies

1. My son, may you prove happier than your father.
[*Ajax*, line 550]

2. Gifts from enemies are no gifts, and bring no good.
[*Ajax*, line 665]

3. Of wonders there are many, but none more wonderful than man.
[*Antigone*, line 333]

4. Death is not the worst thing; rather, when one who craves death cannot attain even that wish.
[*Electra*, line 1007]

5. Not to be born is the best of all; next best is, having been born, to return as quickly as possible whence we came.
[*Oedipus at Colonus*, line 1225. Cf. Heine: 7]

6. Sophocles said that he portrayed men as they ought to be, Euripides portrayed them as they are.
[In Aristotle, *Poetics*, 25]

7. Someone asked Sophocles, 'How do you stand in matters of love? Are you still able to have sex with a woman?' 'Quiet, man,' he replied, 'I've left all that behind me very gladly, as if I'd escaped from a mad and savage master.'
[In Plato, *Republic*, I, 329c]

Soule, John Babsone Lane (1815–1891)
American journalist

1. Go West, young man, go West!
[*Terre Haute* (Indiana) *Express*, 1851]

Souness, Graeme
Scottish footballer and football manager

1. [Response to the accusation that Rangers Football Club refused to sign Catholic players]
How could I carry out a policy where I won't sign a Catholic but I'll go home and live with one?
[In Kenny MacDonald, *Scottish Football Quotations* (1994)]

Southerne, Thomas (1660–1746)
Irish dramatist

1. And when we're worn,
Hack'd, hewn with constant service, thrown aside
To rust in peace, or rot in hospitals.
[*The Loyal Brother* (1682), I]

Southey, Robert (1774–1843)
English poet, essayist, historian, biographer and letter writer; poet laureate from 1813

1. It was a summer evening,
Old Kaspar's work was done,
And he before his cottage door
Was sitting in the sun,
And by him sported on the green
His little grandchild Wilhelmine...

2. 'Now tell us all about the war,
And what they fought each other for.'...

3. But what they fought each other for,
I could not well make out...

4. 'And everybody praised the Duke,
Who this great fight did win.'
'But what good came of it at last?'
Quoth little Peterkin.
'Why that I cannot tell,' said he,
'But 'twas a famous victory.'
['The Battle of Blenheim' (1798)]

5. You are old, Father William, the young man cried,
The few locks which are left you are grey;
You are hale, Father William, a hearty old man,
Now tell me the reason, I pray...

6. In the days of my youth I remembered my God!
And He hath not forgotten my age.
['The Old Man's Comforts, and how he Gained them' (1799). Cf. Carroll: 9]

7. The Monk my son, and my daughter the Nun.
['The Old Woman of Berkeley' (1799)]

8. No stir in the air, no stir in the sea,
The ship was still as she could be...

9. Till the vessel strikes with a shivering shock,–
'Oh Christ! it is the Inchcape Rock!'

Sir Ralph the Rover tore his hair;
He curst himself in his despair.
['The Inchcape Rock' (1803)]

10. Blue, darkly, deeply, beautifully blue.
[*Madoc* (1805), I, 'Madoc in Wales', 5, 'Lincoya']

11. We wage no war with women nor with priests.
[*Madoc* (1805), I, 'Madoc in Wales', 15, 'The Excommunication']

12. What will not woman, gentle woman, dare,
When strong affection stirs her spirit up?
[*Madoc* (1805), II, 'Madoc in Aztlan', 2, 'The Tidings']

13. Curses are like young chickens, they always come home to roost.
[*The Curse of Kehama* (1810), Motto]

14. And Sleep shall obey me,
And visit thee never,
And the Curse shall be on thee
For ever and ever.
[*The Curse of Kehama* (1810), II, 'The Curse']

15. Hark! at the Golden Palaces
The Bramin strikes the hour.
[*The Curse of Kehama* (1810), V, 'The Separation']

16. Thou hast been call'd, O Sleep! the friend of Woe,
But 'tis the happy who have called thee so.
[*The Curse of Kehama* (1810), XV, 'The City of Baly']

17. Their wintry garment of unsullied snow
The mountains have put on.
[*The Poet's Pilgrimage* (1816), I]

18. My name is Death: the last best friend am I.
[*Carmen Nuptiale* (1816), 'The Lay of the Laureate: the Dream']

19. Your true lover of literature is never fastidious.
[*The Doctor* (1812), 17]

20. Show me a man who cares no more for one place than another, and I will show you in that same person one who loves nothing but himself. Beware of those who are homeless by choice!
[*The Doctor* (1812), 34]

21. Live as long as you may, the first twenty years are the longest half of your life.
[*The Doctor* (1812), 130]

22. The death of Nelson was felt in England as something more than a public calamity; men started at the intelligence, and turned pale, as if they had heard of the loss of a dear friend.
[*The Life of Nelson* (1813), 9]

23. The march of intellect.
[*Colloquies on the Progress and Prospects of Society* (1829), 14]

24. She has made me half in love with a cold climate.
[Letter to his brother Thomas, 1797. Cf. Nancy Mitford: 4]

Southwell, Robert (1561–1595)

English poet and Jesuit martyr, noted for his devotional poems

1. As I in hoary Winter's night stood shiveringe in the snowe,
Surpris'd I was with sodayne heat, which made my hart to glowe;
And lifting upp a fearefull eye to vewe what fire was nere,
A pretty Babe all burninge bright, did in the ayre appeare.
['The Burning Babe' (c. 1590)]

Spaak, Paul Henri (1899–1972)

Belgian statesman and lawyer; Prime Minister 1938–39, 1946 and 1947–49; President of the first UN General Assembly

1. Our agenda is now exhausted. The secretary general is exhausted. All of you are exhausted. I find it comforting that, beginning with our very first day, we find ourselves in such complete unanimity.
[Concluding the first General Assembly meeting of the United Nations, 1946]

Spark, Muriel (1918–)

Scottish novelist, poet, dramatist, short-story and autobiographical writer

1. Parents learn a lot from their children about coping with life.
[*The Comforters* (1957), 6]

2. Give me a girl at an impressionable age, and she is mine for life.
[*The Prime of Miss Jean Brodie* (1961), 1]

3. One's prime is elusive. You little girls, when you grow up, must be on the alert to recognise your prime at whatever time of your life it may occur. You must then live it to the full.
[*The Prime of Miss Jean Brodie* (1961), 1]

4. If only you small girls would listen to me I would make of you the crème de la crème.
[*The Prime of Miss Jean Brodie* (1961), 1]

5. Art and religion first; then philosophy; lastly science. That is the order of the great subjects of life, that's their order of importance.
[*The Prime of Miss Jean Brodie* (1961), 2]

6. To me education is a leading out of what is already there in the pupil's soul. To Miss Mackay it is a putting in of something that is not there, and that is not what I call education, I call it intrusion.
[*The Prime of Miss Jean Brodie* (1961), 2]

7. There was a Miss Jean Brodie in her prime.
[*The Prime of Miss Jean Brodie* (1961), last sentence]

8. But I did not remove my glasses, for I had not asked for her company in the first place, and there is a limit to what one can listen to with the naked eye.
[*Voices at Play* (1961), 'The Dark Glasses']

9. It was Edinburgh that bred within me the conditions of exiledom; and what have I been doing since then but moving from exile to exile? It has ceased to be a fate, it has become a calling.
['What Images Return']

10. Do you think it pleases a man when he looks into a woman's eyes and sees a reflection of the British Museum Reading Room?
[In Cowan, *The Wit of Women* (1969)]

Sparrow, John (1906–1992)
English lawyer, Warden of All Souls, Oxford, and writer

1. That indefatigable and unsavoury engine of pollution, the dog.
[Letter to *The Times*, 1975]

Speight, Johnny (1920–)
English television scriptwriter

1. [Said by Alf Garnett, referring to his wife]
You silly moo.
[Catchphrase from *Till Death Do Us Part*, television programme]

2. If Her Majesty stood for Parliament – if the Tory Party had any sense and made Her its leader instead of that grammar school twit Heath – us Tories, mate, would win every election we went in for.
[*Till Death Do Us Part*, television programme]

3. Don't be daft. You don't get any pornography on there, not on the telly. Get filth, that's all. The only place you get pornography is in yer Sunday papers.
[*Till Death Do Us Part*, television programme]

4. Have you noticed, the last four strikes we've had, it's pissed down? It wouldn't be a bad idea to check the weather reports before they pull us out next time.
[*Till Death Do Us Part*, television programme]

Spencer, Herbert (1820–1903)
English evolutionary philosopher and journalist

1. Progress, therefore, is not an accident, but a necessity ... it is a part of nature.
[*Social Statics* (1850), I, 2]

2. A clever theft was praiseworthy amongst the Spartans; and it is equally so amongst Christians, provided it be on a sufficiently large scale.
[*Social Statics* (1850), II, 16]

3. Education has for its object the formation of character.
[*Social Statics* (1850), II, 17]

4. Opinion is ultimately determined by the feelings, and not by the intellect.
[*Social Statics* (1850), IV, 30]

5. No one can be perfectly free till all are free; no one can be perfectly moral till all are moral; no one can be perfectly happy till all are happy.
[*Social Statics* (1850), IV, 30]

6. People are beginning to see that the first requisite to success in life, is to be a good animal.
[*Education* (1861), 2]

7. It cannot but happen ... that those will survive whose functions happen to be most nearly in equilibrium with the modified aggregate of external forces ... This survival of the fittest implies multiplication of the fittest.
[*The Principles of Biology* (1864), I, 3, 12]

8. How often misused words generate misleading thoughts.
[*Principles of Ethics* (1879), I, 2, 8]

9. The Republican form of government is the highest form of government; but because of this it requires the highest type of human nature – a type nowhere at present existing.
[*Essays* (1891), III, 'The Americans']

10. Absolute morality is the regulation of conduct in such a way that pain shall not be inflicted.
[*Essays* (1891), III, 'Prison Ethics']

11. French art, if not sanguinary, is usually obscene.
[In *Home Life with Herbert Spencer* (1906), 4]

12. It was remarked to me ... that to play billiards well was a sign of an ill-spent youth.
[In Duncan, *Life and Letters of Spencer* (1908), 20]

Spencer, Sir Stanley (1891–1959)
English painter, known for his religious subject matter set in a modern context

1. I no more like people personally than I like dogs. When I meet them I am only apprehensive whether they will bite me, which is reasonable and sensible.
[In Collis, *Stanley Spencer* (1962), 17]

2. [Thanking the nurse who had given him his nightly injection, just before he died]
Beautifully done.
[In Collis, *Stanley Spencer* (1962), 19]

Spender, Sir Stephen (1909–)
English poet and critic, associated with 1930s left-wing writers; editor, translator, diarist and autobiographer

1. After the first powerful plain manifesto
The black statement of pistons, without more fuss
But gliding like a queen, she leaves the station.
['The Express' (1933)]

2. I think continually of those who were truly great.

The names of those who in their lives fought for life
Who wore at their hearts the fire's centre.
Born of the sun they travelled a short while towards the sun,
And left the vivid air signed with their honour.
['I think continually of those who were truly great' (1933)]

3. My parents kept me from children who were rough
Who threw words like stones and who wore torn clothes...

4. They threw mud
And I looked another way, pretending to smile.
I longed to forgive them, yet they never smiled.
['My parents kept me from children who were rough' (1933)]

5. Never being, but always at the edge of Being.
[Title of poem, 1933]

6. Eye, gazelle, delicate wanderer,
Drinker of horizon's fluid line.
['Not palaces, an era's crown' (1933)]

7. Pylons, those pillars
Bare like nude, giant girls that have no secret.
['The Pylons' (1933)]

8. What I had not foreseen
Was the gradual day
Weakening the will
Leaking the brightness away.
['What I expected' (1933)]

9. Who live under the shadow of a war,
What can I do that matters?
['Who live under the shadow of a war' (1933)]

10. Their dreams of girls, and their collected
Faith in home, wound up like a little watch.
['The Past Values' (1939)]

11. As she will live who, candle-lit
Floats upon her final breath,
The ceiling of the frosty night
And her high room beneath,
Wearing not like destruction, but
Like a white dress, her death.
['Elegy for Margaret: VI To H.S.']

12. The word bites like a fish.
Shall I throw it back, free
Arrowing to that sea
Where thoughts lash tail and fin?
Or shall I pull it in
To rhyme upon a dish?
['Word']

13. People sometimes divide others into those you laugh at and those you laugh with. The young Auden was someone you could laugh-at-with.
[Address at W.H. Auden's memorial service, Oxford, 1973]

Spenser, Edmund (c. 1522–1599)

English poet, noted for his versification, imagery and allegorical poems; the 'poet's poet'

1. So now they have made our English tongue, a gallimaufray or hodgepodge of al other speches.
[*The Shepheardes Calender* (1579), Dedicatory epistle, to Gabriel Harvey]

2. To be wise and eke to love,
Is graunted scarce to God above.
[*The Shepheardes Calender* (1579), 'March']

3. Bring hether the Pincke and purple Cullambine,
With Gelliflowres:
Bring Coronations, and Sops in wine,
Worne of Paramoures.
Strowe me the ground with Daffadowndillies,
And Cowslips, and Kingcups, and loved Lillies:
The pretie Pawnce,
And the Chevisaunce,
Shall match with the fayre flowre Delice.
[*The Shepheardes Calender* (1579), 'Aprill']

4. And he that strives to touch the starres,
Oft stombles at a strawe.
[*The Shepheardes Calender* (1579), 'Julye']

5. Of such deep learning little had he neede,
Ne yet of Latine, ne of Greeke, that breede
Doubts mongst Divines, and difference of texts,
From whence arise diversitie of sects,
And hatefull heresies.
[*Complaints* (1591), 'Prosopopoia: or Mother Hubberd's Tale']

6. What more felicitie can fall to creature,
Than to enjoy delight with libertie.
[*Complaints* (1591), 'Muiopotmos or the Fate of the Butterflie']

7. The merry Cuckow, messenger of Spring,
His trompet shrill hath thrise already sounded.
[*Amoretti, and Epithalamion* (1595), Sonnet 19]

8. Most glorious Lord of lyfe, that on this day,
Didst make thy triumph over death and sin:
And, having harrowd hell didst bring away
Captivity thence captive us to win...

9. So let us love, deare love, lyke as we ought,
Love is the lesson which the Lord us taught.
[*Amoretti, and Epithalamion* (1595), Sonnet 68]

10. Fresh spring the herald of love's mighty king,
In whose cote armour richly are displayd
All sorts of flowers the which on earth do spring
In goodly colours gloriously arrayd.
[*Amoretti, and Epithalamion* (1595), Sonnet 70]

11. One day I wrote her name upon the strand,
But came the waves and washed it away:
Agayne I wrote it with a second hand,
But came the tyde, and made my paynes his pray.
Vayne man, sayd she, that doest in vaine assay,
A mortall thing so to immortalize,
For I my selfe shall lyke to this decay,
And eek my name bee wyped out lykewize.
Not so, (quod I) let baser things devize
To dy in dust, but you shall live by fame:
My verse your vertues rare shall eternize,
And in the hevens wryte your glorious name.
Where whenas death shall all the world subdew,
Our love shall live, and later life renew.
[*Amoretti, and Epithalamion* (1595), Sonnet 75]

12. The woods shall to me answer and my Eccho ring...

13. Open the temple gates unto my love,
Open them wide that she may enter in...

14. Ah when will this long weary day have end,
And lende me leave to come unto my love?...

15. Song made in lieu of many ornaments,
With which my love should duly have been deckt...

16. Be unto her a goodly ornament,
And for short time an endlesse moniment.
[*Amoretti, and Epithalamion* (1595), 'Epithalamion']

17. Triton blowing loud his wreathed horne...

18. So love is Lord of all the world by right.
[*Colin Clouts Come Home Againe* (1595)]

19. The generall end therefore of all the booke is to fashion a gentleman or noble person in vertuous and gentle discipline.
[*The Faerie Queene* (1596), Preface]

20. Fierce warres and faithfull loves shall moralize my song.
[*The Faerie Queene* (1596), I, Introduction]

21. A Gentle Knight was pricking on the plaine...

22. But on his brest a bloudie Crosse he bore,
The deare remembrance of his dying Lord...

23. A bold bad man, that dar'd to call by name
Great Gorgon, Prince of darknesse and dead night.
[*The Faerie Queene* (1596), I, 1]

24. Her angel's face
As the great eye of heaven shyned bright,
And made a sunshine in the shadie place;
Did never mortall eye behold such heavenly grace.
[*The Faerie Queene* (1596), I, 3]

25. And all the hinder parts, that few could spie,
Were ruinous and old, but painted cunningly.
[*The Faerie Queene* (1596), I, 4]

26. The noble hart, that harbours vertuous thought,
And is with child of glorious great intent,
Can never rest, untill it forth have brought
Th' eternall brood of glorie excellent...

27. A cruell craftie Crocodile,
Which in false griefe hyding his harmefull guile,

Doth weepe full sore, and sheddeth tender teares.
[*The Faerie Queene* (1596), I, 5]

28. Still as he fled, his eye was backward cast,
As if his feare still followed him behind...

29. That darkesome cave they enter, where they find
That cursed man, low sitting on the ground.
Musing full sadly in his sullein mind...

30. Sleepe after toyle, port after stormie seas,
Ease after warre, death after life does greatly please...

31. Death is the end of woes: die soone, O faeries sonne.
[*The Faerie Queene* (1596), I, 9]

32. Upon her eyelids many Graces sate,
Under the shadow of her even browes.
[*The Faerie Queene* (1596), II, 3]

33. And all for love, and nothing for reward.
[*The Faerie Queene* (1596), II, 8]

34. So passeth, in the passing of a day,
Of mortall life the leafe, the bud, the flowre,
Ne more doth flourish after first decay,
That earst was sought to decke both bed and bowre,
Of many a Ladie, and many a Paramowre:
Gather therefore the Rose, whilest yet is prime,
For soone comes age, that will her pride deflowre:
Gather the Rose of love, whilest yet is time,
Whilest loving thou mayst loved be with equall crime...

35. The donghill kind
Delights in filth and fouel incontinence:
Let Grill be Grill, and have his hoggish mind.
[*The Faerie Queene* (1596), II, 12]

36. Hard is to teach an old horse amble trew.
[*The Faerie Queene* (1596), III, 8]

37. And painefull pleasure turnes to pleasing paine.
[*The Faerie Queene* (1596), III, 10. Cf. Leigh Hunt: 8]

38. And as she lookt about, she did behold,
How over that same dore was likewise writ,
Be bold, be bold, and every where *Be bold*...
At last she spyde at that roome's upper end,
Another yron dore, on which was writ,
Be not too bold.
[*The Faerie Queene* (1596), III, 11]

39. Dan Chaucer, well of English undefyled,
On Fame's eternall beadroll worthie to be fyled.
[*The Faerie Queene* (1596), IV, 2]

40. For all that nature by her mother wit
Could frame in earth.
[*The Faerie Queene* (1596), IV, 10]

41. O Sacred hunger of ambitious mindes...

42. A monster, which the *Blatant beast* men call,
A dreadfull feend of gods and men ydrad.
[*The Faerie Queene* (1596), V, 12]

43. The gentle minde by gentle deeds is knowne.
For a man by nothing is so well bewrayd,
As by his manners.
[*The Faerie Queene* (1596), VI, 3]

44. What man that sees the ever-whirling wheele
Of Change, the which all mortall things doth sway,
But that therby doth find, and plainly feele,
How Mutability in them doth play
Her cruell sports, to many men's decay?
[*The Faerie Queene* (1596), VII, 6]

45. For, all that moveth, doth in Change delight:
But thence-forth all shall rest eternally
With Him that is the God of Sabbaoth hight:
O! that great Sabbaoth God, grant me that Sabbaoth's sight.
[*The Faerie Queene* (1596), VIII, 8]

46. That Beautie is not, as fond men misdeeme,
An outward shew of things, that onely seeme...

47. For of the soule the bodie forme doth take:
For soule is forme, and doth the bodie make.
[*Fowre Hymnes* (1596), 'An Hymne in Honour of Beautie']

48. Calme was the day, and through the trembling ayre,
Sweete breathing Zephyrus did softly play...

49. With that I saw two Swannes of goodly hewe,
Come softly swimming downe along the Lee;
Two fairer Birds I yet did never see:
The snow which doth the top of Pindus strew,
Did never whiter shew,
Nor Jove himselfe when he a Swan would be
For love of Leda, whiter did appeare.
Yet Leda was they say as white as he,
Yet not so white as these, nor nothing neare;
So purely white they were,
That even the gentle streame, the which them bare,
Seem'd foule to them, and bad his billowes spare
To wet their silken feathers, least they might
Soyle their fayre plumes with water not so fayre,
And marre their beauties bright,
That shone as heaven's light,
Against their Brydale day, which was not long:
Sweet Themmes, runne softly, till I end my Song.
[*Prothalamion* (1596)]

Spinoza, Baruch (1632–1677)

Dutch moral and metaphysical philosopher, and theologian

1. *Appetitus; qui proinde nihil aliud est quam ipsa hominis essentio.*
Appetite, which is therefore nothing but the very essence of man.
[*Ethics* (1677), III, 'Scholium on Propositio IX']

2. *Nam una eadem res potest eodem tempore bona et mala et etiam indifferans esse, e.g. Musica bona est Melancholico, mala Lugenti; Surdo autem neque bona neque mala.*
One and the same thing can at the same time be good and bad, or even indifferent, for example, music is good to the melancholy, bad to the mourner, and neither good nor bad to the deaf.
[*Ethics* (1677), IV, Praefatio]

3. *Homo sit animale sociale.*
Man is a social animal.
[*Ethics* (1677), IV, 'Scholium on Propositio XXV']

4. *Sentimus experimurque, nos aeternos esse.*
We feel and know by experience that we are eternal.
[*Ethics* (1677), V, 'Scholium on Propositio XXIII']

5. *Sedula curavi, humanas actiones non ridere, non lugere, neque detestare, sed intelligere.*
I have taken great care not to laugh at human actions, not to weep at them, nor to hate them, but to understand them.
[*Tractatus Politicus* (1677), 1, 4]

Spock, Dr Benjamin (1903–)

American paediatrician and influential writer on child care

1. To win in Vietnam, we will have to exterminate a nation.
[*Dr Spock on Vietnam* (1968), 7]

Spooner, William (1844–1930)
English clergyman and university warden
Many of the sayings attributed to Spooner are believed to have been made up by his friends.

1. You will find as you grow older that the weight of rages will press harder and harder upon the employer.
[In William Hayter, *Spooner* (1977), 6]

2. Poor soul, very sad; her late husband, you know, a very sad death – eaten by missionaries – poor soul!
[In William Hayter, *Spooner* (1977), 6]

3. [Announcing hymn in New College chapel]
Kinquering Congs their titles take.
[Attr., 1879]

4. Through a dark glassly . . .
[Attr.]

5. Let us drink to the queer old Dean.
[Attr.]

6. I remember your name perfectly, but I just can't think of your face.
[Attr.]

7. [To an Oxford undergraduate after the First World War]
Was it you or your brother who was killed in the war?
[Attr.]

Sprat, Thomas (1635–1713)
English Bishop of Rochester; preacher, poet and prose writer; Fellow and historian of the Royal Society

1. Poetry is the mother of superstition.
[*The History of the Royal Society* (1667)]

2. [Of the Royal Society]
They have exacted from all their members a close, naked, natural way of speaking; positive expressions; clear senses; a native easiness: bringing all things as near the mathematical plainness, as they can; and preferring the language of artizans, countrymen, and merchants, before that of wits or scholars.
[*The History of the Royal Society* (1667)]

Spring-Rice, Cecil Arthur (1859–1918)
English diplomat and ambassador to the US from 1913

1. I am the Dean of Christ Church, Sir:
There's my wife; look well at her.
She's the Broad and I'm the High;
We are the University.
[In Hiscock (ed.), *The Balliol Rhymes* (1939), 'The Masque of Balliol']

2. I am the Dean, and this is Mrs Liddell;
She the first, and I the second fiddle.
[Unofficially altered first couplet of 'The Masque of Balliol']

Spyri, Johanna (1827–1901)
Swiss writer

1. Oh, I wish that God had not given me what I prayed for! It was not so good as I thought.
[*Heidi* (1880–1881), 11]

Squire, Sir J.C. (1884–1958)
English poet and critic; essayist, journalist, editor and short-story writer

1. God heard the embattled nations sing and shout
'Gott strafe England!' and 'God save the King!'
God this, God that, and God the other thing–
'Good God!' said God, 'I've got my work cut out.'
[*The Survival of the Fittest* (1916), 'Epigrams: 1, The Dilemma']

2. It did not last: the Devil howling 'Ho,
Let Einstein be,' restored the status quo.
['In Continuation of Pope on Newton' (1926). Cf. Pope: 71]

3. But I'm not so think as you drunk I am.
[In Baring, *One Hundred and One Ballades* (1931), 'Ballade of Soporific Absorption']

Stacpoole, H. de Vere (1863–1951)
Irish novelist and physician

1. In home-sickness you must keep moving – it is the only disease that does not require rest.
[*The Bourgeois* (1901)]

Staël, Mme de (Anne-Louise-Germaine Necker) (1766–1817)
French novelist, critic, memoirist, prose writer and hostess

1. *Tout comprendre rend très indulgent.*
Understanding everything makes one very tolerant.
[*Corinne* (1807), IV]

Stalin, Joseph (1879–1953)
Soviet totalitarian dictator, born in Georgia; General Secretary of the Soviet Communist Party 1922–53

1. The state is a machine in the hands of the ruling class for suppressing the resistance of its class enemies.
[*Foundations of Leninism* (1924), 4]

2. The tasks of the party are . . . to be cautious and not allow our country to be drawn into conflicts by warmongers who are accustomed to having others pull the chestnuts out of the fire for them.
[Speech, 1941]

3. History shows that there are no invincible armies.
[Speech on the declaration of war on Germany, 1941]

4. [Reply to Laval, French Foreign Minister, who asked Stalin in 1935 to do something to encourage the Catholic religion in Russia in order to help him gain the support of the Pope]
The Pope! How many divisions has *he* got?
[In W.S. Churchill, *The Gathering Storm* (1948), I, 8]

Stanley, Sir Henry Morton (1841–1904)
Welsh journalist, explorer of Africa, travel writer and politician

1. Dr Livingstone, I presume?
[*How I found Livingstone* (1872), 11]

2. Through the Dark Continent.
[Title of book, 1878]

Stanton, Colonel C.E. (1859–1933)
American soldier

1. [Address at the grave of Lafayette, Paris, 1917]
Lafayette, nous voilà!
Lafayette, we are here!
[*New York Tribune*, 1917]

Stanton, Edwin McMasters (1814–1869)
American lawyer and statesman; Secretary of War 1862–68

1. [Remark on hearing of Lincoln's assassination]
Now he belongs to the ages.
[In I.M. Tarbell, *Life of Abraham Lincoln* (1900), II]

Stanton, Elizabeth Cady (1815–1902)
American suffragist and abolitionist; feminist, editor and writer

1. We hold these truths to be self-evident, that all men and women are created equal.
['Declaration of Sentiments' at First Women's Rights Convention, New York, 1848]

2. I have been into many of the ancient cathedrals – grand, wonderful, mysterious. But I always leave them with a feeling of indignation because of the generations of human beings who have struggled in poverty to build these altars to the unknown god.
[*Diary*, 1882]

3. [On *Genesis*, I]
As to woman's subjection, on which both the canon and the civil law delight to dwell, it is important to note that equal dominion is given to woman over every living thing, but not one word is said giving man dominion over woman.
[*The Woman's Bible* (1895), I]

4. The prolonged slavery of woman is the darkest page in human history.
[In Anthony and Gage (eds), *History of Woman Suffrage* (1881), I, Introduction]

5. Men are uniformly more attentive to women of rank, family, and fortune, who least need their care, than to any other class.
[In Anthony and Gage (eds), *History of Woman Suffrage* (1881), I, Introduction]

6. Womanhood is the great fact in her life; wifehood and motherhood are but incidental relations.
[In Anthony and Gage (eds), *History of Woman Suffrage* (1881), I, Introduction]

7. Woman has been the great unpaid laborer of the world.
[In Anthony and Gage (eds), *History of Woman Suffrage* (1881), I]

8. It is impossible for one class to appreciate the wrongs of another.
[In Anthony and Gage (eds), *History of Woman Suffrage* (1881), I]

Stanton, Frank L. (1857–1927)
American journalist and poet

1. Sweetes' li'l' feller, everybody knows;
Dunno what to call him, but he's mighty lak' a rose!
['Mighty Lak' a Rose', song, 1901]

Stapledon, Olaf (1886–1950)
British philosopher and writer of science fiction

1. That strange blend of the commercial traveller, the missionary, and the barbarian conqueror, which was the American abroad.
[*Last and First Men* (1930), 3]

Staples, James Frederick (1929–)
Australian politician

1. [Said when Deputy President of the Australian Conciliation and Arbitration Commission]
In Canberra if you want a little loyalty you had better buy yourself a dog.
[*Australian Book Review*, 1984]

Stark, Dame Freya (1893–1993)
French-born traveller and writer

1. The beckoning counts, and not the clicking latch behind you.
[*The Sunday Telegraph*, 1993]

Stark, John (1728–1822)
American revolutionary general

1. [Remark before the Battle of Bennington, 1777]
We beat them today, or Molly Stark's a widow!
[In Appletons' *Cyclopaedia of American Biography* (1888), V]

Stead, Christina (1902–1983)
Australian novelist and short-story writer

1. A self-made man is one who believes in luck and sends his son to Oxford.
[*House of All Nations* (1938), 'Credo']

2. When women are free, we'll see other emotions, no love. Love is a slave emotion, like a dog's.
[*For Love Alone* (1944), 15]

3. The rich take their time, the rich marry late so that property will be divided little and late, while the poor rush to marry and divide the little pay that one gets.
[*For Love Alone* (1944), 19]

4. I don't know what imagination is, if not an unpruned, tangled kind of memory.
[*Letty Fox: Her Luck* (1946), 6]

5. A lie is real; it aims at success. A liar is a realist.
[*Letty Fox: Her Luck* (1946), 6]

6. What luck you have, you American women! Men who pay for everything and don't ask for accounts. Yes, it's Protestantism. The men believe they've done their wives insult and injury by sleeping with them. They must pay for ever! They must pay for their mothers because their mothers suffered to have them. And as for the women...
[*Letty Fox: Her Luck* (1946), 14]

7. [On feminism]
I don't believe in segregation of any kind, and I think men and women should unite to fight the battle. All the men I've known have been in favour of women's success.
[Interview with Rodney Wetherell, first broadcast by Australian Broadcasting Commission, 1980]

Steel, Sir David (1938–)
Scottish politician; Liberal Party leader 1976–88

1. Go back to your constituencies and prepare for government!
[Speech to party conference, 1981]

2. I sense that the British electorate is now itching to break out once and for all from the discredited straight-jacket of the past.
[*The Times*, 1987]

Steele, Sir Richard (1672–1729)
Irish-born English essayist, comic dramatist, pamphleteer and politician

1. Women dissemble their Passions better than Men, but ... Men subdue their Passions better than Women.
[*The Lover* (1714), 9]

2. No Woman of spirit thinks a Man hath any Respect for her 'till he hath played the Fool in her Service.
[*The Lover* (1714), 9]

3. I am, dear Prue, a little in Drink but at all times Yr Faithfull Husband.
[Letter to his wife, 1708]

4. It is to be noted, That when any Part of this Paper appears dull, there is a Design in it.
[*The Tatler*, 38, 1709]

5. [Of Lady Hastings]
Tho' her Mien carries much more Invitation than Command, to behold her is an immediate Check to loose Behaviour, and to love her, is a liberal Education.
[*The Tatler*, 49, 1709]

6. Every Man is the Maker of his own Fortune.
[*The Tatler*, 52, 1709]

7. Reading is to the Mind, what Exercise is to the Body ... But as Exercise becomes tedious and painful when we make use of it only as the Means of Health, so Reading is apt to grow uneasy and burdensome, when we apply our selves to it only for our Improvement in Virtue.
[*The Tatler*, 47, 1710]

8. These Ladies of irresistible Modesty are those who make Virtue unamiable.
[*The Tatler*, 217, 1710]

9. The insupportable Labour of doing nothing.
[*The Spectator*, 54, 1711]

10. We were in some little Time fixed in our Seats, and sat with that Dislike which People not too good-natured, usually conceive of each other at first Sight.
[*The Spectator*, 132, 1711]

11. Let your precept be, *Be easy*. That Mind is dissolute and ungoverned, which must be hurried out of itself by loud Laughter or sensual Pleasure, or else be wholly inactive.
[*The Spectator*, 196, 1711]

12. Will Honeycomb calls these over-offended Ladies the outrageously virtuous.
[*The Spectator*, 266, 1712]

13. I have often thought that a Story-teller is born, as well as a Poet.
[*The Guardian*, 42, 1713]

Steffens, Lincoln (1866–1936)
American political analyst, journalist and memoirist

1. [Remark after visiting Russia in 1919]
I have seen the future; and it works.
[Letter to Marie Howe, 1919. Cf. Reginald Hill: 1]

Stein, Gertrude (1874–1946)
American novelist, dramatist, poet, critic and autobiographical writer, noted for her experimental style

1. Rose is a rose is a rose is a rose, is a rose.
[*Sacred Emily* (1913)]

2. She always says she dislikes the abnormal, it is so obvious. She says the normal is so much more simply complicated and interesting.
[*The Autobiography of Alice B. Toklas* (1933)]

3. In the United States there is more space where nobody is than where anybody is. That is what makes America what it is.
[*The Geographical History of America* (1936)]

4. [Remark made in the 1920s]
That's what you are. That's what you all are. All of you young people who served in the war. You are a lost generation.
[In Hemingway, *A Moveable Feast* (1964), 3]

5. [Speaking to a friend she considered knew little about literature]
Besides Shakespeare and me, who do you think there is?
[In Mellow, *Charmed Circle* (1974)]

6. The Jews have produced only three originative geniuses: Christ, Spinoza, and myself.
[In Mellow, *Charmed Circle* (1974)]

7. Just before she [Stein] died she asked, 'What *is* the answer?' No answer came. She laughed and said, 'In that case, what is the question?' Then she died.
[In Sutherland, *Gertrude Stein* (1951), 6]

Stein, Jock (1922–1985)
Scottish football player and manager

1. Let's not lose our dignity.
[Last words]

Steinbeck, John (1902–1968)
American novelist and short-story writer, noted for his stories of farm workers; Nobel prize 1962

1. Cannery Row in Monterey in California is a poem, a stink, a grating noise, a quality of light, a tone, a habit, a nostalgia, a dream.
[*Cannery Row* (1939), Introduction]

2. Okie use' ta mean you was from Oklahoma. Now it means you're a dirty son-of-a-bitch. Okie means you're scum. Don't mean nothing itself, it's the way they say it.
[*The Grapes of Wrath* (1939), 18]

3. [On critics]
Unless the bastards have the courage to give you unqualified praise, I say ignore them.
[In J.K. Galbraith, *A Life in Our Times* (1981)]

4. It is wonderful that even today, with all the competition of radio, television, films, and records, the book has kept its precious character. A book is somehow sacred. A dictator can kill and maim people, can sink to any kind of tyranny, and only be hated. But when books are burnt the ultimate in tyranny has happened. This we cannot forgive.
[Attr.]

Steinem, Gloria (1934–)
American writer, journalist and feminist activist

1. [On transsexualism]
If the shoe doesn't fit, must we change the foot?
[*Outrageous Acts and Everyday Rebellions* (1984)]

2. One day, an army of grey-haired women may quietly take over the earth.
[*Outrageous Acts and Everyday Rebellions* (1984)]

3. Some of us have become the men we wanted to marry.
[*The Observer*, 1982, in Jeffrey Care (ed.), *Sayings of the Eighties* (1989)]

4. A woman needs a man like a fish needs a bicycle.
[Attr.]

Stekel, Wilhelm (1868–1940)
Austrian psychoanalyst and writer, born in Bukovina

1. The mark of the immature man is that he wants to die nobly for a cause, while the mark of the mature man is that he wants to live humbly for one.
[In J.D. Salinger, *The Catcher in the Rye* (1951), 24]

Stendhal (Marie-Henri Beyle) (1783–1842)
French novelist; biographer, critic and soldier

1. *Le romantisme est l'art de présenter aux peuples les oeuvres littéraires qui, dans l'état actuel de leurs habitudes et de leurs*

croyances, sont susceptibles de leur donner le plus de plaisir possible. Le classicisme, *au contraire, leur présente la littérature qui donnait le plus grand plaisir possible à leurs arrière-grand-pères.* Romanticism is the art of presenting people with the literary works which are capable of giving them the greatest possible pleasure, in the present state of their customs and beliefs. Classicism, on the other hand, presents them with the literature that gave the greatest possible pleasure to their great-grandfathers.
[*Racine et Shakespeare* (1823), 3]

2. *Un roman est un miroir qui se promène sur une grande route.*
A novel is a mirror walking along a wide road.
[*Le Rouge et le Noir* (*The Red and the Black*, 1830), 49]

Stenhouse, David (1932–)

1. [On the conservation of biological resources]
I know a man who has a device for converting solar energy into food. Delicious stuff he makes with it, too. Being doing it for years ... It's called a farm.
[*Crisis in Abundance* (1966)]

Stephen, Sir James Fitzjames (1829–1894)
English judge and essayist; uncle of Virginia Woolf

1. The way in which the man of genius rules is by persuading an efficient minority to coerce an indifferent and self-indulgent majority.
[*Liberty, Equality and Fraternity* (1873), ?]

2. Progress has its drawbacks, and they are great and serious; but whatever its value may be, unity in religious belief would further it.
[*Liberty, Equality and Fraternity* (1873), 2]

Stephen, James Kenneth (1859–1892)
English journalist and poet, son of Sir James Fitzjames Stephen

1. Ah! Matt.: old age has brought to me
Thy wisdom, less thy certainty:
The world's a jest, and joy's a trinket:
I knew that once: but now – I think it.
[*Lapsus Calami* (1891), 'Senex to Matt. Prior'. Cf. Gay: 36]

2. Two voices are there: one is of the deep;
It learns the storm-cloud's thunderous melody,
Now roars, now murmurs with the changing sea,
Now bird-like pipes, now closes soft in sleep:
And one is of an old half-witted sheep
Which bleats articulate monotony,
And indicates that two and one are three,
That grass is green, lakes damp, and mountains steep
And, Wordsworth, both are thine.
[*Lapsus Calami* (1891), 'A Sonnet'. Cf. Wordsworth: 41]

3. Will there never come a season
Which shall rid us from the curse
Of a prose which knows no reason
And an unmelodious verse...
When there stands a muzzled stripling,
Mute, beside a muzzled bore:
When the Rudyards cease from kipling
And the Haggards ride no more.
[*Lapsus Calami* (1891), 'To R.K.']

Stephens, James (1882–1950)
Irish poet, novelist and short-story writer

1. Finality is death. Perfection is finality. Nothing is perfect. There are lumps in it.
[*The Crock of Gold* (1912)]

2. Curiosity will conquer fear even more than bravery will.
[*The Crock of Gold* (1912)]

3. A secret is a weapon and a friend. Man is God's secret, Power is man's secret, Sex is woman's secret.
[*The Crock of Gold* (1912)]

4. The lanky hank of a she in the inn over there
Nearly killed me for asking the loan of a glass of beer;
May the devil grip the whey-faced slut by the hair,
And beat bad manners out of her skin for a year.
['A Glass of Beer' (1913)]

5. I heard a sudden cry of pain!
There is a rabbit in a snare...

6. Little one! Oh, little one!
I am searching everywhere!
['The Snare' (1915)]

7. Men come of age at sixty, women at fifteen.
[*The Observer*, 'Sayings of the Week', 1944]

Sterne, Laurence (1713–1768)
Irish-born English novelist, humorist and clergyman, noted for his development of the novel form

1. I live in a constant endeavour to fence against the infirmities of ill health, and other evils of life, by mirth; being firmly persuaded that every time a man smiles, – but much more so, when he laughs, it adds something to this Fragment of Life.
[*Tristram Shandy* (1759–1767), Dedication to Mr Pitt]

2. I wish either my father or my mother, or indeed both of them, as they were in duty both equally bound to it, had minded what they were about when they begot me.
[*Tristram Shandy* (1759–1767), I, 1, opening lines]

3. 'Pray, my dear,' quoth my mother, 'have you not forgot to wind up the clock?' – 'Good G–!' cried my father, making an exclamation, but taking care to moderate his voice at the same time, – 'Did ever woman, since the creation of the world, interrupt a man with such a silly question?'
[*Tristram Shandy* (1759–1767), I, 1]

4. As we jog on, either laugh with me, or at me, or in short, do anything, – only keep your temper.
[*Tristram Shandy* (1759–1767), I, 6]

5. So long as a man rides his hobby-horse peaceably and quietly along the King's highway, and neither compels you or me to get up behind him, – pray, Sir, what have either you or I to do with it?
[*Tristram Shandy* (1759–1767), I, 7]

6. 'Tis no extravagant arithmetic to say, that for every ten jokes, – thou hast got a hundred enemies.
[*Tristram Shandy* (1759–1767), I, 12]

7. 'Tis known by the name of perseverance in a good cause, – and of obstinacy in a bad one.
[*Tristram Shandy* (1759–1767), I, 17]

8. What is the character of a family to an hypothesis? my father would reply.
[*Tristram Shandy* (1759–1767), I, 21]

9. My uncle Toby would never offer to answer this by any other kind of argument, than that of whistling half a dozen bars of *Lillabullero*.
[*Tristram Shandy* (1759–1767), I, 21]

10. Digressions, incontestably, are the sunshine; – they are the life, the soul of reading; – take them out of this book for instance, – you might as well take the book along with them.
[*Tristram Shandy* (1759–1767), I, 22]

11. I should have no objection to this method, but that I think it must smell too strong of the lamp.
[*Tristram Shandy* (1759–1767), I, 23]

12. The desire of knowledge, like the thirst of riches, increases ever with the acquisition of it.
[*Tristram Shandy* (1759–1767), II, 3]

13. Writing, when properly managed, (as you may be sure I think mine is) is but a different name for conversation.
[*Tristram Shandy* (1759–1767), II, 11]

14. 'I'll not hurt thee,' says my uncle Toby, rising from his chair, and going across the room, with the fly in his hand, – 'I'll not hurt a hair of thy head: – Go,' says he, lifting up the sash, and opening his hand as he spoke, to let it escape; – 'go, poor devil, get thee gone, why should I hurt thee? – This world surely is wide enough to hold both thee and me.'
[*Tristram Shandy* (1759–1767), II, 12]

15. Whenever a man talks loudly against religion, – always suspect that it is not his reason, but his passions which have got the better of his creed.
[*Tristram Shandy* (1759–1767), II, 17]

16. 'Sir,' replied Dr Slop, 'it would astonish you to know what improvements we have made of late years in all branches of obstetrical knowledge, but particularly in that one single point of the safe and expeditious extraction of the foetus, – which has received such lights, that, for my part (holding up his hands) I declare I wonder how the world has –.'
'I wish,' quoth my uncle Toby, 'you had seen what prodigious armies we had in Flanders.'
[*Tristram Shandy* (1759–1767), II, 18]

17. It is the nature of an hypothesis, when once a man has conceived it, that it assimilates every thing to itself as proper nourishment; and, from the first moment of your begetting it, it generally grows the stronger by every thing you see, hear, read, or understand. This is of great use.
[*Tristram Shandy* (1759–1767), II, 19]

18. 'Our armies swore terribly in Flanders,' cried my uncle Toby, – 'but nothing to this.'
[*Tristram Shandy* (1759–1767), III, 11]

19. The corregiescity of Corregio.
[*Tristram Shandy* (1759–1767), III, 12. Cf. Thomas Carlyle: 58]

20. Of all the cants which are canted in this canting world, – though the cant of hypocrites may be the worst, – the cant of criticism is the most tormenting!
[*Tristram Shandy* (1759–1767), III, 12]

21. All is not gain that is got into the purse.
[*Tristram Shandy* (1759–1767), III, 30]

22. Heat is in proportion to the want of true knowledge.
[*Tristram Shandy* (1759–1767), IV, Slawkenbergius's Tale]

23. [Of death]
'There is no terror, brother Toby, in its looks, but what it borrows from groans and convulsions – and the blowing of noses, and the wiping away of tears with the bottoms of curtains, in a dying man's room – Strip it of these, what is it?' – ''Tis better in battle than in bed', said my uncle Toby.
[*Tristram Shandy* (1759–1767), V, 3]

24. Prejudice of education, he would say, is the devil, – and the multitudes of them which we suck in with our mother's milk – are the devil and all. – We are haunted with them, brother Toby, in all our lucubrations and researches; and was a man fool enough to submit tamely to what they obtruded upon him, – what would his book be? ... nothing but a farrago of the clack of nurses, and of the nonsense of the old women (of both sexes) throughout the kingdom.
[*Tristram Shandy* (1759–1767), V, 16]

25. There is a North-west passage to the intellectual world.
[*Tristram Shandy* (1759–1767), V, 42]

26. You forget the great Lipsius, quoth Yorick, who composed a work the day he was born; – they should have wiped it up, said my uncle Toby, and said no more about it.
[*Tristram Shandy* (1759–1767), VI, 2]

27. Ask my pen, – it governs me, – I govern not it.
[*Tristram Shandy* (1759–1767), VI, 6]

28. 'The poor soul will die:–'
'He shall not die, by G–', cried my uncle Toby. – The Accusing Spirit, which flew up to heaven's chancery with the oath, blush'd as he gave it in; – and the Recording Angel, as he wrote it down, dropp'd a tear upon the word, and blotted it out for ever.
[*Tristram Shandy* (1759–1767), VI, 8]

29. The excellency of this text is, that it will suit any sermon, – and of this sermon, – that it will suit any text.
[*Tristram Shandy* (1759–1767), VI, 11]

30. To say a man is fallen in love, – or that he is deeply in love, – or up to the ears in love, – and sometimes even over head and ears in it, – carries an idiomatical kind of implication, that love is a thing below a man: – this is recurring again to Plato's opinion, which, with all his divinityship, – I hold to be damnable and heretical; – and so much for that.
Let love therefore be what it will, – my uncle Toby fell into it.
[*Tristram Shandy* (1759–1767), VI, 37]

31. 'My brother Toby,' quoth she, 'is going to be married to Mrs Wadman.'
'Then he will never,' quoth my father, 'be able to lie *diagonally* in his bed again as long as he lives.'
[*Tristram Shandy* (1759–1767), VI, 39]

32. A man should know something of his own country too, before he goes abroad.
[*Tristram Shandy* (1759–1767), VII, 2]

33. 'A soldier,' cried my uncle Toby, interrupting the corporal, 'is no more exempt from saying a foolish thing, Trim, than a man of letters.' – 'But not so often, and please your honour,' replied the corporal.
[*Tristram Shandy* (1759–1767), VIII, 19]

34. Love, an' please your honour, is exactly like war, in this; that a soldier, though he has escaped three weeks complete o' Saturday night, – may nevertheless be shot through his heart on Sunday morning.
[*Tristram Shandy* (1759–1767), VIII, 21]

35. 'I am half distracted, Captain Shandy,' said Mrs Wadman, ... 'a mote – or sand – or something – I know not what, has got into this eye of mine – do look in to it.' ... In saying which, Mrs Wadman edged herself close in beside my uncle Toby, ... 'Do look into it,' – said she...
If thou lookest, uncle Toby, in search of this mote one moment longer – thou art undone.
[*Tristram Shandy* (1759–1767), VIII, 24]

36. An eye full of gentle salutations – and soft responses – ... whispering soft – like the last low accents of an expiring saint ... It did my uncle Toby's business.
[*Tristram Shandy* (1759–1767), VIII, 25]

37. Honours, like impressions upon coin, may give an ideal and local value to a bit of base metal; but Gold and Silver will pass all the world over without any other recommendation than their own weight.
[*Tristram Shandy* (1759–1767), IX, Dedication]

38. Every time I kiss thy hand to bid adieu, and every absence which follows it, are preludes to that eternal separation which we are shortly to make.
[*Tristram Shandy* (1759–1767), IX, 8]

39. Said my mother, 'What is all this story about?' – 'A Cock and a Bull', said Yorick –'And one of the best of its kind, I ever heard.'
[*Tristram Shandy* (1759–1767), IX, 33]

40. They order, said I, this matter better in France.
[*A Sentimental Journey* (1768), first sentence]

41. The whole circle of travellers may be reduced to the following Heads:
Idle Travellers,
Inquisitive Travellers,
Lying Travellers,
Proud Travellers,
Vain Travellers,
Splenetic Travellers,
Then follow The Travellers of Necessity,
The delinquent and felonious Traveller,
The unfortunate and innocent Traveller,
The simple Traveller,
And last of all (if you please)
The Sentimental Traveller.
[*Sentimental Journey* (1768), 'Preface in the Desobligeant']

42. As an Englishman does not travel to see Englishmen, I retired to my room.
[*Sentimental Journey* (1768), 'Preface in the Desobligeant']

43. You need not tell me what the proposal was, said she, laying her hand upon both mine, as she interrupted me. – A man, my good Sir, has seldom an offer of kindness to make to a woman, but she has a presentiment of it some moments before.
[*A Sentimental Journey* (1768), 'The Remise, Calais']

44. Having been in love, with one princess or other, almost all my life, and I hope I shall go on so till I die, being firmly persuaded, that if ever I do a mean action, it must be in some interval betwixt one passion and another.
[*A Sentimental Journey* (1768), 'Montreuil']

45. *Vive l'amour! et vive la bagatelle!*
[Long live love! Long live philandering!]
[*A Sentimental Journey* (1768), 'The Letter']

46. Hail ye small sweet courtesies of life.
[*A Sentimental Journey* (1768), 'The Pulse, Paris']

47. There are worse occupations in this world than feeling a woman's pulse.
[*A Sentimental Journey* (1768), 'The Pulse, Paris']

48. He gave a deep sigh – I saw the iron enter into his soul.
[*A Sentimental Journey* (1768), 'The Captive, Paris']

49. I think there is a fatality in it – I seldom go to the place I set out for.
[*A Sentimental Journey* (1768), 'The Address, Versailles']

50. [Of the French]
They are a loyal, a gallant, a generous, an ingenious, and good tempered people as is under heaven – if they have a fault, they are too serious.
[*A Sentimental Journey* (1768), 'Character, Versailles']

51. I am positive I have a soul; nor can all the books with which materialists have pestered the world ever convince me to the contrary.
[*A Sentimental Journey* (1768), 'Maria']

52. God tempers the wind ... to the shorn lamb.
[*A Sentimental Journey* (1768), 'Maria']

53. Dear sensibility! source inexhausted of all that's precious in our joys, or costly in our sorrows!
[*A Sentimental Journey* (1768), 'The Bourbonnois']

54. If the supper was to my taste – the grace which followed it was much more so.
[*A Sentimental Journey* (1768), 'The Supper']

55. Then shame and grief go with her, and wherever she seeks a shelter, may the hand of justice shut the door against her.
[*The Sermons of Mr Yorick* (1760–1769), 'The Levite and His Concubine']

56. This sad vicissitude of things.
[*The Sermons of Mr Yorick* (1760–1769), 'The character of Shimei']

Stevens, Wallace (1879–1955)
American poet; essayist, dramatist and lawyer

1. The only emperor is the emperor of ice-cream.
['The Emperor of Ice-Cream' (1923)]

2. Poetry is the supreme fiction, madame.
['A High-Toned old Christian Woman' (1923)]

3. In my room, the world is beyond my understanding;
But when I walk I see that it consists of three or four hills and a cloud.
['Of the Surface of Things' (1923)]

4. Just as my fingers on these keys
Make music, so the self-same sounds
On my spirit make a music, too.

Music is feeling, then, not sound.
And thus it is what I feel,
Here in this room, desiring you.

Thinking of your blue-shadowed silk,
Is music.
['Peter Quince at the Clavier' (1923), I]

5. Beauty is momentary in the mind–
The fitful tracing of a portal;
But in the flesh it is immortal.
The body dies; the body's beauty lives.
So evenings die, in their green going,
Aware, interminably flowing.
['Peter Quince at the Clavier' (1923), IV]

6. Complacencies of the peignoir, and late
Coffee and oranges in a sunny chair,
And the green freedom of a cockatoo
Upon a rug mingle and dissipate
The holy hush of ancient sacrifice...

7. Deer walk upon our mountains, and the quail
Whistle about us their spontaneous cries;
Sweet berries ripen in the wilderness;
And, in the isolation of the sky,
At evening, casual flocks of pigeons make
Ambiguous undulations as they sink,
Downward to darkness, on extended wings.
['Sunday Morning' (1923)]

8. I do not know which to prefer,
The beauty of inflections
Or the beauty of innuendoes,

The blackbird whistling
Or just after.
['Thirteen Ways of Looking at a Blackbird' (1923)]

9. For she was the maker of the song she sang.
The ever-hooded, tragic-gestured sea
Was merely a place by which she walked to sing...

10. Oh! Blessed rage for order, pale Ramon.
The maker's rage to order words of the sea,
Words of the fragrant portals, dimly-starred,
And of ourselves and of our origins,
In ghostlier demarcations, keener sounds.
['The Idea of Order at Key West' (1936)]

11. The exceeding brightness of this early sun
Makes me conceive how dark I have become.
['The Sun this March' (1936)]

12. They said, 'You have a blue guitar,
You do not play things as they are.'
The man replied, 'Things as they are
Are changed upon the blue guitar.'
['The Man with the Blue Guitar' (1937)]

13. Two things of opposite natures seem to depend
On one another, as a man depends
On a woman, day on night, the imagined

On the real.
['Notes Toward a Supreme Fiction', II (1948)]

14. If I live according to this law I live
In an immense activity, in which
Everything becomes morning, summer, the hero,
The enraptured woman, the sequestered night,
The man that suffered, lying there at ease.
['A Pastoral Nun' (1948)]

Stevenson, Adlai (1900–1965)

American lawyer and statesman; Democrat presidential candidate, and ambassador to the UN 1961–65

1. As the girl said, 'A kiss on the wrist feels good, but a diamond bracelet lasts forever.'
[Address to Chicago Council on Foreign Relations, 1946. Cf. Loos: 5]

2. Making peace is harder than making war.
[Address to Chicago Council on Foreign Relations, 1946. Cf. Clemenceau: 2]

3. A lie is an abomination unto the Lord, and a very present help in trouble.
[Speech, Springfield, Illinois, 1951. Versions of this saying were current in the 19th century]

4. There is no evil in the atom; only in men's souls.
[Speech, Hartford, Connecticut, 1952]

5. My definition of a free society is a society where it is safe to be unpopular.
[Speech, Detroit, 1952]

6. Let's talk sense to the American people. Let's tell them the truth, that there are no gains without pains.
[Speech, Chicago, 1952]

7. The trouble with this country is that it has a two-party system and a one-party press.
[Speech, 1952]

8. I suppose flattery hurts no one – that is, if he doesn't inhale.
[*Meet the Press*, TV broadcast, 1952]

9. We hear the Secretary of State boasting of his brinkmanship – the art of bringing us to the edge of the abyss.
[Speech, Hartford, Connecticut, 1956]

10. Government by postponement is bad enough, but it is far better than government by desperation.
[*The Observer*, 'Sayings of the Week, 1953]

11. Power corrupts, but lack of power corrupts absolutely.
[*The Observer*, 1963. Cf. First Baron Acton: 2 and William Pitt [1]: 6]

12. [Of the Republican Party]
[Needs to be] dragged kicking and screaming into the twentieth century.
[In K. Tynan, *Curtains* (1961)]

13. An editor is one who separates the wheat from the chaff and prints the chaff.
[In Bill Adler, *The Stevenson Wit* (1966)]

14. A politician is a statesman who approaches every question with an open mouth.
[In L. Harris, *The Fine Art of Political Wit*; also attributed to Arthur Goldberg]

15. Eggheads of the world unite; you have nothing to lose but your yolks.
[Attr.]

Stevenson, Robert Louis (1850–1894)

Scottish novelist, short story writer, poet, essayist and travel writer

1. A faddling hedonist.
[*Travels with a Donkey in the Cévennes* (1879), 'The Boarders']

2. For my part, I travel not to go anywhere, but to go. I travel for travel's sake. The great affair is to move.
[*Travels with a Donkey in the Cévennes* (1879), 'Cheylard and Luc']

3. I own I like definite form in what my eyes are to rest upon; and if landscapes were sold, like the sheets of characters of my boyhood, one penny plain and twopence coloured, I should go the length of the twopence every day of my life.
[*Travels with a Donkey in the Cévennes* (1879), 'Father Apollinaris']

4. In marriage, a man becomes slack and selfish, and undergoes a fatty degeneration of his moral being.
[*Virginibus Puerisque* (1881), Title paper, 1]

5. You have only to look these happy couples in the face, to see they have never been in love, or in hate, or in any other high passion all their days.
[*Virginibus Puerisque* (1881), Title paper, 1]

6. Even if we take matrimony at its lowest, even if we regard it as no more than a sort of friendship recognized by the police.
[*Virginibus Puerisque* (1881), Title paper, 1]

7. A little amateur painting in water-colours shows the innocent and quiet mind.
[*Virginibus Puerisque* (1881), Title paper, 1]

8. Marriage is a step so grave and decisive that it attracts light-headed, variable men by its very awfulness.
[*Virginibus Puerisque* (1881), Title paper, 1]

9. Lastly (and this is, perhaps, the golden rule), no woman should marry a teetotaller, or a man who does not smoke.
[*Virginibus Puerisque* (1881), Title paper, 1]

10. Marriage is like life in this – that it is a field of battle and not a bed of roses.
[*Virginibus Puerisque* (1881), Title paper, 1]

11. Times are changed with him who marries; there are no more by-path meadows, where you may innocently linger, but the road lies long and straight and dusty to the grave.
[*Virginibus Puerisque* (1881), Title paper, 2]

12. To marry is to domesticate the Recording Angel. Once you are married, there is nothing left for you, not even suicide, but to be good.
[*Virginibus Puerisque* (1881), Title paper, 2]

13. The cruellest lies are often told in silence.
[*Virginibus Puerisque* (1881), 'Truth of Intercourse']

14. Old and young, we are all on our last cruise.
[*Virginibus Puerisque* (1881), 'Crabbed Age and Youth']

15. Youth is the time to go flashing from one end of the world to the other both in mind and body; to try the manners of different nations; to hear the chimes at midnight; to see sunrise in town and country; to be converted at a revival; to circumnavigate the metaphysics, write halting verses, run a mile to see a fire, and wait all day long in the theatre to applaud *Hernani*.
[*Virginibus Puerisque* (1881), 'Crabbed Age and Youth']

16. It is better to be a fool than to be dead.
[*Virginibus Puerisque* (1881), 'Crabbed Age and Youth']

17. For God's sake give me the young man who has brains enough to make a fool of himself!
[*Virginibus Puerisque* (1881), 'Crabbed Age and Youth']

18. Books are good enough in their own way, but they are a mighty bloodless substitute for life.
[*Virginibus Puerisque* (1881), 'An Apology for Idlers']

19. Extreme *busyness*, whether at school or college, kirk or market, is a symptom of deficient vitality; and a faculty for idleness implies a catholic appetite and a strong sense of personal identity.
[*Virginibus Puerisque* (1881), 'An Apology for Idlers']

20. There is no duty we so much underrate as the duty of being happy.
[*Virginibus Puerisque* (1881), 'An Apology for Idlers']

21. By the time a man gets well into the seventies his continued existence is a mere miracle.
[*Virginibus Puerisque* (1881), 'Aes Triplex']

22. Even if the doctor does not give you a year, even if he hesitates about a month, make one brave push and see what can be accomplished in a week.
[*Virginibus Puerisque* (1881), 'Aes Triplex']

23. An aspiration is a joy forever.
[*Virginibus Puerisque* (1881), 'El Dorado']

24. To travel hopefully is a better thing than to arrive, and the true success is to labour.
[*Virginibus Puerisque* (1881), 'El Dorado']

25. Politics is perhaps the only profession for which no preparation is thought necessary.
[*Familiar Studies of Men and Books* (1882)]

26. Whitman, like a large shaggy dog, just unchained, scouring the beaches of the world and baying at the moon.
[*Familiar Studies of Men and Books* (1882)]

27. Is there anything in life so disenchanting as attainment?
[*New Arabian Nights* (1882), 'The Suicide Club: The Adventure of the Hansom Cabs']

28. I regard you with an indifference closely bordering on aversion.
[*New Arabian Nights* (1882), 'The Rajah's Diamond: Story of the Bandbox']

29. Tip me the black spot.
[*Treasure Island* (1883), 3]

30. And the parrot would say, with great rapidity, 'Pieces of eight! pieces of eight!' till you wondered that it was not out of breath, or till John threw his handkerchief over the cage.
[*Treasure Island* (1883), 10]

31. Many's the long night I [Ben Gunn] have dreamed of cheese – toasted mostly, and woke up again and here I were . . . You might not happen to have a piece of cheese about you now?
[*Treasure Island* (1883), 15]

32. He who was prepared to help the escaping murderer or to embrace the impenitent thief, found, to the overthrow of all his logic, that he objected to the use of dynamite.
[*More New Arabian Nights: The Dynamiter* (1885), 'The Superfluous Mansion'; with Fanny Stevenson]

33. Am I no a bonny fighter?
[*Kidnapped* (1886), 10]

34. I've a grand memory for forgetting, David.
[*Kidnapped* (1886), 18]

35. I have thus played the sedulous ape to Hazlitt, to Lamb, to Wordsworth, to Sir Thomas Browne, to Defoe, to Hawthorne, to Montaigne, to Baudelaire and to Obermann.
[*Memories and Portraits* (1887), 4, 'A College Magazine']

36. What hangs people . . . is the unfortunate circumstance of guilt.
[*The Wrong Box* (1889), 7; with Lloyd Osbourne]

37. Nothing like a little judicious levity.
[*The Wrong Box* (1889), 7; with Lloyd Osbourne]

38. The harmless art of knucklebones has seen the fall of the Roman Empire and the rise of the United States.
[*Across the Plains* (1892), 'The Lantern-Bearers', 1]

39. The bright face of danger.
[*Across the Plains* (1892), 'The Lantern-Bearers', 4]

40. Everyone lives by selling something.
[*Across the Plains* (1892), 'Beggars', 3]

41. Still obscurely fighting the lost fight of virtue, still clinging, in the brothel or on the scaffold, to some rag of honour, the poor jewel of their souls!
[*Across the Plains* (1892), 'Pulvis et Umbra', 2]

42. To be honest, to be kind – to earn a little and to spend a little less, to make upon the whole a family happier for his presence, to renounce when that shall be necessary and not be embittered, to keep a few friends, but these without capitulation – above all, on the same grim condition, to keep friends with himself – here is a task for all that a man has of fortitude and delicacy.
[*Across the Plains* (1892), 'A Christmas Sermon', 1]

43. Here lies one who meant well, tried a little, failed much: – surely that may be his epitaph, of which he need not be ashamed.
[*Across the Plains* (1892), 'A Christmas Sermon', 4]

44. If your morals make you dreary, depend upon it, they are wrong.
[*Across the Plains* (1892)]

45. It's deadly commonplace, but, after all, the commonplaces are the great poetic truths.
[*Weir of Hermiston* (1896), 6]

46. Fifteen men on the dead man's chest
Yo-ho-ho, and a bottle of rum!
Drink and the devil had done for the rest–
Yo-ho-ho, and a bottle of rum!
[*Treasure Island* (1883), 1]

47. In winter I get up at night
And dress by yellow candle-light.

In summer, quite the other way,–
I have to go to bed by day.

I have to go to bed and see
The birds still hopping on the tree,
Or hear the grown-up people's feet
Still going past me in the street.
[*A Child's Garden of Verses* (1885), 'Bed in Summer']

48. The friendly cow, all red and white,
I love with all my heart:
She gives me cream with all her might,
To eat with apple-tart.
[*A Child's Garden of Verses* (1885), 'The Cow']

49. Children, you are very little,
And your bones are very brittle...

50. If you would grow great and stately,
You must try to walk sedately.
[*A Child's Garden of Verses* (1885), 'Good and Bad Children']

51. The world is so full of a number of things,
I'm sure we should all be as happy as kings.
[*A Child's Garden of Verses* (1885), 'Happy Thought']

52. When I was sick and lay a-bed,
I had two pillows at my head,
And all my toys beside me lay
To keep me happy all the day...

I was the giant great and still
That sits upon the pillow-hill,
And sees before him, dale and plain,
The pleasant land of counterpane.
[*A Child's Garden of Verses* (1885), 'The Land of Counterpane']

53. When I am grown to man's estate
I shall be very proud and great,
And tell the other girls and boys
Not to meddle with my toys.
[*A Child's Garden of Verses* (1885), 'Looking Forward']

54. Must we to bed indeed? Well then,
Let us arise and go like men,
And face with an undaunted tread
The long black passage up to bed.
[*A Child's Garden of Verses* (1885), 'The North-West Passage']

55. The child that is not clean and neat,
With lots of toys and things to eat,
He is a naughty child, I'm sure–
Or else his dear papa is poor.
[*A Child's Garden of Verses* (1885), 'System']

56. A birdie with a yellow bill
Hopped upon the window-sill.
Cocked his shining eye and said:
'Ain't you 'shamed, you sleepy-head?'
[*A Child's Garden of Verses* (1885), 'Time to Rise']

57. A child should always say what's true,
And speak when he is spoken to,
And behave mannerly at table:
At least as far as he is able.
[*A Child's Garden of Verses* (1885), 'Whole Duty of Children']

58. Whenever the moon and stars are set,
Whenever the wind is high,
All night long in the dark and wet,
A man goes riding by.
Late in the night when the fires are out,
Why does he gallop and gallop about?
[*A Child's Garden of Verses* (1885), 'Windy Nights']

59. Go, little book, and wish to all
Flowers in the garden, meat in the hall,
A bin of wine, a spice of wit,
A house with lawns enclosing it,
A living river by the door,
A nightingale in the sycamore!
[*Underwoods* (1887), I, 'Envoy'. Cf. Chaucer: 120]

60. I am a kind of farthing dip,
Unfriendly to the nose and eyes;
A blue-behinded ape, I skip
Upon the trees of Paradise.
[*Underwoods* (1887), 'A Portrait']

61. Under the wide and starry sky
Dig the grave and let me lie.
Glad did I live and gladly die,
And I laid me down with a will.
This be the verse you grave for me:
'Here he lies where he longed to be;
Home is the sailor, home from sea,
And the hunter home from the hill.'
[*Underwoods* (1887), 'Requiem']

62. But all that I could think of, in the darkness and the cold,
Was that I was leaving home and my folks were growing old.
[*Ballads* (1890), 'Christmas at Sea']

63. Let the blow fall soon or late,
Let what will be o'er me;
Give the face of earth around
And the road before me.
Wealth I seek not, hope nor love,
Nor a friend to know me;
All I seek, the heaven above
And the road below me.
[*Songs of Travel* (1896), I, 'The Vagabond']

64. I will make you brooches and toys for your delight
Of bird-song at morning and star-shine at night.
I will make a palace fit for you and me
Of green days in forests and blue days at sea.
I will make my kitchen, and you shall keep your room,
Where white flows the river and bright blows the broom,
And you shall wash your linen and keep your body white
In rainfall at morning and dewfall at night.
[*Songs of Travel* (1896), XI]

65. Bright is the ring of words
When the right man rings them,
Fair the fall of songs
When the singer sings them.
Still they are carolled and said–
On wings they are carried–
After the singer is dead
And the maker buried.
[*Songs of Travel* (1896), XIV]

66. In the highlands, in the country places,
Where the old plain men have rosy faces,
And the young fair maidens
Quiet eyes.
[*Songs of Travel* (1896), XV]

67. Trusty, dusky, vivid, true,
With eyes of gold and bramble-dew,
Steel-true and blade-straight,
The great artificer
Made my mate.
[*Songs of Travel* (1896), XXV, 'My Wife']

68. Sing me a song of a lad that is gone,
Say, could that lad be I?

Merry of soul he sailed on a day
Over the sea to Skye.
[*Songs of Travel* (1896), XLII]

69. Blows the wind today, and the sun and the rain are flying,
Blows the wind on the moors today and now,
Where about the graves of the martyrs the whaups are crying,
My heart remembers how!...

70. Be it granted to me to behold you again in dying,
Hills of home! and to hear again the call;
Hear about the graves of the martyrs the peewees crying,
And hear no more at all.
[*Songs of Travel* (1896), XLV, 'To S.R. Crockett']

71. Life is not all Beer and Skittles. The inherent tragedy of things works itself out from white to black and blacker, and the poor things of a day look ruefully on. Does it shake my cast iron faith? I cannot say it does. I believe in an ultimate decency of things; ay, and if I woke in hell, should still believe it!
[Letter to Sidney Colvin, 1893]

Stocks, Mary, Baroness (1891–1975)
English educationist, broadcaster and biographer

1. Today we enjoy a social structure which offers equal opportunity in education. It is indeed regrettably true that there is no equal opportunity to take advantage of the equal opportunity.
[*Still More Commonplace* (1973), 8]

2. Biographies are like anthologies, especially anthologies of poetry. One's eyes are magnetically directed to what ought to be there but isn't, as well as to what oughtn't to be there but is.
[*Still More Commonplace* (1973), 10]

3. It is clearly absurd that it should be possible for a woman to qualify as a saint with direct access to the Almighty while she may not qualify as a curate.
[Attr.]

Stockwood, Mervyn (1913–)
English Anglican prelate

1. A psychiatrist is a man who goes to the Folies-Bergère and looks at the audience.
[*The Observer*, 1961]

Stoddard, Elizabeth Drew (1823–1902)
American novelist, short-story writer and journalist

1. A woman despises a man for loving her, unless she returns his love.
[Attr.]

Stone, I.F. (1907–1989)
American journalist, editor and writer

1. If you live long enough, the venerability factor creeps in; you get accused of things you never did and praised for virtues you never had.
[In Laurence J. Peter, *Peter's Quotations*]

Stone, Samuel John (1839–1900)
English clergyman, poet and hymn writer

1. The Church's one foundation
Is Jesus Christ her Lord;
She is his new creation
By water and the word.
[Hymn, 1866]

Stoppard, Tom (1937–)
British stage, screen and radio dramatist, born in Czechoslovakia

1. The House of Lords, an illusion to which I have never been able to subscribe – responsibility without power, the prerogative of the eunuch throughout the ages.
[*Lord Malquist and Mr Moon* (1966), VI. Cf. Kipling: 157]

2. We do on the stage the things that are supposed to happen off. Which is a kind of integrity, if you look on every exit being an entrance somewhere else.
[*Rosencrantz and Guildenstern Are Dead* (1967), I]

3. *Guildenstern*: ... Maidens aspiring to godheads–
Rosencrantz: And vice versa.
[*Rosencrantz and Guildenstern Are Dead* (1967), I]

4. I can do you blood and love without the rhetoric, and I can do you blood and rhetoric without the love and I can do you all three concurrent or consecutive but I can't do you love and rhetoric without the blood. Blood is compulsory – they're all blood you see.
[*Rosencrantz and Guildenstern Are Dead* (1967), I]

5. To sum up: your father, whom you love, dies, you are his heir, you come back to find that hardly was the corpse cold before his younger brother popped on to his throne and into his sheets, thereby offending both legal and natural practice. Now why exactly are you behaving in this extraordinary manner?
[*Rosencrantz and Guildenstern Are Dead* (1967), I]

6. Eternity's a terrible thought. I mean, where's it all going to end?
[*Rosencrantz and Guildenstern Are Dead* (1967), II]

7. The bad end unhappily, the good unluckily. That is what tragedy means.
[*Rosencrantz and Guildenstern Are Dead* (1967), II. Cf. Wilde: 90]

8. Life is a gamble, at terrible odds – if it was a bet, you wouldn't take it.
[*Rosencrantz and Guildenstern Are Dead* (1967), III]

9. This is a British murder inquiry and some degree of justice must be seen to be more or less done.
[*Jumpers* (1972), II]

10. Skill without imagination is craftsmanship and gives us many useful objects such as wickerwork picnic baskets. Imagination without skill gives us modern art.
[*Artist Descending a Staircase* (1973)]

11. What is an artist? For every thousand people there's nine hundred doing the work, ninety doing well, nine doing good, and one lucky bastard who's the artist.
[*Travesties* (1975), I]

12. [Referring to foreign correspondents]
He's someone who flies around from hotel to hotel and thinks the most interesting thing about any story is the fact that he has arrived to cover it.
[*Night and Day* (1978), I]

13. The media. It sounds like a convention of spiritualists.
[*Night and Day* (1978), I]

14. I doubt that art needed Ruskin any more than a moving train needs one of its passengers to shove it.
[*The Times Literary Supplement*, 1977]

15. You can only write about what bites you.
[*The Observer*, 1984, in Jeffrey Care (ed.), *Sayings of the Eighties* (1989)]

Storr, Dr Anthony (1920–)
British writer and psychiatrist

1. It is harder to rebel against love than against authority.
[Attr.]

Stout, Rex Todhunter (1886–1975)
American writer of detective fiction

1. There are two kinds of statistics, the kind you look up and the kind you make up.
[*Death of a Doxy*, 9]

2. I like to walk around Manhattan, catching glimpses of its wild life, the pigeons and cats and girls.
[*Three Witnesses*, 'When a Man Murders']

Stow, Randolph (1935–)
Australian poet, anthropological novelist and fantasist

1. Country children have more than they know,
yet have no worldwide Punch and Judy show.
['Country Children' (1957)]

2. The love of man is a weed of the waste places.
One may think of it as the spinifex of dry souls.
['The Land's Meaning' (1969)]

3. His father hadn't been to church since Nan was christened, and his mother only went to weddings and didn't really have any religion except being anti-Catholic.
[*The Merry-go-round in the Sea* (1965), 8]

Stowe, Harriet Beecher (1811–1896)
American novelist, short-story writer, reformer and essayist

1. 'Who was your mother?' 'Never had none!' said the child, with another grin. 'Never had any mother? What do you mean? Where were you born?' 'Never was born!' persisted Topsy.
[*Uncle Tom's Cabin* (1852), 20]

2. 'Do you know who made you?' 'Nobody, as I knows on,' said the child, with a short laugh . . . 'I 'spect I grow'd.'
[*Uncle Tom's Cabin* (1852), 20]

3. ''Cause I's wicked – I is. I's mighty wicked, any how. I can't help it.'
[*Uncle Tom's Cabin* (1852), 20]

4. Whipping and abuse are like laudanum; you have to double the dose as the sensibilities decline.
[*Uncle Tom's Cabin* (1852), 20]

5. The bitterest tears shed over graves are for words left unsaid and deeds left undone.
[*Little Foxes* (1866), 3]

6. [Of *Uncle Tom's Cabin*]
I did not write it. God wrote it. I merely did his dictation.
[Attr.]

Stowell, William Scott, Baron (1745–1836)
English judge and politician, an authority on maritime and international law

1. A dinner lubricates business.
[In Boswell, *The Life of Samuel Johnson* (1791)]

2. [An opinion, given when he was Advocate General]
A precedent embalms a principle.
[Attr. by Disraeli in *Hansard*, 1848]

Strachey, Lytton (1880–1932)
English biographer and critic; member of the Bloomsbury Group

1. [Of Hurrell Froude]
The time was out of joint, and he was only too delighted to have been born to set it right.
[*Eminent Victorians* (1918), 'Cardinal Manning'. Cf. Shakespeare *Hamlet*: 60]

2. Yet her conception of God was certainly not orthodox. She felt towards Him as she might have felt towards a glorified sanitary engineer; and in some of her speculations she seems hardly to distinguish between the Deity and the Drains.
[*Eminent Victorians* (1918), 'Florence Nightingale']

3. [Referring to Prince Albert's plans for the Great Exhibition]
It should not merely be useful and ornamental; it should preach a high moral lesson.
[*Queen Victoria* (1921), 4]

4. Albert was merely a young foreigner, who suffered from having no vices, and whose only claim to distinction was that he had happened to marry the Queen of England.
[*Queen Victoria* (1921), 5]

5. [Reply when asked by a Tribunal what he, as a conscientious objector, would do if he saw a German soldier trying to rape his sister]
I should try and come between them.
[In Michael Holroyd, *Lytton Strachey: A Critical Biography* (1968)]

6. [Last words]
If this is dying, then I don't think much of it.
[In Michael Holroyd, *Lytton Strachey: A Critical Biography* (1968)]

Stravinsky, Igor (1882–1971)
Influential Russian composer and conductor, noted for his ballet scores and stage works; became a French citizen, 1934, and American, 1945; pupil of Rimsky-Korsakov

1. My music is best understood by children and animals.
[*The Observer*, 1961]

2. I had another dream the other day about music critics. They were small and rodent-like with padlocked ears, as if they had stepped out of a painting by Goya.
[*The Evening Standard*, 1969]

3. Rachmaninov's immortalizing totality was his scowl. He was a six-and-a-half-foot-tall scowl.
[In Igor Stravinsky and Robert Craft, *Conversations with Igor Stravinsky* (1958), 2]

4. [On Rachmaninov]
He was the only pianist I have ever seen who did not grimace. That is a great deal.
[In Igor Stravinsky and Robert Craft, *Conversations with Igor Stravinsky* (1958), 2]

5. A good composer does not imitate; he steals.
[In Peter Yates, *Twentieth Century Music* (1967), I, 8]

Streatfield, Sir Geoffrey Hugh Benbow (1897–1978)
British judge

1. I loathe people who keep dogs. They are cowards who haven't got the guts to bite people themselves.
[*A Madman's Diary*]

Stretton, Hugh (1924–)
Australian political scientist and historian

1. People can't change the way they use resources without changing their relations with one another . . . How to

conserve is usually a harder question than whether, or what, to conserve.
[*Capitalism, Socialism and the Environment* (1976)]

2. Is it really good for policy-makers to act as if everything has its price, and as if policies should be judged chiefly by their effects in delivering material benefits to selfish citizens? ... It does not ask those individuals whether they also have other values which are not revealed by their shopping.
[*Capitalism, Socialism and the Environment* (1976)]

Stubbes, Philip (c. 1555–1610)
English Puritan pamphleteer and writer

1. Football ... causeth fighting, brawling, contention, quarrel picking, murder, homicide and great effusion of blood, as daily experience teacheth.
[*Anatomy of Abuses* (1583)]

Su Tung-P'o (Su Shih) (1036–1101)
Chinese poet, writer, painter and public official

1. Families, when a child is born
Want it to be intelligent.
I, through intelligence,
Having wrecked my whole life,
Only hope the baby will prove
Ignorant and stupid.
Then he will crown a tranquil life
By becoming a Cabinet Minister.
[In Arthur Waley, *170 Chinese Poems* (1918), 'On the Birth of his Son']

Suckling, Sir John (1609–1642)
English Cavalier poet and dramatist

1. Why so pale and wan, fond lover?
Prithee, why so pale?
Will, when looking well can't move her,
Looking ill prevail?
Prithee, why so pale?

Quit, quit, for shame, this will not move:
This cannot take her.
If of herself she will not love,
Nothing can make her:
The devil take her!
[*Aglaura* (1637), IV.i, 'Song']

2. At length the candle's out, and now
All that they had not done they do:
What that is, who can tell?
But I believe it was no more
That thou and I have done before
With Bridget, and with Nell...

3. Her feet beneath her petticoat,
Like little mice, stole in and out,
As if they fear'd the light:
But O she dances such a way!
No sun upon an Easter-day
Is half so fine a sight.
['A Ballad upon a Wedding' (1646)]

4. Out upon it, I have loved
Three whole days together;
And am like to love three more
If it prove fair weather.

Time shall moult away his wings,
Ere he shall discover
In the whole wide world again
Such a constant lover...

5. Had it any been but she,
And that very face,
There had been at least ere this
A dozen dozen in her place.
['A Poem with the Answer' (1659)]

6. I prithee send me back my heart,
Since I cannot have thine:
For if from yours you will not part,
Why then shouldst thou have mine?
['Song']

Suetonius (Gaius Suetonius Tranquillus) (c. AD 70–c. 140)
Roman biographer and historian

1. [The gladiators salute to the emperor in the arena]
Ave, Imperator, morituri te salutant.
Hail, Emperor, those about to die salute thee.
[*Life of Claudius*]

Sullivan, Annie (1866–1936)
American lecturer and writer; teacher and companion of Helen Keller

1. It's queer how ready people always are with advice in any real or imaginary emergency, and no matter how many times experience has shown them to be wrong, they continue to set forth their opinions, as if they had received them from the Almighty!
[Letter, 1887]

2. [Of Helen Keller]
She likes stories that make her cry – I think we all do, it's so nice to feel sad when you've nothing particular to be sad about.
[Letter, 1887]

Sullivan, Sir Arthur (1842–1900)
English composer, best known for his operettas written with the librettist W.S. Gilbert

1. [Accused of plagiarism]
We all have the same eight notes to work with.
[Attr.]

Sully, Duc de (Maximilien de Béthune) (1559–1641)
French statesman and financier; minister of Henri IV and memoirist

1. *Les Anglais s'amusent tristement, selon l'usage de leur pays.*
The English enjoy themselves sadly, according to the custom of their country.
[*Memoirs* (1638)]

Surrey, Henry Howard, Earl of (c. 1517–1547)
English poet, translator, courtier and soldier; early writer of sonnets and blank verse; executed

1. The chaste wife wise, without debate;
Such sleeps as may beguile the night;
Content thyself with thine estate;
Neither wish death, nor fear his might.
['The Happy Life' (1547); translation of Martial, X, 47]

2. Calme is the sea, the waves work lesse and lesse:
So am not I, whom love alas doth wring,
Bringing before my face the greatest encrease
Of my desires, whereat I wepe and syng
In joye and wo, as in a doutfull ease.
['A complaint by night of the lover, not beloved']

3. But to the heavens that simple soule is fled:
Which left with such, as covet Christ to know,
Witnesse of faith, that never shall be ded:
Sent for our helth, but not received so.

Thus, for our gilte, this jewel have we lost:
The earth his bones, the heavens possesse his gost.
['Of the death of Sir T.W. [Thomas Wyatt]']

Surtees, R.S. (1805–1864)
English sporting novelist and journalist

1. Every man shouting in proportion to the amount of his subscription.
[*Jorrocks's Jaunts and Jollities* (1838), 1]

2. Champagne certainly gives one werry gentlemanly ideas, but for a continuance, I don't know but I should prefer mild hale.
[*Jorrocks's Jaunts and Jollities* (1838), 9]

3. 'Unting is all that's worth living for – all time is lost wot is not spent in 'unting – it is like the hair we breathe – if we have it not we die – it's the sport of kings, the image of war without its guilt, and only five-and-twenty per cent of its danger.
[*Handley Cross* (1843), 7. Cf. D'Avenant: 4]

4. 'Unting fills my thoughts by day, and many a good run I have in my sleep. Many a dig in the ribs I gives Mrs J when I think they're running into the warmint (renewed cheers). No man is fit to be called a sportsman wot doesn't kick his wife out of bed on a haverage once in three weeks!
[*Handley Cross* (1843), 11]

5. Tell me a man's a fox-hunter, and I loves him at once.
[*Handley Cross* (1843), 11]

6. I'll fill hup the chinks wi' cheese.
[*Handley Cross* (1843), 15]

7. It ar'n't that I loves the fox less, but that I loves the 'ound more.
[*Handley Cross* (1843), 16]

8. Well did that great man, I think it was Sir Walter Scott, but if it warn't, 'twas little Bartley, the bootmaker, say, that there was no young man wot would not rather have a himputation on his morality than on his 'ossmanship.
[*Handley Cross* (1843), 16]

9. Paid for catching my 'oss, 6d.
[*Handley Cross* (1843), 29]

10. Hellish dark, and smells of cheese!
[*Handley Cross* (1843), 50]

11. 'Hurrah! blister my kidneys!' exclaimed he in delight, 'it is a frost! – the dahlias are dead!'
[*Handley Cross* (1843), 59]

12. Three things I never lends – my 'oss, my wife, and my name.
[*Hillingdon Hall* (1845), 33]

13. More people are flattered into virtue than bullied out of vice.
[*The Analysis of the Hunting Field* (1846), 1]

14. The young ladies entered the drawing-room in the full fervour of sisterly animosity.
[*Mr Sponge's Sporting Tour* (1853), 17]

15. Women never look so well as when one comes in wet and dirty from hunting.
[*Mr Sponge's Sporting Tour* (1853), 21]

16. He was a gentleman who was generally spoken of as having nothing a-year, paid quarterly.
[*Mr Sponge's Sporting Tour* (1853), 24]

17. When at length they rose to go to bed, it struck each man as he followed his neighbour upstairs that the one before him walked very crookedly.
[*Mr Sponge's Sporting Tour* (1853), 35]

18. The only infallible rule we know is, that the man who is always talking about being a gentleman never is one.
[*Ask Mamma* (1858), 1]

19. Major Yammerton was rather a peculiar man, inasmuch as he was an ass, without being a fool.
[*Ask Mamma* (1858), 25]

20. No one knows how ungentlemanly he can look, until he has seen himself in a shocking bad hat.
[*Mr Facey Romford's Hounds* (1865), 9]

21. Better be killed than frightened to death.
[*Mr Facey Romford's Hounds* (1865), 32]

22. Thinking that life would be very pleasant if it were not for its enjoyments.
[*Mr Facey Romford's Hounds* (1865), 32]

23. These sort of boobies think that people come to balls to do nothing but dance; whereas everyone knows that the real business of a ball is either to look out for a wife, to look after a wife, or to look after somebody else's wife.
[*Mr Facey Romford's Hounds* (1865), 56]

Suzuki, David (1936–)
Canadian geneticist and broadcaster

1. Science is really in the business of disproving its current models or changing them to conform to new information. In essence, we are constantly proving our latest ideas are wrong.
[*Metamorphosis: Stages in a Life* (1987)]

Suzuki, D.T. (1870–1966)
Japanese Buddhist scholar and main interpreter of Zen to the West

1. When you have *satori* [a mystical experience in Zen] you are able to reveal a palatial mansion made of precious stones on a single blade of grass.
[*Essays in Zen Buddhism* (1927)]

2. The individual ego asserts itself strongly in the West. In the East, there is no ego. The ego is non-existent and, therefore, there is no ego to be crucified.
[*Mysticism Christian and Buddhist, The Eastern and Western Way* (1957), 6]

Svevo, Italo (1861–1928)
Italian novelist

1. There are three things I always forget. Names, faces and – the third I can't remember.
[Attr.]

Swaffer, Hannen (1879–1962)
English journalist and writer

1. Freedom of the press in Britain is freedom to print such of the proprietor's prejudices as the advertisers don't object to.
[In Tom Driberg, *Swaff* (1974), 2]

Swift, Jonathan (Dean Swift) (1667–1745)
Irish satirist, poet, essayist, pamphleteer and Anglican cleric

1. Satire is a kind of glass, wherein beholders do generally discover everybody's face but their own.
[*The Battle of the Books* (1704), Preface]

2. Instead of dirt and poison we have rather chosen to fill our hives with honey and wax; thus furnishing mankind with the two noblest of things, which are sweetness and light.
[*The Battle of the Books* (1704), Preface]

3. It is a maxim, that those to whom everybody allows the second place, have an undoubted title to the first.
[*A Tale of a Tub* (1704), Dedication. Cf. John Webster: 5]

4. Books, like men their authors, have no more than one way of coming into the world, but there are ten thousand to go out of it, and return no more.
[*A Tale of a Tub* (1704), Dedication]

5. Satire, by being levelled at all, is never resented for an offence by any.
[*A Tale of a Tub* (1704), Preface]

6. What though his head be empty, provided his commonplace book be full.
[*A Tale of a Tub* (1704), 7, 'A Digression in Praise of Digressions']

7. Last week I saw a woman flayed, and you will hardly believe how much it altered her person for the worse.
[*A Tale of a Tub* (1704), 9, 'A Digression concerning ... Madness in a Commonwealth']

8. This is the sublime and refined point of felicity, called the possession of being well deceived; the serene peaceful state of being a fool among knaves.
[*A Tale of a Tub* (1704), 9, 'A Digression concerning ... Madness in a Commonwealth']

9. I conceive some scattered notions about a superior power to be of singular use for the common people, as furnishing excellent materials to keep children quiet when they grow peevish, and providing topics of amusement in a tedious winter-night.
[*An Argument Against Abolishing Christianity* (1708)]

10. Laws are like cobwebs, which may catch small flies, but let wasps and hornets break through.
[*A Critical Essay upon the Faculties of the Mind* (1709). Cf. Solon: 1 and Shenstone: 3]

11. There is nothing in this world constant, but inconstancy.
[*A Critical Essay upon the Faculties of the Mind* (1709)]

12. Surely man is a broomstick!
[*A Meditation upon a Broomstick* (1710)]

13. It is the folly of too many to mistake the echo of a London coffee house for the voice of the kingdom.
[*The Conduct of the Allies* (1711)]

14. We have just enough religion to make us hate, but not enough to make us love one another.
[*Thoughts on Various Subjects* (1711)]

15. When a true genius appears in the world, you may know him by this sign, that the dunces are all in confederacy against him.
[*Thoughts on Various Subjects* (1711)]

16. What they do in heaven we are ignorant of; what they do not we are told expressly, that they neither marry, nor are given in marriage.
[*Thoughts on Various Subjects* (1711)]

17. The stoical scheme of supplying our wants, by lopping off our desires, is like cutting off our feet when we want shoes.
[*Thoughts on Various Subjects* (1711)]

18. The reason why so few marriages are happy, is, because young ladies spend their time in making nets, not in making cages.
[*Thoughts on Various Subjects* (1711)]

19. No wise man ever wished to be younger.
[*Thoughts on Various Subjects* (1711)]

20. Few are qualified to shine in company; but it is in most men's power to be agreeable.
[*Thoughts on Various Subjects* (1711)]

21. Every man desires to live long; but no man would be old.
[*Thoughts on Various Subjects* (1711)]

22. Old men and comets have been reverenced for the same reason; their long beards, and pretences to foretell events.
[*Thoughts on Various Subjects* (1711)]

23. Most sorts of diversion in men, children, and other animals, are an imitation of fighting.
[*Thoughts on Various Subjects* (1711)]

24. Proper words in proper places, make the true definition of a style.
[*Letter to a Young Gentleman Lately Entered Into Holy Orders* (1720)]

25. You have but a very few years to be young and handsome in the eyes of the world; and as few months to be so in the eyes of a husband, who is not a fool.
[*Letter to a Young Lady on her Marriage* (1723)]

26. I have heard of a man who had a mind to sell his house, and therefore carried a piece of brick in his pocket, which he shewed as a pattern to encourage purchasers.
[*The Drapier's Letters* (1724), 2]

27. [Of the emperor]
He is taller by almost the breadth of my nail than any of his court, which alone is enough to strike an awe into the beholders.
[*Gulliver's Travels* (1726), 'Voyage to Lilliput', 2]

28. [Describing a watch]
He put this engine to our ears, which made an incessant noise like that of a water-mill; and we conjecture it is either some unknown animal, or the god that he worships; but we are more inclined to the latter opinion.
[*Gulliver's Travels* (1726), 'Voyage to Lilliput', 2]

29. It is alleged, indeed, that the high heels are most agreeable to our ancient constitution: but, however this be, his majesty hath determined to make use of only low heels in the administration of the government.
[*Gulliver's Travels* (1726), 'Voyage to Lilliput', 4]

30. I cannot but conclude the bulk of your natives to be the most pernicious race of little odious vermin that nature ever suffered to crawl upon the surface of the earth.
[*Gulliver's Travels* (1726), 'A Voyage to Brobdingnag', 6]

31. And he gave it for his opinion, that whoever could make two ears of corn or two blades of grass to grow upon a spot of ground where only one grew before, would deserve better of mankind, and do more essential service to his country than the whole race of politicians put together.
[*Gulliver's Travels* (1726), 'A Voyage to Brobdingnag', 7]

32. He had been eight years upon a project for extracting sun-beams out of cucumbers, which were to be put into vials hermetically sealed, and let out to warm the air in raw inclement summers.
[*Gulliver's Travels* (1726), 'A Voyage to Laputa, Balnibarbi, Luggnagg, Glubbdubdrib, and Japan', 5]

33. These unhappy people were proposing schemes for persuading monarchs to choose favourites upon the score of their wisdom, capacity and virtue; of teaching ministers to consult the public good; of rewarding merit, great abilities and eminent services; of instructing princes to know their true interest by placing it on the same foundation with that of their people: of choosing for employments persons qualified to exercise them; with many other wild impossible

chimeras, that never entered before into the heart of man to conceive, and confirmed in me the old observation, that there is nothing so extravagant and irrational which some philosophers have not maintained for truth.
[*Gulliver's Travels* (1726), 'A Voyage to Laputa, Balnibarbi, Luggnagg, Glubbdubdrib, and Japan', 6]

34. He replied that I must needs be mistaken, or that *I said the thing which was not*. (For they have no word in their language to express lying or falsehood.)
[*Gulliver's Travels* (1726), 'A Voyage to the Houyhnhnms', 3]

35. I told him ... that we ate when we were not hungry, and drank without the provocation of thirst.
[*Gulliver's Travels* (1726), 'A Voyage to the Houyhnhnms', 6]

36. My horses understand me tolerably well; I converse with them at least four hours every day. They are strangers to bridle or saddle; they live in great amity with me, and friendship to each other.
[*Gulliver's Travels* (1726), 'A Voyage to the Houyhnhnms', 11]

37. I have been assured by a very knowing American of my acquaintance in London, that a young healthy child well nursed is, at a year old, a most delicious, nourishing, and wholesome food, whether stewed, roasted, baked, or boiled; and I make no doubt that it will equally serve in a fricassee, or a ragout.
[*A Modest Proposal for Preventing the Children of Ireland from being a Burden to their Parents or Country* (1729)]

38. Why, every one as they like; as the good woman said when she kissed her cow.
[*Polite Conversation* (1738), 1]

39. I won't quarrel with my bread and butter.
[*Polite Conversation* (1738), 1]

40. I'm as old as my tongue, and a little older than my teeth.
[*Polite Conversation* (1738), 1]

41. Promises and pie-crusts are made to be broken, they say.
[*Polite Conversation* (1738), 1]

42. She wears her clothes, as if they were thrown on with a pitchfork.
[*Polite Conversation* (1738), 1]

43. Bachelor's fare, bread and cheese, and kisses.
[*Polite Conversation* (1738), 1]

44. I mean, you lie – under a mistake.
[*Polite Conversation* (1738), 1]

45. Faith, that's as well said, as if I had said it myself.
[*Polite Conversation* (1738), 2]

46. He was a bold man that first eat an oyster.
[*Polite Conversation* (1738), 2. Cf. Thomas Fuller {1}: 9]

47. She has more goodness in her little finger, than he has in his whole body.
[*Polite Conversation* (1738), 2]

48. Lord! I wonder what fool it was that first invented kissing!
[*Polite Conversation* (1738), 2]

49. I always love to begin a journey on Sundays, because I shall have the prayers of the church, to preserve all that travel by land, or by water.
[*Polite Conversation* (1738), 2]

50. The Manner whereby the Soul and Body are united, and how they are distinguished, is wholly unaccountable to us. We see but one Part, and yet we know we consist of two; and this is a Mystery we cannot comprehend, any more than that of the Trinity.
['On the Trinity']

51. Philosophy! the lumber of the schools.
['Ode to Sir W. Temple' (1692)]

52. A coming shower your shooting corns presage.
['A Description of a City Shower' (1710)]

53. 'Tis an old maxim in the schools,
That vanity's the food of fools;
Yet now and then your men of wit
Will condescend to take a bit.
['Cadenus and Vanessa' (c. 1712)]

54. I've often wish'd that I had clear,
For life, six hundred pounds a year,
A handsome house to lodge a friend,
A river at my garden's end,
A terrace walk, and half a rood
Of land, set out to plant a wood.
['Imitation of Horace, Satires II, 6' (1714)]

55. Hated by fools, and fools to hate,
Be that my motto and my fate.
['To Mr Delany' (1718)]

56. They never would hear,
But turn a deaf ear,
As a matter they had no concern in.
['Dingley and Brent' (1724)]

57. In Church your grandsire cut his throat;
To do the job too long he tarry'd,
He should have had my hearty vote,
To cut his throat before he marry'd.
['Verses on the Upright Judge' (1724)]

58. *'Libertas et natale solum'*:
Fine words! I wonder where you stole 'em.
['Whitshed's Motto on his Coach' (1724)]

59. Walls have tongues, and hedges ears.
['A Pastoral Dialogue between Richmond Lodge and Marble Hill' (1727)]

60. Nor do they trust their tongue alone,
But speak a language of their own;
Can read a nod, a shrug, a look,
Far better than a printed book;
Convey a libel in a frown,
And wink a reputation down.
['The Journal of a Modern Lady' (1729)]

61. In all distresses of our friends,
We first consult our private ends;
While nature, kindly bent to ease us,
Points out some circumstance to please us...

62. Some great misfortune to portend,
No enemy can match a friend...

63. Poor Pope will grieve a month, and Gay
A week, and Arbuthnot a day.
St John himself will scarce forbear
To bite his pen, and drop a tear.
The rest will give a shrug, and cry,
'I'm sorry – but we all must die!'...

64. Yet malice never was his aim;
He lash'd the vice, but spared the name;
No individual could resent,
Where thousands equally were meant...

65. He gave the little wealth he had
To build a house for fools and mad;

And show'd, by one satiric touch,
No nation wanted it so much.
That kingdom he hath left a debtor,
I wish it soon may have a better.
['Verses on the Death of Dr Swift' (1731)]

66. Thus finishing his grand survey,
The swain disgusted slunk away,
Repeating in his amorous fits,
'Oh! Celia, Celia, Celia shits!'
['The Lady's Dressing Room' (1732)]

67. Then, rising with Aurora's light,
The Muse invoked, sit down to write;
Blot out, correct, insert, refine,
Enlarge, diminish, interline...

68. So geographers, in Afric-maps,
With savage-pictures fill their gaps;
And o'er unhabitable downs
Place elephants for want of towns...

69. He gives directions to the town,
To cry it up, or run it down...

70. So, naturalists observe, a flea
Hath smaller fleas that on him prey;
And these have smaller fleas to bite 'em,
And so proceed *ad infinitum*.
Thus every poet, in his kind,
Is bit by him that comes behind
['On Poetry' (1733). Cf. Augustus de Morgan: 1]

71. It is very warm weather when one is in bed.
[*Journal to Stella*, 8 November 1710]

72. With my own fair hands.
[*Journal to Stella*, 4 January 1711]

73. We are so fond of one another, because our ailments are the same.
[*Journal to Stella*, 1 February 1711]

74. Will she pass in a crowd? Will she make a figure in a country church?
[*Journal to Stella*, 9 February 1711]

75. I love good creditable acquaintance; I love to be the worst of the company.
[*Journal to Stella*, 17 May 1711]

76. He showed me his bill of fare to tempt me to dine with him; Poh, said I, I value not your bill of fare; give me your bill of company.
[*Journal to Stella*, 2 September 1711]

77. We were to do more business after dinner; but after dinner is after dinner – an old saying and a true, 'much drinking, little thinking'.
[*Journal to Stella*, 26 February 1712]

78. If heaven had looked upon riches to be a valuable thing, it would not have given them to such a scoundrel.
[Letter to Miss Vanhomrigh, 1720]

79. I have ever hated all nations, professions and communities, and all my love is towards individuals ... But principally I hate and detest that animal called man; although I heartily love John, Peter, Thomas, and so forth.
[Letter to Pope, 1725]

80. You think, as I ought to think, that it is time for me to have done with the world, and so I would if I could get into a better before I was called into the best, and not die here in a rage, like a poisoned rat in a hole.
[Letter to Bolingbroke, 1729]

81. [Of *A Tale of a Tub*]
Good God! what a genius I had when I wrote that book.
[In Sir Walter Scott, *Works of Swift* (1824), I]

82. [Responding to Lady Carteret's admiration for the quality of the air in Ireland]
For God's sake, madam, don't say that in England for if you do, they will surely tax it.
[In H. Pearson, *Lives of the Wits* (1962)]

83. [Predicting his own mental decline]
I shall be like that tree; and die first at the top.
[Attr.]

84. [Of St Ann's Church, Dublin]
A beggarly people!
A church and no steeple!
[Attr.]

85. I row after health like a waterman, and ride after it like a postboy, and find little success.
[Attr.]

86. [Learning of the arrival of Handel: Swift's last words]
Ah, a German and a genius! a prodigy, admit him!
[Attr.]

87. *Ubi saeva indignatio*
Ulterius cor lacerare nequit.
Where fierce indignation can no longer tear his heart.
[Epitaph]

Swinburne, Algernon Charles (1837–1909)

English lyric poet, critic, dramatist and letter writer

1. They have tied the world in a tether,
They have bought over God with a fee.
['A Song in Time of Order' (1852)]

2. What adders came to shed their coats?
What coiled obscene
Small serpents with soft stretching throats
Caressed Faustine?
['Faustine' (1862)]

3. Swallow, my sister, O sister swallow,
How can thine heart be full of the spring?
A thousand summers are over and dead.
What hast thou found in the spring to follow?
What hast thou found in thine heart to sing?
What wilt thou do when the summer is shed?...

4. Sister, my sister, O fleet sweet swallow,
Thy way is long to the sun and the south;
But I, fulfilled of my heart's desire,
Shedding my song upon height, upon hollow,
From tawny body and sweet small mouth
Feed the heart of the night with fire.

I the nightingale all spring through,
O swallow, sister, O changing swallow,
All spring through till the spring be done,
Clothed with the light of the night on the dew,
Sing, while the hours and the wild birds follow,
Take flight and follow and find the sun...

5. Till life forget and death remember,
Till thou remember and I forget...

6. The small slain body, the flower-like face,
Can I remember if thou forget?...

7. Thou hast forgotten, O summer swallow,
But the world shall end when I forget.
['Itylus' (1864)]

8. Maiden, and mistress of the months and stars
Now folded in the flowerless fields of heaven.
[*Atalanta in Calydon* (1865)]

9. When the hounds of spring are on winter's traces,
The mother of months in meadow or plain
Fills the shadows and windy places
With lisp of leaves and ripple of rain;
And the brown bright nightingale amorous
Is half assuaged for Itylus,
For the Thracian ships and the foreign faces,
The tongueless vigil and all the pain...

10. Bind on thy sandals, O thou most fleet,
Over the splendour and speed of thy feet;
For the faint east quickens, the wan west shivers,
Round the feet of the day and the feet of the night.

Where shall we find her, how shall we sing to her,
Fold our hands round her knees, and cling?
O that man's heart were as fire and could spring to her,
Fire, or the strength of the streams that spring!
For the stars and the winds are unto her
As raiment, as songs of the harp-player;
For the risen stars and the fallen cling to her,
And the southwest-wind and the west-wind sing...

11. And Pan by noon and Bacchus by night,
Fleeter of foot than the fleet-foot kid,
Follows with dancing and fills with delight
The Maenad and the Bassarid;
And soft as lips that laugh and hide
The laughing leaves of the tree divide,
And screen from seeing and leave in sight
The god pursuing, the maiden hid...

12. The wild vine slips with the weight of its leaves,
But the berried ivy catches and cleaves
To the limbs that glitter, the feet that scare
The wolf that follows, the fawn that flies.
[*Atalanta in Calydon* (1865), Chorus: 'When the hounds of spring']

13. Before the beginning of years
There came to the making of man
Time with a gift of tears,
Grief with a glass that ran...

14. They gave him light in his ways,
And love, and a space for delight,
And beauty and length of days,
And night, and sleep in the night...

15. He weaves, and is clothed with derision;
Sows, and he shall not reap;
His life is a watch or a vision
Between a sleep and a sleep.
[*Atalanta in Calydon* (1865), Chorus: 'Before the beginning of years']

16. We have seen thee, O Love, thou art fair; thou art goodly, O Love.
[*Atalanta in Calydon* (1865), Chorus: 'We have seen thee, O Love']

17. For words divide and rend;
But silence is most noble till the end.
[*Atalanta in Calydon* (1865), Chorus: 'Who hath given man speech']

18. Superflux of pain.
['Anactoria' (1866)]

19. We shift and bedeck and bedrape us,
Thou art noble and nude and antique.
['Dolores' (1866), 7]

20. Could you hurt me, sweet lips, though I hurt you?
Men touch them, and change in a trice
The lilies and languors of virtue
For the raptures and roses of vice...

21. O splendid and sterile Dolores,
Our Lady of Pain.
['Dolores' (1866), 9]

22. Ah beautiful passionate body
That never has ached with a heart!
['Dolores' (1866), 11]

23. But sweet as the rind was the core is;
We are fain of thee still, we are fain,
O sanguine and subtle Dolores,
Our Lady of Pain.
['Dolores' (1866), 13]

24. The delight that consumes the desire,
The desire that outruns the delight.
['Dolores' (1866), 14]

25. For the crown of our life as it closes
Is darkness, the fruit thereof dust;
No thorns go as deep as a rose's,
And love is more cruel than lust.
Time turns the old days to derision,
Our loves into corpses or wives;
And marriage and death and division
Make barren our lives.
['Dolores' (1866), 20]

26. What ailed us, O gods, to desert you
For creeds that refuse and restrain?
Come down and redeem us from virtue,
Our Lady of Pain.
['Dolores' (1866), 35]

27. I shall remember while the light lives yet
And in the night time I shall not forget.
['Erotion' (1866)]

28. Here, where the world is quiet;
Here, where all trouble seems
Dead winds' and spent waves' riot
In doubtful dreams of dreams...

29. Pale, beyond porch and portal,
Crowned with calm leaves, she stands
Who gathers all things mortal
With cold immortal hands...

30. We are not sure of sorrow,
And joy was never sure;
To-day will die to-morrow;
Time stoops to no man's lure...

31. From too much love of living,
From hope and fear set free,
We thank with brief thanksgiving
Whatever gods may be
That no man lives forever,
That dead men rise up never;
That even the weariest river
Winds somewhere safe to sea.

Then star nor sun shall waken,
Nor any change of light...

32. Only the sleep eternal
In an eternal night.
['The Garden of Proserpine' (1866)]

33. Yea, is not even Apollo, with hair and harpstring of gold,
A bitter God to follow, a beautiful God to behold?
I am sick of singing: the bays burn deep and chafe: I am fain

To rest a little from praise and grievous pleasure and pain...

34. Wilt thou yet take all, Galilean? but these thou shalt not take,
The laurel, the palms and the paean, the breasts of the nymphs in the brake;
Breasts more soft than a dove's, that tremble with tenderer breath;
And all the wings of the Loves, and all the joy before death...

35. Thou hast conquered, O pale Galilean; the world has grown grey from Thy breath;
We have drunken of things Lethean, and fed on the fullness of death.
Laurel is green for a season, and love is sweet for a day;
But love grows bitter with treason, and laurel outlives not May...

36. For the old faiths loosen and fall, the new years ruin and rend...

37. O ghastly glories of saints, dead limbs of gibbeted Gods!
['Hymn to Proserpine' (1866)]

38. I remember the way we parted,
The day and the way we met;
You hoped we were both broken-hearted,
And knew we should both forget...

39. And the best and the worst of this is
That neither is most to blame,
If you have forgotten my kisses
And I have forgotten your name.
['An Interlude' (1866)]

40. Ah, yet would God this flesh of mine might be
Where air might wash and long leaves cover me;
Where tides of grass break into foam of flowers,
Or where the wind's feet shine along the sea...

41. Until God loosen over sea and land
The thunder of the trumpets of the night.
['Laus Veneris' (1866)]

42. The strong sea-daisies feast on the sun...

43. Content you;
The gate is strait; I shall not be there...

44. I will go back to the great sweet mother,
Mother and lover of men, the sea.
I will go down to her, I and no other,
Close with her, kiss her and mix her with me...

45. I shall sleep, and move with the moving ships,
Change as the winds change, veer in the tide;
My lips will feast on the foam of thy lips,
I shall rise with thy rising and with thee subside...

46. There lived a singer in France of old
By the tideless dolorous midland sea.
In a land of sand and ruin and gold
There shone one woman, and none but she.
['The Triumph of Time' (1866)]

47. O slain and spent and sacrificed
People, the grey-grown speechless Christ.
['Before a Crucifix' (1871)]

48. But God, if a God there be, is the substance of men which is man...

49. Glory to Man in the highest! for Man is the master of things.
['Hymn of Man' (1871)]

50. Shall I strew on thee rose or rue or laurel,
Brother, on this that was the veil of thee?
Or quiet sea-flower moulded by the sea,
Or simplest growth of meadow-sweet or sorrel...

51. Hast thou found place at the great knees and feet
Of some pale Titan-woman like a lover
Such as thy vision here solicited,
Under the shadow of her fair vast head,
The deep division of prodigious breasts,
The solemn slope of mighty limbs asleep?
['Ave atque Vale' (1878)]

52. In a coign of the cliff between lowland and highland,
At the seadown's edge between windward and lee,
Walled round with rocks as an inland island,
The ghost of a garden fronts the sea.

The fields fall southward, abrupt and broken,
To the low last edge of the long lone land.
If a step should sound or a word be spoken,
Would a ghost not rise at the strange guest's hand?
So long have the grey bare walls lain guestless,
Through branches and briars if a man make way,
He shall find no life but the sea-wind's, restless
Night and day...

53. Over the meadows that blossom and wither
Rings but the note of a sea-bird's song;
Only the sun and the rain come hither
All year long...

54. Here now in his triumph where all things falter,
Stretched out on the spoils that his own hand spread,
As a god self-slain on his own strange altar,
Death lies dead.
['A Forsaken Garden' (1878)]

55. Apples of gold for the king's daughter.
['The King's Daughter']

Sylvester, Victor (1902–1978)
British dance-band leader and ballroom dancing teacher

1. Slow, slow, quick, quick, slow [foxtrot tempo].
[Stock phrase]

Symonds, John Addington (1840–1893)
English poet, translator, critic and biographer

1. These things shall be! a loftier race
Than e'er the world hath known shall rise,
With flame of freedom in their souls,
And light of knowledge in their eyes.
[Hymn, 1880]

Symons, Michael Brooke (1945–)
Australian journalist and cookery writer

1. Love is what makes the world go around – that and clichés.
[*Sydney Morning Herald*, 1970]

Synge, J.M. (1871–1909)
Irish dramatist, poet and letter writer

1. Drink a health to the wonders of the western world, the pirates, preachers, poteen-makers, with the jobbing jockies; parching peelers, and the juries fill their stomachs selling judgements of the English law.
[*The Playboy of the Western World* (1907), II]

2. I'd know his way of spitting and he astride the moon.
[*The Playboy of the Western World* (1907), III]

3. A daring fellow is the jewel of the world, and a man did split his father's middle with a single clout should have the bravery of ten, so may God and Mary and St Patrick bless you, and increase you from this mortal day.
[*The Playboy of the Western World* (1907), III]

4. O my grief, I've lost him surely. I've lost the only Playboy of the Western World.
[*The Playboy of the Western World* (1907), final words]

5. 'A man who is not afraid of the sea will soon be drownded,' he said, 'for he will be going out on a day he shouldn't. But we do be afraid of the sea, and we do only be drownded now and again.'
[*The Aran Islands* (1907), II]

6. I have put away sorrow like a shoe that is worn out and muddy, for it is I have had a life that will be envied by great companies.
[*Deirdre of the Sorrows* (1909), III]

7. [To the sister of an enemy of the author who disapproved of *The Playboy of the Western World*]
Lord, confound this surly sister,
Blight her brow with blotch and blister,
Cramp her larynx, lung and liver,
In her guts a galling give her.

Let her live to earn her dinners
In Mountjoy with seedy sinners:
Lord, this judgement quickly bring,
And I'm your servant, J.M. Synge.
['The Curse']

Szasz, Thomas (1920–)
Hungarian-born American psychiatrist, lecturer and writer

1. Men are rewarded and punished not for what they do, but rather for how their acts are defined. This is why men are more interested in better justifying themselves than in better behaving themselves.
[*The Second Sin* (1973)]

2. Traditionally, sex has been a very private, secretive activity. Herein perhaps lies its powerful force for uniting people in a strong bond. As we make sex less secretive, we may rob it of its power to hold men and women together.
[*The Second Sin* (1973)]

3. Masturbation: the primary sexual activity of mankind. In the nineteenth century it was a disease; in the twentieth, it's a cure.
[*The Second Sin* (1973)]

4. Formerly, when religion was strong and science weak, men mistook magic for medicine, now, when science is strong and religion weak, men mistake medicine for magic.
[*The Second Sin* (1973)]

5. A child becomes an adult when he realizes that he has a right not only to be right but also to be wrong.
[*The Second Sin* (1973)]

6. Happiness is an imaginary condition, formerly often attributed by the living to the dead, now usually attributed by adults to children, and by children to adults.
[*The Second Sin* (1973)]

7. The stupid neither forgive nor forget; the naive forgive and forget; the wise forgive but do not forget.
[*The Second Sin* (1973)]

8. Psychiatrists classify a person as neurotic if he suffers from his problems in living, and a psychotic if he makes others suffer.
[*The Second Sin* (1973)]

9. If you talk to God, you are praying; if God talks to you, you have schizophrenia. If the dead talk to you, you are a spiritualist; if God talks to you, you are a schizophrenic.
[*The Second Sin* (1973)]

Szent-Györgyi, Albert von (1893–1986)
Hungarian-born American biochemist; Nobel Prize for medicine, 1937

1. Discovery consists of seeing what everybody has seen and thinking what nobody has thought.
[In I.J. Good (ed.), *The Scientist Speculates* (1962)]

Taber, Robert (20th century)
American writer

1. The guerrilla fights the war of the flea, and his military enemy suffers the dog's disadvantages: too much to defend; too small, ubiquitous, and agile an enemy to come to grips with.
[*The War of the Flea*, 2]

Tabrar, Joseph (1857–1931)
American songwriter

1. Daddy wouldn't buy me a bow-wow, bow-wow.
I've got a little cat
And I'm very fond of that
But I'd rather have a bow-wow now.
['Daddy Wouldn't Buy Me a Bow-wow', song, 1892]

Tacitus (Cornelius Tacitus) (AD c. 56–c. 120)
Roman historian, noted for his prose style

1. *Ubi solitudinem faciunt pacem appellant.*
They create a desert, and call it peace.
[*Agricola*, 30]

2. *Proprium humani ingenii est odisse quem laeseris.*
It is part of human nature to hate those whom you have injured.
[*Agricola*, 42]

3. *Tu vero felix, Agricola, non vitae tantum claritate, sed etiam opportunitate mortis.*
You were indeed fortunate, Agricola, not only in the distinction of your life, but also in the opportune timing of your death.
[*Agricola*, 45]

4. [Of Petronius]
Elegantiae arbiter.
Judge of good taste.
[*Annals*, XVI, 18]

5. *Rara temporum felicitate ubi sentire quae velis et quae sentias dicere licet.*
In the rare good fortune of an age when you may think what you like and say what you think.
[*Histories*, I, 1]

6. [Of the Emperor Galba]
Capax imperii nisi imperasset.
Judged capable of ruling, if only he had not ruled.
[*Histories*, I, 49]

7. *Etiam sapientibus cupido gloriae novissima exuitur.*
The desire for fame is the last thing to be put aside, even by the wise.
[*Histories*, IV, 6]

Taft, William Howard (1857–1930)
American statesman and lawyer; Republican President 1909–13; Chief Justice from 1921, teacher and writer

1. [Referring to his disastrous defeat in the 1912 presidential election]
Well, I have one consolation. No candidate was ever elected ex-president with such a large majority!
[Attr.]

Taine, Hippolyte Adolphe (1828–1893)
French critic, philosopher and historian; leading exponent of Positivism

1. *On peut considérer l'homme comme un animal d'espèce supérieure qui produit des philosophies et des poèmes à peu près comme les vers à soie font leurs cocons et comme les abeilles font leurs ruches.*
Man can be considered as a superior animal who produces philosophies and poems much as silkworms construct their cocoons and bees their hives.
[*La Fontaine et ses Fables* (*La Fontaine and his Fables*, 1860), Preface]

2. *Le vice et la vertu sont des produits comme le vitriol et le sucre.*
Vice and virtues are products like sulphuric acid and sugar.
[*Histoire de la littérature anglaise* (*History of English Literature*, 1863), Introduction]

Talleyrand, Charles-Maurice de (1754–1838)
French statesman; Foreign Minister 1797–1807; memoirist and former prelate

1. [Of the French Revolution]
Qui n'a pas vécu dans les années voisines de 1789 ne sait pas ce que c'est que le plaisir de vivre.
He who has not lived during the years around 1789 cannot know what is meant by the joy of living.
[In M. Guizot, *Mémoires pour servir à l'histoire de mon temps* (1858)]

2. [Comment on Napoleon's defeat at Borodino, 1812]
Voilà le commencement de la fin.
This is the beginning of the end.
[Attr. in Sainte-Beuve, *M. de Talleyrand* (1870). Cf. Winston Churchill: 27]

3. [Remark to a young man who boasted that he did not play whist]
Quelle triste vieillesse vous vous préparez.
What a sad old age you are preparing for yourself.
[In J. Amédée Pichot, *Souvenirs intimes sur M. de Talleyrand* (1870)]

4. [Of America]
I found there a country with thirty-two religions and only one sauce.
[In Pedrazzini, *Autant en apportent les mots*]

5. [Comment on exiled French aristocrats]
Ils n'ont rien appris, ni rien oublié.
They have learnt nothing, and forgotten nothing.
[Attr. Cf. Dumouriez: 1]

6. *Méfiez-vous du premier mouvement; il est toujours généreux.*
Don't trust first impulses; they are always generous.
[Attr. Cf. Montrond: 1]

7. *La parole a été donnée à l'homme pour déguiser sa pensée.*
Speech was given to man to disguise his thoughts.
[Attr. Cf. Voltaire: 17]

8. [Giving his opinion upon what action might impress the French peasantry]
Well, you might try getting crucified and rising again on the third day.
[Attr.]

Tannen, Deborah (1945–)

1. Each person's life is lived as a series of conversations.
[*The Observer*, 'Sayings of the Year', 1992]

Tarkington, Booth (1869–1946)
American novelist and dramatist

1. There are two things that will be believed of any man whatsoever, and one of them is that he has taken to drink.
[*Penrod* (1914), 10]

Tate, Allen (1899–1979)
American poet and critic; novelist, biographer and teacher

1. Row upon row with strict impunity
The headstones yield their names to the element.
['Ode to the Confederate Dead' (1926)]

Tate, Nahum (1652–1715)
Irish poet, dramatist, editor and translator; appointed poet laureate in 1692

1. While shepherds watch'd their flocks by night,
All seated on the ground,
The Angel of the Lord came down,
And glory shone around.
[Hymn, 1702]

Tawney, R.H. (1880–1962)
Indian-born British economic historian and Christian socialist

1. It is a commonplace that the characteristic virtue of Englishmen is their power of sustained practical activity, and their characteristic vice a reluctance to test the quality of that activity by reference to principles.
[*The Acquisitive Society* (1921), 1]

Taylor, A.J.P. (1906–1990)
English historian; journalist, broadcaster, writer and lecturer

1. Communism continued to haunt Europe as a spectre – a name men gave to their own fears and blunders. But the crusade against Communism was even more imaginary than the spectre of Communism.
[*The Origins of the Second World War* (1961), 2]

2. Lenin was the first to discover that capitalism 'inevitably' caused war; and he discovered this only when the First World War was already being fought. Of course he was right. Since every great state was capitalist in 1914, capitalism obviously 'caused' the First World War; but just as obviously it had 'caused' the previous generation of Peace.
[*The Origins of the Second World War* (1961), 6]

3. A racing tipster who only reached Hitler's level of accuracy would not do well for his clients.
[*The Origins of the Second World War* (1961), 7]

4. History gets thicker as it approaches recent times.
[*English History, 1914–1945* (1965), Bibliography]

5. [Of Lord Northcliffe]
He aspired to power instead of influence, and as a result forfeited both.
[*English History, 1914–1945* (1965), 1]

6. [Of Napoleon III]
He was what I often think is a dangerous thing for a statesman to be – a student of history; and like most of those who study history, he learned from the mistakes of the past how to make new ones.
[*The Listener*, 1963]

Taylor, Ann (1782–1866)
and Taylor, Jane (1783–1824)
English writers of poetry and hymns for children

1. Who ran to help me when I fell,
And would some pretty story tell,
Or kiss the place to make it well?
My Mother.
[*Original Poems for Infant Minds* (1804), 'My Mother']

2. Twinkle, twinkle, little star,
How I wonder what you are!
Up above the world so high,
Like a diamond in the sky.
[*Rhymes for the Nursery* (1806), 'The Star'. Cf. Carroll: 18]

3. I thank the goodness and the grace
Which on my birth have smiled,
And made me, in these Christian days,
A happy English child.
[*Hymns for Infant Minds* (1810), 'A Child's Hymn of Praise']

4. 'Tis a *credit* to any good girl to be neat,
But quite a *disgrace* to be fine.
[*Hymns for Sunday Schools* (1810), 'The Folly of Finery']

Taylor, Bayard (1825–1878)
American traveller and writer; poet, journalist, translator, novelist and diplomat

1. Till the sun grows cold,
And the stars are old,
And the leaves of the Judgment Book unfold.
['Bedouin Song' (1855)]

Taylor, Bert Leston (1866–1921)
American journalist and columnist

1. A bore is a man who, when you ask him how he is, tells you.
[*The So-Called Human Race* (1922)]

Taylor, Elizabeth (1912–1975)
English novelist and short-story writer, noted for her observation of middle-class life

1. 'What use will [Greek] be to her when she leaves school? Will it cook her husband's dinner?'
'No, it won't do that, but it will help her to endure doing it, perhaps.'
[*At Mrs Lippincote's* (1945), 12]

2. It is very strange ... that the years teach us patience; that the shorter our time, the greater our capacity for waiting.
[*A Wreath of Roses* (1950), 10]

Taylor, Bishop Jeremy (1613–1667)
English divine, noted for his devotional writings

1. As our life is very short, so it is very miserable, and therefore it is well it is short.
[*The Rule and Exercise of Holy Dying* (1651)]

2. In the matter of interest we are wary as serpents, subtle as foxes, vigilant as the birds of the night, rapacious as kites, tenacious as grappling-hooks and the weightiest anchors, and, above all, false and hypocritical as a thin crust of ice spread upon the face of a deep, smooth, and dissembling pit.
[*XXV Sermons Preached at Golden Grove* (1653)]

3. The union of hands and hearts.
[*XXV Sermons Preached at Golden Grove* (1653)]

4. He that loves not his wife and children, feeds a lioness at home and broods a nest of sorrows.
[*XXV Sermons Preached at Golden Grove* (1653)]

Taylor, John (1580–1653)
English 'water poet' and Thames waterman

1. 'Tis a mad world, my masters.
[*Western Voyage*, 1]

Taylor, Mary
Friend and correspondent of Charlotte Brontë

1. I can hardly explain to you the queer feeling of living as I do in two places at once. One world contains books, England, and all the people with whom I can exchange an idea; the other all that I actually see and hear and speak to. The separation is as complete as between the things in a picture and the things in the room. The puzzle is that both move and act, and [I] must say my say as one of each. The result is that one world at least must think me crazy.
[Letter to Charlotte Brontë, 1848]

Tebbitt, Lord Norman (1931–)
English Conservative politician

1. [Of his father who had grown up during the 1930s]
He didn't riot. He got on his bike and looked for work and he kept looking till he found it.
[Speech, Conservative Party Conference, 1981]

2. I hope Mrs Thatcher will go on until the turn of the century looking like Queen Victoria.
[*The Observer*, 'Sayings of the Week', 1987]

Tecumseh (d. 1812)
Leader of the Shawnees

1. Where today are the Pequot? Where are the Narragansett, the Mohican, the Pokanoket, and many other once powerful tribes of our people? They have vanished before the avarice and the oppression of the White Man, as snow before a summer sun.
[In Dee Brown, *Bury My Heart at Wounded Knee* (1971), 1]

Teilhard de Chardin, Pierre (1881–1955)
French Jesuit priest, palaeontologist and religious philosopher

1. *Vous m'avez dit, mon Dieu, de croire à l'enfer. Mais vous m'avez interdit de penser, avec absolue certitude, d'un seul homme, qu'il était damné.*
You have told me, O God, to believe in hell. But you have forbidden me to think, with absolute certainty, of any man as damned.
[*Le Milieu divin*]

2. *Rien ne vaut la peine d'être trouvé que ce qui n'a jamais existé encore.*
Nothing is worth discovering except that which has not yet existed.
[*La Vision du passé*]

Teller, Edward
Hungarian-born physicist

1. An expert is a man who has made all the mistakes which can be made in a very narrow field.
[Remark, 1972]

Temple, Sir William [1] (1628–1699)
English diplomat and essayist; husband of Dorothy Osborne

1. When all is done, human life is, at the greatest and the best, but like a forward child, that must be play'd with and humoured a little to keep it quiet till it falls asleep, and then the care is over.
[*Miscellanea, The Second Part* (1690), 'Of Poetry']

Temple, William [2] (1881–1944)

English prelate, social reformer, supporter of ecumenicalism, teacher and writer

1. Christianity is the most materialistic of all great religions.
[*Readings in St John's Gospel* (1939)]

2. In place of the conception of the Power-State we are led to that of the Welfare-State.
[*Citizen and Churchman* (1941)]

3. 'Are you not,' a Rugby master had asked him in discussing one of his [schoolboy] essays, 'a little out of your depth here?' 'Perhaps, Sir,' was the confident reply, 'but I can swim.'
[In F.A. Iremonger, *William Temple* (1948)]

4. [Remark to parents when headmaster of Repton School]
Personally, I have always looked on cricket as organized loafing.
[Attr.]

5. It is not the ape, nor the tiger in man that I fear, it is the donkey.
[Attr.]

6. The Church exists for the sake of those outside it.
[Attr.]

7. I believe in the Church, One Holy, Catholic and Apostolic, and I regret that it nowhere exists.
[Attr.]

Tenniel, Sir John (1820–1914)

English caricaturist, book illustrator and Punch *cartoonist*

1. Dropping the pilot.
[Cartoon, depicting Wilhelm II dispensing with Bismarck's services, 1890]

Tennyson, Alfred, Lord (1809–1892)

English poet, noted for his lyric genius; poet laureate from 1850

1. Below the thunders of the upper deep;
Far, far beneath in the abysmal sea,
His ancient, dreamless, uninvaded sleep
The Kraken sleepeth...

2. There hath he lain for ages and will lie
Battening upon huge seaworms in his sleep,
Until the latter fire shall heat the deep.
['The Kraken' (1830)]

3. Airy, fairy Lilian.
['Lilian' (1830)]

4. Weeded and worn the ancient thatch
Upon the lonely moated grange.
She only said, 'My life is dreary,
He cometh not,' she said;
She said, 'I am aweary, aweary,
I would that I were dead!'

Her tears fell with the dews at even;
Her tears fell ere the dews were dried...

5. The blue fly sung in the pane; the mouse
Behind the mouldering wainscot shrieked...

6. She wept, 'I am aweary, aweary,
O God, that I were dead!'
['Mariana' (1830)]

7. Vex not thou the poet's mind
With thy shallow wit:
Vex not thou the poet's mind;
For thou canst not fathom it.
['The Poet's Mind' (1830)]

8. Alone and warming his five wits,
The white owl in the belfry sits.
['Song – The Owl' (1830)]

9. Oh teach me yet
Somewhat before the heavy clod
Weighs on me, and the busy fret
Of that sharp-headed worm begins
In the gross blackness underneath.
['Supposed Confessions of a Second-Rate Sensitive Mind' (1830)]

10. [Of Helen]
A daughter of the gods, divinely tall
And most divinely fair.
['A Dream of Fair Women' (1832)]

11. O Love, O fire! once he drew
With one long kiss my whole soul thro'
My lips, as sunlight drinketh dew.
['Fatima' (1832)]

12. On either side the river lie
Long fields of barley and of rye,
That clothe the wold and meet the sky;
And thro' the field the road runs by
To many-tower'd Camelot...

13. Willows whiten, aspens quiver,
Little breezes dusk and shiver...

14. But who hath seen her wave her hand?
Or at the casement seen her stand?
Or is she known in all the land,
The Lady of Shalott?...

15. Only reapers, reaping early
In among the bearded barley,
Hear a song that echoes cheerly
From the river winding clearly
Down to tower'd Camelot.
['The Lady of Shalott' (1832, revised 1842), Part I]

16. She has heard a whisper say,
A curse is on her if she stay
To look down to Camelot...

17. She hath no loyal knight and true,
The Lady of Shalott...

18. Or when the moon was overhead,
Came two young lovers lately wed;
'I am half sick of shadows,' said
The Lady of Shalott.
['The Lady of Shalott' (1832, revised 1842), Part II]

19. All in the blue unclouded weather
Thick-jewell'd shone the saddle-leather,
The helmet and the helmet-feather
Burn'd like one burning flame together,
As he rode down to Camelot...

20. 'Tirra lirra,' by the river
Sang Sir Lancelot...

21. She left the web, she left the loom,
She made three paces thro' the room
She saw the water-lily bloom,
She saw the helmet and the plume,
She look'd down to Camelot.
Out flew the web and floated wide;
The mirror crack'd from side to side;
'The curse is come upon me,' cried
The Lady of Shalott.
['The Lady of Shalott' (1832, revised 1842), Part III]

22. Lying, robed in snowy white
That loosely flew to left and right–
The leaves upon her falling light–
Thro' the noises of the night
She floated down to Camelot:
And as the boat-head wound along
The willowy hills and fields among,
They heard her singing her last song,
The Lady of Shalott...

23. Who is this? and what is here?
And in the lighted palace near
Died the sound of royal cheer;
And they cross'd themselves for fear,
All the knights at Camelot:
But Lancelot mused a little space;
He said, 'She has a lovely face;
God in his mercy lend her grace,
The Lady of Shalott.'
['The Lady of Shalott' (1832, revised 1842), Part IV]

24. 'Courage!' he said, and pointed toward the land,
'This mounting wave will roll us shoreward soon.'
In the afternoon they came unto a land
In which it seemed always afternoon...

25. Far off, three mountaintops,
Three silent pinnacles of aged snow,
Stood sunset-flushed...

26. Our island home
Is far beyond the wave; we will no longer roam.
['The Lotos-Eaters' (1832, revised 1842)]

27. Music that gentlier on the spirit lies,
Than tir'd eyelids upon tir'd eyes...

28. There is no joy but calm!...

29. Hateful is the dark-blue sky,
Vaulted o'er the dark-blue sea.
Death is the end of life; ah, why
Should life all labour be?
Let us alone. Time driveth onward fast,
And in a little while our lips are dumb.
Let us alone. What is it that will last?
All things are taken from us, and become
Portions and parcels of the dreadful Past...

30. But, propt on beds of amaranth and moly,
How sweet (while warm airs lull us, blowing lowly)
With half-dropt eyelid still,
Beneath a heaven dark and holy,
To watch the long bright river drawing slowly
His waters from the purple hill...

31. The Lotos blows by every winding creek...

32. We have had enough of action, and of motion we,
Rolled to starboard, rolled to larboard, when the surge was seething free,
Where the wallowing monster spouted his foam-fountains in the sea...

33. Live and lie reclined
On the hills like Gods together, careless of mankind.
For they lie beside their nectar, and the bolts are hurl'd
Far below them in the valleys, and the clouds are lightly curl'd
Round their golden houses, girdled with the gleaming world...

34. Surely, surely, slumber is more sweet than toil, the shore
Than labour in the deep mid-ocean, wind and wave and oar;
Oh rest ye, brother mariners, we will not wander more.
['The Lotos-Eaters' (1832, revised 1842), Choric Song]

35. After-dinner talk
Across the walnuts and the wine.
['The Miller's Daughter' (1832, revised 1842)]

36. There lies a vale in Ida, lovelier
Than all the valleys of Ionian hills...

37. O mother Ida, many-fountain'd Ida...

38. Then to the bower they came,
Naked they came to that smooth-swarded bower,
And at their feet the crocus brake like fire,
Violet, amaracus, and asphodel,
Lotos and lilies.
['Oenone' (1832, revised 1842)]

39. I built my soul a lordly pleasure-house,
Wherein at ease for aye to dwell...

40. An English home – gray twilight pour'd
On dewy pastures, dewy trees,
Softer than sleep – all things in order stored,
A haunt of ancient Peace.
['The Palace of Art' (1832, revised 1842)]

41. Her arms across her breast she laid;
She was more fair than words can say:
Bare-footed came the beggar maid
Before the king Cophetua.
In robe and crown the king stept down,
To meet and greet her on her way;
'It is no wonder,' said the lords,
'She is more beautiful than day.'

As shines the moon in clouded skies,
She in her poor attire was seen:
One praised her ankles, one her eyes,
One her dark hair and lovesome mien.
So sweet a face, such angel grace,
In all that land had never been:
Cophetua sware a royal oath:
'This beggar maid shall be my queen!'
['The Beggar Maid' (1833)]

42. Ere leaves are new,
Caught in the frozen palms of Spring.
['The Blackbird' (1833)]

43. Deep on the convent-roof the snows
Are sparkling to the moon:
My breath to heaven like vapour goes:
May my soul follow soon!
['St Agnes' Eve' (1833, revised later)]

44. Battering the gates of heaven with storms of prayer.
['St Simeon Stylites' (1833)]

45. The woods decay, the woods decay and fall,
The vapours weep their burthen to the ground,
Man comes and tills the field and lies beneath,
And after many a summer dies the swan.
Me only cruel immortality
Consumes: I wither slowly in thine arms,
Here at the quiet limit of the world...

46. Why wilt thou ever scare me with thy tears,
And make me tremble lest a saying learnt,
In days far-off, on that dark earth, be true?
'The Gods themselves cannot recall their gifts.'...

47. Of happy men that have the power to die,
And grassy barrows of the happier dead.
['Tithonus' (1833, revised 1864)]

48. A still small voice spake unto me,
'Thou art so full of misery,
Were it not better not to be?'...

49. This truth within thy mind rehearse,
That in a boundless universe
Is boundless better, boundless worse...

50. No life that breathes with human breath
Has ever truly long'd for death.
['The Two Voices' (1833)]

51. It little profits that an idle king,
By this still hearth, among these barren crags,
Match'd with an aged wife, I mete and dole
Unequal laws unto a savage race...

52. I will drink
Life to the lees: all times I have enjoy'd
Greatly, have suffer'd greatly, both with those
That loved me, and alone; on shore, and when
Thro' scudding drifts the rainy Hyades
Vext the dim sea: I am become a name;
For always roaming with a hungry heart
Much have I seen and known; cities of men
And manners, climates, councils, governments,
Myself not least, but honour'd of them all;
And drunk delight of battle with my peers,
Far on the ringing plains of windy Troy.
I am a part of all that I have met;
Yet all experience is an arch wherethro'
Gleams that untravell'd world, whose margin fades
For ever and for ever when I move.
How dull it is to pause, to make an end,
To rust unburnish'd, not to shine in use!
As tho' to breathe were life...

53. This gray spirit yearning in desire
To follow knowledge like a sinking star,
Beyond the utmost bound of human thought...

54. This is my son, mine own Telemachus...

55. There lies the port; the vessel puffs her sail:
There gloom the dark broad seas. My mariners,
Souls that have toil'd, and wrought, and thought with me–
That ever with a frolic welcome took
The thunder and the sunshine, and opposed
Free hearts, free foreheads – you and I are old;
Old age hath yet his honour and his toil;
Death closes all: but something ere the end,
Some work of noble note, may yet be done,
Not unbecoming men that strove with Gods.
The lights begin to twinkle from the rocks:
The long day wanes: the slow moon climbs: the deep
Moans round with many voices. Come, my friends,
'Tis not too late to seek a newer world.
Push off, and sitting well in order smite
The sounding furrows; for my purpose holds
To sail beyond the sunset, and the baths
Of all the western stars, until I die.
It may be that the gulfs will wash us down:
It may be we shall touch the Happy Isles,
And see the great Achilles, whom we knew.
Tho' much is taken, much abides; and tho'
We are not now that strength which in old days
Moved earth and heaven; that which we are, we are;
One equal temper of heroic hearts,
Made weak by time and fate, but strong in will
To strive, to seek, to find, and not to yield.
['Ulysses' (1833)]

56. A land of settled government,
A land of just and old renown,
Where Freedom slowly broadens down
From precedent to precedent.
['You ask me, why, though ill at ease' (c. 1833)]

57. He is but a landscape-painter,
And a village maiden she.
['The Lord of Burleigh' (1833–1834)]

58. Break, break, break,
On thy cold gray stones, O Sea!
And I would that my tongue could utter
The thoughts that arise in me...

59. And the stately ships go on
To their haven under the hill;
But O for the touch of a vanish'd hand,
And the sound of a voice that is still!
['Break, Break, Break' (c. 1834)]

60. Half light, half shade,
She stood, a sight to make an old man young.
['The Gardener's Daughter' (c. 1834)]

61. My strength is as the strength of ten,
Because my heart is pure.
['Sir Galahad' (c. 1834)]

62. Lady Clara Vere de Vere,
Of me you shall not win renown:
You thought to break a country heart
For pastime, ere you went to town.
At me you smiled, but unbeguiled
I saw the snare, and I retired:
The daughter of a hundred Earls,
You are not one to be desired.
['Lady Clara Vere de Vere' (c. 1835), line 1]

63. A simple maiden in her flower
Is worth a hundred coats-of-arms.
['Lady Clara Vere de Vere' (c. 1835), line 15]

64. From yon blue heavens above us bent
The gardener Adam and his wife
Smile at the claims of long descent.
Howe'er it be, it seems to me,
'Tis only noble to be good.
Kind hearts are more than coronets,
And simple faith than Norman blood.
['Lady Clara Vere de Vere' (c. 1835), line 50]

65. Oh! teach the orphan-boy to read,
Or teach the orphan-girl to sew.
['Lady Clara Vere de Vere' (c. 1835), line 69]

66. A happy bridesmaid makes a happy bride.
['The Bridesmaid' (1836–1837)]

67. O plump head-waiter at The Cock,
To which I most resort,
How goes the time? 'Tis five o'clock.
Go fetch a pint of port.
['Will Waterproof's Lyrical Monologue' (c. 1837)]

68. Comrades, leave me here a little, while as yet 'tis early morn:
Leave me here, and when you want me, sound upon the bugle-horn.
['Locksley Hall' (1837–1838), line 1]

69. Here about the beach I wander'd, nourishing a youth sublime
With the fairy tales of science, and the long result of Time.
['Locksley Hall' (1837–1838), line 11]

70. In the Spring a livelier iris changes on the burnish'd dove;
In the Spring a young man's fancy lightly turns to thoughts of love.
['Locksley Hall' (1837–1838), line 19]

71. And our spirits rush'd together at the touching of the lips.
['Locksley Hall' (1837–1838), line 38]

72. As the husband is, the wife is: thou art mated with a clown,
And the grossness of his nature will have weight to drag thee down.

He will hold thee, when his passion shall have spent its novel force,
Something better than his dog, a little dearer than his horse.
['Locksley Hall' (1837–1838), line 47]

73. Cursed be the social wants that sin against the strength of youth!
Cursed be the social lies that warp us from the living truth.
['Locksley Hall' (1837–1838), line 59]

74. Such a one do I remember, whom to look at was to love.
['Locksley Hall' (1837–1838), line 72]

75. This is truth the poet sings,
That a sorrow's crown of sorrow is remembering happier things.
['Locksley Hall' (1837–1838), line 75]

76. Like a dog, he hunts in dreams.
['Locksley Hall' (1837–1838), line 79]

77. O, I see thee old and formal, fitted to thy petty part,
With a little hoard of maxims preaching down a daughter's heart.
['Locksley Hall' (1837–1838), line 93]

78. But the jingling of the guinea helps the hurt that Honour feels.
['Locksley Hall' (1837–1838), line 105]

79. Men, my brothers, men the workers, ever reaping something new:
That which they have done but earnest of the things that they shall do:

For I dipt into the future, far as human eye could see,
Saw the Vision of the world, and all the wonder that would be;

Saw the heavens fill with commerce, argosies of magic sails,
Pilots of the purple twilight, dropping down with costly bales;

Heard the heavens fill with shouting, and there rain'd a ghastly dew
From the nations' airy navies grappling in the central blue;

Far along the world-wide whisper of the south-wind rushing warm,
With the standards of the peoples plunging thro' the thunder-storm;

Till the war-drum throbb'd no longer, and the battle-flags were furl'd
In the Parliament of man, the Federation of the world.
['Locksley Hall' (1837–1838), line 117]

80. The kindly earth shall slumber, lapt in universal law.
So I triumph'd ere my passion sweeping thro' me left me dry,
Left me with the palsied heart, and left me with the jaundiced eye.
['Locksley Hall' (1837–1838), line 130]

81. Science moves, but slowly slowly, creeping on from point to point.
['Locksley Hall' (1837–1838), line 134]

82. Yet I doubt not thro' the ages one increasing purpose runs,
And the thoughts of men are widen'd with the process of the suns.
['Locksley Hall' (1837–1838), line 137]

83. Knowledge comes, but wisdom lingers.
['Locksley Hall' (1837–1838), line 143]

84. I will take some savage woman, she shall rear my dusky race.
['Locksley Hall' (1837–1838), line 168]

85. Not with blinded eyesight poring over miserable books.
['Locksley Hall' (1837–1838), line 172]

86. I the heir of all the ages, in the foremost files of time.
['Locksley Hall' (1837–1838), line 178]

87. Forward, forward let us range,
Let the great world spin for ever down the ringing grooves of change.
['Locksley Hall' (1837–1838), line 181]

88. Better fifty years of Europe than a cycle of Cathay.
['Locksley Hall' (1837–1838), line 184]

89. Come not, when I am dead,
To drop thy foolish tears upon my grave,
To trample round my fallen head,
And vex the unhappy dust thou wouldst not save.
['Come Not, When I Am Dead' (c. 1838)]

90. God made the woman for the man,
And for the good and increase of the world...

91. Slight Sir Robert with his watery smile
And educated whisker.
['Edwin Morris' (1839)]

92. Thro' all the circle of the golden year.
['The Golden Year' (c. 1839)]

93. The long mechanic pacings to and fro,
The set gray life, and apathetic end.
['Love and Duty' (c. 1840)]

94. With twelve great shocks of sound, the shameless noon
Was clash'd and hammer'd from a hundred towers.
['Godiva' (1842)]

95. Bitter barmaid, waning fast!...

96. Let us have a quiet hour,
Let us hob-and-nob with Death...

97. Every moment dies a man,
Every moment one is born.
['The Vision of Sin' (1842). Cf. Babbage: 1]

98. Ah God! the petty fools of rhyme
That shriek and sweat in pigmy wars.
['Literary Squabbles' (1846)]

99. What, it's you,
The padded man – that wears the stays...

100. What profits now to understand
The merits of a spotless shirt–
A dapper boot – a little hand–
If half the little soul is dirt?
['The New Timon, and the Poets' (1846)]

101. With prudes for proctors, dowagers for deans,
And sweet girl-graduates in their golden hair.
[*The Princess* (1847, revised later), Prologue, line 141]

102. I seemed to move among a world of ghosts,
And feel myself the shadow of a dream.
[*The Princess* (1847, revised later), I, line 17]

103. As thro' the land at eve we went,
And pluck'd the ripen'd ears.
We fell out, my wife and I,
O we fell out I know not why,
And kiss'd again with tears.
And blessings on the falling out

That all the more endears,
When we fall out with those we love
And kiss again with tears!
[*The Princess* (1847, revised later), II, Song, added 1850]

104. O hard, when love and duty clash!
[*The Princess* (1847, revised later), II, line 273]

105. Sweet and low, sweet and low,
Wind of the western sea,
Low, low, breathe and blow,
Wind of the western sea!
Over the rolling waters go,
Come from the dying moon, and blow,
Blow him again to me;
While my little one, while my pretty one, sleeps.
[*The Princess* (1847, revised later), III, Song, added 1850]

106. The splendour falls on castle walls
And snowy summits old in story:
The long light shakes across the lakes,
And the wild cataract leaps in glory.
Blow, bugle, blow, set the wild echoes flying,
Blow, bugle; answer, echoes dying, dying, dying.

O hark, O hear! how thin and clear,
And thinner, clearer, farther going!
O sweet and far from cliff and scar
The horns of Elfland faintly blowing!...

107. O love, they die in yon rich sky,
They faint on hill or field or river:
Our echoes roll from soul to soul,
And grow for ever and for ever.
[*The Princess* (1847, revised later), IV, Song, added 1850]

108. Tears, idle tears, I know not what they mean,
Tears from the depth of some divine despair
Rise in the heart, and gather to the eyes,
In looking on the happy Autumn-fields,
And thinking of the days that are no more...

109. So sad, so fresh, the days that are no more.

Ah, sad and strange as in dark summer dawns
The earliest pipe of half-awaken'd birds
To dying ears, when unto dying eyes
The casement slowly grows a glimmering square;
So sad, so strange, the days that are no more.

Dear as remembered kisses after death,
And sweet as those by hopeless fancy feign'd
On lips that are for others: deep as love,
Deep as first love, and wild with all regret;
O Death in Life, the days that are no more.
[*The Princess* (1847, revised later), IV, Song]

110. O Swallow, Swallow, flying, flying South,
Fly to her, and fall upon her gilded eaves,
And tell her, tell her, what I tell to thee.

O tell her, Swallow, thou that knowest each,
That bright and fierce and fickle is the South,
And dark and true and tender is the North...

111. O tell her, Swallow, that thy brood is flown:
Say to her, I do but wanton in the South,
But in the North long since my nest is made.

O tell her, brief is life but love is long.
[*The Princess* (1847, revised later), IV, Song]

112. Man is the hunter; woman is his game:
The sleek and shining creatures of the chase,
We hunt them for the beauty of their skins;
They love us for it, and we ride them down.
[*The Princess* (1847, revised later), V, line 147]

113. Man for the field and woman for the hearth:
Man for the sword and for the needle she:
Man with the head and woman with the heart:
Man to command and woman to obey;
All else confusion.
[*The Princess* (1847, revised later), V, line 437]

114. Home they brought her warrior dead:
She nor swoon'd, nor utter'd cry:
All her maidens, watching, said,
'She must weep or she will die.'...
[*The Princess* (1847, revised later), VI, Song, added 1850]

115. The woman is so hard
Upon the woman.
[*The Princess* (1847, revised later), VI, line 205]

116. Ask me no more: what answer should I give?
I love not hollow cheek or faded eye:
Yet, O my friend, I will not have thee die!
Ask me no more, lest I should bid thee live;
Ask me no more.
[*The Princess* (1847, revised later), VII, Song, added 1850]

117. Now sleeps the crimson petal, now the white;
Nor waves the cypress in the palace walk;
Nor winks the gold fin in the porphyry font:
The fire-fly wakens: waken thou with me.

Now droops the milkwhite peacock like a ghost,
And like a ghost she glimmers on to me.

Now lies the Earth all Danaë to the stars,
And all thy heart lies open unto me.

Now slides the silent meteor on, and leaves
A shining furrow, as thy thoughts in me.

Now folds the lily all her sweetness up,
And slips into the bosom of the lake:
So fold thyself, my dearest, thou, and slip
Into my bosom and be lost in me.
[*The Princess* (1847, revised later), VII, Song]

118. For Love is of the valley, come thou down
And find him; by the happy threshold, he,
Or hand in hand with Plenty in the maize,
Or red with spirted purple of the vats,
Or foxlike in the vine; nor cares to walk
With Death and Morning on the silver horns...

119. Sweet is every sound,
Sweeter thy voice, but every sound is sweet;
Myriads of rivulets hurrying thro' the lawn,
The moan of doves in immemorial elms,
And murmuring of innumerable bees.
[*The Princess* (1847, revised later), VII, Song]

120. No little lily-handed Baronet he,
A great broad-shoulder'd genial Englishman,
A lord of fat prize-oxen and of sheep,
A raiser of huge melons and of pine,
A patron of some thirty charities,
A pamphleteer on guano and on grain.
[*The Princess* (1847, revised later), 'Conclusion', line 84]

121. A life that moves to gracious ends
Thro' troops of unrecording friends,
A deedful life, a silent voice.
['To –, after reading a Life and Letters' (1849)]

122. Believing where we cannot prove...

123. Thou madest man, he knows not why,
He thinks he was not made to die;
And thou hast made him: thou art just...

124. Our little systems have their day;
They have their day and cease to be:
They are but broken lights of thee,
And thou, O Lord, art more than they...

125. Forgive these wild and wandering cries,
Confusions of a wasted youth.
[*In Memoriam A. H. H.* (1850), Prologue]

126. I held it truth, with him who sings
To one clear harp in divers tones,
That men may rise on stepping-stones
Of their dead selves to higher things.
[*In Memoriam A. H. H.* (1850), 1]

127. Old Yew, which graspest at the stones
That name the under-lying dead,
Thy fibres net the dreamless head,
Thy roots are wrapt about the bones.
[*In Memoriam A. H. H.* (1850), 2]

128. O Sorrow, cruel fellowship,
O Priestess in the vaults of Death,
O sweet and bitter in a breath,
What whispers from thy lying lip?

'The stars,' she whispers, 'blindly run;
A web is wov'n across the sky;
From out waste places comes a cry,
And murmurs from the dying sun:

'And all the phantom, Nature, stands–
With all the music in her tone,
A hollow echo of my own,–
A hollow form with empty hands.'

And shall I take a thing so blind,
Embrace her as my natural good;
Or crush her, like a vice of blood,
Upon the threshold of her mind?
[*In Memoriam A. H. H.* (1850), 3]

129. I sometimes hold it half a sin
To put in words the grief I feel;
For words, like Nature, half reveal
And half conceal the Soul within.

But, for the unquiet heart and brain,
A use in measured language lies;
The sad mechanic exercise,
Like dull narcotics, numbing pain.
[*In Memoriam A. H. H.* (1850), 5]

130. And common is the commonplace,
And vacant chaff well meant for grain...

131. Never morning wore
To evening, but some heart did break...

132. His heavy-shotted hammock-shroud
Drops in his vast and wandering grave.
[*In Memoriam A. H. H.* (1850), 6]

133. Dark house, by which once more I stand
Here in the long unlovely street,
Doors, where my heart was used to beat
So quickly, waiting for a hand...

134. But far away
The noise of life begins again,
And ghastly thro' the drizzling rain
On the bald streets breaks the blank day.
[*In Memoriam A. H. H.* (1850), 7]

135. The last red leaf is whirl'd away,
The rooks are blown about the skies.
[*In Memoriam A. H. H.* (1850), 15]

136. And from his ashes may be made
The violet of his native land.
[*In Memoriam A. H. H.* (1850), 18]

137. There twice a day the Severn fills;
The salt sea-water passes by,
And hushes half the babbling Wye,
And makes a silence in the hills.
[*In Memoriam A. H. H.* (1850), 19]

138. I do but sing because I must,
And pipe but as the linnets sing.
[*In Memoriam A. H. H.* (1850), 21]

139. The Shadow cloak'd from head to foot,
Who keeps the keys of all the creeds...

140. And Thought leapt out to wed with Thought
Ere Thought could wed itself with Speech...

And many an old philosophy
On Argive heights divinely sang,
And round us all the thicket rang
To many a flute of Arcady.
[*In Memoriam A. H. H.* (1850), 23]

141. I envy not in any moods
The captive void of noble rage,
The linnet born within the cage,
That never knew the summer woods...

142. I hold it true, whate'er befall;
I feel it, when I sorrow most;
'Tis better to have loved and lost
Than never to have loved at all.
[*In Memoriam A. H. H.* (1850), 27. Cf. Samuel Butler [2]: 20]

143. The time draws near the birth of Christ:
The moon is hid; the night is still;
The Christmas bells from hill to hill
Answer each other in the mist.
[*In Memoriam A. H. H.* (1850), 28]

144. Her eyes are homes of silent prayer.
[*In Memoriam A. H. H.* (1850), 32]

145. And what delights can equal those
That stir the spirit's inner deeps,
When one that loves but knows not, reaps
A truth from one that loves and knows?
[*In Memoriam A. H. H.* (1850), 42]

146. How fares it with the happy dead?
[*In Memoriam A. H. H.* (1850), 44]

147. Short swallow-flights of song, that dip
Their wings in tears, and skim away.
[*In Memoriam A. H. H.* (1850), 48]

148. Be near me when my light is low,
When the blood creeps, and the nerves prick
And tingle; and the heart is sick,
And all the wheels of Being slow.

Be near me when the sensuous frame
Is rack'd with pains that conquer trust;
And Time, a maniac scattering dust,
And Life, a Fury slinging flame.
[*In Memoriam A. H. H.* (1850), 50]

149. Do we indeed desire the dead
Should still be near us at our side?
Is there no baseness we would hide?
No inner vileness that we dread?
[*In Memoriam A. H. H.* (1850), 51]

150. How many a father have I seen,
A sober man, among his boys,
Whose youth was full of foolish noise...

151. Hold thou the good: define it well:
For fear divine Philosophy
Should push beyond her mark, and be
Procuress to the Lords of Hell.
[*In Memoriam A. H. H.* (1850), 53]

152. Oh yet we trust that somehow good
Will be the final goal of ill...

153. That nothing walks with aimless feet;
That not one life shall be destroy'd,
Or cast as rubbish to the void,
When God hath made the pile complete...

154. Behold, we know not anything;
I can but trust that good shall fall
At last – far off – at last, to all,
And every winter change to spring.

So runs my dream: but what am I?
An infant crying in the night:
An infant crying for the light:
And with no language but a cry.
[*In Memoriam A. H. H.* (1850), 54]

155. So careful of the type she seems,
So careless of the single life

156. The great world's altar-stairs
That slope thro' darkness up to God.
[*In Memoriam A. H. H.* (1850), 55]

157. Who trusted God was love indeed
And love Creation's final law–
Tho' Nature, red in tooth and claw
With ravine, shrieked against his creed.
[*In Memoriam A. H. H.* (1850), 56]

158. Peace; come away: the song of woe
Is after all an earthly song:
Peace; come away: we do him wrong
To sing so wildly: let us go...

159. The passing of the sweetest soul
That ever look'd with human eyes.
[*In Memoriam A. H. H.* (1850), 57]

160. O Sorrow, wilt thou live with me
No casual mistress, but a wife.
[*In Memoriam A. H. H.* (1850), 59]

161. His inner day can never die,
His night of loss is always there.
[*In Memoriam A. H. H.* (1850), 66]

162. The mystic glory swims away;
From off my bed the moonlight dies;
And closing eaves of wearied eyes
I sleep till dusk is dipt in gray.
[*In Memoriam A. H. H.* (1850), 67]

163. I dreamed there would be Spring no more,
That Nature's ancient power was lost.
[*In Memoriam A. H. H.* (1850), 69]

164. So many worlds, so much to do,
So little done, such things to be.
[*In Memoriam A. H. H.* (1850), 73]

165. Death has made
His darkness beautiful with thee.
[*In Memoriam A. H. H.* (1850), 74]

166. I care not in these fading days
To raise a cry that lasts not long,
And round thee with the breeze of song
To stir a little dust of praise.
[*In Memoriam A. H. H.* (1850), 75]

167. Laburnums, dropping-wells of fire.
[*In Memoriam A. H. H.* (1850), 83]

168. This truth came borne with bier and pall,
I felt it, when I sorrow'd most,
'Tis better to have loved and lost,
Than never to have loved at all...

169. God's finger touch'd him, and he slept.
[*In Memoriam A. H. H.* (1850), 85]

170. Another name was on the door:
I linger'd; all within was noise
Of songs, and clapping hands, and boys
That crash'd the glass and beat the floor.
[*In Memoriam A. H. H.* (1850), 87]

171. When rosy plumelets tuft the larch,
And rarely pipes the mounted thrush;
Or underneath the barren bush
Flits by the sea-blue bird of March.
[*In Memoriam A. H. H.* (1850), 91]

172. And strangely on the silence broke
The silent-speaking words, and strange
Was love's dumb cry defying change
To test his worth; and strangely spoke

The faith, the vigour, bold to dwell
On doubts that drive the coward back,
And keen thro' wordy snares to track
Suggestion to her inmost cell.

So word by word, and line by line,
The dead man touch'd me from the past,
And all at once it seem'd at last
The living soul was flash'd on mine,

And mine in this was wound, and whirl'd
About the empyreal heights of thought,
And came on that which is, and caught
The deep pulsations of the world,

Aeonian music measuring out
The steps of Time – the shocks of Chance–
The blows of Death. At length my trance
Was cancell'd, stricken thro' with doubt.

Vague words! but, ah, how hard to frame
In matter-moulded forms of speech
Or ev'n for intellect to reach
Thro' memory that which I became:

Till now the doubtful dusk reveal'd
The knolls once more where, couch'd at ease,
The white kine glimmer'd, and the trees
Laid their dark arms about the field:

And suck'd from out the distant gloom
A breeze began to tremble o'er
The large leaves of the sycamore,
And fluctuate all the still perfume,

And gathering freshlier overhead,
Rock'd the full-foliaged elms, and swung
The heavy-folded rose, and flung
The lilies to and fro, and said

'The dawn, the dawn,' and died away;
And East and West, without a breath,
Mixt their dim lights, like life and death,
To broaden into boundless day.
[*In Memoriam A. H. H.* (1850), 95]

173. There lives more faith in honest doubt,
Believe me, than in half the creeds.
[*In Memoriam A. H. H.* (1850), 96]

174. Their meetings made December June,
Their every parting was to die...

175. Though rapt in matters dark and deep
He seems to slight her simple heart...

176. He seems so near and yet so far.
[*In Memoriam A. H. H.* (1850), 97]

177. Ring out, wild bells, to the wild sky,
The flying cloud, the frosty light:
The year is dying in the night;
Ring out, wild bells, and let him die.

Ring out the old, ring in the new,
Ring, happy bells, across the snow:
The year is going, let him go;
Ring out the false, ring in the true.

Ring out the grief that saps the mind,
For those that here we see no more;
Ring out the feud of rich and poor,
Ring in redress to all mankind.

Ring out a slowly dying cause,
And ancient forms of party strife;
Ring in the nobler modes of life,
With sweeter manners, purer laws.

Ring out the want, the care, the sin,
The faithless coldness of the times;
Ring out, ring out my mournful rhymes,
But ring the fuller minstrel in.

Ring out false pride in place and blood,
The civic slander and the spite;
Ring in the love of truth and right,
Ring in the common love of good.

Ring out old shapes of foul disease;
Ring out the narrowing lust of gold;
Ring out the thousand wars of old,
Ring in the thousand years of peace.

Ring in the valiant man and free,
The larger heart, the kindlier hand;
Ring out the darkness of the land,
Ring in the Christ that is to be.
[*In Memoriam A. H. H.* (1850), 106]

178. Not the schoolboy heat,
The blind hysterics of the Celt.
[*In Memoriam A. H. H.* (1850), 109]

179. And thus he bore without abuse
The grand old name of gentleman,
Defamed by every charlatan,
And soil'd with all ignoble use.
[*In Memoriam A. H. H.* (1850), 111]

180. Now fades the last long streak of snow
Now burgeons every maze of quick
About the flowering squares, and thick
By ashen roots the violets blow...

181. And drown'd in yonder living blue
The lark becomes a sightless song.
[*In Memoriam A. H. H.* (1850), 115]

182. Contemplate all this work of Time,
The giant labouring in his youth;
Nor dream of human love and truth,
As dying Nature's earth and lime;
But trust that those we call the dead
Are breathers of an ampler day.
[*In Memoriam A. H. H.* (1850), 118]

183. There rolls the deep where grew the tree.
O earth, what changes hast thou seen!
There, where the long street roars, hath been
The stillness of the central sea.

The hills are shadows, and they flow
From form to form, and nothing stands;
They melt like mist, the solid lands,
Like clouds they shape themselves and go.
[*In Memoriam A. H. H.* (1850), 123]

184. And thou art worthy; full of power;
As gentle; liberal-minded, great,
Consistent; wearing all that weight
Of learning lightly like a flower...

185. One God, one law, one element,
And one far-off divine event,
To which the whole creation moves.
[*In Memoriam A. H. H.* (1850), Epilogue]

186. He clasps the crag with crooked hands;
Close to the sun in lonely lands,
Ring'd with the azure world, he stands.

The wrinkled sea beneath him crawls;
He watches from his mountain walls,
And like a thunderbolt he falls.
['The Eagle' (1851)]

187. Her court was pure; her life serene;
God gave her peace; her land reposed;
A thousand claims to reverence closed
In her as Mother, Wife, and Queen.
['To the Queen' (1851)]

188. Bury the Great Duke
With an empire's lamentation,
Let us bury the Great Duke
To the noise of the mourning of a mighty nation...

189. The last great Englishman...

190. O fall'n at length that tower of strength
Which stood four-square to all the winds that blew!...

191. For this is England's greatest son,
He that gain'd a hundred fights,
Nor ever lost an English gun...

192. In that world-earthquake, Waterloo!...

193. That sober freedom out of which there springs
Our loyal passion for our temperate kings...

194. Who never sold the truth to serve the hour,
Nor palter'd with Eternal God for power...

195. Not once or twice in our rough island-story,
The path of duty was the way to glory...

196. Speak no more of his renown,
Lay your earthly fancies down,
And in the vast cathedral leave him,
God accept him, Christ receive him.
['Ode on the Death of the Duke of Wellington' (1852, revised later)]

197. O love, what hours were thine and mine,
In lands of palm and southern pine;
In lands of palm, of orange-blossom,
Of olive, aloe, and maize and vine.
['The Daisy' (1853)]

198. Half a league, half a league,
Half a league onward,
All in the valley of Death
Rode the six hundred...

199. 'Forward the Light Brigade!'
Was there a man dismay'd?
Not tho' the soldier knew
Some one had blunder'd:
Their's not to make reply,
Their's not to reason why,
Their's but to do and die:
Into the valley of Death
Rode the six hundred.

Cannon to right of them
Cannon to left of them,
Cannon in front of them
Volley'd and thunder'd;
Storm'd at with shot and shell,
Boldly they rode and well,
Into the jaws of Death,
Into the mouth of Hell
Rode the six hundred.
['The Charge of the Light Brigade' (1854)]

200. You'll have no scandal while you dine,
But honest talk and wholesome wine.
['To the Rev. F.D. Maurice' (1854)]

201. I come from haunts of coot and hern,
I make a sudden sally,
And sparkle out among the fern,
To bicker down a valley...

202. I wind about, and in and out,
With here a blossom sailing,
And here and there a lusty trout,
And here and there a grayling,

And here and there a foamy flake
Upon me, as I travel
With many a silvery waterbreak
Above the golden gravel,

And draw them all along, and flow
To join the brimming river,
For men may come and men may go,
But I go on for ever...

203. I slip, I slide, I gloom, I glance,
Among my skimming swallows;
I make the netted sunbeam dance
Against my sandy shallows.
['The Brook' (1855)]

204. Slander, meanest spawn of Hell.
['The Letters' (1855)]

205. Faultily faultless, icily regular, spendidly null,
Dead perfection, no more.
[*Maud* (1855), I, 2]

206. The passionate heart of the poet is whirl'd into folly and vice...

207. And most of all would I flee from the cruel madness of love,
The honey of poison-flowers and all the measureless ill.
[*Maud* (1855), I, 4]

208. That jewell'd mass of millinery,
That oil'd and curl'd Assyrian Bull.
[*Maud* (1855), I, 6]

209. She came to the village church,
And sat by a pillar alone;
An angel watching an urn
Wept over her, carved in stone...

210. I heard no longer
The snowy-banded, dilettante,
Delicate-handed priest intone.
[*Maud* (1855), I, 8]

211. Ah God, for a man with heart, head, hand,
Like some of the simple great ones gone
For ever and ever by,
One still strong man in a blatant land,
Whatever they call him, what care I,
Aristocrat, democrat, autocrat – one
Who can rule and dare not lie.

And ah for a man to arise in me,
That the man I am may cease to be!
[*Maud* (1855), I, 10]

212. Birds in the high Hall-garden
When twilight was falling,
Maud, Maud, Maud, Maud,
They were crying and calling.
[*Maud* (1855), I, 12]

213. Gorgonised me from head to foot
With a stony British stare.
[*Maud* (1855), I, 13]

214. A livelier emerald twinkles in the grass,
A purer sapphire melts into the sea.
[*Maud* (1855), I, 18]

215. Come into the garden, Maud,
For the black bat, night, has flown,
Come into the garden, Maud,
I am here at the gate alone;
And the woodbine spices are wafted abroad,
And the musk of the rose is blown.

For a breeze of morning moves,
And the planet of Love is on high,
Beginning to faint in the light that she loves
On a bed of daffodil sky...

216. All night have the roses heard
The flute, violin, bassoon;
All night has the casement jessamine stirr'd
To the dancers dancing in tune;
Till a silence fell with the waking bird,
And a hush with the setting moon...

217. I said to the rose, 'The brief night goes
In babble and revel and wine.
O young lord-lover, what sighs are those,
For one that will never be thine?
But mine, but mine,' so I sware to the rose,
'For ever and ever, mine.'...

218. But the rose was awake all night for your sake,
Knowing your promise to me;
The lilies and roses were all awake,
They sigh'd for the dawn and thee.

Queen rose of the rosebud garden of girls,
Come hither, the dances are done,
In gloss of satin and glimmer of pearls,
Queen lily and rose in one...

219. There has fallen a splendid tear
From the passion-flower at the gate.
She is coming, my dove, my dear;
She is coming, my life, my fate;

The red rose cries, 'She is near, she is near;'
And the white rose weeps, 'She is late;'
The larkspur listens, 'I hear, I hear;'
And the lily whispers, 'I wait.'

She is coming, my own, my sweet;
Were it ever so airy a tread,
My heart would hear her and beat,
Were it earth in an earthy bed;
My dust would hear her and beat;
Had I lain for a century dead;
Would start and tremble under her feet,
And blossom in purple and red.
[*Maud* (1855), I, 22]

220. O that 'twere possible
After long grief and pain
To find the arms of my true love
Round me once again!
[*Maud* (1855), II, 4]

221. Dead, long dead,
Long dead!
And my heart is a handful of dust,
And the wheels go over my head,
And my bones are shaken with pain,
For into a shallow grave they are thrust,
Only a yard beneath the street,
And the hoofs of the horses beat, beat,
The hoofs of the horses beat,
Beat into my scalp and my brain,
With never an end to the stream of passing feet...

222. For I thought the dead had peace, but it is not so;
To have no peace in the grave, is that not sad?...

223. But the churchmen fain would kill their church,
As the churches have kill'd their Christ...

224. O me, why have they not buried me deep enough?
Is it kind to have made me a grave so rough,
Me, that was never a quiet sleeper.
Somebody, surely, some kind heart will come
To bury me, bury me
Deeper, ever so little deeper.
[*Maud* (1855), II, 5]

225. My life has crept so long on a broken wing
Thro' cells of madness, haunts of horror and fear,
That I come to be grateful at last for a little thing...

226. When the face of night is fair on the dewy downs,
And the shining daffodil dies...

227. It is better to fight for the good, than to rail at the ill;
I have felt with my native land, I am one with my kind,
I embrace the purpose of God, and the doom assign'd.
[*Maud* (1855), III, 6]

228. A lie which is all a lie may be met and fought with outright,
But a lie which is part a truth is a harder matter to fight.
['The Grandmother' (1859)]

229. Form, Form, Riflemen Form!
['Riflemen Form!' (1859)]

230. The voice of the dead was a living voice to me.
['In the Valley of Cauteretz' (1861)]

231. And when they buried him the little port
Had seldom seen a costlier funeral.
['Enoch Arden' (1861–1862)]

232. O you chorus of indolent reviewers.
['Milton: Hendecasyllabics' (1863)]

233. Dreams are true while they last, and do we not live in dreams?
['The Higher Pantheism' (1867)]

234. But I knaw'd a Quaäker feller as often 'as towd ma this:
'Doänt thou marry for munny, but goä wheer munny is!'
['Northern Farmer: New Style' (1869)]

Quotations from *The Idylls of the King* appear in the final order of the work, which is that of the 1889 edition.

235. But thro' all this tract of years
Wearing the white flower of a blameless life,
Before a thousand peering littlenesses,
In that fierce light which beats upon a throne,
And blackens every blot.
[*The Idylls of the King*, Dedication (1862), line 24]

236. From the great deep to the great deep he goes.
[*The Idylls of the King*, 'The Coming of Arthur' (1869), line 410]

237. Blow trumpet, for the world is white with May.
[*The Idylls of the King*, 'The Coming of Arthur' (1869), line 481]

238. Live pure, speak true, right wrong, follow the King–
Else, wherefore born?
[*The Idylls of the King*, 'Gareth and Lynette' (1872), line 117]

239. The city is built
To music, therefore never built at all,
And therefore built for ever.
[*The Idylls of the King*, 'Gareth and Lynette' (1872), line 272]

240. Lead, and I follow.
[*The Idylls of the King*, 'Gareth and Lynette' (1872), line 728 and elsewhere]

241. Our hoard is little, but our hearts are great.
[*The Idylls of the King*, 'The Marriage of Geraint' (1857), line 352]

242. For man is man and master of his fate.
[*The Idylls of the King*, 'The Marriage of Geraint' (1857), line 355]

243. They take the rustic murmur of their bourg
For the great wave that echoes round the world.
[*The Idylls of the King*, 'The Marriage of Geraint' (1857), line 419]

244. It is the little rift within the lute,
That by and by will make the music mute,
And ever widening slowly silence all.
[*The Idylls of the King*, 'Merlin and Vivien' (1856), line 388]

245. And trust me not at all or all in all.
[*The Idylls of the King*, 'Merlin and Vivien' (1856), line 396]

246. Man dreams of Fame while woman wakes to love.
[*The Idylls of the King*, 'Merlin and Vivien' (1856), line 458]

247. Where blind and naked Ignorance
Delivers brawling judgments, unashamed,
On all things all day long.
[*The Idylls of the King*, 'Merlin and Vivien' (1856), line 662]

248. Face-flatterer and backbiter are the same.
[*The Idylls of the King*, 'Merlin and Vivien' (1856), line 822]

249. Elaine the fair, Elaine the loveable,
Elaine, the lily maid of Astolat.
[*The Idylls of the King*, 'Lancelot and Elaine' (1859), line 1]

250. He is all fault who hath no fault at all:
For who loves me must have a touch of earth.
[*The Idylls of the King*, 'Lancelot and Elaine' (1859), line 132]

251. In me there dwells
No greatness, save it be some far-off touch
Of greatness to know well I am not great.
[*The Idylls of the King*, 'Lancelot and Elaine' (1859), line 447]

252. I know not if I know what true love is,
But if I know, then, if I love not him,
I know there is none other I can love.
[*The Idylls of the King*, 'Lancelot and Elaine' (1859), line 672]

253. The shackles of an old love straiten'd him,
His honour rooted in dishonour stood,
And faith unfaithful kept him falsely true.
[*The Idylls of the King*, 'Lancelot and Elaine' (1859), line 870]

254. Never yet
Was noble man but made ignoble talk.
He makes no friend who never made a foe.
[*The Idylls of the King*, 'Lancelot and Elaine' (1859), line 1080]

255. Our bond is not the bond of man and wife.
This good is in it, whatso'er of ill,
It can be broken easier.
[*The Idylls of the King*, 'Lancelot and Elaine' (1859), line 1199]

256. For good ye are and bad, and like to coins,
Some true, some light, but every one of you
Stamp'd with the image of the King.
[*The Idylls of the King*, 'The Holy Grail' (1869), line 25]

257. The cup, the cup itself, from which our Lord
Drank at the last sad supper with his own.
[*The Idylls of the King*, 'The Holy Grail' (1869), line 46]

258. 'God make thee good as thou art beautiful,'
Said Arthur, when he dubb'd him knight.
[*The Idylls of the King*, 'The Holy Grail' (1869), line 136]

259. I will be deafer than the blue-eyed cat,
And thrice as blind as any noonday owl,
To holy virgins in their ecstasies,
Henceforward.
[*The Idylls of the King*, 'The Holy Grail' (1869), line 862]

260. O great and sane and simple race of brutes
That own no lust because they have no law!
[*The Idylls of the King*, 'Pelleas and Ettarre' (1869), line 471]

261. The dirty nurse, Experience, in her kind
Hath foul'd me.
[*The Idylls of the King*, 'The Last Tournament' (1871), line 317]

262. The greater man, the greater courtesy.
[*The Idylls of the King*, 'The Last Tournament' (1871), line 628]

263. Too late, too late! ye cannot enter now.
[*The Idylls of the King*, 'Guinevere' (1859), line 168]

264. The children born of thee are sword and fire,
Red ruin, and the breaking up of laws.
[*The Idylls of the King*, 'Guinevere' (1859), line 422]

265. To love one maiden only, cleave to her,
And worship her by years of noble deeds,
Until they won her; for indeed I knew
Of no more subtle master under heaven
Than is the maiden passion for a maid,
Not only to keep down the base in man,
But teach high thought, and amiable words
And courtliness, and the desire of fame,
And love of truth, and all that makes a man.
[*The Idylls of the King*, 'Guinevere' (1859), line 472]

266. Our fair father Christ.
[*The Idylls of the King*, 'Guinevere' (1859), line 559]

267. He never mocks,
For mockery is the fume of little hearts.
[*The Idylls of the King*, 'Guinevere' (1859), line 627]

268. I thought I could not breathe in that fine air
That pure severity of perfect light–
I yearn'd for warmth and colour which I found
In Lancelot.
[*The Idylls of the King*, 'Guinevere' (1859), line 640]

269. It was my duty to have loved the highest:
It surely was my profit had I known:
It would have been my pleasure had I seen.
We needs must love the highest when we see it,
Not Lancelot, nor another.
[*The Idylls of the King*, 'Guinevere' (1859), line 652]

270. To where beyond these voices there is peace.
[*The Idylls of the King*, 'Guinevere' (1859), line 692]

271. I found Him in the shining of the stars,
I mark'd Him in the flowering of His fields,
But in His ways with men I find Him not.
[*The Idylls of the King*, 'The Passing of Arthur' (1869), line 9]

272. So all day long the noise of battle roll'd
Among the mountains by the winter sea.
[*The Idylls of the King*, 'The Passing of Arthur' (1869), line 170]

273. The bold Sir Bedivere uplifted him
And bore him to a chapel nigh the field,
A broken chancel with a broken cross,
That stood on a dark strait of barren land:
On one side lay the Ocean, and on one
Lay a great water, and the moon was full.
[*The Idylls of the King*, 'The Passing of Arthur' (1869), line 175]

274. An arm
Rose up from out the bosom of the lake,
Clothed in white samite, mystic, wonderful.
[*The Idylls of the King*, 'The Passing of Arthur' (1869), line 197]

275. He, stepping down
By zigzag paths, and juts of pointed rock,
Came upon the shining levels of the lake.
[*The Idylls of the King*, 'The Passing of Arthur' (1869), line 217]

276. Authority forgets a dying king.
[*The Idylls of the King*, 'The Passing of Arthur' (1869), line 289]

277. Clothed with his breath, and looking, as he walk'd,
Larger than human on the frozen hills.
He heard the deep behind him, and a cry
Before.
[*The Idylls of the King*, 'The Passing of Arthur' (1869), line 350]

278. [Sir Bedivere]
'The days darken round me, and the years,
Among new men, strange faces, other minds.'

And slowly answer'd Arthur from the barge:
'The old order changeth, yielding place to new,
And God fulfils himself in many ways,
Lest one good custom should corrupt the world.'
[*The Idylls of the King*, 'The Passing of Arthur' (1869), line 405]

279. I have lived my life, and that which I have done
May He within Himself make pure! but thou,
If thou shouldst never see my face again,
Pray for my soul. More things are wrought by prayer
Than this world dreams of. Wherefore, let thy voice
Rise like a fountain for me night and day.
For what are men better than sheep and goats
That nourish a blind life within the brain,
If, knowing God, they lift not hands of prayer
Both for themselves and those who call them friend?
For so the whole round earth is every way
Bound by gold chains about the feet of God.
But now farewell.
I am going a long way
With these thou seëst – if indeed I go
(For all my mind is clouded with a doubt)–
To the island-valley of Avilion;
Where falls not hail, or rain, or any snow,
Nor ever wind blows loudly; but it lies
Deep-meadow'd, happy, fair with orchard lawns
And bowery hollows crown'd with summer sea,
Where I will heal me of my grievous wound.'

So said he, and the barge with oar and sail
Moved from the brink, like some full-breasted swan
That, fluting a wild carol ere her death,
Ruffles her pure cold plume, and takes the flood
With swarthy webs. Long stood Sir Bedivere
Revolving many memories, till the hull
Looked one black dot against the verge of dawn,
And on the mere the wailing died away.
[*The Idylls of the King*, 'The Passing of Arthur' (1869), line 412]

280. Weird Titan by thy winter weight of years
As yet unbroken, Stormy voice of France!
['To Victor Hugo' (1877)]

281. At Flores in the Azores Sir Richard Grenville lay...

282. And Sir Richard said again: 'We be all good English men.
Let us bang these dogs of Seville, the children of the devil,
For I never turn'd my back upon Don or devil yet.'...

283. And the sun went down, and the stars came out far over the summer sea,
But never a moment ceased the fight of the one and the fifty-three...

284. A day less or more
At sea or ashore,
We die – does it matter when?...

285. Sink me the ship, Master Gunner – sink her, split her in twain!
Fall into the hands of God, not into the hands of Spain!...

286. And they praised him to his face with their courtly foreign grace;
But he rose upon their decks, and he cried:
'I have fought for Queen and Faith like a valiant man and true;
I have only done my duty as a man is bound to do:
With a joyful spirit I Sir Richard Grenville die!'
And he fell upon their decks, and he died...

287. And the little Revenge herself went down by the island crags
To be lost evermore in the main.
['The Revenge' (1878), 14]

288. Tenderest of Roman poets nineteen-hundred years ago,
'Frater Ave atque Vale' – as we wander'd to and fro
Gazing at the Lydian laughter of the Garda Lake below
Sweet Catullus' all-but-island, olive-silvery Sirmio!
['Frater Ave atque Vale' (1880)]

289. Fur hoffens we talkt o' my darter es died o' the fever at fall:
An' I thowt 'twur the will o' the Lord, but Miss Annie she said it wur draäins.
['The Village Wife' (1880)]

290. All the charm of all the Muses often flowering in a lonely word...

291. I salute thee, Mantovano, I that loved thee since my day began,
Wielder of the stateliest measure ever moulded by the lips of man.
['To Virgil' (1882)]

292. For nothing worthy proving can be proven,
Nor yet disproven: wherefore thou be wise,
Cleave ever to the sunnier side of doubt.
['The Ancient Sage' (1885)]

293. You praise when you should blame
The barbarism of wars.
A juster epoch has begun...

294. The song that nerves a nation's heart,
Is in itself a deed.
['The Charge of the Heavy Brigade' (1885), 'Epilogue']

295. What is it all but a trouble of ants in the gleam of a million million of suns?
['Vastness' (1885)]

296. Sunset and evening star,
And one clear call for me!
And may there be no moaning of the bar,
When I put out to sea...

297. Twilight and evening bell,
And after that the dark!
And may there be no sadness of farewell,
When I embark;

For tho' from out our bourne of Time and Place
The flood may bear me far,
I hope to see my Pilot face to face
When I have crost the bar.
['Crossing the Bar' (1889)]

298. Launch your vessel,
And crowd your canvas,
And, ere it vanishes
Over the margin,
After it, follow it,
Follow the Gleam.
['Merlin and the Gleam' (1889)]

299. [Of the critic, Churton Collins]
A louse in the locks of literature.
[In Charteris, *Life and Letters of Sir Edmund Gosse* (1931), 14]

Terence (Publius Terentius Afer) (c. 190–159 BC)
Carthaginian-born Roman comic dramatist

1. *Id arbitror*
Adprime in vita esse utile, ut nequid nimis.
My view is that the golden rule in life is never to have too much of anything.
[*Andria*, line 60]

2. *Hinc illae lacrimae.*
Hence these tears.
[*Andria*, line 126]

3. *Amantium irae amoris integratio est.*
Lovers' quarrels are the renewal of love.
[*Andria*, line 555]

4. *Nullumst iam dictum quod non dictum sit prius.*
Nothing can be said now that has not been said before.
[*Eunuchus*, Prologue, line 41. Cf. La Bruyère: 12]

5. *Homo sum; humani nil a me alienum puto.*
I am a man, I count nothing human indifferent to me.
[*Heauton Timoroumenos*, line 76]

6. *Modo liceat vivere, est spes.*
Where there's life, there's hope.
[*Heauton Timoroumenos*, line 980]

7. *Vos valete et plaudite.*
Farewell, and give us your applause.
[*Heauton Timoroumenos*, line 1067]

8. *Fortis fortuna adiuvat.*
Fortune favours the brave.
[*Phormio*, line 203. Cf. Virgil: 81]

9. *Quot homines tot sententiae: suos quoique mos.*
There are as many opinions as there are people: each has his own point of view.
[*Phormio*, line 454]

Teresa, Mother (Agnes Gouxha Bojaxhui) (1910–)
Roman Catholic missionary to the very poor in India, born in Skopje; Nobel peace prize, 1979

1. ... the poor are our brothers and sisters ... people in the world who need love, who need care, who have to be wanted.
[*Time*, 1975, 'Saints Among Us']

St Teresa of Ávila (c. 1512–1582)
Spanish Carmelite nun, mystic, ascetic and writer

1. *¡Oh, válgame Dios, Señor, cómo apretáis a vuestros amadores!*
Alas, O Lord, how thou dost afflict those who love thee!
[*El castillo interior* or *Las moradas* (*Interior Castle* or *Mansions*, 1577), 'Sixth Mansion', 11]

Terry, Dame Ellen (1847–1928)
English Shakespearean actress, theatrical manager and memoirist

1. Wonderful women! Have you ever thought how much we all, and women especially, owe to Shakespeare for his vindication of women in these fearless, high-spirited, resolute and intelligent heroines?
[*Four Lectures on Shakespeare* (1932), 'The Triumphant Women']

2. Imagination! imagination! I put it first years ago, when I was asked what qualities I thought necessary for success upon the stage.
[*The Story of My Life* (1933), 2]

3. What is a diary as a rule? A document useful to the person who keeps it, dull to the contemporary who reads it, invaluable to the student, centuries afterwards, who treasures it!
[*The Story of My Life* (1933), 14]

Tertullian (Quintus Septimus Florens Tertullianus) (c. AD 160–c. 225)
Carthaginian theologian and Latin Church Father

1. *O testimonium animae naturaliter Christianae.*
O witness of a soul Christian in its very nature.
[*Apologeticus*, 17]

2. *Vide, ut invicem se diligant.*
See how these Christians love one another.
[*Apologeticus*, 39]

3. *Plures efficimur quoties metimur a vobis, semen est sanguis Christianorum.*
As often as we are mown down by you, the more we grow in numbers; the blood of Christians is the seed.
[*Apologeticus*, 50]

4. *Certum est quia impossibile.*
It is certain because it is impossible.
[*De Carne Christi*, 5]

5. *Pervenimus igitur de calcaria, quod dici solet, in carbonarium.*
We come therefore, as the proverb has it, out of the frying pan into the fire [literally, from the limekiln to the charcoal furnace].
[*De Carne Christi*, 6]

Teschemacher, Edward (fl. 19th century)
Lyricist

1. Where my caravan has rested,
Flowers I leave you on the grass.
['Where My Caravan Has Rested']

Tessimond, A.S.J. (1902–1962)
English poet

1. Cats, no less liquid than their shadows,
Offer no angles to the wind.
They slip, diminished, neat, through loopholes
Less than themselves.
[*Cats* (1934)]

Thackeray, William Makepeace (1811–1863)
Indian-born English novelist; journalist and lecturer

1. And this I set down as a positive truth. A woman with fair opportunities, and without an absolute hump may marry *whom she likes*.
[*Vanity Fair* (1847–1848), 4]

2. [Miss Crawley] had been in France – and loved, ever after, French novels, French cookery, and French wines.
[*Vanity Fair* (1847–1848), 10]

3. Some cynical Frenchman has said that there are two parties to a love transaction; the one who loves and the other who condescends to be so treated.
[*Vanity Fair* (1847–1848), 13]

4. Whenever he met a great man he grovelled before him, and my-lorded him as only a free-born Briton can do.
[*Vanity Fair* (1847–1848), 13]

5. If a man's character is to be abused, say what you will, there's nobody like a relation to do the business.
[*Vanity Fair* (1847–1848), 19]

6. Them's my sentiments!
[*Vanity Fair* (1847–1848), 21]

7. Darkness came down on the field and city: and Amelia was praying for George, who was lying on his face, dead, with a bullet through his heart.
[*Vanity Fair* (1847–1848), 32]

8. Nothing like blood, sir, in hosses, dawgs, and men.
[*Vanity Fair* (1847–1848), 35]

9. How to live well on nothing a year.
[*Vanity Fair* (1847–1848), Title of chapter 36]

10. I think I could be a good woman if I had five thousand a year.
[*Vanity Fair* (1847–1848), 36]

11. Ah! *Vanitas Vanitatum!* Which of us is happy in this world? Which of us has his desire? or, having it, is satisfied? –

Come, children, let us shut up the box and the puppets, for our play is played out.
[*Vanity Fair* (1847–1848), 67]

12. He who meanly admires mean things is a Snob.
[*The Book of Snobs* (1848), 2]

13. It is impossible, in our condition of Society, not to be sometimes a Snob.
[*The Book of Snobs* (1848)]

14. Yes, I am a fatal man, Madame Fribsbi. To inspire hopeless passion is my destiny.
[*Pendennis* (1848–50), 23]

15. Remember, it is as easy to marry a rich woman as a poor woman.
[*Pendennis* (1848–1850), 28]

16. The *Pall Mall Gazette* is written by gentlemen for gentlemen.
[*Pendennis* (1848–1850), 32]

17. 'Tis not the dying for a faith that's so hard, Master Harry – every man of every nation has done that – 'tis the living up to it that is difficult.
[*The History of Henry Esmond* (1852), I, 6]

18. 'Tis strange what a man may do, and a woman yet think him an angel.
[*The History of Henry Esmond* (1852), I, 7]

19. We love being in love, that's the truth on't.
[*The History of Henry Esmond* (1852), II, 15]

20. There are some meannesses which are too mean even for man – woman, lovely woman alone, can venture to commit them.
[*A Shabby-Genteel Story* (1852), 3]

21. Runs not a river by my palace wall? Have I not sacks to sew up wives withal?
[*The Rose and the Ring* (1855), 9]

22. 'No business before breakfast, Glum!' says the King. 'Breakfast first, business next.'
[*The Rose and the Ring* (1855), 11]

23. There were three sailors of Bristol City
Who took a boat and went to sea.
But first with beef and captain's biscuits
And pickled pork they loaded she.
There was gorging Jack and guzzling Jimmy,
And the youngest he was little Billee.
Now when they got as far as the Equator
They'd nothing left but one split pea...

24. Says gorging Jim to guzzling Jacky,
We have no wittles, so we must eat *we*...

25. There's little Bill as is young and tender,
We're old and tough – so let's eat *he*...

26. He scarce had said his Catechism,
When up he jumps: 'There's land I see!
There's Jerusalem and Madagascar,
And North and South Amerikey.
There's the British Fleet a-riding at anchor,
With Admiral Napier, K.C.B.'
['Little Billee' (1849)]

27. Werther had a love for Charlotte
Such as words could never utter;
Would you know how first he met her?
She was cutting bread and butter.
Charlotte was a married lady,
And a moral man was Werther,
And for all the wealth of Indies,
Would do nothing for to hurt her.

So he sighed and pined and ogled,
And his passion boiled and bubbled,
Till he blew his silly brains out
And no more was by it troubled.
Charlotte, having seen his body
Borne before her on a shutter,
Like a well-conducted person,
Went on cutting bread and butter.
['Sorrows of Werther' (1855)]

28. One of our chief objectives in this Magazine is the getting out of novel spinning, and back into the world. Don't understand me to disparage our craft, especially *your* wares. I often say I am like the pastrycook, and don't care for tarts, but prefer bread and cheese; but the public love the tarts (luckily for us), and we must bake and sell them.
[Letter to Anthony Trollope, 28 October 1859]

29. When I am in labour with a book I don't quite know what happens.
[Letter to Mrs William Ritchie, May 1863]

30. They tell me not to drink, and I *do* drink ... They tell me not to eat, and I *do* eat.
[*The Letters and Private Papers of William Makepeace Thackeray* (1946), IV]

Thales (c. 624–547 BC)

Ionian philosopher, mathematician and astronomer; one of the earliest Greek scientists

1. [His reply when asked why he chose to carry on living after saying there was no difference between life and death]
Because there is no difference.
[In W. Durant, *The Story of Civilization*, II]

Thatcher, Denis (1915–)

English company director; husband of Margaret Thatcher

1. [Replying to the question 'Who wears the pants in this house?']
I do, and I also wash and iron them.
[*The Times* (Los Angeles), 1981]

Thatcher, Margaret (Margaret Hilda Roberts, Baroness Thatcher) (1925–)

English stateswoman; Conservative Prime Minister 1979–90

1. [Said after receiving school prize, aged nine]
I wasn't lucky. I deserved it.
[Attr.]

2. Let our children grow tall, and some taller than others if they have it in them to do so.
[Speech, US tour, 1975]

3. Britain is no longer in the politics of the pendulum, but of the ratchet.
[Speech, Institute of Public Relations, 1977]

4. U-turn if you want to. The lady's not for turning.
[Speech, Conservative Conference, 1980]

5. Victorian values ... were the values when our country became great.
[Television interview, 1982]

6. I'm not hard – I'm frightfully soft. But I will not be hounded.
[*Daily Mail*, 1972]

7. No one would have remembered the Good Samaritan if he'd only had good intentions. He had money as well.
[*The Observer*, 1980]

8. I don't mind how much my Ministers talk – as long as they do what I say.
[*The Observer*, 1980]

9. The thing I notice is that I tend to look at things much more logically than my colleagues.
[*The Observer*, 1980, in Jeffrey Care (ed.), *Sayings of the Eighties* (1989)]

10. If you are going from A to B you do not always necessarily go in a straight line.
[*The Observer*, 1980, in Jeffrey Care (ed.), *Sayings of the Eighties* (1989)]

11. I love argument, I love debate. I don't expect anyone just to sit there and agree with me, that's not their job.
[*The Times*, 1980]

12. If a woman like Eva Peron with no ideals can get that far, think how far I can go with all the ideals that I have.
[*The Sunday Times*, 1980]

13. The battle for women's rights has been largely won.
[*The Guardian*, 1982]

14. Pennies do not come from heaven. They have to be earned here on earth.
[*The Sunday Telegraph*, 1982]

15. State socialism is totally alien to the British character.
[*The Times*, 1983]

16. I am painted as the greatest little dictator, which is ridiculous – you always take some consultations.
[*The Times*, 1983]

17. Young people ought not to be idle. It is very bad for them.
[*The Times*, 1984]

18. I love being at the centre of things.
[*Reader's Digest*, 1984]

19. I am certain that we will win the election with a good majority. Not that I am ever over-confident.
[*Evening Standard*, 1984]

20. I think I have become a bit of an institution – you know, the sort of thing people expect to see around the place.
[*The Observer*, 1987, in Jeffrey Care (ed.), *Sayings of the Eighties* (1989)]

21. We have become a grandmother.
[*The Observer*, 1989, in Jeffrey Care (ed.), *Sayings of the Eighties* (1989)]

22. [Of her economic policy]
There is no alternative.
[Said on several occasions]

23. There is no such thing as society. There are individual men and women and there are families.
[Attr.]

Thayer, William Makepeace (1820–1898)
American clergyman, writer and biographer

1. From Log Cabin to White House.
[Title of biography of President Garfield, 1881]

Themistocles (c. 528–462 BC)
Athenian statesman and general

1. [Explaining his remark that his young son ruled all Greece]
Athens holds sway over all Greece; I dominate Athens; my wife dominates me; our newborn son dominates her.
[Attr.]

Theodoric (c. 445–526)
Asian King of the Ostragoths from 474

1. [Explaining why he had had a trusted minister, who had said he would adopt his master's religion, beheaded]
If this man is not faithful to his God, how can he be faithful to me, a mere man?
[In E. Guérard, *Dictionnaire Encyclopédique*]

Theroux, Paul (1941–)
American novelist, short-story and travel writer

1. The Japanese have perfected good manners and made them indistinguishable from rudeness.
[*The Great Railway Bazaar* (1975), 2]

2. It is with a kind of perverse pride that the Japanese point out how expensive their country has become. But this is as much a measure of wealth as of inflation.
[*The Great Railway Bazaar* (1975), 26]

3. The ship follows Soviet custom: it is riddled with class distinctions so subtle, it takes a trained Marxist to appreciate them.
[*The Great Railway Bazaar* (1975), 30]

Thiers, Louis Adolphe (1797–1877)
French statesman and historian; first President of the Third Republic 1871–73

1. *Il faut tout prendre au sérieux, mais rien au tragique.*
Everything must be taken seriously, nothing tragically.
[Speech, French National Assembly, 1873]

2. *[Le roi] règne et le peuple se gouverne.*
The king reigns, and the people govern themselves.
[*Le National*, 1830]

3. [Defending his social status after someone had remarked that his mother had been a cook]
She was – but I assure you that she was a very bad cook.
[Attr.]

St Thomas Aquinas (c. 1225–1274)
Italian scholastic philosopher, theologian and Dominican friar; founder of Thomism

1. *Pange, lingua, gloriosi*
Corporis mysterium,
Sanquinisque pretiosi,
Quem in mundi pretium
Fructus ventris generosi
Rex effudit gentium.
Sing, my tongue, of the mystery of the glorious Body, and of the precious Blood which the King of all peoples, the fruit of a noble womb, shed to redeem the world.
['Pange Lingua Gloriosi', Corpus Christi Hymn]

2. *Tantum ergo sacramentum*
Veneremur cernui;
Et antiquum documentum
Novo cedat ritui.
Let us therefore, bowing before Him, reverence this great Sacrament, and let the teaching of old yield to the new rite.
['Pange Lingua Gloriosi', Corpus Christi Hymn]

Thomas, Brandon (1856–1914)
English comedy actor and dramatist

1. Oh, my giddy aunt!
[*Charley's Aunt* (1892)]

2. I'm Charley's aunt from Brazil – where the nuts come from.
[*Charley's Aunt* (1892)]

Thomas, Dylan (1914–1953)
Welsh poet, short-story writer, essayist, radio dramatist and journalist

1. I, born of flesh and ghost, was neither
A ghost nor man, but mortal ghost.
And I was struck down by death's feather.
['Before I knocked' (1933)]

2. The hunchback in the park
A solitary mister
Propped between trees and water...

3. And the wild boys innocent as strawberries.
['The hunchback in the park' (1933)]

4. The force that through the green fuse drives the flower
Drives my green age; that blasts the roots of trees
Is my destroyer.
And I am dumb to tell the crooked rose
My youth is bent by the same wintry fever.
['The force that through the green fuse drives the flower' (1934)]

5. Light breaks where no sun shines;
Where no sea runs, the waters of the heart
Push in their tides.
['Light breaks where no sun shines' (1934)]

6. This bread I break was once the oat,
This wine upon a foreign tree
Plunged in its fruit;
Man in the day or wind at night
Laid the crops low, broke the grape's joy.
['This bread I break' (1936)]

7. Though they go mad they shall be sane,
Though they sink through the sea they shall rise again;
Though lovers be lost love shall not;
And death shall have no dominion.
['And death shall have no dominion' (1936)]

8. The hand that signed the paper felled a city;
Five sovereign fingers taxed the breath,
Doubled the globe of death and halved a country;
These five kings did a king to death...

9. The hand that signed the treaty bred a fever,
And famine grew, and locusts came;
Great is the hand that holds dominion over
Man by a scribbled name.
['The hand that signed the paper' (1936)]

10. And I must enter again the round
Zion of the water bead
And the synagogue of the ear of corn...

11. After the first death, there is no other.
['A Refusal to Mourn the Death, by Fire, of a Child in London' (1946)]

12. It was my thirtieth year to heaven
Woke to my hearing from harbour and neighbour wood
And the mussel pooled and the heron
Priested shore...

13. My birthday began with the water-
Birds and the birds on the winged trees flying my name.

14. Pale rain over the dwindling harbour
And over the sea wet church the size of a snail
With its horns through mist and the castle
Brown as owls
But all the gardens
Of spring and summer were blooming in the tall tales
Beyond the border and under the lark full cloud.
There could I marvel
My birthday
Away but the weather turned around.
['Poem in October' (1946)]

15. It is a winter's tale
That the snow blind twilight ferries over the lakes
And floating fields from the farm in the cup of the vales.
['A Winter's Tale' (1946)]

16. Now as I was young and easy under the apple boughs
About the lilting house and happy as the grass was green...

17. Oh as I was young and easy in the mercy of his means,
Time held me green and dying
Though I sang in my chains like the sea.
['Fern Hill' (1946)]

18. Do not go gentle into that good night,
Old age should burn and rave at close of day;
Rage, rage against the dying of the light...

19. And you, my father, there on the sad height,
Curse, bless, me now with your fierce tears, I pray.
['Do Not Go Gentle into that Good Night' (1952)]

20. Not for the proud man apart
From the raging moon I write
On these spindrift pages
Not for the towering dead
With their nightingales and psalms
But for the lovers, their arms
Round the griefs of the ages,
Who pay no praise or wages
Nor heed my craft or art.
['In My Craft or Sullen Art' (1952)]

21. To begin at the beginning: It is spring, moonless night in the small town, starless and bible-black, the cobblestreets silent and the hunched, courters'-and-rabbits' wood limping invisible down to the sloe-black, slow, black, crowblack, fishingboat-bobbing sea...

22. The boys are dreaming wicked or of the bucking ranches of the night and the jollyrodgered sea...

23. Chasing the naughty couples down the grassgreen gooseberried double bed of the wood...

24. *Mr Pritchard*: I must dust the blinds and then I must raise them.
Mrs Ogmore-Pritchard: And before you let the sun in, mind it wipes its shoes...

25. Sleeping as quiet as death, side by wrinkled side, toothless, salt and brown, like two old kippers in a box...

26. Every night of her married life she has been late for school...

27. Gomer Owen who kissed her once by the pig-sty when she wasn't looking and never kissed her again although she was looking all the time...

28. Here's your arsenic, dear.
And your weedkiller biscuit.
I've throttled your parakeet.
I've spat in the vases.
I've put cheese in the mouseholes.
Here's your...
...nice tea, dear...

29. Oh, isn't life a terrible thing, thank God?...

30. The hands of the clock have stayed still at half past eleven for fifty years. It is always opening time at the Sailors Arms...

31. Which of their gandering hubbies moaned in Milk Wood for your naughty mothering arms and body like a wardrobe, love?...

32. Oh, I'm a martyr to music...

33. Organ Morgan, you haven't been listening to a word I said. It's organ organ all the time with you...

34. ... his nicotine-eggyellow weeping walrus Victorian moustache worn thick and long in memory of Doctor Crippen...

35. Seventeen and never been sweet in the grass ho ho...

36. Portraits of famous bards and preachers, all fur and wool from the squint to the kneecaps...

37. You just wait, I'll sin till I blow up!
[*Under Milk Wood* (1954)]

38. These poems, with all their crudities, doubts, and confusions, are written for the love of Man and in praise of God, and I'd be a damn' fool if they weren't.
[*Collected Poems* (1952), Note]

39. The gong was bombilating, and Mrs Prothero was announcing ruin like a town crier in Pompeii.
[*A Child's Christmas in Wales* (1954)]

40. Years and years and years ago, when I was a boy, when there were wolves in Wales, and birds the colour of red-flannel petticoats whisked past the harp-shaped hills ... when we rode the daft and happy hills bareback, it snowed and it snowed.
[*A Child's Christmas in Wales* (1954)]

41. ... the hockey-legged girls who laughed behind their hands.
[*Adventures in the Skin Trade* (unfinished novel, 1955)]

42. Dylan talked copiously, then stopped.
'Somebody's boring me,' he said, 'I think it's me.'
[In Rayner Heppenstall, *Four Absentees* (1960)]

43. [Referring to Wales]
The land of my fathers. My fathers can have it.
[In John Ackerman, *Dylan Thomas* (1991)]

Thomas, Edward (1878–1917)
English nature poet and critic

1. Yes, I remember Adlestrop–
The name, because one afternoon
Of heat the express train drew up there
Unwontedly. It was late June.
['Adlestrop' (1917)]

2. The past is the only dead thing that smells sweet.
['Early One Morning' (1917]

3. If I should ever by chance grow rich
I'll buy Codham, Cockridden, and Childerditch,
Roses, Pyrgo, and Lapwater,
And let them all to my elder daughter.
['If I should ever by chance' (1917)]

4. There is not any book
Or face of dearest look
That I would not turn from now
To go into the unknown
I must enter, and leave, alone,
I know not how.
['Lights Out' (1917)]

5. Out in the dark over the snow
The fallow fawns invisible go
With the fallow doe;
And the winds blow
Fast as the stars are slow.
['Out in the Dark' (1917)]

6. As well as any bloom upon a flower
I like the dust on the nettles, never lost
Except to prove the sweetness of a shower.
['Tall Nettles' (1917)]

7. Now all roads lead to France
And heavy is the tread
Of the living; but the dead
Returning lightly dance...

8. I love roads:
The goddesses that dwell
Far along them invisible
Are my favourite gods.
['Roads' (1917)]

9. Choose me,
You English words.
['Words' (1917)]

Thomas, Gwyn (1913–1981)
Welsh novelist, radio and stage dramatist and teacher

1. My life's been a meeting, Dad, one long meeting. Even on the few committees I don't yet belong to, the agenda winks at me when I pass.
[*The Keep* (1961), I]

2. I wanted a play that would paint the full face of sensuality, rebellion and revivalism. In South Wales these three phenomena have played second fiddle only to the Rugby Union which is a distillation of all three.
[*Jackie the Jumper* (1962), Introduction, 'Plays and Players']

3. There are still parts of Wales where the only concession to gaiety is a striped shroud.
[*Punch*, 1958]

Thomas, Irene (1920–)
English writer and broadcaster

1. Protestant women may take the Pill. Roman Catholic woman must keep taking The Tablet.
[*The Guardian*, 1990]

2. It should be a very happy marriage – they are both so much in love with *him*.
[Attr.]

3. It was the kind of show where the girls are not auditioned – just measured.
[Attr.]

4. The cello is not one of my favourite instruments. It has such a lugubrious sound, like someone reading a will.
[Attr.]

Thomas, Lewis (1913–)
American pathologist and university administrator

1. Worrying is the most natural and spontaneous of all human functions. It is time to acknowledge this, perhaps even to learn to do it better.
[*More Notes of a Biology Watcher*, 'The Medusa and the Snail']

Thomas, Norman M. (1884–1968)
American Presbyterian minister, socialist, editor and writer

1. [Referring to his lack of success in presidential campaigns]
While I'd rather be right than president, at any time I'm ready to be both.
[In A. Whitman, *Come to Judgment*]

Thomas, R.S. (1913–)
Welsh poet, critic and clergyman

1. We were a people taut for war; the hills
Were no harder, the thin grass
Clothed them more warmly than the coarse
Shirts our small bones.
['Welsh History' (1952)]

2. An impotent people,
Sick with inbreeding,
Worrying the carcase of an old song.
['Welsh Landscape' (1952)]

3. We will listen instead to the wind's text
Blown through the roof, or the thrush's song
In the thick bush that proved him wrong,
Wrong from the start, for nature's truth
Is primary and her changing seasons
Correct out of a vaster reason
The vague errors of the flesh.
[*Song at the Year's Turning* (1955), 'The Minister']

Thompson, E.P. (1924–1993)
British historian and writer

1. [On the Europe debate]
This going into Europe will not turn out to be the thrilling mutual exchange supposed. It is more like nine middle-aged couples with failing marriages meeting in a darkened bedroom in a Brussels hotel for a Group Grope.
[*The Sunday Times*, 1975]

Thompson, Emma (1959–)
Oscar-winning British actress; wife of Kenneth Branagh, actor and film director

1. [Commenting on comparisons between the greatest married screen couple and the more down-to-earth Branagh household]
Olivier was a matinée idol and Leigh was an exquisite creature. Ken is a plumber figure ... when you meet him you think he's come to do the pipes, and I'm a sort of blue-stocking.
[*The List*, 1992]

Thompson, Francis (1859–1907)
English poet, essayist and critic, noted for his religious imagery

1. And thou – what needest with thy tribe's black tents
Who hast the red pavilion of my heart?
['Arab Love Song' (1913)]

2. She went her unremembering way,
She went and left in me
The pang of all the partings gone,
And partings yet to be.
She left me marvelling why my soul
Was sad that she was glad;
At all the sadness in the sweet,
The sweetness in the sad...

3. Nothing begins and nothing ends
That is not paid with moan;
For we are born in others' pain,
And perish in our own.
['Daisy' (1913)]

4. Go, songs, for ended is our brief sweet play;
Go, children of swift joy and tardy sorrow:
And some are sung, and that was yesterday,
And some unsung, and that may be to-morrow.
['Envoy' (1913)]

5. And all man's Babylons strive but to impart
The grandeurs of his Babylonian heart.
['The Heart' (1913)]

6. My days have crackled and gone up in smoke,
Have puffed and burst as sunstarts on a stream.
Yea, faileth now even dream
The dreamer, and the lute the lutanist...

7. I fled Him, down the nights and down the days;
I fled Him, down the arches of the years;
I fled Him, down the labyrinthine ways
Of my own mind; and in the mist of tears
I hid from Him, and under running laughter...

8. But with unhurrying chase,
And unperturbèd pace,
Deliberate speed, majestic instancy,
They beat – and a Voice beat
More instant than the Feet–
'All things betray thee, who betrayest Me.'
['The Hound of Heaven' (1913), I]

9. I said to Dawn: Be sudden – to Eve: Be soon...

10. To all swift things for swiftness did I sue;
Clung to the whistling mane of every wind...

11. Came on the following Feet,
And a Voice above their beat–
'Naught shelters thee, who wilt not shelter Me.'
['The Hound of Heaven' (1913), II]

12. Such is; what is to be?
The pulp so bitter, how shall taste the rind?...

13. Yet ever and anon a trumpet sounds
From the hid battlements of Eternity;
Those shaken mists a space unsettle, then
Round the half-glimpsèd turrets slowly wash again.
['The Hound of Heaven' (1913), IV]

14. 'Tis ye, 'tis your estrangèd faces,
That miss the many-splendoured thing.

But (when so sad thou canst not sadder)
Cry; – and upon thy so sore loss
Shall shine the traffic of Jacob's ladder
Pitched betwixt Heaven and Charing Cross.
['The Kingdom of God' (1913)]

15. Spring is come home with her world-wandering feet.
And all things are made young with young desires...

16. Let even the slug-abed snail upon the thorn
Put forth a conscious horn!
['Ode to Easter' (1913)]

17. Summer set lip to earth's bosom bare,
And left the flushed print in a poppy there...

18. The sleep-flower sways in the wheat its head,
Heavy with dreams, as that with bread:
The goodly grain and the sun-flushed sleeper
The reaper reaps, and Time the reaper.

I hang 'mid men my needless head,
And my fruit is dreams, as theirs is bread:
The goodly men and the sun-hazed sleeper
Time shall reap, but after the reaper
The world shall glean of me, me the sleeper.
['The Poppy' (1913)]

19. What heart could have thought you?–
Past our devisal
(O filigree petal!)
Fashioned so purely,
Fragilely, surely,

From what Paradisal
Imagineless metal,
Too costly for cost?
['To a Snowflake' (1913)]

Thompson, Hunter S. (1939–)
American 'new' journalist and writer

1. Fear and Loathing in Las Vegas.
[Title of two articles in *Rolling Stone*, 1971]

Thompson, William Hepworth (1810–1886)
English Greek scholar, university lecturer and priest

1. [Of Sir Richard Jebb, Professor of Greek at Cambridge]
What time he can spare from the adornment of his person he devotes to the neglect of his duties.
[In M.R. Bobbit, *With Dearest Love to All* (1960)]

Thomson, James [1] (1700–1748)
Scottish poet and dramatist, noted for his nature poetry

1. Oh! Sophonisba! Sophonisba! oh!
[*Sophonisba* (1730), III.ii]

2. When Britain first, at heaven's command,
Arose from out the azure main,
This was the charter of the land,
And guardian angels sung this strain:
'Rule, Britannia, rule the waves;
Britons never will be slaves.'
[*Alfred: A Masque* (1740), II]

3. Delightful task! to rear the tender thought,
To teach the young idea how to shoot...

4. An elegant sufficiency, content,
Retirement, rural quiet, friendship, books.
[*The Seasons* (1746), 'Spring']

5. Ships, dim-discovered, dropping from the clouds.
[*The Seasons* (1746), 'Summer']

6. Autumn nodding o'er the yellow plain
Comes jovial on.

7. While listening senates hang upon thy tongue...

8. For loveliness
Needs not the foreign aid of ornament,
But is when unadorned adorned the most...

9. Poor is the triumph o'er the timid hare!...

10. Find other lands beneath another sun.
[*The Seasons* (1746), 'Autumn']

11. Welcome, kindred glooms!
Congenial horrors, hail!...

12. The redbreast, sacred to the household gods,
Wisely regardful of the embroiling sky,
In joyless fields and thorny thickets leaves
His shivering mates, and pays to trusted man
His annual visit...

13. There studious let me sit,
And hold high converse with the mighty dead.
[*The Seasons* (1746), 'Winter']

14. A pleasing land of drowsyhead it was.
[*The Castle of Indolence* (1748), I]

Thomson, James [2] (1834–1882)
Scottish poet, essayist and journalist

1. ... to cure the pain
Of the headache called thought in the brain.
['L'Ancien Régime' (1880)]

2. For life is but a dream whose shapes return,
Some frequently, some seldom, some by night
And some by day...

3. The City is of Night; perchance of Death,
But certainly of Night; for never there
Can come the lucid morning's fragrant breath
After the dewy dawning's cold grey air...

4. The City is of Night, but not of Sleep;
There sweet sleep is not for the weary brain;
The pitiless hours like years and ages creep,
A night seems termless hell.
[*The City of Dreadful Night* (1880), I]

5. The vilest thing must be less vile than Thou
From whom it had its being, God and Lord!
[*The City of Dreadful Night* (1880), VIII]

6. I find no hint throughout the universe
Of good or ill, of blessing or of curse;
I find alone Necessity Supreme.
[*The City of Dreadful Night* (1880), XIV]

7. Speak not of comfort where no comfort is.
[*The City of Dreadful Night* (1880), XVI]

8. For verily the Tribe is all, and we
Are nothing singly save as parts of it.
[*Weddah and Om-el-Bonain* (1881), 2]

9. The gracious power
Of sleep's fine alchemy...

10. Some dark Presence watching by my bed,
The awful image of a nameless dread.
['Insomnia' (1899)]

Thomson, Joseph (1858–1895)
Scottish explorer of Africa, geologist and writer

1. [His reply when J.M. Barrie asked what was the most hazardous part of his expedition to Africa]
Crossing Piccadilly Circus.
[In D. Dunbar, *J.M. Barrie*]

Thomson, Roy (Baron Thomson of Fleet) (1894–1976)
Canadian-born British newspaper proprietor

1. [To an Edinburgh neighbour just after the opening of Scottish Television, which Thomson had founded, in 1957]
You know, it's just like having a licence to print your own money.
[In R. Braddon, *Roy Thomson of Fleet Street* (1965)]

Thoreau, Henry David (1817–1862)
American essayist, social critic, writer on natural history and follower of Emerson

1. I heartily accept the motto, 'That government is best which governs least'; and I should like to see it acted up to more rapidly and systematically. Carried out, it finally amounts to this, which I also believe, – 'That government is best which governs not at all.'
[*Civil Disobedience* (1849)]

2. Under a government which imprisons any unjustly, the true place for a just man is also a prison.
[*Civil Disobedience* (1849)]

3. It takes two to speak the truth, – one to speak, and another to hear.
[*A Week on the Concord and Merrimack Rivers* (1849)]

4. I have travelled a good deal in Concord.
[*Walden* (1854), 'Economy']

5. The finest qualities of our nature, like the bloom on fruits,

can be preserved only by the most delicate handling. Yet we do not treat ourselves nor one another delicately.
[*Walden* (1854), 'Economy']

6. As if you could kill time without injuring eternity.
[*Walden* (1854), 'Economy']

7. The mass of men lead lives of quiet desperation.
[*Walden* (1854), 'Economy']

8. I have lived some thirty years on this planet, and I have yet to hear the first syllable of valuable or even earnest advice from my seniors.
[*Walden* (1854), 'Economy']

9. Beware of all enterprises that require new clothes.
[*Walden* (1854), 'Economy']

10. It is a characteristic of wisdom not to do desperate things.
[*Walden* (1854), 'Economy']

11. There are now-a-days professors of philosophy but not philosophers.
[*Walden* (1854), 'Economy']

12. The owner of the axe, as he released his hold on it, said that it was the apple of his eye; but I returned it sharper than I received it.
[*Walden* (1854), 'Economy']

13. For more than five years I maintained myself thus solely by the labor of my hands, and I found, that by working about six weeks in a year, I could meet all the expenses of living.
[*Walden* (1854), 'Economy']

14. Time is but the stream I go a-fishing in.
[*Walden* (1854), 'Where I lived, and what I lived for']

15. Our life is frittered away by detail ... Simplify, simplify.
[*Walden* (1854), 'Where I lived, and what I lived for']

16. I would rather sit on a pumpkin and have it all to myself than be crowded on a velvet cushion.
[*Walden* (1854), 'Where I lived, and what I lived for']

17. The three-o'-clock in the morning courage, which Bonaparte thought was the rarest.
[*Walden* (1854), 'Sounds']

18. I never found the companion that was so companionable as solitude.
[*Walden* (1854), 'Solitude']

19. I had three chairs in my house; one for solitude, two for friendship, three for society.
[*Walden* (1854), 'Visitors']

20. Wherever a man goes, men will pursue him and paw him with their dirty institutions, and, if they can, constrain him to belong to their desperate oddfellow society.
[*Walden* (1854), 'The Village']

21. I once had a sparrow alight upon my shoulder for a moment while I was hoeing in a village garden, and I felt that I was more distinguished by that circumstance than I should have been by any epaulet I could have worn.
[*Walden* (1854), 'Winter Animals']

22. Things do not change; we change.
[*Walden* (1854), Conclusion]

23. Whatever sentence will bear to be read twice, we may be sure was thought twice.
[Journal, 1842]

24. Some circumstantial evidence is very strong, as when you find a trout in the milk.
[Journal, 1850]

25. I do not perceive the poetic and dramatic capabilities of an anecdote or story which is told me, its significance, till some time afterwards ... We do not enjoy poetry unless we know it to be poetry.
[Journal, 1856]

26. Not that the story need be long, but it will take a long while to make it short.
[Letter to Harrison Blake, 1857. Cf. Pascal: 1]

27. Any fool can make a rule and every fool will mind it.
[Attr.]

28. [On being urged to make his peace with God]
I did not know that we had ever quarrelled.
[Attr.]

Thorndike, Dame Sybil (1882–1976)
Distinguished English actress

1. [Replying to a query as to whether she had ever considered divorce during her long marriage to Sir Lewis Casson]
Divorce? Never. But murder often!
[Attr.]

Thorpe, Jeremy (1929–)
English politician, leader of the Liberal Party 1967–76, and business consultant

1. [Remark on Macmillan's Cabinet purge, 1962]
Greater love hath no man than this, that he lay down his friends for his life.
[Speech, House of Commons, 1962]

Thurber, James (1894–1961)
American humorist, essayist, short-story writer, illustrator and dramatist

1. I suppose that the high-water mark of my youth in Columbus, Ohio, was the night the bed fell on my father.
[*My Life and Hard Times* (1933), 1]

2. Her own mother lived the latter years of her life in the horrible suspicion that electricity was dripping invisibly all over the house.
[*My Life and Hard Times* (1933), 2]

3. Old Nat Burge sat ... watching the moon come up lazily out of the old cemetery in which nine of his daughters were lying, and only two of them were dead.
[*Let Your Mind Alone* (1937), 'Bateman Comes Home']

4. It is better to have loafed and lost than never to have loafed at all.
[*Fables for Our Time* (1940)]

5. It is not so easy to fool little girls today as it used to be.
[*Fables for Our Time* (1940)]

6. A man should not insult his wife publicly, at parties. He should insult her in the privacy of the home.
[*Thurber Country* (1953)]

7. A man's bed is his resting-place, but a woman's is often her rack.
[*Further Fables for Our Time* (1956)]

8. 'Joe,' I said, 'was perhaps the first great nonstop literary drinker of the American nineteenth century. He made the indulgences of Coleridge and De Quincey seem like a bit of mischief in the kitchen with the cooking sherry.'
[*Alarms and Diversions* (1957), 'The Morbundant Life...']

9. I was seized by the stern hand of Compulsion, that dark, unreasonable Urge that impels women to clean house in the middle of the night.
[*Alarms and Diversions* (1957), 'There's a Time for Flags']

10. There is no safety in numbers, or in anything else.
[*The New Yorker*, 1939, 'The Fairly Intelligent Fly']

11. Early to rise and early to bed makes a male healthy and wealthy and dead.
[*The New Yorker*, 1939, 'The Shrike and the Chipmunks']

12. Then, with that faint fleeting smile playing about his lips, he faced the firing squad; erect and motionless, proud and disdainful, Walter Mitty, the undefeated, inscrutable to the last.
[*The New Yorker*, 1939, 'The Secret Life of Walter Mitty']

13. You can fool too many of the people too much of the time.
[*The New Yorker*, 1939, 'The Owl Who Was God']

14. All right, have it your way – you heard a seal bark.
[Caption to cartoon 'The Seal in the Bedroom', in *The New Yorker*, 1932]

15. The War between Men and Women.
[Title of a series of cartoons in *The New Yorker*, 1934]

16. It's a naïve domestic Burgundy, without any breeding, but I think you'll be amused by its presumption.
[Cartoon caption in *The New Yorker*, 1937]

17. Well, if I called the wrong number, why did you answer the phone?
[Cartoon caption in *The New Yorker*, 1937]

18. He knows all about art, but he doesn't know what he likes.
[Cartoon caption]

19. Perhaps *this* will refresh your memory.
[Cartoon caption; remark by lawyer producing kangaroo in court]

20. Where did you get those big brown eyes and that tiny mind?
[Cartoon caption]

21. You wait here and I'll bring the etchings down.
[Cartoon caption]

22. Progress was all right; only it went on too long.
[Attr.]

23. [On being accosted at a party by a drunk woman who claimed she would like to have a baby by him]
Surely you don't mean by unartificial insemination!
[Attr.]

24. [Remark made about a play]
It had only one fault. It was kind of lousy.
[Attr.]

25. [His last words]
God bless ... God damn.
[Attr.]

Thurlow, Edward, First Baron (1731–1806)
English lawyer and politician; Lord Chancellor 1778–83, 1783–92

1. Did you ever expect a corporation to have a conscience, when it has no soul to be damned, and no body to be kicked?
[Attr.]

Tibullus (Albius Tibullus) (c. 54–19 BC)
Roman poet, noted for his elegiac love poetry

1. *Te spectem, suprema mihi cum venerit hora,*
Et teneam moriens deficiente manu.
May I be looking at you when my last hour has come, and as I die may I hold you with my weakening hand.
[*Elegies*, I, 1, 59]

2. [Of the Nile in Egypt]
Te propter nullos tellus tua postulat imbres,
Arida nec pluvio supplicat herba Iovi.
Because of you your land does not ask for showers, nor does its parched grass pray to Jupiter the Rain-giver.
[*Elegies*, I, 7, 25]

Tichborne, Chidiock (c. 1558–1586)
English Roman Catholic conspirator against Queen Elizabeth

1. My prime of youth is but a frost of cares;
My feast of joy is but a dish of pain;
My crop of corn is but a field of tares;
And all my good is but vain hope of gain.
The day is past, and yet I saw no sun;
And now I live, and now my life is done.
['Elegy', written in the Tower before his execution]

Tickell, Thomas (1686–1740)
English poet and editor

1. There taught us how to live; and (oh! too high
The price for knowledge) taught us how to die.
['On the Death of Mr Addison' (1721)]

Tillich, Paul (1886–1965)
German-born American philosopher and Protestant theologian

1. Neurosis is the way of avoiding non-being by avoiding being.
[*The Courage to Be* (1952)]

2. He who knows about depth knows about God.
[*The Shaking of the Foundations* (1962 edition)]

Tillotson, John (1630–1694)
English prelate, Archbishop of Canterbury

1. It might well seem strange if any man should write a book to prove that an egg is not an elephant, and that a musket-bullet is not a pike.
[*Works*, II, 'A Discourse against Transubstantiation']

Tindal, Matthew (1657–1733)
English deist and writer

1. Matters of fact, which as Mr Budgell somewhere observes, are very stubborn things.
[*The Will of Matthew Tindal* (1733)]

Tintoretto (Jacopo Robusti Tintoretto) (1518–1594)
Italian painter of the late Venetian School, noted for his dramatic religious scenes

1. [Arguing that he be allowed to paint the *Paradiso* at the Doge's palace in Venice, despite his advanced age]
Grant me paradise in this world; I'm not so sure I'll reach it in the next.
[Attr.]

Titus Vespasianus (AD 39–81)
Roman emperor from 79 and public benefactor

1. *Recordatus quondam super cenam, quod nihil cuiquam toto die praestitisset, memorabilem illam meritoque laudatam vocem edidit: 'Amici, diem perdidi.'*
Recalling once after dinner that he had done nothing to help anyone all that day, he gave voice to that memorable and praiseworthy remark: 'Friends, I have lost a day.'
[In Suetonius, *Lives of the Caesars*, 'Titus', VIII]

Tocqueville, Alexis de (1805–1859)
French political historian, liberal politician, lawyer and memoirist

1. *L'esprit français est de ne pas vouloir de* supérieur. *L'esprit anglais de vouloir des* inférieurs. *Le Français lève les yeux sans cesse au-dessus de lui avec inquiétude. L'Anglais les baisse au-dessous de lui avec complaisance. C'est de part et d'autre de l'orgueil, mais entendu de manière différente.*
The French want no-one to be their *superior*. The English want *inferiors*. The Frenchman constantly looks above him with anxiety. The Englishman looks beneath him with complacency. On either side it is pride, but understood in a different manner.
[*Voyage en Angleterre et en Irlande de 1835* (1835)]

2. *Il faut une science politique nouvelle à un monde tout nouveau.*
A new world demands a new political science.
[*De la démocratie en Amérique* (1835–1840)]

Tolkien, J.R.R. (1892–1973)
South African-born British novelist, philologist and Anglo-Saxon scholar

1. In a hole in the ground there lived a hobbit.
[*The Hobbit* (1937), 1]

2. One Ring to rule them all, One Ring to find them,
One Ring to bring them all and in the darkness bind them.
[*The Lord of the Rings* (1954), I]

Tolstoy, Leo (1828–1910)
Great Russian novelist; essayist, short-story writer, philosopher and moralist

1. The chief attraction of military service has been and will remain this compulsory and irreproachable idleness.
[*War and Peace* (1868–1869), VII]

2. Love is God, and when I die it means that I, a particle of love, shall return to the general and eternal source.
[*War and Peace* (1868–1869), VII]

3. Our body is a machine for living. It is geared towards it, it is its nature. Let life go on in it unhindered and let it defend itself, it will be more effective than if you paralyse it by encumbering it with remedies.
[*War and Peace* (1868–1869), X]

4. Pure and complete sorrow is just as impossible as pure and complete joy.
[*War and Peace* (1868–1869), XV]

5. Let me lie down like a stone, O Lord, and rise up like new bread.
[*War and Peace* (1868–1869)]

6. All happy families resemble one another, but every unhappy family is unhappy in its own way.
[*Anna Karenina* (1875–1877), I, 1]

7. He knew that people would be merciless for the very reason that his heart was lacerated. He felt that his fellow-man would destroy him, as dogs kill some poor cur maimed and howling with pain. He knew that his only salvation lay in hiding his wounds, and he had instinctively tried to do this for two days, but now he no longer had the strength to keep up the unequal struggle.
[*Anna Karenina* (1875–1877), V, 21]

8. I sit on a man's back, choking him and making him carry me, and yet assure myself and others that I am very sorry for him and wish to ease his lot any way I can – except by getting off his back.
[*What Then Must We Do?* (1886)]

9. It is amazing how complete is the delusion that beauty is goodness.
[*The Kreutzer Sonata* (1890)]

10. Don't trust your horse in the field, or your wife in the house.
[*The Kreutzer Sonata* (1890)]

11. Art is a human activity which has as its purpose the transmission to others of the highest and best feelings to which men have risen.
[*What is Art?* (1898)]

12. Art is not a handicraft, it is a transmission of feeling which the artist has experienced.
[*What is Art?* (1898)]

13. I am always with myself, and it is I who am my own tormentor.
[*Memoirs of a Madman* (1943)]

14. Historians are like deaf people who go on answering questions that no one has asked them.
[Attr.]

15. History would be an excellent thing if only it were true.
[Attr.]

16. If you want to be happy, be.
[Attr.]

17. [Refusing to reconcile himself with the Russian Orthodox Church as he lay dying]
Even in the valley of the shadow of death, two and two do not make six.
[Attr.]

Tolstoy, Sophie (1844–1919)
Russian diarist and autobiographer; wife of Leo Tolstoy

1. One can't live on love alone; and I am so stupid that I can't do anything but think of him.
[*A Diary of Tolstoy's Wife, 1860–1891*]

2. I am a source of satisfaction to him; a nurse, a piece of furniture, a *woman* – nothing more.
[*A Diary of Tolstoy's Wife, 1860–1891*]

3. He would like to destroy his old diaries and to appear before his children and the public only in his patriarchal robes. His vanity is enormous!
[*A Diary of Tolstoy's Wife, 1860–1891*]

Tomalin, Nicholas (1931–1973)
English journalist

1. The only qualities essential for real success in journalism are rat-like cunning, a plausible manner, and a little literary ability.
[*The Sunday Times Magazine*, 1969]

Tomaschek, Rudolphe (b. c. 1895)
German scientist

1. Modern Physics is an instrument of Jewry for the destruction of Nordic science ... True physics is the creation of the German spirit.
[In W.L. Shirer, *The Rise and Fall of the Third Reich* (1960), 8]

Tomasetti, Glen (1929–)
Australian travelling singer; writer of songs, poetry and plays

1. Don't be too polite, girls, don't be too polite
Show a little fight, girls, show a little fight
Don't be fearful of offending in case you get the sack

Just recognise your value and we won't look back.
['Don't Be Too Polite, Girls', song]

Tomasi, Giuseppe di Lampedusa (1896–1957)
Italian writer

1. *L'Italia era nata in quella accigliata sera a Donnafugata, nata proprio lì in quel paese dimenticato.*
Una fata cattiva però della quale non si conosceva il nome doveva essere stata presente.
Italy was born on that sombre evening at Donnafugata, she was indeed born in that forgotten village.
A bad fairy, however, whose name no one knew must have been there.
[*Il Gattopardo* (*The Leopard*, 1958)]

Toner, Pauline Therese (1935–1989)
Australian politician

1. [The credo of the first woman Minister in the history of the Victorian Parliament]
Why join a women's group to lobby government ministers when you can become a minister yourself?
[*Australian Women's Weekly*, 1982]

Tonna, Charlotte Elizabeth (1790–1846)
British miscellaneous writer

1. Derry's sons alike defy
Pope, traitor, or pretender
Peal to heaven their prentice cry
Their patriot – 'No Surrender!'
['No Surrender']

Toplady, Augustus Montague (1740–1778)
English divine; controversialist and hymn-writer

1. Rock of Ages, cleft for me,
Let me hide myself in Thee...

2. Nothing in my hand I bring,
Simply to Thy Cross I cling;
Naked, come to Thee for dress;
Helpless, look to Thee for grace;
Foul, I to the fountain fly;
Wash me, Saviour, or I die.
[Hymn, 1776]

Tosatti, Giorgio
Italian journalist

1. *Lo sport è sempre stato strumento di lotta politica.*
Sport has always been an instrument for political strife.
[*Corriere della Sera*, 1994]

Toscanini, Arturo (1867–1957)
Italian conductor

1. [Rebuking an incompetent orchestra]
After I die, I shall return to earth as a gatekeeper of a bordello and I won't let any of you – not a one of you – enter!
[In Howard Taubman, *The Maestro: The Life of Arturo Toscanini* (1951)]

2. [Refusing a floral wreath at the end of a performance]
They are for prima donnas or corpses – I am neither.
[In C. Galtey, *The Elephant that Swallowed a Nightingale*]

3. [Criticizing the playing of an Austrian orchestra during rehearsal]
Can't you read? The score demands *con amore*, and what are you doing? You are playing it like married men!
[Attr.]

4. [Rebuking an incompetent woman cellist]
Madame, there you sit with that magnificent instrument between your legs, and all you can do is *scratch* it!
[Attr.]

Tourneur, Cyril (c. 1575–1626)
English dramatist and poet

1. Were't not for gold and women, there would be no damnation.
[*The Revenger's Tragedy* (1607), II.i; also attributed to Middleton]

2. Does the silk-worm expend her yellow labours
For thee? for thee does she undo herself?
[*The Revenger's Tragedy* (1607), III.v; also attributed to Middleton]

Toynbee, Arnold (1889–1975)
English historian and scholar, noted for his analysis of world civilizations

1. America is a large, friendly dog in a very small room. Ever time it wags its tail it knocks over a chair.
[Broadcast news summary, 1954]

2. [Urging the need for a greater British influence in the United Nations Organisation, 1947]
No annihilation without representation.
[Attr.]

Tracy, Spencer (1900–1967)
American film actor; Academy Awards 1937 and 1938

1. [Of leaner times in his life]
There were times my pants were so thin I could sit on a dime and tell if it was heads or tails.
[In L. Swindell, *Spencer Tracy*]

2. [Defending his demand for equal billing with Katherine Hepburn]
This is a movie, not a lifeboat.
[Attr.]

Traherne, Thomas (c. 1637–1674)
English metaphysical religious poet and prose writer; clergyman

1. The hands are a sort of feet, which serve us in our passage towards Heaven, curiously distinguished into joints and fingers, and fit to be applied to any thing which reason can imagine or desire.
[*Meditations on the Six Days of Creation* (1717), VI]

2. You never enjoy the world aright, till the sea itself floweth in your veins, till you are clothed with the heavens, and crowned with the stars: and perceive yourself to be the sole heir of the whole world, and more than so, because men are in it who are every one sole heirs as well as you. Till you can sing and rejoice and delight in God, as misers do in gold, and kings in sceptres, you can never enjoy the world.
[*Centuries of Meditations*, I, 29 (published 1908)]

3. The corn was orient and immortal wheat, which never should be reaped, nor was ever sown. I thought it had stood from everlasting to everlasting.
[*Centuries of Meditations*, III, 3 (published 1908)]

4. The Men! O what venerable and reverend creatures did the aged seem! Immortal Cherubims! And young men glittering and sparkling Angels, and maids strange seraphic pieces of life and beauty! Boys and girls tumbling in the street, and playing, were moving jewels. I knew not that

they were born or should die; but all things abided eternally as they were in their proper places.
[*Centuries of Meditations*, III, 3 (published 1908)]

5. I within did flow
With seas of life, like wine.
['Wonder']

Traill, Catherine Parr (1802–1899)
Canadian pioneer writer and diarist

1. The making and baking of good, nourishing, palatable bread, is perhaps one of the most important duties of the practical housewife.
[*The Female Emigrant's Guide, and Hints on Canadian Housekeeping* (1854)]

Traill, Henry Duff (1842–1900)
English journalist, essayist and biographer

1. Look in my face. My name is Used-to-was;
I am also called Played-out and Done-to-death,
And It-will-wash-no-more.
['After Dilettante Concetti'. Cf. D.G. Rossetti: 12]

Trapp, Joseph (1679–1747)
English poet, pamphleteer, translator and clergyman

1. The King, observing with judicious eyes,
The state of both his universities,
To Oxford sent a troop of horse, and why?
That learned body wanted loyalty;
To Cambridge books, as very well discerning,
How much that loyal body wanted learning.
[Epigram on George I's donation of Bishop Ely's Library to Cambridge University. Cf. Sir William Browne: 1]

Travers, Ben (1886–1980)
English dramatist, screenwriter and novelist

1. One night Mr and Mrs Reginald Bingham went to Ciro's. They had been married only about six months. Mr Bingham had never been to Ciro's before in his life. His surprise, therefore, upon seeing his wife there, was considerable.
[*Mischief* (1926), 1]

Tree, Sir Herbert Beerbohm (1853–1917)
English actor and theatre manager, noted for his productions of Shakespeare; half-brother of Sir Max Beerbohm

1. [Of Israel Zangwill]
He is an old bore; even the grave yawns for him.
[In Hesketh Pearson, *Beerbohm Tree* (1956)]

2. The only man who wasn't spoilt by being lionized was Daniel.
[In Hesketh Pearson, *Beerbohm Tree* (1956)]

3. The national sport of England is obstacle-racing. People fill their rooms with useless and cumbersome furniture, and spend the rest of their lives trying to dodge it.
[In Hesketh Pearson, *Beerbohm Tree* (1956)]

4. When I pass my name in such large letters I blush, but at the same time instinctively raise my hat.
[In Hesketh Pearson, *Beerbohm Tree* (1956)]

5. [Remark to a man carrying a grandfather clock in the street]
My poor fellow, why not carry a watch?
[In Hesketh Pearson, *Beerbohm Tree* (1956)]

6. [Objecting to the presence of a camera while performing in a silent film]
Take that black box away. I can't act in front of it.
[In K. Brownlow, *Hollywood: The Pioneers*]

7. [Directing a group of sophisticated actresses]
Ladies, just a little more virginity, if you don't mind.
[In H. Teichmann, *Smart Aleck*]

Trevelyan, G.M. (1876–1962)
English historian and writer; great-nephew of Macaulay

1. Disinterested intellectual curiosity is the life blood of real civilization.
[*English Social History* (1942)]

2. Education ... has produced a vast population able to read but unable to distinguish what is worth reading.
[*English Social History* (1942)]

Trilling, Lionel (1905–1975)
American literary critic; university lecturer and novelist

1. I asked them to look into the Abyss, and, both dutifully and gladly, they have looked into the Abyss, and the Abyss has greeted them with the grave courtesy of all objects of serious study; saying: 'Interesting, am I not? And *exciting*, if you consider how deep I am and what dread beasts lie at my bottom.'
[*Beyond Culture*. Cf. Nietzsche: 9]

Trollope, Anthony (1815–1882)
English novelist, noted for his portrayal of provincial and political life; short-story writer, biographer, traveller and post office official

1. 'Unhand it, sir!' said Mrs Proudie. From what scrap of dramatic poetry she had extracted the word cannot be said; but it must have rested on her memory, and now seemed opportunely dignified for the occasion.
[*Barchester Towers* (1857), 11]

2. Not only humble but umble, which I look upon to be the comparative, or, indeed, superlative degree.
[*Doctor Thorne* (1858), 4]

3. In these days a man is nobody unless his biography is kept so far posted up that it may be ready for the national breakfast-table on the morning after his demise.
[*Doctor Thorne* (1858), 25]

4. The comic almanacs give us dreadful pictures of January and February; but, in truth, the months which should be made to look gloomy in England are March and April. Let no man boast himself that he has got through the perils of winter till at least the seventh of May.
[*Doctor Thorne* (1858), 47]

5. No man thinks there is much ado about nothing when the ado is about himself.
[*The Bertrams* (1859), 27]

6. Those who have courage to love should have courage to suffer.
[*The Bertrams* (1859), 27]

7. For the most of us, if we do not talk of ourselves, or at any rate of the individual circles of which we are the centres, we can talk of nothing. I cannot hold with those who wish to put down the insignificant chatter of the world.
[*Framley Parsonage* (1860), 10]

8. We cannot bring ourselves to believe it possible that a foreigner should in any respect be wiser than ourselves. If any such point out to us our follies, we at once claim those follies as the special evidences of our wisdom.
[*Orley Farm* (1862), 18]

9. It is because we put up with bad things that hotel-keepers continue to give them to us.
[*Orley Farm* (1862), 18]

10. As for conceit, what man will do any good who is not conceited? Nobody holds a good opinion of a man who has a low opinion of himself.
[*Orley Farm* (1862), 22]

11. To think of one's absent love is very sweet; but it becomes monotonous after a mile or two of a towing-path, and the mind will turn away to Aunt Sally, the Cremorne Gardens, and financial questions. I doubt whether any girl would be satisfied with her lover's mind if she knew the whole of it.
[*The Small House at Allington* (1864), 4]

12. It may almost be a question whether such wisdom as many of us have in our mature years has not come from the dying out of the power of temptation, rather than as the results of thought and resolution.
[*The Small House at Allington* (1864), 14]

13. Never think that you're not good enough yourself. A man should never think that. My belief is that in life people will take you very much at your own reckoning.
[*The Small House at Allington* (1864), 32]

14. With many women I doubt whether there be any more effectual way of touching their hearts than ill-using them and then confessing it. If you wish to get the sweetest fragrance from the herb at your feet, tread on it and bruise it.
[*Miss Mackenzie* (1865), 10]

15. How I did respect you when you dared to speak the truth to me! Men don't know women, or they would be harder to them.
[*The Claverings* (1867), 15]

16. It is a comfortable feeling to know that you stand on your own ground. Land is about the only thing that can't fly away.
[*The Last Chronicle of Barset* (1867), 58]

17. It's dogged as does it. It ain't thinking about it.
[*The Last Chronicle of Barset* (1867), 61]

18. A fainéant government is not the worst government that England can have. It has been the great fault of our politicians that they have all wanted to do something.
[*Phineas Finn* (1869), 13]

19. Mr Turnbull had predicted evil consequences ... and was now doing the best in his power to bring about the verification of his own prophecies.
[*Phineas Finn* (1869), 25]

20. Perhaps there is no position more perilous to a man's honesty than that ... of knowing himself to be quite loved by a girl whom he almost loves himself.
[*Phineas Finn* (1869), 50]

21. Men are so seldom really good. They are so little sympathetic. What man thinks of changing himself so as to suit his wife? And yet men expect that women shall put on altogether new characters when they are married, and girls think that they can do so.
[*Phineas Redux* (1874), 3]

22. It is the necessary nature of a political party in this country to avoid, as long as it can be avoided, the consideration of any question which involves a great change ... The best carriage horses are those which can most steadily hold back against the coach as it trundles down the hill.
[*Phineas Redux* (1874), 4]

23. Is it not singular how some men continue to obtain the reputation of popular authorship without adding a word to the literature of their country worthy of note? ... To puff and get one's self puffed have become different branches of a new profession.
[*The Way We Live Now* (1875), 1]

24. Love is like any other luxury. You have no right to it unless you can afford it.
[*The Way We Live Now* (1875), 84]

25. I feel convinced in my mind that I have been flogged oftener than any human being alive. It was just possible to obtain five scourgings in one day at Winchester, and I have often boasted that I obtained them all.
[*Autobiography* (1883), 1]

26. [Of his headmaster]
He must have known me had he seen me as he was wont to see me, for he was in the habit of flogging me constantly. Perhaps he did not recognize me by my face.
[*Autobiography* (1883), 1]

27. I found that I passed in railway-carriages very many hours of my existence ... I made for myself a little tablet, and found that I could write as quickly in a railway carriage as I could at my desk.
[*Autobiography* (1883), 1]

28. [On Frances Trollope's *Domestic Manners of the Americans*]
What though people had plenty to eat and clothes to wear, if they put their feet upon the tables and did not reverence their betters? The Americans were to her rough, uncouth, and vulgar, – and she told them so.
[*Autobiography* (1883), 2]

29. Take away from English authors their copyrights, and you would very soon take away from England her authors.
[*Autobiography* (1883), 6]

30. Three hours a day will produce as much as a man ought to write.
[*Autobiography* (1883), 15]

31. [Replying to the accusation made by two clergymen that he used the same characters over and over again]
I got up, and standing between them, I acknowledged myself to be the culprit. 'As to Mrs Proudie,' I said, 'I will go home and kill her before the week is over.' And so I did.
[*Autobiography* (1883), 15]

32. Of all the needs a book has the chief need is that it be readable.
[*Autobiography* (1883), 19]

33. I think that Plantagenet Palliser, Duke of Omnium, is a perfect gentleman. If he be not, then I am unable to describe a gentleman.
[*Autobiography* (1883), 20]

Trotsky, Leon (Lev Davidovich Bronstein) (1879–1940)
Ukrainian-born Russian revolutionary and Communist theorist; exiled from the USSR (1929) and assassinated

1. It was the supreme expression of the mediocrity of the apparatus that Stalin himself rose to his position.
[*My Life* (1930), 40]

2. Where force is necessary, one should make use of it boldly, resolutely, and right to the end. But it is as well to know the limitations of force; to know where to combine force with manoeuvre, assault with conciliation.
[*Was nun? (What Next?* 1932)]

3. Revolutions are always verbose.
[*History of the Russian Revolution* (1933), II]

4. Insurrection is an art, and like all arts it has its laws.
[*History of the Russian Revolution* (1933), III]

5. The fundamental premise of a revolution is that the existing social structure has become incapable of solving the urgent problems connected with the development of the nation.
[*History of the Russian Revolution* (1933), III]

6. From being a patriotic myth, the Russian people have become a terrible reality.
[*History of the Russian Revolution* (1933), III]

7. In a serious struggle there is no worse cruelty than to be magnanimous at an inappropriate time.
[*The History of the Russian Revolution* (1933), IV]

8. Old age is the most unexpected of all the things that happen to a man.
[*Diary in Exile* (1959), 8 May 1935]

9. Marxism is above all a method of analysis.
[*Permanent Revolution* (1969)]

10. An ally has to be watched just like an enemy.
[In A. Ulam, *Expansion and Coexistence* (1966)]

11. Lenin's method leads to this: the party organization at first substitutes itself for the party as a whole. Then the central committee substitutes itself for the party organization, and finally a single dictator substitutes himself for the central committee.
[In N. McInnes, *The Communist Parties of Western Europe*, 3]

Troubridge, Sir T. St Vincent (1895–1963)
British army officer

1. There is an iron curtain across Europe.
[*Sunday Empire News*, 1945. Cf. Winston Churchill: 35]

Truman, Harry S. (1884–1972)
American statesman; Democrat President 1945–53, and memoirist

1. If you can't stand the heat, get out of the kitchen.
[*Mr Citizen* (1960), 15]

2. [Referring to Vice-President Nixon's nomination for President]
You don't set a fox to watching the chickens just because he has a lot of experience in the hen house.
[Speech, 1960]

3. [Remark when Russia was invaded by Germany]
If we see that Germany is winning the war we ought to help Russia, and if Russia is winning we ought to help Germany, and in that way let them kill as many as possible.
[*The New York Times*, 1941]

4. The President spends most of his time kissing people on the cheek in order to get them to do what they ought to do without getting kissed.
[*The Observer*, 'Sayings of the Week', 1949]

5. It's a recession when your neighbour loses his job; it's a depression when you lose your own.
[*The Observer*, 'Sayings of the Week', 1958]

6. [Of General MacArthur]
I didn't fire him because he was a dumb son of a bitch, although he was, but that's not against the law for generals. If it was, half to three-quarters of them would be in gaol.
[In Merle Miller, *Plain Speaking* (1974)]

7. [Comment on Senator Fulbright]
An over-educated S.O.B.
[Quoted by Alistair Cooke, BBC broadcast, 1995]

8. Give me a one-handed economist! All my economists say, 'on the one hand ... on the other'.
[In P. Boller, *Presidential Anecdotes*]

9. The buck stops here.
[Sign on his desk]

10. A statesman is a politician who's been dead ten or fifteen years.
[Attr.]

Tuchman, Barbara W. (1912–1989)
American journalist and historian

1. Dead battles, like dead generals, hold the military mind in their dead grip.
[*August 1914* (1962), 2]

Tucholsky, Kurt (1890–1935)
German satirist and writer

1. *Aber der Frieden ist undankbar, und weiss nie, dass er seinen Bestand nur dem Krieg dankt.*
But peace is ungrateful and never knows it only owes its continued existence to war.
[*An Arno Holz* (*To Arno Holz*, 1913)]

2. *Die Frauen haben es ja von Zeit zu Zeit auch nicht leicht. Wir Männer aber müssen uns rasieren.*
Women from time to time don't have it easy either. But we men have to shave.
[*Schnipsel* (*Scraps*, 1973), 'Die Herren Männer' ('Men')]

3. *Das Merkwürdigste an einem Loch ist der Rand. Er gehört noch zum Etwas, sieht aber beständig in das Nichts, eine Grenzwache der Materie.*
The strangest thing about a hole is its edge. It is still part of Something but looks constantly into Nothing, a border guard of matter.
[*Schnipsel* (*Scraps*, 1973), 'Und überhaupt' ('And anyway')]

4. *Es gibt vielerlei Lärme, aber es gibt nur eine Stille.*
There are many sorts of noises, but there is only one silence.
[*Schnipsel* (*Scraps*, 1973), 'Und überhaupt' ('And anyway')]

5. *Das deutsche Schicksal: vor einem Schalter zu stehn.*
Das deutsche Ideal: hinter einem Schalter zu sitzen.
The German fate: standing in front of a counter.
The German ideal: sitting behind a counter.
[*Schnipsel* (*Scraps*, 1973), 'An preussischen Kammern' ('To Prussian Chambers')]

6. *Es gibt ein altes Wort: 'Wenn der Deutsche hinfällt, steht er nicht auf, sondern sieht sich um, wer ihm schadensersatzpflichtig ist.'*
There is an old saying: 'When a German falls over, he doesn't stand up, but looks about to see who is liable to pay him compensation.'
[*Schnipsel* (*Scraps*, 1973), 'An preussischen Kammern' ('To Prussian Chambers')]

7. *Das Englische ist eine einfache, aber schwere Sprache. Es besteht aus lauter Fremdwörtern die falsch ausgesprochen werden.*
English is a simple, yet hard language. It consists entirely of foreign words pronounced wrongly.
[*Schnipsel* (*Scraps*, 1973), 'Die Nation ist das achte Sakrament–!' ('The Nation is the Eighth Sacrament–!')]

8. *Der französische Soldat ist ein verkleideter Zivilist, der deutsche Zivilist ist ein verkleideter Soldat.*
The French soldier is a civilian in disguise, the German civilian is a soldier in disguise.
[*Schnipsel* (*Scraps*, 1973), 'Ozean der Schmerzen' ('Ocean of Pain')]

9. *Humor ist ein Element, das dem deutschen Menschen abhanden gekommen ist.*
Humour is an element which the German man has lost.
[*Schnipsel* (*Scraps*, 1973), 'Was darf die Satire–?' ('What may Satire do–?')]

10. *Was die Kirche nicht verhindern kann, das segnet sie.*
What the church can't prevent, it blesses.
[*Schnipsel* (*Scraps*, 1973), '...es gibt einen kleinen Rest, ausserhalb der Erdenschwere...' ('...there is a little left over, outside gravity...')]

Tucker, Sophie (Sophia Abuza) (1884–1966)
Russian-born American vaudeville singer

1. From birth to eighteen, a girl needs good parents. From eighteen to thirty-five, she needs good looks. From thirty-five to fifty-five, she needs a good personality. From fifty-five on, she needs good cash.
[In Michael Freedland, *Sophie* (1978)]

2. I've been poor and I've been rich. Rich is better.
[In Cowan, *The Wit of Women*]

3. The Last of the Red-Hot Mamas.
[Publicity self-description]

4. Life begins at forty.
[Attr.]

5. [Asked, when aged 80, the secret of longevity]
Keep breathing.
[Attr.]

Tuer, A.W. (1838–1900)
British publisher, editor and writer on books

1. English as she is Spoke.
[Title of Portuguese-English conversational guide]

Tupper, Martin (1810–1889)
English writer; lawyer and inventor

1. It is well to lie fallow for a while.
[*Proverbial Philosophy* (1838), 'Of Recreation']

2. Well-timed silence hath more eloquence than speech.
[*Proverbial Philosophy* (1838), 'Of Discretion']

3. A good book is the best of friends, the same today and for ever.
[*Proverbial Philosophy* (1838), 'Of Reading']

Turenne, Henri de la Tour d'Auvergne, Vicomte (1611–1675)
French marshal, noted for his command during the Thirty Years War

1. *Dieu est toujours pour les gros bataillons.*
God is always on the side of the big battalions.
[Attr. Cf. Anouilh: 5, Bussy-Rabutin: 3 and Voltaire: 9]

Turgenev, Ivan (1818–1883)
Russian novelist, dramatist and short-story writer, noted for his portrayal of provincial life

1. Diary of a Superfluous Man.
[Title of story, 1850]

2. I submit to no man's opinion; I have opinions of my own.
[*Fathers and Sons* (1862), 13]

3. The courage to believe in nothing.
[*Fathers and Sons* (1862), 14]

4. Go and try to disprove death. Death will disprove you, and that's all there is to it!
[*Fathers and Sons* (1862), 27]

5. Death is an old jest but it comes to everyone.
[In Jennifer Johnston, *The Old Jest*]

6. Hardly have I succeeded in reaching a definite position or in stopping at a familiar point of view, when fate drags me down from it.
[Attr.]

Turnbull, Margaret (fl. 1920s–1942)
Scottish-born American novelist, dramatist and screenwriter

1. No man is responsible for his father. That is entirely his mother's affair.
[*Alabaster Lamps* (1925)]

2. When a man confronts catastrophe on the road, he looks in his purse – but a woman looks in her mirror.
[*The Left Lady* (1926)]

Turner, Joseph Mallord William (1775–1851)
Great English landscape painter, water-colourist and illustrator, associated with the Romantic Movement

1. [Responding to a criticism of the fact that he had painted no portholes on the ships in a view of Plymouth]
My business is to paint not what I know, but what I see.
[In G. Painter, *Proust: The Early Years* (1959–1965)]

2. [His customary remark following the sale of one of his paintings]
I've lost one of my children this week.
[In E. Chubb, *Sketches of Great Painters*]

Turner, W.J.R. (1889–1946)
British poet, music critic and journalist, born in Australia

1. Beyond the blue, the purple seas
Beyond the thin horizon's line,
Beyond Antilla, Hebrides,
Jamaica, Cuba, Caribbes
There lies the land of Yucatan.
[*The Hunter and Other Poems* (1916), Title poem]

2. When I was but thirteen or so
I went into a golden land,
Chimborazo, Cotapaxi
Took me by the hand.

My father died, my brother too,
They passed like fleeting dreams.
I stood where Popocatapetl
In the sunlight gleams...

3. Chimborazo, Cotopaxi
They had stolen my soul away!
[*The Hunter and Other Poems* (1916), 'Romance']

4. He carved the red deer and the bull
Upon the smooth cave rock,
Returned from war, with belly full,
And scarred with many a knock,
He carved the red deer and the bull
Upon the smooth cave rock.
[*The Dark Fire* (1918), 'In the Caves of Auvergne']

Tusser, Thomas (c. 1524–1580)
English agricultural writer, poet and musician

1. Sweet April showers
Do spring May flowers.
[*Five Hundred Points of Good Husbandry* (1557)]

2. Yet true it is, as cow chaws cud,
And trees at spring do yield forth bud,
Except wind stands as never it stood,
It is an ill wind turns none to good.
[*Five Hundred Points of Good Husbandry* (1557)]

3. In doing of either, let wit bear a stroke,
For buying or selling of pig in a poke.
[*Five Hundred Points of Good Husbandry* (1557)]

4. The stone that is rolling can gather no moss;
For master and servant oft changing is loss.
[*Five Hundred Points of Good Husbandry* (1557)]

5. A fool and his money be soon at debate.
[*Five Hundred Points of Good Husbandry* (1557)]

6. Make hunger thy sauce, as a medicine for health.
[*Five Hundred Points of Good Husbandry* (1557)]

7. At Christmas play and make good cheer,
For Christmas comes but once a year.
[*Five Hundred Points of Good Husbandry* (1557)]

8. Feb, fill the dyke
With what thou dost like.
[*Five Hundred Points of Good Husbandry* (1557)]

9. Who goeth a borrowing
Goeth a sorrowing.
Few lend (but fools)
Their working tools.
[*Five Hundred Points of Good Husbandry* (1557)]

Tutu, Archbishop Desmond (1931–)

South African Anglican Archbishop and anti-apartheid campaigner; Nobel peace prize 1984

1. It seems that the British Government sees black people as expendable.
[Speech, 1986]

2. It is very difficult now to find anyone in South Africa who ever supported apartheid.
[*The Observer*, 1994]

3. For the Church in any country to retreat from politics is nothing short of heresy. Christianity is political or it is not Christianity.
[*The Observer*, 1994]

Tuwim, Julian (1894–1954)

Polish poet and writer

1. There are two kinds of blood, the blood that flows in the veins and the blood that flows out of them.
[*We, the Polish Jews*]

Twain, Mark (Samuel Langhorne Clemens) (1835–1910)

American humorist and novelist; journalist, lecturer and autobiographer

1. If there was two birds sitting on a fence, he would bet you which one would fly first.
[*The Celebrated Jumping Frog* (1867)]

2. I don't see no p'ints about that frog that's any better'n any other frog.
[*The Celebrated Jumping Frog* (1867)]

3. They spell it Vinci and pronounce it Vinchy; foreigners always spell better than they pronounce.
[*The Innocents Abroad* (1869), 19]

4. Lump the whole thing! say that the Creator made Italy from designs by Michael Angelo!
[*The Innocents Abroad* (1869), 27]

5. This poor little one-horse town.
['The Undertaker's Chat' (1875)]

6. Work consists of whatever a body is obliged to do.
[*The Adventures of Tom Sawyer* (1876), 2]

7. The cross of the Legion of Honour has been conferred upon me. However, few escape that distinction.
[*A Tramp Abroad* (1880), 8]

8. Some of his words were not Sunday-school words.
[*A Tramp Abroad* (1880), 20]

9. All the modern inconveniences.
[*Life on the Mississippi* (1883), 3]

10. Persons attempting to find a motive in this narrative will be prosecuted; persons attempting to find a moral in it will be banished; persons attempting to find a plot in it will be shot.
[*The Adventures of Huckleberry Finn* (1884), Introduction]

11. There was things which he stretched, but mainly he told the truth.
[*The Adventures of Huckleberry Finn* (1884), 1]

12. There was some books . . . One was *Pilgrim's Progress*, about a man that left his family, it didn't say why. I read considerable in it now and then. The statements was interesting, but tough. Another was *Friendship's Offering*, full of beautiful stuff and poetry; but I didn't read the poetry.
[*The Adventures of Huckleberry Finn* (1884), 17]

13. You feel mighty free and easy and comfortable on a raft.
[*The Adventures of Huckleberry Finn* (1884), 18]

14. Hain't we got all the fools in town on our side? and ain't that a big enough majority in any town?
[*The Adventures of Huckleberry Finn* (1884), 26]

15. An experienced, industrious, ambitious, and often quite picturesque liar.
[*Private History of a Campaign that Failed* (1885)]

16. There was worlds of reputation in it, but no money.
[*A Yankee at the Court of King Arthur* (1889), 9]

17. Adam was but human – this explains it all. He did not want the apple for the apple's sake, he wanted it only because it was forbidden.
[*Pudd'nhead Wilson* (1894), 2]

18. Whoever has lived long enough to find out what life is, knows how deep a debt of gratitude we owe to Adam, the first great benefactor of our race. He brought death into the world.
[*Pudd'nhead Wilson* (1894), 3]

19. Cauliflower is nothing but cabbage with a college education.
[*Pudd'nhead Wilson's Calendar* (1894)]

20. All say, 'How hard it is to die' – a strange complaint to come from the mouths of people who have had to live.
[*Pudd'nhead Wilson's Calendar* (1894)]

21. When angry count four; when very angry swear.
[*Pudd'nhead Wilson's Calendar* (1894)]

22. Don't part with your illusions. When they are gone, you may still exist, but you have ceased to live.
[*Pudd'nhead Wilson's Calendar* (1894)]

23. As to the Adjective: when in doubt, strike it out.
[*Pudd'nhead Wilson's Calendar* (1894)]

24. The holy passion of Friendship is of so sweet and steady and loyal and enduring a nature that it will last through a whole lifetime, if not asked to lend money.
[*Pudd'nhead Wilson's Calendar* (1894)]

25. There ain't no way to find out why a snorer can't hear himself snore.
[*Tom Sawyer Abroad* (1894), 10]

26. It is by the goodness of God that in our country we have those three unspeakably precious things: freedom of speech, freedom of conscience, and the prudence never to practise either of them.
[*Following the Equator* (1897)]

27. I admire him [Cecil Rhodes], I frankly confess it; and when his time comes I shall buy a piece of the rope for a keepsake.
[*Following the Equator* (1897)]

28. Man is the Only Animal that Blushes. Or needs to.
[*Following the Equator* (1897)]

29. Soap and education are not as sudden as a massacre, but they are more deadly in the long run.
[*Sketches New and Old* (1900), 'The Facts concerning the Recent Resignation']

30. The radical invents the views. When he has worn them out, the conservative adopts them.
[*Notebooks* (1935)]

31. When people do not respect us we are sharply offended; yet deep down in his heart no man much respects himself.
[*Notebooks* (1935)]

32. Good breeding consists in concealing how much we think of ourselves and how little we think of other persons.
[*Notebooks* (1935)]

33. There are three kinds of lies: lies, damned lies, and statistics.
[*Autobiography* (1959 edition)]

34. I have been told that Wagner's music is better than it sounds.
[*Autobiography* (1959 edition)]

35. When in doubt, tell the truth.
[*Pudd'nhead Wilson's New Calendar*]

36. [Definition of a classic]
Something that everybody wants to have read and nobody wants to read.
['The Disappearance of Literature']

37. The report of my death was an exaggeration.
[Cable, 1897]

38. When I was a boy of 14 my father was so ignorant I could hardly stand to have the old man around. But when I got to be 21, I was astonished at how much he had learned in seven years.
[In Alan L. Mackay, *The Harvest of a Quiet Eye* (1977)]

39. Most people are bothered by those passages in Scripture which they cannot understand; but as for me, I always noticed that the passages in Scripture which trouble me most are those that I do understand.
[In Simcox, *Treasury of Quotations on Christian Themes*]

40. Earned a precarious living by taking in one another's washing.
[Attr. by William Morris]

41. Heaven for climate, hell for society.
[Attr.]

42. I can live for two months on a good compliment.
[Attr.]

43. [Agreeing with a friend's comment that the money of a particular rich industrialist was 'tainted']
That's right. 'Taint yours, and 'taint mine.
[Attr.]

44. [Responding to the question 'In a world without women what would men become?']
Scarce, sir. Mighty scarce.
[Attr.]

45. [Saying how easy it is to give up smoking]
I've done it a hundred times!
[Attr.]

46. A banker is a person who lends you his umbrella when the sun is shining and wants it back the minute it rains.
[Attr.]

Twells, Henry (1823–1900)
British canon and headmaster

1. At even, when the sun was set,
The sick, O Lord, around Thee lay;
O in what divers pains they met!
O with what joy they went away!...

2. Thy touch has still its ancient power;
No word from thee can fruitless fall.
[Hymn, 1868]

Tynan, Kenneth (1927–1980)
English drama critic, producer and essayist

1. A novel is a static thing that one moves through; a play is a dynamic thing that moves past one.
[*Curtains* (1961)]

2. William Congreve is the only sophisticated playwright England has produced; and like Shaw, Sheridan, and Wilde, his nearest rivals, he was brought up in Ireland.
[*Curtains* (1961)]

3. A good drama critic is one who perceives what is happening in the theatre of his time. A great drama critic also perceives what is not happening.
[*Tynan Right and Left* (1967), Foreword]

4. What, when drunk, one sees in other women, one sees in Garbo sober.
[*The Sunday Times*, 1963]

5. A critic is a man who knows the way but can't drive the car.
[*The New York Times Magazine*, 1966]

6. [His reply when asked if he would allow sexual intercourse on stage at the National Theatre]
Oh, I think so, certainly ... I mean, there are few rational people in this world to whom the word 'fuck' is particularly diabolical or revolting or totally forbidden.
[In Paul Ferris, *Sex and the British* (1993); first use of the word 'fuck' on live television]

Tyrrell, George (1861–1909)
Irish theologian; modernist, teacher and writer

1. I never quite forgave Mahaffy for getting himself suspended from preaching in the College Chapel. Ever since his sermons were discontinued, I suffer from insomnia in church.
[In Oliver St John Gregory, *As I Was Going Down Sackville Street*, 25]

Uccello, Paolo (1397–1475)
Florentine painter, noted for his use of perspective

1. What a delightful thing this perspective is!
[In T. Craven, *Men of Art*]

Ulpian, Domitius (d. c. AD 228)
Roman jurist and writer, born in Phoenicia

1. *Volenti non fit iniuria.*
With consent, there is no injury.
[*Corpus Iuris Civilis*, 47, 10]

Umberto I (1844–1900)
King of Italy from 1878; assassinated

1. [After an attempt on his life]
È un incidente del mestiere.
It is one of the hazards of my profession.
[Attr., c. 1897]

Unamuno, Miguel de (1864–1936)
Spanish philosopher, essayist, poet and novelist

1. *No, no quiero ese mundo. Me aturde, me marea y me confunde. Sus hombres y sus cosas revoltean zumbando en torno de mi espíritu y me impiden soñar; son como nube de langosta que me vela mis luceros.*
No, I do not love this world. It perplexes me, makes me feel sick and confuses me. Its men and its things flutter and buzz around my spirit and prevent me from dreaming; they are like a cloud of locusts blocking off my stars.
['Después de una conversación' ('After a Conversation', 1904)]

2. *En cuanto a Alemania, es ésta desde hace algunos años una nación de faquires que se pasan la vida contemplando el ombligo imperial germánico.*
As far as Germany is concerned, for some years now it has been a nation of fakirs who spend their lives contemplating the imperial Germanic navel.
['La supuesta anormalidad española' ('Supposed Spanish Abnormality', 1913)]

3. *No suelen ser nuestras ideas las que nos hacen optimistas o pesimistas, sino que es nuestro optimismo o nuestro pesimismo, de origen fisiológico o patalógico quizás ... el que hace nuestras ideas.*
It is not normally our ideas which make us optimists or pessimists, but it is our optimism or our pessimism, which is perhaps of a physiological or pathological origin ... which makes our ideas.
[*Del sentimiento trágico de la vida* (*The Tragic Sense of Life*, 1913), 'The Man of Flesh and Blood']

4. *El hombre, por ser hombre, por tener conciencia, es ya, respecto al burro o a un cangrejo, un animal enfermo. La conciencia es una enfermedad.*
Man, because he is man, because he is conscious, is, in relation to the ass or to a crab, already a diseased animal. Consciousness is a disease.
[*Del sentimiento trágico de la vida* (*The Tragic Sense of Life*, 1913), 'The Man of Flesh and Blood']

5. *Creer en Dios es anhelar que le haya y es además conducirse como si le hubiera.*
To believe in God is to yearn for his existence and, moreover, it is to behave as if he did exist.
[*Del sentimiento trágico de la vida* (*The Tragic Sense of Life*, 1913), 'From God to God']

6. *Pues bien, mi señor don Miguel, tambíen usted se morirá, tambíen usted, y se volverá a la nada de que salió ... ¡Dios dejará de soñarle!*
Well then, my lord don Miguel, *you also* will die, and return to nothingness from whence you came ... God will stop dreaming you!
[*Niebla* (*Mist*, 1914), 31]

7. *Cúrate de la afección de preocuparte cómo aparezcas a los demás. Cuídate sólo de cómo aparezcas ante Dios, cuídate de la idea que de ti Dios tenga.*
Cure yourself of the disease of worrying about how you appear to others. Concern yourself only with how you appear before God, concern yourself with the idea which God has of you.
[*Vida de Don Quijote y Sancho* (1914 edition), 'Preliminary Essay']

8. *Una fe que no duda es una fe muerta.*
A faith which does not doubt is a dead faith.
[*La agonía del cristianismo* (*The Agony of Christianity*, written 1924, published 1931)]

9. [Of Franco's supporters]
Vencer no es convencer.
To conquer is not to convince.
[Speech at Salamanca University, 1936]

Ungaretti, Giuseppe (1888–1970)
Italian poet

1. *Cessate di uccidere i morti,*
Non gridate più, non gridate.
Stop killing the dead,
Don't shout anymore, don't shout.
[*Il Dolore* (*Pain*, 1942–1946)]

Upanishads (c. 800–300 BC)
Sacred books embodying the doctrines of ancient Hindu philosophy

1. When all desires that dwell within the human heart are cast away, then a mortal becomes immortal and here he attaineth to Brahman.
[*Katha Upanishad*, II, iii, 14]

Updike, John (1932–)
American novelist, short-story writer, poet and critic

1. A healthy male adult bore consumes one and a half times his own weight in other people's patience.
[*Assorted Prose* (1965), 'Confessions of a Wild Bore']

2. In general the churches, visited by me too often on weekdays ... bore for me the same relation to God that billboards did to Coca-Cola: they promoted thirst without quenching it.
[*A Month of Sundays* (1975), 2]

Upton, Ralph R. (1868–1935)

1. [Notice devised in 1912 for American railway crossings]
Stop; look; listen.
[In R. Hyman, *Dictionary of Famous Quotations* (1967)]

Upton, W. (fl. 1788)
British poet and songwriter

1. The lass so neat, with smile so sweet,
Has won my right good will,
I'd crowns resign to call thee mine,
Sweet lass of Richmond Hill.
['The Lass of Richmond Hill' (1789); also attributed to Leonard McNally]

Urey, Harold (1893–1981)
American chemist, discoverer of deuterium; Nobel prize for chemistry 1934

1. The next war will be fought with atom bombs and the one after that with spears.
[*The Observer*, 'Sayings of the Week', 1946]

Urquhart, Sir Thomas (1611–1660)
Scottish prose writer and translator

1. ... an Alcoranal paradise where nothing tending to the pleasure of all the senses was wanting.
[*The Jewel* (1652)]

Ussher, James (1581–1656)
Irish Archbishop of Armagh and scholar

1. [On the Creation]
Which beginning of time according to our Chronologie, fell upon the entrance of the night preceding the twenty third

day of *Octob.* in the year of the Julian Calendar, 710 [i.e. 4004 BC].
[*The Annals of the World* (1658)]

Ustinov, Sir Peter (1921–)
English stage and film actor (Academy Awards 1960 and 1964); director, dramatist, writer and raconteur

1. This is a free country, madam. We have a right to share your privacy in a public place.
[*Romanoff and Juliet* (1956), I]

2. As for being a General, well, at the age of four with paper hats and wooden swords we're all Generals. Only some of us never grow out of it.
[*Romanoff and Juliet* (1956), I]

3. A diplomat these days is nothing but a head-waiter who's allowed to sit down occasionally.
[*Romanoff and Juliet* (1956), I]

4. ... the great thing about history is that it is adaptable.
[*Romanoff and Juliet* (1956), II]

5. Thanks to the movies, gunfire has always sounded unreal to me, even when being fired at.
[*Dear Me* (1977), 7]

6. I am an optimist, unrepentant and militant. After all, in order not to be a fool an optimist must know how sad a place the world can be. It is only the pessimist who finds this out anew every day.
[*Dear Me* (1977), 9]

7. I believe that the Jews have made a contribution to the human condition out of all proportion to their numbers: I believe them to be an immense people. Not only have they supplied the world with two leaders of the stature of Jesus Christ and Karl Marx, but they have even indulged in the luxury of following neither one nor the other.
[*Dear Me* (1977), 19]

8. If Botticelli were alive today he'd be working for *Vogue*.
[*The Observer*, 'Sayings of the Week', 1962]

9. When Mrs Thatcher says she has a nostalgia for Victorian values I don't think she realises that 90 per cent of her nostalgia would be satisfied in the Soviet Union.
[*The Observer*, 1987, in Jeffrey Care (ed.), *Sayings of the Eighties* (1989)]

10. People at the top of the tree are those without qualifications to detain them at the bottom.
[Attr.]

11. Courage is often lack of insight, whereas cowardice in many cases is based on good information.
[Attr.]

Uvavnuk
Inuit singer and shaman

1. The arch of sky and mightiness of storms
Have moved the spirit within me,
Till I am carried away
Trembling with joy.
[In Knud Rasmussen, *Intellectual Culture of the Igulik Eskimos* (1929)]

2. The great sea
Has set me adrift
It moves me as the weed in the river,
Earth and the great weather
Move me,
Have carried me away
And move my inward parts with joy.
[In Knud Rasmussen, *Intellectual Culture of the Igulik Eskimos* (1929)]

Vachell, Horace Annesley (1861–1955)
English novelist, dramatist, memoirist and essayist

1. In nature there are no rewards or punishments; there are consequences.
[*The Face of Clay* (1906), 10]

Vail, Amanda (1921–1966)
American writer

1. Sometimes I think if there was a third sex men wouldn't get so much as a glance from me.
[*Love Me Little* (1957), 6]

Valerius Maximus (fl. c. AD 15)
Roman historian

1. *Provocarem ad Philippum, inquit, sed sobrium.*
Let me appeal to Philip, she said, but to Philip sober.
[*Facta et Dicta Memorabilia*, VI, 2; often quoted as 'Appeal from Philip drunk to Philip sober']

Valéry, Paul (1871–1945)
French Symbolist poet; critic, mathematician and philosopher

1. *Mes vers ont le sens qu'on leur prête.*
My poems mean what people take them to mean.
[*Variété* (*Variety*, 1924)]

2. *Il faut n'appeler 'Science' que l'ensemble des recettes qui réussissent toujours. – Tout le reste est littérature.*
The term Science should only be given to the aggregate of the recipes that are always successful. All the rest is literature.
[*Moralités* (*Moralities*, 1932). Cf. Verlaine: 5]

3. *Ce qui a été cru par tous, et toujours, et partout, a toutes les chances d'être faux.*
What has always been believed by everyone, everywhere, will most likely turn out to be false.
[*Moralités* (*Moralities*, 1932). Cf. St Vincent: 1]

4. *La politique est l'art d'empêcher les gens de se mêler de ce qui les regarde.*
Politics is the art of preventing people from becoming involved in affairs which concern them.
[*Tel quel 2* (*As Such 2*, 1943)]

5. *Le goût est fait de mille dégoûts.*
Taste is created from a thousand distastes.
[*Choses tues* (*Unsaid Things*)]

6. *Les livres ont les mêmes ennemis que lhomme: le feu, l'humide, les bêtes, le temps; et leur propre contenu.*
Books have the same enemies as man: fire, damp, animals, time; and their own contents.
[*Littérature*]

Vallentin, Antonina

1. His imperturbable optimism infected everyone; two little words which he had so frequently employed in talk with French friends in America in the blackest moments of his country's struggle, 'so it goes', '*ça ira*', became fashionable in Paris. Very quickly those two words became the chorus of a Revolutionary song.
[*Mirabeau: Voice of the Revolution*. Cf. Anon: 1]

Vanbrugh, Sir John (1664–1726)
English comic dramatist and baroque architect

1. Thinking is to me the greatest fatigue in the world.
[*The Relapse, or Virtue in Danger* (1696), II.i]

2. Once a woman has given you her heart you can never get rid of the rest of her.
[*The Relapse, or Virtue in Danger* (1696), III.i]

3. No man worth having is true to his wife, or can be true to his wife, or ever was, or ever will be so.
[*The Relapse, or Virtue in Danger* (1696), III.ii]

4. *Belinda*: Ay, but you know we must return good for evil.
Lady Brute: That may be a mistake in the translation.
[*The Provok'd Wife* (1697), I.i]

5. As if a woman of education bought things because she wanted 'em.
[*The Confederacy* (1705), I.i]

6. Jealousy's a city passion; 'tis a thing unknown amongst people of quality.
[*The Confederacy* (1705), I.ii]

7. The want of a thing is perplexing enough, but the possession of it is intolerable.
[*The Confederacy* (1705), I.ii]

8. Much of a muchness.
[*The Provok'd Husband* (1728), I.i; unfinished work completed by Colley Cibber]

Vanderbilt, William H. (1821–1885)
American financier and railway magnate

1. [When asked whether the public should be consulted about luxury trains]
The public be damned! I'm working for my stockholders.
[Remark, 1883]

2. I have had no real gratification or enjoyment of any sort more than my neighbor on the next block who is worth only half a million.
[In B. Conrad, *Famous Last Words* (1961)]

Van der Post, Sir Laurens (1906–)
South African writer; soldier, explorer and novelist

1. People like myself, whose first memory is of a large, black, smiling, crooning, warm, full-bosomed figure bending over his cot and whose friends for years were naked black urchins, know that contact between Europeans and Africans is, whether the individual wishes it or not, a significant, almost measureless two-way flow of traffic.
[*Venture to the Interior* (1952), I]

2. When my forefathers landed more than three hundred years ago in the Cape of Good Hope the colour prejudice was much less marked, and today we have the million 'coloured' people of the Cape colony as proof of it.
[*The Dark Eye in Africa* (1955), II]

3. Africa has always walked in my mind proudly upright, an African giant among the other continents, toes well dug into the final ocean of one hemisphere, rising to its full height in the greying skies of the other; head and shoulders broad, square and enduring, making light of the bagful of blue Mediterranean slung over its back as it marches patiently through time.
[*Flamingo Feather* (1955), 3]

4. Organized religion is making Christianity political rather than making politics Christian.
[*The Observer*, 'Sayings of the Week', 1986]

Vanzetti, Bartolomeo (1888–1927)
Italian-born American anarchist; executed, controversially, for murder

1. [Statement disallowed at his trial]
Sacco's name will live in the hearts of the people and in their gratitude when Katzmann's and yours bones will be dispersed by time, when your name, his name, your laws, institutions, and your false god are but a deem rememoring of a cursed past in which man was wolf to the man.
[In Frankfurter and Jackson, *Letters of Sacco and Vanzetti* (1928)]

2. [Statement after receiving death sentence]
Never in our full life could we hope to do such work for tolerance, for joostice, for man's understanding of man as now we do by accident. Our words – our lives – our pains – nothing! The taking of our lives – lives of a good shoemaker and a poor fish-peddler – all! That last moment belongs to us – that agony is our triumph.
[In Frankfurter and Jackson, *Letters of Sacco and Vanzetti* (1928)]

Vaughan, Charles J. (1816–1897)
English clergyman, teacher and author of religious works

1. [Remark designed to conclude visits by schoolboys too embarrassed to leave]
Must you go? Can't you stay?
[In G.W.E. Russell, *Collections and Recollections* (1898)]

Vaughan, Henry (1622–1695)
Welsh metaphysical poet and physician

1. Wise Nicodemus saw such light
As made him know his God by night.

Most blest believer he!
Who in that land of darkness and blinde eyes
Thy long expected healing wings could see,
When thou didst rise,
And what can never more be done,
Did at mid-night speak with the Sun!...

2. Dear night! this world's defeat;
The stop to busie fools; care's check and curb;
The day of Spirits; my soul's calm retreat
Which none disturb!...

3. There is in God (some say)
A deep, but dazzling darkness; as men here
Say it is late and dusky, because they
See not all clear;
O for that night! where I in him
Might live invisible and dim.
[*Silex Scintillans* (1650–1655), 'The Night']

4. My Soul, there is a countrie
Far beyond the stars,
Where stands a winged Sentry
All skilfull in the wars;
There above noise and danger,
Sweet peace sits crown'd with smiles,
And one born in a Manger
Commands the Beauteous files.
[*Silex Scintillans* (1650–1655), 'Peace']

5. Happy those early dayes, when I
Shin'd in my Angell-infancy.
Before I understood this place
Appointed for my second race,
Or taught my soul to fancy ought
But a white, Celestiall thought,
When yet I had not walkt above

A mile, or two, from my first love,
And looking back (at that short space),
Could see a glimpse of his bright face...

6. When on some gilded Cloud, or flowre
My gazing soul would dwell an houre,
And in those weaker glories spy
Some shadows of eternity...

7. But felt through all this fleshly dresse
Bright shootes of everlastingnesse.
O how I long to travell back
And tread again that ancient track!
That I might once more reach that plaine,
Where first I left my glorious traine,
From whence th' inlightened spirit sees
That shady City of Palme trees...

8. Some men a forward motion love,
But I by backward steps would move,
And when this dust falls to the urn,
In that state I came return.
[*Silex Scintillans* (1650–1655), 'The Retreate']

9. They are all gone into the world of light!
And I alone sit lingring here;
Their very memory is fair and bright,
And my sad thoughts doth clear...

10. I see them walking in an Air of glory,
Whose light doth trample on my days:
My days, which are at best but dull and hoary,
Mere glimering and decays...

11. Dear, beauteous death! the Jewel of the Just,
Shining nowhere, but in the dark;
What mysteries do lie beyond thy dust;
Could man outlook that mark!...

12. And yet, as Angels in some brighter dreams
Call to the soul, when man doth sleep:
So some strange thoughts transcend our wonted theams,
And into glory peep.
[*Silex Scintillans* (1650–1655), 'They Are All Gone']

13. Man is the shuttle, to whose winding quest
And passage through these looms
God order'd motion, but ordain'd no rest.
[*Silex Scintillans* (1650–1655), 'Man']

14. I saw Eternity the other night
Like a great Ring of pure and endless light,
All calm, as it was bright,
And round beneath it, Time in hours, days, years
Driv'n by the spheres
Like a vast shadow mov'd, in which the world
And all her train were hurl'd.
[*Silex Scintillans* (1650–1655), 'The World']

Vaughan, Norman (1927–)
English comic, variety artiste and television performer

1. Dodgy!
[Catchphrase, from 1960s]

2. Swingin'!
[Catchphrase, from 1960s]

Vaughan Williams, Ralph (1872–1958)
English composer of operas, symphonies and choral works

1. [Asked what he thought about music]
It's a Rum Go!
[Attr.]

Vauvenargues, Luc de Clapiers, Marquis de (1715–1747)
French soldier and moralist

1. *Les grandes pensées viennent du coeur.*
Great thoughts come from the heart.
[*Réflexions et Maximes* (1746)]

2. *Pour exécuter de grandes choses, il faut vivre comme si on ne devait jamais mourir.*
In order to achieve great things we must live as though we were never going to die.
[*Réflexions et Maximes* (1746)]

Veblen, Thorstein (1857–1929)
American economist and sociologist

1. Conspicuous consumption of valuable goods is a means of reputability to the gentleman of leisure.
[*The Theory of the Leisure Class* (1899), 4. Cf. Galbraith: 3]

2. The requirement of conspicuous wastefulness is not commonly present, consciously, in our canons of taste, but it is none the less present as a constraining norm, selectively shaping and sustaining our sense of what is beautiful.
[*The Theory of the Leisure Class* (1899), 6]

3. All business sagacity reduces itself in the last analysis to a judicious use of sabotage.
[*The Nature of Peace* (1917)]

4. The outcome of any serious research can only be to make two questions grow where only one grew before.
[*The Place of Science in Modern Civilization* (1919)]

Vega, Garcilaso de la (c. 1501–1536)
Spanish poet

1. *Aquéste es de los hombres el oficio:*
tentar el mal, y si es malo el suceso,
pedir con humildad perdón del vicio.
This is man's rôle: to try evil, and if the outcome be evil, to ask humbly for forgiveness for the act of depravity.
[*Égloga II (Second Eclogue)*, line 823]

Vega Carpio, Félix Lope de (1562–1635)
Prolific and influential Spanish dramatist, poet and novelist

1. *El más discreto hablar*
no es santo como el silencio.
The most wise speech is not as holy as silence.
[*La dama boba* (*The Stupid Lady*, 1613), III, ix]

2. [On learning that he was about to die]
All right, then, I'll say it: Dante makes me sick.
[Attr.]

Vegetius Renatus, Flavius (fl. c. AD 375)
Latin military writer

1. *Qui desiderat pacem, praeparet bellum.*
Let him who desires peace be prepared for war.
[*Epitoma Rei Militaris*, III, Prologue]

Venantius Fortunatus (c. 530–c. 610)
Italian-born Latin poet; Bishop of Poitiers and hymn-writer

1. *Pange, lingua, gloriosi*
Proelium certaminis.
Sing, my tongue, of battle in the glorious conflict.
[Hymn]

2. *Vexilla regis prodeunt,*
Fulget crucis mysterium;
Quo carne carnis conditor

Suspensus est patibulo.
The banners of the king advance, the mystery of the cross shines bright; by which the creator of the flesh hangs in the flesh from the gibbet.
['Vexilla Regis']

3. [Referring to the crucifixion as fulfilment of David's prophecy]
Regnavit a ligno Deus.
God reigned from the wood.
['Vexilla Regis']

Vergniaud, Pierre (1753–1793)
French politician, leader of the Girondists; executed

1. [Remark at his trial, 1793]
Il a été permis de craindre que la Révolution, comme Saturne, dévorât successivement tous ses enfants.
There was reason to fear that the Revolution, like Saturn, would eventually devour all her children one by one.
[In Alphonse de Lamartine, *Histoire des Girondins* (1847)]

Verlaine, Paul (1844–1896)
French lyric poet, associated with the Symbolists, and autobiographical writer

1. *Les sanglots longs*
Des violons
De l'automne
Blessent mon coeur
D'une langueur
Monotone.
The long weeping of autumn violins wounds my heart with a monotonous languor.
['Chanson d'Automne' ('Autumn Song', 1866)]

2. *Il pleure dans mon coeur*
Comme il pleut sur la ville.
Tears fall in my heart as rain falls on the city.
[*Romances sans paroles* (*Songs without Words*, 1874)]

3. *Et, ô ces voix d'enfants chantant dans la coupole!*
And oh those children's voices, singing beneath the cupola!
['Parsifal, A Jules Tellier' (1888)]

4. *Prends l'éloquence et tords-lui son cou!*
Take eloquence and wring its neck.
['Art poétique' (1884)]

5. *Et tout le reste est littérature.*
And all the rest of it is literature.
['Art poétique' (1884). Cf. Valéry: 2]

Verrall, Arthur Woollgar (1851–1912)
English Greek scholar and essayist

1. [Reply to a person who thought the number 58 difficult to remember]
Oh, quite easy! The Septuagint minus the Apostles.
[Attr.]

Vespasian (Titus Flavius Vespasianus) (AD 9–79)
Roman emperor from AD 69; consolidated Roman rule in Britain and Germany

1. *Pecunia non olet.*
Money does not smell.
[In Suetonius, *Lives of the Caesars*, 'Vespasian']

2. [Last words]
Vae, puto deus fio.
Woe is me, I think I am becoming a god.
[In Suetonius, *Lives of the Caesars*, 'Vespasian']

Vicky (Victor Weisz) (1913–1966)
British political cartoonist, born in Germany

1. Introducing Super-Mac.
[Cartoon caption depicting Harold Macmillan as Superman, *Evening Standard*, 1958]

Victoria, Queen (1819–1901)
Queen of Great Britain and Ireland from 1837 and Empress of India from 1876; diarist and writer

1. I sat between the King and Queen. We left supper soon. My health was drunk. I then danced one more quadrille with Lord Paget . . . I was very much amused.
[Journal, 1833]

2. . . . I too well know its truth, from experience, that whenever any poor Gipsies are encamped anywhere and crimes and robberies &c. occur, it is invariably laid to their account, which is shocking; and if they are always looked upon as vagabonds, how can they become good people?
[Journal, 1836]

3. I am sick of all this horrid business of politics, and Europe in general, and I think you will hear of me going with the children to live in Australia, and to think of Europe as the Moon!
[Letter to her daughter, the Princess Royal, 1859]

4. The Queen is most anxious to enlist every one who can speak or write to join in checking this mad, wicked folly of 'Women's Rights', with all its attendant horrors, on which her poor feeble sex is bent, forgetting every sense of womanly feeling and propriety . . . It is a subject which makes the Queen so furious that she cannot contain herself. God created men and women different – then let them remain each in their own position.
[Letter to Sir Theodore Martin, 1870]

5. [On Gladstone's last appointment as Prime Minister]
The danger to the country, to Europe, to her vast Empire, which is involved in having all these great interests entrusted to the shaking hand of an old, wild, and incomprehensible man of 82, is very great!
[Letter to Lord Lansdowne, 1892]

6. [Of Gladstone]
He speaks to Me as if I was a public meeting.
[In G.W.E. Russell, *Collections and Recollections* (1898), 14]

7. We are not amused.
[Attr. in Caroline Holland, *Notebooks of a Spinster Lady* (1919), 21]

8. [Said of the Boer War in 'Black Week', 1899]
We are not interested in the possibilities of defeat; they do not exist.
[In Lady Gwendolen Cecil, *Life of Robert, Marquis of Salisbury* (1931)]

9. [Remark when it was suggested that the statue of Queen Anne outside St Paul's should be moved]
Move Queen Anne? Most certainly not! Why it might some day be suggested that *my* statue should be moved, which I should much dislike.
[Attr.]

10. [Giving her opinion of *King Lear*]
A strange, horrible business, but I suppose good enough for Shakespeare's day.
[Attr.]

11. No pudding and no *fun*!
[Attr.]

Vidal, Gore (1925–)
American novelist, dramatist, essayist, critic and poet

1. The astronauts! ... Rotarians in outer space.
[*Two Sisters* (1970)]

2. Never have children, only grandchildren.
[*Two Sisters* (1970)]

3. He will lie even when it is inconvenient, the sign of the true artist.
[*Two Sisters* (1970)]

4. American writers want to be not good but great; and so are neither.
[*Two Sisters* (1970)]

5. [When asked for his views about corporal punishment] I'm all for bringing back the birch, but only between consenting adults.
[TV interview with David Frost]

6. Whenever a friend succeeds, a little something in me dies.
[*The Sunday Times Magazine*, 1973. Cf. Oscar Wilde: 43]

7. There's a lot to be said for being *nouveau riche* and the Reagans mean to say it all.
[*The Observer*, 1981, in Jeffrey Care (ed.), *Sayings of the Eighties* (1989)]

8. [On being asked if his first sexual experience had been heterosexual or homosexual]
I was too polite to ask.
[*Forum*, 1987, 'First Sex']

9. It is not enough to succeed. Others must fail.
[In G. Irvine, *Antipanegyric for Tom Driberg* (1976)]

Viera Gallo, José Antonio (1943–)
Chilean politician

1. *El socialismo puede llegar sólo en bicicleta.*
Socialism can arrive only by bicycle.
[In Ivan Illich, *Energy and Equity* (1974)]

Vigny, Alfred de (1797–1863)
French Romantic poet, dramatist and novelist

1. *Hélas je suis, Seigneur, puissant et solitaire,*
Laissez-moi m'endormir du sommeil de la terre!
Alas, Lord, I am powerful and alone. Let me sleep the sleep of the earth.
['Moïse' ('Moses', 1822)]

2. *J'aime le son du cor, le soir, au fond des bois.*
I love the sound of the horn, in the evening, in the depths of the woods.
['Le Cor' (1826)]

3. *Dieu! que le son du cor est triste au fond des bois!*
O God! How sad is the sound of the horn in the depths of the woods!
['Le Cor' (1826)]

4. *Seul le silence est grand; tout le reste est faiblesse...*
Fais énergiquement ta longue et lourde tâche...
Puis, après, comme moi, souffre et meurs sans parler.
Silence alone is great; all else is weakness...
Perform with all your heart your long and heavy task...
Then, afterwards, as do I, suffer and die without a word.
['La Mort du loup' ('The Death of the Wolf', 1843)]

5. *J'aime la majesté des souffrances humaines.*
I love the majesty of human suffering.
[*La Maison du Berger* (*The Shepherd's House*, 1844)]

6. *L'armée est une nation dans la nation; c'est un vice de notre temps.*
The army is a nation within the nation; it is one of the vices of our times.
[*Servitude et grandeur militaire* (*The Military Condition*, 1835), I, 2]

7. *Le vrai Dieu, le Dieu fort, est le Dieu des idées.*
The true God, the mighty God, is the God of ideas.
['La Bouteille à la mer' ('The Bottle in the Sea', 1847)]

Villiers, Alan John (1903–1982)
Australian naval commander and writer

1. Only fools and passengers drink at sea.
[*The Observer*, 'Sayings of the Week', 1957]

Villiers de l'Isle-Adam, Philippe-Auguste (1838–1889)
French Symbolist poet, short-story writer, novelist and dramatist

1. *Vivre? Les serviteurs feront cela pour nous.*
Live? The servants will do that for us.
[*Axel* (1890), IV, 2]

Villon, François (b. 1431)
French poet, noted for his ballades and use of jargon

1. *Mais où sont les neiges d'antan?*
But where are the snows of yesteryear?
[*Le Grand Testament* (1461), 'Ballade des dames du temps jadis'; trans. D.G. Rossetti]

2. *En cette foi je veux vivre et mourir.*
In this faith I wish to live and to die.
[*Le Grand Testament* (1461), 'Ballade pour prier Notre Dame']

3. *Frères humains qui après nous vivez,*
N'ayez les coeurs contre nous endurcis,
Car, si pitié de nous pauvres avez,
Dieu en aura plus tôt de vous mercis...
Mais priez Dieu que tous nous veuille absoudre!
Brothers in humanity who live after us, don't let your hearts be hardened against us, for, if you take pity on us poor souls, God will be more likely to have mercy on you. But pray to God that he may be willing to absolve us all!
['Ballade des pendus' ('Ballad of the Hanged Men', 1462)]

Vincent, St (d. c. 450)
Gallo-Roman theologian

1. *Quod semper, quod ubique, quod ab omnibus creditum est.*
What is believed always, everywhere, and by everybody.
[*Commonitoria*, I. Cf. Valéry: 3]

Virgil (Publius Vergilius Maro) (70–19 BC)
Roman epic and pastoral poet, also noted for his verse on husbandry

1. *Tityre, tu patulae recubans sub tegmine fagi*
Silvestrem tenui musam meditaris avena.
Beneath the shade which beechen boughs diffuse,
You, Tit'rus, entertain your sylvan Muse.
[*Eclogues*, I, line 1, trans. Dryden]

2. *Deus nobis haec otia fecit.*
This peace a god has made for us.
[*Eclogues*, I, line 6]

3. *At nos hinc alii sitientis ibimus Afros,*
Pars Scythiam et rapidum Cretae veniemus Oaxen
Et penitus toto divisos orbe Britannos.
But we must go from here, some to arid Africa, some to

Scythia and to Oaxes, swift river of Crete, and to the Britons wholly sundered from all the world.
[*Eclogues*, I, line 64]

4. *Formosum pastor Corydon ardebat Alexim,*
Delicias domini, nec, quid speraret, habebat.
Corydon the shepherd was hotly in love with the beautiful Alexis, his master's darling, but he did not have what he hoped for.
[*Eclogues*, II, line 1]

5. *O formose puer, nimium ne crede colori.*
O beautiful boy, do not put too much trust in your beauty.
[*Eclogues*, II, line 17]

6. *Quem fugis, a! demens? Habitarunt di quoque silvas.*
Ah, madman! Whom are you fleeing? Even the gods have lived in the woods.
[*Eclogues*, II, line 60]

7. *Trahit sua quemque voluptas.*
Each one's pleasure draws him on.
[*Eclogues*, II, line 65]

8. *Malo me Galatea petit, lasciva puella,*
Et fugit ad salices et se cupit ante videri.
Galatea, the playful tease, pelts me with an apple and runs off into the willows hoping to be spotted first.
[*Eclogues*, III, line 64]

9. *Latet anguis in herba.*
A snake lurks in the grass.
[*Eclogues*, III, line 93]

10. *Claudite iam rivos, pueri; sat prata biberunt.*
Now dam the streams, boys; the meadows have drunk their fill.
[*Eclogues*, III, line 111]

11. *Sicelides Musae, paulo maiora canamus.*
Non omnis arbusta iuvant humilesque myricae;
Si canimus silvas, silvae sint consule dignae.
Ultima Cumaei venit iam carminis aetas;
Magnus ab integro saeclorum nascitur ordo.
Iam redit et Virgo, redeunt Saturnia regna;
Iam nova progenies caelo demittitur alto.
Sicilian Muses, let us sing in loftier strain. Trees and the humble tamarisk do not please everyone; if we sing of woods, let the woods be worthy of a consul. The last age of the Cumaean prophetic song has now come. The mighty order of the ages is born anew. Now too the Virgin goddess returns, and the reign of Saturn returns. Now a new race is sent down from heaven on high.
[*Eclogues*, IV, line 1]

12. *Incipe, parve puer, risu cognoscere matrem.*
Begin, baby boy, to recognize your mother with a smile.
[*Eclogues*, IV, line 60]

13. *Incipe, parve puer: cui non risere parentes,*
Nec deus hunc mensa, dea nec dignata cubili est.
Begin, baby boy: the child on whom his parents have not smiled, no god honours with his table, no goddess with her bed.
[*Eclogues*, IV, line 62]

14. *Ambo florentes aetatibus, Arcades ambo,*
Et cantare pares et respondere parati.
Both in the flower of their youth, Arcadians both, matched and ready to start a song and to respond.
[*Eclogues*, VII, line 4]

15. *Saepibus in nostris parvam te roscida mala*
(Dux ego vester eram) vidi cum matre legentem.
Alter ab undecimo tum me iam acceperat annus,
Iam fragilis poteram ab terra contingere ramos.
Ut vidi, ut perii! ut me malus abstulit error!
In our orchard I saw you, a little girl, picking dewy apples with your mother (I was showing you the way). I had just turned twelve years old then, I could just reach the brittle branches even from the ground: as I saw you, how I fell in love! how an awful madness swept me away!
[*Eclogues*, VIII, line 37]

16. *Nunc scio, quid sit Amor.*
Now I know what Love is.
[*Eclogues*, VIII, line 43]

17. *Non omnia possumus omnes.*
We are not all able to do all things.
[*Eclogues*, VIII, line 63]

18. *Et me fecere poetam*
Pierides, sunt et mihi carmina, me quoque dicunt
Vatem pastores; sed non ego credulus illis.
Nam neque adhuc Vario videor nec dicere Cinna
Digna, sed argutos inter strepere anser olores.
Me too the Muses made write verse. I too have songs and the shepherds call me a poet also; but I'm not inclined to believe them. For I don't seem yet to write things as worthy of either Varius or Cinna, but to be a goose honking amongst tuneful swans.
[*Eclogues*, IX, line 32]

19. *Omnia vincit Amor: et nos cedamus Amori.*
Love conquers all: let us also yield to love.
[*Eclogues*, X, line 69]

20. *Ite domum saturae, venit Hesperus, ite capellae.*
Go on home, my full-fed goats, the evening star is coming, go on home.
[*Eclogues*, X, line 77]

21. *Ultima Thule.*
Farthest Thule.
[*Georgics*, I, line 30]

22. *Labor omnia vicit*
Improbus et duris urgens in rebus egestos.
Hard work conquered everything, and need pressing in straitened circumstances.
[*Georgics*, I, line 145]

23. *Nosque ubi primus equis Oriens adflavit anhelis,*
Illic sera rubens accendit lumina Vesper.
And when the rising sun has first breathed on us with his panting horses, over there the glowing evening-star is lighting his late lamps.
[*Georgics*, I, line 250]

24. *Ter sunt conati imponere Pelio Ossam*
Scilicet atque Ossae frondosum involvere Olympum;
Ter pater exstructos disiecit fulmine montis.
Three times did they endeavour to pile Ossa on Pelion, and to roll leafy Olympus on top of Ossa; three times our Father scattered the heaped-up mountains with his thunderbolt.
[*Georgics*, I, line 281]

25. *O fortunatos nimium, sua si bona norint,*
Agricolas!
O happy are farmers, too happy if they knew their blessings.
[*Georgics*, II, line 458]

26. *Felix, qui potuit rerum cognoscere causas.*
Happy the man who could understand the causes of things.
[*Georgics*, II, line 490]

27. *Fortunatus et ille, deos qui novit agrestis.*
Happy too is he who knows the gods of the country.
[*Georgics*, II, line 493]

28. *Optima quaeque dies miseris mortalibus aevi*
Prima fugit; subeunt morbi tristisque senectus
Et labor, et durae rapit inclementia mortis.
In youth alone, unhappy mortals live;
But oh! the mighty bliss is fugitive:
Discoloured sickness, anxious labours, come,
And age and death's inexorable doom.
[*Georgics*, III, line 66, trans. Dryden]

29. *Sed fugit interea, fugit inreparabile tempus.*
But time meanwhile is flying, flying beyond recall.
[*Georgics*, III, line 284]

30. *Hi motus animorum atque haec certamina tanta*
Pulveris exigui iactu compressa quiescunt.
Yet all those dreadful deeds, this deadly fray,
A cast of scattered dust will soon allay.
[*Georgics*, IV, line 86, trans. Dryden]

31. *Non aliter, si parva licet componere magnis,*
Cecropias innatus apes amor urget habendi
Munere quamque suo.
Just so, if one may compare small things with great, an inborn love of gain drives these Attic bees each with its own function.
[*Georgics*, IV, line 176]

32. *At genus immortale manet, multosque per annos*
Stat fortuna domus, et avi numerantur avorum.
But the race remains immortal; for many a year the fortune of the house stands firm, and grandsires' grandsires are numbered in the roll.
[*Georgics*, IV, line 208]

33. *Arma virumque cano, Troiae qui primus ab oris*
Italiam fato profugus Laviniaque venit
Litora, multum ille et terris iactatus et alto
Vi superum, saevae memorem Iunonis ob iram.
Arms and the man I sing who first from the shores of Troy, exiled by fate, came to the Lavinian coast, much buffeted on land and sea by force of the gods through cruel Juno's unrelenting anger.
[*Aeneid*, I, line 1]

34. *Tantaene animis caelestibus irae?*
Can such great anger dwell in heavenly hearts?
[*Aeneid*, I, line 11]

35. *Furor arma ministrat.*
Madness supplies the arms.
[*Aeneid*, I, line 150]

36. *O passi graviora, dabit deus his quoque finem.*
O you who have borne even heavier things, to these too, God will grant an end!
[*Aeneid*, I, line 199]

37. *Forsan et haec olim meminisse iuvabit.*
Perhaps even these things will one day be pleasant to recall.
[*Aeneid*, I, line 203]

38. *Durate, et vosmet rebus servate secundis.*
Endure, and save yourselves for better things.
[*Aeneid*, I, line 207]

39. *Dux femina facti.*
The leader of the enterprise a woman.
[*Aeneid*, I, line 364]

40. *Dixit et avertens rosea cervice refulsit,*
Ambrosiaeque comae divinum vertice odorem
Spiravere; pedes vestis defluxit ad imos,
Et vera incessu patuit dea.
Thus having said, she turned, and made appear
Her neck refulgent, and dishevelled hair,
Which, flowing from her shoulders, reached the ground,
And widely spread ambrosial scents around:
In length of train descends her sweeping gown;
And, by her graceful walk, the Queen of Love is known.
[*Aeneid*, I, line 402, trans. Dryden]

41. *En Priamus. Sunt hic etiam sua praemia laudi,*
Sunt lacrimae rerum et mentem mortalia tangunt.
Behold Priam. Even here virtue has its due rewards, here are tears for misfortune and mortal sorrows touch the heart.
[*Aeneid*, I, line 461]

42. *Di tibi, si qua pios respectant numina, si quid*
Usquam iustitiae est, et mens sibi conscia recti,
Praemia digna ferant.
The gods, if gods to goodness are inclined;
If acts of mercy touch their heavenly mind,
And, more than all the gods, your gen'rous heart,
Conscious of worth, requite its own desert!
[*Aeneid*, I, line 603, trans. Dryden]

43. *Non ignara mali miseris succurrere disco.*
No stranger to misery myself I am learning to befriend the wretched.
[*Aeneid*, I, line 630]

44. *Infandum, regina, iubes renovare dolorem.*
Unspeakable is the grief, O queen, that you bid me renew.
[*Aeneid*, II, line 3]

45. *Quaeque ipse miserrima vidi*
Et quorum pars magna fui.
And the most wretched things which I myself saw and of which I was no small part.
[*Aeneid*, II, line 5]

46. *Equo ne credite, Teucri.*
Quidquid id est, timeo Danaos et dona ferentis.
Trust not the horse, Trojans. Whatever it is, I fear the Greeks even when they bring gifts.
[*Aeneid*, II, line 48]

47. *Crimine ab uno*
Disce omnis.
From the one crime learn the nature of them all.
[*Aeneid*, II, line 65]

48. *Horresco referens.*
I shudder as I tell the tale.
[*Aeneid*, II, line 204]

49. *Tacitae per amica silentia lunae.*
Through the friendly silence of the soundless moonlight.
[*Aeneid*, II, line 255]

50. *Tempus erat, quo prima quies mortalibus aegris*
Incipit et dono divum gratissima serpit.
It was the time when for weary mortals their first sleep begins and steals over them most sweetly.
[*Aeneid*, II, line 268]

51. *Quantum mutatus ab illo*
Hectore, qui redit exuvias indutus Achilli.
How greatly changed from that Hector who returns after donning the spoils of Achilles.
[*Aeneid*, II, line 274]

52. *Venit summa dies et ineluctabile tempus*
Dardaniae. Fuimus Troes, fuit Ilium et ingens
Gloria Teucrorum.
The last day and the inevitable hour has come for Troy. We Trojans are no more, Ilium has passed and the great glory of the Teucer's race.
[*Aeneid*, II, line 325]

53. *Moriamur et in media arma ruamus.*
Una salus victis nullam sperare salutem.
Let us die as we rush into the midst of the battle. The one safe course for the vanquished is to expect no safety.
[*Aeneid*, II, line 353]

54. *Dis aliter visum.*
The gods thought otherwise.
[*Aeneid*, II line 428]

55. *Quid non mortalia pectora cogis,*
Auri sacra fames!
O sacred hunger of pernicious gold!
What bands of faith can impious lucre hold?
[*Aeneid*, III, line 56, trans. Dryden]

56. *Monstrum horrendum, informe, ingens, cui lumen ademptum.*
A monstrous bulk, deformed, deprived of sight.
[*Aeneid*, III, line 658, trans. Dryden]

57. *Agnosco veteris vestigia flammae.*
I feel again a spark of that ancient flame.
[*Aeneid*, IV, line 23]

58. *Quis fallere possit amantem?*
Who may deceive a lover?
[*Aeneid*, IV, line 296]

59. *Nec me meminisse pigebit Elissae,*
Dum memor ipse mei, dum spiritus hos regit artus.
Nor will it irk me to remember Elissa while I am mindful of myself, while the breath of life controls these limbs.
[*Aeneid*, IV, line 335]

60. *Mens immota manet, lacrimae volvuntur inanes.*
His mind remains unmoved; tears are shed in vain.
[*Aeneid*, IV, line 449]

61. *Varium et mutabile semper*
Femina.
Woman is always a fickle and changeable thing.
[*Aeneid*, IV, line 569]

62. *Exoriare aliquis nostris ex ossibus ultor.*
Arise from the ashes of my bones, some unknown avenger!
[*Aeneid*, IV, line 625]

63. *'Moriemur inultae,*
Sed moriamur' ait, 'sic, sic, iuvat ire sub umbras.'
'I shall die unavenged, but let me die,' she cries. 'Thus, thus, it is joy to go to the shades below.'
[*Aeneid*, IV, line 660]

64. *Hos successus alit: possunt, quia posse videntur.*
To these success gives heart: they can because they think they can.
[*Aeneid*, V, line 231]

65. *Bella, horrida bella,*
Et Thybrim multo spumantem sanguine cerno.
I see wars, horrid wars, and the Tiber foaming with much blood.
[*Aeneid*, VI, line 86]

66. *Facilis descensus Averno:*
Noctes atque dies patet atri ianua Ditis;
Sed revocare gradum superasque evadere ad auras,
Hoc opus, hic labor est.
The gates of Hell are open night and day;
Smooth the descent, and easy is the way:
But to return, and view the cheerful skies,
In this the task and mighty labour lies.
[*Aeneid*, VI, line 126, trans. Dryden]

67. *Procul, o procul este, profani.*
Far hence, oh far be souls profane!
[*Aeneid*, VI, line 258]

68. *Ibant obscuri sola sub nocte per umbram*
Perque domos Ditis vacuas et inania regna.
Obscure they went through dreary shades that led
Along the waste dominions of the dead.
[*Aeneid*, VI, line 268, trans. Dryden]

69. *Stabant orantes primi transmittere cursum*
Tendebantque manus ripae ulterioris amore.
They stood begging to be the first to make the voyage across and stretched out their hands in longing for the further shore.
[*Aeneid*, VI, line 313]

70. *Desine fata deum flecti sperare precando.*
Cease to hope that the decrees of the gods can be set aside through prayer.
[*Aeneid*, VI, line 376]

71. *Principio caelum ac terras camposque liquentis*
Lucentemque globum lunae Titaniaque astra
Spiritus intus alit, totamque infusa per artus
Mens agitat molem et magno se corpore miscet.
Know, first, that heaven, and earth's compacted frame,
And flowing waters, and the starry flame,
And both the radiant lights, one common soul
Inspires and feeds, and animates the whole.
This active mind, infused through all the space,
Unites and mingles with the mighty mass.
[*Aeneid*, VI, line 724, trans. Dryden]

72. *Excudent alii spirantia mollius aera,*
(Credo equidem), vivos ducent de marmore voltus;
Orabunt causas melius, caelique meatus
Describent radio et surgentia sidera dicent:
Tu regere imperio populos, Romane, memento
(Hae tibi erunt artes), pacique imponere morem,
Parcere subiectis et debellare superbos.
Let others better mold the running mass
Of metals, and inform the breathing brass,
And soften into flesh a marble face;
Plead better at the bar; describe the skies,
And when the stars descend, and when they rise.
But, Rome, 'tis thine alone, with awful sway,
To rule mankind, and make the world obey,
Disposing peace and war thy own majestic way;
To tame the proud, the fettered slave to free;
These are imperial arts, and worthy thee.
[*Aeneid*, VI, line 847, trans. Dryden]

73. *Heu, miserande puer, si qua fata aspera rumpas,*
Tu Marcellus eris!
Alas, piteous youth, if only you could break the harsh bonds of your fate, you will be Marcellus.
[*Aeneid*, VI, line 882]

74. *Sunt geminae Somni portae; quarum altera fertur*
Cornea, qua veris facilis datur exitus umbris,
Altera candenti perfecta nitens elephanto,
Sed falsa ad caelum mittunt insomnia Manes.
Two gates the silent house of Sleep adorn;
Of polished ivory this, that of transparent horn:
True visions through transparent horn arise;
Through polished ivory pass deluding lies.
[*Aeneid*, VI, line 893, trans. Dryden]

75. *Geniumque loci primamque deorum*
Tellurem nymphasque et adhuc ignota precatur
Flumina.
He prays to the spirit of the place and to Earth, first of the gods; and to the Nymphs and to streams as yet unknown.
[*Aeneid*, VII, line 136]

76. *Flectere si nequeo superos, Acheronta movebo.*
If I cannot make the gods above relent, I shall move Hell.
[*Aeneid*, VII, line 312]

77. *Pedibus timor addidit alas.*
Fear lends wings to his feet.
[*Aeneid*, VIII, line 224]

78. *O mihi praeteritos referat si Iuppiter annos.*
If only Jupiter would bring me back the years that are past.
[*Aeneid*, VIII, line 560]

79. *Quadrupedante putrem sonitu quatit ungula campum.*
The thundering gallop of the horses' hooves is shaking the powdery plain.
[*Aeneid*, VIII, line 596]

80. *Macte nova virtute, puer: sic itur ad astra.*
A blessing, young man, on your youthful valour; this is the way to the stars.
[*Aeneid*, IX, line 641]

81. *Audentis Fortuna iuvat.*
Fortune helps those who dare.
[*Aeneid*, X, line 284. Cf. Terence: 8]

82. *Experto credite.*
Believe one who speaks from experience.
[*Aeneid*, XI, line 283]

Vizinczey, Stephen (1933–)
Hungarian-born writer, editor and broadcaster

1. I was told I am a true cosmopolitan. I am unhappy everywhere.
[*The Guardian*, 1968]

Voltaire (François-Marie Arouet) (1694–1778)
French philosopher, dramatist, poet, historian, novelist, critic and letter writer; outstanding figure of the Enlightenment

1. *La Liberté est née en Angleterre des querelles des tyrans.*
Liberty was born in England from the quarrels of tyrants.
[*Lettres philosophiques* (1734)]

2. *En philosophie, il faut se défier de ce qu'on croit entendre trop aisément, aussi bien que des choses qu'on n'entend pas.*
In philosophy, we must distrust the things we understand too easily as well as the things we don't understand.
[*Lettres philosophiques* (1734)]

3. *Le superflu, chose très nécessaire.*
The superfluous, a very necessary thing.
[*Le Mondain* (1736)]

4. *Le secret d'ennuyer est celui de tout dire.*
The secret of being boring is to say everything.
[*Discours en vers sur l'homme* (1737), 'De la nature de l'homme']

5. *Tous les genres sont bons hors le genre ennuyeux.*
All styles are good except the tedious kind.
[*L'Enfant prodigue* (1738 edition), Preface]

6. *N'ayant jamais pu réussir dans le monde, il se vengeait par en médire.*
Never having been able to succeed in the world, he took his revenge by speaking ill of it.
[*Zadig, ou la Fatalité* (*Zadig, or Fate*, 1747), 4]

7. *C'est une des superstitions de l'esprit humain d'avoir imaginé que la virginité pouvait être une vertu.*
It is one of the superstitions of the human mind to have imagined that virginity could be a virtue.
['The Leningrad Notebooks' (c. 1735–1750). Cf. Voltaire: 34]

8. *Il faut, dans le gouvernement, des bergers et des bouchers.*
In governments there must be both shepherds and butchers.
['The Piccini Notebooks' (c. 1735–1750)]

9. *Dieu n'est pas pour les gros bataillons, mais pour ceux qui tirent le mieux.*
God is not on the side of the big batallions, but of the best marksmen.
['The Piccini Notebooks' (c. 1735–1750). Cf. Anouilh: 5, Bussy-Rabutin: 3 and Turenne: 1]

10. *Ce corps qui s'appelait et qui s'appelle encore le saint empire romain n'était en aucune manière ni saint, ni romain, ni empire.*
This body, which was called and still calls itself the Holy Roman Empire, was by no means Holy, nor Roman, nor an Empire.
[*Essai sur l'histoire générale et sur les moeurs et l'esprit des nations* (1756), 70]

11. *Tout est pour le mieux dans le meilleur des mondes possibles.*
Everything is for the best in the best of all possible worlds.
[*Candide* (1759), 1]

12. *Si nous ne trouvons pas des choses agréables, nous trouverons du moins des choses nouvelles.*
If we do not find anything pleasant, we shall at least find something new.
[*Candide* (1759), 17]

13. [Referring to the execution of the English Admiral Byng for refusing to attack a French fleet]
Dans ce pays-ci il est bon de tuer de temps en temps un amiral pour encourager les autres.
In this country it is considered a good idea to kill an admiral from time to time, to encourage the others.
[*Candide* (1759), 23]

14. *Le travail éloigne de nous trois grand maux: l'ennui, le vice et le besoin.*
Work keeps away those three great evils: boredom, vice, and poverty.
[*Candide* (1759), 30]

15. *Quand l'homme fut mis dans le jardin d'Eden, il y fut mis pour qu'il travaillât; ce qui prouve que l'homme n'est pas né pour le repos.*
– Travaillons sans raisonner ... c'est le seul moyen de rendre la vie supportable.
When man was put in the garden of Eden, he was put there to work; that proves that man was not born for rest.
Let us work without reasoning ... that is the only way to make life bearable.
[*Candide* (1759), 30]

16. *Cela est bien dit, répondit Candide, mais il faut cultiver notre jardin.*
'That is well said,' replied Candide, 'but we must cultivate our garden.'
[*Candide* (1759), 30]

17. *Ils ne servent de la pensée que pour autoriser leurs injustices, et n'emploient les paroles que pour déguiser leurs pensées.*
People use thought only to justify their injustices, and they use words only to disguise their thoughts.
[*Dialogues* (1763), 'Le Chapon et la poularde'. Cf. Talleyrand: 7]

18. *La superstition met le monde entier en flammes; la philosophie les éteint.*
Superstition sets the whole world on fire; philosophy quenches the flames.
[*Dictionnaire philosophique* (1764), 'Superstition']

19. *Toutes les histoires anciennes, comme le disait un de nos beaux esprits, ne sont que des fables convenues.*
All the ancient histories, as one of our wits used to say, are just fables that have been agreed upon.
[*Jeannot et Colin* (1764)]

20. *En effet, l'histoire n'est que le tableau des crimes et des malheurs.*
Indeed, history is nothing but a tableau of crimes and misfortunes.
[*L'Ingénu* (1767), 10]

21. *Le mieux est l'ennemi du bien.*
The best is the enemy of the good.
[*Dictionnaire philosophique* (1770 edition), 'Art dramatique']

22. *La foi consiste à croire ce que la raison ne croit pas ... Il ne suffit pas qu'une chose soit possible pour la croire.*
Faith consists in believing what reason does not believe ... It is not enough that a thing may be possible for it to be believed.
[*Questions sur l'Encyclopédie* (1770–1772)]

23. *Toute Française, à ce que j'imagine, sait, bien ou mal, faire un peu de cuisine.*
Every Frenchwoman, I imagine, knows, well or ill, how to do a little cooking.
[*Oevres Complètes de Voltaire* (1877), X, 'La Bégueule' (written 1772)]

24. *Si Dieu nous a faits à son image, nous le lui avons bien rendu.*
If God has created us in his image, we have repaid him well.
[*Le Sottisier* (c. 1778), 32]

25. *On doit des égards aux vivants; on ne doit aux morts que la vérité.*
We owe respect to the living; we owe nothing but truth to the dead.
[*Oeuvres* (1785), 'Première Lettre sur *Oedipe*', 1]

26. *Si Dieu n'existait pas, il faudrait l'inventer.*
If God did not exist, it would be necessary to invent him.
[*Epîtres*, 'A l'auteur du livre des trois imposteurs']

27. *Divisés d'intérêts, et pour le crime unis.*
Divided by interests, and united in crime.
[*Mérope* (1743), 1]

28. *La crainte suit le crime, et c'est son châtiment.*
Fear follows crime, and is its punishment.
[*Sémiramis* (1748), V]

29. *Le sombre Anglais, même dans ses amours,*
Veut raisonner toujours.
On est plus raisonnable en France.
The gloomy Englishman, even in love, always wants to reason. We are more reasonable in France.
[*Les Originaux, Entrée des Diverses Nations*]

30. *La lâche fuit en vain; la mort vole à sa suite.*
C'est en la défiant que le brave l'évite.
In vain the coward flies, death rushes after him. It is by defying death that the brave man escapes it.
[*Le Triumvirat*, IV]

31. *Sachez que le secret des arts*
Est de corriger la nature.
Know that the secret of the arts is to correct nature.
[*Epîtres*, 'A M. de Verrière']

32. *Quoi que vous fassiez, écrasez l'infâme, et aimez qui vous aime.*
Whatever you do, stamp out infamy, and love the one who loves you.
[Letter to M. d'Alembert, 1762]

33. *Quand la populace se mêle de raisonner, tout est perdu.*
Once the people start to reason, all is lost.
[Letter to Damilaville, 1766]

34. *Il est plaisant qu'on fait une vertu du vice de chasteté; et voilà encore une drôle de chasteté que celle qui mène tout droit les hommes au péché d'Onan, et les filles aux pâles couleurs!*
It is amusing that the vice of chastity is made into a virtue; and it's an odd sort of chastity at that, which leads men straight to the sin of Onan, and girls to the fading of their colours.
[Letter to M. Mariott, 1766. Cf. Voltaire: 7]

35. *Je ne suis pas comme une dame de la cour de Versailles, qui disait: c'est bien dommage que l'aventure de la tour de Babel ait produit la confusion des langues; sans cela tout le monde aurait toujours parlé français.*
I am not like a lady at the court of Versailles, who said: 'What a great pity it is that the adventure at the tower of Babel should have produced the confusion of languages; if it weren't for that, everyone would always have spoken French.'
[Letter to Catherine the Great, 1767]

36. [When asked why no woman had ever written a tolerable tragedy]
The composition of a tragedy requires *testicles*.
[In a letter from Byron to John Murray, 1817]

37. I disapprove of what you say, but I will defend to the death your right to say it.
[Attr.]

38. Marriage is the only adventure open to the cowardly.
[Attr.]

39. [On learning that coffee was considered a slow poison]
I think it must be so, for I have been drinking it for sixty-five years and I am not dead yet.
[Attr.]

40. [Giving a funeral oration]
He was a great patriot, a humanitarian, a loyal friend – provided, of course, that he really is dead.
[Attr.]

41. [Reviewing Rousseau's poem 'Ode to Posterity', c. 1778]
I do not think this poem will reach its destination.
[Attr.]

42. [Turning down an invitation to an orgy, having attended one the previous night for the first time]
Once: a philosopher; twice: a pervert!
[Attr.]

Vorster, John (1915–1983)
South African Nationalist politician; Prime Minister 1966–78 and President 1978–79

1. As far as criticism is concerned, we don't resent that unless it is absolutely biased, as it is in most cases.
[*The Observer*, 'Sayings of the Week', 1969]

Voznesensky, Andrei (1933–)
Russian avant-garde poet

1. The art of creation
is older than the art of killing.
['Poem with a Footnote']

Vukovich, Bill (1918–1955)
American racing driver

1. [Explaining his success in the Indianapolis 500]
There's no secret. You just press the accelerator to the floor and steer left.
[Attr.]

Vulliamy, Ed
British journalist and author

1. [A pacifist until the war in the Balkans forced him to change his convictions]
Ironically, the horrors of war have taught me that there are things that are worse than war, and against them determined

and careful war should be waged, in the name of the innocent and the weak.
[*The Weekend Guardian*, 1992]

Waddell, Helen Jane (1889–1965)
Irish scholar and novelist

1. Would you think Heaven could be so small a thing
As a lit window on the hills at night.
['I Shall Not Go To Heaven']

Wagner Richard (1813–1883)
German Romantic composer of operas; best known for his Ring of the Nibelung cycle

1. *In des Wonnemeeres*
wogendem Schwall,
in der Duft-Wellen
tönendem Schall,
in des Welt-Atems
wehendem All–
ertrinken–
versinken–
unbewusst–
höchste Lust!
In the surging flood
of the sea of bliss,
in the echoing sound
of the fragrant waves,
in the waving universe
of the breath of the world–
drowning–
sinking–
unconscious–
highest pleasure!
[*Tristan und Isolde* (1865), III, 'Liebestod']

Wain, John (1925–)
English poet, associated with the Movement, novelist and literary critic

1. Poetry is to prose as dancing is to walking.
[BBC broadcast, 1976]

Wainewright, Thomas Griffiths (1794–1847)
English convict, writer and artist

1. [On being asked by a caller at Newgate prison how he could have the barbarity to poison such a 'fair, innocent and trusting creature' as his sister-in-law Helen Abercromby]
Upon my soul, I don't know, unless it was because she had such thick legs.
[In W.C. Hazlitt, *Wainewright's Essays* (1880)]

Wales, Princess of (1961–)
Diana Spencer, wife of Charles, Prince of Wales

1. I'm as thick as a plank.
[*The Observer*, 1987, in Jeffrey Care (ed.), *Sayings of the Eighties* (1989)]

2. I would walk miles for a bacon sandwich.
[*The Observer*, 1988, in Jeffrey Care (ed.), *Sayings of the Eighties* (1989)]

Waley, Arthur (1889–1966)
English orientalist

1. What is hard today is to censor one's own thoughts–
To sit by and see the blind man
On the sightless horse, riding into the bottomless abyss.
['Censorship']

Walker, Alice (1944–)
American novelist, poet, short-story writer and essayist

1. I think it pisses God off if you walk by the color purple in a field somewhere and don't notice it.
[*The Color Purple* (1982); film, 1985, scriptwriter Menno Meyjes]

Wall, Max (1908–1990)
English comedian, stage actor and radio performer

1. Wall is the name – Max Wall. My father was the Great Wall of China. He was a brick.
[Opening line of one of his acts]

2. To me Adler will always be Jung.
[Telegram to Larry Adler on his 60th birthday]

Wallace, Edgar (1875–1932)
English novelist, dramatist and journalist, known for his thrillers

1. What is a highbrow? He is a man who has found something more interesting than women.
[*New York Times*, 1932]

2. [Said when a candidate for Parliament]
A writer of crook stories ought never to stop seeking new material.
[In Alan Hodge, *The Long Weekend* (1940)]

Wallace, George (Stevenson) (1895–1960)

1. 'What will you have?' said the waiter,
Reflectively picking his nose.
'I'll have two boiled eggs, you bastard,
You can't get your fingers in those.'
[Attr.]

Wallace, Henry (1888–1965)
American agriculturalist and statesman; Democrat Vice-President 1941–45

1. The century on which we are entering – the century which will come out of this war – can be and must be the century of the common man.
[Speech, 1942]

Wallace, Lew (1827–1905)
American novelist, statesman, soldier and lawyer

1. Beauty is altogether in the eye of the beholder.
[*The Prince of India* (1893)]

Wallace, William Ross (c. 1819–1881)
American lawyer and poet

1. The hand that rocks the cradle
Is the hand that rules the world.
['What Rules the World' (c. 1865)]

Wallace-Crabbe, Chris (1934–)
Australian poet and critic

1. We are the final children of the earth
Whom knowledge has not scarred,
Delighting still in sunlight and green grass
Back in our own backyard:
Gaping, we hear the tales of adulthood
Where life is dour and hard,
Far, far away, beyond some wicked wood.
['Terra Australis']

2. Do not call me a freak,
you scruffy dwarves,

I have designs
on the tattooed lady.
['Squibs in the Nick of Time']

Wallas, Graham (1858–1932)
English political scientist, teacher and socialist

1. The little girl had the makings of a poet in her who, being told to be sure of her meaning before she spoke, said: 'How can I know what I think till I see what I say?'
[*The Art of Thought* (1926)]

Waller, Edmund (1606–1687)
English poet and politician

1. So was the huntsman by the bear oppress'd,
Whose hide he sold – before he caught the beast!
['The Battle of the Summer Islands' (1645). Cf. La Fontaine: 16]

2. Go, lovely Rose!
Tell her, that wastes her time and me,
That now she knows,
When I resemble her to thee,
How sweet and fair she seems to be...

3. Small is the worth
Of beauty from the light retir'd;
Bid her come forth,
Suffer herself to be desir'd,
And not blush so to be admir'd...

4. How small a part of time they share,
That are so wondrous sweet and fair.
['Go, lovely rose!' (1645)]

5. Poets that lasting marble seek
Must carve in Latin or in Greek.
['Of English Verse' (1645)]

6. That which her slender waist confin'd
Shall now my joyful temples bind;
No monarch but would give his crown
His arms might do what this has done.
['On a Girdle' (1645)]

7. Why came I so untimely forth
Into a world which, wanting thee,
Could entertain us with no worth,
Or shadow of felicity?
['To My Young Lady Lucy Sidney' (1645)]

8. Rome, though her eagle through the world had flown,
Could never make this island all her own.
['Panegyric to My Lord Protector' (1655)]

9. The soul's dark cottage, batter'd and decay'd
Lets in new light through chinks that time has made;
Stronger by weakness, wiser men become,
As they draw nearer to their eternal home.
Leaving the old, both worlds at once they view,
That stand upon the threshold of the new.
['Of the Last Verses in the Book' (1685)]

10. Poets lose half the praise they should have got,
Could it be known what they discreetly blot.
['On Roscommon's Translation of Horace']

Walpole, Horace, Fourth Earl of Orford (1717–1797)
English novelist and prose writer; Whig politician, and son of Sir Robert Walpole

1. Alexander at the head of the world never tasted the true pleasure that boys of his own age have enjoyed at the head of a school.
[Letter, 1736]

2. Our supreme governors, the mob.
[Letter to Sir Horace Mann, 1743]

3. [Lovat] was beheaded yesterday, and died extremely well, without passion, affectation, buffoonery or timidity: his behaviour was natural and intrepid.
[Letter to Sir Horace Mann, 1747]

4. [Strawberry Hill] is a little plaything-house that I got out of Mrs Chenevix's shop, and is the prettiest bauble you ever saw. It is set in enamelled meadows, with filigree hedges.
[Letter to Henry Conway, 1747]

5. Every drop of ink in my pen ran cold.
[Letter to George Montagu, 1752]

6. At present, nothing is talked of, nothing admired, but what I cannot help calling a very insipid and tedious performance: it is a kind of novel, called *The Life and Opinions of Tristram Shandy*; the great humour of which consists in the whole narration always going backwards.
[Letter to Sir David Dalrymple, 1760]

7. One of the greatest geniuses that ever existed, Shakespeare, undoubtedly wanted taste.
[Letter to Christopher Wren, 1764]

8. What has one to do, when one grows tired of the world, as we both do, but to draw nearer and nearer, and gently waste the remains of life with friends with whom one began it?
[Letter to George Montagu, 1765]

9. It is charming to totter into vogue.
[Letter to George Selwyn, 1765]

10. Everybody talks of the constitution, but all sides forget that the constitution is extremely well, and would do very well, if they would let it alone.
[Letter to Sir Horace Mann, 1770]

11. [Of the East]
It was easier to conquer it than to know what to do with it.
[Letter to Sir Horace Mann, 1772]

12. The way to ensure summer in England is to have it framed and glazed in a comfortable room.
[Letter to Rev. William Cole, 1774]

13. The next Augustan age will dawn on the other side of the Atlantic. There will, perhaps, be a Thucydides at Boston, a Xenophon at New York, and, in time, a Virgil at Mexico, and a Newton at Peru. At last, some curious traveller from Lima will visit England and give a description of the ruins of St Paul's, like the editions of Balbec and Palmyra.
[Letter to Sir Horace Mann, 1774]

14. Old age is no such uncomfortable thing if one gives oneself up to it with a good grace, and doesn't drag it about 'To midnight dances and the public show'.
[Letter, 1774]

15. This world is a comedy to those that think, and a tragedy to those that feel.
[Letter to Anne, Countess of Upper Ossory, 1776]

16. Tell me, ye divines, which is the most virtuous man, he who begets twenty bastards, or he who sacrifices an hundred thousand lives?
[Letter to Sir Horace Mann, 1778]

17. When will the world know that peace and propagation are the two most delightful things in it?
[Letter to Sir Horace Mann, 1778]

18. The life of any man written under the direction of his family, did nobody honour.
[Letter, 1778]

19. When men write for profit, they are not very delicate.
[Letter to Rev. William Cole, 1778]

20. When people will not weed their own minds, they are apt to be overrun with nettles.
[Letter to Caroline, Countess of Ailesbury, 1779]

21. The wisest prophets make sure of the event first.
[Letter to Thomas Walpole, 1785]

22. [Referring to Boswell's *Tour of the Hebrides*]
It is the story of a mountebank and his zany.
[Letter to Henry Conway, 1785]

23. [Of Sir Joshua Reynolds]
All his own geese are swans, as the swans of others are geese.
[Letter to Anne, Countess of Upper Ossory, 1786]

24. I do not dislike the French from the vulgar antipathy between neighbouring nations, but for their insolent and unfounded airs of superiority.
[Letter, 1787]

25. Lord Rochester's poems have much more obscenity than wit, more wit than poetry, more poetry than politeness.
[*Catalogue of Royal and Noble Authors* (1758)]

26. William Kent leapt the fence, and saw that all Nature was a garden.
[*On Modern Gardening*]

27. [Explaining why he filled his son's glass twice for every glass he drank himself]
Come, Robert, you shall drink twice while I drink once, for I cannot permit the son in his sober senses to witness the intoxication of his father.
[Attr.]

28. They who cannot perform great things themselves may yet have a satisfaction in doing justice to those who can.
[Attr.]

Walpole, Robert, First Earl of Orford (1676–1745)

English Whig statesman, known as first British Prime Minister, 1721–42; father of Horace Walpole

1. The balance of power.
[Speech, House of Commons, 1741]

2. [Remark to Queen Caroline, 1734, on the war of Austrian succession]
Madam, there are fifty thousand men slain this year in Europe, and not one Englishman.
[In John Hervey, *Memoirs* (written 1734–43, published 1848)]

3. [Remark on declaration of war with Spain, 1739]
They now ring the bells, but they will soon wring their hands.
[In W. Coxe, *Memoirs of Sir Robert Walpole* (1798)]

4. [Of fellow-parliamentarians]
All those men have their price.
[In W. Coxe, *Memoirs of Sir Robert Walpole* (1798)]

5. [To Pulteney, Earl of Bath, on their promotion to the House of Lords]
My Lord Bath, you and I are now two as insignificant men as any in England.
[In W. King, *Political and Literary Anecdotes* (1819)]

6. [On being asked whether he would like to be read to]
Anything but history, for history must be false.
[Attr.]

Walsh, William (1663–1708)

English critic, poet and Whig politician

1. And sadly reflecting,
That a lover forsaken
A new love may get,
But a neck when once broken
Can never be set.
['The Despairing Lover']

2. I can endure my own despair,
But not another's hope.
['Song: Of All the Torments']

Walton, Izaak (1593–1683)

English prose writer and biographer

1. And for winter fly-fishing it is as useful as an almanac out of date.
[*The Compleat Angler* (1653), 'Epistle to the Reader']

2. As no man is born an artist, so no man is born an angler.
[*The Compleat Angler* (1653), 'Epistle to the Reader']

3. I shall stay him no longer than to wish him a rainy evening to read this following discourse; and that if he be an honest angler, the east wind may never blow when he goes a-fishing.
[*The Compleat Angler* (1653), 'Epistle to the Reader']

4. I am, Sir, a Brother of the Angle.
[*The Compleat Angler* (1653), I, 1]

5. Sir Henry Wotton ... was also a most dear lover, and a frequent practiser of the art of angling; of which he would say, 'it was an employment for his idle time, which was then not idly spent ... a rest to his mind, a cheerer of his spirits, a diverter of sadness, a calmer of unquiet thoughts, a moderator of passions, a procurer of contentedness; and that it begat habits of peace and patience in those that professed and practised it.'
[*The Compleat Angler* (1653), I, 1]

6. I remember that a wise friend of mine did say, 'that which is everybody's business is nobody's business.'
[*The Compleat Angler* (1653), I, 2]

7. Good company and good discourse are the very sinews of virtue.
[*The Compleat Angler* (1653), I, 2]

8. An excellent angler, and now with God.
[*The Compleat Angler* (1653), I, 4]

9. We may say of angling as Dr Boteler said of strawberries: 'Doubtless God could have made a better berry, but doubtless God never did'; and so (if I might be judge) God never did make a more calm, quiet, innocent recreation than angling.
[*The Compleat Angler* (1653), I, 4]

10. I love such mirth as does not make friends ashamed to look upon one another next morning.
[*The Compleat Angler* (1653), I, 5]

11. A good, honest, wholesome, hungry breakfast.
[*The Compleat Angler* (1653), I, 5]

12. No man can lose what he never had.
[*The Compleat Angler* (1653), I, 5]

13. [On using a live frog to bait a hook]
In so doing, use him as though you loved him.
[*The Compleat Angler* (1653), I, 8]

14. I love any discourse of rivers, and fish and fishing.
[*The Compleat Angler* (1653), I, 18]

15. Look to your health; and if you have it, praise God, and value it next to a good conscience; for health is the second

blessing that we mortals are capable of; a blessing money cannot buy.
[*The Compleat Angler* (1653), I, 21]

16. But God, who is able to prevail, wrestled with him, as the Angel did with Jacob, and marked him; marked him for his own.
[*Life of Donne* (1670 edition)]

17. The great Secretary of Nature and all learning, Sir Francis Bacon.
[*Life of Herbert* (1670 edition)]

Warburton, William (1698–1779)
English theologian and pamphleteer; Bishop of Gloucester from 1759

1. Orthodoxy is my doxy; heterodoxy is another man's doxy.
[In Joseph Priestley, *Memoirs* (1807)]

Ward, Artemus (Charles Farrar Browne) (1834–1867)
American humorist; journalist, editor and lecturer

1. I now bid you a welcome adoo.
[*Artemus Ward, His Book* (1862), 'The Shakers']

2. N.B. This is rote Sarcasticul.
[*Artemus Ward, His Book* (1862), 'A Visit to Brigham Young']

3. I girdid up my Lions & fled the Seen.
[*Artemus Ward, His Book* (1862), 'A Visit to Brigham Young']

4. If you mean gettin hitched, I'M IN!
[*Artemus Ward, His Book* (1862), 'The Showman's Courtship']

5. Did you ever hav the measels, and if so how many?
[*Artemus Ward, His Book* (1862), 'The Census']

6. The female woman is one of the greatest institooshuns of which this land can boste.
[*Artemus Ward, His Book* (1862), 'Woman's Rights']

7. The ground flew up and hit me in the hed.
[*Artemus Ward, His Book* (1862), 'Thrilling Scenes in Dixie']

8. I presunted myself at Betty's bedside late at nite, with considerbul licker koncealed about my persun.
[*Artemus Ward, His Book* (1862), 'Betsy-Jain Re-orgunised']

9. It is a pity that Chawcer, who had geneyus, was so unedicated. He's the wuss speller I know of.
[*Artemus Ward in London* (1867), 4, 'At the Tomb of Shakespeare']

10. I am happiest when I am idle. I could live for months without performing any kind of labour, and at the expiration of that time I should feel fresh and vigorous enough to go right on in the same way for numerous more months.
[*Artemus Ward in London* (1867), 9, 'Pyrotechny']

11. He is dreadfully married. He's the most married man I ever saw in my life.
[*Artemus Ward's Lecture* (1869), 'Brigham Young's Palace']

12. Why is this thus? What is the reason of this thusness?
[*Artemus Ward's Lecture* (1869), 'Heber C. Kimball's Harem']

13. Let us all be happy, and live within our means, even if we have to borrer the money to do it with.
['Science and Natural History']

Ward, Mrs Humphry (Mary Augusta Ward) (1851–1920)
English novelist and social campaigner; niece of Matthew Arnold

1. 'Propinquity does it' – as Mrs Thornburgh is always reminding us.
[*Robert Elsmere* (1888), 2]

Ward, Nathaniel (1578–1652)
English Puritan divine

1. The world is full of care, much like unto a bubble;
Women and care, and care and women, and women and care and trouble.
[Epigram (1647). Cf. Francis Bacon [1]: 131]

Ward, Russel Braddock (1914–)
Australian historian and socio-cultural writer

1. The Australian Legend.
[Title of book, 1958]

Ward, Thomas (1577–1639)

1. Where to elect there is but one,
'Tis Hobson's choice, – take that or none.
[*England's Reformation* (1630), 4]

Warhol, Andy (c. 1926–1987)
American 'pop' artist; painter, graphic designer and film-maker

1. In the future everyone will be world famous for fifteen minutes.
[Catalogue for his exhibition of photographs, Stockholm, 1968]

2. An artist is someone who produces things that people don't need to have but that he – for *some reason* – thinks it would be a good idea to give them.
[*From A to B and Back Again* (1975), 'Atmosphere'. Cf. Thornton Wilder: 1]

Warner, Anna (1827–1915)
American novelist and author of works on religion and gardening; collaborated with her sister, Susan Warner

1. Jesus loves me! this I know,
For the Bible tells me so;
Little ones to Him belong,
They are weak, but He is strong.
[Hymn, 1859]

Warner, Susan (1819–1885)
Popular American novelist and children's writer; collaborated with her sister, Anna Warner

1. Jesus bids us shine
With a pure, clear light,
Like a little candle
Burning in the night.
In this world is darkness;
So let us shine,
You in your small corner,
And I in mine.
[Hymn, 1881]

Warren, Earl (1891–1974)
American lawyer and politician; Chief Justice 1953–69

1. Many people consider the things which government does for them to be social progress, but they consider the things government does for others as socialism.
[*Peter's Quotations*]

Washington, George (1732–1799)
American general and statesman; first US President 1789–97

1. [On being accused of cutting down a cherry tree]
Father, I cannot tell a lie; I did it with my little hatchet.
[Attr., probably apocryphal]

2. Few men have virtue to withstand the highest bidder.
[*Moral Maxims*]

3. To persevere in one's duty and be silent is the best answer to calumny.
[*Moral Maxims*]

4. Influence is not government.
[*Political Maxims*]

5. Associate yourself with men of good quality if you esteem your own reputation; for 'tis better to be alone than in bad company.
[*Rules of Civility and Decent Behaviour*]

6. Labour to keep alive in your breast that little spark of celestial fire, called conscience.
[*Rules of Civility and Decent Behaviour*]

7. The very idea of the power and the right of the People to establish Government, presupposes the duty of every individual to obey the established Government.
[Farewell Address, 1796]

8. 'Tis our true policy to steer clear of permanent alliances, with any portion of the foreign world.
[Farewell Address, 1796]

9. It is not a custom with me to keep money to look at.
[Letter, 1780]

10. Be courteous to all, but intimate with few, and let those few be well tried before you give them your confidence. True friendship is a plant of slow growth, and must undergo and withstand the shocks of adversity before it is entitled to the appellation.
[Letter, 1783]

11. Mankind, when left to themselves, are unfit for their own government.
[Letter, 1786]

12. Liberty, when it begins to take root, is a plant of rapid growth.
[Letter, 1788]

13. I heard the bullets whistle, and believe me, there is something charming in the sound.
[In P. Boller, *Presidential Anecdotes* (1981)]

14. [Order given in 1777]
Put none but Americans on guard tonight.
[Attr.]

Waten, Judah Leon (1911–1985)
Australian novelist

1. The art of politics is to make more friends than enemies.
[Remark to S. Murray-Smith]

Watkyns, Rowland (c. 1616–1664)
British poet

1. I love him not, but shew no reason can
Wherefore, but this, I *do not love* the man.
[*Flamma sine fumo*, 'Antipathy']

Watson, James Dewey (1928–)
American biologist; shared Nobel prize for medicine (1962) for his DNA research

1. The thought could not be avoided that the best home for a feminist was in another person's lab.
[*The Double Helix* (1968), 2]

2. [Referring to Francis Crick]
Already for thirty-five years he had not stopped talking and almost nothing of fundamental value had emerged.
[*The Double Helix* (1968), 8]

Watson, Sir William (1858–1936)
English poet

1. [Of Ireland]
The lovely and lonely bride,
Whom we have wedded but never won.
['Ode on the Coronation of Edward VII' (1902)]

2. The staid conservative,
Came-over-with-the Conqueror type of mind.
['A Study in Contrasts' (1905)]

3. Too long, that some may rest,
Tired millions toil unblest.
['New National Anthem']

Watts, Isaac (1674–1748)
English hymn-writer, poet and minister

1. When I survey the wondrous Cross
On which the Prince of Glory died,
My richest gain I count but loss,
And pour contempt on all my pride...

2. Were the whole realm of Nature mine,
That were an offering far too small;
Love so amazing, so divine,
Demands my soul, my life, my all.
[*Hymns and Spiritual Songs* (1707)]

3. When I can read my title clear
To mansions in the skies,
I'll bid farewell to every fear,
And wipe my weeping eyes.
[*Hymns and Spiritual Songs* (1707)]

4. One sickly sheep infects the flock,
And poisons all the rest.
[*Divine Songs for Children* (1715), 'Against Evil Company']

5. How doth the little busy bee
Improve each shining hour,
and gather honey all the day
From every opening flower!...

6. In works of labour, or of skill,
I would be busy too;
For Satan finds some mischief still
For idle hands to do.
[*Divine Songs for Children* (1715), 'Against Idleness and Mischief'. Cf. Carroll: 4]

7. The tulip and the butterfly
Appear in gayer coats than I:
Let me be dressed fine as I will,
Flies, worms, and flowers, exceed me still.
[*Divine Songs for Children* (1715), 'Against Pride in Clothes']

8. Let dogs delight to bark and bite,
For God hath made them so;
Let bears and lions growl and fight,
For 'tis their nature too...

9. But, children, you should never let
Such angry passions rise;
Your little hands were never made
To tear each other's eyes.
[*Divine Songs for Children* (1715), 'Against Quarrelling']

10. I'll not willingly offend,
Nor be easily offended;
What's amiss I'll strive to mend,
And endure what can't be mended.
[*Divine Songs for Children* (1715), 'Good Resolution']

11. There is a dreadful Hell,
And everlasting pains;
There sinners must with devils dwell
In darkness, fire and chains.
[*Divine Songs for Children* (1715), 'Heaven and Hell']

12. Birds in their little nests agree
And 'tis a shameful sight,
When children of one family
Fall out, and chide, and fight.
[*Divine Songs for Children* (1715), 'Love between Brothers and Sisters']

13. Lord, I ascribe it to Thy Grace,
And not to chance, as others do,
That I was born of Christian race,
And not a Heathen, or a Jew.
[*Divine Songs for Children* (1715), 'Praise for the Gospel']

14. 'Tis the voice of the sluggard; I heard him complain,
'You have wak'd me too soon, I must slumber again'.
As the door on its hinges, so he on his bed,
Turns his sides and his shoulders and his heavy head.
[*Divine Songs for Children* (1715), 'The Sluggard'. Cf. Carroll: 34]

15. There's no repentance in the grave.
[*Divine Songs for Children* (1715), 'Solemn Thoughts of God and Death']

16. Jesus shall reign where'er the sun
Does his successive journeys run;
His Kingdom stretch from shore to shore,
Till moons shall wax and wane no more...

17. Blessings abound where'er He reigns;
The prisoner leaps to lose his chains.
[*The Psalms of David Imitated* (1719), Psalm 72]

18. O God, our help in ages past,
Our hope for years to come,
Our shelter from the stormy blast,
And our eternal home.

Under the shadow of Thy throne
Thy saints have dwelt secure;
Sufficient is Thine arm alone,
And our defence is sure.

Before the hills in order stood,
Or earth received her frame,
From everlasting Thou art God,
To endless years the same.

A thousand ages in Thy sight
Are like an evening gone;
Short as the watch that ends the night
Before the rising sun.

Time, like an ever-rolling stream,
Bears all its sons away;
They fly forgotten, as a dream
Dies at the opening day.
[*The Psalms of David Imitated* (1719), Psalm 90]

Waugh, Auberon (1939–)

English novelist, journalist and critic; eldest son of Evelyn Waugh

1. I can even visit a bank without the usual fantasies of grabbing everything and running for the door. When a woman left her handbag in my house I didn't even look inside it for several days.
[*The Lion's Den* (1973), 'Not to Worry']

2. It is a sad feature of modern life that only women for the most part have time to write novels, and they seldom have much to write about.
[*The Observer*, 1981, in Jeffrey Care (ed.), *Sayings of the Eighties* (1989)]

3. It is one of the tragedies of our time to see women making a nuisance of themselves as welfare officers when they could be employed as nursery maids.
[*The Independent on Sunday*, 1994]

Waugh, Evelyn (1903–1966)

English novelist, journalist, travel writer and diarist; noted for his satire

1. The sound of the English county families baying for broken glass.
[*Decline and Fall* (1928), 'Prelude']

2. I expect you'll be becoming a schoolmaster, sir. That's what most of the gentlemen does, sir, that gets sent down for indecent behaviour.
[*Decline and Fall* (1928), 'Prelude']

3. 'We class schools, you see, into four grades: Leading School, First-rate School, Good School, and School. Frankly,' said Mr Levy, 'School is pretty bad.'
[*Decline and Fall* (1928), I, 1]

4. We schoolmasters must temper discretion with deceit.
[*Decline and Fall* (1928), I, 2]

5. Very hard for a man with a wig to keep order.
[*Decline and Fall* (1928), I, 3]

6. That's the public-school system all over. They may kick you out, but they never let you down.
[*Decline and Fall* (1928), I, 3]

7. I can't quite explain it, but I don't believe one can ever be unhappy for long provided one does just exactly what one wants to and when one wants to.
[*Decline and Fall* (1928), I, 5]

8. Meanwhile you will write an essay on 'self-indulgence'. There will be a prize of half a crown for the longest essay, irrespective of any possible merit.
[*Decline and Fall* (1928), I, 5]

9. For generations the British bourgeoisie have spoken of themselves as gentlemen, and by that they have meant, among other things, a self-respecting scorn of irregular perquisites. It is the quality that distinguishes the gentleman from both the artist and the aristocrat.
[*Decline and Fall* (1928), I, 6]

10. 'The Welsh,' said the Doctor, 'are the only nation in the world that has produced no graphic or plastic art, no architecture, no drama. They just sing,' he said with disgust, 'sing and blow down wind instruments of plated silver.'
[*Decline and Fall* (1928), I, 8]

11. I have noticed again and again since I have been in the Church that lay interest in ecclesiastical matters is often a prelude to insanity.
[*Decline and Fall* (1928), I, 8]

12. I haven't been to sleep for over a year. That's why I go to bed early. One needs more rest if one doesn't sleep.
[*Decline and Fall* (1928), II, 3]

13. There is a species of person called a 'Modern Churchman' who draws the full salary of a beneficed clergyman and need not commit himself to any religious belief.
[*Decline and Fall* (1928), II, 4]

14. I came to the conclusion many years ago that almost all crime is due to the repressed desire for aesthetic expression.
[*Decline and Fall* (1928), III, 1]

15. Anyone who has been to an English public school will always feel comparatively at home in prison.
[*Decline and Fall* (1928), III, 4]

16. He was greatly pained at how little he was pained by the events of the afternoon.
[*Decline and Fall* (1928), III, 4]

17. Instead of this absurd division into sexes they ought to class people as static and dynamic.
[*Decline and Fall* (1928), III, 7]

18. Particularly against books the Home Secretary is. If we can't stamp out literature in the country, we can at least stop it being brought in from outside.
[*Vile Bodies* (1930), 2]

19. When the war broke out she took down the signed photograph of the Kaiser and, with some solemnity, hung it in the menservants' lavatory; it was her one combative action.
[*Vile Bodies* (1930), 3]

20. All this fuss about sleeping together. For physical pleasure I'd sooner go to my dentist any day.
[*Vile Bodies* (1930), 6]

21. When Lord Copper was right he said, 'Definitely, Lord Copper'; when he was wrong, 'Up to a point'.
[*Scoop* (1938), I, 1]

22. Feather-footed through the plashy fen passes the questing vole.
[*Scoop* (1938), I, 1]

23. Pappenhacker says that every time you are polite to a proletarian you are helping to bolster up the capitalist system.
[*Scoop* (1938), I, 2]

24. News is what a chap who doesn't care much about anything wants to read. And it's only news until he's read it. After that it's dead.
[*Scoop* (1938), I, 5]

25. 'I will not stand for being called a woman in my own house,' she said.
[*Scoop* (1938), II, 1]

26. Other nations use 'force'; we Britons alone use 'Might'.
[*Scoop* (1938), II, 5]

27. Lady Peabury was in the morning room reading a novel; early training gave a guilty spice to this recreation, for she had been brought up to believe that to read a novel before luncheon was one of the gravest sins it was possible for a gentlewoman to commit.
[*Work Suspended* (1942)]

28. In the dying world I come from quotation is a national vice. It used to be the classics, now it's lyric verse.
[*The Loved One* (1948)]

29. Enclosing every thin man, there's a fat man demanding elbow-room.
[*Officers and Gentlemen* (1955), Interlude. Cf. Kingsley Amis: 3 and Orwell: 7]

30. Assistant masters came and went ... Some liked little boys too little and some too much.
[*A Little Learning* (1964)]

31. Manners are especially the need of the plain. The pretty can get away with anything.
[*The Observer*, 'Sayings of the Year', 1962]

32. No writer before the middle of the 19th century wrote about the working classes other than as grotesque or as pastoral decoration. Then when they were given the vote certain writers started to suck up to them.
[Interview in the *Paris Review*, 1963]

33. [Remark to Graham Greene, who was planning to write a political novel]
I wouldn't give up writing about God at this stage if I was you. It would be like P.G. Wodehouse dropping Jeeves half-way through the Wooster series.
[In Christopher Sykes, *Evelyn Waugh*]

34. [Of Winston Churchill]
Simply a radio personality who outlived his prime.
[In Christopher Sykes, *Evelyn Waugh*]

35. [Cable sent after he had failed, while a journalist in Ethiopia, to substantiate a rumour that an English nurse had been blown up in an Italian air raid]
Nurse unupblown.
[In R. Claiborne, *Our Marvellous Native Tongue*]

36. [Giving his opinions of warfare after the battle of Crete, 1941]
Like German opera, too long and too loud.
[Attr.]

37. We cherish our friends not for their ability to amuse us, but for our ability to amuse them.
[Attr.]

38. I put the words down and push them a bit.
[Obituary, *New York Times*, 11 April 1966]

Wax, Ruby

Controversial American television chat-show host

1. This 'relationship' business is one big waste of time. It is just Mother Nature urging you to breed, breed, breed. Learn from nature. Learn from our friend the spider. Just mate once and then kill him.
[*Dundee Courier*, 1994]

Weatherly, Frederic Edward (1848–1929)

English songwriter, lawyer and writer

1. Where are the boys of the old Brigade,
Who fought with us side by side?
['The Old Brigade', song, 1886]

2. Roses are flowering in Picardy,
But there's never a rose like you.
['Roses of Picardy', song, 1916]

Webb, Beatrice (née Potter) (1858–1943)

English political and social writer and reformer; wife of Sidney Webb

1. Religion is love; in no case is it logic.
[*My Apprenticeship* (1926), 1]

2. If I ever felt inclined to be timid as I was going into a room full of people, I would say to myself, 'You're the cleverest

member of one of the cleverest families in the cleverest class of the cleverest nation in the world, why should you be frightened?'
[In Bertrand Russell, *Portraits from Memory* (1956)]

Webb, David Allardice (1912–1994)
Irish botanist and academic

1. It is only human to believe that the work which you are doing is more interesting than the next man's; you would presumably not be doing it otherwise. This does no harm so long as you recognise your attitude as subjective. But to objectify and generalise it, and to suggest that anyone who is not working in the same field as yourself is wasting his time is a very different matter.
[Address to the British Association for the Advancement of Science, 1957]

Webb, Sidney (Baron Passfield) (1859–1947)
English social reformer, historian and socialist; husband and collaborator of Beatrice Webb

1. The inevitability of gradualness.
[Presidential address to the annual conference of the Labour Party, 1923]
2. Marriage is the waste-paper basket of the emotions.
[In Bertrand Russell, *Autobiography* (1967), I, 4]
3. Old people are always absorbed in something, usually themselves; we prefer to be absorbed in the Soviet Union.
[Attr.]

Weber, Max (1864–1920)
German economist and sociologist

1. Specialists without spirit, sensualists without heart; this nullity imagines that it has attained a level of civilisation never before achieved.
[*The Protestant Ethic and the Spirit of Capitalism* (1930)]

Webster, Daniel (1782–1852)
American statesman, orator and lawyer; Secretary of State 1841–43, 1850–52

1. The past, at least, is secure.
[Speech, 1830]
2. The people's government, made for the people, made by the people, and answerable to the people.
[Speech, 1830. Cf. Oscar Wilde: 38]
3. Liberty and Union, now and forever, one and inseparable!
[Speech, 1830]
4. On this question of principle, while actual suffering was yet afar off, they [the Colonies] raised their flag against a power, to which, for purposes of foreign conquest and subjugation, Rome, in the height of her glory, is not to be compared; a power which has dotted over the surface of the whole globe with her possessions and military posts, whose morning drum-beat, following the sun, and keeping company with the hours, circles the earth with one continuous and unbroken strain of the martial airs of England.
[Speech, 1834]
5. Thank God, I – I also – am an American!
[Speech, 1843]
6. Inconsistencies of opinion, arising from changes of circumstances, are often justifiable.
[Speech, 1846]
7. The Law: It has honoured us, may we honour it.
[Speech, 1847]
8. I was born an American; I will live an American; I shall die an American.
[Speech, 1850]
9. [Argument on the murder of Captain White, 1830]
Fearful concatenation of circumstances.
[*Writings and Speeches* (1903)]
10. [On being advised not to join the overcrowded legal profession]
There is always room at the top.
[Attr.]

Webster, John (c. 1580–c. 1625)
English dramatist, noted for his tragedies

1. Is not old wine wholesomest, old pippins toothsomest? Does not old wood burn brightest, old linen wash whitest? Old soldiers, sweethearts, are surest, and old lovers are soundest.
[*Westward Hoe* (1607), II.ii]
2. I saw him even now going the way of all flesh, that is to say towards the kitchen.
[*Westward Hoe* (1607), II.ii]
3. Fortune's a right whore:
If she give aught, she deals it in small parcels,
That she may take away all at one swoop.
[*The White Devil* (1612), I.i]
4. 'Tis just like a summer birdcage in a garden; the birds that are without despair to get in, and the birds that are within despair, and are in consumption, for fear they shall never get out.
[*The White Devil* (1612), I.ii]
5. A mere tale of a tub, my words are idle.
[*The White Devil* (1612), II.i. Cf. Swift: 3]
6. Only the deep sense of some deathless shame.
[*The White Devil* (1612), II.ii]
7. Cowardly dogs bark loudest.
[*The White Devil* (1612), III.i]
8. A rape! a rape!...
Yes, you have ravish'd justice;
Forced her to do your pleasure.
[*The White Devil* (1612), III.i]
9. There's nothing sooner dry than women's tears.
[*The White Devil* (1612), V.iii]
10. Call for the robin redbreast and the wren,
Since o'er shady groves they hover,
And with leaves and flowers do cover
The friendless bodies of unburied men.
[*The White Devil* (1612), V.iv]
11. But keep the wolf far thence that's foe to men,
For with his nails he'll dig them up again.
[*The White Devil* (1612), V.iv. Cf. T.S. Eliot: 39]
12. We think caged birds sing, when indeed they cry.
[*The White Devil* (1612), V.iv]
13. And of all axioms this shall win the prize,–
'Tis better to be fortunate than wise.
[*The White Devil* (1612), V.vi]
14. There's nothing of so infinite vexation
As man's own thoughts.
[*The White Devil* (1612), V.vi]
15. My soul, like to a ship in a black storm,
Is driven, I know not whither.
[*The White Devil* (1612), V.vi]

16. Prosperity doth bewitch men, seeming clear;
As seas do laugh, show white, when rocks are near.
[*The White Devil* (1612), V.vi]

17. I have caught
An everlasting cold; I have lost my voice
Most irrecoverably.
[*The White Devil* (1612), V.vi]

18. Vain the ambition of kings
Who seek by trophies and dead things,
To leave a living name behind,
And weave but nets to catch the wind.
[*The Devil's Law-Case* (1623), V.iv]

19. *Ferdinand*: And women like that part which, like the lamprey,
Hath never a bone in't.
Duchess: Fie, sir!
Ferdinand: Nay,
I mean the tongue; variety of courtship:
What cannot a neat knave with a smooth tale
Make a woman believe?
[*The Duchess of Malfi* (1623), I.ii]

20. Unequal nature, to place women's hearts
So far upon the left side.
[*The Duchess of Malfi* (1623), II.v]

21. Why should only I . . .
Be cas'd up, like a holy relic? I have youth
And a little beauty.
[*The Duchess of Malfi* (1623), III.ii]

22. Raised by that curious engine, your white hand.
[*The Duchess of Malfi* (1623), III.ii]

23. O, that it were possible,
We might but hold some two days' conference
With the dead!
[*The Duchess of Malfi* (1623), IV.ii]

24. I am Duchess of Malfi still.
[*The Duchess of Malfi* (1623), IV.ii]

25. Glories, like glow-worms, afar off shine bright,
But, looked too near, have neither heat nor light.
[*The Duchess of Malfi* (1623), IV.ii]

26. I know death hath ten thousand several doors
For men to take their exits.
[*The Duchess of Malfi* (1623), IV.ii]

27. *Ferdinand*: Cover her face; mine eyes dazzle; she died young.
Bosola: I think not so; her infelicity
Seem'd to have years too many.
[*The Duchess of Malfi* (1623), IV.ii]

28. Other sins only speak; murder shrieks out.
[*The Duchess of Malfi* (1623), IV.ii. Cf. Chaucer: 63]

29. Physicians are like kings – they brook no contradiction.
[*The Duchess of Malfi* (1623), V.ii]

30. We are merely the stars' tennis-balls, struck and bandied,
Which way please them.
[*The Duchess of Malfi* (1623), V.iv]

Webster, Noah (1758–1843)
American lexicographer; teacher, writer and lecturer

1. [Responding to his wife's comment that she had been surprised to find him embracing their maid]
No, my dear, it is *I* who am surprised; you are merely astonished.
[Attr.]

Wedgewood, Cicely Veronica (1910–)
English historian of the 17th century

1. . . . truth can neither be apprehended nor communicated . . . history is an art like all other sciences.
[*Truth and Opinion* (1960)]

Wedgwood, Josiah (1730–1795)
English potter, known for his neo-classical design; manufacturer and pamphleteer

1. Am I not a man and a brother?
[Motto adopted by Anti-Slavery Society]

Weil, Simone (1909–1943)
French philosopher, essayist and mystic

1. *La culture est un instrument manié par des professeurs pour fabriquer des professeurs qui à leur tour fabriqueront des professeurs.*
Culture is an instrument wielded by teachers to manufacture teachers, who, in their turn, will manufacture teachers.
[*L'Enracinement* (*The Need for Roots*, 1949)]

2. *Les collectivités ne pensent point.*
Collectivities do not think.
[*Oppression et Liberté* (*Oppression and Freedom*, 1955)]

3. *On pense aujourd'hui à la révolution, non comme à une solution des problèmes posés par l'actualité, mais comme à un miracle dispensant de résoudre les problèmes.*
Nowadays we think of revolution not as the solution to problems posed by current developments but as a miracle which releases us from the obligation to solve these problems.
[*Oppression et Liberté* (*Oppression and Freedom*, 1955)]

Weinreich, Professor Max

1. A language is a dialect that has an army and a navy.
[In Leo Rosten, *The Joys of Yiddish* (1968)]

Weiss, Peter (1916–1982)
German dramatist, painter, film producer and writer

1. *Jeder Tod auch der grausamste*
ertrinkt in der völligen Gleichgültigkeit der Natur
Nur wir verleihen unserm Leben irgendeinen Wert.
Every death, even the cruellest,
drowns in Nature's complete indifference. We are the only ones who bestow a value on our lives.
[*Die Verfolgung und Ermordung Jean Paul Marats* (*The Hunting Down and Murder of Jean Paul Marat*, 1964), I.xii]

2. *So verseucht sind wir von den Gedankengängen*
die Generation von Generation übernahm
dass auch die besten von uns
sich immer noch nicht zu helfen wissen.
We are so poisoned by the ideas which generation handed down to generation that even the best of us still don't know how to help ourselves.
[*Die Verfolgung und Ermordung Jean Paul Marats* (*The Hunting Down and Murder of Jean Paul Marat*, 1964), I.xv]

3. *Wir sind die Erfinder der Revolution*
doch wir können noch nicht damit umgehn.
We invented the revolution but we can't handle it yet.
[*Die Verfolgung und Ermordung Jean Paul Marats* (*The Hunting Down and Murder of Jean Paul Marat*, 1964), I.xv]

4. *Denn was wäre schön diese Revolution*
ohne eine allgemeine Kopulation.
What sort of a state would this revolution be in without general copulation.
[*Die Verfolgung und Ermordung Jean Paul Marats* (*The Hunting Down and Murder of Jean Paul Marat*, 1964), II.xxx]

Weissmuller, Johnny (1904–1984)
American film actor

1. Me Tarzan, you Jane.
[Describing his role in *Tarzan, the Ape Man*, film, 1932]

Welch, Raquel (Raquel Tejada) (1940–)
American film actress

1. The mind can also be an erogenous zone.
[Attr.]

Weldon, Fay (1931–)
British novelist, short-story writer and critic

1. Hilda and Patricia were instructed to come straight home after school, for fear of licentious soldiery.
[*Praxis* (1978)]
2. ... the great wonderful construct which is marriage – a construct made up of a hundred little kindnesses, a thousand little bitings back of spite, tens of thousands of minor actions of good intent – this must not, as an institution, be brought down in ruins.
[*Splitting* (1995)]
3. I don't believe in happiness: why should we expect to be happy? In such a world as this, depression is rational, rage reasonable.
[*The Observer*, 1995]

Welles, Orson (1915–1985)
American actor, director and producer; Academy Awards 1941 and 1970

1. In Italy for thirty years under the Borgias they had warfare, terror, murder, bloodshed – they produced Michelangelo, Leonardo da Vinci and the Renaissance. In Switzerland they had brotherly love, five hundred years of democracy and peace, and what did they produce...? The cuckoo clock.
[*The Third Man*, film, 1949; words added by Welles to Graham Greene's script]
2. I began at the top and I've been working my way down ever since.
[In J.R. Colombo (ed.), *Wit and Wisdom of the Moviemakers* (1979)]
3. [Speaking to an audience after a matinée performance]
I would just like to mention Robert Houdin who in the eighteenth century invented the vanishing bird-cage trick and the theatre matinée – may he rot and perish. Good afternoon.
[In G. Brandreth, *Great Theatrical Disasters*]

Wellington, Arthur Wellesley, Duke of (1769–1852)
Irish-born British field marshal and statesman; Tory Prime Minister 1828–30; famous for his victory over Napoleon at Waterloo, 1815

1. When I reflect upon the characters and attainments of some of the general officers of this army, and consider that these are the persons on whom I am to rely to lead columns against the French, I tremble; and as Lord Chesterfield said of the generals of his day, 'I only hope that when the enemy reads the list of their names, he trembles as I do.'
[Letter to Torrens, 29 August 1810; usually quoted as 'I don't know what effect these men will have upon the enemy, but, by God, they frighten me.']
2. I believe I forgot to tell you I was made a Duke.
[Postscript to a letter to his nephew, Henry Wellesley, 22 May 1814]
3. [Supposedly said during the Battle of Waterloo]
Up guards and at them again!
[Attr.; but see also quote 4]
4. What I must have said and possibly did say was, Stand up, Guards! and then gave the commanding officers the order to attack.
[Letter to J.W. Croker]
5. [Remark at Waterloo]
Hard pounding this, gentlemen; let's see who will pound longest.
[In Sir Walter Scott, *Paul's Letters* (1816), Letter 8]
6. Beginning reform is beginning revolution.
[In Mrs Arbuthnot's Journal, 1830]
7. There is no mistake; there has been no mistake; and there shall be no mistake.
[In Timbs, *Wellingtoniana* (1852)]
8. I always say that, next to a battle lost, the greatest misery is a battle gained.
[In S. Rogers, *Recollections* (1859)]
9. [Of Waterloo]
It has been a damned serious business – Blücher and I have lost 30,000 men. It has been a damned nice thing – the nearest run thing you ever saw in your life ... By God! I don't think it would have done if I had not been there.
[*The Creevey Papers* (1885), X]
10. All the business of war, and indeed all the business of life, is to endeavour to find out what you don't know by what you do; that's what I called 'guessing what was at the other side of the hill'.
[*The Croker Papers* (1885), III]
11. [Of his troops]
The mere scum of the earth.
[In Philip Henry Stanhope, *Notes of Conversations with the Duke of Wellington* (1888)]
12. [Of Napoleon]
I used to say of him that his presence on the field made the difference of forty thousand men.
[In Philip Henry Stanhope, *Notes of Conversations with the Duke of Wellington* (1888)]
13. My rule always was to do the business of the day in the day.
[In Philip Henry Stanhope, *Notes of Conversations with the Duke of Wellington* (1888)]
14. What is the best to be done for the country? How can the Government be carried on?
[In Philip Henry Stanhope, *Notes of Conversations with the Duke of Wellington* (1888)]
15. [On seeing the first Reformed Parliament]
I never saw so many shocking bad hats in my life.
[In Sir William Fraser, *Words on Wellington* (1889)]
16. You must build your House of Parliament upon the river: so ... that the populace cannot exact their demands by sitting down round you.
[In Sir William Fraser, *Words on Wellington* (1889)]
17. Possible? Is anything impossible? Read the newspapers.
[In Sir William Fraser, *Words on Wellington* (1889)]
18. In my situation as Chancellor of the University of Oxford, I have been much exposed to authors.
[In G.W.E. Russell, *Collections and Recollections* (1898)]
19. [Referring to steam locomotives]
I see no reason to suppose that these machines will ever force themselves into general use.
[In J. Gere, *Geoffrey Madan's Notebooks*]

20. [Replying to the observation that the French cavalry had come up very well during the Battle of Waterloo]
Yes, and they went down very well too.
[In A. Bryant, *The Age of Elegance*]

21. [Refusing permission to shoot at Napoleon during the Battle of Waterloo]
It is not the business of generals to shoot one another.
[Attr.]

22. The battle of Waterloo was won on the playing fields of Eton.
[Attr.]

23. I hate the whole race ... There is no believing a word they say – your professional poets, I mean – there never existed a more worthless set than Byron and his friends for example.
[Attr.]

24. [To a man who approached him saying, 'Mr Jones, I believe?']
If you believe that, you'll believe anything.
[Attr.]

25. [Responding to a vicar's enquiry as to whether there was anything he would like his forthcoming sermon to be about]
Yes, about ten minutes.
[Attr.]

26. [Advice when asked by Queen Victoria how to remove sparrows from the Crystal Palace]
Sparrowhawks, Ma'am.
[Attr.]

27. [Reply to a threat of blackmail by Harriette Wilson]
Publish and be damned.
[Attr.]

Wells, Allan (1952–)

Scottish athlete and Olympic champion

1. When the gun goes, you become a different human being.
[*The Observer*, 1981, in Jeffrey Care (ed.), *Sayings of the Eighties* (1989)]

Wells, H.G. (1866–1946)

English novelist, known for his scientific romances and autobiographical writing; short-story, historical and political writer

1. The Social Contract is nothing more or less than a vast conspiracy of human beings to lie to and humbug themselves and one another for the general Good. Lies are the mortar that bind the savage individual man into the social masonry.
[*Love and Mr Lewisham* (1900), 23]

2. They feared the 'low' and they hated and despised the 'stuck up' and so they 'kept themselves to themselves', according to the English ideal.
[*Kipps: the Story of a Simple Soul* (1905), I, 1]

3. I tell you, we're in a blessed drainpipe, and we've got to crawl along it till we die.
[*Kipps: the Story of a Simple Soul* (1905), I, 2]

4. There's no social differences – till women come in.
[*Kipps: the Story of a Simple Soul* (1905), II, 4]

5. I don't 'old with Wealth. What *is* Wealth? Labour robbed out of the poor.
[*Kipps: the Story of a Simple Soul* (1905), II, 4]

6. Everybody hates house-agents because they have everybody at a disadvantage. All other callings have a certain amount of give and take; the house-agent simply takes.
[*Kipps: the Story of a Simple Soul* (1905), III, 1]

7. I was thinking jest what a Rum Go everything is.
[*Kipps: the Story of a Simple Soul* (1905), III, 3]

8. In the Country of the Blind the One-eyed Man is King.
[*The Country of the Blind* (1911)]

9. Moral indignation is jealousy with a halo.
[*The Wife of Sir Isaac Harman* (1914), 9]

10. The War That Will End War.
[Title of book, 1914]

11. He was quite sure that he had been wronged. Not to be wronged is to forgo the first privilege of goodness.
[*Bealby* (1915), IV, 1]

12. He began to think the tramp a fine, brotherly, generous fellow. He was also growing accustomed to something – shall I call it an olfactory bar – that had hitherto kept them apart.
[*Bealby* (1915), VI, 3]

13. The army ages men sooner than the law and philosophy; it exposes them more freely to germs, which undermine and destroy, and it shelters them more completely from thought, which stimulates and preserves.
[*Bealby* (1915), VIII, 1]

14. He had one peculiar weakness; he had faced death in many forms but he had never faced a dentist. The thought of dentists gave him just the same sick horror as the thought of Socialism.
[*Bealby* (1915), VIII, 1]

15. [Of Henry James]
The thing his novel is *about* is always there. It is like a church lit but without a congregation to distract you, with every light and line focused on the high altar. And on the altar, very reverently placed, intensely there, is a dead kitten, an egg-shell, a bit of string.
[*Boon* (1915)]

16. [Of the British officer]
He muffs his real job without a blush, and yet he would rather be shot than do his bootlaces up criss-cross.
[*Mr Britling Sees It Through* (1916), II, 4]

17. Human history becomes more and more a race between education and catastrophe.
[*The Outline of History* (1920), II, 41]

18. In England we have come to rely upon a comfortable time-lag of fifty years or a century intervening between the perception that something ought to be done and a serious attempt to do it.
[*The Work, Wealth and Happiness of Mankind* (1931)]

19. The Shape of Things to Come.
[Title of book, 1933]

20. One thousand years more. That's all *Homo sapiens* has before him.
[In Harold Nicolson, *Diary*]

Wesker, Arnold (1932–)

English dramatist, screenwriter, short-story writer and socialist

1. Don't you sit there and sigh gal like you was Lady Nevershit.
[*Roots* (1959), III]

2. You breed babies and you eat chips with everything.
[*Chips with Everything* (1962), I.ii]

Wesley, Charles (1707–1788)

English divine; Methodist preacher and hymn-writer; brother of John Wesley

1. Vain the stone, the watch, the seal;
Christ has burst the gates of hell.
[*Hymns and Sacred Poems* (1739)]

2. O for a thousand tongues, to sing
My great Redeemer's praise...

3. Jesus! the Name that charms our fears,
That bids our sorrows cease;
'Tis music in the sinner's ears,
'Tis life, and health, and peace...

4. Hear Him, ye deaf; His praise, ye dumb,
Your loosened tongues employ;
Ye blind, behold your Saviour come;
And leap, ye lame, for joy!
[*Hymns and Sacred Poems* (1740)]

5. Jesus, Lover of my soul,
Let me to Thy bosom fly,
While the nearer waters roll,
While the tempest still is high.
[*Hymns and Sacred Poems* (1740)]

6. Gentle Jesus, meek and mild,
Look upon a little child,
Pity my simplicity,
Suffer me to come to Thee.
[*Hymns and Sacred Poems* (1742)]

7. Hark! the herald angels sing,
'Glory to the new-born King,
Peace on earth, and mercy mild,
God and sinners reconciled!'
[In G. Whitefield, *Hymns for Social Worship* (1753)]

Wesley, John (1703–1791)
English theologian and preacher; founder of Methodist Church, 1739; diarist; brother of Charles Wesley

1. [On the Sermon on the Mount]
Thou art guilty of everlasting death. It is the just reward of thy inward and outward wickedness. It is just that the sentence should now take place. Dost thou see, dost thou feel thus? Art thou thoroughly convinced, that thou deservest God's wrath, and everlasting damnation?
[*Fifty Three Sermons* (c. 1748), VII]

2. Let it be observed, that slovenliness is no part of religion; that neither this, nor any text of Scripture, condemns neatness of apparel. Certainly this is a duty, not a sin. 'Cleanliness is, indeed, next to godliness.'
[*Sermons on Several Occasions* (1788), Sermon 88, 'On Dress']

3. I look upon all the world as my parish.
[*Journal*, 1739]

4. I heard a good man say 'Once in seven years I burn all my sermons; for it is a shame if I cannot write better sermons now than I did seven years ago'.
[*Journal*, 1778]

5. Though I am always in haste, I am never in a hurry.
[Letter to Miss March, 1777]

6. Do all the good you can,
By all the means you can,
In all the ways you can,
In all the places you can,
At all the times you can,
To all the people you can,
As long as ever you can.
[*Letters* (1915)]

7. Beware you be not swallowed up in books! An ounce of love is worth a pound of knowledge.
[In R. Southey, *Life of Wesley* (1820)]

8. [On preaching to 'plain people']
We should constantly use the most common, little, easy words (so they are pure and proper) which our language affords.
[In R. Southey, *Life of Wesley* (1820)]

Wesley, Samuel (1662–1735)
English divine and poet; father of John and Charles Wesley

1. Style is the dress of thought; a modest dress,
Neat, but not gaudy, will true critics please.
['An Epistle to a Friend concerning Poetry' (1700)]

2. The poet's fate is here in emblem shown,
He asked for bread, and he received a stone.
['Epigram on Butler's Monument in Westminster Abbey']

West, Mae (1892–1980)
American leading vaudeville and film actress, and scriptwriter

1. 'Goodness, what beautiful diamonds!'
'Goodness had nothing to do with it!'
[*Night After Night*, film, 1932; scriptwriter Vincent Laurence]

2. Why don't you come up sometime, see me?
[*She Done Him Wrong*, film, 1933; script by Mae West from the play *Diamond Lil*. Usually quoted as 'Come up and see me sometime']

3. You're a fine woman, Lou. One of the finest women that ever walked the streets.
[*She Done Him Wrong*, film, 1933]

4. Beulah, peel me a grape.
[*I'm No Angel*, film, 1933]

5. When I'm good I'm very good, but when I'm bad I'm better.
[*I'm No Angel*, film, 1933. Cf. Longfellow: 36 and Max Miller: 1]

6. A man in the house is worth two in the street.
[*Belle of the Nineties*, film, 1934]

7. [Referring to Delilah]
I have a lot of respect for that dame. There's one lady barber that made good.
[*Goin' to Town*, film, 1935]

8. Whenever I'm caught between two evils, I take the one I've never tried.
[*Klondike Annie*, film, 1936; scriptwriters Mae West, Marion Morgan and George B. Dowell]

9. [After her performance in *Catherine the Great*]
I'm glad you like my Catherine. I like her too. She ruled thirty million people and had three thousand lovers. I do the best I can in two hours.
[Speech from the stage]

10. It's hard to be funny when you have to be clean.
[In J. Weintraub (ed.), *The Wit and Wisdom of Mae West* (1967)]

11. It is better to be looked over than overlooked.
[In J. Weintraub (ed.), *The Wit and Wisdom of Mae West* (1967)]

12. I used to be Snow White ... but I drifted.
[In J. Weintraub (ed.), *The Wit and Wisdom of Mae West* (1967)]

13. When women go wrong, men go right after them.
[In J. Weintraub (ed.), *The Wit and Wisdom of Mae West* (1967)]

14. Is that a gun in your pocket or are you just pleased to see me?
[In J. Weintraub, *Peel Me a Grape* (1975)]

15. You can say what you like about long dresses, but they cover a multitude of shins.
[In J. Weintraub, *Peel Me a Grape* (1975)]

West, Nathaniel (Nathan Wallenstein Weinstein) (1903–1940)
American novelist and screenwriter

1. Are you in trouble? Do you need advice? Write to Miss Lonelyhearts and she will help.
[*Miss Lonelyhearts* (1933)]

West, Dame Rebecca (Cicily Isabel Fairfield) (1892–1983)
English novelist, journalist, critic and feminist

1. A life of immorality which involves posing as a page-boy in an Italian hotel must have been something so rich and strange that few of us could forebear to pause and inquire.
[*The Strange Necessity* (1928)]

2. God forbid that any book should be banned. The practice is as indefensible as infanticide.
[*The Strange Necessity* (1928)]

3. The point is that nobody likes having salt rubbed into their wounds, even if it is the salt of the earth.
[*The Salt of the Earth* (1935), 2]

4. There is no such thing as conversation. It is an illusion. There are intersecting monologues, that is all.
[*There is No Conversation* (1935)]

5. But there are other things than dissipation that thicken the features. Tears, for example.
[*Black Lamb and Grey Falcon* (1942), 'Serbia']

6. Just how difficult it is to write biography can be reckoned by anybody who sits down and considers just how many people know the real truth about his or her love affairs.
[*Vogue*, 1952, 'The Art of Scepticism']

7. . . . any authentic work of art must start an argument between the artist and his audience.
[*The Court and the Castle* (1958), I, 1]

8. Margaret Thatcher's great strength seems to be the better people know her, the better they like her. But, of course, she has one great disadvantage – she is a daughter of the people and looks trim, as the daughters of the people desire to be. Shirley Williams has such an advantage over her because she's a member of the upper-middle class and can achieve that kitchen-sink-revolutionary look that one cannot get unless one has been to a really good school.
[Interview with Jilly Cooper, *The Sunday Times*, 1976]

9. [Cable sent to Noël Coward after learning they had both been on a Nazi death list]
My dear – the people we should have been seen dead with.
[*Times Literary Supplement*, 1982]

10. [Defining an anti-feminist]
The man who is convinced that his mother was a fool.
[*The Clarion*]

11. If our divorce laws were improved, we could at least say that if marriage does nobody much good it does nobody any harm.
[*The Clarion*]

12. People call me a feminist whenever I express sentiments that differentiate me from a doormat or a prostitute.
[In Anne Stibbs (ed.), *Hell Hath No Fury*]

Westmorland, John Fane, Tenth Earl of (1759–1841)
English Lord Lieutenant of Ireland, 1790–95; Lord Privy Seal, 1798–1827

1. *Merit*, indeed! . . . We are come to a pretty pass if they talk of *merit* for a bishopric.
[In C. Oman, *The Gascoyne Heiress* (1968), V]

Weston, R.P. (1878–1936) and Lee, Bert (1880–1947)
British songwriters

1. Some soldiers send epistles, say they'd sooner sleep in thistles
Than the saucy, soft, short shirts for soldiers, sister Susie sews.
['Sister Susie's Sewing Shirts for Soldiers', song, 1914]

2. Good-bye-ee! – good-bye-ee!
Wipe the tear, baby dear, from your eye-ee.
Tho' it's hard to part, I know,
I'll be tickled to death to go.
Don't cry-ee! – don't sigh-ee!
There's a silver lining in the sky-ee!–
Bonsoir, old thing! cheerio! chin-chin!
Nahpoo! Toodle-oo! Good-bye-ee!
[Song, 1918]

Wever, Robert (fl. 1550)
British dramatist and poet

1. In a harbour grene aslepe whereas I lay,
The byrdes sang swete in the middes of the day,
I dreamèd fast of mirth and play:
In youth is pleasure, in youth is pleasure.
['Lusty Juventus']

Weygand, Maxime (1867–1965)
French general in Second World War, born in Belgium; surrendered to Germany, 1940

1. [Said of the fall of France]
In three weeks England will have her neck wrung like a chicken.
[In Winston S. Churchill, *Their Finest Hour* (1949). Cf. Winston Churchill: 24]

Wharton, Edith (1862–1937)
American novelist; short-story, travel and autobiographical writer, noted for her portrayal of American society

1. She keeps on being Queenly in her own room with the door shut.
[*The House of Mirth* (1905), II, 1]

2. Mrs Ballinger is one of the ladies who pursue Culture in bands, as though it were dangerous to meet it alone.
[*Xingu and Other Stories* (1916), Title story]

3. An unalterable and unquestioned law of the musical world required that the German text of French operas sung by Swedish artists should be translated into Italian for the clearer understanding of English speaking audiences.
[*The Age of Innocence* (1920), I, 1]

4. Another unsettling element in modern art is that common symptom of immaturity, the dread of doing what has been done before.
[*The Writing of Fiction* (1925), 1]

Wharton, Thomas, First Marquis (1648–1715)
English Whig statesman; Lord Lieutenant of Ireland, 1708–10

1. [Satirical anti-Catholic ballad]
Ho, Brother *Teague*, dost hear de Decree?

Lilli Burlero Bullena-la.
Dat we shall have a new Debity,
Lilli Burlero Bullena-la.
['A New Song' (1687); first published in *Poems on Affairs of State* (1704)]

Whately, Richard (1787–1863)
English philosopher and theologian, educationist and writer; Archbishop of Dublin from 1831

1. Preach not because you have to say something, but because you have something to say.
[*Apophthegms* (1854)]
2. Happiness is no laughing matter.
[*Apophthegms* (1854)]
3. It is a folly to expect men to do all that they may reasonably be expected to do.
[*Apophthegms* (1854)]
4. Honesty is the best policy, but he who is governed by that maxim is not an honest man.
[*Apophthegms* (1854)]
5. [To a meeting of his diocesan clergy]
'Never forget, gentlemen,' he said, to his astonished hearers, as he held up a copy of the 'Authorised Version' of the Bible, 'never forget that this is *not* the Bible,' then, after a moment's pause, he continued, 'This, gentlemen, is only a *translation* of the Bible.'
[In H. Solly, *These Eighty Years* (1893)]

Wheeler, Hugh (1912–1987)
English dramatist, novelist and screenwriter

1. To lose a lover or even a husband or two during the course of one's life can be vexing. But to lose one's teeth is a catastrophe.
[*A Little Night Music* (1974)]

Whewell, William (1794–1866)
English moral philosopher, theologian, mathematician, scientist and translator

1. Hence no force however great can stretch a cord however fine into a horizontal line which is accurately straight: there will always be a bending downwards.
[*Elementary Treatise on Mechanics* (1819); often cited as an instance of accidental metre and rhyme]

Whistler, James McNeill (1834–1903)
American painter and etcher, noted for his portraits and nocturnes, and pamphleteer

1. Art is upon the Town!
[*Mr Whistler's 'Ten O'Clock'* (1885)]
2. Listen! There never was an artistic period. There never was an Art-loving nation.
[*Mr Whistler's 'Ten O'Clock'* (1885)]
3. Nature is usually wrong.
[*Mr Whistler's 'Ten O'Clock'* (1885)]
4. I am not arguing with you – I am telling you.
[*The Gentle Art of Making Enemies* (1890)]
5. *Oscar Wilde*: I wish I had said that.
Whistler: You will, Oscar, you will.
[In Ingleby, *Oscar Wilde* (1907)]
6. [Replying to a sitter's complaint that his portrait was not a great work of art]
Perhaps not, but then you can't call yourself a great work of nature.
[In D.C. Seitz, *Whistler Stories* (1913)]
7. [Replying to a lady inquiring whether he thought genius hereditary]
I cannot tell you that, madam. Heaven has granted me no offspring.
[In D.C. Seitz, *Whistler Stories* (1913)]
8. [To a lady who told him a landscape reminded her of his work]
Yes, madam, Nature is creeping up.
[In D.C. Seitz, *Whistler Stories* (1913)]
9. You shouldn't say it is not good. You should say, you do not like it; and then, you know, you're perfectly safe.
[In D.C. Seitz, *Whistler Stories* (1913)]
10. [Replying to the question 'For two days' labour, you ask two hundred guineas?']
No, I ask it for the knowledge of a lifetime.
[In D.C. Seitz, *Whistler Stories* (1913)]
11. [Replying to the pointed observation that it was as well that we do not see ourselves as others see us]
Isn't it? I know in my case I would grow intolerably conceited.
[In H. Pearson, *The Man Whistler*]
12. [His reply when asked if he agreed that the stars were especially beautiful one night]
Well, not bad, but there are decidedly too many of them, and they are not very well arranged. I would have done it differently.
[Attr.]
13. [Explaining to a snobbish lady why he had been born in such an unfashionable place as Lowell, Massachusetts]
The explanation is quite simple. I wished to be near my mother.
[Attr.]

White, Andrew Dickson (1832–1918)
American educator, historian and diplomat

1. [Refusing to allow the Cornell football team to visit Michigan to play a match]
I will not permit thirty men to travel four hundred miles to agitate a bag of wind.
[In D. Wallechinsky, *The People's Almanac*]

White, E.B. (1899–1985)
American humorist, essayist and children's writer

1. To perceive Christmas through its wrapping becomes more difficult with every year.
[*The Second Tree from the Corner* (1954)]
2. Commuter – one who spends his life
In riding to and from his wife;
A man who shaves and takes a train,
And then rides back to shave again.
['The Commuter' (1982)]

White, Henry Kirke (1785–1806)
English poet

1. Oft in danger, oft in woe,
Onward, Christians, onward go.
[Hymn, 1812]

White, Patrick (1912–1990)
Australian novelist, dramatist and short-story writer, born in England; Nobel prize, 1973

1. Anyone who stares long enough into the distance is bound to be mistaken for a philosopher or mystic in the end.
[*Happy Valley* (1939), 1]

2. The tragedy of domesticity, that avalanche of overcoats and boots.
[*The Aunt's Story* (1948)]

3. Mrs Parker's voice had been scrubbed clean of the emotions.
[*The Tree of Man* (1955), 1]

4. She would imprison the child in her house by force of love.
[*The Tree of Man* (1955), 7]

5. Virtue is, anyway, frequently in the nature of an iceberg, the other parts of it submerged.
[*The Tree of Man* (1955), 16]

6. But bombs *are* unbelievable until they actually fall.
[*Riders in the Chariot* (1961), I, 4]

7. 'I dunno,' Arthur said. 'I forget what I was taught. I only remember what I've learnt.'
[*The Solid Mandala* (1966), 2]

8. Well, good luck to you, kid! I'm going to write the Great Australian Novel.
[*The Vivisector* (1970)]

9. I have never managed to escape being this thing, Myself.
[*The Eye of the Storm* (1973)]

10. Brilliance at its best is a quality of heartless jewels, at its worst of subtle, ultimately self-destructive intrigue.
[*The Eye of the Storm* (1973)]

11. The aged are usually tougher and more calculating than the young, provided they keep enough of their wits about them. How could they have lived so long if there weren't steel buried inside them?
[*The Eye of the Storm* (1973)]

12. And remember Mother's practical ethics: *one can drown in compassion if one answers every call it's another way of suicide.*
[*The Eye of the Storm* (1973)]

13. The ideal Australia I visualised during my exile and which drew me back, was always, I realise, a landscape without figures.
[*Flaws in the Glass* (1981)]

14. Today when science has perfected the techniques of destruction, nuclear warfare could mean the immediate annihilation of what we know as civilisation, followed by a slow infection of those who inhabit the less directly involved surface of this globe – as it revolves in space – swathed in its contaminated shroud.
[Speech to public meeting on nuclear disarmament, Melbourne, 1981]

15. All my novels are an accumulation of detail. I'm a bit of a bower-bird.
[Attr.]

White, W.L. (1900–1973)
American journalist and writer; son of William Allen White

1. They Were Expendable.
[Title of book, 1942]

White, William Allen (1868–1944)
American journalist, editor, novelist and letter writer

1. [Of the Progressive Party, after Theodore Roosevelt's withdrawal from the 1916 US Presidential election]
All dressed up with nowhere to go.
[Attr.]

Whitefield, George (1714–1770)
English evangelist; Methodist preacher and writer of pamphlets, sermons and letters

1. [On Jeremiah VI:14]
You are the children of the devil, if Christ is not in you, if God has not spoken peace to your heart. Poor soul! What a cursed condition you are in. I would not be in your case for ten thousand, thousand worlds.
['The Method of Grace']

2. I had rather wear out than rust out.
[Attr.]

Whitehead, A.N. (1861–1947)
English mathematician and idealist philosopher; collaborated with Bertrand Russell, his former pupil, on Principia Mathematica

1. The safest general characterization of the European philosophical tradition is that it consists of a series of footnotes to Plato.
[*Process and Reality* (1929), II, 1]

2. It is more important that a proposition be interesting than that it be true. This statement is almost a tautology. For the energy of operation of a proposition in an occasion of experience is its interest, and is its importance. But of course a true proposition is more apt to be interesting than a false one.
[*Adventures of Ideas* (1933), IV]

3. It is the essence of life that it exists for its own sake.
[*Nature and Life* (1934)]

4. Philosophy is the product of wonder.
[*Nature and Life* (1934)]

5. There are no whole truths; all truths are half-truths. It is trying to treat them as whole truths that plays the devil.
[*Dialogues* (1954), Prologue]

6. Intelligence is quickness to apprehend as distinct from ability, which is capacity to act wisely on the thing apprehended.
[*Dialogues* (1954)]

7. Art is the imposing of a pattern on experience, and our aesthetic enjoyment is recognition of the pattern.
[*Dialogues* (1954)]

8. The systematic thought of ancient writers is now nearly worthless; but their detached insights are priceless.
[Attr.]

Whitehorn, Katherine (1926–)
English journalist and writer

1. Hats divide generally into three classes: offensive hats, defensive hats, and shrapnel.
[*Shouts and Murmurs* (1963), 'Hats']

2. The Life and Soul, the man who will never go home while there is one man, woman or glass of anything not yet drunk.
[*Sunday Best* (1976), 'Husband-Swapping']

3. It is a pity, as my husband says, that more politicians are not bastards by birth instead of vocation.
[*The Observer*, 1964]

4. The best careers advice to give to the young is 'Find out what you like doing best and get someone to pay you for doing it.'
[*The Observer*, 1975]

5. A good listener is not someone who has nothing to say. A good listener is a good talker with a sore throat.
[Attr.]

Whiteing, Richard (1840–1928)
English journalist and novelist

1. 'Did you hear that fearful cry?'
'Ah! I 'eerd somethink.'
'There's murder going on – a woman, I think.'
'Dessay. It's Sat'dy night.'
[*No 5 John Street* (1899)]

Whitelaw, William (Viscount Whitelaw) (1918–)
English politician and landowner; Conservative Home Secretary, 1979–83

1. I do not intend to prejudge the past.
[*The Times*, 1973]

2. I am not prepared to go about the country stirring up apathy.
[Attr.]

Whiting, William (1825–1878)
English teacher, poet and hymn-writer

1. Eternal Father, strong to save,
Whose arm hath bound the restless wave,
...O hear us when we cry to Thee
For those in peril on the sea.
[Hymn, 1869]

Whitlam, Gough (1916–)
Australian statesman; Labor Party leader, 1967–78, and Prime Minister, 1972–75

1. I do not mind the Liberals, still less do I mind the Country Party, calling me a bastard. In some circumstances I am only doing my job if they do. But I hope you will not publicly call me a bastard, as some bastards in the Caucus have.
[Speech to the Australian Labor Party, 9 June 1974]

2. The challenge for the writer is to adapt his ancient and difficult craft to a generation that is largely insensitive to its virtues and to a popular audience increasingly distracted by the pace, immediacy and materialism of contemporary life.
[Speech to the Australian Society of Authors, Melbourne, 1975]

3. Quite small and ineffectual demonstrations can be made to look like the beginnings of a revolution if the cameraman is in the right place at the right time.
[In Jonathon Green (ed.), *A Dictionary of Contemporary Quotations* (1982)]

Whitman, Walt (1819–1892)
American poet, journalist and essayist, noted for his free verse

1. I celebrate myself, and sing myself,
And what I assume you shall assume...

2. I loafe and invite my soul.
['Song of Myself' (1855), 1]

3. Urge and urge and urge,
Always the procreant urge of the world.
['Song of Myself' (1855), 3]

4. A child said *What is the grass?* fetching it to one with full hands,
How could I answer the child? I do not know what it is any more than he.

I guess it must be the flag of my disposition, out of the hopeful green stuff woven.

Or I guess it is the handkerchief of the Lord,
A scented gift and remembrancer designedly dropt,
Bearing the owner's name someway in the corners, that we may see and remark, and say *Whose?*...
And now it seems to me the beautiful uncut hair of graves.
['Song of Myself' (1855), 6]

5. Has anyone supposed it lucky to be born?
I hasten to inform him or her it is just as lucky to die, and I know it.
['Song of Myself' (1855), 7]

6. I believe a leaf of grass is no less than the journey-work of the stars,
And the pismire is equally perfect, and a grain of sand, and the egg of the wren,
And the tree-toad is a chef-d'oeuvre for the highest,
And the running blackberry would adorn the parlors of heaven.
['Song of Myself' (1855), 31]

7. I think I could turn and live with animals, they are so placid and self-contain'd,
I stand and look at them long and long.

They do not sweat and whine about their condition,
They do not lie awake in the dark and weep for their sins,
They do not make me sick discussing their duty to God,
Not one is dissatisfied, not one is demented with the mania of owning things,
Not one kneels to another, nor to his kind that lived thousands of years ago,
Not one is respectable or unhappy over the whole earth.
['Song of Myself' (1855), 32]

8. Behold, I do not give lectures or a little charity,
When I give I give myself.
['Song of Myself' (1855), 40]

9. My rendezvous is appointed, it is certain,
The Lord will be there and wait till I come on perfect terms,
The great Camerado, the lover true for whom I pine will be there.
['Song of Myself' (1855), 45]

10. I have said that the soul is not more than the body,
And I have said that the body is not more than the soul,
And nothing, not God, is greater than one's self is...

11. In the faces of men and women I see God, and in my own face in the glass,
I find letters from God dropt in the street, and every one is sign'd by God's name,
And I leave them where they are, for I know that wheresoe'er I go,
Others will punctually come for ever and ever.
['Song of Myself' (1855), 48]

12. Do I contradict myself?
Very well then I contradict myself,
(I am large, I contain multitudes).
['Song of Myself' (1855), 51]

13. I sound my barbaric yawp over the roofs of the world.
['Song of Myself' (1855), 52]

14. If anything is sacred the human body is sacred.
['I Sing the Body Electric' (1855)]

15. Youth, large, lusty, loving – youth full of grace, force, fascination,
Do you know that Old Age may come after you with equal grace, force, fascination?
['Youth, Day, Old Age and Night' (1855)]

16. What do you see Walt Whitman?
Who are they you salute, and that one after another salute you?
['Salut au monde' (1856)]

17. Afoot and light-hearted I take to the open road,
Healthy, free, the world before me,
The long brown path before me leading wherever I choose...

18. The earth, that is sufficient,
I do not want the constellations any nearer,
I know they are very well where they are,
I know they suffice for those who belong to them.
['Song of the Open Road' (1856)]

19. Where the populace rise at once against the never-ending audacity of elected persons...

20. Where women walk in public processions in the streets the same as the men,
Where they enter the public assembly and take places the same as the men;
Where the city of the faithfullest friends stands,
Where the city of the cleanliness of the sexes stands,
Where the city of the healthiest fathers stands,
Where the city of the best-bodied mothers stands,
There the great city stands.
['Song of the Broad Axe' (1856)]

21. The earth does not argue,
Is not pathetic, has no arrangements,
Does not scream, haste, persuade, threaten, promise.
Makes no discriminations, has no conceivable failures,
Closes nothing, refuses nothing, shuts none out.
['A Song of the Rolling Earth' (1856)]

22. Out of the cradle endlessly rocking,
Out of the mocking-bird's throat, the musical shuttle...

23. A reminiscence sing.
['Out of the cradle endlessly rocking' (1859)]

24. I hear it was charged against me that I sought to destroy institutions,
But really I am neither for nor against institutions...

25. The institution of the dear love of comrades.
['I hear it was charged against me' (1860)]

26. Me imperturbe, standing at ease in Nature.
['Me imperturbe' (1860)]

27. Camerado, this is no book,
Who touches this touches a man,
(Is it night? Are we here together alone?)
It is I you hold and who holds you,
I spring from the pages into your arms – decease calls me forth.
['So Long!' (1860)]

28. Give me the splendid silent sun with all his beams full-dazzling!
['Give me the splendid silent sun' (1865)]

29. O Captain! My Captain! our fearful trip is done,
The ship has weather'd every rack, the prize we sought is won,
The port is near, the bells I hear, the people all exulting...

30. But O heart! heart! heart!
O the bleeding drops of red,
Where on the deck my Captain lies,
Fallen cold and dead...

31. The ship is anchor'd safe and sound, its voyage closed and done.
From fearful trip the victor ship comes in with object won:
Exult O shores, and ring O bells!
But I with mournful tread,
Walk the deck my Captain lies,
Fallen cold and dead.
['O Captain! My Captain!' (1865)]

32. Come my tan-faced children,
Follow well in order, get your weapons ready,
Have you your pistols? have you your sharp-edged axes?
Pioneers! O pioneers!
['Pioneers! O Pioneers! (1865)]

33. Beautiful that war and all its deeds of carnage must in time be utterly lost,
That the hands of the sisters Death and Night incessantly softly wash again, and ever again, this soil'd world;
For my enemy is dead, a man as divine as myself is dead,
I look where he lies white-faced and still in the coffin – I draw near,
Bend down and touch lightly with my lips the white face in the coffin.
['Reconciliation' (1865)]

34. When lilacs last in the dooryard bloom'd,
And the great stars early droop'd in the western sky in the night,
I mourn'd, and yet shall mourn with ever-returning spring...

35. Come lovely and soothing death,
Undulate round the world, serenely arriving, arriving,
In the day, in the night, to all, to each,
Sooner or later, delicate death.

Prais'd be the fathomless universe,
For life and joy, and for objects and knowledge curious,
And for love, sweet love – but praise! praise! praise!
For the sure-enwinding arms of cool-enfolding death.
['When lilacs last in the dooryard bloom'd' (1865)]

36. Silent and amazed even when a little boy,
I remember I heard the preacher every Sunday put God in his statements,
As contending against some being or influence.
['A Child's Amaze' (1867)]

37. That shadow my likeness that goes to and fro seeking a livelihood, chattering, chaffering,
How often I find myself standing and looking at it where it flits,
How often I question and doubt whether that is really me.
['That shadow my likeness' (1867)]

38. Women sit or move to and fro, some old, some young.
The young are beautiful – but the old are more beautiful than the young.
['Beautiful Women' (1871)]

39. The United States themselves are essentially the greatest poem.
[*Leaves of Grass* (1855 edition), Preface]

40. After you have exhausted what there is in business, politics, conviviality, and so on – have found that none of these finally satisfy, or permanently wear – what remains? Nature remains.
[*Specimen Days and Collect* (1882), 'New Themes Entered Upon']

41. No one will ever get at my verses who insists upon viewing them as a literary performance.
[*November Boughs* (1888), 'A Backward Glance O'er Travel'd Roads']

42. Language ... is not an abstract construction of the learned, or of dictionary-makers, but is something arising out of the

work, needs, ties, joys, affections, tastes, of long generations of humanity, and has its bases broad and low, close to the ground.
[*November Boughs* (1888), 'Slang in America']

43. I no doubt deserved my enemies, but I don't believe I deserved my friends.
[In Bradford, *Biography and the Human Heart*]

Whittier, John Greenleaf (1807–1892)
American Quaker poet, abolitionist and journalist

1. The Indian Summer of the heart!
['Memories' (1841)]

2. For all sad words of tongue or pen,
The saddest are these: 'It might have been!'
['Maud Muller' (1854). Cf. Harte: 1]

3. Up from the meadows rich with corn,
Clear in the cool September morn,

The clustered spires of Frederick stand
Green-walled by the hills of Maryland...

4. Up the street came the rebel tread,
Stonewall Jackson riding ahead...

5. 'Shoot if you must, this old grey head,
But spare your country's flag,' she said.

A shade of sadness, a blush of shame,
Over the face of the leader came...

6. 'Who touches a hair of yon grey head
Dies like a dog! March on!' he said.
['Barbara Frietchie' (1863)]

7. Dear Lord and Father of mankind,
Forgive our foolish ways;
Reclothe us in our rightful mind;
In purer lives Thy service find,
In deeper reverence, praise...

8. Drop Thy still dews of quietness,
Till all our strivings cease;
Take from our souls the strain and stress,
And let our ordered lives confess
The beauty of Thy peace.
['The Brewing of Soma' (1872)]

Whittington, Robert (c. 1480–c. 1530)
English grammarian and translator from Latin

1. [Of Sir Thomas More]
As time requireth, a man of marvellous mirth and pastimes, and sometime of as sad gravity, as who say: a man for all seasons.
[*Vulgaria* (1521), II]

Whitton, Charlotte (1896–1975)
Canadian welfare consultant; first woman mayor of a Canadian city

1. Whatever women do they must do twice as well as men to be thought half as good. Luckily, this is not difficult.
[*Canada Month*, 1963]

Whitty, Larry (1943–)
General Secretary of the Labour Party

1. [Referring to the scandal surrounding the sexual behaviour of Conservative Minister, Cecil Parkinson, and which resulted in his resignation]
He came and he went.
[Remark at Labour Party Conference, 1994]

Whorf, Benjamin (1897–1941)
American anthropological linguist and engineer

1. We dissect nature along lines laid down by our native language ... Language is not simply a reporting device for experience but a defining framework for it.
[In Hoyer (ed.), *New Directions in the Study of Language* (1964)]

Whyte-Melville, George John (1821–1878)
Scottish novelist, poet, field sportsman and army officer

1. Then drink, puppy, drink, and let ev'ry puppy drink,
That is old enough to lap and swallow;
For he'll grow into a hound, so we'll pass the bottle round,
And merrily we'll whoop and we'll holloa.
['Drink, Puppy, Drink']

Wigg, George Edward Cecil, Baron (1900–1983)
English Labour politician, army officer and horse-racing enthusiast

1. For Hon. Members opposite the deterrent is a phallic symbol. It convinces them that they are men.
[*The Observer*, 'Sayings of the Week', 1964]

Wilberforce, Bishop Samuel (1805–1873)
English divine; author of religious works

1. [To T.H. Huxley]
And, in conclusion, I would like to ask the gentleman ... whether the ape from which he is descended was on his grandmother's or his grandfather's side of the family.
[Speech at Oxford, 1860. Cf. T.H. Huxley: 14]

2. If I were a cassowary
On the plains of Timbuctoo,
I would eat a missionary,
Cassock, band, and hymn-book too.
[Attr. impromptu verse; also attributed to W.M. Thackeray]

Wilcox, Ella Wheeler (1850–1919)
American poet and novelist; prolific author of romantic verse

1. We flatter those we scarcely know,
We please the fleeting guest,
And deal full many a thoughtless blow
To those who love us best.
['Life's Scars' (1917)]

2. No question is ever settled
Until it is settled right.
['Settle the Question Right' (1917)]

3. Laugh and the world laughs with you;
Weep, and you weep alone;
For the sad old earth must borrow its mirth,
But has trouble enough of its own.
['Solitude' (1917)]

4. So many gods, so many creeds,
So many paths that wind and wind,
While just the art of being kind
Is all the sad world needs.
['The World's Need' (1917)]

Wilde, Lady Jane (1826–1896)
Irish poet and society hostess; mother of Oscar Wilde

1. There's a proud array of soldiers –
what do they round your door?
They guard our master's granaries
from the thin hands of the poor.
['The Famine Years']

Wilde, Oscar (1854–1900)
Irish poet, comic dramatist, novelist, critic, wit and author of fairy tales

1. One can live for years sometimes without living at all, and then all life comes crowding into one single hour.
[*Vera, or The Nihilist* (1880), IV]

2. No, my Lord Cardinal, I weary of her!
Why, she is worse than ugly, she is good.
[*The Duchess of Padua* (1883), II]

3. We are each our own devil, and we make
This world our hell.
[*The Duchess of Padua* (1883), V]

4. Everybody who is incapable of learning has taken to teaching.
[*The Nineteenth Century*, 1889, 'The Decay of Lying']

5. [George Meredith's] style is chaos, illuminated by flashes of lightning.
[*The Nineteenth Century*, 1889, 'The Decay of Lying']

6. [Of Wordsworth]
He found in stones the sermons he had already hidden there.
[*The Nineteenth Century*, 1889, 'The Decay of Lying']

7. Art never expresses anything but itself.
[*The Nineteenth Century*, 1889, 'The Decay of Lying']

8. The final revelation is that Lying, the telling of beautiful untrue things, is the proper aim of Art.
[*The Nineteenth Century*, 1889, 'The Decay of Lying']

9. Meredith is a prose Browning, and so is Browning. He used poetry as a medium for writing in prose.
[*Intentions* (1891), 'The Critic as Artist', I]

10. As for modern journalism, it is not my business to defend it. It justifies its own existence by the great Darwinian principle of the survival of the vulgarest.
[*Intentions* (1891), 'The Critic as Artist', I]

11. To give an accurate description of what has never occurred is not merely the proper occupation of the historian, but the inalienable privilege of any man of parts and culture.
[*Intentions* (1891), 'The Critic as Artist', I]

12. Education is an admirable thing, but it is well to remember from time to time that nothing that is worth knowing can be taught.
[*Intentions* (1891), 'The Critic as Artist', I]

13. Movement, that problem of the visible arts, can be truly realized by Literature alone. It is Literature that shows us the body in its swiftness and the soul in its unrest.
[*Intentions* (1891), 'The Critic as Artist', II]

14. The man who sees both sides of a question is a man who sees absolutely nothing at all.
[*Intentions* (1891), 'The Critic as Artist', II]

15. A little sincerity is a dangerous thing, and a great deal of it is absolutely fatal.
[*Intentions* (1891), 'The Critic as Artist', II]

16. There is much to be said in favour of modern journalism. By giving us the opinions of the uneducated, it keeps us in touch with the ignorance of the community.
[*Intentions* (1891), 'The Critic as Artist', II]

17. Ah! Don't say that you agree with me. When people agree with me I always feel that I must be wrong.
[*Intentions* (1891), 'The Critic as Artist', II]

18. There is no sin except stupidity.
[*Intentions* (1891), 'The Critic as Artist', II]

19. There is no such thing as a moral or an immoral book. Books are well written, or badly written. That is all.
[*The Picture of Dorian Gray* (1891), Preface]

20. The nineteenth century dislike of Realism is the rage of Caliban seeing his own face in a glass.
[*The Picture of Dorian Gray* (1891), Preface]

21. The moral life of man forms part of the subject matter of the artist, but the morality of art consists in the perfect use of an imperfect medium.
[*The Picture of Dorian Gray* (1891), Preface]

22. All art is quite useless.
[*The Picture of Dorian Gray* (1891), Preface]

23. There is only one thing in the world worse than being talked about, and that is not being talked about.
[*The Picture of Dorian Gray* (1891), 1]

24. Being natural is simply a pose, and the most irritating pose I know.
[*The Picture of Dorian Gray* (1891), 1]

25. A man cannot be too careful in the choice of his enemies.
[*The Picture of Dorian Gray* (1891), 1]

26. The only way to get rid of a temptation is to yield to it.
[*The Picture of Dorian Gray* (1891), 2]

27. It has been said that the great events of the world take place in the brain. It is in the brain, and the brain only, that the great sins of the world take place.
[*The Picture of Dorian Gray* (1891), 2]

28. It is only shallow people who do not judge by appearances.
[*The Picture of Dorian Gray* (1891), 2]

29. I can sympathize with everything, except suffering.
[*The Picture of Dorian Gray* (1891), 3]

30. Women represent the triumph of matter over mind, just as men represent the triumph of mind over morals.
[*The Picture of Dorian Gray* (1891), 4]

31. The real drawback to marriage is that it makes one unselfish. And unselfish people are colourless.
[*The Picture of Dorian Gray* (1891), 6]

32. A cigarette is the perfect type of a perfect pleasure. It is exquisite, and it leaves one unsatisfied. What more can one want?
[*The Picture of Dorian Gray* (1891), 6]

33. It is better to be beautiful than to be good. But . . . it is better to be good than to be ugly.
[*The Picture of Dorian Gray* (1891), 17]

34. Anybody can be good in the country.
[*The Picture of Dorian Gray* (1891), 19]

35. If property had simply pleasures, we could stand it; but its duties make it unbearable. In the interest of the rich we must get rid of it.
[*The Fortnightly Review*, 1891, 'The Soul of Man under Socialism'; published under the pseudonym of Sebastian Melmoth]

36. We are often told that the poor are grateful for charity. Some of them are, no doubt, but the best amongst the poor are never grateful. They are ungrateful, discontented, disobedient, and rebellious. They are quite right to be so.
[*The Fortnightly Review*, 1891, 'The Soul of Man under Socialism'; published under the pseudonym of Sebastian Melmoth]

37. As for the virtuous poor, one can pity them, of course, but one cannot possibly admire them. They have made private

terms with the enemy, and sold their birthright for very bad pottage.
[*The Fortnightly Review*, 1891, 'The Soul of Man under Socialism'; published under the pseudonym of Sebastian Melmoth]

38. Democracy means simply the bludgeoning of the people by the people for the people.
[*The Fortnightly Review*, 1891, 'The Soul of Man under Socialism'; published under the pseudonym of Sebastian Melmoth. Cf. Daniel Webster: 2]

39. He who would be free ... must not conform.
[*The Fortnightly Review*, 1891, 'The Soul of Man under Socialism'; published under the pseudonym of Sebastian Melmoth]

40. A community is infinitely more brutalised by the habitual employment of punishment than it is by the occasional occurrence of crime.
[*The Fortnightly Review*, 1891, 'The Soul of Man under Socialism'; published under the pseudonym of Sebastian Melmoth]

41. Art is the most intense mode of individualism that the world has known.
[*The Fortnightly Review*, 1891, 'The Soul of Man under Socialism'; published under the pseudonym of Sebastian Melmoth]

42. The Lords Temporal say nothing, the Lords Spiritual have nothing to say, and the House of Commons has nothing to say and says it. We are dominated by Journalism.
[*The Fortnightly Review*, 1891, 'The Soul of Man under Socialism'; published under the pseudonym of Sebastian Melmoth]

43. Anybody can sympathise with the sufferings of a friend, but it requires a very fine nature to sympathise with a friend's success.
[*The Fortnightly Review*, 1891, 'The Soul of Man under Socialism'; published under the pseudonym of Sebastian Melmoth. Cf. Vidal: 6]

44. It is absurd to divide people into good and bad. People are either charming or tedious.
[*Lady Windermere's Fan* (1892), I]

45. I couldn't help it. I can resist everything except temptation.
[*Lady Windermere's Fan* (1892), I]

46. Many a woman has a past, but I am told that she has at least a dozen, and that they all fit.
[*Lady Windermere's Fan* (1892), I]

47. Do you know, Mr Hopper, dear Agatha and I are so much interested in Australia. It must be so pretty with all the dear little kangaroos flying about.
[*Lady Windermere's Fan* (1892), II]

48. I am the only person in the world I should like to know thoroughly.
[*Lady Windermere's Fan* (1892), II]

49. We are all in the gutter, but some of us are looking at the stars.
[*Lady Windermere's Fan* (1892), III]

50. There's nothing in the world like the devotion of a married woman. It's a thing no married man knows anything about.
[*Lady Windermere's Fan* (1893), III]

51. *Cecil Graham*: What is a cynic?
Lord Darlington: A man who knows the price of everything and the value of nothing.
[*Lady Windermere's Fan* (1892), III]

52. *Dumby*: Experience is the name every one gives to their mistakes.
Cecil Graham: One shouldn't commit any.
Dumby: Life would be very dull without them.
[*Lady Windermere's Fan* (1892), III]

53. It is not customary in England, Miss Worsley, for a young lady to speak with such enthusiasm of any person of the opposite sex. English women conceal their feelings till after they are married.
[*A Woman of No Importance* (1893), I]

54. The youth of America is their oldest tradition. It has been going on now for three hundred years.
[*A Woman of No Importance* (1893), I]

55. The English country gentleman galloping after a fox – the unspeakable in full pursuit of the uneatable.
[*A Woman of No Importance* (1893), I]

56. Twenty years of romance make a woman look like a ruin; but twenty years of marriage make her something like a public building.
[*A Woman of No Importance* (1893), I]

57. One should never trust a woman who tells one her real age. A woman who would tell one that would tell one anything.
[*A Woman of No Importance* (1893), I]

58. We women adore failures. They lean on us.
[*A Woman of No Importance* (1893), I]

59. *Lord Illingworth*: The soul is born old but grows young. That is the comedy of life.
Mrs Allonby: And the body is born young and grows old. That is life's tragedy.
[*A Woman of No Importance* (1893), I]

60. *Lord Illingworth*: The Book of Life begins with a man and a woman in a garden.
Mrs Allonby: It ends with Revelations.
[*A Woman of No Importance* (1893), I]

61. Nothing is so aggravating as calmness. There is something positively brutal about the good temper of most modern men.
[*A Woman of No Importance* (1893), II]

62. Children begin by loving their parents. After a time they judge them. Rarely, if ever, do they forgive them.
[*A Woman of No Importance* (1893), II]

63. A well-tied tie is the first serious step in life.
[*A Woman of No Importance* (1893), III]

64. [Of society]
To be in it is merely a bore. But to be out of it simply a tragedy.
[*A Woman of No Importance* (1893), III]

65. Moderation is a fatal thing, Lady Hunstanton. Nothing succeeds like excess.
[*A Woman of No Importance* (1893), III]

66. When one is in love one begins by deceiving oneself. And one ends by deceiving others.
[*A Woman of No Importance* (1893), III]

67. You should study the Peerage, Gerald. It is the one book a young man about town should know thoroughly, and it is the best thing in fiction the English have ever done.
[*A Woman of No Importance* (1893), III]

68. *Mrs Allonby*: I delight in men over seventy. They always offer one the devotion of a lifetime.
[*A Woman of No Importance* (1893), IV]

69. Wickedness is a myth invented by good people to account for the curious attractiveness of others.
[*The Chameleon*, 1894, 'Phrases and Philosophies for the Use of the Young']

70. Nothing that actually occurs is of the smallest importance.
[*The Chameleon*, 1894, 'Phrases and Philosophies for the Use of the Young']

71. If one tells the truth, one is sure, sooner or later, to be found out.
[*The Chameleon*, 1894, 'Phrases and Philosophies for the Use of the Young']

72. It is only by not paying one's bills that one can hope to live in the memory of the commercial classes.
[*The Chameleon*, 1894, 'Phrases and Philosophies for the Use of the Young']

73. In examinations the foolish ask questions that the wise cannot answer.
[*The Chameleon*, 1894, 'Phrases and Philosophies for the Use of the Young']

74. The old believe everything: the middle-aged suspect everything: the young know everything.
[*The Chameleon*, 1894, 'Phrases and Philosophies for the Use of the Young']

75. Men can be analysed, women ... merely adored.
[*An Ideal Husband* (1895), I]

76. Questions are never indiscreet. Answers sometimes are.
[*An Ideal Husband* (1895), I]

77. Morality is simply the attitude we adopt towards people whom we personally dislike.
[*An Ideal Husband* (1895), II]

78. Other people are quite dreadful. The only possible society is oneself.
[*An Ideal Husband* (1895), II]

79. To love oneself is the beginning of a lifelong romance, Phipps.
[*An Ideal Husband* (1895), III]

80. Really, if the lower orders don't set us a good example, what on earth is the use of them? They seem, as a class, to have absolutely no sense of moral responsibility.
[*The Importance of Being Earnest* (1895), I]

81. It is very vulgar to talk like a dentist when one isn't a dentist. It produces a false impression.
[*The Importance of Being Earnest* (1895), I]

82. The truth is rarely pure and never simple. Modern life would be very tedious if it were either, and modern literature a complete impossibility!
[*The Importance of Being Earnest* (1895), I]

83. I have invented an invaluable permanent invalid called Bunbury, in order that I may be able to go down into the country whenever I choose.
[*The Importance of Being Earnest* (1895), I]

84. The amount of women in London who flirt with their own husbands is perfectly scandalous. It looks so bad. It is simply washing one's clean linen in public.
[*The Importance of Being Earnest* (1895), I]

85. You don't seem to realise, that in married life three is company and two is none.
[*The Importance of Being Earnest* (1895), I]

86. Ignorance is like a delicate exotic fruit; touch it, and the bloom is gone.
[*The Importance of Being Earnest* (1895), I]

87. To lose one parent may be regarded as a misfortune ... to lose both seems like carelessness.
[*The Importance of Being Earnest* (1895), I]

88. All women become like their mothers. That is their tragedy. No man does. That's his.
[*The Importance of Being Earnest* (1895), I]

89. The old-fashioned respect for the young is fast dying out.
[*The Importance of Being Earnest* (1895), I]

90. The good ended happily, and the bad unhappily. That is what Fiction means.
[*The Importance of Being Earnest* (1895), II. Cf. Stoppard: 7]

91. I hope that you have not been leading a double life, pretending to be wicked and being really good all the time. That would be hypocrisy.
[*The Importance of Being Earnest* (1895), II]

92. Charity, dear Miss Prism, charity! None of us are perfect. I myself am peculiarly susceptible to draughts.
[*The Importance of Being Earnest* (1895), II]

93. I never travel without my diary. One should always have something sensational to read in the train.
[*The Importance of Being Earnest* (1895), III]

94. On an occasion of this kind it becomes more than a moral duty to speak one's mind. It becomes a pleasure.
[*The Importance of Being Earnest* (1895), III]

95. *Cecily*: When I see a spade I call it a spade.
Gwendolen: I am glad to say that I have never seen a spade. It is obvious that our social spheres have been widely different.
[*The Importance of Being Earnest* (1895), III]

96. In matters of grave importance, style, not sincerity, is the vital thing.
[*The Importance of Being Earnest* (1895), IV]

97. Three addresses always inspire confidence, even in tradesmen.
[*The Importance of Being Earnest* (1895), IV]

98. I am not in favour of long engagements. They give people the opportunity of finding out each other's character before marriage, which I think is never advisable.
[*The Importance of Being Earnest* (1895), IV]

99. Untruthful! My nephew Algernon? Impossible! He is an Oxonian.
[*The Importance of Being Earnest* (1895), IV]

100. No woman should ever be quite accurate about her age. It looks so calculating.
[*The Importance of Being Earnest* (1895), IV]

101. This suspense is terrible. I hope it will last.
[*The Importance of Being Earnest* (1895), IV]

102. Where there is sorrow, there is holy ground.
[*De Profundis* (1897)]

103. I became the spendthrift of my own genius and to waste an eternal youth gave me a curious joy.
[*De Profundis* (1897)]

104. Most people are other people. Their thoughts are someone else's opinions, their lives a mimicry, their passions a quotation.
[*De Profundis* (1897)]

105. A thing is not necessarily true because a man dies for it.
[*Sebastian Melmoth* (1904 edition)]

106. [On a notice at a dancing saloon]
I saw the only rational method of art criticism I have ever come across ... 'Please do not shoot the pianist. He is doing

his best.' The mortality among pianists in that place is marvellous.
['Impressions of America' (1906)]

107. One's real life is so often the life that one does not lead.
[L'Envoi to Rose-Leaf and Apple-Leaf]

108. Sing on! Sing on! I would be drunk with life,
Drunk with the trampled vintage of my youth.
['The Burden of Itys' (1881)]

109. And down the long and silent street,
The dawn, with silver-sandalled feet,
Crept like a frightened girl.
['The Harlot's House' (1881)]

110. All her bright golden hair
Tarnished with rust,
She that was young and fair
Fallen to dust.
['Requiescat' (1881)]

111. And yet, and yet,
These Christs that die upon the barricades,
God knows it I am with them, in some things.
['Sonnet to Liberty: Not that I Love Thy Children' (1881)]

112. When a voice behind me whispered low,
'That fellow's got to swing.'...

113. Yet each man kills the thing he loves,
By each let this be heard,
Some do it with a bitter look,
Some with a flattering word,
The coward does it with a kiss,
The brave man with a sword!
[*The Ballad of Reading Gaol* (1898), I]

114. Like two doomed ships that pass in storm
We had crossed each other's way:
But we made no sign, we said no word,
We had no word to say.
[*The Ballad of Reading Gaol* (1898), II]

115. *'He does not win who plays with sin*
In the secret House of Shame'...

116. Something was dead in each of us,
And what was dead was Hope.

For Man's grim Justice goes its way,
And will not swerve aside:
It slays the weak, it slays the strong,
It has a deadly stride...

117. And the wild regrets, and the bloody sweats,
None knew so well as I:
For he who lives more lives than one
More deaths than one must die.
[*The Ballad of Reading Gaol* (1898), III]

118. There is no chapel on the day
On which they hang a man.
[*The Ballad of Reading Gaol* (1898), IV]

119. I know not whether Laws be right,
Or whether Laws be wrong;
All that we know who lie in gaol
Is that the wall is strong;
And that each day is like a year,
A year whose days are long...

120. The vilest deeds like poison-weeds
Bloom well in prison-air;
It is only what is good in Man
That wastes and withers there:
Pale Anguish keeps the heavy gate
And the warder is Despair.
[*The Ballad of Reading Gaol* (1898), V]

121. No publisher should ever express an opinion of the value of what he publishes. That is a matter entirely for the literary critic to decide ... A publisher is simply a useful middle-man. It is not for him to anticipate the verdict of criticism.
[Letter in *St James's Gazette*, 1890]

122. [On the artist James Whistler]
With our James vulgarity begins at home, and should be allowed to stay there.
[Letter to the *World*]

123. Those things which the English public never forgives – youth, power, and enthusiasm.
[In R. Ross (ed.), *Collected Works of Oscar Wilde* (1908), 'The English Renaissance']

124. [Spoken to André Gide]
Voulez-vous savoir le grand drame de ma vie? C'est que j'ai mis mon génie dans ma vie; je n'ai mis que mon talent dans mes oeuvres.
Do you want to know the great tragedy of my life? I have put all of my genius into my life; all I've put into my works is my talent.
[In André Gide, *Oscar Wilde* (1910), 'In Memoriam']

125. [At the New York Customs]
I have nothing to declare except my genius.
[In F. Harris, *Oscar Wilde* (1918)]

126. There seems to be some curious connection between piety and poor rhymes.
[In Lucas (ed.), *A Critic in Pall Mall* (1919)]

127. [From an unpublished character sketch of W.E. Henley]
He has fought a good fight and has had to face every difficulty except popularity.
[In W. Rothenstein, *Men and Memories* (1931)]

128. Work is the curse of the drinking classes.
[In H. Pearson, *Life of Oscar Wilde* (1946)]

129. [Of Bernard Shaw]
He hasn't an enemy in the world, and none of his friends like him.
[In Shaw, *Sixteen Self Sketches* (1949)]

130. [In a lecture on Dickens]
One would have to have a heart of stone to read the death of Little Nell without laughing.
[In H. Pearson, *Lives of the Wits*]

131. [Said to Frank Harris who was listing the houses he had dined at]
Dear Frank, we believe you; you have dined in every house in London – *once*.
[Attr.]

132. I must decline your invitation owing to a subsequent engagement.
[Attr.]

133. I have made an important discovery ... that alcohol, taken in sufficient quantities, produces all the effects of intoxication.
[Attr.]

134. The English have a miraculous power of turning wine into water.
[Attr.]

135. Patriotism is the virtue of the vicious.
[Attr.]

136. [Refusing to attend a function at a club whose members were hostile to him]
I should be like a lion in a cage of savage Daniels.
[Attr.]

137. [Last words, as he lay dying in a drab Paris bedroom]
Either that wallpaper goes, or I do.
[*Time*, 16 January 1984]

Wilder, Billy (1906–)
American film director, producer and screenwriter, born in Austria; Academy Awards 1945, 1960

1. I've met a lot of hardboiled eggs in my time, but you're twenty minutes.
[*Ace in the Hole*, film, 1951; scriptwriters Billy Wilder, Lesser Samuels and Walter Newman]

2. France is a country where the money falls apart in your hands and you can't tear the toilet paper.
[In Halliwell, *Filmgoer's Book of Quotes* (1973)]

3. [Said to Cliff Osmond]
You have Van Gogh's ear for music.
[Attr.]

Wilder, Thornton (1897–1975)
American dramatist, novelist and teacher

1. A living is made, Mr Kemper, by selling something that everybody needs at least once a year. Yes, sir! And a million is made by producing something that everybody needs every day. You artists produce something that nobody needs at any time.
[*The Merchant of Yonkers* (1939), II; later revised and retitled *The Matchmaker*. Cf. Warhol: 2]

2. When you're at war you think about a better life; when you're at peace you think about a more comfortable one.
[*The Skin of Our Teeth* (1942), III]

3. The best part of married life is the fights. The rest is merely so-so.
[*The Matchmaker* (1954), II]

4. Literature is the orchestration of platitudes.
[*Time*, 1953]

Wilhelm I, Kaiser (1797–1888)
King of Prussia from 1861 and first Emperor of Germany, from 1871

1. [Said during his last illness]
I haven't got time to be tired.
[Attr.]

Wilhelm II, Kaiser (1859–1941)
Emperor of Germany and King of Prussia, 1888–1918; forced to abdicate

1. You will be home before the leaves have fallen from the trees.
[Remark to troops leaving for the Front, August 1914]

2. The Admiral of the Atlantic salutes the Admiral of the Pacific.
[Telegram sent to Czar Nicholas II during a naval exercise]

3. I would have liked to go to Ireland, but my grandmother [Queen Victoria] would not let me. Perhaps she thought I wanted to take the little place.
[In H. Montgomery Hyde, *Carson*]

4. [Referring to the British Expeditionary Force in 1914]
A contemptible little army.
[Attr.]

Wilkes, John (1727–1797)
English politician and parliamentary reformer

1. [Reply to Lord Sandwich, who had told him that he would die either on the gallows or of the pox]
That must depend on whether I embrace your lordship's principles or your mistress.
[Attr. in Sir Charles Petrie, *The Four Georges* (1935)]

Wilkinson, Ellen Cicely (1891–1947)
English feminist, trade unionist and Labour politician; Minister of Education 1945–47

1. I should like to help Britain become a Third Programme country.
[*The Observer*, 'Sayings of the Week', 1947]

Willard, Emma Hart (1787–1870)
American teacher and writer; pioneer of women's education

1. Rock'd in the cradle of the deep
I lay me down in peace to sleep
Secure I rest upon the wave
For Thou, O Lord, hast power to save.
I know Thou wilt not slight my call,
For Thou dost note the sparrow's fall
And calm and peaceful is my sleep,
Rock'd in the cradle of the deep.
[Song, 1840]

William I (William the Conqueror) (1027–1087)
Duke of Normandy from 1035 and King of England after defeating Harold II at Hastings

1. [Said after falling over as he came ashore at Pevensey with his army of invasion]
By the splendour of God I have taken possession of my realm; the earth of England is in my two hands.
[Attr.]

William III (William of Orange) (1650–1702)
King of Great Britain and Ireland from 1689

1. Every bullet has its billet.
[In John Wesley, *Journal* (1827), 6 June 1765]

2. [Of Holland, his country of birth]
There is one way never to see it lost, and that is to die in the last ditch.
[In Gilbert Burnet, *History of My Own Time* (1838 edition)]

William of Wykeham (1324–1404)
English Bishop of Winchester from 1367, Chancellor of England 1368–71, and founder of New College, Oxford (1380)

1. Manners maketh man.
[Motto of Winchester College and New College, Oxford]

Williams, Kenneth (1926–1988)
English stage, radio and film actor and comedian

1. The nicest thing about quotes is that they give us a nodding acquaintance with the originator which is often socially impressive.
[*Acid Drops* (1980)]

Williams, Tennessee (Thomas Lanier Williams) (1911–1983)
American dramatist, noted for his dialogue, characterization and Deep South settings; novelist and short-story writer

1. Knowledge – Zzzzzp! Money – Zzzzzp! – Power! That's the cycle democracy is built on!
[*The Glass Menagerie* (1945)]

2. I can't stand a naked light bulb, any more than I can a rude remark or a vulgar action.
[*A Streetcar Named Desire* (1947), II]

3. I have always depended on the kindness of strangers.
[*A Streetcar Named Desire* (1947), II]

4. We have to distrust each other. It's our only defence against betrayal.
[*Camino Real* (1953), Block 10]

5. You can be young without money but you can't be old without it.
[*Cat on a Hot Tin Roof* (1955), I]

6. If people behaved in the way nations do they would all be put in straitjackets.
[BBC interview]

7. [Explaining why he had stopped seeing his psychoanalyst] He was meddling too much in my private life.
[Attr.]

Williams, William Carlos (1883–1963)

American objectivist poet, short-story writer, novelist, essayist, letter writer and paediatrician

1. On a tissue-thin monotone of blue-grey buds
two blue-grey birds, chasing a third,
at full cry! Now they are
flung outward and up – disappearing suddenly!
['Spring Strains' (1917)]

2. so much depends
upon
a red wheel
barrow
glazed with rain
water
beside the white
chickens.
['The Red Wheelbarrow' (1923)]

3. I have eaten
the plums
that were in
the icebox

and which
you were probably
saving
for breakfast

Forgive me
they were delicious
so sweet
and so cold
['This Is Just to Say' (1934)]

4. Is it any better in Heaven, my friend Ford,
Than you found it in Provence?
['To Ford Madox Ford in Heaven' (1944)]

5. Of Asphodel, that greeny flower, . . .
I come, my sweet,
to sing to you . . .

6. As I think of it now,
after a lifetime,
it is as if
a sweet-scented flower
were poised
and for me did open.
Asphodel
has no odor
save to the imagination
but it too
celebrates the light.
['Asphodel, that Greeny Flower' (1955)]

7. Minds like beds always made up,
(more stony than a shore)
unwilling or unable.
[*Paterson* (1946–1958), Preface]

8. . . . no ideas but in things.
[*Paterson* (1946–1958), I, 1]

9. In old age
the mind
casts off
rebelliously
an eagle
from its crag.
[*Paterson* (1946–1958), V, 1]

10. no woman is virtuous
who does not give herself to her lover
– forthwith.
[*Paterson* (1946–1958), V, 3]

Williamson, Malcolm (1931–)

Master of the Queen's Music

1. Lloyd Webber's music is everywhere, but so is Aids.
[Attr.]

Willkie, Wendell (1892–1944)

American lawyer, industrialist and Republican presidential candidate, 1940

1. Freedom is an indivisible word. If we want to enjoy it, and fight for it, we must be prepared to extend it to everyone, whether they are rich or poor, whether they agree with us or not, no matter what their race or the colour of their skin.
[*One World* (1943), 13]

2. The Constitution does not provide for first and second class citizens.
[*An American Program* (1944), 2]

Willmore, Alfred (Michael MacLiammoir) (1899–1978)

Irish actor, painter and writer

1. The Importance of Being Oscar.
[Title of one-man show about Oscar Wilde]

2. All for Hecuba.
[Title of autobiographical volume]

Wilson, A.N. (1950–)

English novelist, biographer and journalist

1. It has to be admitted that Boswell's Scottish life, which he himself found so hellishly boring, reads even more boringly when it is recounted by a painstaking modern scholar from the University of Yale.
[*Penfriends from Porlock* (1988), 'James Boswell']

Wilson, Sir Angus (1913–1991)

English novelist, short-story writer and critic; noted for his social satire

1. 'God knows how you Protestants can be expected to have any sense of direction,' she said. 'It's different with us. I haven't been to mass for years, I've got every mortal sin on my conscience, but I know when I'm doing wrong. I'm still a Catholic.'
[*The Wrong Set* (1949), 'Significant Experience']

2. I have no concern for the common man except that he should not be so common.
[*No Laughing Matter* (1967)]

Wilson, Charles E. (1890–1961)
American industrialist, car manufacturer and politician; Secretary of Defence, 1953–57

1. What is good for the country is good for General Motors, and vice versa.
[Remark to Congressional Committee, 1953]

Wilson, Harold (Baron Wilson of Rievaulx) (1916–1995)
English statesman; Labour party leader, 1963–76, and Prime Minister, 1964–70, 1974–76

1. The little gnomes of Zurich.
[Speech, 1956]

2. [Referring to Christine Keeler]
There is something utterly nauseating about a system of society which pays a harlot 25 times as much as it pays its Prime Minister, 250 times as much as it pays its Members of Parliament, and 500 times as much as it pays some of its ministers of religion.
[Speech, 1963]

3. After half a century of democratic advance, the whole process has ground to a halt with a 14th Earl.
[Speech, 1963. Cf. Sir Alec Douglas-Home: 2]

4. We are redefining and we are restating our socialism in terms of the scientific revolution ... the Britain that is going to be forged in the white heat of this revolution will be no place for restrictive practices or out-dated methods on either side of industry.
[Speech, 1963]

5. A week is a long time in politics.
[Remark, 1964]

6. It does not mean, of course, that the pound here in Britain, in your pocket or purse or in your bank, has been devalued.
[T.V. broadcast, 1967]

7. I believe the greatest asset a head of state can have is the ability to get a good night's sleep.
[Radio broadcast, 1975]

8. [Of Tony Benn]
He immatures with age.
[Attr., BBC programme, 1995]

9. Hence the practised performances of latter-day politicians in the game of musical daggers: never be left holding the dagger when the music stops.
[*The Governance of Britain*, 2]

10. If I had the choice between smoked salmon and tinned salmon, I'd have it tinned. With vinegar.
[*The Observer*, 'Sayings of the Week', 1962]

11. Everybody should have an equal chance – but they shouldn't have a flying start.
[*The Observer*, 'Sayings of the Week', 1963]

12. One man's wage rise is another man's price increase.
[*The Observer*, 'Sayings of the Week', 1970]

13. The monarchy is a labour-intensive industry.
[*The Observer*, 'Sayings of the Week', 1977]

Wilson, Harriette (née Dubochet) (1789–1846)
English courtesan and memoirist

1. I shall not say why and how I became, at the age of fifteen, the mistress of the Earl of Craven.
[*Memoirs* (1825), first sentence]

Wilson, Woodrow (1856–1924)
American statesman; Democrat President 1913–21; helped found the League of Nations; Nobel peace prize, 1919

1. Generally young men are regarded as radicals. This is a popular misconception. The most conservative persons I ever met are college undergraduates.
[Speech, 1905]

2. America lives in the heart of every man everywhere who wishes to find a region where he will be free to work out his destiny as he chooses.
[Speech, 1912]

3. The history of liberty is a history of resistance.
[Speech, 1912]

4. Business underlies everything in our national life, including our spiritual life. Witness the fact that in the Lord's Prayer the first petition is for daily bread. No one can worship God or love his neighbour on an empty stomach.
[Speech, 1912]

5. I fancy that it is just as hard to do your duty when men are sneering at you as when they are shooting at you.
[Speech, 1914]

6. No nation is fit to sit in judgement upon any other nation.
[Speech, 1915]

7. Character is a by-product; it is produced in the great manufacture of daily duty.
[Speech, 1915]

8. We have stood apart, studiously neutral.
[Speech, 1915]

9. There is a price which is too great to pay for peace, and that price can be put in one word. One cannot pay the price of self-respect.
[Speech, 1916]

10. Armed neutrality is ineffectual enough at best.
[Speech, 1917]

11. It must be a peace without victory ... only a peace between equals can last.
[Speech, 1917]

12. The world must be made safe for democracy.
[Speech, 1917]

13. Open covenants of peace, openly arrived at, after which there shall be no private international understandings of any kind, but diplomacy shall proceed always frankly and in the public view.
['Fourteen Points', Speech, 1918]

14. America is the only idealistic nation in the world.
[Speech, 1919]

15. Never murder a man who is committing suicide.
[In John Dos Passos, *Mr Wilson's War* (1917), II, 10]

16. Once lead this people into war and they'll forget there ever was such a thing as tolerance.
[In John Dos Passos, *Mr Wilson's War* (1917), III, 12]

Winchell, Walter (1897–1972)
American drama critic, columnist and broadcaster

1. [Referring to a show starring Earl Carroll]
I saw it at a disadvantage – the curtain was up.
[In A. Whiteman, *Come to Judgement*]

Winchilsea, Anne Finch, Lady (1661–1720)
English poet

1. Now the Jonquille o'ercomes the feeble brain;
We faint beneath the aromatic pain.
['The Spleen' (1701)]

Windham, William (1750–1810)
English statesman and diarist; Secretary of War, 1794–1801

1. Those entrusted with arms ... should be persons of some substance and stake in the country.
[House of Commons, 1807]

Windsor, Duchess of (Wallis Simpson) (1896–1986)
Twice-divorced American socialite; married Edward VIII in 1937 following his abdication

1. I don't remember any love affairs. One must keep love affairs quiet.
[*Los Angeles Times*, 1974]

2. One can never be too thin or too rich.
[Attr.]

Winthrop, Robert Charles (1809–1894)
American orator, lawyer and senator

1. A Star for every State, and a State for every Star.
[Speech on Boston Common, 1862]

Wister, Owen (1860–1938)
American novelist, short-story writer and biographer

1. [To an enemy who had called him a son-of-a-bitch]
When you call me that, *smile*!
[*The Virginian* (1902), 2]

Wither, George (1588–1667)
English poet, pamphleteer and Puritan

1. Shall I, wasting in despair,
Die because a woman's fair?
Or make pale my cheeks with care,
'Cause another's rosy are?
Be she fairer than the day,
Or the flow'ry meads in May;
If she think not well of me,
What care I how fair she be?
['Sonnet' (1622)]

2. Hang sorrow, care will kill a cat,
And therefore let's be merry.
['Christmas']

Wittgenstein, Ludwig (1889–1951)
Austrian-born British philosopher of linguistics; influential on logical positivism

1. The solution of the problem of life is seen in the vanishing of the problem.
[*Tractatus Logico-Philosophicus* (1922)]

2. What can be said at all can be said clearly; and whereof one cannot speak, thereon one must keep silent.
[*Tractatus Logico-Philosophicus* (1922)]

3. Logic must look after itself.
[*Tractatus Logico-Philosophicus* (1922)]

4. In order to draw a limit to thinking, we should have to be able to think both sides of this limit.
[*Tractatus Logico-Philosophicus* (1922)]

5. Philosophy is not a theory but an activity.
[*Tractatus Logico-Philosophicus* (1922)]

6. Philosophy is a struggle against the bewitching of our minds by means of language.
[*Philosophical Investigations* (1953)]

7. If there were a verb meaning 'to believe falsely', it would not have any significant first person, present indicative.
[*Philosophical Investigations* (1953)]

Woddis, Roger
British satirical poet and scriptwriter

1. Men play the game; women know the score.
[*The Observer*, 1982, in Jeffrey Care (ed.), *Sayings of the Eighties* (1989)]

Wodehouse, P.G. (1881–1975)
English humorist; novelist, short-story writer and librettist, noted for his literary skill; American citizen from 1955

1. It is a good rule in life never to apologize. The right sort of people do not want apologies, and the wrong sort take a mean advantage of them.
[*The Man Upstairs* (1914)]

2. His ideas of first-aid stopped short at squirting soda-water.
[*My Man Jeeves* (1919), 'Doing Clarence a Bit of Good']

3. I don't owe a penny to a single soul – not counting tradesmen, of course.
[*My Man Jeeves* (1919), 'Jeeves and the Hard-Boiled Egg']

4. What with excellent browsing and sluicing and cheery conversation and what-not the afternoon passed quite happily.
[*My Man Jeeves* (1919), 'Jeeves and the Unbidden Guest']

5. She fitted into my biggest armchair as if it had been built round her by someone who knew they were wearing armchairs tight about the hips that season.
[*My Man Jeeves* (1919), 'Jeeves and the Unbidden Guest']

6. I spent the afternoon musing on Life. If you come to think of it, what a queer thing Life is! So unlike anything else, don't you know, if you see what I mean.
[*My Man Jeeves* (1919), 'Rallying Round Old George']

7. If I had had to choose between him and a cockroach as a companion for a walking-tour, the cockroach would have had it by a short head.
[*My Man Jeeves* (1919), 'A Spot of Art']

8. All the unhappy marriages come from the husbands having brains. What good are brains to a man? They only unsettle him.
[*The Adventures of Sally* (1920), 10]

9. It was my Uncle George who discovered that alcohol was a food well in advance of modern medical thought.
[*The Inimitable Jeeves* (1923)]

10. She had a penetrating sort of laugh. Rather like a train going into a tunnel.
[*The Inimitable Jeeves* (1923)]

11. Jeeves coughed one soft, low, gentle cough like a sheep with a blade of grass stuck in its throat.
[*The Inimitable Jeeves* (1923)]

12. There was another ring at the front door. Jeeves shimmered out and came back with a telegram.
[*Carry On, Jeeves!* (1925), 'Jeeves Takes Charge']

13. To my daughter Leonora without whose never-failing sympathy and encouragement this book would have been finished in half the time.
[*The Heart of a Goof* (1926), Dedication]

14. Her hair was a deep chestnut, her eyes blue, her nose small and laid back with about as much loft as a light iron.
[*The Heart of a Goof* (1926), 'Chester Forgets Himself']

15. The lunches of fifty-seven years had caused his chest to slip down to the mezzanine floor.
[*The Heart of a Goof* (1926), 'Chester Forgets Himself']

16. While they were content to peck cautiously at the ball, he never spared himself in his efforts to do it a violent injury.
[*The Heart of a Goof* (1926), 'Chester Forgets Himself']

17. The Right Hon was a tubby little chap who looked as if he had been poured into his clothes and had forgotten to say 'When!'
[*Very Good, Jeeves* (1930), 'Jeeves and the Impending Doom']

18. I can honestly say that I always look on Pauline as one of the nicest girls I was ever engaged to.
[*Thank You Jeeves* (1934), 6]

19. It is never difficult to distinguish between a Scotsman with a grievance and a ray of sunshine.
[*Blandings Castle and Elsewhere* (1935), 'The Custody of the Pumpkin']

20. He spoke with a certain what-is-it in his voice, and I could see that, if not actually disgruntled, he was far from being gruntled.
[*The Code of the Woosters* (1938), 1]

21. Slice him where you like, a hellhound is always a hellhound.
[*The Code of the Woosters* (1938), 1]

22. It is no use telling me that there are bad aunts and good aunts. At the core they are all alike. Sooner or later, out pops the cloven hoof.
[*The Code of the Woosters* (1938), 2]

23. Big chap with a small moustache and the sort of eye that can open an oyster at sixty paces.
[*The Code of the Woosters* (1938), 2]

24. There is only one cure for grey hair. It was invented by a Frenchman. It is called the guillotine.
[*The Old Reliable* (1951)]

25. Ice formed on the butler's upper slopes.
[*Pigs Have Wings* (1952)]

26. They tell me I was writing when I was five, but it seems rather extraordinary, doesn't it?
[Television interview with Malcolm Muggeridge, 1965]

27. The stationmaster's whiskers are of a Victorian bushiness and give the impression of having been grown under glass.
[In R. Usborne, *Wodehouse at Work to the End* (1976), 2]

28. Like so many substantial Americans, he had married young and kept on marrying, springing from blonde to blonde like the chamois of the Alps leaping from crag to crag.
[In R. Usborne, *Wodehouse at Work to the End* (1976), 2]

29. Unlike the male codfish which, suddenly finding itself the parent of three million five hundred thousand little codfish, cheerfully resolves to love them all, the British aristocracy is apt to look with a somewhat jaundiced eye on its younger sons.
[In R. Usborne, *Wodehouse at Work to the End* (1976), 5]

30. He was either a man of about a hundred and fifty who was rather young for his years or a man of about a hundred and ten who had been aged by trouble.
[In R. Usborne, *Wodehouse at Work to the End* (1976), 6]

Wolfe, Charles (1791–1823)
Irish poet and clergyman

1. Not a drum was heard, not a funeral note,
As his corse to the rampart we hurried...

2. We buried him darkly at dead of night,
The sods with our bayonets turning...

3. But he lay like a warrior taking his rest,
With his martial cloak around him...

4. We carved not a line, and we raised not a stone–
But we left him alone in his glory.
['The Burial of Sir John Moore at Corunna' (1817)]

Wolfe, James (1727–1759)
English major-general, noted for the capture of Quebec

1. [On the eve of the Battle of Quebec, during which he was fatally wounded]
The General ... repeated nearly the whole of Gray's Elegy ... adding, as he concluded, that he would prefer being the author of that poem to the glory of beating the French tomorrow.
[In J. Playfair, *Biographical Account of J. Robinson* (1815)]

2. [Dying words]
Now God be praised, I will die in peace.
[In J. Knox, *Historical Journal of Campaigns* (1914 edition)]

Wolfe, Thomas (1900–1938)
American novelist, short-story writer and dramatist

1. Most of the time we think we're sick, it's all in the mind.
[*Look Homeward, Angel* (1929), I, 1]

Wolfe, Tom (1931–)
American novelist, 'new' journalist and illustrator

1. Radical chic.
[Title of essay, 1970]

Wolff, Charlotte (1904–1986)
German-born British psychiatrist and writer

1. Women have always been the guardians of wisdom and humanity which makes them natural, but usually secret, rulers. The time has come for them to rule openly, but together with and not against men.
[*Bisexuality: A Study*, 2]

Wollstonecraft, Mary (1759–1797)
English feminist, novelist, essayist, letter writer and teacher; wife of William Godwin and mother of Mary Shelley

1. No man chooses evil because it is evil; he only mistakes it for happiness, the good he seeks.
[*A Vindication of the Rights of Men* (1790)]

2. The woman who has only been taught to please will soon find that her charms are oblique sunbeams, and that they cannot have much effect on her husband's heart when they are seen every day, when the summer is passed and gone. Will she then have sufficient native energy to look into herself for comfort, and cultivate her dormant faculties? or, is it not more rational to expect that she will try to please other men, and, in the emotions raised by the expectation of new conquests, endeavour to forget the mortification her love or pride has received?
[*A Vindication of the Rights of Woman* (1792), 2]

3. She was created to be the toy of man, his rattle, and it must jingle in his ears whenever, dismissing reason, he chooses to be amused.
[*A Vindication of the Rights of Woman* (1792), 2]

4. Taught from their infancy that beauty is woman's sceptre, the mind shapes itself to the body, and roaming round its gilt cage, only seeks to adorn its prison.
[*A Vindication of the Rights of Woman* (1792), 3]

5. The *divine right* of husbands, like the divine right of kings, may, it is hoped, in this enlightened age, be contested without danger.
[*A Vindication of the Rights of Woman* (1792), 3]

6. [Of women]
I do not wish them to have power over men; but over themselves.
[*A Vindication of the Rights of Women* (1792), 4]

7. When a man seduces a woman, it should, I think, be termed a *left-handed* marriage.
[*A Vindication of the Rights of Women* (1792), 4]

8. A king is always a king – and a woman is always a woman; his authority and her sex ever stand between them and rational converse.
[*A Vindication of the Rights of Women* (1792), 4]

Wolsey, Thomas, Cardinal (c. 1475–1530)
English cardinal and statesman; Lord Chancellor under Henry VIII, 1515–29

1. [Remark at Leicester Abbey, 1529]
Father Abbot, I am come to lay my bones amongst you.
[In George Cavendish, *Negotiations of Thomas Wolsey* (1641)]

2. [Remark to Sir William Kingston]
Had I but served God as diligently as I have served the King, he would not have given me over in my grey hairs.
[In George Cavendish, *Negotiations of Thomas Wolsey* (1641)]

Wood, Mrs Henry (née Ellen Price) (1814–1887)
English novelist, short-story writer and editor

1. Dead! and ... never called me mother.
[*East Lynne* (stage adaptation, 1874); the words do not appear in the novel of 1861]

Woodroofe, Thomas (1899–1978)
British naval officer

1. The Fleet's lit up.
[Broadcast commentary on Spithead Naval Review, 1937]

Woolf, Leonard (1880–1969)
English publisher and political writer; husband of Virginia Woolf

1. From the first moment of my existence, perhaps even before I left my mother's womb, I must have been 'a born intellectual'.
[*Sowing* (1960)]

Woolf, Virginia (1882–1941)
English novelist and critic; short-story and letter writer, and diarist; known for her 'stream of consciousness' technique

1. In or about December, 1910, human character changed.
[*Nation and Athenaeum*, 1923, 'Mr Bennett and Mrs Brown']

2. *Middlemarch*, the magnificent book which with all its imperfections is one of the few English novels for grown up people.
[*The Common Reader* (1925), 'George Eliot']

3. Those comfortably padded lunatic asylums which are known, euphemistically, as the stately homes of England.
[*The Common Reader* (1925), 'Lady Dorothy Nevill']

4. Trivial personalities decomposing into the eternity of print.
[*The Common Reader* (1925), 'The Modern Essay']

5. She bore about with her, she could not help knowing it, the torch of her beauty; she carried it erect into any room that she entered; and after all, veil it as she might, and shrink from the monotony of bearing that it imposed on her, her beauty was apparent. She had been admired. She had been loved.
[*To the Lighthouse* (1927), I, 8]

6. So that is marriage, Lily thought, a man and a woman looking at a girl throwing a ball.
[*To the Lighthouse* (1927), I, 13]

7. A Room of One's Own.
[Title of book, 1929]

8. It is the masculine values that prevail. Speaking crudely, football and sport are 'important'; the worship of fashion, the buying of clothes 'trivial' ... This is an important book, the critic assumes, because it deals with war. This is an insignificant book because it deals with feelings of women in a drawing-room ... everywhere and much more subtly the difference of values persists.
[*A Room of One's Own* (1929)]

9. A woman must have money and a room of her own if she is to write fiction.
[*A Room of One's Own* (1929)]

10. Women have served all these centuries as looking-glasses possessing the magic and delicious power of reflecting the figure of man at twice its natural size.
[*A Room of One's Own* (1929)]

11. Why are women ... so much more interesting to men than men are to women?
[*A Room of One's Own* (1929)]

12. I would venture to guess that Anon, who wrote so many poems without signing them, was often a woman.
[*A Room of One's Own* (1929)]

13. Literature is strewn with the wreckage of men who have minded beyond reason the opinions of others.
[*A Room of One's Own* (1929)]

14. I have lost friends, some by death ... others through sheer inability to cross the street.
[*The Waves* (1931)]

15. The poet gives us his essence, but prose takes the mould of the body and mind entire.
[*The Captain's Death Bed* (1950), 'Reading']

16. If you do not tell the truth about yourself you cannot tell it about other people.
[*The Moment and Other Essays*]

17. [Of Joyce's *Ulysses*]
Merely the scratching of pimples on the body of the bootboy at Claridge's.
[Letter to Lytton Strachey, 1922]

Woollcott, Alexander (1887–1943)
American journalist, drama critic, writer and anthologist

1. Subjunctive to the last, he preferred to ask, 'And that, sir, would be the Hippodrome?'
[*While Rome Burns* (1934), 'Our Mrs Parker']

2. All the things I really like to do are either immoral, illegal, or fattening.
[In R.E. Drennan, *Wit's End* (1973)]

3. I must get out of these wet clothes and into a dry Martini.
[Attr.]

4. [On being shown round Moss Hart's elegant country house and grounds]
Just what God would have done if he had the money.
[Attr.]

Wootton, Barbara Frances (Lady Wootton) (1897–1988)
English economist, educationist, social scientist and criminologist

1. Sociology is a lot of waffle. It is using a lot of words to cover up rather obvious remarks.
[*The Observer*, 1984, in Jeffrey Care (ed.), *Sayings of the Eighties* (1989)]

Wordsworth, Dorothy (1771–1855)
English diarist, letter and travel writer; sister of William Wordsworth

1. When we were in the woods beyond Gowbarrow park we saw a few daffodils close to the waterside ... But as we went along there were more and yet more and at last under the boughs of the trees, we saw that there was a long belt of them along the shore, about the breadth of a country turnpike road. I never saw daffodils so beautiful. They grew among the mossy stones about and about them, some rested their heads upon these stones as on pillow for weariness and the rest tossed and reeled and danced and seemed as if they verily laughed with the wind that blew upon them over the lake.
[*Journals*, 'Grasmere Journal', 1802. Cf. William Wordsworth: 120 – 122]

Wordsworth, Dame Elizabeth (1840–1932)
English educationist and writer; great-niece of William Wordsworth

1. If all the good people were clever,
And all clever people were good,
The world would be nicer than ever
We thought that it possibly could.
But somehow, 'tis seldom or never
The two hit it off as they should;
The good are so harsh to the clever,
The clever so rude to the good.
['The Clever and the Good' (1890)]

Wordsworth, Mary (1770–1859)
Wife of William Wordsworth

1. [Rebuking John Keats for interrupting a long monologue by William Wordsworth]
Mr Wordsworth is never interrupted.
[Attr.]

Wordsworth, William (1770–1850)
English Romantic poet, inspired by the Lake District; poet laureate from 1843

1. And three times to the child I said,
'Why, Edward, tell me why?'
['Anecdote for Fathers' (1798)]

2. Nor less I deem that there are powers
Which of themselves our minds impress;
That we can feed this mind of ours
In a wise passiveness.
['Expostulation and Reply' (1798)]

3. 'Tis he whom you so long have lost,
He whom you love, your Idiot Boy.
['The Idiot Boy' (1798)]

4. I have owed to them,
In hours of weariness, sensations sweet,
Felt in the blood, and felt along the heart;
And passing even into my purer mind,
With tranquil restoration: – feelings too
Of unremembered pleasure: such, perhaps,
As have no slight or trivial influence
On that best portion of a good man's life;
His little, nameless, unremembered acts
Of kindness and of love...

5. That blessed mood,
In which the burthen of the mystery,
In which the heavy and the weary weight
Of all this unintelligible world,
Is lightened...

6. We are laid asleep
In body, and become a living soul:
While with an eye made quiet by the power
Of harmony, and the deep power of joy,
We see into the life of things...

7. For nature then
(The coarser pleasures of my boyish days,
And their glad animal movements all gone by,)
To me was all in all. – I cannot paint
What then I was. The sounding cataract
Haunted me like a passion: the tall rock,
The mountain, and the deep and gloomy wood,
Their colours and their forms, were then to me
An appetite, a feeling and a love,
That had no need of a remoter charm,
By thought supplied, nor any interest
Unborrowed from the eye...

8. I have learned
To look on nature, not as in the hour
Of thoughtless youth; but hearing often-times
The still, sad music of humanity,
Nor harsh nor grating, though of ample power
To chasten and subdue. And I have felt
A presence that disturbs me with the joy
Of elevated thoughts; a sense sublime
Of something far more deeply interfused,
Whose dwelling is the light of setting suns,
And the round ocean and the living air,
And the blue sky, and in the mind of man,
A motion and a spirit, that impels
All thinking things, all objects of all thought,
And rolls through all things...

9. Therefore am I still
A lover of the meadows and the woods,
And mountains; and of all that we behold
From this green earth; of all the mighty world
Of eye, and ear, – both what they half create,
And what perceive; well pleased to recognise
In nature and the language of the sense,
The anchor of my purest thoughts, the nurse,
The guide, the guardian of my heart, and soul
Of all my moral being...

10. Nature never did betray
The heart that loved her...

11. Nor greetings where no kindness is, nor all
The dreary intercourse of daily life,
Shall e'er prevail against us, or disturb
Our cheerful faith, that all which we behold
Is full of blessings.
['Lines composed a few miles above Tintern Abbey' (1798)]

12. In that sweet mood when pleasant thoughts
Bring sad thoughts to the mind...

13. And much it grieved my heart to think
What man has made of man...

14. If this belief from heaven be sent,
If such be Nature's holy plan,
Have I not reason to lament
What man has made of man?
['Lines Written in Early Spring' (1798)]

15. Up! up! my friend, and quit your books;
Or surely you'll grow double...

16. Books! 'tis a dull and endless strife:
Come, hear the woodland linnet,
How sweet his music! on my life,
There's more of wisdom in it...

17. One impulse from a vernal wood
May teach you more of man,
Of moral evil and of good,
Than all the sages can...

18. Sweet is the lore which Nature brings;
Our meddling intellect
Misshapes the beauteous forms of things:
We murder to dissect.
['The Tables Turned' (1798)]

19. I've measured it from side to side;
'Tis three feet long, and two feet wide.
['The Thorn' (1798)]

20. A simple child,
That lightly draws its breath,
And feels its life in every limb,
What should it know of death?...

21. I take my little porringer
And eat my supper there...

22. 'But they are dead; those two are dead!
Their spirits are in Heaven!'
'Twas throwing words away; for still
The little Maid would have her will,
And said, 'Nay, we are seven!'
['We are Seven' (1798)]

23. The wiser mind
Mourns less for what age takes away
Than what it leaves behind.
['The Fountain' (1800)]

24. The moving accident is not my trade;
To freeze the blood I have no ready arts:
'Tis my delight, alone in summer shade,
To pipe a simple song for thinking hearts.
['Hart-Leap Well' (1800), II]

25. I chanced to see at break of day
The solitary child.
['Lucy Gray' (1800)]

26. Move along these shades
In gentleness of heart; with gentle hand
Touch – for there is a spirit in the woods.
['Nutting' (1800)]

27. Physician art thou? – one, all eyes,
Philosopher! – a fingering slave,
One that would peep and botanize
Upon his mother's grave?...

28. A reasoning, self-sufficing thing,
An intellectual All-in-all!...

29. But who is He, with modest looks,
And clad in homely russet brown?
He murmurs near the running brooks
A music sweeter than their own.
['A Poet's Epitaph' (1800)]

30. She dwelt among the untrodden ways
Beside the springs of Dove;
A maid whom there were none to praise
And very few to love.

A violet by a mossy stone
Half hidden from the eye!
Fair as a star, when only one
Is shining in the sky.

She lived unknown, and few could know
When Lucy ceased to be;
But she is in her grave, and, oh,
The difference to me!
['She dwelt among the untrodden ways' (1800)]

31. A slumber did my spirit seal;
I had no human fears:
She seemed a thing that could not feel
The touch of earthly years.

No motion has she now, no force;
She neither hears nor sees;
Rolled round in earth's diurnal course,
With rocks, and stones, and trees.
['A slumber did my spirit seal' (1800)]

32. Strange fits of passion have I known:
And I will dare to tell,
But in the lover's ear alone,
What once to me befell...

33. What fond and wayward thoughts will slide
Into a Lover's head!
'O mercy!' to myself I cried,
'If Lucy should be dead!'
['Strange Fits of Passion' (1800)]

34. Three years she grew in sun and shower,
Then Nature said, 'A lovelier flower
On earth was never sown;
This child I to myself will take;
She shall be mine, and I will make
A Lady of my own'.
['Three years she grew' (1800)]

35. 'Tis said that some have died for love.
[''Tis said that some have died' (1800)]

36. But an old age, serene and bright,
And lovely as a Lapland night,
Shall lead thee to thy grave.
['To a Young Lady' (1802)]

37. Sweet Highland Girl, a very shower
Of beauty is thy earthly dower!
['To the Highland Girl of Inversneyde' (1803)]

38. My apprehensions come in crowds;
I dread the rustling of the grass;
The very shadows of the clouds
Have power to shake me as they pass.
['The Affliction of Margaret' (1807)]

39. Who is the happy Warrior? Who is he
That every man in arms should wish to be?
It is the generous spirit, who, when brought
Among the tasks of real life, hath wrought
Upon the plan that pleased his childish thought:
Whose high endeavours are an inward light
That makes the path before him always bright:
Who, with a natural instinct to discern

What knowledge can perform, is diligent to learn.
['Character of the Happy Warrior' (1807)]

40. [On Beaumont's painting of Peele Castle]
Ah! then, if mine had been the Painter's hand,
To express what then I saw; and add the gleam,
The light that never was, on sea or land,
The consecration, and the Poet's dream.
['Elegiac Stanzas' (1807)]

41. Two Voices are there; one is of the Sea,
One of the Mountains; each a mighty voice,
In both from age to age thou didst rejoice,
They were thy chosen music, Liberty!
['England and Switzerland, 1802' (1807). Cf. J.K. Stephen: 2]

42. It is a beauteous evening, calm and free,
The holy time is quiet as a nun,
Breathless with adoration...

43. Dear Child! dear Girl! that walkest with me here
If thou appear untouched by solemn thought,
Thy nature is not therefore less divine.
Thou liest in Abraham's bosom all the year;
And worshipp'st at the temple's inner shrine,
God being with thee when we know it not.
['It is a beauteous evening, calm and free' (1807)]

44. In our halls is hung
Armoury of the invincible Knights of old:
We must be free or die, who speak the tongue
That Shakespeare spake; the faith and morals hold
Which Milton held. – In every thing we are sprung
Of Earth's first blood, have titles manifold.
['It is not to be thought of that the Flood (1807)]

45. I travelled among unknown men
In lands beyond the sea;
Nor, England! did I know till then
What love I bore to thee.
['I travelled among unknown men' (1807)]

46. Jones! as from Calais southward you and I
Went pacing side by side, this public Way
Streamed with the pomp of a too-credulous day.
['Jones! as from Calais' (1807)]

47. Milton! thou shouldst be living at this hour:
England hath need of thee; she is a fen
Of stagnant waters: altar, sword, and pen,
Fireside, the heroic wealth of hall and bower,
Have forfeited their ancient English dower
Of inward happiness...

48. Thy soul was like a star, and dwelt apart.
['Milton! thou shouldst be living at this hour' (1807)]

49. My heart leaps up when I behold
A rainbow in the sky:
So was it when my life began;
So it is now I am a man;
So be it when I shall grow old,
Or let me die!
The Child is father of the Man;
And I could wish my days to be
Bound each to each by natural piety.
['My heart leaps up when I behold' (1807)]

50. Nuns fret not at their convent's narrow room;
And hermits are contented with their cells...

51. In sundry moods, 'twas pastime to be bound
Within the Sonnet's scanty plot of ground;
Pleased if some souls (for such there needs must be)
Who have felt the weight of too much liberty,
Should find some solace there, as I have found.
['Nuns fret not at their convent's narrow room' (1807)]

52. There was a time when meadow, grove, and stream,
The earth, and every common sight,
To me did seem
Apparelled in celestial light,
The glory and the freshness of a dream.
It is not now as it hath been of yore;–
Turn wheresoe'er I may,
By night or day,
The things which I have seen I now can see no more.
['Ode: Intimations of Immortality' (1807), 1]

53. The rainbow comes and goes,
And lovely is the rose,
The moon doth with delight
Look round her when the heavens are bare,
Waters on a starry night
Are beautiful and fair;
The sunshine is a glorious birth:
But yet I know, where'er I go,
That there hath passed away a glory from the earth.
['Ode: Intimations of Immortality' (1807), 2]

54. A timely utterance gave that thought relief,
And I again am strong...

55. The winds come to me from the fields of sleep.
['Ode: Intimations of Immortality' (1807), 3]

56. The sun shines warm,
And the Babe leaps up on his Mother's arm...

57. – But there's a tree of many, one,
A single field which I have lookd upon,
Both of them speak of something that is gone:
The pansy at my feet
Doth the same tale repeat:
Whither is fled the visionary gleam?
Where is it now, the glory and the dream?
['Ode: Intimations of Immortality' (1807), 4]

58. Our birth is but a sleep and a forgetting.
The Soul that rises with us, our life's Star,
Hath had elsewhere its setting,
And cometh from afar;
Not in entire forgetfulness,
And not in utter nakedness,
But trailing clouds of glory do we come
From God, who is our home:
Heaven lies about us in our infancy!
Shades of the prison-house begin to close
Upon the growing Boy,
But he beholds the light, and whence it flows,
He sees it in his joy;
The Youth, who daily farther from the east
Must travel, still is Nature's priest,
And by the vision splendid
Is on his way attended;
At length the Man perceives it die away,
And fade into the light of common day.
['Ode: Intimations of Immortality' (1807), 5]

59. As if his whole vocation
Were endless imitation.
['Ode: Intimations of Immortality' (1807), 7]

60. Thou eye among the blind,
That, deaf and silent, read'st the eternal deep
Haunted for ever by the eternal Mind...

61. Why with such earnest pains dost thou provoke
The years to bring the inevitable yoke,
Thus blindly with thy blessedness at strife?

Full soon thy soul shall have her earthly freight,
And custom lie upon thee with a weight,
Heavy as frost, and deep almost as life!
['Ode: Intimations of Immortality' (1807), 8]

62. O joy! that in our embers
Is something that doth live,
That Nature yet remembers
What was so fugitive!
The thought of our past years in me doth breed
Perpetual benediction...

63. Not for these I raise
The song of thanks and praise;
But for those obstinate questionings
Of sense and outward things,
Fallings from us, vanishings;
Blank misgivings of a creature
Moving about in worlds not realised,
High instincts before which our mortal nature
Did tremble like a guilty thing surprised...

64. Our noisy years seem moments in the being
Of the eternal Silence: truths that wake,
To perish never...

65. Hence in a season of calm weather
Though inland far we be,
Our souls have sight of that immortal sea
Which brought us hither,
Can in a moment travel thither,
And see the children sport upon the shore,
And hear the mighty waters rolling evermore.
['Ode: Intimations of Immortality' (1807), 9]

66. Though nothing can bring back the hour
Of splendour in the grass, of glory in the flower;
We will grieve not, rather find
Strength in what remains behind...

67. In the faith that looks through death,
In years that bring the philosophic mind.
['Ode: Intimations of Immortality' (1807), 10]

68. And O, ye Fountains, Meadows, Hills and Groves,
Forbode not any severing of our loves!
Yet in my heart of hearts I feel your might;
I only have relinquished one delight
To live beneath your more habitual sway...

69. The clouds that gather round the setting sun
Do take a sober colouring from an eye
That hath kept watch o'er man's mortality.
Another race hath been, and other palms are won.
Thanks to the human heart by which we live,
Thanks to its tenderness, its joys and fears,
To me the meanest flower that blows can give
Thoughts that do often lie too deep for tears.
['Ode: Intimations of Immortality' (1807), 11]

70. Stern Daughter of the Voice of God!
O Duty! if that name thou love
Who art a light to guide, a rod
To check the erring and reprove...

71. Me this unchartered freedom tires;
I feel the weight of chance-desires:
My hopes no more must change their name,
I long for a repose that ever is the same...

72. Thou dost preserve the Stars from wrong;
And the most ancient Heavens, through Thee, are fresh and strong.
['Ode to Duty' (1807)]

73. Plain living and high thinking are no more:
The homely beauty of the good old cause
Is gone; our peace, our fearful innocence,
And pure religion breathing household laws.
['O friend! I know not which way I must look' (1807)]

74. Once did she hold the gorgeous East in fee,
And was the safeguard of the West...

75. Venice, the eldest child of Liberty.
She was a maiden city, bright and free...

76. And when she took unto herself a mate,
She must espouse the everlasting Sea...

77. Men are we, and must grieve when even the shade
Of that which once was great is pass'd away.
['On the Extinction of the Venetian Republic' (1807)]

78. Sweetest melodies
Are those by distance made more sweet.
[*Personal Talk* (1807), 'I am not One who much or oft delight']

79. Behold her, single in the field,
Yon solitary Highland lass!...

80. Will no one tell me what she sings?–
Perhaps the plaintive numbers flow
For old, unhappy, far-off things,
And battles long ago...

81. Some natural sorrow, loss, or pain
That has been, and may be again...

82. The music in my heart I bore,
Long after it was heard no more.
['The Reaper' (1807)]

83. There was a roaring in the wind all night;
The rain came heavily and fell in floods;
But now the sun is rising, calm and bright.
['Resolution and Independence' (1807), 1]

84. I thought of Chatterton, the marvellous boy,
The sleepless soul, that perished in his pride;
Of him who walked in glory and in joy,
Following his plough, along the mountain side:
By our own spirits we are deified:
We poets in our youth begin in gladness;
But thereof comes in the end despondency and madness.
['Resolution and Independence' (1807), 7]

85. His words came feebly, from a feeble chest,
But each in solemn order followed each,
With something of a lofty utterance drest–
Choice words, and measured phrase, above the reach
Of ordinary men; a stately speech;
Such as grave Livers do in Scotland use.
Religious men, who give to God and Man their dues.
['Resolution and Independence' (1807), 14]

86. The fear that kills;
And hope that is unwilling to be fed;
Cold, pain, and labour, and all fleshly ills;
And mighty Poets in their misery dead.
– Perplexed, and longing to be comforted,
My question eagerly I did renew.
'How is it that you live, and what is it you do?'
['Resolution and Independence' (1807), 17]

87. The good old rule
Sufficeth them, the simple plan,
That they should take, who have the power,
And they should keep who can.
['Rob Roy's Grave' (1807)]

88. She was a Phantom of delight
When first she gleam'd upon my sight...

89. I saw her upon nearer view,
A Spirit, yet a Woman too!
Her household motions light and free,
And steps of virgin-liberty;
A countenance in which did meet
Sweet records, promises as sweet;
A creature not too bright or good
For human nature's daily food;
For transient sorrows, simple wiles,
Praise, blame, love, kisses, tears, and smiles.

And now I see with eye serene,
The very pulse of the machine;
A being breathing thoughtful breath,
A traveller betwixt life and death;
The reason firm, the temperate will,
Endurance, foresight, strength, and skill;
A perfect woman, nobly plann'd,
To warn, to comfort, and command;
And yet a spirit still, and bright
With something of angelic light.
['She was a Phantom of delight' (1807)]

90. O Man! that from thy fair and shining youth
Age might but take the things Youth needed not!
['The Small Celandine' (1807)]

91. Earth has not anything to show more fair;
Dull would he be of soul who could pass by
A sight so touching in its majesty:
This city now doth, like a garment, wear

The beauty of the morning; silent, bare,
Ships, towers, domes, theatres, and temples lie
Open unto the fields, and to the sky,
All bright and glittering in the smokeless air...

92. Dear God! the very houses seem asleep;
And all that mighty heart is lying still!
['Sonnet composed upon Westminster Bridge' (1807)]

93. Wisdom doth live with children round her knees.
[*Sonnets Dedicated to Liberty and Order* (1807), 4]

94. Happy is he, who, caring not for Pope,
Consul, or King, can sound himself to know
The destiny of Man, and live in hope.
[*Sonnets Dedicated to Liberty and Order* (1807), 5]

95. What, you are stepping westward?
['Stepping Westward' (1807)]

96. Sweet childish days, that were as long
As twenty days are now.
['To a Butterfly' (1807)]

97. O blithe new-comer! I have heard,
I hear thee and rejoice.
O Cuckoo! Shall I call thee bird,
Or but a wandering voice?...

98. Thrice welcome, darling of the spring!
Even yet thou are to me
No bird, but an invisible thing,
A voice, a mystery.
['To the Cuckoo' (1807)]

99. Thou unassuming common-place
Of Nature.
['To the Daisy' (1807)]

100. There's a flower that shall be mine,
'Tis the little Celandine.
['To the Small Celandine' (1807)]

101. Pleasures newly found are sweet
When they lie about our feet.
['To the Same Flower' (1807)]

102. Spade! with which Wilkinson hath tilled his lands,
And shaped these pleasant walks by Emont's side,
Thou art a tool of honour in my hands;
I press thee, through the yielding soil, with pride.
['To the Spade of a Friend' (1807)]

103. Though fallen thyself, never to rise again,
Live, and take comfort. Thou hast left behind
Powers that will work for thee; air, earth, and skies;
There's not a breathing of the common wind
That will forget thee; thou hast great allies;
Thy friends are exultations, agonies,
And love, and man's unconquerable mind.
['To Toussaint L'Ouverture' (1807)]

104. The world is too much with us; late and soon,
Getting and spending, we lay waste our powers:
Little we see in Nature that is ours;
We have given our hearts away, a sordid boon!

This sea that bares her bosom to the moon;
The winds that will be howling at all hours,
And are up-gathered now like sleeping flowers;
For this, for everything, we are out of tune...

105. Great God! I'd rather be
A Pagan suckled in a creed outworn,
So might I, standing on this pleasant lea,

Have glimpses that would make me less forlorn;
Have sight of Proteus rising from the sea,
Or hear old Triton blow his wreathèd horn.
['The world is too much with us' (1807)]

106. All shod with steel
We hissed along the polished ice, in games
Confederate.
['Influence of Natural Objects' (1809) and *The Prelude* (1850), I]

107. Leaving the tumultuous throng
To cut across the reflex of a star;
Image, that, flying still before me, gleamed
Upon the glassy plain.
['Influence of Natural Objects' (1809)]

108. Yet still the solitary cliffs
Wheeled by me – even as if the earth had rolled
With visible motion her diurnal round!
['Influence of Natural Objects' (1809) and *The Prelude* (1850), I]

109. On Man, on Nature and on Human Life,
Musing in solitude...

110. The Mind of Man–
My haunt, and the main region of my song.
[*The Excursion* (1814), Preface]

111. Oh! many are the Poets that are sown
By Nature; men endowed with highest gifts,
The vision and the faculty divine;
Yet wanting the accomplishment of verse...

112. What soul was his, when from the naked top
Of some bold headland, he beheld the sun
Rise up, and bathe the world in light!...

113. The good die first,
And they whose hearts are dry as summer dust
Burn to the socket.
[*The Excursion* (1814), I]

114. [Of Voltaire's *Candide*]
This dull product of a scoffer's pen.
[*The Excursion* (1814), II]

115. Wisdom is oftimes nearer when we stoop
Than when we soar...

116. The intellectual power, through words and things,
Went sounding on, a dim and perilous way!
[*The Excursion* (1814), III]

117. I have seen
A curious child, who dwelt upon a tract
Of inland ground applying to his ear
The convolutions of a smooth-lipped shell;
To which, in silence hushed, his very soul
Listened intensely; and his countenance soon
Brightened with joy; for from within were heard
Murmurings, whereby the monitor expressed
Mysterious union with its native sea...

118. 'Tis a thing impossible, to frame
Conceptions equal to the soul's desires;
And the most difficult of tasks to *keep*
Heights which the soul is competent to gain.
[*The Excursion* (1814), IV]

119. 'To every Form of being is assigned,'
Thus calmly spoke the venerable Sage,
'An *active* Principle.'
[*The Excursion* (1814), IX]

120. I wandered lonely as a cloud
That floats on high o'er vales and hills,
When all at once I saw a crowd,
A host, of golden daffodils;
Beside the lake, beneath the trees,
Fluttering and dancing in the breeze...

121. Ten thousand saw I at a glance,
Tossing their heads in sprightly dance...

122. A poet could not but be gay,
In such a jocund company!
I gazed – and gazed – but little thought
What wealth the show to me had brought:

For oft when on my couch I lie
In vacant or in pensive mood,
They flash upon that inward eye
Which is the bliss of solitude;
And then my heart with pleasure fills,
And dances with the daffodils.
['I wandered lonely as a cloud' (1815 edition). Cf. Dorothy Wordsworth: 1]

123. The gods approve
The depth, and not the tumult, of the soul...

124. Of all that is most beauteous – imaged there
In happier beauty; more pellucid streams,
An ampler ether, a diviner air,
And fields invested with purpureal gleams.
['Laodamia' (1815)]

125. Surprised by joy – impatient as the Wind
I turned to share the transport – Oh! with whom
But thee, deep buried in the silent tomb.
['Surprised by joy' (1815)]

126. There's something in a flying horse,
There's something in a huge balloon;
But through the clouds I'll never float
Until I have a little Boat,
Shaped like the crescent moon.
[*Peter Bell* (1819), Prologue]

127. A primrose by a river's brim
A yellow primrose was to him
And it was nothing more.
[*Peter Bell* (1819), I]

128. I thought of Thee, my partner and my guide,
As being past away – Vain sympathies!
For, backward, Duddon! as I cast my eyes,
I see what was, and is, and will abide;
Still glides the Stream, and shall for ever glide;
The Form remains, the Function never dies...

129. Enough, if something from our hands have power
To live, and act, and serve the future hour;
And if, as toward the silent tomb we go,
Through love, through hope, and faith's transcendent dower,
We feel that we are greater than we know.
['The River Duddon' (1820), After-Thought]

130. A genial hearth, a hospitable board,
And a refined rusticity.
['A genial hearth, a hospitable board' (1822)]

131. Not choice
But habit rules the unreflecting herd.
['Grant that by this unsparing hurricane' (1822)]

132. Isis and Cam, to patient Science dear!
['Open your gates' (1822)]

133. Scorn not the Sonnet; Critic, you have frowned,
Mindless of its just honours; with this key
Shakespeare unlocked his heart.
['Scorn not the Sonnet' (1827)]

134. Ethereal minstrel! pilgrim of the sky!
Dost thou despise the earth where cares abound?...

135. Type of the wise who soar, but never roam;
True to the kindred points of Heaven and Home!
['To a Skylark' (1827)]

136. By grace divine,
Not otherwise, O Nature! We are thine.
['Evening Voluntaries' (1835)]

137. Some happy tone
Of meditation, slipping in between
The beauty coming and the beauty gone.
['Most sweet it is' (1835)]

138. Small service is true service, while it lasts.
['To a Child, Written in her Album' (1835)]

139. Action is transitory, – a step, a blow,
The motion of a muscle, – this way or that–
'Tis done, and in the after-vacancy
We wonder at ourselves like men betrayed:
Suffering is permanent, obscure, and dark,
And shares the nature of infinity.
[*The Borderers* (1842), III]

140. A Poet! – He hath put his heart to school,
Nor dares to move unpropped upon the staff
Which Art hath lodged within his hand – must laugh
By precept only, and shed tears by rule.
['A Poet! He hath put his heart' (1842)]

141. I recoil and droop, and seek repose
In listlessness from vain perplexity,
Unprofitably travelling towards the grave...

142. Made one long bathing of a summer's day...

143. Fair seed-time had my soul, and I grew up
Fostered alike by beauty and by fear...

144. When the deed was done
I heard among the solitary hills
Low breathings coming after me, and sounds
Of undistinguishable motion, steps
Almost as silent as the turf they trod...

145. Though mean
Our object and inglorious, yet the end
Was not ignoble...

146. Dust as we are, the immortal spirit grows
Like harmony in music; there is a dark
Inscrutable workmanship that reconciles
Discordant elements, makes them cling together
In one society...

147. The grim shape
Towered up between me and the stars, and still,
For so it seemed, with purpose of its own
And measured motion like a living thing,
Strode after me...

148. For many days, my brain
Worked with a dim and undetermined sense
Of unknown modes of being...

149. Huge and mighty forms that do not live
Like dying men, moved slowly through the mind
By day, and were a trouble to my dreams.
[*The Prelude* (1850), I]

150. I was taught to feel, perhaps too much,
The self-sufficing power of Solitude...

151. To thee
Science appears but, what in truth she is,
Not as our glory and our absolute boast,
But as a succedaneum, and a prop
To our infirmity.
[*The Prelude* (1850), II]

152. Where the statue stood
Of Newton, with his prism and silent face,
The marble index of a mind for ever
Voyaging through strange seas of Thought, alone.
[*The Prelude* (1850), III]

153. Spirits overwrought
Were making night do penance for a day
Spent in a round of strenuous idleness.
[*The Prelude* (1850), IV]

154. Even forms and substances are circumfused
By that transparent veil with light divine,
And, through the turnings intricate of verse,
Present themselves as objects recognised,
In flashes, and with glory not their own.
[*The Prelude* (1850), V]

155. Whether we be young or old,
Our destiny, our being's heart and home,
Is with infinitude, and only there;
With hope it is, hope that can never die,
Effort, and expectation, and desire,
And something evermore about to be...

156. The unfetter'd clouds, and region of the Heavens,
Tumult and peace, the darkness and the light
Were all like workings of one mind, the features
Of the same face, blossoms upon one tree,
Characters of the great Apocalypse,
The types and symbols of Eternity,
Of first and last, and midst, and without end.
[*The Prelude* (1850), VI]

157. We were brothers all
In honour, as in one community,
Scholars and gentlemen.
[*The Prelude* (1850), IX]

158. In the People was my trust,
And in the virtues which mine eyes had seen...

159. Bliss was it in that dawn to be alive,
But to be young was very heaven...

160. Not in Utopia – subterranean fields, –
Or some secreted island, Heaven knows where!
But in the very world, which is the world
Of all of us, – the place where, in the end
We find our happiness, or not at all!...

161. There is
One great society alone on earth:
The noble Living and the noble Dead.
[*The Prelude* (1850), XI]

162. I shook the habit off
Entirely and for ever, and again
In Nature's presence stood, as now I stand,
A sensitive being, a *creative* soul.
[*The Prelude* (1850), XII]

163. Imagination, which, in truth,
Is but another name for absolute power
And clearest insight, amplitude of mind,
And Reason in her most exalted mood...

164. Instruct them how the mind of man becomes
A thousand times more beautiful than the earth
On which he dwells.
[*The Prelude* (1850), XIV]

165. The Poet writes under one restriction only, namely, that of the necessity of giving pleasure to a human Being possessed of that information which may be expected from him, not as a lawyer, a physician, a mariner, an astronomer or a natural philosopher, but as a Man.
[*Lyrical Ballads* (1802), Preface]

166. I have said that poetry is the spontaneous overflow of powerful feelings: it takes its origin from emotion recollected in tranquillity: the emotion is contemplated till, by a species of reaction, the tranquillity gradually disappears, and an emotion, kindred to that which was before the subject of contemplation, is gradually produced, and does itself actually exist in the mind.
[*Lyrical Ballads* (1802), Preface. Cf. Dorothy Parker: 9]

167. Poetry is the breath and finer spirit of all knowledge; it is the impassioned expression which is in the countenance of all science.
[*Lyrical Ballads* (1802), Preface]

168. There neither is, nor can be, any *essential* difference between the language of prose and metrical compositions.
[*Lyrical Ballads* (1802), Preface]

169. Never forget what I believe was observed to you by Coleridge, that every great and original writer, in proportion as he is great and original, must himself create the taste by which he is to be relished.
[Letter to Lady Beaumont, 1807]

Work, H.C. (1832–1884)
American songwriter and printer

1. 'Hurrah! hurrah! we bring the Jubilee!
Hurrah! hurrah! the flag that makes you free!'
So we sang the chorus from Atlanta to the sea
As we were marching through Georgia.
['Marching Through Georgia', song, 1865]

2. My grandfather's clock was too large for the shelf
So it stood twenty years in the hall...

3. But it stopped short – never to go again–
When the old man died.
['Grandfather's Clock', song, 1876]

Worlock, Derek, Archbishop of Liverpool (1920–)
English prelate and writer

1. [Commenting on rising levels of homelessness]
I am my brother's keeper and he is sleeping pretty rough at the moment.
[*The Sunday Telegraph*, 1990]

Worsthorne, Sir Peregrine (1923–)
English journalist

1. A little more willingness to bore, and much less eagerness to entertain, would do the monarchy no end of good in 1993.
[*The Sunday Telegraph*, 1993]

Wotton, Sir Henry (1568–1639)
English diplomat, traveller and poet

1. He first deceased; she for a little tried
To live without him: liked it not, and died.
['Death of Sir Albertus Moreton's Wife' (c. 1610)]

2. How happy is he born and taught
That serveth not another's will;
Whose armour is his honest thought,
And simple truth his utmost skill!
['The Character of a Happy Life' (1614)]

3. You meaner beauties of the night,
That poorly satisfy our eyes,
More by your number, than your light;
You common people of the skies,
What are you when the moon shall rise?
['On his Mistress, the Queen of Bohemia' (1624)]

4. Virtue is the roughest way,
But proves at night a bed of down.
['Upon the Imprisonment of the Earl of Essex']

5. *Legatus est vir bonus peregre missus ad mentiendum rei publicae causa.*
An ambassador is an honest man sent to lie abroad for the good of his country.
[Written in the Album of Christopher Fleckamore, 1606]

6. In Architecture as in all other *Operative* Arts, the *end* must direct the *Operation*. The *end* is to build well. Well building hath three Conditions: *Commodity*, *Firmness*, and *Delight*.
[*Elements of Architecture* (1624), I]

7. The itch of disputing will prove the scab of churches.
[*A Panegyric to King Charles* (1651)]

Wran, Neville Kenneth (1926–)
Australian lawyer and politician

1. There's what being in the working-class is all about – how to get out of it.
[*Sydney Morning Herald*, 1982]

Wren, Sir Christopher (1632–1723)
English architect, mathematician and astronomer; known for his many buildings replacing those destroyed in the Great Fire of London

1. *Si monumentum requiris, circumspice.*
If you are looking for his memorial, look around you.
[Inscription written by his son, in St Paul's Cathedral, London]

Wright, Frank Lloyd (1869–1959)
Influential American architect and writer, known for his 'organic' architecture

1. The physician can bury his mistakes, but the architect can only advise his client to plant vines.
[*New York Times Magazine*, 1953]

2. The truth is more important than the facts.
[In Simcox, *Treasury of Quotations on Christian Themes*]

3. Give me the luxuries of life and I will willingly do without the necessities.
[Attr.]

Wright, Judith (Judith Arundell Wright McKinney) (1915–)
Australian poet, critic, short-story writer and children's novelist

1. Beside his heavy-shouldered team,
thirsty with drought and chilled with rain,
he weathered all the striding years
till they ran widdershins in his brain.
[*The Moving Image* (1946), 'Bullocky']

2. We meet and part now over all the world;
we, the lost company,
take hands together in the night, forget
the night of our brief happiness, silently.
We, who sought many things, throw all away
for this one thing, one only,
remembering that in the narrow grave
we shall be lonely.

Death marshals up his armies round us now.
Their footsteps crowd too near.
Lock your warm hand above the chilling heart
and for a time I live without my fear.
Grope in the night to find me and embrace,
for the dark preludes of the drums begin,
and round us, round the company of lovers,
death draws his cordons in.
[*The Moving Image* (1946), 'The Company of Lovers']

3. That harsh biblical country of the scapegoat
closed its magnificence finally round his bones
polished by diligent ants.
[*The Moving Image* (1946), 'Remittance Man']

4. South of my days' circle, part of my blood's country,
rises that tableland, high delicate outline
of bony slopes wincing under the winter,
low trees blue-leaved and olive, outcropping granite–
clean, lean, hungry country.
[*The Moving Image* (1946), 'South of My Days']

5. Tunnelling through the night, the trains pass
in a splendour of power, with a sound like thunder
shaking the orchards, waking
the young from a dream, scattering like glass
the old men's sleep; laying
a black trail over the still bloom of the orchards.
The trains go north with guns.
[*The Moving Image* (1946), 'The Trains']

6. Their smooth dark flames flicker at time's own root.
Round them the rising forests of the years
alter the climates of forgotten earth
and silt with leaves the strata of first birth.

Only the antique cycads sullenly
keep the old bargain life has long since broken;
and, cursed by age, through each chill century
they watch the shrunken moon, but never die,

for time forgets the promise he once made,
and change forgets that they are left alone.

Among the complicated birds and flowers
they seem a generation carved in stone.
[*Woman to Man* (1949), 'The Cycads']

7. The eyeless labourer in the night,
the selfless, shapeless seed I hold,
builds for its resurrection day–
silent and swift and deep from sight
foresees the unimagined light.

This is no child with a child's face;
this has no name to name it by;
yet you and I have known it well.
This is our hunter and our chase,
the third who lay in our embrace.

This is the strength that your arm knows,
the arc of flesh that is my breast,
the precise crystals of our eyes.
This is the blood's wild tree that grows
the intricate and folded rose.

This is the maker and the made;
this is the question and reply;
the blind head butting at the dark,
the blaze of light along the blade.
Oh hold me, for I am afraid.
[*Woman to Man* (1949), Title poem]

8. Little nightmare flying-fox
trapped on the cruel barbs of day
has no weapon but a wing
and a tiny scream.
Here's a patch of night, a thing
that looks by daylight like a hoax;
dawn wouldn't let it fly away
with its kin into its dream,
but stabbed with a pin its velvet hand
and hung it in a hostile land.
[*The Two Fires* (1955), 'Flying-Fox on Barbed Wire']

9. And you, who speak in me when I speak well,
withdraw not your grace, leave me not dry and cold.
I have praised you in the pain of love, I would praise you still
in the slowing of the blood, the time when I grow old.
['Prayer']

Wright, Orville (1871–1948)

American aviation pioneer, known for the first powered flight, 1903

1. [Explaining the principles of powered flight]
The airplane stays up because it doesn't have the time to fall.
[Attr.]

Wyatt, Sir Thomas (c. 1503–1542)

English poet, courtier and diplomat

1. And wilt thou leave me thus?
Say nay, say nay, for shame.
['An Appeal' (1557)]

2. What should I say,
Since faith is dead,
And Truth away
From you is fled?
['Farewell' (1557)]

3. They flee from me, that sometime did me seek
With naked foot, stalking in my chamber.
I have seen them gentle, tame, and meek,
That now are wild, and do not remember
That sometime they put themselves in danger
To take bread at my hand...

4. When her loose gown from her shoulders did fall,
And she me caught in her arms long and small,
Therewith all sweetly did me kiss
And softly said, 'Dear heart how like you this?'
['They flee from me' (1557)]

5. My lute, awake! perform the last
Labour that thou and I shall waste,
An end that I have now begun;
For when this song is sung and past,
My lute, be still, for I have done.
['To his Lute' (1557)]

6. Whoso list to hunt, I know where is an hind...

7. There is written her fair neck round about:
Noli me tangere, for Caesar's I am;
And wild for to hold, though I seem tame.
['Whoso list to hunt' (1557)]

Wycherley, William (c. 1640–1716)

English Restoration dramatist and poet

1. Nay, you had both felt his desperate deadly daunting dagger: – there are your d's for you!
[*The Gentleman Dancing-Master* (1672), V]

2. Fy! madam, do you think me so ill bred as to love a husband?
[*Love in a Wood, or, St James's Park* (1672), III]

3. A mistress should be like a little country retreat near the town, not to dwell in constantly, but only for a night and away.
[*The Country Wife* (1675), I]

4. Go to your business, I say, pleasure, whilst I go to my pleasure, business.
[*The Country Wife* (1675), II]

5. With faint praises one another damn.
[*The Plain Dealer* (1677), Prologue]

Wycliffe, John (c. 1329–1384)

English religious reformer; instigator of a complete English translation of the Bible

1. [To the Duke of Lancaster, 1381]
I believe that in the end the truth will conquer.
[In J.R. Green, *Short History of the English People*]

Wylie, Betty Jane

1. A marriage is really a nonstop conversation.
[*All in the Family: A Survival Guide for Living and Loving in a Changing World*]

2. The first time I had hands laid on me in lust, and not in love, it took me a while to know the difference.
[*Beginnings: A Book for Widows*]

Wyndham, George (1863–1913)

English politician and essayist; Conservative Secretary for Ireland, 1900–1905

1. Over the construction of Dreadnoughts ... What the people said was, 'We want eight, and we won't wait.'
[Speech, Wigan, 1909]

Wynne-Tyson, Esme (1898–1972)

British actress, dramatist and writer

1. Scheherazade is the classical example of a woman saving her head by using it.
[Attr.]

Wyntoun, Andrew of (c. 1350–c. 1420)
Scottish poet-historian and prior

1. Quhen Alysandyr oure King wes dede
That Scotland led in luve and le,
Away wes sons of ale and brede,
Of wyne and wax, of gamyn and gle,
Oure gold wes changyd into lede.
Chryst, born into virgynyte,
Succour Scotland, and remede
That stad is in perplexyté.
[*Oryginale Cronykille of Scotland* (1406)]

X, Malcolm (Malcolm Little) (1925–1965)
Afro-American activist leader; assassinated

1. I believe in the brotherhood of all men, but I don't believe in wasting brotherhood on anyone who doesn't want to practise it with me.
[Speech, Harvard Law School, 1964, in Archie Epps, *Malcolm X and the American Negro Revolution* (1965)]

2. We never made one step forward until world pressure put Uncle Sam on the spot ... It has never been out of any internal sense of morality or legality or humanism that we were allowed to advance. You have been as cold as an icicle whenever it comes to the rights of the black man in this country.
[Speech, Harvard Law School, 1964, in Archie Epps, *Malcolm X and the American Negro Revolution* (1965)]

3. The Negro problem has ceased to be a Negro problem. It has ceased to be an American problem and has now become a world problem, a problem for all humanity.
[Speech, Harvard Law School, 1964, in Archie Epps, *Malcolm X and the American Negro Revolution* (1965)]

4. The soul of Africa is still reflected in the music played by the black man. In everything else we do we still are African in color, feeling, everything. And we will always be that whether we like it or not.
[Speech, Harvard Law School, 1964, in Archie Epps, *Malcolm X and the American Negro Revolution* (1965)]

Xenophanes (c. 570–480 BC)
Greek monotheist philosopher and poet, founder of the Eleatic School

1. Ethiopians say that their gods are snub-nosed and black, Thracians that theirs have light blue eyes and red hair.
[In J.H. Lesher, *Xenophanes of Colophon* (1992), Fragment 16]

2. All things are from the earth, and all things come to the earth in the end.
[In J.H. Lesher, *Xenophanes of Colophon* (1992), Fragment 27]

3. And of course the clear and certain truth no man has seen.
[In J.H. Lesher, *Xenophanes of Colophon* (1992), Fragment 34]

Xenophon (c. 430–354 BC)
Greek general, historian and prose writer; disciple of Socrates

1. [The joyful cry of his soldiers after their long march (1000 miles) back to the Aegean from the centre of Persia]
The sea! The sea!
[*Anabasis* IV, 7]

Xerxes (c. 519–465 BC)
King of Persia, 485–465, and leader of a failed expedition against Greece (480–479); assassinated

1. [On surveying his army]
I was thinking, and I was moved to pity that the whole of human life is so short – not one of this great number will be alive a hundred years from now.
[In Heridotus, *Histories*, VII, 46]

Ximénèz, Augustin, Marquis de (1726–1817)
French wit, essayist and poet

1. *Attaquons dans ses eaux*
La perfide Albion!
Let us attack perfidious Albion in her own waters!
[In *Poésies révolutionnaires et contre-révolutionnaires* (1821), I, 'L'Ere des Français']

Yamamoto, Isoroku (1884–1943)
Japanese admiral; devised the attack on Pearl Harbor, 1941

1. [Said after the Japanese attack on Pearl Harbor, 1941]
I fear we have only awakened a sleeping giant, and his reaction will be terrible.
[Attr. by A.J.P. Taylor in *The Listener*, 1976]

Yankwich, Léon R. (1888–1975)
Romanian-born American judge and writer

1. [Decision, State District Court, Southern District of California, June 1928, quoting columnist O.O. McIntyre]
There are no illegitimate children – only illegitimate parents.
[Attr.]

Yeames, W.F. (1835–1918)
Russian-born British historical and subject painter

1. And when did you last see your father?
[Title of painting, 1878]

Yeatman, Robert Julian (1897–1968)
British humorous writer

1. To confess that you are totally ignorant about the Horse, is social suicide: you will be despised by everybody, especially the horse.
[*Horse Nonsense* (1933); with W.C. Sellar]

Yeats, W.B. (1865–1939)
Irish lyric poet and dramatist; editor, essayist, letter writer, autobiographer, a founder of the Irish National Theatre Company and senator; Nobel prize 1923

1. In the Junes that were warmer than these are, the waves were more gay,
When I was a boy with never a crack in my heart.
[In *Irish Monthly*, 1886, 'The Meditation of the Old Fisherman']

2. Come away, O human child!
To the waters and the wild
With a faery, hand in hand,
For the world's more full of weeping than you can understand.
[In *Irish Monthly*, 1886, 'The Stolen Child']

3. Down by the salley gardens my love and I did meet;
She passed the salley gardens with little snow-white feet.
She bid me take love easy, as the leaves grow on the tree;
But I, being young and foolish, with her would not agree.
In a field by the river my love and I did stand,
And on my leaning shoulder she laid her snow-white hand.

She bid me take life easy, as the grass grows on the [illegible]s;
But I was young and foolish, and now am full of t[illegible]
[*The Wanderings of Oisin and Other Poems* (1889), 'Down by the Salley Gardens']

4. I will arise and go now, and go to Innisfree,
And a small cabin build there, of clay and wattles made:
Nine bean-rows will I have there, a hive for the honey-bee,
And live alone in the bee-loud glade.

And I shall have some peace there, for peace comes dropping slow,
Dropping from the veils of the morning to where the cricket sings;
There midnight's all a glimmer, and noon a purple glow,
And evening full of the linnet's wings.

I will arise and go now, for always night and day
I hear lake water lapping with low sounds by the shore;
While I stand on the roadway, or on the pavements grey,
I hear it in the deep heart's core.
[In the *National Observer*, 1890, 'The Lake Isle of Innisfree']

5. When I play on my fiddle in Dooney,
Folk dance like a wave of the sea...

6. For the good are always the merry,
Save by an evil chance,
And the merry love the fiddle,
And the merry love to dance.
[In the *Bookman*, 1892, 'The Fiddler of Dooney']

7. The Light of Lights
Looks always on the motive, not the deed,
The Shadow of Shadows on the deed alone.
Tell them who walk upon the floor of peace
That I would die and go to her I love;
The years like great black oxen tread the world,
And God the herdsman goads them on behind,
And I am broken by their passing feet.
[*The Countess Cathleen* (1892), closing lines]

8. A pity beyond all telling
Is hid in the heart of love.
[*The Countess Kathleen and Various Legends and Lyrics* (1892), 'The Pity of Love']

9. Rose of all Roses, Rose of all the World!
[*The Countess Kathleen and Various Legends and Lyrics* (1892), 'The Rose of Battle']

10. The brawling of a sparrow in the eaves,
The brilliant moon and all the milky sky,
And all that famous harmony of leaves,
Had blotted out man's image and his cry.

A girl arose that had red mournful lips
And seemed the greatness of the world in tears,
Doomed like Odysseus and the labouring ships
And proud as Priam murdered with his peers;

Arose, and on the instant clamorous eaves,
A climbing moon upon an empty sky,
And all that lamentation of the leaves,
Could but compose man's image and his cry.
[*The Countess Kathleen and Various Legends and Lyrics* (1892), 'The Sorrow of Love']

11. Know, that I would accounted be
True brother of a company
That sang, to sweeten Ireland's wrong,
Ballad and story, rann and song...

12. My rhymes more than their rhyming tell
Of things discovered in the deep,
Where only body's laid asleep.
[*The Countess Kathleen and Various Legends and Lyrics* (1892), 'To Ireland in the Coming Times']

13. Come near; I would, before my time to go,
Sing of old Eire and the ancient ways:
Red Rose, proud Rose, sad Rose of all my days.
[*The Countess Kathleen and Various Legends and Lyrics* (1892), 'To the Rose upon the Rood of Time']

14. When you are old and grey and full of sleep,
And nodding by the fire, take down this book,
And slowly read, and dream of the soft look
Your eyes had once, and of their shadows deep;

How many loved your moments of glad grace,
And loved your beauty with love false or true,
But one man loved the pilgrim soul in you,
And loved the sorrows of your changing face;

And bending down beside the glowing bars,
Murmur, a little sadly, how Love fled
And paced upon the mountains overhead
And hid his face amid a crowd of stars.
[*The Countess Kathleen and Various Legends and Lyrics* (1892), 'When You are Old'. Cf. Ronsard: 1]

15. Out-worn heart, in a time out-worn,
Come clear of the nets of wrong and right;
Laugh, heart, again in the grey twilight,
Sigh, heart, again in the dew of the morn.
[In the *National Observer*, 1893, 'Into the Twilight']

16. Land of Heart's Desire,
Where beauty has no ebb, decay no flood,
But joy is wisdom, Time an endless song.
[*The Land of Heart's Desire* (1894)]

17. For they hear the wind laugh and murmur and sing
Of a land where even the old are fair,
And even the wise are merry of tongue.
[*The Land of Heart's Desire* (1894)]

18. When my arms wrap round you I press
My heart upon the loveliness
That has long faded from the world.
[In *The Savoy*, 1896, 'He remembers Forgotten Beauty']

19. A woman of so shining loveliness
That men threshed corn at midnight by a tress...

20. When shall the stars be blown about the sky,
Like the sparks blown out of a smithy, and die?
Surely thine hour has come, thy great wind blows,
Far-off, most secret, and inviolate Rose?
[In *The Savoy*, 1896, 'The Secret Rose']

21. I would that the boar without bristles had come from the West
And had rooted the sun and moon and stars out of the sky.
[In *The Dome*, 1897, 'He mourns for the Change that has come upon him and his Beloved, and longs for the End of the World']

22. I went out to the hazel wood
Because a fire was in my head...

23. Though I am old with wandering
Through hollow lands and hilly lands
I will find out where she has gone,
And kiss her lips and take her hands;
And walk among long dappled grass
And pluck till time and times are done
The silver apples of the moon,
The golden apples of the sun.
[In *The Sketch*, 1897, 'The Song of Wandering Aengus']

24. I have drunk ale from the Country of the Young
And weep because I know all things now.
[In *The Dome*, 1898, 'He Thinks of his Past Greatness when a Part of the Constellations of Heaven']

25. But weigh this song with the great and their pride;
I made it out of a mouthful of air,
Their children's children shall say they have lied.
[In *The Dome*, 1898, 'He thinks of those who have Spoken Evil of his Beloved']

26. Had I the heavens' embroidered cloths,
Enwrought with golden and silver light,
The blue and the dim and the dark cloths
Of night and light and the half-light,
I would spread the cloths under your feet:
But I, being poor, have only my dreams;
I have spread my dreams under your feet;
Tread softly because you tread on my dreams.
[*The Wind Among the Reeds* (1899), 'He wishes for the Cloths of Heaven']

27. A line will take us hours maybe;
Yet if it does not seem a moment's thought,
Our stitching and unstitching has been naught.
[In the *Monthly Review*, 1902, 'Adam's Curse']

28. One woman and two men: that is the quarrel
That knows no mending.
[*Deirdre* (1907)]

29. Now I may wither into the truth.
[In the *English Review*, 1909, 'The Coming of Wisdom with Time']

30. Why should I blame her that she filled my days
With misery, or that she would of late
Have taught to ignorant men most violent ways,
Or hurled the little streets upon the great,
Had they but courage equal to desire?...

31. Why, what could she have done, being what she is?
Was there another Troy for her to burn?
[*The Green Helmet and Other Poems* (Cuala, 1910), 'No Second Troy']

32. But was there ever dog that praised his fleas?
[*The Green Helmet and Other Poems* (Cuala, 1910), 'To a Poet, Who would have me Praise certain Bad Poets, Imitators of His and Mine']

33. When I was young,
I had not given a penny for a song
Did not the poet sing it with such airs
That one believed he had a sword upstairs;
Yet would be now, could I but have my wish,
Colder and dumber and deafer than a fish.
[*The Green Helmet and Other Poems* (Cuala, 1910), 'All Things can Tempt Me']

34. Suddenly I saw the cold and rook-delighting heaven
That seemed as though ice burned and was but the more ice,
And thereupon imagination and heart were driven
So wild that every casual thought of that and this
Vanished, and left but memories, that should be out of season.
[*The Green Helmet and Other Poems* (1912), 'The Cold Heaven']

35. Where, where but here have Pride and Truth,
That long to give themselves for wage,
To shake their wicked sides at youth
Restraining reckless middle-age?
[*The Green Helmet and Other Poems* (1912), 'On hearing that the Students of our New University have joined the Agitation against Immoral Literature']

36. [Of Ireland]
This blind bitter land.
[*The Green Helmet and Other Poems* (1912), 'Words']

37. Was it for this the wild geese spread
The grey wing upon every tide;
For this that all that blood was shed...
All that delirium of the brave?
Romantic Ireland's dead and gone,
It's with O'Leary in the grave.
[In the *Irish Times*, 1913, 'September, 1913']

38. That grammar school of courtesies
Where wit and beauty learned their trade
Upon Urbino's windy hill.
[In the *Irish Times*, 1913, 'To a Wealthy Man who promised a Second Subscription to the Dublin Municipal Gallery if it were proved the People wanted Pictures']

39. I made my song a coat
Covered with embroideries
Out of old mythologies
From heel to throat;
But the fools caught it,
Wore it in the world's eye
As though they'd wrought it.
Song, let them take it
For there's more enterprise
In walking naked.
[*Responsibilities* (1914), 'A Coat']

40. Bald heads forgetful of their sins,
Old, learned, respectable bald heads
Edit and annotate the lines
That young men, tossing on their beds,
Rhymed out in love's despair
To flatter beauty's ignorant ear.

All shuffle there; all cough in ink;
All wear the carpet with their shoes;
All think what other people think;
All know the man their neighbour knows.
Lord, what would they say
Did their Catullus walk that way?
[In *Catholic Anthology* 1914–1915, 1915, 'The Scholars']

41. I have met them at close of day
Coming with vivid faces
From counter or desk among grey
Eighteenth-century houses.
I have passed with a nod of the head
Or polite meaningless words,
Or have lingered awhile and said
Polite meaningless words,
And thought before I had done
Of a mocking tale or a gibe
To please a companion
Around the fire at the club,
Being certain that they and I
But lived where motley is worn:
All changed, changed utterly:
A terrible beauty is born...

42. This other man I had dreamed
A drunken vainglorious lout.
He had done most bitter wrong
To some who are near my heart,
Yet I number him in the song;
He, too, has resigned his part
In the casual comedy;
He, too, has been changed in his turn,
Transformed utterly...

43. Too long a sacrifice
Can make a stone of the heart...

44. And what if excess of love
Bewildered them till they died?...

45. MacDonagh and MacBride
And Connolly and Pearse
Now and in time to be,
Wherever green is worn,
Are changed, changed utterly:
A terrible beauty is born.
[*Easter, 1916* (1916), Title poem]

46. Before I am old
I shall have written him one
Poem maybe as cold
And passionate as the dawn.
[In *Poetry* (Chicago), 1916, 'The Fisherman']

47. I mourn for that most lonely thing; and yet God's will be done:
I knew a phoenix in my youth, so let them have their day.
[In *Poetry* (Chicago), 1916, 'His Phoenix']

48. I think it better that in times like these
A poet's mouth be silent, for in truth
We have no gift to set a statesman right;
He has had enough of meddling who can please
A young girl in the indolence of her youth,
Or an old man upon a winter's night.
[In E. Wharton (ed.), *The Book of the Homeless* (1916), 'On being asked for a War Poem']

49. The trees are in their autumn beauty,
The woodland paths are dry,
Under the October twilight the water
Mirrors a still sky;
Upon the brimming water among the stones
Are nine-and-fifty swans...

50. I have looked upon those brilliant creatures,
And now my heart is sore...

51. Among what rushes will they build,
By what lake's edge or pool
Delight men's eyes when I awake some day
To find they have flown away?
[*The Wild Swans at Coole, Other Verses and a Play* (1917), 'The Wild Swans at Coole']

52. Others because you did not keep
That deep-sworn vow have been friends of mine.
[*The Wild Swans at Coole, Other Verses and a Play* (1917), 'The Deep-sworn Vow']

53. [Of Keats]
I see a schoolboy when I think of him,
With face and nose pressed to a sweet-shop window,
For certainly he sank into his grave
His senses and his heart unsatisfied,
And made – being poor, ailing and ignorant,
Shut out from all the luxury of the world,
The coarse-bred son of a livery-stable keeper–
Luxuriant song.
[*The Wild Swans at Coole, Other Verses and a Play* (1917), 'Ego Dominus Tuus']

54. Always we'd have the new friend meet the old
And we are hurt if either friend seem cold.
[In the *English Review*, 1918, 'In Memory of Major Robert Gregory', II]

55. I am accustomed to their lack of breath,
But not that my dear friend's dear son,
Our Sidney and our perfect man,
Could share in that discourtesy of death.
[In the *English Review*, 1918, 'In Memory of Major Robert Gregory', VI]

56. O heart, we are old;
The living beauty is for younger men:
We cannot pay its tribute of wild tears.
[In the *Little Review*, 1918, 'The Living Beauty']

57. I thought no more was needed
Youth to prolong
Than dumb-bell and foil
To keep the body young.
O who could have foretold
That the heart grows old?
[In the *Little Review*, 1918, 'A Song']

58. I know what wages beauty gives,
How hard a life her servant lives,
Yet praise the winters gone:
There is not a fool can call me friend,
And I may dine at journey's end
With Landor and with Donne.
[*Nine Poems* (1918), 'To a Young Beauty']

59. In courtesy I'd have her chiefly learned;
Hearts are not had as a gift but hearts are earned
By those that are not entirely beautiful...

60. An intellectual hatred is the worst,
So let her think opinions are accursed.
[In *Poetry*, 1919, 'A Prayer for my Daughter']

61. Those that I fight I do not hate,
Those that I guard I do not love;
My country is Kiltartan Cross,
My countrymen Kiltartan's poor,
No likely end could bring them loss
Or leave them happier than before.
Nor law, nor duty bade me fight,
Nor public men, nor cheering crowds,
A lonely impulse of delight
Drove to this tumult in the clouds;
I balanced all, brought all to mind,
The years to come seemed waste of breath,
A waste of breath the years behind
In balance with this life, this death.
[*The Wild Swans at Coole* (1919), 'An Irish Airman Forsees his Death']

62. Turning and turning in the widening gyre
The falcon cannot hear the falconer;
Things fall apart; the centre cannot hold;
Mere anarchy is loosed upon the world,
The blood-dimmed tide is loosed, and everywhere
The ceremony of innocence is drowned;
The best lack all conviction, while the worst
Are full of passionate intensity.

Surely some revelation is at hand;
Surely the Second Coming is at hand.
The Second Coming!...

63. And what rough beast, its hour come round at last,
Slouches towards Bethlehem to be born?
[In *The Dial*, 1920, 'The Second Coming']

64. For it is a ghost's right,
His element is so fine
Being sharpened by his death,
To drink from the wine-breath
While our gross palates drink from the whole wine.
[In the *New Republic*, 1921, 'All Souls' Night']

65. All men are dancers and their tread
Goes to the barbarous clangour of a gong.
[In *The Dial*, 1921, 'Nineteen Hundred and Nineteen', II]

66. We are closed in, and the key is turned
On our uncertainty; somewhere
A man is killed, or a house burned,
Yet no clear fact to be discerned...

67. We had fed the heart on fantasies,
The heart's grown brutal from the fare;
More substance in our enmities
Than in our love.
[In *The Dial*, 1923, 'Meditations in Time of Civil War', VI, 'The Stare's Nest by My Window']

68. A sudden blow: the great wings beating still
Above the staggering girl, her thighs caressed
By the dark webs, her nape caught in his bill,
He holds her helpless breast upon his breast.

How can those terrified vague fingers push
The feathered glory from her loosening thighs?...

69. A shudder in the loins engenders there
The broken wall, the burning roof and tower
And Agamemnon dead.
[In *The Dial*, 1924, 'Leda and the Swan']

70. O chestnut-tree, great-rooted blossomer,
Are you the leaf, the blossom or the bole?
O body swayed to music, O brightening glance,
How can we know the dancer from the dance?
[In *The Dial*, 1927, 'Among School Children']

71. That is no country for old men. The young
In one another's arms, birds in the trees
– Those dying generations – at their song,
The salmon-falls, the mackerel-crowded seas,
Fish, flesh, or fowl, commend all summer long
Whatever is begotten, born, and dies...

72. An aged man is but a paltry thing,
A tattered coat upon a stick, unless
Soul clap its hands and sing, and louder sing
For every tatter in its mortal dress...

73. And therefore I have sailed the seas and come
To the holy city of Byzantium.
[*October Blast* (1927), 'Sailing to Byzantium']

74. What shall I do with this absurdity–
O heart, O troubled heart – this caricature,
Decrepit age that has been tied to me
As to a dog's tail?...

75. It seems that I must bid the Muse go pack,
Choose Plato and Plotinus for a friend
Until imagination, ear and eye,
Can be content with argument and deal
In abstract things; or be derided by
A sort of battered kettle at the heel.
[In the *New Republic*, 1927, 'The Tower', I]

76. Does the imagination dwell the most
Upon a woman won or woman lost?
If on the lost, admit you turned aside
From a great labyrinth out of pride.
[In the *New Republic*, 1927, 'The Tower', II]

77. Death and life were not
Till man made up the whole,
Made lock, stock and barrel
Out of his bitter soul.
[In the *New Republic*, 1927, 'The Tower', III]

78. Odour of blood when Christ was slain
Made all Platonic tolerance vain
And vain all Doric discipline.
[In the *Adelphi*, 1927, 'Two Songs from a Play', II]

79. And God-appointed Berkeley that proved all things a dream...

80. This pragmatical, preposterous pig of a world.
[In *The Exile*, 1928, 'Blood and the Moon', II]

81. What lively lad most pleasured me
Of all that with me lay?
I answer that I gave my soul
And loved in misery,
But had great pleasure with a lad
That I loved bodily.

Flinging from his arms I laughed
To think his passion such
He fancied that I gave a soul
Did but our bodies touch,
And laughed upon his breast to think
Beast gave beast as much.
[*The Winding Stair* (1929), 'A Last Confession']

82. Come, let me sing into your ear;
Those dancing days are gone.
[In the *New Republic*, 1930, 'Those Dancing Days are Gone']

83. Locke sank into a swoon;
The Garden died;
God took the spinning-jenny
Out of his side.
[In the *Dublin Magazine*, 1931, 'Fragments', I]

84. Swift has sailed into his rest;
Savage indignation there
Cannot lacerate his breast.
Imitate him if you dare,
World-besotted traveller; he
Served human liberty.
[In the *Dublin Magazine*, 1931, 'Swift's Epitaph']

85. What were all the world's alarms
To mighty Paris when he found
Sleep upon a golden bed
That first dawn in Helen's arms?
[In the *New Keepsake*, 1931, 'Lullaby']

86. A starlit or a moonlit dome disdains
All that man is,
All mere complexities,
The fury and the mire of human veins.

Before me floats an image, man or shade,
Shade more than man, more image than a shade;
For Hades' bobbin bound in mummy-cloth
May unwind the winding path...

87. That dolphin-torn, that gong-tormented sea.
[*Words for Music Perhaps and Other Poems* (1932), 'Byzantium']

88. Between extremities
Man runs his course.
[*Words for Music Perhaps and Other Poems* (1932), 'Vacillation', I]

89. While on the shop and street I gazed
My body of a sudden blazed;
And twenty minutes more or less
It seemed, so great my happiness,
That I was blessèd and could bless.
[*Words for Music Perhaps and Other Poems* (1932), 'Vacillation', IV]

90. Those great honey-coloured
Ramparts at your ear...

91. Only God, my dear,
Could love you for yourself alone
And not your yellow hair.
[*Words for Music Perhaps and Other Poems* (1932), 'Anne Gregory']

92. I shudder and I sigh to think
That even Cicero
And many-minded Homer were
Mad as the mist and snow.
[*Words for Music Perhaps and Other Poems* (1932), 'Words for Music Perhaps', 'Mad as the Mist and Snow']

93. Scattered on the level grass
Or winding through the grove
Plato there and Minos pass,
There stately Pythagoras
And all the choir of Love.
[*Words for Music Perhaps and Other Poems* (1932), 'Words for Music Perhaps', 'The Delphic Oracle upon Plotinus']

94. The intellect of man is forced to choose
Perfection of the life, or of the work.
[*The Winding Stair and Other Poems* (1933), 'The Choice']

95. A woman can be proud and stiff
When on love intent;
But Love has pitched his mansion in
The place of excrement;
For nothing can be sole or whole
That has not been rent.
[*The Winding Stair and Other Poems* (1933), 'Crazy Jane talks with the Bishop']

96. Nor dread nor hope attend
A dying animal;
A man awaits his end
Dreading and hoping all...

97. He knows death to the bone–
Man has created death.
[*The Winding Stair and Other Poems* (1933), 'Death']

98. Only the dead can be forgiven;
But when I think of that my tongue's a stone.
[*The Winding Stair and Other Poems* (1933), 'A Dialogue of Self and Soul', I]

99. I am content to live it all again
And yet again, if it be life to pitch
Into the frog-spawn of a blind man's ditch,
A blind man battering blind men.
[*The Winding Stair and Other Poems* (1933), 'A Dialogue of Self and Soul', II]

100. The light of evening, Lissadell,
Great windows open to the south,
Two girls in silk kimonos, both
Beautiful, one a gazelle...

101. The innocent and the beautiful
Have no enemy but time.
[*The Winding Stair and Other Poems* (1933), 'In Memory of Eva Gore-Booth and Con Markiewicz']

102. Never to have lived is best, ancient writers say;
Never to have drawn the breath of life, never to have looked into the eye of day;
The second best's a gay goodnight and quickly turn away.
[*The Collected Poems of W.B. Yeats* (1933), 'From Oedipus at Colonus']

103. Now his wars on God begin;
At stroke of midnight God shall win.
['The Four Ages of Man', first published in the *London Mercury*, 1934, then as IX of 'Supernatural Poems' in *Parnell's Funeral and Other Poems* (1935)]

104. Think where man's glory most begins and ends,
And say my glory was I had such friends.
[*A Speech and Two Poems* (1937), 'The Municipal Gallery Revisited']

105. Grant me an old man's frenzy,
Myself I must remake
Till I am Timon or Lear
Or that William Blake
Who beat upon the wall
Till Truth obeyed his call.
[In *Atlantic Monthly* and the *London Mercury*, 1938, 'An Acre of Grass']

106. Maud Gonne at Howth Station waiting a train,
Pallas Athene in that straight back and arrogant head:
All the Olympians; a thing never known again.
[*New Poems* (1938), 'Beautiful Lofty Things']

107. The ghost of Roger Casement
Is beating on the door.
[*New Poems* (1938), 'The Ghost of Roger Casement']

108. The gyres! the gyres! Old Rocky Face, look forth;
Things thought too long can be no longer thought,
For beauty dies of beauty, worth of worth,
And ancient lineaments are blotted out.
[*New Poems* (1938), 'The Gyres']

109. All men have aimed at, found and lost;
Black out; Heaven blazing into the head:
Tragedy wrought to its uttermost...

All things fall and are built again,
And those that build them again are gay.
[In the *London Mercury*, 1938, 'Lapis Lazuli']

110. Parnell came down the road, he said to a cheering man:
'Ireland shall get her freedom and you still break stone.'
[In the *London Mercury*, 1938, 'Parnell']

111. You think it horrible that lust and rage
Should dance attention upon my old age;
They were not such a plague when I was young;
What else have I to spur me into song?
[In the *London Mercury*, 1938, 'The Spur']

112. A statesman is an easy man,
He tells his lies by rote;
A journalist makes up his lies
And takes you by the throat;
So stay at home and drink your beer
And let the neighbours vote,
Said the man in the golden breastplate
Under the old stone Cross.
[In *The Nation*, 1938, 'The Old Stone Cross']

113. Why should not old men be mad?
[*On the Boiler* (1939), 'Why should not Old Men be Mad?']

114. Now that my ladder's gone,
I must lie down where all the ladders start,
In the foul rag-and-bone shop of the heart.
[In *Atlantic Monthly* and the *London Mercury*, 1939, 'The Circus Animals' Desertion']

115. How can I, that girl standing there,
My attention fix
On Roman or on Russian
Or on Spanish politics?
[In *Atlantic Monthly* and the *London Mercury*, 1939, 'Politics']

116. All that I have said and done,
Now that I am old and ill,

Turns into a question till
I lie awake night after night
And never get the answers right.
[In *Atlantic Monthly* and the *London Mercury*, 1939, 'The Man and the Echo']

117. Our master Caesar is in the tent,
Where the maps are spread,
His eyes fixed upon nothing,
A hand under his head.
Like a long-legged fly upon the stream
His mind moves upon silence.
[In the *London Mercury*, 1939, 'Long-legged Fly']

118. There all the golden codgers lay,
There the silver dew.
[In the *London Mercury*, 1939, 'News for the Delphic Oracle', I]

119. From where Pan's cavern is
Intolerable music falls.
Foul goat-head, brutal arm appear,
Belly, shoulder, bum,
Flash fishlike; nymphs and satyrs
Copulate in the foam.
[In the *London Mercury*, 1939, 'News for the Delphic Oracle', III]

120. Pythagoras planned it. Why did the people stare?
His numbers, though they moved or seemed to move
In marble or in bronze, lacked character.
But boys and girls, pale from the imagined love
Of solitary beds, knew what they were,
That passion could bring character enough,
And pressed at midnight in some public place
Live lips upon a plummet-measured face.

No! Greater than Pythagoras, for the men
That with a mallet or a chisel modelled these
Calculations that look but casual flesh, put down
All Asiatic vague immensities,
And not the banks of oars that swam upon
The many-headed foam at Salamis.
Europe put off that foam when Phidias
Gave women dreams and dreams their looking glass...

121. When Pearse summoned Cuchulain to his side,
What stalked through the Post Office? What intellect,
What calculation, number, measurement, replied?
We Irish, born into that ancient sect
But thrown upon this filthy modern tide
And by its formless spawning fury wrecked,
Climb to our proper dark, that we may trace
The lineaments of a plummet-measured face.
[In the *London Mercury*, 1939, 'The Statues']

122. Measurement began our might.
[In the *Irish Times*, *Irish Independent*, and *Irish Press*, 1939, 'Under Ben Bulben', IV]

123. Irish poets, learn your trade,
Sing whatever is well made,
Scorn the sort now growing up
All out of shape from top to toe,
Their unremembering hearts and heads
Base-born products of base beds.
Sing the peasantry, and then
Hard-riding country gentlemen,
The holiness of monks, and after
Porter-drinkers' randy laughter;
Sing the lords and ladies gay
That were beaten into the clay
Through seven heroic centuries.
Cast your mind on other days
That we in coming days may be
Still the indomitable Irishry.
[In the *Irish Times*, *Irish Independent*, and *Irish Press*, 1939, 'Under Ben Bulben', V]

124. Under bare Ben Bulben's head
In Drumcliff churchyard Yeats is laid...
On limestone quarried near the spot
By his command these words are cut:
Cast a cold eye
On life, on death.
Horseman, pass by!
[In the *Irish Times*, *Irish Independent*, and *Irish Press*, 1939, 'Under Ben Bulben', VI (Yeats's epitaph)]

125. Twelve pennies! What better reason for killing a man?
[*The Death of Cuchulain* (1939)]

126. Behind Ireland fierce and militant, is Ireland poetic, passionate, remembering, idyllic, fanciful, and always patriotic.
['Popular Ballad Poetry of Ireland', 1889]

127. When we remember the majesty of Cuchullin and the beauty of sorrowing Deirdre we should not forget that it is that majesty and that beauty which are immortal, and not the perishing tongue that first told of them.
[*United Ireland*, 1892]

128. All folk literature, and all literature that keeps the folk tradition, delights in unbounded and immortal things.
['The Celtic Element in Literature' (1902)]

129. We have no longer in any country a literature as great as the literature of the old world, and that is because the newspapers, all kinds of second-rate books, the preoccupation of men with all kinds of practical changes, have driven the living imagination out of this world.
[In *Samhain*, 1904, 'First Principles']

130. 'In dreams begins responsibility.'
[In *Responsibilities* (1914), Epigraph]

131. We make out of the quarrel with others, rhetoric; but of the quarrel with ourselves, poetry.
[*Per Amica Silentia Lunae* (1917), 'Anima Hominis', V]

132. The poet finds and makes his mask in disappointment, the hero in defeat.
[*Per Amica Silentia Lunae* (1917), 'Anima Hominis', X]

133. [On his Nobel Prize medal]
It shows a young man listening to a Muse, who stands young and beautiful ... and I think as I examine it, 'I was good looking once like that young man, but my verse was full of infirmity, my Muse old as it were; and now I am old and rheumatic, and nothing to look at, but my Muse is young.'
[*The Bounty of Sweden* (1925), 7]

134. A civilisation is a struggle to keep self-control.
[*A Vision* (1925), 'Dove or Swan']

135. [From Yeats's speech on divorce, in which he stressed the contribution made by the Protestant minority to the literary and political life of Ireland]
We against whom you have done this thing are no petty people. We are one of the great stocks of Europe. We are the people of Burke; we are the people of Grattan; we are the people of Swift, the people of Emmet, the people of Parnell. We have created the most of the modern literature of this country. We have created the best of its political intelligence.
[Speech to the Senate, June 1925]

136. It seems to me that true love is a discipline, and it needs so much wisdom that the love of Solomon and Sheba must have lasted, for all the silence of the Scriptures.
[*Estrangement: Being some fifty Thoughts from a Diary kept in the year nineteen hundred and nine* (1926), 7]

137. I think that all happiness depends upon the energy to assume the mask of some other self; that all joyous or creative life is a rebirth as something not oneself, something which has no memory and is created in a moment and perpetually renewed.
[*The Death of Synge and other Passages from an Old Diary* (1928), 6]

138. A good writer should be so simple that he has no faults, only sins.
[*The Death of Synge and other Passages from an Old Diary* (1928), 41]

139. [On George Moore]
He had gone to Paris straight from his father's racing stables ... acquired copious inaccurate French, sat among art students, young writers about to become famous, in some café; a man carved out of a turnip, looking out of astonished eyes.
[*Dramatis Personae* (1935), 7]

140. [On George Moore as a plagiarist]
'The man I object to,' said Moore, 'is the man who plagiarizes without knowing it; I always know; I took ten pages.' To Lady Gregory he said, 'We both quote well, but you always put inverted commas, I never do.'
[*Dramatis Personae* (1935), 20]

141. I once boasted, copying the phrase from a letter of my father's, that I would write a poem 'cold and passionate as the dawn'.
[*Essays and Introductions* (1961), 'A General Introduction for my Work' (1937), 3]

142. The Irish mind has still in country rapscallion or in Bernard Shaw an ancient, cold, explosive, detonating impartiality. The English mind, excited by its newspaper proprietors and its schoolmasters, has turned into a bed-hot harlot.
[*On the Boiler* (1939), 'Ireland after the Revolution', III]

143. When I think of all the books I have read, and of the wise words I have heard spoken, and of the anxiety I have given to parents and grandparents, and of the hopes that I have had, all life weighed in the scales of my own life seems to me preparation for something that never happens.
[*Autobiographies* (1955)]

144. [An imaginary letter, 1931, to a schoolmaster]
My son is now between 9 and 10 and should begin Greek at once ... Do not teach him one word of Latin. The Roman people were the classical decadence, their literature form without matter. They destroyed Milton, the French seventeenth and our eighteenth century...
[In J. Hone, *W.B. Yeats 1865–1939* (1943), 18.7]

145. [Referring to Wilfred Owen]
He is all blood, dirt and sucked sugar stick.
[In D. Wellesley (ed.), *Letters on Poetry from W.B. Yeats to Dorothy Wellesley* (1940), Letter, 21 December 1936]

146. The chief use I can be ... will be by introducing you to some other writers ... one always learns one's business from one's fellow workers.
[In Richard Ellmann, *James Joyce*, Letter to James Joyce]

147. [In conversation with John Sparrow, 1931]
The tragedy of sexual intercourse is the perpetual virginity of the soul.
[Attr. in A. Norman Jeffares, *W.B. Yeats: man and poet* (1949), 10 (i)]

148. [On being told how great an honour it was for himself and his country to win the Nobel Prize]
How much is it, Smyllie, how much is it?
[Attr. in W.R. Rodgers (ed.), *Irish Literary Portraits* (1972)]

149. [Of George Eliot]
She is magnificently ugly – deliciously hideous ... now in this vast ugliness resides a most powerful beauty which, in a very few minutes steals forth and charms the mind.
[Attr.]

150. [Speaking to playwright, Denis Johnston]
It's not a writer's business to hold opinions.
[Attr.]

151. *O'Connor*: How are you?
W.B.Y.: Not very well, I can only write prose today.
[Attr.]

Yeltsin, Boris (1931–)

Russian politician; former Communist, elected President of Russia in 1990

1. I am for the market, not for the bazaar.
[*The Times*, 1992]

2. Some soldiers were picking potatoes, while others didn't feel like fighting.
[In *Newsweek*, 1994, 'The Struggle for Russia']

3. Truth is truth, and the truth will overcome the left, the right and the centre.
[Interview in *Newsweek*, 1994]

4. History will record that the twentieth century essentially ended on 19–21 August 1991]
[Article in *Newsweek*, 1994]

Yevtushenko, Yevgeny (1933–)

Russian lyric poet, noted for his political outspokenness

1. The hell with it. Who never knew
the price of happiness will not be happy.
['Lies' (1955)]

2. Priests preached that Galileo
was the most foolish and harmful ever.
But, as time does prove,
the most foolish is the most clever...

3. Talent is talent, slandered it's no worse,
and those who cursed are forgotten
but remembered are those who were cursed.
['A Career' (1957)]

4. No Jewish blood runs among my blood,
but I am as bitterly and hardly hated
by every anti-semite
as if I were a Jew. By this
I am a Russian.
['Babi Yar' (1961)]

5. In the final analysis, humanity has only two ways out – either universal destruction or universal brotherhood.
[*Yevtushenko Poems* (1966), 'The Spirit of Elbe (To My American Readers)']

6. A tremendous part in strengthening friendship between our peoples must be played by art, whose eternal role is the uniting of human hearts in the name of goodness and justice.
[*Yevtushenko Poems* (1966), 'The Spirit of Elbe (To My American Readers)']

York, Duchess of (1959–)
Sarah Ferguson, wife of Andrew, Duke of York

1. A woman should have a trim waist, a good 'up top' and enough down the bottom, but not too big!
[*The Observer*, 1986, in Jeffrey Care (ed.), *Sayings of the Eighties* (1989)]

Young, Andrew (1807–1889)
Scottish poet and head teacher

1. There is a happy land,
Far, far away,
Where saints in glory stand,
Bright, bright as day.
[Hymn, 1838]

Young, Andrew John (1885–1971)
Scottish poet, churchman and botanist

1. Sometimes an autumn leaf
That falls upon the ground,
Gives the heart a wound
And wakes an ancient grief.
['The Leaf' (1910)]

2. But moon nor star-untidy sky
Could catch my eye as that star's eye;
For still I looked on that same star,
That fitful, fiery Lucifer,
Watching with mind as quiet as moss
Its light nailed to a burning cross.
['The Evening Star' (1922)]

Young, Edward (1683–1765)
English 'graveyard' poet, tragic dramatist and satirist; clergyman and royal chaplain

1. Life is the desert, life the solitude;
Death joins us to the great majority.
[*The Revenge* (1721), IV]

2. Some, for renown, on scraps of learning dote,
And think they grow immortal as they quote.
[*Love of Fame, the Universal Passion* (1725–1728), Satire 1]

3. Be wise with speed;
A fool at forty is a fool indeed.
[*Love of Fame, the Universal Passion* (1725–1728), Satire 2]

4. With skill she vibrates her eternal tongue,
For ever most divinely in the wrong.
[*Love of Fame, the Universal Passion* (1725–1728), Satire 6, 'On Women']

5. How commentators each dark passage shun,
And hold their farthing-candle to the sun.
[*Love of Fame, the Universal Passion* (1725–1728), Satire 7]

6. Tir'd nature's sweet Restorer, balmy Sleep!
He, like the World, his ready visit pays
Where Fortune smiles; the wretched he forsakes...

7. Night, sable Goddess! from her Ebon throne,
In rayless Majesty, now stretches forth
Her leaden Scepter o'er a slumbering world...

8. We take no note of Time
But from its Loss...

9. Be wise today, 't is madness to defer...

10. Procrastination is the Thief of Time...

11. At thirty man suspects himself a Fool;
Knows it at forty, and reforms his Plan;
At fifty chides his infamous Delay,
Pushes his prudent Purpose to Resolve;
In all the magnanimity of Thought
Resolves; and re-resolves; then dies the same...

12. All men think all men Mortal, but themselves.
[*Night-Thoughts on Life, Death and Immortality* (1742–1746), 'Night 1']

13. Sweet Harmonist! and Beautiful as sweet!
And young as beautiful! and Soft, as young!
And Gay as soft! and Innocent as gay!
[*Night-Thoughts on Life, Death and Immortality* (1742–1746), 'Night 3, Narcissa']

14. Shall our pale, wither'd Hands be still stretch'd out,
Trembling, at once, with Eagerness and Age?
With Avarice, and Convulsions grasping hard?
Grasping at Air! for what has Earth beside?
Man wants but Little; nor that Little, long...

15. A God All mercy, is a God unjust.
[*Night-Thoughts on Life, Death and Immortality* (1742–1745), 'Night 4, The Christian Triumph']

16. By Night an Atheist half believes a God.
[*Night-Thoughts on Life, Death and Immortality* (1742–1745), 'Night 5, The Relapse']

17. To know the World, not love her, is thy point;
She gives but little, nor that little long.
[*Night-Thoughts on Life, Death and Immortality* (1742–1745), 'Night 8, Virtue's Apology']

Young, George W. (1846–1919)
British writer

1. Your lips, on my own, when they printed 'Farewell',
Had never been soiled by the 'beverage of hell';
But they come to me now with the bacchanal sign,
And the lips that touch liquor must never touch mine.
['The lips that touch liquor must never touch mine' (c. 1870); also attrib. in a different form to Harriet Glazebrook, 1874]

Young, Michael (Baron Young of Dartington) (1915–)
British educationist, writer, sociologist and lawyer; President of the Consumers' Association from 1965

1. The Rise of the Meritocracy.
[Title of book, 1958]

Young, William Blamire (1862–1935)
Australian painter and poster artist

1. A mad little maid is Rose Madder,
As bad as they make 'em and badder.
At her window one night
Was the scandalous sight
Of a lad and, God help us, a ladder.
[In R.H. Croll, *I Recall*]

Zamoyski, Jan (1541–1605)
Polish Chancellor and army leader

1. The king reigns, but does not govern.
[Speech, Polish Parliament, 1605]

Zangwill, Israel (1864–1926)
English writer and Jewish spokesman; novelist, dramatist, poet, essayist and journalist; teacher and Zionist

1. Scratch the Christian and you find the pagan – spoiled.
[*Children of the Ghetto* (1892)]

2. Let us start a new religion with one commandment, 'Enjoy thyself'.
[*Children of the Ghetto* (1892)]

3. America is God's Crucible, the great Melting-Pot where all the races of Europe are melting and re-forming!
[*The Melting Pot* (1908), I]

4. The law of dislike for the unlike will always prevail. And whereas the unlike is normally situated at a safe distance, the Jews bring the unlike into the heart of every milieu, and must there defend a frontier line as large as the world.
[Speech, 1911, 'The Jewish Race']

Zanuck, Darryl F. (1902–1979)
American film production executive

1. For God's sake, don't say yes until I've finished talking.
[In Philip French, *The Movie Moguls* (1969), 5]

Zanzotto, Andrea (1921–)
Italian poet

1. *Sappiate scrivere ma non leggere, non importa.*
Know how to write but not to read, it doesn't matter.
[*L'Elegia in petèl, da La Beltà* (Beauty, 1968)]

Zapata, Emiliano (1879–1919)
Mexican revolutionary leader; assassinated

1. [On the maderistas who, in Zapata's view, had betrayed the Mexican revolutionary cause]
Muchos de ellos, por complacer a tiranos, por un puñado de monedas, o por cohecho o soborno, están derramando la sangre de sus hermanos.
Many of them, in order to please tyrants, for a handful of coins, or by bribery or corruption, are causing their brothers' blood to be shed.
[*Plan de Ayala*, 28 November 1911]

Zappa, Frank (1940–)
American musician, songwriter and record producer

1. Most people wouldn't know music if it came up and bit them on the ass.
[Attr.]

2. A composer? What the fuck do they do? All the good music's already been written by people with wigs and stuff.
[Attr.]

Zarnack, August (1777–1827)

1. *O Tannenbaum, O Tannenbaum,*
Wie treu sind deine Blätter!
O Christmas tree, O Christmas tree,
How faithful are thy branches!
[Adaptation of an old folk-song, 1820]

Ze Ami (1363–1443)
Japanese playwright, theorist and director of Noh theatre

1. The true aim [of art] is faithfully to represent whatever is imitated.
[*Fúshi kaden* (1400–1418)]

2. In the act of imitation there is the level of no-imitation. When the act of imitation is perfectly accomplished and the actor becomes the thing itself, the actor will no longer have the desire to imitate.
[*Fúshi kaden* (1400–1418)]

3. Know that all beautiful things that are seen and heard represent *yugen*. One that enters the realm of *yugen* is he who makes this his own working principle and becomes that which embodies *yugen*.
[*Fúshi kaden* (1400–1418)]

Zhirinovsky, Vladimir (b. 1946–)
Russian nationalist politician

1. The whole nation, I promise you, will experience an orgasm next year.
[In *Newsweek*, 1994]

2. I will bring Russia up off her knees.
[In *Newsweek*, 1994]

Zola, Emile (1840–1902)
Leading French naturalist novelist, short-story writer and critic; champion of Dreyfus

1. *Des hommes poussaient, une armée noire, vengeresse, qui germait lentement dans les sillons, grandissant pour les récoltes du siècle futur, et dont la germination allait faire bientôt éclater la terre.*
Men were growing, a black army, vengeful, slowly sprouting along the furrows, growing towards the harvests of the coming century, whose germination soon would burst open the earth.
[*Germinal* (1885), VII, 6]

2. *Ne me regardez plus comme ça, parce que vous allez vous user les yeux.*
Stop looking at me like that, or you'll wear your eyes out.
[*La Bête Humaine* (1889–1890), 5]

3. *Le seul intérêt à vivre est de croire à la vie, de l'aimer et de mettre toutes les forces de son intelligence à la mieux connaître.*
The only interest in living comes from believing in life, from loving life and using all the power of your intelligence to know it better.
[*Le Docteur Pascal* (1893), 2]

4. [Article on the Dreyfus affair]
La vérité est en marche, et rien ne l'arrètera.
Truth is on the move and nothing can stop it.
[In *La Vérité en marche* (1901), 'M. Scheurer-Kestner', 1897]

5. *Je n'ai pas voulu que mon pays restât dans le mensonge et l'injustice ... Un jour, la France me remerciera d'avoir aidé à sauver son honneur.*
I did not want my country to languish in lies and injustice ... One day, France will thank me for helping to save her honour.
[In *La Vérité en marche* (1901), 'Déclaration au jury', 1898]

6. *J'accuse.*
I accuse.
[Title of open letter to the President of the Republic, 1898, accusing those in power of making Dreyfus a scapegoat in order to protect the real traitor]

Zukor, Adolph (1873–1976)
American pioneering film producer, born in Hungary; Academy Award 1948 for his services to the industry

1. The public is never wrong.
[In Halliwell, *Filmgoer's Book of Quotes* (1973)]

APPENDIX:
MEMORABLE TITLES AND SLOGANS

FILMS

The films below are listed alphabetically by title, followed by the director's name and the date of release.

The Abominable Dr Phibes, Robert Fuest (1971)
Absolute Beginners, Julien Temple (1986)
Accident, Joseph Losey (1967)
Accidental Hero, Stephen Frears (1992)
The Accused, Jonathan Kaplan (1988)
Aces High, Jack Gold (1976)
Adolf Hitler – My Part in His Downfall, Norman Cohen (1972)
The African Queen, John Huston (1951)
The Agony and the Ecstasy, Carol Reed (1965)
Airplane, Abrahams/Zucker/Zucker (1980)
The Alamo, John Wayne (1960)
Alexander Nevsky, Sergei Eisenstein (1938)
Alfie, Lewis Gilbert (1966)
Alice Doesn't Live Here Anymore, Martin Scorsese (1974)
Alien, Ridley Scott (1979)
Aliens, James Cameron (1986)
All About Eve, Joseph L Mankiewicz (1950)
All Quiet on the Western Front, Lewis Milestone (1930)
All the King's Men, Robert Rossen (1949)
All the President's Men, Alan J Pakula (1976)
All This and Heaven Too, Anatole Litvak (1940)
Amadeus, Milos Forman (1984)
American Gigolo, Paul Schraeder (1980)
American Graffiti, George Lucas (1973)
An American in Paris, Vincente Minnelli (1951)
An American Werewolf in London, John Landis (1981)
The Amityville Horror, Stuart Rosenberg (1979)
Anatomy of a Murder, Otto Preminger (1959)
And God Created Woman, Roger Vadim (1988)
Angel Heart, Alan Parker (1987)
Angel on My Shoulder, Archie Mayo (1946)
Angels With Dirty Faces, Michael Curtiz (1938)
The Angry Silence, Guy Green (1960)
Animal Crackers, Victor Heerman (1930)
Annie Get Your Gun, George Sidney (1950)
Annie Hall, Woody Allen (1977)
The Apartment, Billy Wilder (1960)
Apocalypse Now, Francis Ford Coppola (1979)
April in Paris, David Butler (1952)
Arabesque, Stanley Donen (1966)
Arachnophobia, Frank Marshall (1990)
Around the World in Eighty Days, Michael Anderson (1956)
The Asphalt Jungle, John Huston (1950)
The Attack of the Fifty Foot Woman, Nathan Hertz (1958)
Attack of the Killer Tomatoes, John de Bello (1978)

Babette's Feast, Gabriel Axel (1987)
Baby Boom, Charles Shyer (1987)
Baby Doll, Elia Kazan (1956)
Back to the Future, Robert Zemeckis (1985)
Bad Day at Black Rock, John Sturges (1955)
Bambi, *{Walt Disney animation}* (1942)
The Bank Wagon, Vincente Minnelli (1953)
Barbarella, Roger Vadim (1967)
The Barretts of Wimpole Street, Sidney Franklin (1934)
Barry Lyndon, Stanley Kubrick (1975)
Barton Fink, Joel Coen (1991)
Basic Instinct, Paul Verhoeven (1992)
Batman, Tim Burton (1989)
Battle of the Bulge, Ken Annakin (1965)
The Battleship Potemkin, Sergei Eisenstein (1925)
The Beast from Twenty Thousand Fathoms, Eugène Lourié (1953)
Beau Brummell, Harry Beaumont (1924)
Beau Geste, Herbert Brenon (1926)
The Beautiful Blonde from Bashful Bend, Preston Sturgess (1949)
Becket, Peter Glenville (1964)
The Bed Sitting Room, Richard Lester (1969)
Bedknobs and Broomsticks, Robert Stevenson (1971)
Beetlejuice, Tim Burton (1988)
The Beguiled, Don Siegel (1971)
Behold a Pale Horse, Fred Zinnemann (1964)
Belle de Jour, Luis Buñuel (1967)
La Belle et la Bête, Jean Cocteau (1946)
The Belles of St Trinian's, Frank Launder (1954)
The Belly of an Architect, Peter Greenaway (1987)
Beloved Infidel, Henry King (1959)
Ben Hur, William Wyler (1959)
Bequest to the Nation, James Cellan Jones (1973)
The Best Things in Life are Free, Michael Curtiz (1956)
The Best Years of Our Lives, William Wyler (1946)
La Bête Humaine, Jean Renoir (1938)
Betty Blue, Jean-Jacques Beineix (1986)
Beverly Hills Cop, Martin Brest (1984)
Bicycle Thieves, Vittorio de Sica (1948)
Big, Penny Marshall (1988)
The Big Chill, Lawrence Kasdan (1983)
The Big Easy, Jim McBride (1986)
The Big Sky, Howard Hawks (1952)
The Big Sleep, Howard Hawks (1946)
Bill and Ted's Excellent Adventure, Stephen Herek (1989)
Billion Dollar Brain, Ken Russell (1967)
Billy Liar, John Schlesinger (1963)
Billy the Kid and the Green Baize Vampire, Alan Clarke (1985)
Birdman of Alcatraz, John Frankenheimer (1961)
The Birds, Alfred Hitchcock (1963)
The Birth of a Nation, DW Griffith (1915)
The Bitter Tea of General Yen, Frank Capra (1932)
Black Narcissus, Powell/Pressburger (1946)
The Black Stallion, Carroll Ballard (1979)
Black Widow, Bob Rafelson (1986)
The Blackboard Jungle, Richard Brooks (1955)
Blade Runner, Ridley Scott (1982)
The Blob, Chuck Russell (1988)
Blood and Sand, Rouben Mamoulian (1941)
Bloodbath at the House of Death, Ray Cameron (1983)
Blood Simple, Joel Coen (1985)
Blow Up, Michelangelo Antonioni (1966)
The Blue Angel, Josef von Sternberg (1930)
The Blue Lamp, Basil Dearden (1949)
Bob and Carol and Ted and Alice, Paul Mazursky (1969)
The Body Snatcher, Robert Wise (1945)
Bonnie and Clyde, Arthur Penn (1967)
Boomerang, Elia Kazan (1947)
Born Free, James Hill (1965)
Born on the Fourth of July, Oliver Stone (1989)
Boys' Town, Norman Taurog (1938)
The Brave Don't Cry, Philip Leacock (1952)
Bread and Chocolate, Franco Brusati (1973)
Breakfast at Tiffany's, Blake Edwards (1961)
Breathless {A Bout de Souffle}, Jean-Luc Godard (1960)
The Bride of Frankenstein, James Whale (1935)
The Bridge on the River Kwai, David Lean (1957)
A Bridge Too Far, Attenborough/Hayers (1977)
Brief Encounter, David Lean (1945)
Brighton Rock, John Boulting (1947)
Bring Me the Head of Alfredo Garcia, Sam Peckinpah (1974)
Bringing Up Baby, Howard Hawks (1938)
Broadway Danny Rose, Woody Allen (1984)
Broadway Melody, Harry Beaumont (1929)
Broken Blossoms, DW Griffith (1919)
Buffalo Bill, William Wellman (1944)
Buffet Froid, Bertrand Blier (1979)
Bugsy Malone, Alan Parker (1976)
Bullitt, Peter Yates (1968)
Bunny Lake is Missing, Otto Preminger (1965)
Buster, David Green (1988)
Butch Cassidy and the Sundance Kid, George Roy Hill (1969)

Cabaret, Bob Fosse (1972)
The Cabinet of Dr Caligari, Robert Wiene (1919)
The Caine Mutiny, Edward Dmytryk (1954)
Calamity Jane, David Butler (1953)
Canadian Mounties vs Atomic Invaders {serial}, Franklin Adreon (1953)
Cape Fear, Martin Scorsese (1992)
Captain America {serial}, English/Clifton (1944)
Captains Courageous, Victor Fleming (1937)
The Captive Heart, Basil Dearden (1946)
Carlton-Browne of the FO, Dell/Boulting (1958)
Carmen Jones, Otto Preminger (1954)
The Carpetbaggers, Edward Dmytryk (1964)
Carrie, Brian de Palma (1976)
Carry on Sergeant {First 'Carry On' film}, Gerald Thomas (1958)
The Cars That Ate Paris, Peter Weir (1974)
Carve Her Name With Pride, Lewis Gilbert (1958)
Casablanca, Michael Curtiz (1942)
The Cat and the Canary, Paul Leni (1927)
A Certain Smile, Jean Negulesco (1958)
Champagne Charlie, Alberto Cavalcanti (1944)
The Chant of Jimmie Blacksmith, Fred Schepisi (1978)
Charade, Stanley Donen (1963)
The Charge of the Light Brigade, Michael Curtiz (1936)
Chariots of Fire, Hugh Hudson (1981)
Charlie Chan Carries On {First Charlie Chan film}, – (1931)
Chase a Crooked Shadow, Michael Anderson (1957)
Un Chien Andalou, Luis Buñuel (1928)
Child's Play, Tom Holland (1988)
Chinatown, Roman Polanski (1974)
Chitty Chitty Bang Bang, Ken Hughes (1968)
Christ Stopped at Eboli, Francesco Rosi (1979)
Citizen Kane, Orson Welles (1941)
City Lights, Charles Chaplin (1931)

Clash of the Titans, Desmond Davis (1981)
Cleopatra, Joseph L Mankiewicz [and others] (1963)
Closely Observed Trains, Jiri Menzel (1966)
The Cockeyed Cowboys of Calico County, Tony Leader (1969)
Cockleshell Heroes, Jose Ferrer (1955)
Cocoon, Ron Howard (1985)
The Colditz Story, Guy Hamilton (1954)
Colonel Redl, Istvan Szabo (1984)
The Color of Money, Martin Scorsese (1986)
The Color Purple, Steven Spielberg (1985)
Come Back to the Five and Dime, Jimmy Dean, Jimmy Dean, Robert Altman (1983)
Comfort and Joy, Bill Forsyth (1984)
Commando, Mark L Lester (1985)
The Commitments, Alan Parker (1991)
The Company of Wolves, Neil Jordan (1984)
Compulsion, Richard Fleischer (1959)
The Computer Wore Tennis Shoes, Robert Butler (1970)
Conan the Barbarian, John Milius (1981)
Confessions of a Nazi Spy, Anatole Litvak (1939)
A Connecticut Yankee in King Arthur's Court, Tay Garnett (1948)
Cool Hand Luke, Stuart Rosenberg (1967)
The Cotton Club, Francis Ford Coppola (1984)
Cousin, Cousine, Jean-Charles Tacchella (1975)
The Creature from the Black Lagoon, Jack Arnold (1954)
Crocodile Dundee, Peter Faiman (1986)
The Cruel Sea, Charles Frend (1953)
Cry Freedom, Richard Attenborough (1987)
The Crying Game, Neil Jordan (1992)
A Cry in the Dark, Fred Schepisi (1988)
Curse of the Mummy's Tomb, Michael Carreras (1964)

Daddy Longlegs, Alfred Santell (1931)
The Dam Busters, Michael Anderson (1954)
Dance With a Stranger, Mike Newell (1985)
Dances With Wolves, Kevin Costner (1990)
The Dark Crystal, Jim Henson (1982)
David Copperfield, George Cukor (1934)
Day for Night, François Truffaut (1973)
The Day of the Jackal, Fred Zinnemann (1973)
The Day the Earth Caught Fire, Val Guest (1961)
The Day the Earth Stood Still, Robert Wise (1951)
The Day the Fish Came Out, Michael Cacoyannis (1967)
Days of Wine and Roses, Blake Edwards (1962)
Dead Men Don't Wear Plaid, Carl Reiner (1982)
Deadlier Than the Male, Ralph Thomas (1967)
Death Race 2000, Paul Bartel (1975)
Death Wish, Michael Winner (1974)
The Deer Hunter, Michael Cimino (1978)
Delicatessen, Jeunet/Caro (1992)
Deliverance, John Boorman (1972)
Desperately Seeking Susan, Susan Seidelman (1985)
Destry Rides Again, George Marshall (1939)
Diamonds Are Forever, Guy Hamilton (1971)
Diary of a Mad Housewife, Frank Perry (1970)
Die Hard, John McTiernan (1988)
Dirty Dancing, Emile Ardolino (1987)
The Dirty Dozen, Robert Aldrich (1967)
Dirty Harry, Don Siegel (1971)
The Discreet Charm of the Bourgeoisie, Luis Buñuel (1972)
Distant Voices, Still Lives, Terence Davies (1988)
Divorce American Style, Bud Yorkin (1967)
Divorce Italian Style, Pietro Germi (1961)
Doc Savage, Man of Bronze, Michael Anderson (1975)
Doctor in the House, Ralph Thomas (1954)
Dr Strangelove; or, How I Learned to Stop Worrying and Love the Bomb, Stanley Kubrick (1963)
Dr Terror's House of Horrors, Freddie Francis (1965)
Dog Day Afternoon, Sidney Lumet (1975)
La Dolce Vita, Federico Fellini (1960)
Don't Look Now, Nicolas Roeg (1973)
Double Indemnity, Billy Wilder (1944)
Down and Out in Beverly Hills, Paul Mazursky (1986)
The Draughtsman's Contract, Peter Greenaway (1982)
Dressed to Kill, Brian de Palma (1980)
Driving Miss Daisy, Bruce Beresford (1989)
Drowning By Numbers, Peter Greenaway (1988)
Duck Soup, Leo McCarey (1933)
Duel in the Sun, King Vidor [and others] (1946)
Dumbo {Walt Disney animation}, Ben Sharpsteen (1941)

E.T. , Steven Spielberg (1982)
The Eagle Has Landed, John Sturges (1976)
Easy Rider, Dennis Hopper (1969)
Eat the Peach, Peter Ormrod (1986)
Educating Rita, Lewis Gilbert (1983)
Edward Scissorhands, Tim Burton (1990)
Effi Briest, Rainer Werner Fassbinder (1974)
El Cid, Anthony Mann (1961)
Elephant Boy, Robert Flaherty (1937)
The Elephant Man, David Lynch (1980)
The Elusive Pimpernel, Powell/Pressburger (1950)
Elvira Madigan, Bo Widerberg (1967)
Emmanuelle, Just Jaeckin (1974)
Empire of the Sun, Steven Spielberg (1987)
The Empire Strikes Back, Irvin Kershner (1980)
L'Enfant Sauvage, François Truffaut (1969)
Les Enfants du Paradis, Marcel Carné (1945)
The Enforcer, Bretaigne Windust (1950)
Enter the Dragon, Tony Richardson (1960)
Eraserhead, David Lynch (1976)
Every Which Way But Loose, James Fargo (1978)
Everything You Always Wanted to Know About Sex, Woody Allen (1972)
The Evil Dead, Sam M Raimi (1980)
Excalibur, John Boorman (1981)
Executive Suite, Robert Wise (1954)
The Exorcist, William Friedkin (1973)
Expresso Bongo, Val Guest (1959)
The Exterminating Angel, Luis Buñuel (1962)
The Exterminator, James Glickenhaus (1980)
Eyes of Laura Mars, Irvin Kershner (1978)

The Fabulous Baker Boys, Steve Kloves (1989)
A Face in the Crowd, Elia Kazan (1957)
Fahrenheit 451, François Truffaut (1966)
Fail Safe, Sidney Lumet (1964)
Fame, Alan Parker (1980)
Fanfan la Tulipe, Christian-Jaque (1951)
Fanny, Joshua Logan (1960)
Fanny and Alexander, Ingmar Bergman (1982)
Fanny by Gaslight, Anthony Asquith (1944)
Fantasia {Walt Disney animation}, Supervisor: Ben Sharpsteen (1940)
Farewell, My Lovely, Edward Dmytryk (1944)
The Fast Lady, Ken Annakin (1962)
Fatal Attraction, Adrian Lyne (1987)
Faust, F W Murnau (1926)
La Femme du Boulanger, Marcel Pagnol (1938)
Ferris Bueller's Day Off, John Hughes (1986)
A Few Good Men, Rob Reiner (1992)
Finian's Rainbow, Francis Ford Coppola (1968)
A Fish Called Wanda, Charles Crichton (1988)
A Fistful of Dollars, Sergio Leone (1964)
Fitzcarraldo, Werner Herzog (1982)
Five Easy Pieces, Bob Rafelson (1970)
Five Graves to Cairo, Billy Wilder (1943)
Flash Gordon {serials}, Stephani/Beebe/Hill/Taylor (1936–1940)
Flashdance, Adrian Lyne (1983)
Flipper, James B Clark (1963)
The Fly, David Cronenberg (1986)
Flying Down to Rio, Thorton Freeland (1933)
The Fog, John Carpenter (1979)
Folies Bergère, Roy del Ruth (1935)
Footlight Parade, Lloyd Bacon (1933)
For a Few Dollars More, Sergio Leone (1965)
For Me and My Gal, Busby Berkeley (1942)
For Queen and Country, Martin Stellman (1988)
For Your Eyes Only, John Glen (1981)
Forbidden Planet, Fred M Wilcox (1956)
Foreign Correspondent, Alfred Hitchcock (1940)
Fort Apache, John Ford (1948)
Forty-Second Street, Lloyd Bacon (1933)
The Four Feathers, Zoltan Korda (1939)
The Four Horsemen of the Apocalypse, Rex Ingram (1921)
Frankenstein, James Whale (1931)
Freebie and the Bean, Richard Rush (1974)
The French Connection, William Friedkin (1971)
Friday the Thirteenth, Sean S Cunningham (1980)
Fried Green Tomatoes at the Whistle Stop Café, John Avent (1991)
Fritz the Cat {animation}, Ralph Bakshi (1971)
From Here to Eternity, Fred Zinneman (1953)
From Russia With Love, Terence Young (1963)
The Front Page, Lewis Milestone (1931)
Full Metal Jacket, Stanley Kubrick (1987)
Fun With Dick and Jane, Ted Kotcheff (1976)
Funny Face, Stanley Donen (1956)
Funny Girl, William Wyler (1968)
Fury, Fritz Lang (1936)

G Men, William Keighley (1935)
Gandhi, Richard Attenborough (1982)
Gaslight, Thorold Dickinson (1939)
The Gay Divorcee, Mark Sandrich (1934)
The General, Buster Keaton (1926)
The General Died at Dawn, Lewis Milestone (1936)
Geneviève, Henry Cornelius (1953)
Georgy Girl, Silvio Narizzano (1966)
The Getting of Wisdom, Bruce Beresford (1977)
Ghostbusters, Ivan Reitman (1984)
Giant, George Stevens (1956)
Gigi, Vincente Minnelli (1958)
Gilda, Charles Vidor (1946)
The Glen Miller Story, Anthony Mann (1953)
The Godfather, Francis Ford Coppola (1972)
Godzilla, Inoshiro Honda (1955)

Gold Diggers of 1933, Mervyn Le Roy (1933)
The Gold Rush, Charles Chaplin (1925)
Goldfinger, Guy Hamilton (1964)
The Goldwyn Follies, George Marshall (1938)
Gone With the Wind, Victor Fleming (1939)
The Good Die Young, Lewis Gilbert (1954)
The Good Earth, Sidney Franklin (1937)
Good Morning, Vietnam, Barry Levinson (1987)
The Good, the Bad and the Ugly, Sergio Leone (1966)
Goodbye Mr Chips, Sam Wood (1939)
The Goonies, Richard Donner (1985)
Gorillas in the Mist, Michael Apted (1988)
The Gospel According to St Matthew, Pier Paolo Pasolini (1964)
Gothic, Ken Russell (1986)
The Graduate, Mike Nicholls (1967)
Le Grand Chemin, Jean Loup Hubert (1988)
Grand Hotel, Edmund Goulding (1932)
La Grande Illusion, Jean Renoir (1937)
The Grapes of Wrath, John Ford (1940)
Grease, Randal Kleiser (1978)
The Great Dictator, Charles Chaplin (1940)
The Great Escape, John Sturges (1963)
Great Expectations, David Lean (1946)
The Great Gatsby, Jack Clayton (1974)
The Great Race, Blake Edwards (1965)
Greed, Erich von Stroheim (1923)
The Green Berets, John Wayne (1968)
Gregory's Girl, Bill Forsyth (1980)
Gremlins, Joe Dante (1984)
Greyfriars Bobby, Don Chaffey (1960)
Greystoke: The Legend of Tarzan, Lord of the Apes, Hugh Hudson (1984)
The Group, Sidney Lumet (1966)
Guess Who's Coming to Dinner, Stanley Kramer (1967)
The Guinea Pig, Roy Boulting (1948)
Gumshoe, Stephen Frears (1971)
Gunfight at the OK Corral, John Sturges (1957)
The Gunfighter, Henry King (1950)
Gunga Din, George Stevens (1939)
The Guns of Navarone, J Lee-Thompson (1961)

Hail the Conquering Hero, Preston Sturges (1944)
Halloween, John Carpenter (1978)
The Hand that Rocks the Cradle, Curtis Hanson (1992)
Hannah and Her Sisters, Woody Allen (1985)
A Hard Day's Night, Richard Lester (1964)
Harvey, Henry Koster (1950)
Hatter's Castle, Lance Comfort (1941)
The Heart is a Lonely Hunter, Robert Ellis Miller (1968)
Heat and Dust, James Ivory (1982)
Heatwave, Phillip Noyce (1982)
Heaven Can Wait, Ernest Lubitsch (1943)
Heidi, Allan Dwan (1937)
Heimat, Edgar Reitz (1984)
The Heiress, William Wyler (1949)
Hell's Angels, Howard Hughes (1930)
Hellzapoppin, H C Potter (1942)
Henry VIII and His Six Wives, Waris Hussein (1972)
Here We Go Round the Mulberry Bush, Clive Donner (1967)
High Noon, Fred Zinnemann (1952)
High Plains Drifter, Clint Eastwood (1972)
High Sierra, Raoul Walsh (1941)
High, Wide and Handsome, Rouben Mamoulian (1937)
A High Wind in Jamaica, Alexander Mackendrick (1965)
Hiroshima Mon Amour, Alain Resnais (1959)
His Girl Friday, Howard Hawks (1940)
History of the World Part One, Mel Brooks (1981)
Hobson's Choice, David Lean (1953)
Holiday, George Cukor (1938)
Holiday Inn, Mark Sandrich (1942)
Hombre, Martin Ritt (1967)
Home Alone, Chris Columbus (1990)
Honey, I Shrunk the Kids, Joe Johnston (1989)
Hope and Glory, John Boorman (1987)
Hotel, Richard Quine (1967)
The House of Seven Gables, Joe May (1940)
House of Wax, André de Toth (1953)
The House on 92nd Street, Henry Hathaway (1945)
How Green Was My Valley, John Ford (1941)
How the West Was Won, Hathaway/Ford/Marshall (1962)
How to Marry a Millionaire, Jean Negulesco (1953)
How to Murder Your Wife, Richard Quine (1964)
How to Steal a Million, William Wyler (1966)
How to Succeed in Business Without Really Trying, David Swift (1967)
Huckleberry Finn, Norman Taurog (1931)
Hud, Martin Ritt (1963)
The Human Jungle, Joseph M Newman (1954)
Humoresque, Jean Negulesco (1947)
The Hunchback of Notre Dame, William Dieterle (1939)
Hush Hush Sweet Charlotte, Robert Aldrich (1964)
The Hustler, Robert Rossen (1961)

I Am a Fugitive From a Chain Gang, Mervyn Le Roy (1932)
I Can Get It For You Wholesale, Michael Gordon (1951)
I Could Go On Singing, Ronald Neame (1963)
I Married a Monster From Outer Space, Gene Fowler Jnr (1958)
I Never Promised You a Rose Garden, Anthony Page (1977)
I Was a Male War Bride, Howard Hawks (1949)
I Was a Teenage Werewolf, Gene Fowler Jnr (1957)
I Was Monty's Double, John Guillermin (1958)
Ice Cold in Alex, J Lee-Thompson (1958)
If It's Tuesday, This Must Be Belgium, Mel Stuart (1969)
I'll Never Forget Whatshisname, Michael Winner (1967)
I'm All Right Jack, John Boulting (1959)
I'm Dancing As Fast As I Can, Jack Hofsiss (1982)
I'm No Angel, Wesley Ruggles (1933)
The Immigrant, Charles Chaplin (1917)
In Cold Blood, Richard Brooks (1967)
In Like Flint, Gordon Douglas (1967)
In the Heat of the Night, Norman Jewison (1967)
In Which We Serve, Noel Coward (1942)
The Incredible Journey, Fletcher Markle (1963)
The Incredible Melting Man, William Sachs (1977)
The Incredible Shrinking Man, Jack Arnold (1957)
Indecent Proposal, Adrian Lyne (1993)
Indiana Jones and the Temple of Doom, Steven Spielberg (1984)
The Informer, John Ford (1935)
The Inn of the Sixth Happiness, Mark Robson (1958)
Intermezzo, Gregory Ratoff (1939)
Intolerance, D W Griffith (1916)
Invasion of the Body Snatchers, Don Siegel (1956)
The Invisible Man, James Whale (1933)
The Ipcress File, Sidney J Furie (1965)
It Always Rains on Sunday, Robert Hamer (1947)
It Came From Outer Space, Jack Arnold (1953)
The Italian Job, Peter Collinson (1969)
It's a Mad Mad Mad Mad World, Stanley Kramer (1963)
It's a Wonderful Life, Frank Capra (1946)
Ivan the Terrible, Sergei Eisenstein (1942-6)

Jabberwocky, Terry Gilliam (1977)
Jagged Edge, Richard Marquand (1985)
Jailhouse Rock, Richard Thorpe (1957)
Jason and the Argonauts, Don Chaffey (1963)
Jaws, Steven Spielberg (1975)
The Jazz Singer, Alan Crosland (1927)
Jean de Florette, Claude Berri (1986)
Jesse James, Henry King (1938)
Jeux Interdits, René Clément (1952)
Jew Suss, Veit Harlan (1940)
Jezebel, William Wyler (1938)
Johnny Belinda, Jean Negulesco (1948)
The Jolson Story, Alfred E Green (1946)
Jour de Fête, Jacques Tati (1948)
Le Jour Se Lève, Marcel Carné (1939)
Journey to the Centre of the Earth, Henry Levin (1959)
Judgment at Nuremberg, Stanley Kramer (1961)
Jules et Jim, François Truffaut (1962)
The Jungle Book, Zoltan Korda (1942)
Jurassic Park, Steven Spielberg (1993)

The Karate Kid, John G Avildsen (1984)
Kelly's Heroes, Brian G Hutton (1970)
The Kentucky Fried Movie, John Landis (1977)
Kes, Ken Loach (1969)
Key Largo, John Huston (1948)
The Kid, Charles Chaplin (1921)
The Killers, Robert Siodmak (1946)
The Killing Fields, Roland Joffe (1984)
Kind Hearts and Coronets, Robert Hamer (1949)
King Kong, Merian C Cooper (1933)
King of Comedy, Martin Scorsese (1982)
King of Kings, Cecil B de Mille (1927)
King of the Rocket Men {serial}, Fred Brannon (1949)
Kipps, Carol Reed (1941)
Kiss of Death, Henry Hathaway (1947)
Kiss of the Spider Woman, Hector Babenco (1985)
Klute, Alan J Pakula (1971)
The Knack, Richard Lester (1965)
Kramer Versus Kramer, Robert Benton (1979)

The L-Shaped Room, Bryan Forbes (1962)
The Lacemaker, Claude Goretta (1977)
Lacombe, Lucien, Louis Malle (1974)
Lady and the Tramp {Walt Disney animation}, Hamilton Luske (1955)
Ladyhawke, Richard Donner (1985)
Lady Killer, Roy del Ruth (1933)
The Ladykillers, Alexander Mackendrick (1955)
Lady Sings the Blues, Sidney J Furie (1972)
The Lady Vanishes, Alfred Hitchcock (1938)

The Lady With a Lamp, Herbert Wilcox (1951)
The Land That Time Forgot, Kevin Connor (1974)
Lassie Come Home, Fred M Wilcox (1943)
The Last Emperor, Bernardo Bertolucci (1987)
The Last Picture Show, Peter Bogdanovich (1971)
Last Tango in Paris, Bernardo Bertolucci (1972)
The Last Temptation of Christ, Martin Scorsese (1988)
Last Year in Marienbad, Alain Resnais (1961)
The Lavender Hill Mob, Charles Crichton (1951)
Lawrence of Arabia, David Lean (1962)
The League of Gentlemen, Basil Dearden (1960)
Legal Eagles, Ivan Reitman (1986)
Lethal Weapon, Richard Donner (1987)
A Letter to Brezhnev, Chris Bernard (1985)
The Life and Death of Colonel Blimp, Powell/Pressburger (1943)
The Life and Times of Judge Roy Bean, John Huston (1972)
Life at the Top, Ted Kotcheff (1965)
Limelight, Charles Chaplin (1952)
Lisztomania, Ken Russell (1975)
Little Caesar, Mervyn Le Roy (1930)
Live and Let Die, Guy Hamilton (1973)
Live Now, Pay Later, Jay Lewis (1962)
The Living Daylights, John Glen (1987)
Local Hero, Bill Forsyth (1983)
Lolita, Stanley Kubrick (1962)
London Belongs to Me, Sidney Gilliat (1948)
The Loneliness of the Long Distance Runner, Tony Richardson (1962)
Lonely Are the Brave, David Miller (1962)
The Lonely Passion of Judith Hearne, Jack Clayton (1987)
The Long Goodbye, Robert Altman (1973)
The Long Good Friday, John Mackenzie (1980)
The Long Hot Summer, Martin Ritt (1958)
Looking for Mr Goodbar, Richard Brooks (1977)
Look Who's Talking, Amy Heckerling (1989)
The Lost Boys, Joel Schumacher (1987)
Lost Horizon, Frank Capra (1937)
The Lost Weekend, Billy Wilder (1945)
Love and Pain and the Whole Damn Thing, Alan J Pakula (1972)
Love at First Bite, Stan Dragoti (1979)
The Love Bug, Robert Stevenson (1968)
Love Is a Many Splendored Thing, Henry King (1955)
Love Me or Leave Me, Charles Vidor (1955)
Love Me Tender, Robert D Webb (1956)
Love Story, Arthur Hiller (1970)
Love With the Proper Stranger, Robert Mulligan (1964)
The Loved One, Tony Richardson (1965)
Lust for Life, Vincente Minnelli (1956)

Ma Nuit Chez Maud, Eric Rohmer (1969)
MacKenna's Gold, J Lee-Thompson (1969)
The Mackintosh Man, John Huston (1973)
Mad Max, George Miller (1979)
Madame Curie, Mervyn Le Roy (1944)
Madame Dubarry {Passion}, Ernst Lubitsch (1919)
Madame X, Sam Wood (1937)
The Magic Toyshop, David Wheatley (1986)
The Magnificent Ambersons, Orson Welles (1942)
The Magnificent Seven, John Sturges (1960)
Magnum Force, Ted Post (1973)
The Maltese Falcon, John Huston (1941)
Mammy, Michael Curtiz (1930)
A Man About the House, Leslie Arliss (1947)
A Man and a Woman, Claude Lelouch (1966)
A Man Called Horse, Elliot Silverstein (1970)
The Man in the Iron Mask, James Whale (1939)
The Man in the White Suit, Alexander Mackendrick (1951)
Man of Aran, Robert Flaherty (1934)
Man of Iron, Andrzej Wajda (1981)
Man of Marble, Andrzej Wajda (1978)
The Man Who Broke the Bank at Monte Carlo, Stephen Roberts (1935)
The Man Who Fell to Earth, Nicolas Roeg (1976)
The Man Who Knew Too Much, Alfred Hitchcock (1934)
The Man Who Never Was, Ronald Neame (1955)
The Man Who Shot Liberty Valance, John Ford (1962)
The Man Who Would Be King, John Huston (1975)
The Man With the Golden Arm, Otto Preminger (1956)
The Manchurian Candidate, John Frankenheimer (1962)
Mandy, Alexander Mackendrick (1952)
Manhattan, Woody Allen (1979)
Manon des Sources, Claude Berri (1987)
Marathon Man, John Schlesinger (1976)
The Mark of Zorro, Rouben Mamoulian (1940)
Marnie, Alfred Hitchcock (1964)
Mary Poppins, Robert Stevenson (1964)
*M*A*S*H*, Robert Altman (1970)
Mask, Peter Bogdanovich (1985)
The Mask of Fu Manchu, Charles Brabin (1932)
The Masque of the Red Death, Roger Corman (1964)
Masquerade, Basil Dearden (1985)
Mata Hari, George Fitzmaurice (1931)
A Matter of Life and Death, Powell/Pressburger (1946)
Mayerling, Anatole Litvak (1935)
McCabe and Mrs Miller, Robert Altman (1971)
Mean Streets, Martin Scorsese (1973)
Meet John Doe, Frank Capra (1941)
Meet Me in St Louis, Vincente Minnelli (1944)
Memphis Belle, Michael Caton-Jones (1990)
The Men, Fred Zinnemann (1950)
Metropolis, Fritz Lang (1926)
Midnight Cowboy, John Schlesinger (1969)
Midnight Express, Alan Parker (1978)
Mildred Pierce, Michael Curtiz (1945)
Le Million, René Clair (1931)
Miracle on 34th Street, George Seaton (1947)
The Misfits, John Huston (1961)
The Mission, Roland Joffe (1986)
Mississippi Burning, Alan Parker (1988)
Mr Blandings Builds His Dream House, H C Potter (1948)
Mr Deeds Goes to Town, Frank Capra (1936)
Mr Skeffington, Vincent Sherman (1944)
Mrs Miniver, William Wyler (1942)
Mr Smith Goes to Washington, Frank Capra (1939)
Modern Times, Charles Chaplin (1936)
The Molly Maguires, Martin Ritt (1970)
Mon Oncle, Jacques Tati (1956)
Mona Lisa, Neil Jordan (1986)
Monkey Business, Norman Z McLeod (1931)
Monsieur Hulot's Holiday, Jacques Tati (1953)
Monty Python and the Holy Grail, Gilliam/Jones (1975)
Monty Python's Life of Brian, Terry Jones (1979)
Monty Python's The Meaning of Life, Terry Jones (1983)
The Moon and Sixpence, Albert Lewin (1943)
Moonraker, Lewis Gilbert (1979)
Morgan – A Suitable Case for Treatment, Karel Reisz (1966)
Morning Glory, Lowell Sherman (1933)
Morocco, Josef von Sternberg (1930)
Morons From Outer Space, Michael Hodges (1985)
Mother Riley Meets the Vampire, John Gilling (1952)
Moulin Rouge, John Huston (1952)
The Mouse That Roared, Jack Arnold (1959)
My Beautiful Laundrette, Stephen Frears (1985)
My Brilliant Career, Gillian Armstrong (1979)
My Darling Clementine, John Ford (1946)
My Life as a Dog, Lasse Hallstrom (1985)
My Little Chickadee, Edward Cline (1939)
My Stepmother is an Alien, Richard Benjamin (1988)
The Mysterious Dr Fu Manchu, Rowland V Lee (1929)

The Naked City, Jules Dassin (1948)
The Naked Jungle, Byron Haskin (1954)
Nanook of the North, Robert Flaherty (1921)
National Lampoon's Animal House, John Landis (1978)
National Velvet, Clarence Brown (1945)
Naughty Marietta, W S Van Dyke (1935)
Network, Sidney Lumet (1976)
Never Give a Sucker an Even Break, Edward Cline (1941)
Never on Sunday, Jules Dassin (1959)
New York, New York, Martin Scorsese (1977)
A Night at the Opera, Sam Wood (1935)
A Nightmare on Elm Street, Wes Craven (1984)
Night of the Living Dead, Tom Savini (1990)
Nine and a Half Weeks, Adrian Lyne (1986)
Ninotchka, Ernst Lubitsch (1939)
No Way to Treat a Lady, Jack Smight (1968)
None But the Brave, Frank Sinatra (1965)
None But the Lonely Heart, Clifford Odets (1944)
North By Northwest, Alfred Hitchcock (1959)
Northwest Frontier, J Lee-Thompson (1959)
Nosferatu, F W Murnau (1921)
Notorious, Alfred Hitchcock (1946)
Now Voyager, Irving Rapper (1942)

O Lucky Man, Lindsay Anderson (1973)
Obsession, Brian de Palma (1976)
Octopussy, John Glen (1983)
Odd Man Out, Carol Reed (1946)
An Officer and a Gentleman, Taylor Hackford (1982)
Old Mother Riley, Maclean Rogers (1937)
Old Yeller, Robert Stevenson (1957)
Oliver!, Carol Reed (1968)
The Omen, Richard Donner (1976)
On Golden Pond, Mark Rydell (1981)
On the Waterfront, Elia Kazan (1954)
Once Upon a Time in the West, Sergio Leone (1969)
One Flew Over the Cuckoo's Nest, Milos Forman (1975)

One Million Years BC, Don Chaffey (1966)
Only Two Can Play, Sidney Gilliat (1962)
Only When I Larf, Basil Dearden (1968)
Ordinary People, Robert Redford (1980)
Orient Express, Paul Martin (1934)
Orphée, Jean Cocteau (1949)
Out of Africa, Sydney Pollack (1985)
The Outlaw Josey Wales, Clint Eastwood (1976)

Panic in the Streets, Elia Kazan (1950)
Paper Moon, Peter Bogdanovich (1973)
Les Parapluies de Cherbourg, Jacques Demy (1964)
Paris, Texas, Wim Wenders (1984)
Passport to Pimlico, Henry Cornelius (1949)
Paths of Glory, Stanley Kubrick (1957)
Peggy Sue Got Married, Francis Ford Coppola (1986)
Pépé le Moko, Julien Duvivier (1936)
Performance, Nicolas Roeg (1970)
The Perils of Pauline {serial}, Ray Taylor (1934)
Persona, Ingmar Bergman (1966)
Personal Services, Terry Jones (1987)
Phantom of the Opera, Rupert Julian (1925)
The Philadelphia Story, George Cukor (1940)
Picnic at Hanging Rock, Peter Weir (1975)
Pillow Talk, Michael Gordon (1959)
The Pink Panther, Blake Edwards (1963)
Pinocchio {animation}, Supervisors: Sharpsteen/Luske (1940)
A Place in the Sun, George Stevens (1951)
Planet of the Apes, Franklin Shaffner (1968)
Platoon, Oliver Stone (1986)
Play It Again Sam, Herbert Ross (1972)
Play Misty for Me, Clint Eastwood (1971)
Playtime, Jacques Tati (1968)
Please Don't Eat the Daisies, Charles Walters (1960)
The Ploughman's Lunch, Richard Eyre (1983)
Police Academy, Hugh Wilson (1984)
Poltergeist, Tobe Hooper (1982)
Portrait of Jennie, William Dieterle (1948)
The Poseidon Adventure, Ronald Neame (1972)
Postcards from the Edge, Mike Nichols (1990)
A Prayer for the Dying, Mike Hodges [disowned released version] (1987)
Predator, John McTiernan (1987)
Pretty in Pink, Howard Deutsch (1986)
Pretty Woman, Garry Marshall (1990)
Prick Up Your Ears, Stephen Frears (1987)
The Prince and the Showgirl, Laurence Olivier (1957)
Private Benjamin, Howard Zieff (1980)
A Private Function, Malcolm Mowbray (1984)
The Private Life of Henry VIII, Alexander Korda (1933)
The Private Lives of Elizabeth and Essex, Michael Curtiz (1939)
Psycho, Hitchock/Bass (1960)
The Public Enemy, William Wellman (1931)
The Purple Rose of Cairo, Woody Allen (1984)
Puttin' on the Ritz, Edward Sloman (1930)

Quai des Brumes, Marcel Carné (1938)
Quartet, Smart/French/Crabtree/Annakin (1948)
The Quatermass Experiment, Val Guest (1955)
Les Quatre Cents Coups, François Truffaut (1958)
Queen Christina, Rouben Mamoulian (1933)
Quo Vadis, Mervyn Le Roy (1951)

Raffles, George Fitzmaurice (1930)
Raging Bull, Martin Scorsese (1980)
Raiders of the Lost Ark, Steven Spielberg (1981)
Rain Man, Barry Levinson (1988)
Raise the Titanic!, Jerry Jameson (1980)
Rambo: First Blood, George Pan Cosmatos (1985)
Rancho Notorious, Fritz Lang (1952)
Razorback, Russell Mulcahy (1984)
Reach for the Sky, Lewis Gilbert (1956)
Reap the Wild Wind, Cecil B de Mille (1942)
Rear Window, Alfred Hitchcock (1954)
Rebel Without a Cause, Nicholas Ray (1955)
The Red Balloon, Albert Lamorisse (1955)
The Red Shoes, Powell/Pressburger (1948)
Reds, Warren Beatty (1981)
La Règle du Jeu, Jean Renoir (1939)
Repulsion, Roman Polanski (1965)
La Retour de Martin Guerre, Daniel Vigne (1982)
Return of the Jedi, Richard Marquand (1983)
Riff Raff, J Walter Ruben (1935)
Rififi, Jules Dassin (1955)
Rio Bravo, Howard Hawks (1959)
Road to Singapore {First of 'Road' series}, Victor Schertzinger (1940)
The Roaring Twenties, Raoul Walsh (1939)
Robocop, Paul Verhoeven (1987)
Rocco and His Brothers, Luchino Visconti (1960)
Rocky, John G Avildsen (1976)
Rollerball, Norman Jewison (1975)
Roman Holiday, William Wyler (1953)
Romancing the Stone, Robert Zemeckis (1984)
La Ronde, Max Ophuls (1950)
Ruggles of Red Gap, Leo McCarey (1935)
Rumble Fish, Francis Ford Coppola (1983)
Run Wild, Run Free, Richard C Sarafian (1969)
The Running Man, Carol Reed (1963)

Sailor Beware, Gordon Parry (1956)
The Sailor Who Fell From Grace With the Sea, Lewis John Carlino (1976)
The St Valentine's Day Massacre, Roger Corman (1967)
Sally in Our Alley, Maurice Elvey (1931)
Sammy and Rosie Get Laid, Stephen Frears (1987)
Saturday Night Fever, John Badham (1978)
Scarface, Howard Hawks (1932)
Scott of the Antarctic, Charles Frend (1948)
Seance on a Wet Afternoon, Bryan Forbes (1964)
The Secret of My Success, Herbert Ross (1987)
Sergeant Pepper's Lonely Hearts Club Band, Michael Schultz (1978)
Seven Brides for Seven Brothers, Stanley Donen (1954)
Seven Samurai, Akira Kurasawa (1954)
The Seventh Seal, Ingmar Bergman (1957)
The Seventh Veil, Compton Bennett (1945)
Sex and the Single Girl, Richard Quine (1964)
Sex, Lies and Videotape, Steven Soderbergh (1989)
Sexton Blake and the Hooded Terror, George King (1938)
Shane, George Stevens (1953)
Shanghai Express, Josef von Sternberg (1932)
She Done Him Wrong, Lowell Sherman (1933)
She Wore a Yellow Ribbon, John Ford (1949)
The Sheik, George Melford (1921)
She'll Be Wearing Pink Pajamas, John Goldschmidt (1985)
The Shining, Stanley Kubrick (1980)
Ship of Fools, Stanley Kramer (1965)
The Ship That Died of Shame, Relph/Dearden (1955)
The Sign of the Cross, Cecil B de Mille (1932)
The Silence of the Lambs, Jonathan Demme (1991)
Silkwood, Mike Nichols (1983)
The Singer Not the Song, Roy Baker (1960)
Singin' in the Rain, Gene Kelly (1952)
Single White Female, Barbet Shroeder (1992)
Smokey and the Bandit, Hal Needham (1977)
Snow White and the Seven Dwarfs {animation}, David Hand (1937)
Some Like it Hot, Billy Wilder (1959)
Someone to Watch Over Me, Ridley Scott (1987)
The Sons of Katie Elder, Henry Hathaway (1965)
The Sound of Music, Robert Wise (1965)
Spartacus, Stanley Kubrick (1960)
Spellbound, Alfred Hitchcock (1945)
Splendor in the Grass, Elia Kazan (1961)
Stagecoach, John Ford (1939)
A Star is Born, William A Wellman (1937)
Star Trek: The Motion Picture, Robert Wise (1979)
Star Wars, John Barry (1977)
The Stepford Wives, Bryan Forbes (1974)
The Sting, George Roy Hill (1973)
Stir Crazy, Sidney Poitier (1980)
Sunday, Bloody Sunday, John Schlesinger (1971)
Sunset Boulevard, Billy Wilder (1950)
Superman , Richard Donner (1978)
Support Your Local Gunfighter, Burt Kennedy (1971)
Suppose They Gave a War and Nobody Came, Hy Averback (1969)
Suspicion, Alfred Hitchcock (1941)
Sweet Smell of Success, Alexander Mackendrick (1957)

The Talk of the Town, George Stevens (1942)
Taras Bulba, J Lee-Thompson (1962)
Tarzan the Tiger {serial}, Henry McRae (1929)
Taxi Driver, Martin Scorsese (1976)
Tea for Two, David Butler (1950)
Teenage Mutant Ninja Turtles, Steve Barron (1990)
Teen Wolf, Rod Daniel (1985)
Tell Them Willie Boy is Here, Abraham Polonsky (1969)
The Terminator, James Cameron (1984)
Terms of Endearment, James L Brooks (1983)
The Texas Chainsaw Massacre, Tobe Hooper (1974)
That Was Then...This is Now, Christopher Cain (1985)
Thelma and Louise, Ridley Scott (1991)
There's No Business Like Show Business, Walter Lang (1954)
They Died With Their Boots On, Raoul Walsh (1941)
They Shoot Horses, Don't They?, Sydney Pollack (1969)
The Thief of Baghdad, Powell/Berger/Whelan (1940)
The Thin Man, W S Van Dyke (1934)
Things to Come, William Cameron Menzies (1936)
This Land is Mine, Jean Renoir (1943)
This Sporting Life, Lindsay Anderson (1963)
Thoroughly Modern Millie, George Roy Hill (1967)
Those Magnificent Men in Their Flying Machines,

STAGE AND TELEVISION PLAYS, MUSICALS, REVUES

or How I Flew From London to Paris in Twenty-five Hours and Eleven Minutes, Ken Annakin (1965)
Those Were the Days, Thomas Bentley (1934)
Three Coins in the Fountain, Jean Negulesco (1954)
The Three Faces of Eve, Nunnally Johnson (1957)
Three Into Two Won't Go, Peter Hall (1969)
Three Men and a Baby, Leonard Nimoy (1987)
Throw Momma From the Train, Danny deVito (1987)
Tin Pan Alley, Walter Lang (1940)
The Titfield Thunderbolt, Charles Crichton (1952)
To Sir With Love, James Clavell (1967)
Tombstone {The Town Too Tough to Die}, William McGann (1942)
Tommy {Rock Opera}, Ken Russell (1975)
Too Hot to Handle, Jack Conway (1938)
Tootsie, Sydney Pollack (1982)
Top Gun, Tony Scott (1986)
Top Hat, Mark Sandrich (1935)
Topper, Norman Z MacLeod (1937)
A Touch of Class, Melvin Frank (1973)
The Towering Inferno, John Guillermin (1974)
Town Without Pity, Gottfried Reinhardt (1961)
Trading Places, John Landis (1983)
The Treasure of the Sierra Madre, John Huston (1948)
A Tree Grows in Brooklyn, Elia Kazan (1945)
Triumph of the Will, Leni Riefenstahl (1936)
Truly, Madly, Deeply, Anthony Minghella (1990)
Tugboat Annie, Mervyn Le Roy (1933)
Tunes of Glory, Ronald Neame (1960)
Twelve O'Clock High, Henry King (1949)
2001: A Space Odyssey, Stanley Kubrick (1968)

The Unbearable Lightness of Being, Philip Kaufman (1987)
Up the Down Staircase, Robert Mulligan (1967)

Vertigo, Alfred Hitchcock (1958)
Victim, Basil Dearden (1961)
Viva Zapata, Elia Kazan (1952)
Voyage to the Bottom of the Sea, Irwin Allen (1961)

The Wages of Fear, Henri-Georges Clouzot (1953)
Walk on the Wild Side, Edward Dmytryk (1962)
The War of the Roses, Danny deVito (1989)
Wayne's World, Penelope Spheeris (1992)
The Way to the Stars, Anthony Asquith (1945)
The Way We Were, Sydney Pollack (1973)
Went the Day Well?, Alberto Cavalcanti (1942)
Whatever Happened to Baby Jane?, Robert Aldrich (1962)
What's New Pussycat?, Clive Donner (1965)
What's Up, Doc?, Peter Bogdanovich (1972)
When Harry Met Sally, Rob Reiner (1989)
Where Were You When the Lights Went Out?, Hy Averback (1968)
Whisky Galore, Alexander Mackendrick (1948)
Whistle Down the Wind, Bryan Forbes (1961)
White Heat, Raoul Walsh (1949)
Who Framed Roger Rabbit?, Robert Zemeckis (1988)
The Wicked Lady, Leslie Arliss (1945)
The Wild Bunch, Sam Peckinpah (1969)
The Wild One, Laslo Benedek (1954)
The Witches of Eastwick, George Miller (1987)
Witness, Peter Weir (1985)
The Wizard of Oz, Victor Fleming (1939)
Women on the Verge of a Nervous Breakdown, Pedro Almodóvar (1988)
The World According to Garp, George Roy Hill (1982)
Written on the Wind, Douglas Sirk (1956)

X – The Man With X-Ray Eyes, Roger Corman (1963)

A Yank at Oxford, Jack Conway (1938)
Yankee Doodle Dandy, Michael Curtiz (1942)
The Year of Living Dangerously, Peter Weir (1982)
Yellow Submarine, George Dunning (1968)

Ziegfeld Follies, Vincente Minnelli (1944)
Zombies of the Stratosphere, Fred Brannon (1952)
Zorba the Greek, Michael Cacoyannis (1964)
Zorro Rides Again {serial}, Witney/English (1937)

STAGE AND TELEVISION PLAYS, MUSICALS, REVUES

Titles listed alphabetically, followed by playwright's name.

Section 1 – 1892–1925

The Admirable Crichton, J M Barrie
All God's Chillun Got Wings, Eugene O'Neill
Androcles and the Lion, George Bernard Shaw
Anna Christie, Eugene O'Neill
Arms and the Man, George Bernard Shaw
Back to Methuselah, George Bernard Shaw
A Bill of Divorcement, Clemence Dane
Blithe Spirit, Noel Coward
Candida, George Bernard Shaw
Captain Brassbound's Conversion, George Bernard Shaw
The Cat and the Canary, John Willard
Charley's Aunt, Brandon Thomas
Chu Chin Chow, Asche/Norton
The Dance of Death, August Strindberg
Dear Brutus, J M Barrie
Desire Under the Elms, Eugene O'Neill
The Devil's Disciple, George Bernard Shaw
The Doctor's Dilemma, George Bernard Shaw
The Enchanted Cottage, Arthur Pinero
The Gay Lord Quex, Arthur Pinero
The Girl of the Golden West, David Belasco
The Glass Slipper, Ferenc Molnar
The Hairy Ape, Eugene O'Neill
Hay Fever, Noel Coward
Heartbreak House, George Bernard Shaw
Hindle Wakes, Stanley Houghton
Hobson's Choice, Harold Brighouse
The Importance of Being Earnest, Oscar Wilde
John Bull's Other Island, George Bernard Shaw
Juno and the Paycock, Sean O'Casey
The Last of Mrs Cheyney, Frederick Lonsdale
Liliom, Ferenc Molnar
The Madras House, Harley Granville-Barker
Major Barbara, George Bernard Shaw
Man and Superman, George Bernard Shaw
Midsummer Madness, Clifford Bax
No, No, Nanette, Mandel/Harback/Caesar/Youmans
Passing of the Third Floor Back, Jerome K Jerome
Peg o' My Heart, J Hartley Manners
Playboy of the Western World, J M Synge
Pygmalion, George Bernard Shaw
Quality Street, J M Barrie
Saint Joan, George Bernard Shaw
The Second Mrs Tanqueray, Arthur Pinero
See Naples and Die, Elmer Rice
The Shadow of a Gunman, Sean O'Casey
Six Characters in Search of an Author, Luigi Pirandello
Smilin' Through, Allan L Martin
The Vortex, Noel Coward
The Voysey Inheritance, Harley Granville-Barker
What Every Woman Knows, J M Barrie
When We Were Twenty-One, H V Esmond
A Woman of No Importance, Oscar Wilde
You Never Can Tell, George Bernard Shaw

Section 2 – 1926–1944

The Amazing Dr Clitterhouse, Barrie Lyndon
The Apple Cart, George Bernard Shaw
Arsenic and Old Lace, Joseph Kesselring
The Ascent of F6, Auden/Isherwood
The Barratts of Wimpole Street, Rudolf Besier
Bitter Sweet, Noel Coward
Blood Wedding, Federico Garcia Lorca
Canaries Sometimes Sing, Frederick Lonsdale
Cavalcade, Noel Coward
The Constant Wife, W Somerset Maugham
The Corn is Green, Emlyn Williams
Dear Octopus, Dodie Smith
Design for Living, Noel Coward
Dinner at Eight, Kaufman/Ferber
The Dog Beneath the Skin, Auden/Isherwood
The Dybbuk, Solomon Ansky
Easy Virtue, Noel Coward
The Family Reunion, T S Eliot
French Without Tears, Terance Rattigan
The Front Page, MacArthur/Hecht
The Ghost Train, Arnold Ridley
Goodbye Mr Chips, Hilton/Burnham
The Good Woman of Setzuan, Bertholt Brecht
The Greeks Had a Word for It, Zoe Akins
I Have Been Here Before, J B Priestley
Journey's End, R C Sheriff
The Lady With a Lamp, Reginald Berkeley
Life of Galileo, Bertholt Brecht
The Little Foxes, Lillian Hellman
Little Orphant Annie, Robert H McLaughlin
Love on the Dole, Gow/Greenwood
The Man Who Came to Dinner, Kaufman/Hart
Mother Courage and Her Children, Bertholt Brecht
Mourning Becomes Electra, Eugene O'Neill
A Murder Has Been Arranged, Emlyn Williams
Murder in the Cathedral, T S Eliot
Night Music, Clifford Odets
Night Must Fall, Emlyn Williams
None But the Brave, Merivale/Fleming
Page Miss Glory, Shrank/Dunning
Pink String and Sealing Wax, Roland Pertwee
The Plough and the Stars, Sean O'Casey
Porgy and Bess, Heywood/Heywood
Private Lives, Noel Coward
The Silver Tassie, Sean O'Casey
Ten Little Indians or And Then There Were None, Agatha Christie

They Came By Night, Barrie Lyndon
This Happy Breed, Noel Coward
The Threepenny Opera, Brecht/Weill
Time and the Conways, J B Priestley
Tobacco Road, Jack Kirkland
Too True to be Good, George Bernard Shaw
When We Are Married, J B Priestley
Whistling in the Dark, Gross/Carpenter
You Can't Take It With You, Hart/Kaufman

Section 3 – 1945–1964

Alfie, Bill Naughton
All About Eve, Joseph L Mankiewicz
All the King's Men, Robert Penn Warren
All That Fall, Samuel Beckett
The American Dream, Edward Albee
The Amorous Prawn, Anthony Kimmins
Anne of a Thousand Days, Maxwell Andersen
Annie Get Your Gun, Rodgers/Hammerstein/Berlin
Baby Doll, Tennessee Williams
The Ballad of the Sad Café, Edward Albee
Barefoot in the Park, Neil Simon
Bell, Book and Candle, John van Druten
Beyond the Fringe , Bennett/Cook/Moore
Billy Budd, Guy Williams
Billy Liar, Waterhouse/Hall
The Birthday Party, Harold Pinter
The Bishop's Bonfire, Sean O'Casey
Brigadoon, Lerner/Loewe
Brothers-in-Law, Ted Willis
The Browning Version, Terence Rattigan
Bus Stop, William M Inge
The Caine Mutiny, Herman Wouk
Call Me Madam, Lindsay/Crouse/Berlin
Camelot, Alan Jay Lerner
Camino Real, Tennessee Williams
The Caretaker, Harold Pinter
Cat on a Hot Tin Roof, Tennessee Williams
The Caucasian Chalk Circle, Bertholt Brecht
Chicken Soup With Barley, Arnold Wesker
Chips With Everything, Arnold Wesker
Come Blow Your Horn, Neil Simon
The Country Girl, Clifford Odets
The Crucible, Arthur Miller
Damn Yankees, Adler Ross
The Dark at the Top of the Stairs, William M Inge
The Dark is Light Enough, Christopher Fry
Death of a Salesman, Arthur Miller
The Deep Blue Sea, Terence Rattigan
The Devils, John Whiting
Dial M for Murder, Frederick Knott
The Dumb Waiter, Harold Pinter
The Eagle Has Two Heads, Jean Cocteau
The Entertainer, John Osborne
Entertaining Mr Sloane, Joe Orton
Fiddler on the Roof, Stein/Bock/Harwick
Fings Ain't Wot They Use T'Be, Frank Norman
Five Finger Exercise, Peter Shaffer
Flower Drum Song, Rodgers/Hammerstein
A Funny Thing Happened on the Way to the Forum, Shevelove/Gelbart
The Glass Menagerie, Tennessee Williams
The Grass is Greener, Williams/Williams
Guys and Dolls, Loesser/Burrows/Swerling
The Happiest Days of Your Life, John Dighton
Happy Days, Samuel Beckett
The Hasty Heart, John Patrick
Hello, Dolly!, Stewart/Herman
Home is the Hero, Walter Macken
Home is the Hunter, Helen MacInnes
The Hostage, Brendan Behan
How to Succeed in Business Without Really Trying, Burrows/Weinstock/Gilbert/Loesser
I Can Get It For You Wholesale, Jerome Weidman
The Iceman Cometh, Eugene O'Neill
I Love Lucy, Christopher Serkel
I'm Talking About Jerusalem, Arnold Wesker
Inadmissable Evidence, John Osborne
Inherit the Wind, Lawrence/Lee
An Inspector Calls, J B Priestley
Irma la Douce, Alexander Breffori
The Killing of Sister George, Frank Marcus
The King and I, Rodgers/Hammerstein
Kismet, Wright/Forrest
Kiss Me Kate, Spewack/Spewack/Porter
The Lady's Not For Burning, Christopher Fry
Lock Up Your Daughters, Miles/Johnson/Bart
The Long and the Short and the Tall, Willis Hall
Long Day's Journey Into Night, Eugene O'Neill
Look Back in Anger, John Osborne
The Maids, Jean Genet
A Man For All Seasons, Robert Bolt
The Matchmaker, Thornton Wilder
Me and My Girl, Rose/Furber/Gay
Meet Me in St Louis, Christopher Serkel
Member of the Wedding, Carson McCullers
Miss Lonelyhearts, Howard Teichman
A Moon for the Misbegotten, Eugene O'Neill
The Mouse That Roared, Christopher Serkel
The Mousetrap, Agatha Christie
My Fair Lady, Lerner/Loewe
Next Time I'll Sing to You, James Saunders
The Night of the Iguana, Tennessee Williams
No Room at the Inn, Joan Temple
Oh, What a Lovely War!, Charles Chilton
Oklahoma!, Riggs/Rodgers/Hammerstein
Once More, With Feeling, Harry Kurnitz
One Flew Over the Cuckoo's Nest, Dale Wasserman
Orpheus Descending, Tennessee Williams
Our Town, Thornton Wilder
Paint Your Wagon, Lerner/Loewe
The Pajama Game, Abbott/Bessell/Adler/Ross
Pal Joey, O'Hara/Rodgers/Hart
Past Imperfect, Williams/Williams
A Phoenix Too Frequent, Christopher Fry
Pillow Talk, Christopher Serkel
The Pope's Wedding, Edward Bond
Present Laughter, Noel Coward
Privates on Parade, Peter Nichols
The Quare Fellow, Brendan Behan
Quatermass and the Pit, Nigel Kneale
Rattle of a Simple Man, Charles Dyer
The Reluctant Debutante, William Douglas Home
The Resistible Rise of Artuor Ui, Bertholt Brecht
A Resounding Tinkle, N F Simpson
Ring Round the Moon, Jean Anouilh
Roar Like a Dove, Lesley Storm
Romanoff and Juliet, Peter Ustinov
Rookery Nook, Ben Travers
Roots, Arnold Wesker
The Rose Tattoo, Tennessee Williams
The Royal Hunt of the Sun, Peter Shaffer
Sailor, Beware!, Philip King
Saint's Day, John Whiting
Salad Days, Reynolds/Slade
Say It With Flowers, Glenn Hughes
The Secret Life of Walter Mitty, James Thurber
See How They Run, Philip King
Sergeant Musgrave's Dance, John Arden
The Servant of Two Masters, Carlo Goldoni
The Seven Year Itch, George Axelrod
Showboat, Kern/Hammerstein
Simple Spymen, John Chapman
Six Characters in Search of an Author, Luigi Pirandello
The Solid Gold Cadillac, Teichman/Kauffman
The Sound of Music, Lindsay/Crouse
South Pacific, Osborn/Rodgers/Hammerstein
Splendour in the Grass, William Inge
Spring and Port Wine, Bill Naughton
Stage Door, Edna Ferber
Stop the World I Want to Get Off, Newley/Bricusse
A Streetcar Named Desire, Tennessee Williams
Suddenly Last Summer, Tennessee Williams
Summer of the Seventeenth Doll, Ray Lawler
Sweet Bird of Youth, Tennessee Williams
Tea and Sympathy, Robert W Anderson
The Teahouse of the August Moon, John Patrick
The Tender Trap, Charles Walters
The Tenth Man, Paddy Chayefsky
There's a Girl in My Soup, Terence Frisby
This Happy Breed, Noel Coward
The Tiger At the Gates or The Trojan War Will Not Take Place, Jean Giraudoux
A Tree Grows in Brooklyn, Smith/Abbott
The Trip to Bountiful, Horton Foote
Twelve Angry Men, Reginald Rose
Under Milkwood, Dylan Thomas
The Unsinkable Molly Brown, Morris/Willson
Venus Observed, Christopher Fry
A View from the Bridge, Arthur Miller
Waiting for Godot, Samuel Beckett
West Side Story, Arthur Laurents
Who's Afraid of Virginia Woolf, Edward Albee
The Winslow Boy, Terence Rattigan
Witness for the Prosecution, Agatha Christie
Woman in a Dressing Gown, Ted Willis
Zip Goes a Million, Littler/Mashwitz/Posford

Section 4 – 1965–1985

Abigail's Party, Mike Leigh
Absent Friends, Alan Ayckbourn
Absurd Person Singular, Alan Ayckbourn
Accidental Death of an Anarchist, Dario Fo
AC/DC, Hugh Williams
Amadeus, Peter Shaffer
American Buffalo, David Mamet
And a Nightingale Sang, C P Taylor
Barbarians, Barrie Keeffe
The Bedsitting Room, Spike Milligan
Bent, Martin Sherman
A Bequest to the Nation, Terence Rattigan
Blood Brothers, Willy Russell
The Boys in the Band, Mart Crowley
Brief Lives, John Aubrey
Brighton Beach Memoirs, Neil Simon
Brimstone and Treacle, Dennis Potter
Butley, Simon Gray
La Cage Aux Folles, Jean Poiret
California Suite, Neil Simon
Can't Pay? Won't Pay!, Dario Fo
Can You Hear Me at the Back?, Brian Clark
Cathy Come Home, Jeremy Sandford
Cats, Andrew Lloyd Webber
The Changing Room, David Storey
Children of a Lesser God, Mark Medoff
A Chorus Line, Kirkwood/Dante
Close the Coalhouse Door, Alan Plater
Conduct Unbecoming, Barry England
The Contractor, David Storey
Crimes of the Heart, Beth Henley
Cuttin' a Rug, John Byrne
A Day in Hollywood, A Night in the Ukraine, Vosburgh/Lazarus

A Day in the Death of Joe Egg, Peter Nicholls
Dog Days, Simon Gray
The Dog It Was That Died, Tom Stoppard
Don't Just Lie There, Say Something, Michael Pertwee
The Dresser, Ronald Harwood
Duet for One, Tom Kempinski
Easy Street, John Waddington-Feather
Edna, The Inebriate Woman, Jeremy Sandford
Educating Rita, Willy Russell
The Effect of Gamma Rays on Man-in-the-Moon Marigolds, Paul Zindel
The Elephant Man, Bernard Pomerance
Equus, Antony Shaffer
Every Good Boy Deserves Favour, Stoppard/Previn
Evita, Andrew Lloyd Webber
A Flea in Her Ear, Georges Feydeau
Fur Coat and No Knickers, Mike Harding
Gimme Shelter, Barrie Keeffe
Godspell, Tebelak/Schwartz
Good and Faithful Servant, Joe Orton
The Greeks, John Barton
Half a Sixpence, Cross/Heneker
How the Other Half Loves, Alan Ayckbourn
Inadmissible Evidence, John Osborne
Jamie the Saxt, Robert McLellan
Jesus Christ Superstar, Lloyd-Webber/Rice
Joseph and the Amazing Technicolor Dreamcoat, Lloyd-Webber/Rice
Jumpers, Tom Stoppard
The Killing of Sister George, Frank Marcus
The Knack, Ann Jellicoe
Last of the Red-Hot Lovers, Neil Simon
Let's Get a Divorce, Goldsby/Goldsby
Life Class, David Storey
The Lion in Winter, James Goldman
A Little Night Music, Wheeler/Sondheim
The Little Shop of Horrors, Ashman/Menken
Lloyd George Knew My Father, William Douglas-Home
Loot, Joe Orton
Luther, John Osborne
Mame, Lawrence/Lee/Herman
The Man Most Likely To..., Joyce Rayburn
Man of La Mancha, Dale Wasserman
Maria Marten or Murder in the Red Barn, Brian Burton
Melancholy Bay, S K Adams
A Murder is Announced, Agatha Christie
My Giddy Aunt, Ray Cooney
The National Health, Peter Nichols
Night Must Fall, Emlyn Williams
No Man's Land, Harold Pinter
No Sex Please – We're British, Marriott/Foot
The Norman Conquests, Alan Ayckbourn
The Odd Couple, Neil Simon
Once a Catholic, Mary O'Malley
A Patriot for Me, John Osborne
Piaf, Pam Gems
Pravda, Howard Brenton
P'Tang, Yang, Kipperbang, Jack Rosenthal
The Real Inspector Hound, Tom Stoppard
Richard's Cork Leg, Brendan Behan
Ring Round the Moon, Christopher Fry
The Rocky Horror Show, Richard O'Brien
Rosencrantz and Guildenstern Are Dead, Tom Stoppard
The Ruffian on the Stair, Joe Orton
Run For Your Wife, Ray Cooney
Same Time, Next Year, Bernard Slade
Savages, Christopher Hampton
Say Who You Are, Waterhouse/Hall
Shut Your Eyes and Think of England, Chapman/Marriott
The Slab Boys, John Byrne
Slag, David Hare
Sleuth, Antony Shaffer
Still Life, John Byrne
Sweeney Todd, the Demon Barber of Fleet Street, Pitt/ Wheeler
Sweet Charity, Neil Simon
They're Playing Our Song, Neil Simon
To Have and Have Not, Jules Furthman
Travesties, Tom Stoppard
Trumpets and Raspberries, Dario Fo
Unman, Wittering and Zigo, Giles Cooper
Vivat! Vivat Regina!, Robert Bolt
A Voyage Round My Father, John Mortimer
Wait Until Dark, Frederick Knott
What the Butler Saw, Joe Orton
Whose Life Is It Anyway?, Brian Clark
Wise Child, Simon Gray
You Know I Can't Hear You When the Water's Running, Robert Anderson
Zigger Zagger, Peter Terson
Zoo Zoo Widdershins Zoo, Kevin Barry Laffan

Section 5 – 1986–95

The Clown Prince, Bill Hayden
Death and the Maiden, Ariel Dorfman
Good, C P Taylor
Hindle Wakes, Stanley Houghton
The Hired Man, Howard Goodall
Ilsa, Queen of the Nazi Love Camp, Blake Brooker
Jeffrey Bernard is Unwell, Keith Waterhouse
Les Liaisons Dangereuses, Christopher Hampton
Lettice and Lovage, Peter Shaffer
A Nice Little Earner, Arnold Evans
Passion Play, Peter Nichols
Rita, Sue and Bob Too, Andrea Dunbar
Serious Money, Caryl Churchill
Shirley Valentine, Willy Russell
Tom and Viv, Michael Hastings

SONGS

Titles listed alphabetically followed by composer/lyricist with date of release.

'A' You're Adorable, Kaye/Wise/Lippman (1948)
After The Ball, Harris (1892)
After You've Gone, Creamer/Layton (1918)
Ain't It Grand To Be Bloomin' Well Dead, Sarony (1932)
The Air That I Breathe, Hammond/Hazelwood (1974)
Alexander's Ragtime Band, Berlin (1911)
Alice Blue Gown, Tierney/McCarthy (1919)
Alice Where Art Thou?, Ascher/Guernsey (1861)
All I Do Is Dream Of You, Brown/Freed (1934)
All I Have To Do Is Dream, Bryant (1958)
All Kinds Of Everything, Lindsay/Smith (1970)
All My Loving, Lennon/McCartney (1963)
All Of Me, Simons/Marks (1931)
All Or Nothing At All, Lawrence/Altman (1940)
All Shook Up, Presley/Blackwell (1957)
All The Way, Van Heusen/Cahn (1957)
Almost Like Being In Love, Loewe/Lerner (1947)
Amapola, Lacalle (1924)
America, Bernstein/Sondheim (1957)
American Pie, McLean (1971)
Among My Souvenirs, Nicholls/Leslie (1927)
And Her Mother Came Too, Novello/ Titheradge (1921)
And I Love You So, McLean (1970)
Annie's Song, Denver (1974)
Anniversary Song, Jolson/Chaplin (1946)
Anniversary Waltz, Franklin/Dubin (1941)
Another Suitcase In Another Hall, Lloyd Webber/Rice (1978)
Any Old Iron?, Collins/Sheppard/Terry (1911)
Anyone Who Had A Heart, Bacharach/David (1963)
Anything Goes, Porter (1934)
Anything You Can Do I Can Do Better, Berlin (1946)
April Love, Fain/Webster (1957)
April Showers, Silvers/ De Sylva (1921)
Aquarius, MacDermot/Ragni/Rado (1967)
Are You Lonesome Tonight?, Turk/Handman (1926)
Around The World, Young/Adamson (1956)
Arrivederci Roma, Rascel/Garinei/Giovannini/ Sigman (1954)
As Long As He Needs Me, Bart (1960)
As Time Goes By, Hupfeld (1931)
A-Tisket A-Tasket, Fitzgerald/Feldman (1938)
Auf Wiederseh'n Sweetheart, Storch/Sexton/ Turner (1949/1952)
Autumn Leaves, Kosma/Prevert [Fr] (1947)/ Mercer [Eng] (1950)
Avalon, Jolson/Rose (1920)

Baby Face, Davis/Akst (1926)
Baby Love, Holland/Holland/Dozier (1964)
Bachelor Boy, Richard/Welch (1962)
Bali Ha'i, Rodgers/Hammerstein (1949)
Ballad Of Davy Crockett, Burns/Blackburn (1955)
Banana Boat Song, Darling/Carey/Arkin (1956)
Band Of Gold, Taylor/Musel (1955)
Band On The Run, McCartney (1974)
Battle Of New Orleans, Driftwood (1957)
Because, D'Hardelot/Teschemaker (1902)
Begin The Beguine, Porter (1935)
Behind Closed Doors, O'Dell (1973)
The Bells Of St Mary's, Adams/Furber (1917)
Be My Love, Brodzsky/Cahn (1950)
The Best Things In Life Are Free, Henderson/ De Sylva/Brown (1927)
Bewitched, Bothered and Bewildered, Rodgers/ Hart (1941)
Beyond The Blue Horizon, Whiting/Robin (1930)
Beyond The Sea {La Mer}, Trenet (1947)
The Biggest Aspidistra In The World, Harper/ Haines/Connor (1938)
Big Spender, Coleman/Fields (1965)
Bill Bailey, Won't You Please Come Home, Cannon (1902)
Bits And Pieces, Clark/smith (1963)
Blame It On The Bossa Nova, Mann/Weill (1962)
Bless 'Em All, Hughes/Lake/Stillman (1940)
Bless This House, Taylor/Morghan (1922)
Bless Your Beautiful Hide, De Paul/Mercer (1954)
Blowing Bubbles, Kenbrovin/Kellette (1919)
Blowin' In The Wind, Dylan (1962)
Blue Bayou, Orbison/Melson (1963)
Blueberry Hill, Lewis/Stock/Rose (1940)
Blue Moon, Rodgers/Hart (1934)
Blue Skies, Berlin (1926)

Bohemian Rhapsody, Mercury (1975)
Boiled Beef and Carrots, Collins/Murray (1910)
Born Free, Barry/Black (1966)
Breaking Up Is Hard To Do, Sedaka/Greenfield (1959)
Bridge Over Troubled Water, Simon/Garfunkel (1969)
Bright Eyes, Bart (1980)
Brother Can You Spare A Dime?, Gorney/Harburg (1932)
Build Me Up Buttercup, Macaulay/D'Abo (1968)
Burlington Bertie From Bow, Hargreaves (1915)
Bus Stop, Gouldman (1966)
Buttons And Bows, Livingston/Evans (1948)
Bye Bye Baby, Gaudio/Crewe (1964)
Bye Bye Blackbird, Henderson/Dixon (1926)
Bye Bye Love, Bryant/Bryant (1957)
By The Light Of The Silvery Moon, Edwards/Madden (1909)

California Dreamin', Phillips/Phillips (1965)
California Here I Come, Jolson/De Sylva/Meyer (1924)
Can't Buy Me Love, Lennon/McCartney (1964)
Can't Help Falling In Love, Weiss/Peretti/Creatore (1961)
Can't Help Lovin' Dat Man, Kern/Hammerstein (1927)
Can't Take My Eyes Off You, Gaudio/Crewe (1967)
Cara Mia, Lange/Trapani (1954)
Carolina Moon, Davis/Burke (1928)
Carrie-Anne, Clarke/Hicks/Nash (1967)
Carry Me Back To Old Virginny, Bland (1878)
Casey Jones, Newton/Seibert (1909)
Catch A Falling Star, Vance/Pockriss (1957)
A Certain Smile, Fain/Webster (1958)
Champagne Charlie, Lee/Whymark (1867)
Chances Are, Allen/Stillman (1957)
Chantilly Lace, Richardson (1958)
Charmaine, Rapee/Pollack (1926)
Chattanooga Choo Choo, Warren/Gordon (1941)
Cheek To Cheek, Berlin (1935)
Cherry Pink And Apple Blossom White, Louiguy/Larue/David (1950/1951)
Chicago, Fisher (1922)
Chinatown, My Chinatown, Schwartz/Jerome (1906)
Claire, O'Sullivan (1972)
Climb Ev'ry Mountain, Rodgers/Hammerstein (1959)
Close To You, David/Bacharach (1963)
Come Fly With Me, Van Heusen/Cahn (1958)
Come Rain Or Come Shine, Arlen/Mercer (1946)
Comin' In On A Wing And A Prayer, McHugh/Adamson (1943)
Congratulations, Martin/Coulter (1968)
Could It Be Magic, Manilow/Anderson (1973)
Count Your Blessings Instead Of Sheep, Berlin (1952)
Cracklin' Rosie, Diamond (1970)
Cruisin' Down The River, Beadell/Tollerton (1945)
Cry, Kohlman (1951)
Cryin', Orbison/Melson (1961)
Crying In The Chapel, Glenn (1953)
Cry Me A River, Hamilton (1953)
Cuddle Up A Little Closer, Lovey Mine, Hoschna/Harbach (1908)

Daddy Wouldn't Buy Me A Bow Wow, Tabrar (1892)
Dancing In The Dark, Schwartz/Dietz (1931)
Danny Boy, Weatherly (1913)
Daydream Believer, Stewart (1967)
Days Of Wine And Roses, Mancini/Mercer (1962)
The Deck Of Cards, Tyler (1948)
Deep In The Heart Of Texas, Swander/Hershey (1941)
Deep Purple, De Rose/Parish (1934)
Delaware, Gordon (1960)
Diamonds Are A Girl's Best Friend, Styne/Robin (1949)
Diamonds Are Forever, Barry/Black (1971)
Diana, Anka (1957)
Diane, Pollack/Radge (1927)
D-I-V-O-R-C-E, Braddock/Putnam (1968)
Does The Spearmint Lose Its Flavour, Breuer/Rose/Bloom (1924)
Doin' What Comes Natur'lly, Berlin (1946)
Donna, Valens (1958)
Don't Blame Me, McHugh/Fields (1932)
Don't Cry For Me Argentina, Lloyd Webber/Rice (1975)
Don't Let's Be Beastly To The Germans, Noel Coward (1943)
Don't Put Your Daughter On The Stage, Mrs Worthington, Coward (1935)
Don't Sit Under The Apple Tree, Brown/Tobias/Stept (1942)
Do-Re-Mi, Rogers/Hammerstein (1959)
Down At The Old Bull And Bush, Von Tilzer/Hunting/Krone/Stirling (1903)
Downtown, Hatch (1964)
Do You Want To Know A Secret?, Lennon/McCartney (1963)
Dream A Little Dream Of Me, Schwandt/Andre/Kahn (1931)
Dream Lover, Darin (1959)

Easter Parade, Berlin (1933)
East Of The Sun, Bowman (1934)
Edelweiss, Rodgers/Hammerstein (1959)
Eleanor Rigby, Lennon/McCartney (1966)
Embraceable You, Gershwin/Gershwin (1930)
The End Of The World, Kent/Dee (1962)
Eternally, Chaplin/Parsons (1953)
Evergreen, Streisand/Williams (1976)
Everybody Loves Somebody, Lane/Taylor (1948)
Everybody's Doing It, Berlin (1911)
Everything I Have Is Yours, Lane/Adamson (1933)
Everything's Coming Up Roses, Styne/Sondheim (1959)
Exodus, Gold/Boone (1961)
Eye Of The Tiger, Sullivan/Peterik (1982)

Falling In Love Again, Hollander/Lerner (1930)
Falling In Love With Love, Rogers/Hart (1938)
Fascinating Rhythm, Gershwin/Gershwin (1924)
Fascination, Marchetti/Manning (1957)
Feelings, Albert/Kaiserman (1974)
Ferry Cross The Mersey, Marsden (1964)
50 Million Frenchmen Can't Be Wrong, Fisher/Rose/Raskin (1927)
The First Time Ever I Saw Your Face, McColl (1972)
Five Foot Two, Eyes Of Blue, Henderson/Lewis/Young (1925)
The Five Pennies, Fine (1959)
Flower Of Scotland, Williamson (c.1960)
Fly Me To The Moon, Howard (1954)
The Folks Who Live On The Hill, Kern/Hammerstein (1937)
Fools Rush In, Bloom/Mercer (1940)
For Me And My Gal, Meyer/Leslie/Goetz (1917)
For The Good Times, Kristofferson (1970)
Friendly Persuasion, Tiomkin/Webster (1956)
From Here To Eternity, Karger/Wells (1953)
From Russia With Love, Bart (1964)
From This Moment On, Porter (1950)

Georgia On My Mind, Carmichael/Gorrell (1930)
Get Me To The Church On Time, Loewe/Lerner (1956)
Getting To Know You, Rodgers/Hammerstein (1951)
Gigi, Loewe/Lerner (1958)
Gilly Gilly Ossenfeffer Katzenellen Bogen By The Sea, Hoffmann/Manning (1954)
The Girl That I Marry, Berlin (1946)
Give Me The Moonlight, Von Tilzer/Brown (1917)
Give My Regards To Broadway, Cohan (1904)
God Save The Queen, Carey/Bull (–)
Good Bye-ee, Weston/Lee (1918)
Goodbye, Good Luck, God Bless You, Ball/Brennan (1916)
The Good Life, Distel/Reardon (1963)
Good Morning Starshine, MacDermot/Ragni/Rado (1969)
Goodnight Sweetheart, Noble/Campbell/Connelly/Vallee (1931)
Goody, Goody, Mercer/Malneck (1936)
Granada, Lara/ Dodd [Eng]/Lara[Sp] (1932)
The Great Pretender, Ram (1955)
Green, Green Grass Of Home, Putman (1967)
The Green Leaves Of Summer, Tiomkin/Webster (1960)
Groovy Kind Of Love, Wine/Bayer (1966)
Guantanamera, Seeger/Angulo (1966)

Half a Sixpence, Heneker (1962)
Halfway To Paradise, Coffin/King (1961)
Happy Days Are Here Again, Ager/Yellen (1929)
Happy Talk, Rogers/Hammerstein (1949)
Has Anybody Here Seen Kelly?, Murphy/Letters/Moore/McKenna (1909)
Have You Ever Been Lonely?, De Rose/Brown (1932)
Hear My Song, Violetta, Luckesch/ Klose/Bernier/Emmerich [Eng]/Klose/Carosio [Ger] (1938)
Heart And Soul, Carmichael/Loesser (1938)
Heatwave, Berlin (1933)
Hello Dolly, Herman (1963)
Hello, Hello, Who's Your Lady Friend?, David/Lee/Fragson (1914)
Hello Young Lovers, Rodgers/Hammerstein (1951)
Help Me Make It Through The Night, Kristofferson (1970)
Hernando's Hideaway, Adler/Ross (1954)
He's Got The Whole World, Love (1957)
Hey Good Lookin', Porter (1942)
High Noon, Tiomkin/Washington (1952)
Hi Lili, Hi Lo, Kaper/Deutsch (1952)
How About You?, Lane/Freed (1941)
How Are Things In Glocca Morra?, Lane/Harburg (1947)
How Deep Is The Ocean?, Berlin (1932)
How High The Moon, Lewis/Hamilton (1940)
How To Handle A Woman, Loewe/Lerner (1960)
How Ya Gonna Keep 'Em Down On The Farm, Donaldson/Lewis/Young (1919)
A Hymn To Him, Loewe/Lerner (1956)

I Believe, Drake/Graham/Shirl/Stillman (1983)
I Belong To Glasgow, Fyffe (1920)
I Can't Give You Anything But Love, McHugh/Fields (1928)
I Can't Stop Loving You, Gibson (1962)
I Could Have Danced All Night, Loewe/Lerner (1956)
I Do Like To Be Beside The Seaside, Glover-Kind (1909)
I Don't Know How To Love Him, Lloyd Webber/Rice (1971)
I Don't Know Why, Ahlert/Turk (1931)
I Feel Pretty, Bernstein/Sondheim (1957)
I Get A Kick Out Of You, Porter (1934)
I Got Plenty O' Nuttin', Gershwin/Heyward (1935)
I Got Rhythm, Gershwin (1930)
I Left My Heart In San Francisco, Cory/Cross (1954)
I Love A Lassie, Lauder/Grafton (1906)
I Love Paris, Porter (1953)
I Never Knew, Fiorito/Kahn (1925)
I Only Have Eyes For You, Warren/Dubin (1934)
I Saw Mommy Kissing Santa Claus, Connor (1952)
I Should Have Known Better, Lennon/McCartney (1964)
I Taut I Taw A Puddy-Tat, Livingston/Foster (1950)
I Wanna Be Loved By You, Stothart/Ruby/Kalmar (1928)
I Want A Girl, Just Like The Girl That Married Dear Old Dad, Von Tilzer/Dillon (1911)
I Want To Be Happy, Youmans/Caesar (1924)
I Want To Hold Your Hand, Lennon/McCartney (1964)
I Was Standing At The Corner Of The Street, Formby/Hunt (1910)
I Whistle A Happy Tune, Rodgers/Hammerstein II (1951)
I Wonder Who's Kissing Her Now?, Howard/Orlob/Hough/Adams (1909)
I'd Do Anything, Bart (1963)
I'd Like To Teach The World To Sing, Davis/West/Backer (1971)
If Ever I Would Leave You, Loewe/Lerner (1960)
If I Had A Hammer, Hays/Seeger (1958)
If I Knew You Were Comin' I'd've Baked A Cake, Hoffman/Merrill/Watts (1950)
If I Loved You, Rodgers/Hammerstein II (1945)
If I Ruled The World, Ornadel/Bricusse (1963)
If I Were A Rich Man, Bock/Harnick (1964)
If You Knew Susie Like I Know Susie, De Sylva/Meyer (1925)
If You Were The Only Girl In The World, Ayer/Grey (1916)
I'll Be Seeing You, Fain/Kahal (1938)
I'll Be With You In Apple Blossom Time, Von Tilzer/Fleeson (1920)
I'll Be Your Sweetheart, Dacre (1900)
I'll Get By, Ahlert/Turk (1928)
I'll See You Again, Coward (1929)
I'll See You In My Dreams, Jones/Kahn (1924)
I'll String Along With You, Warren/Dubin (1934)
I'll Take You Home Again Kathleen, Westendorf (1876)
I'm Always Chasing Rainbows, Carroll/McCarthy (1918)
I'm Forever Blowing Bubbles, Kenbrovin/Kellette (1918)
I'm Gonna Wash That Man Right Outta My Hair, Rodgers/Hammerstein II (1949)
I'm In Love With A Wonderful Guy, Rodgers/Hammerstein II (1949)
I'm In The Mood For Love, McHugh/Fields (1935)
I'm Looking Over A Four Leaf Clover, Woods/Dixon (1927)
I'm Sitting On Top Of The World, Henderson/Lewis/Young (1925)
In The Good Old Summertime, Evans/Shields (1902)
In The Mood, Razaf/Garland (1939)
In The Quartermaster's Store, Trad. Adapted by Box/Cox/Reed (1940)
It Ain't Necessarily So, Gershwin/Gershwin (1935)
It Had To Be You, Jones/Kahn (1924)
It's A Long Way To Tipperary, Judge/Williams (1912)
It's A Lovely Day Tomorrow, Berlin (1940)
It's Nice To Get Up In The Morning, Lauder (1913)
It's Only A Paper Moon, Arlen/Harbour/Rose (1933)
Itsy Bitsy Teenie Weenie Yellow Polka Dot Bikini, Vance/Pockriss (1960)
I've Got A Lovely Bunch Of Coconuts, Heatherton (1948)
I've Got My Love To Keep Me Warm, Berlin (1937)
I've Got You Under My Skin, Porter (1936)
I've Grown Accustomed To Her Face, Loewe/Lerner (1956)

Jeanie With The Light Brown Hair, Foster (1854)
Jeepers Creepers, Warren/Mercer (1938)
Jesus Christ Superstar, Lloyd Webber/Rice (1971)
Jimmy Crack Corn, Emmett (1846)
Jingle Bells, Pierpont (1857)
John Brown's Body, Music based on *Glory Glory Hallelujah*, Hall/Brownell/Bishop (1861)
June Is Bustin' Out All Over, Rodgers/Hammerstein II (1945)
Just A Closer Walk With Thee, Foley (1950)
Just In Time, Styne/Comden/Green (1956)
Just One Of Those Things, Porter (1935)

Keep The Home Fires Burning, Novello/Ford (1915)
Keep Right On To The End Of The Road, Lauder (1924)
Kiss Me, Honey, Honey, Kiss Me, Timothy/Julien (1958)
Kisses Sweeter Than Wine, Newman/Campbell (1951)
K-K-K-Katy, O'Hara/O'Hara [Eng]/Bollaert [Fr] (1918)
Knees Up Mother Brown, Weston/Lee/Taylor (1938)

The Lady Is A Tramp, Rodgers/Hart (1937)
The Lambeth Walk, Furber/Gay/Rose (1937)
Land Of My Fathers, James/James[Welsh]/Stephens [Eng](1856)
Last Night On The Back Porch – I Loved Her Best Of All, Brown/Schraubstader (1923)
The Last Time I Saw Paris, Kern/Hammerstein II (1940)
Lay, Lady, Lay, Dylan (1969)
Leaning On A Lamp Post, Gay (1937)
Let It Be, Lennon/McCartney (1970)
Let Me Call You Sweetheart, Whitson/Friedman (1910)
Let The Rest Of The World Go By, Ball/Brennan (1919)
Let The Sunshine In, MacDermot/Ragni/Rado (1969)
Let's All Go Down The Strand, Castling/Murphy (1910)
Let's Do It, Porter (1928)
Let's Face The Music And Dance, Berlin (1936)
Let's Twist Again, Appell/Mann (1961)
Life Is Just A Bowl of Cherries, Henderson/Brown (1931)
A Life On The Ocean Wave, Russell/Sargent (1838)
Lili Marlene, Leip/Schultze/Connor (1944)
Lily Of Laguna, Stuart (1912)
Lipstick On Your Collar, Goehring/Lewis (1959)
Little Brown Jug, Winner (1869)
Little Dolly Daydream, Stuart (1900)
Little Donkey, Boswell (1959)
The Little Drummer Boy, Simeone/Onorati (1959)
Little Things Mean A Lot, Lindeman/Stutz (1954)
Living Doll, Bart (1959)
Lloyd George Knew My Father, Unknown/Sullivan (–)
Loch Lomond, Traditional (c.1880)
Look For The Silver Lining, Kern/De Sylva (1920)
Love And Marriage, Van Heusen/Cahn (1955)
Love Is A Many Splendored Thing, Fain/Webster (1955)
Love Is Like A Violin, Laparcerie/Kennedy (1945)
Love Letters In The Sand, Coots/Kenny/Kenny (1931)
Love Me Or Leave Me, Donaldson/Kahn (1928)
Love Me Tender, Presley/Matson (1956)
Love Story Theme, Sigman/Lai (1920)
Luck Be A Lady, Loesser (1950)
Lullaby Of Broadway, Warren/Dubin (1935)

Ma! He's Making Eyes At Me, Conrad/Clare (1921)
Macnamara's Band, O'Connor/Stamford (1917)
Mack The Knife, Weill/Blitzstein[Eng]/Brecht [Ger] (1928)
Mad Dogs And Englishmen, Coward (1931)
Mademoiselle From Armentières, Gitz/Rowland (1918)
Magic Moments, Bacharach/David (1958)
Mairzy Doats, Drake/Hoffman/Livingston (1943)
Make Believe, Kern/Hammerstein II (1927)
Makin' Whoopee, Donaldson/Kahn (1928)
Mame, Herman (1966)
The Man I Love, Gershwin/Gershwin (1924)
The Man That Broke The Bank At Monte Carlo, Gilbert (1892)
Marching Through Georgia, Work (1865)
Maria, Bernstein/Sondheim (1957)
La Marseillaise, De Lisle (1792)
Mary's Boy Child, Hairston (1956)
Maybe It's Because I'm A Londoner, Gregg (1949)
Me And My Shadow, Jolson/Dreyer/Rose (1927)
Meet Me In St Louis, Louis, Mills/Sterling (1904)
Meet Me Tonight In Dreamland, Friedman/Slater (1909)

Memory, Lloyd Webber/Eliot (1982)
La Mer, Trenet (1939)
Mexicali Rose, Tenny/Stone (1923)
Miss Otis Regrets, Porter (1934)
Mister Sandman, Ballard (1954)
Misty, Garner/Burke (1954)
Mona Lisa, Livingston/Evans (1950)
Moon River, Mancini/Mercer (1961)
Moonlight And Roses, Black/Moret (1925)
Mountain Greenery, Rodgers/Hart (1926)
Mrs Robinson, Simon (1968)
Music, Maestro, Please, Wrubel/Magidson (1938)
My Ain Folk, Lemon/Mills (1905)
My Favourite Things, Rodgers/Hammerstein II (1959)
My Foolish Heart, Young/Washington (1949)
My Funny Valentine, Rodgers/Hart (1937)
My Heart Belongs To Daddy, Porter (1938)
My Melancholy Baby, Burnett/Norton (1912)

Nellie Dean, Armstrong (1906)
New York, New York, Bernstein/Comden/Green (1945)
Nice Work If You Can Get It, Gershwin/Gershwin (1937)
Night And Day, Porter (1932)
A Nightingale Sang In Berkeley Square, Maschwitz/Sherwin/Strachey (1940)
No Two People, Loesser (1952)

O Mein Papa, Burkhard/Burkhard [Ger]/Turner/Parsons [Eng] (1953)
Oh! Susanna (Foster1848)
Oh What A Beautiful Mornin', Rodgers/Hammerstein II (1943)
Oh You Beautiful Doll, Ayer/Brown (1911)
Oklahoma, Rodgers/Hammerstein II (1943)
Old Black Joe, Foster (1860)
Old Folks At Home, Foster (1851)
The Old Rugged Cross, Bennard (1913)
Old Soldiers Never Die, Westphal (1939)
Ol' Man River, Kern/Hammerstein II (1927)
On A Slow Boat To China, Loesser (1948)
On Moonlight Bay, Wenrich/Madden (1912)
On Mother Kelly's Doorstep, Stevens (1925)
On The Road To Mandalay, Speaks/Kipling (1907)
On The Street Where You Live, Loewe/Lerner (1956)
On The Sunny Side Of The Street, McHugh/Fields (1930)
On Top Of Old Smokey, Trad. arr Barovick (1951)
One Alone, Romberg/Hammerstein II/Marbach (1926)
One For My Baby, Arlen/Mercer(1943)
Only You, Ram/Rand (1955)
Over The Rainbow, Arlen/Warburg (1939)

Pack Up Your Troubles, Powell/Asaf (1915)
Pennies From Heaven, Johnston/Burke (1936)
People, Styne/Merrill (1964)
Pop Goes The Weasel, Twiggs [attr] (1853)
Praise The Lord And Pass The Amunition, Loesser (1942)
Puff The Magic Dragon, Lipton/Yarrow (1963)

Que Será, Será, Livingston/Evans (1956)

Ragtime Cowboy Joe, Muir/Clarke/Abrahams (1912)
Raindrops Keep Fallin' On My Head, Bacharach/David (1970)
Ramblin' Rose, Sherman/Sherman (1962)
Ramona, Wayne/Gilbert (1927)
Red Sails In The Sunset, Williams/Kennedy (1935)
Release Me, Miller/Stevenson (1954)
Roamin' In The Gloamin', Lauder (1911)
Rock-A-Bye Your Baby With A Dixie Melody, Schwartz/Lewis/Young (1918)
Rock Around The Clock, Freedman/De Knight (1955)
Rock Of Ages, Hasting/Toplady (1832)
Rocked In The Cradle Of The Deep, Knight/Willard (1840)
Roll Out The Barrel, Brown/Timm/Vejvoda (1939)
Rose Marie, Friml/Harbach/Hammerstein II (1924)
Roses Of Picardy, Wood/Weatherly (1916)
Rudolph The Red-Nosed Reindeer, Marks (1949)
Rule Britannia, Arne/Thomson/Mallet (c.1740)

Sally, Haines/Leon/Towers (1931)
San Antonio Rose, Wills (1938)
Save The Last Dance For Me, Pomus/Shuman (1960)
Scarborough Fair, Simon/Garfunkel (1966)
Scarlet Ribbons, Danzig/Segal (1949)
Scottish Soldier, Stewart/MacFadyen (1961)
The Second Time Around, Van Heusen/Cahn (1960)
See What The Boys In The Back Room Will Have, Hollander/Loesser (1939)
Send In The Clowns, Sondheim (1973)
Sergeant Pepper's Lonely Hearts Club Band, Lennon/McCartney (1967)
Seventy-Six Trombones, Willson (1957)
The Shadow Of Your Smile, Mandel/Webster (1965)
She Didn't Say Yes, Kern/Harbach (1931)
She's Only A Bird In A Gilded Cage, Von Tilzer/Lamb (1900)
Shine On Harvest Moon, Bayes/Norworth (1908)
Show Me The Way To Go Home, Connolly/Campbell (1925)
Silver Threads Among The Gold, Danks/Rexford (1873)
Singin' In The Rain, Herb/Freed (1929)
Sister Susie's Sewing Shirts For Soldiers, Darewski/Weston (1914)
Sit Down, You're Rockin' The Boat, Loesser (1950)
Smoke Gets In Your Eyes, Kern/Harbach (1933)
Softly, As In A Morning Sunrise, Hammerstein II/Romberg (1928)
The Soldier's Song, Kearney/Heeney (1907)
Some Day My Heart Will Awake, Novello (1949)
Some Enchanted Evening, Rodgers/Hammerstein II (1949)
Some Of These Days, Brooks (1910)
Someone To Watch Over Me, Gershwin/Gershwin (1926)
Somewhere, Bernstein/Sondheim (1957)
Song Of The Clyde, Gourlay/Yeudall (1958)
Sonny Boy, Jolson/De Sylva/Brown/Henderson (1928)
Spanish Eyes, Kaempfert/Snyder/Singleton(1965)
Speak Softly Love, Rota/Kusik (1972)
A Spoonful of Sugar, Sherman/Sherman (1964)
St Louis Blues, Handy (1914)
Stand By Your Man, Wynette/Sherrill (1968)
The Star Spangled Banner, Smith/Key (1814)
Stars Fell On Alabama, Perkins/Parish (1934)
Stay As Sweet As You Are, Revel/Gordon (1934)
Stop Yer Tickling, Jock!, Lauder/Folley (1904)
Stormy Weather, Arlen/Koehler (1933)
The Story Of My Life, Bacharach/David (1957)
Stranger In Paradise, Wright/Forrest (1954)
Strangers In The Night, Kaempfert/Snyder/Singleton (1966)
Strollin', Reader (1959)
Summertime, Gershwin/Heyward (1935)
Supercalifragilisticexpialidocious, Sherman/Sherman (1964)
The Surry With The Fringe On Top, Rodgers/Hammerstein II (1943)
Swanee, Gershwin/Caesar (1919)
Sweet Georgia Brown, Casey/Pinkard (1925)
Sweet Rosie O'Grady, Nugent (1896)
'Swonderful, Gershwin/Gershwin (1927)

Take My Breath Away, Moroder/Whitlock (1986)
Tammy, Livingston/Evans (1957)
Tangerine, Schertzinger/Mercer (1942)
Ta-Ra-Ra-Boom-De-Ay, Sayers (1891)
Tea For Two, Youmans/Caesar (1924)
The Teddy Bear's Picnic, Bratton/Kennedy (1913)
Teenager In Love, Pomus/Shuman (1959)
The Tender Trap, Van Heusen/Cahn (1955)
Tennessee Waltz, Stewart/King (1948)
Thank Heaven For Little Girls, Loewe/Lerner (1958)
Thanks For The Memory, Rainger/Robin (1937)
That Doggie In The Window, Merrill (1953)
That'll Be The Day, Holly/Petty (1957)
That Old Black Magic, Arlen/Mercer (1943)
There Is Nothin' Like A Dame, Rodgers/Hammerstein II (1949)
There's A Rainbow Round My Shoulder, Jolson/Rose/Dreyer (1928)
There's A Small Hotel, Rodgers/Hart (1936)
There's No Business Like Show Business, Berlin (1946)
Those Foolish Things, Strachey/Link/Marvell (1936)
They Can't Take That Away From Me, Gershwin/Gershwin (1937)
They Didn't Believe Me, Kern/Reynolds (1914)
This Can't Be Love, Rodgers/Hart (1938)
This Is A Lovely Way To Spend An Evening, McHugh/Adamson (1943)
This Nearly Was Mine, Rodgers/Hammerstein II (1949)
Three Coins In The Fountain, Styne/Cahn (1954)
Three Little Fishes, Dowell (1939)
Till There Was You, Willson (1957)
Tip Toe Through The Tulips, Burke/Dubin (1926)
Tomorrow Is A Lovely Day, Berlin (1940)
Tonight, Bernstein/Sondheim (1957)
Too Marvellous For Words, Whiting/Mercer (1937)
Toot Toot Tootsie, Kahn/Erdman/Russo (1922)
The Touch Of Your Hand, Kern/Harbach (1933)
The Trolley Song, Martin/Blane (1944)
Tulips From Amsterdam, Arnie/Neumann/Bader [Ger]/Martyn [Eng] (1956)
True Love, Porter(1956)
Try A Little Tenderness, Woods/Campbell/Connelly (1932)

The Twelfth Of Never, Livingston/Webster (1952)
Two Lovely Black Eyes, Coborn (1886)
Two Sleepy People, Carmichael/Loesser (1938)

The Ugly Duckling, Loesser (1952)
Una Paloma Blanca, Bouwens (1975)
Unchained Melody, North/Zaret (1955)
Underneath The Arches, Flanagan/McCarthy (1932)
Under the Bridges Of Paris, Scott/Rodor/Cochram (1931)
Unforgettable, Gordon (1951)
Up A Lazy River, Carmichael/Arodin (1931)

The Very Thought Of You, Noble (1934)
Vilia, Lehr/Ross (1907)
Volare, Modugno/Modugno/Migliacci [Ita]/Parish[Eng]

Wait 'Til The Sun Shines, Nellie (Von Tilzer/Sterling1905)
Walkin' My Baby Back Home, Turk/Ahlert/Richman (1930)
Waltzing Matilda, Cowan/Paterson [based on trad.] (1903)
Washing On The Siegfried Line, Kennedy/Carr (1939)
Way Down Yonder In New Orleans, Creamer/Layton (1922)
A Wee Deoch-An-Doris, Grafton/Lauder (1911)
We'll Gather Lilacs, Novello (1945)
We'll Keep A Welcome, Jones/Joshua/Harper (1949)
We'll Meet Again, Burnett/Griffin (1939)
We're Off To See The Wizard, Arlen/Harburg (1939)
We Saw The Sea, Berlin (1936)
What A Friend We Have In Jesus, Converse/Bonar (1876)
What Do You Want To Make Those Eyes At Me For?, McCarthy/Johnson/Monaco (1916)
What Is This Thing Called Love?, Porter (1930)
What Kind Of Fool Am I?, Bricusse/Newley (1962)
What'll I Do?, Berlin (1924)
What's New Pussycat?, Bacharach/David (1965)
When I Fall In Love, Heyman/Young (1951)
When I Grow Too Old To Dream, Romberg/Hammerstein II (1935)
When I'm Cleaning Windows, Gifford/Cliffe/Formby (1937)
When I'm Sixty-Four, Lennon/McCartney (1967)
When Irish Eyes Are Smiling, Ball/Olcott/Graff (1912)
When Johnny Comes Marching Home, Gilmore (1863)
When The Boys Come Home, Speaks/Hay (1917)
When The Lights Go On Again, Seiler/Marcus/Benjamin (1942)
When The Midnight Choo-Choo Leaves For Alabam', Berlin (1912)
When The Red, Red, Robin, Woods (1926)
When The Saints Go Marching In, Black/Purvis (1896)
When They Sound The Last All Clear, Charles/Elton (1941)
When You And I Were Young, Maggie, Butterfield/Johnson (1866)
When You Were Sweet Sixteen, Thornton (1898)
When You Wish Upon A Star, Harline/Washington (1940)
When You're All Dressed Up And No Place To Go, Hein/Burt (1913)
When You're Smiling, Fisher/Goodwin/Shay (1928)
Where Did You Get That Hat?, Sullivan (1888)
Where Have All The Flowers Gone?, Seeger (1961)
Where The Blue Of The Night Meets The Gold Of The Day, Turk/Crosby/Ahlert (1931)
White Christmas, Berlin (1942)
The White Cliffs Of Dover, Kent/Burton (1942)
Who Do You Think You Are Kidding Mr Hitler?, Perry/Taverner (1971)
Who's Sorry Now?, Snyder/Kalmar/Ruby (1923)
Who Wants To Be A Millionaire?, Porter (1956)
Wish Me Luck As You Wave Me Goodbye, Parr-Davies/Park (1939)
With A Song In My Heart, Rodgers/Hart (1929)
Wonderful Copenhagen, Loesser (1952)
Wunderbar, Porter (1948)

Yellow Rose of Texas, George [trad.] (1955)
Yes, Sir, That's My Baby, Donaldson/Kahn (1925)
Yes! We Have No Bananas, Silver/Cohn (1923)
Yesterday, Lennon/McCartney (1965)
You Are My Lucky Star, Brown/Freed (1935)
You Are My Sunshine, Davis/Mitchell (1940)
You Do Something To Me, Porter (1929)
You Made Me Love You, Monaco/McCarthy (1913)
You Make Me Feel So Young, Myrow/Gordon (1946)
You Must Have Been A Beautiful Baby, Warren/Mercer (1938)
You Need Hands, Bygraves (1958)
You'll Never Walk Alone, Rodgers/Hammerstein II (1945)
You Were Meant For Me, Brown/Freed (1929)
Young At Heart, Richards/Leigh (1954)
Younger Than Springtime, Rodgers/Hammerstein II (1949)
You're The Top, Porter (1934)

Zing Went The Strings Of My Heart, Hanley (1935)
Zip-A-Dee-Doo-Dah, Wrubel/Gilbert (1947)

SLOGANS

Slogans promoting products and services

Access takes the waiting out of wanting
[Access credit card, UK, c. 1973]

Access – your flexible friend
[Access credit card, UK, 1981]

I like Aeroplane Jelly . . . Aeroplane Jelly for me,
I like it for dinner, I like it for tea
[Originally sung by five year old Joy King, it began in 1938 and was in use in the 1980s]

That'll do nicely, Sir!
[Television advertisement for American Express card, UK, late 1970s onwards]

Don't leave home without it
[American Express card, USA, 1981]

Apple – The Power to be Your best
[Apple Corporation, USA, 1986]

You too can have a body like mine
[Charles Atlas body-building courses]

The greatest show on earth
[Barnum and Bailey's circus, from 1881]

Worth a guinea a box
[Beechams pills, c. 1940]

That's a h**l of a way to run a railroad!
[Slogan for the Boston and Maine Railroad, derived from a cartoon, c. 1932, showing two trains about to collide. A signalman comments: Tch-tch – what a way to run a railroad!]

Bounty – The Taste of Paradise
[Long-running slogan for Bounty chocolate bars]

Alas! My poor brother
[Caption to a picture of a sorrowful bull looking at a jar of Bovril meat extract, 1896]

The two infallible powers. The Pope and Bovril
[Bovril meat extract, late 1890s]

I hear they want more
[One apprehensive bull to another, 1903; Bovril meat extract]

Bovril – prevents that sinking feeling
[Bovril meat extract, 1920]

Let the train take the strain
[British Rail, 1970]

Inter-City makes the going easy, and the coming back.
[British Rail, from 1972]

This is the age of the train
[British Rail, 1980]

We're Getting There
[British Rail, 1980's]

It's good to talk
[British Telecom, 1994]

And all because the lady loves Milk Tray
[Cadbury's Milk Tray chocolates, 1968 onwards]

Everyone's a fruit and nut case
[Cadbury's Fruit and Nut chocolate, 1964 onwards]

Perfume worth 9 guineas an ounce
[Camay soap, c. 1956]

You'll look a little lovelier each day
With fabulous pink Camay
[Camay soap, c. 1960]

Milk from contented cows
[Carnation Milk, 1906]

Is it true . . . blondes have more fun?
[Lady Clairol, c. 1965]

It's the real thing
[Coca-Cola, 1970]

I'd like to buy the world a Coke
[Coca-Cola, 1971]

Things go better with Coke
[Coca-Cola, 1963]

Cool as a mountain stream
[Consulate menthol cigarettes]

If we don't have the lowest fare, we probably don't fly there
[Continental Airlines, USA]

Don't just book it – Thomas Cook it
[Thomas Cook Travel Agents]

Thank Crunchie it's Friday
[Crunchie chocolate bars]

Trust Dettol to protect your family's health
[Dettol antiseptic/disinfectant, 1978]

Kills all known germs
[Domestos bleach, 1959]

I'm only here for the beer
[Double Diamond beer]

Drinka Pinta Milka Day
[British Milk Marketing Board, 1958]

Go to work on an egg
[British Egg Marketing Board]

Happiness is egg-shaped
[British Egg Marketing Board]

You can rely on the lion
[British Egg Marketing Board]

The Esso sign means happy motoring
[Advertising jingle for Esso, UK, 1950s]

Put a tiger in your tank
[Esso, USA, 1964]

You only fit double glazing once, so fit the best
[Everest Double Glazing, UK]

Now hands that do dishes can be soft as your face
[Jingle for Fairy washing up liquid]

Say it with flowers
[Advertisement for the Society of American florists, late 1920s]

High o'er the fence leaps Sunny Jim
'Force' is the food that raises him.
[Force breakfast cereal, 1903]

They're g-r-r-r-eat!
[Long-running slogan for Kellogg's Frosties cereal]

Desperation, Pacification, Expectation, Acclamation, Realization
[Fry's Chocolate, UK, post First World War, on advertisements featuring the 'five boys']

The greatest motion picture ever made
[Promotional slogan for the film *Gone with the Wind*, 1939]

Guinness is good for you.
[Guinness, 1930s]

My goodness, my Guinness
[Guinness, 1930s]

Pure Genius
[Guinness, 1994]

Don't be vague – ask for Haig
[Haig whisky, c. 1936]

Happiness is a cigar called Hamlet
[Hamlet cigars, UK]

Does she . . . or doesn't she?
[Harmony hairspray 1980s]

If you want to get ahead, get a hat
[UK Hat Council, 1965]

Heineken refreshes the parts other beers cannot reach
[Heineken lager, 1975 onwards]

Beanz means Heinz
[Heinz baked beans]

Make today a Heinz Souperday
[Heinz soups, 1968]

Let Hertz put you in the driver's seat
[Hertz car rental, 1962]

It beats as it sweeps as it cleans
[Advertising slogan for Hoover vacuum cleaners, 1919]

Horlicks guards against night starvation
[Horlicks milk drink]

It's fingerlickin' good
[Kentucky Fried Chicken Co., USA, 1950s]

You press the button, and we'll do the rest
[Kodak cameras and film]

Never knowingly undersold
[John Lewis stores, c. 1920]

The mint with the hole
[Life-Savers, USA, 1920; Rowntree's Polo mints, U.K. from 1947]

Lucozade refreshes you through the ups and downs of the day
[Beecham Foods c. 1978]

Nine out of ten screen stars use Lux toilet soap
[Lux soap, USA, late 1920s]

Out of the strong came forth sweetness
[Lyle's Golden Syrup; from the Bible, Judges 14:14]

Test drive a Mackintosh
[Apple Corporation, USA, 1984]

Chocolates with the less fattening centres
[Maltesers chocolates, UK, 1965]

A Mars a day helps you work, rest and play
[Mars bars, from 1960]

The right one
[Martini, UK, 1970]

Any time, any place, anywhere
[Martini, UK, 1970s]

For Mash Get Smash
[Smash instant mashed potato]

Good to the last drop
[Remark made by Theodore Roosevelt, 1907, about Maxwell House coffee; later used as an advertising slogan]

Murray Mints! Murray Mints!
Too-good-to-hurry-Mints
[Advertising jingle for Murray Mints, UK from late 1950s]

Naughty but nice
[Slogan promoting the sale of cream cakes]

All human life is there
[Slogan promoting the *News of the World*]

Mean! Moody! Magnificent!
[Promotional slogan for the film *The Outlaw*, 1943]

We are the Ovaltineys
Happy girls and boys
[Advertisement for Ovaltine]

Oxo is British – Made in Britain – By a British Company – with British Capital and British Labour
[Early advertising slogan for Oxo, UK]

Oxo gives a meal man-appeal
[Oxo, 1958]

Ask the man who owns one
[Packard, USA, 1902]

Keep that schoolgirl complexion
[Palmolive soap, 1917, in Nigel Rees]

Since when I have used no other
[Pears' Soap, 1884]

He won't be happy till he gets it
[Pears' Soap]

Top breeders recommend it
[Pedigree Chum dog food, UK, 1964]

The tea you can really taste
[Brooke Bond PG Tips]

P-p-p-pick up a Penguin
[Penguin chocolate biscuits]

You'll wonder where the yellow went
When you brush your teeth with Pepsodent
[Advertising jingle for Pepsodent toothpaste, USA, 1950s]

Persil washes whiter – and it shows
[Long-running Persil soap powder slogan]

Everything you hear is true
[Pioneer hi-fi equipment, 1970s]

Player's please
[John Player and Sons cigarettes]

What is home without Plumtree's Potted Meat? Incompleat [*sic*]
[Early 1900s]

Someone, somewhere wants a letter from you
[Post Office campaign, 1960s]

Snap! Crackle! Pop!
[Kellogg's Rice Crispies, USA, c. 1928]

It's a lot less bovver with a hover
[Qualcast Lawnmowers, UK]

Don't forget the fruit gums, Mum
[Rowntree's Fruit Gums, 1958 onwards]

Have a break, have a Kit-Kat
[Rowntree's Kit-Kat chocolate bars, from c. 1955]

They laughed when I sat down at the piano. But when I started to play!
[Advertisement for US School of Music, 1920s]

Sch. . .you know who
[Schweppes mineral drinks, 1960s]

Some day all watches will be made this way
[Slogan used by Seiko for its first quartz watches, late 1960s]

Man invented time – Seiko perfected it
[Seiko watches, 1980s]

Complete satisfaction or your money cheerfully refunded
[Selfridge's department store]

The customer is always right.
[Selfridge's department store]

You can be sure of Shell
[Shell UK, c. 1931]

Senior Service satisfy
[Senior Service cigarettes]

Every picture tells a story
[Advertisement for Sloane's Backache and Kidney Pills, showing someone bending over in pain]

Can you tell Stork from butter?
[Stork margarine]

You're never alone with a Strand
[Strand cigarettes]

Tell 'em about the honey, Mummy
[Kellogg's Sugar Puffs]

Tetley make tea-bags make tea
[Tetley's tea]

Top people take the Times
[Slogan promoting *The Times* newspaper, 1957]

Which twin has the Toni?
[Toni home perms, USA, 1951]

Treats. Melt in your mouth, not in your hand
[Treats chocolates]

Tunes help you breathe more easily
[Tunes throat lozenges]

Virginia is for lovers
[Tourist board slogan, Virginia, USA]

You've come a long way baby
[Virginia Slims cigarettes]

Think small
[Volkswagen, USA, from c. 1959]

Stop me and buy one
[Wall's ice-cream, 1922]

They came as a boon and a blessing to men,
The Pickwick, the Owl, and the Waverley Pen.
[Waverley pens]

Where's the beef?
[Wendy's Hamburgers]

Breakfast of champions
[Wheaties cereal, USA, 1950]

Eight out of ten cats prefer Whiskas
[Whiskas catfood, 1970s]

We're with the Woolwich
[Woolwich Equitable Building Society, UK, from late 1970s]

Nothing over sixpence
[Woolworth stores, UK, from 1909]

Let your fingers do the walking
[Yellow Pages, from American Telephone and Telegraph Company, 1960s]

Slogans promoting political parties and social change

One man, one vote
[Campaign run by Major John Cartwright (1740–1824) against plural voting]

No taxation without representation
[In use before the American War of Independence, 1775–1783]

Liberté! Egalité! Fraternité! Liberty! Equality! Brotherhood!
[French Revolution, 1793]

Ulster will fight, and Ulster will be right
[Ulster Volunteers opposed to Irish Home Rule, 1913–1914, from a letter by Lord Randolph Churchill, 1886]

Votes for Women
[Suffragette Movement, 1905, in Emmeline Pankhurst, *My Own Story* (1914)]

Are we downhearted? No!
[World War I, based on remark of Joseph Chamberlain]

Your King and Country need you
[World War I]

Kraft durch Freude. Strength through joy
[German Labour Front, 1933]

Ein Reich, Ein Volk, Ein Führer. One realm, one people, one leader
[Nazi Party, 1934]

Dig for victory
[Ministry of Agriculture, 1939]

Is your journey really necessary?
[World War II]

Careless talk costs lives
[British Ministry of Information, World War II]

A bayonet is a weapon with a worker at each end
[Pacifist movement, 1940]

Coughs and sneezes spread diseases
[Ministry of Health, c. 1942]

No names, no pack drill
[Used frequently in both World Wars]

With thumb in bum and mind in neutral
[US navy catchphrase, 1940s]

Fair shares for all
[Labour Party; devised by Douglas Jay, 1946]

The family that prays together stays together
[Devised by Al Scalpone for the Roman Catholic Family Rosary Crusade, 1947]

I like Ike
[US button badge, first used in 1947, to support Eisenhower]

Keep Britain tidy
[British government, 1950s]

Ban the bomb
[Current from 1953 onwards]

Better red than dead
[British nuclear disarmament movement; 'Better dead than red' was also in common use]

Life's better with the Conservatives
[Conservative Party, 1959]

Make love, not war
[Common in the mid-1960s]

Flower Power
[Hippy slogan, 1960s]

Let's go with Labour
[Labour Party, 1964]

In your heart you know he's right
[Goldwater Presidential campaign, 1964]

Don't ask a man to drink and drive
[Road safety campaign, 1964]

Thirteen Wasted Years
[Unofficial Labour Party slogan prior to 1964 General Election]

Prosperity With a Purpose
[Conservative Party, 1964]

Let's Go With Labour For The New Britain
[Labour Party, 1964]

Think For Yourself – Vote Liberal
[Liberal Party, 1964]

Black is beautiful
[US civil rights movement, 1966]

I'm backing Britain
[Slogan, 1968; campaign to support UK economy after devaluation of sterling]

Would you buy a used car from this man?
[Campaign slogan directed against Richard Nixon, 1968]

Power to the People
[Black Panther movement, 1969]

Out of the closets and into the streets
[Gay Liberation movement, USA c. 1969]

Burn Your Bra
[Attributed, erroneously, to feminist movement, USA, 1970s]

It smells like you're kissing an old ashtray
[Health Education Council anti-smoking campaign, c. 1970]

(Of the Conservatives)
Yesterday's men (they failed before!).
[Labour party, 1970]

What a Life!
[Liberal Party, 1970]

A Better Tomorrow
[Conservative Party, 1970]

Now Britain's Strong – Let's Make It Great To Live In
[Labour Party, 1970]

Clunk, Click, every trip
[Road safety campaign promoting the use of seat belts, 1971]

Dull it isn't
[Recruiting advertisement for the Metropolitan Police, 1972]

England Expects – Scotland's Oil
[Scottish National Party, 1973]

Let Us Work Together
[Labour Party, 1974]

Change the Face of Britain
[Liberal Party election manifesto, 1974]

Putting Britain First
[Conservative Party, 1974]

Scotland a Nation Once Again
[Scottish National Party, 1977]

Labour isn't working
[Conservative Party, 1978]

Lavorare meno – Lavorare tutti. Work less – work for everybody
[From a collection of slogans used by students and workers during the 70s demonstrations]

Be all you can be
[Scottish Health Education Council, 1980s]

Choose Life, Not Drugs
[Scottish Health Education Council, 1980s]

Britain is Great Again, Don't Let Labour Wreck It
[Conservative Party, 1987]

Don't Die of Ignorance
[Department of Health AIDS campaign, 1987]

Meet the Challenge, Make the Change
[Labour Party, 1989]

Green Policies in a Nutshell
[Green Party, 1992]

Independence in Europe: Make It Happen Now
[Scottish National Party, 1992]

Changing Britain for Good
[Liberal Democrat Party, 1992]

It's Time to Get Britain Working Again
[Labour Party, 1992]

The Best Future for Britain
[Conservative Party, 1992]

Good Health is Good Business
[Health and Safety Executive, 1993]

INDEX

INDEX

second a. and the child's COWARD 34
that the players cannot a. AGATE 3
those who *a.* rightly who carry off ARISTOT 4
To see him a. COLERIDGE:ST 83
what a., That roars so SHAK:HAM 139
Where we are free to a. ARISTOT 9
Act of Settlement: six horses through the A.o.S. RICE:S 1
acting:
A. is therefore the lowest MOORE:G 2
A. without design LAO 1
Be not too tame neither* SHAK:HAM 107
danger chiefly lies in a. well CHURCH:C 12
Speak the speech* SHAK:HAM 106
when he was off, he was a. GOLDS 39
action:
A. is but coarsened thought AMIEL 1
A. is transitory WORDS:W 139
A., of one alone DE GAU 1
cold for a. SHAK:HEN.V 5
end of man is an A. CARLYLE:T 9
gratuitous a. GIDE 1
have had enough of a. TENNY 32
heavenly gifts is the man of a. PEREZ 2
Let a single complete a. BOIL 5
made to follow a course of a. CONF 7
not knowledge but a. HUX:TH 6
prefer thought to a. BALZ 4
rarer a. is In virtue SHAK:TEM 28
Suit the a. to the word SHAK:HAM 107
true men of a. in our time AUD 64
actions:
a. are a kind of words EMER 29
a. determine our dispositions ARISTOT 7
A. speak louder than words PROV 3
best of our a. tend BUTLER:S[1] 39
Great a. speak great FLETCH:J 13
in his a. be so ill MASSIN 5
my a. are my ministers' CHARLES II 8
active: a. think they are better CANET 4
activity:
A. is the only road SHAW 54
live In an immense a. STEVENS 14
power of sustained practical a. TAWN 1
actor:
a. becomes the thing itself ZE AMI 2
a. He had certain qualifications HOPP 1
a.'s a guy who, if BRANDO 1
Anybody may see he is an a. FIELDING 31
can really *like* an a. HITCH 3
Like a dull a. now SHAK:COR 16
Scratch an a. PARKER:D 36
to get an a. to be a cowboy FORD:J[2] 1
well-grac'd a. leaves SHAK:RIC.II 42
whole world plays the a. ANON 255
actors:
A. don't pretend to be MALOUF 1
a. or spectators? SHELLEY:PB 114
A. should be treated like cattle HITCH 4
A. speak of things imaginary BETT 1
Assembled like amateur a. ELIOT:TS 78
best a. in the world SHAK:HAM 84
question a. most often get asked DUND 1
send me some good a. – cheap BAYLIS 1
actress:
Next worst to an a. CARY:J 2
you'll find an a. PARKER:D 36
actresses: a. excite my amorous propensities JOHNSON:S 90
acts:
a. being seven ages SHAK:AS 34
a. his own creations BROWNING:R 4
great length for two a. more SHAW 123
how he a. when he loses money PROV 194
speedy end to the a. of God DE VR 5
ad infinitum: so proceed *a.i.* SWIFT 69
Adam:
A. Had 'em ANON 51
A. lay I-bowndyn ANON 52
A. the goodliest man MILT 194
A. was a gardener KIP 140
A. was but human TWAIN 17
compared to A.'s dream KEATS 118
flower of A.'s bastards BYR 240
gardener A. and his wife TENNY 64
gratitude we owe to A. TWAIN 18
Old A., the carrion crow BEDD 3
penalty of A. SHAK:AS 11
That A. was not Adamant HOOD 18
they hold up A.'s profession SHAK:HAM 179
When A. delved ANON 116
Whilst A. slept ANON 120
whipp'd th' offending A. SHAK:HEN.V 3
added: things shall be a. unto you BIBLE 396
adder: that brings forth the a. SHAK:JUL 19
adders:
a. came to shed SWIN 2
long'd to eat a.' heads SHAK:WIN 24
addiction:
Every form of a. is a bad JUNG:Carl 6
prisoners of a. ILL 4
terminal point of a. is what AUD 68
Addington: Pitt is to A. CANN 3
Addison:
A. approved Cannot be wrong BUDG 1
nights to the volumes of A. JOHNSON:S 44
address: a. will soon be Annihilation DANTON 3
addresses: Three a. always inspire WILDE:O 97
adieu:
A., a., kind friends ANON 46
A., she cries GAY 40
bid you a welcome adoo WARD:A 1
up into a loose a. SHAK:TRO 20
adipose tissue: personal issue of a.t. COWARD 23
adjective: A.: when in doubt TWAIN 23
adjourn: a. this meeting to some other SMITH:Ad 15
Adler: A. will always be Jung WALL 2
Adlestrop: I remember A. THOMAS:E 1
administered: best administer'd is best POPE 99
administrator: a. in a bureaucratic world MCLUH 11
admiral:
A. of the Atlantic salutes the A. WILHELM II 2
good idea to kill an a. VOLT 13
still call me 'A.' ANON 234
admirals: A. all, for England's NEWBOLT 1
admiralty: blood be the price of a. KIP 88
admiration:
a. onely of weak minds MILT 266
disease of a. MACAULAY:TB 25
admire:
a. without desiring BRADLEY:FH 4
fools a. POPE 22
Not to a. is all BYR 209
Not to a. is all the art HORACE 85
admired:
have been a. by their servants MONTAIGNE 20
She had been a. WOOLF:V 5
admirers: he became his a. AUD 36
admires: who meanly a. mean things THACK 12
admit: Never a. the pain GILMORE 1
admittance: No a. till the week after CARROLL 87
ado: when the a. is about himself TROLL 5
adolescence:
I would there were no age* SHAK:WIN 9
suffering from petrified a. BEVAN 8
adolescent: a., and therefore bound to LESSING:D 3
Adonais:
soul of A., like a star SHELLEY:PB 127
weep for A. SHELLEY:PB 106
What A. is SHELLEY:PB 125
Adonis: A. from his native Rock MILT 128
adoration: Breathless with a. WORDS:W 42
adore: may command where I a. SHAK:TWE 34
adored: women . . . merely a. WILDE:O 75
adorned:
a. with furs and feathers ADDIS 29
unadorned a. the most THOMS:Ja[1] 8
adrenal glands: larger cerebrums and smaller a.g. MENCK 8
Adriatic: spouseless A. mourns BYR 98
ads:
A. are the cave art MCLUH 7
He watched the a. NASH 18
adult:
be an a. is to be alone ROSTAND:J 2
child becomes an a. when SZASZ 5
What is an a.? BEAUV 4
adulteration: Not quite adultery, but a. BYR 226
adulterer: statue of the onehandled a. JOYCE:J 20
adultery:
A. in your heart is committed JOHN PAUL 1
a. Is much more common BYR 163
commit a. again if God moves me DRING 1
commit a. at one end CARY:J 1
committed a. in my heart CARTER:J 2
Die for a.? SHAK:KING L 67
Do not a. commit CLOUGH 20
Not quite a., but adulteration BYR 226
taken in a. than in provincialism HUX:A 6
Tasmanians, who never committed a. MAUGH 22
Thou shalt not commit a. BIBLE 103
adultress: good eye at an A. AUSTEN 74
adults: only between consenting a. VIDAL 5
advance:
a. in another direction RIPPON 1
a. or die BYR 93
in this world to a. GILB:WS 86
retrograde if it does not a. GIBBON:E 11
somewhat to a. POPE 149
that they are twenty years in a. HOBS 1
too much in a. of the time SHAW 132
advancement: progressive a. of civilization GALLACH 1
advantage:
them as take a. that get a. ELIOT:G 8
undertaking of Great A. ANON 172
when to forego an a. DISR:B 100
you have the a. of me MARX:G 6
adventure:
A. must be held in delicate DUKES 1
most beautiful a. in life FROH 1
only a. open to the cowardly VOLT 38
thrift and a. seldom go CHURCH:JJ 2
To die will be an awfully big a. BARRIE 8
adversity:
a. doth best discover virtue BACON:F[1] 34
a. is not without comforts BACON:F[1] 33
a. is the blessing BACON:F[1] 31
A.'s sweet milk SHAK:ROM 34
bread of a. BIBLE 316
cross'd with a. SHAK:TWO 11
great men contending with a. BURTON:Ro 14
hundred that will stand a. CARLYLE:T 50
old companions in a. BRYANT 1
Sweet are the uses of a. SHAK:AS 12
advertise:
call him and a. him PRAY 61
Don't tell! they'd a. DICKIN:E 3
It pays to a. ANON 208
advertisement:
one effective a. that will take in HUX:A 9
promise, is the soul of an a. JOHNSON:S 31
advertisements:
A. contain the only truths JEFFERSON 13
ideals of a nation by its a. DOUGLAS:N 1
advertising:
A. is the most fun you can DELLA 1
A. may be described as LEACOCK 8
Half the money I spend on a. LEVERHU 1
advice:
A. is seldom welcome CHESTERFIELD 11
even earnest a. from my seniors THOREAU 8
intended to give you some a. HARRIS:G 1
Love be controll'd by a.? GAY 13
matrimony I never give any a. CHESTERFIELD 28
nothing so generously as a. LA ROCHE 17
people are with a. SULLI:AN 1
To ask a. is in nine cases COLLINS:JC 1
woman seldom asks a. before ADDIS 24
advices: lengthen'd, sage a. BURNS:R 85
advocaat: a., a drink made from lawyers COREN 2
advocates: best of all a. CATUL 12
Aegean: Among the A. isles ARNOLD:M 30
aerials: had my [tv] a. removed MUGG 7
Aeschylus: sublime simplicity of A. COLERIDGE:ST 92
Aesop: A. was writing for the tortoise BROOKN 1
aesthetic:
A. enjoyment is a sudden discharge ORTEGA G 2
degree of my a. emotion BELL:C 2
desire for a. expression WAUGH:E 14
high a. band GILB:WS 33
high a. line GILB:WS 30
aesthetics: long-haired a. GILB:WS 29
aetheist: a., who finds creation so perfect PROUST 9
Afaq: A. to Knight at the Nursery End JOHNSTON:B 3
affair: a. had to begin after lunch GREENE:G 18

affairs:
long as he's Minister for Foreign A. MACLAINE 1
must keep love a. quiet WINDSOR 1
affectation: wits to sophistry and a. BACON:F[1] 2
affecting: A. to seem unaffected CONG 59
affection:
a. beaming in one eye DICKENS 108
a. stirs her spirit up? SOUTHEY 12
heard Of any true a. MIDD 1
more a. than she feels AUSTEN 79
what unrequited a. is DICKENS 140
affections:
a. dark as Erebus SHAK:MERC 51
history of the a. IRV 1
holiness of the Heart's a. KEATS 119
lovers' souls descend T'a. DONNE 37
old offences of a. new SHAK:SON 51
young a. runs to waste BYR 105
affinity: betray a secret a. HAZL 15
afflict: dost a. those who love thee TERESA of A. 1
affliction:
A. is enamour'd of thy parts SHAK:ROM 32
life but a veil of a.? SMOL 13
water of a. BIBLE 316
affluent: A. Society GALB 1
afford:
Can't a. them, Governor SHAW 107
no right to it unless you can a. TROLL 24
only what you can a. to lose PROV 232
parties could any way a. it EDGE 1
afraid:
a. to go home in the dark HENRY:O 5
be not a. BIBLE 128, 414
do what you are a. to do EMER 21
I am devilishly a. DRYD 96
in short, I was a. ELIOT:TS 9
it is a. of itself HAZL 14
neither tarnished nor a. CHAND 5
not a. of God, a. of me POPE 154
not that I'm a. to die ALLEN:W 8
they were sore a. BIBLE 448
to keep myself from being a. DRYD 97
Who's A. of Virginia Woolf? ALBEE 1
Afric: Where A.'s sunny fountains HEB 2
Africa:
A. has always walked VAN DER P. 3
A. is good PLOM 7
A. is not a white man's PLOM 10
all A. and her prodigies in us BROWNE:T 10
Death-light of A. CHESTERTON 20
familiar with A. than my own body ORTON 1
I speak of A. SHAK:HEN.IV[2] 50
looking far away into A. DICKENS 176
sloggin' over A. KIP 111
something new out of A. PLINY 1
soul of A. is still reflected X 4
That was the A. we knew PLOM 3
Voice of Mother A. MTS 2
African:
decorate it in true A. style BIKO 2
we are still A. in color, feeling X 4
Africans: contact between Europeans and A. VAN DER P 1
after:
A. you, Claude ITMA 4
men go right a. them WEST:M 13
after-dinner: a. talk TENNY 35
after-silence: a. on the shore BYR 46
afternoon:
rude multitude call the a. SHAK:LOV 20
seemed always a. TENNY 24
summer a.; to me those have always JAMES:H 23
Afton: Flow gently, sweet A. BURNS:R 72
again:
been, and may be a. WORDS:W 81
Cuts off the country of A. MUIR:E 1
I do it a. and a. CARROLL 9
against:
a. everything all the time KENNEDY:RF 1
A. whom? ADL:A 3
every man's hand a. him BIBLE 48
He said he was a. it COOL 5
not with me is a. me BIBLE 411
who can be a. us? BIBLE 513
Agamemnon:
A. cried aloud ELIOT:TS 30
And A. dead YEATS 69
looked upon the face of A. SCHLIEM 1
Aganippe: never drank of A. well SIDNEY:P 9
age:
a. and death's inexorable VIRGIL 28
A. cannot wither her SHAK:ANT 28
a. from folly could not give SHAK:ANT 18
A., I do abhor thee SHAK:POET 2
a. might but take the things WORDS:W 90
a. of chivalry is gone BURKE:E 55
a. of ease GOLDS 23
A. only matters when PICAS 7
a. or a little money will not cure DURA 1
A. shall not weary them BINY 1
a. which forgives itself SHAW 68
A. will not be defied BACON:F[1] 95
A.'s icy caves SHELLEY:PB 81
apt to forget my a. QUEN 1
arrogance of a. must submit BURKE:E 86
As full of grief as a. SHAK:KING L 30
at my a., I am delighted REAG 5
child blown up by a. BEAUV 4
complain of the a. we live in BURKE:E 12
Crabbed a. and youth SHAK:POET 1
Damn the a. LAMB:Ch 44
dawn an a., More fortunate ARNOLD:M 36
Decrepit a. that has been tied YEATS 74
Drives my green a. THOMAS:D 4
each a. is a dream that is dying O'SHAUGH 1
evening of my a. ROWE 3
Every a. has a kind of universal DRYD 134
Every a. hath its book KORAN 3
Everything comes with a. MOLIERE 16
from a. to a. endure KETHE 2
golden a. was never the present FRANKLIN:B 12
He hath not forgotten my a. SOUTHEY 6
He immatures with a. WILSON:Harold 8
He is of a.; ask him BIBLE 483
He is of no a. COLERIDGE:ST 94
He was not of an a. JONS 43
His wealth a well-spent a. CAMPION 4
I can tell a woman's a. GILB:WS 56
I will not make a. an issue REAG 3
if only a. could EST 1
in a. I bud again HERB:G 46
in a. we seem MELV 4
less for what a. takes away WORDS:W 23
Let a. approve of youth BROWNING:R 190
man's a. is like to be DENH 3
Men come of a. at sixty STEPHENS 7
my a. is as a lusty winter SHAK:AS 17
not necessarily improve with a. HALL:P 1
pays us but with a. and dust RALE 9
quite accurate about her a. WILDE:O 100
soone comes a. SPENS 34
Soul of the A. JONS 39
subject of her a. with ambiguity RUBINS 1
Than settled a. his sables SHAK:HAM 175
thou a. unbred SHAK:SON 46
Unregarded a. in corners thrown SHAK:AS 15
When the a. is in SHAK:MUCH 22
who tells one her real a. WILDE:O 57
woes that wait on a.? BYR 72
worth an a. without a name MORD 1
yet some smack of a. SHAK:HEN.IV[2] 6
aged:
a. are usually tougher WHITE:P 11
a. man is but a paltry thing YEATS 72
beauty Of an a. face CAMPBELL:Jo 1
deliciously a. and sad SHAW 72
don't object to an a. parent DICKENS 212
I saw an a. a. man CARROLL 81
Match'd with an a. wife TENNY 51
reverend creatures did the a. seem TRAH 4
this a. man his right PEELE 2
ageing:
see also **aging**
But Time, to make me* HARDY:T 12
every year grows dim* CONRAD 8
His golden locks* PEELE 2
matters when one is a. PICAS 7
My days are in the yellow* BYR 241
so many a. college people NAB 4
The years as they come* HORACE 109
three parts iced over* ARNOLD:M 85
Till recently I was fit for* HORACE 46
Time doth transfix* SHAK:SON 24
When forty winters shall* SHAK:SON 2
Years steal Fire* BYR 75
Agenbite: A. of inwit JOYCE:J 23
agenda:
a. winks at me THOMAS:G 1
Our a. is now exhausted SPAAK 1
agent: is the poor a. despis'd SHAK:TRO 27
ages:
acts being seven a. SHAK:AS 34
A. of hopeless end MILT 154
army a. men sooner WELLS:HG 13
as our diff 'rent a. move PRIOR 3
God, our help in a. past WATTS 18
he belongs to the a. STANTON:Ed 1
Make the mighty a. CARNEY 1
order of the a. is born anew VIRGIL 11
Rock of A., cleft for me TOP 1
thousand a. in Thy sight WATTS 18
aggravating: She was an a. child BELLOC 25
aggregate: large a. of little things MORE:H 2
aggressors: defeat the US a. MAO 4
Agincourt: affright the air at A.? SHAK:HEN.V 2
aging:
see also **ageing**
A. seems to be the only available AUBER 2
agley: gang aft a. BURNS:R 32
agnostic:
appropriate title of 'a.' HUX:TH 9
compliment to be called an a. DARROW 3
agony:
a., and that has ending BROOKE 24
a. is abated MACAULAY:TB 1
By thine A. and bloody Sweat PRAY 34
conquers a. BYR 108
intense the a. BRONTE:E 4
that a. is our triumph VANZ 2
agree:
all things differ, all a. POPE 31
Don't say that you a. WILDE:O 17
How a. the kettle and BIBLE 367
how could so many a. BACON:F[1] 26
sense unless they a. with us LA ROCHE 30
sit there and a. with me THATCH:M 11
trade can ne'er a. GAY 45
agreeable:
men's power to be a. SWIFT 20
multiplicity of a. consciousness JOHNSON:S 132
My idea of an a. person DISR:B 42
people to be very a. AUSTEN 71
think himself a most a. AUSTEN 43
agreed:
a. to none of it in private AUSTEN 56
except they be a.? BIBLE 356
agreement:
accept our views we shall be in full a. DAYAN 1
a. with hell GARRIS 3
agreements: experience of gentlemen's a. CHIF 1
Agricola: indeed fortunate, A. TAC 3
agricultural: a. labourers round here commute POWELL:A 4
agriculture: taxes must . . . fall upon a. GIBBON:E 6
ague: I am not a.-proof SHAK:KING L 66
ahead: don't know who's a. SNAGGE 1
aid:
lend us Thine a. HEB 1
whence doth come mine a. SCOTTISH 2
without large-scale outside a., Russia NIX 14
Aids: everywhere, but so is A. WILLIAMSON 1
ail: what can a. thee, knight-at-arms KEATS 79
ailments: our a. are the same SWIFT 73
aim:
a. a little above it LONGFEL 35
at which all things a. ARISTOT 2
not always a. his bow HORACE 23
pays for setting an impossible a. GREENE:G 7
they have an a. MORA 1
two things to a. at in life SMITH:LP 1
aimed: a. at, found and lost YEATS 109
aimeth: Who a. at the sky HERB:G 10
aimless: nothing walks with a. feet TENNY 153
aims:
other a. than my delight HARDY:T 20
who a. but at a bush SIDNEY:P 12
Ainslie Gotto: its name is A.G. ERWIN 1
ain't: as it isn't, it a. CARROLL 52
air:
a., a charter'd libertine SHAK:HEN.V 4
a. a solemn stillness GRAY:T 16
A. arched, enormous SLESS 3

am:
I A. THAT I A. BIBLE 88
I a. the way I a. PREVERT 2
I think, therefore I a. DESCA 2
infinite I A. COLERIDGE:ST 73
must take me as I a. COMPT 11
what I a., none cares CLARE:J 8
amaranth:
beds of a. and moly TENNY 30
fields Of a. lie DE LA M 4
There are no fields of a. LANDOR 17
Amaranthus: Bid A. all his beauty MILT 55
Amaryllis: sport with A. in the shade MILT 49
amateur:
a. is an artist who supports SHAHN 1
a. status must be strictly GRAVES:R 9
Assembled like a. actors ELIOT:TS 78
take part as an a. AUBER 1
amateurs:
disease that afflicts a. CHESTERTON 37
nation of a. ROSE 2
Amazon:
I've never sailed the A. KIP 107
She was an A. BLANCH 1
ambassador: a. is an honest man sent WOTTON 5
ambassadors: A. cropped up like hay GILB:WS 111
amber:
A. scent of odorous perfume MILT 289
in a. to observe the forms POPE 120
ambergris: Proclaim the a. on shore MARV 6
ambiguities: life. There are always a. GRANT:C 2
ambiguity: Seven Types of A. EMPS 1
ambiguous: made myself sufficiently a. PID 1
ambition:
a. can creep as well BURKE:E 80
A., in a private man MASSIN 14
A. is the growth of ev'ry clime BLAKE:W 5
A. should be made of sterner SHAK:JUL 50
a. to be a wag JOHNSON:S 269
fling away a. SHAK:HEN.VIII 12
Ill-weav'd a. SHAK:HEN.IV[1] 90
Let not A. mock GRAY:T 17
lilies of a. still spring DOUGLAS:K 4
lowliness is young a.'s ladder SHAK:JUL 20
not with a. join'd CONG 48
That makes a. virtue SHAK:OTH 43
Vain the a. of kings WEBSTER:J 18
Vaulting a., which o'er-leaps SHAK:MAC 24
Was this a.? SHAK:JUL 51
Who doth a. shun SHAK:AS 26
ambitions:
abandon your a. that they become KENEAL 1
All a. are lawful except CONRAD 13
ambitious:
as he was a., I slew him SHAK:JUL 46
Brutus says he was a. SHAK:JUL 49
especially a. young men ALCOTT:LM 3
amble: teach an old horse a. trew SPENS 36
amen:
A. I heard me cry HODG 4
'A.' stuck in my throat SHAK:MAC 39
Glorious the catholic a. SMART 3
sound of a great A. PROC 2
America:
A.! A.! God shed BATES:KL 1
a. i love you land CUMM 2
A. is a country of young men EMER 67
A. is a land where boys MADAR 1
A. is a large, friendly dog TOYN 1
A. is God's Crucible ZANG 3
A. is just ourselves, with ARNOLD:M 62
A. is the only idealistic nation WILSON:W 14
A. is the only nation in history CLEMENCE 5
A. lives in the heart of every WILSON:W 2
A., thou half-brother BAILEY 1
A. was thus clearly top SELL 10
A. . . . where law and custom RUSS:B 13
ask not what A. will do KENNEDY:JF 2
brutal dirty culture you have in North A. DURRELL:L 5
business of A. is business COOL 2
every man . . . in A. to see it GOLDWYN 6
God's own country* ANON 189
handed our sword to A. RUTS 1
in A. the successful writer LEWIS:S 1
lawfulness of their conquering A. JOHNSON:S 124
lost in the living rooms of A. MCLUH 9
makes A. what it is STEIN:G 3
more absolute silence of A. LAWR:DH 14
my A.! my new-found-land DONNE 7
owe to the discovery of A. HELPS 2
rejoice that A. has resisted PITT:W[1] 3
than *whole A.* BURKE:E 28
Whatever A. hopes to bring to pass EISEN 1
You cannot conquer A. PITT:W[1] 10
Young man, there is A. BURKE:E 26
youth of A. is their oldest WILDE:O 54
American:
all mankind, *except an A.* JOHNSON:S 202
A. girls turn into A. women HAMP 3
A. heiress wants to buy a man MCCARTHY:M 2
A. professors like their literature LEWIS:S 4
A. system of rugged individualism HOOV 2
A. writers want to be not good VIDAL 4
fallen in love with A. names BENET 1
I also – am an A. WEBSTER:D 5
I was born an A. WEBSTER:D 8
in an A. ship LOND 2
intelligence of the A. people MENCK 19
not a Virginian, but an A. HENRY:P 2
not about to send A. boys JOHNSON:LB 1
represented the modern A. woman MCCARTHY:M 3
which was the A. abroad STAPLED 1
Americanism:
A. with its sleeves rolled MCCARTHY:J[2] 1
can be no fifty-fifty A. ROOS:T 9
hyphenated A. ROOS:T 6
Americans:
A. are polite by telling the truth BRADB 4
A. have little faith EMER 90
A. have taken umbrage PUNCH 13
A. say, 'How much time have ATWOOD 9
A. were to her rough, uncouth TROLL 28
A., while willing, even eager FITZGER:FS 6
Good A., when they die APPLETON:TG 1
hand in hand, brave A. DICKIN:J 1
none but A. on guard WASH 14
worse Than ignorant A. MASSIN 9
amiability: found to have gained in a. BUTLER:S[2] 24
amiable: with any thing that is a. CONG 67
amiably-disposed: You're a a. young man DICKENS 47
amicably: a. if they can QUINCY 1
amice: with Pilgrim steps in a. gray MILT 276
Amin, Idi: village tyrant . . . a black* HILLS 1
ammunition:
one who has run out of a. KISS 5
pass the a. FORGY 1
amo:
A., amas, I love a lass O'KEEFFE:J 1
'a.' I love BROWNING:R 111
among: A. them, but not of them BYR 95
amor: *A. vincit omnia* CHAUC 11
amorous:
be a., but chaste BYR 13
excite my a. propensities JOHNSON:S 90
offence from am'rous causes POPE 36
tangl'd in A. Nets MILT 264
amour:
beginning of an A. BEHN 7
Vive l'amour STERNE 45
amphibii: These rational a. go MARV 34
amputate: Thank God they had to a. SASS 1
Amurath: Not A. an A. succeeds SHAK:HEN.IV[2] 48
amuse:
Just a talent to a. COWARD 17
our ability to a. them WAUGH:E 37
amused:
a. by its presumption THURB 16
be a. at what you read MONTAGUE 2
how to be a. rather than shocked BUCK 5
I was very much a. VICT 1
We are not a. VICT 7
amusement:
providing topics of a. SWIFT 9
write for the general a. SCOTT:W 84
amusements:
no a. in England but vice SMITH:Syd[1] 38
tolerable but for its a. LEWIS:GC 1
amusing:
a. herself with me more MONTAIGNE 15
a. with numerous errors GOLDS 48
anaesthetic:
a. from which none LARK 9
like being put under a. DORS 2
anagram: but mild a. DRYD 65
Anak: sons of A. BIBLE 116
analogy: Though a. is often misleading BUTLER:S[2] 36
analysed: Men can be a. WILDE:O 75
analysis: method of a. TROT 9
analytics: Sweet A. MARLOWE 29
anapaests: swift A. throng COLERIDGE:ST 57
anarchist: set up a small a. community BENNETT:AI 3
anarchists: worst a. are the magistrates SHAW 81
anarchy:
a. and competition the laws RUSKIN 15
a. is loosed upon the world YEATS 62
a. prevails in my kitchen JOHNSON:S 268
Charybdis of a. and despotism SHELLEY:PB 166
cure of a. BURKE:E 36
grieved under a *democracy*, call it *a.* HOBB 11
shapeless lump, like A. DRYD 40
anatomy:
A mere a. SHAK:COM 7
eat the rest of th' a. SHAK:TWE 45
ancestor: I am my own a. JUNOT 1
ancestors:
a. were hunting the wild boar BENJ:JP 1
a. . . . were probably chained together HUGHES:B 4
look backward to their a. BURKE:E 53
obscure of all classes, our a. CHESTERTON 41
they will make fine a. FORRO 1
wisdom of our a. to guide BURKE:E 15
ancestral: works his a. lands HORACE 60
ancestry:
boasts his a., praises SEN 6
by a delusion about its a. INGE 11
I can trace my a. back GILB:WS 62
anchor:
a. of my purest thoughts WORDS:W 9
Let us weigh a. BAUD 8
anchored: anchor'd safe and sound WHITMAN 31
ancient:
A. person of my heart ROCHES 11
a. times are only old HARDY:T 53
It is an a. Mariner COLERIDGE:ST 10
ancients:
a. without idolatry CHESTERFIELD 12
what unsuspected a. say DRYD 71
and: learn a great deal more about 'a.' EDDI 1
Anderson: John A. my jo BURNS:R 79
Andrea del Sarto: A.d.S. appears for a moment BEERB 14
ands: If ifs and a. PEAC 18
Andy: Our A.'s gone with cattle LAWS 3
anecdotage: man fell into his a. DISR:B 39
angel:
A. faces smile NEWM:JH 16
a. is nobody in particular SHAW 60
a. of death has been abroad BRIGHT 1
A. of Death spread his BYR 40
A. of the Lord came down TATE:N 1
a. of the Lord came upon BIBLE 448
a. satyr walks these hills KILV 4
a. to pass, flying slowly FIRB 2
a. watching an urn TENNY 209
a. writing in a book HUNT:L 4
beautiful and ineffectual a. ARNOLD:M 84
better a. is a man SHAK:SON 60
clip an A.'s wings KEATS 108
domesticate the Recording A. STEVENSON:RL 12
drive an a. from your door BLAKE:W 24
Her a.'s face SPENS 24
is a. yet in this SHAK:HAM 147
Is man an ape or an a.? DISR:B 67
Look homeward A. now MILT 56
Lost A. of a ruined Paradise SHELLEY:PB 110
ministering a. thou SCOTT:W 29
minist'ring a. shall my sister SHAK:HAM 186
more a. she SHAK:OTH 64
no child is born an a. SMITH:Syd[2] 1
Recording A., as he wrote STERNE 28
Recording A. think seriously about BENTLEY:N 2
She drew an a. down DRYD 115
such a. grace TENNY 41
This was the A. of History GOEB 4

up-lifted A. trumpets blow MILT 64
What a. wakes me SHAK:MID 27
White as an a. is the English BLAKE:W 27
woman yet think him an a. THACK 18
You may not be an a. DUBIN 1
young 'ooman a Wenus or a a. DICKENS 28
angelic: With something of a. light WORDS:W 89
angels:
A. affect us oft DONNE 25
a. all are Tories BYR 149
a. all were singing out of BYR 145
A. are bright still SHAK:MAC 91
A. bending near the earth SEARS 1
A. came and ministered BIBLE 382
A. can fly because CHESTERTON 43
A. from an evil sprite DONNE 7
a. heave up Sir Launcelot MALORY 15
A. in some brighter dreams VAUGHAN:H 12
A. may be familiar PATMO 2
a. of God ascending and BIBLE 60
A., Progenie of Light MILT 218
a. tremble round POPE 64
A. would be Gods POPE 84
band of A. coming after ANON 42
entertained a. unawares BIBLE 560
flights of a. sing thee SHAK:HAM 201
Four a. to my bed ADY 1
Four a. to my bed ANON 81
give his a. charge over thee BIBLE 226
Go with me like good a. SHAK:HEN.VIII 3
God and a. to be lookers on BACON:F[1] 10
Hark the herald a. sing ANON 67
hear the a. sing SEARS 1
if a. fight SHAK:RIC.II 23
little lower than the a. BIBLE 199
makes the a. weep SHAK:MEA 13
not A., but *Anglicans* SELL 3
Now walk the a. MARLOWE 12
on the side of the a. DISR:B 67
sorrow for a. BROWNING:R 55
Tears such as A. weep MILT 138
they have the countenance of a. GREG I 1
Though women are a. BYR 3
'twixt Air and A.' purity DONNE 26
Where A. fear to tread POPE 28
Where A. tremble GRAY:T 35
anger:
a. dwell in heavenly hearts? VIRGIL 34
A. invests with such a lovely SIDNEY:P 8
A. is a brief madness HORACE 83
A. is never without an Argument HALIF 10
A. is one of the sinews FULLER:T[1] 6
A. makes dull men witty BACON:F[1] 128
carries a. as the flint SHAK:JUL 74
disappointment give rise to a. HUME 3
Juno's unrelenting a. VIRGIL 33
Your heart of a. BAXTER:JK 1
angle:
Brother of the A. WALT 4
Give me mine a. SHAK:ANT 30
angler:
excellent a., and now with God WALT 8
no man is born an a. WALT 2
angles: Offer no a. to the wind TESS 1
Angles: they were called A. GREG I 1
Anglican: English literature and the A. Church PYM 1
Anglicans: *not* Angels, but *A.* SELL 3
angling:
a. or float fishing I can only JOHNSON:S 270
innocent recreation of a. WALT 9
Anglo-Saxon:
Come in, you A. swine BEHAN:Br 9
those are A. attitudes CARROLL 74
angry:
a. at a slander makes it true JONS 26
a. man always thinks he can do ALBERTA 1
a. on the right grounds ARISTOT 10
A. Young Man PAUL 1
a. young men FEAR 1
Be ye a., and sin not BIBLE 534
I was a. with my friend BLAKE:W 76
When he was a. BECKF 1
when very a. swear TWAIN 21
within me, that's a. with me BROWNE:T 5
anguish:
A. keeps the heavy gate WILDE:O 120
a. of all sizes HERB:G 20
solitary hidden a. ELIOT:G 16
that divinest a. BRONTE:E 5
animal:
a. of no character FONTAINE 1
a. – or vegetable – or mineral? CARROLL 80
attend A dying a. YEATS 96
Be a good a. LAWR:DH 1
curled-up a. generosities ROWB 1
He was into a. husbandry LEHRER 2
Man is a social a. SPIN 3
Man is not a solitary a. RUSS:B 18
success in life, is to be a good a. SPENCER:H 6
Whenever you observe an a. CANET 1
woman as a beautiful, romantic a. ADDIS 29
animality: a. either objectionable or funny LEWIS:CS 2
animals:
All a. are equal, but some ORWELL 20
A. are always loyal FOY 1
A. are such agreeable friends ELIOT:G 2
a. went in one by one ANON 2
a. were created solely PEAC 1
a. will not look AUD 21
best understood by children and a. STRAV 1
distinguish us from other a. BEAUMA 3
how to make use of a. MACHIA 7
I could turn and live with a. WHITMAN 7
if we stop loving a. SOLZ 2
animates: feeds and a. the whole VIRGIL 71
animosities: a. are mortal NORTH:C 7
animosity: full fervour of sisterly a. SURT 14
Anjou: sweetness of A. DU BEL 3
ankles: One praised her a. TENNY 41
Anna Livia: tell me all about A.L. JOYCE:J 33
Annabel Lee: By the name of A.L. POE 7
annals:
a. are blank in history-books CARLYLE:T 59
simple a. of the poor GRAY:T 17
Annan: A. water's wading deep BALL 1
Anne Hathaway: reproductions of A.H.'s cottage LANCAS 2
Anne of Cleves: a Flanders mare* HENRY VIII 2
Annie:
A.'s wond'rous bonnie BALL 1
for bonnie A. Laurie DOUGLAS:W 1
annihilation:
address will soon be A. DANTON 3
doomed to complete a. DARW:C 11
No a. without representation TOYN 2
Oblivion is a kind of A. BROWNE:T 63
one immortality And one a. SHELLEY:PB 134
anniversaries: secret a. of the heart LONGFEL 34
annoy: He only does it to a. CARROLL 12
annoyance: Shadow of a. SHELLEY:PB 98
annoying: not a. somebody, you're not ATWOOD 7
annuity:
a. is a very serious business AUSTEN 6
Buy an a. cheap DICKENS 112
annus: *A. horribilis* ELIZ II 3
anointed: as he hadde been enoynt CHAUC 13
anointest: thou a. my head with oil BIBLE 206
anon: guess that A. ... was often a woman WOOLF:V 12
another:
I would have given you a. JARRY 1
When comes such a.? SHAK:JUL 59
answer:
a. came there none CARROLL 59
a. came there none SCOTT:W 44
A. each other in the mist TENNY 143
a. is blowin' in the wind DYL 1
dusty a. gets the soul MERED:G 29
How could I a. the child? WHITMAN 4
man's a waitin' for a a. DICKENS 147
nobody asks, nobody needs to a. JUNG:Carl 1
reduced the a. to shillings CARROLL 37
silver a. rang ... 'Not Death BROWNING:EB 9
soft a. turneth away BIBLE 261
than the wisest man can a. COLTON 4
way to the pertinent a. BRONO 4
What *is* the a.? STEIN:G 7
why did you a. the phone? THURB 17
would not stay for an a. BACON:F[1] 114
answered:
A. him brotherly GRAVES:R 4
I came, and no one a. DE LA M 7
answering: without being paid for a. HELLMAN 3
answerphone: a. installed on his six-yard line DUFFY:J 1
answers:
A. sometimes are WILDE:O 76
Kinde are her answeres CAMPION 7
learned the a., all the a. MACLEISH 3
never get the a. right YEATS 116
ant:
a. Appears a monstrous COTTON 1
a. herself cannot philosophize HUX:JS 3
a.'s a centaur POUND 35
Go to the a., thou sluggard BIBLE 253
ant-hill: epoch of the a. AMIEL 2
antagonist: Our a. is our helper BURKE:E 66
antediluvian: one of your a. families CONG 29
antelope: deer and the a. play HIGL 1
anthem: heavenly a. drowns BRIDGES:M 1
anthologies: Biographies are like a. STOCKS 2
antic:
old father a. the law? SHAK:HEN.IV[1] 7
put an a. disposition on SHAK:HAM 58
Antichrist: like A. in that lewd hat JONS 25
anticipate: What we a. seldom occurs DISR:B 11
anti-clerical: understand a. things BELLOC 45
antidote: she is the a. to desire CONG 58
anti-everythings: hungry, savage a. HOLMES:OW 2
antipathies: Violent a. are always suspicious HAZL 15
antipathy:
Dread is a sympathetic a. KIERK 5
strong A. of Good to Bad POPE 153
Antipodean: upside-downe Antipodian tricke BROME:R 3
Antipodes: like A. in shoes MARV 34
antiquarian: a. is a rugged being JOHNSON:S 201
antiquates: Time, which a. antiquities BROWNE:T 53
antique:
a. lady, much decayed HAMIL:E 1
group that's quite a. BYR 181
noble and nude and a. SWIN 19
traveller from an a. land SHELLEY:PB 21
antiquities:
A. are history defaced BACON:F[1] 7
Time, which antiquates a. BROWNE:T 53
antiquity:
about you blasted with a.? SHAK:HEN.IV[2] 12
elaborate, and finisht piece of all a. ADDIS 2
I will write for A. LAMB:Ch 44
little skill in a. inclines a man FULLER:T[1] 2
reflected all respect for a. DISR:B 15
anti-Semite: A. is a man so absorbed BELLOC 44
anti-semitism: weren't any a. I wouldn't think MILLER:A 8
antithesis: one vile A. POPE 127
Antony:
A., Enthron'd i' th' market-place SHAK:ANT 26
bear the weight of A. SHAK:ANT 21
buried by her A. SHAK:ANT 80
every one an A. SHAK:ANT 30
my lord Is A. again SHAK:ANT 41
my oblivion is a very A. SHAK:ANT 19
none but A. Should conquer A. SHAK:ANT 55
quick spirit that is in A. SHAK:JUL 5
there were an A. SHAK:JUL 58
would catch another A. SHAK:ANT 78
ants:
bones polished by diligent a. WRIGHT:J 3
If a. are such busy workers DRES 1
trouble of a. in the gleam TENNY 295
anvil:
Be the a. or the hammer GOET 4
England's on the a. KIP 135
heart is an a. unto sorrow MARLOWE 26
anxiety: to buy off a. BETJ 39
anybody:
Is there a. there? DE LA M 6
Then no one's a. GILB:WS 113
anything:
a. goes PORTER:C 3
mention what the a. is RUSS:B 4
there's a. that you want LENNON 2
anywhere: a. I damn well please BEVIN 1
apart:
Lying a. now JENN:E 1
We have stood a. WILSON:W 8
apartheid: who ever supported a. TUTU 2
apathetic: gray life and a. end TENNY 93

apathy: country stirring up a. WHITELAW 2
ape:
a. from which he is descended WILB 1
a. the magnanimity of love MERED:G 17
blue-behinded a., I skip STEVENSON:RL 60
gorgeous buttocks of the a. HUX:A 46
having an a. for his grandfather HUX:TH 14
How like us is the a. EMPS 4
Is man an a. or an angel? DISR:B 67
Jesus and a nameless a. MACDIAR 14
like an a. an apple SHAK:HAM 151
Naked A. MORRIS:D 1
never an a. or a bear POUND 16
played the sedulous a. STEVENSON:RL 35
take their manners from the A. BELLOC 2
Tulia's a. a marmasyte ANON 69
ape-like: a. virtues without which CONNOLLY:C 1
Apella: A. the Jew may believe it HORACE 69
apes:
a. are a. JONS 13
lead a. in hell SHAK:TAM 5
person and the peple his a. CHAUC 32
aphorism: corroboration of this a. in the records SMITH:FE 1
aphorists: a. read as if they had all CANET 2
aphrodisiac:
Fame is a powerful a. GREENE:G 17
Power is the ultimate a. KISS 8
Apollo:
A. does not always aim HORACE 23
A. hunted Daphne so MARV 16
bright A.'s lute SHAK:LOV 16
burnèd is A.'s laurel MARLOWE 46
Apollyon:
A. straddled quite over BUNYAN 8
his name is A. BUNYAN 7
apologise: I never a. SHAW 5
apologize:
Never a. FISHER:JA 1
rule in life never to a. WODE 1
apologizing: ever a. for his occupation MENCK 3
apology: a. before you be accused CHARLES I 1
apoplexy: a. . . . is a kind of lethargy SHAK:HEN.IV[2] 7
apostles:
A. of Freedom are ever idolised CONNOLLY:J 1
arises in the midst of his a. HUGHES:B 6
company of the A. PRAY 8
Septuagint minus the A. VERR 1
apostolic: a. blows and knocks BUTLER:S[1] 12
apothecary:
expires in the arms of an a. SMITH:Syd[1] 2
starved a. than a starved poet LOCKHART 1
apparel:
a. oft proclaims the man SHAK:HAM 30
true man's a. fits SHAK:MEA 32
apparelled: apparell'd like the spring SHAK:PER 1
apparition:
a., sole of men SHELLEY:PB 66
Cirencester, was an a. AUBREY 13
Like a fleeting a. PUSH 1
apparitions: a. which *are*, and then CARLYLE:T 42
appeal: He has a gay a. COWARD 22
appear:
how you a. before God UNA 7
Things are entirely what they a. SARTRE 1
appearance:
insinuating a. are seldom associated CONF 1
pleased by their a. OSB:J 5
secret of a successful a. SITWELL:E 16
appearances:
A. are deceptive PROV 19
A. are not held to be a clue COMPT 7
contrive To save appeerances MILT 229
Keep up a. CHURCH:C 2
Never judge from a. PROV 284
no trusting a. SHERIDAN:RB 28
who do not judge by a. WILDE:O 28
appeasement: of armaments by political a. LOTH 1
appeaser: a. is one who feeds a CHURCH:W 72
appendix: The rest of me is a mere a. DOYLE:AC 36
appetite:
A. comes with eating RAB 3
a. may sicken SHAK:TWE 1
A., which is therefore nothing SPIN 1
Doth not the a. alter? SHAK:MUCH 15
his a. Is more to bread SHAK:MEA 2
satisfying a voracious a. FIELDING 24
appetites:
Subdue your a., my dears DICKENS 68
wrecched worldes a. CHAUC 122
applaud:
A. us when we run BURKE:E 96
go out front and a. yourself ROGERS:W 8
Till thou a. the deed SHAK:MAC 67
applause:
attentive to his own a. POPE 121
gain a. which he cannot keep JOHNSON:S 3
give us your a. TEREN 7
in the sunshine and with a. BUNYAN 13
apple:
appil that he tok ANON 52
a. a day keeps the doctor PROV 20
Eve and the a. was the first great BRIDIE 4
for an a. damn'd mankind OTWAY 2
goodly a. rotten SHAK:MERC 16
honest state before the a. LAWR:DH 41
pelts me with an a. and runs VIRGIL 8
there vor me the a. tree BARNES:W 1
want the a. for the a.'s sake TWAIN 17
apple-dumplings: pure mind who refuses a. LAMB:Ch 7
apple-pie:
A was an a. ANON 55
a. without some cheese PROV 21
apple-tart: carv'd like an a.? SHAK:TAM 11
apples:
A. of gold for the king's SWIN 55
a. on the Dead Sea's BYR 82
comfort me with a. BIBLE 294
egg right through to the a. HORACE 65
girl, picking dewy a. VIRGIL 15
golden a. of the sun YEATS 23
moon-washed a. of wonder DRINK 1
Over which red a. shone MORRIS:W 10
Ripe a. drop about MARV 17
silver a. of the moon YEATS 23
small choice in rotten a. SHAK:TAM 2
Stolen, stolen, be your a. HUNT:L 2
application:
observation lays in the a. DICKENS 137
What use is a. COLETTE 3
applications: No a. can be received here SHERIDAN:RB 45
applied: no a. sciences PASTEUR 2
appointing: men a. men who remind BAKEW 1
appointment:
a. by the corrupt few SHAW 51
Every time I make an a. LOUIS XIV 3
appreciate: I never 'a'. PICAS 5
appreciation: dependence on the a. of others CONNOLLY:C 7
apprehension a. of the good SHAK:RIC.II 12
apprehensions: a. come in crowds WORDS:W 38
approve: men of sense a. POPE 22
April:
A. is the cruellest month ELIOT:TS 34
A. of your youth adorns HERB:E 1
A.'s in the west wind MASE 5
he smells A. and May SHAK:MERR 11
lovely A. of her prime SHAK:SON 3
March winds and A. showers PROV 268
Now that A.'s here BROWNING:R 49
proud-pied A., dress'd SHAK:SON 43
Sweet A. showers TUSS 1
that Aprill with his shoures CHAUC 1
uncertain glory of an A. SHAK:TWO 5
April-fools: One of love's A. CONG 4
aprons: made themselves a. BIBLE 18
aquavitae: great god of *A.* FERGUSS:R 1
Aquitaine: prince of A., with the ruined NERV 1
Arab:
A. who build himself a hut FRANCE 2
A.'s Farewell to his Horse NORT 2
shook hands with a friendly A. MILLIG 2
Arabia: spell of far A. DE LA M 5
Araby: burns in glorious A. DARLEY 1
Aral Sea: shine upon the A.S. ARNOLD:M 34
arbiter: high A. Chance governs all MILT 172
arbitrary: *Supream Power must be A.* HALIF 3
arbitrator: old common a., Time SHAK:TRO 23
arboreal: probably a. in its habits DARW:C 6
Arcadians: A. both VIRGIL 14
archaeologist: a. is the best husband CHRIS 7
archangel: A. a little damaged LAMB:Ch 41
archbishop: sign of an a. is a double-cross DIX:GEA 1
Archbishop of Canterbury: that is the A.o.C. SMITH:Syd[1] 24
archduke: Like an a. in the gutter SLESS 7
archer:
A. his sharpe Arrowes tryes? SIDNEY:P 5
mark the a. little meant SCOTT:W 52
arches:
down the a. of the years THOMP:F 7
Underneath the a. FLANA 1
architect:
a. can only advise his client WRIGHT:FL 1
a. of his own destiny APPI 1
architectooralooral: drawd too a. DICKENS 213
architecture:
a. a kind of petrified music GOET 35
A. as in all other *Operative* WOTTON 6
A. is . . . petrified music SCHELL 1
Has the age of a. passed GOGOL 2
Rise and Fall of English A. BETJ 38
wondrous a. of the world MARLOWE 9
work of a. on this continent PRINGLE:JMD 1
archways: ripple under a. HARDY:T 9
archy: wotthehell a. wotthehell MARQUIS 3
arcs: earth the broken a. BROWNING:R 166
ardour: a. hidden in my veins RACINE 6
are:
know that which we a. BYR 236
that which we a., we a. TENNY 55
Argentina: In A. they throw themselves DIET 4
Argo: A loftier A. cleaves SHELLEY:PB 154
argosies:
a. of magic sails TENNY 79
a., with portly sail SHAK:MERC 1
argue:
a. freely according to conscience MILT 321
good people a. over principles EBNER 1
he could a. still GOLDS 29
It is as absurd to a. men NEWM:JH 1
only d–d fools who a. FISHER:JA 1
argues: heart a., not the mind ARNOLD:M 38
argufies: What a. sniv'ling DIBDIN:C 1
arguing:
Be calm in a. HERB:G 8
in a. with the inevitable LOWELL:JR 9
not a. with you – I am telling WHIST 4
argument:
All a. is against it JOHNSON:S 196
A., but seldom with a good HALIF 10
a. is a whore and a cuckold SHAK:TRO 9
a. of the broken pane of glass PANK:E 6
be content with a. YEATS 75
half truth in a. LEACOCK 9
heard great a. FITZGER:E 17
It would be a. for a week SHAK:HEN.IV[1] 29
no a. but force BROWNE:W[2] 1
not to stir without great a. SHAK:HAM 157
only once in the use of an a. BENNETT:Ar 9
their swords for lack of a. SHAK:HEN.V 18
this is a rotten a. ANON 246
argumentative: wife to be of studious or a. JOHNSON:S 218
arguments:
able to hold all a. BACON:F[1] 54
A. out of a pretty mouth ADDIS 30
a. which influenced FERGUSS:J 1
Arian: upon the subject of the A. heresy JOHNSON:S 218
arise:
I a. and unbuild it again SHELLEY:PB 56
I will a. and go now YEATS 4
aristocracy:
a. in a republic is like MITFORD:N 6
a. means government by the badly CHESTERTON 54
a. the most democratic MACAULAY:TB 31
a. to what is decent HOPE:An 5
a. would be biologically sound HALDA 4
aristocrat: A. who banks with Coutts GILB:WS 105
aristocratic: a. class from the Philistines ARNOLD:M 68
aristocrats: a. will hang ANON 1
Aristotle: teacher of those who know* DANTE 5
arithmetic: branches of A. – Ambition CARROLL 28

ark:
for him an a. of bulrushes BIBLE 81
into the a., the male BIBLE 36
Wisdom makes him an A. DONNE 96
arm:
a. clothed in white samite MALORY 3
a. of the Lord revealed? BIBLE 327
a. Rose up from out TENNY 274
Don't carry away that a. RAG 1
long a. of coincidence CHAMBERS 1
must lose my right a. NELS 4
one a. bent across your SASS 10
peculiar flourish of his right a. DICKENS 219
Sufficient is Thine a. WATTS 18
With pliant a. thy glassy GRAY:T 4
armadillos: yellow lines and dead a. HIGH 1
Armageddon: warheads for the domestic A. LEONARD:H 1
Armagh: look north towards A. KAV 1
Armalite: A. in this hand MORRISON:D 1
armchairs: wearing a. tight about the hips WODE 5
armed:
a. prophets were victorious MACHIA 4
Thrice is he a. BILL 1
We are in a. conflict EDEN:A 2
We should be a. O'BRIEN:E 3
Armentiers: Mademoiselle from A. ROWL:E 1
armes: *Aux a., citoyens* ROUG 2
armies:
are no invincible a. STALIN 3
a. but flocks of sheep? CERV 4
a. swore terribly in Flanders STERNE 18
embattled A. clad in iron MILT 283
ignorant a. clash by night ARNOLD:M 47
Napoleon's a. always used to march SELL 9
prodigious a. we had in Flanders STERNE 16
Arminian: A. clergy PITT:W[1] 8
armistice: short a. with truth BYR 191
armour:
a. is his honest thought WOTTON 2
Christian's a. bright COWP 8
Conceit is the finest a. JEROME:JK 3
Like to the A. iron brace BLAKE:W 91
no a. against fate SHIRL 3
upon us the a. of light PRAY 42
whole a. of God BIBLE 537
armourers:
a. accomplishing the knights SHAK:HEN.V 25
Now thrive the a. SHAK:HEN.V 10
armpits: like smelling their own a. MILLER:J 1
arms:
A., and the man I sing DRYD 82
A. and the man I sing VIRGIL 33
a. control means some kind of deodorant SCHROED 1
a. is not spending money alone EISEN 2
a. ye forge, another bears SHELLEY:PB 52
artiste with short a. can never BERNH 1
as happy in the a. of a chambermaid JOHNSON:S 207
as the everlasting a. BIBLE 127
caught in her a. long WYATT 4
challenge this world in a. EISEN 3
defie th' Omnipotent to A. MILT 110
Excites us to a. DRYD 93
find the a. of my true love TENNY 220
he laid down his a. HOOD 3
his a. hang down to laugh ELIOT:TS 28
Imparadis't in one anothers a. MILT 197
it hath very long a. HALIF 11
Let a. yield to the toga CIC 5
lord of folded a. SHAK:LOV 8
made A. ridiculous MILT 283
Madness supplies the a. VIRGIL 35
naughty mothering a. THOMAS:D 31
never would lay down my a. PITT:W[1] 9
take a. against a sea SHAK:HAM 97
Those entrusted with a. WINDHAM 1
To a., citizens ROUG 2
To war and a. I fly LOVELACE 7
took up a. with more justice LUCAN 1
army:
a. ages men sooner WELLS:HG 13
a. . . . goes on its belly FRED 5
a. is a nation within the VIGNY 6
a. loses if it does not win KISS 1
a. marches on its stomach NAPO I 16
a. of lions led by asses CHAMP 1
a. of unalterable law MERED:G 33
backbone of the A. KIP 82
black a., vengeful ZOLA 1
brought the A. home GUED 4
contemptible little a. WILHELM II 4
don't want to use the a. LINC 15
German a. was stabbed in the back HIND 1
honour of the British A. KITCHEN 2
hum of either a. stilly SHAK:HEN.V 25
I hear an a. charging JOYCE:J 44
Like a mighty a. BARING-G 3
Arques: we fought at A. and you HENRI 2
arranged:
It can be a. GALLICO 1
they are not very well a. WHIST 12
Arras: As they slogged up to A. SASS 9
arrest:
didn't create you to a. me PEEL:AW 1
Is strict in his a. SHAK:HAM 197
One does not a. Voltaire DE GAU 11
arrive: to a. where we started ELIOT:TS 109
arrived:
a., and to prove it, I'm here BYG 2
fact that he has a. to cover it STOP 12
arrogance:
a. of age must submit BURKE:E 86
A. to dare to be drunk HALIF 13
arrow:
A. from the Almighties Bow BLAKE:W 115
Every a. that flies feels LONGFEL 35
shot an a. into the air LONGFEL 16
shot my a. o'er the house SHAK:HAM 194
arrows:
Archer his sharpe Arrowes tryes? SIDNEY:P 5
Bring me my A. of desire BLAKE:W 98
children as living a. are sent GIBRAN 1
arse:
a. upon which everyone has CUMM 3
child's head up the horse's a. COWARD 33
never see my a. again AUBREY 2
Sit on your a. for fifty MACNEICE 3
arsenal: great a. of democracy ROOS:FD 11
arsenals:
a. of divine vengeance HOUSM 54
not only urinals but also a. HOUDE 1
arsenic:
A. and Old Lace KESS 1
Here's your a., dear THOMAS:D 28
art:
all the adulteries of a. JONS 23
almost lost in A. COLLINS:Will 1
a. achieves a purpose CONSTANT 1
A. and religion first SPARK 5
a., as far as it can, imitates DANTE 8
a., by being publicly exhibited ALBERT 1
a. can only be learned in BUTLER:S[2] 4
a. constantly aspires PATER 3
A. does not reproduce KLEE 1
a. for a.'s sake PATER 6
A. for a.'s sake, without CONSTANT 1
a. had once worshipped something other HUX:A 12
a. has something to do with BELLOW 1
A. is a human activity TOLS:L 11
A. is a jealous mistress EMER 49
a. is an investment that hangs ALEX:H 1
a. is, as it were, God's grandchild DANTE 8
A. is either a plagiarist GAUG 1
a. is in limiting GOET 33
A. is incapable of bearing the burden ORTEGA G 4
A. is long LONGFEL 2
A. is meant to disturb BRAQ 1
A. is not a handicraft TOLS:L 12
A. is not a mirror MAYA 1
A. is not a study of positive SAND 1
a. is not a weapon KENNEDY:JF 6
A. is not essential where Nature GRACIAN 1
a. is quite useless WILDE:O 22
A. is ruled uniquely CROCE 1
a. is serene SCHILL 3
a. is significant deformity FRY:R 1
A. is the imposing of a pattern WHITEHEAD 7
A. is the most beautiful of all lies DEBU 1
A. is the most intense mode WILDE:O 41
A. is the only thing that can BOWEN:El 6
A. is upon the Town WHIST 1
A. is vice DEGAS 1
a. itself is nature SHAK:WIN 18
a. Lawful as eating SHAK:WIN 33
a. like all other sciences WEDGEWOOD 1
a. made tongue-tied SHAK:SON 30
A. most cherishes BROWNING:R 138
A. must be parochial MOORE:G 3
A. never expresses anything but WILDE:O 7
A. stopped short GILB:WS 32
a. that is interested in itself SANT 4
a., whose eternal role YEV 6
aspires . . . to the condition of a. CONRAD 1
believe in A. for A.'s sake FORST 19
by the Satans, for the Depression of A. BLAKE:W 97
cave a. of the twentieth century MCLUH 7
collective work of a. of the twentieth BRONO 5
don't want a., they want football RUCK 1
doubt that a. needed Ruskin STOP 14
emotion in the form of a. ELIOT:TS 113
enemy of good a. than the pram CONNOLLY:C 6
every a. is its intensity KEATS 123
Fine a. is that in which RUSKIN 9
French a., if not sanguinary SPENCER:H 11
glib and oily a. SHAK:KING L 4
glory and good of A. BROWNING:R 205
great a. by a deliberate attempt ELIOT:TS 120
half a trade and half an a. INGE 3
history of a. is the history BUTLER:S[2] 28
I will use no a. SHAK:HAM 65
in a. the best is good GOET 27
It is a. that *makes* life JAMES:H 22
it makes things visible* KLEE 1
it's clever, but is it A.? KIP 44
It's pretty, but is it A.? KIP 43
knows all about a. THURB 18
models destroy genius and a. HAZL 8
morality of a. consists in WILDE:O 21
my job and my a. MONTAIGNE 12
nature's handmaid a. DRYD 7
new visions of a. MORRELL 1
next to Nature, A. LANDOR 9
Nor heed my craft of a. THOMAS:D 20
ornaments their want of a. POPE 13
people start on all this A. HERB:AP 7
proper aim of A. WILDE:O 8
purpose of a. to give it shape ANOU 4
revenge of the intellect upon a. SONT 1
sacrificed to their a. EMER 76
sensitive one is to great a. BEERB 13
symbol of Irish a. JOYCE:J 12
than to suppress a work of a. BORO 1
than when A. Is too precise HERR 16
Thought and a. only develop GUER 1
unsettling element in modern a. WHARTON:E 4
without skill gives us modern a. STOP 10
work of a. must start an argument WEST:R 7
you are only interested in a. SHAW 130
art-loving: never was an A. nation WHIST 2
arthritis: a., and I don't deserve that BENNETT:Ar 1
Arthur:
He's in A.'s bosom SHAK:HEN.V 13
talks of A.'s death SHAK:KING J 17
article: snuff'd out by an a. BYR 223
artificer: Old father, old a. JOYCE:J 9
artificial: All things are a. BROWNE:T 11
artillery:
love's great a. CRASH 4
shot With the self-same a.? LOVELACE 1
artisan: give employment to the a. BELLOC 32
artist:
amateur is an a. who supports SHAHN 1
a. And you know what CARY:J 2
a. does not have to fight to eat GUER 1
a. is someone who produces WARHOL 2
a. is the one that can make a puzzle KRAUS 6
a., like the God of creation JOYCE:J 8
a. may not be a democrat MARON 1
a. may not be a judge CHEK 16
a. must be in his work FLAU 4
a. starts saving the world FRIEL 2
a. will be judged only by CONNOLLY:C 17
a. writes his own autobiography ELLIS:H 1
As an *a.*, one has no home NIET 23
be more of an a. KEATS 167
God is only another a. PICAS 4
grant the a. his subject JAMES:H 8
great a. dies with me NERO 1

I, too, am an a. CORR 1
Never trust the a. LAWR:DH 9
one lucky bastard who's the a. STOP 11
Portrait of the A. as a Young Man JOYCE:J 1
successful a. would have no trouble NOLAN 1
true a. will let his wife starve SHAW 31
artistic:
a. temperament is a disease CHESTERTON 37
never was an a. period WHIST 2
artists:
A. are not engineers KENNEDY:JF 6
A. must be sacrificed EMER 76
Great a. have no homeland MUSSET 5
relation to the dead poets and a. ELIOT:TS 114
arts:
a. aspire to the condition of music SANT 12
brought the a. into rustic Latium HORACE 94
cry both a. and learning down QUAR 15
entwine our a. with laughters JOYCE:J 37
famed in all great a. ARNOLD:M 7
foiled by woman's a. BLAKE:W 7
gentle a. which refine and humanize DICKENS 135
grew the a. of war and BYR 192
had I but followed the a. SHAK:TWE 4
liberal a. refines behaviour OSB:J 12
liberal without the manual a. JOHNSON:S 39
must learn both a. CARLYLE:T 69
secret of the a. is to correct VOLT 31
spoiled by going into the a. GAUG 2
Ten thousand baneful a. GOLDS 34
The Cinderella of the A. MONROE:H 1
these are imperial a. VIRGIL 72
Women are like the A. DONNE 4
ascendancy: supreme acts of a. CRISP 10
ascended: He a. in the sky CALVINO 1
ascends: who a. to mountain-tops BYR 87
ascension: glorious Resurrection and A. PRAY 34
ascetic: a. rocks and the sensual whirlpools MERED:G 13
ash:
A. on an old man's sleeve ELIOT:TS 103
Oak, and A., and Thorn KIP 122
ashamed:
afraid of death, as a. thereof BROWNE:T 16
a. of our finest actions LA ROCHE 33
a. with the noble shame KINGSLEY:C 9
more things a man is a. of SHAW 30
ashes:
A. and sparks, my words SHELLEY:PB 46
a. to a. PRAY 92
a. where once I was fire BYR 155
For the a. of his fathers MACAULAY:TB 47
from his a. may be made TENNY 136
Her a. new create another SHAK:HEN VIII 21
into a. all my lust MARV 31
Leave the fire a. BROWNING:R 187
monograph of the a. of one hundred DOYLE:AC 10
Scatter my A. GRAHAM:J 2
slept among his a. cold KEATS 78
sour grapes and a. ASHFORD 11
splendid in a. BROWNE:T 62
turn the universe to a. CEL 1
turn to a. on the lips MOORE:T 23
was burnt to a. GRAHAM:H 4
Asia:
army on the mainland of A. MONTGOM:BL 3
A. has been insatiable KIP 12
nor A. two Kings ALEX 2
There is too much A. KIP 12
Asia Minor: faraway A.M., slides of which JOYCE:J 26
Asian: what A. boys ought to be doing JOHNSON:LB 1
ask:
all I at present a. HAZL 39
A., and it shall be given BIBLE 400
a. him how he is, tells you TAYL:BL 1
A. me no more TENNY 116
Aske me no more CAREW:T 6
But Were Afraid to A. REUB 1
greatest fool may a. more COLTON 4
he see you now, a. why? AUD 52
I was too polite to a. VIDAL 8
If I a. Him to receive me NEALE 5
reluctant to a., because this is Japan HODS 1
We a. and a. ARNOLD:M 5
asked:
glad that they have been a. OSB:J 4
You a. for it, George Dandin MOLIERE 19
asking: a. too much CANN 7
asks: nobody a., nobody needs to answer JUNG:Carl 1
asleep:
asked her once, 'Are you a.?' MULD 1
a. before you finish saying it ROWL:H 5
Got 'tween a. and wake? SHAK:KING L 7
laid a. In body WORDS:W 6
only body's laid a. YEATS 12
quiet till it falls a. TEMPLE:W[1] 1
too young to fall a. for ever SASS 11
asp: with the 'a.' as with Antony BYR 245
asparagus:
like a. in May GILB:WS 111
only necessary to mention A. DICKENS 195
aspect: Meet in her a. BYR 41
aspen: aspes leef she gan to quake CHAUC 112
aspens: a. quiver TENNY 13
aspersion: a. upon my parts of speech SHERIDAN:RB 10
Asphodel:
A. has no odor save WILLIAMS:WC 6
A., that greeny flower WILLIAMS:WC 5
aspirates: taking a couple of a. SMITH:FE 8
aspiration: a. is a joy forever STEVENSON:RL 23
aspirations:
talk to you of their a. SMITH:LP 5
young have a. SAKI 5
aspire: a. to higher things SIDNEY:P 1
aspirin: Live on a. and beer SLESS 7
ass:
a. was feared far and wide FONTAINE 1
a., without being a fool SURT 19
enamour'd of an a. SHAK:MID 40
every a. thinks he may kick PARR 1
great Caesar a. Unpolicied SHAK:ANT 75
him egregiously an a. SHAK:OTH 23
kiss my a. in Macy's window JOHNSON:LB 5
law is such an A. CHAPMAN:G 9
Love a woman? You're an a. ROCHES 8
seeing an asse eat figs NASHE 4
Wild A. stamps FITZGER:E 12
With the jawbone of an a. BIBLE 135
write me down an a. SHAK:MUCH 28
assassinates: satisfied until somebody a. him KAUFMANN 2
assassination:
absolutism moderated by a. ANON 206
A. is the extreme form of censorship SHAW 100
A. is the shortest way MOLIERE 20
If th' a. Could trammel up SHAK:MAC 23
assault: as soon as a a. Plush DICKIN:E 12
assay: Th'a. so hard CHAUC 99
asses:
army of lions led by a. CHAMP 1
bridge of a. EUC 2
Mankind are the a. BYR 137
assume:
A. a virtue SHAK:HAM 147
never a. that which is incapable LEWES 2
what I a. you shall a. WHITMAN 1
assurance:
a. sits As a silk hat ELIOT:TS 45
make a. double sure SHAK:MAC 83
Assyrian: A. came down BYR 39
Astaire, Fred: Can't act, can't sing* ANON 166
Astolat: lily maid of A. TENNY 249
astonish: intend to a. God Almighty FORBES:JN 1
astonished: you are merely a. WEBSTER:N 1
astonishment: not so much a. SARGENT:M 1
astray:
like sheep have gone a. BIBLE 329
one that has been led a. MILT 82
quite a liberty in going a. ELIOT:G 3
astrology:
obedience of planetary influence* SHAK:KING L 9
predictions of a. BACON:F[1] 94
astronauts: a.! . . . Rotarians in outer VIDAL 1
astronomers: Confounding her a. HODG 1
astute: not more a. than all the others LA ROCHE 32
asunder:
let no man put a. PRAY 87
no man ever shall put a. SHAW 98
asylum:
lunatic a. run by lunatics LLOYD GEO 9
lunatics have taken over the a. ROWL:R 1
asylums: comfortably padded lunatic a. WOOLF:V 3
Atahualpa: who strangled A. MACAULAY:TB 5
Atalanta: wit; . . . made of A.'s heels SHAK:AS 46
ate:
a. but little meat MALORY 14
a. when we were not hungry SWIFT 35
atheism:
a. is against, not only BURKE:E 62
honest a. for my money OTWAY 6
inclineth man's mind to a. BACON:F[1] 36
miracle to convince a. BACON:F[1] 35
owlet A. COLERIDGE:ST 4
atheist:
a. is a man who has no invisible BUCHAN 3
a.-laugh's a poor exchange BURNS:R 47
be an a. if the king were LA BRU 2
By Night an A. half believes YOUNG:E 16
female a. talks you dead JOHNSON:S 62
happens to be an a. HAYD 1
He was an embittered a. ORWELL 1
I am still an a., thank God BUNUEL 1
scepticism kept her from being an a. SARTRE 10
very *chic* for an a. RUSS:B 23
worst moment for the a. ROSSET:DG 14
Athenaeum: leaving the A. with jugs HERB:AP 18
Athens:
Another A. shall arise SHELLEY:PB 157
A. arose SHELLEY:PB 152
A. holds sway over all Greece THEM 1
A. the eye of Greece MILT 273
Atkins: it's 'Thank you, Mister A.' KIP 64
Atlantic:
Admiral of the A. salutes WILHELM II 2
A. Ocean beat Mrs Partington SMITH:Syd[1] 11
steep Atlantick stream MILT 20
where the A. raves ARNOLD:M 30
atom:
carbon a. possesses certain exceptional JEANS 1
no evil in the a. STEVENSON:A 4
split the a. by firing HAY:W 1
atom bomb: best defence against the a.b. ANON 165
atom bombs: next war will be fought with a.b. UREY 1
atomic:
lunatics or suicides . . . could want an a. war KHRU 8
only effect the a. age has had BOYD:MAB 1
way to win an a. war BRADLEY:OM 2
atomies: easy to count a. SHAK:AS 42
atoms:
A. of Democritus BLAKE:W 101
fortuitous concurrence of a. PALMERS 2
ATS: beefy A. Without their hats BETJ 14
attack:
A. is the best form of defence PROV 24
I shall a. FOCH 1
attacked: a. it defends itself ANON 169
attainment: so disenchanting as a.? STEVENSON:RL 27
attempt:
a., and not the deed SHAK:MAC 36
A. the end HERR 43
attempted: Something a., something done LONGFEL 12
attendant: Am an a. lord ELIOT:TS 10
attention:
arrest of a. in the midst BELLOW 1
a. must finally be paid MILLER:A 2
close the Valves of her a. DICKIN:E 11
the a. of the nation is concentrated BAGE 11
attentive: more a. to women of rank STANTON:El 5
Attic:
A. Bird Trills MILT 273
A. shape KEATS 92
A. wit PLINY 4
back safely to A. shores HORACE 3
gain drives these A. bees VIRGIL 31
glory of the A. stage ARNOLD:M 6
attics: a. explored in solitude LEWIS:CS 6
Attila: A. with a cold PORTER:PNF 1
attire:
a. be comely, but not LYLY 1

Not the sort of a. for a gentleman SHARPE 2
attitude: lies in men's a. to women BRITT 2
Attlee: He is a modest man* CHURCH:W 66
attorney:
believed the gentleman was an *a.* JOHNSON:S 147
office boy to an A.'s GILB:WS 11
smartness of an a.'s clerk DISR:B 91
that journey you find your a. GILB:WS 51
attracted: believe that they are a. by God INGE 7
attraction: feels the a. of earth LONGFEL 35
attractiveness: account for the curious a. WILDE:O 69
attribute: a. to God himself SHAK:MERC 44
Auburn: Sweet A. GOLDS 19
Auchtermuchty: Tak' A. for a name MACDIAR 10
auctioneer: saleroom and varnishing a. CARLYLE:T 58
audacity:
Arm me, a. SHAK:CYM 1
a. of elected persons WHITMAN 19
To be tactful in a. COCT 1
Auden:
He didn't love God* ANON 192
young A. was someone SPEND 13
audience:
a. want to be surprised BERNARD:T 1
fit a. find MILT 225
auditioned: not a. – just measured THOMAS:I 3
augury: we defy a. SHAK:HAM 193
Augustan: next A. age will dawn WALP:H 13
Augustus:
A. was a chubby lad HOFFMAN:H 1
When A. drank FRED 1
auld: a. lang syne BURNS:R 71
aunt:
Charley's a. from Brazil THOMAS:B 2
I had an A. in Yucatan BELLOC 9
my giddy a. THOMAS:B 1
Aunt Edna: A.E. is universal RATT 2
Aunt Jennifer: A.J.'s tigers prance across RICH 1
aunts:
are bad a. and good a. WODE 22
Old-fashion'd halls, dull a. POPE 65
songs for me and my a. SHAK:WIN 12
Aurora: A.'s harbinger SHAK:MID 33
Aussie: hard-swearing A.' to the end HASKELL 1
Austen, Jane:
J.A. knew much more about men CHESTERTON 47
Perpendicular, precise* MITFORD:MR 2
prettiest, silliest, most* MITFORD:MR 1
Austerlitz: rises the sun of A. NAPO I 10
Australia:
Advance A. – you are theirs ANON 123
Advance A. fair MCCOR 1
A., an area famed among nuclear scientists DAGG 1
A. FOR THE AUSTRALIANS MEU 1
A. is a lucky country HORNE:DR 1
A. is the only country in the world ESSON 1
A. was like sunshine and fresh BRAGG 1
A. was the next large rectangular GREEN:Mar 1
despair about the cultural scene in A. HELPMAN 1
destiny of A. in the hollow CALWELL 2
Distance Shaped A.'s History BLAIN 2
guess that he was born in A. SHAW 82
hostility to A. ... shown by English MURRAY:LA 7
I am A.'s lorikeet KEV 1
ideal A. I visualised WHITE:P 13
irony alive in A. are taxi-drivers HUMPH 8
Liberals in A. are really Conservatives LENIN 7
most valuable acquisition* PHILLIP 1
mystical A., where reside MCAULEY 3
nation of punters and party-goers* HOGAN 1
paid to A. was the imminent Japanese invasion HUMPH 5
peculiar capitalist country* LENIN 6
physical mastering of A. was BLAIN 1
simply a nation of *Drunkards** CLARKE:M 4
weary aloofness of A. LAWR:DH 7
with the children to live in A. VICT 3
Australian:
A. Aborigine and the Irish being BATES:DM 2
A.-born, A.-bred ANON 53
A. bush – the nurse and tutor LAWS 1
A. Cultural Cringe PHILLIPS:AA 1
A. earth a battle-station PALMER:V 1
A. native can withstand all BATES:DM 1
A. often speaks without DINN 1
A. town-dweller spent a century BOYD:RGP 1
A. world is peopled HARRIS:M 3
A. worships the Goddess of Sport KINGLAKE 1
inside every A. there's an Irishman ROYCE 1
into the wide sea of A. bush ELLIS:H 8
moods of A. egalitarianism HORNE:DR 2
seek amid A. fields BROWN:FM 1
The A. Legend WARD:RB 1
under an A. sun without water HENN 1
write the Great A. Novel WHITE:P 8
Australians:
A. can express mutual affection HARRIS:M 2
they clearly require the most space* GALB 8
Austria: A. will astonish the world SCHWARZ 1
Austrian: A. army, awfully ANON 54
author:
a. is concealed behind the door JOHNSON:S 108
a. of peace PRAY 22
a. to get at *his* meaning RUSKIN 18
a. who speaks about his own DISR:B 74
a.'s name on the title-page EMER 86
but a shrimp of an a. GRAY:T 42
expected to see an a. PASC 4
indeed to be an a. HAZL 27
man were a. of himself SHAK:COR 15
more than wit to be an a. LA BRU 13
next in merit to the a. LANDOR 18
prefer being the a. of that poem WOLFE:J 1
same steps as the A. KEATS 134
so that you know the a. knew GOET 30
truth about its a. CHESTERTON 36
authoress: who ever dared to be an a. AUSTEN 76
authority:
a. be a stubborn bear SHAK:WIN 30
A. forgets a dying king TENNY 276
a. from God to do mischief MAYHEW:J 1
defiance of established a. AREN 3
Dress'd in a little brief a. SHAK:MEA 13
Madmen in a. KEYN 9
No morality can be founded on a. AYER 2
Nothing destroyeth a. so BACON:F[1] 59
one a. on my plays PINT 5
rejection of a. can sometimes result D'SOU 2
reproofs from a. ought BACON:F[1] 74
authorize: not have it enforced is to a. RICHELIEU:A 1
Authorized Version: never include the A.V. QUIL 2
authors:
A. are easy to get on with JOS 1
chief glory ... arises from its a. JOHNSON:S 9
damn those a. whom they CHURCH:C 18
faults of great a. COLERIDGE:ST 96
From English a. their copyrights TROLL 29
He invades a. DRYD 137
let great a. have their due BACON:F[1] 4
much exposed to a. WELLING 18
praise of ancient a. HOBB 14
reciprocal civility of a. is one JOHNSON:S 17
trouble with our younger a. MAUGH 24
We a., ma'am DISR:B 98
authorship:
phantasies that surround a. BRITT 1
reputation of popular a. TROLL 23
autobiography: artist writes his own a. ELLIS:H 1
autocrat: a.: that's my job CATHERINE 1
automatics: a. acquired in the holidays SEARLE 2
autumn:
A. nodding o'er THOMS:Ja[1] 6
breath of A.'s being SHELLEY:PB 40
I saw old A. in the misty HOOD 1
long weeping of a. violins VERL 1
Season of mists* KEATS 109
trees are in their a. beauty YEATS 49
autumn-evenings: When the long dark a. come BROWNING:R 89
autumnal:
deep, a. tone SHELLEY:PB 45
seen in one A. face DONNE 10
avarice:
A., the spur of industry HUME 6
beyond the dreams of a. MOORE:E 2
low drudgery of a. BURKE:E 3
must take up with a. BYR 172
Ave: *A. Maria* ANON 160
avenge: A. O Lord thy slaughter'd MILT 99
avenger: some unknown a. VIRGIL 62
average: ideal, the absolutely a. man ECO 1
aversion: matrimony to begin with a little a. SHERIDAN:RB 5
Avon:
Sweet Swan of A. JONS 45
where lucid A. stray'd GRAY:T 34
awake:
A., my heart BRIDGES:R 2
a. while sleeping, and MONTAIGNE 18
Smiles a. you DEK 3
to stay a. for it all day NIET 5
When you're lying a. GILB:WS 50
awakened: a. a sleeping giant YAM 1
away:
a. to marry LEIGH 1
big one that got a. DENNIS:N 1
further a. than anywhere else RAPH 2
He got a. CIC 9
someone takes them a. MITFORD:N 7
wish he'd stay a. MEARNS 1
awe:
a. into the beholders SWIFT 27
keep even kings in a. DAVEN:C 1
aweary:
Cassius is a. of the world SHAK:JUL 73
I am a., a. TENNY 6
awful:
many kinds of a. men COPE 4
Oh, you *are* a. EMERY 1
this is an a. place SCOTT:Rob 1
awoke:
a. and found it truth KEATS 118
a. one morning and found BYR 256
axe:
a. for the frozen sea within KAF 13
a.'s edge did try MARV 2
head off with a golden a. SHAK:ROM 33
Hurt not the Ax CHARLES I 3
Lay then the a. to the root PAINE 5
Lizzie Borden took an a. ANON 80
axes: you your sharp-edged a.? WHITMAN 32
axioms: A. in philosophy are not a. KEATS 134
axis: exposure of the underbelly of the A. CHURCH:W 28
axle: glowing A. doth allay MILT 20
aye: Charybdis of A. and No NEWM:JH 11
Ayr:
A. Watter is its name PATERSON:A 1
Auld A. BURNS:R 84
Ayrian: This A. Eightfold Path BUDDHA 2
Azores: Flores in the A. TENNY 281
azure:
A. hath a canker POUND 41
a. sister of the Spring SHELLEY:PB 40
Ring'd with the a. world TENNY 186
robes the mountain in its a. CAMPBELL:T 2
B: B bit it ANON 55
baa: B.! B.! B.! KIP 52
babble:
learned b. of the saleroom CARLYLE:T 58
to b. and to talk is most SHAK:MUCH 20
babbled: babbl'd of green fields SHAK:HEN.V 13
babe:
B. all burninge bright SOUTHW 1
B. leaps up on WORDS:W 56
Becomes a B. in Eternity BLAKE:W 87
'E acts like a b. KIP 69
to bring the b. to rest EDWARDS:R 1
Babel: tower of B. should have produced VOLT 35
babes:
B. reduced to misery BLAKE:W 65
Out of the mouth of b. BIBLE 197
babies:
bit the b. in the cradles BROWNING:R 25
putting milk into b. CHURCH:W 32
who hates dogs and b. ROSTEN 1
baboon:
hoaryheaded and toothless b. CARLYLE:T 60
Into b. and monkey SHAK:TIM 3
baby:
b. beats the nurse SHAK:MEA 1
B. in an ox's stall? BETJ 24
b. out with the bathwater PROV 83
Begin b. boy to recognize VIRGIL 12
Down will come b. NURS 60
Every b. ... is a finer one DICKENS 83

hope the b. will prove Ignorant SU 1
loud noise at one end* KNOX:R 4
price you pay for having a b. BURCHI 2
Rock-a-bye b. BLAKE:CD 1
That great b. you see SHAK:HAM 83
throw out the bath along with the b. KRAUS 3
When the first b. laughed BARRIE 6
wrap the b. bunting in NURS 5
you come from, b. dear? MACDON:G 2
Babylon:
B. in all its desolation DAVIES:SB 1
B. is fallen BIBLE 582
By the rivers of B. BIBLE 244
Ere B. was dust SHELLEY:PB 66
How many miles to B.? NURS 19
I was a King in B. HENL 7
Babylons: all man's B. strive THOMP:F 5
Bacchus:
B. that first from out MILT 19
Not charioted by B. KEATS 93
baccy: 'B. for the Clerk KIP 121
Bach:
If B. wriggles BUTLER:S[2] 10
you play B. *your* way LANDON 1
bachelor:
b. lives like a king LOWRY:LS 1
B.'s fare, bread and cheese SWIFT 43
I am a b., I live ANON 31
nor a b. too near ROWL:H 4
pleasant dining with a b. GASK 5
bachelors:
reasons for b. to go out ELIOT:G 20
Two old B. were living LEAR 29
baching: that word is 'b.' JACOMB 1
back:
b. to plasters, pills LOCKHART 1
b. us or sack us CALLA 2
borne b. ceaselessly into FITZGER:FS 9
boys in the b. rooms BEAV 2
Come b., come b., Horatius MACAULAY:TB 51
hard to get it b. in HALDE 1
I go, I come b. ITMA 5
I sit on a man's b. TOLS:L 8
Not to go b., is POPE 149
One who never turned his b. BROWNING:R 213
Scratch my b. and I'll PROV 339
those before cried 'B.!' MACAULAY:TB 50
turned his b. on a big one HUGHES:Th 5
whirl'd them to the b. o'beyont SCOTT:W 71
will you no come b. again? HOGG 4
backbiter: face-flatterer and b. are the same TENNY 248
backfire: new regime will have caused a b. ECO 2
backgammon: sport I ever mastered was b. JERROLD 11
backing: Plague upon such b. SHAK:HEN.IV[1] 37
backs: b. between your knees CORY 4
backward:
b. ran sentences GIBBS 1
eye was b. cast SPENS 28
I by b. steps would move VAUGHAN:H 8
life goes not b. GIBRAN 1
backwards:
I'm walking b. till Christmas MILLIG 5
Life can only be understood b. KIERK 1
Long ones, b. JOHNSTON:B 2
bacon:
b. was nat fet for hem CHAUC 78
b.'s not the only thing KINGSMILL 1
foundation be b. and eggs HERB:AP 20
think there's b. and there's not even CERV 9
walk miles for a b. sandwich WALES 2
Bacon:
all learning, Sir Francis B. WALT 17
When their lordships asked B. BENTLEY:EC 9
bad:
as b. as b. can be JOHNSON:S 242
b. as they make 'em YOUNG:WB 1
b. die late DEF 8
b. end unhappily STOP 7
b. girls go everywhere BROWN:HG 1
b. she was horrid LONGFEL 36
b. she was very very popular MILLER:M 1
b.'s the best of us FLETCH:J 8
bold b. man SPENS 23
brave b. man CLAREN 5
Defend the b. against the worse DAY LEWIS 5
Good and b. are but names EMER 8
How sad and b. and mad BROWNING:R 173
Mad, b. and dangerous COPE 3
Mad, b., and dangerous LAMB:Car 1
made the world ugly and b. NIET 17
never so good or so b. MACKINT 2
not really b. at heart BELLOC 25
same time be good and b. SPIN 2
so b. but it might have been worse PROV 300
so much b. in the best ANON 98
strong Antipathy of Good to B. POPE 153
they say it's not as b. as they say ANON 150
To make b. good SHAK:MEA 31
was b., she was horrid NURS 71
what I feel really b. about FRAYN 2
When b. men combine BURKE:E 16
when I'm b. I'm better WEST:M 5
badge:
It is the B. of Men DAVIDS 1
Red B. of Courage CRANE:S 1
suff'rance is the b. SHAK:MERC 17
badness:
All good and no badnes SKEL:J 4
b. of her b. when she's BARRIE 16
bag:
b. and baggage GLAD 2
not with b. and baggage SHAK:AS 40
take out of the b., Mamma? PUNCH 16
to agitate a b. of wind WHITE:AD 1
bagatelle: *vive la b.* STERNE 45
baggage: believe the b. loves me CONG 3
bagpipe: when the b. sings SHAK:MERC 40
bags:
rattling of a thousand douche b. LOWRY:M 1
steal the b. to hold the crumbs ISH 1
Three b. full NURS 2
bagwash: thought's daily b FAIRBURN 1
bairn:
b. brocht up in vanitie BOYD:MA 1
bonnie broukit b. MACDIAR 2
hed the speech o a b. BIBLE 594
bairnie: Singin' till a b. MACDIAR 17
bairns: kind to fou folk and b. PROV 150
bait: swallowed b., On purpose SHAK:SON 56
baked: You have b. me too brown CARROLL 34
baker:
b. rhymes for his pursuit BROWNING:R 208
b., The candlestick-maker NURS 63
Baker Street: B.S. irregulars DOYLE:AC 6
bakers: B. and brewers, bouchers LANGLAND 7
Bakewell: every fool in B. at Buxton RUSKIN 31
balance: In b. with this life YEATS 61
balanced: I b. all YEATS 61
balances: Thou art weighed in the b. BIBLE 351
bald:
b. and discontented BYR 244
b. as the bare mountain ARNOLD:M 83
Go up, thou b. head BIBLE 168
His heed was balled CHAUC 13
rather like going b. LARK 12
respectable b. heads YEATS 40
two b. men over a comb BORGES 5
baldness:
b. full of grandeur ARNOLD:M 83
felicity on the far side of b. SMITH:LP 15
Baldwin, Stanley:
A large pipe and thick country* DOUGLAS-H:A 4
Not even a public figure* CURZON 3
bales: undid his corded b. ARNOLD:M 30
Balfour: Mr B.'s poodle LLOYD GEO 2
Balkans: damned silly thing in the B. BISM 9
ball:
after the b. HARRIS:C 1
business of a b. is either to look out SURT 23
content to peck cautiously at the b. WODE 16
Hitler has only got one b. ANON 19
leave the b. in the back of the net DUFFY:J 1
little b. of feather and bone HARDY:T 5
looking at a girl throwing a b. WOOLF:V 6
never thrown a b. in my life DISR:B 84
On a round b. A workman DONNE 70
Urge the flying b. GRAY:T 5
ballad:
air is full of b. notes LANG:A 3
I love a b. in print SHAK:WIN 24
I met with a b. CALVER 4
ballad-mongers: these same metre b. SHAK:HEN.IV[1] 60
ballads:
fuss of b. than of blueprints COPE 1
permitted to make all the b. FLETCH:A 1
ballet:
enter the School of the Imperial B. PAVLO 1
more than one to make a b. DE VALO 1
ballets: Aren't all b. sexy? HELPMAN 3
balloon:
if the moon's a b. CUMM 1
something in a huge b. WORDS:W 126
ballot: b. is stronger than the bullet LINC 2
ballot box: with a b.b. in this hand MORRISON:D 1
balls:
our rackets to these b. SHAK:HEN.V 9
things they did with b. and bats SASS 8
thousand lost golf b. ELIOT:TS 73
Tosser of b. in the sun DEU 1
balm:
all our calm is in that b. NORT 3
B. of hurt minds SHAK:MAC 40
b. of woe SIDNEY:P 6
b. th'hydroptic earth hath drunk DONNE 54
New rubd with Baume MILT 147
no b. in Gilead? BIBLE 338
not the b., the sceptre, and SHAK:HEN.V 35
odorous gumms and balme MILT 188
out a b. upon the world KEATS 102
wash the b. off from SHAK:RIC.II 23
Balmain: like a bushfire behind B. SLESS 8
Balmoral: don't often invite me to B. FRASER:GM 1
baloney: it's still b. SMITH:Alf 3
Balzac: All B.'s novels occupy BROWNING:R 79
bamboo: Under the b. tree ELIOT:TS 69
banal: Frumpish and b. MUGG 1
Banbury: To B. came I BRATH 1
band:
Can e'er untie the filial b. SCOTT:W 11
running of a b. and you got plenty DAVIS:M 1
when the b. begins to play KIP 64
when the wearied B. HUX:A 44
bandages: only a few light b. RUNYON 3
banditti: that black b., the City Guard FERGUSS:R 1
bands: pursue Culture in b. WHARTON:E 2
bandstand: Silver music from the b. BETJ 19
Bandusia: spring of B. HORACE 42
bandy: Do you b. looks with me SHAK:KING L 13
bane: Deserve the precious b. MILT 143
bang:
If the big b. does come OSB:J 7
Kiss Kiss B. B. KAEL 1
Not with a b. but a whimper ELIOT:TS 59
banish: B. plump Jack SHAK:HEN.IV[1] 53
banished: Alone, a b. man BALL 39
banjo: wid my b. on my knee FOST:SC 1
bank:
b. and shoal of time SHAK:MAC 23
b. was green DUNB 2
b. was mightier than PLOM 5
broke the b. at Monte Carlo GILB:F 1
cried all the way to the b. LIB 1
deposit in my name at a Swiss b. ALLEN:W 10
don't trust a b. that would lend BENCH 5
entangled b., clothed with many DARW:C 4
George goes to sleep at a b. JEROME:JK 6
I know a b. where SHAK:MID 20
pregnant b. swelled up DONNE 33
robbing a b. compared to founding BRECHT 5
tyrannize over his b. balance KEYN 8
bank manager: don't think my b.m. understands FOLL 1
banker:
b. is a person who lends TWAIN 46
thought he saw a B.'s Clerk CARROLL 95
banks:
cashiers of the Musical B. BUTLER:S[2] 2
country in possession of the B. LAWS 4
Ye b. and braes BURNS:R 96
banned: any book should be b. WEST:R 2
banner:
b. waved without a blast SCOTT:W 6
b. with the strange device LONGFEL 6
'Tis the star-spangled b. KEY:FS 1
banners:
all thy b. wave CAMPBELL:T 20

b. of the king advance VENAN 2
Confusion on thy b. GRAY:T 28
bannocks: b. and a share of cheese RAMS 2
banquet-hall: Some b. deserted MOORE:T 21
Bapaume: riddled corpses round B. SASS 2
bar:
b. in Lower Thames Street ELIOT:TS 48
Get up and b. the door BALL 22
harbour b. be moaning KINGSLEY:C 15
Mute at the b. CHURCH:C 5
shall I call it an olfactory b. WELLS:HG 12
When I have crost the b. TENNY 297
When I went to the B. GILB:WS 47
Barabbas:
B. was a publisher CAMPBELL:T 25
will always save B. COCT 2
Barbara Allen: Her name was B.A. BALL 3
barbarians:
become of us without any b.? CAVAFY 1
former, in my own mind, *the B.* ARNOLD:M 68
his young b. all at play BYR 110
into B., Philistines, and Populace ARNOLD:M 62
barbaric: sound my b. yawp WHITMAN 13
barbarism:
b. of wars TENNY 293
directly from b. to degeneration CLEMENCE 5
barbarisms: clear it from colloquial b. JOHNSON:S 4
barbarity:
act with the b. of tyrants SMITH:Syd[1] 1
Sooner b. than boredom GAUT 2
Barbarossa: When B. commences HITL 11
barbarous: times b. and gothic FRANCE 4
barbeque: one moment, at a b. DAWE 2
barber:
b.'s chair, that fits all SHAK:ALL 5
I must to the b.'s SHAK:MID 36
imprudently married the b. FOOTE 3
one lady b. that made good WEST:M 7
barbs: trapped on the cruel b. of day WRIGHT:J 8
bard:
blame not the b. MOORE:T 11
Hear the voice of the B. BLAKE:W 62
If the B. was weatherwise COLERIDGE:ST 53
This goat-footed b. KEYN 6
bards:
B. of Passion and of Mirth KEATS 55
b. sublime, Whose distant LONGFEL 15
bare: Though I go b. ANON 21
barefaced: barefac'd on the bier SHAK:HAM 168
barefoot:
shoemaker's son always goes b. PROV 345
that makes shoes go b. BURTON:Ro 5
bare-footed: B. came the beggar maid TENNY 41
bargain:
Necessity never made a good b. FRANKLIN:B 5
never was a better Bargayne SIDNEY:P 3
barge: b. she sat in SHAK:ANT 25
bark:
b. of wisdom's tree CONF 20
come out as I do and *b.* JOHNSON:S 230
Cowardly dogs b. loudest WEBSTER:J 7
dog and b. yourself? PROV 432
fatall and perfidious B. MILT 51
If the dog b., go in PROV 185
my b. is on the sea BYR 130
spirit like a charmed b. SHELLEY:PB 19
star to every wand'ring b. SHAK:SON 52
Though his b. cannot SHAK:MAC 6
watch-dog's honest b. BYR 168
barking:
b. at those who refuse DIOG 3
B. dogs seldom bite PROV 28
Barkis: B. is willin' DICKENS 144
barley:
A-shearing at her b. BALL 31
fields of b. and of rye, TENNY 12
In among the bearded b. TENNY 15
Sitting on a heap of B. LEAR 12
barley-bree: ay we'll taste the b. BURNS:R 76
barleycorn:
Inspiring, bold John B. BURNS:R 87
John B. should die BURNS:R 1
barmaid: Bitter b., waning fast TENNY 95
baronet:
B.'s rank is exceedingly GILB:WS 92
No little lily-handed B. TENNY 120
baronetage: any book but the B. AUSTEN 65
baronets: All b. are bad GILB:WS 84
baroque: B. is over HEMINGWAY 3
barracking: already begun a lifetime's b. DAWE 1
barrel: already had a whole b. CHEK 13
barrel-organ: kind of human b. DICKENS 131
barreltone: base b. voice JOYCE:J 21
barren:
dark strait of b. land TENNY 273
I am but a b. stock ELIZ:I 9
live a b. sister SHAK:MID 1
Make b. our lives SWIN 25
barricades: Christs that die upon the b. WILDE:O 111
Barrie: clatter of Sir James B.'s cans GUED 2
barrow: b. and the camp abide KIP 108
barrows: grassy b. of the happier dead TENNY 47
bars: Nor iron b. a cage LOVELACE 5
barter: founded on compromise and b. BURKE:E 37
base:
All that is b. shall die BUCHANAN 6
art thou b., common and popular? SHAK:HEN.V 28
b. barreltone voice JOYCE:J 21
b. old man FRY:C 5
keep down the b. in man TENNY 265
To what b. uses we may SHAK:HAM 184
Wherefore b.? SHAK:KING L 7
baseball: sensible as b. in Italian MENCK 21
baseness: no b. we would hide? TENNY 149
bases: b. broad and low, close WHITMAN 42
bashfulness: b. in every thing that regards religion ADDIS 23
basil: Hung over her sweet b. KEATS 30
basil-pot: To steal my b. away KEATS 31
basilisk: b. is sure to kill GAY 24
Basingstoke: hidden meaning – like 'B.' GILB:WS 93
basket: all your eggs in one b. PROV 80
basnet: my b. a widow's curch? BALL 30
Basques: say about the B. CHAMFORT 6
bass-viol: mid burn the old b. HARDY:T 10
bassoon: he heard the loud b. COLERIDGE:ST 13
bastard:
all my eggs in one b. PARKER:D 25
Because I am a b. HEMINGWAY 12
getter of more b. children SHAK:COR 14
Let us pray to God ... the b. BECKETT 12
not publicly call me a b. WHITLAM 1
we knocked the b. off HILLARY 1
Why b.? SHAK:KING L 7
bastards:
b. by birth instead of vocation WHITEHORN 3
flower of Adam's b. BYR 240
for the getting a hundred b. SHAK:MEA 29
I wish the b. dead SHAK:RIC.III 12
peopled with good blokes and b. HARRIS:M 3
some call nature's b. SHAK:WIN 17
stand up for b. SHAK:KING L 8
who begets twenty b. WALP:H 16
bat:
black b., night, has flown TENNY 215
On the b.'s back I do SHAK:TEM 31
They came to see me b. GRACE 1
Twinkle, twinkle, little b. CARROLL 18
weak-eyed b. With short COLLINS:Will 6
batallions: not on the side of the big b. VOLT 9
bath:
B. twice a day to be really BURGESS:A 4
soaping her breasts in the b. EWART 1
sore labour's b. SHAK:MAC 40
take a b. without wearing a bathrobe RUSS:B 21
throw out the b. along with the baby KRAUS 3
Bath:
ever be tired of B.? AUSTEN 61
no deception of our doings at B. SMOL 11
bath-house: country b., with spiders DOST 2
bathed: b. in the Poem Of the Sea RIMB 1
bathing: long b. of a summer's day WORDS:W 142
bathroom:
fierce and revolutionary in a b. LINK 2
hangs up behind the b. door HEMINGWAY 6
man in the b. cupboard EWART 1
baths:
Having b. in Camden Town BETJ 22
In b. to steep him JONS 34
Two walking b. CRASH 15
bathtub: b. lined with white POUND 13
bathwater: baby out with the b. PROV 83
baton: marshal's b. in his knapsack NAPO I 8
bats:
b. in the belfry PHILLPOTS 1
b. with baby faces ELIOT:TS 53
Do b. eat cats? CARROLL 2
Flittering b. JOYCE:J 35
like b. amongst birds BACON:F[1] 111
things they did with balls and b. SASS 8
batsman: Holding, the b.'s Willey JOHNSTON:B 1
battalions:
But in b. SHAK:HAM 163
on the side of the big b. PROV 149
on the side of the big b. TURE 1
batter: B. my heart DONNE 87
batteries: dispose of their mercury b. NICHOL 1
battle:
Agreed to have a b. CARROLL 51
b. ceased for lack CORNEILLE 2
b. fares like to the morning's SHAK:HEN.VI[3] 2
b. of Britain is about to begin CHURCH:W 15
b. rages loud and long CAMPBELL:T 7
b. there was which I saw MCLENN 1
better in b. than in bed STERNE 23
Done is a battell on the dragon DUNB 18
drunk delight of b. TENNY 52
Each b. sees the other's SHAK:HEN.V 25
few die well that die in b. SHAK:HEN.V 32
field of b. and not a bed STEVENSON:RL 10
foremost in b. was Mary Ambree BALL 37
from b. and murder PRAY 33
half the b. GOLDS 72
into the midst of b. VIRGIL 53
mighty b. were we defeated LIVY 2
Money is the sinews of b. RAB 7
next to a b. lost WELLING 8
noise of b. roll'd TENNY 272
nor the b. to the strong BIBLE 287
out of b. I escaped OWEN:W 11
sends his nation into b. MEIR 1
Sing, my tongue, of b. VENAN 1
the Lord mighty in b. BIBLE 208
to b. for freedom and truth IBS 10
When the b.'s lost and won SHAK:MAC 1
battle-flags: b. were furl'd TENNY 79
battledore: B. and shuttlecock's a wery good game DICKENS 14
battlefield: most beautiful b. I've ever seen NAPO I 14
battlements:
hid b. of Eternity THOMP:F 13
o're the Crystal B. MILT 144
battles:
b. long ago WORDS:W 80
blood and b. was my youth ARNOLD:M 32
Dead b., like dead generals TUCHMAN 1
opening b. of all subsequent wars ORWELL 12
bauble:
Pleas'd with this b. still POPE 98
that fool's b., the mace CROMWELL 7
bawcock: King's a b. SHAK:HEN.V 29
bawdy-house: pretence of keeping a b. JOHNSON:S 215
bawled: every soul b. out, Well done COWP 54
bay: b. the moon SHAK:JUL 69
bay tree: himself like a green b.t. BIBLE 209
bayed: b. the whispering wind GOLDS 24
bayonets: build himself a throne of b. INGE 5
bays: palm, the oak, or b. MARV 12
bazaar: for the market, not for the b. YELT 1
BBC:
B. is full of men appointing BAKEW 1
enabled the B. to make broadcasting REITH 1
be:
Car'd not to b. at all MILT 150
it'll b., it'll b. ANON 1
less what we may b. BYR 236
let them b. as they are CLEMENT 1
something better not to b. BYR 21
To b. at all is to b. religious BUTLER:S[2] 38
To b., or not to b. SHAK:HAM 97

Were it not better not to b.? TENNY 48
What must b., must b. PROV 418
What will b., shall b.? MARLOWE 32
When not to b. receives SHAK:SON 54
Where ought I to b.? CHESTERTON 57
be-all: b. and the end-all here SHAK:MAC 23
beach:
about the b. I wander'd TENNY 69
know this b. like the back HOLT 2
lie on the b. and stare REED:R 2
Ninety-Mile B. was obviously named MCDER 1
not the only pebble on the b. BRAIS 1
warm sea-scented b. BROWNING:R 58
way to the b. you had RICHARDSON:HH 1
You walk in the sky's b. SLESS 3
beaches:
scouring the b. of the world STEVENSON:RL 26
we shall fight on the b. CHURCH:W 13
Beachy Head: by way of B.H. CHESTERTON 8
beacon-light: b. is quenched in smoke SCOTT:W 14
beacons:
b. burn again HOUSM 1
b. of wise men HUX:TH 4
star B. from the abode SHELLEY:PB 127
bead: Venomous B. SELL 4
beadroll: Fame's eternall b. SPENS 39
beads:
bedes, gauded al with grene CHAUC 11
glass b. are to African traders CRISP 4
beadsman:
B., after thousand aves KEATS 78
b. now that was your knight PEELE 2
beak:
b. of the goose is no longer PROV 29
thy b. from out my heart POE 5
beaker: b. full of the warm South KEATS 93
Beale: Miss Buss and Miss B. ANON 82
beam: Eternal Coeternal b. MILT 175
beaming: Lesbia hath a b. eye MOORE:T 8
beamish:
b. nephew CARROLL 90
my b. boy CARROLL 46
beams:
all his b. full-dazzling WHITMAN 28
borrowed b. of moon and stars DRYD 69
bean:
dined on one pea and one b. LEAR 32
home of the b. and the cod BOSSI 1
not-too-French French b. GILB:WS 33
beanflowers: b.' boon BROWNING:R 103
bear:
authority be a stubborn b. SHAK:WIN 30
b. another's misfortunes perfectly POPE 181
B. of Very Little Brain MILNE 11
b. with a sore head MARR 2
Exit, pursued by a b. SHAK:WIN 8
habits from the B. BELLOC 2
has been eaten by the b. HOUSM 49
How a b. likes honey? MILNE 9
huntsman by the b. oppress'd WALLER 1
is a bush suppos'd a b.? SHAK:MID 43
like the rugged Russian b. SHAK:MAC 72
Man is born to b. HOMER 15
Moppsikon Floppsikon b. LEAR 31
More can I b. than you SHAK:HEN.VI[2] 7
my safe old b. BETJ 33
never an ape or a b. POUND 16
never to sell the b.'s skin FONTAINE 16
No dancing b. was so genteel COWP 1
not made by nature to b. AUR 9
oft out-watch the B. MILT 84
rather b. with you than SHAK:AS 19
Silly old B. MILNE 10
sing the savageness out of a b. SHAK:OTH 48
We've fought the B. before HUNT:GW 1
who did most, shall b. most BROWNING:R 150
bear-baiting: Puritan hated b. MACAULAY:TB 33
beard:
all built their nests in my b. LEAR 1
b. full of butterflies GARC 2
b. full of butterflies LORCA 3
b. the lion in his den SCOTT:W 26
brave b. curled CHESTERTON 20
grey b. and glittering eye COLERIDGE:ST 10
I have a b. coming SHAK:MID 8
icicle on a Dutchman's b. SHAK:TWE 43
pluck me by the b. SHAK:KING L 53
singeing of the King of Spain's B. DRAKE 2
take the Turk by the b.? SHAK:HEN.V 47
wears a b., a bow tie, two-toned CAINE 1
bearded: refuge of b. Trotskyite HOWK 1
beards:
b. forbid me to interpret SHAK:MAC 8
We'll grow our b. FLAU 1
beareth: B. all things BIBLE 522
bears:
long b., and pretences SWIFT 22
wandering b. may come with buns ISH 1
bearskin: love scene on a b. rug HUX:A 30
beast:
b. but a just b. ANON 161
B. gave b. as much YEATS 81
b. of prey is unmistakable NIET 2
b. With many heads SHAK:COR 12
beest is deed he hath no peyne CHAUC 44
beste, out of thy stal CHAUC 125
Blatant b. men call SPENS 42
either a b. or a god ARISTOT 15
either a wild b., or a god BACON:F[1] 65
evil b. hath devoured him BIBLE 69
gentle Bible b. MUIR:E 4
How like a b. was I COWP 4
I have a b. on my back DOUGLAS:K 3
No b. so fierce SHAK:RIC.III 4
noise in the b.'s belly MALORY 2
questing b. that had in shape MALORY 4
regardeth the life of his b. BIBLE 258
what rough b. YEATS 63
You b. RICHARDS:F 1
beastie: cowrin, tim'rous b. BURNS:R 31
beasties: long leggety b. ANON 187
beasts: like brute b. PRAY 81
beat:
b. keep time with little steps ANDER 4
b. my people to pieces BIBLE 302
b. of a horse's feet KIP 132
b. of her unseen feet SHELLEY:PB 55
Go mad, and b. their wives CALVER 2
hearts with just one b. HALM 1
We b. them today, or Molly STARK:J 1
beaten:
b. till they know What wood BUTLER:S[1] 21
I was b. up by Quakers ALLEN:W 5
maker is hymself ybeten CHAUC 106
beating:
b. in the void his luminous ARNOLD:M 84
b. of war drums KOES 4
b. up a man physically and b. him MACKEN 7
hear the b. of his wings BRIGHT 1
Beattock: Pulling up B. AUD 16
beauing: B., belle-ing ANON 56
beauteous:
All b. things for which CORY 3
How b. mankind is SHAK:TEM 32
love all b. things BRIDGES:R 4
beauties:
forgotten crowd Of common b. CAREW:T 4
in your b. orient deepe CAREW:T 6
meaner b. of the night WOTTON 3
small proportions we just b. see JONS 48
thousand b. are gone down POUND 4
With spoils of meaner B. LOVELACE 9
beautification:
A face made up* CRASH 8
adulteries of art* JONS 23
painting a face and not washing* FULLER:T[1] 1
putting on a false complexion* FERG:R 3
They're painted to the eyes* DOBSON:HA 3
beautified:
'b.' is a vile phrase SHAK:HAM 66
b. with our feathers GREENE:R 2
beautiful:
all b. things that are seen and ZE AMI 3
All that is b. shall abide BUCHANAN 6
b., and therefore to be woo'd SHAK:HEN.VI[1] 4
B. as sweet YOUNG:E 13
b. cannot be the way COUS 1
b. God to behold? SWIN 33
b. has its origin in the death RODO 1
b. through love SHELLEY:PB 85
believe to be b. MORRIS:W 11
better to be b. than to be good WILDE:O 33
comes up more b. HORACE 52
good is the b. PLATO 4
How b. upon the mountains BIBLE 326
I see, not feel, how b. COLERIDGE:ST 54
It was b. and simple HENRY:O 3
most b. things in the world RUSKIN 4
most b. woman I've ever seen MARX:G 1
name of which was B. BUNYAN 5
old are more b. WHITMAN 38
one was b. BYR 43
own that thou art b. SHELLEY:PB 128
She is more b. than day TENNY 41
Small is b. PROV 348
theory that his wife is b. MENCK 6
those that are not entirely b. YEATS 59
to him ceases to be b. SAINTE-B 3
to me The entirely b. AUD 13
too b. to live DICKENS 73
When a woman isn't b. CHEK 7
will always make it b. CONSTABLE:J 2
world over to find the b. EMER 27
beautifully:
B. done SPENCER:S 2
Print it as it stands – b. JAMES:H 10
beautitude: Unknown, yet known b. DOBSON:R 1
beauty:
absence of flaw in b. ELLIS:H 6
After the wildest b. OWEN:W 12
astonishment at its own b. MANS:K 10
Beautie is not, as fond SPENS 46
B. and Truth, though never found BUCHANAN 1
b. being the best of all BRIDGES:R 1
B. by Constraint possessing GAY 3
B. cannot keep her lustrous KEATS 93
b. cold and austere RUSS:B 2
b. coming and the b. gone WORDS:W 137
b. dies of b. YEATS 108
b. does not lead to extravagance PERIC 2
b. draws us with POPE 44
B. endures for only as long SAP 3
b. faded has no second PHILIPS:A 1
b. fires the blood DRYD 118
B. for some provides escape HUX:A 46
B. from order springs KING:W 1
b. from the light retir'd WALLER 3
b. has no ebb YEATS 16
B. in distress is much the BURKE:E 6
B. is altogether in the eye HUNG 1
B. is altogether in the eye WALLACE:L 1
B. is as useful as usefulness HUGO 6
B. is but a flower NASHE 1
b. is imperceptible to all but him GREER 7
B. is in the eye PROV 30
B. is momentary in the mind STEVENS 5
B. is nature's brag MILT 39
B. is nature's coyn MILT 38
b. is only sin deep SAKI 2
B. is only skin-deep PROV 31
B. is the child of love ELLIS:H 2
B. is the lover's gift CONG 44
B. is the product of harmony SCHILL 11
b. is thy earthly dower WORDS:W 37
B. is truth, truth b. KEATS 92
b. is woman's sceptre WOLLST 4
B. itself doth of itself SHAK:POET 4
b. lives with kindness SHAK:TWO 12
b. made The bright world SHELLEY:PB 103
b. making beautiful old SHAK:SON 48
b. of a face is a frail MOLIERE 29
b. of a thousand stars MARLOWE 39
b. Of an aged face CAMPBELL:Jo 1
b. of Thy peace WHITTIER 8
B. provoketh thieves SHAK:AS 9
b. remains RENOIR:PA 2
B. should never be half way KEATS 128
B. smiling in her tears CAMPBELL:T 5
B. stands In th'admiration MILT 266
b. summoned Greece to arms MARLOWE 14
B., that dost consecrate SHELLEY:PB 13
b., that hath not some strangeness BACON:F[1] 39
b., though injurious, hath MILT 291
b. to delight DAVIES:J 1
B. too rich for use SHAK:ROM 7
b. truly blent SHAK:TWE 15
B. was, nothing ever ran GALS 4
b., which a picture cannot BACON:F[1] 38

B.'s but skin deep DAVIES:J 5
B.'s ensign yet SHAK:ROM 43
b.'s ignorant ear YEATS 40
b.'s rose might never die SHAK:SON 1
body's b. live STEVENS 5
clear perception of its B. KEATS 148
close relationship with B. KEATS 123
daughters Have stolen their b. CAMPBELL:G 2
delusion that b. is goodness TOLS:L 9
dreamed that life was B. HOOP 1
each mind perceives a different b. HUME 8
Everything has its b. CONF 25
Exuberance is B. BLAKE:W 50
fatal gift of b. BYR 100
first in b. should be KEATS 53
fortune contributes to B. ASQU:M 1
found England a land of b. JOAD 3
friend of B. in distress? BYR 19
Ghosts of B. glide POPE 138
girls' hearts is their own b. OSB:J 9
He hath a daily b. SHAK:OTH 59
he not been a thing of b. GILB:WS 21
horror and its b. are divine SHELLEY:PB 47
I have lov'd the principle of b. KEATS 164
If I could write the b. SHAK:SON 5
If you get simple b. BROWNING:R 113
in hearing their b. praised OSB:J 5
its own b. is the mind BYR 106
Like a spirit of pure b. PUSH 1
living b. is for younger YEATS 56
looked on B. bare MILLAY 6
Love built on b. DONNE 3
more than they love b. CASSON 1
no b. that we should desire BIBLE 328
no woman ... b. without a fortune FARQ 13
poetic b. ARNOLD:M 79
power of b. I remember DRYD 117
put too much trust in your b. VIRGIL 5
rarest gift To B. MERED:G 22
redemption of all things by B. SHAW 94
she dwells with B. KEATS 96
She walks in b. BYR 41
soul of her b. and love SHELLEY:PB 92
such b. as a woman's eye? SHAK:LOV 15
Such seems your b. still SHAK:SON 46
terrible b. is born YEATS 45
They grew in b., side HEMA 5
thing of b. is a joy KEATS 34
'Tis b. calls LEE:N 1
unmask her b. to the moon SHAK:HAM 28
was b.'s summer dead SHAK:SON 46
What ills from b. spring JOHNSON:S 70
what wages b. brings YEATS 58
whence arises all that Order and B. NEWT:I 2
whose b. is past change HOPK:GM 7
wit and b. learned their trade YEATS 38
youth And a little b. WEBSTER:J 21
beauty spots: land of b.s. JOAD 3
beaver: Harry with his b. on SHAK:HEN.IV[1] 76
because: B. it was he MONTAIGNE 7
Bechstein: pawn the B. grand COWARD 26
Becket, Thomas: this turbulent priest?* HENRY II 1
beckoning: b. counts, and not STARK:F 1
becks: Nods, and B. MILT 66
become: we b. more like ourselves HALL:P 1
becomes: nothing so b. a man SHAK:HEN.V 17
bed:
Ample make this B. DICKIN:E 15
Are a' the weans in their b. MILLER:W 1
Are the children all in b.? NURS 82
at night a b. of down WOTTON 4
b. be blest that I lie on ADY 1
B. be blest that I lie on ANON 81
b. by night GOLDS 31
b. for a year when he is forty SHAW 137
B. ... is the poor man's opera HUX:A 42
better in battle than in b. STERNE 23
big enough for the b. of Ware SHAK:TWE 44
black passage up to b. STEVENSON:RL 54
Books and bimbos can be taken to b. BENJ:W 1
bounced out of b. MILNE 4
bracken made their b. GLOVER 1
come to b. in boots HERB:AP 2
Creep into thy narrow b. ARNOLD:M 48
cup of tea than go to b. with someone BOY 1
deep in my b. I turn JENN:E 3
deep peace of the double b. CAMPBELL:Mrs P 2
double b. of the wood THOMAS:D 23
drunk to b. SHAK:ANT 6
each in a separate b. JENN:E 1
Each within our narrow b. CASWALL 2
Early to b. and early to rise PROV 88
Every b. is narrow MILLAY 3
fit a b. for this huge birth CRASH 12
From his brimstone b. COLERIDGE:ST 40
go to b. in another world HENS 1
go to b. with a woman whose troubles ALG 2
go to b. with the lamb BRET 6
Go to b. with the lamb PROV 154
grave as little as my b. KEN 2
have to go to b. by day STEVENSON:RL 47
heat of luxurious b. SHAK:MUCH 25
home, weary to b. PEPYS 2
I drunk him to his b. SHAK:ANT 31
I hate to go to b. BANK 1
I in my b. again ANON 114
I took her into b. ANON 31
I toward thy b. FLECKER 13
keeping open b. HUX:A 8
kick his wife out of b. on a haverage SURT 4
lie *diagonally* in his b. STERNE 31
make my b. soon BALL 33
making your b. with idols? JEROME 1
man's b. is his resting-place THURB 7
my second best b. SHAK:MISC 1
Never go to b. mad DILL 2
nicer to stay in b. LAUD 3
night the b. fell on my father THURB 1
no goddess with her b. VIRGIL 13
old men, safe in b. HOPE:AI 3
pluck me from my naked b.? KYD 1
Presence watching by my b. THOMS:Ja[2] 10
rise and early to b. THURB 11
spare b. for my friends PEPYS 19
take up thy b., and walk BIBLE 479
This b. thy centre is DONNE 62
to b. Says Sleepy-head NURS 7
To b., to b., to b. SHAK:MAC 105
to come home to an unmade b. DIET 2
to more than one a b. DONNE 55
union of your b. with weeds SHAK:TEM 25
used to go to b. early PROUST 2
warm weather when one is in b. SWIFT 71
When boyes go first to b. HERB:G 38
Who goes to b. with whom SAYERS 4
whole world out of b. MASE 14
bed-time: I would 'twere b. SHAK:HEN.IV[1] 85
bedbug: b. on which a sensitive man O'CONOR 1
bedfellows:
acquaints a man with strange b. SHAK:TEM 17
Poverty has strange b. BULWER 3
Bedivere: bold Sir B. uplifted him TENNY 273
bedlam: anxiety is to keep out of b. CARLYLE:JW 6
bedroom:
darkened b. in a Brussels hotel THOMP:EP 1
everything changes in the beddaroom O'FAOL 3
French widow in every b. HOFFNUNG 1
take care of the b. bit HALL:Je 1
beds:
Avoid damp b. ANON 125
b. for all who come ROSSET:C 15
beat them to their b. SHAK:ANT 45
getting into other people's b. MOUNT 3
hearers weeping to their b. SHAK:RIC.II 41
make thee b. of roses MARLOWE 51
Minds like b. always made WILLIAMS:WC 7
propt on b. of amaranth TENNY 30
when I came unto my b. SHAK:TWE 59
bedside:
presunted myself at Betty's b. WARD:A 8
very good b. manner PUNCH 22
bedstead: make any one go to sleep, that b. DICKENS 48
bee:
b. has quit the clover KIP 148
b. were crossed with a Friesian GOGA 6
b.'s kiss, now BROWNING:R 16
busy b. has no time for sorrow BLAKE:W 36
doth the little busy b. WATTS 5
in my bosom, like a b. LODGE:T 1
in the bag of one b. BROWNING:R 212
Murmured like a noontide b. SHELLEY:PB 147
sting like a b. ALI 1
Where the b. sucks SHAK:TEM 31
bee-loud: alone in the b. glade YEATS 4
beech-tree: Under yonder b. MERED:G 30
beechen: shade which b. boughs diffuse VIRGIL 1
beef:
b. make Britons fight PRIOR 8
fed on b. and beer MARLBOR:J 1
great meals of b. and iron SHAK:HEN.V 24
I am a great eater of b. SHAK:TWE 3
Mortal loads of b. and beer ROS 1
roast b. in a violent perspiration CLARKE:M 3
roast b. of England FIELDING 3
beefsteak: English an article as a b. HAWT 5
beehive: What is not good for the b. AUR 11
Beelzebub: B. called for his syllabub SITWELL:E 4
been:
as we had never b. LUCRET 8
b. and gone and done? GILB:WS 3
b., and may be again WORDS:W 81
what has b., has b. DRYD 76
what we have b. makes us ELIOT:G 38
beens: one of the *has* b. HONE 1
beer:
all b. and skittles CALVER 8
b. and skittles, or something better HUGHES:Th 2
B. makes you feel as LAWS 7
chronicle small b. SHAK:OTH 21
Did you ever taste b.? DICKENS 96
fed on beef and b. MARLBOR:J 1
felony to drink small b. SHAK:HEN.VI[2] 9
Life ain't all b. and skittles DU MAU:G 1
Life is not all B. and Skittles STEVENSON:RL 71
Live on aspirin and b. SLESS 7
loan of a glass of b. STEPHENS 4
Mortal loads of beef and b. ROS 1
muddy ecstasies of b. CRAB 1
not all b. and skittles PROV 239
of two foaming glasses of b. CLARK:M 2
poor creature, small b. SHAK:HEN.IV[2] 25
quarts of Ludlow b. HOUSM 29
to desire small b.? SHAK:HEN.IV[2] 24
who drink b. will think b. IRV 3
You may talk o' gin and b. KIP 54
bees:
As B. In spring time MILT 147
b. are stirring COLERIDGE:ST 66
b. who have lost their queen FRY:C 14
cannot be good for the b. AUR 11
gain drives these Attic b. VIRGIL 31
hive of silvery b. LEAR 17
murmuring of innumerable b. TENNY 119
No b., no honey PROV 291
so work the honey b. SHAK:HEN.V 7
they rob the Hybla b. SHAK:JUL 79
yellow b. in the ivy-bloom SHELLEY:PB 74
Beethoven: B.'s Fifth Symphony is the most FORST 2
beetle:
b. wheels his droning GRAY:T 16
b. winds His small COLLINS:Will 6
cohabit with a rhinoceros b. LOWER 1
shard-borne b. with his SHAK:MAC 66
beetles:
B. black, approach not SHAK:MID 22
scarce so gross as b. SHAK:KING L 65
special preference for b. HALDA 5
before:
All be as b., Love BROWNING:R 165
I have been here b. ROSSET:DG 5
not dead – but gone b. ROGERS:S 4
nothin' much b. KIP 55
those b. cried 'Back!' MACAULAY:TB 50
befriend: learning to b. the wretched VIRGIL 43
beg: more alms they can b. GAND:I 4
began:
left off before you b. CONG 9
that's how it all b. KIP 41
beggar:
b. maid shall be my queen TENNY 41
behold desert a b. born SHAK:SON 30
best beggere in his hous CHAUC 16
dies like a b. LOWRY:LS 1
He's an absent-minded b. KIP 97
Patience, the b.'s virtue MASSIN 12

beggared:
'Beggar'd by fools DRYD 48
It beggar'd all description SHAK:ANT 25
beggars:
B. can't be choosers PROV 32
b. would ride PROV 189
When b. die SHAK:JUL 30
beggary:
b. he was never born to SHAK:MEA 27
b. in the love SHAK:ANT 2
no vice but b. SHAK:KING J 8
begged: Homer b. his Bread ANON 94
begin:
B. at the beginning CARROLL 40
let it b. here PARKER:John 1
man will b. with certainties BACON:F[1] 5
She refused to b. the 'Beguine' COWARD 30
Then I'll b. LIST 1
to b. with the beginning BYR 158
When they b. the beguine PORTER:C 5
beginning:
As it was in the b. MASS 5
As it was in the b. PRAY 7
Before the b. of years SWIN 13
b., a muddle, and an end LARK 10
b. and the ending BIBLE 572
b. is half of the business HORACE 82
b. is often the end ELIOT:TS 108
b. of any great matter DRAKE 1
film should have a b., a middle GODA 2
has a b., a middle ARISTOT 20
In my b. is my end ELIOT:TS 92
In my end is my b. ELIOT:TS 100
In my end is my b. MARY QUEEN OF S 2
In the b. God created BIBLE 2
In the b. was the word BIBLE 471
In the b. was the Word ELIOT:TS 26
In the b. was the Word MASS 22
never had b. took HERB:E 2
Nothing so difficult as a b. BYR 200
perhaps, the end of the b. CHURCH:W 27
This is the b. of the end TALL 2
true b. of our end SHAK:MID 46
beginnings:
ends and the b. still constitute DOST 3
ends by our b. know DENH 3
From small b. come great PROV 138
mighty things from small b. DRYD 7
begins: b. to live, b. to die QUAR 11
begot:
about when they b. me STERNE 2
b. Within a pair of minutes KYD 4
Mother on his Father him b. BLAKE:W 102
begotten: was b. by despair MARV 7
beguile:
draught might b. for an hour ANON 68
lady to b. BALL 35
beguine:
She refused to begin the 'B.' COWARD 30
When they begin the b. PORTER:C 5
begun: Not b. at all until half done KEATS 115
behave:
How well did I b. HOUSM 10
nowadays to b. like men MACKEN 3
she b. like a nice man? EVANS:E 1
behaved: people b. in the way nations do WILLIAMS:T 6
behaving: b. in this extraordinary manner? STOP 5
behaviour:
immediate Check to loose B. STEELE 5
liberal arts refines b. OSB:J 12
moral b. varies in inverse HUX:A 35
upon his good b. BYR 206
beheaded: was b. yesterday WALP:H 3
behind:
about six hours b. it HOBS 1
B. ever great man is an exhausted FAIRBAIRN:S 1
b. her stands his wife MARX:G 29
b. them ... there is nothing SARTRE 1
Get thee b. me BIBLE 418
less than 'arf o' that b. KIP 55
no bosom and no b. SMITH:Ste 2
put b. him he put out of existence DICKENS 219
Scratches its innocent b. AUD 15
those b. cried 'Forward!' MACAULAY:TB 50
behold:
B. the man BIBLE 613
Lord, b. us with Thy blessing BUCKO 1
to b. from far LUCRET 5
beholder: altogether in the eye of the b. HUNG 1
beige: It's b.! My color DE WOL 1
being:
always at the edge of B. SPEND 5
and have our b. BIBLE 503
Harmonious hymn of b. roll HODG 4
light in the darkness of mere b. JUNG:Carl 5
non-being by avoiding b. TILLICH 1
To Real B. we go back PLOT 1
unknown modes of b. WORDS:W 148
Belbroughton Road: B.R. is bonny BETJ 18
Belfast: be kind to B. CRAIG:MJ 1
belfry:
bats in the b. PHILLPOTS 1
white owl in the b. sits TENNY 8
Belgium: B. recovers in full measure ASQU:HH 2
Belgrade: by battery besieged B. ANON 54
Belial:
B., in act more graceful MILT 152
sons of B. had a glorious DRYD 50
wander forth the Sons Of B. MILT 129
belief:
all b. is for it JOHNSON:S 196
b. certainly seems to get stronger GREENE:G 20
b. is not true because AMIEL 4
illogical b. in the occurrence MENCK 2
many different kinds of b. KANT 9
unity in religious b. would further STEPHEN:FJ 2
beliefs:
dust of exploded b. MADAN 2
holding two contradictory b. ORWELL 35
believe:
Apella the Jew may b. it HORACE 69
being born to b. DISR:B 65
B. a woman or an epitaph BYR 10
b. also in me BIBLE 487
b., because they so were bred DRYD 89
b., falsely, to be the truth HAMP 2
B. it or not RIPLEY 1
B. me, you who come HORACE 26
b. more than they need DRYD 71
B. nothing of what you hear PROV 33
b. that, you'll b. anything WELLING 24
b. what I do b. more JENKINS:D 1
can b. what we choose NEWM:JH 19
can't b. impossible things CARROLL 65
courage to b. in nothing TURG 3
generally b. what they wish CAES:GJ 2
have to b. in yourself CHAPLIN 3
how much to b. of my own stories IRV 5
I b., and take it ELIZ I 8
I b. in God the Father PRAY 19
I b. in Michael Angelo SHAW 94
I b. in one God MASS 10
I b. in one God PRAY 66
I can b. in them all SHAW 85
I do b. her, though SHAK:SON 59
I do not b. in Belief FOR 15
I will not b. BIBLE 493
If you b., clap your hands BARRIE 9
leads you to B. a Lie BLAKE:W 108
Lord, I b. BIBLE 443
luck whether you b. in it or not BOHR 2
may b. ... but can never know LEVIN 3
must b. what you ought NEWM:JH 20
professing to b. what one does PAINE 9
public will b. anything SITWELL:E 11
They b. God to be there JOHNSON:S 142
They didn't b. me ROUR 1
to b. concerning God CATEC 2
To b. in God is to yearn UNA 5
undesirable to b. a proposition RUSS:B 9
Unless you b., you will not AUGUS 10
verb meaning 'to b. falsely' WITT 7
what reason does not b. VOLT 22
what we b. is not necessarily true BELL:C 3
Will neer B. do what BLAKE:W 92
you'll b. in me, I'll b. in you CARROLL 79
believed:
b. always, everywhere VINCE 1
If you b. in me HARBU 2
not seen, and yet have b. BIBLE 494
two things that will be b. of any TARK 1
What has always been b. VALERY 3
believers: So long as there are earnest b. BAGE 26
believes:
each b. his own POPE 5
true he more readily b. BACON:F[1] 21
believeth:
b. all things BIBLE 522
whosoever b. in him BIBLE 477
believing:
b. their own lies ARB 1
B. where we cannot prove TENNY 122
no b. a word they say WELLING 23
Seeing is b. PROV 341
torture them, into b. NEWM:JH 1
bell:
B., book, and candle SHAK:KING J 11
b.-swarmèd HOPK:GM 12
Ding, dong, b. NURS 9
for whom the *b.* tolls DONNE 100
heart as sound as a b. SHAK:MUCH 17
I shall b. the cat DOUGLAS:Arc 1
merry as a marriage b. BYR 76
sullen b., Rememb'red tolling SHAK:HEN.IV[2] 4
surly sullen b. SHAK:SON 32
that sauncing b. RALE 4
Thrice rung the b. POPE 37
tinkledy-binkledy-winkled a b. LEAR 25
Twilight and evening b. TENNY 297
Who will b. the cat? DESCH 1
bell-man: stayed up till the b. came PEPYS 1
bellman: fatal b. SHAK:MAC 35
bellows: My b. too have lost ANON 139
bells:
belles ryngeth to evensonge HAWES 2
b. all peal the hour of nine NEIL 1
b. have knoll'd to church SHAK:AS 33
b. in your parlours SHAK:OTH 19
b. of Hell go ting-a-ling ANON 32
b. on her toes NURS 58
B. Put out their Tongues DICKIN:E 8
b. they sound so clear HOUSM 11
Christmas b. from hill to hill TENNY 143
Christmas morning b. say 'Come!' BETJ 24
church b. hollowing out BETJ 33
floating many b. down CUMM 5
From the b., b., b. POE 10
heavy with b. BETJ 21
Like sweet b. jangled SHAK:HAM 104
loved the ringing of church b. CHEK 15
noisy b., be dumb HOUSM 12
Ring out, wild b. TENNY 177
St Giles's b. BETJ 13
Say the b. of St Clement's NURS 49
silver b. and cockle shells NURS 40
who lives between five b. SLESS 4
belly:
army ... goes on its b. FRED 5
banish hunger by rubbing the b. DIOG 6
best fits a little bellie HERR 37
Dragging its slimy b. ELIOT:TS 43
eye is bigger than the b. PROV 112
fellow with the great b. SHAK:HEN.IV[2] 10
filled his b. with the husks BIBLE 463
great pod of her b. swelled HOPE:Al 2
he who does not mind his b. JOHNSON:S 127
in the b. of the fish BIBLE 359
noise in the beast's b. MALORY 2
O bely! O stynkyng cod CHAUC 69
overfilled b. will not study PROV 197
room for the bouncing B. JONS 37
something a round b. SHAK:HEN.IV[2] 13
wears his wit in his b. SHAK:TRO 7
Whose God is their b. BIBLE 540
belly-tension: b. between a man and a woman GIBBONS:S 4
belong: know how to b. to oneself MONTAIGNE 10
belongs: it b. to Him CHAPLIN 1
beloved:
never be belovd by Men BLAKE:W 85
What is thy b. more BIBLE 298
below: Faithful, b. DIBDIN:C 4
belt: see a b. without hitting ASQU:M 5
Belvoir: B.'s lordly terraces MACAULAY:TB 42
bench:
drowsy B. protect CRAB 4
suppose I am on the B. SMITH:FE 5

bend:
B. what is stiff LANGTON 2
Better b. the neck PROV 41
bends:
b. with the remover SHAK:SON 52
Though she b. him LONGFEL 22
benediction: breed Perpetual b. WORDS:W 62
benefit-club: b. for mutual flattery COLERIDGE:ST 5
benevolence:
b. of mankind does most good BAGE 19
b. of the passive order MERED:G 6
Bengal: In B., to move at all COWARD 21
benison: For a Benizon to fall HERR 4
Benn, Tony: He immatures with age* WILSON:Harold 8
Berkeley:
Bishop B. destroyed this world SMITH:Syd[1] 7
God-appointed B. YEATS 79
Berkeley Square: rested and sang in B.S. ARLEN 1
Berlin: new West-B. out of Bosnia COHN 1
Berliner: *Ich bin ein B.* KENNEDY:JF 4
Bermudas: Where the remote B. ride MARV 4
Bernard: B. the monk ne saugh nat CHAUC 93
berries: I come to pluck your B. MILT 42
berry:
God could have made a better b. BUTLER:W 1
sweeter than the B. GAY 2
Bertie: I'm Burlington B. HARG 1
beside: thou art b. thyself BIBLE 506
best:
All is b. MILT 301
all our b. men are dead PUNCH 26
b. all died LEVI:P 2
b. and the last BROWNING:R 182
b. be the enemy of the good JENKINS:R 2
b. ends by the b. means HUTCHES 1
b. good man ROCHES 6
b. is good enough GOET 27
b. is the b., though QUIL 1
b. is the enemy of the good VOLT 21
b. is yet to be BROWNING:R 184
b. lack all conviction YEATS 62
b., the wisest and most PLATO 6
b. things come in small PROV 35
b. things in life are free PROV 36
carries out, in the b. possible way GINZ 1
do the b. I can in two hours WEST:M 9
done our b. and worst, and parted BROOKE 14
Everything is for the b. VOLT 11
Fear not to touch the b. RALE 3
He is doing his b. WILDE:O 106
in the b. of all possible worlds; and the CAB 3
last and b. MILT 248
learn and propagate the b. ARNOLD:M 57
low-voiced B. is killed HARDY:T 6
not to seem but to be the b. AESC 8
where the b. is like the worst KIP 62
best man: trouble with being b.m. MURRAY:LA 4
best-seller: b. was a book which somehow BOORS 1
bestride: b. the narrow world SHAK:JUL 11
bet:
b. you which one would fly TWAIN 1
b., you wouldn't take it STOP 8
Somebody b. on the bay FOST:SC 3
Betelgeux: Aldebaran and B. shone HARDY:T 51
Bethel: God of B. DODDR 1
Bethlehem:
Beth-lehem Ephrata, though thou be little BIBLE 360
little town of B. BROOKS:P 1
Slouches towards B. YEATS 63
betray:
All things b. thee THOMP:F 8
b. The heart that loved her WORDS:W 10
guts to b. my country FORST 17
she'll b. more men SHAK:OTH 60
too late that men b. GOLDS 18
betrayal:
Just for a handful of silver* BROWNING:R 53
only defence against b. WILLIAMS:T 4
possible to succeed without b.? RENOIR:J 1
Three Judases, each one* SHAK:RIC.II 26
betrayed:
b. by what is false within MERED:G 24
Betrothed, betrayer, and betray'd SCOTT:W 62
but by ourselves, b. CONG 7
should have b. our soldiers CHURCH:W 61
betrayer: Betrothed, b., and betray'd SCOTT:W 62
betrothed: B., betrayer, and betray'd SCOTT:W 62
better:
admit it's getting b. LENNON 6
always be trying to get the b. LAMB:Ch 14
b. day, the worse dead HENRY:M 1
b. For being a little bad SHAK:MEA 40
Did I say 'b.'? SHAK:JUL 71
do not pretend to anything b. GWENN 1
done b. in my day KEPP:A 1
for b. for worse PRAY 84
gave up hope I feel so much b. OSB:J 13
He is no b. AUSTIN:A 1
I get b. and b. COUE 1
I see the b. way OSB:J 22
I took thee for thy b. SHAK:HAM 138
if I could get into a b. SWIFT 80
It is a far, far b. thing DICKENS 204
it is much b. than likely? BRONTE:P 2
little b. than one of the wicked SHAK:HEN.IV[1] 11
nae b. than he should be BURNS:R 39
no b. than you should be BEAUMO 8
pity those who are b. off POUND 15
prefer that which is truly b. MILT 313
save yourselves for b. things VIRGIL 38
she'd b. CARLYLE:T 64
shortly see b. days BEHN 4
something b. not to be BYR 21
spake worse, 'twere b. JONS 9
was a b. man than you HOMER 13
way to the B. there be HARDY:T 6
We have seen b. days SHAK:TIM 10
Were it not b. not to be? TENNY 48
When you meet someone b. CONF 16
You're a b. man than I am KIP 58
betters:
chew the fat about their b. CAMPBELL:R 5
set them above their b. MENCK 12
between:
a damn what goes on in b. BEECHAM 3
try and come b. them STRACH 5
bewildered: b. once for three days BOONE 1
bewitched:
bewitch'd with the rogue's company SHAK:HEN.IV[1] 27
You're a b. girl COWARD 16
bewitching: b. of our minds by means WITT 6
beyond: is there anything b.? BROOKE 16
bias:
b. against *understanding* BIRT 1
free from political b. ORWELL 24
biased: resent that unless it is absolutely b. VORS 1
Bible:
B. as if it was a constable's KINGSLEY:C 1
B. clash and contradict itself DOW 1
B. is literature, not dogma SANT 11
B. made England HUGO 10
B. only is the religion of Protestants CHILLING 1
B. tells me so WARNER:A 1
big ha-B. BURNS:R 13
Both read the B. day & night BLAKE:W 106
English B., a book which MACAULAY:TB 6
hanged with the B. under AUBREY 3
it was called The B. MAYER 1
only a *translation* of the B. WHATE 5
studie was but litel on the B. CHAUC 23
that book is the B. ARNOLD:M 52
bible-black: starless and b. THOMAS:D 21
Bibles:
B., Billet-doux POPE 39
we have the B. GEO:D 2
bicycle:
b. made for two DAC 1
crossing Salisbury Plain on a b. GILB:WS 52
lean our b. against a hedge FRY:C 1
like a fish needs a b. STEINEM 4
Socialism can arrive only by b. VIERA 1
Tomorrow the b. races AUD 20
bicycles: mixed up with the personalities of their b. O'BRIEN:F 4
bid: B. me to live HERR 29
bidder: withstand the highest b. WASH 2
bier: barefac'd on the b. SHAK:HAM 168
big:
because he was too b. for them BULM 1
b. words for little matters JOHNSON:S 130
just sit and be b. FITZGER:FS 2
on the side of the b. squadrons BUSSY 3
thought of b. men and little men JOHNSON:S 164
Big-Sea-Water: By the shining B. LONGFEL 20
bigger:
b. they come FITZSIM 1
seems no b. than his head SHAK:KING L 65
bigot: courteous exterior of a b. EASTM 1
bike: got on his b. and looked TEB 1
bill:
Among the defects of the B. RUSS:J[2] 3
b. of indemnity ... for raid KRUG 1
b. will hold more MERRITT 1
I love you' on the back of the b. MARX:G 17
showed me his b. of fare SWIFT 76
unpaid b., Despair SHELLEY:PB 161
Bill: Roaring B. (who killed him) BELLOC 42
billabong: camped by a b. PATERSON:AB 3
billboard: b. lovely as a tree NASH 10
billet: Every bullet has its b. WILLIAM III 1
billet-doux: Bibles, B. POPE 39
billiard: elliptical b. balls GILB:WS 74
billiards: play b. well was a sign SPENCER:H 12
billion: b. dollar country? FOST:C 1
billow: A breaking b. SHELLEY:PB 117
billows: b. smooth and bright CARROLL 53
bills:
have the b. to prove it LERN 9
inflammation of his weekly b. BYR 186
she sends in terrific b. ANTRIM 1
wife and children but as b. BACON:F[1] 84
Billy:
Silly B. HEAL 3
way for B. and me HOGG 7
Who's Silly B. now? GLOU:WF 1
youngest he was little Billee THACK 23
billy-can: I'll get a good black b. DENNIS:CJ 3
bimbos: Books and b. can be taken to bed BENJ:W 1
bind: In body and in soul can b. SCOTT:W 9
Binnorie: *bonnie mill-dams o' B.* BALL 9
biographies:
B. are like anthologies STOCKS 2
essence of innumerable b. CARLYLE:T 32
biography:
B. and memoirs can never be wholly POWELL:A 8
B. at its best is a form DAVIES:R 2
B. is about chaps BENTLEY:EC 1
b. is kept so far posted up TROLL 3
B. of great men CARLYLE:T 45
how difficult it is to write b. WEST:R 6
no history; only b. EMER 3
Nobody can write the life* JOHNSON:S 152
nothing but b. DISR:B 9
One of the new terrors* ARB 4
There is no life* CARLYLE:T 36
well-written Life is* CARLYLE:T 23
birch:
all for bringing back the b. VIDAL 5
go by climbing a b. tree FROST:R 4
bird:
b. in the hand is worth two PROV 45
b. of dawning singeth SHAK:HAM 10
b. of loudest lay SHAK:POET 3
b. of night did sit SHAK:JUL 17
B. of Time has but FITZGER:E 4
b. of wonder dies SHAK:HEN.VIII 21
b. That flutters least COWP 85
B. thou never wert SHELLEY:PB 94
b. would trust Her household HERB:G 21
early b. catches the worm PROV 87
For the death of a singing b.? DUTT 1
forgets the dying b. PAINE 4
hear the b.'s song without EMER 62
I Know Why the Caged B. Sings ANGELOU 1
immortal B. KEATS 93
Irks care the crop-full b.? BROWNING:R 185
It was the carol of a b. BYR 50
like a b. on the wing BOULTON:HE 1
Like that self-begott'n b. MILT 298
My heart is like a singing b. ROSSET:C 2
No b., but an invisible thing WORDS:W 98
No b. soars too high BLAKE:W 38

rare b. upon the earth JUV 11
regretted that he was not a b. ROCHE 3
secular b. ages of lives MILT 299
Shall I call thee b.? WORDS:W 97
song of night's sweet b. SHELLEY:PB 123
Stirred for a b. HOPK:GM 11
wakeful B. Sings darkling MILT 177
widow b. sate mourning SHELLEY:PB 150
would I were thy b. SHAK:ROM 19
young b. in this bush LEAR 2

bird of paradise:
b.o.p. among carrion crows HUGHES:B 7
If you cannot catch a b.o.p. KHRU 11

bird-song: b. at morning STEVENSON:RL 64

birdcage:
bird-cage played with toasting forks BEECHAM 9
summer b. in a garden WEBSTER:J 4

birdie: b. with a yellow bill STEVENSON:RL 56

birds:
all the b. are flown CHARLES I 2
And no b. sing KEATS 79
b. are on the wing COLERIDGE:ST 66
B. build HOPK:GM 31
B. do it PORTER:C 1
B. in the high Hall-garden TENNY 212
B. of a feather flock PROV 46
b. of the air Fell to sighing NURS 85
b., sit brooding SHAK:LOV 25
b. the colour of red-flannel THOMAS:D 40
charm of earliest B. MILT 199
Fine feathers make fine b. PROV 119
If b. confabulate or no COWP 88
lytell byrdes swetely dyde HAWES 1
Melodious b. sing madrigals MARLOWE 50
Near all the b. Will sing BROWNING:EB 16
nest of singing b. JOHNSON:S 88
no b. as happy as we LEAR 22
pipe of half awaken'd b. TENNY 109
sing like b. i' th' cage SHAK:KING L 79
song of the b. for mirth GUR 1
suffers little b. to sing SHAK:TIT 3
sweet b.' marriage hymns ELIOT:G 46
think caged b. sing WEBSTER:J 12
time of the singing of b. BIBLE 295
two blue-grey b., chasing WILLIAMS:WC 1
Two little dicky b. NURS 81
very merciful to the b. ANON 260

birk: ane there sprang a b. BALL 40

Birmingham:
I wanted to go to B. LLOYD:M 1
mayor of B. in an off-year LLOYD GEO 15
night we went to B. CHESTERTON 8
not great hopes from B. AUSTEN 55

Birnam wood:
Great B.w. to high Dunsinane SHAK:MAC 84
Till B.w. remove to Dunsinane SHAK:MAC 108

birth:
at my b. The frame SHAK:HEN.IV[1] 55
at the hour of our b. ELIOT:TS 64
B., and copulation, and death ELIOT:TS 68
b. and death, are not experienced MANN:T 7
b. is but a sleep and a forgetting WORDS:W 58
b. to eighteen, a girl needs TUCK 1
bring this monstrous b. to the world's SHAK:OTH 18
first time that we smell the air* SHAK:KING L 74
fit a bed for this huge b. CRASH 12
for the dead b. is certain BHAG 2
I had seen b. and death ELIOT:TS 63
Land of our b. KIP 116
leaves his well belov'd imprisonment* DONNE 79
long descent of b. MILT 284
My mother groand* BLAKE:W 75
no cure for b. and death SANT 7
quaking muscles in the act of b. HOPE:Al 2
sudden and portentous b. SCOTT:W 28
There was a B., certainly ELIOT:TS 63

birth control: Rome to discuss b.c. SABIA 1

birth-rate: provoke the world into a rising b. FRY:C 11

birthday:
b. of my life Is come ROSSET:C 3
My b. began with water-Birds THOMAS:D 13
remembers a woman's b. but never FROST:R 21

birthright:
b. for very bad pottage WILDE:O 37
his b. for a mess of potage BIBLE 54
sold his b. unto Jacob BIBLE 56

biscuit:
b., or confectionary plum COWP 90
dry as the remainder b. SHAK:AS 31
fellow even enjoy a b. PORTL 1
he took a captain's b. DICKENS 107

biscuit box: It didn't look like a b.b. COWARD 2

bishop:
another B. dead MELBOU 8
b. kick a hole in a stained CHAND 2
How can a b. marry? SMITH:Syd[1] 22
Make him a b. CHESTERFIELD 35
No b., no king JAMES VI/I 4
symbol of a b. is a crook DIX:GEA 1
think of contradicting a B. JOHNSON:S 240

bishopric: talk of *merit* for a b. WESTMOR 1

bishops:
B. like best in their Clergy SMITH:Syd[1] 4
b. were seen leaving the Athenaeum HERB:AP 18
Send down upon our B. PRAY 26

bit:
b. by him that comes behind SWIFT 70
b. him till he bled HOFFMAN:H 3
came up and b. them on the ass ZAPPA 1
for requital b. his fingers CHILLING 2
went mad and b. the man GOLDS 15

bitch:
if the b. bark, go out PROV 185
old b. gone in the teeth POUND 29

bitches:
Come on, you sons of b. DALY:D 1
Now we are all sons of b. BAIN 1

bite:
apprehensive whether they will b. me SPENCER:S 1
Barking dogs seldom b. PROV 28
b. every time for fishermen MORTON:JB 3
b. some of my other generals GEO II 2
b. the hand that fed them BURKE:E 81
don't b. anyone LAMB:Ch 32
guts to b. people STREAT 1
helped him b. it PEREL 3
man recovered of the b. GOLDS 16
read those books which b. KAF 12

bites:
dead woman b. not GRAY:P 1
feeds the hand that b. him PETER 2
man b. a dog that is news BOGART:JB 1
only write about what b. you STOP 15
when a man b. a dog DANA 2

biting:
b. rascals DIOG 3
b. the hand that lays GOLDWYN 5
His b. is immortal SHAK:ANT 69
you don't stop b. your fingernails ROGERS:W 9

bitter:
b. God to follow SWIN 33
something b. that is a torment LUCRET 11

bittern: He heard the b. call GRAVES:R 4

bitterness: must have no hatred or b. CAVELL 1

black:
a b. Nero HILLS 1
any colour so long as it's b. FORD:H 2
be the heavens with b. SHAK:HEN.VI[1] 1
big b. boundin' beggar KIP 50
b. and merciless things JAMES:H 20
b. and white, cut and dried JACK:R 1
b. as a tar-barrel CARROLL 51
b., as if bereav'd of light BLAKE:W 27
b. as our loss SITWELL:E 8
B. as the Pit from pole HENL 1
b. hat – which isn't there BOWEN:L 2
b. it stood as Night MILT 167
b. kitten's fault entirely CARROLL 42
b. man ... one destiny FANON 1
b. men fought on the coast MACAULAY:TB 8
b. ram is tupping SHAK:OTH 4
B. schoolchildren started rioting PATON 4
b. sheep in every flock PROV 375
b. South Africans said to white PATON 5
B.'s not so b. CANN 5
cannot change from b. to white HOFFMAN:H 6
devil damn thee b. SHAK:MAC 109
don't believe in b. majority rule SMITH:I 1
for I am b. SHAK:OTH 38
future is ... b. BALD:J 5
gods are snub-nosed and b. XENOPHAN 1
here in b. and white JONS 5
I am b., but comely BIBLE 293
I am b., but O! my soul BLAKE:W 27
I'm b. an' I'm proud DOYLE: R 1
music played by the b. man X 4
not as a b. but as a man PLOM 9
not so b. as he is painted PROV 69
readst b. where I read White BLAKE:W 106
rights of the b. man in this country X 2
sees b. people as expendable TUTU 1
she is become as b. SHAK:TWO 13
Take them down in b. and white BYROM 4
Tip me the b. spot STEVENSON:RL 29
Two lovely b. eyes COBORN 1
Walk the b. path CAMPBELL:ATA 1
what b. hours we have spent HOPK:GM 26
you always wear b.? CHEK 1

black-eyed: black-ey'd Susan came aboard GAY 37

Black Marias: Where the B.M. clatter SLESS 7

black widow: B.W., death LOWELL:R 3

blackberries:
prove a micher and eat b.? SHAK:HEN.IV[1] 49
reasons were as plentiful as b. SHAK:HEN.IV[1] 42
sit round it and pluck b. BROWNING:EB 21

blackberry: b. would adorn the parlors WHITMAN 6

blackbird:
b. whistling Or just after STEVENS 8
b.'s tune BROWNING:R 103

blackbirds:
Four and twenty b. NURS 66
full of b. than of cherries ADDIS 26

blackened: face b. by charcoal EDGE 8

blackens:
b. all the water about him ADDIS 25
b. every blot TENNY 235

blacker: Leaving a b. air HARDY:T 43

blackguard:
b. may be slow to think KIP 9
fellow is a b. HORACE 67
Sesquipedalian b. CLOUGH 2

blackie: I could hear a b. sing PATERSON:A 2

blackman: Until we give back to the B. HERB:X 3

blackness:
gross b. underneath TENNY 9
Some nocturnal b. HARDY:T 34

Blackpool:
little stick of B. rock FORMBY 2
seaside place called B. EDGAR 1

blacks: or to fleece the b. CAMPBELL:R 1

bladder: blows a man up like a b. SHAK:HEN.IV[1] 48

blade:
B. on the feather CORY 4
bloody blameful b. SHAK:MID 47
His b. struck the water COKE:D 1
magic b., begins to rust DAVIDS 5
trenchant b., Toledo trusty BUTLER:S[1] 14
vorpal b. went snicker-snack CARROLL 46

Blake: B. was no good because BUTLER:S[2] 30

blame:
b. not the bard MOORE:T 11
Bricks of b. pave the floor KENNELLY 3
know who are to b. PLATO 5
neither is most to b. SWIN 39
poor wot gets the b. ANON 38
responsibility but not the b. SEMP 1

blameless: white flower of a b. life TENNY 235

bland: demeanour nobly b. GILB:WS 107

blank verse:
b.v. has suffered not only ELIOT:TS 112
even road of a b.v. SHAK:MUCH 33
much b.v., and blanker BYR 151

blankets: rough male kiss of b. BROOKE 20

blanks: historians left b. POUND 32

blaring: two weeks of blotching and b. CARLYLE:T 72

blasphemies: great truths begin as b. SHAW 115

blasphemy: in the soldier is flat b. SHAK:MEA 14

blast: wert thou in the cauld b. BURNS:R 121

blasted:
b. with excess of light GRAY:T 35
no sooner blown but b. MILT 2

blaze:
b. Is infinite, eternal LOWELL:R 3
unclouded b. of living light BYR 34
blazed: My body of a sudden b. YEATS 89
blazes: b., and expires BYR 17
bleak: seeing it b., knowing it is so O'KEEFFE:G 1
bled: God b., but with man's blood HUGHES:Te 5
bleed:
and then we b. SHELLEY:PB 58
do we not b.? SHAK:MERC 32
I b. SHELLEY:PB 45
lay me downe and b. BALL 46
shall Caesar b. in sport SHAK:JUL 38
bleeding: thou b. piece of earth SHAK:JUL 43
blemish: no b. but the mind SHAK:TWE 53
bless:
B. relaxes BLAKE:W 49
B. the Lord, all the works BIBLE 606
B. the Lord, O my soul BIBLE 231
b. them that curse you BIBLE 387
b. ye the Lord PRAY 12
b. you real good GRAHAM:B 1
except thou b. me BIBLE 65
Lord b. thee, and keep BIBLE 114
blessed:
B. are the poor in spirit BIBLE 384
b. be the name of the Lord BIBLE 181
B. is he that cometh MASS 14
B. is the man who expects nothing POPE 183
b. them unawares COLERIDGE:ST 27
call her b. BIBLE 277
His b. part to heaven SHAK:HEN.VIII 15
I was b. and could bless YEATS 89
more b. to give than BIBLE 504
whom thou blessest is b. BIBLE 118
blesses: church can't prevent, it b. TUCHOL 10
blesseth: It b. him that gives SHAK:MERC 44
blessing:
b. money cannot buy WALT 15
b. will not feed PROV 47
continual dew of thy b. PRAY 26
earnest in the pursuit of the b. AUSTEN 37
enjoy but half the B. GAY 3
God had made her for a b. BRIDGES:R 12
Lord, behold us with Thy b. BUCKO 1
Lord, dismiss us with Thy b. BUCKO 2
taken away thy b. BIBLE 59
blessings:
B. abound where'er WATTS 17
b. in disguise HERV 1
from whom all b. flow KEN 3
glasse of b. standing by HERB:G 43
too happy if they knew their b. VIRGIL 25
blest:
always To be b. POPE 83
I *have been* b. BYR 28
It is twice b. SHAK:MERC 44
blether: seek out friens to hae a b. GARIO 1
blight: b. man was born for HOPK:GM 17
blind:
Altho' a poor b. boy CIB 8
among the b. the one-eyed ERAS 1
b. as any noonday owl TENNY 259
B. as the nineteen hundred SITWELL:E 8
b., behold your Saviour WESLEY:C 4
b. from sheer supremacy KEATS 51
b. man battering b. men YEATS 99
b. man in a dark room BOWEN:L 2
b. man On the sightless horse WALEY 1
B. with thine hair the eyes SHELLEY:PB 146
country of the b., the one-eyed PROV 201
Country of the B. the One-eyed WELLS:HG 8
deaf man to a b. woman COLERIDGE:ST 98
halt, and the b. BIBLE 461
I have a right to be b. NELS 8
I was eyes to the b. BIBLE 190
if love be b. SHAK:ROM 29
If the b. lead the b. BIBLE 416
Love is b. PROV 250
Painting is a b. man's profession PICAS 1
splendid work for the b. SASS 6
Thou b. fool, Love SHAK:SON 58
though she is b. BACON:F[1] 64
to her faults a little b. PRIOR 4
unbelief is b. MILT 34
will accompany my being b. PEPYS 25
wing'd Cupid painted b. SHAK:MID 5
Ye b. guides BIBLE 427
blind-worm: b.'s sting SHAK:MAC 79
blindfold: b. and alone KIP 152
blindness:
eye for an eye leads only to more b. ATWOOD 5
incurable disease – colour b. DE BL 2
triple sight in b. keen KEATS 32
blinds:
b. let through the day HOUSM 35
drawing-down of b. OWEN:W 3
must dust the b. THOMAS:D 24
blinked: other fellow just b. RUSK 1
blinking: b. sort o' place HARDY:T 65
bliss:
B. in our brows' bent SHAK:ANT 17
b. is not an ideal of reason KANT 5
B. was it in that dawn WORDS:W 159
certainty of waking b. MILT 27
deprived of everlasting b.? MARLOWE 34
each to his point of b. BROWNING:R 154
enjoy their fill Of b. on b. MILT 197
flood of the sea of b. WAG 1
Land of Perfect B. SHINRAN 1
men call domestic b. PATMO 10
mighty b. is fugitive VIRGIL 28
moment may with b. repay CAMPBELL:T 22
mutual and partak'n b. MILT 38
promise of pneumatic b. ELIOT:TS 33
sum of earthly b. MILT 235
blithe:
be you b. and bonny SHAK:MUCH 13
buxom, b., and debonair MILT 66
Hail to thee, b. spirit SHELLEY:PB 94
blitz: b. of a boy is Timothy Winters CAUS 1
blizzard: willingly to his death in a b. ATK:EL 1
bloated: To swell one b. Chief's BYR 59
block:
chopper on a big black b. GILB:WS 70
old b. itself BURKE:E 105
blockhead:
bookful b. POPE 27
No man but a b. ever wrote JOHNSON:S 184
talking b. FARQ 12
when a b.'s insult points JOHNSON:S 63
blocks: You b., you stones SHAK:JUL 2
blokes: peopled with good b. and bastards HARRIS:M 3
blond: magnificent *b. beast* NIET 2
blonde:
b. to make a bishop kick CHAND 2
springing from b. to b. WODE 28
blondes: Gentlemen Prefer B. LOOS 1
blood:
achieved by 'b. and iron' BISM 7
beauty fires the b. DRYD 118
b. and battles was my youth ARNOLD:M 32
B. and soil DARRE 1
b. and talk of modesty MIDD 6
b. be the price of admiralty KIP 88
b. Came gargling from OWEN:W 5
b., dirt and sucked sugar YEATS 145
B. is compulsory STOP 4
b. is nipp'd SHAK:LOV 25
B. is thicker than water PROV 48
b. Is very snow-broth SHAK:MEA 4
b. more stirs SHAK:HEN.IV[1] 21
b. of Christians is the seed TERT 3
b. on my hands than water GREENE:G 14
b. Spoke in her cheeks DONNE 77
b. will have b. SHAK:MAC 74
b. with guilt is bought SHELLEY:PB 69
b.'s a rover HOUSM 4
by crikey b. will tell MARQUIS 2
by man shall his b. be shed BIBLE 42
causing their brothers' b. to be ZAPA 1
drop my b. for drachmas SHAK:JUL 72
examine well your b. SHAK:MID 1
Flesh and B. can't bear it BYROM 3
flesh and b. so cheap HOOD 21
fountain fill'd with b. COWP 5
get b. out of a stone PROV 440
give me B. DICKENS 160
good enough to shed his b. ROOS:T 3
guiltless of his country's b. GRAY:T 20
I smell the b. of an Englishman NURS 11
I smell the bloud of an English-man NASHE 5
idea of tasting your menstrual b. GREER 5
in b. down Palace walls BLAKE:W 74
in b. Stepp'd in so far SHAK:MAC 75
'Let there be b.!' says man BYR 216
like it for cooling the b. FLAND 1
lose more b. with love SHAK:MUCH 2
Make thick my b. SHAK:MAC 20
moment when the moon was b. CHESTERTON 1
most noble b. of all SHAK:JUL 40
my b. . . . will contribute to the growth GAND:I 2
never end this life of b. ARNOLD:M 32
no getting b. out of a turnip MARR 3
Nothing like b. THACK 8
nothing to offer but b., toil CHURCH:W 11
odour of b. when Christ YEATS 78
old man to have had so much b. SHAK:MAC 100
part of my b.'s country WRIGHT:J 4
poison the whole b. stream EMPS 3
precious B. which the King THOMAS AQ 1
reaped in b. BLAKE:W 10
red with guiltless b. SHELLEY:PB 5
rivers of b., and years of desolation JEFFERSON 14
sanction to the trade of b.? SHELLEY:PB 1
smell the b. of a British man SHAK:KING L 51
smell the b. still SHAK:MAC 102
sprung Of Earth's first b. WORDS:W 44
stench of b. makes sick BLAKE:W 3
still the b. is strong GALT 1
still the b. is strong SCOTT:W 66
summon up the b. SHAK:HEN.V 17
that all that b. was shed YEATS 37
that sheds his b. with me SHAK:HEN.V 40
thick man's b. with cold COLERIDGE:ST 20
Tiber foaming with much b. POWELL:E 1
Tiber foaming with much b. VIRGIL 65
to Heaven for Human b. BLAKE:W 83
to shed innocent b. BIBLE 332
trading on the b. of my men LEE:RE 3
two kinds of b., the b. that flows TUWIM 1
voice of thy brother's b. crieth BIBLE 28
walks again on the Seas of B. SITWELL:E 9
washed in the b. of the Lamb? HOFFMAN 1
We be of one b. KIP 14
Whoso sheddeth man's b. BIBLE 42
with b. Of human sacrifice MILT 126
with the b. of patriots and tyrants JEFFERSON 10
without letting b. SHAK:RIC.II 2
young b. must have its course KINGSLEY:C 19
blood-thirsty: b. clinging to life ARNOLD:M 55
bloodless: b. lay the untrodden snow CAMPBELL:T 19
bloody:
b., bold, and resolute SHAK:MAC 82
b., but unbowed HENL 1
last act is b. PASC 9
No more b. wars MARY QUEEN CON 4
often wipe a b. nose GAY 47
What b. man is that? SHAK:MAC 2
bloom:
b. of young Desire GRAY:T 33
breath and the b. of the year BROWNING:R 212
How can ye b. BURNS:R 96
hung with b. along the bough HOUSM 3
Life's a piece in b. HENL 3
sort of b. on a woman BARRIE 10
sweet of earliest b. COLLINS:Will 2
with the b. go I. ARNOLD:M 42
Bloom: When in doubt persecute B. JOYCE:J 25
blossom:
b. as the rose BIBLE 317
b. in purple and red TENNY 219
b. into a Duchess AILES 1
b. that hangs on the bough SHAK:TEM 31
full spring-tide of b. BETJ 18
Love's perfect b. PATMO 2
blossoms:
in the b. of my sin SHAK:HAM 48
thousand B. within the Day FITZGER:E 5
blot:
Art to b. POPE 146
B. out, correct SWIFT 67
scarce received from him a b. HEMING 2
what they discreetly b. WALLER 10
blotching: two weeks of b. and blaring CARLYLE:T 72

blotted:
b. from life's page BYR 72
b. it out for ever STERNE 28
had b.-out a thousand AUBREY 11
Would he had b. a thousand JONS 54
blow:
been struck a deep mortal b. AESC 3
b. and whistle at the same PLAU 4
B. him again to me TENNY 105
b. in cold blood SHAW 58
B. me about in winds SHAK:OTH 68
b. them at the moon SHAK:HAM 149
b., thou winter wind SHAK:AS 35
b. up the universe unawares RUTH 2
first b. is half GOLDS 72
hand that gave the b. DRYD 60
he was but a word and a b. BUNYAN 10
perhaps return the b. CANN 6
take one b., and turn HOLMES:OW 8
who does not return your b. SHAW 69
who gets his b. in fust BILL 1
bloweth: wind b. where it listeth BIBLE 476
blowing: blowin' in the wind DYL 1
blown: no sooner b. but blasted MILT 2
blows:
apostolic b. and knocks BUTLER:S[1] 12
b. hot and cold AESOP 6
B. out his brains upon the flute BROWNING:R 208
blubbered: blubber'd is that pretty face PRIOR 9
bludgeoning: b. of the people by WILDE:O 38
blue:
b. above the trees KEATS 30
B., b. is the grass POUND 8
b. days at sea STEVENSON:RL 64
b. remembered hills HOUSM 24
deeply, beautifully b. SOUTHEY 10
Little boy b. NURS 33
no objection to the b. stocking JEFFREY 2
that b. is all in a rush HOPK:GM 8
too expressive to be b. ARNOLD:M 11
'Twas Presbyterian true b. BUTLER:S[1] 10
blue-stocking: I'm a sort of b. THOMP:Em 1
blueprint: fatal blue-print And he signed it BUZZ 1
blueprints: fuss of ballads than of b. COPE 1
blues: I got the Weary B. HUGHES:L 1
blunder: so grotesque a b. BENTLEY:EC 8
blundered: Someone had blunder'd TENNY 199
blunders:
escaped making the b. HELPS 3
one of Nature's agreeable b. COWLEY:H 1
bluntness: having been prais'd for b. SHAK:KING L 25
blush:
b. is no language ELIOT:G 44
b. to find it Fame POPE 152
born to b. unseen GRAY:T 20
her b. is guiltiness SHAK:MUCH 25
If not, with a b. retire DICKENS 230
not b. so to be admir'd WALLER 3
see a young man b. CATO 3
She look'd down to b. SCOTT:W 22
would it bring a b. into the cheek DICKENS 220
blushed:
blush'd at herself SHAK:OTH 7
saw her God and b. CRASH 1
blushes: Only Animal that B. TWAIN 28
blushing:
b. into the very whites of DICKENS 34
B. is becoming GOLDO 1
take b. either for a sign CONG 38
Bo-peep:
As if they started at B. HERR 33
Little B. has lost NURS 32
Boadicea: some bargain basement B. HEAL 5
boar: b. without bristles had YEATS 21
boar-pig: little tidy Bartholomew b. SHAK:HEN.IV[2] 28
board: wasn't any B., and now HERB:AP 10
boardrooms: in b. more important CASSIDY 1
boards: all the b. did shrink COLERIDGE:ST 19
boast: B. not thyself of to morrow BIBLE 272
boasteth: then he b. BIBLE 266
boastful:
b. of her hoard GOLDS 8
b. soldier PLAU 3
boastings: b. as the Gentiles use KIP 93
boat:
as well, if the B. went even HALIF 1
beautiful pea-green b. LEAR 18
best fits a little B. HERR 37
deposit us in Charon's b. HORACE 20
frail b. to the cruel sea HORACE 4
My b. is on the shore BYR 130
My b. sails freely SHAK:OTH 25
On a slow b. to China LOES 1
Speed, bonny b. BOULTON:HE 1
Until I have a little B. WORDS:W 126
boating: Jolly b. weather CORY 4
boatman: B., do not tarry CAMPBELL:T 11
boats:
b. against the current FITZGER:FS 9
messing about in b. GRAHAME 2
We seek happiness in b. HORACE 87
bobbin: Hades' b. bound in mummy-cloth YEATS 86
bodice: lace my b. blue HUNTER:A 1
bodies:
b. of those that made EDWARDS:J 1
b. why do we forebear? DONNE 36
friendless b. of unburied men WEBSTER:J 10
go forth ... with well-developed b. FORST 14
our dead b. must tell the tale SCOTT:Rob 3
Pile the b. high at Austerlitz SANDBURG 2
rent our b. for sexual services SCOTT:V 1
to your scattered b. go DONNE 82
bodkin: With a bare b.? SHAK:HAM 97
Bodleian: so describe the B. library HOUSM 54
body:
Absence of b. PUNCH 4
Absent in b. BIBLE 519
ask me for my b. as a plaything SHAW 99
beautiful and passionate b. SWIN 22
b. is a machine for living TOLS:L 3
B. is a portion of Soul BLAKE:W 32
b. is born young WILDE:O 59
b. is his book DONNE 38
b. is not more than the soul WHITMAN 10
b. like a wardrobe THOMAS:D 31
b. of a weak and feeble woman ELIZ I 3
b. of man is capable of much CAB 2
b. will be guarded from LOWELL:A 1
b.'s beauty lives STEVENS 5
b.'s delicate SHAK:KING L 40
brief loan of his own b. CAB 2
commit his b. to the deep PRAY 95
commit his b. to the ground PRAY 92
examining every part of my b. JOHN PAUL 2
familiar with Africa than my own b. ORTON 1
filling some other B. KEATS 145
Gin a b. meet BURNS:R 119
Hail the true b. ANON 5
healthy mind in a healthy b. JUV 23
Her b. looms above him CAMPBELL:R 4
her b. thought DONNE 77
His b. is perfectly spherical LEAR 6
human b. is sacred WHITMAN 14
If I had the use of my b. BECKETT 13
Make less thy b. hence SHAK:HEN.IV[2] 54
My b. of a sudden blazed YEATS 89
My b. turns to you HEWETT 3
mystery of the glorious B. THOMAS AQ 1
mystical b. of thy Son PRAY 60
Naught broken save this b. BROOKE 24
nothing the b. suffers MERED:G 14
Over my dead b. KAUFMANN 3
own and control her own b. SANG 1
patch up thine old b. SHAK:HEN.IV[2] 28
provinces of his b. revolted AUD 36
revoltingly tufted areas of the b. FRY:S 4
soul and b. part like friends CRASH 16
soul, how small a b. holds JUV 22
soule the bodie forme doth SPENS 47
Thersites' b. is as good SHAK:CYM 16
Thy b. is all vice JOHNSON:S 92
To keep the b. young YEATS 57
whereby the Soul and B. are united SWIFT 50
Why be given a b. MANS:K 1
with my b. I thee worship PRAY 86
Boer War: bungled, unwise war* PLOM 1
bog: This Bolshevik b. MACDIAR 21
Bogart: After that he thinks he's B. CHASEN 1
boggy: dark, b., dirty GOLDS 71
Bognor: Bugger B. GEO V 5
Bogside: PARAS THIRTEEN B. NIL ANON 231
bogus: She's genuinely b. HASS 1
boil:
b. breaking forth BIBLE 93
We b. at different degrees EMER 58
boiler: United States is like a gigantic b. GREY 2
boilers: fire the b. on what lonely HEWETT 1
boils: watched pot never b. PROV 413
bois: along the B. Bou-long GILB:F 1
bold:
Be not too b. SPENS 38
b. bad man SPENS 23
righteous are b. as a lion BIBLE 274
This b. bad man SHAK:HEN.VIII 5
boldest: b. measures are the safest LIVY 3
boldness:
B. be my friend SHAK:CYM 1
B., more b., always b. DANTON 1
Familiarity begets b. MARM 2
Bolingbroke:
this canker, B.? SHAK:HEN.IV[1] 20
Who now reads B.? BURKE:E 61
bollocks: 'B.' *sotto voce* to the bishops HAILS 4
Bolshevik: This B. bog MACDIAR 21
bolts: fool b. pleasure ANTRIM 2
bomb:
best defence against the atom b. ANON 165
blown to bits by a terrorist b. EAMES:R 1
b. them into the Stone Age LEMAY 1
climber with a b. in his pocket ORWELL 9
Don't let anyone b. me BETJ 8
hydrogen b. is history's exclamation point MCLUH 15
bombast: b. out a blanke verse GREENE:R 2
bombazine: B. would have shown a deeper GASK 6
bombed:
ARP'd or b. out of existence MACMILL:H 2
I'm glad we've been b. ELIZ:QM 1
bomber: b. will always get through BALD:S 2
bombing: begin b. in five minutes REAG 2
bombs:
b. *are* unbelievable until WHITE:P 6
b., you're going to hit civilians GOLDWATER 2
Come, friendly b. BETJ 6
next war will be fought with atom b. UREY 1
bon mot: produce an occasional *b.m.* BALZ 12
Bonar Law: Unknown Prime Minister* ASQU:HH 3
bond:
Englishman's word is his b. PROV 96
not the b. of man and wife TENNY 255
take a b. of fate SHAK:MAC 83
word is as good as his b. PROV 175
bondage:
B. is hoarse SHAK:ROM 18
b. which is Freedom's self SHELLEY:PB 6
out of the house of b. BIBLE 103
whole eternity in b. ADDIS 6
bondmaid: b. who sat in our hall PRINGLE:T 3
bondman:
Check'd like a b. SHAK:JUL 73
so base that would be a b.? SHAK:JUL 47
bonds:
garters to be b. and shackles BACON:F[1] 82
people to dissolve the political b. JEFFERSON 1
without b. and without depth BORCH 1
bondsmen: Hereditary B. BYR 69
bone:
as curs mouth a b. CHURCH:C 8
B. and Skin, two millers thin BYROM 3
B. of my B. thou art MILT 250
b. of my bones BIBLE 14
dog deserves a good b. PROV 152
every b. a-stare BROWNING:R 95
nearer the b., the sweeter PROV 279
boneless: 50 years to see the b. wonder CHURCH:W 7
bones:
be he that moves my b. SHAK:MISC 2
Bleach the b. of comrades HOUSM 22
b. are very brittle STEVENSON:RL 49
b. polished by diligent ants WRIGHT:J 3
brittle strength of b. MILT 127
can these b. live? BIBLE 346
canoniz'd b., hearsed in death SHAK:HAM 36
England keep my b. SHAK:KING J 19
from the ashes of my b. VIRGIL 62
he hadde pigges b. CHAUC 32

I'll grind his b. NURS 11
lay my b. amongst you WOLSEY 1
lovely in her b. ROETH 2
memory of some b. SLESS 5
mock'd the dead b. SHAK:RIC.III 9
Of his b. are coral SHAK:TEM 11
roots are wrapt about the b. TENNY 127
sit in my b. SMITH:Syd[1] 27
stones may break my b. PROV 353
to subsist in b. BROWNE:T 56
weave their thread with b. SHAK:TWE 28
whose b. Lie scatter'd MILT 99
ye dry b. BIBLE 347
bonfire: To the dodecaphonic b. MACDIAR 25
bong-tree: land where the B. grows LEAR 19
bonhomie: Overcame his natural b. BENTLEY:EC 6
bonkers: it will be stark, staring b. HAILS 2
bonnet:
follow the b. of Bonny Dundee SCOTT:W 67
Off goes his b. SHAK:RIC.II 13
bonnets: Blue B. are bound for the Border SCOTT:W 59
bonnie: My B. lies over the ocean ANON 29
Bononcini: Some say, that Signor B. BYROM 2
booby: give her b. for another? GAY 43
boojum:
If your Snark be a B. CARROLL 90
Snark *was* a B. CARROLL 92
book:
all the needs a b. has TROLL 32
any b. should be banned WEST:R 2
as a moral or an immoral b. WILDE:O 19
away and write a b. about it BRAB 1
bad b. is as much of a labour HUX:A 22
better than a printed b. SWIFT 60
b. belongs to the very few NIET 19
b. is somehow sacred STEINB 4
b. is the best of friends TUP 3
b. is the world's most patient FRYE:N 1
B. learning certainly increases knowledge KANT 10
b. may be amusing GOLDS 48
b. must be the axe KAF 13
B. of Life begins with WILDE:O 60
b. of my enemy has been remaindered JAMES:B 2
B. of Songs and Sonnets here SHAK:MERR 2
b. that made this great war LINC 29
b. to kill time for those MACAULAY:R 8
b. where men May read SHAK:MAC 21
b. would have been finished in half WODE 13
b. written against fame EMER 86
B.'s a b., although BYR 8
Booke is the pretious life-blood MILT 313
can't tell a b. by its cover PROV 446
Charlotte has been writing a b. BRONTE:P 2
cover of an old b. FRANKLIN:B 21
dainties that are bred in a b. SHAK:LOV 10
Death put down his b. AUD 23
delight me for to print My b. HERR 3
do not throw this b. about BELLOC 33
each b. should be a new beginning HEMINGWAY 11
Every age hath its b. KORAN 3
Farewel my bok CHAUC 94
first praises a good b. LANDOR 18
flicks through every b. HANDKE 1
Go, litel bok CHAUC 120
Go, little b. STEVENSON:RL 59
got around to reading the b. MARX:G 21
great b. is like great evil CALLIM 2
greatest b. of English prose? QUIL 2
half a library to make one b. JOHNSON:S 168
He gets at the substance of a b. KNOW 1
his commonplace b. be full SWIFT 6
If a b. is worth reading RUSKIN 23
I'll drown my b. SHAK:TEM 30
in him to write one b. MAUGH 15
Is it a b. you would even wish GRIFFITH-J 1
leaves of the Judgment B. unfold TAYL:B 1
like a b. in breeches SMITH:Syd[1] 29
little volume, but large b. CRASH 3
making of a b. ... is a craft LA BRU 13
man behind the b. EMER 43
most valuable b. by chance GRAY:T 41
motives for reading a b. RUSS:B 16
My b. is licentious MARTIAL 1
name out of the b. of life BIBLE 575
Never judge a b. by its cover LEB 1
never read a b. before reviewing SMITH:Syd[1] 35
no b. – it is a plaything PEAC 10
no doubt in this b. KORAN 1
Not on his picture, but his b. JONS 51
one English b. and one only ARNOLD:M 52
only b. that ever took him out of bed JOHNSON:S 144
possession of a b. becomes BURGESS:A 7
read the b. of fate SHAK:HEN.IV[2] 32
reader seldom peruses a b. ADDIS 14
reader that makes the good b. EMER 66
review a bad b. without showing off AUD 60
shut the b. and sit him SHAK:HEN.IV[2] 33
There is a b. KEBLE 5
thick, square b. GLOU:W 1
this B., the most valuable thing CORON 1
until he has written a b. JOW 2
warmth, sleep, and a b. HAZL 39
What is the use of a b. CARROLL 1
When I am in labour with a b. THACK 29
who art able to write a B. CARLYLE:T 12
who destroyes a good Booke MILT 312
Who is worthy to open the b. BIBLE 578
without mentioning a single b. REED:H 6
would look at the best b. RUSKIN 22
writing in a b. of gold HUNT:L 4
written b. will be brought CEL 2
bookful: b. blockhead POPE 27
books:
against b. the Home Secretary is WAUGH:E 18
attention to the inside of b. CHESTERFIELD 21
be not swallowed up in b. WESLEY:J 7
B. and bimbos can be taken to bed BENJ:W 1
B. and friends should be few PROV 49
B. and marriage do not go well MOLIERE 31
B. are a load of crap LARK 6
B. are good enough in their STEVENSON:RL 18
B. are just trees with squiggles INNES 1
B., are like men their authors SWIFT 4
B. are made ... like the pyramids FLAU 6
B. are not seldom talismans COWP 81
b. are weapons ROOS:FD 15
b. arranged three by three PROUST 13
b. by which the printers FULLER:T[1] 4
B. cannot always please CRAB 12
b. consum'd the midnight oil GAY 42
B. Do Furnish a Room POWELL:A 6
B. have the same enemies as man VALERY 6
b. in the running brooks SHAK:AS 12
B. must follow sciences BACON:F[1] 17
b. never die ROOS:FD 15
B. ... propose to *instruct* or to *amuse* DEQ 8
B. that you may carry to JOHNSON:S 260
b., the arts, the academes SHAK:LOV 17
B. think for me LAMB:Ch 22
b., those spiritual repasts LAMB:Ch 6
B.! 'tis a dull and endless WORDS:W 16
b. were sweet unreproaching GOLDS 53
B. will speak plain BACON:F[1] 46
cannot learn men from b. DISR:B 2
Collection of B. CARLYLE:T 48
Deep verst in b. and shallow MILT 275
do *you* read b. *through*? JOHNSON:S 159
Few b. today are forgivable LAING 3
few friends, and many b. COWLEY:A 5
From my b. surcease POE 3
Give me B., fruit KEATS 160
God has written all the b. BUTLER:S[2] 31
his b. were read BELLOC 36
I have read all the b. MALLAR 2
I mean your *borrowers of b.* LAMB:Ch 18
If my b. had been any worse CHAND 7
I'll burn my b. MARLOWE 41
indiscriminate reviewing of b. ORWELL 38
keep my b. at the British Museum BUTLER:S[2] 12
Many are engaged in writing b. ELIOT:TS 72
many b. there is no end BIBLE 290
Medicine for the soul* DIOD 1
my b. be then the eloquence SHAK:SON 9
nation, care about b.? RUSKIN 20
needed not the spectacles of b. DRYD 135
never read b. – I *write* them PUNCH 18
No furniture as charming as b. SMITH:Syd[1] 20
not contain the b. that should BIBLE 495
Of writing many b. there is no end BROWNING:EB 15
On bokes for to rede I me CHAUC 94
only b. that influence us FORST 12
only b., Were woman's looks MOORE:T 15
out of olde bokes CHAUC 100
poring over miserable b. TENNY 85
proper study of mankind is b. HUX:A 2
quit your b. WORDS:W 15
rather studied b. than men BACON:F[1] 19
Read any good b., lately? HORNE:K 1
read those b. which bite KAF 12
reading of all good b. DESCA 3
Some b. are to be tasted BACON:F[1] 107
Some b. are undeservedly forgotten AUD 61
speaks about his own b. DISR:B 74
stranger commodity ... than b. LICHT 3
there, where they Burn b. HEINE 1
They do most by B. BROWNE:T 66
They lard their lean b. BURTON:Ro 2
This, b. can do CRAB 8
thumb each other's b. RUSKIN 21
To read too many b. is harmful MAO 7
Twenty bookes, clad in black CHAUC 19
bookseller: he once shot a b. CAMPBELL:T 24
booksellers:
Ask the b. of London BURKE:E 61
b. are generous liberal-minded JOHNSON:S 104
Not men, nor gods, nor b. HORACE 115
bookshop: second-hand b. is the sign MURD:WLF 1
boon: Is life a b.? GILB:WS 95
boot:
B., saddle, to horse BROWNING:R 14
b. stamping on a human face ORWELL 36
dapper b. TENNY 100
bootboy: body of the b. at Claridge's WOOLF:V 17
booted: ready b. and spurred to ride MACAULAY:TB 35
Booth: B. died blind LIND:V 1
bootlaces: shot than do his b. up criss-cross WELLS:HG 16
boots:
always have one's b. on MONTAIGNE 2
avalanche of overcoats and b. WHITE:P 2
b. are heavy on the floor AUD 19
B.–b.–b.–b KIP 111
come to bed in b. HERB:AP 2
dae it wi' your b. on ANON 202
elastic-sided b. and made-up bow ties SHARPE 2
gentleman: look at his b. SHAW 106
legs when I take my b. off DICKENS 140
Murray or thick b. behind CALVER 9
to the top of his army b. LLOYD GEO 16
truth has got its b. on CALLA 1
went to school without any b. BULM 1
what thick b. DICKENS 208
booze:
heavy on the b. BAXTER:JK 2
wee reliefs we ha'e in b. MACDIAR 12
bordello: to earth as a gatekeeper of a b. TOSC 1
border:
Blue Bonnets are bound for the B. SCOTT:W 59
thin, flowery b. LAMB:Ch 36
bore:
B.: A person who BIER 1
b. is a man who TAYL:BL 1
Every hero becomes a b. EMER 42
healthy male adult b. consumes UPDIKE 1
If you want to b. an Irishman SHAW 138
in it is merely a b. WILDE:O 64
It b. thy fruit and mine KYD 5
little more willingness to b. WORST 1
no greater b. than the travel b. SACK 1
old folks who are quite a b. PARNELL:A 1
proof that God is a b. MENCK 10
borealis: like the B. race BURNS:R 86
bored:
better for aged diplomats to be b. AUSTIN:WR 1
b. as enthusiasm would permit GOSSE 1
b. by the very people whom we LA ROCHE 31
Bores and *B.* BYR 231
he b. for England MUGG 6
too short – to get b.? NIET 11
wanted to be b. to death DE VR 3

boredom:
B. is a sign of satisfied ignorance BRIDIE 3
b. is the very source of death HUGO 5
effect of b. on a large scale INGE 9
Sooner barbarity than b. GAUT 2
borer: make a square meal for a b. SEMP 3
bores:
B. and *Bored* BYR 231
B. have succeeded to dragons DISR:B 6
Nancy-boys and crashing B. CAMPBELL:R 5
Borgias: under the B. they had warfare, terror WELLES 1
boring:
being b. is to say everything VOLT 4
Life, friends, is b. BERR 1
Somebody's b. me THOMAS:D 42
born:
All men are b. good CONF 18
best never to have been b. HEINE 7
better to be b. lucky PROV 203
b. about three of the clock SHAK:HEN.IV[2] 13
b., and once is enough ELIOT:TS 68
b. at the age of twelve GARL 1
b., bred, and hanged ANON 136
B. but to die POPE 89
b. free and equal ANON 153
b. free as Caesar SHAK:JUL 8
b. in 1896, and my parents were ACK 1
b. in a cellar CONG 22
b. in a merry hour SHAK:MUCH 10
b. King of the Jews? BIBLE 375
b. . . . not for ourselves alone PLATO 2
b. of the Virgin Mary ANON 5
B. on a Monday NURS 67
b. out of my due time MORRIS:W 5
b. three thousand years old DELAN 1
b. to a kiss and a smile FENT 2
b. to be forgot COWP 18
b. to himself alone QUAR 2
b. to set it right SHAK:HAM 60
b. when I was consul CIC 18
b. with your legs apart ORTON 5
can't be b., unless it's pretty nigh DICKENS 163
distant countrie I was b. BALL 27
Every moment is one b. TENNY 97
Godolphin Horne was Nobly B. BELLOC 13
greatest offence is to have been b. CALD 1
he's just b. SMITH:Syd[2] 1
hundred years before he is b. INGE 10
I am not yet b. MACNEICE 12
I was b. an American WEBSTER:D 8
I was b. in the year 1632 DEF 1
if anyone is b. to obey COMPT 3
Man was b. free ROUSS:JJ 1
neither of us had been b. NAPO I 9
Never was b. STOWE 1
No child is b. a criminal SMITH:Syd[2] 1
none of woman b. SHAK:MAC 82
not aware of being b. LA BRU 4
Not to be b. is the best AUD 9
Not to be b. is the best SOPH 5
Not to be b., or being b. BACON:F[1] 133
one and one-sixteenth is b. BABB 1
powerless to be b. ARNOLD:M 35
some are b. posthumously NIET 24
sucker b. every minute BARNUM 1
Then surely I was b. CHESTERTON 1
time to be b. BIBLE 281
took the trouble to be b. BEAUMA 4
unto us a child is b. BIBLE 308
we are b. in others' pain THOMP:F 3
When we are b., we cry SHAK:KING L 75
why was I b. with a different face? BLAKE:W 79
why wasn't I b. old and ugly? DICKENS 91
work the day he was b. STERNE 26
borne: I have b., and and b. SHAK:HEN.IV[2] 20
borogoves: mimsy were the b. CARROLL 45
borrow:
borrer the money to do it WARD:A 13
men who b., and *the men* LAMB:Ch 16
vainly had I sought to b. POE 3
borrowed: dress me In b. robes SHAK:MAC 13
borrower:
Every man is a b. EMER 65
Neither a b. nor a lender SHAK:HAM 30
borrowers: I mean your *b. of books* LAMB:Ch 18
borrowing:
b. dulls the edge SHAK:HAM 30
b. only lingers and lingers SHAK:HEN.IV[2] 17
founded on b. and debt IBS 3
goes a b. goes a sorrowing FRANKLIN:B 16
goeth a b. Goeth a sorrowing TUSS 9
implore you for five pounds* BURNS:R 129
Bosnia: new West-Berlin out of B. COHN 1
bosom:
b. black as death SHAK:HAM 131
b. to hang jewels upon DICKENS 190
Cleanse the stuff'd b. SHAK:MAC 111
Cover that b. MOLIERE 7
from out the b. of the lake TENNY 274
He's in Arthur's b. SHAK:HEN.V 13
in my b., like a bee LODGE:T 1
in your fragrant bosome dyes CAREW:T 8
into the b. of the sea SHAK:HEN.VI[2] 6
Let me to thy b. fly WESLEY:C 5
no b. and no behind SMITH:Ste 2
slips into the b. of the lake TENNY 117
Thou liest in Abraham's b. WORDS:W 43
unadornèd b. of the Deep MILT 18
wring his b. GOLDS 18
bosomed: Boosom'd high in tufted Trees MILT 71
boss: got the b.'s job at last ANON 265
bossing: nobody b. you about ORWELL 6
Bossuet: excite the horror of B. MACAULAY:TB 3
Boston:
B. man is the east wind APPLETON:TG 2
cows laid out B. EMER 50
solid man of B. LONGFEL 28
this is good old B BOSSI 1
bo'sun: b. tight GILB:WS 2
Boswell:
admitted that B.'s Scottish life WILSON:AN 1
B. is a very clubbable man JOHNSON:S 239
Boswelliana: exposed to the *Lues B.* MACAULAY:TB 25
botanise: to b. in the swamp CHESTERTON 48
botanize: b. Upon his mother's grave? WORDS:W 27
botany: learnt that bottinney means a knowledge DICKENS 70
botched: For a b. civilization POUND 29
both:
b. in the same minute KEATS 158
I'm ready to be b. THOMAS:NM 1
Botticelli:
B. were alive today UST 8
B.'s a *cheese* PUNCH 27
bottle:
a little for the b. DIBDIN:C 6
b. pointing to the north SAKI 14
leave the b. on the chimley-piece DICKENS 113
like magic in a pint b. DICKENS 195
My b. of salvation RALE 2
thy dog, thy b., and thy wife POPE 103
bottles: new wine into old b. without bursting ATT 1
bottom:
enough down the b., but not too YORK 1
sit down on my botom to answer FLEM:M 3
warmth is mainly at the b. COUN 1
will reach the b. first? GRAHAM:H 1
woman had a b. of good sense JOHNSON:S 222
bottomless: b. lake as a luxury HARPER 1
bottoms: we clap on Dutch b. CANN 7
boue: made most of mine *de la b.* NAPO I 7
bough:
blossom that hangs on the b. SHAK:TEM 31
danced at the end of a b. LEAR 30
Touch not a single b. MORRIS:GP 1
When the b. bends BLAKE:CD 1
boughs:
b. which shake against SHAK:SON 33
soul into the b. does glide MARV 20
bought:
b. over God with a fee SWIN 1
b. things because she wanted VANB 5
he is b., will stay b. CAMERON 1
Boulogne: was an old man of B. ANON 106
bounce: plural and they b. LUTY 2
bound:
But hath his b., in earth SHAK:COM 1
She made a sudden b. COLERIDGE:ST 32
boundaries: b. beyond which and short HORACE 63
boundary: has a right to fix the b. PARNELL:CS 1
boundless:
b. better, b. worse TENNY 49
what we see Is b. SHELLEY:PB 23
bounds: flaming b. of Place GRAY:T 35
bounties: morning b. ere I left COWP 90
bountiful: My Lady B. FARQ 10
bounty:
goat is the b. of God BLAKE:W 41
My b. is as boundless SHAK:ROM 16
those his former b. fed DRYD 108
bouquet: b. is better than the taste POTTER:S 7
bourg: rustic murmur of their b. TENNY 243
bourgeois:
b. are other people RENARD 1
B. . . . is an epithet of the riff-raff HOPE:An 5
How beastly the b. is LAWR:DH 34
shocked them, the *b.* PRIV 1
bourgeoisie:
British B. Is not born SITWELL:O 1
For generations the British b. WAUGH:E 9
bousing: b. at the nappy BURNS:R 83
bow:
As unto the b. the cord LONGFEL 22
B., ye tradesmen GILB:WS 42
Bring me my B. of burning BLAKE:W 98
certain man drew a b. BIBLE 167
I do set my b. in the cloud BIBLE 43
Lord of his unerring b. BYR 113
not always aim his b. HORACE 23
Thou shalt not b. down BIBLE 103
To draw the b., to ride BYR 237
two strings to my b. FIELDING 2
vain the B. BLAKE:W 80
bow-wow:
Big B. strain I can do myself SCOTT:W 95
Daddy wouldn't buy me a b. TABRAR 1
not for his *b. way* PEMB:10th Earl 1
bow-wows: gone to the demnition b. DICKENS 87
bowdlerize: to b. political history is not AUD 67
bowels: Have you no b. GAY 25
bower: to the b. they came TENNY 38
bower-bird: I'm a bit of a b. WHITE:P 15
bowl:
b. of lather on which a mirror JOYCE:J 10
fill the flowing b. ANON 8
inverted B. we call The Sky FITZGER:E 27
just a b. of cherries PROV 238
Or Love in a golden b.? BLAKE:W 28
bowler: b.'s Holding, the batsman's JOHNSTON:B 1
bowling green: Some recommend the b.g. GREEN:Mat 1
bows: b. Of double-fatal yew SHAK:RIC.II 25
box:
B. about: 'twill come to AUBREY 7
b. is only temporary PLATH 4
b. where sweets compacted HERB:G 32
shut up the b. and the puppets THACK 11
Take that black b. away TREE 6
to no B. his being owes CRASH 9
boxty: can't make b., you'll never get ANON 57
boy:
Altho' a poor blind b. CIB 8
between b. and man SHAK:TWE 12
blitz of a b. is Timothy Winters CAUS 1
b. playing on the sea-shore NEWT:I 5
b. stood on the burning HEMA 1
b. the promise of a man DUMAS:A[F] 3
b.'s will is the wind's will LONGFEL 25
compound a b. SHAK:HEN.V 47
horrid wicked b. HOFFMAN:H 2
It's a b. GUEST 1
Little b. blue NURS 33
Little B. kneels MILNE 8
little b. named baby tuckoo JOYCE:J 2
love, your Idiot B. WORDS:W 3
Mad about the b. COWARD 22
purblind, wayward b. SHAK:LOV 8
see his b. as he really is LEACOCK 5
Speak roughly to your little b. CARROLL 12
thing of duty is a b. for ever O'BRIEN:F 6
want a b., dae it wi' your boots ANON 202
was and a little tiny b. SHAK:TWE 59
What a good b. am I NURS 34

where is my wandering b. ANON 88
who would not be a b.? BYR 66
You silly twisted b. MILLIG 7
boyhood: In the lost b. of Judas RUSS:GW 1
boys:
B. are capital fellows LAMB:Ch 12
B. do not grow up gradually CONNOLLY:C 9
b. get at one end they lose JOHNSON:S 176
b. in the back rooms BEAV 2
b. innocent as strawberries THOMAS:D 3
b. of the old Brigade WEATH 1
b. plan for what they will GILMAN 1
Christian b. I can scarcely ARNOLD:T 1
Deceive b. with toys LYS 1
fond of children (except b.) CARROLL 96
I don't often eat b. JOHNSTON:Jen 1
liked little b. too little and some WAUGH:E 30
not about to send American b. JOHNSON:LB 1
only know two sorts of b. DICKENS 61
they were small b.? O'BRIEN:F 5
Three merry b. FLETCH:J 7
To please the b. JUV 21
were b. when I was a boy BELLOC 31
What are little b. made of? NURS 83
When boyes go first to bed HERB:G 38
bracelet:
b. of bright hair DONNE 55
safire b. lasts forever LOOS 5
brach:
b. may stand by th' fire SHAK:KING L 14
Verity, you b. MASSIN 10
bracken: b. made their bed GLOVER 1
Bradford:
silk hat on a B. millionaire ELIOT:TS 45
there goes John B. BRADF 1
Bradshaw: vocabulary of B. is nervous DOYLE:AC 29
brag: Beauty is nature's b. MILT 39
Brahman: here he attaineth to B. UPA 1
Brahmin: hymn the B. sings EMER 99
brain:
Bear of Very Little B. MILNE 11
B.: An apparatus with which BIER 2
b. is a device to keep the ears DE VR 1
b. : it's my second favourite ALLEN:W 6
b. of a four-year-old boy MARX:G 9
b. of feathers POPE 165
b. only, that the great sins WILDE:O 27
b. Worked with a dim WORDS:W 148
dry b. in a dry season ELIOT:TS 25
feared it might injure the b. CARROLL 9
glean'd my teeming b. KEATS 21
I am a b., Watson DOYLE:AC 36
keep his little b. attic stocked DOYLE:AC 15
mere incurious b. BRENN 2
More b., O Lord MERED:G 26
My b. I'll prove the female SHAK:RIC.II 44
ran widdershins in his b. WRIGHT:J 1
rare bits of b. lie here ROS 1
tares of mine own b. BROWNE:T 15
that cobweb of the b. BUTLER:S[1] 20
brains:
blew his silly b. out THACK 27
b. enough to make a fool STEVENSON:RL 17
b. out of a brass knob DICKENS 193
b. ta'en out and butter'd SHAK:MERR 13
exercises of his b. GILB:WS 48
girl with b. ought to do something LOOS 3
Had their b. knocked out SHELLEY:PB 38
his b. go to his head ASQU:M 7
I mix them with my b. OPIE 1
needs one's b. all the time POUND 18
scorne with vulgar braines to dwell SIDNEY:P 9
steal away their b. SHAK:OTH 28
unhinged the b. of better BROWNE:T 6
What good are b. to a man? WODE 8
with no b. at all HERB:AP 5
brainsickly: So b. of things SHAK:MAC 42
bramble-bush: alphabet as if it had been a b. DICKENS 206
brambles: b. like tall cedars show COTTON 1
bramin: B. strikes the hour SOUTHEY 15
branch:
B. shall grow out of BIBLE 309
Cut is the b. that might MARLOWE 46
Every b. big with it HARDY:T 45
branches:
some b. rotted and falling POUND 14
Thy b. ne'er remember KEATS 19
brand: b. sae drap with bluid? BALL 18
brandy:
B. for the Parson KIP 121
get me a glass of b. GEO IV 1
hero must drink b. JOHNSON:S 210
brass:
become as sounding b. BIBLE 522
evil manners live in b. SHAK:HEN.VIII 18
inform the breathing b. VIRGIL 72
Since b., nor stone SHAK:SON 29
This be your wall of b. HORACE 77
wall all Germany with b. MARLOWE 31
brave:
All that delirium of the b.? YEATS 37
b. bad man CLAREN 5
b. man with a sword WILDE:O 113
b. towards God, and BACON:F[1] 118
B. with the needlework BROWNING:R 83
e'en the valiant more b. DIBDIN:C 8
Fears of the b. JOHNSON:S 69
Fortune favours the b. TEREN 8
going to do something b. HOWARD:M 1
home of the b. KEY:FS 1
How sleep the b. COLLINS:Will 3
In the b. days of old MACAULAY:TB 49
I've very b. generally CARROLL 61
many b. men before Agamemnon HORACE 57
None but the b. deserves DRYD 105
O b. new world SHAK:TEM 32
partly b. and partly good RICH 2
passing b. to be a King MARLOWE 8
Then I was clean and b. HOUSM 10
Toll for the b. COWP 15
tomorrow to be b. ARMST:J 1
Whither depart the souls of the b. CLOUGH 18
bravely: live b. in another country MIDD 5
braver: I have done one b. thing DONNE 67
bravery: With all her b. on MILT 289
bravest: b. by far ANON 95
brawl: killed in a pub b. in a suburb JAMES:PD 1
brazenness: B. and public liberties CERV 20
Brazil:
B. – where the nuts come THOMAS:B 2
In B. they throw flowers DIET 4
I've never reached B. KIP 107
breach:
not yet A b., but an expansion DONNE 69
Once more unto the b. SHAK:HEN.V 17
bread:
All b. is not baked in one PROV 6
asked for b., and he received WESLEY:S 2
better than no b. PROV 157
bones to make my b. NURS 11
b. and cheese, and kisses SWIFT 43
b. and circuses JUV 20
b. I break was once the oat THOMAS:D 6
B. is the staff of life PROV 50
b. of adversity BIBLE 316
Bring us in no browne bred ANON 58
but one halfpennyworth of b. SHAK:HEN.IV[1] 54
Cast thy b. upon the waters BIBLE 288
dole b. is bitter b. HEWETT 4
Dry b. at home is better PROV 86
Eating b. and honey NURS 66
first petition is for daily b. WILSON:W 4
for The Royal slice of b.? MILNE 3
give b. with one fish-ball LANE 1
He took the B. and brake it ELIZ I 8
Honest b. is very well JERROLD 2
in breaking of b. BIBLE 470
loaf of b.,, the walrus said CARROLL 57
looked to government for b. BURKE:E 81
looking for better b. CERV 2
Man doth not live by b. only BIBLE 123
Man shall not live by b. alone BIBLE 380
never ate his b. in tears GOET 6
nourishing, palatable b. TRAILL:CP 1
Once the b. has been eaten CERV 16
our daily b. BIBLE 391
quarrel with my b. and butter SWIFT 39
shalt thou eat b. BIBLE 24
She was cutting b. and butter THACK 27
smell of b. and butter BYR 134
that b. should be so dear HOOD 21
Their learning is like b. JOHNSON:S 170
this day our daily b. MASS 15
this day our daily b. PRAY 6
trees were b. and cheese ANON 71
unleavened b. BIBLE 96
who are winning the b. by it BUTLER:S[2] 4
Who ground the flour for b. KEES 1
breadfruit: Where the b. fall ELIOT:TS 69
breadth: Let me have length and b. BALL 16
break:
B., b., b., On thy TENNY 58
thyself must b. at last ARNOLD:M 48
breakdown: Madness need not be all b. LAING 5
breakers: I wanton'd with thy b. BYR 120
breakfast:
All too soon the tiny b. BETJ 23
b. that a laird might please RAMS 2
credit for b. in the morning RHYS 2
Hope is a good b. BACON:F[1] 127
Laugh before b., you'll cry PROV 226
No business before b. THACK 22
not reheat his sins for b. DIET 1
One doth but b. here HENS 1
that I b. on gin HERB:AP 1
Where shall we our b. take? BALL 58
wholesome, hungry b. WALT 10
breakfast-table: b. on the morning after his demise TROLL 3
breakfast-time: in matrimony is b. HERB:AP 15
breakfasted: b. with you and shall sup BRUCE:R 1
breaking:
By b. of windows MORE:H 4
I'm b. it in for a friend MARX:G 23
in b. of bread BIBLE 470
breaks:
something twangs and b. MACNEICE 9
world b. everyone HEMINGWAY 1
breast:
And calms the troubled b. NEWT:J 2
b. at their ripening wept HOPE:Al 2
brest surcharged with musick SIDNEY:P 11
By thy cold b. BYR 121
coming harvest in its b. CAMPBELL:R 4
depth of her glowing b. SHELLEY:PB 92
fill thy brest with glorie HERB:G 4
her helpless b. upon his b. YEATS 68
his boiling bloody b. SHAK:MID 47
on Madeline's fair b. KEATS 70
soothe a savage b. CONG 33
sulk upon my mothers b. BLAKE:W 75
victor sunk upon her b. DRYD 111
With sweetness fills the b. CASWALL 1
breastplate:
man in the golden b. YEATS 112
stronger b. than a heart SHAK:HEN.VI[2] 4
breasts:
chiaroscuro Of your naked b. MALLEY 3
division of prodigious b. SWIN 51
freed some b. from the domination GREER 4
Sestos and Abydos of her b. DONNE 18
she hath no b. BIBLE 299
soaping her b. in the bath EWART 1
such b. must suckle slaves BYR 197
breath:
accustomed to their lack of b. YEATS 55
Although thy b. be rude SHAK:AS 35
b. and the bloom of the year BROWNING:R 212
b. can make them GOLDS 21
b. of her false mouth SHELLEY:PB 131
b. of life BIBLE 9
b. of worldy men SHAK:RIC.II 23
b. to heaven like vapour TENNY 43
Could ever yet cut b.? SHAK:WIN 32
Floats upon her final b. SPEND 11
Had borne my b. away HOOD 9
hear her tender-taken b. KEATS 113
if every b. were as terrible SHAK:MUCH 7
last b. be drawn through LAMB:Ch 49
noise and smoky b. SMITH:Alex 2
Save your b. to cool PROV 337
such is the b. of Kings SHAK:RIC.II 8
Sweet is the b. of morn MILT 199
through Mists of human b. DAVEN:W 3
waste of b. the years YEATS 61
Where b. most breathes SHAK:SON 36
while you have it use your b. FLETCH:J 5
world will hold its b. HITL 11
breathe:
As tho' to b. were life TENNY 52
b. not his name MOORE:T 12

So long as men can b. SHAK:SON 6
yearning to b. free LAZ 1
breathed:
b. in the face of the foe BYR 40
b. into his nostrils BIBLE 9
He b. upon dead bodies EMER 75
breathers: b. of an ample day TENNY 182
breathes: B. there the man SCOTT:W 10
breathing:
b. English air BROOKE 25
In the sound his b. kept SHELLEY:PB 73
Keep b. TUCK 5
stops b. anywhere else FOUCA 1
'Tis her b. that Perfumes the chamber SHAK:CYM 2
breathings: Low b. coming after me WORDS:W 144
bred:
b. amongst the weeds and tares BROWNE:T 15
man's b. out Into baboon SHAK:TIM 3
so ill b. as to love a husband? WYCH 2
Bredon:
In summertime on B. HOUSM 11
'Tis Summer Time on B. KINGSMILL 2
breech: turned up his b. against the Standard AUBREY 2
breeches:
b. were blue COLERIDGE:ST 41
like a book in b. SMITH:Syd[1] 29
made themselves b. BIBLE 18
breed:
b. babies and you eat WESK 2
b. in your closet like rattlesnakes MCLEAN:S 1
b. of their horses and dogs PENN 3
not b. one work that wakes HOPK:GM 31
breeder: be a b. of sinners? SHAK:HAM 100
breeding:
Good b. consists in concealing TWAIN 32
sign of guilt, or of ill-b. CONG 38
spoiled i' the b. BROME:R 2
breeks: b. aff a wild Highlandman SCOTT:W 85
breeze:
b. is on the sea SCOTT:W 60
fair b. blew COLERIDGE:ST 18
hay harvest b. CORY 4
breezes:
interfered with by the first b. O'BRIEN:F 3
Little b. dusk and shiver TENNY 13
sunset b. shiver NEWBOLT 7
To feel no other b. KEATS 15
Breffney: little waves of B. go GORE 1
breid:
Gie us our b. BIBLE 589
sanna live on b. alane BIBLE 588
Brer Fox: B.F., he lay low HARRIS:JC 2
brethren: for we be b. BIBLE 45
brevity:
B. is the soul of lingerie PARKER:D 13
B. is the soul of wit SHAK:HAM 63
do my best to equal his b. FORD:GR 1
Its body b. COLERIDGE:ST 58
brewers: Bakers and b., bouchers LANGLAND 7
brewery: take me to a b. ANON 72
brews: many a peer of England b. HOUSM 28
briars: binding with b. my joys BLAKE:W 72
bribe:
b. . . . changes a relation GREENE:G 13
doing nothing for a b. SHAK:CYM 10
insulted with a very considerable b. GILB:WS 66
taking of a B. or Gratuity PENN 4
Too poor for a b. GRAY:T 37
bribes:
How many b. he had taken BENTLEY:EC 9
man open to b. GREENE:G 6
our fingers with base b.? SHAK:JUL 68
bribing: Money is good for b. REIN 1
brick:
b. in his pocket as a JOHNSON:S 35
carried a piece of b. in his pocket SWIFT 26
'Eave 'arf a b. at 'im PUNCH 6
found it b. and left it marble CAES:A 1
He was a b. WALL 1
bricks:
can't make b. without straw PROV 442
Red b. in the suburbs CRAIG:MJ 1
Throw b. at your father instead BEHAN:Br 1
bride:
barren B. POPE 132
b. at the altar SCOTT:W 55
bridesmaid makes a happy b. TENNY 66
I brought the handsomest b. PRINGLE:T 3
I drew my b. PATMO 3
like a blooming Eastern b. DRYD 105
lovely and lonely b. WATSON:W 1
my life and my b. POE 9
Never turns him to the b. HOUSM 8
proud b. of a ducal coronet DICKENS 127
though a Virgin, yet a B. CAREW:T 5
unravish'd b. of quietness KEATS 92
young b. and her bridegroom POUND 41
bride-bed: thought thy b. to have deck'd SHAK:HAM 187
bridegroom:
funeral train which the b. sees CLOUGH 16
I will be A b. in my death SHAK:ANT 53
Like a b. from his room AYT 3
bridesmaid: happy b. makes a happy TENNY 66
bridge:
b. of asses EUC 2
b. over troubled water SIMON:P 3
Don't cross the b. till PROV 77
How well Horatius kept the b. MACAULAY:TB 54
keep the b. with me? MACAULAY:TB 48
on the b. at midnight ANON 38
promise to build a b. even KHRU 4
Railway B. of the Silv'ry Tay MCGON 2
stood on the b. at midnight LONGFEL 38
Who needs a b. or dam? COPE 1
Bridge of Sighs:
on the B.o.S. BYR 96
over the B.o.S. into eternity KIERK 3
bridled: millions ready saddled and b. MACAULAY:TB 35
brief:
b. . . . As woman's love SHAK:HAM 115
I labour to be b. HORACE 101
brier:
grows a bonny b. bush HOGG 2
out of the other a b. BALL 40
brier-patch: Bred en bawn in a b. HARRIS:JC 3
briers: full of b. is this working-day SHAK:AS 8
brigade: boys of the old B. WEATH 1
brigands: B. demand your money or BUTLER:S[2] 54
bright:
All things b. and beautiful ALEX:CF 1
B. as the day GRANVILLE 2
B., b. as day YOUNG:A 1
creature not too b. or good WORDS:W 89
Dark with excessive b. MILT 178
I've got B.'s disease PEREL 4
brightest:
B. and best of the sons HEB 1
though the b. fell SHAK:MAC 91
brightness:
B. falls from the air NASHE 1
b. of this early sun STEVENS 11
Cloth'd with transcendent b. MILT 112
ere life hath lost its b.? HAST:F 1
Leaking the b. away SPEND 8
sunrise brings back the b. BLUN 1
brilliance: B. at its best is a quality WHITE:P 10
brilliant:
b. to the top of his army LLOYD GEO 16
envy of b. men BEERB 6
less b. pen than mine BEERB 20
looked upon those b. creatures YEATS 50
brillig: 'Twas b. CARROLL 45
brimstone: From his b. bed COLERIDGE:ST 40
bring:
being provoked to b. up PEPYS 23
why didn't you b. him CUNARD 1
bringing:
b. me up by hand, gave her no DICKENS 209
they're b. them home DAWE 3
brink: eternity, and you are on the b. ANON 140
brinkmanship: boasting of his b. STEVENSON:A 9
Bristol: three sailors of B. City THACK 23
Britain:
battle of B. is about to begin CHURCH:W 15
B. first, at heaven's command THOMS:Ja[1] 2
B. is A world by itself SHAK:CYM 7
B. set the world a-blaze GILB:WS 49
end of B. as an independent GAIT 2
hail, happy B. SOMER 2
Hath B. all the sun SHAK:CYM 12
In B. our institutions evolve HAMIL:WW 2
three things against living in B. EDMOND 2
when B. had a savage culture BANDA 1
Britannia:
B. needs no bulwarks CAMPBELL:T 8
B., rule the waves THOMS:Ja[1] 2
free B., bears BYR 65
brither: lo'ed him like a very b. BURNS:R 85
brithers: b. be for a' that BURNS:R 116
British:
breaking the mould of B. politics JENKINS:R 3
B., and therefore uneasy LESSING:D 3
B. Bourgeoisie Is not born SITWELL:O 1
B. Government sees black people TUTU 1
B. love permanence more CASSON 1
B. management doesn't seem CHARLES:Prince 2
B. Public, ye who like me not BROWNING:R 192
B. say, 'Jolly good story' ATWOOD 9
B. subject, in whatever land PALMERS 1
dismissed by the B. electorate CHURCH:W 51
For generations the B. bourgeoisie WAUGH:E 9
my life for the B. female? CLOUGH 14
reflections on the greatness of the *B.* ADDIS 22
smell the blood of a B. man SHAK:KING L 51
socialism is totally alien to the B. THATCH:M 15
stony B. stare TENNY 213
we are B. – thank God MONTGOM:BL 4
world less known by the B. BORR 3
British Empire:
B.E. and its Commonwealth CHURCH:W 14
B.E. and the United States will have CHURCH:W 17
leave the destinies of the B.E. DISR:B 63
liquidation of the B.E. CHURCH:W 29
provinces of the B.e. SMITH:Ad 14
British Museum:
keep my books at the B.M. BUTLER:S[2] 12
reflection of the B.M. Reading Room? SPARK 10
room somewhere in the B.M. PRIEST 2
very learned B.M. assistant POUND 10
Briton:
glory in the name of B. GEO III 1
only a free-born B. can do THACK 4
Britons:
beef make B. fight PRIOR 8
B. alone use 'Might' WAUGH:E 26
B. never will be slaves THOMS:Ja[1] 2
B. were only natives at that time SELL 2
B. wholly sundered from all VIRGIL 3
brittle: b. glory shineth SHAK:RIC.II 39
broad:
B. before and b. behind BETJ 2
She is a smart old b. RUNYON 8
She's the B. SPRING 1
broadcasting: enabled the BBC to make b. REITH 1
brocade: honour, or her new b. POPE 45
broccoli: I do not like b. BUSH 1
Brodie: Miss Jean B. in her prime SPARK 7
brogues: not fit to tie his b. SCOTT:W 97
broke:
all of us bottomly b. KERO 1
b. underestimating the intelligence MENCK 19
broke out: he b.o. CIC 9
broken:
b. open on the most scientific PEAC 11
It can be b. easier TENNY 255
Naught b. save this body BROOKE 24
pie-crusts are made to be b. SWIFT 41
broken-hearted:
Half b. BYR 54
hoped we were both b. SWIN 38
There's a b. woman HAYES 1
We had ne'er been b. BURNS:R 93
brokenhearted: to bind up the b. BIBLE 333
broker: more than that of an honest b. BISM 5
bronchitis: theatre unless he or she has b. AGATE 1
Brontës: burst by the B. CHESTERTON 47
bronze: monument more lasting than b. HORACE 48
brooches: I will make you b. STEVENSON:RL 64

brook:
b. was full of breamis DUNB 2
b. was troubled MASE 15
noise like of a hidden b. COLERIDGE:ST 31
Where the b. and river meet LONGFEL 8
brooks:
b. too broad for leaping HOUSM 26
I sing of *B.* HERR 7
sedged b. are Thames's ARNOLD:M 43
Shallow brookes murmur moste SIDNEY:P 2
broom: bright blows the b. STEVENSON:RL 64
broomstick: Surely man is a b. SWIFT 12
broth:
b. without any bread NURS 72
Too many cooks spoil the b. PROV 398
brothel: metaphysical b. for emotions KOES 1
brothel-house: hang me up at the door of a b. SHAK:MUCH 2
brothels:
B. with bricks of Religion BLAKE:W 41
Keep thy foot out of b. SHAK:KING L 45
brother:
Am I my b.'s keeper? BIBLE 27
Am I not a man and a b.? WEDGWOOD 1
And hurt my b. SHAK:HAM 194
Be my b., or I shall CHAMFORT 9
Big B. is watching you ORWELL 27
b., good morning BELLOC 6
b. of death exacteth a third BROWNE:T 42
B. of the Angle WALT 4
B. to Death DANI 1
father died, my b. too TURNER:WJR 2
Had it been his b. ANON 132
hand of every man's b. BIBLE 41
have him than his b. MARV 35
lawless linsy-woolsy b. BUTLER:S[1] 19
looked into his b.'s face O'FAOL 2
my b.; be he ne'er so vile SHAK:HEN.V 40
my b., hail and farewell CATUL 20
my b. is a hairy man BIBLE 57
no b. near the throne POPE 121
Still to my b. turns GOLDS 4
Strong B. in God BELLOC 39
Thy b. came with subtilty BIBLE 59
to be the white man's b. KING:ML 5
voice of thy b.'s blood crieth BIBLE 28
you or your b. who was killed SPOON 7
brotherhood:
And crown thy good with b. BATES:KL 1
b. of man under ROCKE 1
I don't believe in wasting b. X 1
Love the b. BIBLE 567
sweet a b. in song KEATS 1
thy b. of Cain BYR 121
universal destruction or universal b. YEV 5
brotherly:
Answered him b. GRAVES:R 4
Let b. love continue BIBLE 559
brothers:
agree like b. SHAK:HEN.VI[2] 9
All men become b. SCHILL 7
all the b. were valiant NEWC 1
b. all In honour WORDS:W 157
b. and their murder'd man KEATS 29
causing their b.' blood to be shed ZAPA 1
forty thousand b. Could not SHAK:HAM 188
make b. and sisters hate each other JOHNSON:S 86
Men, my b. TENNY 79
Romans were like b. MACAULAY:TB 49
we band of b. SHAK:HEN.V 40
brothers-in-law: aren't all b. POWELL:A 3
Brougham: Lord B.'s face has this BAGE 3
brought: things b. to one on a tray BOWEN:S 1
brow:
Blight her b. with blotch SYNGE 7
b. with homely biggen bound SHAK:HEN.IV[2] 44
Consul's b. was sad MACAULAY:TB 46
I see a lily on thy b. KEATS 80
manly b. Consents to death BYR 108
parallels in beauty's b. SHAK:SON 24
show thy dang'rous b. SHAK:JUL 22
southward-facing b. ARNOLD:M 30
That great b. BROWNING:R 91
wanton with a velvet b. SHAK:LOV 9
Your bonnie b. was brent BURNS:R 79
brown:
b., The b. of her MEW 1
clad in homely russet b.? WORDS:W 29
in some b. study LYLY 2
wide b. land for me MACKELL 1
You have baked me too b. CARROLL 34
Brown: John B.'s body lies HALL:CS 1
browner: tinge with a b. shade GIBBON:E 29
Browning:
B. He used poetry as a medium WILDE:O 9
Mrs B.'s death is rather a relief FITZGER:E 35
take the safety-catch off my B. JOHST 1
Tennyson and B. are poets ELIOT:TS 117
brows:
b. with roses and with DRYD 105
Gathering her b. like gathering BURNS:R 83
shadow of her even browes SPENS 32
browsing: with excellent b. and sluicing WODE 4
bruise: It shall b. thy head BIBLE 22
bruised: b. in a new place IRV 6
Brunetto: *you* here, Advocate B.? DANTE 10
Brunswick: Sate B.'s fated chieftan BYR 78
brush:
Daft as a b. PLATT 12
never b. their hair BELLOC 2
Brussels: darkened bedroom in a B. hotel THOMP:EP 1
brutal: apparently rude and b. natures MANNING 2
brutalised: community is infinitely more b. WILDE:O 40
brutality:
industry without art is b. RUSKIN 28
love this woman with the greatest b. NEWBY 1
brute:
B. heart of a b. PLATH 2
Feed the b. DU MAU:G 4
Feed the b. PUNCH 25
such a cross-grained b.? GOLDS 74
woman that was a b. SHELLEY:PB 20
Brute:
Et tu B.? CAES:GJ 7
Et tu, B.? SHAK:JUL 35
brutes:
B. never meet GOLDS 2
Exterminate all the b. CONRAD 4
had been b. without you OTWAY 4
not made to live as b. DANTE 13
simple race of b. TENNY 260
brutish: nasty, b., and short HOBB 7
Brutus:
B. is an honourable man SHAK:JUL 48
'B.' will start a spirit SHAK:JUL 12
You too, B.? CAES:GJ 7
bubble:
B. on the stream CLARE:J 1
b. winked at me HERF 1
empty b. GRAIN:J 1
Honour but an empty b. DRYD 109
Like the b. on the fountain SCOTT:W 39
now a b. burst POPE 82
world's a b. BACON:F[1] 131
bubble-mouthing: b., fog-blathering FRY:C 5
bubbles: beaded b. winking at KEATS 93
buck: b. stops here TRU 9
buckets:
dropping b. into empty wells COWP 67
well that owes two b. SHAK:RIC.II 35
Buckingham: so much for B. CIB 2
Buckingham Palace: changing guard at B.P. MILNE 1
buckles: Silver b. on his knee NURS 3
buckram:
eleven b. men grown out SHAK:HEN.IV[1] 41
Four rogues in b. SHAK:HEN.IV[1] 40
bud:
be a b. again KEATS 73
B., and yet a *Rose full-blowne* HERR 5
b. may have a bitter taste COWP 11
I'll nip him in the b. ROCHE 2
in age I b. again HERB:G 46
This b. of love SHAK:ROM 15
budding: b. Miss is very charming BYR 134
budge: b. for no man's pleasure SHAK:ROM 26
buds:
darling b. of May SHAK:SON 6
green b. hang in the elm HOUSM 42
monotone of blue-grey b. WILLIAMS:WC 1
spare the b. MARV 29
buff: bide by the b. and the blue BURNS:R 100
buffalo:
home where the b. roam HIGL 1
thought he saw a B. CARROLL 94
buffaloes: flower-fed b. of the spring LIND:V 4
Buffs: Steady the B. KIP 8
bug:
b. with gilded wings POPE 125
snug as a b. in a rug FRANKLIN:B 25
bugger:
B. Bognor GEO V 5
Poor b. me, Gurindji EGAN 1
buggered: I'm absolutely b. JONES:P 1
buggering: Keep B. On CHURCH:W 69
buggers: Land of B. MACNAM 1
bugle:
Blow, b., blow TENNY 106
came a Wind like a B. DICKIN:E 20
bugle-horn:
One blast upon the b. SCOTT:W 43
sound upon the b. TENNY 68
bugles:
b. calling for them OWEN:W 2
Here no b. sound reveillé SCOTT:W 37
What are the b. blowin' for? KIP 47
bugloss: b. paints the sterile soil CRAB 2
bugs: b. that secretly bite ANTI 1
build:
Birds b. – but not I b. HOPK:GM 31
b. 'em up with worn-out tools KIP 127
b. stately, sooner than to garden BACON:F[1] 69
that b. them again are gay YEATS 109
they labour in vain that b. BIBLE 243
think that we b. for ever RUSKIN 3
time to b. BIBLE 281
to b. in Hell MILT 145
to b. the house of death MONTAIGNE 4
When we mean to b. SHAK:HEN.IV[2] 18
builded: b. better than he knew EMER 92
builders: b. have very high flights MARLBOR:S 1
building:
castle or b. not in decay BACON:F[1] 89
her something like a public b. WILDE:O 56
it's a very old b. OSB:J 9
principal beauty in b. FULLER:T[1] 5
stole thence The life o' th' b. SHAK:MAC 54
tall b., with a tower and bells CRAB 13
Well b. hath three Conditions WOTTON 6
buildings:
plenty of ruined b. MACDIAR 22
sad when I look at new b. GOGOL 2
builds: What is he that b. stronger SHAK:HAM 180
built:
b. in such a logical way HOLMES:OW 5
B. in th' eclipse MILT 51
city is b. To music TENNY 239
he is almost lost that b. it BROWNE:T 59
Rome was not b. in a day PROV 335
Unless the Lord has b. the house BIBLE 604
bulb: stand a naked light b. WILLIAMS:T 2
bull:
bee were crossed with a Friesian b. GOGA 6
Cock and a B.', said Yorick STERNE 39
curl'd Assyrian b. TENNY 208
Irish b. is always pregnant MAHAF 2
savage b. doth bear the yoke SHAK:MUCH 3
take the b. between the teeth GOLDWYN 9
they are gone to milk the b. JOHNSON:S 117
bullet:
ballot is stronger than the b. LINC 2
b. has got its commission DIBDIN:C 7
b. that is to kill me has NAPO I 17
Every b. has its billet WILLIAM III 1
bullets:
b. made of platinum BELLOC 4
heard the b. whistle WASH 13
Sharp b. are preferable BISM 1
bullfighting: B. is the only art HEMINGWAY 2
bullfrog: left with a puffing b. BROWN:Geoff 1
bullied:
than b. out of vice SURT 13
who never b. a little b. HUGHES:Th 5
bullocks: yoke of b. at Stamford Fair? SHAK:HEN.IV[2] 35
bulls: Strong b. of Bashan BIBLE 205
bully:
let a b. come into your JOHNSON:LB 2
love this lovely b. SHAK:HEN.V 29

bulrushes: for him an ark of b. BIBLE 81
bulwark: floating b. of the island BLACKS 3
bulwarks:
Britannia needs no b. CAMPBELL:T 8
b. which stand against ruthless power AUNG 1
bum: then slip I from her b. SHAK:MID 13
bump:
mind . . . fetched up with a b. ORWELL 34
not to b. into the furniture LUNT 1
that go b. in the night ANON 187
bumpy: going to be a b. night DAVIS:B 1
bunch: b. of other men's flowers MONTAIGNE 21
buns:
Hot cross b. NURS 18
wandering bears may come with b. ISH 1
Bunyan: of genius in literature – B. ARNOLD:M 77
burbled: b. as it came CARROLL 46
burden: Take up the White Man's b. KIP 99
bureaucracy: cannot understand the b. SHAW 51
bureaucratic: administrator in a b. world MCLUH 11
Burgundy: naïve domestic B. THURB 16
burial:
groaning for b. SHAK:JUL 44
precious Death and B. PRAY 34
burial-ground: b. God's-Acre LONGFEL 7
buried:
ane was b. in Marie's BALL 40
bodies are b. in peace BIBLE 372
b. him darkly at dead of night WOLFE:C 2
b. in a good old age BIBLE 47
b. in so sweet a place SHELLEY:PB 105
b. in the king's high way SHAK:RIC.II 31
not b. me deep enough? TENNY 224
They were b. side by side MCGUAIG 1
This living b. man DONNE 21
To be b. while alive POE 13
twenty generations lie b. MACAULAY:TB 11
Burke:
We are the people of B. YEATS 135
Who, too deep for his* GOLDS 37
Burlington: I'm B. Bertie HARG 1
burn:
beacons b. again HOUSM 1
better to marry than to b. BIBLE 520
b. a Poland winter SHAK:COM 4
B. to the socket WORDS:W 113
b. your house down to cook CHAMFORT 8
eventually they b. people HEINE 1
I rage, I melt, I b. GAY 1
I'll b. my books MARLOWE 41
mid b. the old bass-viol HARDY:T 10
We b. daylight SHAK:MERR 5
burning:
b. fiery furnace BIBLE 348
B. for b. BIBLE 104
firebrand plucked out of the b. BIBLE 356
smell of b. fills the startled BELLOC 30
vain is now the b. KEATS 20
Burns:
excellence of B. is, indeed CARLYLE:T 26
into Parliament, much as Robert B. CARLYLE:T 55
Lovely B. has charms BURNS:R 61
burnt:
play with fire you get b. PROV 192
was b. to ashes GRAHAM:H 4
burnt-out: b. ends of smoky days ELIOT:TS 15
burr: I am a kind of b. SHAK:MEA 36
burrow: always so near his b. MEY:H 1
burrows: b. of the Nightmare AUD 7
burrs:
Do roses stick like b.? BROWNING:R 159
stick on conversation's b. HOLMES:OW 3
burst:
B. smilingly SHAK:KING L 82
b. while drinking a seidlitz ANON 134
Let me not b. in ignorance SHAK:HAM 36
Burton: why was B. built on Trent? HOUSM 28
bury:
B. my heart at Wounded Knee BENET 2
B. the Great Duke TENNY 188
b. whom he help'd to starve POPE 123
dead b. their dead BIBLE 404
feel disposed to b. for nothing DICKENS 116
I b. some of you DONNE 40
want one to b. my sister MITFORD:JL 1
bus:
Can it be a Motor B.? GODLEY 1
canny shove yer granny aff a b. ANON 124
Clerk Descending from the b. CARROLL 95
he missed the b. CHAMBERLAIN:N 6
Threepenny-b. young man GILB:WS 37
tumbled off a b. GRAHAM:H 2
bush:
Australian b. – the nurse and tutor LAWS 1
b. has friends to meet him PATERSON:AB 2
B., the dusty loam HARDY:T 15
b. was not consumed BIBLE 84
b. will never suit you PATERSON:AB 5
every common b. afire BROWNING:EB 21
four times as big as the b. LEAR 2
into the wide sea of Australian b. ELLIS:H 8
is a b. suppos'd a bear? SHAK:MID 43
leap over a b. is better than CERV 7
Spirit of the B. walked down CUS 1
Thorough b., thorough brier SHAK:MID 12
worth two in the b. PROV 45
bush-boy: B. alone by my side PRINGLE:T 1
bushfire: like a b. behind Balmain SLESS 8
bushmen: b. love hard riding PATERSON:AB 4
busier: he semed bisier than he was CHAUC 21
business:
All the b. of war WELLING 10
any b. done during the remainder SHERIDAN:RB 45
be about my Father's b.? BIBLE 451
been a damned serious b. WELLING 9
B. as usual CHURCH:W 4
B. as usual SELF 1
b. give the people a square deal ROOS:T 12
B. . . . may bring money AUSTEN 53
b. of America is b. COOL 2
b. of consequence do it BARH 2
b. sagacity reduces itself VEB 3
B. underlies everything WILSON:W 4
B. was his aversion EDGE 4
convenience of the b. of the day BURKE:E 11
did my uncle Toby's b. STERNE 36
dinner lubricates b. STOWELL 1
do b. in great waters BIBLE 234
do more b. after dinner SWIFT 77
do the b. of the day in the day WELLING 13
everybody's b. is nobody's b. WALT 6
full of careful b. SHAK:RIC.II 19
go to my pleasure, b. WYCH 4
If everybody minded their own b. CARROLL 11
learns b. from one's fellow YEATS 146
love will yield to b. OSB:J 8
Mind your own b. PROV 273
No b. before breakfast THACK 22
No praying, it spoils b. OTWAY 5
On a thousand b. women BETJ 22
person on b. from Porlock COLERIDGE:ST 62
requisite in b. than dispatch ADDIS 12
To b. that we love SHAK:ANT 42
totter on in bus'ness POPE 114
Treasury is the spring of b. BAGE 7
young b. and professional men of EDWARD VIII 1
businessman: I wasn't a b. BERLU 1
buskin: hear thy b. tread JONS 42
Buss: Miss B. and Miss Beale ANON 82
bust:
give a b. of marriages BYR 184
have a b. made of them GOLDWYN 7
hero's b. is bigger than MARX:G 30
raise the tardy b. JOHNSON:S 67
Uncorseted, her friendly b. ELIOT:TS 33
bustle: B. in a House DICKIN:E 18
busts: picture plac'd the b. between CHESTERFIELD 32
busy:
bustle of the b. BURNS:R 124
b., and you will be safe OSB:J 8
English are b. MONTESQU 6
thou knowest how b. I must be ASTLEY 1
busyness: Extreme *b.*, whether at school STEVENSON:RL 19
but: There is always a 'b.' BRONTE:A 2
butcher:
b., the baker, The candlestick NURS 63
I want to know a b. paints BROWNING:R 208
son of a first rate b. ASHFORD 8
butchered: Butcher'd to make a Roman BYR 110
butchers:
Even b. weep GAY 16
gentle with these b. SHAK:JUL 43
must be both shepherds and b. VOLT 8
sacrificers, but not b. SHAK:JUL 23
supposed to become policemen or b. CONNOLLY:C 4
butler: Ice formed on the b.'s upper WODE 25
butlers:
b. and no friends POUND 15
B. ought To know their place BELLOC 19
butt: knocks you down with the b. GOLDS 77
Butt: open for this little B. ANON 129
butt-end: knock me down with the b. CIB 7
butter:
B. and eggs and a pound CALVER 4
b. in a lordly dish BIBLE 132
b. that makes the temptation JERROLD 2
b. will only make us fat GOER 1
b. would not melt in her mouth MACKLIN 1
b. wouldn't melt in her mouth LANCH 1
b.'s spread too thick CARROLL 58
do like a little bit of b. MILNE 5
It was the *best* b. CARROLL 17
quarrel with my bread and b. SWIFT 39
We can manage without b. GOEB 3
buttercup:
b. Had blessed with gold OWEN:W 10
I'm called Little B. GILB:WS 6
buttercups:
b. fried with fish LEAR 27
b., the little children's dower BROWNING:R 50
buttered:
always on the b. side PAYN 1
butter'd his hay SHAK:KING L 27
b. scones and crumpets ELIOT:TS 20
butterflies:
All the b. and cockyolybirds KINGSLEY:C 7
beard full of b. GARC 2
beard full of b. LORCA 3
b. are already yellow POUND 6
b. are free DICKENS 172
I look for b. CARROLL 82
tearing wings off dying b. HAYD 2
butterfly:
affected, husband-hunting b. MITFORD:MR 1
b., a cabbage-white GRAVES:R 7
b. dreaming I am a man CHUANG 1
b. upon the road KIP 34
Float like a b. ALI 1
tulip and the b. WATTS 7
Who breaks a b. POPE 125
buttock: by boiling his b. AUBREY 5
buttocks:
chair, that fits all b. SHAK:ALL 5
gorgeous b. of the ape HUX:A 46
button:
Pray you undo this b. SHAK:KING L 85
we are not the very b. SHAK:HAM 76
we don't care a b. LEAR 16
button-moulder: I am a b. IBS 2
button-stick: I've a tongue like a b. KIP 46
buttons: had a soul above b. COLMAN:G[2] 2
buttress: regarded as a b. of the church MELBOU 11
butts: beast with many heads b. SHAK:COR 12
butty: He's an oul' b. o' mine O'CAS 1
buxom: b., blithe, and debonair MILT 66
Buxton: every fool in B. can be at RUSKIN 31
buy:
b. a world of happy days SHAK:RIC.III 8
b. Codham, Cockridden THOMAS:E 3
b. it first HEMING 1
Did b. each other SHAK:TRO 20
I will b. with you SHAK:MERC 14
nobody would b. him BAGE 3
not going to b. repentance DEMOS 3
What would you b.? BEDD 4
buyer: it is naught, saith the b. BIBLE 266
buying:
b. and the selling, and the strife BUCHANAN 4
worth reading, it is worth b. RUSKIN 23
buzz: I heard a Fly b. DICKIN:E 7
buzzard: he was nothing but a b. ANON 85
buzzards: B. are all gentlemen BROME:R 2
buzzing: What is he b. in my ears? BROWNING:R 172

by-and-by: In the sweet b. BENNETT:SF 1
bygones: Let b. be b. PROV 233
byle: His b. was black CHAUC 62
by-product:
Character is a b. WILSON:W 7
something you get as a b. HUX:A 25
Byron:
B. is only great as a poet GOET 32
Mad, bad, and dangerous* LAMB:Car 1
more worthless set than B. and his friends WELLING 23
words: B. is dead CARLYLE:JW 4
Byronic: to think all poets were B. COPE 3
Byzantium:
come To the holy city of B. YEATS 73
Soldan of B. is smiling CHESTERTON 18
C: C cut it ANON 55
C Major:
C M. of this life BROWNING:R 169
write Even yet in C m. MACDIAR 25
cabbage:
c. nor a woman for five years GUNN:J 2
c. with a college education TWAIN 19
Rehashed c. has proved fatal JUV 16
cabbage-leaf: to cut a c., to make FOOTE 3
cabbages:
c. – and kings CARROLL 56
find me planting my c. MONTAIGNE 3
cabin:
average c. of a life BROWNING:R 78
From Log C. to White House THAY 1
Make me a willow c. SHAK:TWE 16
small c. build there YEATS 4
cabin-boy: C. did swim all to BALL 24
cabinet:
consequence of C. government BAGE 8
Or c. of *pleasure* HERB:G 34
this C. of Mediocrities DISR:B 13
cable: chord, nor c. can so forcibly BURTON:Ro 21
Cabots: C. talk only to God BOSSI 1
cabs: busy driving c. and cutting hair BURNS:G 1
cackle: cut The c. and pursue MACDIAR 24
cadence: harsh c. of a rugged line DRYD 73
Cadiz Bay: reeking into C.B. BROWNING:R 51
Caesar:
Broad-fronted C. SHAK:ANT 22
C. bears such rebel blood SHAK:JUL 33
C. had his Brutus HENRY:P 1
C. hath wept SHAK:JUL 50
C. is more dangerous than he SHAK:JUL 31
C. is turn'd to hear SHAK:JUL 3
C., now be still SHAK:JUL 87
C. was a man of great common SHAW 24
C.'s wife must be above PROV 51
C.'s wife must be above suspicion CAES:GJ 5
call great C. ass Unpolicied SHAK:ANT 75
Did I the tired C. SHAK:JUL 8
Either C. or nothing BORGIA 1
for always I am C. SHAK:JUL 15
for C.'s I. am WYATT 7
Here was a C. SHAK:JUL 59
I am C.'s daughter JULIA 2
I come to bury C. SHAK:JUL 48
Imperious C., dead SHAK:HAM 185
in envy of great C. SHAK:JUL 88
master C. is in the tent YEATS 117
melt their sweets On blossoming C. SHAK:ANT 47
Not that I lov'd C. less SHAK:JUL 45
shall C. bleed in sport SHAK:JUL 38
So long as C.'s self is God's? CRASH 5
sometimes forgets that he is C. JULIA 2
that C. might be great CAMPBELL:T 6
Then fall, C. SHAK:JUL 35
'Tis paltry to be C. SHAK:ANT 62
unto C. the things which are C.'s BIBLE 426
upon Dead C.'s trencher SHAK:ANT 39
What C. did DONNE 76
where some buried C. bled FITZGER:E 13
Caesars:
many C. Ere such another SHAK:CYM 7
now no kings nor C. POUND 5
Cafe Royal: upper room in the C.R. BAGN 1
cage:
cannot c. the minute MACNEICE 4
keeps a lady in a c. CHESTERTON 11
linnet born within the c. TENNY 141
Nor iron bars a c. LOVELACE 5
Robin Red breast in a C. BLAKE:W 82
there's no c. to him HUGHES:Te 1
caged: I Know Why the C. Bird Sings ANGELOU 1
cages: making nets, not in making c. SWIFT 18
Cain:
C. went out from the presence BIBLE 31
Had C. been Scot CLEVE:J 1
Like C., I am marked HALL:Rad 1
Lord set a mark upon C. BIBLE 30
Of C. and his brother, Abel COLERIDGE:ST 42
thy brotherhood of C. BYR 121
cake:
Bake me a c. as fast NURS 50
geological home-made c. DICKENS 106
Let them eat c. MARIE 1
cakes:
in the manufacture of little c. FOUR 2
Land o' C. BURNS:R 74
no more c. and ale? SHAK:TWE 22
Calais:
find 'C.' lying in my heart MARY I 1
Jones! as from C. WORDS:W 46
to shew light at C. JOHNSON:S 123
calamities: c. of life were shared among DEF 2
calamity:
third day a c. PROV 123
wedded to c. SHAK:ROM 32
calculate: c. the Starrs MILT 229
calculating: looks so c. WILDE:O 100
calculation: c. shining out of the other DICKENS 108
calculus:
bumpkin c. of Time SLESS 5
C. racked him BROWNING:R 119
integral and differential c. GILB:WS 24
Caledonia:
C.! stern and wild SCOTT:W 11
support C.'s cause BURNS:R 100
Caledonian: Firm and erect the C. stood HOME 4
calendar: year of the Julian C., 710 USSH 1
calf:
Bring hither the fatted c. BIBLE 464
c. won't get much sleep ALLEN:W 9
When he killed a c. AUBREY 10
calf's-skin: hang a c. on those recreant SHAK:KING J 9
Caliban:
'Ban 'Ban, Ca – C. SHAK:TEM 19
C. seeing his own face WILDE:O 20
Calibans: with C. SHAK:TEM 7
call:
C. me by the old familiar HOLL:HS 1
c. me that, *smile* WIST 1
C. of the Wild LOND 1
c. ye upon him while BIBLE 330
Don't c. us ANON 179
I know not what to c. you ELIZ I 14
May I c. you 338? COWARD 31
one clear c. for me TENNY 296
only c. me thine COLERIDGE:ST 45
they come when you do c. for them? SHAK:HEN.IV[1] 57
What shall I c. thee? BLAKE:W 21
wild c. and a clear c. MASE 2
callans: c. cryin i the Temple BIBLE 591
called:
I've been c. many things BANK 3
many are c. BIBLE 425
calligraphy: c. . . . indulges in cursive MURA 2
calm:
all is c. again GAY 7
all our c. is in that balm NORT 3
Be c. in arguing HERB:G 8
c. the troubled mind CONG 62
for a c. unfit DRYD 38
no joy but c. TENNY 28
to c. contending kings SHAK:POET 6
calmness:
Calmnesse is great advantage HERB:G 9
gay c. of the Pagan OUIDA 1
so aggravating as c. WILDE:O 61
calms: And c. the troubled breast NEWT:J 2
calumniate: c. boldly BACON:F[1] 29
calumnies: C. are answered best JONS 17
calumny:
silent is the best answer to c. WASH 3
thou shalt not escape c. SHAK:HAM 101
Calvin: C., oat-cakes, and sulphur SMITH:Syd[1] 18
Calvinistic: We have a C. creed PITT:W[1] 8
Calwell: C.'s three great loves were FREUDEN 2
Cam: Isis and C., to patient Science WORDS:W 132
Camberley: nine o'clock C. BETJ 21
Cambridge:
After C. – unemployment EWART 2
C. has seen Wordsworth drunk HOUSM 58
C. people rarely smile BROOKE 11
C. science and a sausage ANON 230
city of perspiring dreams* RAPH 1
happen in C. almost every NAB 2
it's either Oxford or C. SNAGGE 1
To C. books TRAPP 1
to C. books he sent BROWNE:W[2] 1
visit C. first BAED 1
Camden Town: Having baths in C.T. BETJ 22
came:
He c. and he went WHITTY 1
I c.; I saw; God conquered JOHN III SOB 1
I c., I saw, I conquered CAES:GJ 4
I c., saw, and overcame SHAK:HEN.IV[2] 40
Tell them I c. DE LA M 7
came-over-with-the-conqueror: C. type of mind WATSON:W 2
camel:
breaks the c.'s back PROV 224
C. came chewing milkweed KIP 21
C. humphed himself KIP 22
C.'s hump is an ugly lump KIP 102
easier for a c. to go through BIBLE 445
swallow a c. BIBLE 427
Take my c., dear MACAULAY:R 5
'tis like a c. indeed SHAK:HAM 126
Camelot:
cackling home to C. SHAK:KING L 24
To many-tower'd C. TENNY 12
camera:
c. cannot lie EVANS:H 1
c. with its shutter open ISH 2
camerado:
C., this is no book WHITMAN 27
great C. WHITMAN 9
cameraman: c. is in the right place WHITLAM 3
camp: waiting on the Common outside the c. GREENE:G 8
Campbell: do not Maister or C. me SCOTT:W 75
Campbell-Bannerman, H.: about whom all is forgotten* BENTLEY:N 1
Campbells: C. are comin' ANON 7
Campden Hill: strikes the stars on C.H. CHESTERTON 3
camphire: all c. and frankincense CONG 57
camps: Courts and c. are the only places CHESTERFIELD 5
can:
c. because they think they c. VIRGIL 64
c. must be so sweet HOPK:GM 1
I c.; C. something, hope HOPK:GM 20
Pass me the c. HOUSM 31
You c. and you can't DOW 1
You c., for you ought to GOET 9
youth replies, 'I c.' EMER 100
Canada: C. is a country so square BENNER 1
Canadians: C. ask, 'Can it happen here?' ATWOOD 9
canal:
fishing in the dull c. ELIOT:TS 43
swimming along the old c. BETJ 11
Canberra: C. – the accent is on the Can DENMAN:GM 1
cancel: c. all our vows DRAYT 9
cancers: because women have C. KEATS 137
candid: be c. where we can POPE 79
candidates: C. should not attempt more than six BELLOC 46
candle:
At length the c.'s out SUCK 2
burning a farthing c. at Dover JOHNSON:S 123
c. burns at both ends MILLAY 1
c. sing'd the moth SHAK:MERC 31
c. to light you to bed NURS 49
farthing-c. to the sun YOUNG:E 5
hold a c. to my shames? SHAK:MERC 25
How far that little c. SHAK:MERC 52
lights a c. to the sun FLETCH:A 2
Like a little c. WARNER:S 1

one c. in my darkness SASS 19
out, brief c. SHAK:MAC 113
set a c. in the sun BURTON:Ro 20
this day light such a c. LAT 2
Two old chairs, and half a c. LEAR 7
white c. In a holy place CAMPBELL:Jo 1
candle-light:
Can I get there by c.? NURS 19
Colours seen by c. BROWNING:EB 5
Fire and fleet and candle-lighte BALL 36
candlelights: stately and daintily as c. BACON:F[1] 115
candles:
c. burn their sockets HOUSM 35
Night's c. are burnt SHAK:ROM 35
Their c. are all out SHAK:MAC 31
candlestick-maker: butcher, the baker, The c. NURS 63
candy:
c. deal of courtesy SHAK:HEN.IV[1] 23
C. Is dandy NASH 3
canker:
c. lives in sweetest bud SHAK:SON 17
killing as the C. to the Rose MILT 47
this c., Bolingbroke? SHAK:HEN.IV[1] 20
worm, the c., and the grief BYR 241
Cannery Row: C.R. in Monterey STEINB 1
Cannes: C. is where you lie REED:R 2
cannibal: sleep with a sober c. MELV 2
cannibalism: everything would be lawful, even c. DOST 4
cannikin: why clink the c.? BROWNING:R 47
cannon:
C. to right of them TENNY 199
then the c. CHESTERTON 20
cannon-ball: c. took off his legs HOOD 3
cannons: land, where the c. bloom? KAST 1
canoe:
man paddle his own c. MARR 1
on the floor of a narrow c. ELIOT:TS 49
canoes: shod their heads in their c. MARV 34
canonized: many (questionless) c. on earth BROWNE:T 14
canopies: c. of costly state SHAK:HEN.IV[2] 30
Canossa: We won't go to C. BISM 4
cans: clatter of Sir James Barrie's c. GUED 2
cant:
c. of criticism is the most tormenting STERNE 20
Clear your *mind* of c. JOHNSON:S 237
Don't c. in defence of savages JOHNSON:S 245
we have nothing but c., c., c. PEAC 9
canteen: double drills and no c. KIP 57
canvass: ordeal of a political c. SHERMAN 3
canyon: In a cavern, in a c. MONTROSE 1
cap: riband in the c. of youth SHAK:HAM 175
capability:
c. and godlike reason SHAK:HAM 156
Negative C. KEATS 124
caparisons: C. don't become a young woman SHERIDAN:RB 13
cape: person in the Spanish c. ELIOT:TS 29
Cape of Good Hope: me to double the C.o.G.H. BACON:F[1] 23
Capella: star called C. was yellow HARDY:T 51
capers:
c. nimbly in a lady's chamber SHAK:RIC.III 2
He c., he dances SHAK:MERR 11
true lovers run into strange c. SHAK:AS 23
capital:
before a jury for a c. crime JOHNSON:S 183
high C., where kingly Death SHELLEY:PB 108
not want C. in Heaven ELIOT:TS 19
capitalism:
c. 'inevitably' caused war TAYL:AJP 2
C. is the exploitation of man ANON 167
C., wisely managed, can probably KEYN 4
European c. may crash LENIN 12
fight c. even if it kills me PANK:S 2
form of c. will make way ORTEGA S 1
give a definition of c. HAMP 3
one of the chief bulwarks of c. KELLER 1
unacceptable face of c. HEATH 2
Under c. we have a state LENIN 3
well paid watch-dogs of C. GONNE 1
capitalist:
bolster up the c. system WAUGH:E N
C. production creates MARX:K 6
Governments in a c. society CONNOLLY:J 2
peculiar c. country LENIN 6
to the c. mode of production MARCUSE 1
Capitol: Who was't betrayed the C.? OTWAY 3
capitulate: I will not c. JOHNSON:S 249
capon: Madeira and a cold c.'s leg? SHAK:HEN.IV[1] 14
capons: you cannot feed c. so SHAK:HAM 110
caps: They threw their c. SHAK:COR 3
captain:
C.! My C. WHITMAN 29
c. of the Hampshire grenadiers GIBBON:E 23
C. of the Pinafore GILB:WS 7
C.'s hand on his shoulder NEWBOLT 10
I am the c. of my soul HENL 2
in the c.'s but a choleric word SHAK:MEA 14
captains:
C. and the Kings depart KIP 91
c. courageous whom death BALL 37
C. of industry CARLYLE:T 53
captived: body in the walls c. RALE 7
captives: proclaim liberty to the c. BIBLE 333
Capulet: no longer be a C. SHAK:ROM 10
Capulets: than in the tomb of the C. BURKE:E 84
car:
afford to keep a motor c.? SHAW 121
buy a second-hand c. from this man? SAHL 2
c. comes up, with lamps HARDY:T 43
c. has become the carapace MCLUH 6
c. rattling o'er the stony BYR 77
gilded C. of Day MILT 20
loving relationship with his c. MOFF 1
motor c. is our supreme form of privacy MCLUH 8
caravan:
Put up your c. HODG 6
Where my c. has rested TESCH 1
caravans: With c., but never an ape POUND 16
caravanserai: in this batter'd C. FITZGER:E 11
carbon: c. atom possesses certain exceptional JEANS 1
carboniferous: In the C. Epoch KIP 150
carbuncle: c. on the face of a much-loved CHARLES:Prince 4
carbuncular: young man's c. ELIOT:TS 45
carcase: c. of an old song THOMAS:RS 2
carcasses: dead c. of unburied men SHAK:COR 10
card:
He's a cheery old c. SASS 9
We must speak by the c. SHAK:HAM 181
cardinal:
Jackdaw sat on the C.'s chair BARH 3
unbecoming for a c. to ski badly JOHN PAUL 3
cards:
Fate shuffles the c. SCHOP 3
have patience, and shuffle the c. CERV 21
Lucky at c., unlucky PROV 256
Never play c. with a man called ALG 2
not learned to play at c. JOHNSON:S 85
old Age of C. POPE 138
play'd At c. for kisses LYLY 3
wicked pack of c. ELIOT:TS 36
care:
absolute paternal c. ELIOT:TS 97
asleep, and then the c. is over TEMPLE:W[1] 1
begone, dull C. ANON 6
Can a woman's tender c. COWP 7
c. kill'd a cat SHAK:MUCH 32
C. Sat on his faded cheek MILT 137
c. will kill a cat WITHER 2
c.'ll kill a cat JONS 1
Careless she is with artful c. CONG 59
Deliberation sat and publick c. MILT 158
efter ioy oftymes cummis cair HENRYS 3
fig for c. HEYW:J 2
great deal too much, c. of me EDGE 6
Heaven's peculiar c. SOMER 2
I c. for nobody BICK 3
I shan't c. or ho HARDY:T 11
in thee to kill c. SHAK:MUCH 32
Irks c. the crop-full bird? BROWNING:R 185
meant I did not c. for them HARTL 1
Nor c. beyond today GRAY:T 7
now with me past c. SHAK:RIC.II 22
rider's back sits dismal C. HORACE 28
Sport that wrincled C. derides MILT 67
Take c. of the pence, and PROV 362
taken better c. of myself BLAKE:E 1
this life if, full of c. DAVIES:WH 2
tiresome verse-reciter, C. SHELLEY:PB 161
to c. and not to c. ELIOT:TS 66
Took great C. of his Mother MILNE 2
'twas nipt With c. MIDD 1
women and c. and trouble WARD:N 1
career:
c. open to talent NAPO I 7
c. that made the Recording Angel BENTLEY:N 2
having a c. of my own BALF 5
ideal of a manly c. DISR:B 24
my brilliant c. FRANKLIN:M 1
stake my entire political c. OWEN:D 2
structural approach to c. PRAT 1
which might damage his c. BARRIE 11
careful:
can't be good, be c. PROV 190
So c. of the type TENNY 155
careless:
c. of mankind TENNY 33
C. she is with artful care CONG 59
So c. of the single life TENNY 155
carelessness:
lose both seems like c. WILDE:O 87
With carefullest c. BETJ 20
cares:
c. can make the sweetest GREENE:R 1
c. that infest the day LONGFEL 14
deprest with c. GAY 20
If no one c. for me BICK 3
one c. for none of them AUSTEN 75
poor devil has ended his c. BROWNING:R 135
war'ly c. an' war'ly men BURNS:R 4
with caris cald and kene HENRYS 1
cargo: With a c. of ivory MASE 9
caribous: c. lie around and snooze COWARD 21
caricatures: c. are the most penetrating HUX:A 23
Carlisle:
roused the burghers of C. MACAULAY:TB 42
You may go to C.'s ANST 1
Carlyle:
He had his talents* CARLYLE:JW 1
let C. and Mrs C. marry BUTLER:S[2] 51
carnage: c. and his conquests cease BYR 24
carnal:
Heathen in the c. part POPE 131
satisfy men's c. lusts PRAY 81
carnation:
could never abide c. SHAK:HEN.V 15
with a c. up my nose MACKINN 1
carnations: c. and streak'd gillyvors SHAK:WIN 17
carol:
fluting a wild c. TENNY 279
It was the c. of a bird BYR 50
carolings: So little cause for c. HARDY:T 17
carpenter:
Walrus and the C. CARROLL 55
You may scold a c. JOHNSON:S 111
carpet:
after a bit the c. ends CHURCH:W 48
All wear the c. YEATS 40
carpet-mongers: bookful of these quondam c. SHAK:MUCH 33
carpets:
damned tartan c. always put me off FRASER:GM 1
long c. rose along KEATS 77
carriage:
C. held but just Ourselves DICKIN:E 13
I can't afford a c. DAC 1
like a horse and c. CAHN 1
very small second-class c. GILB:WS 51
women of good c. SHAK:ROM 5
carried: we are c. high BERNARD:Ch 1
carrion: c. comfort, Despair HOPK:GM 20
carry:
c. everything before me DISR:B 48
c. them in his bosom BIBLE 322
for to c. me home ANON 42
cars:
even the c. are half-timbered HUMPH 4
giant finned c. nose forward LOWELL:R 13
Carter: Jimmy C. had the air of a man SIMON:G 1
Carthage:
C. must be destroyed CATO 1

mighty C., raised higher HORACE 36
carve:
carf biforn his fader CHAUC 7
c. in Latin or in Greek WALLER 5
c. on every tree SHAK:AS 36
Let's c. him as a dish SHAK:JUL 24
not c. heads upon cherry-stones JOHNSON:S 244
To c. out dials SHAK:HEN.VI[3] 3
carved: c. the red deer and the bull TURNER:WJR 4
carver: was the c. happy RUSKIN 1
carving: Now it is time for c. POUND 21
Cary Grant: Old C.G. fine GRANT:C 1
case:
c. is concluded AUGUS 12
c. is still before the court HORACE 104
c. will be thrown out with HORACE 70
Clutching a little c. AUD 11
casement:
at the c. seen her stand? TENNY 14
c. high and triple-arch'd KEATS 69
c. ope at night KEATS 89
Full on this c. shone KEATS 70
Casement: ghost of Roger C. YEATS 107
casements: Charm'd magic c. KEATS 93
cash:
c. payment has become the sole CARLYLE:T 40
fifty-five on, she needs good c. TUCK 1
from hand to hand of c. SICK 1
only the poor who pay c. FRANCE 11
pay you c. to go away KIP 137
take the C. in hand FITZGER:E 9
cashiered: shall ... be C. ANON 156
cask: oldest c. is opened MACAULAY:TB 54
Cassius: C. has a lean and hungry SHAK:JUL 14
cassowary: If I were a c. WILB 2
cast:
more he c. away BUNYAN 28
set my life upon a c. SHAK:RIC.III 21
To c. into my teeth SHAK:JUL 73
caste: harsh fetters of Colour and C.? PRINGLE:T 4
castle:
c. Brown as owls THOMAS:D 14
c. or building not in decay BACON:F[1] 89
Cowards c. CHAPMAN:G 1
Englishman's home is his c. PROV 95
I'm the king of the c. NURS 25
Little war that c. knew MORRIS:W 10
splendour falls on c. walls TENNY 106
strong c. is our God LUTHER 4
This c. hath a pleasant seat SHAK:MAC 22
castled: c. crag of Drachenfels BYR 88
Castlereagh:
He had a mask like C. SHELLEY:PB 37
intellectual eunuch C. BYR 157
castles:
c. I have, are built with air JONS 15
C. in the air – they're so easy IBS 16
make castels thanne in Spayne CHAUC 104
castration: c. may be the solution LEWIS:W 3
casualty: first c. when war comes JOHNSON:H 1
casuists: soundest C. doubt POPE 76
cat:
call his c. Pusset HARE:ME 2
care kill'd a c. SHAK:MUCH 32
care'll kill a c. JONS 1
care will kill a c. WITHER 2
c. and the fiddle NURS 16
c. has nine lives PROV 52
c. in profound meditation ELIOT:TS 86
c. may look at a king CARROLL 22
c. may look at a king PROV 53
C. of such deceitfulness ELIOT:TS 84
c. that likes to Gallop SMITH:Ste 5
c. that walks alone BEAV 5
C., the Rat, and Lovell COLLINGBO 1
C. who walks by himself KIP 27
c. will mew SHAK:HAM 190
c.'s away, the mice will play PROV 426
Curiosity killed the c. PROV 63
Hanging of his c. on Monday BRATH 1
he is a very fine c. JOHNSON:S 236
I shall bell the c. DOUGLAS:Arc 1
if your mother's c. had but kitten'd SHAK:HEN.IV[1] 55
Lat take a c. CHAUC 53
made a c. laugh PLAN 1
more than one way to skin a c. PROV 371
More ways of killing a c. KINGSLEY:C 2
Old Foss is the name of his c. LEAR 6
part to tear a c. in SHAK:MID 7
piss and vinegar like a barber's c. DAVIES:R 1
pussy c., Where have you been? NURS 55
Runcible C. with crimson whiskers LEAR 26
see how the c. jumps SCOTT:W 96
see the c. i' the dairy ELIOT:G 12
Self-reliant like the c. MOORE:M 5
smile of a cosmic Cheshire c. HUX:JS 1
some of the tranquillity of the c. ROWB 1
vigilant as a c. to steal cream SHAK:HEN.IV[1] 79
wasn't room to swing a c. DICKENS 164
What C.'s averse to fish? GRAY:T 13
When I play with my c. MONTAIGNE 15
Who will bell the c.? DESCH 1
catalogue:
dull c. of common things KEATS 108
in the c. ye go for men SHAK:MAC 61
cataract:
sounding c. Haunted me WORDS:W 7
wild c. leaps in glory TENNY 106
cataracts: c. ablaze with Heaven HARRISON 1
catastrophe:
c. of the old comedy SHAK:KING L 10
I'll tickle your c. SHAK:HEN.IV[2] 21
man confronts c. on the road TURNBULL 2
race between education and c. WELLS:HG 17
catch-22: simplicity of this clause of C. HELLER 3
catch: hard to c. and conquer MERED:G 31
catched: wise, and not be c. PEPYS 14
catcher: I'd just be the c. in the rye SALIN 4
catechisms: To know but C. and Alphabets DONNE 76
category-habits: Philosophy is the replacement of c. RYLE 2
caterpillar: catterpiller chooses the fairest BLAKE:W 48
caterpillars:
become the c. of the island SCOTT:W 93
c. of the commonwealth SHAK:RIC.II 21
two religious c. MARLOWE 24
catharsis: it effects a c. ARISTOT 18
Cathay: than a cycle of C. TENNY 88
cathedral:
Heft Of C. Tunes DICKIN:E 4
in the vast c. leave him TENNY 196
cathedrals: been into many of the ancient c. STANTON:El 2
Catherine: glad you like my C. WEST:M 9
Catholic:
doing wrong. I'm still a C. WILSON:Ang 1
I cannot be a good C. NORF 1
I have a C. soul ERAS 5
Roman C. Church is getting nearer PAIS 1
Roman C. woman must keep taking THOMAS:I 1
to be a C. unless they had to GREENE:G 19
won't sign a C. but I'll go home SOUN 1
Catholics:
C. and Communists have committed GREENE:G 14
C. and Protestants you meet ALLING 4
Cato:
C. gives his little senate POPE 30
vanquished pleased C. LUCAN 1
What C. did BUDG 1
cats:
All c. are grey in the dark PROV 7
and killed the c. BROWNING:R 25
C. is 'dogs' and rabbits is PUNCH 10
c. most appreciate in a human HOUSE 1
C., no less liquid TESS 1
Do c. eat bats? CARROLL 2
greater c. with golden eyes SACK 3
hole nacyon Of cattes SKEL:J 2
monkeys and c. – all human life JAMES:H 4
Naming of C. is a difficult ELIOT:TS 85
three black c. Watch DE LA M 12
where c. are c. MARQUIS 1
wild c. in a red-hot iron cage BROWNING:R 97
cattle:
Actors should be treated like c. HITCH 4
call the c. home KINGSLEY:C 13
c. rise and listen KINGSMILL 2
c. then are sick KINGSMILL 2
for these who die as c.? OWEN:W 1
Our Andy's gone with c. LAWS 3
Catullus:
C. gives his greatest thanks CATUL 12
their C. walk that way? YEATS 40
caught:
Ah ha! Y'are c. SHAK:ANT 30
better than any that've been c. PROV 377
cauldron:
Fire burn, and c. bubble SHAK:MAC 78
Round about the c. go SHAK:MAC 78
cauliflower: C. is nothing but cabbage with TWAIN 19
cause:
beauty of the good old c. WORDS:W 73
c. of cheering us all up BENNETT:Ar 2
c. that cannot lose FRY:C 18
c. that perishes with them? CLOUGH 18
failure to discover the c. JAMES:PD 1
help the just c. MORE:H 4
in the armour of a righteous c. BRYAN 2
It is the c. SHAK:OTH 60
know c., or just impediment PRAY 79
Obstinacy in a bad c., is but BROWNE:T 12
Our c. is just DICKIN:J 2
set the c. above NEWBOLT 8
victorious c. pleased the gods LUCAN 1
causes:
any good, brave c. left OSB:J 7
home of lost c. ARNOLD:M 56
is the knowledge of c. BACON:F[1] 124
malice, to breed c. JONS 21
thread of c. was spinning from eternity AUR 13
understand the c. of things VIRGIL 26
caution: c. in love is perhaps the most fatal RUSS:B 14
cavaliero: he was a perfect c. BYR 132
cavaliers:
C. (Wrong but Wromantic) SELL 6
former were called c. FIELDING 17
cave:
c. art of the twentieth century MCLUH 7
darkesome c. they enter SPENS 29
In this our pinching c. SHAK:CYM 11
lone c.'s stillicide HARDY:T 9
misty eastern c. SHELLEY:PB 145
Upon the smooth c. rock TURNER:WJR 4
vacant interlunar c. MILT 281
cave-dwellers: produced a wilderness of c. HOWARD:P 2
Cave of Adullam: his political C.o.A. BRIGHT 3
cavern: In a c., in a canyon MONTROSE 1
caverns:
c. measureless to man COLERIDGE:ST 63
Gluts twice ten thousand c. KEATS 18
Sand-strewn c., cool ARNOLD:M 1
caves:
Ages's icy c. SHELLEY:PB 81
c. in which his shadow will be NIET 15
Ring from their marble c. DRUMMOND OF H 3
those c. of ice COLERIDGE:ST 63
unfathom'd c. of ocean GRAY:T 20
caviare: 'twas c. to the general SHAK:HAM 86
cavity: filling his last c. ANON 144
Cawdor:
Glamis thou art, and C. SHAK:MAC 19
Thane of C. lives SHAK:MAC 13
cease:
did not c. while he stayed HAZL 23
fears that I may c. to be KEATS 21
To c. upon the midnight KEATS 93
Cecco: must have another C. SFORZA 1
cedar:
c. tall and slender O'KEEFFE:J 1
grow like a c. in Lebanon BIBLE 228
ceiling:
engraved in the lines of the c. ELUARD 1
stood up and spat on the c. ANON 105
celandine: 'Tis the little C. WORDS:W 100
celebrities: like they knew they were c. SALIN 3
celebrity:
c. is a person who is known BOORS 2
c. is a person who works hard ALLEN:F 1
celery:
thousand people crunching c. SHAW 134
thrives in the dark. Like c. HUX:A 11

Celia:
C, C. shits SWIFT 66
C. (since thou art so proud) CAREW:T 4
celibacy:
c. has no pleasures JOHNSON:S 24
c. is almost always a muddy PEAC 3
cell:
Each in his narrow c. GRAY:T 16
Thou hast given me a c. HERR 2
cellar:
born in a c. CONG 22
Born in a c. . . . and living FOOTE 2
cello: c. is not one of my favourite THOMAS:I 4
cells: gray c., It is up to them CHRIS 1
Celt: blind hysterics of the C. TENNY 178
Celts: Never C. They're stringy JOHNSTON:Jen 1
cemetery:
c. in which nine of his daughters THURB 3
c. is an open space among SHELLEY:PB 105
cenotaph: laugh at my own c. SHELLEY:PB 56
censer: c. in a barber's SHAK:TAM 11
censor:
c. one's own thoughts WALEY 1
Deleted by French c. BENNETT:JG 1
censorship: Assassination is the extreme form of c. SHAW 100
censure:
c. freely who have written POPE 6
c. of a man's self is oblique JOHNSON:S 204
c., without hope of praise JOHNSON:S 5
Take each man's c. SHAK:HAM 30
centaur: mortal c., man and wife? BYR 211
centaurs: from the waist they are c. SHAK:KING L 68
centre:
c. cannot hold YEATS 62
love being at the c. of things THATCH:M 18
May sit i' th' center MILT 30
My c. is giving way FOCH 1
poor c. of a man's actions BACON:F[1] 121
cents: won't need the ten c. MARX:G 14
centuries:
All c. but this GILB:WS 65
forty c. are looking down NAPO I 4
century:
c. of the common man WALLACE:H 1
history of the first half of this c. BEECHAM 7
screaming into the twentieth c. STEVENSON:A 12
screaming into the twenty-first c. PORTER:G 1
Cerberus: Of C., and blackest midnight MILT 65
cereal: what breakfast c. is made of? DAH 1
cerebration: well of unconscious c. JAMES:H 16
cerebrums: larger c. and smaller adrenal glands MENCK 8
ceremonial: c. purposes the otherwise HERB:AP 19
ceremony:
It useth an enforced c. SHAK:JUL 66
No c. that to great ones SHAK:MEA 10
thrice gorgeous c. SHAK:HEN.V 35
Ceres:
C. reassume the land POPE 73
cost C. all that pain MILT 191
certain:
c. because it is impossible TERT 4
c. but death and taxes PROV 299
Nothing more c. than incertainties BARNF 1
one thing is c. FITZGER:E 16
certainties:
hot for c. in this MERED:G 29
man will begin with c. BACON:F[1] 5
certainty:
c. lay, in everyday work CAMUS 5
not to seek tranquility in c. BOYD:W 2
prefer complexity to c. BISS 1
quit a c. for an uncertainty JOHNSON:S 32
Cervantes:
C. is never petulant MACAULAY:TB 3
C. on his galley sets CHESTERTON 22
C. smiled Spain's chivalry BYR 229
cesspool: c. into which all the loungers DOYLE:AC 3
chafe: He that lets Another c. HERB:G 9
chaff:
c. well meant for grain TENNY 130
like c. in my Mouth KEATS 166
prints the c. STEVENSON:A 13
chaffinch: c. sings on the orchard bough BROWNING:R 49
chain:
c. is no stronger than its PROV 54
c. that is round us now CORY 4
c., which reacheth down BURTON:Ro 19
ends of an invisible c. LERM 1
flesh to feel the c. BRONTE:E 4
remove a lengthening c. GOLDS 4
Their land from error's c. HEB 2
chained: ancestors . . . were probably c. together HUGHES:B 4
chains:
Adamantin c. and penal Fire MILT 110
Bound by gold c. TENNY 279
c. and calls them Liberty BUCHANAN 8
c. and I grew friends BYR 51
C. and slaverie BURNS:R 107
everywhere he is in c. ROUSS:JJ 1
leaps to lose his c. WATTS 17
nothing to lose but its c. MARX:K/ENG 3
often better to be in c. KAF 6
sang in my c. like the sea THOMAS:D 17
Shake your c. to earth SHELLEY:PB 39
woman must wear c. FARQ 12
chair:
age of the editorial c. MCLUH 3
C. she sat in ELIOT:TS 40
c., that fits all buttocks SHAK:ALL 5
rack of a too easy c. POPE 173
Seated in thy silver c. JONS 11
tail it knocks over a c. TOYN 1
tavern c. was the throne JOHNSON:S 272
up a c. to the writing desk ANON 205
With one enormous c. LERN 2
chairs:
c. are being brought in AUD 55
three c. in my house THOREAU 19
Two old c., and half a candle LEAR 7
chaise-longue: hurly-burly of the c. CAMPBELL:Mrs P 2
chalk: like making c. marks on water FRAME 1
challenge: I used to c. . . . everything BERLING 1
cham: great C. of literature SMOL 15
chamber: And in my lady's c. NURS 14
Chamberlain:
good mayor of Birmingham* LLOYD GEO 15
Listening to a speech by C. BEVAN 5
chambermaid: as happy in the arms of a c. JOHNSON:S 207
chambermaids: worms that are thy c. SHAK:ROM 44
chambers:
four c., the right ventricle BRIDIE 1
perfum'd c. of the great SHAK:HEN.IV[2] 30
chameleon: c.'s dish SHAK:HAM 110
chameleons: C. feed on light SHELLEY:PB 33
champagne:
C. certainly gives one SURT 2
his feet in a bucket of c. KELLY:B 1
not a c. teetotaller SHAW 11
simply sent c. and women O'ROUR 2
water flowed like c. EVAR 1
with a pint of imperial c. GALS 3
with c. and a chicken MONTAGU 1
chance:
bludgeonings of c. HENL 1
c. favours only the prepared PASTEUR 1
C. might be God's pseudonym FRANCE 5
dice will never eliminate c. MALLAR 3
Everybody should have an equal c. WILSON:Harold 11
Have a care o' th' main c. BUTLER:S[1] 25
high Arbiter C. governs all MILT 172
Necessitie and C. Approach not MILT 226
No gifts from c. ARNOLD:M 4
to thee ane blissed c. DUNB 15
why take the c. REAG 12
chancel:
broken c. with a broken TENNY 273
Strange sounds along the c. pass'd SCOTT:W 6
chancellor: rather susceptible C. GILB:WS 43
Chancellor of the Exchequer: C.o.t.E. is a man whose duties LOWE 2
change:
accept the things I cannot c. NIEB 2
certain relief in c. IRV 6
C. and decay in all around LYTE 1
C. as the winds c. SWIN 45
C. is inevitable DISR:B 68
C. is not made without inconvenience HOOK 3
c. itself can give no more SEDLEY 6
c. of nuisances is as good as LLOYD GEO 13
ever-whirling wheele of C. SPENS 44
extreams by c. more fierce MILT 165
I c., but I cannot die SHELLEY:PB 56
I would c. still less BROWNING:R 73
Keep the c., my dear EVANS:E 2
lamentable c. SHAK:KING L 55
learned that c. comes slowly MCCART 1
leave it to a torrent of c. CHESTERTON 42
more things c. KARR 1
moveth, doth in C. delight SPENS 45
must often c. who would be constant CONF 26
necessary not to c. FALK 1
Neither to c., nor falter SHELLEY:PB 87
not boast that I do c. SHAK:SON 55
not necessary to c. FALK 1
point, however, is to c. it MARX:K 2
preferable to c. and disturbance MONTAIGNE 19
question which involves a great c. TROLL 22
ringing grooves of c. TENNY 87
that I would c. with him? ADAMS:FP 3
things do not c.; we c. THOREAU 22
Times c. and we c. ANON 243
'tis Nature's law to c. ROCHES 9
to c. my state with kings SHAK:SON 11
universe is c. AUR 6
wind of c. is blowing MACMILL:H 7
with fear of c. Perplexes MILT 136
without the means of some c. BURKE:E 51
women set out to try to c. a man DIET 5
Women to c. their shapes SHAK:TWO 15
changed:
all things are c. BACON:F[1] 3
c., c. utterly YEATS 45
changit right clean in another kind JAMES I 3
He, too, has been c. YEATS 42
living creatures are c. LUCRET 6
so c. that my oldest creditors FOX:HS 1
we shall all be c. BIBLE 526
changelessness:
Five decades hardly* HARDY:T 53
The great inviolate place* HARDY:T 59
changes:
what c. hast thou seen TENNY 183
world's a scene of c. COWLEY:A 2
changing:
ever c., like a joyless eye SHELLEY:PB 101
oft c. is loss TUSS 4
What man thinks of c. himself TROLL 21
Chankly Bore: Hills of the C.B. LEAR 9
channel: c. of no-meaning NEWM:JH 11
Channel:
brush the C. with his sleeve SCHLIEF 1
Butting through the C. MASE 9
drum them up the C. NEWBOLT 5
you are crossing the C. GILB:WS 51
Channel Fleet: C.F. been knocked to atoms SMITH:Syd[1] 5
chant: How can ye c. BURNS:R 96
chaos:
advantages of c.? MANN:T 4
Be no longer a C. CARLYLE:T 15
C., an ill-formed OSB:J 17
c., illuminated by flashes WILDE:O 5
C. is come again SHAK:OTH 31
C.! is restor'd POPE 175
C. often breeds life ADAMS:H 4
C. Umpire sits MILT 172
Frighted the Reign of C. MILT 131
God dawned on C. SHELLEY:PB 113
like a cloak of c. GUNN:T 3
means of overcoming c. RICHARDS:IA 1
stillness in the midst of c. BELLOW 1
chapel:
Devil always builds a c. DEF 10
gates of this C. were shut BLAKE:W 71
no c. on the day WILDE:O 118
through the c. of my soul HODG 4
chapman: When c. billies leave BURNS:R 83
Chapman: Mr C.'s yea was yea BENTLEY:EC 2
chapter: c. of accidents is a very long CHESTERFIELD 27
character:
As to the poetical C. KEATS 147
c. comes second ARISTOT 19

c. dead at every word SHERIDAN:RB 22
C. in the headlong rush GOET 5
C. is a by-product WILSON:W 7
c. is destiny ELIOT:G 19
C. is like a tree LINC 22
C. is nature in the highest EMER 36
December 1910, human c. changed WOOLF:V 1
each other's c. before marriage WILDE:O 98
entailing Divergence of C. DARW:C 4
fashion is the beginning of c. MURRAY:LA 3
leave my c. behind me SHERIDAN:RB 23
object the formation of c. SPENCER:H 3
passion could bring c. YEATS 120
reganing my c. I despare FLEM:M 2
that children are true judges of c. AUD 58
time to influence the c. INGE 10
true index of a man's c. CONNOLLY:C 15
Ulysses is the strongest c. FLAU 2
What is c. but the determination JAMES:H 7

characters:
can be not only those c. CERV 1
c. in one of my novels FITZGER:FS 16
c. of hell to trace GRAY:T 30
Every man has three c. KARR 3
judge either of the feelings or of the c. EDGE 2
Most women have no C. POPE 130
new c. when they are married TROLL 21
No Man's Land with only two c. ADAMOV 1
not be a judge of his c. CHEK 16
Write the c. in dust SCOTT:W 63
your c. talk like typewriters CAMPBELL:Mrs P 4

charge:
C., Chester, c. SCOTT:W 30
c. with all thy chivalry CAMPBELL:T 20
I am in c. at the White House HAIG:A 1

charges: ought warily to begin c. BACON:F[1] 61

Charing Cross:
betwixt Heaven and C.C. THOMP:F 14
C.C., to see Major-General PEPYS 4

chariot:
Bring me my C. of Fire BLAKE:W 98
slap-up gal in a bang-up c. DICKENS 225
Swing low sweet c. ANON 442
Time's wingèd c. MARV 31
Why is his c. so long in BIBLE 133

charities:
cold c. of man to man CRAB 3
patron of some thirty c. TENNY 120

charity:
a little earth for c. SHAK:HEN.VIII 14
and have not c. BIBLE 522
be a c. in sin SHAK:MEA 17
C. and beating begins FLETCH:J 4
C. and Mercy. Not unholy DICKENS 109
C. begins at home BROWNE:T 36
C. begins at home PROV 55
C., dear Miss Prism WILDE:O 92
c. envieth not BIBLE 522
c. never faileth BIBLE 522
C. shall cover the multitude BIBLE 568
C. suffereth long BIBLE 522
c. vaunteth not itself BIBLE 522
dollars spent in so-called c. CARNEG:A 2
doughterly loue and deere charitie MORE:T 2
faith, hope, c. BIBLE 523
feigned c. of the rich man ROUSS:JJ 4
greater humility or c. in Him ANDREW 1
greatest of these is c. BIBLE 523
In c. there is no excess BACON:F[1] 70
living need c. more ARNOLD:G 1
Mankind's concern is C. POPE 99
not give lectures or a little c. WHITMAN 8
voice of Christian c. BURKE:E 50
with c. for all LINC 13
without c. are nothing worth PRAY 46

charity-boy: as the c. said ven he got DICKENS 24

charlatans: c. kill us LA BRU 15

Charlemagne: When Charlemain with all his Peerage MILT 135

Charles: By headless C. BYR 38

Charles I:
C. perished for resisting NAPO I 11
fair and fatal king* JOHNSON:L 5
saddest of all Kings* JOHNSON:L 4

Charles the First:
It was used by C.t.F. COWARD 27
King C.t.F. walked and talked ANON 209

Charles II:
C. was always very merry SELL 7
merry monarch* ROCHES 12
Whose word no man* ROCHES 13

Charlie:
C. he's my darling BURNS:R 109
C. he's my darling HOGG 3
C. is my darling NAIRNE 3
easier to lo'e Prince C. MACDIAR 20
live or die wi' C. HOGG 6
live or die with C. SCOTT:W 61

Charlotte:
C. has been writing a book BRONTE:P 2
Werther had a love for C. THACK 27

charm:
every c. to nature owing PHILIPS:A 2
It's a sort of bloom* BARRIE 10
no need of a remoter c. WORDS:W 7
of hard words like a c. OSB:D 1
Oozing c. from every pore LERN 4
What c. can soothe GOLDS 18

charmed: c. it with smiles and soap CARROLL 91

charmer:
c. whose dimples we prize SHERIDAN:RB 25
Were t'other dear c. away GAY 28

charming:
at least they're never c. EWART 3
c. people have something CONNOLLY:C 7
Ever c., ever new DYER:J[1] 2
People are either c. or tedious WILDE:O 44

charms:
c. all other maids surpass MACNALL 1
C. by accepting POPE 139
C. strike the sight POPE 54
her c. are oblique sunbeams WOLLST 2
lass that has acres o' c. BURNS:R 120
Lifeless C. GAY 3
steals forth and c. the mind YEATS 149
those endearing young c. MOORE:T 3

Charon: deposit us in C.'s boat HORACE 20

charry: see the c. hung with snow HOUSM 3

Chartres: like the Virgin, build C. ADAMS:H 8

Chartreuse: system that produced green C. SAKI 1

chase:
c., the sport of kings SOMER 1
Thy c. had a beast in view DRYD 129
thy c. is done SCOTT:W 37

chasm: deep romantic c. COLERIDGE:ST 63

chassis: worl's in a terrible state o' c. O'CAS 2

chaste:
Be thou as c. SHAK:HAM 101
c., and twenty-three BYR 161
C. as the icicle SHAK:COR 18
c. as unsunn'd snow SHAK:CYM 6
If I pronounce it c. GILB:WS 35
My English text is c. GIBBON:E 28
My life is c., my muse OSB:J 10
Nor ever c., except DONNE 89
sacred poet ought to be c. CATUL 8
she has lost her c. flower CATUL 15
wol nat kepe me chaast CHAUC 77

chasteneth: the Lord loveth he c. BIBLE 558

chastised:
chastis'd with the sober eye Of dull SHAK:ANT 63
father hath c. you with whips BIBLE 160

chastity:
all c. and odour CONG 57
c. and continence, but not yet AUGUS 3
C. faces them JENN:E 1
'Tis c., my brother MILT 32
vice of c. is made into VOLT 34

Chatham: Because you're in C. ANON 162

chats: even spoiled the women's c. BROWNING:R 25

chatter:
hare-brained c. of irresponsible DISR:B 77
idle c. of a transcendental GILB:WS 31
leave the world to c. DANTE 15
put down the insignificant c. TROLL 7

Chatterton: I thought of C. WORDS:W 84

Chaucer:
C., well of English undefyled SPENS 39
He is a perpetual fountain* DRYD 146
He lacks the high seriousness* ARNOLD:M 80
he was the lodesterre* LYD 2
Here is God's plenty* DRYD 145
It is a pity that Chawcer WARD:A 9
worshipful father and first* CAX

chavender: There is a fine stuffed c. ST-LEG 1

cheap:
costs to look this c. PART 1
flesh and blood so c. HOOD 21
King to have things done as c. PEPYS 8
Man's life is c. as beast's SHAK:KING L 29
sell it c. COHEN 1
sold c. what is most dear SHAK:SON 51

cheapness: tawdry c. Shall outlast POUND 28

Cheapside:
As if C. were mad COWP 52
in C. shall my palfrey SHAK:HEN.VI[2] 9
surprised in C. AUBREY 2

cheat:
c. a man is nothing GAY 23
c. at cards genteelly BOSW 2
detecting what I think a c. JOHNSON:S 162
it's so lucrative to c. CLOUGH 20
sweet c. gone DE LA M 21

cheated:
c. into some fine passages KEATS 150
to be exceedingly c. at EVELYN 3

cheating: c. between two periods of fighting BIER 9

check:
c. enclosed PARKER:D 33
dreadful is the c. BRONTE:E 4

checkmate: cheating c. GRAVES:R 5

cheek:
Care sat on his faded c. MILT 137
c. that doth not fade KEATS 59
C. where grows More CRASH 9
cherry, cherry was her c. BALL 2
Feed on her damask c. SHAK:TWE 31
give this C. a little Red POPE 116
Hee that loves a Rosie cheeke CAREW:T 2
her c. upon her hand SHAK:ROM 9
Her c. was soft as silk PAIN 1
hit on one c., he will turn MARSD 1
on thy c. a fading rose KEATS 80
one who offers his c. PROV 199
slapped our c. would get his head KHRU 1
turn the other c. HOLMES:OW 8
yellow C. of hers FITZGER:E 3

cheeks:
c. of sorry grain MILT 39
Fat ruddy c. Augustus HOFFMAN:H 1
starv'd the roses in her c. SHAK:TWO 13

cheer:
Be of good c. BIBLE 414
c. up, my lads GARRICK 4
c. us when we recover BURKE:E 96
Come c. up, my lads ROSSET:C 1
Died the sound of royal c. TENNY 23
Don't c., men PHILIP:JW 1
Greet the unseen with a c. BROWNING:R 214
hoarse, half-human c. DAVIDS 3
scarce forbear to c. MACAULAY:TB 53
to c. but not inebriate BERK 3
why can't he just c. up? MOTION 1

cheerful:
c. as any man could do PEPYS 4
c. look makes a dish HERB:G 56
entertain a c. disposition SHAK:RIC.II 18
God loveth a c. giver BIBLE 529

cheerfulness:
c. as their main characteristic BATES:DM 2
c. was always breaking in EDWARDS:O 2

cheeriness:
chintzy, chintzy c. BETJ 1
cult of c. and manliness ORWELL 10

cheering: cause of c. us all up BENNETT:Ar 2

cheerio: c.! chin-chin WESTON 2

cheerioh: And 'c.' and 'cheeri-bye' BETJ 14

cheese:
bannocks and a share of c. RAMS 2
born i' the rotten c. ELIOT:G 9
Botticelli's a c. PUNCH 27
bread and c., and kisses SWIFT 43
c. and garlic in a windmill SHAK:HEN.IV[1] 63
C. – milk's leap toward FADI 3
do not like green c. CHESTERTON 52
dreamed of c. – toasted STEVENSON:RL 31

eggs and a pound of c. CALVER 4
fill hup the chinks wi' c. SURT 6
Hellish dark, and smells of c. SURT 10
like some valley c. AUD 53
no end of Stilton C. LEAR 17
that produces 265 kinds of c. DE GAU 2
what a swiss c. would think MARQUIS 6
cheeses: ate the c. out of the vats BROWNING:R 25
Chelsea: dressed up as people in C. MURD:I 3
Cheltenham: killed by drinking C. waters ANON 111
chemical: up-to-date in their c. knowledge HALDA 2
cheque:
Bringing the c. and the postal AUD 16
Mrs Claypool's c. will come back MARX:G 15
political blank c. GOSC 1
cheque book: Have you brought the c.b. BUTLER:S[2] 55
chequer-board: C. of Nights and Days FITZGER:E 25
cherchez: *C. la femme* DUMAS:A[P] 2
cherish:
c. those hearts that hate SHAK:HEN.VIII 12
to love and to c. PRAY 84
To love, c., and to obey PRAY 85
cheroot: whackin' white c. KIP 59
cherries:
just a bowl of c. PROV 238
There C. grow, which none CAMPION 9
cherry:
c., c. was her cheek BALL 2
Like a double c. SHAK:MID 30
ruddier than the C. GAY 2
cherry-isle: There's the Land, or Cherry-Ile HERR 10
cherry orchard: c.o. is mine CHEK 12
cherry-ripe: Cherrie-ripe, Ripe, Ripe HERR 10
cherry-stones:
not carve heads upon c. JOHNSON:S 244
people do like carved cherrystones BROWNING:R 216
cherub: C.'s face POPE 128
cherubim: C. does cease to sing BLAKE:W 83
cherubins: quiring to the young-ey'd c. SHAK:MERC 50
chess: devil played at c. with me BROWNE:T 40
chess-board:
c. is the world HUX:TH 1
We called the c. white BROWNING:R 81
chest:
caused his c. to slip down WODE 15
c. of drawers by day GOLDS 31
Fifteen men on the dead man's c. STEVENSON:RL 46
Chesterton: dared attack my C. BELLOC 29
chestnut:
c. casts his flambeaux HOUSM 31
showers betumble the c. HARDY:T 40
chestnut-tree:
c., great-rooted blossomer YEATS 70
Under a spreading c. LONGFEL 11
chestnuts:
sailor's wife had c. SHAK:MAC 5
there the c., summer through BROOKE 6
chevalier:
Young C. BURNS:R 109
young C. HOGG 3
young C. NAIRNE 3
chewing: c. little bits of String BELLOC 15
chianti: bottles of C. to make into lamps SHAFF 1
chiaroscuro: c. Of your naked breasts MALLEY 3
chic: Radical c. WOLFE:Tom 1
chicken:
character called the Game C. DICKENS 135
c. in his pot every Sunday HENRI 1
c. whose head has been cut MITFORD:N 6
Mere c. feed MARX:G 3
Some c.! Some neck CHURCH:W 24
with champagne and a c. MONTAGU 1
chickens:
all my pretty c. and their dam SHAK:MAC 97
beside the white c. WILLIAMS:WC 2
could Christ himself get all the c. DONNE 107
count their c. ere they're hatched BUTLER:S[1] 28
Don't count your c. PROV 76
set a fox to watching the c. TRU 2
would have raised c. MOSES 1
chief:
Hail to the C. SCOTT:W 38
To swell one bloated C.'s BYR 59
chief justice: C.J. was rich, quiet MACAULAY:TB 10
chiefs: mighty C. untimely slain HOMER 1
chieftain:
c. o' the puddin-race BURNS:R 35
Sate Brunswick's fated c. BYR 78
chield: c.'s amang you takin notes BURNS:R 75
child:
act and the c.'s throat COWARD 34
Around the c. bent all the three LANDOR 6
beautiful – a faery's c. KEATS 80
because I'm nobody's c.? CASE 1
but getting wenches with c. SHAK:WIN 9
c. becomes an adult when SZASZ 5
c. belongs to its father ACHEBE 1
c. blown up by age BEAUV 4
c. cannot possibly go on KEMBLE 1
c. imposes on the man DRYD 89
C. is father of the Man WORDS:W 49
c. ought to be of the party AUSTEN 7
c. should always say what's STEVENSON:RL 57
c. that is not clean and neat STEVENSON:RL 55
c. that took one peep of Life ANON 129
c. who knows poems RILKE 1
c.'s head up the horse's arse COWARD 33
dauntless c. stretched forth GRAY:T 34
every c. born therein shall be RUSKIN 27
fetch a c. of five MARX:G 11
flourish in a C. of Six BELLOC 14
Give me a c. for the first seven PROV 146
gobbled up the infant c. HOUSM 49
gods' help, a spirited c. HORACE 34
grave Proves the c. ephemeral AUD 13
Half devil and half c. KIP 99
happy English c. TAYL:Ann 3
healthy c. well nursed is SWIFT 37
heard one calling, *C.* HERB:G 42
Here a little c. I stand HERR 4
How could I answer the c.? WHITMAN 4
I was a c. and she was a c. POE 8
I would not *coddle* the c. JOHNSON:S 140
imprison the c. ... by force of love WHITE:P 4
it didn't seem right to the c. EDGAR 1
knows his own c. SHAK:MERC 21
life is ... but like a forward c. TEMPLE:W[1] 1
making love is c.'s play MITFORD:N 1
Monday's c. is fair of face NURS 41
mother's sake the c. was dear COLERIDGE:ST 3
No c. is born a criminal SMITH:Syd[2] 1
no c. with a c.'s face WRIGHT:J 7
not care for the c.'s rattle JOHNSON:S 134
On a cloud I saw a c. BLAKE:W 13
One stops being a c. PAVE 1
only one pretty c. in the world PROV 385
painted c. of dirt POPE 125
right to a c. with the obligation SHAW 97
room up of my absent c. SHAK:KING J 12
She was an aggravating c. BELLOC 25
simple c., That lightly draws WORDS:W 20
slayeth the c. in the womb POUND 41
solitary c. WORDS:W 25
spare the rod, and spoil the c. BUTLER:S[1] 26
spoil the c. PROV 350
To have a thankless c. SHAK:KING L 21
Train up a c. BIBLE 267
unto us a c. is born BIBLE 308
who shall teach the C. to Doubt BLAKE:W 90
wife sing to her c. EDWARDS:R 1
Wretched C. expires BELLOC 17
Child Rowland: C.R. to the dark tower came SHAK:KING L 51
child-wife: It's only my c. DICKENS 165
childbirth:
Death and taxes and c.? MITCH:M 2
preserved you in the great danger of C. PRAY 93
childhood:
careless c. stray'd GRAY:T 3
C. is the kingdom where MILLAY 8
c. moving like a sigh AUD 29
c. shews the man MILT 272
Old age is a second c. ARISTOP 3
what a lousy c. was like SALIN 1
Womanhood and c. fleet LONGFEL 8
childish:
C., but very Natural COLERIDGE:ST 47
glamour Of c. days LAWR:DH 31
More c. valorous MARLOWE 15
childishness:
It does from c. SHAK:ANT 18
second c. and mere SHAK:AS 34
childless:
C. and crownless BYR 104
proceeded from c. men BACON:F[1] 92
children:
all c. of our environment LAWL 1
Anybody who hates c. FIELDS 6
Are the c. all in bed? NURS 82
banished c. of Eve ANON 37
be called the c. of God BIBLE 384
being deprived of c. ANON 110
best understood by c. and animals STRAV 1
c. at play are not merely MONTAIGNE 6
C. begin by loving WILDE:O 62
c. born of thee are sword TENNY 264
c. casual as birds AUD 32
c. died in the streets AUD 10
c. I might have had? LOWRY:M 1
c. of a larger growth CHESTERFIELD 16
c. of one family Fall out WATTS 12
c. of the devil TENNY 282
C. of the future Age BLAKE:W 77
c. stood watching them KINGSLEY:C 15
C. sweeten labours BACON:F[1] 91
C. that resemble both their Parents HALIF 7
c., tossed to and fro BIBLE 532
c. walking two & two BLAKE:W 23
c., were sooner allured ASCHAM 3
c. will not leave unless I do ELIZ:QM 2
C., you are very little STEVENSON:RL 49
c.'s c. shall say they have lied YEATS 25
Country c. have more than STOW 1
Do you hear the c. weeping BROWNING:EB 2
dogs that of their c. PENN 3
fond of c. (except boys) CARROLL 96
from c. who were rough SPEND 3
get their c. out of the house CLARK:K 2
He that hath wife and c. BACON:F[1] 80
Her c. arise up BIBLE 277
I *see* ... the faces of the little c. EAMES:R 1
I love all my c. CARTER:L 2
I never knows the c. MARR 6
if you're fond of c. JOS 1
known as the C.'s Hour LONGFEL 26
like to have four healthy c. BURNET 2
little c. cried in the streets MOTLEY 1
live with c. round her knees WORDS:W 93
look at my c. I say CARTER:L 1
lost one of my c. this week TURNER:JMW 2
love c. – especially when MITFORD:N 7
make sure my c. are frightened of me GEO V 3
materials to keep c. quiet SWIFT 9
Men are but c. of a larger DRYD 29
Never have c., only grandchildren VIDAL 2
not much about having c. LODGE:D 1
playing at c.'s games from the beginning CHESTERTON 33
provide for, the fatherless c. PRAY 36
provoke not your c. BIBLE 536
raising c. To feed ruddy Lions? EDGAR 2
see his c. fed PUD 2
She had so many c. NURS 72
Suffer the little c. BIBLE 444
terrible c. GAV 1
that c. are true judges of character AUD 58
that loves not his wife and c. TAYL:Jer 4
they started life as c. AMIS:K 4
thou shalt bring forth c. BIBLE 23
To bear many c. is considered GAND:I 4
too easy for c., and too SCHNAB 2
too good to waste on c. SHAW 131
Two c. playing by a stream PARNELL:A 1
unfavourable to the rearing of c. SMITH:Ad 4
violations committed by c. on c. BOWEN:El 1
voices of c. are heard BLAKE:W 22
watch our fair-haired c. play CAMPBELL:G 4
We are the final c. WALLACE-C 1
We have no c., except me BEHAN:Br 10
who ought to have c. BUTLER:S[2] 53
who shall return us the c.? KIP 146
wife and c. are a kind of discipline BACON:F[1] 83
wife and c. but as bills BACON:F[1] 84

with c. you never know where FOY 1
write for c. just as GORKY 13
You are c. of the devil WHITEF 1
Your c. are not your c. GIBRAN 1
chilly:
c. day for Willie ANON 79
feel c. and grown old BROWNING:R 158
Chimborazo: C., Cotopaxi TURNER:WJR 3
chime:
set a c. of words SMITH:LP 16
soft c. had stroked the air JONS 49
chimera: c. bombinating in a vacuum RAB 1
chimeras:
dire C. and enchanted Iles MILT 34
other wild impossible c. SWIFT 33
chimes: hear the c. of midnight STEVENSON:RL 15
chimney:
HORSES WEDGED IN A C. MORTON:JB 4
olde men from the C. corner SIDNEY:P 15
Who smoked like a c. BARH 7
chimney-piece: Buffalo Upon the c. CARROLL 94
chimney-sweepers:
As c., come to dust SHAK:CYM 17
How the C. cry BLAKE:W 74
chimneys:
good grove of c. MORRIS:C 2
your c. I sweep & BLAKE:W 18
chin: Pillows his c. upon an Orient MILT 12
china:
C. that's ancient and blue LANG:A 4
ye break my best blue c. HARDY:T 11
China:
Hooligan was probably invented in C. SAKI 4
infusion of a C. plant ADDIS 17
On a slow boat to C. LOES 1
one who treads the Wall Of C. PATMO 1
tho' C. fall POPE 140
Till C. and Africa meet AUD 6
Chinese:
C. wouldn't dare to COWARD 20
Nothing and no one can destroy the C. BUCK 4
chinks: c. that time has made WALLER 9
chinook: break loose, like the c. LOWELL:R 14
chintzy: c., c. cheeriness BETJ 1
chip: c. on each shoulder ALLEN:D 1
chips: eat c. with everything WESK 2
chisel: Usura rusteth the c. POUND 40
chivalry:
age of c. is gone BURKE:E 55
age of c. is never past KINGSLEY:C 12
age of c. is past DISR:B 6
courteous exterior of a bigot* EASTMAN 1
have a truant been to c. SHAK:HEN.IV[1] 84
He loved chivalrie CHAUC 3
his infernal, cursed c. CERV 11
learn the noble acts of c. CAX 3
nine-tenths of the law of c. SAYERS 1
save fallen C. BYR 60
smiled Spain's c. away BYR 229
Chloe: C. is my real flame PRIOR 6
chloroform: Politics is the c. of the Irish GOGA 4
choice:
being just the terrible c. BROWNING:R 203
in the worth and c. JONS 10
is c., it can only be bad PROUST 12
small c. in rotten apples SHAK:TAM 2
takes your c. PUNCH 2
'Tis Hobson's c. WARD:T 1
you takes your c. ANON 266
choir:
all the c. of Love YEATS 93
sweet singing in the c. ANON 20
wailful c. the small gnats KEATS 109
choirs: Bare ruin'd c. SHAK:SON 33
choke: for nothing but to c. a man JONS 3
cholera: those sins which had caused the c.? KINGSLEY:C 2
choose:
c. by show SHAK:MERC 29
C. One – Then – close DICKIN:E 11
man is forced to c. YEATS 94
right to c. FAUST 1
they c. each other MACHIA 1
what we c. to believe NEWM:JH 19
choosing: just c. so BROWNING:R 170
chop:
if it doesn't, c. it down ANON 201
Some day you'll eat a pork c. CAMPBELL:Mrs P 1
chopcherry: c. ripe within PEELE 4
Chopin: gap between Dorothy and C. ADE 2
chopper:
c. on a big black block GILB:WS 70
c. to chop off your head NURS 49
chops:
C. and tomata sauce DICKENS 36
One c. the wood, the other PROV 308
chord:
c. in unison with what we hear COWP 78
c., nor cable can so forcibly draw BURTON:Ro 21
feel for the common c. BROWNING:R 169
struck one c. of music PROC 2
chore: see his c. done by the gods EMER 57
chortled: He c. in his joy CARROLL 46
Christ:
Came C. the tiger ELIOT:TS 22
C. cannot save thy soul MARLOWE 36
C. follows Dionysus POUND 28
C. his *John* HERB:G 7
C. in this country would DE BL 1
C. receive him TENNY 196
C., Spinoza, and myself STEIN:G 6
C. took the kindness BROWNING:R 200
Christe receive thy saule BALL 36
cold C. and tangled Trinities KIP 36
Cristes loore and his apostles CHAUC 28
do all things through C. BIBLE 543
dreamed that C. has died in vain? SITWELL:E 9
fair father C. TENNY 266
grey-grown speechless C. SWIN 47
I am all at once what C. is HOPK:GM 29
poore man is C.'s stamp HERB:G 11
rejoice in C. even more LUTHER 7
Ring in the C. that is to be TENNY 177
wars as the kingdom of C. MONTESQU 2
We withstood C. then? BROWNING:R 124
Where C. erecteth his Church BANC 1
Christ-Church:
festal light in C. ARNOLD:M 25
I am the Dean of Christ Church SPRING 1
must study at C. and All-Souls JOHNSON:S 136
Christ Jesus: C.J., that can speak to thy condition FOX:G 1
christened: pleasing you when she was christen'd SHAK:AS 45
Christian:
cannibal than a drunken C. MELV 2
C. decision to find the world NIET 17
C. ideal has not been tried CHESTERTON 44
C. socialist who happens to be HAYD 1
C.'s armour bright COWP 8
decently and like a C. SHERIDAN:RB 12
good C. at her heart POPE 131
hard it is To be a C. BROWNING:R 67
hearing the C. religion doubted BUTLER:S[2] 15
horror and darkness fell upon C. BUNYAN 19
I dye a C. CHARLES I 5
I hate him for he is a C. SHAK:MERC 15
I was born of C. race WATTS 13
in what peace a C. can die ADDIS 41
no more wit than a C. SHAK:TWE 3
Onward! C. soldiers BARING-G 2
persuadest me to be a C. BIBLE 507
poor tiger that hadn't *got* a C. PUNCH 15
Pure eyes and C. hearts KEBLE 5
Scratch the C. and you ZANG 1
soul C. in its very nature TERT 1
souls of C. peoples CHESTERTON 16
three Jews, and three C. men CAX 2
to form C. men ARNOLD:T 2
true warfaring C. MILT 313
voice of C. charity BURKE:E 50
you were a C. slave HENL 7
Christian Science: C.S. explains all cause and effect EDDY 1
Christianity:
C. has done a great deal for love FRANCE 7
C. is not so much as a subject BUTLER:J 1
C. is part of the laws HALE:M 1
C. is political TUTU 3
C. is the most materialistic TEMPLE:W[2] 1
C. the *one* great curse NIET 22
from C. and journalism BALF 4
His C. was muscular DISR:B 44
local cult called C. HARDY:T 72
loving C. better than Truth COLERIDGE:ST 81
Muscular C. ANON 217
of death C. has made a terror OUIDA 1
organization that conquered the world* BARTON 1
religion is making C. political VAN DER P 4
Christians:
blood of C. is the seed TERT 3
C. awake BYROM 1
C. have burnt each other BYR 165
how these C. love one another TERT 2
Onward, C., onward go WHITE:HK 1
Christmas:
At C. I no more desire a rose SHAK:LOV 2
at Home the C. Day is breaking wan KIP 33
Bloody C., here again COPE 7
C. bells from hill to hill TENNY 143
C. brought his sports again SCOTT:W 25
C. come but once a year PROV 56
C. comes but once a year TUSS 7
C. Day in the morning ANON 4
C. Day in the Workhouse SIMS 1
C. Eve, and twelve of the clock HARDY:T 31
C. is coming ANON 60
C. morning bells say 'Come!' BETJ 24
C. to a child is the first terrible FRY:S 1
C. tree, O C. tree ZAR 1
C., with roast beef in a violent CLARKE:M 3
dreaming of a white C. BERLIN:Ir 2
Happy C. to all MOORE:CC 2
I'm walking backwards till C. MILLIG 5
keep our C. merry still SCOTT:W 24
perceive C. through its wrapping WHITE:EB 1
shopping days to C. SELF 2
that C. should fall out in ADDIS 20
'Twas the night before C. MOORE:CC 1
twelfth day of C. NURS 80
who sent me the insulting C. card GROS 5
Christopher Robin:
C.R. Has Fallen Down-Stairs MORTON:JB 1
C.R. is saying his prayers MILNE 8
C.R. went down with Alice MILNE 1
Christs: C. that die upon the barricades WILDE:O 111
Christ's College: *lady* of C.C. AUBREY 4
chronicle: make her c. as rich SHAK:HEN.V 6
chronicles: brief c. of the time SHAK:HAM 88
chronometers: Two c. the captain had SLESS 2
chrysolite: entire and perfect c. SHAK:OTH 65
chub: chavender, or c. ST-LEG 1
chubby: Augustus was a c. lad HOFFMAN:H 1
chuck: C. it, Smith CHESTERTON 16
church:
best harmony in a C. MILT 316
brings his politics to c. BYROM 6
Broad of C. and broad BETJ 2
c. and no steeple SWIFT 84
c. can't prevent, it blesses TUCHOL 10
C. exists for the sake of those outside TEMPLE:W[2] 6
c. for peace BROWNING:R 41
c. lit but without a congregation WELLS:HG 15
C. tumbled down SMITH:Syd[1] 5
C.'s one foundation STONE:SJ 1
Come all to c. HOUSM 12
English C. shall be free MAGNA 1
equall are within the churches HERB:G 12
Every blackning C. appalls BLAKE:W 74
figure in a country c.? SWIFT 74
free C. in a free State CAVOUR 1
get me to the c. on time LERN 5
Here is the c., and here NURS 15
Here's a c.! ... Let's go in DICKENS 214
his C. lewd Hirelings climbe MILT 187
holy Catholick C. PRAY 19
I believe in the C. TEMPLE:W[2] 7
I like the silent c. EMER 12
if at the C. they would give us BLAKE:W 73
Moves the C. of God BARING-G 3
nearer the C. the further ANDREW 4
never passes a c. without JOHNSON:S 112
not saints that go to c. PROV 5
not the C. as his mother CYP 1
obstacle in the path to equality* DEVL 1
one Catholick and Apostolick C. PRAY 66
regarded as a buttress of the c. MELBOU 11
see a c. by daylight SHAK:MUCH 5

state of Christ's C. militant PRAY 67
suffer from insomnia in c. TYR 1
there of necessity is the C. AMB 1
this rock I will build my c. BIBLE 417
to c. as he goes to the bathroom BLY 1
waiting at the c. LEIGH 1
wet c. the size of a snail THOMAS:D 14
What is a c.? CRAB 13
Where Christ erecteth his C. BANC 1
Church of England:
and they're head of the C.o.E. ARCHER 1
C.o.E. . . . is no doubt a compromise SHORTHOU 1
profession of the C.o.*E*. CHARLES I 5
Protestant religion but the C.o.E. FIELDING 22
Church of Ireland: A C.o.I. resurrection BETJ 17
churches:
c. built to please BURNS:R 26
c. have kill'd their Christ TENNY 223
c., visited by me too often UPDIKE 2
prove the scab of c. WOTTON 7
Churchill:
Simply a radio personality* WAUGH:E 34
suffering from petrified adolescence* BEVAN 8
young man of promises* BALF 6
churchman: person called a 'Modern C.' WAUGH:E 13
churchmen: c. fain would kill their TENNY 223
churchyard:
corner of a little country church-yard BURKE:E 84
devil in the same c. BANC 1
lie in Mellstock c. now HARDY:T 8
palsy-stricken, c. thing KEATS 67
worse taste, than in a c. JOW 3
churchyards: When c. yawn SHAK:HAM 128
cicadas: din of c. Seeps BAS 2
Cicero:
opinion can alienate C. MACAULAY:TB 3
what C. said DONNE 76
cigar:
good c. is a Smoke KIP 31
good five cent c. MARSHALL:TR 1
He smokes a fifty-cent c. ADAMS:FP 2
sweet post-prandial c. BUCHANAN 5
cigarette: c. is the perfect type WILDE:O 32
cigars: sacred rite smoking c. CHURCH:W 64
Cinara: reign of my dear C. HORACE 50
cincinnatus: C. of the West BYR 37
cinder: dry a c. this world DONNE 72
Cinderella: The C. of the Arts MONROE:H 1
cinders:
I've made the c. fly KIP 46
Sat among the c. NURS 36
cinema: c. is truth twenty-four times GODA 1
ciphers: We are mere c. HORACE 81
circle:
c. of the golden year TENNY 92
c. of which the centre is everywhere ANON 219
firmness makes my c. just DONNE 69
God is a c. EMPE 1
weave a c. round him COLERIDGE:ST 63
wheel is come full c. SHAK:KING L 81
whole c. be completed HUME 3
circles:
c. around and around KAV 3
c. can never make a square GOLDS 54
circuitous: foiled c. wanderer ARNOLD:M 34
circular: Within this c. idea HUME 17
circumcised: c. Herbert Samuel they threw LLOYD GEO 11
circumlocution: C. Office was beforehand DICKENS 186
***circumspice:** C., si Monumentum requiris* BARH 1
circumstance:
Eternal artistries in C. HARDY:T 69
fell clutch of c. HENL 1
I am myself and my c. ORTEGA G 3
no c., however trifling GOLDS 45
slave of c. And impulse BYR 140
circumstances:
arising from changes in c. WEBSTER:D 6
Fearful concatenation of c. WEBSTER:D 9
circus: doing in the bloody c.? MAX 1
circuses: bread and c. JUV 20
Ciro: Reginald Bingham went to C.'s TRAV 1
cistern:
c. contains BLAKE:W 44
c. for foul toads SHAK:OTH 52
cisterns: noises of gurgling c. LEWIS:CS 6
citadel: suburb of thir Straw-built Cittadel MILT 147
citadels: vain c. that are not walled OWEN:W 13
cities:
C. and their civilities PATMO 1
C. and Thrones and Powers KIP 119
c. had rubbed him smooth GREENE:G 2
C. rise again KIP 119
five c., like teeming sores HOPE:Al 1
human c. torture BYR 91
Seven c. warr'd for Homer HEYW:T 2
Towred C. please us then MILT 73
citizen:
c. of no mean city BIBLE 505
c. of the world SOC 1
he is a c. of the world BACON:F[1] 72
humblest c. of all the land BRYAN 2
I am a c. of the world DIOG 4
I am a Roman c. CIC 10
that I am a c. of the world EINS 9
citizens: for first and second class c. WILKIE 2
city:
Back from the C. of Sleep KIP 95
Behold now this vast C. MILT 318
briskly to infect a c. AUD 11
c. as a whole is the school of Hellas PERIC 3
c. consists of men NICIAS 1
C.! I am true son SMITH:Alex 2
c. is barren DICKENS 178
c. is built To music TENNY 239
c. is not a concrete jungle MORRIS:D 2
C. is of Night THOMS:Ja[2] 3
c. now doth, like a garment WORDS:W 91
c. of perspiring dreams RAPH 1
c. of the soul BYR 103
c. where everyone is an exile GILMAN 3
c. with her dreaming spires ARNOLD:M 41
crowded c.'s horrible street BROWNING:R 46
Despising For you the c. SHAK:COR 1
dull and witless c. BRIDIE 2
except the Lord keep the c. BIBLE 243
fallen, that great c. BIBLE 582
first c. Cain COWLEY:A 11
hope of the C. of God MASE 13
in populous C. pent MILT 244
Jealousy's a c. passion VANB 6
live in a c. COLTON 5
long in c. pent KEATS 2
maiden c., bright and free WORDS:W 75
nation, not a c. DISR:B 37
no continuing c. BIBLE 561
no mean c. BIBLE 505
populous and a smoky c. SHELLEY:PB 48
Provided that the C. of London remains CHAMBERLAIN:J 1
rose-red c. BURGON 1
second grandest c. in Scotland MCGON 1
several villages is the c. state ARISTOT 12
shady C. of Palme trees VAUGHAN:H 6
Soft morning, c. JOYCE:J 41
Stands Saint Kieran's C. fair ROLL:TW 1
suffer me not to see Thy Holy C. RICHARD 2
Sun-girt C. SHELLEY:PB 28
there the great c. stands WHITMAN 20
this great hive, the c. COWLEY:A 4
Towery c. and branchy HOPK:GM 12
Unless the Lord guards the c. BIBLE 604
Unreal C. ELIOT:TS 37
why not their c. too? BYR 31
Zion, c. of our God NEWT:J 1
city-builder: whom they name C. CARLYLE:T 12
civet: Give me an ounce of c. SHAK:KING L 68
civics: talk on 'Sex and C.' BETJ 29
civil:
c. to folk he ne'er saw ANST 1
dire effects from c. discord ADDIS 10
too c. by half SHERIDAN:RB 12
When c. fury grew high BUTLER:S[1] 1
civil rights: We never made one step forward* X 2
civil servant:
c.s. has the ability . . . to correctly KELLY:B 1
professional c.s. will step in RUTH 3
civil service: taken over by the C.S. CROSSMAN 1
civilian:
forget about this c. GOLDWATER 2
German c. is a soldier TUCHOL 8
• **civilisation:**
see also **civilization**
born the sweetness of c. HUGO 8
c. had been left in female PAG 1
c. is a struggle to keep YEATS 134
educated c. can remove PHILIP:R 1
he cannot withstand c. BATES:DM 1
I had left c. behind GREENE:G 15
civilised:
see also **civilized**
connive in c. outrage HEAN 3
civilities: bandy c. with my Sovereign JOHNSON:S 135
civility:
C. cost nothing and MONTAGU 5
C. costs nothing PROV 57
reciprocal c. of authors is one JOHNSON:S 17
use the c. of my knee BROWNE:T 1
civilization:
see also **civilisation**
As c. advances, poetry MACAULAY:TB 18
C. degrades the many ALCOTT:B 2
c. . . . has not yet fully recovered POPP 2
C. is a method of living ADAMS:H 2
c. is founded on the shambles JAMES:W 2
C. is paralysis GAUG 3
dark c. that I had abandoned LEVI:C 1
For a botched c. POUND 29
great elements of modern c. CARLYLE:T 24
I am the c. they are fighting GARROD 1
in c. to appeal to a Yeti HILLARY 3
progressive advancement of c. GALLACH 1
resources of c. against its enemies GLAD 3
without the usual interval of c. CLEMENCE 5
civilized:
see also **civilised**
better phrase is the c. society JENKINS:R 1
force another to be c. MILL 20
proved that I was in a c. society PARK 1
Woman will be the last thing c. MERED:G 1
civilizers: two c. of man DISR:B 74
civilizes: sex whose presence c. COWP 28
claes:
Craft maun hae c. PROV 61
some upo' their c. BURNS:R 48
claim: It is the last territorial c. HITL 8
clairvoyante: Madame Sosostris, famous c. ELIOT:TS 36
clan: Your c. will pay me back PARKER:D 10
Clancy: C. of The Overflow PATERSON:AB 1
clap:
Don't c. too hard OSB:J 9
If you believe, c. your hands BARRIE 9
in the cheaper seats c. LENNON 11
Clarence: Duke of C. . . . drowned in a barrel FABY 3
claret:
C. is the liquor for boys JOHNSON:S 210
dozen of C. on my tomb KEATS 159
his c. good HOME 4
look for the second cheapest c. POTTER:S 6
clarets: racehorses and the cheaper c. SAKI 6
Claridge's: body of the bootboy at C. WOOLF:V 17
clarion: sound the c. MORD 1
clasp: I shall c. thee again BROWNING:R 183
class:
Because there's no fourth c. SANT 13
c. distinctions so subtle, it takes THER 3
c. of all classes similar to RUSS:B 1
c. people as static and dynamic WAUGH:E 17
c. struggle necessarily leads MARX:K 8
constitute a special c. BREN 9
designated us as an *inferior gender c.* DWO 1
Discussion in c., which means NAB 5
Every c. is unfit to govern ACTON:Baron 1
for first and second c. citizens WILKIE 2
history of c. struggles MARX:K/ENG 2
Like many of the Upper C. BELLOC 40
lower c., I am in it DEBS 1
machine for the suppression of one c. LENIN 3
machine in the hands of the ruling c. STALIN 1
navy always travels first c. FISHER:JA 3
not confined to any one c. ANON 237
one c. to appreciate the wrongs STANTON:El 8
one c. you do *not* belong to MIKES 4
some social and c. pigeonhole HOWARD:P 1
They are the real c. traitors PARS 1
women as a servant c. PANK:E 4

young Englishman of our upper c. ARNOLD:M 66
classes:
back the masses against the c. GLAD 5
divisible into two great c. BEERB 21
extinction of all the privileged c. COOL 1
lower c. had such white skins CURZON 4
not interested in c. LEWIS:JL 1
prove the upper c. COWARD 24
classic:
C. learning lost POPE 172
Something that everybody wants* TWAIN 36
tread on c. ground ADDIS 34
What avails the c. bent KIP 151
classical:
c. mind at work PIR 4
C. quotation is the *parole* JOHNSON:S 223
classicism:
c. I call health GOET 36
C. . . . presents them with STEND 1
classics:
high seriousness of the great c. ARNOLD:M 80
task of editing the c. HOUSM 53
Than the c. in paraphrase POUND 27
Claudel: will pardon Paul C. AUD 42
Claus of Innsbruck: C.o.I. cast in bronze BROWNING:R 23
Claverhouse: 'twas Claver'se who spoke SCOTT:W 67
clavers: Mang heaps o' c. BURNS:R 29
claws:
been a pair of ragged c. ELIOT:TS 7
c. that catch CARROLL 45
neatly spreads his c. CARROLL 4
clay:
C. lies still HOUSM 4
for this the c. grew tall OWEN:W 7
knowest Who hast made the C. KIP 36
of c. and wattles made YEATS 4
Potter and c. endure BROWNING:R 189
clean:
c. house in the middle of the night THURB 9
c., verb active DICKENS 69
funny when you have to be c. WEST:M 10
I shall be made c. BIBLE 598
one more thing to keep c. FRY:C 7
people are too c. LINK 2
Then I was c. and brave HOUSM 10
cleaning: C. your house while your kids DILL 1
cleanliness:
by his c. a cook must KING:W 3
city of the c. of the sexes WHITMAN 20
C. is, indeed, next WESLEY:J 2
cleansed:
be c. from all their sins PRAY 57
I shall be c. MASS 1
clear:
c. to all the other people ROOS:E 1
not c. is not French RIVAR 1
clearing: c. up the obscure corners HUX:TH 12
clearing-house: c. of the world CHAMBERLAIN:J 1
Clee: C. to heaven the beacon HOUSM 1
clemency: C. is also a revolutionary DESM 1
Clementine: my darling C. MONTROSE 1
Cleopatra:
C.'s nose had been shorter PASC 5
every man's C. DRYD 30
gone to gaze on C. SHAK:ANT 26
I will be C. SHAK:ANT 41
pleased with less than C. DRYD 28
Some squeaking C. boy SHAK:ANT 67
clergy:
been a virtue with the Roman c. KINGSLEY:C 8
Bishops like best in their C. SMITH:Syd[1] 4
c. are men FIELDING 10
in spite of what the c. JOW 5
without the benefit o' the C. CONG 21
clergyman: Once a c. always a c. ANON 226
clergymen:
men, women, and c. SMITH:Syd[1] 25
To have with c. to do DOYLE:F 1
cleric: C. before, and Lay behind BUTLER:S[1] 19
clerk:
C. ther was of Oxenford also CHAUC 18
difference 'twixt the Priest and Clark HERR 40
less illustrious, goes the c. COWP 19
thought he saw a Banker's C. CARROLL 95
clerks:
clerkes been noght wisest men CHAUC 72
clerkes preise wommen but a lite CHAUC 35
clever:
all c. people were good WORDS:E 1
c. enough for us in Dublin MAHAF 1
c. woman to manage a fool KIP 1
it's c., but is it Art? KIP 44
let who can be c. KINGSLEY:C 17
most foolish is the most c. YEV 2
never develop a reputation of being c. FRANKLIN:M 2
not very c., but I'm quite intelligent BOGARDE 2
we are all c. here FOAKES 1
we are all c. here JACK:FJF 1
cleverest: c. member of one of the c. WEBB:B 2
cleverness: c. is to be able to conceal it LA ROCHE 24
cliché:
between a c. and an indiscretion MACMILL:H 11
between the c. and the indiscretion RUNCIE:Rob 1
c. is dead poetry BREN 7
clichés:
go around – that and c. SYMONS 1
Let's have some new c. GOLDWYN 11
client: am mistaken, is our c. DOYLE:AC 33
cliffs:
c. of fall Frightful, sheer HOPK:GM 23
down cloudy c. ARNOLD:M 30
solitary c. Wheeled by me WORDS:W 108
climate:
c. more uncertain than CONG 66
heaven for c. TWAIN 41
If it's Heaven for c. BARRIE 2
in love with a cold c. SOUTHEY 24
in the c. or the company JOHNSON:S 256
Love in a Cold C. MITFORD:N 4
place, the c. and the people EDMOND 2
climb:
c. not at all ELIZ I 7
c. upward on the miseries CONRAD 13
Fain would I c. RALE 13
Man can c. to the highest summits SHAW 10
whose last steps I c. SHELLEY:PB 136
climbed: curiosity, one c. on ANNE 2
climber: c. with a bomb in his pocket ORWELL 9
climbing: thou c. sorrow SHAK:KING L 26
clime:
change their c. not their frame HORACE 87
that sweet golden c. BLAKE:W 70
this the Soil, the C. MILT 121
clinging: c. onto it for dear life COMPT 13
clink:
I'm here in the C. KIP 46
why c. the cannikin? BROWNING:R 47
Clive: What I like about C. BENTLEY:EC 3
cloak:
knyf under the cloke CHAUC 47
like a c. of chaos GUNN:T 3
martial c. around him WOLFE:C 3
thy old c. about thee ANON 18
travel forth without my c. SHAK:SON 15
clock:
Church c. at ten to three? BROOKE 13
c. has stopped in the dark ELIOT:TS 81
c. struck one NURS 17
c. talked to c. SLESS 1
c. that clicked behind the door GOLDS 31
c. which has stopped but EBNER 2
count the slow c. POPE 65
cuckoo c. was invented solely COREN 3
forgot to wind up the c.? STERNE 3
grandfather's c. was too large WORK 2
open with a c. striking SHERIDAN:RB 34
Past one of the c. PEPYS 1
they produce . . . ? The cuckoo c. WELLES 1
to stop the church c. KILV 2
turned into a sort of c. HUX:TH 2
watch the c. for you SHAK:SON 22
clocks:
c. the tongues of bawds SHAK:HEN.IV[1] 3
c. were striking thirteen ORWELL 26
hands of c. in railway stations CONNOLLY:C 9
morning c. will ring HOUSM 6
strange women and grandfather c. NASH 24
clod:
become A kneaded c. SHAK:MEA 24
c. of wayward marl? SHAK:MUCH 4
if a *c.* be washed away DONNE 100
uncultured, polo-playing c. PHILIP 5
clods: breaks the c. and tosses ADDIS 1
clog: c. the foot of a flea SHAK:TWE 45
clogs:
age to quit their cloggs MILT 95
c. of that which else might SHELLEY:PB 84
c. to c. takes only three generations PROV 137
cloister:
in shady c. mew'd SHAK:MID 1
walk the studious Cloyster's pale MILT 89
cloisters: quiet collegiate c. CLOUGH 17
Clootie: Nick, or C. BURNS:R 10
close:
breathless hush in the C. NEWBOLT 10
still hasten to a c. COWP 26
close-lipped: c. patience for our only friend ARNOLD:M 27
close-up: c. of a woman past sixty ASTOR:N 2
closed: went to Philadelphia but it was c. FIELDS 4
closer: c. together the further LERM 1
closet: world, and not in a c. CHESTERFIELD 2
cloth:
coat according to your c. PROV 64
not mean to abuse the c. FIELDING 26
On a c. untrue GILB:WS 74
cloth of gold: For c.o.g. you cease GILB:WS 112
clothed:
Cloth'd with transcendent brightness MILT 112
C., and in his right mind BIBLE 441
weaves, and is c. SWIN 15
clothes:
been poured into his c. WODE 17
fun you can have with your c. on DELLA 1
get out of these wet c. BENCH 1
if it is our c. which fit us EBNER 6
in cloathes a wantonnesse HERR 15
just take the girl's c. off CHAND 6
Loves but their oldest c. DONNE 68
On the state of her c. NASH 12
out of these wet c. and into WOOLL 3
she has bought her wedding c. ADDIS 24
spoiling her nice new c. NURS 36
taking her c. off at the same COLETTE 2
That liquefaction of her c. HERR 38
that require new c. THOREAU 9
wears her c., as if SWIFT 42
who wore torn c. SPEND 3
years hang like old c. MOORE:B 1
clothing:
C. for the soul divine BLAKE:W 86
Gave thee c. of delight BLAKE:W 15
sheep in sheep's c. GOSSE 2
cloths: heaven's embroidered c. YEATS 26
cloud:
c. in stead MILT 177
c. takes all away SHAK:TWO 5
c. that's almost in shape of a camel? SHAK:HAM 126
c. that's dragonish SHAK:ANT 49
c. which had outwept SHELLEY:PB 110
did a sable c. MILT 25
Every c. has a silver lining PROV 98
first c. so terrible and still CAMPBELL:R 4
I wandered lonely as a c. WORDS:W 120
I wield the flail* SHELLEY:PB 54
in a pillar of a c. BIBLE 100
like a fiend hid in a c. BLAKE:W 75
On a c. I saw a child BLAKE:W 13
region c. hath mask'd him SHAK:SON 15
so great a c. of witnesses BIBLE 557
Stooping through a fleecy c. MILT 82
swift c. to fly with thee SHELLEY:PB 44
three or four hills and a c. STEVENS 3
When the c. is scattered SHELLEY:PB 159
wrapt in c. of sorrowe CAMPION 2
cloudcuckooland: What do you think of 'C.'? ARISTOP 2
clouds:
C. and eclipses stain SHAK:SON 17
c. are lightly curl'd TENNY 33
c. are once again gathering GORKY 2
dappled seaborne c. JOYCE:J 6
let base c. o'ertake SHAK:SON 16

it needn't c. to that CARROLL 70
Let 'em all c. KNIGHT 1
men may c. and men TENNY 202
One to c., and one to go CARROLL 75
Shape of Things to C. WELLS:HG 19
suppose it has to c. to this KELLY:N 3
Take things as they c. PROV 363
'tis not to c. SHAK:HAM 193
ve must all c. to it DICKENS 54
way to suppose what may c. HALIF 14
Why don't you c. up sometime WEST:M 2
will it c. without warning AUD 26
Will ye no c. back again? NAIRNE 1
will you no c. back again? HOGG 4
you c. from, baby dear? MACDON:G 2

comedies:
c. are ended by a marriage BYR 185
C. of manners swiftly become COWARD 13

comedy:
All I need to make a c. CHAPLIN 2
at a c. we only look HUX:A 40
catastrophe of the old c. SHAK:KING L 10
c. in long-shot CHAPLIN 6
C. ... is an unnatural act FELD 1
C. is if I walk into an open BROOKS:M 2
C. is medicine GRIFFITHS 1
c. is over LEONCAV 1
C. ... is society protecting PRIEST 1
c. to those that think WALP:H 15
fine c. this world would be DIDE 4
most Lamentable C. SHAK:MID 6

comes:
c. again in the morning SHERIDAN:RB 21
Everything c. to him who waits PROV 108
just as it c. dear? BETJ 27

comes down: one 'c.d.' from Jimmy's university OSB:J 4

cometh: no man c. unto the Father BIBLE 489

comets:
country c., that portend MARV 23
Old men and c. have been SWIFT 22

comfit-maker: swear like a c.'s wife SHAK:HEN.IV[1] 66

comfort:
a' the c. we're to get BURNS:R 123
carrion c., Despair HOPK:GM 20
carry their c. about with them ELIOT:G 17
c. and relieve them PRAY 39
c. like cold porridge SHAK:TEM 13
c. me with apples BIBLE 294
C.'s a cripple DRAYT 2
here's my c. SHAK:TEM 18
I beg cold c. SHAK:KING J 20
not ecstasy but it was c. DICKENS 195
Of c. no man speak SHAK:RIC.II 27
Speak not of c. THOMS:Ja[2] 7
thy rod and thy staff they c. BIBLE 206
What would c. the one GAY 30
who cherishes the love of c. CONF 8

comfortable:
slip into something more c. HARLOW 1
to be baith grand and c. BARRIE 3

comfortably: Are you sitting c.? LIST 1

comforted:
for they shall be c. BIBLE 384
longing to be c. WORDS:W 86

comforting: where is your c.? HOPK:GM 22

comfortless: leave us not c. PRAY 50

comforts:
c. we despise SHAK:ANT 54
fail, and c. flee LYTE 1
loves and c. should increase SHAK:OTH 22

comic: business of a c. poet CONG 14

coming:
cold c. they had of it ANDREW 3
cold c. we had of it ELIOT:TS 60
c. events cast their shadows CAMPBELL:T 21
c. of the King of Heaven ANON 59
It's comin' yet BURNS:R 116
of the c. of the Lord HOWE 1
one way of c. into the world SWIFT 4

command:
hast c. of every part HERR 31
Man to c. and woman TENNY 113
may c. where I adore SHAK:TWE 34
move only in c. SHAK:MAC 107
one dreams of being in c. SARTRE 11
to sue than to c. SCOTT:W 36
why people c. rather badly COMPT 3

commanded: God so c. MILT 246

commandment:
his c. is fulfill'd SHAK:HAM 202
religion with one c. ZANG 2

commandments:
Fear God, and keep his c. BIBLE 291
perfectly to keep the c. CATEC 4
set my ten c. in your face SHAK:HEN.VI[2] 2
Where there aren't no Ten C. KIP 62

commands:
I gave c. BROWNING:R 22
wise man who c. himself HORACE 73

commend: forced to c. her highly PEPYS 11

commendeth: obliquely c. himself BROWNE:T 64

commends: hurts me most who lavishly c. CHURCH:C 1

comment: C. is free SCOTT:CP 1

commentators: c. each dark passage shun YOUNG:E 5

comments: made our c. before us DONA 1

commerce:
C. its god LINK 3
c. the fault of the Dutch CANN 7
disinterested c. between equals GOLDS 58
equal to the whole of that c. BURKE:E 26
heavens fill with c. TENNY 79
honour sinks where c. GOLDS 7
only one rule of c. QUES 1

commercial: memory of the c. classes WILDE:O 72

commercial traveller: blend of the c.t., the missionary STAPLED 1

commisar: New C. is but old Czar MONRO 1

commissary: Destiny the C. of God DONNE 20

commission: bullet has got its c. DIBDIN:C 7

commit: didn't c. when he had the opportunity ROWL:H 3

commitment: difference between involvement and c.? NAV 1

committee:
c. is a cul-de-sac ANON 171
group of the unwilling* HARK 1
written by a c. MAYER 1

committees: c. of the rich to manage CONNOLLY:J 2

commodity:
C., Firmness, and Delight WOTTON 6
C., the bias of the world SHAK:KING J 7

common:
according to the c. weal JAMES VI/I 5
art thou base, c. and popular? SHAK:HEN.V 28
century of the c. man WALLACE:H 1
c. as the air GRANVILLE 2
c. interest always will prevail DRYD 52
c. people of the skies WOTTON 3
dull catalogue of c. things KEATS 108
happiness of the c. man BEVER 1
loathe all things held in c. CALLIM 1
man of c. opinions BAGE 1
morality of the c. man has NIET 1
nor lose the c. touch KIP 128
not in the roll of c. men SHAK:HEN.IV[1] 56
not jump with c. spirits SHAK:MERC 29
nothing c. did or mean MARV 2
one want for a c. good MARLOWE 22
saying in c. talk, should be admitted ADDIS 3
should not be so c. WILSON:Ang 2
steals a c. from a goose ANON 65
steals the c. from the goose ANON 77
the c. task KEBLE 1
to make it too c. SHAK:HEN.IV[2] 15
treat c. things in an original way HORACE 106
trust a good deal to c. fame EMER 83
vulgar flight of c. souls MURPHY:A 1

common-looking: Lord prefers c. people LINC 20

Common Prayer: Because they hated C.P. JORD 1

common sense:
betray'd me into c.s. POPE 162
common-sense and plain dealing EMER 28
c.s., and relatively clean MORTIM 1
C.s. is the best distributed thing DESCA 1
C.s. is the collection of prejudices EINS 19
gift To Beauty, C.S. MERED:G 22

commonalty: a very dog to the c. SHAK:COR 1

commonplace:
common is the c. TENNY 130
c. people see no difference PASC 2
'C.,' said Holmes DOYLE:AC 1
great minds in the c. HUBB 2
his c. book be full SWIFT 6
so unnatural as the c. DOYLE:AC 11
unassuming common-place Of Nature WORDS:W 99

commonplaces: c. are the great poetic truths STEVENSON:RL 45

Commons:
C., faithful to their system MACKINT 1
first week in the C. is like JACK:G 1

commonwealth:
caterpillars of the c. SHAK:RIC.II 21
Empire is a C. of Nations ROSE 1
my heart for the C.'s broke LAWS 6
service and conduct of the c. BURKE:E 17

commonwealths: To raise up c. DRYD 37

communicate: c. Something between breaths ASHBERY 1

communicating: c. of a man's self BACON:F[1] 67

communication: c. with the eternal spring RENAN 2

communion:
C. of Saints PRAY 19
lost c. with God CATEC 3
one c. and fellowship PRAY 60
one equal c. and Identity DONNE 110
partakers of the holy C. PRAY 61
They pluck't c. tables down JORD 1

communism:
arrested under the Suppression of C. Act DE BL 1
C. is like prohibition ROGERS:W 6
C. is Soviet power plus LENIN 9
C. is the complete opposite ANON 167
in Russia, c. is a dead dog SOLZ 10
nearer to c. every day PAIS 1
Russian C. is the illegitimate child ATT 2
spectre of C. MARX:K/ENG 1
spectre of c. TAYL:AJP 1

communist: What is a c.? ELLIOTT:E 2

Communist Party: Its relationship to democratic* BEVAN 9

communists: Catholics and C. have committed GREENE:G 14

communities: to both c. in the other part ROBINS:M 1

community:
[European] C. that its enlargement HEATH 1
not a nation but a c. of thieves HERB:X 3
part of the c. of Europe GLAD 7

commute: agricultural labourers round here c. POWELL:A 4

commuter: C. – one who spends WHITE:EB 2

companion:
last C.: Wine BELLOC 39
send the Prince a better c. SHAK:HEN.IV[2] 14

companions:
c. for middle age BACON:F[1] 85
old c. in adversity BRYANT 1
Shun evil c. PALMER:HR 2

company:
alone than in bad c. WASH 5
always except the present c. O'KEEFFE:J 2
bad c. leads to the gallows MACHIA 3
c. breaks up CERV 16
conversation in a mixed c. CHESTERFIELD 29
crowd is not c. BACON:F[1] 66
give me your bill of c. SWIFT 76
Good c. and good discourse WALT 7
in the climate or the c. JOHNSON:S 256
it's Hell for c. BARRIE 2
love and good c. FARQ 17
lovers of low c. BURKE:E 95
married life three is c. WILDE:O 85
oother compaignye in youthe CHAUC 25
Our c. absorbs the cost ANON 228
out of the Lady's c. SHADWE 3
Take the tone of the c. CHESTERFIELD 8
Tell me the c. you keep CERV 22
they get one into disreputable c. SHAW 133
villainous c., hath been the spoil SHAK:HEN.IV[1] 72
we, the lost c. take hands WRIGHT:J 2
what I call good c. AUSTEN 66

compare:
Shall I c. thee to SHAK:SON 6

there's none than can c. ANON 40
comparisons:
c. are odious DONNE 6
c. are odorous SHAK:MUCH 21
Comparisouns doon offte gret LYD 3
compass:
heart shall be The faithful c. GAY 38
my life is run his c. SHAK:JUL 82
compasses: stiff twin c. are two DONNE 69
compassion:
C. is not a sloppy KINN 1
one can drown in c. WHITE:P 12
compensation: who is liable to pay him c. TUCHOL 6
competency: c. lives longer SHAK:MERC 11
competition:
anarchy and c. the laws RUSKIN 15
Approves all forms of c. CLOUGH 21
complacencies: C. of the peignoir STEVENS 6
complain:
hardly knows to whom to c. FIRB 1
Never c. and never explain BALD:S 7
Never c., never explain DISR:B 96
Only the weak c. GILMORE 1
complainers: loudest c. for the public BURKE:E 10
complaining: but the voice of c. MORRIS:W 7
complaint:
C. is cheap GILMORE 1
how is the old c.? DISR:B 95
most fatal c. of all HILT 1
Nobody, and that's my c. MARX:G 5
complete: man who is c. in himself HORACE 73
complexion:
his c. is perfect gallows SHAK:TEM 2
his gold c. dimm'd SHAK:SON 6
putting on a false c. FERG:R 3
complexity: prefer c. to certainty BISS 1
compliance: timely c., prevented him FIELDING 16
complication: arrived at through c. SAND 3
complies: He that c. against his will BUTLER:S[1] 35
compliment:
farewell c. SHAK:ROM 13
two months on a good c. TWAIN 42
compliments: it must be c. AUSTEN 34
compose: Never c. anything unless HOLST 1
composed:
c. a work the day STERNE 26
conceived and c. in the soul ARNOLD:M 82
composer:
c.? What the fuck do they do? ZAPPA 2
good c. does not imitate STRAV 5
compositions: c. spring from my sorrows SCHUB 1
comprehend: less the greater c.? DRYD 70
compromise:
founded on c. and barter BURKE:E 37
Man accepts the c. KIP 134
that's his idea of a c. HUGHES:Th 3
compromises: arrive at certain c. MOLIERE 10
compulsion:
give no man a reason upon c. SHAK:HEN.IV[1] 42
Made happy by c. COLERIDGE:ST 60
stern hand of C. THURB 9
computer:
c. in his head SMITHERS 1
giving this c. to the last Luddite OND 2
comrades:
Bleach the bones of c. HOUSM 22
institution of the dear love of c. WHITMAN 25
comradeship: no c. between men and women LAWR:DH 3
concatenation: Fearful c. of circumstances WEBSTER:D 9
concealed: that more may be c. DARLING:CJ 3
concealing: hazard of c. BURNS:R 46
concealment: c., like a worm i' SHAK:TWE 31
conceit:
C. is the finest armour JEROME:JK 3
could never forgive any c. DRYD 144
conceited:
do any good who is not c.? TROLL 10
I would grow intolerably c. WHIST 11
never any pity for c. people ELIOT:G 17
conceits: best c. do prove DRAYT 4
conceivable: on every c. occasion MILLIG 8
conceive:
be the heart to c. JUNIUS 7
Madame, I cannot c. MACDON:JA 1
conceived:
c. and composed in the soul ARNOLD:M 82
c. by the Holy Ghost PRAY 19
concentrates: c. his mind wonderfully JOHNSON:S 191
conception:
if the dad is present at the c. ORTON 2
Immaculate C. was spontaneous PARKER:D 16
conceptions: C. equal to the soul's desires WORDS:W 118
concepts: simplest c. repeated a thousand HITL 1
concerns: think onely what c. thee MILT 231
concertina: I've a head like a c. KIP 46
concessions: c. of the weak are BURKE:E 25
conciseness: accuracy must be sacrificed to c. JOHNSON:S 33
conclaves: Kingly c. stern SHELLEY:PB 69
conclusion:
I could but spot a c. NASH 20
the other is a c. JOHNSON:S 100
ultimate c. in unmitigated KIP 134
conclusions:
arrive at their c. – largely KIP 125
comin' to c. MACDIAR 13
draw from it narrow c. MILL 27
sufficient c. from insufficient BUTLER:S[2] 2
who jump to c. rarely alight GUED 5
concord:
in pleasing c. end MILT 292
lover of c. PRAY 22
sweet milk of c. SHAK:MAC 94
travelled a good deal in C. THOREAU 4
concrete: city is not a c. jungle MORRIS:D 2
concubines: Twenty-two acknowledged c. GIBBON:E 5
concurrence: fortuitous c. of atoms PALMERS 2
condemn: C. the fault and not SHAK:MEA 9
condemned: Condemn'd alike to groan GRAY:T 8
condense: make a creature of you. C. EDWARDS:EH 1
condescend: c. to take a bit SWIFT 53
condescension: c. to their colonials NASH 1
condition:
Christ Jesus that can speak to thy c. FOX:G 1
c. rather than a profession GRAVES:R 11
devils in life and c. ASCHAM 2
observe the c. of the people JUNIUS 2
What, *me?* In *my* c.? ITMA 8
conditions:
all sorts and c. of men PRAY 38
create new c. of life MORRELL 1
people live in such awful c.? GEO V 2
condolement: persever In obstinate c. SHAK:HAM 19
condoms: without c. at the weekend will have to wait ANON 158
conduct:
C. . . . to the prejudice ANON 173
principle of the rules of c. MILL 66
what is c.? ARNOLD:M 74
conference:
c. a ready man BACON:F[1] 108
naked into the c. chamber BEVAN 3
two days' c. With the dead WEBSTER:J 23
confess:
c. our manifold sins PRAY 3
confessing that I have nothing to c. BURNEY 3
I c. to almighty God MASS 6
make him c. the truth HOUSE 2
confessed: half absolv'd who has confess'd PRIOR 7
confide:
c. their views to none KIP 125
seldom c. in those who are better CAMUS 17
confidence:
by c. grows weak DONNE 73
c. is a plant of slow growth PITT:W[1] 4
greatest success is c. EMER 51
total c. in my ability HAWKE 3
confident: Flushed and c. IBS 13
confiscation: We have legalized c. DISR:B 70
conflict:
in this c. of opinions JOHNSON:S 263
Never in the field of human c. CHURCH:W 16
We are in armed c. EDEN:A 2
conform:
either c., or be more wise PEPYS 14
free . . . must not c. WILDE:O 39
rebel and c. at the same time CRISP 1
conformable: c. to her self NEWT:I 1
conformers: mere c. to commonplace MILL 18
confounded: let me never be c. PRAY 11
confounding: Neither c. the Persons PRAY 30
confused:
harmoniously confus'd POPE 31
isn't c. here doesn't really understand ANON 157
confusion:
C., now hath made his masterpiece SHAK:MAC 54
C. on thy banners wait GRAY:T 28
C. to his enemies ANON 15
C. worse confounded MILT 174
except my own c. KERO 2
confusions: C. of a wasted youth TENNY 125
Congo: From the mouth of the C. LIND:V 2
congregation: latter has the largest c. DEF 10
congregations: Curates, and all C. PRAY 26
congress: C. is going nowhere LIGNE 1
Congreve: C. is the only sophisticated playwright TYNAN 2
congs: Kinquering C. their titles take SPOON 3
conjecture: not beyond all c. BROWNE:T 55
conjunction: c. of the mind MARV 8
conked out: he c.o. on November 15th LE MES 1
connect: Only c. the prose FORST 5
connecting-rod: stride o' yon connectin'-rod KIP 71
connoisseurs: Stockholm's place for c. ALLB 1
connubiality: wictim o' c. DICKENS 17
conquer:
Antony Should c. Antony SHAK:ANT 55
c. him that did his master c. SHAK:ANT 38
easier to c. it than WALP:H 11
go forth and c. a crown O'SHAUGH 1
hard to catch and c. MERED:G 31
In this sign thou shalt c. CONSTANTINE 1
slain me you will c. France JOAN 1
To c. is not to convince UNA 9
We'll fight and we'll c. GARRICK 4
When we c. without danger CORNEILLE 1
conquered:
c. and peopled half the world SEEL 1
hast c., O pale Galilean SWIN 35
I came; I saw; God c. JOHN III SOB 1
I came, I saw, I c. CAES:GJ 4
I will be c. JOHNSON:S 249
not ye c. one? ALEX 5
organization that c. the world BARTON 1
perpetually to be c. BURKE:E 27
You have c., Galilean JULIAN 1
conquering:
not c. but fighting well COUB 1
See, the c. hero MORELL 1
so sharp the conquerynge CHAUC 99
conqueror:
C. or City-Burner CARLYLE:T 12
Every other c. of every BURKE:E 97
proud foot of a c. SHAK:KING J 21
We came in with the C. BROME:R 2
conquest:
C.'s crimson wing GRAY:T 28
How to divide the c. SHAK:SON 18
shameful c. of itself SHAK:RIC.II 17
subdue By C. farr MILT 270
To joy in c. is LAO 2
conquests:
Are all thy c., glories SHAK:JUL 39
carnage and his c. cease BYR 24
spread her c. farther BURNS:R 103
conscience:
argue freely according to c. MILT 321
catch the c. of the King SHAK:HAM 95
celestial fire, called c. WASH 6
c. does make cowards SHAK:HAM 97
C. has no more to do with gallantry SHERIDAN:RB 2
c. hath a thousand SHAK:RIC.III 17
C. is but a word SHAK:RIC.III 19
C. is the inner voice MENCK 5
c. with injustice is corrupted SHAK:HEN.VI[2] 4
dilemmas of c. and egotism SNOW 1
expect a corporation to have a c. THURL 1

have nothing on your c. HORACE 77
Hebraism, *strictness of c.* ARNOLD:M 71
his c. Has crept too near SHAK:HEN.VIII 4
plural of c. is conspiracy HENDER:A 1
save free c. from the paw MILT 98
some c. of what they did CROMWELL 2
still and quiet c. SHAK:HEN.VIII 11
uncreated c. of my race JOYCE:J 9
uncreated c. of the race HEAN 9
war has a bad c. KEY:E 5
who is ridden by a c. NASH 15
will not cut my c. to fit HELLMAN 2
conscious: be c. is not to be in time ELIOT:TS 90
consciousness:
centre of the c. of the human GINSBERG 1
C. is a disease UNA 4
Hellenism is *spontaneity of c.* ARNOLD:M 71
multiplicity of agreeable c. JOHNSON:S 132
consecrate: we cannot c. LINC 11
consecration: c., and the Poet's dream WORDS:W 40
consent:
deep c. of all great men RUSKIN 11
whispering 'I will ne'er c.' BYR 167
with c., there is no injury ULP 1
consenting:
c. language of the heart GAY 5
only between c. adults VIDAL 5
consequence:
If it's business of c. do it BARH 2
it's of no c., thank 'ee DICKENS 136
consequences:
Logical c. are the scarecrows HUX:TH 4
prevent it and to damn the c. MILNER 1
there are c. INGER 1
there are c. VACH 1
Turnbull had predicted evil c. TROLL 19
conservation:
spare that tree* MORRIS:GP 1
We are living beyond* MEAD 1
What would the world be* HOPK:GM 18
without the means of its c. BURKE:E 51
conservatism:
barren thing this C. DISR:B 19
C. discards Prescription DISR:B 15
c. is based upon the idea CHESTERTON 42
What is c.? LINC 7
conservative:
c. adopts them TWAIN 30
C. government is an organized DISR:B 54
fear it would make me c. FROST:R 10
most c. persons I ever met WILSON:W 1
Or else a little C. GILB:WS 48
propriety be called the C., party CROKER 1
sound C. government DISR:B 16
conservatives:
C. ... being ... the stupidest party MILL 26
They are c. after dinner EMER 40
conserve: How to c. is usually a harder STRETT 1
considerable: appear c. in his native place JOHNSON:S 150
consideration: C. like an angel SHAK:HEN.V 3
consimility: wonderfull c. of phansey AUBREY 12
consistency:
C. is contrary to nature HUX:A 26
foolish c. is the hobgoblin EMER 10
idea of c. is exploded BURKE:E 11
consolation: Kate of my c. SHAK:TAM 7
console: c. us when we fall BURKE:E 96
consort: complete c. dancing together ELIOT:TS 123
conspiracy:
c. against the public SMITH:Ad 5
c., Sham'st thou to show SHAK:JUL 22
not a Party, it is a c. BEVAN 9
Open-ey'd c. SHAK:TEM 16
plural of conscience is c. HENDER:A 1
Society everywhere is in c. EMER 6
conspirators: All the c. save SHAK:JUL 88
constable: it was a c.'s handbook KINGSLEY:C 1
constabulary: When c. duty's to be GILB:WS 27
constancy:
but c. in a good BROWNE:T 12
C. alone is strange ROCHES 9
c. lives in realms above COLERIDGE:ST 61
c. to a bad, ugly woman BYR 147
Hope c. in wind BYR 10
infernal c. of the women SHAW 15
no object worth its c.? SHELLEY:PB 101
to establish dangerous c. DONNE 46
constant:
c. as the northern star SHAK:JUL 34
c. do remain to keep SHAK:JUL 34
C., in Nature were inconstancy COWLEY:A 2
C. in nothing but inconstancy BARNF 1
C. you are SHAK:HEN.IV[1] 34
if thou wilt be c. then GRAHAM:J 1
must often change who would be c. CONF 26
nothing in this world is c. SWIFT 11
nothing is c. HERAC 1
to one thing c. never SHAK:MUCH 13
were man But c. SHAK:TWO 16
Constantinople: Russians shall not have C. HUNT:GW 1
constellations:
do not want the c. any nearer WHITMAN 18
strange-eyed c. reign HARDY:T 16
constituencies: your c. and prepare for government STEEL 1
constituency:
not be in my c. MENZ 1
that as a primary c. SNY 2
constituents: service to my c. if I went into shops GAREL 1
constitution:
C. does not provide WILKIE 2
c. is extremely well WALP:H 10
c. that does not follow the custom PERIC 1
country has its own c. ANON 206
invoke the genius of the C. PITT:W[1] 11
little bit about the c. BREZ 1
principle of the English c. BLACKS 4
principles of a free c. GIBBON:E 2
very essence of the c. JUNIUS 3
constitutional:
exercise their c. right LINC 9
symptom of c. liberty GIBBON:E 7
construct: wonderful c. which is marriage WELD 1
constructs: worse. It c. it COMPT 1
construe: c. things after their fashion SHAK:JUL 18
consul: born when I was c. CIC 18
consuls: Let the c. see to it ANON 168
consultations: always take some c. THATCH:M 16
consume:
born to c. the fruits HORACE 81
c. all you have corrupted OSB:J 23
c. little more than the poor SMITH:Ad 2
lest I c. thee BIBLE 109
consumer: c. society there are inevitably ILL 4
consumer goods: spending father's earnings on c.g. GREER 2
consumes: creature that c. without producing ORWELL 16
consummation:
c. comes HARDY:T 23
c. Devoutly to be wish'd SHAK:HAM 97
consumption:
Conspicuous c. of valuable goods VEB 1
C. has no pity For DALTON W 1
contagion:
C. to this world SHAK:HAM 128
dare the vile c. of the night? SHAK:JUL 26
contemned: still contemn'd and flatter'd SHAK:KING L 55
contemplation:
C. makes a rare turkey-cock SHAK:TWE 33
C.'s sober eye GRAY:T 10
For c. hee MILT 192
mind serene for c. GAY 50
contemporary: I am no one's c. MANDELS 1
contempt:
breeds not c. but acceptance HATTER 1
c. and anger of his lip SHAK:TWE 41
Familiarity breeds c. PROV 115
for c. too high COWLEY:A 13
only an Object of C. AUSTEN 5
pour c. on all my pride WATTS 1
contend: Let's c. no more BROWNING:R 165
content:
c. surpassing wealth SHELLEY:PB 32
C. thyself with thine SURREY 1
c. with his fortunes fit SHAK:KING L 39
He has eneuch that is c. DUNB 16
her c. so absolute SHAK:OTH 22
lot is happy to one who is c. BOET 2
religion teaches us c. DRYD 14
sweet c. DEK 2
sweet C.! where doth BARNES:B 1
That is the land of lost c. HOUSM 24
contented:
c., don't show it JEROME:JK 5
C. wi' little and cantie BURNS:R 110
most enjoy c. least SHAK:SON 11
no one lives c. with his lot HORACE 61
contention: Let the long c. cease ARNOLD:M 48
contentment:
c. depends not on COLTON 8
freedom reign c. fails GOLDS 7
what c. for? MILT 234
continence:
chastity and c., but not yet AUGUS 3
perversion known as c. HUX:A 7
continent:
C. will not suffer England DISR:B 52
destiny to overspread the c. O'SULL 2
failed in discovering the ... southern C. COOK:J 1
man is a piece of *C.* DONNE 100
Through the Dark C. STANLEY 2
contingent: play of the c. and the unforeseen FISHER:HAL 1
continuity:
Like Leaves on Trees* HOMER 7
pass on the torch of life* LUCRET 6
this will go onward the same* HARDY:T 30
contraception: story about oral c. ALLEN:W 14
contraceptive: best c. is a glass of cold water ANON 164
contraceptives:
C. should be used MILLIG 8
Skullion had little use for c. SHARPE 2
contract:
labour c. into which men enter CHURCH:W 1
nature is tugging at every c. EMER 55
Social C. is nothing more WELLS:HG 1
verbal c. is worth more GOLDWYN 4
contradict:
Do I c. myself? WHITMAN 12
I never c. DISR:B 87
Never c. FISHER:JA 1
truth which you cannot c. PLATO 15
contradicted: I dogmatize and am c. JOHNSON:S 263
contradicting: as soon think of c. a Bishop JOHNSON:S 240
contradiction:
C. for its own dear sake COWP 24
c. in terms SHAW 117
c. in terms SIMPSON:NF 2
everlasting c. to himself HAZL 21
they brook no c. WEBSTER:J 29
Woman's at best a C. POPE 141
contradictions:
bundle of c. COLTON 6
one chain of c. CLARE:J 2
contraire: falleth al the effect c. CHAUC 105
contraries: Without C. is no progression BLAKE:W 31
contrary:
everythink goes contrairy with me DICKENS 141
On the c. IBS 17
contrive: head to c. GIBBON:E 8
controlled: events have c. me LINC 18
controls: c. the past ... c. the future ORWELL 32
controversy: c. is either superfluous NEWM:JH 3
convenient: never any c. time MITCH:M 2
convent:
C. girls never leave the church DALP 1
C. of the Sacred Heart ELIOT:TS 30
high up in the c. wall AUD 25
convention:
like a c. of spiritualists STOP 13
To the Lords of C. SCOTT:W 67
conventionality: C. is not morality BRONTE:C 3
convents: C., bosom'd deep in vines POPE 171
conversation:
best of life is c. EMER 51
cheery c. and what-not WODE 4
C. has a kind of charm SEN 4
c. interrupted three years HEMINGWAY 4

my own definition of c. ARNOLD:M 57
People ask you for c. MAUGH 2
criticize: c. What you can't understand DYL 3
criticizing:
c. without actually listening POTTER:S 3
pleasure of c. takes away LA BRU 14
critics:
before You trust in c. BYR 10
Cosmopolitan c. DISR:B 76
c. are all ready made BYR 9
C. like me shall make POPE 170
failed; therefore they turn c. COLERIDGE:ST 70
know how foolish c. can be BURGESS:A 6
lot of c. is to be remembered MOORE:G 1
men who have failed in literature* DISR:B 41
music c. They were small STRAV 2
Turned C. next POPE 8
writer what he thinks about c. HAMP 5
crocodile:
cruell craftie C. SPENS 27
feeds a c. – hoping that CHURCH:W 72
How doth the little c. CARROLL 4
What manner o' thing is your c.? SHAK:ANT 35
crocodiles: wisdom of the c. BACON:F[1] 123
crocus: c. brake like fire TENNY 38
Cromwell:
brave bad man* CLAREN 5
C.; the Philistine of genius ARNOLD:M 77
His grandeur he derived* DRYD 1
restless C. could not cease MARV 1
ruin that C. knocked about LLOYD:M 2
set up C. and his heir JORD 1
Some C. guiltless GRAY:T 20
crony: against government by c. ICK 1
crook:
I am not a c. NIX 8
such a thumping c. BETJ 15
symbol of a bishop is a c. DIX:GEA 1
writer of c. stories ought never WALLACE:E 2
crooked:
as c. as corkscrews AUD 9
c. be made straight ELIOT:TS 82
c. shall be made straight BIBLE 320
formed out of timber as c. KANT 1
There was a c. man NURS 70
to set the c. straight? MORRIS:W 5
With your c. heart AUD 8
croquet: c. matches in summer AUD 25
cross:
bloudie Crosse he bore SPENS 22
by thy C. and Passion PRAY 34
chancel with a broken c. TENNY 273
C. hangs upside-down in water SLESS 4
c. him in nothing SHAK:ANT 15
croys of latoun ful of stones CHAUC 32
Don't c. the bridge till PROV 77
for love Upon a crois CHAUC 122
I survey the wondrous C. WATTS 1
If you bear the c. willingly KEMP 12
I'll c. it SHAK:HAM 7
mystery of the c. shines bright VENAN 2
nailed to a burning c. YOUNG:AJ 2
no c., no crown PENN 1
Road to Freedom is via the C. LUTHULI 1
sheer inability to c. the street WOOLF:V 14
sparkling C. she wore POPE 40
standing beside the c., weeping JACOP 1
There's a little marble c. HAYES 1
to Thy C. I cling TOP 2
triumphall rasit is of the croce DUNB 18
Under the old stone C. YEATS 112
With the C. of Jesus BARING-G 2
Ye soldiers of the C. DUFFI 1
cross-breed: unhappy c. DISR:B 19
cross-gartered: see thee ever cross-garter'd SHAK:TWE 36
cross-grained: ever such a c. brute? GOLDS 74
crossed: c. be uncrossed ELIOT:TS 82
crosses:
Are they clinging to their c. CHESTERTON 15
Between the c., row on row MCCRAE 1
c. from his sovereign hand HERV 1
tumbled down the c. JORD 1
crossing: before c. a one-way street PETER 3
crossroads: at the c. and in the alleyways CATUL 14
crotchets: thou hast some c. in thy head SHAK:MERR 6
crow:
c. doth sing as sweetly SHAK:MERC 53
C. went on laughing HUGHES:Te 4
c. will tumble up and down CLARE:J 11
flew down a monstrous c. CARROLL 51
Old Adam, the carrion c. BEDD 3
risen to hear him c. ELIOT:G 10
thenk upon the crowe CHAUC 54
there is an upstart C. GREENE:R 2
crowd:
A c. is not company BACON:F[1] 66
can make a c. of men BEERB 11
c., and buzz, and murmurings COWLEY:A 4
C. not your table KING:W 2
Far from the madding c.'s GRAY:T 22
fear or favour of the c. KIP 117
frightful c. DANTE 11
I hate the c. LANDOR 13
I hate the unholy c. HORACE 27
these faces in the c. POUND 17
Will she pass in a c.? SWIFT 74
crowded: c. on a velvet cushion THOREAU 16
Crowdieknowe: men o' C. MACDIAR 3
crowding: come c. in so fast DRYD 143
crowds:
C. without company GIBBON:E 21
If you can talk with c. KIP 128
supplies c. for all occasions SIMPLE 1
crown:
both divide the c. DRYD 115
brow of labour this c. of thorns BRYAN 1
C. him with many crowns BRIDGES:M 1
c. is merely a hat FRED 2
C. is . . . the 'fountain of honour' BAGE 7
c. of our life as it closes SWIN 25
c. thy good with brotherhood BATES:KL 1
down and broke his c. NURS 27
fruition of an earthly c. MARLOWE 9
golden c. like a deep well SHAK:RIC.II 35
hairy gold c. on 'er 'ead? KIP 67
head that wears a c. SHAK:HEN.IV[2] 31
influence of the C. has increased DUNNI 1
monarch but would give his c. WALLER 6
no cross, no c. PENN 1
no man wears a c. LONG 2
power of the c., almost dead BURKE:E 14
presented him a kingly c. SHAK:JUL 51
Sceptre and c. Must tumble SHIRL 3
strike his father's c. SHAK:HEN.V 9
to an incorruptible C. CHARLES I 5
verse is not a c. HERB:G 29
within the hollow c. SHAK:RIC.II 28
crown-imperial: oxlips, and The c. SHAK:WIN 20
crowned:
Crown'd and again discrown'd JOHNSON:L 4
Crown'd with rank fumiter SHAK:KING L 64
crowns:
c. are empty things DEF 14
c. resign to call thee mine UPTON:W 1
Give c. and pounds HOUSM 9
I'd c. resign MACNALL 2
Not thrones and c., but men ELLIOTT:E 1
there are c. to be broke SCOTT:W 67
crows: bird of paradise among carrion c. HUGHES:B 7
crows feet: Til crowes f. be growen CHAUC 109
crucible: America is God's C. ZANG 3
crucified:
c. when alive CONNOLLY:J 1
try getting c. and rising TALL 8
Was c., dead, and buried PRAY 19
Where the dear Lord was c. ALEX:CF 5
crucify:
choose someone to c. COCT 2
c. mankind upon a cross BRYAN 1
Do you want to c. the boy? GRADE 3
would not even c. him CARLYLE:T 66
cruel:
being reputed as a c. man MACHIA 5
C. he looks, but calm SHELLEY:PB 67
c., only to be kind SHAK:HAM 148
c. story runs on wheels OUIDA 2
Here is c. Frederick HOFFMAN:H 2
you c. men of Rome SHAK:JUL 2
cruelty:
C. has a Human Heart BLAKE:W 121
English are known for their c. ROUSS:E 1
Fear is the parent of c. FROUDE 3
top-full Of direst c. SHAK:MAC 20
cruet: as the neck of a vinegar c. JOHNSON:S 79
cruise: all on our last c. STEVENSON:RL 14
cruising: c. trip that was so much fun FITZGER:FS 12
crumbling: C. between the fingers MACNEICE 9
crumbs:
picker up of learning's c. BROWNING:R 105
steal the bags to hold the c. ISH 1
crumpet: Improved Hot Muffin and C. DICKENS 65
crumpets: buttered scones and c. ELIOT:TS 20
crumpetty: longer I live on this C. Tree LEAR 28
Crusoe: Where are you, Robin C.? DEF 3
crust: c. So fresh HOPK:GM 1
cry:
a c. Before TENNY 277
at least they can c. RHYS 3
bubbling c. BYR 176
c. that lasts not long TENNY 166
despairing c. of an Italian prostitute HUGHES:B 1
dismal c. rose slowly BROWNING:EB 4
don't you c. for me FOST:SC 1
especially when they c., for then MITFORD:N 7
for fear of having to c. BEAUMA 2
hear us when we c. to Thee WHITING 1
I c. unto thee BIBLE 247
likes stories that make her c. SULLI:An 2
make 'em c. READE 2
no language but a c. TENNY 154
our c. come unto thee PRAY 78
that we still should c. BACON:F[1] 133
To c. it up SWIFT 69
too old to c., but it hurt LINC 27
truth without making anybody c. FELL 2
when indeed they c. WEBSTER:J 12
When we are born, we c. SHAK:KING L 75
will c. on Sunday RACINE 5
you'll c. before supper PROV 226
crying:
fellow c. in Martin Place MURRAY:LA 2
infant c. in the night TENNY 154
no use c. over spilt milk MAUGH 3
no use c. over spilt milk PROV 206
one c. in the wilderness BIBLE 377
we came c. hither SHAK:KING L 74
crystal: Ring out ye Crystall sphears MILT 8
Cuba: humiliate Fidel is to humiliate C. ALEA 1
cuckold: make her husband a c. SHAK:OTH 58
cuckoo:
as the c. is in June SHAK:HEN.IV[1] 69
c. clock was invented solely COREN 3
C.-echoing HOPK:GM 12
C.! Shall I call thee bird WORDS:W 97
c. shouts all day HOUSM 38
c. then on every tree SHAK:LOV 24
c.'s parting cry ARNOLD:M 42
Cuckow, messenger of Spring SPENS 7
hedge-sparrow fed the c. so long SHAK:KING L 18
Lhude sing cuccu ANON 41
pleasant c., loud and long DAVIES:WH 6
rainbow and a c.'s song DAVIES:WH 5
Responsive to the c.'s GRAY:T 9
they produce . . . ? The c. clock WELLES 1
weather the c. likes HARDY:T 40
cuckoo-buds: c. of yellow hue SHAK:LOV 24
cucumber: c. should be well sliced JOHNSON:S 80
cucumbers: extracting sun-beams out of c. SWIFT 32
cud:
chew the c. and are silent BURKE:E 60
he cheweth not the c. BIBLE 111
cuddling: c., you should buy a puppy BURCHI 1
cudgel:
grievous crab-tree c. BUNYAN 16
What wood a c.'s of by th' blow BUTLER:S[1] 21
cue: with a twisten c. GILB:WS 74
cuff: Anything said off the c. SKEL:R 1
cuisine: C. is when things taste LEITH 1
cully: Woman's c. made CONG 7
cult:
c. of cheeriness and manliness ORWELL 10
c. of personality KHRU 1
local c. called Christianity HARDY:T 72

What's a c.? ALTMAN 1
cultivate: we must c. our garden VOLT 16
cultivated: c. entirely by the spade MILL 2
cultivation: c. has considerable breadth HIGIN 1
cultural:
Australian C. Cringe PHILLIPS:AA 1
despair about the c. scene in Australia HELPMAN 1
culture:
brutal dirty c. you have in North America DURRELL:L 5
Creative c. is infinitely porous FRYE:N 3
C. being a pursuit of our ARNOLD:M 61
C., I reach for my revolver GOER 2
'c.' . . . I take the safety-catch JOHST 1
C. is an instrument wielded WEIL 1
C. is the openness of the individual BELLOW 5
C. isn't something that comes MENAND 2
c. of poverty suffer much less FRIEL 1
C., the acquainting ourselves with ARNOLD:M 72
everyone's c. is different MENAND 2
great aim of c. ARNOLD:M 63
half-cultures do not make a c. KOES 2
In a statesman so-called 'c.' MUSSO:B 5
man of c. rare GILB:WS 30
men of c. are the true apostles ARNOLD:M 65
pursue C. in bands WHARTON:E 2
cultures: Decadent c. usually fall KENNY:Mar 1
cumber: I c. you goode Margaret MORE:T 2
cunning:
C. is the dark sanctuary CHESTERFIELD 30
that c. men pass for wise BACON:F[1] 49
cup:
come, fill the C. FITZGER:E 4
Come fill up my c. SCOTT:W 56
c. itself, from which our Lord TENNY 257
drunk their C. a Round FITZGER:E 14
Fill high the c. BYR 196
fill the C. Before FITZGER:E 2
leave a kiss upon the c. JONS 36
let this c. pass BIBLE 432
made puddings in his tea c. CARLYLE:JW 1
my c. overflows SCOTTISH 1
my c. runneth over BIBLE 206
Perfect the c. as planned BROWNING:R 190
prayed my c. might pass KIP 147
tak' a c. o' kindness BURNS:R 71
There's Death in the c. BURNS:R 117
'twixt the c. and the lip PROV 379
cupboard:
man in the bathroom c. EWART 1
our c. of *food* Or cabinet HERB:G 34
skeleton in the c. PROV 100
The c. was bare NURS 47
cupboards:
c. bursting with skeletons ORWELL 11
her c. opened HARDY:T 61
Cupid:
C. blind did rise LYLY 4
C. is a knavish lad SHAK:MID 34
for the sign of blind C. SHAK:MUCH 2
giant-dwarf, Dan C. SHAK:LOV 8
silent note which C. strikes BROWNE:T 29
wing'd C. painted blind SHAK:MID 5
***cupiditas:** Radix malorum est C.* CHAUC 67
cups:
c., That cheer but not COWP 72
flowing c. /With pleasant liquors MILT 214
frequent c. prolong POPE 50
cur:
c. can lend three thousand SHAK:MERC 18
half lurcher and half c. COWP 75
I spurn thee like a c. SHAK:JUL 33
spurn a stranger c. SHAK:MERC 18
curate:
as if a c. has been taken out SMITH:Syd[1] 16
compassion in the very name of C. SMITH:Syd[1] 3
may not qualify as a c. STOCKS 3
shabby c. who has strayed AUD 65
signify their names to the C. PRAY 61
To sit upon the c.'s knee CHESTERTON 23
curates:
abundant shower of c. BRONTE:C 5
C., and all Congregations PRAY 26
C., long dust, will come BROOKE 9
preached to death by wild c. SMITH:Syd[1] 32
curators: more philosophical than all the c. FRANCE 2
curch: my basnet a widow's c.? BALL 30
curds:
Eating her c. and whey NURS 35
queen of c. and cream SHAK:WIN 22
cure:
age or a little money will not c. DURA 1
c., on exercise depend DRYD 122
c. the disease and kill BACON:F[1] 68
death is the c. of all BROWNE:T 31
labour against our own c. BROWNE:T 31
no C. for this Disease BELLOC 16
no c. for this sort of madness SMITH:FE 2
Past c. I am SHAK:SON 63
Prevention is better than c. PEAC 4
Prevention is better than c. PROV 324
Work is the grand c. CARLYLE:T 62
cured:
can't be c., must be endured PROV 417
certainly c. you, Mahaffy SALM 2
look forward to being c. of MANK 1
cures:
cuts must have desperate c. PROV 67
Like c. like HAHN 1
2 c. for love COPE 8
curfew:
C. tolls the knell GRAY:T 16
far-off Curfeu sound MILT 82
curfew-tide: Yet at mothy c. HARDY:T 9
curiosities: c. would be quite forgot AUBREY 1
curiosity:
C. is the key to creativity MORITA 1
C. killed the cat PROV 63
C. will conquer fear STEPHENS 2
Disinterested intellectual c. is the life TREV 1
full of 'satiable curtiosity KIP 24
Love, c., freckles PARKER:D 3
curious:
only c. in proportion to one's level ROUSS:JJ 3
That was the c. incident DOYLE:AC 25
curiouser: C. and c. CARROLL 3
curl:
she had a little c. NURS 71
Who had a little c. LONGFEL 36
Who had a little c. MILLER:M 1
curled: c. up on the floor HARTE 3
curlers: you couldn't wear c. in bed O'BRIEN:E 2
curly: C. locks, C. locks NURS 8
currency:
Debasing the moral c. ELIOT:G 45
party to debasing the c. KEYN 13
current:
boats against the c. FITZGER:FS 9
c. in this place damm'd up SHAK:HEN.IV[1] 59
c. of his feeling failed AUD 36
take the c. when it serves SHAK:JUL 76
thing is c., it creates currency MCLUH 12
currents: Cold c. thrid, and turn HARDY:T 21
curs:
as c. mouth a bone CHURCH:C 8
common cry of c. SHAK:COR 10
c. of low degree GOLDS 14
curse:
bless them that c. you BIBLE 387
c. be ended ELIOT:TS 82
C. God, and die BIBLE 183
c. is come upon me TENNY 21
c. is on her if she stay TENNY 16
c. of hell frae me sall ye BALL 19
c. on the fairest joys BLAKE:W 48
C. shall be on thee SOUTHEY 14
do not matter a tinker's c. SHINWELL 1
How the youthful Harlots c. BLAKE:W 74
I know how to c. SHAK:TEM 8
open foe may prove a c. GAY 44
Rise up, and c. Him BROOKE 1
under his wrath and c. CATEC 3
cursed:
c. and kicked the stairs MILLAY 2
C. be the social wants TENNY 73
He c. him in sleeping BARH 5
remembered are those who were c. YEV 3
She curs'd Cole Porter too COWARD 30
to all succeeding ages curst DRYD 38
whom thou cursest is c. BIBLE 118
curses:
C. are like young chickens SOUTHEY 13
C. not loud but deep SHAK:MAC 110
fling the c. on his neighbours BRONTE:E 9
Not all the c. which the Furies MARLOWE 3
rigg'd with c. dark MILT 51
curst: c. be he that moves my SHAK:MISC 2
curtain:
Bring down the c. RAB 9
disadvantage – the c. was up WINCHELL 1
Drew Priam's c. SHAK:HEN.IV[2] 3
I face the final c. ANKA 1
Iron C. GOEB 2
iron c. across Europe TROU 1
Iron C. has descended across CHURCH:W 35
Spread thy close c. SHAK:ROM 29
curtains:
fringed c. of thine eye SHAK:TEM 12
Nottingham lace of the c. BETJ 3
curtiosity: full of 'satiable c. KIP 24
curtsies:
dream on c. straight SHAK:ROM 5
Low-crooked c. SHAK:JUL 33
curtsy: C. while you're thinking CARROLL 47
curveship: c. lend a myth to God CRANE:H 2
Curzon: name is George Nathaniel C. ANON 86
cushion:
crowded on a velvet c. THOREAU 16
C. and soft Dean invite POPE 72
Custer: as true for Crazy Horse as it was for C. FRASER:GM 2
custom:
C. calls me to't SHAK:COR 6
c. is no argument HARDY:T 54
c. lie upon thee with a weight WORDS:W 61
c. loathesome to the eye JAMES VI/I 2
c. More honour'd in SHAK:HAM 35
C. reconciles us to everything BURKE:E 7
C. that is before all law DANI 3
C., that unwritten law DAVEN:C
C., then, is the great guide HUME 9
Hath not old c. SHAK:AS 11
old C. SHELLEY:PB 11
one good c. should corrupt TENNY 278
That monster c. SHAK:HAM 147
What c. hath endear'd BAILLIE 1
customers:
raising up a people of c. SMITH:Ad 7
When you are skinning your c. KHRU 5
cut:
c. and dried, yaa-boo JACK:R 1
Nor c. each other's throats GOLDS 2
Two things should be c. COWARD 34
unkindest c. of all SHAK:JUL 55
your servant's c. in half GRAHAM:II 3
cutlets: suggested we should play 'C.' GROS 3
cutpurse: c. of the empire SHAK:HAM 143
cuts:
C. off so many years SHAK:JUL 37
Desperate c. must have desperate PROV 67
cutty-sark: 'Weel done, C.' BURNS:R 89
cycads: Only the antique c. WRIGHT:J 6
cycle-clips: c. in awkward reverence LARK 1
cygnets: swan her downy c. save SHAK:HEN.VI[1] 3
cymbal: tinkling c. BIBLE 522
Cynara: faithful to thee, C. DOWS 1
cynic: precepts from the Cynick Tub MILT 37
cynicism:
C. is an unpleasant way HELLMAN 1
C. is intellectual dandyism MERED:G 8
c. of real life can't be outdone CHEK 13
cynosure: C. of neighbouring eyes MILT 71
cypress:
correct in c. wood PARKER:D 8
c. and myrtle Are emblems BYR 22
in sad c. let me be laid SHAK:TWE 29
Cyprus: rings black C. with a lake FLECKER 8
Cythera: It's C., they tell us BAUD 7
czar: but old C. writ large MONRO 1
dactyl: with D. trisyllable COLERIDGE:ST 57
dad:
fuck you up, your mum and d. LARK 8
girls in slacks remember D. BETJ 24
if the d. is present at the conception ORTON 2
daddy: D. wouldn't buy me a bow-wow TABRAR 1
daemon: Some D. stole my pen POPE 162
daffadillies: D. fill their cups with tears MILT 55
daffadowndillies: Strowe me the ground with D. SPENS 3
daffadowndilly: Diaphenia, like the d.

darken:
days d. round me TENNY 278
never d. my towels again MARX:G 13
darkening: sky is d. like a stain AUD 27
darkest:
d. hour is just before the dawn PROV 64
d. just before the day FULLER:T[1] 8
d. spot . . . is a small luminous screen DEBR 1
darkling:
as on a d. plain ARNOLD:M 47
D. I listen KEATS 93
we were left d. SHAK:KING L 18
darkly: d. looked he at the wall MACAULAY:TB 46
darkness:
cast away the works of d. PRAY 42
d. comprehended it not BIBLE 472
d. deepens; Lord LYTE 1
d. falls at Thy behest ELLER 1
d. has been filled with the light KELLER 2
D. is more productive of sublime BURKE:E 8
d. of man's heart GOLDI 2
d. over the land of Egypt BIBLE 94
d. was upon the face BIBLE 2
d. which may be felt BIBLE 94
Dawn on our d. HEB 1
Death has made his d. beautiful TENNY 165
deep, but dazzling d. VAUGHAN:H 3
did the act of d. SHAK:KING L 44
encounter d. as a bride SHAK:MEA 22
everlasting d. shall have an inchoation DONNE 108
horror and d. fell upon Christian BUNYAN 19
horror of great d. BIBLE 46
horror of outer d. after GORDON:AM 2
instruments of d. tell us truths SHAK:MAC 14
into the d. of the grave MILLAY 7
leaves the world to d. GRAY:T 16
light in the d. of mere being JUNG:Carl 5
Lighten our d. PRAY 29
lump bred up in d. KYD 4
nightly roll into d. HARDY:T 58
pass'd the door of D. FITZGER:E 24
people that walked in d. BIBLE 307
prince of d. is a gentleman SHAK:KING L 48
race that long in d. pin'd SCOTTISH 3
shores of d. there is light KEATS 32
sink, Downward to d. STEVENS 7
Swaddled with d. ELIOT:TS 22
talks of d. at noon-day COWP 37
Terror of darknesse CHAPMAN:G 4
they appear in the d. GUNN:T 3
thro' d. up to God TENNY 156
Universal D. buries All POPE 175
what has light to do with d. JEROME 1
year Of now done d. HOPK:GM 21
darling:
Better be an old man's d. PROV 39
d. of my heart CAREY 2
D. of the Gods was born MARV 28
D. of the music-halls SMITH:FE 6
he's a darlin' man O'CAS 1
darn: d. is premeditated poverty SHUTER 1
dart: shook a dreadful D. MILT 167
dastard: d. in war SCOTT:W 19
date: keep them up to d. SHAW 96
dates:
all three d. on their slates CARROLL 37
very few D. in this History AUSTEN 1
daub: d. the wall of a jakes SHAK:KING L 23
daughter:
d. of a hundred Earls TENNY 62
d. of debate ELIZ I 13
d. of Earth and Water SHELLEY:PB 56
d. of the gods TENNY 10
D. of the Moon, Nokomis LONGFEL 20
d. went through the river BUNYAN 31
death of your d. would have been AUSTEN 25
Duke-and-a-Duchess's d. BARH 10
ever rear a d. GAY 11
fairer d. of a fair mother HORACE 14
farmer's d. hath soft brown hair CALVER 4
I am Caesar's d. JULIA 2
King of Spain's d. Came NURS 21
landlord's black-eyed d. NOY 3
let them all to my elder d. THOMAS:E 3
Marrying off your d. is a piece SAIK 1
my d. is only half-Jewish MARX:G 20
My father had a d. lov'd SHAK:TWE 31
One fair d., and no more SHAK:HAM 85
preaching down a d.'s heart TENNY 77
she is a d. of the people WEST:R 8
skipper had taken his little d. LONGFEL 9
Sole D. of his voice MILT 246
Stern D. of the Voice of God WORDS:W 70
this Lord Ullin's d. CAMPBELL:T 12
whipped her little d. NURS 36
daughterly: doughterly loue and deere MORE:T 2
daughters:
all the d. of my father's SHAK:TWE 32
d. Have stolen their beauty CAMPBELL:G 2
d. of the uncircumcised triumph BIBLE 151
d. ride away ELIOT:TS 71
d. were then both abed AUBREY 6
fairest of her D. Eve MILT 194
nine of his d. were lying THURB 3
Three d. married AUSTEN 30
Tigers, not d. SHAK:KING L 61
Words are men's d. MADDEN 1
words are the d. of the earth JOHNSON:S 6
dauntless: so d. in war SCOTT:W 18
dauphin: kingdom of daylight's d. HOPK:GM 10
David:
D. and the Sybil foretell CEL 1
D. danced before the Lord BIBLE 155
D. had his Jonathan HERB:G 7
D. his ten thousands BIBLE 149
Great D.'s greater Son MONTGOM:J 1
King D. wrote the Psalms NAY 1
Once in royal D.'s city ALEX:CF 4
David Copperfield: all that D.C. kind of crap SALIN 1
Davy: Humphrey D. Abominated gravy BENTLEY:EC 4
dawn:
brown fog of a winter d. ELIOT:TS 37
carch and to reflect the d. MACAULAY:TB 15
cold And passionate as the d. YEATS 46, 141
darkest hour is just before the d. PROV 64
d. an age, More fortunate ARNOLD:M 36
d. comes up like thunder KIP 59
D. in New York has LORCA 2
d. is my brother BELLOC 6
D. on our darkness HEB 1
d. was contagious O'BRIEN:F 3
d., with silver-sandalled feet WILDE:O 109
D.'s Left Hand FITZGER:E 2
Dim d. behind the tamarisks KIP 32
first d. in Helen's arms? YEATS 85
grey d. breaking MASE 1
grey d. is breaking CRAW 1
I have seen d. and sunset MASE 6
in that d. to be alive WORDS:W 159
in whom I greet a new d. BANV 1
Rosy-fingered d. HOMER 2
said to D.: Be sudden THOMP:F 9
sigh'd for the d. and thee TENNY 218
dawneth: darkest just before the day d. FULLER:T[1] 8
dawning:
bird of d. singeth SHAK:HAM 10
brightness Of the winter d. BRIDGES:R 7
d.'s cold grey air THOMS:Ja[2] 3
in the d. passing through HARDY:T 39
day:
as gain each d. that Fortune HORACE 11
As we were saying the other d. LEON 1
Believe every d. that has dawned HORACE 84
better d., the worse dead HENRY:M 1
breaks the blank d. TENNY 134
bright d. is done SHAK:ANT 66
broaden into boundless d. TENNY 172
d. and night shall not cease BIBLE 40
d. begins to droop BRIDGES:R 15
d. brought back my night MILT 103
D. decreed by Fates HOMER 9
d. in thy courts is better BIBLE 222
d. is a miniature eternity EMER 88
d. is at hand BIBLE 518
d. is for honest men EUR 2
d. is gone KEATS 110
D. joins the past Eternity BYR 99
d. less or more TENNY 284
d. of glory has arrived ROUG 1
d. of his death was a dark AUD 35
d. of wrath CEL 1
d. oot o' Aiberdeen ANON 175
d. returns too soon BYR 129
d. stood distinct in the sky HARDY:T 57
d. that comes betwixt CAREY 3
d. that hath no *pridie* DONNE 104
d. Thou gavest, Lord ELLER 1
d.'s at the morn BROWNING:R 9
d.'s out and the labour done BROWNING:EB 18
daye very meete and MORE:T 2
death will have his d. SHAK:RIC.II 24
describe a whole d. in heaven SHAW 102
do the business of the d. in the d. WELLING 13
done better in my d. KEPP:A 1
each d. dies with sleep HOPK:GM 24
each d. is like a year WILDE:O 119
ebbs out life's little d. LYTE 1
enjoy bright d. MILT 30
ever I had seen that d. SHAK:HAM 24
Every d., in every way COUE 1
every d. is the best d. EMER 63
every dog has his d. BORR 9
first d. a guest PROV 123
first, last, everlasting d. DONNE 27
frabjous d. CARROLL 46
gilded Car of D. MILT 20
Go ahead – make my d. REAG 9
go w'en de great d. comes HARRIS:JC 11
had spent one whole d. well KEMP 10
hard d.'s night LENNON 4
have known a better d. SCOTT:W 1
I have lost a d. TITUS 1
in the d. of judgment PRAY 34
inner d. can never die TENNY 161
jocund d. Stands tiptoe SHAK:ROM 35
let them have their d. YEATS 47
long d. done HENL 6
long d. wanes TENNY 55
morning were the first d. BIBLE 3
Night and d. PORTER:C 2
Now the d. is over BARING-G 1
Now's the d. BURNS:R 107
only twenty-four hours in the d. PROV 368
perfect d. nor night SHAK:HEN.VI[3] 2
posteriors of this d. SHAK:LOV 20
So foul and fair a d. SHAK:MAC 7
something for a rainy d. PROV 218
Spirit on the Lord's d. BIBLE 573
succeeds thy little d. PEAC 17
such a merry d. once or twice PEPYS 24
Sufficient unto the d. BIBLE 397
Sweet d., so cool HERB:G 32
thanks for another d. of loving GIBRAN 2
There's night and d., brother BORR 5
to undo the time of d. FAIRBURN 2
twelfth d. of Christmas NURS 80
what a beautiful d. HAMMER 3
what a d. may bring forth BIBLE 272
Without all hope of d. MILT 280
Would seem a winter's d. ROCHES 10
you must be a d. yourself EMER 62
day-labour: Doth God exact d. MILT 100
day-returns: but d. from now on LEONARD:H 2
day-star: So sinks the d. MILT 57
daybreak: vision Of d. SASS 17
daylight:
doesn't do a man any good, d. FRY:C 13
dropping of the d. in the West BROWNING:R 21
kingdom of d.'s dauphin HOPK:GM 10
long and lone d. SHELLEY:PB 145
night . . . is but the d. sick SHAK:MERC 54
We burn d. SHAK:MERR 5
days:
As thy d., so shall BIBLE 126
broader lands and better d. CHURCH:W 17
D. and moments quickly CASWALL 2
D. and months are itinerants BAS 3
d. are fallen in the long wet FAIRBURN 3
d. are in the yellow leaf BYR 241
D. are where we live LARK 5
d. darken round me TENNY 278
d. have crackled and gone THOMP:F 6
d. of Methuselah were nine BIBLE 33
d. of swine amd Porsches HILL:Reg 2
d. of wine and roses DOWS 3
D. Steal on us BYR 124
d. that are no more TENNY 108
d. when I was dear to you HORACE 39
drawing d. out SHAK:JUL 36

fall'n on evil dayes MILT 224
Few and evil have the d. BIBLE 78
full of d., riches and BIBLE 174
glamour Of childish d. LAWR:DH 31
good d. hasten and depart MARTIAL 5
Half our d. we pass BROWNE:T 42
happy those early dayes VAUGHAN:H 5
his d. are as grass BIBLE 232
in six d. the Lord made BIBLE 103
live laborious dayes MILT 49
longest d., sooner or later must ORCZY 2
look'd on better d. SHAK:AS 33
most wasted of all d. CHAMFORT 1
of few d., and full of trouble BIBLE 188
shortly see better d. BEHN 4
Shuts up the story of our d. RALE 9
South of my d.' circle WRIGHT:J 4
Sweet childish d. WORDS:W 96
Ten D. that Shook the World REED:Joh 1
These are not dark d. CHURCH:W 23
Thirty d. hath September ANON 109
treat the d. respectfully EMER 62
We have seen better d. SHAK:TIM 10
ye Nights and D. PRAY 15
dazzled:
d. by the ways of God LIND:V 1
D. like slate roofs in sun DAY LEWIS 6
de: doctrine of the enclitic *D.* BROWNING:R 121
De Vere: why not of D.V.? CREWE 1
dead:
A living d. man SHAK:COM 7
all our best men are d. PUNCH 26
all the D., lie down DICKIN:E 8
already been d. for a year LEHRER 3
any man fears to be d. BACON:F[1] 126
as d. as if he'd been wrong ANON 146
beest is deed he hath no peyne CHAUC 44
better day, the worse d. HENRY:M 1
Blend the living with the d. CASWALL 2
By the incurious d. DEU 1
cheer a d. man's sweetheart HOUSM 18
cold, pure, and very d. LEWIS:S 4
Come not, when I am d. TENNY 89
converse with the mighty d. THOMS:Ja[1] 13
D.! and ... never called WOOD 1
D. and living were nearly one SASS 18
D. battles, like d. generals TUCHMAN 1
d. bequeathed them life SASS 14
d., but in the Elysian fields DISR:B 83
d. don't die. They look on LAWR:DH 40
d. ere his prime MILT 42
D., for a ducat SHAK:HAM 136
D. from the waist down BROWNING:R 121
d. man touch'd me TENNY 172
D. men tell no tales PROV 65
d. or my watch has stopped MARX:G 16
d. rest well CLARE:J 4
d. Returning lightly dance THOMAS:E 7
d. shall live DRYD 95
d., the sweet musician LONGFEL 23
d. there is no rivalry MACAULAY:TB 3
d. thing, upside down DUTT 1
d. who will not fight GREN 1
d. whose pupils we have been BUTLER:S[2] 49
d. woman bites not GRAY:P 1
d., you're made for life HENDRIX 1
democracy of the d. CHESTERTON 41
dew on the face of the d. BEERS 1
Down among the d. men DYER:J[2] 1
drank it, and fell d. DICKENS 145
everything in me Was d. CERN 2
fares it with the happy d.? TENNY 146
Fifteen men on the d. man's chest STEVENSON:RL 46
for the d. birth is certain BHAG 2
frightful when one's d. POPE 116
generally shammin' when 'e's d. KIP 49
Half d. and half alive BETJ 1
have been seen d. with WEST:R 9
he breathed upon d. bodies EMER 75
He is d. and gone SHAK:HAM 159
healthy and wealthy and d. THURB 11
Hector is d. SHAK:TRO 26
I am d., and laid ANON 118
I am d. he will be very glad HOLL:H 1
I saw a d. man win a fight BALL 8
I speak for 60,000 d. HUGHES:B 2
idolised when d. CONNOLLY:J 1
If Lucy should be d. WORDS:W 33
In the long run we are all d. KEYN 1
it will remain here d. BETHU 1
I've just read that I am d. KIP 158
just the d. on holiday MAET 2
kissed by the English d. OWEN:W 8
lasting mansions of the d. CRAB 9
Let the d. bury their d. BIBLE 404
Mistah Kurtz – he d. CONRAD 6
more to say when I am d. ROBINS:EA 1
my enemy is d. WHITMAN 33
mysel' were d. and gane BALL 63
Never speak ill of the d. PROV 288
noble Living and the noble D. WORDS:W 161
not d. – but gone before ROGERS:S 4
not only d., but damned DISR:B 81
on his face, d., with a bullet THACK 7
only d. thing that smells sweet THOMAS:E 2
only two of them were d. THURB 3
Over my d. body KAUFMANN 3
owe nothing but truth to the d. VOLT 25
Past bury its d. LONGFEL 3
place was rotten with d. SASS 3
provided ... that he is really d. VOLT 40
quite forever d. CONG 35
Rejoice ye d. BRIDGES:R 13
sculptur'd d., on each side KEATS 62
sea gave up the d. BIBLE 584
Sea shall give up her d. PRAY 95
she has been d. many times PATER 2
she is d.; she's d. DONNE 72
sheeted d. Did squeak SHAK:HAM 5
sight of his d. wife HARRISON 1
simplify me when I'm d. DOUGLAS:K 1
Smiling the boy fell d. BROWNING:R 17
Stop killing the d. UNG 1
talk with the departed d. SHELLEY:PB 14
th' unhonour'd D. GRAY:T 25
That's where the d. men lie BOA 1
There are no d. MAET 1
they told me you were d. CORY 1
thought the d. had peace TENNY 222
to be said For being d. BENTLEY:EC 3
took their orders and are d. HOPE:Al 3
took their wages and are d. HOUSM 37
two days' conference With the d. WEBSTER:J 23
Tyrawley and I have been d. CHESTERFIELD 34
waste dominions of the d. VIRGIL 68
wench is d. MARLOWE 25
what was d. was Hope WILDE:O 116
Where d. men meet BUTLER:S[2] 50
wife, or himself must be d. AUSTEN 73
would that I were d. TENNY 4
you remind me of the d. SASS 11
dead-born: fell *d. from the press* HUME 15
dead march: you can hear the D.M. play KIP 48
Dead Sea:
apples on the D.S.'s shore BYR 82
D.S. fruits, that tempt MOORE:T 23
deadener: habit is a great d. BECKETT 9
deadlock: Holy D. HERB:AP 12
deadly:
has a d. stride WILDE:O 116
invaluable at first, and d. afterwards BAGE 21
more d. than the male KIP 133
deaf:
d. man to a blind woman COLERIDGE:ST 98
He is as d. as a door BRET 5
hear Him, ye d. WESLEY:C 4
I'm de'f in one year HARRIS:JC 5
turn a d. ear SWIFT 56
deafened: wit I e'er was deafen'd with BYR 239
deafer:
d. than a fish YEATS 33
d. than the blue-eyed cat TENNY 259
deafness:
mother's d. is very trifling AUSTEN 45
tale, sir, would cure d. SHAK:TEM 5
deal:
better to d. by speech BACON:F[1] 88
business give the people a square d. ROOS:T 12
given a square d. afterwards ROOS:T 3
New D. for the American people ROOS:FD 4
dealer: d. in magic and spells GILB:WS 5
dean:
Cushion and soft D. invite POPE 72
drink to the queer old D. SPOON 5
I am the D. of Christ Church SPRING 1
no dogma, no D. DISR:B 82
sly shade of a Rural D. BROOKE 9
Dean: was an old person of D. LEAR 32
de-anglicise: In order to d. ourselves HYDE:D 1
deans: dowagers for d. TENNY 101
dear:
dangerously d. BYR 33
days when I was d. to you HORACE 39
D. 338171 COWARD 31
d. to me in the middle of my LAWR:DH 20
what you do not need is d. CATO 5
dearer: d. was the mother COLERIDGE:ST 3
dearie: For thinking on my d. BURNS:R 77
dearth: d. of noble natures KEATS 35
death:
After the first d., there is THOMAS:D 11
age and d.'s inexorable VIRGIL 28
all Life d. does end HOPK:GM 24
allotted d. and hell MARLOWE 43
anaesthetic from which* LARK 9
Angel of D. spread his BYR 40
any man's *d.* diminishes *me* DONNE 100
apprehends d. no more dreadfully SHAK:MEA 33
arms of cool-enfolding d. WHITMAN 35
back resounded D. MILT 170
bargain to engrossing d. SHAK:ROM 44
Be absolute for d. SHAK:MEA 18
be so the moment after d. HAWT 6
been accused of every d. CAP 1
Birth, and copulation, and d. ELIOT:TS 68
birth and d., are not experienced MANN:T 7
born with a sense of d.? BUNIN 2
brother of d. exacteth a third BROWNE:T 42
Brother to D. DANI 1
Brought D. into the World MILT 106
brought d. into the world TWAIN 18
build your ship of d. LAWR:DH 37
but D. who comes at last SCOTT:W 16
but one life and one d. BROWNING:R 126
by defying d. that the brave VOLT 30
can this be d.? POPE 69
certain but d. and taxes PROV 299
comes first – d. or glory ANON 207
covenant with d. GARRIS 3
dance along D.'s icy brink EL-YEZ 1
day of his d. was a dark AUD 35
Dear, beauteous d. VAUGHAN:H 11
d., a necessary end SHAK:JUL 30
d. after life does greatly SPENS 30
D. and his brother Sleep SHELLEY:PB 9
d. and i will coquette MARQUIS 4
D. and taxes and childbirth? MITCH:M 2
D., as the Psalmist saith SHAK:HEN.IV[2] 35
d. bandaged my eyes BROWNING:R 182
D. be not proud DONNE 83
d. but a negligible accident? HOLL:HS 1
D. closes all TENNY 55
D. cometh soon or late MACAULAY:TB 47
d. complete the same BROWNING:R 190
D. devours all lovely things MILLAY 3
D. does not necessarily diminish PATTEN 5
D. does not take the wise man FONTAINE 15
d. exempts him LUCRET 8
D. goes dogging everywhere HENL 3
d. grippeth right hard SEN 8
d. ... had been his next-door neighbour SCOTT:W 82
D. has a thousand doors MASSIN 13
D. has done all d. can BROWNING:R 70
D. has made his darkness beautiful TENNY 165
D. hath so many doors FLETCH:J 20
D. hath ten thousand WEBSTER:J 26
d. I was to dee BALL 43
D., in itself, is nothing DRYD 23
D. in the front BYR 71
d. into the world BIBLE 365
D. is a fearful thing SHAK:MEA 24
D. is a great leveller PROV 66
D. is an old jest TURG 5
d. is as a lover's pinch SHAK:ANT 74
d. is but a groom DONNE 74
D. is dead, not he SHELLEY:PB 122
d. is most in apprehension SHAK:MEA 21
D. is my neighbour now EVANS:E 4
d. is no such terrible enemy BACON:F[1] 51
D. is not the worst thing SOPH 4
D. is nothing at all HOLL:HS 1

D. is one of two things SOC 4
d. is slumber SHELLEY:PB 15
D. is still working like a mole HERB:G 27
D. is the best exit CHEV:M 3
d. is the cure of all BROWNE:T 31
D. is the easy way out BELL:I 1
D. is the end of life TENNY 29
D. is the end of woes SPENS 31
D. is the only grammatically PATTEN 1
D. is the privilege of human ROWE 5
D. is the remedy CHAMFORT 3
D. is the veil which those SHELLEY:PB 83
d. is the worst thing that LERM 2
D. . . . It's the only thing HUX:A 34
d. itself must be, Like all SHELLEY:PB 93
D. joins us to the great YOUNG:E 1
D. Keeps his pale court SHELLEY:PB 108
D. lays his icy hand SHIRL 3
D. lies dead SWIN 54
D. lies on her SHAK:ROM 40
d. lives, and Nature MILT 166
d. makes equal the high HEYW:J 2
D. marshals up his armies WRIGHT:J 2
D. must be distingushed from dying SMITH:Syd[1] 41
d. of Little Nell without laughing WILDE:O 130
d. of your daughter would have been AUSTEN 25
D. only this mysterious JUV 22
D. opens unknown doors MASE 16
D. put down his book AUD 23
d. reveals the eminent SHAW 65
d. shall have no dominion THOMAS:D 7
D. stands above me LANDOR 4
D. strikes with impartial foot HORACE 5
d., the grand physician CLARE:J 4
d. the journey's end DRYD 126
d., the poor man's dearest friend BURNS:R 9
d. they were not divided BIBLE 152
d., thou shalt die DONNE 84
d., To die and know it LOWELL:R 3
d. ; to this a thousand doors SEN 5
D. took him by the heart OWEN:W 4
D. unloads thee SHAK:MEA 19
d. was in all our hearts SASS 18
D. , whene'er he call GILB:WS 95
D., where is thy sting-a-ling ANON 32
d., where is thy sting? BIBLE 527
D.! where is thy sting? POPE 69
D., where is thy sting? ROSS:R 1
d., which has eclipsed the gaiety JOHNSON:S 57
d. who had the soldier singled DOUGLAS:K 2
D. will be amazed CEL 2
D. will come SHELLEY:PB 148
d. will disappear with EDDY 2
D. will disprove you TURG 3
D. will find me long before BROOKE 2
d. will have his day SHAK:RIC.II 24
d. will take us in tow DIBDIN:C 7
D. without more words SIEY 2
d.'s a great disguiser SHAK:MEA 34
d.'s counterfeit SHAK:MAC 55
d.'s dreadful doom ANON 54
d.'s own hand is warmer MAUGH 27
d.'s pale flag SHAK:ROM 43
D.'s second self SHAK:SON 33
D.'s self is sorry JONS 34
D.'s shadow at the door BLUN 1
Deeth is an ende CHAUC 50
deposit us in Charon's boat* HORACE 20
direful d. indeed FLEM:M 1
disqualified by the accident of d. CHESTERTON 41
dread of something after d. SHAK:HAM 97
dull cold ear of D.? GRAY:T 18
eloquent, just and mighty D. RALE 10
encounter darkness as a bride* SHAK:MEA 22
enormously improved by d. SAKI 21
ever truly long'd for d. TENNY 50
Every d., even the cruellest WEISS 1
except d. and taxes FRANKLIN:B 27
extent of injustice in your d. CANET 6
fain die a dry d. SHAK:TEM 3
Fear of d. is worse than d. PROV 116
fed on the fulness of d. SWIN 35
feed on D., that feeds SHAK:SON 62
find d. so terrible SEV 1
first day of our Jubilee is d. BROWNE:T 17
follow my own d. step by JOHN XXIII 2
for restful d. I cry SHAK:SON 30
for us in d. to fear? LUCRET 8
from sudden d. PRAY 33
Game, That must be lost* BEAUMO 6
go we know not where* SHAK:MEA 24
great leap in the dark* HOBB 16
guilty of everlasting d. WESLEY:J 1
harbingers of d. PEG 1
He hath shook hands with time* FORD:J[1] 7
he paid the debt of nature* FABY 1
hob-and-nob with D. TENNY 96
I am become d., the destroyer BHAG 3
I could not look on D. KIP 152
I could not stop for D. DICKIN:E 13
I had seen birth and d. ELIOT:TS 63
I should be glad of another d. ELIOT:TS 63
I will be A bridegroom in my d. SHAK:ANT 53
I will dare E'en D. HERR 31
idea of D. saves him FORST 6
idea of its d. as a species KOES 7
If there wasn't d. SMITH:Ste 6
in love with easeful D. KEATS 93
in the hour of d. PRAY 34
in this administration of d. BOLL 1
into the Dust descend* FITZGER:E 15
Into the jaws of D. TENNY 199
Into the valley of D. TENNY 199
is d. itself a farewell? BALZ 6
It come equally to us all* DONNE 101
It is the only disease* MANK 1
Jewel of the Just* VAUGHAN:H 11
keep a league till d. SHAK:RIC.II 40
killed than frightened to d. SURT 21
kiss of d. SMITH:Alf 1
kiss the image of my d. DRUMMOND OF H 2
knocking at D.'s door DORSET 1
knows d. to the bone YEATS 97
last gift in d. CATUL 20
laws of d. RUSKIN 15
least of all evils* BACON:F[1] 125
life forget and d. remember SWIN 5
lightning before d. SHAK:ROM 42
Like a white dress, her d. SPEND 11
lively form of d. KYD 2
living d. MILT 282
lovely and soothing d. WHITMAN 35
make d. proud to take us SHAK:ANT 60
make one in love with d. SHELLEY:PB 105
man after his deeth moot wepe CHAUC 44
Man has created d. YEATS 97
mankind would abolish d. LAWR:DH 13
manly brow Consents to d. BYR 108
marriage and d. and division SWIN 25
masters the fear of d. BACON:F[1] 51
Men fear d. as children BACON:F[1] 50
Men love d. DWO 6
midst of life we are in d. PRAY 91
Morning after D. DICKIN:E 18
most beautiful adventure in life* FROH 1
much possessed by d. ELIOT:TS 31
must hate and d. return? SHELLEY:PB 158
My name is D. SOUTHEY 18
name that sat on him was D. BIBLE 579
neither d., nor life BIBLE 514
neither wish d., nor fear SURREY 1
new terrors of d. ARB 4
no cure for birth and d. SANT 7
no hope of d. for these souls DANTE 3
Nor shall D. brag SHAK:SON 6
not d. but dying, which is terrible FIELDING 32
Not D., but Love BROWNING:EB 9
Not one returns to tell us* FITZGER:E 24
not so much afraid of d. BROWNE:T 16
of d. Christianity has made a terror OUIDA 1
only a need for d. KAF 2
only the stroke of d. BACON:F[1] 126
opportune timing of your d. TAC 3
overcome the sharpness of d. PRAY 10
precious D. and Burial PRAY 34
Priestess in the vaults of D. TENNY 128
privilege of putting him to d. SMITH:Syd[1] 2
ranks of d. you'll find him MOORE:T 10
Reaper whose name is D. LONGFEL 39
remedy for everything, except d. CERV 17
report of my d. was an exaggeration TWAIN 37
Riddles of d. Thebes never SHELLEY:PB 156
room Do we take up in d. SHIRL 1
ruffian on the stair* HENL 3
sans Singer, and – sans End* FITZGER:E 15
shall be destroyed is d. BIBLE 525
Sleep is a d. BROWNE:T 35
so like d., I dare not trust BROWNE:T 34
solving d. and to overcoming PASTER 1
sooner forget the d. of their father MACHIA 6
stories of the d. of kings SHAK:RIC.II 28
strong and long-liv'd d. DONNE 97
struck down by d.'s feather THOMAS:D 1
sundown splendid and serene* HENL 6
swallow up d. in victory BIBLE 315
Swarm over, D. BETJ 6
swoon to d. KEATS 113
that discourtesy of d. YEATS 55
the distinguished thing* JAMES:H 24
There is d. in the pot BIBLE 169
there is mettle in d. SHAK:ANT 11
There is no terror* STERNE 23
there's always d. NAPO I 18
There's D. in the cup BURNS:R 117
thick shapes of human d. SHELLEY:PB 70
This fell sergeant D. SHAK:HAM 197
thou art D.'s fool SHAK:MEA 18
thou owest God a d. SHAK:HEN.IV[1] 85
thou wast not born for d. KEATS 93
Through D. and birth, to a diviner SHELLEY:PB 81
through the d. of some of her MASE 12
Thy brother D. came SHELLEY:PB 147
tie that only d. can sever MAUGH 8
till d. us do part PRAY 84
'tis d. to us L'EST 2
to build the house of d. MONTAIGNE 4
To certain d. by certain shame KIP 129
triumph over d. and sin SPENS 8
Under the ribs of D. MILT 36
Universe of d. MILT 166
unsubstantial D. is amorous SHAK:ROM 44
valley of the shadow of d. BIBLE 206
wages of sin is d. BIBLE 511
walk in d.'s dark vale SCOTTISH 1
wanted to be bored to d. DE VR 3
way to dusty d. SHAK:MAC 113
we shall meet again after d. GREG:Lady 4
What has this bugbear d. LUCRET 7
What should I know of d.? WORDS:W 20
which is born d. is certain BHAG 2
who craves d. cannot attain SOPH 4
whom d. could not daunte BALL 37
worst friend and enemy is but D. BROOKE 24
yet afraid of d. CHURCH:C 21

death-bill: d. must be passed off hand BYR 250

death penalty: want to abolish the d.p. KARR 2

death warrant: this morning I signed my d.w. COLLINS:Mic 1

deathless: lightly of my d. friends SASS 13

deaths:
After so many d. I live HERB:G 46
Any amusing d. lately? BOWRA 2
More d. than one must die WILDE:O 117
our own d. that we mourn BREN 6

deaths head: Call in thy d.h. there HERB:G 42

debate:
daughter of d. ELIZ I 13
to a noisy d. in an ale-house HAZL 6

debauchee: *D.*: One who has so BIER 3

debity: we shall have a new D. WHARTON:T 1

debonair: buxom, blithe, and d. MILT 66

debonaire: kaught is d. CHAUC 105

debt:
founded on borrowing and d. IBS 3
in love, and in d., and in drink BROME:A 1
midst of life we are in d. MUM 1
National D. is a very Good Thing SELL 8
paid the d. of nature FABY 1
pay a d. to pleasure too? ROCHES 7
promise made is a d. unpaid SERVICE 3

debts:
forgive us our d. BIBLE 391
He that dies pays all d. SHAK:TEM 23

decadent: D. cultures usually fall KENNY:Mar 1

decades:
D. have an delusive edge MACAULAY:R 1
Five d. hardly modified HARDY:T 53

decay:
By laws of space and time d. CORY 3

castle or building not in d. BACON:F[1] 89
Change and d. in all around LYTE 1
d. no flood YEATS 16
embody the national d. MUGG 4
flavour of mild d. HOLMES:OW 6
how soon a d. DONNE 109
men d. GOLDS 21
muddy vesture of d. SHAK:MERC 50
quick a growth to meet D. HERR 32
shall thy work d.? DONNE 80
things are subject to d. DRYD 62
decayed:
antique lady, much d. HAMIL:E 1
you are sufficiently d.? GILB:WS 83
decease: d. calls me forth WHITMAN 27
deceit:
am not up to small d. HARTE 2
men favour the d. DRYD 21
temper discretion with d. WAUGH:E 4
deceitful: heart is d. above all BIBLE 340
deceitfulness: Cat of such d. ELIOT:TS 84
deceits: from all the d. of the world PRAY 33
deceive:
all to d. one's self DEMOS 1
D. boys with toys LYS 1
first we practise to d. SCOTT:W 27
nor ever d. me MCCUAIG 1
Oh, don't d. me ANON 10
Who may d. a lover? VIRGIL 58
deceived:
by bad Women been deceiv'd MILT 285
deceiv'd The Mother of Mankinde MILT 109
possession of being well d. SWIFT 8
deceiver: I'm a gay d. COLMAN:G[2] 7
deceivers: Men were d. ever SHAK:MUCH 13
deceiving:
begins by d. oneself WILDE:O 66
d., could no longer harm ELIOT:TS 94
nearly d. your friends CORNFORD:Fran 4
She d., I believing SEDLEY 3
December:
D.'s bareness everywhere SHAK:SON 42
In drear-nighted D. KEATS 19
meetings made D. June TENNY 174
rain and wind beat dark D. SHAK:CYM 11
Seek roses in D. BYR 10
Decembers: fifteen wild D. BRONTE:E 6
decencies: Content to dwell in D. POPE 135
decency:
believe in an ultimate d. STEVENSON:RL 71
D. is Indecency's Conspiracy SHAW 64
owe the comparative d. of our lives ORWELL 2
want of D. is want of Sense ROSCOM 2
decent:
aristocracy to what is d. HOPE:An 5
d. means poor PEAC 8
decently:
behaves d. when they have power AMIS:K 5
d. and like a Christian SHERIDAN:RB 12
done d. and in order BIBLE 524
deception:
Truth lives on in d. SCHILL 9
Violence everywhere leads to d. SAINT-P 1
decide: Who shall d. POPE 76
decimal: imposed the d. system NAPO I 3
decision:
by d. more imbroils MILT 172
going to make 'a realistic d.' MCCARTHY:M 1
questions of will or d. CHOM 2
decisions: never taken any d. SIMON:G 1
deck:
d. put on its leaves FLECKER 10
master on his spar-strewn d. ARNOLD:M 15
on the d. my Captain lies WHITMAN 30
stood on the burning d. HEMA 1
to d. her mistress' head BYR 53
Who on a tilting d. sings DAY LEWIS 3
Declaration of Independence: D.o.I. bear no relation to MARTIN 4
declare: d. except my genius WILDE:O 125
decline:
D.-and-Fall-Off DICKENS 216
idea of writing the d. and fall GIBBON:E 24
declined: dear Carrie rightly d. GROS 3
declines: Professionally he d. and falls DICKENS 218
decorum:
athwart Goes all d. SHAK:MEA 1
hunt D. down BYR 15
Let them prate about d. BURNS:R 27
old Lie: *Dulce et d. est* OWEN:W 5
decoyed: see these poor fools d. PEPYS 16
decree: dost hear de D.? WHARTON:T 1
dedicate: we cannot d. LINC 11
dedicated: never d. to something you PIR 1
deductions: long train of d. DOYLE:AC 2
dee: I'll lay me doun and d. DOUGLAS:W 1
Dee: Across the sands of D. KINGSLEY:C 13
deed:
attempt, and not the d. SHAK:MAC 36
d. is all GOET 19
d. of dreadful note SHAK:MAC 66
d. whereat valour will weep SHAK:COR 23
d. without a name SHAK:MAC 81
Don't take the will for the d. MUM 2
Fit for the d. I had to do CARROLL 72
I have done the d. SHAK:MAC 38
If one good d. in all my life SHAK:TIT 4
matchless d.'s achiev'd SMART 3
one that will do the d. SHAK:LOV 9
Poor in d. and rich HOLD 1
tak the dede LYD 4
deeds:
attention on their d. EINS 3
d. left undone STOWE 5
D., not words FLETCH:J 16
d. which should not pass BYR 89
Make d. ill done SHAK:KING J 18
Our d. determine us ELIOT:G 6
Our d. still travel with us ELIOT:G 38
tell of the thrice famous d. MACAULAY:TB 39
virtuous d. that some knights CAX 3
deep:
commit his body to the d. PRAY 95
D. calleth unto d. BIBLE 213
d. Moans round TENNY 55
d. places of the earth BIBLE 229
d. where Holland lies GOLDS 9
d. yet clear DENH 1
From the great d. to the TENNY 236
He heard the d. behind him TENNY 277
Her home is on the d. CAMPBELL:T 8
his wonders in the d. BIBLE 234
home on the rolling d. SARGENT:E 1
in the lowest d. a lower MILT 184
latter fire shall heat the d. TENNY 2
lie too d. for tears WORDS:W 69
not buried me d. enough? TENNY 224
one is of the d. STEPHEN:JK 2
read'st the eternal d. WORDS:W 60
remorseless d. Clos'd o'er MILT 48
Rock'd in the cradle of the d. WILLARD 1
seem so d. as they are LANDOR 14
singularly d. young man GILB:WS 32
Still waters run d. PROV 355
too d. for his hearers GOLDS 37
unadornèd bosom of the D. MILT 18
upon the face of the d. BIBLE 2
deeper: Diving d. than anyone else HUX:A 36
deer:
d. and the antelope play HIGL 1
D. walk upon our mountains STEVENS 7
running of the d. ANON 20
stricken d., that left the herd COWP 66
Time's d. is slain MUIR:E 1
defeat:
After Alamein we never had a d. CHURCH:W 59
d. is an orphan CIANO 1
d. is an orphan KENNEDY:JF 12
D. of Germany means the d. ROOS:FD 16
d. without a war CHURCH:W 9
hero in d. YEATS 132
in d., defiance CHURCH:W 49
In d., unbeatable CHURCH:W 67
in the possibilities of d. VICT 8
know we should d. you KIP 137
man is not made for d. HEMINGWAY 9
defeated:
d., yearning to get out MURRAY:LA 6
History to the d. May say AUD 21
mighty battle we were d. LIVY 2
what he is going to do if d. OWEN:D 3
defeats: Victories and d. for the bigshots BRECHT 11
defect: fair d. of Nature? MILT 254
defence:
at one gate to make d. MILT 287
Attack is the best form of d. PROV 24
D., not defiance ANON 176
d. of the indefensible ORWELL 37
immediate d. of the United States ROOS:FD 17
make a d. or apology before CHARLES I 1
only d. is in offence BALD:S 2
think of the d. of England BALD:S 5
defend:
d. ourselves with guns not butter GOEB 3
d. to the death your right VOLT 37
d. us from all perils PRAY 29
D. us thy humble servants PRAY 22
God d. me from my friends PROV 147
had promised to d. MACAULAY:TB 8
defended: God abandoned, these d. HOUSM 37
defender: Our Shield and D. GRANT:R 1
defending: sake of d. those who Do BLAKE:W 111
defends: attacked it d. itself ANON 169
defer: 'tis madness to d. YOUNG:E 9
defiance:
Defence, not d. ANON 176
d. in their eye GOLDS 10
in defeat, d. CHURCH:W 49
definite: d. maybe GOLDWYN 10
deformed: None can be call'd deform'd but SHAK:TWE 53
deformity:
art is significant d. FRY:R 1
I – that am rudely stamp'd* SHAK:RIC.III 2
defrauding: as the d. of the State PENN 4
dégagé: half so d. COWP 1
degeneration:
directly from barbarism to d. CLEMENCE 5
fatty d. of his moral being STEVENSON:RL 4
degradation: d. after an interview with a doctor JAMES:A 2
degree:
Observe d., priority, and place SHAK:TRO 3
Take but d. away SHAK:TRO 5
when d. is shak'd SHAK:TRO 4
degrees: Good d. are good for nothing EWART 2
deid:
Gey few, and they're a' d. ANON 194
y'er a lang time d. ANON 163
deil:
D.'s Awa' wi' th' Exciseman BURNS:R 99
tae be tempit bi the D. BIBLE 588
deils: clever D. he'll mak them BURNS:R 58
deity:
between the D. and the Drains STRACH 2
D. offended BURNS:R 47
delay:
hasten is now To d. MALLEY 3
In d. there lies no SHAK:TWE 19
reluctant amorous d. MILT 193
delayed: d. till I am indifferent JOHNSON:S 95
delaying: by d. saved the situation EMPS 5
delays: d. are dangerous in war DRYD 10
delectable: They came to the D. Mountains BUNYAN 17
Delia:
D., when her beauty's flown FERG:R 3
While D. is away JAGO 1
deliberates: woman that d. is lost ADDIS 9
deliberation:
D. is the work of many DE GAU 1
D. sat and publick care MILT 158
delicate:
body's d. SHAK:KING L 40
Young ladies are d. plants AUSTEN 54
delicately: ourselves nor one another d. THOREAU 5
delice: with the fayre flowre D. SPENS 3
delicious: 'tis d. to hate you MOORE:T 2
delight:
All for your d. SHAK:MID 46
beauty to d. DAVIES:J 1
Commodity, Firmness, and D. WOTTON 6
d., . . . in the real misfortunes BURKE:E 4
d. is a delicate growth HARDY:T 6
d. is in proper young men BURNS:R 21
d. that consumes the desire SWIN 24
enjoy d. with libertie SPENS 6
little visible d., but necessary BRONTE:E 11
My d. and thy d. BRIDGES:R 14
my d. on a shining night ANON 33
my ever new d. MILT 208
never too late for d. MOORE:T 18

other aims than my d. HARDY:T 20
relinquished one d. WORDS:W 68
She was a Phantom of d. WORDS:W 88
space for d. SWIN 14
Spirit of D. SHELLEY:PB 138
Teach us D. in simple KIP 118
to d. Thou have paid DE LA M 20
turn d. into a sacrifice HERB:G 1
unrest which men miscall d. SHELLEY:PB 121
very temple of D. KEATS 96
delighted:
d. to be anywhere REAG 5
d. us long enough AUSTEN 18
delights:
king of intimate d. COWP 73
midst of the fountain of d. rises LUCRET 11
To scorn d. MILT 49
Delilah: lady barber that made good* WEST:M 7
delinquencies: naturally indulge in a few d. ELIOT:G 3
delirium: All that d. of the brave? YEATS 37
deliver:
d. me from myself BROWNE:T 39
Good Lord, d. us PRAY 33
They call us to d. HEB 2
deliverance: give you safe d. PRAY 93
deliverer: Ask for this great D. now MILT 278
delivers: Man Who D. the Goods MARSH:W 1
delivery: Punctual D. Company DICKENS 65
Delphos: steep of D. leaving MILT 11
deluded: we are all d. thus SHELLEY:PB 58
déluge: *Après nous le d.* POMPA 1
delusion: announce but that addled d. ELIOT:G 26
demagogues: found among d. MACAULAY:TB 36
demand: foresee the d. situation for any KELLY:B 1
demesne: private *pagus* and d. AUD 54
democracies:
in d. it is the only sacred thing FRANCE 10
to d. against despots DEMOS 2
democracy:
cycle d. is built on WILLIAMS:T 1
d. because power is in the hands PERIC 1
D. is only an experiment INGE 4
D. is the name we give the people FLERS 1
D. means government by discussion ATT 3
D. means government by the uneducated CHESTERTON 54
D. means simply the bludgeoning WILDE:O 38
d. of the dead CHESTERTON 41
d. was ... the most aristocratic MACAULAY:TB 31
extreme d. or absolute oligarchy ARISTOT 16
form of government but d. PLATO 12
great arsenal of d. ROOS:FD 11
grieved under a *d.*, call it *anarchy* HOBB 11
justice makes d. possible NIEB 1
made safe for d. WILSON:W 12
No one pretends that d. is perfect CHURCH:W 37
perfect d. is therefore BURKE:E 63
political experiment of d. SHAW 28
Scandal is the manure of d. FO 1
Two cheers for D. FORST 18
democrat: artist may not be a d. MARON 1
democratic: no such thing as a d. gentleman FURP 3
Democritus:
Atoms of D. BLAKE:W 101
D. would laugh HORACE 95
demon-lover: woman wailing for her d. COLERIDGE:ST 63
demonstrandum: *Quod erat d.* EUC 1
demonstrations: ineffectual d. can be made WHITLAM 3
demonstrators: weeks by tens of thousands of d. KISS 7
Demosthenes: D. never comes unseasonably MACAULAY:TB 3
demure: Sober, steadfast, and d. MILT 79
denial: with d. vain, and coy MILT 43
denied:
d. none of it aloud AUSTEN 56
if it be but half d. BUTLER:S[1] 33
denies: spirit that constantly d. GOET 13
Denmark:
look like a friend on D. SHAK:HAM 16
Prince of D. being left out SCOTT:W 90
rotten in the state of D. SHAK:HAM 39
sure it may be so in D. SHAK:HAM 52
Than is the throne of D. SHAK:HAM 13
dentist:
he had never faced a d. WELLS:HG 14
sooner go to my d. WAUGH:E 20
vulgar to talk like a d. WILDE:O 81
dentists: as our feeling for d. CHAMFORT 2
dentopedology: D. is the science of opening PHILIP 6
deny:
d. the possibility of anything HUX:TH 13
D. yourself GOET 14
I never d. DISR:B 87
Room to d. ourselves KEBLE 1
teaches to d. that faintly QUAR 1
deoch-an-duoris: Just a wee d. LAUD 2
deodorant: arms control means some kind of d. SCHROED 1
depart:
D., – be off HOLMES:OW 13
D., I say AMERY 2
now it is time to d. SOC 6
thy servant d. in peace BIBLE 609
departed:
all but he d. MOORE:T 21
D. never to return BURNS:R 97
Lord was d. from him BIBLE 137
departure: if not the arrival, the d. PROV 156
dependent: d. on what happens to her ELIOT:G 27
depends: d. on what you mean by JOAD 4
deportment: everywhere, for his D. DICKENS 175
deposit: d. in my name at a Swiss bank ALLEN:W 10
depraved: ever became d. in an instant JUV 5
depravity: d. of inanimate things HAMIL:G 1
depressed: heart of a man is depressed GAY 20
depression:
d. is rational, rage reasonable WELD 2
d. when you lose your own TRU 5
depth:
about d. knows about God TILLICH 2
d., and not the tumult WORDS:W 123
far beyond my d. SHAK:HEN.VIII 10
in the d. be praise NEWM:JH 17
without bonds and without d. BORCH 1
depths:
Out of the d. I have cried BIBLE 605
Plunge it in the d. HORACE 52
deputy: d. elected by the Lord SHAK:RIC.II 23
Derby: blue ribbon of the turf* DISR:B 33
Derby, Lord: A very weak-minded fellow* HAIG:D 1
derelicts: Like d. in my tempests BARKER:G 1
derision:
clothed with d. SWIN 15
music of d. GIBBONS:O 2
Derry: D.'s sons alike defy TONNA 1
Descartes: cannot forgive D. PASC 6
descent:
claims of long d. TENNY 64
long d. of birth MILT 284
Smooth the d. VIRGIL 66
describe: d. the undescribable BYR 101
description:
answered the d. to a T. FARQ 3
d. of the rising sun SHERIDAN:RB 34
d. of what has never occurred WILDE:O 11
from the truth of the d. SCOTT:W 95
descriptions: describe with his d. AUSTEN 35
desert:
beyond High Park's a d. to you ETH 4
create a d., and call it peace TAC 1
D. and reward ... seldom keep RICHARDSON:S 1
d. shall rejoice BIBLE 317
d. sighs in the bed AUD 7
d. were a Paradise BURNS:R 122
D. were my dwelling-place BYR 115
every man after his d. SHAK:HAM 89
Keep your heart a d. MUSSO:B 11
Life is the d. YOUNG:E 1
never will d. Mr Micawber DICKENS 150
requite its own d. VIRGIL 42
scare myself with my own d. FROST:R 9
straight in the d. a highway BIBLE 320
waste its sweetness on the d. GRAY:T 20
water but the d. BYR 105
wide d. where no life is found HOOD 2
your d. speaks loud SHAK:MEA 37
deserted: D. at his utmost need DRYD 108
deserts:
D. of vast eternity MARV 31
In the d. of the heart AUD 43
deserve:
I don't d. this BENNY 1
we'll d. it ADDIS 4
deserved:
don't believe I d. my friends WHITMAN 43
I d. it THATCH:M 1
deserves: She d. More worlds DRYD 25
deserving: where is my d.? SHAK:SON 38
design:
appears dull, there is a D. STEELE 4
d. might cover their face POUND 38
his vast D. unfold MARV 27
I see the whole d. BROWNING:R 186
designs:
d. on the tattooed lady WALLACE-C 2
d. were strictly honourable FIELDING 28
ladder of all high d. SHAK:TRO 4
Lofty d. must close in BROWNING:R 122
to his own dark d. MILT 120
utility of Japanese d. MORITA 2
desire:
air suffuses with d. ATWOOD 3
bloom of young D. GRAY:T 33
depth and dream of my d. KIP 36
d. for preventing the things one says PROUST 10
D. Gratified Plants fruits BLAKE:W 58
d. is got without content SHAK:MAC 64
D. makes everything blossom PROUST 1
d. of Man being Infinite BLAKE:W 12
d. of the moth for SHELLEY:PB 144
d. should so many years outlive SHAK:HEN.IV[2] 29
d. that outruns the delight SWIN 24
Dost thou d. her foully SHAK:MEA 15
have few things to d. BACON:F[1] 58
immoderate d. of humane learning DONNE 111
in the image of his own d. LAVER 1
kindle soft d. DRYD 114
Land of Heart's D. YEATS 16
lineaments of Gratified D. BLAKE:W 60
man's d. is for the woman COLERIDGE:ST 85
mixing Memory and d. ELIOT:TS 34
most transient flicker of d. MULK 1
One is to lose your heart's d. SHAW 47
sated, d. begins to pall PETRO 5
she is the antidote to d. CONG 58
that the d. is boundless SHAK:TRO 11
who restrain d., do so because BLAKE:W 32
wonder and wild d. BROWNING:R 194
desired:
many boys have d. it CATUL 15
Suffer herself to be desir'd WALLER 3
desires:
all d. known PRAY 63
by lopping off our d. SWIFT 17
Conceptions equal to the soul's d. WORDS:W 118
d. and petitions of thy servants PRAY 27
d. are limited by his perceptions BLAKE:W 11
d., like fell and cruel hounds SHAK:TWE 2
d. of the heart are as crooked AUD 9
d. which thereof did ensue DONNE 14
doing what one d. MILL 21
from whom all holy d. PRAY 28
nurse unacted d. BLAKE:W 51
Question your d. SHAK:MID 1
When all d. that dwell UPA 1
who d. but acts not BLAKE:W 34
with briars my joys & d. BLAKE:W 72
young with young d. THOMP:F 15
desiring:
d. the things they fear MALLET:R 1
D. this man's art SHAK:SON 11
desk: but a d. to write upon BUTLER:S[1] 22
desks: Stick close to your d. GILB:WS 14
desolation:
Love in d. masked SHELLEY:PB 117
rivers of blood, and years of d. JEFFERSON 14
despair:
Bid me despaire HERR 31

can endure my own d. WALSH 2
carrion comfort, D. HOPK:GM 20
D. bolts up my doors RALE 8
d., disguised as a virtue BIER 8
D. is the price one pays GREENE:G 7
D. yawns HUGO 5
Do not d., not even about KAF 3
Giant D. had a wife BUNYAN 15
Interpreters and prophets of d. JOHNSON:L 2
know no mithridatum of d. HARRIS:M 1
near neighbour to d. ARNOLD:M 27
Never d. under Teucer's HORACE 8
never hoped can never d. SHAW 22
now fiercer by d. MILT 150
owner whereof was Giant D. BUNYAN 14
quality of his d. CONNOLLY:C 17
rackt with deep despaire MILT 116
unpaid bill, D. SHELLEY:PB 161
very life in our d. BYR 81
warder is D. WILDE:O 120
was begotten by d. MARV 7
what resolution from despaire MILT 119

desperate:
D. cuts must have d. PROV 67
Tempt not a desp'rate man SHAK:ROM 41
wisdom not to do d. things THOREAU 10

desperation:
better than government by d. STEVENSON:A 10
lives of quiet d. THOREAU 7

despise:
know them best d. BURNS:R 59
to hate and to d. myself? HAZL 31

despised:
d. and rejected of men BIBLE 328
d. as well as served it BUTLER:S[2] 35
heartily d. by a street boy HUX:TH 11

despises:
d. all, displeases all ALBERTA 2
d. God PLUT 2
is the thing that she d. CONG 60

despoil: tremble and d. SHELLEY:PB 43

despond: name of the slough was D. BUNYAN 3

despondency:
in the end d. and madness WORDS:W 84
last words of Mr D. BUNYAN 31
SPREAD ALARM AND D. PEN 1

despotism:
Charybdis of anarchy and d. SHELLEY:PB 166
crushes individuality is d. MILL 16
d. tempered by epigrams CARLYLE:T 22

destination: think this poem will reach its d. VOLT 41

destinies: Persuasions and veiled D. SHELLEY:PB 111

destiny:
architect of his own d. APPI 1
as if I were walking with d. CHURCH:W 50
belief in a brute fate or D. EMER 79
black man ... one d. FANON 1
D. the Commissary of God DONNE 20
free to work out his d. WILSON:W 2
his d. and his doom DUTT 4
His own funereal d. BYR 52
know The d. of Man WORDS:W 94
Our d., our being's heart WORDS:W 155
Riddle of d. LAMB:Ch 30

destroy:
age shall be able to d. OSB:J 24
became necessary to d. it ANON 254
power to d. themselves HORACE 117
Whom God wishes to d. DUPO 1
whom God wishes to d. EUR 3
whom the gods wish to d. CONNOLLY:C 5

destroyed: I shall not be d. for ever ANON 44

destroyer:
D. and preserver SHELLEY:PB 40
d. of worlds BHAG 3

destruction:
by d. dwell SHAK:MAC 64
Dealing d. ANON 54
desire for d. is, at the same BAK 1
D. in the rear BYR 71
d. of our world will not DARW:C 11
D. with d. to destroy MILT 255
perfected the techniques of d. WHITE:P 14
time for the d. of error AUD 54
universal d. or universal brotherhood YEV 5

destructive:
been not creative, but d. CHEK 5
In the d. element immerse CONRAD 2
smiling, d. man LEE:N 3

detail:
frittered away by d. THOREAU 15
Merely corroborative d. GILB:WS 78

details: reveres d. and never quite LEWIS:S 2

detection: D. is, or ought to be DOYLE:AC 4

detective: thinking about writing a d. story SAYERS 2

determined: D., dared, and done SMART 3

deterrent: d. is a phallic symbol WIGG 1

detest: they d. at leisure BYR 228

detested: I have d. you long enough POUND 21

detraction: D. is but baseness' varlet JONS 13

Deutschland: *D. über alles* HOFFMAN von 1

devalued: or in your bank, has been d. WILSON:Harold 6

development:
contributions to human d. ARNOLD:M 70
d. is allowed to multiply NAIRN 1
psychic d. of an individual FREUD:S 1

devil:
A walking the D. is gone COLERIDGE:ST 40
Abasht the D. stood MILT 205
but the world, the flesh, and the d. MURRAY:D 1
can the d. speak true? SHAK:MAC 12
children of the d. TENNY 282
crafts and assaults of the d. PRAY 33
defy the d. SHAK:TWE 47
D. a monk would be MOTT 1
D. always builds a chapel DEF 10
d. and all his works PRAY 74
d. Be sometime honour'd SHAK:MEA 38
d. can cite Scripture SHAK:MERC 16
d. doesn't exist, and man has DOST 5
D. finds mischief still MADAN 1
d. finds work for idle hands PROV 68
D., having nothing else BELLOC 35
d. in the same churchyard BANC 1
d. is always blaming someone KENNELLY 3
d. is asleep or having trouble PEARY 1
d. is not so black PROV 69
D. knows how to row COLERIDGE:ST 36
d. looks after his own PROV 70
d. played at chess with me BROWNE:T 40
D. sa deavit was DUNB 1
d. should have all the good tunes HILL:Row 1
d. take her SUCK 1
D. to pay MOORE:T 24
D. turned precisian? MASSIN 10
D. watches all opportunities CONG 5
d.'s most devilish when respectable BROWNING:EB 20
do the d.'s work for nothing FIELDING 12
dream of the d. BARH 5
Drink and the d. has done for STEVENSON:RL 46
During the intervals the d. is busy ANON 181
each our own d. WILDE:O 3
favourable reference to the D. CHURCH:W 58
first Whig was the D. JOHNSON:S 205
given up believing in the d. when KNOX:R 1
Half d. and half child KIP 99
he counteracts the D. SMART 1
He who sups with the d. PROV 170
how the d. they got there? POPE 120
Is the d. to have all the passions SHAW 33
language of the D. CARLYLE:T 7
long spoon that must eat with the d. SHAK:COM 5
make a moral of the d. SHAK:HEN.V 27
not serve God if the d. bid SHAK:OTH 5
of the D.'s party without knowing BLAKE:W 33
Resist the d. BIBLE 564
shame the d. PROV 366
sugar o'er The d. himself SHAK:HAM 96
ten for the d.'s own sel PROV 309
Through envy of the d. BIBLE 365
when the d. drives PROV 281
who cleft the D.'s foot DONNE 56
world, the flesh, and the d. PRAY 33
You are children of the d. WHITEF 1
Your adversary the d. BIBLE 569

devils:
d. being offended SHAK:OTH 19
d. in life and condition ASCHAM 2
known that as many d. would LUTHER 2
no good casting out d. LAWR:DH 24
One more d.'-triumph BROWNING:R 55
they were d. incarnate SHAK:HEN.V 15

devisal: Past our d. THOMP:F 19

Devonshire: this dull *Devon-shire* HERR 9

devotion:
abstracted d. should not be encouraged JOHNSON:S 133
d. of a married woman WILDE:O 50
d. to something afar SHELLEY:PB 144
last full measure of d. LINC 11
one the d. of a lifetime WILDE:O 68
Open and obvious d. from any KIP 5

devour:
eventually d. all her children VERG 1
seeking whom he may d. BIBLE 569

devoured: evil beast hath d. him BIBLE 69

devourers: become so great d. MORE:T 1

devout:
d. in dishabilly FARQ 8
less a man for being d. MOLIERE 8

dew:
continual d. of thy blessing PRAY 26
dark with d. DE LA M 15
d. her orbs upon SHAK:MID 12
d. on the face of the dead BEERS 1
d. shall weep thy fall HERB:G 32
d. will rust them SHAK:OTH 6
fades awa' like morning d. BALL 62
from the foggy, foggy d. ANON 31
Hear noises in the d. NEIL 3
In the heart of d. we lie CAMPBELL:G 4
Like the d. on the mountain SCOTT:W 39
rain'd a ghastly d. TENNY 79
roses newly wash'd with d. SHAK:TAM 6
rough with hoary d. BROWNING:R 50
smell the d. and rain HERB:G 46
swish of a skirt in the d. KIP 132
There the silver d. YEATS 118
to meet the morning d. ARNOLD:M 44
ye Showers and D. PRAY 14

dew-bespangling: D. Herbe and tree HERR 22

dew-drop: fragile d. on its perilous KEATS 8

dewfall: d. at night STEVENSON:RL 64

dews:
Her tears fell with the d. TENNY 4
Thy still d. of quietness WHITTIER 8
ye D. and Frosts PRAY 15

dewy: full of d. wine KEATS 93

dexterity: Your d. seems a happy compound DISR:B 91

diagonally: lie *d.* in his bed STERNE 31

dialect:
d. I understand very little PEPYS 13
d. that has an army WEIN 1
D. words – those terrible HARDY:T 62
purify the d. of the tribe ELIOT:TS 104

dials: d. the signs of leaping-houses SHAK:HEN.IV[1] 3

diamond:
d. and safire bracelet lasts LOOS 5
d. bracelet lasts forever STEVENSON:A 1
imitation rough d. ASQU:M 6
immortal d. HOPK:GM 29
Like a d. in the sky TAYL:Ann 2
rough than the polished d. CHESTERFIELD 20
wrenched from her brow a d. READE 1

diamonds:
enough to give him the d. back GABOR 1
what beautiful d. WEST:M 1

diapason: d. closing full in Man DRYD 91

Diaphenia: D., like the daffadowndilly CONSTABLE:H 1

diaries:
like to destroy his old d. TOLS:S 3
Only good girls keep d. BANK 8

diary:
D. of a Superfluous Man TURG 1
never travel without my d. WILDE:O 93
What is a d. as a rule? TERRY 3

dice:
d. will never eliminate chance MALLAR 3
God does not play d. EINS 18

dickens: what the d. his name is SHAK:MERR 10

Dickens:
put to D. as children BENNETT:Al 4

that D.' world is not lifelike CECIL 1
dictates: d. to me slumbring MILT 238
dictation: merely did his d. STOWE 6
dictator:
painted as the greatest little d. THATCH:M 16
single d. substitutes himself TROT 11
dictators:
D. needed a talking cinema BROWN:Geoff 1
D. ride to and fro upon tigers CHURCH:W 47
dictatorship: d. of the proletariat MARX:K 8
dictionaries:
To make d. is dull work JOHNSON:S 10
unhappy mortals is the writer of d. JOHNSON:S 5
writer of d., a harmless JOHNSON:S 12
dictionary: but a walking dictionarie CHAPMAN:G 5
did:
he d. for them both with his plan SASS 9
who d. most, shall bear most BROWNING:R 150
diddle:
Hey d. d. NURS 16
High d. d. GILB:WS 35
didgeridoo: Play your d., Blue HARRIS:R 1
didgeridoos: Between the mouth-organs and the d. HOPE:Al 4
die:
about to d. salute thee SUET 1
all shall d. SHAK:HEN.IV[2] 35
all that lives must d. SHAK:HAM 17
as I d. may I hold you TIB 1
as natural to d. as to be BACON:F[1] 52
as though we were never going to d. VAUV 2
asked this man to d. AUD 52
at the altar d. HODG 4
begins to d. QUAR 11
being born to d.? BACON:F[1] 133
believes he shall ever d. HAZL 32
better to d. on your feet IBA 2
bid me d. HERR 31
but to do and d. TENNY 199
by feigned deaths to d. DONNE 63
can't d. . . . except when the tide's DICKENS 163
Dar'st thou d.? SHAK:MEA 21
decent thing to do is to d. BUTLER:S[2] 52
d. and be a riddance DICKENS 143
D. and become GOET 23
D., and endow a College POPE 77
d., and go we know not SHAK:MEA 24
D. because a woman's fair? WITHER 1
d. before they sing COLERIDGE:ST 49
d. but once to serve ADDIS 8
d. by famine d. by inches HENRY:M 3
d., dear, d. BEDD 2
d. first at the top SWIFT 83
d. in music SHAK:OTH 67
d. in the last ditch WILLIAM III 2
D. in the lost, lost fight CLOUGH 18
d. in their glory and never HOUSM 14
d. is cast CAES:GJ 3
D., my dear Doctor PALMERS 5
d. nobly for a cause STEK 1
D. not, poor death DONNE 83
D. of the absolute paternal ELIOT:TS 97
d. on the spot rather than give JOFF 1
d. upon a kiss SHAK:OTH 71
d. with harness on SHAK:MAC 114
d. young than to outlive POWER:M 1
Doth d. unknown SEN 8
dreading still to d. BYR 124
Dye and Lye and Sleep together ANON 137
Easy live and quiet d. SCOTT:W 58
Everybody has got to d. SAROY 1
fain d. a dry death SHAK:TEM 3
faint hope that he will d. EMER 53
fated not to d. DRYD 84
few d. well that d. in battle SHAK:HEN.V 32
fish d. belly-upward GIDE 3
for these who d. as cattle? OWEN:W 1
for to morrow we shall d. BIBLE 314
forgets that he can d. BROWNE:T 18
good d. early DEF 8
good d. first WORDS:W 113
good d. young PROV 151
great enough to d. for HAMMAR 1
Grieve not that I d. young HAST:F 1
harder lesson! how to d. PORTEUS 3
have been learning how to d. LEONARDO 2
he was not made to d. TENNY 123
hero to those who d. young RILKE 2
hire other people to d. for them PROV 188
honourable to d. for one's country HORACE 30
How hard it is to d. TWAIN 20
How often are we to d. POPE 184
how to d. by killing others CHATEAU 2
I d. As often as from thee DONNE 48
I d. because I do not d. JOHN OF C 1
I d. happy FOX:CJ 3
I dye a Christian CHARLES I 5
I have seen her d. twenty SHAK:ANT 11
I shall not wholly d. HORACE 49
I should d. before I wake ANON 61
I will d. in peace WOLFE:J 2
I will not have thee d. TENNY 116
I would like my love to d. BECKETT 14
If I d. in the service of this nation GAND:I 2
If I should d. BROOKE 25
If souls can d. as well LUCRET 7
If we are mark'd to d. SHAK:HEN.V 38
If you don't work, you d. KIP 150
I'll d. for him to-morrow BALL 5
in what peace a Christian can d. ADDIS 41
it was sure to d. MOORE:T 22
just as lucky to d. WHITMAN 5
know What 'tis to d. BEAUMO 6
let me d. drinking MAP 1
let me d. with kissing MARLOWE 13
let the idea d. instead of you? LEWIS:W 2
Let us determine to d. here BEE 1
live forever or d. in the HELLER 2
live or d. wi' Charlie HOGG 6
Lives to d. another day HOUSM 27
lot of money to d. comfortably BUTLER:S[2] 26
make a malefactor d. sweetly DRYD 142
make those – d. for theirs MICHAEL 1
man can d. but once PROV 259
men that d. at morn HOUSM 5
More deaths than one must d. WILDE:O 117
most grand to d. MASE 16
Muse forbids to d. HORACE 56
Must d. for love SHAK:ALL 2
my resolution is to D. MILT 249
never let my country d. for me KINN 4
Never say d. PROV 287
not d. but in Jerusalem SHAK:HEN.IV[2] 47
not d. here in a rage SWIFT 80
not d. in that man's company SHAK:HEN.V 40
not d. when the trees were green CLARE:J 9
not so difficult to d. BYR 127
not that I'm afraid to d. ALLEN:W 8
not to live, but to d. in BROWNE:T 32
Now that I come to d. BROWNING:R 172
Of easy ways to d. SHAK:ANT 79
Old soldiers never d. PROV 306
Only we d. in earnest RALE 5
or bravely d.? POPE 58
pie in the sky when you d. HILL:J 1
Remember man that thou must d. ANON 141
resolved to d.in a tavern ARCHPOET 1
ride on to d. MILM 1
safely home and d. – in bed SASS 5
See Naples and d. PROV 342
seems it rich to d. KEATS 93
shall d. unavenged VIRGIL 63
she must weep or she will d. TENNY 114
sit him down and d. SHAK:HEN.IV[2] 33
sooner d. than think RUSS:B 29
sorry – but we all must d. SWIFT 63
stand the hazard of the d. SHAK:RIC.III 21
suddenly we d. PUSH 8
suffer and d. without a word VIGNY 4
taught us how to d. TICK 1
tend not to d. fighting ORWELL 15
that have the power to d. TENNY 47
That we shall d., we know SHAK:JUL 36
they d. to vex me MELBOU 8
this is how you d. CHANEL 5
thou must d. HERB:G 32
time to d. BIBLE 281
To d. for faction DRYD 58
To d., to sleep SHAK:HAM 97
To d. will be an awfully big adventure BARRIE 8
To live and d. for thee HERR 31
tomorrow I shall d. LESSING:GE 2
Tomorrow let us do or d. CAMPBELL:T 10
unlamented let me d. POPE 2
We d. – does it matter when? TENNY 284
we d. in earnest GIBBONS:O 3
We must be free or d. WORDS:W 44
We shall d. alone PASC 10
What I shall d. to want SHAK:TEM 20
when they d., go to Paris APPLETON:TG 1
when you d., your memorie d. SIDNEY:P 17
when you have to d. MOLIERE 22
who lives is born to d. DRYD 126
Who saw him d.? NURS 85
who would wish to d.? BORR 5
Whom the gods love d. BYR 203
whom the gods love d. young PROV 389
with you I would willingly d. HORACE 40
without Thee I dare not d. KEBLE 3
yet d. we must SHAK:HEN.VI[3] 7
youth that must fight and d. HOOV 4
died:
been the same since God d. MILLAY 9
children who d. for our lands KIP 146
d. as he lived – at sea ANON 193
d. extremely well WALP:H 3
d. in order completely to be a creator MANN:T 2
d. last night of my physician PRIOR 15
d. like a Duke-and-a-Duchess's BARH 10
d. to save their country CHESTERTON 28
d. to succour me BALL 25
dreamed that Christ has d. in vain? SITWELL:E 9
Had I but d. an hour before SHAK:MAC 56
he d. in a good old age BIBLE 174
it d. of grieving KEATS 57
Laodameia d.; Helen d. LANDOR 16
liked it not, and d. WOTTON 1
love me who have d. for thee BROWNING:R 108
My love has d. for me to-day BALL 5
said that some have d. for love WORDS:W 35
she damned near d. ANON 31
she d. singing it SHAK:OTH 55
she d. young WEBSTER:J 27
should have d. hereafter SHAK:MAC 113
so groan'd and dy'd GAY 46
there they d. for me HOUSM 36
thought I should 'ave d. CHEV:A 2
What millions d. CAMPBELL:T 6
Who d. to save us all ALEX:CF 5
Would God I had d. for thee BIBLE 158
dies:
d. thus rich d. disgraced CARNEG:A 3
Every moment d. a man BABB 1
Every moment d. a man TENNY 97
he d. in suffering LA BRU 4
He that d. pays all debts SHAK:TEM 23
king never d. BLACKS 2
kingdom where nobody d. MILLAY 8
little something in me d. VIDAL 6
matters not how a man d. JOHNSON:S 143
no man d. for love DRYD 31
not necessarily true beacause a man d. WILDE:O 105
One d. only once MOLIERE 1
the giant d. GREEN:Mat 1
to one who d. unshriven PEREL 5
who d. fighting has GREN 1
Who d. if England live? KIP 145
who either marries or d., is sure AUSTEN 46
whom the gods love d. young PLAU 2
diest: Where thou d., will I die BIBLE 139
diet:
d. unparalleled DICKENS 66
diete was accordant to hir cote CHAUC 61
part of a balanced d. LEB 2
Praise is the best d. SMITH:Syd[1] 26
dieu: *D. et mon droit* RICHARD 1
differ: all things d., all agree POPE 31
difference:
Because there is no d. THALES 1
d. significant to no-one BOYD:RGP 1
internal d., Where DICKIN:E 4
made the d. of forty thousand WELLING 12
much d. . . . either in the climate JOHNSON:S 256
while to know the d. WYLIE 2
differences: no social d. – till women come WELLS:HG 4
different: for something completely d. MONTY 1

differentiate: sentiments that d. me from a doormat WEST:R 12
differently:
I would have done it d. WHIST 12
they do things d. there HARTL 2
difficult:
D. things take a long ANON 177
found d.; and left untried CHESTERTON 44
piece gets d. make faces SCHNAB 3
Why be d. when with a little GRAIN:P 1
difficulties:
D., Lions, or Vanity-Fair BUNYAN 27
Ten thousand d. do not NEWM:JH 13
these little local d. MACMILL:H 5
difficulty:
d. for every solution SAMUEL 6
every d. except popularity WILDE:O 127
diffidence:
in the d. that faltered POUND 37
wife, and her name was D. BUNYAN 15
dig:
d. him up and throw stones SHAW 74
d. till you gently perspire KIP 104
forbear, To d. the dust SHAK:MISC 2
he'll d. them up again WEBSTER:J 11
pen rests. I'll d. with it HEAN 1
digest:
inwardly d. them PRAY 43
just d. in its waistcoat SHERIDAN:RB 44
digestion:
d. is the great secret of life SMITH:Syd[1] 13
good d. wait on appetite SHAK:MAC 70
digestions: Few radicals have good d. BUTLER:S[2] 27
digged: d. a pit before me BIBLE 217
digging: are in one, stop d. HEAL 8
dignity:
below the d. of history MACAULAY:TB 30
d. compos'd and high exploit MILT 152
d. tends to increase in inverse HUX:A 32
find d. and greatness COWARD 6
in the d. of thinking beings JOHNSON:S 42
Let's not lose our d. STEIN:J 1
maintained the d. of history BOLI 4
room with silent d. GROS 4
digression:
Leave that ungodly d. ELIZ I 11
there began a lang d. BURNS:R 55
digressions: D. ... are the sunshine STERNE 10
dilettante: snowy-banded d. TENNY 210
diligence: D. is the mother of good fortune CERV 23
dim:
D., as the borrowed beams DRYD 69
live invisible and d. VAUGHAN:H 3
dime:
can you spare a d.? HARBU 1
sit on a d. and tell if it was heads TRACY 1
dimensions: dream of new d. GRAVES:R 4
dimples: charmer whose d. we prize SHERIDAN:RB 25
dimply: d. damsel PHILIPS:A 2
din: Within thy central d. SMITH:Alex 2
dine:
d. exact at noon POPE 65
I may d. at journey's end YEATS 58
I shall d. late LANDOR 20
If wife should d. at Edmonton COWP 56
no scandal while you d. TENNY 200
that jury-men may d. POPE 48
Whaur sall we gang and d. BALL 59
dined:
d. in every house in London WILDE:O 131
harm me, I have d. today SMITH:Syd[1] 31
in love, or had not d. POPE 110
just d. off her husband DURRELL:L 7
More d. against than dining BOWRA 1
diner-out: philosophic d. BROWNING:R 178
diners-out: d. from whom we guard MACAULAY:TB 57
dingo: Yellow-Dog D. behind KIP 106
dingy: looks d. on the surface PIR 4
dining:
pleasant d. with a bachelor GASK 5
while they thought of d. GOLDS 37
dining-room: d. will be well lighted LANDOR 20
dinner:
after d. is after d. SWIFT 77
always willing to come to d. RUNYON 10
best number for a d. party is two GUL 1
could not have had a better d. JOHNSON:S 129
d. lubricates business STOWELL 1
d. of herbs where love BIBLE 262
doubtful of his d. JOHNSON:S 46
fill the interval between d. and supper JOHNSON:S 149
good d. and feasting reconciles PEPYS 15
good d. upon his table JOHNSON:S 261
not a d. to *ask* a man to JOHNSON:S 128
not sufficient for a kite's d. QUAR 5
than he does of his d. JOHNSON:S 259
They would ask him to d. CARLYLE:T 66
three hours' march to d. HAZL 18
want d. do not ring the bell BAGE 25
What gat ye to your d. BALL 34
your d. that is eloquent MARTIAL 6
dinner-bell: tocsin of the soul – the d. BYR 207
dinners:
Let her live to earn her d. SYNGE 7
London d. evaporate in whispers SMITH:Syd[1] 21
Diogenes:
D. struck the father BURTON:Ro 23
I am D. the Cynic DIOG 3
I would be D. ALEX 4
tub was large enough for D. COLTON 8
Dionysus: Christ follows D. POUND 28
dip: kind of farthing d. STEVENSON:RL 60
diplomacy:
D. is letting someone else PEARS:LB 1
Dollar d. ANON 178
diplomat:
d. is a man who always remembers FROST:R 21
d. these days is nothing but UST 3
When a d. says yes DENNING 2
diplomats: better for aged d. to be bored AUSTIN:WR 1
Dirce: With D. in one boat LANDOR 8
direct:
d. and honest is not safe SHAK:OTH 45
understanding to d. JUNIUS 7
direction:
all leading in your d. HORACE 79
looking together in the same d. SAINT-EX 1
directions:
gives d. to the town SWIFT 69
rode madly off in all d. LEACOCK 4
directors: D. [are] always biting GOLDWYN 5
dirge:
d. of her certain ending SHAK:POET 7
d. Of the dying year SHELLEY:PB 41
forms unseen their d. is sung COLLINS:Will 4
with d. in marriage SHAK:HAM 12
dirt:
d. doesn't get any worse CRISP 3
eternal vigilance as eternal d. ORWELL 3
if d. were trumps LAMB:Ch 46
If half the little soul is d.? TENNY 100
painted child of d. POPE 125
Throw d. enough, and some PROV 390
dirty:
creature's at his d. work POPE 118
d. and charging high prices ELIOT:TS 61
d., dangerous way GOLDS 70
Wash what is d. LANGTON 2
disadvantage: d. – the curtain was up WINCHELL 1
disagree: men onely d. MILT 162
disagreeable: I'm such a d. man GILB:WS 55
disappeared:
d. in the dead of winter AUD 35
he d. CIC 9
disappears: d., and comes no more ARNOLD:M 15
disappoint: can't abide to d. *myself* GOLDS 67
disappointment:
d. give rise to anger HUME 3
his mask in d. YEATS 132
must D. all I endeavour end? HOPK:GM 30
disapproves: Dr Johnson condemns whatever he d. BURNEY 7
disarm: d. the strong and arm FRANCE 9
disaster:
meet with Triumph and D. KIP 127
The irretrievable d. BRIDGES:R 11
disasters:
d. in his morning face GOLDS 28
d., it was done with flair HAYD 3
disastrous: between the d. and the unpalatable GALB 7
disbelief: willing suspension of d. COLERIDGE:ST 75
disc jockeys: wriggling ponces of the spoken* BRIDS 1
disciples: d. to desire the multitudes HARDWO 1
discipline:
D. must be maintained DICKENS 179
good order and military d. ANON 173
lack of fear – is a result of d. NIX 17
merciless d. reigns PAVLO 1
vain all Doric d. YEATS 78
vertuous and gentle d. SPENS 19
wife and children are a kind of d. BACON:F[1] 83
disclaim: d. all my paternal care SHAK:KING L 2
disclose: not d. at too early CAUD 1
Discobolus: The D. hath no gospel BUTLER:S[2] 47
discoloured: discolour'd through our Passions POPE 109
discommendeth: He who d. others BROWNE:T 64
discontent:
contented sort of d. KEATS 107
winter of our d. SHAK:RIC.III 1
discontented:
d. with the divine discontent KINGSLEY:C 9
hundred men d. LOUIS XIV 3
discontents: More d. I never had HERR 9
discord:
dire effects from civil d. ADDIS 10
eke d. doth sow ELIZ I 13
So musical a d. SHAK:MID 41
discordant: D. harmony HORACE 88
discords: D. make the sweetest airs BUTLER:S[1] 31
discourse:
d. The freezing hours SHAK:CYM 11
fittest for d. DRYD 72
Good company and good d. WALT 7
rather hear thy d. than see a play BURTON:Ro 18
to punctuate my d. COLERIDGE:ST 91
discourtesy: that d. of death YEATS 55
discoverers: They are ill d. that think BACON:F[1] 9
discovering:
failed in d. the ... southern Continent COOK:J 1
Nothing is worth d. except TEIL 2
discovery:
D. consists of seeing SZENT 1
never made a mistake never made a d. SMILES 2
portals of d. JOYCE:J 22
Scientific d. is a private event MEDA 1
so ungrudgingly of his d. SAKI 17
discretion:
better part of valour is d. SHAK:HEN.IV[1] 92
come to the years of d. PRAY 77
d. be your tutor SHAK:HAM 107
Philosophy is nothing but d. SELD 10
temper d. with deceit WAUGH:E 4
discriminate:
If one cannot d. between HOUSM 50
Not to d. every moment PATER 5
discussion:
continue our d. in eternity SERVET 1
D. in class, which means NAB 5
government by d. ATT 3
disdain: little d. is not amiss CONG 46
disease:
Confront d. at its onset PERS 3
cure the d. and kill BACON:F[1] 68
desperate d. requires FAWK 1
d. of modern life ARNOLD:M 28
hath his favourite d. FIELDING 21
I've got Bright's d. PEREL 4
Life is an incurable d. COWLEY:A 10
long d., my Life POPE 119
means the d. is incurable CHEK 11
no Cure for this D. BELLOC 16
remedy is worse than the d. BACON:F[1] 101
diseases:
collected lists of fatal d. HELLER 6

D. desperate grown SHAK:HAM 152
scientific treatment for all d. SHAW 92
disfigure: d. us that our nearest friends BROWNE:T 16
disgrace:
d. to our family name MARX:G 8
in d. with Fortune and men's SHAK:SON 11
male-driven male d. CLARE:A 3
quite a *d.* to be fine TAYL:Ann 4
disguise:
naked is the best d. CONG 20
on earth goes about in d. O'FAOL 1
disguised: men are d. by sobriety DEQ 3
disguises: troublesom d. which wee wear MILT 201
disgust: People look at you with such d. SHADBO 1
dish:
discovery of a new d. does more BRILL 1
d. ran away with the spoon NURS 16
d. that tastes better cold PROV 332
Serve up in a clean d. LEAR 35
side d. he hadn't ordered LARD 1
Wasn't that a dainty d. NURS 66
woman is a d. for the gods SHAK:ANT 71
dishabilly: devout in d. FARQ 8
dishes:
d. were ill-sorted DRYD 144
Home-made d. that drive one HOOD 17
nothing but spicy d. LENIN 14
thorn twig for clettering d. GIBBONS:S 5
Thou shalt not wash d. NURS 8
dishonour: fears d. more than death HORACE 58
disinterested: there are d. actions GIDE 2
disk: D. of fire somewhat like a Guinea? BLAKE:W 112
dislike:
D. which People not too good-natured STEELE 10
must not d. people MACNEICE 15
disliked:
get ourselves rather d. POUND 23
I have always d. myself CONNOLLY:C 8
dislikings: made up of likings and d. LAMB:Ch 9
dismal: d. cry rose slowly BROWNING:EB 4
dismay: Let nothing you d. ANON 13
dismayed: neither be thou d. BIBLE 128
dismiss: Lord, d. us with Thy blessing BUCKO 2
dismissed:
d. by the British electorate CHURCH:W 51
you are d. MASS 19
dismount:
they dare not d. CHURCH:W 47
tiger is afraid to d. PROV 169
Disney: makes D. the most significant LOW 2
disobedience:
By one man's d. lost MILT 262
Man's First D. MILT 106
disobey: Naughty girl to d. NURS 42
disorder:
Her last d. mortal GOLDS 1
policeman is there to *preserve* d. DALEY 1
sweet d. in the dresse HERR 15
dispatch: requisite in business than d. ADDIS 12
displeasing: aristocratic pleasure of d. HUX:A 27
disposes:
God d. KEMP 8
God d. PROV 262
disposition:
must be the flag of my d. WHITMAN 4
put an antic d. on SHAK:HAM 58
dispositions: actions determine our d. ARISTOT 7
dispossess: d. the swain GOLDS 22
dispraised: of such To be d. JONS 9
disproportion: Foul d. SHAK:OTH 37
dispute: D. it like a man SHAK:MAC 98
disputing: itch of d. will prove WOTTON 7
Disraeli: He is a self-made man* BRIGHT 6
disreputable: they get one into d. company SHAW 133
dissect: We murder to d. WORDS:W 18
dissent:
dissidence of d. BURKE:E 30
Paradise of D. PIKE 1
dissipation:
d. without pleasure GIBBON:E 21
other things than d. that thicken WEST:R 5
distance:
by d. made more sweet WORDS:W 78
d. isn't important DU DEF 1
d. lends enchantment to the view CAMPBELL:T 2
Tyranny of D. BLAIN 2
distant:
Man is d. PRINGLE:T 2
prospect of a d. good DRYD 89
distastes: from a thousand d. VALERY 5
distempered: physic to the d. mind AESC 7
distinction: few escape that d. TWAIN 7
distinctiveness: vice of d. to become queer HOPK:GM 33
distinguish: wisdom to d. the one from NIEB 2
distinguished:
at last, the d. thing JAMES:H 24
be d. above others HOMER 8
distracted: I shall go d. AUSTEN 30
distress: incapable of her own d. SHAK:HAM 176
distressed: Art thou sore d.? NEALE 4
distribute: not know how to d. it SITTING 1
distribution: same d. of the necessaries SMITH:Ad 2
distrust:
d. the things we understand too VOLT 2
stay together, but we d. BRADB 5
We have to d. each other WILLIAMS:T 4
What is it? D. DEMOS 2
distrusting: more shame in d. one's friends LA ROCHE 14
disturbance:
no d. in the world CHARLES I 5
preferable to change and d. MONTAIGNE 19
ditch:
both shall fall into the d. BIBLE 416
die in the last d. WILLIAM III 2
environed with a great d. CROMWELL 10
if he wasn't as dull as d. water DICKENS 227
Rather a d. in Egypt SHAK:ANT 63
Who needs a d.? COPE 1
ditchers: d., and grave-makers SHAK:HAM 179
ditches: of Dutchmen and of d. BYR 219
ditchwater: Is d. dull? CHESTERTON 55
ditties: wonderful deathless d. O'SHAUGH 1
ditty: He play'd an ancient d. KEATS 75
diuturnity: D. [long-lastingness] is a dream BROWNE:T 61
divan: Enacted on this same d. ELIOT:TS 46
diver:
d.'s brilliant bow AUD 7
Don't forget the d. ITMA 3
diversion: Most sorts of d. in men SWIFT 23
diversity: make the world safe for d. KENNEDY:JF 3
divide:
both d. the crown DRYD 115
D. and rule GOET 25
D. and rule PROV 71
d. with the poor the produce SMITH:Ad 2
joins it, to d. POPE 52
divided:
D. by interests VOLT 27
D. by the morning tea MACNEICE 11
d. we fall PROV 409
expect it will cease to be d. LINC 4
dividend: no d. from time's tomorrows SASS 7
dividends: comfortable man, with d. LONGFEL 28
dividing:
by d. we fall DICKIN:J 1
nor d. the Substance PRAY 30
divine:
good d. that follows his own SHAK:MERC 12
Hand that made us is d. ADDIS 40
horror and its beauty are d. SHELLEY:PB 47
More needs she the d. SHAK:MAC 106
Touch the unknowable D. NEIL 1
When d. souls appear EMER 89
wrote that monarchs were d. KIP 141
divinely: d. tall And most d. fair TENNY 10
divineness: some participation of d. BACON:F[1] 8
diviner: d. than a loveless god BROWNING:R 65
diving: D. deeper than anyone else HUX:A 36
divinity:
d. of – another Jew? HEINE 9
d. that shapes our ends SHAK:HAM 191
something in it of d. BROWNE:T 30
such d. doth hedge a king SHAK:HAM 165
surely a piece of d. in us BROWNE:T 33
wingy mysteries in d. BROWNE:T 6
division:
D. is as bad ANON 84
equal d. of unequal earnings ELLIOTT:E 2
marriage and death and d. SWIN 25
divisions: How many d. has *he* got? STALIN 4
divorce:
D.? Never THORN 1
long d. of steel SHAK:HEN.VIII 3
Seal then this bill of my D. DONNE 92
divorcees: family of d., and they're head ARCHER 1
dizziness: Love is like a d. HOGG 8
dizzy: d. 'tis to cast one's eyes SHAK:KING L 65
do:
all wanted to d. something TROLL 18
but to d. and die TENNY 199
Can I d. you now HANDL 1
Can I d. you now, sir? ITMA 2
Canst thou d. likewise? DICKENS 230
Didn't they d. well FORSY 1
d. all things through Christ BIBLE 543
D. as I say, not as I d. PROV 72
D. as I say, not as I d. SELD 12
d. as much of it as you can HOLMES:H 1
D. as we say BOCCAC 1
D. as you would be done by CHESTERFIELD 7
D. as you would be done by PROV 73
d. as you're bid EDGE 3
d. it with thy might BIBLE 286
d. it with thy whole might CARLYLE:T 15
d. not d. to others CONF 12
D. not d. unto others SHAW 48
d. only one thing at once SMILES 1
D. other men DICKENS 111
d. those things which at present KEYN 3
d. what you are afraid to d. EMER 21
D. what you will RAB 8
d. your worst, and we will d. CHURCH:W 22
Doe all things like a man HERB:G 5
Don't d. anything for people until SCOTT:Rose 1
either d., or die FLETCH:J 11
finding out what will not d. SMILES 2
Go, and d. thou likewise BIBLE 458
HOW NOT TO D. IT DICKENS 186
I can d. no other LUTHER 8
I dare say she will d. BROOKE 15
I didn't want to d. it MCCARTHY:J[1] 1
I don't mind if I d. ITMA 6
I'll d., I'll d., and I'll d. SHAK:MAC 5
I'll d.'t before I speak SHAK:KING L 4
it won't d. JOHNSON:S 125
less one has to d. CHESTERFIELD 31
let me d. it now GREL 1
Let us d., or die BURNS:R 108
let us d. something today COLLINGWOOD:Ad 1
Let's d. it PORTER:C 1
long as they d. what I say THATCH:M 8
Love and d. what you like AUGUS 11
must d. twice as well as men WHITTON 1
Never d. things by halves PROV 283
not knowing what they d. SHAK:MUCH 23
one that will d. the deed SHAK:LOV 9
People don't d. such things IBS 14
shall we d. the thing you ken ANON 92
This will never d. JEFFREY 1
To be is to d. KENNELLY 1
to d. anything for oneself MAUGH 14
To d. it as for thee HERB:G 50
to d. were as easy as to know SHAK:MERC 12
to know what to d. with it WALP:H 11
Tomorrow let us d. or die CAMPBELL:T 10
tomorrow what you can d. today PROV 286
true and d. what is right HUX:TH 2
We cannot d. it, Sir, because CARROLL 71
well done, d. it yourself PROV 193
what a man would d. BROWNING:R 149
What are we going to d.? AUD 56
What can I d. that matters? SPEND 9
what d. I d. with *this*? EDWARD VIII 6
What'll we d. with ourselves FITZGER:FS 7
which he/she has been called to d. GINZ 1
who can d. all things well? CHURCH:C 13

write what men d., and not BACON:F[1] 11
Doasyouwouldbedoneby: her name is Mrs D. KINGSLEY:C 6
doc: cards with a man called D. ALG 2
docks: by what dry d. HEWETT 1
doctor:
degradation after an interview with a d. JAMES:A 2
d. full of phrase ARNOLD:M 50
d. who cannot tell them SHAW 101
God and the d. we alike adore OWEN:J 1
keeps the d. away PROV 20
Knocked down a d.? SIMPSON:NF 2
out-liv'd the d.'s pill GAY 24
Than fee the d. DRYD 122
therein D. but himself MILT 286
doctors:
better have d. well off SHAW 95
budge d. of the Stoick furr MILT 37
D. allow us to die LA BRU 15
more old drunkards than old d. FRANKLIN:B 32
more old drunkards than old d. PROV 367
when D. disagree POPE 76
doctrinally: d. inexplicable but it goes on MUGG 8
doctrine:
d. could be held by no sane BROWNING:R 101
d. so illogical and so dull KEYN 2
lov'd the d. for the teacher's DEF 9
Not for the d., but the music POPE 18
prove their d. orthodox BUTLER:S[1] 12
Though all the windes of doctrin MILT 322
with every wind of d. BIBLE 532
doctrines:
By d. fashioned GOLDS 25
What makes all d. plain BUTLER:S[1] 32
documents: more d. than he can really use JAMES:H 19
dodger: *sobriquet* of 'The Artful D.' DICKENS 56
dodgers: dodgerest of the d. DICKENS 229
dodgy: D. VAUGHAN:N 1
dodo: D. never had a chance CUPPY 1
doers: be ye d. of the word BIBLE 562
does:
d. well what one loves COLETTE 3
'Tis not what man d. BROWNING:R 149
dog:
a very d. to the commonalty SHAK:COR 1
Am I a d., that thou BIBLE 148
and he my d. SHAK:HEN.IV[2] 10
beaten d. beneath the hail POUND 36
better buy yourself a d. STAPLES 1
Beware of the d. PETRO 1
d. did nothing in the night-time DOYLE:AC 25
D. does not eat d. PROV 74
d. – he *shat* in the tuckerbox ANON 3
d. it was that dy'd GOLDS 16
d. must to kennel SHAK:KING L 14
d. returneth to his vomit BIBLE 271
d. starvd at his Masters gate BLAKE:W 83
d., to gain some private ends GOLDS 15
d. will have his day SHAK:HAM 190
engine of pollution, the d. SPARROW 1
ever d. that praised his fleas? YEATS 32
every d. has his day BORR 9
Every d. has his day PROV 99
every d. his day KINGSLEY:C 19
Give a d. a bad name PROV 143
good d. deserves a good bone PROV 152
hair of the d. that bit you PROV 361
Hath a d. money? SHAK:MERC 18
hear my d. bark at a crow SHAK:MUCH 1
help a lame d. over a stile CHILLING 2
honour the very flea of his d. JONS 4
I had rather be a d. SHAK:JUL 69
If the d. bark, go in PROV 185
If you call a d. *Hervey* JOHNSON:S 89
in Russia, communism is a dead d. SOLZ 10
keep the D. far hence ELIOT:TS 39
little d. laughed NURS 16
living d. is better BIBLE 285
Love me, love my d. PROV 253
man bites a d. that is news BOGART:JB 1
my poor d. Tray CAMPBELL:T 1
portrait of a d. that I know JOHNSON:S 262
shaggy d., just unchained STEVENSON:RL 26
Something better than his d. TENNY 72
suffers the d.'s disadvantages TABER 1
tail must wag the d. KIP 44
teach an old d. new tricks PROV 445
thy d., thy bottle, and thy wife POPE 103
to a d. for a new year's gift SHAK:MERR 13
To his d., every man is Napoleon HUX:A 47
when a man bites a d. DANA 2
whose d. are you? POPE 155
Why keep a d. and bark PROV 432
You call'd me d. SHAK:MERC 18
dog-star: D. rages POPE 117
dogged: It's d. as does it TROLL 17
doggie: d. in front has suddenly COWARD 32
doggy: go on with their d. life AUD 15
dogma:
d. of the Ghost in the Machine RYLE 3
no d., no Dean DISR:B 82
stigma . . . serve to beat a d. GUED 3
teach a d. new tricks PARKER:D 31
dogmas: d. or goals are in doubt PIR 1
dogmatize: I d. and am contradicted JOHNSON:S 263
dogs:
all their running d. MAO 4
all things as straw d. LAO 4
As many d. there be GOLDS 14
attentive to the feelings of d. ELIOT:G 36
bang these d. of Seville TENNY 282
Barking d. seldom bite PROV 28
breed of their horses and d. PENN 3
Cats is 'd.' PUNCH 10
Cowardly d. bark loudest WEBSTER:J 7
curious habits of d. POUND 20
d. bark at me as SHAK:RIC.III 2
d. delight to bark WATTS 8
D., easily won to fawn SHAK:RIC.II 26
Don't let's go to the d. HERB:AP 4
fought the d. and killed BROWNING:R 25
From d. that would devour PSALMS 1
Goethe had an aversion to d. NERV 3
hates children and d. can't be all FIELDS 6
Lame d. over stiles KINGSLEY:C 18
lamp-post how it feels about d. HAMP 5
Let sleeping d. lie PROV 234
let slip the d. of war SHAK:JUL 44
like dancing d. JOHNSON:S 174
loathe people who keep d. STREAT 1
Mad d. and Englishmen COWARD 20
more I admire d. SEV 2
Unmiss'd but by his d. COWP 33
who hates d. and babies ROSTEN 1
woman who is really kind to d. BEERB 9
doileys: I'm soiling the d. BETJ 27
doing:
about the manner of d. it HAZL 37
joy's soul lies in the d. SHAK:TRO 2
one way of *d.* things rightly RUSKIN 10
see what she's d. PUNCH 14
stop everyone from d. it HERB:AP 6
without any hope of d. it well CHESTERTON 59
dolce vita: 'La d.v.' was a pathetic and awkward title FELL 3
dole: d. bread is bitter bread HEWETT 4
doll: worthier than the d. in the d.'s house DICKENS 228
dollar:
almighty d. IRV 7
almighty d. is the only ANON 155
D. diplomacy ANON 178
rely on the power of a d. EMER 90
dollars:
d. spent in so-called charity CARNEG:A 2
What's a thousand d.? MARX:G 3
Dolores:
sanguine and subtle D. SWIN 23
splendid and sterile D. SWIN 21
dolour: have wept to see the d. MALORY 11
dolphin: D., you only guide me LOWELL:R 17
dolphin-like: His delights Were d. SHAK:ANT 64
dolphin-torn: d., that gong-tormented sea YEATS 87
dome:
starlit or a moonlit d. YEATS 86
That sunny d. COLERIDGE:ST 63
domestic:
d. as a plate MILLAY 2
D. happiness, thou only bliss COWP 65
d. matters are no less importunate MONTAIGNE 8
d. sort which never stirs SHERIDAN:RB 27
men call d. bliss PATMO 10
warheads for the d. Armageddon LEONARD:H 1
domesticate: d. the Recording Angel STEVENSON:RL 12
domesticated: she has been d. like a cat DARK 2
domesticity: d., that avalanche of overcoats WHITE:P 2
domestics: repeat itself in the conduct of her d. BEETON
dominance: nail in the coffin of male d. FIGES 1
dominant: idea of man as the d. mammal BURNET 1
domination: fought against white d. MANDELA:N 2
dominion:
death shall have no d. THOMAS:D 7
equal d. is given to woman STANTON:EI 3
hand that holds d. THOMAS:D 9
it and the d. of the world MAHAN 1
their love of d. HUME 7
truly sorry man's d. BURNS:R 31
dominions:
d., on which the sun NORTH:C 3
waste d. of the dead VIRGIL 68
dominoes: d. set up. You knock over EISEN 4
don:
elderly homosexual d. and asked to spy FRY:S 2
Remote and ineffectual D. BELLOC 29
Don John of Austria:
D.J.o.A. is going to the war CHESTERTON 19
D.J.o.A. Is riding to the sea CHESTERTON 20
D.J.o.A. rides homeward CHESTERTON 22
done:
be seen to be d. HEWART 1
Beautifully d. SPENCER:S 2
been and gone and d.? GILB:WS 3
but what we have d. KEMP 3
Determined, dared, and d. SMART 3
Do as you would be d. by PROV 73
do not want d. to yourself CONF 12
d. cannot be undone PROV 419
d. instead of not doing POUND 37
dread of doing what has been d. WHARTON:E 4
Easier said than d. PROV 89
ever be d. for the first time CORNFORD:FM 1
he has d. it all himself BARRIE 13
I had d. all I could JOHNSON:S 94
I have d. the deed SHAK:MAC 38
If it were d. when 'tis d. SHAK:MAC 23
much is to be d. and little JOHNSON:S 271
must be seen to be d. OSB:J 11
nothing d. while anything was LUCAN 3
nothing d. while aught remains ROGERS:S 3
Nothing to be d. BECKETT 2
only see what remains to be d. CURIE 4
reward of a thing well d. EMER 41
seldom, if ever d. COWARD 21
So little d. TENNY 164
So little d., so much to do RHODES 4
Something attempted, something d. LONGFEL 12
surprised to find it d. at all JOHNSON:S 126
thank God I have d. with him JOHNSON:S 99
they d. the old woman in SHAW 109
thou hast not d. DONNE 95
want a thing well d., do it PROV 193
way to get thing d. is not JOW 7
we have d. those things which we PRAY 4
What have I d. for you HENL 8
what he might have d. with us CLOUGH 24
What is this that thou hast d.? BIBLE 20
What's d. cannot be undone SHAK:MAC 105
What's d. is d. SHAK:MAC 65
dong: D. with the Luminous Nose LEAR 10
donkey:
I tried eatin' d. too NEVILL 1
that I fear, it is the d. TEMPLE:W[2] 5
that's a dead d. DICKENS 53
donkeys:
lions led by d. HOFFMAN:M 1
two china condiment d. SHAFF 1
Donne:
D. . . . deserved hanging JONS 52
D., I suppose, was such ELIOT:TS 32

D., whose muse on COLERIDGE:ST 64
D.'s verses are like the peace JAMES VI/I 6
Here lyes a King* CAREW:T 1
John D., Anne D., Un-done DONNE 112
read D. you must measure *time* COLERIDGE:ST 78
thought to D. was an experience ELIOT:TS 117
with Landor and with D. YEATS 58
dons: little d. I complain about PRIEST 4
donsmanship: *D.* – the art of criticizing POTTER:S 3
don't-knows: One day the d. will get in MILLIG 12
doom:
d. falls pitiless and dark RUSS:B 6
even to the edge of d. SHAK:SON 52
great d.'s image SHAK:MAC 55
his destiny and his d. DUTT 4
to th' crack of d.? SHAK:MAC 86
doomed:
Doom'd for a certain term SHAK:HAM 41
doom'd to death DRYD 84
doomsday:
D. is near SHAK:HEN.IV[1] 77
every day is D. EMER 63
threaten that they have D. weapons LAING 1
door:
Another name was on the d. TENNY 170
at any d. I knock HORACE 74
came out by the same D. FITZGER:E 17
d. is what a dog is NASH 21
d. stood open at our feast COLERIDGE:M 3
D. to which I found no Key FITZGER:E 19
every d. is shut but one COWP 9
For barring of the d. BALL 21
Get up and bar the d. BALL 22
hand of justice shut the d. STERNE 55
He is as deaf as a d. BRET 5
in at the palace d. one day DICKENS 5
in her own room with the d. shut WHARTON:E 1
in interest a knock at the d. LAMB:Ch 19
knock on my d. in the morning AUD 26
knocking at Death's d. DORSET 1
knocking at preferment's d. ARNOLD:M 21
Knocking on the moonlit d. DE LA M 6
lie I by the chancel d. ANON 128
made my sin their d.? DONNE 95
No d. can keep them out HERB:G 24
one d. shuts, another PROV 424
open d. for all nations' trade BERE 1
opening of a D. DICKIN:E 19
Shut the d. after you EDGE 3
Shut the d., Wales BRUM 4
shut the stable d. after the horse PROV 210
stand at the d., and knock BIBLE 577
When poverty comes in at the d. PROV 425
wolf is at the d. GILMAN 1
wrong side of the d. CHESTERTON 6
doorkeeper: d. in the house of my God BIBLE 222
doormat: from a d. or a prostitute WEST:R 12
doors:
Death has a thousand d. MASSIN 13
Death opens unknown d. MASE 16
death; to this a thousand d. SEN 5
Despair bolts up my d. RALE 8
d. of perception were cleansed BLAKE:W 53
d. to let out life FLETCH:J 20
D., where my heart TENNY 133
exit d. are all in order SHAW 123
Little Girls is slamming D. BELLOC 24
opening the d. very often AUSTEN 49
shut their d. against SHAK:TIM 7
ten thousand several d. WEBSTER:J 26
Th' infernal dores MILT 171
ye everlasting d. BIBLE 208
doorstep: I don't have a d. low enough BOLTE 1
doorway: lilacs in the d. bloom'd WHITMAN 34
doots: hae ma d. aboot the meenister PUNCH 21
Dorchester:
end up with drinks at the D. GAIT 3
Safe in the D. Hotel BETJ 24
Doric: vain all D. discipline YEATS 78
Doris Day: knew D.D. before she was a virgin MARX:G 28
dotage:
lose myself in d. SHAK:ANT 9
streams of d. flow JOHNSON:S 69
dote: d. on her for anything SHAK:KING L 12
Dotheboys: Squeer's Academy, D. Hall DICKENS 66
dots: what those damned d. mean CHURCH:Lord R 5
double:
D., d. toil and trouble SHAK:MAC 78
d. the vision my Eyes do see BLAKE:W 78
surely you'll grow d. WORDS:W 15
double-bed: d. of a world FRY:C 3
double-cross: sign of an archbishop is a d. DIX:GEA 1
double-entendre: horrible d. ANON 106
doublet:
d. all unbrac'd SHAK:HAM 61
d. of changeable taffeta SHAK:TWE 30
he bought his d. in Italy SHAK:MERC 13
doublethink: *D.* means the power of holding ORWELL 35
doubt:
curiosity, freckles, and d. PARKER:D 3
difficulties do not make one d. NEWM:JH 13
does not d. is a dead faith UNA 8
dogmas or goals are in d. PIR 1
d. diversified by faith BROWNING:R 81
D. everything at least once LICHT 2
Frets d. the maw-crammed BROWNING:R 185
Humility is only d. BLAKE:W 107
I show you d. BROWNING:R 84
in d. to act or rest POPE 89
let us never, never d. BELLOC 8
mair I am in d. DUNB 13
more faith in honest d. TENNY 173
never d. I love SHAK:HAM 67
never stand to d. HERR 43
night of d. and sorrow BARING-G 5
no d. in this book KORAN 1
No possible d. whatever GILB:WS 102
not enabled to d. thee KNOX:R 3
overcompensates a secret d. HUX:A 17
soundest Casuists d. POPE 76
stricken thro' with d. TENNY 172
sunnier side of d. TENNY 292
time will d. of Rome BYR 204
troubled with religious d. CHESTERTON 23
when all men d. you KIP 127
when in d., strike it out TWAIN 23
When in d., tell the truth TWAIN 35
When in d., win the trick HOYLE 1
wherefore didst thou d.? BIBLE 415
who shall teach the Child to D. BLAKE:W 90
doubter: I am the d. and the doubt EMER 99
Doubting-Castle: castle, called D. BUNYAN 14
doubts:
breede D. mongst Divines SPENS 5
d. that drive the coward TENNY 172
he shall end in d. BACON:F[1] 5
His d. are better than most HARDWI 1
To saucy d. and fears SHAK:MAC 69
who D. from what he sees BLAKE:W 92
douche: rattling of a thousand d. bags LOWRY:M 1
dough: chilled d. of his flesh HARRISON 1
doughnuts: d. turn out like Fanny's CRAD 1
Douglas:
doughty D. bound him to ride BALL 7
Like D. conquer, or like D. die HOME 3
dove:
d. descending breaks ELIOT:TS 107
d. found no rest BIBLE 38
hawk at eagles with a d.? HERB:G 17
I had wings like a d. BIBLE 216
patient as the female d. SHAK:HAM 189
sweet d. died KEATS 57
dove-cote: like an eagle in a d. SHAK:COR 22
Dover:
burning a farthing candle at D. JOHNSON:S 123
There's mile-stones on the D. road DICKENS 192
think of the chalk cliffs of D. BALD:S 5
doves:
d. opposed the air strike BARTL 1
harmless as d. BIBLE 407
hurricane of black d. LORCA 2
moan of d. in immemorial TENNY 119
dovetailedness: kind of universal d. DICKENS 81
dowagers: d. for deans TENNY 101
dowel: D., Dobet and Dobest LANGLAND 1
dower:
faith's transcendent d. WORDS:W 129
forfeited their ancient English d. WORDS:W 47
truth, then, be thy d. SHAK:KING L 2
down:
been working my way d. WELLES 2
D., wanton, d. GRAVES:R 6
Go d. like lumps of lead HODG 3
He did again get d. COWP 57
meet 'em on your way d. MIZ 1
neither up nor d. NURS 45
never let you d. WAUGH:E 6
soft young d. of her MEW 1
that is d. needs fear BUNYAN 26
they must be kept d. MARLBOR:S 1
went d. very well too WELLING 20
down under: had carried us safely *d.u.* FROUDE 4
downhearted: We are not d. CHAMBERLAIN:J 4
downhill: d. path is easy ROSSET:C 17
Downs: All in the D. the fleet GAY 37
downstairs:
I'll kick you d. CARROLL 10
why did you kick me d.? BICK 5
downward: thoughts Were always d. bent MILT 142
downwards:
look no way but d. BUNYAN 22
will always be a bending d. WHEW 1
doxy: Orthodoxy is my d. WARB 1
dozen:
d., and that they all fit WILDE:O 46
d. d. in her place SUCK 5
Dr Fell: I do not love you, D.F. BROWN:T 2
Drachenfels: castled crag of D. BYR 88
drachmas: drop my blood for d. SHAK:JUL 72
drag:
Gestapo in d. ALLEN:D 6
Put on the d. SMITH:Syd[1] 6
drag-net: swept like a d. DRYD 144
dragon:
between the d. and his wrath SHAK:KING L 3
Dare the unpastured d. SHELLEY:PB 115
Done is a battell on the d. DUNB 18
d. on time's hoard LOWELL:R 15
ev'ning D. came MILT 297
O to be a d. MOORE:M 7
dragon-fly:
d. Hangs like a blue thread ROSSET:DG 9
With the d. on the river BROWNING:EB 22
dragonflies: d. draw flame HOPK:GM 19
drain: have to put it down the d. HERB:AP 11
drainage: which does not require main d. BRIEN 1
drainpipe:
we're in a blessed d. WELLS:HG 3
wrong end of a municipal d. LLOYD GEO 10
drains:
between the Deity and the D. STRACH 2
she said it wur draäins TENNY 289
very pale owing to the d. ASHFORD 3
Drake: D. he's in his hammock NEWBOLT 4
dram: Tak aff your d. BURNS:R 38
drama:
d.'s laws the d.'s patrons give JOHNSON:S 65
good d. critic is one who perceives TYNAN 3
What is d. but life with HITCH 1
dramatist:
d. only wants more liberties JAMES:H 19
d. who had discovered himself SAKI 17
dramatize: D., d. JAMES:H 17
***Drang:** Sturm und D.* KLIN 1
drank:
d. it, and fell dead DICKENS 145
d. it when we met the gas KIP 147
d. without provocation SWIFT 35
ne d., till he was dead MALORY 14
They all d. his health FARRAR 3
welle than of the tonne She d. CHAUC 34
drapery: with the d. of his figures COLERIDGE:ST 94
draught:
does not think of the d. AUSTEN 49
nauseous d. of life go ROCHES 1
O, for a d. of vintage KEATS 93
such a d. of woe? SHELLEY:PB 118
draughts:
peculiarly susceptible to d. WILDE:O 92

two reasons for d. PEAC 4
unhappy brains for d. SHAK:OTH 24
With constant d. fresh COWLEY:A 6
drinks:
'e d. like a beast KIP 69
end up with d. at the Dorchester GAIT 3
drip: d. after d. hollows out LUCRET 4
dripping:
Come d. along BETJ 12
Constant d. wears away PROV 60
drive: easy to lead, but difficult to d. BROUGHAM 2
driver: he remained in the d.'s seat BEAV 4
driveth: he d. furiously BIBLE 172
driving:
d. briskly in a post-chaise JOHNSON:S 190
like the d. of Jehu BIBLE 172
drizzle: blasted Henglish d. KIP 61
droit: *Dieu et mon d.* RICHARD 1
drollery: fatal d. called a representative DISR:B 29
dromedary: muse on d. trots COLERIDGE:ST 64
drone: lazy yawning d. SHAK:HEN.V 7
drop:
dark d., the trapped sky HEAN 2
One d. would save my soul MARLOWE 40
should like very well to d. JOHNSON:S 220
than to d. thy 'H's' CALVER 3
tune in, and d. out LEARY 1
we d. like the fruits MERED:G 16
dropped: not wish to be d. by JOHNSON:S 220
droppingdown-deadness: d. of manner SMITH:Syd[1] 4
drops:
changed into little water d. MARLOWE 45
d. on gate-bars hang HARDY:T 42
These are gracious d. SHAK:JUL 55
dross:
all is d. that is not Helena MARLOWE 38
rest is d. POUND 34
stoops not to shows of d. SHAK:MERC 26
drought: thirsty with d. and chilled WRIGHT:J 1
droving: D. songs are very pretty LAWS 4
drown:
left her to d. ION 1
what pain it was to d. SHAK:RIC.III 9
drownded: only be d. now and again SYNGE 5
drowned:
found him drown'd in Yarrow BALL 44
waiting for people who had d. LLOSA 1
drowning:
d. man will clutch at a straw PROV 85
He hath no d. mark SHAK:TEM 2
not waving but d. SMITH:Ste 4
drowns: d. things weighty and solid BACON:F[1] 93
drowsy:
d. numbness pains my sense KEATS 93
d. syrups of the worlds SHAK:OTH 41
dull ear of a d. man SHAK:KING J 13
drowsyhead: pleasing land of d. THOMS:Ja[1] 14
drugs: d. cause cramp PARKER:D 5
drum:
Bang, whang, whang, goes the d. BROWNING:R 164
Beats like a fatalistic d. ELIOT:TS 17
dispirit every d. FINCH 1
d. them up the Channel NEWBOLT 5
Dumb as a d. vith a hole DICKENS 21
follow an antique d. ELIOT:TS 106
melancholy as an unbrac'd d. CENT 1
Music of a *distant* D. FITZGER:E 9
My pulse like a soft d. KING:H 2
Not a d. was heard WOLFE:C 1
sound of a cowhide d. MTS 2
Take my d. to England NEWBOLT 5
drum-beat: morning d., following the sun WEBSTER:D 4
drummer: Far I hear the steady d. HOUSM 21
drumming: in the valley d., d.? AUD 18
drums:
beat the d. DRYD 106
beat the d. MORELL 1
beating of war d. KOES 4
de bangin' er de d.? HARRIS:JC 11
D. in his ear SHAK:ROM 5
when the d. begin to roll KIP 65
drunk:
anything not yet d. WHITEHORN 2
Arrogance to dare to be d. HALIF 13
Be not d. with wine BIBLE 535
drink, and no be d. BURNS:R 62
d. to bed SHAK:ANT 6
d. too much or womanized BROWN:Geor 1
d. with sight of power KIP 93
Every month one should get d. PROV 327
glass won't get someone d. CHEK 13
I d. him to his bed SHAK:ANT 31
meadows have d. their fill VIRGIL 10
not genteel when he gets d. BOSW 2
not so think as you d. I am SQUIRE 3
not the art of getting d. JOHNSON:S 211
partly she was d. BURNS:R 24
Poland became d. FRED 1
reasonable, must get d. BYR 179
Then hasten to be d. DRYD 121
this meeting is d. DICKENS 33
to be d. Among whispers ELIOT:TS 25
would be d. with life WILDE:O 108
drunkard:
Reel in a d. CHURCH:C 3
rolling English d. made CHESTERTON 7
drunkards:
more old d. than old doctors FRANKLIN:B 32
more old d. than old doctors PROV 367
MSS as d. use lamp-posts HOUSM 51
simply a nation of *D.* CLARKE:M 4
drunken:
but as a d. sleep SHAK:MEA 33
cannibal than a d. Christian MELV 2
do with the d. sailor ANON 49
I had d. in my dreams COLERIDGE:ST 29
drunkenness:
dronkenesse is verray sepulture CHAUC 70
D. is a temporary suicide RUSS:B 17
d. of things being various MACNEICE 1
d., which is the root of all JAMES VI/I 1
d. would be the supremely valid JAMES:W 3
drunks: d., the angry penguins HARRIS:M 1
dry:
d. as the remainder biscuit SHAK:AS 31
d. brain in a d. season ELIOT:TS 25
I am so d. ANON 72
in a d. and thirsty land BIBLE 218
into a d. martini BENCH 1
old man in a d. month ELIOT:TS 21
sooner d. than women's tears WEBSTER:J 9
dryad: light-wingèd D. of the trees KEATS 93
Dryden:
D. and Pope are not classics ARNOLD:M 81
D. taught to join POPE 145
father of English criticism* JOHNSON:S 51
poetry of D., Pope, and all their ARNOLD:M 82
Dublin:
centre of paralysis* JOYCE:J 47
clever enough for us in D. MAHAF 1
D. street names that in JOYCE:J 48
D., though a place much JOHNSON:S 247
history of my country and I chose D. JOYCE:J 47
In D.'s fair city ANON 24
walk the streets of D. O'BRIEN:RB 1
Dubliners: D. are the niggers of Ireland DOYLE: R 1
duchess:
blossom into a D. AILES 1
chambermaid as of a D. JOHNSON:S 207
D.! The D.! CARROLL 7
Hell! said the D. CHRIS 2
I am D. of Malfi still WEBSTER:J 24
That's my last D. BROWNING:R 18
duck:
As the D. and the Kangaroo? LEAR 11
looks like a d., walks like a d. MCCARTHY:J[2] 3
duckling: Ugly D. ANDER 1
ducks:
Four d. on a pond ALLING:W 2
your precious 'lame d.' GALS 2
duddies: coost her d. to the wark BURNS:R 88
due:
give to every one his d. JUST 1
let great authors have their d. BACON:F[1] 4
dues: to God and man their d. WORDS:W 85
dugs: old man with wrinkled d. ELIOT:TS 45
duke:
Bury the Great D. TENNY 188
d. costs as much to keep LLOYD GEO 3
D. of dark corners SHAK:MEA 35
D. of Plaza-Toro GILB:WS 101
forgot to tell you I was made a D. WELLING 2
She bears a d.'s revenues SHAK:HEN.VI[2] 1
Duke of Argyll: D.o.A. is a nobleman of very HIGIN 1
Duke of York: grand old D.o.Y. NURS 45
dukes:
D. were three a penny GILB:WS 111
Lord Angelo d. it well SHAK:MEA 27
dulce: old Lie: *D. et decorum est* OWEN:W 5
dulcimer: damsel with a d. COLERIDGE:ST 63
dull:
Anger makes d. men witty BACON:F[1] 128
appears d., there is a Design STEELE 4
d. man writing broken English NAB 1
D. 'mongst the dullest CHURCH:C 5
d., naturally d. JOHNSON:S 122
d. product of a scoffer's pen WORDS:W 114
d. without a single absurdity GOLDS 48
He was d. in a new way JOHNSON:S 166
her name was D. BUNYAN 24
How d. it is to pause TENNY 52
if he wasn't as d. as ditch water DICKENS 227
life with the d. bits cut out? HITCH 1
songs provide the d. with wit MAUGH 18
tell them that they are d. SHELLEY:PB 128
To make dictionaries is d. work JOHNSON:S 10
very d. without them WILDE:O 52
who can be d. in Fleet Street LAMB:Ch 35
you are very d. CARROLL 27
dullness: D. ever loves a joke POPE 164
dumb:
D. as a drum vith a hole DICKENS 21
D. As old medallions MACLEISH 1
face is a d. recommendation PUB 1
His praise, ye d. WESLEY:C 4
otherwise I will be d. KEATS 149
dumb-bell: Than d. and foil YEATS 57
dumbness: man's d. is wonderful HARDY:T 50
dumbs: now he is one of the d. LEAR 4
dumplings: I want d. FERD:AUS 1
dumps: one in doleful d. SHEALE 1
dumpy: I hate a d. woman BYR 162
dunce:
dearest, you're a d. JOHNSON:S 224
Excels a d. that has been kept COWP 36
Satan thou art but a D. BLAKE:W 110
Still D. the second reigns POPE 158
duncery: inquisitorious and tyrannical d. MILT 304
dunces: d. are all in confederacy SWIFT 15
Dundee:
follow the bonnet of Bonny D. SCOTT:W 67
stay langer in bonny D. SCOTT:W 56
dune: summit of the great d. RICHARDSON:HH 1
Dunfermline: king sits in D. town BALL 47
dung:
d. about with an air of gracefulness ADDIS 1
Fulfilled of dong and of corrupcion CHAUC 69
dungeon:
D. horrible MILT 111
D., that I'm rotting in CANN 9
Himself in his own d. MILT 30
Shalt never be my d. SHELLEY:PB 149
What other d. is so dark HAWT 4
dungeons: Brightest in d., Liberty BYR 48
dunghill:
donghill kind SPENS 35
d. hard by his own COLERIDGE:ST 42
Dunmowe: men han in Essex at D. CHAUC 78
Dunsinane:
Birnam wood to high D. SHAK:MAC 84
Till Birnam wood remove to D. SHAK:MAC 108
duodecimos: humbler band of d. CRAB 10
dupe: d. of friendship, and the HAZL 31
duration: fallacy in d. BROWNE:T 56
dusky: she shall rear my d. race TENNY 84
dust:
and come to d. SHAK:CYM 17
d. and silence of the upper MACAULAY:TB 17
d., defiled wi' sin BURNS:R 20
D. hath closed Helen's eye NASHE 1
D. in the air suspended ELIOT:TS 103
d. of exploded beliefs MADAN 2
d. of great persons' graves DONNE 101

d. on antique time SHAK:COR 6
d. returneth to d. again GORDON:AM 2
d. should mingle with kindred d. BURKE:E 84
d. that is a little gilt SHAK:TRO 16
d. thou art BIBLE 25
D. thou art, to d. returnest LONGFEL 1
d. to d. PRAY 92
Excuse my d. PARKER:D 15
fear in a handful of d. ELIOT:TS 35
forbear, To dig the d. SHAK:MISC 2
formed man of the d. BIBLE 9
from d. I sprung BYR 136
heap of d. alone remains POPE 61
into the D. descend FITZGER:E 15
Less than the d. HOPE:L 1
life in the handful of d. CONRAD 8
My d. would hear her TENNY 219
not worth the d. SHAK:KING L 60
pays us but with age and d. RALE 9
piece of valiant d. SHAK:MUCH 4
provoke the silent d. GRAY:T 18
raised a d. and then complain BERK 1
richer d. concealed BROOKE 25
scattered d. will soon allay VIRGIL 30
This quiet D. was Gentlemen DICKIN:E 16
Thou'lt recollect my D. GRAHAM:J 2
to make d. of all things BROWNE:T 53
unto d. shalt thou return BIBLE 25
vex the unhappy d. TENNY 89
victory without the d. of racing HORACE 76
we are but d. and shadow HORACE 55
what a d. do I raise BACON:F[1] 120
Write the characters in d. SCOTT:W 63
dust-heap: great d. called 'history' BIRR 1
dusty: d. answer gets the soul MERED:G 29
Dutch:
'swop' for my dear old D. CHEV:A 1
we clap on D. bottoms CANN 7
Dutchman: never see a D. in his own house GOLDS 76
Dutchmen: water-land of D. BYR 219
duties:
devotes to the neglect of his d. THOMP:WH 1
discharge my d. as King EDWARD VIII 2
d. make it unbearable WILDE:O 35
New occasions teach new d. LOWELL:JR 2
duty:
as keen a sense of d. GILB:WS 21
dare to do our d. LINC 8
declares that it is his d. SHAW 22
discussing their d. to God WHITMAN 7
do their d., they need not BLAKE:W 20
Do your d., and put yourself CORNEILLE 3
Do your d. bravely KITCHEN 2
Do your d. in all things LEE:RE 2
do your d. when men are sneering WILSON:W 5
d., d. must be done GILB:WS 89
d. God requires of man CATEC 2
D.! if that name thou love WORDS:W 70
d. of being happy STEVENSON:RL 20
d. was his destiny and DUTT 4
d. was the way to glory TENNY 195
EVERY MAN TO DO HIS D. NELS 14
first d. is towards the people SALIS 3
first d. to serve society JOHNSON:S 133
found that life was D. HOOP 1
gratifying feeling that our d. GILB:WS 106
great manufacture of daily d. WILSON:W 7
he had a d. to perform GIBBON:E 17
here a divided d. SHAK:OTH 10
I have done my d. NELS 16
I've done my d. FIELDING 6
Love is then our d. GAY 22
merely performing a d. BOLL 1
only done my d. TENNY 286
persevere in one's d. and be WASH 3
raised to the concepts of d. and law KANT 12
thing of d. is a boy for ever O'BRIEN:F 6
this is the whole d. of man BIBLE 291
When D. whispers low EMER 100
when love and d. clash TENNY 104
dwarf:
d. sees farther than the giant COLERIDGE:ST 79
my d. shall dance JONS 20
dwarfish: d. whole COLERIDGE:ST 58
dwarfs:
d. on the shoulders of giants BERNARD:Ch 1
d. trying to grill a whale PRIEST 5
little d. creep out CHESTERTON 21
State which d. its men MILL 23
dwell:
d. in the house of the Lord BIBLE 206
d. in the tents of wickedness BIBLE 222
dwelling: d. is the light of setting suns WORDS:W 8
dwells: he d. not in his own MILT 230
dwelt:
and d. among us BIBLE 473
dreamt that I d. in marble BUNN 1
d. among the untrodden ways WORDS:W 30
dying:
achieve it by not d. ALLEN:W 15
act of d. is not of importance JOHNSON:S 143
as a d. man to d. men BAXTER:R 2
attend A d. animal YEATS 96
behold you again in d. STEVENSON:RL 70
coming to that Holy room* DONNE 94
doubly d., shall go down SCOTT:W 11
d. as fast as my enemies . . . could wish HUME 16
d., bless the hand that DRYD 60
D. is a very dull MAUGH 25
D. Is an art PLATH 3
d. lady, lean and pale SHELLEY:PB 102
d. now and done for BETJ 32
d. of a hundred good symptoms POPE 185
d. On a log DICKENS 11
D., we live BROWNING:R 209
forgive my friends for d. SMITH:LP 3
I am d., Egypt SHAK:ANT 56
I could not see to see* DICKIN:E 7
I think you're dyin' BALL 4
If this is d., then STRACH 6
if you don't mind some people d. FERL 1
Leaving is d. a little HARA 1
living indisposeth us for d. BROWNE:T 54
may feel that he is d. CALIG 2
met'st with things d. SHAK:WIN 11
not death but d., which is terrible FIELDING 32
not the d. for a faith that's so hard THACK 17
pain, the bliss of d. POPE 68
poor devils are d. PHILIP:JW 1
such a celerity in d. SHAK:ANT 11
there's no more d. then SHAK:SON 62
They're d. just the same HALL:Rod 1
Time held me green and d. THOMAS:D 17
Tomorrow will be d. HERR 26
Two things for d. people BYR 174
unconscionable time d. CHARLES II 7
dyingness: sort of d. CONG 47
dyke: Feb, fill the d. TUSS 8
dynamite:
not a man, I'm d. NIET 26
objected to the use of d. STEVENSON:RL 32
E: $E = mc^2$ EINS 1
each:
e. according to his abilities MARX:K 7
e. according to his needs BAK 2
Ech man for hymself CHAUC 43
eagle:
By all the e. in thee CRASH 11
E. has landed ARMST:N 1
E. know what is in the pit? BLAKE:W 28
E. mewing her mighty youth MILT 320
e. suffers little birds SHAK:TIT 3
e. through the world has flown WALLER 8
gaze an e. blind SHAK:LOV 16
hooded e. among blinking owls SHELLEY:PB 62
like an e. in a dove-cote SHAK:COR 22
lover looked like an e. ANON 85
upon my e.'s wings I bore DRYD 27
with e. eyes He star'd KEATS 4
eagles:
hawk at e. with a dove? HERB:G 17
mount up with wings as e. BIBLE 324
Where are the e. and the trumpets? ELIOT:TS 20
ear:
beauty's ignorant e. YEATS 40
cleave the general e. SHAK:HAM 91
close at the eare of Eve MILT 204
divinity more than the e. discovers BROWNE:T 30
dull cold e. of Death? GRAY:T 18
dull e. of a drowsy man SHAK:KING J 13
e. of man hath not seen SHAK:MID 42
flea in his e. ARMIN 1
give e. unto my voice BIBLE 247
Give every man thy e. SHAK:HAM 30
God's own e. List'ns MILT 220
I was all eare MILT 36
lover's e. will hear SHAK:LOV 16
mighty world Of eye, and e. WORDS:W 9
more is meant than meets the e. MILT 87
Oon ere it herde CHAUC 114
reasonable good e. in music SHAK:MID 37
shall see the golden E. POPE 73
sow by the right e. HENRY VIII 1
through the channels of the e. AUD 12
turn a deaf e. SWIFT 56
Van Gogh's e. for music WILDER:B 3
Why an E., a whirlpool BLAKE:W 30
with a flea in's e. FLETCH:J 17
earl: ground to a halt with a 14th E. WILSON:Harold 3
Earl of Murray: They hae slain the E.o.M. BALL 11
earlier: Here's one I made e. BLUE P 1
earls: daughter of a hundred E. TENNY 62
early:
e. bird catches the worm PROV 87
E. in the morning our song HEB 4
E. in the morning? ANON 49
E. one morning ANON 10
E. to bed FRANKLIN:B 19
E. to bed and e. to rise PROV 88
E. to rise and e. THURB 11
had it been e., had been kind JOHNSON:S 95
nobody who does not rise e. will ever JOHNSON:S 76
you've gut to git up airly LOWELL:JR 4
earn:
I e. that I eat SHAK:AS 38
week I e. my salary KENNEDY:JF 10
earned:
gives us what we have e. BREN 5
have to be e. here THATCH:M 14
I've e. everything I've got NIX 8
earnest:
I am in e. GARRIS 1
it is time to be in e. JOHNSON:S 41
Only we die in e. RALE 5
we die in e. GIBBONS:O 3
ears:
E. like bombs CAUS 1
e. like errant wings CHESTERTON 1
e. yielding like swinging doors DOUGLAS:K 3
Folds his e. like hands in prayer CAMPBELL:G 1
lend me your e. SHAK:JUL 48
Look with thine e. SHAK:KING L 69
put this engine to our e. SWIFT 28
rodent-like with padlocked e. STRAV 2
seven good e. BIBLE 72
to keep the e. from grating DE VR 1
tongues, and hedges e. SWIFT 59
Walls have e. PROV 411
What is he buzzing in my e.? BROWNING:R 172
earth:
a little e. for charity SHAK:HEN.VIII 14
All e. can take SHELLEY:PB 157
all the e. were paper white LYLY 8
All things are from the e. XENOPHAN 2
didi thee fel the e. move? HEMINGWAY 7
dim spot, Which men call E. MILT 16
E. Be but the shaddow MILT 217
e. covereth QUAR 12
e. does not argue WHITMAN 21
e. doth like a snake renew SHELLEY:PB 153
E. felt the wound MILT 247
E. has not anything to show WORDS:W 91
e. his sober Inne CAMPION 4
e. is all the home I have AYT 5
e. is becoming poorer and uglier CHEK 5
E. is but a star FLECKER 3
e. is like a child who knows RILKE 1
e. is not too low HERB:G 24
e. is the Lord's BIBLE 207
E. laughs in flowers EMER 94
E., lie heavily upon ROSSET:C 9
e. shall be filled AINGER:AC 1
E. stood hard as iron ROSSET:C 18

e., that is sufficient WHITMAN 18
e. to e. PRAY 92
e. Was feverous SHAK:MAC 52
e. was without form BIBLE 2
e., what changes hast thou TENNY 183
E.'s crammed with heaven BROWNING:EB 21
E.'s the right place for love FROST:R 4
feel the e. itself has stopped MANS:K 10
feels the attraction of e. LONGFEL 35
flowery lap of e. ARNOLD:M 8
foundations of the e.? BIBLE 192
get away from e. awhile FROST:R 4
God gives all men all e. KIP 110
going the way of all the e. BIBLE 130
going to and fro in the e. BIBLE 179
have a touch of e. TENNY 250
He always loved the e. CALVINO 1
Help to make e. happy CARNEY 2
I will move the e. ARCHIM 1
in the e. beneath BIBLE 103
inherit the e., but not the mineral rights GET 3
let the E. bless the Lord PRAY 16
Lie heavy on him, E. EVANS:A 1
man appears on e. for a little BEDE 1
Man marks the e. with ruin BYR 117
Moving the e. brings harm DONNE 69
naked e. is warm with spring GREN 1
On the bare e. expos'd DRYD 108
poetry of e. is never dead KEATS 14
put a girdle round about the e. SHAK:MID 19
replenish the e. BIBLE 8
round e.'s imagined corners DONNE 82
spent and unconsidered E. KIP 119
there is our e. here BROWNING:R 60
they shall inherit the e. BIBLE 384
this goodly frame, the e. SHAK:HAM 80
This litel spot of erthe CHAUC 121
thou bleeding piece of e. SHAK:JUL 43
though the e. be removed BIBLE 215
two paces of the vilest e. SHAK:HEN.IV[1] 90
Wasting the E. MILT 162
we shall stay on e. PREVERT 1
When e. was nigher heaven BROWNING:R 11
when e.'s foundations fled HOUSM 37
While the e. remaineth BIBLE 40
whole e. is the sepulchre PERIC 4
Yours is the E. KIP 128

earthquake:
after the e. a fire BIBLE 166
gloom of e. and eclipse SHELLEY:PB 29
story that starts with an e. GORKY 20

ease:
age of e. GOLDS 23
as much at his e. SMITH:Ad 11
E. after warre SPENS 30
standing at e. in Nature WHITMAN 26
Studious of elegance and e. GAY 51
Virtue shuns e. MONTAIGNE 13

easel: Get thee to thy e. ELIOT:G 47

easing: call it e. the Spring REED:H 4

east:
E. is E. KIP 39
E., west, home's best PROV 90
e. wind made flesh APPLETON:TG 2
faint e. quickens SWIN 10
fiery portal of the e. SHAK:RIC.II 29
gorgeous E. with richest hand MILT 148
hold the gorgeous E. in fee WORDS:W 74
I' th' E. my pleasure lies SHAK:ANT 29
If you've 'eard the E. a-callin' KIP 60
in the E., there is no ego SUZ:DT 2
It is the e. SHAK:ROM 8
on the e. of Eden BIBLE 31
practice of politics in the E. DISR:B 10
recruity goes out to the E. KIP 69
somewheres e. of Suez KIP 62
wind's in the e. DICKENS 171
with his back to the E. COLERIDGE:M 3

East End: I can look the E.E. in the face ELIZ:QM 1

eastern: Right against the E. gate MILT 69

Eastertide: Wearing white for E. HOUSM 3

eastwards: life had retreated e. LAWR:DH 10

easy:
e. after the first one HALL:A 1
E. come, e. go PROV 91
I was young and e. THOMAS:D 16
It's either e. or impossible DAL 3
precept be, *Be e.* STEELE 11
She bid me take love e. YEATS 3
too e. for children, and too SCHNAB 2

eat:
cannot e. your money MCLEAN:J 1
can't e. sun ANON 259
e. and drink; for to morrow BIBLE 314
e. exceedingly, and prophesy JONS 28
E. in the evening BLAKE:W 45
E. not of it raw BIBLE 96
e. the fat of the land BIBLE 76
e. the rest of th' anatomy SHAK:TWE 45
E. to live and not PROV 92
e. to live, not live to e. MOLIERE 21
E. with the rich SMITH:LP 8
I did e. BIBLE 19
I e. like a vulture MARX:G 26
I e. well, and I drink MORTON:T 2
I will not e. with you SHAK:MERC 14
I'll e. my head DICKENS 60
neither should he e. BIBLE 546
Never e. anything at one PIG 1
Never e. at a place called ALG 2
not e. but little meat ANON 21
not to e., and I *do* e. THACK 30
sat down to e. and to BIBLE 108
she pluck'd, she e. MILT 247
So I did sit and e. HERB:G 55
substantial happiness, to *e* POPE 67
Tell me what you e. BRILL 2
that it will e. him last CHURCH:W 72
they will e. like wolves SHAK:HEN.V 24
thou shalt not e. of it BIBLE 11
We e. before we talk ATWOOD 6
we must e. *we* THACK 24
with the victims he intends to e. BUTLER:S[2] 45
ye shall e. it in haste BIBLE 97
You can e. grass COAT 1

eaten:
e. by missionaries SPOON 2
e. me out of house and home SHAK:HEN.IV[2] 22
has been e. by the bear HOUSM 49
They have e. me alive HARW 1
They'd e. every one CARROLL 59

eater: of the e. came forth meat BIBLE 134

eaters: Great e. and great sleepers are not HENRI 3

eating:
E. is our earliest metaphor ATWOOD 6
E. out keeps you thin RENDELL 1
E. people is wrong FLAND 2
loves to commit to e. RUNYON 7
not to know what he is e. LAMB:Ch 8
sign something is e. us DE VR 2

eats: whatever Miss T e. DE LA M 14

eaves: instant clamorous e. YEATS 10

ebbing:
Do chase the e. Neptune SHAK:TEM 29
more steady than an e. FORD:J[1] 9

***ecce:** E. homo* BIBLE 613

eccentric: tutor of e. minds LAWS 1

eccentricities: E. of genius, Sam DICKENS 25

Ecclefechan: kent that E. stood MACDIAR 10

ecclesiastic: E. tyranny's the worst DEF 13

ecclesiastical: lay interest in e. matters WAUGH:E 11

echo:
e. arose from the suicide's GILB:WS 82
e. in a Marabar cave FORST 8
e. of a London coffee house for SWIFT 13
e. to the sense POPE 20
In worship of an e. BYR 94
It gives a very e. to the seat SHAK:TWE 25
last turn'd Air, the E. POPE 172
left an e. in the sense JONS 49
my Eccho ring SPENS 12
Sweet E., sweetest Nymph MILT 26
tear the cave where E. lies SHAK:ROM 18

echoes:
he e. me SHAK:OTH 32
On Fontarabian e. borne SCOTT:W 31
Only the e. which he DRUMMOND OF H 3
Our e. roll from soul TENNY 106
set the wild e. flying TENNY 106
stage but e. back the public JOHNSON:S 65

eclipse:
almost to doomsday with e. SHAK:HAM 6
Built in th' e. MILT 51
E. first, the rest nowhere O'KELLY 1
gloom of earthquake and e. SHELLEY:PB 29
moon hath her e. endur'd SHAK:SON 50
total E. Without all hope MILT 280

eclipses: Clouds and e. stain SHAK:SON 17

economic:
bottom of the e. pyramid ROOS:FD 3
e. documents I have to have a box DOUGLAS-H:A 1
e. ones are incomprehensible DOUGLAS-H:A 3
quote Shakespeare in an e. crisis PHILIP 8

economics:
e. as if people mattered SCHUM 1
know now that it is bad e. ROOS:FD 6

economist:
Give me a one-handed e. TRU 8
he was a first-rate political e. SHAW 104
I am a strict e. BURNS:R 125
slaves of some defunct e. KEYN 9
sorry for the death of a political e. BAGE 4

economists:
e. have about the status JONES:BO 1
E. set themselves too easy KEYN 1
form of employment for e. GALB 11

economy:
E. is going without something HOPE:An 1
for fear of Political E. SELL 8
general e. and particular expenditure EDEN:A 3
no e. where there is no efficiency DISR:B 86

ecstasies: Dissolve me into extasies MILT 90

ecstasy:
Blasted with e. SHAK:HAM 104
not e. but it was comfort DICKENS 195
seraph-wings of Extasy GRAY:T 35
think thereof without an e.? BROWNE:T 8
to maintain this e. PATER 4
very e. of love SHAK:HAM 62
What wild e.? KEATS 92

eczema: too often hides e. CAMUS 14

Eden:
attempt a picnic in E. BOWEN:El 7
garden eastward in E. BIBLE 9
happier E. shall enjoy MILT 197
on the east of E. BIBLE 31
tales Told in dim E. DE LA M 4
This other E. SHAK:RIC.II 17
Through E. took their solitarie MILT 261
voice that breathed o'er E. KEBLE 6
With loss of E. MILT 106

Eden, Anthony:
he bored for England* MUGG 6
Not a gentleman* RUSS:B 30

edge:
always at the e. of Being SPEND 5
to the e. of the abyss STEVENSON:A 9

edifice: E. too large for him to fill MILT 230

edit: E. and annotate the lines YEATS 40

edition: If life had a second e. CLARE:J 13

editor: e. is one who separates STEVENSON:A 13

editorial: age of the e. chair MCLUH 3

editors: e. are well under thirty ANON 182

Edmonton:
If wife should dine at E. COWP 56
Unto the Bell at E. COWP 49

educate:
and ... to e. our party DISR:B 69
e. a man you e. an individual MACIVER 1
schoolboys that e. my son EMER 85

educated:
e. civilisation can remove PHILIP:R 1
e. into believing there are BELLOW 6
e. man's BROWNING:R 204
only creature which must be e. KANT 11
supposed to be An e. man HEAN 4

educating: E. the natives of Borrioboola-Gha DICKENS 170

education:
advantages of an e. is simply coming SKIN:BF 1
all this fuss about e. MELBOU 10
borne out of a good e. MACHIA 10
chief hand in their own e. SCOTT:W 94
E. – At Mr Wackford Squeer's DICKENS 66
e. at the Colleges of Unreason BUTLER:S[2] 1
E. forms the common mind POPE 112
E. has for its object SPENCER:H 3
E. ... has produced a vast TREV 2
e. is a leading out SPARK 6
E. is casting false pearls CODY 1
E. is simply the soul of a society

CHESTERTON 53
E. is something that tempers DIOG 5
E. is what most people receive KRAUS 5
E. is what survives SKIN:BF 2
E. made us what HELV 1
E. makes a people easy BROUGHAM 2
e. most have been misled DRYD 89
e. of the heart SCOTT:W 92
e. of the people of this country DISR:B 75
E. that which fits a man MILT 310
E.: That which discloses BIER 4
escaping regular e. MACDIAR 29
great minds is the best kind of e. BUCHAN 2
honesty is the beginning of e. RUSKIN 26
If e. cannot help separate D'SO 1
love her, is a liberal E. STEELE 5
no public institutions for the e. of women SMITH:Ad 10
part of e. BACON:F[1] 112
part of every Englishman's e. HUGHES:Th 2
Prejudice of e. . . . is the devil STERNE 24
race between e. and catastrophe WELLS:HG 17
roots of e. are bitter ARISTOT 23
Soap and e. are not as sudden TWAIN 29
state e. relinquishing its role PARS 2
thank your e. JONS 21
vertuous and noble e. MILT 309
woman of e. bought things VANB 5
Edward: by the blood of Kind E. ANON 45
Edward the Confessor: E.t.C. Slept under the dresser BENTLEY:EC 5
Edward VIII: From his childhood onward* HARDIE 1
Edwardian: left over from the E. Wilderness OSB:J 6
eel: have seen but an e. DICKENS 178
eels:
as the cockney did to the e. SHAK:KING L 27
I gat e. boil'd in broo' BALL 34
e'en: pike out his bonny blue e. BALL 59
effect: little e. after much labour AUSTEN 77
effervesced: waited till it had e. ANON 134
efficiency: no economy where there is no e. DISR:B 86
efficient:
be e. if you're going to be lazy CONRAN 2
being e. . . . makes everybody hate you EDWARDS:B 1
sorts of people: the e. and the inefficient SHAW 78
effort: e. very nearly killed her BELLOC 21
egalitarianism: moods of Australian e. HORNE:DR 2
Egdon:
glory of the E. waste HARDY:T 58
yet E. remained HARDY:T 59
egg:
afraid you've got a bad e. PUNCH 28
as an e. is full of meat SHAK:ROM 25
beauty of a Poached E. KITCHIN 1
e. boiled very soft AUSTEN 39
e. I laid was a hen ERAS 7
e. right through to the apples HORACE 65
e.'s way of making another e. BUTLER:S[2] 8
Everything is from an e. HARV 1
fatal e. by pleasure laid COWP 34
goodness of a good e. DANA 1
goose that lays the golden e. PROV 221
like eating an e. without salt KIP 7
radish and an e. COWP 74
See this e. DIDE 1
sitting on one addled nest-e. ELIOT:G 26
that an e. is not an elephant TILLOT 1
throw an e. into an electric fan HERF 2
eggheads: E. of the world unite STEVENSON:A 15
eggs:
All e. are not hatched DONNE 107
all my e. in one bastard PARKER:D 25
all your e. in one PROV 80
but to roast their e. BACON:F[1] 122
e. and buttercups fried LEAR 27
foundation be bacon and e. HERB:AP 20
Lays e. inside a paper bag ISH 1
lays sentences like e. CANET 3
met a lot of hardboiled e. WILDER:B 1
omelette without breaking e. PROV 441
teach your grandmother to suck e. PROV 82
Think of ham and e. NAV 1
to cook himself a couple of e. CHAMFORT 8
eglantine:
and with e. SHAK:MID 20
grew lush e. SHELLEY:PB 90
hawthorn, and the pastoral e. KEATS 93
ego:
becomes the extension of a man's e. GREER 8
In the East, there is no e. SUZ:DT 2
too much E. in your Cosmos KIP 11
egoist:
E.: A person of low taste BIER 5
e. does not tolerate egoism ROUX 3
Should I call myself an e.? HARTL 1
egotism:
dilemmas of conscience and e. SNOW 1
e. out of its depth KEITH:P 1
egotistical: any more e. than possible HAWKE 3
Egypt:
arose up a new king over E. BIBLE 80
darkness over the land of E. BIBLE 94
E.'s might is tumbled COLERIDGE:M 1
firstborn in the land of E. BIBLE 97
Israel was in E. land ANON 50
not at war with E. EDEN:A 2
out of the land of E. BIBLE 103
there was a great cry in E. BIBLE 98
there was corn in E. BIBLE 73
wonders in the land of E. BIBLE 91
Egyptian: E. Temple dedicated to an ox GOLDS 76
Egyptians:
how the E. worshipped an insect DISR:B 92
they spoiled the E. BIBLE 99
eight:
Pieces of e.! pieces of e. STEVENSON:RL 30
want e., and we won't wait WYND 1
eight o'clock: It's past e.o. NURS 82
eighteen: I knew almost as much at e. JOHNSON:S 119
eightfold: This Ayrian E. Path BUDDHA 2
eighty: In a dream you are never e. SEXT 1
Einstein:
E. – the greatest Jew since HALDA 1
Let E. be SQUIRE 2
Eire: Sing of old E. YEATS 13
elbow: My right e. has a fascination GILB:WS 76
elbow-room: fat man demanding e. WAUGH:E 29
elbows:
graceful with her e. on the table JAMES:H 15
Knees & e. are only glued together BLAKE:W 93
elder:
but five days e. than ourselves BROWNE:T 8
e. man not at all BACON:F[1] 81
I said an e. soldier SHAK:JUL 71
scent of e. bushes AUD 25
take An e. than herself SHAK:TWE 26
elderly: e. man of 42 ASHFORD 1
elders: good at listening to their e. BALD:J 3
eldest: e. of things MILT 173
Eldorado: banal E. of all the old BAUD 7
elected:
audacity of e. persons WHITMAN 19
e. ex-president with such a large majority TAFT 1
will not serve if e. SHERMAN 2
election:
certain that we will win the e. THATCH:M 19
doctrine of Particular E. DOW 1
e. by the incompetent many SHAW 51
e. is coming ELIOT:G 24
guts to call an e. BARNES:J 1
right of e. is the very essence JUNIUS 3
elections: no go the e. MACNEICE 3
electorate:
dismissed by the British e. CHURCH:W 51
e. is now itching to break out STEEL 2
electric:
dark interludes in the e. display O'NEILL 1
tried to mend the E. Light BELLOC 32
electrician: E. is no longer there BELLOC 30
electricity: suspicion that e. was dripping THURB 2
electrification: Soviet power plus the e. LENIN 9
elegance: Studious of e. and ease GAY 51
elementary: 'E.,' said he DOYLE:AC 22
elements:
become our E. MILT 157
Blow, winds, and crack* SHAK:KING L 32
e. So mix'd in him SHAK:JUL 88
Rumble thy bellyful* SHAK:KING L 33
elephant:
E.'s Child – who was full KIP 24
got an e. by the hind leg LINC 14
great masterpiece, an E. DONNE 22
shot an e. in my pajamas MARX:G 2
thought he saw an E. CARROLL 93
unwieldy E. To make them MILT 196
elephants:
Place e. for want of towns SWIFT 68
Women and e. never forget SAKI 8
elevate: E. them guns a little lower JACK:A 2
eleven:
he tells you he's only e. GILB:WS 51
like a bunch of 11-year-olds LYNNE 1
elf: not a modest maiden e. HARDY:T 4
elfland: horns of E. faintly TENNY 106
Elginbrodde: Here lie I, Martin E. MACDON:G 1
Elinor Glyn: E.G. on a tiger-skin? ANON 122
Eliot, George:
No wonder G.E.'s husband MORRIS:J 1
She is magnificently ugly* YEATS 149
untied by G.E. CHESTERTON 47
Elissa: irk me to remember E. VIRGIL 59
élite: actually wrong with an e. CHARLES:Prince 6
Elizabeth: E. the Last KEV 1
Elizabeth II: Frumpish and banal* MUGG 1
Elliot: ELLIOT OF KELLYNCH-HALL AUSTEN 65
ellum: E. she hateth mankind KIP 123
elm: green buds hang in the e. HOUSM 42
elms:
Beneath those rugged e. GRAY:T 16
doves in immemorial e. TENNY 119
elocution:
demands e. rather than reason PARKMAN 1
distrust more than my e. HOBB 13
elope: must e. methodically GOLDS 64
elopement: was an e. down in Mullingar ANON 104
eloquence:
e. is *heard* MILL 25
embellisher of ornate e. CAX 1
finest e. is that which gets LLOYD GEO 6
Greeks the gift of e. HORACE 111
intoxicated with my own e. DISR:B 8
she uttereth piercing e. SHAK:TAM 6
Take e. and wring its neck VERL 4
Talking and e. are not the same JONS 56
eloquent:
e. in a more sublime MACAULAY:TB 21
Even silence may be e. CONG 6
elsewhere: would not be e. for thousands NELS 7
Elsinore: stormy deep, E. CAMPBELL:T 9
elucescebat: E. quoth our friend? BROWNING:R 45
elves: e. of hills, brooks SHAK:TEM 29
Elvis: don't blame E. for eating it BARE 1
Elysian: dead, but in the E. fields DISR:B 83
Elysium: What E. have ye known KEATS 25
emancipate: proposal is made to e. BYR 250
emancipation:
by e. the adoption of the masculine GREER 6
e. of women is practically the greatest KEY:E 1
embalmer: e. of the still midnight KEATS 91
embalming: For my E. (Sweetest) HERR 12
embarrassed: too e. to say so PARKER:D 21
embarrassment: e. of riches ALLA 1
embassy: E. residence, subject, of course ANNEN 1
embers:
fill him full of smoke and e. JONS 3
glowing E. through the room MILT 83
in our e. Is something WORDS:W 62
emblem: fate is here in e. shown WESLEY:S 2
embrace:
guarded from e. LOWELL:A 1
none I think do there e. MARV 31
pity, then e. POPE 95
third who lay in our e. WRIGHT:J 7
time to e. BIBLE 281
embraces: age in her e. passed ROCHES 10
embracing: e. each other's waist GOZ 1
Embro: E. to the ploy GARIO 1
embroideries: coat Covered with e. YEATS 39

embroidery: A little daily e. ELIOT:G 25
emerald:
E. findeth no Memling POUND 41
e. twinkles in the grass TENNY 214
Emerald Isle: cause, or the men, of the E.I. DREN 1
emergency: one e. following upon another FISHER:HAL 1
Emerson, R.W.: hoaryheaded and toothless baboon* CARLYLE:T 60
emigration:
e. Has proved most useful BARRIN 1
The last of England* BROWN:FM 1
Emily: up roos Emelye CHAUC 48
eminence: that bad e. MILT 148
eminency: some e. in ourselves HOBB 1
eminent: death reveals the e. SHAW 65
Emmas: If there were more E. NELS 10
emolument: positions of considerable e. GAIS 1
emotion:
degree of my aesthetic e. BELL:C 2
e. in the form of art ELIOT:TS 113
e. recollected in tranquillity WORDS:W 166
epigram for the death of an e. NIET 13
escape from e. ELIOT:TS 116
less bounding at e. new ARNOLD:M 44
Love is a slave e. STEAD 2
emotional: cultivate the e. sense HEYS 1
emotions:
e. are not skilled workers MALLEY 2
e. from A to B PARKER:D 26
grounds for the noble e. RUSKIN 6
metaphysical brothel for e. KOES 1
poet is not to find new e. ELIOT:TS 115
scrubbed clean of e. WHITE:P 3
emperor:
by e. and clown KEATS 93
E. has nothing on ANDER 2
e. of ice-cream STEVENS 1
Hail, E. SUET 1
emperors: e. can't do it all themselves BRECHT 12
empire:
e. founded by war MONTESQU 3
E. is a Commonwealth of Nations ROSE 1
e. is no more than DRYD 44
great e. and little minds BURKE:E 43
Holy, nor Roman, nor an E. VOLT 10
How is the E.? GEO:V 6
it may make us an E. yet KIP 115
lost an E. and not yet found a role ACHESON 2
preserve the unity of the e. BURKE:E 42
rod of e. might have GRAY:T 19
the metropolis of the e.? COBBETT 2
trample an e. down O'SHAUGH 1
way she disposed of an e. HARLE 1
Westward the course of e. BERK 6
empires:
day of E. has come CHAMBERLAIN:J 3
e. of the future are e. of the mind CHURCH:W 33
hatching vain E. MILT 159
proud e., pass away ELLER 2
employ: whole e. of body and POPE 94
employed:
more innocently e. than in JOHNSON:S 165
total of those e. is governed PARKIN 2
employment:
e. for his idle time WALT 5
form of e. for economists GALB 11
give e. to the artisan BELLOC 32
happily known as gainful e. ACHESON 1
man who gives me e. GEO:H 1
pleasantness of an e. does not AUSTEN 8
employments: How various his e. COWP 71
emptiness:
little e. of love BROOKE 23
smiles his e. betray POPE 126
empty:
E. vessels make the most PROV 93
rich he hath sent away e. BIBLE 608
empty-handed: go for wool and come back e.? CERV 2
emulation: pale and bloodless e. SHAK:TRO 6
enchanted: Enter these e. woods MERED:G 34
enchanter: from an e. fleeing SHELLEY:PB 40
enchantment: distance lends e. to the view CAMPBELL:T 2
encompassed: walls encompass'd but one man? SHAK:JUL 13
encourage: to e. the others VOLT 13
encyclopaedia: whole E. behind the rest LAMB:Ch 11
end:
as an e. withal, never merely KANT 6
boys get at one e. they lose JOHNSON:S 176
come to the e.: then stop CARROLL 40
do us no e. of good KIP 114
e. crowns all SHAK:TRO 23
e. in sight was a vice BROWNING:R 155
e. is when all things return BALZ 3
e. is where we start from ELIOT:TS 108
e. justifies the means BUSEN 1
e. justifies the means PROV 94
e. must direct the *Operation* WOTTON 6
e. of man is an Action CARLYLE:T 9
e. of the way inescapable PASTER 1
e. of the world, and Melbourne sure is JILL 1
e. of this day's business SHAK:JUL 81
e. to the beginnings of all wars. ROOS:FD 13
e. Was not ignoble WORDS:W 145
God be at my e. ANON 66
God will grant an e. VIRGIL 36
great e. of life is not knowledge HUX:TH 6
have planned at the e. CANET 6
he shall e. in doubts BACON:F[1] 5
in my beginning is my e. ELIOT:TS 92
In my e. is my beginning ELIOT:TS 100
In my e. is my beginning MARY QUEEN OF S 2
likeways is the hend of all DICKENS 118
Look at the e. of work BROWNING:R 131
make an e. the sooner BACON:F[1] 56
makes me e., where I begun DONNE 69
man awaits his e. YEATS 96
Man's chief e. is to glorify CATEC 1
move softly towards the e. JOHN XXIII 2
no e. of things in the heart POUND 7
not even the beginning of the e. CHURCH:W 27
now the e. is near ANKA 1
one must consider the e. FONTAINE 18
perhaps, the e. of the beginning CHURCH:W 27
reserved for some e. or other CLIVE 1
same thing at the e. BROWNING:R 74
take account of the e. ANON 233
then the e. is known SHAK:JUL 81
there shall I e. SHAK:JUL 82
therefore she had a good e. MALORY 8
there's an e. on't JOHNSON:S 137
there's an e. on't JOHNSON:S 161
This is the beginning of the e. TALL 2
This was the e., Echecrates PLATO 6
To the preposterousest e. BUTLER:S[1] 39
true beginning of our e. SHAK:MID 46
Waiting for the e., boys EMPS 4
what e. the gods have in store HORACE 12
where's it all going to e.? STOP 6
Whoever wills the e. KANT 4
will come to a bad e. BEERB 6
endearing: those e. young charms MOORE:T 3
endeavour: should our e. be so lov'd SHAK:TRO 27
endeavours:
high e. are an inward light WORDS:W 39
my e. are unlucky explorers DOUGLAS:K 4
endeth: e. wrecchedly CHAUC 58
ending:
marked out for ... an unhappy e. JAMES:H 21
Never e., still beginning DRYD 109
endings: Fuckin' e., man, they LEONARD:E 2
endow: e. a College, or a Cat POPE 77
ends:
are men's e. mark'd SHAK:RIC.II 15
best e. by the best means HUTCHES 1
e. and the beginnings still constitute DOST 3
e. by our beginnings know DENH 3
no e. nor beginnings DONNE 110
Out to the undiscovered e. BELLOC 27
yours e. with you IPH 1
endure:
E., and save yourselves VIRGIL 38
e. Their going hence SHAK:KING L 78
e. what can't be mended WATTS 10
first e., the pity POPE 95
flattering some Men to e. them HALIF 12
hard to e. is sweet to recall PROV 420
help her to e. doing it TAYL:E 1
Let us e. an hour HOUSM 25
endured:
can't be cured, must be e. PROV 417
much is to be e., and little JOHNSON:S 23
endureth: e. all things BIBLE 522
enemies:
Books have the same e. as man VALERY 6
careful in the choice of his e. WILDE:O 25
Confusion to his e. ANON 15
do not have to forgive my e. NARV 1
e.: – all stupid men EBNER 1
e. of Freedom do not argue INGE 8
Even a paranoid can have e. KISS 3
friendship with thine e. SHAK:JUL 42
Gifts from e. are no gifts SOPH 2
hast got a hundred e. STERNE 6
have been mortal e. LESAGE 1
in the presence of mine e. BIBLE 206
judge me by the e. I have made ROOS:FD 14
Love your e. BIBLE 453, 387
smote his e. in the hinder BIBLE 220
trophies unto the e. of truth BROWNE:T 3
enemy:
best be the e. of the good JENKINS:R 2
best is the e. of the good VOLT 21
better class of e. MILLIG 1
dangerous than an open e. BACON:F[1] 18
e. – and that is life ANOU 3
e. cannot be allowed to interfere BETHU 1
e. faints not CLOUGH 10
e. reads the list of their names WELLING 1
e. who speaks ill of your king NELS 2
fears his e., but despises PLUT 2
gall and wormwood to an e. BYR 84
he's an e. to mankind SHAK:TWE 47
I am the e. you killed OWEN:W 14
kisses of the e. are deceitful BIBLE 273
last e. that shall be destroyed BIBLE 525
learn even from an e. OSB:J 21
man is his own worst e. PROV 103
Man is not the e. PAINE 6
my E. for Friendships sake BLAKE:W 105
my e. is dead WHITMAN 33
nearest and dearest e.? SHAK:HEN.IV[1] 70
no e. but time YEATS 101
no e. to learning CONG 49
No e. can match a friend SWIFT 62
Our friends, the e. BERA 1
peach for your e. PROV 317
two points nearer the e. BEAT 1
worst friend and e. is but Death BROOKE 24
energies: vital e. to the oppressor JOHNSTONE:Jil 2
energy:
converting solar e. into food STENHO 1
E. = mass x EINS 1
E. is the only life BLAKE:W 32
e. of his mind prevailed LUCRET 1
enfant terrible: *e.t.* of literature and science BUTLER:S[2] 9
enfants:
Allons, e. de la patrie ROUG 1
e. terribles GAV 1
enforced: not have it e. is to authorize RICHELIEU:A 1
engaged: nicest girls I was ever e. to WODE 18
engagement: owing to a subsequent e. WILDE:O 132
engagements: not in favour of long e. WILDE:O 98
engine:
curious e., your white hand WEBSTER:J 22
found out the excellent e. JONS 37
put this e. to our ears SWIFT 28
two-handed e. at the door MILT 54
Wit's an unruly e. HERB:G 6
engine drivers: Do e.d. ... eternally wish O'BRIEN:F 5
engineer:
e. Hoist with his own petar SHAK:HAM 149
e. is nobody EMER 60
engineering: hard if you choose e. COPE 2
engineers: e. scrape by COPE 1
engines:
E. more een than ever MARV 11
e. to play a little BURKE:E 49
scape By all his Engins MILT 145

England:
aboriginal E. still lingers LAWR:DH 12
as the stately homes of E. WOOLF:V 3
back to thy stately homes of E. LAWR:DH 19
Be E. what she will CHURCH:C 19
between France and E. is – the sea JERROLD 4
Bible made E. HUGO 10
Coastwise Lights of E. KIP 80
Common Law of E. has been HERB:AP 13
don't say that in E. SWIFT 82
E.! awake! awake! BLAKE:W 118
E.! did I know till then WORDS:W 45
E. does not love coalitions DISR:B 59
E. EXPECTS EVERY MAN NELS 14
E., farewell SHELLEY:PB 149
E. forget her precedence MILT 308
E.! full of sinne HERB:G 4
E. has been in a dreadful state DICKENS 183
E. has saved herself PITT:W[2] 2
E. hath need of thee WORDS:W 47
E., home and beauty BRAHAM 1
E. in reversion his SHAK:RIC.II 13
E. is a garden KIP 138
E. is in my two hands WILLIAM I 1
E. is not all the world MARY QUEEN OF S 1
E. is not the jewelled isle ORWELL 11
E. is the mother of Parliaments BRIGHT 2
E. keep my bones SHAK:KING J 19
E. made Shakespeare HUGO 10
E., must be like being married HALS:M 3
E., my E.? HENL 8
E. shall bide till Judgement KIP 124
E. should be free MAGEE 1
E. since gentlemen came up SHAK:HEN.VI[2] 8
E., that was wont to conquer SHAK:RIC.II 17
E. to be a downright hive CUNNING:PM 1
E., which the bulwarks of the sea BOSSU 1
E. will have her neck wrung WEY 1
E., with all thy faults COWP 61
E.'s being hammered KIP 135
E.'s greatest son TENNY 191
E.s green & pleasant bowers BLAKE:W 119
found E. a land of beauty JOAD 3
further off from E. CARROLL 33
get me to E. once again BROOKE 10
God punish E. FUNKE 1
Happy is E. KEATS 15
hear our noble E.'s praise MACAULAY:TB 39
heart of E. DRAYT 5
history of E. is emphatically MACAULAY:TB 14
I am in E., everywhere BROWNE:T 24
in E. nobody goes to the theatre AGATE 1
In E.s green & pleasant land BLAKE:W 98
knuckle-end of E. SMITH:Syd[1] 18
Liberty was born in E. VOLT 1
martial airs of E. WEBSTER:D 4
Men of E., wherefore plough SHELLEY:PB 51
men that worked for E. CHESTERTON 27
no amusements in E. but vice SMITH:Syd[1] 38
occurred nowhere but in E. CONRAD 7
Oh, to be in E. BROWNING:R 49
On E.s pleasant pastures seen BLAKE:W 98
one of the stately homos of E. CRISP 6
only seeing a worse E. JOHNSON:S 199
open my legs and think of E. HILLING 1
plan on going to E. HUDS:B 1
poison E. at her roots BOTT:G 1
poorest he that is in E. RAINBO 1
road that leads him to E. JOHNSON:S 114
royal navy of E. hath ever been BLACKS 3
Rule all E. under a Hog COLLINGBO 1
Speak for E., Arthur AMERY 1
Stately Homes of E. COWARD 24
stately Homes of E. HEMA 3
Stately Homes of E. ope CAMPBELL:R 5
strong arm of E. will protect him PALMERS 1
Such night in E. ne'er had MACAULAY:TB 40
suffer E. to be the workshop DISR:B 52
ten thousand of those men in E. SHAK:HEN.V 37
That is forever E. BROOKE 25
The last of E. BROWN:FM 1
There'll always be an E. PARKER:R 1
think of the defence of E. BALD:S 5
This E. never did SHAK:KING J 21
this realm, this E. SHAK:RIC.II 17
use to the landscape of E. AUSTEN 3
Walk upon E.s mountains BLAKE:W 98
way to ensure summer in E. WALP:H 12
we are the people of E. CHESTERTON 24
weave old E.s winding Sheet BLAKE:W 92
When does this place get to E.? LILL 2
Who dies if E. live? KIP 145
who only E. know? KIP 45
With E.'s own coal KIP 136
Ye Mariners of E. CAMPBELL:T 7
you cannot leave E. PORTER:PNF 3
You gentlemen of E. PARKER:M 2
youth of E. are on fire SHAK:HEN.V 10

English:
Allah created the E. mad KIP 113
and the King's E. SHAK:MERR 4
angel is the E. child BLAKE:W 27
anything but the most dignified E. DAY 1
As long as there is E. spoken GOGA 3
attitude of the E. . . . toward E. history HALS:M 2
been raped and speaks E.? ANON 191
Breeds hard E. men KINGSLEY:C 16
credulity of an E. jury HILL:Reg 3
dull man writing broken E. NAB 1
E. an article as a beefsteak HAWT 5
E. are best at everything GOLDI 1
E. are busy MONTESQU 6
E. are known for their cruelty ROUSS:E 1
E. are polite by telling lies BRADB 4
E. . . . are rather a foul-mouthed HAZL 20
E. are very little indeed inferior NORTH:C 2
E. as she is Spoke TUER 1
E. Church shall be free MAGNA 1
E. enjoy themselves sadly SULLY 1
E. have a miraculous power WILDE:O 134
E. have hot-water bottles MIKES 2
E. have no family feelings COMPT 4
E. home TENNY 40
E. is a very adaptable NARA 1
E. is simple, yet hard TUCHOL 7
E. literature is always in danger BREN 7
E. manners are far more frightening JARRELL 2
E. may not like music BEECHAM 2
E. mind, excited by YEATS 142
E., not the Turkish court SHAK:HEN.IV[2] 48
E. public never forgives WILDE:O 123
E. style, familiar but not JOHNSON:S 44
E. think of an opinion as HALS:M 4
E. want *inferiors* TOC 1
For undemocratic reasons* KIP 125
greatest book of E. prose? QUIL 2
happy E. child TAYL:Ann 3
He mobilized the E. language MURROW 1
hear abuse of the E. PICCO 1
In an E. lane BROWNING:R 102
In an E. ship, they say LOND 2
in favour of boys learning E. CHURCH:W 43
kissed by the E. dead OWEN:W 8
love nor favour an Englishe man BOORDE 2
My country is the E. language DOBBS 1
My native E. SHAK:RIC.II 5
not the expression in E. ARNOLD:M 59
Opera in E. is MENCK 21
ornate eloquence in our E. CAX 1
our E. tongue, a gallimaufray SPENS 1
Owing to the weather, E. Social life MACAULAY:R 3
pause to consider the E. NASH 1
principle of the E. constitution BLACKS 4
provinces where they still speak E. GUINN 1
rolling E. drunkard made CHESTERTON 7
Roman-Saxon-Danish-Norman E. DEF 12
seven feet of E. ground HARO 1
shooting mothers of E.-speaking children GOGA 3
so gret diversite In Englissh CHAUC 120
sort of E. up with which CHURCH:W 65
sound of the E. county families WAUGH:E 1
speak E. when our backs are turned CRISP 7
talent of our E. nation DRYD 32
till the E. grew polite KIP 112
To make his Englissh sweete CHAUC 17
to the dominion of the E. ANON 186
trick of our E. nation SHAK:HEN.IV[2] 15
under an E. heaven BROOKE 25
We be all good E. men TENNY 282
when you can't think of the E. CARROLL 49
Whom the E. call 'the Queen' LAWS 2
You E. words THOMAS:E 9

Englishman:
born an E. and remained one BEHAN:Br 3
broad-shoulder'd genial E. TENNY 120
E. . . . always wants to reason VOLT 29
E. believes be heresy? SHAW 117
E. has all the qualities of a poker O'CONNELL 1
E. . . . is afraid to feel FORST 13
E. is content to say nothing JOHNSON:S 214
E. never enjoys himself HERB:AP 16
E. thinks he is moral SHAW 41
E.'s heaven-born privilege ARNOLD:M 69
E.'s home is his castle PROV 95
E.'s way of speaking LERN 1
E.'s word is his bond PROV 96
Every time an E. opens his mouth HOWARD:P 1
good part of every E.'s education HUGHES:Th 2
He is an E. GILB:WS 17
He remains an E. GILB:WS 18
I smell the blood of an E. NURS 11
I smell the bloud of an English-man NASHE 5
impossible for an E. to open his mouth SHAW 105
in the E. a combination of qualities DICKENS 221
last great E. TENNY 189
never find an E. in the wrong SHAW 14
not one E. WALP:R 2
one *E.* could beat three *Frenchmen* ADDIS 22
religious rights of an E. JUNIUS 1
Remember that you are an E. RHODES 2
there's an Irishman fighting an E. ROYCE 1
thorough an E. as ever coveted KINGSLEY:C 5
to produce ennui in an E. HALS:M 1
vain, ill-natur'd thing, an E. DEF 11
weet an E. to the skin RAMS 4
What E. will give his mind to politics SHAW 121
young E. of our upper class ARNOLD:M 66

Englishmen:
absurd nature of E. PEPYS 9
characteristic virtue of E. TAWN 1
create Frenchmen in the image of E. CHURCH:W 31
does not travel to see E. STERNE 42
E. are distinguished by NASH 1
E. meet, their first talk JOHNSON:S 30
first to his English-men? MILT 317
Honest E. KINGSLEY:C 18
Mad dogs and E. COWARD 20
proper drink of E. BORR 8

Englishwoman: E. is so refined SMITH:Ste 2

enigma: mystery inside an e. CHURCH:W 10

enjoy:
after that, to e. it SMITH:LP 1
English e. themselves sadly SULLY 1
e. both operations at once CARY:J 1
e. it while I can SMOL 3
E. thyself ZANG 2
have to go out and e. it SMITH:LP 14
in winter e. BLAKE:W 34
Let me e. the earth no less HARDY:T 20
most e. contented least SHAK:SON 11
never e. the world aright TRAH 2
to e. him forever CATEC 1
Who can e. alone MILT 234

enjoyed: little to be e. JOHNSON:S 23

enjoying: always to be e. himself BENTLEY:EC 11

enjoyment:
capacity for innocent e. GILB:WS 26
Was it done with e. RUSKIN 1

enjoyments: pleasant if it were not for its e. SURT 22

enjoys: Englishman never e. himself HERB:AP 16

enmities:
e. of twenty generations lie MACAULAY:TB 11
More substance in our e. YEATS 67

enmity: covert e. SHAK:HEN.IV[2] 1

ennui: to produce e. in an Englishman HALS:M 1

Enoch: E. walked with God BIBLE 32

enormity: womb and bed of e. JONS 27

enough:
never know what is e. unless BLAKE:W 46
Once is more than e. BIRCH 1
Was it not e.? SHAW 99

enrich: e. unknowing nations DANI 2

enriched: on every side enrich'd MARLOWE 21

Ensham: Above by E. ARNOLD:M 43
ensign:
Beauty's e. yet SHAK:ROM 43
Th' Imperial E. MILT 130
enslave: impossible to e. BROUGHAM 2
enslaved: spirits are e. which serve SHELLEY:PB 77
entente: *La cordiale e.* LOUIS PHIL 1
enter:
Abandon all hope, you who e. DANTE 2
King of England cannot e. PITT:W[1] 2
ye cannot e. now TENNY 263
enterprise:
e. is sick SHAK:TRO 4
Glorious Enterprize MILT 113
enterprises: impediments to great e. BACON:F[1] 80
entertain:
less eagerness to e. WORST 1
There e. him all the Saints MILT 58
entertained: e. angels unawares BIBLE 560
entertainment:
late e. this week cost PEPYS 24
some other custom of e. SHAK:OTH 24
enthrall: Except you e. me DONNE 89
enthusiasm:
bored as e. would permit GOSSE 1
ever achieved without e. EMER 26
enthusiasts: so few e. can be trusted BALF 3
entrails: Examining one's e. while fighting HEAL 6
entrance:
being an e. somewhere else STOP 2
one e. quite shut out MILT 177
entwine: e. itself verdantly still MOORE:T 3
envied: Better be e. than pitied PROV 40
envious: To silence e. tongues SHAK:HEN.VIII 12
environment:
all children of our e. LAWL 1
which was the e. and which was President JARRELL 1
envy:
at a guard with e. SHAK:MEA 2
e. is a kind of praise GAY 48
e. of brilliant men BEERB 6
e. of less happier lands SHAK:RIC.II 17
extinguisheth e. BACON:F[1] 53
from e., hatred, and PRAY 33
in e. of great Caesar SHAK:JUL 88
mutual e. of the living HOBB 14
not through e. of thy happy KEATS 93
prisoners of e. ILL 4
Stirrd up with E. and Revenge MILT 109
Through e. of the devil BIBLE 365
Too low for e. COWLEY:A 13
wound of spiteful e. RALE 7
ephemeral: Everything is e. AUR 7
epigram: What is an e.? COLERIDGE:ST 58
epigrams: despotism tempered by e. CARLYLE:T 22
epilogue: good play needs no e. SHAK:AS 73
epiphany: By an e. he meant JOYCE:J 43
epistles: Some soldiers send e. WESTON 1
epitaph:
better have a bad e. SHAK:HAM 88
if ye carve my e. aright BROWNING:R 43
epitaphs: nice derangement of e. SHERIDAN:RB 10
epitome: all mankind's e. DRYD 47
Epsom salts: but stuck to E.s. ANON 127
equal:
All animals are e., but some ORWELL 20
all e. when it comes DONNE 101
all men are created e. JEFFERSON 2
all men are created e. LINC 11
all men are created free and e. LINC 5
all men are e. is a proposition HUX:A 14
all shall e. be GILB:WS 105
death makes e. the high HEYW:J 2
e. division of unequal earnings ELLIOTT:E 2
e. in dignity and rights ANON 153
e. to all things GOLDS 37
equall are within the churches HERB:G 12
Everybody should have an e. chance WILSON:Harold 11
in the dust be e. made SHIRL 3
men and women are created e. STANTON:El 1
no e. opportunity STOCKS 1
no friends not e. to yourself CONF 2
one e. eternity DONNE 110
rule of e. justice MILL 29
that all men are created e. KING:ML 1
equality:
be no talk of the e. of the sexes HUGHES:B 7
Either one of mankind* CONDOR 1
E. may perhaps be a right BALZ 8
e. pulls everyone down MURD:I 5
e. until women themselves help ANTH 2
never be e. in the servant's hall BARRIE 5
principle of perfect e. MILL 28
true apostles of e. ARNOLD:M 65
We wish, in a word, e. BAK 2
equally: all e. wise – e. foolish EINS 13
equals:
disinterested commerce between e. GOLDS 58
least of all between e. BACON:F[1] 62
equanimity: e. bordering on indifference GILB:WS 115
equator:
quarrellin wi' the equawtor NORTH:C 5
united nation than the E. CHURCH:W 8
equinox: when was the e.? BROWNE:T 60
equivocate: I will not e. GARRIS 1
equivocation: e. will undo us SHAK:HAM 181
equivocator: come in, e. SHAK:MAC 49
Eremite: patient, sleepless E. KEATS 113
Erin: warriors of E. in their famous ROLL:TW 1
erogenous: mind can also be an e. zone WELCH 1
err:
Better to e. with Pope BYR 11
mortal, and may e. SHIRL 2
most may e. as grossly DRYD 53
To e. is human POPE 25
To e. is human PROV 395
Who e. each other must respect PATMO 2
wiser than the wise may e. AESC 5
errand: What thy e. here below? LAMB:Ch 30
errands: Meet to be sent on e. SHAK:JUL 64
erred:
have e. exceedingly BIBLE 150
We have e., and strayed PRAY 4
Wisest Men have errd MILT 285
erring: check the e. and reprove WORDS:W 70
error:
All men are liable to e. LOCKE 5
assured by spectacular e. GALB 12
but for a typographical e. PARKER:D 22
E. has never even come METT 2
e. is immense BOLI 1
e. is ineradicable MAUGH 17
E. of opinion may be tolerated JEFFERSON 6
harder struggle with e. SCHILL 8
hateful e., melancholy's SHAK:JUL 83
If this be e. SHAK:SON 52
made the e. double CLARE:J 3
makes Errour a fault HERB:G 8
maxim is often a brilliant e. MALES 1
mountainous e. be too highly SHAK:COR 6
only one innate e. SCHOP 9
show a man that he is in an e. LOCKE 4
stronger than all the hosts of e. BRYAN 2
Their land from e.'s chain HEB 2
time for the destruction of e. AUD 54
errors:
E., like straws DRYD 24
E. look so very ugly ELIOT:G 3
His e. are volitional JOYCE:J 22
knows some of the worst e. HEIS 1
more harmful than reasoned e. HUX:TH 7
vague e. of the flesh THOMAS:RS 3
errs: e. as long as he strives GOET 11
erump: evade, – e. HOLMES:OW 13
eruption: strange e. to our state SHAK:HAM 3
Esau:
E. my brother is a hairy BIBLE 57
E. selleth his birthright BIBLE 54
E. was a cunning hunter BIBLE 55
hands are the hands of E. BIBLE 58
escape:
Beauty for some provides e. HUX:A 46
can't e. it some time LERM 2
e. being this thing, Myself WHITE:P 9
E. me? Never – Beloved BROWNING:R 132
help those we love to e. HUGEL 1
escaped: he e. CIC 9
Eskdale: march, E. and Liddesdale SCOTT:W 59
espouse: e. the everlasting Sea WORDS:W 76
essays: volume of e. and offer it COLLINGWOOD:RG 2
establishment: 'E.' in this country is today more powerful FAIRL 1
estate:
any man with a good e. CONG 25
has become a fourth e. MACAULAY:TB 9
my e. is time GOET 24
noon estaat assureth to be weel CHAUC 40
reck'n not in high e. MILT 284
relief of man's e. BACON:F[1] 6
there sat a *Fourth E.* CARLYLE:T 49
they had his e. DRYD 48
estate workers: He is used to dealing with e.w. DOUGLAS-H:C 1
estates: Unto the deid gois all Estatis DUNB 9
esteems: shipwreck of my life's e. CLARE:J 8
état: *L'é. c'est moi* LOUIS XIV 5
etchings: I'll bring the e. down THURB 21
eternal:
abode where the E. are SHELLEY:PB 127
by experience that we are e. SPIN 4
e. summer in his soul HOLMES:OW 9
lose not the things e. PRAY 52
portion of the E. SHELLEY:PB 119
eternity:
All things from e. are of similar AUR 4
Becomes a Babe in E. BLAKE:W 87
conjecture about e. is a waste CRISP 9
day is a miniature e. EMER 88
Deserts of vast e. MARV 31
E. – by term DICKIN:E 9
E. in an hour BLAKE:W 82
E. is in love with BLAKE:W 36
E. shut in a span CRASH 13
E. was in our lips SHAK:ANT 17
E. was in that moment CONG 8
E.'s a terrible thought STOP 6
from here to E. KIP 52
Heads Were toward E. DICKIN:E 14
heard E. drip water MACDIAR 11
hid battlements of E. THOMP:F 13
I am in e., and you are ANON 140
image of e. BYR 119
kill time without injuring e. THOREAU 6
Lives in e.'s sun rise BLAKE:W 59
Lovers' hours be full e. DONNE 48
nothing of a god but e. SHAK:COR 21
one equal e. DONNE 110
over the Bridge of Sighs into e. KIERK 3
prepared for you from all e. AUR 13
saw E. the other night VAUGHAN:H 14
sells e. to get a toy? SHAK:POET 5
small parenthesis in e. BROWNE:T 65
Some shadows of e. VAUGHAN:H 6
speak of e. without a solecism BROWNE:T 8
spiders in all the corners – that's e. DOST 2
sweet e. of love HERR 8
That ope's the Palace of E. MILT 17
thievish progress to e. SHAK:SON 35
through nature to e. SHAK:HAM 17
types and symbols of E. WORDS:W 156
white radiance of E. SHELLEY:PB 126
ether: An ampler e. WORDS:W 124
etherised: patient e. upon a table ELIOT:TS 3
Ethiopian: Can the E. change his skin BIBLE 339
Eton:
cheer for an E. crew CORY 4
won on the playing-fields of E. ORWELL 12
won on the playing fields of E. WELLING 22
Etrurian: In Vallombrosa, where th' E. shades MILT 125
Ettrick: march, E. and Teviotdale SCOTT:W 59
Euclid:
E. alone had looked MILLAY 6
into the fifth proposition of E. DOYLE:AC 4
eunuch:
intellectual e. Castlereagh BYR 157
kind of moral e. SHELLEY:PB 50
prerogative of the e. throughout Time's e. STOP 1
Time's e. HOPK:GM 31
eureka: *E.!* I've got it! ARCHIM 2
Euripides:
E. portrayed them SOPH 6
passionate outpourings of E. COLERIDGE:ST 92
Europe:
Better fifty years of E. TENNY 88
E. is disclosed as a prone HARDY:T 71

E. there are now only small LEF 1
ever another war in E. BISM 9
glory of E. is extinguished BURKE:E 55
going into E. will not turn out THOMP:EP 1
going out all over E. GREY 1
Going to E. ... was about as final HAZZ 2
hack through a window on E. PUSH 6
kind of United States of E. CHURCH:W 36
lasting solution is that E. itself LOTH 1
one of the great stocks of E. YEATS 135
part of the community of E. GLAD 7
regard the history of E. GOLDS 46
rights of the smaller nationalities of E. ASQU:HH 2
save E. by her example PITT:W[2] 2
think of E. as the Moon VICT 3
To make peace in E. possible BENES 1
to re-enter E. ACHES 2
We are part of the community of E. SALIS 2

European: E. a job was an income MORLEY:JD 1

European Community: end of Britain as an independent* GAIT 2

Europeanism: Their E. is nothing but imperialism HEAL 4

Europeans:
contact between E. and Africans VAN DER P 1
second-hand E. pullulate HOPE:Al 1
You are learned E. MASSIN 9

Eurydice: His half regain'd E. MILT 76

Euston:
flushpots of E. JOYCE:J 32
now we three in E. waiting-room CORNFORD:Fran 3

euthanasia: E. is a long, smooth-sounding word BUCK 3

evacuations: Wars are not won by e. CHURCH:W 55

evasion: e. of whoremaster man SHAK:KING L 9

Eve:
banished children of E. ANON 37
close at the eare of E. MILT 204
E. and the apple was the first great BRIDIE 4
E. from his side arose ANON 120
E. ministerd naked MILT 214
fairest of her Daughters E. MILT 194
to E.: Be soon THOMP:F 9

eve-jar: spins the brown e. MERED:G 32

evening:
along the road of e. DE LA M 10
And yet the E. listens KEATS 24
beauteous e., calm and free WORDS:W 42
came still E. on MILT 198
Come in the e. DAVIS:T 1
Eat in the e. BLAKE:W 45
e. and the morning were the first BIBLE 3
e. has already drawn in QUAS 1
e. is spread out against ELIOT:TS 3
e. of my age ROWE 3
into the corners of the e. ELIOT:TS 4
quiet-coloured end of e. BROWNING:R 134
shade the e. of life GIBBON:E 29
Shadows of the e. BARING-G 1
welcome peaceful ev'ning COWP 72

evening star:
E. Starr Love's Harbinger MILT 258
e.s. is coming VIRGIL 20
evening-star is lighting his late VIRGIL 23

evenings: plan your projects in the e. COPE 2

evensong:
belles ryngeth to evensonge HAWES 2
full-hearted e. Of joy HARDY:T 17

event:
How much the greatest e. FOX:CJ 1
prophets make sure of the e. WALP:H 21

eventide: fast falls the e. LYTE 1

events:
coming e. cast their shadows CAMPBELL:T 21
e. have controlled me LINC 18
E. in the past may roughly INGE 6
spirits Of great e. stride COLERIDGE:ST 48
three e. in a man's life LA BRU 4

ever:
I go on for e. TENNY 202
it may be for e. CRAW 1

Everest:
as though it were Mount E. HUX:A 33
Between you and your E. DAY LEWIS 1
E. is now littered with junk HILLARY 4
skied down Mount E. in the nude MACKINN 1
summit of E. was hardly the place HILLARY 2

evergreen: touched with salt and e. LOWELL:R 9

everlasting: stood from e. to e. TRAH 3

everlastingness: bright shootes of everlastingnesse VAUGHAN:H 6

every: E. day, in e. way COUE 1

everybody:
E. was up to something COWARD 14
know e. CHESTERFIELD 25

everyday:
e. affair life is LAF 1
familiar merely with the e. DOST 3

everyman: E., I will go with thee ANON 62

everyone:
When e. is wrong LA CHAU 1
WRONG to do what e. else POTTER:S 6

everything:
cannot all do e. LUCIL 1
e. about something HUX:TH 16
e. in its place SMILES 3
e. in the world is good for DRYD 61
e. the concern of everyone SOLZ 7
let us be e. POTTIER 1
Life, the Universe and E. ADAMS:D 1
robbed a man of *e.* he's no longer SOLZ 5
They told me I was e. SHAK:KING L 66

everywhere: Out of the e. into here MACDON:G 2

evidence:
e. against their own Understanding HALIF 9
e. of things not seen BIBLE 556
it's not e. DICKENS 39
presented in e. and explained PARKER:Hub 1
Some circumstantial e. is very strong THOREAU 24

evil:
by curse Created e. MILT 166
chooses e. because it is e. WOLLST 1
deliver us from e. BIBLE 391
deliver us from e. MASS 15
deliver us from e. PRAY 6
do e., that good may come BIBLE 509
dreadful wood Of conscious e. AUD 31
enslaved which serve things e. SHELLEY:PB 77
E. be thou my Good MILT 185
E. be to him who e. thinks ANON 222
e., can be as gratuitous as good GIDE 2
e. is wrought by want HOOD 25
e. on the ground of expediency ROOS:T 11
e. that men do lives SHAK:JUL 48
E. tumbles in, unaware BURGESS:A 3
fall'n on e. dayes MILT 224
Familiarity with e. breeds not HATTER 1
fear of one e. often leads BOIL 7
From all e. and mischief PRAY 33
great book is like great e. CALLIM 2
I will fear no e. BIBLE 206
is the greatest good and e.? LERM 1
know all the e. he does LA ROCHE 25
made e. wrangling with the e. MUIR:E 2
man's heart is e. from his youth BIBLE 39
may look e. in theory BURKE:E 100
must return good for e. VANB 4
necessary for the triumph of e. BURKE:E 107
No e. can befall a good man SOC 5
no e. in the atom STEVENSON:A 4
overcome e. by means of SARTRE 4
preserve thee from all e. BIBLE 240
Put off the e. hour PROV 326
root of all e. BIBLE 549
still to find means of e. MILT 118
supernatural source of e. is not necessary CONRAD 12
them that call e. good BIBLE 304
There are no e. people BULG 2
try e., and if the outcome VEGA 1
we are the origin of all coming e. JUNG:Carl 9
what all the blessed e.'s for BROWNING:R 85
Whenever God prepares e. ANON 262
within them which tells them it is e. NEWM:JH 14
word-and-thought-defying banality of e. AREN 1

evils:
business is the choice of e. BENTH 2
Don't let us make imaginary e. GOLDS 60
great e. we submit HAZL 13
I'm caught between two e. WEST:M 8
least of all e. BACON:F[1] 125
live only by fighting e. BERLIN:Is 2
must expect new e. BACON:F[1] 77
Of two e. the lesser is KEMP 13
they are necessary e. JOHNSON:S 38

evolution: e. of the human race will not DARW:CG 1

ewes: my e. breed not BARNF 4

exact:
e. without vulgarity ELIOT:TS 123
greatness not to be e. BURKE:E 19

exaggeration: report of my death was an e. TWAIN 37

exalt: praise him and e. him BIBLE 606

examinations:
E. are formidable even to COLTON 4
In e. the foolish ask WILDE:O 73

example:
E. is always more efficacious JOHNSON:S 25
E. is the school BURKE:E 79
e. To a' Thy flock BURNS:R 20
noble ensample to his sheep CHAUC 26

examples:
Good e. are borne out of MACHIA 10
philosophy teaching from e. DION 1

excel:
Always to e. HOMER 8
daring to e. CHURCH:C 12
different men e. CHURCH:C 13
thou shalt not e. BIBLE 79

excellence:
dispute each other's e. in FOUR 2
limited e. at twenty-one FITZGER:FS 3

excellences: e. carried to an excess COLERIDGE:ST 96

excellent: in the knowledge of what is e. ALEX 3

excelsior: strange device, E. LONGFEL 6

exception:
believed an e. would be made SAROY 1
e. proves the rule PROV 109
make an e. in your case MARX:G 19

excess:
be blamed, but the e. SELD 3
carried to e. are wrong CHURCH:C 11
excellences carried to an e. COLERIDGE:ST 96
e. is quite delightful ANOU 1
Give me e. of it SHAK:TWE 1
have the courage of your e. MANS:K 7
Nothing in e. ANON 139
Nothing succeeds like e. WILDE:O 65
road of e. leads to the palace BLAKE:W 34
so much poverty and e. PENN 2
There is moderation even in e. DISR:B 1
wasteful and ridiculous e. SHAK:KING J 16

exchange: dote upon the e. SHAK:MUCH 8

exchequer bond: In a five per cent E.B. ELIOT:TS 19

excise: *E.* A hateful tax levied JOHNSON:S 11

exciseman: Deil's Aw' wi' th' E. BURNS:R 99

excited: artistically or sexually e. by any FAIRBAIRN:N 3

exciting: too excitin' to be pleasant DICKENS 14

excrement: in The place of e. YEATS 95

excursions: e. in my own mind COLERIDGE:ST 69

excuse:
coy e. MILT 43
E. I HUMPH 1
I will not e. GARRIS 1
just using that as an e. MARX:G 12
not a single e. KIP 115

execute:
hand to e. GIBBON:E 8
hand to e. JUNIUS 7

execution:
daily led to e. RALE 14
effective as their stringent e. GRANT:US 3
e. confin'd SHAK:TRO 11
smok'd with bloody e. SHAK:MAC 3

executioner: I am mine own *E.* DONNE 99

executioners: victims who respect their e. SARTRE 9

executions:
e. are intended to draw spectators JOHNSON:S 273
taste for marriages and public e. DISR:B 43

executive:
power is nominated by the e. GIBBON:E 2
salary of the chief e. GALB 9
weakest e. in the world DISR:B 53

executors: Let's choose e. SHAK:RIC.II 27
exercise:
all, e. GREEN:Mat 1
by temp'rance and by e. POPE 129
cure, on e. depend DRYD 122
every faculty . . . strengthens by e. BRONTE:A 3
E. is bunk FORD:H 3
feel like e., I lie down HUTCHINS 1
sad mechanic e. TENNY 129
exertion: e. is too much for me PEAC 6
exhalation: fall like a bright e. SHAK:HEN.VIII 9
exhausted: Our agenda is now e. SPAAK 1
exhaustion: sense of premature or projected e. BOYD:W 1
exile:
bind your sons to e. KIP 99
moving from e. to e.? SPARK 9
therefore I die in e. GREG VII 1
where everyone is an e. GILMAN 3
whose e. Hath emptied heav'n MILT 139
exiledom: within me the conditions of e. SPARK 9
exiles:
e. from our father's land GALT 1
Paradise of e., Italy SHELLEY:PB 24
Which none save e. feel AYT 4
exist:
behave as if he did e. UNA 5
He doesn't e. BECKETT 12
he need not e. in order to save DE VR 4
I e. by what I think SARTRE 2
impression that we e.? BECKETT 7
that he doesn't e. PRIEST 7
Why do you and I e.? JOHNSON:S 208
existed:
he had not lived, merely e. BUNIN 1
that which has not yet e. TEIL 2
existence:
aim of human e. is to kindle JUNG:Carl 5
also the right to our e. HALL:Rad 2
ARP'd or bombed out of e. MACMILL:H 2
continued e. is a mere miracle STEVENSON:RL 21
how e. could be cherished BRONTE:E 8
individual e. goes out in a lonely JAMES:W 2
Let us contemplate e. DICKENS 110
struggle for e. DARW:C 3
there is quite enough e. SARTRE 3
woman's whole e. BYR 171
existing: at the same time not e. HUGHES:S 1
exists:
e. for its own sake WHITEHEAD 3
regret that it nowhere e. TEMPLE:W[2] 7
exit:
Death is the best e. CHEV:M 3
E., pursued by a bear SHAK:WIN 8
every e. being an entrance somewhere STOP 2
exits:
For men to take their e. WEBSTER:J 26
their e. and their entrances SHAK:AS 34
exorciser: No e. harm thee SHAK:CYM 17
expect:
folly to e. men to do all WHATE 3
more of mankind I e. less JOHNSON:S 238
expectation:
distinction between hope and e. ILL 3
dream and a folly of e. BROWNE:T 61
e. whirls me round SHAK:TRO 10
Singing songs of e. BARING-G 5
sits E. in the air SHAK:HEN.V 10
expectations: between our talents and our e. BONO 1
expected: least e. generally happens DISR:B 11
expects: Blessed is the man who e. nothing POPE 183
expediency:
always be sacrificed to e. MAUGH 6
evil on the ground of e. ROOS:T 11
politicians by e. BELLOCH 1
expedient: not a principle, but an e. DISR:B 55
expendable: They Were E. WHITE:WL 1
expenditure:
annual e. nineteen nineteen DICKENS 151
general economy and particular e. EDEN:A 3
expense:
e. damnable CHESTERFIELD 36
relations must cause no e. COMPT 4
expensive:
from E. Sins refrain DRYD 49
Japanese point out how e. their THER 2
obtrusively e. goods GALB 3
experience:
all e. is an arch TENNY 52
can go beyond his e. LOCKE 3
dirty nurse, E. TENNY 261
everyone's e. is different MENAND 2
E. is a good teacher ANTRIM 1
e. is dangerous HIPP 1
E. is never limited JAMES:H 6
E. is the best teacher PROV 110
E. is the child of Thought DISR:B 2
E. is the mother of wisdom PROV 111
E. is the name every one WILDE:O 52
E. isn't interesting till it BOWEN:El 4
E. keeps a dear school FRANKLIN:B 10
e. of women which extends DOYLE:AC 5
E. teaches slowly FROUDE 2
E., though noon auctoritee CHAUC 76
e. to make me sad SHAK:AS 54
I have e. CONG 37
knowledge too but recorded e. CARLYLE:T 31
land of the individual e. SCHREIN 1
light which e. gives COLERIDGE:ST 90
man of no e. CURZON 3
Old Age, and E., hand in hand ROCHES 3
one who speaks from e. VIRGIL 82
part of e. BACON:F[1] 112
reality of e. JOYCE:J 9
triumph of hope over e. JOHNSON:S 148
worth a life's e. HOLMES:OW 14
experienced: becomes real till it is e. KEATS 155
experiences: meet the real e. of life KEY:E 2
experientia: E. does it DICKENS 148
experiment:
e. to the birth of a theory EINS 16
full tide of successful e. JEFFERSON 4
great social and economic e. HOOV 1
man who never tried an e. DARW:E 2
expert:
E. beyond experience ELIOT:TS 32
e. is a man who has made TELL 1
e. is a man who has made all BOHR 1
e. is a man who knows HEIS 1
e. is one who knows more BUTLER:NM 2
experts: never should trust e. SALIS 1
expiate: I have something to e. LAWR:DH 33
expire: I tremble, I e. SHELLEY:PB 135
expires: Wretched Child e. BELLOC 17
explain:
e. a thing till all men POPE 163
e. it away in the morning HUDS:B 2
I can't e. *myself* CARROLL 8
Never complain and never e. BALD:S 7
Never complain, never e. DISR:B 96
Never e. FISHER:JA 1
Never e. GRAYS 1
spoil it by trying to e. it SHERIDAN:RB 14
way to e. it is to do it CARROLL 5
explained: has been e. to him three times PROV 217
explanation:
inaccuracy sometimes saves tons of e. SAKI 24
minimum of fuss and no e. BLY 1
wish he would explain his E. BYR 156
explanations:
death is less hideous than e. LEWIS:DBW
I do loathe e. BARRIE 1
exploit: dignity compos'd and high e. MILT 152
exploration:
Polar e. is at once CHERRY 1
We shall not cease from e. ELIOT:TS 109
explorers: my endeavours are unlucky e. DOUGLAS:K 4
export: integrate the current e. drive BETJ 36
exposed: intellect is improperly e. SMITH:Syd[1] 23
exposes: who e. himself when he is intoxicated JOHNSON:S 211
exposure: unseemly e. of the mind HAZL 33
ex-president: elected e. with such a large majority TAFT 1
expressed: ne'er so well express'd POPE 14
expression:
executive e. of human immaturity BRITT 3
impassioned e. which is in WORDS:W 167
not the e. in English ARNOLD:M 59
expressions: grant me some wild e. FARQ 5
expressive:
e. systems which possess PAZ 1
too e. to be blue ARNOLD:M 11
extempore: pouring out his e. stuff SMITH:R 1
extend: So let e. thy mind MILT 272
exterminate:
destiny of science to e. PEAC 12
E. all the brutes CONRAD 4
have to e. a nation SPOCK 1
extinct: purpose of becoming e. CUPPY 1
extinction: E. of less-improved forms DARW:C 4
extol:
extoll Him first, him last MILT 210
How shall we e. thee BENS:AC 1
extraordinary:
this is an e. man JOHNSON:S 241
work of one e. man HUBB 3
extravagance:
beauty does not lead to e. PERIC 2
owe something to e. CHURCH:JJ 2
extravagant: nothing so e. and irrational SWIFT 33
extreme: Either extreame, of love, or hate CAREW:T 3
extremes:
extreams by change more fierce MILT 165
E. meet MERCIER 1
'E. meet', as the whiting HOOD 32
result from either of these e. ARISTOT 16
(to show his judgement) in e. DRYD 48
extremism: E. in the defence of liberty GOLDWATER 1
extremities: Between e. man runs YEATS 88
exuberance: E. is Beauty BLAKE:W 50
ex-wife: e. searching for a new lover CONNOLLY:C 11
eye:
altogether in the e. of the beholder HUNG 1
Beauty is altogether in the e. WALLACE:L 1
blacking the Corporal's e. KIP 46
can listen to with naked e. SPARK 8
Cast a cold e. YEATS 124
defiance in their e. GOLDS 10
Every Tear from Every E. BLAKE:W 87
e. among the blind WORDS:W 60
e. for an e. leads only to more ATWOOD 5
E. for e. BIBLE 104
e. full of gentle salutations STERNE 36
e. is bigger than the belly PROV 112
e. of heaven shines SHAK:SON 6
e. of heaven to garnish SHAK:KING J 16
e. of man hath not heard SHAK:MID 42
E. of newt, and toe SHAK:MAC 79
e. that can open an oyster WODE 23
e. that marks the perfect liar BENET 3
e. was backward cast SPENS 28
e., whose bend doth awe SHAK:JUL 9
e. will mark Our coming BYR 168
flash upon that inward e. WORDS:W 122
fringed curtains of thine e. SHAK:TEM 12
good e. at an Adultress AUSTEN 74
has got into this e. of mine STERNE 35
He had but one e. DICKENS 67
him with his glittering e. COLERIDGE:ST 11
If thine e. offend thee BIBLE 420
in the e. of the beholder PROV 30
left me with a jaundiced e. TENNY 80
Lesbia hath a beaming e. MOORE:T 8
less in this than meets the e. BANK 9
love-light in your e. BLACKWOOD 1
man who looks you straight in the e. FAD 4
mighty world Of e., and ear WORDS:W 9
mild and magnificent e. BROWNING:R 54
Mine e. and heart are at SHAK:SON 18
more than meets the e. KIP 138
neither e. to see nor tongue LENT 1
not Man a microscopic e.? POPE 85
road from the e. to the heart CHESTERTON 30
Russian e. Is underlined ELIOT:TS 33
see with, not thro the E. BLAKE:W 108
sniv'ling and piping your e.? DIBDIN:C 1
squenes the e. SHAK:KING L 47
such beauty as a woman's e.? SHAK:LOV 15
through the e. of a needle BIBLE 445
to the jaundic'd e. POPE 26
unforgiving e. SHERIDAN:RB 26
Who sees with equal e. POPE 82
with his e. on the object ARNOLD:M 51

with its soft black e. DICKENS 95
with its soft black e. MOORE:T 22
With my inward E. 'tis an old BLAKE:W 78
With my little e. NURS 85
with that e. no one could answer BAGE 3
ye of day CHAUC 97
eye-ball:
e. – like a bastion's mole SMART 2
e. to e. and I think RUSK 1
eyeballs: turn your e. black and blue BEHAN:Br 9
eyeing: gain a happiness in e. HUX:A 46
eyeless: E. in Gaza MILT 278
eyelids:
e. are a little weary PATER 1
e. many Graces sate SPENS 32
tir'd e. upon tir'd eyes TENNY 27
When she raises her e. COLETTE 2
With e. heavy and red HOOD 19
eyes:
From women's e. this doctrine SHAK:LOV 17
advantage both of E. and Voice MARV 10
all e. else dead coals SHAK:WIN 31
as many e. as thou hast wounds SHAK:JUL 42
big brown e. and that tiny mind? THURB 20
Black E., red Lips MARV 11
Bright as the sun, her e. POPE 42
but black e. and lemonade MOORE:T 19
close my e., open my legs HILLING 1
close your e. with holy dread COLERIDGE:ST 63
Closed his e. in endless night GRAY:T 35
cold commemorative e. ROSSET:DG 13
Cynosure of neighbouring e. MILT 71
death bandaged my e. BROWNING:R 182
deep upon her peerless e. KEATS 96
Drink to me only with thine e. JONS 36
encounter of assailing e. SHAK:ROM 3
e. are bright with it KEATS 154
e. are homes of silent prayer TENNY 144
e. are lenses through which DOUGLAS:K 3
e. are quickened so with grief GRAVES:R 1
e. are the window of the soul PROV 113
e. are the windows of the soul BEERB 7
e. as wise, but kindlier BROOKE 15
e. drop out LOCKER 1
e. grew dross of lead BROWNING:R 119
e. have seen what my hand LOWELL:R 17
E., look your last SHAK:ROM 44
e. met the e. of a mate CLARK:M 2
e. more bright Than stars DRYD 15
e. of gold and bramble-dew STEVENSON:RL 67
e. purging thick amber SHAK:HAM 73
E. too expressive to ARNOLD:M 11
e. were blind with stars HODG 5
e. were deeper than the depth ROSSET:DG 1
e. were made to look SHAK:ROM 26
e., Which Star-like sparkle HERR 19
fair maidens Quiet e. STEVENSON:RL 66
five e. smouldering DE LA M 12
From women's e. this doctrine SHAK:LOV 14
Gasp and Stretch one's E. BELLOC 21
Get thee glass e. SHAK:KING L 73
girl with kaleidoscope e. LENNON 7
girl with the pair of blue e. SHERIDAN:RB 25
God be in my e. ANON 66
Have e. to wonder SHAK:SON 49
he set her both his e. LYLY 4
her e. were wild KEATS 80
his e. Were with his heart BYR 110
His flashing e. COLERIDGE:ST 63
I was e. to the blind BIBLE 190
I will lift up mine e. BIBLE 239
I'd say I had e. again SHAK:KING L 57
keep her lustrous e. KEATS 93
kindling her undazl'd e. MILT 320
light that lies In woman's e. MOORE:T 15
Look into that man's e. LAW 4
look Your e. had once YEATS 14
Love in her sunny e. COWLEY:A 1
Love looks not with the e. SHAK:MID 5
lover's e. will gaze an eagle SHAK:LOV 16
made the e. dazzle but I? HERB:G 54
mine e. dazzle WEBSTER:J 27
Mine e. do itch SHAK:OTH 57
Mine e. have seen the glory HOWE 1
Mine e. have seen the glory KING:ML 3
mouth shut and your e. open PROV 219
My e. are dim ANON 30
night has a thousand e. BOUR 1
Night hath a thousand e. LYLY 7
no e. but constitutional e. LINC 25
no e., but fountains KYD 2
old e. Were very blue DENNIS:CJ 3
one of his e. became so terrible BECKF 1
only e., you see my wision's limited DICKENS 40
pair of sparking e. GILB:WS 108
pearls that were his e. SHAK:TEM 11
pick out mine e. with a ballad-maker's SHAK:MUCH 2
Pure e. and Christian hearts KEBLE 5
Seal her sweet e. ROSSET:C 9
see the whites of their e. PUT 1
shut her wild wild e. KEATS 84
Soft e. look'd love to e. BYR 76
sparkles that flash from their e. DRYD 112
Suddenly discovering in the e. POUND 10
swimmingness in the e. CONG 47
tear each other's e. WATTS 9
that your e. might be shining LAWR:TE 1
their e. are burning AUD 19
therefore want no e. SHAK:KING L 56
Thou turn'st my e. SHAK:HAM 141
two grey e. with lids SHAK:TWE 15
Two lovely black e. COBORN 1
West in her e. COLERIDGE:M 3
what dost thou to mine e. SHAK:SON 58
While I have e. to see HERR 30
whose e. are full of sand KEYES 1
will lift mine e. SCOTTISH 2
Will you put out mine e. SHAK:KING J 15
with eagle e. He star'd KEATS 4
with his half-shut e. POPE 51
With magic in my e. HARDY:T 3
woollen e. looked sad BETJ 33
worship of his e. JOYCE:J 5
you'll wear your e. out ZOLA 2
your e. are lode-stars SHAK:MID 4
Eyre: E. was an unlucky man DUTT 4
Fabian: F. Society writ large HAMIL:WW 2
Fabians: good man fallen among F. LENIN 10
fable: life's sweet f. ends CRASH 16
fables: f. that have been agreed upon VOLT 19
face:
Accustomed to her f. LERN 7
Am I in f. today? GOLDS 68
beauty Of an aged f. CAMPBELL:Jo 1
blubber'd is that pretty f. PRIOR 9
boot stamping on a human f. ORWELL 36
brittle as the glory is the f. SHAK:RIC.II 39
can't think of your f. SPOON 6
caricature of a f. GILB:WS 80
cold, Exhausted f. SASS 10
Cover her f. WEBSTER:J 27
design might cover their f. POUND 38
did not recognize me by my f. TROLL 26
disasters in his morning f. GOLDS 28
draw a full f. DRYD 141
everybody's f. but their own SWIFT 1
everyone has the f. he deserves ORWELL 40
f. and nose pressed YEATS 53
f. blackened by charcoal EDGE 8
f. made up Out of no CRASH 8
F. of a country lout LAWS 5
f. One would meet KEATS 60
f. that launch'd a thousand MARLOWE 38
f. that left no portraiture SASS 17
f. that she keeps in a jar LENNON 5
f. the index of a feeling mind CRAB 24
f., with Nature's own hand SHAK:SON 7
False f. must hide SHAK:MAC 30
features of my father's f. BYR 47
fyr-reed cherubynnes f. CHAUC 29
garden of your f. HERB:E 1
Give me them that will f. me SHAK:HEN.IV[1] 37
glimpse of his bright f. VAUGHAN:H 5
God hath given you one f. SHAK:HAM 102
Has he not a rogue's f.? CONG 21
He hides a smiling f. COWP 10
He shows his honest f. DRYD 106
Her angel's f. SPENS 24
homely f. and no figure ANTRIM 3
honest, sonsie f. BURNS:R 35
I am the family f. HARDY:T 36
I never forget a f. MARX:G 19
Knight of the Sad F. CERV 5
languid patience of thy f. COLERIDGE:ST 1
Look on her f. and you'll forget POPE 43
Looks the whole world in the f. LONGFEL 13
Lord make his f. shine BIBLE 114
made with my f. on it CHARLES F 1
maun f. God mysel' MACDIAR 1
mind's construction in the f. SHAK:MAC 18
mist in my f. BROWNING:R 181
Moses hid his f. BIBLE 86
moste kisse worthy f. SIDNEY:P 8
My f. is my fortune NURS 84
oil to make his f. shine BIBLE 233
one f. he has got is so SNOW 5
one to f. the world with BROWNING:R 141
Over the f. of the leader WHITTIER 5
painting a f. and not washing FULLER:T[1] 12
pardon'd all except her f. BYR 210
plummet-measured f. YEATS 120
poorest way to f. life ROOS:T 19
prepare a f. to meet ELIOT:TS 5
pretty f. is a dumb PUB 1
responsible for the f. he has CAMUS 13
seen God f. to f. BIBLE 66
she has a lovely f. TENNY 23
So sweet a f. TENNY 41
sorrows of your changing f. YEATS 14
still and lovely f. DE LA M 1
There is a Garden in her f. CAMPION 9
thy f. Bears a command SHAK:COR 13
to negotiate with my f.? SHAK:TWE 15
two strong men stand f. to f. KIP 39
why was I born with a different f.? BLAKE:W 79
with how meane a f. SIDNEY:P 5
ye have a singing f. FLETCH:J 12
Your f. . . . is as a book SHAK:MAC 21
face-flatterer: F. and backbiter are the same TENNY 248
faced: f. the possibility of not returning EAR 2
faces:
almost everywhere two f. DRYD 139
among so many millions of f. BROWNE:T 26
Bid them wash their f. SHAK:COR 5
change their f. wi' their clo'es FERG:R 2
f. are but a gallery BACON:F[1] 66
five or six f. in front of a mirror GLOVER 3
grace-proud f. BURNS:R 33
grind the f. of the poor? BIBLE 302
I *see* . . . the f. of the little children EAMES:R 1
In the f. of men and women WHITMAN 11
innocent f. clean BLAKE:W 23
know the f. I shall see ROSSET:DG 10
laces And sweet pretty f. NURS 83
make f. and produce laughter JOHNSON:S 174
Mild monastic f. CLOUGH 17
nice clean f. BARH 4
old familiar f. LAMB:Ch 31
our dewy dreaming f. HEAN 6
owners of their f. SHAK:SON 41
piece gets difficult make f. SCHNAB 3
plain men have rosy f. STEVENSON:RL 66
Private f. in public AUD 4
these f. in the crowd POUND 17
we hid as it were our f. BIBLE 328
facetious:
foolish because I am f. SMITH:Syd[1] 15
to be f. it is not necessary ROGERS:T 1
fact:
ever turn it into a f. BALZ 8
fatal futility of F. JAMES:H 11
find the historical f. ELIOT:TS 75
hypothesis by an ugly f. HUX:TH 3
Matters of f. . . . are very stubborn TIND 1
when a f. appears opposed DOYLE:AC 2
faction:
grow up there From F. MILT 149
it made them a f. MACAULAY:TB 32
To die for f. DRYD 58
Whig. The name of a f. JOHNSON:S 16
whisper of a f. should prevail RUSS:J[2] 1
factions: cannot revive old f. ELIOT:TS 106
facts:
deny the f. but to re-allocate RYLE 1
f. are chiels that winna BURNS:R 40
f. are f. and flinch not BROWNING:R 196
f. are lost forever MAIL 1
f. are sacred SCOTT:CP 1
F. do not cease to exist HUX:A 16

F. were never pleasing BARRIE 15
intelligent anticipation of f. CURZON 1
report the f. ROGERS:W 10
Stick to F., sir DICKENS 185
to his imagination for his f. SHERIDAN:RB 42
faculties:
each according to his f. BAK 2
very f. of eyes and ears SHAK:HAM 91
votaries of the use of their f. SMOL 4
faculty: every f. . . . strengthens by exercise BRONTE:A 3
fade:
F. far away KEATS 93
She cannot f. KEATS 92
they simply f. away PROV 306
faded:
f. away in a wall BETJ 12
f. on the crowing SHAK:HAM 10
fades:
f. awa' like morning dew BALL 62
Now f. the glimmering landscape GRAY:T 16
fading:
F. in music SHAK:MERC 33
f. pleasure brings SIDNEY:P 1
she's f. down the river NEWBOLT 7
faery:
see also **fairy**
beautiful – a f.'s child KEATS 80
in f. lands forlorn KEATS 93
sing A f.'s song KEATS 82
With a f., hand in hand YEATS 2
fail:
f. conventionally than to KEYN 7
no such word As – *f.* BULWER 2
Others must f. VIDAL 9
probability that we may f. LINC 6
sooner f. than not be among KEATS 142
We shall not flag or f. CHURCH:W 13
we'll not f. SHAK:MAC 28
failed:
men who have f. in literature DISR:B 41
tried a little, f. much STEVENSON:RL 43
failing:
every f. but their own BYR 27
she had ae f. BURNS:R 61
failings: no f. which were not owing BURKE:E 22
failure:
f.'s no success at all DYL 6
forty million reasons for f. KIP 115
I'll show you a f. ROCKWE 1
utterly unspoiled by f. COWARD 38
Women don't forgive f. CHEK 3
failures:
Half the f. in life arise HARE:J 2
women adore f. WILDE:O 58
faint: Many f. with toil SHELLEY:PB 2
fainted: we f. Alternately on a Sofa AUSTEN 4
fainting: F. in coils CARROLL 29
faints: sense f. picturing them SHELLEY:PB 42
fair:
All is f. in love and war PROV 9
all's f. in love and war FORREST 2
anything to show more f. WORDS:W 91
care I how f. she be? WITHER 1
every f. from f. some time SHAK:SON 6
f. as any may be PEELE 1
F. be their wives DUNB 12
F. is foul, and foul is f. SHAK:MAC 1
F. is too foul an epithet MARLOWE 11
F., kind, and true, have SHAK:SON 47
F. laughs the Morn GRAY:T 31
f. sex is your department DOYLE:AC 28
F. stood the wind for France DRAYT 6
F. though you are DRYD 15
false because she's f.? DONNE 12
Fat, f. and forty O'KEEFFE:J 3
Fat, f., and forty SCOTT:W 86
fayr as is the rose in May CHAUC 98
find how to make it f. BROWNING:R 77
hand that hath made you f. SHAK:MEA 25
I have been to Ludlow f. HOUSM 29
I have sworn thee f. SHAK:SON 63
like the morning f. GRANVILLE 2
Ludlow come in for the f. HOUSM 13
more f. than words can say TENNY 41
most divinely f. TENNY 10
Outward be f. CHURCH:C 2
settle what's right and f. HUGHES:Th 3
Shee f., divinely f. MILT 245
so long at the f. NURS 44
so wondrous sweet and f. WALLER 4
This isn't f. dealing KIP 142
where God doth admit the f. HERB:E 3
fair play:
laws were made to keep f.p. BLAKE:W 2
sport has nothing to do with f.p. ORWELL 39
fairer:
f. far in May JONS 48
I can't say f. than that GILB:WS 87
You shall be yet for f. SHAK:ANT 5
fairest:
f. of Creation MILT 248
f. of her Daughters Eve MILT 194
fairies:
Do you believe in f.? BARRIE 9
f. at the bottom of our garden FYLE 1
She is the f.' midwife SHAK:ROM 5
since the f. left off dancing SELD 8
that was the beginning of f. BARRIE 6
fairness: fairnes bot ane faiding flour HENRYS 4
fairy:
see also **faery**
Airy, f. Lilian TENNY 3
By f. hands their knell COLLINS:Will 4
enough to wrap a f. in SHAK:MID 20
f. gifts fading away MOORE:T 3
f. kind of writing DRYD 99
f. somewhere that falls down BARRIE 7
loveliest f. in the world KINGSLEY:C 6
'tis almost f. time SHAK:MID 50
W. Lilly believes it was a f. AUBREY 13
fairy tale:
fairy-tale written by God's fingers ANDER 3
f.t. that I cannot get out HEINE 4
fairy tales: With the f.t. of science TENNY 69
faith:
Americans have little f. EMER 90
break f. with us who die MCCRAE 2
can't be too decisive in our f. BROWNING:R 82
collected F. in home SPEND 10
constitutes poetic f. COLERIDGE:ST 75
disturb Our cheerful f. WORDS:W 11
does not doubt is a dead f. UNA 8
Draw near with f. PRAY 71
f. and fire within us HARDY:T 27
f. can impious lucre hold? VIRGIL 55
F. consists in believing what VOLT 22
f. diversified by doubt BROWNING:R 81
f., hope, charity BIBLE 523
f., howp, luve BIBLE 594
F. is defying BARNF 4
F. is the substance of things BIBLE 556
f. of the Saviour made landfall BOSSU 1
f. shines equal BRONTE:E 1
f. than Norman blood TENNY 64
f. that looks through death WORDS:W 67
f. unfaithful kept him TENNY 253
f. unhappily forsworn SHAK:SON 30
F. will move mountains PROV 114
F. without works is dead BIBLE 563
f.'s transcendent dower WORDS:W 129
good fight of f. BIBLE 550
His f. perhaps in some COWLEY:A 8
I have kept the f. BIBLE 553
illogical belief in the* MENCK 2
In this f. I wish to live VILLON 2
just shall live by f. BIBLE 508
Kept f. with me HARDY:T 47
life is a profession of f. AMIEL 3
Life without f. is an arid COWARD 9
lived by hearsay, and f. BUNYAN 33
more f. in honest doubt TENNY 173
not found so great f. BIBLE 403
not the dying for a f. that's so hard THACK 17
other f. than my f. in human beings BUCK 2
plain and simple f. SHAK:JUL 66
reason is itself a matter of f. CHESTERTON 39
scientific f.'s absurd BROWNING:R 68
Sea of F. ARNOLD:M 47
shake a man's f. in himself SHAW 9
Since f. is dead WYATT 2
staff of f. to walk upon RALE 2
still by f. he trod LIND:V 1
sudden explosions of f. BREN 2
thou of little f. BIBLE 415
to prove that f. exists BROWNING:R 84
vain f., and courage vain MACAULAY:TB 55
whoever is moved by *F.* HUME 11
whummlin the f. o haill faimlies BIBLE 596
With Punic f. SALL 9
Woman's f. SCOTT:W 63
yive I feyth and ful CHAUC 94
faith-healer: was a f. of Deal ANON 103
faithful:
be mentally f. to himself PAINE 9
come, all ye f. OAK 1
done had you been f.? RACINE 3
Ever faithfull, ever sure MILT 1
F. are the wounds of a friend BIBLE 273
F., below DIBDIN:C 4
f. of thy word GRAHAM:J 1
f. to thee, Cynara DOWS 1
how can he be f. to me THEO 1
seldom strictly f. if they are CAMPBELL:R 6
So f. in love SCOTT:W 18
faithfully: Yours f., God ANON 61
faithfulness: thy f. every night BIBLE 227
faithless: F. as the winds or seas SEDLEY 1
faiths:
men's f. are wafer-cakes SHAK:HEN.V 16
old f. loosen and fall SWIN 36
falcon:
dapple-dawn-drawn F. HOPK:GM 10
f., tow'ring in her pride SHAK:MAC 59
Jentyll as fawcoun Or hawke SKEL:J 5
falcons: rapid f. in a snare MERED:G 28
Falklands: F. thing was a fight between BORGES 5
fall:
All things f. and are built YEATS 109
And must they f.? BYR 59
By dividing we f. DICKIN:J 1
console us when we f. BURKE:E 96
divided we f. PROV 409
doesn't have time to f. WRIGHT:O 1
down needs fear no f. BUNYAN 26
f. Frightful, sheer HOPK:GM 23
f. Like a bright exhalation SHAK:HEN.VIII 9
f. not out by the way BIBLE 77
fear I to f. RALE 13
going to f. like rain AUD 27
haughty spirit before a f. BIBLE 263
how soon the f. of the leaf DONNE 109
I f. upon the thorns of life SHELLEY:PB 45
in this we stand or f. MILT 216
It had a dying f. SHAK:TWE 1
mankind by their f. lost CATEC 3
meditated on the F. BETJ 29
raise up them that f. PRAY 35
shall not f. on the ground without BIBLE 408
take warning by the f. BALL 6
unbelievable until they actually f. WHITE:P 6
We all f. down NURS 59
we f. to rise BROWNING:R 213
what a f. was there SHAK:JUL 55
you f., pick up something AVE 1
fall out: F.o., and chide, and fight WATTS 12
fallacy: characterize as 'Pathetic F.' RUSKIN 7
fallen:
F. from his high estate DRYD 108
How are the mighty f. BIBLE 154
How art thou f. from heaven BIBLE 312
lay mightily f. HOMER 12
not f. on top of us CANET 5
say a man has f. in love STERNE 30
they are f. themselves BIBLE 217
though f., great BYR 68
falling:
by oft f. LAT 1
day when heaven was f. HOUSM 37
f. with a f. state POPE 30
it is their way of f. GIDE 3
fallow:
f. fawns invisible go THOMAS:E 5
well to lie f. for a while TUP 1
falls: When a German f. over TUCHOL 6
false:
all was f. and hollow MILT 152
betrayed by what is f. within MERED:G 24
breath of her f. mouth SHELLEY:PB 131
f. because she's fair? DONNE 12
F., ere I come, to two DONNE 58
F. face must hide SHAK:MAC 30
f. were once true EMER 56
fram'd to make women f. SHAK:OTH 17
If she be f. SHAK:OTH 39

In friendship f. DRYD 41
likely turn out to be f. VALERY 3
maiden gloriously f. HORACE 41
man who is f. to his friends BERK 5
Ring out the f. TENNY 177
True and *f.* are attributes HOBB 2
falsehood:
F. has a perennial spring BURKE:E 20
goodly outside f. hath SHAK:MERC 16
its f. would be more miraculous HUME 12
Let her and F. grapple MILT 322
no protection against f. HOUSM 50
smallest foundation to f. GOLDS 54
to express lying or f. SWIFT 34
To unmask f. SHAK:POET 6
falsehoods: one of those convenient f. PLATO 8
falser: f. than vows made in wine SHAK:AS 52
Falstaff: F. sweats to death SHAK:HEN.IV[1] 30
falter:
F., are lost ARNOLD:M 49
hesitate and f. life away ARNOLD:M 26
Famagusta: dipping deep For F. FLECKER 8
fame:
blush to find it F. POPE 152
damn'd to everlasting f. POPE 105
damn'd to F. POPE 167
desire for f. is the last thing TAC 7
establishment of my f. GIBBON:E 27
exceedest the f. that I heard BIBLE 175
f. ? an empty bubble GRAIN:J 1
F. and tranquility cannot dwell MONTAIGNE 11
F. is a food DOBSON:HA 5
F. is a powerful aphrodisiac GREENE:G 17
F. is at best POPE 67
F. is like a river BACON:F[1] 93
F. is love disguised SHELLEY:PB 34
F. is no plant MILT 50
f. is not achieved by sitting DANTE 12
F. is the spur MILT 49
F., like a wayward girl KEATS 90
F., like water, bears up CALD 5
F.? It's glory in small HUGO 1
F.'s eternall beadroll SPENS 39
for his f. the ocean sea BARNF 2
Fortune and to F. unknown GRAY:T 26
full of phrase and f. ARNOLD:M 50
grant an honest f. POPE 55
her f. survives MILT 299
immoderate passion for f. BURKE:E 22
Let f., that all hunt SHAK:LOV 1
love and f. to nothingness KEATS 23
Man dreams of F. TENNY 246
nor yet a fool to f. POPE 119
openeth the fate to good f. BACON:F[1] 53
Posthumous f. is not particularly HUX:TH 15
trust a good deal to common f. EMER 83
What rage for f. attends PINDAR:P 1
while f. elates thee MOORE:T 6
you shall live by f. SPENS 11
your f. is bright BRIDGES:R 13
familiar:
Don't let us be f. CONG 53
F. acts are beautiful SHELLEY:PB 85
f. things are made new JOHNSON:S 55
makes a f. word new HORACE 102
makes f. objects be as if SHELLEY:PB 164
old f. faces LAMB:Ch 31
familiarity:
F. begets boldness MARM 2
F. breeds contempt PROV 115
F. with evil breeds not HATTER 1
families:
f. last not three oaks BROWNE:T 57
Good f. are generally worse HOPE:An 7
happy f. resemble one another TOLS:L 6
in the best-regulated f. DICKENS 161
in the best regulated f. PROV 2
Mothers of large f. BELLOC 5
old f. should stick together HUGHES:B 4
one of your antediluvian f. CONG 29
to run in f. LEWES 1
family:
bloodiness of f. life MITCH:Ju 1
brought up a large f. GOLDS 49
character of a f. to an hypothesis? STERNE 8
children of one f. Fall out WATTS 12
dead heart of the f. GREER 2
English have no f. feelings COMPT 4
f. happier for his presence STEVENSON:RL 42
f. pride is something inconceivable GILB:WS 62
f., with its narrow privacy LEACH 1
f. with the wrong members ORWELL 11
I am the f. face HARDY:T 36
my f. begins with me IPH 1
One extinguished f. waits BETJ 17
prolong f. connection unduly BUTLER:S[2] 25
remaining years among his f. DU BEL 2
that his f. was not unworthy DISR:B 34
trouble in running a f. MONTAIGNE 8
written under the direction of his f. WALP:H 18
famine:
die by f. die by inches HENRY:M 3
f. in his face CHURCH:C 5
from plague, pestilence, and f. PRAY 33
famous:
Be f. then By wisdom MILT 272
earth is the sepulchre of f. men PERIC 4
f. by my sword GRAHAM:J 1
f. for fifteen minutes WARHOL 1
found myself f. BYR 256
get rich, get f. and get laid GEL 3
I am just f. MURD:I 1
Let us now praise f. men BIBLE 370
fan:
always use so large a f. CARROLL 83
f. spread and streamers out CONG 41
no greater f. of the opposite sex LERN 9
throw an egg into an electric f. HERF 2
fan vaulting: 'F.v.' . . . an architectural device LANCAS 1
fanatic: f. is a man who consciously HUX:A 17
fanaticism: F. consists in redoubling SANT 1
fanatics: F. have their dreams KEATS 99
fancied: didn't love God, he just f. ANON 192
fancies:
F. that broke through language BROWNING:R 188
Our f. are more giddy SHAK:TWE 26
fancy:
Did your f. ever stray GAY 17
Ever let the F. roam KEATS 58
f. cannot cheat so well KEATS 93
f. dies In the cradle SHAK:MERC 34
f. is indeed no other COLERIDGE:ST 74
f. is taken by a young man CAUD 1
F. is the Sails KEATS 117
f.'s maze and clue COLERIDGE:ST 64
In the Spring a young man's f. TENNY 70
keep your f. free HOUSM 9
makes f. lame COWP 41
now the f. passes by HOUSM 10
odiferous flowers of f. SHAK:LOV 12
see The f. out-work nature SHAK:ANT 25
So full of shapes is f. SHAK:TWE 1
sweet and bitter f. SHAK:AS 62
where is f. bred SHAK:MERC 34
wonderfull consimility of phansey AUBREY 12
fanned: fann'd by Conquest's GRAY:T 28
Fanny:
doughnuts turn out like F.'s CRAD 1
F. by Gaslight SADL 1
fans: divers-colour'd f., whose wind SHAK:ANT 25
fantasies:
exchange of two f. CHAMFORT 5
fed the heart on f. YEATS 67
twilight Phantasies SHELLEY:PB 111
fantastic:
In a light fantastick round MILT 22
light fantastick toe MILT 67
fantasy: I *am* a f. MONROE:M 2
far:
F. and few, f. and few LEAR 13
F., f. ahead CLOUGH 8
F. from us be that fate OSB:J 1
F. hence, oh f. be souls VIRGIL 67
how f. one can go too f. COCT 1
Over the hills and f. away GAY 18
She is f. from the land MOORE:T 14
so near and yet so f. TENNY 176
think how f. I can go THATCH:M 12
thus f. shalt thou go. PARNELL:CS 1
to behold from f. LUCRET 5
far-off: unhappy, f. things WORDS:W 80
far-reaching: f. in purpose HOOV 1
Faraday: I must remain plain Michael F. FARA 1
farce:
f. is played out RAB 9
F. is the essential theatre CRAIG:G 1
longest running f. in the West End SMITH:C 1
not as hard as f. GWENN 1
pet-lamb in a sentimental f. KEATS 98
second as f. MARX:K 3
wine was a f. POWELL:A 2
fare:
F. thee well! and if for ever BYR 45
F. thee well, for I must ANON 46
fewer the better f. PROV 277
showed me his bill of f. SWIFT 76
farewell:
Arab's F. to his Horse NORT 2
bid the company f. RALE 12
F. the tranquil mind SHAK:OTH 43
is death itself a f.? BALZ 6
my brother, hail and f. CATUL 20
No-more, Too-late, F. ROSSET:DG 12
farewells:
As many f. as be stars SHAK:TRO 20
Everlasting f. DEQ 5
farm:
It's called a f. STENHO 1
keep a f. and carters SHAK:HAM 70
snug little f. the Earth COLERIDGE:ST 40
farmer:
better f. ne'er brush'd dew BYR 146
f. sowing his corn NURS 73
f. that hanged himself SHAK:MAC 48
f.'s daughter hath soft brown hair CALVER 4
Never you marry A f.'s boy MCCUAIG 2
farmers:
embattled f. stood EMER 98
f., flourish and complain CRAB 7
happy are f. VIRGIL 25
now the f. swear KINGSMILL 2
farmland: f. as a dark HEAN 5
farms:
flat earth of empty f. SLESS 3
lass wi' the weel-stockit f. BURNS:R 120
pleasant Villages and Farmes MILT 244
what f. are those? HOUSM 24
farmyard: f. world of sex GRANVILLE-B 2
farrago: f. of the clack of nurses STERNE 24
farrier: Felix Randal the f. HOPK:GM 13
fart: f. and chew gum at the same JOHNSON:LB 6
farthing:
for a f. less ADDIS 11
kind of f. dip STEVENSON:RL 60
steal one poor f. NEWM:JH 4
two sparrows sold for a f.? BIBLE 408
farthing-candle: f. to the sun YOUNG:E 5
farthings:
Latin word for three f. SHAK:LOV 7
You owe me five f. NURS 49
farts: enjoy the smell of their own f. AUD 63
fascination: There's a f. frantic GILB:WS 83
fascism:
century of F. MUSSO:B 8
F. is a religion MUSSO:B 8
F. is not an article for export MUSSO:B 6
fascist: Every woman adores a F. PLATH 2
fashion:
as out of the f. CIB 1
defiance of f. is the beginning MURRAY:LA 3
dress is very independent of f. GASK 2
Every man after his f. PROV 102
F. – a word which knaves CHURCH:C 9
F. is architecture CHANEL 3
F. is reduced to a question CHANEL 4
f.'s brightest arts decoy GOLDS 32
glass of f. SHAK:HAM 104
highflyer at F. DICKENS 217
in the first style of f. AUSTEN 11
laws of markets and f. ALBERT 1
men in shape and f. ASCHAM 2
fashionable: ever to be f. is ominous SANT 5
fast:
move very f. to even stand still KENNEDY:JF 9
never be done too f. GOLDS 64
Now can I break my f. SHAK:TWO 8
will not f. in peace CRAB 5
faster:
nobody walks much f. CARROLL 77
Will you walk a little f.? CARROLL 31
world would go round a deal f. CARROLL 11

one universal passion: f. SHAW 13
Perfect love casteth out f. BIBLE 571
quite unaccustomed to f. ANON 95
Severity breedeth f. BACON:F[1] 74
stopped being an object of *f.* NIET 14
They hate whom they f. ENN 3
thing we have to f. is f. ROOS:FD 5
whom shall I f.? BIBLE 597
why f. we to become? SHELLEY:PB 125
with Hope farewel F. MILT 185
without f. and without blame BAYA 1
feared:
f. nor flattered and flesh DOUGLAS:J 1
seeks to be f. rather than RUSS:B 15
She fear'd no danger DRYD 83
tell thee what is to be fear'd SHAK:JUL 15
fears:
all our hopes and f. BUTLER:J 2
Applying f. to hopes SHAK:SON 53
f. his enemy, but despises PLUT 2
f. may be liars CLOUGH 10
F. of the brave JOHNSON:S 69
forgot the taste of f. SHAK:MAC 112
Happy is the man who f. the Lord BIBLE 601
Present f. Are less SHAK:MAC 16
sum of their f. CHURCH:W 70
tie up thy f. HERB:G 42
feast:
at a great f. of languages SHAK:LOV 19
door stood open at our f. COLERIDGE:M 3
look makes a dish a f. HERB:G 56
perpetual f. of nectar'd sweets MILT 33
sat at any good man's f. SHAK:AS 33
When I make a f. HARI 1
feasting: f. reconciles everybody PEPYS 15
feasts:
nights and f. divine HORACE 72
Table of Moveable F. PRAY 1
feather:
He stuck a f. in his hat BANGS 2
little ball of f. and bone HARDY:T 5
moulted f., an eagle-f. BROWNING:R 137
slow on the f. CORY 4
struck down by death's f. THOMAS:D 1
feather-footed: F. through the plashy fen WAUGH:E 22
feathered: feather'd race with pinions FRERE 1
feathers:
beautified with our f. GREENE:R 2
Fine f. make fine birds PROV 119
mune shak's her gowden f. MACDIAR 2
feats: f. of broil and battle SHAK:OTH 7
feature: every f. works AUSTEN 42
features:
dissipation that thicken the f. WEST:R 5
f. of my father's face BYR 47
incisive f. bound in stale MERED:G 12
Feb: F., fill the dyke TUSS 8
fed:
bite the hand that f. them BURKE:E 81
f. on beef and beer MARLBOR:J 1
F. the same flock MILT 44
see his children f. PUD 2
federation: F. of the world TENNY 79
fee: serve for meat and f. BALL 28
feeble: not enough to help the f. SHAK:TIM 1
feed:
blessing will not f. PROV 47
cannot f. the hungry on statistics LLOYD GEO 1
f. his flock like a shepherd BIBLE 322
f. on Death, that feeds SHAK:SON 62
F. the brute DU MAU:G 4
F. the brute PUNCH 25
f. thee out of my own vitals? CONG 23
he that doth me f. HERB:G 47
feeding: F. your face comes first BRECHT 3
feeds:
F. beast as man SHAK:ANT 3
f. the hand that bites him PETER 2
f. the poor as he f. dogs ROUSS:JJ 4
one that f. On abjects SHAK:JUL 65
feel:
also f. it as a man SHAK:MAC 98
dislike what I fancy I f. ANON 103
f. a feeling which I f. RIDD 1
I f. it more than other people DICKENS 142
I only f. BYR 4
Speak that we f. SHAK:KING L 87
tragedy to those that f. WALP:H 15
feelies: Going to the F. this evening HUX:A 30
feeling:
current of his f. failed AUD 36
exposing states of f. HARRIS:M 2
f. is bad form FORST 13
f. of a Former world BYR 249
f. that I could last forever CONRAD 8
f. which I feel you all feel RIDD 1
formal f. comes DICKIN:E 5
mess of imprecision of f. ELIOT:TS 98
petrifies the f. BURNS:R 46
probably is there more true f. JOW 3
sensible To f. as to sight? SHAK:MAC 33
transmission of f. which the artist TOLS:L 12
feelings:
English women conceal their f. WILDE:O 53
express f. which are not in actual emotions ELIOT:TS 115
fate and f. are the names of but NOVA 2
First f. are always the most LOUIS XIV 2
highest and best f. to which men TOLS:L 11
judge either of the f. or of the characters EDGE 2
fees: who straight dream on f. SHAK:ROM 5
feet:
always land on someone's f. PARKER:D 26
bathe those beauteous f. FLETCH:P 4
beat of her unseen f. SHELLEY:PB 55
better to die on your f. IBA 2
chance to sit down and rest your f. EDWARD VIII 4
couldn't feel my f. CERN 1
cutting off our f. when SWIFT 17
did those f. in ancient time BLAKE:W 98
fall at her flying feete CAMPION 2
Fear lends wings to his f. VIRGIL 77
f. beneath her petticoat SUCK 3
f. firmly planted in the air ROOS:FD 9
f. firmly planted in the air SCAN 1
f. of him that bringeth BIBLE 326
f. was I to the lame BIBLE 190
Her pretty f. Like snailes HERR 33
his f. in a bucket of champagne KELLY:B 1
Its f. were tied KEATS 57
Keep Thou my f. NEWM:JH 15
laith she should weet her f. BALL 1
let my due f. never fail MILT 89
little snow-white f. YEATS 3
nothing walks with aimless f. TENNY 153
Scots lords at his f. BALL 51
seven f. of English ground HARO 1
splendour and speed of thy f. SWIN 10
stream of passing f. TENNY 221
Their f. run to evil BIBLE 332
those little silver f. MARV 24
Thus I set my printless f. MILT 41
walk'd those blessed f. SHAK:HEN.IV[1] 2
wash their f. in soda water ELIOT:TS 44
with flying f. BYR 77
with their f. forward BROWNE:T 51
your f. are always in the water AMES 2
felicity:
Absent thee from f. SHAK:HAM 199
likely to mar the general f.? BUTLER:S[2] 44
pleyn felicite That is in hevene CHAUC 121
shadow of f.? WALLER 7
fell:
f. among thieves BIBLE 456
f. to earth, I knew not LONGFEL 16
from Morn to Noon he f. MILT 144
he f. like a stick PAINE 8
men f. out they knew not why BUTLER:S[1] 1
my uncle Toby f. into it STERNE 30
We f. out, my wife TENNY 103
fella: F. belong Mrs Queen PHILIP 1
fellow: you're a f. DICKENS 12
fellow-feeling: f. makes one wond'rous kind GARRICK 3
fellows: I say you f. RICHARDS:F 1
fellowship:
f. with essence KEATS 36
one communion and f. PRAY 60
felon: When a f.'s not engaged GILB:WS 26
female:
fault of the f. character SCHOP 8
f., and obliged to repudiate LESSING:D 3
f. impersonators are women BENNER 1
f. mind is not capable KNOX:V 2
F. of sex it seems MILT 289
f. of the species is more KIP 133
f. person RILKE 4
f. to that of neuter being BERNARD:Jes 1
left in f. hands, we would PAG 1
my life for the British f.? CLOUGH 14
pious friendships of the f. CONG 40
seldom f. in a world of males PITTER 1
unlearned and uninformed f. AUSTEN 76
females: masters to their f. SHAK:COM 1
feminine:
f. in all of us GOET 21
she's of the f. gender O'KEEFFE:J 1
feminism:
Above the titles of wife* LIVER 2
American women are kept from growing* FRIEDAN 1
As a woman of letters I fight for* DWO 4
claim our right as women* PANK:C 2
cover for lesbian homosexuality* FAIRBAIRN:N 4
Every man, deep down* SOLAN 1
expect women to accept it* PANK:E 2
F. is the theory: lesbianism ATK:T 1
If civilization is to advance* PANK:E 4
If women understand by emancipation* GREER 6
in the schoolroom more than* ANTH 3
object to being defined by* FOLL 1
one word is said giving man* STANTON:El 3
principle which regulates* MILL 28
The vote, I thought* O'BRIEN:E 3
When modern woman discovered* FIGES 1
will never be complete equality* ANTH 2
women their rights* ANTH 1
feminist:
best home for a f. WATSON:JD 1
Fat is a F. Issue ORB 1
not a f., I'm a person FRIEDAN 2
feminists:
F. who still sleep with men JOHNSTONE:Jil 2
they just become f. DALP 1
feminization: f. of the white European LEWIS:W 3
femme: *Cherchez la f.* DUMAS:A[P] 2
fen:
Feather-footed through the plashy f. WAUGH:E 22
f. Of stagnant waters WORDS:W 47
fence:
don't pull down the f. PROV 255
f. strong enough I'll sit on it SMITH:C 2
so long on the f. that the iron LLOYD GEO 12
fences:
Good f. make good neighbours FROST:R 3
Good f. make good neighbours PROV 153
ferlie: f. he spied wi' BALL 54
fern-seed: We have the receipt of f. SHAK:HEN.IV[1] 26
ferry: To row us o'er the f. CAMPBELL:T 11
Fesole: from the top of F. MILT 124
fetlocks: f. shag and long SHAK:POET 11
fettered: so f. fast we are BROWNING:R 71
fetters:
harsh f. of Colour and Caste? PRINGLE:T 4
These strong Egyptian f. SHAK:ANT 9
fettle: f. for the great grey drayhorse HOPK:GM 14
fever:
enigma of the f. chart ELIOT:TS 96
f. call'd 'Living' POE 12
He had a f. SHAK:JUL 9
wakes the f. in my bones KIP 61
weariness, the f., and the fret KEATS 93
fever-trees: all set about with f. KIP 25
fevers: Time and f. burn away AUD 13
few:
A f. honest men are better CROMWELL 1
as against the privileged f. ROOS:E 3
by so many to so f. CHURCH:W 16
Far and f., far and f. LEAR 13
F. and evil have the days BIBLE 78
f. are chosen BIBLE 425
Gey f., and they're a' deid ANON 194
we happy f. SHAK:HEN.V 40
fewer:
f. men, the greater share SHAK:HEN.V 38
f. the better fare PROV 277
feynd: F. is slee DUNB 8

Fhairshon: F. swore a feud AYT 1
fib: Destroy this f. or sophistry POPE 118
fickle:
Whatever is f., freckled HOPK:GM 7
Woman is always a f. VIRGIL 61
fickleness: f. of the women I love SHAW 15
fiction:
as an improbable f. SHAK:TWE 48
best thing in f. the English WILDE:O 67
clad in eternall F. CHAPMAN:G 8
form of continuous f. BEVAN 7
if she is to write f. WOOLF:V 9
in a f., in a dream SHAK:HAM 90
make f. of the truth FRY:C 20
Poetry is the supreme f. STEVENS 2
Stranger than f. BYR 234
That is what F. means WILDE:O 90
Truth is stranger than f. PROV 403
fictions: Who sayes that f. onely HERB:G 25
fiddle:
cat and the f. NURS 16
consider your puny little f. BEETH 4
f., sir, and spade SCOTT:W 79
good tune played on an old f. BUTLER:S[2] 19
good tune played on an old f. PROV 378
I the second f. SPRING 2
important beyond all this f. MOORE:M 2
merry love the f. YEATS 6
play on my f. in Dooney YEATS 5
fiddled: f. whisper music ELIOT:TS 53
fiddler:
f.'s old tune MORRIS:W 9
f.'s standing by ANON 9
fiddlers: called for his f. three NURS 46
fiddles: some are fond of f. MASE 8
fiddling:
end up f. with the tea lady HEWITT:LS 1
My master's lost his f. stick NURS 6
Fidel: humiliate F. is to humiliate ALEA 1
Fidele: fair F.'s grassy tomb COLLINS:Will 2
fidgety: f. Phil, He won't sit still HOFFMAN:H 5
field:
a man of the f. BIBLE 55
corner of a foreign f. BROOKE 25
faire felde ful of folke LANGLAND 3
For Vaguery in the F. OSB:J 1
He rush'd into the f. BYR 79
man for the f. and woman TENNY 113
ponder the warm f. OWEN:W 10
single f. which I have look'd WORDS:W 57
single in the f. WORDS:W 79
that lay f. to f. BIBLE 303
What though the f. be lost? MILT 115
fieldmice: f. bawk talk JOYCE:J 35
fields:
back her folded f. JOYCE:J 36
Farewel happy f. MILT 122
f. from Islington to Marybone BLAKE:W 114
f. invested with purpureal WORDS:W 124
f. of barley and of rye TENNY 12
f. of corn where Troy once OSB:J 15
floating f. from the farm THOMAS:D 15
flowerless f. of heaven SWIN 8
holy f. Over whose acres SHAK:HEN.IV[1] 2
I am gone into the f. SHELLEY:PB 161
In f. where roses fade HOUSM 26
in the flowering of His f. TENNY 271
out of olde feldes CHAUC 100
Poetic f. encompass me ADDIS 34
There are no f. of amaranth LANDOR 17
fiend:
F. of the Fell ELIOT:TS 83
F. Walkd up and down MILT 179
foul F. coming over the field BUNYAN 7
frightful f. Doth close COLERIDGE:ST 34
Like a f. hid in a cloud BLAKE:W 75
fierce:
extreams by change more f. MILT 165
F. as ten Furies MILT 167
look not so f. on me MARLOWE 45
No beast so f. SHAK:RIC.III 4
fierceness: fiercenesse makes Errour a fault HERB:G 8
fiercer: now f. by despair MILT 150
fife:
fill the f. MORD 1
That practised on a f. CARROLL 93
tootle-te-tootle, the f. BROWNING:R 164
fifteen:
age of f., the mistress of the Earl WILSON:Harr 1
f.-year-old boy until *they die* ROTH 1
to the maiden of bashful f. SHERIDAN:RB 24
women at f. STEPHENS 7
fifth:
came f. and lost the job JOYCE:J 19
f. column MOLA 1
f. of the people are against KENNEDY:RF 1
fifties: These are the tranquilized *F.* LOWELL:R 5
fifty:
corpulent gentleman of f. HUNT:L 7
f. and I haven't seen a thing SATIE 2
F. springs are little room HOUSM 3
Love is lame at f. years HARDY:T 19
wants a woman of f. to be sweet LAST 1
fifty-fifty: can be no f. Americanism ROOS:T 9
fig:
Peel a f. for your friend PROV 317
We don't care a f. LEAR 16
fig leaves:
rather too fond of f.l. HUX:A 24
sewed f.l. together BIBLE 18
fig-tree: Train up a f. DICKENS 133
fight:
and f. like devils SHAK:HEN.V 24
better to f. for the good TENNY 227
dead who will not f. GREN 1
Die in the lost, lost f. CLOUGH 18
don't want to f., but, by jingo HUNT:GW 1
f. again to save the Party GAIT 1
f. and not to heed LOY 1
f. between two bald men BORGES 5
f. for their country, children SALL 6
f. it out on this line GRANT:US 1
F. the good f. MONSELL 1
F. the good f. of faith BIBLE 550
Good at a f. MOORE:T 24
I have fought a good f. BIBLE 553
I saw a dead man win a f. BALL 8
Ile rise and f. againe BALL 46
Let's f. till six CARROLL 62
live to f. another day PROV 163
lost f. of virtue STEVENSON:RL 41
man may f., and no BURNS:R 62
may f. and not be slain SCOTT:W 65
must f. on to the end HAIG:D 2
never a moment ceased the f. TENNY 283
no circumstances f. for its King ANON 244
no stomach to this f. SHAK:HEN.V 40
nor duty bade me f. YEATS 61
not the f. that crowns us HERR 42
not yet begun to f. JONES:JP 1
Our cock won't f. BEAV 1
Show a little f., girls TOMASET 1
sleep before you f. ARMST:J 1
Stay up and f. DILL 2
that I f. I do not hate YEATS 61
they shall f. against thee BIBLE 335
those that fly, may f. again BUTLER:S[1] 34
thought it wrong to f. BELLOC 42
we shall f. on the beaches CHURCH:W 13
We'll f. and we'll conquer GARRICK 4
who bade me f. had told me EWER 1
youth that must f. and die HOOV 4
fighter:
Am I no a bonny f.? STEVENSON:RL 33
I was ever a f. BROWNING:R 182
fighters:
flak and the nightmare f. JARRELL 3
Writers as a rule don't make f. BERNARD:Jef 1
fighteth: none other that f. for us PRAY 21
fighting:
cheating between two periods of f. BIER 9
f. man shall from the sun GREN 1
finest f. machine the world MONASH 1
imitation of f. SWIFT 23
others didn't feel like f. YELT 2
tend not to die f. ORWELL 15
want of f. was grown rusty BUTLER:S[1] 14
What are we f. for? SERVICE 5
who dies f. has GREN 1
worth the f. for HEMINGWAY 8
fights:
He that f. and runs away PROV 163
knows what he f. for and loves CROMWELL 2
married life is the f. WILDER:T 3
figments: making f. feel HARDY:T 74
figs:
f. grew upon thorn CHESTERTON 1
f. off the tree in the very early DAVID 3
Green bursting f. ARNOLD:M 30
seeing an asse eat f. NASHE 4
figure:
despair of ever making a f. BURNS:R 124
f. in a country church? SWIFT 74
homely face and no f. ANTRIM 3
figures:
his f. seem to breathe FIELDING 9
landscape without f. WHITE:P 13
prove anything by f. CARLYLE:T 38
those thieves, the nine f. DICKENS 206
with the drapery of his f. COLERIDGE:ST 94
files:
Commands the Beauteous f. VAUGHAN:H 4
foremeost f. of time TENNY 86
filial: Can e'er untie the f. band SCOTT:W 11
fill: world can never f. COWP 3
filled: they shall be f. BIBLE 384
filling:
f. his last cavity ANON 144
f. the world, and emptying SCOTT:W 79
film:
bad f. twice as bad GORKY 21
f. should have a beginning GODA 2
film acting: be someone else in front* COLTRANE 1
films:
f. They are too exciting BERR 2
Now I go to f. alone HUDS:L 1
filth: Delights in f. and fouel SPENS 35
filths: F. savour but themselves SHAK:KING L 61
final: This is the f. struggle POTTIER 1
finality:
F. is death STEPHENS 1
F. is not the language of politics DISR:B 60
finals: This is called F. LODGE:D 3
financial: free from all f. dealing HORACE 60
Finchley: Lord F. tried to mend BELLOC 32
find:
by searching f. out God? BIBLE 186
f. it after many days BIBLE 288
f. out what you don't know WELLING 10
I do not search; I f. PICAS 8
To strive, to seek, to f. TENNY 55
We always f. something BECKETT 7
Where does she f. them? PARKER:D 32
wilt thou f. their like agen? SCOTT:W 15
finders: F. keepers PROV 118
finds: he, Who f. himself ARNOLD:M 13
fine:
F. feathers make f. birds PROV 119
F. words butter no parsnips PROV 120
particularly f., strike it out JOHNSON:S 160
quite a *disgrace* to be f. TAYL:Ann 4
fine arts: Considered as One of the F.A. DEQ 9
fineries: rejected those pleasures and f. SOC 7
finery: I hate that Persian f. HORACE 17
fines: Let us have f. for platitudes NEIL 4
finest:
One of the f. women that ever walked WEST:M 3
this is our f. shower OSB:J 10
This was their f. hour CHURCH:W 14
finger:
Better a f. aff RAMS 5
God's f. touch'd him TENNY 169
least pain in our little f. HAZL 35
more goodness in her little f. SWIFT 47
Moving F. writes FITZGER:E 26
Old Harry's got a f. in it ELIOT:G 15
Press'd her cold f. closer KEATS 45
fingernails:
paring his f. JOYCE:J 8
you don't stop biting your f. ROGERS:W 9
fingers:
can't get your f. in those WALLACE:G 1
do dead men's f. call them SHAK:HAM 176
F. were made before forks PROV 121
Five sovereign f. taxed THOMAS:D 8
in the cool stream thy f. ARNOLD:M 23
My f. into glue CARROLL 84
my f. wandered idly PROC 1
Rings on her f. and NURS 58
ten poor idiot f. RANS 2
terrified vague f. YEATS 68

What did my f. do PLATH 1
With f. weary and worn HOOD 19
finish:
have resolved to f. it CHAMBERLAIN:N 5
pace when approaching the f.? DIOG 1
we will f. the job CHURCH:W 21
finished:
finish'd gentleman from top BYR 227
It is f. BIBLE 614
married. Then he's f. GABOR 3
never getting f. HARDY:T 66
tasks are pleasant when they are f. CIC 2
until it be thoroughly f. DRAKE 1
fir: f. trees dark and high HOOD 10
fire:
Adamantin chains and penal F. MILT 110
after the f. a still small voice BIBLE 165
All things, oh priests, are on f. BUDDHA 1
at their hearts the f.'s centre SPEND 2
before the f. of life LANDOR 9
brach may stand by th' f. SHAK:KING L 14
Bring me my Chariot of F. BLAKE:W 98
broad gate and the great f. SHAK:ALL 9
coals of f. upon his head BIBLE 269
Disk of f. somewhat like a Guinea? BLAKE:W 112
dropping-wells of f. TENNY 167
every time She shouted 'F.!' BELLOC 23
faith and f. within us HARDY:T 27
Fell in the f. GRAHAM:H 4
Fight f. with f. PROV 117
F. and fleet and candle-lighte BALL 36
F. and people do in this GREV 3
F. answers f. SHAK:HEN.V 25
F. burn, and cauldron SHAK:MAC 78
F. in the heavens, and f. BRENN 1
f. is quite put out DONNE 71
f. our souls to regale BLAKE:W 73
f. was furry as a bear SITWELL:E 1
f. was in my head YEATS 22
f. which in the heart ARNOLD:M 12
F. – without hatred RIVERA 1
frighted with false f. SHAK:HAM 120
gentle f. flickers under my skin SAP 1
gulfs of liquid f. SHAK:OTH 68
hand dare seize the f.? BLAKE:W 68
heart of the night with f. SWIN 4
heretic that makes the f. SHAK:WIN 6
I am f. and air SHAK:ANT 73
I shall be found by the f. BROWNING:R 90
in a pillar of f. BIBLE 100
knowest Who hast made the F. KIP 36
latter f. shall heat the deep TENNY 2
learning to make f. ATWOOD 2
Leave the f. ashes BROWNING:R 187
little f. is quickly trodden SHAK:HEN.VI[3] 6
Love set his f. in my hands BRENN 3
Love's f. heats water SHAK:SON 65
Luve is ane fervent f. SCOTT:A 1
Many irons in the f. PROV 266
My f.'s extinct ANON 139
no smoke without f. PROV 382
Not till the f. is dying MERED:G 18
our neighbour's house is on f. BURKE:E 49
out of the frying pan into the f. TERT 5
pale martyr in his shirt of f. SMITH:Alex 1
play with f. you get burnt PROV 192
right Promethean f. SHAK:LOV 17
roast with f. BIBLE 96
run a mile to see a f. STEVENSON:RL 15
true Promethean f. SHAK:LOV 14
two irons in the f. BEAUMO 2
warm him at his f. HERB:G 9
will set a house on f. BACON:F[1] 122
world will end in f. FROST:R 6
You must not take for f. SHAK:HAM 32
you play with f. openly ROOS:FD 1
Youk'n hide de fier HARRIS:JC 10
your neighbour's wall catches f. HORACE 90
fire-folk: f. sitting in the air HOPK:GM 9
fire-irons: St Preux never kicked the f. CARLYLE:JW 1
fire station: vast municipal f.s. CHARLES:Prince 4
firearms: f. were strictly forbidden SEARLE 2
firebrand: f. plucked out of the burning BIBLE 356
Fireforefiddle: F., the Fiend of the Fell ELIOT:TS 83
fires:
Great f. flare up FRANCIS:ST 1
Husbands are like f. GABOR 2
Keep the home f. burning FORD:L 1
violent f. soon burn out SHAK:RIC.II 16
fireside:
glass of wine by his own f. SHERIDAN:RB 41
make a happy f. clime BURNS:R 73
Sit by the f. with Sorrow SHELLEY:PB 161
to leave their own f. AUSTEN 43
winter talk by the f. BACON:F[1] 94
firm: we're a f. GEO VI 2
firmament:
f. sheweth his handywork BIBLE 203
spacious f. on high ADDIS 39
firmness: *Commodity, F., and Delight* WOTTON 6
first:
better to be f. with an ugly woman BUCK 1
ever be done for the f. time CORNFORD:FM 1
f. by whom the new POPE 17
F. come, f. served PROV 122
F. impressions are the most lasting PROV 124
f. in war, f. in peace LEE:Hen 1
f. shall be last BIBLE 424
f. step is the hardest PROV 125
F. things f. PROV 126
he'd have been here f. CARROLL 77
killed by the clash of the F. HARDY:T 6
navy always travels f. class FISHER:JA 3
rather be the f. man here CAES:GJ 6
there is no last nor f. BROWNING:R 13
undoubted title to the f. SWIFT 3
what to put f. PASC 3
first-aid: ideas of f. stopped short WODE 2
first-rate:
powers of a f. man BAGE 2
test of a f. work BENNETT:Ar 8
firstborn:
against all the first-born of Egypt SHAK:AS 27
smite all the f. in the land BIBLE 97
fish:
anyway the f. were biting ION 1
bonnie f. and halesome farin' NAIRNE 2
buttercups fried with f. LEAR 27
dumber and deafer than a f. YEATS 33
F. and guests smell in three PROV 127
F. die belly-upward GIDE 3
F. fuck in it FIELDS 5
f. in the sea better than any PROV 377
F. is plentiful and cheap LEAR 8
F. not with this SHAK:MERC 6
F. out of water SHADWE 3
F. say, they have their stream BROOKE 16
f. with the worm that SHAK:HAM 154
half f. and half women LLOSA 1
husband, is a poor f. DENNIS:N 1
I sent a message to the f. CARROLL 71
in the belly of the f. BIBLE 359
It's no f. ye're buying SCOTT:W 72
kept the poor f. alive CLAYTON 1
like a f. needs a bicycle STEINEM 4
like f. in a private pond SAIK 2
no more land, say f. BROOKE 18
rivers, and f. and fishing WALT 14
shortage of coal and f. at the same BEVAN 1
smell of f. there is sometimes KILV 2
so free as a f. RUSKIN 12
There's a f. that *talks* DE LA M 11
This is a pretty kettle of f. MARY QUEEN CON 2
white wine came up with the f. MANK 3
word bites like a f. SPEND 12
fish-ball: give bread with one f. LANE 1
fish-knives: Phone for the f. BETJ 26
fishbone: monument sticks like a f. LOWELL:R 12
fished: He f. by obstinate isles POUND 26
fishers:
F. of men BIBLE 383
Three f. went sailing KINGSLEY:C 15
fishes:
f. first to shipping did DRYD 7
F., that tipple in the deep LOVELACE 4
looked around at the little f. LONG 1
marvel how the f. live SHAK:PER 4
So are the f. CHURCH:W 19
uncommunicating muteness of f. LAMB:Ch 15
welcomes little f. in CARROLL 4
When f. flew CHESTERTON 1
fishified: flesh, how art thou f. SHAK:ROM 21
fishing:
f. in the dull canal ELIOT:TS 43
float f. I can only compare JOHNSON:S 270
Fly f. may be a very pleasant JOHNSON:S 270
stream I go a-f. in THOREAU 14
when he goes a-f. WALT 3
fishmen: Where f. lounge at noon ELIOT:TS 48
fishmonger:
she was a f. ANON 24
you are a f. SHAK:HAM 71
fishpond: great f. (the sea) DEK 4
fishy:
proof that something's f. BRECHT 9
something f. about the French COWARD 7
fist:
His withered f. still knocking DORSET 1
shake hands with a clenched f. GAND:I 1
fists: f. in my torn pockets RIMB 2
fit:
dozen, and that they all f. WILDE:O 46
It isn't f. for humans now BETJ 6
only the F. survive SERVICE 1
seldom f. so exactly SMITH:Syd[1] 8
when the f. was on him SHAK:JUL 9
Why then I'll f. you KYD 6
fitchew: f. nor the soiled horse SHAK:KING L 68
fitness: no test of f. for it is ever SHAW 124
fits: cope him in these sullen f. SHAK:AS 14
fittest:
Survival of the F. DARW:C 2
survival of the f. implies multiplication SPENCER:H 7
fitting: It is right and f. MASS 13
Fitzgerald:
F. strung them LOWELL:JR 7
shall hoarse F. bawl BYR 6
five-and-twenty: reputation of f. DRYD 9
five-pound note:
gen'l'm'n said to the fi' pun' n. DICKENS 22
get a f. n. as one got a light JAMES:H 12
Wrapped up in a f.n. LEAR 18
fizz: sheer necessity of f. BELLOC 10
flag:
death's pale f. SHAK:ROM 43
f. has braved, a thousand CAMPBELL:T 7
f. of all the free CHESTERTON 20
f. that makes you free WORK 1
keep the red f. flying CONNELL 1
must be the f. of my disposition WHITMAN 4
old f. flyin' NEWBOLT 6
raised their f. against a power WEBSTER:D 4
spare your country's f. WHITTIER 5
to the f. be true CORY 4
We shall not f. or fail CHURCH:W 13
flag-flapper: Jelly-bellied f. KIP 17
flagons: Stay me with f. BIBLE 294
flair: disasters, it was done with f. HAYD 3
flak: I woke to black f. JARRELL 3
flakes: f. have lost their way HARDY:T 45
flame:
by adding fuel to the f.? MILT 294
Chloe is my real f. PRIOR 6
clasped the f. into my heart BRENN 3
Fan the sinking f. of hilarity DICKENS 93
feed his sacred f. COLERIDGE:ST 50
f. creeps in at every hole PEELE 3
f. of incandescent terror ELIOT:TS 107
f. which does not go out RENOIR:PA 1
Kindled a f. I still deplore GARRICK 5
like one burning f. TENNY 19
man's sensuous f. of life LAWR:DH 2
spark of that ancient f. VIRGIL 57
Still plays about the f. GAY 10
this hard, gemlike f. PATER 4
flamens: Here lyes two *F.* CAREW:T 1
flames:
f. flicker at time's own root WRIGHT:J 6
from those f. No light MILT 111
his f. must waste away CAREW:T 2
thou King of f. CHAPMAN:G 4
Went by her like thin f. ROSSET:DG 4
With rich f. BROWNE:T 49
Flanders:
armies swore terribly in F. STERNE 18
brought him a F. mare HENRY VIII 2
F. fields the poppies blow MCCRAE 1
prodigious armies we had in F. STERNE 16
flannel: Get her a f. waistcoat GASK 3

flannelled: f. fools at the wicket KIP 101
flap-dragon: easier swallowed than a f. SHAK:LOV 19
flare: f. was up in the gym BETJ 11
flash:
f. cut him, and he lies ANON 130
sparkles that f. from their eyes DRYD 112
Flashman: F. was a formidable enemy HUGHES:Th 1
flask: at about forty cents a f. LEACOCK 3
flat:
life extremely f. GILB:WS 58
Very f., Norfolk COWARD 3
flats: f. are rather flatter SLESS 7
flatter:
before you f. a man JOHNSON:S 267
f. beauty's ignorant ear YEATS 40
f. those we scarcely know WILCOX 1
Regard me as I do not f. SHAK:COR 8
flattered:
being then most f. SHAK:JUL 25
feared nor f. any flesh DOUGLAS:J 1
He that loves to be f. SHAK:TIM 2
More people are f. into virtue SURT 13
flatterer:
brave beast is no f. JONS 55
every f. lives at the expense FONTAINE 4
Self-love is the greatest f. LA ROCHE 3
flatterers: I tell him he hates f. SHAK:JUL 25
flattering:
f. some Men to endure them HALIF 12
f. unction to your soul SHAK:HAM 145
talent of f. with delicacy AUSTEN 17
you think him worth f. SHAW 77
flatters: lie that f. I abhor COWP 43
flattery:
benefit-club for mutual f. COLERIDGE:ST 5
Everyone likes f. DISR:B 89
feyned flaterye and japes CHAUC 32
F. wearis ane furrit gown DUNB 6
gained by every sort of f. CHESTERFIELD 26
is paid with f. JOHNSON:S 15
sincerest form of f. COLTON 3
sincerest form of f. PROV 196
suppose f. hurts no one STEVENSON:A 8
This is no f. SHAK:AS 11
to tout for f. COLLINS:JC 1
your f. is worth his having JOHNSON:S 267
Flaubert: true Penelope was F. POUND 26
flaunt: if you've got it, f. it BROOKS:M 1
flautists: f. are most obviously the ones JENN:P 1
flaw: absence of f. in beauty ELLIS:H 6
flayed: saw a woman f. SWIFT 7
flaying: f. would be fair HOUSM 48
flea:
clog the foot of a f. SHAK:TWE 45
English literature's performing f. O'CAS 8
f. hath smaller fleas SWIFT 69
f. in his ear ARMIN 1
guerilla fights the war of the f. TABER 1
honour the very f. of his dog JONS 4
precedency between a louse and a f. JOHNSON:S 235
with a f. in's ear FLETCH:J 17
fleas:
ever dog that praised his f.? YEATS 32
F. know not whether LANDOR 15
f. that tease in the High BELLOC 38
Great f. have little f. MORGAN:A 1
fled:
f. away into the storm KEATS 77
f. Him, down the nights THOMP:F 7
flee:
f. from the wrath to come? BIBLE 378
f., howling in terror POUND 24
They f. from me WYATT 3
wicked f. when no man pursueth BIBLE 274
fleece: or to f. the blacks CAMPBELL:R 1
fleet:
All in the Downs the f. GAY 37
as we took care of our f. ADDIS 22
Fire and f. and candle-lighte BALL 36
F. the time carelessly SHAK:AS 1
F.'s lit up WOODRO 1
Spanish f. thou *canst* not see SHERIDAN:RB 35
speed toward the Japanese f. HALS:WF 1
Fleet Street: who can be dull in F.S. LAMB:Ch 35
flesh:
All f. is grass BIBLE 321
all f. shall see it together BIBLE 320
but the f. is weak BIBLE 433
but the world, the f., and the devil MURRAY:D 1
chilled dough of his f. HARRISON 1
Could not all this f. SHAK:HEN.IV[1] 91
creator of the f. hangs in the f. VENAN 2
delicate white human f. FIELDING 24
f., alas, is sad MALLAR 2
F. and Blood can't bear it BYROM 3
f. and blood so cheap HOOD 21
f., how art thou fishified SHAK:ROM 21
f. is bruckle DUNB 8
f. makes all BURGESS:A 2
f. of my f. BIBLE 14
going the way of all f. WEBSTER:J 2
gone the way of all f. CONG 68
Leave the f. to the fate BROWNING:R 148
make your f. creep DICKENS 9
man and wife one f. CONG 17
men are f. and blood SHAK:JUL 34
more f. than another man SHAK:HEN.IV[1] 74
my f. longeth for thee BIBLE 218
my gross f. sinks SHAK:RIC.II 47
not against f. and blood BIBLE 538
painful Covenants of f. HEAN 6
pound of f. which I demand SHAK:MERC 42
sweeter the f. PROV 279
take off my f. and sit SMITH:Syd[1] 27
that I am is f. and spirit AUR 1
they shall be one f. BIBLE 15
thorn in the f. BIBLE 530
too solid f. would melt SHAK:HAM 21
vague errors of the f. THOMAS:RS 3
we sat by the f. pots BIBLE 102
Why a little curtain of f. BLAKE:W 30
Word was made f. BIBLE 473
WORD WAS MADE F. MASS 23
world, the f., and the devil PRAY 33
fleshed: flesh'd Thy maiden sword SHAK:HEN.IV[1] 93
flibbertigibbet: foul fiend F. SHAK:KING L 47
flicks: f. through every book HANDKE 1
flies:
as f. hanging in heat GUNN:T 1
As f. to wanton boys SHAK:KING L 59
f. through the air with LEYB 1
may catch small f. SWIFT 10
more f. with a spoonful of honey HENRI 6
murmurous haunt of f. KEATS 93
small f. were caught BACON:F[1] 30
time's f. SHAK:TIM 9
flight:
honest idiocy of f. GRAVES:R 7
on tip-toe for a f. KEATS 7
Swift be thine approaching f. SHELLEY:PB 148
Swift be thy f. SHELLEY:PB 145
flights: builders have very high f. MARLBOR:S 1
fling: I'll have a f. FLETCH:J 18
flirt: f. with their own husbands WILDE:O 84
flirtation:
Merely innocent f. BYR 226
most significant word *f.* CHESTERFIELD 33
float: best fits a little F. HERR 37
flock:
Fed the same f. MILT 44
feed his f. like a shepherd BIBLE 322
f. in woolly fold KEATS 61
flocks: My f. feed not BARNF 4
Flodden: Of F.'s fatal field SCOTT:W 33
flog: f. the rank and file ARNOLD:T 1
flogged: f. oftener than any human TROLL 25
flogging:
habit of f. me constantly TROLL 26
There is now less f. JOHNSON:S 176
flood:
After us the f. POMPA 1
f. could not wash away CONG 29
giant race before the f. DRYD 130
Let it roll on full f. CHURCH:W 17
taken at the f. SHAK:JUL 76
thorough f., thorough fire SHAK:MID 12
flooded: Streets f. Please advise BENCH 4
floodgate: F. of the deeper heart FLECKN 1
floods:
Beside the haystack in the f.? MORRIS:W 1
moon, the governess of f. SHAK:MID 16
She quells the f. below CAMPBELL:T 8
floor:
I could f. them all DISR:B 48
nicely sanded f. GOLDS 31
oiled his way around the f. LERN 4
floors: across the f. of silent seas ELIOT:TS 7
flop: f. in favour of your husband DICKENS 201
Flopsy: F., Mopsy, Cottontail POTTER:B 1
Flora: Tasting of F. KEATS 93
Florence:
lily of F. blossoming LONGFEL 27
Rode past fair F. KEATS 29
Flores: F. in the Azores TENNY 281
Florrie: not Flo but always F. HARRISON 1
flotsam: f. from a former passion JENN:E 1
flour:
There's weevils in the f. HEWETT 4
Who ground the f. for bread KEES 1
flourisheth:
flower of the field, so he f. BIBLE 232
She florysheth new and new SKEL:J 6
flout: F. 'em and scout 'em SHAK:TEM 22
flow:
could I f. like thee DENH 1
F. gently, sweet Afton BURNS:R 72
flower:
Beauty is but a f. NASHE 1
Both in the f. of their youth VIRGIL 14
constellated f. that never sets SHELLEY:PB 89
creep from f. to f. SHELLEY:PB 12
every f. that sad embroidery MILT 55
fairnes bot and faiding flour HENRYS 4
f. in his hand when he awoke COLERIDGE:ST 71
f. of light JONS 48
f. secretly springs up CATUL 15
F. that once hath blown FITZGER:E 16
f. that smiles to-day SHELLEY:PB 137
flow'r with base infection SHAK:SON 41
God took our flour ANON 126
green fuse drives the f. THOMAS:D 4
Heaven in a Wild F. BLAKE:W 82
little western f. SHAK:MID 18
look like th'innocent f. SHAK:MAC 21
meanest f. that blows can give WORDS:W 69
no stronger than a f.? SHAK:SON 29
of glory in the f. WORDS:W 66
one f. in all this arid SASS 19
same f. that smiles today HERR 26
seeing the f. fade away JOHNSON:S 199
she has lost her chaste f. CATUL 15
single f. could impress you KAW 1
summer's flow'r is to the summer sweet SHAK:SON 41
sweet will be the f. COWP 11
white f. of a blameless life TENNY 235
flower-pots: Water your damned f. BROWNING:R 36
flower show: just miss the prizes at the f.s. BRONO 2
flowering:
f. in a lonely word TENNY 290
in the f. of His fields TENNY 271
flowers:
All sorts of f. the which SPENS 10
break into foam of f. SWIN 40
bunch of other men's f. MONTAIGNE 21
Earth laughs in f. EMER 94
floures gynnen for to sprynge CHAUC 94
Flours of all hue MILT 189
f. and fruits of love BYR 241
f. appear on the earth BIBLE 295
f. are wide-awake MCAULEY 3
f. but fading seen PEELE 2
F. I leave you on the grass TESCH 1
F. in the garden STEVENSON:RL 59
f. of the forest are a' wade COCKBURN:A 1
F. of the Forest are a' wede ELLIOT:J 1
f. that bloom in the spring GILB:WS 79
f. that grow between LONGFEL 39
forgets the f. at his feet BENTH 3
Gather the f., but MARV 29
gathered f. are dead FLECKER 14
got me f. to straw HERB:G 19
Here's flow'rs for you SHAK:WIN 19
hush'd, cool-rooted f. KEATS 86
In Brazil they throw f. DIET 4
it won't be f. AUD 27
Larded with sweet f. SHAK:HAM 160

Letting a hundred f. blossom MAO 2
No f., by request AINGER:C 1
odiferous f. of fancy SHAK:LOV 12
showers bring forth May f. PROV 268
spring May f. TUSS 1
thise floures white and rede CHAUC 95
time did becken to the f. HERB:G 37
Tomorrow is all like sweet f. BURGESS:A 1
too soon for f. DE LA M 23
Where have all the f. gone? SEEG 1
where Proserpin gathering flours MILT 191
flowery:
f. way that leads SHAK:ALL 9
walk your f. way GILB:WS 33
flown: find they have f. away? YEATS 51
flowret: meanest f. of the vale GRAY:T 39
fluffy: f., just f., with no brains HERB:AP 5
flush: pint and f. two gallons PHILIP 2
flushed: F. and confident IBS 13
flushing: constant sound of f. BETJ 198
flushpots: f. of Euston JOYCE:J 32
flute:
Blows out his brains upon the f. BROWNING:R 208
many a f. of Arcady TENNY 140
soft complaining f. DRYD 94
flutes:
as the sound of lyres and f. PATER 2
F. and soft Recorders MILT 132
to the tune of f. kept stroke SHAK:ANT 25
fluttered: which f. on the grate COLERIDGE:ST 8
fluttering: F. and dancing in the breeze WORDS:W 120
flutters: That f. least is longest on COWP 85
fly:
Angels can f. because CHESTERTON 43
as pigs have to f. CARROLL 26
blue f. sung in the pane TENNY 5
curious, thirsty f. OLD 1
F. away, Peter NURS 81
f. sat upon the axletree BACON:F[1] 120
f., Sir, may sting a stately JOHNSON:S 96
f. that sips treacle GAY 24
f. to India for gold MARLOWE 30
hatchet to remove a f. PROV 75
I heard a F. buzz DICKIN:E 7
I will f. to thee KEATS 93
If God had intended us to f. FLAND 3
long-legged f. upon the stream YEATS 117
Man is not a f. POPE 85
Pigs might f. PROV 320
rainbow smashing a dry f. LOWELL:R 15
said a spider to a f. HOWITT 1
they ever f. by twilight BACON:F[1] 111
those that f., may fight again BUTLER:S[1] 34
Thou shalt f. CLEESE 1
to f. is safe COWP 70
with the f. in his hand STERNE 14
fly fishing: F.f. may be a very pleasant JOHNSON:S 270
fly-fishing: for winter f. it is as useful WALT 1
flyer: sober and no high f. PEPYS 12
flying:
art of f. straight GRAVES:R 7
shouldn't have a f. start WILSON:Harold 11
flying-fishes: Where the flyin'-fishes play KIP 59
flying-fox: f. trapped on the cruel WRIGHT:J 8
foal: F. of an oppressed race COLERIDGE:ST 1
foam:
dank with f. KINGSLEY:C 13
f. Of perilous seas KEATS 93
Like the f. on the river SCOTT:W 39
morning rolls them in the f. SLESS 6
satyrs Copulate in the f. YEATS 119
through sheets of f. ARNOLD:M 30
white f. flew COLERIDGE:ST 18
foe:
breathed in the face of the f. BYR 40
erect and manly f. CANN 6
first f. in the field LOVELACE 7
His f. was folly HOPE:An 8
one worthy man my f. POPE 124
open f. may prove a curse GAY 44
The f.! they come BYR 80
To match another f. CAMPBELL:T 7
who never made a f. TENNY 254
wish my deadly f., no worse BRET 1
foeman: f. bares his steel GILB:WS 25
foemen: f. worthy of their steel SCOTT:W 42
foes:
if his f. pursue him still SHAK:POET 12
judge of a man by his f. CONRAD 3
foetus: expeditious extraction of the f. STERNE 16
fog:
brown f. of a winter dawn ELIOT:TS 37
feel the f. in my throat BROWNING:R 181
f. comes on little cat feet SANDBURG 1
f. of the good man's mind BROWNING:R 63
Light rinses f. from colours KAV 4
London particular . . . A f. DICKENS 168
yellow f. that rubs its back ELIOT:TS 4
fogs: f. prevail upon the day DRYD 63
foil: shining from shook f. HOPK:GM 5
fold: f. stands empty SHAK:MID 15
folds: lull the distant f. GRAY:T 16
foliage: sapless f. of the ocean SHELLEY:PB 43
Folies-Bergère: F. and looks at the audience STOCKWOOD 1
folio: for whole volumes in f. SHAK:LOV 3
folios: mighty f. first CRAB 10
folk:
All f. literature YEATS 128
nowt so queer as f. PROV 383
folk-dancing: except incest and f. BAX 1
folks:
my f. were growing old STEVENSON:RL 62
old f. at home FOST:SC 4
some f. rail against other f. FIELDING 15
follies:
f. as the special evidences TROLL 8
f. of the town crept slowly GOLDS 65
f. of the wise JOHNSON:S 69
f. which a man regrets ROWL:H 3
paint the vices and f. CONG 14
follow:
expect to see when I f. DOYLE:AC 32
f. someone who puts you right AUR 12
F. the Gleam TENNY 298
F. up! F. up! F. up! BOWEN:EE 1
I f. but myself SHAK:OTH 2
Lead, and I f. TENNY 240
made to f. a course of action CONF 7
must f. them; I am their leader LAW 2
Pay, pack, and f. BURTON:Ri 1
followed:
first he folwed it hymselve CHAUC 28
they f. dancing BROWNING:R 29
following:
luxury of f. neither UST 7
should be f. them LEDRU 1
follows: yet she f. LONGFEL 22
folly:
Accounted dangerous f. SHAK:MAC 88
age from f. could not give SHAK:ANT 18
f., doctor-like SHAK:SON 30
f. without father bred MILT 77
f.'s all they've taught me MOORE:T 15
F.'s at full length CHESTERFIELD 32
fool according to his f. BIBLE 270
fool returneth to his f. BIBLE 271
greatest f. of all MOLIERE 14
harmlesse follie of the time HERR 23
He knew human f. AUD 10
His foe was f. HOPE:An 8
knavery and f. to excuse CHURCH:C 9
lovely woman stoops to f. ELIOT:TS 47
lovely woman stoops to f. GOLDS 18
Mix a little f. with your plans HORACE 59
odd and unworthy piece of f. BROWNE:T 28
persist in his f. he would become BLAKE:W 39
shoot f. as it flies POPE 79
slightest f. That ever love SHAK:AS 22
'Tis f. to be wise GRAY:T 8
uses his f. like a stalking-horse SHAK:AS 72
usually ends in f. COLERIDGE:ST 89
whirl'd into f. and vice TENNY 206
food:
brightest where f. is best PROV 227
Continent people have good f. MIKES 1
converting solar energy into f. STENHO 1
fake f. under plastic trees SKY 1
f. a tragedy POWELL:A 2
F. for powder SHAK:HEN.IV[1] 80
F. is an important part LEB 2
F. will Win the War HOOV 5
is better f. in heaven LLEW 1
Music is the f. of love PROV 278
nourishing, and wholesome f. SWIFT 37
sincerer than the love of f. SHAW 32
tinned f. is a deadlier weapon ORWELL 4
wholsom f. is caught without a net BLAKE:W 37
Why has he no f.? GEL 2
food poisoning: F.p. . . . probably poses a greater MOHL 1
fool:
A motley f. SHAK:AS 28
Answer a f. according BIBLE 270
Any f. can make a rule THOREAU 27
ass, without being a f. SURT 19
at his end shall be a f. BIBLE 341
be a damn'd f. if they weren't THOMAS:D 38
be a f. POPE 91
be a f. than to be dead STEVENSON:RL 16
being a f. among knaves SWIFT 8
Better a witty f. SHAK:TWE 8
Better be a f. than a knave PROV 38
brains enough to make a f. STEVENSON:RL 17
Call me not f. till heaven SHAK:AS 28
can f. too many of the people THURB 13
cannot f. all of the people LINC 24
clever woman to manage a f. KIP 1
convinced that his mother was a f. WEST:R 10
Dost thou call me f. SHAK:KING L 16
every F. is not a Poet POPE 74
excess of wisdom is made a f. EMER 34
first wisdom, to be f. no more HORACE 75
f. all of the people all of ADAMS:FP 1
f. and his money are soon PROV 128
f. and his money be soon TUSS 5
f. at forty is a f. indeed PROV 129
f. at forty is a f. indeed YOUNG:E 3
f. in the eye of the world CONG 30
f. . . . is a man who never tried DARW:E 2
f. is happy that he POPE 96
f. me to the top of my bent SHAK:HAM 127
f. must now and then COWP 23
f. of love HAZL 31
f. returneth to his folly BIBLE 271
f. sees not the same tree BLAKE:W 35
f. there was and he made KIP 94
f. to make me merry SHAK:AS 54
f. will always find a greater f. BOIL 8
greatest f. may ask more COLTON 4
haste of a F. is the slowest thing SHADWE 2
heart of the f. MILT 286
hes become the Golden F. BLAKE:W 104
I am fortune's f. SHAK:ROM 28
I have played the f. BIBLE 150
I met a f. i' th' forest SHAK:AS 28
intermittent f., full of lucid CERV 18
knowledgeable f. is more foolish MOLIERE 30
longer I live the more f. ANON 119
man suspects himself a F. YOUNG:E 11
more of the f. than of the wise BACON:F[1] 40
no f. like an old f. PROV 380
not so easy to f. little girls THURB 5
One f. . . . in every married FIELDING 35
played the F. in her Service STEELE 2
Send a f. to the market PROV 344
silent and be thought a f. LINC 26
so is the laughter of the f. BIBLE 283
So true a f. is love SHAK:SON 22
this your all-licens'd f. SHAK:KING L 17
twenty minutes to make a f. of him ROWL:H 2
who will not laugh is a f. SANT 9
wisest f. in Christendom HENRI 5
worm at one end and a f. at JOHNSON:S 270
foolish:
disguises from the f. their lack BIER 4
exempt from saying a f. STERNE 33
f. because I am facetious SMITH:Syd[1] 15
f. fond old man SHAK:KING L 77
f. thing was but a toy SHAK:TWE 59
f. when he had not a pen JOHNSON:S 216
most f. is the most clever YEV 2
never said a f. thing ROCHES 13
not denyin' the women are f. ELIOT:G 13
foolishest: f. act a wise man commits BROWNE:T 28
foolishness: not the one who commits an act of f. GRACIAN 3
fools:
all the f. in town on our side? TWAIN 14
coxcombs Nature meant but f. POPE 7

she f. the stars KEATS 30
forgotten:
always a f. thing CHESTERTON 6
at least have f. it MATT 1
f. even by God BROWNING:R 5
f. man at the bottom ROOS:FD 3
f. nothing and learnt nothing DUMO 1
f. what I have done for him? LOUIS XIV 4
He hath not f. my age SOUTHEY 6
I am all f. SHAK:ANT 19
I have not f. much MAYN 1
Long absent, soon f. PROV 245
man about whom all is f. BENTLEY:N 1
Nobody is f. DISR:B 93
Soon learnt, soon f. PROV 349
fork:
Every f. like a white web-foot HARDY:T 45
odd F. in Being's Road DICKIN:E 9
forks:
Fingers were made before f. PROV 121
pursued it with f. and hope CARROLL 91
their knives and f. like dumb-bells MACNEICE 16
forlorn:
F.! the very word KEATS 93
I wait f. ARNOLD:M 35
form:
ev'ry respect but the f. GAY 25
f. rebellious to work GAUT 1
F. remains WORDS:W 128
F., Riflemen F. TENNY 229
like definite f. in what my eyes STEVENSON:RL 3
mould of f. SHAK:HAM 104
no f. nor comeliness BIBLE 327
'significant f.' was f. behind which BELL:C 1
formed: f., as notes of music SHELLEY:PB 129
forms: measured f., are everything MELV 7
fornication:
F.: but that was in another MARLOWE 25
From f., and all other PRAY 33
forsaken:
Most choice, f. SHAK:KING L 6
why hast thou f. me? BIBLE 437
fort: Hold the f. BLISS 1
Fortescue: Was Charles Augustus F. BELLOC 12
forth: Come f., Lazarus JOYCE:J 19
fortissimo: At last, *f.!* MAHL 1
fortitude: What f. the Soul contains DICKIN:E 19
fortress: This f. built by Nature SHAK:RIC.II 17
fortunate: better to be f. than wise WEBSTER:J 13
fortune:
Blind F. still Bestows her gifts JONS 7
Crool Forchin's dirty left DENNIS:CJ 1
Diligence is the mother of good f. CERV 23
Disdaining F. SHAK:MAC 3
do f. what she can DRAYT 3
F. always favours fools GAY 52
F. and hire flae wheel CHAUC 40
f. contributes to Beauty ASQU:M 1
F. favours fools PROV 134
F. favours the brave TEREN 8
F. helps those who dare VIRGIL 81
F. ... is friendly to the young MACHIA 8
F. is full of fresh variety BARNF 1
f. is in his own hands BACON:F[1] 63
F. is merry SHAK:JUL 61
f. of the house stands firm VIRGIL 32
F., that favours fools JONS 24
F.'s a right whore WEBSTER:J 3
given hostages to f. BACON:F[1] 80
happily upon a plentiful f. JOHNSON:S 116
he shall see F. BACON:F[1] 64
Health and high f. till we meet SCOTT:W 51
he's but F.'s knave SHAK:ANT 62
how does f. banter us BOLI 6
I am f.'s fool SHAK:ROM 28
I can enjoy her while* DRYD 77
Ill f. seldom comes alone DRYD 120
In the secret parts of F.? SHAK:HAM 76
leads on to f. SHAK:JUL 76
Maker of his own F. STEELE 6
mock the good housewife F. SHAK:AS 2
My face is my f. NURS 84
no woman ... beauty without a f. FARQ 13
not so many men of large f. AUSTEN 31
not the method of making a f. GRAY:T 37
On f.'s cap we are not SHAK:HAM 76
people of f. may naturally indulge ELIOT:G 3
possession of a good f. AUSTEN 12
share in the good f. of the mighty BRECHT 18
sphear of f. raises MILT 284
sustain good f. than bad LA ROCHE 5
Thus trails our f. in MARLOWE 21
to F. and to Fame unknown GRAY:T 26
what's one woman's f. HARDY:T 75
when we are sick in f. SHAK:KING L 9
You fools of f. SHAK:TIM 9
fortunes:
content with his f. fit SHAK:KING L 39
it troubleth men's f. BACON:F[1] 79
you'll ne'er mend your f. MORE:H 4
forty:
bed for a year when he is f. SHAW 137
Fat, fair and f. O'KEEFFE:J 3
Fat, fair, and f. SCOTT:W 86
fool at f. YOUNG:E 3
fool at f. is a fool indeed PROV 129
From f. to fifty a man PINE 2
girls we loved Are over f. CAMPBELL:G 2
Life begins at F. PITK 1
Life begins at f. PROV 237
Life begins at f. TUCK 4
look young till f. DRYD 9
man over f. is a scoundrel SHAW 67
Pushing f.? She's clinging COMPT 13
than to be f. years old HOLMES:OW 17
turning f. and taking my time LLOYD:H 1
forward:
Great Leap F. MAO 3
looking f. to the past OSB:J 5
one step f., two steps LENIN 1
Take a step f., lads CHILDERS 2
those behind cried 'F.!' MACAULAY:TB 50
forwards: it must be lived f. KIERK 1
Foss: Old F. is the name of his cat LEAR 6
Foster: Doctor F. went to Gloucester NURS 10
foster-child: Thou f. of silence KEATS 92
fostered: F. alike by beauty WORDS:W 143
fou:
amna' f. sae muckle as tired MACDIAR 4
between a f. man and a fasting SCOTT:W 88
f., we're sometimes capernoity FERGUSS:R 1
getting f. and unco happy BURNS:R 83
I was na f. BURNS:R 15
kind to f. folk and bairns PROV 150
some are f. o' love divine BURNS:R 50
They had been f. for weeks BURNS:R 85
we're nae that f. BURNS:R 76
fought:
As if men f. upon the earth SCOTT:W 28
better to have f. and lost CLOUGH 9
f. a long hour by Shrewsbury SHAK:HEN.IV[1] 94
f. for nothing – and I won HOT 2
f. for Queen and Faith TENNY 286
F. was this noble fray DRAYT 7
f. with us upon Saint Crispin's SHAK:HEN.V 40
I have f. a good fight BIBLE 553
what they f. each other for SOUTHEY 3
Women had always f. for men PANK:E 5
foul:
as f. As Vulcan's stithy SHAK:HAM 109
f. and most unnatural murder SHAK:HAM 43
f. deed shall smell SHAK:JUL 44
F. deeds will rise SHAK:HAM 27
Murder most f. SHAK:HAM 44
thank the gods I am f. SHAK:AS 50
foul-mouthed: rather a f. nation HAZL 20
found:
Hast thou f. me BIBLE 166
have it f. out by accident LAMB:Ch 28
man who has f. himself out BARRIE 14
someone else who f. you like this RICHELIEU:A-E 1
sooner or later, to be f. out WILDE:O 71
foundation:
end of our f. is BACON:F[1] 124
Good order is the f. BURKE:E 68
foundations:
when earth's f. fled HOUSM 37
when I laid the f. of the earth? BIBLE 192
fount: Slow, slow, fresh f. JONS 8
fountain:
at the f.'s sliding foot MARV 20
Back to the burning f. SHELLEY:PB 119
f. fill'd with blood COWP 5
f. from the which my current SHAK:OTH 52
f. momently was forced COLERIDGE:ST 63
f. of all goodness PRAY 25
f. of honour BAGE 7
f. of the water of life BIBLE 585
f. overflows BLAKE:W 44
healing f. start AUD 43
like a f. troubled SHAK:TAM 14
midst of the f. of delights rises LUCRET 11
perpetual f. of good sense DRYD 146
fountains:
and silver f. mud SHAK:SON 17
f. fraught with tears KYD 2
f. of divine philosophy SHELLEY:PB 7
large streams from little f. EVER 1
no more, sad f. ANON 47
Where Afric's sunny f. HEB 2
whose f. are within COLERIDGE:ST 55
founts: White f. falling CHESTERTON 18
four:
Don't be a gang of f. MAO 8
F. things greater than all KIP 40
4-H Club: formed their own 4-H C. AGNEW 2
four-square: stood f. to all the winds TENNY 190
fourth:
has become a f. estate MACAULAY:TB 9
mother needed a f. at meals LILL 1
there sat a *F. Estate* CARLYLE:T 49
fowl:
broiled f. and mushrooms DICKENS 6
tame villatic F. MILT 297
You elegant f. LEAR 19
fowls:
all small fowlys singis on DOUGLAS:G 1
here the foules synge CHAUC 94
fox:
attributes of the f. and the lion MACHIA 7
f. came home MASE 15
f. from his lair in the GRAVES:JW 1
f. knows many things ARCHIL 1
f. obscene to gaping POPE 32
gentleman galloping after a f. WILDE:O 55
Russell the f. stirte up CHAUC 65
set a f. to watching the chickens TRU 2
that I loves the f. less SURT 7
fox-hunter: Tell me a man's a f. SURT 5
foxes:
f. have a sincere interest ELIOT:G 24
f. stunk and litter'd GRAY:T 40
many f. grow grey FRANKLIN:B 12
Take us the f. BIBLE 296
foxlike: f. in the vine TENNY 118
fragrance: f. from the herb at your feet TROLL 14
frailest: Why choose you the f. SHELLEY:PB 160
frailty:
f. of the mind CONG 48
F., thy name is woman SHAK:HAM 21
more flesh ... therefore more f. SHAK:HEN.IV[1] 74
noblest f. of the mind DRYD 3
frame:
all the Human F. requires BELLOC 17
shakes this fragile F. HARDY:T 12
framed: have it f. and glazed WALP:H 12
frames: finest collection of f. DAVY 1
France:
all roads lead to F. THOMAS:E 7
between F. and England is – the sea JERROLD 4
Fair blows the wind for F. MARLOWE 27
Fair stood the wind for F. DRAYT 6
F., famed in all great ARNOLD:M 7
F. has more need of me NAPO I 5
F. is a country where the money WILDER:B 2
F. is adequately secured ASQU:HH 2
F., mother of arts DU BEL 1
F. put agents into New Zealand LANGE 1
F. was long a despotism CARLYLE:T 22
F. will say that I am a German EINS 9
full pride of F. SHAK:HEN.V 5
nearer is to F. CARROLL 33
One day, F. will thank me ZOLA 5
since I saw the queen of F. BURKE:E 55
slain me you will conquer F. JOAN 1
Stormy voice of F. TENNY 280
this matter better in F. STERNE 40

warmer F. With all her vines COWP 62
We are more reasonable in F. VOLT 29
Francesca: F. di Rimini GILB:WS 36
frank: f. words in our respective languages COOK:P 1
Frankie: F. and Johnny were lovers ANON 11
frankincense: all camphire and f. CONG 57
Franklin: body of Benjamin F., printer FRANKLIN:B 21
fraud:
Force, and f., are in war HOBB 8
Grown old in f. CHURCH:C 5
fray:
eager for the f. CIB 4
Fought was this noble f. DRAYT 7
freak: Do not call me a f. WALLACE-C 2
freaks: Nature is full of f. EMER 68
freckled:
f. like a pard KEATS 103
Whatever is fickle, f. HOPK:GM 7
freckles:
curiosity, f., and doubt PARKER:D 3
In those f. live SHAK:MID 12
Fred: since 'tis only F. ANON 132
Frederick:
clustered spires of F. WHITTIER 3
Here is cruel F. HOFFMAN:H 2
free:
all men are created f. and equal LINC 5
be f. themselves must strike BYR 69
best things in life are f. PROV 36
born f. and equal ANON 153
definition of a f. society STEVENSON:A 5
England should be f. MAGEE 1
English Church shall be f. MAGNA 1
feel mighty f. and easy TWAIN 13
flag of all the f. CHESTERTON 20
flag that makes you f. WORK 1
f. as nature first made DRYD 12
f. as the sons of the waves GARRICK 4
F. at last KING:ML 2
f. behave much as the respectable AUD 28
f. Church in a f. State CAVOUR 1
f. man how to praise AUD 43
f. . . . must not conform WILDE:O 39
f. passage and freedom of action QUES 1
f. to work out his destiny WILSON:W 2
have to believe in f. will SING 1
he that ay hass levyt f. BARB 2
I only ask to be f. DICKENS 172
keep your fancy f. HOUSM 9
Man was born f. ROUSS:JJ 1
men everywhere could be f. LINC 17
men naturally were born f. MILT 324
Mother of the F. BENS:AC 1
never be f. until the last king DIDE 6
No f. man shall be taken MAGNA 2
no such thing as a f. lunch FRIEDMAN 1
no such thing as a f. lunch HEINL 1
No woman can call herself f. SANG 1
O'er the land of the f. KEY:FS 1
of these no man is f. SHAK:WIN 4
only less f. Than thou SHELLEY:PB 44
people are f. to do as HOFFER 1
perfectly f. till all are f. SPENCER:H 5
so f. as a fish RUSKIN 12
So f. we seem BROWNING:R 71
Thou art f. ARNOLD:M 5
truth shall make you f. BIBLE 481
We must be f. or die WORDS:W 44
Where we are f. to act ARISTOT 9
Who then is f.? HORACE 73
wholly slaves or wholly f. DRYD 86
yearning to breathe f. LAZ 1
free-loader: f. is a confirmed guest RUNYON 10
free will: conclusion upon F.W. and predestination CHURCH:W 44
freedom:
access of psychological f. MANN:WE 1
ambassadors of f. to women PANK:C 3
Apostles of F. are ever idolised CONNOLLY:J 1
are fit to use their f. MACAULAY:TB 20
bondage which is F.'s self SHELLEY:PB 6
enemies of F. do not argue INGE 8
establish our true f. MONTAIGNE 9
evils which newly acquired f. MACAULAY:TB 19
flame of f. in their souls SYMONDS 1
fredome is a noble thing BARB 1
F. and slavery are mental states GAND:M 2
F. and whisky BURNS:R 38
F. as free lances MACNEICE 5
F. has a thousand charms COWP 44
f. has never existed MUSSO:B 1
F. is an indivisible word WILKIE 1
F. is Slavery ORWELL 30
F. is the recognition of necessity ENGELS 3
F. is the right to do MONTESQU 4
F. of action, f. of movement GOUR 1
f. of action to all buyers QUES 1
f. of speech, f. of TWAIN 26
F. of the press in Britain SWAFF 1
F. only, which no good man ANON 186
F. shriek'd CAMPBELL:T 4
F. slowly broadens down TENNY 56
F., the seven pillared LAWR:TE 1
F., what liberties are taken GEO:D 1
F.'s just another word KRIS 1
I desire their Liberty and F. CHARLES I 4
I gave my life for f. EWER 1
If I have f. in my love LOVELACE 5
In giving f. to the slave LINC 10
is f. there will be no state LENIN 4
Let f. reign MANDELA:N 7
Let f. ring SMITH:Sam 1
live in f. everich in his kind JAMES I 1
None can love f. heartilie MILT 323
Once f. has exploded in the soul SARTRE 5
only f. can make security POPP 4
Perfect f. is reserved COLLINGWOOD:RG 1
Regain'd my f. with a sigh BYR 51
Road to F. is via the Cross LUTHULI 1
stride is wildernesses of f. HUGHES:Te 1
think fredome mar to pryss BARB 3
this participation of f. BURKE:E 42
this uncharted f. tires WORDS:W 71
to battle for f. and truth IBS 10
together we can do for the f. KENNEDY:JF 2
took my f. away long ago SOLZ 4
Was F.'s home BYR 25
what is F.? COLERIDGE:H 1
What stands if F. fall? KIP 145
who deny f. to others LINC 3
whose service is perfect f. PRAY 22
wind of nationalism and f. BALD:S 4
Your f. and mine cannot be MANDELA:N 3
freedoms:
four essential human f. ROOS:FD 12
There are f. MUSSO:B 1
freemasonry: kind of bitter f. BEERB 8
freemen: only f., are the only slaves MASSIN 7
freeze: F., f., thou bitter sky SHAK:AS 35
freezing: As F. persons, recollect DICKIN:E 6
freezings: What f. have I felt SHAK:SON 42
freight: soul shall have her earthly f. WORDS:W 61
French:
copious inaccurate F. YEATS 139
Deleted by F. censor BENNETT:JG 1
dislike the F. from the vulgar WALP:H 24
Every F. soldier carries NAPO I 8
F. art, if not sanguinary SPENCER:H 11
F. soldier is a civilian in disguise TUCHOL 8
F. to men CHARLES V 3
F. want no-one to be their *superior* TOC 1
Frenssh of Parys was to hire unknowe CHAUC 9
how it's improved her F. GRAHAM:H 5
Imagine the Lord talking F. DAY 1
loved, ever after, F. novels, F. THACK 2
may be tolerated by the F. MONTGOM:BL 4
not clear is not F. RIVAR 1
only unite the F. under the threat DE GAU 2
regius professor of F. letters JOYCE:J 24
some are fond of F. MASE 7
Someone who speaks F. COLETTE 7
something fishy about the F. COWARD 7
something Vichy about the F. NOVEL 1
Speak in F. when you can't CARROLL 49
they are too serious* STERNE 50
varicose veins or F. foreign LEVIN 1
would always have spoken F. VOLT 35
Frenchies: F. seek him everywhere ORCZY 1
Frenchman:
F. must be always talking JOHNSON:S 214
hate a F. as you hate the devil NELS 2
Frenchmen:
create F. in the image of Englishmen CHURCH:W 31
million F. *can* be wrong GUINAN 1
million F. can't be wrong ANON 185
Frenchwoman: Every F., I imagine, knows VOLT 23
frenzy:
Daemoniac Phrenzie MILT 256
Grant me an old man's f. YEATS 105
fresh:
fressh as is the month of May CHAUC 5
looking as f. as paint SMED 1
fret: weariness, the fever, and the f. KEATS 93
Freud: F. is that he never played DODD 1
friar: Frere ther was, a wantowne CHAUC 14
friars: These f. are cunning MACHIA 2
Friday:
on a F. fil al this meschaunce CHAUC 66
takes my man F. with me DEF 5
who laughs on F. RACINE 5
friend:
Codlin's the f. DICKENS 94
devoted F. – but not a Wife CARLYLE:JW 2
every friendless name the f. JOHNSON:S 228
every mess I finds a f. DIBDIN:C 2
Faithful are the wounds of a f. BIBLE 273
false f. is more dangerous BACON:F[1] 18
Fav'rite has no f. GRAY:T 14
f. in need is a f. indeed PROV 136
f. in power is a f. lost ADAMS:H 2
f. is a person with whom EMER 17
f. may well be reckoned EMER 18
f. of Beauty in distress? BYR 19
f. of every country CANN 4
F. of my better days HALLE 1
f. rememb'red not SHAK:AS 35
f. unseen FLECKER 2
F. we have in Jesus SCRIV 1
from the candid f. CANN 6
good f., but bad acquaintance BYR 188
good-natured f. or another SHERIDAN:RB 30
guide, philosopher, and f. POPE 107
He was my f., faithful SHAK:JUL 49
homes without a f. CLARE:J 5
I was angry with my f. BLAKE:W 76
In every f. we lose a part POPE 184
last best f. SOUTHEY 18
lay down his wife for a f. JOYCE:J 24
look like a f. on Denmark SHAK:HAM 16
makes no f. who never TENNY 254
might give my life for my f. SMITH:LP 9
mine own familiar f. BIBLE 211
new f. meet the old YEATS 54
No enemy can match a f. SWIFT 62
no f. like a sister ROSSET:C 5
not a f. to close his eyes DRYD 108
oldest and least presentable f. ALLING:M 1
One f. in a lifetime is much ADAMS:H 5
Peel a fig for your f. PROV 317
pretended f. is worse GAY 44
rejoin its f., and it would be EMER 16
single soul dwelling in two bodies* ARISTOT 24
suspicious f. POPE 121
Thou art not my f. EMER 95
to the f. be kind DUNB 3
truest f. to thy lover MALORY 16
('twas all he wish'd) a f. GRAY:T 27
use a f. as I use Thee HERB:G 36
way to have a f. is to be one EMER 19
Whenever a f. succeeds VIDAL 6
Who's your fat f.? BRUM 2
With one chained f. SHELLEY:PB 130
woman can only become a man's f. CHEK 6
worst f. and enemy is but Death BROOKE 24
friendless: every f. name the friend JOHNSON:S 228
friendly:
f. terms with the victims BUTLER:S[2] 45
so large, So f., and so rich AUD 57
sort of f. acquaintance we have AUSTEN 34
friends:
all distresses of our f. SWIFT 61
best of f. must part ANON 46
best of f. must part PROV 34
better to drop thy f. CALVER 3
cast of his f. as a huntsman GOLDS 40
Change f. DE GAU 7
choice of f. COWLEY:A 14
city of the faithfullest f. WHITMAN 20
comes to meet one's f. BURNEY 1

don't believe I deserved my f. WHITMAN 43
dreads, but more his f. CHURCH:C 1
few f., and many books COWLEY:A 5
first speech are old f. CATHERWOOD 1
forgive my f. for dying SMITH:LP 3
freendes everych oother moot obeye CHAUC 36
F. and loves we have none MASE 13
f. are exultations, agonies WORDS:W 103
F. are God's apology KINGSMILL 4
f. by choice DELIL 1
f. forsake me like CLARE:J 8
f. hear no more of him? SHELLEY:PB 63
f., laymen and clerical LEAR 6
f. of every country save DISR:B 76
F., Romans, countrymen SHAK:JUL 48
F. who set forth ARNOLD:M 49
glory was I had such f. YEATS 104
God defend me from my f. PROV 147
Good thoughts his onely friendes CAMPION 4
had been f. in youth COLERIDGE:ST 61
hat – and a few f. PARKER:D 23
hath f. in the garrison HALIF 2
have guessed you were f. BRADB 6
I let down my f. NIX 16
in the house of my f. BIBLE 362
keep f. with himself STEVENSON:RL 42
laughter and the love of f. BELLOC 27
laughter, learnt of f. BROOKE 25
lay down his f. for his life THORPE 1
lay down his life for his f. BIBLE 490
left to treat my f. MALLET:D 1
lightly of my deathless f. SASS 13
like him with f. possess'd SHAK:SON 11
lost f., some by death WOOLF:V 14
make more f. than enemies WATEN 1
man who is false to his f. BERK 5
misfortunes of our closest f. LA ROCHE 2
Money can't buy f. MILLIG 1
more shame in distrusting one's f. LA ROCHE 14
no f. not equal to yourself CONF 2
none of his f. like him WILDE:O 129
not in the multitude of f. JONS 10
Old f. are best SELD 2
opened a tavern for his f. DOUGLAS:N 2
ought to forgive our f. MEDICI:C 1
Our f., the enemy BERA 1
rememb'ring my good f. SHAK:RIC.II 20
soul and body part like f. CRASH 16
trencher f. SHAK:TIM 9
troops of unrecording f. TENNY 121
until his f. came to comfort him KIERK 2
want of f., and empty purse BRET 1
wary of him. We're f. BRECHT 10
we have f. and no butlers POUND 15
we will part good f. MARR 4
Win F. and Influence People CARNEG:D 1
with a little help from my f. LENNON 9
friendship:
basis of true f. SALL 2
cultivate your f. of his own accord JOHNSON:S 226
dupe of f., and the HAZL 31
elegance of female f. JOHNSON:S 27
extend the hand of f. ROBINS:M 1
f. from knowledge BUSSY 2
F. is a disinterested commerce GOLDS 58
f. is a plant of slow growth WASH 10
F. is constant in all other SHAK:MUCH 6
F. is Love without his wings BYR 1
F. is not always the sequel JOHNSON:S 59
F. is of so sweet and steady TWAIN 24
F. is tested in the thick years HUMPH 10
F. is unnecessary LEWIS:CS 1
F. needs a certain parallelism ADAMS:H 5
F. oft has made my heart to ake BLAKE:W 105
F. often ends in love COLTON 7
f. recognized by the police STEVENSON:RL 6
f. with thine enemies SHAK:JUL 42
hedge between keeps f. PROV 162
honest f. with all nations JEFFERSON 5
In f. false DRYD 41
keep his f. in constant repair JOHNSON:S 103
little f. in the world BACON:F[1] 62
Love is f. plus sex ELLIS:H 9
Most f. is feigning SHAK:AS 35
swear an eternal f. CANN 8
wanted f. and got friendliness MALAM 1
way of f.'s gone HERB:G 7
wing of f. never moults DICKENS 92
woman's f. ever ends in GAY 8
friendships:
F. begin with liking ELIOT:G 43
have no true f. BACON:F[1] 28
pious f. of the female CONG 40
friens: seek out f. to hae a blether GARIO 1
frightened:
killed than f. to death SURT 21
make sure my children are f. of me GEO V 3
upon the stage is not f. FIELDING 30
frightful: f. when one's dead POPE 116
Frigidaire: his faithful F. SLESS 7
fringe: lunatic f. in all reform ROOS:T 13
fritillaries: what white, what purple f. ARNOLD:M 43
fritters: best f. that ever I eat PEPYS 5
frivolity:
chatter of irresponsible f. DISR:B 77
gay without f. ARNOLD:M 36
frocks: streets alive with summer f. HEWETT 1
frog:
A f. dives BAS 1
better'n any other f. TWAIN 2
Expiring f. DICKENS 11
f. he would a-wooing go NURS 12
public – like a F. DICKIN:E 3
frog-spawn: f. of a blind man's ditch YEATS 99
frogs:
F. and snails And puppy-dogs' NURS 83
f. do not die in sport BION 1
frolick: f., while 'tis May GRAY:T 11
fromage: big f. in this family NASH 23
front:
All Quiet on the Western F. REM 1
to which f. these were sent OWEN:W 9
frontier:
f. of my Person goes AUD 54
on the edge of a new f. KENNEDY:JF 1
frontiers: all f., are sacred MUSSO:B 3
frost:
forms Of the radiant f. SHELLEY:PB 140
f. performs its secret COLERIDGE:ST 7
like an untimely f. SHAK:ROM 40
secret ministry of f. COLERIDGE:ST 9
Thaw not the f. which binds SHELLEY:PB 106
third day comes a f. SHAK:HEN.VIII 10
ye F. and Cold PRAY 15
frosts: ye Dews and F. PRAY 15
frosty: F., but kindly SHAK:AS 17
froth: idlest f. amid the boundless BRONTE:E 2
frown:
Convey a libel in a f. SWIFT 60
trembled with fear at your f.? ENGL 1
frowned: dismal tidings when he f. GOLDS 28
frowns: killed by f. and smiles SHELLEY:PB 70
frozen: Torrid or the f. Zone CAREW:T 3
frugal: She had a f. mind COWP 51
fruit:
fill all f. with ripeness KEATS 109
f. burnisht with Gold'n MILT 188
f. is sweet ARISTOT 23
f. of good works PRAY 58
F. Of that Forbidd'n Tree MILT 106
f. that can fall without MONTAGU 2
give them f. for their songs ADDIS 26
humid nightblue f. JOYCE:J 27
It bore thy f. and mine KYD 5
my f. is dreams THOMP:F 18
pluck the f. of today HORACE 13
Sorrow's most detested f. BYR 82
Too late for f. DE LA M 23
weakest kind of f. SHAK:MERC 43
will long for the f. at last SHERIDAN:RB 6
fruit-tree: some f.'s mossy root MARV 20
fruitful: Be f., and multiply BIBLE 8
fruitfulness: mists and mellow f. KEATS 109
fruition: f. of an earthly crown MARLOWE 9
fruits:
By their f. ye shall know BIBLE 402
Dead Sea f., that tempt MOORE:T 23
first partaker of the f. BIBLE 552
flowers and f. of love BYR 241
Forbidden f. are sweet PROV 131
kindly f. of the earth PRAY 37
frumpish: F. and banal MUGG 1
fry: owene grece I made him frye CHAUC 80
Fry: Roger F. whom I love MARSH 1
frying-pan: blackened f. over a primus DAVID 2
frying pan:
f.p. full of abominable loves AUGUS 2
out of the f.p. into the fire TERT 5
fubbed: have been f. off, and f. off SHAK:HEN.IV[2] 20
fuck:
couldn't write f. on a dusty venetian BROWNE:Co 1
fish f. in it FIELDS 5
word 'f.' is particularly diabolical TYNAN 6
fucking: all this cold-hearted f. LAWR:DH 18
fudging: fed up with f. and nudging OWEN:D 1
fuel:
by adding f. to the flame? MILT 294
Gathering f. in vacant lots ELIOT:TS 16
Fulbright, Senator: over-educated S.O.B.* TRU 7
fulfil: F. now, O Lord the desires PRAY 27
full:
fu' man's a true man PROV 141
f. man doesn't understand the wants PROV 140
f. of days, riches and BIBLE 174
without o'erflowing f. DENH 1
full-stop: grammatically correct f. PATTEN 1
fun:
desire to have all the f. is nine-tenths SAYERS 1
f. enough for far into BETJ 32
f. you can have with your clothes on DELLA 1
I must pay for my f. KIP 85
little f., to match the sorrow DU MAU:G 2
most f. I ever had without laughing ALLEN:W 12
much more f. than f. COWARD 36
No pudding and no *f.* VICT 11
noted for fresh air and f. EDGAR 1
taken my f. where I've KIP 85
teems with quiet f. CHESTERTON 55
the people have f. MONTESQU 5
they often have a lot more f. FRIEL 1
To come and spoil the f. CARROLL 54
We are not here for f. HERB:AP 14
function:
F. never dies WORDS:W 128
relieved and f. achieved MENCK 15
fundamental: There is . . . no other F. HALIF 3
funeral:
be jolly at my f. MOUNT 2
can't be reminded of your own f. BEHAN:Br 7
down on him for the f. expenses JEROME:JK 8
f. bak'd-meats Did coldly SHAK:HAM 24
F. marches to the grave LONGFEL 2
f. train which the bridegroom sees CLOUGH 16
go to a f. when you wish MANN:T 6
his obscure f. SHAK:HAM 173
may have to pay for the f. PROV 59
misbehaved once at a f. LAMB:Ch 39
not a f. note WOLFE:C 1
present is the f. of the past CLARE:J 7
seen a costlier f. TENNY 231
to speak in Caesar's f. SHAK:JUL 48
With mirth in f. SHAK:HAM 12
funerals:
attend the f. of our friends BREN 6
don't go to other men's f. DAY 2
funny:
Everything is f. as long as ROGERS:W 2
F.-peculiar or f.-ha-ha? HAY:I 1
F. without being vulgar GILB:WS 117
hard to be f. when you have WEST:M 10
just as f. as politicians ROOS:T 18
Whatever is f. is subversive ORWELL 13
fur:
all f. and wool THOMAS:D 36
f. side inside ANON 117
my f. and whiskers CARROLL 7
with her on some other f.? ANON 122
Furies: See the F. arise DRYD 112
furnace:
As one great F. flam'd MILT 111
burning fiery f. BIBLE 348
Heat not a f. for your foe SHAK:HEN.VIII 1
limekiln to the charcoal f. TERT 5
furnaces: fatal when f. burn AUD 1
furnish: Books Do F. a Room POWELL:A 6
furnished: how sparsely f. it is PERS 4
furniture:
No f. so charming as books SMITH:Syd[1] 20
not to bump into the f. LUNT 1
nurse, a piece of f., a *woman* TOLS:S 2

re-arrange the f. on the deck MORTON:R 1
useless and cumbersome f. TREE 3
furrow:
crush'd beneath the f.'s BURNS:R 53
f. followed free COLERIDGE:ST 18
must plough my f. alone ROSE 3
plough traces the f. MUSSO:B 2
furrows: time's f. I behold SHAK:SON 8
further:
f. away than anywhere else RAPH 2
f. in, the more you pay ANON 128
f. one goes, the less LAO 3
fury:
blind F. with th' abhorred shears MILT 49
f. and the mire of human YEATS 86
f. of a patient man DRYD 55
f. of the many-headed monster MASSIN 1
Life, a F. slinging flame TENNY 148
no f. like a non-combatant MONTAGUE 1
no f. like an ex-wife searching CONNOLLY:C 11
Nor Hell a f. CONG 34
When civil f. grew high BUTLER:S[1] 1
fusees: they who use f. CALVER 2
fuss: minimum of f. and no explanation BLY 1
fustest: I got there f. FORREST 1
future:
do not dream about the f. HAMMAR 2
drew into itself the f. HUX:A 21
extravagent hopes of the f. BURKE:E 12
fight against the f. GLAD 1
f. conquers it because it swallows ORTEGA G 7
f. contained in time past ELIOT:TS 87
f. is always a closed book DOYLE:AC 37
f. is . . . black BALD:J 5
f. is purchased by the present JOHNSON:S 273
F. is something which everyone LEWIS:CS 4
f. is the only kind of property CAMUS 11
f. is the shadow PROUST 5
f. It comes soon enough EINS 11
F. : That period of time in which BIER 6
f. to the divine Providence BACON:F[1] 12
hopes of f. years LONGFEL 17
I dipt into the f. TENNY 79
love demands some f. CAMUS 6
makes no preparation for the f. DISR:B 15
menace of the f. that makes cowards DIX:D 2
plan the f. by the past BURKE:E 72
prick with a limited f. HAWKE 2
seen the f. and it sucks HILL:Reg 1
seen the f. ; and it works STEFF 1
seen the f. and it's here GZO 1
Trust no F. LONGFEL 3
want a picture of the f. ORWELL 36
would divine the f. CONF 21
futurity: let f. shift for itself SMOL 3
fuzzy-wuzzy: 'ere's to you F. KIP 50
fwowed: Tonstant Weader f. up PARKER:D 11
gabble: to g. like tinkers SHAK:TWE 21
gaberdine: spit upon my Jewish g. SHAK:MERC 17
Gael: sleep of the sons of the G. SCOTT:W 46
Gaels: great G. of Ireland CHESTERTON 5
gai: toujours g. toujours g. MARQUIS 4
gaiety:
concession to g. is a striped THOMAS:G 3
eclipsed the g. of nations JOHNSON:S 57
gain:
All is not g. that is got STERNE 21
broke the Sabbath, but for G. DRYD 49
For g., not glory POPE 142
for the g. of a few POPE 182
g. drives these Attic bees VIRGIL 31
Glory, and g., th' industrious POPE 164
if he shall g. the whole world BIBLE 418
No pain, no g. FONDA 2
richest g. I count but loss WATTS 1
vain hope of g. TICH 1
Who stands to g.? CIC 14
gains:
Light g. make heavy purses BACON:F[1] 43
no g. without pains STEVENSON:A 6
gait:
eev'n step and musing gate MILT 80
forc'd g. of a shuffling nag SHAK:HEN.IV[1] 61
gaiters: All is gas and g. DICKENS 85
gal: slap-up g. in a bang-up chariot DICKENS 225
Galatians: There's a great text in G. BROWNING:R 37
gale: g., it plies the saplings HOUSM 20
gales: cool g. shall fan the glade POPE 3
Galilean:
Pilot of the G. lake MILT 52
thou yet take all, G. SWIN 34
You have conquered, G. JULIAN 1
Galileo: If G. had said in verse HARDY:T 76
gall:
g. and wormwood to an enemy BYR 84
I am g. HOPK:GM 27
no g., no glory PENN 1
to g. a new-heal'd wound SHAK:HEN.IV[2] 11
wormwood and the g. BIBLE 344
gallant:
died a very g. gentleman ATK:EL 1
He was a braw g. BALL 12
gallantry: What men call g. BYR 163
galleon: moon was a ghostly g. NOY 2
galleons: where are the g. of Spain? DOBSON:HA 4
galleys: Their g. blaze BYR 31
galliard: sing and dance a g. ANON 45
gallimaufry: English tongue, a gallimaufray SPENS 1
gallop:
G. about doing good SMITH:Ste 5
thundering g. of the horse's VIRGIL 79
Why does he g. and g. STEVENSON:RL 58
galloped: I g., Dirck g. BROWNING:R 52
gallows:
bad company leads to the g. MACHIA 3
his complexion is perfect g. SHAK:TEM 2
It grew a g. KYD 5
see nothing but the g. BURKE:E 57
Shall there be g. standing SHAK:HEN.IV[1] 7
gallows-maker: g.; for that frame SHAK:HAM 180
gallows-tree:
Jack on the g. SCOTT:W 48
Under the G. FLETCH:J 7
galumphing: He went g. back CARROLL 46
gamble: Life is a g., at terrible STOP 8
gambler: G. by the State Licenced BLAKE:W 92
game:
g. is done! I've won COLERIDGE:ST 21
g. . . . is never lost till won CRAB 23
g. of the few BERK 4
g., That must be lost BEAUMO 6
how you played the G. RICE:G 1
I don't like this g. MILLIG 4
love the g. beyond NEWBOLT 8
men play the g. WODDIS 1
more than a g. HUGHES:Th 4
play the g. NEWBOLT 10
pretend that politics is a g. PARKIN 3
silly g. where nobody wins FULLER:T[2] 1
start some g. on these lone HAZL 18
The g.'s afoot SHAK:HEN.V 20
time to win this g. DRAKE 4
turned to jollitie and g. MILT 259
gamecock: Luther hatched a g. ERAS 7
gamekeeper:
and the g. below CONNOLLY:C 20
shot by his g. ANON 143
games:
any sinful g. HARTE 2
desire to enjoy the g. of the rich HORNE:DR 2
g. should be seen as MONTAIGNE 6
I don't play little girls' g. CROMP 2
in g. Confederate WORDS:W 106
playing at children's g. from the beginning CHESTERTON 33
gamesmanship: G. or, the Art of Winning POTTER:S 1
gamesome: I am not g. SHAK:JUL 5
gaming: Man is a g. animal LAMB:Ch 14
gammon: What a world of g. and spinnage DICKENS 157
gander: Goosey, goosey g. NURS 14
gang:
Don't be a g. of four MAO 8
old g. CHURCH:Lord R 1
Ganges: by the Indian G.' side MARV 30
gangsters: nations have always acted like g. KUB 1
gaol: world's thy g. DONNE 9
gap:
g. between Dorothy and Chopin ADE 2
made a g. in nature SHAK:ANT 26
That g. is the grave AUD 1
gap-toothed: Gat-tothed I was CHAUC 82
gaping: g. wretches of the sea HUNT:L 3
Garbo: one sees in G. sober TYNAN 4
garden:
all Nature was a g. WALP:H 26
Almighty first planted a g. BACON:F[1] 69
Come into the g., Maud TENNY 215
England is a g. KIP 138
G. called Gethsemane KIP 147
G. died YEATS 83
g. eastward in Eden BIBLE 9
g. is a lovesome thing BROWN:TE 2
G. of your face HERB:E 1
g., That grows to seed SHAK:HAM 21
ghost of a g. fronts the sea SWIN 52
Glory of the G. it abideth KIP 139
Glory of the G. lies KIP 138
God the first g. made COWLEY:A 11
God walking in the g. BIBLE 18
have a g. of my own MARV 25
How does your g. grow? NURS 40
I went to the G. of Love BLAKE:W 71
man and woman in a g. WILDE:O 60
My heart shall be thy g. MEY:A 1
nearer God's heart in a g. GUR 1
see the g. and God there BROWNING:R 115
small house, and a large g. have COWLEY:A 5
sunlight on the g. MACNEICE 4
There is a G. in her face CAMPION 9
value my g. more ADDIS 26
we must cultivate our g. VOLT 16
garden party: have a g.p. with a man dead MANS:K 3
garden-state: that happy g. MARV 21
gardener:
Adam was a g. KIP 140
come the G. in white FLECKER 14
g. Adam and his wife TENNY 64
g. does not scent his roses COCT 3
talk to my g., I'm convinced RUSS:B 35
gardeners:
gard'ners, ditchers, and grave-makers SHAK:HAM 179
our wills are g. SHAK:OTH 14
gardens:
all the g. Of spring and summer THOMAS:D 14
closing time in the g. of the West CONNOLLY:C 17
Down by the salley g. YEATS 3
g. bright with sinuous rills COLERIDGE:ST 63
imaginary g. with real toads MOORE:M 1
In the g. of the night BRIDGES:R 14
Our bodies are our g. SHAK:OTH 14
sweetest delight of g. BROWNE:T 47
gare:* *idées au-dessus de sa g. RATT 1
garland: wither'd is the g. SHAK:ANT 58
garlanded: g. with carven imag'ries KEATS 69
garlands:
fantastic g. did she make SHAK:HAM 176
weave the g. of repose MARV 12
garlic:
continue to wear a clove of g. O'BRIEN:CC 1
loved he garleek, oynons CHAUC 30
garment:
Language is called the G. CARLYLE:T 6
left his g. in her hand BIBLE 70
not know the G. from the Man BLAKE:W 110
remove any g. consistent with HEWETT 2
garments:
hanging g. of Marylebone JOYCE:J 32
Stuffs out his vacant g. SHAK:KING J 12
garnish: g. it when it's orf HARN 1
garret: Born in the g. BYR 53
Garrick, David:
abridgment of all that was pleasant* GOLDS 38
On the stage he was* GOLDS 39
Garrick Club: G.C. excluded lunatics, gays MORTIM 2
garrison: hath friends in the G. HALIF 2
garter: I like the G. MELBOU 4
garters:
girdles and g. to be bonds BACON:F[1] 82
thine own heir-apparent g. SHAK:HEN.IV[1] 28

gas:
All is g. and gaiters DICKENS 85
G. smells awful PARKER:D 5
g. was on in the Institute BETJ 11
ship our masks in case of g. KIP 147
gas-lights: g. flare and flutter SLESS 7
gash: g. Is added to her wounds SHAK:MAC 92
gashouse: round behind the g. ELIOT:TS 43
Gaskell: No quailing, Mrs G. BRONTE:P 1
gaslight: Fanny by G. SADL 1
gasp: G. and Stretch one's Eyes BELLOC 21
gate:
A-sitting on a g. CARROLL 81
at one g. to make defence MILT 287
broad g. and the great fire SHAK:ALL 9
G. bear no proportion with the Building HOWELL 1
g. is strait SWIN 43
here at the g. alone TENNY 215
Hun is at the g. KIP 144
keeps the g. of hell SHAK:OTH 53
lead you in at Heavens g. BLAKE:W 117
no latch ter de golden g.? HARRIS:JC 11
not how strait the g. HENL 2
Right against the Eastern g. MILT 69
sat by the celestial g. BYR 144
stood at the g. of the year HASKINS 1
this is the g. of heaven BIBLE 62
world to my neighbour's g. MERED:G 35
would burst the Iron G. BROOKE 1
gatekeeper: to earth as a g. of a bordello TOSC 1
gates:
at heaven's g. she claps LYLY 6
Battering the g. of heaven TENNY 44
burst the g. of hell WESLEY:C 1
g. of heaven opened against him MALORY 15
g. of Hell are open night VIRGIL 66
g. of hell shall not prevail BIBLE 417
g. of this Chapel were shut BLAKE:W 71
g. the silent house of Sleep VIRGIL 74
iron g. of life MARV 32
Open the temple g. SPENS 13
Op'n, ye everlasting G. MILT 228
shut the g. of mercy GRAY:T 21
your heads, O ye g. BIBLE 208
gateways: through the g. of the mind SASS 17
gather: G. ye Rose-buds HERR 26
gathered:
I am g. to thy heart MEY:A 3
two or three are g. together PRAY 27
where two or three are g. together BIBLE 421
***gaudeamus:** G. igitur* ANON 12
gaudy:
doff't her gawdy trim MILT 5
g., blabbing, and remorseful SHAK:HEN.VI[2] 6
have one other g. night SHAK:ANT 40
Gaul: G. is divided into three parts CAES:GJ 1
Gaullist: G. only little by little DE GAU 5
Gaunt:
G.'s embattled pile MACAULAY:TB 42
seige of the city of G. BALL 37
gauntlet: g. with a gift in't BROWNING:EB 17
gave:
That we g., we have ANON 145
The Lord g. BIBLE 181
Gaveston: frantic for my G. MARLOWE 26
gay:
flutter of the G. BURNS:R 124
foremost of our g. young fellows FERGUS 1
G. as soft YOUNG:E 13
G. gilded scenes ADDIS 34
G. men generally are ... more loyal to masculinity FRYE:M 1
g. without frivolity ARNOLD:M 36
He has a g. appeal COWARD 22
impiously g. CRAB 11
life on the whole is far from g. LEAR 28
making G. *rich* and Rich *g.* JOHNSON:S 52
that build them again are g. YEATS 109
would not, if I could, be g. ROGERS:S 2
Gay: making G. *rich* and Rich *g.* JOHNSON:S 52
gays: excluded lunatics, g. and women MORTIM 2
Gaza: Eyeless in G. MILT 278
gaze:
g. an eagle blind SHAK:LOV 16
quiet sufferance of his g. JOYCE:J 5
stand at g. GRAVES:R 6
Stand fixt in stedfast g. MILT 7
gazed:
And still they g. GOLDS 29
Too much gaz'd at? KEATS 59
gazelle:
both Beautiful, one a g. YEATS 100
never nurs'd a dear g. MOORE:T 22
never nursed a dear g. DICKENS 95
gazes: what does ho see when he g. HARDY:T 25
gazing:
didn't know that everybody was g. DICKENS 34
why stand ye g. up into heaven? BIBLE 496
geck: most notorious g. and gull SHAK:TWE 56
geese:
for this the wild g. spread YEATS 37
g. are getting fat ANON 60
G. are swans ARNOLD:M 48
his own g. are swans WALP:H 23
More g. than men now live ANON 63
wild g. that the creeping SHAK:MID 28
gem:
g. of purest ray GRAY:T 20
Gemme of all joy DUNB 11
gems: Rich and rare were the g. MOORE:T 13
gender:
designated us as an *inferior g. class* DWO 1
she's of the feminine g. O'KEEFFE:J 1
general:
first twentieth-century g. SMITHERS 1
G. notions are generally wrong MONTAGU 4
g.'s disdain'd By him SHAK:TRO 6
'twas caviare to the g. SHAK:HAM 86
General Motors: country is good for G.M. WILSON:CE 1
generalizations: All g. are dangerous DUMAS:A[F] 2
generalize: To G. is to be an Idiot BLAKE:W 95
generals:
bite some of my other g. GEO II 2
business of g. to shoot one another WELLING 21
Despite of all your g. LANDOR 7
not against the law for g. TRU 6
Our Gen'rals now, retir'd POPE 148
Russia has two g. in whom NICHOLAS 1
wooden swords we're all G. UST 2
generation:
castigator of the young g. HORACE 109
Each g. imagines itself ORWELL 41
g. carved in stone WRIGHT:J 6
g. even more vicious HORACE 38
g. without bonds and without BORCH 1
minds of my g. destroyed GINSBERG 1
pride in this coming g. ROOS:FD 1
unto the third and fourth g. BIBLE 103
You are a lost g. STEIN:G 4
generations:
blind And fleeting g. SHELLEY:PB 104
clogs to clogs takes only three g. PROV 137
G. have trod HOPK:GM 5
G. pass while some tree stands BROWNE:T 57
How does it affect seven g. RIF 1
see three g. of one house POUND 14
Ten g. failed to alter HARDY:T 53
Those dying g. YEATS 71
three g. 'from shirt-sleeves BUTLER:NM 1
generosities: curled-up animal g. ROWB 1
generous:
be g. rather than just MENZ 2
every sort of g. and honest feeling BURKE:E 17
G. people make bad shopkeepers BALZ 9
genius:
all of my g. into my life WILDE:O 124
creates a g. to do it EMER 91
declare except my g. WILDE:O 125
difference between talent and g. ALCOTT:LM 3
Eccentricities of g., Sam DICKENS 25
feminine of g. FITZGER:E 36
g. a better discerning GOLDS 36
G. and the mortal instruments SHAK:JUL 21
g., but with absolutely no talent LEONARD:H 3
G. does what it must MERED:O 1
G. ... has been defined as BUTLER:S[2] 29
g. is a mind of large general JOHNSON:S 49
G. is an infinite capacity PROV 142
G. is merely a greater aptitude BUFF 2
g. is no more than a girl POUND 33
G. is of no country CHURCH:C 7
G. is one per cent inspiration EDIS 1
g. makes no mistakes JOYCE:J 22
g. ... only means an infinite capacity HOPK:JE 1
g. that could cut a Colossus JOHNSON:S 244
G. walks along a line GOLDS 43
'G.' (which means transcendent CARLYLE:T 57
German and a g. SWIFT 86
if a man have a g. EMER 49
invoke the g. of the Constitution PITT:W[1] 11
kind of universal g. DRYD 134
models destroy g. and art HAZL 8
no man of g. who had not to pay BEERB 15
now they call me a g. SARAS 1
Philistine of g. ARNOLD:M 77
Ramp up my g. JONS 12
spendthrift of my own g. WILDE:O 103
stupendous g. damned fool BYR 252
talent instantly recognizes g. DOYLE:AC 30
think yourself a great g. BEAUMA 4
true for all men, – that is g. EMER 4
unseen G. of the Wood MILT 88
what a g. I had SWIFT 81
When a true g. appears SWIFT 15
when was g. found respectable? BROWNING:EB 19
'women of g.' require very special JEWS 1
works of g. are the first things KEATS 126
geniuses:
G. don't die DALEY 2
only three originative g. STEIN:G 6
genteel:
beast to the truly g. HARDY:T 62
No dancing bear was so g. COWP 1
not g. when he gets drunk BOSW 2
gentle:
Do not go g. THOMAS:D 18
g. minde by g. deeds SPENS 43
g. yet not dull DENH 1
His life was g. SHAK:JUL 88
is gentil that dooth gentil CHAUC 89
Jentyll as fawcoun Or hawke SKEL:J 5
gentleman:
almost a definition of a g. NEWM:JH 5
Be a little g. HOFFMAN:H 4
character of an officer and a g. ANON 156
every Jack became a g. SHAK:RIC.III 6
fat g. in such a passion about? SHAW-L 1
fine old English g. ANON 28
finish'd g. from top BYR 227
g.: look at his boots SHAW 106
g. needs not know Latin MATT 1
g. to haul and draw DRAKE 3
grand old name of g. TENNY 179
he cannot make a G. BURKE:E 89
I am a g. SHAK:TWE 17
I am a g. SHAW 39
I am a g., though spoiled BROME:R 2
I am not quite a g. ASHFORD 2
last g. in Europe LEVERS 1
no such thing as a democratic g. FURP 3
Not a g.; dresses too well RUSS:B 30
Not the sort of attire for a g. SHARPE 2
Once a g., and always a g. DICKENS 197
Plantagenet Palliser ... is a perfect g. TROLL 33
quality that distinguishes the g. WAUGH:E 9
talking about being a g. never is SURT 18
This squash, this g. SHAK:WIN 3
to fashion a g. SPENS 19
too pedantic for a g. CONG 31
what a g. is to a gent BALD:S 9
Who was then a g.? ANON 116
gentleman-rankers: G. out on the spree KIP 52
gentlemanly: werry g. ideas SURT 2
gentlemen:
difficult to behave like g. MACKEN 3
distinguish God's g. from Fashion's EMER 37
England since g. came up SHAK:HEN.VI[2] 8
experience of g.'s agreements CHIF 1
G. Prefer Blondes LOOS 1
g. were not seamen MACAULAY:TB 34
God Almighty's g. DRYD 51
Good-morning, g. both ELIZ I 10
no ancient g. but gard'ners SHAK:HAM 179
not to forget we are g. BURKE:E 17
one of nature's G. LINT 1
Three jolly g. DE LA M 13
while the G. go by KIP 121

written by g. for g. THACK 16
You g. of England PARKER:M 2
gentleness: Let g. my strong enforcement SHAK:AS 33
gentlewomen: Cherubic Creatures – These G. DICKIN:E 12
gently:
g. down hill SMITH:Syd[1] 6
g. scan your brother BURNS:R 37
genuine: a lace for the g. MOORE:M 2
genuineness: G. only thrives in the dark HUX:A 11
geographers: g., in Afric-maps SWIFT 68
geography: G. is about Maps BENTLEY:EC 1
geology: happens to the world's g. MACDIAR 23
geometrician: God is like a skilful G. BROWNE:T 38
geometricians: we are g. only by chance JOHNSON:S 53
geometry:
G. . . . is the only science HOBB 3
no royal road to g. EUC 4
George the First: G.t.F. was always reckoned LANDOR 5
George the Second: viler G.t.S. LANDOR 5
George the Third:
Any good of G.t.T.? LANDOR 5
G.t.T. Ought never BENTLEY:EC 8
George III:
A better farmer ne'er* BYR 146
An old, mad, blind* SHELLEY:PB 53
Georges: be praised, the G. ended LANDOR 5
Georgia: As we were marching through G. WORK 1
Georgian: sweet laxative of G. strains CAMPBELL:R 5
Georgie: G. Porgie, pudding NURS 13
geranium: shakes a dead g. ELIOT:TS 17
German:
failing in the G. people than they SCHOP 5
G. and a genius SWIFT 86
G. army was stabbed in the back HIND 1
G. civilian is a soldier in TUCHOL 8
G. fate: standing in front TUCHOL 5
G. ideal: sitting behind TUCHOL 5
G. language is the most profound KRAUS 7
G. to my horse CHARLES V 3
Humour is an element which the G. TUCHOL 9
physics is the creation of the G. TOMASCH 1
wee, wee G. lairdie CUNNING:A 3
When a G. falls over TUCHOL 6
Germans:
appallingly thorough these G. HUX:A 36
bomb the G. BETJ 8
G. So they will end by ruining MUSSO:B 10
G., you too are Poor in deed HOLD 1
jab the life out of G. SASS 20
Germany:
country is at war with G. CHAMBERLAIN:N 4
Defeat of G. means ROOS:FD 16
G. . . . has been a nation of fakirs UNA 2
G. above all else HOFFMAN von 1
G., united Fatherland BECH 1
G. will claim me EINS 9
G. will either be a world power HITL 4
If we see that G. is winning TRU 3
Nazi G. had become a menace NEVINS 1
'Radical Nationalism' . . . is in today's G. GLOTZ 1
wall all G. with brass MARLOWE 31
germination: whose g. soon would burst open ZOLA 1
Gestapo: G. in drag ALLEN:D 6
get:
g. what you think you want CLARE:A 1
on where you want to g. to CARROLL 13
quite enough to g., sir DICKENS 39
time to g. BIBLE 281
What g. we? ANDREW 2
get up:
G.u., g.u. for shame HERR 21
G.u., sweet-Slug-a-bed HERR 22
I hate to g.u. BANK 1
getaways: History is full of ignominious g. ORWELL 15
Gethsemane: Garden called G. KIP 147
getting on: Gospel of G.O. SHAW 2
gewgaw: This g. world DRYD 28
geyser: From the g. ventilators BETJ 22
ghost:
Alas, poor g. SHAK:HAM 40
dogma of the G. in the Machine RYLE 3
g. of a garden fronts the sea SWIN 52
G. of a land by the g. of KEND 1
g. of Roger Casement YEATS 107
g. of the deceased *Roman empire* HOBB 12
g. orbiting forever LOWELL:R 16
heavens possess his gost SURREY 3
it is a g.'s right YEATS 64
It is an honest g. SHAK:HAM 54
lat thy gost thee lade CHAUC 125
lighte goost ful blisfully CHAUC 121
make a g. of him that SHAK:HAM 38
My g., my self HARW 2
neither A g. nor man THOMAS:D 1
Poor Slender's g. SHEN 2
raise up the g. of a rose BROWNE:T 47
talk with some old lover's g. DONNE 50
There needs no g. SHAK:HAM 53
thought to please my g. MENCK 16
Turn thou g. that way DONNE 98
Vex not his g. SHAK:KING L 86
We saw the g. of Captain Webb BETJ 12
What beck'ning g. POPE 56
Your g. will walk BROWNING:R 102
ghost town: I've always wanted to see a g.t. BYG 1
ghosties: From ghoulies and g. ANON 187
ghosts:
All argument is against it* JOHNSON:S 196
among a world of g. TENNY 102
g. from an enchanter fleeing SHELLEY:PB 40
g. gliding between the lines IBS 5
G. glut the throat of hell BLAKE:W 3
G. of Beauty glide POPE 138
g. . . . Troop home to churchyards SHAK:MID 33
I sought for g. SHELLEY:PB 14
make the g. gaze SHAK:ANT 52
ghoulies: From g. and ghosties ANON 187
giant:
awakened a sleeping g. YAM 1
g.'s shoulder to mount on COLERIDGE:ST 79
I was the g. great and still STEVENSON:RL 52
To have a g.'s strength SHAK:MEA 12
giants:
not g., but windmills CERV 3
on the shoulders of g. BERNARD:Ch 1
standing on the shoulders of g. NEWT:I 3
there we saw the g. BIBLE 116
There were g. in the earth BIBLE 35
when the war of the g. is over CHURCH:W 63
Giant's Causeway: Worth seeing? yes* JOHNSON:S 212
Gibbon: G. moved to flutes COLMAN:G[2] 8
gier-eagle: Strong, the g. on his sail SMART 2
gift:
as men a g. BROWNING:R 127
gauntlet with a g. in't BROWNING:EB 17
gave him the lead g. JEFFERS 2
G., like genius . . . only means HOPK:JE 1
Heav'n's last best g. MILT 208
last g. in death CATUL 20
look a g. horse in the mouth PROV 285
rarest g. To Beauty MERED:G 22
worth more than the g. CORNEILLE 5
You have a g. JONS 21
your g. survived it all AUD 38
gift-horse: To look a g. in the mouth BUTLER:S[1] 17
gifts:
cannot recall their g. TENNY 45
fairy g. fading away MOORE:T 3
Fortune still Bestows her g. JONS 7
G. from enemies are no g. SOPH 2
God's g. put man's best g. BROWNING:EB 12
Greeks even when they bring g. VIRGIL 46
imperfection of all the g. of life CONRAD 14
makes use of its heavenly g. PEREZ 2
plenteously with heavenly g. PRAY 24
rarer g. than gold BROOKE 19
Rich g. wax poor SHAK:HAM 99
They presented unto him g. BIBLE 376
use the g. of the gods wisely HORACE 58
Win her with g. SHAK:TWO 9
giggle: All G., Blush BYR 134
gild:
G., but to flout SCOTT:W 5
g. the faces of the grooms SHAK:MAC 43
To g. refined gold BYR 190
To g. refined gold SHAK:KING J 16
gilded: Gay g. scenes ADDIS 34
gilding:
bear to swallow without g. JOHNSON:S 258
g. the eastern hemisphere SHERIDAN:RB 34
Gilead: no balm in G.? BIBLE 338
Gilpin:
And G., long live he COWP 58
John G. was a citizen COWP 48
gilt:
dust that is a little g. SHAK:TRO 16
g. farthing for a gold coin CARLYLE:T 8
gin:
G. by pailfuls SCOTT:W 48
G. was mother's milk SHAW 110
that I breakfast on g. HERB:AP 1
You may talk o' g. and beer KIP 54
ginger: all 'ot sand and g. KIP 49
Giotto: G.'s tower LONGFEL 27
gipsies:
same the g. wore ARNOLD:M 22
whenever any poor G. are encamped VICT 2
gipsying: go a-g. through the world with LAMB:Ch 27
giraffe: Swelling to maculate g. ELIOT:TS 28
girded: g. with praise GRANT:R 1
girder: difference between joist and g.? ALLEN:D 3
girdle:
folds of a bright g. ARNOLD:M 47
put a g. round about the earth SHAK:MID 19
girdles: g. and garters to be bonds BACON:F[1] 82
girl:
A g. like I. LOOS 2
big mountainous sports g. BETJ 10
birth to eighteen, a g. needs TUCK 1
Every little g. knows about love SAG 2
genius is no more than a g. POUND 33
g. at an impressionable age SPARK 2
g. the threat of a woman DUMAS:A[F] 3
g. with brains ought to do something LOOS 3
g. with the pair of blue eyes SHERIDAN:RB 25
having made a young g. miserable FRANKLIN:B 24
Home is the g.'s prison SHAW 66
I shall find some g. perhaps BROOKE 15
just like a little g. DYL 8
lady and the daring young g. GOZ 1
little cottage g. PAIN 1
looking at a g. throwing a ball WOOLF:V 6
No, no, my g. JOHNSON:S 125
policeman and a pretty g. CHAPLIN 2
sits with a pretty g. for an hour EINS 17
Sweet Highland G. WORDS:W 37
There was a little g. LONGFEL 36
There was a little g. MILLER:M 1
We all love a pretty g. BICK 4
You speak like a green g. SHAK:HAM 31
young g. stood beside me NEIL 5
girl-graduates: sweet g. in their golden TENNY 101
girlfriend: problem someone has with his g. MARCUSE 1
girls:
American g. turn into American HAMP 3
bad g. go everywhere BROWN:HG 1
both crazy about g. MARX:G 27
Even respectable g. delight OSB:J 5
g. are so queer ALCOTT:LM 2
g.' hearts is their own beauty OSB:J 9
G. in our town HUDS:B 1
g. in slacks remember Dad BETJ 24
g. plan for whom they will GILMAN 1
g. we loved Are over forty CAMPBELL:G 2
g. we was all of us ladies MARQUIS 2
I don't play little g.' games CROMP 2
I was fit for the g. HORACE 46
not so easy to fool little g. THURB 5
Only good g. keep diaries BANK 8
there were more g. JACK:G 1
What are little g. made of? NURS 83
with the g. be handy BANGS 1
Wretched *un-idea'd* g. JOHNSON:S 93
GIs: Overpaid, overfed, oversexed* ANON 229
Gissing: G. . . . struck me as quite particularly JAMES:H 21

Gitche Gumee: By the shore of G.G. LONGFEL 20
give:
g. and not to count LOY 1
G. crowns and pounds HOUSM 9
G. me your tired LAZ 1
good idea to g. them WARHOL 2
more blessed to g. than BIBLE 504
receive but what we g. COLERIDGE:ST 56
such as I have g. I thee BIBLE 497
What I desire to g. SHAK:TEM 20
When I g. I g. myself WHITMAN 8
given:
accordance with what one has g. BALZ 1
g. unsought is better SHAK:TWE 42
giver: God loveth a cheerful g. BIBLE 529
givers: when g. prove unkind SHAK:HAM 99
gives:
She g. but little YOUNG:E 17
two favours who g. quickly PUB 2
When a father g. to his son PROV 423
whoever g., takes liberty DONNE 91
giving:
excuse for never g. me anything SHAW 108
Godlike in g. MOORE:T 24
I am not in the g. vein SHAK:RIC.III 13
manner of g. is worth CORNEILLE 5
gizzard: wife has something in her g. PEPYS 23
gizzards: carving knives Into their g. CALVER 2
glacier:
edge of a receding g. ATWOOD 2
g. knocks in the cupboard AUD 7
glad:
be g. who will be so MEDICI:L 1
G. to death's mystery HOOD 24
too soon made g. BROWNING:R 21
gladdies: Wave your g., possums HUMPH 3
glade:
alone in the bee-loud g. YEATS 4
cool gales shall fan the g. POPE 3
gladness:
g. of her g. BARRIE 16
our brightest blazes of g. JOHNSON:S 28
serve the Lord with g. BIBLE 600
Teach me half the g. SHELLEY:PB 100
Without g. availis no tresour DUNB 5
gladsome: Let us with a gladsom mind MILT 1
Gladstone:
A sophisticated rhetorician* DISR:B 79
G. read Homer for fun CHURCH:W 41
G.'s always having the ace LABOU 1
Mr G. may perspire CHURCH:Lord R 2
old man in a hurry* CHURCH:Lord R 3
old, wild, and incomprehensible* VICT 5
Glamis:
G. hath murder'd sleep SHAK:MAC 41
G. thou art, and Cawdor SHAK:MAC 19
glance:
How such a g. came BROWNING:R 19
mutual g. of great politeness BYR 150
glare: strange unheavenly g. BRIDGES:R 7
Glasgow:
Beautiful city of G. MCGON 1
never played the G. Empire Saturday DODD 1
glass:
argument of the broken pane of g. PANK:E 6
baying for broken g. WAUGH:E 1
brittle crazie glasse HERB:G 28
but she made mouths in a g. SHAK:KING L 34
dome of many-coloured g. SHELLEY:PB 126
double g. o' the inwariable DICKENS 27
Drink not the third glasse HERB:G 2
g. Wherein the noble youth SHAK:HEN.IV[2] 26
g. won't get someone drunk CHEK 13
Grief with a g. that ran SWIN 13
having been grown under g. WODE 27
if you break the bloody g. MACNEICE 3
like it out of a thin g. PINT 1
liked the Sound of Broken G. BELLOC 40
man that looks on glasse HERB:G 51
My g. is not large MUSSET 1
My g. shall not persuade SHAK:SON 8
prove an excuse for the g. SHERIDAN:RB 24
Satire is a kind of g. SWIFT 1
set you up a g. Where SHAK:HAM 135
Thou art thy mother's g. SHAK:SON 3
Through Optic G. the Tuscan Artist MILT 124
when he looked into the g. DISR:B 34
Your own g. shows you SHAK:SON 45
glasses:
At girls who wear g. PARKER:D 7
broke our painted g. JORD 1
dark g. to avoid being recognized ALLEN:F 1
forget both pairs of g. NASH 24
with plenty of looking g. ASHFORD 6
glazed: have it framed and g. WALP:H 12
gleam: Follow the G. TENNY 298
gleams: g. of a remoter world SHELLEY:PB 15
glean:
thou shouldst but g. HOOD 12
world shall g. of me THOMP:F 18
glee:
They fill'd one home with g. HEMA 5
to the brim with girlish g. GILB:WS 67
glen: Down the rushy g. ALLING:W 1
Glenartney: lone G.'s hazel shade SCOTT:W 35
Gleniffer: We ca' the place G. PATERSON:A 1
glens: silence of the g. SMITH:Alex 2
glib: g. and oily art SHAK:KING L 4
glimpses: g. of the moon SHAK:HAM 36
glisters:
All that g. is not gold SHAK:MERC 27
Nor all, that g., gold GRAY:T 15
glittering: how that g. taketh me HERR 38
glitters: All that g. is not gold PROV 14
gloaming:
In the g., O, my darling ORRED 1
Roamin' in the gloamin' LAUD 1
gloat: Hear me g. KIP 16
global: image of a g. village MCLUH 2
globe: rattle of a g. to play DRYD 28
***gloire:** jour de g. est arrivé* ROUG 1
gloom:
amid the encircling g. NEWM:JH 15
g. of earthquake and eclipse SHELLEY:PB 29
I g., I glance TENNY 203
inspissated g. JOHNSON:S 138
mournful g. For that MILT 121
Teach light to counterfeit a g. MILT 83
There g. the dark broad seas TENNY 55
glooms: Welcome, kindred g. THOMS:Ja[1] 11
glories:
G., like glow-worms WEBSTER:J 25
g. of our blood and state SHIRL 3
ghastly g. of saints SWIN 37
I see Heaven's g. shine BRONTE:E 1
thy G. end HOMER 9
glorify: g. God, and to enjoy him CATEC 1
glorious:
g. by my pen GRAHAM:J 1
G. the sun in mid career SMART 3
G. things of thee NEWT:J 1
gloriously: maiden g. false HORACE 41
glory:
brittle g. shineth SHAK:RIC.II 39
chief g. of every people JOHNSON:S 9
comes first – death or g. ANON 207
day of g. has arrived ROUG 1
die in their g. and never HOUSM 14
drown'd my G. in a Shallow Cup FITZGER:E 31
duty was the way to g. TENNY 195
earth are full of thy g. MASS 14
eternall brood of glorie SPENS 26
fill thy brest with glorie HERB:G 4
filled with the g. of God AINGER:AC 1
for the g. of the Creator BACON:F[1] 6
G., and gain, th' industrious POPE 164
G. be to God on high MASS 8
G. be to the Father MASS 5
G. be to the Father PRAY 7
g. dropped from their youth BROWNING:R 153
g. in small change HUGO 1
g. is departed BROWNING:R 39
g. is departed from Israel BIBLE 141
g. is naught GOET 19
g., jest, and riddle of the world POPE 90
g., jest, and terror of mankind MINIF 1
g. leads the way LEE:N 1
G., like the phoenix BYR 17
g. of great men must LA ROCHE 21
G. of the Garden it abideth KIP 139
G. of the Garden lies KIP 138
g. of the Lord shall be BIBLE 320
g. of the Lord shone round BIBLE 448
g., or the grave CAMPBELL:T 20
g. shone around TATE:N 1
g. smear'd in dust and blood SHAK:HEN.VI[3] 7
g. that shall be revealed PRAY 44
g. that was Greece POE 1
G., the grape, love, gold BYR 179
g. thrill is o'er MOORE:T 7
G. to God in the highest BIBLE 450
G. to Man in the highest SWIN 49
g. was I had such friends YEATS 104
G.'s grave BYR 25
Go where g. waits thee MOORE:T 6
greatest g. of a woman PERIC 5
heavens declare the g. of God BIBLE 203
his g. among the heathen BIBLE 230
hope of g. PRAY 40
I felt it was g. BYR 142
I go on to g. DUNC 5
into g. peep VAUGHAN:H 12
Land of Hope and G. BENS:AC 1
left him alone in his g. WOLFE:C 4
madness is the g. of SHAK:TIM 6
Mine eyes have seen the g. HOWE 1
Mine eyes have seen the g. KING:ML 3
My gown of g. RALE 2
No flowery path leads to g. FONTAINE 6
no gall, no g. PENN 1
of g. in the flower WORDS:W 66
passes the g. of the world ANON 239
paths of g. lead but GRAY:T 17
peacock is the g. of God BLAKE:W 41
prospect of g. gives me strength PROP 4
quickly the g. in this world passes KEMP 4
race of g. run MILT 288
short of the g. of God BIBLE 510
sudden g. arising from some HOBB 1
there hath passed away a g. WORDS:W 53
to g. we steer GARRICK 4
To the greater g. of God ANON 149
trailing clouds of g. WORDS:W 58
uncertain g. of an April SHAK:TWO 5
walking in an air of g. VAUGHAN:H 10
Where is it now, the g. WORDS:W 57
Who is this King of g.? BIBLE 208
whose g. is in their shame BIBLE 540
with g. not their own WORDS:W 154
with inward g. crowned SHELLEY:PB 32
wretchedness that g. brings SHAK:TIM 11
youth are the days of our g. BYR 141
gloss: so fine a g. on things? BROWNING:R 180
Gloucester: Doctor Foster went to G. NURS 10
glove:
he play'd at the gluve BALL 13
iron hand in a velvet g. CHARLES V 1
that I were a g. SHAK:ROM 9
gloves:
through the fields in g. CORNFORD:Fran 1
with my g. on my hand HARG 1
wore g. in my cap SHAK:KING L 44
glow: g. in the heart that with every CONRAD 8
glow-worm: glowworm shows the matin SHAK:HAM 50
glow-worms:
Glories, like g. WEBSTER:J 25
Ye living lamps* MARV 23
glowed: G. on the marble ELIOT:TS 40
glowing: g. like the vital morn SHELLEY:PB 9
glue:
My fingers into g. CARROLL 84
thought it was sniffing g. KENNELLY 4
glutton: glotoun of wordes LANGLAND 4
gluttony: G. is an emotional escape DE VR 2
gnat:
small grey-coated g. SHAK:ROM 5
strain at a g. BIBLE 427
gnats: small g. mourn KEATS 109
gnomes: little g. of Zurich WILSON:Harold 1
go:
best thing to be up and g. EMPS 2
do not g., For weariness DONNE 63
G., and do thou likewise BIBLE 458
g. away at any rate ANON 83
G. from me JOHNSON:L 1
g. we know not where SHAK:MEA 24
g. with the one I love BRECHT 17
g. into the house of the Lord BIBLE 241
G. ye into all the world BIBLE 446
going to where I have to g. ROETH 1
I g. – I come back HANDL 1

I g., I come back ITMA 5
I like to g. by myself HAZL 16
I need not g. HARDY:T 18
I shall g. to him BIBLE 157
I will arise and g. now YEATS 4
I will not let thee g. BIBLE 65
I will not let thee g. BRIDGES:R 5
In the name of God, g. AMERY 2
In the name of God, g. CROMWELL 6
It's a Rum G. VAUGHAN W 1
Let my people g. ANON 50
Let my people g. BIBLE 92
Must you g.? VAUGHAN:CJ 1
no g. the merrygoround MACNEICE 2
One to come, and one to g. CARROLL 75
They g. out when unattended GABOR 2
think how far I can g. THATCH:M 12
time for you to g. HORACE 98
we think you ought to g. RUBENS 1
what a Rum G. everything is WELLS:HG 7
you couldn't g. on SMITH:Ste 6

goal:
g. but no way of reaching it KAF 11
good Will be the final g. TENNY 152
The g. stands up HOUSM 17

goals:
dogmas or g. are in doubt PIR 1
muddied oafs at the g. KIP 101

goat:
g. with a puzzled face HOPE:Al 4
lust of the g. is the bounty BLAKE:W 41

goats: separate me from the g. CEL 3

god:
brought to a dying g. HEINE 5
diviner than a loveless g. BROWNING:R 65
either a wild beast, or a g. BACON:F[1] 65
g. of war is drunk with blood BLAKE:W 3
g. pursuing, the maiden hid SWIN 11
g. self-slain on his own SWIN 54
grete g. of Loves name CHAUC 92
Imaging a g. is the resort HULME 1
mortal g., to which we owe HOBB 10
presents the g. unshorne HERR 21
stops being a g. for his wife PALAC 2
think I am becoming a g. VESP 2
to be equal to a g. CATUL 13
whose g. is in the skies SHAW 59

God:
about depth knows about G. TILLICH 2
Act of G. was defined HERB:AP 17
afraid to look upon G. BIBLE 86
been the same since G. died MILLAY 9
believe in G. in spite of JOW 5
believe that they are attracted by G. INGE 7
better to have no opinion of G. BACON:F[1] 110
bought over G. with a fee SWIN 1
but served G. as diligently WOLSEY 2
canna sair G. and Gowd baith BIBLE 590
cannot have G. as his father CYP 1
cannot serve G. and mammon BIBLE 394
Chance might be G.'s pseudonym FRANCE 5
choose a Jewish G., But spurn BROWNE:Ce 1
closer walk with G. COWP 2
concerning the man that trusteth in G. HOOK 1
cope without recourse to G. BONHOEF 2
daily, nearer G. KEBLE 1
despises G. PLUT 2
didn't love G., he just fancied ANON 192
Doth G. exact day-labour MILT 100
ever mention G. any more MILLER:A 4
Fear G., and keep his BIBLE 291
Fear G., and take your own BORR 10
Fear G. Honour the king BIBLE 567
final proof of G.'s omnipotence DE VR 4
for they shall see G. BIBLE 384
From everlasting Thou art G. WATTS 18
further from G. ANDREW 4
glad ... that he thanks G. for any thing JOHNSON:S 99
glorify G., and to enjoy him CATEC 1
go unto the altar of G. MASS 4
G. abandoned, these defended HOUSM 37
G. accept him TENNY 196
G. All mercy, is a G. unjust YOUNG:E 15
G. always seeth you BAXTER:R 1
G. and angels to be lookers on BACON:F[1] 10
G. and my right RICHARD 1
G. and sinners reconciled WESLEY:C 7
G. and the doctor we alike adore OWEN:J 1
G. be in my head ANON 66
G. be with you till RANK 1
G. being with thee WORDS:W 43
G. bled, but with man's blood HUGHES:Te 5
G. bless ... G. damn THURB 25
G. bless us every one DICKENS 100
G. Calls Me G. SAMP 1
G. can stand being told PRIEST 7
G. commonly gives wealth to LUTHER 6
G. creates men MACHIA 1
G. dawned on Chaos SHELLEY:PB 113
G. disposes KEMP 8
G. disposes PROV 262
G. does not play dice EINS 18
G. for Harry, England SHAK:HEN.V 20
G. fulfils himself in many TENNY 278
G. had never spoken anything DAY 1
G. has not said a word BROWNING:R 35
G. has written all the books BUTLER:S[2] 31
G. hath made the pile complete TENNY 153
G. helps them that help PROV 148
G., if a G. there be SWIN 48
G., if there be a G. ANON 223
G. is a circle EMPE 1
G. is a good fellow HUGHES:Te 3
G. is a Spirit BIBLE 478
G. is absence SARTRE 8
G. is always on the side PROV 149
G. is an inhuman concept DURREN 2
G. is an unutterable Sigh ELLIS:H 5
G. is dead: but men's NIET 15
G. is dead NERV 2
G. is forgotten JORD 2
G. is his own interpreter COWP 13
G. is like a skilful Geometrician BROWNE:T 38
G. is love BIBLE 570
G. is Love, I dare say BUTLER:S[2] 32
G. is near PRINGLE:T 2
G. is no respecter of persons BIBLE 500
G. is normally on the side BUSSY 3
G. is not a man BIBLE 119
G. is nothing more than an exalted father FREUD:S 2
G. is on everyone's side ANOU 5
G. is only another artist PICAS 4
G. is our refuge BIBLE 215
G. is the immemorial refuge MENCK 12
G. is the perfect poet BROWNING:R 4
G. is thy Law MILT 199
G. is working His purpose out AINGER:AC 1
G. moves in a mysterious way COWP 12
G. must be a person NIET 20
G. never wrought miracle to BACON:F[1] 35
G. of life, and poesy BYR 113
G. of love my shepherd is HERB:G 47
G. of our fathers KIP 91
G. of Things as They are KIP 89
G. only a mistake made NIET 27
G. ought surely to shut HARDY:T 38
G. reigned from the wood VENAN 3
G. save the king BIBLE 143
G. save the king HOGG 5
G. saw that it was good BIBLE 4
G. shall win YEATS 103
G. shed His grace on thee BATES:KL 1
G. si Love FORST 9
G. so commanded MILT 246
G. so loved the world BIBLE 477
G. the herdsman goads YEATS 7
G. this, G. that SQUIRE 1
G., to me, it seems, is a verb FULLER:RB 1
G. took him BIBLE 32
G. walking in the garden BIBLE 18
G. was rarely mentioned CLARK:M 1
G. wasn't too bad a novelist BARTH:J 1
G. went on sleeping HUGHES:Te 4
G. were suddenly condemned to live DUMAS:A[F] 1
G. who allowed us to prove BONH 1
G. who has endowed us with sense GALI 2
G. will forgive me HEINE 10
G. will provide himself BIBLE 52
G. will save the Queen HOUSM 2
G. will stop dreaming you UNA 6
G. won't, and we can't CLOUGH 22
G.'s *first* mistake NIET 21
G.'s grandchild DANTE 8
G.'s in his heaven BROWNING:R 9
G.'s name hold in reverence PALMER:HR 2
G.'s own country ANON 189
'G.'s police' – wives and little children CHIS 1
G.'s sons are things MADDEN 1
good G. prepare me PEPYS 25
Had I but serv'd my G. SHAK:HEN.VIII 13
had no more use for G. PASC 6
hands of the living G. BIBLE 555
Has G. then forgotten LOUIS XIV 4
Have G. to be his guide BUNYAN 26
Heart within, and G. o'erhead LONGFEL 3
here in the sight of G. PRAY 80
Here is G.'s plenty DRYD 145
honest G.'s the noblest work BUTLER:S[2] 40
How odd Of G. EWER 2
hungry and inactive, G. can only appear ASTUR 1
I believe in G. the Father PRAY 19
I believe in one G. MASS 10
I believe in one G. PRAY 66
I came; I saw; G. conquered JOHN III SOB 1
I find letters from G. dropt WHITMAN 11
I found G. there BROWNING:R 64
I know I am G. BARNES:P 1
I neglect G. and his Angels DONNE 105
I remembered my G. SOUTHEY 6
If G. be for us BIBLE 513
If G. cannot do this, then BALD:J 4
If G. did not exist VOLT 26
If G. has created us in his image VOLT 24
If you don't find a G. by five o'clock JOW 8
Inclines to think there is a G. CLOUGH 25
intend to astonish G. Almighty FORBES:JN 1
Just are the ways of G. MILT 286
Just what G. would have done WOOLL 4
justify G.'s ways to man HOUSM 28
Kindly Call Me G. SAMP 1
lay wrestling with (my G.!) HOPK:GM 21
Let us pray to G. ... the bastard BECKETT 12
like G.'s own head COLERIDGE:ST 17
lively Oracles of G. CORON 1
Lord G. is crafty EINS 8
Lord G. of your fathers BIBLE 89
Lord thy G. am a jealous G. BIBLE 103
Lord thy G. is a jealous G. BIBLE 122
Lord thy G. is with thee BIBLE 128
lost communion with G. CATEC 3
made him know his G. by night VAUGHAN:H 1
man is as G. made him CERV 12
man with G. is always KNOX:J 3
maun face G. mysel' MACDIAR 1
men that G. made mad CHESTERTON 5
might have become a g. RUSS:B 23
mighty G. BIBLE 308
mighty G., is the G of ideas VIGNY 7
mills of G. grind slowly LOGAU 1
My G. and King HERB:G 24
My G., my King HERB:G 26
nature of G. is a circle ANON 219
none other but the house of G. BIBLE 62
Not only is there no G. ALLEN:W 2
not serve G. if the devil bid SHAK:OTH 5
now G. alone knows KLOP 1
Of what I call G. BROWNING:R 202
Our G.'s forgotten QUAR 3
Praise G. from whom KEN 3
proof that G. is a bore MENCK 10
put G. in his statements WHITMAN 36
Read G. aright QUAR 10
reason and the will of G. prevail ARNOLD:M 64
see G. made and eaten BROWNING:R 44
seen G. face to face BIBLE 66
she for G. in him MILT 192
So near is G. to man EMER 100
speedy end to the acts of G. DE VR 5
strong castle is our G. LUTHER 4
Teach me, my G. and King HERB:G 50
than a bogus g. MACNEICE 7
thank G. for fucking up my life HUGHES:S 1
Thanks be to G. MASS 9
that is really your G. LUTHER 3
There is no G. BIBLE 200
There is no G. CLOUGH 24
They believe G. to be there JOHNSON:S 142
Thou, my G., art in't HERR 3
thou owest G. a death SHAK:HEN.IV[1] 85

Thou shalt have one G. only CLOUGH 19
thy G. my G. BIBLE 139
to believe concerning G. CATEC 2
To believe in G. is to yearn UNA 5
to represent G. to the nation HIGT 1
To see G. only DONNE 93
Tomorrow I will be sweet G. PLATH 4
too much respect for the idea of G. DUH 1
Trust in G., and do the Right MACLEOD:N 1
'Twas G. the word that spake ELIZ I 8
unto G. the things that are G.'s BIBLE 426
Very G. of Very G. PRAY 66
want to take in G. LOWELL:JR 4
whan G. first maked man CHAUC 64
What G. does, He does well FONTAINE 8
What G. hath wrought MORSE 1
What hath G. wrought BIBLE 120
when I reflect that G. is just JEFFERSON 3
where G. doth admit the fair HERB:E 3
who think not G. at all MILT 286
Who trusted G. TENNY 157
whom G. hath joined together PRAY 87
Whom G. wishes to destroy DUPO 1
with the grandeur of G. HOPK:GM 5
with the idea which G. has of you UNA 7
woman is the work of G. BLAKE:W 41
words *G., Immortality, Duty* ELIOT:G 48
worship one G. in Trinity PRAY 30
wouldn't give up writing about G. WAUGH:E 33
Yellow G. forever gazes down HAYES 1
Yours faithfully, G. ANON 61
God's-acre: burial-ground G. LONGFEL 7
goddamn: Lhude sing G. POUND 12
goddess:
G., excellently bright JONS 11
Virgin g. returns VIRGIL 11
goddesses:
G. are possible now ATWOOD 3
like the immortal g. to look upon HOMER 6
goddessess: g. that dwell Far THOMAS:E 8
godfather: so noble a god-father SHAK:POET 8
godheads: Maidens aspiring to g. STOP 3
godless: decent g. people ELIOT:TS 73
godly: g., righteous, and sober life PRAY 5
Godot: waiting for G. BECKETT 4
gods:
alien people clutching their g. ELIOT:TS 63
alle hire goddes may availle CHAUC 122
And the temples of his G.? MACAULAY:TB 47
Angels would be G. POPE 84
are not three G. PRAY 31
bow to the G. of his Wives MILT 265
By the nine g. he swore MACAULAY:TB 45
creates G. by the dozen MONTAIGNE 17
dead limbs of gibbeted Gods SWIN 37
do not know whether there are g. DIOG 7
fear first in the world made g. JONS 14
g. are snub-nosed and black XENOPHAN 1
g. have lived in the woods VIRGIL 6
g. have no more power SARTRE 5
G. they had tried of every DRYD 36
g. thought otherwise VIRGIL 54
g. to goodness are inclined VIRGIL 42
he is living with the g. who AUR 10
He seems equal to the g. SAP 1
into the hands of the g. CORNEILLE 3
knows the g. of the country VIRGIL 27
large utterance of the early G. KEATS 46
Leave the rest to the g. HORACE 10
Little Tin G. on Wheels KIP 35
man's ignorance of the g. BUTLER:S[2] 6
no g. and precious few HENDER:H 1
No weekends for the g. LOWELL:R 16
not know much about g. ELIOT:TS 101
not resort to the g. POLY 1
On the hills like G. together TENNY 33
Shall weigh your G. and you KIP 100
So many g. WILCOX 4
These by the g., O israel BIBLE 107
Thou shalt have no other g. BIBLE 103
To my own G. I go KIP 36
Twa g. guides me BOYD:MA 1
use the gifts of the g. wisely HORACE 58
what end the g. have in store HORACE 12
What men or g. are these? KEATS 92
Whom the g. love die BYR 203
whom the g. love die young PROV 389
whom the g. love dies young PLAU 2
Whom the g. wish to destroy CONNOLLY:C 5
Ye shall be as g. BIBLE 17
Goebbels: G. Has no balls at all ANON 19
goes:
anything g. PORTER:C 3
he g. and knows 'em DICKENS 70
it g. of a night SHERIDAN:RB 21
so it g., *ça ira* VALL 1
goest:
whither thou g. BIBLE 139
whithersoever thou g. BIBLE 128
Goethe: G. had an aversion to dogs NERV 3
going:
endure Their g. hence SHAK:KING L 78
g. one knows not where MASE 4
g. to and fro in the earth BIBLE 179
knowing to what he was g. HARDY:T 37
thy g. out and thy coming in BIBLE 240
upon the order of your g. SHAK:MAC 73
Where are you g. ? BIBLE 612
Where are you g. to, my NURS 84
gold:
All that glisters is not g. SHAK:MERC 27
All that glitters is not g. PROV 14
all the g. that the goose could give AESOP 3
Apples of g. for the king's SWIN 55
Barbaric Pearl and g. MILT 148
Bow of burning g. BLAKE:W 98
burned g. was his colour CHAUC 62
but litel g. in cofre CHAUC 19
comes back, it's not g. LOWER 2
desired are they than g. BIBLE 204
female heart can g. despise? GRAY:T 13
fly to India for g. MARLOWE 30
gilt farthing for a g. coin CARLYLE:T 8
glistering g. but more to shine BRADST 3
G.? a transient GRAIN:J 1
g. and silver becks me SHAK:KING J 11
g., frankincense, and myrrh BIBLE 376
g. in phisik is a cordial CHAUC 24
G. is for the mistress KIP 126
g. like fire blazing PINDAR 1
g. to ayery thinness beat DONNE 69
G. undiscovered HORACE 33
g. wes changyd into lede WYNT 1
hair and harpstring of g. SWIN 33
he lovede g. in special CHAUC 24
hunger of pernicious g. VIRGIL 55
If g. ruste, what shal CHAUC 27
led by the nose with g. SHAK:WIN 30
narrowing lust of g. TENNY 177
next, my g. JONS 16
Nor all, that glisters, g. GRAY:T 15
Plate sin with g. SHAK:KING L 72
saint-seducing g. SHAK:ROM 3
shower of g. most things CARLYLE:T 17
so pale, is yet of g. CRAB 21
streets are paved with g. COLMAN:G[2] 3
streets of London are paved with g. PROV 357
That turneth all to g. HERB:G 52
To gild refined g. BYR 190
To gild refined g. SHAK:KING J 16
to turn smoke into g. ELIZ I 15
travell'd in realms of g. KEATS 3
trodd'n G. MILT 142
trusted with untold g. SCOTT:W 99
Were't not for g. and women TOUR 1
what survives is g. BROWNING:R 187
what's become of all the g. BROWNING:R 158
writing in a book of g. HUNT:L 4
gold-diggings: G., deserted, like huge HORNE:RH 2
golden:
burnisht with Gold'n Rinde MILT 188
circle of the g. year TENNY 92
give you the end of a g. string BLAKE:W 117
g. age was never the present FRANKLIN:B 13
G. days of my springtime? PUSH 4
g. lamps in a green night MARV 5
G. lie the meadows MERED:G 3
G. opes MILT 52
hand that lays the g. egg GOLDWYN 5
hands on that G. Key MILT 17
Happy the g. mean MASSIN 7
He has observd the G. Rule BLAKE:W 104
Or Love in a g. bowl? BLAKE:W 28
Poets only deliver a g. SIDNEY:P 14
there are no g. rules SHAW 49
went into a g. land TURNER:WJR 2
Whosoever loves the g. mean HORACE 22
golden-calf: g. of Self-love CARLYLE:T 28
Goldsmith:
Here lies Nolly G. GARRICK 6
No man was more foolish* JOHNSON:S 216
Oliver G., A Poet, Naturalist JOHNSON:S 189
Such men as G. ought not BLAKE:W 94
golf:
form of moral effort* LEACOCK 6
G. is a thoroughly national LANG:A 6
g. its anodyne LINK 3
G. may be played on Sunday LEACOCK 6
play g. ye maun hae a heid MACDON:CB 1
thousand lost g. balls ELIOT:TS 73
Golgotha: memorize another G. SHAK:MAC 4
gondola:
Didst ever see a G.? BYR 131
g. of London DISR:B 38
think you have swam in a g. SHAK:AS 55
gone:
g., and for ever SCOTT:W 39
g. with the wind DOWS 1
He has g. from us for ever LONGFEL 23
lost and g. forever MONTROSE 1
Now thou art gon MILT 45
They'd g., and you could only CARR 1
what haste I can to be g. CROMWELL 14
Goneril: Quite a sweet little G. BAYLIS 2
gong:
barbarous clangour of a g. YEATS 65
g. was bombilating THOMAS:D 39
gong-tormented: that g. sea YEATS 87
gongs:
Strong g. groaning CHESTERTON 19
struck regularly, like g. COWARD 5
good:
acknowledge the g. they have CHAMFORT 2
All g. and no badnes SKEL:J 4
All g. things must come PROV 8
All g. things which exist MILL 17
all G. to me is lost MILT 185
All men are born g. CONF 18
And crown thy g. with brotherhood BATES:KL 1
any g. thing therefore GREL 1
Anybody can be g. in the country WILDE:O 34
apprehension of the g. SHAK:RIC.II 12
Be g., sweet maid KINGSLEY:C 17
be rather than to seem g. SALL 5
Beneath the G. how far GRAY:T 36
best be the enemy of the g. JENKINS:R 2
best g. man ROCHES 6
best is the enemy of the g. VOLT 21
better to be g. than to be ugly WILDE:O 33
better to fight for the g. TENNY 227
but to be g. STEVENSON:RL 12
can't be g., be careful PROV 190
captive g. attending SHAK:SON 30
creature not too bright or g. WORDS:W 89
do a g. action by stealth LAMB:Ch 28
Do all the g. you can WESLEY:J 6
do evil, that g. may come BIBLE 509
Do g. by stealth POPE 152
do g. to them that hate BIBLE 387
do g. to them which hate BIBLE 453
do us no end of g. KIP 114
don't look too g. KIP 127
dreamed of g. shall exist BROWNING:R 167
everything in the world is g. for DRYD 61
few Know their own g. DRYD 78
for g. men to do nothing BURKE:E 107
for the g. of the community CARNEG:A 1
foundation of all g. things BURKE:E 68
General G. is the plea of the Scoundrel BLAKE:W 116
God saw that it was g. BIBLE 4
G. and bad are but names EMER 8
g. – and not too long in coming BUTLER:S[2] 41
g. are always the merry YEATS 6
g. as thou art beautiful TENNY 258
G., but not religious-g. HARDY:T 48
g., but they were *too* g. SALIN 3
g. deed in a naughty world SHAK:MERC 52
g. die early DEF 8
g. die first WORDS:W 113
g. die young PROV 151
g. dog deserves a g. bone PROV 152
g. end happily, and WILDE:O 90

g. end unluckily STOP 7
G. examples are borne out of MACHIA 10
g. except out of necessity MACHIA 9
G. fences make g. neighbours PROV 153
g. for the country is g. for WILSON:CE 1
g. has been beforehand NEWM:JH 14
g. has been well said to be ARISTOT 2
g. is oft interred with SHAK:JUL 48
g. is the beautiful PLATO 4
g. isn't enough ... to rule ALAS 2
G. isn't the word GILB:WS 116
g. man, and did g. things HARDY:T 64
G. men must not obey EMER 38
g. must associate BURKE:E 16
g. never will be our task MILT 117
g. of subjects is the end DEF 14
g. of the people is the chief law CIC 3
g. people's wery scarce DICKENS 1
g., she was very, very g. NURS 71
g. sometime Accounted dangerous SHAK:MAC 88
g. the gods provide thee DRYD 109
g. they inculcate must live after SAKI 20
g. thing come out of Nazareth? BIBLE 474
G. things, if they are short GRACIAN 5
g. time that was had by all DAVIS:B 2
G. Time Was Had By All SMITH:Ste 1
g. to be merry and wise ANON 27
G., to forgive BROWNING:R 209
g. Will be the final goal TENNY 152
G. without effort BYR 114
greatest g. CIC 4
He wos wery g. to me DICKENS 174
Hold thou the g. TENNY 151
If all the g. people were clever WORDS:E 1
If it's a g. one MURD:WLF 2
I'm as g. as you be EMER 78
in dreams doing g. is not wasted CALD 3
is no g.: I'll sell him LEACOCK 5
is the greatest g. and evil? LERM 1
know better what is g. for people JAY 1
knowing g. and evil BIBLE 17
loves what he is g. at SHADWE 4
luxury of doing g. CRAB 22
luxury of doing g. GOLDS 5
man *a g. man*, upon easier JOHNSON:S 238
May symply gud man callyt be BARB 4
Men are never so g. or so MACKINT 2
Men are so seldom really g. TROLL 21
Men have never been g. BARTH:K 1
Men we like are g. for every thing HALIF 15
might act for my g. COMPT 8
minds having what is too g. AUSTEN 37
must first be wise and g. MILT 96
must return g. for evil VANB 4
my g. is but vain hope TICH 1
my religion is to do g. PAINE 7
never had it so g. MACMILL:H 4
never hear g. of themselves PROV 243
Never think that you're not g. enough TROLL 13
No evil can befall a g. man SOC 5
No g. can come of it SCOTT:CP 2
no g. For which to strive MILT 149
no g. he must be pole-axed CHURCH:W 54
no g. to fight the evil with BURGESS:A 3
noble type of g. LONGFEL 24
nor g. Compensate bad BROWNING:R 203
not so g. as I thought SPYRI 1
nothing either g. or bad SHAK:HAM 77
Nothing is so g. as it seems ELIOT:G 22
one want for a common g. MARLOWE 22
only g. things the world MUSSET 4
out of g. still to find means MILT 118
partly brave and partly g. RICH 2
people who say he is very g. GRAVES:R 10
prospect of a distant g. DRYD 89
same time be g. and bad SPIN 2
she was g. as she was fair ROGERS:S 1
so much g. in the worst ANON 98
some are less g. PICAS 6
strong Antipathy of G. to Bad POPE 153
suppose the people g. ROBES 2
surprised at hearing of a g. action KEATS 163
them that call evil g. BIBLE 304
There's a g. time coming MACKAY 1
They love the G. BROOKE 12
thus a *G. Thing* for everyone SELL 5
Time makes ancient g. uncouth LOWELL:JR 2
to be not g. but great VIDAL 4
to be obscurely g. ADDIS 7
to do g. to rogues is to throw CERV 8
to enjoy what is g. GOET 27
to the public g. Private respects MILT 290
too g. for the Pill HUDS:B 2
too much of a g. thing PROV 436
trust that g. shall fall TENNY 154
universal licence to be g. COLERIDGE:H 1
what g. came of it SOUTHEY 4
what is g. for them CROMWELL 12
When she was g. LONGFEL 36
When she was g. MILLER:M 1
who go about doing g. CREIGH 1
work together for g. to them BIBLE 512
worse than ugly, she is g. WILDE:O 2
good-humour: G. can prevail POPE 54
good morrow: g.m. to our waking souls DONNE 42
good night:
bid the world Good-night HERR 28
gay goodnight and quickly turn away YEATS 102
gives the stern'st good-night SHAK:MAC 35
G.n., ladies SHAK:HAM 162
G.n., sweet prince SHAK:HAM 201
His happy good-night air HARDY:T 17
My last g.n. KING:H 1
to all a goodnight MOORE:CC 2
To all, to each, a fair g. n. SCOTT:W 34
Good Samaritan: would have remembered the G.S. THATCH:M 7
goodbye:
G. to All That GRAVES:R 8
Good-bye-ee! – good-bye-ee WESTON 2
Good bye is not worth while HARDY:T 29
Good-bye, proud world EMER 95
single kiss or a good-bye? PATMO 8
goodliest: g. person that ever came MALORY 16
goodliness: g. thereof is as the flower BIBLE 321
goodman: When our gudeman's awa' ANON 102
goodness:
delusion that beauty is g. TOLS:L 9
felt how awful g. is MILT 205
forgo the first privilege of g. WELLS:HG 11
fountain of all g. PRAY 25
gods to g. are inclined VIRGIL 42
g. and mercy shall follow me BIBLE 206
g., beautiful today, will remain SAP 3
G. does not more certainly LANDOR 22
G. has nothing to do with it WEST:M 1
g., in her person shin'd MILT 102
g. never fearful SHAK:MEA 26
g. of a good egg DANA 1
g. seems of almost supernatural GREENE:G 20
inclination to g. is imprinted BACON:F[1] 71
invisible G., which alone CARLYLE:T 28
more g. in her little finger SWIFT 47
my criterion of g. BURNS:R 131
nourish us with all g. PRAY 55
thirst for g. as for drink FERG:R 2
True g. springs from a man's CONF 18
Whose g. faileth never BAKER 1
goods:
G. may be most their own CHARLES I 4
he's got the g. HENRY:O 4
Man Who Delivers the G. MARSH:W 1
with all my worldly g. PRAY 86
goodwill:
good will toward men BIBLE 450
in peace, g. CHURCH:W 49
goose:
all the gold that the g. could give AESOP 3
beak of the g. is no longer PROV 29
every g. a swan KINGSLEY:C 19
every g. can PLUT 1
g. honking amongst tuneful VIRGIL 18
G., if I had you upon SHAK:KING L 24
g. that lays the golden egg PROV 221
got'st thou that g. look? SHAK:MAC 109
Leda's g. a swan ANON 69
steals a g. from off ANON 65
steals the g. from off ANON 77
Gorbachev: This man has a nice smile* GROM 1
gordian: She was a g. shape KEATS 103
gore: hope it mayn't be human g. DICKENS 88
gored:
Gor'd mine own thoughts SHAK:SON 51
you tossed and g. several BOSW 1
gorgon:
Great G., Prince of darknesse SPENS 23
think of myself as the G. Zola NASH 23
gormandizing: Leave g. SHAK:HEN.IV[2] 54
gormed: I'm G. DICKENS 166
gosling: such a g. to obey instinct SHAK:COR 15
gospel:
g. according to Jean Jacques CARLYLE:T 19
g. is their maw MILT 98
g. Of the radio-phonograph AUD 49
G.'s pearls upon our coast MARV 6
preach the g. to every BIBLE 446
Preferrest thou the g. of Montreal BUTLER:S[2] 47
goss-hawk: well's me o' my g. BALL 20
gossip:
At last the secret is out* AUD 24
babbling g. of the air SHAK:TWE 16
g., g. from all the nations AUD 17
G. is a sort of smoke ELIOT:G 39
I believe they talked of me* FARQ 14
murdered reputations of the week* CONG 36
talk about the rest of us* ANON 98
who wins; who's in, who's out* SHAK:KING L 79
gossips: No one g. about other RUSS:B 7
got:
G. 'tween asleep and wake? SHAK:KING L 7
haven't g. me yet BENS:EF 1
if you've g. it, flaunt it BROOKS:M 1
I've g. it ARCHIM 2
Gotham: G.'s three Wise Men we be PEAC 14
Gottingen: -NIVERSITY OF G. CANN 9
Gounod: G., who was pleased to express MELBA 4
gourd: swell the g. KEATS 109
gout:
drink, combined with g. GILB:WS 103
give them the g. MONTAGU 6
that old enemy the g. HOOD 14
govern:
all will g. in turn LENIN 5
easy to g., but impossible BROUGHAM 2
Every class is unfit to g. ACTON:Baron 1
g. by means of popular assemblies FOX:CJ 2
G. two millions of men BURKE:E 34
He would that g. others MASSIN 3
kings to g. wrong POPE 169
No king could g. DRYD 36
No man is good enough to g. LINC 1
people g. themselves THIERS 2
reigns, but does not g. ZAM 1
To g. is to make choices LEVIS 2
governed:
many are g. by the few HUME 5
not so well g. as they ought HOOK 2
government:
against g. by crony ICK 1
All g. ... is founded on compromise BURKE:E 37
all g. is evil O'SULL 1
best g. is that which governs least O'SULL 1
better than g. by desperation STEVENSON:A 10
can the G. be carried on? WELLING 14
consequence of Cabinet g. BAGE 8
constituencies and prepare for g. STEEL 1
Democracy means g. by the uneducated CHESTERTON 54
drollery called a representative g. DISR:B 29
duty of g. to protect all PAINE 2
fainéant g. is not the worst g. TROLL 18
false system of g. PAINE 6
fancy giving money to the G. HERB:AP 11
Forms of G. let fools contest POPE 99
Good g. could never be a substitute CAMPBELL-B 1
G. and cooperation are in all RUSKIN 15
G. at Washington lives GARF 1
g. by discussion ATT 3
g. does for others as socialism WARR 1
G., even in its best state PAINE 1
G., in due course, acted GILES 1
G. is a contrivance of human BURKE:E 54
g. is best which governs not THOREAU 1
g. is not to do things which KEYN 3
g. it deserves MAIS 1
g. of the people, by the LINC 11
G. of the United States is a device COOL 1

g. organization could do it CARTER:J 3
g. shall be upon his shoulder BIBLE 308
g. that is big enough to give GOLDWATER 3
g. that should ask me for a pardon DEBS 2
g. which robs Peter SHAW 125
heels in the administration of g. SWIFT 29
In every g., though terrors GOLDS 12
Influence is not g. WASH 4
just watch the g. and report ROGERS:W 10
land of settled g. TENNY 56
looked to g. for bread BURKE:E 81
Many forms of g. have been tried CHURCH:W 37
No G. can be long secure DISR:B 14
no go the G. grants MACNEICE 3
object of g. in peace and BEVER 1
oppressive g. is more to be feared CONF 19
people in the processes of g. GORB 1
people's g., made for WEBSTER:D 2
reproach to religion and g. PENN 2
Republican form of g. is the highest SPENCER:H 9
right of the People to establish G. WASH 7
share in G. (Sir) that is nothing CHARLES I 4
there has been no G. DICKENS 183
under one form of g. rather than JOHNSON:S 153
unfit for their own g. WASH 11
virtue of paper g. BURKE:E 24
want of g., is any new kind HOBB 11
what she would have thought of a Labour G. GEO V 1
why Monarchy is a strong g. BAGE 10
without party Parliamentary g. DISR:B 71
worst g. is the most moral MENCK 11
Your sister is given to g. DICKENS 207
governments:
Bad g. preserve nothing LEWIS:N 1
G. don't retreat RIPPON 1
g. had better get out of the way EISEN 5
G. in a capitalist society CONNOLLY:J 2
g. there must be both shepherds VOLT 8
Never trust g. absolutely PASS 1
peoples and g. have never learned HEG 2
teach g. humanity PAINE 5
governors: supreme g., the mob WALP:H 2
gowd:
canna sair God and G. baith BIBLE 590
man's the g. for a' that BURNS:R 115
Gower: moral G. CHAUC 123
gown:
ease a heart, like a satin g. PARKER:D 1
loose g. from her shoulders WYATT 4
My g. of glory RALE 2
sweet little Alice blue g. MCCARTHY:J[1] 2
gowns: furr'd g. hide all SHAK:KING L 71
Goya: out of a painting by G. STRAV 2
grace:
behold such heavenly g. SPENS 24
By g. divine, Not otherwise WORDS:W 136
does it with a better g. SHAK:TWE 20
for the means of g. PRAY 40
God in his mercy lend her g. TENNY 23
God shed His g. on thee BATES:KL 1
g. before Milton LAMB:Ch 6
G. is given of God CLOUGH 4
g. of God there goes John BRADF 1
g. of our Lord Jesus Christ BIBLE 587
G. under pressure HEMINGWAY 14
g. which followed it was STERNE 54
graceful, graceless G. BYR 238
grant us the help of thy g. PRAY 51
Have g. and favour in them SHAK:OTH 54
heaven such g. did lend her SHAK:TWO 12
here's g. and a cod-piece SHAK:KING L 35
his G. to an acorned hog BROWNING:R 123
moments of glad g. YEATS 14
such angel g. TENNY 41
Such g. had kings BROWNING:R 12
trust him for his g. COWP 10
with sory g. CHAUC 71
withdraw not your g. WRIGHT:J 9
graceful: g. with her elbows on the table JAMES:H 15
gracehoper: G. was always jigging JOYCE:J 40
graceless: G., Pointless, Feckless GIBBONS:S 3
graces:
Envy, Malice, are his G. LANDOR 6
g. and your gifts to tell SHAK:SON 45
G. do not seem to be native CHESTERFIELD 20
hauf-mile g. BURNS:R 33
inherit Heaven's g. SHAK:SON 41
Sweet G.: Faith, Hope LANDOR 6
gradualness: inevitability of g. WEBB:S 1
graffitti: daub the wall of a jakes* SHAK:KING L 23
grail: going to do with the G. BEERB 17
grain:
see a World in a G. of Sand BLAKE:W 82
which g. will grow SHAK:MAC 9
grammar:
am above g. SIG 1
erecting a g. school SHAK:HEN.VI[2] 11
g., and nonsense GOLDS 36
G., which can govern MOLIERE 27
Grammere, that grounde is LANGLAND 5
to posterity talking bad g. DISR:B 101
grammar school:
g.s. boys who with impure MACNEICE 16
g.s. of courtesies YEATS 38
grammar schools: death of the g.s. PARS 2
grammarians: inquisitive tribe of g. ANTI 1
grammars: What sairs your grammers BURNS:R 17
grammatical: 'g.' cannot be identified with 'meaningful' CHOM 1
gramophone: puts a record on the g. ELIOT:TS 47
gramophones: waxworks inhabited by g. DE LA M 22
granary: careless on a g. floor KEATS 109
grand: to be baith g. and comfortable BARRIE 3
Grand Canal: husband fell into the G.C. MORRIS:J 1
grandchild: God's g. DANTE 8
grandchildren:
have fourteen kidnapped g. GET 2
Never have children, only g. VIDAL 2
grandeur:
g. he derived from Heaven DRYD 1
g. is a dream COWP 68
g. that was Rome POE 1
nigh is g. to our dust EMER 100
Scotia's g. springs BURNS:R 14
with the g. of God HOPK:GM 5
grandeurs: g. of his Babylonian heart THOMP:F 5
grandfather:
don't know who my g. was LINC 21
having an ape for his g. HUX:TH 14
grandmother:
teach your g. to suck eggs PROV 82
walk over my g. if necessary COLSON 1
We have become a g. THATCH:M 21
grandsire: like his g. cut in alabaster? SHAK:MERC 4
grandsires: g.' g. are numbered VIRGIL 32
grandson: to know what his g. will be LINC 21
granites: g. which titanic wars OWEN:W 11
granny: canny shove yer g. aff a bus ANON 124
Grant: Old Cary G. fine GRANT:C 1
granted:
capacity for taking things for g. HUX:A 39
Never take anything for g. DISR:B 64
grants: no go the Government g. MACNEICE 3
grape:
broke the g.'s joy THOMAS:D 6
burst Joy's g. against KEATS 96
For one sweet g. who SHAK:POET 5
Glory, the g., love, gold BYR 179
G. that can with Logic FITZGER:E 22
peel me a g. WEST:M 4
trod on a g. as I came in EVANS:E 2
When your g. was green BRAY 2
grapes:
fathers have eaten sour g. BIBLE 345
Freighted with amber g. ARNOLD:M 30
g. are sour AESOP 2
g. of wrath are stored HOWE 1
sour g. and ashes ASHFORD 11
grasp:
G. it like a man of mettle HILL:A 1
G. not at much HERB:G 39
reach should exceed his g. BROWNING:R 72
grasping:
G. at Air YOUNG:E 14
shadow of an idea without g. BOWEN:El 5
grass:
All flesh is g. BIBLE 321
Blue, blue is the g. POUND 8
child said *What is the g.?* WHITMAN 4
destroy a blade of g. BOTT:G 1
dread the rustling of the g. WORDS:W 38
fallen in the long wet g. FAIRBURN 3
g. below – above the vaulted CLARE:J 8
g. is returning HORACE 53
g., it grew as scant BROWNING:R 94
g. stuck in its throat WODE 11
g. will grow in the street HOOV 3
green g. growing over me BALL 63
happy as the g. was green THOMAS:D 16
his days are as g. BIBLE 232
I am like the g. POUND 9
I am paler than g. SAP 1
I am the g.; I cover all SANDBURG 2
I fall on g. MARV 17
isn't g. to graze a cow BETJ 6
know the g. beyond the door ROSSET:DG 5
leaf of g. is no less WHITMAN 6
lift me from the g. SHELLEY:PB 36
never been sweet in the g. THOMAS:D 35
nor does its parched g. pray TIB 2
Of splendour in the g. WORDS:W 66
on a single blade of g. SUZ:DT 1
snake lurks in the g. VIRGIL 9
spears are like the summer g. BLAKE:W 8
tides of g. break into SWIN 40
two blades of g. SWIFT 31
when the g. is green. KIP 130
You can eat g. COAT 1
grasshoppers:
g. under a fern make BURKE:E 60
in our own sight as g. BIBLE 116
grate: which fluttered on the g. COLERIDGE:ST 8
grateful:
g. at last for a little thing TENNY 225
poor are never g. WILDE:O 36
gratifying: g. feeling that our duty GILB:WS 106
gratitude:
g. is merely a secret hope LA ROCHE 27
g. to most benefactors CHAMFORT 2
to merit anyone's g. CATUL 17
Grattan: We are the people of G. YEATS 135
gratuitous:
evil, can be as g. as good GIDE 2
g. action GIDE 1
gratuity: taking of a Bribe or G. PENN 4
grave:
a-mouldering in the g. HALL:CS 1
alive he'd turn in his g. GORKY 15
baith in ae g. laid BALL 32
be no meeting past the g. HUX:H 1
Between himself and the g. PATTEN 2
Between the cradle and the g. DYER:J[1] 1
botanize Upon his mother's g.? WORDS:W 27
dark inn, the g. SCOTT:W 53
Dig the g. and let me lie STEVENSON:RL 61
digs my g. at each remove HERB:G 27
dread The g. as little KEN 2
even the g. yawns TREE 1
foolish tears upon my g. TENNY 89
from the cradle to the g. SHELLEY:PB 86
gone wild into his g. SHAK:HEN.IV[2] 49
g. doth gape For thee SHAK:HEN.IV[2] 54
g. is not its goal LONGFEL 1
g. Proves the child ephemeral AUD 13
G., thy victoree? ANON 32
g. where English oak HARRIS:JC 4
g., where is thy victory? BIBLE 527
G.! where is thy victory? POPE 69
g.'s a fine and private MARV 31
help him to his g. SHAK:RIC.II 14
her heart in his g. is lying MOORE:T 14
In cold g. she was lain BALL 61
In ev'ry g. make room DAVEN:W 1
into the darkness of the g. MILLAY 7
kind of healthy g. SMITH:Syd[1] 14
lead but to the g. GRAY:T 17
like Alcestis from the g. MILT 101
little little g. SHAK:RIC.II 31
narrow g. we shall be lonely WRIGHT:J 2
No g. upon the earth shall SHAK:ANT 80
no peace in the g. TENNY 222
no repentance in the g. WATTS 15
not rest in an English g. BYR 254

Peace is in the g. SHELLEY:PB 71
pompous in the g. BROWNE:T 62
pot of honey on the g. MERED:G 21
receive no letters in the g. JOHNSON:S 251
renowned be thy g. SHAK:CYM 17
revel on the g. Of Liberty SHELLEY:PB 10
see myself go into my g. PEPYS 25
sleeping enough in the g. PROV 386
soldier's g. BYR 242
statue to o'erlook my g. BROWNING:R 99
straight and dusty to the g. STEVENSON:RL 11
tends the g. of Mad Carew HAYES 1
thank God for the quiet g. KEATS 170
That gap is the g. AUD 1
third thought shall be my g. SHAK:TEM 33
This G.'s the second Marriage-Bed CRASH 6
Thy victory, O G.? ROSS:R 1
travelling towards the g. WORDS:W 141
vast and wandering g. TENNY 132
When my g. is broke up DONNE 55
wise because you are g. SMITH:Syd[1] 15
with sorrow to the g. BIBLE 75
Without a g. BYR 118

grave-digger: if I were a g. JERROLD 6

grave-makers: ditchers, and g. SHAK:HAM 179

gravender: Wherein I eat my g. ST-LEG 1

graves:
about the g. of the martyrs STEVENSON:RL 69
beautiful uncut hair of g. WHITMAN 4
g. have yawn'd SHAK:JUL 29
g. stood tenantless SHAK:HAM 5
have no g. as yet CHESTERTON 27
in the g. of deceased languages DICKENS 130
into their voluntarie g. HERB:G 38
Let's talk of g. SHAK:RIC.II 27
ourselves dishonourable g. SHAK:JUL 11
Their g. are sever'd, far HEMA 5
who crouch in narrow g. KEYES 1

graveyard: to be raining on the g. BECKETT 14

gravity:
alters the centre of g. CARLYLE:T 16
G. is only the bark CONF 20
g. should be in two people CHEK 17
What doth g. out of his bed SHAK:HEN.IV[1] 47
You have risen by your g. SMITH:Syd[1] 40

gravy:
Humphrey Davy Abominated g. BENTLEY:EC 4
person who disliked g. SMITH:Syd[1] 21
rich wot gets the g. ANON 38

gray:
see also **grey**
grow g. with fear SHELLEY:PB 43
head grown g. in vain SHELLEY:PB 121
set g. life TENNY 93
ye bring down my g. hairs BIBLE 75

Gray, Thomas: He was dull in a new way* JOHNSON:S 166

Gray's Elegy: nearly the whole of G.E. WOLFE:J 1

grayling: here and there a g. TENNY 202

grease:
owene grece I made him frye CHAUC 80
servility slides by on g. LOWELL:R 13
she's the kitchen-wench, and all g. SHAK:COM 4

greasy: g. Joan doth keel the pot SHAK:LOV 25

great:
age of g. men is going AMIEL 2
All my shows are g. GRADE 1
All rising to g. place BACON:F[1] 75
Behind every g. man is an exhausted FAIRBAIRN:S 1
capable of doing anything g. HENRI 3
compare small things with g. VIRGIL 31
disbelief in g. men CARLYLE:T 44
Everything g. . . . is done by neurotics PROUST 8
far above the G. GRAY:T 36
glory of g. men must LA ROCHE 21
g. as is my grief SHAK:RICH II 30
g. enough to die for HAMMAR 1
g., ere fortune made him DRYD 1
g. has been done by youth DISR:B 17
G. have kindness in reserve POPE 123
g. in what is small LAO 1
g. man helped the poor MACAULAY:TB 49
G. men are almost always bad ACTON:Baron 2
G. men are but life-sized BEERB 18
G. men are the guide-posts BURKE:E 21
g. men have their poor relations DICKENS 181
g. men of history are frauds LAW 3
g. minds in the commonplace HUBB 2
g. object of which he has no idea BAGE 23
g. ones eat up the little SHAK:PER 4
g. seemed to him little MACAULAY:TB 28
G. things are done BLAKE:W 99
g. without a foe BYR 114
he is always g. DRYD 135
heights by g. men reached LONGFEL 19
History of the G. Men CARLYLE:T 41
Lives of g. men all remind LONGFEL 4
made many people think him g. JOHNSON:S 166
made me too g. for my house BACON:N 1
Man is only truly g. DISR:B 21
many lunatics and most of the g. men RUSS:B 15
met a g. man he grovelled THACK 4
No g. man lives in vain CARLYLE:T 45
not little, nor too g. POMF 1
nothing g. but man HAMIL:W 2
Nothing g. was ever achieved EMER 26
once was g. is pass'd away WORDS:W 77
Rightly to be g. SHAK:HAM 157
rudely g. POPE 89
see g. men contending with adversity BURTON:Ro 14
Some are born g. SHAK:TWE 35
That he is grown so g.? SHAK:JUL 12
the g. no heart LA BRU 9
those who were truly g. SPEND 2
Thou wouldst be g. SHAK:MAC 19
to achieve g. things VAUV 2
To be g. is to be misunderstood EMER 11
to be not good but g. VIDAL 4
who cannot perform g. things WALP:H 28
with small men no g. thing MILL 23

great-aunt: g. or uncle, whose existence HAZL 11

Great Britain:
G.B. should free herself SMITH:Ad 14
most valuable acquisition G.B. PHILLIP 1
success of G.B. in defending ROOS:FD 17
taken refuge in G.B. DUH 2

great-grandfather: g. was but a water-man BUNYAN 12

great-heart: One G. BUNYAN 25

Great Wall: G.W. . . . is the only man-made structure GALB 10

greater:
behold a g. SHAK:JUL 15
Four things g. than all KIP 40
g. man, the g. courtesy TENNY 262
that he is g. than they RUSKIN 11
we are g. than we know WORDS:W 129

greatest:
g. happiness for the g. numbers HUTCHES 2
g. happiness of the g. number BENTH 4
I am the g. ALI 2
not be among the g. KEATS 142
There sunk the g. BYR 83

greatness:
Be not afraid of g. SHAK:TWE 35
farewell, to all my g. SHAK:HEN.VIII 10
find dignity and g. COWARD 6
get out with my g. intact ALI 4
G. consists in bringing FIELDING 18
G. knows itself SHAK:HEN.IV[1] 81
g. of the world in tears YEATS 10
G., with private men MASSIN 7
intended g. for men ELIOT:G 35
moment of my g. flicker ELIOT:TS 9
of all g. not to be exact BURKE:E 19
Only real g. can be so PASTER 3
some far-off touch Of g. TENNY 251
some have g. thrust upon 'em SHAK:TWE 35
Than g. going off SHAK:ANT 48
Unhappiness . . . comes of his G. CARLYLE:T 14
wedding g. with balance MURRAY:LA 6
without ideals and without g. CAMUS 2

Greece:
Athens holds sway over all G. THEM 1
Captive G. captivated her savage HORACE 94
Fair G.! Sad relic BYR 68
for G. a tear BYR 194
glory that was G. POE 1
G. is fallen COLERIDGE:M 1
G. might still be free BYR 193
isles of G. BYR 192

greedy: thank goodness, I am g. PUNCH 19

Greek:
Because he was a G. SHELLEY:PB 168
can say a word against G. SHAW 83
carve in Latin or in G. WALLER 5
G. as a treat CHURCH:W 43
G. of grammar and factions O'CONNOR 1
hungry G. exactly knows JUV 6
it was G. to me SHAK:JUL 16
loving, natural, and G. BYR 181
pages of your G. models HORACE 110
questioned him in G. CARROLL 94
small Latin, and less G. JONS 41
study of G. literature GAIS 1
'tis known he could speak G. BUTLER:S[1] 2
understand G. and Latin DRYD 74
when his wife talks G. JOHNSON:S 261

Greeks:
For G. a blush BYR 194
G. even when they bring gifts VIRGIL 46
G. pay the penalty HORACE 80
Let *G.* be *G.* BRADST 2
To the G. the Muse gave HORACE 111

green:
all ye G. Things upon the Earth PRAY 17
am'rous as this lovely g. MARV 15
As g. as emerald COLERIDGE:ST 14
But not quite so g. KIP 3
children are heard on the g. BLAKE:W 22
dry smooth-shaven G. MILT 82
dye one's whiskers g. CARROLL 83
g. days in forests STEVENSON:RL 64
g. fuse drives the flower THOMAS:D 4
g. grow the rushes ANON 22
G. I love you g. GARC 1
G. I love you g. LORCA 1
g. the golden tree GOET 17
g. Thought in a g. Shade MARV 19
horses can eat g. shit and be strong DAVIS:M 2
in their g. going STEVENS 5
laid him on the g. BALL 11
Learn of the g. world POUND 35
Making the g. one red SHAK:MAC 45
only g. was the cutting grass NEIL 2
out of the hopeful g. stuff woven WHITMAN 4
particularly peaceful or particularly g. BUCH 1
precipices show untrodden g. KEATS 32
remember Their g. felicity KEATS 19
roots, and ever g. PEELE 2
see the g. man pass HOFFMAN:H 12
Time held me g. and dying THOMAS:D 17
tunnel of g. gloom BROOKE 6
wearin' o' the G. ANON 23
When I was g. in judgement SHAK:ANT 23
Wherever g. is worn YEATS 45
You speak like a g. girl SHAK:HAM 31

green-coat: shoot the sleepy, g. man HOFFMAN:H 14

greener: in a cleaner, g. land KIP 61

Greenland: From G.'s icy mountains HEB 2

greenly: We have done but g. SHAK:HAM 164

greenness: have recover'd greennesse? HERB:G 45

Greensleeves: G. was all my joy ANON 14

greenwood:
I must to the g. go BALL 39
Under the g. tree SHAK:AS 24

greet:
How should I g. thee? BYR 55
it gars me g. BURNS:R 85

greeting: g. a corpse would give to BALD:S 3

greetings:
g. where no kindness is WORDS:W 11
perhaps the g. are meant for me BEETH 2

grenades: g., and other novelties BETHU 1

grenadier: for the British G. ANON 40

Grenville: Sir Richard G. lay TENNY 281

grew:
Three years she g. WORDS:W 34
where only one g. before SWIFT 31

grey:
see also **gray**
All cats are g. in the dark PROV 7
amber locks to g. DRAYT 1
g., but not with years BYR 49
G., dear friend, is all theory GOET 17

Many a head has turned g. MULL 1
Too lovely to be g. ARNOLD:M 11
greyhound: fawning g. then did proffer SHAK:HEN.IV[1] 23
greyhounds: like g. in the slips SHAK:HEN.V 20
grief:
acquainted with g. BIBLE 328
As full of g. as age SHAK:KING L 30
But only time for G. HOOD 22
Can I see anothers g. BLAKE:W 25
Every one can master a g. SHAK:MUCH 18
eyes are quickened so with g. GRAVES:R 1
From perfect g. there need ROSSET:DG 6
G. and disappointment give rise HUME 3
G. brought to numbers DONNE 66
G. fills the room up SHAK:KING J 12
g. flieth to it BACON:F[1] 51
G. for awhile is blind SHELLEY:PB 68
G. is a species of idleness JOHNSON:S 73
G. is itself a med'cine COWP 21
g. itself be mortal SHELLEY:PB 114
G. never mended no broken DICKENS 1
g. returns with the revolving SHELLEY:PB 112
g. still treads upon CONG 11
g. that develops the powers PROUST 15
g. that does not speak SHAK:MAC 96
g. That fame can never heal AYT 4
g. that we are quite unable MANN:T 8
G. with a glass that ran SWIN 13
heart which g. hath canker'd CALVER 1
hopeless g. is passionless BROWNING:EB 6
in false griefe hyding SPENS 27
into the bottom of my g.? SHAK:ROM 37
journeyman to g.? SHAK:RIC.II 10
Patch g. with proverbs SHAK:MUCH 29
Pitched past pitch of g. HOPK:GM 22
put in words the g. TENNY 129
reason to be fond of g. SHAK:KING J 12
shame and g. go with her STERNE 55
Should be past g. SHAK:WIN 7
Silence augmenteth g. GREV 1
silent manliness of g. GOLDS 35
Smiling at g. SHAK:TWE 31
spider g. swings in his bitter DAWE 3
There's g. in the taste of it HEWETT 4
thirsty g. in wine we steep LOVELACE 4
'tis unmanly g. SHAK:HAM 19
To cure this deadly g. SHAK:MAC 97
Unspeakable is the g. VIRGIL 44
wakes an ancient g. YOUNG:AJ 1
Was ever g. like mine? HERB:G 16
woman's g. is like a summer storm BAILLIE 2
worm, the canker, and the g. BYR 241
griefs:
All our sins and g. to bear SCRIV 1
But not my g. SHAK:RIC.II 36
cutteth g. in halves BACON:F[1] 67
Drinking my g. SHAK:RIC.II 35
Great g., I see SHAK:CYM 15
he hath borne our g. BIBLE 328
like g. are silent MARM 1
lion g. loped from AUD 23
silent g. which cut FORD:J[1] 8
solitary g. JOHNSON:L 3
grievance: Scotsman with a g. and a ray WODE 19
grieve:
g. at grievances foregone SHAK:SON 12
g. not over that which is unavoidable BHAG 2
G. not that I die young HAST:F 1
Poor Pope will g. a month SWIFT 63
than a nation g. DRYD 45
grieving:
it died of g. KEATS 57
Margaret, are you g. HOPK:GM 15
grill: Let G. be G. SPENS 35
grim: g., g. grew his countenance BALL 14
grimace: ever seen who did not g. STRAV 4
grin:
cheerfully he seems to g. CARROLL 4
ending with the g. CARROLL 14
Nature wears one universal g. FIELDING 4
opens on her like a g. ELIOT:TS 17
rustic, woodland g. PAIN 1
with a lipless g. ELIOT:TS 31
grind:
g. the faces of the poor? BIBLE 302
life is one demd horrid g. DICKENS 86
they g. extremely small LOGAU 1
grinning: to mock your own g. SHAK:HAM 183
Grishkin: G. is nice ELIOT:TS 33
grist: All's g. that comes to PROV 12
groan:
bitter g. of a Martyrs woe BLAKE:W 115
Condemn'd alike to g. GRAY:T 8
hear each other g. KEATS 93
groaned: so groan'd and dy'd GAY 46
groans: alike are the g. of love LOWRY:M 2
grocer: God made the wicked G. CHESTERTON 10
Gromboolian: Over the great G. plain LEAR 9
Gromyko: be the G. of the Labour party HEAL 7
groom:
by his dogs and by his g. COWP 33
death is but a g. DONNE 74
prince as soon as his g. JONS 55
grooms:
gild the faces of the g. SHAK:MAC 43
G. besmear'd with Gold MILT 213
grooves:
moves In predestinate g. HARE:ME 1
ringing g. of change TENNY 87
they tend to think in g. MORGAN:E 1
grope: for a Group G. THOMP:EP 1
Grosvenor Gallery: greenery-yallery, G.G. GILB:WS 38
grotesque:
from the g. to the horrible DOYLE:AC 34
so g. a blunder BENTLEY:EC 8
Groucho: G. is not my real name MARX:G 23
ground:
choose thy g. BYR 242
every rood of g. maintained GOLDS 21
for an acre of barren g. SHAK:TEM 3
found six feet of g. HOUSM 36
gain a little patch of g. SHAK:HAM 155
g. flew up and hit me WARD:A 7
g., the books, the academes SHAK:LOV 14
In his own g. POPE 1
is sorrow, there is holy g. WILDE:O 102
lose to-morrow and the g. won ARNOLD:M 26
on the g. while you're still around ALI 3
seven feet of English g. HARO 1
stand on your own g. TROLL 16
thou standest is holy g. BIBLE 85
'tis haunted, holy g. BYR 70
grounds: round the g. for a second time? PEAC 2
groups: g. that no British Prime Minister BALD:S 12
grove: good g. of chimneys MORRIS:C 2
groves:
feels as if it was g. DICKENS 191
truth among the g. of Academe HORACE 96
grow:
All g. by slow degrees CALVER 2
Boys do not g. up gradually CONNOLLY:C 9
g. up with the country GREEL 1
watch them g. and thrive HARW 1
growed: I'spect I grow'd STOWE 2
growing:
g. up into a pretty woman AUSTEN 32
it will be g., Jock SCOTT:W 78
growl: but sit and g. JOHNSON:S 230
growled: It cracked and g. COLERIDGE:ST 15
grown:
g. and take our place KIP 116
having been g. under glass WODE 27
I am g. to man's estate STEVENSON:RL 53
grows: Nothing g. well in the shade BRANC 1
growth: quick a g. to meet Decay HERR 32
grub:
gravender, or g. ST-LEG 1
poor g., poor pay LON 2
Grubby: John G., who was short and stout CHESTERTON 23
grudge: feed fat the ancient g. SHAK:MERC 15
grudges: We collect g. LEONARD:H 1
gruel:
g. spooned up off a dirty floor BARL 1
Make the g. thick SHAK:MAC 80
started off living on g. PEREL 1
grumble:
g. with the rest JEROME:JK 5
nothing whatever to g. at GILB:WS 58
grumbling: g. grew to a mighty rumbling BROWNING:R 28
Grundy: what will Mrs G. zay? MORTON:T 1
grunting: other does the g. PROV 308
gruntled: far from being g. WODE 20
guard:
border g. of matter TUCHOL 3
changing g. at Buckingham Palace MILNE 1
G. dies and does not surrender CAMB 1
none but Americans on g. WASH 14
that I g. I do not love YEATS 61
who will g. the guards JUV 14
guardian: constitutional g. I GILB:WS 43
guards:
Stand up, G. WELLING 4
Unless the Lord g. the city BIBLE 604
Up g. and at them WELLING 3
gude: There's a g. time coming SCOTT:W 74
gudeman: he was g. to me BARNARD:A 1
gudgeon: this fool g. SHAK:MERC 6
gudgeons: swallow g. ere they're catched BUTLER:S[1] 28
guerilla:
g. fights the war of the flea TABER 1
g. wins if he does not lose KISS 1
to turn her into an urban g. HUMPH 9
guessing: g. what was at the other side WELLING 10
guest:
awaited the expected g. ELIOT:TS 45
g. always brings pleasure PROV 156
please the fleeting g. WILCOX 1
poor nigh-related g. COLERIDGE:ST 68
speed the parting g. HOMER 18
speed the parting g. POPE 66
guests:
Fish and g. smell in three PROV 127
g. few and select LANDOR 20
g. must be chosen as carefully SAKI 14
hosts and g. BEERB 21
to the g. rather than to the cooks MARTIAL 8
you to mix with my g. MELBA 3
guide:
g., philosopher, and friend POPE 107
Have God to be his g. BUNYAN 26
Pleasure after all is a safer g. BUTLER:S[2] 17
thy lab'ring steps to g. LUCRET 5
guide-posts: g. and landmarks in the state BURKE:E 21
guides: Ye blind g. BIBLE 427
guiding-star: g. of a whole brave nation MOTLEY 1
guile:
packed with g. BROOKE 11
There is no g. or warp PLATH 1
unfathom'd gulfs of g. BYR 121
guillotine: It is called the g. WODE 24
guilt:
art can wash her g. away? GOLDS 18
blood with g. is bought SHELLEY:PB 69
Calls g., in first confusion CLOUGH 25
depressing to admit g. AREN 2
dwell on g. and misery AUSTEN 36
free from g. or pain SHELLEY:PB 84
G. in his heart CHURCH:C 5
g. is avenged on earth GOET 7
Life without industry is g. RUSKIN 28
put on a dress of g. MCGOUGH 1
reason to grow pale with g. HORACE 77
sign of g., or of ill-breeding CONG 38
thief doth fear each bush* SHAK:HENVI[3] 8
unfortunate circumstance of g. STEVENSON:RL 36
upright and untainted by g. HORACE 15
guiltier: G. than him they try SHAK:MEA 6
guiltiness: her blush is g. SHAK:MUCH 25
guiltless:
g. of his country's blood GRAY:T 20
Whose guiltlesse hart is free CAMPION 3
guilts: Close pent-up g. SHAK:KING L 37
guilty:
better that ten g. persons escape BLACKS 5
gratifying to feel g. if you haven't AREN 2
g. creatures, sitting SHAK:HAM 94
g. of everlasting death WESLEY:J 1
g. party is acquitted PUB 3
How can a man be g. KAF 7
innocent until he is proved g. PROV 105
Let no g. man escape GRANT:US 2
Lose all their g. stains COWP 5
no g. man is acquitted JUV 24
started like a g. thing SHAK:HAM 9

Suspicion always haunts the g. SHAK:HEN.VI[3] 8
they arouse g. thoughts MOLIERE 7
guinea:
Disc of fire somewhat like a G.? BLAKE:W 112
g. helps the hurt TENNY 78
rank is but the g.'s stamp BURNS:R 115
guinea-pig:
G., there's a tasty dish NEVILL 1
life a g. up by the tail LOCKER 1
guineas: two hundred g. for flinging a pot RUSKIN 30
Guinness: can't drink G. from a thick PINT 1
guitar:
changed upon the blue g. STEVENS 12
sang to a small g. LEAR 18
Tune the Italian spark's g. PRIOR 8
gum: fart and chew g. at the same JOHNSON:LB 6
gums:
blue g. are growing O'HAG 1
odorous gumms and balme MILT 188
gun:
bare-legg'd beggarly son of a g. CALVER 6
difference between a g. and a tree POUND 46
escape from rope and g. GAY 24
ever lost an English g. TENNY 191
g. goes, you become a different WELLS:A 1
holy text of pike and g. BUTLER:S[1] 11
I have no g., but I can spit AUD 54
Is that a g. in your pocket WEST:M 14
out of the barrel of a g. MAO 1
rid of the g. it is necessary MAO 6
Gundagai:
Along the road to G. O'HAG 1
five miles from G. ANON 3
gunfire: g. has always sounded unreal UST 5
Gung Ho: *G.H.* Work Together ALLEY 1
Gunga Din: better man than I am G.D. KIP 58
gunpowder:
G., Printing, and the Protestant CARLYLE:T 24
gun powder ran out at the heels FOOTE 3
G., treason and plot NURS 53
guns:
but for these vile g. SHAK:HEN.IV[1] 19
elevate them g. a little lower JACK:A 2
G. aren't lawful PARKER:D 5
g. boom far CHESTERTON 19
G. will make us powerful GOER 1
loaded g. with boys CRAB 25
monstrous anger of the g. OWEN:W 1
trains go north with g. WRIGHT:J 5
when the g. begin to shoot KIP 66
Gurindji: Poor bugger me, G. EGAN 1
gurly: g. grew the sea BALL 14
gush: G.! – flush the man HOPK:GM 4
guts:
Grace under pressure* HEMINGWAY 14
his g. in his head SHAK:TRO 7
In her g. a galling give her SYNGE 7
lug the g. into SHAK:HAM 150
modified in the g. of the living AUD 37
sheep's g. should hale souls SHAK:MUCH 12
gutter:
Homesickness for the g. AUGIER 1
love sitting in the g. SHADBO 1
We are all in the g. WILDE:O 49
guy: County G., the hour is nigh SCOTT:W 60
gym: flare was up in the g. BETJ 11
gypsies:
Play with the g. in the wood NURS 42
quiet, pilfering, unprotected* CLARE:J 6
gypsy: Time, you old g. man HODG 6
gyres: The g.! the g.! YEATS 108
haberdasher: brother-in-law is h. to Mr Spurgeon BUTLER:S[2] 47
habit:
h. is a great deadener BECKETT 9
h. of which he is deeply CRISP 8
h. rules the unreflecting WORDS:W 131
H. with him was all CRAB 15
I shook the h. off WORDS:W 162
Memory and h. are the harbingers PEG 1
Moral virtue is the child of h. ARISTOT 5
order breeds h. ADAMS:H 4
use doth breed a h. SHAK:TWO 14
habits:
consider the curious h. POUND 20
Curious things, h. CHRIS 3
h. from the Bear BELLOC 2
h. that carry them far apart CONF 13
Old h. die hard PROV 304
Small h., well pursued MORE:H 3
hack: Do not h. me MONMOU 1
Hackney: see to 'Ackney Marshes BATEM 1
haggard: If I do prove her h. SHAK:OTH 38
Haggards: H. ride no more STEPHEN:JK 3
haggis: Him H. – velly goot MACDIAR 5
haggis-eater: redshank Norland h. HALLI 1
hags: black, and midnight h. SHAK:MAC 81
Haig, Douglas: brilliant to the top of* LLOYD GEO 16
hail:
flail of the lashing h. SHELLEY:PB 54
H. holy queen ANON 37
H. Mary ANON 160
H. the true body ANON 5
H. to the Chief SCOTT:W 38
my brother, h. and farewell CATUL 20
hair:
And not your yellow h. YEATS 91
beautiful uncut h. of graves WHITMAN 4
Blind with thine h. the eyes SHELLEY:PB 146
bracelet of bright h. DONNE 55
bright h. uplifted from the head SHELLEY:PB 41
busy driving cabs and cutting h. BURNS:G 1
draws us with a single h. POPE 44
drew me backward by the h. BROWNING:EB 9
Every h. of the bear reproduced HUX:A 30
excellent head of h. SHAK:TWE 4
golden h. Tarnished WILDE:O 110
h. has become very white CARROLL 9
h. of the dog that bit you PROV 361
h. soft-lifted KEATS 109
h. that lay along her back ROSSET:DG 2
h. to stand on end SHAK:HAM 42
h. was the most important thing O'BRIEN:E 2
his floating h. COLERIDGE:ST 63
lass wi' tousie h. MACDIAR 17
letting down your golden h. HORACE 7
lie tangled in her h. LOVELACE 3
long black h. out tight ELIOT:TS 53
make your h. curl GILB 88
mother bids me bind my h. HUNTER:A 1
must sugar my h. CARROLL 34
My h. is grey BYR 49
never brush their h. BELLOC 2
never pin up my h. with prose CONG 42
only one cure for grey h. WODE 24
prison for the colour of his h. HOUSM 48
Ralph the Rover tore his h. SOUTHEY 9
red Lips, and curled H. MARV 11
scant as h. In leprosy BROWNING:R 94
Shall I part my h. behind? ELIOT:TS 11
smoothes her h. with automatic ELIOT:TS 47
stars in her h. were seven ROSSET:DG 1
That subtle wreath of h. DONNE 39
thy amber-dropping h. MILT 40
tie up my bonny brown h. NURS 44
to her *with a single h.* DRYD 81
touches a h. of yon old grey head WHITTIER 6
with such h., too BROWNING:R 158
You have lovely h. CHEK 7
hairbreadth: h. scapes i' th' imminent SHAK:OTH 8
hairs:
any h. but these POPE 53
sad, last grey h. KEATS 93
ye bring down my gray h. BIBLE 75
hairy:
h. quadruped DARW:C 6
marvellous h. about the face SHAK:MID 36
my brother is a h. man BIBLE 57
half:
ae h. of the warld thinks the SCOTT:W 889
dearer h. MILT 209
H. past six JOYCE:J 49
h. that's got my keys GRAHAM:H 3
H. the world is laughing at the other GRACIAN 2
h. there when I am ill LAWR:DH 39
h. was not told me BIBLE 160
h. way up the social ladder LILL 3
if it be but h. denied BUTLER:S[1] 33
not told h. of what I saw POLO 1
half-a-dozen: h. of the other MARR 6
half-educated: *liked* being h. DURRELL:G 1
half-Jewish: my daughter is only h. MARX:G 20
half-knowledge: remaining content with h. KEATS 124
half-timbered: even the cars are h. HUMPH 4
half-way:
H. House to Rome PUNCH 3
Halfway through the journey of DANTE 1
run h. to meet it JERROLD 7
halfpenny: if you haven't got a ha'penny ANON 60
halitosis: h. of the intellect ICK 2
hall: stood twenty years in the h. WORK 2
Hall: Mr H.'s nay was nay BENTLEY:EC 2
halloo: H. your name SHAK:TWE 16
hallow: we cannot h. this ground LINC 11
hallowed:
H. be thy name BIBLE 391
So h. and so gracious SHAK:HAM 10
halls:
dwelt in marble h. BUNN 1
Old-fashion'd h., dull aunts POPE 65
once through Tara's h. MOORE:T 7
your dreary marble h. CALVER 10
halo: Is a h.? FRY:C 7
halt:
ground to a h. with a 14th Earl WILSON:Harold 3
h., and the blind BIBLE 461
halves:
h. of one august event HARDY:T 23
Never do things by h. PROV 283
ham: Think of h. and eggs NAV 1
hamburger: h. in one hand, and a grandson DAWE 2
hame:
It's h. and it's h. CUNNING:A 1
thou must bring her h. BALL 48
Hamelin: H. Town's in Brunswick BROWNING:R 24
Hamlet:
announced the tragedy of H. SCOTT:W 90
Bear H. like a soldier SHAK:HAM 203
good juggler to a bad H. COCHRAN 1
H. is the strongest character FLAU 2
I am not Prince H. ELIOT:TS 10
I saw *H.* Prince of Denmark EVELYN 5
Lord H. is a prince SHAK:HAM 68
man who could not make up* DENT 1
hammer: Yet I'll h. it out SHAK:RIC.II 44
hammered:
England's being h. KIP 135
hammer'd from a hundred towers TENNY 94
hammock: Drake he's in his h. NEWBOLT 4
hammock-shroud: heavy-shotted h. TENNY 132
Hampden:
had a head to contrive* CLAREN 2
some village-H. GRAY:T 20
Hampshire: captain of the H. grenadiers GIBBON:E 23
hams: together with most weak h. SHAK:HAM 73
hand:
at the right h. of the Father MASS 10
attentive to the minute h. MACCARTHY:D 1
bird in the h. is worth two PROV 45
blood Clean from my h.? SHAK:MAC 45
By God's Almighty H. CAMPBELL:Ja 1
curious engine, your white h. WEBSTER:J 22
death's own h. is warmer MAUGH 27
emprison her soft h. KEATS 96
every man's h. against him BIBLE 48
extend the h. of friendship ROBINS:M 1
feeds the h. that bites him PETER 2
gie's a h. o' thine BURNS:R 70
h. dare seize the fire? BLAKE:W 68
h. for h. BIBLE 104
h. in h. they passd MILT 194
h. is not able to taste SHAK:MID 42
h. more instrumental SHAK:HAM 13
h. that fired the shot BALL 25
h. that gave the blow DRYD 60
h. that hath made you fair SHAK:MEA 25
h. that holds dominion THOMAS:D 9
h. that kings Have lipp'd SHAK:ANT 32
h. that lays the golden egg GOLDWYN 5
H. that made us is divine ADDIS 40
h. that rocks the cradle WALLACE:WR 1

h. that rocks the cradle rules PROV 159
h. that signed the paper THOMAS:D 8
h. that waited for the heart's ELIOT:G 16
h. to execute GIBBON:E 8
h. to execute JUNIUS 7
h. to execute any mischief CLAREN 2
having put his h. to the plough BIBLE 454
Heaving up my either h. HERR 4
her h., In whose comparison SHAK:TRO 1
Here's my h. SHAK:TEM 21
holds him with his skinny h. COLERIDGE:ST 11
I fear thy skinny h. COLERIDGE:ST 23
in a big round h. GILB:WS 12
In his h. are the deep places BIBLE 229
iron h. in a velvet glove CHARLES V 1
join h. in h., brave Americans DICKIN:J 1
lays his icy h. on kings SHIRL 3
lend thy guiding h. MILT 277
Let not thy left h. know BIBLE 390
lifted h. between the mind HEWITT:J 1
Love took my h. HERB:G 54
mine had been the Painter's h. WORDS:W 40
my h. a needle better fits BRADST 1
my knee, my hat, and h. BROWNE:T 1
on the right h. of God PRAY 19
One lovely h. she stretched CAMPBELL:T 14
or the print of a h. HARDY:T 77
put your h. into the h. of God HASKINS 1
right h. shall work it all off SCOTT:W 98
seen what my h. did LOWELL:R 17
spirit-small h. propping it BROWNING:R 91
still the upper h. COWARD 24
there's a h., my trusty BURNS:R 70
This is the h. that wrote it CRANMER 1
thrust my h. into his side BIBLE 493
touch of a vanish'd h. TENNY 59
use ... but of my left h. MILT 302
waves her lily h. GAY 40
What dread h.? BLAKE:W 68
What immortal h. or eye BLAKE:W 67
Whatsoever thy h. findeth BIBLE 286
who will stand on either h. MACAULAY:TB 48
handbag:
shifts her h. from my side MTS 1
woman left her h. in my house WAUGH:A 1
handclasp: h.'s a little stronger CHAPMAN:A 1
Handel: Compar'd to H.'s a mere ninny BYROM 2
handiwork: beyond or above his h. JOYCE:J 8
handkerchief:
conditions in the h. industry CONNOLLY:C 16
h. of the Lord WHITMAN 4
handle:
all ready to h. honesty SHAW 89
I polished up the h. GILB:WS 11
stick with an 'orse's 'ead 'andle EDGAR 1
handled: h., not embraced DUKES 1
handles: Quit the h. KINGSFORD 1
handling: make a slip in h. us KIP 143
handmaid:
but an h. to religion BACON:F[1] 13
Riches are a good h. BACON:F[1] 25
hands:
Before rude h. have touch'd JONS 46
Cold h., warm heart PROV 58
cold immortal h. SWIN 29
couldn't find my h. CERN 1
devil finds work for idle h. PROV 68
don't raise your h. because I AUD 65
England is in my two h. WILLIAM I 1
Farewell, my poor h. RACH 1
finds mischief still for h. MADAN 1
From the hard h. of peasants SHAK:JUL 72
h. are a sort of feet TRAH 1
h. are the h. of Esau BIBLE 58
h. before knives PROV 121
h. guiding where I stumble SASS 13
h. laid on me in lust, and not WYLIE 2
h. of the living God BIBLE 555
H., that the rod of empire GRAY:T 19
his h. the print of the nails BIBLE 493
horny h. of toil LOWELL:JR 1
I warmed both h. LANDOR 9
into the h. of God TENNY 285
into thy h. I commend BIBLE 469
large and sinewy h. LONGFEL 11
Laying on of H. PRAY 76
Let us hold h. and look BETJ 15
Licence my roving h. DONNE 7
little h. were never made WATTS 9
long h. slowly twining over DICKENS 154
Many h. make light work PROV 265
not without men's h. ELIOT:G 47
not your h. be weak BIBLE 176
Our h. will never meet again HOOD 28
Pale h. I loved HOPE:L 2
Pale h., pink tipped HOPE:L 3
played with both h. in the pocket SATIE 3
plunge your h. in water AUD 7
Shake h. for ever DRAYT 9
shake h. with a clenched fist GAND:I 1
shook h. with a friendly Arab MILLIG 2
shook h. with time FORD:J[1] 7
thought it out with both h. SAYERS 3
Tomorrow my h. will be bound BAILLY 1
union of h. and hearts TAYL:Jer 3
Wash your h. SHAK:MAC 104
what coarse h. he has DICKENS 208
will soon wring their h. WALP:R 3
will these h. ne'er be clean? SHAK:MAC 101
With my own fair h. SWIFT 72
handshake: adds a firm h. FAD 4
handsome:
few years to be young and h. SWIFT 25
h. in three hundred pounds SHAK:MERR 12
H. is as h. does PROV 158
He was a h., well-shaped man AUBREY 9
handsomest: h. man that ever cut a throat CHURCH:W 73
handwriting: enjoy the sight of their own h. AUD 63
hang:
bad name and h. him PROV 143
drops on gate-bars h. HARDY:T 42
enough rope and he'll h. himself PROV 144
H. thyself in thine SHAK:HEN.IV[1] 28
h. us now in Shrewsbury HOUSM 5
H. yourself, brave Crillon HENRI 2
man and wife ... power to h. one another FARQ 18
must all h. together FRANKLIN:B 28
On which they h. a man WILDE:O 118
something in them to h. him RICHELIEU:A 2
wretches h. that jury-men POPE 48
hangdog: creature with a h. face SLESS 2
hanged:
farmer that h. himself SHAK:MAC 48
going to see me h. CROMWELL 13
hang'd a man for the getting a hundred SHAK:MEA 29
h., all in the same parish ANON 136
h. By men like that? DOWL 1
h. with the Bible under AUBREY 3
have a man h., and then MOLIERE 23
If I were h. on the highest KIP 42
my poor fool is hang'd SHAK:KING L 85
not hang'd for stealing Horses HALIF 6
see Major-General Harrison h. PEPYS 4
to be h. for nonsense DRYD 58
when a man knows he is to be h. JOHNSON:S 191
hanget: he was h. BRAX 2
hanging:
bare h. DRYD 142
cured by h. from a string KINGSMILL 1
h. a man who does not object SHAW 12
H. is too good for him BUNYAN 11
h. isn't bad enough HOUSM 48
h.-look to me CONG 21
H. of his cat on Monday BRATH 1
h. prevents a bad marriage SHAK:TWE 7
keep h. him until he MILLIG 11
nane the waur o' a h. BRAX 3
they're hangin' Danny Deever KIP 48
they're hangin' men an' women ANON 23
hangman:
grave-digger, or even a h. JERROLD 6
louse for the h. JONS 1
naked to the h.'s noose HOUSM 6
hangover: single malt h. BELL:I 1
hangs: What h. people STEVENSON:RL 36
Hanover: By famous H. city BROWNING:R 24
Hansard: H. is history's ear SAMUEL 3
hansel: h. of this guid new year DUNB 15
happen:
Canadians ask, 'Can it h. here?' ATWOOD 9
It Can't H. Here LEWIS:S 3
let it h. QUES 1
happened:
most of which had never h. CHURCH:W 56
this site in 1897 nothing h. ANON 227
wonder what h. to him COWARD 29
happening: perceives what is not h. TYNAN 3
happens:
all that h., h. as it should AUR 5
h. anywhere LARK 2
h. in the next world to one PEREL 5
Nothing h. to any thing AUR 9
what h., let us bear DRYD 126
what h. where it isn't RUSS:B 8
happier:
prove h. than your father SOPH 1
remembering h. things TENNY 75
seek No h. state MILT 203
that I am h. than I know? MILT 233
happiest: h. women, like the h. nations ELIOT:G 18
happily: live very h. upon a plentiful JOHNSON:S 116
happiness:
all the h. mankind can DRYD 5
boring about somebody else's h. HUX:A 1
day or brief time of h. ARISTOT 3
Domestic h., thou only bliss COWP 65
don't have h. you send out REED:R 1
fill the hour – that is h. EMER 33
greatest h. for the greatest HUTCHES 2
greatest h. of the greatest number BENTH 4
greatest h. of the whole PLATO 9
h. ? A Bubble on CLARE:J 1
H. alone is beneficial PROUST 15
H. consists in the multiplicity JOHNSON:S 132
h. destroyed by preparation AUSTEN 52
H. in marriage is entirely AUSTEN 15
H. is a mystery like religion CHESTERTON 35
H. is an imaginary condition SZASZ 6
H. is like coke HUX:A 25
H. is no laughing matter WHATE 2
h. is no longer a possibility RUSS:B 35
h. is to admire without desiring BRADLEY:FH 4
h. of the common man BEVER 1
H.! our being's end POPE 101
h. through another man's eyes SHAK:AS 64
h. too swiftly flies GRAY:T 8
It is a flaw In h. KEATS 26
life, liberty, and the pursuit of h. JEFFERSON 2
lifetime of h. SHAW 29
no more right to consume h. SHAW 7
Perfect h., even in memory AUSTEN 48
remembrance of h. when in misery DANTE 6
so great my h. YEATS 89
so much h. is produced as by JOHNSON:S 179
than h. makes them good LANDOR 22
We find our h. WORDS:W 160
We seek h. in boats HORACE 87
Were the h. of the next world BROWNE:T 52
Wherein lies h.? KEATS 36
Who never knew the price of h. YEV 1
Withdraws into its h. MARV 18
you'll give h. and joy to many BEETH 3
happy:
all be as h. as kings STEVENSON:RL 51
as h. as one hopes LA ROCHE 1
be h. while we are young ANON 12
Be h. while y'er leevin ANON 163
be worthy of being h. KANT 7
bother about whether you are h. SHAW 103
call him not h. but lucky SOLON 2
days are few, is to be h. BRECHT 2
deserves to be called h. HORACE 58
Don't worry, be h. BABA 1
duty of being h. STEVENSON:RL 20
equally *satisfied*, but not equally *h.* JOHNSON:S 132
frightening will to be h.? SAG 1
h. are farmers, too h. VIRGIL 25
h. as the grass was green THOMAS:D 16
h. could I be with either GAY 28
h. families resemble one another TOLS:L 6
h. for having been h. SMITH:Syd[1] 10
H. is the man who fears BIBLE 601
h. is the rose distill'd SHAK:MID 1
h. people are married women MENCK 20
h. that he knows no more POPE 96

H. Though Married HARDY:EJ 1
h. unless they hate some other RUSS:B 32
h. will it be for us to reside HARDWO 1
Help to make earth h. CARNEY 2
here in order to be h. SCHOP 9
How h. some o'er others SHAK:MID 5
I've had a h. life HAZL 40
lot is h. to one who is content BOET 2
Made h. by compulsion COLERIDGE:ST 60
make men h. and to keep HORACE 85
making of an old woman h. FRANKLIN:B 24
misfortune is to have been h. BOET 1
perfectly h. till all are h. SPENCER:H 5
somewhere, may be h. MENCK 4
There is a h. land YOUNG:A 1
think I'd be h. about that? REAG 7
This h. breed of men SHAK:RIC.II 17
Thrice h. he MARV 33
want to be h., be TOLS:L 16
want to be h., pretend PALAC 1
what would make one h. MENAGE 1
why should we expect to be h.? WELD 2
yourself whether you are h. MILL 30
Happy Isles: we shall touch the H.I. TENNY 55
harbour:
h. bar be moaning KINGSLEY:C 15
H. floats In air SLESS 4
In a h. grene aslepe WEVER 1
Pale rain over the dwindling h. THOMAS:D 14
where doth thine h. hold? BARNES:B 1
hard:
'H.,' replied the Dodger DICKENS 57
never think I have hit h., unless JOHNSON:S 167
not as h. as farce GWENN 1
Nothing's so h., but search HERR 43
woman is so h. upon TENNY 115
hard-faced: lot of h. men who look BALD:S 10
harder: h. they fall FITZSIM 1
hardness: without h. will be sage ARNOLD:M 36
Hardy: H. went down to botanise CHESTERTON 48
hare:
h. Fold his ears like CAMPBELL:G 1
h. limp'd trembling KEATS 61
it is the h. who wins BROOKNER 1
little h. came, hop, hop HOFFMAN:H 13
outcry of the hunted H. BLAKE:W 83
run with the h. and hunt PROV 438
than to start a h. SHAK:HEN.IV[1] 21
triumph o'er the timid h. THOMS:Ja[1] 9
hare-brained: h. chatter of irresponsible DISR:B 77
hare-lip: makes the h. SHAK:KING L 47
hares: merry brown h. came leaping KINGSLEY:C 14
hark:
H., h.! the lark SHAK:CYM 4
H., my soul COWP 6
harlot:
Every H. was a Virgin once BLAKE:W 110
pays a h. 25 times as much WILSON:Harold 2
Portia is Brutus' h. SHAK:JUL 27
prerogative of the h. BALD:S 1
prerogative of the h. KIP 157
turned into a bed-hot h. YEATS 142
harlots:
H. cry from Street to Street BLAKE:W 92
How the youthful H. curse BLAKE:W 74
harm:
Fate cannot h. me SMITH:Syd[1] 31
most harme to the mene peple LANGLAND 7
No people do so much h. CREIGH 1
power to do me h. SHAK:OTH 66
prevent h. to others MILL 8
to do h. Is often laudable SHAK:MAC 88
harmless: h. as doves BIBLE 407
harmonies: tumult of thy mighty h. SHELLEY:PB 45
harmonious: Such h. madness SHELLEY:PB 100
harmoniously: h. confus'd POPE 31
harmony:
Beauty is the product of h. SCHILL 11
best h. in a Church MILT 316
Discordant h. HORACE 88
famous h. of leaves YEATS 10
from heavenly h. DRYD 91
h. is in immortal souls SHAK:MERC 50
heaven drowsy with the h. SHAK:LOV 16
I am disposed to h. LAMB:Ch 2
other h. of prose DRYD 143
thir motions harmonie Divine MILT 220
touches of sweet h. SHAK:MERC 50
with your ninefold h. MILT 8
harness:
die with h. on our back SHAK:MAC 114
hear the h. jingle HOUSM 15
right *soupçon* of h. SAKI 13
wait in heavy h. KIP 99
harp:
hang my h. on a weeping ANON 46
h. that once through MOORE:T 7
h. with a solemn sound BIBLE 227
heart and h. have lost a string BYR 74
high-born Hoël's h. GRAY:T 29
No h. like my own CAMPBELL:T 1
wild h. slung behind him MOORE:T 10
harps:
hanged our h. upon the willows BIBLE 245
To touch their h. of gold SEARS 1
harpsichon: daughter ... play on the h. PEPYS 11
harpsichord: sound of the h. resembles BEECHAM 9
harpy: labeled h., shrew and whore RICH 2
Harris:
Bother Mrs H. DICKENS 125
words she spoke of Mrs H. DICKENS 126
Harrow: H. may be more clever CORY 4
Harrow-on-the-Hill: H.'s a rocky island BETJ 25
harrowed: having harrowd hell SPENS 8
harrowing: Only a man h. clods HARDY:T 30
Harry: Such a King H.? DRAYT 7
hart:
As pants the h. BRADY 1
As the h. panteth after BIBLE 212
was I turn'd into a h. SHAK:TWE 2
harvest:
coming h. in its breast CAMPBELL:R 4
h. is past BIBLE 337
hay h. breeze CORY 4
in h. teach BLAKE:W 34
no h. but a thorn HERB:G 40
Share my h. and my home HOOD 12
shine on, h. moon NORWORTH 1
thin h. waves its wither'd CRAB 2
harvests:
Deep H. bury all his pride POPE 73
h. of the coming century ZOLA 1
has: one of the *h.* beens HONE 1
haste:
always in h., I am never in a hurry WESLEY:J 5
H. makes waste PROV 160
h. of a Fool is the slowest thing SHADWE 2
H. still pays h. SHAK:MEA 39
h. to shed innocent blood BIBLE 332
Make h. slowly ERAS 4
Men love in h. BYR 228
More h., less speed PROV 276
This sweaty h. SHAK:HAM 4
what h. I can to be gone CROMWELL 14
Without h., but without rest GOET 40
hasten: h. is now To delay MALLEY 3
hat:
black h. – which isn't there BOWEN:L 2
forbade me to put off my h. FOX:G 3
get away with a h. like that LOOS 7
h. and wig will soon be here COWP 55
h. of antique shape ARNOLD:M 22
h. that lets the rain in FRED 2
He weareth a runcible h. LEAR 6
hit a woman with his h. on ALLEN:F 2
I put my h. upon my head JOHNSON:S 72
in a shocking bad h. SURT 20
In his h. a Railway-Ticket LEAR 12
lay a h. – and a few PARKER:D 23
like Antichrist in that lewd h. JONS 25
like the brim of a sundowner's h. BOYD:RGP 2
my knee, my h., and hand BROWNE:T 1
No h. upon his head SHAK:HAM 61
recollect where he laid his h. JOHNSON:S 233
silk h. on a Bradford millionaire ELIOT:TS 45
touching of the h. is a very rare KINGSLEY:H 2
Where did you get that h.? ROLM 1
without pulling off his h. JOHNSON:S 112
hatched:
All eggs are not h. DONNE 107
h. o'er again, an' h. different ELIOT:G 5
hatches: continually under h. KEATS 132
hatchet:
did it with my little h. WASH 1
h. to remove a fly PROV 75
hate:
been in love, or in h. STEVENSON:RL 5
being efficient ... makes everybody h. you EDWARDS:B 1
bother with people I h. HART 1
cherish those hearts that h. SHAK:HEN.VIII 12
enough religion to make us h. SWIFT 14
fools to h. SWIFT 55
glance of supernatural h. BYR 148
grown past h. GILMORE 2
happy unless they h. some other RUSS:B 32
h. him through the glass BLUN 2
h. of those below BYR 87
h. provided that they fear ACC 1
h. that which we often fear SHAK:ANT 16
h. those whom you have injured TAC 2
he ruled by getting people to h. JUNG:Chang 1
I h. all that don't love me FARQ 4
I h. and I love CATUL 19
I h. everyone equally FIELDS 7
If h. killed men BROWNING:R 36
If we h. a person, we h. HESSE 1
implacable in h. DRYD 41
love him whom thou dost h. SHAK:SON 39
men h. one another so MELBOU 9
Men will not h. you Enough ELIOT:TS 75
must h. and death return? SHELLEY:PB 158
no h. lost between us MIDD 4
nought I did in h. SHAK:OTH 69
roughness breedeth h. BACON:F[1] 74
scarcely h. any one that we know HAZL 29
Take away this murdherin' h. O'CAS 4
They h. whom they fear ENN 3
time to h. BIBLE 281
'tis delicious to h. you MOORE:T 2
to h. and to despise myself? HAZL 31
too much not to h. him RACINE 1
Two Minutes H. ORWELL 31
who h. you don't win unless you h. NIX 10
hated:
I never h. a man enough GABOR 1
loved well because he h. BROWNING:R 140
hater:
h. he came SHELLEY:PB 20
he was a very good h. JOHNSON:S 254
haters: Where the h. meet BROWNING:R 46
hates:
h. me because I'm so universally liked DE VR 6
who h. dogs and babies ROSTEN 1
hating:
don't give way to h. KIP 127
h., my boy, is an art NASH 9
h. such a hateless thing SHELLEY:PB 65
they [blacks] are turned to h. PATON 2
hatless: young man lands h. BETJ 5
hatred:
from envy, h., and malice PRAY 33
intellectual h. is the worst YEATS 60
love to h. turned CONG 34
more like h. than like friendship LA ROCHE 10
must have no h. or bitterness CAVELL 1
ox and h. therewith BIBLE 262
Passionate h. can give meaning HOFFER 2
Yet live in h., enmitie MILT 162
hats:
nests inside men's Sunday h. BROWNING:R 25
offensive h., defensive h., and shrapnel WHITEHORN 1
so many shocking bad h. in my life WELLING 15
They wat their h. BALL 50
Haughey: Mr H. buried at midnight O'BRIEN:CC 1
haughtiness: h. of soul ADDIS 5
haughty: h. spirit before a fall BIBLE 263
haundit: be h. owre tae the haithen BIBLE 592
haunt: all the h. be ours SHAK:ANT 52
haunted:
'tis h., holy ground BYR 70
women who h. you were not MULK 1
haunts: from h. of coot and hern TENNY 201
hautboys: give the h. breath DRYD 106
haute couture: H.c. is finished CHANEL 4
have:
H. more than thou showest SHAK:KING L 15

If you h. it BARRIE 10
We shall h. them PETAIN 1
have-his-carcase: h., next to the perpetual DICKENS 50
haves: H. and the Have-nots CERV 19
havoc: Cry 'H.!' SHAK:JUL 44
hawk:
h. at eagles with a dove? HERB:G 17
h. to fetch the wild-fowl BALL 59
I know a h. from a handsaw SHAK:HAM 82
Jentyll as fawcoun Or hawke SKEL:J 5
hawks:
Dark h. hear us JOYCE:J 35
h. favoured an air strike BARTL 1
hawthorn:
flowers Stream from the h. HOUSM 31
h. bush a sweeter shade SHAK:HEN.VI[3] 4
h. hedge puts forth its buds BROOKE 5
Under the H. in the dale MILT 70
White h., and the pastoral KEATS 93
hay:
butter'd his h. SHAK:KING L 27
dance the antic h. MARLOWE 28
dance the h., the h. BRET 3
eating h. when you're faint CARROLL 76
h. harvest breeze CORY 4
Live on h. HILL:J 1
Make h. while the sun shines PROV 258
sweet h., hath no fellow SHAK:MID 38
that's what h. looks like MARY QUEEN CON 1
we lie tumbling in the h. SHAK:WIN 12
When the muir-men win their h. BALL 7
world is a bundle of h. BYR 137
Hayden, Bill: prick with a limited future* HAWKE 2
haystack: Beside the h. in the floods? MORRIS:W 1
hazard:
Men that h. all SHAK:MERC 26
occupational h. of being a wife ANNE 4
hazards: one of the h. of my profession UMB 1
haze:
lives in a sort of rosy h. MURD:I 3
seaward h. HARDY:T 25
hazel:
I went out to the h. wood YEATS 22
plump the h. shells KEATS 109
he:
Because it was h. MONTAIGNE 7
every h. has got him ANON 9
meant both 'h.' and 'she' MILNE 19
poorest h. that is in England RAINBO 1
Who h.? ROSS:HW 1
head:
after his h. was cut off ANON 209
all that by shaking his h.? SHERIDAN:RB 37
Australia in the hollow of your h. CALWELL 2
bear with a sore h. MARR 2
bowed his comely h. MARV 3
can't make a h. and brains DICKENS 193
child's h. up the horse's arse COWARD 33
crawled h. downward down ELIOT:TS 53
cuts the wrong man's h. off DICKENS 20
darling black h. my heart above FERGUS 1
examined your son's h. MUIR:F 1
excellent h. of hair SHAK:TWE 4
gently lay my h. BROWNE:T 35
God be in my h. ANON 66
greatest asset a h. of state WILSON:Harold 7
hard of h., blunt of speech HILL:Reg 4
h. bit off by it young SHAK:KING L 18
h. grown gray in vain SHELLEY:PB 121
h. is a thoroughly inefficient MAUGH 16
h. is bloody, but unbowed HENL 1
h. is not more native SHAK:HAM 13
h. is the most important MANS:K 9
h. like yours, I'd have it circumcised ALLEN:D 2
h. of a family off DICKENS 4
h. off with a golden axe SHAK:ROM 33
h. to contrive CLAREN 2
h. to contrive GIBBON:E 8
h. upon which all 'the ends PATER 1
heart runs away with his h. COLMAN:G[2] 6
Heaven blazing into the h. YEATS 109
his brains go to his h. ASQU:M 7
his guts in his h. SHAK:TRO 7
If you can keep your h. KIP 127
I'll eat my h. DICKENS 60
incessantly stand on your h. CARROLL 9
it hanging on the h. HARRIS:R 1
I've a h. like a concertina KIP 46
keep a level h. HORACE 19
Lay your sleeping h. AUD 13
like God's own h. COLERIDGE:ST 17
make you shorter by the h. ELIZ I 12
Man with the h. and woman TENNY 113
Many a h. has turned grey MULL 1
maugree his heed CHAUC 42
must not stroke anyone's h. LENIN 11
my h. is bending low FOST:SC 6
My ho h. halls JOYCE:J 35
never broke any man's h. SHAK:HEN.V 23
Off with his h. CARROLL 21
Off with his h. CIB 2
Off with his h. SHAK:RIC.III 11
old h. on young shoulders EMER 68
one small h. could carry GOLDS 29
pur-boil'd H. upon a Stake GRAHAM:J 2
repairs his drooping h. MILT 57
saving her h. by using it WYNNE 1
shake his sapient h. ARNOLD:M 50
She had the h. DICKENS 179
short in the h. ANON 53
should have his h. examined GOLDWYN 2
show my h. to the people DANTON 4
stand. 'On my h.' DISR:B 49
stars with my exalted h. HORACE 2
Such as take lodgings in a h. BUTLER:S[1] 9
tell which was the h. BRIGHT 4
thing under your hat a h.? HOLB 1
to get one's h. cut off CARROLL 60
touches a hair of yon old grey h. WHITTIER 6
turns no more his h. COLERIDGE:ST 34
Uneasy lies the h. SHAK:HEN.IV[2] 31
What though his h. be empty SWIFT 6
which way the h. lies RALE 11
without either its h. or its point JERROLD 12
head-in-air: Little Johnny H. HOFFMAN:H 7
head-waiter:
h. who's allowed to sit down UST 3
plump h. at The Cock TENNY 67
headache:
h. called thought in the brain THOMS:Ja[2] 1
I happen to have a h. CARROLL 61
headaches: In h. and in worry AUD 7
headland: naked top Of some bold h. WORDS:W 112
headless: By h. Charles BYR 38
headline: fit this sensational h. MORTON:JB 4
headlong: H. themselves they threw MILT 223
headmaster:
peculiar behaviour from a h. NICHOLS:B 1
Was not my father the h.? GREENE:G 15
headmasters: H. have powers CHURCH:W 42
heads:
h. are like a stomach and intestines SCHOP 6
H., h....! ... five children – mother DICKENS 4
shod their h. in their canoes MARV 34
stood them on their h. BARRIE 15
Tossing their h. in sprightly dance WORDS:W 121
Two h. are better than PROV 406
your h., O ye gates BIBLE 208
headstones: h. yield their names TATE:A 1
headstrong: h. as an allegory SHERIDAN:RB 11
heady: H., not strong POPE 168
heal:
h. but by degrees? SHAK:OTH 30
h. what is wounded LANGTON 2
Physician, h. thyself BIBLE 452
time to h. BIBLE 281
healer:
compassion of the h.'s art ELIOT:TS 96
It is not a great h. COMPT 9
Time is a great h. PROV 393
healing:
no h. has been necessary COMPT 9
not heroics but h. HARDING:WG 1
time for the h. of the wounds MANDELA:N 6
with h. in his wings BIBLE 363
With h. in His wings COWP 14
heals: h. his wounds NEWT:J 2
health:
character is the h. of his wife CONNOLLY:C 15
double h. to thee BYR 130
H. and high fortune till we meet SCOTT:W 51
H. is better than wealth PROV 161
h. is the second blessing WALT 15
h. unbought DRYD 122
H. unto his Majesty ANON 15
I have nor hope nor h. SHELLEY:PB 32
in sickness and in h. PRAY 84
My h. was drunk VICT 1
row after h. like a waterman SWIFT 85
that will his h. deny DYER:J[2] 1
healths: drink our h. at dinner KIP 33
healthy:
be h. that makes a life MARTIAL 7
h. and wealthy and dead THURB 11
H. by temp'rance, and by exercise POPE 129
h., wealthy and wise PROV 88
heap:
make one h. of all your winnings KIP 127
struck all of a h. SHERIDAN:RB 1
hear:
Can you h. me, mother? POWELL:S 1
cannot choose but h. COLERIDGE:ST 11
can't h. out'n de udder HARRIS:JC 5
h. more of him later LAW 4
h. my Thisby's face SHAK:MID 48
h. no more at all STEVENSON:RL 70
h. the word of the Lord BIBLE 347
h. us, good Lord PRAY 35
Lord, h. our prayers PRAY 78
she is sure to h. AUSTEN 45
sure to h. of it from one damned SHERIDAN:RB 30
To h., to see, to feel BYR 67
two counties he can h. GRAVES:R 2
you will h. me DISR:B 51
heard:
have ye not h.? BIBLE 323
h. no more in Heav'n MILT 221
H., not regarded SHAK:HEN.IV[1] 69
I h. it all HODG 4
I will be h. GARRIS 1
then is h. no more SHAK:MAC 113
You ain't h. nothin' yet JOLS 1
hearers:
not h. only BIBLE 562
send the h. weeping SHAK:RIC.II 41
want attentive and favourable h. HOOK 2
heareth: thy servant h. BIBLE 140
hearing:
if he thought he was within h. JOHNSON:S 219
passionate my sense of h. SHAK:LOV 6
hearken: h. than the fat of rams BIBLE 145
hearsay: lived by h., and faith BUNYAN 33
hearse:
strew the Laureat Herse MILT 55
Underneath this sable h. BROWNE:W[1] 1
undertakers – walk before the h. GARRICK 1
hearses: frequent h. shall besiege POPE 59
Hearst: Look at Patty H. Those parents HUMPH 9
heart:
Absence makes the h. grow PROV 1
Absence makes the h. grow fonder BAYLY 2
always roaming with a hungry h. TENNY 52
as the h. grows older HOPK:GM 16
Awake, my h. BRIDGES:R 2
awful warmth about my h. KEATS 141
Batter my h. DONNE 87
be the h. to conceive JUNIUS 7
Because my h. is pure TENNY 61
begins in the h. of a man CATHER 1
blind side of the h. CHESTERTON 6
broken h. lies here MACAULAY:TB 56
Bury my h. at Wounded Knee BENET 2
Call home the h. DRAYT 10
calm sunshine of the h. CONSTABLE:J 4
Cold hands, warm h. PROV 58
dark as one's own h. HAWT 4
darkness of man's h. GOLDI 2
Dere's where my h. FOST:SC 4
desires of the h. are as crooked AUD 9
dooth myn herte boote CHAUC 79
education of the h. SCOTT:W 92
Feed the h. of the night SWIN 4
find 'Calais' lying in my h. MARY I 1
From all blindness of h. PRAY 33
from the h., goes to the h. COLERIDGE:ST 101

give me back my h. BYR 20
give me back my h. GRANVILLE 3
glow in the h. that with every CONRAD 8
God be in my h. ANON 66
grandeurs of his Babylonian h. THOMP:F 5
harden Pharaoh's h. BIBLE 91
he tears out the h. KNOW 1
hear it in the deep h.'s core YEATS 4
h. aboon them a' BURNS:R 30
h. and harp have lost a string BYR 74
h. and my flesh crieth out BIBLE 221
h. and stomach of a king ELIZ I 3
h. and voice would fail me CLARI 1
h. argues, not the mind ARNOLD:M 38
h. as sound as a bell SHAK:MUCH 17
h. ay's the part BURNS:R 16
h. be still as loving BYR 128
h., Closed up tight CHON 1
h. could never speak MUIR:E 7
h. for every fate BYR 130
h. grown cold SHELLEY:PB 121
h. has its reasons PASC 11
h. is a lonely hunter MACLEOD:F 1
h. is a small thing QUAR 5
h. is an anvil unto sorrow MARLOWE 26
h. is deceitful above all BIBLE 340
h. is Highland GALT 1
h. is Highland SCOTT:W 66
h. is inditing a good BIBLE 214
h. is like Indian rubber BRONTE:A 1
h. is on the left MOLIERE 18
h. is restless till it finds AUGUS 1
h. is slow to learn MILLAY 5
h. less bounding ARNOLD:M 44
h. let me more have pity on HOPK:GM 25
h. Must bear the longest HERB:G 24
h. of a man is deprest GAY 20
h. of lead POPE 165
H. of Man, we are told, is deceitful BRIDIE 1
H. of oak are our ships GARRICK 4
h. of the wise, like a mirror CONF 22
h. runs away with his head COLMAN:G[2] 6
h. shall be The faithful compass GAY 38
H. speaks to h. NEWM:JH 22
h. that has truly lov'd MOORE:T 4
h. that thought the thought BALL 25
h. the keener ANON 248
h. to resolve GIBBON:E 8
h. untravell'd fondly turns GOLDS 4
h. was pierced through the ear SHAK:OTH 12
h. was warm and gay HAMMER 2
h. which grief hath canker'd CALVER 1
H. within, and God o'erhead LONGFEL 3
h.'s grown brutal YEATS 67
h.'s in the right place MAUGH 16
h.'s renying BARNF 4
her h. in his grave is lying MOORE:T 14
His flaw'd h. SHAK:KING L 82
Home is where the h. is PROV 174
humble and a contrite h. KIP 91
I am gathered to thy h. MEY:A 3
I had lock'd my h. BALL 63
I would eat his h. SHAK:MUCH 27
If thou wilt ease thine h. BEDD 1
If thy h. fails thee, climb not ELIZ I 7
In my h. of h. SHAK:HAM 108
in politics there is no h. NAPO I 13
Indian Summer of the h. WHITTIER 1
Keep your h. a desert MUSSO:B 11
Land of H.'s Desire YEATS 16
Left me with a palsied h. TENNY 80
looke in thy h. and write SIDNEY:P 4
loosed our h. in tears ARNOLD:M 8
Lord looketh on the h. BIBLE 146
lose her h., or necklace POPE 45
loving h. to thee HERR 29
make stone of the h. YEATS 43
Makes my h. go pit-a-pat BROWNING:R 27
maketh the h. sick BIBLE 259
man after his own h. BIBLE 144
Many a h. is aching HARRIS:C 1
may not follow their own h. SCHILL 2
me 'eart 'as got The pip DENNIS:CJ 1
merry h. doeth good BIBLE 264
merry h. goes all the day SHAK:WIN 15
mighty h. is lying still WORDS:W 92
mind is always fooled by the h. LA ROCHE 16
My h. aches KEATS 93
my h. for the Commonwealth's broke LAWS 6
My h. in hiding Stirred HOPK:GM 11
my h. is a handful of dust TENNY 221
My h. is heavy GOET 18
My h. is like a singing bird ROSSET:C 2
My h. is turn'd to stone SHAK:OTH 47
My h. leaps up when I behold WORDS:W 49
my h. not badly shaken KAV 2
my h. puts forth its pain BROOKE 5
My h. shall be thy garden MEY:A 1
my h. waketh BIBLE 297
my h. was in the sea BARNARD:A 1
My h. was wandering BRENN 3
My h. would hear her TENNY 219
My h.'s in the Highlands BURNS:R 80
My h.'s in the Highlands SCOTT:W 47
my h.'s right there JUDGE 1
My true Love hathe my harte SIDNEY:P 3
naked thinking h. DONNE 29
never a crack in my h. YEATS 1
never has ached with a h. SWIN 22
no end of things in the h. POUND 7
nor his h. to report SHAK:MID 42
not your h. be troubled BIBLE 487
on my h. they tread SHAK:RIC.II 31
Once a woman has given you her h. VANB 2
only had to examine my own h. DE VALE 1
Open my h. and you will see BROWNING:R 104
out-worn h. YEATS 15
put his h. to school WORDS:W 140
put in a h. o' stane BALL 53
red pavilion of my h.? THOMP:F 1
road from the eye to the h. CHESTERTON 30
secret anniversaries of the h. LONGFEL 34
seems to slight her simple h. TENNY 175
send me back my h. SUCK 6
She had A h. – how shall I say? BROWNING:R 21
She wants a H. POPE 134
shut out of mine own h. BRENN 4
since man's h. is small KIP 110
smoke and flame I lost my h. HOUSM 47
some h. did break TENNY 131
stab'd me to the H. GAY 1
sure of his unspotted h. PEELE 2
Sweeping up the H. DICKIN:E 18
sweet concurrence of the H. HERR 1
Take any h. GILB:WS 23
Take h. of grace GILB:WS 22
Tears fall in my h. VERL 2
That the h. grows old? YEATS 57
Then burst his mighty h. SHAK:JUL 55
then my h. with pleasure fills WORDS:W 122
there will your h. be also BIBLE 393
thou hast cleft my h. SHAK:HAM 146
thou hast my h. PRIOR 11
thought my shrivel'd h. HERB:G 45
thy h. lies open unto me TENNY 117
tie my h. upon my sleeve DAVIDS 1
twist the sinews of thy h.? BLAKE:W 68
untroubled h. of stone CAMPBELL:T 3
want to break my h.?' 'Yes,' said Seth GIBBONS:S 2
waters of the h. Push in THOMAS:D 5
way to a man's h. FERN 1
way to a man's h. is through PROV 414
We hear the h. break MUIR:E 7
wear him In my h.'s core SHAK:HAM 108
wear my h. upon my sleeve SHAK:OTH 3
Were not my h. at rest SEDLEY 5
What h. could have thought you? THOMS:F 19
Whatever your h. clings to LUTHER 3
Whose guiltlesse hart is free CAMPION 3
wilt thou cure thine h. BEDD 2
With a h. for any fate LONGFEL 5
with my h. in't SHAK:TEM 21
with the h. that one can see SAINT-EX 3
With your crooked h. AUD 8
woman with the h. TENNY 113
would not have such a h. SHAK:MAC 103
Your h. of anger BAXTER:JK 1
heart-ache: say we end the h. SHAK:HAM 97
heart-break: h. in the heart of things GIBS 1
heart-easing: tell the most h. things KEATS 13
heart-strings: griefs which cut the h. FORD:J[1] 8
heartburn: I am h. HOPK:GM 27
hearth:
from an unextinguished h. SHELLEY:PB 46
genial h. WORDS:W 130
Save the Cricket on the h. MILT 83
woman for the h. TENNY 113
hearth-stane: His clean h. BURNS:R 11
hearts:
at their h. the fire's centre SPEND 2
cold h. and muddy understandings BURKE:E 56
don't let your h. be hardened VILLON 2
draw H. after them MILT 264
few h. and intellects like hers MILL 24
finite h. that yearn BROWNING:R 162
first in the h. of his countrymen LEE:Hen 1
Graft in our h. the love PRAY 55
h. are dry as summer dust WORDS:W 113
h. are earned YEATS 59
h. I lost my own to HOUSM 36
H. just as pure and fair GILB:WS 46
h. that honour could not move BROOKE 23
h., that once beat high MOORE:T 7
h. That spaniel'd me SHAK:ANT 47
joining of h. and house-keepings DICKENS 62
Kind h. are more than coronets TENNY 64
Lift up your h. MASS 12
live in h. we leave behind CAMPBELL:T 18
Neither have the h. to stay BUTLER:S[1] 36
our h. are great TENNY 241
Our h. are out of order LAWS 3
Our h. are young LANG:A 5
Poore h., that humbly sue CAREW:T 9
Pure eyes and Christian h. KEBLE 5
Queen of H. She made NURS 56
simple song for thinking h. WORDS:W 24
take away our h. o' stone O'CAS 4
to place women's h. So far WEBSTER:J 20
two h. beating each to each BROWNING:R 58
Two h. that beat as one LOVELL:M 1
Two h. with just one HALM 1
union of hands and h. TAYL:Jer 3
uniting of human h. YEV 6
unto whom all h. be open PRAY 63
We have given our h. away WORDS:W 104
When h. have once mingled SHELLEY:PB 160
wot's hidden in each other's h. DICKENS 119
you hard h. SHAK:JUL 2
heat:
don't like the h., get out PROV 191
h. another h. expels SHAK:TWO 7
H. is in proportion STERNE 22
If you can't stand the h. TRU 1
Lap your loneliness in h. BETJ 23
Not the schoolboy h. TENNY 178
one heate (all know) doth CHAPMAN:G 2
heat-waves: where the h. dance for ever BOA 1
heath:
h., with withering brake CRAB 2
h. wore the appearance HARDY:T 57
Little rose on the h. GOET 1
said to understand the h. HARDY:T 58
There's the wind on the h. BORR 6
Heath: grammar school twit H. SPEIGHT 2
heathen:
'eathen in 'is blindness KIP 81
H. in the carnal part POPE 131
his glory among the h. BIBLE 230
not a H., or a Jew WATTS 13
Why do the h. rage BIBLE 196
You're a pore benighted 'eathen KIP 50
heather:
know I how the H. looks DICKIN:E 17
Names canna mak the h. Bloom PATERSON:A 1
heaven:
all Heav'n before mine eyes MILT 90
All I seek, the h. above STEVENSON:RL 63
all of h. we have below ADDIS 33
All places are distant from H. BURTON:Ro 16
All this and h. too HENRY:M 4
an humbler Heav'n POPE 83
and a h. to throne in SHAK:COR 21
any writer will get into h. CLARK:M 3
at h.'s gates she claps LYLY 6
Battering the gates of h. TENNY 44
become the hoped-for h. MILL 24
Beneath a h. dark and holy TENNY 30
betwixt H. and Charing Cross THOMP:F 14
bid him go to H., to H. he goes JUV 7
blue liberality of h.? BROWNING:R 206
bring up the rear in h. BROWNE:T 22
builds a H. in Hells despair BLAKE:W 63

cold and rook-delighting h. YEATS 34
come to model Heav'n MILT 229
day when h. was falling HOUSM 37
describe a whole day in h. SHAW 102
do in h. we are ignorant of SWIFT 16
Down from the verge of Heav'n MILT 223
Earth's crammed with h. BROWNING:EB 21
exile Hath emptied Heav'n MILT 139
Father, who art in h. MASS 15
flowerless fields of h. SWIN 8
gates of h. opened against him MALORY 15
God's in his h. BROWNING:R 9
Guesses at H. KEATS 99
hath in hevene or helle ybe CHAUC 93
He ascended into h. PRAY 19
heard no more in Heav'n MILT 221
H. and earth shall pass BIBLE 429
h. be in these lips MARLOWE 38
H. blazing into the head YEATS 109
H. could be so small a thing WAD 1
H. for climate TWAIN 41
H. in a Wild Flower BLAKE:W 82
H. is empty NERV 2
H. lies about us WORDS:W 58
h. still guards the right SHAK:RIC.II 23
h. that leads men SHAK:SON 56
H. vows to keep him JONS 34
H.'s light forever shines SHELLEY:PB 126
H.'s peculiar care SOMER 2
h.'s vault should crack SHAK:KING L 83
Heav'n has no rage CONG 34
Heav'n is for thee too high MILT 231
Heav'n's wide pathles way MILT 82
His looks do menace h. MARLOWE 6
I see H.'s glories shine BRONTE:E 1
Is it any better in H. WILLIAMS:WC 4
know I'm farther off from heav'n HOOD 10
lead you in at H. gate BLAKE:W 117
Let h. exist BORGES 1
Love is h., and h. is love SCOTT:W 8
Made life a h. on earth KEPP:C 1
make a Heav'n of Hell MILT 122
Man is H.'s masterpiece QUAR 9
Marriage is . . . excluded from h. BUTLER:S[2] 44
Marriages are made in h. PROV 269
new h. and a new earth BIB:REV 13
new h., new earth SHAK:ANT 2
not want Capital in H. ELIOT:TS 19
One h., one hell BROWNING:R 126
One H., one Hell SHELLEY:PB 134
open face of h. KEATS 2
open the Kingdom of H. to all PRAY 10
or H. can give SHELLEY:PB 157
Or what's a h. for? BROWNING:R 72
Our Father which art in H. PREVERT 1
Parting is all we know of h. DICKIN:E 22
Pennies from H.? BURKE:J 1
Persian's H. is easily made MOORE:T 19
Puts all H. in a Rage BLAKE:W 82
quincunx of h. runs low BROWNE:T 45
Sends ane to H. BURNS:R 19
Starrie Cope of h. MILT 207
starry h. above me KANT 8
steep and thorny way to h. SHAK:HAM 29
Strike h. on the face SHAK:MAC 90
than serve in Heav'n MILT 123
that's the way to heav'n POPE 65
theirs is the kingdom of h. BIBLE 384
then the heav'n espie HERB:G 51
There may be h. BROWNING:R 60
there shall be no Cloud nor Sun* DONNE 110
There's h. above BROWNING:R 6
things are the sons of h. JOHNSON:S 6
think about going to h. CARLYLE:JW 6
this is the gate of h. BIBLE 62
trouble deaf h. SHAK:SON 11
under an English h. BROOKE 25
waitest for the spark from h. ARNOLD:M 26
waiting for the spark from h. ARNOLD:M 24
Warring in Heav'n against MILT 183
water'd h. with their tears BLAKE:W 69
Waves that Beat on H. Shore BLAKE:W 88
we know the way to h. ELS 1
we shall practise in h. BROWNING:R 138
why stand ye gazing up into h.? BIBLE 496
without a thought of H. or Hell BROWNE:T 19
heavenly: H. Hurt DICKIN:E 4
heavens:
h. declare the glory of God BIBLE 203
h. my wide roof-tree AYT 5
h. possesse his gost SURREY 3
h. rain odours on you SHAK:TWE 39
heav'ns are not too high HERB:G 24
promise h. free from strife CORY 2
spangled h., a shining frame ADDIS 39
When I consider thy h. BIBLE 198
heaventree: h. of stars hung with JOYCE:J 27
heavier: borne even h. things VIRGIL 36
heaviness: h. foreruns the good event SHAK:HEN.IV[2] 39
heavy: h., but no less divine BYR 198
Hebraism:
H. and Hellenism – between these ARNOLD:M 70
H., *strictness of conscience* ARNOLD:M 71
Hebrew: between H. and Olympian revelations GLAD 9
Hebrides:
beyond the stormy H. MILT 56
in dreams behold the H. GALT 1
in dreams behold the H. SCOTT:W 66
seas colder than the H. FLECKER 6
Hector:
great H.'s Life HOMER 14
greatly changed from that H. VIRGIL 51
H. is dead SHAK:TRO 26
Hecuba:
All for H. WILLM 2
What's H. to him SHAK:HAM 90
hedge:
clipped h. is to a forest JOHNSON:S 252
h. between keeps friendship PROV 162
voice will run From h. to h. KEATS 14
hedge-crickets: H. sing KEATS 109
hedge-sparrow: h. fed the cuckoo so long SHAK:KING L 18
hedgehog:
h. one *big* one ARCHIL 1
h. travels furtively HARDY:T 34
hedgehogs:
begin throwing h. under me KHRU 7
Thorny h. SHAK:MID 21
hedges:
meadows, with filigree h. WALP:H 4
tongues, and h. ears SWIFT 59
hedonist: faddling h. STEVENSON:RL 1
heel: lifted up his h. against BIBLE 211
heels:
high h. are most agreeable SWIFT 29
Time wounds all h. ANON 250
Time wounds all h. MARX:G 22
heffalump: decided to catch a H. MILNE 12
heid: play golf ye maun hae a h. MACDON:CB 1
heifer:
h. lowing at the skies KEATS 92
Mullingar h. was beef ANON 104
height:
Great is the h. that I must PROP 4
such infinities of h. SLESS 3
three years old is half his h. LEONARDO 3
to the Holiest in the h. NEWM:JH 17
heights:
difficult task to *keep* H. WORDS:W 118
h. by great men reached LONGFEL 19
let us suffer on the h. HUGO 4
struggle itself towards the h. CAMUS 3
heir:
h. of all the ages TENNY 86
heire of my invention prove SHAK:POET 8
heiress: American h. wants to buy a man MCCARTHY:M 2
heirs:
And to your h. for ever SHAK:JUL 59
make us h. of all eternity SHAK:LOV 1
Helen:
Dust hath closed H.'s eye NASHE 1
first dawn in H.'s arms? YEATS 85
H., as befits her name AESC 2
H., thy beauty is POE 1
H., whose beauty MARLOWE 14
like another H. DRYD 113
Past ruin'd Ilion H. lives LANDOR 2
white H. bears Child BROOKE 4
wish I were where H. lies BALL 25
Helena: all is dross that is not H. MARLOWE 38
helicopters: they are all my h. JOHNSON:LB 7
hell:
agreement with h. GARRIS 3
all H. broke loose? MILT 206
all we need of h. DICKIN:E 22
allotted death and h. MARLOWE 43
bells of H. go ting-a-ling ANON 32
Better to reign in H. MILT 123
blame pave the floor of h. KENNELLY 3
Bloody h., Ma'am, what's he ANDREWS 1
builds a H. in Heavens despite BLAKE:W 64
burst the gates of h. WESLEY:C 1
characters of h. to trace GRAY:T 30
come hot from h. SHAK:JUL 44
corn and begin raising h. LEASE 1
entrance leads to H. MILT 34
even if my place be h. BORGES 1
first to tell me about H. BETJ 34
gates of H. are open night VIRGIL 66
gates of h. shall not prevail BIBLE 417
Ghosts glut the throat of h. BLAKE:W 3
go through h. to get it MARQUIS 11
hath in hevene or helle ybe CHAUC 93
having harrowd h. SPENS 8
He descended into h. PRAY 19
h. for society TWAIN 41
H. hath no limits MARLOWE 35
H. I suffer seems a Heav'n MILT 184
H. is a city much like London SHELLEY:PB 48
H. is murky SHAK:MAC 100
H. is oneself ELIOT:TS 110
H. is other people SARTRE 6
H., . . . is to love no longer BERNAN 1
H. is when you get CLARE:A 1
H. of Heav'n MILT 122
H.! said the Duchess CHRIS 2
h. to ships, a h. to men AESC 2
H. trembl'd at the hideous MILT 170
I myself am h. LOWELL:R 6
If Hitler invaded H. CHURCH:W 58
If there is a h. upon earth BURTON:Ro 13
I'll get a swig in H. KIP 57
improving his prisons in H. COLERIDGE:ST 44
in a Printing house in H. BLAKE:W 54
injur'd Lover's H. MILT 215
Into the mouth of H. TENNY 199
it is all h. SHERMAN 1
keeps the gate of h. SHAK:OTH 53
lead apes in h. SHAK:TAM 5
leads men to this h. SHAK:SON 56
make a h. of this world BECKF 2
make This world our h. WILDE:O 3
My self am H. MILT 184
never mentions H. to ears POPE 72
Nor H. a fury CONG 34
One heaven, one h. BROWNING:R 126
One Heaven, one H. SHELLEY:PB 134
out of H. leads up to Light MILT 161
pains of h. for ever CATEC 3
place is too cold for h. SHAK:MAC 50
prince of h. Hath risen LUTHER 5
Procuress to the Lords of H. TENNY 151
Raises from H. a Human Soul BLAKE:W 84
road to h. is paved with good PROV 334
saw there was a way to H. BUNYAN 20
Sent to H., Sir JOHNSON:S 243
shall move H. VIRGIL 76
so wicked as Lord George H. BEERB 3
stirrup-pump can extinguish h. REED:H 2
that riches grow in H. MILT 143
The h. I am ANON 76
There is a dreadful H. WATTS 11
There is wishful thinking in H. LEWIS:CS 3
there must be h. BROWNING:R 60
though h. should bar the way NOY 4
Thyself to be thy proper H. BYR 121
to build in H. MILT 145
to make the earth my h. SHAK:RIC.III 14
told me . . . to believe in h. TEIL 1
where we are is H. MARLOWE 35
Which way I flie is H. MILT 184
Why this is h. MARLOWE 34
woke in h., should still believe STEVENSON:RL 71
working definition of h. SHAW 139
yettis of h. ar brokin DUNB 18
Hellas: city as a whole is the school of H. PERIC 3
Hellenism:
governing idea of H. ARNOLD:M 71

Hebraism and H. – between these ARNOLD:M 70
Hellespont: have pass'd the H. BYR 177
hellhound: h. is always a h. WODE 21
helm: Pleasure at the h. GRAY:T 31
helmet:
h. and the helmet-feather TENNY 19
h. now shall make a hive PEELE 2
help:
did his best to h. the people HUX:TH 15
encumbers him with h.? JOHNSON:S 95
God, our h. in ages past WATTS 18
God will not h. him MENCK 13
gods h. those who h. themselves AESOP 4
h. us, this and every KEBLE 2
H. yourself, and heaven will FONTAINE 2
know how to h. themselves WEISS 2
knowledge that they will h. EPI 1
make him an h. meet BIBLE 12
many of your countrymen cannot h. JOHNSON:S 106
My h. cometh from BIBLE 239
never try to begin to h. HUGEL 1
Our h. is in the Name of the Lord PRAY 78
They look on and h. LAWR:DH 40
very present h. in time of trouble ANON 148
very present h. in trouble BIBLE 215
very present h. in trouble STEVENSON:A 3
what is past my h. FLETCH:J 21
what's past h. SHAK:WIN 7
Who ran to h. me TAYL:Ann 1
with a little h. from my friends LENNON 9
helped: We shall have h. it DICKENS 203
helper: Our antagonist is our h. BURKE:E 66
helpers: When other h. fail LYTE 1
helpless: h. man, in ignorance sedate JOHNSON:S 71
helplessness: h. being foreign to snorters GUNN:J 1
helps:
Every little h. PROV 101
God h. them that help PROV 148
helter skelter: H.s., hang sorrow JONS 1
Hemingway, Ernest: He has never been known to* FAULK 2
hemlock:
hand him h. for his wage MARQUIS 8
of h. I had drunk KEATS 93
hen:
better take a wet h. KHRU 11
h. is only an egg's way BUTLER:S[2] 8
nat of that text a pulled h. CHAUC 12
hen house: lot of experience in the h.h. TRU 2
hen-pecked: have they not hen-peck'd you BYR 160
Henry:
H.[1] . . . caught his death FABY 2
heartless H. lies BYR 38
strictly a Hoorah H. RUNYON 6
hens: hennes for to doon al his plesaunce CHAUC 62
herald:
H. sad and trumpet SHAK:POET 3
Homer the h. of your valour ALEX 1
herald-angels: Hark! the h. sing WESLEY:C 7
heraldry: boast of h. GRAY:T 17
herb:
call it h. of grace SHAK:HAM 170
fragrance from the h. at your feet TROLL 14
from some single h. or tree MARV 12
sour h. of grace SHAK:RIC.II 34
herbs:
dinner of h. where love BIBLE 262
runs either to h. or to weeds BACON:F[1] 87
with bitter h. BIBLE 96
herd:
elevates above the vulgar h. GAIS 1
Leave untended the h. SCOTT:W 55
lowing h. wind slowly GRAY:T 16
herd-instinct: h. in the individual NIET 16
herdsman: God the h. goads YEATS 7
here:
destiny – are *h.* and *now* HAMMAR 2
hell, Ma'am, what's he doing h.? ANDREWS 1
H. I am, and h. I stay MACMAH 1
H. or nowhere is the whole EMER 80
h. today and gone tomorrow BEHN 8
h. we are again KNIGHT 1
H.'s tae us ANON 194
I have been h. before ROSSET:DG 5
It Can't Happen H. LEWIS:S 3
We're h. because we're h. ANON 48
you h., Advocate Brunetto? DANTE 10
hereafter: 'Tis not h. SHAK:TWE 19
hereditary: I am the family face* HARDY:T 36
hereditary principle: his qualifications? – ONE!* BROUGH 1
heredity: A person may be indebted* HAZL 11
heresies:
Religions are kept alive by h. BREN 2
truths to begin as h. HUX:TH 8
heresy:
Englishman believes be h.? SHAW 117
h. signifies no more than HOBB 5
upon the subject of the Arian h. JOHNSON:S 218
heretic: h. that makes the fire SHAK:WIN 6
heretics: Poor H. in love DONNE 46
heritage:
I have a goodly h. BIBLE 201
lov'st well is thy true h. POUND 34
hermit: dwell a weeping h. there COLLINS:Will 4
hermits: h. are contented with WORDS:W 50
hero:
better to be the widow of a h. IBA 3
Came the h. from his prison AYT 3
close is the h. to those who die RILKE 2
Every h. becomes a bore EMER 42
fight for an idea like a h. SHAW 43
god-like h. sate DRYD 105
H. can be Poet, Prophet CARLYLE:T 47
h. is the Conqueror Worm POE 2
h. must drink brandy JOHNSON:S 210
h. perish POPE 82
h.'s bust is bigger than MARX:G 30
No man is a h. to his valet CORNUEL 1
See, the conquering h. MORELL 1
truth about its h. CHESTERTON 36
very valet seem'd a h. BYR 132
Herod: it out-herods H. SHAK:HAM 106
heroes:
and return home as h. DAVISON:RK 1
bastards, but not h. HARRIS:M 3
fit country for h. to live in LLOYD GEO 5
h. that it deserves FELL 1
no gods and precious few h. HENDER:H 1
speed glum h. up the line SASS 4
their h. and villains from fiction AUD 67
thin red line of 'eroes KIP 65
Unhappy the country that needs h. BRECHT 6
heroic:
denigrate the h. aspect of man MACKEN 6
finisht A life H. MILT 300
H. times have passed GAM 1
pinch, human beings are h. ORWELL 14
something more than h. ROOS:FD 2
heroics: not h. but healing HARDING:WG 1
heroine: when a h. goes mad SHERIDAN:RB 38
heroines: resolute and intelligent h.? TERRY 1
heroing: H. is one of the shortest-lived ROGERS:W 7
heroism: fathered by our h. ELIOT:TS 24
heron:
haunts of coot and hern TENNY 201
h. Priested shore THOMAS:D 12
Herostratus: H. lives that burnt BROWNE:T 59
herring:
buy my caller herrin'? NAIRNE 2
roast thee like a herrin BURNS:R 90
herself: that which in h. she prizes CONG 60
Hervey: If you call a dog *H.* JOHNSON:S 89
hesitate: h. and falter life away ARNOLD:M 26
hesitates:
He who h. is lost PROV 166
She wavers, she h. RACINE 9
hesitation: call the way is h. KAF 11
Hesperides: ladies of th' H. MILT 267
Hesperus:
H. entreats thy light JONS 11
It was the schooner H. LONGFEL 9
heterodoxy: H. is another man's doxy WARB 1
hew: Not h. him as a carcase SHAK:JUL 24
hewers: let them be h. of wood BIBLE 129
hexameter: In the h. rises COLERIDGE:ST 46
heyday: h. in the blood SHAK:HAM 140
Hic jacet: two narrow words *H.j.* RALE 10
hickory: H., dickory, dock NURS 17
hid:
to keep that h. DONNE 67
we h. as it were our faces BIBLE 328
hide:
h. is sure to flatten 'em BELLOC 4
h. of an elephant to publish DAVISON:FD 2
H. their diminisht heads MILT 182
Let me h. myself in thee TOP 1
rub each other's coarse h. BUCHN 1
run, but he can't h. LOUIS:J 1
Tan me h. when I'm dead HARRIS:R 1
tattoo his bloody h. ANON 3
There's nothing much to h. HUMPH 2
Whose h. he sold WALLER 1
hideous: deliciously h. YEATS 149
high:
for contempt too h. COWLEY:A 13
from h. Life h. Characters POPE 111
Hold the heye wey CHAUC 125
I'm the H. SPRING 1
we are carried h. BERNARD:Ch 1
high jinks: forgotten pastime of *H.J.* SCOTT:W 70
high-mindedness: joss-sticks and honourable h. BRAM 1
High Park: beyond H.P.'s a desert to you ETH 4
highbrow:
h. is the kind of person HERB:AP 21
What is a h.? WALLACE:E 1
highbrows: article denouncing 'h.' ORWELL 10
Highbury: H. bore me ELIOT:TS 49
higher: aspire to h. things SIDNEY:P 1
highest: needs must love the h. TENNY 269
highflyer: h. at Fashion DICKENS 217
Highgate: barking dogs by H. Pond BETJ 19
highland:
heart is H. SCOTT:W 66
solitary H. lass WORDS:W 79
Sweet H. Girl WORDS:W 37
the heart is H. GALT 1
Highlandmen: breeks aff a wild H. SCOTT:W 85
highlands:
Farewell to the H. BURNS:R 81
In the h., in the country STEVENSON:RL 66
My heart's in the H. BURNS:R 80
My heart's in the H. SCOTT:W 47
Ye H. and ye Lawlands BALL 11
highway:
broad h. of the world SHELLEY:PB 130
straight in the desert a h. BIBLE 320
travelled each and evr'y high-way ANKA 1
highwayman: h. came riding NOY 2
hilarity:
Fan the sinking flame of h. DICKENS 93
His h. was like a scream GREENE:G 9
hill:
h. will not come to Mahomet BACON:F[1] 41
hunter home from the h. STEVENSON:RL 61
I climbed a h. as light HODG 2
I stood upon that silent h. HODG 5
nurst upon the self-same h. MILT 44
On a huge h., Cragged DONNE 2
On the idle h. of summer HOUSM 21
Over h., over dale SHAK:MID 12
There is a green h. ALEX:CF 5
tip-toe upon a little h. KEATS 5
hill-side: h.'s dew-pearled BROWNING:R 9
hills:
angel satyr walks these h. KILV 4
as immutable as the H. KIP 3
blue remembered h. HOUSM 24
dwindled h. are small and bare SLESS 3
Green-walled by the h. of Maryland WHITTIER 3
h. are alive with HAMMER 5
h. are shadows TENNY 183
H. of home STEVENSON:RL 70
H. of the Chankly Bore LEAR 9
H. peep o'er h. POPE 11
h. whose heads touch SHAK:OTH 8
I to the h. will lift SCOTTISH 2
makes a silence in the h. TENNY 137
mine eyes unto the h. BIBLE 239
My black h. have never KAV 1
On the h. like Gods together TENNY 33
Over the h. and far away GAY 18
Over the h. and far away NURS 78
Shine forth upon our clouded h.? BLAKE:W 98
strength of the h. is his BIBLE 229

three or four h. and a cloud STEVENS 3
to be out on the h. alone KILV 3
Who owns them hungry h. KAV 2
yon are the h. o' Heaven BALL 14
him:
all cried, 'That's h.!' BARH 6
H. first, h. last MILT 210
it belongs to H. CHAPLIN 1
with men I find H. not TENNY 271
Himalayas: Those H. of the mind DAY LEWIS 1
himself:
centre of a man's actions, h. BACON:F[1] 121
Ech man for hymself CHAUC 43
end by loving h. COLERIDGE:ST 81
gesture by the individual to h. GALB 9
he has done it all h. BARRIE 13
he speaks so much of h. BACON:F[1] 55
he, Who finds h. ARNOLD:M 13
more interested in h. than BIER 5
than kan hymselven knowe CHAUC 59
that chiefly owes h. unto h. BROWNE:T 66
To be h. IBS 1
Who lives unto h. QUAR 2
hind:
h. that would be mated SHAK:ALL 2
know where is an h. WYATT 6
hinder:
enemies in the h. parts BIBLE 220
h. parts, that few could spie SPENS 25
weep upon your h. parts HUX:A 45
hindsight: very *best*, 20–20 h. PIR 2
hinges: on thir h. grate MILT 171
Hippocrene: blushful H. KEATS 93
hippopotamus:
found it was A H. CARROLL 95
shoot the H. BELLOC 4
hips: hold their h. and laugh SHAK:MID 13
hirelings: into his Church lewd H. climbe MILT 187
hiss:
dismal universal h. MILT 253
they h. in their hair DRYD 112
historian:
abilities are not requisite for an H. JOHNSON:S 113
h., essentially, wants more documents JAMES:H 19
h. is a prophet SCHLEG 2
h. of the Roman empire GIBBON:E 23
life of the h. must be short GIBBON:E 27
one safe rule for the h. FISHER:HAL 1
historians:
alter the past, h. can BUTLER:S[2] 13
H. are like deaf people TOLS:L 14
h. left blanks POUND 32
H. repeat each other BALF 7
H. tell stories GON 1
how men who are not h. behave FORST 12
These gentle h. BURKE:E 74
to be left to h. MACLEOD:I 1
historical: find the h. fact ELIOT:TS 75
histories:
ancient h. ... are just fables VOLT 19
H. make men wise BACON:F[1] 109
history:
a h. in all men's lives SHAK:HEN.IV[2] 34
Antiquities are h. defaced BACON:F[1] 7
beginning and end of h. are *prophetic* SCHLEG 1
below the dignity of h. MACAULAY:TB 30
end of a thousand years of h. GAIT 2
English ... toward English h. HALS:M 2
fix the period in the h. GIBBON:E 4
great deal of h. to produce JAMES:H 2
great dust-heap called 'h.' BIRR 1
greatest week in the h. NIX 4
have no h. ELIOT:G 18
H. a distillation of rumour CARLYLE:T 18
h. as a sort of poker game BLUE:L 1
h. becomes more and more a race WELLS:HG 17
H. came to a SELL 10
H. does not repeat itself BALF 7
H., faced with courage ANGELOU 2
H. gets thicker TAYL:AJP 4
H. has many cunning passages ELIOT:TS 23
H. is a nightmare from which JOYCE:J 16
h. is an art like WEDGEWOOD 1
H. is an endless repetition DURRELL:L 6
H. is full of ignominious getaways ORWELL 15
H. ... is, indeed, little more GIBBON:E 3
H. is more or less bunk FORD:H 1
h. is nothing but a tableau VOLT 20
h. is on our side KHRU 2
H. is past politics SEEL 2
H. is Philosophy teaching by examples BOLI 2
H. is philosophy teaching from DION 1
h. is that it is adaptable UST 4
H. is the essence of innumerable CARLYLE:T 32
H. is too serious to MACLEOD:I 1
h. must be false WALP:R 6
h. of art is the h. of revivals BUTLER:S[2] 28
h. of class struggles MARX:K/ENG 2
h. of England is emphatically MACAULAY:TB 14
h. of every country begins CATHER 1
h. of the first half of this century BEECHAM 7
h. of the human spirit ARNOLD:M 72
H. of the world is but the Biography CARLYLE:T 45
h. of the world is its judgement SCHILL 1
H. repeats itself PROV 171
H. tells me nothing that AUSTEN 78
H. to the defeated May say AUD 21
H. would be an excellent TOLS:L 15
hysterical hypochondriacs of h. AGNEW 2
I belong to h. PASO 1
maintained the dignity of h. BOLI 4
Man is a h.-making creature AUD 66
men could learn from h. COLERIDGE:ST 90
My h., my love, Is but AUD 30
need all of h. in order ORTEGA G 8
never learned anything from h. HEG 2
no h.; only biography EMER 3
No man knows my h. SMITH:Jos 1
Political h. is far too criminal AUD 67
powdered h. – add hot water HALS:M 5
Pride in your h. is MACNEICE 13
product of h. CARLYLE:T 31
Read no h. DISR:B 9
Real solemn h. AUSTEN 62
regard the h. of Europe GOLDS 46
seems h. is to blame JOYCE:J 14
Thames is liquid h. BURNS:J 1
There is no h. of mankind POPP 3
This was the Angel of H. GOEB 4
to bowdlerize political h. is not AUD 67
to the minute hand of h. MACCARTHY:D 1
Universal H., the h. of what CARLYLE:T 41
very few Dates in this H. AUSTEN 1
War makes rattling good h. HARDY:T 73
welding of their later h. HARDY:T 23
what *is* h.? PASTER 1
history-books: annals are blank in h. CARLYLE:T 59
hit:
h. a woman with his hat on ALLEN:F 2
never h. soft ROOS:T 14
never think I have h. hard, unless JOHNSON:S 167
write a h. the same way LERN 8
hitched: mean gettin h., I'M IN WARD:A 4
hither: Let him come h. BUNYAN 30
Hitler:
between the Holy Spirit and a picture of H. GRASS 2
H. Has only got one ball ANON 19
H. showed surprising loyalty to Mussolini BULLOCK 2
H. thought he might get away CHAMBERLAIN:N 6
If H. invaded Hell CHURCH:W 58
people H. never understood BULLOCK 1
reached H.'s level of accuracy TAYL:AJP 3
That garrulous monk* MUSSO:B 7
wouldn't believe H. was dead SCHACHT 1
hitting: h. the mean and the right ARISTOT 8
hive:
helmet now shall make a h. PEELE 2
h. for the honey-bee YEATS 4
this great h., the city COWLEY:A 4
hoard:
boastful of her h. GOLDS 8
Our h. is little TENNY 241
hob-and-nob: h. with Death TENNY 96
hobbit: there lived a h. TOLK 1
hobby-horse:
h. is forgot SHAK:HAM 113
rides his h. peacably STERNE 5
hobgoblin: h. of little minds EMER 10
Hobson: 'Tis H.'s choice WARD:T 1
hock: weak h. and seltzer BETJ 3
hockey-legged: h. girls who laughed THOMAS:D 41
Hodge: Will H. for ever be HARDY:T 16
hodgepodge: h. of al other speches SPENS 1
hoe: darned long row to h. LOWELL:JR 5
hog:
all England under a H. COLLINGBO 1
his Grace to an acorned h. BROWNING:R 123
never get the whole h. LAWR:DH 26
to go the whole h. MARR 4
hogshead: fighting with daggers in a h. SCOTT:W 91
hoi polloi: *h.p.*, 'tis no matter DRYD 136
hoist: engineer H. with his own petar SHAK:HAM 149
hold:
as I die may I h. you TIB 1
first cries 'H. enough!' SHAK:MAC 116
h. me, for I am afraid WRIGHT:J 7
h. thee but by thy granting? SHAK:SON 38
to h. thee and me STERNE 14
holdfast: H. is the only dog SHAK:HEN.V 16
Holding: bowler's H., the batsman's JOHNSTON:B 1
holds: Guess now who h. thee? BROWNING:EB 9
hole:
happens to the h. when the cheese BRECHT 14
h. is the accident of a day SHUTER 1
h. where the tail came through COLERIDGE:ST 41
if you knows of a better 'ole BAIR 1
smallest h. that a man can hide CHESTERTON 38
stop a h. to keep the wind SHAK:HAM 185
thing about a h. is its edge TUCHOL 3
holes: follow the first law of h. HEAL 8
holiday:
he speaks h. SHAK:MERR 11
h. of fools CHESTERFIELD 22
I am in a h. humour SHAK:AS 56
Is this a h.? SHAK:JUL 1
it's a regular h. to them DICKENS 49
just the dead on h. MAET 2
On a Sunshine Holyday MILT 72
perpetual h. is a good working SHAW 139
to make a Roman h. BYR 110
working is her h. CERV 14
holidays:
Term, h., term, h. LEWIS:CS 7
treats itself to so many h. KINGLAKE 1
year were playing h. SHAK:HEN.IV[1] 16
holiest: to the H. in the height NEWM:JH 17
holiness:
h. of the Heart's affections KEATS 119
put off H. BLAKE:W 120
Holland:
deep where H. lies GOLDS 9
H. ... lies so low HOOD 33
hollow:
all was false and h. MILT 152
Australia in the h. of your head CALWELL 2
Let me slumber in the h. GORDON:AM 3
We are the h. men ELIOT:TS 56
holly:
heigh-ho, the h. SHAK:AS 35
h. and the ivy ANON 20
h. bears the crown ANON 20
Hollywood:
not have been invited to H. CHAND 7
of a H. director toward love HALS:M 2
Strip the phony tinsel off H. LEVANT 2
holocaust: lay ere while a H. MILT 298
holy:
every thing that lives is H. BLAKE:W 56
every thing that lives is h. BLAKE:W 61
H., fair, and wise SHAK:TWO 12
h. land of Walsinghame RALE 6
H., nor Roman, nor an Empire VOLT 10
h. time is quiet as a nun WORDS:W 42
Is this a h. thing to see BLAKE:W 65
suffer me not to see Thy H. City RICHARD 2
thou standest is h. ground BIBLE 85
Holy Ghost:
by the coming of the H.G. PRAY 34

this is h. life KEATS 38
title h. being, which precedes LIVER 2
To step aside is h. BURNS:R 37
human nature:
freckled H.N. DICKIN:E 12
h.n. is finer KEATS 131
I got disappointed in h.n. DONL 1
in h.n. generally more BACON:F[1] 40
new edition of h.n. HAZL 27
no h.n., since there is no God SARTRE 7
observer of h.n., sir DICKENS 5
requires the highest type of h.n. SPENCER:H 9
unfortunate than my Treatise of H.N. HUME 15
human race:
forget the h.r. BYR 115
He held the H.R. in Scorn BELLOC 13
h.r. to which so many of my readers CHESTERTON 33
h.r. was most happy GIBBON:E 4
Nought can deform the H.R. BLAKE:W 91
humane: Any man of h. sentiments SMOL 7
humanities: H. live for ever NORTH:C 7
humanity:
h. as a whole is changeful CHESTERTON 32
H. is beastly and stupid FRASER:GM 2
H. must perforce prey SHAK:KING L 62
one immortal blemish of h. NIET 22
second duty is to all h. SALIS 3
still, sad music of h. WORDS:W 8
teach governments h. PAINE 5
unremitting h. soon had me BENNETT:Al 4
wearisome Condition of H. GREV 2
humans: It isn't fit for h. now BETJ 6
Humber: I by the tide Of H. MARV 30
humble:
Be it ever so h. PAYNE 1
He that is h. ever shall BUNYAN 26
h. knowledge of thyself is a surer KEMP 2
It is difficult to be h. DOBR 1
I've never had a h. opinion BAEZ 1
Not only h. but umble TROLL 2
There's a star to guide the h. MACLEOD:N 1
To God be hummle DUNB 3
use such names and not be h.? SASS 14
We are so very umble DICKENS 153
We live in a numble abode DICKENS 152
humbled: h., kiss the rod SHAK:TWO 4
humbleness: in humblesse hym acquite As womman CHAUC 35
humblest: I am the umblest person going DICKENS 152
humbly: wants to live h. for one STEK 1
humbug:
'Bah!' said Scrooge, 'H.!' DICKENS 98
h. in a Pickwickian point of view DICKENS 3
Hume:
fate from the hand of Mr H. SMITH:Syd[1] 7
That constituted H. HUME 17
humiliation:
h. of an aged scholar COLLINGWOOD:RG 2
moment of greatest h. PANK:C 1
valley of H. BUNYAN 6
humility:
greater h. or charity in Him ANDREW 1
H. is only doubt BLAKE:W 107
pride that apes h. COLERIDGE:ST 43
humming: your little h. at the piano CAMPBELL:Mrs P 4
humour:
absence of h. makes life COLETTE 6
H. is an element which the German TUCHOL 9
it is my h. SHAK:MERC 39
most perfect h. and irony BUTLER:S[2] 7
phrase 'unconscious h.' is the one BUTLER:S[2] 11
the ridiculous, but no sense of h. ALBEE 2
will own up to a lack of h.? COLBY 1
Wit and H. are no more HAD 1
hump:
Camel's h. is an ugly lump KIP 102
h. that is black and blue KIP 103
humphed: Camel h. himself KIP 22
Humpty: H. Dumpty sat on a wall NURS 20
Hun: H. is at the gate KIP 144
Huncamunca: sun my self in H.'s eyes FIELDING 5
hunchback: h. in the park THOMAS:D 2
hundred:
alive a h. years from now XERX 1
as but a h. of us remain ANON 186
done it a h. times TWAIN 45
His h.'s soon hit BROWNING:R 120
h. years of fine writing HAZL 30
now it will tell a h. years hence BUTLER:S[2] 37
same a h. years hence DICKENS 71
uttered it a h. times HOLMES:OW 11
hundred and fifty: h.a.f. who was rather young WODE 30
hundred thousand: I was on a basic £100,000 a year SAUN 1
Hungarian: not enough to be H. KORDA 1
hunger:
banish h. by rubbing the belly DIOG 6
H. allows no choice AUD 44
h. and thirst after righteousness BIBLE 384
H. finds no fault with the cookery PROV 179
H. is the best sauce CERV 13
H. is the best sauce PROV 180
h. of ambitious mindes SPENS 41
h. of pernicious gold VIRGIL 55
h., thirst, forced marches GARI 1
idle if h. didn't pinch ELIOT:G 28
make h. thy sauce TUSS 6
religion to a man with bodily h. SHAW 86
theft from those who h. EISEN 2
hungry:
cannot feed the h. on statistics LLOYD GEO 1
He hath filled the h. BIBLE 608
Hongry rooster don't cackle HARRIS:JC 9
h. and inactive, God can only appear ASTUR 1
h. as a hunter LAMB:Ch 33
she makes h. SHAK:ANT 28
too h. For dinner at eight HART 1
understand the wants of the h. PROV 140
hunt:
animated when they h. in a pack HUME 2
h. a poetaster down BYR 18
h. with the hounds PROV 438
To h., and vote BYR 154
Whoso list to h. WYATT 6
Hunt: You will see H. SHELLEY:PB 62
hunted: others by their h. expression LEWIS:CS 5
hunter:
Esau was a cunning h. BIBLE 55
heart is a lonely h. MACLEOD:F 1
horn of the h. is heard CRAW 1
hungry as a h. LAMB:Ch 33
h. home from the hill STEVENSON:RL 61
H. of the East FITZGER:E 1
Man is the h. TENNY 112
Nimrod the mighty h. BIBLE 44
Hunter Dunn: Miss J. H.D. BETJ 20
hunters:
H. and lovers see best DUTT 3
h. ben nat hooly men CHAUC 12
hunting:
a-h. we will go FIELDING 7
Daddy's gone a-h. NURS 5
Detested sport* COWP 69
discourse was about h. PEPYS 13
ever to call h. one of them JOHNSON:S 255
Good h. KIP 15
H. he lov'd SHAK:POET 9
I went h. wild OWEN:W 12
passion *for h. something* DICKENS 58
'Unting fills my thoughts SURT 4
'Unting is all that's worth SURT 3
We daren't go a-h. ALLING:W 1
wet and dirty from h. SURT 15
Where hae ye been h. BALL 33
hunting-grounds: h. for the poetic imagination ELIOT:G 31
huntress: Queen and h. JONS 11
hunts: he h. in dreams TENNY 76
huntsman:
h. by the bear oppress'd WALLER 1
H., rest SCOTT:W 37
hurled:
Hurld headlong flaming MILT 110
Swift to be hurl'd HOOD 24
hurlyburly: When the h.'s done SHAK:MAC 1
hurricane: h. on the way – well don't worry FISH 1
hurry:
always in haste, I am never in a h. WESLEY:J 5
No one to h. us COWARD 19
old man in a h. CHURCH:Lord R 3
So who's in a h.? BENCH 7
hurt:
don't know can't h. you PROV 421
guinea helps the h. TENNY 78
Heavenly H. DICKIN:E 4
h. but I am not slain BALL 46
h. too much to laugh LINC 27
I'll not h. thee STERNE 14
They that have power to h. SHAK:SON 41
Those have most power to h. us BEAUMO 4
who shall h. the little Wren BLAKE:W 85
wish to h. BRONO 1
hurting:
once it has stopped h. BOWEN:El 6
You are hurtig be KIP 26
hurts:
h. me most who lavishly commends CHURCH:C 1
it h. not me CONG 49
husband:
all times Yr Faithfull H. STEELE 3
archaeologist is the best h. CHRIS 7
As the h. is, the wife is TENNY 72
bad h. and an ill provider EMER 49
easier to be a lover than a h. BALZ 12
good works in her H. MILT 242
have my h., but not my horse LAWR:DH 15
H., I come SHAK:ANT 73
h. in these circumstances? GAY 25
h., is a poor fish DENNIS:N 1
h. is a whole-time job BENNETT:Ar 3
just dined off her h. DURRELL:L 7
life her h. makes for her ELIOT:G 34
monstrous animal a h. and wife FIELDING 29
My h. is dead MARX:G 12
Never trust a h. too far ROWL:H 4
nothing but his being my h. CONG 32
so ill bred as to love a h.? WYCH 2
that one is the h. BLACKS 6
Thy h. is thy lord SHAK:TAM 15
'twas not Her h.'s presence BROWNING:R 20
unawares to look at her h. AUSTEN 72
with the words, 'My h. and I' ELIZ II 1
woman oweth to her h. SHAK:TAM 16
husband-hunting: affected, h. butterfly MITFORD:MR 1
husbandman: h. that laboureth BIBLE 552
husbandry:
He was into animal h. LEHRER 2
There's h. in heaven SHAK:MAC 31
husbands:
divine right of h. WOLLST 5
for most h. to hear GAY 30
Housbondes at chirche dore she CHAUC 25
H. are like fires GABOR 2
reasons for h. to stay at home ELIOT:G 20
When h., or when lap-dogs POPE 52
women pushing their h. along DEWAR 1
hush:
breathless h. in the Close NEWBOLT 10
h. with the setting moon TENNY 216
husks: filled his belly with the h. BIBLE 463
hut: Love in a h. KEATS 105
huts: still be living in grass h. PAG 1
hyacinth: every H. the Garden wears FITZGER:E 13
Hyacinth: Children with H.'s temperament SAKI 23
hydrogen bomb: h.b. is history's exclamation point MCLUH 15
hydrostatics: gives me the h. to such a degree SHERIDAN:RB 9
Hymen: As H.'s lamps shall light you SHAK:TEM 25
hymn:
Aisle. Altar. H. MUIR:F 2
Harmonious h. of being roll HODG 4
h. the Brahmin sings EMER 99
lass was singing a h. BETJ 11
hymns:
Chanting faint h. SHAK:MID 1
happy h. of farmers KINGSMILL 2
My poems are h. of praise SITWELL:E 10
Singing h. unbidden SHELLEY:PB 97
sings h. at heaven's gate SHAK:SON 11
sweet birds' marriage h. ELIOT:G 46
Hynde Horn: it's H.H. fair BALL 27
hyperbole: speaking in perpetual h. BACON:F[1] 78

hyperbolical: Out, h. fiend SHAK:TWE 54
hyphenated:
h. Americanism ROOS:T 6
h. by a drawn sword FURP 3
hypochondriacs: hysterical h. of history AGNEW 2
hypocrisy:
government is an organized h. DISR:B 54
Hypocrisie, the onely evil MILT 181
H. is a homage that vice LA ROCHE 22
H. is the most difficult MAUGH 12
love is taught h. BYR 164
pride, vain-glory, and h. PRAY 33
thy shut soul's h. BYR 121
we call it h. BUTLER:S[2] 16
hypocrite:
h. lecteur ELIOT:TS 39
H. reader BAUD 2
No man is a h. in his pleasures JOHNSON:S 246
hypocritical: learns by being h. KERR:Jea 3
hypotenuse: about the square of the h. GILB:WS 24
hypothesis:
character of a family to an h.? STERNE 8
destroy a favourite h. every day LORENZ 1
It is the nature of an h. STERNE 17
no need of that h. LAP 1
slaying of a beautiful h. HUX:TH 3
hypothetics: taken the highest degrees in h. BUTLER:S[2] 1
hyssop:
sprinkle me with h. BIBLE 598
Sprinkle me with h. MASS 1
hysterica passio: H.p. – down SHAK:KING L 26
hysterics: blind h. of the Celt TENNY 178
I:
A girl like I LOOS 2
I am the state LOUIS XIV 5
infinite I AM COLERIDGE:ST 73
It is I DE LA M 2
what I am, none cares CLARE:J 8
Iago: conceiving an I. as an Imogen KEATS 147
iambics:
I. march from short COLERIDGE:ST 57
not escape my i. CATUL 21
Iberians: dark I. come ARNOLD:M 30
Ibo: I. the art of conversation ACHEBE 2
ice:
hissed along the polished i. WORDS:W 106
i. burned and was but YEATS 34
I. formed on the butler's upper WODE 25
i. in June BYR 10
i., mast-high came floating COLERIDGE:ST 14
i. was all around COLERIDGE:ST 15
In skating over thin i. EMER 20
it is good to break the i. BACON:F[1] 46
penny i. and cold meat GILB:WS 51
those caves of i. COLERIDGE:ST 63
To smooth the i. SHAK:KING J 16
white lies to i. a wedding cake ASQU:M 3
ye I. and Snow PRAY 15
ice-cream: emperor of i. STEVENS 1
ice cream: I.c. is the most evocative POOLE:SC 1
iceberg:
grew the I. too HARDY:T 23
Virtue is . . . in the nature of an i. WHITE:P 5
icebox: eaten the plums that were in the i. WILLIAMS:WC 3
iced: three parts i. over ARNOLD:M 85
Iceland: not so bad as I. JOHNSON:S 247
icicle:
Chaste as the i. SHAK:COR 18
i. on a Dutchman's beard SHAK:TWE 43
icicles:
hang them up in silent i. COLERIDGE:ST 9
When i. hang SHAK:LOV 25
icy: thrust his i. fingers SHAK:KING J 20
id: PUT THE I. BACK IN YID ROTH 2
Ida:
mother I. TENNY 37
There lies a vale in I. TENNY 36
idea:
Between the i. And the reality ELIOT:TS 58
end by ruining our i. MUSSO:B 10
fight for an i. like a hero SHAW 43
good i. but it won't work ROGERS:W 6
i. isn't responsible for MARQUIS 9
i., when you only have one i. ALAIN 1
let the i. die instead of you? LEWIS:W 2
live in the shadow of an i. BOWEN:El 5
mind treats a new i. the way MEDA 2
object of which he has no i. BAGE 23
one i., and that is the wrong one JOHNSON:S 146
one i., – and that was wrong DISR:B 27
pain of a new i. BAGE 20
teach the young i. how THOMS:Ja[1] 3
terrible in the simplicity of his i. CONRAD 10
with the i. which God has of you UNA 7
Within this circular i. HUME 17
would be an excellent i. GAND:M 3
ideal:
German i.: sitting behind TUCHOL 5
i. for which I am prepared MANDELA:N 2
I. mankind would abolish death LAWR:DH 13
softly sleeps the calm I. DICKENS 122
Television puts forward, as an i. ECO 1
ideals:
Away with all i. LAWR:DH 23
enemy of progressive i. BELLOW 4
i. of a nation by its advertisements DOUGLAS:N 1
shoes with broken high i. MCGOUGH 1
with all the i. that I have THATCH:M 12
without i. and without greatness CAMUS 2
ideas:
cannot resist the invasion of i. HUGO 2
Colourless green i. CHOM 1
cul-de-sac down which i. ANON 171
God, is the God of i. VIGNY 7
heterogenous i. are yoked by violence JOHNSON:S 48
i. by which they have once won GALB 4
i. grow better when transplanted HOLMES:OW JR 2
i., not vested interests KEYN 10
i. simply pass through BRADLEY:FH 5
i. which generation handed WEISS 2
i. would simply drive it frantic MENCK 14
It is the same with i. MACDON:R 1
mixture of sound and original i. MACMILL:H 12
no i. but in things WILLIAMS:WC 8
optimism or our pessimism . . . which makes our i. UNA 3
own i. and other people's values BREN 4
proving our latest i. are wrong SUZ:D 1
put trust in i. EMER 46
reality by means of i. ORTEGA G 6
scarifying the edges of i. FAIRBURN 1
those who love i. and those ALAIN 1
words are but the signs of i. JOHNSON:S 6
idées: *i. au-dessus de sa gare* RATT 1
identification: form of i. with a people BOLL 2
ideology: I. is a special way of relating HAVEL 1
ides:
Beware the i. of March SHAK:JUL 3
i. of March are come SHAK:JUL 32
idioms: licentious i. JOHNSON:S 4
idiot:
i. race, to honour lost BURNS:R 59
i. who praises GILB:WS 65
love, your I. Boy WORDS:W 3
portrait of a blinking i. SHAK:MERC 30
tale Told by an i. SHAK:MAC 113
To Generalize is to be an I. BLAKE:W 95
idiots: fatuity of i. SMITH:Syd[1] 1
idle:
be not i. BURTON:Ro 26
devil finds work for i. hands PROV 68
For i. hands to do WATTS 5
happiest when I am i. WARD:A 10
i. as a painted ship COLERIDGE:ST 19
i. if hunger didn't pinch ELIOT:G 28
If you are i., be not solitary JOHNSON:S 74
most i. and unprofitable GIBBON:E 14
most 'scrutiating idle KIP 21
Never be completely i. KEMP 9
Never less i. than when free CIC 6
that have not learnt how to be i. MADAN 1
whom the world Calls i. COWP 71
with i. state GRAY:T 28
Young people ought not to be i. THATCH:M 17
idleness:
compulsory and irreproachable i. TOLS:L 1
faculty for i. implies a catholic STEVENSON:RL 19
Grief is a species of i. JOHNSON:S 73
I. is only the refuge CHESTERFIELD 22
My i. doth hatch SHAK:ANT 10
Pains and Penalties of i. POPE 173
passed a day in i. CATO 2
restless i. occupies us HORACE 87
round of strenuous i. WORDS:W 153
unyok'd humour of your i. SHAK:HEN.IV[1] 15
idler: is, or hopes to be, an i. JOHNSON:S 29
idlers: number of well-to-do i. MARX:K 5
idling: enjoy i. thoroughly unless JEROME:JK 1
idol: There's a one-eyed yellow i. HAYES 1
idolatry:
god of my i. SHAK:ROM 14
god of our i., the press COWP 38
There is no i. in the Mass JOHNSON:S 142
idolised: i. when dead CONNOLLY:J 1
idols:
I. I have loved so long FITZGER:E 31
making your bed with i.? JEROME 1
worship the national i. SHAW 50
if:
I. you can keep your head KIP 127
much virtue in I. SHAK:AS 71
ifs:
If i. and ands were pots PEAC 18
If i. and ands were pots PROV 184
ignoble:
end Was not i. WORDS:W 145
made i. talk TENNY 254
ignominy: Thy i. sleep with thee SHAK:HEN.IV[1] 91
ignorance:
blind and naked I. TENNY 247
Boredom is a sign of satisfied i. BRIDIE 3
But an exchange of i. BYR 125
distinguished for i. DISR:B 27
I. is like a delicate exotic WILDE:O 86
I. is not innocence but sin BROWNING:R 207
I. is Strength ORWELL 30
I., madam, sheer i. JOHNSON:S 101
i. must necessarily be infinite POPP 5
in i. sedate JOHNSON:S 71
in touch with the i. of the community WILDE:O 16
keeping women in a state of i. KNOX:V 1
man's i. of the gods BUTLER:S[2] 6
more than Gothic i. FIELDING 25
names To hide its i. SHELLEY:PB 4
no sin but i. MARLOWE 19
Oppress'd with i. DONNE 75
Pompous I. sits enthroned BRIDIE 2
smallest allowance for i. HUX:TH 1
where i. is bliss GRAY:T 8
you understand a writer's i. COLERIDGE:ST 72
Your i. cramps my conversation HOPE:An 6
ignorant:
Confound the i. SHAK:HAM 91
father was so i. I could hardly TWAIN 38
hope the baby will prove I. SU 1
i. man always loves that LOM 1
In language, the i. DUPPA 1
many i. men are sure DARROW 3
right of the i. man to be CARLYLE:T 39
surprised at everything when you were *i.* DURRELL:G 1
they should always be i. AUSTEN 63
ignore: happy with nothing to i. NASH 8
ignored: better than to be i. MACMILL:H 8
Iliad: greater than the I. is about PROP 3
Ilium: I. has passed VIRGIL 52
ill:
half there when I am i. LAWR:DH 39
I. fares the land GOLDS 21
I. fortune seldom comes alone DRYD 120
i. he cannot cure a name ARNOLD:M 50
i., It has a frightened look SITWELL:O 1
Never speak i. of the dead PROV 288
old and i. and terrified BETJ 32
revenge by speaking i. of it VOLT 6
sauf us frae the I. Ane BIBLE 589
to do i. our soul delight MILT 117
ill-breeding: sign of guilt, or of i. CONG 38
ill-fed: it is i., ill-killed JOHNSON:S 242
ill-housed: i., ill-clad, ill-nourished ROOS:FD 8
ill-luck: so fond of i. that they run JERROLD 7
ill-tempered: think him i. and queer LEAR 3

ill-treated: This is for all i. fellows HOUSM 41
ill-usage: complaints of i. contemptible MELBOU 1
ill-using: i. them and the confessing TROLL 14
illegal:
immoral, i., or fattening WOOLL 2
President does it, that means it is not i. NIX 11
illegitimacy: stain of i. AUSTEN 57
illegitimate:
only i. parents YAN 1
that all Scots are i. MUIR:E 8
illiberal: I may be i. PEEL:R 1
illiteracy: ratio of literacy to i. is constant MORA 5
illiterate:
I. him . . . quite from your memory SHERIDAN:RB 4
repartee of the i. BRIEN 2
illiterates: i. can read and write MORA 5
illness: I. is the night-side of life SONT 4
ills:
bear those i. we have SHAK:HAM 97
have they of i. to come GRAY:T 7
i. enow To be a woman DONNE 23
to hastening i. a prey GOLDS 21
What i. from beauty spring JOHNSON:S 70
when nae real i. perplex BURNS:R 58
illusion:
i. of an identity HAVEL 1
nothing but sophistry and i. HUME 13
thankful for i. CLOUGH 25
The Great I. ANGELL 1
visible universe was an i. BORGES 3
illusions:
Don't part with your i. TWAIN 22
Indulgin' in i. MACDIAR 13
lose i. as we get older SMITH:Syd[1] 24
illustrious: less i., goes the clerk COWP 19
image:
Before me floats an i. YEATS 86
Best I. of my self MILT 209
blotted out man's i. YEATS 10
If God has created us in his i. VOLT 24
in the i. of his own desire LAVER 1
make man in our i. BIBLE 6
Met his own i. SHELLEY:PB 66
more i. than shade YEATS 86
Scatter'd his Maker's i. DRYD 34
Stamp'd with the i. of the King TENNY 256
transitory is but an i. GOET 20
unto thee any graven i. BIBLE 103
imaged: I. as we HARDY:T 24
images:
express the i. of their minds BACON:F[1] 92
i. according to a stopwatch IGNAT 1
imaginary:
Don't let us make i. evils GOLDS 60
i. relish is so sweet SHAK:TRO 10
things real as if they were i. BETT 1
imagination:
driven the living i. out YEATS 129
good i. and a pile of junk EDIS 2
hunting-grounds for the poetic i. ELIOT:G 31
if i. amend them SHAK:MID 49
I. droops her pinion BYR 201
i.! I put it first TERRY 2
i. is, if not an unpruned STEAD 4
I. is more important EINS 7
I. is not required JOHNSON:S 113
I. may be compared to Adam's KEATS 118
i. of a boy is healthy KEATS 133
i. of man's heart is evil BIBLE 39
i. resembled the wings MACAULAY:TB 7
I. the Rudder KEATS 117
I., which, in truth WORDS:W 163
I. without skill gives us STOP 10
I.'s struggles, far KEATS 38
lady's i. is very rapid AUSTEN 16
literalists of the i. MOORE:M 1
no better way of exercising the i. GIR 2
nothing but his i. SHAW 75
paint her in my i. the way CERV 10
primary i. I hold COLERIDGE:ST 73
refined play of the i. BURKE:E 3
ruled uniquely by i. CROCE 1
save those that have no i.? SHAW 118
Such tricks hath strong i. SHAK:MID 43
to his i. for his facts SHERIDAN:RB 42
to sweeten my i. SHAK:KING L 68
truth of I. KEATS 119
upon the force of i. DRYD 99
Were it not for i. JOHNSON:S 207
What the i. seizes as Beauty KEATS 119
where does i. start ROBINS:RE 1
whispering chambers of I. DICKENS 122
imagine: people i. a vain thing? BIBLE 196
imagined: now proved was once only imagin'd BLAKE:W 43
imaging: I. a god is the resort HULME 1
imagining: bright world of my i.? KELLER 2
imaginings: less than horrible i. SHAK:MAC 16
imitate:
good composer does not i. STRAV 5
I. him if you dare YEATS 84
obliged to i. himself REYN:J 3
usually i. each other HOFFER 1
imitated:
i. humanity so abominably SHAK:HAM 107
one who can be i. by none CHATEAU 1
represent whatever is i. ZE AMI 1
imitation:
fruit of i. and thoughtlessness? CERN 3
i. is perfectly accomplished ZE AMI 2
I. is the sincerest form COLTON 3
I. is the sincerest form PROV 196
Were endless i. WORDS:W 59
imitator:
happy i. of Nature HEMING 2
professed i. of Horace DRYD 138
imitators: i., you slavish herd HORACE 93
immature: mark of the i. man STEK 1
immatures: He i. with age WILSON:Harold 8
immaturity: executive expression of human i. BRITT 3
immensity:
I. cloistered in thy dear DONNE 79
into the vortex of i. DICKENS 122
immodest: I. words admit no defence ROSCOM 2
immoral:
i., illegal, or fattening WOOLL 2
nothing then would be i. DOST 4
people looked on it as i. GALS 4
worse than i., it's a mistake ACHES 3
immorality: most rigid code of i. BRADB 2
immortal:
imagine that I was i.? LOUIS XIV 8
i. diamond HOPK:GM 29
I have I. longings SHAK:ANT 72
I. in his own despite POPE 142
I., though no more BYR 68
I. youth to mortal maids LANDOR 2
Know thyself first i. CHAUC 101
majesty and that beauty which are i. YEATS 127
make me i. with a kiss MARLOWE 38
race remains i. VIRGIL 32
robbed us of i. things MERED:G 25
Sire of an i. strain SHELLEY:PB 107
then a mortal becomes i. UPA 1
thing i. as itself? SHAK:HAM 37
unbounded and i. things YEATS 128
What i. hand or eye BLAKE:W 67
immortality:
achieve i. through my work ALLEN:W 15
achieve it by not dying* ALLEN:W 15
cruel i. Consumes TENNY 45
destroy in mankind the belief in i. DOST 4
Drowned in brief i. CAMPBELL:G 4
I long to believe in i. KEATS 165
i. can always be assured by spectacular GALB 12
I. is the only thing which doesn't KRAUS 2
like a load of i. KEATS 141
millions long for i. who don't know ERTZ 1
Nor shall Death brag* SHAK:SON 6
Nurslings of i. SHELLEY:PB 74
one i. And one annihilation SHELLEY:PB 134
they gave, their i. BROOKE 19
those who fully admit the i. DARW:C 11
Your monument shall be* SHAK:SON 36
immortalize: mortall thing so to i. SPENS 11
immunity: is how the i. was given HAVERS 1
immutable: as i. as the hills KIP 3
Imogen: conceiving an Iago as an I. KEATS 147
impartiality: explosive, detonating i. YEATS 142
impeach: I i. him in the name BURKE:E 104
impeachment: own the soft i. SHERIDAN:RB 16
impediment: know cause, or just i. PRAY 79
impediments: i. to great enterprises BACON:F[1] 80
imperative: This i. is *categorical* KANT 3
imperfect: i., unfinished, inartistic JAMES:H 3
imperfection: i. itself may have its ideal DEQ 10
imperfections:
all my i. on my head SHAK:HAM 48
pass my i. by EVER 1
imperial:
I. fiddlestick CARROLL 43
These are i. arts VIRGIL 72
We have had an I. lesson KIP 115
imperialism:
I. is a paper tiger MAO 5
i. with an inferiority complex HEAL 4
imperially: Learn to think I. CHAMBERLAIN:J 2
imperious: combine a pose i. GILB:WS 107
imperium:* *I. et Libertas DISR:B 80
impersonators: female i. are women BENNER 1
impertinent: ask an i. question BRONO 4
imperturbe: Me i. WHITMAN 26
importance:
I. of Being Oscar WILLM 1
occurs is of the smallest i. WILDE:O 70
important:
i. things are invisible SAINT-EX 3
recognize . . . the really i. moments CHRIS 4
to puff and look i. KIP 137
imports: biased for and against free i. SAKI 16
importune: too proud to i. GRAY:T 37
impose: you to i. on him, knows you BLAKE:W 45
impossibe: certain because it is i. TERT 4
impossibilities:
not i. enough in Religion BROWNE:T 6
Probable i. are always to be ARISTOT 22
impossibility:
by despair Upon i. MARV 7
That fond i. LOVELACE 8
impossible:
i. ? It will be done CALON 1
i. takes a little longer ANON 177
In two words: im possible GOLDWYN 13
Is anything i.? WELLING 17
is i., he is very probably wrong CLARKE:AC 1
It's either easy or i. DAL 3
pays for setting an i. aim GREENE:G 7
six i. things before breakfast CARROLL 65
you can make yourself i.? GRAIN:P 1
impotent: i. people THOMAS:RS 2
imprecision:
Decay with i. ELIOT:TS 91
mess of i. of feeling ELIOT:TS 98
impression:
creating a public i. of himself MENZ 2
produces a false i. WILDE:O 81
impressionable: girl at an i. age SPARK 2
impressions:
First i. are the most lasting PROV 124
i. not so lasting CHOP 2
imprison: i. the child . . . by force of love WHITE:P 4
imprisoned:
imprison'd in the viewless winds SHAK:MEA 24
you suffer'd me to be imprison'd SHAK:TWE 56
imprisonment: leaves his well belov'd i. DONNE 79
improbable:
however i., must be the truth DOYLE:AC 7
in the occurrence of the i. MENCK 2
preferred to i. possibilities ARISTOT 22
improper:
I only hope it is not i. GASK 5
i. thoughts about their neighbours BRADLEY:FH 3
impropriety: I. is the soul of wit MAUGH 5
improvement:
intellectual i. arises from leisure JOHNSON:S 158
most schemes of political i. JOHNSON:S 141
improving: i., and that's your own self HUX:A 37
imprudent: Nobody could be so i. AUSTEN 50
impudence: pride and i., in faction knit JONS 50
impulse:
lonely i. of delight YEATS 61
One i. from a vernal wood WORDS:W 17
slave of circumstance And i. BYR 140
impulses:
Beware of first i. MONTROND 1

Don't trust first i. TALL 6
impure: To the Puritan all things are i. LAWR:DH 21
in:
come and take him i. FROST:R 11
i. us that we can be without us BROWNE:T 41
many hoof-marks going i. AESOP 5
mean gettin hitched, I'M I. WARD:A 4
such as are i. the institution EMER 44
inaccuracy:
I hate i. BUTLER:S[2] 34
i. sometimes saves tons of explanation SAKI 24
inactive: hungry and i., God can only ASTUR 1
inactivity: wise and masterly i. MACKINT 1
inane: Pinnacled dim in the intense i. SHELLEY:PB 84
inanimate: depravity of i. things HAMIL:G 1
inarticulate:
largely i. KIP 125
raid on the i. ELIOT:TS 98
speak for the i. BEAV 6
inbreeding: Sick with i. THOMAS:RS 2
incapacity: dark sanctuary of i. CHESTERFIELD 30
incarnations: glimmering I. Of hopes SHELLEY:PB 111
incense:
blest unfabled I. Tree DARLEY 1
gods themselves throw i. SHAK:KING L 80
incense-smoke: thick stupefying i. BROWNING:R 44
incentive: keep alive the i. to push on HAMMAR 2
incertainties: Nothing more certain than i. BARNF 1
incest: except i. and folk-dancing BAX 1
inch:
every i. a king SHAK:KING L 67
i. and he'll take a yard PROV 145
Inchcape Rock: it is the I.R. SOUTHEY 9
incident:
That was the curious i. DOYLE:AC 25
What is i. but the illustration JAMES:H 7
inclined: he i. unto me BIBLE 210
include: i. me out GOLDWYN 1
income:
Annual i. twenty pounds DICKENS 151
desire ... to live beyond its i. BUTLER:S[2] 23
fanned by an adequate i. COLLINS:Wilk 1
£40,000 a year a moderate i. LAMBTON 1
good i. is of no avail SMITH:LP 2
large i. is the best recipe AUSTEN 33
private i. one has better things KINGSMILL 3
75% on the last slice of their i. HEAL 1
income tax: I.t. has made more liars ROGERS:W 1
incomes: live beyond their i. nowadays SAKI 12
incommunicable: burden of the i. DEQ 7
incompetence: rise to his level of i. PETER 1
incompetent:
election by the i. many SHAW 51
last refuge of the i. HARDIN 1
refuge of the i. MENCK 12
incomplete: man in love is i. GABOR 3
incomprehensible: old, wild and i. VICT 5
inconceivable: family pride is something i GILB:WS 62
inconstancy:
constant, but i. SWIFT 11
Constant, in Nature were i. COWLEY:A 2
Constant in nothing but i. BARNF 1
inconstant:
I loved you i. RACINE 3
i. woman GAY 33
incontinence: filth and fouel i. SPENS 35
inconveniences: All the modern i. TWAIN 9
inconvenient: it is confoundedly i. SMITH:Syd[1] 34
incorruptible: sea-green I. CARLYLE:T 21
increase:
good and i. of the world TENNY 90
we desire i. SHAK:SON 1
incredulity: *Incredulitie*, the wit of Fooles CHAPMAN:G 1
increment: Unearned i. MILL 3
incubate: forgets to i. them CANET 3
indecent:
not necessary to be i. ROGERS:T 1
sent down for i. behaviour WAUGH:E 2
indecision: nothing is habitual but i. JAMES:W 1
indefensible: defence of the i. ORWELL 37
indemnity: i. ... for raid by Dr Jameson KRUG 1
independence:
first of earthly blessings, i. GIBBON:E 26
i. of solitude EMER 9
separate and equal station to which* JEFFERSON 1
independent:
To be poor and i. COBBETT 4
Why was an i. wish BURNS:R 8
with an i. air GILB:F 1
index:
i. of a feeling mind CRAB 24
So essential did I consider an I. CAMPBELL:Baron 1
thunders in the i.? SHAK:HAM 139
why there is no table or I. HOWELL 1
India:
driven out of I. this day BURKE:E 97
final message of I. FORST 9
fly to I. for gold MARLOWE 30
From I.'s coral strand HEB 2
I. is a geographical term CHURCH:W 8
no politician in I. daring enough GAND:I 3
people of I., whose rights BURKE:E 104
Indian:
Go, like the I. POPE 103
I. Summer of the heart WHITTIER 1
only good I. is a dead I. SHERIDAN:PH 4
poor I. whose untutor'd POPE 83
indictment: i. against an whole people BURKE:E 32
indifference:
equanimity bordering on i. GILB:WS 115
i. and a coach and six COLMAN:G[1] 1
i. closely bordering on aversion STEVENSON:RL 28
morn and cold i. came ROWE 1
Nature's complete i. WEISS 1
so fatal to religion as i. BURKE:E 87
indifferent:
be i. to them SHAW 25
count nothing human i. to me TEREN 5
delayed till I am i. JOHNSON:S 95
i. in a week AUD 41
It is simply i. HOLMES:JH 1
we are the most i. BIAGI 2
indigestion: complains of moral i. ANTRIM 2
indignation:
i. can no longer tear his heart SWIFT 87
i. will prompt my verse JUV 3
mists of righteous i. MUGG 2
Moral i. is jealousy with WELLS:HG 9
indiscretion:
at least one blazing i. MORLEY:Lord[2] 1
between a cliché and an i. MACMILL:H 11
between the cliché and the i. RUNCIE:Rob 1
Green i. FORD:J[1] 4
lover without i. HARDY:T 55
indispensables: one of those i. of whom HUX:A 5
indistinct: host with someone i. ELIOT:TS 30
individual:
each i. act spontaneously LAWR:DH 23
i. existence goes out in a lonely JAMES:W 2
injustice done to an i. JUNIUS 8
liberty of the i. must be MILL 14
not the i. but the species JOHNSON:S 20
psychic development of an i. FREUD:S 1
upon i. initiative and exertion PAVLO 2
individualism:
American system of rugged i. HOOV 2
most intense mode of i. WILDE:O 41
individuality:
ceases to possess i. MILL 15
crushes i. is despotism MILL 16
No-one can escape from his i. SCHOP 1
individuals:
all my love is towards i. SWIFT 79
worth of the i. composing MILL 22
indolence: steep'd in honied i. KEATS 97
indoors: given us i. and out-of-doors MACAULAY:R 2
indulgence: might expect more i. GOLDS 61
industrial: advance of the i. world LAWR:DH 4
industrial relations: I.r. are like sexual relations FEATH 1
industrialization: Trade's unfeeling train* GOLDS 22
industry:
Avarice, the spur of i. HUME 6
Captains of i. CARLYLE:T 53
i. will improve them REYN:J 1
i. without art is brutality RUSKIN 28
inebriate: to cheer but not i. BERK 3
inelegance: continual state of i. AUSTEN 70
inequalities: pub uniquely represents ... the precise i. HOWK 2
ineradicable: error is i. MAUGH 17
inevitability: i. of gradualness WEBB:S 1
inevitable:
accept the i. and go with it GONNE 2
in arguing with the i. LOWELL:JR 9
not believe in i. war LAW 1
inexactitude: terminological i. CHURCH:W 1
inexplicable: doctrinally i. but it goes on MUGG 8
infallible: No man is i. PROV 294
infamous: rich, quiet, and i. MACAULAY:TB 10
infamy: stamp out i. VOLT 32
infancy:
Nations, like men, have their i. BOLI 3
shadow-peopled I. SHELLEY:PB 81
wayward was thy i. SHAK:RIC.III 14
infant:
describe the i. phenomenon DICKENS 80
gobbled up the i. child HOUSM 49
i. crying in the night TENNY 154
i., Mewling and puking SHAK:AS 34
Sooner murder an i. BLAKE:W 51
infanticide: as indefensible as i. WEST:R 2
infantry: small i. Warr'd on by Cranes MILT 134
infect: briskly to i. a city AUD 11
infection: Against i. and the hand SHAK:RIC II 17
infelicity: i. Seem'd to have years WEBSTER:J 27
inferior:
feel i. without your consent ROOS:E 2
Had I been in anything i. BRONTE:C 1
loves most is the i. one MANN:T 1
pleasing i. people CLOUGH 13
inferiority: Wherever an i. complex exists JUNG:Carl 8
inferiors:
admit that he has no social i. RUSS:B 19
English want *i.* TOC 1
I. agitate in order that ARISTOT 17
infidelity:
at least, half i. BURKE:E 87
I. does not consist in believing PAINE 9
infidels: kiss, and I. adore POPE 40
infinite:
appear to man as it is, i. BLAKE:W 53
for both are i. SHAK:ROM 16
i. can never meet MARV 8
king of i. space SHAK:HAM 78
possession is I. & himself I. BLAKE:W 12
silence of these i. spaces PASC 8
there is an I. in him CARLYLE:T 14
infinitive: when I split an i. CHAND 8
infinitude: with i., and only there WORDS:W 155
infinity:
Hold I. in the palm BLAKE:W 82
i. torments me MUSSET 2
infirmities: devoid of all these i. of human SMOL 7
infirmity:
feblit with infirmitie DUNB 7
last i. of Noble mind MILT 49
inflame: It will i. you SHAK:JUL 53
inflammation: i. of his weekly bills BYR 186
inflation:
I. in the Sixties was a nuisance LEVIN 1
little i. is like being a little HENDER:L 1
inflicted: By man on man i. COLERIDGE:ST 2
influence:
acquisition of unwarranted i. EISEN 6
aspired to power instead of i. TAYL:AJP 5
can only i. the strong ASQU:M 2
I. is not government WASH 4
Spheres of i. ANON 242
under the name of I. BURKE:E 14
Win Friends and I. People CARNEG:D 1
influenza: no i. in my young days BENNETT:Ar 1
information:
For your i., let me ask MCLUH 13

I only ask for i. DICKENS 155
know where we can find i. JOHNSON:S 171
referendum on women's access to i. CLARE:A 3
informed: far better i. SMITH:FE 7
infortune: worste kynde of i. CHAUC 113
infusion: i. of a China plant ADDIS 17
ingenious: i, sober, nor kind ANON 135
ingle: wee bit i., blinkin BURNS:R 11
ingle-nook: In the teashop's i. BETJ 15
ingots: don't go to market with i. CHAMFORT 4
ingrateful: That makes i. man SHAK:KING L 32
ingratitude:
by the magnitude of her i. SCHWARZ 1
I hate i. more SHAK:TWE 52
I., more strong than traitors' SHAK:JUL 55
I., thou marble-hearted fiend SHAK:KING L 19
no limits to human i. GARC 1
repay an obligation is a form of i. LA ROCHE 23
unkind As man's i. SHAK:AS 35
ingratitudes: great-siz'd monster of i. SHAK:TRO 14
inhale: if he doesn't i. STEVENSON:A 8
inherit:
not just what we i. from our mothers IBS 5
they shall i. the earth BIBLE 384
inheritance:
Come for your i. and you may PROV 59
pernicious i. GAIUS 1
wide and broad is my i. GOET 24
inherited: from us what we have i. BREN 5
inhibitions: cultivate a few i. LOOS 9
inhuman: God is an i. concept DURREN 2
inhumanity:
essence of i. SHAW 25
Man's i. to man BURNS:R 7
iniquity:
laid on him the i. of us all BIBLE 329
my measure of i. BURNS:R 131
injured:
hate those whom you have i. TAC 2
injur'd Lover's Hell MILT 215
know that he hath i. you FIELDING 19
sense of injur'd merit MILT 114
injuries: adding insult to i. MOORE:E 1
injury:
efforts to do it a violent i. WODE 16
i. is much sooner forgotten CHESTERFIELD 4
least i. you can do him JAMES:H 1
Recompense i. with justice CONF 9
repaying i. with kindness LAO 1
with consent, there is no i. ULP 1
injustice:
any amount of i. to be had KELLY:N 2
conscience with i. is corrupted SHAK:HEN.VI[2] 4
don't suffer from i. seem incapable MENAND 1
extent of i. in your death CANET 6
fear of suffering i. LA ROCHE 12
i. done to an individual JUNIUS 8
i. is the fundamental fault SCHOP 8
i. makes democracy necessary NIEB 1
i. of it is almost perfect OSB:J 8
protect him against i. and wrong PALMERS 1
see i. done HOUSM 25
suffers from their i. MENCK 9
threatened with a great i. CARLYLE:JW 5
injustices:
established i. are sanctioned FRANCE 9
to justify their i. VOLT 17
ink:
all the sea were i. ANON 71
all the sea were i. LYLY 8
buried in the i. that writes CLARE:J 14
he hath not drunk i. SHAK:LOV 10
i. in my pen ran cold WALP:H 5
i. were temp'red with Love's SHAK:LOV 16
inmost: see the i. part of you SHAK:HAM 135
inn:
Do you remember an I. Miranda? BELLOC 37
earth his sober Inne CAMPION 4
find a chamber in the i. ANON 59
incognito of an i. HAZL 19
Make my house your i. MOORE:M 4
no room for them in the i. BIBLE 447
not an i., but an hospital BROWNE:T 32
old i., and the lights MORRIS:W 9
produced as by a good tavern or i. JOHNSON:S 179
soul's second i. DONNE 21
To gain the timely i. SHAK:MAC 68
warmest welcome, at an i. SHEN 1
world's an i. DRYD 126
innards: at war with my i. MACHA 1
inner: Holy Spirit in the i. man PRAY 90
Innisfree: go to I. YEATS 4
innocence:
badge of lost i. PAINE 1
business to lose i. BOWEN:El 7
ceremony of i. is drowned YEATS 62
dallies with the i. of love SHAK:TWE 28
in total i. DANTE 7
i. and health GOLDS 21
I. is a kind of insanity GREENE:G 11
i. is at last becoming RACINE 2
i. is closing up his eyes DRAYT 9
i. itself has many a wile BYR 164
I. itself sometimes hath need PROV 200
I. thy sister dear MARV 13
Valour and I. Have latterly KIP 129
wept for the end of i. GOLDI 2
What we chang'd Was i. SHAK:WIN 1
innocent:
Be i. of the knowledge SHAK:MAC 67
boys i. as strawberries THOMAS:D 3
I am i. of the blood BIBLE 435
i. as gay YOUNG:E 13
i. until he is proved guilty PROV 105
than one i. suffer BLACKS 5
to shed i. blood BIBLE 332
innocuous: lambent but i. GOUL 1
innovator: time is the greatest i. BACON:F[1] 77
inns: go to i. to dine CHESTERTON 10
inquest: together like the Coroner's I. CONG 36
inquiries: suspended my religious i. GIBBON:E 18
Inquisition: I. might have left him HARDY:T 76
insane:
eaten on the i. root SHAK:MAC 11
i. take themselves quite seriously BEERB 22
insanity:
Innocence is a kind of i. GREENE:G 11
often a prelude to i. WAUGH:E 11
inscriptions: lapidary i. a man is not JOHNSON:S 175
inscrutable:
fathom the i. workings SMITH:FE 5
i. to the last THURB 12
insect:
how the Egyptians worshipped an i. DISR:B 92
into a monstrous verminous i. KAF 9
insects:
loud and troublesome i. BURKE:E 60
million i. in every drop SMITH:Syd[1] 12
insemination: don't mean by unartificial i. THURB 23
insensibility:
It argues an i. LAMB:Ch 4
stark i. JOHNSON:S 87
state of such i. AUSTEN 21
inside:
finding other people i. them MALOUF 1
look i. myself I am afraid JOAD 1
person sitting i. is making fun CANET 1
insight:
Courage is often lack of i. UST 11
moment's i. is sometimes HOLMES:OW 14
insights: detached i. are priceless WHITEHEAD 8
insignificance:
natural, sterling i. AUSTEN 11
of the utmost i. CURZON 3
insignificant: i. men as any in England WALP:R 5
insinuating: i. appearance are seldom associated CONF 1
insolence:
flown with i. and wine MILT 129
i. is not invective DISR:B 58
i. of wealth will creep out JOHNSON:S 203
wretch who supports the i. JOHNSON:S 15
insomnia:
cure for i. is to get a lot of sleep FIELDS 3
reader suffering from an ideal i. JOYCE:J 31
suffer from i. in church TYR 1
insouciance: life in nonchalance and i. NASH 14
inspiration:
Genius is one per cent i. EDIS 1
i. comes, and then it goes MILLAIS 1
I. is the act of drawing up ANON 205
Ninety per cent of i. is PROV 290
no more i. in her than SHAW 37
where i. is what's needed? COLETTE 3
inspire: feel not what they i. SHELLEY:PB 167
inspired:
conscious of being i. by God BEETH 4
i. at nine o'clock every morning DE VR 8
That I am i. and please HORACE 51
inspires: common soul I. and feeds VIRGIL 71
instability: to dissimulate their i. HOUSM 51
instinct:
all healthy i. for it BUTLER:S[2] 33
i. for being unhappy highly developed SAKI 11
I. is a great matter SHAK:HEN.IV[1] 45
reasons for what we believe upon i. BRADLEY:FH 1
such a gosling to obey i. SHAK:COR 15
instincts:
High i. before which our mortal WORDS:W 63
true to your animal i. LAWR:DH 1
institute: gas was on in the I. BETJ 11
institution:
Any i. which does not ROBES 2
I have become a bit of an i. THATCH:M 20
i. of the dear love of comrades WHITMAN 25
It's an i. HUGHES:Th 4
institutions:
In Britain our i. evolve HAMIL:WW 2
no public i. for the education of women SMITH:Ad 10
paw him with their dirty i. THOREAU 20
working of great i. is mainly SANT 10
instructing: same time as i. him HORACE 112
instruction: wiser than the horses of i. BLAKE:W 46
instructor: grand I., Time BURKE:E 90
instructors: We are the Tiger i. ANON 113
instrument:
Call me what i. you will SHAK:HAM 125
Language is only the i. of science JOHNSON:S 6
magnificent i. between your legs TOSC 4
tune the I. here DONNE 94
Upon an i. of ten strings BIBLE 227
instruments: thousand twangling i. SHAK:TEM 24
insult:
adding i. to injuries MOORE:E 1
one more i. to God BROWNING:R 55
should i. her in the privacy THURB 6
sooner forgotten than an i. CHESTERFIELD 4
when a blockhead's i. points JOHNSON:S 63
insulted:
i. in places where the average Negro DAVIS:S 1
not i., I beg his pardon BRAHMS 1
who allows himself to be i. CORNEILLE 8
insured: i. for the accidents that are most likely COREN 4
insurrection:
I. is an art TROT 4
nature of an i. SHAK:JUL 21
to the next i. of the negroes JOHNSON:S 194
integrity:
I. without knowledge is weak JOHNSON:S 26
virgin white i. DONNE 24
intellect:
enough i. not enough literature HOUSM 53
halitosis of the i. ICK 2
i. is improperly exposed SMITH:Syd[1] 23
i. Misshapes the beauteous WORDS:W 18
march of i. SOUTHEY 23
put on I. BLAKE:W 120
revenge of the i. upon art SONT 1
voice of the i. is a soft FREUD:S 5
intellects:
few hearts and i. like hers MILL 24
highest i., like the tops MACAULAY:TB 15
intellectual:
Disinterested i. curiosity is the life TREV 1
if my wife wasn't an i. SHORTIS 1
i. All-in-all WORDS:W 28
i. and don't carry wood SCHWEITZ 1
i. eunuch Castlereagh BYR 157
i. improvement arises from leisure JOHNSON:S 158
i. nature is necessary JOHNSON:S 53
i. = one who splits himself CAMUS 1
i. power, through words and WORDS:W 116

Man is an i. animal HAZL 21
must have been 'a born i.' WOOLF:L 1
never an i. BANK 3
no i. society can flourish JOHNSON:P 1
North-west passage to the i. world STERNE 25
this i. being MILT 153
without some i. intention RUSKIN 2
word *i.* suggests straight AUD 45
ye lords of ladies i. BYR 160
intellectuals:
comic about i. when they meet FRISCH 1
I. are people who believe BREN 4
treachery of the i. BENDA 1
intelligence:
arresting the human i. long enough LEACOCK 8
filled with the light of i. KELLER 2
I. is quickness to apprehend WHITEHEAD 6
i. of the American people MENCK 19
lack of i. is its father LA BRU 6
The people have little i. LA BRU 9
intelligencies: we are The i. DONNE 36
intelligent:
i. are to the intelligentsia BALD:S 9
not very clever, but I'm quite i. BOGARDE 2
we are not i. GILB:WS 54
intelligentsia: intelligent are to the i. BALD:S 9
intelligible: best to aim at being i. HOPE:An 3
intemperance: brisk i. of youth GIBBON:E 16
intensity:
every art is its i. KEATS 123
full of passionate i. YEATS 62
intent:
glorious great i. SPENS 26
His first avow'd i. BUNYAN 30
Th'entente is al CHAUC 119
intention: good i. was never reached CERV 23
intentions:
devour second i. RAB 1
to hell is paved with good i. PROV 334
inter: In hugger-mugger to i. him SHAK:HAM 164
interchange: quiet i. of sentiments JOHNSON:S 173
intercourse:
dreary i. of daily life WORDS:W 11
I. as an act often expresses DWO 2
i. between tyrants and slaves GOLDS 58
the tragedy of sexual i. YEATS 147
interest:
common i. always will prevail DRYD 52
five per cent is the natural i. MACAULAY:TB 26
In the matter of i. we are wary TAYL:Jer 2
not my i. to pay the principal SHERIDAN:RB 47
interested:
always been i. in people MAUGH 23
man is more i. in a woman DIET 3
proceedings i. him no more HARRIS:JC 3
interesting:
important that a proposition be i. WHITEHEAD 1
i. by those who take an interest DALTON 1
something more i. than women WALLACE:E 1
statements was i., but tough TWAIN 12
who are in i. situations AUSTEN 46
Why are women ... so much more i. WOOLF:V 11
interests:
Divided by i. VOLT 27
power of vested i. is vastly KEYN 10
interference: No i. ARG 1
interim: i. is Like a phantasma SHAK:JUL 21
interludes: dark i. in the electric display O'NEILL 1
international: I. will be the human race POTTIER 1
interpenetrate: where men and sea i. CONRAD 7
interpretation:
bearing some other i. DOYLE:AC 2
I. is the revenge SONT 1
satisfaction with my i. MELBA 4
interpreted: merely i. the world MARX:K 2
interpreter:
God is his own i. COWP 13
i. is the hardest to be understood SHERIDAN:RB 31
interrupt:
i. a man with such a silly STERNE 3
shouldn't i. my interruptions ELIOT:TS 111
interrupted: saying when I was i. CONNOR 1
interstices: with i. between the intersections JOHNSON:S 13
interval:
fill the i. between dinner and supper JOHNSON:S 149
i. without an opera NEWM:E 1
save to enjoy the i. SANT 7
intervals: i. the devil is busy ANON 181
interview: strange and fatal i. DONNE 14
intestines: product of the smaller i. CARLYLE:T 30
intolerant: Time that is i. AUD 41
intoxicated:
man i. with God NOVA 1
once i. with power BURKE:E 70
who exposes himself when he is i. JOHNSON:S 211
intoxication:
all the effects of i. WILDE:O 133
best of life is but i. BYR 179
witness the i. of his father WALP:H 27
intransigent: dislike people ... because they are i. MACNEICE 15
intrigue: i. of a Greek of the lower empire DISR:B 91
intrigues: I. half-gather'd CRAB 14
introduction: one is an i. to any literary work JOHNSON:S 100
intrude: hope I don't i.? POOLE:J 1
intruders: i. on his ancient home ARNOLD:M 30
intrusion: I call it i. SPARK 6
invalid: invaluable permanent i. WILDE:O 83
invaluable: i. at first, and deadly afterwards BAGE 21
invariable: double glass o' the inwariable DICKENS 27
invasion:
can resist the i. of an army HUGO 2
waiting for the long-promised i. CHURCH:W 19
invent:
be necessary to i. him VOLT 26
To i., you need a good imagination EDIS 2
invented: good many that haven't been i. CARROLL 68
invention:
Beggars i. and makes COWP 41
heire of my i. prove SHAK:VEN 1
I. breeds i. EMER 59
it is a happy i. ANON 236
jerks of i.? SHAK:LOV 12
Necessity is the mother of i. PROV 280
vigor of his own i. SIDNEY:P 13
Woman's virtue is man's greatest i. SKIN:CO 1
inventions: lazybones can produce labour-saving i. GRASS 1
inventive: i. faculty on the stern condition DICKENS 232
inventor: return To plague th' i. SHAK:MAC 23
inventoried: It shall be i. SHAK:TWE 15
invents: Everything one i. is true FLAU 3
inverted commas:
absence of i.c. FAD 2
you always put i.c. YEATS 140
investment: art is an i. that hangs ALEX:H 1
invisible:
all things visible and i. PRAY 66
Am I i.? FRY:C 6
important things are i. SAINT-EX 3
i., As a nose SHAK:TWO 6
I., except to God MILT 181
live i. and dim VAUGHAN:H 3
we walk i. SHAK:HEN.IV[1] 26
yet she is not i. BACON:F[1] 64
invitation:
decline your i. owing to a subsequent WILDE:O 132
i. which dear Carrie rightly GROS 3
invited: People were not i. FITZGER:FS 4
involved: i. in affairs which concern them VALERY 4
involvement: difference between i. and commitment? NAV 1
invulnerable: as the air, i. SHAK:HAM 8
inward:
move my i. parts with joy UVA 2
with i. glory crowned SHELLEY:PB 32
inwit: Agenbite of i. JOYCE:J 23
Iohannes fac totum: being an absolute *I.f.t.* GREENE:R 2
Iona: warmer among the ruins of I. JOHNSON:S 40
Ionian:
I. white and gold ELIOT:TS 49
isle under I. skies SHELLEY:PB 133
ira: '*ça i.*', became fashionable VALL 1
Iranian: I. moderate is one who has run out KISS 5
Ireland:
Behind I. fierce and militant YEATS 126
best traitors I. has ever had DEVL 1
great Gaels of I. CHESTERTON 5
have liked to go to I. WILHELM II 3
How's poor ould I. ANON 23
I'll not forget old I. BLACKWOOD 3
I. has her madness AUD 38
I. is the old sow JOYCE:J 7
I. shall get her freedom YEATS 110
land whose countryside would be* DEVALE 2
lovely and lonely bride* WATSON:W 1
majority of the people of Northern I. ANON 257
Not in vain is I. pouring CHILD 1
problem with I. is that it's LEONARD:H 3
romantic I.'s dead and gone YEATS 37
sang to sweeten I.'s wrong YEATS 11
territory consists of the whole island of I. ANON 218
This blind bitter land* YEATS 36
very name of I. is mentioned SMITH:Syd[1] 1
we take power in I. MORRISON:D 1
what have I got for I.? COLLINS:Mic 1
iris:
i. blooms, Remember COLERIDGE:M 2
one vast I. of the West BYR 99
Irish:
apologise to I. women CLARE:A 3
Australian Aborigine and the I. being BATES:DM 2
dislike only *some* I. BEHAN:Br 6
I. and the Jews have a psychosis BEHAN:Br 8
I. are a fair people JOHNSON:S 163
I. are great talkers EWART 3
I. are the niggers of Europe DOYLE: R 1
I. bull is always pregnant MAHAF 2
I. hate work KENNELLY 1
I. mind has still YEATS 142
I. poets, learn your trade YEATS 123
I. were not English GALLANT 1
I., with their glowing hearts CHILD 1
know what the I. people wanted DE VALE 1
Let the I. vessel lie AUD 40
More I. than the I. ANON 196
Not men and women in an I. street ALLING 4
Politics is the chloroform of the I. GOGA 4
still an I. rebel to the backbone DUFFY:CG 1
symbol of I. art JOYCE:J 12
That is the I. question DISR:B 53
We I., born into that ancient YEATS 121
Irishman:
Every I. ... has a potato HARE:J 4
If you want to bore an I. SHAW 138
I.'s heart is nothing but SHAW 75
there's an I. fighting an Englishman ROYCE 1
Irishry: indomitable I. YEATS 123
iron:
achieved by 'blood and i.' BISM 7
beat the i. while it is hot DRYD 103
I also wash and i. them THATCH:D 1
I. Curtain GOEB 2
i. curtain across Europe TROU 1
I. Curtain has descended across CHURCH:W 35
i. enter into his souls STERNE 48
i. gates of life MARV 32
i. hand in a velvet glove CHARLES V 1
i. has entered his soul LLOYD GEO 12
I. – is master of them KIP 126
I. shuts amain MILT 52
my i.'s gone ANON 139
religion's i. age SHELLEY:PB 5
smoothing i. like a plane HEAN 8
sound of i. on stone DE LA M 9
Strike while the i. is hot PROV 358

no right to bring me up by j. DICKENS 209
Jerusalem:
absence from J. of a lunatic asylum ELLIS:H 7
J. the golden BERNARD:Cl 1
J. the golden NEALE 3
J. thy Sister calls BLAKE:W 118
not die but in J. SHAK:HEN.IV[2] 47
on our gate tae J. BIBLE 592
there J.s pillars stood BLAKE:W 114
There's J. and Madagascar THACK 26
thries hadde she been at J. CHAUC 25
was J. builded here BLAKE:W 98
Jesse: rod out of the stem of J. BIBLE 309
jesses: j. were my dear heart-strings SHAK:OTH 38
jest:
bitter is a scornful j. JOHNSON:S 63
Death is an old j. TURG 5
fellow of infinite j. SHAK:HAM 183
glory, j., and riddle of the world POPE 90
glory, j., and terror of mankind MINIF 1
good j. for ever SHAK:HEN.IV[1] 29
J. and youthful jollity MILT 66
j. unseen, inscrutable SHAK:TWO 6
j. without the smile COLERIDGE:ST 68
J.'s prosperity lies in the ear SHAK:LOV 23
Life is a j. GAY 36
true word is spoken in j. PROV 264
use myself in j. DONNE 63
jesters: shallow j. and rash SHAK:HEN.IV[1] 68
jests: to his memory for his j. SHERIDAN:RB 42
Jesu: J., the very thought CASWALL 1
Jesuit: thing, a tool, a J. KINGSLEY:C 3
***Jésus:** bon Sansculotte J.* DESM 2
Jesus:
Friend we have in J. SCRIV 1
Gentle J., meek and mild WESLEY:C 6
How sweet the Name of J. NEWT:J 2
J. and a nameless ape MACDIAR 14
J. bids us shine WARNER:S 1
J. calls us; o'er the ALEX:CF 3
J. Christ her little child ALEX:CF 4
J. Christ his only Son PRAY 19
J. Christ were to come to-day CARLYLE:T 66
J. cried HUGO 8
J., Lover of my soul WESLEY:C 5
J. loves me WARNER:A 1
J. loves you more than SIMON:P 2
J. shall reign where'er WATTS 16
J. speaks COWP 6
J.! the Name that charms WESLEY:C 3
J. was not by nature the marrying MONTEF 1
J. wept BIBLE 485
J.! with all thy faults BUTLER:S[2] 42
more popular than J. Christ LENNON 12
question of J. Christ as leader HUGHES:B 6
sweet reasonableness of J. ARNOLD:M 76
think J. was God or not SHAW 104
This J. will not do BLAKE:W 109
thou shalt call his name J. BIBLE 374
wasn't a woman who betrayed J. CARSWELL 1
With the Cross of J. BARING-G 2
Jew:
because I was not a J. NIEM 1
coloured, one-eyed J. DAVIS:S 2
difficult for a J. to be converted HEINE 9
divinity of – another J.? HEINE 9
Germany will declare that I am a J. EINS 9
greatest J. since Jesus HALDA 1
Hath not a J. eyes? SHAK:MERC 32
he is poor they call him a J. HEINE 8
I am a J. else SHAK:HEN.IV[1] 39
J. cannot help feeling superior BELLOC 44
J.-ish, not the whole hog MILLER:J 2
Liver of blaspheming J. SHAK:MAC 80
luxury that a J. can never allow MEIR 5
must the J. be merciful SHAK:MERC 44
not a Heathen, or a J. WATTS 13
where a J. feels even slightly uneasy JOHNSON:P 1
jewel:
j. in an Ethiop's ear SHAK:ROM 7
J. of the Just VAUGHAN:H 11
No j. is like Rosalinde SHAK:AS 39
poor j. of their souls STEVENSON:RL 41
stage's j. JONS 34
this j. have we lost SURREY 3
jewellery:
Never wear artistic j. COLETTE 4
rattle your j. LENNON 11
jewelry: remember to hang on to her j. LOOS 6
jewels:
bosom to hang j. upon DICKENS 190
Dumb j. often in their silent SHAK:TWO 9
j. for a set of beads SHAK:RIC.II 31
quality of heartless j. WHITE:P 10
Jewish:
choose A J. God, But spurn BROWNE:Ce 1
Final Solution to the J. question GOEB 1
home for the J. people BALF 2
J. man with parents alive ROTH 1
wouldn't think of myself as J. MILLER:A 8
Jewry: Modern Physics is an instrument of J. TOMASCH 1
Jews:
born King of the J.? BIBLE 375
game played between J. and God BLUE:L 1
Irish and the J. have a pyschosis BEHAN:Br 8
Jewish God, But spurn the J. BROWNE:Ce 1
J., a headstrong, moody DRYD 36
J. bring the unlike into ZANG 4
J. have made a contribution UST 7
J. have produced only three STEIN:G 6
J. might kiss, and Infidels POPE 40
three paynims, three J. CAX 2
To choose The J. EWER 2
Jill: J. came tumbling after NURS 27
Jim: Lucky J. AMIS:K 1
jingo: by j., if we do HUNT:GW 1
job:
European a j. was an income MORLEY:JD 1
got the boss's j. at last ANON 265
If a j.'s worth doing PROV 181
Living is both my j. MONTAIGNE 12
need another j. as well COPE 2
to do one's j. well CAMUS 5
We have finished the j. HAILE 1
we will finish the j. CHURCH:W 21
Job:
blessed the latter end of J. BIBLE 195
describing the afflictions of J. BACON:F[1] 32
Doth J. fear God for nought? BIBLE 180
I am as poor as J. SHAK:HEN.IV[2] 9
J. endured everything KIERK 2
jocundity: jasper of jocunditie DUNB 11
jog:
as a man might *j. on* with LAMBTON 1
j. on, the footpath way SHAK:WIN 15
John: No, J.! No, J. ANON 34
John-a-dreams: Like J. SHAK:HAM 92
John Barleycorn:
Inspiring, bold J.B. BURNS:R 87
J.B. should die BURNS:R 1
John Brown: J.B.'s body lies HALL:CS 1
John Bull: greatest of all is J.B. BYR 137
John Gilpin: J.G. was a citizen COWP 48
John Highlandman: my braw J.H. BURNS:R 23
John of Gaunt: Old J.o.G. SHAK:RIC.II 1
John Peel: D'ye ken J.P. GRAVES:JW 1
Johnny:
For J. head-in-air PUD 1
J. was as brave a knight BALL 28
Little J. Head-In-Air HOFFMAN:H 7
Johnson: Lyndon B. J. always thought that Australia GREEN:Mar 1
Johnson, Dr:
Cham of literature, Samuel J. SMOL 15
Dr J.'s morality was as English HAWT 5
Dr J.'s sayings would not appear PEMB:10th Earl 1
freedom with which Dr J. condemns BURNEY 7
J. marched to kettle-drums COLMAN:G[2] 8
J.'s stule was grand COLMAN:G[2] 8
no arguing with J. GOLDS 77
old lion* PARR 1
old philosopher is still* MACAULAY:TB 12
join:
j. the regions they divide POPE 35
j. together this Man and this PRAY 80
joined:
j. that they cannot be separated SMITH:Syd[1] 28
not lawfully be j. together PRAY 82
What God hath j. together SHAW 98
whom God hath j. together PRAY 87
joins: j. it, to divide POPE 52
joint: j., and not an entertainment HAMMO 1
joist: difference between j. and girder? ALLEN:D 3
joke:
coarse j. proclaims that we LEWIS:CS 2
get a j. well into a Scotch SMITH:Syd[1] 17
good deed to forget a poor j. BRAC 1
It's our only j. BARRIE 13
j. is ultimately a custard pie ORWELL 13
j.'s a very serious thing CHURCH:C 16
rich man's j. is always funny BROWN:TE 1
thing about a j. with a double meaning BARKER:R 1
jokes:
difference of taste in j. ELIOT:G 40
Forgive, O Lord, my little j. FROST:R 15
hackney'd j. from Miller BYR 9
no more j. in Music-halls SASS 2
no-one dares makes bad j. MANN:T 6
ten j., – thou hast got a hundred STERNE 6
joking:
way of j. is to tell the truth SHAW 76
wine and generous j. NEIL 4
jollity:
Jest and youthful j. MILT 66
turned to jollitie and game MILT 259
jolly:
lead a j. life like that DENNIS:CJ 3
some credit in being j. DICKENS 105
jollyrodgered: j. sea THOMAS:D 22
Jonah:
J. was in the belly BIBLE 359
lot fell upon J. BIBLE 358
Jones: J.! as from Calais WORDS:W 46
Joneses: drag the J. down to my level CRISP 2
jonquil: Jonquille o'ercomes the feeble WINCHIL 1
jonquils: land-locked pools of j. BETJ 18
Jonson:
Ben J. his best piece of poetrie JONS 33
He invades authors* DRYD 137
J. knew the critic's part COLLINS:Will 1
J.'s learned Sock be on MILT 74
Master J. ... was built far higher FULLER:T[1] 11
Next these, learn'd J. DRAYT 12
not only a professed imitator* DRYD 138
rare Ben J. JONS 57
Jordan: I looked over J. ANON 42
Joseph: Israel loved J. more BIBLE 67
Josephine:
court of the Empress J. GILB:WS 32
Not tonight, J. NAPO I I 12
joss-sticks: j. and honourable high-mindedness BRAM 1
jostling: not done by J. in the Street BLAKE:W 99
jot: care for public opinion a J.? LEAR 34
***jour:** j. de gloire est arrivé* ROUG 1
journalism:
As for modern j. WILDE:O 10
bias in television j. BIRT 1
essential for real success in j. TOMAL 1
from Christianity and j. BALF 4
in favour of modern j. WILDE:O 16
J. is a literary genre GARC 3
j. what will be grasped CONNOLLY:C 2
We are dominated by J. WILDE:O 42
journalist:
functions of the modern j. CURZON 1
j. makes up his lies YEATS 112
that's what makes a j. KRAUS 4
journalists:
J. are people who take in ELD 1
J. say a thing that BENNETT:Ar 4
no j. is even better BENTLEY:N 3
journey:
death the j.'s end DRYD 126
dreariest and the longest j. SHELLEY:PB 130
I have a long j. RALE 12
I may dine at j.'s end YEATS 58
itinerants on an eternal j. BAS 3
j. in my head SHAK:SON 10
j. is not long FORD:J[1] 6
j. of a thousand miles LAO 5
love to begin a j. on Sundays SWIFT 49
Our j. had advanced DICKIN:E 9
Whenever I prepare for a j. MANS:K 6
Where the travellers j. is done BLAKE:W 70
Will the day's j. take the whole ROSSET:C 14

wondering j. from the East MUIR:E 4
worst time of the year, to take a j. ANDREW 3
journeying: third-class seat sat the j. boy HARDY:T 37
journeyman: j. to grief? SHAK:RIC.II 10
journeys:
I shall make Speedier j. DONNE 63
J. end in lovers meeting SHAK:TWE 19
jousted: J. in Aspramont or Montalban MILT 135
Jove:
lovelier than the love of J. MARLOWE 2
starry threshold of J.'s Court MILT 15
joy:
a defeated j. SHAK:HAM 12
all the j. before death SWIN 34
asks, if this be j. GOLDS 32
aspiration is a j. forever STEVENSON:RL 23
beauty is a j. for ever KEATS 34
broke the grape's j. THOMAS:D 6
burst J.'s grape against KEATS 96
Converting j. to pain? CAMPION 7
dreme of joye CHAUC 104
dwell in doubtful j. SHAK:MAC 64
efter ioy oftymes cummis cair HENRYS 3
for ever in j. BROWNING:R 147
Gemme of all j. DUNB 11
good tidings of great j. BIBLE 449
He chortled in his j. CARROLL 46
headlong j. is ever on the wing MILT 61
j. delights in j. SHAK:SON 4
J., fair ray of the gods SCHILL 7
j. in the making BRIDGES:R 4
j. is but a dish of pains TICH 1
J. is my name BLAKE:W 21
j. is wisdom YEATS 16
J. rul'd the day DRYD 128
J. shall be in heaven BIBLE 462
j. was never sure SWIN 30
J., whose hand is ever KEATS 96
j. without canker or cark LANG:A 4
J. without labour is base RUSKIN 24
j.'s a trinket STEPHEN:JK 1
laugh with the voice of j. BLAKE:W 26
let j. be unconfined BYR 77
lost a j. for it worth HERB:G 13
Man was made for J. & Woe BLAKE:W 86
meant by the j. of living TALL 1
mother's pride, a father's j. SCOTT:W 45
move my inward parts with j. UVA 2
My scrip of j. RALE 2
no j. but calm TENNY 28
often does the evening cup of j. HOGG 9
sees in it his j. WORDS:W 58
snatch a fearful j. GRAY:T 6
sons of god shouted for j. BIBLE 193
spot Of j. into the Duchess' BROWNING:R 20
stern j. which warriors feel SCOTT:W 42
Strength through j. LEY 1
Surprised by j. WORDS:W 125
To j. in conquest is LAO 2
unbodied j. whose race SHELLEY:PB 96
Where J. for ever dwells MILT 122
Where's all the j. and mirth KEPP:C 1
who are capable of J. SMITH:LP 8
who binds to himself a j. BLAKE:W 59
with what j. they went away TWELLS 1
without the aid of j. BRONTE:E 8
world of capability For j. BROWNING:R 100
Joyce, James: And when you saw him* HEMINGWAY 4
joyful: J. and triumphant OAK 1
joys:
all that's precious in our j. STERNE 53
buy the j. o'er dear BURNS:R 91
come to those unspeakable j. PRAY 60
Earth's j. grow dim LYTE 1
Great j., like griefs MARM 1
it redoubleth j. BACON:F[1] 67
J. impregnate BLAKE:W 42
j. of all his life were said KEATS 63
j. of parents are secret BACON:F[1] 90
minds me o' departed j. BURNS:R 97
our j. are but fantastical DONNE 11
present j. are more to flesh DRYD 88
sacred j. of home MORE:H 2
season made for j. GAY 22
vain deluding joyes MILT 77
where true j. are to be found PRAY 49
wild j. of living BROWNING:R 146
with briars my j. & desires BLAKE:W 72
Juantorena: J. opens wide his legs ANON 152
jubilee:
first day of our J. is death BROWNE:T 17
we bring the J. WORK 1
Judas:
flowering J. ELIOT:TS 22
In the lost boyhood of J. RUSS:GW 1
thrice worse than J. SHAK:RIC.II 26
judge:
Forbear to j. SHAK:HEN.VI[2] 5
Half as sober as a j. LAMB:Ch 45
I'll be j., I'll be jury CARROLL 6
J. betweene the hie and lowe SIDNEY:P 6
j. human beings more by MAUR 1
j. is condemned when PUB 3
j. is not supposed to know PARKER:Hub 1
j. knows nothing unless PROV 217
j. me by the enemies I have made ROOS:FD 14
J. not BIBLE 398
j. not me CAMDEN:W 1
J. not the play before QUAR 6
J. not the preacher HERB:G 14
j. of a man by his foes CONRAD 3
J. of good taste TAC 4
J. That no king can corrupt SHAK:HEN.VIII 8
j. the quick and the dead PRAY 19
neutrality of an impartial j. BURKE:E 73
Never j. from appearances PROV 284
not be a j. of his characters CHEK 16
prince and a j. over us? BIBLE 82
sober as a j. FIELDING 8
sole j. of truth POPE 90
To j. great and high MONTAIGNE 1
wags that j. by rote OTWAY 1
who do not j. by appearances WILDE:O 28
world we know j. wisely? BENTLEY:EC 10
judged:
that ye be not j. BIBLE 398
whereby the world will be j. CEL 2
judgement:
see also **judgment**
acquitted in his own j. JUV 24
but in permanently suspended j. BOYD:W 2
by the lawful j. of his peers MAGNA 2
common pursuit of true j. ELIOT:TS 119
critical j. is so exquisite FRY:C 17
Don't wait for the Last J. CAMUS 16
history of the world is its j. SCHILL 1
j. in discerning what is true BACON:F[1] 54
j. is difficult HIPP 1
j. of persons was penetrating BENTLEY:EC 11
j. of the world is sure AUGUS 6
No nation is fit to sit in j. WILSON:W 6
Nor is the people's j. DRYD 53
their j. is a mere lottery DRYD 136
wait till J. break DICKIN:E 15
your fear in passing j. is greater BRUNO 1
judgements:
see also **judgments**
j. as our watches POPE 5
selling j. of the English law SYNGE 1
judges:
hundred j. have declared QUIL 1
hungry J. soon the sentence POPE 48
J. are guided by the law BELLOCH 1
j. of fact, though not PULT 1
j. seem the well paid watch-dogs GONNE 1
not my Accuser, but my j. NEWM:JH 7
When j. steal themselves SHAK:MEA 15
judging:
in writing or in j. ill POPE 4
not a matter of j. him but killing DANTON 1
we consider j. others MOLIERE 17
judgment:
see also **judgement**
angry with his j. for not BROWNE:T 2
I expect a j. Shortly DICKENS 169
in j. old SHAK:MERC 28
in the day of j. PRAY 34
J. drunk COWP 37
j. I had increases DRYD 143
j., thou art fled SHAK:JUL 52
leaves of the J. Book unfold TAYL:B 1
reserve thy j. SHAK:HAM 30
vulgarize the day of j. JERROLD 5
What j. shall I dread SHAK:MERC 41
judgments:
see also **judgements**
Delivers brawling j. TENNY 247
jug:
it git loose fum de j. HARRIS:JC 8
One old j. without a handle LEAR 7
juggler:
good j. to a bad Hamlet COCHRAN 1
least perceive a j.'s sleight BUTLER:S[1] 27
Julia:
in silks my *J.* goes HERR 38
Where's my *J.*'s lips doe smile HERR 10
Juliet: J. is the sun SHAK:ROM 8
Jumblies: lands where the J. live LEAR 13
jumbuck: Down came a j. PATERSON:AB 3
jump:
j. the life to come SHAK:MAC 23
not j. with common spirits SHAK:MERC 29
jumps: see how the cat j. SCOTT:W 96
June:
ice in J. BYR 10
meetings made December J. TENNY 174
needs not J. for beauty's ARNOLD:M 41
old sophistries of J. DICKIN:E 2
Junes: J. that were warmer than these YEATS 1
Jung: Adler will always be J. WALL 2
jungle:
city is not a concrete j. MORRIS:D 2
it is watchful as the j. BROD 1
this is the Law of the J. KIP 78
juniper-tree: leopards sat under a j. ELIOT:TS 67
junk:
imagination and a pile of j. EDIS 2
What j. BLUCH 1
Juno:
J. when she walks JONS 47
J.'s unrelenting anger VIRGIL 33
Jupiter: rage of thundering J. MARLOWE 4
jurisprudence: gladsome light of J. COKE:E 3
jury:
acquitted by a Limerick j. ADAMS:R[1] 1
credulity of an English j. HILL:Reg 3
I'll be judge, I'll be j. CARROLL 6
j. eagerly wrote all three CARROLL 37
j., passing on the prisoner's SHAK:MEA 6
Trial by j. itself DENMAN:T 1
jury-men: that j. may dine POPE 48
just:
all j. works do proceed PRAY 28
be generous rather than j. MENZ 2
Be j., and fear not SHAK:HEN.VIII 12
cause we believe to be j. LINC 6
I should be j. HERB:G 21
Jewel of the J. VAUGHAN:H 11
J. are the ways of God. MILT 286
j. men but little ROUX 2
j. shall live by faith BIBLE 508
ninety and nine j. persons BIBLE 462
Only the actions of the j. SHIRL 4
Our cause is j. DICKIN:J 2
path of the j. is BIBLE 252
place for a j. man is also a prison THOREAU 2
rain it raineth on the j. BOWEN:L 1
raise me with the J. GRAHAM:J 2
sendeth rain on the j. BIBLE 388
slept the sleep of the j. RACINE 10
Thou art indeed j., Lord HOPK:GM 30
thou art j. TENNY 123
whatsoever things are j. BIBLE 542
when I reflect that God is j. JEFFERSON 3
juster:
j. epoch has begun TENNY 293
that I j. am SEDLEY 5
justice:
doing j. to those who can WALP:H 28
don't want j., I want mercy HUGHES:B 5
God's j., if it makes no haste PETERS 1
grim J. goes its way WILDE:O 116
hand of j. shut the door STERNE 55
j., In fair round belly SHAK:AS 34
J. is not a mincer DURREN 1
j. is open to all – like the Ritz BING 1
J. is something terrible DURREN 6
J. is the constant and perpetual JUST 1
J. is the means whereby FRANCE 9
J. is truth in action DISR:B 57
j. makes democracy possible NIEB 1
j. should not only be done HEWART 1
J., though she's painted blind BUTLER:S[1] 37
'J.' was done HARDY:T 67
Let there be j. FERD 1

Let there be j. for all MANDELA:N 7
like the old line about j. OSB:J 11
love of j. in most men LA ROCHE 12
memory of j. to fade COETZ 1
our j. sees as in a mirror PETERS 1
price of j. is eternal publicity BENNETT:Ar 7
pursue j. with wisdom PLATO 14
Revenge is a kind of wild j. BACON:F[1] 96
rule of equal j. MILL 29
sad-ey'd j. SHAK:HEN.V 7
some degree of j. must be STOP 9
such a thing as j. in the English KELLY:N 2
sword of j. first lay down DEF 14
temper so J. with Mercie MILT 252
This even-handed j. SHAK:MAC 23
Thou shalt have j. SHAK:MERC 47
Though j. be thy plea SHAK:MERC 44
Thwackum was for doing j. FIELDING 23
truly and indifferently minister j. PRAY 69
We love j. greatly ROUX 2
what you think j. requires MANS:W 1
When mercy seasons j. SHAK:MERC 44
Where J. naked is AUD 6
which is the j. SHAK:KING L 69
you have ravish'd j. WEBSTER:J 8
justification: carry its j. in every line CONRAD 1
justified: half as good as j. BUTLER:S[1] 33
justify:
justifie the wayes of God to men MILT 108
j. God's ways to man HOUSM 28
to j. their injustices VOLT 17
justifying: interested in better j. themselves SZASZ 1
kafir: why He made the k. BOSMAN 1
Kaiser: down the signed photograph of the K. WAUGH:E 19
kaleidoscope: girl with k. eyes LENNON 7
kalends:
Kalendis are begun JAMES I 2
paid at the Greek K. CAES:A 2
kames: gowd k. in their hair BALL 51
kangaroo:
As the Duck and the K.? LEAR 11
ever tried to lasso a k.? SAV 1
Old Man K. first KIP 106
Tie me k. down HARRIS:R 1
kangaroos: little k. flying about WILDE:O 47
Kansas: K. had better stop raising LEASE 1
Kant: K. on the handle-bars BETJ 9
Karoo: meaning of the broad K. HARDY:T 15
Karshish: K., the picker up BROWNING:R 105
Kaspar: Old K.'s work was done SOUTHEY 1
Kate:
Kiss me, K. SHAK:TAM 9
none of us car'd for K. SHAK:TEM 18
You are call'd plain K. SHAK:TAM 7
Kathleen: K. Mavourneen CRAW 1
Katy: K-K-K., beautiful K. O'HARA 1
kauri: k., the giant timber tree MANDER 1
KBO: We must just K. CHURCH:W 69
Kean, Edmund: To see him act* COLERIDGE:ST 83
Keats:
I see a schoolboy* YEATS 53
K., who was ignorant of Greek SHELLEY:PB 168
K., who was kill'd off BYR 223
Mister John K. five feet high KEATS 138
Shelley and K. were the last HALDA 2
What porridge had John K.? BROWNING:R 144
Who killed John K.? BYR 139
keel: No k. has ever ploughed SHELLEY:PB 132
keener: k. with constant use IRV 2
keep:
k. something to yoursel BURNS:R 45
k. thee in all thy ways BIBLE 226
K. we must, if k. we can HOUSM 34
may k. that will and can HOUSM 32
Pound a week and his k. LAWS 5
they should k. who can WORDS:W 87
keeper:
Am I my brother's k.? BIBLE 27
k. is only a poacher turned KINGSLEY:C 4
k. Stands up to keep HOUSM 17
keepeth: he that k. thee BIBLE 239
Kelly: anybody here seen K.? MURPHY:A 1
Kempenfelt: When K. went down COWP 17
ken: k. aathing hauflinsweys BIBLE 594
Kensal Green: Paradise by way of K.G. CHESTERTON 9
Kent: everybody knows K. DICKENS 7
Kentish Town: courts of K.T. BETJ 19
Kentucky: old K. Home far away FOST:SC 5
kernel:
this k., This squash SHAK:WIN 3
when he hath the k. eat DONNE 31
kettle:
back to the tea-k. DISR:B 56
battered k. at the heel YEATS 75
How agree the k. and BIBLE 367
Polly put the k. on NURS 54
Polly put the ket-tle on DICKENS 89
This is a pretty k. of fish MARY QUEEN CON 2
took a k. large and new CARROLL 72
Kew:
down to K. in lilac-time NOY 1
Richmond and K. Undid me ELIOT:TS 49
key:
all of us looking for the k. BENNETT:Al 1
hands on that golden K. MILT 17
k. is turned On our uncertainty YEATS 66
this k. Shakespeare unlocked WORDS:W 133
keys:
half that's got my k. GRAHAM:H 3
His k. were rusty BYR 144
k. of all the creeds TENNY 139
Thou hast the k. of Paradise DEQ 4
Two massy Keyes MILT 52
Khatmandu: idol to the north of K. HAYES 1
kick:
every ass thinks he may k. PARR 1
I'll k. you downstairs CARROLL 10
k. against the pricks BIBLE 499
scarcely k. to come to the top KEATS 136
They may k. you out WAUGH:E 6
why did you k. me downstairs? BICK 5
without wanting to k. his face HAMP 4
kicked:
any that was k. up stairs HALIF 16
cursed and k. the stairs MILLAY 2
kicking: dragged k. and screaming into STEVENSON:A 12
kicky-wicky: hugs his k. here SHAK:ALL 6
kid:
Dandl'd the K. MILT 196
Here's lookin' at you, k. BOGART:H 2
lie down with the k. BIBLE 310
not seethe a k. BIBLE 106
kidlings: K. blithe and merry GAY 2
kidnapped:
finally realize that I'm k. ALLEN:W 13
have fourteen k. grandchildren GET 2
kidney: man of my k. SHAK:MERR 15
kidneys: Hurrah! blister my k. SURT 11
Kilbride: met a child Eily K. KENNELLY 4
kill:
animals never k. for sport FROUDE 5
brother, or I shall k. you CHAMFORT 9
can't step up and k. a woman BENCH 3
care will k. a cat WITHER 2
could only k. you once CARLYLE:T 61
did not k. me HOUSM 47
have to k. a man it costs nothing CHURCH:W 57
have to k. more women and children BALD:S 2
he is genuinely anxious to k. KIP 9
He would k. Himself DUMAS:A[F] 1
I will go home and k. her TROLL 31
k. a king and marry SHAK:HAM 137
k. a Man as k. a good Book MILT 312
k. a man than a hawk JEFFERS 1
k. a wife with kindness SHAK:TAM 10
K. me to-morrow SHAK:OTH 62
K. not the goose that lays PROV 221
K. one man, and you ROSTAND:J 1
k. sick people MARLOWE 23
K. the other guy before he DEMP 1
k. the patient BACON:F[1] 68
k. the poor creature at once GASK 3
k. thee, And love thee after SHAK:OTH 60
k. thee with much cherishing SHAK:ROM 19
k. time without injuring eternity THOREAU 6
let them k. as many as possible TRU 3
must men k. SHELLEY:PB 158
next year I'll k. myself RHYS 2
Otherwise k. me MACNEICE 12
sin to k. a mockingbird LEE:Har 1
They k. us for their sport SHAK:KING L 59
they k. you a new way ROGERS:W 3
Thou shalt not k. BIBLE 103
Thou shalt not k. CLOUGH 20
time to k. BIBLE 281
To k. a human being is JAMES:H 1
killed:
Better be k. than frightened SURT 21
effort very nearly k. her BELLOC 21
I am the enemy you k. OWEN:W 14
I don't mind your being k. KITCHEN 1
k. by frowns and smiles SHELLEY:PB 70
k. in a pub brawl in a suburb JAMES:PD 1
Roaring Bill (who k. him) BELLOC 42
so many people k. AUSTEN 75
Woman K. with Kindness HEYW:T 1
you or your brother who was k. SPOON 7
killer: lover and k. are mingled DOUGLAS:K 2
killeth: letter k. BIBLE 528
killing:
how to die by k. others CHATEAU 2
k. as the Canker to the Rose MILT 47
K. Is the ultimate simplification MACDIAR 27
K. noe Murder SEXBY 1
man is k. time LOWELL:R 7
More ways of k. a cat KINGSLEY:C 2
never of k. for their country RUSS:B 33
Stop k. the dead UNG 1
What better reason for k. YEATS 125
kills:
it k. something precious COMPT 8
man k. the thing he loves WILDE:O 113
time quietly k. them BOUC 1
ways By which Time k. us SITWELL:O 2
Kilmeny: K. had been she knew HOGG 1
kilt: standing knock-kneed in a k. FRASER:GM 1
Kiltartan: My country is K. Cross YEATS 61
kilted: she has k. her green kirtle BALL 52
kimonos: Two girls in silk k. YEATS 100
kin:
A little more than k. SHAK:HAM 14
k. and kith Were more fun NASH 2
little less than 'k.' BARH 9
kind:
All that k. HORACE 64
coarsely k. JOHNSON:S 228
fellow-feeling makes one wond'rous k. GARRICK 3
had it been early, had been k. JOHNSON:S 95
I am one with my k. TENNY 227
ingenious, sober, nor k. ANON 135
Is she k. as she is fair? SHAK:TWO 12
just the art of being k. WILCOX 4
just try to be ***kind*** FOAKES 1
k. to fou folk and bairns PROV 150
k. to you when you were young BIRL 1
less than k. SHAK:HAM 14
people will always be k. SASS 6
people you've been k. to MARSHALL:Al 1
rather more than 'k.' BARH 9
to the friend be k. DUNB 3
Too k. – too k. NIGHT 2
try to be *k.* – a little k. JACK:FJF 1
kindest: k. man that ever struck MALORY 16
kindle:
cannot k. when we will ARNOLD:M 12
k. soft desire DRYD 114
kindled: k. by unexpected sparks JOHNSON:S 28
kindness:
acts Of k. and of love WORDS:W 4
Christ took the k. BROWNING:R 200
depended on the k. of strangers WILLIAMS:T 3
generates k. and consolidates JOHNSON:S 85
greetings where no k. is WORDS:W 11
have k. in reserve POPE 123
kill a wife with k. SHAK:TAM 10
k., being rude to him DANTE 14
K. in another's trouble GORDON:AM 1
Little deeds of k. CARNEY 2
milk of human k. BURKE:E 74
milk of human k. SHAK:MAC 19
recompense k. with k. CONF 9
repaying injury with k. LAO 1
round with the milk of human k. GUED 2
shew forth thy loving k. BIBLE 227
tak a cup o' k. BURNS:R 71
value on spontaneous k. JOHNSON:S 226
Woman Killed with K. HEYW:T 1

kindnesses: made up of a hundred little k. WELD 1
kinds: There are two k. of people PAP 1
kine: seven fat k. BIBLE 71
king:
a' for our rightfu' k. BURNS:R 111
against Heav'n's matchless K. MILT 183
All the k.'s horses NURS 20
anointed thee k. over Israel BIBLE 156
bachelor lives like a k. LOWRY:LS 1
banners of the k. advance VENAN 2
born K. of the Jews? BIBLE 375
cat may look at a k. CARROLL 22
cat may look at a k. PROV 53
coming of the K. of Heaven ANON 59
despised, and dying k. SHELLEY:PB 53
discharge my duties as K. EDWARD VIII 2
every inch a k. SHAK:KING L 67
Every man a k. LONG 2
fair and fatal k. JOHNSON:L 5
Fear God. Honour the k. BIBLE 567
follow the K. TENNY 238
God bless the K. BYROM 5
God save the k. BIBLE 143
God save the k. HOGG 5
he might hae been a k. BALL 12
heart and stomach of a k. ELIZ I 3
hew wood than be a k. CHARLES X 1
I am a K. CIB 8
I was a K. in Babylon HENL 7
I'm the k. of the castle NURS 25
kind of K. for me GILB:WS 110
k., and officers of sorts SHAK:HEN.V 7
K. asked The Queen MILNE 3
K. born of all England MALORY 1
k. can do no wrong BLACKS 4
K. – even in your underpants FULDA 1
k. has been very good to me BOLE 1
k. is a thing men have made SELD 4
k. is always a k. WOLLST 8
K. is but a man as I SHAK:HEN.V 31
k. may make a nobleman BURKE:E 89
k. must learn to stoop LEOP 1
k. my brother's wreck ELIOT:TS 43
k. never dies BLACKS 2
k. of intimate delights COWP 73
K. of Love my Shepherd is BAKER 1
k. of shreds and patches SHAK:HAM 144
K. Over himself SHELLEY:PB 84
K. over the Water ANON 210
k. reigns THIERS 2
k. reigns, but does not ZAM 1
k. sees thee still HERB:G 5
K. to have things done as cheap PEPYS 8
k. was in his counting-house NURS 66
K. will not leave the country ELIZ:QM 2
K.'s a bawcock SHAK:HEN.V 29
K.'s a K. DRAYT 3
K.'s life is moving peacefully DAWS 1
lad that's born to be k. BOULTON:HE 1
lessened my esteem of a k. PEPYS 7
little profits that an idle k. TENNY 51
mockery k. of snow SHAK:RIC.II 38
Mrs Simpson's pinched our k. ANON 67
My dead K. JOYCE:J 3
My God and K. HERB:G 24
My God, my K. HERB:G 26
my life to make you K. CHARLES II 6
No bishop, no k. JAMES VI/I 4
not sing *God save the K.* BURNS:R 114
Offends no K., and is a K. CHAPMAN:G 3
painting the k.'s robe GRAVES:R 5
passing brave to be a K. MARLOWE 8
played the K. as though FIELD 2
recognise a true k. CORNEILLE 4
skipping K. SHAK:HEN.IV[1] 68
so much a k. as a Monarch SELL 7
Stamp'd with the image of the K. TENNY 256
still am I k. of those SHAK:RIC.II 36
such divinity doth hedge a k. SHAK:HAM 165
This hath not offended the k. MORE:T 6
Till the K. enjoys his own again PARKER:M 1
to serve my k. and country NELS 11
Under which k. SHAK:HEN.IV[2] 51
unjust and wicked k. SEN 7
until the last k. is strangled DIDE 6
What a k., what a court ABELA 2
What must the K. do now? SHAK:RIC.II 31
When I am k., dilly NURS 30
Who is this K. of glory? BIBLE 208
whom the k. delighteth to honour BIBLE 178
worse k. never left a realm BYR 146
worship the K. GRANT:R 1
King Cole: Old K.C. Was a merry NURS 46
King George: K.G. will be able to read that HANC:J 1
King John: K.J. was not a good man MILNE 16
King Richard: K.R. doth himself appear SHAK:RIC.II 29
kingdom:
For thine is the k. BIBLE 391
I never gave you k. SHAK:KING L 33
In a k. by the sea POE 7
k. for a stage SHAK:HEN.V 1
k. of heaven is like to a grain BIBLE 412
K. stretch from shore WATTS 16
k. where nobody dies MILLAY 8
large k. for a little grave SHAK:RIC.II 31
mercy upon this afflicted K. GRAHAM:J 3
my k. for a horse SHAK:RIC.III 20
of such is the k. of God BIBLE 444
Seek ye first the k. of God BIBLE 396
theirs is the k. of heaven BIBLE 384
thine is the k. PRAY 6
Thy K. come BIBLE 391
thy k. come MASS 15
Thy k. come PRAY 6
Thy k. is divided BIBLE 352
wars as the k. of Christ MONTESQU 2
kingdoms:
goodly states and k. seen KEATS 3
k. are clay SHAK:ANT 3
kingfish: I'm the K. LONG 1
kingfisher: It was the Rainbow gave* DAVIES:WH 1
kingfishers: As k. catch fire HOPK:GM 19
kingly:
his State Is K. MILT 100
K. conclaves stern SHELLEY:PB 69
kings:
accounted poet k. KEATS 13
all be as happy as k. STEVENSON:RL 51
and ruin k. DRYD 37
Beside the scheme of k. HARDY:T 75
but the breath of k. BURNS:R 14
cabbages – and k. CARROLL 56
Captains and the K. depart KIP 91
dread and fear of k. SHAK:MERC 44
either philosophers became k. PLATO 10
Howsoever their k. go mad HORACE 80
K. and such like are just as funny ROOS:T 18
K. are but slaves of their rank SCHILL 2
K. are by God appointed ANON 25
K. are earth's gods SHAK:PER 3
K. are naturally lovers of BURKE:E 95
k. crept out again BROWNING:EB 1
K. govern by means of FOX:CJ 2
k. have cares GREENE:R 1
K. it makes gods SHAK:RIC.III 16
K. may be blest BURNS:R 86
k. of the sea ARNOLD:M 2
K. seek their Subjects good HERR 39
K. will be tyrants from policy BURKE:E 58
nor Asia two K. ALEX 2
now no k. nor Caesars POUND 5
part which laws or k. can cause GOLDS 12
passion for our temperate k. TENNY 193
puller down of k. SHAK:HEN.VI[3] 5
Punctuality is the politeness of k. LOUIS XVIII 1
Right Divine of k. POPE 169
saddest of all K. JOHNSON:L 4
soon be only five k. left FAROUK 1
sport of k. SOMER 1
stories of the death of k. SHAK:RIC.II 28
subjects is the end of k. DEF 14
Such grace had k. BROWNING:R 12
such is the breath of K. SHAK:RIC.II 8
three k. into the east BURNS:R 1
to calm contending k. SHAK:POET 6
to change my state with k. SHAK:SON 11
'Twixt K. & Tyrants there's HERR 39
Vain the ambition of k. WEBSTER:J 18
walk with K. KIP 128
way of making k. MELBOU 7
what have k. that privates have not SHAK:HEN.V 34
what they show to k. CRAB 8
kinky: more k. than a prince chasing a swan HELPMAN 3
kinquering: K. Congs their titles take SPOON 3
kinship: any k. with the stars MERED:G 18
Kipling: Pardoned K. and his views AUD 42
kippers: two old k. in a box THOMAS:D 25
Kirconnell: On fair K. lea BALL 25
kirk: Marie Hamilton's to the k. BALL 41
kiss:
add to that k. a score HERR 14
Ae fond k. BURNS:R 92
born to a k. and a smile FENT 2
Colder thy k. BYR 54
coughs when you would k. AUD 7
coward does it with a k. WILDE:O 113
die upon a k. SHAK:OTH 71
drew With one long k. TENNY 11
Each k. a heart-quake BYR 180
effrontery to k. me on the lips ELIZ:QM 5
first k. is magic CHAND 6
I dare not ask a kisse HERR 36
I k. his dirty shoe SHAK:HEN.V 29
kis the steppes CHAUC 120
k., a sigh, and so away CRASH 16
k. again with tears TENNY 103
k. before they are married SHAK:HEN.V 48
K. her until she be wearied SHELLEY:PB 146
k. is but a k. now MERED:G 21
k. is still a k. HUP 1
K. K. Bang Bang KAEL 1
k. Long as my exile SHAK:COR 17
k. me and never no more MALORY 11
K. me as if you made believe BROWNING:R 16
K. me, Kate SHAK:TAM 9
k. me with the kisses of his BIBLE 292
k. my ass in Macy's window JOHNSON:LB 5
k. my *Julia's* dainty leg HERR 34
k. my Lord before I die MARLOWE 13
k. of death SMITH:Alf 1
k. of the sun for pardon GUR 1
k. on the wrist feels good STEVENSON:A 1
k. the image of my death DRUMMOND OF H 2
k. the place to make it well? TAYL:Ann 1
k. thy hand to bid adieu STERNE 38
K. till the cow comes home BEAUMO 3
k. without a squeeze PROV 21
k.'s strength, I think it must be reckon'd BYR 180
last lamenting k. DONNE 98
leave a k. upon the cup JONS 36
let us k. and part DRAYT 9
Let's k. afresh HERR 14
lover's k. may play CRASH 9
make me immortal with a k. MARLOWE 38
man may k. a bonie lass BURNS:R 62
man may k. a bonny lass SCOTT:W 65
must not k. and tell CONG 24
needes must kisse againe SIDNEY:P 8
never canst thou k. KEATS 92
nor k. before folks CONG 53
Onely to kisse that Aire HERR 36
part at last without a k.? MORRIS:W 1
Quit in a single k.? BRIDGES:R 5
saw you take his k. PATMO 5
seal with a righteous k. SHAK:ROM 44
single k. of a good-bye? PATMO 8
so k. on HERR 14
spend that k. Which is my heaven SHAK:ANT 75
swear to never k. the girls BROWNING:R 114
take occasion to k. SHAK:AS 57
When women k. MENCK 22
wrong in a connubial k. BYR 184
kissed:
childish face up to be k. MCAULEY 2
had I a wist, before I kist BALL 63
Hasn't been k. for forty years ROWL:E 1
He k. likewise the maid COWP 96
Jenny k. me HUNT:L 5
kiss'd thee ere I kill'd SHAK:OTH 71
k. . . . by a man who *didn't* wax KIP 7
k. by the English dead OWEN:W 8
k. her little sister MONTROSE 3
k. her once by the pig-sty THOMAS:D 27
k. his hand to me and died HOUSM 47
k. his sad Andromache CORNFORD:Fran 3
k. it and then fled SHELLEY:PB 88

K. the girls and made them NURS 13
k. the maiden all forlorn NURS 73
she k. 'her cow SWIFT 38
We have kiss'd away Kingdoms SHAK:ANT 36
Wherever one wants to be k. CHANEL 2
kisses:
a-wastin' Christian k. KIP 59
bread and cheese, and k. SWIFT 43
Dear as remembered k. TENNY 109
Give me a thousand k. CATUL 6
I understand thy k. SHAK:HEN.IV[1] 64
k. of the enemy are deceitful BIBLE 273
littered with remembered k. MACNEICE 6
love in k. rain SHELLEY:PB 36
one who k., and one who offers PROV 199
play'd At cards for k. LYLY 3
poor half-k. kill me DRAYT 10
Stolen k. much completer HUNT:L 2
thousand k. the poor last SHAK:ANT 56
With k. four KEATS 84
you have forgotten my k. SWIN 39
kissing:
K. don't last MERED:G 4
k., kind-hearted gentleman COWP 96
K. with golden face SHAK:SON 14
K. your hand may make LOOS 5
let me die with k. MARLOWE 13
President spends most of his time k. TRU 4
that first invented k. SWIFT 48
when the k. had to stop? BROWNING:R 157
kit-bag: troubles in your old k. ASAF 1
kitchen:
anarchy prevails in my k. JOHNSON:S 268
heat, get out of the k. TRU 1
in a k. bred BYR 53
like the heat, get out of the k. PROV 191
to say towards the k. WEBSTER:J 2
waiting at the k-k-k-k. door O'HARA 1
kitchen-cabals: K., and nursery-mishaps CRAB 14
kitchen-sink-revolutionary: k. look WEST:R 8
kitchen-wench: she's the k., and all grease SHAK:COM 4
Kitchener: if K. was not a great man ASQU:M 4
kite:
K. swoops down a furlong KIP 79
not sufficient for a k.'s dinner QUAR 5
kith: kin and k. Were more fun NASH 2
kitten:
black k.'s fault entirely CARROLL 42
My imperial k. CARROLL 43
rather be a k. and cry SHAK:HEN.IV[1] 60
kittens:
sewing-basket after half a dozen k. RAD 1
Three little k. they lost NURS 76
Kitty: K., a fair, but frozen GARRICK 5
kiwi: K. is the ugliest bird POWER:JJ 1
kleptomaniac: suddenly I remembered: k. MORA 3
knapsack: marshal's baton in his k. NAPO I 18
knave:
he's an arrant k. SHAK:HAM 53
neat k. with a smooth tale WEBSTER:J 19
petty sneaking K. I knew BLAKE:W 103
knavery: k. and folly to excuse CHURCH:C 9
knaves:
all men should be k. ROCHES 5
being a fool among k. SWIFT 8
call'd them untaught k. SHAK:HEN.IV[1] 17
He calls the k., Jacks DICKENS 208
We are arrant k., all SHAK:HAM 100
knee:
bend The supple k.? MILT 222
k. is a joint, and not HAMMO 1
little abune her k. BALL 52
my k., my hat, and hand BROWNE:T 1
To sit upon the curate's k. CHESTERTON 23
tribute of his supple k. SHAK:RIC.II 13
knee-cap: soul started at the k. LEWIS:W 6
kneel: they should k. for peace SHAK:TAM 17
kneeling: K. ne're spoil'd silk stocking HERB:G 12
kneels:
Little Boy k. MILNE 8
Not one k. to another WHITMAN 7
knees:
bring Russia up off her k. ZHI 2
creeps rustling to her k. KEATS 71
heart, not in the k. JERROLD 1
into the water up to her k.? MARX:G 20
K. & elbows are only glued together BLAKE:W 93
knocked everything but the k. HAMMO 2
live with children round her k. WORDS:W 93
now serve on his k. PEELE 2
sit on Sweeney's k. ELIOT:TS 29
Sweeney spreads his k. ELIOT:TS 28
the rest on his k. DICKENS 194
they are all on their k. HARDY:T 31
to live on your k. IBA 2
weakest saint upon his k. COWP 8
woo her with too slavish k. KEATS 90
work is done upon his k. KIP 140
knell:
By fairy hands their k. COLLINS:Will 4
Curfew tolls the k. GRAY:T 16
k. That summons thee SHAK:MAC 34
strikes like a rising k. BYR 76
thy k. who shall survive? HARDY:T 24
knew:
he k. nothing yet BEHN 6
he nothing k. MILT 274
I k. all that he k. BRONTE:C 1
I k. almost as much at eighteen JOHNSON:S 119
I k. you once BROWNING:R 191
if we k. one, we k. two EDDI 1
k. exactly what they were doing GLASH 1
k. thee but to love thee HALLE 1
k. you had it in you PARKER:D 24
knife:
keeps them on the k. ANON 70
k. was at my throat GREG:Lady 3
last twist of the k. ELIOT:TS 18
smylere with the knyf CHAUC 47
strike with our spirit's k. SHELLEY:PB 120
War to the k. PALAF 1
wound, the k. is lost in it SHELLEY:PB 64
you are the k. which I plunge KAF 14
knight:
beadsman now that was your k. PEELE 2
courteoust k. that ever bare MALORY 16
Gentle K. was pricking on the plaine SPENS 21
K. of the Sad Face CERV 5
k. without fear and BAYA 1
lies a new-slain k. BALL 59
no loyal k. and true TENNY 17
parfit gentil knyght CHAUC 4
shortest k. of the year RICHARDS:G 1
Knight: Afaq to K. at the Nursery End JOHNSTON:B 3
knighthood: k., their resolve buckled GRANT:BA 1
knights:
deeds that some k. used CAX 3
K. of Logres, or of Lyones MILT 267
knits: Nothing k. man to man SICK 1
knitter:
beautiful little k. SITWELL:E 13
Like a k. drowsed HARDY:T 70
knitters: spinsters and the k. SHAK:TWE 28
knives:
carving k. Into their gizzards CALVER 2
hands before k. PROV 121
their k. and forks like dumb-bells MACNEICE 16
knob: brains out of a brass k. DICKENS 193
knock:
at any door I k. HORACE 74
exceed in interest a k. LAMB:Ch 19
k., and it shall be opened BIBLE 400
K. at a Starre HERR 35
k. him down first, and pity JOHNSON:S 182
k. on my door in the morning AUD 26
right to k. him down for it JOHNSON:S 213
stand at the door, and k. BIBLE 577
you k. it is never at home COWP 29
knock-kneed: standing k. in a kilt FRASER:GM 1
knocked:
have, with decency, k. POUND 37
K. down a doctor? SIMPSON:NF 2
K. 'em in the Old Kent Road CHEV:A 2
k. everything but the knees HAMMO 2
we k. the bastard off HILLARY 1
knocker: tye up the k. POPE 117
knockers: K., larrikins, and chromos ANON 123
knocking:
Here's a k. indeed SHAK:MAC 48
k. at preferment's door ARNOLD:M 21
K. on the moonlit door DE LA M 6
Wake Duncan with thy k. SHAK:MAC 47
Whence is that k.? SHAK:MAC 44
knocks: Opportunity seldom k. twice PROV 314
knot:
k. be unknotted ELIOT:TS 82
k. intrinsicate Of life SHAK:ANT 75
last k. that love could tye CRASH 6
too hard a k. for me SHAK:TWE 18
knotted: Sat and k. all the while SEDLEY 2
know:
All that we k. is BYR 63
all ye need to k. KEATS 92
better people k. her, the better WEST:R 8
can believe . . . but can never k. LEVIN 3
don't k. can't hurt you PROV 421
find out what you don't k. WELLING 10
fine thing it is, to k. something MOLIERE 25
get to k. him better COPE 8
God, thou, and I, do k. SHAK:RIC.II 7
he that aspired to K. BROWNING:R 3
how may I k. him MILT 233
I do not k. myself GOET 37
I k. who I am CERV 1
k. better what is good for people JAY 1
k. everybody CHESTERFIELD 25
k. how not to k. the things MOLIERE 26
k. it about the right person MUM 3
k. much about science but I k. what AMIS:M 1
k. not what, we k. not where DRYD 23
k. nothing whatever about you DOYLE:AC 23
k. the man their neighbour YEATS 40
k. the World, not love her YOUNG:E 17
K. then thyself POPE 89
K. thyself ANON 211
K. thyself PROV 223
'K. thyself' is a most superfluous COMPT 2
k. to k. no more MILT 203
K. what thou canst work at CARLYLE:T 11
Let not thy left hand k. BIBLE 390
no one would k. anything BJEL:J 1
one wanted much to k. EWART 2
ourselves to k. POPE 107
People of quality k. everything MOLIERE 2
saying you want to k., you k. DICKENS 187
should like to k. thoroughly WILDE:O 48
teacher of those who k. DANTE 5
than kan hymselven knowe CHAUC 59
they k. not what they do BIBLE 468
they merely k. more SAKI 23
To k. her was to love her ROGERS:S 1
truly to k. is everlasting life PRAY 59
We all *k.* what light is JOHNSON:S 187
We k. a subject ourselves JOHNSON:S 171
we k. damn all MONSAR 1
we k. what we are SHAK:HAM 161
weep because I k. all things YEATS 24
What do I k.? MONTAIGNE 16
What I don't k. isn't knowledge BEECHING 1
which you yourselves do k. SHAK:JUL 57
would k., and not be known COLTON 5
know-all: Old man K. died las' year HARRIS:JC 6
knowed: all that there is to be k. GRAHAME 4
knowing:
k. a little is more agreeable MENEN 1
k. what should not be known FLECKER 15
past k. to what he was going HARDY:T 37
she have the misfortune of k. AUSTEN 63
worth k. is mostly uncertain INGE 6
knowledge:
After such k., what ELIOT:TS 23
age in which useless k. was JOAD 2
all k. to be my province BACON:F[1] 129
but k. in the making MILT 319
chapter of k. is a very short CHESTERFIELD 27
close the five ports of k. BROWNE:T 45
desire of k. . . . increases STERNE 12
discern What k. can perform WORDS:W 39
finer spirit of all k. WORDS:W 167
first the literature of *k.* DEQ 12
follow k. like a sinking star TENNY 53
for the k. of a lifetime WHIST 10
fret not after k. KEATS 24
He that increaseth k. BIBLE 280
humble k. of thyself is a surer KEMP 2

if a little k. is dangerous HUX:TH 5
if a little k. was a dangerous SHARPE 3
If it rained k., I'd hold out JOHNSON:S 209
intimate k. of its ugly side BALD:J 2
K. advances by steps MACAULAY:TB 2
k. can only be finite POPP 5
K. comes TENNY 83
K. dwells In heads replete COWP 79
K. enormous makes a God KEATS 54
k. has not scarred WALLACE-C 1
k. is bought in the market CLOUGH 4
K. is not happiness BYR 125
K. is of two kinds JOHNSON:S 171
K. is power PROV 222
K. is power if you know MUM 3
'K. is power' is the finest RENAN 1
K. is proud that he COWP 80
K. itself is power BACON:F[1] 1
k. of the world is only to be CHESTERFIELD 2
k. too but recorded experience CARLYLE:T 31
k. we have lost in information? ELIOT:TS 70
k. without integrity is dangerous JOHNSON:S 26
light of k. in their eyes SYMONDS 1
love is worth a pound of k. WESLEY:J 7
men naturally desire k. ARISTOT 1
method in which k. is transmitted BLAKE:W 54
no k. that is not power EMER 69
No man's k. here can go LOCKE 3
Not for the k. in thy mind DAVIES:WH 4
not k. but action HUX:TH 6
only road to k. SHAW 54
our k. fatal DURREN 3
Out-topping k. ARNOLD:M 5
pangs us fou o' k. BURNS:R 49
pursue virtue and k. DANTE 13
receive the new k. BROWNING:R 57
rich storehouse for the glory* BACON:F[1] 6
river of k. has too often turned JEANS 2
so little k. to such great ELIOT:TS 121
Still climbing after k. MARLOWE 9
to communicate k. DEQ 8
too high The price of k. TICK 1
tree of k. of good and evil BIBLE 10
true antithesis to k. DEQ 8
want of true k. STERNE 22
What I don't know isn't k. BEECHING 1
Woman's happiest k. MILT 199
words without k.? BIBLE 191

knowledgeable: k. fool is more foolish MOLIERE 30

knowledges: General K. are those K. that Idiots BLAKE:W 95

known:
apart from the k. and the unknown PINT 3
be k., and not know COLTON 5
don't choose to have it k. CHESTERFIELD 34
Have ye not k.? BIBLE 323
I have k. them all already ELIOT:TS 6
is she k. in all the land TENNY 14
k. for his well-knownness BOORS 2
k. to them in breaking BIBLE 470
K. unto God. KIP 30
should have knowne no more HOBB 15
thing never k. again YEATS 106
things I shouldn't have k. at all COWARD 1
to be done and little to be k. JOHNSON:S 271

knows:
happy that he k. no more POPE 96
he goes and k. 'em DICKENS 70
He k. the world and does not FONTAINE 5
hope that no one else k. COMPT 2
k. nothing whatever about Thee KNOX:R 3
k. too much, he tells too HOPE:Al 5
less one k. LAO 3
no man truly k. another BROWNE:T 27
now God alone k. KLOP 1
She k. her man DRYD 81
She k. wot's wot DICKENS 44
that loves but k. not, reaps TENNY 145
thinks he k. everything SHAW 90
you to impose on him, k. you BLAKE:W 45

Knox, John: neither feared nor flattered* DOUGLAS:J 1

knuckle-end: k. of England SMITH:Syd[1] 18

knucklebones: harmless art of k. STEVENSON:RL 38

kopje-crest: His landmark is a k. HARDY:T 14

Kosciusko: as K. fell CAMPBELL:T 4

Kraft: *K. durch Freude* LEY 1

Kraken: K. sleepeth TENNY 1

Kubla Khan: Xanadu did K.K. COLERIDGE:ST 63

kudos: great k. leaving this muck alone MURD:R 1

Kurtz: Mistah K. – he dead CONRAD 6

lab: in another person's l. WATSON:JD 1

label: rag of a l. to cover himself HUX:TH 9

laborare: *L. est orare* ANON 212

laboratorium: *L. est oratorium* NEED:J 1

laborer: great unpaid l. of the world STANTON:El 7

laborious: live l. dayes MILT 49

labour:
all l. Mars what it does SHAK:ANT 52
Australian L. Party does not even call LENIN 7
be the Gromyko of the L. party HEAL 7
bleeding brow of l. this crown BRYAN 1
builders l. in vain BIBLE 604
By l. and intent study MILT 303
day's out and the l. done BROWNING:EB 18
devices for cheapening l. MORRIS:W 12
grotesque chaos of a L. council KINN 2
Honest l. bears a lovely DEK 2
l. and not to ask LOY 1
l. and the wounds are vain CLOUGH 10
l. contract into which men enter CHURCH:W 1
L. is not fit to govern CHURCH:W 5
L. of doing nothing STEELE 9
L. robbed out of the poor WELLS:HG 5
L. without joy is base RUSKIN 24
little effect after much l. AUSTEN 77
many still must l. BYR 29
Mountains will be in l. HORACE 107
relaxation from one kind of l. FRANCE 1
rest from l. – the sweetest time BLAKE:W 9
Should life all l. be? TENNY 29
Six days shalt thou l. BIBLE 103
that there is a model L. voter KINN 3
they l. in vain that build BIBLE 243
to l. and to wait LONGFEL 5
true success is to l. STEVENSON:RL 24
votes L. ought to be locked up MONTGOM:BL 2
We l. soon BURNS:R 123
what she would have thought of a L. Government GEO V 1
ye that l. and are heavy laden BIBLE 410
youth of l. GOLDS 23

labour-intensive: monarchy is a l. industry WILSON:Harold 13

labour-saving: lazybones can produce l. inventions GRASS 1

labourer:
eyeless l. in the night WRIGHT:J 7
for a l. to take his pension RUSKIN 14
l. is worthy of his hire BIBLE 455

labouring:
Sleep is sweet to the l. man BUNYAN 18
women l. of child PRAY 36

laburnums: L., dropping-wells of fire TENNY 167

labyrinth:
dreamt I was in the l. MUIR:E 3
turned aside From a great l. YEATS 76

lace:
Arsenic and Old L. KESS 1
l. my bodice blue HUNTER:A 1

laces:
L. for a lady KIP 121
Ribbons and l. And sweet NURS 83

lad:
could that l. be I? STEVENSON:RL 68
l. and, God help us YOUNG:WB 1
lively l. most pleasured me YEATS 81
once I was a little l. DENNIS:CJ 3

ladder:
God help us, a l. YOUNG:WB 1
half way up the social l. LILL 3
he dreamed, and behold a l. BIBLE 60
l. of all high designs SHAK:TRO 4
Now that my l.'s gone YEATS 114
Talk to him of Jacob's l. JERROLD 9
traffic of Jacob's l. THOMP:F 14
We are dropping down the l. KIP 53
Wiv a l. and some glasses BATEM 1
young ambition's l. SHAK:JUL 20

ladies:
Fair Spanish L. ANON 64
I am parshial to l. ASHFORD 2
if l. be but young SHAK:AS 31
L. of th' Hesperides MILT 267
nothing but of l.? SHAK:TWE 54
old l. of both sexes DICKENS 189
when he has l. to please AUSTEN 42
ye lords of l. intellectual BYR 160
Young l. are delicate plants AUSTEN 54

ladle: popped into my casting l. IBS 2

lads:
l. in their hundreds HOUSM 13
l. that will die in their glory HOUSM 14
l. that will never be old HOUSM 13
lie as l. would choose HOUSM 18

lady:
ain't a l. livin' in the land CHEV:A 1
antique l., much decayed HAMIL:E 1
but-not-altogether-satisfactory l. POUND 13
cannot reform a l. of many lovers KIP 12
Colonel's L. an' Judy O'Grady KIP 86
I met a l. in the meads KEATS 80
keeps a l. in a cage CHESTERTON 11
l. doth protest too much SHAK:HAM 116
l. in the case BYR 205
l. of Christ's College AUBREY 4
L. of Shalott? TENNY 14
l. sweet and kind ANON 97
L. with a Lamp shall stand LONGFEL 24
l.'s not for turning THATCH:M 4
l.'s ta'en anither mate BALL 59
lang will his L. Look BALL 13
make A Lady of my own WORDS:W 34
nicest old l. I ever met FAULK 2
once a l. always game MARQUIS 2
out of the L.'s company SHADWE 3
shrewd l. and the daring GOZ 1
six times with the same single l. BYR 225
There is a l. in the case GILB:WS 114
till the fat l. sings ANON 238
When a l. says no DENNING 2
when a l.'s in the case GAY 49
why the l. is a tramp HART 1
With the l. inside ANON 107

Lady Chatterley: like L.C. above the waist CONNOLLY:C 20

Lady Hamilton: Take care of poor L.H. NELS 15

lady-smocks: l. all silver-white SHAK:LOV 24

ladybird: L., l., Fly away home NURS 29

ladylike: wouldn't be too l. in love HERB:AP 9

Lafayette: L., we are here STANTON:CE 1

lag-end: entertain the l. of my life SHAK:HEN.IV[1] 82

laggard: l. in love SCOTT:W 19

laid:
get rich, get famous and get l. GEL 3
l. end to end PARKER:D 14
l. on with a trowel SHAK:AS 3

lain: in lovely muck I've l. HOUSM 29

Laird o' Drum: L.o.D. is a-wooing gane BALL 31

lairdie: wee, wee German l. CUNNING:A 3

laisser-faire: *L.*, No interference ARG 1

laissez:
L. faire, l. passer GOUR 1
L. faire, l. passer QUES 1

laity: To tell the l. our love DONNE 69

lake:
bottomless l. as a luxury HARPER 1
from out the bosom of the l. TENNY 274
I hear l. water lapping YEATS 4
shining levels of the l. TENNY 275
should like a great l. of ale BRIGID 1
slips into the bosom of the l. TENNY 117

Lake Leman: L.L. woos me BYR 90

Lake of Geneva: open onto the L.o.G. KEATS 151

Lalage: sweetly talking L. HORACE 16

lamb:
Did he who made the L. BLAKE:W 69
go to bed with the l. BRET 6
Go to bed with the l. PROV 154
goes out like a l. PROV 267
L. of God, who takest MASS 17
l. shall be without blemish BIBLE 95
L. upon his throne BRIDGES:M 1
Little L., who made thee BLAKE:W 15
Mary had a little l. NURS 39
Pipe a song about a L. BLAKE:W 13

provide himself a l. BIBLE 52
Receive the L. of God to dwell BLAKE:W 119
shall dwell with the l. BIBLE 310
skin of an innocent l. SHAK:HEN.VI[2] 10
That leads me to the L. COWP 2
to the shorn l. STERNE 52
unless the l. is inside LAWR:DH 27
was the holy L. of God BLAKE:W 98
washed in the blood of the L.? HOFFMAN 1
yoked with a l. SHAK:JUL 74
Lamb: at first, 1, Mr C. L. LAMB:Ch 37
lambent: l. but innocuous GOUL 1
Lambeth: doin' the L. walk FURBER 1
lambs:
as twinn'd l. that did frisk SHAK:WIN 1
full-grown l. loud bleat KEATS 109
gather the l. with his arm BIBLE 322
l. could not forgive DICKENS 126
poor little l. who've lost KIP 52
lame:
feet was I to the l. BIBLE 190
help a l. dog over a stile CHILLING 2
leap, ye l., for joy WESLEY:C 4
makes fancy l. COWP 41
your precious 'l. ducks' GALS 2
lamenting: he was left l. CAMPBELL:T 15
Lammas: It fell about the L. tide BALL 7
lamp:
It is a dying l. SHELLEY:PB 117
Lady with a L. shall stand LONGFEL 24
largest l. is lit MACAULAY:TB 54
let my L. at midnight hour MILT 84
smell too strong of the l. STERNE 11
Thy word is a l. unto BIBLE 238
When the l. is shattered SHELLEY:PB 159
lamp-post:
l. how it feels about dogs HAMP 5
leaning on the l. FORMBY 1
lamp-posts: MSS as drunkards use l. HOUSM 51
lamprey: surfeit of l. FABY 2
lamps:
As Hymen's l. shall light you SHAK:TEM 25
filled their l. With everlasting MILT 24
golden l. in a green night MARV 5
Heav'n's great l. do dive CATUL 5
l. are going out all over GREY 1
L. for my gloom SASS 13
old l. for new ones? ARAB 1
Ye living l. MARV 23
Yew alone burns l. of peace DE LA M 17
Lancaster: time-honoured L. SHAK:RIC.II 1
lance: my l. a wand of the willow BALL 30
Lancelot:
L. mused a little space TENNY 23
love that constrained L. DANTE 7
land:
Allabout l. belongin' to we EGAN 1
always l. on someone's feet PARKER:D 26
and possessed his l. BIBLE 117
Ceres reassume the l. POPE 73
dunno what a lovely l. it is HERB:X 1
eat the fat of the l. BIBLE 76
Ghost of a l. by the ghost KEND 1
Ill fares the l. GOLDS 21
in a cleaner, greener l. KIP 61
Into the l. of my dreams KING:S 1
I've seen the promised l. KING:ML 3
l. celebrated in song BAUD 7
l. flowing with milk BIBLE 87
L. is about the only thing TROLL 16
l. no one can define BURNE 1
L. o' Cakes BURNS:R 74
l. of beauty spots JOAD 3
L. of brown heath SCOTT:W 11
L. of Heart's Desire YEATS 16
L. of Hope and Glory BENS:AC 1
L. of our birth KIP 116
L. of Perfect Bliss SHINRAN 1
l. was forever GIBBON:LG 1
l. was ours before we were FROST:R 12
l. where nothing happens HUMPH 2
l., where the cannons bloom? KAST 1
Marching to the Promised L. BARING-G 5
mire Of the last l. BROOKE 2
more I loved my native l. BELLOY 1
my own, my native l. SCOTT:W 10
new people takes the l. CHESTERTON 25
not fit to live on l. JOHNSON:S 176
now they have the l. GEO:D 2
O'er the l. of the free KEY:FS 1
piece of l. not so very large HORACE 71
seems a moving L. MILT 227
She is far from the l. MOORE:T 14
Sweet l. of liberty SMITH:Sam 1
That is the l. of lost content HOUSM 24
There is a happy l. YOUNG:A 1
There shall be no more l. BROOKE 18
There's l. I see THACK 26
There's the L., or Cherry-Ile HERR 10
think there is no l. BACON:F[1] 9
This blind bitter l. YEATS 36
this dear dear l. SHAK:RIC.II 17
to enjoy thy l. SHAK:KING J 1
to see the nakedness of the l. BIBLE 74
To the l. o' the leal NAIRNE 5
under The l. you used to plough HOUSM 16
Usurp the l. GOLDS 22
went into a golden l. TURNER:WJR 2
Where lies the l. CLOUGH 8
wide brown l. for me MACKELL 1
wilful, lavish l. MACKELL 2
land-breeze: l. shook the shrouds COWP 16
landed: Eagle has l. ARMST:N 1
landlady: l. of a boarding-house is a parallelogram LEACOCK 2
landlord:
better have a rich l. SHAW 95
l. does not intend to repair ADAMS:JQ 2
l. fill the flowing bowl ANON 8
l.'s black-eyed daughter NOY 3
landmarks:
guide-posts and l. in the state BURKE:E 21
l. from the wisdom of BURKE:E 15
Landor: with L. and with Donne YEATS 58
lands:
broader l. and better days CHURCH:W 17
in faery l. forlorn KEATS 93
l. I was to travel in BALL 43
l. were fairly portioned MACAULAY:TB 49
l. where the Jumblies live LEAR 13
other l. beneath another sun THOMS:Ja[1] 10
works his ancestral l. HORACE 60
landscape:
fades the glimmering l. GRAY:T 16
l. without figures WHITE:P 13
use to the l. of England AUSTEN 3
will the l. tire the view? DYER:J[1] 2
landscape-painter: He is but a l. TENNY 57
landsmaul: mearbound to the march of a l. JOYCE:J 42
lane:
In an English l. BROWNING:R 102
l. to the land of the dead AUD 7
long l. that has no turning PROV 202
While there's a country l. PARKER:R 1
language:
arrest the decay of the l. HYDE:D 1
bad l. disdain PALMER:HR 2
between the l. of prose and metrical WORDS:W 168
broke through l. and escaped BROWNING:R 188
consenting l. of the heart GAY 5
countries separated by the same l. SHAW 126
else in our l. should perish MACAULAY:TB 6
English have no respect for their l. SHAW 105
enrichment of our native l. DRYD 104
essentially they are all l. PAZ 1
Finality is not the l. of politics DISR:B 60
German l. is the most profound KRAUS 7
He mobilized the English l. MURROW 1
in l. strange she said KEATS 83
In l., the ignorant DUPPA 1
laboured to refine our l. JOHNSON:S 4
l. all nations understand BEHN 3
l. charged with meaning to POUND 42
l. convey more than CONNOLLY:C 10
L. has not the power CLARE:J 14
l. he was the lodesterre LYD 2
l. is a dialect that has WEIN 1
L. is a kind of human reason LEVI-ST 1
L. is called the Garment of Thought CARLYLE:T 6
L. is fossil poetry EMER 32
L. . . . is not an abstract WHITMAN 42
L. is not simply a reporting WHORF 1
L. is only the instrument of science JOHNSON:S 6
L. is the dress of thought JOHNSON:S 50
l. of the Devil CARLYLE:T 7
l. of the heart POPE 129
l. of the liberal dead PORTER:PNF 3
l. of the unheard KING:ML 4
l. performs what is required CONNOLLY:C 3
l. that would make your hair curl GILB:WS 88
liberation of l. is rooted in DALY:M 1
most human thing we have is l. FONTANE 1
natural l. of the heart SHADWE 1
Newspeak was the official l. ORWELL 29
obscurity of a learned l. GIBBON:E 28
Our l. sunk under him ADDIS 21
poetical l. of an age should be HOPK:GM 34
preferring the l. of artizans SPRAT 2
room for but one l. ROOS:T 16
some entrance into the l. BACON:F[1] 112
speak a l. of their own SWIFT 60
spontaneous l. of my head BURNS:R 132
There's l. in her eye SHAK:TRO 21
thunder In such lovely l. LAWR:DH 35
use any l. you choose GILB:WS 50
use in measured l. lies TENNY 129
what l. an opera is sung in APPLETON:EV 1
Worships l. and forgives AUD 41
writing in its l.; even if you BOLL 2
You taught me l. SHAK:TEM 8
languages:
all world l. die O'CONNOR 1
among the ruined l. AUD 32
at a great feast of l. SHAK:LOV 19
be silent in several l. HARBO 1
frank words in our respective l. COOK:P 1
in the graves of deceased l. DICKENS 130
l. are the pedigree of nations JOHNSON:S 78
not acquainted with foreign l. knows nothing GOET 29
produced the confusion of l. VOLT 35
She took and gave l. PRIOR 2
languid: art thou l. NEALE 4
languor: L. cannot be SHELLEY:PB 98
languors: lilies and l. of virtue SWIN 20
lanky: l. hank of she STEPHENS 4
Laodameia: L. died; Helen LANDOR 16
lap:
asked Carrie to sit on his l. GROS 3
flowery l. of earth ARNOLD:M 8
head upon the l. of Earth GRAY:T 26
lap-dogs: l. breathe their last POPE 52
Lapland: lovely as a L. night WORDS:W 36
laps: tumbling into some men's l. BACON:F[1] 16
lapse: Liquid L. of murmuring streams MILT 232
larch: plumelets tuft the l. TENNY 171
lard: They l. their lean books BURTON:Ro 2
lards: l. the lean earth SHAK:HEN.IV[1] 30
large:
I am l., I contain multitudes WHITMAN 12
l. as life and twice CARROLL 78
so l., So friendly, and so rich AUD 57
too l. to hang on a watch-chain ANON 253
large-brained: Thou l. woman BROWNING:EB 7
large-hearted: woman and l. man BROWNING:EB 7
lark:
bisy larke, messager CHAUC 45
Ethereal minstrel* WORDS:W 134
How at heaven's gates* LYLY 6
l. at heaven's gate sings SHAK:CYM 4
l. becomes a sightless song TENNY 181
l.-charmèd HOPK:GM 12
l. from her light wing CRAW 1
l. shall sing me hame CUNNING:A 2
l., that tirra-lirra chants SHAK:WIN 12
l.'s on the wing BROWNING:R 9
late l. twitters HENL 4
Like to the l. at break SHAK:SON 11
No l. more blithe than he BICK 2
rise with the l. BRET 6
rise with the l. PROV 154
Some late l. singing HENL 6
swallow for the holy l. BROWNING:EB 16
larks:
hear the l. so high HOUSM 11
mounting l. their notes POPE 34
larkspur: l. listens TENNY 219
Lars Porsena: L.P. of Clusium MACAULAY:TB 45

Las Vegas: Fear and Loathing in L.V. THOMP:HS 1
lascivious: l. pleasing of a lute SHAK:RIC.III 2
lash: rum, sodomy and the l. CHURCH:W 68
lass:
cam' wi' a l., and it'll gang JAMES V 1
Drink to the l. SHERIDAN:RB 24
every l. a queen KINGSLEY:C 19
l. so neat UPTON:W 1
l. that has acres o' charms BURNS:R 120
l. that loves a sailor DIBDIN:C 9
lies A l. unparallel'd SHAK:ANT 76
solitary Highland l. WORDS:W 79
lasses:
An' then she made the l. BURNS:R 5
An' 'twere na for the l. BURNS:R 2
Come l. and lads ANON 9
He dearly lov'd the l. BURNS:R 5
lassie: young l. Do wi' an auld man BURNS:R 95
lassitude: I yield now to l. GOGA 1
lasso: ever tried to l. a kangaroo? SAV 1
last:
best and the l. BROWNING:R 182
cobbler stick to his l. PROV 235
day that has dawned is your l. HORACE 84
Don't say my l. PARKES 1
each act as if it were your l. AUR 2
feeling that I could l. forever CONRAD 8
is sweetest l. SHAK:RIC.II 15
It will l. my time CARLYLE:T 35
l. and best MILT 248
L. came, and l. did go MILT 52
l. is commonly best BURTON:Ro 8
l. of life for which the first BROWNING:R 184
l. shall be first BIBLE 424
l. thing I shall do PALMERS 5
l. thing one finds out PASC 3
l. to lay the old aside POPE 17
live this day, as if thy l. KEN 2
Nice guys finish l. DURO 1
terrible I hope it will l. WILDE:O 101
there is no l. nor first BROWNING:R 13
they l. while they l. DE GAU 3
to be but the l. man BROWNE:T 22
last-supper: L.-carved-on-a-peach-stone LANCAS 1
latch:
clicking l. behind you STARK:F 1
no l. ter de golden gate? HARRIS:JC 11
late:
Better l. than never PROV 43
damned fella will be l. MITFORD:N 5
Never too l. to learn PROV 289
not too l. tomorrow ARMST:J 1
she has been l. for school THOMAS:D 26
sinners'll be kotched out l. HARRIS:JC 11
that leaves him out so l. FROST:R 11
'Tis not too l. to seek a newer TENNY 55
too l. all my life-time COWLEY:H 2
Too l. I came to love you AUGUS 5
Too l., too l. TENNY 263
we have met too l. JOYCE:J 53
worse when it comes l. JERROLD 3
later: It is l. than you think SERVICE 4
latest: say my l. PARKES 1
lather: bowl of l. on which a mirror JOYCE:J 10
Latin:
All the L. I construe BROWNING:R 111
gentleman needs not know L. MATT 1
He speaks L. SHAK:HEN.VI[2] 12
L. of clotted syntax O'CONNOR 1
learn L. as an honour CHURCH:W 43
Remuneration! O, that's the L. SHAK:LOV 7
say something stupid in L. CERV 26
small L., and less Greek JONS 41
teach him one word of L. YEATS 144
you understand L., Mr Bonniface? FARQ 16
Latin-bred: wench, a prophetess, and a L. HERB:G 60
Latins: L. are tenderly enthusiastic DIET 4
Latium: brought the arts into rustic L. HORACE 94
laudanum: Whipping and abuse are like l. STOWE 4
lauds: Laudes to theyr maker HAWES 1
laugh:
Anything awful makes me l. LAMB:Ch 39
behind her a meaning l. EWART 1
day one did not l. CHAMFORT 1
Democritus would l. HORACE 95
do we not l.? SHAK:MERC 32
his arms hang down to l. ELIOT:TS 28
hurt too much to l. LINC 27
I did l. sans intermission SHAK:AS 30
l. aloud in unison CATUL 9
L. and be well GREEN:Mat 1
L. and grow fat PROV 225
L. and the world laughs WILCOX 3
l. At gilded butterflies SHAK:KING L 79
l. at them in our turn? AUSTEN 27
L. before breakfast, you'll cry PROV 226
l. broke into a thousand BARRIE 6
l. By precept only WORDS:W 140
L.! I thought I should CHEV:A 2
l. that spoke the vacant GOLDS 24
l. uproariously in youth BROOKE 12
L. where we must POPE 79
l. with me, or at me STERNE 4
made a cat l. PLAN 1
Make 'em laugh READE 2
make her l. at that SHAK:HAM 183
make myself l. at everything BEAUMA 2
making decent people l. MOLIERE 5
man cannot make him l. SHAK:HEN.IV[2] 41
man of quality than to l. CONG 16
must l. before one is happy LA BRU 7
no girl wants to l. all LOOS 8
nobody has ever heard me l. CHESTERFIELD 14
not to l. at human actions SPIN 5
nothing to l. at at all EDGAR 1
penetrating sort of l. WODE 10
sillier than a silly l. CATUL 10
time to l. BIBLE 281
to know when to l. OWEN:Rod 1
unextinguishable l. in heaven BROWNE:T 43
When the green woods l. BLAKE:W 26
Who but must l.? POPE 122
who will not l. is a fool SANT 9
laugh-at-with: someone you could l. SPEND 13
laughed:
Few women care to be l. at AYCK 1
good thing to be l. at MACMILL:H 8
he l., respectable senators AUD 10
heartily and wholly l. CARLYLE:T 1
I laugh'd him out of patience SHAK:ANT 31
laugh'd with counterfeited glee GOLDS 28
l. and kissed his hand HOUSM 47
l. consumedly FARQ 14
When the first baby l. BARRIE 6
who l. behind their hands THOMAS:D 41
laughing:
always l. at a man without AUSTEN 24
cannot forbear l. and jeering PEPYS 9
Crow went on l. HUGHES:Te 4
Half the world is l. at the other GRACIAN 2
Happiness is no l. matter WHATE 2
l. Devil in his sneer BYR 30
l. immoderately at stated intervals SMITH:Syd[1] 17
L. in spite of her tears HOMER 10
l. is heard on the hill BLAKE:W 22
laughs:
Earth l. in flowers EMER 94
he l. much louder than MILLAY 9
more so, when he l. STERNE 1
who l. at other people MOLIERE 3
who l. on Friday RACINE 5
laughter:
Born with the gift of l. SABA 1
by the faculty of l. ADDIS 27
died with extreme l. NASHE 4
Give me the bonus of l. BETJ 37
ill-bred, as audible l. CHESTERFIELD 14
l. and the love of friends BELLOC 27
l. for a month SHAK:HEN.IV[1] 29
L. holding both his sides MILT 67
L. is brightest where food PROV 227
L. is nothing else but sudden HOBB 1
L. is pleasant, but PEAC 6
L. is the best medicine PROV 228
l., learnt of friends BROOKE 25
l. tinkled among the teacups ELIOT:TS 13
l. With some pain SHELLEY:PB 99
make faces and produce l. JOHNSON:S 174
out of itself by loud L. STEELE 11
Porter-drinkers' randy l. YEATS 123
present l. SHAK:TWE 19
Seismic with l. BARKER:G 2
so is the l. of the fool BIBLE 283
twinkling l. of the waves AESC 6
under running l. THOMP:F 7
weeping and the l. DOWS 3
worst returns to l. SHAK:KING L 55
laughters:
entwine our arts with l. JOYCE:J 37
tears and l. for all time BROWNING:EB 8
Launcelot: angels heave up Sir L. MALORY 15
laundry: Widow Twankey's Nuclear L. ART 1
laundry-list: l. and I will set it to music ROSSINI 2
Laura:
L. had been Petrarch's wife BYR 184
Rose-cheekt Lawra, come CAMPION 6
laurel:
burnèd is Apollo's l. MARLOWE 46
l. crown to praise CIC 5
l. for the perfect prime ROSSET:C 11
L. is green for a season SWIN 35
rose or rue or l. SWIN 50
she might l. grow MARV 16
laurels: l. all are cut HOUSM 30
Laurie: for bonnie Annie L. DOUGLAS:W 1
lavatories: nose nailed to other people's l. SITWELL:E 17
lavatory:
hung it in the menservants' l. WAUGH:E 19
I go to the l. ANON 203
lavat'ry makes you fear COWARD 27
to build a l. for a cockroach SEMP 3
lavender:
Hot l., mints SHAK:WIN 19
L. water tinged with pink LEAR 23
L.'s blue, dilly dilly NURS 30
law:
Any l. which violates ROBES 1
army of unalterable l. MERED:G 33
because they have no l. TENNY 260
Borne under one L. GREV 2
built with stones of L. BLAKE:W 41
by the l. of the land MAGNA 2
Common L. of England has been HERB:AP 13
duty even to break the l. PANK:E 1
Every l. is an evil BENTH 2
fantastic will is the man's l. BROWNING:R 107
follow the first l. of holes HEAL 8
forgotten more l. than you MAYN 1
God is thy L. MILT 199
good of the people is the chief l. CIC 3
Ignorance of the l. excuses no SELD 5
ignorance of the l. is not punished BENTH 7
I'll find them l. BRAX 4
impersonal and unrecompensing L. ELIOT:G 48
is the l. so general a study BURKE:E 31
it is no l. ROBES 1
it is of no force in l. COKE:E 1
judgements of the English l. SYNGE 1
Judges are guided by the l. BELLOCH 1
Just to the windward of the l. CHURCH:C 15
lapt in universal l. TENNY 80
l. does not concern itself PROV 229
l. doth give it SHAK:MERC 46
l. doth punish man ANON 77
l. ends, there tyranny begins PITT:W[1] 5
L. ends, Tyranny begins LOCKE 6
l. hath not been dead SHAK:MEA 11
l. is a ass DICKENS 64
L. is a bottomless pit ARB 2
l. is above you DENNING 1
l. is an infraction of liberty BENTH 2
l. is made solely to exploit BRECHT 4
l. is such an Ass CHAPMAN:G 9
L. : It has honoured us WEBSTER:D 7
l. itself creates the sides DWO 3
L. of England is a very strang DARLING:CJ 5
l. of nature, and of nations BURKE:E 103
l. to weed it out BACON:F[1] 96
l. which governs all l. BURKE:E 103
l.'s grave study six COKE:E 6
l.'s made to take care ELIOT:G 14
lesser breeds without the L. KIP 93
live L. to our selves MILT 246
Love is a greater l. unto itself BOET 3
Love is a gretter lawe CHAUC 41
maxim to become a general l. KANT 2
moral l. within me KANT 8

mysterious L., true sourse MILT 202
Necessity gives the l. without PUB 4
not a single l. connected PEEL:R 1
not make a scarecrow of the l. SHAK:MEA 5
nothing is l. that is not reason POWELL:J 1
old father antic the l.? SHAK:HEN.IV[1] 7
One l. for the Lion & Ox BLAKE:W 55
one l. for the rich, and another PROV 384
our hearts to keep this l. PRAY 64
pass a l. and not have it RICHELIEU:A 1
People crushed by l. BURKE:E 85
perfection of our l. ANON 188
raised to the concepts of duty and l. KANT 12
Reason is the life of the l. COKE:E 2
their l.'s their will SHAK:PER 3
There is no universal l. LAWR:DH 23
this is the L. of the Jungle KIP 78
This is the L. of the Yukon SERVICE 1
this is the royal L. CORON 1
very good l. for all that SCOTT:W 69
Who to himselfe is l. CHAPMAN:G 3
windy side of the l. SHAK:TWE 49
within the purlieus of the l. ETH 1
Wrest once the l. SHAK:MERC 45
law-givers: My l. are Erasmus FORST 16
lawful: everything would be l., even cannibalism DOST 4
lawn:
L. as white as driven SHAK:WIN 23
Out on the l. I lie AUD 22
lawns: house with l. enclosing it STEVENSON:RL 59
Lawrence: how well he knew D.H. L. QUEN 1
laws:
are the absurdities of our l. HERV:Lord 2
Bad l. are the worst sort BURKE:E 47
breaking up of l. TENNY 264
Christianity is part of the l. HALE:M 1
do is to uphold the l. COETZ 1
do whatever the l. permit MONTESQU 4
do with the l. but to obey HORS 1
foreign l. of God and man HOUSM 34
If l. are their enemies BURKE:E 85
If one were to study all the l. GOET 31
in all things the l. of life RUSKIN 15
L. are always useful to those ROUSS:JJ 2
L. are generally found to be nets SHEN 3
L. are like cobwebs SWIFT 10
L. are like spider's webs SOLON 1
L. are silent in war CIC 13
L., by which their Life CHARLES I 4
L. grind the poor GOLDS 11
L., like houses, lean BURKE:E 82
l. of England are at SHAK:HEN.IV[2] 52
l. of God and man and metre LOCKHART 2
l. of God, the l. of man HOUSM 32
l. of poetic truth ARNOLD:M 79
l. of the Persians and the Medes BIBLE 177
l. were like cobwebs BACON:F[1] 30
L. were made to be broken NORTH:C 4
l. were made to keep fair play BLAKE:W 2
not care who should make the l. FLETCH:A 1
not obey the l. too well EMER 38
obedient to their l., we lie SIMONID 1
or breaking of l. MORE:H 4
part which l. or kings can cause GOLDS 12
religion breathing household l. WORDS:W 73
repeal of bad or obnoxious l. GRANT:US 3
Unequal l. unto a savage TENNY 51
where the peasantry make the l. ESSON 1
whether L. be right WILDE:O 119
you do not make the l. but GRIM 1
lawsuit:
L.: A machine which BIER 7
priest, don't begin a l. PROV 433
lawyer:
as a l. interprets reality GIR 2
l. with his briefcase can steal PUZO 2
saw a L. killing a viper COLERIDGE:ST 42
trusting in the Lord and a good l. NORTH:O 1
what a l. tells me I *may* do BURKE:E 33
lawyers:
drink made from l. COREN 2
L. are the only persons in whom BENTH 7
l. in the vacation SHAK:AS 47
let's kill all the l. SHAK:HEN.VI[2] 9
laxative: sweet l. of Georgian strains CAMPBELL:R 5
lay:
Cleric before, and L. behind BUTLER:S[1] 19
he l. low HARRIS:JC 2
I'll l. me doun and dee DOUGLAS:W 1
l. a hat – and a few PARKER:D 23
l. interest in ecclesiastical WAUGH:E 11
lays:
know wot l. afore us DICKENS 123
ways of constructing tribal l. KIP 76
Lazarus: Come forth, L. JOYCE:J 19
laziness:
blow away all the l. CHEK 8
through its opposite, l. CERV 23
lazy:
be efficient if you're going to be l. CONRAN 2
L. and silly SITWELL:E 5
L. folkes' stummocks don't git HARRIS:JC 7
Longing to be A l. lady SITWELL:E 7
L.B.J.: All the way with L.B.J. HOLT 1
Le Mesurier: John L.M. wishes it to be known LE MES 1
lead:
easy to l., but difficult to drive BROUGHAM 2
eyes grew dross of l. BROWNING:R 119
gave him the l. gift JEFFERS 2
gently l. those that are with BIBLE 322
Go down like lumps of l. HODG 3
L., and I follow TENNY 240
L., kindly Light NEWM:JH 15
L. us, Heavenly Father EDMES 1
little l. best fits HERR 37
scald like molten l. SHAK:KING L 76
This is the Hour of L. DICKIN:E 6
thy friends are lapp'd in l. BARNF 3
Unite and l. GOET 25
when we think we l. BYR 143
leader:
I am their l. LEDRU 1
l. of the enterprise a woman VIRGIL 39
l. who doesn't hesitate MEIR 1
must follow them; I am their l. LAW 2
Over the face of the l. WHITTIER 5
question of Jesus Christ as l. HUGHES:B 6
leader-writers: God exists only for l. GREENE:G 10
leaders:
least praise to have pleased l. HORACE 89
not the l. of a revolution CONRAD 11
on peoples by their own l. MCMILL:J 1
supplied the world with two l. UST 7
leadership:
approach to l. until they have lost BEVER 2
L. counts for something MONASH 1
party about its future l. MACMILL:H 9
leadeth: l. me beside the still waters BIBLE 206
leaf:
how soon the fall of the l. DONNE 109
If I were a dead l. SHELLEY:PB 44
last red l. is whirl'd TENNY 135
no l. upon the forest bare SHELLEY:PB 150
November's l. is red SCOTT:W 12
Sometimes an autumn l. YOUNG:AJ 1
thou cursed l. BURNS:R 51
wet l. clings to the threshold POUND 19
where the dead l. fell KEATS 44
league:
Half a l. onward TENNY 197
She hadna sail'd a l. BALL 14
leak: One l. will sink a ship BUNYAN 23
leal: To the land o' the l. NAIRNE 5
lean:
has a l. and hungry look SHAK:JUL 14
leene was his hors CHAUC 18
Never trust a l. meritocracy MURRAY:LA 6
leaning:
encourage a will to l. ASCHAM 4
L. over the lip DAY LEWIS 6
leap:
giant l. for mankind ARMST:N 2
Great L. Forward MAO 3
great l. in the dark HOBB 16
l. over a bush is better than CERV 7
look before you ere you l. BUTLER:S[1] 25
Look before you l. PROV 247
made a l. into the dark BROWN:T 1
more worthy to l. in SHAK:JUL 85
leaping: l. from rock up to rock BROWNING:R 146
leaps: Two l. the water ALLING:W 3
Lear: pleasant to know Mr L. LEAR 3
learn:
cannot l. men from books DISR:B 2
gladly wolde he lerne CHAUC 20
In seed time l. BLAKE:W 34
l. about women from me KIP 85
l. by going to where I have ROETH 1
l. even from an enemy OSB:J 21
l. something about everything HUX:TH 16
l. wisdom even from one's enemies ARISTOP 1
Live and l. PROV 244
Never too late to l. PROV 289
through so much, to l. so little DICKENS 24
We l. so little DAVIES:J 2
We live and l. POMF 2
when will you ever l.? SEEG 1
Where there is much desire to l. MILT 319
while they teach, men l. SEN 1
who know how to l. ADAMS:H 7
learned:
been l. has been forgotten SKIN:BF 2
I l. about women from 'er KIP 84
l. lumber in his head POPE 27
l. was far more than he could stand MORA 2
make the l. smile POPE 16
obscurity of a l. language GIBBON:E 28
of the opinion with the l. CONG 2
Things l. on earth BROWNING:R 138
without ever having l. MOLIERE 2
learning:
a' the l. I desire BURNS:R 18
Book l. certainly increases knowledge KANT 10
cry both arts and l. down QUAR 15
deep l. little had he neede SPENS 5
enough of l. to misquote BYR 9
grow old ever l. SOLON 3
have been l. how to die LEONARDO 2
immoderate desire of humane l. DONNE 111
incapable of l. has taken to teaching WILDE:O 4
L. hath gained most FULLER:T[1] 4
l. lightly like a flower TENNY 184
L., that cobweb of the brain BUTLER:S[1] 20
l. was painfully beaten into PEAC 5
l., what a thing it is SHAK:TAM 4
L. will be cast into the mire BURKE:E 59
L. without thought CONF 4
little l. is a dangerous POPE 10
love he bore to l. GOLDS 28
loyal body wanted l. TRAPP 1
more l. than is taught in books GREG:LADY 2
much l. doth make thee mad BIBLE 506
no enemy to l. CONG 49
nonsense and l. GOLDS 36
on scraps of l. dote YOUNG:E 2
picker up of l.'s crumbs BROWNING:R 105
progeny of l. SHERIDAN:RB 7
saw L. fall, and Rome POPE 29
Swallow all your l. CHESTERFIELD 25
that is what l. is LESSING:D 4
Their l. is like bread JOHNSON:S 170
Then l. is most excellent FOOTE 1
to attain good l. ASCHAM 3
Wear your l., like your watch CHESTERFIELD 13
Whence is thy l.? GAY 42
learnt:
forgotten nothing and l. nothing DUMO 1
l. nothing and forgotten TALL 5
only remember what I've l. WHITE:P 7
leather: l. orb flew like a heavy bird JOYCE:J 4
leave:
be ready to l. MONTAIGNE 2
forever take our l. RILKE 3
I l. my love alone SHAK:SON 30
I will take my l. of you SHAK:HAM 75
l. a thing alone you l. it CHESTERTON 42
L. her to heaven SHAK:HAM 49
L. it alone QUES 1
l. me here a little TENNY 68
L. off first BIBLE 369
l. to come unto my love? SPENS 14
L. well alone PROV 231
l. what with his toil he DRYD 39
Love me, and never l. me MCCUAIG 1
Oh, never l. me ANON 10
so leased to l. a place CERN 4
will ye l. to your ain mither BALL 19
wilt thou l. me thus? WYATT 1

leaves:
famous harmony of l. YEATS 10
handling the l., will long SHERIDAN:RB 6
home before the l. have fallen WILHELM II 1
lamentation of the l. YEATS 10
laughing l. of the tree divide SWIN 11
l. are coming back HORACE 53
l. fall early this autumn POUND 6
L. of Life keep falling FITZGER:E 6
L. on Trees the Race of Man HOMER 7
l. Scurry into heaps POUND 19
l. they were crispèd and sere POE 6
sweetest l. yet folded BYR 235
tender l. of hope SHAK:HEN.VIII 10
thick on Severn snow the l. HOUSM 20
With vine l. in his hair IBS 13
leaving:
Became him like the l. SHAK:MAC 18
L. is dying a little HARA 1
Lebanon:
grow like a cedar in L. BIBLE 228
silken Samarcand to cedar'd L. KEATS 74
lecherous: l. as a sparwe CHAUC 29
lechery: Still wars and l. SHAK:TRO 24
lecture: I will read to thee A l. DONNE 47
lectures: not give l. or a little charity WHITMAN 8
led:
l. by the nose with gold SHAK:WIN 30
L. go KIP 26
tenderly be l. by th' nose SHAK:OTH 18
leeches: that l. have red blood CUV 1
leek: if you can mock a l. SHAK:HEN.V 44
leers: Sighs and l. And crocodile NURS 83
left:
better to be l. than never CONG 39
dream of being l. fifty thousand MILNE 20
l. off before you began CONG 9
l. over from last year HARRIS:G 1
Let them be l. HOPK:GM 18
loved her, then he l. her ANON 38
So far upon the l. side WEBSTER:J 20
That we l., we lost ANON 145
use ... but of my l. hand MILT 302
we only are l. ARNOLD:M 49
What is there l. to be said? FAIRBURN 2
leg:
here I leave my second l. HOOD 4
honest woman and a broken l. CERV 14
kiss my *Julia*'s dainty l. HERR 34
literary man – *with* a wooden l. DICKENS 215
long time upon one l. PLUT 1
upon one l., and play the tambourine DICKENS 82
what l. you shall put into your JOHNSON:S 121
legacy:
l. from a rich relative work SMITH:FE 2
told anyone you have left him a l. BUTLER:S[2] 52
legality: from any taint of l. KNOX:PC 1
legends: Men must have l. MURRAY:LA 1
legion:
L. that was never 'listed KIP 77
My name is L. BIBLE 440
To the l. of the lost ones KIP 51
Legion of Honour: L.o.H. has been conferred upon me TWAIN 7
legions:
moving l. mingled in the war LUCRET 5
puissant L. whose exile MILT 139
legislation:
foundation of morals and l. BENTH 4
good l. is borne out of MACHIA 10
legislator:
l. of mankind JOHNSON:S 21
people is the true l. BURKE:E 83
legislators: unacknowledged l. of the world SHELLEY:PB 167
legislature: sentiments that no l. can manufacture BAGE 6
legs:
better to view her l. NORM 1
born with your l. apart ORTON 5
cannon-ball took off his l. HOOD 3
ever recuvver the use of his l. DICKENS 74
fold his l. and have out his talk JOHNSON:S 197
Four l. good, two l. bad ORWELL 17
have to run your l. off BRECHT 1
His l. bestrid the ocean SHAK:ANT 64
l. when I take my boots off DICKENS 140
Like asure were his legges CHAUC 62
Long in the l. ANON 53
Matching their lily-white l. CLOUGH 1
never have stood upon his l. DICKENS 101
not pleasure in the l. BIBLE 249
open my l. and think of England HILLING 1
she had such thick l. WAINE 1
Stands on his hinder l. SHAK:POET 12
Taste your l. SHAK:TWE 38
to lie between maids' l. SHAK:HAM 111
Two vast and trunkless l. SHELLEY:PB 22
Walk under his huge l. SHAK:JUL 11
wide his l. and shows his class ANON 152
with your l. ungainly huddled SASS 10
woman – with beautiful l. DIET 3
Leicester Square: Farewell L.S. JUDGE 1
leiff: Now l. thi myrth BLIND 1
leisure:
I am quite at l. AUSTEN 29
Increased means and increased l. DISR:B 73
intellectual improvement arises from l. JOHNSON:S 158
l. answers l. SHAK:MEA 39
l. to be good GRAY:T 1
l. to think about going to heaven CARLYLE:JW 6
No blessed l. for Love HOOD 22
reputability to the gentleman of l. VEB 1
they detest at l. BYR 228
lemon: in the squeezing of a l. GOLDS 70
lemon-trees: land, where the l. bloom? GOET 8
lemonade: but black eyes and l. MOORE:T 19
lend:
Few l. (but fools) TUSS 9
glaidly len' and borrow DUNB 3
I l. it instantly HERB:G 36
if not asked to l. money TWAIN 24
I'll l. you thus much moneys? SHAK:MERC 18
L. less than thou owest SHAK:KING L 15
L. only what you can afford PROV 232
men who l. LAMB:Ch 16
lenders: thy pen from l.' books SHAK:KING L 45
lendings: Off, off, you l. SHAK:KING L 46
lends: never l. – my 'oss, my wife SURT 12
length: Let me have l. and breadth BALL 16
Lenin: L.'s method leads to this TROT 11
Lent: Marry in L., and you'll PROV 271
Lenten: L. ys come with love ANON 78
leopard:
l. shall lie down with BIBLE 310
or the l. his spots? BIBLE 339
leopards: three white l. sat ELIOT:TS 67
leprosy:
It is full of l. DAM 1
scant as hair In l. BROWNING:R 94
Lesbia:
L. hath a beaming eye MOORE:T 8
L. let us live and love CATUL 5
L. whom Catullus has loved CATUL 14
L. with her sparrow MILLAY 3
lesbian:
cover for l. homosexuality FAIRBAIRN:N 4
L. officer with the thin lips GREENE:G 8
lesbianism: l. is the practice ATK:T 1
lesbians: Until all women are l. JOHNSTONE:Jil 1
Lesley: saw ye bonie L. BURNS:R 103
less:
Even l. am I HOPE:L 1
l. in this than meets the eye BANK 9
L. is more MIES 1
l. one has to do CHESTERFIELD 31
L. than the dust HOPE:L
l. the greater comprehend? DRYD 70
more about l. and l. MAYO 1
more and more about l. and l. BUTLER:NM 2
rather than be l. Car'd not MILT 150
You mean you can't take *l.* CARROLL 19
lessen: they l. from day to day CARROLL 30
lesser: l. is always to be chosen KEMP 13
lesson:
harder l.! how to die PORTEUS 3
l. which the Lord us SPENS 9
no end of a l. KIP 114
We have had an Imperial l. KIP 115
lessons: reason they're called l. CARROLL 30
let: l. them all to my elder daughter THOMAS:E 3
let go:
I've learned to l.g. HARRISON 2
Led go KIP 26
lethal: a lot was l. SHARPE 3
Lethe: go not to L. KEATS 94
letter:
carry a l. to my love BALL 20
deal by speech than by l. BACON:F[1] 88
forgetting to write the l. BEECHER 1
I have made this l. longer PASC 1
king has written a braid l. BALL 48
l. delivered to the wrong MUGG 5
l. from his wife CARROLL 93
l. killeth BIBLE 528
thou unecessary l. SHAK:KING L 23
letter writing:
great art o' letter writin' DICKENS 30
habit the pleasure of which* ADAMS:A 2
way of wasting time* MORLEY:Lord[1] 1
letters:
I find l. from God dropt WHITMAN 11
learning the remaining twenty-two l. ORWELL 19
l. for a spy KIP 121
L. for the rich, l. for AUD 16
l., methinks, should be OSB:D 1
l. mingle souls DONNE 8
L. of thanks, l. from AUD 17
l., soft interpreters PRIOR 5
love the l. of his name BROWNING:R 145
man of l., of the kind PETRO 4
masters to learn their l. LOWE 1
name in such large l. I blush TREE 4
no body knows how to write l. CONG 42
pause awhile from l. JOHNSON:S 67
persecuted with l. CONG 42
receive no l. in the grave JOHNSON:S 251
woman of l. I fight for my kind DWO 4
letting:
come from l. people off MURD:I 2
then the l. go DICKIN:E 6
levee: l. from a couch in some CONG 50
level: rise to his l. of incompetence PETER 1
leveller: Death is a great l. PROV 66
levellers: l. wish to level *down* JOHNSON:S 120
levels:
Life l. all men SHAW 65
shining l. of the lake TENNY 275
leviathan: draw out l. with an hook? BIBLE 194
Leviathan:
generation of that great L. HOBB 10
There L. Hugest MILT 227
levity:
have sunk by my l. SMITH:Syd[1] 40
little judicious l. STEVENSON:RL 37
lexicographer:
doomed at last to wake a l. JOHNSON:S 8
L. A writer of dictionaries JOHNSON:S 12
l. can only hope to escape JOHNSON:S 5
lexicography: not yet so lost in l. JOHNSON:S 6
lexicon:
In the l. of youth BULWER 2
Two men wrote a l. ANON 112
liaison: partly a l. man BETJ 36
liar:
boy they called me a l. SING 2
easy virtue and a proved l. HAILS 1
eye that marks the perfect l. BENET 3
I am the club L. SAKI 22
l. gone to burning hell SHAK:OTH 64
l. is a realist STEAD 5
l. is worse than a thief PROV 236
l. must have a good memory QUINT 1
only answered 'Little L.!' BELLOC 23
quite picturesque l. TWAIN 15
liars:
All writers are l. CLARK:M 3
Income tax has made more l. ROGERS:W 1
L. ought to have good memories SIDNEY:A 1
prove the greatest l. DRAYT 4
libation: pouring a l. to some god SOC 8
libel:
action against his countenance for l. DICKENS 59
Convey a l. in a frown SWIFT 60
libellous: truth is always l. FINEY 1

liberal:
either a little L. GILB:WS 48
ineffectual l.'s problem FRAYN 2
Just like an old l. PLOM 5
language of the l. dead PORTER:PNF 3
l. without the manual arts JOHNSON:S 39
panted for a l. profession COLMAN:G[2] 2
liberalism: By l. I don't mean PATON 3
liberality: blue l. of heaven? BROWNING:R 206
liberals:
L. affer a mixture of sound MACMILL:H 12
L. in Australia are really Conservatives LENIN 7
liberate: we shall l. this country MANDELA:W 1
liberation:
l. of language is rooted in the l. DALY:M 1
vegetable creep of women's l. GREER 4
libertas: *L. et natale solum* SWIFT 58
liberties:
Brazenness and public l. CERV 20
extending the l. of his country BROUGHAM 1
more l. than he can really take JAMES:H 19
people never give up their l. BURKE:E 98
what l. are taken in thy name GEO:D 1
libertine: puff'd and reckless l. SHAK:HAM 29
liberty:
Abstract l., like other BURKE:E 29
brightest in dungeons, L. BYR 48
cause of a single life, is l. BACON:F[1] 82
chains and calls them L. BUCHANAN 8
dead to all the feelings of l. PITT:W[1] 3
distinction between l. and slavery CAMDEN:Lord 1
eldest child of L. WORDS:W 75
enjoy delight with libertie SPENS 6
Extremism in the defence of l. GOLDWATER 1
Give me l., or give HENRY:P 3
Give me the l. to know MILT 321
he Served human l. YEATS 84
history of l. is a history of resistance WILSON:W 3
hour of virtuous l. ADDIS 6
I desire their L. and Freedom CHARLES I 4
I must have l. Withal SHAK:AS 32
If men are to wait for l. MACAULAY:TB 20
interfering with the l. of action MILL 7
Know no such l. LOVELACE 3
lamp of l. will burn LINC 5
law is an infraction of l. BENTH 2
L. and Union, now and forever WEBSTER:D 3
l. cannot long exist BURKE:E 46
l. connected with order BURKE:E 92
L. consists in doing MILL 21
l.! how many crimes ROLAND 1
L. is l., not equality or BERLIN:Is 1
L. means responsibility SHAW 52
l. of the individual must be MILL 14
l. of the press is the *Palladium* JUNIUS 1
l. plucks justice by SHAK:MEA 1
l., shall I leave thee? CONG 52
L. to be saucy HALIF 4
l. to man is eternal vigilance CURRAN 1
L., too, must be limited BURKE:E 45
L. was born in England VOLT 1
L. when it begins to take WASH 12
L.'s a glorious feast BURNS:R 26
L.'s in every blow BURNS:R 108
life, l., and the pursuit of happiness JEFFERSON 2
loudest yelps for l. among JOHNSON:S 43
love of l. is the love HAZL 10
loving-jealous of his l. SHAK:ROM 19
man, and lackith l. JAMES I 1
mansion house of l. MILT 318
moral, regulated l. BURKE:E 48
Mountain Nymph, sweet L. MILT 67
people contend for their L. HALIF 5
preferring Hard l. MILT 156
price of l. is not so much eternal ORWELL 3
primordial condition of l. BAK 2
proclaim l. to the captives BIBLE 333
revel on the grave Of L. SHELLEY:PB 10
spirit of divinest L. COLERIDGE:ST 6
such refreshing airs of l. BURKE:E 1
Sweet land of l. SMITH:Sam 1
symptom of constitutional l. GIBBON:E 7
taking quite a l. in going astray ELIOT:G 3
to seek power and to lose l. BACON:F[1] 73
tree of l. must be refreshed JEFFERSON 10
true that l. is precious LENIN 13
voice of l. be mute? CUMM 2
weight of too much l. WORDS:W 51
were thy chosen music, L. WORDS:W 41
when they cry libertie MILT 96
whoever gives, takes l. DONNE 91
Wommen, of kynde, desiren libertee CHAUC 36
Liberty-Hall: This is L., gentlemen GOLDS 73
libraries:
books out of circulating l. RUSKIN 21
I love l., but I will be damned NEED:RJ 1
spend altogether on our l. RUSKIN 20
library:
circulating l. in a town SHERIDAN:RB 6
half a l. to make one book JOHNSON:S 168
l. is thought in cold storage SAMUEL 4
l. of sixty-two thousand GIBBON:E 5
lumber-room of his library DOYLE:AC 15
My l. Was dukedom SHAK:TEM 6
so describe the Bodleian l. HOUSM 54
take choice of all my l. SHAK:TIT 2
licence:
L. they mean MILT 96
not freedom, but l. MILT 323
poets . . . have always had l. HORACE 99
universal l. to be good COLERIDGE:H 1
licencers: work of twenty l. MILT 315
licentious:
all l. passages are left GIBBON:E 28
for fear of l. soldiery WELD 1
My book is l. MARTIAL 1
lichen: Yellow l. on the stone MORRIS:W 10
licht:
l., at enlichtens ilka man BIBLE 593
l. that bends owre a' thing MACDIAR 17
Welcum the lord of lycht DOUGLAS:G 1
lick:
cannot l. his own fingers SHAK:ROM 38
no time to l. it into form BURTON:Ro 3
licked: They l. the platter clean NURS 28
Liddell:
right part wrote L. ANON 112
this is Mrs L. SPRING 2
Liddesdale: march, Eskdale and L. SCOTT:W 59
lids: l. are like the lilac flower PLATH 1
lie:
abomination unto the Lord* ANON 148
Better a l. that heals PROV 37
Better a noble l. DAVIES:R 3
Cannot come, l. follows PROUST 16
fain wad l. doun BALL 33
give the world the l. RALE 3
here let her l. DRYD 132
I cannot tell a l. WASH 1
I l. down alone HOUSM 44
if a l. may do thee grace SHAK:HEN.IV[1] 95
invent a new l. when an old MAUGH 11
leads you to Believe a L. BLAKE:W 108
l. as lads would choose HOUSM 18
l. as quietly among the graves EDWARDS:J 1
l. can be half-way round CALLA 1
L. Circumstantial SHAK:AS 70
L. Direct SHAK:AS 70
l. down until the feeling passes HUTCHINS 1
l. even when it is inconvenient VIDAL 3
L. follows by post BERE 2
l. has become not just a moral SOLZ 9
L. heavy on him, Earth EVANS:A 1
l. in dealing with citizens PLATO 7
l. in the Soul is a true l. JOW 1
l. is an abomination unto STEVENSON:A 3
l. on the beach and stare REED:R 2
l. shall rot PATMO 9
l. that flatters I abhor COWP 43
l. that sinketh in BACON:F[1] 117
l. usefully should l. seldom HERV:Lord 1
l. where shades of darkness DE LA M 18
l. which is part a truth TENNY 228
l. with your legs ungainly SASS 10
Love is just another dirty l. HEMINGWAY 6
misleading impression, not a l. ARMST:R 1
not built to comprehend a l. KIP 143
not wenen every thing a lye CHAUC 93
Nothing can need a ly HERB:G 3
obedient to their laws, we l. SIMONID 1
only l. he had ever told RUSS:B 24
sense to know how to l. well BUTLER:S[2] 39
sent to l. abroad for the good WOTTON 5
something given to l. SHAK:ANT 70
stand up and l. like white men O'ROUR 1
Take the saving l. from IBS 12
that he should l. BIBLE 119
to l. between maids' legs SHAK:HAM 111
together Lye Gray Age ANON 137
truth in masquerade* BYR 222
Truth is the safest l. PROV 404
victim to a big l. more easily HITL 2
what is a l.? BYR 222
what they know to be a l. HAMP 2
Who can rule and dare not l. TENNY 211
Who loves to l. with me SHAK:AS 24
you l. – under a mistake SWIFT 44
lied: children shall say they have l. YEATS 25
liege: L. of all loiterers SHAK:LOV 8
lies:
Art is the most beautiful of all l. DEBU 1
As many l. as will lie SHAK:TWE 44
believing their own l. ARB 1
compulsory, force-feeding of l. SOLZ 8
Cursed be the social l. TENNY 73
don't deal in l. KIP 127
good memory after telling l. CORNEILLE 6
just hear the l. trickling out SALM 1
l. about his wooden horse FLECKER 11
l. are often told in silence STEVENSON:RL 13
L. are the mortar that bind WELLS:HG 1
l., damned l. and statistics DISR:B 90
L., damned l., and statistics TWAIN 33
make a man confess the l. HOUSE 2
Matilda told such Dreadful L. BELLOC 21
need l. . . . in order to live NIET 28
only l. are invented BRAQ 2
open truth to cover l. CONG 20
Optimistic l. have such immense SHAW 101
questions and hear no l. PROV 23
Rest is L. FITZGER:E 16
spring of endless l. COWP 38
tells his l. by rote YEATS 112
This poet l. SHAK:SON 5
Through polished ivory pass deluding l. VIRGIL 74
white l. to ice a wedding cake ASQU:M 3
wish I were where Helen l. BALL 25
lieth: To say that a man l. BACON:F[1] 118
life:
all l. comes crowding into WILDE:O 1
all L. death does end HOPK:GM 24
all l. weighed in the scales YEATS 143
all of l. is a dream CALD 4
alone L., Joy, Empire SHELLEY:PB 87
Anythin' for a quiet l. DICKENS 51
art of drawing sufficient conclusions* BUTLER:S[2] 22
As our l. is very short TAYL:Jer 1
at war you think about a better l. WILDER:T 2
average cabin of a l. BROWNING:R 78
bear a charmed l. SHAK:MAC 115
before the fire of l. LANDOR 9
believe in the l. to come? BECKETT 11
believing in l., from loving l. ZOLA 3
best portion of a good man's l. WORDS:W 4
bitterness of l. CARROLL 93
blood-thirsty clinging to l. ARNOLD:M 55
bloodiness of family l. MITCH:Ju 1
Book of L. begins with WILDE:O 60
Bread is the staff of l. PROV 50
brief is l. but love is long TENNY 111
busy scenes of crowded l. JOHNSON:S 66
but one l. and one death BROWNING:R 126
cats – all human l. is there JAMES:H 4
compare human l. to a large Mansion KEATS 135
consider how my l. is spent NASH 4
deedful l. TENNY 121
devils in l. and condition ASCHAM 2
discovered the secret of l. CREWE 1
disease of modern l. ARNOLD:M 28
dreamed that l. was Beauty HOOP 1
dreary intercourse of daily l. WORDS:W 11
drink L. to the lees TENNY 52
drink of l. again HOUSM 42
ebbs out l.'s little day LYTE 1
enjoy l., or better to endure JOHNSON:S 60
essence of l. that it exists for WHITEHEAD 3
every man wastes part of his l. JOHNSON:S 3
Every man's l. is a fairy-tale ANDER 3
everyday affair l. is LAF 1
experience of l. has been drawn from l. BEERB 10

get about ten percent out of l. DUNC 3
giveth his l. for the sheep BIBLE 484
great end of l. is not knowledge HUX:TH 6
great l. if you don't weaken BUCHAN 1
half of my own l. HORACE 3
have everlasting l. BIBLE 477
He that findeth his l. BIBLE 409
heat of l. in the handful CONRAD 8
her l. began BROWNING:R 151
his l., I'm sure, was COWLEY:A 8
holding up the nothingness of l.? BYR 215
home l. of our own dear Queen ANON 199
How good is man's l. BROWNING:R 147
how short is the longest L. KEATS 165
human l. is so short XERX 1
I gave my l. for freedom EWER 1
I have measured out my l. ELIOT:TS 6
I mean a Future L. BUTLER:J 2
I require the l. of man BIBLE 41
If l. had a second edition CLARE:J 13
imperfection of all the gifts of l. CONRAD 14
in all things the laws of l. RUSKIN 15
in mourning for my l. CHEK 1
In the midst of l. we are in death PRAY 91
intend to lead a new l. PRAY 71
Is l. a boon? GILB:WS 95
Is L. much, or no? HARDY:T 38
Is there another L.? KEATS 168
isn't l. a terrible thing THOMAS:D 29
it exists for the good l. ARISTOT 12
It is art that *makes* l. JAMES:H 22
It is not a L. at all GLAD 8
It may be l., but ain't HERB:AP 3
it might well prolong his l. DARLING:CJ 1
It's an easy l. BUZO 1
I've had a happy l. HAZL 40
jump the l. to come SHAK:MAC 23
King's l. is moving peacefully DAWS 1
large as l. and twice CARROLL 78
last of l. for which the first BROWNING:R 184
later l. renew SPENS 11
lay down his friends for his l. THORPE 1
lay down his l. for his friends BIBLE 490
lead a jolly l. like that DENNIS:CJ 3
lead to a Struggle for L. DARW:C 4
L., a Fury slinging flame TENNY 148
L. and death is cat and dog FRY:C 3
L. and Soul, the man who will WHITEHORN 2
L. and their Goods may be CHARLES I 4
L. begins at forty PROV 237
L. can only be understood backwards KIERK 1
l. delights in l. BLAKE:W 61
l. everlasting PRAY 19
L. exists in the universe only JEANS 1
L. for l. BIBLE 104
L. Force supplies us with its own SHAW 71
l. forget and death remember SWIN 5
L., friends, is boring BERR 1
L. gets better As I grow older DOBSON:R 2
l. goes not backward GIBRAN 1
l. hath been one chain CLARE:J 2
l. hovers like a star BYR 236
l. is ... but like a forward child TEMPLE:W[1] 1
L. is a gamble, at terrible STOP 8
l. is a glorious cycle PARKER:D 4
L. is a jest GAY 36
L. is a maze in which CONNOLLY:C 13
L. is a pill which none JOHNSON:S 258
l. is a profession of faith AMIEL 3
l. is a watch or a vision SWIN 15
L. is all a variorum BURNS:R 27
L. is an incurable disease COWLEY:A 10
l. is but a day KEATS 8
L. is but an empty dream LONGFEL 1
l. is colour and warmth GREN 1
L. is falling sideways COCT 4
L. is just a bowl of cherries PROV 238
L. is just one damned O'MALLEY:FW 1
L. is just one damned thing HUBB 1
L. is like a sewer LEHRER 1
l. is lived as a series of conversations TANN 1
L. is made up of marble HAWT 3
L. is made up of sobs HENRY:O 1
L. is mostly froth GORDON:AM 1
L. ... is much too short to be taken BENTLEY:N 4
l. Is nobler than attending SHAK:CYM 10
L. is not a spectacle or a feast SANT 14
L. is not all beer and skittles PROV 239
l. is not confined to him LUCRET 9
L. is not meant to be easy FRASER:M 1
l. is one dem'd horrid grind DICKENS 86
l. ... is one prolonged effort HUX:A 4
L. is real! L. is earnest LONGFEL 1
L. is serious SCHILL 3
L. is short HIPP 1
L. is sweet PROV 240
L. is sweet, brother BORR 5
L. is the desert YOUNG:E 1
l. is theatrical EMER 65
l. is thorny COLERIDGE:ST 61
L. is too short to stuff CONRAN 1
L. is what happens to you LENNON 10
l. is what thinking makes of it AUR 6
L. isn't all beer and skittles HUGHES:Th 2
l. ... it's rather like opening a tin BENNETT:Al 1
L. itself is but the shadow BROWNE:T 44
l. leaks away AUD 7
L. levels all men SHAW 65
l., liberty, and the pursuit of happiness JEFFERSON 2
L., like a dome of many-coloured SHELLEY:PB 126
l. of man Less a span BACON:F[1] 131
l. of man, solitary, poor HOBB 7
l. on the ocean wave SARGENT:E 1
l. seems to have no plots COMPT 12
l. so fast doth fly DAVIES:J 2
l., that insane dream BROWNING:R 69
L., the Universe and Everything ADAMS:D 1
l., time's fool SHAK:HEN.IV[1] 89
l., 'tis all a cheat DRYD 21
L., to be sure, is nothing much HOUSM 46
L. we have lost in living? ELIOT:TS 70
l. with the dull bits cut out? HITCH 1
L. without faith is an arid COWARD 9
L. without industry is guilt RUSKIN 28
L. would be tolerable but LEWIS:GC 1
l. would pass in front of him ALLEN:D 4
L.'s a piece in bloom HENL 3
L.'s brief span forbids HORACE 6
L.'s but a walking shadow SHAK:MAC 113
L.'s more amusing than LANG:A 5
light of his l. as if gone out CARLYLE:T 63
live a l. half dead MILT 282
lived a l. that's full ANKA 1
living sepulchre of l. CLARE:J 7
Loathing our l. BYR 124
long disease, my L. POPE 119
long littleness of l. CORNFORD:Fran 2
long process of getting tired* BUTLER:S[2] 21
love of l. is necessary to the vigorous JOHNSON:S 2
lyf so short, the CHAUC 99
Made l. a heaven on earth? KEPP:C 1
make your l. interesting DICKENS 112
Man's l. was spacious ELIOT:G 46
man's sensuous flame of l. LAWR:DH 2
Men deal with l. as children COWP 31
might give my l. for my friend SMITH:LP 9
money or your l.; women require BUTLER:S[2] 54
My l. closed twice DICKIN:E 22
my l. for the British female? CLOUGH 14
My l. is chaste, my muse OSB:J 10
My l. is dreary TENNY 4
my l. is pure MARTIAL 1
My l. is run his compass SHAK:JUL 82
my l. to make you King CHARLES II 6
My lines and l. are free HERB:G 40
Nae spark of l. was there BALL 2
nauseous draught of l. go ROCHES 1
no one loses any other l. AUR 3
Nobody can write the l. of a man JOHNSON:S 152
not been leading a double l. WILDE:O 91
not only live his personal l. MANN:T 5
Nothing in his l. Became him SHAK:MAC 18
now my l. is done TICH 1
on the ocean of l. we pass LONGFEL 31
One l. for each to give KIP 145
one l. to lose for my country HALE:N 1
One's real l. is so often WILDE:O 107
Only a l. lived for others EINS 5
Organic l. we are told RUSS:B 5
our little l. Is rounded SHAK:TEM 27
part of l.'s rich pageant MARSHALL:Ar 1
pass on the torch of l. LUCRET 6
pathway of l. unnoticed HORACE 91
pointless l. is an early GOET 3
powerless l. is Man's l. RUSS:B 6
prepare for l. ELIOT:TS 18
put l. before honour JUV 18
Railing at l., and yet CHURCH:C 21
really don't know l. at all MITCH:Jo 1
Rushes l. in a race MERED:G 16
saves a man's l. against his will HORACE 117
sech is l. DICKENS 118
see into the l. of things WORDS:W 6
set gray l. TENNY 93
set my l. at a pin's fee SHAK:HAM 37
set my l. on any chance SHAK:MAC 62
shade the evening of l. GIBBON:E 29
She bid me take l. easy YEATS 3
slits the thin-spun l. MILT 49
spare all ... take my l. FARQ 19
spirit giveth l. BIBLE 528
state in which much is to be endured JOHNSON:S 23
stuff l. is made of FRANKLIN:B 11
such is L. DICKENS 210
Such is l. KELLY:N 3
sweet is this human l. CORY 2
swift flight of a lone sparrow* BEDE 1
take my l. and all SHAK:MERC 48
tenant of the room* HENL 3
thank God for fucking up my l. HUGHES:S 1
that is l. without theory DISR:B 9
that loseth his l. for my sake BIBLE 409
their lost l. is so low DANTE 3
There is no l. of a man CARLYLE:T 36
thing That none but fools would keep* SHAK:MEA 18
this gives l. to thee SHAK:SON 6
this is human l. KEATS 38
those who live Call L. SHELLEY:PB 30
Thou art my l. QUAR 13
Thou art my l., my love HERR 31
Three fourths of l. ARNOLD:M 74
time of l. is short SHAK:HEN.IV[1] 87
'Tis the sunset of l. gives me CAMPBELL:T 21
To lengthen thy l. FRANKLIN:B 3
to out-do the l. JONS 51
Tomorrow's l. is too late MARTIAL 2
took one peep of L. ANON 129
transience of l. has always exasperated BEHAN:Bea 1
tree of l. also BIBLE 10
truly to know is everlasting l. PRAY 59
unexamined l. is not a l. worth SOC 3
value of l. does not lie MONTAIGNE 5
way, the truth, and the l. BIBLE 489
weary of the study of real l. BRONTE:C 2
well-written L. is almost CARLYLE:T 23
What a minefield L. is FRY:C 19
what a queer thing L. is WODE 6
What is l.? A frenzy CALD 4
what is L.? – an hour glass CLARE:J 1
What is our l.? GIBBONS:O 2
What is this l. if DAVIES:WH 2
when l.'s sweet fable ends CRASH 16
Where all l. dies MILT 166
where l. is more like l. O'CAS 7
Where there's l., there's hope TEREN 6
While there's l. there's hope PROV 429
will he give for his l. BIBLE 182

life-in-death: Nightmare L. was she COLERIDGE:ST 20

lifeboat: movie, not a l. TRACY 2

lifetime: for the knowledge of a l. WHIST 10

lift:
I will l. up mine eyes BIBLE 239
L. her with care HOOD 23
l. itself in homage SHELLEY:PB 142
l. me as a wave, a leaf SHELLEY:PB 45
l. me from the grass SHELLEY:PB 36
L. not the painted veil SHELLEY:PB 30
L. up your heads BIBLE 208
one sitting that you cannot l. PIG 1

light:
against the dying of the l. THOMAS:D 18
Apparelled in celestial l. WORDS:W 52
as l. fell short HODG 2
bathe the world in l. WORDS:W 112

blasted with excess of l. GRAY:T 35
by one another's l. PATTEN 4
caught . . . in a noose of L. FITZGER:E 1
certain Slant of l. DICKIN:E 4
Clasp'd by the golden l. HOOD 11
consider how my l. is spent MILT 100
dimm religious l. MILT 90
dissolving verticals of l. SLESS 4
do your teeth with the l. on JENKIN 1
Don't turn down the l. HENRY:O 5
drainless shower of l. is Poesy KEATS 12
festal l. in Christ-Church ARNOLD:M 25
filled with the l. of intelligence KELLER 2
flower of l. JONS 48
For that celestial l.? MILT 121
from heaven the beam of your l. LANGTON 1
gave him a l. in his ways SWIN 14
Giving more l. than heat SHAK:HAM 32
gone into the world of l. VAUGHAN:H 9
Hail, holy L. MILT 175
happy Realms of L. MILT 112
have seen a glorious l. SCOTTISH 3
he beholds the l. WORDS:W 58
He that has l. within MILT 30
Heaven's l. forever shines SHELLEY:PB 126
high endeavours are an inward l. WORDS:W 39
I travel l. FRY:C 4
if once we lose this l. JONS 19
In a l. fantastick round MILT 22
It gives a lovely l. MILLAY 1
It is the l. of Terewth DICKENS 177
it too celebrates the l. WILLIAMS:WC 6
Lead, kindly L. NEWM:JH 15
leaping l. for you discovers AUD 12
let me not be l. SHAK:MERC 55
let perpetual l. shine MASS 20
Let there be l. BIBLE 2
Let there be l. SHELLEY:PB 152
'Let there be l.!' said God BYR 216
Lets in new l. WALLER 9
L. and Mrs Humphrey Ward CHESTERTON 17
l., and will aspire SHAK:POET 10
l. at the end of the tunnel LOWELL:R 18
l. better than any lights BURNE 1
L. breaks where no sun THOMAS:D 5
l. broke in upon BYR 50
l. but the shadow of God BROWNE:T 44
l. dissolved in star-showers SHELLEY:PB 31
l. enough for wot I've got DICKENS 63
l. fantastick toe MILT 67
L. half-believers ARNOLD:M 26
l. in the darkness of mere being JUNG:Carl 5
l. in the dust lies SHELLEY:PB 159
L. . . . is a principal beauty FULLER:T[1] 5
L. is the first of painters EMER 1
l. of his life as if gone out CARLYLE:T 63
L. of L. PRAY 66
L. of Lights YEATS 7
L. rinses fog from colours KAV 4
l., she said, not of the sky NEIL 5
L. she was and MONTROSE 2
l. shineth in darkness BIBLE 472
l. so dim he would not CHEV:M 1
L. that Failed KIP 10
l. that I may tread safely HASKINS 1
l. that led astray BURNS:R 34
l. that lies In woman's eyes MOORE:T 15
l. to shine upon the road COWP 2
l. unto my path BIBLE 238
l. we sought is shining ARNOLD:M 45
l. which experience gives COLERIDGE:ST 90
Lord is the source of my l. BIBLE 597
More l. GOET 41
morning l. creaks down again SITWELL:E 3
Newtons Particles of l. BLAKE:W 101
Nicodemus saw such l. VAUGHAN:H 1
out of Hell leads up to L. MILT 161
Progenie of L. MILT 218
purple l. of Love GRAY:T 33
pursuit of sweetness and l. ARNOLD:M 64
Put out the l. SHAK:OTH 60
resistance to l. and its children ARNOLD:M 67
Ring of pure and endless l. VAUGHAN:H 14
rule of streaming l. MILT 29
seen a great l. BIBLE 307
set is our little l. CATUL 5
severity of perfect l. TENNY 268
shining l., that shineth more BIBLE 252
shores of darkness there is l. KEATS 32
so l. a foot SHAK:ROM 24
Sometimes a l. surprises COWP 14
stand a little out of my l. DIOG 2
such glimmerings of l. BURKE:E 1
Teach l. to counterfeit a gloom MILT 83
There is a l., a step, a call NEIL 6
this day l. such a candle LAT 2
Thou art my l. QUAR 13
to shew l. at Calais JOHNSON:S 123
tried to mend the Electric L. BELLOC 32
unclouded blaze of living l. BYR 34
upon us the armour of l. PRAY 42
We all *know* what l. is JOHNSON:S 187
we grow toward the l. SARTON 2
what has l. to do with darkness JEROME 1
What l. through yonder SHAK:ROM 8
what's the use of l.? PASO 1
which are sweetness and l. SWIFT 2

Light Brigade: Forward the L.B. TENNY 199
lightening: lightning before death SHAK:ROM 42
lightfoot: many a l. lad HOUSM 26
lighthouse: took the sitivation at the l. DICKENS 51
lightly: take themselves l. CHESTERTON 43
lightning:
at l. and lashed rod HOPK:GM 3
Bring in the bottled l. DICKENS 84
coruscations of summer l. GOUL 1
From l. and tempest PRAY 33
illuminated by flashes of l. WILDE:O 5
its own internal l. blind SHELLEY:PB 62
known the l.'s hour DAY LEWIS 2
man who was killed by l. ANON 130
Postillion Struck by L. BOGARDE 1
Shakespeare by flashes of l. COLERIDGE:ST 83
Then flash'd the living l. POPE 52
to keep the l. out ISH 1
Too like the l. SHAK:ROM 15
lights:
all the l. wax dim HERR 11
Coastwise L. of England KIP 80
God made two great l. BIBLE 5
l. around the shore ROSSET:DG 5
l. begin to twinkle TENNY 55
spent l. quiver and gleam ARNOLD:M 1
like:
awful! But I l. you EMERY 1
Dear heart how l. you this? WYATT 4
doing as they l. without detriment MILL 19
every one as they l. SWIFT 38
finally l. it RIMSK 1
got to l. the little swine DARLING:J 1
I do not l. you MARTIAL 3
I don't know what I l. BLACK 1
I know what I l. BEERB 12
I said there was nothing *l.* it CARROLL 76
L. breeds l. PROV 241
L. cures l. HAHN 1
l. doing best and get someone to pay WHITEHORN 4
L. doth quit l. SHAK:MEA 39
L. father, l. son PROV 242
Men we l. are good for every thing HALIF 15
no more l. people personally SPENCER:S 1
not look upon his l. again SHAK:HAM 25
now she is l. everyone else DE GAU 6
say, you do not l. it WHIST 9
some of them I don't l. CARTER:L 2
sort of thing they l. LINC 19
think they ought to l. it SHAW 40
To l. and dislike the same SALL 2
wha's l. us ANON 194
what we l. is not necessarily good BELL:C 3
wilt thou find their l. agen? SCOTT:W 15
liked:
Because I l. you better HOUSM 45
easier we're l. PUSH 3
How I like to be l. LAMB:Ch 42
I've never l. them MAUGH 23
l., but he's not well l. MILLER:A 1
likeness:
after our l. BIBLE 6
l. of an old fat man SHAK:HEN.IV[1] 50
never got a l. once BRAY 1
shadow of my l. that goes WHITMAN 37
likes:
doesn't know what he l. THURB 18
She l. her self CONG 60
that somebody l. me PRIEST 3
likewise:
Canst thou do l.? DICKENS 230
Go, and do thou l. BIBLE 458
liking: saves me the trouble of l. them AUSTEN 71
likings: made up of l. and dislikings LAMB:Ch 9
lilac: Just now the l. is in bloom BROOKE 8
lilac-time: down to Kew in l. NOY 1
lilacs:
l. in the doorway bloom'd WHITMAN 34
L. out of the dead land ELIOT:TS 34
lilies:
Consider the l. of the field BIBLE 395
had three l. in her hand ROSSET:DG 1
l. and languors of virtue SWIN 20
l. of all kinds SHAK:WIN 20
l. of ambition still spring DOUGLAS:K 4
L. that fester smell SHAK:SON 41
L. without, roses within MARV 26
Roses and white Lillies grow CAMPION 9
Lillabullero: half a dozen bars of *L.* STERNE 9
Lilli Burlero: *L.B. Bullena-la* WHARTON:T 1
Lillie: born Beatrice Gladys L. LILL 1
lilting: I've heard them l. ELLIOT:J 1
lily:
How sweet the l. grows HEB 5
I see a l. on thy brow KEATS 80
in the morning glows the l. FLECKER 12
l. maid of Astolat TENNY 249
l. of a day JONS 48
l. of Florence blossoming LONGFEL 27
l. whispers TENNY 219
paint the l. BYR 190
seen but a bright l. grow JONS 46
to paint the l. SHAK:KING J 16
Lily:
Daisy and L. SITWELL:E 5
L. O'Grady SITWELL:E 7
limb:
Care I for the l. SHAK:HEN.IV[2] 36
perils both of wind and l. BUTLER:S[1] 18
limbecks: Distill'd from l. foul SHAK:SON 53
limbo: L. large and broad MILT 180
limbs:
dead l. of gibbeted Gods SWIN 37
great smooth marbly l. BROWNING:R 43
life controls these l. VIRGIL 59
l. of a poet HORACE 66
solemn slope of mighty l. SWIN 51
stir no l. in any other measure DONNE 108
Whose l. were made SHAK:HEN.V 19
lime: sprinkle the l. like rain HOUSM 42
lime-tree: l. bower my prison COLERIDGE:ST 51
limekiln: from the l. to the charcoal TERT 5
limelight: always backing into the l. BERNE 1
Limerick: acquitted by a L. jury ADAMS:R[1] 1
limericks: Whose l. never would scan ANON 108
limit:
act a slave to l. SHAK:TRO 11
find the l. of yourself MANS:K 7
quiet l. of the world TENNY 45
to draw a l. to thinking WITT 4
use me to the l. ROOS:T 10
who does not know how to l. himself BOIL 6
limiting: l. and isolating oneself GOET 33
limits:
l. within which a human soul may SCHREIN 1
stony l. cannot hold love out SHAK:ROM 12
limousine:
All we want is a l. MACNEICE 2
One perfect l. PARKER:D 6
Limpopo:
grey-green, greasy L. River KIP 25
L. and Tugela churned PLOM 2
Lincoln:
at the back o' merry L. BALL 26
L. sped the message on MACAULAY:TB 42
Linden:
down low in L. Lea BARNES:W 1
L., when the sun was low CAMPBELL:T 19
Lindesay: Sir David L. of the Mount SCOTT:W 17
line:
creep in one dull l. POPE 18
Drinker of horizon's fluid l. SPEND 6
fight it out on this l. GRANT:US 1
Genius walks along a l. GOLDS 43

l. going for a stroll KLEE 2
l. is length without breadth EUC 3
l. too labours POPE 21
l. will take us hours YEATS 27
lives along the l. POPE 86
necessarily go in a straight l. THATCH:M 10
not a l. has yet been written EMER 87
speed glum heroes up the l. SASS 4
Thin red l. of 'eroes KIP 65
thin red l. tipped with RUSS:WH 1
thought I heard a l. I wrote KAUFMANN 1

lineages: only two l. in the world CERV 19

lineaments:
in my l. they trace BYR 47
l. of Gratified Desire BLAKE:W 60

linen:
He did not love clean l. JOHNSON:S 110
l. to keep the neighbours' eyes off DICKENS 191
Love is like l. FLETCH:P 1
not l. you're wearing out HOOD 20
old l. was whitest? WEBSTER:J 1
very fine l., plenty of it BRUM 1
wash your dirty l. in public PROV 84
washing one's clean l. in public WILDE:O 84

lines:
As l. (so loves) oblique MARV 8
consisted of l. like these CALVER 4
hangman's-knot of sinking l. LOWELL:R 17
l. are fallen unto me BIBLE 201
My l. and life are free HERB:G 40
silken l., and silver hooks DONNE 28
six l. together without a fault JOHNSON:S 139
six l. written by the most honest RICHELIEU:A 2
walk on the l. or the squares MILNE 6
yellow l. and dead armadillos HIGH 1

lingerie: Brevity is the soul of l. PARKER:D 13

lingering: Something l. GILB:WS 77

lining:
Every cloud has a silver l. PROV 98
l. of his coffers shall make SHAK:RIC.II 14
silver l. in the sky-ee WESTON 2
There's a silver l. FORD:L 1
Turn forth her silver l. MILT 25

link:
no stronger than its weakest l. PROV 54
silver l. SCOTT:W 9

linnet:
full of the l.'s wings YEATS 4
hear the woodland l. WORDS:W 16
I heard a l. courting BRIDGES:R 3
l. born within the cage TENNY 141

linnets: pipe but as the l. sing TENNY 138

linsey-wolsey: l. brothers POPE 166

linsy-woolsy: lawless l. brother BUTLER:S[1] 19

lion:
attributes of the fox and the l. MACHIA 7
beard the l. in his den SCOTT:W 26
better than a dead l. BIBLE 285
from the L. mouth PSALMS 1
great big L. called Wallace EDGAR 1
I hear the l. roar COWP 9
l. among ladies is a most SHAK:MID 23
l. and the calf shall lie down ALLEN:W 9
L. and the Lizard keep FITZGER:E 12
l. and the unicorn Were fighting NURS 31
l. griefs loped from AUD 23
l. in a cage of savage Daniels WILDE:O 136
l. shall eat straw BIBLE 12
make the l. lie down with LAWR:DH 27
March comes in like a l. PROV 267
Now that the old l. is dead PARR 1
Now the hungry l. roars SHAK:MID 51
One law for the L. & Ox BLAKE:W 55
Only the L. and the Cock GOGA 1
righteous are bold as a l. BIBLE 274
roaring l., walketh about BIBLE 569
rouse the l. from his lair SCOTT:W 64
Sporting the L. rampd MILT 196
Strong is the l. SMART 2
Thou wear a l.'s hide SHAK:KING J 9
To rouse a l. than SHAK:HEN.IV[1] 21
wrath of the l. is the wisdom BLAKE:W 41

lioness:
feeds a l. at home TAYL:Jer 4
l. hath whelped in the streets SHAK:JUL 29

lionized: who wasn't spoilt by being l. TREE 2

lions:
army of l. led by asses CHAMP 1
children To feed ruddy L.? EDGAR 2
Difficulties, L., or Vanity-Fair BUNYAN 27
Every Wolfs & L. howl BLAKE:W 84
girdid up my L. and fled WARD:A 3
laughing l. must come NIET 8
like l. to the roaring slaughter CUMM 2
l. led by donkeys HOFFMAN:M 1
Rise like L. SHELLEY:PB 39
two l. litter'd in one day SHAK:JUL 31
yellow l. come out CAMPBELL:ATA 2
young l. of the Daily Telegraph ARNOLD:M 54

lip:
bit his l. in a manner PEREL 3
gnaw you so your nether l.? SHAK:OTH 61
Keep a stiff upper l. CARY:P 1
l. mature is ever new? KEATS 59
red was on your l. BLACKWOOD 1
'twixt the cup and the l. PROV 379

Lippo: brother L., by your leave BROWNING:R 110

lips:
at the touching of the l. TENNY 71
Black Eyes, red L. MARV 11
claycauld were her rosy l. BALL 2
Fled not his thirsting l. SHELLEY:PB 7
heaven be in these l. MARLOWE 38
Her l. were red COLERIDGE:ST 20
Here hung those l. SHAK:HAM 183
l. are not yet unsealed BALD:S 6
l. as soft, but true BROOKE 15
l. cannot fail of taking BURGOY 1
l. of dying men ARNOLD:M 31
l. of lurid blue SHELLEY:PB 9
l. say, 'God be pitiful' BROWNING:EB 3
l. suck forth my soul MARLOWE 38
l. that touch liquor YOUNG:GW 1
L., where all Day CRASH 9
love to the l. we are near MOORE:T 16
man of unclean l. BIBLE 305
meet on l. of living men BUTLER:S[2] 50
On l. that are for others TENNY 109
put my l. to it when I am so dispoged DICKENS 113
red mournful l. YEATS 10
take those l. away SHAK:MEA 30
that those l. had language COWP 89
to tilt with l. SHAK:HEN.IV[1] 33
two l. indifferent red SHAK:TWE 15
very good words for the l. DICKENS 196
When the l. have spoken SHELLEY:PB 159
Where's my *Julia*'s l. doe smile HERR 10
whole soul thro' My l. TENNY 11

liquidation: over the l. of the British Empire CHURCH:W 29

liquidity: purpose in l. BROOKE 17

liquor:
considerbul licker koncealed WARD:A 8
drynke licour of the vyne CHAUC 68
Good l., I stoutly maintain GOLDS 36
lads for the l. are there HOUSM 13
Licker talks mighty loud HARRIS:JC 8
Life's L. in its Cup FITZGER:E 2
lips that touch l. YOUNG:GW 1
l. Is quicker NASH 3
Livelier l. than the Muse HOUSM 28
other such spiritual l. BYR 148

liquors:
grateful l. glide POPE 50
Hot and rebellious l. SHAK:AS 16
With pleasant l. crownd MILT 214

lisped: Somwhat he lipsed CHAUC 17

list: I've got a little l. GILB:WS 64

listen:
can l. to with naked eye SPARK 8
privilege of wisdom to l. HOLMES:OW 16
Stop; look; l. UPTON:RR 1
they will l. today KHRU 9
world should l. then SHELLEY:PB 100

listened: very soul L. intensely WORDS:W 117

listener: good l. is a good talker with WHITEHORN 5

listeners:
L. never hear good PROV 243
least stir made the l. DE LA M 8

listening:
disease of not l. SHAK:HEN.IV[2] 8
good at l. to their elders BALD:J 3

People l. without hearing SIMON:P 1
still l. when the song has ended SAINT-LA 1

literacy: ratio of l. to illiteracy is constant MORA 5

literalists: l. of the imagination MOORE:M 1

literary:
disgusted with l. Men KEATS 116
educated l. and scientific opinion ARNOLD:M 58
great nonstop l. drinker THURB 8
l. man – *with* a wooden leg DICKENS 215
l. man Who played with spoons BROWNING:R 87
L. men are . . . a perpetual CARLYLE:T 25
little about their jobs as the l. ones ESSON 2
lowest class is *l. footmen* HAZL 38
Majesty is the head of the l. DISR:B 85
quotation is the *parole* of l. men JOHNSON:S 223
viewing them as a l. performance WHITMAN 41
with St Paul are l. terms ARNOLD:M 73

literary criticism:
L.c. provides the test LEAV 1
You *may* abuse a tragedy* JOHNSON:S 111

literature:
about l. except how to enjoy HELLER 4
All folk l. YEATS 128
All the rest is l. VALERY 2
Bible is l., not dogma SANT 11
Bounded by English l. and the Anglican PYM 1
created the most of the modern l. YEATS 135
English l. is always in danger BREN 7
English l.'s performing flea O'CAS 8
enough intellect nor enough l. HOUSM 53
failed in l. and art DISR:B 41
first the l. of *knowledge* DEQ 12
great as the l. of the old world YEATS 129
great Cham of l. SMOL 15
Great l. is simply language POUND 42
history to produce a little l. JAMES:H 2
l. a quotation EMER 65
l. clear, cold, pure, and LEWIS:S 4
L. flourishes best INGE 3
l. has truly told us EMER 87
l. is a drug BORR 7
L. is an epiphenomenon of the action BURGESS:A 2
L. is mostly about having sex LODGE:D 1
l. is my mistress CHEK 14
L. is news that STAYS POUND 45
L. is the art of writing CONNOLLY:C 2
L. is the orchestration of platitudes WILDER:T 4
l. seeks to communicate power DEQ 8
louse in the locks of l. TENNY 299
lover of l. is never fastidious SOUTHEY 19
newest works, in l., the oldest BULWER 5
once the itch of l. comes LOVER 1
Philistine of genius in l. ARNOLD:M 77
rest of it is l. VERL 5
such thing as 'pure' l.? PALMER:N 1
survive very well without l. SARTRE 12
time for the era of world l. GOET 34
truly realized by L. alone WILDE:O 13
visions of art and l. MORRELL 1

littlans: lairnt the mouths o l. and pap-bairns BIBLE 591

little:
aggregate of l. things MORE:H 2
big words for l. matters JOHNSON:S 130
but l. in our love SHAK:TWE 31
Every l. helps PROV 101
From having too l. to do KIP 102
he's left a lot of l. things KIP 97
it was a very l. one MARR 5
L., but to the purpose BYR 218
L. man, l. man ELIZ I 16
l. more, and how much BROWNING:R 92
l. seemed to him great MACAULAY:TB 28
l. streame best fits HERR 37
L. things affect l. minds DISR:B 26
l. things are infinitely DOYLE:AC 13
Man wants but l. GOLDS 17
Man wants but L. YOUNG:E 14
Man wants but l. here below BUTLER:S[2] 41
not l., nor too great POMF 1
So l. done BELL:AG 2
So l. done, so much to do RHODES 4

though she be but l., she is fierce SHAK:MID 32
thought of big men and l. men JOHNSON:S 164
littleness:
long l. of life CORNFORD:Fran 2
own l. than disbelief CARLYLE:T 44
littlenesses: thousand peering l. TENNY 235
liturgy: Popish l. PITT:W[1] 8
live:
always getting ready to l. EMER 81
available way to l. a long AUBER 2
Bid me to l., and I will l. HERR 29
blundering people will l. on SANDBURG 3
can't l. on love alone TOLS:S 1
Come l. with me MARLOWE 49
desire ... to l. beyond its income BUTLER:S[2] 23
do not l. Like dying men WORDS:W 149
don't know how to l. right HORACE 98
don't l. it, it won't come out PARKER:C 1
don't think men and women are meant to l. DORS 1
don't wish to l. any longer MAUGH 27
Easy l. and quiet die SCOTT:W 58
Eat to l. and not l. to eat PROV 92
eat to l., not l. to eat MOLIERE 21
he forgets to l. LA BRU 4
He that begins to l. QUAR 11
he'd learn how to l. BROWNING:R 117
How can I l. without thee MILT 249
How is it that you l. WORDS:W 86
I l. not in myself BYR 91
I l. on BROOKE 3
I would l. to study BACON:F[1] 24
If you l. long enough STONE:IF 1
just shall l. by faith BIBLE 508
known I was gonna l. this long BLAKE:E 1
let me l. to-night SHAK:OTH 62
let me l., unseen POPE 2
let us l. and love CATUL 5
L. all you can JAMES:H 14
L. among men as if God SEN 3
L. and learn PROV 244
l., and move, and have BIBLE 503
l. and shame the land HOUSM 46
L. as I lived BYR 136
l. as if we were going to l. forever BREN 3
l. bravely in another country MIDD 5
l. by positive goals BERLIN:Is 2
l. cleanly, as a nobleman SHAK:HEN.IV[1] 96
l. each day as it comes DIX:D 2
l. forever or die in the HELLER 2
l. in hearts we leave behind CAMPBELL:T 18
l. in proportion to the extent ORTEGA G 5
l. it all again And yet again YEATS 99
l. it to the full SPARK 3
l. more nearly as KEBLE 2
l. or die wi' Charlie HOGG 6
L. ? The servants will do that VILLIERS DE 1
l. this day, as if thy last KEN 2
l. today MARTIAL 2
l. too long DANI 4
l. we how we can SHAK:HEN.VI[3] 7
l. well on nothing a year THACK 9
l. with me, and be my love DONNE 28
l. with thee, and be thy love RALE 1
long to l. PRAY 24
longer I l. the more fool ANON 119
love first and l. incidentally FITZGER:Z 1
man desires to l. long SWIFT 21
Man doth not l. by bread only BIBLE 123
Man shall not l. by bread alone BIBLE 380
neither l. with you – nor without MARTIAL 9
not to l., but to die in BROWNE:T 32
nothing but a Rage to l. POPE 133
one bare hour to l. MARLOWE 40
so long as you both shall l.? PRAY 83
Teach him how to l. PORTEUS 3
Teach me to l. KEN 2
teaching nations how to l. MILT 308
Tell me whom you l. with CHESTERFIELD 6
that l. to please must please to l. JOHNSON:S 65
thou wilt l. again NIET 29
To l. and die for thee HERR 31
To l. is like love BUTLER:S[2] 33
to l. on your knees IBA 2
tried To l. without him WOTTON 1
wants to l. humbly for one STEK 1
We l. and learn POMF 2
what thou livst L. well MILT 257
while you l., you l. in love SIDNEY:P 17
who l. in the past must yield BENNETT:Ar 12
With you I should love to l. HORACE 40
without Thee I cannot l. KEBLE 3
You might as well l. PARKER:D 5
you shall l. by fame SPENS 11
You still shall l. SHAK:SON 36
lived:
he had not l., merely existed BUNIN 1
I have l. many lives SLESS 4
I have liv'd long enough SHAK:MAC 110
I l. SIEY 1
liv'd comfortably so long together GAY 12
liv'd light in the spring ARNOLD:M 10
l. better than I have done MALORY 5
l. by hearsay, and faith BUNYAN 33
L. on; and so did I COLERIDGE:ST 25
Never to have l. is best YEATS 102
who l. for joys in vain CLARE:J 4
liver:
l. cannot exist without the lungs DALAI 1
l. is on the right MOLIERE 18
L. of blaspheming Jew SHAK:MAC 80
Liverpool: L. is at the present moment the centre GINSBERG 1
livery: light and careless l. SHAK:HAM 175
lives:
all that l. must die SHAK:HAM 17
can make our l. sublime LONGFEL 4
cat has nine l. PROV 52
every thing that l. is Holy BLAKE:W 56
every thing that l. is holy BLAKE:W 61
Every thing that l., L. not BLAKE:W 29
He that l. in hope danceth HERB:G 59
He that l. long suffers much PROV 164
If two l. join BROWNING:R 93
leave their little l. in air POPE 34
levys at ess that frely levys BARB 1
l. are merely strange dark O'NEILL 1
l. by the sword dies by PROV 167
L. of great men all remind LONGFEL 4
l. of quiet desperation THOREAU 7
L. to die another day HOUSM 27
l. wandering lost in the labyrinth ORTEGA G 9
l. your wishes never led AUD 33
moments of other people's l. PIR 3
not how a man dies, but how he l. JOHNSON:S 143
One really l. nowhere BURNEY 6
sacrifices an hundred thousand l.? WALP:H 16
short, brutal l. RAMEY 1
spend the best part of their l. LA BRU 3
Then chiefly l. HERB:G 32
who bestow a value on our l. WEISS 1
who l. between five bells SLESS 4
who l. more l. than one WILDE:O 117
Who l. unto himself, he l. QUAR 2
woman who l. for others LEWIS:CS 5
liveth: he that l., and was dead BIBLE 574
living:
aren't any l. people in it CHEK 2
before l. he'd learn how to live BROWNING:R 117
Blend the l. with the dead CASWALL 2
Dead and l. were nearly one SASS 18
fever call'd 'L.' POE 12
from existence is *l. dangerously* NIET 18
From too much love of l. SWIN 31
get so good a l. at home? BURKE:R 1
habit of l. indisposeth us BROWNE:T 54
had prepared Podduyev for l. SOLZ 1
he is l. with the gods who AUR 10
L. and partly l. ELIOT:TS 74
l. are just the dead on MAET 2
l. beyond our means MEAD 1
L. is an art HUX:A 31
L. is an illness CHAMFORT 3
L. is both my job MONTAIGNE 12
l. is made ... by selling something WILDER:T 1
l. know No bounds SHIRL 1
l. to some purpose PAINE 11
l. up to it that is difficult THACK 17
L., we fret BROWNING:R 209
lose the reasons for l. JUV 18
making a l., which is rather a nouciance NASH 14
man became a l. soul BIBLE 9
meant by the joy of l. TALL 1
noble L. and the noble Dead WORDS:W 161
only interest in l. comes ZOLA 3
owe respect to the l. VOLT 25
Plain l. and high thinking WORDS:W 73
poor could make a wonderful l. PROV 188
They have their l. to earn DUKES 3
Which l. failed to give HARDY:T 7
world owes me a l. DISN 1
wrong way of l. DURRELL:L 6
Year of L. Dangerously KOCH 1
living rooms: lost in the l.r. of America MCLUH 9
Livingstone: Dr L. I presume? STANLEY 1
Lizzie Borden: L.B. took an axe ANON 80
Llewellyn: soft L.'s lay GRAY:T 29
Lloyd George:
He couldn't see a belt* ASQU:M 5
L.G. spoke for a hundred BENNETT:Ar 9
This goat-footed bard* KEYN 6
When he's alone in a room* KEYN 12
Lloyd Webber: L.W.'s music is everywhere WILLIAMSON 1
loaf:
Half a l. is better than no PROV 157
Here with a L. FITZGER:E 8
loafed: better to have l. and lost THURB 4
loan: l. oft loses both itself SHAK:HAM 30
loathe: my relief Must be to l. her SHAK:OTH 38
loathing: Fear and L. in Las Vegas THOMP:HS 1
loaves:
halfpenny l. sold for SHAK:HEN.VI[2] 9
they that did eat of the l. BIBLE 442
lob: l. as far as doing anything useful RUNYON 6
lobelias: land of l. and tennis ELIOT:TS 73
lobster: like a l. boil'd, the morn BUTLER:S[1] 23
lobsters: I have a liking for l. NERV 3
local: l., but prized elsewhere AUD 53
locality: l. is 'choice' SLESS 7
Loch Lomomd: bonnie banks of Loch Lomon' ANON 36
Lochaber: Farewell to L. RAMS 1
Lochinvar: young L. is come out of the west SCOTT:W 18
lock: it's broken the l. AUD 19
Locke: L. sank into a swoon YEATS 83
locks:
amber l. to grey DRAYT 1
Curly l., Curly l. NURS 8
l. of the approaching storm SHELLEY:PB 41
l. were like the raven BURNS:R 79
l. were yellow as gold COLERIDGE:ST 20
never shake Thy gory l. SHAK:MAC 71
shaking her invincible l. MILT 320
locksmiths: Love laughs at l. PROV 251
locomotives: where the l. sing LIND:V 4
locust: years that the l. hath BIBLE 354
locusts:
cloud of l. blocking off my stars UNA 1
luscious as l. SHAK:OTH 16
lode-stars: your eyes are l. SHAK:MID 4
lodestar: language he was the lodesterre LYD 2
lodger: l. in my own house GOLDS 58
lodgers: l. rather odd SLESS 7
lodgest: where thou l., I will lodge BIBLE 139
lodging: may He give us a safe l. NEWM:JH 2
lodgings: Such as take l. in a head BUTLER:S[1] 9
lo'ed: Better l. ye canna be NAIRNE 1
loft: as much l. as a light iron WODE 14
lofty: L. designs must close in BROWNING:R 122
log:
dying On a l. DICKENS 11
fall a l. at last JONS 48
l. was burning brightly GODWIN 1
logic:
l. and metaphysics are true AYER 1
L. must look after itself WITT 2
L., of course CLOUGH 3
unto logyk hadde longe ygo CHAUC 18
logically: look at things much more l. THATCH:M 9
loins:
shudder in the l. engenders YEATS 69

With your l. girded BIBLE 97
Loire: my Gallic L. DU BEL 3
loitered: So have I l. my life away HAZL 24
loiterers: Liege of all l. SHAK:LOV 8
loitering: Alone and palely l.? KEATS 79
Lolita: L., light of my life NAB 3
lollipop: Monkey with l. paws LEAR 17
Lombardy: waveless plain of L. SHELLEY:PB 27
London:
As L. is to Paddington CANN 3
Behold now this vast City* MILT 318
best club in L. DICKENS 223
chief advantage of L. MEY:H 1
Crowds without company* GIBBON:E 21
drinks a tumbler of L. water SMITH:Syd[1] 12
dull and witless city* BRIDIE 2
Earth hath not anything* WORDS:W 91
gondola of L. DISR:B 38
Hell is a city much like L. SHELLEY:PB 48
I wander thro' each charter'd* BLAKE:W 74
in L. only is a trade DRYD 20
it isn't far from L. NOY 1
I've been to L. To look NURS 55
L.; a nation, not a city DISR:B 37
L. doth pour out her citizens SHAK:HEN.V 42
L. is a fine town COLMAN:G[2] 3
L. is a modern Babylon DISR:B 32
L. particular ... A fog DICKENS 168
L.! Pompous Ignorance sits BRIDIE 2
L., small and white MORRIS:W 6
L., that great cesspool DOYLE:AC 3
L., that great sea SHELLEY:PB 61
L., thou art of townes DUNB 10
L., thou art the flower DUNB 10
L.'s lasting shame GRAY:T 32
lungs of L. PITT:W[1] 12
Mr Weller's knowledge of L. DICKENS 15
nails can reach the length o' Lunnon SCOTT:W 76
Nobody is healthy in L. AUSTEN 41
One road leads to L. MASE 10
people of L. with one voice CHURCH:W 22
Provided that the City of L. remains CHAMBERLAIN:J 1
rainy Sunday in L. DEQ 2
seeing L., I have seen as much JOHNSON:S 81
society to be found out of L. HAZL 12
streets of L. are paved with gold PROV 357
the metropolis of the empire?* COBBETT 2
vilest alleys of L. DOYLE:AC 14
What junk* BLUCH 1
When a man is tired of L. JOHNSON:S 192
London Bridge:
crowd flowed over L.B. ELIOT:TS 37
L.B. is falling down NURS 38
L.B. was a greater piece ADDIS 22
on a broken arch of L.B. MACAULAY:TB 27
Londoner: L. who stole spoons HANC:WK 1
lone: I am a l. lorn creetur DICKENS 141
loneliness:
Lap your l. in heat BETJ 23
L. is the poverty of self SARTON 1
Pray that your l. may spur you HAMMAR 1
lonely:
All the l. people LENNON 5
less l. than when completely CIC 6
l. for unrealistic things O'BRIEN:E 4
Lovely in a l. place DE LA M 1
narrow grave we shall be l. WRIGHT:J 2
She left l. for ever ARNOLD:M 2
So l. 'twas that God COLERIDGE:ST 37
troubled with her l. life PEPYS 10
we are very l. BUCHN 1
lonelyhearts: Write to Miss L. WEST:N 1
lonesome:
l. man on a rainy day FRANKLIN:B 31
one, that on a l. road COLERIDGE:ST 34
lonesomeness: starlight lit my l. HARDY:T 2
long:
delighted us l. enough AUSTEN 18
How l., O Lord, how l.? SHAW 119
In the l. run we are all dead KEYN 1
It cannot hold you l. GOLDS 13
it went on too l. THURB 22
L. in the legs ANON 53
L. ones, backwards JOHNSTON:B 2
l. or short permit to Heav'n MILT 257
l. while to make it short THOREAU 26
longe I to goe to God MORE:T 2
Nor wants that little l. GOLDS 17
short and the l. of it SHAK:MERR 8
They are not l. DOWS 3
Long: presuming Emperor L. has an intellect ICK 2
longer:
it just seems l. FREUD:C 1
stay l. in an hour than others HOWELLS 1
was wished l. by its readers JOHNSON:S 257
Longford: thought of Lord L. coming to visit INGRAMS 3
longing:
dry love and barren l.? LAVIN 1
l. ling'ring look behind? GRAY:T 24
longings: I have Immortal l. SHAK:ANT 72
longueurs: it has its *l.* RIVAR 2
look:
cannot l. after himself JOT 1
don't l. too good KIP 127
How do you l. when I'm sober? LARD 2
like the owner of the l. COCKBURN:H 1
longing ling'ring l. behind? GRAY:T 24
l. after our people SCOTT:Rob 2
l., and pass on DANTE 4
l. at me – in that tone of voice PUNCH 24
l. at was to love TENNY 74
l. before you ere you leap BUTLER:S[1] 25
L. before you leap PROV 247
l. long and carefully at ourselves MOLIERE 17
l. makes a dish a feast HERB:G 56
l. no way but downwards BUNYAN 22
l. on both indifferently SHAK:JUL 7
L. on the bright side PROV 248
L. thy last on all things DE LA M 20
not l. upon his like again SHAK:HAM 25
People l. at you with such disgust SHADBO 1
sit and l. at it for hours JEROME:JK 7
Stop; l.; listen UPTON:RR 1
They l. on and help LAWR:DH 40
looked:
better to be l. over than overlooked WEST:M 11
his wife l. back BIBLE 50
no sooner look'd but they lov'd SHAK:AS 63
She should never have l. BROWNING:R 15
looker on: God and angels to be l.o. BACON:F[1] 10
looking:
advantages of l. at mankind BYR 255
Here's lookin' at you, kid BOGART:H 2
l. at you when my last TIB 1
l. one way, and rowing BUNYAN 12
love is not l. into one another's SAINT-EX 1
she was l. all the time THOMAS:D 27
somebody may be l. MENCK 5
would not be l. for me PASC 15
looking-glass:
and dreams their looking glass YEATS 120
cracked lookingglass of a servant JOYCE:J 12
since she did neglect her l. SHAK:TWO 13
looking-glasses: Women have served ... as l. WOOLF:V 10
looks:
her l. went everywhere BROWNING:R 21
Her l. were free COLERIDGE:ST 20
His l. do menace heaven MARLOWE 6
l. both ways before crossing PETER 3
l. commercing with the skies MILT 80
L. the whole world in the face LONGFEL 13
only books, Were woman's l. MOORE:T 15
side-long l. of love GOLDS 20
Stolen l. are nice in chapels HUNT:L 2
thy l. canst clear the darken'd MARLOWE 4
loom: she left the l. TENNY 21
looney: misfits, l. tunes and squalid REAG 4
loopholes: through l. Less than themselves TESS 1
lord:
Because you are a great l. BEAUMA 4
English l. should lightly BALL 30
Great l. of all things POPE 90
had been a L. among wits JOHNSON:S 97
L. High Everything Else GILB:WS 59
l. of the fowl and the brute COWP 46
L. of thy presence SHAK:KING J 1
l. on yon sea-side BALL 35
Lord:
Bless the L., all the works BIBLE 606
bless ye the L. PRAY 12
cometh in the name of the L. MASS 14
Dear L. and Father of mankind WHITTIER 7
Good L., deliver us PRAY 33
good L. will forgive me CATHERINE 1
Happy is the man who fears the L. BIBLE 601
help is in the Name of the L. PRAY 78
I am my L.'s DODDR 2
I never knew the L. at all BETJ 13
I replied, *My L.* HERB:G 42
Imagine the L. talking French DAY 1
L., art more than they TENNY 124
L. be with thee BIBLE 147
L. be with you MASS 2
L. began to wake PSALMS 2
L. bless thee, and keep BIBLE 114
L. have mercy on your soul CHAPLIN 1
L. is a man of war BIBLE 101
L. is great BIBLE 230
L. is in this place BIBLE 61
L. is my shepherd BIBLE 206
L. looketh on the heart BIBLE 146
L. loveth he chasteneth BIBLE 558
L. mighty in battle BIBLE 208
L. reigneth BIBLE 173
L. seeth not as man BIBLE 146
L. survives the rainbow LOWELL:R 4
L. was departed from him BIBLE 137
L. was not in the wind BIBLE 165
L. watch between me BIBLE 64
L. went before them BIBLE 100
L. will be there and wait WHITMAN 9
Love is our L.'s meaning JULIANA 2
names of those who love the L. HUNT:L 4
of the coming of the L. HOWE 1
one L. Jesus Christ PRAY 66
Praise the L., all nations BIBLE 603
remembrance of his dying L. SPENS 22
sole L. Of life and death CRASH 14
Suppose you saw the L. BAXTER:R 1
the L. bless you real good GRAHAM:B 1
The L. God made them all ALEX:CF 1
the L. is with thee ANON 160
unhouse and house the L. HOPK:GM 2
Unless the L. has built BIBLE 604
Lord Chancellor: made by the L.C. ... without JOHNSON:S 180
Lord Randal: L.R., my son? BALL 33
lords:
About the 'l. o' the creation' BURNS:R 55
For the l. who lay ye low? SHELLEY:PB 51
Great l. have pleasures MONTESQU 5
L. are Lordliest in thir wine MILT 295
l. of human kind pass by GOLDS 10
Scots l. at his feet BALL 51
To the L. of Convention SCOTT:W 67
lordships: l. on a hot summer afternoon ANON 246
Lorenzini: murmur goes round L.'s MURRAY:LA 2
lorikeet: I am Australia's l. KEV 1
lose:
l. and start again KIP 127
l. both seems like carelessness WILDE:O 87
l. her heart, or necklace POPE 45
l. it that do buy it SHAK:MERC 2
l. thee were to loose myself MILT 251
l. to-morrow and the ground won ARNOLD:M 26
l. what he never had WALT 12
nothing left to l. KRIS 1
still the strongest l. DRYD 16
time to l. BIBLE 281
way to l. him SHAK:ANT 15
loser:
Show me a good and gracious l. ROCKWE 1
Show me a good l. NEWM:P 1
losers:
all are l. CHAMBERLAIN:N 1
l. weepers PROV 118
losest: for fear thou l. all HERB:G 39
losing:
l. party never appears right BURKE:E 69
l. when I saw my self to win SHAK:SON 53
loss:
breathe a word about your l. KIP 127
deeper sense of l. GASK 6
l. they were afraid of AUD 3
night of l. is always there TENNY 161
losses: All l. are restor'd SHAK:SON 12
lost:
All is not l. MILT 115

all was l. MILT 247
better to have loved and l. TENNY 142, 168
he is almost l. that built it BROWNE:T 59
l. and gone forever MONTROSE 1
l. are like this HOPK:GM 28
l. evermore in the main TENNY 287
l., that is unsought CHAUC 107
More was l. there than life LUCAN 4
never l. till won CRAB 23
never to have l. at all BUTLER:S[2] 20
Not l. but gone before NORT 3
Nothing is l. that's wrought DAVIDS 2
Praising what is l. SHAK:ALL 10
recover what has been l. ELIOT:TS 99
see is l. consider to be l. CATUL 7

lot:
a l. was lethal SHARPE 3
better l., is unknown to anyone SOC 6

Lothario: That false L. ROWE 2
lotos: L. blows by every winding TENNY 31
lots: So they cast l. BIBLE 358
lottery: first prize in the l. of life RHODES 2
Lotus Sutra: faith in the L.S. is in winter NICHI 1
Lou: lady that's known as L. SERVICE 2
louder: l. he talked of his honor EMER 52
Louis: Son of Saint L., ascend FIRM 1
Louis XVI: L. for not resisting NAPO I 11
loungers: l. of the Empire are irresistibly DOYLE:AC 3
lounging: Lounjun 'roun' en suffer'n' HARRIS:JC 4

louse:
l. for the hangman JONS 1
l. in the locks of literature TENNY 299
precedency between a l. and a flea JOHNSON:S 235

lousy: It was kind of l. THURB 24
lout: Face of a country l. LAWS 5
louts: oafish l. remember Mum BETJ 24
Lovat, Lord: handsomest man that ever cut a throat* CHURCH:W 73

love:
acts Of kindness and of l. WORDS:W 4
against the reasons of my L. KEATS 162
all for l. and a little DIBDIN:C 6
all for the l. of you DAC 1
All is fair in l. and war PROV 9
All l. is sweet SHELLEY:PB 79
all made of sighs and tears* SHAK:AS 65
all the choir of L. YEATS 93
almost with a husband and wife l. LAWR:DH 42
'amo' I l. BROWNING:R 111
And all for l. SPENS 33
and L. the night DRYD 128
ape the magnanimity of l. MERED:G 17
are but Ministers of L. COLERIDGE:ST 50
be my l. MARLOWE 49
be wise and eke to l. SPENS 2
beautiful through l. SHELLEY:PB 85
beauty on my l. depends SHAK:SON 44
Because we freely l. MILT 216
been in l., or in hate STEVENSON:RL 5
beginning and the decline of l. LA BRU 8
believe in rheumatism and true l. EBNER 4
best l. affairs are those LIND:N 3
both so much in l. with *him* THOMAS:I 2
boy's l. SHAK:KING L 52
brief ... As woman's l. SHAK:HAM 115
brief is life but l. is long TENNY 111
but not for l. SHAK:AS 58
can't do l. and rhetoric STOP 4
can't live on l. alone TOLS:S 1
choose l. by another's eyes SHAK:MID 3
Common as light is l. SHELLEY:PB 79
could not l. thee (Dear) so much LOVELACE 7
course of true l. may be expected MARTIN 1
course of true l. never did SHAK:MID 2
crime to l. too well? POPE 57
cruel madness of l. TENNY 207
Deep as first l. TENNY 109
demand that men l. their neighbour BRECHT 8
didn't l. God, he just fancied ANON 192
difficult to l. mankind unless KINGSMILL 3
dost afflict those who l. thee TERESA of A. 1
doughterly loue and deer MORE:T 2
dream of human l. and truth TENNY 182
dry l. and barren longing? LAVIN 1
Dull sublunary lovers l. DONNE 69
Ends all our month-long l. BRIDGES:R 5
ever been in l., me boys PATTER 1
ever tire of l. or rhyme COPE 5
Every little girl knows about l. SAG 2
Except for l.'s sake only BROWNING:EB 11
excess of l. bewildered them YEATS 44
facile show of l. MURA 2
faith, howp, luve BIBLE 594
fallen in l. with a girl in a light CHEV:M 1
fallen was in l. dance JAMES I 3
feeling of falling in l. DORS 2
fell in l. with himself at first POWELL:A 1
fit L. for Gods MILT 245
flowers and fruits of l. BYR 241
fool of l. HAZL 31
for a good man's l. SHAK:AS 51
for ever wilt thou l. KEATS 92
Forgets the shows of l. SHAK:JUL 6
From too much l. of living SWIN 31
give up a long established l. CATUL 18
give up another person's l. LEWIS:W 1
go with the one I l. BRECHT 17
God is l. BIBLE 570
God is L., I dare say BUTLER:S[2] 32
God of l. my shepherd is HERB:G 47
Greater l. hath no man BIBLE 490
Hail wedded L. MILT 202
he best to l. is CHAUC 122
he was the Queen's luve BALL 13
help those we l. to escape HUGEL 1
hid in the heart of l. YEATS 8
his dark secret l. BLAKE:W 66
How do I l. thee? BROWNING:EB 13
how I fell in l. VIRGIL 15
How shall I know your true l. RALE 6
How should I your true l. know SHAK:HAM 158
how these Christians l. one another TERT 2
how they could l. ANON 11
hundred, pure l., for thee FERGUS 1
I am in l., you say CLOUGH 15
I am sick of l. BIBLE 294
I *do not l.* the man WATKYNS 1
I do not l. thee NORT 1
I hate all that don't l. me FARQ 4
I hate and I l. CATUL 19
I knew it was l. BYR 142
I l. all that thou lovest SHELLEY:PB 139
I l. not Man the less BYR 116
I l. thee true KEATS 83
I l. them all MELBOU 9
I l. you' on the back of the bill MARX:G 17
I perish for her l. CAMPION 2
I went to the Garden of L. BLAKE:W 71
I would like my l. to die BECKETT 14
I would L. infinitely BROWNING:R 3
idealize l. too much JOW 4
If I have freedom in my l. LOVELACE 5
if l. be blind SHAK:ROM 29
If l. were all COWARD 17
if she made wery fierce l. DICKENS 44
if they cannot but admit l. BACON:F[1] 79
If yet I have not all thy l. DONNE 49
I'm tired of L. BELLOC 34
important thing in the world is l. BREN 1
imprison the child ... by force of l. WHITE:P 4
in l., and in debt, and in drink BROME:A 1
In l. as in sport GRAVES:R 9
In l., one endures more NIET 20
in l. with all sorts of girls CHARLES:Prince 5
in l. with l. itself AUGUS 2
institution of the dear l. of comrades WHITMAN 25
is not L. a Hercules SHAK:LOV 16
King of L. my Shepherd is BAKER 1
knew thee but to l. thee HALLE 1
know whose l. would follow me KIP 42
lease of my l. control SHAK:SON 50
Leave me, O L. SIDNEY:P 1
leave to come unto my l.? SPENS 14
less we l. a woman PUSH 3
let brotherly l. continue BIBLE 559
let the warm L. in KEATS 89
Let those l. now ANON 174
let us also yield to l. VIRGIL 19
let us live and l. CATUL 5
let's fall in l. PORTER:C 1
little emptiness of l. BROOKE 23
little words of l. CARNEY 2
live with thee, and be thy l. RALE 1
Long live l. STERNE 45
look at was to l. TENNY 74
lost to L. and Truth KIP 53
L. a woman? You're an ass ROCHES 8
l. a womman that she woot CHAUC 107
L., all alike DONNE 60
l. all beauteous things BRIDGES:R 4
L. alters not with his SHAK:SON 52
l., an abject intercourse GOLDS 58
L. and a cottage COLMAN:G[1] 1
L. and do what you like AUGUS 11
l. and fame to nothingness KEATS 23
l. and good company FARQ 17
L. and I were well acquainted GILB:WS 4
L. and marriage CAHN 1
l. and murder will out CONG 19
L. and scandal are FIELDING 1
l. as a man but detest MARSH 1
l. as I have loved BYR 136
L., as it exists in society CHAMFORT 5
l. bade me welcome HERB:G 53
L. be controll'd by advice? GAY 13
l. ... become a relationship RILKE 4
L. built on beauty DONNE 3
l. but only her BYR 115
l. but you alone BALL 38
'l. by making a sin of it FRANCE 7
l. can do with a teined thread BURTON:Ro 21
L. ceases to be a pleasure BEHN 5
L. conquers all PROV 249
L. conquers all VIRGIL 19
l. Creation's final law TENNY 157
L., curiosity, freckles PARKER:D 3
l. demands some future CAMUS 6
l. exalts the mind DRYD 118
l. exists all right ANOU 3
l. first, and live incidentally FITZGER:Z 1
l., first learned in SHAK:LOV 16
l. flies out the window PROV 425
L. gilds the scene SHERIDAN:RB 17
L. goes toward l. SHAK:ROM 17
L. has no other desire GIBRAN 2
L. has pitched his mansion YEATS 95
L.! has she done this LYLY 4
l. he laugh'd to scorn SHAK:POET 9
l. her, is a liberal Education STEELE 5
l. him whom thou dost hate SHAK:SON 39
L., I l. thee not SHAK:HEN.IV[1] 33
L. in a Cold Climate MITFORD:N 4
L. in a hut KEATS 105
L. in desolation masked SHELLEY:PB 117
L. in friendship – never COLTON 7
L. in her sunny eyes COWLEY:A 1
L., in my bosom LODGE:T 1
L. in this part of the world BYR 253
L. is a boy BUTLER:S[1] 26
L. is a circle that doth HERR 8
L. is a greater law unto itself BOET 3
L. is a gretter lawe CHAUC 41
L. is a passion that hath friends HALIF 2
L. is a slave emotion STEAD 2
L. is a spirit all compact SHAK:POET 10
l. is a thing that can never PARKER:D 4
L. is always a bit deceitful GORKY 1
l. is better than wine BIBLE 292
L. is blind PROV 250
L. is blind SHAK:MERC 24
L. is denying BARNF 4
L. is enough MORRIS:W 7
L., ... is exactly like war STERNE 34
L. is friendship plus sex ELLIS:H 9
L. is God TOLS:L 2
l. is heaven and heaven is l. SCOTT:W 8
L. is just another dirty lie HEMINGWAY 6
L. is lame at fifty years HARDY:T 19
L. is like a dizziness HOGG 8
L. is like any other luxury TROLL 24
L. is like linen FLETCH:P 1
L. is like the measles JEROME:JK 2
L. is Lord of all the world SPENS 18
l. is lost HERB:G 7
l. is lost but upon God DUNB 14
l. is maister where he wile GOW 1
L. is mor than gold LYD 1
L. is moral even without legal KEY:E 4
l. is more cruel than lust SWIN 25
L. is not l. Which SHAK:SON 52

l. is not looking into one another's SAINT-EX 1
l. is not secure CHESTERTON 6
l. is of man's life a thing BYR 171
L. is of the valley TENNY 118
L. is our Lord's meaning JULIANA 2
l. is sweet for a day SWIN 35
L. is swift of foot HERB:G 49
l. is taught hypocrisy BYR 164
L. is the lesson which SPENS 9
L. is . . . the gift of oneself ANOU 2
L. is then our duty GAY 22
L. is what makes the world SYMONS 1
L. itself shall slumber SHELLEY:PB 143
L. laughs at locksmiths PROV 251
l. likes stratagem and subterfuge BROWNING:R 193
L., l., l. – all the wretched cant GREER 3
L. makes the world go round PROV 252
L. me, and never leave me MCCUAIG 1
L. me, l. my dog PROV 253
l. me little, so you l. me long HERR 18
l. me who have died for thee BROWNING:R 108
L. means never having SEGAL 1
L. means the pre-cognitive flow LAWR:DH 41
l. might take no end HERB:E 2
l. nothing in the world so well SHAK:MUCH 26
l. of beauty does not lead PERIC 2
l. of finished years ROSSET:C 4
l. of liberty is the l. HAZL 10
l. of life is necessary to the vigorous JOHNSON:S 2
l. of man is a weed STOW 2
L. of Pleasure, and the L. POPE 136
l. of power is the l. HAZL 10
l. one another or die AUD 44
l. oneself is the beginning WILDE:O 79
L. rules the court SCOTT:W 8
l. scene on a bearskin rug HUX:A 30
L. seeketh not Itself to please BLAKE:W 63
L. seeketh only Self to please BLAKE:W 64
L. set his fire in my hands BRENN 3
l. should act so inconsistent SMOL 4
l. slights it BACON:F[1] 51
L. so amazing, so divine WATTS 2
l., so much refin'd DONNE 69
L. sometimes would contemplate DONNE 51
L. sought is good SHAK:TWE 42
L. sounds the Alarms GAY 4
L. springs from blindness BUSSY 2
L. still has something of the Sea SEDLEY 4
l. takes wit away DIDE 2
l. that can be reckon'd SHAK:ANT 2
L. that dare not speak DOUGLAS:Alf 1
L., that had robbed us MERED:G 25
l. that loves a scarlet coat HOOD 5
l. that makes the world go round CARROLL 24
l. that moves the sun DANTE 19
L. that never told can be BLAKE:W 57
L. the Beloved Republic FORST 18
L. the brotherhood BIBLE 567
L., the human form divine BLAKE:W 17
l. the one who loves you VOLT 32
l. thee better after death BROWNING:EB 14
l. thee for a heart that's DAVIES:WH 4
l. this woman with the greatest brutality NEWBY 1
l. those whom they do not marry MARTIN 3
L., thou art absolute CRASH 14
l. thy neighbour BIBLE 113
l. thy neighbour as thyself BIBLE 422
L. thyself last SHAK:HEN.VIII 12
L. to be the object of l. FIELDING 33
l. to hatred turned CONG 34
l. to matrimony, in a moment AUSTEN 16
l. to the lips we are near MOORE:T 16
L. took my hand HERB:G 54
L. warps the mind a little CRAB 26
L.! was thought a crime BLAKE:W 77
l. we swore would last DAY LEWIS 4
l. which was more than l. POE 8
l. Wi' a scunner in't MACDIAR 19
l. will change in growing old BRIDGES:R 10
L. will find a way PROV 254
l. will yield to business OSB:J 8
L. with unconfined wings LOVELACE 3
L. without his wings BYR 1
L. wol nat been constreyned CHAUC 36
L. would prove so hard BRIDGES:R 11
L. you for yourself alone YEATS 91
L. your enemies BIBLE 387, 453
L. your neighbour, but don't PROV 255
L. your neighbour is not merely sound LLOYD GEO 8
l.'s a malady without DRYD 123
L.'s a man of warre HERB:G 49
L.'s but a frailty of the mind CONG 48
l.'s great artillery CRASH 4
L.'s like the measles JERROLD 3
L.'s mysteries in souls do grow DONNE 38
L.'s not l. When it's mingled SHAK:KING L 5
L.'s not so pure DONNE 51
L.'s not Time's fool SHAK:SON 52
L.'s passives are his activ'st CRASH 10
L.'s pleasure only lasts FLOR 1
l.'s sad satiety SHELLEY:PB 98
l.'s sorrow lasts FLOR 1
L.'s sweetest Part, Variety DONNE 45
l.'s the noblest frailty DRYD 3
L.'s tongue is in FLETCH:P 3
l.'s young dream MOORE:T 9
Luve is ane fervent fire SCOTT:A 1
Luve is patientfu BIBLE 594
Luve will venture in BURNS:R 102
lyric L. BROWNING:R 194
made l. to ten thousand women SIMEN 1
make l., hopefully, to all KEEN 2
make l. to you at five o'clock BANK 5
make not a bond of l. GIBRAN 3
making l. all the time BEAUMA 3
making l. is child's play MITFORD:N 1
man moot nedes l. CHAUC 42
mantrap of l. FRY:C 12
me and my true l. will never ANON 36
Men l. in haste BYR 228
mightie l. HERB:G 35
mind where people make l. CAMPBELL:Mrs P 3
mischievous devil L. is BUTLER:S[2] 32
money can't buy me l. LENNON 3
more like hatred than like friendship* LA ROCHE 10
more l. and knowledge of you SHAK:AS 7
more of l. than matrimony GOLDS 52
Music is the food of l. PROV 278
Must die for l. SHAK:ALL 2
must keep l. affairs quiet WINDSOR 1
Must not Trifle with L. MUSSET 6
My l. admits no qualifying SHAK:TRO 19
My l. has died for me to-day BALL 5
my l. is come to me ROSSET:C 2
My l. is of a birth so rare MARV 7
my l. is slain DONNE 15
my l. were in my arms ANON 114
My l.'s a noble madness DRYD 26
my luve's like a red, red, rose BURNS:R 113
naked name of l. SHAK:TWO 8
names of those who l. the Lord HUNT:L 4
Need we say it was not l. MILLAY 4
never doubt I l. SHAK:HAM 67
never yet the one true l. O'BRIEN:E 1
new l. may get WALSH 1
No l. like the first l. PROV 293
no l. lost between us GOLDS 75
no man dies for l. DRYD 31
none other I can l. TENNY 252
Nor l., nor pitty knew CAREW:T 9
not as l. is nowadays MALORY 9
not enough to make us l. SWIFT 14
not l. thee if I l. thee not HERB:G 22
Now I know what L. is VIRGIL 16
of a Hollywood director toward l. HALS:M 2
of herself she will not l. SUCK 1
off with the old l. ANON 27
office and affairs of l. SHAK:MUCH 6
often make l. but I never talk PROUST 7
One of l.'s April-fools CONG 4
Or bid me l. HERR 29
Or L. in a golden bowl? BLAKE:W 28
ounce of L. is worth a pound WESLEY:J 7
Our l. and toil KIP 116
our l. hath no decay DONNE 27
Our l. shall live SPENS 11
over shoes in l. SHAK:TWO 2
Pains of l. be sweeter DRYD 11
pangs of disappointed l. ROWE 4
Partly wi' l. o'ercome BURNS:R 24
passing the l. of women BIBLE 153
past making l. PRIOR 3
Perfect l. casteth out fear BIBLE 571
purple light of L. GRAY:T 33
putting L. away DICKIN:E 18
regain L. once possesst MILT 291
remembrance of my former l. SHAK:TWO 7
right true end of l. DONNE 17
Rites Mysterious of connubial L. MILT 201
said that some have died for l. WORDS:W 35
say a man has fallen in l. STERNE 30
secret sympathy* SCOTT:W 9
see now l. perfect too BROWNING:R 186
separate us from the l. of God BIBLE 514
shackles of an old l. TENNY 253
She bid me take l. easy YEATS 3
She never told her l. SHAK:TWE 31
sincerer than the l. of food SHAW 32
sinews of l. FARQ 1
so ill bred as to l. a husband? WYCH 2
So sweet l. seemed BRIDGES:R 10
So true a fool is l. SHAK:SON 22
soft interpreters of l. PRIOR 5
soul of her beauty and l. SHELLEY:PB 92
sports of l. JONS 18
spring of l. gushed COLERIDGE:ST 27
subject but eternal L. SHELLEY:PB 78
Such ever was l.'s way BROWNING:R 175
sweet eternity of l. HERR 8
Sweet L. of youth BRONTE:E 7
sweets and bitters of l. BYR 2
tell me the truth about l. AUD 26
temple gates unto my l. SPENS 13
tests of generous l. BURNS:R 127
That cordial drop* ROCHES 1
that dares l. attempt SHAK:ROM 12
that he excludeth L.? HERB:E 3
their death-mark'd l. SHAK:ROM 2
There shall be no l. lost JONS 6
They l. us for it TENNY 112
Thou blind fool, L. SHAK:SON 58
Thou doubtful pleasure* GRANVILLE 5
through our l. MALORY 10
Thy l. to me was wonderful BIBLE 153
'Till I the prince of l. beheld BLAKE:W 1
time to l. BIBLE 281
to be crossed in l. a little AUSTEN 22
To be wise and l. SHAK:TRO 12
To hell with l. HEMINGWAY 6
To know her was to l. her ROGERS:S 1
to l. and be loved by me POE 7
to l. and to cherish PRAY 84
To l., cherish, and to obey PRAY 85
To live is like l. BUTLER:S[2] 33
to manage l. BUTLER:S[1] 38
To see her is to l. her BURNS:R 103
to see her was to l. her BURNS:R 93
to speak what l. indites CLARE:J 14
to tell the laity our l. DONNE 69
To think of one's absent l. TROLL 11
Too late I came to l. you AUGUS 5
towards the wilder shores of l. BLANCH 1
true l. is a discipline YEATS 136
True l. never grows cold PROV 401
True l.'s the gift which God SCOTT:W 9
Try thinking of l. or something FRY:C 16
Turning mortal for thy l. SHAK:LOV 13
turns to thoughts of l. TENNY 70
'Twixt women's l. and men's DONNE 26
2 cures for l. COPE 8
two parties to a l. transaction THACK 3
unlucky in l. PROV 256
vanity and l.; these are their CHESTERFIELD 23
vegetable l. should grow MARV 30
very ecstasy of l. SHAK:HAM 62
walk, the Queen of L. VIRGIL 40
water cools not l. SHAK:SON 65
We have seen thee, O L. SWIN 16
We l. being in l. THACK 19
we may perfectly l. thee PRAY 63
What is commonly called l. FIELDING 24
What is l.? HALM 1
what is l.? RALE 4
What is l.? SHAK:TWE 19
What thing is l. for PEELE 3
What will survive of us is l. LARK 4
whatever that may mean* CHARLES:Prince 3
when I l. thee not SHAK:OTH 31
when l. and duty clash TENNY 104

When l. begins to sicken SHAK:JUL 66
When l., converted SHAK:SON 19
when l. for you died, I should BROOKE 3
When l. grows diseased ETH 2
when L. speaks SHAK:LOV 16
When my l. swears SHAK:SON 59
where there is no l. BACON:F[1] 66
who dare not say they l. SIDNEY:P 7
whom l. alas doth wring SURREY 2
Why do you l. me? POUND 9
with l. and wine at once oppressed DRYD 111
with l. from me to you LENNON 2
withstand L.'s shock GOGA 1
woman wakes to l. TENNY 246
women who have never had a l. affair LA ROCHE 11
Women who l. the same man BEERB 8
wonder and wild desire* BROWNING:R 194
world and l. were young RALE 1
worship romantic l. for the wrong HAZZ 1
wouldn't be too ladylike in l. HERB:AP 9
yet I l. her till I die ANON 97
You cannot call it l. SHAK:HAM 140
You made me l. you MCCARTHY:J[1] 1
your true l.'s coming SHAK:TWE 19
love call: l.c. of two pieces of sandpaper O'REILLY 1
love-cars: I watched for l. LOWELL:R 6
love-in-idleness: maidens call it l. SHAK:MID 18
love-knot: Plaiting a dark red l. NOY 3
love-light: l. in your eye BLACKWOOD 1
love-lyrics: write so many l. POUND 33
love-making: L. is such a non-verbal MCCULL 1
love-match: l. was the only thing for happiness EDGE 1
love-quarrels: L. oft in pleasing concord MILT 292
love-rhymes: Regent of l. SHAK:LOV 8
love-sick: Twenty l. maidens GILB:WS 28
loved:
ashamed of having l. one another LA ROCHE 9
Better lo'ed you'll never be HOGG 4
better to have l. and lost BUTLER:S[2] 20
better to have l. and lost TENNY 142, 168
Had we never lov'd BURNS:R 93
has caused manny a lady to be l. DUNNE 1
I saw and l. GIBBON:E 19
lov'd not wisely SHAK:OTH 70
l. her, then he left her ANON 38
l. him too much not to RACINE 1
l. well because he hated BROWNING:R 140
l. you without words PUSH 2
Might she have l. me? BROWNING:R 130
most lov'd, despis'd SHAK:KING L 6
never lov'd, has never liv'd GAY 9
never to have been l. CONG 39
no sooner look'd but they lov'd SHAK:AS 63
nor no man ever lov'd SHAK:SON 52
Once she had l. her fellow HARTL 3
pressed me to say why I l. him MONTAIGNE 7
quite l. by a girl whom he almost TROLL 20
She had been l. WOOLF:V 5
She lov'd me for the dangers SHAK:OTH 9
so l., yet so mistaken BROWNING:R 215
That I l. bodily YEATS 81
that lov'd not at first sight? SHAK:AS 53
that l. not at first sight? MARLOWE 47
This man l. *me* LANDOR 10
thou, and I Did, till we lov'd? DONNE 41
Thou hast not lov'd SHAK:AS 22
Twice or thrice had I l. DONNE 25
use him as though you l. him WALT 13
we l. in vain BYR 4
Weel l. by mony men BALL 29
who thought she l. me BECKETT 14
yesterday I l. LESSING:GE 2
lovelier: l. than the love of Jove MARLOWE 2
loveliest:
l. and best FITZGER:E 14
l. vision far KEATS 87
loveliness:
He is a portion of the l. SHELLEY:PB 124
l. that has long faded YEATS 18
there is a l. that burns HEWETT 3
thy l. fade as it will MOORE:T 3
who l. within Hath found DONNE 68
woman of so shining l. YEATS 19
years have stolen all her l. FAIRBURN 3
Lovell: Cat, the Rat, and L. COLLINGBO 1
lovely:
It's all been rather l. LE MES 2
l. and a fearful thing BYR 182
l. beyond any singing PATON 1
l. woman stoops to folly GOLDS 18
more l. and more temperate SHAK:SON 6
whatsoever things are l. BIBLE 542
wouldn't it be loverly? LERN 2
lover:
abhor, too, the roaming l. CALLIM 1
All mankind love a l. EMER 15
All the world loves a l. PROV 15
as true a l. As ever sigh'd SHAK:AS 21
easier to be a l. than a husband BALZ 12
give herself to her l. WILLIAMS:WC 10
give repentance to her l. GOLDS 18
injur'd L.'s Hell MILT 215
It was a l. and his lass SHAK:AS 67
Jesus, L. of my soul WESLEY:C 5
l. and killer are mingled DOUGLAS:K 2
l. looked like an eagle ANON 85
l. of the meadows and the woods WORDS:W 9
l., Sighing like furnace SHAK:AS 34
l. true for whom I pine WHITMAN 9
l. without indiscretion HARDY:T 55
my fause l. stole my rose BURNS:R 98
one was round her l. CAMPBELL:T 14
resolve the propositions of a l. SHAK:AS 42
satisfied with her l.'s mind TROLL 11
says to her eager l. CATUL 16
searching for a new l. CONNOLLY:C 11
she was a true l. MALORY 8
Such a constant l. SUCK 4
talk with some old l.'s ghost DONNE 50
truest l. of a sinful man MALORY 16
Who may deceive a l.? VIRGIL 58
lovers:
as I am all true l. are SHAK:TWE 25
awkwardness l. feel in being alone LA BRU 8
cannot reform a lady of many l. KIP 12
Dull sublunary l. love DONNE 69
had three thousand l. WEST:M 9
Hello, young l. HAMMER 4
Journeys end in l. meeting SHAK:TWE 19
l. cannot see SHAK:MERC 24
L.' hours be full eternity DONNE 48
L. lying two and two HOUSM 8
L.' quarrels are the renewal TEREN 3
L. remember everything OSB:J 16
l. see best in the dark DUTT 3
l.' souls descend T'affections DONNE 37
old l. are soundest WEBSTER:J 1
one makes l. as fast CONG 45
pair of star-cross'd l. SHAK:ROM 1
smiles at l.' perjuries OSB:J 6
These l. fled KEATS 77
Thy l. were all untrue DRYD 129
true l. run into strange capers SHAK:AS 23
Two l. walking PARNELL:A 1
two young l. lately wed TENNY 18
What need l. wish for more? SEDLEY 3
whether they were l. or not CERV 9
loves:
all she l. is love BYR 183
all the wings of the L. SWIN 34
As lines (so l.) oblique MARV 8
believe the baggage l. me CONG 3
Chang'd l. are but DONNE 31
Fierce warres and faithfull l. SPENS 20
Friends and l. we have none MASE 13
girl whom he almost l. TROLL 20
If country l. such sweet GREENE:R 1
Jesus l. me WARNER:A 1
l. and comforts should increase SHAK:OTH 22
L. but their oldest clothes DONNE 68
l. him still the better GOLDS 57
l. into corpses or wives SWIN 25
l. you more than you will know SIMON:P 2
man kills the thing he l. WILDE:O 113
no creature l. me SHAK:RIC.III 18
plurality of l. no crime DONNE 16
rarely that a man l. MACDIAR 26
She l. you, yeh LENNON 1
show a woman when he l. her BROWNING:R 141
taken in by what one l. MOLIERE 9
that a man swear he l. me SHAK:MUCH 1
that l. but knows not, reaps TENNY 145
that l. not his wife and children TAYL:Jer 4
truly l. on to the close MOORE:T 4
Two l. I have SHAK:SON 60
who l. most is the inferior MANN:T 1
lovest: What thou l. well remains POUND 34
loveth:
He made and l. all COLERIDGE:ST 38
He that l. not knoweth not God BIBLE 570
the Lord l. he chasteneth BIBLE 558
loving:
begin by l. their parents WILDE:O 62
despises a man for l. her STOD 1
end by l. himself COLERIDGE:ST 81
For l., and for saying so DONNE 65
for l. himself better than me? BACON:F[1] 97
I ain't had no lovin' NORWORTH 1
l. thee above all things PRAY 54
L. your neighbour as much CLEESE 1
machine for l. in MCGREG 1
most l. mere folly SHAK:AS 35
perfectly sore with l. her DICKENS 139
thanks for another day of l. GIBRAN 2
that of l. longest AUSTEN 69
we [whites] are turned to l. PATON 2
low:
I never stoop'd so l. DONNE 52
lovers of l. company BURKE:E 95
l. on whom assurance sits ELIOT:TS 45
Sweet and l. TENNY 105
That l. man seeks a little BROWNING:R 120
They feared the 'l.' WELLS:HG 2
too l. for envy COWLEY:A 13
wilt thou weep when I am l.? BYR 5
lower:
a little l. than the angels BIBLE 199
l. orders don't set us WILDE:O 80
lowly:
be lowlie wise MILT 231
better to be l. born SHAK:HEN.VIII 6
In l. pomp ride on MILM 1
sooner found in l. sheds MILT 28
loyalties:
impossible l. ARNOLD:M 56
l. which centre upon number one CHURCH:W 54
loyalty:
I want *l.* JOHNSON:LB 5
learned body wanted l. TRAPP 1
l. you had better buy STAPLES 1
Party l. brings the greatest LA BRU 5
room for but one l. ROOS:T 16
Lucasta:
L. that bright northern star LOVELACE 2
my L. might I crave LOVELACE 6
lucid: fool, full of l. intervals CERV 18
Lucifer:
for ever damned with L. MARLOWE 33
starred night Prince L. uprose MERED:G 33
That fitful, fiery L. YOUNG:AJ 2
luck:
all the day you'll have good l. PROV 340
believes in l. and sends his STEAD 1
far too much l. in it NAPO III 2
Has he l.? NAPO I 15
l. whether you believe in it BOHR 2
nae l. about the house ANON 102
watching his l. was his light-o'-love SERVICE 2
luckiest: l. people in the world MERRILL 1
lucky:
Australia is a l. country HORNE:DR 1
better to be born l. PROV 203
call him not happy but l. SOLON 2
just as l. to die WHITMAN 5
L. at cards, unlucky PROV 256
L. Jim AMIS:K 1
Third time l. PROV 388
we only have to be l. once ANON 251
lucrative: it's so l. to cheat CLOUGH 20
lucre: faith can impious l. hold? VIRGIL 55
Lucy: If L. should be dead WORDS:W 33
Luddite: giving this computer to the last L. OND 2
Ludlow:
I have been to L. fair HOUSM 29
L. come in for the fair HOUSM 13
lugger: forcing her on board the l. JOHNSTONE:Jon 1
Luke: L., the beloved physician BIBLE 544
lukewarm: Because thou art l. BIBLE 576

madness:
awful m. swept me VIRGIL 15
cruel m. of love TENNY 207
Great wits are sure to m. DRYD 38
in the end despondency and m. WORDS:W 84
Like m. is the glory SHAK:TIM 6
M. in great ones must not SHAK:HAM 105
M. need not be all breakdown LAING 5
m. of many POPE 182
M. supplies the arms VIRGIL 35
m. was not of the head BYR 36
m. wherein now he raves SHAK:HAM 69
Moche mirthe and no madnes SKEL:J 4
Money is our m. LAWR:DH 28
Moon-struck m. MILT 256
My love's a noble m. DRYD 26
no cure for this sort of m. SMITH:FE 2
noble mind is here o'erthrown* SHAK:HAM 104
that fine m. DRAYT 11
that way m. lies SHAK:KING L 41
Though this be m. SHAK:HAM 74
Thro' cells of m. TENNY 225
To define true m. SHAK:HAM 64
uproar is always akin to m. ALCU 1
work like m. in the brain COLERIDGE:ST 61
Madonna: vein o'er the M.'s breast BROWNING:R 42
madrigals:
melodious birds sing m. MARLOWE 50
namby-pamby m. of love GIFF 1
Maeonides: old M. the blind FLECKER 1
Mafia:
M. is rational BOCCA 2
successful member of the M. NOLAN 1
magazines: what it says in the women's m. GABOR 4
Magdalen:
fourteen months at M. College GIBBON:E 14
manufactures of the monks of M. GIBBON:E 15
maggot:
blown me full of m. ostentation SHAK:LOV 21
how to create a m. MONTAIGNE 17
m. must be born i' ELIOT:G 9
maggots:
M. half-form'd in rhyme POPE 158
m. in your brains FLETCH:J 10
magic:
dealer in m. and spells GILB:WS 5
mistook m. for medicine SZASZ 4
That old black m. MERCER 2
This rough m. SHAK:TEM 30
With m. in my eyes HARDY:T 3
magistrate: m. corruptible ROBES 2
magistrates: worst anarchists are the m. SHAW 81
Magna Carta: Bible under one arm and M.C. AUBREY 3
Magna Charter: M.C. was ... the cause of Democracy SELL 5
magnanimity:
ape the m. of love MERED:G 17
in victory, m. CHURCH:W 49
M. in politics is not seldom BURKE:E 43
you might curb your m. KEATS 167
magnanimous: m. at an inappropriate time TROT 7
magnate: but a business m. BERLU 1
magnetism: doubt as to animal m. COLERIDGE:ST 86
magnificent:
m., but it is not war BOSQ 1
more than m. – it's mediocre GORKY 16
magnify:
m. him for ever PRAY 14
soul doth m. the Lord BIBLE 607
worthily m. thy holy Name PRAY 63
Magnus: walls Of M. Martyr hold ELIOT:TS 49
magpie: big bellied m. legged KELLY:N 1
magpies:
m. call you Jack MCAULEY 3
wardle doodle The m. said GLOVER 1
Magus: M. Zoroaster SHELLEY:PB 66
Mahaffy: never quite forgave M. TYR 1
Mahomet:
M. must go to the mountain PROV 186
M. will go to the hill BACON:F[1] 41
maid:
be a m. in the living room HALL:Je 1
fair, but frozen m. GARRICK 5
going to, my pretty m.? NURS 84
I once was a m. BURNS:R 21
I'll die your m. SHAK:TEM 21
m. not vendible SHAK:MERC 7
M. of Athens, ere we BYR 20
She could not live a m. PEELE 4
There was a fair m. dwellin' BALL 3
Yonder a m. and her wight HARDY:T 30
maiden:
god pursuing, the m. hid SWIN 11
kissed the m. all forlorn NURS 73
Listen to a m.'s prayer SCOTT:W 40
m. gloriously false HORACE 41
m. passion for a maid TENNY 265
m. That is makeles ANON 26
m. virtue rudely strumpeted SHAK:SON 30
pursued a m. and clasped SHELLEY:PB 58
scanter of your m. presence SHAK:HAM 33
she lost her m. name ANON 38
simple m. in her flower TENNY 63
to the m. of bashful fifteen SHERIDAN:RB 24
undergo such m. pilgrimage SHAK:MID 1
What shall be the m.'s fate? SCOTT:W 4
you use a poor m. so? ANON 10
maidenhead: he rafte hire maydenhed CHAUC 87
maidens:
all the m. pretty COLMAN:G[2] 3
M. aspiring to godheads STOP 3
M., like moths, are ever caught BYR 56
Twenty love-sick m. GILB:WS 28
maids:
m. are May SHAK:AS 59
m. doe woe the Batchelors BROME:R 3
pretty m. all in a row NURS 40
seven m. with seven mops CARROLL 55
Three little m. from school GILB:WS 67
mail:
like a rusty m. SHAK:TRO 15
Night M. crossing the Border AUD 16
maimed: poor, and the m. BIBLE 461
main:
flooding in, the m. CLOUGH 11
lost evermore in the m. TENNY 287
rages like the troubled m. GAY 7
Maine: in M. things bend LOWELL:R 9
Maisie: Proud M. is in the wood SCOTT:W 57
maister: do not M. or Campbell me SCOTT:W 75
maisters: Nae man can sair two m. BIBLE 590
majestic: Majestick though in ruin MILT 158
majesties: hope Your M. sleep well CAMPBELL:G 3
majesty:
full of the M.: of thy Glory PRAY 8
health unto his M. ANON 15
Her M. is not a subject DISR:B 94
If Her M. stood for Parliament SPEIGHT 2
Infinite M. PRAY 9
M. is the head of the literary DISR:B 85
m. of human suffering VIGNY 5
m. Which living failed HARDY:T 7
sex to which Your M. belongs? RHODES 3
This earth of m. SHAK:RIC.II 17
Major: John M. was drowning, his whole ALLEN:D 4
major-general: model of a modern M. GILB:WS 24
majorities: Wisdom goes by m. MERED:G 2
majority:
big enough m. in any town? TWAIN 14
compact liberal m. IBS 9
God is always in the m. KNOX:J 3
indifferent and self-indulgent m. STEPHEN:FJ 1
joined the great m. PETRO 2
m. has the might IBS 8
m. is always the best repartee DISR:B 30
silent m. of Americans to stand up NIX 7
silent m. of my fellow Americans NIX 5
To her divine M. – Present DICKIN:E 10
majors: with scarlet M. at the Base SASS 4
make:
cannot m. him out at all BELLOC 7
does not usually m. anything PHELPS 1
m. that, which was nothing, All DONNE 70
Nothing can m. her SUCK 1
Scotsman on the m. BARRIE 12
white man knows how to m. SITTING 1
who made the Lamb m. thee? BLAKE:W 69
make-believe: it wouldn't be m. HARBU 2
make up: offend and m.u. at pleasure RICHARDSON:S 3
makeless: maiden That is makeles ANON 26
maker:
m. and the made WRIGHT:J 7
M. of heaven and earth PRAY 19
M. of his own Fortune STEELE 6
Scatter'd his M.'s image DRYD 34
makes:
all that m. a man TENNY 265
It is art that *m.* life JAMES:H 22
one pleases one m. more CONG 45
what we have been m. us ELIOT:G 38
making:
joy in the m. BRIDGES:R 4
m. things which he does not want HOPE:An 4
malady: love's a m. without DRYD 123
male:
especially the m. of the species LAWR:DH 34
M. and female created he BIBLE 7
male-driven m. disgrace CLARE:A 3
more deadly than the m. KIP 133
nail in the coffin of m. dominance FIGES 1
preserve one last m. thing LAWR:DH 15
males: six of them left ... and all m. BENNETT:Al 6
Malfi: I am Duchess of M. still WEBSTER:J 24
Malherbe: At last came M. BOIL 3
malice:
from envy, hatred, and m. PRAY 33
leaven of m. and wickedness PRAY 48
M. is of low stature HALIF 11
m. mingles with a little wit DRYD 87
m. never was his aim SWIFT 64
m., to breed causes JONS 21
With m. toward none LINC 13
malignity: motive hunting of motiveless m. COLERIDGE:ST 95
mallard: remembrance of the m. ANON 45
mallow: slimy m. waves her silky CRAB 2
Mallow: live the rakes of M. ANON 56
Malmesey: drowned in a barrel of M. FABY 3
malt:
gud m. and makis ill drink ANON 115
m. does more than Milton HOUSM 28
Malvern: May morwenyng on Maluerne LANGLAND 6
mama: m. of dada FAD 1
mamas: Last of the Red-Hot M. TUCK 3
mammal: man as the dominant m. BURNET 1
mammon:
Better authentic m. MACNEICE 7
cannot serve God and m. BIBLE 394
easy for the devil M. GONNE 1
M. led them on MILT 142
M. wins his way BYR 56
man:
all that makes a m. TENNY 265
Am I not a m. and a brother? WEDGWOOD 1
another m. within me BROWNE:T 5
Before you call him a m.? DYL 1
Behind every great m. is an exhausted FAIRBAIRN:S 1
Behold the m. BIBLE 613
better angel is a m. SHAK:SON 60
bold bad m. SHAK:HEN.VIII 5
boxty, you'll never get a m. ANON 57
brave bad m. CLAREN 5
detest that animal called m. SWIFT 79
Doe all things like a m. HERB:G 5
eight years with a strange m. IBS 4
Eustace is a m. no longer KINGSLEY:C 3
formed m. of the dust BIBLE 9
from pig to m., and from m. to pig ORWELL 21
Get a new m. SHAK:TEM 19
He was her m. ANON 11
I am a m. TEREN 5
I love not M. the less BYR 116
It's that m. again ITMA 1
Little m., little m. ELIZ I 16
Little M., What Now? FALL 1
lonesome m. on a rainy day FRANKLIN:B 31
make a m. a woman PEMB:2nd Earl 1
make a m. of her son ROWL:H 2
make m. in our image BIBLE 6
m. alone is, I believe, the creator GORKY 12
m. appears on earth for a little BEDE 1

m. as he is *not* to be LAMB:Ch 48
M. delights not me SHAK:HAM 80
m. for all seasons WHITTING 1
M. for the field and woman TENNY 113
m. he must go with a woman KIP 74
m. in the house WEST:M 6
m. is a dangerous creature ADAMS:A 1
M. is a lump DONNE 96
M. is . . . a mediocre creature MOLIERE 12
M. is a noble animal BROWNE:T 62
M. is a tool-making animal FRANKLIN:B 29
M. is a wolf to m. PLAU 1
M. is a woman CHESTERTON 32
M. is all symmetrie HERB:G 33
m. is and will always be a wild DARW:CG 1
m. is as God made him CERV 12
m. is as old as he's feeling COLLINS:Mor 1
m. is distinguished from all other ADDIS 27
M. is God's secret STEPHENS 3
M. is Heaven's masterpiece QUAR 9
m. is his own worst enemy PROV 103
M. is m.'s A.B.C. QUAR 10
M. is Nature's sole mistake GILB:WS 57
M. is not the enemy of M. PAINE 6
M. is one world, and hath Another HERB:G 35
m. . . . is *so* in the way GASK 1
M. is the hunter TENNY 112
M. is the master of things SWIN 49
M. is the measure of all things PROT 1
M. is what he eats FEU 1
m. of infinite-resource-and-sagacity KIP 20
m. of many thoughts BYR 122
m. perfect to the last detail HORACE 68
m. proposes, but God KEMP 8
M. proposes, God disposes PROV 262
m. remains Sceptreless, free SHELLEY:PB 84
m. shall have his mare SHAK:MID 35
m. the living sepulchre CLARE:J 7
M. to command and woman TENNY 113
m. to m. the world o'er BURNS:R 116
M. was formed for society BLACKS 1
m. who stood at the gate HASKINS 1
M. will go down into the pit BALF 1
m. with God is always KNOX:J 3
M. with the head and woman TENNY 113
m.'s the gowd for a' that BURNS:R 115
my only study, is m. BORR 2
not the m. I was HORACE 50
only repelled by m. INGE 7
outward semblance of a m. DICKENS 35
presumptuous m. CANN 1
She knows her m. DRYD 81
she was taken out of M. BIBLE 14
smiling, destructive m. LEE:N 3
So unto the m. is woman LONGFEL 22
social, friendly, honest m. BURNS:R 28
strain of m.'s bred out SHAK:TIM 3
substance of men which is m. SWIN 48
That say thou art a m. SHAK:TWE 6
that the m. I am may cease TENNY 211
they be M. and Wife together PRAY 88
this m. Is now become a god SHAK:JUL 8
This was a m. SHAK:JUL 88
Thou art the m. BIBLE 156
true study of m. is m. CHARR 1
WAS MADE M. MASS 10
we find a m. PASC 4
We know nothing of m. JUNG:Carl 9
whan God first maked m. CHAUC 64
What a piece of work is m. SHAK:HAM 80
What is m., that thou BIBLE 198
What m. has made of m. WORDS:W 13
What m. Knows anything of women? KENNELLY 2
when a m. should marry? BACON:F[1] 81
you'll be a M., my son KIP 128
young m. hid with me DICKENS 205
You're a better m. than I am KIP 58
man-at-arms: m. must now serve PEELE 2
man of war: Love's a man of warre HERB:G 49
manacles: mind-forg'd m. I hear BLAKE:W 74
management: British m. doesn't seem CHARLES:Prince 2
Mandalay: Come you back to M. KIP 59
mandarin: M. style . . . is beloved CONNOLLY:C 10
Manderley: dreamt I went to M. again DU MAU:D 1
mandoline: pleasant whining of a m. ELIOT:TS 48
mandrake:
Get with child a m. root DONNE 56
quiet m., rest DONNE 21
mane: whistling m. of every wind THOMP:F 10
manger:
In a m. for His bed ALEX:CF 4
not too cleanly, m.? CRASH 12
still lodge Him in the m. ANON 59
mangle: immense pecuniary M. DICKENS 199
mangrove: m. swamps where the python COWARD 21
Manhattan: like to walk around M. STOUT 2
manhood:
M. a struggle DISR:B 18
M.'s dark and tossing waves SHELLEY:PB 81
strife comes with m. SCOTT:W 50
manhoods: hold their m. cheap SHAK:HEN.V 40
maniac: m. scattering dust TENNY 148
manifesto: first powerful plain m. SPEND 1
mankind:
all m., *except an American* JOHNSON:S 202
difficult to love m. unless KINGSMILL 3
giant leap for m. ARMST:N 2
Ideal m. would abolish death LAWR:DH 13
M. are the asses BYR 137
proper study of M. POPE 89
What m. desires, and what JUV 4
manliness:
cult of cheeriness and m. ORWELL 10
silent m. of grief GOLDS 35
Manlius: when M. was consul HORACE 45
manly: m. part is to do EMER 48
manna:
his Tongue Dropd M. MILT 152
m. to the hungry soul NEWT:J 2
We loathe our m. DRYD 66
manned: when with one man mann'd DONNE 7
manner:
m. of his speech SHAK:ANT 24
m. rude and wild BELLOC 1
to the m. born SHAK:HAM 35
very good bedside m. PUNCH 22
manners:
All m. make a tincture POPE 109
As by his m. SPENS 43
beat bad m. out of her STEPHENS 4
English m. are far more frightening JARRELL 2
evil m. live in brass SHAK:HEN.VIII 18
Good m. are made up EMER 72
Japanese have perfected good m. THER 1
M. are especially the need WAUGH:E 31
M. maketh man PROV 261
M. maketh man WILLIAM of WYK 1
m. of a dancing master JOHNSON:S 98
m. of a Marquis with GILB:WS 85
no longer any m. COWARD 13
not men but m. FIELDING 13
people have good table m. MIKES 1
take their m. from the Ape BELLOC 2
we've no m. SHAW 19
What times! What m. CIC 8
mansion:
life to a large M. of Many KEATS 135
Love has pitched his m. YEATS 95
made his everlasting m. SHAK:TIM 13
m. house of liberty MILT 318
m. made of precious stones SUZ:DT 1
upon thy fading m. spend? SHAK:SON 61
mansions:
Father's house are many m. BIBLE 488
lasting m. of the dead CRAB 9
mantle:
morn, in russet m. clad SHAK:HAM 11
o're the dark her Silver M. MILT 198
twitch'd his M. blew MILT 60
Mantovano: I salute thee, M. TENNY 291
mantrap: m. of love FRY:C 12
manufacture: great m. of daily duty WILSON:W 7
manure:
It is its natural m. JEFFERSON 10
Scandal is the m. of democracy FO 1
manuscripts: M. don't burn BULG 3
many:
decidedly too m. of them WHIST 12
in favour of the m. ROOS:E 3
m. are called BIBLE 425
m. men, m. women, and JOHNSON:S 107
m. still must labour BYR 29
Ye are m. – they are few SHELLEY:PB 39
many-splendoured: miss the m. thing THOMP:F 14
Mao:
M. had created a moral wasteland JUNG:Chang 1
restless fight promoter* JUNG:Chang 1
map:
picture of a relief m. of Ireland ASTOR:N 2
Roll up that m. PITT:W[2] 3
Marathon:
gain force upon the plain of M. JOHNSON:S 40
M. looks on the sea BYR 193
marble:
dwelt in m. halls BUNN 1
found it brick and left it m. CAES:A 1
into flesh a m. face VIRGIL 72
made up of m. and mud HAWT 3
m. to retain BYR 133
Not m. nor the gilded SHAK:SON 21
Poets that lasting m. seek WALLER 5
this in m. BEAUMO 7
your dreary m. halls CALVER 10
marbles: Eyetalian m. in the City Hall CRAIG:MJ 1
Marcellus: you will be M. VIRGIL 73
march:
day's m. nearer home MONTGOM:J 2
dinna ye m. forward in order? SCOTT:W 59
long majestic M. POPE 145
M. in a slow procession FINCH 1
m. of intellect SOUTHEY 23
m. of mind has marched in PEAC 11
m. of the human mind BURKE:E 35
m. of the retreating world OWEN:W 13
m. on their stomachs, shouting SELL 9
mearbound to the m. of a landsmaul JOYCE:J 42
Men who m. away HARDY:T 27
three hours' m. to dinner HAZL 18
March:
droghte of M. hath perced CHAUC 1
in the mad M. days MASE 9
M. comes in like a lion PROV 267
M. winds and April showers PROV 268
sea-blue bird of M. TENNY 171
That highte M. CHAUC 64
marched: m. breast forward BROWNING:R 213
marches: Funeral m. to the grave LONGFEL 2
marching:
As we were m. through Georgia WORK 1
M. as to war BARING-G 2
M. to the Promised Land BARING-G 5
'Tis the people m. on MORRIS:W 8
mare:
brought him a Flanders m. HENRY VIII 2
lend me your grey m. BALL 64
man shall have his m. SHAK:MID 35
Remember Tam o' Shanter's m. BURNS:R 91
mares: Mackerel sky and m.' tails PROV 257
Margaret:
It is M. you mourn for HOPK:GM 17
merry Margarete, This midsomer SKEL:J 5
margin: through a meadow of m. SHERIDAN:RB 19
Marie: I am M. of Roumania PARKER:D 4
Marie Hamilton: M.H.'s to the kirk gane BALL 41
Maries: Yestreen the Queen had four M. BALL 43
marigold: m., that goes to bed SHAK:WIN 19
marijuana: curlicues of m. in his hair LOWELL:R 5
mariner:
It is an ancient M. COLERIDGE:ST 10
m. with the gentleman DRAKE 3
mariners: Ye M. of England CAMPBELL:T 7
mark:
hundred m. is a long one SHAK:HEN.IV[2] 20
If you would hit the m. LONGFEL 35
it is an ever-fixed m. SHAK:SON 52
Lord set a m. upon Cain BIBLE 30
Mark Antony: Who lost M.A. the world? OTWAY 3
marked:
Like Cain, I am m. HALL:Rad 1
m. him for his own WALT 16

market:
don't go to m. with ingots CHAMFORT 4
for the m., not for the bazaar YELT 1
Send a fool to the m. PROV 344
market-gardener: sure to marry a m. DICKENS 95
Market Harborough: in M.H. Where ought I CHESTERTON 57
markets:
great m. by the sea FLECKER 3
great new m. out of nothing ENGELS 1
laws of m. and fashion ALBERT 1
marking: malady of not m. SHAK:HEN.IV[2] 8
marks:
bears the m. of the last person HAIG:D 1
m. and scars I carry with me BUNYAN 32
M. of weakness, m. of woe BLAKE:W 74
marksmen: of the best m. VOLT 9
marl: Over the burning Marle MILT 124
Marlborough: From Marlb'rough's eyes JOHNSON:S 69
Marlowe:
M.'s mighty line JONS 40
Neat M. bathed DRAYT 11
marmalade:
m. skies LENNON 7
never heard of m. KENNELLY 4
Oxford gave the world m. ANON 230
Marmion: last words of M. SCOTT:W 30
marmoset: Tulia's ape a marmasyte ANON 69
marquis:
Abducted by a French *M.* GRAHAM:H 5
manners of a M. with GILB:WS 85
marred: married is a man that's m. SHAK:ALL 7
marriage:
be incontinent before m. SHAK:AS 63
Before m. a man will lie awake ROWL:H 5
Books and m. do not go well MOLIERE 31
Courtship to m., as a very witty CONG 13
drawback of m. is that it makes WILDE:O 31
frighten her into m. JOHNSTONE:Jon 1
furnish forth the m. tables SHAK:HAM 24
hanging prevents a bad m. SHAK:TWE 7
Happiness in m. is entirely AUSTEN 15
if m. does nobody much good WEST:R 11
if you think there is any in m. GAY 26
In m., a man becomes slack STEVENSON:RL 4
Is not m. an open question EMER 44
isn't that a definition of m.? BRADB 5
it is a field of battle* STEVENSON:RL 10
It resembles a pair of shears* SMITH:Syd[1] 28
Let it be rather a moving sea* GIBRAN 3
long monotony of m.? GIBBONS:S 4
Love and m. CAHN 1
M., Agnes, is not a joke MOLIERE 4
m. and death and division SWIN 25
m. depends on the first night BALZ 2
m. has been made in heaven SAKI 16
M. has many pains JOHNSON:S 24
m. in the vulgar, weak sense BRONTE:C 6
M. is a framework to preserve DAVIES:R 6
M. is a step so grave STEVENSON:RL 8
M. is an insult MURRAY:J 1
M. is ... excluded from heaven BUTLER:S[2] 44
m. is immoral without love KEY:E 4
m. is not a house or even ATWOOD 1
M. is nothing but a civil SELD 7
M. is popular because SHAW 55
m. is really a nonstop conversation WYLIE 1
M. is the greatest earthly happiness DISR:B 50
M. is the only adventure VOLT 38
M. is the result of the longing CAMPBELL:Mrs P 2
M. is the waste-paper basket WEBB:S 2
m. makes man and wife CONG 17
M. may often be a stormy lake PEAC 3
M., which is necessarily overt DUBY 1
m. with his brother's wife SHAK:HEN.VIII 4
m. without love FRANKLIN:B 4
more for a m. than a ministry BAGE 13
most happy m. I can picture COLERIDGE:ST 98
one way to have a happy m. EASTWOOD 1
rob a lady ... by way of m. FIELDING 28
So that is m. WOOLF:V 6
sweet birds' m. hymns ELIOT:G 46
termed a *left-handed* m. WOLLST 7
to live in a state of m. that we JOHNSON:S 151
to the m. of true minds SHAK:SON 52
twenty years of m. make her WILDE:O 56
two to make a m. a success SAMUEL 5
Was m. ever out of fashion? BUTLER:S[1] 30
we will have no more m. SHAK:HAM 103
with dirge in m. SHAK:HAM 12
wo that is in mariage CHAUC 76
woman dictates before m. ELIOT:G 30
Women at m. move BERNARD:Jes 1
wonderful construct which is m. WELD 1
won't be a stylish m. DAC 1
marriage-bed: This Grave's the second M. CRASH 6
marriage-procession: fall in with the m.? CLOUGH 16
marriages:
early m. of silly children MARTIN 2
give a bust of m. BYR 184
good m., but no delightful LA ROCHE 18
loudly against second m. FIELDING 34
M. are made in heaven PROV 269
M. would in general be as happy JOHNSON:S 180
not against hasty m. COLLINS:Wilk 1
taste for m. and public executions DISR:B 43
unhappy m. come from husbands WODE 8
why so few m. are happy SWIFT 18
married:
as if we had been m. a great while CONG 53
At leisure marry'd CONG 11
be m. Without a wife? NURS 37
Being m. six times shows MAIL 3
complains of in the m. state HUME 7
countenance of a new-m. couple LAMB:Ch 1
cut his throat before he marry'd SWIFT 57
defined by whether I am m. FOLL 1
delight we m. people have PEPYS 16
devotion of a m. woman WILDE:O 50
don't sleep with happily m. men EKL 2
Every night of her m. life THOMAS:D 26
feelings till after they are m. WILDE:O 53
for a wench who is just m. GAY 15
happy people are m. women MENCK 20
Happy Though M. HARDY:EJ 1
He is dreadfully m. WARD:A 11
I have m. a wife BIBLE 460
I m. beneath me ASTOR:N 1
if ever we had been m.? GAY 12
I'm getting m. in the morning LERN 5
I'm to be m. to-day GILB:WS 40
incomplete until he has m. GABOR 3
kiss before they are m. SHAK:HEN.V 48
learn what it is I'll get m. again EASTWOOD 1
M. a Wife he finds out BLAKE:W 93
m. and brought up a large GOLDS 49
m. before three and twenty AUSTEN 23
m., charming, chaste BYR 161
m. in an afternoon as she SHAK:TAM 13
m. is a man that marr'd SHAK:ALL 7
m. life is the fights WILDER:T 3
m. life three is company WILDE:O 85
m. pair whose dream is o'er PARNELL:A 1
m. past redemption DRYD 18
m. the man all tattered NURS 73
m., there is nothing left STEVENSON:RL 12
m. to a single life CRASH 2
m. to a stupid but exquisitely HALS:M 3
M. women are kept women SMITH:LP 6
Marry'd in haste CONG 11
Mocks m. men SHAK:LOV 24
mostly m. people CLOUGH 25
never m., and that's his hell BURTON:Ro 12
no taste when you m. me SHERIDAN:RB 20
one fool ... in every m. FIELDING 35
playing it like m. men TOSC 3
Reader, I m. him BRONTE:C 4
she has m. a sot POUND 8
Some were m., which was bad KIP 13
thankfu' ye're no m. to her BRAX 1
thankful for not having m. MARTIN 5
that are going to be m. GOLDS 64
to be m. to a Poem KEATS 157
Trade Unionism of the m.? SHAW 45
we will be m. a Sunday SHAK:TAM 9
Wen you're a m. man[en]Samivel DICKENS 24
When m. people don't get on MAUGH 8
woman is m. before she well MARTIN 2
woman's business to get m. SHAW 36
marries:
much signify whom one m. ROGERS:S 6
When a man m., dies SHELLEY:PB 63
who either m. or dies, is sure AUSTEN 46
marrow: Spending his manly m. SHAK:ALL 6
marry:
about to m. – 'Don't' PUNCH 1
as easy to m. a rich woman THACK 15
away to m. LEIGH 1
become the men we wanted to m. STEINEM 3
better to m. than to burn BIBLE 520
every woman should m. DISR:B 40
happened to m. the Queen of England STRACH 4
if you do *not* m. Mr Collins AUSTEN 19
m. a man out of pity ASQU:M 2
m. him to a puppet SHAK:TAM 3
M. in haste PROV 270
M. in Lent, and you'll PROV 271
M. in May, rue for aye PROV 272
m. thee, purely to be rid CONG 12
m. those whom they do not love MARTIN 3
m. with his brother SHAK:HAM 137
may m. *whom she likes* THACK 1
neither m., nor are given SWIFT 16
Never you m. A farmer's boy MCCUAIG 2
nill you, I will m. you SHAK:TAM 8
no woman should m. a teetotaller STEVENSON:RL 9
not to m. ladies in very high positions AMIN 1
poor rush to m. STEAD 3
prepared to m. again GILB 44
see what some girls m. ROWL:H 1
Those who m. God GREENE:G 12
To m. is to domesticate STEVENSON:RL 12
when a man should m.? BACON:F[1] 81
while ye may, goe m. HERR 27
why they m. them LONGFEL 37
You can just m. her FRENCH 1
You will m. a boy I choose SETH 1
marrying:
advantage about m. a princess CHARLES:Prince 7
keep people from m. Protestants GALLANT 1
married young and kept on m. WODE 28
M. a punk SHAK:MEA 41
M. off your daughter is a piece SAIK 1
not by nature the m. sort? MONTEF 1
they aren't the m. brand KIP 74
Mars:
M. is braw in crammasy MACDIAR 2
Next July we collide with M.? PORTER:C 7
Marsala: drinks a good deal of M. LEAR 5
marshal: m.'s baton in his knapsack NAPO I 8
martial:
m. airs of England WEBSTER:D 4
Sonorous mettal blowing M. MILT 131
Martin Place: fellow crying in M.P. MURRAY:LA 2
martini:
into a dry m. BENCH 1
into a dry m. WOOLL 3
martlet:
like the m., Builds SHAK:MERC 29
temple-haunting m., does SHAK:MAC 22
martyr:
bitter groan of a M.s woe BLAKE:W 115
deye a m., go to hevene CHAUC 115
I am the M. of the People CHARLES I 4
I'm a m. to music THOMAS:D 32
pale m. in his shirt of fire SMITH:Alex 1
martyrdom:
it were a m. to live BROWNE:T 52
M. is the test JOHNSON:S 213
m. must run its course AUD 15
not the gift of m. DRYD 85
martyrs:
about the graves of the m. STEVENSON:RL 69
noble army of M. PRAY 8
stones and clouts make m. BROWNE:T 50
marvellous:
has done m. things BIBLE 599
propensity of mankind towards the m. HUME 10
Marx:
M. been Groucho instead of BERLIN:Ir 3
M. in the saddle-bag BETJ 9
Marxian: M. socialism must always remain KEYN 2

Marxism:
M. exists in 19th-century thought FOUCA 1
M. is above all a method TROT 9
Marxist: takes a trained M. to appreciate THER 3
Mary:
born of the Virgin M. ANON 5
Hail M. ANON 160
M. had a little lamb NURS 39
M., M., quite contrary NURS 40
M. was that Mother mild ALEX:CF 4
My M.'s asleep BURNS:R 72
Philip and M. on a shilling BUTLER:S[1] 29
sweet Highland M. BURNS:R 101
Mary Ambree: foremost in battle was M.A. BALL 37
mary-buds: winking M. begin SHAK:CYM 4
Mary Jane: *What* is the matter with M.J.? MILNE 7
Mary Queen of Scots: The daughter of debate* ELIZ I 13
Maryland: Green-walled by the hills of M. WHITTIER 3
Marylebone: hanging garments of M. JOYCE:J 32
masculine:
adoption of the m. role GREER 6
makes me feel m. to tell you HELLMAN 3
m. values that prevail WOOLF:V 8
With Spirits M. MILT 254
mask:
He had a m. like Castlereagh SHELLEY:PB 37
his m. in disappointment YEATS 132
loathsome m. has fallen SHELLEY:PB 84
m., and antique Pageantry MILT 74
m. from the face of the Pharisee BRONTE:C 3
m. of some other self YEATS 136
No m. like open truth CONG 20
sometimes hath need of a m. PROV 200
masks: ship our m. in case of gas KIP 147
masons: singing m. building roofs SHAK:HEN.V 7
mass:
blessed mutter of the m. BROWNING:R 44
ill-formed and unordered m. OSB:J 17
mingles with the mighty m. VIRGIL 71
Paris is well worth a m. HENRI 4
two thousand years of m. HARDY:T 46
masses:
back the m. against the classes GLAD 5
huddled m. yearning to LAZ 1
obedience of enormous m. BAGE 9
mast: m. burst open with a rose FLECKER 10
master:
be The m. of himself MASSIN 3
from mad and savage m. SOPH 7
Has a new m. SHAK:TEM 19
I am the m. of my fate HENL 2
manners of a dancing m. JOHNSON:S 98
m. is first seen in self-limitation GOET 10
m. of his passions is Reason's CONNOLLY:C 19
m. of none PROV 216
m. on his spar-strewn deck ARNOLD:M 15
m.'s lost his fiddling stick NURS 6
only The M. shall praise us KIP 89
Sworn to no m. HORACE 74
that man is my m. GEO:H 1
to become the m., the politician DE GAU 10
which I would fain call m. SHAK:KING L 11
With her great M. so to sympathize MILT 5
masterpiece:
m. of nature EMER 18
Man is Heaven's m. QUAR 9
masters:
are m. of their fates SHAK:JUL 11
Assistant m. came and went WAUGH:E 30
both ill m. be GREV 3
By studying the m. ABEL 1
for the ease of the m. SMITH:Ad 8
good servants, but bad m. L'EST 1
m. to their females SHAK:COM 1
m. willingly concede to slaves CAMUS 11
No man can serve two m. BIBLE 394
Old M.: how well they understood AUD 14
prevail on our future m. to LOWE 1
show themselves m. of their own persons PERIC 3
'The m.' have been abolished NIET 1
their Victory but new M. HALIF 5
We are the m. at the moment SHAWC 1
masturbation:
don't knock m. ALLEN:W 11
M: the primary sexual SZASZ 3
m. of war RAE 1
match:
made 'em to m. the men ELIOT:G 13
spurt of a lighted m. BROWNING:R 58
To m. another foe CAMPBELL:T 7
matches:
boxes of m. and our necklaces MANDELA:W 1
have to have a box of m. DOUGLAS-H:A 1
mate:
bold m. of Henry Morgan MASE 8
great artificer Made my m. STEVENSON:RL 67
lady's ta'en anither m. BALL 59
m. once and then kill him WAX 1
met the eyes of a m. over the top CLARK:M 2
oddy knocky seeing like a m. BURGESS:A 1
walk'd without a m. MARV 21
Who shall be the maiden's m.? SCOTT:W 4
mated: thou art m. with a clown TENNY 72
material: stop seeking new m. WALLACE:E 2
materialism: sink in the mire of m. MOLTKE 1
materialistic: only really m. people MCCARTHY:M 2
maternal: I am not particularly m. ANNE 4
mateship: M. is an informal male-bonding DIXS 1
mathematics:
How are you at M.? MILLIG 6
ignorant of m. enter here PLATO 16
laws of m. refer to reality EINS 15
M. may be defined RUSS:B 3
M., rightly viewed RUSS:B 2
mystical m. of the city BROWNE:T 46
pregnancy by a resort to m. MENCK 7
pure m. consists entirely RUSS:B 4
Matilda:
M. told such Dreadful Lies BELLOC 21
Waltzing M. PATERSON:AB 3
matinée: theatre m. – may he rot WELLES 3
mating: Only in the m. season MILLIG 3
matrimony:
any one much improved by m. BYR 244
barrier against M. KEATS 144
critical period in m. is HERB:AP 15
first experience with m. DUNC 4
in the holy estate of M.? PRAY 83
love to m., in a moment AUSTEN 16
M., as the origin of change AUSTEN 38
m. I never give any advice CHESTERFIELD 28
m. to begin with a little aversion SHERIDAN:RB 5
more of love than m. GOLDS 52
take m. at its lowest STEVENSON:RL 6
woman in holy M. PRAY 80
matron: m.'s glance that would GOLDS 20
matter:
Does it m.? SASS 6
few things m. at all BALF 8
gravell'd for lack of m. SHAK:AS 57
M. . . . a convenient formula RUSS:B 8
Much m. decocted FULLER:T[1] 10
speculations upon m. are voluntary JOHNSON:S 53
sum of m. remains exactly BACON:F[1] 3
triumph of m. over mind WILDE:O 30
'twas no m. what he said BYR 220
what can the m. be? NURS 44
What is M.? – Never mind PUNCH 7
What is the m. with Mary Jane? MILNE 7
wretched m. and lame Meeter MILT 104
mattering: go on m. once it has stopped BOWEN:El 6
matters:
Between what m. and what seems BENTLEY:EC 10
What can I do that m.? SPEND 9
Matthew:
M., Mark, Luke, and John ADY 1
M., Mark, Luke and John ANON 81
maturing: think my mind is m. late NASH 19
matzo: another part of the m. you can eat? MONROE:M 3
Maud:
Come into the garden, M. TENNY 215
M. was my hateful nurse BETJ 34
Maud Gonne: M.G. at Howth Station YEATS 106
maunder: Let her m. and mumble CARLYLE:T 68
mausoleums: designing m. for his enemies LINK 1
mawkishness: thence proceeds m. KEATS 133
maxim:
m. is often a brilliant error MALES 1
m. to become a general law KANT 2
useless as a general m. MACAULAY:TB 13
Maxim gun: we have got The M.G. BELLOC 11
maxims: with a little hoard of m. TENNY 77
may:
moonlight-coloured m. SHELLEY:PB 90
what a lawyer tells me I *m.* do BURKE:E 33
May:
bring forth M. flowers PROV 268
cast a clout till M. be out PROV 282
darling buds of M. SHAK:SON 6
fayr as is the rose in M. CHAUC 98
fressh as is the month of M. CHAUC 5
fruit and flourish in M. MALORY 7
gathering nuts in M. ANON 17
In depraved M. ELIOT:TS 22
in the merry month of M. BALL 3
In the merry month of M. BRET 2
Is the merry month of M. BALL 45
leads with her The Flowry M. MILT 91
Marry in M., rue for aye PROV 272
M. month flaps its glad HARDY:T 33
M. morwenyng on Maluerne LANGLAND 6
mid-M.'s eldest child KEATS 93
spring M. flowers TUSS 1
sweet than M. day morn MACNALL 1
there's an end of M. HOUSM 31
weel-far'd M. BALL 29
world is white in M. TENNY 237
maybe: definite m. GOLDWYN 10
maying: let's goe a M. HERR 24
mayor:
m. of Birmingham in an off-year LLOYD GEO 15
M. was dumb BROWNING:R 31
maypole:
away to the M. hie ANON 9
organ and the m. JORD 1
maze: Life is a m. in which CONNOLLY:C 13
mazes:
in wandring m. lost MILT 163
voice through m. running MILT 75
me:
because it was m. MONTAIGNE 7
He certainly never was m. MANDELS 1
This is on m. PARKER:D 20
What's in it for m.? DE VR 7
with love from m. to you LENNON 2
meadow: painted m. ADDIS 35
meadow-sweet: simplest growth of m. or sorrel SWIN 50
meadows:
enamelled m., with filigree WALP:H 4
lover of the m. and the woods WORDS:W 9
m. have drunk their fill VIRGIL 10
M. trim with Daisies pied MILT 71
no more by-path m. STEVENSON:RL 11
meal:
handful of m. in a barrel BIBLE 162
make a square m. for a borer SEMP 3
no man gets a full m. JOHNSON:S 170
meals:
great m. of beef and iron SHAK:HEN.V 24
lessen thy m. FRANKLIN:B 3
m. can . . . be cooked with the sole DAVID 2
m. require ingenious organization DAVID 1
mother needed a fourth at m. LILL 1
mean:
at least I m. what I say CARROLL 16
depends on what you m. by JOAD 4
Don't m. nothing itself STEINB 2
Down these m. streets CHAND 5
ever I do a m. action STERNE 44
Happy the golden m. MASSIN 7
I m. this most sincerely GREEN:H 1
m. man is always full of CONF 6
nothing common did or m. MARV 2
people take them to m. VALERY 1
to be seated in the m. SHAK:MERC 11
too m. even for man THACK 20
virtuous person with a m. mind BAGE 24
what does it m.? AUD 56

whatever that may m. CHARLES:Prince 3
who meanly admires m. things THACK 12
Whosoever loves the golden m. HORACE 22
meander: slow M.'s margent green MILT 26
meandering: m. with a mazy motion COLERIDGE:ST 63
meaner: m. things are within her reach ELIOT:G 27
meaning:
author to get at *his* m. RUSKIN 18
belief that words have a m. OGDEN 1
charged with m. to the utmost POUND 42
hidden m. – like 'Basingstoke' GILB:WS 93
Love is our Lord's m. JULIANA 2
m.'s press and screw COLERIDGE:ST 64
thing about a joke with a double m. BARKER:R 1
To find its m. is my meat BROWNING:R 116
meanings:
two m. packed up into one word CARROLL 69
Where the M. are DICKIN:E 4
wrestle With words and m. ELIOT:TS 93
means:
best ends by the best m. HUTCHES 1
end justifies the m. BUSEN 1
in persons of small m. ELIOT:G 3
Increased m. and increased leisure DISR:B 73
it m. just what I choose CARROLL 67
live within our m., even WARD:A 13
living beyond our m. MEAD 1
make it by any m. HORACE 78
m. of rising in the world JOHNSON:S 172
m. they have used to obtain LA ROCHE 21
m. which lies within his power KANT 4
never merely as a m. KANT 6
Private M. is dead SMITH:Ste 3
meant:
m. well, tried a little STEVENSON:RL 43
more is m. than meets the ear MILT 87
mearbound: m. to the march of a landsmaul JOYCE:J 42
measles:
Love is like the m. JEROME:JK 2
Love's like the m. JERROLD 3
measels, and if so how many? WARD:A 5
measure:
man is the m. of all things PROT 1
M. still for M. SHAK:MEA 39
There is m. in all things HORACE 63
To lead but one m. SCOTT:W 21
Wielder of the stateliest m. TENNY 291
you must move in m. ELIOT:TS 105
measured:
m. it from side to side WORDS:W 19
not auditioned – just m. THOMAS:I 3
measurement: m. began our might YEATS 122
measures:
in short m., life may JONS 48
standardization of weights and m. NAPO I 3
Who m. right DAVIDS 4
measuring: Aeonian music m. out TENNY 172
meat:
appointed to buy the m. SELD 4
deliver m. to a woman who BENNETT:Al 5
dined upon cold m. PEPYS 18
eaters of m. in general ROUSS:E 1
its meaning is my m. and drink BROWNING:R 116
little m. best fits HERR 37
little of solid m. for men DRYD 144
loves the m. in his youth SHAK:MUCH 15
m. doth this our Caesar feed SHAK:JUL 12
m. in the hall STEVENSON:RL 59
much m. in God's storehouse PROV 372
not eat but little m. ANON 21
of the eater came forth m. BIBLE 134
One man's m. LUCRET 10
One man's m. is another PROV 312
serve for m. and fee BALL 28
snewed in his hous of mete CHAUC 22
Some hae m. and cannot eat BURNS:R 78
tearing his m. like a tiger MACAULAY:TB 12
meat-fly: Thackeray settled like a m. RUSKIN 29
Mecca:
not M. It just smells like it SIMON:N 1
some to Meccah turn FLECKER 13
mechanical: Being m., you ought not SHAK:JUL 1
medals: no more bloody m. MARY QUEEN CON 4
meddle:
m. and muddle DERB 2
Wha daur m. wi' me ANON 220
meddling:
enough of m. YEATS 48
m. too much in my private life WILLIAMS:T 7
Medes: given to the M. and Persians BIBLE 352
media:
get rid of all the m. BJEL:J 1
m. It sounds like STOP 13
medicine:
Comedy is m. GRIFFITHS 1
Grief is itself a med'cine COWP 21
Laughter is the best m. PROV 228
med'cine the less SHAK:CYM 15
M. for the soul DIOD 1
M. is my lawful wife CHEK 14
m. thee to that sweet sleep SHAK:OTH 41
m. worse than the malady FLETCH:J 15
mistake m. for magic SZASZ 4
no other m. But only hope SHAK:MEA 18
practise m. using a completely MOLIERE 18
Medicine Hat: plumed war-bonnet of M.H. BENET 1
medicines:
med'cines of our great revenge SHAK:MAC 97
m. to make me love him SHAK:HEN.IV[1] 27
worthlessness of the most m. FRANKLIN:B 2
mediocre:
man is . . . a m. creature MOLIERE 12
more than magnificent – it's m. GORKY 16
Some men are born m. HELLER 5
women want m. men MEAD 2
mediocrities: this Cabinet of M. DISR:B 13
mediocrity:
m. is the apparatus that Stalin TROT 1
M. knows nothing higher DOYLE:AC 30
real m. of her circumstances SMITH:Ad 14
welcomes Pretentious M. BRIDIE 2
meditate: m. on thee in the night BIBLE 219
meditation:
cat in profound m. ELIOT:TS 86
disposed to abstracted m. JOHNSON:S 46
let us all to m. SHAK:HEN.VI[2] 5
Some happy tone Of m. WORDS:W 137
Mediterranean:
bagful of blue M. VAN DER P. 3
had ever taken from the M. SHAFF 1
summer dreams The blue M. SHELLEY:PB 42
to see the shores of the M. JOHNSON:S 186
medium:
consequences of any m. MCLUH 5
m. is the message MCLUH 4
perfect use of an imperfect m. WILDE:O 21
meek:
believing the m. shall inherit SMITH:FE 1
Blessed are the m. BIBLE 384
m. do not inherit the earth LASKI 1
stuff about the m. inheriting HAWKE 4
meekness: to fight for their m. LASKI 1
meenister: hae ma doots aboot the m. PUNCH 21
meet:
be delighted to m. him CUNARD 1
If we do m. again SHAK:JUL 80
infinite can never m. MARV 8
M. in her aspect BYR 41
m. thee in that hollow vale KING:H 1
never the twain shall m. KIP 39
part to m. again GAY 38
run half-way to m. it JERROLD 7
till we m. again RANK 1
We m. and part now WRIGHT:J 2
we shall m. again after death GREG:Lady 4
when Men & Mountains m. BLAKE:W 99
when shall we two m. again HEWETT 1
When you m. someone better CONF 16
Yet m. we shall BUTLER:S[2] 50
meeting:
adjourn this m. to some other SMITH:Ad 15
as if I was a public m. VICT 6
be no m. past the grave HUX:H 1
My life's been a m. THOMAS:G 1
this m. is drunk DICKENS 33
To the Saturday evening m. BETJ 12
meetings: m. made December June TENNY 174
megalomaniac: m. differs from the narcissist RUSS:B 15
melancholy:
black *sun* of *m.* NERV 1
found in a m. man's heart BURTON:Ro 13
Full of spirit's m. BROWNING:EB 4
had this trick of m. SHAK:ALL 8
Hail divinest M. MILT 78
I inherited a vile m. JOHNSON:S 77
(like all morals) m. BYR 208
loathed M, Of Cerberus MILT 65
m. as an unbrac'd drum CENT 1
m. is, which can transform FORD:J[1] 11
M. mark'd him GRAY:T 26
moping Melancholie MILT 256
Most musicall, most m. MILT 81
Naught so sweet as M. BURTON:Ro 1
no sentimental m. in him KINGSLEY:C 10
Pale M. sate retir'd COLLINS:Wilk 7
pleasing fit of m. MILT 35
rare recipe for m. LAMB:Ch 35
soothe her m. GOLDS 18
stool there to be m. upon? JONS 2
such a charm in m. ROGERS:S 2
suck m. out of a song SHAK:AS 25
sweet as lovely m. FLETCH:J 22
Veil'd M. KEATS 96
when the m. fit shall fall KEATS 96
Melba, Nellie: she remained a 'dinkum* HASKELL 1
Melbourne:
M. sure is the right place to film it JILL 1
people of M. Are frightfully BEVEN 1
meliorist: not an optimist but a m. ELIOT:G 49
mellow: Indeed is too m. for me MONTAGU 2
Mellstock: lie in M. churchyard now HARDY:T 8
melodies: Heard m. are sweet KEATS 92
melodious:
meed of som m. tear MILT 42
Move in m. time MILT 8
melody:
blund'ring kind of m. DRYD 56
ful of hevenyssh melodie CHAUC 121
melon-flower: brighter than this gaudy m. BROWNING:R 50
melons:
raiser of huge m. TENNY 120
Stumbling on m. MARV 17
Melrose: thou would'st view fair M. SCOTT:W 5
melt:
I rage, I m., I burn GAY 1
m. into sorrow BYR 22
m. with ruth MILT 56
melting-pot: great M. ZANG 3
member: he is a m. of *parliament* BURKE:E 94
members:
m. are not formidable as BYR 243
m. one of another BIBLE 533
memoirs:
m. can never be wholly true POWELL:A 8
m. of a thousand years KEATS 112
memorandum:
don't make a m. of it CARROLL 44
m. is written not to inform ACHES 4
memorial:
frail m., but sincere COWP 91
looking for his m., look around WREN 1
which have no m. BIBLE 371
memories:
Liars ought to have good m. SIDNEY:A 1
m.: a heap of tumbling stories DEU 2
M. are hunting horns APOLL 1
more m. then if I had lived BAUD 5
night of m. and of sighs LANDOR 1
Vanished, and left but m. YEATS 34
memorize: only m. and mumble SASS 14
memory:
Everyone complains of his m. LA ROCHE 15
Fond M. brings the light MOORE:T 20
from the table of my m. SHAK:HAM 51
good m. after telling lies CORNEILLE 6
grand m. for forgetting STEVENSON:RL 34
great man's m. may outlive SHAK:HAM 112
hath my night of life some m. SHAK:COM 8
His m. is going JOHNSON:S 233
I claim Only a m. BROWNING:R 128
Illiterate him . . . quite from your m. SHERIDAN:RB 4
liar must have a good m. QUINT 1
man with a m. at a drinking bout PROV 195
M. and habit are the harbingers PEG 1

m. be green SHAK:HAM 12
m. emancipated from the order COLERIDGE:ST 74
M. fades DE LA M 19
m. of yesterday's pleasures DONNE 106
m. that only works backwards CARROLL 64
Midnight shakes the m. ELIOT:TS 17
mist of m. broods LANG:A 3
mixing M. and desire ELIOT:TS 34
no force can abolish m. ROOS:FD 15
Perhaps *this* will refresh your m. THURB 19
poet's m. has fled PUSH 5
Quick, thy tablets, M. ARNOLD:M 3
rather be a brilliant m. EAMES:E 1
Small things can pit the m. MCAULEY 2
Some women'll stay in a man's m. KIP 29
tangled kind of m. STEAD 4
to his m. for his jests SHERIDAN:RB 42
What did they know about m.? LAVIN 1

men:
become the m. we wanted to marry STEINEM 3
enemies: – all stupid m. EBNER 1
I don't think m. and women are meant to live DORS 1
If any young m. come AUSTEN 29
in their right place they are wonderful* FRANKLIN:M 3
made 'em to match the m. ELIOT:G 13
many kinds of awful m. COPE 4
many m., many women, and JOHNSON:S 107
m. all so good for nothing AUSTEN 62
m. and we know not how BROWNE:T 41
m. and women should unite STEAD 7
m. and women with our race KIP 116
m. appointing m. who remind BAKEW 1
M. are but children of a larger DRYD 29
M. are clumsy, stupid creatures FRANKLIN:M 3
m. are designed for short RAMEY 1
M. are m., but Man CHESTERTON 32
M. are made by nature unequal FROUDE 1
M. can be analysed WILDE:O 75
M. have precedency BRADST 2
M. ... have to be weighed COLERIDGE:ST 100
m. in a world of m. KIP 83
m. in women do require? BLAKE:W 60
m. must work KINGSLEY:C 15
M., my brothers TENNY 79
M. of few words SHAK:HEN.V 22
M. of little showing KIP 98
m. that God made mad CHESTERTON 5
m., women and, clergymen SMITH:Syd[1] 25
M. would be Angels POPE 84
M.'s m.: gentle or simple ELIOT:G 42
mens, dey does de walkin' HARRIS:JC 14
no comradeship between m. and women LAWR:DH 3
not m. but manners FIELDING 13
nowadays to behave like m. MACKEN 3
race of m. is almost extinct LAWR:DH 5
same as m. WHITMAN 20
that I am not as other m. BIBLE 465
twelve m. from the bottom ranks BARTON 1
unnecessary things are m. ROCHES 14
War between M. and Women THURB 15
We are all the President's m. KISS 2
We are still the property of m. BARRE 1
What are young m. made of? NURS 83
What m. or gods are these? KEATS 92
where m. and sea interpenetrate CONRAD 7
while there are m. And malice JONS 21
with and not against men WOLFF 1
written by m. physicians LIVER 1
you are m. of stones SHAK:KING L 83

men-children: Bring forth m. only SHAK:MAC 29
menace: His looks do m. heaven MARLOWE 6
mend:
amiss I'll strive to m. WATTS 10
To m. it or be rid on't SHAK:MAC 62
we can't m. it CLOUGH 22
mendacities: Better m. Than the classics POUND 27
mended: Least said soonest m. PROV 230
Mendip: from M.'s sunless caves MACAULAY:TB 41
mene: M., M., TEKEL, UPHARSIN BIBLE 350
Menelaus: M. bold Waxed garrulous BROOKE 4
menstrual: idea of tasting your m. blood GREER 5
mental: sort of m. rebellion ORWELL 13
mental deficiency: speech is a symptom of m.d. BAGE 22
mention: we never m. her BAYLY 1
mentioned: than m. not at all PINDAR:P 1
Menzies: M. never made the mistake FREUDEN 1
mercenary: Followed their m. calling HOUSM 37
merchant: m., to secure his treasure PRIOR 6
merchantman: monarchy is a m. AMES
mercies: Thanks for m. past received BUCKO 2
merciful:
Blessed are the m. BIBLE 384
very m. to the birds ANON 260
merciless:
black and m. things JAMES:H 20
people would be m. TOLS:L 7
mercury:
Licked the m. right off ANON 79
m. sank in the mouth AUD 35
Mercury: words of M. are harsh SHAK:LOV 26
mercy:
acts of m. touch their heavenly VIRGIL 42
Charity and M. Not unholy DICKENS 109
dimensions of this m. are above CROMWELL 4
don't want justice, I want m. HUGHES:B 5
emboldens sin so much as m. SHAK:TIM 8
God All m., is a God YOUNG:E 15
God ha' m. on such as we KIP 52
hand folks over to God's m. ELIOT:G 11
Have m. upon all Jews, Turks PRAY 47
Have m. upon us miserable sinners PRAY 32
leaving m. to Heaven FIELDING 23
Lord have m. on your soul CHAPLIN 1
Lord, have m. upon us MASS 7
Lord, have m. upon us PRAY 11, 20
may have m. upon mine SHAK:TWE 50
M. and truth are met BIBLE 223
M. has a human heart BLAKE:W 17
M. I asked, m. I found CAMDEN:W 1
M. I to others show POPE 156
m. is the greatest sign CORNEILLE 4
M. ... laboured much BUNYAN 29
m. upon this afflicted Kingdom GRAHAM:J 3
mother of m. ANON 37
Peace on earth, and m. mild WESLEY:C 7
quality of m. is not strain'd SHAK:MERC 44
shewing m. unto thousands BIBLE 103
shut the gates of m. GRAY:T 21
so good a grace As m. SHAK:MEA 10
temper so Justice with Mercie MILT 252
that is M.'s door COWP 9
they shall obtain m. BIBLE 384
When m. seasons justice SHAK:MERC 44
merde: *M.* CAMB 2
Meredith:
M. climbed towards the sun CHESTERTON 48
M. is a prose Browning WILDE:O 9
merit:
irrespective of any possible m. WAUGH:E 8
m. wins the soul POPE 54
m.'s all his own CHURCH:C 10
no damned m. in it MELBOU 4
sense of injur'd m. MILT 114
talk of *m.* for a bishopric WESTMOR 1
think we honour m. POPE 24
What is m.? PALMERS 3
meritocracy: Rise of the M. YOUNG:M 1
mermaid:
A seeming m. steers SHAK:ANT 26
m. on a dolphin's back SHAK:MID 17
Mermaid Tavern: Choicer than the M.T. KEATS 25
mermaids: I have heard the m. singing ELIOT:TS 11
mermen: M. swing them to and fro DARLEY 2
merrier: more the m. PROV 277
merrily: M., m. shall I live now SHAK:TEM 31
merriment:
m. of parsons is mighty offensive JOHNSON:S 221
Riot, and ill-manag'd M. MILT 23
merry:
Charles II was always very m. SELL 7
God rest you m. ANON 13
good are always the m. YEATS 6
It's guid to be m. BURNS:R 100
m. as a marriage bell BYR 76
m. heart doeth good BIBLE 264
m. heart goes all the day SHAK:WIN 15
never m. world in England SHAK:HEN.VI[2] 8
never was a m. world since SELD 8
such a m. day once or twice PEPYS 24
tonight we'll m., m. be ANON 8
merrygoround: no go the m. MACNEICE 2
merryman: song of a m. GILB:WS 97
mess:
another fine m. you've gotten HARDY:O 1
every m. I finds a friend DIBDIN:C 2
made a m. of again by officials ADEN 1
mess-bills: M. exceeding his pay COWARD 29
message:
ask me to take a m. to Albert DISR:B 102
electric m. came AUSTIN:A 1
I sent a m. to the fish CARROLL 71
medium is the m. MCLUH 4
messages: fair speechless m. SHAK:MERC 10
messenger:
messager of day CHAUC 45
He's an Anglo-Saxon M. CARROLL 74
m. of Satan BIBLE 530
other M.'s called Hatta CARROLL 75
messing: m. about in boats GRAHAME 2
met:
day and the way we m. SWIN 38
Ill m. by moonlight SHAK:MID 14
m. a man who wasn't there MEARNS 1
m. them at close of day YEATS 41
never be m. with again CARROLL 90
We have m. too late JOYCE:J 53
When first we m. we did not BRIDGES:R 11
metal: Sonorous mettal blowing Martial MILT 131
metals: mold the running mass Of m. VIRGIL 72
metaphor: all m. is poetry CHESTERTON 31
metaphysic: As m. wit can fly BUTLER:S[1] 8
metaphysical:
m. need is only a need KAF 2
termed the *m.* poets JOHNSON:S 47
metaphysicians: tempted to say about m. CHAMFORT 6
metaphysics:
logic and m. are true AYER 1
M. is the finding of bad reasons BRADLEY:FH 1
metempsychosis: Pythagoras' m. MARLOWE 44
meteor:
cloud-encircled m. of the air SHELLEY:PB 62
M. streaming to the wind MILT 130
slides the silent m. on TENNY 117
meter: wretched matter and lame Meeter MILT 104
method: yet there is m. in't SHAK:HAM 74
Methodist: morals of a M. GILB:WS 85
methods: You know my m., Watson DOYLE:AC 21
Methuselah: days of M. were nine hundred BIBLE 33
metre:
laws of God and man and m. LOCKHART 2
m.-making argument, that makes EMER 30
stretched m. of an antique SHAK:SON 5
Metro-Goldwyn-Mayer: age of twelve on a M. lot GARL 1
metropolis: the m. of the empire? COBBETT 2
mettle: m. of your pasture SHAK:HEN.V 19
meum: *distinctions of m. and tuum* LAMB:Ch 17
Mexico: Poor M., so far from God DIAZ 1
mezzanine: slip down to the m. floor WODE 15
mice:
cat's away, the m. will play PROV 426
little m., stole in and out SUCK 3
o' m. an' men BURNS:R 32
Three blind m. NURS 75
Michael Angelo:
Enter M.A. BEERB 14
I believe in M.A. SHAW 94
Italy from designs by M.A. TWAIN 4
might be the name of M.A. REYN:J 4
Michelangelo: Talking of M. ELIOT:TS 4
miching: this is m. mallecho SHAK:HAM 114
micht: Gif thou has m. DUNB 16
Mickey Mouse: love M.M. more than any woman DISN 2
mickle:
Many a m. makes a muckle PROV 263
Mony a m. maks a muckle CERV 15

microbe: M. is so very small BELLOC 7
microscopic: not Man a m. eye? POPE 85
microwave: had a m. to heat things SMITH:D 1
midday: We spend our m. sweat QUAR 7
midden: m. whose odours will madden AUD 1
middle:
cannot steer A m. course MASSIN 8
in the m. of my being LAWR:DH 20
m. course between the throne CHARLES X 2
m. state is to be praised ARISTOT 8
m. state, Neither too MALLET:D 1
m. station had the fewest disasters DEF 2
M. Way MACMILL:H 1
m. way is the safest OSB:J 19
split his father's m. with a single SYNGE 3
who stay in the m. of the road BEVAN 6
middle age:
companions for m.a. BACON:F[1] 85
last enchantments of the M.A. ARNOLD:M 56
Our hearts are young* LANG:A 5
pleasures of m.a. is to *find out* POUND 44
restraining reckless middle-age? YEATS 35
When forty winters shall* SHAK:SON 2
middle-aged:
consolations of m. reformers SAKI 20
m. couples with failing marriages THOMP:EP 1
m. suspect everything WILDE:O 74
only the m. who are really conscious SAKI 5
middle class:
any harm in being m.c. HAILS 3
belonging to the lower-m.c. MIKES 4
he's up agen m.c. morality SHAW 108
M.C. was quite prepared BELLOC 20
specially suits our m. ARNOLD:M 67
what goes on in a middle-class family ELIZ:QM 3
middle classes: bow, ye lower m.c. GILB:WS 42
middle-sized: m. are alone entangled SHEN 3
Middlemarch:
M., the magnificent book WOOLF:V 2
Rosamond Vincy, in M., frightens me ELIOT:TS 122
Middleton: M.'s Rouseabout LAWS 5
midge:
lightly skims the m. BETJ 14
Spins like a fretful m. ROSSET:DG 3
midnight:
at m. when the noon-heat HARDY:T 9
at mid-night speak with the Sun VAUGHAN:H 1
budding morrow in m. KEATS 32
came upon a m. clear SEARS 1
consum'd the m. oil GAY 42
embalmer of the still m. KEATS 91
hear the chimes of m. STEVENSON:RL 15
her woes at m. rise LYLY 5
iron tongue of m. SHAK:MID 50
m. never come MARLOWE 40
M. shakes the memory ELIOT:TS 17
m.'s all a glimmer YEATS 4
mock the m. bell SHAK:ANT 40
Of Cerberus, and blackest m. MILT 65
on the bridge at m. ANON 38
our m. oil QUAR 7
stood on the bridge at m. LONGFEL 38
tea solaces the m. JOHNSON:S 18
'Tis the year's m. DONNE 53
To cease upon the m. KEATS 93
troubled m. and the noon's ELIOT:TS 2
upon a m. dreary POE 3
upper room at m. AUD 49
midst: there am I in the m. BIBLE 421
midwife: She is the fairies' midwife SHAK:ROM 5
mid-winter: In the bleak m. ROSSET:C 18
might:
as our m. lessens ANON 248
beauty should be first in m. KEATS 53
Britons alone use 'M.' WAUGH:E 26
do it with thy m. BIBLE 286
faith that right makes m. LINC 8
if it was so, it m. be CARROLL 52
It m. have been HARTE 1
It m. have been WHITTIER 2
majority has the m. IBS 8
measurement began our m. YEATS 122
m. half slumb'ring KEATS 12
Puts invincible m. MILT 293
to do with m. and main EMER 48
might-have-been: my name is M. ROSSET:DG 12
mightier: make thee m. yet BENS:AC 1
mightiest: 'Tis m. in the m. SHAK:MERC 44
mighty:
God who made thee m. BENS:AC 1
How are the m. fallen BIBLE 154
m. man lay mightily HOMER 12
m. men which were of old BIBLE 35
share in the good fortune of the m. BRECHT 18
the Lord m. in battle BIBLE 208
thou art m. yet SHAK:JUL 84
To quell the m. of the Earth MILT 293
Milan: he wants M., and so do I CHARLES V 2
mild: brought reg'lar and draw'd m. DICKENS 115
mildest: m. manner'd man That ever BYR 187
mildews: m. the white wheat SHAK:KING L 47
mile:
As men Do walk a m. BEAUMO 5
compel thee to go a m. BIBLE 386
miss is as good as a m. PROV 274
mile-stones: There's m. on the Dover road DICKENS 192
miles:
How many m. to Babylon? NURS 19
m. to go before I sleep FROST:R 7
militant:
m. movement was established PANK:E 5
part in this m. movement PANK:C 2
state of Christ's Church m. PRAY 67
militarism: M. ... is one of the chief bulwarks KELLER 1
military:
chief attraction of m. service TOLS:L 1
good order and m. discipline ANON 173
m. mind in their dead grip TUCHMAN 1
to be left to the m. CLEMENCE 6
When the m. man approaches SHAW 44
milk:
cow enjoys on giving m. MENCK 15
cow when m. is so cheap? PROV 431
drunk the m. of Paradise COLERIDGE:ST 63
find a trout in the m. THOREAU 24
flowing with m. and honey BIBLE 87
fostre hym wel with m. CHAUC 53
land flow with m. and honey GOGA 6
little drop of m. PAIN 1
m. comes frozen home SHAK:LOV 25
m. my ewes and weep SHAK:WIN 26
m. of human kindness BURKE:E 74
m. of human kindness SHAK:MAC 19
M. of the elderly OSLER 1
m.'s leap toward immortality FADI 3
no use crying over spilt m. MAUGH 3
no use crying over spilt m. PROV 206
putting m. into babies CHURCH:W 32
round with the m. of human kindness GUED 2
she gave him m. BIBLE 132
sincere m. of the word BIBLE 566
Skim m. masquerades GILB:WS 15
swanning around buying pints of m. GAREL 1
sweet m. of concord SHAK:MAC 94
take my m. for gall SHAK:MAC 20
they are gone to m. the bull JOHNSON:S 117
With m. and honey blest BERNARD:Cl 1
With m. and honey blest NEALE 3
milk-soup: M. men call domestic bliss PATMO 10
milked: awaited their turn to be m. GIBBONS:S 3
milking:
at our yowe-m. ELLIOT:J 1
I'm going a-m., sir NURS 84
milkmaid: M. singeth blithe MILT 70
milkweed: Camel came chewing m. KIP 21
mill:
at the M. with slaves MILT 278
grist that comes to the m. PROV 12
In Hans' old M. DE LA M 12
water glideth by the m. SHAK:TIT 1
Mill : John Stuart M., By a mighty effort BENTLEY:EC 6
mill-stones: Turned to m. as they fell SHELLEY:PB 38
mill-wheel: Except the m.'s sound SHELLEY:PB 150
millenium: of a description of the *M.* HAZL 28
miller:
Than wots the m. of SHAK:TIT 1
There was a jolly m. BICK 2
Miller: M. is not really a writer BREN 8
millers: Bone and Skin, two m. thin BYROM 3
millinery: jewell'd mass of m. TENNY 208
million:
aiming at a m., Misses BROWNING:R 120
man who has a m. dollars ASTOR:JJ 1
m. is made by producing something WILDER:T 1
who is worth only half a m. VANDERB 2
millionaire:
be in the room with a m. SMITH:LP 9
Endowed by the ruined m. ELIOT:TS 97
He must be a m. GILB:F 1
M. That is my religion SHAW 84
silk hat on a Bradford m. ELIOT:TS 45
Who Wants to be a M.? PORTER:C 9
millions:
our yearly multiplying m. O'SULL 2
Thirty m., mostly fools CARLYLE:T 71
Tired m. toil unblest WATSON:W 3
What m. died CAMPBELL:T 6
mills:
Among these dark Satanic M.? BLAKE:W 98
m. of God grind slowly LOGAU 1
Milton:
acrimonious and surly republican* JOHNSON:S 54
Chinese Wall of M. ELIOT:TS 112
lady of Christ's College* AUBREY 4
making up of a Shakespeare or a M. COLERIDGE:ST 97
M. almost requires a solemn LAMB:Ch 23
M. ... was a genius that JOHNSON:S 244
M.'s the prince of poets BYR 198
Nor second He* GRAY:T 35
Poet blind, yet bold* MARV 27
reason M. wrote in fetters BLAKE:W 33
Shakespeare and M. are forgotten PORS 1
Some mute inglorious M. GRAY:T 20
something relevant about M.'s SAINTS 1
mimickry: M., which is the common CHESTERFIELD 19
mimicry: their lives a m. WILDE:O 104
mimsy: m. were the borogoves CARROLL 45
mince: They dined on m. LEAR 21
mind:
abandon his m. to it JOHNSON:S 234
beauty is the m. diseased BYR 106
better than presence of m. PUNCH 4
between the m. and truth HEWITT:J 1
big brown eyes and that tiny m.? THURB 20
brilliant m. until he makes it up ASQU:M 9
broad of m. BETJ 2
buckle and bow the m. BACON:F[1] 8
calm the troubled m. CONG 62
certain unsoundness of m. MACAULAY:TB 16
classical m. at work PIR 4
clear, attentive m. Has no SNY 1
Clear your *m.* of cant JOHNSON:S 237
Clothed, and in his right m. BIBLE 441
concentrates his m. wonderfully JOHNSON:S 191
conjunction of the m. MARV 8
depths of his own oceanic m. COLERIDGE:ST 94
empires of the m. CHURCH:W 33
empty m. Colliding with the lush ASHBERY 1
energy of his m. prevailed LUCRET 1
excursions in my own m. COLERIDGE:ST 69
first damages his m. ANON 262
first destroys their m. DRYD 90
fixt m. And high disdain MILT 114
fog of the good man's m. BROWNING:R 63
frailty of the m. CONG 48
gentle minde by gentle SPENS 43
golden m. stoops not SHAK:MERC 26
he who does not m. his belly JOHNSON:S 127
healthy m. in a healthy body JUV 23
His m. is open BRADLEY:FH 5
His m. moves upon silence YEATS 117
human m. in ruins DAVIES:SB 1
hundred-horse-power m. BALD:S 8
I don't m. if I do ITMA 6
in a fit of absence of m. SEEL 1
index of a feeling m. CRAB 24
Intense irradiation of a m. SHELLEY:PB 62

it's all in the m. WOLFE:Tho 1
know the *m.* of a woman is to LAWR:DH 41
last infirmity of Noble m. MILT 49
let the m. be a thoroughfare KEATS 161
like workings of one m. WORDS:W 156
love exalts the m. DRYD 118
Love warps the m. a little CRAB 26
make up one's m. about nothing KEATS 161
man but chang'd his m. POPE 110
man that has a m. and knows it SHAW 120
man who could not make up his m. DENT 1
man's unconquerable m. WORDS:W 103
march of m. has marched in PEAC 11
march of the human m. BURKE:E 35
m. and hand went together HEMING 2
m. as narrow as the neck JOHNSON:S 79
m. can also be an erogenous zone WELCH 1
m. ... fetched up with a bump ORWELL 34
m. for ever Voyaging WORDS:W 152
M., from pleasure less MARV 18
m. has a thousand eyes BOUR 2
m. has mountains HOPK:GM 23
m. is a tool, a machine DOST 7
m. is always fooled by the heart LA ROCHE 16
m. is free DRAYT 3
m. is its own place MILT 122
m. is the guide and ruler SALL 7
m. lays down its burden CATUL 9
m. of man becomes A thousand WORDS:W 164
M. of Man – My haunt WORDS:W 110
m. of the oppressed BIKO 1
m. quite vacant is a m. COWP 40
m. remains unmoved VIRGIL 60
m. serene for contemplation GAY 50
m. shapes itself to the body WOLLST 4
m. swings between sense and nonsense JUNG:Carl 3
m. treats a new idea the way MEDA 2
m. Was changit right clean JAMES I 3
m.'s construction in the face SHAK:MAC 18
moral duty to speak one's m. WILDE:O 94
moved slowly through the m. WORDS:W 149
my m. baulks at it COMPT 1
My m. to me a kingdom DYER:E 1
my m. was still unpledged EUR 1
no blemish but the m. SHAK:TWE 53
not any subsistence without a m. BERK 2
Not for the knowledge of thy m. DAVIES:WH 4
not m. any thing at all AUSTEN 21
nothing great but m. HAMIL:W 2
old age the m. casts off WILLIAMS:WC 9
out of m. because I am out of sight? HOLL:HS 1
out of sight is out of m. CLOUGH 7
Out of sight, out of m. PROV 315
pleased to call his m. BETHE 1
prepare the m. of the country DISR:B 69
raise and erect the m. BACON:F[1] 8
satisfied with her lover's m. TROLL 11
seasons in the m. of man KEATS 27
She had a frugal m. COWP 51
So let extend thy m. MILT 272
squares of his m. were empty AUD 36
steals forth and charms the m. YEATS 149
steam-wheels of the m. SHELLEY:PB 59
stress on not changing one's m. MAUGH 1
think my m. is maturing late NASH 19
this tormented m. tormenting yet HOPK:GM 25
thoroughness of a m. that reveres LEWIS:S 2
Those Himalayas of the m. DAY LEWIS 1
through the gateways of the m. SASS 17
thy m. all virtue JOHNSON:S 92
to change your m. and follow AUR 12
to cover his m. decently SMITH:Syd[1] 23
triumph of m. over matter WILDE:O 30
unbends the m. like them GAY 21
unbent her m. afterwards LAMB:Ch 13
unseemly exposure of the m. HAZL 33
until reeled the m. GIBBS 1
Upon the threshold of her m.? TENNY 128
Vex not thou the poet's m. TENNY 7
virtuous person with a mean m. BAGE 24
we can feed this m. of ours WORDS:W 2
what a noble m. is here SHAK:HAM 104
What is M.? – No matter PUNCH 7
When the m.'s free SHAK:KING L 40
Woman's m. oft' shifts GAY 7

minds:
bewitching of our m. by means WITT 6
express the images of their m. BACON:F[1] 92
for a time close to great m. BUCHAN 2
great empire and little m. BURKE:E 43
hobgoblin of little m. EMER 10
hunger of ambitious mindes SPENS 41
Little m. are interested in HUBB 2
Little things affect little m. DISR:B 26
M. are not ever craving CRAB 12
M. like beds always made WILLIAMS:WC 7
m. of my generation destroyed GINSBERG 1
not weed their own m. WALP:H 20
purest and most thoughtful m. RUSKIN 5
refuge of weak m. CHESTERFIELD 22
spurre of all great mindes CHAPMAN:G 7
taken out of men's m., vain BACON:F[1] 116
to have aspiring m. MARLOWE 9
to the marriage of true m. SHAK:SON 52
wars begin in the m. ANON 240
weak m. Led captive MILT 266
Women never have young m. DELAN 1

mine:
abandoned m. shaft – *in France* NICHOL 1
For ever and ever, m. TENNY 217
He is m. for ever BAKER 1
he was but one hour m. SHAK:SON 15
she is m. for life SPARK 2
then shouldst thou have m.? SUCK 6
What thou art is m. MILT 251
What's m. is yours SHAK:MEA 42
While he is m., and I HERB:G 47
whisper softly 'I am m.' HUDS:L 1
would she were m. LODGE:T 2

minefield: What a m. Life is FRY:C 19
miner: Dwelt a m., Forty-niner MONTROSE 1
mineral:
animal – or vegetable – or m.? CARROLL 80
inherit the earth, but not the m. rights GET 3

miners:
because m. sweat their guts out ORWELL 2
rugged m. poured to war MACAULAY:TB 41
Vatican, the Treasury and the M. BALD:S 12

Minerva: M. when she talks JONS 47
mines: one yard below their m. SHAK:HAM 149
mining-claims: snakeskin-titles of m. BENET 1
minion: I a salaried m. GILB:WS 63
minister:
can become a m. yourself? TONER 1
designated as a 'stickit m.' SCOTT:W 68
m. kiss't the fiddler's wife BURNS:R 82
m. to a mind diseas'd SHAK:MAC 111
tranquil life By becoming a Cabinet M. SU 1
wisdom of a great m.? JUNIUS 4
Yes, M.! No, M.! CROSSMAN 1

ministers: my actions are my m.' CHARLES II 8
ministry:
acquainted with the merit of a m. JUNIUS 2
m. of all talents ANON 216
more for a marriage than a m. BAGE 13

Minnehaha: M., Laughing Water LONGFEL 21
minnows: this Triton of the m.? SHAK:COR 9
minorities: M. ... are almost always SMITH:Syd[1] 36
minority:
efficient m. to coerce STEPHEN:FJ 1
m., however fervent its cause, prevails NIX 5
m. is always right IBS 8
not enough people to make a m. ALTMAN 1

minstrel:
Ethereal m. WORDS:W 134
M. Boy to the war MOORE:T 10
M. was infirm and old SCOTT:W 1
ring the fuller m. in TENNY 177
wandering m. I GILB:WS 60

mintage: coiner the m. of man HOUSM 14
minute:
both in the same m. KEATS 158
cannot cage the m. MACNEICE 4
good m. goes BROWNING:R 161
In a m. there is time ELIOT:TS 6
m.'s success pays the failure BROWNING:R 211
not a m. on the day COOK:AJ 1
sucker born every m. BARNUM 1

minutes:
about ten m. WELLING 25
and m. capons SHAK:HEN.IV[1] 3
first ninety m. are the most ROBSON 1
five m. too late all my COWLEY:H 2
I give myself two m. DISR:B 95
our m. hasten to their end SHAK:SON 23
rate of sixty m. an hour LEWIS:CS 4
see the m. how they run SHAK:HEN. VI[3] 3
set with sixty diamond m. MANN:H 2
some of them are about ten m. DYL 9
take care of m. CHESTERFIELD 10
think for two m. together SMITH:Syd[1] 9
three m. is a long time HOUSM 52
you're twenty m. WILDER:B 1

minx: whether I am a M., or a Sphinx DICKENS 224
miracle:
continued existence is a mere m. STEVENSON:RL 21
continued m. in his own person HUME 11
God never wrought m. to BACON:F[1] 35
m. of our age CAREW:R 1
m. of rare device COLERIDGE:ST 63
sufficient to establish a m. HUME 12
would seem a M. DONNE 102

miracles:
M. can be made, but only AGNEL 1
m. do not happen ARNOLD:M 78
there will have to be m. GREENE:G 4

mire:
Is there then no m.? ROCHES 7
m. of human veins YEATS 86

mirror:
deceiving m. of self-love MASSIN 4
faithful m. up to man LLOYD:R 1
five or six faces in front of a m. GLOVER 3
hold ... the m. up to nature SHAK:HAM 107
in a m. and see an old bastard ALLEN:D 5
Little Willy from his m. ANON 79
m. crack'd from side to side TENNY 21
m. walking along a wide road STEND 2
woman looks in her m. TURNBULL 2

mirrors:
M. and fatherhood are abominable BORGES 3
Over the m. meant To glass HARDY:T 21

mirth:
Bards of Passion and of M. KEATS 55
Him serve with m. KETHE 1
I'll use you for my m. SHAK:JUL 70
m. and fun grew fast BURNS:R 88
m. as does not make friends ashamed WALT 10
m. may molest us on Monday NEAV 1
m. of cracker-barrel men BENET 3
M. that has no bitter KIP 118
Moche mirthe and no madnes SKEL:J 4
must borrow its m. WILCOX 3
Now leiff thi myrth BLIND 1
Our m. the music GIBBONS:O 2
Present m. hath present SHAK:TWE 19
Prime Minister of M. ROBEY 1
song of the birds for m. GUR 1
very tragical m. SHAK:MID 45
where's all the joy and m. KEPP:C 1
Who buys a minute's m. SHAK:POET 5
With m. in funeral SHAK:HAM 12

misbeliever: You call me m. SHAK:MERC 17
miscarriage:
disgraced by m. JOHNSON:S 5
success and m. are empty sounds JOHNSON:S 102

miscarriages: pregnancies and at least four m. BEECHAM 10
mischief:
authority from God to do m. MAYHEW:J 1
bringing all manner of m. FIELDING 18
devil finds m. still MADAN 1
foundation of lasting m. JOHNSON:S 86
From all evil and m. PRAY 33
hand to execute any m. CLAREN 2
M., thou art afoot SHAK:JUL 60
neglect may breed m. FRANKLIN:B 18
Satan finds some m. still WATTS 5
To m. trained CHURCH:C 5

mischiefs: M. feed Like beasts JONS 22
miser:
sensible reflection in a m. CHESTERFIELD 9
unsun'd heaps Of M.'s treasure MILT 31

miserable:
being m. is to have leisure SHAW 103
God would make a man m. CHARLES II 2
made a young girl m. FRANKLIN:B 24
members are poor and m. SMITH:Ad 3

m. unless you think it so BOET 2
pretend to be m. PALAC 1
two people m. instead of four BUTLER:S[2] 51
miseries:
climb upward on the m. CONRAD 13
heap m. upon us yet entwine JOYCE:J 37
liable to all the m. in this life CATEC 3
long to see the m. of the world JOHNSON:S 19
to whom the m. of the world KEATS 101
misery:
amount of m. which it is his duty LOWE 2
deep wide sea of M. SHELLEY:PB 26
dwell on guilt and m. AUSTEN 36
gave to Mis'ry all he had GRAY:T 27
M. acquaints a man SHAK:TEM 17
m. still delights to trace COWP 92
No stranger to m. VIRGIL 44
relation of distant m. GIBBON:E 9
she filled my days With m. YEATS 30
Thou art so full of m. TENNY 48
misfits: strangest collection of m. REAG 3
misfortunes:
bear another's m. perfectly POPE 181
easy to bear the m. of others PROV 204
He'll hae m. BURNS:R 30
if a man talks of his m. JOHNSON:S 217
make m. more bitter BACON:F[1] 91
m. and pains of others BURKE:E 4
m. hardest to bear LOWELL:JR 8
m. of our closest friends LA ROCHE 2
tableau of crimes and m. VOLT 20
misgovernment:
augur m. at a distance BURKE:E 31
refuge of cheap m. SHAW 28
mishap: there be they on whom m. CALVER 7
miskent: warld m. him BIBLE 593
mislead: One to m. the public ASQU:HH 5
misleading:
least m. thing we have BUTLER:S[2] 36
m. impression, not a lie ARMST:R 1
misquotation: M. is the pride and privilege PEARS:H 1
misquotations: M. are the only quotations PEARS:H 2
misquote: enough of learning to m. BYR 9
miss:
count and calls her 'M.' CHESTERTON 11
m. for pleasure GAY 35
m. is as good as a mile PROV 274
m. the one before it CHESTERTON 58
Miss Muffet: Little M.M. Sat on a tuffet NURS 35
Miss Otis: M.O. regrets PORTER:C 4
Miss T: whatever M.T eats DE LA M 14
missed:
Scepter, oftest better misst MILT 268
who never would be miss'd GILB:WS 64
wonder what you've m. AUD 7
misses: sadly m. family and friends LE MES 1
missing:
M. so much CORNFORD:Fran 1
Only one being is m. LAMAR 1
mission: Never have a M. DICKENS 182
missionaries: eaten by m. SPOON 2
missionary:
blend of the commercial traveller, the m. STAPLED 1
I would eat a m. WILB 2
not be confused with m. work KISS 6
Mississippi: I have seen the M. BURNS:J 1
mis-spent: Redeem thy m. time KEN 1
missus: The M. my Lord PUNCH 20
mist:
broke into a m. with bells BROWNING:R 143
grey m. on the sea's face MASE 1
M. enveloped me CERN 1
m. in my face BROWNING:R 181
m. is dispell'd when a woman GAY 20
m. retreating from the morning CLARE:J 1
Out of the m. and hum ARNOLD:M 33
Scots m. will weet an Englishman RAMS 4
Thee is m. on the mountain SCOTT:W 46
mistake:
all forms of m., prophecy ELIOT:G 32
God's *first* m. NIET 21
he never overlooks a m. HUX:TH 1
made a new m. instead COPE 4
Man is Nature's sole mistake GILB:WS 57
m. made by God NIET 27
m. to theorize before one DOYLE:AC 19
never do right by m. JUNIUS 5
never made a m. never made a discovery SMILES 2
There is no m.: there has been no WELLING 7
worse than a crime; it is a m. BOULAY 1
worse than immoral, it's a m. ACHES 3
you lie – under a m. SWIFT 44
mistaken:
possible you may be m. CROMWELL 3
so loved, yet so m. BROWNING:R 215
mistakes:
all the m. which can be made BOHR 1
all the m. which can be made TELL 1
Canberra, even the m. are planned FITZGER:AJ 1
every one gives to their m. WILDE:O 52
few m. they have ever avoided CHURCH:W 34
from the m. of the past how to TAYL:AJP 6
genius makes no m. JOYCE:J 22
I hope you will excuse m. DICKENS 75
man who makes no m. PHELPS 1
plenty of m. if you've lived REAG 10
mistress:
age of fifteen, the m. of the Earl WILSON:Harr 1
In ev'ry port a m. GAY 39
lordship's principles or your m. WILKES 1
m. I am ashamed to call ELIZ I 14
M. moderately fair COWLEY:A 5
m. of a household considers BEETON 1
M. of herself, tho' China POPE 140
m. should be like a little country WYCH 3
new m. now I chase LOVELACE 7
No casual m., but a wife TENNY 160
no M. but their Muse DONNE 51
teeming M., but a barren POPE 132
worst m. BACON:F[1] 25
mistresses:
better price than old m. BEAV 7
I shall have m. GEO II 1
m. with great smooth marbly BROWNING:R 43
one wife and hardly any m. SAKI 9
Wives are young men's m. BACON:F[1] 85
mists:
golden m. are born SHELLEY:PB 139
m. a space unsettle THOMP:F 13
m. and mellow fruitfulness KEATS 109
through M. of human breath DAVEN:W 3
misty: ful m. morwe CHAUC 111
misunderstood: To be great is to be m. EMER 11
mittens:
skin he made him m. ANON 117
they lost their m. NURS 76
Mitty: Walter M., the undefeated THURB 12
mix: I m. them with my brains OPIE 1
mixed grill: not to look like a m.g. COWARD 15
mixer: Keep Paddy behind the big m. MCALP 1
moan:
made sweet m. KEATS 81
make delicious m. KEATS 88
That is not paid with m. THOMP:F 3
we cast away m. SHAK:HAM 172
moanday: All m., tearsday JOYCE:J 38
moaning:
harbour bar be m. KINGSLEY:C 15
m. on ilka green loaning ELLIOT:J 1
no moaning of the bar TENNY 296
moat: m. flowing with fright MTS 3
mob:
M., Parliament, Rabble COBBETT 1
supreme governors, the m. WALP:H 2
mobs: suppose there are two m.? DICKENS 10
mock:
M. on M. on BLAKE:W 100
m. the midnight bell SHAK:ANT 40
m. your own grinning SHAK:HAM 183
They m. the air GRAY:T 28
mockery:
Like all the rest, a m. SHELLEY:PB 93
m. is the fume of little TENNY 267
vain blows malicious m. SHAK:HAM 8
mocking-bird: Out of the m.'s throat WHITMAN 22
mockingbird: sin to kill a m. LEE:Har 1
models:
Rules and m. destroy genius HAZL 8
they have no other m. BALD:J 3
moderate: Iranian m. is one who has run out KISS 5
moderation:
abstain totally than to use m. AUGUS 8
astonished at my own m. CLIVE 2
M. in all things PROV 275
m. in war is imbecility MACAULAY:TB 24
M. is a fatal thing WILDE:O 65
m., . . . is a sort of treason BURKE:E 44
There is m. even in excess DISR:B 1
modern: they knew that it was m. ELIOT:TS 1
moderns: Speak of the m. without CHESTERFIELD 12
modest:
good deal to be m. about CHURCH:W 66
no talent and is m. about it AGATE 2
modester: People ought to be m. CARLYLE:T 67
modesty:
blood and talk of m. MIDD 6
Enough for m. – no more BUCHANAN 3
had time to cultivate m. SITWELL:E 15
Ladies of irresistible M. STEELE 8
maiden m. would float face HUX:A 45
m. may more betray SHAK:MEA 15
True m. will there GILB:WS 98
Mohicans: Last of the M. COOPER:JF 1
mole:
Death is still working like a m. HERB:G 27
m. cinque-spotted SHAK:CYM 3
Well said, old m. SHAK:HAM 55
wilt thou go ask the M. BLAKE:W 28
molehills: M. seem mountains COTTON 1
Moloch: First M., horrid King MILT 126
moly: beds of amaranth and m. TENNY 30
mom: eat at a place called M.'s ALG 2
moment:
Eternity was in that m. CONG 8
Every m. dies a man BABB 1
Every m. dies a man TENNY 97
force the m. to its crisis? ELIOT:TS 8
last m. belongs to us VANZ 2
m. may with bliss repay CAMPBELL:T 22
m. of my greatness flicker ELIOT:TS 9
m. of time make us GAY 29
say to the m.: 'Linger GOET 15
sonnet is a m.'s monument ROSSET:DG 7
moments:
delicate and evanescent of m. JOYCE:J 43
had left were m. CAMUS 6
little m. Humble though CARNEY 1
m. big as years KEATS 47
m. of other people's lives PIR 3
m. quickly flying CASWALL 2
take care of the m., the years EDGE 7
Wagner has beautiful m. ROSSINI 1
Mona: M. did research in PLOM 6
Mona Lisa:
Hers is the head* PATER 1
lotta cats copy the M.L. ARMST:L 1
She has the smile* DURRELL:L 7
She is older than the rocks* PATER 2
Monan: moon on M.'s rill SCOTT:W 35
monarch:
becomes The throned m. SHAK:MERC 44
cuckold to make him a m.? SHAK:OTH 58
every hereditary m. was insane BAGE 15
merry m., scandalous ROCHES 12
m. of a shed GOLDS 8
m. of all I survey COWP 46
so much a king as a M. SELL 7
monarchs:
m. to behold SHAK:HEN.V 1
Perplexes M. MILT 136
when fate summons, m. must DRYD 62
wrote that m. were divine KIP 141
monarchy:
discontented under *m.*, call it HOBB 11
do the m. no end of good WORST 1
essential to a true m. BAGE 6
m. is a labour-intensive industry WILSON:Harold 13
m. is a merchantman AMES 1
take in the M. along with feeding HAMIL:WW 1
under a constitutional m. BAGE 12
why M. is a strong government BAGE 10
monastic: Mild m. faces CLOUGH 17

Moors: these M. are changeable SHAK:OTH 16
moose: strong as a bull m. ROOS:T 10
mops: seven maids with seven m. CARROLL 55
Mopsy: Flopsy, M., Cottontail POTTER:B 1
moral:
All good m. philosophy BACON:F[1] 13
as a m. or an immoral book WILDE:O 19
by nature not a m. being KANT 12
complains of m. indigestion ANTRIM 2
Debasing the m. currency ELIOT:G 45
Everything's got a m. CARROLL 23
fatty degeneration of his m. being STEVENSON:RL 4
find a m. in it will be banished TWAIN 10
His M. pleases POPE 143
kind of m. eunuch SHELLEY:PB 50
make a m. of the devil SHAK:HEN.V 27
Men made the m. code PANK:E 2
m. as soon as one is unhappy PROUST 6
m. behaviour varies in inverse HUX:A 35
M. indignation is jealousy with WELLS:HG 9
m. law within me KANT 8
m. life of man forms part WILDE:O 21
m. (like all morals) BYR 208
m. principles are idle fancies SADE 1
M. virtue is the child of habit ARISTOT 5
M. virtues we acquire through practice ARISTOT 6
m. when he is only uncomfortable SHAW 41
no sense of m. responsibility WILDE:O 80
perfectly m. till all are m. SPENCER:H 5
preach a high m. lesson STRACH 3
story with a bad m. HARDY:T 49
To point a m. JOHNSON:S 68
moralist: no sterner m. than Pleasure BYR 189
moralists: We are perpetually m. JOHNSON:S 53
morality:
Dr Johnson's m. was as English HAWT 5
Good-bye, moralitee HERB:AP 7
have a himputation on his m. SURT 8
he's up agen middle class m. SHAW 108
imperative may be called that of *m.* KANT 3
m. for m.'s sake COUS 1
M. is simply the attitude WILDE:O 77
M. is the herd-instinct in NIET 16
m. is the regulation of conduct SPENCER:H 10
M. is the tendency to throw KRAUS 3
m. of the common man has NIET 1
m. touched by emotion ARNOLD:M 75
M. which is based on ideas LAWR:DH 6
M.'s a gesture BOLT 1
No m. can be founded on authority AYER 2
periodical fits of m. MACAULAY:TB 22
principles of public m. BURKE:E 11
some people talk of m. EDGE 5
There is *master-m.* and *slave-m.* NIET 12
two kinds of m. side by side RUSS:B 12
unawares M. expires POPE 174
morals:
basing m. on myth SAMUEL 1
foundation of m. and legislation BENTH 4
Have you no m., man? SHAW 107
If your m. make you dreary STEVENSON:RL 44
teach the m. of a whore JOHNSON:S 98
the m. of a Methodist GILB:WS 85
more:
easy to take *m.* than nothing CARROLL 19
I have m. DONNE 95
I want some m. DICKENS 55
knows m. and m. about less MAYO 1
Less is m. MIES 1
little m., and how much BROWNING:R 92
m. and m. about less and less BUTLER:NM 2
m. he cast away, the m. BUNYAN 28
m. I give to thee, The m. SHAK:ROM 16
m. I see of men, the less BYR 246
m. the merrier PROV 277
M. WILL MEAN WORSE AMIS:K 2
no m. of that, Hal SHAK:HEN.IV[1] 46
she'll vish there wos m. DICKENS 30
some m. than others COWARD 8
there is no m. to say SHAK:TRO 26
More, Thomas: man for all seasons* WHITTING 1
Morgan: bold mate of Henry M. MASE 8
morganatic: rumours of a m. alliance HARDIE 1
mori: *Pro patria m.* OWEN:W 5
morn:
Fair laughs the M. GRAY:T 31
From m. to night, my friend ROSSET:C 14
from M. To Noon he fell MILT 144
incense-breathing M. GRAY:T 16
m. and cold indifference came ROWE 1
m. From black to red began BUTLER:S[1] 23
m., in russet mantle clad SHAK:HAM 11
m. not waking till she sings LYLY 6
m. went out with sandals gray MILT 59
new m. she saw not KEATS 30
salute the happy m. BYROM 1
Son of M. in weary Nights BLAKE:W 110
Sweet is the breath of m. MILT 199
this the happy m. MILT 3
morning:
Almost at odds with m. SHAK:MAC 74
beauty of the m.; silent, bare WORDS:W 91
best of the sons of the m. HEB 1
caught this m. m.'s minion HOPK:GM 10
cold and frosty m. ANON 17
cold, frosty, windy m. PEPYS 1
Drinking in the m. is the best RAB 5
Each m. sees some task LONGFEL 12
Early in the m.? ANON 49
Early in the m. our song HEB 4
Early one m. ANON 10
Everything becomes m. STEVENS 14
explain it away in the m. HUDS:B 2
Full many a glorious m. SHAK:SON 14
great m. of the world SHELLEY:PB 113
hour in the m. is worth two PROV 178
I scent the m. air SHAK:HAM 47
In the m. of the world BROWNING:R 11
lead to sorrow in the m. HOGG 9
like to have the m. well-aired BRUM 3
like to the m.'s war SHAK:HEN.VI[3] 2
M. after Death DICKIN:E 18
m. fair Came forth MILT 276
M. in the Bowl of Night FITZGER:E 1
m. stars sang together BIBLE 193
M.'s at seven BROWNING:R 9
Never glad confident m. BROWNING:R 56
rainbow in the m. is the shepherd's PROV 329
slantwise At everyone's m. DOBSON:R 2
Soft m., city JOYCE:J 41
Take 'old o' the Wings o' the Mornin' KIP 68
Think in the m. BLAKE:W 45
'Tis always m. somewhere HORNE:RH 1
Up in the m. early BURNS:R 67
what a beautiful mornin' HAMMER 3
mornings: Frank Sargeson works in the m. SARGESON 2
morns: M. abed and daylight HOUSM 4
Moro: M.'s kidnapping, Italy looked BOCCA 1
moron: See the happy m. ANON 93
morris dancers: bearded Trotskyite M.d. HOWK 1
morrow:
budding m. in midnight KEATS 32
m. shall take thought for BIBLE 397
morsel:
I found you as a m. cold SHAK:ANT 39
m. for a monarch SHAK:ANT 22
mortal:
All men are m. PROV 10
all men M., but themselves YOUNG:E 12
been struck a deep m. blow AESC 3
desperately m. SHAK:MEA 33
gathers all things m. SWIN 29
Her last disorder m. GOLDS 1
I had begotten a m. GOET 39
I presume you're m. SHIRL 2
more than an ordinary mortall AUBREY 8
m. god, to which we owe HOBB 10
raised a m. to the skies DRYD 115
shuffled off this m. coil SHAK:HAM 97
then a m. becomes immortal UPA 1
Turning m. for thy love SHAK:LOV 13
mortality:
All beauteous things* CORY 3
changing year and the passing* HORACE 54
Days and moments* CASWALL 2
insensible of m. SHAK:MEA 33
it smells of m. SHAK:KING L 68
M. weighs heavily KEATS 17
nothing serious in m. SHAK:MAC 56
Old m. BROWNE:T 48
One doth but breakfast here* HENS 1
There are no fields of amaranth* LANDOR 17
urns and sepulchres of m. CREWE 1
We are all being gathered* HORACE 20
we are but dust and shadow* HORACE 55
mortals: what fools these m. be SHAK:MID 29
mortis: *Timor m. conturbat me* DUNB 7
Moscow: One is don't march on M. MONTGOM:BL 3
Moses: M. hid his face BIBLE 86
mosquitoes: crossing salmon with m. MORTON:JB 3
moss:
can gather no m. TUSS 4
miles of golden m. AUD 50
most:
make the m. of what PINDAR 2
make the m. on 'em DICKENS 1
mote: this m. one moment longer STERNE 35
motes: thikke as m. in the sonne-beem CHAUC 86
moth:
candle sing'd the m. SHAK:MERC 31
desire of the m. for the star JOYCE:J 51
like a m., the simple maid GAY 10
m. and rust doth corrupt BIBLE 392
m. in his brother's parachute SIMPSON:NF 1
m.'s kiss, first BROWNING:R 16
moth-balls: exuded a flavour of m. MUGG 4
mother:
back to the great sweet m. SWIN 44
convinced that his m. was a fool WEST:R 10
dearer was the m. COLERIDGE:ST 3
deceiv'd The M. of Mankinde MILT 109
Don't tell my m. HERB:AP 1
Don't tell my m. I'm in politics ANON 180
entirely his m.'s affair TURNBULL 1
every m. has it PROV 385
fairer daughter of a fair m. HORACE 14
gave her m. forty whacks ANON 80
his m. would let him or no NURS 12
His m.'s against Him HUGHES:Te 3
It cannot Be call'd our m. SHAK:MAC 95
little did my m. ken BALL 43
May you be the m. of a bishop BEHAN:Br 11
mighty M. did unveil GRAY:T 34
m. bids me bind my hair HUNTER:A 1
m., do not cry FARM 1
m. is only brought unlimited satisfaction FREUD:S 4
m. is supreme ACHEBE 1
M. is the dead heart GREER 2
m. is there to protect you ACHEBE 1
m., m., make my bed BALL 4
M. o' mine KIP 42
m. of all living BIBLE 26
m. of mercy ANON 37
M. of the Free BENS:AC 1
M. on his Father him begot BLAKE:W 102
m. who talks about her own children DISR:B 74
m. will be there HERB:AP 4
m.'s life made me a man MASE 12
m.'s pride, a father's joy SCOTT:W 45
My M. TAYL:Ann 1
my m. didna speak BARNARD:A 1
My m., drunk or sober CHESTERTON 29
My m. groand BLAKE:W 75
never called me m. WOOD 1
Never had any m.? STOWE 1
Never throw stones at your m. BEHAN:Br 1
recognize your m. with a smile VIRGIL 12
sorrowing M. was standing JACOP 1
Thou art thy m.'s glass SHAK:SON 3
thy dear m. any courtesy SHAK:COR 20
Thy m. a lady, both lovely SCOTT:W 49
titles of wife and m. LIVER 2
Took great care of his M. MILNE 2
were she ten times our m. SHAK:HAM 122
Where a M. laid her Baby ALEX:CF 4
wish either my father or my m. STERNE 2
wished to be near my m. WHIST 13
yet was ever found a m. GAY 43
Mother Hubbard: Old M.H. Went to the cupboard NURS 47
mother-in-law:
as long as your m. is alive JUV 13
became T S Eliot's m. BENNETT:Al 5
place everyone should send his m. BOTH 1
place to drop one's m. FOCH 4
untutored savage contemplates his m. FRAZ 1

motherhood: wifehood and m. are but incidental STANTON:El 6
mothering: naughty m. arms THOMAS:D 31
mothers:
city of the best-bodied m. WHITMAN 20
mock their anxious m. CAMPBELL:G 2
M. of large families BELLOC 5
shooting m. of English-speaking children GOGA 3
weakened-genitive-organed m. O'MALLEY:K 1
women become like their m. WILDE:O 88
mothers-in-law: Two m. RUSS:J[2] 5
moths: Maidens, like m., are ever caught BYR 56
mothy: m. and warm HARDY:T 34
motion:
Between the m. And the act ELIOT:TS 58
Devoid of sense and m.? MILT 153
enough of action and of m. TENNY 32
God order'd m. VAUGHAN:H 13
measured m. like a living thing WORDS:W 147
m. and a spirit, that impels WORDS:W 8
next to the perpetual m. DICKENS 50
sounds Of undistinguishable m. WORDS:W 144
motions: secret m. of things BACON:F[1] 124
motive:
Looks always on the m. YEATS 7
noble in m. and far-reaching HOOV 1
Persons attempting to find a m. TWAIN 10
motives:
if the world could see the m. LA ROCHE 33
m. meaner than your own BARRIE 17
motley:
A m. fool SHAK:AS 28
lived where m. is worn YEATS 41
made myself a m. SHAK:SON 51
M.'s the only wear SHAK:AS 30
wear not m. in my brain SHAK:TWE 10
motor car: m.c. is our supreme form of privacy MCLUH 8
motorcycle: son would have his m. ELIOT:TS 71
motorcycles: On m., up the road GUNN:T 1
motors: sound of horns and m. ELIOT:TS 44
motto: Be that my m. and my fate SWIFT 55
mottoes: Rather than the m. on sundials POUND 26
mould:
Breaking the m. of British politics JENKINS:R 3
If you cannot m. yourself KEMP 7
then smashed the m. ARIO 1
moulded: men are m. out of faults SHAK:MEA 40
moulds: distain your m. frae mine BALL 32
mouldy: blue m. for the want of that pint JOYCE:J 28
Moulmein: by the old M. Pagoda KIP 59
moulting: when they're m. NASH 13
mount:
merely seek to m. us BARRE 1
m. up with wings as eagles BIBLE 324
mountain:
alone on a great m. KILV 3
if I never see another m. LAMB:Ch 34
I've been to the m. top KING:ML 3
Land of the m. and the flood SCOTT:W 11
Mahomet must go to the m. PROV 186
m. and hill shall be made BIBLE 320
m. in labour made such a FONTAINE 13
robes the m. in its azure CAMPBELL:T 2
Up the airy m. ALLING:W 1
mountain-goat: damned and luxurious m. SHAK:HEN.V 41
mountain-peaks: Over all the m. there is quiet GOET 22
mountain-tops:
Flatter the m. SHAK:SON 14
who ascends to m. BYR 87
mountains:
could remove m. BIBLE 522
Faith will move m. PROV 114
From Greenland's icy m. HEB 2
High m. are a feeling BYR 91
M. are the beginning and the end RUSKIN 8
m. by the winter sea TENNY 272
M. divide us GALT 1
m. look on Marathon BYR 193
m. whitened endlessly GLOVER 2
M. will be in labour HORACE 107
scatter the heaped-up m. VIRGIL 24
They came to the Delectable M. BUNYAN 17
though the m. be carried into BIBLE 215
To the M. of the Moon LIND:V 2
upon Englands m. green BLAKE:W 98
when Men & M. meet BLAKE:W 99
you m., you see it all CANET 5
mountebank: story of a m. and his zany WALP:H 22
mourn:
Blessed are they that m. BIBLE 384
I'll sit and m. all at BALL 61
in summer skies to m. KEATS 26
It is Margaret you m. for HOPK:GM 17
Man was made to m. BURNS:R 6
m. with ever-returning spring WHITMAN 34
No longer m. for me SHAK:SON 32
time to m. BIBLE 281
To m. avails not HOMER 15
mourned: by strangers mourn'd POPE 60
mourner:
be ev'ry m.'s sleep tonight KEBLE 4
only constant m. o'er BYR 26
mourners: Most musical of m. SHELLEY:PB 106
mourning:
in m. for my life CHEK 1
m. is perhaps not so much MANN:T 8
m. of a mighty nation TENNY 188
m. that either his mother AUSTEN 73
with my m., very handsome PEPYS 21
mourns: M. less for what age takes WORDS:W 23
mous: hae the m. o them steikit BIBLE 596
mouse:
always leave room for the m. SAKI 25
appetit hath he to ete a mous CHAUC 53
if that she saugh a mous CHAUC 10
killing of a m. on Sunday BRATH 1
m. Behind the mouldering TENNY 5
m. ran up the clock NURS 17
m.'s limp tail hanging MOORE:M 5
Not a m. stirring SHAK:HAM 2
other caught a M. LEAR 29
ridiculous m. will be born HORACE 107
she gave birth to a m. FONTAINE 13
mouse-trap: 'The M.' SHAK:HAM 117
mousseline: Supplants the *m.* of Cos POUND 28
moustache:
Big chap with a small m. WODE 23
man who *didn't* wax his m. KIP 7
outside with a big black m. MARX:G 7
walrus Victorian m. worn THOMAS:D 34
mouth:
butter would not melt in her m. MACKLIN 1
every question with an open m. STEVENSON:A 14
Every time an Englishman opens his m. HOWARD:P 1
fig-leaves – especially over the m. HUX:A 24
God be in my m. ANON 66
impossible for an Englishman to open his m. SHAW 105
Into the m. of Hell TENNY 199
I've a m. like an old potato KIP 46
look a gift horse in the m. PROV 285
met in her m. – or anywhere LANCH 1
m. of honey, with the thyme FERGUS 1
m. of the Lord hath spoken BIBLE 320
m. shut and your eyes open PROV 219
No m. has the might to set JOYCE:J 42
opening your m. and putting PHILIP 6
Out of the m. of babes BIBLE 197
puff of vapour from his m. BROWNING:R 106
purple-stainèd m. KEATS 93
slap-dash down in the m. CONG 10
To look a gift-horse in the m. BUTLER:S[1] 17
was whispering in her m. MARX:C 1
mouth-organs: Between the m. and the didgeridoos HOPE:Al 4
mouthed: first mouth'd SHAK:HAM 151
mouthful: made it out of a m. of air YEATS 25
mouths:
Blind mouthes MILT 53
but she made m. in a glass SHAK:KING L 34
by examining his wives' m. RUSS:B 20
enemy in their m. to steal SHAK:OTH 28
lairnt the m. o littlans and pap-bairns BIBLE 591
less than the number of m. LEDDA 1
make m. upon me SHAK:MID 31
m. a sentence, as curs CHURCH:C 8
m. were made for tankards MASE 8
whose ready m. are stopped KEYES 1
move:
But it does m. GALI 1
did thee feel the earth m.? HEMINGWAY 7
Everything is on the m. HERAC 1
great affair is to m. STEVENSON:RL 2
I propose to m. immediately GRANT:US 4
I will m. the earth ARCHIM 1
Let's all m. one place on CARROLL 20
M. those ten thousand horses GRIFFITH 2
m. with the moving ships SWIN 45
moved:
day he m. out was terrible COPE 6
mooved more than with a Trumpet SIDNEY:P 16
m. more ways than one ROETH 2
moveless: With m. hands and face HARDY:T 25
movement:
detest as a m. MARSH 1
intelligent may begin a m. CONRAD 11
M., that problem of the visible WILDE:O 13
There was m. at the station PATERSON:AB 4
movers: we are the m. and shakers O'SHAUGH 1
moves: If it m., shoot it ANON 201
movie: m., not a lifeboat TRACY 2
moving: movin' up an' down again KIP 111
mower: M. whets his sithe MILT 70
Mozart:
M. was my age he had already LEHRER 3
sonatas of M. are unique SCHNAB 2
MPs:
dull M. in close proximity GILB:WS 48
in that House M. divide GILB:WS 48
Mrs Dale's Diary: 'M.D.D.'. I try never to miss ELIZ:QM 3
MSS: M. as drunkards use lamp-posts HOUSM 51
much:
do as m. of it as you can HOLMES:H 1
doesn't say m. for you MARX:G 1
have too m. of anything TEREN 1
How m. is it, Smyllie YEATS 148
I don't think m. of it STRACH 6
just so m., no more BROWNING:R 160
knows too m., tells too m. HOPE:Al 5
M. of a muchness VANB 8
so m. to do BELL:AG 2
so m. to do RHODES 4
so m. to do TENNY 164
won't be m. for us CARROLL 95
muchness: they're much of a m. ELIOT:G 42
muck:
great kudos leaving this m. alone MURD:R 1
in lovely m. I've lain HOUSM 29
money is like m. BACON:F[1] 100
sing 'em m. MELBA 2
muck-rake: with a m. in his hand BUNYAN 22
muck-rakes: men with the m. are often ROOS:T 5
muckle:
Many a mickle makes a m. PROV 263
Mony a mickle maks a m. CERV 15
mud:
dripping of water on m. FAIRBURN 1
made most of mine ... out of m. NAPO I 7
made up of marble and m. HAWT 3
Me name is M. DENNIS:CJ 1
m., glorious m. FLAND 1
One sees the m. LANGBRI 1
muddier: coming up m. HUX:A 36
muddle:
beginning, a m., and an end LARK 10
manage somehow to m. through BRIGHT 7
meddle and m. DERB 2
Mudie: British Museum and M.'s BUTLER:S[2] 12
muffin:
Improved Hot M. and Crumpet DICKENS 65
One caught a M. LEAR 29
mug: Guinness from a thick m. PINT 1
muir-men: When the m. win their hay BALL 7
Mulberry Garden: M.G., now the onely place EVELYN 3
Mulciber: Men call'd him M. MILT 144
mule: m. of politics DISR:B 19
mules: m. of politics POWER:JO 1

Mulligan: Stately, plump Buck M. JOYCE:J 10
Mullingar: elopement down in M. ANON 104
multiplication: M. is vexation ANON 84
multiplicity: life in m. AMIEL 2
multiplied: not be needlessly m. OCCAM·1
multiply: forth to m. in Yorkshire HILL:Reg 4
multiplying: our yearly m. millions O'SULL 2
multitude:
fool m. SHAK:MERC 29
giddy m. MASSIN 1
hoofs of a swinish m. BURKE:E 59
m.; that numerous piece of BROWNE:T 25
Nouns of number, or m. COBBETT 1
multitudes:
I am large, I contain m. WHITMAN 12
m. to digest themselves into HARDWO 2
Weeping, weeping m. ELIOT:TS 20
mum:
fuck you up, your m. and dad LARK 8
M.'s the word COLMAN:G[2]
oafish louts remember M. BETJ 24
mumble:
Let her maunder and m. CARLYLE:T 68
only memorize and m. SASS 14
Those who m. do not pray DUTT 2
mumbo-jumbo:
get M. out of the world MORRIS:W 13
M. will hoo-doo you LIND:V 3
mune: m. shak's her gowden feathers MACDIAR 2
murder:
But m. often THORN 1
does the same as m. him HORACE 117
foul and midnight murther GRAY:T 32
foul and most unnatural m. SHAK:HAM 43
from battle and m. PRAY 33
hear war called m. MACDON:R 2
I met M. on the way SHELLEY:PB 37
Killing noe M. SEXBY 1
love and m. will out CONG 19
Men especially love m. DWO 6
Mordre wol out CHAUC 63
Most sacrilegious m. hath SHAK:MAC 54
m. a man who is committing suicide WILSON:W 15
m. back into the home HITCH 2
m. cannot be hid SHAK:MERC 22
M. Considered as One of the Fine DEQ 9
M., like talent, seems LEWES 1
M. most foul SHAK:HAM 44
m. of men is disgusting EINS 10
m. shrieks out WEBSTER:J 28
m., though it have no tongue SHAK:HAM 94
once indulges himself in m. DEQ 11
One m. made a villain PORTEUS 1
rape and m. ... fill the fantasies CRISP 10
So it was m. MARX:G 12
Sooner m. an infant BLAKE:W 51
There's m. going on WHITEING 1
This is a British m. inquiry STOP 9
Thou shalt do no m. PRAY 65
time to m. and create ELIOT:TS 5
We m. to dissect WORDS:W 18
murdered:
brothers and their murder'd man KEATS 29
man who m. both his parents LINC 23
murderer:
An honourable m. SHAK:OTH 69
deaf and viperous m. SHELLEY:PB 118
first m. lay upon the earth HOPE:Al 2
help the escaping m. STEVENSON:RL 32
man is a common m. SAKI 19
murderers: m. take the first step KARR 2
murmur:
m. of a summer's day ARNOLD:M 20
rustic m. of their bourg TENNY 243
murmured: M. like a noontide bee SHELLEY:PB 147
murmuring: m. of innumerable bees TENNY 119
murmurs: hollow m. died away COLLINS:Will 7
murrain: Usura is a m. POUND 39
Murray: M. or thick boots behind CALVER 9
Murrumbidgee: and the M.'s flowing O'HAG 1
muscles:
m. on his brawny arms LONGFEL 11
quaking m. in the act of birth HOPE:Al 2
muse:
bid the M. go pack YEATS 75
entertain your sylvan M. VIRGIL 1
M. forbids to die HORACE 56
M. invoked, sit down to write SWIFT 67
m. on dromedary trots COLERIDGE:ST 64
my m. is playful OSB:J 10
my M. is young YEATS 133
no Mistress but their M. DONNE 51
with the worst-natur'd m. ROCHES 6
museum: become a m. man PRIEST 2
mush: with m. and slush OWEN:D 1
mushroom:
m. of a night's growth DONNE 104
m. On whom the dew FORD:J[1] 3
shape of a supramundane m. LAUR:WL 1
too short to stuff a m. CONRAN 1
mushrooms: silver-hatted m. make NEIL 3
music:
Aeonian m. measuring out TENNY 172
All m. but its own BRIDGES:M 1
all the m. in her tone TENNY 128
between classical m. and jazz PREVIN 1
brest surcharged with musick SIDNEY:P 11
can't listen to m. too oftem LENIN 11
city is built To m. TENNY 239
dagger when the m. stops WILSON:Harold 9
die in m. SHAK:OTH 67
English may not like m. BEECHAM 2
Fading in m. SHAK:MERC 33
fiddled whisper m. ELIOT:TS 53
Fled is that m. KEATS 93
good m.'s already been written ZAPPA 2
he hears no m. SHAK:JUL 15
heavy part the m. bears JONS 8
His voice in all her m. SHELLEY:PB 123
hope danceth without m. HERB:G 59
how potent cheap m. is COWARD 4
How sour sweet m. SHAK:RIC.II 45
I shall be made thy M. DONNE 94
If m. be the food SHAK:TWE 1
I'm a martyr to m. THOMAS:D 32
In sweet m. is such art SHAK:HEN.VIII 7
Intolerable m. falls YEATS 119
kind of petrified m. GOET 35
know m. if it came up and bit ZAPPA 1
laundry-list and I will set it to m. ROSSINI 2
let the sounds of m. Creep SHAK:MERC 50
lie on a sofa and listen to m. BOWEN:S 1
Like m. on my heart COLERIDGE:ST 35
little m. out of doors KEATS 160
madder m. and stronger wine DOWS 2
magic worlds of poetry and m. MORRELL 1
make the m. mute TENNY 244
making m. throatily and palpitatingly HUX:A 10
man that hath no m. SHAK:MERC 51
Mind the m. and the step BANGS 1
more or less lascivious m. MENCK 1
M. alone with sudden CONG 62
M. and women I cannot but PEPYS 17
M. begins to atrophy POUND 43
m. critics. They were small STRAV 5
M. has charms to soothe CONG 33
M. helps not the tooth-ache HERB:G 58
m. in my heart I bore WORDS:W 82
m. in the sinner's ears WESLEY:C 3
M. is essentially useless SANT 3
M. is feeling, then STEVENS 4
m. is good to the melancholey SPIN 2
M. is the food of love PROV 278
M. is your own experience PARKER:C 1
m. of derision GIBBONS:O 2
m. of forfended spheres PATMO 1
m. of men's lives SHAK:RIC.II 45
m. of the languid hours LANG:A 1
M. oft hath such a charm SHAK:MEA 31
m. played by the black man X 4
M. shall untune the sky DRYD 95
m. sweeter than their own WORDS:W 29
M. that gentlier on the spirit TENNY 27
M., the greatest good ADDIS 33
m. to attending ears SHAK:ROM 18
M., when soft voices die SHELLEY:PB 143
m. wherever there is a harmony BROWNE:T 29
m., yearning like a God KEATS 65
My m. is best understood by children STRAV 1
Not for the doctrine, but the m. POPE 18
now the m. of the spheres DAVIDS 2
Of m. Dr Johnson JOHNSON:S 264
only Jimmy had stuck to m. JOYCE:NB 1
own Musicke when they stray CAMPION 7
passion cannot M. raise DRYD 92
peculiar m. – wild, melancholy BRONTE:C 8
read m. but can't hear it BEECHAM 8
reasonable good ear in m. SHAK:MID 37
seduction of martial m. BURNEY 8
She shall have m. wherever NURS 58
Silent musick CAMPION 6
Silver m. from the bandstand BETJ 19
solemn service of m. to be LAMB:Ch 23
some are all for m. MASE 8
soul of m. shed MOORE:T 7
still, sad m. of humanity WORDS:W 8
stops when the m. stops HELPMAN 2
they quiver with the same m. GIBRAN 4
This m. crept by me SHAK:TEM 10
thou hast thy m. too KEATS 109
understood m. unless he was a scientist BUCK 6
uproar's your only m. KEATS 125
Van Gogh's ear for m. WILDER:B 3
vulgar and tavern m. BROWNE:T 30
Wagner's m. is better than it sounds TWAIN 34
We are the m. makers O'SHAUGH 1
were thy chosen m., Liberty WORDS:W 41
why hear'st thou m. sadly? SHAK:SON 4
with m. loud and long COLERIDGE:ST 63
with the sound of m. HAMMER 5
Your voice is m. BEERB 12
music-hall: M. songs provide the dull MAUGH 18
music-halls:
Darling of the m. SMITH:FE 6
no more jokes in m. SASS 2
musical:
cashiers of the M. Banks BUTLER:S[2] 2
Most musicall, most melancholy MILT 81
m. as is Apollo's lute MILT 33
Silence more m. ROSSET:C 10
We were none of us m. GASK 4
musician: dead, the sweet m. LONGFEL 23
musicians: we m. know BROWNING:R 168
musicologist: m. is a man who can read BEECHAM 8
musing: M. in solitude WORDS:W 109
musk: m. of the rose is blown TENNY 215
musk-roses: sweet m. SHAK:MID 20
musket-bullet: that a m. is not a pike TILLOT 1
mussel: m. pooled and the heron THOMAS:D 12
mussels: gaping m., left upon the mud CRAB 16
Musset: Alfred de M. Used to call HARE:ME 2
Mussolini:
remove the sound from M. BROWN:Geoff 1
showed surprising loyalty to M. BULLOCK 2
This whipped jackal* CHURCH:W 25
must:
It m. be BEETH 1
'm.' is not to be used to princes ELIZ I 16
What m. be, m. be PROV 418
whispers low, 'Thou m.' EMER 100
mustard: like to a grain of m. seed BIBLE 412
mustn't: tell her she m. PUNCH 14
mutability:
endure but M. SHELLEY:PB 17
M. in them doth play SPENS 44
strange m. of human affairs DICKENS 5
mute: care of natures that are m. MERED:G 23
muteness: uncommunicating m. of fishes LAMB:Ch 15
mutiny: refuse to go it is m. HERV:Lord 2
muttering: m. grew to a grumbling BROWNING:R 28
mutton:
boiled leg of m. with the usual DICKENS 43
introduce you to that leg of m. CARROLL 88
Old was his m. HOME 4
mutton-pies: I make them into m. CARROLL 82
muzzle: shalt not m. the ox BIBLE 125
my-lorded: m. him as only a free-born THACK 4
Myfanwy: my staunch M. BETJ 9
myriad: There died a m. POUND 29
myriads: united voice of m. GOLDS 54
myrtle:
all the m. and turkey part AUSTEN 33
cypress and m. Are emblems BYR 22
m. and ivy of sweet BYR 141
m. mixed in my path BROWNING:R 142
myself:
busy thinking about m. SITWELL:E 15
celebrate m., and sing m. WHITMAN 1

more I loved my n. land BELLOY 1
My n. land – Good Night BYR 58
my own, my n. land SCOTT:W 10
used to our ideas about the n. LESSING:D 1
natives:
Britons were only n. at that time SELL 2
Educating the n. of Borrioboola-Gha DICKENS 170
nativity: At my n. The front SHAK:HEN.IV[1] 55
nattering: n. nabobs of negativism AGNEW 1
natura: CONTRA N. POUND 41
natural:
Being n. is simply a pose WILDE:O 24
I do it more n. SHAK:TWE 20
in this more than n. SHAK:HAM 81
N. Selection DARW:C 1
prevents us from being n. so much LA ROCHE 34
twice as n. CARROLL 78
natural science: N.s. does not simply describe HEIS 2
nature:
Accuse not N. MILT 236
against n. not to go out MILT 311
All N. seems at work COLERIDGE:ST 66
all N. was a garden WALP:H 26
Allow not n. more SHAK:KING L 29
Art is not essential where N. GRACIAN 1
art itself is n. SHAK:WIN 18
arts is to correct n. VOLT 31
Beauty is n.'s brag MILT 39
Beauty is n.'s coyn MILT 38
cruel works of n. DARW:C 10
debt of n. FABY 1
drive out N. with a pitchfork HORACE 86
every charm to n. owing PHILIPS:A 2
fair defect of N.? MILT 254
fools call N. BROWNING:R 202
frame of n. round him break ADDIS 38
fresh from Natur's mould DICKENS 120
fulfils great N.'s plan BURNS:R 28
goal of the conquest of n. CARSON 2
good painters imitated n. CERV 25
great n.'s second course SHAK:MAC 40
great Secretary of N. WALT 17
grow ... into another n. SIDNEY:P 13
happy N. to explore POPE 96
In n. there are neither rewards INGER 1
In n. there are no rewards VACH 1
in our life alone does N. live COLERIDGE:ST 56
It can't be N. CHURCH:C 20
law of n., and of nations BURKE:E 103
looks through N., up to POPE 106
made one with N. SHELLEY:PB 123
man belongs to n. GREY OWL 1
Man is N.'s sole mistake GILB:WS 57
man's n. runs either to herbs BACON:F[1] 87
masterpiece of N. EMER 18
masters n. not by force BRIDGES:R 16
N. abhors a vacuum RAB 4
N., and N.'s laws lay POPE 71
n. by her mother wit SPENS 40
N. does not make progress LINN 1
n. doth nothing in vain NEWT:I 2
N. first made him ARIO 1
n., heartless, witless n. HOUSM 39
N. in you stands on the very SHAK:KING L 28
N. is a temple BAUD 3
N. is but a name for an effect COWP 82
N. is but Art POPE 88
N. is creeping up WHIST 8
N. is fine in love SHAK:HAM 167
N. is full of freaks EMER 68
N. is often hidden BACON:F[1] 86
n. is the art of God BROWNE:T 11
N. is unforgiving HUGO 7
N. is usually wrong WHIST 3
N. is very consonant NEWT:I 1
n. learning how to write CLARKE:M 1
N. made man happy ROUSS:JJ 5
n. makes the whole world kin SHAK:TRO 16
n. must obey necessity SHAK:JUL 77
N. never did betray WORDS:W 10
N. never makes excellent LOCKE 2
N. remains WHITMAN 40
N. that fram'd us MARLOWE 9
N. that is above all art DANI 3
N. to him was almost lost COLLINS:Will 1
N.! We are thine WORDS:W 136
N. wears one universal grin FIELDING 4
n. Whom passion could not SHAK:OTH 51
N. with a poet's eye CAMPBELL:T 5
N. yet remembers WORDS:W 62
N.'s ancient power was lost TENNY 163
N.'s complete indifference WEISS 1
n.'s handmaid art DRYD 7
n.'s infinite book of secrecy SHAK:ANT 4
N.'s mystic book MARV 33
n.'s truth Is primary THOMAS:RS 3
next to N., Art LANDOR 9
one of N.'s agreeable blunders COWLEY:H 1
one of N.'s Gentlemen LINT 1
one of the forces of n. MICHEL 1
opinion of their position in n. MAUGH 17
rest on N. fix COKE:E 6
rinnin coonter to natur NORTH:C 5
secret aims Of n. BRIDGES:R 1
sights of N. made me rejoice CURIE 2
simply *because it is n.* SCHILL 10
spokesman for wild n. SNY 2
standing at ease in N. WHITMAN 26
such be N.'s holy plan WORDS:W 14
Sweet is the lore which N. WORDS:W 18
'Tes the hand of N. GIBBONS:S 4
Then n. rul'd GAY 5
'tis N.'s law to change ROCHES 9
'tis their n. too WATTS 8
touched the hem of N.'s shift SHELLEY:PB 50
When N. has work to be done EMER 91
Who can fence in Mother N.? CERV 9
whole realm of N. mine WATTS 2
Whose body N. is POPE 87
With N.'s pride MARLOWE 6
write as the interpreter of n. JOHNSON:S 21
yourself a great work of n. WHIST 6
natures:
care of n. that are mute MERED:G 23
Men's n. are alike CONF 13
other naturs thinks different DICKENS 114
strife Of little n. BUCHANAN 4
naught: it is n., saith the buyer BIBLE 266
naughty:
good deed in a n. world SHAK:MERC 52
N. girl to disobey NURS 42
nauseous: n. draught of life go ROCHES 1
naval: talk to me about n. tradition CHURCH:W 68
nave: from the n. to th' chaps SHAK:MAC 3
navel:
ended at the n. LEWIS:W 6
imperial Germanic n. UNA 2
navel-cord: wind-toughened n. KAV 3
navies: nations' airy n. TENNY 79
navigators: side of the ablest n. GIBBON:E 10
navy:
It is upon the N. CHARLES II 1
joined the N. to see BERLIN:Ir 1
n. always travels first class FISHER:JA 3
N.'s here PARKER:Johnny 1
royal n. of England hath ever BLACKS 3
Ruler of the Queen's Navee GILB:WS 11
Nazareth: good thing come out of N.? BIBLE 474
Nazi:
come to terms with their N. past BUCH 1
N. Germany had become a menace NEVINS 1
Nazis: N. came for the Communists NIEM 1
Neanderthal: wouldn't take N. Man five years SNOW 3
near:
Be n. me TENNY 148
so n. and yet so far TENNY 176
nearer:
n. by not keeping still GUNN:T 2
N. to thee ADAMS:SF 1
nearest: n. and dearest enemy? SHAK:HEN.IV[1] 70
nearsighted: I am also n. AUD 69
neat:
n., clean, shaved CHAND 1
Still to be n. JONS 23
necessaries: made between luxuries and n. GALB 6
necessary:
little visible delight, but n. BRONTE:E 11
Make yourself n. to somebody EMER 54
they are n. evils JOHNSON:S 38
wondrous n. man MIDD 7
necessities:
art of our n. is strange SHAK:KING L 38
dispense with its n. MOTLEY 2
willingly do without the n. WRIGHT:FL 3
necessity:
alone N. Supreme THOMS:Ja[2] 6
grim N. SHAK:RIC.II 40
maken virtu of necessitee CHAUC 51
nature must obey n. SHAK:JUL 77
Necessitie and Chance Approach not MILT 226
N. gives the law without PUB 4
N. hath no law CROMWELL 8
N. is the mother of invention PROV 280
N. is the plea for every PITT:W[2] 1
N. makes an honest man DEF 7
N. never made a good bargain FRANKLIN:B 5
no virtue in n. SHAK:RIC.II 11
recognition of n. ENGELS 3
Thy n. is yet greater SIDNEY:P 18
neck:
Better bend the n. PROV 41
England will have her n. wrung WEY 1
especially from the n. down RUNYON 3
Her n. refulgent VIRGIL 40
in equipping us with a n. KOES 6
my n. is very short MORE:T 5
n. God made for other HOUSM 6
n. when once broken WALSH 1
Roman people had only one n. CALIG 1
Some chicken! Some n. CHURCH:W 24
Take eloquence and wring its n. VERL 4
necking: named it n. was a poor judge MARX:G 24
necklace: lose her heart, or n. POPE 45
necklaces: boxes of matches and our n. MANDELA:W 1
necks: Will ye submit your n. MILT 222
necktie: left my n. God knows where HOUSM 29
nectar:
draws n. in a sieve COLERIDGE:ST 67
To comprehend a n. DICKIN:E 1
nectarine: n. and curious peach MARV 17
need:
many things I have no n. of SOC 2
metaphysical n. is only a n. KAF 2
n. of a world of men BROWNING:R 62
reason not the n. SHAK:KING L 29
what you do not n. is dear CATO 5
needle:
blunteth the n. POUND 39
for the n. she TENNY 113
my hand a n. better fits BRADST 1
Plying her n. and thread HOOD 19
through the eye of a n. BIBLE 445
touched it with a n. PLAU 6
needlework: n. of Noodledom BROWNING:R 83
needs:
each according to his n. BAK 2
each according to his n. MARX:K 7
everybody n. at least once WILDER:T 1
N. must when the devil PROV 281
n. that challenge this world EISEN 3
nefarious: pity she is so n. RUNYON 8
negation: creates ... its own n. MARX:K 6
negativism: nattering nabobs of n. AGNEW 1
neglect:
becomes more irksome with n. ADAMS:A 2
devotes to the n. of his duties THOMP:WH 1
I n. God and his Angels DONNE 105
most tender mercy is n. CRAB 4
n. may breed mischief FRANKLIN:B 18
punished for n. JOHNSON:S 5
sweet n. more taketh me JONS 23
negligent: I may be n. SHAK:WIN 4
negotiate: to n. with my face? SHAK:TWE 15
negotiations: Man propounds n. KIP 134
negro:
insulted in places where the average N. DAVIS:S 1
makes a N. unpleasant to white MENCK 9
N. problem has ceased to be a N. X 3
negroes:
liberty among the drivers of n.? JOHNSON:S 43
poor are the n. of Europe CHAMFORT 7
providing the infant n. ... with flannel DICKENS 23

to the next insurrection of the n. JOHNSON:S 194
neigh: people expect me to n. ANNE 3
neighbor: more than my n. on the next block VANDERB 2
neighbour:
coveted his n.'s goods KINGSLEY:C 5
death ... had been his next-door n. SCOTT:W 82
Death is my n. now EVANS:E 4
demand that men love their n. BRECHT 8
love thy n. as thyself BIBLE 113, 422
love your crooked n. AUD 8
Love your n., but don't PROV 255
Love your n. is not merely sound LLOYD GEO 8
Loving your n. as much CLEESE 1
man their n. knows YEATS 40
neighed after his n.'s wife BIBLE 336
nor anything that is thy n.'s BIBLE 103
our n.'s house is on fire BURKE:E 49
policy of the good n. ROOS:FD 7
that he might rob a n. MACAULAY:TB 8
world to my n.'s gate MERED:G 35
your n.'s wall catches fire HORACE 90
neighbours:
common hatred of its n. INGE 11
fences make good n. FROST:R 3
fling the curses on his n. BRONTE:E 9
Good fences make good n. PROV 153
Good n. I have had ELIZ I 2
improper thoughts about their n. BRADLEY:FH 3
make sport for our n. AUSTEN 27
what is happening to our n. CHAMBERLAIN:J 4
neighed: n. after his neighbour's wife BIBLE 336
neither: 'Tis n. here nor there SHAK:OTH 57
Nell: death of Little N. without laughing WILDE:O 130
Nelly: Let not poor N. starve CHARLES II 5
Nelson:
death of N. was felt SOUTHEY 22
explain to them the *N. touch* NELS 1
keep the N. touch NEWBOLT 3
onehandled adulterer* JOYCE:J 20
To N.'s peerless name NEWBOLT 1
nemo: *N. me impune lacessit* ANON 220
neo-Gothic: n., you know BEECHAM 1
nephew: beamish n. CARROLL 90
nepotism: son-in-law also rises* KNOPF 1
Neptune:
Do chase the ebbing N. SHAK:TEM 29
influence N.'s empire stands SHAK:HAM 6
N.'s park SHAK:CYM 8
Notice N., though Taming BROWNING:R 23
Nero: a black N. HILLS 1
nerves:
feels for my poor n. AUSTEN 20
N. sit ceremonious DICKIN:E 5
strengthens our n. BURKE:E 66
Nervii: day he overcame the N. SHAK:JUL 54
nervous breakdowns: symptoms of approaching n.b. RUSS:B 31
nest:
broods a n. of sorrows TAYL:Jer 4
Her soft and chilly n. KEATS 72
leaves the well-built n. SHELLEY:PB 160
n. of singing birds JOHNSON:S 88
nests:
all built their n. in my beard LEAR 1
n. inside men's Sunday hats BROWNING:R 25
net:
leave the ball in the back of the n. DUFFY:J 1
N. Anything reticulated or JOHNSON:S 13
Whizzing them over the n. BETJ 10
nets:
making n., not in making cages SWIFT 18
n. of such a texture SHEN 3
n. to catch the wind WEBSTER:J 18
tangl'd in Amorous N. MILT 264
nettle:
Out of this n., danger SHAK:HEN.IV[1] 31
Tender-hearted stroke a n. HILL:A 1
nettles:
apt to be overrun with n. WALP:H 20
like the dust on the n. THOMAS:E 6
neurosis: N. is the way of avoiding TILLICH 1
neurotic: n. if he suffers from his problems SZASZ 8
neurotics: Everything great ... is done by n. PROUST 8
neuter: female to that of n. being BERNARD:Jes 1
neutral: studiously n. WILSON:W 8
neutrality:
Armed n. is ineffectual WILSON:W 10
Just for a word – 'n.' BETHM 1
n. of an impartial judge BURKE:E 73
never: Better late than n. PROV 43
Never Never: Out on the wastes of the N.N. BOA 1
nevermore: Quoth the Raven, 'N.' POE 5
nevershit: like you was Lady N. WESK 1
new:
at least find something n. VOLT 12
Ever charming, ever n. DYER:J[1] 2
first by whom the n. POPE 17
it remains forever new HEINE 3
N. things are made familiar JOHNSON:S 55
n. world demands a n. political TOC 2
old yield to the n. rite THOMAS AQ 2
ring in the n. TENNY 177
shock of the n. DUNL 1
something n. out of Africa PLINY 1
sun shone ... on the nothing n. BECKETT 1
yielding place to n. TENNY 278
new-born:
I with things n. SHAK:WIN 11
use of a n. child? FRANKLIN:B 30
New South Wales: Go out and govern N.S.W. BELLOC 20
New World: called the N.W. into existence CANN 10
new year: hansel of this guid n.y. DUNB 15
New York:
dawn in N.Y. has LORCA 2
four hundred people in N.Y. society MCALL 1
N.Y. ... is not Mecca SIMON:N 1
N.Y. ... that unnatural city GILMAN 3
New Yorker: Read *The N.Y.* AUD 47
New Zealand:
approaching N.Z. Please move your watches ANON 151
France put agents into N.Z. LANGE 1
In your atlas two islands* CURNOW 2
it seemed to be shut* FREUD:C 2
New Zealanders:
don't exactly hate N.Z. ADAMS:P 1
N.Z. are a rough mob LEE:JA 1
N.Z. are the most balanced ALLEN:D 1
news:
All the n. that's fit to print OCHS 1
bad n. infects the teller SHAK:ANT 8
Bad n. travels fast PROV 25
bites a man that is not n. DANA 2
bringer of unwelcome n. SHAK:HEN.IV[2] 4
evil n. rides post MILT 296
good n. baits MILT 296
good n. yet to hear CHESTERTON 9
Have you n. of my boy KIP 153
if there was any n. in the paper AUSTEN 9
Ill n. hath wings DRAYT 2
man bites a dog that is n. BOGART:JB 1
master-passion is the love of n. CRAB 6
nearly time for the n. ELIOT:TS 80
never good To bring bad n. SHAK:ANT 33
n. coverage that's got so much better CHESTERTON 61
N. is a genre IGNAT 1
n. much older than their ale GOLDS 30
n. that stays n. POUND 45
N. value RALPH 1
No n. is good n. PROV 296
only n. until he's read it WAUGH:E 24
They brought me bitter n. CORY 1
newspaper:
art of n. paragraphing MARQUIS 10
n. ... be compared to a stagecoach FIELDING 20
n. ... is a nation talking MILLER:A 7
n. is of necessity something SCOTT:CP 1
Once a n. touches a story MAIL 1
Reading someone else's n. BRADB 3
rule never to look into a n. SHERIDAN:RB 29
truths to be relied on in a n. JEFFERSON 13
newspapers:
form of continuous fiction* BEVAN 7
N. always excite curiosity LAMB:Ch 21
plenty of n. with plenty of people MURD:R 2
Read the n. WELLING 17
wall of n. and FORST 1
Newspeak: N. was the official language ORWELL 29
Newton:
Let N. be POPE 71
N., with his prism WORDS:W 152
N.s Particles of light BLAKE:W 101
Newtons: five hundred Sir Isaac N. COLERIDGE:ST 97
newts: N. and blind-worms SHAK:MID 21
nexus: sole n. of man to man CARLYLE:T 40
nice:
Be n. to people on your MIZ 1
haven't anything n. to say LONGWORTH 2
how nasty the n. people can be POWELL:A 5
N. but nubbly KIP 19
N. guys finish last DURO 1
nicely-nicely: N. dies of will be over-feeding RUNYON 7
nicest: n. child I ever knew BELLOC 12
Nicholas Nye: Old N.N. DE LA M 15
nicht:
braw brecht moonlecht necht LAUD 2
Change n. into day NORTH:C 5
efter sic a n. MACDIAR 16
Nick: N., or clootie BURNS:R 10
nickel: care if it doesn't make a n. GOLDWYN 6
nickname: n. is the heaviest stone HAZL 7
Nicodemus: N. saw such light VAUGHAN:H 1
niece: sister's husband's n. CARROLL 94
nieve: His n. a nit BURNS:R 36
Niger: on the left bank of the N. DICKENS 170
niggers:
gone whar de good n. go FOST:SC 2
Irish are the n. of Europe DOYLE: R 1
night:
acquainted with the n. FROST:R 8
ain't a fit n. out FIELDS 1
alone, upon the alps at n. DURRELL:L 1
black bat, n., has flown TENNY 215
choose An everlasting n. DONNE 93
Come, civil n. SHAK:ROM 29
dark n. of the soul FITZGER:FS 12
day brought back my n. MILT 103
deep of n. is crept SHAK:JUL 77
drown'd with us in endlesse n. HERR 24
dusky n. rides down FIELDING 7
Every n. of her married life THOMAS:D 26
Every nighte and alle BALL 36
eyeless labourer in the n. WRIGHT:J 7
face of n. is fair TENNY 226
Feed the heart of the n. SWIN 4
for a n. and away WYCH 3
From morn to n., my friend ROSSET:C 14
gentle into that good n. THOMAS:D 18
genuine n. admits no ray DRYD 63
go bump in the n. ANON 187
going to be a bumpy n. DAVIS:B 1
hard day's n. LENNON 4
hath my n. of life some memory SHAK:COM 8
have one other gaudy n. SHAK:ANT 40
horror of a profoundly dark n. RACINE 8
In an eternal n. SWIN 32
In the forests of the n. BLAKE:W 67
instalment of n. which had HARDY:T 57
It was mirk, mirk n. BALL 57
last out a n. in Russia SHAK:MEA 8
Long n. succeeds PEAC 17
long out-living n. MILT 61
love-performing n. SHAK:ROM 29
loving, black-brow'd n. SHAK:ROM 30
made him know his God by n. VAUGHAN:H 1
make the n. joint-labourer SHAK:HAM 4
Making n. hideous SHAK:HAM 36
marriage depends on the first n. BALZ 2
meaner beauties of the n. WOTTON 3
middle of the n. CARROLL 53
moonless n. in the small town THOMAS:D 21
Morning in the Bowl of N. FITZGER:E 1
my delight on a shining n. ANON 33
N. and day PORTER:C 2
n. cometh BIBLE 482
n. do penance for a day WORDS:W 153
n. for thieves EUR 2
n. has a thousand eyes BOUR 1
n. has been long GILB:WS 53

N. hath a thousand eyes LYLY 7
n. . . . is but the daylight sick SHAK:MERC 54
N. is drawing nigh BARING-G 1
n. is far spent BIBLE 518
N. is growing gray? HARDY:T 27
N. makes no difference HERR 40
n. of loss is always there TENNY 161
n. of memories and of sighs LANDOR 1
n. of time far surpasseth BROWNE:T 60
N., sable Goddess YOUNG:E 7
n. seems termless hell THOMS:Ja[2] 4
n. that should banish GODWIN 1
n.! this world's defeat VAUGHAN:H 2
n. was made for loving BYR 129
n. with different stars SACK 3
N. with her train of stars HENL 5
n.'s black agents SHAK:MAC 67
not yet the N. BETJ 13
Oft, in the stilly n. MOORE:T 20
Our first n. years ago HEAN 6
Out of the n. that covers HENL 1
perils and dangers of this n. PRAY 29
Red sky at n., shepherd's PROV 331
Sable-vested N. MILT 173
Sleep in the n. BLAKE:W 45
sleep one ever-during n. CATUL 5
Spirit of N. SHELLEY:PB 145
Such n. in England ne'er had MACAULAY:TB 40
tender is the n. KEATS 93
Then it will be *good* n. SHELLEY:PB 57
There's n. and day, brother BORR 5
thievish N. MILT 24
Thro' the noises of the n. TENNY 22
Through the n. of doubt BARING-G 5
'Twas the n. before Christmas MOORE:CC 1
watch the n. and wait HOUSM 7
were the world's last n.? DONNE 86
What hath n. to do with sleep? MILT 21
what of the n.? BIBLE 313
with us perpetual n. JONS 19
womb of uncreated n. MILT 153
Work, for the n. is coming COG 1
yet it is not n. BYR 99
night-side: Illness is the n. of life SONT 4
night watchman: steady work – the n.w. BANK 2
nightblue: humid n. fruit JOYCE:J 27
nightgown: and in his n. NURS 82
nightingale:
A voice and nothing more* ANON 258
all but the wakeful N. MILT 198
brown bright n. amorous SWIN 9
envie no man's n. HERB:G 26
it was the n. SHAK:ROM 35
light-wingèd Dryad of the trees* KEATS 93
little brown n. bills his best HARDY:T 40
n. all spring through SWIN 4
N. cries to the Rose FITZGER:E 3
n. does sit so late MARV 23
n., if she should sing SHAK:MERC 53
n. in the sycamore STEVENSON:RL 59
N. that in the Branches FITZGER:E 33
N., that on yon bloomy MILT 92
N. when May is past CAREW:T 7
roar you an 'twere any n. SHAK:MID 10
sings as sweetly as a n. SHAK:TAM 6
spoils the singing of the n. KEATS 26
'tis the ravish'd n. LYLY 5
told in London about a n. ARLEN 1
Where the n. doth sing KEATS 56
nightingales:
By Eve's n. DE LA M 4
n. are singing near ELIOT:TS 30
nightmare:
Between dream and n. CAMPBELL:ATA 1
burrows of the N. AUD 7
N. LIFE-IN-DEATH was she COLERIDGE:ST 20
nights:
I walk abroad o' n. MARLOWE 23
Love not such n. as these SHAK:KING L 36
never spent the n. of sorrow GOET 6
n. and feasts divine HORACE 72
n. are longest there SHAK:MEA 8
n. are wholesome SHAK:HAM 10
They shorten tedious n. CAMPION 8
weariest n., the longest ORCZY 2
ye N. and Days PRAY 15
nihilist: cannot be a part-time n. CAMUS 12
nihilistic: say that my works are n. KAW 2
Nile:
allegory on the banks of the N. SHERIDAN:RB 11
barged down the N. last night BROWN:JM 1
I dipped my pen in the N. FENT 2
know the sources of the N. ELIOT:G 31
pour the waters of the N. CARROLL 4
nimini-pimini: pronouncing to yourself n. BURGOY 1
Nimrod: N. the mighty hunter BIBLE 44
nine men's morris: n.m.m. is fill'd up with mud SHAK:MID 15
ninepence: but n. in ready money ADDIS 31
ninety: n. and nine just persons BIBLE 462
Nineveh:
Built N. with our sighing O'SHAUGH 1
Quinquireme of N. MASE 9
Niobe: N. of nations BYR 104
nip: I'll n. him in the bud ROCHE 2
nipping: n. and an eager air SHAK:HAM 34
nipple: pluck'd my n. from his boneless SHAK:MAC 28
Nixon:
between N. and the White House KENNEDY:JF 7
to get N. re-elected COLSON 1
won't have N. to kick around NIX 1
no:
can't say 'N.' in any PARKER:D 18
everlasting N. CARLYLE:T 10
man who says n. CAMUS 9
N., John! N., John ANON 34
N., n., my girl JOHNSON:S 125
N. sun – n. moon HOOD 26
say N. when they mean Yes ALCOTT:LM 2
says n., he is not a diplomat DENNING 2
we are able to say N. ARISTOT 9
No-more: N., Too-late, Farewell ROSSET:DG 12
Noah:
cataclysm but one poor N. HUX:A 43
God remembered N. BIBLE 37
N. begat Shem, Ham, and BIBLE 34
N. he often said CHESTERTON 13
nobility:
N. has its obligations LEVIS 1
N. is a graceful ornament BURKE:E 64
n. is exempt from fear SHAK:HEN.VI[2] 7
only true n. is virtue JUV 17
still our old n. MANNERS 1
nobiscum: What gets God by *n.*? ANDREW 2
noble:
all were n., save Nobility BYR 60
dearth of n. natures KEATS 35
except for a n. purpose HERB:AP 16
last infirmity of N. mind MILT 49
Man is a n. animal BROWNE:T 62
n. and nude and antique SWIN 19
n. grounds for the n. emotions RUSKIN 6
n. in motive and far-reaching HOOV 1
n. Living and the n. Dead WORDS:W 161
n. man but made ignoble TENNY 254
n. savage ran DRYD 12
n. type of good LONGFEL 24
N. values, in the end MONTH 1
not Be n. to myself SHAK:ANT 65
not birth that makes us n. FLETCH:J 13
'Tis only n. to be good TENNY 64
nobleman: king may make a n. BURKE:E 89
nobleness:
allied with perfect n. ARNOLD:M 52
inform Thy thoughts with n. SHAK:COR 19
nobles: n. by the right of an earlier MACAULAY:TB 21
noblesse: *N. oblige* LEVIS 1
noblest:
honest God's the n. work BUTLER:S[2] 40
n. offspring is the last BERK 6
n. work of God POPE 104
nobly:
Godolphin Horne was N. Born BELLOC 13
Made us n. wild HERR 41
N., n. Cape St Vincent BROWNING:R 51
Spurn not the n. born GILB:WS 45
nobody:
because I'm n.'s child? CASE 1
I'm N.! Who are you? DICKIN:E 3
n. comes, n. goes BECKETT 5
N. is on my side AUSTEN 20
N. tells me anything GALS 1
there's n. at home POPE 75
nocht: man that will n. HENRYS 2
nocturnal: Some n. blackness HARDY:T 34
nod: n. is as good as a wink PROV 292
Nod:
dwelt in the land of N. BIBLE 31
Old N., the shepherd DE LA M 10
nodded: While I n., nearly napping POE 3
noddle: barmie n.'s working prime BURNS:R 41
nods:
N., and Becks MILT 66
whenever the good Homer n. HORACE 113
noise:
all within was n. TENNY 170
barbarous n. environs me MILT 95
Damn'd would make no n. HERR 13
Empty vessels make the most n. PROV 93
let us make a joyful n. BIBLE 229
little noiseless n. KEATS 6
loud n. at one end KNOX:R 4
love the n. it makes BEECHAM 2
more n. they make in pouring POPE 179
most sublime n. that ever FORST 2
never valued till they make a n. CRAB 25
n. in the beast's belly MALORY 2
n. like of a hidden brook COLERIDGE:ST 31
n. like that of a water-mill SWIFT 28
n. of battle roll'd TENNY 272
n. of life begins again TENNY 134
n. so slight it would surpass GRAVES:R 2
n. turns up my giddy brain MARLOWE 26
nothingness of scorn and n. CLARE:J 8
The *n.*, my dear ANON 221
when every n. appals me? SHAK:MAC 44
noises:
isle is full of n. SHAK:TEM 24
Thro' the n. of the night TENNY 22
noisy:
n. man is always in the right COWP 25
people would be just as n. CROMWELL 13
Nokomis: Daughter of the Moon, N. LONGFEL 20
nomadic: discomfort of a n. existence SACK 2
nominated: will not accept if n. SHERMAN 2
non-combatant: no fury like a n. MONTAGUE 1
non-commissioned: Army is the N. man KIP 82
non sequitur: conclusion was *n.s.* FIELDING 26
non-smoking: one of the n. sort LIND:N 1
non-violence:
N. is the first article of my faith GAND:M 1
n. without wanting to kick his HAMP 4
nonchalance: life in n. and insouciance NASH 14
nonconformist: man must be a n. EMER 7
nonpareil: Colour-Serjeant of the N. DICKENS 184
nonsense:
his n. suited their n. CHARLES II 4
lump of clotted n. DRYD 140
mind swings between sense and n. JUNG:Carl 3
n. of the old women STERNE 24
round the corner of n. COLERIDGE:ST 93
to be hanged for n. DRYD 58
noodledom: needlework of N. BROWNING:R 83
noon:
Act in the n. BLAKE:W 45
from Morn to N. he fell MILT 144
lady sing at the n. MORRIS:W 2
midnight and the n.'s repose ELIOT:TS 2
n. a purple glow YEATS 4
shameless n. Was clash'd TENNY 94
noon-day: talks of darkness at n. COWP 37
noon-heat: n. breathes it back HARDY:T 9
noontide: With throbbings of n. HARDY:T 12
nooses: N. give PARKER:D 5
Norfolk:
bear him up the N. sky BETJ 4
Very flat, N. COWARD 3
normal:
knowing, The n. thing to do KOCAN 1
n. is so much more simply STEIN:G 2
on the very type of the n. JAMES:H 18
Thank God we're n. OSB:J 10
normalcy: not nostrums but n. HARDING:WG 1
Noroway: To N. o'er the faem BALL 48
north:
Ask where's the N.? POPE 95

journey n. has the quality of dream ATWOOD 4
n. focuses our anxieties ATWOOD 4
n. of my lady's opinion SHAK:TWE 43
n. wind doth blow NURS 43
n. wind doth blow PROV 298
true and tender is the N. TENNY 110
Without sharp N. DONNE 43
North: to the last be Christopher N. NORTH:C 6
north star: she would infect the n.s. SHAK:MUCH 7
north-west: N. passage to the intellectual world STERNE 25
northern:
constant as the n. star SHAK:JUL 34
Prater of the *n.* race CHURCH:C 5
Northumbrian: N. Shades, which overlook AKEN 1
Norval: My name is N. HOME 1
nose:
And pecked off her n. NURS 66
Any n. May ravage BROWNING:R 8
big n. is the proper sign ROSTAND:E 2
blow his n. without moralizing CONNOLLY:C 16
Cleopatra's n. had been shorter PASC 5
cut off your n. to spite PROV 78
Dong with the Luminous N. LEAR 10
down his innocent n. SHAK:AS 13
Entuned in hir n. CHAUC 9
final cause of the human n. COLERIDGE:ST 82
hadde a semely n. CHAUC 74
Her n. and chin they threaten BURNS:R 104
indebted for a n. or an eye HAZL 11
Just as I'm picking my n.? AUD 26
Marian's n. looks red SHAK:LOV 25
n. nailed to other people's lavatories SITWELL:E 17
N. of Turk SHAK:MAC 80
n. small and laid back WODE 14
n. was as sharp as a pen SHAK:HEN.V 13
often wipe a bloody n. GAY 47
On his n. there was a Cricket LEAR 12
Pope ... he was picking his n. SHEN 4
provided he minds his n. LEAR 24
Reflectively picking his n. WALLACE:G 1
ring at the end of his n. LEAR 19
see further than his own n. FONTAINE 17
see what is in front of one's n. ORWELL 23
tenderly be led by th' n. SHAK:OTH 18
Tickling a parson's n. SHAK:ROM 5
turn up your n. rather than wipe LICHT 1
who gave thee this jolly red n.? BEAUMO 1
with a carnation up my n. MACKINN 1
noses:
For wearing our own n. SHAK:CYM 7
We must have bloody n. SHAK:HEN.IV[1] 34
nostalgia:
n. nurtured from childhood? SAG 1
n. would be satisfied in the Soviet Union UST 9
nostalgic: most n. people on earth HYDE:R 1
nostril: Why a N. wide inhaling BLAKE:W 30
nostrums: not n. but normalcy HARDING:WG 1
not:
easier to say what it is n. JOHNSON:S 187
I would prefer n. to MELV 5
said the thing which was n. SWIFT 34
note:
best fits my little n. HERR 37
silent n. which Cupid strikes BROWNE:T 29
notes:
chield's amang you takin n. BURNS:R 75
mixtur-maxtur o n. BIBLE 595
N. are often necessary JOHNSON:S 38
n. by distance made COLLINS:Will 7
n. I handle no better SCHNAB 1
rough n. and our dead bodies SCOTT:Rob 3
same eight n. to work with SULLI:Ar 1
thinks two n. a song DAVIES:WH 6
nothing:
burden it is to have n. to do BOIL 2
but don't say nothin' HAMMER 1
courage to believe in n. TURG 3
for good men to do n. BURKE:E 107
gives to airy n. SHAK:MID 43
he n. knew MILT 274
I ... I ... have n. MORA 1
I have n. to say CAGE 1
I said there was n. *like* it CARROLL 76
infinite deal of n. SHAK:MERC 8
Is it n. to you BIBLE 343
Labour of doing n. STEELE 9
learnt n. and forgotten n. TALL 5
live well on n. a year THACK 9
lives doing n. for each other CROSBY 1
looks constantly into N. TUCHOL 3
make that, which was n., All DONNE 70
n. a-year, paid quarterly SURT 16
n. at all to be done FAIRBURN 2
N. can be created from n. LUCRET 3
n. can be known BYR 63
n. done while aught remains ROGERS:S 3
N. happens, nobody comes BECKETT 5
n. is but what is not SHAK:MAC 16
n. is had for n. CLOUGH 5
N. is so good as it seems ELIOT:G 22
n. left to lose KRIS 1
N., like something, happens LARK 2
N. to be done BECKETT 2
n. to do about anything ELIOT:TS 80
N. to do but work KING:B 1
n. to offer anybody KERO 2
n. to say and I want to communicate HIRST 1
n. to say, say n. COLTON 2
N. ventured, n. gained PROV 302
N. will come of n. SHAK:KING L 1
Nothink for nothink 'ere PUNCH 11
say n., when he has n. to say JOHNSON:S 214
space in which there is absolutely n. DESCA 4
this site in 1897 n. happened ANON 227
To do n. and get something DISR:B 24
to do n. for ever and ever ANON 131
To whom n. is given FIELDING 11
We are n.; less than n. LAMB:Ch 5
we said n., all the day DONNE 35
who do n. are never wrong BANV 2
You ain't heard nothin' yet JOLS 1
You ain't seen n. yet REAG 8
nothingness:
holding up the n. of life? BYR 215
love and fame to n. do sink KEATS 23
never Pass into n. KEATS 34
n. of scorn and noise CLARE:J 8
nothings:
Invulnerable n. SHELLEY:PB 120
such labour'd n. POPE 16
notice: man who used to n. HARDY:T 33
noticeboard: *The Times* is a tribal n. ANON 249
noticed: though little notic'd here COWP 91
notions: General n. are generally wrong MONTAGU 4
nouns: N. of number, or multitude COBBETT 1
nourish: n. us with all goodness PRAY 55
nouveau riche: lot to be said for being *n.r.* VIDAL 7
novel:
because a n.'s invented POWELL:A 8
getting out of n. spinning THACK 28
given away by a N. KEATS 157
good n. tells us the truth CHESTERTON 36
in advance we may hold a n. JAMES:H 5
it is a kind of n. WALP:H 6
it is only a n. AUSTEN 58
not a n. to be tossed PARKER:D 30
n. is a mirror walking STEND 2
n. is a static thing TYNAN 1
n. is the one bright book LAWR:DH 25
n. of the nineteenth century was female CHESTERTON 46
n. tells a story FORST 10
read a n. before luncheon WAUGH:E 27
sex n. is now normal SHAW 129
supersede the last fashionable n. MACAULAY:TB 59
thin as a cigarette paper to write a n. DAVISON:FD 2
thing his n. is *about* is always there WELLS:HG 15
When I want to read a n. DISR:B 99
write a n. unless one has something SAYERS 5
write the Great Australian N. WHITE:P 8
novelist:
being a n., I consider myself LAWR:DH 26
completely forbidden to the n. GARC 3
God wasn't too bad a n. BARTH:J 1
No poet or n. wishes AUD 63
n. is ... more fully at home NAB 6
novelists:
many reasons why n. write FOW 2
n. stories of the present GON 1
novels:
factor common to all n. FORST 11
few English n. for grown up WOOLF:V 2
my n. are an accumulation of detail WHITE:P 15
N. are as useful as Bibles EMER 51
time to write n. WAUGH:A 2
novelties: grenades, and other n. BETHU 1
novelty: N., n., n. HOOD 30
November:
no leaves, no birds, – N. HOOD 27
N.'s sky is chill SCOTT:W 12
remember the Fifth of N. NURS 53
now:
destiny – are *here* and *n.* HAMMAR 2
If it be n. SHAK:HAM 193
If not n. when? HILLEL 2
is n., and ever shall be MASS 5
is n., and ever shall be PRAY 7
Leave N. for dogs and apes BROWNING:R 118
nowhere: dressed up with n. to go WHITE:Wil 1
noxious: Of all n. animals KILV 1
nuclear:
Australia, an area famed among n. scientists DAGG 1
enemy of the n. threat LANGE 1
n. warfare could mean WHITE:P 14
this issue, the n. defence of Britian OWEN:D 2
Widow Twankey's N. Laundry ART 1
nude:
keep one from going n. KING:B 1
noble and n. and antique SWIN 19
trouble with n. dancing HELPMAN 2
nudging: fed up with fudging and n. OWEN:D 1
nuisance:
exchange of one n. for another ELLIS:H 4
Inflation in the Sixties was a n. LEVIN 1
not make himself a n. MILL 14
nuisances: change of n. is as good as LLOYD GEO 13
number:
if I called the wrong n. THURB 17
it is a very interesting n. RAMAN 1
Not on the n., but the choice COWLEY:A 14
Nouns of n., or multitude COBBETT 1
number one:
always took care of n.o. MARR 1
Look after n.o. PROV 246
loyalties which centre upon n.o. CHURCH:W 54
numbered: n. in case they get lost MILLIG 9
numbers:
add to golden n. DEK 2
Here are only n. ratified SHAK:LOV 12
I lisp'd in n. POPE 119
Round n. are always false JOHNSON:S 195
safety in n. PROV 374
secret magic of n. BROWNE:T 9
There is no safety in n. THURB 10
numbness: drowsy n. pains my sense KEATS 93
nun:
endure the livery of a n. SHAK:MID 1
extremely rowdy N. COWARD 28
my daughter the N. SOUTHEY 7
pensive N., devout and pure MILT 79
nunc dimittis: sweetest canticle is *N.d.* BACON:F[1] 53
nunnery: Get thee to a n. SHAK:HAM 100
nuns: N. fret not at their WORDS:W 50
nuptials: prone to any iteration of n. CONG 56
nurse:
always keep a-hold of N. BELLOC 18
beggar's n. and Caesar's SHAK:ANT 62
definition of what a n. NIGHT 1
dirty n., Experience TENNY 261
hateful n. who smelt of soap BETJ 34
n., a piece of furniture, a *woman* TOLS:S 2
n. unacted desires BLAKE:W 51
N. unupblown WAUGH:E 35
sleep, Nature's soft n. SHAK:HEN.IV[2] 30
sucks the n. asleep? SHAK:ANT 75
to fawn upon a n. SHAK:RIC.II 6
will scratch the n. SHAK:TWO 4
nursed: nurst upon the self-same hill MILT 44
nurseries: n. of all vice and immorality FIELDING 14
nursery:
n. of future revolutions BURKE:E 52

n. still leaps out BYR 134
nursery maids: could be employed as n.m. WAUGH:A 3
nurses:
farrago of the clack of n. STERNE 24
old men's n. BACON:F[1] 85
nursling: n. of the Sky SHELLEY:PB 56
nut: I had a little n. tree NURS 21
nutrition: draw n., propagate POPE 92
nuts:
Brazil – where the n. come THOMAS:B 2
gathering n. in May ANON 17
may be n. for Mary Ann ANON 138
N.! MCAULIFFE 1
nutshell: bounded in a n. SHAK:HAM 78
nymph:
here's to the n. with but one SHERIDAN:RB 25
n., with long dishevelled SHAK:POET 10
o: Within this wooden O SHAK:HEN.V 2
oafs: muddied o. at the goals KIP 101
oak:
Heart of o. are our ships GARRICK 4
hollow o. our palace is CUNNING:A 5
no epitaph of that O. DONNE 101
nodosities of the o. without its BURKE:E 106
O., and Ash, and Thorn KIP 122
owl lived in an o. NURS 86
thunders from her native o. CAMPBELL:T 8
win the palm, the o. MARV 12
oaks:
families last not three o. BROWNE:T 57
Great o. from little acorns PROV 155
lie like one of those old o. BURKE:E 75
Little strokes fell great o. FRANKLIN:B 14
Tall o., branch-charmèd KEATS 48
Tall o. from little acorns EVER 1
oar: imprint of an o. upon CHOP 2
oars: o. were silver SHAK:ANT 25
oat-cakes: Calvin, o., and sulphur SMITH:Syd[1] 18
Oates: gentleman, Captain L.E.G. O. ATK:EL 1
oath:
good mouth-filling o. SHAK:HEN.IV[1] 67
gretteste ooth was but by Seinte Loy CHAUC 8
If ever I utter an o. SHAW 116
inscriptions a man is not upon o. JOHNSON:S 175
who triumphs by breaking an o. PLUT 2
oaths:
but men with o. LYS 1
Full of stange o. SHAK:AS 34
O. are but words BUTLER:S[1] 24
o. are straws SHAK:HEN.V 16
swore as many o. as I spake SHAK:KING L 44
oats: *O.* A grain, which in England JOHNSON:S 14
Obadiah: O. Bind-their-kings MACAULAY:TB 38
obedience:
keeps men in o. BURTON:Ro 24
might expect more o. GOLDS 61
O. is woman's earthly duty SCHILL 5
o. of distant provinces MACAULAY:TB 29
o. of enormous masses BAGE 9
Rebellion to tyrants is o. BRADSH:J 1
obey:
aways implicitly o. orders NELS 2
easy to o., if one dreams SARTRE 11
if anyone is born to o. COMPT 3
in all my best o. you SHAK:HAM 20
make the world o. VIRGIL 72
not o. the laws too well EMER 38
o. is better than sacrifice BIBLE 145
o. the established Government WASH 7
people wouldn't o. the rules BENNETT:Al 3
To love, cherish, and to o. PRAY 85
way parents o. their children EDWARD VIII 5
woman to o. TENNY 113
obeyed: o. as a son GIBBON:E 20
obeys:
most, when she o. POPE 139
she o. him LONGFEL 22
obituaries: many o. with a lot of pleasure DARROW 1
object: My o. all sublime GILB:WS 73
objects: Hallowed be o. ORTEGA G 1
oblations: accept our alms and o. PRAY 68
obligation:
haste to repay an o. LA ROCHE 23
not always the sequel of o. JOHNSON:S 59
obligations: Nobility has its o. LEVIS 1
obliged: whatever a body is o. to do TWAIN 6
obliging: so o., that he ne'er obliged POPE 121
oblivion:
drink o. of a day MERED:G 19
formless ruin of o. SHAK:TRO 22
long journey towards o. LAWR:DH 37
my o. is a very Antony SHAK:ANT 19
o. blindly scattereth her poppy BROWNE:T 58
O. is a kind of Annihilation BROWNE:T 63
o. which awaits the uncreative HALDA 1
obnoxious: o. to each carping tongue BRADST 1
obscene:
is usually o. SPENCER:H 11
not at all o. MACMAN 1
obscenity:
more o. than wit WALP:H 25
trembles on the brink of o. LONGFORD 2
whale-white o. MACDIAR 7
obscure:
Because I never am o. MACMAN 1
I become o. HORACE 101
palpable o. MILT 160
obsequies: they solemnized their o. BROWNE:T 49
observance: upon the o. of trifles DOYLE:AC 9
observation:
bearings of this o. lays DICKENS 137
in the field of o. chance PASTEUR 1
Let o. with extensive view JOHNSON:S 66
strange places cramm'd With o. SHAK:AS 31
observations: o. which ourselves we POPE 108
observe: see, but you do not o. DOYLE:AC 18
observer: He is a great o. SHAK:JUL 15
obstacle: o. in the path to equality DEVL 1
obstacle-racing: sport of England is o. TREE 3
obstetrical: all branches of o. knowledge STERNE 16
obstinacy:
O. in a bad cause, is but BROWNE:T 12
o. in a bad one STERNE 7
obstinate: O. people may be subdivided ARISTOT 11
obvious: lay in never despising the o. FREUDEN 1
occasion: on O.'s forelock watchful wait MILT 270
occasions:
New o. teach new duties LOWELL:JR 2
o. do inform against me SHAK:HAM 156
occupation:
Absence of o. is not rest COWP 40
ever apologizing for his o. MENCK 3
occupations: let us love our o. DICKENS 102
occurs: Nothing that actually o. WILDE:O 70
ocean:
Amidst an o. of delight DRAYT 10
deep and dark blue O. BYR 117
His legs bestrid the o. SHAK:ANT 64
hungry o. gain SHAK:SON 27
I have loved thee, O. BYR 120
life on the o. wave SARGENT:E 1
Make the mighty o. CARNEY 1
o. Is folded and hung AUD 6
o. leans against the land GOLDS 9
o. of truth lay all undiscovered NEWT:I 5
O.'s child, and then SHELLEY:PB 28
old O. smiles MILT 186
On one side lay the O. TENNY 273
on the o. of life we pass LONGFEL 31
Ransack the o. for orient pearl MARLOWE 30
sapless foliage of the o. SHELLEY:PB 43
They didn't think much to the O. EDGAR 1
Upon a painted o. COLERIDGE:ST 19
oceans: Portable, and compendious o. CRASH 15
o'clock:
If you are asked what o. CHESTERFIELD 13
It shall be what o. SHAK:TAM 12
Octob.: third day of *O.* USSH 1
October: night in the lonesome O. POE 6
odd:
How o. Of God EWER 2
It's a very o. thing DE LA M 14
Nothing *o.* will do long JOHNSON:S 178
odds:
o. is gone SHAK:ANT 58
Than facing fearful o. MACAULAY:TB 47
ode: I intended an O. DOBSON:HA 1
odour:
all chastity and o. CONG 57
Stealing and giving o. SHAK:TWE 1
odours:
heavens rain o. on you SHAK:TWE 39
o. from the spicie shoare MILT 186
O., when sweet violets SHELLEY:PB 143
with o. sweet MILT 4
odyssey: surge and thunder of the O. LANG:A 1
odysseys: last of all our O. BELLOC 28
Oedipuses: peculiar family, the O. BEERB 23
off:
come from letting people o. MURD:I 2
O. with his head CARROLL 21
O. with his head CIB 2
o. with the old love ANON 27
sooner it is o. the better NELS 4
to get one's head cut o. CARROLL 60
offence:
After o. returning MILT 291
greatest o. is to have been born CALD 1
my o. is rank SHAK:HAM 130
o. from am'rous causes POPE 36
offences:
more o. at my beck SHAK:HAM 100
old o. of affections new SHAK:SON 51
offend:
I'll not willingly o. WATTS 10
o. and make up at pleasure RICHARDSON:S 3
we come not to o. SHAK:MID 46
offended:
for him have I o. SHAK:JUL 47
This hath not o. the king MORE:T 6
offender: love the o. POPE 62
offenders: society o. who might well GILB:WS 64
offensive: You are extremely o. SMITH:FE 4
offer:
nothing to o. anybody KERO 2
nothing to o. but blood, toil CHURCH:W 11
o. he can't refuse BRANDO 2
o. he can't refuse PUZO 1
offering:
o. far too small WATTS 2
o. too little and asking CANN 7
offertory: he song an offertorie CHAUC 33
office:
can't run an o. without the secretaries FONDA 1
find a set of maxims in o. BURKE:E 11
man who has no o. SHAW 73
participation of o. is a matter of right JEFFERSON 12
that the o. sanctifies the holder ACTON:Baron 2
office boy: o.b. to an Attorney's GILB:WS 11
office boys: By o.b. for o.b. SALIS 4
officer:
art thou o. SHAK:HEN.V 28
character of an o. and a gentleman ANON 156
dashing Swiss o.' is one such RUSS:J[1] 1
good o. without being a gentleman NELS 9
officers:
better known as o. of Justice KELLY:N 1
some of the general o. of this army WELLING 1
offices: o. both private and publick MILT 310
official:
high o., all allow, Is grossly HERB:AP 10
O. dignity tends to increase in HUX:A 32
What is o. is uncontestable FRY:C 8
officials: made a mess of again by o. ADEN 1
offspring:
Heaven has granted me no o. WHIST 7
noblest o. is the last BERK 6
sourse Of human ofspring MILT 202
O'Grady: Lily O. SITWELL:E 7
oil:
consum'd the midnight o. GAY 42
'incomparable o.', Macassar BYR 159
lamps With everlasting o. MILT 24
little o. in a cruse BIBLE 162
o. to make his face shine BIBLE 233
with boiling o. in it GILB:WS 77
oiled: o. his way around the floor LERN 4
ointment: plasters, pills, and o. boxes LOCKHART 1
okie: O. use' ta mean STEINB 2
old:
adherence to the o. and tried LINC 7
all that the young can do for the o. SHAW 96

as o. as my tongue SWIFT 40
as o. as the woman he feels MARX:G 25
become O. in their youth BYR 126
Better be an o. man's darling PROV 39
both were o. BROOKE 4
comic to hear oneself called o. JAMES:A 1
Darling, I am growing o. REX 1
Do they know they're o. JENN:E 1
Don't let the o. folks know HERB:AP 1
even the o. are fair YEATS 17
feel chilly and grown o. BROWNING:R 158
foolish fond o. man SHAK:KING L 77
Grant me an o. man's frenzy YEATS 105
Grow o. along with me BROWNING:R 184
grow o. ever learning SOLON 3
growing o. in drawing nothing up COWP 67
Growing o. is like being increasingly POWELL:A 7
Grown o. before my time ROSSET:C 11
half as o. as Time BURGON 1
half as o. as time PLOM 4
he is o. and she a shade LANDOR 8
his o. times are still new HARDY:T 53
I am o. with wandering YEATS 23
Is not o. wine wholesomest WEBSTER:J 1
It was too o. for him DICKENS 145
lads that will never be o. HOUSM 13
last to lay the o. aside POPE 17
love every thing that's o. GOLDS 66
love will change in growing o. BRIDGES:R 10
make an o. man young TENNY 60
man is as o. as he feels PROV 260
man is as o. as he's feeling COLLINS:Mor 1
my folks were growing o. STEVENSON:RL 62
nicest o. lady I ever met FAULK 2
no country for o. men YEATS 71
no man would be o. SWIFT 21
not persuade me I am o. SHAK:SON 8
not so o., and not so GILB:WS 44
Not yet o. enough for a man SHAK:TWE 12
o. and ill and terrified BETJ 32
o. are more beautiful WHITMAN 38
o. believe everything WILDE:O 74
o. folks who are quite a bore PARNELL:A 1
o. have reminiscences of what SAKI 5
o. have rubbed it into the young MAUGH 13
o. head on young shoulders EMER 68
o. is having lighted rooms LARK 7
o. know what they want SMITH:LP 13
o. man in a dry month ELIOT:TS 21
o. man in a hurry CHURCH:Lord R 3
o. man to have had so much blood SHAK:MAC 100
o. man to learn wisdom AESC 4
O. men and comets have been SWIFT 22
O. men are dangerous SHAW 114
o. men have grey beards SHAK:HAM 73
O. men in country houses BETJ 5
o. men, safe in bed HOPE:Al 3
o. men shall dream dreams BIBLE 355
o. men's dream DRYD 43
O. people are always absorbed WEBB:S 3
o. ways are the safest COKE:E 7
o., wild and incomprehensible VICT 5
O. women sit, stiffly DEU 2
o. yield to the new rite THOMAS AQ 2
off with the o. love ANON 27
our midnight o. QUAR 7
Ring out the o. TENNY 177
should not o. men be mad? YEATS 113
so o., and so profane SHAK:HEN.IV[2] 53
Some day before I'm o. KIP 107
suppose an o. man decayed JOHNSON:S 233
temple half as o. as time ROGERS:S 5
than to be forty years o. HOLMES:OW 17
that o. man I used to know CARROLL 85
they done the o. woman in SHAW 109
They shall grow not o. BINY 1
they think he is growing o. IRV 4
Though I look o. SHAK:AS 16
too o. for me to have any effect JOYCE:J 53
too o. to cry, but it hurt LINC 27
too o. to fawn upon SHAK:RIC.II 6
too o. to go again to my travels CHARLES II 10
Very o. are we men DE LA M 4
when they get to feeling o. BROOKE 12
When you are o. and grey YEATS 14
why wasn't I born o. and ugly? DICKENS 91
woman as o. as she looks COLLINS:Mor 1
woman as o. as she looks PROV 260
you and I are o. TENNY 55
You are o., Father William CARROLL 9
You are o., Father William SOUTHEY 5
you never can be o. SHAK:SON 46
young reject the o. with more CHEV:M 3

old age:
accept the inevitable and go* GONNE 2
age is full of care* SHAK:POET 1
both worlds at once they view* WALLER 9
buried in a good o.a. BIBLE 47
dance attention upon my o.a. YEATS 111
grow virtuous in their o.a. POPE 178
grown peaceful as o.a. BROWNING:R 73
I must reluctantly observe* GIBBON:E 29
In life's last scene* JOHNSON:S 69
lag-end of my life* SHAK:HEN.IV[1] 82
most fatal complaint of all* HILT 1
Nature in you stands on the very* SHAK:KING L 28
O.A. a regret DISR:B 18
Old-age, a second child CHURCH:C 21
O.A., and Experience, hand in hand ROCHES 3
O.a. brings along with its EMER 84
o.a. has brought to me Thy wisdom STEPHEN:JK 1
O.a. hath yet his honour TENNY 55
O.a. is a second childhood ARISTOP 3
o.a. is always fifteen years older BARU 2
O.a. is no such uncomfortable WALP:H 14
O.a. is not an illness SARTON 2
O.a. is the most unexpected TROT 8
o.a., is the one thing for which no preparation DEWEY 1
O.a. is woman's hell LENCLOS 1
O.A. may come after you WHITMAN 15
o.A. of Cards POPE 138
o.a., serene and bright WORDS:W 36
O.a. should burn and rave THOMAS:D 18
O.a. takes away from us BREN 5
o.a. the mind casts off WILLIAMS:WC 9
o.a. to be my best performance CHEV:M 3
prefer o.a. to the alternative CHEV:M 2
sad o.a. you are preparing TALL 3
son of his o.a. BIBLE 67
terrifying is oncoming o.a. GOGOL 1
That time of year* SHAK:SON 33
that which should accompany o.a. SHAK:MAC 110
There is a wicked inclination* JOHNSON:S 233
Though now this grained face* SHAK:COM 8
'Tis well an o.a. is out DRYD 129
weariness and sadness of o.a. MAUGH 27
What is the worst of woes* BYR 72
when I shall be able* DONNE 108
When the age is in* SHAK:MUCH 22
years have stolen all her loveliness* FAIRBURN 3

old-fashioned:
afterwards be always o. SANT 5
O. ways which no longer apply ADDAMS 1

Old Kent Road: Knocked 'em in the O.K.R. CHEV:A 2
old maid: Being an o.m. is like death FERB 1
old masters: Buy o.m. BEAV 7
Old Testament: blessing of the O.T. BACON:F[1] 31

older:
grow o., you feel you are also LAUR:M 1
Life gets better As I grow o. DOBSON:R 2
little o. than my teeth SWIFT 40
O. men declare war HOOV 4
o. she gets, the more interested CHRIS 7
o. than the rocks PATER 2
to go on getting o. ADEN 2
was of an o. generation LUCIL 1

oldest: o. hath borne SHAK:KING L 87

O'Leary:
Till Art O. returns CHON 1
with O. in the grave YEATS 37

olfactory: shall I call it an o. bar WELLS:HG 12
oligarchy: extreme democracy or absolute o. ARISTOT 16
olive: O. Grove of Academe MILT 273
olives: pungent taste of these black o. DURRELL:L 2
Olympian: between Hebrew and O. revelations GLAD 9
Olympians: All the O. YEATS 106
Olympic games: O.g. it is not the handsomest ARISTOT 4

Olympus:
leafy O. on top of Ossa VIRGIL 24
O.' faded hierarchy KEATS 87

Omar: diver O. plucked them LOWELL:JR 7
omelette: make an o. without breaking PROV 441

omen:
gods avert this o. CIC 11
no O. but his Country's Cause HOMER 11

omnibuses: had only ridden more in o. HELPS 3
omnipotence: final proof of God's o. DE VR 4

omnipotent:
defie th' O. to Arms MILT 110
O. but friendless SHELLEY:PB 75

omniscience:
his specialism is o. DOYLE:AC 31
o. is his foible SMITH:Syd[1] 33

omniverbivorous: I am o. by nature HOLMES:OW 12

on:
First they get *o.* ROLL:H 1
O., Stanley, o. SCOTT:W 30
This is o. me PARKER:D 20

Onan: straight to the sin of O. VOLT 34

once:
every house in London – *o.* WILDE:O 131
if it were done but o. DONNE 102
O. is more than enough BIRCH 1

one:
All for o., o. for all DUMAS:A[P] 1
all our means to make us o. DONNE 34
always took care of number o. MARR 1
animals went in o. by o. ANON 2
big o. that got away DENNIS:N 1
can't have o. without CAHN 1
do only o. thing at once SMILES 1
How to be o. up POTTER:S 2
I am o. with my kind TENNY 227
I was out by o. GREENE:G 16
in a procession of o. DICKENS 121
o. and the fifty-three TENNY 283
O. for sorrow, two for mirth PROV 309
O. God, o. law TENNY 185
O. near o. is too far BROWNING:R 93
O., two, buckle my shoe NURS 48
Only o. being is missing LAMAR 1
that o. is the husband BLACKS 6
we are o. MILT 251

one-and-twenty: I was o. HOUSM 9

one-eyed:
o., blinking sort o' place HARDY:T 65
o. man is king ERAS 1
o. man is king PROV 201
O. Man is King WELLS:HG 8
There's a o. yellow idol HAYES 1

one-horse: poor little o. town TWAIN 5
onehandled: statue of the o. adulterer JOYCE:J 20

oneself:
know how to belong to o. MONTAIGNE 10
limiting and isolating o. GOET 33
possible society is o. WILDE:O 78
to do anything for o. MAUGH 14
Why not be o.? SITWELL:E 16

onion: tears live in an o. SHAK:ANT 13

onward:
O.! Christian soldiers BARING-G 2
O., Christians, o. go WHITE:HK 1
'O.', the sailors cry BOULTON:HE 1
upward still, and o. LOWELL:JR 2

ooze:
o. and bottom of the sea SHAK:HEN.V 6
o. of the past NAB 6
o. of their pasture-ground ARNOLD:M 1

oozings: watchest the last o. KEATS 109
opal: thy mind is a very o. SHAK:TWE 30

open:
His mind is o. BRADLEY:FH 5
O. sesame ARAB 2
Op'n, ye everlasting Gates MILT 228
this thing o. – whatever it is PHILIP 7

opening: It is always o. time THOMAS:D 30
opens: o. on her like a grin ELIOT:TS 17

opera:
first rule in o. MELBA 1
German o., too long and WAUGH:E 36
O. in English is MENCK 21

CONNOLLY:C 16
Oscar:
Importance of Being O. WILLM 1
You will, O. WHIST 5
Ossa: pile O. on Pelion VIRGIL 24
ostentation:
blown me full of maggot o. SHAK:LOV 21
for use rather than o. GIBBON:E 5
slightest touch of o. PEREZ 1
ostrich:
o. burying its head MANS:K 9
resembled the wings of an o. MACAULAY:TB 7
Strong the tall o. SMART 2
Othello: O.'s occupation's gone SHAK:OTH 43
other:
did lots of o. things too JOYCE:J 50
I can do no o. LUTHER 8
most people are o. people WILDE:O 104
one without the o. CAHN 1
O. people are quite dreadful WILDE:O 78
that I am not as o. men BIBLE 465
wonderful things for o. people KERR:Jea 1
others:
but by o.' seeing SHAK:SON 54
do not do to o. CONF 12
how can you expect o. KEMP 7
woman who lives for o. LEWIS:CS 5
otherwise: some are o. SMOL 1
ought:
hadn't o. to be HARTE 1
tell me I o. to do BURKE:E 33
what o. to be there but isn't STOCKS 2
what things they o. to do PRAY 45
Oun: Properly based *O.* BROWNING:R 121
ours: They were not o. OWEN:W 9
ourselves:
born . . . not for o. alone PLATO 2
but by o., betrayed CONG 7
find a parallel in o. HUME 1
in o., are triumph and defeat LONGFEL 33
look long and carefully at o. MOLIERE 17
not within o. doesn't upset HESSE 1
o. to know POPE 107
we become more like o. HALL:P 1
ousel: o. cock, so black SHAK:MID 27
out:
I was o. by one GREENE:G 16
never be allowed o. in private CHURCH:R 1
o. of the war, o. of debt EMER 84
o. of thee shall he come BIBLE 360
o. wish to get in EMER 44
shall never be put o. LAT 2
ten thousand to go o. of it SWIFT 4
that leaves him o. so late FROST:R 11
went o., like all good things DISR:B 47
out-of-doors: given us indoors and o.
MACAULAY:R 2
out-argue: we will o. them JOHNSON:S 198
outcast: beweep my o. state SHAK:SON 11
outcome: regardless of the possible o. MEIR 2
outcries: What o. pluck me KYD 1
outlive: o. all one loved POWER:M 1
outrage:
connive in civilised o. HEAN 3
o. it is against simple men KETT 1
outshine:
didst o. Myriads MILT 112
T' o. each other LUCRET 5
outside:
I am just going o. OAT 1
wait till I get you o. MARX:G 6
outsoared: o. the shadow of our night
SHELLEY:PB 121
outspoken: O. by whom? PARKER:D 35
out-vote: Though we cannot o. JOHNSON:S 198
outvoted: they o. me LEE:N 4
outward:
more the o. man decayeth PRAY 90
O. be fair CHURCH:C 2
o. shew of things SPENS 46
out-worn: O. heart YEATS 15
oven:
flesh went in an o. HARRISON 1
not baked in one o. PROV 6
Put it in the o. for baby NURS 50
over:
o., and can't be helped DICKENS 20
oversexed, and o. here ANON 229
pleasure of having it o. HOOD 16
they're both of them o. GILB:WS 53
overboard:
throw the ocacasional man o. GILMORE 1
told him not to go o. HAIN 1
overcame: day he o. the Nervii SHAK:JUL 54
overcoat:
is to put on your o. LOWELL:JR 9
o. also was entering RIMB 2
overcoats: avalanche of o. and boots WHITE:P 2
overcome:
Man is something to be o. NIET 4
what is else not to be o.? MILT 115
overcomes: who o. By force MILT 140
over-confident: Not that I am ever o.
THATCH:M 19
over-educated: I've o. myself COWARD 1
overgrown: o. with azure moss SHELLEY:PB 42
overloaded: patient while they are being o.
KINGSLEY:C 1
overlooked: better to be looked over than o.
WEST:M 11
overpaid:
Is grossly o. HERB:AP 10
O., overfed, oversexed ANON 229
overpaying: o. him but he's worth it GORKY 19
over-prepared: I had o. the event POUND 11
over-run: to o. Large Countries MILT 270
oversimplification: art of systematic o. POPP 7
overtake: had the misfortune to o. BIER 3
overtakers: o. who keep the undertakers PITTS 1
overthrown: o. More than your enemies
SHAK:AS 6
overtook: soon as the man o. me BUNYAN 10
overtures: tried to resist his o. PEREL 2
Ovid:
O., the soft philosopher DRYD 102
Venus clerk, Ovide CHAUC 92
owe:
can't pay, why I can o. HEYW:J 2
don't o. a penny to a single WODE 3
owed: so much o. by so many CHURCH:W 16
Owen, Wilfrid: He is all blood, dirt and*
YEATS 145
owes:
chiefly o. himself unto himself BROWNE:T 66
o. not any man LONGFEL 13
owl:
by a mousing o. hawk'd SHAK:MAC 59
curves of the white o. MERED:G 32
It was the o. that shriek'd SHAK:MAC 35
nightly sings the staring o. SHAK:LOV 25
O. and the Pussy-Cat went to sea LEAR 18
o. does to the moon complain GRAY:T 16
o., for all his feathers KEATS 61
they brought an O. LEAR 17
white o. in the belfry sits TENNY 8
wise old o. lived in NURS 86
owlet: o. Atheism COLERIDGE:ST 4
owls: O. might have hooted GRAY:T 40
own:
apart from my o.? GABOR 5
at least it is my o. MUSSET 1
don't 'o.' a country by signing GORDIM 2
man's o., is absolutely his o. CAMDEN:Lord 1
we o. thee Lord ANON 43
own-alone: All by my o. self HARRIS:JC 15
owning: mania of o. things WHITMAN 7
owns: property o. them INGER 2
ox:
Egyptian Temple dedicated to an o. GOLDS 76
Manningtree o. with the pudding
SHAK:HEN.IV[1] 51
One law for the Lion & O. BLAKE:W 55
o. goeth to the slaughter BIBLE 254
shalt not muzzle the o. BIBLE 125
stalled o. and hatred BIBLE 262
stands like an o. in the furrow KIP 142
who the O. to wrath has movd BLAKE:W 85
oxen:
lands with his own o. HORACE 60
see the o. kneel HARDY:T 32
years like great black o. YEATS 7
Oxford:
Beautiful city! so venerable* ARNOLD:M 56
best shearers' cooks are O. men ARCHIB 1
better run over to O. MAHAF 1
clever men at O. GRAHAME 4
Half-Way House to Rome, O. PUNCH 3
I have never seen O. since NEWM:JH 12
it's either O. or Cambridge SNAGGE 1
King to O. sent a troop BROWNE:W[2] 1
new North O. air BETJ 18
nice sort of place, O. SHAW 34
O. gave the world marmalade ANON 230
O. is on the whole more attractive BAED 1
O. that has made me insufferable BEERB 4
poetry, which is in O. DRYD 19
secret in the O. sense FRANKS 1
sends his son to O. STEAD 1
stage-coach from London to O. HAZL 6
To O. sent a troop of horse TRAPP 1
To the University of O. GIBBON:E 14
Towery city and branchy* HOPK:GM 12
Oxford Street: O.S., stony-hearted stepmother
DEQ 1
oxlips:
bold o., and The crown-imperial
SHAK:WIN 20
o. and the nodding violet SHAK:MID 20
Oxonian: He is an O. WILDE:O 99
oxtail: to the University of O. JOYCE:J 24
Oxus: O., forgetting the bright ARNOLD:M 34
oyster:
made an uncommon fine o. DICKENS 19
open an o. at sixty paces WODE 23
o. may be crossed in love SHERIDAN:RB 39
pearl in your foul o. SHAK:AS 69
that first eat an o. SWIFT 46
world's mine o. SHAK:MERR 7
oyster-wench: his bonnet to an o.
SHAK:RIC.II 13
oysters:
all the little O. stood CARROLL 56
first ventured on eating o. FULLER:T[1] 9
He had often eaten o. GILB:WS 1
Poverty and o. always seem DICKENS 18
Ozymandias: My name is O. SHELLEY:PB 22
pace:
Creeps in this petty p. SHAK:MAC 113
don't like the p. you are driving
SMITH:Syd[1] 6
slacken my p. when approaching DIOG 1
paces: made three p. thro' the room TENNY 21
Pacific: He star'd at the P. KEATS 4
pacifism: did not justify the sacrifice* PANK:S 1
pacifist: I am an absolute p. EINS 10
pacings: long mechanic p. TENNY 93
pack:
animated when they hunt in a p. HUME 2
p., and take a train BROOKE 10
p. up your troubles ASAF 1
Pay, p., and follow BURTON:Ri 1
pack-drill: No names, no p. PROV 295
pack-horse: posterity is a p. DISR:B 62
packhorses: p. And hollow pamper'd
SHAK:HEN.IV[2] 27
pact: p. with you, Walt Whitman POUND 21
padded: p. man – that wears TENNY 99
Paddington: As London is to P. CANN 3
paddle:
man p. his own canoe MARR 7
Mummy's leave to p. KIP 20
paddles: Can't you 'ear their p. chunkin' KIP 59
paddocks: Cold as P. though they be HERR 4
Paddy: Keep P. behind the big mixer MCALP 1
padlock: clap your p. – on her mind PRIOR 4
pagan:
find the p. – spoiled ZANG 1
gay calmness of the P. OUIDA 1
P. suckled in a creed outworn WORDS:W 105
page:
I turn the p. BROWNING:R 90
on a beautiful quarto p. SHERIDAN:RB 19
page-boy: posing as a p. in an Italian hotel
WEST:R 1
pageant:
part of life's rich p. MARSHALL:Ar 1
this insubstantial p. faded SHAK:TEM 27
pageantry: mask, and antique P. MILT 74
pages:
almost turned down the p. POUND 11
Turn the p. of your Greek HORACE 110
Pagets: none of the P. can read MELBOU 10
pagoda: By the old Moulmein P. KIP 59
pagus: private *p.* and demesne AUD 54
paid:
as they are being p. in or p. out HUX:JS 2
cannot be p. for in money COMPT 6

long ez mine's p. punctooal LOWELL:JR 6
might as well get p. for it DUND 1
p. at the Greek Kalends CAES:A 2
That is not p. with moan THOMP:F 3
we ha' p. in full KIP 88
well p. that is well satisfied SHAK:MERC 49
Ye are not p. to think KIP 72
pain:
After great p. DICKIN:E 5
almost to amount to p. HUNT:L 8
but relieved their p. GOLDS 26
but the intermission of p. SELD 11
Converting joy to p.? CAMPION 7
costs worlds of p. MASE 14
delight in others' p. BYR 121
disinclination to inflict p. MERED:G 6
faint beneath the aromatic p. WINCHIL 1
free from guilt or p. SHELLEY:PB 84
heard a sudden cry of p. STEPHENS 5
I feel no p. dear mother ANON 72
I'have no p., dear mother FARM 1
I love to give p. CONG 43
in rest from p. DRYD 5
intoxication with p. BRONO 1
its pleasures to another's p. COWP 69
least p. in our little finger HAZL 35
leaves behind it the p. ANON 68
like a God in p. KEATS 65
mosaics of p. DEU 2
Never admit the p. GILMORE 1
Never p. to tell thy love BLAKE:W 57
no living thing to suffer p. SHELLEY:PB 68
No p., no gain FONDA 2
No p., no palm PENN 1
No pleasure without p. PROV 297
one who never inflicts p. NEWM:JH 5
Our Lady of P. SWIN 21
P. acute, yet dead MANG 2
p. of a new idea BAGE 20
p. passes, but the beauty RENOIR:PA 2
p. shall not be inflicted SPENCER:H 10
purchase P. with all that Joy POPE 133
shame nor physical p. KEY:E 3
she hasn't a p. MILNE 7
stranger yet to p. GRAY:T 3
Superflux of p. SWIN 18
sure she felt no p. BROWNING:R 34
Sweet is pleasure after p. DRYD 107
tender for another's p. GRAY:T 8
thou certain p. GRANVILLE 5
tongueless vigil and all the p. SWIN 9
turnes to pleasing paine SPENS 37
Unnumber'd hours of p. CAMPBELL:T 22
wait for the p. to pass CARR 1
we are born in others' p. THOMP:F 3
we remember the p. CHAMFORT 2
what p. it is to part GAY 19
wicked to deserve such p. BROWNING:R 96
pained: p. at how little he was p. WAUGH:E 16
painful: one is as p. as the other BACON:F[1] 52
pains:
capacity for taking p. PROV 142
infinite capacity for taking p. HOPK:JE 1
misfortunes and p. of others BURKE:E 4
no gains without p. STEVENSON:A 6
P. of love be sweeter DRYD 11
p. that conquer trust TENNY 148
p. unfelt produce LUCRET 5
pleasure in poetic p. COWP 63
paint:
flinging a pot of p. in the public's RUSKIN 30
fresh p. on the captains' LOWELL:R 10
looking as fresh as p. SMED 1
p. her in my imagination the way CERV 10
p. my picture freely like me CROMWELL 11
p. not what I know, but TURNER:JMW 1
p. the lily BYR 190
p. the sable skies DRUMMOND OF H 1
p. the souls of men BROWNING:R 112
who p. 'em truest ADDIS 37
wife works to enable him to p. SHAHN 1
painted:
As if p. in honey CONSTABLE:J 5
Nature's own hand p. SHAK:SON 7
not so young as they are p. BEERB 1
old, but p. cunningly SPENS 25
p. child of dirt POPE 125
That fears a p. devil SHAK:MAC 43
They're p. to the eyes DOBSON:HA 3
Upon a p. ocean COLERIDGE:ST 19
painter:
could have become a real p. HOK 1
mine had been the P.'s hand WORDS:W 40
p. dips His pencil in SHELLEY:PB 29
those scenes made me a p. CONSTABLE:J 1
vast commendation of a p. FIELDING 9
painters:
good p. imitated nature CERV 25
hate all Boets and Bainters GEO I 1
Light is the first of p. EMER 1
P. and poets . . . have always had licence HORACE 99
p., poets and builders MARLBOR:S 1
Poets and p. are outside the class BREN 9
painting:
It's either easy or impossible* DAL 3
keep p. till I feel like pinching RENOIR:PA 3
knew as much about p. as I LANDS 1
p. in water-colours shows the innocent STEVENSON:RL 7
P. is a blind man's profession PICAS 1
P. thy outward walls SHAK:SON 61
paintings:
all the allegorical p. JOHNSON:S 262
I have heard of your p. SHAK:HAM 102
paints: I want to know a butcher p. BROWNING:R 208
pair:
Happy, happy, happy, p. DRYD 105
p. so famous SHAK:ANT 80
there's a p. of us? DICKIN:E 3
Why not import a p. KERR:Jo 1
pajamas: How he got into my p. MARX:G 2
Pakistan: You wouldn't have that in P. BUZO 1
pal: Quietly sweating p. to p. HUX:A 44
palace:
Be thine own p. DONNE 9
in at the p. door one day DICKENS 5
in blood down P. walls BLAKE:W 74
p. and a prison on each BYR 96
P. in smoky light POUND 31
p. is more than a house COLERIDGE:ST 87
purple-linèd p. of sweet sin KEATS 106
river by my p. wall? THACK 21
That ope's the P. of Eternity MILT 17
very stately p. before him BUNYAN 5
palaces:
Mid pleasures and p. PAYNE 1
old p. and towers Quivering SHELLEY:PB 42
p. of kings are built upon PAINE 1
ploughs down p. CAMPBELL:R 3
palate: P., the hutch of tasty HOPK:GM 1
pale:
Art thou p. for weariness SHELLEY:PB 101
look not so p. SHAK:MAC 104
P. grew thy cheek BYR 54
Prithee, why so p.? SUCK 1
turn not p., beloved snail CARROLL 33
very p. owing to the drains ASHFORD 3
Palestine: establishment in P. of a national home BALF 2
pall:
brows shall be their p. OWEN:W 3
Scepter'd P. com sweeping MILT 85
Pall Mall: shady side of P.M. MORRIS:C 1
Pall Mall Gazette: *P.M.G.* is written by gentlemen THACK 16
Pallas Athene: P.A. in that straight back YEATS 106
Palliser: Plantagenet P. . . . is a perfect gentleman TROLL 33
pallor: p. of girls' brows OWEN:W 3
palm:
bear the p. alone SHAK:JUL 10
flourish like the p. tree BIBLE 228
Hard as the p. of ploughman SHAK:TRO 1
lands of p. and southern pine TENNY 197
No pain, no p. PENN 1
shady City of Palme trees VAUGHAN:H 6
to have an itching p. SHAK:JUL 67
who has won it bear the p. JORT 1
win the p., the oak MARV 12
palm-oil: proverbs are the p. ACHEBE 2
palms:
frozen p. of Spring TENNY 42
other p. are won WORDS:W 69
palsy: brought palsey to bed POUND 41
pampered: God's p. people DRYD 36
pamphleteer: p. on guano TENNY 120
pan: Put on the p. Says Greedy NURS 7
Pan:
doing, the great god P. BROWNING:EB 22
From where P.'s cavern YEATS 119
great god P. is dead PLUT 3
P. did after Syrinx speed MARV 16
P. is dead BROWNING:EB 4
panache: My p. ROSTAND:E 3
pandemonium: Pandaemonium, the high Capitol MILT 146
Pandora's box: open that P.b. you never BEVIN 2
pangs:
P. are in vain KEATS 20
p. of disappointed love ROWE 4
panic: Don't p. ADAMS;D 3
Panjandrum: grand P. himself FOOTE 3
pans: were pots and p. PEAC 18
pansies: p., that's for thoughts SHAK:HAM 169
pansy: Pansie freakt with jet MILT 55
pant:
I p., I sink, I tremble SHELLEY:PB 135
to p. beneath thy power SHELLEY:PB 44
pantaloon: lean and slipper'd p. SHAK:AS 34
panteth: so p. my soul after thee BIBLE 212
pantheist: p. not only sees the god LAWR:DH 11
pantomime: smell of oranges and wee-wee* ASK 1
pants:
deck your lower limbs in p. NASH 16
fast thick p. were breathing COLERIDGE:ST 63
times my p. were so thin TRACY 1
pap-bairns: lairnt the mouths o littlans and p. BIBLE 591
papacy:
God has given us the p. LEO 1
P. is no other than the *ghost* HOBB 12
paper:
all the earth were p. white LYLY 8
all the world were p. ANON 71
both sides of the p. at once SELL 11
fellows when the p. was blank? ALLEN:F 3
hand that signed the p. THOMAS:D 8
he hath not eat p. SHAK:LOV 10
if there was any news in the p. AUSTEN 9
just for a scrap of p. BETHM 1
thin as a cigarette p. to write a novel DAVISON:FD 1
worth more than the p. GOLDWYN 4
paper-mill: thou hast built a p. SHAK:HEN.VI[2] 11
paper work: keep the p.w. down to a minimum ORTON 4
papers: produced two clear p. CARLYLE:T 72
parables: troubled to invent p.? HARDY:T 49
parachute:
moth in his brother's p. SIMPSON:NF 1
p. to open here after 10p.m. BYG 1
parade: from the Fifth Kiev machine-gun p. FAIRBAIRN:N 3
paradise:
Alcoranal p. where nothing URQ 1
All P. opens DISR:B 4
Beautiful as a wreck of P. SHELLEY:PB 133
enjoy p. in the next BECKF 2
Grant me p. in this world TINT 1
hast thou to say of 'P. found'? ELWOOD 1
Lost Angel of a ruined P. SHELLEY:PB 110
Paradis stood formed in hire CHAUC 117
P. by way of Kensal Green CHESTERTON 9
p. for a sect KEATS 99
P. of Dissent PIKE 1
P. of Fools MILT 180
pass through P. in a dream COLERIDGE:ST 71
Recoverd P. to all mankind MILT 262
ruins of the bowers of p. PAINE 1
Same old glimpse of P. LAMP 1
that working man's p. KINGSLEY:H 1
Thou hast the keys of P. DEQ 4
To him are opening p. GRAY:T 39
Upon the trees of P. STEVENSON:RL 60
paradises:
All p. . . . want for one thing NIET 21
Two P. 'twere in one MARV 22
paradox:
Man is an embodied p. COLTON 6
P. with him was only Truth LE GAL 1
paradoxical: Whoever is faced with the p.

DURREN 4
paragraphing: art of newspaper p. MARQUIS 10
parallel:
find a p. in ourselves HUME 1
ours so truly p. MARV 8
parallelogram: landlady of a boarding-house is a p. LEACOCK 2
parallelograms: My Princess of P. BYR 251
parallels: delves the p. in beauty's SHAK:SON 24
paralysis: seemed to me the centre of p. JOYCE:J 47
paramours: his sistres and his p. CHAUC 62
paranoid: Even a p. can have enemies KISS 3
paraphrase: Than the classics in p. POUND 27
paras: P. THIRTEEN BOGSIDE NIL ANON 231
parcel: not ask me to do up a p. SMITH:LP 9
parcels:
best things come in small p. PROV 35
p. of the dreadful Past TENNY 29
parching: p. Air Burns frore MILT 164
parchment:
features bound in stale p. MERED:G 12
p., being scribbl'd o'er SHAK:HEN.VI[2] 10
pardon:
cannot beg for p. MACNEICE 4
God may p. you ELIZ I 17
government that should ask me for a p. DEBS 2
I p. that man's life SHAK:KING L 67
kiss of the sun for p. GUR 1
p., who have done the wrong DRYD 13
thousand Ta's and P.'s BETJ 30
pardoned:
pardon'd all except her face BYR 210
P. in heaven BROWNING:R 57
to be praised than to be p. JONS 54
pardons:
P. him for writing well AUD 42
pardoun, comen from Rome CHAUC 31
parent:
don't object to an aged p. DICKENS 212
lose one p. may be regarded WILDE:O 87
parentage:
P. is a very important profession SHAW 124
What is your p.? SHAK:TWE 17
parenthesis: world is but a small p. BROWNE:T 65
parents:
begin by loving their p. WILDE:O 62
defying their p. and copying CRISP 1
Don't be too hard on p. COMPT 5
grave his p. stand PATTEN 2
Jewish man with p. alive ROTH 1
joys of p. are secret BACON:F[1] 90
man who murdered both his p. LINC 23
only illegitimate p. YAN 1
P. are the last people BUTLER:S[2] 53
P. first season us HERB:G 20
p. have not smiled VIRGIL 13
p. kept me from children SPEND 3
P. learn a lot from their children SPARK 1
resemble both their P. HALIF 7
resurrection of their p. GIBBON:E 25
sacrifice, and p.' tears MILT 126
sort of people our p. warned us JOHN:A 1
stranger to one of your p. AUSTEN 19
that p. could get their children out CLARK:K 2
way p. obey their children EDWARD VIII 5
what p. were created for NASH 8
Paris:
I love P. in the springtime PORTER:C 7
Is P. burning? HITL 10
last time I saw P. HAMMER 2
P. is a movable feast HEMINGWAY 10
P. is well worth a mass HENRI 4
P. slept on by Scamander BROOKE 4
Take back your P. MOLIERE 15
when they die, go to P. APPLETON:TG 1
parish:
all the world as my p. WESLEY:J 3
deserved well of his p. RUSKIN 14
hanged, all in the same p. ANON 136
p. of rich women AUD 38
park:
Over p., over pale SHAK:MID 12
p., a policeman and a pretty CHAPLIN 2
parliament:
Impression of P. upon me BYR 243
In the P. of man TENNY 79
into P., much as Robert Burns CARLYLE:T 55
Mob, P., Rabble COBBETT 1
p. can do anything PEMB:2nd Earl 1
p. is a *deliberative* assembly BURKE:E 94
P. to do things at eleven at night SHAW 88
parliamentarian: only safe pleasure for a p. CRIT 1
parliaments:
England is the mother of P. BRIGHT 2
we shall have no more P. JONS 31
parlour:
queen was in the p. NURS 66
Will you walk into my p.? HOWITT 1
Parnassus: my chiefe P. be SIDNEY:P 10
Parnell:
he had fits of depression* O'BRIEN:RB 1
P. came down the road YEATS 110
Poor P.! he cried loudly JOYCE:J 3
parochial:
p. in the beginning MOORE:G 3
scorning p. ways HARDY:T 28
worse than provincial – he was p. JAMES:H 3
parodies: P. and caricatures are the most HUX:A 23
parody: devil's walking p. CHESTERTON 1
parritch: healsome p., chief o' BURNS:R 12
parrots: p. seek the river-side KIP 32
Parsee: P. from whose hat the rays KIP 23
parsley:
depth which the p. had sunk DOYLE:AC 27
p. to stuff a rabbit SHAK:TAM 13
parsnips:
Fine words butter no p. PROV 120
fine words butter no p. SCOTT:W 83
Ten frozen p. RANS 2
parson:
Blanky, cranky p. ANON 121
coughing drowns the p.'s SHAK:LOV 25
like a p.'s damn HARDY:T 56
Once a p. always a p. PROV 307
p. and the p.'s wife CLOUGH 25
p. leaves the Christian in the lurch BYROM 6
P. left conjuring SELD 8
There goes the p. COWP 19
Tickling a p.'s nose SHAK:ROM 5
parsons: merriment of p. is mighty offensive JOHNSON:S 221
part:
best of friends must p. PROV 34
every man must play a p. SHAK:MERC 3
forgotten this day we must p.? CRAW 1
He, too, has resigned his p. YEATS 42
I have forgot my p. SHAK:COR 16
In every friend we lose a p. POPE 184
let us kiss and p. DRAYT 9
more willingly p. withal SHAK:HAM 75
p. at last without a kiss? MORRIS:W 1
p. of all that I have met TENNY 52
p. to meet again GAY 38
p. to tear a cat in SHAK:MID 7
shee hath don her p. MILT 236
take your own p. BORR 10
to both communities in the other p. ROBINS:M 1
We meet and p. now WRIGHT:J 2
We see but one P. SWIFT 50
We two now p. PATMO 7
what pain it is to p. GAY 19
parted:
done our best and worst, and p. BROOKE 14
Mine never shall be p. MILT 250
remember the way we p. SWIN 38
When we two p. BYR 54
Parthenophil: P. is lost FORD:J[1] 1
partial: p. for th' Observer's sake POPE 108
particularize: To p. is the Alone Distinction BLAKE:W 95
particulars:
do it in Minute P. BLAKE:W 116
P. are not to be examined JOHNSON:S 37
parties:
one of those p. which got out of hand BRUCE:L 1
P. must ever exist BURKE:E 39
two p. to a love transaction THACK 3
parting:
every p. was to die TENNY 174
let this p. grieve thee ANON 46
P. is all we know of heaven DICKIN:E 22
P. is such sweet sorrow SHAK:ROM 19
p. there is an image of death ELIOT:G 1
P.'s well-paid PATMO 6
rive not more in p. SHAK:ANT 48
then this p. was well made SHAK:JUL 80
partings: pang of all the p. gone THOMP:F 2
Partington: Atlantic Ocean beat Mrs P. SMITH:Syd[1] 11
partisanship: P. is our great curse ROBINS:JH 1
partition: Lodg'd in a small p. MILT 230
partner: but I have a p. DICKENS 159
partridge:
Always p. ANON 256
As the p. sitteth on eggs BIBLE 341
p. in a pear tree NURS 80
p. with a pint of imperial GALS 3
parts:
hinder p., that few could spie SPENS 25
P. of it are excellent PUNCH 28
p. of one stupendous whole POPE 87
Today we have naming of p. REED:H 3
party:
ancient forms of p. strife TENNY 177
and . . . to educate our p. DISR:B 69
children's p. taken over FITZGER:FS 11
each p. is worse than the other ROGERS:W 5
existence the stupidest p. MILL 26
fight again to save the P. GAIT 1
He's been true to *one* p. LOWELL:JR 3
mind which creates p. strife ARISTOT 17
none was for a p. MACAULAY:TB 49
not a P., it is a conspiracy BEVAN 9
p. is not to be brought down HAILS 1
P. is organized opinion DISR:B 66
P. loyalty brings the greatest LA BRU 5
p. of order or stability MILL 12
p. organization at first substitutes TROT 11
passion and p. blind COLERIDGE:ST 90
purpose in having a p.? O'ROUR 2
sooner every p. breaks up AUSTEN 47
Stick to your p. DISR:B 97
tasks of the p. are STALIN 2
What a swell p. this is PORTER:C 7
within the p. about its future MACMILL:H 9
without p. Parliamentary government DISR:B 71
party-goers: nation of punters and p. HOGAN 1
party-spirit: P., which at best POPE 182
pass:
I shall not p. this way GREL 1
I will p. nor turn my face BROWNING:R 191
it didn't p. from me KIP 147
let us p. on BURKE:E 96
look, and p. on DANTE 4
They shall not p. IBA 1
They shall not p. NIV 1
when thou shalt strangely p. SHAK:SON 19
Will she p. in a crowd? SWIFT 74
passage:
free p. and freedom of action QUES 1
North-west p. to the intellectual world STERNE 25
passages:
Bright p. that strike your mind BYROM 4
cheated into some fine p. KEATS 150
passed:
p. by on the other side BIBLE 457
would have p. in any case BECKETT 6
passengers: fools and p. drink at sea VILLIERS 1
passes: Men seldom make p. PARKER:D 7
passing:
but see her p. by ANON 97
in the dawning p. through HARDY:T 39
p. of the sweetest soul TENNY 159
So be my p. HENL 6
passing-bells: p. for these who die OWEN:W 1
passion:
All breathing human p. KEATS 92
Bards of P. and of Mirth KEATS 55
be cheated into p. DRYD 68
betwixt one p. and another STERNE 44
by thy Cross and P. PRAY 34
commanded By such poor p. SHAK:ANT 59
fat gentleman in such a p. about? SHAW-L 1
her first p. woman loves BYR 183
his p. boiled and bubbled THACK 27
in a P. you Good may do BLAKE:W 92
in any other high p. STEVENSON:RL 5
Infinite p. BROWNING:R 162
inspire hopeless p. THACK 14
it did relieve my p. much SHAK:TWE 24

p. you in the grave SHELLEY:PB 161
poor grub, poor p. LOND 2
saved the sum of things for p. HOUSM 37
shorter hours and better p. ANON 75
someone to p. you for doing it WHITEHORN 4
They must p. for ever STEAD 6
Who p. no praise or wages THOMAS:D 20
wonders what's to p. HOUSM 35
Your clan will p. me back PARKER:D 10
paying: only by not p. one's bills WILDE:O 72
payment:
cash p. has become the sole CARLYLE:T 40
p. of half twenty shillings BURKE:E 18
paynims: three p., three Jews CAX 2
pays:
He who p. the piper PROV 168
p. a harlot 25 times as much WILSON:Harold 2
p. us poor beggars in red KIP 67
pea:
dined on one p. and one bean LEAR 32
nothing left but one split p. THACK 23
pea-green: beautiful p. boat LEAR 18
peace:
all her paths are p. BIBLE 250
and give thee p. BIBLE 114
arts of p. are great BLAKE:W 4
author of p. PRAY 22
babble of a God of p. SHELLEY:PB 5
beauty of Thy p. WHITTIER 8
begat habits of p. and patience WALT 5
beyond these voices there is p. TENNY 270
burns lamps of p. DE LA M 17
certaine knot of p. SIDNEY:P 6
cherish a just and lasting p. LINC 13
church for p. BROWNING:R 41
come ye in p. here SCOTT:W 20
deep p. of the double bed CAMPBELL:Mrs P 2
desert, and call it p. TAC 1
desires p. be prepared for war VEGET 1
Despair of p. as long JUV 13
Eternal p. is a dream MOLTKE 1
for ever hold his p. PRAY 82
from a deep dream of p. HUNT:L 4
Give p. in our time PRAY 21
give us p. MASS 17
greatness and p. again COWARD 6
haunt of ancient P. TENNY 40
I speak of p. while SHAK:HEN.IV[2] 1
I will die in p. WOLFE:J 2
If these should hold their p. BIBLE 466
in His will lies our p. DANTE 17
in p., goodwill CHURCH:W 49
In p., Love tunes SCOTT:W 8
in time of p. thinks of war ANON 190
in what p. a Christian can die ADDIS 41
ingeminate the word *P.*, *P.*, CLAREN 3
inglorious arts of p. MARV 1
it is no longer p. RUSS:J[2] 2
Just to disturb the p. SALL 3
lazy P. Will hide DAVEN:W 4
Let there be p. for all MANDELA:N 7
live in p. with men MACHA 1
made p. between us LESAGE 1
makes a good p. HERB:G 57
Making p. is harder than STEVENSON:A 2
May they rest in p. MASS 21
mutual cowardice keeps us in p. JOHNSON:S 206
my everlasting p. Is broken HOOD 7
My heart asks for p. PUSH 8
My p. is lost GOET 18
Nation shall speak p. unto RENDALL 1
no p. in the grave TENNY 222
no p. . . . unto the wicked BIBLE 325
Nor p. within nor calm SHELLEY:PB 32
not p. at any price JERROLD 10
old as we to keep the p. SHAK:ROM 4
on earth p., good will BIBLE 450
on earth p. to men MASS 8
only a p. between equals WILSON:W 11
Open covenants of p. WILSON:W 13
or a bad p. FRANKLIN:B 26
Our p. betrayed us MUIR:E 2
p. above all earthly dignities SHAK:HEN.VIII 11
p. and propagation are the two most WALP:H 17
p. at the last NEWM:JH 2
P. be to this house PRAY 89
P. be unto you BIBLE 610
P. cannot be kept by force EINS 6
P. : come away TENNY 158
p. comes dropping slowly YEATS 4
P., commerce, and honest JEFFERSON 5
p. does nothing to relieve COWP 30
p. for our time CHAMBERLAIN:N 2
p. from twelve till two COWARD 21
p. had made Ben Adhem bold HUNT:L 4
p. has been broken anywhere ROOS:FD 10
p. has broken out BRECHT 16
p., I hope, with honour DISR:B 78
P. : In international affairs BIER 9
p. in Shelley's mind SHELLEY:PB 162
P. is a very apoplexy SHAK:COR 14
P. is in the grave SHELLEY:PB 71
P. is indivisible LIT 1
P. is poor reading HARDY:T 73
p. is ungrateful and never TUCHOL 1
P. its ten thousands PORTEUS 2
p. of God, which passeth BIBLE 541
p. of the Lord be always MASS 16
P. on earth, and mercy mild WESLEY:C 7
p. propaganda makes war seem LAWR:DH 29
p. sits crown'd with smiles VAUGHAN:H 4
p. that passeth all understanding MAYHEW:C 1
P., the human dress BLAKE:W 17
P. to corrupt no less MILT 260
p. – until we meet again ANON 142
p. we seek, founded upon decent EISEN 3
p. which the world cannot give PRAY 28
P. with Germany and Japan CHURCH:W 63
p. with honour CHAMBERLAIN:N 2
p. with honour CIC 16
p. without victory WILSON:W 11
people want p. so much EISEN 5
period of cold p. LIE 1
poor, and mangled P. SHAK:HEN.V 45
potent advocates of p. GEO V 4
practising upon his p. SHAK:OTH 23
Prince of P. BIBLE 308
Sent down the meek-eyd P. MILT 6
She strikes a universall P. MILT 6
So enamoured on p. CLAREN 4
soft phrase of p. SHAK:OTH 7
solitude, and calls it – p. BYR 24
they should kneel for p. SHAK:TAM 17
This p. a god has made VIRGIL 2
those who could make a good p. CHURCH:W 46
thy servant depart in p. BIBLE 609
time of p. BIBLE 281
To make p. in Europe possible BENES 1
Universal p. is declared ELIOT:G 24
Uproar the universal p. SHAK:MAC 94
we have to win the p. CLEMENCE 3
when there was p., he was for p. AUD 48
work us a perpetual p. MILT 3
working for perpetual p. KETT 1
peaceably:
p. if we can CLAY 1
world may be so p. ordered PRAY 53
peaceful:
grown p. as old age BROWNING:R 73
particularly p. or particularly green BUCH 1
peacefully: moving p. towards its close DAWS 1
peacemaker: If is the only peace-maker SHAK:AS 71
peacemakers: Blessed are the p. BIBLE 384
peach:
Do I dare to eat a p.? ELIOT:TS 11
nectarine and curious p. MARV 17
p. for your enemy PROV 317
peach-stone: Last-supper-carved-on-a-p. LANCAS 1
peaches: poetry in p. GRANVILLE-B 1
peacock:
droops the milkwhite p. TENNY 117
Eyed like a p. KEATS 103
Mor the P. flutters KIP 79
pride of the p. is the glory BLAKE:W 41
Proude as a pecocke BRADSH:H 1
peak: small things from the p. CHESTERTON 51
peanut-butter: p. sandwiches day after day HUMPH 9
pear: partridge in a p. tree NURS 80
pearl:
Barbaric P. and gold MILT 148
hang a p. in every cowslip's SHAK:MID 12
named the infant 'P.' HAWT 1
p. in your foul oyster SHAK:AS 69
Ransack the ocean for orient p. MARLOWE 30
threw a p. away SHAK:OTH 70
pearls:
cast ye your p. before swine BIBLE 399
false p. before real swine CODY 1
Gospel's p. upon our coast MARV 6
p. of thought in Persian gulfs LOWELL:JR 7
p. that were his eyes SHAK:TEM 11
search for p. must dive DRYD 24
pears: French wither'd p. SHAK:ALL 3
peartree: glassy p. leaves and blooms HOPK:GM 8
peas:
always eat p. with honey ANON 70
anybody likes green p. CLINT 1
first green p. LONGFEL 28
peasant:
For Pheasant *read* P., throughout SELL 12
p. in his little acres KAV 3
toe of the p. comes so near SHAK:HAM 182
what a rogue and p. slave SHAK:HAM 90
Yonder p., who is he? NEALE 2
peasanthood: wallow in their p. PARS 1
peasantry:
bold p. GOLDS 21
obstinate about being p. FITZGER:FS 6
where the p. make the laws ESSON 1
peasants: From the hard hands of p. SHAK:JUL 72
pebble:
casting of this p. from my hand CARLYLE:T 16
finding a smoother p. NEWT:I 5
not the only p. on the beach BRAIS 1
peccavi:
P.! I have sinned NAPIER 1
P. – I've Scinde wrote PUNCH 7
peck: content to p. cautiously at the ball WODE 16
pecker: want his p. in my pocket JOHNSON:LB 5
pedant: precious apothegmaticall P. NASHE 5
pedantic:
acquired a certain p. presumption PEREZ 1
too p. for a gentleman CONG 31
pedants:
Plague take all your p. BROWNING:R 40
Which learned p. much affect BUTLER:S[1] 5
pedestal:
ideal woman to put on a p. NORM 1
place my wife under a p. ALLEN:W 1
Women must come off the p. RHON 1
pedestrians: only two classes of p. DEWAR 2
peel: p. me a grape WEST:M 4
peeled: Peel'd, patch'd, and pyebald POPE 166
peep show: ticket for the p.s. MACNEICE 2
peepers: where'd you get them p.? MERCER 1
peer: many a p. of England brews HOUSM 28
peerage:
gained a p., or Westminster Abbey NELS 5
want a p., I shall buy one NORTHCLIFFE 2
You should study the P. WILDE:O 67
peers: important p. were most important BAGE 16
peewees: p. crying STEVENSON:RL 70
Pegasus: And thought it P. KEATS 10
peignoir: Complacencies of the p. STEVENS 6
Pekingese: why try to look like a P.? SITWELL:E 16
pelf: what they call p. CLOUGH 23
pelican:
have me turn p. CONG 23
Pluffskin, P. jee LEAR 22
wonderful bird is the p. MERRITT 1
Pelion: pile Ossa on P. VIRGIL 22
pen:
Ask my p., – it governs STERNE 27
before my p. has glean'd KEATS 21
but the scratching of a p. LOVER 1
foolish when he had not a pen JOHNSON:S 216
glorious by my p. GRAHAM:J 1
have my veto p. drawn REAG 9
His fingers held the p. COWP 17
I dipped my p. in the Nile FENT 2
I made a rural p. BLAKE:W 14
ink in my p. ran cold WALP:H 5
legs which prevents his holding a p. DICKENS 74

less brilliant p. than mine BEERB 20
more cruel the p. is than the sword BURTON:Ro 11
p. is mightier than the sword BULWER 1
Some Daemon stole my p. POPE 162
squat p. rests HEAN 1
virtue hath my p. SHAK:SON 36
penalized: p. for a crime you haven't POWELL:A 7
penalty: p. of Adam SHAK:AS 11
penance:
making night do p. for a day WORDS:W 153
man hath p. done COLERIDGE:ST 33
pence:
loss of p., full well he knew COWP 53
Take care of the p., and PROV 362
pencil: p. of the Holy Ghost hath BACON:F[1] 32
pendulum:
ominous vibration of a p.? JUNIUS 4
politics of the p. but of THATCH:M 3
penguin: And the p. call ELIOT:TS 69
penguins: angry p. of the night HARRIS:M 1
penitence: distinguish p. from love? POPE 62
penitent: Restore thou them that are p. PRAY 4
penitentiary: world for a p. and himself DENNIS:CJ 4
penned: excellently well penn'd SHAK:TWE 13
pennies:
P. do not come from heaven THATCH:M 14
P. from Heaven? BURKE:J 1
Twelve p. What better reason YEATS 125
penny:
bad p. always turns up PROV 26
I spent a p. of it NURS 24
In for a p., in for PROV 198
Not a p. off the pay COOK:AJ 1
not a peny hadde in wolde CHAUC 103
p. saved is a p. earned PROV 318
P. wise, pound foolish PROV 319
Please to put a p. in ANON 60
pens: other p. dwell on guilt AUSTEN 36
pension:
for a labourer to take his p. RUSKIN 14
hang your hat on a p. MACNEICE 3
p. list of the republic a roll CLEVE:G 1
till I made his p. jingle COWP 94
wild as p. plans COPE 3
pentameter: In the p. aye falling COLERIDGE:ST 46
peonies: wealth of globèd p. KEATS 96
people:
All p. that on earth KETHE 1
And the *p.* ANON 221
belongs to the p. who inhabit LINC 9
better for these p. never to have COOK:J 3
bludgeoning of the p. by the p. WILDE:O 38
blundering p. will live on SANDBURG 3
cannot fool all of the p. LINC 24
Eating p. is wrong FLAND 2
from the p., and for the p., all springs DISR:B 3
good of the p. is the chief law CIC 3
government by the p. themselves CAMPBELL-B 1
government of the p., by the p. LINC 11
I am for p. CHAPLIN 4
I am the Martyr of the P. CHARLES I 4
I would be of the p. LA BRU 9
In the P. was my trust WORDS:W 158
it's p. I can't stand SCHULTZ 1
kind of p. do they think CHURCH:W 26
Let my p. go ANON 50
Let my p. go BIBLE 92
look after our p. SCOTT:Rob 2
makes the p.'s wrongs his own DRYD 52
most p. are other p. WILDE:O 104
name we give the p. when we need FLERS 1
new p. takes the land CHESTERTON 25
no more like p. personally SPENCER:S 1
no vision, the p. perish BIBLE 275
Nor is the p.'s judgement DRYD 53
observe the condition of the p. JUNIUS 2
par in favour of the p. BURKE:E 13
P. are either charming or tedious WILDE:O 44
p. are never in the wrong BURKE:E 13
p. govern themselves THIERS 2
p. is the true legislator BURKE:E 83
p. keep even kings DAVEN:C 1
p. standing in the corners COREN 5
P. who need p. MERRILL 1
p. will at once put everyone in GORB 1
p.'s government, made for WEBSTER:D 2
place, the climate and the p. EDMOND 2
sort of p. our parents warned us JOHN:A 1
suppose the p. good ROBES 2
The p., Lord, the p. ELLIOTT:E 1
The p.'s prayer DRYD 43
There are two kinds of p. PAP 1
thy p. shall be my p. BIBLE 139
'Tis the p. marching on MORRIS:W 8
voice of the p. has BACON:F[1] 26
voice of the p. is the voice ALCU 1
We are for our own p. GALLACH 1
we are the p. of England CHESTERTON 24
We'll ne'er forget the P. BURNS:R 114
wrong p. going hungry OSB:J 8
ye are the p. BIBLE 187
peopled:
conquered and p. half the world SEEL 1
world must be p. SHAK:MUCH 16
peoples:
p. and governments have never learned HEG 2
silent, sullen p. KIP 100
pepper:
peck of pickled p. NURS 52
P. and vinegar besides CARROLL 57
Pequod: P.'s sea wings, beating LOWELL:R 1
Pequot: Where today are the P.? TEC 1
percentage: It's a reasonable p. BECKETT 3
perception:
agent of all human p. COLERIDGE:ST 73
between the p. that something ought WELLS:HG 18
If the doors of p. were cleansed BLAKE:W 53
perceptions: desires are limited by his p. BLAKE:W 11
perdition: bottomless p. MILT 110
perfect:
Be ye therefore p. BIBLE 389
man p. to the last detail HORACE 68
Man's as p. as he ought POPE 81
never made the full and p. man SMITH:Alex 3
Nothing is p. STEPHENS 1
Nothing is p. from every point HORACE 25
perfectibility: who speak of p. as a dream MILL 1
perfection:
ascertain what p. is ARNOLD:M 63
contains p.'s germ SHELLEY:PB 3
Dead p., no more TENNY 205
let us speak of p. POUND 23
make defect p. SHAK:ANT 27
P. is finality STEPHENS 1
P. is the child of Time HALL:Jo 2
P., of a kind, was AUD 10
P. of life, or of work YEATS 94
p. wrongfully disgrac'd SHAK:SON 30
pursuit of our total p. ARNOLD:M 61
pursuit of p., then, is ARNOLD:M 64
right praise and true p. SHAK:MERC 53
very pink of p. GOLDS 69
What's come to p. perishes BROWNING:R 138
perfections:
in the world but your p. CONG 1
own compleat P. MILT 213
perfidious: p. Albion XIM 1
performance:
All words, And no p. MASSIN 6
and the p. so loathed? SHAK:TRO 27
but it takes away the p. SHAK:MAC 51
her p. keeps no day CAMPION 7
highly overrated p. DUNC 4
p., as he is now, nothing SHAK:HEN.VIII 17
so many years outlive p.? SHAK:HEN.IV[2] 29
perfume:
Amber scent of odorous p. MILT 289
disappeared with a curious p. AUBREY 13
fluctuate all the still p. TENNY 172
perfumes: All the p. of Arabia SHAK:MAC 102
perhaps: grand P. BROWNING:R 80
peril: those in p. on the sea WHITING 1
perils:
p. and dangers of this night PRAY 29
p. both of wind and limb BUTLER:S[1] 18
peripatetics: p. Of long-haired GILB:WS 29
periphrastic: p. study ELIOT:TS 93
periscope: turn yourself into a p. LEE:JA 1
perish:
I p. for her love CAMPION 2
no vision, the people p. BIBLE 275
not p., but have everlasting BIBLE 477
p. in our own THOMP:F 3
P. the thought CIB 3
shall p. with the sword BIBLE 434
Than many p. for a private MARLOWE 22
perished:
all else p., and he remained BRONTE:E 11
We p., each alone COWP 93
perishes: nothing really p. BACON:F[1] 3
periwig: new p., make a great PEPYS 21
perjuries: smiles at lovers' p. OSB:J 6
perjury: P. is often bold and open DARLING:CJ 4
permanence:
British love p. more CASSON 1
place had an ancient p. HARDY:T 59
permissive: p. society has been allowed to JENKINS:R 1
pernicious: p. inheritance GAIUS 1
perpendicular: P., precise and taciturn MITFORD:MR 2
persecute: When in doubt p. Bloom JOYCE:J 25
persecutest: why p. thou me? BIBLE 498
persecution:
P. is a bad and indirect BROWNE:T 13
P. produced its natural effect MACAULAY:TB 32
Religious p. may shield itself BURKE:E 99
truth put down by p. MILL 13
Persepolis: ride in triumph through P.? MARLOWE 8
perseverance:
name of p. in a good cause STERNE 7
P. . . . Keeps honour bright SHAK:TRO 15
persevere: grace ay for to p. DUNB 15
Persian:
I hate that P. finery HORACE 17
P.'s Heaven is easily made MOORE:T 19
Persians: antique P. taught three BYR 237
persistence: dominant's p. till it must BROWNING:R 156
person:
frontier of my P. goes AUD 54
he is no more a p. AUD 34
only p. in the world I should like WILDE:O 48
p. and a smooth dispose SHAK:OTH 17
p. you and I took me for CARLYLE:JW 3
there's no sich a p. DICKENS 125
personal:
No p. consideration GRANT:US 2
not only live his p. life MANN:T 5
personalities:
mixed up with the p. of their bicycles O'BRIEN:F 4
Trivial p. decomposing WOOLF:V 4
personality:
attempt to express his own p. ELIOT:TS 120
cult of p. KHRU 1
dominant p. doesn't believe JAMES:B 1
escape from p. ELIOT:TS 116
Simply a radio p. WAUGH:E 34
persons:
made up of several p. MAUGH 19
Neither confounding the P. PRAY 30
perspective: delightful thing this p. UCC 1
perspiration:
his p. was but ichor BYR 148
ninety-nine per cent p. EDIS 1
per cent of inspiration is p. PROV 290
perspire:
dig till you gently p. KIP 104
he never seemed to p. FITZGER:FS 1
Mr Gladstone may p. CHURCH:Lord R 2
persuade: Wit to p. DAVIES:J 1
persuaders: Hidden P. PACK 1
persuading: p. others, we convince ourselves JUNIUS 6
persuasion: alone is not truth, but p. MACAULAY:TB 37
persuasions: Winged P. and veiled SHELLEY:PB 111
Pertelote: faire damoysele P. CHAUC 62
pertness: half P., and half Pout BYR 134
perturbed: rest, p. spirit SHAK:HAM 59
perverse: women are born so p. BRIDGES:R 12
perversion: War is . . . the universal p. RAE 1

You are p. out a-doors SHAK:OTH 19
You furnish the p. HEAR 1
picturesque: p. has taken us in MUSSO:B 4
pie:
don't want no p. in the sky ALI 3
p. in the sky when you die HILL:J 1
put into a p. by Mrs McGregor POTTER:B 2
you shall have no p. NURS 76
pie-crusts: Promises and p. are made SWIFT 41
piebald: Peel'd, patch'd, and pyebald POPE 166
piece: all of a p. throughout DRYD 129
pieces:
P. of eight! p. of eight STEVENSON:RL 30
'Tis all in p. DONNE 71
pieman: Simple Simon met a p. NURS 65
pies: one of Bellamy's veal p. PITT:W[2] 4
piety:
between p. and poor rhymes WILDE:O 126
mistaken and over-zealous p. BURKE:E 99
to p. more prone ALEX:W 1
whose p. would not grow warmer JOHNSON:S 40
piffle: as p. before the wind ASHFORD 7
pig:
from p. to man, and from man to p. ORWELL 21
into as a p. and come out BIER 7
love not a gaping p. SHAK:MERC 40
preposterous p. of a world YEATS 80
selling of p. in a poke TUSS 3
Stole a p. and away NURS 79
This little p. went to NURS 74
pig-sticking: p. in *quite* the wrong way COWARD 29
pigeon:
Father, the Son, and the P. ANON 74
I am p.-liver'd SHAK:HAM 93
p. that cannot follow you MONTALE 1
pigeonhole: some social and class p. HOWARD:P 1
pigeons: p. make Ambiguous undulations STEVENS 7
piggy: wise friend called P. GOLDI 2
pigmy:
p.'s straw does pierce it SHAK:KING L 72
shriek and sweat in p. wars TENNY 98
pigs:
As naturally as p. squeak BUTLER:S[1] 2
as p. have to fly CARROLL 26
he hadde pigges bones CHAUC 32
P. might fly PROV 320
whether p. have wings CARROLL 56
pike: holy text of p. and gun BUTLER:S[1] 11
pikes: Trail all your p. FINCH 1
pile:
God hath made the p. complete TENNY 153
P. it high, sell it cheap COHEN 1
pilfering: p., unprotected race CLARE:J 6
pilgrim:
Forth, p., forth CHAUC 125
loved the p. soul YEATS 14
Never tired p.'s limbs CAMPION 5
Onward goes the p. band BARING-G 5
p. of the sky WORDS:W 134
To be a p. BUNYAN 30
with P. steps in amice gray MILT 276
pilgrimage:
quiet P. CAMPION 4
through this weary p. DODDR 1
thus I'll make my p. RALE 2
pilgrimages: longen folk to goon on p. CHAUC 2
pilgrims: we been pilgrymes, passynge CHAUC 50
pill:
Life is a p. which none JOHNSON:S 258
need another p. to calm me SKY 1
out-liv'd the doctor's p. GAY 24
Protestant women may take the P. THOMAS:I 1
too good for the P. HUDS:B 2
pillar:
be regarded as a p. MELBOU 11
in a p. of a cloud BIBLE 100
p. o' Thy temple BURNS:R 20
P. of State MILT 158
p. of the world transform'd SHAK:ANT 1
sat by a p. alone TENNY 209
she became a p. of salt BIBLE 50
pillared: Freedom, the seven p. LAWR:TE 1
pillars:
antick P. massy proof MILT 90
builded over with p. of gold BLAKE:W 114
hewn out her seven p. BIBLE 255
pillicock: P. sat on P.-hill SHAK:KING L 43
pillions: ride away on casual p. ELIOT:TS 71
pillow:
feather p., bears the marks HAIG:D 1
like a p. on a bed DONNE 33
sigh'd upon a midnight p. SHAK:AS 21
softer p. than my heart BYR 257
pillow-hill: sits upon the p. STEVENSON:RL 52
pillows: To their deaf p. SHAK:MAC 106
pilot:
daring p. in extremity DRYD 38
Dropping the p. TENNIEL 1
P. of the Galilean lake MILT 52
P. that weathered the storm CANN 2
see my P. face to face TENNY 297
pilotage: lives in learning p. MERED:G 36
pilots: P. of the purple twilight TENNY 79
pimpernel: That demned, elusive P.? ORCZY 1
pimples:
Merely scratching of p. WOOLF:V 17
p., warts, and everything CROMWELL 11
pin:
If I sit on a p. ANON 103
little p. Bores through SHAK:RIC.II 28
might have heard a p. drop ROGERS:S 7
Not p. pricks DAU 2
p., but without either its head JERROLD 12
pinn'd it wi' a siller p. BALL 63
See a p. and pick it up PROV 340
set my life at a p.'s fee SHAK:HAM 37
Stay not for th' other p. HERB:G 13
pin-up: typical p. for men is Miss FAUST 2
pinch: death is as a lover's p. SHAK:ANT 74
pinches: Phoebus' amorous p. SHAK:ANT 22
pinching: painting till I feel like p. RENOIR:PA 3
pine:
p. away for having lost it PERS 2
p. for what is not SHELLEY:PB 99
p. within and suffer dearth SHAK:SON 61
This spray of Western p. HARRIS:JC 4
pine-apple: very p. of politeness SHERIDAN:RB 8
pine-trees: black and gloomy p. LONGFEL 20
pined: She pin'd in thought SHAK:TWE 31
pink:
Bring hether the Pincke SPENS 3
Strike me p., I'd sooner ANON 121
very p. of courtesy SHAK:ROM 22
very p. of perfection GOLDS 69
pinnacles: silent p. of aged snow TENNY 25
pins: files of P. extend POPE 39
pint:
get a quart into a p. pot PROV 439
mouldy for the want of that p. JOYCE:J 28
P. OF PLAIN IS YOUR ONLY MAN O'BRIEN:F 2
put a quart in a p. cup GILMAN 2
pioneering: P. does not pay CARNEG:A 4
pioneers: P.! O p. WHITMAN 32
pious:
p. man is one who LA BRU 2
p. person who mistakes the world DENNIS:CJ 4
pipe:
Blow your pipe there till BROWNING:R 30
He called for his p. NURS 46
his p. might fall out FORST 13
my small P. best fits HERR 37
p. for Fortune's finger SHAK:HAM 108
p. of half-awaken'd birds TENNY 109
P. to the spirit ditties KEATS 92
p., with solemn interposing COWP 27
put that in your p. BARH 8
quite a three-p. problem DOYLE:AC 17
Rumour is a p. SHAK:HEN.IV[2] 2
thy small p. Is as SHAK:TWE 6
piper:
Followed the P. for their lives BROWNING:R 29
He who pays the p. PROV 168
ten to wan the p. is a Cockney MACDIAR 5
Tom, he was a p.'s son NURS 78
Tom, Tom, the p.'s son NURS 79
pipers:
five-and-thirty p. AYT 1
Wi' a hundred p. an' a' NAIRNE 4
pipes:
from the dirty tobacco-p. ELIOT:G 39
Grate on their scrannel P. MILT 54
gurgling cisterns and p. LEWIS:CS 6
he's come to do the p. THOMP:Em 1
p. that supply the bathroom burst COWARD 27
piping: P. down the valleys wild BLAKE:W 13
pipkin: This little P. fits HERR 37
Pippa: P. passes BEERB 14
pippins: old p. toothsomest? WEBSTER:J 1
pips: until the p. squeak GED 1
pirate: To be a P. King GILB:WS 20
pismire: p. is equally perfect WHITMAN 6
piss:
full of p. and vinegar like a barber's DAVIES:R 1
isn't worth a pitcher of p. GARN 1
pissing: inside the tent p. out JOHNSON:LB 8
pistol:
p. let off at the ear LAMB:Ch 25
when his p. misses fire GOLDS 77
pistols: Have you your p.? WHITMAN 32
piston: snorting steam and p. stroke MORRIS:W 6
pistons: black statement of p. SPEND 1
pit:
Black as the P. from pole HENL 1
digged a p. before me BIBLE 217
Eagle know what is in the p.? BLAKE:W 28
have beat us to the p. SHAK:JUL 85
Man will go down into the p. BALF 1
pitch:
bumping p. and a blinding NEWBOLT 10
He that toucheth p. BIBLE 366
pitch and toss: risk it on one turn of p. KIP 127
pitcher: isn't worth a p. of piss GARN 1
pitchfork:
drive out nature with a p. HORACE 86
thrown on with a p. SWIFT 42
use my wit as a p. LARK 3
pitied: Better be envied than p. PROV 40
pitiful: God be p. BROWNING:EB 3
pits: You are the p. of the world MCEN 1
Pitt:
Pilot that weathered* CANN 2
P. is to Addington CANN 3
watchman on the lonely tower* SCOTT:W 13
pity:
best can p. who has felt GAY 6
cherish p., lest you drive BLAKE:W 24
dint of p. SHAK:JUL 55
heart let me more have p. on HOPK:GM 25
Heaven and Earth have no p. LAO 4
in myself no p. to myself? SHAK:RIC.III 18
know what 'tis to p. SHAK:AS 33
knows some touch of p. SHAK:RIC.III 4
Nor love, nor pitty knew CAREW:T 9
pitee renneth soon in gentil CHAUC 46
P., a human face BLAKE:W 17
p. beyond all telling YEATS 8
P. from blust'ring wind LOVELACE 6
p. him afterwards JOHNSON:S 182
P. is but one remove RICHARDSON:S 2
p. is felt to be a sign of scorn NIET 14
p., like a naked new-born SHAK:MAC 24
p. of war OWEN:W 13
p. sitting in the clouds SHAK:ROM 37
P. the planet LOWELL:R 16
p., then embrace POPE 95
p. 'tis 'tis true SHAK:HAM 65
Poetry is in the p. OWEN:W 15
take p. on us poor souls VILLON 2
the p. of it SHAK:OTH 49
place:
any means get Wealth and P. POPE 150
cares no more for one p. SOUTHEY 20
dozen dozen in her p. SUCK 5
everybody allows the second p. SWIFT 3
everything in its p. and nothing over BEVAN 5
fill up a p., which may be better SHAK:AS 5
flaming bounds of P. and Time GRAY:T 35
give him a placy p. CAREY 1
give p. to better men CROMWELL 9
go to the p. I set out for STERNE 49
grown and take our p. KIP 116
his p. know him any more BIBLE 185
know the p. for the first ELIOT:TS 109
Let's all move one p. on CARROLL 20

love a p. the less for having AUSTEN 68
Never the time and the p. BROWNING:R 210
no p., that they may be placed alone BIBLE 303
out of p. you see it better PICAS 3
p. by which she walked STEVENS 9
p. for everything, and everything SMILES 3
p., that great object SMITH:Ad 1
p., the climate and the people EDMOND 2
p. whereon thou standest BIBLE 85
pleasure of putting her in her p. SITWELL:E 18
superior to time and p. JOHNSON:S 21
the Lord is in this p. BIBLE 61
this is an awful p. SCOTT:Rob 1
time and p. for everything PROV 369
to keep in the same p. CARROLL 48
When does this p. get to England? LILL 2

places:
all p. are alike to me KIP 27
All p. are distant from Heaven BURTON:Ro 16
Certain p. seem to exist mainly DIDI 1
in two p. at once TAYL:M 1
Others will fill our p. CORY 4
spiritual wickedness in high p. BIBLE 538

plackets:
Dread prince of p. SHAK:LOV 8
thy hand out of p. SHAK:KING L 45

plagiarist: p. or a revolutionist GAUG 1
plagiarizes: p. without knowing it YEATS 140
plagiary: learned p. of all DRYD 138

plague:
from p., pestilence, and famine PRAY 33
From winter, p. and pestilence NASHE 3
p. had deprived us all CAMUS 6
p. o' both your houses SHAK:ROM 27
p. of opinion SHAK:TRO 17

plain:
as on a darkling p. ARNOLD:M 47
Cannot a p. man live SHAK:RIC.III 5
especially the need of the p. WAUGH:E 31
From many a palmy p. HEB 2
Gentle Knight was pricking on the plaine SPENS 21
make it p. upon tables BIBLE 361
Over the Gromboolian p. LEAR 9
PINT OF P. IS YOUR ONLY MAN O'BRIEN:F 2
p. blunt man SHAK:JUL 56
p. to uninstructed people HUX:TH 12

plain-speaking: favourite apology for p. DICKENS 173
plainness: in this p. Harbour more craft SHAK:KING L 25

plains:
ringing p. of windy Troy TENNY 52
sunlit p. extended PATERSON:AB 2

plaisters: for which there are no p. GARRICK 2

plan:
boys p. for what they will GILMAN 1
he did for them both with his p. SASS 9
new and original p. GILB:WS 47
such be Nature's holy p. WORDS:W 14

Plancus: P. was consul HORACE 43
planes: clear and gliding p. SLESS 3

planet:
it fell on the wrong p. BRAUN 1
new p. swims into his ken KEATS 4
not born under a rhyming p. SHAK:MUCH 34
Pity the p. LOWELL:R 16
p. of Love is on high TENNY 215

planetary: obedience of p. influence SHAK:KING L 9

planets:
other p. circle other suns POPE 80
P. in thir stations list'ning MILT 228
starrie spheare Of P. MILT 220

plank: I'm as thick as a p. WALES 1

plans:
best p. have always been wrecked BRECHT 12
busy making other p. LENNON 10

plant:
Fixed like a p. POPE 92
p. and flower of light JONS 48
p. that you don't want SIMM 1
p. whose virtues have not EMER 77
Sensitive P. in a garden SHELLEY:PB 91
time to p. BIBLE 281

Plantagenet: most of all, where is P.? CREWE 1
plantation: longing for de old p. FOST:SC 4

plants:
p. left over from the Edwardian OSB:J 6
p. suck in the earth COWLEY:A 6

plasters: p., pills, and ointment boxes LOCKHART 1

plate:
domestic as a p. MILLAY 2
like the silver p. on a coffin CURRAN 2

plates:
As p. dropp'd from his pocket SHAK:ANT 64
They are rattling breakfast p. ELIOT:TS 12

platinum: bullets made of p. BELLOC 4

platitude:
p. is simply a truth repeated BALD:S 11
stroke a p. until it purrs MARQUIS 10

platitudes:
Let us have fines for p. NEIL 4
Literature is the orchestration of p. WILDER:T 4
p. with courtesy and propriety PALAC 3

Plato:
attachment *à la* P. GILB:WS 33
Choose P. and Plotinus YEATS 75
Good-bye now, P. MACNEICE 8
P. is dear to me ARISTOT 25
P. is never sullen MACAULAY:TB 3
prefer to be wrong with P. CIC 17
series of footnotes to P. WHITEHEAD 1

Platonic: all P. tolerance vain YEATS 78

platter:
Displays her cleanly p. GOLDS 8
They licked the p. clean NURS 28

plaudits: Not in the shouts and p. LONGFEL 33

play:
Absurdist p. takes place in No Man's ADAMOV 1
All work and no p. PROV 16
better at a p. MOORE:T 24
Better than going to a p. CHARLES II 9
Boys and girls come out to p. NURS 4
daughter ... p. on the harpsichon PEPYS 11
Every thing that heard him p. SHAK:HEN.VIII 7
full house till the end of the p. BOIL 5
go to p. with the Poor SMITH:LP 8
good p. needs no epilogue SHAK:AS 73
home and p. it on the piano? HUGHES:B 3
Is there no p. SHAK:MID 44
Judge not the p. before QUAR 6
little victims p. GRAY:T 7
not easy to act in your p. CHEK 2
not p. things as they are STEVENS 12
old playe began to disgust EVELYN 5
or a' the p. was play'd BALL 50
our p. is played out THACK 11
p. a song for me DYL 7
p. is a dynamic thing TYNAN 1
p. is stopped, the child cannot KEMBLE 1
p. is the tragedy POE 2
p. it BOGART:H 1
P. it, Sam BERG 1
p. of passion GIBBONS:O 2
p. on SHAK:TWE 1
p. to you, 'tis death L'EST 2
P. up! p. up! and p. the game NEWBOLT 10
p.'s the thing SHAK:HAM 95
Publishing a p. is reversing SHAFF 3
rather hear thy discourse than see a p. BURTON:Ro 18
rose up to p. BIBLE 108
see that Interesting P. BELLOC 22
They will not let my p. run DENNIS:J 2
watch our fair-haired children p. CAMPBELL:G 4
what's a p. without a woman KYD 7
when the band begins to p. KIP 64
you cannot p. upon me SHAK:HAM 125
you p. Bach *your* way LANDON 1
You would p. upon me SHAK:HAM 124
young and old com forth to p. MILT 72

play-bills: no time to read p. BURNEY 1
playboy: P. of the Western World SYNGE 4

played:
He play'd so truly JONS 34
how you p. the Game RICE:G 1
p. with both hands in the pocket SATIE 3
this were play'd upon a stage SHAK:TWE 48

playedst: Thou play'dst most foully for't SHAK:MAC 60

player:
p. on the other side is hidden HUX:TH 1
poor p., That struts SHAK:MAC 113

players:
men and women merely p. SHAK:AS 34
P., Sir! I look upon them JOHNSON:S 174

playing:
add to p. your instrument the running DAVIS:M 1
p. it like married men TOSC 3

playing-fields: won on the p. of Eton ORWELL 12
playing fields: won on the p.f. of Eton WELLING 22

plays:
don't want to see p. about rape COOK:P 3
He loves no p. SHAK:JUL 15
write three p. and then stop SHAW 16

plaything: child's a p. for an hour LAMB:M 1
plaything-house: little p. that I got WALP:H 4

playthings:
Great princes have great p. COWP 76
Old boys have their p. FRANKLIN:B 15

pleasance: ywhet with fals plesaunce CHAUC 91

pleasant:
abridgment of all that was p. GOLDS 38
few think him p. enough LEAR 3
one day be p. to recall VIRGIL 37
p. if it were not for its enjoyments SURT 22
so many p. things are GASK 5
tasks are p. when they are finished CIC 2

pleasantness: Her ways are ways of p. BIBLE 250

please:
can't p. everyone PROV 443
coy, and hard to p. SCOTT:W 29
endeavour to p. everybody CHESTERFIELD 25
ferforth yeven hym to plese CHAUC 90
greatest rule of all is not to p. MOLIERE 6
I am to do what I p. FRED 4
more hard to p. himself DRYD 20
Myself alone I seek to p. GAY 51
no God could p. DRYD 36
Nothing can p. many, and p. long JOHNSON:S 34
only been taught to p. WOLLST 2
p. all the people all CONNOR 1
p. the fleeting guest WILCOX 1
p. thee, both in will and deed PRAY 51
seeketh not Itself to p. BLAKE:W 63
seeketh only Self to p. BLAKE:W 64
she never fails to p. SEDLEY 1
some circumstance to p. us SWIFT 61
That I am inspired and p. HORACE 51
that live to p. must p. to live JOHNSON:S 65
'twas natural to p. DRYD 35
when he has ladies to p. AUSTEN 42

pleased:
All seemed well pleas'd MILT 219
are you just p. to see me? WEST:M 14
in whom I am well p. BIBLE 379
least praise to have p. leaders HORACE 89
pleas'd us, had he pleas'd us less ADDIS 32

pleasing:
p. consists in being pleased HAZL 3
p. inferior people CLOUGH 13

pleasure:
aching P. nigh KEATS 96
capable of much curious p. CAB 2
did p. me in his top-boots MARLBOR:S 2
Each one's p. draws him on VIRGIL 7
fatal egg by p. laid COWP 34
fool bolts p. ANTRIM 2
go to my p., business WYCH 4
highest p. WAG 1
I' th' East my p. lies SHAK:ANT 29
In youth is p. WEVER 1
Love of P., and the Love POPE 136
make a bait if p. HERB:G 1
miss for p. GAY 35
necessity of giving p. WORDS:W 165
No p. without pain PROV 297
no sterner moralist than P. BYR 189
painefull p. turnes to pleasing SPENS 37
pay a debt to p. too? ROCHES 7
only safe p. for a parliamentarian CRIT 1
only sensual p. without vice JOHNSON:S 264
Or cabinet of *p.* HERB:G 34
P. after all is a safer guide BUTLER:S[2] 17
p. all they find GREEN:Mat 3

p. truth and p. beauty ARNOLD:M 79
poetical:
As to the p. Character KEATS 147
gods had made thee p. SHAK:AS 48
heard you are p. FLETCH:J 14
p. language of an age should be HOPK:GM 34
that werges on the p. DICKENS 29
worn-out p. fashion ELIOT:TS 93
poetry:
A criticism of life under the* ARNOLD:M 79
as much as mincing p. SHAK:HEN.IV[1] 61
at all like the p. women generally BRONTE:C 8
Ben Jonson his best piece of poetrie JONS 33
censorships that p. exists to dispel BOLA 1
cradled into p. by wrong SHELLEY:PB 25
dig up the p. of others ANTI 1
enjoy p. unless we know it to be p. THOREAU 25
Fleshly School of P. BUCHANAN 2
gave p. a proper rhythm BOIL 3
genuine p. is conceived ARNOLD:M 82
grand style arises in p. ARNOLD:M 53
he drops into p. DICKENS 218
I can repeat p. as well CARROLL 70
I didn't read the p. TWAIN 12
it doth raise and erect the mind* BACON:F[1] 8
Language is fossil p. EMER 32
Made p. a mere mechanic COWP 45
magic worlds of p. and music MORRELL 1
means of overcoming chaos* RICHARDS:IA 1
more p. than politeness WALP:H 25
never written any p. CHESTERTON 40
only p. we can admit PLATO 13
p. almost necessarily declines MACAULAY:TB 18
p. as a medium for writing in prose WILDE:O 9
p. begins to atrophy POUND 43
P. comes not as naturally KEATS 129
p., for those who know ROUX 1
p. he invented was easy AUD 10
p. in peaches GRANVILLE-B 1
P. is a comforting piece of fiction MENCK 1
P. is a kind of ingenious nonsense BARROW 1
P. is a way of taking life by FROST:R 19
P. is as exact a science FLAU 3
P. is certainly something more COLERIDGE:ST 87
P. is defined by its energies BOLA 1
P. is in the pity OWEN:W 15
P. is like painting HORACE 114
P. is not a turning loose ELIOT:TS 116
P. is nothing but time PAZ 2
P. is opposed to science COLERIDGE:ST 80
p. is *overheard* MILL 25
p. is something more philosophical ARISTOT 21
P. is the breath and finer WORDS:W 167
P. is the mother of superstition SPRAT 1
P. is the record of the happiest SHELLEY:PB 165
p. is the spontaneous overflow WORDS:W 166
P. is the supreme fiction STEVENS 2
P. is to prose as dancing WAIN 1
P. is what is lost in translation FROST:R 20
P. is when some of them fall BENTH 6
P. like politics maun MACDIAR 24
p. makes nothing happen AUD 39
p. of earth is never dead KEATS 14
p. of heaven BYR 92
p. reminds him of the richness KENNEDY:JF 5
P. should be great and unobtrusive KEATS 127
P. should surprise by a fine excess KEATS 128
p. sinks and swoons under LANDOR 19
p. = the best words in the best COLERIDGE:ST 84
p., 'The Cinderella MONROE:H 1
p., which is in Oxford DRYD 19
p.'s a mere drug FARQ 2
Polar Star of P. KEATS 117
quarrel with ourselves, p. YEATS 131
reach to as high a summit in P. KEATS 146
read p., they are radicals EMER 40
religious p. . . . is likely to be most HOUSM 55
resuscitate the dead art Of p. POUND 25
She that with p. is won BUTLER:S[1] 22
think p. has given me up LARK 12
truest p. is the most feigning SHAK:AS 49
What is p.? BYR 249
What is p.? RUSKIN 6
when p. has a meaning HOUSM 56
where is p. to be found? JOHNSON:S 56
poets:
All p. are mad BURTON:Ro 6
be among the English P. KEATS 143
drawing-rooms has spoiled more p. BEER 1
Giddy fantastic P. DONNE 1
hate all Boets and Bainters GEO I 1
Irish p. learn your trade YEATS 123
Let p. have the licence HORACE 117
many are the P. that are sown WORDS:W 111
painters, p. and builders MARLBOR:S 1
placate the sensitive race of p. HORACE 97
P. and painters are outside the class BREN 9
p. any use as government ministers ALAS 2
P. are . . . the trumpets SHELLEY:PB 167
P. are the unacknowledged legislators SHELLEY:PB 167
p. better prove SHAK:SON 13
p. exploding like bombs AUD 20
P.' food is love SHELLEY:PB 33
p. . . . have always had licence HORACE 99
p. have morals and manners HARDY:T 54
P. lose half the praise WALLER 10
P. only deliver a golden SIDNEY:P 14
P. painful vigils keep POPE 160
p. steal from Homer BURTON:Ro 8
P. that lasting marble seek WALLER 5
prince of p. BYR 198
relation to the dead p. and artists ELIOT:TS 114
so many p. end up rich COPE 1
Souls of p. dead KEATS 25
Tenderest of Roman p. TENNY 288
termed the *metaphysical* p. JOHNSON:S 47
that p. should be second rate HORACE 115
to think all p. were Byronic COPE 3
true P. must be truthful OWEN:W 16
very Janus of p. DRYD 139
We p. in our youth begin WORDS:W 84
Which only p. know COWP 63
worst of all p. CATUL 12
would be theft in other p. DRYD 137
point:
make a p. than make a friend CURTIN 1
Not to put too fine a p. DICKENS 173
without either its head or its p. JERROLD 12
wrong, 'Up to a p.' WAUGH:E 21
point of view: each has his own p.o.v. TEREN 9
points: just score more p. MOURIE 1
points of view: two p.o.v. – mine, and one that is GORT 1
poison:
Adonais has drunk p. SHELLEY:PB 118
another's p. LUCRET 10
coward's weapon, p. FLETCH:P 2
drank the p. and his spirit HOME 4
Expect p. from standing water BLAKE:W 46
go about and p. wells MARLOWE 23
If you p. us SHAK:MERC 32
meat is another man's p. PROV 312
p. England at her roots BOTT:G 1
p. in jest SHAK:HAM 117
p. the whole blood stream EMPS 3
sweet p. for the age's tooth SHAK:KING J 3
sweet poyson of mis-used Wine MILT 19
to *p. the wells* NEWM:JH 6
Turning to p. while KEATS 96
Vitality of p. BYR 81
poison-flowers: honey of p. TENNY 207
poison-gas: We've got as far as p. HARDY:T 46
poison-weeds: vilest deeds like p. WILDE:O 120
poisoned:
ingredience of our poison'd chalice SHAK:MAC 23
p. by its own secretions BREN 7
poisons:
p. all the rest WATTS 4
use in medicine for p. EMER 47
poke:
selling of pig in a p. TUSS 3
to p. poor Billy GRAHAM:H 4
poker:
p. game played between Jews and God BLUE:L 1
qualities of a p. except its O'CONNELL 1
Poland:
burn a P. winter SHAK:COM 4
P. became drunk FRED 1
polar: P. exploration is at once CHERRY 1
pole:
all sights from p. to p. ARNOLD:M 40
Beloved from p. to p. COLERIDGE:ST 28
pole-axed: no good he must be p. CHURCH:W 54
Poles: few virtues that the P. do not CHURCH:W 34
police:
do the P. in different voices DICKENS 222
'God's p.' – wives and little children CHIS 1
I'll send for the P. CARROLL 94
lying when one speaks to the p. PHILIPPE 1
occupation we encourage among p. officers ORTON 4
officers of Justice or Victorian p. KELLY:N 1
Only the Thought P. mattered ORWELL 28
Polis as Polis, in this city O'CAS 5
South African P. would leave no stone SHARPE 1
policeman:
Ask a P'liceman ROGERS:EW 1
go back with P. Day KIP 95
It would not do for a p. NIGHT 1
park, a p. and a pretty CHAPLIN 2
p. is there to *preserve* disorder DALEY 1
p.'s lot is not GILB:WS 27
terrorist and p. both come CONRAD 9
policemen:
how young the p. look HICKS 1
P. are numbered in case MILLIG 9
supposed to become p. or butchers CONNOLLY:C 4
policies: cannot restore old p. ELIOT:TS 106
policy:
Kings will be tyrants from p. BURKE:E 58
p. must be based on *it* RUSKIN 25
take his p. home and play it HUGHES:B 3
polish: p. it at leisure DRYD 103
polite:
Americans are p. by telling the truth BRADB 4
costs nothing to be p. CHURCH:W 57
Don't be too p., girls TOMASET 1
don't have the time to be p. MONTESQU 6
English are p. by telling lies BRADB 4
eventually, he *becomes* p. KERR:Jea 3
every time you are p. to a proletarian WAUGH:E 23
I was too p. to ask VIDAL 8
p. meaningless words YEATS 41
till the English grew p. KIP 112
You're exceedingly p. GILB:WS 9
politeness:
mutual glance of great p. BYR 150
Punctuality is the p. of kings LOUIS XVIII 1
Punctuality is the p. of princes PROV 325
very pine-apple of p. SHERIDAN:RB 8
political:
addiction of p. groups to the ideas GALB 4
by nature a p. animal ARISTOT 13
Christianity is p. TUTU 3
created the best of its p. intelligence YEATS 135
demands a new p. science TOC 2
for fear of P. Economy SELL 8
formation of the p. will of the entire HITL 5
free from p. bias ORWELL 24
he was a first-rate p. economist SHAW 104
healthy state of p. life MILL 12
history of p. power POPP 3
most schemes of p. improvement JOHNSON:S 141
ordeal of a p. canvass SHERMAN 3
people to dissolve the p. bonds JEFFERSON 1
points clearly to a p. career SHAW 90
P. activity is essentially absurd HORNE:DR 3
P. history is far too criminal AUD 67
p. ones are insoluble DOUGLAS-H:A 3
P. oratory is the art PALAC 3
P. power grows out MAO 1
p. speech and writing ORWELL 37
religion is making Christianity p. VAN DER P 4
sorry for the death of a p. economist BAGE 4
stake my entire p. career OWEN:D 2
stomach is not a good p. adviser EINS 2
to bowdlerize p. history is not AUD 67
we are not p. whores MUSSO:B 9
politician:
at home you're just a p. MACMILL:H 6
honest p. is one who CAMERON 1

like a scurvy p. SHAK:KING L 73
no p. in India daring enough GAND:I 3
p. is a statesman who POMPI 1
p. is a statesman who approaches STEVENSON:A 14
p. is an arse upon CUMM 3
p. never believes what he says DE GAU 8
p. poses as the servant DE GAU 10
which makes the p. wise POPE 51
politicians:
anxious dwarfs trying* PRIEST 5
great fault of our p. TROLL 18
just as funny as p. ROOS:T 18
more p. are not bastards by birth WHITEHORN 3
not get it from their p. MACMILL:H 13
Old P. chew on wisdom POPE 114
P. are the same everywhere KHRU 4
p. by expediency BELLOCH 1
P. cannot help being clowns HORNE:DR 3
whole race of p. put together SWIFT 31
politics:
breaking the mould of British p. JENKINS:R 3
brings his p. to church BYROM 6
don't concern themselves with p. CAMUS 2
Don't tell my mother I'm in p. ANON 180
executive expression of human immaturity* BRITT 3
Finality is not the language of p. DISR:B 60
From p., it was an easy step AUSTEN 64
gallantry than it has with p. SHERIDAN:RB 2
holy mistaken zeal in p. JUNIUS 6
horrid business of p. VICT 3
in p. there is no heart NAPO I 13
In p., what begins COLERIDGE:ST 89
Magnanimity in p. is not seldom BURKE:E 43
mule of p. DISR:B 19
mules of p. POWER:JO 1
no longer in the p. of the pendulum THATCH:M 3
nothing to do with p. is itself a political ORWELL 24
Or on Spanish p.? YEATS 115
Philistine of genius in p. ARNOLD:M 77
p. and little else beside CAMPBELL:R 1
P. and the pulpit are terms BURKE:E 50
P. are now nothing more JOHNSON:S 172
p. are too serious a matter to be left DE GAU 9
p. by other means CLAUS 1
P. is both fraud and vision HORNE:DR 4
P. is not a precise science BISM 2
P. is not a science BISM 6
P. is not the art of the possible GALB 7
P. is perhaps the only profession STEVENSON:RL 25
P. is supposed to be the second oldest REAG 1
P. is the art of preventing VALERY 4
P. is the chloroform of the Irish GOGA 4
P. is the doctrine of what is possible BISM 3
p. is to make more friends WATEN 1
p. maun cut The cackle MACDIAR 24
p. present history SEEL 2
P. we bar GILB:WS 54
practice of p. in the East DISR:B 10
pretend that p. is a game PARKIN 3
systematic organization of hatreds* ADAMS:H 1
week is a long time in p. WILSON:Harold 5
What Englishman will give his mind to p. SHAW 121
polities: shall the saner, softer p. HARDY:T 13
polka: See me dance the p. SITWELL:E 6
Poll: talk'd like poor P. GARRICK 6
poll-taxes: p. never produced the sum SMITH:Ad 13
pollution: engine of p., the dog SPARROW 1
Polly:
Little P. Flinders Sat among NURS 36
P. is a sad slut GAY 11
P. put the ket-tle on DICKENS 89
P. put the kettle on NURS 54
polo-playing: uncultured, p. clod PHILIP 5
polygamy:
Before p. was made a sin DRYD 33
chaste Poligamie CAREW:T 5
pommie: P. his fare home to England KENEAL 1
pomp:
all his p., without his force BURKE:E 106
all our p. of yesterday KIP 92
easie yoke Of servil P. MILT 156
In lowly p. ride on MILM 1
P. ascended jubilant MILT 228
p. of pow'r GRAY:T 17
possess'd with double p. SHAK:KING J 16
puts all the p. to flight POPE 64
Vain p. and glory SHAK:HEN.VIII 10
what is p. SHAK:HEN.VI[3] 7
Pompey: Knew you not P.? SHAK:JUL 2
pompous: p. in the grave BROWNE:T 62
Poms:
second-hand, recycled P. ADAMS:P 1
seem to be bloody P. CHARLES:Prince 1
ponces: wriggling p. of the spoken word BRIDS 1
pond: Into the ancient p. BAS 1
poniards: She speaks p. SHAK:MUCH 7
pony: I had a little p. NURS 22
poodle: Mr Balfour's p. LLOYD GEO 2
pool: plunge in a p.'s living water BROWNING:R 146
pools: Where the p. are bright HOGG 7
poop: p. was beaten gold SHAK:ANT 25
poor:
apt the p. are to be proud SHAK:TWE 40
As for the virtuous p. WILDE:O 37
be p., I'm honest MIDD 3
Blessed are the p. in spirit BIBLE 384
by heavens he must be p. KAV 2
divide with the p. the produce SMITH:Ad 2
does the p. man two favours PUB 2
else his dear papa is p. STEVENSON:RL 55
even p. in thanks SHAK:HAM 79
feeds the p. as he feeds ROUSS:JJ 4
go to play with the P. SMITH:LP 8
greater part of the members are p. SMITH:Ad 3
grind the faces of the p.? BIBLE 302
he is p. they call him a Jew HEINE 8
how p. a thing is man DANI 5
I am as p. as Job SHAK:HEN.IV[2] 9
I can dare to be p. GAY 32
I should love to be p. ANOU 1
in the p. country no pauper NEIL 2
inconvenient to be p. COWP 22
Labour robbed out of the p. WELLS:HG 5
laboured much for the P. BUNYAN 29
Laws grind the p. GOLDS 11
live by robbing the p. SHAW 39
man is the worse for being p. SHAW 95
most rich, being p. SHAK:KING L 6
murmuring p. CRAB 5
no right to the property of the p. RUSKIN 16
only the p. who pay cash FRANCE 12
Only the p. will help the p. HARDY:F 1
open to the p. and the rich ANON 188
Plenty has made me p. OSB:J 20
p. always ye have BIBLE 486
p. and have a rotten time COPE 5
p., and the maimed BIBLE 461
p. are never grateful WILDE:O 36
p. are our brothers and sisters TERESA 1
p. are the negroes of Europe CHAMFORT 7
p. but she was honest ANON 38
p. could make a wonderful living PROV 188
p.-folk maun be wretches BURNS:R 56
p. have become poorer SHELLEY:PB 166
P. in deed and rich HOLD 1
p. know that it is money BREN 1
P. little rich girl COWARD 16
p. man at his gate ALEX:CF 2
p. man is despised JEROME:JK 4
p. man loved the great MACAULAY:TB 49
p. may lie to himself HORV 1
p. person has hope KERR:Jea 2
p. rush to marry STEAD 3
p. who got away MURRAY:LA 7
p. wot gets the blame ANON 38
poore man is Christ's stamp HERB:G 11
Resolve not to be p. JOHNSON:S 229
RICH AND THE P. DISR:B 25
save the p., feel for the p. LANDON 1
simple annals of the p. GRAY:T 17
so p. that he cannot have a chicken HENRI 1
space that many p. supplied GOLDS 33
thin hands of the p. WILDE:J 1
To be p. and independent COBBETT 4
Too p. for a bribe GRAY:T 37
When that the p. have cried SHAK:JUL 50
poorer: for richer for p. PRAY 84
poorest:
p. he that is in England RAINBO 1
p. man may in his cottage PITT:W[1] 2
poorly: P. (poor man) he liv'd FLETCH:P 5
pop:
into p. because I want to get rich GEL 3
Too much religion makes me go p. RUNCIE:Ros 1
pop-star: girls react to the p. as a person FAUST 2
pope:
P.! How many divisions STALIN 4
remember I am the P. JOHN XXIII 1
Pope:
Better to err with P. BYR 11
Dryden and P. are not classics ARNOLD:M 81
If P. be not a poet JOHNSON:S 56
P. . . . he was picking his nose SHEN 4
P. composes with his eye ARNOLD:M 51
poetry of Dryden, P., and all their ARNOLD:M 82
Poor P. will grieve a month SWIFT 63
popery:
disguised his p. to the last CHARLES II 2
never be in danger of P. ADDIS 22
popinjay: So pest'red with a p. SHAK:HEN.IV[1] 18
popish: P. liturgy PITT:W[1] 8
poplars: p. are felled COWP 47
Popocatapetl: P. In the sunlight gleams TURNER:WJR 2
poppies:
Drows'd with the fume of p. KEATS 109
In Flanders fields the p. blow MCCRAE 1
p. was nothing to it DICKENS 48
poppy:
flushed print in a p. THOMP:F 17
not p., nor mandragora SHAK:OTH 41
oblivion blindly scattereth her p. BROWNE:T 58
populace:
give the name of *P.* ARNOLD:M 69
into Barbarians, Philistines, and P. ARNOLD:M 62
popular:
art thou base, common and p.? SHAK:HEN.V 28
bad she was very very p. MILLER:M 1
worse I do, the more p. I get KENNEDY:JF 11
popularity:
every difficulty except p. WILDE:O 127
P. is a Crime from the Moment HALIF 8
population:
only talked of p. GOLDS 49
P., when unchecked MALT 1
porcelain: dainty rogue in p. MERED:G 7
porch: he'll be on your p. JOHNSON:LB 2
porcupines: throw two p. under you KHRU 7
Porlock: person on business from P. COLERIDGE:ST 62
porn: want your p. in black and white ALLB 1
pornographic: so exciting as p. books HUX:A 20
pornography:
gives p. a bad name BARNES:C 1
p. is in yer Sunday papers SPEIGHT 3
P. is the attempt to insult LAWR:DH 22
porpoise: There's a p. close behind CARROLL 31
porpoises: If p. were really so smart LEONARD:E 1
porridge:
breath to cool your p. PROV 337
comfort like cold p. SHAK:TEM 13
What p. had John Keats? BROWNING:R 144
porringer: take my little p. WORDS:W 21
Porsches: days of swine and P. HILL:Reg 2
Porson: P. sober HOUSM 58
port:
Any p. in a storm PROV 17
Go fetch a pint of p. TENNY 67
In every p. a wife DIBDIN:C 2
In every p. he finds a wife BICK 1
In ev'ry p. a mistress GAY 39
It would be p. if it could BENTLEY:R 2
Let him drink p. HOME 4
p. after stormie seas SPENS 30
p. for men JOHNSON:S 210
p. in every storm PROV 336
Pride in their p. GOLDS 10
Still bent to make some p. ARNOLD:M 15
There lies the p. TENNY 55
portal: wondrous p. opened wide

BROWNING:R 32
portcullis: Let the p. fall SCOTT:W 26
portents: These are p. SHAK:OTH 61
porter:
all p. and skittles DICKENS 49
just as well for a p. NIGHT 1
mister p., what shall I do LLOYD:M 1
Porter : moon shone bright on Mrs P. ELIOT:TS 44
porter-drinkers: P.' randy laughter YEATS 123
porters: poor mechanic p. crowding SHAK:HEN.V 7
portion: best p. of a good man's life WORDS:W 4
portmanteau: You see it's like a p. CARROLL 69
portrait:
Every man's work ... is always a p. BUTLER:S[2] 14
only two styles of p. painting DICKENS 72
paint a p. I lose a friend SARGENT:JS 1
p. of a blinking idiot SHAK:MERC 30
p. of a dog that I know JOHNSON:S 262
P. of the Artist as a Young Man JOYCE:J 1
portraits: P. of famous bards THOMAS:D 36
portrayed: p. men as they ought SOPH 6
ports: close the five p. of knowledge BROWNE:T 45
pose: Being natural is simply a p. WILDE:O 24
posies: thousand fragrant p. MARLOWE 51
position:
Every p. must be held HAIG:D 2
Holders of one p. AUD 3
p. ridiculous CHESTERFIELD 36
p. will be held BETHU 1
positive:
live by p. goals BERLIN:Is 2
p. men are the most credulous POPE 180
Power of P. Thinking PEALE 1
possess:
if you did not p. me PASC 15
p. The things I seek SHELLEY:PB 141
to feel and to p. BYR 67
possessing: too dear for my p. SHAK:SON 38
possession:
one equal p. DONNE 110
P. is nine points of the law PROV 321
p. makes everything wither PROUST 1
p. of it is intolerable VANB 7
P. without obligation MERED:G 10
possessions:
All my p. for a moment ELIZ I 18
behind the great p. JAMES:H 20
Covetous of others' p., prodigal SALL 1
than the loss of their p. MACHIA 6
useful to those who have p. ROUSS:JJ 2
who has many p. happy HORACE 58
possessor: Receive thy new P. MILT 122
possessors: p. seldom outlast LOWELL:R 11
possibilities:
believe only p., is not faith BROWNE:T 20
preferred to improbable i. ARISTOT 22
possibility: deny the p. of anything HUX:TH 13
possible:
doctrine of what is p. BISM 3
effecting of all things p. BACON:F[1] 124
In two words: im p. GOLDWYN 13
most of what is p. PINDAR 2
p., it has been done CALON 1
p. was every instant made HUX:A 21
scientist states that something is p. CLARKE:AC 1
with God all things are p. BIBLE 423
possums: Wave your gladdies, p. HUMPH 3
post:
against a p. when he was drunk SHAK:HEN.V 23
p. o're Lands and Ocean MILT 100
whose p. lay in the rear ROSSET:C 1
post-chaise: driving briskly in a p. JOHNSON:S 190
post office: What stalked through the P.O.? YEATS 121
postboy: Never ... see ... a dead p. DICKENS 53
poster: at least, a great p. ASQU:M 4
posterity:
give a hoot about p. COWARD 11
not look forward to p. BURKE:E 53
p. is a pack-horse DISR:B 62
see P. do something for us ADDIS 28
Think of your p. ADAMS:JQ 1
Trustees of P. DISR:B 28
What has p. done for us? ROCHE 1
postgraduate: p. student is a lonely forlorn LODGE:D 3
posthumously: some are born p. NIET 24
postillion: P. Struck by Lightning BOGARDE 1
postponed: doesn't tolerate being p. KRAUS 2
postponement: Government by p. is bad enough STEVENSON:A 10
postscript: most material in the p. BACON:F[1] 48
posy: made a posie while the day HERB:G 37
pot:
don't make them in the one p. JOYCE:J 13
greasy Joan doth keel the p. SHAK:LOV 25
kettle and the earthen p. BIBLE 367
quart into a pint p. PROV 439
There is death in the p. BIBLE 169
treasures from an earthen p. HERB:G 14
watched p. never boils PROV 413
potage:
see also **pottage**
birthright for a mess of p. BIBLE 54
potations:
dull and deep p. GIBBON:E 16
forswear thin p. SHAK:HEN.IV[2] 43
potato:
I've a mouth like an old p. KIP 46
jumped out of a rotten p. NURS 63
mashed p. is one of the great BARE 1
p. in his head HARE:J 4
take him like a sweet p. MARQUIS 8
Though the p. is an excellent root DAVIES:D 1
potatoes: Tired of digging p. HARDY:T 1
potions: What p. have I drunk SHAK:SON 53
Potomac:
All quiet along the P. MCCLELL 1
quiet along the P. to-night BEERS 1
pots: were p. and pans PEAC 18
pottage:
see also **potage**
birthright for very bad p. WILDE:O 37
potter:
Hand then of the P. shake? FITZGER:E 29
P. and clay endure BROWNING:R 189
Who *is* the P. FITZGER:E 30
poultice: silence, like a p., comes HOLMES:OW 1
poultry:
A p. matter MARX:G 3
prolonging the lives of the p. ELIOT:G 24
pound:
penny, in for a p. PROV 198
P. a week and his keep LAWS 5
p. here in Britain, in your WILSON:Harold 6
P. notes are the best religion BEHAN:Br 5
p. of flesh which I demand SHAK:MERC 42
see who will p. longest WELLING 5
pounds:
About two hundred p. a year BUTLER:S[1] 32
being left fifty thousand p. MILNE 20
draw for a thousand p. ADDIS 31
handsome in three hundred p. SHAK:MERR 12
implore you for five p. BURNS:R 129
only ask you for twenty-five p. SHERIDAN:RB 46
p. will take care of themselves PROV 362
six hundred p. a year SWIFT 54
pour: poure on him all we can HERB:G 43
pouring: more noise they make in p. POPE 179
pout: half Pertness, and half P. BYR 134
poverty:
bear about luckless p. JUV 7
culture of p. suffer much less FRIEL 1
depths of helpless p. JUV 8
Do you call p. a crime? SHAW 91
If p. is the mother of crime LA BRU 6
In honoured p. thy voice SHELLEY:PB 18
it is confoundedly inconvenient* SMITH:Syd[1] 34
Loneliness is the p. of self SARTON 1
Not taught to endure p. HORACE 1
P. and oysters always seem DICKENS 18
P. has strange bedfellows BULWER 3
P. is a great enemy JOHNSON:S 229
P. is an anomaly to rich BAGE 25
P. is no disgrace SMITH:Syd[1] 34
P. is not a crime PROV 322
p. that knows the destitution ANON 110
P., though it does not prevent SMITH:Ad 4
p.'s catching BEHN 1
she scorns our p. SHAK:HEN.VI[2] 1
so much p. and excess PENN 2
state of pretentious p. JUV 9
struggled in p. to build STANTON:El 2
to a state of extreme p. MARX:G 4
When p. comes in at the door PROV 425
worst of our crimes is p. SHAW 79
worth by p. depress'd JOHNSON:S 64
poverty-stricken: P. in the midst of great riches HORACE 44
powder:
drinking a seidlitz p. ANON 134
Food for p. SHAK:HEN.IV[1] 80
keep your p. dry BLACKER 1
powders: Puffs, P., Patches POPE 39
power:
absolute p. corrupts ACTON:Baron 2
all p. is a trust DISR:B 3
another name for absolute p. WORDS:W 163
aspired to p. instead of influence TAYL:AJP 5
at the present possessors of p. BURKE:E 12
balance of p. WALP:R 1
behaves decently when they have p. AMIS:K 5
Between his p. and thine JONS 14
bulwarks which stand against ruthless p. AUNG 1
certainty of p. DAY LEWIS 2
corridors of p. SNOW 1
Corridors of P. SNOW 6
disastrous rise of misplaced p. EISEN 6
drunk with sight of p. KIP 93
except my own p. in the theatre GIEL 1
for men, sex is p. FAUST 3
gives to every p. a double p. SHAK:LOV 16
greater the p., the more BURKE:E 91
history of political p. POPP 3
If p. change purpose SHAK:MEA 2
Knowledge is p. PROV 222
'Knowledge is p.' is the finest RENAN 1
Knowledge itself is p. BACON:F[1] 1
lack of p. corrupts absolutely STEVENSON:A 11
legislative p. is nominated GIBBON:E 2
literature of *p.* DEQ 12
literature seeks to communicate p. DEQ 8
love of p. is the love HAZL 10
Nature's ancient p. was lost TENNY 163
no hopes but from p. BURKE:E 85
no knowledge that is not p. EMER 69
no longer in your p. SOLZ 5
no more than p. in trust DRYD 44
once intoxicated with p. BURKE:E 70
only purpose for which p. MILL 8
Political p. grows out MAO 1
pomp of pow'r GRAY:T 17
P. dwells apart SHELLEY:PB 16
P. Girt round with weakness SHELLEY:PB 117
p. ... is ever grasping ADAMS:A 1
p. is in the hands not of the few PERIC 1
P. is man's secret STEPHENS 3
P. is so apt to be insolent HALIF 4
P. is the ultimate aphrodisiac KISS 8
p. men have over women DWO 2
p. narrows the areas of man's KENNEDY:JF 5
p. of no calamity while death BROWNE:T 18
p. over men; but over themselves WOLLST 6
p. should always be distrusted JONES:W 1
P. wears down the man who doesn't ANDREO 1
p. without responsibility BALD:S 1
P. without responsibility KIP 157
reinforcement of the p. of the State CAMUS 10
shadow of some unseen P. SHELLEY:PB 12
smallest amount of p. to be nice CLARE:A 2
some P. the giftie gie us BURNS:R 52
something from our hands have p. WORDS:W 129
superior p. to be of singular use SWIFT 9
Supream P. must be Arbitrary HALIF 3
that have the p. to die TENNY 47
that p. to do me harm SHAK:OTH 66
'tis the supreme of p. KEATS 12
to erect such a common p. HOBB 10
to seek p. and to lose liberty BACON:F[1] 73
Unlimited p. is apt to corrupt PITT:W[1] 6
untimely interchange of p. BACON:F[1] 59

whole world wants: p. BOULTON:M 1
with Eternal God for p. TENNY 194
Women and Horses and P. and War KIP 40
powerful:
be p. rather than charming RUSS:B 15
I am p. and alone VIGNY 1
powerless: p. to be born ARNOLD:M 35
powers:
Cities and Thrones and P. KIP 119
p. that be are ordained BIBLE 517
P. that will work for thee WORDS:W 103
we lay waste our p. WORDS:W 104
practical: power of sustained p. activity TAWN 1
practice:
in p., though not in principle AUSTEN 28
Moral virtues we acquire through p. ARISTOT 6
My p. is never very absorbing DOYLE:AC 16
p. drives me mad ANON 84
principles without having good p.? JOHNSON:S 84
practise:
able to p. five things CONF 14
P. what you preach PROV 323
prudence never to p. either TWAIN 26
we p. but seldom preach RUSS:B 12
practised:
For thirty-seven years I've p. SARAS 1
practis'd what he preach'd ARMST:J 2
seeing it p. BUTLER:S[2] 15
praise:
alms of thy superfluous p. DRAYT 8
can p. too much JONS 38
clerkes preise wommen but a lite CHAUC 35
Damn with faint p. POPE 121
disprais'd were no small p. MILT 269
dispraised, is the most perfect p. JONS 9
envy is a kind of p. GAY 48
free man how to p. AUD 43
girded with p. GRANT:R 1
give you unqualified p. STEINB 2
His p. forth tell KETHE 1
I will p. any man SHAK:ANT 34
I would p. you still WRIGHT:J 9
In deeper reverence, p. WHITTIER 7
lack tongues to p. SHAK:SON 49
laurel crown to p. CIC 5
Let us now p. famous men BIBLE 370
little dust of p. TENNY 166
man's self is oblique p. JOHNSON:S 204
My great Redeemer's p. WESLEY:C 2
named thee but to p. HALLE 1
no such whetstone ... as is p. ASCHAM 4
not be dieted with p. KEATS 98
paint 'em truest p. 'em ADDIS 37
p. at morning what POPE 23
P. God from whom KEN 3
p. him and exalt him BIBLE 606
p. him, and magnify PRAY 14
P. is the best diet SMITH:Syd[1] 26
p. of the Lord is drummed into you PEV 1
p. ourselves in other men POPE 24
P. the Lord, all nations BIBLE 603
P. to the Holiest NEWM:JH 17
Refusal of p. reveals LA ROCHE 20
right p. and true perfection SHAK:MERC 53
sickens at another's p. CHURCH:C 14
there were none to p. WORDS:W 30
they only want p. MAUGH 2
They p. those works MARTIAL 4
We p. thee, God ANON 43
We p. thee, O God PRAY 8
Who pay no p. or wages THOMAS:D 20
worthy of p. the Muse forbids HORACE 56
wretched lust of p. POPE 55
praised:
greatly to be p. BIBLE 230
p. for virtues you never STONE:IF 1
they p. him to his face TENNY 286
to be p. than to be pardoned JONS 54
praises:
boldly sound your own p. BACON:F[1] 29
faint p. one another damn WYCH 5
sing p. unto thy name BIBLE 227
who p. everybody p. nobody JOHNSON:S 193
praising:
advantage of doing one's p. BUTLER:S[2] 18
P. all alike GAY 34
pram: than the p. in the hall CONNOLLY:C 6
prance: if a man has a mind to *p.* JOHNSON:S 136
pranks:
his p. have been too broad SHAK:HAM 134
let God see the p. SHAK:OTH 36
pray:
All p. in their distress BLAKE:W 16
going to p. for you at St Paul's SMITH:Syd[1] 42
I'd as lief p. with Kit Smart JOHNSON:S 109
Let us p. MASS 11
Let us p. to God ... the bastard BECKETT 12
look at the senators and I p. HALE:EE 1
more nearly as we p. KEBLE 2
necessary to p. to the gods SOC 8
P. without ceasing BIBLE 545
remained to p. GOLDS 27
starve and p., for that's POPE 65
Watch and p. ELLIOT:C 1
prayed: not given me what I p. for SPYRI 1
prayer:
back to early p. CHURCH:C 3
be set aside through p. VIRGIL 70
Because they hated Common P. JORD 1
Everything to God in p. SCRIV 1
eyes are homes of silent p. TENNY 144
Four spend in p. COKE:E 6
home-brew'd p. GREEN:Mat 2
In P. the Lips ne're act HERR 1
let the p. re-echo LINLEY 1
Listen to a maiden's p. SCOTT:W 40
More things are wrought by p. TENNY 279
most perfect p. LESSING:GE 1
P. makes the Christian's COWP 8
P. the Churches banquet HERB:G 23
sleep with a p. for the beloved GIBRAN 2
storms of p. TENNY 44
swears a p. or two SHAK:ROM 5
The people's p. DRYD 43
troubles me in my p. DONNE 106
Work is p. ANON 212
prayer-books: pray'r-books are the toys of age POPE 98
prayers:
Christopher Robin is saying his p. MILNE 8
feed on p. PEELE 2
Lord, hear our p. PRAY 78
not trust it without my p. BROWNE:T 34
P. grow like windless trees DUTT 2
p. in the hall and some whiskey ASHFORD 5
p. of good CERV 7
three-mile p. BURNS:R 33
prayeth: p. best, who loveth best COLERIDGE:ST 38
praying:
No p., it spoils business OTWAY 5
talk to God, you are p. SZASZ 9
that's past p. for SHAK:HEN.IV[1] 40
prays:
p. to the spirit of the place VIRGIL 75
to deny that faintly p. QUAR 1
preach:
could na p. for thinkin o't BURNS:R 82
Practise what you p. PROV 323
P. not because you have WHATE 1
p. the gospel to every BIBLE 446
we p. but do not practise RUSS:B 12
preached:
Deserves to be p. to death SMITH:Syd[1] 32
p. as never sure to preach BAXTER:R 2
p. him and Christ BROWNING:R 101
practis'd what he preach'd ARMST:J 2
preacher:
Judge not the p. HERB:G 14
p. every Sunday put God WHITMAN 36
preachers:
P. say, Do as I say SELD 12
p. too often speak of BETT 1
preaching:
God calleth p. folly HERB:G 14
woman's p. is like a dog's JOHNSON:S 126
preamble: long p. of a tale CHAUC 85
precedency:
Men have p. BRADST 2
p. between a louse and a flea JOHNSON:S 235
precedent:
From p. to p. TENNY 56
p. embalms a principle STOWELL 2
precedents: as well to create good p. BACON:F[1] 76
precepts: p. for the teacher's sake FARQ 6
precincts: left the warm p. GRAY:T 24
precious:
all that's p. in our joys STERNE 53
can make vile things p. SHAK:KING L 38
it kills something p. COMPT 8
precipice:
edge of a p. upon a dark night BRAM 2
p. in front, wolves behind ERAS 2
precipices: p. show untrodden green KEATS 32
precise:
Perpendicular, p. and taciturn MITFORD:MR 2
p. but not pedantic ELIOT:TS 123
too p. in every part HERR 16
precisian: devil turned p.? MASSIN 10
predestination:
conclusion upon Free Will and P. CHURCH:W 44
P. in the stride KIP 71
predicament: it is a p. SANT 14
predictions: p. of astrology BACON:F[1] 94
prefabricated: better word than 'p.' CHURCH:W 62
prefer: I would p. not to MELV 5
preferment:
knocking at p.'s door ARNOLD:M 21
so I got p. ANON 25
pregnancies: I took note of six p. BEECHAM 10
pregnancy:
avoid p. by a resort to MENCK 7
occupational hazard of being a wife* ANNE 4
one solution: it's called p. NIET 6
pregnant:
Irish bull is always p. MAHAF 2
like being a little p. HENDER:L 1
worry about *getting* p. NICHOLS:P 1
prejudge: not intend to p. the past WHITELAW 1
prejudice:
Conduct ... to the p. ANON 173
dislike for the unlike* ZANG 4
do I behold with p. the French BROWNE:T 23
full of vulgar p. BUCHANAN 7
P. of education ... is the devil STERNE 24
Scottish p. in my veins BURNS:R 126
to cure us of the p. HAZL 30
prejudices:
be above national p. NORTH:C 2
bundle of p. – made up LAMB:Ch 9
discipline his personal p. ELIOT:TS 119
exploded systems and obsolete p. SMITH:Ad 9
honest p. which naturally cleave ADDIS 22
merely rearranging their p. JAMES:W 5
narrow p. of an islander BYR 255
p. acquired by age eighteen EINS 19
p. as the advertisers don't object SWAFF 1
reason to strengthen their own p. DUKES 2
prelaty: impertinent yoke of p. MILT 304
prentice: Her p. han' she try'd BURNS:R 5
preparation:
dreadful note of p. SHAK:HEN.V 25
foolish p. AUSTEN 52
no p. is thought necessary STEVENSON:RL 25
p. for something that never happens YEATS 143
p. for this hour and this trial CHURCH:W 50
such p. there is sure to be failure CONF 23
prepare:
good God p. me PEPYS 25
P. ye the way of the Lord BIBLE 320
P. ye the way of the Lord BIBLE 377
Whenever I p. for a journey MANS:K 6
preposterousest: To the p. end BUTLER:S[1] 39
prerogative:
dead and rotten as P. BURKE:E 14
p. of the harlot BALD:S 1
p. of the harlot KIP 157
presbyter: New P. is but Old Priest MILT 93
Presbyterian:
'Twas P. true blue BUTLER:S[1] 10
virtues of a Scottish P., but none CAMPBELL:M 1
presbyterianism: not a religion for gentlemen* CHARLES II 3
presence:
better than p. of mind PUNCH 4
conspicuous by its p. RUSS:J[2] 3
p. on the field made the difference WELLING 12
p. that disturbs me WORDS:W 8

P. watching by my bed THOMS:Ja[2] 10
present:
act in the living P. LONGFEL 3
All p. and correct ANON 154
always except the p. company O'KEEFFE:J 2
an un-birthday p. CARROLL 66
but p. in spirit BIBLE 519
his p. is futurity HARDY:T 53
No time like the p. MANLEY 1
No time like the p. PROV 303
offers no redress for the p. DISR:B 15
p. cannot be revealed MCLUH 14
P. has latched its postern HARDY:T 33
p. is the funeral of the past CLARE:J 7
p. joys are more to flesh DRYD 88
P. mirth hath p. SHAK:TWE 19
p. stood still HUX:A 21
surface of the p. than in NAB 6
things p., worst SHAK:HEN.IV[2] 19
things which are just in p. BACON:F[1] 12
though the p. I regret CONG 61
who controls the p. ORWELL 32
presentiment: but she has a p. STERNE 43
presents: P. . . . endear Absents LAMB:Ch 3
preserve:
Bad governments p. nothing LEWIS:N 1
The Lord shall p. thee BIBLE 240
preserver: Destroyer and p. SHELLEY:PB 40
president:
in America anyone can be P. FORD:GR 3
P. does it, that means it is not illegal NIX 11
p. of the United States and I am not going to eat BUSH 1
P. should on no account be allowed ADAMS:D 2
P. spends most of his time kissing TRU 4
p. who might have been CARTER:J 1
rather be right than be P. CLAY 2
rather be right than p. THOMAS:NM 1
slept more than any other P. MENCK 17
told that anybody could become P. DARROW 2
We are all the P.'s men KISS 2
press:
fell *dead-born from the p.* HUME 15
Flee fro the prees CHAUC 124
Freedom of the p. in Britain SWAFF 1
god of our idolatry, the p. COWP 38
I have misused the King's p. SHAK:HEN.IV[1] 78
liberty of the p. is the *Palladium* JUNIUS 1
Never lose your temper with the P. PANK:C 4
not say that our P. is obscene LONGFORD 2
one-party p. STEVENSON:A 7
p.: slow dripping of water FAIRBURN 1
P. was squared BELLOC 20
press conference: this is my last p.c. NIX 1
pressure:
grace under p. HEMINGWAY 14
world p. put Uncle Sam X 2
presume: P. not that I am the thing SHAK:HEN.IV[2] 55
presumption:
acquired a certain pedantic p. PEREZ 1
amused by its p. THURB 16
surquidrie and foul presumpcioun CHAUC 105
pretend:
do not p. to anything better GWENN 1
p. to be someone else COLTRANE 1
pretender: who P. is, or who is King BYROM 5
pretexts: Tyrants seldom want p. BURKE:E 71
pretty:
all the maidens p. COLMAN:G[2] 3
growing up into a p. woman AUSTEN 32
It is a p., p. thing PEELE 3
It is a p. thing GREENE:R 1
It's p., but is it Art? KIP 43
only one p. child in the world PROV 385
p. can get away with anything WAUGH:E 31
p. women to deserve them AUSTEN 31
uncommon p. young woman ELIOT:G 4
prevail:
Should strive and should p. NEWM:JH 18
they shall not p. against thee BIBLE 335
prevent: p. it and to damn the consequences MILNER 1
prevention:
P. is better than cure PEAC 4
P. is better than cure PROV 324
preventive: P. action was like p. war HAGG:W 1
pre-war: take his p. mentality into BENES 1
prey:
bent on his p. MILT 179
Humanity must perforce p. SHAK:KING L 62
soon must be his p. SHELLEY:PB 28
takes its p. to privacy MOORE:M 5
to hastening ills a p. GOLDS 21
yet a p. to all POPE 90
Priam: proud as P. murdered YEATS 10
Priapus: P. in the shrubbery ELIOT:TS 13
price:
another man's p. increase WILSON:Harold 12
as if everything has its p. STRETT 2
bought it at any p. CLAREN 4
cannot pay the p. of self-respect WILSON:W 9
her p. is far above rubies BIBLE 276
no point in lying about the p. CERV 9
p. of everything and the value WILDE:O 51
those men have their p. WALP:R 4
prices:
dirty and charging high p. ELIOT:TS 61
some contrivance to raise p. SMITH:Ad 5
prick:
If you p. us SHAK:MERC 32
p. with a limited future HAWKE 2
prickly pear: Here we go round the p.p. ELIOT:TS 57
pricks: kick against the p. BIBLE 499
pride:
great labyrinth out of p. YEATS 76
high-blown p. SHAK:HEN.VIII 10
kind of p. of stomach BURNS:R 125
mother's p., a father's joy SCOTT:W 45
poet's inward p. DAY LEWIS 2
p. and impudence, in faction knit JONS 50
p., but understood in a different TOC 1
P., Envy, Malice, are LANDOR 6
P. goeth before destruction BIBLE 263
P. in their port GOLDS 10
P. in your history is MACNEICE 13
p. Is skilful to invent SHELLEY:PB 4
p. of the peacock is the glory BLAKE:W 41
p. that apes humility COLERIDGE:ST 43
p. that puts this country ANON 18
P., the never-failing vice POPE 9
p., vain-glory, and hypocrisy PRAY 33
rank p., and haughtiness ADDIS 5
Shame is P.'s cloke BLAKE:W 40
So sleeps the p. MOORE:T 7
priest:
Delicate-handed p. TENNY 210
difference 'twixt the P. and Clark HERR 40
Old P. writ Large MILT 93
on the p.'s table you'll find it PROV 187
p. all shaven and shorn NURS 73
p. continues what the nurse DRYD 89
p. lays his curse on the fairest BLAKE:W 48
rather go with sir p. SHAK:TWE 51
rid me of this turbulent p.? HENRY II 1
Than he listen'd to the p. BALL 41
That whisky p. GREENE:G 3
true God's P. CAREW:T 1
With a Scotsman or a p., don't begin PROV 433
with the entrails of the last p. DIDE 6
priestcraft: ere p. did begin DRYD 33
priestess: P. in the vaults of Death TENNY 128
priesthood: perpetual p. CARLYLE:T 25
priests:
like to associate with a lot of p. BELLOC 45
pay a million p. to bring HARDY:T 46
p. are only men BROWNING:R 193
p. by the imposition of MACAULAY:TB 21
p. dare babble of a God SHELLEY:PB 5
P. in black gowns were BLAKE:W 72
P. of a fearful sacrament JOHNSON:L 2
with women nor with p. SOUTHEY 11
prima donnas: for p.d. or corpses TOSC 2
prime:
dead ere his p. MILT 42
goe, while we are in our p. HERR 23
lost but once your p. HERR 27
One's p. is elusive SPARK 3
return the glory of your p.? SHELLEY:PB 136
splendour of its p. SHELLEY:PB 157
prime minister:
buried the Unknown P.M. ASQU:HH 3
Is Mr Macmillan the best p.m. BUTLER:RA 1
next P.M. but three BELLOC 20
no British P.M. should provoke BALD:S 12
of the P.M. of 1944? CHARM 1
or a turned out P.M. MELBOU 1
P.M. exercises his greatest MENZ 2
P.M. of Mirth ROBEY 1
that of P.M. is filled by fluke POWELL:E 2
when a British P.M. sneezed LEVIN 2
prime ministers:
P.M. and such as they GILB:WS 111
which P.M. have never yet been CHURCH:W 42
primrose:
p. by a river's brim WORDS:W 127
P. first-born child FLETCH:J 19
p. path of dalliance SHAK:HAM 29
p. way to th' everlasting SHAK:MAC 50
rathe P. that forsaken dies MILT 55
silken P. fading timelessly MILT 2
primroses:
pale p., That die SHAK:WIN 20
p. gather'd at midnight KEATS 42
p. make a capital salad DISR:B 35
prince:
born to the hopes of a p. FENT 2
Dread p. of plackets SHAK:LOV 8
great P. in prison lies DONNE 37
p. as soon as his groom JONS 55
p. chasing a swan around HELPMAN 3
p. of darkness is a gentleman SHAK:KING L 48
P. of Denmark being left out SCOTT:W 90
p. of hell Hath risen LUTHER 5
P. of Peace BIBLE 308
p. of poets BYR 198
p. out of thy star SHAK:HAM 68
'Till I the p. of love beheld BLAKE:W 1
Who made thee a p. BIBLE 82
Prince Consort: P.C. standing knock-kneed FRASER:GM 1
Prince of Wales:
danced with the P.o.W. FARJ 1
God bless the P.o.W. LINLEY 1
nimble-footed madcap P.o.W. SHAK:HEN.IV[1] 75
Prince Regent: corpulent gentleman of fifty* HUNT:L 7
princes:
blaze forth the death of p. SHAK:JUL 30
Great p. have great playthings COWP 76
mine were p. of the earth BENJ:JP 1
P. and lords may flourish GOLDS 21
p. are come home again SHAK:KING J 21
P. do but play us DONNE 61
p. to act SHAK:HEN.V 1
Put not your trust in p. BIBLE 248
that hangs on p.' favours SHAK:HEN.VIII 10
princess:
advantage about marrying a p. CHARLES:Prince 7
fitting for a p. SHAK:ANT 77
I love the Far-away P. ROSTAND:E 1
principle:
An *active* P. WORDS:W 119
does everything on p. SHAW 14
furnish the p. for doing it BURKE:E 11
in practice, though not in p. AUSTEN 28
most useful thing about a p. MAUGH 6
nor my p. to pay the interest SHERIDAN:RB 47
not a p., but an expedient DISR:B 55
precedent embalms a p. STOWELL 2
remark any passion or p. in others HUME 1
subjects are rebels from p. BURKE:E 58
That's a p. in life SHAW 20
principles:
by reference to p. TAWN 1
Damn your p. DISR:B 97
easier to fight for one's p. than ADL:A 1
good people argue over p. EBNER 1
invariably from the highest p. FARRAR 1
lordship's p. or your mistress WILKES 1
may be very sincere in good p. JOHNSON:S 84
moral p. are idle fancies SADE 1
P. are only excuses MACKEN 2
p. as light as my purse MANS:K 4
shews that he has good p. JOHNSON:S 112
their p. are the same JOHNSON:S 227
unfixed in p. and place DRYD 38
win for our p. is ROOS:FD 2
print:
big p. giveth and the fine SHEALE 1

decomposing into the eternity of p. WOOLF:V 4
delight me for to p. My book HERR 3
licence to p. your own money THOMS:R 1
monotony Of ugly p. marks POUND 3
or the p. of a hand HARDY:T 77
P. it as it stands JAMES:H 10
p. of a man's naked foot DEF 4
see one's name in p. BYR 8
seeing our names in p. CHESTERTON 26
to see their names in p. ELIOT:TS 72
printing:
caused p. to be us'd SHAK:HEN.VI[2] 11
Gunpowder, P., and the Protestant CARLYLE:T 24
had invented the Art of P. CARLYLE:T 2
If we think to regulat P. MILT 315
in a P. house in Hell BLAKE:W 54
prints:
sporting p. in the hall AUD 25
sporting p. of Aunt Florence's COWARD 25
priorities: p. is the religion of Socialism BEVAN 10
prism: especially prunes and p. DICKENS 196
prison:
Came the hero from his p. AYT 3
comparatively at home in p. WAUGH:E 15
compare This p. where I live SHAK:RIC.II 44
great Prince in p. lies DONNE 37
Home is the girl's p. SHAW 66
I was in p., and ye came BIBLE 431
in a brazen p. live ARNOLD:M 14
is in a maximum security p. GREER 1
let's away to p. SHAK:KING L 79
lime-tree bower my p. COLERIDGE:ST 51
opening of the p. to them BIBLE 333
part of mankind is in p. BELLOW 2
place for a just man is also a p. THOREAU 2
seeks to adorn its p. WOLLST 4
soul in p., I am not free DEBS 1
Stone walls do not a p. LOVELACE 5
world itself is but a large p. RALE 14
prison-air: Bloom well in p. WILDE:O 120
prison-house:
Shades of the p. begin WORDS:W 58
tell the secrets of my p. SHAK:HAM 42
prison-wall: nought beyond their p. ARNOLD:M 14
prisoner:
object to your being taken p. KITCHEN 1
poor p. in his twisted gyves SHAK:ROM 19
p. is happy, why lock SHAW 46
p. leaps to lose WATTS 17
prysoner's release SIDNEY:P 6
upon myself as a p. of war PANK:E 3
prisoners:
all p. and captives PRAY 36
Let them bring me p. BRAX 4
P. and warders – we are all of one DOWL 1
p. of addiction and the p. of envy ILL 4
still p. of our colonial history HAWKE 1
prisons:
improving his p. in Hell COLERIDGE:ST 44
Madhouses, p., whore-shops CLARE:J 2
P. are built with stones of Law BLAKE:W 41
privacy:
minutes of undisturbed p. PARKER:D 27
right to share your p. UST 1
private:
agreed to none of it in p. AUSTEN 56
at a p. view in the morning EDWARD VII 1
first consult our p. ends SWIFT 61
honour is a p. station ADDIS 7
invade the sphere of p. life MELBOU 5
Its p. life is a disgrace ANON 89
meddling too much in my p. life WILLIAMS:T 7
never be allowed out in p. CHURCH:R 1
perish for a p. man MARLOWE 22
P. faces in public AUD 4
p. goods have full sway GALB 5
P. Means is dead SMITH:Ste 3
P. respects must yield MILT 290
p. station GAY 50
to cancel p. crimes DRYD 42
privates: her p. we SHAK:HAM 76
privilege:
find often a defender of p. BEVER 3
forgo the first p. of goodness WELLS:HG 11
p. I claim for my own sex AUSTEN 69
p. of doing as he likes ARNOLD:M 69
war on all undeserved p. LEVI:P 1
What a p. to carry SCRIV 1
privileged:
as against the p. few ROOS:E 3
ascent of the p. LEVI:P 1
extinction of all the p. classes COOL 1
privileges: extension of all women's p. FOUR 1
prize:
first p. in the lottery of life RHODES 2
game beyond the p. NEWBOLT 8
leave so rich a p. MARLOWE 3
Men p. the thing ungain'd SHAK:TRO 2
P. contended was great Hector's HOMER 14
p. we sought is won WHITMAN 29
prizes:
continues to offer glittering p. SMITH:FE 3
just miss the p. at the flower show BRONO 2
that which in herself she p. CONG 60
P.R.O.: liaison man and partly a P.R.O. BETJ 36
probability: p. is the very guide of life BUTLER:J 3
probiscis: sinewy p. did remissly lie DONNE 22
problem:
quite a three-pipe p. DOYLE:AC 17
solution of the p. of life WITT 1
we have a p. LOVELL:J 1
world p., a p. for all humanity X 3
you're part of the p. CLEAV 1
problems: only those p. it can solve MARX:K 4
proboscis: wreath'd His Lithe P. MILT 196
proceedings: subsequent p. interested him HARRIS:JC 3
proceeds: good conscience on the p. SMITH:LP 4
procession:
in a p. of one DICKENS 121
March in a slow p. FINCH 1
proclamation: Thou art the p. DONNE 78
procrastination:
P. is the Thief of Time YOUNG:E 10
the breeding-ground of all p. BOYD:W 1
to incivility and p. DEQ 11
procreant: p. urge of the world WHITMAN 3
procreate: we might p. like trees BROWNE:T 28
proctors: With prudes for p. TENNY 101
procuress: P. to the Lords of Hell TENNY 151
prodigies: all Africa and her p. in us BROWNE:T 10
prodigy: p., I admit him SWIFT 86
produce: p. it, in God's name CARLYLE:T 15
production: Capitalist p. creates MARX:K 6
productions: These modern p. ELIOT:TS 83
profane: Coldly p. CRAB 11
profession:
charm'd me from my p. SHAK:TIM 12
It is his p. HEINE 10
most ancient p. in the world KIP 6
one of the hazards of my p. UMB 1
ornament to her p. BUNYAN 29
panted for a liberal p. COLMAN:G[2] 2
second oldest p. REAG 1
without the sign Of your p.? SHAK:JUL 1
professional:
p. is someone whose wife works SHAHN 1
young business and p. men of EDWARD VIII 1
professionally: P. he declines and falls DICKENS 218
professions: All p. are conspiracies SHAW 93
professor:
p. is one who talks in AUD 70
regius p. of French letters JOYCE:J 24
professors: If the science p. knew as little ESSON 2
profit:
balance between p. and honesty HUME 4
no p. but the name SHAK:HAM 155
No p. grows where SHAK:TAM 1
p. is not always what motivates GIDE 2
When men write for p. WALP:H 19
who has mixed p. with pleasure HORACE 112
winds will blow the p. MACNEICE 3
profited: What is a man p. BIBLE 418
profiteth: it p. me nothing BIBLE 522
profits:
little p. that an idle king TENNY 51
p. most who serves best SHELD 1
p. of the mind, study SHAK:MEA 4
progress:
calls each fresh link P. BUCHANAN 8
exchange of one nuisance* ELLIS:H 4
history of p. MACAULAY:TB 14
make our P. slow DAVEN:W 3
nations trek from p. OWEN:W 13
Our p. through the world LONGFEL 32
party of p. or reform MILL 12
p. depends on the unreasonable man SHAW 62
P. has its drawbacks STEPHEN:FJ 2
P. is a comfortable disease CUMM 4
p. is based upon a universal BUTLER:S[2] 23
P. . . . is not an accident SPENCER:H 1
p. of a deathless soul DONNE 19
P. was all right THURB 22
spoke of P. spiring round CHESTERTON 17
progressive:
enemy of p. ideals BELLOW 4
may be p. for a certain MILL 15
prohibit: very thing you wish to p. RICHELIEU:A 1
prohibition: social and economic experiment* HOOV 1
projects: plan your p. in the evenings COPE 2
proles: p. are not human beings ORWELL 33
proletarian:
every time you are polite to a p. WAUGH:E 23
substitution of the p. for LENIN 2
proletariat:
dictatorship of the p. MARX:K 8
p. has nothing to lose MARX:K/ENG 3
prologue:
What's past is p. SHAK:TEM 15
witty p. to a very dull Play CONG 13
prologues: p. precede the piece GARRICK 1
promiscuity: keeping open bed* HUX:A 8
promise:
p., is the soul of an advertisement JOHNSON:S 31
p. made is a debt unpaid SERVICE 3
time forgets the p. WRIGHT:J 6
promised:
I've seen the p. land KING:ML 3
Marching to the P. Land BARING-G 5
promises:
may obtain thy p. PRAY 54
P. and pie-crusts are made SWIFT 41
p. were, as he then was SHAK:HEN.VIII 17
rake the p. to himself BRONTE:E 9
promising: they first call p. CONNOLLY:C 5
promontory:
on the p. which I named BROWNING:R 99
once I sat upon a p. SHAK:MID 17
promoted: P. everybody GILB:WS 110
promotion: will sweat but for p. SHAK:AS 18
promptly: in due course, acted p. GILES 1
pronounce:
p. foreign names as he chooses CHURCH:W 71
p. with the vulgar FRANKLIN:B 8
pronouncing: p. to yourself nimini-pimini BURGOY 1
proof:
Dost thou ask p.? ARNOLD:M 45
enjoy is feeling p. against it ADAMS:R[2] 1
give me the ocular p. SHAK:OTH 44
which is incapable of p. LEWES 2
proofs: how would I correct the p. CLARE:J 13
prop: p. To our infirmity WORDS:W 151
propaganda:
peace p. makes war seem LAWR:DH 29
P. is that branch CORNFORD:Fran 4
propagate: p., and rot POPE 92
propagated: beings could be p. by cutting HALDA 4
propagation:
peace and p. are the two most WALP:H 17
Was all our p. DONNE 34
proper:
delight is in p. young men BURNS:R 21
P. words in p. places SWIFT 24
very p., so far as it goes DICKENS 76
property:
Get hold of portable p. DICKENS 211
give me a little snug p. EDGE 5
If p. had simply pleasures WILDE:O 35
no right to the p. of the poor RUSKIN 16
P. has its duties DRUMMOND:T 1
p. owns them INGER 2
Time is my p. GOET 24
We are still the p. of men BARRE 1
What is p.? PROUD 1

prophecies: verification of his own p. TROLL 19
prophecy:
all forms of mistake, p. ELIOT:G 32
trumpet of a p. SHELLEY:PB 46
urn Of bitter p. SHELLEY:PB 158
prophesy:
eat exceedingly, and p. JONS 28
man may p. SHAK:HEN.IV[2] 34
your daughters shall p. BIBLE 355
prophet:
historian is a p. SCHLEG 2
p. is not without honour BIBLE 413
p. new inspir'd SHAK:RIC.II 16
P. of the Utterly Absurd KIP 75
sons of the p. ANON 95
there is a p. in Israel BIBLE 170
What-you-may-call-it is his p. DICKENS 138
prophetess:
more than a p. – a uncommon pretty ELIOT:G 4
wench, a p., and a Latin-bred HERB:G 60
prophetic:
beginning and end of history are *p.* SCHLEG 1
O my p. soul SHAK:HAM 46
prophets:
armed p. were victorious MACHIA 4
Beware of false p. BIBLE 401
ceased to pose as its p. POPP 6
fellowship of the P. PRAY 8
Is Saul also among the p.? BIBLE 142
p. make sure of the event WALP:H 21
propinquity: P. does it WARD:MRS H 1
proportion: strangeness in the p. BACON:F[1] 39
proportions: it is a matter of p. CHANEL 3
proposal: Your p. comes too late LEAR 8
proposed: He p. seven times DICKENS 194
proposes:
man p., but God disposes KEMP 8
Man p., God disposes PROV 262
proposition:
important that a p. be interesting WHITEHEAD 1
such a p. is true of *anything* RUSS:B 4
undesirable to believe a p. RUSS:B 9
propositions: resolve the p. of a lover SHAK:AS 42
propriety:
humanity's sense of p. RENARD 3
p. of some persons seems BRADLEY:FH 3
prose:
anything except bad p. CHURCH:W 2
Good p. is like a window pane ORWELL 25
greatest book of English p.? QUIL 2
I can only write p. today YEATS 151
I love thee in p. PRIOR 11
make it P. again POPE 170
never pin up my hair with p. CONG 42
Not verse now, only p. BROWNING:R 90
other harmony of p. DRYD 143
Poetry is to p. as dancing WAIN 1
proper antithesis to p. COLERIDGE:ST 80
P. is architecture HEMINGWAY 3
p. is verse BYR 12
P. is when all the lines BENTH 6
P. on certain occasions LANDOR 19
p. takes the mould of the body WOOLF:V 15
p. which knows no reason STEPHEN:JK 3
p. = words in their best order COLERIDGE:ST 84
speaking p. without knowing it MOLIERE 24
unattempted yet in P. or Rime MILT 107
Proserpin: where P. gathering flours MILT 191
prospect:
can't exactly be joyful at the p. CLARK:K 3
Though every p. pleases HEB 3
prosperity:
han ben in prosperitee CHAUC 113
one man who can stand p. CARLYLE:T 50
P. doth best discover vice BACON:F[1] 34
P. doth bewitch men WEBSTER:J 16
P. is like the tide HERB:X 2
P. is not without many fears BACON:F[1] 33
P. is the blessing BACON:F[1] 31
P.'s the very bond of love SHAK:WIN 27
troubill efter grit prosperitie HENRYS 3
prostate: equivalent of a p. operation MUGG 7
prostitute:
despairing cry of an Italian p. HUGHES:B 1
don't think a p. is more moral PHILIP 4
from a doormat or a p. WEST:R 12
I puff the p. away DRYD 77
prostitutes: small nations like p. KUB 1
prostitution:
for me, it is my profession* GWENN 1
P. gives her an opportunity HELLER 7
protect: I'll p. it now MORRIS:GP 1
protecting: p. itself – with a smile PRIEST 1
protection:
P. is not a principle DISR:B 55
P. is not only dead DISR:B 81
protest: lady doth p. too much SHAK:HAM 116
Protestant:
I am the *P.* whore GWYN 2
Printing, and the P. Religion CARLYLE:T 24
P., is he wants aid DISR:B 36
P. with a horse BEHAN:Br 2
P. women may take the Pill THOMAS:I 1
Thy P. to be HERR 29
protestantism:
chief contribution of P. MENCK 10
p., even the most cold BURKE:E 30
Yes, it's P. STEAD 6
Protestants:
Bible only is the religion of P. CHILLING 1
Catholics and P. you meet ALLING 4
keep people from marrying P. GALLANT 1
Proteus: sight of P. rising from WORDS:W 105
protozoon: philosopher, not the p., who gives RUSS:B 5
proud:
all the p. shall be POPE 61
apt the poor are to be p. SHAK:TWE 40
he was very p. and stiff CARROLL 73
kaught is p. CHAUC 105
p. and yet a wretched thing DAVIES:J 3
p. as Priam murdered YEATS 10
P. me no prouds SHAK:ROM 36
P. word you never spoke LANDOR 10
too p. to importune GRAY:T 37
we ain't p., because ma says DICKENS 77
Why were they p.? KEATS 28
proudest: when the spirit is p. PANK:C 1
prove:
Believing where we cannot p. TENNY 122
don't get a chance to p. it MURRAY:LA 4
if thou wouldst p. me CONSTABLE:H 1
let us p., While we can JONS 18
p. anything by figures CARLYLE:T 38
ther be no man it preve CHAUC 93
proved:
now p. was once only imagin'd BLAKE:W 43
Which was to be p. EUC 1
proven: nothing worthy proving can be p. TENNY 292
proverb:
P. is no p. to you till KEATS 155
p. is one man's wit RUSS:J[2] 4
p. is something musty SHAK:HAM 123
proverbs:
King Solomon wrote the P. NAY 1
Patch grief with p. SHAK:MUCH 29
p. are the palm-oil ACHEBE 2
p. provide them with wisdom MAUGH 18
provide: God will p. himself BIBLE 52
provided: Micawber's expression, 'P. for' DICKENS 162
providence:
future to the divine P. BACON:F[1] 12
inscrutable workings of P. SMITH:FE 5
may assert Eternal P. MILT 108
P. thir guide MILT 261
P. will put a speedy end DE VR 5
There's a P. in it all DICKENS 54
provider: bad husband and an ill p. EMER 49
province: p. they have desolated GLAD 2
provinces:
obedience of distant p. MACAULAY:TB 29
p. where they still speak English GUINN 1
provincial: worse than p. – he was parochial JAMES:H 3
provincialism: taken in adultery than in p. HUX:A 6
provisoes: I hate your odious p. CONG 55
provocations: resent little p. HAZL 13
provoke: p. not your children BIBLE 536
provoked: being p. to bring up PEPYS 23
provokes: it p. the desire SHAK:MAC 51
prow:
their head the p. DRYD 7
Youth on the p. GRAY:T 31
prude: twenty is not the time to be a p. MOLIERE 16
prudence:
effect of p. on rascality SHAW 60
P. is a rich ugly old maid BLAKE:W 34
p. never to practise either TWAIN 26
prudent: o'er stocked with p. men DRYD 67
prudes:
Cease, ye p. BURNS:R 61
With p. for proctors TENNY 101
pruner: blind swipe of the p. LOWELL:R 16
prunes: especially p. and prism DICKENS 196
pruninghooks: spears into p. BIBLE 301
Prussia:
military domination of P. ASQU:HH 2
War is P.'s national industry MIR 1
Prussians: others may be Prooshans DICKENS 114
prussic acid: She drank P.a. BARH 10
psalm: practising the hundreth p. BYR 152
psalmist: sweet p. of Israel BIBLE 159
psalms:
Church with p. must shout HERB:G 24
King David wrote the P. NAY 1
unto him with p. BIBLE 229
psaltery: upon the p. BIBLE 227
pseudonym: Chance might be God's p. FRANCE 5
psyche: His p. should be studied JUNG:Carl 9
Psyche: Your mournful P. KEATS 95
psychiatrist:
Any man who goes to a p. GOLDWYN 2
p. is a man who goes STOCKWOOD 1
psychical: chances For P. Research COWARD 28
psychology: P. is the Theology of the 20th century HOT 1
psychopathologist: p. the unspeakable MAUGH 4
psychosis: Irish and the Jews have a p. BEHAN:Br 8
psychotic:
on whom the label 'p.' LAING 1
p. if he makes others suffer SZASZ 8
pub:
killed in a p. brawl in a suburb JAMES:PD 1
pavender or p. ST-LEG 1
p. uniquely represents ... the precise inequalities HOWK 2
someone take me to a p.? CHESTERTON 17
public:
abuse in p. and to read BORR 1
as if I was a p. meeting VICT 6
Brazenness and p. liberties CERV 20
British P., ye who like me not BROWNING:R 192
conspiracy against the p. SMITH:Ad 5
creating a p. impression of himself MENZ 2
in p. affairs, no state so bad MONTAIGNE 19
man assumes a p. trust JEFFERSON 7
no right to strike against the p. safety COOL 3
not describe holding p. office ACHESON 1
principles of p. morality BURKE:E 11
p. be damned VANDERB 1
p. faces in private AUD 4
p. is always right DE MIL 1
P. is an old woman CARLYLE:T 68
p. is never wrong ZUK 1
p. – like a Frog DICKIN:E 3
P. scandal is what constitutes offence MOLIERE 11
p. will believe anything SITWELL:E 11
should be true to the p. BERK 5
three things which the p. will HOOD 30
to the p. good Private respects MILT 290
ungrateful animal than the P. HAZL 14
where p. services have failed to keep GALB 5
With p. zeal to cancel private DRYD 42
worth doing is worth doing in p. ORTON 6
write for the p. and have no CONNOLLY:C 18
public school:
no one can enjoy a p.s. CONNOLLY:C 1
p.s. where a little learning PEAC 5
public-school system all over WAUGH:E 6
vulgarity with a P.S. accent LEAV 3
who has been to an English p.s. WAUGH:E 15
public schools:
fill the p.s. with silk MARLOWE 31

P.s. are the nurseries FIELDING 14
publican: How like a fawning p. SHAK:MERC 15
publicity:
Any p. is good p. PROV 18
p. rather than of poetry LEAV 2
price of justice is eternal p. BENNETT:Ar 7
publish:
hide of an elephant to p. DAVISON:FD 2
P. and be damned WELLING 27
p. and be sued INGRAMS 2
p. it not in the streets BIBLE 151
p., right or wrong BYR 7
published: can destroy what you haven't p. HORACE 116
publisher:
Barabbas was a p. CAMPBELL:T 25
p. is simply a useful middle-man WILDE:O 121
publishers: fear of life become p. CONNOLLY:C 4
publishing: P. a play is reversing SHAFF 3
pudding:
Manningtree ox with the p. SHAK:HEN.IV[1] 51
No p. and no *fun* VICT 11
P. and beef make Britons PRIOR 8
puddings: made p. in his tea cup CARLYLE:JW 1
puddle: He stepped in a p. NURS 10
puff:
p. and get one's self puffed TROLL 23
solemn interposing p. COWP 27
To p. and look important KIP 137
puffed: is not p. up BIBLE 522
puffing: p. is of various sorts SHERIDAN:RB 31
puffs: P., Powders, Patches POPE 39
pull: P. down thy vanity POUND 35
puller: p. down of kings SHAK:HEN.VI[3] 5
pulp:
p. so bitter THOMP:F 12
savourie p. they chew MILT 195
pulpit: Politics and the p. are terms BURKE:E 50
pulsations: deep p. of the world TENNY 172
pulse:
feel that p. no more MOORE:T 7
feeling a woman's p. STERNE 47
My p. like a soft drum KING:H 2
pride in taking your own p. MACNEICE 13
two people with one p. MACNEICE 10
pumice: Beside a p. isle SHELLEY:PB 42
pumpkin:
put her in a p. shell NURS 51
rather sit on a p. THOREAU 16
pumpkins: Where the early p. blow LEAR 7
pun:
could make so vile a p. DENNIS:J 1
exhaled in a p. LAMB:Ch 49
Pistol let off at the ear* LAMB:Ch 25
punctilio: None of your dam p. MERED:G 15
punctuality:
P. is the politeness of kings LOUIS XVIII 1
P. is the politeness of princes PROV 325
punctuation: place the p. where he pleases SHERIDAN:RB 48
Punic: With P. faith SALL 9
punished:
p. everlastingly JOHNSON:S 243
p. for their sins, but by them HUBB 4
p. not for what they do SZASZ 1
punishment:
also the p. of a crime MANNING 1
corporal p. is as humiliating for him KEY:E 3
habitual employment of p. WILDE:O 40
it shall suffer first p. CRANMER 1
Juridical p. for crime scares DOST 8
My p. is greater than BIBLE 29
power of p. is to silence JOHNSON:S 61
p. fit the crime GILB:WS 73
p. in itself is evil BENTH 1
p. is prevention from evil MANN:H 1
punishments:
charged with p. the scroll HENL 2
no rewards or p. VACH 1
sanguinary p. which corrupt PAINE 5
punk: Marrying a p. SHAK:MEA 41
punt:
better fun to p. than to SAYERS 1
slow p. swings round ARNOLD:M 23
story get out of the p. JOYCE:J 34
punters: nation of p. and party-goers HOGAN 1
pupil: far in years to be a p. SHAK:RIC.II 6
pupils:
dead whose p. we have been BUTLER:S[2] 49
it kills all its p. BERLIOZ 1
puppet: marry him to a p. SHAK:TAM 3
puppets:
shut up the box and the p. THACK 11
We are p. on strings BUCHN 2
puppy: drink, p., drink WHYTE 1
purchasing: I am not worth p. REED:Jos 1
pure:
Because my heart is p. TENNY 61
Blessed are the p. BIBLE 384
hundred, p. love, for thee FERGUS 1
live p. TENNY 238
my life is p. MARTIAL 1
not quite – so p. as you BUTLER:S[2] 46
particularly p. young man GILB:WS 33
p. as the driven slush BANK 4
Unto the p. all things are p. BIBLE 554
what God declares P. MILT 201
whatsoever things are p. BIBLE 542
Whoever is not racially p. HITL 3
Pure: real Simon P. CENT 2
pureness: p. of living and truth PRAY 48
purer: live the p. with the other SHAK:HAM 146
purest: p. and most thoughtful minds RUSKIN 5
purge:
I'll p., and leave sack SHAK:HEN.IV[1] 96
Let's p. this choler SHAK:RIC.II 2
purged: purg'd the air of pestilence SHAK:TWE 2
Puritan:
P. hated bear-baiting MACAULAY:TB 33
To the P. all things are impure LAWR:DH 21
puritanism: P. – The haunting fear MENCK 4
purity:
P. is the feminine HARE:J 3
'twixt Air and Angels' p. DONNE 26
purlieus: within the p. of the law ETH 1
purple:
I never saw a P. Cow BURGESS:G 1
p. light of Love GRAY:T 33
p. patches are often stitched in HORACE 100
Ran p. to the Sea MILT 128
So cool a p. KEATS 40
walk by the color p. WALK 1
purpose:
creature hath a p. KEATS 154
except for a noble p. HERB:AP 16
far-reaching in p. HOOV 1
God is working His p. out AINGER:AC 1
If people want a sense of p. MACMILL:H 13
Infirm of p. SHAK:MAC 43
man who is tenacious of p. HORACE 31
one increasing p. runs TENNY 82
Sole p. of visit HARDING:G 1
purposes: execute thir aerie p. MILT 127
purse:
fill thy p. with money SHAK:OTH 16
gain that is got into the p. STERNE 21
he looks at his p. TURNBULL 2
My p., my person SHAK:MERC 9
Put money in thy p. SHAK:OTH 15
steals my p. steals trash SHAK:OTH 34
this consumption of the p. SHAK:HEN.IV[2] 17
want of friends, and empty p. BRET 1
purses: Light gains make heavy p. BACON:F[1] 43
pursued: you who are the p. SHAW 35
pursues: still the world p. ELIOT:TS 41
push:
real since the Big P. LODGE:D 3
Than tarry till they p. us SHAK:JUL 85
Pusset: call his cat P. HARE:ME 2
pussy:
beautiful P. you are LEAR 18
I love my little p. NURS 23
p. cat, Where have you been? NURS 55
P.'s in the well NURS 9
pussy-cat: Owl and the P. went to sea LEAR 18
put: up with which I will not p. CHURCH:W 65
puzzle: make a p. out of the solution KRAUS 6
Pye: shine with P. BYR 11
pygmies: wars of the p. will begin CHURCH:W 63
pyjamas: in p. for the heat LAWR:DH 32
pylons: P., those pillars Bare SPEND 7
pyramid:
bottom of the economic p. ROOS:FD 3
Under a Star-ypointing P.? MILT 14
pyramidally: be but p. extant BROWNE:T 56
pyramids:
from the top of these p. NAPO I 4
p. built up with newer SHAK:SON 55
p. . . . have forgotten the names FULLER:T[1] 7
Pyramus:
Cruel Death of P. and Thisby SHAK:MID 6
P. is a sweet-fac'd man SHAK:MID 11
Pyrenees:
P. no longer exist LOUIS XIV 1
tease in the High P. BELLOC 38
Pythagoras:
mystical way of P. BROWNE:T 9
opinion of P. concerning wild fowl? SHAK:TWE 55
P.' metempsychosis MARLOWE 44
P. planned it YEATS 120
P. was misunderstood EMER 11
python:
bought a P. from a man BELLOC 9
swamps where the p. romps COWARD 21
quack: potent q., long versed CRAB 4
quad:
always about in the Q. ANON 61
no one about in the Q. KNOX:R 2
quadruped: hairy q. DARW:C 6
quadrupeds: horses, are q. MUIR:F 4
quaffing: q., and unthinking time DRYD 127
quail: q. Whistle about us STEVENS 7
quailing: No q., Mrs Gaskell BRONTE:P 1
quails: we long for q. DRYD 66
quake: aspes leef she gan to q. CHAUC 112
Quakers:
I was beaten up by Q. ALLEN:W 5
sedate, sober, silent* HOOD 31
qualifications:
what are his q.? – ONE! BROUGH 1
without q. to detain them UST 10
qualifying: love admits no q. dross SHAK:TRO 19
qualities:
display q. which he does not possess JOHNSON:S 3
have the weaknesses of their q. BALZ 10
q. that you lacked ELIOT:TS 75
Q. too elevated often CHAMFORT 4
quality:
People of q. know everything MOLIERE 2
unknown amongst people of q. VANB 6
quangle-wangle: Q. Quee LEAR 28
quarks: Three q. for Muster Mark JOYCE:J 39
quarrel:
Beware Of entrance to a q. SHAK:HAM 30
find q. in a straw SHAK:HAM 157
hath his q. just SHAK:HEN.VI[2] 4
have therefore a perpetual q. BURKE:E 38
hourly carp and q. SHAK:KING L 17
In a false q. there is SHAK:MUCH 31
lover's q. with the world FROST:R 13
of the q. with others, rhetoric YEATS 131
only one to make a q. INGE 1
q. in a far-away country CHAMBERLAIN:N 3
q. That knows no mending YEATS 28
q. with my bread and butter SWIFT 39
Take up our q. with the foe MCCRAE 2
takes two to make a q. PROV 212
that hath his q. just BILL 1
They quite forgot their q. CARROLL 51
very pretty q. as it stands SHERIDAN:RB 14
quarrelled:
know that we had ever q. THOREAU 28
who has q. with his wife PEAC 7
quarrels:
from the q. of tyrants VOLT 1
Lovers' q. are the renewal TEREN 3
q. of popes and kings AUSTEN 62
Q. would not last long LA ROCHE 35
Thy head is as full of q. SHAK:ROM 25
who in q. interpose GAY 47
quart:
put a q. in a pint cup GILMAN 2
q. into a pint pot PROV 439
quarterly:
'I', says the Q. BYR 139
nothing a-year, paid q. SURT 16
quean: flaunting, extravagant q.

SHERIDAN:RB 24
Quebec: Long live free Q. DE GAU 4
queen:
beggar maid shall be my q. TENNY 41
ever raised To toast the Q. HEAN 7
every lass a q. KINGSLEY:C 19
Fella belong Mrs Q. PHILIP 1
from this enchanting q. break SHAK:ANT 10
God will save the Q. HOUSM 2
Hail holy q. ANON 37
happened to marry the Q. of England STRACH 4
he slides like a q. GRAVES:R 5
he was the Q.'s luve BALL 13
home life of our own dear Q. ANON 199
I'll q. it no inch farther SHAK:WIN 26
Most Gracious Q., we thee ANON 83
Mother, Wife, and Q. TENNY 187
Q. and her lands BALL 42
Q. and huntress JONS 11
Q. asked The Dairymaid MILNE 3
Q. lily and rose in one TENNY 218
q. of curds and cream SHAK:WIN 22
Q. of Hearts She made NURS 56
q. of Scots is lighter ELIZ I 9
q. was in the parlour NURS 66
remembrance of a weeping q. SHAK:RIC.II 34
right-down regular Royal Q. GILB:WS 104
seen the mobled q. SHAK:HAM 87
since I saw the q. of France BURKE:E 55
To look at the q. NURS 55
walk, the Q. of Love VIRGIL 40
Whom the English call 'the Q.' LAWS 2
would be a q. for life POPE 137
Yestreen the Q. had four Maries BALL 43
Queen Anne:
Move Q.A.? VICT 9
Tell 'em Q.A.'s dead COLMAN:G[2] 4
Queen Caroline: Most Gracious Queen* ANON 83
Queen Elizabeth:
No scandal about Q.*E.* SHERIDAN:RB 31
perfidious Succubus was that Q.E. BURNS:R 128
that bright Occidental Star, Q.E. BIBLE 1
Queen Mab: Q.M. hath been with you SHAK:ROM 5
Queen Mother: 'Hop in,' said the Q.M. CAMPBELL:G 3
Queen of Hearts: Q.o.H., she made some tarts CARROLL 36
queenly: Q. in her own room WHARTON:E 1
queens:
Q. have died young NASHE 1
Q. hereafter shall be glad DRAYT 8
queer:
drink to the q. old Dean SPOON 5
name him as a q. is going too far DUNS 1
nowt so q. as folk PROV 383
Q. are the ways of a man HARDY:T 25
q. save thee and me OWEN:Rob 1
think him ill-tempered and q. LEAR 3
Queer Street: Q.S. is full of lodgers DICKENS 226
queerer: q. than we *can* suppose HALDA 3
quench: rivers cannot q. SHAK:HEN.VI[3] 6
quest: what thy q.? BRIDGES:R 9
questing: twenty couple of hounds q. MALORY 4
question:
Answer to the Great Q. of ADAMS:D 1
Ask a silly q. and you'll get PROV 22
ask an impertinent q. BRONO 4
dare I q. with my jealous SHAK:SON 22
drop a q. on your plate ELIOT:TS 5
every q. with an open mouth STEVENSON:A 14
let me ask you a q. MCLUH 13
No q. is ever settled WILCOX 2
not a wise q. for me EDEN:A 1
Others abide our q. ARNOLD:M 5
Q. and answer is not a civilized O'BRIAN 1
q. that we do not know MACLEISH 3
that case, what is the q.? STEIN:G 7
that is the q. SHAK:HAM 97
that q.'s out of my part SHAK:TWE 14
timid q. will always receive DARLING:CJ 2
who sees both sides of a q. WILDE:O 14
with such a silly q.? STERNE 3
questioning: Q. is not the mode of conversation JOHNSON:S 181
questionings: obstinate q. Of sense WORDS:W 63
questions:
all q. are open BELL:C 3
answering q. that no-one has asked TOLS:L 14
Ask no q. and hear PROV 23
Discourst in three quaestions SEXBY 1
don't ask impertinent q. DARW:E 1
foolish ask q. that the wise WILDE:O 73
I have answered three q. CARROLL 10
make two q. grow VEB 4
Q. are never indiscreet WILDE:O 76
Them that asks no q. KIP 121
There are innumerable q. JOHNSON:S 208
who asks the right q. LEVI-ST 2
queue: orderly q. of one MIKES 3
quibble: q. is to Shakespeare what JOHNSON:S 36
quick:
less q. to spring again ARNOLD:M 44
q., I know not how GREV 1
quickness: too much Q. ever to POPE 133
quiet:
after-tram-ride q. BETJ 19
All q. along the Potomac MCCLELL 1
All Q. on the Western Front REM 1
In q. she reposes ARNOLD:M 18
in the awful q. then HODG 4
let us have a q. hour TENNY 96
my scallop-shell of q. RALE 2
Q., all it hath a mind BROWNING:R 171
q. along the Potomac to-night BEERS 1
q., have I found thee MARV 13
Q. takes back her folded JOYCE:J 36
Q. to quick bosoms is BYR 85
Q., vast and slumbrous HARPUR 1
thank God for the q. grave KEATS 170
There is q. everywhere HARPUR 1
quietly:
inability to stay q. in a room PASC 7
lie as q. among the graves EDWARDS:J 1
quietness:
in all godly q. PRAY 53
Thy still dews of q. WHITTIER 8
unravish'd bride of q. KEATS 92
quills: tender stops of various Q. MILT 59
quince: mince, and slices of q. LEAR 21
quincunx: q. of heaven runs low BROWNE:T 45
quinquireme: Q. of Nineveh MASE 9
quip: Q. Modest SHAK:AS 70
quips:
Q. and Cranks, and wanton MILT 66
thy q. and thy quiddities? SHAK:HEN.IV[1] 6
quiver: they q. with the same music GIBRAN 4
quotation:
Classical q. is the *parole* JOHNSON:S 223
Every q. contributes something JOHNSON:S 7
literature a q. EMER 65
q. is a national vice WAUGH:E 28
spring of happy q. MONTAGUE 2
their passions a q. WILDE:O 104
quotations:
book that furnishes no q. PEAC 10
I hate q. EMER 82
one's q. very slightly wrong RIB 1
only q. that are never misquoted PEARS:H 2
recommend him by select q. JOHNSON:S 35
to read books of q. CHURCH:W 45
quote:
grow immortal as they q. YOUNG:E 2
I often q. myself SHAW 127
we all q. EMER 73
quoter: first q. of it EMER 74
quotes:
nicest think about q. WILLIAMS:K 1
widely-read man never q. PEARS:H 1
rabbit:
Gone to get a r. skin NURS 5
parsley to stuff a r. SHAK:TAM 13
r. has a charming face ANON 89
There is a r. in a snare STEPHENS 5
rabbits: there were four little R. POTTER:B 1
Rabelais:
Irresistible as R. BARKER:G 2
soul of R. dwelling in a dry COLERIDGE:ST 88
race:
All is r. DISR:B 31
Another r. hath been WORDS:W 69
Another R. the following Spring HOMER 7
black man ... one destiny* FANON 1
challenge me the r. MARV 24
giant r. before the flood DRYD 130
idiot r., to honour lost BURNS:R 59
men and women with our r. KIP 116
new r. is sent down from heaven VIRGIL 11
nothing but the r. reports ELIOT:TS 72
pernicious r. of little odious SWIFT 30
pilfering, unprotected r. CLARE:J 6
r. is not to the swift BIBLE 287
r. of glory run MILT 288
r. that binds Its body BUCHANAN 8
r. that long in darkness pin'd SCOTTISH 3
Rushes life in a r. MERED:G 16
she shall rear my dusky r. TENNY 84
slinks out of the r. MILT 313
Slow and steady wins the r. LLOYD:R 2
Such is the r. of Man GRAY:T 10
till thou run out thy r. MILT 62
what avails the sceptred r. LANDOR 1
racehorses: r. and the cheaper clarets SAKI 6
races: white r. are really pinko-gray FORST 7
Rachel: served seven years for R. BIBLE 63
Rachmaninov:
He was the only pianist* STRAV 4
R.'s immortalizing totality STRAV 3
racially: Whoever is not r. pure HITL 3
racing: victory without the dust of r. HORACE 76
racism:
had Aborigines working for him* BJEL:FI 1
harsh fetters of Colour* PRINGLE:T 4
they're all the same* BOSMAN 1
world problem, a problem for all* X 3
rack:
Leave not a r. behind SHAK:TEM 27
upon the r. of this tough world SHAK:KING L 86
woman's is often her r. THURB 7
rackets: our r. to these balls SHAK:HEN.V 9
radiance:
r. rare and fathomless HARDY:T 3
strains of this trail, have r.? CAUL 1
radical:
I never dared be r. FROST:R 10
R. chic WOLFE:Tom 1
r. invents the views TWAIN 30
r. is a man with both feet ROOS:FD 9
radicals:
Few r. have good digestions BUTLER:S[2] 27
read poetry, they are r. EMER 40
young men are regarded as r. WILSON:W 1
radio:
I had the r. on MONROE:M 1
proliferation of r. and television HOWARD:P 2
Simply a r. personality WAUGH:E 34
radio-phonograph: gospel Of the r. AUD 49
radish:
like a fork'd r. SHAK:HEN.IV[2] 38
r. and an egg COWP 74
raft:
easy and comfortable on a r. TWAIN 13
republic is a r. AMES 2
rag:
bloomin' old r. over 'ead KIP 68
r. and bone and a hank KIP 94
that Shakespeherian R. ELIOT:TS 42
rag-and-bone: r. shop of the heart YEATS 114
rag-time: roaring, epic, r. tune LIND:V 2
rage:
depression is rational, r. reasonable WELD 2
Heav'n has no r. CONG 34
horrible that lust and r. YEATS 111
I r., I melt, I burn GAY 1
not die here in a r. SWIFT 80
nothng but a R. to live POPE 133
Puts all Heaven in a R. BLAKE:W 82
r. against the dying THOMAS:D 18
r. of thundering Jupiter MARLOWE 4
swell the soul to r. DRYD 114
void of noble r. TENNY 141
Why do the heathen r. BIBLE 196
writing increaseth r. GREV 1
rages:
r., like the troubled main GAY 7
weight of r. will press harder SPOON 1
raggedness: loop'd and window'd r. SHAK:KING L 42

readers:
enable the r. better to enjoy JOHNSON:S 60
give their r. sleep POPE 160
r. to become more indolent GOLDS 44
trade a hundred contemporary r. KOES 5
was wished longer by its r. JOHNSON:S 257
readeth: he may run that r. BIBLE 361
readiness: r. is all SHAK:HAM 193
reading:
art of r. is to skip HAMER 1
as much pleasure in the r. QUAR 4
distinguish what is worth r. TREV 2
easy writing's vile hard r. SHERIDAN:RB 40
got around to r. the book MARX:G 21
I prefer r. SMITH:LP 11
invincible love of r. GIBBON:E 13
like the picture of somebody r. KEATS 151
lose no time in r. it DISR:B 88
mad with too much r. PETRO 3
R. is sometimes an ingenious HELPS 1
R. is to the Mind, what Exercise STEELE 7
R. isn't an occupation we encourage ORTON 4
R. maketh a full man BACON:F[1] 108
r. of all good books DESCA 3
substitute for r. it BURGESS:A 7
There is an art of r. D'ISR:I 1
What exactly is she r.? EVANS:E 3
worth r., it is worth buying RUSKIN 23
writer's time is spent in r. JOHNSON:S 168
reads:
He r. much SHAK:JUL 15
Who often r. will CRAB 18
Who r. Incessantly MILT 275
ready:
necessity of being *r.* increases LINC 15
r. whenever fate calls SOC 7
We always are r. GARRICK 4
ready-made: Why not 'r.'? CHURCH:W 62
Reagan: R. cannot tell the difference SAHL 1
Reagans: R. mean to say it all VIDAL 7
real:
becomes r. till it is experienced KEATS 155
r. things inspires terror MCLUH 11
things r. as if they were imaginary BETT 1
To R. Being we go back PLOT 1
what is r. is rational HEG 1
realism: dislike of R. is the rage WILDE:O 20
realist: liar is a r. STEAD 5
realistic: going to make 'a r. decision' MCCARTHY:M 1
reality:
Cannot bear very much r. ELIOT:TS 88
document a hidden r. SONT 3
laws of mathematics refer to r. EINS 15
paradoxical exposes himself to r. DURREN 4
parts for the time with r. CHURCH:W 20
r. by means of ideas ORTEGA G 6
R. invents me GUIL 1
sense of ultimate r. BELL:C 1
shadows and types to the r. NEWM:JH 21
study of positive r. SAND 1
realize: saw it but did not r. it PEAB 1
realms:
r. and islands were As plates SHAK:ANT 64
travell'd in r. of gold KEATS 3
reap:
as you sow, you are like to r. BUTLER:S[1] 25
shall r. in joy BIBLE 242
that shall he also r. BIBLE 531
they shall r. the whirlwind BIBLE 353
We r. our sowing DU MAU:G 2
Where I r. thou shouldst HOOD 12
reaped: r. in blood BLAKE:W 10
reaper: R. whose name is Death LONGFEL 39
reapers: Only r., reaping early TENNY 15
reaping:
ever r. something new TENNY 79
No, r. BOTT:HW 1
That grew the more by r. SHAK:ANT 64
reaps: ye sow, another r. SHELLEY:PB 52
rear:
boldly bring I up the r. MARSH:RAK 1
bring up the r. in heaven BROWNE:T 22
expect to r. healthy, vigorous O'MALLEY:K 1
whose post lay in the r. ROSSET:C 1
reason:
all r. is against it BUTLER:S[2] 33
bound To rules of r. HERB:G 20
but a woman's r. SHAK:TWO 3
cloath'd in r.'s garb MILT 155
divorced old barren R. FITZGER:E 21
Englishman . . . always wants to r. VOLT 29
finite r. reach Infinity? DRYD 70
give no man a r. upon compulsion SHAK:HEN.IV[1] 42
Human r. won KHRU 6
if it be against r. COKE:E 1
Is r. to the soul DRYD 69
let r. mitigate our Care HOMER 15
let us r. together JOHNSON:LB 3
men have lost their r. SHAK:JUL 52
neither rhyme nor r. MORE:T 3
noble and most sovereign r. SHAK:HAM 104
nothing is law that is not r. POWELL:J 1
our R. is the Law MILT 246
Passion conquers R. still POPE 78
passions is R.'s slave CONNOLLY:C 19
private r. for this AUD 25
pursue my r. to an *O altitudo* BROWNE:T 7
r. abuseth me. KYD 3
r. against the reasons of my Love KEATS 162
R., an *ignis fatuus* ROCHES 2
r. and the will of God prevail ARNOLD:M 64
r. doth buckle and bow BACON:F[1] 8
R. has moons HODG 1
R. in her most exalted mood WORDS:W 163
r. is insufficient to convince HUME 11
R. is itself a matter of faith CHESTERTON 39
r. is past care SHAK:SON 63
R. is the bound or outward BLAKE:W 32
R. is the life of the law COKE:E 2
r. of the strongest FONTAINE 12
r. to strengthen their own prejudices DUKES 2
right deed for the wrong r. ELIOT:TS 76
start to r., all is lost VOLT 33
Tam tint his r. BURNS:R 89
That takes the r. prisoner? SHAK:MAC 11
Their's not to r. why TENNY 199
What can we r. POPE 79
what r. does not believe VOLT 22
who listens to R. is lost SHAW 63
Will know the r. why HAWKER 1
worse appear The better r. MILT 152
reasonable:
figure of 'The R. Man' HERB:AP 13
no r. man could have expected HERB:AP 17
rather be right than r. NASH 17
the r. is an invention of man FRY:C 2
We are more r. in France VOLT 29
reasonableness: sweet r. of Jesus ARNOLD:M 76
reasoners: plausible r. are not always HAZL 36
reasoning:
contain any abstract r. HUME 13
in dirt the r. engine lies ROCHES 3
reas'ning but to err POPE 89
R. is thundering in its crater POTTIER 1
r., self-sufficing thing WORDS:W 28
truth by consecutive r. KEATS 120
reasons:
five r. we should drink ALDRICH 1
for r. of state PLATO 7
Good r. must . . . give place SHAK:JUL 75
heart has its r. PASC 11
Metaphysics is the finding of bad r. BRADLEY:FH 1
never give your r. MANS:W 1
R. are not like garments ESSEX 1
r. were as plentiful as blackberries SHAK:HEN.IV[1] 42
rebel:
both young and old r. SHAK:RIC.II 25
harder to r. against love STORR 1
No one can go on being a r. DURRELL:L 3
r. and conform at the same time CRISP 1
still an Irish r. to the backbone DUFFY:CG 1
street came the r. tread WHITTIER 4
What is a r.? CAMUS 9
rebellion:
little r. now and then JEFFERSON 9
R. lay in his way SHAK:HEN.IV[1] 83
R. to tyrants is obedience BRADSH:J 1
rum, Romanism, and r. BURCHA 1
sensuality, r., and revivalism THOMAS:G 2
sort of mental r. ORWELL 13
within me a sentiment of r. BERLING 1
rebels: subjects are r. from principle BURKE:E 58
rebirth: r. in the Land of Perfect Bliss SHINRAN 1
rebounds: hit hard, unless it r. JOHNSON:S 167
rebuild: to r. it on the old plan MILL 4
rebuke: standing r. MENCK 9
recall:
hard to endure is sweet to r. PROV 420
one day be pleasant to r. VIRGIL 37
recalled:
spoke can never be recall'd ROSCOM 1
word once out cannot be r. HORACE 116
receive:
If I ask Him to r. me NEALE 5
r. but what we give COLERIDGE:ST 56
receiver:
r. is always thought as bad CHESTERFIELD 18
seems to have left the r. off KOES 3
receives: one r. only in accordance BALZ 1
recession: r. when your neighbour loses TRU 5
recipes: r. that are always successful VALERY 2
recirculation: by a commodius vicus of r. JOYCE:J 30
reckoning:
No reck'ning made SHAK:HAM 48
very much at your own r. TROLL 13
recognised: objects r., In flashes WORDS:W 154
recognize: did not r. me by my face TROLL 26
recognized: dark glasses to avoid being r. ALLEN:F 1
recoils: back on it self r. MILT 241
recommendation:
r. than their own weight STERNE 37
Self-praise is no r. PROV 343
reconciles:
feasting r. everybody PEPYS 15
r. Discordant elements WORDS:W 146
reconciliation:
minute of r. is worth more GARC 2
temple of silence and r. MACAULAY:TB 11
record: puts a r. on the gramophone ELIOT:TS 47
recorders: Flutes and soft R. MILT 132
recover:
cheer us when we r. BURKE:E 96
things one does not r. from ANON 110
recreation: man has made of it a r. POST 2
recreations: must regulat all r. MILT 315
rectitude: unctuous r. of my countrymen RHODES 1
reculer: *r. pour mieux r.* MAYHEW:C 2
red:
bleeding drops of r. WHITMAN 30
give this Cheek a little R. POPE 116
grace To get very r. BENTLEY:EC 9
hectic r. SHELLEY:PB 40
In coats of r. DE LA M 13
keep the r. flag flying CONNELL 1
pays us poor beggars in r. KIP 67
r. men scalped each other MACAULAY:TB 8
r. with guiltless blood SHELLEY:PB 5
roising reid to rotting sall HENRYS 4
Thin r. line of 'eroes KIP 65
thin r. line tipped with RUSS:WH 1
true colour, which is r. SAINTE-B 2
wine when it is r. BIBLE 268
red brick: not even r.b., but white tile OSB:J 4
red-hot: Last of the R. Mamas TUCK 3
Red Sea: sands upon the R.s. shore BLAKE:W 101
redbreast:
r., sacred to the household THOMS:Ja[1] 12
r. sit and sing COLERIDGE:ST 9
red-breast: r. whistles KEATS 109
redeem: down and r. us from virtue SWIN 26
redeemer:
know that my r. liveth BIBLE 189
My great R.'s praise WESLEY:C 2
so great a r. MASS 24
redemption:
inestimable love in the r. PRAY 40
Our great r. from above MILT 3
r. of all things by Beauty SHAW 94
redress: things past r. are now SHAK:RIC.II 22
reed:
but for a r. MARV 16
he is a thinking r. PASC 12
Love tunes the shepherd's r. SCOTT:W 8
maiden and clasped a r. SHELLEY:PB 58
r. is as the oak SHAK:CYM 17
reeds: Down in the r. by the river? BROWNING:EB 22
reef: Time is the r. upon which COWARD 10

reel: R. in a drunkard CHURCH:C 3
reeling: R. and Writhing CARROLL 28
references: always to verify your r. ROUTH 1
refined:
Englishwoman is so r. SMITH:Ste 2
Horror so r. DICKIN:E 12
r. out of existence JOYCE:J 8
reflect: r. all objects without being CONF 22
reflecting: r. the figure of man at twice WOOLF:V 10
reflection:
God looks at his r. RENAN 2
man of r. discovers Truth PEREZ 2
R., you may come to-morrow SHELLEY:PB 161
reform:
All r. except a moral one CARLYLE:T 34
Beginning r. is beginning revolution WELLING 6
lunatic fringe in all r. ROOS:T 13
party of progress or r. MILL 12
reformation:
plotting some new r. DRYD 32
reforming of R. it self MILT 317
reformers: consolations of middle-aged r. SAKI 20
refresh: r. it when it was dry PRAY 41
refreshment: greatest r. to the spirits BACON:F[1] 69
refuge:
eternal God is thy r. BIBLE 127
God is our r. BIBLE 215
last r. of the incompetent HARDIN 1
r. of the incompetent MENCK 12
r. of weak minds CHESTERFIELD 22
refurbishment: need for, uh, elements of r. ANNEN 1
refusal: her r., through her skill CONG 63
refuse:
offer he can't r. BRANDO 2
offer he can't r. PUZO 1
Which he did thrice r. SHAK:JUL 51
refute: I r. it *thus* JOHNSON:S 131
regards: r. that stands Aloof SHAK:KING L 5
regency: We're R. Rakes COWARD 23
regeneration: madness and despair to the r. CONRAD 10
regime: new r. will have caused a backfire ECO 2
regiment:
led his r. from behind GILB:WS 100
Monstrous R. of Women KNOX:J 1
R. 'an pokes the 'eathen out KIP 81
region: Is this the R. MILT 121
register: r. of the crimes, follies GIBBON:E 3
regret:
I r. a little BROWNING:R 73
man's r. is no more PORTER:PNF 1
wild with all r. TENNY 109
regular: brought reg'lar and draw'd mild DICKENS 115
regulate: must regulat all recreations MILT 315
rehearsing: R. a play is making SHAFF 3
reheat: not r. his sins for breakfast DIET 1
reid: roising r. to rotting sall HENRYS 4
reign:
Better to r. in Hell MILT 123
friendless is to r. SHELLEY:PB 75
His r. on earth begun MONTGOM:J 1
Jesus shall r. where'er WATTS 16
Long to r. over us HOGG 5
reigned:
God r. from the wood VENAN 3
I have r. with your loves ELIZ I 4
reigneth: The Lord r. BIBLE 173
reigns: r., but does not govern ZAM 1
reincarnation: nine reasons for r. MILLER:H 1
reindeer:
Herds of r. move AUD 50
R. are coming to drive AUD 5
reinforcement: r. we may gain from Hope MILT 119
rejoice:
Making all the vales r.? BLAKE:W 15
r. in Christ even more LUTHER 7
R. in the Lord, all ye lands BIBLE 600
R. with them that do r. BIBLE 515
R. ye dead BRIDGES:R 13
rejoiced: spirit hath r. in God BIBLE 607
rejuvenate: only way ... to r. oneself GOET 26
related: r. persons living under one MACAULAY:R 4
relation:
nobody like a r. to do THACK 5
poor r. – is the most irrelevant LAMB:Ch 24
relations:
God's apology for r. KINGSMILL 4
great men have their poor r. DICKENS 181
Industrial r. are like sexual r. FEAT 1
Personal r. are the important thing FORST 4
R. are made by fate DELIL 1
r. must cause no expense COMPT 4
relationship:
'r.' business is one big waste WAX 1
r. which is one of person to RILKE 4
'special r.' with the United States ACHESON 2
relationships: free from ambivalence of all human r. FREUD:S 4
relativity:
If my theory of r. is proven EINS 9
That's r. EINS 17
relaxation: r. from one kind of labour FRANCE 1
relent: make the gods above r. VIRGIL 76
relic: cas'd up, like a holy r.? WEBSTER:J 21
relics:
other's hands these r. came DONNE 40
unhonour'd his r. are laid MOORE:T 12
relieve: miss an opportunity to r. yourself EDWARD VIII 4
religion:
airy subtleties in r. BROWNE:T 6
any r. except being anti-Catholic STOW 3
Art and r. first SPARK 5
As to r., I hold it to be PAINE 2
bashfulness in every thing that regards r. ADDIS 23
Brothels with bricks of R. BLAKE:W 41
but an handmaid to r. BACON:F[1] 13
enough r. to make us hate SWIFT 14
for r. when in rags BUNYAN 13
fundamental principle of my r. NEWM:JH 10
I know no other r. NEWM:JH 10
in England but vice and r. SMITH:Syd[1] 38
increase in us true r. PRAY 55
indirect way to plant r. BROWNE:T 13
Let there be no violence in r. KORAN 2
Men will wrangle for r. COLTON 1
men's minds about to r. BACON:F[1] 36
more fierce in its r. NEWM:JH 9
must be r. for r.'s sake COUS 1
my r. is to do good PAINE 7
mystery begins, r. ends? BURKE:E 2
no reason to bring r. O'CAS 6
not a r. for gentlemen CHARLES II 3
not impossibilities enough in R. BROWNE:T 6
One r. is as true as another BURTON:Ro 25
only one (true) r. KANT 9
Organized r. is making Christianity VAN DER P 4
persuasion to evil was r. LUCRET 2
Philistine of genius in r. ARNOLD:M 77
Pound notes are the best r. BEHAN:Br 5
reject me on account of my r. BELLOC 43
r. and matrimony I never give CHESTERFIELD 28
r. and policy must be based RUSKIN 25
R. blushing veils POPE 174
r. breathing household laws WORDS:W 73
r. but a childish toy MARLOWE 19
r. is allowed to invade MELBOU 5
R. is an illusion FREUD:S 3
R. is by no means a proper CHESTERFIELD 29
R. is love WEBB:B 1
R. is the opium MARX:K 1
r. must still be allowed to be CHESTERFIELD 24
r. of feeble minds BURKE:E 65
r. teaches us content DRYD 14
r. to a man with bodily hunger SHAW 86
r. was made to root out MONTAIGNE 14
r. was strong and science SZASZ 4
r. with one commandment ZANG 2
r. without science EINS 4
R.'s in the heart, not JERROLD 1
r.'s iron age SHELLEY:PB 5
reproach to r. and government PENN 2
respect the other fellow's r. MENCK 6
rum and true r. BYR 173
sense are really but of one r. SHAFT 1
Sensible men are all of the same r. DISR:B 45
so fatal to r. as indifference BURKE:E 87
take my r. from the priest GOLDS 78
talks loudly against r. STERNE 15
There is only one r. SHAW 17
Too much r. makes me go pop RUNCIE:Ros 1
true meaning of r. ARNOLD:M 75
When I mention r., I mean FIELDING 22
religions:
R. are kept alive by heresies BREN 2
r. we call false EMER 56
sort of collector of r. SHAW 85
thirty-two r. and only one sauce TALL 4
religious:
abolishing R. Houses and leaving AUSTEN 3
constitution a r. animal BURKE:E 62
hope I will be r. again FLEM:M 2
R. persecution may shield itself BURKE:E 99
r. poetry ... is likely to be most HOUSM 55
suspended my r. inquiries GIBBON:E 18
to be r. more or less BUTLER:S[2] 38
two r. caterpillars MARLOWE 24
remain: it will r. here dead BETHU 1
remaindered: book of my enemy has been r. JAMES:B 2
remained: all else perished, and he r. BRONTE:E 11
remarkable: there is nothing left r. SHAK:ANT 58
remedies:
If many r. are suggested CHEK 11
r. oft in ourselves SHAK:ALL 4
will not apply new r. BACON:F[1] 77
remedy:
r. for everything, except death CERV 17
r. is worse than the disease BACON:F[1] 101
sharp r., but a sure RALE 15
Things without all r. SHAK:MAC 65
unfailing r. – the Tankard CALVER 1
remember:
Can I r. if thou forget? SWIN 6
cannot r. the past are condemned SANT 2
can't r. how They go CALVER 5
convenient to r. him DISR:B 93
Haply I may r. ROSSET:C 13
I r., I r. HOOD 9
I r. thee upon my bed BIBLE 219
if thou wilt, r. ROSSET:C 12
iris blooms, R. COLERIDGE:M 2
Let them taste and r. PLOM 8
Lovers r. everything OSB:J 16
not r. what I must be SHAK:RIC.II 30
only r. what I've learnt WHITE:P 7
R. man that thou must die ANON 141
R. me when I am gone ROSSET:C 7
r. of this unstable world MALORY 6
r. The Fifth of November NURS 53
r. what is past HALIF 14
r. while the light lives SWIN 27
should r. and be sad ROSSET:C 8
still r. me MOORE:T 6
that no man r. me HARDY:T 63
third I can't r. SVEVO 1
till thou r. and I forget SWIN 5
To r. with tears ALLING:W 2
We will r. them BINY 1
Yet will I r. thee COWP 7
remembered:
By this may I r. be ANON 118
I have made myself remember'd KEATS 164
I r. my God SOUTHEY 6
never said anything that was r. DISR:B 23
none are undeservedly r. AUD 61
photograph, even a smell r. GREENE:G 6
r. day and night BRIDGES:R 13
R., if outlived DICKIN:E 6
r. Perishing be? DE LA M 19
remembering:
r. happier things TENNY 75
succeed in r. only the simplest HITL 1
remembers: it remembren, whan it passed is CHAUC 113
remembrance:
appear almost a R. KEATS 128
Makes the r. dear SHAK:ALL 10
r. of a weeping queen SHAK:RIC.II 34
r. of happiness when in misery DANTE 6
r. of his dying Lord SPENS 22
r. of my former love SHAK:TWO 7
r. of things past SHAK:SON 12
rosemary, that's for r. SHAK:HAM 169

to drive away R. KEATS 111
reminded: more frequently require to be r. JOHNSON:S 1
reminds: weep, for it r. me so CARROLL 85
reminiscence: r. sing WHITMAN 23
reminiscences:
old have r. SAKI 5
R. make one feel SHAW 72
remorse:
Farewel R. MILT 185
rather feel r. than know KEMP 1
R., the fatal egg COWP 34
remote: R., unfriended GOLDS 3
remuneration: R.! O, that's the Latin SHAK:LOV 7
Renaissance: R. was simply the green end FOW 1
rend: time to r. BIBLE 281
render: R. therefore unto Caesar BIBLE 426
rendezvous: My r. is appointed WHITMAN 9
renewal:
grass is returning* HORACE 53
You may drive out Nature* HORACE 86
renounced: r. everything but MURRAY:D 1
renouncement: By your r. an immortal SHAK:MEA 3
renown:
I that gave thee thy renowne CAREW:T 4
men of r. BIBLE 35
rent:
last out my month's r. RHYS 2
r. is always high SLESS 7
That has not been r. YEATS 95
they r. out my room ALLEN:W 13
Rentacrowd: R. Ltd, the enterprising SIMPLE 1
repair: landlord does not intend to r. ADAMS:JQ 2
repartee:
majority is always the best r. DISR:B 30
r. of the illiterate BRIEN 2
repay: I will r. BIBLE 516
repeated: simplest concepts r. a thousand HITL 1
repelled: only r. by man INGE 7
repent:
earnestly r. of your sins PRAY 71
I hardly ever r. NASH 4
marble caves r., r. DRUMMOND OF H 3
no strength to r. SHAK:HEN.IV[1] 71
r. at leisure PROV 270
they r. in haste CONG 11
we may r. at leisure CONG 11
weak alone r. BYR 32
you'll live to r. PROV 271
repentance:
but sinners to r. BIBLE 406
give r. to her lover GOLDS 18
morning cool r. came SCOTT:W 73
no r. in the grave WATTS 15
not going to buy r. DEMOS 3
R. is but want of power DRYD 125
R. is the virtue of weak DRYD 4
Where pleasure and r. dwell RALE 4
Winter Garment of R. FITZGER:E 4
repented: r. but of three things CATO 2
Repin: word goes round R.'s MURRAY:LA 2
reply:
loving and a fair r. SHAK:HAM 20
R. Churlish SHAK:AS 70
Their's not to make r. TENNY 199
report:
r. the facts ROGERS:W 10
Who hath believed our r.? BIBLE 327
who knows how he may r. MILT 294
reporter:
I am a r. GREENE:G 10
r. can invent things GARC 3
r. is a man who has renounced MURRAY:D 1
reports: Bring me no more r. SHAK:MAC 108
repose:
be his last r. ANON 120
earned a night's r. LONGFEL 12
r. that ever is the same WORDS:W 71
seek not yet r. ELLIOT:C 1
seek r. In listlessness WORDS:W 141
weave the garlands of r. MARV 12
reposes: In quiet she r. ARNOLD:M 18
repossess: r. their native seat? MILT 139
represent: r. whatever is imitated ZE AMI 1
representation:
No annihilation without r. TOYN 2
r. of visible things LEONARDO 1
Taxation and r. are inseparable CAMDEN:Lord 1
Taxation without r. OTIS 1
representations: just r. of general nature JOHNSON:S 34
representative:
indignity of being your r. BELLOC 43
Your r. owes you BURKE:E 93
reproche: *sans peur et sans r.* BAYA 1
reproductions: r. of Anne Hathaway's cottage LANCAS 2
reproof: R. Valiant SHAK:AS 70
reproofs: r. from authority ought BACON:F[1] 75
reprove: check the erring and r. WORDS:W 70
reptile: r. all the rest POPE 128
republic:
Love the Beloved R. FORST 18
R. is a government in which BAGE 11
r. is a raft AMES 2
republican:
acrimonious and surly r. JOHNSON:S 54
R. form of government is the highest SPENCER:H 9
republicans:
assure me that you are all R. REAG 11
from very little r. EMER 78
We are R. and don't propose BURCHA 1
reputation:
delicate as the r. of a woman BURNEY 2
for the r. to fail conventionally KEYN 7
I have lost my r. SHAK:OTH 27
it ruins a woman's r. COLETTE 4
r. in it, but no money TWAIN 16
r. like its shadow LINC 22
r. of five-and-twenty DRYD 9
sold my R. for a Song FITZGER:E 31
spotless r.; that away SHAK:RIC.II 3
Until you've lost your r. MITCH:M 1
wink a r. down SWIFT 60
word a r. dies POPE 47
reputations:
home of ruined r. ELIOT:G 29
sit upon the murdered r. CONG 36
reputed: only are r. wise SHAK:MERC 5
request: ruined at our own r. MORE:H 1
requiem: high r. become a sod KEATS 93
research:
chances For Psychical R. COWARD 28
our r. dangerous DURREN 3
outcome of any serious r. VEB 4
R.! A mere excuse JOW 6
r. in original sin PLOM 6
r. is always incomplete PATTIS 1
researcher: morning exercise for a r. LORENZ 1
resemblance: straight its own r. find MARV 18
resent: r. that unless it is absolutely biased VORS 1
reserved: r. for some end or other CLIVE 1
reside: happy it will be for us to r. HARDWO 1
resigned: I am not r. MILLAY 7
resist: r. everything except temptation WILDE:O 45
resistance:
history of liberty is a history of r. WILSON:W 3
r. against her is vain MARV 10
resolution:
In war, r. CHURCH:W 49
road to r. lies by doubt QUAR 14
what r. from despaire MILT 119
resolve:
heart to r. GIBBON:E 8
not shaken from his firm r. HORACE 31
resolves: R.; and re-r.; then dies YOUNG:E 11
resort: not r. to the gods POLY 1
resource centre: ever walk into a 'R.C.' NEED:RJ 1
resources: priceless and irreplaceable r. MEAD 1
respect:
any nation except their r. CHURCH:W 18
equal r. for all men ADAMS:H 2
fellow of a good r. SHAK:JUL 86
Is there no r. of place? SHAK:TWE 21
old-fashioned r. for the young WILDE:O 89
owe r. to the living VOLT 25
R. was mingled with surprise SCOTT:W 42
r. you when you dared to speak TROLL 15
too much r. upon the world SHAK:MERC 2
Who err each other must r. PATMO 2
respectable:
devil's most devilish when r. BROWNING:EB 20
Not one is r. or unhappy WHITMAN 7
R. means rich PEAC 8
riff-raff apply to what is r. HOPE:An 5
when was genius found r.? BROWNING:EB 19
respecter: God is no r. of persons BIBLE 500
respects: no man much r. himself TWAIN 31
responsibility:
heavy burden of r. EDWARD VIII 2
In dreams begins r. YEATS 130
Liberty means r. SHAW 52
no sense of moral r. WILDE:O 80
no sense of r. at the other KNOX:R 4
r. but not the blame SEMP 1
r. without power, the prerogative STOP 1
responsible: to be r. and wrong CHURCH:W 38
rest:
crept silently to R. FITZGER:E 14
Eclipse first, the r. nowhere O'KELLY 1
evening's r. from labour BLAKE:W 9
God be the r. BROWNING:R 183
Grant them eternal r. MASS 20
I will give you r. BIBLE 410
it is a far, far better r. DICKENS 204
man was not born for r. VOLT 15
May they r. in peace MASS 21
more r. if one doesn't sleep WAUGH:E 12
not to seek for r. LOY 1
ordain'd no r. VAUGHAN:H 13
r. for the people of God BROWNING:R 139
R. in peace – until ANON 142
she's at r., and so am I DRYD 132
shortly be with them that r. MILT 288
till it finds r. in thee AUGUS 1
will not let them r. KEATS 101
Without haste, but without r. GOET 40
yet 'tis r. HUX:H 1
restless: r. idleness occupies us HORACE 87
restorer: nature's sweet R. YOUNG:E 6
restrictive: no place for r. practices WILSON:Harold 4
resurrection:
certain hope of the R. PRAY 92
glorious R. and Ascension PRAY 34
R. of the body PRAY 19
r. of their parents GIBBON:E 25
symbol of his r. PROUST 13
retainer: not to play The Old R. BELLOC 19
reticence: R., in three volumes GLAD 8
reticulated: Anything r. or decussated JOHNSON:S 13
retire:
R. me to my Milan SHAK:TEM 33
should r. at half-past eight? MILLAY 2
Skilld to r. MILT 264
retired: R. to their tea and scandal CONG 15
retirement:
Absence of occupation* COWP 40
R., rural quiet THOMS:Ja[1] 4
short r. urges sweet returne MILT 243
there must be no r. HAIG:D 2
retiring: r. at high speed toward HALS:WF 1
retort: R. Courteous SHAK:AS 70
retreat:
Governments don't r. RIPPON 1
like a little country r. WYCH 3
make an honourable r. SHAK:AS 40
not r. a single inch GARRIS 1
retreating:
Have you seen yourself r.? NASH 16
march of the r. world OWEN:W 13
retrograde:
be not r. JONS 12
r. if it does not advance GIBBON:E 11
return:
But to r., and view VIRGIL 66
he shall not r. to me BIBLE 157
I shall r. MACAR 1
In that state I came r. VAUGHAN:H 8
never must r. MILT 45
None that go r. again HOUSM 22
r. To plague th' inventor SHAK:MAC 23
r. to the general and eternal TOLS:L 2
returned: no one r. the same HAZZ 2
returning:
faced the possibility of not r. EAR 2
R. were as tedious as go SHAK:MAC 75

returns: they say no one r. CATUL 3
reunion: r. a foretaste of resurrection SCHOP 7
reveal: What does he then but r. Himself MILT 317
reveillé: Here no bugles sound r. SCOTT:W 37
revelations:
ends with R. WILDE:O 60
pretending to extraordinary r. BUTLER:J 4
revelry: sound of r. by night BYR 76
revels: What r. are in hand? SHAK:MID 44
revenge:
little R. herself went down TENNY 287
man that studieth r. BACON:F[1] 98
med'cines of our great r. SHAK:MAC 97
R., at first though sweet MILT 241
R. is a dish that tastes better PROV 332
R. is a kind of wild justice BACON:F[1] 96
R. is sweet PROV 333
R. proves its own executioner FORD:J[1] 5
R. triumphs over death BACON:F[1] 51
shall we not r.? SHAK:MERC 32
so long as I have my r. CYR 1
Stirrd up with Envy and R. MILT 109
Sweet is r. BYR 169
took his r. by speaking ill VOLT 6
tribal, intimate r. HEAN 3
revenged: reveng'd on the whole pack SHAK:TWE 58
revenges: time brings in his r. SHAK:TWE 57
revenue: Instead of a standing r. BURKE:E 38
revenues: she bears a duke's r. SHAK:HEN.VI[2] 1
Revere: midnight ride of Paul R. LONGFEL 29
reverence:
In deeper r., praise WHITTIER 7
little more r., please SARGENT:M 1
myn herte have hem in r. CHAUC 94
reverently: r., discreetly, advisedly PRAY 81
reverse:
nothing will r. and return GOGOL 1
which a minute will r. ELIOT:TS 6
review:
r. a bad book without showing off AUD 60
so long writing my r. MARX:G 21
reviewers:
chorus of indolent r. TENNY 232
R. are usually people COLERIDGE:ST 70
reviewing:
indiscriminate r. of books ORWELL 38
never read a book before r. SMITH:Syd[1] 35
revivalism: sensuality, rebellion, and r. THOMAS:G 2
revivals: history of art is the history of r. BUTLER:S[2] 28
revolution:
fear that the R., like Saturn VERG 1
fundamental premise of a r. TROT 5
impossible without a violent r. LENIN 2
invented the r. but we WEISS 3
No, Sire, it is a r. LA ROCHEFOUCAULD-L 1
not the leaders of a r. CONRAD 11
reform is beginning r. WELLING 6
R. a parent of settlement BURKE:E 52
r. be in without general copulation WEISS 4
Russian r. accomplished by you LENIN 12
see the r. of the times SHAK:HEN.IV[2] 32
socialism in terms of the scientific r. WILSON:Harold 4
think of r. not as the solution WEIL 3
time hath his r. CREWE 1
revolutionaries: first thing r. . . . give up HILL:Reg 5
revolutionary:
chorus of a R. song VALL 1
Every r. ends as an oppressor CAMUS 8
feed people with r. slogans KHRU 9
fierce and r. in a bathroom LINK 2
I would be a r. myself GEO V 2
r. is merely a climber with a bomb ORWELL 9
r. right to dismember LINC 9
r. simpleton is everywhere LEWIS:W 5
revolutionists: age fatal to R. DESM 2
revolutions:
herald of all r. EMER 14
nursery of future r. BURKE:E 52
R. are always verbose TROT 3
r. are not to be evaded DISR:B 20
r. have led to a reinforcement CAMUS 10
R. may spring from trifles ARISTOT 14
r. never go backward SEW 1
share in two r. PAINE 11
revolver: Culture, I reach for my r. GOER 2
reward:
Desert and r. . . . seldom keep RICHARDSON:S 1
not to ask for any r. LOY 1
nothing for r. SPENS 33
r. of a thing well done EMER 41
rewarded:
be plenteously r. PRAY 58
courage, I r. it NAPO I 7
r. and punished not for what SZASZ 1
rewards: no r. or punishments VACH 1
Reynolds, Joshua:
acquainted with such men as R. BLAKE:W 94
Artists as R., are at all times BLAKE:W 97
He shifted his trumpet* GOLDS 41
When Sir J.R. died BLAKE:W 96
Rheims: Lord Archbishop of R. BARH 3
rhetoric:
can't do love and r. STOP 4
For r. he could not ope BUTLER:S[1] 3
of the quarrel with others, r. YEATS 131
rhetorician: r.'s rules Teach nothing BUTLER:S[1] 4
rheumatic: r. diseases do abound SHAK:MID 16
rheumatism:
believe in r. and true love EBNER 4
occurred to me to complain of r. SAKI 15
Rhine:
henceforth wash the river R.? COLERIDGE:ST 65
R. circle fair Wertenberg MARLOWE 31
You think of the R. BALD:S 5
rhinoceros: arm'd r. SHAK:MAC 72
Rhodesia: black majority rule in R. SMITH:I 1
Rhodope: Brighter than is the silver R. MARLOWE 2
rhyme:
ever tire of love or r. COPE 5
I r. for fun BURNS:R 42
In a sort of Runic r. POE 10
making beautiful old r. SHAK:SON 48
more tired of R. BELLOC 34
neither r. nor reason MORE:T 3
petty fools of r. TENNY 98
punish me with losse of ryme HERB:G 26
R. is the rock on which DRYD 57
r. the rudder is of verses BUTLER:S[1] 15
r. themselves into ladies' SHAK:HEN.V 46
R.'s sturdy cripple COLERIDGE:ST 64
Rime being no necessary MILT 104
Ryme thee to good HERB:G 1
sense always should agree with r. BOIL 4
taen the fit o' r. BURNS:R 41
To r. upon a dish? SPEND 12
unattempted yet in Prose or Rime MILT 107
rhymes:
baker r. for his pursuit BROWNING:R 208
between piety and poor r. WILDE:O 126
rhyming:
modern bondage of rimeing MILT 105
more than their r. tell YEATS 12
not born under a r. planet SHAK:MUCH 34
rymyng is nat worth a toord CHAUC 75
veins of r. mother-wits MARLOWE 1
rhythm:
ceaselessly creative r. PAZ 2
gave poetry a proper r. BOIL 3
some in sprung r. HOPK:GM 32
Rialto: many a time and oft In the R. SHAK:MERC 17
rib: r., which the Lord God had BIBLE 13
riband:
for a r. to stick in his coat BROWNING:R 53
r. in the cap of youth SHAK:HAM 175
ribbon: blue r. of the turf DISR:B 33
ribbons:
bunch of blue r. NURS 44
R. and laces And sweet NURS 83
Wi' r. on her breast BALL 41
ribs:
breaking of r. was sport SHAK:AS 4
Under the r. of Death MILT 36
rice:
pound of R., and a Cranberry LEAR 17
Same old r. LAMP 1
rice pudding: *lovely r.p. for dinner again* MILNE 7
rich:
as easy to marry a r. woman THACK 15
be r. and free BURKE:E 77
be r. in things or in the freedom ILL 2
be too thin or too r. WINDSOR 2
committees of the r. to manage CONNOLLY:J 2
desire to enjoy the games of the r. HORNE:DR 2
dies thus r. dies disgraced CARNEG:A 3
Eat with the r. SMITH:LP 8
ever by chance grow r. THOMAS:E 3
feigned charity of the r. man ROUSS:JJ 4
forbids the r. as well as FRANCE 8
get r., get famous and get laid GEL 3
have to live with r. people SMITH:LP 7
I am becoming disgustingly r. EBDEN 1
If the r. could hire other people PROV 188
If thou art r., thou'rt poor SHAK:MEA 19
Let him be r. and wearie HERB:G 44
making Gay r. and R. *gay* JOHNSON:S 52
most r., being poor SHAK:KING L 6
no sin but to be r. SHAK:KING J 8
not really a r. man GET 1
one law for the r., and another PROV 384
Poor in deed and r. HOLD 1
Poor little r. girl COWARD 16
R. and rare were the gems MOORE:T 13
R. AND THE POOR DISR:B 25
r. are different from us FITZGER:FS 13
r. are the scum of the earth CHESTERTON 49
r. beyond the dreams MOORE:E 2
r. enough to pay over 75 HEAL 1
r. have become richer SHELLEY.PB 166
r. have butlers and no POUND 15
r. have no right to the property RUSKIN 16
r. he hath sent away empty BIBLE 608
r. in a more precious MACAULAY:TB 21
R. in the simple worship KEATS 33
R. is better TUCK 2
r. man has his motor car ADAMS:FP 2
r. man in his castle ALEX:CF 2
r. man to enter into BIBLE 445
r. man's joke is always funny BROWN:TE 1
r. men rule the law GOLDS 11
R. men's houses are seldom ASQU:M 1
r. only select from the heap SMITH:Ad 2
r. take their time STEAD 3
r. with forty pounds GOLDS 25
r. wot gets the gravy ANON 38
Sincerely Want to be R.? CORNFELD 1
so large, So friendly, and so r. AUD 57
tell you about the very r. FITZGER:FS 10
that r. men usually hate PETRO 4
victim of a r. man's ANON 38
well off as if he were r. ASTOR:JJ 1
Richard:
R.'s himself again CIB 4
scowl on gentle R. SHAK:RIC.II 42
Richardson:
heart in one letter of R.'s JOHNSON:S 155
were to read R. for the story JOHNSON:S 156
richer: for r. for poorer PRAY 84
riches:
embarrassment of r. ALLA 1
enjoyment of r. consists in the parade SMITH:Ad 6
he that getteth r. BIBLE 341
how folk live that hae r. BURNS:R 56
in the midst of great r. HORACE 44
infinite r. in a little ROM SEGAL 2
Infinite r. in a little room MARLOWE 20
R. are a good handmaid BACON:F[1] 25
R. are for spending BACON:F[1] 60
R. are needless then MILT 268
R. have wings COWP 68
r. of heav'n's pavement MILT 142
r. sall return to thee DUNB 16
r. that bring more trouble? HORACE 29
r., there is no real excuse BACON:F[1] 99
That r. grow in Hell MILT 143
upon r. to be valuable SWIFT 78
richly: lady r. left SHAK:MERC 10
Richmond:
R. and Kew Undid me ELIOT:TS 49
Sweet lass of R. Hill MACNALL 2
Sweet lass of R. Hill UPTON:W 1
richness:
all in a rush With r. HOPK:GM 8
r. is made day by day ALBERO 1

richt:
curst conceit o' bein' r. MACDIAR 6
Yer a' recht, that's a' LAUD 2
ricks: r. stand grey to the sun KIP 148
rickshaw: no go the r. MACNEICE 2
rid:
he was glad to get r. of it MARX:G 9
purely to be r. of thee CONG 12
riddle:
glory, jest, and r. of the world POPE 90
r. wrapped in a mystery CHURCH:W 10
riddles: R. of death Thebes never SHELLEY:PB 156
ride:
And r. mankind EMER 97
cannot r. two horses MAX 1
physical courage to r. a horse LEACOCK 3
R. on! r. on in majesty MILM 1
r. slowly towards the sea CHESTERTON 25
we r. them down TENNY 112
when he next doth r. abroad COWP 58
rider:
proud r. on so proud a back SHAK:POET 11
r.'s back sits dismal Care HORACE 28
rides:
Alone he r., alone JOHNSON:L 5
He who r. a tiger PROV 169
Who r. so late GOET 2
ridicule: way it exposes men to r. JUV 7
ridiculous:
fine sense of the r., but no sense ALBEE 2
from the sublime to the r. NAPO I 6
sublime and the r. are often so nearly PAINE 10
Sublime to the R. GRAHAM:H 2
sublime to the r. is only a step PROV 139
riding:
fate of a nation was r. LONGFEL 30
man goes r. by STEVENSON:RL 58
riff-raff: r. apply to what is respectable HOPE:An 5
riflemen: Form, R. Form TENNY 229
rifles: stuttering r.' rapid rattle OWEN:W 1
rigged: rigg'd with curses dark MILT 51
riggish: when she is r. SHAK:ANT 28
right:
all come r. in the wash PROV 214
all goes r. and nothing GILB:WS 58
all is r. as r. GILB:WS 61
All's r. with the world BROWNING:R 9
almost always in the r. SMITH:Syd[1] 36
also the r. to our existence HALL:Rad 2
always in the r. COWLEY:A 8
are exclusively in the r. HUX:A 15
be r., by chance COWP 23
been, a man of the r. MOSLEY 1
born to set it r. SHAK:HAM 60
born to set it r. STRACH 1
claim our r. as women PANK:C 2
convincing myself that I am r. AUSTEN 10
death your r. to say it VOLT 37
divine r. of husbands WOLLST 5
Equality may perhaps be a r. BALZ 8
everyone is r. LA CHAU 1
exercise their constitutional r. LINC 9
faith that r. makes might LINC 8
find out that one WAS r. POUND 44
God and my r. RICHARD 1
great r. of an excessive wrong BROWNING:R 198
heaven still guards the r. SHAK:RIC.II 23
I had been r. all along DULL 1
I'm all r. BONE 1
it didn't seem r. to the child EDGAR 1
It is r. and fitting MASS 13
It must be r.: I've done it CRAB 15
Man's r. on this earth BRECHT 2
may not always be right GOLDWYN 14
men go r. after them WEST:M 13
minority is always r. IBS 8
more attraction than abstract r. HAZL 1
never do r. by mistake JUNIUS 5
noisy man is always in the r. COWP 25
not r. that matters, but victory HITL 9
only r. is what is after my own EMER 8
our country, r. or wrong DECA 1
put the r. man in the r. place JEFFERSON 15
rather be r. than be President CLAY 2
rather be r. than president THOMAS:NM 1
rather be r. than reasonable NASH 17
r. deed for the wrong reason ELIOT:TS 76
R. Divine of kings POPE 169
r. he said, 'Definitely WAUGH:E 21
r. not only to be right SZASZ 5
r. of the ignorant man to be CARLYLE:T 39
r. people are rude MAUGH 9
r. was r., and there CRAB 20
r. will prevail CHAMBERLAIN:N 5
r. wrong TENNY 238
Roundheads (R. but Repulsive) SELL 6
see what is r. and not to do CONF 27
set r. what is astray LANGTON 2
settle what's r. and fair HUGHES:Th 3
they are both r. EBNER 1
To do a great r. SHAK:MERC 45
Trust in God, and do the R. MACLEOD:N 1
Two wrongs do not make a r. PROV 407
Up you, Jack, I'm all r. ANON 113
we've got to do the r. things GOLDI 1
Whatever is, is r. POPE 88
When r., to be kept r. SCHURZ 1
which was r. in his own eyes BIBLE 138
Who measures r. DAVIDS 4
with firmness in the r. LINC 13
wrong because not all was r. CRAB 17
right-hand: setting me on the r. CEL 3
right of way: died maintaining his r.o.w. ANON 146
righteous:
Be not r. over much BIBLE 284
godly, r., and sober life PRAY 5
not come to call the r. BIBLE 406
r. are bold as a lion BIBLE 273
r. man who is tenacious HORACE 31
r. shall flourish BIBLE 228
When the r. man turneth away BUTLER:S[2] 24
Ye must leave r. ways behind BUDDHA 3
righteousness:
hunger and thirst after r. BIBLE 384
I have loved r. GREG VII 1
r. and peace have kissed BIBLE 223
R. is the end ROOS:T 17
Sun of r. arise BIBLE 363
That is the path of r. BALL 56
what r. really is ARNOLD:M 76
Within the paths of r. SCOTTISH 1
rightly: those who *act* r. who carry off ARISTOT 4
rights:
Creator with certain unalienable r. JEFFERSON 2
equal in dignity and r. ANON 153
fight for their own human r. PANK:E 5
in perpetuity the r. of the people COOL 1
Men their r. ANTH 1
r. of the black man in this country X 2
religious r. of an Englishman JUNIUS 1
second thing is other people's r. HILL:Reg 5
sovereign has . . . three r. BAGE 12
votes against another's r. CONDOR 1
wicked folly of 'Women's R.' VICT 4
women their r. ANTH 1
women's r. has been largely won THATCH:M 13
rigol: from this golden r. hath SHAK:HEN.IV[2] 45
riled: no sense In gittin' r. HARRIS:JC 5
rime: r. was on the spray HARDY:T 2
rind:
now shall taste the r.? THOMP:F 12
sweet as the r. was SWIN 23
rinderpest: made the kafir and the r. BOSMAN 1
ring:
Bright is the r. of words STEVENSON:RL 65
he rid at the r. BALL 12
One R. to rule them all TOLK 2
r. at the end of his nose LEAR 19
r. is worn away by use OSB:J 14
r. on her wand she bore MOORE:T 13
R. out, wild bells TENNY 177
r. so worn CRAB 21
They now r. the bells WALP:R 3
till I have taken off my r. RAG 1
want dinner do not r. the bell BAGE 25
what shall we do for a r.? LEAR 19
With this R. I thee wed PRAY 86
ring-bo-ree: forty bottles of R. LEAR 17
ringing: r. the Old Year out GODWIN 1
ringleaders: fling the r. from the Tarpeian ARNOLD:T 1
ringlets: green sour r. make SHAK:TEM 29
rings: R. on her fingers and NURS 58
Ringsend: I will live in R. GOGA 2
Rio: rolling down to R. KIP 107
riot:
fierce blaze of r. SHAK:RIC.II 16
R., and ill-manag'd Merriment MILT 23
r. is at bottom the language KING:ML 4
Riot Act: When . . . two or three hundred* HERV:Lord 2
rioters: two or three thousand r. HERV:Lord 2
rioting:
As for r., the old Roman ARNOLD:T 1
Black schoolchildren started r. PATON 4
riots: not-to-be-endured r. SHAK:KING L 17
ripe: we r. and r. SHAK:AS 29
ripeness: R. is all SHAK:KING L 78
rise:
Early to r. and early THURB 11
men may r. on stepping-stones TENNY 126
Must r. at five CLARKE:J 1
nobody who does not r. early will ever JOHNSON:S 76
r. up like new bread TOLS:L 5
R. up, you damned souls POTTIER 1
r. with the lark BRET 6
r. with the lark PROV 154
r. with thy rising SWIN 45
stoop to r. MASSIN 2
to r., it stoops BROWNING:R 175
we fall to r. BROWNING:R 213
risen: You have r. by your gravity SMITH:Syd[1] 40
rises: Hoo-ray and up she r. ANON 49
rising:
All r. to great place BACON:F[1] 75
means of r. in the world JOHNSON:S 172
risk: lend money to such a poor r. BENCH 5
rite: No noble r. SHAK:HAM 173
rites:
of payens corsed olde r. CHAUC 122
R. Mysterious of connubial Love MILT 201
Ritz: open to all – like the R. BING 1
rivalry: dead there is no r. MACAULAY:TB 3
river:
Away, you rolling r. ANON 35
bridge even when there's no r. KHRU 4
build your House of Parliament upon the r. WELLING 16
either side the r. lie TENNY 12
even the weariest r. SWIN 31
Fame is like a r. BACON:F[1] 93
From many an ancient r. HEB 2
into the same r. HERAC 2
last r. poisoned MCLEAN:J 1
living r. by the door STEVENSON:RL 59
majestic r. floated on ARNOLD:M 33
Ol' man r. HAMMER 1
one more r. to cross ANON 2
reynynge ryver bee CHATT 1
r. at my garden's end SWIFT 54
r. Is a strong brown god ELIOT:TS 101
r. is within us ELIOT:TS 102
r. jumps over the mountain AUD 6
r. of knowledge has too often turned JEANS 2
r.-rounded HOPK:GM 12
Runs not a r. by my palace THACK 21
sacred r. ran COLERIDGE:ST 63
she's fading down the r. NEWBOLT 7
through the r. singing BUNYAN 31
Time is like a r. made up AUR 8
Up the r. and o'er the lea HOGG 7
Where the brook and r. meet LONGFEL 8
white flows the r. STEVENSON:RL 64
riverrun: r., past Eve and Adam's JOYCE:J 30
rivers:
By the r. of Babylon BIBLE 244
object is worth r. of blood JEFFERSON 14
r., and fish and fishing WALT 14
R. are damp PARKER:D 5
r. cannot quench SHAK:HEN.VI[3] 6
road:
along the r. of evening DE LA M 10
And the r. below me STEVENSON:RL 63
Golden R. to Samarkand FLECKER 15
good to be out on the r. MASE 4
hard-beaten r. to his house EMER 83
it is on the r. and coming DICKENS 202

life's r., so dim and dirty BYR 138
light to shine upon the r. COWP 2
long, laborious r. HARDY:T 60
My r. leads me seawards MASE 10
no r. or ready way to virtue BROWNE:T 21
odd Fork in Being's R. DICKIN:E 9
on the r. to understanding AESC 1
one, that on a lonesome r. COLERIDGE:ST 34
only monument the asphalt r. ELIOT:TS 73
Only things in the middle of the r. HIGH 1
Our r. is steaming HEAN 5
returns to tell us of the R. FITZGER:E 24
r. from the eye to the heart CHESTERTON 30
r. is rough and long BRONTE:A 4
r. lies long and straight STEVENSON:RL 11
r. of excess leads to the palace BLAKE:W 34
r. that leads him to England JOHNSON:S 114
r. that runs from Ixopo PATON 1
r. that turning always MUIR:E 1
r. To bring us, daily KEBLE 1
r. to hell is paved with good PROV 334
r. to resolution lies by doubt QUAR 14
'r. was a ribbon of moonlight NOY 2
r. wind up-hill all the way? ROSSET:C 14
rolling English r. CHESTERTON 7
sad r. lies so clear PATMO 7
some call it the r. to heaven BALL 56
take to the open r. WHITMAN 17
They are upon the r. COWP 55
Upon the upland r. BAXTER:JK 1
was once a r. through the woods KIP 131
who stay in the middle of the r. BEVAN 6
who takes no private r. POPE 106
winding r. before me HAZL 18
ye'll tak' the high r. ANON 36
yon braid, braid r. BALL 56

roads:
all r. lead to France THOMAS:E 7
All r. lead to Rome PROV 11
How many r. must DYL 1
I love r. THOMAS:E 8
Most r. lead men homewards MASE 11
New r.: new ruts CHESTERTON 62
r. 'not adopted' BETJ 21
Two r. diverged FROST:R 5
when the r. were dry MORRIS:W 2

roam:
we will no longer r. TENNY 26
who soar, but never r. WORDS:W 135

roamed: How sweet I roam'd BLAKE:W 1

roaming:
abhor, too, the r. lover CALLIM 1
always r. with a hungry heart TENNY 52
Roamin' in the gloamin' LAUD 1

roar:
called upon to give the r. CHURCH:W 40
let him r. again SHAK:MID 9
long, withdrawing r. ARNOLD:M 47
Swinging slow with sullen r. MILT 82
they r. their ribs out GILB:WS 99

roared:
how the poor souls r. SHAK:WIN 10
r. and howled COLERIDGE:ST 15

roarers: cares these r. for the name SHAK:TEM 1

roareth: What is this that r. GODLEY 1

roaring:
magnificent r. of the young lions ARNOLD:M 54
was a r. in the wind WORDS:W 83

roast:
R. me in sulphur SHAK:OTH 68
r. with fire BIBLE 96
strove to rule the r. PRIOR 14

rob:
r. a lady ... by way of marriage FIELDING 28
R. me, but bind me not DONNE 44
r. the Hybla bees SHAK:JUL 79
that he might r. a neighbour MACAULAY:TB 8

robbed:
he's not robb'd at all SHAK:OTH 42
robb'd that smiles SHAK:OTH 11
r. a man of *everything* he's no longer SOLZ 5
We was r. JACOBS:J 1
You have all r. Him SIMEON 1

robbery:
for their r. have SHAK:MEA 15
scandal, as in that of r. CHESTERFIELD 18

Robbins: President R. was so well adjusted JARRELL 1

robed: R. and furr'd gowns hide SHAK:KING L 71

robes: r. ye weave, another wears SHELLEY:PB 52

Robespierre: sea-green Incorruptible* CARLYLE:T 21

Robey: R. is the Darling of the music-halls SMITH:FE 6

robin:
Call for the r. redbreast WEBSTER:J 10
R. Red breast in a Cage BLAKE:W 82
Robyn Redbrest He shall be the preest SKEL:J 3
Sweet R. sits in the bush SCOTT:W 57
what will poor r. do then? NURS 43
Who killed Cock R.? NURS 85

Robin : R.'s not near KEPP:C 1

Robin Adair: R.A. KEPP:C 1

Robin Gray: auld R.G., he was BARNARD:A 1

Robin Hood: *Here lies bold R.H.* BALL 16

Robinson: Here's to you, Mrs R. SIMON:P 2

robot: modern conception of a r. CHURCH:W 52

Rochester: Lord R.'s poems have much WALP:H 25

rock:
leaping from r. up to r. BROWNING:R 146
my r., and my fortress BIBLE 202
r. of Ages, cleft for me TOP 1
Rhyme is the r. on which DRYD 57
upon this r. I will build BIBLE 417

rock-a-bye:
R. baby BLAKE:CD 1
R., baby NURS 60

rocked: She r. it, and rated it EDWARDS:R 1

rocket: he rose like a r. PAINE 8

rocking horse: sway'd about upon a r.h. KEATS 10

rocks:
ascetic r. and the sensual whirlpools MERED:G 13
bold anfractuous r. ELIOT:TS 27
full speed ahead for the r. GILMORE 1
'mid these dancing r. COLERIDGE:ST 63
rifted R. whose entrance MILT 34
when I throw r. at seabirds NASH 22

rod:
at lightning and lashed r. HOPK:GM 3
He that spareth his r. BIBLE 260
humbled, kiss the r. SHAK:TWO 4
r. and thy staff they comfort BIBLE 206
r. Becomes more mock'd SHAK:MEA 1
r. out of the stem of Jesse BIBLE 309
r. produces an effect which JOHNSON:S 86
r. To check the erring WORDS:W 70
spare the r., and spoil BUTLER:S[1] 26
Spare the r. and spoil PROV 350
Wisdom be put in a silver r.? BLAKE:W 28

rode: r. madly off in all directions LEACOCK 4

Roderick:
Saxon, – I am R. Dhu SCOTT:W 41
where was R. then? SCOTT:W 43

rogue:
dainty r. in porcelain MERED:G 7
Has he not a r.'s face? CONG 21
r. and peasant slave SHAK:HAM 90
r. is married to a whore KIP 87

rogues:
cannot move without r. EMER 47
to do good to r. is to throw CERV 8

roll:
Let it r. on full flood CHURCH:W 17
nightly r. into darkness HARDY:T 58
r. of the world eastward HARDY:T 51
R. on, thou deep BYR 117

rolling:
He jus' keeps rollin' HAMMER 1
r. down to Rio KIP 107
r. English road CHESTERTON 7

Rolls Royce: Goes the green R.R. SLESS 7

ROM: infinite riches in a little R. SEGAL 2

Roman:
after the high R. fashion SHAK:ANT 60
been a virtue with the R. clergy KINGSLEY:C 8
Before the R. came to Rye CHESTERTON 7
Butcher'd to make a R. BYR 110
ghost of the deceased *R. empire* HOBB 12
historian of the R. empire GIBBON:E 23
Holy, nor R., nor an Empire VOLT 10
I am a R. citizen CIC 10
I'm a R. for that FARQ 15
live in the R. fashion AMB 2
more an antique R. than a Dane SHAK:HAM 198
R. by a R. Valiantly vanquish'd SHAK:ANT 57
R. Conquest was, however, a *Good* SELL 2
R. meal COWP 74
R. people had only one neck CALIG 1
R. people were the classical decadence YEATS 144
R. state survives by its ENN 2
R. thought hath struck him SHAK:ANT 7
R.'s life, a R.'s arms MACAULAY:TB 52
so rude that would not be a R.? SHAK:JUL 47
Tenderest of R. poets TENNY 288
Than such a R. SHAK:JUL 69
This was the noblest R. SHAK:JUL 88
worship which prevailed in the R. GIBBON:E 1

Roman Catholic:
I'll show you a R.C. ELLIS:B 1
like you, your holiness, is a R.C. CHURCH:R 2
R.C. Church is getting nearer PAIS 1

romance:
beginning of a lifelong r. WILDE:O 79
cloudy symbols of a high r. KEATS 22
not a little given to r. EVELYN 2
R. at short notice SAKI 18
steam spoils r. at sea? KIP 73
Twenty years of r. make WILDE:O 56

romances: R. paint at full length BYR 84

Romanism: rum, R., and rebellion BURCHA 1

Romans:
R. call it stoicism ADDIS 5
R. were like brothers MACAULAY:TB 49

romantic:
mustn't be r. about money SHAW 38
worship r. love for the wrong HAZZ 1

romanticism:
r. disease GOET 36
R. is the art of presenting STEND 1

Rome:
All roads lead to R. PROV 11
comen from R. al hoot CHAUC 31
grandeur that was R. POE 1
Half-Way House to R. PUNCH 3
happy R., born when I CIC 18
high and palmy state of R. SHAK:HAM 5
hook-nos'd fellow of R. SHAK:HEN.IV[2] 40
I lov'd R. more SHAK:JUL 45
If you are in R. AMB 2
in R. comes at a price JUV 10
lay thou on for R. MACAULAY:TB 43
Now is it R. indeed SHAK:JUL 13
R. has spoken AUGUS 12
R. hath lost her crown COLERIDGE:M 1
R. ... like its own Monte Testaceo CLOUGH 12
R.! my country BYR 103
R., though her eagle through WALLER 8
R., 'tis thine alone VIRGIL 72
R. was not built in a day PROV 335
R.'s gross yoke BROWNING:R 66
R.'s just a city like anywhere BURGESS:A 5
saw Learning fall, and R. POPE 29
soon or late comes round by R. BROWNING:R 199
stones of R. to rise SHAK:JUL 58
than second in R. CAES:GJ 6
time will doubt of R. BYR 204
wealth and noise of R. HORACE 47
when R. falls – the World BYR 112
you cruel men of R. SHAK:JUL 2

Romeo:
repetition of my R.'s name SHAK:ROM 18
wherefore art thou R.? SHAK:ROM 10

Rommel: finish with this chap R. MONTGOM:BL 1

romping: hear them r. overhead GORDON:AM 3

Ronsard: R. sang of me RON 1

rood:
every r. of ground maintained GOLDS 21
Throw away thy r. HERB:G 48

roof:
heavens my wide r.-tree AYT 5
no r. to shroud his head HEYW:T 2
through its gorgeous r. BROWNING:R 6
until my r. whirl around JONS 20

roofs: galvanized-iron r. on their front verandahs BOYD:RGP 2

rook:
last r. Beat its straight COLERIDGE:ST 52
r.-racked HOPK:GM 12
rooks:
r. are blown about the skies TENNY 135
r. came home in scramble HODG 2
r. in families homeward HARDY:T 42
room:
All I want is a r. somewhere LERN 2
always r. at the top PROV 376
always r. at the top WEBSTER:D 10
coming to that Holy r. DONNE 94
have money and a r. of her own WOOLF:V 9
How little r. Do we take SHIRL 1
In ev'ry grave make r. DAVEN:W 1
in her own r. with the door shut WHARTON:E 1
In my r. the world is STEVENS 3
Infinite riches in a little r. MARLOWE 20
little to have chang'd our r. DONNE 75
no r. for them in the inn BIBLE 447
one little r., an everywhere DONNE 42
r. for the bouncing Belly JONS 37
r. in this country for but one ROOS:T 16
R. of One's Own WOOLF:V 7
R. to deny ourselves KEBLE 1
r. with a view – and you COWARD 19
tell when you walk into a r. JOHNSON:LB 4
upper r. at midnight AUD 49
who sneaked into my r. MARX:G 5
Who's in the next r.? HARDY:T 39
will just be one little r. DOST 2
rooms:
boys in the back r. BEAV 2
lighted r. Inside your head LARK 7
weep in empty r. COLERIDGE:M 2
Roosevelt: R. were alive he'd turn GORKY 15
roost: always come home to r. SOUTHEY 13
rooster: Hongry r. don't cackle HARRIS:JC 9
root:
eaten on the insane r. SHAK:MAC 11
flames flicker at time's own r. WRIGHT:J 6
Lay then the axe to the r. PAINE 5
r. of all evil BIBLE 549
Thy r. is ever in its grave HERB:G 32
rooted: r. the sun and moon YEATS 21
roots:
feel the r. of the house move HUGHES:Te 2
grow out of his r. BIBLE 309
r., and ever green PEELE 2
r. are wrapt about the bones TENNY 127
r. that can be pulled up ELIOT:G 43
send my r. rain HOPK:GM 31
stirring Dull r. ELIOT:TS 34
rope:
escape from r. and gun GAY 24
Give a thief enough r. PROV 144
Not yet a r. to hang ANON 15
piece of r. for a keepsake TWAIN 27
Thy r. of sands HERB:G 41
Rosaleen: My Dark R. MANG 1
Rosalinde: No jewel is like R. SHAK:AS 39
rose:
As though a r. should shut KEATS 73
At Christmas I no more desire a r. SHAK:LOV 2
At last he r. MILT 60
blossom as the r. BIBLE 317
Bud, and yet a *R. full-blowne* HERR 5
English unofficial r. BROOKE 7
fayr as is the r. in May CHAUC 98
fresh lap of the crimson r. SHAK:MID 16
Gather the R. of love SPENS 34
glut thy sorrow on a morning r. KEATS 96
Go, lovely R. WALLER 2
happy is the r. distill'd SHAK:MID 1
He wears the r. Of youth SHAK:ANT 37
he's mighty lak' a r. STANTON:FL 1
intricate and folded r. WRIGHT:J 7
killing as the Canker to the R. MILT 47
last r. of summer MOORE:T 17
leaves the R. of Yesterday? FITZGER:E 7
Little r. on the heath GOET 1
little white r. of Scotland MACDIAR 28
lovely is the r. WORDS:W 53
mad little maid is R. Madder YOUNG:WB 1
musk of the r. is blown TENNY 215
my fause lover stole my r. BURNS:R 98
my luve's like a red, red, r. BURNS:R 113
ne're the R. without the Thorn HERR 6
never a r. like you WEATH 2
never blows so red The R. FITZGER:E 13
No thorns go as deep as a r.'s SWIN 25
on thy cheek a fading r. KEATS 80
One perfect r. PARKER:D 6
opened up like a flowering r. MUSSO:V 1
pluck a white r. with me SHAK:HEN.VI[1] 2
pluck the r. And love it more BROWNING:R 161
raise up the ghost of a r. BROWNE:T 47
ravage with impunity a r. BROWNING:R 8
red r. from off this thorn SHAK:HEN.VI[1] 2
r. By any other name SHAK:ROM 11
R. crossed the road DOBSON:HA 1
R. is a r. is a r. STEIN:G 1
R. leaves, when the r. SHELLEY:PB 143
r. like a nymph to the bath SHELLEY:PB 92
R. of all Roses YEATS 9
r. of the rosebud garden TENNY 218
r. or rue or laurel SWIN 50
R., thou art sick BLAKE:W 66
r. with all its sweetest leaves BYR 235
r. without a thorn MACNALL 1
Roves back the r. DE LA M 3
sad R. of all my days YEATS 13
secret, and inviolate R.? YEATS 20
supplication to the r. FLECKER 12
Sweet r., whose hue HERB:G 32
tell the crooked r. THOMAS:D 4
third day he r. again MASS 10
third day he r. again PRAY 19
thought came like a full-blown r. KEATS 66
tiger sniffs the r. SASS 15
twilight dim with r. DE LA M 10
unblown r. HEAN 5
under the r. BICK 4
where a late r. may linger HORACE 18
without Thorn the R. MILT 189
You r. o' the wrong side to-day BROME:R 1
Rose Aylmer: R.A., all were thine LANDOR 1
rose-buds: Gather ye R. while ye may HERR 26
rose buds: R.b. fill'd with snow CAMPION 9
rose-red:
r. city 'half as old BURGON 1
r. sissy half as old PLOM 4
rose-water: pour r. over a toad JERROLD 8
rosemary:
r., that's for remembrance SHAK:HAM 169
there's r. and rue SHAK:WIN 16
Rosencrantz: R. and Guildenstern are dead SHAK:HAM 202
roses:
ash the burnt r. leave ELIOT:TS 103
brightening r. of the sky CAMPBELL:T 5
days of wine and r. DOWS 3
Do r. stick like burrs? BROWNING:R 159
Each Morn a thousand R. FITZGER:E 7
Flung r., r. riotously DOWS 1
In fields where r. fade HOUSM 26
It was the time of r. HOOD 8
Lilies without, r. within MARV 26
lived as long as r. MALHER 1
make thee beds of r. MARLOWE 51
not a bed of r. STEVENSON:RL 10
Plant no r. at my head ROSSET:C 12
raptures and r. of vice SWIN 20
Ring-a-ring o' r. NURS 59
R. and white Lillies grow CAMPION 9
R. are flowering in Picardy WEATH 2
r. for the flush of youth ROSSET:C 11
R. have thorns SHAK:SON 17
R. newly wash'd with dew SHAK:TAM 6
r., r., all the way BROWNING:R 142
scent of the r. will hang MOORE:T 5
Seek r. in December BYR 10
She wore a wreath of r. BAYLY 3
starv'd the r. in her cheeks SHAK:TWO 13
Strew on her r. ARNOLD:M 18
two dozen r. to Room MARX:G 17
Two red r. across the moon MORRIS:W 3
rosy: lives in a sort of r. haze MURD:I 3
rot:
Here continueth to r. ARB 3
propagate, and r. POPE 92
r. in hospitals SOUTHER 1
we r. and r. SHAK:AS 29
Rotarians: R. in outer space VIDAL 1
rotten: r. in the state of Denmark SHAK:HAM 39
rottenfulness: r. is terrific RICHARDS:F 2
rottenness: r. begins in his conduct JEFFERSON 11
rouble: r. is just a sweetie paper RUTS 1
rough:
R. he may be DICKENS 120
r. places plain BIBLE 320
rough-hew: R. them how we will SHAK:HAM 191
roughness: r. breedeth hate BACON:F[1] 74
Roumania: I am Marie of R. PARKER:D 4
round:
heaven, a perfect r. BROWNING:R 166
In a light fantastick r. MILT 22
must enter again the r. THOMAS:D 10
R. and r. the garden NURS 61
R. and r. the rugged rock NURS 62
R. the world forever ARNOLD:M 1
roundabouts:
gain on the r. PROV 422
What's lost upon the r. CHALM 1
Roundheads: R. (Right but Repulsive) SELL 6
rouse:
If anything might r. him OWEN:W 6
No more shall r. them GRAY:T 16
What will it take to r. us? BELLOW 2
rouseabout: Middleton's R. LAWS 5
Rousseau: shall not ask Jean Jacques R. COWP 88
rout: pleasures of having a r. HOOD 16
rover: laughing fellow r. MASE 3
roving: we'll go no more a r. BYR 128
row:
darned long r. to hoe LOWELL:JR 5
Devil knows how to r. COLERIDGE:ST 36
r. after health like a waterman SWIFT 85
r. one way and look another BURTON:Ro 4
To r. us o'er the ferry CAMPBELL:T 11
we'll r., r. for ever CORY 4
rowing: one way, and r. another BUNYAN 12
Rowland: Child R. to the dark tower came SHAK:KING L 51
rowley: With a r., powley, gammon NURS 12
royal:
more r. than we are ELIZ II 5
To have prov'd most r. SHAK:HAM 203
Royal Commission: R.C. is a broody hen FOOT 1
Royal George: Down went the R.G. COWP 16
Royal Society: honour which the R.S. desires to FARA 1
royalist: more of a r. than the King ANON 213
royalties:
fond of fresh air and r. ASHFORD 9
my r. are lean MACMAN 1
royalty: R. is a government in which BAGE 11
rub:
there's the r. SHAK:HAM 97
try to r. up against money RUNYON 4
What r. or what impediment SHAK:HEN.V 45
rubber: heart is like Indian r. BRONTE:A 1
rubbers: *makkin it a r.' howff* BIBLE 591
rubbishing: reciprocal banter or r. HARRIS:M 2
rubies:
her price is far above r. BIBLE 276
R. unparagon'd SHAK:CYM 2
rubs: Leave no r. nor botches SHAK:MAC 63
ruby: That *Rubie* which you weare HERR 20
rudder:
Grasping the r. hard ARNOLD:M 15
rhyme the r. is of verses BUTLER:S[1] 15
snatched his r. ARNOLD:M 30
Their tail the r. DRYD 7
ruddier: r. than the Cherry GAY 2
rude:
apparently r. and brutal natures MANNING 2
kindness, being r. to him DANTE 14
manner r. and wild BELLOC 1
right people are r. MAUGH 9
Some of which were rather r. COWARD 25
rudeness: indistinguishable from r. THER 1
rudest: r. work that tells a story RUSKIN 2
Rudyards: R. cease from kipling STEPHEN:JK 3
rue:
I'll set a bank of r. SHAK:RIC.II 34
King shall r. SHAK:RIC.II 7
Marry in May, r. for aye PROV 272
rose or r. or laurel SWIN 50
R., even for ruth SHAK:RIC.II 34

s. for at least fifty years CHURCH:W 61
safeguard: s. of the West WORDS:W 74
safety:
pluck this flower, s. SHAK:HEN.IV[1] 31
public s. be the supreme law SELD 9
s. in numbers PROV 374
s. is in our speed EMER 20
source of my light and my s. BIBLE 597
There is no s. in numbers THURB 10
to expect no s. VIRGIL 53
safety-catch: take the s. off my Browning JOHST 1
sage:
often when they find a s. MARQUIS 8
without hardness will be s. ARNOLD:M 36
said:
as well s., as if I had s. it SWIFT 45
Do not ask who s. KEMP 5
Easier s. than done PROV 89
Everything has been s. already LA BRU 12
if I s. so; it was so GOLDS 47
Least s. soonest mended PROV 230
much might be s. on both sides ADDIS 19
never s. anything that was remembered DISR:B 23
not know what they have s. CHURCH:W 3
s. at all can be s. clearly WITT 2
that has not been s. before TEREN 4
thing well s. will be DRYD 133
thought cannot wisely be s. PEAC 16
wish I had s. that WHIST 5
sail:
Hoist your s. when the wind PROV 172
Never weather-beaten s. CAMPION 5
S. and s., with unshut eye ARNOLD:M 1
s. beyond the sunset TENNY 55
s. on, O Ship of State LONGFEL 17
she comes i' faith full s. CONG 41
shook out more s. ARNOLD:M 30
Two towers of s. CLOUGH 6
vessel puffs her s. TENNY 55
sailed:
s. away for a year and a day LEAR 19
She hadna sail'd a league BALL 14
you never s. with *me* before JACK:A 1
sailing: s. Like a stately Ship MILT 289
sailor:
do with the drunken s. ANON 49
drowned Phoenician S. ELIOT:TS 36
ever s. free to choose KIP 154
Home is the s. STEVENSON:RL 61
lass that loves a s. DIBDIN:C 9
No man will be a s. who has JOHNSON:S 105
S. men 'ave their faults JACOBS:WW 1
s. tells stories of winds PROP 1
s.'s wife had chestnuts SHAK:MAC 5
sailors:
convoys of dead s. come SLESS 6
S. have a port in every storm PROV 336
Spanish s. with bearded LONGFEL 25
three s. of Bristol City THACK 23
sails:
argosies of magic s. TENNY 79
lofty ships carry low s. PROV 257
still the s. made on COLERIDGE:ST 31
saint:
able to corrupt a s. SHAK:HEN.IV[1] 10
accents of an expiring s. STERNE 36
before we *know* he is a s. GREENE:G 4
Follow your S. CAMPION 2
my late espoused S. MILT 101
Poet and S. COWLEY:A 9
reel out a s. CHURCH:C 3
S. in Crape is twice a S. POPE 111
seem a s. when most SHAK:RIC.III 7
she cou'd make of me a s. CONG 64
that I may see my s. JONS 16
to catch a s., With saints SHAK:MEA 16
'twould a s. provoke POPE 115
vices of the s. EMER 24
weakest s. upon his knees COWP 8
Wednesday wencher and a Sunday s. ELLIS:B 1
woman to qualify as a s. STOCKS 3
worst of Madmen is a S. POPE 151
St Andrews: S.A. by the Northern Seas LANG:A 2
Saint Crispin: Upon S.C.'s day DRAYT 7
St Dunstan: push him all the way to S.D.'s COWARD 32
Saint George: S.G., that swing'd the dragon SHAK:KING J 4
St Ives:
As I was going to S.I. NURS 1
Vicar of S.I. says the smell KILV 2
St James: ladies of S.J.'s DOBSON:HA 3
Saint Kieran: Stands S.K.'s City fair ROLL:TW 1
St Lawrence: I have seen the S.L. BURNS:J 1
St Nicholas: S.N. soon would be there MOORE:CC 1
St Pancras: equivalent of the towers of S.P. BEECHAM 1
St Paul:
description of the ruins of S.P.'s WALP:H 13
Say I am designing S.P.'s BENTLEY:EC 7
sketch the ruins of S.P.'s MACAULAY:TB 27
stunk and litter'd in S.P.'s GRAY:T 40
with S.P. are literary terms ARNOLD:M 73
St Peter: hooted in S.P.'s Quire GRAY:T 40
Saint Peter: S.P. sat by the celestial gate BYR 144
Saint Praxed: S.P.'s ever was the church BROWNING:R 41
St Swithin's Day: S.S.D., if thou dost rain PROV 359
St Trinian:
Maidens of S.T.'s SEARLE 4
Terror of S.T.'s SEARLE 1
sainted: thing enskied and s. SHAK:MEA 3
saintly: tell the s. from the suburban AUD 28
saints:
All are not s. that go PROV 5
be ready to receive Thy s.? SHAW 119
Communion of S. PRAY 19
ghastly glories of s. SWIN 37
is the death of his s. BIBLE 236
s. in your injuries SHAK:OTH 19
shall never be S. in Heaven BROWNE:T 14
slaughter'd S., whose bones MILT 99
There entertain him all the S. MILT 58
Thy s. have dwelt secure WATTS 18
Where s. in glory stand YOUNG:A 1
Where the s. have trod BARING-G 3
With the s. in church DANTE 11
salad:
My s. days SHAK:ANT 23
wholesome s. from the brook COWP 83
salads: S., and eggs, and lighter PRIOR 8
Salamanca: I love the University of S. JOHNSON:S 124
salary:
he had a s. to receive GIBBON:E 17
s. of the chief executive GALB 9
week I earn my s. KENNEDY:JF 10
salesman: s. has got to dream MILLER:A 3
Salisbury Plain: crossing S.P. on a bicycle GILB:WS 52
salley: Down by the s. gardens YEATS 3
sally: make a sudden s. TENNY 201
Sally: none like pretty S. CAREY 2
salmon:
between smoked s. and tinned s. WILSON:Harold 10
crossing s. with mosquitoes MORTON:JB 3
first s. and the first LONGFEL 28
It was the s. DICKENS 8
s. are striking back ELIZ:QM 4
s. jumping and falling LOWELL:R 14
s. sing in the street AUD 6
saumon to be served up in its integrity NORTH:C 1
salmon-fishers: now the s. moist MARV 34
saloons: Solomon of s. BROWNING:R 178
salt:
Better s. than sour PROV 44
like eating an egg without s. KIP 7
Most women turn to s. MANS:K 8
nobody likes having s. rubbed WEST:R 3
running s. and snow DUG 1
s. have lost his savour BIBLE 385
s. of broken tears SHAK:TRO 20
s. of the earth SHELLEY:PB 62
she became a pillar of s. BIBLE 50
touched with s. and evergreen LOWELL:R 9
With a grain of s. PLINY 3
Ye are the s. of the earth BIBLE 385
saltness: relish of the s. of time SHAK:HEN.IV[2] 6
saltpetre: villainous s. should be digg'd SHAK:HEN.IV[1] 19
salty: how s. other people's bread DANTE 18
salus: *S. populi suprema lex* SELD 9
salutations: eye full of gentle s. STERNE 36
salute:
about to die s. thee SUET 1
Who are they you s. WHITMAN 16
saluting: s. strange women NASH 24
salvation:
Him that brought s. down SMART 3
My bottle of s. RALE 2
no s. outside the Church CYP 2
Outside the church there is no s. AUGUS 7
s. lay in hiding his wounds TOLS:L 7
s. of mankind lies only SOLZ 7
shew forth his s. BIBLE 230
wilfully seeks her own s.? SHAK:HAM 178
Work out your own s. BIBLE 539
working out your own s. ROOS:FD 1
Wot prawce selvytion SHAW 87
Samarcand: silken S. to cedar'd Lebanon KEATS 74
Samarkand: Golden Road to S. FLECKER 15
same:
all comes to the s. thing BROWNING:R 74
all look just the s. REYN:M 1
all say *the s.* MELBOU 2
all the s. in a hundred years PROV 215
Ever the s. ELIZ I 5
he is much the s. AUSTIN:A 1
more they remain the s. KARR 1
s. the whole world over ANON 38
they're all the s. BOSMAN 1
To endless years the s. WATTS 18
we're all made the s. COWARD 8
world would not be the s. OPP 2
samite: Clothed in white s. TENNY 274
sample: a chosen s. BURNS:R 20
Samson:
S. hath quit himself MILT 300
S., the strongest of the children BLAKE:W 7
Samuel: circumcised Herbert S. they threw LLOYD GEO 11
sanction: s. to the trade of blood? SHELLEY:PB 1
sanctuaries: s. in which exploded systems SMITH:Ad 9
sanctuary: dark s. of incapacity CHESTERFIELD 30
sand:
all 'ot s. an' ginger KIP 49
handfuls of s. in their eyes HOFFMAN:ETA 1
Little grains of s. CARNEY 1
see a World in a Grain of S. BLAKE:W 82
Such quantities of s. CARROLL 55
throw the s. against the wind BLAKE:W 100
sandal: bright and battering s. HOPK:GM 14
sandals:
Bind on thy s. SWIN 10
morn went out with s. gray MILT 59
sandalwood: S., cedarwood MASE 9
sandbags: trodden s. loosely filled SASS 3
Sandford: down by S., yields ARNOLD:M 43
sandpaper: love call of two pieces of s. O'REILLY 1
sands:
Across the s. of Dee KINGSLEY:C 13
And looks at the s. HARDY:T 25
Come unto these yellow s. SHAK:TEM 9
Footprints on the s. of time LONGFEL 4
level s. stretch far SHELLEY:PB 22
on the s. with printless foot SHAK:TEM 29
s. upon the Red sea shore BLAKE:W 101
sane:
held by no s. man BROWNING:R 101
s. man and I will cure him JUNG:Carl 10
sang:
Ful weel she soong the service CHAUC 9
he s. his didn't CUMM 5
it may turn out a s. BURNS:R 44
s. in my chains like the sea THOMAS:D 17
s. themselves to s. HODG 2
s. to a small guitar LEAR 18
s. to sweeten Ireland's wrong YEATS 11
S. with a fountain's panache DAY LEWIS 6
sing a s. at least BURNS:R 60
Thus s. the uncouth Swain MILT 59
sanitary towel: Golden S.T. Award Presentation OSB:J 12
sanitas: *S. sanitatum et omnia s.* MENAGE 1

sank:
And s. her in the sea BALL 15
she s. by the Low-lands low BALL 24
sans:
S. teeth, s. eyes SHAK:AS 34
S. Wine, s. Song FITZGER:E 15
Santa Claus: Nobody shoots at S.C. SMITH:Alf 2
sap: world's whole s. is sunk DONNE 54
sapient:
s. sutlers of the Lord ELIOT:TS 26
shake his s. head ARNOLD:M 50
sapphire: s. melts into the sea TENNY 214
Sarah: it ceased to be with S. BIBLE 49
sarcasm: S. I now see to be CARLYLE:T 7
sarcasticul: This is rote S. WARD:A 2
sardines:
like opening a tin of s. BENNETT:Al 1
think s. will be thrown CANT 1
Sargent: musical Malcolm S. BEECHAM 5
sark: linket at it in her s. BURNS:R 88
sat:
last person who s. on him HAIG:D 1
You have s. too long here AMERY 2
You have s. too long here CROMWELL 6
Satan:
Auld Hornie,, S. BURNS:R 10
beat down S. under our feet PRAY 35
Get thee behind me, S. BIBLE 418
messenger of S. BIBLE 530
S. exalted sat MILT 148
S. finds some mischief still WATTS 5
S. glowr'd, and fidg'd BURNS:R 89
S. thou art but a Dunce BLAKE:W 110
Satanic Verses: With *The S.V.* and Salman Rushdie SIDD 1
Satans: Hired by the S., for the Depression BLAKE:W 97
satellite: under some outcast s. BRENN 2
satiety: love's sad s. SHELLEY:PB 98
satin:
always goes into white s. SHERIDAN:RB 38
ease a heart, like a s. gown PARKER:D 1
satire:
difficult *not* to write s. JUV 1
let s. be my song BYR 7
purpose of s. .... is aggression LEWIS:W 7
S., by being levelled at all SWIFT 5
S. is a kind of glass SWIFT 1
S. should, like a polished MONTAGU 3
Verse s. indeed is all QUINT 2
satirical: Shall this s. collection fill JUV 4
satirist: be the second English Satyrist HALL:Jo 1
satisfaction:
ready ... to give you s. GAY 26
source of s. to him TOLS:S 2
satisfied:
equally *s.*, but not equally *happy* JOHNSON:S 132
s. with what is assigned to him AUR 10
well paid that is well s. SHAK:MERC 49
satisfies: Where most she s. SHAK:ANT 28
satori: When you have *s.* SUZ:DT 1
Saturday:
Dessay. It's Sat'dy night WHITEING 1
S. and Monday CAREY 3
Saturn:
reign of S. returns VIRGIL 11
sat gray-hair'd S. KEATS 43
satyr:
angel s. walks these hills KILV 4
stoic or a s. PINE 2
sauce:
First father of s. JONS 37
Hunger is the best s. CERV 13
Hunger is the best s. PROV 180
Make hunger thy s. TUSS 6
thirty-two religions and only one s. TALL 4
sauces: manner in which s. are prepared ACTON:E 1
sauf: s. us frae the Ill Ane BIBLE 589
Saul:
Is S. also among the prophets? BIBLE 142
S. and Jonathan were lovely BIBLE 152
S. hath slain his thousands BIBLE 149
S., S., why persecutest BIBLE 498
sausage:
come out as a s. BIER 7
s. and thinks of Picasso HERB:AP 21
took from her pocket a s. READE 1
savage:
I will take some s. woman TENNY 84
noble s. ran DRYD 12
not allow it to be s. OSB:J 11
when Britain had a s. culture BANDA 1
who has not wept is a s. SANT 9
savaged: being s. by a dead sheep HEAL 2
savages:
Bring your s. with you CLEMENCE 4
Don't cant in defence of s. JOHNSON:S 245
savant: Every time I talk to a s. RUSS:B 35
save:
cannot s. it I cannot s. myself ORTEGA G 3
enough to s. one's own BROWNING:R 133
Eternal Father, strong to s. WHITING 1
he need not exist in order to s. DE VR 4
himself he cannot s. BIBLE 436
Lord, hast power to s. WILLARD 1
s. those that have no imagination? SHAW 118
s. yourselves for better things VIRGIL 38
To s. your world you asked AUD 52
Whenever you s. five shillings KEYN 11
Who died to s. us all ALEX:CF 5
wilt thou s. the people? ELLIOTT:E 1
saved:
He s. others BIBLE 436
only s. by being dammed HOOD 33
only s. the world CHESTERTON 28
s., and he knows it KINGSLEY:C 10
s. herself by her exertions PITT:W[2] 2
s. the sum of things for pay HOUSM 37
we are not s. BIBLE 337
We could have s. sixpence BECKETT 10
What must I do to be s.? BIBLE 502
saves: s. a man's life against his will HORACE 117
savings: don't make many s. on that SAUN 1
saviour:
But it's 'S. of 'is country' KIP 66
faith of the S. made landfall BOSSU 1
no S. here or in Science Fiction PORTER:PNF 1
saw:
I came, I s.; God conquered JOHN III SOB 1
I came, I s., I conquered CAES:GJ 4
I s. and loved GIBBON:E 19
I s. no one DOYLE:AC 32
monk ne saugh nat all CHAUC 93
more he s. the less NURS 86
s. it but did not realize PEAB 1
Saxon: leave the S. alone KIP 142
say:
all s. *the same* MELBOU 2
as long as they do what I s. THATCH:M 8
because you have something to s. WHATE 1
careful indeed what we s. CONF 24
death your right to s. it VOLT 37
Do as I s., not SELD 12
I have nothing to s. CAGE 1
it's the way they s. it STEINB 2
know what they are going to s. CHURCH:W 3
more to s. when I am dead ROBINS:EA 1
Mrs Poyser 'has her s. out' ELIOT:G 7
nothing to s. about myself PINT 7
nothing to s. and I want to communicate HIRST 1
nothing to s., s. nothing COLTON 2
Quhat s. they? Lat thame s. KEITH:G 1
s. nothing but what hath been said BURTON:Ro 8
s. nothing, when he has nothing JOHNSON:S 214
s. something about me MELBA 5
s. what you have to s. in twenty minutes BRAB 1
s. what you think TAC 5
there is no more to s. SHAK:TRO 26
think till I see what I s.? WALLAS 1
you should s. what you mean CARROLL 16
saying:
As we were s. the other day LEON 1
asleep before you finish s. it ROWL:H 5
bear s. the same things over DUND 1
keep on s. it long enough BENNETT:Ar 4
not worth s. is made into a song BEAUMA 1
S. is one thing, and doing PROV 338
says:
desire for preventing the things one s. PROUST 10
s. little, thinks less FARQ 11
s. what he thinks and feels BRYAN 3
scab: prove the s. of churches WOTTON 7
scabbard: he threw away the s. CLAREN 1
scabs: Make yourselves s.? SHAK:COR 2
scaffold:
between the throne and the s. CHARLES X 2
To the s. and the doom AYT 3
scale: be on a sufficiently large s. SPENCER:H 2
scallop-shell: Give me my s. of quiet RALE 2
scalps: thin and hairless s. SHAK:RIC.II 25
scaly: s. Horrour of his foulded MILT 10
scan: Whose limericks never would s. ANON 108
scandal:
case of s., as in that CHESTERFIELD 18
No s. about Queen *Elizabeth* SHERIDAN:RB 31
no s. while you dine TENNY 200
Public s. is what constitutes offence MOLIERE 11
Retired to their tea and s. CONG 15
S. is the manure of democracy FO 1
scandalous: not dead, are always s. BEAUV 1
scapegoat:
biblical country of the s. WRIGHT:J 3
for a s. into the wilderness BIBLE 112
scar:
lives join, there is oft a s. BROWNING:R 93
We can find no s. DICKIN:E 4
scarce: Mighty s. TWAIN 44
scare: s. myself with my own desert FROST:R 9
scarecrow: not make a s. of the law SHAK:MEA 5
scarecrows: s. of fools and the beacons HUX:TH 4
scarlet:
Cowards in s. GRANVILLE 1
His sins were s. BELLOC 36
In S. town BALL 3
raise the s. standard high CONNELL 1
though clothed in s. JONS 13
Though your sins be as s. BIBLE 300
scars: s. that never felt a wound SHAK:ROM 8
scathed: did not appear to be s. CROMP 2
scatter: S., as from the unextinguished SHELLEY:PB 46
scene:
as well imagine the s. COMPT 1
Love gilds the s. SHERIDAN:RB 17
two people were on a s. CHAND 9
scenery:
end of all natural s. RUSKIN 8
S. is fine KEATS 131
scenes:
busy s. of crowded life JOHNSON:S 66
I'll come no more behind your s. JOHNSON:S 90
those s. made me a painter CONSTABLE:J 1
Through all the changing s. BRADY 2
scent:
Amber s. of odorous perfume MILT 289
How hot the s. is GRAVES:R 3
I s. the morning air SHAK:HAM 47
s. of the roses will hang MOORE:T 5
scents: spread ambrosial s. VIRGIL 40
sceptic:
too much of a s. to deny HUX:TH 13
What ever s. could inquire for BUTLER:S[1] 7
scepticism:
s. kept her from being an atheist SARTRE 10
s. of everything with credulity POWYS 1
sceptre:
His s. shows the force SHAK:MERC 44
S. and crown Must tumble SHIRL 3
stretches forth Her leaden Scepter YOUNG:E 7
To gain a Scepter MILT 268
schedule: My s. is already full KISS 4
Scheherazade: S. is the classical example WYNNE 1
Scheld: by the lazy S. GOLDS 3
schemes: best-laid s. BURNS:R 32
schizophrenia:
God talks to you, you have s. SZASZ 9
S. cannot be understood LAING 2
scholar:
by a painstaking modern s. WILSON:An 1
humiliation of an aged s. COLLINGWOOD:RG 2
humour of a s. BACON:F[1] 104
not fit to be deemed a s. CONF 8
s., and a ripe and good one

SHAK:HEN.VIII 19
s., he can do almost nothing LIPP 1
S. travels yet ARNOLD:M 45
Scholler, all earths volumes CHAPMAN:G 5
what ills the s.'s life assail JOHNSON:S 67
scholars:
only two kinds of s. ALAIN 1
S., ... as a rule study with SCHOP 6
S. dispute, and the case HORACE 104
scholarship: foolery of s. for s.'s sake HUX:A 38
school:
at their first secondary s. LYNNE 1
be a theme at s. JUV 21
erecting a grammar s. SHAK:HEN.VI[2] 11
grammar s. of courtesies YEATS 38
he had been to night s. ADE 1
like snail Unwillingly to s. SHAK:AS 34
S. is pretty bad WAUGH:E 3
she has been late for s. THOMAS:D 26
toward s. with heavy looks SHAK:ROM 17
vicious till he's been to a good s. SAKI 10
was whipt at s. DRYD 80
school-days: Thy s. frightful SHAK:RIC.III 14
schoolboy:
A s.'s tale BYR 62
I see a s. YEATS 53
Not the s. heat TENNY 178
s. rallies the ranks NEWBOLT 11
whining school-boy, with his satchel SHAK:AS 34
schoolboys: s. that educate my son EMER 85
schoolgirl:
Pert as a s. GILB:WS 67
priggish s., captain of the hockey ALTRIN 1
schoolgirls: s. hastening through the light NEIL 1
schoolmaster:
expect you'll be becoming a s. WAUGH:E 2
I pay the s. EMER 85
s. is abroad BROUGHAM 1
schoolmastering: perish than to continue s. CARLYLE:T 65
schoolmasters:
Let school-masters puzzle GOLDS 36
s. Deliver us to laws HERB:G 20
s. must temper discretion WAUGH:E 4
schoolroom: in the s. more than ANTH 3
schools:
bewilder'd in the maze of s. POPE 7
death of the grammar s. PARS 2
hundred s. of thought contend MAO 2
jargon o' your s. BURNS:R 17
lernis ouir mekle at the sculis LIND:D 3
lumber of the s. SWIFT 51
We class s. WAUGH:E 3
schulin': Gie him the s. BURNS:R 58
sciatica: S.: he cured it AUBREY 5
science:
about s. but I know what I like AMIS:M 1
Cometh al this newe s. CHAUC 100
destiny of s. to exterminate PEAC 12
dismal s. CARLYLE:T 54
Fair S. frown'd not GRAY:T 26
force s. down the throats PORTER:G 1
great step in experimental s. BRIDIE 4
great tragedy of S. HUX:TH 3
In everything that relates to s. LAMB:Ch 11
In s., read ... the newest works BULWER 5
in the countenance of all s. WORDS:W 167
Language is only the instrument of s. JOHNSON:S 6
never that s. was the only career JOLIOT 1
only applications of s. PASTEUR 2
S. appears but, what WORDS:W 151
s. But an exchange of BYR 125
S. falsely so called BIBLE 551
s. has become terrible DURREN 3
S. has nothing to be ashamed of BRONO 6
s. is essentially international CURIE 1
S. is for those who learn ROUX 1
S. is his forte SMITH:Syd[1] 33
S. is really in the business SUZ:D 1
s. is so long to learn HIPP 1
S. may be described POPP 7
S. moves, but slowly TENNY 81
S. must begin with myths POPP 8
s. reassures BRAQ 1
S. struck the thrones SHELLEY:PB 76
S. the principal thing in my son's ARNOLD:T 3
s. to take an interest in the administration RUTH 3
S. without religion EINS 4
term S. should only be given VALERY 2
That is the essence of s. BRONO 4
to patient S. dear WORDS:W 132
when s. is strong and religion SZASZ 4
Why does ... s. ... bring us so little happiness? EINS 12
With the fairy tales of s. TENNY 69
science fiction:
guy in a s.f. movie who is the first FRYE:D 1
S.f. is no more written for scientists ALDISS 1
sciences:
art like all other s. WEDGEWOOD 1
Books must follow s. BACON:F[1] 17
in s. untaught BYR 123
no applied s. PASTEUR 2
S. aspire to the condition of mathematics SANT 12
That great mother of s. BACON:F[1] 22
scientific:
as if they were s. terms ARNOLD:M 73
broken open on the most s. PEAC 11
educated literary and s. opinion ARNOLD:M 58
S. discovery is a private event MEDA 1
s. faith's absurd BROWNING:R 68
socialism in terms of the s. revolution WILSON:Harold 4
Traditional s. method had PIR 2
where we do our s. work NEED:J 1
scientist: s. states that something is possible CLARKE:AC 1
scientists:
and statesmen, but the s. AUD 64
Curse the s., and all science COOK:J 2
in the company of s., I feel AUD 65
incredulity at the illiteracy of s. SNOW 2
s. who stir the embers LEVIN 3
scintillations: Let the s. of your wit GOUL 1
scissor-man: long, red-legged s. HOFFMAN:H 9
scoff:
came to s., remained GOLDS 27
some that came to s. AYT 2
scoffer: dull product of a s.'s pen WORDS:W 114
scones: buttered s. and crumpets ELIOT:TS 20
'Sconset: our Atlantic wall Off 'S. LOWELL:R 1
score:
just s. more points MOURIE 1
women know the s. WODDIS 1
scorer: when the One Great S. comes RICE:G 1
scorn:
deal of s. looks beautiful SHAK:TWE 41
figure for the time of s. SHAK:OTH 52
little s. is alluring CONG 46
nothingness of s. and noise CLARE:J 8
sound Of public s. MILT 253
scorned:
like a woman scorn'd CONG 34
s. the love she bought me MOORE:T 15
scornful: bitter is a s. jest JOHNSON:S 63
scorpion:
s. in his neighbour's underwear SIMPSON:NF 1
s. on a stone PLOM 3
scorpions: chastise you with s. BIBLE 161
Scot:
Had Cain been S. CLEVE:J 1
Hauf a soul a S. maun use MACDIAR 13
Trust your no Skott BOORDE 1
scot-free: You will get off s. HORACE 70
Scotch:
credit it to them to be S. MAUGH 21
indeed inferior to the S. NORTH:C 2
into a S. understanding SMITH:Syd[1] 17
S. may be compared to a tulip GOLDS 76
Scotchman:
considering that he is a S. HIGIN 1
Much may be made of a S. JOHNSON:S 157
noblest prospect which a S. ever JOHNSON:S 114
one S. but what was a man of sense LOCKIER 1
what it is that makes a S. happy JOHNSON:S 83
Scotchmen: all my life to like S. LAMB:Ch 10
Scotia: S.'s grandeur springs BURNS:R 14
Scotland:
As if it felt with S. SHAK:MAC 90
for poor auld S.'s sake BURNS:R 60
I do indeed come from S. JOHNSON:S 106
I'll be in S. afore ye ANON 36
in S. supports the people JOHNSON:S 14
knuckle-end of England* SMITH:Syd[1] 18
land of Calvin, oat-cakes* SMITH:Syd[1] 18
lay the scene in S. five hundred HAZL 28
second grandest city in S. MCGON 1
Seeing S., Madam, is only JOHNSON:S 199
shiver'd was fair S.'s spear SCOTT:W 33
Stands S. where it did? SHAK:MAC 95
Succour S., and remede WYNT 1
swordless S., sadder than LINK 3
wad ha'e S. to my eye MACDIAR 10
We left fair S.'s strand BURNS:R 111
Scots:
blow the S. back again FAWK 2
lots and lots against the S. EWART 3
nothing the S. like better PICCO 1
S. lords at his feet BALL 51
S. mist will weet an Englishman RAMS 4
S. to have attained the liberal JOHNSON:S 39
S., wha hae BURNS:R 107
seven dozen of S. at a breakfast SHAK:HEN.IV[1] 35
that all S. are illegitimate MUIR:E 8
they're never charming* EWART 3
Scotsman:
moral attribute of a S. BARRIE 11
S. on the make BARRIE 12
S. with a grievance and a ray WODE 19
With a S. or a priest, don't begin PROV 433
Scott: wrong part wrote S. ANON 112
Scott, Walter:
He writes as fast* HAZL 25
His works (taken together)* HAZL 27
His worst is better* HAZL 26
Sir Walter would make a bad* HAZL 28
scotticism: a palpable S. NORTH:C 6
Scottish:
dysposicion of a Scottysh man BOORDE 2
Lutherans are like S. people KEIL 1
S. poet maun assume MACDIAR 15
scoundrel:
given them to such a s. SWIFT 78
last refuge of a s. JOHNSON:S 169
scoured: s. to nothing with perpetual SHAK:HEN.IV[2] 16
scourge: S. of God, must die MARLOWE 17
scowl:
s. on gentle Richard SHAK:RIC.II 42
six-and-a-half-foot-tall s. STRAV 3
scratch:
all you can do is *s.* TOSC 4
does not have any real s. RUNYON 2
S. an actor PARKER:D 36
S. my back and I'll s. PROV 339
S. the Christian and you ZANG 1
scratches: When Ah itchez, Ah scratchez NASH 12
scratching: but the s. of a pen LOVER 1
scream:
an' thcream till I'm thick CROMP 1
brazen s. distracts DWO 4
like a s. from a crevasse GREENE:G 9
screaming: I am s. out loud DICKENS 75
screech: song that was more of a s. SHELLEY:PB 20
screen:
darkest spot ... is a small luminous s. DEBR 1
wide s. just makes a bad film GORKY 21
screenwriter: behind every successful s. MARX:G 29
scribble: Always s., s., s., GLOU:W 1
scribbles: think something of my s. CATUL 1
scribblings: strange s. of nature CLARKE:M 1
scrip: with s. and scrippage SHAK:AS 40
scripture:
devil can cite S. SHAK:MERC 16
I will better it in S. OVER 2
passages in S. which trouble me TWAIN 39
scriptures:
holy S. to be written PRAY 43
Let us look at the S. SELD 1
S. principally teach CATEC 2
scroll:
charged with punishments the s. HENL 2
long-cramped s. BROWNING:R 130
scrotumtightening: s. sea JOYCE:J 11
scrub: s. has a charm of its own FURP 2
scruples: He without benefit of s. NASH 15
scrupulosity: washed himself with oriental s.

JOHNSON:S 58
scrutiny: S. . . . can be just as efficient ELIZ II 2
sculptor: last refuge of the s. PLOM 11
scum:
mere s. of the earth WELLING 11
rich are the s. of the earth CHESTERTON 49
scunner: love Wi' a s. in't MACDIAR 19
Scylla:
S. and Charybdis of anarchy SHELLEY:PB 166
S. and Charybdis of Aye and No NEWM:JH 11
scythe:
bate his s.'s keen edge SHAK:LOV 1
poor crooked s. and spade SHIRL 3
Scythian: whitest snow on S. Hills MARLOWE 2
sea:
all at last return to the s. CARSON 1
all the s. were ink ANON 71
all the s. were ink LYLY 8
Alone on a wide, wide s. COLERIDGE:ST 24
Alone on a wide wide s. COLERIDGE:ST 37
bathed in the Poem Of the S. RIMB 1
beneath in the abysmal s. TENNY 1
crown'd with summer s. TENNY 279
died as he lived – at s. ANON 193
dominion of the s. COV 1
Down to a sunless s. COLERIDGE:ST 63
down to the s. in ships BIBLE 234
espouse the everlasting S. WORDS:W 76
far over the summer s. TENNY 283
flood of the s. of bliss WAG 1
fools and passengers drink at s. VILLIERS 1
frail boat to the cruel s. HORACE 4
frozen s. within us KAF 13
gaping wretches of the s. HUNT:L 3
goes to s. for nothing but DONNE 17
great fishpond (the s.) DEK 4
great s. Has set me adrift UVA 2
gurly grew the s. BALL 14
home from the s. STEVENSON:RL 61
if Ye take away the s. KIP 70
image of eternity* BYR 119
In a solitude of the s. HARDY:T 21
in the s. of life enisled ARNOLD:M 16
Into that silent s. COLERIDGE:ST 18
jollyrodgered s. THOMAS:D 22
kings of the s. ARNOLD:M 2
Learn the secret of the s.? LONGFEL 40
let nae the s. come in BALL 49
life's wild restless s. ALEX:CF 3
lonely s. and the sky MASE 1
lover of men, the s. SWIN 44
magic of the s. LONGFEL 25
man who is not afraid of the s. SYNGE 5
mirrors of the s. are strewn FLECKER 7
moving s. between the shores GIBRAN 3
never go to s. GILB:WS 14
never sick at s. GILB:WS 8
not having been at s. JOHNSON:S 200
of a sudden came the s. BROWNING:R 62
Our heritage the s. CUNNING:A 5
Out of the s. came he COLERIDGE:ST 12
plants his footsteps in the s. COWP 12
ride slowly towards the s. CHESTERTON 25
salt, estranging s. ARNOLD:M 17
s. gave up the dead BIBLE 583
s. grew civil at her song SHAK:MID 17
s. is all about us ELIOT:TS 102
s. is calm to-night ARNOLD:M 46
s. is his BIBLE 229
s. mock'd them SHAK:WIN 10
S. of Faith ARNOLD:M 47
s. rendered inaccessible BOSSU 1
S. shall give up her dead PRAY 95
s. was made his tomb BARNF 2
serpent-haunted s. FLECKER 4
settle somewhere near the s.? KIP 154
sheet and a flowing s. CUNNING:A 4
sight of that immortal s. WORDS:W 65
snotgreen s. JOYCE:J 11
sound is the sound of the s. ELIOT:TS 69
spouts out a S. MILT 227
swaying sound of the s. AUD 12
that gong-tormented s. YEATS 87
The s.! The s. XENOPHON 1
there was no more s. BIB:REV 13
they can see nothing but s. BACON:F[1] 9
They went to s. in a sieve LEAR 14
those in peril on the s. WHITING 1
thousand furlongs of s. for SHAK:TEM 3
to throw water into the s. CERV 8
touch of the s. is sensuous CHOP 1
triumphant s. Whose rocky SHAK:RIC.II 17
union with its native s. WORDS:W 117
voice of the s. speaks CHOP 1
wan grassy s. SITWELL:E 5
We saw the s. BERLIN:Ir 1
went by s. when I might CATO 2
what comes over the s. CURNOW 1
what it says . . . The s. DICKENS 129
where men and s. interpenetrate CONRAD 7
white horses of the winter s. GLOVER 2
why the s. is boiling hot CARROLL 56
wife ingenrit of the s. BOYD:MA 1
Winds somewhere safe to s. SWIN 31
wine-dark s. HOMER 4
Within a walk of the s. BELLOC 31
world's tempestuous s. EDMES 1
sea-beasts: s. ranged all round ARNOLD:M 1
sea-change: suffer a s. SHAK:TEM 11
sea-daisies: s. feast on the sun SWIN 42
sea-flower: s. moulded by the sea SWIN 50
sea-life: When men come to like a s.
JOHNSON:S 176
sea-sand:
As is the ribbed s. COLERIDGE:ST 23
name upon The soft s. LANDOR 12
sea-shore: boy playing on the s. NEWT:I 5
sea sickness: it's as universal as s.s. SHAW 42
sea-side: lord on yon s. BALL 35
sea-tides: s. tossing free LONGFEL 25
sea-worm: s. crawls – grotesque HARDY:T 21
sea-worms: Battening upon huge seaworms
TENNY 2
seabirds: when I throw rocks at s. NASH 22
seafogs: s. lap and cling KIP 109
seagull: remember when you shot a s.? CHEK 4
seagulls: When the s. follow the trawler CANT 1
seal:
opened the seventh s. BIBLE 581
s. with a righteous kiss SHAK:ROM 44
you heard a s. bark THURB 14
sealing wax: shoes – and ships – and s.w.
CARROLL 56
seals:
loose the s. thereof? BIBLE 579
s. must live as long LOWELL:R 8
S. of love SHAK:MEA 30
seam: And sew a fine s. NURS 8
seaman: s. to be an officer NELS 9
seamen: s. were not gentlemen
MACAULAY:TB 34
search:
I do not s.; I find PICAS 8
s. will find it out HERR 43
they are not worth the s. SHAK:MERC 8
searching:
by s. find out God? BIBLE 186
I am s. everywhere STEPHENS 6
still s. what we know not MILT 316
seas:
Beyond the blue, the purple s.
TURNER:WJR 1
bluest of s., which broke its
RICHARDSON:HH 1
dangers of the s. PARKER:M 2
foam Of perilous s. KEATS 93
hushed the shrunken s. ELIOT:TS 29
multitudinous s. incarnadine SHAK:MAC 45
must go down to the s. again MASE 1
s. but join the regions POPE 35
s. colder than the Hebrides FLECKER 6
s. do laugh WEBSTER:J 16
s. of life, like wine TRAH 5
snarled and yelping s. ELIOT:TS 27
there gloom the dark broad s. TENNY 55
through friendly s. they FLECKER 9
walks again on the S. of Blood SITWELL:E 9
season:
by s. season'd are SHAK:MERC 53
Compels me to disturb your s. MILT 42
each thing that in s. grows SHAK:LOV 2
ghastly s. it's been for you Spanish BANK 6
in the s. of the year ANON 33
it is but for a s. HOUSM 25
little s. of love and laughter GORDON:AM 2
no s. knows, nor clime DONNE 60
Only in the mating s. MILLIG 3
s. made for joys GAY 22
S. of mists and mellow KEATS 109
To every thing there is a s. BIBLE 281
seasons:
all s. shall be sweet COLERIDGE:ST 9
for S.; not Eternities MERED:G 20
four s. in the mind KEATS 27
in vain the envious s. roll HOLMES:OW 9
interested in the changing s. SANT 6
man for all s. WHITTING 1
those vernal s. of the yeer MILT 311
we see The s. alter SHAK:MID 16
seat:
he remained in the driver's s. BEAV 4
I'd have a private S. POMF 1
Not a s. but a springboard CHURCH:W 30
offering my s. to three ladies CHESTERTON 60
S. of pleasure DRYD 101
s. Where love is thron'd SHAK:TWE 25
seat belts: Fasten your s.b. DAVIS:B 1
seclusion: place of s. and solitude
MONTAIGNE 9
second:
everybody allows the s. place SWIFT 3
On s. thoughts, they knew exactly GLASH 1
round the grounds for a s. time? PEAC 2
than s. in Rome CAES:GJ 6
second-hand:
buy a s. car from this man? SAHL 2
s. bookshop is the sign MURD:WLF 1
second-rate:
creed of a s. man BAGE 2
s. people who share its luck HORNE:DR 1
that poets should be second rate HORACE 115
secrecy:
for s., No lady closer SHAK:HEN.IV[1] 34
nature's infinite book of s. SHAK:ANT 4
S. the Human Dress BLAKE:W 121
secret:
At last the s. is out AUD 24
discovered the s. of life CREWE 1
honour than s. wickedness CERV 20
I know that's a s. CONG 26
Learn the s. of the sea? LONGFEL 40
s. in the Oxford sense FRANKS 1
s. is a weapon and a friend STEPHENS 3
S. sits in the middle FROST:R 14
There is always a wicked s. AUD 25
Three may keep a s. FRANKLIN:B 6
trusted a woman with a s. CATO 2
when it ceases to be a s. BEHN 5
secretaries: can't run an office without the s.
FONDA 1
secretary:
great S. of Nature WALT 17
word processor if he has an efficient s.
DAVIES:R 7
secrets:
from whom no s. are hid PRAY 63
s. are edged tools DRYD 8
s. of th' Abyss to spy GRAY:T 35
S. with girls CRAB 25
something that elicits s. SEN 4
tell the s. of my prison-house SHAK:HAM 42
sect:
It found them a s. MACAULAY:TB 32
loving his own s. COLERIDGE:ST 81
of no s. am I HORACE 74
paradise for a s. KEATS 99
serious, sad-coloured s. HOOD 31
Slave to no s. POPE 106
sects:
arise diversitie of s. SPENS 5
Founders of s. and systems BYR 86
Two-and-Seventy jarring S. FITZGER:E 22
secure:
s. amidst a falling world ADDIS 38
where a man can feel really s. GREER 1
securities: sooner trust to two s.
CHESTERFIELD 24
security:
freedom can make s. secure POPP 4
Its business was s. HAGG:W 1
S. Is mortals' chiefest SHAK:MAC 77
watchword is s. PITT:W[1] 13
sedan-chair: in a flood of tears and a s.
DICKENS 42
sedative: *s.* of lust CHILEBI 1
sedge: s. has wither'd from KEATS 79
seduce: did not s., she ravished MERED:G 11

seducer: strong s., opportunity DRYD 17
seduces: When a man s. a woman WOLLST 7
seduction:
delusive s. of martial music BURNEY 8
In s., the rapist often bothers DWO 5
see:
All I can s. is my own BATMAN 1
can't s. what he sees in her HERB:AP 8
did not s., or would not BYR 166
I could not s. to s. DICKIN:E 7
I do not ask to s. NEWM:JH 15
I s., not feel, how beautiful COLERIDGE:ST 54
I'll s. you again COWARD 18
I'm damned if I s. it NEWBOLT 2
no man s. me, and live BIBLE 110
out of place you s. it better PICAS 3
rather s. than be one BURGESS:G 1
se, and eek for to CHAUC 81
s. beyond our bourn KEATS 26
s., but you do not observe DOYLE:AC 18
s. further than his own nose FONTAINE 17
s. into the life of things WORDS:W 6
s. not what they s.? SHAK:SON 58
s. oursels as ithers s. us BURNS:R 52
s. the things thou dost not SHAK:KING L 73
s. thee in my touch SHAK:KING L 57
s. things which are underground CERV 6
s. thro' all things POPE 51
s. what is in front of one's nose ORWELL 23
s. with, not thro the Eye BLAKE:W 108
them they'll s. nae mair BALL 51
think till I s. what I say? WALLAS 1
To s. and be seen DRYD 79
To s. her is to love her BURNS:R 88
to s. her was to love her BURNS:R 93
to s. it like it is NIX 2
see-saw:
His wit all s. POPE 127
S., Margery Daw NURS 64
seed:
blood of Christians is the s. TERT 3
good s. on the land CAMPBELL:Ja 1
In s. time learn BLAKE:W 34
s. o' a' the men that in MACDIAR 9
s. of ruin in himself ARNOLD:M 39
s. ye sow, another reaps SHELLEY:PB 52
shapeless s. I hold WRIGHT:J 7
spills his s. on the ground PARKER:D 34
seeds: look into the s. of time SHAK:MAC 9
seedtime:
Fair seed-time had my soul WORDS:W 143
Ought I to regret my s.? LOWELL:R 5
s. and harvest BIBLE 40
seeing:
one way of *s.* them RUSKIN 10
S. is believing PROV 341
s. what everybody has seen SZENT 1
Thinking is s. BALZ 5
seek:
early will I s. thee BIBLE 218
s., and ye shall find BIBLE 400
s. it, ere it come to light COWP 87
S. ye the Lord while BIBLE 330
To strive, to s., to find TENNY 55
We s. him here, we s. him ORCZY 1
seekest: s. thou great things BIBLE 342
seeks: What the superior man s. CONF 11
seem:
between what I s. and what HAWT 2
Men should be that they s. SHAK:OTH 33
not always what they s. PROV 387
not what they s. LONGFEL 1
things, that onely seeme SPENS 46
seemed: all s., but were not all MILT 219
seeming:
these keep S. and savour SHAK:WIN 16
thing I am by s. otherwise SHAK:OTH 20
seems: I know not s. SHAK:HAM 18
seen:
be s. to be done HEWART 1
come that they may be s. OSB:J 3
must be s. to be done OSB:J 11
not s., and yet have believed BIBLE 494
T' have s. what I have s. SHAK:HAM 104
things a' didn't wish s. HARDY:T 61
things which I have s. I now WORDS:W 52
You ain't s. nothing yet REAG 8
sees:
not everyone s. it CONF 25
that Which s. is truly seen SNY 1
seidlitz: drinking a s. powder ANON 134
Seine: Today I spat in the S. PATTON 1
seldom: s., if ever done COWARD 21
select: should s. Out of the crowd SHELLEY:PB 130
selection: Natural S. DARW:C 1
self:
affirmation of the right of s. KEY:E 1
All by my own-alone s. HARRIS:JC 15
Best Image of my s. MILT 209
concentred all in s. SCOTT:W 11
greater than one's s. is WHITMAN 10
improving, and that's your own s. HUX:A 37
inexorable as one's s. HAWT 4
it has no s. KEATS 147
Loneliness is the poverty of s. SARTON 1
mask of some other s. YEATS 137
never to think of one's s. CLOUGH 23
sad s. hereafter kind HOPK:GM 25
seeketh only S. to please BLAKE:W 64
S. is hateful PASC 14
She likes her s. CONG 60
to thine own s. be true SHAK:HAM 30
Vile s. gets in BURNS:R 20
self-centred: Writers are too s. CONDON 1
self-consciousness: certain inarticulate S. CARLYLE:T 11
self-control: struggle to keep s. YEATS 134
self-denial: S. is not a virtue SHAW 60
self-destructive: ultimately s. intrigue WHITE:P 10
self-esteem: profits more Than s. MILT 237
self-expression: being void of s. KIP 125
self-indulgence:
favourite form of s. MAUGH 7
write an essay on 's.' WAUGH:E 8
self-interest:
heedless s. was bad morals ROOS:FD 6
S. speaks every kind LA ROCHE 7
self-love:
deceiving mirror of s. MASSIN 4
golden-calf of S. CARLYLE:T 28
S. and Social be the same POPE 100
S. is the greatest flatterer LA ROCHE 3
S. seems so often unrequited POWELL:A 1
Sin of s. possesseth SHAK:SON 25
you are sick of s. SHAK:TWE 11
self-lovers: nature of extreme s. BACON:F[1] 122
self-made:
He is a s. man, and worships BRIGHT 6
s. man is one who STEAD 1
s. man who owed his lack HELLER 1
self-praise: S. is no recommendation PROV 343
self-protection: their number, is s. MILL 7
self-realization: s. cannot be the supreme RUSS:B 18
self-reliant: S. like the cat MOORE:M 5
self-reproach: not abolish, of bitter s. DEQ 6
self-respect: cannot pay the price of s. WILSON:W 9
self-revelation: terrible *fluidity* of s. JAMES:H 13
self-righteousness: S. is not religion BRONTE:C 3
self-sufficiency:
ground maintained its man* GOLDS 21
limit of virtual s. ARISTOT 12
self-sufficient: need to because he is s. ARISTOT 15
selfish:
s. being all my life AUSTEN 28
sensible people are s. EMER 55
What a s. woman CHURCH:JJ 1
sell:
is no good: I'll s. him LEACOCK 5
Pile it high, s. it cheap COHEN 1
selling:
buying and the s., and the strife BUCHANAN 4
Everyone lives by s. STEVENSON:RL 40
selves: their sweating s. HOPK:GM 28
semblance: outward s. of a man DICKENS 35
semi-colon: better a s. than a full stop MCAULEY 4
semicolon: doesn't know how to use a s. CONRAN 3
seminary: Come from a ladies' s. GILB:WS 68
senate:
his little s. laws POPE 30
in the s. loud CHURCH:C 5
senates: listening s. hang upon THOMS:Ja[1] 7
senators:
green-rob'd s. of mighty woods KEATS 48
look at the s. and I pray HALE:EE 1
s. burst with laughter AUD 10
send:
Here I am; s. me BIBLE 306
S. me nor this DONNE 64
whom shall we s. MILT 160
Seneca: S. cannot be too heavy SHAK:HAM 84
seniors: teach you to speak to your s. CLARK:K 1
sensation: first s. on entering a wood EMER 87
sensational: something s. to read in the train WILDE:O 93
sensations: S. rather than of Thoughts KEATS 121
sense:
Batteries of alluring S. MARV 9
Between good s. and good taste LA BRU 10
but their s. is shut SHAK:MAC 99
cultivate the emotional s. HEYS 1
Devoid of s. and motion? MILT 153
echo to the s. POPE 20
endowed us with s., reason and GALI 2
for it is not s. CHURCH:C 20
good s. unless they agree LA ROCHE 30
it must be good s. COLERIDGE:ST 87
Let no night Seal thy s. DE LA M 20
men of s. approve POPE 22
men of s. never tell it SHAFT 1
mind swings between s. and nonsense JUNG:Carl 3
never deviates into s. DRYD 63
no substitute for s. ELIOT:TS 32
perpetual fountain of good s. DRYD 146
Scotchman but what was a man of s. LOCKIER 1
s. always should agree with rhyme BOIL 4
s. beneath is rarely found POPE 15
s. faints picturing them SHELLEY:PB 42
s. is with their senses MERED:G 27
stings and motions of the s. SHAK:MEA 4
Take care of the s. CARROLL 25
woman had a bottom of good s. JOHNSON:S 222
senseless: worse than s. things SHAK:JUL 2
senses: Oot o' the way, my s. five MACDIAR 1
sensibility:
Dear s. STERNE 53
dissociation of s. set in ELIOT:TS 118
sensible: S. men never tell DISR:B 45
sensitive:
s. being WORDS:W 162
s. one is to great art BEERB 13
sensual:
ascetic rocks and the s. whirlpools MERED:G 13
only s. pleasure without vice JOHNSON:S 264
sensualists: s. without heart WEBER 1
sensuality: face of s., rebellion THOMAS:G 2
sent: say I s. thee thither SHAK:HEN.VI[3] 9
sentence:
in any way accept, the s. PANK:E 3
It ends an age-long s. MCLUH 15
mouths a s., as curs CHURCH:C 8
My s. is for op'n warr MILT 151
S. first – verdict afterwards CARROLL 41
structure of the normal British s. CHURCH:W 43
sentences:
backward ran s. GIBBS 1
Don't keep finishing your s. LONS 1
lays s. like eggs CANET 3
sentiment:
corrupted by s. GREENE:G 6
read him for the s. JOHNSON:S 156
S. was the more dangerous GREENE:G 6
sentimental: no s. melancholy in him KINGSLEY:C 10
sentimentalist: of all mortals is the s. CARLYLE:T 33
sentimentality:
S. is a superstructure covering JUNG:Carl 7
S. is only sentiment that rubs MAUGH 20
sentiments:
high s. always win ORWELL 14
quiet interchange of s. JOHNSON:S 173
s. that no legislature can manufacture BAGE 6
Them's my s. THACK 6

sentinel:
scarce worth the s. GOLDS 51
s. stars set their watch CAMPBELL:T 23
sentry: Where stands a winged S. VAUGHAN:H 4
separate: s. us from the love of God BIBLE 514
separated: joined that they cannot be s. SMITH:Syd[1] 28
separation:
causes which impel them to the s. JEFFERSON 1
preludes to that eternal s. STERNE 38
prepare for a s. QUINCY 1
s. gives a foretaste of death SCHOP 7
s. to have killed him DARLING:CJ 1
Septuagint: S. minus the Apostles VERR 1
sepulchre:
earth is the s. of famous men PERIC 4
living s. of life CLARE:J 7
s. there by the sea POE 9
sera: Che s., s. MARLOWE 32
seraphim: bright S. in burning row MILT 64
seraphs: where S. might despair BYR 56
serene: mind s. for contemplation GAY 50
serenity: s. to accept the things NIEB 2
serf:
eager to be s. FITZGER:FS 6
surly patience of the s. CAMPBELL:R 3
sergeant:
blustering s. with the big bust GREENE:G 8
Cheer for the S.'s weddin' KIP 87
This fell s. Death SHAK:HAM 197
serious:
much more s. than that SHANK 1
they are too s. STERNE 50
You cannot be s. MCEN 2
seriously:
Everything must be taken s. THIERS 1
insane take themselves quite s. BEERB 22
seriousness: high s. of the great classics ARNOLD:M 80
sermon:
honest and painful s. PEPYS 6
it will suit any s. STERNE 29
Perhaps, turn out a s. BURNS:R 44
who a s. flies HERB:G 1
sermons:
found in stones the s. WILDE:O 6
S. and soda-water the day after BYR 178
S. in stones SHAK:AS 12
seven years I burn all my s. WESLEY:J 4
serpent:
But be the s. under't SHAK:MAC 21
gold and flowing s. LAWR:DH 20
infernal S.; hee it was MILT 109
s. beguiled me BIBLE 21
s. smile BYR 121
S. suttl'st beast MILT 240
s. was more subtil than any BIBLE 16
sharper than a s.'s tooth DICKENS 227
Where's my s. of old Nile? SHAK:ANT 21
serpents:
coiled obscene Small s. SWIN 2
ye therefore wise as s. BIB:MATT 34
servant:
cracked lookingglass of a s. JOYCE:J 12
good and faithful s. ANON 143
good and faithful s. BIBLE 430
good s. does not all commands SHAK:CYM 18
obligation to become the s. of a man SHAW 97
s. to be bred at an University CONG 31
s.'s too often a negligent BARH 2
thy s. depart in peace BIBLE 609
thy s. heareth BIBLE 140
women as a s. class PANK:E 4
Your s.'s cut in half GRAHAM:H 3
servants:
both good s., both ill GREV 3
good s., but bad masters L'EST 1
great place are thrice s. BACON:F[1] 73
have been admired by their s. MONTAIGNE 20
Live? The s. will do that VILLIERS DE 1
prefer hiring their s. for life CARLYLE:T 70
When domestic s. are treated SHAW 57
servant's hall: never be equality in the s.h. BARRIE 5
serve:
also s. who only stand MILT 100
be willing faithfully to s. CROMWELL 5
die but once to s. ADDIS 8
Freely we s. MILT 216
let me not s. so DONNE 5
No man can s. two masters BIBLE 394
opportunity to s. our country SMITH:John 1
Or s. and lose GOET 4
s. for meat and fee BALL 28
s. the Lord with gladness BIBLE 600
s. Thee as Thou deservest LOY 1
s. thee with a quiet mind PRAY 57
S. up in a clean dish LEAR 35
than s. in Heav'n MILT 123
to s. my king and country NELS 11
will not s. if elected SHERMAN 2
served:
being s. up for my guests GREG:Lady 3
but s. God as diligently WOLSEY 2
serves: profits most who s. best SHELD 1
service:
All s. ranks the same BROWNING:R 13
Ful weel she soong the s. CHAUC 9
He's out on active s. KIP 97
It did me yeoman's s. SHAK:HAM 192
make the s. greater than SHAK:TRO 8
places the nation at his s. POMPI 1
played the Fool in her S. STEELE 2
shrink from the s. of their country PAINE 3
small s. is true s. WORDS:W 138
Weary and old with s. SHAK:HEN.VIII 10
When s. sweat for duty SHAK:AS 18
whose s. is perfect freedom PRAY 22
serviettes: kiddies have crumpled the s. BETJ 26
servile: easie yoke Of servil Pomp MILT 156
servility: s. of mankind towards MILL 6
serving-man: s., proud in heart SHAK:KING L 44
serving-men: I keep six honest s. KIP 105
servitors: nimble and airy s. MILT 307
servitude: laws of s. began DRYD 12
sesquipedalian: S. blackguard CLOUGH 2
setter: s. up and puller down SHAK:HEN.VI[3] 5
settled:
People wish to be s. EMER 25
place that is not yet safely s. OND 1
Thank God, that's s. SHERIDAN:RB 43
that cannot be honourably s. BRAM 2
Until it is s. right WILCOX 2
settlement: Revolution a parent of s. BURKE:E 52
seven:
deadly s. it is the least SHAK:MEA 23
s. fat kine BIBLE 71
s. good ears BIBLE 72
we are s. WORDS:W 22
Seven Dials: lowly air Of S.D. GILB:WS 46
sevens: doing things in s. MURRAY:G 1
seventeen: S. and never been sweet THOMAS:D 35
seventies:
I'm living in the s. SKY 1
man gets well into the s. STEVENSON:RL 21
seventy:
Being s. is not a sin MEIR 3
delight in men over s. WILDE:O 68
Oh, to be s. again HOLMES:OW JR 3
To be s. years young HOLMES:OW 17
sever:
how soon we must s.? CRAW 1
nothing in life shall s. CORY 4
To s. for years BYR 54
severance: God their s. ruled ARNOLD:M 17
severe: man s. he was GOLDS 28
severity:
S. breedeth fear BACON:F[1] 74
set in with its usual s. COLERIDGE:ST 99
Severn:
out to S. strode CHESTERTON 7
thick on S. snow the leaves HOUSM 20
twice a day the S. fills TENNY 137
Seville: bang these dogs of S. TENNY 282
sew: time to s. BIBLE 281
sewage: s. has probably kept CLAYTON 1
sewer:
into an open s. and die BROOKS:M 2
Life is like a s. LEHRER 1
to keep this place a s. CACC 1
sewers: S. annoy the Aire MILT 244
sewing: Ah, Bottomley, s.? BOTT:HW 1
sewing-basket: s. after half a dozen kittens RAD 1
sex:
As we make s. less secretive SZASZ 2
Can either S. assume MILT 127
condition of our s. is so deplorable PANK:E 1
Continental people have s. life MIKES 2
difference of s., if there is any ANTH 3
disgrace to their Whole S. CLARK:R 1
dislike a s. to which Your Majesty RHODES 3
epitome of her s. BYR 245
fair s. is your department DOYLE:AC 28
farmyard world of s. GRANVILLE-B 2
for men, s. is power FAUST 3
formed for the ruin of our s. SMOL 2
How wonderful s. can be LAWR:DH 17
I haven't had enough s. BETJ 40
if there was a third s. VAIL 1
Is s. dirty? ALLEN:W 3
It was the most fun I ever had* ALLEN:W 12
Know About S., But Were Afraid REUB 1
legal subordination of one s. MILL 28
Like sunshine through* LAWR:DH 17
Literature is mostly about having s. LODGE:D 1
Love is friendship plus s. ELLIS:H 9
meant us to have group s. BRADB 7
Money . . . was exactly like s. BALD:J 1
more fundamental than s. DENNIS:N 2
never separated s. from feeling NIN 1
no greater fan of the opposite s. LERN 9
No s. without responsibility LONGFORD 1
no very high opinion of the s. BYR 248
Once people had s. BURCHI 2
pleasure is momentary* CHESTERFIELD 36
practically conceal its s. NASH 5
privilege I claim for my own s. AUSTEN 69
S. exists on both sides of the law DWO 3
S. is a human activity like any FAIRBAIRN:N 1
S. is between the ears NEWBOLD 1
S. is one of the nine reasons MILLER:H 1
S. is something I really don't understand SALIN 3
S. is woman's secret STEPHENS 3
s. isn't too bad either PINT 4
s., it's too boring DURRELL:L 4
s. novel is now normal SHAW 129
S. that is not an evidence DAVIES:R 4
S. . . . was meant to be short, nasty BURCHI 1
s., whatever it may consist in, must BLACKWELL 1
s. whose presence civilizes COWP 28
s. with someone I love ALLEN:W 11
soft, unhappy s. BEHN 9
still able to have s. SOPH 7
talk on 'S. and Civics' BETJ 29
weaker s. ALEX:W 1
women are a s. by themselves BEERB 2
Women complain about s. LANDERS 1
sex-war: In the s. thoughtlessness CONNOLLY:C 12
sexes:
absurd division into s. WAUGH:E 17
be no talk of the equality of the s. HUGHES:B 7
city of the cleanliness of the s. WHITMAN 20
more difference within the s. COMPT 10
old ladies of both s. DICKENS 189
three s. – men, women, and clergymen SMITH:Syd[1] 25
sexism:
Can anything be more absurd* KNOX:V 1
designated us as an *inferior gender class** DWO 1
I am obnoxious to each* BRADST 1
that one is the husband* BLACKS 6
To promote a Woman* KNOX:J 2
We are still the property* BARRE 1
sexton:
s. toll'd the bell HOOD 6
that bald s. Time SHAK:KING J 10
sexual:
S. pleasure seems to consist in ORTEGA G 2
throatily and palpitatingly s. HUX:A 10
women have always faced s. facts MACKEN 4
sexual act: s.a. is a comic operation MACKEN 8
sexual intercourse:
foolishest act a wise man commits* BROWNE:T 28
Intercourse as an act often expresses* DWO 2
tragedy of s.i. YEATS 147

shackles: garters to be bonds and s. BACON:F[1] 82
shade:
boundless contiguity of s. COWP 60
clutching the inviolable s. ARNOLD:M 29
crowd into a s. POPE 3
Dancing in the Chequer'd s. MILT 72
fleeting image of a s. SHELLEY:PB 103
he is old and she a s. LANDOR 8
in the s. of a big tree BRANC 1
not wish to put anyone in the s. BULOW 1
old sit under the s. on it DICKENS 133
S. more than man YEATS 86
s. which beechen boughs diffuse VIRGIL 1
sly s. of a Rural Dean BROOKE 9
sport with Amaryllis is the s. MILT 49
shades:
joy to go to the s. VIRGIL 63
s. whom we have held as foes BUTLER:S[2] 49
shadow:
beyond the s. of a dream KEATS 37
caves in which his s. will be NIET 15
Earth Be but the shaddow MILT 217
fair sunne, unhappy shadowe CAMPION 1
Falls the S. ELIOT:TS 58
feel myself the s. of a dream TENNY 102
Follow a s. JONS 35
future is the s. PROUST 5
Grasp at the s. and lose AESOP 1
grow not in each other's s. GIBRAN 5
Life itself is but the s. BROWNE:T 44
Like a vast s. mov'd VAUGHAN:H 14
mere s. of a mighty name LUCAN 2
S. cloak'd from head TENNY 139
s. is what we think LINC 22
s. of my likeness that goes WHITMAN 37
S. of Shadows YEATS 7
s. of some unseen Power SHELLEY:PB 12
Then falls thy s. DOWS 2
under the s. of a war SPEND 9
we are but dust and s. HORACE 55
shadow-show: nothing but a Magic S. FITZGER:E 23
shadowing: not to employ any depth of s. DRYD 141
shadowless: Stand s. like Silence HOOD 1
shadows:
am half sick of s. TENNY 18
Come like s. SHAK:MAC 85
coming events cast their s. CAMPBELL:T 21
Earth's s. fly SHELLEY:PB 126
Fills the s. and the windy places SWIN 9
From s. and types NEWM:JH 21
hills are s. TENNY 183
If we s. have offended SHAK:MID 53
In ancient s. and twilights RUSS:GW 1
in this kind are but s. SHAK:MID 49
Old sins cast long s. PROV 305
s. cast from the fire PLATO 11
s., not substantial things SHIRL 3
s. now so long do grow COTTON 1
S. of the evening BARING-G 1
s., that showed at noon LEE:N 2
Some s. of eternity VAUGHAN:H 6
Styl'd but the s. of us men? JONS 35
very s. of the clouds WORDS:W 38
Where the coolest s. sleep HARPUR 1
shadowy: with a s. third BROWNING:R 93
Shadrach: S., Meshach, and Abednego BIBLE 349
shady:
Silly and s. SITWELL:E 7
sunny place for s. people COWARD 37
shaft: many a s., at random sent SCOTT:W 52
Shafto: Bobby S.'s gone to sea NURS 3
shag: common cormorant or s. ISH 1
shag-eared: thou shag-ear'd villain SHAK:MAC 89
shake:
power to s. me as they pass WORDS:W 38
S. hands for ever DRAYT 9
this god did s. SHAK:JUL 9
Shake-scene: lonely S. in the country GREENE:R 2
shaken: So s. as we are SHAK:HEN.IV[1] 1
shakers: we are the movers and s. O'SHAUGH 1
Shakespeare:
Besides S. and me STEIN:G 5
Corneille is to S. JOHNSON:S 252
delicious, nourishing S. HALS:M 5
despise S. when I measure SHAW 74
England made S. HUGO 10
Far from the sun* GRAY:T 34
For there is an upstart Crow* GREENE:R 2
good enough for S.'s day VICT 10
He is of no age* COLERIDGE:ST 94
He is the very Janus* DRYD 139
He was a handsome, well-shaped* AUBREY 9
He was (indeed) honest* JONS 54
He was not of an age* JONS 43
He was the man who of all* DRYD 135
making up of a S. or a Milton COLERIDGE:ST 97
monument, without a tomb* JONS 39
myriad-minded S. COLERIDGE:ST 76
never has a man turned so little* ELIOT:TS 121
perhaps understand S. KEATS 130
Playing S. is very tiring HULL 1
quibble is to S. what JOHNSON:S 36
quote S. in an economic crisis PHILIP 8
S., and found it so intolerably dull DARW:C 8
S. and Milton are forgotten PORS 1
S. by flashes of lightning COLERIDGE:ST 83
S., I come DREIS 1
S. is charged with debts EMER 75
S. . . . is really very good GRAVES:R 10
S. led a life of Allegory KEATS 153
S. made use of it first SHERIDAN:RB 36
S. never had six lines together JOHNSON:S 139
S., on whose forehead climb BROWNING:EB 8
S., undoubtedly wanted taste WALP:H 7
S. unlocked his heart WORDS:W 133
S. wanted Art JONS 52
S. was not a whit more intelligible COLERIDGE:ST 94
S. (whom you and ev'ry) POPE 142
S. with the English man of war FULLER:T[1] 11
S.'s genius has been cultivated CHESTERFIELD 15
Soul of the Age* JONS 39
Sweet Swan of Avon* JONS 45
sweetest Shakespear, Fancy's childe MILT 74
talk of my being like S. SCOTT:W 97
To S. gave as much DRYD 131
was for gentle S. cut JONS 51
We all talk S. AUSTEN 35
What needs my Shakespear MILT 14
Whaur's yer Wully S. noo? ANON 261
When I read S. LAWR:DH 35
women especially owe to S. TERRY 1
Shakespearian:
S. way wherewith to take POWYS 1
that Shakespeherian Rag ELIOT:TS 42
shaking: all that by s. his head? SHERIDAN:RB 37
shall: His absolute 'shall'? SHAK:COR 9
shallow:
S. brookes murmur moste SIDNEY:P 2
s. draughts intoxicate the brain POPE 10
s. in himself MILT 275
s. streams run dimpling POPE 126
Shalott: Lady of S.? TENNY 14
shambles: civilization is founded on the s. JAMES:W 2
shame:
all a bleedin' s.? ANON 38
as if the s. would outlive him KAF 8
ashamed with the noble s. KINGSLEY:C 9
blush of s. WHITTIER 5
erring sister's s. BYR 27
live and s. the land HOUSM 46
now bound in with s. SHAK:RIC.II 17
secret House of S. WILDE:O 115
send them sorowe and s. SKEL:J 2
sense of some deathless s. WEBSTER:J 6
s. and grief go with her STERNE 55
S. is Pride's cloke BLAKE:W 40
s. nor physical pain KEY:E 3
s. say what it will SHAK:HAM 177
To certain death by certain s. KIP 129
To s. unvulnerable SHAK:COR 19
unto a s. That was perpetuall PSALMS 2
Upon his brow s. is asham'd SHAK:ROM 31
whose glory is in their s. BIBLE 540
womman cast hir s. away CHAUC 84
shameless: most s. thing in the world BURKE:E 63
shames: hold a candle to my s.? SHAK:MERC 25
shamming: generally shammin' when 'e's dead KIP 49
shank:
his shrunk s. SHAK:AS 34
spindle s. a guid whip-lash BURNS:R 36
shanks: Her dry s. twitch BROOKE 4
Shannon: green banks of S. CAMPBELL:T 1
shape:
art thou, execrable s.? MILT 168
grim s. Towered up WORDS:W 147
if s. it might be calld MILT 167
in what s. they choose MILT 127
men in s. and fashion ASCHAM 2
purpose of art to give it s. ANOU 4
S. of Things to Come WELLS:HG 19
share the selfsame s. MACDIAR 14
shapeless: s. lump, like Anarchy DRYD 40
shapely: It is s., it wiggles, and it's name ERWIN 1
shapes:
dream whose s. return THOMS:Ja[2] 2
So full of s. is fancy SHAK:TWE 1
Women to change their s. SHAK:TWO 15
share: I turned to s. the transport WORDS:W 125
sharp: s. remedy, but a sure RALE 15
sharper: returned it s. than I received THOREAU 12
shave:
we men have to s. TUCHOL 2
which one to s. GLOVER 3
shaved: clean, s. and sober CHAND 1
shaves: who s. and takes a train WHITE:EB 2
shaving: when I am s. of a morning HOUSM 57
Shaw: Mr S. is (I suspect) the only CHESTERTON 40
Shaw, Bernard:
good man fallen among* LENIN 10
He hasn't an enemy* WILDE:O 129
shay: wonderful one-hoss s. HOLMES:OW 5
she:
chaste, and unexpressive s. SHAK:AS 36
lanky hank of s. STEPHENS 4
meant both 'he' and 's.' MILNE 19
That not impossible s. CRASH 7
she-who-must-be-obeyed: S. HAGG:R 1
shear: s. the fleeces or to CAMPBELL:R 1
shearers: best s.' cooks are Oxford men ARCHIB 1
shears:
blind Fury with th' abhorred s. MILT 49
resembles a pair of s. SMITH:Syd[1] 28
sheath:
His sword was in the s. COWP 17
We shall never s. the sword ASQU:HH 2
sheathed: sheath'd their swords for lack SHAK:HEN.V 18
shed:
monarch of a s. GOLDS 8
prepare to s. them SHAK:JUL 54
Stood a lowly cattle s. ALEX:CF 4
sheds: sooner found in lowly s. MILT 28
sheep:
armies but flocks of s.? CERV 4
Baa, baa, black s. NURS 2
being savaged by a dead s. HEAL 2
black s. in every flock PROV 375
Bo-peep has lost her s. NURS 32
for the s. to pass resolutions INGE 1
giveth his life for the s. BIBLE 484
hungry S. look up. MILT 54
in s.'s clothing BIBLE 401
Let us return to our s. ANON 235
like lost s. PRAY 4
like s. have gone astray BIBLE 329
little black s. who've gone KIP 52
looking on their silly s. SHAK:HEN.VI[3] 4
Mountain s. are sweeter PEAC 15
noble ensample to his s. CHAUC 26
one is of an old half-witted s. STEPHEN:JK 2
One sickly s. infects WATTS 4
s. bringeth no gain POUND 39
s. in s.'s clothing GOSSE 2
s. show me a place CEL 3
s., that used to be so MORE:T 1
s. with a blade of grass stuck WODE 11
s.'s guts should hale souls SHAK:MUCH 12
s.'s in the meadows NURS 33
standing a s. on its hind legs BEERB 11

30 S. came on board CLARK:R 2
sheep-bells: s. and the ship-bells ring KIP 109
sheep-hook: how to hold a S. MILT 53
sheet:
although the s. were big enough SHAK:TWE 44
wet s. and a flowing CUNNING:A 4
sheets: cool kindliness of s. BROOKE 20
shelf: silence of the upper s. MACAULAY:TB 17
shell:
convolutions of a smooth-lipped s. WORDS:W 117
doth not fling away the s.? DONNE 31
Shelley:
beautiful and ineffectual angel* ARNOLD:M 84
did you once see S. plain BROWNING:R 136
peace in S.'s mind SHELLEY:PB 162
S. and Keats were the last HALDA 2
S. dream's his white JOHNSON:L 6
S., whom envy never touched SHELLEY:PB 168
shells: silver bells and cockle s. NURS 40
shelter:
I'd s. thee BURNS:R 121
s. from the stormy blast WATTS 18
who wilt not s. Me THOMP:F 11
Shem: S., Ham, and Japheth BIBLE 34
Shenandoah: S., I long to hear you ANON 35
shepherd:
As sweet unto a s. GREENE:R 1
Dick the s. blows SHAK:LOV 25
fairest s. on our green PEELE 1
feed his flock like a s. BIBLE 322
God of love my s. is HERB:G 47
good s. giveth his life BIBLE 484
King of Love my S. is BAKER 1
Lord's my s. SCOTTISH 1
Old Nod, the s. DE LA M 10
rainbow in the morning is the s.'s PROV 329
Red sky at night, s.'s PROV 331
s. his sheep PROP 1
S. I take thy word MILT 28
S. tells his tale MILT 70
S.'s warning ANON 91, 90
slighted S.'s trade MILT 49
they call you, s. ARNOLD:M 19
truth in every s.'s tongue RALE 1
weather the s. shuns HARDY:T 41
shepherdess: s. of sheep MEY:A 4
shepherds:
must be both s. and butchers VOLT 8
While s. watch'd their flocks TATE:N 1
Sheridan: dull, naturally dull* JOHNSON:S 122
Sheriffmuir: I'm sure, that at S. MCLENN 1
sherris-sack: good s. hath a twofold SHAK:HEN.IV[2] 42
sherry:
in the kitchen with the cooking s. THURB 8
s. in the cupboard BETJ 35
very fond of brown s. CHESTERTON 52
shield:
broken was her s. SCOTT:W 33
His ponderous s. MILT 124
Our S. and Defender GRANT:R 1
shieling:
From the lone s. GALT 1
lone s. of the misty island SCOTT:W 66
shift: let me s. for myself MORE:T 4
shilling:
happen to have the s. about you SHERIDAN:T 1
Philip and Mary on a s. BUTLER:S[1] 29
Shillin' a day KIP 63
splendid s. PHILIPS:J 1
to sell for one s. LEAR 20
shillings:
payment of half twenty s. BURKE:E 18
Whenever you save five s. KEYN 11
shimmered: Jeeves s. out and came WODE 12
shimmy: Put thy s. on LAWR:DH 19
shine:
afar off s. bright WEBSTER:J 25
Few are qualified to s. SWIFT 20
Forever singing as they s. ADDIS 40
glistering gold but more to s. BRADST 3
How late they start to s. GUNN:T 3
Jesus bids us s. WARNER:S 1
not to s. in use TENNY 52
S. forth upon our clouded hills? BLAKE:W 98
s. on, harvest moon NORWORTH 1
that's where I s. BENCH 8
they s. on all alike POPE 42
shined: goodness, in her person shin'd MILT 102
shines:
more it's shook it s. HAMIL:W 1
s. only on the waves behind COLERIDGE:ST 90
So s. a good deed SHAK:MERC 52
shingles: naked s. of the world ARNOLD:M 47
shining:
in the s. of the stars TENNY 271
s. prospects rise ADDIS 34
S. with all his might CARROLL 53
shins: cover a multitude of s. WEST:M 15
ship:
all I ask is a tall s. MASE 1
being in a s. is being in a jail JOHNSON:S 105
brake that gallant s. in twain BALL 15
build your s. of death LAWR:DH 37
come to the aid of a sinking s. ANON 247
Don't give up the s. LAWR:J 1
happy and an efficient s. MOUNT 1
idle as a painted s. COLERIDGE:ST 19
In an English s., they say LOND 2
It was so old a s. FLECKER 10
Like a stately S. Of Tarsus MILT 289
One leak will sink a s. BUNYAN 23
sail on, O S. of State LONGFEL 17
s., an isle FLECKER 7
s. has weather'd every rack WHITMAN 29
s. have I got in the North BALL 23
s. is floating in the harbour SHELLEY:PB 132
s. so slow would pass MUIR:E 5
s. that goes DIBDIN:C 9
s. was still as she SOUTHEY 8
spoil the s. for a ha'porth PROV 81
There was a s. COLERIDGE:ST 11
to make an end of the s. SHAK:WIN 10
whale s. was my Yale MELV 3
Whither, O splendid s. BRIDGES:R 9
Women Wair out of the S. CLARK:R 1
shipmates: much more Agreable Ship mates CLARK:R 2
ships:
distant, storm-beaten s. MAHAN 1
down to the sea in s. BIBLE 234
got the s., we've got the men HUNT:GW 1
I spied three s. ANON 4
launch'd a thousand s. MARLOWE 38
little s. of England brought GUED 4
lofty s. carry low sails PROV 257
mighty s. ten thousand ton HODG 3
mystery of the s. LONGFEL 25
old s. sail like swans FLECKER 8
s., becalmed at eve CLOUGH 6
S., dim-discovered THOMS:Ja[1] 5
S. that pass in the night LONGFEL 31
shoes – and s. – and sealing wax CARROLL 56
something wrong with our bloody s. BEAT 1
stately s. are twirled HODG 3
thousand s. to Tenedos MARLOWE 14
two doomed s. that pass WILDE:O 114
watch the s. of England go KIP 80
shipwreck:
escaped the s. of time BACON:F[1] 7
s. of my ill adventured youth DANI 1
s. of my life's esteems CLARE:J 8
shires: for them from sad s. OWEN:W 2
shirt:
In your s. and your socks GILB:WS 52
merits of a spotless s. TENNY 100
no s. or collar ever comes back LEACOCK 7
pale martyr in his s. of fire SMITH:Alex 1
shirt-sleeves: from s. to s. BUTLER:NM 1
shirts:
coarse S. our small bones THOMAS:RS 1
s. for soldiers, sister Susie WESTON 1
shit:
he's a worthless piece of s. SOLAN 1
you do when you s.? CARU 1
shits: Celia, Celia s. SWIFT 66
shiver: You create a new s. HUGO 9
shock:
One must s. the bourgeois BAUD 9
s. of the new DUNL 1
s. them and keep them SHAW 96
short, sharp s. GILB:WS 70
we shall s. them SHAK:KING J 21
shock-headed: see S. Peter HOFFMAN:H 15
shocked:
how to be amused rather than s. BUCK 5
s. them, the *bourgeois* PRIV 1
shocks:
thousand natural s. SHAK:HAM 97
twelve great s. of sound TENNY 94
shoddy: Up goes the price of s. GILB:WS 112
shoe:
I kiss his dirty s. SHAK:HEN.V 29
If the s. doesn't fit STEINEM 1
Into a left-hand s. CARROLL 84
My dame has lost her s. NURS 6
One, two, buckle my s. NURS 48
s. be Spanish or neats-leather BUTLER:S[1] 21
want of a nail the s. was lost PROV 135
woman who lived in a s. NURS 72
shoelace:
like a s. from its mouth MOORE:M 5
tying a s. by fogged HARRIS:M 1
shoemaker: s.'s son always go barefoot PROV 345
shoes:
feet when we want s. SWIFT 17
Him that makes s. go barefoot BURTON:Ro 5
his s. were far too tight LEAR 12
mind it wipes its s. THOMAS:D 24
over s. in love SHAK:TWO 2
Put off thy s. BIBLE 85
s. – and ships – and sealing wax CARROLL 56
s. at the door, sleep ELIOT:TS 18
s. exhaled the right *soupçon* SAKI 13
s. from the shoemaker GOLDS 78
s. were number nine MONTROSE 2
s. with broken high ideals MCGOUGH 1
shook:
more it's s. it shines HAMIL:W 1
Ten Days that S. the World REED:Joh 1
shoon:
night in her silver s. DE LA M 16
wat their cork-heel'd s. BALL 50
shoot:
business of generals to s. one another WELLING 21
do not s. the pianist WILDE:O 106
If it moves, s. it ANON 201
S. if you must WHITTIER 5
s. me in my absence BEHAN:Br 4
s. the way you shout ROOS:T 8
They S. Horses, Don't They? MCCOY 1
they shout and they s. INGE 8
They up and s. themselves BROOKE 12
young idea how to s. THOMS:Ja[1] 3
shooting:
S. is a popular sport ANON 237
sometimes to s. short ARISTOT 8
war minus the s. ORWELL 39
shoots:
Nobody s. at Santa Claus SMITH:Alf 2
Who s. at the midday sun SIDNEY:P 12
shop:
little back s., all our own MONTAIGNE 9
s. is closing down MACNEICE 8
shop-keepers: s. are very seldom so disinterested ADAMS:S 1
shopkeepers:
Generous people make bad s. BALZ 9
government is influenced by s. SMITH:Ad 7
shopocracy: hear you abuse the s. NORTH:C 8
shopping:
salvation? Go s. MILLER:A 6
s. days to Christmas SELF 2
s. sense is important DAVID 1
shops:
service to my constituents if I went into s. GAREL 1
shun the awful s. CHESTERTON 10
shore:
adieu! my native s. BYR 57
after-silence on the s. BYR 46
control Stops with the s. BYR 117
false, impossible s. ARNOLD:M 15
heron Priested s. THOMAS:D 12
longing for the further s. VIRGIL 69
meet on that beautiful s. BENNETT:SF 1
Not on sad Stygian s. BUTLER:S[2] 49
Over som wide-water'd shoar MILT 82
rapture on the lonely s. BYR 116
safely to behold from s. LUCRET 5
s. of the sounding sea HOMER 5
swerve of s. to bend of bay JOYCE:J 30

to gain his natal s. HOMER 16
unknown and silent s. LAMB:Ch 29
Waves that Beat on Heavens S. BLAKE:W 88
shoreless: s. watery wild ARNOLD:M 16
shores:
back safely to Attic s. HORACE 3
betwixt their s. to be ARNOLD:M 17
on the edge of alien s. HOPE:Al 1
s. of darkness there is light KEATS 32
towards the wilder s. of love BLANCH 1
shorn: went home s. BROWNING:R 177
short:
falls s., 'tis Nature's fault CHURCH:C 10
if you find it wond'rous s. GOLDS 13
it is well it is s. TAYL:Jer 1
long while to make it s. THOREAU 26
Most of them ... are rather s. BEERB 18
nasty, brutish, and s. HOBB 7
s. and the long of it SHAK:MERR 8
s., are twice as good GRACIAN 5
s. enough and ugly enough ALLEN:W 4
s. in the head ANON 53
too s. to be taken seriously BENTLEY:N 4
shorten: s. I the stature of my soul MERED:G 19
shorter:
had time to make it s. PASC 1
make you s. by the head ELIZ I 12
shorthand: seriously about taking up s. BENTLEY:N 2
shot:
hand that fired the s. BALL 25
I have had them all s. NARV 1
long s., Watson DOYLE:AC 24
may nevertheless be s. through STERNE 34
s. at for sixpence a-day DIBDIN:C 5
s. by his gamekeeper ANON 143
s. heard round the world EMER 98
s. than do his bootlaces up criss-cross WELLS:HG 16
s. With the self-same artillery? LOVELACE 1
young Sahib s. divinely ANON 260
shoulder: giant's s. to mount on COLERIDGE:ST 79
shoulder-blade:
left s. that is a miracle GILB:WS 76
my touch on your s. BETJ 9
shoulders:
s. held the sky suspended HOUSM 37
standing on the s. of giants NEWT:I 3
shout:
Don't s. anymore UNG 1
no use raising a s. AUD 56
shoot the way you s. ROOS:T 8
s. that tore Hell's Concave MILT 131
S. with the largest DICKENS 10
they s. and they shoot INGE 8
You needn't s. so loud CARROLL 73
shouted:
sons of God s. for joy BIBLE 193
went and s. in his ear CARROLL 73
shouteth: s. by reason of wine BIBLE 220
shouting:
Every man s. in proportion SURT 1
tumult and the s. dies KIP 91
shouts: Not in the s. and plaudits LONGFEL 33
shoveling: s. the walk before it stops snowing DILL 1
show:
heart, that makes no s. DONNE 29
midnight dances and the public s. WALP:H 14
often think of it As a s. HARDY:T 38
outward shew of things SPENS 46
s. ain't over till ANON 238
show business: two reasons why I'm in s.b. GRAB 1
shower:
a falling s. SHELLEY:PB 117
prove the sweetness of a s. THOMAS:E 6
s. of your shooting corns presage SWIFT 52
This is our finest s. OSB:J 10
showers:
land does not ask for s. TIB 2
March winds and April s. PROV 268
s. betumble the chestnut HARDY:T 40
small s. last long SHAK:RIC.II 16
Sweet April s. TUSS 1
ye S. and Dew PRAY 14
shows: All my s. are great GRADE 1
shreds:
king of s. and patches SHAK:HAM 144
thing of s. and patches GILB:WS 60
shrew:
how to tame a s. SHAK:TAM 10
labeled harpy, s. and whore RICH 2
Shrewsbury: vanes of S. gleam HOUSM 19
shriek:
solitary s. BYR 176
With hollow shreik MILT 11
shrieking: With s. and squeaking BROWNING:R 25
shrimp:
but a s. of an author GRAY:T 42
until a s. learns to whistle KHRU 10
shrine: Open the s. that I may see JONS 16
shroud:
gaiety is a striped s. THOMAS:G 3
in a s. Of thoughts BYR 95
stiff dishonoured s. ELIOT:TS 30
swathed in its contaminated s. WHITE:P 14
White his s. as SHAK:HAM 160
Who ever comes to s. me DONNE 39
shrouds: land-breeze shook the s. COWP 16
shrubbery: Priapus in the s. ELIOT:TS 13
shrunk: S. to this little measure? SHAK:JUL 39
shuffling: forc'd gait of a s. nag SHAK:HEN.IV[1] 61
shunting: more of my life to s. and hooting BURR 1
shut:
God ought surely to s. HARDY:T 38
S. the door after you EDGE 3
was there it seemed to be s. FREUD:C 2
shutters: close the s. fast COWP 72
shuttle: Man is the s. VAUGHAN:H 13
shuttlecock: Battledore and s.'s a wery good game DICKENS 14
shy: we are not s. GILB:WS 71
shyness: S. is just egotism out of KEITH:P 1
Siberia: In S.'s wastes No tears MANG 2
Sibyl: S. without the inspiration BURKE:E 106
Sicily: Sertes and soft S. ARNOLD:M 30
sick:
all s. persons PRAY 36
an' thcream till I'm thick CROMP 1
choose to be at when he is s. JOHNSON:S 232
Created sicke GREV 2
grievously s. man NEWT:J 2
I am s. of love BIBLE 294
I was s. and lay a-bed STEVENSON:RL 52
I'm more than a little s. KIP 46
made one s. of it RUSKIN 29
make a man s. to hear her PEPYS 11
never s. at sea GILB:WS 8
nothing but to make him s. DONNE 17
report That I am sudden s. SHAK:ANT 14
s., and ye visited me BIBLE 431
s., O Lord, around thee TWELLS 1
s. of an old passion DOWS 1
s. or are you sullen? JOHNSON:S 250
s. way down inside MCCARTHY:J[2] 2
they all make me s. MITFORD:N 2
time we think we're s. WOLFE:Tho 1
were you not extremely s.? PRIOR 13
you are s. of self-love SHAK:TWE 11
sicken: When love begins to s. SHAK:JUL 66
sickle: bending s.'s compass come SHAK:SON 52
sickness:
in s. and in health PRAY 84
s. enlarges the dimensions LAMB:Ch 26
Sidcup: only I could get down to S. PINT 2
side:
Hear the other s. AUGUS 9
in beauty, s. by s. HEMA 5
knows only his own s. MILL 10
Look on the bright s. PROV 248
Nobody is on my s. AUSTEN 20
not on the s. of the big batallions VOLT 9
on our s. to-day MACAULAY:TB 44
on the s. of the big battalions PROV 149
on the s. of the big battalions TURE 1
on the s. of the big squadrons BUSSY 3
on the s. of those who have plenty ANOU 5
passed by on the other s. BIBLE 457
perpetually on the wrong s. NASH 21
pierce my s. DONNE 85
sounded for him on the other s. BUNYAN 32
thrust my hand into his s. BIBLE 493
Time is on our s. GLAD 1
to move over to the other s. REED:H 7
what was at the other s. of the hill WELLING 10
You rose o' the wrong s. to-day BROME:R 1
side-long: s. looks of love GOLDS 20
sides:
assume that everything has two s. ROBINS:JH 1
at life from both s. now MITCH:Jo 1
both s. of the paper at once SELL 11
have seen both s. AUBREY 6
much might be said on both s. ADDIS 19
say that she supported both s. MACDON:R 3
who sees both s. of a question WILDE:O 14
sideways: I have no s. CHESTERTON 56
siege:
envious s. Of wat'ry Neptune SHAK:RIC.II 17
stay the s. of loving terms SHAK:ROM 3
siesta: Englishmen detest a S. COWARD 20
sieve:
draws nectar in a s. COLERIDGE:ST 67
in a s. I'll thither sail SHAK:MAC 5
They went to sea in a s. LEAR 14
sigh:
Don't you sit there and s. WESK 1
hapless Soldiers s. BLAKE:W 74
He took her with a s. BLAKE:W 57
passing tribute of a s. GRAY:T 23
she look'd up to s. SCOTT:W 22
s. is just a s. HUP 1
S. is the Sword of an Angel King BLAKE:W 115
s. like Tom o' Bedlam SHAK:KING L 10
s. no more SHAK:MUCH 13
s. that silence heaves KEATS 6
s. to those who love BYR 130
unutterable S. in the Human Heart ELLIS:H 5
sighed:
Sigh'd and look'd, and sigh'd again DRYD 110
s. as a lover GIBBON:E 20
s. for the love of GILB:WS 97
wept not greatly, but s. MALORY 13
sighing:
plague of s. and grief SHAK:HEN.IV[1] 48
Sorrow and s. shall flee BIBLE 318
sighs:
all made of s. and tears SHAK:AS 65
for my pains a world of s. SHAK:OTH 9
S. and leers And crocodile NURS 83
S. are the natural language SHADWE 1
Sorrow, with her family of S. SHELLEY:PB 111
sovereign of s. and groans SHAK:LOV 8
sight:
admit them in your s. AUSTEN 26
It is not yet in s. SHERIDAN:RB 35
of each other at first S. STEELE 10
out of mind because I am out of s.? HOLL:HS 1
out of s. is out of mind CLOUGH 7
Out of s., out of mind PROV 315
s. to make an old man TENNY 60
that lov'd not at first s.? SHAK:AS 53
that loved not at first s.? MARLOWE 47
triple s. in blindness keen KEATS 32
sightless: blind man On the s. horse WALEY 1
sights: all s. from pole to pole ARNOLD:M 40
sign:
In this s. thou shalt conquer CONSTANTINE 1
s. documents which they do not HURST 1
signal: I really do not see the s. NELS 8
signed:
fatal blue-print. And he s. it BUZZ 1
hand that s. the paper THOMAS:D 8
signifying: S. nothing SHAK:MAC 113
signing: s. his name and forgetting to write BEECHER 1
signs: S. are taken for wonders ELIOT:TS 22
silence:
a talent for s. HUNT:L 6
air rings with s. BAS 2
answered best with s. JONS 17
being Of the eternal S. WORDS:W 64
dust and s. of the upper MACAULAY:TB 17
easy step to s. AUSTEN 64
eternal s. of these infinite PASC 8
Even s. may be eloquent CONG 6
He went off in s. along HOMER 5
His mind moves upon s. YEATS 117
His s. will sit drooping SHAK:HAM 189
I ha'e S. left MACDIAR 16

in that s. we the tempest DRYD 2
lies are often told in s. STEVENSON:RL 13
like S. listening To s. HOOD 1
maintaining the 'conspiracy of s.' COMTE 1
makes a s. in the hills TENNY 137
more absolute s. of America LAWR:DH 14
not as holy as s. VEGA CAR 1
occasional flashes of s. SMITH:Syd[1] 30
only one s. TUCHOL 4
Out of s. mystery comes DARK 1
padlock of s. on mental wealth BRONTE:C 1
power of punishment is to s. JOHNSON:S 61
rest is s. SHAK:HAM 200
sigh that s. heaves KEATS 6
S. alone is great VIGNY 4
s. also does not necessarily ELIOT:G 26
S. and sleep like fields DE LA M 4
S. augmenteth grief GREV 1
S. between them like a thread JENN:E 1
s. fell with the waking TENNY 216
S. invaded the suburbs AUD 36
S. is as full of potential wisdom HUX:A 19
S. is become his mother GOLDS 63
S. is deep as Eternity CARLYLE:T 37
S. is divine, yet also CARLYLE:T 69
S. is golden PROV 346
s. is golden PROV 352
s. is most noble SWIN 17
S. is only commendable SHAK:MERC 7
S. is the perfectest herald SHAK:MUCH 8
S. is the safest policy LA ROCHE 13
S. is the virtue of fools BACON:F[1] 27
s., like a poultice, comes HOLMES:OW 1
S. more musical ROSSET:C 10
s. of the glens SMITH:Alex 2
s. of the soundless moonlight VIRGIL 49
S. ruled this land DARK 1
s. sank Like music COLERIDGE:ST 35
s. surged softly backward DE LA M 9
S. was pleas'd MILT 198
s. was the song of love ROSSET:DG 9
s. where hath been no sound HOOD 2
small change of s. MERED:G 5
Still-born S. FLECKN 1
temple of s. and reconciliation MACAULAY:TB 11
there was a s. in heaven BIBLE 581
thou foster-child of s. KEATS 92
time to keep s. BIBLE 281
'Tis visible s. ROSSET:DG 8
To s. envious tongues SHAK:HEN.VIII 12
Well-timed s. hath more eloquence TUP 2
who shall s. all the airs MILT 315
will s. him at once CHESTERFIELD 35
With s. and tears BYR 55
silences: s. Of dreadful things AUD 32
silencing: justified in s. that one MILL 9
silent:
be s. in several languages HARBO 1
be s. is the best answer to calumny WASH 3
I like the s. church EMER 12
impossible to be s. BURKE:E 101
like griefs are s. MARM 1
mornings are strangely s. CARSON 3
one must keep s. WITT 2
remain s. and be thought LINC 26
S. as the sleeve-worn stone MACLEISH 1
s. majority of Americans to stand up NIX 7
s. majority of my fellow Americans NIX 5
s. manliness of grief GOLDS 35
S., upon a peak in Darien KEATS 4
talents were of the more s. BYR 213
unlocked her s. throat GIBBONS:O 1
why art thou s. CRAW 1
silk:
make his couche of s. CHAUC 53
rustling in unpaid-for s. SHAK:CYM 10
Thinking of your blue-shadowed s. STEVENS 4
silk-worm: s. expend her yellow labours TOUR 2
silken: s. terms precise SHAK:LOV 21
silks: in s. my *Julia* goes HERR 38
sillier: nothing s. than a silly laugh CATUL 10
silly:
Lazy and s. SITWELL:E 5
S. and shady SITWELL:E 7
S. Billy HEAL 3
to be s. at the right moment HORACE 59
You were s. like us AUD 38
Siloam: By cool S.'s shady HEB 5
Silurist: Here sleeps the S. SASS 17
silver:
for a handful of s. he left us BROWNING:R 53
night in her s. shoon DE LA M 16
o're the dark her S. Mantle MILT 198
Selling the family s. MACMILL:H 10
S. and gold have I none BIBLE 497
s. for the maid KIP 126
s. lining in the sky-ee WESTON 2
S. threads among the gold REX 1
Turn forth her s. lining MILT 25
Wisdom be put in a s. rod? BLAKE:W 28
silver-sweet: s. sound lovers' tongues SHAK:ROM 18
similes:
most unsavoury s. SHAK:HEN.IV[1] 8
your land of s. MCAULEY 3
Simon:
real S. Pure CENT 2
Simple S. met a pieman NURS 65
simple:
Delight in s. things KIP 118
It was beautiful and s. HENRY:O 3
simpler: recommended something s. ALF 1
simplest: s. concepts repeated a thousand HITL 1
simpleton: revolutionary s. is everywhere LEWIS:W 5
simplicity:
makes s. a grace JONS 23
O holy s. HUSS 1
Pity my s. WESLEY:C 6
sacred s. rather than wordy JEROME 2
S. is the most deceitful mistress ADAMS:H 6
s. of the three per cents DISR:B 46
s. that I see in some SASS 19
terrible in the s. of his idea CONRAD 10
truth and s. are the best strategy LA BRU 1
simplify:
s. me when I'm dead DOUGLAS:K 1
S., s. THOREAU 15
Simpson: Mrs S.'s pinched our king ANON 67
simulacrum: sun itself is but the dark *s.* BROWNE:T 44
sin:
All s. tends to be addictive AUD 68
be a charity in s. SHAK:MEA 17
black and soft as s. CHESTERTON 21
commit one single venial s. NEWM:JH 4
cunning s. cover itself SHAK:MUCH 24
England! full of sinne HERB:G 4
Excepting Original S. CAMPBELL:T 17
He said he was against it* COOL 5
He that is without s. BIBLE 480
How shall I lose the s. POPE 62
I'll s. till I blow up THOMAS:D 37
I'm living in s. HERB:AP 1
in secret s. CHURCH:C 2
it is no s. SHAK:MEA 23
keep us this day without s. PRAY 11
made my s. their door? DONNE 95
no s. but ignorance MARLOWE 19
no s. except stupidity WILDE:O 18
not win who plays with s. WILDE:O 115
Nothing emboldens s. so SHAK:TIM 8
one s. will destroy a sinner BUNYAN 23
palace of sweet s. KEATS 106
Plate s. with gold SHAK:KING L 72
research in original s. PLOM 6
she knew no s. DRYD 83
S. brought death EDDY 2
s. in secret is no s. MOLIERE 11
S. is behovely JULIANA 1
s. strongly, but believe LUTHER 7
s. that amends is but SHAK:TWE 9
s. with Elinor Glyn ANON 122
smacking of every s. SHAK:MAC 93
Some rise by s. SHAK:MEA 7
sometimes s.'s a pleasure BYR 170
sorrow dogging sinne HERB:G 20
straight to the s. of Onan VOLT 34
take me away from my s. QUEV 1
To s. in loving virtue SHAK:MEA 16
triumph over death and s. SPENS 8
wages of s. is death BIBLE 511
waive the quantum o' the s. BURNS:R 46
want of power to s. DRYD 125
we fall into no s. PRAY 23
We wallow in our s. ANON 59
Wilt thou forgive that s. DONNE 95
your s. will find you out BIBLE 121
Sinatra: now have the 'Frank S.' doctrine GERAS 1
sincere: may be very s. in good principles JOHNSON:S 84
sincerely: I mean this most s. GREEN:H 1
sincerity:
little s. is a dangerous WILDE:O 15
no longer be written with s. PROUST 17
sinews:
one of the s. of the soul FULLER:T[1] 6
s. of war, unlimited money CIC 12
Stiffen the s. SHAK:HEN.V 17
strung with poets' s. SHAK:TWO 10
twist the s. of thy heart? BLAKE:W 68
sinful: any s. games HARTE 2
sing:
And no birds s. KEATS 79
Bifore the theves he may synge JUV 19
but s. because I must TENNY 138
cannot s. the old songs now CALVER 5
Cherubim does cease to s. BLAKE:W 83
die before they s. COLERIDGE:ST 49
found in thine heart to s.? SWIN 3
I cannot s. the old songs CLARI 1
I know ye s. well FLETCH:J 12
I s. of *Brooks*, of *Blossomes* HERR 7
I'll s. you twelve O ANON 22
lady s. at the noon MORRIS:W 2
let me s. and die BYR 197
let us s. in loftier strain VIRGIL 11
let us s. unto the Lord BIBLE 229
Lhude s. Goddamn POUND 12
made blind Homer s. to me? MARLOWE 37
safe I S. with mortal voice MILT 224
s. A faery's song KEATS 82
s. 'em muck MELBA 2
S. 'Hey to you GILB:WS 34
s. like birds i' th' cage SHAK:KING L 79
S., my tongue, of battle VENAN 1
S. of old Eire YEATS 13
s., that I may seem valiant DRYD 96
s. the Lord's song in a strange BIBLE 246
s. the savageness out of a bear SHAK:OTH 48
S. thou smoothly with thy CAMPION 6
S. to the Lord a new song BIBLE 599
s. unto the Lord a new BIBLE 230
S. whatever is well made YEATS 123
They just s. WAUGH:E 10
think caged birds s. WEBSTER:J 12
What shall we s.? GLOVER 2
Whilst thus I s. CIB 8
who used to s. in the water DICKENS 103
Who would not s. for Lycidas? MILT 42
wife s. to her child EDWARDS:R 1
world in ev'ry corner s. HERB:G 24
singe: That it do s. yourself SHAK:HEN.VIII 1
singeing: s. of the King of Spain's Beard DRAKE 2
singer:
After the s. is dead STEVENSON:RL 65
idle s. of an empty day MORRIS:W 4
lived a s. in France of old SWIN 46
none hear Beside the s. LANDOR 3
s. not the song ANON 39
S. of sweet Colonus ARNOLD:M 6
Thou the s. GILB:WS 41
singers:
Long ago he was one of the s. LEAR 4
sweetest of all s. LONGFEL 23
singing:
angels all were s. out of BYR 145
clear voice suddenly s. AUD 25
Evryone suddenly burst out s. SASS 12
Forever s. as they shine ADDIS 40
heard her s. her last song TENNY 22
I am sick of s. SWIN 33
I heard a maid s. ANON 10
lovely beyond any s. PATON 1
Singin' till a bairnie MACDIAR 17
s. beneath the cupola VERL 3
s. in the rain FREED 1
s. in their glory move MILT 58
S., it's the same thing CARU 1
S. so rarely SCOTT:W 57
s. still dost soar SHELLEY:PB 95
sweet s. in the choir ANON 20
There is delight in s. LANDOR 3
through the river s. BUNYAN 31

time of the s. of birds BIBLE 295
to love a woman for s. SHAK:KING L 12
waves of thy sweet s. SHELLEY:PB 19, 80
singing-boys: six little S. BARH 4
single:
cause of a s. life, is liberty BACON:F[1] 82
continued s. and only talked GOLDS 49
in s. blessedness SHAK:MID 1
married women and s. men MENCK 20
otherwise might've died s. DUNNE 1
s. in the field WORDS:W 79
s. life, it's more airy ANON 263
s. man in possession of a good AUSTEN 12
s. men, though they be BACON:F[1] 83
six times with the same s. lady BYR 225
they come not s. spies SHAK:HAM 163
singles: What strenuous s. we played BETJ 20
singly: we Are nothing s. THOMS:Ja[2] 8
sings:
I Know Why the Caged Bird S. ANGELOU 1
no one tell me what she s.? WORDS:W 80
S. for his supper NURS 37
till the fat lady s. ANON 238
Who on a tilting deck s. DAY LEWIS 3
singularity:
into the trick of s. SHAK:TWE 36
S. is almost invariably a clue DOYLE:AC 8
sinister: strange and s. embroidered on JAMES:H 18
sink:
One leak will s. a ship BUNYAN 23
s. is the great symbol MITCH:Ju 1
sinking:
kind of alacrity in s. SHAK:MERR 14
S. from thought to thought POPE 161
sinned:
all have s. BIBLE 510
I have s. exceedingly MASS 6
More sinn'd against than sinning SHAK:KING L 37
Peccavi! I have s. NAPIER 1
Peccavi – I've Scinde wrote PUNCH 7
sinner:
Be a s. and sin strongly LUTHER 7
I of her a s. CONG 64
music in the s.'s ears WESLEY:C 3
over one s. that repenteth BIBLE 462
s., lov'st thou me? COWP 6
sinners:
be a breeder of s.? SHAK:HAM 100
but s. to repentance BIBLE 406
God and s. reconciled WESLEY:C 7
Have mercy upon us miserable s. PRAY 32
s. are still in bed resting RUNYON 9
s. must with devils dwell WATTS 11
s., plunged beneath that flood COWP 5
s.'ll be kotched out late HARRIS:JC 11
Why do s.' ways prosper? HOPK:GM 30
sinning:
good shape for more s. RUNYON 9
nothing so artificial as s. LAWR:DH 16
sins:
Albion's s. are crimson-dy'd BLAKE:W 6
All our s. and griefs to bear SCRIV 1
away the s. of the world MASS 17
Be all my s. rememb'red SHAK:HAM 98
being weighed with his s. KAF 5
brain only, that the great s. WILDE:O 27
Commit The oldest s. SHAK:HEN.IV[2] 46
Compound for s., they are inclin'd BUTLER:S[1] 13
cover the multitude of s. BIBLE 568
earnestly repent of your s. PRAY 71
Few love to hear the s. SHAK:PER 2
Forgiveness of S. PRAY 19
His s. were scarlet BELLOC 36
manifold s. and wickedness PRAY 3
no faults, only s. YEATS 138
not reheat his s. for breakfast DIET 1
Old s. cast long shadows PROV 305
Other s. only speak WEBSTER:J 28
pay for the s. of your fathers HORACE 37
punished for their s., but by them HUBB 4
root of all s. JAMES VI/I 1
some are thinkin' on their s. BURNS:R 48
they know our s. MACHIA 2
those s. which had caused the cholera? KINGSLEY:C 2
Though your s. be as scarlet BIBLE 300
under the weight of our s. PRAY 94
weep for her s. at the other CARY:J 1
sip:
can't be tasted in a s. DICKENS 96
s. is the most that mortals ALCOTT:B 1
sipped: s., not swallowed at a gulp DUKES 1
Sir-come-spy-me: Monument, S. BARH 1
sire:
S. of an immortal strain SHELLEY:PB 107
thy s. was a knight SCOTT:W 49
sirens:
Blest pair of S. MILT 63
S. Dear me! s., of course DICKENS 103
What song the S. sang BROWNE:T 55
Sirius: sovereign brilliancy of S. HARDY:T 51
Sirmio:
olive-silvery S. TENNY 288
S., bright eye CATUL 9
sissy: s. half as old as time PLOM 4
sister:
confound this surly s. SYNGE 7
erring s.'s shame BYR 27
Had it been his s. ANON 132
kissed her little s. MONTROSE 3
My s. and my s.'s child COWP 50
no friend like a s. ROSSET:C 5
s., good night BELLOC 6
s.'s husband's niece CARROLL 94
sometime s., now our queen SHAK:HAM 12
We have a little s. BIBLE 299
Your s. is given to government DICKENS 207
sisterly: full fervour of s. animosity SURT 14
sisters:
all the s. virtuous NEWC 1
his s., and his cousins GILB:WS 10
his sustres and his paramours CHAUC 62
little s. to all the world DIX:D 1
make brothers and s. hate each other JOHNSON:S 86
S. are women first KIP 2
s. under their skins KIP 86
Sphear-born harmonious S. MILT 63
twa s. lived in a bower BALL 9
Sisyphus: imagine S. happy CAMUS 3
sit:
Don't you s. there and sigh WESK 1
He won't s. still HOFFMAN:H 5
nobody can tell you when to s. EISEN 7
s. down, unless you're a king HULL 1
S. on your arse for fifty MACNEICE 3
So I did s. and eat HERB:G 55
Though I s. down now DISR:B 51
To s. upon a hill SHAK:HEN.VI[3] 3
sitting:
Are you s. comfortably? LIST 1
most of my work s. down BENCH 8
no reason for s. in one place rather ELIOT:G 37
situation: s. excellent. I shall attack FOCH 1
situations: those who are in interesting s. AUSTEN 46
Sitwell: substitute *Dame* Edith for Dr S. SITWELL:E 14
Sitwell, Edith: She's genuinely bogus* HASS 1
Sitwells: S. belong to the history of LEAV 2
six:
All's set at s. and seven ANON 59
Couldn't we make do with *s.*? GRADE 2
Half past s. JOYCE:J 49
not attempt more than s. BELLOC 46
s. of one and half-a-dozen MARR 6
sixpence:
bang – went saxpence PUNCH 9
I love s. NURS 24
I only got s. PUNCH 16
nothing over s. BEVAN 5
Sing a song of s. NURS 66
We could have saved s. BECKETT 10
sixth: Welcome the sixte CHAUC 77
sixty: Men come of age at s. STEPHENS 7
skating: In s. over thin ice EMER 20
skeleton: Every family has a s. PROV 100
skeletons: cupboards bursting with s. ORWELL 11
ski: unbecoming for a cardinal to s. badly JOHN PAUL 3
Skiddaw: S. saw the fire that burned MACAULAY:TB 42
skied: s. down Mount Everest in the nude MACKINN 1
skies:
common people of the s. WOTTON 3
exchange thy sullen s. COWP 62
I looked to these very s. BROWNING:R 64
I'll meet the raging of the s. CAMPBELL:T 13
marmalade s. LENNON 7
paint the sable s. DRUMMOND OF H 1
s. are not cloudy all day HIGL 1
s. they were ashen POE 6
some watcher of the s. KEATS 4
whose god is in the s. SHAW 59
skill:
God gives s. ELIOT:G 47
S. comes so slow DAVIES:J 2
S. without imagination is craftsmanship STOP 10
skimble-skamble: such a deal of s. stuff SHAK:HEN.IV[1] 62
skin:
belonging only to the s. MOLIERE 29
Bone and S., two millers thin BYROM 3
Ethiopian change his s. BIBLE 339
guard his own s. and perforate KIP 9
more than one way to s. a cat PROV 371
on the s. beneath the s. DAVIES:J 5
Shed s. will never fit LOWELL:R 11
s. as thin as a cigarette paper to write DAVISON:FD 1
s. he made him mittens ANON 117
s. was white as leprosy COLERIDGE:ST 20
stuff my s. so full ANON 21
skinning: When you are s. your customers KHRU 5
skins:
beauty of their s. TENNY 112
contact of two s. CHAMFORT 5
lower classes had such white s. CURZON 4
skip: reading is to s. judiciously HAMER 1
skipper:
s. had taken his little daughter LONGFEL 9
where will I get a gude s. BALL 47
skipping: what a pretty s. grace MARV 24
skirt: swish of a s. in the dew KIP 132
skittles:
all beer and s. CALVER 8
all porter and s. DICKENS 49
beer and s., or something better HUGHES:Th 2
Life is not all Beer and S. STEVENSON:RL 71
not all beer and s. PROV 239
skull:
pushed up a knob of s. SLESS 3
s. beneath the skin ELIOT:TS 31
s. that housed white angels SASS 17
stupid s. was choking full BUCHANAN 7
skunk: indignity of being the s. MANDELA:N 5
skunks: only s. that search LOWELL:R 6
skuttle fish: put me in mind of the s.f. ADDIS 25
sky:
above the vaulted s. CLARE:J 8
arch of s. and mightiness UVA 1
bear him up the Norfolk s. BETJ 4
blue ethereal s. ADDIS 39
blue s. over my head HAZL 18
brightening roses of the s. CAMPBELL:T 5
dark drop, the trapped s. HEAN 2
Hateful is the dark-blue s. TENNY 29
He ascended in the s. CALVINO 1
I stared into the s. HODG 5
inverted Bowl we call The S. FITZGER:E 27
lonely sea and the s. MASE 1
Mackerel s. and mares' tails PROV 257
November's s. is chill SCOTT:W 12
On a bed of daffodil s. TENNY 215
pie in the s. when you die HILL:J 1
red s. at night ANON 91
Red s. at night PROV 331
shoulders held the s. suspended HOUSM 37
s. is darkening like a stain AUD 27
s. is overcast DAY LEWIS 4
s. is saffron-yellow KIP 32
strips of the s. fallen SHELLEY:PB 55
Surrender to the s. BAXTER:JK 1
Under the wide and starry s. STEVENSON:RL 61
wrote my will across the s. LAWR:TE 1
You walk in the s.'s beach SLESS 3
Skye:
Over the sea to S. BOULTON:HE 1
Over the sea to S. STEVENSON:RL 68

skylark:
despise the s.'s song? BRONTE:A 4
Hail to thee, blithe Spirit* SHELLEY:PB 94
S. wounded in the wing BLAKE:W 83
slacks: girls in s. remember Dad BETJ 24
slag: She was a s., he was HEINE 6
slain:
fifty thousand men s. WALP:R 2
is my most noble lord s. MALORY 10
it does not slay, nor is it s. BHAG 1
might see him s. MORRIS:W 1
Saul hath s. his thousands BIBLE 149
s. by a fair cruel maid SHAK:TWE 29
s. me you will conquer France JOAN 1
slander:
angry at a s. makes it true JONS 26
left no s. unspoken HUGHES:Th 1
no s. in an allow'd fool SHAK:TWE 11
S., meanest spawn TENNY 204
slang: All s. is metaphor CHESTERTON 31
slap-dash: s. down in the mouth CONG 10
slap-up: s. gal in a bang-up chariot DICKENS 225
slate:
fine s. pleases me DU BEL 3
wiping something off a s. KIP 97
write his thoughts upon a s. HOOD 29
slates: In and out the slipping s. BETJ 17
slaughter:
like lions to the roaring s. CUMM 2
name to aid the s. PANK:S 1
ox goeth to the s. BIBLE 254
through s. to a throne GRAY:T 21
slave:
Be not the s. of Words CARLYLE:T 4
Being your s. SHAK:SON 22
design'd yon lordling's s. BURNS:R 8
fettered s. to free VIRGIL 72
has been s. to thousands SHAK:OTH 34
Here I stand, your s. SHAK:KING L 33
In giving freedom to the s. LINC 10
Madman or s., must man ARNOLD:M 15
No more s. States CHASE 1
passions is Reason's s. CONNOLLY:C 19
pleasures without being a s. CAMUS 4
s. at another's plough HOMER 17
s. of circumstance And impulse BYR 140
S. to no sect POPE 106
soundly as the wretched s. SHAK:HEN.V 35
than a young man's s. PROV 39
That is not passion's s. SHAK:HAM 108
unambitious s., Like thou SHELLEY:PB 10
would have made him a s. BURKE:E 18
you were a Christian s. HENL 7
slavery:
because they impose s. RUSS:B 11
classified as s. in the extreme CHURCH:W 1
distinction between liberty and s. CAMDEN:Lord 1
Freedom and s. are mental states GAND:M 2
prolonged s. of woman STANTON:El 4
s. of being waited upon MACKEN 1
s. of the tea and coffee COBBETT 3
S. they can have everywhere BURKE:E 41
so dreadful as voluntary s. DICKIN:J 2
state of S. in which GILL 1
slaves:
at the Mill with s. MILT 278
Britons never will be s. THOMS:Ja[1] 2
intercourse between tyrants and s. GOLDS 58
Kings are but s. of their rank SCHILL 2
land of s. shall ne'er BYR 197
masters willingly concede to s. CAMUS 11
only freemen, are the only s. MASSIN 7
s. of some defunct economist KEYN 9
s. with weary footsteps SHELLEY:PB 130
such breasts must suckle s. BYR 197
to submit to be s. PITT:W[1] 3
wholly s. or wholly free DRYD 86
slay:
it does not s., nor is it slain BHAG 1
s., and s., and s. MACAULAY:TB 44
slays: War its thousands s. PORTEUS 2
sledge: My s. and anvil lie ANON 139
sleek-headed: S. men SHAK:JUL 14
sleep:
after-dinner's s., Dreaming SHAK:MEA 20
and get some s. LOOS 9
at eve the Prince of S. DE LA M 1
azure-lidded s. KEATS 74
Back from the City of S. KIP 95
balmy S. YOUNG:E 6
Be but to s. and feed? SHAK:HAM 156
Be ev'ry mourner's s. tonight KEBLE 4
Between a s. and a s. SWIN 15
birth is but a s. and a forgetting WORDS:W 58
bless whoever invented s. CERV 24
but as a drunken s. SHAK:MEA 33
calm and peaceful is my s. WILLARD 1
Care-charmer S. DANI 1
Care-charming s. FLETCH:J 2
Death and his brother S. SHELLEY:PB 9
Do I wake or s.? KEATS 93
don't s. with happily married men EKL 2
dreamless, uninvaded s. TENNY 1
Dye and Lye and S. together ANON 137
each day dies with s. HOPK:GM 24
embalmer of the still midnight* KEATS 91
exposition of s. come upon me SHAK:MID 39
Feminists who still s. with men JOHNSTONE:Jil 2
first s. should be his last ANON 120
first sweet s. of night SHELLEY:PB 35
from the fields of s. WORDS:W 55
gates the silent house of S. VIRGIL 74
gentle s. from Heaven COLERIDGE:ST 28
George goes to s. at a bank JEROME:JK 6
get a good night's s. WILSON:Harold 7
give their readers s. POPE 160
giveth His beloved s. HUX:H 1
great gift of s. HENL 5
grey and full of s. YEATS 14
hope Your Majesties s. well CAMPBELL:G 3
hour's s. before midnight, is worth PROV 311
How do people go to s.? PARKER:D 12
How s. the brave COLLINS:Will 3
I lay me down to s. ANON 61
I might s. out this great gap SHAK:ANT 20
I s., but my heart BIBLE 297
I s. on the coals DICKENS 146
I s. out the thought SHAK:WIN 14
ideas s. furiously CHOM 1
In s. a king SHAK:SON 38
in soot I s. BLAKE:W 18
Let me s. the s. of the earth VIGNY 1
make any one go to s., that bedstead DICKENS 48
medicine thee to that sweet s. SHAK:OTH 41
more dark is the s. SCOTT:W 46
more rest if one doesn't s. WAUGH:E 12
One short s. past DONNE 84
Only s. BROWNING:R 165
Only the s. eternal SWIN 32
sang themselves to s. HODG 2
season of all natures, s. SHAK:MAC 76
Shake off this downy s. SHAK:MAC 55
She looks like s. SHAK:ANT 78
Silence and s. like fields DE LA M 4
Six hours in s. COKE:E 6
s. before evening PATER 5
s. before you fight ARMST:J 1
s. between term and term SHAK:AS 47
s., dear, s. BEDD 1
S. I can get nane BURNS:R 77
S. in the night BLAKE:W 45
s. in the night SWIN 14
S. is a death BROWNE:T 35
S. is good, death is HEINE 7
s. is not for the weary brain THOMS:Ja[2] 4
S. is sweet to the labouring man BUNYAN 18
s.! it is a gentle thing COLERIDGE:ST 28
s. like a top DAVEN:W 2
s. may I nocht DUNB 13
s., Nature's soft nurse SHAK:HEN.IV[2] 30
S. no more SHAK:MAC 40
s. not so sound, as sweet HERR 17
S. on, blest pair MILT 203
S. on, my Love KING:H 1
s. one ever-during night CATUL 5
s. provides relief CHAMFORT 3
S. shall neither night SHAK:MAC 6
S. shall obey me SOUTHEY 14
S. that knits up SHAK:MAC 40
s. that knows not breaking SCOTT:W 37
S.! the friend of Woe SOUTHEY 16
s. the s. of death? BLAKE:W 118
s. thegither at the foot BURNS:R 79
s. till dusk is dipt in gray TENNY 162
S. upon a golden bed YEATS 85
S. will come SHELLEY:PB 148
s. with a prayer for the beloved GIBRAN 2
s. with a sober cannibal MELV 2
s.'s fine alchemy THOMS:Ja[2] 9
Sleepe after toyle SPENS 30
Sleepe, the certain knot SIDNEY:P 6
slept the s. of the just RACINE 10
such as s. o' nights SHAK:JUL 14
talks in someone else's s. AUD 70
This s. is sound indeed SHAK:HEN.IV[2] 45
thy deep and dreamless s. BROOKS:P 1
Thy sweet child S. SHELLEY:PB 147
time enough to s. HOUSM 4
time when I shall s. BRONTE:E 3
To die, to s. SHAK:HAM 97
To s., perchance to SHAK:HAM 97
Visit the soul in s. SHELLEY:PB 15
We shall not all s. BIBLE 526
weary mortals their first s. VIRGIL 50
What hath night to do with s.? MILT 21
when you s. you remind me SASS 11
whom they s. beside HOUSM 8
yet I would not s. SHAK:MAC 32
sleep-flower: s. sways in the wheat THOMP:F 18
sleepers:
Great eaters and great s. are not HENRI 3
s. in that quiet earth BRONTE:E 12
snorted we in the Seven S. den? DONNE 41
sleepeth: s., and must be awaked BIBLE 164
sleeping:
All this fuss about s. together WAUGH:E 20
art tha' sleepin' there below? NEWBOLT 4
God went on s. HUGHES:Te 4
happy no-time of his s. OWEN:W 4
He cursed him in s. BARH 5
injury by s. with them STEAD 6
king of s. in the blood SHAK:HEN.IV[2] 7
like s. with someone else's wife BRADB 3
S. as quiet as death THOMAS:D 25
s. enough in the grave PROV 386
S. is no mean art NIET 5
s. pretty rough at the moment WORL 1
s. while awake MONTAIGNE 18
slepyng hound to wake CHAUC 110
sleepless: S. as the river under thee CRANE:H 2
sleeps:
Now s. the crimson petal TENNY 117
She s. alone at last BENCH 2
S. in Elysium SHAK:HEN.V 35
while my pretty one, s. TENNY 105
sleepwalker: with the certainty of a s. HITL 6
sleepy-head: Ain't you 'shamed you s.? STEVENSON:RL 56
sleeve:
brush the Channel with his s. SCHLIEF 1
knits up the ravell'd s. SHAK:MAC 40
tie my heart upon my s. DAVIDS 1
wear my heart upon my s. SHAK:OTH 3
sleeves: Tie up my s. with ribbons HUNTER:A 1
sleigh: on an ebony s. AUD 5
sleight:
by the s. of men BIBLE 532
more th' admire his s. of hand BUTLER:S[1] 27
Slender: Poor S.'s ghost SHEN 2
slept:
s. among his ashes cold KEATS 78
s. like a rock or a man HUGHES:L 1
s. more than any other President MENCK 17
though it hath s. SHAK:MEA 11
thought he thought I s. PATMO 5
slice:
No matter how thin you s. it SMITH:Alf 3
S. him where you like WODE 21
slides: s. of which will now be shown JOYCE:J 26
slight: seems to s. her simple heart TENNY 175
slimy:
s. things did crawl COLERIDGE:ST 29
thousand thousand s. things COLERIDGE:ST 25
sling: like a stone from a s. ANON 100
slings: s. and arrows of outrageous SHAK:HAM 97
slip:
I s., I slide TENNY 203
make a s. in handling us KIP 143
many a s. 'twixt the cup PROV 379
Since he gave us all the s.? BROWNING:R 38
slipper: s. knock'd the ground POPE 37

slippers:
he walks in his golden s. BUNYAN 13
Same old s. LAMP 1
slit: S. your girl's and swing KINGSMILL 1
slitty-eyed: you'll all be s. PHILIP 3
sloe: lush-kept plush-capped s. HOPK:GM 4
slog: foot–s.–s.–s. KIP 111
slogans: feed people with revolutionary s. KHRU 9
sloth:
cares and woe of s. SHELLEY:PB 2
peaceful sloath MILT 155
resty s. Finds the down SHAK:CYM 13
Sinne, but most of s. HERB:G 4
too much time in studies, is s. BACON:F[1] 104
slough: name of the s. was Despond BUNYAN 3
Slough:
bombs, and fall on S. BETJ 6
was an old person of S. LEAR 30
slovenliness: s. is no part of religion WESLEY:J 2
slow:
but ain't it s.? HERB:AP 3
I am s. of speech BIBLE 90
S. and steady wins the race LLOYD:R 2
S. but sure wins PROV 347
S., s., quick, quick SYL 1
Wisely and s. SHAK:ROM 20
slug-horn: s. to my lips I set BROWNING:R 98
sluggard:
foul s.'s comfort CARLYLE:T 35
Go to the ant, thou s. BIBLE 253
S. cradle CHAPMAN:G 1
'Tis the voice of the s. WATTS 14
slugs: S. leave their lair COLERIDGE:ST 66
sluicing: with excellent browsing and s. WODE 4
slum: if you've seen one city s. AGNEW 1
slumber:
abed and daylight s. HOUSM 4
death is s. SHELLEY:PB 15
keepeth thee will not s. BIBLE 239
Let me s. in the hollow GORDON:AM 3
Love itself shall s. SHELLEY:PB 143
s. did my spirit seal WORDS:W 31
s. is more sweet than toil TENNY 34
slumbers:
Golden s. kiss DEK 3
imagine unquiet s. for the sleepers BRONTE:E 12
infant's s., pure and light KEBLE 4
slush:
pure as the driven s. BANK 4
with mush and s. OWEN:D 1
slut:
I am not a s. SHAK:AS 50
Polly is a sad s. GAY 11
sly: Tough, and de-vilish s. DICKENS 128
small:
best things come in s. parcels PROV 35
compare s. things with great VIRGIL 31
feel so s. and sweet PATMO 6
From s. beginnings come great PROV 138
How s. is man GILMORE 3
Is it so s. a thing ARNOLD:M 10
It's a s. world PROV 209
make us feel s. in the right way FORST 21
S. have paid for the folly FONTAINE 7
S. is beautiful PROV 348
S. is Beautiful SCHUM 1
S. matters win great BACON:F[1] 44
s. proportions we just beauties see JONS 48
Too s. to live in ANON 253
what the s. man seeks CONF 11
with s. men no great thing MILL 23
smaller: We often need someone s. FONTAINE 10
Smart: I'd as lief pray with Kit S. JOHNSON:S 109
smattering: s. of everything DICKENS 2
smell:
because of the s. and squashiness O'CONOR 1
Cheard with the grateful s. MILT 186
enjoy the s. of their own farts AUD 63
even a s. remembered GREENE:G 6
guests s. in three days PROV 127
he too Would like a s. ANON 126
once more s. the dew HERB:G 46
shares man's s. HOPK:GM 5
s. too strong of the lamp STERNE 11
world would s. like what it is SHELLEY:PB 62
would s. as sweet SHAK:ROM 11
smelling: like s. their own armpits MILLER:J 1
smells:
he s. April and May SHAK:MERR 11
it s. to heaven SHAK:HAM 130
only dead thing that s. sweet THOMAS:E 2
smile:
Angel faces s. NEWM:JH 16
born to a kiss and a s. FENT 2
call me that, *s.* WIST 1
Cambridge people rarely s. BROOKE 11
Did he s. his work to see? BLAKE:W 69
His s. explained everything GREENE:G 1
I dare not beg a s. HERR 36
I hear a s. CROSS 1
make the learned s. POPE 16
nice s., but he has got iron GROM 1
one vast substantial s. DICKENS 99
protecting itself – with a s. PRIEST 1
recognize your mother with a s. VIRGIL 12
serpent s. BYR 121
should forget and s. ROSSET:C 8
s. dwells a little longer CHAPMAN:A 1
s. his face into more lines SHAK:TWE 46
s. I could feel in my hip pocket CHAND 3
s. of a cosmic Cheshire cat HUX:JS 1
s. of a woman who has just dined DURRELL 7
s. on her lips and a tear SCOTT:W 22
s. on the face of the tiger ANON 107
s. to those who hate BYR 130
smiled a kind of sickly s. HARTE 3
Then shalt thou see me s. ROSSET:DG 13
watery s. And educated TENNY 91
we shall s. SHAK:JUL 80
with s. so sweet UPTON:W 1
smiled:
I remember how you s. LANDOR 12
I smil'd and wond'red SHAK:MEA 16
parents have not s. VIRGIL 13
Voltaire s. HUGO 8
yet they never s. SPEND 4
smiler: smylere with the knyf CHAUC 47
smiles:
charmed it with s. and soap CARROLL 91
corner of the world s. HORACE 21
every time a man s. STERNE 1
killed by frowns and s. SHELLEY:PB 70
making practis'd s. SHAK:WIN 2
Seldom he s. SHAK:JUL 15
S. awake you DEK 3
s. his emptiness betray POPE 126
s., miles and miles BROWNING:R 134
s. to-day To-morrow dies SHELLEY:PB 137
s., Wan as primroses KEATS 42
Then all s. stopped BROWNING:R 22
There's daggers in men's s. SHAK:MAC 58
thy own sweet s. I see COWP 89
to all she s. extends POPE 41
Venus when she s. JONS 47
Wreathed S. MILT 66
smilest: Thou s. and art still ARNOLD:M 5
smiling:
He hides a s. face COWP 10
S. at grief SHAK:TWE 31
S. the boy fell dead BROWNING:R 17
With gently s. jaws CARROLL 4
smite: caitiff s. the other too HOLMES:OW 8
smith:
first s. was the first murd'rer's son COWP 77
s., a mighty man LONGFEL 11
Smith:
Chuck it, S. CHESTERTON 16
conceal him by naming him S. HOLMES:OW 7
that I am the son of Adam S. SMITH:Syd[1] 39
wind, I'll call it F.E. S. HEWART 2
Smithfield: S. muses to the Ear POPE 157
smithy:
forge in the s. of my soul JOYCE:J 9
village s. stands LONGFEL 11
smock: Whan she cast of hir smok CHAUC 84
smoke:
Above the smoak and stirr MILT 16
corrupted by this stinking s. JAMES VI/I 3
counties overhung with s. MORRIS:W 6
doctor has always told me to s. SATIE 1
dunnest s. of hell SHAK:MAC 20
fill him full of s. and embers JONS 3
good cigar is a S. KIP 31
He smoorit them with s. DUNB 1
horrible Stygian s. JAMES VI/I 2
in their rotten s.? SHAK:SON 16
no s. without fire PROV 382
notice imploring you to s. PRIEST 2
only s. on special occasions ANON 225
or a man who does not s. STEVENSON:RL 9
salt-caked s. stack MASE 9
s. across an azure sky PUSH 5
s. that rubs its muzzle ELIOT:TS 4
s. torn from the fumy engine MUIR:E 6
to turn s. into gold ELIZ I 15
you gwine do wid de s.? HARRIS:JC 10
your pipe ... and s. it BARH 8
smoked: Who s. like a chimney BARH 7
smoking:
acquired his power of s. LAMB:Ch 47
custom loathesome to the eye* JAMES VI/I 2
If you resolve to give up s. FREUD:C 1
place for penalties for s. NEIL 4
This vice brings in one hundred* NAPO III 1
What a blessing this s. is HELPS 2
smoking-room: sometimes in a s., one learns KIP 125
smoky: noise and s. breath SMITH:Alex 2
smoorit: He s. them with smoke DUNB 1
smooth:
cities had rubbed him s. GREENE:G 2
I am a s. man BIBLE 57
person and a s. dispose SHAK:OTH 17
s. him fair DARLEY 2
smote: s. his enemies in the hinder BIBLE 220
smudge: wears man's s. HOPK:GM 5
smug: s. and thoroughly uncomfortable POUND 22
snail:
creeping like s. Unwillingly SHAK:AS 34
slug-abed s. upon the thorn THOMP:F 16
s., which everywhere doth DONNE 9
s.'s on the thorn BROWNING:R 9
turn not pale, beloved s. CARROLL 33
wet church the size of a s. THOMAS:D 14
snails: Frogs and s. And puppy-dogs' NURS 83
snake:
dangerous than a garter s. BROWN:JM 1
earth doth like a s. renew SHELLEY:PB 153
scotch'd the s., not kill'd SHAK:MAC 65
s. came to my water-trough LAWR:DH 32
S. is living yet BELLOC 9
s. lurks in the grass VIRGIL 9
s. throws her enamell'd skin SHAK:MID 20
snakes:
See the s. that they rear DRYD 112
spotted s. with double tongue SHAK:MID 21
snap-dragon: s. growing on the walls NEWM:JH 12
snapper-up: s. of unconsidered trifles SHAK:WIN 13
snare:
I saw the s. TENNY 62
s. in which the feet of women ADDAMS 1
There is a rabbit in a s. STEPHENS 5
world's great s. uncaught? SHAK:ANT 45
Snark:
If your S. be a Boojum CARROLL 90
S. *was* a Boojum CARROLL 92
sneer:
face it with a s. ROOS:T 19
laughing Devil in his s. BYR 30
teach the rest to s. POPE 121
Who can refute a s.? PALEY 1
sneering:
do your duty when men are s. WILSON:W 5
S. doesn't become either SHAW 112
sneery: looked very s. ASHFORD 10
sneeze:
like having a good s. LAWR:DH 38
you s., You might damage LEAR 30
sneezed:
Not to be s. at COLMAN:G[2] 5
when a British Prime minister s. LEVIN 2
sneezes: beat him when he s. CARROLL 12
snickersnee: I drew my s. GILB:WS 75
sniffles: with s. predominating HENRY:O 1
snip: Here's s. and nip and SHAK:TAM 11
sniper: s. turned over the dead O'FAOL 2
snivelling: S. snufflebusters SEMP 2
snob:
admires mean things is a S. THACK 12

not to be sometimes a S. THACK 13
snored: simply sat and s. CHESTERTON 17
snorer: why a s. can't hear himself TWAIN 25
snores: S. out the watch of night SHAK:HEN.IV[2] 44
snorters: helplessness being foreign to s. GUNN:J 1
snotgreen: s. sea JOYCE:J 11
snouted: world 'as got me s. DENNIS:CJ 1
snow:
as s. before a summer sun TEC 1
bloodless lay the untrodden s. CAMPBELL:T 19
Drifts the appalling s. AUD 7
Earth in forgetful s. ELIOT:TS 34
Every branch big* HARDY:T 45
frolic architecture of the s. EMER 96
garment of unsullied s. SOUTHEY 17
He sends the s. in winter CAMPBELL:Ja 1
I love s. SHELLEY:PB 140
last long streak of s. TENNY 180
mark'd but the fall o' the s. JONS 46
mockery king of s. SHAK:RIC.II 38
pale Virgin shrouded in s. BLAKE:W 70
recollect the S. DICKIN:E 6
Rose buds fill'd with s. CAMPION 9
running salt and s. DUG 1
see the cherry hung with s. HOUSM 3
silent pinnacles of aged s. TENNY 25
s. came flying BRIDGES:R 6
s. disfigured the public statues AUD 35
S. has fallen, s. on s. ROSSET:C 18
s. of ferne yere CHAUC 118
S. upon the Desert's FITZGER:E 10
we shall have s. PROV 298
When the s. lay round about NEALE 1
Whiter than new s. SHAK:ROM 30
wish a s. in May's SHAK:LOV 2
ye Ice and S. PRAY 15
Snow White: used to be S.W. . . . but I drifted WEST:M 12
snowed:
it s. and it s. THOMAS:D 40
snewed in his hous of mete CHAUC 22
snowing: shoveling the walk before it stops s. DILL 1
snows:
are the s. of yesteryear VILLON 1
s. Are sparkling to the moon TENNY 43
s. have fled HORACE 53
snowy:
S., Flowy, Blowy ELLIS:G 1
s. summits old in story TENNY 106
snuff:
enjoy another pinch of s. BAILLY 1
only took s. GOLDS 41
You abuse s. COLERIDGE:ST 82
snufflebusters: Snivelling s. SEMP 2
snug:
give me a little s. property EDGE 5
lie I as s. as they ANON 128
s. as a bug in a rug FRANKLIN:B 25
s. little Island DIBDIN:T 1
so: if I said s.; it was s. GOLDS 47
soap:
charmed it with smiles and s. CARROLL 91
hands with invisible s. HOOD 15
hateful nurse who smelt of s. BETJ 34
S. and education are not as sudden TWAIN 29
used your s. two years ago PUNCH 23
soar:
singing still dost s. SHELLEY:PB 95
S. not too high MASSIN 2
Thou canst not s. SHELLEY:PB 119
who s., but never roam WORDS:W 135
soars: if he s. with his own wings BLAKE:W 38
S.O.B.: over-educated S.O.B. TRU 7
sobbing: na solace mycht his s. ces HENRYS 1
sober:
at least not s. JOHNSON:S 77
be compulsorily s. MAGEE 1
clean, shaved and s. CHAND 1
godly, righteous, and s. life PRAY 5
Half as s. as a judge LAMB:Ch 45
How do you look when I'm s.? LARD 2
ingenious, s., nor kind ANON 135
No s. man dances CIC 15
sleep with a s. cannibal MELV 2
s. and no high flyer PEPYS 12
s. as a judge FIELDING 8
s., as a Scot ne'er was MACDIAR 8
s. man, among his boys TENNY 150
S., steadfast, and demure MILT 79
that will go to bed s. FLETCH:J 6
to Philip s. VALERIUS 1
Tomorrow we'll be s. ANON 8
Sobranies: Balkan S. in a wooden box BETJ 35
sobriety: men are disguised by s. DEQ 3
sobs: Life is made up of s. HENRY:O 1
social:
admit that he has no s. inferiors RUSS:B 19
Cursed be the s. wants TENNY 73
half way up the s. ladder LILL 3
Man is a s. animal SPIN 3
no s. differences – till women come WELLS:HG 4
Owing to the weather, English S. life MACAULAY:R 3
Self-love and S. be the same POPE 100
S. Contract is nothing more WELLS:HG 1
s. structure has become incapable TROT 5
some s. and class pigeonhole HOWARD:P 1
social science:
nor commit A s.s. AUD 46
S.S., – not a 'gay science' CARLYLE:T 54
socialism:
government does for others as s. WARR 1
Marxian S. must always remain KEYN 2
nothing in S. that a little age DURA 1
priorities is the religion of S. BEVAN 10
S. can arrive only by bicycle VIERA 1
S. does not mean much more ORWELL 6
s. in terms of the scientific revolution WILSON:Harold 4
s. is totally alien to the British THATCH:M 15
s. would not lose its human face DUBC 1
Under s. *all* will govern LENIN 5
worst advertisement for S. is its adherents ORWELL 5
socialist:
Christian s. who happens to be HAYD 1
construct the s. order LENIN 12, 8
socialists:
We are all s. now EDWARD VIII 8
We are all S. now HARC 1
society:
Affluent S. GALB 1
definition of a free s. STEVENSON:A 5
desperate oddfellow s. THOREAU 20
Education is simply the soul of a s. CHESTERTON 53
first duty to serve s. JOHNSON:S 133
hell for s. TWAIN 41
kindness and consolidates s. JOHNSON:S 85
make a man unfit for s. CHAMFORT 4
Man seeketh in s. comfort BACON:F[1] 14
Man was formed for s. BLACKS 1
no intellectual s. can flourish where JOHNSON:P 1
no such thing as s. THATCH:M 23
One great s. alone on earth WORDS:W 161
Open S. and its Enemies POPP 1
permissive s. has been allowed to JENKINS:R 1
person who cannot live in s. ARISTOT 15
s. corrupts him ROUSS:JJ 5
S. everywhere is in conspiracy EMER 6
S. goes on and on MACDON:R 1
S. is no comfort SHAK:CYM 14
s. to be found out of London HAZL 12
s., where none intrudes BYR 116
Soul selects her own S. DICKIN:E 10
the tribal or 'closed' s. POPP 2
When s. requires to be rebuilt MILL 4
sociology: S. is a lot of waffle WOOT 1
sock: s. is a highly sensitive conjugal KAUFMAN 1
socks:
s. compelled one's attention SAKI 13
when thy s. were on JONS 42
Socrates: easily contradict S. PLATO 15
sod:
Green s. above lie light ANON 147
high requiem become a s. KEATS 93
under my head a s. BALL 16
soda-water:
Sermons and s. the day after BYR 178
stopped short at squirting s. WODE 2
soda water: wash their feet in s.w. ELIOT:TS 44
sodomy: rum, s. and the lash CHURCH:W 68
sods: s. with our bayonets turning WOLFE:C 2
sofa:
lie on a s. and listen to music BOWEN:S 1
rather lie on a s. than sweep CONRAN 2
soft:
S., as young YOUNG:E 13
wisdom does not make us s. PERIC 2
softly: S. come and s. go ORRED 1
softness: For s. shee MILT 192
soger: s. frae the wars returns BURNS:R 112
soil:
Before the s. hath smutch'd it? JONS 46
Blood and s. DARRE 1
s. Is bare now HOPK:GM 5
this the S., the Clime MILT 121
soirée: friendly swarry, consisting of DICKENS 43
solace: na s. mycht his sobbing ces HENRYS 1
solar:
converting s. energy into food STENHO 1
crash of the whole s. CARLYLE:T 61
sold:
I'd not have s. her for it SHAK:OTH 65
s. a goodly manor for a song SHAK:ALL 8
s. cheap what is most dear SHAK:SON 51
s. well simply because it was selling BOORS 1
soldan: S. of Byzantium is smiling CHESTERTON 18
soldier:
as a s. of the King KITCHEN 2
boastful s. PLAU 3
can always tell an old s. SHAW 3
chocolate cream s. SHAW 4
death who had the s. singled DOUGLAS:K 2
Drinking is the s.'s pleasure DRYD 107
For a s. I listed DIBDIN:C 5
for not having been a s. JOHNSON:S 200
French s. is a civilian in disguise TUCHOL 8
I said an elder s. SHAK:JUL 71
in the s. is flat blasphemy SHAK:MEA 14
never expect a s. to think SHAW 26
No s. can fight unless MARLBOR:J 1
our s. slighted JORD 2
S. armd with Sword & Gun BLAKE:W 89
s. counts his wounds PROP 1
s., Full of strange oaths SHAK:AS 34
S. of the Great War Known KIP 30
S., rest SCOTT:W 37
s.'s grave BYR 242
s.'s life is terrible hard MILNE 1
s.'s pole is fall'n SHAK:ANT 58
summer s. PAINE 3
would himself have been a s. SHAK:HEN.IV[1] 19
soldier-saints: s., who row on row BROWNING:R 154
soldiers:
English s. fight like lions HOFFMAN:M 1
god of s. SHAK:COR 19
hapless S. sigh BLAKE:W 74
Old s. never die PROV 306
Old s., sweethearts WEBSTER:J 1
Only the scarlet s. AUD 18
Onward! Christian s. BARING-G 2
our s. slighted QUAR 3
proud array of s. WILDE:J 1
shirts for s., sister Susie WESTON 1
should have betrayed our s. CHURCH:W 61
S. are citizens of death's SASS 7
S. are dreamers SASS 8
S. of the ploughshare as well RUSKIN 13
some s. were picking potatoes YELT 2
steel my s.' hearts SHAK:HEN.V 36
What is the world, O s.? DE LA M 2
Ye s. of the Cross DUFFI 1
soldiery: for fear of licentious s. WELD 1
sole:
no rest for the s. of her foot BIBLE 38
nothing can be s. or whole YEATS 95
solecism: speak of eternity without a s. BROWNE:T 8
solemn:
air a s. stillness GRAY:T 16
untouched by s. thought WORDS:W 43
solicitor: can only go to his s. DISR:B 36
solitary:
Be not s. BURTON:Ro 26
if you are s., be not idle JOHNSON:S 74
Man is not a s. animal RUSS:B 18
s. child WORDS:W 25

s. Highland lass WORDS:W 79
To wander s. there MARV 22
took their solitarie way MILT 261
waste And s. places SHELLEY:PB 23
solitude:
God is the s. of man SARTRE 8
I love tranquil s. SHELLEY:PB 141
In a s. of the sea HARDY:T 21
In s. what happiness MILT 234
independence of s. EMER 9
makes a s., and calls it BYR 24
Musing in s. WORDS:W 109
passing sweet, is s. COWP 42
place of seclusion and s. MONTAIGNE 9
resonance of his s. CONNOLLY:C 17
self-sufficing power of S. WORDS:W 150
so companionable as s. THOREAU 18
S. gives rise to what is original MANN:T 3
S. is the fate of all outstanding SCHOP 2
s. is the richness of self SARTON 1
s. sometimes is best MILT 243
s.! where are the charms COWP 46
this delicious s. MARV 14
this s. Through which we go DE LA M 2
Whosoever is delighted in s. BACON:F[1] 65
worst s., to have no BACON:F[1] 28
Solomon:
heart Of wisest S. MILT 265
King S. wrote the Proverbs NAY 1
S. his son reigned BIBLE 174
S. of saloons BROWNING:R 178
than the felicities of S. BACON:F[1] 32
Solomon Grundy: S.G., Born on a Monday NURS 67
solution:
difficulty for every s. SAMUEL 6
Final S. to the Jewish question GOEB 1
If you're not part of the s. CLEAV 1
lasting s. is that Europe itself LOTH 1
people were a kind of s. CAVAFY 1
s. of the problem of life WITT 1
think of revolution not as the s. WEIL 3
Solzhenitsyn: not since we voted to expel S. ANON 159
somebody:
dreary – to be – S. DICKIN:E 3
s. must, or the thing HOPE:An 2
When everyone is somebodee GILB:WS 113
someone:
happening to s. else ROGERS:W 2
next morning that it was s. else ROGERS:S 6
Somerset House: aphorism in the records of S.M. SMITH:FE 1
something:
Everybody was up to s. COWARD 14
learn s. about everything HUX:TH 16
Time for a little s. MILNE 13
somewhat: More than S. RUNYON 1
son:
Absalom, my s., my s. BIBLE 158
bare-legg'd beggarly s. of a gun CALVER 6
England's greatest s. TENNY 191
examined your s.'s head MUIR:F 1
Fitzdotterel's eldest s. BROUGH 1
Forgive your s. JOYCE:J 46
gave his only begotten S. BIBLE 477
Great David's greater S. MONTGOM:J 1
her S. was hanging there JACOP 1
make a man of her s. ROWL:H 2
My s. is still my s. GILMORE 2
only-begotten S. of God PRAY 66
only S., Sir, might expect GOLDS 61
our newborn s. dominates THEM 1
satisfaction by her relation to a s. FREUD:S 4
she shall bring forth a s. BIBLE 374
s. of his old age BIBLE 67
S. of Morn in weary Nights BLAKE:W 110
struck the father when the s. swore BURTON:Ro 23
Take now thy s. BIBLE 51
This is my beloved S. BIBLE 379
two-legged thing, a s. DRYD 39
unto us a s. is given BIBLE 308
what's a s.? KYD 4
When a father gives to his s. PROV 423
wise s. maketh a glad father BIBLE 257
your s.'s tender years JUV 25
son-in-law:
different s. might have described LOWER 1
s. also rises KNOPF 1
son of a bitch:
because he was a dumb s.o.a.b. TRU 6
over-educated S.O.B. TRU 7
son-of-a-bitch: poor s. PARKER:D 29
song:
acquaints His soul with s. BROWNING:R 208
all this for a s.? BURL 1
Any little old s. HARDY:T 44
can hear the monks' s. CANUTE 1
carcase of an old s. THOMAS:RS 2
chorus of a Revolutionary s. VALL 1
despise the skylark's s.? BRONTE:A 4
ditto, ditto my s. GILB:WS 53
end of ane old s. OGIL 1
Everything ends with a s. BEAUMA 5
Give ear unto my s. GOLDS 13
given a penny for a s. YEATS 33
govern thou my S. MILT 225
Hear a s. that echoes cheerly TENNY 15
hear the bird's s. without EMER 62
heard her singing her last s. TENNY 22
I have a s. to sing GILB:WS 96
I made my s. a coat YEATS 39
I the s. GILB:WS 41
in suffering what they teach in s. SHELLEY:PB 25
In the triumph s. BARING-G 4
It's the s. of a merryman GILB:WS 97
listening when the s. has ended SAINT-LA 1
Lord's s. in a strange land? BIBLE 246
low lone s. CARP 1
Luxuriant s. YEATS 53
maker of the s. she sang STEVENS 9
my s. begins and endeth SIDNEY:P 11
my s. comes native KEATS 24
not love wine, woman and s. LUTHER 9
not worth saying is made into a s. BEAUMA 1
oaten stop, or pastoral s. COLLINS:Will 5
On wings of s. HEINE 2
One grand sweet s. KINGSLEY:C 17
our s. shall rise to thee HEB 4
own accord my s. used to OSB:J 11
pipe that s. again BLAKE:W 13
play a s. for me DYL 7
ready to start a s. VIRGIL 14
shall moralize my s. SPENS 20
Short swallow-flights of s. TENNY 147
simple s. for thinking hearts WORDS:W 24
Sing a s. of sixpence NURS 66
Sing to the Lord a new s. BIBLE 599
sold a goodly manor for a s. SHAK:ALL 8
S. charms the Sense MILT 163
S. made in lieu SPENS 15
s. of a lad that is gone STEVENSON:RL 68
s. of canaries Never varies NASH 13
s. of night's sweet bird SHELLEY:PB 123
s. of the birds for mirth GUR 1
s. that nerves a nation's TENNY 294
s. that was more of a screech SHELLEY:PB 20
s. too daring PRIOR 1
suck melancholy out of a s. SHAK:AS 25
swear to the truth of a s.? PRIOR 10
sweet a brotherhood in s. KEATS 1
sweetest passage of a s. MEY:A 2
sweetest s. ear ever BYR 50
tedious S. should here have MILT 13
That glorious s. of old SEARS 1
That old and antique s. SHAK:TWE 24
That s. to-night Will not go SHAK:OTH 55
thinks two notes a s. DAVIES:WH 6
Time an endless s. YEATS 16
to spur me into s.? YEATS 111
unto the Lord a new s. BIBLE 230
weigh this s. with the great YEATS 25
What s. the Sirens sang BROWNE:T 55
when this s. is sung and past WYATT 5
songs:
all their s. are sad CHESTERTON 5
best of all trades, to make s. BELLOC 26
Book of S. and Sonnets here SHAK:MERR 2
cannot sing the old s. now CALVER 5
despairing s. are the most beautiful MUSSET 3
dirty s. and dreary BROOKE 23
Droving s. are very pretty LAWS 4
Fair the fall of s. STEVENSON:RL 65
give them fruit for their s. ADDIS 26
Go, s., for ended THOMP:F 4
He koude songes make CHAUC 6
I cannot sing the old s. CLARI 1
I wrote my happy s. BLAKE:W 14
lean and flashy s. MILT 54
matchless s. does mediate MARV 23
Music-hall s. provide the dull MAUGH 18
Sing no sad s. for me ROSSET:C 12
Singing s. of expectation BARING-G 5
S. consecrate to truth SHELLEY:PB 18
s. for me and my aunts SHAK:WIN 12
s. not heard before HORACE 27
s. that voices never shared SIMON:P 1
s. they have sung For a HAMMER 5
sweetest s. are those that tell SHELLEY:PB 99
sonnet:
it turned to a S. DOBSON:HA 1
Scorn not the S. WORDS:W 133
s. is a moment's monument ROSSET:DG 7
S.'s scanty plot of ground WORDS:W 51
sure I shall turn s. SHAK:LOV 3
sonnets:
s. turn'd to holy psalms PEELE 2
write ten passably effective S. HUX:A 9
written s. all his life? BYR 184
sons:
best of the s. of the morning HEB 1
Come on, you s. of bitches DALY:D 1
free as the s. of the waves GARRICK 4
Get you the s. your HOUSM 2
God's s. are things MADDEN 1
have further s. to their name EDGAR 2
If I had a thousand s. SHAK:HEN.IV[2] 43
jaundiced eye on its younger s. WODE 29
Now we are all s. of bitches BAIN 1
s. and your daughters shall BIBLE 355
s. of the prophet ANON 95
Their s., they gave BROOKE 19
things are the s. of heaven JOHNSON:S 6
three stout and stalwart s. BALL 65
soon:
Come s., s. SHELLEY:PB 148
S. learnt, s. forgotten PROV 349
soot:
in s. I sleep BLAKE:W 18
s. cannot spoil your white BLAKE:W 19
soothe: s. a savage breast CONG 33
soothed: sooth'd his soul to pleasures DRYD 109
soothes:
It s. his sorrows NEWT:J 2
saddens while it s. BROWNING:R 59
sophistries: old s. of June DICKIN:E 2
sophistry:
Destroy this fib or s. POPE 118
nothing but s. and illusion HUME 13
wits to s. and affectation BACON:F[1] 2
Sophocles:
S. is the most perfect COLERIDGE:ST 92
S. said that he portrayed SOPH 6
Sophonisba: Oh! S. THOMS:Ja[1] 1
sops: S. in wine SPENS 3
Sordello: hear S.'s story told BROWNING:R 7
sore: perfectly s. with loving her DICKENS 139
sores: vile, incurable s. OWEN:W 5
sorrel: simplest growth of meadow-sweet or s. SWIN 50
sorrow:
any s. like unto my s. BIBLE 343
busy bee has no time for s. BLAKE:W 36
Ere the s. comes with years? BROWNING:EB 2
Give s. words SHAK:MAC 96
glut thy s. on a morning rose KEATS 96
Hang s. WITHER 2
hang s., care'll kill a cat JONS 1
heart in an anvil unto s. MARLOWE 26
In s. thou shalt bring forth BIBLE 23
is s., there is holy ground WILDE:O 102
knowledge increaseth s. BIBLE 280
lead to s. in the morning HOGG 9
melt into s. BYR 22
mused on s. but its own CAMPBELL:T 3
natural s., loss, or pain WORDS:W 81
never spent the nights of s. GOET 6
night of doubt and s. BARING-G 5
No s. is deeper than the remembrance DANTE 6
Nought but vast s. was there DE LA M 21
One for s., two for mirth PROV 309
Parting is such sweet s. SHAK:ROM 19
Pure and complete s. is just TOLS:L 4
put away s. like a shoe SYNGE 6
send the sorowe and shame SKEL:J 2

Sit by the fireside with S. SHELLEY:PB 161
so beguile thy s. SHAK:TIT 2
S. and sighing shall flee BIBLE 318
S., cruel fellowship TENNY 128
s. dogging sinne HERB:G 20
s. for angels BROWNING:R 55
S. is tranquillity PARKER:D 9
s. never comes too late. GRAY:T 8
S., wilt thou live with me TENNY 160
S., with her family of Sighs SHELLEY:PB 111
S. without labour is base RUSKIN 24
s.'s crown of s. TENNY 75
S.'s most detested fruit BYR 82
swerd of sorowe CHAUC 91
This s.'s heavenly SHAK:OTH 60
To S., I bade good-morrow KEATS 41
useless and hopeless s. JOHNSON:S 75
We are not sure of s. SWIN 30
wear a golden s. SHAK:HEN.VIII 6
with s. to the grave BIBLE 75
wrapt in cloud of sorrowe CAMPION 2
Write s. on the bosom SHAK:RIC.II 27
your s. is not dead MILT 57

sorrows:
and s. end SHAK:SON 12
bids our s. cease WESLEY:C 3
broods a nest of s. TAYL:Jer 4
carried our s. BIBLE 328
compositions spring from my s. SCHUB 1
costly in our s. STERNE 53
Half the s. of women ELIOT:G 23
It soothes his s. NEWT:J 2
man of s. BIBLE 328
mortal s. touch the heart VIRGIL 41
my s. are at an end GAY 15
S. bring forth BLAKE:W 42
s. of your changing face YEATS 14
Telling one's s. often brings CORNEILLE 7
There are few s. SMITH:LP 2
When s. come SHAK:HAM 163
world's great s. were born RUSS:GW 1

sorry:
Better be safe than s. PROV 42
never having to say you're s. SEGAL 1
s. for it when she's dead BEHAN:Br 1

sorts:
all s. and conditions of men PRAY 38
takes all s. to make a world PROV 211

Sosostris: Madame S., famous clairvoyante ELIOT:TS 36

sot: she has married a s. POUND 8

sothfastnesse: dwelle with s. CHAUC 124

soufflé: Can a s. rise twice? KEATING 1

sought:
She s. him east BALL 44
unknowing what he s. DRYD 119
worthy to be s. BUCHANAN 1
yet in love He s. me BAKER 1

soul:
be still, my s. HOUSM 25
become a living s. WORDS:W 6
change and migration of the s. SOC 4
chosen thus to fling his s. HARDY:T 17
Christ cannot save thy s. MARLOWE 36
Christe receive thy saule BALL 36
Clothing for the s. divine BLAKE:W 86
common s. Inspires and feeds VIRGIL 71
dark night of the s. FITZGER:FS 12
dim Windows of the S. BLAKE:W 108
eager s., biting for anger FULLER:T[1] 3
Education is simply the s. of a society CHESTERTON 53
eternal summer in his s. HOLMES:OW 9
eyes are the window of the s. PROV 113
eyes are the windows of the s. BEERB 7
eyes into my very s. SHAK:HAM 141
Fair seed-time had my s. WORDS:W 143
fine point of his s. taken off KEATS 122
first offshoot (S.) PLOT 1
For my unconquerable s. HENL 1
Hark, my s. COWP 6
Hauf a s. a Scot maun use MACDIAR 13
He fancied that I gave a s. YEATS 81
His s. is marching on HALL:CS 1
I am the captain of my s. HENL 2
I gave you your own s. SHAW 99
I have a Catholic s. ERAS 5
I have freed my s. BERNARD:St 1
If half the little s. is dirt? TENNY 100
Impropriety is the s. of wit MAUGH 5
In mystery our s. ARNOLD:M 12
iron enter into his s. STERNE 48
It is the s. that sees CRAB 27
leaves s. free a little BROWNING:R 76
Life and S., the man who will WHITEHORN 2
limed s. SHAK:HAM 131
limits within which a human s. SCHREIN 1
lips suck forth my s. MARLOWE 38
living s. was flash'd on mine TENNY 172
loafe and invite my s. WHITMAN 2
Lord have mercy on your s. CHAPLIN 1
lose his own s.? BIBLE 418
May my s. follow soon TENNY 43
Medicine for the s. DIOD 1
mighty s., how small a body JUV 22
mount, my s. SHAK:RIC.II 47
my s. drew back HERB:G 53
My s. he doth restore SCOTTISH 1
My s. in agony COLERIDGE:ST 24
my s. is white BLAKE:W 27
My s., like to a ship WEBSTER:J 15
my s. shall be healed MASS 18
my s. thirsteth for thee BIBLE 218
My s.'s in arms CIB 4
never once possess our s. ARNOLD:M 40
No coward s. is mine BRONTE:E 1
not the tumult of the s. WORDS:W 123
One drop would save my s. MARLOWE 40
Onely a sweet and vertuous s. HERB:G 32
Out of his bitter s. YEATS 77
passing of the sweetest s. TENNY 159
Poor intricated s. DONNE 103
Poor s., the centre SHAK:SON 61
positive I have a s. STERNE 51
progress of a deathless s. DONNE 19
Raises from Hell a Human S. BLAKE:W 84
rapt s. sitting in thine eyes MILT 80
record one lost s. more BROWNING:R 55
save my s., if I have a s. ANON 223
save my soule By thy myght PSALMS 1
shorten I the stature of my s. MERED:G 19
so panteth my s. after thee BIBLE 212
S. and body part like friends CRASH 16
s. but flown beyond MARLOWE 18
s. Christian in its very nature TERT 1
S. clap its hands YEATS 72
s. doth magnify the Lord BIBLE 607
s. dwelling in two bodies ARISTOT 24
s. into the boughs does glide MARV 20
s. is an enchanted boat SHELLEY:PB 80
s. is born old WILDE:O 59
s. is dead that slumbers LONGFEL 1
s. is immortal and capable PLATO 14
s. is not more than the body WHITMAN 10
s. lies buried in the ink CLARE:J 14
s. may but ascend MARLOWE 43
s. may not profit by MERED:G 14
s. must feed on something MCAULEY 1
s. of her beauty and love SHELLEY:PB 92
s. of man, like unextinguished SHELLEY:PB 82
S. of mighty Chiefs HOMER 1
S. of the Age JONS 39
S. selects her own Society DICKIN:E 10
s. shall have her earthly freight WORDS:W 61
s. Smoothed itself out BROWNING:R 130
s. started at the knee-cap LEWIS:W 6
s. that knew not fear DAVIDS 3
S. that rises with us WORDS:W 58
S., the body's guest RALE 3
s.'s dark cottage WALLER 9
s.'s second inn DONNE 21
soule is forme, and doth SPENS 47
strains that might create a s. MILT 36
That puff of vapour* BROWNING:R 106
Thou art a s. in bliss SHAK:KING L 76
through the chapel of my s. HODG 4
thy s. shall be required BIBLE 459
Thy s. the fixt foot DONNE 69
Thy s. was like a star WORDS:W 48
'tis my outward s. DONNE 39
two to bear my s. away ADY 1
What fortitude the S. contains DICKIN:E 19
What s. is without faults? RIMB 3
What s. was his WORDS:W 112
when a single S. does fence MARV 9
whereby the S. and Body are united SWIFT 50
whole s. thro' My lips TENNY 11
whose s. is not a clod KEATS 100
writhe in – is my s. MACDIAR 7

soul-making: vale of S. KEATS 156

soul-sides: Boasts two s. BROWNING:R 141

sould: hides a dark s. MILT 30

souls:
between the shores of your s. GIBRAN 3
beyond the reaches of our s.? SHAK:HAM 36
far be s. profane VIRGIL 67
fire our s. to regale BLAKE:W 73
If s. can die as well LUCRET 7
left your s. on earth KEATS 55
lovers' s. descend T'affections DONNE 37
Most people sell their s. SMITH:LP 4
our soules for to beye CHAUC 122
paint the s. of men BROWNING:R 112
poor jewel of their s. STEVENSON:RL 41
s. but the shadows of the living BROWNE:T 44
s. dwell in the house of tomorrow GIBRAN 1
s. have sight of that immortal sea WORDS:W 65
s. I could not save HOUSM 36
s. mounting up to God ROSSET:DG 4
s. of Christian peoples CHESTERTON 16
s. of women are so small BUTLER:S[1] 40
spinifex of dry s. STOW 2
take pity on us poor s. VILLON 2
they have no s. COKE:E 4
times that try men's s. PAINE 3
to play with s. BROWNING:R 133
two s. which dwell, alas GOET 12
Two s. with but a single LOVELL:M 1
Two s. with just one HALM 1
vulgar flight of common s. MURPHY:A 1
When divine s. appear EMER 89
Where s. do couch on flowers SHAK:ANT 52
whilst our s. negotiate DONNE 35
Whither depart the s. of the brave CLOUGH 18

sound:
all is not s. JONS 23
evening s. was smooth MUIR:E 5
full of s. and fury SHAK:MAC 113
My love to thee is s. SHAK:LOV 22
other not very s. SMOL 8
remove the s. from Mussolini BROWN:Geoff 1
self-same s. On my spirit STEVENS 4
something direful in the s. AUSTEN 55
s. is the s. of the sea ELIOT:TS 69
s. must seeem an echo POPE 20
s. of iron on stone DE LA M 9
Sweet is every s. TENNY 119
sweet s. That breathes upon SHAK:TWE 1
this, the s. and rumour? MORRIS:W 8
To heal the blows of s. HOLMES:OW 1
twelve great shocks of s. TENNY 94

sound bite: TV s.b. also makes it impossible JACK:R 1

sounding: Went s. on WORDS:W 116

sounds:
concord of sweet s. SHAK:MERC 51
s. will take care of themselves CARROLL 25
Strange s. along the chancel pass'd SCOTT:W 6
sympathy with s. COWP 78

soup:
Beautiful S., so rich CARROLL 35
do not take s. at luncheon CURZON 2
licked the s. from the cooks' BROWNING:R 125
take the nasty s. away HOFFMAN:H 1

soups: live on good s. MOLIERE 28

sour:
Better salt than s. PROV 44
fathers have eaten s. grapes BIBLE 345
grapes are s. AESOP 2
green s. ringlets make SHAK:TEM 29
prove in digestion s. SHAK:RIC.II 9

source: Tell it to forget the s. MERED:G 32

sourest: turn s. by their deeds SHAK:SON 41

Souter Johnny: at his elbow, S.J. BURNS:R 85

south:
beaker full of the warm S. KEATS 93
but not in the S. POTTER:S 5
fierce and fickle is the S. TENNY 110
S. of my days' circle WRIGHT:J 4
You come to the S. Country SLESS 3

South Africa:
anyone in S.A. who ever supported TUTU 2
Christ in this country* DEBL 1
era came to an end in S.A. PATON 5
S.A., renowned both far CAMPBELL:R 1

South African: S.A. Police would leave no stone

SHARPE 1
South Africans:
black S.A. said to white PATON 5
society in which all S.A. MANDELA:N 4
south-wind: s. rushing warm TENNY 79
Southey: He had written much* BYR 151
sovereign:
bandy civilities with my S. JOHNSON:S 135
s. has ... three rights BAGE 12
s. of sighs and groans SHAK:LOV 8
Subject and S. are clean different CHARLES I 4
sovereignty:
exclusive national s. has passed BOUT 1
idea of absolute national s. MCMILL:J 1
That is the top of s. KEATS 52
Wommen desiren to have sovereynetee CHAUC 88
Soviet: Communism is S. power plus LENIN 9
Soviet Union:
absorbed in the S.U. WEBB:S 3
nostalgia would be satisfied in the S.U. UST 9
sow:
as you s., you are like to reap BUTLER:S[1] 25
old s. that eats her farrow JOYCE:J 7
s. by the right ear HENRY VIII 1
s. that hath overwhelm'd SHAK:HEN.IV[2] 5
They that s. in tears BIBLE 242
soweth: whatsoever a man s. BIBLE 531
Soweto: S. on June 16, 1976 PATON 4
sown: They have s. the wind BIBLE 353
sows: S., and he shall not reap SWIN 15
space:
clearly require the most s. GALB 8
foot less of s. and it would BENCH 6
more s. where nobody is STEIN:G 3
never knew the depth of s. GILMORE 3
puzzles me more than time and s. LAMB:Ch 38
s. for delight SWIN 14
S. may produce new Worlds MILT 141
s. that many poor supplied GOLDS 33
s. was the uncontrollable mystery MCLUH 1
star-cold and the dread of s. BRENN 2
vacuum or s. in which there is DESCA 4
yields The s. to dwell in BROWN:FM 1
spaces: silence of these infinite s. PASC 8
spaceship: passenger on the s., Earth FULLER:RB 2
spade:
fiddle, sir, and s. SCOTT:W 79
have never seen a s. WILDE:O 95
nominate a s. a s. JONS 12
poor crooked scythe and s. SHIRL 3
S.! with which Wilkinson WORDS:W 102
spades: let S. be trumps POPE 49
Spain:
King of S.'s daughter came NURS 21
Love-light of S. CHESTERTON 20
make castels thanne in Spayne CHAUC 104
not into the hands of S. TENNY 285
singeing of the King of S.'s Beard DRAKE 2
slow old tunes of S. MASE 6
S. forming a head HARDY:T 71
where are the galleons of S.? DOBSON:HA 4
spam: they offered s. MALAM 1
Spaniards: thrash the S. too DRAKE 4
Spanish:
Fair S. ladies ANON 64
I must learn S. BROWNING:R 48
season it's been for you S. dancers BANK 6
some are fond of S. wine MASE 7
S. fleet thou *canst* not see SHERIDAN:RB 35
speak S. to God CHARLES V 3
stupid in Latin as well as in S. CERV 26
spare:
I can't s. this man LINC 28
s. all I have FARQ 19
s. the rod, and spoil BUTLER:S[1] 26
s. time and in his working GILL 1
s. your country's flag WHITTIER 5
spareth: He that s. his rod BIBLE 260
spark:
ae s. o' Nature's fire BURNS:R 18
s. of inextinguishable thought SHELLEY:PB 163
s. of than ancient flame VIRGIL 57
s. Struck out from a LONGFEL 30
Vital s. of heav'nly flame POPE 68
waitest for the s. from heaven ARNOLD:M 26
waiting for the s. from heaven ARNOLD:M 24
sparkles:
but s. near the brim BYR 75
s. that flash from their eyes DRYD 112
sparks:
as the s. fly upward BIBLE 184
Ashes and s., my words SHELLEY:PB 46
kindled by unexpected s. JOHNSON:S 28
painted with unnumb'red s. SHAK:JUL 34
s. blown out of a smithy YEATS 20
sparrow:
beloved's s. is dead CATUL 2
brawling of a s. YEATS 10
For the sowle of Phyllyp Sparrowe SKEL:J 1
I, said the S. NURS 85
lecherous as a sparwe CHAUC 29
providence in the fall of a s. SHAK:HAM 193
s. alight upon my shoulder THOREAU 21
s. fall POPE 82
s. hath found an house BIBLE 221
swift flight of a lone s. BEDE 1
sparrow-grass: Hit look lak sparrer-grass HARRIS:JC 13
sparrowhawks: S., Ma'am WELLING 26
sparrows:
note the s. fall WILLARD 1
two s. sold for a farthing? BIBLE 408
Spartan: remnant of our S. dead BYR 195
Spartans: Go, tell the S. SIMONID 1
spat:
Today I s. in the Seine PATTON 1
up and s. on the ceiling ANON 105
spats: walked in, complete with s. SAYERS 2
spawn:
meanest s. of Hell TENNY 204
to s. and die LOWELL:R 14
speak:
did he stop and s. to you BROWNING:R 136
difficult to s., and impossible BURKE:E 101
got it, so that we can s. FONTANE 1
heart could never s. MUIR:E 7
I only s. right on SHAK:JUL 57
I s. for 60,000 dead HUGHES:B 2
I s. it like a native MILLIG 6
if they s. first CONG 2
let him now s. PRAY 82
moral duty to s. one's mind WILDE:O 94
never s. well of one another JOHNSON:S 163
no one to s. up for anyone NIEM 1
one that can s. so well MASSIN 5
province of knowledge to s. HOLMES:OW 16
rather s. ill of oneself LA ROCHE 19
s., and to s. well, are two JONS 56
s. as the common people ASCHAM 1
S. for England, Arthur AMERY 1
s. for the inarticulate BEAV 6
s. in public on the stage EVER 1
S. less than thou knowest SHAK:KING L 15
S., Lord BIBLE 140
S. of me as I am SHAK:OTH 70
s. one moment before they think LA BRU 11
S. roughly to your little boy CARROLL 12
S. softly and carry a big stick ROOS:T 2
S. that we feel SHAK:KING L 87
S. to dead walls RALE 8
s. to God as if men were SEN 3
s. true TENNY 238
s. very well in the House of Commons DISR:B 7
s. when he is spoken to STEVENSON:RL 57
S. when you are spoken to PROV 351
S. when you're spoken to CARROLL 86
Strive to s. big SHAK:RIC.II 25
teach you to s. to your seniors CLARK:K 1
time to s. BIBLE 281
time to think before I s. DARW:E 1
To s. and purpose not SHAK:KING L 4
whereof one cannot s. WITT 2
who s. in me when I s. well WRIGHT:J 9
would not cease to s. CRAB 19
speakers: you imperfect s. SHAK:MAC 10
speaking:
By drowning their s. BROWNING:R 25
equal his brevity and plain s. FORD:GR 1
naked, natural way of s. SPRAT 2
s. absolutely classifies him LERN 1
speaks:
he s. so much of himself BACON:F[1] 55
No man s. concerning another JOHNSON:S 219
s. without obviously opening DINN 1
she never s. well of me CONG 3
spear:
Bring me my S. BLAKE:W 98
shiver'd was fair Scotland's s. SCOTT:W 33
S., to equal which MILT 124
spear-men: stubborn s. still made good SCOTT:W 32
spears:
one after that with s. UREY 1
sheen of their s. was BYR 39
s. are like the summer grass BLAKE:W 8
s. into pruninghooks BIBLE 301
stars threw down their s. BLAKE:W 69
specialist: S. – A man who knows MAYO 1
specialists:
All other men are s. DOYLE:AC 31
S. without spirit WEBER 1
trouble with s. is MORGAN:E 1
species:
not the individual but the s. JOHNSON:S 20
s. I wouldn't mind seeing vanish BENNETT:Al 6
specious: may look s. in theory BURKE:E 100
specs: not brought my s. with me ANON 30
spectacles:
needed not the s. of books DRYD 135
without a pair Of s. HOFFMAN:H 12
spectator: rather as a s. of mankind ADDIS 15
spectators:
actors or s.? SHELLEY:PB 114
gave pleasure to the s. MACAULAY:TB 33
spectre:
s. of Communism MARX:K/ENG 1
s. of Communism TAYL:AJP 1
speculation: fine subject for s. HAZL 22
speculations: Not wrung from s. BROWNE:T 15
speculative: made myself a s. statesman ADDIS 15
speech:
aspersion upon my parts of s. SHERIDAN:RB 10
better to deal by s. BACON:F[1] 88
but a choice of s. AUD 30
common and continuous s. is BAGE 22
Consul's s. was low MACAULAY:TB 46
dreamt that I was making a s. DEVON:SCC 1
false are attributes of s. HOBB 2
first s. are old friends CATHERWOOD 1
German s. the most shallow KRAUS 7
hed the s. o a bairn BIBLE 594
high s., and make a s. AUBREY 10
I am slow of s. BIBLE 90
law and rule of s. HORACE 103
loath to cast away my s. SHAK:TWE 13
manner of his s. SHAK:ANT 24
most wise s. is not VEGA CAR 1
nor the power of s. To stir SHAK:JUL 57
Our concern was s. ELIOT:TS 104
perfect plainness of s. ARNOLD:M 52
Speak the s. SHAK:HAM 106
s. created thought SHELLEY:PB 76
s. flow'd fair and free SCOTT:W 36
S. is human CARLYLE:T 69
S. is often barren ELIOT:G 26
s. is shallow as Time CARLYLE:T 37
S. is silver PROV 352
S. is the small change MERED:G 5
S. than to give evidence HALIF 9
s. they have resolved not ELIOT:G 23
S. was given to man TALL 7
stately s. WORDS:W 85
true use of s. GOLDS 42
speeches:
hodgepodge of al other speches SPENS 1
preparing his improptu s. SMITH:FE 9
too busy making s. to think RUSS:B 26
wise s. of fools FULLER:T[1] 1
speed:
full s. ahead for the rocks GILMORE 1
More haste, less s. PROV 276
not rather to s. up? DIOG 1
quench its s. i' the slushy BROWNING:R 58
safety is in our s. EMER 20
S., bonny boat BOULTON:HE 1
s. the parting guest HOMER 18
s. the parting guest POPE 66
s. was faster than light BULLER 1
spell:
never s. a word wrong JEFFERSON 8
s. better than they pronounce TWAIN 3

s. of far Arabia DE LA M 5
unless he first s. Man QUAR 10
Who lies beneath your s.? HOPE:L 2
speller:
taste and fancy of the s. DICKENS 37
wass s. I know of WARD:A 9
Spence:
see also **Spens**
ballad of Sir Patrick S. COLERIDGE:ST 53
spend:
I'm going to s., s., s. NICHOLSON 1
whatever you have, s. less JOHNSON:S 229
spending:
Riches are for s. BACON:F[1] 60
S. again what is already SHAK:SON 34
spends: save only that thou spendis DUNB 4
spendthrift: s. of my own genius WILDE:O 103
Spens:
see also **Spence**
lies good Sir Patrick S. BALL 51
Spenser: sage and serious Poet S. MILT 314
spent:
had s. one whole day well KEMP 10
That we s., we had ANON 145
spermatozoa: million million s. HUX:A 43
spheres:
Ring out ye Crystall sphears MILT 8
S. of influence ANON 242
trepidation of the s. DONNE 69
spherical: His body is perfectly s. LEAR 6
spice:
Sugar and s. And all NURS 83
very s. of life COWP 64
spices: will be No S. wanting HERR 12
spicy:
nothing but s. dishes LENIN 14
odours from the spicie shoare MILT 186
spider:
Laws are like s.'s webs SOLON 1
said a s. to a fly HOWITT 1
s.'s touch POPE 86
There came a big s. NURS 35
spiders:
country bath-house, with s. DOST 2
I saw the s. marching through LOWELL:R 2
Weaving s., come not SHAK:MID 22
spies:
As if we were God's s. SHAK:KING L 79
Ye are s. BIBLE 74
spill: let them not s. me MACNEICE 12
spilling: universe were bent on s. it MAUGH 3
spin:
Let the great world s. TENNY 87
tell me, can she s.? JAMES I 4
spinach: What a world of gammon and spinnage DICKENS 157
spinifex: s. of dry souls STOW 2
spinner: stoppeth the s.'s cunning POUND 39
spinning-jenny: God took the s. YEATS 83
Spinoza:
Christ, S., and myself STEIN:G 6
S. is a man intoxicated NOVA 1
spinsters:
based upon dreams of s. RUSS:B 13
s. and the knitters SHAK:TWE 28
spires:
city with her dreaming s. ARNOLD:M 41
clustered s. of Frederick WHITTIER 3
What s., what farms HOUSM 24
Ye distant s. GRAY:T 2
spirit:
And with thy s. MASS 2
be filled with the S. BIBLE 535
break a man's s. is devil's work SHAW 9
but present in s. BIBLE 519
expense of s. in a waste SHAK:SON 56
fleeting S.! wand'ring Fire HAD 1
Give me the s. SHAK:HEN.IV[2] 36
Hail to thee, blithe S. SHELLEY:PB 94
history of the human s. ARNOLD:M 72
Holy S. may in all things PRAY 56
I commend my s. BIBLE 469
I will pour out my s. BIBLE 355
immortal s. grows Like harmony WORDS:W 146
in the S. on the Lord's day BIBLE 573
Like a s. of pure beauty PUSH 1
motion and a s., that impels WORDS:W 8
poison and his s. died HOME 4
quick s. that is in Antony SHAK:JUL 5
save the s. of man, is divine? BYR 23
slumber did my s. seal WORDS:W 31
s., antithetically mixt BYR 83
s. be thine BROWNING:R 148
s. bloweth and is still ARNOLD:M 12
s. burning but unbent BYR 32
s. giveth life BIBLE 528
s. hath rejoiced in God BIBLE 607
s. indeed is willing BIBLE 433
s. is the true self CIC 7
s. like a charmed bark SHELLEY:PB 19
S. of Delight SHELLEY:PB 138
s. of health or goblin SHAK:HAM 36
S. of Night SHELLEY:PB 145
s. of the chainless mind BYR 48
s. that constantly denies GOET 13
S., yet a Woman too WORDS:W 89
strongest and the fiercest S. MILT 150
that I am is flesh and s. AUR 1
there is a s. in the woods WORDS:W 26
too much S. to be e'er POPE 133
Wild S., which art moving SHELLEY:PB 40
spirits:
By our own s. we are deified WORDS:W 84
call s. from the vasty deep SHAK:HEN.IV[1] 57
choice and master s. SHAK:JUL 41
fiery s. blaze POPE 50
greatest refreshment to the s. BACON:F[1] 69
our s. rush'd together TENNY 71
s. are enslaved which serve SHELLEY:PB 77
S. of well-shot woodcock BETJ 4
Would ruffle up your s. SHAK:JUL 58
spiritual: Millions of s. Creatures MILT 200
spiritualist: you are a s. SZASZ 9
spiritualists: like a convention of s. STOP 13
spit:
I have no gun, but I can s. AUD 54
S. in my face you Jews DONNE 85
s. on all things faire CHAPMAN:G 1
s. on me Wednesday last SHAK:MERC 18
s. upon my Jewish gaberdine SHAK:MERC 17
spiteful: write when I feel s. LAWR:DH 38
spits: Who s. against the wind PROV 430
spitting: know his way of s. SYNGE 2
spleen:
excite your languid s. GILB:WS 33
mind's wrong biass, S. GREEN:Mat 1
S. can subsist on any HAZL 9
splendid: s. in ashes BROWNE:T 62
splendour:
Of s. in the grass WORDS:W 66
Pavilioned in s. GRANT:R 1
reflected in more-than-oriental-s. KIP 23
s. falls on castle walls TENNY 106
s. of a sudden thought BROWNING:R 174
spliced: to be s. in the humdrum way BRONTE:C 7
split:
s. it so it will stay s. CHAND 8
they only s. it? HAY:W 1
spoil:
Spare the rod and s. PROV 350
spare the rod, and s. BUTLER:S[1] 26
To come and s. the fun CARROLL 54
spoiler: worst, dull s., who BYR 64
spoils:
carried off the finest s. ELLIS:H 3
s. were fairly sold MACAULAY:TB 49
to the victor belong the s. MARCY 1
With s. of meaner Beauties LOVELACE 9
spoilt: who wasn't s. by being lionized TREE 2
spoke:
carl spak oo thing CHAUC 39
he saw the less he s. NURS 86
sometimes no one s. to him MILNE 16
s. among your wheels FLETCH:J 9
spoken:
never have s. yet CHESTERTON 24
Speak when you're s. to CARROLL 86
When the lips have s. SHELLEY:PB 159
spokesman: s. for wild nature SNY 2
spondee: Slow s. stalks COLERIDGE:ST 57
spontaneity:
Hellenism is *s. of consciousness* ARNOLD:M 71
S. is only a term for BUTLER:S[2] 6
spoon:
ate with a runcible s. LEAR 21
dish ran away with the s. NURS 16
long s. that must eat with the devil SHAK:COM 5
one s. less than the number LEDDA 1
should have a long s. PROV 170
trifle with the s. POPE 65
spoons:
better count your s. SMITH:LP 5
faster we counted our s. EMER 52
literary man Who played with s. BROWNING:R 87
locks up its s. and packs SHAW 44
Londoner who stole s. HANC:WK 1
my life with coffee s. ELIOT:TS 6
we guard our s. MACAULAY:TB 57
sport:
animals never kill for s. FROUDE 5
Australian worships the Goddess of S. KINGLAKE 1
Detested s. That owes its COWP 69
ended his s. with Tess HARDY:T 67
for the s. of Kings DAVEN:W 4
frogs do not die in s. BION 1
In love as in s. GRAVES:R 9
make s. for our neighbours AUSTEN 27
ribs was s. for ladies SHAK:AS 4
some feeling of the s. SHAK:MEA 29
S. has always been an instrument TOSA 1
s. has nothing to do with fair play ORWELL 39
s. I ever mastered was backgammon JERROLD 11
S. is a loathsome and dangerous HUMPH 6
s. of kings SOMER 1
S. that wrincled Care derides MILT 67
s. with Amaryllis in the shade MILT 49
they kill us for their s. SHAK:KING L 59
To s. would be as tedious SHAK:HEN.IV[1] 16
what sort of s. has Lord ANON 260
sporting:
s. prints in the hall AUD 25
s. prints of Aunt Florence's COWARD 25
sports:
big mountainous s. girl BETJ 10
joy Of youthful s. BYR 120
s. of love JONS 18
sportsman: s. wot doesn't kick his wife SURT 4
spot:
one s. shall prove beloved KIP 110
Out, damned s. SHAK:MAC 100
Tip me the black s. STEVENSON:RL 29
with a s. I damn him SHAK:JUL 63
spots:
or the leopard his s.? BIBLE 339
turns to one mass of s. SEARLE 3
spotted: hoping to be s. first VIRGIL 8
spouse: thy s., so bright and clear DONNE 90
spouts: s. out a Sea MILT 227
sprat: s. to catch a mackerel PROV 391
sprats: open the kegs of salted s. BROWNING:R 25
spread: not good except it be s. BACON:F[1] 100
spreading: s. himself like a green bay BIBLE 209
spring:
apparell'd like the s. SHAK:PER 1
azure sister of the S. SHELLEY:PB 40
be S. no more TENNY 163
call it easing the S. REED:H 4
can S. be far behind? SHELLEY:PB 46
commonly called the s. COWP 95
deep of the Pierian s. DRAYT 12
dream of S. COLERIDGE:ST 66
eternal s. in which God looks RENAN 2
ever bid the S. adieu KEATS 92
found in the s. to follow? SWIN 3
frozen palms of S. TENNY 42
hopelessly in love with s. SANT 6
hounds of s. are on winter's SWIN 9
In the S. a young man's fancy TENNY 70
lap of the new come s.? SHAK:RIC.II 43
less quick to s. again ARNOLD:M 44
liv'd light in the s. ARNOLD:M 10
melted into s. BRONTE:E 6
mourn with ever-returning s. WHITMAN 34
no second s. PHILIPS:A 1
rifle all the breathing s. COLLINS:Will 2
S. brings back her gently CATUL 11
s., full of sweete dayes HERB:G 32
S. has come again RILKE 1
S. is come home THOMP:F 15

s. now comes unheralded CARSON 3
s. of Bandusia HORACE 42
s. of endless lies COWP 38
S. should vanish with FITZGER:E 33
S. still makes s. in the mind EMER 93
S., sweet laxative of Georgian CAMPBELL:R 5
s. the herald of love's SPENS 10
S., the sweet s. NASHE 2
s. will surely come to him NICHI 1
Sweet lovers love the s. SHAK:AS 67
There had made a lasting s. SHAK:HEN.VIII 7
thy s. is gone GRAY:T 11
Treasury is the s. of business BAGE 7
We have as short a S. HERR 32
welcome, darling of the s. WORDS:W 98
Whenever s. breaks through COWARD 18
You doe bring In the S. HERR 25
springboard: Not a seat but a s. CHURCH:W 30
springtime:
Golden days of my s.? PUSH 4
S.'s Harbinger FLETCH:J 19
sprites: one Of sprites and goblins SHAK:WIN 5
spue: s. thee out of my mouth BIBLE 576
spur:
Fame is the s. MILT 49
no s. To prick the sides SHAK:MAC 24
spurre of all great mindes CHAPMAN:G 7
spurn: s. a stranger cur SHAK:MERC 18
spurred: ready booted and s. to ride MACAULAY:TB 35
spurs: Let the boy win his s. EDWARD III 1
spurts: They move forward in s. CONNOLLY:C 9
spy:
asked to s. for or against my country FRY:S 2
letters for a s. KIP 121
sent to s. out the land BIBLE 115
S. Who Came In From The Cold LE CAR 1
squad: awkward s. fire over me BURNS:R 130
squalor: private opulence and public s. GALB 5
squandering: s. wealth was his peculiar DRYD 48
square:
business give the people a s. deal ROOS:T 12
given a s. deal afterwards ROOS:T 3
main s. of its capital occupied for eight KISS 7
you broke a British s. KIP 50
square-riggers: s. used to whiten LOWELL:R 11
squares:
s. of his mind were empty AUD 36
walk on the lines or the s. MILNE 6
squash: s. is before 'tis a peascod SHAK:TWE 12
squashiness: because of the smell and s. O'CONOR 1
squat: urban, s., and packed BROOKE 11
squatter: who shall cheek the s. LAWS 3
squeaking: With shrieking and s. BROWNING:R 25
squeamish: let's not get overly s. KRIEG 1
Squeer: S.'s Academy, Dotheboys Hall DICKENS 66
squeezed: s. – until the pips squeak GED 1
squeezing: in the s. of a lemon GOLDS 70
squire:
Bless the s. and his relations DICKENS 102
gave the image of a yeoman s. DOUGLAS-H:A 4
squires: last sad s. ride slowly CHESTERTON 25
squirrel: Made by the joiner s. SHAK:ROM 5
stabbed:
German army was s. in the back HIND 1
stab'd me to the Heart GAY 1
stability: party of order or s. MILL 12
stable: shut the s. door after the horse PROV 210
stadium: no go the s. MACNEICE 3
staff:
I'll break my s. SHAK:TEM 30
s. of faith to walk upon RALE 2
very s. of my age SHAK:MERC 20
your s. in your hand BIBLE 97
stag:
runnable s. DAVIDS 6
s. at eve had drunk his fill SCOTT:W 35
stage:
All the world's a s. SHAK:AS 34
but on the s. DRYD 31
do on the s. the things STOP 2
drown the s. with tears SHAK:HAM 91
glory of the Attic s. ARNOLD:M 6
How others on our s. DONNE 76
kingdom for a s. SHAK:HEN.V 1
leave the loathèd s. JONS 50
necessary for success upon the s. TERRY 2
On the s. he was natural GOLDS 39
people on the s. are making PARKER:Hen 1
shake a s. JONS 42
speak in public on the s. EVER 1
s. but echoes back the public JOHNSON:S 65
s., where every man SHAK:MERC 3
s.'s jewel JONS 34
Then to the well-trod s. MILT 74
this great s. of fools SHAK:KING L 75
this were play'd upon a s. SHAK:TWE 48
upon the s. is not frightened FIELDING 30
wonder of our s. JONS 39
stage-coach:
outside of a s. from London HAZL 6
travel faster than a s. GOLDS 63
stagflation: sort of 's.' situation MACLEOD:I 2
stain:
any other s. on your character ADAMS:R[1] 1
s. her honour, or POPE 45
world's slow s. SHELLEY:PB 121
stair:
As I was going up the s. MEARNS 1
but a s. Betwixt us MEW 1
by a winding s. BACON:F[1] 75
ruffian on the s. HENL 3
staircase: S. wit DIDE 3
stairs:
And threw him down the s. NURS 14
any that was kicked up s. HALIF 16
climb and descend unfamiliar s. DANTE 18
cursed and kicked the s. MILLAY 2
rotten-runged rat-riddled s.? BROWNING:R 135
Up s. and down s. MILLER:W 1
stairway: s. which leads to a dark gulf CHURCH:W 48
Stalin: mediocrity is the apparatus that S. TROT 1
stalking-horse:
make truth serve as a s. BOLI 5
uses his folly like a s. SHAK:AS 72
stamp: s. to be made with my face CHARLES F 1
stand:
Here I s. LUTHER 8
I s. alone, and think KEATS 23
If she can s. it, I can BOGART:H 1
in this we s. or fall MILT 216
intended *to s.* 'On my head' DISR:B 49
it's people I can't s. SCHULTZ 1
no time to s. and stare? DAVIES:WH 2
s., s. at the window AUD 8
S. stable here AUD 12
s. up and be counted NIX 7
s. up for Jesus DUFFI 1
S. up, Guards WELLING 4
United we s. PROV 409
who only s. and waite MILT 100
who will s. on either hand MACAULAY:TB 48
standard:
raise the scarlet s. high CONNELL 1
turned up his Breech against the S. AUBREY 2
standards: With the s. of the people TENNY 79
standing: I'm s. on both of them GRAB 1
standpoint: Give me a proper s. ARCHIM 1
stands: What s. if Freedom fall? KIP 145
stane: put in a heart o' s. BALL 53
stanneris: s. clear as stern DUNB 2
star:
across the reflex of a s. WORDS:W 107
Bright s., would I were KEATS 113
catch a falling s. DONNE 56
constant as the northern s. SHAK:JUL 34
curb a runaway young s. BYR 145
desire of the moth for the s. JOYCE:J 51
evening s. is coming VIRGIL 20
evening-s. is lighting his late VIRGIL 23
Evening Starr Love's Harbinger MILT 258
follow knowledge like a sinking s. TENNY 53
hitch his wagon to a s. EMER 57
Knock at a Starre HERR 35
like a falling Starr MILT 144
love a bright particular s. SHAK:ALL 1
moist s. SHAK:HAM 6
morning S., Dayes harbinger MILT 91
My only *s.* is dead NERV 1
on the change of a s. SHAK:KING L 9
our life's S. WORDS:W 58
seen his s. in the east BIBLE 375
s. Beacons from the abode SHELLEY:PB 127
s. danc'd, and under that SHAK:MUCH 10
S. for every State WINTH 1
s. of two beside COLERIDGE:ST 26
s. to every wand'ring bark SHAK:SON 52
s. to steer her by MASE 1
s., which on a steeple MOORE:M 6
Sunset and evening s. TENNY 296
that bright Occidental S. BIBLE 1
There's a s. to guide the humble MACLEOD:N 1
Twinkle, twinkle, little s. TAYL:Ann 2
violate a S. DICKIN:E 12
with one bright s. COLERIDGE:ST 22
Star Chamber: make a S.C. matter of it SHAK:MERR 1
star-shine: s. at night STEVENSON:RL 64
star-spangled: 'Tis the s. banner KEY:FS 1
stare:
beach and s. at the stars REED:R 2
no time to stand and s.? DAVIES:WH 2
S., in the basin AUD 7
stony British s. TENNY 213
stared: I s. into the sky HODG 5
stares: s. long enough into the distance WHITE:P 1
starless: s. and bible-black THOMAS:D 21
starlight:
Into the frosty s. ARNOLD:M 33
s. lit my lonesomeness HARDY:T 2
starry:
s. heaven above me KANT 8
Starrie Cope of heaven MILT 207
Waters on a s. night WORDS:W 53
stars:
all night by troops of s. COLERIDGE:ST 59
and one the s. LANGBRI 1
any kinship with the s. MERED:G 18
beach and stare at the s. REED:R 2
beauty of a thousand s. MARLOWE 39
bright, patient s. KEATS 50
calculate the Starrs MILT 229
cloud of locusts blocking off my s. UNA 1
cut him out in little s. SHAK:ROM 30
erratik sterres CHAUC 121
eyes were blind with s. HODG 5
fleet of s. is anchored FLECKER 6
glory of the everlasting s. PATERSON:AB 2
he made the s. also BIBLE 5
heaventree of s. hung with JOYCE:J 27
His s. eternally HARDY:T 16
in the shining of the s. TENNY 271
Look at the s. HOPK:GM 9
morning s. sang together BIBLE 193
new-bathed s. Emerge ARNOLD:M 34
night with different s. SACK 3
Night with her train of s. HENL 5
not in our s. But in ourselves SHAK:JUL 11
opposition of the s. MARV 8
preserve the S. from wrong WORDS:W 72
puts the S. to Flight FITZGER:E 1
ready to ascend to the s. DANTE 16
sentinel s. set their watch CAMPBELL:T 23
seven s. go squawking AUD 6
silent s. go by BROOKS:P 1
some of us are looking at the s. WILDE:O 49
Starrs Hide their diminisht MILT 182
s. above us, govern SHAK:KING L 63
s. are dead AUD 21
s. are shining bright SHELLEY:PB 35
s. be blown about the sky YEATS 20
s. come down from the rafters AUD 9
s. early droop'd in the western WHITMAN 34
s. grew bright MASE 15
s. in her hair were seven ROSSET:DG 1
s. in their courses fought BIBLE 131
s. may see and be NORT 1
s. peep behind SHELLEY:PB 55
s. rush out COLERIDGE:ST 21
S., s., And all eyes else SHAK:WIN 31
s. that reigned at my nativity MARLOWE 43
s. threw down their spears BLAKE:W 69
s. went out and so did HUGHES:L 1
s., Which are the brain MERED:G 33
s.! which are the poetry BYR 92
S. with deep amaze MILT 7
steeped in s. RIMB 1
strikes the s. on Campden Hill CHESTERTON 3

strives to touch the starres SPENS 4
Tempt not the s. FORD:J[1] 2
this is the way to the s. VIRGIL 80
thus close up the s. MILT 24
touch the s. with my exalted HORACE 2
We should be like s. FRY:C 10
what is the s.? O'CAS 3
yoke of inauspicious s. SHAK:ROM 44
start:
If I'm late s. without me BANK 5
shouldn't have a flying s. WILSON:Harold 11
s. again at your beginnings KIP 127
started: s. like a guilty thing SHAK:HAM 9
starts: Was everything by s. DRYD 47
starve:
bury whom he help'd to s. POPE 123
Let not poor Nelly s. CHARLES II 5
s. and pray, for that's POPE 65
starved:
pleasure to be s. DRAYT 10
s. apothecary than a s. poet LOCKHART 1
starving:
only s. some of the time FERL 1
Why is he s. to death? GEL 2
state:
all were for the s. MACAULAY:TB 49
as the defrauding of the S. PENN 4
done the s. some service SHAK:OTH 70
duty of a S. is to see that every child RUSKIN 27
falling with a falling s. POPE 30
for reasons of s. PLATO 7
free Church in a free S. CAVOUR 1
greatest asset a head of s. WILSON:Harold 7
his S. Is Kingly MILT 100
I am the s. LOUIS XIV 5
in himself was all his s. MILT 213
in the establishment of the s. PLATO 9
is freedom there will be no s. LENIN 4
no harm come to the s. ANON 168
no such thing as the S. AUD 44
Our S. cannot be severd MILT 251
Pillar of S. MILT 158
Predicts the ruin of the S. BLAKE:W 83
reinforcement of the power of the S. CAMUS 10
several villages is the city s. ARISTOT 12
S. for every Star WINTH 1
s. is a machine in the hands STALIN 1
s. is not abolished ENGELS 2
S. which dwarfs its men MILL 23
strange eruption to our s. SHAK:HAM 3
time for the s. to sacrifice itself DURREN 5
to ruin or to rule the s. DRYD 41
woman gives to the S. a support ANON 204
worth of a S. MILL 22
stately:
as the s. homes of England WOOLF:V 3
back to thy s. homes of England LAWR:DH 19
one of the s. homos of England CRISP 6
S. Homes of England COWARD 24
s. homes of England HEMA 3
S. Homes of England ope CAMPBELL:R 5
statements: put God in his s. WHITMAN 36
states:
debt have been small s. INGE 2
goodly s. and kingdoms seen KEATS 3
Northern S. will manage somehow BRIGHT 7
She is all S. DONNE 61
S., like men, have their growth LANDOR 23
statesman:
abroad you're a s. MACMILL:H 6
constitutional s. is in general BAGE 1
definition of a constitutional s. BAGE 2
gift to set a s. right YEATS 48
In a s. so-called 'culture' MUSSO:B 5
s. is a politician who POMPI 1
s. is a politician who's been dead TRU 10
s. is an easy man YEATS 112
Too nice for a s. GOLDS 37
statesmen:
adored by little s. EMER 10
village s. talked GOLDS 30
station:
at the wayside s. MUIR:E 6
isn't that sort of s. RATT 1
private s. GAY 50
she leaves the s. SPEND 1
There was movement at the s. PATERSON:AB 4
stations: always know our proper s. DICKENS 102
statisticians: shalt not sit With s. AUD 46
statistics:
cannot feed the hungry on s. LLOYD GEO 1
damned lies, and s. TWAIN 33
lies, damned lies and s. DISR:B 90
Proved by s. that some cause AUD 51
study s., for these are the measure NIGHT 3
two kinds of s. STOUT 1
statue:
ask why I have no s. CATO 4
No s. has ever been put SIB 1
s. inside every block of stone? ORWELL 7
s. of the onehandled adulterer JOYCE:J 20
s. to o'erlook my grave BROWNING:R 99
that *my* s. should be moved VICT 9
statues:
like sepulchral s. lay DONNE 35
snow disfigured the public s. AUD 35
worth a million s. CUMM 6
stature:
shorten I the s. of my soul MERED:G 19
soul of the same s. MONTAIGNE 1
staves: thou comest to me with s.? BIBLE 148
stay:
Can't you s.? VAUGHAN:CJ 1
fond of asking peaple to s. ASHFORD 1
here I s. MACMAH 1
Neither have the hearts to s. BUTLER:S[1] 36
or s. and die SHAK:ROM 35
s. longer in an hour than others HOWELLS 1
S. up and fight DILL 2
we shall s. on earth PREVERT 1
when you can't s. so long SICK 2
Stay-at-home: Sweet S. DAVIES:WH 3
staying: Tell the people I'm s. PED 1
stays: that wears the s. TENNY 99
steadfast:
Sober, s., and demure MILT 79
S., like Russia PUSH 7
would I were s. as thou KEATS 113
steadily: Who saw life s. ARNOLD:M 6
steady: Slow and s. wins the race LLOYD:R 2
steak: wanted s. and they offered MALAM 1
steaks: smells of s. in passageways ELIOT:TS 15
steal:
Days S. on us BYR 124
lawyer with his briefcase can s. PUZO 2
s. away their brains SHAK:OTH 28
s. *for* me will s. *from* me ROOS:T 15
s. one poor farthing NEWM:JH 4
Thou shalt not s. BIBLE 103
Thou shalt not s. CLOUGH 20
to s. away your hearts SHAK:JUL 56
stealing:
not hang'd for s. Horses HALIF 6
S. and giving odour SHAK:TWE 1
steals:
does not imitate; he s. STRAV 5
s. a common from a goose ANON 65
s. my purse s. trash SHAK:OTH 34
s. something from the thief SHAK:OTH 11
s. the common from the goose ANON 77
steam:
All the s. in the world could not ADAMS:H 8
exceptin' always S. KIP 71
Shovelling white s. AUD 16
snorting s. and piston stroke MORRIS:W 6
s. spoils romance at sea? KIP 73
steam-engine: He traces the s. always DISR:B 56
steam-wheels: s. of the mind SHELLEY:PB 59
steamer: in a s. from Harwich GILB:WS 51
steamers: going to, all you Big S. KIP 136
steed:
as a s. That knows his rider BYR 73
Border his s. was the best SCOTT:W 18
I set her on my pacing s. KEATS 82
mounted on her milk-white s. BALL 55
s. flying fearless and fleet LONGFEL 30
S. threatens s. SHAK:HEN.V 25
steeds: They'll have fleet s. that follow SCOTT:W 23
steel:
All shod with s. WORDS:W 106
brandish'd s. Which smok'd SHAK:MAC 3
clad in compleat s. MILT 32
foeman bares his s. GILB:WS 25
Give them the cold s. ARMIS 1
s. my soldiers' hearts SHAK:HEN.V 36
To lift shrewd s. SHAK:RIC.II 23
weren't s. buried inside WHITE:P 11
steeple:
church and no s. SWIFT 84
shadow of the s. CLOUGH 25
steeple-jack: s. placing danger-signs MOORE:M 6
steeples:
have drench'd our s. SHAK:KING L 32
Talk about the pews and s. CHESTERTON 16
steer:
accelerator to the floor and s. left VUK 1
cannot s. A middle course MASSIN 8
s. too nigh the sands DRYD 38
S. two points nearer BEAT 1
steersman: good s. when the vessel's crank MERED:G 36
Stein: wonderful family called S. ANON 101
Stein, Gertrude: mama of dada* FAD 1
stenches: two and seventy s. COLERIDGE:ST 65
step:
begin with a single s. LAO 5
eev'n s. and musing gate MILT 80
first s. is the hardest PROV 125
first s. that is difficult DU DEF 1
one s. enough for me NEWM:JH 15
One s. forward, two steps LENIN 1
one small s. for a man ARMST:N 2
s. is short from GRAHAM:H 2
sublime to the ridiculous is only a s. PROV 139
Take a s. forward, lads CHILDERS 2
To s. aside is human BURNS:R 37
You cannot s. twice HERAC 2
Stephen: On the Feast of S. NEALE 1
stepping: s. where his comrade fell SCOTT:W 32
stepping-stones: men may rise on s. TENNY 126
steps:
countest the s. of the Sun BLAKE:W 70
kis the steppes CHAUC 120
s. Almost as silent WORDS:W 144
thy lab'ring s. to guide LUCRET 5
Thy s. retrace GILB:WS 22
With how sad s. O Moone SIDNEY:P 5
with wandring s. and slow MILT 261
would ask the number of s. JERROLD 9
sterility: her womb convey s. SHAK:KING L 20
stern:
lantern on the s. COLERIDGE:ST 90
s. to view GOLDS 28
sterner: made of s. stuff SHAK:JUL 50
stick:
he fell like a s. PAINE 8
I shall s. SHAK:MEA 36
meant us to s. it out KOES 6
set one's teeth and s. it out MONASH 2
some of it will s. BACON:F[1] 29
some will s. PROV 390
Speak softly and carry a big s. ROOS:T 2
s. with an 'orse's 'ead 'andle EDGAR 1
thrown against the Wall, he would s. BURT 1
sticks: S. and stones may break PROV 353
stiff:
he was very s. and proud CARROLL 73
two things I like s. MELBA 6
stiff-necked: s. and perverse in the resistance ARNOLD:M 67
stiffnecked: thou art a s. people BIBLE 109
stifling: s. it would be an evil MILL 11
stigma: s. . . . serve to beat a dogma GUED 3
stile:
help a lame dog over a s. CHILLING 2
I'm sitting on the s. BLACKWOOD 2
stiles: Lame dogs over s. KINGSLEY:C 18
still:
be s., my soul HOUSM 25
best be s. ARNOLD:M 48
he can't Sit s. MILLAY 9
He won't sit s. HOFFMAN:H 5
How s. we see thee lie BROOKS:P 1
nearer by not keeping s. GUNN:T 2
s. and lovely face DE LA M 1
s. point of the turning world ELIOT:TS 89
stillness:
air a solemn s. GRAY:T 16
English s. was so soft LAWR:DH 14
horrid s. first invades DRYD 2
modest s. and humility SHAK:HEN.V 17
s. in the midst of chaos BELLOW 1

s. where our spirits walk SASS 16
What a mighty s. broods HARPUR 1
wilful s. entertain SHAK:MERC 5
world in solemn s. lay SEARS 1
stilly: Oft, in the s. night MOORE:T 20
Stilton: no end of S. Cheese LEAR 17
sting:
death, where is thy s.? BIBLE 527
Death! where is thy s.? POPE 69
Death, where is thy s.? ROSS:R 1
pluck out the s. from the brain? ANON 68
put their lives into the s. EMER 76
stings: that stinks and s. POPE 125
stink: stand by th' fire and s. SHAK:KING L 14
stinks:
several s. COLERIDGE:ST 65
that s. and stings POPE 125
What writers talk s. KAF 1
stir:
Never the least s. DE LA M 8
No s. in the air SOUTHEY 8
s. it and stump it GILB:WS 86
stirred: all night long we have not s. BROWNING:R 35
stirring: s. times we live in HARDY:T 52
stirrup:
Betwixt the s. and the ground CAMDEN:W 1
heard his foot upon the s. DE LA M 9
I sprang to the s. BROWNING:R 52
stirrup-pump: s. can extinguish hell REED:H 2
stirrups: Spurning of his s. CHESTERTON 20
stitch:
s. in time saves nine PROV 356
S.,! s.,! s.! In poverty HOOD 19
stock: see how his s. goes on COLERIDGE:ST 40
stock exchange: S.E. scribblers forget MURRAY:LA 2
stockholders: I'm working for my s. VANDERB 1
Stockholm: S.'s place for connoisseurs ALLB 1
stocking:
Kneeling ne're spoiled silk s. HERB:G 12
no objection to the blue s. JEFFREY 2
stockings:
commended thy yellow s. SHAK:TWE 36
did you change your s.? AUSTEN 54
s. fouled, Ungart'red SHAK:HAM 61
s. were hung by the chimney MOORE:CC 1
stocks:
one of the great s. of Europe YEATS 135
s. were sold BELLOC 20
stockwhip: Wrap me up in my s. LAWS 6
stoic:
doctors of the Stoick furr MILT 37
s. or a satyr PINE 2
stoicism: Romans call it s. ADDIS 5
stole:
Londoner who s. spoons HANC:WK 1
wonder where you s. 'em SWIFT 58
stolen:
he that has s. the treasure CONG 27
S. sweets are always sweeter HUNT:L 2
S. sweets are best CIB 6
S. waters are sweet BIBLE 256
stoles: nice white s. BARH 4
stomach:
army marches on its s. NAPO I 16
burst s. like a cave DOUGLAS:K 2
but a Lutheran s. ERAS 5
empty s. is not a good political EINS 2
healthy s. is nothing if not BUTLER:S[2] 27
his neighbour on an empty s. WILSON:W 4
hit the pit of my s. with a click JOYCE:J 28
hungry s. will not listen FONTAINE 14
It's all s. MILLAIS 1
man's heart is through his s. PROV 414
no s. for such meat DOBSON:HA 5
no s. to this fight SHAK:HEN.V 40
s., gentlemen, a *s.* HUNTER:W 1
s. must just digest SHERIDAN:RB 44
s. sets us to work ELIOT:G 28
s. thinks her throat is cut RUNYON 5
think rationally on an empty s. REITH 2
wine for thy s.'s sake BIBLE 548
stomach-aches: tuned like fifty s. DICKENS 99
stomachs: Lazy folkes' stummocks don't git HARRIS:JC 7
stone:
are themselves as s. SHAK:SON 41
bread, and he received a s. WESLEY:S 2
conscious s. to beauty grew EMER 92
drip hollows out a s. LUCRET 4
dripping wears away the s. PROV 60
famous s. That turneth all HERB:G 52
Fling but a s. GREEN:Mat 1
generation carved in s. WRIGHT:J 6
get blood out of a s. PROV 440
give them the s. MONTAGU 6
head s. of the corner BIBLE 237
let him first cast a s. BIBLE 480
Let me lie down like a s. TOLS:L 5
Like a rolling s.? DYL 5
like a s. from a sling ANON 100
make s. of the heart YEATS 43
rain maketh a hole in the s. LAT 1
standing like a s. wall BEE 1
s. that is rolling can gather TUSS 4
s. the twenty-first BROWNING:R 170
s. which the builders refused BIBLE 237
them not make me a s. MACNEICE 12
This precious s. set in SHAK:RIC.II 17
Two things stand like s. GORDON:AM 1
untroubled heart of s. CAMPBELL:T 3
Virtue is like a rich s. BACON:F[1] 37
water hollow out a s. OSB:J 14
you still break s. YEATS 110
Stone Age:
bomb them into the S.A. LEMAY 1
Where a S.A. people breeds BETJ 16
Stonehenge: bring S. to Nyasaland BANDA 1
stones:
boys throw s. at frogs BION 1
cold gray s., O Sea TENNY 58
dig him up and throw s. SHAW 74
found in s. the sermons WILDE:O 6
Hearing the s. cry out HUGHES:Te 2
labour of an age in piled S.? MILT 14
Never throw s. at your mother BEHAN:Br 1
no ruined s. MACDIAR 22
not s., but men SHAK:JUL 53
stained s. kissed by the English OWEN:W 8
s. and clouts make martyrs BROWNE:T 50
S. have been known to move SHAK:MAC 74
s. of Rome to rise SHAK:JUL 58
s. prate of my whereabout SHAK:MAC 34
s. would immediately cry out BIBLE 466
that spares these s. SHAK:MISC 2
you are men of s. SHAK:KING L 83
stonewall: I want you all to s. it NIX 9
stool:
for three-foot s. mistaketh SHAK:MID 13
s. there to be melancholy upon? JONS 2
stoop:
nearer when we s. Than WORDS:W 115
s. to rise MASSIN 2
stooped: I never stoop'd so low DONNE 52
stooping: s. through a fleecy cloud MILT 82
stop:
I could not s. for Death DICKIN:E 13
oaten s., or pastoral song COLLINS:Will 5
s. everyone from doing it HERB:AP 6
S. ; look; listen UPTON:RR 1
s. to busie fools VAUGHAN:H 2
stopped:
He kindly s. for me DICKIN:E 13
s. short – never to go WORK 3
stopper: Pull out the s. LERN 5
stoppeth: he s. one of three COLERIDGE:ST 10
stopping: I'm not s. PLATT 2
stops: not everything s. when the music HELPMAN 2
stopwatch: images according to a s. IGNAT 1
store: cares were to increase his s. HOME 1
storehouse: s. for the glory of the Creator BACON:F[1] 6
stories:
how much to believe of my own s. IRV 5
likes s. that make her cry SULLI:An 2
sailor tells s. of winds PROP 1
s. do recount what life MURA 1
With dismal s. BUNYAN 30
storm:
After a s. comes a calm PROV 4
Any port in a s. PROV 17
As drives the s. HORACE 74
directs the s. ADDIS 36
fled away into the s. KEATS 77
He mounts the s. POPE 93
locks of the approaching s. SHELLEY:PB 41
lost in the s. ARNOLD:M 49
not in the s. nor in BYR 46
Now sinks the s. GAY 7
pelting of this pitiless s. SHAK:KING L 42
Pilot that weathered the s. CANN 2
port in every s. PROV 336
rides upon the s. COWP 12
S. and stress KLIN 1
s. has gone over me BURKE:E 75
S. in a Teacup BERNARD:WB 1
s. is long past the ocean will KEYN 1
storms:
He sought the s. DRYD 38
mightiness of s. UVA 1
outward s. the strongest DONNE 73
sudden s. are short SHAK:RIC.II 16
stormy: winter's morn, on a s. day LEAR 15
story:
British say, 'Jolly good s.' ATWOOD 9
cruel s. runs on wheels OUIDA 2
don't just *get* a s. MAUGH 26
don't like my s. get out JOYCE:J 34
earns a place i' th' s. SHAK:ANT 38
Every picture tells a s. PROV 107
old s., yet it remains HEINE 3
only one s., the s. of your life FRYE:N 2
place where a s. ended ELIOT:TS 103
saddest s. I have ever heard FORD:FM 1
Shuts up the s. of our days RALE 9
Still is the s. told MACAULAY:TB 54
s. always old and always new BROWNING:R 197
s. is about you HORACE 62
s. is ripe to tell AUD 24
s. is the old s. MACAULAY:TB 58
s. that starts with an earthquake GORKY 20
s. with a bad moral HARDY:T 49
Tell me the old, old s. HANK 1
To tell my s. SHAK:HAM 199
story-teller: S. is born, as well STEELE 13
stout:
Athenaeum with jugs of s. HERB:AP 18
Collapse of the S. Party ANON 252
stoutness: no objection to s. GILB:WS 39
stove: sit on a hot s. for a minute EINS 17
strabismus: Dr S. (Whom God Preserve) MORTON:JB 3
Stradivari: make Antonio S.'s violins ELIOT:G 47
straight:
crooked shall be made s. BIBLE 320
line which is accurately s. WHEW 1
make his paths s. BIBLE 377
make s. in the desert BIBLE 320
necessarily go in a s. line THATCH:M 10
No s. thing can ever be KANT 1
nothing ever ran quite s. GALS 4
straight-jacket: discredited s. of the past STEEL 2
strain:
from our souls the s. and stress WHITTIER 8
no, but s. HOPK:GM 31
strains:
s. of unpremeditated art SHELLEY:PB 94
s. such as would have won MILT 76
s. that might create a soul MILT 36
strait:
dark s. of barren land TENNY 273
driven Into a desperate s. MASSIN 8
straits: echoing s. between us ARNOLD:M 16
strand:
knits me to thy rugged s. SCOTT:W 11
Was walking on the s. BALL 48
wrote her name upon the s. SPENS 11
Strand:
I walk down the S. HARG 1
I walked into the S. JOHNSON:S 72
strands: these last s. of man HOPK:GM 20
strange:
at everything that looks s. PEPYS 9
be very s. and well-bred CONG 53
eight years with a s. man IBS 4
it's a jolly s. world BENNETT:Ar 5
Lord's song in a s. land? BIBLE 246
s. and sinister embroidered on JAMES:H 18
this is wondrous s. SHAK:HAM 56
'Tis s. – but true BYR 234
strangely: when thou shalt s. pass SHAK:SON 19
stranger:
entertain Him always like a s. ANON 59

From the wiles of a s. NASH 2
I, a s. and afraid HOUSM 33
No s. to misery VIRGIL 43
On earth I am a s. grown BURNS:R 94
s., and ye took me in BIBLE 431
s. in a strange land BIBLE 83
s. On the dark earth GOET 23
S. than fiction BYR 234
s. to my heart and me SHAK:KING L 2
s. to one of your parents AUSTEN 19
s. yet to pain GRAY:T 3
This s. is a theologian DIDE 5
To entertain this starry s.? CRASH 12

strangers:
By s. honour'd and by s. POPE 60
depended on the kindness of s. WILLIAMS:T 3
gracious and courteous to s. BACON:F[1] 72
not forgetful to entertain s. BIBLE 560
we may be better s. SHAK:AS 44

Stratford:
as S. trades on Shakespeare BURGESS:A 5
S. . . . suggests powdered history HALS:M 5

straw:
can't make bricks without s. PROV 442
drowning man will clutch at a s. PROV 85
Headpiece filled with s. ELIOT:TS 56
last s. breaks the camel's PROV 224
Oft stombles at a strawe SPENS 4
pigmy's s. does pierce it SHAK:KING L 72
tickled with a s. POPE 97

strawberries:
boys innocent as s. THOMAS:D 3
feed upon s., Sugar and cream NURS 8
great s. at the mouth ELIZ I 6
S. swimming in cream PEELE 4

strawberry: s. beside him and picks it HODS 3
stray: Did your fancy ever s. GAY 17

strayed:
foolish oft I s. BAKER 1
We have erred, and s. PRAY 4

stream:
ever-flowing s. of time CARSON 1
little streame best fits HERR 37
purling s. ADDIS 35
scoop the brimming s. MILT 195
Still glides the S. WORDS:W 128
s. I go a-fishing in THOREAU 14
s. My great example DENH 1
Time, like an ever-rolling s. WATTS 18
we knew all that s. POUND 9

streamers: fan spread and s. out CONG 41

streams:
coil of his crystalline s. SHELLEY:PB 42
Gilding pale s. SHAK:SON 14
Large s. from little fountains EVER 1
Liquid Lapse of murmuring S. MILT 232
more pellucid s. WORDS:W 124
Stillest s. Oft water fairest COWP 85

street:
before crossing a one-way s. PETER 3
crowded city's horrible s. BROWNING:R 46
long unlovely s. TENNY 133
not done by Jostling in the S. BLAKE:W 99
sheer inability to cross the s. WOOLF:V 14
s. and pavement mute HARDY:T 45
they don't do it in the s. CAMPBELL:Mrs P 3
trampled edges of the s. ELIOT:TS 12
worth two in the s. WEST:M 6
yard beneath the s. TENNY 221

street-car: when a s. is going in the right JEFFE 1
street-lamp: s. sputtered ELIOT:TS 17

streets:
Down these mean s. CHAND 5
ebb and flow of s. SMITH:Alex 2
little children cried in the s. MOTLEY 1
On the bald s. TENNY 134
s. alive with summer frocks HEWETT 1
s. are paved with gold COLMAN:G[2] 3
S. flooded. Please advise BENCH 4
s. of London are paved with gold PROV 357
that ever walked the s. WEST:M 3
through s. broad and narrow ANON 24

strength:
As thy days, so shall thy s. BIBLE 126
find S. in what remains WORDS:W 66
full of the s. of five BETJ 10
grew from s. to s. ELIOT:G 46
His s. the more is BUNYAN 30
my s., in whom I will trust BIBLE 202
prospect of glory gives me s. PROP 4
sin against the s. of youth TENNY 73
s. by limping sway disabled SHAK:SON 30
s. is as the s. of ten TENNY 61
s. of the hills is his BIBLE 229
S. through joy LEY 1
that tower of s. TENNY 190
Though s. may be lacking OSB:J 13
To have a giant's s. SHAK:MEA 12
triumphant conviction of s. CONRAD 8
Union is s. PROV 408
what is s. without a double MILT 279

strengthen: s. such as do stand PRAY 35

stress:
from our souls the strain and s. WHITTIER 8
Storm and s. KLIN 1

stretch: s. out to th' crack SHAK:MAC 86
stretched: was things which he s. TWAIN 11

stride:
has a deadly s. WILDE:O 116
s. is wildernesses of freedom HUGHES:Te 1

strife:
anguish'd glance upon the s. ANON 129
cast aside all sturt, and stryfe LIND:D 2
In Place of S. CASTLE 1
Let there be no s. BIBLE 45
madding crowd's ignoble s. GRAY:T 22
no s. can grow up there MILT 149
none was worth my s. LANDOR 9
or a double s.? BACON:F[1] 132
s. comes with manhood SCOTT:W 50

strike:
by and by it will s. SHAK:TEM 14
care that you s. it in anger SHAW 58
no right to s. against the public safety COOL 3
particularly fine, s. it out JOHNSON:S 160
s. not awry MORE:T 5
S. while the iron is hot PROV 358
twenty-four-hour s. is like MUIR:F 3

strikes:
It s. where it doth love SHAK:OTH 60
last four s. . . . it's pissed down? SPEIGHT 4

string:
chewing little bits of S. BELLOC 15
give you the end of a golden s. BLAKE:W 117
heart and harp have lost a s. BYR 74
I'll s. along with you DUBIN 1
of my own only the s. MONTAIGNE 21

strings:
as the s. of the lute are alone GIBRAN 4
There are s. . . . in the human DICKENS 90
two s. to my bow FIELDING 2
untun'd golden s. all women MARLOWE 48

strip: S. thy own back SHAK:KING L 70
stripe: s. for s. BIBLE 104
stripes: Whom s. may move SHAK:TEM 7
stripper: Men react impersonally to the s.'s FAUST 2

strive:
Should s. and should prevail NEWM:JH 18
To s., to seek, to find TENNY 55

strivings: all our s. cease WHITTIER 8

stroke:
he will hear the s. of eight HOUSM 7
must not s. anyone's head LENIN 11

strokes:
Little s. fell great oaks FRANKLIN:B 14
redoubled s. upon the foe SHAK:MAC 4

strong:
Be s. and of good courage BIBLE 128
Be ye s. BIBLE 176
disarm the s. and arm FRANCE 9
I again am s. WORDS:W 54
nor the battle to the s. BIBLE 287
of the s. came forth sweetness BIBLE 134
only the S. shall thrive SERVICE 1
s. as iron bands LONGFEL 11
s. at the broken places HEMINGWAY 1
s. enough to bear the sufferings LA ROCHE 4
S. is the horse SMART 2
S. without rage DENH 1
those who think they are s. BID 1
wants that little s. HOLMES:OW 4
weak, but He is s. WARNER:A 1

stronger:
no s. than a flower? SHAK:SON 29
S. by weakness WALLER 9
s. than all the hosts of error BRYAN 2

strongest:
reason of the s. FONTAINE 12
still the s. lose DRYD 16
s. man in the world IBS 11
s. shall stand the most weak BROWNING:R 150

strove:
I s. with none LANDOR 9
men that s. with Gods TENNY 55

struck:
been s. a deep mortal blow AESC 3
s. all of a heap SHERIDAN:RB 1
s. regularly, like gongs COWARD 5

structure:
good s. in a winding stair? HERB:G 25
social s. has become incapable TROT 5

struggle:
lead to a S. for Life DARW:C 4
s. between you and the world KAF 10
s. for existence DARW:C 3
s. for room and food MALT 2
s. is my life MANDELA:N 1
s. itself towards the heights CAMUS 3
s. naught availeth CLOUGH 10
This is the final s. POTTIER 1
'Tis vain to s. BYR 136
to-day the s. AUD 20
worn down by the s. with want SCHILL 8

strumpet:
half some sturdy s. HARDY:T 4
Into a s.'s fool SHAK:ANT 1

struts: Stoutly s. his Dames before MILT 68
Stuarts: like all good things, with the S. DISR:B 47
stubbornness: even his s., his checks SHAK:OTH 54
stuck: only say 'he s. it in her' so MCCULL 1
stuck up: despised the 's.u.' WELLS:HG 2

student:
probably be a s. forever CHEK 10
whether the s. can do a greater LIPP 1

students:
s. come with so much MCLUH 10
to notice the existence of s. NAB 4

studies:
acquired from reading critical s. SOLZ 6
Crafty men contemn s. BACON:F[1] 105
still air of delightfull s. MILT 305
S. serve for delight BACON:F[1] 103
too much time in s., is sloth BACON:F[1] 104

studious:
s. let me sit THOMS:Ja[1] 13
wife to be of s. or argumentative JOHNSON:S 218

study:
belly will not s. willingly PROV 197
By labour and intent s. MILT 303
in some brown s. LYLY 2
much s. is a weariness BIBLE 290
my only s., is man BORR 2
not s. to live BACON:F[1] 24
proper s. of Mankind POPE 89
proper s. of mankind is books HUX:A 2
result of previous s.? AUSTEN 17
s. had made him very lean HOOD 13
s. what you most affect SHAK:TAM 1
true s. of man is man CHARR 1

studying: By s. the masters ABEL 1
stuff: s. my skin so full ANON 21
stuffed: We are the s. men ELIOT:TS 56

stumble:
do not s. MACLEOD:N 1
they s. that run fast SHAK:ROM 20

stumbled: I s. when I saw SHAK:KING L 56
stumbles: Oft stombles at a strawe SPENS 4
stumps: fought upon his s. SHEALE 1
stung: S. by the splendour of BROWNING:R 174

stupid:
appear s. are s., as are half GRACIAN 4
say something s. in Latin CERV 26
s. neither forgive nor forget SZASZ 7

stupider: feel you are also growing s. LAUR:M 1
stupidest: existence the s. party MILL 26

stupidity:
no sin except s. WILDE:O 18
struggle in vain with s. SCHILL 6
s. and wickedness of his own kind SADE 3
Such an excess of s. JOHNSON:S 122

Sturm: *S. und Drang* KLIN 1
sturt: cast aside all s., and stryfe LIND:D 2
sty: absence is No better than a s.? SHAK:ANT 58
Stygian: Not on sad S. shore BUTLER:S[2] 49
style:
author arrives at a good s. CONNOLLY:C 3
grand s. arises in poetry ARNOLD:M 53
he would do it in high s. AUBREY 10
in so strange a s. POPE 16
Mandarin s. . . . is beloved CONNOLLY:C 10
only secret of s. ARNOLD:M 86
Poor s. reflects imperfect thought RENARD 4
S. is the dress of thought WESLEY:S 1
s. is the essence of man BUFF 1
s. is the man PROV 360
S., like sheer silk CAMUS 14
s., not sincerity, is the vital WILDE:O 96
Theirs for their s. SHAK:SON 13
true definition of s. SWIFT 24
styles: All s. are good except the tedious VOLT 5
suavity: such deceitfulness and s. ELIOT:TS 84
subdue: s. By Conquest farr MILT 270
subject:
every s.'s soul is his own SHAK:HEN.V 33
grant the artist his s. JAMES:H 8
Her Majesty is not a s. DISR:B 94
know what it is to be a s. ELIZ I 2
S. and a Soveraign are clean different CHARLES I 4
s. but eternal Love SHELLEY:PB 78
subjects:
good of s. is the end DEF 14
order of the great s. SPARK 5
s. are rebels from principle BURKE:E 58
s.' feet May hourly trample SHAK:RIC.II 31
to s., what they show to kings CRAB 8
subjunctive: S. to the last WOOLL 1
sublime:
from the s. to the ridiculous NAPO I 6
Howls the s. DICKENS 122
most s. act is to set another BLAKE:W 39
object all s. GILB:WS 73
s. and the ridiculous are often PAINE 10
s. dashed to pieces COLERIDGE:ST 93
S. to the Ridiculous GRAHAM:H 2
s. to the ridiculous is only a step PROV 139
to maintain 'the s.' POUND 25
submission:
appetite for s. afterwards ELIOT:G 30
s., with which men resign HUME 5
Yeilded with coy s. MILT 193
submitting: by s. sways POPE 139
subordinate: safer to be in a s. position KEMP 6
subordination: legal s. of one sex MILL 28
subscribers: delete me from your list of s. KIP 158
subscription:
to the amount of his s. SURT 1
You owe me no s. SHAK:KING L 33
subsistence:
not any s. without a mind BERK 2
S. only increases MALT 1
substance:
More s. in our enmities YEATS 67
nor dividing the S. PRAY 30
What is your s. SHAK:SON 20
substitute: bloodless s. for life STEVENSON:RL 18
subtilty: Thy brother came with s. BIBLE 59
subtle: not be s. but neither are men GABOR 4
subtleties:
Destroyed by s. these women MERED:G 27
wrung from speculations and s. BROWNE:T 15
Subtopia: hope that it will stick – S. NAIRN 1
suburb:
stare At the new s. BETJ 5
s. of thir Straw-built Cittadel MILT 147
suburban: tell the saintly from the s. AUD 28
suburbia:
emasculated garden, a five-roomed* BOYD:RGP 1
I come from s. RAPH 2
suburbs:
Silence invaded the s. AUD 36
s. Of your good pleasure? SHAK:JUL 27
succedaneum: s., and a prop WORDS:W 151
succeed:
If at first you don't s. HICKSON 1
If at first you don't s. PROV 183
Never having been able to s. VOLT 6
not enough to s. VIDAL 9
possible to s. without betrayal? RENOIR:J 1
than to s. unconventionally KEYN 7
ugly enough to s. ALLEN:W 4
succeeds:
he s., the merit's CHURCH:C 10
Nothing s. like excess WILDE:O 65
Whenever a friend s. VIDAL 6
success:
affected by the question of the s. MEIR 2
can guarantee s. in war CHURCH:W 53
ecstacy is s. in life PATER 4
greatest s. is confidence EMER 51
in mortals to command s. ADDIS 4
minute's s. pays the failure BROWNING:R 211
necessary for s. upon the stage TERRY 2
no s. like failure DYL 6
Nothing succeeds like s. PROV 301
owed his lack of s. to nobody HELLER 1
road to s. is filled with women DEWAR 1
s. and miscarriage are empty sounds JOHNSON:S 102
S. . . . demands strange sacrifices HUX:A 18
s. depends upon previous CONF 23
s. hide its emptiness HAMMAR 2
s. in life, is to be a good animal SPENCER:H 6
S. is counted sweetest DICKIN:E 1
Sweet Smell of S. LEHMAN 1
sympathise with a friend's s. WILDE:O 43
To these s. gives heart VIRGIL 64
to vulgar judgements – s. BURKE:E 69
true s. is to labour STEVENSON:RL 24
what good s. soever QUAR 12
worship of the bitch-goddess *s.* JAMES:W 4
successes: look back on a long line of s. EBNER 2
successful: do all we can to appear s. LA ROCHE 8
successive: fall s., and s. rise HOMER 7
suck: Doth s. his sweet LODGE:T 1
Suck-a-thumb: naughty little S. HOFFMAN:H 11
sucker: s. born every minute BARNUM 1
suckle: To s. fools SHAK:OTH 21
sucks: s. the nurse asleep? SHAK:ANT 75
suction: good power o' s., Sammy DICKENS 19
sue:
Less used to s. SCOTT:W 36
not born to s. SHAK:RIC.II 4
Poore hearts, that humbly s. CAREW:T 9
sued: publish and be s. INGRAMS 2
Suez: somewheres east of S. KIP 62
Suez Canal: S.C. was flowing through my EDEN:C 1
suffer:
Better one s. DRYD 45
let us s. on the heights HUGO 4
s. and die without a word VIGNY 4
S. me to come to thee WESLEY:C 6
S. or triumph GOET 4
S. the little children BIBLE 444
To s. in one's whole self LAWR:DH 39
today I s. LESSING:GE 2
Two Ways: One is to s. KIERK 4
sufferance: suff'rance is the badge SHAK:MERC 17
suffered: professor of the fact that another s. KIERK 7
suffering:
all been s., nothing but s. AUSTEN 68
created for this sort of s. KEATS 168
Harsh s. is her sorry fate SCHILL 5
learn in s. what they teach SHELLEY:PB 25
lounjoun 'roun' en suffer'n' HARRIS:JC 4
loved the s. many BENTH 5
majesty of human s. VIGNY 5
man who fears s. MONTAIGNE 22
not s. in itself but the pointlessness NIET 3
s. inflicted on peoples MCMILL:J 1
S. is permanent WORDS:W 139
s. they were never wrong AUD 14
Suff'ring is the Lover's Part GAY 3
sympathize with everything, except s. WILDE:O 29
wisdom comes through s. AESC 1
sufferings:
endured the s. of the troops SASS 21
to bear the s. of others LA ROCHE 4
To each his suff'rings GRAY:T 8
suffers: He that lives long s. much PROV 164
sufficeth: it s. me MALORY 5
sufficiency: elegant s. THOMS:Ja[1] 4
sufficient:
S. unto the day BIBLE 397
whole world is not s. QUAR 5
whom shall we find S.? MILT 160
suffrage: new order in history: *universal s.* SAND 2
suffragette: legitimate child of the 's.' LEWIS:W 4
suffragettes: we s. aspire to be PANK:C 3
sugar:
blood, dirt and sucked s. stick YEATS 145
If sack and s. be a fault SHAK:HEN.IV[1] 52
must s. my hair CARROLL 34
S. and spice And all NURS 83
s. o'er The devil SHAK:HAM 96
suicide:
arose from the s.'s grave GILB:WS 82
by s., a bag of gold, or BRAM 2
committed s. twenty-five years after BEAV 3
Drunkenness is a temporary s. RUSS:B 17
have forgiven him – s. PARKES 2
Longest s. note ever ANON 214
mild s. LEWIS:W 1
murder a man who is committing s. WILSON:W 15
thought of s. is a great comfort NIET 10
suicides: lunatics or s. . . . could want an atomic war KHRU 8
suit:
I s. *me a lot* better LAST 1
not have chosen a s. by it CHEV:M 1
silk s., which cost me much PEPYS 3
So fatal to my s. GARRICK 5
Your s. is granted, said HERB:G 18
suitors: See s. following, and not look SHAK:OTH 21
sukebind: when the s. hangs heavy GIBBONS:S 4
sullen:
sadly in his sullein mind SPENS 29
sick or are you s.? JOHNSON:S 250
sulphur: Calvin, oat-cakes, and s. SMITH:Syd[1] 18
sultan: S. after S. with his Pomp FITZGER:E 11
sultana: nibble at the old s.? BRAY 2
sultry: common where the climate's s. BYR 163
sum:
Make up my s. SHAK:HAM 188
s. of earthly bliss MILT 235
Sumatra: giant rat of S. DOYLE:AC 35
summer:
Come, S., come the sweet seasoun JAMES I 2
compare thee to a s.'s day? SHAK:SON 6
Eternal s. gilds them BYR 192
eternal s. in his soul HOLMES:OW 9
far over the s. sea TENNY 283
Indian S. of the heart WHITTIER 1
long bathing of a s.'s day WORDS:W 142
Made glorious s. SHAK:RIC.III 1
murmur of a s.'s day ARNOLD:M 20
ofte a myrie someris day CHAUC 111
On the idle hill of s. HOUSM 21
peak of s.'s past DAY LEWIS 4
somer, oure governour CHAUC 96
somer seson when soft LANGLAND 2
s. afternoon; to me those have always JAMES:H 23
s. all the year round ORWELL 8
s. clothe the general earth COLERIDGE:ST 9
S. has o'erbrimmed KEATS 109
S. has set in with its COLERIDGE:ST 99
S. hath his joyes CAMPION 8
s. is ended BIBLE 337
S. is icumen in ANON 41
s. talk stopped AUD 55
s.'s evening, in his tent SHAK:JUL 54
s.'s flow'r is to the s. SHAK:SON 41
s.'s lease hath all too SHAK:SON 6
S.s pleasures they are gone CLARE:J 10
swallow does not make a s. ARISTOT 3
swallow does not make a s. PROV 313
sweet as s. SHAK:HEN.VIII 19
This will be a long, hot s. DOCH 1
thy eternal s. shall not SHAK:SON 6
'Tis S. Time on Bredon KINGSMILL 2
twefith hour of unrelenting s. KEYES 1
way to ensure s. in England WALP:H 12

surprised:
I who am s. WEBSTER:N 1
s. at everything when you were ignorant DURRELL:G 1
s. – but by things that they expect BERNARD:T 1
surquidry: surquidrie and foul presumpcioun CHAUC 105
surrender:
daring of a moment's s. ELIOT:TS 54
patriot – 'No S.' TONNA 1
S. to the sky BAXTER:JK 1
unconditional and immediate s., GRANT:US 4
we shall never s. CHURCH:W 13
survey: monarch of all I s. COWP 46
surveyors: there are worse s. EMER 50
survival:
S. of the Fittest DARW:C 2
s. of the fittest implies multiplication SPENCER:H 7
s. of the vulgarest WILDE:O 10
things that give value to s. LEWIS:CS 1
without victory there is no s. CHURCH:W 12
survive:
significant in us will s. PALMER:V 1
s. even more easily without man SARTRE 12
thy knell who shall s.? HARDY:T 24
What will s. of us is love LARK 4
Susan: black-ey'd S. came aboard GAY 37
Susie: sister S. sews WESTON 1
suspect:
Always s. everybody DICKENS 97
s. is better to be moving KAF 5
s. The thoughts of others SHAK:MERC 19
suspects: Round up the usual s. RAINS 1
suspense: s. is terrible. I hope WILDE:O 101
suspicion:
Caesar's wife must be above s. CAES:GJ 5
S. always haunts the guilty SHAK:HEN.VI[3] 8
wife must be above s. PROV 51
suspicions: S. amongst thoughts BACON:F[1] 111
Sussex: S. songs be sung BELLOC 31
sutlers: sapient s. of the Lord ELIOT:TS 26
swaddling: not yet out of his s. clouts SHAK:HAM 83
swaggering: By s. could I never thrive SHAK:TWE 59
swagman: Once a jolly s. PATERSON:AB 3
swain: dispossess the s. GOLDS 22
swallow:
bear to s. without gilding JOHNSON:S 258
chaffering s. for the holy lark BROWNING:EB 16
just don't s. it SEC 1
One s. does not make ARISTOT 3
One s. does not make PROV 313
summer s. SWIN 7
s. a nest for herself BIBLE 221
S., flying, flying South TENNY 110
s. gudgeons ere they're catched BUTLER:S[1] 28
s. has set her six young BROWNING:R 176
S., my sister SWIN 3
s. twitt'ring from GRAY:T 16
swallow-flights: Short s. of song TENNY 147
swallows:
and all the s. BROWNING:R 49
gathering s. twitter KEATS 109
swamp: to botanise in the s. CHESTERTON 48
swamps: mangrove s. where the python COWARD 21
swan:
black s. of trespass MALLEY 1
I will play the s. SHAK:OTH 67
Leda's goose a s. ANON 69
like a black s. JUV 11
pale s. in her wat'ry nest SHAK:POET 7
silver s., who living GIBBONS:O 1
sleeping s., doth float SHELLEY:PB 80
some full-breasted s. TENNY 279
summer dies the s. TENNY 45
s. her downy cygnets save SHAK:HEN.VI[1] 3
s. sail with her young MERED:G 25
Sweet S. of Avon JONS 45
What time is the next s.? SLEZ 1
swan-like: He makes a s. end SHAK:MERC 33
Swann: no more talk of S. PROUST 4
swans:
Are nine-and-fifty s. YEATS 49
honking amongst tuneful s. VIRGIL 18
s. are geese ARNOLD:M 48
s. of others are geese WALP:H 23
S. sing before they die COLERIDGE:ST 49
two Swannes of goodly hewe SPENS 49
swashing: s. and a martial outside SHAK:AS 10
Swat: Is the Akond of S.? LEAR 33
swats: cog o' guid s. BURNS:R 110
sway: Love of S. POPE 136
swear:
By the time you s. you're his PARKER:D 2
Do not s. at all SHAK:ROM 14
now the farmers s. KINGSMILL 2
s. like a comfit-maker's wife SHAK:HEN.IV[1] 66
S. me, Kate, like a lady SHAK:HEN.IV[1] 67
s. not by the moon SHAK:ROM 14
To s. against the truth SHAK:SON 64
when very angry s. TWAIN 21
sweat:
blood, toil, tears and s. CHURCH:W 11
By thine Agony and bloody S. PRAY 34
In the s. of thy face BIBLE 24
rank s. of an enseamed bed SHAK:HAM 142
s. and whine about their condition WHITMAN 7
We spend our midday s. QUAR 7
will s. but for promotion SHAK:AS 18
sweated: s. through his apostolic skin BYR 148
sweating:
made, but only by s. AGNEL 1
Quietly s. palm to palm HUX:A 44
their s. selves HOPK:GM 28
sweats:
Falstaff s. to death SHAK:HEN.IV[1] 30
S. in the eye of Phoebus SHAK:HEN.V 35
Sweeney:
Apeneck S. spreads his knees ELIOT:TS 28
bring S. to Mrs Porter ELIOT:TS 44
sit on S.'s knees ELIOT:TS 29
sweep: your chimneys I s. & BLAKE:W 18
sweeping: S. up the Heart DICKIN:E 18
sweet:
All is not s. JONS 23
As s. unto a shepherd GREENE:R 1
by distance made more s. COLLINS:Will 7
by distance made more s. WORDS:W 78
feel so small and s. PATMO 6
how it was s. BROWNING:R 173
Is trifle sufficient for s.? BETJ 27
made this life more s. SHAK:AS 11
never been s. in the grass THOMAS:D 35
So s. love seemed BRIDGES:R 10
so wondrous s. and fair WALLER 4
Stolen waters are s. BIBLE 255
S. and low TENNY 105
s. as summer SHAK:HEN.VIII 19
s. as the rind was SWIN 23
S. is every sound TENNY 119
s. is this human life CORY 45
S. though in sadness SHELLEY:PB 45
s. to taste prove in digestion SHAK:RIC.II 9
s. will be the flower COWP 11
wants a woman of fifty to be s. LAST 1
would smell as s. SHAK:ROM 11
sweet-apple: Just as the s. reddens SAP 2
sweet-shop: pressed to a s. window YEATS 53
sweeten: not s. this little hand SHAK:MAC 102
sweeteners: best s. of tea FIELDING 1
sweeter: s. than the Berry GAY 2
sweetest:
is s. last SHAK:RIC.II 15
s. hours that e'er I spend BURNS:R 3
s. things turn sourest SHAK:SON 41
sweetheart:
cheer a dead man's s. HOUSM 18
s. of the sun HOOD 11
sweetmeats: whole pyramids of s. DRYD 144
sweetness:
linckd s. long drawn out MILT 74
of the strong came forth s. BIBLE 134
pursuit of s. and light ARNOLD:M 64
s. in the sad THOMP:F 2
waste its s. on the desert GRAY:T 20
which are s. and light SWIFT 2
With s. fills the breast CASWALL 1
sweets:
all its s. are gone KEATS 110
bag of boiled s. CRIT 1
brought'st thy s. along with thee HERB:G 19
melt their s. On blossoming Caesar SHAK:ANT 47
perpetual feast of nectar'd s. MILT 33
Stolen s. are always sweeter HUNT:L 2
Stolen s. are best CIB 6
S. with s. war not SHAK:SON 4
where s. compacted lie HERB:G 32
Wilderness of s. MILT 211
swell: s. the soul to rage DRYD 114
swelling: She's a swellin' wisibly DICKENS 32
swept: S. it for half a year CARROLL 55
swift:
Love is s. of foot HERB:G 49
race is not to the s. BIBLE 287
Swift:
Cousin S., you will never DRYD 147
S. expires a driv'ler JOHNSON:S 69
S. has sailed into YEATS 84
S. was *anima Rabelaisii* COLERIDGE:ST 88
We are the people of S. YEATS 135
swiftness:
for s. did I sue THOMP:F 10
with s. of the tigress OWEN:W 13
swig: I'll get a s. in Hell KIP 57
swim:
boys that s. on bladders SHAK:HEN.VIII 10
but I can s. TEMPLE:W[2] 3
swimmer: strong s. in his agony BYR 176
swimming: like teach s. from a book COOGAN 1
swimming pool: Walk across my s.p. RICE:T 1
swimmingness: s. in the eyes CONG 47
swindles: as all truly great s. HENRY:O 3
swine:
cast ye your pearls before s. BIBLE 399
days of s. and Porsches HILL:Reg 2
false pearls before real s. CODY 1
got to like the little s. DARLING:J 1
Nor yet feed the s. NURS 8
s., though he divide the hoof BIBLE 111
s. to show you where the truffles ALBEE 3
swing:
Gaping at the lady in the s. ELIOT:TS 13
s. for it KINGSMILL 1
S. low sweet chariot ANON 42
S., s. together CORY 4
That fellow's got to s. WILDE:O 112
wasn't room to s. a cat DICKENS 164
swinging:
Swingin' VAUGHAN:N 2
S. slow with sullen roar MILT 82
swings:
lose on the s. you gain PROV 422
pulls up on the s. CHALM 1
swish: s. of a skirt in the dew KIP 132
Swiss:
dashing S. officer' is one such RUSS:J[1] 1
practical people the S. NICHOL 1
what a s. cheese would think MARQUIS 6
Switzerland: S. they had brotherly love WELLES 1
swoon: s. to death KEATS 113
sword:
believed he had a s. upstairs YEATS 33
brave man with a s. WILDE:O 113
fair s. in that hand MALORY 3
famous by my s. GRAHAM:J 1
father's s. he has girded MOORE:T 10
flesh'd Thy maiden s. SHAK:HEN.IV[1] 93
from the s. (Lord) save PSALMS 1
gave them a s. and they stuck it in NIX 12
hack thy s. as thou hast SHAK:HEN.IV[1] 44
handed our s. to America RUTS 1
hides a s. from hilts SHAK:HEN.V 10
his S. the brave Man draws HOMER 11
His s. was in the sheath COWP 17
Hold then my s. SHAK:JUL 86
hyphenated by a drawn s. FURP 3
is the s. that defends it MUSSO:B 2
Islam unashamedly came with a s. RUNCIM 1
lives by the s. dies by the s. PROV 167
Man for the s. TENNY 113
more cruel the pen is than the s. BURTON:Ro 11
My s., I give to him BUNYAN 32
my S. sleep in my hand BLAKE:W 98
nation shall not lift up s. BIBLE 301
out this s. of this stone MALORY 1
pen is mightier than the s. BULWER 1

tameless: t., and swift, and proud SHELLEY:PB 45
tangerine: t. trees and marmalade skies LENNON 7
tango: takes two to t. PROV 213
tank: see a T. come down the stalls SASS 2
tankard: unfailing remedy – the T. CALVER 1
tankards: mouths were made for t. MASE 8
Tannenbaum: *T., O T.* ZAR 1
Tao: this is the method of T. LAO 1
taper:
Out went the t. KEATS 68
t. to the outward room DONNE 74
to the sun my little t. BYR 224
tapping: suddenly there came a t. POE 3
tapsalteerie: May a' gae t. BURNS:R 4
tar:
ship for a ha'porth of t. PROV 81
thumb-nail dipped in t. PATERSON:AB 1
Tar-baby:
T. ain't sayin' nuthin' HARRIS:JC 2
what he call a T. HARRIS:JC 1
tar-barrel: black as a t. CARROLL 51
Tara: once through T.'s halls MOORE:T 7
tares:
bred amongst the weeds and t. BROWNE:T 15
clasping t. cling round CRAB 2
tarnished: neither t. nor afraid CHAND 5
Tarquin: great house of T. MACAULAY:TB 45
tarry:
Boatman, do not t. CAMPBELL:T 11
You may for ever t. HERR 27
tart: lost us the t.'s vote DEVON:EWSC 1
tartan: damned t. carpets always put me off FRASER:GM 1
Tartar: T.'s lips SHAK:MAC 80
tarts:
public love the t. THACK 28
she made some t. CARROLL 36
She made some t. NURS 56
Tarzan: Me T., you Jane WEISSMU 1
task:
all with weary t. fordone SHAK:MID 51
long day's t. is done SHAK:ANT 51
morning sees some t. begin LONGFEL 12
My t. accomplished HENL 6
the common t. KEBLE 1
There is but one t. for all KIP 145
thy worldly t. hast done SHAK:CYM 17
tasks: t. are pleasant when they are finished CIC 2
taskwork: some unmeaning t. give ARNOLD:M 14
Tasmania: Farewell T.'s isle MACNAM 1
Tasmanians: T., who never committed adultery MAUGH 22
tassie: fill it in a silver t. BURNS:R 66
taste:
bad t. is better than no t. BENNETT:Ar 11
bad t. of the smoker ELIOT:G 39
Between good sense and good t. LA BRU 10
bouquet is better than the t. POTTER:S 7
carries his own inch-rule of t. ADAMS:H 3
difference of t. in jokes ELIOT:G 40
Every one to his t. PROV 106
Ghastly Good T. BETJ 38
Judge of good t. TAC 4
Let them t. and remember PLOM 8
must himself create the t. WORDS:W 169
never t. who always drink PRIOR 16
no t. when you married me SHERIDAN:RB 20
t. as old as cold water DURRELL:L 2
T. does not come by chance REYN:J 5
T. is created from a thousand VALERY 5
T. is the feminine of genius FITZGER:E 36
t. with a distemper'd appetite SHAK:TWE 11
T. your legs SHAK:TWE 38
There's grief in the t. of it HEWETT 4
things t. like what they are LEITH 1
willing to t. any drink once CAB 1
worse t., than in a churchyard JOW 3
tasted: can't be t. in a sip DICKENS 96
tastes:
no accounting for t. PROV 373
t. greatly alter JOHNSON:S 134
t. may not be the same SHAW 48
that t. woman, ruin meets GAY 24
ta-ta: T. for now ITMA 7
taters: Here's t. hot BARE 2
tattered:
man all t. and torn NURS 73
Through tatter'd clothes small vices SHAK:KING L 71
tatters: You left us in t. HARDY:T 1
Tattersall: At T.'s, men look up MURRAY:LA 2
tattooed: designs on the t. lady WALLACE-C 2
taught:
afterward he taughte CHAUC 26
forget what I was t. WHITE:P 7
needs what we have t. her GAY 11
t. us how to die TICK 1
They t. me all I knew KIP 105
thirty not wanting to be t. SELL 13
worth knowing can be t. WILDE:O 12
tautology: great Prophet of T. DRYD 64
tavern:
creaking couplets in a t. BYR 6
opened a t. for his friends DOUGLAS:N 2
produced as by a good t. or inn JOHNSON:S 179
resolved to die in a t. ARCHPOET 1
So is the London T. ANON 188
t. chair was the throne JOHNSON:S 272
There is a t. in the town ANON 46
taverns: knew the tavernes wel CHAUC 15
tawdry: t. cheapness Shall outlast POUND 28
tax:
be a crushing t. on bachelors SHAW 27
hateful t. levied upon commodities JOHNSON:S 11
they will surely t. it SWIFT 82
to say to the t. increasers REAG 9
To t. and to please BURKE:E 23
taxation:
T. and representation are inseparable CAMDEN:Lord 1
T. without representation OTIS 1
taxed:
either t., insured, ARP'd MACMILL:H 2
schoolboy whips his t. top SMITH:Syd[1] 2
taxes:
certain but death and t. PROV 299
collect legal t. from illegal CAP 3
Death and t. and childbirth? MITCH:M 2
except death and t. FRANKLIN:B 27
people overlaid with t. BACON:F[1] 113
t. must ... fall upon agriculture GIBBON:E 6
true ... as t. is DICKENS 156
taxi: every human activity inside a t. BRIEN 1
taxing: more or less of a t. machine LOWE 2
Tay: Railway Bridge of the Silv'ry T. MCGON 2
Te Deum:
Sings its own seablown T.D. BETJ 17
T.D. laudamus ANON 43
tea:
after t. and cakes and ices ELIOT:TS 8
best sweeteners of t. FIELDING 1
cup of t. than go to bed with someone BOY 1
Divided by the morning t. MACNEICE 11
glad I was not born before t. SMITH:Syd[1] 43
if this is coffee, I want t. ARMOUR 1
is there honey still for t.? BROOKE 13
Make me some fresh t. AUD 56
nice t., dear THOMAS:D 28
Retired to their t. and scandal CONG 15
slavery of the t. and coffee COBBETT 3
spill her solitary T. POPE 65
swallowing his t. in oceans MACAULAY:TB 12
take – and sometimes T. POPE 46
Take some more t. CARROLL 19
T., although an Oriental CHESTERTON 12
t. is a powerful champion GLAD 4
want my cup of t. PAIN 1
we drink too much t. PRIEST 6
We'll all have t. NURS 54
When I makes t. I makes t. JOYCE:J 13
While there's t. there's hope PINE 1
with t. amuses the evening JOHNSON:S 18
tea-drinker: hardened and shameless t. JOHNSON:S 18
tea lady: end up fiddling with the t.l. HEWITT:LS 1
tea-rose: t. tea-gown, etc POUND 28
teach:
For every person wishing to t. SELL 13
gladly teche CHAUC 20
in harvest t. BLAKE:W 34
no matter what you t. them ... first JOHNSON:S 121
Oh t. me yet TENNY 9
t. an old dog new tricks PROV 445
t. an old horse amble trew SPENS 36
T. me, my God and King HERB:G 50
t. others who themselves POPE 6
while they t., men learn SEN 1
years t. much EMER 35
teacher:
doctrine for the t.'s sake DEF 9
Experience is a good t. ANTRIM 1
Experience is the best t. PROV 110
neither their t. nor they know NAB 5
t. of those who know DANTE 5
teachers:
t. can only help the work MONTESS 1
wielded by t. to manufacture t. WEIL 1
teaches: He who cannot, t. SHAW 53
teaching: incapable of learning has taken to t. WILDE:O 4
teacup:
A Storm in a T. BERNARD:WB 1
crack in the tea-cup opens AUD 7
teacups: laughter tinkled among the t. ELIOT:TS 13
Teague: Ho, Brother *T.* WHARTON:T 1
team:
Is my t. ploughing HOUSM 15
quite get into the first t. BRONO 2
tear:
all he had, a t. GRAY:T 27
dropp'd a t. upon the word STERNE 28
droppe the byrnie teare CHATT 1
Every T. from Every Eye BLAKE:W 87
fallen a splendid t. TENNY 219
Forbade the rising t. to flow SCOTT:W 3
meed of som melodious t. MILT 42
persuasive language of a t. CHURCH:C 22
shed a bitter t. CARROLL 55
shed one English t. MACAULAY:TB 56
t. blinded his e'e BALL 48
T. him for his bad verses SHAK:JUL 62
t. in her eye SCOTT:W 22
T. is an Intellectual thing BLAKE:W 115
Thinking every t. a gem SHELLEY:PB 38
unanswerable t. BYR 33
Wipe the t., baby dear WESTON 2
tears:
big round t. Cours'd SHAK:AS 13
bitterest t. shed over graves STOWE 5
Come back in t. ROSSET:C 4
dip Their wings in t. TENNY 147
drop, slow t. FLETCH:P 4
foolish t. upon my grave TENNY 89
foolish t. would flow CLARI 1
fountains fraught with t. KYD 2
frequent t. have run The colours BROWNING:EB 10
full of t. am I SHAK:RIC.II 35
God shall wipe away all t. BIBLE 580
God will wipe away t. BIBLE 315
Hence these t. TEREN 2
Her t. fell with the dews TENNY 4
here are t. for misfortune VIRGIL 41
hired t. BROWNE:T 49
His big t. SHELLEY:PB 38
If you have t. SHAK:JUL 54
in a flood of t. and a sedan-chair DICKENS 42
in t. amid the alien corn KEATS 93
in the mist of t. I hid THOMP:F 7
Iron t. down Pluto's cheek MILT 86
keep time with my salt t. JONS 8
kiss again with t. TENNY 103
land of t. SAINT-EX 2
Laughing in spite of her t. HOMER 10
leers And crocodile t. NURS 83
lie too deep for t. WORDS:W 69
loosed our heart in t. ARNOLD:M 8
Mine eyes are full of t. SHAK:RIC.II 37
mine own t. Do scald SHAK:KING L 76
No t. in the writer FROST:R 16
Nor all thy T. wash FITZGER:E 26
now with your fierce t. THOMAS:D 19
sacrifice, and parents' t. MILT 126
scare me with thy t. TENNY 45
shed t. by rule WORDS:W 140
sheddeth tender teares SPENS 27
Som natural t. they dropd MILT 261
sooner dry than women's t. WEBSTER:J 9

t. and laughters for all time BROWNING:EB 8
t. are shed in vain VIRGIL 60
T. fall in my heart VERL 2
T., idle t. TENNY 108
t. live in an onion SHAK:ANT 13
T. of eternity, and sorrow HOUSM 41
t. of it are wet SHAK:ANT 35
t. scald and start AUD 8
t. shall drown the wind SHAK:MAC 24
T. such as Angels weep MILT 138
T. were to me what CRISP 4
t. when they would devour BACON:F[1] 123
that's wrought with t. DAVIDS 2
they are cruel t. SHAK:OTH 60
They that sow in t. BIBLE 242
Time with a gift of t. SWIN 13
To these crocodile's t., they will add BURTON:Ro 22
tribute of wild t. YEATS 56
washed clear with t. DIX:D 1
water's heaven with their t. BLAKE:W 69
wipe the t. for ever MILT 58
world as a vale of t.? BROWNING:R 172
wrong'd orphan's t. MASSIN 11

teas: T., Where small talk SHELLEY:PB 49
teashop: In the t.'s ingle-nook BETJ 15
teatray: Like a t. in the sky CARROLL 18
tedious:
except the t. kind VOLT 5
People are either charming or t. WILDE:O 44
t. As a tired horse SHAK:HEN.IV[1] 63
t. as a twice-told tale SHAK:KING J 13
teeth:
born with natural false t. ROBINS:R 1
children's t. are set on edge BIBLE 345
do your t. with the light on JENKIN 1
feel the t. of time SIMPSON:RA 1
he has got iron t. GROM 1
I'll dispose of my t. PEREL 1
keep their t. clean SHAK:COR 5
little older than my t. SWIFT 40
lose one's t. is a catastrophe WHEEL 1
No t., no t. POTTER:B 3
old bitch gone in the t. POUND 29
set my t. nothing on edge SHAK:HEN.IV[1] 61
set one's t. and stick it out MONASH 2
take the bull between the t. GOLDWYN 9
taking out his false t. and hurling them DOYLE:AC 12
t. like splinters CAUS 1
tell him to his t. SHAK:HAM 174
To cast into my t. SHAK:JUL 73
women have fewer t. RUSS:B 20
teetotaller:
I'm only a beer t. SHAW 11
no woman should marry a t. STEVENSON:RL 9
tehee: 'T.!' quod she CHAUC 57
telegrams:
outer life of t. and anger FORST 4
t. tremble like leaves DAWE 3
Telemachus: mine own T. TENNY 54
telephone:
He really needs a t. PARKER:D 21
watch a silent t. HUDS:L 1
telephone number: your dreams, your t.n. ARNO 2
television:
bias in t. journalism BIRT 1
do it on t. CRISP 8
proliferation of radio and t. HOWARD:P 2
see bad t. for nothing? GOLDWYN 12
T. brought the brutality MCLUH 9
T. has brought murder back HITCH 2
T. has done more for the unification BIAGI 1
T. is an invention that permits FROST:D 1
T. is for appearing on COWARD 40
T. is more interesting COREN 5
T. puts forward, as an ideal ECO 1
T.? The word is half Latin SCOTT:CP 2
through the spirit of t. PASO 2
tell:
about to t. me something CONG 9
do not t. them so CHESTERFIELD 1
had to t. him who we were SITWELL:E 12
have to t. him who you are PECK 1
How could they t.? PARKER:D 17
let them t. thee tales SHAK:RIC.II 41
must not kiss and t. CONG 24
not easy to *t.* what it is JOHNSON:S 187
shudder as I t. the tale VIRGIL 48
t. him to his teeth SHAK:HAM 174
t. it like it is NIX 2
T. it not in Gath BIBLE 151
t. you three times is true CARROLL 89
would t. one anything WILDE:O 57
telling:
not arguing with you – I am t. you WHIST 4
tale never loses in the t. PROV 364
T. one's sorrows often brings CORNEILLE 7
tells:
ask him how he is, t. you TAYL:BL 1
Nobody t. me anything GALS 1
telly: We saw you on the t. CRISP 8
Téméraire: She's the Fighting T. NEWBOLT 7
Tempe: did in shade of T. sit SIDNEY:P 9
temper:
brutal about the good t. WILDE:O 61
I should lose my t. LOUIS XIV 7
made thee To t. man OTWAY 4
Never lose your t. with the Press PANK:C 4
no one could answer for his t. BAGE 3
only keep your t. STERNE 4
tart t. never mellows IRV 2
temperament:
artistic t. is a disease CHESTERTON 37
Children with Hyacinth's t. SAKI 23
temperance:
by temp'rance and by exercise POPE 129
t. would be difficult JOHNSON:S 266
this t., not compleat MILT 287
temperate: t. affords me none CAREW:T 3
tempest:
From lightning and t. PRAY 33
should not have meddled with a t. SMITH:Syd[1] 11
silence we the t. fear DRYD 2
While the t. still is high WESLEY:C 5
tempest-tost: Yet it shall be t. SHAK:MAC 6
tempests: looks on t. and is never SHAK:SON 52
tempit: tae be t. bi the Deil BIBLE 588
temple:
Egyptian T. dedicated to an ox GOLDS 76
Open the t. gates SPENS 13
t. half as old as time ROGERS:S 5
t. of silence and reconciliation MACAULAY:TB 11
very t. of Delight KEATS 96
temple-bells: t. are callin' KIP 62
temples: And the t. of his Gods? MACAULAY:TB 47
tempt:
bad for me do not t. me SHAW 122
not t. the Lord thy God BIBLE 381
off to t. My Lady Poltagrue BELLOC 35
T. me no more DAY LEWIS 2
T. not a desp'rate man SHAK:ROM 41
temptation:
butter that makes the t. JERROLD 2
dying out of the power of t. TROLL 12
get rid of a t. is to yield WILDE:O 26
I never resist t. SHAW 122
insist on their resisting t.? KNOX:V 1
last t. is the greatest treason ELIOT:TS 76
lead us not into t. MASS 15
lead us not into t. BIBLE 391
lead us not into t. PRAY 6
maximum of t. with SHAW 55
not over-fond of resisting t. BECKF 3
oughtn't to yield to t. HOPE:An 2
resist everything except t. WILDE:O 45
to get the better of t. GRAHAM:CS 1
to t. slow SHAK:SON 41
Yield not to t. PALMER:HR 1
temptations:
in spite of all t. GILB:WS 18
t. both in wine and women KITCHEN 2
tempted:
annoyance, t. him BELLOC 35
'Tis one thing to be t. SHAK:MEA 6
tempter: t. of the tempted SHAK:MEA 15
tempts: all that t. your wand'ring eyes GRAY:T 15
ten:
t. for the devil's own sel PROV 309
They are only t. NORTHCLIFFE 1
ten percent: get about t.p. out of life DUNC 3
1066: 1. and All That SELL 1
tenacious: man who is t. of purpose HORACE 31
tenant: t. of the room HENL 3
tender:
Bill as is young and t. THACK 25
t. for another's pain GRAY:T 8
t. is the night KEATS 93
t. passion is much overrated DUKES 3
tenderly: Take her up t. HOOD 23
tenderness:
My t. thenceforth escaped MCAULEY 2
pain of too much t. GIBRAN 2
sometimes obtained, it is human t. CAMUS 7
tamed with t. RENARD 2
t. and tact which was more MANNING 2
t. becomes me best CONG 47
t. is not so oft called BACON:F[1] 83
t. of patient minds OWEN:W 3
Want of t. is want of parts JOHNSON:S 145
tenders: shoal of fools for t. CONG 41
tenement: weak, frail, decayed t. ADAMS:JQ 2
tennis:
land of lobelias and t. flannels ELIOT:TS 73
playing t. with the net down FROST:R 18
tennis-balls:
merely the stars' t. WEBSTER:J 30
T., my liege SHAK:HEN.V 8
Tennyson:
Lawn T., gentleman poet JOYCE:J 18
T. and Browning are poets ELIOT:TS 117
T. goes without saying BUTLER:S[2] 30
tenor: kept the noiseless t. GRAY:T 22
tenses: Using t. to divide time FRAME 1
tension:
t. between standing apart and GORDIM 3
t. relieved and function MENCK 15
tent:
inside the t. pissing out JOHNSON:LB 8
nightly pitch my moving t. MONTGOM:J 2
rent in my wind-built t. SHELLEY:PB 55
Sits in yon western t. COLLINS:Will 6
stately t. of war MARLOWE 1
tenth: This Submerged T. BOOTH 1
tents:
dwell in the t. of wickedness BIBLE 222
dwelling in t. BIBLE 55
Ha' done with the T. of Shem KIP 148
Israels t. do shine so bright BLAKE:W 101
never dwelt in t. have no idea SACK 2
thy tribe's black t. THOMP:F 1
Terewth: It is the light of T. DICKENS 177
term: T., holidays, term, holidays LEWIS:CS 7
terms: T. like grace, new birth ARNOLD:M 73
tern: leave no t. unstoned NASH 22
terrible:
isn't life a t. thing THOMAS:D 29
t. as hell MILT 167
t. children GAV 1
terribles: *enfants t.* GAV 1
terrier: t. that was so covered with hair BRIGHT 4
terrified: t. and tight BETJ 32
territorial: It is the last t. claim HITL 8
territory: It comes with the t. MILLER:A 3
terror:
flame of incandescent t. ELIOT:TS 107
glory, jest, and t. of mankind MINIF 1
T. of darknesse CHAPMAN:G 4
T. of St Trinian's SEARLE 1
T. the Human Form Divine BLAKE:W 121
There is no t. STERNE 23
Thy t., O Christ HOPK:GM 3
terrorism: that t. could be so powerful BOCCA 1
terrorist:
blown to bits by a t. bomb EAMES:R 1
t. and policeman both come CONRAD 9
this country and commit t. activities DAVISON:RK 1
terrorists: all t., at the invitation GAIT 3
Tess: ended his sport with T. HARDY:T 67
Testaceo: like its own Monte T. CLOUGH 12
testament: blessing of the Old T. BACON:F[1] 31
testicles: tragedy requires *t.* VOLT 36
tether: tied the world in a t. SWIN 1
tethered: t. to a punctual snorin' MACDIAR 8
Teucer:
glory of T.'s race VIRGIL 52
under T.'s leadersip and protection HORACE 8
Teviotdale: march, Ettrick and T. SCOTT:W 59

text:
it will suit any t. STERNE 29
neat rivulet of t. SHERIDAN:RB 19
return to your t. ELIZ I 11
texts: difference of t. SPENS 5
Thackeray: T. settled like a meat-fly RUSKIN 29
Thames:
brooks are T.'s tributaries ARNOLD:M 43
clear T. bordered by its MORRIS:W 6
flights upon the banks of T. JONS 45
shall I see the T. again? BETJ 14
stripling T. at Bab-lock-hithe ARNOLD:M 23
Sweet Themmes, runne softly SPENS 49
T. is liquid history BURNS:J 1
T. was the noblest river ADDIS 22
where the charter'd T. does flow BLAKE:W 74
Thane of Cawdor: T.o.C. lives SHAK:MAC 13
Thane of Fife: T.o.F. had a wife SHAK:MAC 101
thank:
I t. thee that I am not BIBLE 465
T. me no thankings SHAK:ROM 36
thanked:
She t. men, – good BROWNING:R 21
When I'm not thank'd at all FIELDING 6
thankful: t. and has nobody to thank ROSSET:DG 14
thankless: To have a t. child SHAK:KING L 21
thanks:
give t. unto thee, O Lord PRAY 73
glad . . . that he t. God for any thing JOHNSON:S 99
T. be to God MASS 9
t. for another day of loving GIBRAN 2
to give t. unto the Lord BIBLE 227
thatch:
t. Smokes in the sun-thaw COLERIDGE:ST 9
worn the ancient t. TENNY 4
Thatcher, Margaret:
hope Mrs T. will go on until the turn TEB 2
Mrs T. says she has a nostalgia UST 9
M.T.'s great strength seems WEST:R 8
some bargain basement Boadicea* HEAL 5
Thatcherism: unruly children of T. PARS 1
theatre:
Aunt was off to the T. BELLOC 22
except my own power in the t. GIEL 1
go to the t. to be entertained COOK:P 3
I do try with the t. RAME 1
in this t. of man's life it is BACON:F[1] 10
problems of the modern t. RATT 2
t. unless he or she has bronchitis AGATE 1
T.'s certainly not what ELIOT:TS 83
theatre director: T.d.: a person engaged AGATE 3
theatrical: find happiness in t. life PAVLO 1
theft:
clever t. was praiseworthy SPENCER:H 2
not likewise answer 'T.' PROUD 1
t. from those who hunger EISEN 2
would be t. in other poets DRYD 137
theme:
be a t. at school JUV 21
t. too great PRIOR 1
themselves:
become t. by finding MALOUF 1
kept t. to t. WELLS:HG 2
theologian: This stranger is a t. DIDE 5
theologians: t. have employed as if ARNOLD:M 73
theology:
golden rule in T. MILT 316
overturns all the schools of t. DIDE 1
theorem: About binomial t. I'm GILB:WS 24
theorize: mistake to t. before one DOYLE:AC 19
theory:
important for a t. to be shapely HAMP 1
may look specious in t. BURKE:E 100
t. can be proved by experiment EINS 16
there:
Because it is t. MALLORY 1
I just don't want to be t. ALLEN:W 8
I shall not be t. SWIN 43
met a man who wasn't t. MEARNS 1
She won't be t. MILLER:A 9
you were not t. HENRI 2
thermodynamics: describe the Second Law of T. SNOW 2
Thermopylae: make a new T. BYR 195
Thersites: T.' body is as good SHAK:CYM 16
they: every one else is T. KIP 155
thick:
I'm as t. as a plank WALES 1
lay it on so t. and exactly BUTLER:S[2] 18
through t. and thin DRYD 56
Through t. and thin she follow'd BUTLER:S[1] 18
thicken: dissipation that t. the features WEST:R 5
thief:
embrace the impenitent t. STEVENSON:RL 32
first cries out stop t. CONG 27
Give a t. enough rope PROV 144
man's apparel fits your t. SHAK:MEA 32
Opportunity makes a t. BACON:F[1] 130
slag, he was a t. HEINE 6
steals something from the t. SHAK:OTH 11
suttel t. of youth MILT 94
t. doth fear each bush SHAK:HEN.VI[3] 8
t. said the last kind word BROWNING:R 200
this first grand t. MILT 187
which is the t.? SHAK:KING L 69
thieves:
Beauty provoketh t. SHAK:AS 9
Bifore the theves he may synge JUV 19
fell among t. BIBLE 456
honour among t. PROV 370
night for t. EUR 2
not a nation but a community of t. HERB:X 3
number of t. there CUNNING:PM 1
One of the t. was saved BECKETT 3
t. break through and steal BIBLE 392
T. for their robbery have SHAK:MEA 15
Twenty Thousand T. LAMBERT 1
thighs: glory from her loosening t.? YEATS 68
thimbles: sought it with t. CARROLL 91
thin:
can never be too t. or WINDSOR 2
Eating out keeps you t. RENDELL 1
Enclosing every t. man WAUGH:E 29
No matter how t. you slice it SMITH:Alf 3
t. man inside every fat man ORWELL 7
t. mankind GOLDS 34
t. one is wildly signalling CONNOLLY:C 14
thine: No thing is t. DUNB 4
thing:
between a t. and a thought PALMER:S 1
he is not quite the t. AUSTEN 49
t. that ends all other deeds SHAK:ANT 62
Thou art the t. itself SHAK:KING L 46
too much of a good t. PROV 436
things:
All t. bright and beautiful ALEX:CF 1
all t. to all men BIBLE 521
begin to see t. as they really are FONTEN 2
do all t. through Christ BIBLE 543
First t. first PROV 126
God's sons are t. MADDEN 1
more t. in heaven and earth SHAK:HAM 57
nor t. present, nor t. BIBLE 514
sorry Scheme of T. FITZGER:E 34
such t. to be TENNY 164
Take t. as they come PROV 363
The t. that are not? SHAK:JUL 83
t. are the sons of heaven JOHNSON:S 6
thingummy: T., and What-you-may-call-it is DICKENS 138
think:
always talk, who never t. PRIOR 16
because I t. him so SHAK:TWO 3
Before him I may t. aloud EMER 17
can't t. of your face SPOON 6
comedy to those that t. WALP:H 15
don't *t.* foolishly JOHNSON:S 237
effort and preparation to t. RUSS:B 26
have sufficient time to t. HEATH 3
I exist by what I t. SARTRE 2
I t., therefore I am DESCA 2
know what I t. till I see WALLAS 1
Learn to t. Imperially CHAMBERLAIN:J 2
not so t. as you drunk I am SQUIRE 3
not t. so, exactly CLOUGH 15
now – I t. it STEPHEN:JK 1
She *could* not think CRAB 19
so we've got to t. RUTH 1
sooner die than t. RUSS:B 29
they did not stop to t. CUMM 2
they tend to t. in grooves MORGAN:E 1
t. as wise men do ASCHAM 1
t. continually of those SPEND 2
t. for two minutes together SMITH:Syd[1] 9
T. in the morning BLAKE:W 45
t. of me when I'm dead COWARD 11
t. on these things BIBLE 542
t. rationally on an empty stomach REITH 2
t. what other people t. YEATS 40
those who greatly t. POPE 58
to t. like other people SHELLEY:MW 1
too busy making speeches to t. RUSS:B 26
try to t. it through again GOET 38
what a swiss cheese would t. MARQUIS 6
When I t., I must speak SHAK:AS 43
Who t. too little DRYD 46
whom it hurts to t. HOUSM 28
with which we t. that we t. BIER 2
Ye are not paid to t. KIP 72
you can't make her t. PARKER:D 19
you may t. what you like TAC 5
thinker: God lets loose a t. EMER 22
thinkers: not always the justest t. HAZL 36
thinking:
ain't t. about it TROLL 17
but t. makes it so SHAK:HAM 77
Everything worth t. has already been GOET 38
great deal of wishful t. DEMOS 1
in the dignity of t. beings JOHNSON:S 42
keeps the unhappy from t. DIBDIN:C 8
life is what t. makes of it AUR 6
many people think they are t. JAMES:W 5
modes of t. are different JOHNSON:S 227
much drinking, little t. SWIFT 77
Plain living and high t. WORDS:W 73
Power of Positive T. PEALE 1
There is wishful t. in Hell LEWIS:CS 3
t. for myself at all GILB:WS 13
T. hurts HORV 2
T. is seeing BALZ 5
T. is the desire to gain reality ORTEGA G 6
T. is to me the greatest fatigue VANB 1
t. man's Tory BARNARD:R 1
t. what nobody has thought SZENT 1
to draw a limit to t. WITT 4
to prevent oneself t. HUX:A 4
too much T. to have POPE 133
thinks:
He t. too much SHAK:JUL 14
never t. of me ANON 46
other naturs t. different DICKENS 114
says little, T. less FARQ 11
t. too little or too much POPE 89
third:
t. thing, that makes it water LAWR:DH 36
T. time lucky PROV 388
t. who lay in our embrace WRIGHT:J 7
Who is the t. who walks ELIOT:TS 52
with a shadowy t. BROWNING:R 93
third-class: t. seat sat the journeying boy HARDY:T 37
Third Programme: become a T.P. country WILKIN 1
thirldom: cowpyt to foule thyrldome BARB 2
thirst:
drink for the t. to come RAB 2
man can raise a t. KIP 62
never know what t. is HENN 1
promoted t. without quenching UPDIKE 2
t. goes RAB 3
t. that from the soul doth rise JONS 36
thirsteth: my soul t. for thee BIBLE 218
thirsting: Fled not his t. lips SHELLEY:PB 7
thirsty:
t., to cure it PEAC 4
t. with drought and chilled WRIGHT:J 1
thirteen: clocks were striking t. ORWELL 26
thirtieth: my t. year to heaven THOMAS:D 12
thirty:
At t. man suspects YOUNG:E 11
Don't trust anyone over t. RUBIN 1
I am past t. ARNOLD:M 85
T. days hath September ANON 109
under t. and intend to remain so ANON 182
thistles:
sooner sleep in t. WESTON 1
t. stretch their prickly arms CRAB 2
thocht: vexit am with heavy t. DUNB 13
Thomas: True T. lay on Huntlie BALL 54
Thomas, Dylan: ribald, inspired urchin* DAY LEWIS 6

Thoreau: Whatever question there may be* JAMES:H 3
thorn:
left the t. wi' me BURNS:R 98
ne're the Rose without the T. HERR 6
no harvest but a t. HERB:G 40
Oak, and Ash, and T. KIP 122
pluck out one t. of many? HORACE 98
t. in the flesh BIBLE 530
t. twig for clettering dishes GIBBONS:S 5
without T. the Rose MILT 189
thorns:
crackling of t. under a pot BIBLE 283
I fall upon the t. of life SHELLEY:PB 45
No t. go as deep as a rose's SWIN 25
no t., no throne PENN 1
t. should never be plucked KEY:E 2
t. that in her bosom SHAK:HAM 49
thorough: appallingly t. these Germans HUX:A 36
thoroughfare: This world nys but a thurghfare CHAUC 50
thoroughness: t. of a mind that reveres LEWIS:S 2
thou: T. that in the Heavens BURNS:R 19
thought:
all capable of original t. MENCK 14
armour is his honest t. WOTTON 2
as in uffish t. he stood CARROLL 46
be sure was t. twice THOREAU 23
between a thing and a t. PALMER:S 1
called the Garment of T. CARLYLE:T 6
constitution of their modes of t. MILL 31
device for avoiding t. HELPS 1
does not seem a moment's t. YEATS 27
gave t. relief WORDS:W 54
gods t. otherwise VIRGIL 54
grateful t. raised to heaven LESSING:GE 1
he thoghte another CHAUC 39
headache called t. in the brain THOMS:Ja[2] 1
heart that t. the t. BALL 25
her body t. DONNE 77
hit on the same t. SHERIDAN:RB 36
holy and good t. BIBLE 373
hundred schools of t. contend MAO 2
I t. he t. I slept PATMO 5
it is due to patient t. NEWT:I 4
may be t. cannot wisely PEAC 16
My t. is *me* SARTRE 2
no t. for the morrow BIBLE 397
oft was t., but ne'er POPE 14
One t. fills immensity BLAKE:W 44
Only the T. Police mattered ORWELL 28
passion-winged Ministers of t. SHELLEY:PB 109
pearls of t. in Persian gulfs LOWELL:JR 7
People use t. only to VOLT 17
Perish the t. CIB 3
pleasures of t. surpass CLOUGH 23
Poor style reflects imperfect t. RENARD 4
prefer t. to action BALZ 4
rear the tender t. THOMS:Ja[1] 3
residual fraction is t. SANT 10
Roman t. hath struck him SHAK:ANT 7
Sinking from t. to t. POPE 161
sleep out the t. of it SHAK:WIN 14
souls with just one t. HALM 1
spark of inextinguishable t. SHELLEY:PB 163
splendour of a sudden t. BROWNING:R 174
Style is the dress of t. WESLEY:S 1
Things t. too long YEATS 108
This t. is as a death SHAK:SON 28
T. and art only develop GUER 1
t. become concrete AMIEL 1
t. came like a full-blown rose KEATS 66
t. does not become a young woman SHERIDAN:RB 3
t. in cold storage SAMUEL 4
T. is free SHAK:TEM 22
t. is often original HOLMES:OW 11
T. is the child of Action DISR:B 2
t. it out with both hands SAYERS 3
T. leapt out to wed with T. TENNY 140
T. must be divided against HUX:A 27
t. of ancient writers is now WHITEHEAD 8
t. of thee MEY:A 2
T. shall be the harder ANON 248
t. three times before taking CONF 17
t. to Donne was an experience ELIOT:TS 117
t. which saddens while BROWNING:R 59
t. without learning CONF 4
T. would destroy GRAY:T 8
Three minutes' t. would suffice HOUSM 52
through strange seas of T. WORDS:W 152
throw the t. away HOUSM 45
tire the night in t. QUAR 7
To believe your own t. EMER 4
unmeaning thing they call a t. POPE 19
untouched by solemn t. WORDS:W 43
utmost bound of human t. TENNY 53
very t. of Thee CASWALL 1
want of T., As well as want HOOD 25
What heart could have t. you? THOMP:F 19
white, Celestiall t. VAUGHAN:H 5
with but a single t. LOVELL:M 1
without a t. of Heaven or Hell BROWNE:T 19
working-house of t. SHAK:HEN.V 42
thoughtless: full many a t. blow WILCOX 1
thoughtlessness:
fruit of imitation and t.? CERN 3
t. is the weapon of the male CONNOLLY:C 12
thoughts:
anchor of my purest t. WORDS:W 9
censor one's own t. WALEY 1
deadly rhythm of their private t. CHAND 4
fond and wayward t. will WORDS:W 33
Give thy t. no tongue SHAK:HAM 30
Good t. his onely friendes CAMPION 4
Gor'd mine own t. SHAK:SON 51
Great t. come from the heart VAUV 1
in a shroud Of t. BYR 95
joy Of elevated t. WORDS:W 8
man of many t. BYR 122
man's own t. WEBSTER:J 14
misused words generate misleading t. SPENCER:H 8
my sad t. doth clear VAUGHAN:H 9
my t. are not your t. BIBLE 331
no t. and be able to express KRAUS 4
not make t. your aim KIP 127
On second t., they knew exactly GLASH 1
ought to control our t. DARW:C 5
pansies, that's for t. SHAK:HAM 169
pleasant t. Bring sad t. WORDS:W 12
Poor in deed and rich in t. HOLD 1
second and sober t. HENRY:M 2
some strange t. transcend VAUGHAN:H 12
they arouse guilty t. MOLIERE 7
they have their own t. GIBRAN 1
thinking Thy t. after Thee KEPL 1
T. are not subject to duty LUTHER 1
t. beyond the reaches SHAK:HAM 36
t. in my brain inhearse SHAK:SON 37
T. of a dry brain ELIOT:TS 25
t. of men are widen'd TENNY 82
t. of youth are long LONGFEL 25
t. that wander through Eternity MILT 153
t., the slaves of life SHAK:HEN.IV[1] 89
T. vagrant as the wind FORD:J[1] 4
t. which have their natural colour SAINTE-B 2
to disguise his t. TALL 7
to disguise their t. VOLT 17
To understand God's t. NIGHT 3
turns to t. of love TENNY 70
United t. and counsels MILT 113
write his t. upon a slate HOOD 29
thousand:
about five t. men BIBLE 442
good woman if I had five t. THACK 10
made love to ten t. women SIMEN 1
t. years in thy sight BIBLE 224
t. years more. That's all WELLS:HG 20
thousands:
go out and get t. GORKY 21
T. at his bidding speed MILT 100
t. equally were meant SWIFT 64
thraldom: single t., or a double BACON:F[1] 132
thrall: Hath thee in t. KEATS 85
thread:
love can do with a twined t. BURTON:Ro 21
t. of causes was spinning from eternity AUR 13
t. of his verbosity SHAK:LOV 18
threads: Silver t. among the gold REX 1
three:
at t. years old is half LEONARDO 3
Gaul is divided into t. parts CAES:GJ 1
married life t. is company WILDE:O 85
One of the t. to share it? SHAK:JUL 64
rule of t. doth puzzle ANON 84
Though he was only t. MILNE 2
thought t. times before taking CONF 17
When shall we t. meet again? SHAK:MAC 1
three-and-thirty: I have dragg'd to t. BYR 138
three-cornered: is it those t. things? BARRIE 4
three o'clock: always t.o. in the morning FITZGER:FS 12
three per cents: simplicity of the t.p.c. DISR:B 46
threepenny: T.-bus young man GILB:WS 37
threescore: years are t. years and ten BIBLE 225
threshold:
dares not cross the t. PITT:W[1] 2
starry t. of Jove's Court MILT 15
Upon the t. of her mind? TENNY 128
wear on a t. or the print HARDY:T 77
wet leaf clings to the t. POUND 19
whining at the t. GILMAN 1
threw:
t. away the wrong bit LLOYD GEO 11
t. me in front of the Judges BETJ 28
thrift: t. and adventure seldom go CHURCH:JJ 2
thrive:
He that would t. CLARKE:J 1
wive an' t. baith in ae RAMS 3
throat:
act and the child's t. COWARD 34
cut his t. before he marry'd SWIFT 57
feel the fog in my t. BROWNING:R 181
Ghosts glut the t. of hell BLAKE:W 3
good talker with a sore t. WHITEHORN 5
handsomest man that ever cut a t. CHURCH:W 73
if I am to have my t. cut EDGE 8
looking down the t. of Old Time DICKENS 231
procession marching down your t. O'SULL 3
rather felt you round my t. HOPE:L 3
stomach thinks her t. is cut RUNYON 5
three times her little t. around BROWNING:R 34
T. of Warr had ceast to roar MILT 259
t. 'tis hard to slit KINGSMILL 1
unlocked her silent t. GIBBONS:O 1
throats:
My sore-t. ... are always worse AUSTEN 67
Nor cut each other's t. GOLDS 2
throne:
between the t. and the scaffold CHARLES X 2
build himself a t. of bayonets INGE 5
drive everyone before the t. CEL 2
first by the t. BROWNING:R 57
High on a T. of Royal State MILT 148
honour'd for his burning t. SHAK:MEA 38
Lamb upon his t. BRIDGES:M 1
like a burnished t. ELIOT:TS 40
no brother near the t. POPE 121
no thorns, no t. PENN 1
something behind the t. PITT:W[1] 7
tavern chair was the t. JOHNSON:S 272
that you gave up a t. for her EDWARD VIII 7
This royal t. of kings SHAK:RIC.II 17
through slaughter to a t. GRAY:T 21
Thy t. shall never ELLER 2
Whoso mounts the t. BROWNING:R 145
thrones:
Cities and T. and Powers KIP 119
Not t. and crowns, but men ELLIOTT:E 1
throng:
Join our happy t. BARING-G 4
Leaving the tumultuous t. WORDS:W 107
throstle: t. with his note so true SHAK:MID 27
throw:
In Argentina they t. themselves DIET 4
t. a prince as soon as JONS 55
t. all away for this one WRIGHT:J 2
throwed: Tonstant Weader fwowed up PARKER:D 11
thrown:
All *this* t. away for *that* MARY QUEEN CON 3
should be t. with great force PARKER:D 30
t. out, as good for nothing JOHNSON:S 80
thrush:
aged t., frail, gaunt HARDY:T 17
pipes the mounted t. TENNY 171
t.; he sings each song BROWNING:R 50
Thuammuz: T. came next behind MILT 128
Thule: Farthest T. VIRGIL 21

t. meanwhile is flying VIRGIL 29
T. past and t. future ELIOT:TS 90
T. present and t. past ELIOT:TS 87
t. quietly kills them BOUC 1
t. seemed finished ere MUIR:E 5
T. shall throw a dart BROWNE:W[1] 1
T. stays, *we* go DOBSON:HA 2
T. stoops to no man's lure SWIN 30
T. that is intolerant AUD 41
t., that takes survey SHAK:HEN.IV[1] 89
T., the avenger BYR 107
T., the devourer of all OSB:J 23
T. the suttel theef MILT 94
T., thou must untangle SHAK:TWE 18
t. to be born BIBLE 281
t. to begin a new DRYD 129
t. to every purpose BIBLE 281
t. to murder and create ELIOT:TS 5
t. to spare From company HARDY:T 18
T. travels in divers paces SHAK:AS 47
T. was away MACNEICE 10
t. was out of joint STRACH 1
T. watches from the shadow AUD 7
T. we may comprehend BROWNE:T 8
T. went over them a hundred SLESS 1
T., which antiquates antiquities BROWNE:T 53
T., which takes in trust RALE 9
t. will come DISR:B 48
T. will have his fancy AUD 7
T. will run back MILT 9
T. will tell PROV 394
T. with a gift of tears SWIN 13
T. wounds all heels ANON 250
T. wounds all heels MARX:G 22
T., you old gypsy man HODG 6
T.'s deer is slain MUIR:E 1
T.'s eunuch HOPK:GM 31
T.'s noblest offspring BERK 6
T.'s wheel runs back BROWNING:R 189
T.'s winged chariot MARV 31
T.'s thievish progress SHAK:SON 35
to undo the t. of day FAIRBURN 2
twice daily indicated the right t. EBNER 2
tyme, that may not sojourne CHAUC 102
tyme ylost may nought recovered CHAUC 116
undiminished by the ravages of t.? HORACE 38
waste my t. making money AGAS 1
way of having a bad t. CHERRY 1
ways By which T. kills us SITWELL:O 2
We have short t. to stay HERR 32
when our t.'s come DIBDIN:C 7
When t. is broke SHAK:RIC.II 45
which are the rags of t. DONNE 60
wisest of counsellors, T. PERIC 6
With leaden foot t. creeps JAGO 1
women for the most part have t. to write WAUGH:A 2
You cannot conquer T. AUD 7
time-lag: comfortable t. of fifty years WELLS:HG 18
times:
all t. when old are good BYR 153
best of t., it was the worst of t. DICKENS 198
done it a hundred t. TWAIN 45
faithless coldness of the t. TENNY 177
get together and forget the old t. FENT 1
Heroic t. have passed GAM 1
My t. be in Thy hand BROWNING:R 190
Our t. are in His hand BROWNING:R 184
ruins of forgotten t. BROWNE:T 48
stirring t. we live in HARDY:T 52
T. change, and we change ANON 243
t. that try men's souls PAINE 3
What t.! What manners CIC 8
Times: *The T.* is a tribal noticeboard ANON 249
***timor:** T. mortis conturbat me* DUNB 7
tin:
Little T. Gods on Wheels KIP 35
wid a pocket full of t. FOST:SC 3
tinker:
do not matter a t.'s curse SHINWELL 1
T., Tailor, Soldier NURS 77
tinkers:
be no trade for t. PROV 184
be no work for t. PEAC 18
tinklings: drowsy t. lull GRAY:T 16
tinned:
have it t. With vinegar WILSON:Harold 10
t. food is a deadlier weapon ORWELL 4
tins: we open t. GALS 6
tinsel: real t. underneath LEVANT 2
tint: take on the t. of any country NARA 1
Tinto: that bit hillock's T. PATERSON:A 1
tip-toe:
on t. for a flight KEATS 7
t. upon a little hill KEATS 5
tippenny: Wi' t., we fear nae BURNS:R 87
Tipperary: long way to T. JUDGE 1
tipping: allow t. on the boat? MARX:G 14
tippled: t. drink more fine KEATS 25
tipster: t. who only reached Hitler's level TAYL:AJP 3
tipsy: never gets t. at all LEAR 5
tire: ever t. of love or rhyme COPE 5
tired:
amna' fou' sae muckle as t. MACDIAR 4
Give me your t. LAZ 1
haven't got time to be t. WILHELM I 1
He was so t. ROLFE 1
I'm t. of Love BELLOC 34
long process of getting t. BUTLER:S[2] 21
Thou are t. ARNOLD:M 48
Tir'd with all these SHAK:SON 30
t. of London, he is t. of life JOHNSON:S 192
when one grows t. of the world WALP:H 8
woman who was always t. ANON 131
Tiresias:
I T. have foresuffered ELIOT:TS 46
I T., old man ELIOT:TS 45
tirra-lirra: 'T.', by the river TENNY 20
tissue: t. of crimes, follies GOLDS 46
Titan-woman: some pale T. like a lover SWIN 51
Titanic: furniture on the deck of the *T.* MORTON:R 1
Titian: much at heart about T. RUSKIN 11
title:
feel his t. Hang loose SHAK:MAC 107
require to possess a t. MILL 19
t.'s uncommonly dear GILB:WS 92
To guard a t. SHAK:KING J 16
When I can read my t. clear WATTS 3
titles:
All thy other t. thou hast SHAK:KING L 16
decliner of honours and t. EVELYN 1
Kinquering Congs their t. take SPOON 3
T. are shadows DEF 14
T. distinguish the mediocre SHAW 56
titwillow: Willow, t., t. GILB:WS 81
toad:
as intelligent as Mr T. GRAHAME 4
I had rather be a t. SHAK:OTH 38
pour rose-water over a t. JERROLD 8
Squat like a T. MILT 204
t. beneath the harrow knows KIP 34
Why should I let the t. *work* LARK 3
toads:
cistern for foul t. SHAK:OTH 52
imaginary gardens with real t. MOORE:M 1
t. carbonado'd SHAK:WIN 24
T. in a poisoned tank BROWNING:R 97
toast:
ever raised To t. the Queen HEAN 7
never had a piece of t. PAYN 1
refus'd to pledge my t. PRIOR 14
t. that pleased the most DIBDIN:C 9
tobacco:
I am going to leave off t. LAMB:Ch 40
in a t. trance ELIOT:TS 14
rare, superexcellent t. BURTON:Ro 17
taking their roguish t. JONS 3
tawney weed t. JONS 29
t., the ruin and overthrow of BURTON:Ro 17
You ain't got any t. LIND:N 1
tobacco-shop: Lend me a little t. POUND 18
tocsin: t. of the soul BYR 207
today:
can call to-day his own DRYD 75
here t. and gone tomorrow BEHN 8
I have lived to-day DRYD 75
in to-day already walks to-morrow COLERIDGE:ST 48
let us do something t. COLLINGWOOD:Ad 1
live t. MARTIAL 2
Never do to-day PUNCH 5
pluck the fruit of t. HORACE 13
t. I suffer LESSING:GE 2
to-day the struggle AUD 20
To-day will die to-morrow SWIN 30
tomorrow what you can do t. PROV 286
vital, beautiful day: t. MALLAR 1
Why fret ... if TO-DAY be sweet FITZGER:E 20
toe:
clerical, printless t. BROOKE 9
Had taken him in *t.* HOOD 14
looking to his great t. JONS 53
t. of the peasant comes so near SHAK:HAM 182
toes:
bells on her t. NURS 58
How cold my t. MILNE 17
No harm Can come to his t. LEAR 24
Pobble who has no t. LEAR 23
tread in the bus on my t.? AUD 26
toga: Let arms yield to the t. CIC 5
together:
get t. and forget the old times FENT 1
hardly sufficient to keep them t. JOHNSON:S 151
Let us remain t. still SHELLEY:PB 57
never again so much t. MACNEICE 11
Stand t. yet not too near GIBRAN 5
start t. and finish t. BEECHAM 3
stay t., but we distrust BRADB 5
toil:
bleared, smeared with t. HOPK:GM 5
day in t. QUAR 7
Horny-handed sons of t. KEAR 1
horny hands of t. LOWELL:JR 1
Many faint with t. SHELLEY:PB 2
mock their useful t. GRAY:T 17
Our love and t. KIP 116
Remark each anxious t. JOHNSON:S 66
they t. not, neither BIBLE 395
time is filched by t. DAVIDS 5
Tired millions t. unblest WATSON:W 3
t. and not to seek LOY 1
t. and trouble DRYD 109
toilet paper: can't tear the t.p. WILDER:B 2
toiling: t. upward in the night LONGFEL 19
toils: unnumber'd t. he bore HOMER 16
Tokay: T. And sherry BETJ 35
told:
best being plainly t. SHAK:RIC.III 15
I. t. my love BLAKE:W 57
like to be t. the worst CHURCH:W 6
not t. half of what I saw POLO 1
portentous phrase, 'I t. you so' BYR 233
t. so as to be understood BLAKE:W 52
t. you from the beginning? BIBLE 323
went and t. the sexton HOOD 6
Toledo: T. trusty BUTLER:S[1] 14
tolerance:
all Platonic t. vain YEATS 78
T. is the virtue of the weak SADE 2
t. which borders on insult ROSTAND:J 3
was such a thing as t. WILSON:W 16
tolerant: Steven's mind was so t. SMITH:T 1
toll: T. for the brave COWP 15
tolls: it *t.* for thee DONNE 100
Tolstoy: not to read T.'s novels SOLZ 6
Tom:
Poor T.'s a-cold SHAK:KING L 49
so no more of T. BYR 221
T., he was a piper's son NURS 78
T., T., the piper's son NURS 79
Tom Bowling: lies poor T.B. DIBDIN:C 3
Tom Cobbleigh: Uncle T.C. and all BALL 64
Tom Jones: romance of *T.J.* GIBBON:E 12
Tom Pearse: T.P., T.P., lend me BALL 64
tom-tit: by a river a little t. GILB:WS 81
tomato sauce: Chops and tomata sauce DICKENS 36
tomb:
brak' their livin' t. MACDIAR 15
Call'd vulgarly a t. HUME 17
fair Fidele's grassy t. COLLINS:Will 2
in this our living T. DONNE 75
Making their t. the womb SHAK:SON 37
sea was made his t. BARNF 2
t. by the side of the sea POE 9
T. hideth trouble POUND 5
tombs:
Some hang above the t. COLERIDGE:M 2
to gaping t. retires POPE 32
Tommy: it's T. this, an' T. that KIP 64
Tommy Tucker: Little T.T. Sings NURS 37
Tomnoddy: My Lord T. is thirty-four

BROUGH 1
tomorrow:
Avoid enquiring into what will be t. HORACE 11
Boast not thyself of to morrow BIBLE 272
borrow trouble by dreading t. DIX:D 2
can put off till t. PUNCH 5
for to morrow we shall die BIBLE 314
in next week t. GRAHAME 3
in to-day already walks to-morrow. COLERIDGE:ST 48
little trust as possible in t. HORACE 13
Never put off till t. PROV 286
no t. hath, nor yesterday DONNE 27
that may be to-morrow. THOMP:F 4
To-morrow, and to-morrow SHAK:MAC 113
T. do thy worst DRYD 75
T. for the young AUD 20
t. has no certainty MEDICI:L 1
t. I shall die LESSING:GE 2
T. is all like sweet flowers BURGESS:A 1
t. is another day MITCH:M 3
T. is another day PROV 396
T. never comes PROV 397
t. shall not drive it out DONNE 104
t. to be brave ARMST:J 1
T. will be dying HERR 26
T.'s life is too late MARTIAL 2
to-morrow's uprising to deeds MORRIS:W 9
tomorrows: no dividend from time's t. SASS 7
tone:
look at me – in that t. of voice PUNCH 24
Take the t. of the company CHESTERFIELD 8
tones: t. as dry and level AUD 51
tongs: have the t. and the bones SHAK:MID 37
tongue:
become his mother t. GOLDS 63
eye to see not t. to speak LENT 1
falser t., That utter'd all DONNE 13
fellows of infinite t. SHAK:HEN.V 46
Had t. at will SHAK:OTH 21
his T. Dropd Manna MILT 152
His t. is growing hotter LAWS 3
his t. is the clapper SHAK:MUCH 17
his t. to conceive SHAK:MID 42
hold your t., and let me love DONNE 30
I must hold my t. SHAK:HAM 22
ignorant of their Mother T. DRYD 74
In their Mother T. PRAY 75
iron t. of midnight SHAK:MID 50
I've a t. like a button-stick KIP 46
Kepe wel thy tonge CHAUC 54
Licked its t. into the corners ELIOT:TS 4
Love's t. is in FLETCH:P 3
man keip weil ane toung LIND:D 1
my t. is frozen SAP 1
My t. swore EUR 1
my t.'s a stone YEATS 98
mysmetre to defaute of tonge CHAUC 120
obnoxious to each carping t. BRADST 1
of a slow t. BIBLE 90
of less truth than t. SHAK:SON 5
One t. is sufficient for a woman MILT 325
perishing t. that first told YEATS 127
put a t. In every wound SHAK:JUL 58
senates hang upon thy t. THOMS:Ja[1] 7
she had a t. with a tang SHAK:TEM 18
still t. makes a wise head PROV 354
T.; well that's a wery good DICKENS 13
t. is the only edged tool IRV 2
t. is the pen of a ready BIBLE 214
t. to persuade CLAREN 2
t.'s sweet air more tuneable SHAK:MID 4
treasure of our t. DANI 2
trust their t. alone SWIFT 60
understanding, but no t. SHAK:HAM 26
use of my oracular t. SHERIDAN:RB 10
vibrates her eternal t. YOUNG:E 4
Why a T. impress'd BLAKE:W 30
would that my t. could utter TENNY 58
Your t. shall be split NURS 69
tongue-tied: art made t. SHAK:SON 30
tongues:
Bells Put out their T. DICKIN:E 8
Finds t. in trees SHAK:AS 12
for a thousand t., to sing WESLEY:C 2
lack t. to praise SHAK:SON 49
thousand several t. SHAK:RIC.III 17
t. of men and of angels BIBLE 522
t., the voice of souls SHAK:SON 31
Walls have t., and hedges SWIFT 59
whispering t. can poison truth COLERIDGE:ST 61
Wild t. that have not Thee KIP 93
tonic: wicked as a ginless t. COPE 3
tonight: Not t., Josephine NAPO I 12
Too-late: No-more, T., Farewell ROSSET:DG 12
took:
'E went an' t. KIP 90
He t. her with a sigh BLAKE:W 57
I t. thee for thy better SHAK:HAM 138
person you and I t. me for CARLYLE:JW 3
tool: t. of honour in my hands WORDS:W 102
tool-making: Man is a t. animal FRANKLIN:B 29
tool-using: Man is a T. Animal CARLYLE:T 3
tools:
always blames his t. PROV 27
build 'em up with worn-out t. KIP 127
Give us the t. CHURCH:W 21
nothing but to name his t. BUTLER:S[1] 4
Their working t. TUSS 9
t. to work withal LOWELL:JR 1
what shall we do with the t.? HAILE 1
Without T. he is nothing CARLYLE:T 3
tooth:
alwey a coltes t. CHAUC 82
pulling out her own rotten t. DI PIET 1
set my pugging t. on edge SHAK:WIN 12
sharper than a serpent's t. DICKENS 227
t. for t. BIBLE 104
toothache:
could endure the t. patiently SHAK:MUCH 30
Music helps not the tooth-ache HERB:G 58
that sleeps feels not the t. SHAK:CYM 19
toothbrush: t. is airing BETJ 18
toothpaste:
can't put t. back NIX 18
Once the t. is out HALDE 1
top:
always room at the t. PROV 376
always room at the t. WEBSTER:D 10
die first at the t. SWIFT 83
I began at the t. WELLES 2
looking at the men at the t. COLBY 2
People at the t. of the tree UST 10
T. of the world CAGNEY 1
top-boots: did pleasure me in his t. MARLBOR:S 2
top-mast: He strack the t. BALL 15
topics: but two t., yourself and me JOHNSON:S 188
torch:
pass on the t. of life LUCRET 6
t.; be yours to hold MCCRAE 2
t. of her beauty; she carried it WOOLF:V 5
Truth, like a t. HAMIL:W 1
torches:
our little t. at his fire COKAYNE 1
teach the t. to burn SHAK:ROM 7
torchlight: t. procession marching O'SULL 3
Tories:
angels all are T. BYR 149
are T. born wicked ANON 215
T. own no argument BROWNE:W[2] 1
torment:
measure of our t. is KIP 53
t. of the night's untruth DANI 1
tormented: this t. mind tormenting yet HOPK:GM 25
tormentor: I who am my own t. TOLS:L 13
torments:
how many t. lie CIB 5
t. also may in length MILT 157
torpedo: aerial t. right in the centre MUSSO:V 1
torpedoes: damn the t. FARRA 1
torrid: T. or the frozen Zone CAREW:T 3
tortoise:
'Tortis' is an insect PUNCH 10
T. because he taught us CARROLL 27
writing for the t. market BROOKNER 1
torture: t. them, into believing NEWM:JH 1
tory: t. rory ranter boys FIELDING 17
Tory:
hatred for the T. Party BEVAN 2
I may be a T. PEEL:R 1
thinking man's T. BARNARD:R 1
T. men and Whig measures DISR:B 16
wise T. and a wise Whig JOHNSON:S 227
toss-pots: t. still had drunken heads SHAK:TWE 59
tossed: you t. and gored several BOSW 1
total: What's the demd t.? DICKENS 79
totter:
t. into vogue WALP:H 9
t. on in bus'ness POPE 114
touch:
anyone can say he is out of t. DOUGLAS-H:C 1
Do not t. me BIBLE 615
He wants the natural t. SHAK:MAC 87
nor lose the common t. KIP 128
nothing, Can t. him further SHAK:MAC 65
see thee in my t. SHAK:KING L 57
t. has still its ancient power TWELLS 2
t. was as electric poison SHELLEY:PB 131
touched: dead man touch'd me TENNY 172
touches: t. this t. a man WHITMAN 27
tough:
going gets t., the t. get KENNEDY:JP 1
statements was interesting, but t. TWAIN 12
t., is J. B. DICKENS 128
toujours: t. gai t. gai MARQUIS 4
tourist:
loathsome is the British t. KILV 1
most noxious is a t. KILV 1
tourists: t. . . . take in the Monarchy HAMIL:WW 1
towels: never darken my t. again MARX:G 13
tower:
be as steady as a t. DANTE 15
Child Rowland to the dark t. came SHAK:KING L 51
that t. of strength TENNY 190
yonder ivy-mantled tow'r GRAY:T 16
towers:
hammer'd from a hundred t. TENNY 94
in Heav'n high Towrs MILT 145
ye antique t. GRAY:T 2
Ye t. of Julius GRAY:T 32
towery: T. city and branchy HOPK:GM 12
town:
comin of the endless t. MURRAY:LA 5
country in the t. MARTIAL 10
country t., and imagines it sleepy BROD 1
down to the end of the t. MILNE 2
follies of the t. crept slowly GOLDS 64
he studies it in the t. COWP 39
I, like an usurpt t. DONNE 88
lived in a pretty how t. CUMM 5
man made the t. COWP 59
poor little one-horse t. TWAIN 5
save the t., it became necessary ANON 254
sounding through the t. BALL 13
spreading of the hideous t. MORRIS:W 6
was the good t. once MUIR:E 2
wenche in every toun CHAUC 68
What's this dull t. to me? KEPP:C 1
town-crier: lief the t. spoke my lines SHAK:HAM 106
town crier: like a t.c. in Pompeii THOMAS:D 39
town-dweller: Australian t. spent a century BOYD:RGP 1
towns: Place elephants for want of t. SWIFT 68
toy:
created to be the t. of man WOLLST 3
foolish thing was but a t. SHAK:TWE 59
sells eternity to get a t.? SHAK:POET 5
toys:
All is but t. SHAK:MAC 56
Deceive boys with t. LYS 1
Not to meddle with my t. STEVENSON:RL 53
pray'r-books are the t. of age POPE 98
then cast their t. away COWP 31
t. for your delight STEVENSON:RL 64
toyshop: moving T. of their heart POPE 38
traces: leaves t. of what he created BRONO 3
track:
There's a t. winding back O'HAG 1
tread again that ancient t. VAUGHAN:H 6
you t. him everywhere DRYD 138
trade:
all is seared with t. HOPK:GM 5
Every man to his t. PROV 104
half a t. and half an art INGE 3
heel of the North-East T. KIP 149
not your t. to make tables JOHNSON:S 111
now There isn't any T. HERB:AP 10

trees:
all the t. are green KINGSLEY:C 19
all the t. were bread ANON 71
Amidst their tall ancestral t. HEMA 3
argument of t. were done SLESS 3
Books are just t. with squiggles INNES 1
Boosom'd high in tufted T. MILT 71
fake food under plastic t. SKY 1
He lived on the t. CALVINO 1
I love t. revealed KAV 4
not die when the t. were green CLARE:J 9
O look at the t. BRIDGES:R 8
Of all the t. in England DE LA M 17
Of all the t. that grow KIP 122
Orpheus with his lute made t. SHAK:HEN.VIII 7
Saw infant t. fill out ELIOT:G 46
tangerine t. and marmalade skies LENNON 7
t. are in their autumn beauty YEATS 49
T., where you sit POPE 3
Upon the t. of Paradise STEVENSON:RL 60
we might procreate like t. BROWNE:T 28
you lover of t. BROWNING:R 102
Trelawney: And shall T. die? HAWKER 1
tremble:
t. and despoil SHELLEY:PB 43
Where Angels t. GRAY:T 35
tremblers: boding t. learned to trace GOLDS 28
trenches: deep t. in thy beauty's SHAK:SON 2
Trent:
'er the wide vale of T. MACAULAY:TB 42
silver T. shall run SHAK:HEN.IV[1] 59
why was Burton built on T.? HOUSM 28
trespass: black swan of t. MALLEY 1
trespasses:
forgive us our t. MASS 15
forgive us our t. PRAY 6
tress: at midnight by a t. YEATS 19
trial:
only a t. if I recognise it KAF 4
purifies us is triall MILT 313
strains of this t., have radiance? CAUL 1
T. by jury itself DENMAN:T 1
Truth fears no t. PROV 402
triangle: eternal t. ANON 183
triangles: If t. created a god MONTESQU 1
tribal: ways of constructing t. lays KIP 76
tribe:
custom of his t. and island SHAW 21
may his t. increase HUNT:L 4
verily the T. is all THOMS:Ja[2] 8
tribes: two mighty t., the *Bores* BYR 231
tribulation: In all time of our t. PRAY 34
tribunal: t. now Higher than God's BROWNING:R 204
tribute: passing t. of a sigh GRAY:T 23
trick:
I know a t. worth two SHAK:HEN.IV[1] 24
pleasure to t. the trickster FONTAINE 3
When in doubt, win the t. HOYLE 1
tricks:
such Affected T. BELLOC 14
teach a dogma new t. PARKER:D 31
teach an old dog new t. PROV 445
Their t. an' craft BURNS:R 25
Women are like t. CONG 28
tried:
take the one I've never t. WEST:M 8
t. a little, failed much STEVENSON:RL 43
t. before a jury for a capital JOHNSON:S 183
Triermain: valiant Knight of T. SCOTT:W 44
trifle:
As 'twere a careless t. SHAK:MAC 18
Is t. sufficient for sweet? BETJ 27
object of domestic art called t. HOLMES:OW 15
trifles:
concern itself about t. PROV 229
man of sense only t. with them CHESTERFIELD 17
Revolutions may spring from t. ARISTOT 14
She who t. with all GAY 41
snapper-up of unconsidered t. SHAK:WIN 13
upon the observance of t. DOYLE:AC 9
trimmer: *T.* signifieth no more HALIF 1
trinities: cold Christ and tangled T. KIP 36
trinity:
T. had never been unkind NEWM:JH 12
worship one God in T. PRAY 30
trip:
fearful t. is done WHITMAN 29
T. no further SHAK:TWE 19
triple: t. cord, which no man BURKE:E 76
triste: jamais t. archy MARQUIS 3
tristesse: *Adieu t. Bonjour t.* ELUARD 1
Tristram Shandy:
The Life and Opinions of T.S. WALP:H 6
T.S. did not last JOHNSON:S 178
Triton:
T. blow his wreathèd horn WORDS:W 105
T. blowing loud SPENS 17
triumph:
meet with T. and Disaster KIP 127
One more devils'-t. BROWNING:R 55
Poor is the t. o'er the timid THOMS:Ja[1] 9
ride in t. through Persepolis? MARLOWE 8
Small trade and no t. CURNOW 2
that agony is our t. VANZ 2
t. is without glory CORNEILLE 1
t. over death and sin SPENS 8
We shall not see the t. DICKENS 203
triumphant: Joyful and t. OAK 1
triumphs:
at all t. but his own CHURCH:C 4
little t. o'er GRAY:T 38
who t. by breaking an oath PLUT 2
trivial:
contests arise from t. things POPE 36
The t. round KEBLE 1
wonder That such t. people LAWR:DH 35
trivialities: tormenting the people with t. NAPO I 3
trochee: T. trips from long COLERIDGE:ST 57
trod: Generations have t. HOPK:GM 5
trodden: I have t. the winepress alone BIBLE 334
Trojan: what T. 'orses will jump out BEVIN 2
Trojans: We T. are no more VIRGIL 52
trolley-bus: T. and windy street BETJ 23
trolley buses: kissing of the t.b. hissing BETJ 25
troops: endured the sufferings of the t. SASS 21
trope: out there flew a t. BUTLER:S[1] 3
trophies:
among her cloudy t. hung KEATS 96
hang their old T. o'er POPE 148
t. unto the enemies of truth BROWNE:T 3
tropics: nuisance of the t. BELLOC 10
trot: don't t. it out and about COLETTE 1
troth: plight thee my t. PRAY 84
Trotskyite: refuge of bearded T. HOWK 1
trouble:
ain't see no t. yit HARRIS:JC 12
borrow t. by dreading tomorrow DIX:D 2
have your t. doubl'd DEF 6
it keeps her out of t. HELLER 7
Kindness in another's t. GORDON:AM 1
lot of t. in his life, most of CHURCH:W 56
Man is born unto t. BIBLE 184
of few days, and full of t. BIBLE 188
telling one's t. does not PAVE 1
to read when they're in t. HOUSM 41
transcendent capacity of taking t. CARLYLE:T 57
transient, shining t. GRAIN:J 1
troubill efter grit prosperitie HENRYS 3
t. enough of its own WILCOX 3
t. of ants in the gleam TENNY 295
t. shared is a t. halved PROV 400
women and care and t. WARD:N 1
troubles:
All the t. of men are caused PASC 7
Don't meet t. half way PROV 79
pack up your t. ASAF 1
t. enough, for one BROWNING:R 139
woman whose t. are greater ALG 2
trousers:
bottoms of my t. rolled ELIOT:TS 11
never have his best t. on IBS 10
wear white flannel t. ELIOT:TS 11
trout:
find a t. in the milk THOREAU 24
good fresh t. for supper LLEW 1
there a lusty t. TENNY 202
Where the grey t. lies HOGG 7
trouts: t. are tickled best BUTLER:S[1] 41
trowel:
laid on with a t. SHAK:AS 3
lay it on with a t. DISR:B 89
lays it on with a t. CONG 18
Troy:
another T. for her to burn? YEATS 31
corn where T. once was OSB:J 15
fired another T. DRYD 113
half his T. was burnt SHAK:HEN.IV[2] 3
heard T. doubted BYR 204
hour has come for T. VIRGIL 52
no more the tale of T. SHELLEY:PB 155
ringing plains of windy T. TENNY 52
tale of T. divine MILT 85
T. but a heap of smouldering POUND 31
T. town COLERIDGE:M 1
Troys: hundred T. 'Twixt noon and supper BROOKE 4
truant:
every t. knew GOLDS 28
have a t. been to chivalry SHAK:HEN.IV[1] 84
t. disposition SHAK:HAM 23
true:
always t. to you, darlin' PORTER:C 6
always think what is t. and do HUX:TH 2
angry at a slander makes it t. JONS 26
as long as it isn't t. HEPB 1
can the devil speak t.? SHAK:MAC 12
Dare to be t. HERB:G 3
discerning what is t. BACON:F[1] 54
fu' man's a t. man PROV 141
He's been t. to *one* party LOWELL:JR 3
if only it were t. TOLS:L 15
kept him falsely t. TENNY 253
let us be t. To one another ARNOLD:M 47
long enough it *will* be t. BENNETT:Ar 4
man had rather were t. BACON:F[1] 21
man worth having is t. to his wife VANB 3
Many a t. word is spoken PROV 264
not necessarily t. because a man dies WILDE:O 105
not t. because it is useful AMIEL 4
Really do come t. HARBU 4
ring in the t. TENNY 177
she were t., when you met DONNE 58
should be t. to the public BERK 5
such a proposition is t. of *anything* RUSS:B 4
tell you three times is t. CARROLL 89
'Tis easy to be t. SEDLEY 6
to thine own self be t. SHAK:HAM 30
T. and *false* are attributes HOBB 2
t. ... as taxes is DICKENS 156
t. as the stars above ANON 11
t. as truth's simplicity SHAK:TRO 13
t. for all men, – that is genius EMER 4
t. to their own ends BACON:F[1] 79
whatever for supposing it t. RUSS:B 9
Whatsoever things are t. BIBLE 542
whether what we say is t. RUSS:B 3
truer:
nothing's t. than them DICKENS 156
t. than tongue confess HOPK:GM 3
truffles: swine to show you where the t. ALBEE 3
trump: speaking t. of future fame BYR 14
trumpet:
anon a t. sounds THOMP:F 13
blow your own t. GILB:WS 86
dreads the final T. HARDY:T 4
He shifted his t. GOLDS 41
mooved more than with a T. SIDNEY:P 16
shrill t. sounds CIB 4
trompet shrill hath thrise SPENS 7
t., at whose voice DONNE 78
t. in terrible tones went ENN 1
t. of a prophecy SHELLEY:PB 46
t. shall be heard on high DRYD 95
t. will fling out a stupendous CEL 2
t.'s loud clangour DRYD 93
t.'s silver sound is still SCOTT:W 14
trumpets:
blow Your t., Angels DONNE 82
de blowin' er de trumpits HARRIS:JC 11
foie gras to the sound of t. SMITH:Syd[1] 37
let the t. sound SCOTT:W 64
silver, snarling t. KEATS 64
Sound the t. DRYD 106
Sound the t. MORELL 1
then the t. CHESTERTON 20
thunder of the t. of the night SWIN 41
t. sounded for him BUNYAN 32
t. which sing to battle SHELLEY:PB 167
up-lifted Angel t. blow MILT 64
Where are the eagles and the t.? ELIOT:TS 20

trumps:
ace of t. up his sleeve LABOU 1
if dirt were t. LAMB:Ch 46
Let Spades be t. POPE 49
trunk: So large a t. before BELLOC 3
trust:
advisable to t. nobody CHRIS 5
built An absolute t. SHAK:MAC 18
Don't t. anyone over thirty RUBIN 1
Don't t. your horse in the field TOLS:L 10
If you can t. yourself KIP 127
in t. I have found treason ELIZ I 2
In the People was my t. WORDS:W 158
man assumes a public t. JEFFERSON 7
men dare t. themselves SHAK:TIM 5
Never t. a husband too far ROWL:H 4
Never t. the man who hath FIELDING 19
Put not your t. in princes BIBLE 248
put too much t. in your beauty VIRGIL 5
put t. in ideas EMER 46
t. anyone who wears a beard CAINE 1
T., his sworn brother SHAK:WIN 28
t. in God SMITH:Syd[1] 19
T. in God, and do the Right MACLEOD:N 1
t. me not at all or all TENNY 245
T. your no Skott BOORDE 1
trusted:
in thee have I t. PRAY 11
Let no such man be t. SHAK:MERC 51
t. with untold gold SCOTT:W 99
unsafe to be t. with our selves? CONG 66
trusteth: concerning the man that t. in God HOOK 1
trusting: t. in the Lord and a good lawyer NORTH:O 1
truth:
alone is not t., but persuasion MACAULAY:TB 37
Any fool can tell the t. BUTLER:S[2] 39
as dangerous to persist in the t. BELLOW 3
as it is not founded on t. SITWELL:E 11
awoke and found it t. KEATS 118
Beauty and T., though never found BUCHANAN 1
Beauty is t., t. beauty KEATS 92
believe, falsely, to be the t. HAMP 2
between the mind and t. HEWITT:J 1
bright countenance of t. MILT 305
bring t. to light SHAK:POET 6
but things like t. CHAPMAN:G 6
casualty when war comes is t. JOHNSON:H 1
certain t. no man has seen XENOPHAN 3
choose varieties of t. FRAME 2
dared to speak the t. to me TROLL 15
dearer still is t. ARISTOT 25
divine melodious t. KEATS 56
dream of human love and t. TENNY 182
economical with the t. ARMST:R 1
feel certain of any t. KEATS 148
find the t., to speak the t. and NIX 2
For t. to o'erpeer SHAK:COR 6
from the t. of the description SCOTT:W 95
further to discover t. BACON:F[1] 4
give thee that due, Utt'ring bare t. SHAK:SON 31
good novel tells us the t. CHESTERTON 36
good that came of telling t. DRYD 98
Great is T., and mighty BIBLE 364
great is t., and shall prevail BROOKS:T 1
half t. in argument LEACOCK 9
half-truths do not make a t. KOES 2
he must speak t. SHAK:KING L 25
hear the t. you've spoken KIP 127
heavenly t. imparts KEBLE 5
help separate t. from falsehood D'SOU 1
how many people know the real t. WEST:R 6
however improbable, must be the t. DOYLE:AC 7
I have look'd on t. SHAK:SON 51
I mean the t. untold OWEN:W 13
If one tells the t., one WILDE:O 71
If ... t. cannot be told SOLZ 3
in the end the t. will conquer WYCLIFFE 1
indisputable air of T. CARLYLE:T 26
Is there in t. no beautie? HERB:G 25
It is t. that is shamefaced DARLING:CJ 4
kept a Strict Regard for T. BELLOC 21
kept thy pure t. MILT 99
laws of poetic t. ARNOLD:M 79
lost to Love and T. KIP 53
mainly he told the t. TWAIN 11
make fiction of the t. FRY:C 20
make him confess the t. HOUSE 2
make t. serve as a stalking-horse BOLI 5
man of reflection discovers T. PEREZ 2
nature's t. Is primary THOMAS:RS 3
never sold the t. to serve TENNY 194
Nobody speaks the t. BOWEN:El 2
not tell the t. about yourself WOOLF:V 16
ocean of t. lay all undiscovered NEWT:I 5
of less t. than tongue SHAK:SON 5
open t. to cover lies CONG 20
owe nothing but t. to the dead VOLT 25
philosophers have not maintained for t. SWIFT 33
possession of t. as of a city BROWNE:T 4
put him in possession of t. LOCKE 4
reasoned into t. DRYD 68
relationship with Beauty and t. KEATS 123
ride and speak the t. BYR 237
see t. dawn together? BROWNING:R 76
seeming t. which cunning SHAK:MERC 35
seven years for not telling the t. DARLING:CJ 5
short armistice with t. BYR 191
simple t. his utmost skill WOTTON 2
simple t. must be abus'd SHAK:RIC.III 5
sole judge of t. POPE 90
still closing up t. to t. MILT 316
swear to the t. of a song? PRIOR 10
takes two to speak the t. THOREAU 3
tell how the t. may be SCOTT:W 7
tell me the t. about love AUD 26
Tell the t. and shame PROV 366
tell t., and shame the devil SHAK:HEN.IV[1] 38
telling the disreputable t. BENET 3
that I have pleaded t. SHAK:HEN.VI[1] 2
they worship T. BROOKE 12
Till T. obeyed his call YEATS 105
time-servers for t. MILL 18
to battle for freedom and t. IBS 10
to be a clue to the t. COMPT 7
to murder, for the t. ADL:A 1
trophies unto the enemies of t. BROWNE:T 3
Trouthe is the hyest thyng CHAUC 38
trouthe thee shal delivere CHAUC 125
true as t.'s simplicity SHAK:TRO 13
t. among the groves of Academe HORACE 96
t. and beauty on my love SHAK:SON 44
t. and simplicity are the best LA BRU 1
t. at all times firmly KETHE 2
T. away From you is fled? WYATT 2
T. be in the field MILT 322
t. by consecutive reasoning KEATS 120
t. can neither be apprehended WEDGEWOOD 1
T. can never be told so BLAKE:W 52
T. exists BRAQ 2
T. fears no trial PROV 402
T., for its own sake, had KINGSLEY:C 8
T. from his lips prevailed GOLDS 27
t. goes naked PROV 62
t., has any inherent power MILL 13
t. has got its boots on CALLA 1
t. in action DISR:B 57
t. in beauty dy'd SHAK:SON 44
t. in every shepherd's tongue RALE 1
t. in masquerade BYR 222
t. is a naked and open BACON:F[1] 115
t. is always libellous FINEY 1
t. is always strange BYR 234
t. is bleeding at the bottom of KENNELLY 3
t. is great, and shall PATMO 9
t. is more important than the facts WRIGHT:FL 2
t. is often a terrible weapon ADL:A 1
T. is on the move ZOLA 4
t. is rarely pure and never WILDE:O 82
t. is spoken, that more DARLING:CJ 3
T. is stranger than fiction PROV 403
T. is the cry of all BERK 4
T. is the safest lie PROV 404
t. is too simple SAND 3
T. is within ourselves BROWNING:R 2
t. lies somewhere, is we COWP 32
T. lies within a little BOLI 1
T., like a torch HAMIL:W 1
T. lives on in deception SCHILL 9
t. miscall'd simplicity SHAK:SON 30
t. of Imagination KEATS 119
t. put down by persecution MILL 13
t. repeated until people BALD:S 11
t. shall be thy warrant RALE 3
t. shall make you free BIBLE 481
t. shines athwart the lies BROWNING:R 66
T., Sir, is a cow JOHNSON:S 117
T. sits upon the lips ARNOLD:M 31
T. standing on its head to LE GAL 1
T. stands, and he that will DONNE 2
t. stands barrit at the dure DUNB 6
t. that wounds PROV 37
t. that's told with bad intent BLAKE:W 86
T. the masculine HARE:J 3
t., then, be thy dower SHAK:KING L 2
T., when witty HARE:J 1
t. which is clearly understood PROUST 17
t. which makes men free AGAR 1
t. which men prefer not to hear AGAR 1
t. which you cannot contradict PLATO 15
T. will come to light SHAK:MERC 22
t. will influence half a score BOLI 7
T. will out PROV 405
t. will overcome the left YELT 3
t. within thy mind rehearse TENNY 49
t. without making anybody cry FELL 2
T.'s a dog must to SHAK:KING L 14
unpleasant way of saying the t. HELLMAN 1
utter what he thinks t. JOHNSON:S 213
warp us from the living t. TENNY 73
way of joking is to tell the t. SHAW 76
way, the t., and the life BIBLE 489
We grope for T. DAVEN:W 3
What is T.? BACON:F[1] 114
What is t.? BIBLE 491
When I tell any T. it is not for BLAKE:W 111
When in doubt, tell the t. TWAIN 35
whispering tongues can poison t. COLERIDGE:ST 61
who would keep abreast of T. LOWELL:JR 2
Wine brings out the t. PLINY 2
wither into t. YEATS 29
truthful:
ever t. about his own life GRANT:C 2
my name is T. James HARTE 2
true Poets must be t. OWEN:W 16
truths:
Advertisements contain the only t. JEFFERSON 13
all t. are half-truths WHITEHEAD 5
bear all naked t. KEATS 52
great t. begin as blasphemies SHAW 115
instruments of darkness tell us t. SHAK:MAC 14
Irrationally held t. may be more HUX:TH 7
man of two t. MURD:I 4
more *home* t. are to be learnt HAZL 6
tell him disagreeable t. BULWER 4
three fundamental t. BELL:C 3
t. that wake WORDS:W 64
t. to begin as heresies HUX:TH 8
Two t. are told SHAK:MAC 15
try:
then proceed to t. him MOLIERE 23
t. everything once BAX 1
T., t. again HICKSON 1
t., t., t. again PROV 183
trying:
goes on t. other things PICAS 4
there is only the t. ELIOT:TS 99
tu:
Et t. Brute? CAES:GJ 7
Et t., Brute? SHAK:JUL 35
tub:
mere tale of a t. WEBSTER:J 5
Three men in a t. NURS 63
t. was large enough for Diogenes COLTON 8
tubby: Hon was a t. little chap WODE 17
tuberculosis: Mankind is responsible for t. PHILIP:R 1
tuckerbox: dog – he *shat* in the t. ANON 3
tuckets: Then the t. CHESTERTON 20
tuckoo: little boy named baby t. JOYCE:J 2
Tugela: Limpopo and T. churned PLOM 2
tulip:
number the streaks of the t. JOHNSON:S 20
t. and the butterfly WATTS 7
t. planted in dung GOLDS 76

tulips: t. bloom as they are told BROOKE 7
tumbler: t. ca'd the Premier BURNS:R 22
tumbling: we lie t. in the hay SHAK:WIN 12
tumult:
calls us; o'er the t. ALEX:CF 3
t. and the shouting dies KIP 91
tun: t. of man is thy companion SHAK:HEN.IV[1] 50
tune:
all the t. that he could play NURS 78
away from the t. that they play KIP 68
good t. played on an old fiddle BUTLER:S[2] 19
good t. played on an old fiddle PROV 378
How dost thou like this t.? SHAK:TWE 25
I am incapable of a t. LAMB:Ch 2
pays the piper calls the t. PROV 168
t. is catching AUD 9
Turn on, t. in LEARY 1
we are out of t. WORDS:W 104
tuned: t. like fifty stomach-aches DICKENS 99
tunes:
devil should have all the good t. HILL:Row 1
Heft Of Cathedral T. DICKIN:E 4
misfits, looney t. and squalid REAG 4
slow old t. of Spain MASE 6
tunnel:
light at the end of the t. LOWELL:R 18
t. of green gloom BROOKE 6
tunnelling: T. through the night WRIGHT:J 5
tunnies: t. steep'd in brine ARNOLD:M 30
turbid: t. look the most profound LANDOR 14
turbot: price of a large t. for it RUSKIN 22
turd: rymyng is nat worth a toord CHAUC 75
tureen: Waiting is a hot t. CARROLL 35
turf:
bless the t. that wraps COLLINS:Will 4
blue ribbon of the t. DISR:B 33
Green be the t. above HALLE 1
green t. beneath my HAZL 18
smooth green miles of t. HOUSM 40
Turk:
malignant and a turban'd T. SHAK:OTH 70
Nose of T. SHAK:MAC 80
out-paramour'd the T. SHAK:KING L 44
take the T. by the beard? SHAK:HEN.V 47
T. a man and a brother? ERAS 6
turkey:
all the myrtle and t. part AUSTEN 33
It *was* a T. DICKENS 101
Turkey : a grievously sick man* NICHOLAS 2
turkey-cock: Contemplation makes a rare t. SHAK:TWE 33
turn:
Even a worm can t. PROV 97
I do not hope to t. again ELIOT:TS 65
leaves no t. unstoned SHAW 128
One good t. deserves PROV 310
T. on, tune in LEARY 1
world would begin to t. the other BENNETT:Ar 12
turned:
In case anything t. up DICKENS 149
One who never t. his back BROWNING:R 213
t. his back on a big one HUGHES:Th 5
turning:
lady's not for t. THATCH:M 4
long lane that has no t. PROV 202
there's no t. back ROSSET:C 17
wrong t. before we have learnt CONNOLLY:C 13
turnip:
man carved out of a t. YEATS 139
no getting blood out of a t. MARR 3
rather Have a t. than his father JOHNSON:S 253
turnpike: I consider supper as a t. EDWARDS:O 1
turns: world t. on the other side JENN:E 3
turret: washed me out of the t. JARRELL 3
turrets: half-glimpsed t. slowly wash THOMP:F 13
turtle:
love of the t. BYR 22
t. lives 'twixt plated NASH 5
voice of the t. is heard BIBLE 295
Tuscan: Through Optic Glass the T. Artist MILT 124
Tusculum: I will lay on for T. MACAULAY:TB 43
tussis: *T.* attacked him BROWNING:R 119
tuum: distinctions of *meum* and *t.* LAMB:Ch 17
twaddle:
Better to write t. MANS:K 11
flat, prosaic t. MACAULAY:TB 58
twain: go with him t. BIBLE 386
twang: most melodious t. AUBREY 13
twangs: something t. and breaks MACNEICE 9
Tweedledum:
T. and Tweedledee CARROLL 51
'Twixt T. and Tweedledee BYROM 2
twelve:
born at the age of t. GARL 1
I'll sing you t. O ANON 22
t. great shocks of sound TENNY 94
t. honest men have decided PULT 1
t. men from the bottom ranks BARTON 1
who needs *t.* GRADE 2
Why only t.? GORKY 21
twentieth century: t.c. essentially ended on YELT 4
twenty:
At t. years of age FRANKLIN:B 9
just as well be t. PICAS 7
Let t. pass BROWNING:R 170
t. is not the time to be a prude MOLIERE 16
T. will not come again HOUSM 3
twenty-four-hour: t. strike is like the t. flu MUIR:F 3
twenty-one: limited excellence at t. FITZGER:FS 3
twenty-three: chaste, and t. BYR 161
twenty-two: tramp of the t. men BOWEN:EE 1
twice:
My life closed t. DICKIN:E 22
T. would have been quite CONF 17
will bear to be read t. THOREAU 23
twice-told: tedious as a t. tale SHAK:KING J 13
twig:
Just as the T. is bent POPE 112
thorn t. for clettering dishes GIBBONS:S 5
twilight:
disastrous t. sheds MILT 136
dreaming through the t. ROSSET:C 13
Pilots of the purple t. TENNY 79
snow blind t. ferries THOMAS:D 15
they ever fly by t. BACON:F[1] 111
T. and evening bell TENNY 297
t., and the sunless day BYR 175
t. dim with rose DE LA M 10
T. gray Had in her sober MILT 198
t. of such day SHAK:SON 33
twilights: In ancient shadows and t. RUSS:GW 1
twin: Don't tell my t. HERB:AP 1
twinkle:
T., t., little bat CARROLL 18
T., t., little star TAYL:Ann 2
twins: threw the t. she nursed GRAHAM:H 1
twisted: You silly t. boy MILLIG 7
two:
be at the expense of t.? CLOUGH 19
can t. do against so many? SHAW 136
Can t. walk together BIBLE 356
formula 'T. and t. is five' DOST 1
must have *t.* you know CARROLL 75
prejudice runs in favour of t. DICKENS 67
Sitting t. and t., boys EMPS 4
takes t. to make a quarrel PROV 212
takes t. to speak the truth THOREAU 3
takes t. to tango PROV 213
t. and t. do not make six TOLS:L 17
T. of a trade can ne'er GAY 45
t. people with one pulse MACNEICE 10
t. to make a marriage a success SAMUEL 5
went in t. and t. BIBLE 36
where t. or three are gathered BIBLE 421
two-and-twenty: sweet t. BYR 141
two-party: t. system and a one-party STEVENSON:A 7
twopence: t. every day of my life STEVENSON:RL 3
Tyburn-face: damn'd T. CONG 21
types:
by device of *Movable T.* CARLYLE:T 2
From shadows and t. NEWM:JH 21
typewriter: someone has given a t. BREN 8
typewriters:
written on t. by other t. JARRELL 4
your characters talk like t. CAMPBELL:Mrs P 4
typographical: but for a t. error PARKER:D 22
tyrannize: t. over his bank balance than KEYN 8
tyranny:
call it *t.* HOBB 11
Ecclesiastic t.'s the worst DEF 13
long dark night of t. MURROW 1
there t. begins PITT:W[1] 5
T. comes from no other PLATO 12
t. in every tainted breeze BURKE:E 31
t. it is far easier to act AREN 4
t. may result from either ARISTOT 16
T. of Distance BLAIN 2
t. of the prevailing opinion MILL 5
without representation is t. OTIS 1
worst sort of t. BURKE:E 47
tyrant:
A village t. HILLS 1
became a T. in his Stead BLAKE:W 81
glare of the threatening t. HORACE 31
let no t. reap SHELLEY:PB 52
little T. of his fields GRAY:T 20
t. kings, or t. laws GOLDS 12
tyrants:
act with the barbarity of t. SMITH:Syd[1] 1
all men would be t. DEF 15
from the quarrels of t. VOLT 1
intercourse between t. and slaves GOLDS 58
Kings will be t. from policy BURKE:E 58
once the oppressed, now the t. KEYN 5
please t., for a handful of coins ZAPA 1
Rebellion to t. is obedience BRADSH:J 1
'Twixt Kings & T. there's HERR 39
T. seldom want pretexts BURKE:E 71
where men are t. SAINT-P 1
with the blood of patriots and t. JEFFERSON 10
Tyrawley: T. and I have been dead CHESTERFIELD 34
Tyrian:
silver-white, and budded T. KEATS 86
some grave T. trader ARNOLD:M 30
U: U. and Non-U ROSS:ASC 1
u-turn: U. if you want THATCH:M 4
ugliness: u. I mean is skin deep BOYD:RGP 3
ugly:
better to be good than to be u. WILDE:O 33
intimate knowledge of its u. side BALD:J 2
made the world u. and bad NIET 17
magnificently u. YEATS 148
no u. women, only lazy RUBINS 2
There is nothing u. CONSTABLE:J 2
u. enough to succeed ALLEN:W 4
why wasn't I born old and u.? DICKENS 91
worse than u., she is good WILDE:O 2
Ullin: this Lord U.'s daughter CAMPBELL:T 12
Ulpian: U. at the best BROWNING:R 45
ultima: *U. Thule* VIRGIL 21
Ulva: chief of U.'s isle CAMPBELL:T 12
Ulysses:
A new U. leaves SHELLEY:PB 154
Happy the man who like U. DU BEL 2
His naked U. CHAPMAN:G 8
U. is the strongest character FLAU 2
umbrage: Americans have taken u. PUNCH 13
umbrella:
lends you his u. when the sun TWAIN 46
u. might pacify barbarians PLOM 5
unjust steals the just's u. BOWEN:L 1
umbrellas: all men ... who possess u. FORST 3
umpire: chaos U. sits MILT 172
unadvisedly: u., lightly, or wantonly PRAY 81
unaffected: Affecting to seem u. CONG 59
unanimity: ourselves in such complete u. SPAAK 1
unanxious: I want to be u. BETJ 39
unarm: U., Eros SHAK:ANT 51
unattempted: u. yet in Prose or Rime MILT 107
unattractive:
most u. old thing GILB:WS 80
not against the u. GREENE:G 5
unbecoming: Not u. men that strove TENNY 55
unbelief:
Blind u. is sure to err COWP 13
help thou mine u. BIBLE 443
Help thou mine u. BUTLER:S[2] 43
help thou my u. FORST 15
u. is blind MILT 34
unblemished: U. let me live POPE 55
unborn: U. TOMORROW FITZGER:E 20

unbounded: delights in u. and immortal things YEATS 128
unbuild: arise and u. it again SHELLEY:PB 56
unbutton: Come, u. here SHAK:KING L 46
uncertain: U., coy SCOTT:W 29
uncertainty:
Greeks knew not: u. BORGES 2
key is turned On our u. YEATS 66
quit a certainty for an u. JOHNSON:S 32
uncharitableness: malice, and all u. PRAY 33
unchivalrous: feeling just a bit u. BENCH 3
unclean:
he is u. to you BIBLE 111
man of u. lips BIBLE 305
uncomely: u. as well in mind BACON:F[1] 102
uncomfortable: smug and thoroughly u. POUND 22
uncorseted: U., her friendly bust ELIOT:TS 33
uncos: saw the u. at he wrocht BIBLE 591
uncouth:
find out His u. way? MILT 160
thus sang the u. Swain MILT 59
uncouther: better the u. BROWNING:R 159
unction: flattering u. to your soul SHAK:HAM 145
under-achiever: he's an u. ALLEN:W 7
underbelly: exposure of the u. of the Axis CHURCH:W 28
underground: see things which are u. CERV 6
underlings: in ourselves, that we are u. SHAK:JUL 11
underpants: King – even in your u. FULDA 1
undersized: He's a bit u. GILB:WS 51
understand:
And he didn't u. me HEG 3
better to u. little FRANCE 11
by what they failed to u. MOORE:G 1
fellow countrymen become harder to u. SOLZ 3
if he could make *me* u. ROOS:E 1
isn't confused here doesn't really u. ANON 157
less they u., The more BUTLER:S[1] 27
may not be made to u. CONF 7
none could u. what she said BUNYAN 31
One has to u. the country LESSING:D 1
said to u. one another CHAMFORT 6
things we u. too easily VOLT 2
u. something you've understood LESSING:D 4
wot do they u.? KIP 61
you believe, you will not u. AUGUS 10
understandeth: Who u. thee not SHAK:LOV 11
understanding:
bias against *u.* BIRT 1
cod passes all u. LUTY 1
evidence against their own U. HALIF 9
friendly u. that exists LOUIS PHIL 1
not by force but by u. BRIDGES:R 16
on the road to u. AESC 1
peace that passeth all u. MAYHEW:C 1
they pass all u. JAMES VI/I 6
u., but no tongue SHAK:HAM 26
U. everything makes STAEL 1
u. May begin, and in doing ASHBERY 1
u. to direct JUNIUS 7
u. will sometimes almost extinguish HOUSM 56
which passeth all u. BIBLE 541
with all thy getting get u. BIBLE 251
woman of mean u. AUSTEN 13
wonderfully obstructs the u. BACON:F[1] 20
world is beyond my u. STEVENS 3
understandings: cold hearts and muddy u. BURKE:E 56
understands: learnt how he u. himself BRADLEY:FH 2
understood:
be u., and not be believ'd BLAKE:W 52
fought with what she partly u. RICH 2
That thow be understonde CHAUC 120
three men who have ever u. PALMERS 4
undertake: nothing he would not u. SMITH:Syd[1] 5
undertakers:
nothing against u. personally MITFORD:JL 1
overtakers who keep the u. PITTS 1
u. – walk before the hearse GARRICK 1
Wot 'ud become of the u. DICKENS 54
undertaking:
no such u. has been received CHAMBERLAIN:N 4
u. of Great Advantage ANON 172
underwear: scorpion in his neighbour's u. SIMPSON:NF 1
undesirable: I know an u. character FRY:C 15
undo:
for thee does she u. herself? TOUR 2
to u. what has been done AGATH 1
undone:
anything was left u. LUCAN 3
done cannot be u. PROV 419
left u. those things PRAY 4
not to leave 't u., but SHAK:OTH 36
some to be u. DRYD 79
Things hitherto u. should be given BEERB 16
u. vast BROWNING:R 131
undressed: I u. her from behind? MANI 1
undrest: u. at Church FARQ 8
unearned: U. increment MILL 3
uneatable: pursuit of the u. WILDE:O 55
unemployed:
help the u. is not the same SAMUEL 2
U. at last FURP 1
unemployment:
After Cambridge – u. EWART 2
It is not only an offence* BRAS 1
unable to find work, u. results HOOV 6
unequal: Men are made by nature u. FROUDE 1
unexpected: moment foreseen may be u. ELIOT:TS 77
unexpectedness: character which I call *u.* PEAC 2
unfeeling: Th' u. for his own GRAY:T 8
unfit: for all things u. GOLDS 37
unforeseen: play of the contingent and the u. FISHER:HAL 1
unforgetful: teach the u. to forget ROSSET:DG 11
unforgiveness: alp of u. grew PLOM 1
unfurnished: head That's to be let u. BUTLER:S[1] 9
ungentlemanly: knows how u. he can look SURT 20
unhand: U. it, sir TROLL 1
unhanged: not three good men unhang'd in England SHAK:HEN.IV[1] 36
unhappiness:
U. .... comes of his Greatness CARLYLE:T 14
U. is best defined BONO 1
unhappy:
better that some should be u. JOHNSON:S 185
can never be very u. GAY 33
ever be u. for long provided WAUGH:E 7
I am u. everywhere VIZ 1
instinct for being u. highly developed SAKI 11
keeps the u. from thinking DIBDIN:C 8
Let us all be u. on Sunday NEAV 1
make us u. forever GAY 29
moral as soon as one is u. PROUST 6
never as u. as one thinks LA ROCHE 1
their remaining years u. LA BRU 3
till his death Be called u. BROWNING:EB 18
u., didn't know what to do MILLER:A 6
u. family is u. in its own TOLS:L 6
u., far-off things WORDS:W 80
unheard:
language of the u. KING:ML 4
those u. Are sweeter KEATS 92
unholy: I hate the u. crowd HORACE 27
unhoming: Men move u. FRY:C 14
unicorn:
lion and the u. Were fighting NURS 31
U. among the cedars AUD 29
unicorns: from the horns of Unicornes PSALMS 1
un-idea'd: Wretched *u.* girls JOHNSON:S 93
uniform:
Every u. corrupts one's character FRISCH 2
scarlet coat Should be more u. HOOD 5
u. 'e wore KIP 55
u. must work its way with the women DICKENS 46
uniformity: use be preferred before u. BACON:F[1] 42
unimportance: understand the u. of events ELIOT:TS 79
unimportant:
This is a comparatively u. time BARNES:J 1
*Un*important, of course, I meant CARROLL 38
unintelligent: anything so u., so unapt ARNOLD:M 66
uninterested: can exist in an u. person CHESTERTON 34
uninteresting: on earth as an u. subject CHESTERTON 34
union:
Liberty and U., now and forever WEBSTER:D 3
struggle is to save the U. LINC 17
u. in partition SHAK:MID 30
u. is complete DICKIN:J 2
U. is strength PROV 408
u. of hands and hearts TAYL:Jer 3
u. of this ever diverse MERED:G 28
u. of your bed with weeds SHAK:TEM 25
unite: U. and lead GOET 25
united:
u. in crime VOLT 27
U. we stand PROV 409
United States:
see also US; USA
British Empire and U.S. will have to CHURCH:W 17
Government of the U.S. is a device COOL 1
humiliate the U.S. Only Americans can NIX 6
immediate defence of the U.S. ROOS:FD 17
kind of U.S. of Europe CHURCH:W 36
so near to the U.S. DIAZ 1
'special relationship' with the U.S. ACHESON 2
U.S. has to move very fast KENNEDY:JF 9
U.S. is like a gigantic boiler GREY 2
U.S. is the glory, jest MINIF 1
U.S. themselves are essentially WHITMAN 39
unities: u., sir, ... are a completeness DICKENS 81
uniting:
By u. we stand DICKIN:J 1
u. of human hearts YEV 6
unity:
all things return to u. BALZ 3
confound All u. on earth SHAK:MAC 94
Trinity in U. PRAY 30
u. in religious belief would further STEPHEN:FJ 2
universal:
lapt in u. law TENNY 80
new order in history: *u. suffrage* SAND 2
There is no u. law LAWR:DH 23
u. destruction or u. brotherhood YEV 5
u. frame began DRYD 91
U. peace is declared ELIOT:G 24
universals: no u. in this man's town MACNEICE 8
universe:
don't pretend to understand the U. CARLYLE:T 67
I accept the u. CARLYLE:T 64
I am specializing in the u. COOK:P 2
Life, the U. and Everything ADAMS:D 1
To mingle with the U. BYR 116
u. is change AUR 6
u. is expanding and contracting DE VR 7
u. is not hostile HOLMES:JH 1
u. is the property of every EMER 2
U. of death MILT 166
visible u. was an illusion BORGES 3
universities:
discipline of colleges and u. SMITH:Ad 8
sanctuaries in which exploded* SMITH:Ad 9
state of both his u. TRAPP 1
u. are so full of knowledge MCLUH 10
u. chiefly valued for being old LODGE:D 2
U. incline wits to sophistry BACON:F[1] 2
university:
'comes down' from Jimmy's u. OSB:J 4
reform the u. without attending ILL 1
servant to be bred at an U. CONG 31
true U. of these days CARLYLE:T 48
u. in order to become a successful writer BRITT 1
u., where it was carefully taken PEAC 5
We are the U. SPRING 1
unjust:
a God u. YOUNG:E 15
u. steals the just's umbrella BOWEN:L 1
unkind: deform'd but the u. SHAK:TWE 53
unkindest: u. cut of all SHAK:JUL 55
unknelled: unknell'd, uncoffin'd, and unknown BYR 118
unknowing:
Alike u. and unknown BURNS:R 94
u. what he sought DRYD 119

unknown:
apart from the known and the u. PINT 3
but keep 't u. SHAK:OTH 36
gently into the u. GONNE 2
To go into the u. THOMAS:E 4
tread safely into the u. HASKINS 1
u. regions preserved ELIOT:G 31
Unknowe, unkist CHAUC 107
unlabelled: to go about u. HUX:TH 10
unlamented: u. let me die POPE 2
unlike: dislike for the u. will always ZANG 4
unlocked: all unlock'd to your occasions SHAK:MERC 9
unlucky:
so u. that he runs into MARQUIS 7
u. in love PROV 256
unmapped: u. country within us ELIOT:G 41
unmarried: man's to keep u. SHAW 36
unmask: u. her beauty to the moon SHAK:HAM 28
unmoved:
mind remains u. VIRGIL 60
U., cold SHAK:SON 41
unnatural: U. deeds Do breed SHAK:MAC 106
unnecessary:
unfit, to do the u. HARK 1
U. things are men ROCHES 14
unpaid:
great u. laborer of the world STANTON:El 7
u. for goods cheers the heart DONL 2
unpalatable: between the disastrous and the u. GALB 7
unpleasant: them do too many u. things HARTL 3
unpopular: safe to be u. STEVENSON:A 5
unprepared: Magnificently u. CORNFORD:Fran 2
unprigs: one u. oneself RIB 1
unquiet: sole u. thing COLERIDGE:ST 8
unreason: education at the Colleges of U. BUTLER:S[2] 1
unreasonable: progress depends on the u. man SHAW 62
unremembered: nameless, u. acts WORDS:W 4
unrest: u. which men miscall delight SHELLEY:PB 121
unrighteous: not to speak of u. ways BUDDHA 3
unsatisfied: it leaves one u. WILDE:O 32
unsavoury: most u. similes SHAK:HEN.IV[1] 8
unseen:
Greet the u. with a cheer BROWNING:R 214
left u. a wonderful piece SHAK:ANT 12
U. before by Gods KEATS 49
unselfish: u. people are colourless WILDE:O 31
unsettled: they are u. is there any hope EMER 25
unsex: u. me here SHAK:MAC 20
unshorn: presents the god unshorne HERR 21
unshriven: to one who dies u. PEREL 5
unsought: lost, that is u. CHAUC 107
unspeakable:
both u. ANDREW 1
u. in full pursuit WILDE:O 55
unspoiled: utterly u. by failure COWARD 38
unstable:
remember of this u. world MALORY 6
U. as water BIBLE 79
untangle: Time, thou must u. SHAK:TWE 18
unthinking: quaffing, and u. time DRYD 127
untimely: Why came I so u. forth WALLER 7
untried: found difficult; and left u. CHESTERTON 44
untrue: man who's u. to his wife AUD 45
untruth:
accessory to u. EVANS:H 1
tell one wilful u. NEWM:JH 4
torment of the night's u. DANI 1
untruthful: U.! My nephew Algernon WILDE:O 99
untune: u. that string SHAK:TRO 5
untuned: untun'd golden strings all women MARLOWE 48
unwashed:
great U. BROUGHAM 3
lean unwash'd artificer SHAK:KING J 17
unwilling: u., picked from the unfit HARK 1
unwind: u. the winding path YEATS 86
unworthiness: mine u., that dare not SHAK:TEM 20
unworthy: that his family was not u. DISR:B 34
up:
best thing to be u. and go EMPS 2
Getting u. in the morning is no RAB 5
How to be one u. POTTER:S 2
In winter I get u. at night STEVENSON:RL 47
neither u. nor down NURS 45
nice to get u. in the mornin' LAUD 3
people on your way u. MIZ 1
same thing, only u. CARU 1
Stand u., Guards WELLING 4
U. guards and at them WELLING 3
U., lad HOUSM 4
was a pity to get u. MAUGH 10
you've gut to git u. airly LOWELL:JR 4
up-tails: u. all JONS 1
upbringing: u. a nun would envy ORTON 1
upper:
Like many of the U. Class BELLOC 40
prove the u. classes COWARD 24
young Englishman of our u. class ARNOLD:M 66
upper crust:
The other, u.c. GILB:WS 19
These men are all u.c. here HALIB 1
upright:
man of life u. CAMPION 3
u. and untainted by guilt HORACE 15
wisest and the most u. man PLATO 6
uprisings: u. which are unduly damned MACHIA 10
uproar: u.'s your only music KEATS 125
upset: how it did u. me LEIGH 1
upside-down: upside-downe Antipodian tricke BROME:R 3
upstairs:
U. and downstairs and in NURS 82
u. into the world CONG 22
upward:
hold to the u. way PLATO 14
u. still, and onward LOWELL:JR 2
urban: u., squat, and packed BROOKE 11
Urbino: Upon U.'s windy hill YEATS 38
urge: procreant u. of the world WHITMAN 3
urinals: not only u. but also arsenals HOUDE 1
urine:
Cannot contain their u. SHAK:MERC 40
his u. in congeal'd ice SHAK:MEA 28
urn: storied u. or animated bust GRAY:T 18
urs: with those dreadful *u.* HOLMES:OW 3
us: Not unto u., Lord BIBLE 602
US:
see also **United States**
defeat the U. aggressors MAO 4
USA: God bless the U. AUD 57
usage: is u. so wills it HORACE 103
use:
exclusively for the u. of man PEAC 1
for u. rather than ostentation GIBBON:E 5
force themselves into general u. WELLING 19
I cannot u. a friend HERB:G 36
not to shine in u. TENNY 52
to people who have no u. for them HOPE:An 4
u. be preferred before uniformity BACON:F[1] 42
u. doth breed a habit SHAK:TWO 14
u. him as though you loved him WALT 13
u. me to the limit ROOS:T 10
used: since then I have u. no other PUNCH 23
Used-to-was: My name is U. TRAILL:HD 1
useful:
Beauty is as u. as usefulness HUGO 6
do not know to be u. MORRIS:W 11
not merely be u. and ornamental STRACH 3
u. becomes beautiful when it RODO 1
useless:
in the world are the most u. RUSKIN 4
U. each without the other LONGFEL 22
uses:
for mean or no u. LOCKE 2
u. to his Lord best known MILT 230
Usher's Well: lived a wife at U.W. BALL 65
usquabae: Wi' u., we'll face BURNS:R 87
usura: With u. POUND 38
Utopia: than a principality in U. MACAULAY:TB 4
utterance:
large u. of the early Gods KEATS 46
timely u. gave thought WORDS:W 54
uttered: u. it a hundred times HOLMES:OW 11
v:
put it down a we DICKENS 38
spell it with a V or a W? DICKENS 37
vacancies: how are v. to be obtained? JEFFERSON 12
vacant:
laugh that spoke the v. GOLDS 24
V. heart and hand and eye SCOTT:W 58
vacuum:
chimera bombinating in a v. RAB 1
Nature abhors a v. RAB 4
v. can only exist FITZGER:Z 3
v. or space in which there is DESCA 4
vaguery: For V. in the Field OSB:J 1
vain:
all is v. ROSSET:DG 11
so v. that we are even concerned EBNER 5
V. are the thousand creeds BRONTE:E 2
v. faith, and courage v. MACAULAY:TB 55
v. is now the burning KEATS 20
v., unnecessary things ROCHES 14
vain-glory: pride, v., and hypocrisy PRAY 33
vale:
cool sequester'd v. GRAY:T 22
meet thee in that hollow v. KING:H 2
shady sadness of a v. KEATS 43
There lies a v. in Ida TENNY 36
v. of Soul-making KEATS 156
world as a v. of tears? BROWNING:R 172
valentine:
Never sign a walentine with your own DICKENS 31
send myself a v. HUDS:L 1
vales: Making all the v. rejoice? BLAKE:W 15
valet: No man is a hero to his v. CORNUEL 1
valiant:
As he was v., I honour SHAK:JUL 46
piece of v. dust SHAK:MUCH 4
v., but not too venturous LYLY 1
v. man and true TENNY 286
valley:
Every v. shall be exalted BIBLE 320
great things from the v. CHESTERTON 51
Into the v. of Death TENNY 199
Love is of the v. TENNY 118
That v. is fatal AUD 1
v. of Humiliation BUNYAN 6
v. of the shadow of death BIBLE 206
valleys: Piping down the v. wild BLAKE:W 13
Vallombrosa: In V., where th' Etrurian shades MILT 125
valorous: More childish v. MARLOWE 15
valour:
better part of v. is discretion SHAK:HEN.IV[1] 92
birthplace of v. BURNS:R 81
Deliberat v. breath'd MILT 133
Like v.'s minion, carv'd SHAK:MAC 3
My v. is certainly going SHERIDAN:RB 15
no true v. SHAK:MUCH 31
this v. comes of sherris SHAK:HEN.IV[2] 42
V. and Innocence Have latterly KIP 129
v. will weep SHAK:COR 23
Wherever v. true GILB:WS 98
Who would true v. see BUNYAN 30
value:
everything and the v. of nothing WILDE:O 51
Just recognise your v. TOMASET 1
News v. RALPH 1
things that give v. to survival LEWIS:CS 1
who bestow a v. on our lives WEISS 1
valued: never v. till they make a noise CRAB 25
values:
Counterfeit v. always resemble AUD 28
masculine v. that prevail WOOLF:V 8
Noble v., in the end MONTH 1
nostalgia for Victorian v. UST 9
own ideas and other people's v. BREN 4
Victorian v. . . . were the v. THATCH:M 5
valves: close the V. of her attention DICKIN:E 11
Van Dycks: though the V.D. have to go COWARD 26
Van Gogh: V.G.'s ear for music WILDER:B 3
Vanbrugh: V.'s house of clay EVANS:A 1
vanes: v. of Shrewsbury gleam HOUSM 19
vanish: suddenly v. away CARROLL 90
vanished:
it v. quite slowly CARROLL 14
V., and left but memories YEATS 34

vanishing: do not find these v. acts SMITH:LP 3
vanities: Guides us by v. ELIOT:TS 23
vanity:
administering to the v. of others AUSTEN 63
all is v. BIBLE 278
All is v. and vexation BIBLE 279
all things are v. BIBLE 611
bairn brocht up in vanitie BOYD:MA 1
Every day when he looked into* DISR:B 34
His v. is enormous TOLS:S 3
hom fro worldly vanyte CHAUC 122
Pull down thy v. POUND 35
speckl'd v. Will sicken MILT 9
that v. in years? SHAK:HEN.IV[1] 51
There was never yet fair* SHAK:KING L 34
v. and love; these are their CHESTERFIELD 23
V., like murder, will out COWLEY:H 3
V. of vanities BIBLE 278, 611
v.'s the food of fools SWIFT 53
Which is your partickler wanity DICKENS 52
vanity-fair:
Difficulties, Lions, or V. BUNYAN 27
It beareth the name of V. BUNYAN 9
vanquish: v., not my Accuser NEWM:JH 7
vanquished:
one safe course for the v. VIRGIL 53
Roman by a Roman Valiantly vanquish'd SHAK:ANT 57
v., not the victor, who has ELLIS:H 3
v. pleased Cato LUCAN 1
Woe to the v. LIVY 1
vapour:
puff of v. from his mouth BROWNING:R 106
v. sometime like a bear SHAK:ANT 49
vapours: pestilent congregation of v. SHAK:HAM 80
variety:
Her infinite v. SHAK:ANT 28
Love's sweetest Part, V. DONNE 45
order in v. we see POPE 31
source of pleasure is v. JOHNSON:S 45
V. is the soul of pleasure BEHN 2
V.'s the very spice COWP 64
variorum: Life is all a v. BURNS:R 27
various: man so v. that he seem'd DRYD 47
varletry: v. Of censuring Rome? SHAK:ANT 63
vase: you may shatter the v. MOORE:T 5
vastness: I feel but v. on my face BRENN 2
Vatican: V., the Treasury and the miners BALD:S 12
Vaughan, Henry: sleeps the Silurist* SASS 17
vaunting: V. aloud MILT 116
Vega: V. conspicuous overhead AUD 22
vegetable:
animal – or v. – or mineral? CARROLL 80
content with a v. love GILB:WS 33
in matters v. GILB:WS 24
passion of a v. fashion GILB:WS 33
v. love should grow MARV 30
vegetarianism:
I figure if horses can eat* DAVIS:M 2
in favour of v. while the wolf INGE 1
vegetarians: V. have wicked, shifty MORTON:JB 2
vegetate:
one does but v. BURNEY 6
v. in a village COLTON 5
wish to v. like the country HAZL 17
veil:
Death is the v. which those SHELLEY:PB 83
Lift not the painted v. SHELLEY:PB 30
sheweth himself without a Vail HALIF 13
transparent v. with light divine WORDS:W 154
v. from the hidden beauty SHELLEY:PB 164
V. past which I could not see FITZGER:E 19
wrapped in a gauzy v. SHELLEY:PB 102
vein: v. o'er the Madonna's breast BROWNING:R 42
veins:
ardour hidden in my v. RACINE 6
mire of human v. YEATS 86
Open all my V. GRAHAM:J 2
petrol in his v. SMITHERS 1
varicose v. or French foreign LEVIN 1
v. of rhyming mother-wits MARLOWE 1
velvet:
iron hand in a v. glove CHARLES V 1
v. that is black and soft CHESTERTON 21
venerability: v. factor creeps in STONE:IF 1
venetian blind: write fuck on a dusty v.b. BROWNE:Co 1
vengeance:
arsenals of divine v. HOUSM 54
hand of V. found the bed BLAKE:W 81
Nor one feeling of v. DREN 1
sudden v. waits POPE 59
V., deep-brooding o'er SCOTT:W 3
V. is mine BIBLE 516
vengefulness: fainted on his v. MERED:G 17
veni: V., vidi, vici CAES:GJ 4
Venice:
I stood in V. BYR 96
lust and dark wine of V. MORRIS:J 1
Ocean's nursling, V. SHELLEY:PB 27
V.' pride is nought COLERIDGE:M 1
V., the eldest child WORDS:W 75
Where V. sate in state BYR 97
ventilators: From the geyser v. BETJ 22
ventured: Nothing v., nothing gained PROV 302
Venus:
callin' a young 'ooman a Wenus DICKENS 28
V. in all her power RACINE 6
V. when she smiles JONS 47
verandahs: galvanized-iron roofs on their front v. BOYD:RGP 2
verb:
brave, attentive v. JENN:E 2
God, to me, it seems, is a v. FULLER:RB 1
V. is God HUGO 3
v. meaning 'to believe falsely' WITT 7
verbosity:
exuberance of his own v. DISR:B 79
thread of his v. SHAK:LOV 18
Verdi: strains of V. will come back MARX:G 15
verdict: Sentence first – v. afterwards CARROLL 41
verdure: no other v. than its own KEATS 15
Vere:
God bless Captain V. MELV 6
Lady Clara V. de V. TENNY 62
verity: V., you brach MASSIN 10
vermin:
race of little odious v. SWIFT 30
they are lower than v. BEVAN 2
vernal: those v. seasons of the yeer MILT 311
verse:
blank v. has suffered not only ELIOT:TS 115
bombast out a blanke v. GREENE:R 2
Book of V. – and Thou FITZGER:E 8
even road of a blank v. SHAK:MUCH 33
full sail of his great v. SHAK:SON 37
give up v., my boy POUND 30
Good light v. is better EWART 3
hoarse, rough v. POPE 21
Lies the subject of all v. BROWNE:W[1] 1
much blank v., and blanker BYR 151
My v. again shall gild DRAYT 1
my v. was full of infirmity YEATS 133
Not v. now, only prose BROWNING:R 90
pleasures that to v. belong KEATS 1
Sisters, Voice and Vers MILT 63
subject for immortal v. DAY LEWIS 5
that fetters it in v. DONNE 66
this unpolished rugged v. DRYD 72
v. is merely prose BYR 12
v. is not a crown HERB:G 29
v. that gives Immortal youth LANDOR 2
V. will seem prose BUCKINGHAM AND 1
wanting the accomplishment of v. WORDS:W 111
was trying to say was v. OSB:J 11
Writing free v. is like playing FROST:R 18
verser: Hearken unto a V. HERB:G 1
verses:
ever get at my v. WHITMAN 41
How many v. have I thrown LANDOR 11
Tear him for his bad v. SHAK:JUL 62
versions: hundred v. of it SHAW 17
vertical: v. man AUD 2
vertigo: whirl around With the *v.* JONS 20
vesper: black v.'s pageants SHAK:ANT 49
vessel:
empty v. that yet may be drawn LAO 6
gilded V. goes GRAY:T 31
steersman when the v.'s crank MERED:G 36
Thou show'st a noble v. SHAK:COR 13
V. of a more ungainly Make FITZGER:E 29
vessels: Empty v. make the most noise PROV 93
vest: Casting the body's v. aside MARV 20
vestry: see you in the v. SMITH:Syd[1] 22
vet: I told him consult a v. KENNY:Mat 1
veterans: World its V. rewards POPE 138
veto: have my v. pen drawn REAG 9
vex:
they die to v. me MELBOU 8
V. not thou the poet's mind TENNY 7
v. the unhappy dust TENNY 89
vexation: nothing so infinite as v. WEBSTER:J 14
viable: v. from ten o'clock till five BETJ 36
vibrated: better not be wibrated DICKENS 90
vibration: brave V. each way free HERR 38
Vicar of Bray: I will be the V.o.B., Sir ANON 25
vice:
art is v. DEGAS 1
can apprehend and consider v. MILT 313
characteristic v. a reluctance to test TAWN 1
end in sight was a v. BROWNING:R 155
good old-gentlemanly v. BYR 172
in England but v. and religion SMITH:Syd[1] 38
lash'd the v., but spared SWIFT 64
never-failing v. of fools POPE 9
Prosperity doth best discover v. BACON:F[1] 34
raptures and roses of v. SWIN 20
scarce weed out the v. GOLDS 56
than bullied out of v. SURT 13
That v. pays homage to virtue BUTLER:S[2] 16
This v. brings in one hundred NAPO III 1
Thy body is all v. JOHNSON:S 92
To sanction V. BYR 15
V. and virtues are products TAINE 2
V. is a monster of so POPE 95
V. is its own reward CRISP 5
V. is often clothed in virtue's PROV 410
whirl'd into folly and v. TENNY 206
vices:
first virtue, v. to abhor HORACE 75
made to root out v. MONTAIGNE 14
one of the v. of our times VIGNY 6
Our *v.* and ***virtues*** couple HALIF 7
paint the v. and follies of CONG 14
pleasant v. Make instruments SHAK:KING L 81
redeemed his v. with his virtues JONS 54
that my v. telleth me CHAUC 83
Through tatter'd clothes small v. SHAK:KING L 71
Unnatural v. Are fathered ELIOT:TS 24
v. of the saint EMER 24
Vichy: something V. about the French NOVEL 1
vicious:
v. man, but very kind to me JOHNSON:S 89
v. till he's been to a good school SAKI 10
vicissitude: sad v. of things STERNE 56
victim:
first insults the v. CRAB 4
v. must be found GILB:WS 64
v. of a rich man's ANON 48
wictim o' connubiality DICKENS 17
victims:
little v. play GRAY:T 7
They are its v. CONRAD 11
v. who respect their executioners SARTRE 9
with the v. he intends to eat BUTLER:S[2] 45
victor:
to the v. belong the spoils MARCY 1
vanquished v. sunk DRYD 111
Victoria Station: ticket at V.S. and go BEVIN 1
Victorian:
nostalgia for V. values UST 9
V. values ... were THATCH:M 5
victories: V. and defeats for the bigshots BRECHT 11
victorious:
If we are v. against the Romans PYR 1
O'er a' the ills o' life v. BURNS:R 86
v. cause pleased the gods LUCAN 1
victory:
Before Alamein we never had a v. CHURCH:W 59
every v. turns into a defeat BEAUV 3
grave, where is thy v.? BIBLE 527
Grave! where is thy v.? POPE 69
in v., magnanimity CHURCH:W 49
in v., unbearable CHURCH:W 67
no substitute for v. MACAR 2
not right that matters, but v. HITL 9

swallow up death in v. BIBLE 315
Thy v., O Grave? ROSS:R 1
'twas a famous v. SOUTHEY 4
v. at all costs CHURCH:W 12
v. finds a hundred fathers CIANO 1
V. has a thousand fathers KENNEDY:JF 12
V. is not a name strong enough NELS 6
v. without the dust of racing HORACE 76
Westminster Abbey or v. NELS 3
without v. there is no survival CHURCH:W 12
victuals:
I live on broken wittles DICKENS 146
to please About their v. CALVER 8
Vietnam:
North V. cannot defeat or humiliate NIX 6
To win in V. SPOCK 1
V. was lost in the living rooms MCLUH 9
Vietnam war: It is worse than immoral* ACHES 3
view:
lends enchantment to the v. CAMPBELL:T 2
room with a v. – and you COWARD 19
will the landscape tire the v.? DYER:J[1] 2
Worm's eye v. HAST:H 1
views:
radical invents the v. TWAIN 30
take short v. AUD 47
Take short v. SMITH:Syd[1] 19
vigil: tongueless v. and all the pain SWIN 9
vigilance: liberty to man is eternal v. CURRAN 1
vigilant: v. as a cat to steal cream SHAK:HEN.IV[1] 79
vigorous: His v. warmth did, variously DRYD 34
Viking: fear now that the V. hordes ANON 99
vile:
goodness to the v. seem v. SHAK:KING L 61
make v. things precious SHAK:KING L 38
only man is v. HEB 3
'Tis better to be v. SHAK:SON 54
vileness: No inner v. that we dread? TENNY 149
vilest:
v. deeds like poison-weeds WILDE:O 120
v. specimens of human MACAULAY:TB 36
v. thing must be less vile THOMS:Ja[2] 5
v. things Become themselves SHAK:ANT 28
village:
image of a global v. MCLUH 2
loveliest v. of the plain GOLDS 19
some v.-Hampden GRAY:T 20
vegetate in a v. COLTON 5
v. statesmen talked GOLDS 30
villages: pleasant V. and Farmes MILT 244
villain:
alone the v. of the earth SHAK:ANT 44
Bloody, bawdy v. SHAK:HAM 93
condemns me for a v. SHAK:RIC.III 17
determined to prove a v. SHAK:RIC.III 3
smiling, damned v. SHAK:HAM 52
v. with a smiling cheek SHAK:MERC 16
villains:
their heroes and v. from fiction AUD 67
v. on necessity SHAK:KING L 9
villainy: clothe my naked v. SHAK:RIC.III 7
Vinci: spell it V. and pronounce TWAIN 3
vindicate: v. the ways of God to man POPE 79
vindictiveness: v. of the female CONNOLLY:C 12
vine:
advise his client to plant v. WRIGHT:FL 1
Daughter of the V. to Spouse FITZGER:E 21
drynke licour of the vyne CHAUC 68
foxlike in the v. TENNY 118
luscious clusters of the v. MARV 17
mantling V. MILT 190
patterned with the v. and grapes FLECKER 9
v. slips with the weight SWIN 12
wild Thyme and the gadding V. MILT 46
With v. leaves in his hair IBS 13
vinegar:
as the neck of a v. cruet JOHNSON:S 79
full of piss and v. like a barber's DAVIES:R 1
Pepper and v. besides CARROLL 57
vines: foxes, that spoil the v. BIBLE 296
vintage:
He is trampling out the v. HOWE 1
O, for a draught of v. KEATS 93
vintners: wonder what the V. buy FITZGER:E 32
violations: v. committed by children BOWEN:El 1
violence:
essence of war is v. MACAULAY:TB 24
heterogeneous ideas are yoked by v. JOHNSON:S 48
Let there be no v. in religion KORAN 2
never be by v. constrained ELIZ I 1
offer it the show of v. SHAK:HAM 8
sentence of manifest v. MCLUH 15
V. everywhere leads to deception SAINT-P 1
V. is the last refuge HARDIN 1
V. is the repartee of BRIEN 2
v. masquerading as love LAING 4
v. of the enemy PRAY 94
violent:
v. delights have v. ends SHAK:ROM 23
v. feelings ... produce in us RUSKIN 7
violently: v. if they must QUINCY 1
violet:
nodding v. grows SHAK:MID 20
She is the vyolet SKEL:J 6
throw a perfume on the v. SHAK:KING J 16
v. by a mossy stone WORDS:W 30
v. of his native land TENNY 136
v. smells to him as it SHAK:HEN.V 31
violets:
By ashen roots the v. blow TENNY 180
do not like to mix v. DISR:B 35
fast fading v. KEATS 93
I forgot the v. LANDOR 24
I would give you some v. SHAK:HAM 170
May v. spring SHAK:HAM 186
pied wind-flowers and v. SHELLEY:PB 89
v. dim, But sweeter SHAK:WIN 20
when sweet v. sicken SHELLEY:PB 143
Who are the v. now SHAK:RIC.II 43
violins:
long weeping of autumn v. VERL 1
make Antonio Stradivari's v. ELIOT:G 47
viper: saw a Lawyer killing a v. COLERIDGE:ST 42
vipers:
generation of v. BIBLE 378
To extirpate the v. AYT 1
Virgil:
V. seems to have composed ARNOLD:M 51
V. was no good because BUTLER:S[2] 30
virgin:
bashful v.'s side-long looks GOLDS 20
before she became a v. LEVANT 1
born of the V. Mary ANON 5
Born of the V. Mary PRAY 19
Every Harlot was a V. once BLAKE:W 110
in My v. womb ha'e met MACDIAR 9
knew Doris Day before she was a v. MARX:G 28
pale V. shrouded in snow BLAKE:W 70
should have stayed a v. CARTER:L 1
though a V., yet a Bride CAREW:T 5
V. goddess returns VIRGIL 11
v. territory for whorehouses CAP 2
v. while she remains intact CATUL 15
v. white integrity DONNE 24
withering on the v. thorn SHAK:MID 1
virgin-knot: If thou dost break her v. SHAK:TEM 25
Virginia creeper: stucco houses in V.c. BETJ 19
Virginian: not a V., but an American HENRY:P 2
Virginians: There is Jackson with his V. BEE 1
virginity:
horror of eternal v. SMOL 6
just a little more v. TREE 7
No, no for my v. PRIOR 13
perpetual v. of the soul YEATS 147
That long preserved v. MARV 31
that v. could be a virtue VOLT 7
your old v. SHAK:ALL 3
virgins: v. are soft as the roses BYR 23
virtue:
admire Vertue, who follow not MILT 263
adversity doth best discover v. BACON:F[1] 34
Assume a v. SHAK:HAM 147
been a v. with the Roman clergy KINGSLEY:C 8
blunder'd on some v. unawares CHURCH:C 6
characteristic v. of Englishmen TAWN 1
clothed in v.'s habit PROV 410
constitutes perfect v. CONF 14
down and redeem us from v. SWIN 26
Even here v. has its due VIRGIL 41
first upgrowth of all v. KINGSLEY:C 9
first v., vices to abhor HORACE 75
fugitive and cloister'd vertue MILT 313
greatest offence against v. HAZL 34
Haggard with v. BROOKE 4
lilies and languors of v. SWIN 20
lost fight of v. STEVENSON:RL 41
maiden v. rudely strumpeted SHAK:SON 30
make V. unamiable STEELE 8
maken vertu of necessitee CHAUC 51
Moral v. is the child of habit ARISTOT 5
More people are flattered into v. SURT 13
only reward of v. is v. EMER 19
only true nobility is v. JUV 17
Patience, the beggar's v. MASSIN 12
pursue v. and knowledge DANTE 13
rarer action is In v. SHAK:TEM 28
ready way to v. BROWNE:T 21
see v. and pine away PERS 2
Silence is the v. of fools BACON:F[1] 27
some by v. fall SHAK:MEA 7
some v., v. to commend CONG 65
That vice pays homage to v. BUTLER:S[2] 16
they rise by v.'s aid JUV 8
thy mind all v. JOHNSON:S 92
Trade Unionism of the married* SHAW 45
very sinews of v. WALT 7
V .? A fig SHAK:OTH 14
v. and not birth FLETCH:J 13
V. is ... in the nature of an iceberg WHITE:P 5
V. is bold SHAK:MEA 26
V. is like a rich stone BACON:F[1] 37
V. is not left to stand CONF 5
V. is the fount whence MARLOWE 10
V. is the roughest way WOTTON 4
v. only makes our bliss POPE 107
V. she finds too painful POPE 135
V. ... should be accommodating MOLIERE 13
V. shuns ease MONTAIGNE 13
v. that brings in as much NAPO III 1
V. that transgresses is but SHAK:TWE 9
v. which requires to be GOLDS 51
v.'s still far too small COLETTE 1
Wertu withoutys warians BLIND 2
without eradicating the v. GOLDS 56
woman of easy v. and a proved HAILS 1
Woman's v. is man's greatest invention SKIN:CO 1
Young men have more v. JOHNSON:S 118
virtues:
all the v. but one DU MAU:G 3
few v. that the Poles do not CHURCH:W 34
in war the two cardinal v. HOBB 8
makes some v. impracticable JOHNSON:S 229
Moral v. we acquire through practice ARISTOT 6
other people's secret v. RUSS:B 7
Our *vices* and *v.* couple HALIF 7
redeemed his vices with his v. JONS 54
spend in discovering his v. LYTTON 1
Vice and v. are products TAINE 2
v. of society are the vices EMER 24
v. We write in water SHAK:HEN.VIII 18
v. Will plead like angels SHAK:MAC 24
Whenever there are such great v. BRECHT 9
world to hide v. in? SHAK:TWE 5
virtuous:
Be in general v. FRANKLIN:B 23
grow v. in their old age POPE 178
Ladies the outrageously v. STEELE 12
no woman is v. who does not WILLIAMS:WC 10
v. maid Subdues me SHAK:MEA 16
v. men pass mildly away DONNE 69
v. person with a mean mind BAGE 24
which is the most v. man WALP:H 16
Who can find a v. woman? BIBLE 276
virus: v. is only doing its job CRON 1
visage:
Of his v. children were aferd CHAUC 29
shattered v. lies SHELLEY:PB 21
visages: v. Do cream and mantle SHAK:MERC 5
visible:
all things v. and invisible PRAY 66
Ineluctable modality of the v. JOYCE:J 17
it makes things v. KLEE 1
little v. delight, but necessary BRONTE:E 11
representation of v. things LEONARDO 1

if you w. at midnight KIP 121
Lord began to w. PSALMS 2
slepyng hound to w. CHAUC 110
w. in a fright BARH 5
w. us, and we drown ELIOT:TS 11
we w. eternally DONNE 84
You will w., and remember BROWNING:R 109
waked:
wak'd herself with laughing SHAK:MUCH 11
You have wak'd me too soon WATTS 14
wakes: What angel w. me SHAK:MID 27
waking: w. from a troubled dream HAWT 6
Wales:
Nobody ever beats W. at rugby MOURIE 1
One road leads to W. MASE 10
Shut the door, W. BRUM 4
South W. these three phenomena THOMAS:G 2
there were wolves in W. THOMAS:D 40
W. where the only concession THOMAS:G 3
walk:
Can two w. together BIBLE 356
closer w. with God COWP 2
I w. abroad o' nights MARLOWE 23
learn to w. before we can PROV 416
may w. uncowed KIP 117
must try to w. sedately STEVENSON:RL 50
take up thy bed, and w. BIBLE 479
W. across my swimming pool RICE:T 1
w., and not faint BIBLE 324
w. at least before they dance POPE 149
w. in death's dark vale SCOTTISH 1
w. in fear and dread COLERIDGE:ST 34
w. miles for a bacon sandwich WALES 2
W.! Not bloody likely SHAW 111
w. o'er the western wave SHELLEY:PB 145
w. on the lines or the squares MILNE 6
W. on the Wild Side ALG 1
W. the black path CAMPBELL:ATA 1
w., the Queen of Love VIRGIL 40
w. with Kings KIP 128
Where'er you w. POPE 3
Will you w. a little faster? CARROLL 31
Within a w. of the sea BELLOC 31
walked:
As I walk'd through the wilderness BUNYAN 1
him that walk'd the waves MILT 57
one before him w. very crookedly SURT 17
people that w. in darkness BIBLE 307
walking:
A w. the Devil is gone COLERIDGE:ST 40
another one w. beside you ELIOT:TS 52
as if I were w. with destiny CHURCH:W 50
children w. two & two BLAKE:W 23
I nauseate w. CONG 51
I'm w. backwards till Christmas MILLIG 5
It is solved in w. ANON 241
w. in an Air of glory VAUGHAN:H 10
w. up and down in it BIBLE 179
walks:
Juno when she w. JONS 47
left you all his w. SHAK:JUL 59
nothing w. with aimless feet TENNY 153
She w. in beauty BYR 41
Some, hilly w. GREEN:Mat 1
W. the night in her DE LA M 16
w. upon the wind POPE 93
wall:
daub the w. of a jakes SHAK:KING L 23
doesn't love a w. FROST:R 2
faded away in a w. BETJ 12
father was the Great W. of China WALL 1
Man is a great w. builder MTS 3
standing like a stone w. BEE 1
This be your w. of brass HORACE 77
thrown against the W., he would stick BURT 1
w. of newspapers and FORST 1
Watch the w., my darling KIP 121
weakest goes to the w. PROV 415
white-washed w. GOLDS 31
Without a city w. ALEX:CF 5
your neighbour's w. catches fire HORACE 90
Wallace: story of W. poured a Scottish BURNS:R 126
Waller: W. was smooth POPE 145
wallet: Time hath, my lord, a w. SHAK:TRO 14
wallpaper: w. goes, or I do WILDE:O 137
walls:
Painting thy outward w. SHAK:SON 61
Speak to dead w. RALE 8
Stone w. do not a prison LOVELACE 5
these w., thy sphere DONNE 62
w. are hung with velvet CHESTERTON 21
W. have ears PROV 411
W. have tongues, and hedges SWIFT 59
wooden w. are the best w. COV 1
walnuts: Across the w. and the wine TENNY 35
walrus: W. and the Carpenter CARROLL 55
Walsinghame: holy land of W. RALE 6
waltz: Swoons to a w. HUX:A 44
waltzing: W. Matilda PATERSON:AB 3
waly: w., w., up the bank BALL 62
wan: so w. with care SHAK:HEN.IV[1] 1
wand:
thine opiate w. SHELLEY:PB 146
waving wide her mirtle w. MILT 6
wander:
I w. in the ways of men BURNS:R 94
we will not w. more TENNY 34
Whither shall I w.? NURS 14
whither w. you? SHAK:MID 12
wandered: I w. lonely as a cloud WORDS:W 120
wanderer:
foiled circuitous w. ARNOLD:M 34
weary, wayworn w. bore POE 1
wandering:
bind The w. sense CONG 62
for weyrynesse of wandryng LANGLAND 6
From w. on a foreign strand SCOTT:W 10
Half to forget the w. FLECKER 5
I am old with w. YEATS 23
poor w. one GILB:WS 22
W. between two worlds ARNOLD:M 35
Wand'ring from clime to clime HOMER 16
where is my w. boy ANON 88
Worchyng and wandryng as LANGLAND 3
wanderings: He chid their w. GOLDS 26
want:
better one w. for a common MARLOWE 22
don't know what they w. MARQUIS 11
get what you think you w. CLARE:A 1
I shall not w. BIBLE 206
I'll not w. SCOTTISH 1
making things which he does not w. HOPE:An 4
Not what they w. but what CROMWELL 12
Ring out the w. TENNY 177
there's anything that you w. LENNON 2
to get what you w. SMITH:LP 1
until you know what they w. SCOTT:Rose 1
w. of a thing is perplexing VANB 7
w. something you probably won't w. HOPE:An 1
What I shall die to w. SHAK:TEM 20
worn down by the struggle with w. SCHILL 8
wanted:
I have w. only one thing HAZL 24
no man is w. much EMER 39
wanting: and art found w. BIBLE 351
wanton:
Down, w., down GRAVES:R 6
I do but w. in the South TENNY 111
w. with a velvet brow SHAK:LOV 9
wantonness:
in cloathes a wantonnesse HERR 15
sad as night Only for w. SHAK:KING J 14
wantons: play the w. with our woes SHAK:RIC.II 32
wants:
everything that he w., and nothing HUGHES:Th 3
exactly what one w. to do and when WAUGH:E 7
provide for human *w.* BURKE:E 54
scheme of supplying our w. SWIFT 17
understand the w. of the hungry PROV 140
war:
ain't gonna be no w. MACMILL:H 3
All is fair in love and w. PROV 9
all lost the w. LAWR:DH 8
All the business of w. WELLING 10
all this w. been wrought MALORY 10
anybody who wasn't against w. LOW 1
at w. with my innards MACHA 1
at w. you think about a better life WILDER:T 2
beating of w. drums KOES 4
beautiful that w. and all its WHITMAN 33
broken the second rule of w. MONTGOM:BL 3
bungled, unwise w. PLOM 1
can guarantee success in w. CHURCH:W 53
capitalism 'inevitably' caused w. TAYL:AJP 2
civil w., the general must know REED:H 7
Come in your w. array SCOTT:W 54
come ye in w. SCOTT:W 20
condemn recourse to w. KELLO 1
condition which is called w. HOBB 6
country is at w. with Germany CHAMBERLAIN:N 4
dejected men of w. FINCH 1
desires peace be prepared for w. VEGET 1
devil's madness – W. SERVICE 5
done very well out of the w. BALD:S 10
Don't you know there's a w. HATTON 1
easier to make w. than CLEMENCE 2
empire founded by w. MONTESQU 3
endless warr still breed MILT 97
essence of w. is violence MACAULAY:TB 24
ever another w. in Europe BISM 9
every w. they kill you a new way ROGERS:W 3
everything in w. is barbaric KEY:E 6
first in w. LEE:Hen 1
Food will Win the W. HOOV 5
god of w. is drunk with blood BLAKE:W 3
guerilla fights the w. of the flea TABER 1
He that makes a good w. HERB:G 57
hear w. called murder MACDON:R 2
I don't care for w. NAPO III 2
I have seen w. and faced KETT 1
I wage w. CLEMENCE 1
I'll furnish the w. HEAR 1
Image of w., without its guilt SOMER 1
In starting and waging a w. HITL 9
in the midst of a cold w. BARU 1
in time of peace thinks of w. ANON 190
In w., he mounts SCOTT:W 8
In w., resolution CHURCH:W 49
in w. the two cardinal virtues HOBB 8
In w., three-quarters depends NAPO I 1
In w., whichever side CHAMBERLAIN:N 1
infection and the hand of w. SHAK:RIC.II 17
Laws are silent in w. CIC 13
learn w. any more BIBLE 301
Let me have w. SHAK:COR 14
Little w. that castle knew MORRIS:W 10
looks on w. as all glory SHERMAN 1
Lord is a man of w. BIBLE 101
lost the w. in an afternoon JELL 1
lunatics or suicides ... could want an atomic w. KHRU 8
magnificent, but it is not w. BOSQ 1
make w. on the living, not CHARLES V 4
masturbation of w. RAE 1
moderation in w. is imbecility MACAULAY:TB 24
My sentence is for op'n warr MILT 151
nature of w. consisteth HOBB 6
never be a perfect w. BRECHT 13
never understood this liking for w. BENNETT:Al 2
never was a good w. FRANKLIN:B 26
next w. will be fought with atom bombs UREY 1
no discharge in the w. KIP 111
no less than Warr to waste MILT 260
not a business in which one* MONASH 2
not at w. with Egypt EDEN:A 2
not believe in inevitable w. LAW 1
Older men declare w. HOOV 4
Once lead this people into w. WILSON:W 16
owes its continued existence to w. TUCHOL 1
pattern called a w. LOWELL:A 1
people taut for w. THOMAS:RS 1
pity of w. OWEN:W 13
politics by other means* CLAUS 1
Shakes Pestilence and Warr MILT 169
signs of w. about his aged SHAK:RIC.II 19
sinews of w., unlimited money CIC 12
small w. on the heels LOWELL:R 16
Stand up and take the w. KIP 144
stately tent of w. MARLOWE 1
steel couch of w. SHAK:OTH 13
tell us all about the w. SOUTHEY 2
that first invented w. MARLOWE 7
there was w., he went AUD 48
they'll start another w. HERB:AP 11
things that are worse than w. VULL 1
This w., like the next w. LLOYD GEO 14

Those who can win a w. CHURCH:W 46
Throat of Warr had ceast to roar MILT 259
time of w. BIBLE 281
To w. and arms I fly LOVELACE 7
too long since there's been a w. BRECHT 7
under the shadow of a w. SPEND 9
voices prophesying w. COLERIDGE:ST 63
wage no w. with women SOUTHEY 11
W. always finds a solution BRECHT 15
W., and the pity of W. OWEN:W 15
W. between Men and Women THURB 15
w. can only be abolished through MAO 6
W. even to the knife BYR 61
w. has a bad conscience KEY:E 5
w. has its laws NEWM:JH 6
W. hath no fury MONTAGUE 1
W., he sung, is toil DRYD 109
W. is . . . the universal perversion RAE 1
W. is being deliberately prolonged SASS 21
w. is easy to begin but difficult SALL 8
W. is much too serious CLEMENCE 6
W. is Peace ORWELL 30
W. is Prussia's national industry MIR 1
W. is sweet to those ERAS 3
W. is the trade of kings DRYD 100
W. is w. ORWELL 18
W. is waged by men MANNING 1
w. : it ruins conversation FONTEN 1
W. its thousands slays PORTEUS 2
W. lays a burden COWP 30
w., let it begin here PARKER:John 1
W. makes rattling good history HARDY:T 73
W. minus the shooting ORWELL 39
w. on all undeserved privilege LEVI:P 1
w. settles *nothing* CHRIS 6
W. That Will End W. WELLS:HG 10
W. to the knife PALAF 1
W., w. is still the cry BYR 61
W. will never cease until MENCK 8
way of ending w. is to lose ORWELL 22
way to win an atomic w. BRADLEY:OM 2
well that w. is so terrible LEE:RE 1
when the blast of w. SHAK:HEN.V 17
when the w. of the giants is over CHURCH:W 63
Without w., the world would sink MOLTKE 1
witnesses to the desolation of w. GEO V 4
wrong w., at the wrong place BRADLEY:OM 1
your lordship that this is w. ADAMS:CF 1
war-drum: w. throbb'd no longer TENNY 79
war-war: jaw-jaw is better than to w. CHURCH:W 39
warble: W., child SHAK:LOV 6
warbler:
Attic w. pours GRAY:T 9
ev'ry w. has his tune COWP 45
warbles: W. his native Wood-notes wilde MILT 74
warbling: w. his Dorick lay MILT 59
Ward: Light and Mrs Humphrey W. CHESTERTON 17
warder:
w. is Despair WILDE:O 120
w. silent on the hill SCOTT:W 14
warders: Prisoners and w. – we are all of one DOWL 1
wardrobe:
body like a w. THOMAS:D 31
silken dalliance in the w. SHAK:HEN.V 10
Ware:
I should dine at W. COWP 56
was an old person of W. LEAR 31
warfare:
thing as legitimate w. NEWM:JH 6
thy w. o'er SCOTT:W 37
warheads: w. for the domestic Armageddon LEONARD:H 1
Waring: What's become of W.? BROWNING:R 38
warm:
Be w., but pure BYR 13
Cold hands, w. heart PROV 58
It is w. work NELS 7
she's w. SHAK:WIN 33
This is too w. work NELS 13
to w. without heating BERK 3
w. days will never cease KEATS 109
w. him at his fire HERB:G 9
w. the air in raw inclement SWIFT 32
w. what is cold LANGTON 2
warming pan: she has crept under The w.p. NURS 29
warmongers: drawn into conflicts by w. STALIN 2
warms: It w. the very sickness SHAK:HAM 174
warmth:
awful w. about my heart KEATS 141
brings back her gentle w. CATUL 11
His vigorous w. did, variously DRYD 34
w. is mainly at the bottom COUN 1
yearn'd for w. and colour TENNY 268
warning:
come without w. DAVIS:T 1
will it come without w. AUD 26
warp:
there is no guile or w. PLATH 1
Weave the w. GRAY:T 30
warrant: truth shall be thy w. RALE 3
warring: W. in Heav'n against MILT 183
warrior:
he lay like a w. WOLFE:C 3
Home they brought her w. TENNY 114
Who is the happy W.? WORDS:W 39
warriors: see thy W. fall HOMER 9
wars:
all their w. are merry CHESTERTON 5
barbarism of w. TENNY 293
cluck'd thee to the w. SHAK:COR 20
end to the beginnings of all w. ROOS:FD 13
Fierce warres and faithfull loves SPENS 20
levie cruel warres MILT 162
many civil w. as the kingdom MONTESQU 2
my w. were global REED:H 5
never can work W. overthrow BLAKE:W 80
No more bloody w. MARY QUEEN CON 4
see w., horrid w. VIRGIL 65
shriek and sweat in pigmy w. TENNY 98
stick i' th' w. SHAK:COR 19
Still w. and lechery SHAK:TRO 24
Thy w. brought nothing DRYD 129
took away the occasion of all w. FOX:G 2
w. and rumours of w. BIBLE 428
W. are not won by evacuations CHURCH:W 55
w. begin in the minds ANON 240
w. not their own CURNOW 2
w. of the pygmies will begin CHURCH:W 63
w. on God begin YEATS 103
w. or pestilences, in every page AUSTEN 62
warts: pimples, w., and everything CROMWELL 11
Warwick: impudent and shameless W. SHAK:HEN.VI[3] 5
wary: be w. of him, good Roman HORACE 67
was:
if it w. so, it might be CARROLL 52
What w., again may be BROWNING:R 195
wash:
all come right in the w. PROV 214
Bid them w. their faces SHAK:COR 5
henceforth w. the river Rhine? COLERIDGE:ST 65
I also w. and iron them THATCH:D 1
incessantly softly w. again WHITMAN 33
W. him bloodless DARLEY 2
w. me and I shall be made BIBLE 598
W. me, Saviour, or I die TOP 2
w. their feet in soda water ELIOT:TS 44
W. what is dirty LANGTON 2
w. your dirty linen in public PROV 84
wash-tub: they trod in the w. CLOUGH 1
washed:
w. himself with oriental scrupulosity JOHNSON:S 58
w. his hands before BIBLE 435
washing:
Always w., and never HARDY:T 66
country w. BRUM 1
take in one another's w. and then sell ELD 1
taking in one another's w. TWAIN 40
w. his hands with invisible HOOD 15
w. one's clean linen in public WILDE:O 84
washing-day: being w., dined upon cold meat PEPYS 18
washing-up: make them do the w. COPE 7
Washington: Government at W. lives GARF 1
Washington, George:
Cincinnatus of the West* BYR 37
citizen, first in war* LEE:Hen 1
Father of his Country* ANON 184
waspish: When you are w. SHAK:JUL 70
wassailing: Here we come a-w. ANON 16
waste:
gently w. the remains of life WALP:H 8
Haste makes w. PROV 160
now doth time w. me SHAK:RIC.II 46
wail my dear time's w. SHAK:SON 12
w. And solitary places SHELLEY:PB 23
w. my time making money AGAS 1
W. not, want not PROV 412
w. remains and kills EMPS 3
w. without sail on it KEND 1
weary w. of hours SHELLEY:PB 8
were I in the wildest w. BURNS:R 122
waste-paper: w. basket of the emotions WEBB:S 2
wasteful: w. and ridiculous excess SHAK:KING J 16
wastefulness: requirement of conspicuous w. VEB 2
wastes:
every man w. part of his life JOHNSON:S 3
W. without springs CLARE:J 5
wasting: delightful way of w. time MORLEY:Lord[1] 1
Wat: poor W., far off SHAK:POET 12
watch:
as a w. in the night BIBLE 224
dead or my w. has stopped MARX:G 16
done far better by a w. BELLOC 41
for the w. to babble and SHAK:MUCH 20
One to w., and one ADY 1
some must w. SHAK:HAM 121
W. and pray ELLIOT:C 1
w. return'd a silver sound POPE 37
w. the night and wait HOUSM 7
why not carry a w.? TREE 5
wound up like a little w. SPEND 10
your w., in a private pocket CHESTERFIELD 13
watch-chain: too large to hang on a w. ANON 253
watch-charm: wear me, like a w. FITZGER:Z 2
watch-dog:
w.'s honest bark BYR 168
w.'s voice that bayed GOLDS 24
watch-dogs: well paid w. of Capitalism GONNE 1
watcher: some w. of the skies KEATS 4
watches:
Correct our w. by the public ELIOT:TS 14
judgements as our w. POPE 5
w. forward two hours – and back 20 years ANON 151
watchful: it is w. as the jungle BROD 1
watchmaker: I should have become a w. EINS 14
watchman:
w. on the lonely tower SCOTT:W 13
w. waketh but in vain BIBLE 243
W., what of the night? BIBLE 313
watchword: w. is security PITT:W[1] 13
water:
A little w. clears us SHAK:MAC 46
and drawers of w. BIBLE 129
as ready by w. as by land ELS 1
As w. is in w. SHAK:ANT 50
benison of hot w. BROOKE 21
best contraceptive is a glass of cold w. ANON 164
best w. is the newest BLAKE:W 49
biggest waste of w. PHILIP 2
blackens all the w. about him ADDIS 25
By w. and the word STONE:SJ 1
can lead a horse to w. PROV 437
changed into little w. drops MARLOWE 45
deeds Shall be in w. writ BEAUMO 7
don't care where the w. goes CHESTERTON 13
Drink no longer w. BIBLE 548
drinks a tumbler of London w. SMITH:Syd[1] 12
dripping of w. on mud FAIRBURN 1
Expect poison from standing w. BLAKE:W 46
Fish fuck in it* FIELDS 5
fountain of the w. of life BIBLE 585
good Shall come of w. BROOKE 17
He asked w. BIBLE 132
heard Eternity drip w. MACDIAR 11
Human beings were invented by w. ROBB 1

I came like W., and FITZGER:E 18
if he wasn't as dull as ditch w. DICKENS 227
In imperceptible w. HOOD 15
in the w. under the earth BIBLE 103
into the w. up to her knees? MARX:G 20
it is w. I dream of CAMPBELL:ATA 2
King over the W. ANON 210
Laughing W. LONGFEL 21
like making chalk marks on w. FRAME 1
Little drops of w. CARNEY 1
o'er the w. to Charlie HOGG 6
Oft w. fairest meadows COWP 85
passed a lot of w. since then GORKY 18
plunge in a pool's living w. BROWNING:R 146
should go across salt w. DICKENS 200
Smooth runs the w. SHAK:HEN.VI[2] 3
sound of the w. BAS 1
third thing, that makes it w. LAWR:DH 36
tickled best in muddy w. BUTLER:S[1] 41
To fetch a pail of w. NURS 27
to throw w. into the sea CERV 8
Too much of w. hast thou SHAK:HAM 177
touch wine, it turns into w. AGA 1
Two leaps the w. ALLING:W 3
under W. I would scarcely kick KEATS 136
Unstable as w. BIBLE 79
virtues We write in w. SHAK:HEN.VIII 18
w. but the desert BYR 105
w. cools not love SHAK:SON 65
w. flowed like champagne EVAR 1
w. hollow out a stone OSB:J 14
W. is best PINDAR 1
w. is on the Bishop's board CHESTERTON 14
w., is unsuitable in colour HERB:AP 19
W. like a stone ROSSET:C 18
w. Mirrors a still sky YEATS 49
w. of affliction BIBLE 316
w. still keeps falling over CHURCH:W 60
W., w., every where COLERIDGE:ST 19
w. what is dry LANGTON 2
W. your damned flower-pots BROWNING:R 36
watir that doun renneth CHAUC 102
when I makes w. I makes w. JOYCE:J 13
When the hot w. gives out POUND 13
whose name was writ in w. KEATS 169
written by drinkers of w. HORACE 92
You will do your work on w. KIP 54
Zion of the w. bead THOMAS:D 10
water-beetles: turn into luminous w. SLESS 8
water-birds: My birthday began with w. THOMAS:D 13
water-colours: painting in w. shows the innocent STEVENSON:RL 7
water-drops: women's weapons, w. SHAK:KING L 31
water-flags: saw the w. in flower PATMO 3
water-flies: let the w. Blow me SHAK:ANT 63
water-lily: saw the w. bloom TENNY 21
water-mill: noise like that of a w. SWIFT 28
water nymph: modest w.n. saw her God CRASH 1
water-tower: great grey w. CHESTERTON 3
watered: water'd heaven with their tears BLAKE:W 69
waterfall: From the w. he named her LONGFEL 21
Watergate: I screwed up on W. NIX 13
Waterloo:
every man meets his W. PHILLIPS:W 1
W. was won on the playing fields WELLING 22
world-earthquake, W. TENNY 192
waterman:
great-grandfather was but a water-man BUNYAN 12
row after health like a w. SWIFT 85
watermen: w., that row one way BURTON:Ro 4
waters:
all that move in the W. PRAY 18
as the w. cover the sea AINGER:AC 1
beside the still w. BIBLE 206
By what strange w. HEWETT 1
Cast thy bread upon the w. BIBLE 288
chittering w. of JOYCE:J 35
do business in great w. BIBLE 234
hear the mighty w. rolling WORDS:W 65
killed by drinking Cheltenham w. ANON 127
luminous home of w. ARNOLD:M 34
moved upon the face of the w. BIBLE 2
Once more upon the w. BYR 73
Over the waste of w. BYR 175
quiet w. by SCOTTISH 1
Still w. run deep PROV 355
Stolen w. are sweet BIBLE 255
Though thou the w. warp SHAK:AS 35
To the w. and the wild YEATS 2
trespass on alien w. MALLEY 1
w. at their priestlike task KEATS 113
w. of the heart Push in THOMAS:D 5
W. on a starry night WORDS:W 53
W. that be above the Firmament PRAY 13
w. wild went o'er his child CAMPBELL:T 15
While the nearer w. roll WESLEY:C 5
world of w. dark and deep MILT 176
waterspouts: at the noise of thy w. BIBLE 213
waterweed: smells Of w. fungus HEAN 2
watery: shoreless w. wild ARNOLD:M 16
Watson: Mr W., come here BELL:AG 1
wattle:
w. Scatters its pollen MCAULEY 3
where the w. blossoms wave GORDON:AM 3
Wattle: ever hear of Captain W.? DIBDIN:C 6
wattles: of clay and w. made YEATS 4
Waugh, Evelyn:
E.W. who, like you CHURCH:R 2
letter delivered to* MUGG 5
wave:
All sunk beneath the w. COWP 15
all thy banners w. CAMPBELL:T 20
blue w. rolls nightly BYR 39
I wish you A w. o' th' sea SHAK:WIN 21
mounting w. will roll us TENNY 24
pliant arm thy glassy w. GRAY:T 4
seen her w. her hand? TENNY 14
w. to pant beneath thy SHELLEY:PB 44
waves:
Britannia, rule the w. THOMS:Ja[1] 2
free as the sons of the w. GARRICK 4
him that walk'd the w. MILT 57
I see the w. upon the shore SHELLEY:PB 31
light-hearted masters of the w. ARNOLD:M 30
Like as the w. make towards SHAK:SON 23
little w. of Breffney go GORE 1
longed-for dash of w. ARNOLD:M 34
tired w., vainly breaking CLOUGH 11
twinkling laughter of the w. AESC 6
w. bound beneath me BYR 73
w. her lily hand GAY 40
w. of thy sweet singing SHELLEY:PB 19, 80
W. that Beat on Heavens Shore BLAKE:W 88
w., they were fiddlin' and small EDGAR 1
w. were more gay YEATS 1
w. work lesse and lesse SURREY 2
Wealdstone turned to w. BETJ 25
What are the wild w. saying CARP 1
What the W. were always saying DICKENS 132
waving: not w. but drowning SMITH:Ste 4
wax:
have to make him out of w. SFORZA 1
W. to receive BYR 133
wax-works: W. weren't made to be CARROLL 50
waxworks: w. inhabited by gramophones DE LA M 22
way:
a will there's a w. PROV 428
All the w. with L.B.J. HOLT 1
dirty, dangerous w. GOLDS 71
easy is the w. VIRGIL 66
every one to his own w. BIBLE 329
going the w. of all flesh WEBSTER:J 2
going the w. of all the earth BIBLE 130
gone the w. of all flesh CONG 68
High w., since you my chiefe SIDNEY:P 10
hold to the upward w. PLATO 14
I did it my w. ANKA 1
knows the w. but can't drive TYNAN 5
Long is the w. And hard MILT 161
Love will find a w. PROV 254
making, breaking, shaping w. DOBSON:R 1
middle w. is the safest OSB:J 19
one w. in to life, but many SEN 2
one w. of *doing* things rightly RUSKIN 10
plods his weary w. GRAY:T 16
Prepare ye the w. of the Lord BIBLE 320
Prepare ye the w. of the lord BIBLE 377
ready w. to virtue BROWNE:T 21
someone else have your w. PEARS:LB 1
Think the w. we go is right PATTEN 4
this is the w. to the stars VIRGIL 80
Thou art my w. QUAR 13
w. for Billy and me HOGG 7
w. home's the farthest w. QUAR 14
W. is like an empty vessel LAO 6
w. of a man with a maid KIP 149
w., the truth, and the life BIBLE 489
woman has her w. HOLMES:OW 10
Wayne: John W. is dead ANON 76
ways:
consider her w. BIBLE 253
dwelt among the untrodden w. WORDS:W 30
great and gracious w. PATMO 8
He had his little w. MILNE 16
Her w. are w. of pleasantness BIBLE 250
justifie the wayes of God to men MILT 108
leave righteous w. behind BUDDHA 3
neither are your w. my w. BIBLE 331
old w. are the safest COKE:E 7
There be triple w. to take KIP 149
wayward: w. is this foolish love SHAK:TWO 4
we:
people like us are W. KIP 155
Put it down a w. DICKENS 38
still it is not w. CHESTERTON 25
weader: Tonstant W. fwowed up PARKER:D 11
weak:
but the flesh is w. BIBLE 433
by confidence grows w. DONNE 73
concessions of the w. are BURKE:E 25
I am w. and weary HANK 1
Only the w. complain GILMORE 1
surely the W. shall perish SERVICE 1
They are w., but He WARNER:A 1
to be w. is miserable MILT 117
w. alone repent BYR 32
w. from your loveliness BETJ 20
w. have one weapon BID 1
w. in courage is strong BLAKE:W 47
w. minds Led captive MILT 266
w. need the strong to look HAWKE 4
w. one is singled SHELLEY:PB 160
weak-hearted: comfort and help the w. PRAY 35
weaken: great life if you don't w. BUCHAN 1
weaker:
the w. gain DRYD 16
to the w. side inclin'd BUTLER:S[1] 37
weakest:
Trample on the w. SEARLE 4
w. goes to the wall PROV 415
w. kind of fruit SHAK:MERC 43
weakness:
An amiable w. FIELDING 27
Marks of w. BLAKE:W 74
no act of w. can be tolerated JOFF 1
Stronger by w. WALLER 9
weaknesses:
have the w. of their qualities BALZ 10
his w. are great KIP 97
touch his w. with a delicate GOLDS 56
Wealdstone: to the W. turned to waves BETJ 25
wealth:
any means get W. and Place POPE 150
don't 'old with W. WELLS:HG 5
Health is better than w. PROV 161
His w. a well-spent age CAMPION 4
honour, and pursuit of w. LUCRET 5
If we command our w. BURKE:E 77
ignorance of w. GOLDS 21
in all time of our w. PRAY 34
insolence of w. will creep out JOHNSON:S 203
no w. but life RUSKIN 17
Order is w. SMILES 3
Outshon the w. of Ormus MILT 148
poore man's w. SIDNEY:P 6
Surplus w. is a sacred trust CARNEG:A 1
W. has never been sufficient GALB 3
w. is a sacred thing FRANCE 10
W. is not without its advantages GALB 2
w. to those coarse asses LUTHER 6
w. ye find, another keeps SHELLEY:PB 52
Where w. accumulates GOLDS 21
Where w. and freedom reign GOLDS 7
wealthy:
business of the w. man BELLOC 32
healthy and w. and dead THURB 11
some are immoderately w. ARISTOT 16

weaned:
had been w. on a pickle LONGWORTH 1
were we not wean'd till then? DONNE 41
weapon:
Grab the nearest w. SEARLE 4
his w. wit HOPE:An 8
no w. but a wing WRIGHT:J 8
weapons:
books are w. ROOS:FD 15
get your w. ready WHITMAN 32
hang my w. and my lyre HORACE 46
not by w. of war but by wheat EISEN 3
threaten that they have Doomsday w. LAING 1
w. of war perished BIBLE 154
women's w., water-drops SHAK:KING L 31
wear:
better to w. out than CUMB 1
man may w. it on both sides SHAK:TRO 17
qualities as would w. well GOLDS 50
rather w. out than rust out WHITEF 2
too costly to w. every day SHAK:MUCH 9
wearies: It w. me SHAK:MERC 1
weariness:
Art thou pale for w. SHELLEY:PB 101
W. Can snore SHAK:CYM 13
w., the fever, and the fret KEATS 93
wearinesse May tosse him to HERB:G 44
wearing:
not linen you're w. out HOOD 20
the worse for w. ESSEX 1
wearin' o' the Green ANON 23
w. my powder-blue suit CHAND 1
wears: so w. she to him SHAK:TWE 26
weary:
Art thou w. NEALE 4
full w. of her watch EDWARDS:R 1
home, w. to bed PEPYS 2
I am weak and w. HANK 1
I got the W. Blues HUGHES:L 1
I sae w. fu' o' care BURNS:R 96
I was w. and ill at ease PROC 1
plods his w. way GRAY:T 16
w., let him sit HERB:G 30
W. with toil SHAK:SON 10
world is w. of the past SHELLEY:PB 158
weasel:
Methinks it is like a w. SHAK:HAM 126
Pop goes the w. MANDALE 1
w. under the cocktail cabinet PINT 6
weather:
after all the w. was ideal MANS:K 2
blue unclouded w. TENNY 19
check the w. reports before they SPEIGHT 4
come like a change in the w.? AUD 26
Come wind, come w. BUNYAN 30
first talk is of the w. JOHNSON:S 30
hard grey w. Breeds KINGSLEY:C 16
Ill is the w. that bringeth no DEK 1
Jolly boating w. CORY 4
Mackerel sky and mares'* PROV 257
no such thing as bad w. RUSKIN 31
not in fine w. CLOUGH 3
notice what the w. was like CHEK 9
Owing to the w., English Social life MACAULAY:R 3
Rain before seven: fine* PROV 328
rainbow in the morning* ANON 90
rainbow in the morning* PROV 329
red sky at night* ANON 91
Red sky at night PROV 331
roof of blue Italian w. SHELLEY:PB 60
St Swithin's Day, if thou dost* PROV 359
waiting for the w. to break PINT 2
warm w. when one is in bed SWIFT 71
W. and rain have undone it KIP 131
w. the cuckoo likes HARDY:T 40
w. the shepherd shuns HARDY:T 41
w. turned around THOMAS:D 14
w., when it is not rainy BYR 135
weder gynneth clere CHAUC 108
What dreadful hot w. AUSTEN 70
winter and rough w. SHAK:AS 24
won't hold up the w. MACNEICE 3
weather-eye: Keep your w. open PROV 220
weather forecast: w.f. seemed to be some kind of spoof LODGE:D 4
weather-wise:
If the Bard was weatherwise COLERIDGE:ST 53
Some are w. FRANKLIN:B 7
weathercock: sad as Widdercock in Wind HENRYS 5
weave:
ever will so w. HARDY:T 70
W. a circle round him COLERIDGE:ST 63
W. the warp GRAY:T 30
w. their thread with bones SHAK:TWE 28
weaves: w., and is clothed SWIN 15
weaving: work at the w. trade ANON 31
web:
gives the w. and the pin SHAK:KING L 47
She left the w. TENNY 21
what a tangled w. we weave SCOTT:W 27
web-foot: Every fork like a white w. HARDY:T 45
Webb:
Captain W. the Dawley man BETJ 11
with the windows shut, reading Mary W. DOUGLAS-H:A 4
wed:
And think to w. it SHAK:ALL 1
December when they w. SHAK:AS 59
w. again, and made the error CLARE:J 3
With this Ring I thee w. PRAY 86
wedded:
Hail w. Love MILT 202
I have w. fyve CHAUC 77
w. but never won WATSON:W 1
w. to calamity SHAK:ROM 32
wedding:
as she did her w. gown GOLDS 50
Cheer for the Sergeant's weddin' KIP 87
dance bare-foot on her w. SHAK:TAM 5
Let's have a w. DICKENS 214
she has bought her w. clothes ADDIS 24
you may get the w. dresses ready BYR 225
wedding-day: To-morrow is our w. COWP 49
wedding-guest:
W. here beat his breast COLERIDGE:ST 14
W. stood still COLERIDGE:ST 11
wedding-ring: small circle of a w. CIB 5
weddings:
w. always make me cry BEHAN:Br 7
w. is sadder than funerals BEHAN:Br 7
wedlock:
W. indeed hath oft compared DAVIES:J 4
w.'s the devil BYR 3
Wednesday: upon W. in Wheeson week SHAK:HEN.IV[2] 23
wee-things: expectant w., toddlin BURNS:R 11
wee-wee: smell of oranges and w. ASK 1
weed:
basest w. outbraves SHAK:SON 41
fat w. That roots SHAK:HAM 45
gather honey from the w. SHAK:HEN.V 27
not w. their own minds WALP:H 20
Pernicious w. COWP 28
salt w. sways in the stream ARNOLD:M 1
scarce w. out the vice GOLDS 56
w. is simply a plant SIMM 1
w. of the waste places STOW 2
w. that grows in every soil BURKE:E 41
What is a w.? EMER 77
weeds:
all the idle w. that grow SHAK:KING L 64
bred amongst the w. and tares BROWNE:T 15
buy your self w. GAY 27
Long live the w. HOPK:GM 18
Rank w., that every art CRAB 2
runs either to herbs or to w. BACON:F[1] 87
w. will overrun the fields HOOV 3
Worthless as withered w. BRONTE:E 2
week:
can be accomplished in a w. STEVENSON:RL 21
greatest w. in the history NIX 4
in next w. tomorrow GRAHAME 3
Middle of Next W. CARROLL 94
w. is a long time in politics WILSON:Harold 5
weekends:
No w. for the gods LOWELL:R 16
try getting a plumber on w. ALLEN:W 2
weep:
Bid me to w., and I will w. HERR 30
Could scarcely cry, 'w. w. BLAKE:W 18
deeth moot wepe and pleyne CHAUC 44
Even butchers w. GAY 16
I'll w. what's left away SHAK:COM 3
makes the angels w. SHAK:MEA 13
No, I'll not w. SHAK:KING L 31
She must w. or she will die TENNY 114
Some w. in empty rooms COLERIDGE:M 2
That he should w. for her? SHAK:HAM 90
time to w. BIBLE 281
'Tis that I may not w. BYR 202
w. and know why HOPK:GM 16
w. because I know all things YEATS 24
w. for Adonais SHELLEY:PB 106
w. for her sins at the other CARY:J 1
w., for it reminds me so CARROLL 85
W. for the lives AUD 33
W. no more, my lady FOST:SC 5
w. to have that which it SHAK:SON 28
w. upon your hinder parts HUX:A 45
w. with them that w. BIBLE 515
W. you no more, sad ANON 47
Who would not w.? POPE 122
wilt thou w. when I am low? BYR 5
women must w. KINGSLEY:C 15
you w. alone WILCOX 3
weeping:
all night in a forest, w. MALORY 12
Do you hear the children w. BROWNING:EB 2
Doth that bode w.? SHAK:OTH 57
hearers w. to their beds SHAK:RIC.II 41
I have full cause of w. SHAK:KING L 31
long w. of autumn violins VERL 1
two w. motions CRASH 15
w. and the laughter DOWS 3
world's more full of w. YEATS 2
weet: w. an Englishman to the skin RAMS 4
weevils: There's w. in the flour HEWETT 4
weigh: w. your Gods and you KIP 100
weighed:
being w. with his sins KAF 5
Men ... have to be w. COLERIDGE:ST 100
Thou art w. in the balances BIBLE 351
weight:
heavy w. of hours SHELLEY:PB 45
recommendation than their own w. STERNE 37
weary w. Of all this unintelligible WORDS:W 5
w. of rages will press harder SPOON 1
w. of this sad time SHAK:KING L 87
willing to pull his w. ROOS:T 1
weights: standardization of w. and measures NAPO I 3
weighty: reserve the more w. voice BACON:F[1] 47
weird: home of the w. LAWS 1
welcome:
bear w. in your eye SHAK:MAC 21
bid you a w. adoo WARD:A 1
hath outstay'd his w. COLERIDGE:ST 68
Love bade me w. HERB:G 53
warmest w., at an inn SHEN 1
W. the coming HOMER 18
W. the coming POPE 66
welcomes: w. at once all the world ANST 1
welding: w. of their later history HARDY:T 23
welfare-state: led to that of the W. TEMPLE:W[2] 2
welkin: let the w. roar SHAK:HEN.IV[2] 27
well:
all shall be w. JULIANA 1
All's w. that ends w. PROV 13
At last I am going to be w. SCAR 1
bleeding at the bottom of the w. KENNELLY 3
Didn't they do w. FORSY 1
do I drink from every w. CALLIM 1
does w. what one loves COLETTE 3
I eat w., and I drink w. MORTON:T 2
must do twice as w. as men WHITTON 1
never do anything w. till HAZL 37
not feeling very w. myself PUNCH 26
one of my w. looking days GOLDS 68
Pussy's in the w. NURS 9
She's perfectly w. MILNE 7
w. That owes two buckets SHAK:RIC.II 35
who can do all things w.? CHURCH:C 13
well-aired: like to have the morning w. BRUM 3
well-bred:
be very strange and w. CONG 53
proof that you are w. HALS:M 1
well connected: virtuous scorn The w.c. GILB:WS 45
well-dressed:
being w. gives a feeling of inward EMER 71
sense of being w. gives FORBES:CF 1

well-favoured: w. man is the gift SHAK:MUCH 19
well-informed: To come with a w. mind AUSTEN 63
Wellington, Duke of:
England's greatest son* TENNY 191
last great Englishman* TENNY 189
tower of strength* TENNY 190
wells:
could not keep me from w. HEAN 2
dropping buckets into empty w. COWP 67
go about and poison w. MARLOWE 23
to *poison the w.* NEWM:JH 6
Welsh:
devil understands W. SHAK:HEN.IV[1] 65
W. ... are the only nation WAUGH:E 10
Welshman:
care and valour in this W. SHAK:HEN.V 30
Taffy was a W. NURS 68
Welsted: Flow, W., flow POPE 168
Wenceslas: Good King W. looked out NEALE 1
wench:
besides, the w. is dead MARLOWE 25
He loved a w. well AUBREY 8
stuff fit only for a w. MASE 7
Take heed of a young w. HERB:G 60
wenche in every toun CHAUC 68
wencher: Wednesday w. and a Sunday saint ELLIS:B 1
wenches: but getting w. with child SHAK:WIN 9
Wenlock Edge:
On W.E. the wood's HOUSM 20
W.E. was umbered HOUSM 40
Wensbeck: W.'s limpid streams AKEN 1
went:
have loved the way you w. DAWE 2
He came and he w. WHITTY 1
wept:
have w. to see the dolour MALORY 11
he w. well SHELLEY:PB 38
he w. with joy to hear BLAKE:W 13
Jesus w. BIBLE 485
long before had w. EDWARDS:R 1
Now turned aside and w. AYT 2
times that I have w. MUSSET 4
w. for my departed youth POWER:M 2
w. not greatly, but sighed MALORY 13
who has not w. is a savage SANT 9
were: if it w. so, it would be CARROLL 52
Wertenberg: Rhine circle fair W. MARLOWE 31
Werther: W. had a love for Charlotte THACK 27
Weser:
river W., deep and wide BROWNING:R 24
Until they came to the river W. BROWNING:R 29
Wesley: John W.'s conversation is good JOHNSON:S 197
west:
Cincinnatus of the W. BYR 37
dropping of the daylight in the W. BROWNING:R 21
gathered to the quiet w. HENL 6
Go W., young man GREEL 1
Go W., young man SOULE 1
I dearly like the w. BURNS:R 65
in the gardens of the W. CONNOLLY:C 17
one vast Iris of the W. BYR 99
safeguard of the W. WORDS:W 74
she sought him w. BALL 44
That's where the W. begins CHAPMAN:A 1
wan w. shivers SWIN 10
warm wind, the w. wind MASE 5
W. in her eyes COLERIDGE:M 3
W. is W. KIP 39
w. yet glimmers SHAK:MAC 68
wild W. Wind SHELLEY:PB 40
without declining W. DONNE 43
western:
All Quiet on the W. Front REM 1
Playboy of the W. World SYNGE 4
w. wind was wild KINGSLEY:C 13
wonders of the w. world SYNGE 1
Westminster Abbey:
gained a peerage, or W.A. NELS 5
That temple of silence* MACAULAY:TB 11
W.A. or victory NELS 3
westward:
w., look, the land CLOUGH 11
W. the course of empire BERK 6
you are stepping w.? WORDS:W 95
wet:
bereft Of w. and wildness? HOPK:GM 18
out of these w. clothes and into WOOLL 3
wether: tainted w. of the flock SHAK:MERC 43
whacks: gave her mother forty w. ANON 80
whale:
against tide, th' enormous w. SMART 2
dwarfs trying to grill a w. PRIEST 5
Very like a w. SHAK:HAM 126
w. ship was my Yale MELV 3
whales:
great w. come sailing by ARNOLD:M 1
ye W., and all PRAY 18
wharves: black w. and the slips LONGFEL 25
what:
He knew w.'s w. BUTLER:S[1] 8
She knows wot's wot DICKENS 44
W. and Why and When KIP 105
w. is which and which MILNE 15
what's-his-name: there is no W. DICKENS 138
whatsoever: W. things are true BIBLE 542
whaups: w. are crying STEVENSON:RL 69
wheat: orient and immortal w. TRAH 3
wheel:
ever-whirling wheele of Change SPENS 44
Time's w. runs back BROWNING:R 189
w. is come full circle SHAK:KING L 81
you who turn the w. ELIOT:TS 51
wheelbarrow:
depends upon a red wheel barrow WILLIAMS:WC 2
she wheeled a w. ANON 24
wheels:
all the w. of Being slow TENNY 148
cruel story runs on w. OUIDA 2
Little Tin Gods on W. KIP 35
round went the w. COWP 52
why tarry the w. of his chariots? BIBLE 133
when:
clothes and had forgotten to say 'W.!' WODE 17
have they fixed the where and w.? HAWKER 1
If not how w.? HILLEL 2
where:
don't know w. he are PATERSON:AB 1
have they fixed the w. and when? HAWKER 1
on w. you want to get to CARROLL 13
wherefore: For every why he had a w. BUTLER:S[1] 7
whetstone: w., to sharpen good wit ASCHAM 4
which: what is w. and w. MILNE 15
whiffling: w. through the tulgey wood CARROLL 46
Whig:
first W. was the Devil JOHNSON:S 205
ridiculous for a W. to pretend JOHNSON:S 82
Tory men and W. measures DISR:B 16
W. The name of a faction JOHNSON:S 16
wise Tory and a wise W. JOHNSON:S 227
you are a vile W. JOHNSON:S 154
Whigs: W. admit no force BROWNE:W[2] 1
whimper: Not with a bang but a w. ELIOT:TS 59
whimsies: they have my w. PRIOR 11
whine: sweat and w. about their condition WHITMAN 7
whining: w. at the threshold GILMAN 1
whip:
Don't forget your w. NIET 7
he brings down the w. LESSING:D 2
Smack went the w. COWP 52
W. me, ye devils SHAK:OTH 68
whipped:
child is afraid of being w. JOHNSON:S 86
She w. him, she lashed him NURS 22
She w. them all soundly NURS 72
was whipt at school DRYD 80
w. her little daughter NURS 36
whipping:
W. and abuse are like laudanum STOWE 4
who shall scape w.? SHAK:HAM 89
whips:
father hath chastised you with w. BIBLE 161
w. and scorns of time SHAK:HAM 97
whirled: whirl'd them to the back o' beyont SCOTT:W 71
whirligig: thus the w. of time SHAK:TWE 57
whirlpools: ascetic rocks and the sensual w. MERED:G 13
whirlwind:
Rides in the w. ADDIS 36
sweeping W.'s sway GRAY:T 31
they shall reap the w. BIBLE 353
with winter and w. and wail KEND 1
whisker:
educated w. TENNY 91
W. and claw, they crouch DE LA M 12
whiskers:
dye one's w. green CARROLL 83
my fur and w. CARROLL 7
Runcible cat with crimson w. LEAR 26
w. are of a Victorian bushiness WODE 27
whisky:
Freedom and w. BURNS:R 38
not with unmeasured w. SCOTT:W 99
one of them is malt w. MCNEILL 1
One w. is all right COOPER:D
That w. priest GREENE:G 3
torchlight procession marching down* O'SULL 3
whisper:
busy w. circling GOLDS 28
There's a w. down the field KIP 148
w. of a faction should prevail RUSS:J[2] 1
whispered: it's w. everywhere CONG 26
whispering:
They've a way of w. to me HARDY:T 9
was w. in her mouth MARX:C 1
w., with white lips BYR 80
whisperings:
Foul whisp'rings are abroad SHAK:MAC 106
It keeps eternal w. KEATS 18
whispers: to be drunk Among w. ELIOT:TS 22
whistle:
blow and w. at the same PLAU 4
clear as a w. BYROM 7
he could w. them back GOLDS 40
heard the bullets w. WASH 13
I'd w. her off SHAK:OTH 38
joly w. wel ywet CHAUC 73
let it w. as it will SCOTT:W 24
until a shrimp learns to w. KHRU 10
w. an' I'll come to ye BURNS:R 106
W. and she'll come FLETCH:J 3
W. o'er the lave BURNS:R 68
whistled:
He w. a tune to the window NOY 3
w. as he went DRYD 119
whistles:
w. blow forlorn HOUSM 5
W. o're the Furrow'd Land MILT 70
w. thrice COLERIDGE:ST 21
whistling:
W. aloud to bear his courage BLAIR 1
W. to keep myself DRYD 97
W. to th' air SHAK:ANT 26
with the w. of a name POPE 105
white:
cannot change from black to w. HOFFMAN:H 6
earth were paper w. LYLY 8
force of w. men's wills GORDIM 1
fought against w. domination MANDELA:N 2
here in black and w. JONS 5
How ill w. hairs become SHAK:HEN.IV[2] 53
my soul is w. BLAKE:W 27
nor w. so very w. CANN 5
not a w. man's country PLOM 10
oppression of the W. Man TEC 1
readst black where I read W. BLAKE:W 106
So purely w. they were SPENS 49
stand up and lie like w. men O'ROUR 1
Take them down in black and w. BYROM 4
Take up the W. Man's burden KIP 99
they shall be as w. as snow BIBLE 300
to be the w. man's brother KING:ML 5
Two Wongs do not make a W. CALWELL 1
Wearing w. for Eastertide HOUSM 3
When the w. man came GEO:D 2
W. as an angel is the English BLAKE:W 27
w. as driven snow SHAK:WIN 23
w., clear w., inside KIP 56
W. Horse of the W. Horse Vale CHESTERTON 4
w. man knows how to make SITTING 1
w. man like him or not MACIN 1
w. man's foot hath never passed PRINGLE:T 1
w. races are really pinko-gray FORST 7
W. shall not neutralize BROWNING:R 203

world is w. in May TENNY 237
White: Mr W. has three disastrous faults HOPE:AI 5
White House:
between Nixon and the W.H. KENNEDY:JF 7
From Log Cabin to W.H. THAY 1
I am in charge at the W.H. HAIG:A 1
no whitewash at the W.H. NIX 15
whitebait: w. with moonlight eyes HULME 2
Whitehall: gentleman in W. really does know JAY 1
whiter:
made w. than snow BIBLE 598
W. than new snow SHAK:ROM 30
whites:
all w. are ink SHAK:TRO 1
see the w. of their eyes PUT 1
whitest: w. man I know JOYCE:J 26
whitethroat: w. builds, and all BROWNING:R 49
whitewash: no w. at the White House NIX 15
whither:
knows not w. nor why MASE 4
W., O splendid ship BRIDGES:R 9
whiting: w. said with its tail HOOD 32
Whitlam: [Gough W.] had many geniuses HAYD 3
whitlow: leather-faced old w. LOWER 1
Whitman:
beautiful old Walt W. GARC 2
pact with you, Walt W. POUND 21
Walt W. who laid end to end LODGE:D 5
What do you see Walt W.? WHITMAN 16
W., like a large shaggy STEVENSON:RL 26
Whittington: Turn again, W. ANON 111
who:
And w. were you? SITWELL:E 12
I know w. I am CERV 1
W. he? ROSS:HW 1
w. loses and w. wins SHAK:KING L 79
W., or why, or which LEAR 33
w.'s for you and w.'s JOHNSON:LB 4
W.'s in the next room? HARDY:T 39
will tell you w. you are CHESTERFIELD 6
whole:
dwarfish w. COLERIDGE:ST 58
nothing can be sole or w. YEATS 95
one stupendous w. POPE 87
seeing the w. of them RUSKIN 10
Till man made up the w. YEATS 77
till the w. has been surveyed JOHNSON:S 37
w. is that which has ARISTOT 20
w. need not a physician BIBLE 405
whom: 'W. are you?' said he ADE 1
whooping: out of all w. SHAK:AS 41
whooping cough: It would cure the w.c. ANON 79
whore:
care for the young man's w. JOHNSON:S 134
cunning w. of Venice SHAK:OTH 53
dost thou lash that w.? SHAK:KING L 70
Fortune's a right w. WEBSTER:J 3
I am the Protestant w. GWYN 2
I' th' posture of a w. SHAK:ANT 67
labeled harpy, shrew and w. RICH 2
prove my love a w. SHAK:OTH 44
rogue is married to a w. KIP 87
teach the morals of a w. JOHNSON:S 98
'TIS PITY SHE'S A W.? FORD:J[1] 10
W. & Gambler by the State BLAKE:W 92
w. in the bedroom HALL:Je 1
With a red-headed w. GOGA 2
w.'s oath SHAK:KING L 52
woman's a w., and there's an end JOHNSON:S 161
whore-shops: Madhouses, prisons, w. CLARE:J 2
whorehouse: play the piano in a w. ANON 180
whorehouses: virgin territory for w. CAP 2
whoremaster: evasion of w. man SHAK:KING L 9
whores:
brought w. for Eleusis POUND 41
we are not political w. MUSSO:B 9
w. dropping in for a word POUND 18
why:
For every w. he had a wherefore BUTLER:S[1] 7
he see you now, ask w.? AUD 52
knows not whither nor w. MASE 4
Never mind the w. and wherefore GILB:WS 16
w. and wherefore in all SHAK:HEN.V 43
W., Edward, tell me w.? WORDS:W 1
wicked:
born w., and grow worse ANON 215
I's mighty w. STOWE 3
little better than one of the w. SHAK:HEN.IV[1] 11
no peace . . . unto the w. BIBLE 325
pretending to be w. and being WILDE:O 91
seen the w. in great power BIBLE 209
so w. as Lord George Hell BEERB 3
w. as a ginless tonic COPE 3
w. flee when no man pursueth BIBLE 274
w. to deserve such pain BROWNING:R 96
worse than w. . . . vulgar PUNCH 17
wickedness:
capable of every w. CONRAD 12
dwell in the tents of w. BIBLE 222
honour than secret w. CERV 20
leaven of malice and w. PRAY 48
manifold sins and w. PRAY 3
spiritual w. in high places BIBLE 538
stupidity and w. of his own kind SADE 3
That is the path of w. BALL 56
W. is a myth invented WILDE:O 69
w. of a woman BIBLE 368
w. of the world is so great BRECHT 1
w. that hinders loving BROWNING:R 140
wicket: flannelled fools at the w. KIP 101
wicket-gate: Do you see yonder w.? BUNYAN 2
widdershins: ran w. in his brain WRIGHT:J 1
Widdicombe Fair: to go to W.F. BALL 64
wider: W. still and w. BENS:AC 1
widow:
Black W., death LOWELL:R 3
better to be the w. of a hero IBA 3
dear, will be my w. GUIT 1
'eard o' the W. at Windsor KIP 67
French w. in every bedroom HOFFNUNG 1
Here's to the w. of fifty SHERIDAN:RB 24
or Molly Stark's a w. STARK:J 1
Some undone w. sits MASSIN 11
w. bird sate mourning SHELLEY:PB 150
widow-maker: go with the old grey W.? KIP 120
widows:
be wery careful o' widders DICKENS 16
do like other w. GAY 27
fatherless children, and w. PRAY 36
New w. howl SHAK:MAC 90
When w. exclaim FIELDING 34
wife:
A-making man's w. BROWNING:R 115
all the world and his w. ANST 1
As the husband is, the w. is TENNY 72
away from his w. for seven years DARLING:CJ 1
behind her stands his w. MARX:G 29
Caesar's w. must be above PROV 51
Caesar's w. must be above suspicion CAES:GJ 5
changing himself so as to suit his w.? TROLL 21
character is the health of his w. CONNOLLY:C 15
chaste w. wise SURREY 1
chose my w. as she did GOLDS 50
damn'd in a fair w. SHAK:OTH 1
devoted Friend – but not a W. CARLYLE:JW 2
dwindle into a w. CONG 54
either to look out for a w. SURT 23
Giant Despair had a w. BUNYAN 15
had a w. and children BYR 174
Had a w. and couldn't keep NURS 51
He that hath w. and children BACON:F[1] 80
Here lies my w. ANON 133
his w. looked back BIBLE 50
I have a w., and so forth CONG 37
I would love to have a w. EKL 1
If w. should dine at Edmonton COWP 56
In every port a w. DIBDIN:C 2
In every port he finds a w. BICK 1
in the same manner at your w. JOHN PAUL 1
kick his w. out of bed on a haverage SURT 4
kill a w. with kindness SHAK:TAM 10
lay down his w. for a friend JOYCE:J 24
light w. doth make SHAK:MERC 55
like sleeping with someone else's w. BRADB 3
lived a w. at Usher's Well BALL 65
man who's untrue to his w. AUD 45
man worth having is true to his w. VANB 3
Married a W. he finds out BLAKE:W 93
Match'd with an aged w. TENNY 51
must be in want of a w. AUSTEN 12
my 'oss, my w., and my name SURT 12
my true and honourable w. SHAK:JUL 27
my w. dominates me THEM 1
My w. won't let me LEIGH 1
neighed after his neighbour's w. BIBLE 336
No casual mistress, but a w. TENNY 160
not insult his w. publicly THURB 6
not the bond of man and w. TENNY 255
nothing against Nick's w. GOOD 1
occupational hazard of being a w. ANNE 4
one w. and hardly any mistresses SAKI 9
One w. is too much GAY 30
or your w. in the house TOLS:L 10
place my w. under a pedestal ALLEN:W 1
roaring of the wind is my w. KEATS 144
seeing his w. there, was considerable TRAV 1
shall cleave unto his w. BIBLE 15
sight of his dead w. HARRISON 1
steer clear of a w. SMOL 10
stops being a god for his w. PALAC 2
that loves not his w. and children TAYL:Jer 4
theory that his w. is beautiful MENCK 6
they be Man and W. together PRAY 88
thy dog, thy bottle, and thy w. POPE 103
titles of w. and mother LIVER 2
to have or have no w. BACON:F[1] 132
to thy wedded w. PRAY 83
trouble with his w., or we PEARY 1
when his w. talks Greek JOHNSON:S 261
who has quarrelled with his w. PEAC 7
whose w. shall I take? MOORE:T 25
w. and children are a kind of discipline BACON:F[1] 83
w. and children but as bills BACON:F[1] 84
w. for breed GAY 35
w. ingenrit of the sea BOYD:MA 1
w. Must lie content SIMPSON:RA 1
w. to be of studious or JOHNSON:S 218
w. was pretty, trifling CRAB 19
with someone other than your w. FAIRBAIRN:N 1
wyf wol laste CHAUC 56
wifehood: w. and motherhood are but incidental STANTON:EI 6
wig:
hat and w. will soon be here COWP 55
man with a w. to keep order WAUGH:E 5
wiggles: shapely, it w., and its name ERWIN 1
wight: Yonder a maid and her w. HARDY:T 30
wigwam: Stood the w. of Nokomis LONGFEL 20
wild:
Call of the W. LOND 1
chance to talk a little w. SHAK:HEN.VIII 2
its w. life, the pigeons STOUT 2
Made us nobly w. HERR 41
three w. lads SCOTT:W 48
To the waters and the w. YEATS 2
Walk on the W. Side ALG 1
walking by his w. lone KIP 28
w. as pension plans COPE 3
w. for to hold WYATT 7
W. he may be DICKENS 120
w. with all regret TENNY 109
will always be a w. animal DARW:CG 1
wild-fowl: not a more fearful w. SHAK:MID 23
wildcats: w. in your kitchens SHAK:OTH 19
Wilde, Oscar: last gentleman in Europe* LEVERS 1
wilderness:
As I walk'd throught the w. BUNYAN 1
for a scapegoat into the w. BIBLE 112
him that crieth in the w. BIBLE 320
lodge in some vast w. COWP 60
one crying in the w. BIBLE 377
To be a little w. MARV 25
Walked in the w. GRAVES:R 4
weeds and the w. yet HOPK:GM 18
W. is Paradise enow FITZGER:E 8
W. of sweets MILT 211
wildernesses: stride is w. of freedom HUGHES:Te 1
wildness: bereft Of wet and w.? HOPK:GM 18
wiles:
Cranks, and wanton W. MILT 66
W. More unexpert MILT 151

honest talk and wholesome w. TENNY 200
I don't see any w. CARROLL 15
I rather like bad w. DISR:B 22
I'll not look for w. JONS 36
inflict the torture of bad w. CLARKE:M 2
It wasn't the w. DICKENS 8
kept the good w. until now BIBLE 475
last Companion: W. BELLOC 39
Look not upon the w. BIBLE 268
Lords are Lordliest in thir w. MILT 295
madder music and stronger w. DOWS 2
Mr Weston's good w. AUSTEN 44
new w. into old bottles without bursting ATT 1
not love w., woman and song LUTHER 9
pass the rosy w. DICKENS 93
seas of life, like w. TRAH 5
some are fond of Spanish w. MASE 7
strong wyn, reed as blood CHAUC 30
Sure there was w. HERB:G 40
sweet poyson of mis-used W. MILT 19
sweet white w. MASE 9
Sweet w. of youth BROOKE 19
thirsty grief in w. we steep LOVELACE 4
This w. upon a foreign tree THOMAS:D 6
to be rinsed with w. HOPK:GM 1
to forgo the pleasures of w. JOHNSON:S 149
touch w., it turns into water AGA 1
turning w. into water WILDE:O 134
use a little w. for thy stomach's BIBLE 548
when w. redeems the sight CRANE:H 1
white w. came up with the fish MANK 3
w., Alive with sparkles KEATS 40
w. and women, mirth BYR 178
W. brings out the truth PLINY 2
W. has play'd the Infidel FITZGER:E 32
w. in rivers SCOTT:W 48
w. is a good familiar creature SHAK:OTH 29
W. is a mocker BIBLE 265
w. is in, the wit is out BECON 1
w. is in, the wit is out PROV 427
w. is never sly SLESS 7
w. list is just out of sight POTTER:S 6
W. lov'd I deeply SHAK:KING L 44
w. of life is drawn SHAK:MAC 56
W. of Life keeps oozing FITZGER:E 6
w. that maketh glad BIBLE 233
w. was a farce POWELL:A 2
with love and w. at once oppressed DRYD 111
Work should begin with w. NEIL 4
yon cup of Samian w. BYR 197
wine-jar: trusty w., born with me HORACE 45
wine-pots: broken and castaway w. CLOUGH 12
winepress: I have trodden the w. alone BIBLE 334
wing:
Brush winter from its w. CLARE:J 11
Conquest's crimson w. GRAY:T 28
damp my intended w. MILT 239
flits by on leathern w. COLLINS:Will 6
headlong joy is ever on the w. MILT 61
I've got to take under my w. GILB:WS 80
no weapon but a w. WRIGHT:J 8
Not knowst 'ou w. from tail POUND 36
so long on a broken w. TENNY 225
wings:
all the w. of the Loves SWIN 34
bug with gilded w. POPE 125
clip an Angel's w. KEATS 108
dip Their w. in tears TENNY 147
exulting on triumphant w. POPE 33
Fear lends w. to his feet VIRGIL 77
gates she claps her w. LYLY 6
great w. beating still YEATS 68
hear the beating of his w. BRIGHT 1
his luminous w. in vain ARNOLD:M 84
I had w. like a dove BIBLE 216
if he soars with his own w. BLAKE:W 38
Ill news hath w. DRAYT 2
On w. of song HEINE 2
resembled the w. of an ostrich MACAULAY:TB 7
Riches have w. COWP 68
Sailing on obscene w. COLERIDGE:ST 4
seraph-w. of Extasy GRAY:T 35
spread his w. on the blast BYR 40
Take 'old o' the W. o' the Mornin' KIP 68
tearing w. off dying butterflies HAYD 2
upon my eagle's w. I bore DRYD 27
viewless w. of Poesy KEATS 93
whirr of the w. of a pigeon MONTALE 1
w. are no longer w. to fly ELIOT:TS 66
w. prevent him from walking BAUD 1
with healing in his w. BIBLE 363
With healing in His w. COWP 14
with their woven w. SHAK:MERC 1
wink:
never a w. too soon HOOD 9
nod is as good as a w. PROV 292
w. a reputation down SWIFT 60
w. and hold out mine iron SHAK:HEN.V 11
w. the other eye GILB:F 1
w. your eye at some homely MENCK 16
Winkie:
Wee Willie W. rins through MILLER:W 1
Wee Willie W. runs through NURS 82
winners: there are no w. CHAMBERLAIN:N 1
winning:
glory of the w. MERED:G 31
not the w. but the taking part COUB 1
nothing worth the wear of w. BELLOC 27
They are too busy w. BROOKNER 1
W. Games without actually POTTER:S 1
winnings: make one heap of all your w. KIP 127
winnowing: soft-lifted by the w. wind KEATS 109
wins: Slow but sure w. PROV 347
Winston:
first time you meet W. LYTTON 1
W. with his hundred-horse-power BALD:S 8
winter:
bid the w. come SHAK:KING J 20
brightness Of the w. dawning BRIDGES:R 7
Brush w. from its wing CLARE:J 11
disappeared in the dead of w. AUD 35
English w. BYR 230
every w. change to spring TENNY 154
From w., plague and pestilence NASHE 3
furious w. blowing RANS 1
If W. comes, can Spring SHELLEY:PB 46
in w. enjoy BLAKE:W 34
In w. I get up at night STEVENSON:RL 47
In w.'s tedious nights SHAK:RIC.II 41
It is a w.'s tale THOMAS:D 15
It was not in the w. HOOD 8
It was the W. wilde MILT 5
my age is as a lusty w. SHAK:AS 17
No one thinks of w. KIP 130
notice whether it is w. or summer CHEK 9
One w.'s morn, on a stormy LEAR 15
Our severest w. COWP 95
sad tale's best for w. SHAK:WIN 5
say that they enjoy the w. ADAMS:R[2] 1
There was no w. in't SHAK:ANT 64
through the perils of w. till TROLL 4
very dead of W. ANDREW 3
very dead of w. ELIOT:TS 60
w. and rough weather SHAK:AS 24
w. hath my absence been SHAK:SON 42
W. his delights CAMPION 8
W. is come and gone SHELLEY:PB 112
W. is icummen in POUND 12
w. is past BIBLE 295
W. kept us warm ELIOT:TS 34
w. of our discontent SHAK:RIC.III 1
W. slumbering in the open COLERIDGE:ST 66
W. suddenly was changed SHELLEY:PB 88
with w. and whirlwind and wail KEND 1
Would seem a w.'s day ROCHES 10
winters: forty w. shall besiege SHAK:SON 2
wiped: should have w. it up STERNE 26
wires: Across the w. the electric message AUSTIN:A 1
wisdom:
all men's w. RUSS:J[2] 4
bark of w.'s tree CONF 20
chew on w. past POPE 114
contrivance of human w. BURKE:E 54
criterion of w. to vulgar judgements BURKE:E 69
excess of w. is made a fool EMER 34
Experience is the mother of w. PROV 111
first w., to be fool no more HORACE 75
full of potential w. and wit HUX:A 19
joy is w. YEATS 16
learn w. even from one's enemies ARISTOP 1
lion is the w. of God BLAKE:W 41
little w. the world is ruled? OXEN 1
Lord is the beginning of w. BIBLE 235
more of w. in it WORDS:W 16
nine-tenths of w. ROOS:T 7
old man to learn w. AESC 4
proverbs provide them with w. MAUGH 18
pursue justice with w. PLATO 14
Seed of W. did I sow FITZGER:E 18
teach Eternal W. how to rule POPE 91
Vain w. all MILT 163
W. and Wit are little seen CHESTERFIELD 32
W. be put in a silver rod? BLAKE:W 28
w. comes through suffering AESC 1
W. denotes the pursuing HUTCHES 1
w. does not make us soft PERIC 2
W. doth live with children WORDS:W 93
W. goes by majorities MERED:G 2
W. hath builded her house BIBLE 255
W. in minds attentive COWP 79
W. is humble that he knows COWP 80
W. is oftimes nearer WORDS:W 115
W. is the principal thing BIBLE 251
w. is worth nothing PLATO 1
w. lingers TENNY 83
W. makes him an Ark DONNE 96
w. of our ancestors to guide us BURKE:E 15
w. of the crocodiles BACON:F[1] 123
w. shall die with you BIBLE 187
w. to distinguish the one from NIEB 2
w. we have lost in knowledge? ELIOT:TS 70
without a double share Of w. MILT 279
wise:
All things w. and wonderful ALEX:CF 1
be lowlie w. MILT 231
be w. and eke to love SPENS 2
be w. today YOUNG:E 9
Be w. with speed YOUNG:E 3
beacons of w. men HUX:TH 4
being darkly w. POPE 89
being w. in time ROOS:T 7
came w. men from the east BIBLE 375
dare to be w. HORACE 82
even the w. are merry YEATS 17
follies of the w. JOHNSON:S 69
Gotham's three W. Men we be PEAC 14
Had you been as w. as bold SHAK:MERC 28
heart of the w., like a mirror CONF 22
more than woman to be w. MOORE:T 1
must first be w. and good MILT 96
no w. man who will quit a certainty JOHNSON:S 32
Nor ever did a w. one ROCHES 13
Obscurely w. JOHNSON:S 228
Penny w., pound foolish PROV 319
So w. so young SHAK:RIC.III 10
Some folks are w. SMOL 1
still tongue makes a w. head PROV 354
talks, and is extremely w. HUX:JS 3
'Tis folly to be w. GRAY:T 8
to be w. after the event PROV 205
To be w. and love SHAK:TRO 12
valorous than manly w. MARLOWE 15
we are all equally w. EINS 13
we were very, very w. COLERIDGE:M 3
What all the w. men promised MELBOU 3
which discloses to the w. BIER 4
Who can be w., amaz'd SHAK:MAC 57
w. because you are grave SMITH:Syd[1] 15
w. enough to play the fool SHAK:TWE 37
w. father that knows SHAK:MERC 21
w. For saying nothing SHAK:MERC 5
w. forgive but do not forget SZASZ 7
w. man is not the man LEVI-ST 2
w. man who commands himself HORACE 73
w. man will make more BACON:F[1] 45
w. men buy them PROV 130
w. son maketh a glad father BIBLE 257
word to the w. is enough PLAU 5
wys is he that kan hymselven CHAUC 59
ye therefore w. as serpents BIBLE 407
wisely:
Be w. worldly QUAR 8
behave w. once they have exhausted EBAN 1
not w. but too well SHAK:OTH 70
W. and slow SHAK:ROM 20
wiseman: met him was Mr Worldly W. BUNYAN 4
wiser:
Be w. than other people CHESTERFIELD 1
not the w. grow POMF 2
sadder and a w. man COLERIDGE:ST 39

that they are w. than they MAUGH 13
to be guided by the w. CARLYLE:T 39
w. than the wise may err AESC 5
w. today than he was POPE 177
wisest:
clerkes been noght w. men CHAUC 72
than the w. man can answer COLTON 4
w. and the most upright man PLATO 6
w. fool in Christendom HENRI 5
W. Men Have errd MILT 285
w. of counsellors, time PERIC 6
wish: Thy own w. w. I thee SHAK:LOV 5
wishes:
all their country's w. blest COLLINS:Will 3
If w. were horses PROV 189
wishful:
great deal of w. thinking DEMOS 1
There is w. thinking in Hell LEWIS:CS 3
wit:
and a little tiny w. SHAK:KING L 39
As metaphysic w. can fly BUTLER:S[1] 8
Attic w. PLINY 4
Brevity is the soul of w. SHAK:HAM 63
fancy W. will come POPE 75
fashion a w. out of two half-wits KINN 5
full of potential wisdom and w. HUX:A 19
he shoots his w. SHAK:AS 72
his weapon w. HOPE:An 8
His w. all see-saw POPE 127
His w. invites you COWP 29
His w. was in his own power JONS 54
I had but a little w. ANON 119
idea of w. is laughing immoderately SMITH:Syd[1] 17
Impropriety is the soul of w. MAUGH 5
In thee was wyt, fredom BLIND 2
Incredulitie, the w. of Fooles CHAPMAN:G 1
let w. bear a stroke TUSS 3
loudest w. I e'er BYR 239
love takes w. away DIDE 2
mechanic part of w. ETH 3
men of w. Will condescend SWIFT 53
mingled with a little w. DRYD 87
more w. than poetry WALP:H 25
Muse gave native w. HORACE 111
nature by her mother w. SPENS 40
neither a w. in his own eyes CONG 30
neither w., nor words SHAK:JUL 57
no more w. than a Christian SHAK:TWE 3
one man's w. and all RUSS:J[2] 4
only a w. among Lords JOHNSON:S 97
Pickepurse of an other's w. SIDNEY:P 9
pleasant smooth w. AUBREY 9
rather commendation of w. BACON:F[1] 54
scintillations of your w. GOUL 1
show a ready w. all day long BALZ 12
songs provide the dull with w. MAUGH 18
spice of w. STEVENSON:RL 59
Staircase w. DIDE 3
too proud for a w. GOLDS 37
trade in courtesies and w. HERB:G 30
Universal Monarchie of w. CAREW:T 1
use my w. as a pitchfork LARK 3
Usurp the chair of w. JONS 50
watch of his w. SHAK:TEM 14
wears his w. in his belly SHAK:TRO 7
whetstone, to sharpen good w. ASCHAM 4
wine is in, the w. is out PROV 427
Wisdom and W. are little seen CHESTERFIELD 32
w. and beauty learned their trade YEATS 38
W. and Humour are no more HAD 1
w. enough to run away BUTLER:S[1] 36
w. in all languages DRYD 133
W. is Nature to advantage POPE 14
w. is out SHAK:MUCH 22
W. is the epigram for NIET 13
w. its soul COLERIDGE:ST 58
w. ; . . . made of Atalanta's heels SHAK:AS 46
w. Makes such a wound SHELLEY:PB 64
W. to persuade DAVIES:J 1
W. will shine Through DRYD 73
w. with jealous eye surveys CHURCH:C 14
W.'s a feather POPE 104
W.'s an unruly engine HERB:G 6
W.'s false mirror POPE 107
W.'s forge and fire-blast COLERIDGE:ST 64
Your w.'s too hot SHAK:LOV 4
witch: not suffer a w. to live BIBLE 105
witchcraft:
Eye of newt* SHAK:MAC 79
Liver of blaspheming* SHAK:MAC 80
no w. charm thee SHAK:CYM 17
Round about the cauldron go* SHAK:MAC 78
This only is the w. SHAK:OTH 9
witches:
know, that there are w. BROWNE:T 37
w. don't go in much for PRAT 1
witching: very w. time of night SHAK:HAM 128
with:
He that is not w. me BIBLE 411
I am w. thee, saith the Lord BIBLE 335
w. them, in some things WILDE:O 111
withdraw: thou (*Anthea*) must w. HERR 11
withdrawal: there will be no further w. MONTGOM:BL 1
wither:
Age cannot w. her SHAK:ANT 28
It needs must w. SHAK:OTH 60
w. slowly in thine arms TENNY 45
withered:
It could not wither'd be JONS 36
wither'd in my hand HERB:G 37
wither'd is the garland SHAK:ANT 58
withers: our w. are unwrung SHAK:HAM 118
within:
he never went w. COWLEY:A 1
that w. which passes show SHAK:HAM 18
There is another man w. me BROWNE:T 5
when the fight begins w. himself BROWNING:R 86
w. would fain go out DAVIES:J 4
you were w. me AUGUS 5
without:
get on quite as well w. them HUX:A 5
things I'd be better w. PARKER:D 3
w. would fain go in DAVIES:J 4
withstand: w. Barabbas now BROWNING:R 124
witness:
cam tae beir w. tae the licht BIBLE 593
on hand to w. it HOWARD:M 1
thou shalt not bear false w. BIBLE 103
witnesses:
multitude of silent w. GEO V 4
so great a cloud of w. BIBLE 557
wits:
bathing place of w. SIDNEY:P 6
Great w. are sure to madness DRYD 38
stolen his w. away DE LA M 5
Universities incline w. to sophistry BACON:F[1] 2
warming his five w. TENNY 8
wittiest: is the w. of all things HARE:J 1
witty:
Anger makes dull men w. BACON:F[1] 128
Better a w. fool SHAK:TWE 8
not only w. in myself SHAK:HEN.IV[2] 5
stumbling on something w. AUSTEN 24
wive: w. an' thrive baith in ae RAMS 3
wives:
bow to the Gods of his W. MILT 265
done their w. insult and injury STEAD 6
Fair be their w. DUNB 12
Go mad, and beat their w. CALVER 2
Like strawberry w. ELIZ I 6
man so happy in *three w.* LAMB:M 2
met a man with seven w. NURS 1
My tall dead w. BARKER:G 1
not sacks to sew up w. THACK 21
Old w.' fables BIBLE 547
others were only my w. GUIT 1
sky changes when they are w. SHAK:AS 59
w. and mothers . . . of those who do GRIM 1
w. are on hand from bridal SAIK 2
W. are young men's mistresses BACON:F[1] 85
w. in the patriarch's days HARDY:T 28
w. lie uppermost BROME:R 3
wizards: Star-led wisards MILT 4
Wodehouse:
like P.G. W. dropping Jeeves WAUGH:E 33
literature's performing flea* O'CAS 8
woe:
bitter groan of a Martyrs w. BLAKE:W 115
Can I see anothers w. BLAKE:W 25
deep, unutterable w. AYT 4
every w. a tear can BYR 27
fig for w. HEYW:J 2
Man was made for Joy & W. BLAKE:W 86
marks of w. BLAKE:W 74
pity who has felt the w. GAY 6
such a draught of w.? SHELLEY:PB 118
thurghfare ful of wo CHAUC 50
to feel another's W. POPE 156
trappings and the suits of w. SHAK:HAM 18
wo that is in mariage CHAUC 76
W. weeps out her division JONS 8
woes:
Death is the end of w. SPENS 31
her w. at midnight rise LYLY 5
Long exercised in w. HOMER 16
play the wantons with our w. SHAK:RIC.II 32
self-consumer of my w. CLARE:J 8
Spring Of W. unnumber'd HOMER 1
Whatever mitigates the w. BURNS:R 131
w. which Hope thinks infinite SHELLEY:PB 87
woke: Happy till I w. again HOUSM 29
wolf:
Every W.s & Lions howl BLAKE:W 84
grim Woolf with privy paw MILT 54
keep the w. far thence WEBSTER:J 11
like the w. on the fold BYR 39
Man is a w. to man PLAU 1
man was w. to the man VANZ 1
trusts in the tameness of a w. SHAK:KING L 52
w. also shall dwell with BIBLE 310
w. behowls the moon SHAK:MID 51
w. is at the door GILMAN 1
w. that follows SWIN 12
wolf's-bane: W., tight-rooted KEATS 94
wolves:
herded w., bold only SHELLEY:PB 116
hireling w. whose gospel MILT 98
howling of Irish w. SHAK:AS 66
precipice in front, w. behind ERAS 2
there were w. in Wales THOMAS:D 40
they are ravening w. BIBLE 401
they will eat like w. SHAK:HEN.V 24
W. tear out his heart DONNE 13
woman:
As a single w. with a child EKL 1
as far as one w. can forgive GAY 14
as old as the w. he feels MARX:G 25
better to be first with an ugly w. BUCK 1
bettre than a good womman? CHAUC 55
body of a weak and feeble w. ELIZ I 3
but a w.'s reason SHAK:TWO 3
cabbage nor a w. for five years GUNN:J 2
called a w. in my own house WAUGH:E 25
callin' a young 'ooman a Wenus DICKENS 28
Can a w.'s tender care COWP 7
can't step up and kill a w. BENCH 3
civil and obliging young w. AUSTEN 5
clever w. has millions of born enemies EBNER 1
constancy to a bad, ugly w. BYR 147
created w. in the image LAVER 1
damnable, deceitful w. OTWAY 3
dead w. bites not GRAY:P 1
dear, deluding w. BURNS:R 43
delightful to be a w. SCHREIN 2
dispell'd when a w. appears GAY 20
easier ways to destroy a w. FRENCH 1
educate a w. you educate MACIVER 1
equal dominion is given to w. STANTON:El 3
ever let a w. in my life LERN 3
Every w. knows that BARRIE 13
every w. should marry DISR:B 40
excellent thing in w. SHAK:KING L 84
fair defect of Nature* MILT 254
fat white w. whom nobody CORNFORD:Fran 1
fellow has got himself another w. FAIRBAIRN:N 2
female w. is one of the greatest WARD:A 6
foiled by w.'s arts BLAKE:W 7
for the sake of such a w. HOMER 6
gentle w., dare SOUTHEY 12
God made w. for the man TENNY 90
good thing when it an't a w.'s DICKENS 13
good w. if I had five thousand THACK 10
greatest glory of a w. PERIC 5
growing up into a pretty w. AUSTEN 32
harm to a w.'s honour than secret CERV 20
hit a w. with his hat on ALLEN:F 2
honest w. and a broken leg CERV 14
I grant I am a w. SHAK:JUL 28
I will take some savage w. TENNY 84
ideal w. to put on a pedestal NORM 1

inconstant w. GAY 33
it ruins a w.'s reputation COLETTE 4
just like a w. DYL 8
keep up with a young 'ooman o' large property DICKENS 45
know a w. until you've met MAIL 2
know the *mind* of a w. is to LAWR:DH 41
leader of the enterprise a w. VIRGIL 39
let not me play a w. SHAK:MID 8
like a w. scorn'd CONG 34
little w. who wrote the book LINC 29
Look for the w. DUMAS:A[P] 2
Love a w.? You're an ass ROCHES 8
love and good company improves a w. FARQ 17
lovely w. in a rural spot HUNT:L 1
lovely w. stoops to folly ELIOT:TS 47
lovely w. stoops to folly GOLDS 18
made he a w. BIBLE 13
make a man a w. PEMB:2nd Earl 1
make a w. look like a ruin WILDE:O 56
man he must go with a w. KIP 74
man is more interested in a w. DIET 3
more than w. to be wise MOORE:T 1
most beautiful w. I've ever seen MARX:G 1
most pernicious w. SHAK:HAM 52
nakedness of w. is the work BLAKE:W 41
Nature's agreeable blunders* COWLEY:H 1
never be by W. lovd BLAKE:W 85
No more but e'en a w. SHAK:ANT 59
no w. . . . beauty without a fortune FARQ 13
No w. can call herself free SANG 1
no w. is virtuous who does not WILLIAMS:WC 10
No where Lives a w. true DONNE 57
none of w. born SHAK:MAC 82
not love wine, w. and song LUTHER 9
nothing Of w. in me SHAK:ANT 68
nurse, a piece of furniture, a w. TOLS:S 2
Obedience is w.'s earthly duty SCHILL 5
Once a w. has given you her heart VANB 2
One is not born a w. BEAUV 2
One w. and two men YEATS 28
opinion is about a w. JAMES:H 9
perfect w., nobly plann'd WORDS:W 89
prolonged slavery of w. STANTON:El 4
promote a W. to bear rule KNOX:J 2
represented the modern American w. MCCARTHY:M 3
she is a w. RACINE 9
she shall be called W. BIBLE 14
show a w. when he loves her BROWNING:R 141
silliest w. can manage a clever KIP 1
So unto the man is w. LONGFEL 22
softening in the presence of a w. BYR 248
support of the w. I love EDWARD VIII 2
that tastes w., ruin meets GAY 24
There shone one w. SWIN 46
they done the old w. in SHAW 109
think my self a very bad w. ADDIS 11
Thou large-brained w. BROWNING:EB 7
thought does not become a young w. SHERIDAN:RB 3
to a w., but a kind of ghost DONNE 29
very honest w., but SHAK:ANT 70
very ordinary little w. BETJ 15
wait long for a w. worthy GORKY 1
wants a w. of fifty to be sweet LAST 1
wasn't a w. who betrayed Jesus CARSWELL 1
What a selfish w. CHURCH:JJ 1
What does a w. want? FREUD:S 6
what is w.? COWLEY:H 1
what's a play without a w. KYD 7
When a w. behaves like a man EVANS:E 1
Who can find a virtuous w.? BIBLE 276
Who takes a w. must GAY 24
wickedness of a w. BIBLE 368
Wilt thou have this W. PRAY 83
w. accepted cooking as a chore POST 2
w. alone, can venture to commit THACK 20
w., and therefore to be won SHAK:HEN.VI[1] 4
w. as a beautiful, romantic animal ADDIS 29
w. as old as she looks COLLINS:Mor 1
w. be more like a man? LERN 6
w. becomes the extension of a man's GREER 8
w. can be stiff and proud YEATS 95
w. can hardly ever choose ELIOT:G 27
w. can only become a man's friend CHEK 6
w. colour'd ill SHAK:SON 60
w. dictates before marriage ELIOT:G 30
w. for the hearth TENNY 113
w. gives to the State a support ANON 204
w. governs America MADAR 1
w. had a bottom of good sense JOHNSON:S 222
w. had better show more AUSTEN 79
W. has been the great unpaid STANTON:El 7
W. has haunted me these two KEATS 140
w. has her way HOLMES:OW 10
w. I was, the w. I am, and the w. EDMOND 1
W.! in our hours of ease SCOTT:W 29
w. is a dish for the gods SHAK:ANT 71
w. is a foreign land PATMO 4
W. is always a fickle VIRGIL 61
w. is always a w. WOLLST 8
W. is at heart a rake POPE 137
w. is his game TENNY 112
w. is infallibly to be gained CHESTERFIELD 26
w. is only a w. KIP 31
w. is so hard upon the w. TENNY 115
w. is the worst GRANVILLE 4
w., let her be as good ELIOT:G 34
w.! lovely w. OTWAY 4
w. mov'd is like a fountain SHAK:TAM 14
w. must wear chains FARQ 12
w. of easy virtue and a proved HAILS 1
w. of education bought things VANB 5
w. of letters I fight for my kind DWO 4
w. of loving BAUD 6
w. of mean understanding AUSTEN 13
w. oweth to her husband SHAK:TAM 16
w., partly brave and partly RICH 2
w., rules us still MOORE:T 26
W. sat, in unwomanly rags HOOD 19
w. seldom asks advice before ADDIS 24
w. should be informed MOLIERE 26
w. should still be forced to bear DUNC 2
w. that deliberates is lost ADDIS 9
w. that was a brute SHELLEY:PB 20
w. that you forsake her KIP 120
w. to obey TENNY 113
w. twenty years to make a man ROWL:H 2
w. wakes to love TENNY 246
W. was God's *second* mistake NIET 21
w. well reputed SHAK:JUL 28
w. who did not care KIP 94
w. who has only had one LA ROCHE 11
w. who is really kind to dogs BEERB 9
w. who lives for others LEWIS:CS 5
w. whose troubles are greater ALG 2
w. will always sacrifice herself MAUGH 7
W. will be the last thing civilized MERED:G 1
w. with the heart TENNY 113
w. with the West COLERIDGE:M 3
w. won or w. lost? YEATS 76
W.'s at best a Contradiction POPE 141
w.'s business to get married SHAW 36
w.'s desire is rarely other COLERIDGE:ST 85
W.'s faith, and w.'s trust SCOTT:W 63
w.'s friendship ever ends in GAY 8
w.'s grief is like a summer storm BAILLIE 2
w.'s is often her rack THURB 7
W.'s mind oft' shifts GAY 7
w.'s place is in the home PROV 434
w.'s preaching is like a dog's JOHNSON:S 126
W.'s virtue is man's greatest invention SKIN:CO 1
w.'s whole existence BYR 171
w.'s whole life is a history IRV 1
w.'s work is never done PROV 435
wrapp'd in a w.'s hide SHAK:HEN.VI[3] 1

womanhood:
Heroic w. LONGFEL 24
W. and childhood fleet LONGFEL 8
W. is the great fact STANTON:El 7

womanized: drunk too much or w. too much BROWN:Geor 1

womankind:
packs off its w. SHAW 44
think better of W. than to suppose KEATS 138
thinks the worst he can of w. HOME 2

womb:
cloistered in thy dear w. DONNE 79
from his mother's w. Untimely SHAK:MAC 115
fruit of thy w., Jesus ANON 160, 37
her w. convey sterility SHAK:KING L 20
in My virgin w. ha'e met MACDIAR 9
In the dark w. where MASE 12
Making their tomb the w. SHAK:SON 37
slayeth the child in the w. POUND 41
w. of uncreated night MILT 153

wombat: fat-necked w. headed KELLY:N 1

wombs: w. the tiring houses be GIBBONS:O 2

women:
after the manner of w. BIBLE 49
All generations of w. KEES 1
ambassadors of freedom to w. PANK:C 3
American w. are kept from growing to FRIEDAN 1
apologise to Irish w. CLARE:A 3
As the weird w. promis'd SHAK:MAC 60
asham'd that w. are so simple SHAK:TAM 17
because w. have Cancers KEATS 137
Blessed art thou among w. ANON 160
but say so of w. too BYR 246
by bad W. been deceiv'd MILT 285
Certain w. should be struck COWARD 5
claim our right as w. PANK:C 2
clerkes preise wommen but a lite CHAUC 35
dotages of human kind, wine and w. BURTON:Ro 10
emancipation of w. is practically the greatest KEY:E 1
English w. conceal their feelings WILDE:O 53
excluded lunatics, gays and w. MORTIM 2
experience of w. which extends DOYLE:AC 5
extension of all w.'s privileges FOUR 1
Gave w. dreams YEATS 120
gets off with w. because he can't LEHMANN 1
grey-haired w. may quietly take over STEINEM 2
half fish and half w. LLOSA 1
Half the sorrows of w. ELIOT:G 23
hands of men who don't like w. CHANEL 4
happiest w. ELIOT:G 18
hardly any w. at all AUSTEN 62
I learned about w. from 'er KIP 84
I must have w. GAY 21
in favour of w.'s success STEAD 7
keeping w. in a state of ignorance KNOX:V 1
knew how w. pass the time HENRY:O 2
know w., or they would be harder TROLL 15
learn about w. from me KIP 85
lies in men's attitude to w. BRITT 2
love of w.! it is known BYR 182
Married w. are kept w. SMITH:LP 6
men and w. are created equal STANTON:El 1
men and w. should unite STEAD 7
men, w., and clergymen SMITH:Syd[1] 25
Monstrous Regiment of W. KNOX:J 1
more attentive to w. of rank STANTON:El 5
Most w. have no Characters POPE 130
Most w. turn to salt MANS:K 8
Music and w. I cannot but PEPYS 17
no comradeship between men and w. LAWR:DH 3
no social differences – till w. come WELLS:HG 4
old w. (of both sexes) STERNE 24
On a thousand business w. BETJ 22
One of the finest w. that ever walked WEST:M 3
only advantage w. have over men RHYS 3
Other w. cloy The appetites SHAK:ANT 28
pretty w. to deserve them AUSTEN 31
proclaiming that w. are brighter LOOS 10
proper function of w. ELIOT:G 20
referendum on w.'s access to information CLARE:A 3
saluting strange w. NASH 24
simply sent champagne and w. O'ROUR 2
snare in which the feet of w. ADAMS:H 1
Some w.'ll stay in a man's memory KIP 29
something more interesting than w. WALLACE:E 1
souls of w. are so small BUTLER:S[1] 40
stir up the zeal of w. MILL 32
sung w. in three cities POUND 1
Their tricks an' craft* BURNS:R 25
then God help all w. CAMPBELL:Mrs P 1
Though w. are angels BYR 3
untun'd golden strings all w. MARLOWE 48
vegetable creep of w.'s liberation GREER 4
wage no war with w. SOUTHEY 11
War between Men and W. THURB 15
Were't not for gold and w. TOUR 1

What are young w. made of? NURS 83
What man knows anything of w.? KENNELLY 2
Why are w. . . . so much more interesting WOOLF:V 11
Why join a w.'s group to lobby TONER 1
Why need the other w. know BROWNING:R 75
wicked folly of 'W.'s Rights' VICT 4
wimmen, dey does de talkin' HARRIS:JC 14
with w. has *one* solution NIET 6
With w. the heart argues ARNOLD:M 38
w. adore failures WILDE:O 58
w. and care and trouble WARD:N 1
W. and elephants never forget SAKI 8
W. and Horses and Power and War KIP 40
w. are a sex by themselves BEERB 2
W. are angels, wooing SHAK:TRO 2
w. are born so perverse BRIDGES:R 12
W. are false in countries SAINT-P 1
w. are glad that they have been asked OSB:J 4
W. are like the Arts DONNE 4
W. are like tricks CONG 28
W. are much more like each other CHESTERFIELD 23
w. are victims of external impositions BUTT 1
w. as a servant class PANK:E 4
W. at marriage move BERNARD:Jes 1
w. become like their mothers WILDE:O 88
w. cannot escape it GIBBONS:S 4
W. . . . care fifty times more BAGE 13
W. complain about sex LANDERS 1
W. dissemble their Passions better STEELE 1
w. do in men require? BLAKE:W 60
W. do not find it difficult MACKEN 3
w. do they must do twice WHITTON 1
W. don't forgive failure CHEK 3
w. especially, owe to Shakespeare TERRY 1
w. for long miserable ones RAMEY 1
w. for the most part have time WAUGH:A 2
w. go wrong, men go WEST:M 13
W. had always fought for men PANK:E 5
W. hate a debt BROWNING:R 127
W. have always been the guardians WOLFF 1
w. have always faced sexual facts MACKEN 4
W. . . . have never separated sex NIN 1
W. have no surnames LAUR:M 2
w. making a nuisance WAUGH:A 3
w. . . . merely adored WILDE:O 75
w. Must be half-workers? SHAK:CYM 5
W. must come off the pedestal RHON 1
w. must weep KINGSLEY:C 15
W. never have young minds DELAN 1
W. never look so well as SURT 15
'w. of genius' require very special JEWS 1
w. pushing their husbands along DEWAR 1
W. represent the triumph of matter WILDE:O 30
w. set out to try to change a man DIET 5
w. shall put on altogether new TROLL 21
W. should talk an hour BEAUMO 5
W. tell men things that DAVIES:R 5
w. their rights ANTH 1
w. themselves help to make laws ANTH 2
W., then, are only children CHESTERFIELD 16
w. to change their shapes SHAK:TWO 15
W. Wair out of the Ship CLARK:R 1
w. walk in public processions WHITMAN 20
W. want mediocre men MEAD 2
W. what they are BRADST 2
W., when nothing else MILT 265
w. who are severe OSB:J 2
w. who haunted you were not MULK 1
W. who love the same man BEERB 8
W. would rather be right NASH 17
w.'s attitude to themselves BRITT 2
w.'s rights has been largely won THATCH:M 13
Wommen desiren to have sovereynetee CHAUC 88
Wommen, of kynde, desiren libertee CHAUC 36
You are pictures out a-doors* SHAK:OTH 19
You should be w. SHAK:MAC 8
won:
gaily you w. BETJ 20
game is done! I've w. COLERIDGE:ST 21
Greetings, we have w. PHEI 1
Human reason w. KHRU 6
She is w.! we are gone SCOTT:W 23
some say that they wan MCLENN 1
Things w. are done SHAK:TRO 2
which hail'd the wretch who w. BYR 109
wonder:
all the w. that would be TENNY 79
boneless w. sitting on the Treasury Bench CHURCH:W 7
Have eyes to w. SHAK:SON 49
How I w. what you're at CARROLL 18
moon-washed apples of w. DRINK 1
Philosophy is the product of w. WHITEHEAD 4
still the w. grew GOLDS 29
w. and wild desire BROWNING:R 194
w. of an hour BYR 62
w. to myself a lot MILNE 15
wonderful:
most w. w. SHAK:AS 41
name shall be called W. BIBLE 308
none more w. than man SOPH 3
right place they are w. FRANKLIN:M 3
with any thing that is w. CONG 67
w. things for other people KERR:Jea 1
wonders:
all w. in one sight CRASH 13
his w. in the deep BIBLE 234
Signs are taken for w. ELIOT:TS 22
We carry within us the w. BROWNE:T 10
w. of the western world SYNGE 1
W. will never cease DUDL 1
Wongs: two W. do not make a White CALWELL 1
woo:
April when they w. SHAK:AS 59
Come, w. me SHAK:AS 56
maids doe woe the Batchelors BROME:R 3
w. a fair young maid ANON 31
w. her with too slavish knees KEATS 90
wood:
beyond some wicked w. WALLACE-C 1
changed into blocks of w. BROWNING:R 31
dark impenetrable w. SCOTT:W 32
dreadful w. Of conscious evil AUD 31
Heap on more w. SCOTT:W 24
hew w. than be a king CHARLES X 1
intellectual and don't carry w. SCHWEITZ 1
let them be hewers of w. BIBLE 129
old w. burn brightest WEBSTER:J 1
One chops the w., the other PROV 308
One impulse from a vernal w. WORDS:W 17
set out to plant a w. SWIFT 54
soft w. staying bright LOWELL:R 9
unseen Genius of the W. MILT 88
What w. a cudgel's of by th' blow BUTLER:S[1] 21
w.'s in trouble HOUSM 20
You are not w. SHAK:JUL 53
wood-notes: Warbles his native W. wilde MILT 74
woodbine:
luscious w SHAK:MID 20
well-attir'd W. MILT 55
w. spices are wafted TENNY 215
woodcock:
as a w., to mine own springe SHAK:HAM 195
Spirits of well-shot w. BETJ 4
woodcocks: springes to catch w. SHAK:HAM 32
woodland: bit of w. beside HORACE 71
woodman: W., spare that tree MORRIS:GP 1
woods:
are the w. for me? BLUN 3
but the w. of complaining MORRIS:W 7
Enter these enchanted w. MERED:G 34
fresh W. and Pastures new MILT 60
gods have lived in the w. VIRGIL 6
green-rob'd senators of mighty w. KEATS 48
in these wilde W. forlorn? MILT 249
oozy w. which wear SHELLEY:PB 43
pleasure in the pathless w. BYR 116
there is a spirit in the w. WORDS:W 26
through the Wet Wild W. KIP 28
was once a road through the w. KIP 131
We'll to the w. no more HOUSM 30
When the green w. laugh BLAKE:W 26
w. are lovely, dark FROST:R 7
w. be worthy of a consul VIRGIL 11
w. decay and fall TENNY 45
w. have no voice MORRIS:W 7
w. shall to me answer SPENS 12
woodshed: Something nasty in the w. GIBBONS:S 1
woodspurge: w. has a cup of three ROSSET:DG 6
woodworm: w. obligingly held hands DU MAU:D 2
woof: broken the w. of my tent's SHELLEY:PB 55
wooing:
all the trouble of w. AUBREY 6
time I've lost in w. MOORE:T 15
women are angels, w. SHAK:TRO 2
w. mind shall be express'd SHAK:LOV 22
wool:
all fur and w. THOMAS:D 36
go for w. and come back empty-handed? CERV 2
Have you any w.? NURS 2
If such as came for w. BROWNING:R 177
w. comes not to market POUND 39
Woolf, Virginia:
beautiful little knitter* SITWELL:E 13
Who's Afraid of V.W.? ALBEE 1
woollen: Odious! in w. POPE 115
Woolworth: finest that W.'s could sell EDGAR 1
Woolworths: like paying a visit to W. BEVAN 5
word:
be ye doers of the w. BIBLE 562
by every w. that proceedeth BIBLE 123, 380
By water and the w. STONE:SJ 1
common w. exact without vulgarity ELIOT:TS 123
Englishman's w. is his bond PROV 96
every w. stabs SHAK:MUCH 7
flowering in a lonely w. TENNY 290
fool can play upon the w. SHAK:MERC 38
For one w. a man is often CONF 24
he was but a w. and a blow BUNYAN 10
hear the w. of the Lord BIBLE 347
I kept my w. DE LA M 7
In the beginning was the W. BIBLE 471
In the beginning was the W. ELIOT:TS 26
In the beginning was the W. MASS 22
make the written w. as unlike CONNOLLY:C 10
makes a familiar w. new HORACE 102
making the w. flesh SHAFF 3
Many a true w. is spoken PROV 264
many a w., at random spoken SCOTT:W 52
nat a w. wol he faille CHAUC 60
never been known to use a w. FAULK 3
No man should break his w. of honour BULG 1
no such w. As – *fail* BULWER 2
No w. from thee can fruitless TWELLS 2
not the w. because we have so much ARNOLD:M 59
one Peculiar w. LANDOR 11
Proud w. you never spoke LANDOR 10
Shepherd I take thy w. MILT 28
sincere milk of the w. BIBLE 566
suffer and die without a w. VIGNY 4
surprised to be taken at his w. DE GAU 8
thy true and lively W. PRAY 70
Thy w. is a lamp unto BIBLE 238
time lies in one little w. SHAK:RIC.II 8
torture one poor w. DRYD 65
two meanings packed up into one w. CARROLL 69
We had no w. to say WILDE:O 114
When *I* use a w. CARROLL 67
Woord is but wynd LYD 4
w. appears at just GOET 16
w. bites like a fish SPEND 12
w. even may be a spark SHELLEY:PB 163
w. is as good as his bond PROV 175
w. is the Verb HUGO 3
w. no man relies on ROCHES 13
w. once out cannot be recalled HORACE 116
w. to the wise is enough PLAU 5
W. was God BIBLE 471
W. was God MASS 22
W. was made flesh BIBLE 473
W. WAS MADE FLESH MASS 23
w. which meant both 'he' and 'she' MILNE 19
w. within a w. ELIOT:TS 22
word processor: No one needs a w.p. if he has DAVIES:R 7
words:
Actions speak louder than w. PROV 3
All w., And no performance MASSIN 6

alms-basket of w. SHAK:LOV 19
barren superfluity of w. GARTH 1
Be not the slave of W. CARLYLE:T 4
belief that w. have a meaning OGDEN 1
best w. in the best COLERIDGE:ST 84
big w. for little matters JOHNSON:S 130
Bright is the ring of w. STEVENSON:RL 65
but w. are w. SHAK:OTH 12
Choice w., and measured phrase WORDS:W 85
common, little, easy w. WESLEY:J 8
danger as long, smooth w. BUCK 3
Don't listen to their w. EINS 3
dressing old w. new SHAK:SON 34
empty w. of a dream BRIDGES:R 4
Fine w. and an insinuating CONF 1
Fine w. butter no parsnips PROV 120
fine w. butter no parsnips SCOTT:W 83
foreign w. pronounced wrongly TUCHOL 7
frank w. in our respective languages COOK:P 1
get as many w. into the last ANON 108
glotoun of wordes LANGLAND 4
He w. me, girls SHAK:ANT 65
hear what comfortable w. PRAY 72
I fear those big w. JOYCE:J 15
I hate false w. LANDOR 21
ill and unfit choice of w. BACON:F[1] 20
Immodest w. admit no defence ROSCOM 2
In two w.: im possible GOLDWYN 13
know the ten-dollar w. HEMINGWAY 13
knowing the force of w. CONF 15
large confusing w. AUD 32
learn the use of living w. DE LA M 22
lets thy w. be few BIBLE 282
little w. of love CARNEY 2
long list of unmentionable w. CLARK:M 1
long w. Bother me MILNE 11
matter decocted into a few w. FULLER:T[1] 10
Melting melodious w. HERR 13
Men of few w. SHAK:HEN.V 22
misused w. generate misleading thoughts SPENCER:H 8
my w. among mankind SHELLEY:PB 46
my w. are my own CHARLES II 8
my w. shall not pass away BIBLE 429
not Sunday-school w. TWAIN 8
of all w. of tongue HARTE 1
palm-oil with which w. are eaten ACHEBE 2
polite meaningless w. YEATS 41
Proper w. in proper places SWIFT 24
put the w. down and push WAUGH:E 38
set a chime of w. SMITH:LP 16
simpler and better w. HEMINGWAY 13
soups, not on fine w. MOLIERE 28
such w. as are poisonous HOLMES:OW 12
Thanks to w., we have been HUX:A 41
threw w. like stones SPEND 3
'Twas throwing w. away WORDS:W 22
two narrow w., *Hic jacet* RALE 10
two w. have undone the world SELD 1
upleasant'st w. That ever SHAK:MERC 37
use w. only to disguise VOLT 17
utter confused w. BAUD 3
very good w. for the lips DICKENS 196
who adds 'in other w.' MORLEY:R 1
Who danced on a plume of w. DAY LEWIS 6
Winged w. HOMER 3
w. a foot and a half long HORACE 105
W. are . . . the most powerful drug KIP 156
W. are also actions EMER 29
w. are but the signs of ideas JOHNSON:S 6
W. are like leaves POPE 15
W. are men's daughters MADDEN 1
W. are physic AESC 7
w. are quick and vain SHELLEY:PB 68
w. are the daughters of the earth JOHNSON:S 6
W. are wise men's counters HOBB 4
w. but wind BUTLER:S[1] 24
w. cloath'd in reason's MILT 155
w. divide and rend SWIN 17
w. in their best order COLERIDGE:ST 84
w. left unsaid and deeds STOWE 5
w., like Nature, half reveal TENNY 129
w. . . . like so many nimble MILT 307
W. may be false and full SHADWE 1
w. move slowly POPE 21
w. never seen in each other's LODGE:D 5
w. of a dead man AUD 37
w. of learned length GOLDS 29
w. of Mercury are harsh SHAK:LOV 26
W. of the fragrant portals STEVENS 10
w. once spoke can never ROSCOM 1
W. strain, Crack ELIOT:TS 91
w. that are only fit for the Bible FRY:C 9
W. to the heat of deeds SHAK:MAC 34
w. very little she heeded PRIOR 2
w. which have now dropped HORACE 103
w. will never hurt me PROV 353
w. without knowledge? BIBLE 191
W. without thoughts never SHAK:HAM 133
W., w., mere w. SHAK:TRO 25
W. w. or I shall burst FARQ 5
W., w., w. SHAK:HAM 72
wrestle With w. and meanings ELIOT:TS 93
write four w., I shall strike BOIL 1
You English w. THOMAS:E 9
your w. before you speak GRAVES:R 2
Wordsworth: hand up Dorothy W.'s skirt COREN 1

Wordsworth, William:
He spoke, and loosed* ARNOLD:M 8
His expression may often* ARNOLD:M 83
Let simple W. chime BYR 16
Mr W. is never interrupted WORDS:M 1
W., both are thine STEPHEN:JK 2
W. drunk, and Porson sober HOUSM 58
W. – stupendous genius BYR 252
wore: w. Enough for modesty BUCHANAN 3
work:
All Nature seems at w. COLERIDGE:ST 66
All out of w. SHAK:HEN.V 5
All w. and no play PROV 16
apportioning of wages to w. CARLYLE:T 51
believe that the w. which you are WEBB:DA 1
Blessed is he who has found his w. CARLYLE:T 52
certainty lay, in everyday w. CAMUS 5
completed a w., which neither OSB:J 24
day's w. is a day's w. SHAW 1
days when w. was scrappy CHESTERTON 26
devil finds w. for idle hands PROV 68
dirty w. for the rest RUSKIN 19
do the devil's w. for nothing FIELDING 12
Do the w. that's nearest KINGSLEY:C 18
done to find them w. EDWARD VIII 3
Every man's w. . . . is always a portrait BUTLER:S[2] 14
except by dint of hard w. PAVLO 2
fact that one does not w. BRAS 1
for a man life means w. CHURCH:JJ 3
form rebellious to w. GAUT 1
good idea but it won't w. ROGERS:W 6
Gung Ho W. Together ALLEY 1
Habit of w. is growing BENNETT:Ar 10
he can't w. any faster NURS 64
I haven't had time to w. KERO 1
I like w.; it fascinates me JEROME:JK 7
If any would not w. BIBLE 546
If you don't w., you die KIP 150
interest in my w. when I don't like it? BACON:F[2] 1
Irish hate w. KENNELLY 1
Let us w. without reasoning VOLT 15
little w., a little play DU MAU:G 2
Look at the end of w. BROWNING:R 131
Many hands make light w. PROV 265
Measure not the w., Until BROWNING:EB 18
men must w. KINGSLEY:C 15
more we w. and the less KIP 115
most of my w. sitting down BENCH 8
must hate to w. for a living ROWL:H 1
My W. is done ANON 139
no one shall w. for money KIP 89
no w., no money PROV 291
not breed one w. that wakes HOPK:GM 31
Nothing to do but w. KING:B 1
Old Kaspar's w. was done SOUTHEY 1
poor pay, and easy w. LOND 2
prejudice against w. CHEK 8
put a man out of w. for a day KEYN 11
say hard w. never hurt REAG 12
Six Days' w., a World MILT 228
stomach sets us to w. ELIOT:G 28
strive on to finish the w. LINC 13
That do no w. to-day SHAK:HEN.V 37
that one's w. is terribly important RUSS:B 31
their w. continueth KIP 98
there is always w. LOWELL:JR 1
To live is to w. KENNELLY 1
To w. my mind SHAK:SON 10
unable to find w., unemployment results HOOV 6
volume of w. were to increase PARKIN 2
When nature has w. to be done EMER 91
when no man can w. BIBLE 482
who lives by his own w. COLLINGWOOD:RG 1
woman's w. is never done PROV 435
words of counsel – w., w., w. BISM 8
W. apace, apace DEK 2
w. conquered everything VIRGIL 22
W. consists of whatever TWAIN 6
W. expands so as to fill PARKIN 1
W., for the night is coming COG 1
w. hard at w. worth doing ROOS:T 4
w. i' th' earth so fast? SHAK:HAM 55
W. is much more fun COWARD 36
W. is prayer ANON 212
W. is the curse of the drinking WILDE:O 128
W. is the grand cure CARLYLE:T 62
W. keeps away those three VOLT 14
w. of some noble note TENNY 55
W. should begin with wine NEIL 4
w. together for good to them BIBLE 512
W. without hope COLERIDGE:ST 67
w., w. till we die LEWIS:CS 7
You will do your w. on water KIP 54
your w. shall be rewarded BIBLE 176
yourself a great w. of nature WHIST 6
worked:
men that w. for England CHESTERTON 27
w. my way up from nothing MARX:G 4
workers:
business from one's fellow w. YEATS 146
men the w. TENNY 79
w. of the country, are our friends SHINWELL 1
W. of the world, unite MARX:K/ENG 3
workhouse:
Christmas Day in the W. SIMS 1
woman's w. SHAW 66
working:
every one will be w. CHEK 8
for the joy of w. KIP 89
spare time and in his w. GILL 1
Worchyng and wandyring as LANGLAND 3
w. about six weeks in a year THOREAU 13
w. is her holiday CERV 14
working-class:
being in the w. is all about WRAN 1
w. which, raw and half-developed ARNOLD:M 69
working class: w.c. can kiss my arse ANON 265
working classes:
w.c. other than as grotesque WAUGH:E 32
wept for the sad lot of the w.c. LIND:N 2
working-day: full of briers is this w. world SHAK:AS 8
working-days: might have another for w. SHAK:MUCH 9
working-house: w. of thought SHAK:HEN.V 42
working man: that w.m.'s paradise KINGSLEY:H 1
workings: like w. of one mind WORDS:W 156
workman: bad w. always blames PROV 27
workmanship:
w. that reconciles Discordant WORDS:W 146
w. triumphed over the material OSB:J 18
works:
all the w. of the Lord BIBLE 606
all ye W. of the Lord PRAY 12
Faith without w. is dead BIBLE 563
Frank Sargeson w. in the mornings SARGESON 2
into my w. is my talent WILDE:O 124
Look on my w. SHELLEY:PB 22
shortest w. are always FONTAINE 9
W. done least rapidly BROWNING:R 138
workshop:
England to be the w. of the world DISR:B 52
other nation may be its w. CHAMBERLAIN:J 1
world:
A foutra for the w. SHAK:HEN.IV[2] 50
all the w. and his wife ANST 1
all the w. as my parish WESLEY:J 3
all the w. in ev'ry corner HERB:G 24
All the w. is queer OWEN:Rob 1
All the w. loves a lover PROV 15
all the w. were paper ANON 71

All the w.'s a stage SHAK:AS 34
All's right with the w. BROWNING:R 9
as good be out of the w. CIB 1
bestride the narrow w. SHAK:JUL 11
But in the very w. WORDS:W 160
but the w., the flesh, and the devil MURRAY:D 1
challenge this w. in arms EISEN 3
dry a cinder this w. DONNE 72
end of the w., and Melbourne sure is JILL 1
fals w. is but transitory DUNB 8
fled From this vile w. SHAK:SON 32
glad one loves His w. BROWNING:R 10
gleams of a remoter w. SHELLEY:PB 15
Go ye into all the w. BIBLE 446
God so loved the w. BIBLE 477
great w. Shall so wear out SHAK:KING L 68
had my w. as in my tyme CHAUC 79
Half the w. is laughing at the other GRACIAN 2
happens in the next w. to one PEREL 5
I do not love this w. UNA 1
I have not loved the w. BYR 94
I never have sought the w. JOHNSON:S 231
if he shall gain the whole w. BIBLE 418
If the w. should crack HORACE 32
In a w. I never made HOUSM 33
In search of this new W. MILT 160
In the morning of the w. BROWNING:R 11
in verse that the w. moved HARDY:T 76
it's a jolly strange w. BENNETT:Ar 5
It's a small w. PROV 209
know the W., not love her YOUNG:E 17
knowledge of the w. is only to be CHESTERFIELD 2
Let the great w. spin TENNY 87
let the w. slide HEYW:J 2
little w. made cunningly DONNE 81
lost the w. for love DRYD 124
Love makes the w. go round PROV 252
love that makes the w. go round CARROLL 24
Mad W., My Masters BRET 4
made the w. ugly and bad NIET 17
make a hell of this w. BECKF 2
Man is one w., and hath Another HERB:G 35
march of the retreating w. OWEN:W 13
mighty w. Of eye, and ear WORDS:W 9
My country is the w. PAINE 7
nature makes the whole w. kin SHAK:TRO 16
need of a w. of men BROWNING:R 62
need to create an alternative w. FOW 2
new w. demands a new political TOC 2
new w. may be safer DONNE 73
O brave new w. SHAK:TEM 32
O w.! O life! O time! SHELLEY:PB 136
one to face the w. with BROWNING:R 141
one way of coming into the w. SWIFT 4
only places to learn the w. CHESTERFIELD 5
only saved the w. CHESTERTON 28
organization that conquered the w. BARTON 1
Our country is the w. GARRIS 2
Our ingress into the world LONGFEL 32
out of the w. with their feet BROWNE:T 51
preposterous pig of a w. YEATS 80
quiet limit of the w. TENNY 45
re-invent the w. BARTH:J 1
remember of this unstable w. MALORY 6
responsible for such an absurd w. DUH 1
Ring'd with the azure w. TENNY 186
rising w. of waters dark MILT 176
roll of the w. eastward HARDY:T 51
same the whole w. over ANON 38
secure amidst a falling w. ADDIS 38
see a W. in a Grain of Sand BLAKE:W 82
see the w. as one GILMORE 2
seek a newer w. TENNY 55
seek the empty w. again? BRONTE:E 5
setting the w. to rights MOLIERE 14
shows how small the w. is GROS 2
Six Days' work, a W. MILT 228
support the w. KAF 10
take thought for the whole w. LAWR:DH 4
takes all sorts to make a w. PROV 211
Ten Days that Shook the W. REED:Joh 1
There is a w. elsewhere SHAK:COR 11
There is no other w. EMER 80
There lies that solid w. AUD 30
These laid the w. away BROOKE 19
This gewgaw w. DRYD 28
This is a puzzling w. ELIOT:G 15
This is the way the w. ends ELIOT:TS 59
this little w. SHAK:RIC.II 17
This w. is bad enough CLOUGH 22
This w. nys but a thurghfare CHAUC 50
This w.'s no blot for us BROWNING:R 116
this w.'s spent DONNE 71
Thus runs the w. away SHAK:HAM 121
tied the w. in a tether SWIN 1
'Tis a mad w. TAYL:Jo 1
To save your w. you asked AUD 52
Top of the w. CAGNEY 1
warm kind w. is all I know CORY 2
What is the w., O soldiers? DE LA M 2
What is this w.? CHAUC 49
when all the w. is young KINGSLEY:C 19
whole w. is not sufficient QUAR 5
w. and its ways BROWNING:R 152
w. and love were young RALE 1
W. 'as got me snouted DENNIS:CJ 1
W. be worth thy winning DRYD 109
w. breaks everyone HEMINGWAY 1
w. can never fill COWP 3
w. forgetting POPE 63
w. gives way and dies MACNEICE 9
w. go well with thee ANON 46
w. has grown grey SWIN 35
w. is a beautiful place FERL 1
w. is a bundle of hay BYR 137
w. is a fine place HEMINGWAY 8
w. is an old woman CARLYLE:T 8
w. is beyond my understanding STEVENS 3
w. is but a small parenthesis BROWNE:T 65
w. is charged with the grandeur HOPK:GM 5
W. is crazier and more MACNEICE 1
w. is disgracefully managed FIRB 1
w. is too much with us WORDS:W 104
w. is weary of the past SHELLEY:PB 158
w. may end to-night? BROWNING:R 129
w. may talk of hereafter COLLINGWOOD:Ad 1
w. must be peopled SHAK:MUCH 16
W. owes me a living DISN 1
w. shall end when I forget SWIN 7
w. surely is wide enough STERNE 14
w., that passeth soone CHAUC 122
w., the flesh, and the devil PRAY 33
w. to hide virtues in? SHAK:TWE 5
W. was all before them MILT 261
w. was made for me SMOL 3
w. was too little for Alexander COLTON 8
w. will end in fire FROST:R 6
w. will hold its breath HITL 11
w. without end MASS 5
w. without end PRAY 7
w. would go round a deal faster CARROLL 11
w. would not be the same OPP 2
w. would smell like what it is SHELLEY:PB 62
W., you have kept faith HARDY:T 47
w.'s a bubble BACON:F[1] 131
w.'s a jest STEPHEN:JK 1
W.'s an inn DRYD 126
w.'s mine oyster SHAK:MERR 7
yet abide the W. DICKIN:E 21
your whole w. is bereft LAMAR 1

World War: casualty list of the W.W. CAP 1

world-wide: first act of a w. tragedy GORKY 2

worldly:
Be wisely w. QUAR 8
met him was Mr W. Wiseman BUNYAN 4

worlds:
best of all possible w. VOLT 11
both w. at once they view WALLER 9
in the best of all possible w.; and the CAB 3
infinite number of w. ALEX 5
More w. than I can lose DRYD 25
So many w. TENNY 164
Space may produce new W. MILT 141
Wandering between two w. ARNOLD:M 35
w. revolve like ancient women ELIOT:TS 16
wrecched worldes appetites CHAUC 122

worm:
bit the W., God's only son HUGHES:Te 4
but as a crushed w.? PUNCH 20
cut w. forgives the plow BLAKE:W 34
early bird catches the w. PROV 87
Even a w. can turn PROV 97
hero is the Conqueror W. POE 2
invisible w. BLAKE:W 66
like a w. i' th' bud SHAK:TWE 31
loving w. within its clod BROWNING:R 65
nakid as a w. was she CHAUC 103
needlessly sets foot upon a w. COWP 84
rather tough w. in GILB:WS 81
tread by chance upon a w. PARKER:D 10
w'en he fine a wum HARRIS:JC 9
w. at one end and a fool at JOHNSON:S 270
w. beneath the sod SHELLEY:PB 142
W. nor snail do no SHAK:MID 22
w. that hath eat of a king SHAK:HAM 154
w. that never dies BROOKE 18
w., the canker, and the grief BYR 241
W.'s eye view HAST:H 1

worms:
convocation of politic w. SHAK:HAM 153
made w.' meat of me SHAK:ROM 27
most exclusive w. PARKER:D 8
nor w. forget DICKENS 126
prodded with it at the w. BENS:EF 1
with vilest w. to dwell SHAK:SON 32
w. do not possess any sense of DARW:C 9
w. have eaten them, but not SHAK:AS 58
w. that are thy chambermaids SHAK:ROM 44
would not even feed your w. BYR 254

Worms: set on me in W. as there are LUTHER 2

wormwood:
gall and w. to an enemy BYR 84
w. and the gall BIBLE 344

worrit: w. to make the days pass ELIOT:G 21

worry:
Don't w., be happy BABA 1
no one to w. us COWARD 19

worrying:
What's the use of w.? ASAF 1
W. is the most natural THOMAS:L 1

worse:
altered her person for the w. SWIFT 7
better day, the w. dead HENRY:M 1
Defend the bad against the w. DAY LEWIS 5
did other things which were w. KIP 13
fear of finding something w. BELLOC 18
for better for w. PRAY 84
greater feeling to the w. SHAK:RIC.II 12
I follow the w. OSB:J 22
make the w. appear The better MILT 152
MORE WILL MEAN W. AMIS:K 2
often even w. CERV 12
so bad but it might have been w. PROV 300
spake w., 'twere better JONS 9
the w. for wearing ESSEX 1
w. I do, the more popular KENNEDY:JF 11
w. than I have power to tell SHAK:RIC.II 25
w. when it comes late JERROLD 3

worship:
come to w. him BIBLE 375
In w. of an echo BYR 94
only object of w. ANON 155
Rich in the simple w. KEATS 33
various modes of w. GIBBON:E 1
with my body I thee w. PRAY 86
w. him in spirit and BIBLE 478
W. is transcendent wonder CARLYLE:T 43
w. of his eyes JOYCE:J 5
w. the King GRANT:R 1
w. the national idols SHAW 50

worshipped: worship'd Stocks and Stones MILT 99

worships: Everybody w. me COWARD 12

worst:
do your w., and we will do CHURCH:W 22
done our best and w., and parted BROOKE 14
full look at the W. HARDY:T 6
His w. is better than HAZL 26
like to be told the w. CHURCH:W 6
love to be the w. SWIFT 75
No w., there is none HOPK:GM 22
thinks the w. he can of womankind HOME 2
we knew the w. too young KIP 53
where the best is like the w. KIP 62
w. is not So long as SHAK:KING L 58
w. is yet to come JOHNSON:PC 1
w. speak something good HERB:G 14
w. survived LEVI:P 2

worth:
Advise if this be w. MILT 159
charter of thy w. gives SHAK:SON 38
Conscious of w. VIRGIL 42
Everything w. thinking has already been GOET 38

I am not w. purchasing REED:Jos 1
in the w. and choice JONS 10
man w. having is true to his wife VANB 3
man's w. something BROWNING:R 86
not w. going to see JOHNSON:S 212
not w. the dust SHAK:KING L 60
nothing that is w. knowing WILDE:O 12
praises others' w. SEN 6
Slow rises w. by poverty JOHNSON:S 64
ways have a certain w. BROWNING:R 152
what is W. in anything BUTLER:S[1] 16
who is w. only half a million VANDERB 2
w. doing has been done BEERB 16
w. doing is w. doing in public ORTON 6
w. doing, it is w. doing badly CHESTERTON 45
w. doing, it's w. doing well PROV 181
w. knowing is mostly uncertain INGE 6
w. more than ever I yet PEPYS 20
w. more than the paper GOLDWYN 4
w. of a State MILL 22
worthless:
he's a w. piece of shit SOLAN 1
more w. set than Byron and his friends WELLING 23
produced us, more w. still HORACE 38
W. as withered weeds BRONTE:E 2
worthy:
be w. of being happy KANT 7
foemen w. of their steel SCOTT:W 42
labourer is w. of his hire BIBLE 455
Lord, I am not w. MASS 18
one w. man my foe POPE 124
She was a w. womman CHAUC 25
there be nine w. CAX 2
Who is w. to open the book BIBLE 578
wotthehell: w. archy w. MARQUIS 3
would:
He w., wouldn't he? RICE-D 1
if it were so, it w. be CARROLL 52
wound:
Earth felt the w. MILT 247
heal me of my grievous w. TENNY 279
knife see not the w. SHAK:MAC 20
put a tongue In every w. SHAK:JUL 58
to gall a new-healed w. SHAK:HEN.IV[2] 11
What w. did ever heal SHAK:OTH 30
Willing to w. POPE 121
wit Makes such a w. SHELLEY:PB 64
w. for w. BIBLE 104
W. with a touch that's MONTAGU 3
wounded:
w. in the house of my BIBLE 362
w. is the wounding heart CRASH 10
Wounded Knee: Bury my heart at W.K. BENET 2
wounds:
as many eyes as thou hast w. SHAK:JUL 42
bind up the nation's w. LINC 13
Faithful are the w. of a friend BIBLE 273
gash Is added to her w. SHAK:MAC 92
heals his w. NEWT:J 2
keeps his own w. green BACON:F[1] 98
not to heed the w. LOY 1
salvation lay in hiding his w. TOLS:L 7
soldier counts his w. PROP 1
These w. I had on Crispian's SHAK:HEN.V 40
time for the healing of the w. MANDELA:N 6
Time w. all heels ANON 250
Time w. all heels MARX:G 22
to bathe in reeking w. SHAK:MAC 4
wowser: ineffably pious person* DENNIS:CJ 4
wowsers: W., whinger, ratbags ANON 123
wrang: gang a kennin w. BURNS:R 37
wrangs: forgie us the w. BIBLE 589
wrap:
enough to w. a fairy in SHAK:MID 20
W. me up in my stockwhip LAWS 6
wrapping: perceive Christmas through its w. WHITE:EB 1
wrath:
between the dragon and his w. SHAK:KING L 3
day of w. CEL 1
Eternal wrauth Burnd after MILT 223
flee from the w. to come?, BIBLE 378
from thy w. PRAY 33
grapes of w. are stored HOWE 1
heavy w. of God MARLOWE 42
Nursing her w. BURNS:R 83
sun go down upon your w. BIBLE 534
thou deservest God's w. WESLEY:J 1
Throw away thy w. HERB:G 48
told my w., my w. did end BLAKE:W 76
turneth away w. BIBLE 261
tygers of w. are wiser BLAKE:W 46
under his w. and curse CATEC 3
who the Ox to w. has movd BLAKE:W 85
w. of the lion is the wisdom BLAKE:W 41
wreath:
homeward with a w. CHESTERTON 22
sent thee late a rosy w. JONS 36
She wore a w. of roses BAYLY 3
wreck:
Beautiful as a w. of Paradise SHELLEY:PB 133
w. and helmsman loom ARNOLD:M 15
wrecks:
thousand fearful w. SHAK:RIC.III 9
Vomits its w. SHELLEY:PB 61
w. of a dissolving dream SHELLEY:PB 153
Wrekin: forest fleece the W. heaves HOUSM 20
wren:
bore this w., till I was DRYD 27
w. goes to 't SHAK:KING L 67
w., The most diminutive SHAK:MAC 87
w. with little quill SHAK:MID 27
Wren:
considered Sir Christopher W. BARH 1
Sir Christopher W. Said BENTLEY:EC 7
youth, Mr Christoper W. EVELYN 4
wrestle: w. not against flesh BIBLE 538
wrestled: you have w. well SHAK:AS 6
wrestles: w. with us strengthens our BURKE:E 66
wrestling: lay w. with (my God!) HOPK:GM 21
wretch:
w. that dare not die BURNS:R 64
which hail'd the w. who won BYR 109
wretched:
learning to befriend the w. VIRGIL 43
most w. things which I myself VIRGIL 45
proud and yet a w. thing DAVIES:J 3
skilled to raise the w. GOLDS 25
w. he forsakes YOUNG:E 6
wretchedness: fierce w. that glory brings SHAK:TIM 11
wretches:
gaping w. of the sea HUNT:L 3
poor-folk maun be w. BURNS:R 56
to feel what w. feel SHAK:KING L 42
wring: will soon w. their hands WALP:R 3
wrinkle:
What stamps the w. deeper BYR 72
with the first w. DRYD 9
wrinkles: Which w. will devour NASHE 1
writ:
deeds Shall be in water w. BEAUMO 7
I never w. SHAK:SON 52
write:
able neither to read nor w. HAZL 5
away and w. a book about it BRAB 1
Better to w. for yourself CONNOLLY:C 18
Better to w. twaddle MANS:K 11
couldn't w. fuck on a dusty venetian BROWNE:Co 1
does not w. himself down HAZL 25
effect men w. in place lite CHAUC 119
frustrate of his hope to w. well MILT 306
He that will w. well ASCHAM 1
how to w. but not to read ZANZ 1
I live and w. HERB:G 46
I will w. for Antiquity LAMB:Ch 44
I w. of *Youth*, of *Love* HERR 7
If I could w. the beauty SHAK:SON 5
if she is to w. fiction WOOLF:V 9
Learn to w. well BUCKINGHAM AND 2
limit himself does not know how to w. BOIL 6
looke in thy heart and w. SIDNEY:P 4
make me w. too much DANI 4
man may w. at any time JOHNSON:S 91
might w. such stuff for ever JOHNSON:S 234
much as a man ought to w. TROLL 30
Muse invoked, sit down to w. SWIFT 67
nature learning how to w. CLARKE:M 1
only w. about what bites you STOP 15
read a novel I w. one DISR:B 99
seldom much to w. about WAUGH:A 2
When men w. for profit WALP:H 19
will sometimes wish to w. CRAB 18
w. about it, and about it POPE 163
w. and read comes by nature SHAK:MUCH 19
w. for children just as GORKY 13
w. for the general amusement SCOTT:W 84
w. for the sake of writing KEATS 149
w. four words, I shall strike BOIL 1
w., I know not what GREV 1
w. in the wind CATUL 16
W. the vision BIBLE 361
w. what men do, and not BACON:F[1] 11
w. when I feel spiteful LAWR:DH 38
w. when I'm inspired DE VR 8
W. with the learned FRANKLIN:B 8
writer:
alone cannot make a w. EMER 43
challenge for the w. is to adapt WHITLAM 2
every great and original w. WORDS:W 169
good w. should be so simple YEATS 138
grown up they call me a w. SING 2
in America the successful w. LEWIS:S 1
involved; that is what makes a w. GORDIM 3
loose, plain, rude w. BURTON:Ro 7
No tears in the w. FROST:R 16
not a w.'s business to hold opinions YEATS 150
original w. is not the one who refrains CHATEAU 1
play the role of a w. BELLOW 3
university in order to become a successful w. BRITT 1
w. of crook stories ought never WALLACE:E 2
w. of it be a black man or a fair ADDIS 14
w. what he thinks about critics HAMP 5
w.'s ambition should be KOES 5
w.'s life is solitary, often bitter BELLOW 3
w.'s only responsibility is FAULK 1
w.'s time is spent in reading JOHNSON:S 168
you understand a w.'s ignorance COLERIDGE:ST 72
writers:
All w. are liars CLARK:M 3
American w. want to be not good VIDAL 4
As w. become more numerous GOLDS 44
Clear w., like clear fountains LANDOR 14
read all w. twice KRAUS 1
What w. talk stinks KAF 1
W. are too self-centred CONDON 1
W. as a rule don't make fighters BERNARD:Jef 1
W., like teeth, are divided BAGE 5
w. started to suck up WAUGH:E 32
W. who stand out BEAUV 1
w. would express thoughts FRANCE 4
writes: w. as fast as they can read HAZL 25
writhe: w. from the waist upwards DICKENS 154
writhing: Reeling and W. CARROLL 28
writing:
dull man w. broken English NAB 1
easy w.'s vile hard reading SHERIDAN:RB 40
end of w. is to enable the readers JOHNSON:S 60
fairy kind of w. DRYD 99
fine w. is next to fine doing KEATS 139
future of my kind of w.? PYM 1
hundred years of fine w. HAZL 30
I had in the w. QUAR 4
incurable itch for w. JUV 15
look on w. as an escape PALMER:N 1
man is weary of w. BAUD 6
Many are engaged in w. books ELIOT:TS 72
not chuse this manner of w. MILT 302
Of w. many books there is no end BROWNING:EB 15
Pardons him for w. well AUD 42
want of skill Appear in w. POPE 4
wish I had the gift of w. GALS 5
wouldn't give up w. about God WAUGH:E 33
w. an exact man BACON:F[1] 108
w. comes from art POPE 20
w. in its language; even if you BOLL 2
w. increaseth rage GREV 1
W. . . . is a mechanic part of wit ETH 3
W. . . . is an act of faith ATWOOD 10
w. is different deep in the heart KAW 2
w. that was written BIBLE 350
w. when I was five WODE 26
W. when properly managed STERNE 13
writing-book: You have lost your w. HOFFMAN:H 8

written:
be w. among the laws BIBLE 177
because someone has w. about them DIDI 1
demanded to be w. MAUGH 26
don't care what is w. HEPB 1
make the w. word as unlike CONNOLLY:C 10
perhaps leave something w. MILT 303
What I have w. I have w. BIBLE 492
What is w. without effort JOHNSON:S 265
w. by a committee MAYER 1
w. by drinkers of water HORACE 92
w. under the direction of his family WALP:H 18
wrong:
absent are always in the w. DEST 1
After all, I may be w. RUSS:B 34
all was w. because not all CRAB 17
always in the w. DRYD 47
anxious to do the w. thing correctly SAKI 3
as dead as if he'd been w. ANON 146
can go w., it will ANON 200
can go w., it will PROV 182
Cavaliers (W. but Wromantic) SELL 6
could not endure being w. CAMUS 15
do a little w. SHAK:MERC 45
feel that something has gone w. POTTER:S 2
From w. to w. the exasperated ELIOT:TS 105
great right of an excessive w. BROWNING:R 198
he done her w. ANON 11
he has been in the w. ROCHES 3
I am never w. GOLDWYN 14
king can do no w. BLACKS 4
know when I'm doing w. WILSON:Ang 1
million Frenchmen can be w. GUINAN 1
million Frenchmen can't be w. ANON 185
most divinely in the w. YOUNG:E 4
never find an Englishman in the w. SHAW 14
one idea, – and that was w. DISR:B 27
one that is probably w. GORT 1
One w. more to man BROWNING:R 55
only thing that I ever did w. ANON 31
only w. what is against it EMER 8
own he has been in the w. POPE 177
pardon, who have done the w. DRYD 13
prefer to be w. with Plato CIC 17
preserve the Stars from w. WORDS:W 72
protect him against injustice and w. PALMERS 1
proving our latest ideas are w. SUZ:D 1
public is never w. ZUK 1
reason to fear I may be w.? AUSTEN 10
right w. TENNY 238
suffer w. no more MACAULAY:TB 45
support me when I am in the w. MELBOU 6
that you do w. by design JUNIUS 5
to be responsible and w. CHURCH:W 38
When everyone is w., everyone LA CHAU 1
when w., to be put right SCHURZ 1
Where is the w. I did them? BROWNING:R 177
who do nothing are never w. BANV 2
who does, not suffers w. SHELLEY:PB 67
women go w., men go WEST:M 13
W. dressed out in pride HAZL 1
w. for years AUD 3
w. people going hungry OSB:J 8
w. to have *thought* that I was w. DULL 1
w., 'Up to a point' WAUGH:E 21
w. war, at the w. place BRADLEY:OM 1
You w. me every way SHAK:JUL 71
wrongdoing: W. can only be avoided SOLON 4
wronged:
Not to be w. is to forgo WELLS:HG 11
not w. feel the same indignation SOLON 4
wronging: w. the ancientry, stealing SHAK:WIN 9
wrongs:
innumerable multitude of W. COLERIDGE:ST 2
makes the people's w. his own DRYD 52
mass of public w. KYD 2
Two w. do not make a right PROV 407
wrote:
as though I w. with acid MANS:K 5
because I w. the damned things PINT 5
can't believe I w. it GER 1
ever w. except for money JOHNSON:S 184
God w. it STOWE 6
thought I heard a line I w. KAUFMANN 1
wroth: be w. with one we love COLERIDGE:ST 61
wrought:
first he wroghte CHAUC 26
What God hath w. MORSE 1
What hath God w. BIBLE 120
wurd: Yon is a true w. BIBLE 596
wurds: moubandna your w. plain BIBLE 595
Wye: half the babbling W. TENNY 137
Wykehamist: rather dirty W. BETJ 2
Wynken: W., Blynken, and Nod FIELD 1
Xanadu: X. did Kubla Khan COLERIDGE:ST 63
xiphias: Shoots x. to his aim SMART 2
yaa-boo: cut and dried, y. JACK:R 1
yacht: I had to sink my y. FITZGER:FS 14
yaks: lot of y. jumping about BEECHAM 4
Yankee Doodle: Y.D. came to town BANGS 2
yard:
bully come into your front y. JOHNSON:LB 2
inch and he'll take a y. PROV 145
man maketh ofte a yerde CHAUC 106
yarn: all I ask is a merry y. MASE 3
yarooh: Y.! RICHARDS:F 1
Yarrow:
found him drown'd in Y. BALL 44
On the bonny banks o' Y.? BALL 17
yawns:
Despair y. HUGO 5
even the grave y. TREE 1
yawp: sound my barbaric y. WHITMAN 13
yea:
everlasting Y. CARLYLE:T 13
Let your y. be y. BIBLE 565
year:
away for a y. and a day LEAR 19
breath and the bloom of the y. BROWNING:R 212
circle of the golden y. TENNY 92
dirge Of the dying y. SHELLEY:PB 41
Is the yeare onely lost HERB:G 40
it isn't this time of y. GOGA 5
my most immemorial y. POE 6
ringing the Old Y. out GODWIN 1
stood at the gate of the y. HASKINS 1
That time of y. thou mayst SHAK:SON 33
'Tis the y.'s midnight DONNE 53
y. has shot her yield KIP 148
y. is dying in the night TENNY 177
Y. of Living Dangerously KOCH 1
y. Of now done darkness HOPK:GM 21
y., so it seems, is going to lose SAINTE-B 1
y. whose days are long WILDE:O 119
y.'s at the spring BROWNING:R 9
yearning: yearnin' fer – I dunno wot DENNIS:CJ 1
years:
all the same in a hundred y. PROV 215
Before the beginning of y. SWIN 13
bring me back the y. that are past VIRGIL 78
come to the y. of discretion PRAY 77
down the arches of the y. THOMP:F 7
few y. to be young and handsome SWIFT 25
first twenty y. are the longest SOUTHEY 21
golden y. return SHELLEY:PB 153
He that cuts off twenty y. SHAK:JUL 37
It may be for y., and it CRAW 1
It ran a hundred y. HOLMES:OW 5
love of finished y. ROSSET:C 4
new y. ruin and rend SWIN 36
nor the years condemn BINY 1
now it will tell a hundred y. hence BUTLER:S[2] 37
number of y. but in the use MONTAIGNE 5
Our noisy y. seem moments WORDS:W 63
remaining y. among his family DU BEL 2
same a hundred y. hence DICKENS 71
thousand y. in thy sight BIBLE 224
thousand y. more. That's all WELLS:HG 20
To be seventy y. young HOLMES:OW 17
touch of earthly y. WORDS:W 31
y. are gliding by HORACE 24
y. are threescore y. and ten BIBLE 225
y. as they come bring HORACE 109
y. hang like old clothes MOORE:B 1
y. like great black oxen YEATS 7
Y. steal Fire BYR 75
y. teach much EMER 35
y. that pass by are also travellers BAS 3
y. that the locust hath BIBLE 354
y. will take care of themselves EDGE 7
yeas: In russet y. SHAK:LOV 22
Yeats:
churchyard Y. is laid YEATS 124
William Y. is laid to rest AUD 40
yellow:
looks y. to the jaundic'd POPE 26
y. fog that rubs its back ELIOT:TS 4
Y. God forever gazes down HAYES 1
y. like ripe corn ROSSET:DG 2
y. lines and dead armadillos HIGH 1
Yellow River: Y.R. down our throats PRIEST 6
yelps: loudest y. for liberty among JOHNSON:S 43
yeoman:
gave the image of a y. squire DOUGLAS-H:A 4
It did me y.'s service SHAK:HAM 192
yes:
don't say y. until I've finished ZANU 1
say y. O at lightning HOPK:GM 3
says y., she is no lady DENNING 2
y. I said y. I will Y. JOYCE:J 29
yesterday:
but as y. when it is past BIBLE 224
Climbing out of Y. with sticky SLESS 2
that was y. THOMP:F 4
until it has become y. MCLUH 14
y. doth not usher it in DONNE 104
Y. I loved LESSING:GE 2
yesterdays: all our y. have lighted SHAK:MAC 113
yeti: in civilization to appeal to a Y. HILLARY 3
yetts: yettis of hell ar brokin DUNB 18
yew:
Beneath a church-yard y. SHEN 2
bows of double-fatal y. SHAK:RIC.II 25
never a spray of y. ARNOLD:M 18
Old Y., which graspest TENNY 127
Y. alone burns lamps DE LA M 17
yew-tree: that y.'s shade GRAY:T 16
Yid: PUT THE ID BACK IN Y. ROTH 2
yield:
just to y. to it GRAHAM:CS 1
to find, and not to y. TENNY 55
Y. not to temptation PALMER:HR 1
yielded: Yeilded with coy submission MILT 193
yoke:
best Bear his milde yoak MILT 100
bring the inevitable y. WORDS:W 61
country sinks beneath the y. SHAK:MAC 92
easie y. Of servil Pomp MILT 156
impertinent y. of prelaty MILT 304
savage bull doth bear the y. SHAK:MUCH 3
So unaccustomed to the y. COWP 4
teach us to cast off this Y.? MILT 222
y. of inauspicious stars SHAK:ROM 44
yoked: y. with a lamb SHAK:JUL 74
yolk: y. runs down the waistcoat DICKENS 78
yolks: nothing to lose but your y. STEVENSON:A 15
Yonghy-Bonghy-Bo: Lived the Y. LEAR 7
yore: as it hath been of y. WORDS:W 52
Yorick: Alas, poor Y. SHAK:HAM 183
York: by this sun of Y. SHAK:RIC.III 1
Yorkshire: forth to multiply in Y. HILL:Reg 4
you:
because of y. HORACE 51
for y. but not for me ANON 32
With y. I should love to live HORACE 40
Y. too, Brutus? CAES:GJ 7
young:
A y. man not yet BACON:F[1] 81
ale from the Country of the Y. YEATS 24
all that the y. can do for the old SHAW 96
America is a country of y. men EMER 67
be happy while we are y. ANON 12
Bill as is y. and tender THACK 25
both were y. and one BYR 43
can be y. without money WILLIAMS:T 5
care for the y. man's whore JOHNSON:S 134
compliment him about looking y. IRV 4
crime of being a y. man PITT:W[1] 1
die y. than to outlive POWER:M 1
few years to be y. and handsome SWIFT 25
for ever y. KEATS 92
Fortune . . . is friendly to the y. MACHIA 8
gods love die y. BYR 203
good die y. PROV 151
greatest reverence to the y. JUV 25

Grieve not that I die y. HAST:F 1
hero to those who die y. RILKE 2
how y. the policemen look HICKS 1
hundred and fifty who was rather y. WODE 30
I was y. and easy THOMAS:D 16
I was y. and foolish YEATS 3
if he be *caught* y. JOHNSON:S 157
let me perish y. BYR 136
look y. till forty DRYD 9
make an old man y. TENNY 60
No y. man believes HAZL 32
nor y. enough for a boy SHAK:TWE 12
not so y. as they are painted BEERB 1
old-fashioned respect for the y. WILDE:O 89
Portrait of the Artist as a Y. Man JOYCE:J 1
she died y. WEBSTER:J 27
So y. and so untender? SHAK:KING L 2
Take heed of a y. wench HERB:G 60
To be seventy years y. HOLMES:OW 17
to be y. was very heaven WORDS:W 159
To find a y. fellow that CONG 30
To keep the body y. YEATS 57
Tomorrow for the y. AUD 20
too y. to fall asleep for ever SASS 11
vile and right the y. are PORTER:H 1
we knew the worst too y. KIP 53
We were y., we were merry COLERIDGE:M 3
what it was like to feel y. OSB:J 3
when all the world is y. KINGSLEY:C 19
whom the gods love die y. PROV 389
whom the gods love dies y. PLAU 2
world and love were y. RALE 1
yonge, fresshe folkes CHAUC 122
you yet call yourself y.? SHAK:HEN.IV[2] 12
y. always have the same problem CRISP 1
y. are beautiful WHITMAN 38
y. are sad and bewildered SMITH:LP 13
y. as beautiful YOUNG:E 13
y. blood must have its course KINGSLEY:C 19
y. girl stood beside me NEIL 5
y. have aspirations that never SAKI 5
y. heart beating under EMER 68
Y. in limbs SHAK:MERC 28
y. In one another's arms YEATS 71
y. know everything WILDE:O 74
y. man hid with me DICKENS 205
y. men are regarded as radicals WILSON:W 1
y. men glittering and sparkling TRAH 4
Y. men have more virtue JOHNSON:S 118
Y. men make great mistakes JOW 4
Y. men of the times BANV 1
y. men shall see visions BIBLE 355
y. men's vision DRYD 43
y. 'neath wrinkled rind LANG:A 5
Y. people ought not to be idle THATCH:M 17
y. with y. desires THOMP:F 15
younger:
do not get any y. REED:H 1
ever wished to be y. SWIFT 19
it seems to get y. and y. SHAW 135
jaundiced eye on its y. sons WODE 29
let thy love be y. SHAK:TWE 27
trouble with our y. authors MAUGH 24
youngest: loved the y. above a' BALL 10
yours: Unalterably, never y. DICKENS 127
yourself:
consequence do it y. BARH 2
do not want done to y. CONF 12
have to believe in y. CHAPLIN 3
Keep y. *to* y. DICKENS 26
see to everything y. MELBA 1
well done, do it y. PROV 193
youth:
April of your y. adorns HERB:E 1
Both in the flower of their y. VIRGIL 14
brisk intemperance of y. GIBBON:E 16
Confusions of a wasted y. TENNY 125
Crabbed age and y. SHAK:POET 1
Creator in the days of thy y. BIBLE 289
days of our y. are BYR 141
Eagle mewing her mighty y. MILT 320
great has been done by y. DISR:B 17
He wears the rose Of y. SHAK:ANT 37
How lovely is y. MEDICI:L 1
I knew a phoenix in my y. YEATS 47
I remember my y. CONRAD 8
ideal state if it came a little later* ASQU:HH 4
If only y. knew EST 1
Immortal y. to mortal maids LANDOR 2
In flow'r of y. DRYD 105
In the lexicon of y. BULWER 2
In y. alone, unhappy mortals VIRGIL 28
In y. is pleasure WEVER 1
In y. we are MELV 4
I've done it from my y. CRAB 15
Know of your y. SHAK:MID 1
laugh uproariously in y. BROOKE 12
my heart another y. SHAK:SON 51
my ill adventured y. DANI 1
nourishing a y. sublime TENNY 69
remembreth me Upon my yowthe CHAUC 79
riband in the cap of y. SHAK:HAM 175
roses for the flush of y. ROSSET:C 11
shake their wicked sides at y. YEATS 35
sign of an ill-spent y. SPENCER:H 12
sin against the strength of y. TENNY 73
So long as y. and thou are SHAK:SON 8
spirit of y. in every thing SHAK:SON 43
suttel thief of y. MILT 94
Sweet Love of y. BRONTE:E 7
Sweet wine of y. BROOKE 19
That miracle of a y. EVELYN 4
things Y. needed not WORDS:W 90
Thou hast nor y. nor age SHAK:MEA 20
thoughts of y. are long LONGFEL 25
to be taught by y. BURKE:E 86
too good to waste on children* SHAW 131
trampled vintage of my y. WILDE:O 108
waste an eternal y. gave WILDE:O 103
wept for my departed y. POWER:M 2
when I was a hot-blooded y. HORACE 43
when Y. and Pleasure meet BYR 77
Where y. grows pale KEATS 93
y. And a little beauty WEBSTER:J 21
y., I do adore thee SHAK:POET 2
y. I shall not taste HARW 2
Y. is a blunder DISR:B 18
y. is but a frost of cares TICH 1
Y. is full of pleasance SHAK:POET 1
Y. is something very new CHANEL 1
y. is the season of credulity PITT:W[1] 4
Y. is the time to go flashing STEVENSON:RL 15
y. is vain COLERIDGE:ST 61
Y., large, lusty, loving WHITMAN 15
Y. means love BROWNING:R 193
Y. of a Nation are the Trustees DISR:B 28
y. of America is their oldest WILDE:O 54
y. of England are on fire SHAK:HEN.V 10
Y. of Frolics POPE 138
y. of labour GOLDS 23
Y. on the prow GRAY:T 31
Y. pined away with desire BLAKE:W 70
Y. shows but half BROWNING:R 184
y. that must fight and die HOOV 4
y. waneth by increasing PEELE 2
y. was full of foolish noise TENNY 150
Y., what men's age DENH 3
Y., which is forgiven SHAW 68
Y. will be served BORR 9
y. will be still in our faces CORY 4
Y. will come here and beat IBS 15
Y. will stand foremost SHELLEY:PB 151
y. would be an ideal state if ASQU:HH 4
Y.'s a stuff will not SHAK:TWE 19
Y.'s smooth ocean SHELLEY:PB 81
Y.'s sweet-scented manuscript FITZGER:E 33
Y.'s the season made GAY 22
youths: Y. green and happy CLOUGH 25
Yucatan:
I had an Aunt in Y. BELLOC 9
lies the land of Y. TURNER:WJR 1
yugen: enters the realm of *y.* ZE AMI 3
Yukon: this is the Law of the Y SERVICE 1
zany: story of a mountebank and his z. WALP:H 22
zeal:
holy mistaken z. in politics JUNIUS 6
passion and think it z. KEMP 11
zealous: very z. man BUNYAN 27
zebra:
Striped like a z. KEATS 103
z. stripes along his jaw ELIOT:TS 28
zed: Thou whoreson z. SHAK:KING L 23
zenith: Dropd from the Z. MILT 144
Zenocrate:
entertain divine Z. MARLOWE 12
fair Z., divine Z. MARLOWE 11
Z., lovelier than the love MARLOWE 2
zephyr: soft the Z. blows GRAY:T 31
Zephyrus: Z. did softly play SPENS 48
Zeus: Z. who leads mortals AESC 1
Zion:
we remembered Z. BIBLE 244
Z., city of our God NEWT:J 1
Z. of the water bead THOMAS:D 10
zone: Torrid or the frozen Z. CAREW:T 3
zoo: human z. MORRIS:D 2
Zoroaster: Magus Z. SHELLEY:PB 66
Zuleika: Z., on a desert island BEERB 5
Zurich: little gnomes of Z. WILSON:Harold 1